HALSBURY'S
Laws of England

FIFTH EDITION
2015

Volume 92

This is volume 92 of the Fifth Edition of Halsbury's Laws of England, containing the title SENTENCING.

This title replaces the SENTENCING AND DISPOSITION OF OFFENDERS title contained in volume 92 (2010) and the Additional Materials booklet *Sentencing and Disposition of Offenders (Release and Recall of Prisoners)*.

Volume 92 (2010) and the Additional Materials booklet *Sentencing and Disposition of Offenders (Release and Recall of Prisoners)* may now be archived.

For a full list of volumes comprised in a current set of Halsbury's Laws of England please see overleaf.

Fifth Edition volumes:

1 (2008), 2 (2008), 3 (2011), 4 (2011), 5 (2013), 6 (2011), 7 (2015), 8 (2015), 9 (2012), 10 (2012), 11 (2009), 12 (2009), 13 (2009), 14 (2009), 15 (2009), 16 (2011), 17 (2011), 18 (2009), 19 (2011), 20 (2014), 21 (2011), 22 (2012), 23 (2013), 24 (2010), 25 (2010), 26 (2010), 27 (2015), 28 (2015), 29 (2014), 30 (2012), 31 (2012), 32 (2012), 33 (2013), 34 (2011), 35 (2015), 36 (2015), 37 (2013), 38 (2013), 38A (2013), 39 (2014), 40 (2014), 41 (2014), 41A (2014), 42 (2011), 43 (2011), 44 (2011), 45 (2010), 46 (2010), 47 (2014), 47A (2014), 48 (2008), 49 (2008), 49 (2015), 50 (2008), 51 (2013), 52 (2014), 53 (2014), 54 (2008), 55 (2012), 56 (2011), 57 (2012), 58 (2014), 58A (2014), 59 (2014), 59A (2014), 60 (2011), 61 (2010), 62 (2012), 63 (2012), 64 (2012), 65 (2015), 66 (2015), 67 (2008), 68 (2008), 69 (2009), 70 (2012), 71 (2013), 72 (2015), 73 (2015), 74 (2011), 75 (2013), 76 (2013), 77 (2010), 78 (2010), 79 (2014), 80 (2013), 81 (2010), 82 (2010), 83 (2010), 84 (2013), 84A (2013), 85 (2012), 86 (2013), 87 (2012), 88 (2012), 88A (2013), 89 (2011), 90 (2011), 91 (2012), 92 (2015), 93 (2008), 94 (2008), 95 (2013), 96 (2012), 97 (2015), 97A (2014), 98 (2013), 99 (2012), 100 (2009), 101 (2009), 102 (2010), 103 (2010), 104 (2014)

Consolidated Index and Tables:

2015 Consolidated Index (A–E), 2015 Consolidated Index (F–O), 2015 Consolidated Index (P–Z), 2016 Consolidated Table of Statutes, 2016 Consolidated Table of Statutory Instruments, etc, 2015 Consolidated Table of Cases (A–G), 2015 Consolidated Table of Cases (H–Q), 2015 Consolidated Table of Cases (R–Z, ECJ Cases)

Updating and ancillary materials:

2015 Annual Cumulative Supplement; Monthly Current Service; Annual Abridgments 1974–2014

October 2015

HALSBURY'S
Laws of England

Volume 92

2015

Members of the LexisNexis Group worldwide

United Kingdom	LexisNexis, a Division of Reed Elsevier (UK) Ltd, Lexis House, 30 Farringdon Street, LONDON, EC4A 4HH, and 9–10, St Andrew Square, EDINBURGH, EH2 2AF
Australia	Reed International Books Australia Pty Ltd trading as LexisNexis, Chatswood, New South Wales
Austria	LexisNexis Verlag ARD Orac GmbH & Co KG, Vienna
Benelux	LexisNexis Benelux, Amsterdam
Canada	LexisNexis Canada, Markham, Ontario
China	LexisNexis China, Beijing and Shanghai
France	LexisNexis SA, Paris
Germany	LexisNexis GmbH, Dusseldorf
Hong Kong	LexisNexis Hong Kong, Hong Kong
India	LexisNexis India, New Delhi
Italy	Giuffrè Editore, Milan
Japan	LexisNexis Japan, Tokyo
Malaysia	Malayan Law Journal Sdn Bhd, Kuala Lumpur
New Zealand	LexisNexis New Zealand Ltd, Wellington
Singapore	LexisNexis Singapore, Singapore
South Africa	LexisNexis, Durban
USA	LexisNexis, Dayton, Ohio

FIRST EDITION	*Published in 31 volumes between 1907 and 1917*
SECOND EDITION	*Published in 37 volumes between 1931 and 1942*
THIRD EDITION	*Published in 43 volumes between 1952 and 1964*
FOURTH EDITION	*Published in 56 volumes between 1973 and 1987, with reissues between 1988 and 2008*
FIFTH EDITION	*Published between 2008 and 2014, with reissues from 2014*

A CIP Catalogue record for this book is available from the British Library.

ISBN 13 (complete set, standard binding): 9781405734394

ISBN 13: 9781405798587

ISBN 978-1-4057-9858-7

9 781405 798587

Typeset by Letterpart Limited, Caterham on the Hill, Surrey CR3 5XL
Printed and bound by CPI Group (UK) Ltd, Croydon, CR0 4YY
Visit LexisNexis at www.lexisnexis.co.uk

Editors of this Volume

SIMON CADDE, LLB

AMANDA WRIGHT, LLB

Commissioning Editor

CLAIRE TURPIN, LLB, MSc

Indexer

JAMES A. WARD, BA, LLB,
a Solicitor of the Senior Courts of England and Wales

Managing Editor

HELEN HALVEY, LLB

SENTENCING

Consultant Editor

ROBERT BANKS, BSc (Hons),
Barrister

Consultant Editor (Part 13)

JASON ELLIOTT, MA (Oxon),
Barrister

The law stated in this volume is in general that in force on 1 September 2015,
although subsequent changes have been included wherever possible.

Any future updating material will be found in the Current Service and annual
Cumulative Supplement to Halsbury's Laws of England.

TABLE OF CONTENTS

HOW TO USE HALSBURY'S LAWS OF ENGLAND

Volumes

Each text volume of Halsbury's Laws of England contains the law on the titles contained in it as at a date stated at the front of the volume (the operative date).

Information contained in Halsbury's Laws of England may be accessed in several ways.

First, by using the tables of contents.

Each volume contains both a general Table of Contents, and a specific Table of Contents for each title contained in it. From these tables you will be directed to the relevant part of the work.

Readers should note that the current arrangement of titles can be found in the Current Service.

Secondly, by using tables of statutes, statutory instruments, cases or other materials.

If you know the name of the Act, statutory instrument or case with which your research is concerned, you should consult the Consolidated Tables of statutes, cases and so on (published as separate volumes) which will direct you to the relevant volume and paragraph.

(Each individual text volume also includes tables of those materials used as authority in that volume.)

Thirdly, by using the indexes.

If you are uncertain of the general subject area of your research, you should go to the Consolidated Index (published as separate volumes) for reference to the relevant volume(s) and paragraph(s).

(Each individual text volume also includes an index to the material contained therein.)

Updating publications

The text volumes of Halsbury's Laws should be used in conjunction with the annual Cumulative Supplement and the monthly Noter-Up.

The annual Cumulative Supplement

The Supplement gives details of all changes between the operative date of the text volume and the operative date of the Supplement. It is arranged in the same volume, title and paragraph order as the text volumes. Developments affecting particular points of law are noted to the relevant paragraph(s) of the text volumes.

For narrative treatment of material noted in the Cumulative Supplement, go to the Annual Abridgment volume for the relevant year.

Destination Tables

In certain titles in the annual *Cumulative Supplement,* reference is made to Destination Tables showing the destination of consolidated legislation. Those Destination Tables are to be found either at the end of the titles within the annual *Cumulative Supplement,* or in a separate *Destination Tables* booklet provided from time to time with the *Cumulative Supplement.*

The Noter-Up

The Noter-Up is contained in the Current Service Noter-Up booklet, issued monthly and noting changes since the publication of the annual Cumulative Supplement. Also arranged in the same volume, title and paragraph order as the text volumes, the Noter-Up follows the style of the Cumulative Supplement.

For narrative treatment of material noted in the Noter-Up, go to the relevant Monthly Review.

REFERENCES AND ABBREVIATIONS

ACT	Australian Capital Territory
A-G	Attorney General
Admin	Administrative Court
Admlty	Admiralty Court
Adv-Gen	Advocate General
affd	affirmed
affg	affirming
Alta	Alberta
App	Appendix
art	article
Aust	Australia
B	Baron
BC	British Columbia
C	Command Paper (of a series published before 1900)
c	chapter number of an Act
CA	Court of Appeal
CAC	Central Arbitration Committee
CA in Ch	Court of Appeal in Chancery
CB	Chief Baron
CCA	Court of Criminal Appeal
CCR	County Court Rules 1981 (as subsequently amended)
CCR	Court for Crown Cases Reserved
CJEU	Court of Justice of the European Union
C-MAC	Courts-Martial Appeal Court
CO	Crown Office
COD	Crown Office Digest
CPR	Civil Procedure Rules
Can	Canada
Cd	Command Paper (of the series published 1900–18)
Cf	compare
Ch	Chancery Division
ch	chapter
cl	clause
Cm	Command Paper (of the series published 1986 to date)

Cmd	Command Paper (of the series published 1919–56)
Cmnd	Command Paper (of the series published 1956–86)
Comm	Commercial Court
Comr	Commissioner
Court Forms (2nd Edn)	Atkin's Encyclopaedia of Court Forms in Civil Proceedings, 2nd Edn. See note 2 post.
CrimPR	Criminal Procedure Rules
DC	Divisional Court
DPP	Director of Public Prosecutions
EAT	Employment Appeal Tribunal
EC	European Community
ECJ	Court of Justice of the European Community (before the Treaty of Lisbon (OJ C306, 17.12.2007, p 1) came into force on 1 December 2009); European Court of Justice (after the Treaty of Lisbon (OJ C306, 17.12.2007, p 1) came into force on 1 December 2009)
EComHR	European Commission of Human Rights
ECSC	European Coal and Steel Community
ECtHR Rules of Court	Rules of Court of the European Court of Human Rights
EEC	European Economic Community
EFTA	European Free Trade Association
EGC	European General Court
EWCA Civ	Official neutral citation for judgments of the Court of Appeal (Civil Division)
EWCA Crim	Official neutral citation for judgments of the Court of Appeal (Criminal Division)
EWHC	Official neutral citation for judgments of the High Court
Edn	Edition
Euratom	European Atomic Energy Community
EU	European Union
Ex Ch	Court of Exchequer Chamber
ex p	ex parte
Fam	Family Division
Fed	Federal
Forms & Precedents (5th Edn)	Encyclopaedia of Forms and Precedents other than Court Forms, 5th Edn. See note 2 post.
GLC	Greater London Council
HC	High Court
HC	House of Commons

HK	Hong Kong
HL	House of Lords
IAT	Immigration Appeal Tribunal
ILM	International Legal Materials
INLR	Immigration and Nationality Law Reports
IRC	Inland Revenue Commissioners
Ind	India
Int Rels	International Relations
Ir	Ireland
J	Justice
JA	Judge of Appeal
Kan	Kansas
LA	Lord Advocate
LC	Lord Chancellor
LCC	London County Council
LCJ	Lord Chief Justice
LJ	Lord Justice of Appeal
LoN	League of Nations
MR	Master of the Rolls
Man	Manitoba
n	note
NB	New Brunswick
NI	Northern Ireland
NS	Nova Scotia
NSW	New South Wales
NY	New York
NZ	New Zealand
OHIM	Office for Harmonisation in the Internal Market
OJ	The Official Journal of the European Community published by the Office for Official Publications of the European Community
Ont	Ontario
P	President
PC	Judicial Committee of the Privy Council
PEI	Prince Edward Island
Pat	Patents Court
q	question
QB	Queen's Bench Division
QBD	Queen's Bench Division of the High Court
Qld	Queensland
Que	Quebec
r	rule

RDC	Rural District Council
RPC	Restrictive Practices Court
RSC	Rules of the Supreme Court 1965 (as subsequently amended)
reg	regulation
Res	Resolution
revsd	reversed
Rly	Railway
s	section
SA	South Africa
S Aust	South Australia
SC	Supreme Court
SI	Statutory Instruments published by authority
SR & O	Statutory Rules and Orders published by authority
SR & O Rev 1904	Revised Edition comprising all Public and General Statutory Rules and Orders in force on 31 December 1903
SR & O Rev 1948	Revised Edition comprising all Public and General Statutory Rules and Orders and Statutory Instruments in force on 31 December 1948
SRNI	Statutory Rules of Northern Ireland
STI	Simon's Tax Intelligence (1973–1995); Simon's Weekly Tax Intelligence (1996-current)
Sask	Saskatchewan
Sch	Schedule
Sess	Session
Sing	Singapore
TCC	Technology and Construction Court
TS	Treaty Series
Tanz	Tanzania
Tas	Tasmania
UDC	Urban District Council
UKHL	Official neutral citation for judgments of the House of Lords
UKPC	Official neutral citation for judgments of the Privy Council
UN	United Nations
V-C	Vice-Chancellor
Vict	Victoria
W Aust	Western Australia
Zimb	Zimbabwe

NOTE 1. A general list of the abbreviations of law reports and other sources used in this work can be found at the beginning of the Consolidated Table of Cases.

NOTE 2. Where references are made to other publications, the volume number precedes and the page number follows the name of the publication; eg the reference '12 Forms & Precedents (5th Edn) 44' refers to volume 12 of the Encyclopaedia of Forms and Precedents, page 44.

NOTE 3. An English statute is cited by short title or, where there is no short title, by regnal year and chapter number together with the name by which it is commonly known or a description of its subject matter and date. In the case of a foreign statute, the mode of citation generally follows the style of citation in use in the country concerned with the addition, where necessary, of the name of the country in parentheses.

NOTE 4. A statutory instrument is cited by short title, if any, followed by the year and number, or, if unnumbered, the date.

TABLE OF STATUTES

TABLE OF STATUTORY INSTRUMENTS

TABLE OF CRIMINAL PROCEDURE

Criminal Procedure Rules 2015, SI 2015/1490 (CrimPR)

Criminal Practice Directions 2015 [2015] EWCA Crim 1567, [2015] All ER (D) 134 (Sep)

TABLE OF CASES

PARA

Decisions of the European Court of Justice are listed below numerically. These decisions are also included in the preceding alphabetical list.

SENTENCING

(7)   Fine Defaulters and Contemnors 729

      (i)   Prisoner Committed or Detained on or after 4 April
              2005 729

      (ii)   Prisoner Committed or Detained before 4 April 2005 731

(8)   Conditions of Release; Supervision 733

      (i)   Prisoner serving Indeterminate Sentence 733

      (ii)   Prisoner serving Determinate Sentence for Offence
              Committed on or after 4 April 2005 735

              A.   Duration of Licences 735

              B.   Licence Conditions 736

      (iii)   Prisoner serving Determinate Sentence for Offence
              Committed before 4 April 2005 738

      (iv)   Supervision after Release 741

(9)   Discharge 746

(10) Removal of Prisoners from the United Kingdom 747

      (i)   Life Sentence Prisoners 747

      (ii)   Fixed-term Prisoners 749

              A.   Offences Committed on or after 4 April 2005 749

              B.   Offences Committed before 4 April 2005 751

1. SENTENCING POWERS OF COURTS

(1) CROWN COURTS

1. Sentencing powers of Crown Court. Almost all available forms of sentence may be passed by the Crown Court[1], although certain forms of sentence are available only in the cases of offenders of specified ages, or are subject to restrictions upon their use in relation to offenders within specified limits of age[2]. A magistrates' court may also commit an offender to the Crown Court for sentence where it considers its own sentencing powers inadequate in light of the seriousness of the either-way offence[3] or where he has indicated that he would plead guilty to an either-way offence and the court has committed in to trial in the Crown Court for related offences[4]. The Crown Court also has jurisdiction under vagrancy laws[5] and in respect of a person who has been conditionally discharged and then committed of a further offence[6]. There is a right of appeal to the Crown Court against most sentences and orders made by the magistrates' courts and licensing, local and other authorities[7]. The Crown Court may impose unlimited fines[8].

1   There are some limited exceptions to the Crown Court's powers: it may not, for example, make a referral order under the Powers of Criminal Courts (Sentencing) Act 2000 s 16(1) (see PARA 156). In the principal legislation governing the sentencing of offenders (ie the Powers of Criminal Courts (Sentencing) Act 2000 and the Criminal Justice Act 2003 Pt 12 (ss 142–305)) 'court' does not generally include the Court Martial (see the Powers of Criminal Courts (Sentencing) Act 2000 s 163(1) (amended by the Armed Forces Act 2006 Sch 16 para 168, though not so as to affect the substance of the definition) or a Service Court (see the Criminal Justice Act 2003 s 305(1) (amended by the Armed Forces Act 2006 Sch 16 para 231, so as to enable a contrary intention to be expressed in the Armed Forces Act 2006))). In the Criminal Justice Act 2003 'service court' means the Court Martial, the Summary Appeal Court, the Service Civilian Court, the Court Martial Appeal Court and the Supreme Court on an appeal brought from the Court Martial Appeal Court: s 305(1) (definition substituted by the Armed Forces Act 2006 Sch 16 para 231). As to the establishment and procedure of the Court Martial see ARMED FORCES vol 3 (2011) PARAS 633–655; as to the establishment and procedure of the Summary Appeal Court see ARMED FORCES vol 3 (2011) PARAS 624–632; as to the establishment and procedure of the Service Civilian Court see ARMED FORCES vol 3 (2011) PARAS 681–688; as to the Court Martial Appeal Court and the Supreme Court on an appeal brought from the Court Martial Appeal Court see ARMED FORCES vol 3 (2011) PARAS 656–680.
2   Cases involving children or young persons may be remitted to youth courts for sentencing: see the Powers of Criminal Courts (Sentencing) Act 2000 s 8; and CHILDREN AND YOUNG PERSONS vol 10 (2012) PARA 1221. As to the determination of a person's age see the Children and Young Persons Act 1933 s 99; and CHILDREN AND YOUNG PERSONS vol 10 (2012) PARA 1206.
3   See the Powers of Criminal Courts (Sentencing) Act 2000 ss 3, 3A; and CRIMINAL PROCEDURE vol 27 (2015) PARAS 292–294. There are corresponding provisions in respect of children and young persons: see ss 3B, 3C; and CRIMINAL PROCEDURE vol 27 (2015) PARAS 234, 235. As to sentencing on committal see s 5; and PARA 549. As to the information to be supplied on committal for sentence see the Criminal Procedure Rules 2015, SI 2015/1490, r 28.10.
4   See the Powers of Criminal Courts (Sentencing) Act 2000 s 4; and CRIMINAL PROCEDURE vol 27 (2015) PARA 295. There are corresponding provisions in respect of children and young persons: see s 4A; and CRIMINAL PROCEDURE vol 27 (2015) PARA 236.
5   See the Vagrancy Act 1824; and CRIMINAL LAW vol 26 (2010) PARA 772 et seq.
6   See the Powers of Criminal Courts (Sentencing) Act 2000 ss 6, 7, 13; and PARAS 455, 456, 549.
7   See COURTS AND TRIBUNALS vol 24 (2010) PARAS 723–724.
8   See the Criminal Law Act 1977 s 32(1); and PARA 174.

(2) MAGISTRATES' COURTS

2. Sentencing powers of magistrates' courts. Magistrates' courts[1] have power to fine and to imprison certain offenders. Provision in connection with the imposition of fines is made by statute[2]. The minimum and maximum terms of imprisonment or detention which may be imposed by a magistrates' court are to be found in the enactment creating the offence, subject to the provisions described below[3].

Until a day to be appointed[4] a magistrates' court does not have power to impose imprisonment[5] or detention in a young offender institution[6] for more than six months in respect of any one offence[7], and unless expressly excluded, this restriction applies even if the offence in question is one for which a person would otherwise be liable on summary conviction to imprisonment or detention in a young offender institution for more than six months[8]. However, any power of a magistrates' court to impose a term of imprisonment for non-payment of a fine[9], or for want of sufficient goods to satisfy a fine, is not limited[10] to six months[11].

It is provided that until a day to be appointed[12], on summary conviction in the magistrates' court of any of the listed offences triable either way[13] a person is liable to imprisonment for a term not exceeding six months or to a fine[14] not exceeding the prescribed sum or both[15]; as from that day the maximum term of imprisonment under this provision is increased to 12 months[16]. It is also provided that magistrates' courts may impose unlimited fines for either way offences, for offences for which no minimum fine is specified, and for offences in relation to which a maximum fine of £5,000 is specified[17].

Where a magistrates' court imposes imprisonment or detention for two or more offences, the court may make the terms concurrent or consecutive with an aggregate maximum (excluding a suspended sentence) of 12 months for two or more offences triable either way and six months for other offences[18].

Where any person disobeys an order of a magistrates' court made under any Act[19] to do anything other than the payment of money, or to abstain from doing anything, he is punishable in the manner prescribed by statute, or if no punishment is prescribed, he may be ordered to pay a sum[20] for every day during which he is in default or a sum not exceeding a prescribed maximum[21], or he may be committed to custody until he has remedied his default or for a period not exceeding two months[22]. These powers may be exercised either of the magistrates' court own motion or by order on complaint[23].

A magistrates' court must not impose imprisonment for less than five days[24].

Magistrates' courts like Crown Courts have the power to remit cases involving children and young persons to youth courts for sentence[25].

1   As to the meaning of 'magistrates' court' see MAGISTRATES vol 71 (2013) PARA 470.

2   See PARAS 174–184.

3   See the text and notes 4–25.

4   The Powers of Criminal Courts (Sentencing) Act 2000 s 78 (see the text and notes 5–11) is prospectively repealed by the Criminal Justice Act 2003 Sch 37 Pt 7; and in the Powers of Criminal Courts (Sentencing) Act 2000 s 78(1), (2) the references to 'detention in a young offender institution' are prospectively repealed by the Criminal Justice and Court Services Act 2000 Sch 7 para 177, Sch 8). At the date at which this volume states the law no day had been appointed for the coming into force of these repeals.

5   For these purposes 'impose imprisonment' means pass a sentence of imprisonment or fix a term of imprisonment for failure to pay any sum of money, or for want of sufficient distress to satisfy any sum of money or for failure to do or abstain from doing anything required to be done or left undone: Powers of Criminal Courts (Sentencing) Act 2000 s 78(6) (prospectively repealed: see note 4). Any reference in the Powers of Criminal Courts (Sentencing) Act 2000 to an 'offence punishable with imprisonment' is to be construed without regard to any prohibition or restriction imposed by or under the Powers of Criminal Courts (Sentencing) Act 2000 or any other Act on the imprisonment of young offenders: s 164(2).

In the event of the magistrates' court deciding against the defendant, it has power to commit him to prison in all cases in which the statute giving occasion for the information or complaint authorises imprisonment, either in the first instance or in default of his doing any act (see e g the Magistrates' Courts Act 1980 s 63(3)) or paying any sum of money which the justices have ordered him to do or pay. As to enforcement of payment orders generally see MAGISTRATES vol 71 (2013) PARA 634 et seq.

6   As to detention in a young offender institution see PARAS 16–17.

7   Powers of Criminal Courts (Sentencing) Act 2000 s 78(1) (prospectively repealed and repealed in part: see note 4). Section 78(1) is without prejudice to the Magistrates' Courts Act 1980 s 133 (consecutive terms of imprisonment and totality: see PARA 555): Powers of Criminal Courts (Sentencing) Act 2000 s 78(3) (as so prospectively repealed).

8   Powers of Criminal Courts (Sentencing) Act 2000 s 78(2) (prospectively repealed and repealed in part: see note 4).

9   For these purposes 'fine' includes a pecuniary penalty but does not include a pecuniary forfeiture or pecuniary compensation: Powers of Criminal Courts (Sentencing) Act 2000 s 78(5) (prospectively repealed: see note 4). As to imprisonment for non-payment of fines see MAGISTRATES vol 71 (2013) PARA 667 et seq.

10   Ie by virtue of the Powers of Criminal Courts (Sentencing) Act 2000 s 78(1): see the text and notes 4–6.

11   Powers of Criminal Courts (Sentencing) Act 2000 s 78(4) (prospectively repealed (see note 4); s 78(4) amended, and s 78(4A) added, by the Tribunals, Courts and Enforcement Act 2007 Sch 13 paras 131, 132). The reference in the Powers of Criminal Courts (Sentencing) Act 2000 s 78(4) to 'want of sufficient goods to satisfy a fine' is a reference to circumstances where there is power to use the procedure in the Tribunals, Courts and Enforcement Act 2007 Sch 12 to recover the fine from a person but it appears, after an attempt has been made to exercise the power, that the person's goods are insufficient to pay the amount outstanding (as defined by Sch 12 para 50(3)): Powers of Criminal Courts (Sentencing) Act 2000 s 78(4A) (as so added).

12   The Magistrates' Courts Act 1980 s 32(1) (see the text and notes 15–16) is prospectively amended by the Criminal Justice Act 2003 s 282. At the date at which this volume states the law no day had been appointed for the coming into force of this amendment.

13   Ie the offences listed in the Magistrates' Courts Act 1980 Sch 1: see CRIMINAL PROCEDURE vol 27 (2015) PARA 179. As to the meaning of 'offence triable either way' see CRIMINAL PROCEDURE vol 27 (2015) PARA 178; MAGISTRATES vol 71 (2013) PARA 511. A magistrates' court does not have power to impose imprisonment for an offence listed in Sch 1 if the Crown Court would not have that power in the case of an adult convicted on indictment: s 32(1)(a).

14   'Fine' includes a pecuniary penalty but does not include a pecuniary forfeiture or pecuniary compensation: Magistrates' Courts Act 1980 s 32(9).

15   Magistrates' Courts Act 1980 s 32(1) (prospectively amended: see note 12). The Magistrates' Courts Act 1980 s 32 extends, subject to modifications, to the Isle of Man and to Guernsey: see the Criminal Justice Act 1982 (Isle of Man) Order 1983, SI 1983/1898; and the Criminal Justice Act 1982 (Guernsey) Order 1992, SI 1992/3202.

16   Magistrates' Courts Act 1980 s 32(1) (prospectively amended: see note 12).

17   See the Legal Aid, Sentencing and Punishment of Offenders Act 2012 s 85(1), (2); and PARA 176. The court's power to impose unlimited fines has been excluded in relation to a number of specified offences involving the evasion of VAT, excise and other duties: see the Legal Aid, Sentencing and Punishment of Offenders Act 2012 (Fines on Summary Conviction) Regulations 2015, SI 2015/664; and PARA 176.

     See also the Magistrates' Courts Act 1980 s 32(2), which provides that for any offence triable either way which is not listed in Sch 1 (see CRIMINAL PROCEDURE vol 27 (2015) PARA 179), being an offence under a 'relevant enactment' (ie an enactment contained in the Criminal Law Act 1977 or in an Act passed before or in the same session as that Act: Magistrates' Courts Act 1980 s 32(9)), the maximum fine which may be imposed on summary conviction is the prescribed sum unless the offence is one for which by virtue of an enactment other than the Magistrates' Courts Act 1980 s 32(2) a larger fine may be imposed on summary conviction. Section 32(2) does not apply on summary conviction of:

     (1)   offences under the Misuse of Drugs Act 1971 s 5(2) (having possession of a controlled drug) (see CRIMINAL LAW vol 26 (2010) PARA 723) where the controlled drug in relation to which the offence was committed was a Class B or Class C drug (Magistrates' Courts Act 1980 s 32(5)(a));

     (2)   offences under the following provisions of the Misuse of Drugs Act 1971, where the controlled drug in relation to which the offence was committed was a Class C drug (Magistrates' Courts Act 1980 s 32(5)(b)):

(a) s 4(2) (production, or being concerned in the production, of a controlled drug) (see CRIMINAL LAW vol 26 (2010) PARA 725);

(b) s 4(3) (supplying or offering a controlled drug or being concerned in the doing of either activity by another) (see CRIMINAL LAW vol 26 (2010) PARA 725);

(c) s 5(3) (having possession of a controlled drug with intent to supply it to another) (see CRIMINAL LAW vol 26 (2010) PARA 725);

(d) s 8 (being the occupier, or concerned in the management, of premises and permitting or suffering certain activities to take place there) (see CRIMINAL LAW vol 26 (2010) PARA 730);

(e) s 12(6) (contravention of direction prohibiting practitioner etc from possessing, supplying etc controlled drugs) (see MEDICAL PRODUCTS AND DRUGS vol 75 (2013) PARA 519); or

(f) s 13(3) (contravention of direction prohibiting practitioner etc from prescribing, supplying etc controlled drugs) (see MEDICAL PRODUCTS AND DRUGS vol 75 (2013) PARA 520).

For these purposes 'controlled drug', 'Class B drug' and 'Class C drug' have the same meanings as in the Misuse of Drugs Act 1971 s 2(1) (see MEDICAL PRODUCTS AND DRUGS vol 75 (2013) PARA 481): Magistrates' Courts Act 1980 s 32(8).

Section 32(3) provides that where by virtue of any relevant enactment a person summarily convicted of an offence triable either way would, apart from s 32, be liable to a maximum fine of one amount in the case of a first conviction and of a different amount in the case of a second or subsequent conviction, s 32(2) applies irrespective of whether the conviction is a first, second or subsequent one. Section 32(4) provides that s 32(2) does not affect so much of any enactment as (in whatever words) makes a person liable on summary conviction to a fine not exceeding a specified amount for each day on which a continuing offence is continued after conviction or the occurrence of any other specified event.

Section 32(6) provides that where, as regards any offence triable either way, there is under any enactment (however framed or worded) a power by subordinate instrument to restrict the amount of the fine which on summary conviction can be imposed in respect of that offence: (1) s 32(2) does not affect or override any restriction imposed in the exercise of that power (s 32(6)(a)); and (2) the amount to which that fine may be restricted in the exercise of that power is any amount less than the maximum fine which could be imposed on summary conviction in respect of the offence apart from any restriction so imposed (s 32(6)(b)).

18 See the Magistrates' Courts Act 1980 s 133; and PARA 555.

19 Ie any Act passed after 31 December 1879 (the commencement of the Summary Jurisdiction Act 1879 (repealed)).

20 Ie a sum not exceeding £50: Magistrates' Courts Act 1980 s 63(3)(a).

21 Magistrates' Courts Act 1980 s 63(3)(a), (5). The prescribed maximum referred to in the text is £5,000: s 63(3)(a) (amended by the Criminal Justice Act 1991 Sch 4 Pt I); although see the text and note 17. Section 63(3) provides that person who is ordered to pay a sum for every day during which he is in default must not by virtue of the Magistrates' Courts Act 1980 s 63 be ordered to pay more than £1,000 for doing or abstaining from doing the same thing contrary to the order. This is without prejudice to the operation of s 63 in relation to any subsequent default: s 63(3). Any sum ordered to be paid under s 63(3) is, for the purposes of the Magistrates' Courts Act 1980, treated as adjudged to be paid by a conviction of a magistrates' court: s 63(4).

22 Magistrates' Courts Act 1980 s 63(3)(b), (5). A person who is committed to custody until he has remedied his default must not by virtue of s 63 be committed for more than two months in all for doing or abstaining from doing the same thing contrary to the order: s 63(3). This is without prejudice to the operation of s 63 in relation to any subsequent default: s 63(3). Appeal against an order or decision under s 63(3) lies to the High Court: see the Administration of Justice Act 1960 s 13(5)(c); and CONTEMPT OF COURT vol 22 (2012) PARA 118.

Where a parent in whose favour there was a custody order failed to comply with an access order, it was held that the parent could be committed to prison for failing to comply with the access order: see *Re K (a minor)* [1977] 2 All ER 737, [1977] 1 WLR 533n, DC. However, before a breach of an order for access could be punished under the Magistrates' Courts Act 1980 s 63(3) it had to be shown that the breach was deliberate: *P v W (Access Order: Breach)* [1984] Fam 32, sub nom *P v W* [1984] 1 All ER 866, DC. Access and custody orders were replaced with residence orders and contact orders by the Children Act 1989: see CHILDREN AND YOUNG PERSONS vol 9 (2012) PARAS 287, 290.

23 See the Contempt of Court Act 1981 s 17(1); and CONTEMPT OF COURT vol 22 (2012) PARA 80.

24 See the Magistrates' Courts Act 1980 s 132; and PARA 28.

25 See the Powers of Criminal Courts (Sentencing) Act 2000 s 8; PARA 1; and CHILDREN AND YOUNG PERSONS vol 10 (2012) PARA 1221.

3. Magistrates' powers of detention for short periods. Where a magistrates' court[1] that has power to commit to prison a person convicted of an offence, or would have that power but for the statutory provisions relating to the restrictions on the power to impose imprisonment for default[2] or the supervision of pending payments[3], it may order him to be detained within the precincts of the courthouse or at any police station until such hour, not later than 8 o'clock in the evening of the day on which the order is made[4], as the court may direct, and, if it does so, must not, where it has power to commit him to prison, exercise that power[5].

A magistrates' court that has power to commit to prison a person in default of payment of a sum adjudged to be paid by a summary conviction, or would have that power but for the statutory provisions relating to the restrictions on the power to impose imprisonment for default[6] or the supervision of pending payments[7] may issue a warrant for his detention in a police station, and, if it does so, must not, where it has power to commit him to prison, exercise that power[8]. A warrant under these provisions authorises the person executing it to arrest the defaulter and take him to a police station[9], and requires the officer in charge of the station to detain him there until 8 o'clock in the morning of the day following that on which he is arrested, or, if he is arrested between midnight and 8 o'clock in the morning, until 8 o'clock in the morning of the day on which he is arrested[10]. The officer may release the defaulter at any time within four hours before 8 o'clock in the morning if the officer thinks it expedient to do so in order to enable him to go to his work or for any other reason appearing to the officer to be sufficient[11].

1 As to the meaning of 'magistrates' court' see MAGISTRATES vol 71 (2013) PARA 470.
2 Ie but for the Magistrates' Courts Act 1980 s 82: see MAGISTRATES vol 71 (2013) PARAS 650, 674.
3 Ie but for the Magistrates' Courts Act 1980 s 88: see MAGISTRATES vol 71 (2013) PARAS 687–689.
4 A court must not make an order under these provisions which will deprive the offender of a reasonable opportunity of returning to his abode on the day of the order: Magistrates' Courts Act 1980 s 135(2). See note 5.
5 Magistrates' Courts Act 1980 s 135(1). Until a day to be appointed ss 135, 136 have effect in relation to a person aged 18 or over but less than 21 as if references to prison were references to detention under the Powers of Criminal Courts (Sentencing) Act 2000 s 108 (detention of persons aged 18 to 20 for default: see PARA 551): Magistrates' Courts Act 1980 ss 135(3), 136(4) (added by the Criminal Justice Act 1982 Sch 14 para 58; amended by the Criminal Justice Act 1991 Sch 8 para 6 and the Powers of Criminal Courts (Sentencing) Act 2000 Sch 9 para 77; prospectively repealed by the Criminal Justice and Court Services Act 2000 Sch 7 Pt II paras 58, 67, 68, Sch 8). At the date at which this volume states the law no day had been appointed for the coming into force of this repeal. As to the determination of a person's age see the Children and Young Persons Act 1933 s 99; and CHILDREN AND YOUNG PERSONS vol 10 (2012) PARA 1206.
　　The age of an offender at the relevant time is deemed to be that which appears to the court after considering any available evidence to be his age at that time: Magistrates' Courts Act 1980 s 150(4); Powers of Criminal Courts (Sentencing) Act 2000 s 164(1); Criminal Justice Act 2003 s 305(2). The time at which a person attains a particular age expressed in years is the commencement of the relevant anniversary of the date of his birth: see the Family Law Reform Act 1969 s 9(1); and CHILDREN AND YOUNG PERSONS vol 9 (2012) PARA 2. Where a court passes sentence on the assumption that the offender is of a particular age, having considered the available evidence, the sentence will not be unlawful if it is subsequently established that he is of a different age: *R v Farndale* (1973) 58 Cr App Rep 336, CA; *R v Brown* (1989) 11 Cr App Rep (S) 263, [1989] Crim LR 750, CA.
6 See note 2.

7   See note 3.
8   Magistrates' Courts Act 1980 s 136(1). See note 5.
9   Magistrates' Courts Act 1980 s 136(2)(a) (substituted by the Access to Justice Act 1999). See note 5.
10 Magistrates' Courts Act 1980 s 136(2)(b). See note 5.
11 Magistrates' Courts Act 1980 s 136(3). See note 5.

4.   Restrictions on magistrates' powers of imprisonment for failure to pay fines. On convicting an offender of an offence a magistrates' court[1] may not, in general, issue a warrant of commitment[2] for default in paying a sum adjudged to be paid unless the offender appears to have sufficient means to pay the sum forthwith, he is unlikely to remain in the United Kingdom for long enough to enable payment of the sum to be enforced by other methods, or the magistrates' court is sentencing him to immediate imprisonment or detention for that or another offence or he is already serving a sentence of custody for life, or a term of imprisonment or detention[3]. The maximum term for which a person may be committed to prison under a warrant of commitment for default in paying a sum adjudged to be paid by a conviction or order must not in general exceed the period applicable to the case[4].

Where a magistrates' court would have power to commit to prison a person under the age of 18[5] for a default consisting in failure to pay or satisfy a sum adjudged to be paid by a conviction, the magistrates' court may make an order requiring the defaulter's parent or guardian to enter into a recognisance to ensure that the defaulter pays so much of that sum as remains unpaid or an order directing so much of that sum as remains unpaid to be paid by the defaulter's parent or guardian instead of by the defaulter[6].

1   As to the meaning of 'magistrates' court' see MAGISTRATES vol 71 (2013) PARA 470.
2   As to warrants of commitment see CRIMINAL PROCEDURE vol 27 (2015) PARA 94; and as to the issue of warrants of commitment see MAGISTRATES vol 71 (2013) PARA 667 et seq. A magistrates' court must not, in advance of the issue of a warrant of commitment, fix a term of imprisonment which is to be served by an offender in the event of a default in paying a sum adjudged to be paid by a conviction, except where it has power to issue a warrant of commitment forthwith, but postpones issuing the warrant: see the Magistrates' Courts Act 1980 s 82(2); and MAGISTRATES vol 71 (2013) PARA 650.
3   See the Magistrates' Courts Act 1980 s 82(1); and MAGISTRATES vol 71 (2013) PARA 650. In any Act, 'United Kingdom' means Great Britain and Northern Ireland (see the Interpretation Act 1978 s 5, Sch 1); and 'Great Britain' means England, Scotland and Wales (see the Union with Scotland Act 1706, preamble art I; Interpretation Act 1978 s 22(1), Sch 2 para 5(a)). Neither the Channel Islands nor the Isle of Man are within the United Kingdom. See further CONSTITUTIONAL AND ADMINISTRATIVE LAW vol 10 (2014) PARA 3.
     In any Act, unless the contrary intention appears, 'England' means, subject to any alteration of the boundaries of local government areas, the areas consisting of the counties established by the Local Government Act 1972 s 1 (see LOCAL GOVERNMENT vol 69 (2009) PARAS 5, 22), and Greater London and the Isles of Scilly: see the Interpretation Act 1978 s 5, Sch 1. As to local government areas in England see LOCAL GOVERNMENT vol 69 (2009) PARA 22 et seq; and as to boundary changes see LOCAL GOVERNMENT vol 69 (2009) PARA 54 et seq. As to Greater London see LONDON GOVERNMENT vol 71 (2013) PARA 14. 'Wales' means the combined areas of the counties created by the Local Government Act 1972 s 20 (as originally enacted) (see LOCAL GOVERNMENT vol 69 (2009) PARAS 5, 37), but subject to any alteration made under s 73 (consequential alteration of boundary following alteration of watercourse: see LOCAL GOVERNMENT vol 69 (2009) PARA 90): see the Interpretation Act 1978 Sch 1 (definition substituted by the Local Government (Wales) Act 1994 s 1(3), Sch 2 para 9).
4   See the Magistrates' Courts Act 1980 s 76(3); and MAGISTRATES vol 71 (2013) PARAS 634, 678.
5   As to the determination of a person's age see the Children and Young Persons Act 1933 s 99; and CHILDREN AND YOUNG PERSONS vol 10 (2012) PARA 1206.
6   See the Magistrates' Courts Act 1980 s 81; and MAGISTRATES vol 71 (2013) PARA 683.

2. CUSTODIAL POWERS

(1) ATTENDANCE CENTRE ORDERS

5.   Attendance centre orders.   Until a day to be appointed[1] where:

(1)   a court[2] would have (or, as from a day to be appointed, has or would have) power[3] to commit a person aged under 21 (or, as from a day to be appointed, 16) years of age[4] to prison in default of payment of any sum of money or for failing to do or abstain from doing anything required to be done or left undone[5]; or

(2)   a court has power to commit a person aged at least 21 but under 25 to prison in default of payment of any sum of money[6],

the court may, if it has been notified by the Secretary of State[7] that an attendance centre[8] is available for the reception of persons of his description, order him to attend at such a centre, to be specified in the order, for such number of hours[9] as may be so specified[10]. Such an order is referred to[11] as an attendance centre order[12]. A court may make an attendance centre order in respect of an offender before a previous attendance centre order made in respect of him has ceased to have effect, and may determine the number of hours to be specified in the order without regard to the number specified in the previous order[13] or to the fact that that order is still in effect[14].

The times at which an offender is required to attend at an attendance centre must be such as, so far as practicable, avoid:

(a)   any conflict with his religious beliefs or with the requirements of any other youth community order to which he may be subject[15]; and

(b)   any interference with the times, if any, at which he normally works or attends school or any other educational establishment[16].

The first such time must be a time at which the centre is available for the attendance of the offender in accordance with the notification of the Secretary of State and must be specified in the order[17]; and the subsequent times must be fixed by the officer in charge of the centre, having regard to the offender's circumstances[18]. An offender may not, however, be required to attend at an attendance centre on more than one occasion on any day, or for more than three hours on any occasion[19].

1   The Powers of Criminal Courts (Sentencing) Act 2000 s 60 (see the text and notes 2–19) is repealed by the Criminal Justice and Immigration Act 2008 s 6(1), Sch 28 Pt 1): however at the date at which this volume states the law only the repeal of the Powers of Criminal Courts (Sentencing) Act 2000 s 60(1)(a) had been brought into force. Section 60(1)(b), (4) are also prospectively amended, and s 60(1)(c) is prospectively repealed, by the Criminal Justice and Court Services Act 2000 Sch 7 paras 160, 173; and by the Criminal Justice Act 2003 Sch 32 para 102(1), (2), Sch 37 Pt 7, but at the date at which this volume states the law no day had been appointed for the coming into force of those amendments and repeals.

2   As to the meaning of 'court' see PARA 1 note 1.

3   Ie but for the Powers of Criminal Courts (Sentencing) Act 2000 s 89 (see PARA 551).

4   As to the determination of a person's age see the Children and Young Persons Act 1933 s 99; and **CHILDREN AND YOUNG PERSONS** vol 10 (2012) PARA 1206. Until a day to be appointed, in the exercise of jurisdiction to commit for contempt of court or any kindred offence the court may not deal with the offender by making an attendance centre order under the Powers of Criminal Courts (Sentencing) Act 2000 s 60 if it appears to the court, after considering any available evidence, that he is under 17 years of age: Contempt of Court Act 1981 s 14(2A) (added by the Criminal Justice Act 1982 Sch 14 para 60; prospectively repealed by the Criminal Justice and Immigration Act 2008 Sch 4 para 25, Sch 28 Pt 1). At the date at which this volume states the law no day had been appointed for the purposes of this repeal.

5   Powers of Criminal Courts (Sentencing) Act 2000 s 60(1)(b) (prospectively amended and repealed: see note 1). Where an offender has been so ordered to attend at an attendance centre in default of payment of any sum of money:

(1)   on payment of the whole sum to any person authorised to receive it, the attendance centre order ceases to have effect (s 60(12)(a) (as so prospectively repealed)); and

(2)   on payment of a part of the sum to any such person, the total number of hours for which the offender is required to attend at the centre is to be reduced proportionately, that is to say by such number of complete hours as bears to the total number of hours proportion most nearly approximating to, without exceeding, the proportion which the part bears to such sum (s 60(12)(b) (as so prospectively repealed)).

6   Powers of Criminal Courts (Sentencing) Act 2000 s 60(1)(c) (prospectively repealed: see note 1).

7   In any enactment, 'Secretary of State' means one of Her Majesty's principal secretaries of state: see the Interpretation Act 1978 s 5, Sch 1; and STATUTES AND LEGISLATIVE PROCESS vol 96 (2012) PARA 1209. As to the office of Secretary of State see CONSTITUTIONAL AND ADMINISTRATIVE LAW vol 20 (2014) PARA 153.

8   As to the meaning of 'attendance centre' and the provision of attendance centres see PRISONS AND PRISONERS vol 85 (2012) PARA 515. An attendance centre order may not be made unless the court is satisfied that the attendance centre to be specified in it is reasonably accessible to the person concerned, having regard to his age, the means of access available to him and any other circumstances: Powers of Criminal Courts (Sentencing) Act 2000 s 60(6) (prospectively repealed: see note 1).

9   The aggregate number of hours for which an attendance centre order may require an offender to attend at an attendance centre may not be less than 12 except where: (1) he is under 14 years of age (Powers of Criminal Courts (Sentencing) Act 2000 s 60(3)(a) (prospectively repealed: see note 1)); and (2) the court is of the opinion that 12 hours would be excessive, having regard to his age or any other circumstances (s 60(3)(b) (as so prospectively repealed)). Until a day to be appointed the aggregate number of hours may not exceed 12 except where the court is of the opinion, having regard to all the circumstances, that 12 hours would be inadequate; and in that case may not exceed 24 hours where the offender is under 16 years of age (s 60(4)(a) (as so prospectively amended and prospectively repealed)) or 36 hours where the offender is aged 16 or over but under 21 or (where head (2) in the text applies) under 25 (s 60(4)(b) (as so prospectively amended and prospectively repealed)). As from that day it is instead provided that the aggregate number of hours may not exceed 12 except where the court is of the opinion, having regard to all the circumstances, that 12 hours would be inadequate; and in that case the aggregate number of hours may not exceed 24: s 60(4) (as so prospectively amended and prospectively repealed).

10   Powers of Criminal Courts (Sentencing) Act 2000 s 60(1) (prospectively repealed: see note 1). Where a court makes an attendance centre order, the designated officer of the court must deliver or send a copy of the order to the officer in charge of the attendance centre specified in it (s 60(11)(a) (s 60(11) amended by SI 2001/618; SI 2005/886; and as so prospectively repealed)), and must also deliver a copy to the offender or send a copy by registered post or the recorded delivery service addressed to the offender's last or usual place of abode (Powers of Criminal Courts (Sentencing) Act 2000 s 60(11)(b) (as so amended and prospectively repealed)).

11   Ie in the Powers of Criminal Courts (Sentencing) Act 2000.

12   Powers of Criminal Courts (Sentencing) Act 2000 s 60(2) (prospectively repealed: see note 1).

13   Powers of Criminal Courts (Sentencing) Act 2000 s 60(5)(a) (prospectively repealed: see note 1).

14   Powers of Criminal Courts (Sentencing) Act 2000 s 60(5)(b) (prospectively repealed: see note 1).

15   Powers of Criminal Courts (Sentencing) Act 2000 s 60(7)(a) (amended by the Criminal Justice Act 2003 Sch 32 para 102(1), (4); and prospectively repealed (see note 1)).

16   Powers of Criminal Courts (Sentencing) Act 2000 s 60(7)(b) (prospectively repealed: see note 1).

17   Powers of Criminal Courts (Sentencing) Act 2000 s 60(8) (prospectively repealed: see note 1).

18   Powers of Criminal Courts (Sentencing) Act 2000 s 60(9) (prospectively repealed: see note 1).

19   Powers of Criminal Courts (Sentencing) Act 2000 s 60(10) (prospectively repealed: see note 1).

6.   Breach of attendance centre orders. Until a day to be appointed[1] where an attendance centre order is in force[2] and it appears on information to a justice that the offender[3]:

(1)   has failed to attend in accordance with the order[4]; or

(2)   while attending, has committed a breach of the rules[5] which cannot be adequately dealt with under those rules[6],

the justice may issue a summons requiring the offender to appear at the place and time specified in the summons or, if the information is in writing and on oath, may issue a warrant for the offender's arrest[7].

If it is proved to the satisfaction of the magistrates' court before which an offender appears or is brought that he has failed without reasonable excuse to attend in accordance with the order or has committed a breach of the rules, that court:

(a)   may impose on him a fine[8];

(b)   if the attendance centre order was made by a magistrates' court[9], may deal with him, for the offence in respect of which the order was made, in any way in which he could have been dealt with for that offence by the court which made the order if the order had not been made[10]; and

(c)   if the order was made by the Crown Court, may commit him in custody or release him on bail until he can be brought or appear before the Crown Court[11].

1   As from a day to be appointed the Powers of Criminal Courts (Sentencing) Act 2000 Sch 5 (see the text and notes 2–11; and PARA 7) is repealed by the Criminal Justice and Immigration Act 2008 s 6(1), Sch 28 Pt 1. At the date at which this volume states the law no such day had been appointed.

2   As to the meaning of 'attendance centre' and the provision of attendance centres see PRISONS AND PRISONERS vol 85 (2012) PARA 515. As to the making etc of attendance centre orders see PARA 5.

3   References in the Powers of Criminal Courts (Sentencing) Act 2000 Sch 5 to an 'offender' include a person who has been ordered to attend an attendance centre for such a default or failure as is mentioned in s 60(1)(b) or s 60(1)(c) (see PARA 5): Sch 5 para 7(1) (prospectively repealed: see note 1).

4   Powers of Criminal Courts (Sentencing) Act 2000 Sch 5 para 1(1)(a) (Sch 5 para 1(1) amended by the Domestic Violence, Crime and Victims Act 2004 Sch 5 para 6; prospectively repealed (see note 1)).

5   Ie rules made under the Criminal Justice Act 2003 s 222(1)(d) or (e) (relating to the provision and carrying on of attendance centres, and to the attendance of persons subject to activity requirements or attendance centre requirements at places at which they are required to attend, including hours of attendance, reckoning days of attendance and the keeping of attendance records: see PARA 137).

6   Powers of Criminal Courts (Sentencing) Act 2000 Sch 5 para 1(1)(b) (Sch 5 paras 1(1)(b), 2(5)(b), 3(3)(b) amended by the Criminal Justice Act 2003 Sch 32 paras 90, 126; prospectively repealed (see note 1)).

7   Powers of Criminal Courts (Sentencing) Act 2000 Sch 5 para 1(1) (as amended and prospectively repealed: see notes 1, 4, 6). Any summons or warrant so issued must direct the offender to appear or be brought:

   (1)   before a magistrates' court acting in the local justice area in which the offender resides (Sch 5 para 1(2)(a) (Sch 5 para 1(2) substituted by the Domestic Violence, Crime and Victims Act 2004 Sch 5 para 6; and amended by SI 2005/886; as so prospectively repealed)); or

   (2)   if it is not known where the offender resides, before a magistrates' court acting in the local justice area in which is situated the attendance centre which the offender is required to attend by the order or by virtue of an order under the Powers of Criminal Courts (Sentencing) Act 2000 Sch 5 para 5(1)(b) (see PARA 7) (Sch 5 para 1(2)(b) (as so substituted, amended and prospectively repealed)).

   In proceedings before the Crown Court for failure to attend an attendance centre or a breach of the rules, any question whether there has been a failure to attend or a breach of the rules is to be determined by the court and not by the verdict of the jury: Sch 5 para 3(4) (as so prospectively repealed).

8   Powers of Criminal Courts (Sentencing) Act 2000 Sch 5 para 2(1)(a) (prospectively repealed: see note 1). The fine may not exceed £1,000: Sch 5 para 2(1)(a) (as so prospectively repealed). Any exercise by a court of this power is without prejudice to the continuation of the attendance centre order: Sch 5 para 2(2) (as so prospectively repealed). Such a fine is deemed, for the purpose of any enactment, to be a sum adjudged to be paid by a conviction: Sch 5 para 2(3) (as

so prospectively repealed). The court may order that a fine imposed under these provisions be paid by the offender's parent or guardian: see s 137; and CHILDREN AND YOUNG PERSONS vol 10 (2012) PARAS 1249, 1250.

9   Where an attendance centre order has been made on appeal, for these purposes it is deemed:
     (1)   if it was made on appeal brought from a magistrates' court, to have been made by that magistrates' court (Powers of Criminal Courts (Sentencing) Act 2000 Sch 5 para 6(1)(a) (prospectively repealed: see note 1)); and
     (2)   if it was made on an appeal brought from the Crown Court or from the criminal division of the Court of Appeal, to have been made by the Crown Court (Sch 5 para 6(1)(b) (as so prospectively repealed)).

10   Powers of Criminal Courts (Sentencing) Act 2000 Sch 5 para 2(1)(b) (prospectively repealed: see note 1). Where a person has been ordered to attend an attendance centre for such a default or failure as is mentioned in s 60(1)(b) or s 60(1)(c) (see PARA 5), Sch 5 para 2(1)(b) instead provides that the court may deal with the offender in any way in which he could have been dealt with by the court which made the order if the order had not been made: Sch 5 para 7(2)(a) (as so prospectively repealed). In relation to an attendance centre order made on appeal (see note 9), Sch 5 para 2(1)(b) instead provides that the court may deal with the offender, for the offence in respect of which the order was made, in any way in which he could have been dealt with for that offence by the court which made the order: Sch 5 para 6(2) (as so prospectively repealed).

Where a magistrates' court deals with an offender under Sch 5 para 2(1)(b) it must revoke the attendance centre order if it is still in force: Sch 5 para 2(4) (as so prospectively repealed). In dealing with an offender under Sch 5 para 2(1)(b) a magistrates' court:
     (1)   must take into account the extent to which the offender has complied with the requirements of the attendance centre order (Sch 5 para 2(5)(a) (as so prospectively repealed)); and
     (2)   in the case of an offender who has wilfully and persistently failed to comply with those requirements, may impose a custodial sentence notwithstanding anything in the Criminal Justice Act 2003 s 152(2) (see PARA 536) (Powers of Criminal Courts (Sentencing) Act 2000 Sch 5 para 2(5)(b) (as amended (see note 6); as so prospectively repealed)).

Head (2) above does not apply where a person has been ordered to attend an attendance centre for such a default or failure as is mentioned in s 60(1)(b) or s 60(1)(c) (see PARA 5): Sch 5 para 7(2)(b) (as so prospectively repealed). Procedural provision in connection with failure to comply is made by the Criminal Procedure Rules 2015, SI 2015/1490, rr 32.1–32.4.

A person sentenced under the Powers of Criminal Courts (Sentencing) Act 2000 Sch 5 para 2(1)(b) for an offence may appeal to the Crown Court against sentence: Sch 5 para 2(6) (as so prospectively repealed).

11   Powers of Criminal Courts (Sentencing) Act 2000 Sch 5 para 2(1)(c) (prospectively repealed: see note 1). A magistrates' court which deals with an offender's case under Sch 5 para 2(1)(c) must send to the Crown Court a certificate signed by a justice of the peace giving particulars of the offender's failure to attend or, as the case may be, the breach of the rules which he has committed (Sch 5 para 2(7)(a) (as so prospectively repealed)), together with such other particulars of the case as may be desirable (Sch 5 para 2(7)(b) (as so prospectively repealed)); and a certificate purporting to be so signed is admissible as evidence of the failure or the breach before the Crown Court (Sch 5 para 2(7) (as so prospectively repealed)).

Where, by virtue of Sch 7 para 2(1)(c) the offender is brought or appears before the Crown Court and it is proved to the satisfaction of the court that he has failed without reasonable excuse to attend in accordance with the order (Sch 5 para 3(1)(a) (as so prospectively repealed)) or has committed a breach of the rules (Sch 5 para 3(1)(b) (as so prospectively repealed)), that court may deal with him, for the offence in respect of which the order was made, in any manner in which it could have dealt with him for that offence if it had not made the order (Sch 5 para 3(1) (as so prospectively repealed)). Where a person has been ordered to attend an attendance centre for such a default or failure as is mentioned in s 60(1)(b) or s 60(1)(c), Sch 5 para 3(1) instead provides that the court may deal with the offender in any way in which he could have been dealt with by the court which made the order if the order had not been made: Sch 5 para 7(2)(a) (as so prospectively repealed). In dealing with an offender under Sch 5 para 3(1) the Crown Court must take into account the extent to which the offender has complied with the requirements of the attendance centre order (Sch 5 para 3(3)(a) (as so prospectively repealed)) and in the case of an offender who has wilfully and persistently failed to comply with those requirements, may impose a custodial sentence notwithstanding anything in the Criminal Justice Act 2003 s 152(2): Powers of Criminal Courts (Sentencing) Act 2000 Sch 5 para 3(3)(b) (as amended (see note 6); as so prospectively repealed)). Schedule 5 para 3(3)(b) does not apply where a person has been ordered to attend an attendance centre for such a default or failure as is mentioned in s 60(1)(b) or s 60(1)(c): Sch 5 para 7(2)(b) (as so prospectively repealed). Where the court deals with the offender under Sch 5 para 3(1) it must revoke the attendance centre order if it is still in force: Sch 5 para 3(2) (as so prospectively repealed).

7. Amendment and revocation of attendance centre orders. Until a day to be appointed[1] on the application of the offender[2] or of the officer in charge of the relevant attendance centre[3], an attendance centre order which is in force may be amended by an appropriate magistrates' court[4]. The power so to vary an attendance centre order is a power by order:

(1)   to vary the day or hour specified in the order for the offender's first attendance at the relevant attendance centre[5]; or

(2)   to substitute for the relevant attendance centre an attendance centre which the court is satisfied is reasonably accessible to the offender, having regard to his age, the means of access available to him and any other circumstances[6].

An attendance centre order which is in force may be revoked by an appropriate court[7] on an application made by the offender or the officer in charge of the relevant attendance centre[8]. The power so to revoke an attendance centre order is a power conferred:

(a)   on a magistrates' court to revoke an attendance centre order made by such a court[9]; or

(b)   on the Crown Court to revoke an attendance centre order made by the Crown Court[10],

and includes power to deal with the offender, for the offence in respect of which the order was made, in any way in which he could have been dealt with for that offence by the court which made the order if the order had not been made[11].

1   As from a day to be appointed the Powers of Criminal Courts (Sentencing) Act 2000 Sch 5 (see the text and notes 2–11; and PARA 6) is repealed by the Criminal Justice and Immigration Act 2008 s 6(1), Sch 28 Pt 1. At the date at which this volume states the law no such day had been appointed.

2   As to the meaning of 'offender' see PARA 6 note 3.

3   As to the meaning of 'attendance centre' and the provision of attendance centres see PRISONS AND PRISONERS vol 85 (2012) PARA 515. As to the making etc of attendance centre orders see PARA 5. For these purposes, 'relevant attendance centre', in relation to an attendance centre order, means the attendance centre specified in the order or substituted for the attendance centre so specified by an order made by virtue of the Powers of Criminal Courts (Sentencing) Act 2000 Sch 5 para 5(1)(b) (see the text and note 6): Sch 5 paras 4(6), 5(4) (prospectively repealed: see note 1).

4   Powers of Criminal Courts (Sentencing) Act 2000 Sch 5 para 5(1) (prospectively repealed: see note 1). 'Appropriate magistrates' court' means a magistrates' court acting in the local justice area in which the relevant attendance centre is situated (Sch 5 para 5(2)(a) (Sch 5 paras 4(2)(b)(i), (7)(a), 5(2)(a), (3) amended by SI 2005/886; as so prospectively repealed)) or (except where the attendance centre order was made by the Crown Court) the magistrates' court which made the order (Powers of Criminal Courts (Sentencing) Act 2000 Sch 5 para 5(2)(b) (as so prospectively repealed)). Where a magistrates' court dealing with an offender under Sch 5 para 2(1)(a) (see PARA 6) would not otherwise have the power to amend the order under Sch 5 para 5(1)(b) (see head (2) in the text), Sch 5 para 5(1)(b) has effect as if references to an appropriate magistrates' court were references to the court dealing with the offender: Sch 5 para 2(5A) (added by the Domestic Violence, Crime and Victims Act 2004 Sch 5 para 6(1), (4); as so prospectively repealed).

      Procedural provision in connection with the revocation or amendment of an attendance centre order is made by the Criminal Procedure Rules 2015, SI 2015/1490, rr 32.1–32.4.

5   Powers of Criminal Courts (Sentencing) Act 2000 Sch 5 para 5(1)(a) (prospectively repealed: see note 1). It is the duty of the designated officer of the court which makes an order under Sch 5 para 5(1) to deliver a copy to the offender or send a copy by registered post or the recorded delivery service addressed to the offender's last or usual place of abode (Sch 5 para 5(3)(a) (as

amended and prospectively repealed: see notes 1, 4)) and to deliver or send a copy: (1) if the order is made by virtue of head (1) in the text, to the officer in charge of the relevant attendance centre (Sch 5 para 5(3)(b)(i) (as so amended and prospectively repealed)); and (2) if it is made by virtue of head (2) in the text, to the officer in charge of the attendance centre which the order as amended will require the offender to attend (Sch 5 para 5(3)(b)(ii) (as so amended and prospectively repealed)).

6   Powers of Criminal Courts (Sentencing) Act 2000 Sch 5 para 5(1)(b) (prospectively repealed: see note 1). As to the determination of a person's age see the Children and Young Persons Act 1933 s 99; and CHILDREN AND YOUNG PERSONS vol 10 (2012) PARA 1206. See note 5.

7   Ie: (1) where the court which made the order was the Crown Court and there is included in the order a direction that the power to revoke the order is reserved to that court, the Crown Court (Powers of Criminal Courts (Sentencing) Act 2000 Sch 5 para 4(2)(a) (prospectively repealed: see note 1)); and (2) in any other case, either of the following: (a) a magistrates' court acting in the local justice area in which the relevant attendance centre is situated (Sch 5 para 4(2)(b)(i) (as amended (see note 4); as so prospectively repealed)); (b) the court which made the order (Sch 5 para 4(2)(b)(ii) (as so prospectively repealed)).

8   Powers of Criminal Courts (Sentencing) Act 2000 Sch 5 para 4(1) (prospectively repealed: see note 1).

9   Powers of Criminal Courts (Sentencing) Act 2000 Sch 5 para 4(3)(a) (prospectively repealed: see note 1).

10 Powers of Criminal Courts (Sentencing) Act 2000 Sch 5 para 4(3)(b) (prospectively repealed: see note 1).

11 Powers of Criminal Courts (Sentencing) Act 2000 Sch 5 para 4(3) (prospectively repealed: see note 1). Where a person has been ordered to attend an attendance centre for such a default or failure as is mentioned in s 60(1)(b) or s 60(1)(c) (see PARA 5), Sch 5 para 4(3) instead provides that the court may deal with the offender in any way in which he could have been dealt with by the court which made the order if the order had not been made: Sch 5 para 7(2)(a) (as so prospectively repealed). In relation to an attendance centre order made on appeal, Sch 5 para 4(3) instead provides that the court's power thereunder includes power to deal with the offender, for the offence in respect of which the order was made, in any way in which he could have been dealt with for that offence by the court which made the order: Sch 5 para 6(2) (as so prospectively repealed). As to the court by which an attendance centre order made on appeal is deemed to have been made for these purposes see Sch 5 para 6(1); and PARA 6 note 9.

A person sentenced by a magistrates' court under Sch 5 para 4(3) for an offence may appeal to the Crown Court against sentence: Sch 5 para 4(4) (as so prospectively repealed). The proper officer of a court which makes an order revoking an attendance centre order must:

(1)   deliver a copy of the revoking order to the offender or send a copy by registered post or the recorded delivery service addressed to the offender's last or usual place of abode (Sch 5 para 4(5)(a) (as so prospectively repealed)); and

(2)   deliver or send a copy to the officer in charge of the relevant attendance centre (Sch 5 para 4(5)(b) (as so prospectively repealed)).

'Proper officer' means: (a) in relation to a magistrates' court, the designated officer for that court (Sch 5 para 4(7)(a) (as amended (see note 4); as so prospectively repealed)); and (b) in relation to the Crown Court, the appropriate officer (Sch 5 para 4(7)(b) (as so prospectively repealed)).

(2) DETENTION OF YOUNG PERSONS

(i) Serious Offenders

8.   Detention of serious offenders aged under 18.   Where a person aged under 18[1] is convicted on indictment of:

(1)   an offence punishable in the case of a person aged 21[2] or over with imprisonment for 14 years or more, not being an offence the sentence for which is fixed by law[3];

(2)   an offence[4] of sexual assault[5];

(3)   a child sex offence[6] committed by a child or young person[7];

(4)   an offence[8] of sexual activity with a child family member[9];

(5)   an offence[10] of inciting a child family member to engage in sexual activity[11]; or

(6)   a specified firearms offence in specified circumstances[12],

and the court is of the opinion that neither a youth rehabilitation order[13] nor a detention and training order[14] is suitable[15], the court may sentence the offender to be detained for such period, not exceeding the maximum term of imprisonment with which the offence is punishable in the case of a person aged 21[16] or over, as may be specified in the sentence[17].

A person sentenced to be so detained is liable to be detained under such conditions as the Secretary of State[18] may direct[19], or as the Secretary of State may arrange with any person[20].

1   As to the determination of a person's age see the Children and Young Persons Act 1933 s 99; and CHILDREN AND YOUNG PERSONS vol 10 (2012) PARA 1206. The relevant age is the offender's age at the time of conviction, rather than his age at the time of sentence: *R v Robinson* [1993] 2 All ER 1, 96 Cr App Rep 418, CA.
2   As from a day to be appointed this age limit is reduced to 18: see the Powers of Criminal Courts (Sentencing) Act 2000 s 91(1)(a), (3) (prospectively amended by the Criminal Justice and Court Services Act 2000 Sch 7 paras 160, 181). At the date at which this volume states the law no such day had been appointed.
3   Powers of Criminal Courts (Sentencing) Act 2000 s 91(1)(a) (prospectively amended: see note 2).
4   Ie an offence under the Sexual Offences Act 2003 s 3 (see CRIMINAL LAW vol 25 (2010) PARA 182).
5   Powers of Criminal Courts (Sentencing) Act 2000 s 91(1)(b) (s 91(1)(b), (c) substituted, and s 91(1)(d), (e) added, by the Sexual Offences Act 2003 Sch 6 para 43(1), (2)).
6   Ie an offence under the Sexual Offences Act 2003 s 13 (see CRIMINAL LAW vol 25 (2010) PARA 190).
7   Powers of Criminal Courts (Sentencing) Act 2000 s 91(1)(c) (as substituted: see note 5).
8   Ie an offence under the Sexual Offences Act 2003 s 25 (see CRIMINAL LAW vol 25 (2010) PARAS 204, 206).
9   Powers of Criminal Courts (Sentencing) Act 2000 s 91(1)(d) (as added: see note 5).
10 Ie an offence under the Sexual Offences Act 2003 s 26 (see CRIMINAL LAW vol 25 (2010) PARAS 204, 206).
11 Powers of Criminal Courts (Sentencing) Act 2000 s 91(1)(e) (as added: see note 5).
12 Powers of Criminal Courts (Sentencing) Act 2000 s 91(1A)–(1C) (s 91(1A), (5) added, and s 91(3), (4) amended, by the Criminal Justice Act 2003 Sch 32 paras 90, 110; Powers of Criminal Courts (Sentencing) Act 2000 s 91(1A)(b), (5) amended, and s 91(1B), (1C) added, by the Violent Crime Reduction Act 2006 Sch 1 para 7). The specified firearms offences and circumstances are:
    (1)   any offence under the Firearms Act 1968 s 5(1)(a), (ab), (aba), (ac) (ad), (ae), (af) or (c) or s 5(1A)(a) (see CRIMINAL LAW vol 25 (2010) PARA 613) committed after 22 January 2004 at a time (for the purposes of s 51A(3)) when the person was aged 16 or over and where the court is of the opinion mentioned in s 51A(2) (exceptional circumstances which justify its not imposing required custodial sentence: see CRIMINAL LAW vol 25 (2010) PARA 613) (Powers of Criminal Courts (Sentencing) Act 2000 s 91(1A) (as so added and amended));
    (2)   any offence under the Firearms Act 1968 that is listed in s 51A(1A)(b), (e) or (f) (minimum sentences for certain offences: see CRIMINAL LAW vol 25 (2010) PARAS 628–631, 633–635) committed in respect of a firearm or ammunition specified in s 5(1)(a), (ab), (aba), (ac), (ad), (ae), (af) or (c) or s 5(1A)(a) after 6 April 2007 at a time (for the purposes of the Firearms Act 1968 51A(3): see CRIMINAL LAW vol 25 (2010) PARAS 614, 616, 628) when the person was aged 16 or over and where the court is of the opinion mentioned in s 51A(2) (Powers of Criminal Courts (Sentencing) Act 2000 s 91(1B) (as so added)); and
    (3)   any offence under the Violent Crime Reduction Act 2006 s 28 (using someone to mind a weapon: see CRIMINAL LAW vol 26 (2010) PARA 656) where s 29(3) (minimum sentences in certain cases: see CRIMINAL LAW vol 26 (2010) PARA 656) applies and the court is of the opinion mentioned in s 29(6) (exceptional circumstances which justify not imposing the minimum sentence: see CRIMINAL LAW vol 26 (2010) PARA 656) (Powers of Criminal Courts (Sentencing) Act 2000 s 91(1C) (as so added)).

22 January 2004 is the date on which the Firearms Act 1968 s 51A was brought into force by the Criminal Justice Act 2003 (Commencement No 2 and Saving Provisions) Order 2004, SI 2004/81. 6 April 2007 is the date on which the Violent Crime Reduction Act 2006 s 30 was brought into force by the Violent Crime Reduction Act 2006 (Commencement No 2) Order 2007, SI 2007/858.

Where the Firearms Act 1968 s 51A(2) or the Violent Crime Reduction Act 2006 s 29(6) requires the imposition of a sentence of detention under the Powers of Criminal Courts (Sentencing) Act 2000 s 91 for a term of at least the term provided for in those provisions the court must sentence the offender to be detained for such period, of at least the term so provided for but not exceeding the maximum term of imprisonment with which the offence is punishable in the case of a person aged 18 or over, as may be specified in the sentence: Powers of Criminal Courts (Sentencing) Act 2000 s 91(5) (as so added and amended).

13 As to youth rehabilitation orders see PARAS 73–99.

14 As to detention and training orders see PARAS 9–15. In exceptional circumstances the court may pass a sentence of less than two years under the Powers of Criminal Courts (Sentencing) Act 2000 s 91 where a detention and training order would not be appropriate: see *R (on the application of D) v Manchester City Youth Court* [2001] EWHC 860 (Admin), [2002] 1 Cr App Rep (S) 573; and in connection with detention and training orders and the Powers of Criminal Courts (Sentencing) Act 2000 s 91 see also *R (on the application of W) v Thetford Youth Justices* [2002] EWHC 1252 (Admin), [2003] 1 Cr App Rep (S) 323; *R (on the application of W) v Southampton Youth Court* [2002] EWHC 1640 (Admin), [2003] 1 Cr App Rep (S) 455; *R v Thomas* [2004] EWCA Crim 2199, sub nom *R v Jahmarl* [2005] 1 Cr App Rep (S) 534.

15 'Suitable' refers to the type of sentence, not merely its length: *R v B (a minor) (sentence: jurisdiction)* [1999] 1 WLR 61, sub nom *R v Brown* [1998] Crim LR 588, CA.

16 As from a day to be appointed this age limit is reduced to 18: see note 2.

17 Powers of Criminal Courts (Sentencing) Act 2000 s 91(3) (as amended (see note 12); further amended by the Criminal Justice and Immigration Act 2008 Sch 4 paras 51, 56). A sentence of detention under the Powers of Criminal Courts (Sentencing) Act 2000 s 91 is a 'custodial sentence' for the purposes of the Powers of Criminal Courts (Sentencing) Act 2000 (see s 76; and PARA 9 note 15) and this power is therefore subject, in particular, to the Criminal Justice Act 2003 ss 152, 153 (see PARAS 29, 536): Powers of Criminal Courts (Sentencing) Act 2000 s 91(4) (as so amended). Although it is not necessary, in order to invoke the provisions of the Powers of Criminal Courts (Sentencing) Act 2000 s 91, for a crime to be one of exceptional gravity (see *R v Fairhurst* [1987] 1 All ER 46, 84 Cr App Rep 19, [1987] Crim LR 60, CA), the power to make an order for detention is a 'long stop reserved for very serious offences': *R (on the application of the Crown Prosecution Service) v Redbridge Youth Court* [2005] EWHC 1390 (Admin), 169 JP 393, DC. In assessing the seriousness of an offence the court may take account of associated offences: see *R v AM* [1998] 2 Cr App Rep (S) 128; *R v Mills* [1998] 2 Cr App Rep (S) 128, [1998] Crim LR 220, CA.

As to the principles to be applied in considering whether a youth court should commit a juvenile for trial with a view to a sentence of detention under the Powers of Criminal Courts (Sentencing) Act 2000 s 91 see *R (on the application of H) v Southampton Youth Court* [2004] EWHC 2912 (Admin), 169 JP 37, [2005] Crim LR 395, [2004] All ER (D) 38 (Dec). As to the court's obligation to have regard to a young offender's welfare see *R v Secretary of State for the Home Department, ex p Furber* [1998] 1 All ER 23, [1998] 1 Cr App Rep (S) 208, DC (approved in *R v M* [1998] 2 All ER 939, [1999] 1 Cr App Rep 9, [1998] Crim LR 512, CA).

A judge imposing a sentence under these provisions must have regard to the period during which the offender's activities might be a source of danger to the public: *R v Storey* [1973] 3 All ER 562, 57 Cr App Rep 840, CA. In a proper case, a sentence of general deterrence may be passed: *R v Ford* (1976) 62 Cr App Rep 303, [1976] Crim LR 391, CA; *R v Nightingale* (1984) 6 Cr App Rep (S) 65, [1984] Crim LR 373, CA; but this is subject to the Criminal Justice Act 2003 s 153(2) (see PARA 29). For guidelines on the use of this provision see *R v AM* [1998] 1 WLR 363, [1998] 2 Cr App Rep 57, CA.

The powers under the Powers of Criminal Courts (Sentencing) Act 2000 s 91 are limited to those convicted in the Crown Court; they may not be exercised by a youth court, nor by the Crown Court on a committal for sentence from a youth court: *R v McKenna* (1985) 7 Cr App Rep (S) 348, [1986] Crim LR 195, CA.

18 As to the Secretary of State see PARA 5 note 7.

19 Powers of Criminal Courts (Sentencing) Act 2000 s 92(1)(a). A person detained pursuant to the directions or arrangements made by the Secretary of State under s 92 is deemed to be in legal custody: s 92(2).

20 Powers of Criminal Courts (Sentencing) Act 2000 s 92(1)(b). See note 19.

(ii) Detention and Training Orders

9. Power to make orders. Where a child or young person[1] is convicted of an offence which is punishable with imprisonment in the case of a person aged 21[2] or over[3] the court[4] may make a detention and training order[5], which is an order that the offender in respect of whom it is made is to be subject, for the term specified in the order, to a period of detention and training followed by a period of supervision[6]. There are two circumstances in which the court may make such an order:

(1) where it is of the opinion that that the offence, or the combination of the offence and one or more offences associated[7] with it, was so serious[8] that neither a fine[9] alone nor a community sentence[10] can be justified for the offence[11]; or

(2) (except where the court is required to make a custodial order in the case of an offence involving threats with knives or other offensive weapons[12]) where it is of the opinion that the offender has failed either to express his willingness to comply with a requirement which is proposed by the court to be included in a community order and which requires an expression of such willingness or to comply with a pre-sentence drug testing order[13].

However, a court may not make a detention and training order:

(a) in the case of an offender under the age of 15 at the time of the conviction, unless it is of the opinion that he is a persistent offender[14];

(b) in the case of an offender under the age of 12 at that time unless:

(i) it is of the opinion that only a custodial sentence[15] will be adequate to protect the public from further offending by him[16]; and

(ii) the offence was committed on or after such date as the Secretary of State[17] may by order[18] appoint[19].

1   Ie any person under 18: Powers of Criminal Courts (Sentencing) Act 2000 s 100(1)(a). As to the determination of a person's age see the Children and Young Persons Act 1933 s 99; and CHILDREN AND YOUNG PERSONS vol 10 (2012) PARA 1206. A detention and training order may be made in relation to an offender who was under 18 when proceedings were begun notwithstanding that he has attained the age of 18 at the time of conviction: *Aldis v DPP* [2002] EWHC 403 (Admin), [2002] 2 Cr App Rep (S) 400, DC (referring to the Children and Young Persons Act 1963 s 29(1) (see CHILDREN AND YOUNG PERSONS vol 10 (2012) PARA 1201)).

2   As from a day to be appointed this age limit is reduced to 18: see the Powers of Criminal Courts (Sentencing) Act 2000 s 100(1)(a) (prospectively amended by the Criminal Justice and Court Services Act 2000 Sch 7 paras 160, 184). At the date at which this volume states the law no such day had been appointed.

3   Powers of Criminal Courts (Sentencing) Act 2000 s 100(1)(a) (prospectively amended: see note 2).

4   As to the meaning of 'court' see PARA 1 note 1.

5   Powers of Criminal Courts (Sentencing) Act 2000 s 100(1) (s 100(1) amended, s 100(1)(b) substituted, by the Criminal Justice Act 2003 Sch 32 paras 90, 111(2)). The power to make a detention and training order is subject to the Powers of Criminal Courts (Sentencing) Act 2000 s 90 (see PARA 38) and s 91 (see PARA 8), and to the Criminal Justice Act 2003 s 226 (see PARA 34) and s 226B (see PARAS 18–20): Powers of Criminal Courts (Sentencing) Act 2000 s 100(1) (as so amended; s 100(1) further amended, s 100(1A) added, by the Legal Aid, Sentencing and Punishment of Offenders Act 2012 Sch 21 paras 7, 13, Sch 26 paras 9, 11). A detention and training order is a 'custodial sentence' for the purposes of the Powers of Criminal Courts (Sentencing) Act 2000 (see s 76; and note 15) and the court must therefore comply with the Criminal Justice Act 2003 ss 152, 153, 158 (see PARAS 536, 29, 578). See also PARA 537.

6   Powers of Criminal Courts (Sentencing) Act 2000 s 100(3). The supervision of children and young persons sentenced to a detention and training order is a 'youth justice service' for the purposes of the Crime and Disorder Act 1998 ss 39–41: see s 38(4)(h); and CHILDREN AND YOUNG PERSONS vol 10 (2012) PARA 1192.

7   An offence is associated with another if the offender is convicted of it in the proceedings in which he is convicted of the other offence, or (although convicted of it in earlier proceedings) is sentenced for it at the same time as he is sentenced for that offence or the offender admits the commission of it in the proceedings in which he is sentenced for the other offence and requests the court to take it into consideration in sentencing him for that offence: Powers of Criminal Courts (Sentencing) Act 2000 s 161(1); Criminal Justice Act 2003 s 305(1). An offence dealt with by a conditional discharge may be an associated offence of another offence for which the offender is subsequently sentenced if the sentencing court imposes a sentence for the former offence on the same occasion: *R v Godfrey* (1993) 14 Cr App Rep (S) 804, [1993] Crim LR 540, CA. An offence for which a suspended sentence has been passed is not an associated offence of another offence committed during the operational period of the suspended sentence: *R v Cawley* (1994) 15 Cr App Rep (S) 25, CA.

8   As to the seriousness of an offence see *R v Howells* [1999] 1 All ER 50, [1999] 1 Cr App Rep 98, CA; and see also *R v Oliver, R v Little* [1993] 2 All ER 9, 96 Cr App Rep 426, CA; *R v Cunningham* [1993] 2 All ER 15, [1993] 1 WLR 183, CA; *R v Cox* [1993] 2 All ER 19, 96 Cr App Rep 452, CA; *R v Baverstock* [1993] 2 All ER 32, 96 Cr App Rep 435, CA; *R v Ollerenshaw* [1999] 1 Cr App Rep (S) 65, [1998] Crim LR 515, CA. As to the principles for determining the seriousness of an offence see PARA 586.

9   See PARA 174.

10   As to the meaning of 'community sentence' see PARA 42.

11   Powers of Criminal Courts (Sentencing) Act 2000 s 100(1)(b) (as substituted: see note 5); Criminal Justice Act 2003 s 152(2).

12   Ie where in the case of an offence the sentence falls to be imposed under either the Prevention of Crime Act 1953 s 1(2B) or s 1A(5) (see CRIMINAL LAW) or the Criminal Justice Act 1988 ss 139(6B), 139A(5B), 139AA(7) (see CRIMINAL LAW): Powers of Criminal Courts (Sentencing) Act 2000 s 100(1A) (as added (see note 5); substituted by the Criminal Justice and Courts Act 2015 Sch 5 para 5).

13   Powers of Criminal Courts (Sentencing) Act 2000 s 100(1)(b) (as amended and substituted: see note 5); Criminal Justice Act 2003 s 152(3).

14   Powers of Criminal Courts (Sentencing) Act 2000 s 100(2)(a). In determining whether an offender under 15 could be considered as a 'persistent offender', account may be taken of offences in respect of which he has been cautioned or given a reprimand or warning (*R v AD* [2001] 1 Cr App Rep (S) 202, CA) or of offences subsequent to the index offence (*R v B* [2001] 1 Cr App Rep (S) 389, CA), and the matter should be looked at according to the 'good sense of the court' (*R v B*). An offender with no previous conviction who is convicted on the same occasion of a number of offences committed within a short period of time may be a persistent offender (*R v S (A)* [2001] 1 Cr App Rep (S) 62, CA); see, however, *R v G* [2008] EWCA Crim 2112, [2008] All ER (D) 39 (Sep); and *R v L* [2012] EWCA Crim 1336, [2013] 1 Cr App Rep (S) 317. It is wrong to impose a detention and training order on a person aged 15, for an offence committed when he was 14, for which he would not have qualified at 14 because he was not a persistent offender: *R v LM* [2002] EWCA Crim 3047, [2003] 2 Cr App Rep (S) 124, [2003] Crim LR 205, CA.

15   In the Powers of Criminal Courts (Sentencing) Act 2000 and the Criminal Justice Act 2003 'custodial sentence' means, by virtue of the Powers of Criminal Courts (Sentencing) Act 2000 s 76(1) (amended by the Criminal Justice Act 2003 Sch 32 paras 90, 108; by the Legal Aid, Sentencing and Punishment of Offenders Act 2012 Sch 21 para 10; prospectively amended by the Criminal Justice and Court Services Act 2000 Sch 7 paras 160, 176, Sch 8) and the Criminal Justice Act 2003 s 305(1):

   (1)   a sentence of imprisonment (see the Powers of Criminal Courts (Sentencing) Act 2000 s 89(1)(a); and PARA 551);
   (2)   a sentence of detention under s 90 (see PARA 38) or s 91 (see PARA 8);
   (3)   a sentence of detention for public protection under the Criminal Justice Act 2003 s 226 (see PARA 34);
   (4)   a sentence of detention under s 226B (see PARAS 18–20) or s 228 (repealed); and
   (5)   a detention and training order under the Powers of Criminal Courts (Sentencing) Act 2000 s 100,
   and until a day to be appointed can also mean:
   (a)   a sentence of custody for life under s 93 or s 94 (see PARAS 36, 37); and

(b)   a sentence of detention in a young offender institution (under s 96 (see PARA 16) or
        otherwise).

At the date at which this volume states the law no such day had been appointed. In these
provisions 'sentence of imprisonment' does not include a committal for contempt of court or
any kindred offence: s 76(2).

16 Powers of Criminal Courts (Sentencing) Act 2000 s 100(2)(b)(i). Where a custodial sentence is
    appropriate but a detention and training order is not available, a sentence under s 91 (see PARA
    8) may be appropriate: see *R (on the application of W) v Thetford Youth Justices* [2002] EWHC
    1252 (Admin), [2003] 1 Cr App Rep (S) 323.
17 As to the Secretary of State see PARA 5 note 7.
18 At the date at which this volume states the law no such order had been made.
19 Powers of Criminal Courts (Sentencing) Act 2000 s 100(2)(b)(ii).

10.   Making the order. The term of a detention and training order[1] made in
respect of an offence (whether by a magistrates' court or otherwise) must[2] be 4,
6, 8, 10, 12, 18 or 24 months[3]. However, the term of a detention and training
order may not exceed the maximum term of imprisonment that the Crown Court
could (in the case of an offender aged 21[4] or over) impose for the offence[5], and
as from a day to be appointed the term may not exceed six months where the
offence is a summary offence[6] and the maximum term of imprisonment that a
court could (in the case of an offender aged 18 or over) impose for the offence is
51 weeks[7].

A court making a detention and training order may order that its term is to
commence on the expiry of the term of any other detention and training order
made by that or any other court[8]. However, a court must not make in respect of
an offender a detention and training order the effect of which would be that he
would be subject to detention and training orders for a term which exceeds 24
months[9], and a court making a detention and training order must not order that
its term is to commence on the expiry of the term of a detention and training
order under which the period of supervision has already begun[10]. Where the term
of the detention and training orders to which an offender would otherwise be
subject exceeds 24 months, the excess must be treated as remitted[11].

Where a detention and training order (the 'new order') is made in respect of
an offender who is subject to a detention and training order under which the
period of supervision has begun (the 'old order'), the old order must be
disregarded in determining:

(1)   for the purposes of the restriction on the accumulation of orders for a
        term exceeding 24 months[12], whether the effect of the new order would
        be that the offender would be subject to detention and training orders
        for a term which exceeds 24 months[13]; and

(2)   for the purposes of the provision relating to the excess of the detention
        and training orders that is treated as remitted where the total term
        exceeds 24 months[14], whether the term of the detention and training
        orders to which the offender would otherwise[15] be subject exceeds 24
        months[16].

In determining the term of a detention and training order for an offence, the
court must take account[17] of any period for which the offender has been
remanded in custody[18] or on bail subject to a qualifying curfew condition and an
electronic monitoring condition[19] in connection with the offence, or any other
offence the charge for which was founded on the same facts or evidence[20].
However, this does not apply where a court proposes to make detention and
training orders in respect of an offender for two or more offences, in which event
in determining the total term of the detention and training orders it proposes to

make in respect of the offender the court must take account of the total period (if any) for which he has been remanded[21] in custody in connection with any of those offences, or any other offence the charge for which was founded on the same facts or evidence[22]. Once a period of remand has been taken account of in relation to a detention and training order made in respect of an offender for any offence or offences, it may not subsequently be taken account of in relation to such an order made in respect of the offender for any other offence or offences[23].

1   As to the making of a detention and training order see PARA 9.
2   Ie subject to the Powers of Criminal Courts (Sentencing) Act 2000 s 101(2) (and, as from a day to be appointed, s 101(2A) (see the text and notes 6–7)).
3   Powers of Criminal Courts (Sentencing) Act 2000 s 101(1) (s 101(1) prospectively amended, s 101(2A) prospectively added, by the Criminal Justice Act 2003 s 298(1)). At the date at which this volume states the law no day had been appointed for the coming into force of these amendments. An offender who has pleaded guilty to any offence and who is liable to a term of detention under the Powers of Criminal Courts (Sentencing) Act 2000 s 91 for that offence may properly have that plea reflected by the imposition of a detention and training order for the maximum term: *R v March* [2002] EWCA Crim 551, [2002] 2 Cr App Rep (S) 448, [2002] Crim LR 509. In connection with the 24-month upper limit see further *R v Fairhurst* [1987] 1 All ER 46, 84 Cr App Rep 19, [1987] Crim LR 60, CA; *R v AM* [1998] 2 Cr App Rep (S) 128.
4   As to the determination of a person's age see the Children and Young Persons Act 1933 s 99; and CHILDREN AND YOUNG PERSONS vol 10 (2012) PARA 1206. As from a day to be appointed this age limit is reduced to 18: see the Powers of Criminal Courts (Sentencing) Act 2000 s 101(2) (prospectively amended by the Criminal Justice and Court Services Act 2000 Sch 7 paras 160, 185). At the date at which this volume states the law no such day had been appointed.
5   Powers of Criminal Courts (Sentencing) Act 2000 s 101(2) (prospectively amended: see note 4).
6   Powers of Criminal Courts (Sentencing) Act 2000 s 101(2A)(a) (prospectively added: see note 3).
7   Powers of Criminal Courts (Sentencing) Act 2000 s 101(2A)(b) (prospectively added: see note 3).
8   Powers of Criminal Courts (Sentencing) Act 2000 s 101(3). A court may impose a consecutive detention and training order notwithstanding that the aggregate term is not a period specified in s 101(1) (see the text and notes 1–3): *R v Norris* [2001] 1 Cr App Rep (S) 401, [2001] Crim LR 48, CA. A sentence imposed, or other order made, by the Crown Court when dealing with an offender takes effect from the beginning of the day on which it is imposed, unless the court otherwise directs: see the Powers of Criminal Courts (Sentencing) Act 2000 s 154(1); and PARA 27.
    Where a court makes a detention and training order in the case of an offender who is subject to a period of detention under s 104(3)(a) (see PARA 13), the detention and training order takes effect at the beginning of the day on which it is made (ss 104(5A), 104B(1)(a) (ss 104(5A), 104B added by the Legal Aid, Sentencing and Punishment of Offenders Act 2012 s 80(1), (5), (7)) or if the court so orders, at the time when the period of detention under the Powers of Criminal Courts (Sentencing) Act 2000 s 104(3)(a) ends (s 104B(1)(b) (as so added)). Where a court orders an offender who is subject to a detention and training order to be subject to a period of detention under s 104(3)(a) for a failure to comply with requirements under a different detention and training order, the period of detention takes effect as follows:
    (1)   if the offender has been released by virtue of s 102(2), (3), (4) or (5) (see PARA 11), at the beginning of the day on which the order for the period of detention is made (s 104B(2)(a) (as so added)); and
    (2)   if not, either as mentioned in s 104B(2)(a) or, if the court so orders, at the time when the offender would otherwise be released by virtue of s 102(2), (3), (4) or (5) (s 104B(2)(b) (as so added)).
    As to when the sentence of detention takes effect where a court passes a sentence of detention in a young offender institution in the case of an offender who is subject to a detention and training order see s 106(1); and PARA 15.
9   Powers of Criminal Courts (Sentencing) Act 2000 s 101(4).
10 Powers of Criminal Courts (Sentencing) Act 2000 s 101(6). As to the period of supervision see s 103(1); and PARA 12.
11 Powers of Criminal Courts (Sentencing) Act 2000 s 101(5).
12 Ie for the purposes of the Powers of Criminal Courts (Sentencing) Act 2000 s 101(4) (see the text and note 9).

13 Powers of Criminal Courts (Sentencing) Act 2000 s 101(7)(a).
14 Ie for the purposes of the Powers of Criminal Courts (Sentencing) Act 2000 s 101(5) (see the text and note 11).
15 Ie apart from the Powers of Criminal Courts (Sentencing) Act 2000 s 101(5).
16 Powers of Criminal Courts (Sentencing) Act 2000 s 101(7)(b).
17 It is considered neither appropriate nor desirable to calculate mathematically the total term by reference to a few days in custody, but weeks or months spent in custody should reduce the sentence to reflect that period: *R v B* [2000] Crim LR 870, CA; *R v Inner London Crown Court, ex p N and S* [2000] Crim LR 871, DC. Accordingly, the court should as a matter of good practice indicate in advance its intention to make such an order so as to be informed of any time in custody on remand: *R v Haringey Youth Court, ex p A* (2000) Times, 30 May, DC. A period totalling 24 months may be upheld on appeal despite a guilty plea and a significant period in custody if the court could otherwise have imposed a term of detention under the Powers of Criminal Courts (Sentencing) Act 2000 s 91 (see PARA 8): *R v Fieldhouse* [2001] 1 Cr App Rep (S) 104, [2000] Crim LR 1020, CA.
18 Any reference in the Powers of Criminal Courts (Sentencing) Act 2000 s 101(8) or s 101(9) (see the text and notes 19–22) to an offender being remanded in custody is a reference to him being:
    (1)   held in police detention (s 101(11)(a));
    (2)   remanded in or committed to custody by an order of a court (s 101(11)(b));
    (3)   remanded to youth detention accommodation under the Legal Aid, Sentencing and Punishment of Offenders Act 2012 s 91(4) (see CHILDREN AND YOUNG PERSONS) (Powers of Criminal Courts (Sentencing) Act 2000 s 101(11)(c) (substituted by the Legal Aid, Sentencing and Punishment of Offenders Act 2012 Sch 12 paras 42, 43(a))); or
    (4)   remanded, admitted or removed to hospital under the Mental Health Act 1983 s 35, s 36, s 38 (see PARAS 474–476) or s 48 (see MENTAL HEALTH AND CAPACITY vol 75 (2013) PARA 893) (Powers of Criminal Courts (Sentencing) Act 2000 s 101(11)(d)).
    A person is 'in police detention' for these purposes:
    (a)   at any time when he is in police detention for the purposes of the Police and Criminal Evidence Act 1984 (see POLICE AND INVESTIGATORY POWERS vol 84A (2013) PARA 504) (Powers of Criminal Courts (Sentencing) Act 2000 s 101(12)(a)); and
    (b)   at any time when he is detained under the Terrorism Act 2000 s 41 (see POLICE AND INVESTIGATORY POWERS vol 84A (2013) PARA 736) (Powers of Criminal Courts (Sentencing) Act 2000 s 101(12)(b) (amended by the Terrorism Act 2000 Sch 15 para 20(1), (3))).
19 See PARA 136.
20 Powers of Criminal Courts (Sentencing) Act 2000 s 101(8) (s 101(8), (9) amended by the Criminal Justice and Immigration Act 2008 s 22(6)). The Powers of Criminal Courts (Sentencing) Act 2000 s 101(8) requires periods of custody to be taken into account but does not require the sentence to be reduced by the exact period of custody (which wold be inconsistent with the intentions of the legislation, under which the periods to which a person may be sentenced under a detention and training order are specified in blocks (see the Powers of Criminal Courts (Sentencing) Act 2000 s 101(1); and the text and notes 1–3)): see (inter alia) *R v B* [2001] 1 Cr App Rep (S) 303, CA; *R v March* [2002] EWCA Crim 551, [2002] 2 Cr App Rep (S) 448; *R v Eagles* [2006] EWCA Crim 2368, [2007] 1 Cr App Rep (S) 612.
21 Ie as mentioned in the Powers of Criminal Courts (Sentencing) Act 2000 s 101(8) (see the text and notes 17–20).
22 Powers of Criminal Courts (Sentencing) Act 2000 s 101(9) (as amended: see note 20).
23 Powers of Criminal Courts (Sentencing) Act 2000 s 101(10).

11.   The period of detention and training. An offender must serve the period of detention and training under a detention and training order[1] in such youth detention accommodation[2] as may be determined by the Secretary of State[3]. The period of detention and training under a detention and training order is[4] one-half of the term of the order[5]: however:

(1)   the Secretary of State may at any time release the offender if he is satisfied that exceptional circumstances exist which justify the offender's release on compassionate grounds[6];

(2)   the Secretary of State may release the offender either at any time during the period of one month ending with the half-way point of the term of

the order (in the case of an order for a term of eight months or more but less than 18 months) or at any time during the period of two months ending with that point (in the case of an order for a term of 18 months or more)[7]; and

(3)   if a youth court so orders on an application made by the Secretary of State for the purpose, the Secretary of State must release the offender either one month after the half-way point of the term of the order (in the case of an order for a term of eight months or more but less than 18 months) or one month or two months after that point (in the case of an order for a term of 18 months or more)[8].

An offender detained in pursuance of a detention and training order is deemed to be in legal custody[9].

1   As to the making of a detention and training order see PARA 9. As to the period of detention and training see the text and note 5. As to the treatment of time spent in custody on remand see *R v Inner London Crown Court, ex p N and S* [2000] Crim LR 871, DC; *R v Fieldhouse* [2001] 1 Cr App Rep (S) 104, [2000] Crim LR 1020, CA.

2   For the purposes of the Powers of Criminal Courts (Sentencing) Act 2000 s 102 (see the text and notes 3–9), s 104 (see PARA 13) and s 105 (see PARA 14) 'youth detention accommodation' means, by virtue of s 107(1) (ss 102(1), (4), 107(1) amended by the Offender Management Act 2007 ss 33(1), 34(1), (2), (6), Sch 5 Pt 3; Powers of Criminal Courts (Sentencing) Act 2000 s 107(1) amended by the Criminal Justice and Courts Act 2015 Sch 9 para 12):

    (1)   a secure training centre (see PRISONS AND PRISONERS vol 85 (2012) PARA 491);
    (2)   a secure college (see PRISONS AND PRISONERS);
    (3)   a young offender institution (see PRISONS AND PRISONERS vol 85 (2012) PARA 487);
    (4)   accommodation provided by or on behalf of a local authority for the purpose of restricting the liberty of children and young persons (see CHILDREN AND YOUNG PERSONS vol 10 (2012) PARA 807 et seq);
    (5)   accommodation provided for that purpose under the Children Act 1989 s 82(5) (financial support by the Secretary of State: see CHILDREN AND YOUNG PERSONS vol 9 (2012) PARA 174); or
    (6)   such other accommodation or descriptions of accommodation as the Secretary of State may by order specify.

    At the date at which this volume states the law no such order had been made.

3   Powers of Criminal Courts (Sentencing) Act 2000 s 102(1) (as amended: see note 2). As to the Secretary of State see PARA 5 note 7. Where at any time an offender is subject concurrently to a detention and training order and to a period of detention under s 104(3)(a) (see PARA 13), the offender is to be treated for the purposes of s 102 as if he were subject only to the detention and training order (although this does not require the offender to be released in respect of either the order or the period of detention unless and until the offender is required to be released in respect of each of them): ss 104(5A), 104B(3), (4) (ss 104(5A), 104B added by the Legal Aid, Sentencing and Punishment of Offenders Act 2012 s 80(1), (5), (7)).

4   Ie subject to the Powers of Criminal Courts (Sentencing) Act 2000 s 102(3)–(5) (see the text and notes 6–8).

5   Powers of Criminal Courts (Sentencing) Act 2000 s 102(2). For the purposes of references in s 102, s 103 (see PARA 12), s 104, s 105 and s 106B to the 'term' of a detention and training order, consecutive terms of such orders and terms of such orders which are wholly or partly concurrent are to be treated as a single term if either the orders were made on the same occasion or, where they were made on different occasions, the offender has not been released (by virtue of s 102(2), (3), (4) or (5)) at any time during the period beginning with the first and ending with the last of those occasions: ss 101(13), 107(2) (amended by the Offender Rehabilitation Act 2014 s 6(1), (2), Sch 3 paras 10, 12).

6   Powers of Criminal Courts (Sentencing) Act 2000 s 102(3).
7   Powers of Criminal Courts (Sentencing) Act 2000 s 102(4) (as amended: see note 2).
8   Powers of Criminal Courts (Sentencing) Act 2000 s 102(5).
9   Powers of Criminal Courts (Sentencing) Act 2000 s 102(6).

12.   Period of supervision of offender subject to detention and training order. The period of supervision of an offender who is subject to a detention and training order[1] begins with the offender's release, whether at the half-way point of the term of the order[2] or otherwise, and ends when the term of the order ends[3]. However, the Secretary of State[4] may by order provide that the period of supervision ends at such point during the term of a detention and training order as may be specified in his order[5].

During the period of supervision, the offender must be under the supervision of:

(1)   an officer of a local probation board or an officer of a provider of probation services[6]; or

(2)   a member of a youth offending team[7];

and the category of person to supervise the offender must be determined from time to time by the Secretary of State[8].

The offender must be given a notice from the Secretary of State specifying the category of person for the time being responsible for his supervision[9] and any requirements with which he must for the time being comply[10].

1   As to the making of a detention and training order see PARA 9.
2   As to the term of a detention and training order see PARA 11 note 5.
3   Powers of Criminal Courts (Sentencing) Act 2000 s 103(1). Where at any time an offender is subject concurrently to a detention and training order and to a period of detention under s 104(3)(a) (see PARA 13), the offender is to be treated for the purposes of s 103 as if he were subject only to the detention and training order (although this does not require the offender to be released in respect of either the order or the period of detention unless and until the offender is required to be released in respect of each of them): ss 104(5A), 104B(3), (4) (ss 104(5A), 104B added by the Legal Aid, Sentencing and Punishment of Offenders Act 2012 s 80(1), (5), (7)).
4   As to the Secretary of State see PARA 5 note 7.
5   Powers of Criminal Courts (Sentencing) Act 2000 s 103(2) (s 103(2), (5)(b) amended, ss 103(2A), 107(3) added, by the Offender Rehabilitation Act 2014 s 6(1), (3), Sch 3 para 12). An order under the Powers of Criminal Courts (Sentencing) Act 2000 s 103(2) may not include provision about cases in which the offender is aged 18 or over at the half-way point of the term of the detention and training order and the order was imposed in respect of an offence committed on or after the day on which the Offender Rehabilitation Act 2014 s 6(4) comes into force (Powers of Criminal Courts (Sentencing) Act 2000 s 103(2A) (as so added)): for the purposes of s 103(2A), where an offence is found to have been committed over a period of 2 or more days, or at some time during a period of 2 or more days, it must be taken to have been committed on the last of those days (s 107(3) (as so added)). At the date at which this volume states the law no order had been made under s 103(2). As to the determination of a person's age see the Children and Young Persons Act 1933 s 99; and CHILDREN AND YOUNG PERSONS vol 10 (2012) PARA 1206.
6   Powers of Criminal Courts (Sentencing) Act 2000 s 103(3)(a) (s 103(3)(a), (4) amended, s 103(4A) added, by the Criminal Justice and Court Services Act 2000 Sch 7 para 4(1), (2); and by SI 2008/912; Powers of Criminal Courts (Sentencing) Act 2000 s 103(4) further amended by SI 2005/886). As to local probation boards and providers of probation services see PARAS 666–687. Where the supervision is to be provided by an officer of a local probation board, the officer must be an officer appointed for or assigned to the local justice area within which the offender resides for the time being, and where the supervision is to be provided by an officer of a provider of probation services, the officer must be an officer acting in the local justice area within which the offender resides for the time being: Powers of Criminal Courts (Sentencing) Act 2000 s 103(4), (4A) (as so amended and added).
7   Powers of Criminal Courts (Sentencing) Act 2000 s 103(3)(c). As to youth offending teams see CHILDREN AND YOUNG PERSONS vol 10 (2012) PARA 1193. Where supervision is to be provided by a member of a youth offending team that member must be a member of a youth offending team established by, or a social worker of, the local authority within whose area the offender resides for the time being: Powers of Criminal Courts (Sentencing) Act 2000 s 103(5)(b) (as amended: see note 5).
8   Powers of Criminal Courts (Sentencing) Act 2000 s 103(3)(a), (c) (s 103(3)(a) as amended: see note 6).
9   Powers of Criminal Courts (Sentencing) Act 2000 s 103(6)(a). Such a notice must be given to the offender before the commencement of the period of supervision and before any alteration in the matters specified in s 103(6) comes into effect: s 103(7).
10   Powers of Criminal Courts (Sentencing) Act 2000 s 103(6)(b). See note 9.

13. Breach of supervision requirements of detention and training order.
Where a detention and training order[1] is in force in respect of an offender and it
appears on information to a justice of the peace[2] that the offender has failed to
comply with the specified requirements[3], the justice:

(1) may issue a summons requiring the offender to appear at the place and
time specified in the summons[4]; or

(2) if the information is in writing and on oath, may issue a warrant for the
offender's arrest[5].

If it is proved to the satisfaction of the youth court before which an offender
appears or is brought[6] that he has failed to comply with those specified
requirements[7], that court may, either before or after the end of the term of the
detention and training order[8]:

(a) order the offender to be detained, in such youth detention
accommodation[9] as the Secretary of State[10] may determine, for such
period, not exceeding a specified maximum[11], as the court may
specify[12];

(b) order the offender to be subject to such period of supervision, not
exceeding a specified maximum[13], as the court may specify[14]; or

(c) impose on the offender a fine[15].

An offender may appeal to the Crown Court against any such order[16].

1 As to the making of a detention and training order see PARA 9. Where at any time an offender is
subject concurrently to a detention and training order and to a period of detention under the
Powers of Criminal Courts (Sentencing) Act 2000 s 104(3)(a) (see the text and notes 6–12), the
offender is to be treated for the purposes of s 104 as if he were subject only to the detention and
training order (although this does not require the offender to be released in respect of either the
order or the period of detention unless and until the offender is required to be released in respect
of each of them): ss 104(5A), 104B(3), (4) (s 104(3)(a) substituted, ss 104(3)(aa), (3A)–(3D),
(4A), (5A), 104A, 104B added, s 104(6) amended, by the Legal Aid, Sentencing and Punishment
of Offenders Act 2012 s 80)). See also the Powers of Criminal Courts (Sentencing) Act 2000
s 104B(1), (2); and PARA 10 note 8.

2 Any summons or warrant issued under these provisions must direct the offender to appear or be
brought:
(1) before a youth court acting in the local justice area in which the offender resides
(Powers of Criminal Courts (Sentencing) Act 2000 s 104(2)(a) (s 104(1) amended,
s 104(2) substituted, by the Domestic Violence (Crime and Victims) Act 2004 Sch 5
para 2; Powers of Criminal Courts (Sentencing) Act 2000 s 104(2) amended by
SI 2005/886)); or
(2) if it is not known where the offender resides, before a youth court acting in the same
local justice area as the justice who issued the summons or warrant (Powers of Criminal
Courts (Sentencing) Act 2000 s 104(2)(b) (as so substituted and amended)).

3 Ie those under the Powers of Criminal Courts (Sentencing) Act 2000 s 103(6)(b) (see PARA 12).

4 Powers of Criminal Courts (Sentencing) Act 2000 s 104(1)(a) (as amended: see note 2).

5 Powers of Criminal Courts (Sentencing) Act 2000 s 104(1)(b) (as amended: see note 2).

6 Ie appears or is brought under the Powers of Criminal Courts (Sentencing) Act 2000 s 104.

7 See note 3.

8 Powers of Criminal Courts (Sentencing) Act 2000 s 104(3C) (as added: see note 1).

9 As to the meaning of 'youth detention accommodation' see PARA 11 note 2.

10 As to the Secretary of State see PARA 5 note 7.

11 Ie not exceeding a period which is the shorter of three months and the period beginning with the
date of the offender's failure and ending with the last day of the term of the detention and
training order: Powers of Criminal Courts (Sentencing) Act 2000 s 104(3A) (as added: see
note 1). For the purposes of s 104(3A) a failure that is found to have occurred over two or more
days is to be taken to have occurred on the first of those days: s 104(3B) (as so added). A period
of detention or supervision ordered under s 104(3) begins on the date the order is made, and
may overlap to any extent with the period of supervision under the detention and training order:
s 104(3D) (as so added).

12 Powers of Criminal Courts (Sentencing) Act 2000 s 104(3)(a) (as substituted: see note 1). An
offender so detained is deemed to be in legal custody: s 104(4). Where an order under

s 104(3)(a) is made in the case of a person who has attained the age of 18, the order has effect to require the person to be detained in prison for the period specified by the court: s 104(4A) (as so added). As to the determination of a person's age see the Children and Young Persons Act 1933 s 99; and CHILDREN AND YOUNG PERSONS vol 10 (2012) PARA 1206.

The Secretary of State may by regulations make provision about the interaction between a period of detention under the Powers of Criminal Courts (Sentencing) Act 2000 s 104(3)(a) and a custodial sentence in a case where:

(1)   an offender who is subject to such a period of detention becomes subject to a custodial sentence (s 104B(5)(a) (as so added)); or

(2)   an offender who is subject to a custodial sentence becomes subject to such a period of detention (s 104B(5)(b) (as so added)).

The provision that may be made by regulations under s 104B(5) includes:

(a)   provision as to the time at which the period of detention under s 104(3)(a) or the custodial sentence is to take effect (s 104B(6)(a) (as so added));

(b)   provision for the offender to be treated, for the purposes of the enactments specified in the regulations, as subject only to the period of detention or the custodial sentence (s 104B(6)(b) (as so added));

(c)   provision about the effect of enactments relating to the person's release from detention or imprisonment in a case where that release is not to take effect immediately by virtue of provision in the regulations (s 104B(6)(c) (as so added)).

At the date at which this volume states the law no such regulations had been made.

13   See note 10.

14   Powers of Criminal Courts (Sentencing) Act 2000 s 104(3)(aa) (as added: see note 1). See s 104(3D); and note 11. Where an offender is subject to a period of supervision by virtue of an order under s 104(3)(aa) he must be under the supervision of:

(1)   an officer of a local probation board or an officer of a provider of probation services (ss 103(3)(a), 104A(1) (s 103(3)(a), (4) amended, s 103(4A) added, by the Criminal Justice and Court Services Act 2000 Sch 7 para 4(1), (2); and by SI 2008/912; Powers of Criminal Courts (Sentencing) Act 2000 s 103(4) further amended by SI 2005/886); Powers of Criminal Courts (Sentencing) Act 2000 s 104A as so added)); or

(2)   a member of a youth offending team (s 103(3)(c)),

and the category of person to supervise the offender must be determined from time to time by the Secretary of State (s 103(3)). The offender must be given a notice from the Secretary of State specifying the category of person for the time being responsible for his supervision (s 103(6)(a)) and any requirements with which he must for the time being comply (s 103(6)(b)). Such a notice must be given to the offender as soon as reasonably practicable after the order under s 104(3)(aa) is made and before any alteration in the matters specified in s 103(6) comes into effect: ss 103(7), 104A(2) (s 104A as so added).

As to local probation boards and providers of probation services see PARAS 666–687. As to youth offending teams see CHILDREN AND YOUNG PERSONS vol 10 (2012) PARA 1193. Where supervision is to be provided by an officer of a local probation board, the officer must be an officer appointed for or assigned to the local justice area within which the offender resides for the time being, and where the supervision is to be provided by an officer of a provider of probation services, the officer must be an officer acting in the local justice area within which the offender resides for the time being: s 103(4), (4A) (as so amended and added). Where supervision is to be provided by a member of a youth offending team that member must be a member of a youth offending team established by, or a social worker of, the local authority within whose area the offender resides for the time being: s 103(5)(b) (as so amended).

Where an offender is subject to a period of supervision by virtue of an order under s 104(3)(aa) and it appears on information to a justice of the peace that the offender has failed to comply with s 103(6)(b) above, the justice:

(a)   may issue a summons requiring the offender to appear at the place and time specified in the summons (ss 104(1)(a), 104A(3), (4)(a) (s 104(1)(a) as amended (see note 2); s 104A(3) as so added)); or

(b)   if the information is in writing and on oath, may issue a warrant for the offender's arrest (s 104(1)(b) (as so amended)).

If it is proved to the satisfaction of the youth court before which an offender appears or is brought under s 104 that he has failed to comply with s 103(6)(b), that court may, either before or after the end of the term of the period of supervision under s 104(3)(aa) (ss 104(3C), 104A(4)(b) (as so added)):

(i)   order the offender to be detained, in such youth detention accommodation as the Secretary of State may determine, for such period (not exceeding a period which is the shorter of three months and of the period beginning with the date of the offender's failure and ending with the last day of the term of the term of the period of supervision under s 104(3)(aa)) as the court may specify (ss 104(3)(a), 104(3A) (as so substituted and added);

(ii)   order the offender to be subject to such period of supervision (not exceeding the period referred to above), as the court may specify (s 104(3)(aa) (as so added)); or

(iii) impose on the offender a fine (s 104(3)(b)).

As to the bringing of offenders before a court pursuant to s 104 see s 104(2); and note 2. For the purposes of s 104(3A) a failure that is found to have occurred over two or more days is to be taken to have occurred on the first of those days: s 104(3B) (as so added). A period of detention or supervision ordered under s 104(3) begins on the date the order is made, and may overlap to any extent with the period of supervision under s 104(3)(aa): ss 104(3D), 104A(4)(c) (as so added). An offender detained pursuant to s 104(3)(a) is deemed to be in legal custody: s 104(4). Where an order under s 104(3)(a) is made in the case of a person who has attained the age of 18, the order has effect to require the person to be detained in prison for the period specified by the court: s 104(4A) (as so added).

15   Powers of Criminal Courts (Sentencing) Act 2000 s 104(3)(b). The fine must not exceed level 3 on the standard scale: s 104(3)(b). As to the standard scale, the statutory maximum, the prescribed sum, and magistrates' powers to levy unlimited fines see PARA 176. A fine so imposed is deemed, for the purposes of any enactment, to be a sum adjudged to be paid by a conviction: s 104(5). The court may order that a fine imposed under these provisions be paid by the offender's parent or guardian: see s 137; and CHILDREN AND YOUNG PERSONS vol 10 (2012) PARAS 1249–1250.

16   Powers of Criminal Courts (Sentencing) Act 2000 s 104(6) (as amended: see note 1).

14.   Offences during currency of detention and training order.

If after the release of a person subject to a detention and training order[1] but before the date on which the term of the order[2] ends that person commits an offence punishable with imprisonment in the case of a person aged 21 or over[3] (the 'new offence'), and, whether before or after that date, he is convicted of the new offence[4], the court[5] by or before which he is convicted of the new offence may, whether or not it passes any other sentence on him, order him to be detained in such youth detention accommodation[6] as the Secretary of State[7] may determine for the whole or any part of the period which begins with the date of the court's order[8] and is equal in length to the period between the date on which the new offence was committed and the date on which the term of the order ends[9]. The court has the same powers in respect of a person who has been made subject to a period of supervision[10] after failing to comply with the supervision requirements[11] of a detention and training order[12].

The period for which such a person is so ordered to be detained must, as the court may direct, either be served before and be followed by, or be served concurrently with, any sentence imposed for the new offence[13] and in either case must be disregarded in determining the appropriate length of that sentence[14]. Where the new offence is found to have been committed over a period of two or more days, or at some time during a period of two or more days, it is deemed to have been committed on the last of those days[15].

1   As to the making of a detention and training order see PARA 9. Where at any time an offender is subject concurrently to a detention and training order and to a period of detention under the Powers of Criminal Courts (Sentencing) Act 2000 s 104(3)(a) (see PARA 13), the offender is to be treated for the purposes of s 105 as if he were subject only to the detention and training order (although this does not require the offender to be released in respect of either the order or the period of detention unless and until the offender is required to be released in respect of each of them): ss 104(5A), 104B(3), (4) (ss 104(5A), 104A, 104B added by the Legal Aid, Sentencing and Punishment of Offenders Act 2012 s 80(1), (5), (7)).

2   As to the term of a detention and training order see PARA 11 note 5.

3   Powers of Criminal Courts (Sentencing) Act 2000 s 105(1)(a). As from a day to be appointed this age limit is reduced to 18: see s 105(1)(a) (prospectively amended by the Criminal Justice and Court Services Act 2000 Sch 7 paras 160, 186). At the date at which this volume states the

law no such day had been appointed. As to the determination of a person's age see the Children and Young Persons Act 1933 s 99; and CHILDREN AND YOUNG PERSONS vol 10 (2012) PARA 1206.

4   Powers of Criminal Courts (Sentencing) Act 2000 s 105(1)(b).
5   As to the meaning of 'court' see PARA 1 note 1.
6   As to the meaning of 'youth detention accommodation' see PARA 11 note 2.
7   As to the Secretary of State see PARA 5 note 7.
8   Powers of Criminal Courts (Sentencing) Act 2000 s 105(2)(a) (s 105(2), (3) amended by the Offender Management Act 2007 s 34). The Powers of Criminal Courts (Sentencing) Act 2000 s 105(2) is subject to s 8(6): see s 105(2); and CHILDREN AND YOUNG PERSONS vol 10 (2012) PARA 1221. A person so detained is deemed to be in legal custody: s 105(5).
9   Powers of Criminal Courts (Sentencing) Act 2000 s 105(2)(b) (as amended: see note 8).
10 Ie under the Powers of Criminal Courts (Sentencing) Act 2000 s 104(3)(aa) (see PARA 13).
11 Ie the requirements of the Powers of Criminal Courts (Sentencing) Act 2000 s 103(6)(b) (see PARA 12).
12 See the Powers of Criminal Courts (Sentencing) Act 2000 s 104A(5) (as added: see note 1).
13 Powers of Criminal Courts (Sentencing) Act 2000 s 105(3)(a) (as amended: see note 8).
14 Powers of Criminal Courts (Sentencing) Act 2000 s 105(3)(b) (as amended: see note 8).
15 Powers of Criminal Courts (Sentencing) Act 2000 s 105(4).

15.   Interaction with other sentences.   Until a day to be appointed[1], where a court[2] passes a sentence of detention in a young offender institution[3] in the case of an offender who is subject to a detention and training order[4], the sentence takes effect as follows:
(1)   if the offender has been released by virtue of the provision made for the release of such offenders[5], at the beginning of the day on which it is passed[6]; and
(2)   if not, either as mentioned in head (1) above or, if the court so orders, at the time when the offender would otherwise be released by virtue of those specified provisions[7].
Where at any time an offender is subject concurrently to a detention and training order and a sentence of detention in a young offender institution he is treated for the purposes of the provisions relating to place of detention[8], return to detention[9] and to release, licences, supervision and recall[10] as if he were subject only to the one of them that was imposed on the later occasion[11]. However, this does not require the offender to be released in respect of either the order or the sentence unless and until he is required to be released in respect of each of them[12].
Where, by virtue of any enactment giving a court power to deal with a person in a way in which a court on a previous occasion could have dealt with him, a detention and training order for any term is made in the case of a person who has attained the age of 18, the person is treated as if he had been sentenced to detention in a young offender institution (or, as from a day to be appointed, imprisonment) for the same term[13].
Where a court passes a sentence of detention[14] in the case of an offender who is subject to a detention and training order, the sentence takes effect as follows:
(a)   if the offender has at any time been released by virtue of the provision made for the release of such offenders[15], at the beginning of the day on which the sentence is passed[16]; and
(b)   if not, either as mentioned in head (a) above or, if the court so orders, at the time when the offender would otherwise be released by virtue of those specified provisions[17].
Where a court makes a detention and training order in the case of an offender who is subject to a sentence of detention, the order takes effect as follows:
(i)   if the offender has at any time been released under the provisions

relating to release on licence of fixed-term prisoners[18], at the beginning of the day on which the order is made[19]; and

(ii) if not, either as mentioned in head (i), above or, if the court so orders, at the time when the offender would otherwise be released by virtue of those provisions[20].

Where at any time an offender is subject concurrently to a detention and training order, and to a sentence of detention, he is to be treated[21] as if he were subject only to the sentence of detention[22]. However, this does not require the offender to be released in respect of either the order or the sentence unless and until he is required to be released in respect of each of them[23].

1 As from a day to be appointed the Powers of Criminal Courts (Sentencing) Act 2000 s 106(1) (see the text and notes 2–7) is repealed (except in relation to any order made, or having effect as if made, under s 102(1) (see PARA 11)) by the Criminal Justice and Court Services Act 2000 Sch 7 paras 160, 187(a), Sch 8. At the date at which this volume states the law no such day had been appointed.

2 As to the meaning of 'court' see PARA 1 note 1.

3 See PARA 16.

4 See PARA 9.

5 Ie by virtue of the Powers of Criminal Courts (Sentencing) Act 2000 s 102(2), (3), (4) or (5) (see PARA 11).

6 Powers of Criminal Courts (Sentencing) Act 2000 s 106(1)(a) (prospectively repealed: see note 1).

7 Powers of Criminal Courts (Sentencing) Act 2000 s 106(1)(b) (prospectively repealed: see note 1).

8 Ie the Powers of Criminal Courts (Sentencing) Act 2000 s 102–105 (see PARAS 11–14) and s 98 or the Criminal Justice and Court Services Act 2000 s 61 (not yet in force) (see PARA 36): Powers of Criminal Courts (Sentencing) Act 2000 s 106(4) (s 106(4) amended by the Criminal Justice and Courts Act 2015 s 15(3); Powers of Criminal Courts (Sentencing) Act 2000 s 106(4), (6) prospectively amended by the Criminal Justice and Court Services Act 2000 Sch 7 para 187(c), (d)). At the date at which this volume states the law no day had been appointed for these amendments to come into effect.

9 Ie the Powers of Criminal Courts (Sentencing) Act 2000 Pt V Ch IV (ss 116, 117) (repealed with savings).

10 Ie the Criminal Justice Act 2003 Pt 12 Ch 6 (ss 237–268) (see PARAS 688–745).

11 Powers of Criminal Courts (Sentencing) Act 2000 s 106(4) (prospectively amended: see note 8).

12 Powers of Criminal Courts (Sentencing) Act 2000 s 106(5).

13 Powers of Criminal Courts (Sentencing) Act 2000 s 106(6) (prospectively amended: see note 8). As to the determination of a person's age see the Children and Young Persons Act 1933 s 99; and **CHILDREN AND YOUNG PERSONS** vol 10 (2012) PARA 1206.

14 For these purposes 'sentence of detention' means (by virtue of the Powers of Criminal Courts (Sentencing) Act 2000 s 106A(1) (s 106A added by the Criminal Justice Act 2003 Sch 32 paras 90, 113; Powers of Criminal Courts (Sentencing) Act 2000 s 106A(1), (8) amended by the Armed Forces Act 2006 Sch 16 para 165); Powers of Criminal Courts (Sentencing) Act 2000 s 106A(1) further amended by the Legal Aid, Sentencing and Punishment of Offenders Act 2012 Sch 21 paras 7, 14, Sch 22 paras 14, 16):

(1) a sentence of detention under the Powers of Criminal Courts (Sentencing) Act 2000 s 91 (see PARA 8) or the Armed Forces Act 2006 s 209 (see **ARMED FORCES** vol 3 (2011) PARA 611); or

(2) a sentence of detention under the Criminal Justice Act 2003 s 226B (see PARAS 18–20) or s 228 (repealed),

and references in the Powers of Criminal Courts (Sentencing) Act 2000 s 106A to a sentence of detention under the Criminal Justice Act 2003 s 226B or s 228 include such a sentence passed as a result of the Armed Forces Act 2006 s 221A or s 222 (see **ARMED FORCES** vol 3 (2011) PARA 611).

15 See note 5.

16 Powers of Criminal Courts (Sentencing) Act 2000 s 106A(2)(a) (as added: see note 14).

17 Powers of Criminal Courts (Sentencing) Act 2000 s 106A(2)(b) (as added: see note 14). Where an order for release in respect of a person serving a detention and training order is made by a youth court under the Powers of Criminal Courts (Sentencing) Act 2000 s 102(5) (see PARA 11) in the case of a person in respect of whom a sentence of detention is to take effect as mentioned

in the Powers of Criminal Courts (Sentencing) Act 2000 s 106A(2)(b), the order must be expressed as an order that the period of detention attributable to the detention and training order is to end at the time determined under the provisions relating to such release: s 106A(4) (as so added).

18   Ie under the Criminal Justice Act 2003 Pt 12 Ch 6.

19   Powers of Criminal Courts (Sentencing) Act 2000 s 106A(3)(a) (as added: see note 14).

20   Powers of Criminal Courts (Sentencing) Act 2000 s 106A(3)(b) (as added: see note 14). In determining for these purposes the time when an offender would otherwise be released under the Criminal Justice Act 2003 Pt 12 Ch 6, the provisions of s 246 (power of Secretary of State to release prisoners on licence before he is required to do so: see PARA 715) are to be disregarded: Powers of Criminal Courts (Sentencing) Act 2000 s 106A(5) (as so added). Where by virtue of these provisions a detention and training order made in the case of a person who is subject to a sentence of detention under the Criminal Justice Act 2003 s 228 (repealed) is to take effect at the time when he would otherwise be released under Pt 12 Ch 6, any direction by the Parole Board under s 247(2)(b) (repealed) in respect of him is to be expressed as a direction that the Board would, but for the detention and training order, have directed his release under s 247: Powers of Criminal Courts (Sentencing) Act 2000 s 106A(6) (as so added).

21   Ie for the purposes of the Powers of Criminal Courts (Sentencing) Act 2000 ss 92 (see PARA 8), ss 102–105 (see PARAS 11–14), the Criminal Justice Act 2003 s 235, Pt 12 Ch 6, and the Armed Forces Act 2006 ss 210, 214 (see ARMED FORCES vol 3 (2011) PARA 611): Powers of Criminal Courts (Sentencing) Act 2000 s 106A(8) (as added and amended: see note 14).

22   Powers of Criminal Courts (Sentencing) Act 2000 s 106A(7) (as added: see note 14).

23   Powers of Criminal Courts (Sentencing) Act 2000 s 106A(9) (as added: see note 14).

(iii) Detention in a Young Offender Institution

16. Power to order detention. Until a day to be appointed[1], where a person aged at least 18 but under 21[2] is convicted of an offence which is punishable with imprisonment in the case of a person aged 21 or over[3], the court[4] must pass a sentence of detention in a young offender institution[5] if it is of the opinion:

(1)   that the offence, or a combination of the offence and one or more offences associated[6] with it, was so serious that only such a sentence could be justified for it[7]; or

(2)   where the offence was a violent or sexual offence, that only such a sentence would be adequate to protect the public from serious harm from him[8],

or if the offender fails to express his willingness to comply with a requirement which is proposed by the court to be included in a supervision order[9] and which requires an expression of such willingness[10].

As from a day to be appointed no court is to pass a sentence of detention in a young offender institution[11].

1   As from a day to be appointed the Powers of Criminal Courts (Sentencing) Act 2000 s 96 (see the text and notes 2–10) is repealed by the Criminal Justice and Court Services Act 2000 Sch 7 paras 160, 182, Sch 8. At the date at which this volume states the law no such day had been appointed.

2   As to the determination of a person's age see the Children and Young Persons Act 1933 s 99; and CHILDREN AND YOUNG PERSONS vol 10 (2012) PARA 1206.

3   Powers of Criminal Courts (Sentencing) Act 2000 s 96(a) (prospectively repealed: see note 1).

4   As to the meaning of 'court' see PARA 1 note 1.

5   Ie subject to the Powers of Criminal Courts (Sentencing) Act 2000 s 90 (see PARA 38), s 93 (see PARA 36) and s 94 (see PARA 37): s 96 (prospectively repealed: see note 1). As to the suspension of a sentence of detention in a young offender institution see the Criminal Justice Act 2003 s 189; and PARA 100.

6   As to an 'associated offence' see PARA 9 note 7.

7   Powers of Criminal Courts (Sentencing) Act 2000 s 79(2)(a), 96(b) (s 96 prospectively repealed: see note 1). Section 79 was repealed as from 4 April 2005 by the Criminal Justice Act 2003 Sch 37 Pt 7, other than in relation to an offence committed before 4 April 2005 (see the

Criminal Justice Act 2003 (Commencement No 8 and Transitional and Saving Provisions) Order 2005, SI 2005/950, Sch 2 para 5(1), (2)(c)(xii), (3)).

8 Powers of Criminal Courts (Sentencing) Act 2000 s 79(2)(b) (repealed with savings: see note 7); s 96(b) (prospectively repealed: see note 1).

9 See PARA 495.

10 Powers of Criminal Courts (Sentencing) Act 2000 s 79(3)(a) (amended by the Criminal Justice and Court Services Act 2000 Sch 7 para 1; repealed with savings (see note 7)); Powers of Criminal Courts (Sentencing) Act 2000 s 96(b) (prospectively repealed: see note 1).

11 Criminal Justice and Court Services Act 2000 s 61(1) (not yet in force): see also PARA 36.

17. Term of detention. Until a day to be appointed[1] the maximum term of detention in a young offender institution[2] that a court[3] may impose for an offence is the same as the maximum term of imprisonment that it may impose for that offence[4], although a court may not pass sentence[5] for an offender's detention in a young offender institution for less than 21 days[6]. Where an offender is convicted of more than one offence for which he is liable to a sentence of detention in a young offender institution, or an offender who is serving such a sentence is convicted of one or more further offences for which he is liable to such a sentence, the court has the same power to pass consecutive sentences of detention in a young offender institution as if they were sentences of imprisonment[7]; and where an offender aged 21 or over[8] who is serving a sentence of detention in a young offender institution is convicted of one or more further offences for which he is liable to imprisonment, the court has the power to pass one or more sentences of imprisonment to run consecutively upon the sentence of detention in a young offender institution[9].

1 As from a day to be appointed the Powers of Criminal Courts (Sentencing) Act 2000 s 97 (see the text and notes 2–9) is repealed by the Criminal Justice and Court Services Act 2000 Sch 7 paras 160, 182, Sch 8. At the date at which this volume states the law no such day had been appointed.

2 As to the power to order detention see PARA 16.

3 As to the meaning of 'court' see PARA 1 note 1.

4 Powers of Criminal Courts (Sentencing) Act 2000 s 97(1) (prospectively repealed: see note 1).

5 'Sentence' refers to the sentence imposed for a particular offence, rather than to the total sentence produced by aggregating more than one custodial term: *R v Dover Youth Court, ex p K (A Minor)* [1998] 4 All ER 24, [1999] 1 Cr App Rep (S) 263, DC.

6 Powers of Criminal Courts (Sentencing) Act 2000 s 97(2) (prospectively repealed (see note 1); amended by the Criminal Justice and Courts Act 2015 s 15(2)).

7 Powers of Criminal Courts (Sentencing) Act 2000 s 97(4) (prospectively repealed: see note 1).

8 As to the determination of a person's age see the Children and Young Persons Act 1933 s 99; and CHILDREN AND YOUNG PERSONS vol 10 (2012) PARA 1206.

9 Powers of Criminal Courts (Sentencing) Act 2000 s 97(5) (prospectively repealed: see note 1).

(3) EXTENDED SENTENCES

(i) Statutory Framework

18. Extended sentences of imprisonment and detention. The court[1] may impose extended sentences of imprisonment (where the offender is aged 18 or over[2]) or detention (where the offender is under 18) for specified violent or sexual offences[3]. An extended sentence of imprisonment or detention is a sentence of imprisonment or detention the term of which is equal to the aggregate of the appropriate custodial term[4] and a further period (the 'extension period') for which the offender is to be subject to a licence[5]. The extension period must be a period of such length as the court considers necessary for the purpose of protecting members of the public from serious harm[6] occasioned by the commission by the offender of further specified offences[7]: it must not exceed five years (in the case of a specified violent offence)[8] or eight years (in the case of a specified sexual offence)[9] and as from a day to be appointed must be at least one year[10]. The term of an extended sentence of imprisonment imposed under these provisions in respect of an offence must not exceed the term that, at the time the offence was committed, was the maximum term permitted for the offence[11], and the term of an extended sentence of detention imposed under these provisions in respect of an offence must not exceed the term that, at the time the offence was committed, was the maximum term of imprisonment permitted for the offence in the case of a person aged 18 or over[12].

1   As to the meaning of 'court' see PARA 1 note 1.
2   As to the determination of a person's age see the Children and Young Persons Act 1933 s 99; and CHILDREN AND YOUNG PERSONS vol 10 (2012) PARA 1206.
3   See the Criminal Justice Act 2003 ss 226A, 226B; the text and notes 4–12; and PARAS 19–20. As to the specified violent and sexual offences for these purposes see PARAS 23, 24. References to a specified offence, a specified violent offence and a specified sexual offence include an offence that was abolished before 4 April 2005 (ss 226A(10)(a), 226B(8)(a) (ss 226A, 226B added by the Legal Aid, Sentencing and Punishment of Offenders Act 2012 s 124)), and would have constituted such an offence if committed on the day on which the offender was convicted of the offence (Criminal Justice Act 2003 ss 226A(10)(b), 226B(8)(b) (as so added)). See also s 232A; and PARA 35 note 4.
     4 April 2005 is the date on which Pt 12 Ch 5 (ss 224–236), which makes provision in connection with the sentencing of dangerous offenders, was brought into force by virtue of the Criminal Justice Act 2003 (Commencement No 8 and Transitional and Saving Provisions) Order 2005, SI 2005/950. The sentencing of dangerous offenders in respect of serious offences committed before that date continues to be governed by the former statutory provisions which were repealed and replaced by the Criminal Justice Act 2003 (in particular, the Powers of Criminal Courts Act 2000 ss 80, 85, 109) and which have been expressly saved, by virtue of the Criminal Justice Act 2003 (Commencement No 8 and Transitional and Saving Provisions) Order 2005, SI 2005/950, Sch 2 para 5(1), (2)(c)(xii), (3), in relation to pre-4 April 2005 offences.
     Extended sentences of imprisonment and detention under the Criminal Justice Act 2003 s 226A, 226B replace imprisonment and detention for public protection under ss 225, 226, which had effect until 3 December 2012 and were abolished pursuant to the Legal Aid, Sentencing and Punishment of Offenders Act 2012 s 123(a), (b).
4   Criminal Justice Act 2003 ss 226A(5)(a), 226B(3)(a) (as added: see note 3). The 'appropriate custodial term' is the term of imprisonment or detention that would (apart from the Criminal Justice Act 2003 s 226A or (as the case may be) s 226B) be imposed in compliance with s 153(2) (see PARA 29: ss 226A(6), 226B(4) (as so added). Where the offence was committed before 4 April 2005 (see note 3), the relevant term of imprisonment or detention is not required to have been imposed in compliance with s 153(2): ss 226A(11)(b), 226B(9)(b) (as so added).
5   Criminal Justice Act 2003 ss 226A(5)(b), 226B(3)(b) (as added: see note 3).
6   As to the meaning of 'serious harm' see PARA 22.
7   Criminal Justice Act 2003 ss 226A(7), 226B(5) (as added: see note 3). This is expressed to be subject to s 226A(7A)–(9) or (as the case may be) s 226B(5A)–(7): see the Criminal Justice Act 2003 ss 226A(7), 226B(5) (as so added; ss 226A(7), 226B(5) amended, ss 226A(7A), 226B(5A) added, by the Offender Rehabilitation Act 2014 s 8(1)–(3)); and the text and notes 8–12.
8   Criminal Justice Act 2003 ss 226A(8)(a), 226B(6)(a) (as added: see note 3).
9   Criminal Justice Act 2003 ss 226A(8)(b), 226B(6)(b) (as added: see note 3).
10   Criminal Justice Act 2003 ss 226A(7A), 226B(5A) (as added: see notes 3, 7).
11   Criminal Justice Act 2003 s 226A(9) (as added: see note 3).
12   Criminal Justice Act 2003 s 226B(7) (as added: see note 3).

19. Circumstances in which an extended sentence of imprisonment may be imposed.   The court[1] may impose an extended sentence of imprisonment where[2]:

    (1)   a person aged 18 or over[3] is convicted of a specified offence (whatever the date on which the offence was committed)[4];

(2)   the court considers that there is a significant risk to members of the public of serious harm[5] occasioned by the commission by the offender of further specified offences[6];

(3)   the court is not required[7] to impose a sentence of imprisonment for life[8]; and

(4)   either:

    (a)   at the time the offence was committed, the offender had been convicted of an offence for which, being a 'second listed offence'[9], the court is required to impose a life sentence[10]; or

    (b)   if the court were to impose an extended sentence of imprisonment, the term that it would specify as the appropriate custodial term would be at least four years[11].

1   As to the meaning of 'court' see PARA 1 note 1.
2   Criminal Justice Act 2003 s 226A(4) (s 226A added by the Legal Aid, Sentencing and Punishment of Offenders Act 2012 s 124). As to extended sentences of imprisonment see PARA 18.
3   As to the determination of a person's age see the Children and Young Persons Act 1933 s 99; and CHILDREN AND YOUNG PERSONS vol 10 (2012) PARA 1206.
4   Criminal Justice Act 2003 s 226A(1)(a) (as added: see note 2). As to the specified violent and sexual offences for these purposes see PARAS 23, 24; and see in particular PARA 18 note 3. These provisions apply in respect of an offence whether it was committed before or after 3 December 2012 (ie the date on which s 226A was brought into force by virtue of the Legal Aid, Sentencing and Punishment of Offenders Act 2012 (Commencement No 4 and Saving Provisions) Order 2012, SI 2012/2906): Criminal Justice Act 2003 s 226A(1)(a) (as so added).
5   As to a 'significant risk of serious harm' see PARA 22.
6   Criminal Justice Act 2003 s 226A(1)(b) (as added: see note 2).
7   Ie, in relation to an offence committed on or after 4 April 2005, by the Criminal Justice Act 2003 s 224A (see PARA 35) or s 225(2) (see PARA 37): s 226A(1)(c), (11)(a) (as added: see note 2). In connection with the sentencing of dangerous offenders for offences committed pre- and post-4 April 2005 see PARA 18 note 3.
8   Criminal Justice Act 2003 s 226A(1)(c) (as added: see note 2).
9   Ie an offence listed in the Criminal Justice Act 2003 Sch 15B (see PARA 25).
10   Criminal Justice Act 2003 s 226A(1)(d), (2) (as added: see note 2).
11   Criminal Justice Act 2003 s 226A(3) (as added: see note 2).

20. Extended sentences for persons aged under 18. The court[1] may impose an extended sentence of detention where[2]:

(1)   a person aged under 18[3] is convicted of a specified offence (whatever the date on which the offence was committed)[4];

(2)   the court considers that there is a significant risk to members of the public of serious harm[5] occasioned by the commission by the offender of further specified offences[6];

(3)   (in respect of an offence committed on or after 4 April 2005 only[7]) the court is not required[8] to impose a sentence[9] of detention for life[10]; and

(4)   if the court were to impose an extended sentence of detention, the term that it would specify as the appropriate custodial term would be at least four years[11].

1   As to the meaning of 'court' see PARA 1 note 1.
2   Criminal Justice Act 2003 s 226B(2) (s 226B added by the Legal Aid, Sentencing and Punishment of Offenders Act 2012 s 124). As to extended sentences of detention see PARA 18.
3   As to the determination of a person's age see the Children and Young Persons Act 1933 s 99; and CHILDREN AND YOUNG PERSONS vol 10 (2012) PARA 1206.
4   Criminal Justice Act 2003 s 226B(1)(a) (as added: see note 2). As to the specified violent and sexual offences for these purposes see PARAS 23, 24; and see in particular PARA 18 note 3. These provisions apply in respect of an offence whether it was committed before or after 3 December 2012 (ie the date on which s 226B was brought into force by virtue of the Legal Aid, Sentencing

and Punishment of Offenders Act 2012 (Commencement No 4 and Saving Provisions) Order 2012, SI 2012/2906): Criminal Justice Act 2003 s 226B(1)(a) (as so added).
5   As to a 'significant risk of serious harm' see PARA 22.
6   Criminal Justice Act 2003 s 226B(1)(b) (as added: see note 2).
7   In connection with the sentencing of dangerous offenders for offences committed pre- and post-4 April 2005 see PARA 18 note 3.
8   Ie by the Criminal Justice Act 2003 s 226(2) (see PARA 34): s 226B(1)(c) (as added: see note 2).
9   Ie under the Powers of Criminal Courts (Sentencing) Act 2000 s 91 (see PARA 8).
10 Criminal Justice Act 2003 s 226B(1)(c), (9)(a) (as added: see note 2).
11 Criminal Justice Act 2003 s 226B(1)(d) (as added: see note 2).

(ii) Interpretation of Provisions governing Sentencing of Dangerous Offenders

21.   Serious offences.   An offence is a 'serious offence' for the purposes of the statutory provisions governing the sentencing of dangerous offenders[1] if, and only if, it is a violent and/or sexual offence specified for those purposes[2] and is usually[3] punishable in the case of a person aged 18 or over[4] by either:

(1)   imprisonment for life[5];
(2)   imprisonment for a determinate period of ten years or more[6]; or
(3)   until a day to be appointed[7], in the case of a person aged at least 18 but under 21, custody for life or detention in a young offender institution[8] for a determinate period of ten years or more[9].

1   Ie for the purposes of the Criminal Justice Act 2003 Pt 12 Ch 5 (ss 224–236): see PARAS 18–20, 22–25, 33–34.
2   Criminal Justice Act 2003 s 224(1), (2)(a). As to the violent and sexual offences specified for these purposes see Schs 15, 15A, 15B; and PARAS 23–25.
3   Ie apart from the Criminal Justice Act 2003 s 224A (see PARA 35): s 224(2)(b) (amended by the Legal Aid, Sentencing and Punishment of Offenders Act 2012 Sch 19 paras 8, 16).
4   As to the determination of a person's age see the Children and Young Persons Act 1933 s 99; and CHILDREN AND YOUNG PERSONS vol 10 (2012) PARA 1206.
5   Criminal Justice Act 2003 s 224(2)(b)(i).
6   Criminal Justice Act 2003 s 224(2)(b)(ii).
7   Ie until the date on which the Criminal Justice and Court Services Act 2000 s 61 (see PARA 36) comes into force.
8   See PARAS 16–17.
9   Criminal Justice Act 2003 s 224(2)(b)(i), (ii) (amended by SI 2005/643).

22.   Significant risk of serious harm.   For the purposes of the statutory provisions governing the sentencing of dangerous offenders[1] 'serious harm' means death or serious personal injury, whether physical or psychological[2]. Where a person has been convicted of a specified offence[3] and it falls to a court[4] to assess[5] whether there is a significant risk to members of the public of serious harm occasioned by the commission by that person of further such offences[6] the court in making the assessment:

(1)   must take into account all such information as is available to it about the nature and circumstances of the offence[7];
(2)   may take into account all such information as is available to it about the nature and circumstances of any other offences of which the offender has been convicted by a court anywhere in the world[8];
(3)   may take into account any information which is before it about any pattern of behaviour of which any of the offences mentioned above forms part[9]; and
(4)   may take into account any information about the offender which is before it[10].

'Significant risk' to members of the public from serious harm by the commission of further specified offences requires significant risk to be shown in relation to two matters: the commission of further specified, but not necessarily serious, offences; and the causing thereby of serious harm to members of the public[11]. These provisions do not allow the court to decide that a defendant is guilty of separate offences with which he has not been charged[12], although a court is not precluded from considering evidence of previous misconduct which would amount to a criminal offence but for which the offender has not been convicted[13].

1   Ie for the purposes of the Criminal Justice Act 2003 Pt 12 Ch 5 (ss 224–236): see PARAS 18–21, 23–25, 33–34.

2   Criminal Justice Act 2003 s 224(3).

3   Criminal Justice Act 2003 s 229(1)(a). See PARA 21; and as to the violent and sexual offences specified for these purposes see Schs 15, 15A, 15B; and PARAS 23–25.

4   As to the meaning of 'court' see PARA 1 note 1.

5   Ie under any of the Criminal Justice Act 2003 ss 225–228: see PARAS 33–34.

6   Criminal Justice Act 2003 s 229(1)(b).

7   Criminal Justice Act 2003 s 229(2)(a) (s 229(2) amended, s 229(2)(aa), (2A) added, by the Criminal Justice and Immigration Act 2008 s 17, Sch 28 Pt 2).

8   Criminal Justice Act 2003 s 229(2)(aa) (as added: see note 7). Such offences need not be the 'specified' offences referred to in note 3: a pattern of minor previous offences of gradually escalating seriousness may be significant for establishing an offender's dangerousness: see *R v Johnson* [2006] EWCA Crim 2486 at [10], [2007] 1 All ER 1237 at [10], [2007] 1 WLR 585 at [10]. The reference in the Criminal Justice Act 2003 s 229(2)(aa) to a 'conviction by a court' includes a reference to a conviction of an offence in any service disciplinary proceedings and a conviction of a service offence within the meaning of the Armed Forces Act 2006 ('conviction' here including anything that under s 376(1), (2) (see ARMED FORCES vol 3 (2011) PARA 508) is to be treated as a conviction): Criminal Justice Act 2003 s 229(2A) (as so added; s 229(2A) amended, s 229(2B) added, by the Coroners and Justice Act 2009 Sch 22 para 95). It is stated that for this purpose 'service disciplinary proceedings' means any proceedings under the Army Act 1955, the Air Force Act 1955, or the Naval Discipline Act (whether before a court-martial or before any other court or person authorised thereunder to award a punishment in respect of any offence) and any proceedings before a Standing Civilian Court (Criminal Justice Act 2003 s 229(2B) (as so added)): however, owing to the repeal of the Service Discipline Acts and the abolition of the Standing Civilian Court it is submitted that for the meaning of 'service disciplinary proceedings' reference should instead be made to the definition contained in the Rehabilitation of Offenders Act 1974 (see s 2(5); and ARMED FORCES vol 3 (2011) PARA 429). 'Conviction' includes the recording of a finding that a charge in respect of the offence has been proved: Criminal Justice Act 2003 s 229(2B) (as so added).

9   Criminal Justice Act 2003 s 229(2)(b) (as amended: see note 7). It is not a prerequisite to a finding of dangerousness under s 229 that the offender should be an individual with previous convictions — a man of good character may properly qualify under these provisions — but nor does the existence of previous offences compel such a finding: *R v Johnson* [2006] EWCA Crim 2486 at [7], [10], [2007] 1 All ER 1237 at [7], [10], [2007] 1 WLR 585 at [7], [10]. There is also no reason in principle why an offence to be taken into consideration which is of a more serious nature than the offence charged should not result in a higher sentence than otherwise would be the case: *R v Lavery* [2008] EWCA Crim 2499, [2009] 3 All ER 295, 172 JP 561. See also *R v S, R v A, R v C* [2008] EWCA Crim 2789, [2009] 2 Cr App Rep (S) 128, [2008] All ER (D) 254 (Nov) (practice of not applying provisions relating to sentence of imprisonment for public protection where conduct encompassed within offences committed before creation of that sentence is of greater gravity than that of later offences unsound).

10 Criminal Justice Act 2003 s 229(2)(c). Such information might include social and economic factors in relation to the defendant including accommodation, employability, education, associates, relationships and drug or alcohol abuse, and the defendant's attitude towards offending and supervision: *R v Lang* [2005] EWCA Crim 2864, [2006] 2 All ER 410, [2006] 1 WLR 2509. See also *A-G's Reference (No 145 of 2006), R v Carter* [2007] EWCA Crim 692, (2007) Times, 20 March, [2007] All ER (D) 86 (Mar), (pre-sentence report should be obtained when considering risk offender poses to the public); and *R v Frota* [2007] EWCA Crim 2602, [2007] All ER (D) 442 (Nov).

11 *R v Lang* [2005] EWCA Crim 2864, [2006] 2 All ER 410, [2006] 1 WLR 2509 (the risk must be 'significant' ie 'noteworthy, of considerable amount or importance'); *R v Johnson* [2006] EWCA Crim 2486 at [5]–[6], [2007] 1 All ER 1237 at [5]–[6], [2007] 1 WLR 585 at [5]–[6]. The fact that no actual harm has been caused by the offender to date does not mean that the risk he will cause serious harm in the future is negligible (*R v Johnson* at [10]; *R v Watty* [2007] EWCA Crim 123, [2007] 2 Cr App Rep (S) 280 (repetitive sexual offending with relatively low or no serious harm does not of itself indicate a significant risk of serious harm in the future); see also *R v Shaffi* [2006] EWCA Crim 418, [2006] 2 Cr App Rep (S) 606). The court will be guided, but not bound by, the assessment of risk in pre-sentence reports; if the judge contemplates differing from the assessment, counsel should be given the opportunity of addressing the point: *R v Lang*; see also *R v Blacklock* [2006] EWCA Crim 1740, [2006] All ER (D) 361 (Jun). The court should guard against assuming that there is a significant risk of serious harm merely because the foreseen specified offence is serious: *R v Lang*. Where the foreseen specified offence is not serious, there will be comparatively few cases in which a risk of serious harm can properly be regarded as significant, and it will usually be unreasonable to conclude that the assumption applies unless information as to the offences, pattern of behaviour, and offender shows a significant risk of serious harm from further offences: *R v Lang*. In relation to particularly young offenders, an indeterminate sentence may be inappropriate even where a serious offence has been committed and there is a significant risk of serious harm from further offences: *R v Lang*. Courts should usually give reasons for their conclusions: in particular, that there was or was not a significant risk of further offences or serious harm: *R v Lang*. Courts should, in giving reasons, identify the information which they have taken into account: *R v Lang*. See also *R v Pedley* [2009] EWCA Crim 840, [2009] 1 WLR 2517, [2010] 1 Cr App Rep (S) 132 (in addressing the question whether the risk of serious harm is significant the judge is entitled to balance the probability of harm against the nature of it if it occurs).

12 *R v Farrar* [2006] EWCA Crim 3261, [2007] 2 Cr App Rep (S) 202, [2007] Crim LR 308. See also *R v Johnson* [2006] EWCA Crim 2486 at [10], [2007] 1 All ER 1237 at [10], [2007] 1 WLR 585 at [10]; *A-G's Reference (No 134 of 2006), R v Bennett (Adam)* [2007] EWCA Crim 309, [2007] 2 Cr App Rep (S) 332; *R v Poynton* [2007] EWCA Crim 1805, [2007] All ER (D) 158 (Aug); *R v Lewis* [2007] EWCA Crim 2015, [2008] 1 Cr App Rep (S) 367, [2007] All ER (D) 40 (Sep).

13 *R v Considine, R v Davis* [2007] EWCA Crim 1166, [2007] 3 All ER 621, [2008] 1 WLR 414.

23. Specified violent offences. The offences which are specified for the purposes of the statutory provisions dealing with the sentencing of dangerous offenders[1] are divided into two categories, 'specified violent offences' and 'specified sexual offences'[2].

The specified violent offences are:

(1) manslaughter[3];

(2) kidnapping[4];

(3) false imprisonment[5];

(4) soliciting murder[6];

(5) threats to kill[7];

(6) wounding with intent to cause grievous bodily harm[8];

(7) malicious wounding[9];

(8) attempting to choke, suffocate or strangle in order to commit or assist in committing an indictable offence[10];

(9) using chloroform, etc, to commit or assist in the committing of any indictable offence[11];

(10) maliciously administering poison, etc, so as to endanger life or inflict grievous bodily harm[12];

(11) abandoning children[13];

(12) causing bodily injury by explosives[14];

(13) using explosives, etc, with intent to do grievous bodily harm[15];

(14) placing explosives with intent to do bodily injury[16];

(15) setting spring guns, etc, with intent to do grievous bodily harm[17];

(16) endangering the safety of railway passengers[18];

(17) injuring persons by furious driving[19];
(18) assaulting an officer preserving a wreck[20];
(19) assault with intent to resist arrest[21];
(20) assault occasioning actual bodily harm[22];
(21) causing an explosion likely to endanger life or property[23];
(22) attempting to cause explosion, or making or keeping explosives, with intent to endanger life or property[24];
(23) making or possession of explosive under suspicious circumstances[25];
(24) child destruction[26];
(25) cruelty to children[27];
(26) infanticide[28];
(27) possession of a firearm with intent to endanger life[29];
(28) possession of a firearm with intent to cause fear of violence[30];
(29) use of a firearm to resist arrest[31];
(30) possession of a firearm when committing or being arrested for a violent offence[32];
(31) carrying a firearm with criminal intent[33];
(32) robbery or assault with intent to rob[34];
(33) burglary with intent to inflict grievous bodily harm on a person[35];
(34) burglary with intent to do unlawful damage to a building or anything in it[36];
(35) aggravated burglary[37];
(36) aggravated vehicle-taking[38] involving an accident which caused the death of any person[39];
(37) arson[40];
(38) destroying or damaging property[41] other than an offence of arson[42];
(39) hostage-taking[43];
(40) hijacking of ships or aircraft[44];
(41) destroying, damaging or endangering the safety of aircraft[45];
(42) other acts endangering or likely to endanger the safety of aircraft[46];
(43) offences in relation to the carrying of certain dangerous articles on aircraft or in aviation installations[47];
(44) ill-treatment of mentally-disordered persons[48];
(45) female genital mutilation[49];
(46) riot[50];
(47) violent disorder[51];
(48) affray[52];
(49) torture[53];
(50) causing death by dangerous driving[54];
(51) causing death by driving (disqualified drivers)[55];
(52) causing death by careless driving when under the influence of drink or drugs[56];
(53) endangering safety at aerodromes[57];
(54) seizing or exercising control of fixed platforms[58];
(55) destroying fixed platforms or endangering their safety[59];
(56) other acts endangering or likely to endanger safe navigation[60];
(57) offences involving threats to ships or fixed platforms[61];
(58) offences relating to Channel Tunnel trains and the tunnel system[62];
(59) putting people in fear of violence[63];
(60) stalking involving fear of violence or serious alarm or distress[64];
(61) racially or religiously aggravated assaults[65];

(62)   racially or religiously aggravated public order offences[66];

(63)   weapons training for terrorism purposes[67];

(64)   directing terrorist organisations[68];

(65)   possessing articles for terrorist purposes[69];

(66)   inciting terrorism overseas[70];

(67)   genocide, crimes against humanity, war crimes and related offences[71], other than an offence involving murder[72];

(68)   use of nuclear weapons[73];

(69)   assisting or inducing certain weapons-related acts overseas[74];

(70)   use of noxious substances or things to cause harm or intimidate[75];

(71)   causing or allowing a child or vulnerable adult to die or suffer serious physical harm[76];

(72)   preparation of terrorist acts[77];

(73)   training for terrorism[78];

(74)   making or possession of radioactive device or material[79];

(75)   use of radioactive device or material for terrorist purposes[80];

(76)   terrorist threats relating to radioactive devices[81];

(77)   slavery, servitude and forced or compulsory labour[82]; and

(78)   human trafficking[83].

Aiding, abetting, counselling or procuring the commission of any of these offences[84], an attempt[85], conspiracy[86] or incitement[87] to commit any such offence or murder, is also a specified violent offence for these purposes, as is an offence of encouraging or assisting the commission of an offence[88] in relation to which any such offence, or murder, is the offence (or one of the offences) which the person intended or believed would be committed[89].

Provision is made for the assessment and management of the risks posed by persons who have been convicted and sentenced for, or (in certain circumstances) found to be not guilty and been made the subject of a hospital or guardianship order in consequence of, a specified violent offence, and other persons who, by reason of offences committed by them, are considered by the responsible authority to be persons who may cause serious harm to the public[90].

1   Ie for the purposes of the Criminal Justice Act 2003 Pt 12 Ch 5 (ss 224–236): see PARAS 18–22, 33–34.

2   Criminal Justice Act 2003 s 224(1), (2)(a), (3), Sch 15 Pt 1 (paras 1–65). For the specified sexual offences see PARA 24.

3   Criminal Justice Act 2003 Sch 15 para 1. As to the offence of manslaughter see CRIMINAL LAW vol 25 (2010) PARA 93.

4   Criminal Justice Act 2003 Sch 15 para 2. As to the offence of kidnapping see CRIMINAL LAW vol 25 (2010) PARA 146.

5   Criminal Justice Act 2003 Sch 15 para 3. As to the offence of false imprisonment see CRIMINAL LAW vol 25 (2010) PARA 145.

6   Criminal Justice Act 2003 Sch 15 para 4. As to the offence of soliciting murder (ie an offence under the Offences Against the Person Act 1861 s 4) see CRIMINAL LAW vol 25 (2010) PARA 114.

7   Criminal Justice Act 2003 Sch 15 para 5. As to this offence (ie an offence under the Offences Against the Person Act 1861 s 16) see CRIMINAL LAW vol 25 (2010) PARA 115.

8   Criminal Justice Act 2003 Sch 15 para 6. As to the offence of wounding with intent to cause grievous bodily harm (ie an offence under the Offences Against the Person Act 1861 s 18) see CRIMINAL LAW vol 25 (2010) PARA 128.

9   Criminal Justice Act 2003 Sch 15 para 7. As to the offence of malicious wounding (ie an offence under the Offences Against the Person Act 1861 s 20) see CRIMINAL LAW vol 25 (2010) PARA 130.

10   Criminal Justice Act 2003 Sch 15 para 8. As to this offence (ie an offence under the Offences Against the Person Act 1861 s 21) see CRIMINAL LAW vol 25 (2010) PARA 131.

11   Criminal Justice Act 2003 Sch 15 para 9. As to this offence (ie an offence under the Offences Against the Person Act 1861 s 22) see CRIMINAL LAW vol 25 (2010) PARA 132.

12 Criminal Justice Act 2003 Sch 15 para 10. As to this offence (ie an offence under the Offences Against the Person Act 1861 s 23) see CRIMINAL LAW vol 25 (2010) PARA 133.

13 Criminal Justice Act 2003 Sch 15 para 11. As to this offence (ie an offence under the Offences Against the Person Act 1861 s 27) see CRIMINAL LAW vol 25 (2010) PARA 153.

14 Criminal Justice Act 2003 Sch 15 para 12. As to this offence (ie an offence under the Offences Against the Person Act 1861 s 28) see CRIMINAL LAW vol 25 (2010) PARA 135.

15 Criminal Justice Act 2003 Sch 15 para 13. As to this offence (ie an offence under the Offences Against the Person Act 1861 s 29) see CRIMINAL LAW vol 25 (2010) PARA 136.

16 Criminal Justice Act 2003 Sch 15 para 14. As to this offence (ie an offence under the Offences Against the Person Act 1861 s 30) see CRIMINAL LAW vol 25 (2010) PARA 140.

17 Criminal Justice Act 2003 Sch 15 para 15. As to this offence (ie an offence under the Offences Against the Person Act 1861 s 31) see CRIMINAL LAW vol 25 (2010) PARA 141.

18 Criminal Justice Act 2003 Sch 15 para 16. As to this offence (ie an offence under the Offences Against the Person Act 1861 s 32) see CRIMINAL LAW vol 25 (2010) PARA 142.

19 Criminal Justice Act 2003 Sch 15 para 17. As to this offence (ie an offence under the Offences Against the Person Act 1861 s 35) see ROAD TRAFFIC vol 90 (2011) PARA 775.

20 Criminal Justice Act 2003 Sch 15 para 18. As to this offence (ie an offence under the Offences Against the Person Act 1861 s 37) see SHIPPING AND MARITIME LAW vol 94 (2008) PARA 1228.

21 Criminal Justice Act 2003 Sch 15 para 19. As to this offence (ie an offence under the Offences Against the Person Act 1861 s 38) see CRIMINAL LAW vol 26 (2010) PARA 693.

22 Criminal Justice Act 2003 Sch 15 para 20. As to this offence (ie an offence under the Offences Against the Person Act 1861 s 47) see CRIMINAL LAW vol 25 (2010) PARA 159.

23 Criminal Justice Act 2003 Sch 15 para 21. As to this offence (ie an offence under the Explosive Substances Act 1883 s 2) see CRIMINAL LAW vol 25 (2010) PARA 137.

24 Criminal Justice Act 2003 Sch 15 para 22. As to this offence (ie an offence under the Explosive Substances Act 1883 s 3) see CRIMINAL LAW vol 25 (2010) PARA 138.

25 Criminal Justice Act 2003 Sch 15 para 22A (added by the Criminal Justice and Courts Act 2015 s 2(2)). As to this offence (ie an offence under the Explosive Substances Act 1883 s 4) see CRIMINAL LAW vol 26 (2010) PARA 666.

26 Criminal Justice Act 2003 Sch 15 para 23. As to this offence (ie an offence under the Infant Life (Preservation) Act 1929 s 1) see CRIMINAL LAW vol 25 (2010) PARA 118.

27 Criminal Justice Act 2003 Sch 15 para 24. As to this offence (ie an offence under the Children and Young Persons Act 1933 s 1) see CRIMINAL LAW vol 25 (2010) PARA 153; and CHILDREN AND YOUNG PERSONS vol 9 (2012) PARA 635.

28 Criminal Justice Act 2003 Sch 15 para 25. As to this offence (ie an offence under the Infanticide Act 1938 s 1) see CRIMINAL LAW vol 25 (2010) PARA 113.

29 Criminal Justice Act 2003 Sch 15 para 26. As to this offence (ie an offence under the Firearms Act 1968 s 16) see CRIMINAL LAW vol 26 (2010) PARA 628.

30 Criminal Justice Act 2003 Sch 15 para 27. As to this offence (ie an offence under the Firearms Act 1968 s 16A) see CRIMINAL LAW vol 26 (2010) PARA 629.

31 Criminal Justice Act 2003 Sch 15 para 28. As to this offence (ie an offence under the Firearms Act 1968 s 17(1)) see CRIMINAL LAW vol 26 (2010) PARA 630.

32 Criminal Justice Act 2003 Sch 15 para 29. As to this offence (ie an offence under the Firearms Act 1968 s 17(2), Sch 1) see CRIMINAL LAW vol 26 (2010) PARA 631.

33 Criminal Justice Act 2003 Sch 15 para 30. As to this offence (ie an offence under the Firearms Act 1968 s 18) see CRIMINAL LAW vol 26 (2010) PARA 633.

34 Criminal Justice Act 2003 Sch 15 para 31. As to this offence (ie an offence under the Theft Act 1968 s 8) see CRIMINAL LAW vol 25 (2010) PARA 289.

35 Criminal Justice Act 2003 Sch 15 para 32(a). As to this offence (ie an offence under the Theft Act 1968 s 9) see CRIMINAL LAW vol 25 (2010) PARA 290.

36 Criminal Justice Act 2003 Sch 15 para 32(b). As to this offence (ie an offence under the Theft Act 1968 s 9) see CRIMINAL LAW vol 25 (2010) PARA 290.

37 Criminal Justice Act 2003 Sch 15 para 33. As to the offence of aggravated burglary (ie an offence under the Theft Act 1968 s 10) see CRIMINAL LAW vol 25 (2010) PARA 291.

38 As to the offence of aggravated vehicle-taking (ie an offence under the Theft Act 1968 s 12A) see CRIMINAL LAW vol 25 (2010) PARA 295.

39 Criminal Justice Act 2003 Sch 15 para 34.

40 Criminal Justice Act 2003 Sch 15 para 35. As to the offence of arson (ie an offence under the Criminal Damage Act 1971 s 1) see CRIMINAL LAW vol 25 (2010) PARA 327.

41 Ie an offence under the Criminal Damage Act 1971 s 1(2) (see CRIMINAL LAW vol 25 (2010) PARA 329).

42 Criminal Justice Act 2003 Sch 15 para 36.

43 Criminal Justice Act 2003 Sch 15 para 37. As to the offence of hostage-taking (ie an offence under the Taking of Hostages Act 1982 s 1) see CRIMINAL LAW vol 25 (2010) PARA 416.

44 Criminal Justice Act 2003 Sch 15 paras 38, 51. As to the offence of hijacking an aircraft (ie an offence under the Aviation Security Act 1982 s 1) see AIR LAW vol 2 (2008) PARA 624; and as to the offence of hijacking a ship (ie an offence under the Aviation and Maritime Security Act 1990 s 9) see SHIPPING AND MARITIME LAW vol 94 (2008) PARA 1210.

45 Criminal Justice Act 2003 Sch 15 para 39. As to this offence (ie an offence under the Aviation Security Act 1982 s 2) see AIR LAW vol 2 (2008) PARA 628.

46 Criminal Justice Act 2003 Sch 15 para 40. As to this offence (ie an offence under the Aviation Security Act 1982 s 3) see AIR LAW vol 2 (2008) PARA 629.

47 Criminal Justice Act 2003 Sch 15 para 41. As to this offence (ie an offence under the Aviation Security Act 1982 s 4) see AIR LAW vol 2 (2008) PARA 630.

48 Criminal Justice Act 2003 Sch 15 para 42. As to this offence (ie an offence under the Mental Health Act 1983 s 127) see MENTAL HEALTH AND CAPACITY vol 75 (2013) PARA 1010.

49 Criminal Justice Act 2003 Sch 15 paras 43, 61–63. As to offences involving female genital mutilation see the Female Genital Mutilation Act 2003 s 1 (female genital mutilation), s 2 (assisting a girl to mutilate her own genitalia) and s 3 (assisting a non-United Kingdom person to mutilate overseas a girl's genitalia); and CRIMINAL LAW vol 25 (2010) PARAS 168–169. The Criminal Justice Act 2003 Sch 15 para 43 refers to this offence as being committed under the Prohibition of Female Circumcision Act 1985 s 1 (repealed), but the offence of female circumcision (or female genital mutilation) is now committed under the Female Genital Mutilation Act 2003 s 1 (see CRIMINAL LAW vol 25 (2010) PARA 168).

50 Criminal Justice Act 2003 Sch 15 para 44. As to the offence of riot (ie an offence under the Public Order Act 1986 s 1) see CRIMINAL LAW vol 25 (2010) PARA 487.

51 Criminal Justice Act 2003 Sch 15 para 45. As to the offence of violent disorder (ie an offence under the Public Order Act 1986 s 2) see CRIMINAL LAW vol 25 (2010) PARA 488.

52 Criminal Justice Act 2003 Sch 15 para 46. As to the offence of affray (ie an offence under the Public Order Act 1986 s 3) see CRIMINAL LAW vol 25 (2010) PARA 489.

53 Criminal Justice Act 2003 Sch 15 para 47. As to the offence of torture (ie an offence under the Criminal Justice Act 1988 s 134) see CRIMINAL LAW vol 25 (2010) PARA 172.

54 Criminal Justice Act 2003 Sch 15 para 48. As to this offence (ie an offence under the Road Traffic Act 1988 s 1) see ROAD TRAFFIC vol 90 (2011) PARA 720.

55 Criminal Justice Act 2003 Sch 15 para 48A (added by the Criminal Justice and Courts Act 2015 Sch 6 para 11). As to this offence (ie an offence under the Road Traffic Act 1988 s 3ZC) see ROAD TRAFFIC.

56 Criminal Justice Act 2003 Sch 15 para 49. As to this offence (ie an offence under the Road Traffic Act 1988 s 3A) see ROAD TRAFFIC vol 90 (2011) PARA 731.

57 Criminal Justice Act 2003 Sch 15 para 50. As to this offence (ie an offence under the Aviation and Maritime Security Act 1990 s 1) see AIR LAW vol 2 (2008) PARA 631.

58 Criminal Justice Act 2003 Sch 15 para 52. As to this offence (ie an offence under the Aviation and Maritime Security Act 1990 s 10) see SHIPPING AND MARITIME LAW vol 94 (2008) PARA 1211.

59 Criminal Justice Act 2003 Sch 15 para 53. As to this offence (ie an offence under the Aviation and Maritime Security Act 1990 s 11) see SHIPPING AND MARITIME LAW vol 94 (2008) PARA 1212.

60 Criminal Justice Act 2003 Sch 15 para 54. As to this offence (ie an offence under the Aviation and Maritime Security Act 1990 s 12) see SHIPPING AND MARITIME LAW vol 94 (2008) PARA 1213.

61 Criminal Justice Act 2003 Sch 15 para 55. As to this offence (ie an offence under the Aviation and Maritime Security Act 1990 s 13) see SHIPPING AND MARITIME LAW vol 94 (2008) PARA 1214.

62 Criminal Justice Act 2003 Sch 15 para 56. The offences referred to in the text are offences under the Channel Tunnel (Security) Order 1994, SI 1994/570, Pt II.

63 Criminal Justice Act 2003 Sch 15 para 57. As to this offence (ie an offence under the Protection from Harassment Act 1997 s 4) see CRIMINAL LAW vol 25 (2010) PARA 164.

64 Criminal Justice Act 2003 Sch 15 para 57 (amended by the Protection of Freedoms Act 2012 Sch 9 para 147). As to this offence (ie an offence under the Protection from Harassment Act 1997 s 4A) see CRIMINAL LAW.

65 Criminal Justice Act 2003 Sch 15 para 58. As to this offence (ie an offence under the Crime and Disorder Act 1998 s 29) see CRIMINAL LAW vol 25 (2010) PARA 166.

66 Criminal Justice Act 2003 Sch 15 para 59. The offences referred to in the text are offences under the Public Order Act 1986 s 4 or s 4A (see CRIMINAL LAW vol 25 (2010) PARAS 490, 491) which

fall within the Crime and Disorder Act 1998 s 31(1)(a) or (b) (see CRIMINAL LAW vol 25 (2010) PARA 493): Criminal Justice Act 2003 Sch 15 para 59.

67   Criminal Justice Act 2003 Sch 15 para 59A (Sch 15 paras 59A–59D, 60A–60C, 63B–63F added by the Coroners and Justice Act 2009 s 138). As to this offence (ie an offence under the Terrorism Act 2000 s 54) see CRIMINAL LAW vol 25 (2010) PARA 401.

68   Criminal Justice Act 2003 Sch 15 para 59B (as added: see note 67). As to this offence (ie an offence under the Terrorism Act 2000 s 56) see CRIMINAL LAW vol 25 (2010) PARA 403.

69   Criminal Justice Act 2003 Sch 15 para 59C (as added: see note 67). As to this offence (ie an offence under the Terrorism Act 2000 s 57) see CRIMINAL LAW vol 25 (2010) PARA 404.

70   Criminal Justice Act 2003 Sch 15 para 59D (as added: see note 67). As to this offence (ie an offence under the Terrorism Act 2000 s 59) see CRIMINAL LAW vol 25 (2010) PARA 415.

71   Ie an offence under the International Criminal Court Act 2001 s 51 or s 52 (see INTERNATIONAL RELATIONS LAW vol 61 (2010) PARAS 454. 455).

72   Criminal Justice Act 2003 Sch 15 para 60.

73   Criminal Justice Act 2003 Sch 15 para 60A (as added: see note 67). As to this offence (ie an offence under the Anti-terrorism, Crime and Security Act 2001 s 47) see ARMED CONFLICT AND EMERGENCY vol 3 (2011) PARA 92.

74   Criminal Justice Act 2003 Sch 15 para 60B (as added: see note 67). As to this offence (ie an offence under the Anti-terrorism, Crime and Security Act 2001 s 50) see ARMED CONFLICT AND EMERGENCY vol 3 (2011) PARA 97.

75   Criminal Justice Act 2003 Sch 15 para 60C (as added: see note 67). As to this offence (ie an offence under the Anti-terrorism, Crime and Security Act 2001 s 113) see CRIMINAL LAW vol 25 (2010) PARA 134.

76   Criminal Justice Act 2003 Sch 15 para 63A (added by the Domestic Violence, Crime and Victims Act 2004 Sch 10 para 65; amended by the Domestic Violence, Crime and Victims (Amendment) Act 2012 Schedule para 6). As to this offence (ie an offence under the Domestic Violence, Crime and Victims Act 2004 s 5) see CRIMINAL LAW vol 25 (2010) PARA 117.

77   Criminal Justice Act 2003 Sch 15 para 63B (as added: see note 67). As to this offence (ie an offence under the Terrorism Act 2006 s 5) see CRIMINAL LAW vol 25 (2010) PARA 375.

78   Criminal Justice Act 2003 Sch 15 para 63C (as added: see note 67). As to this offence (ie an offence under the Terrorism Act 2006 s 6) see CRIMINAL LAW vol 25 (2010) PARA 375.

79   Criminal Justice Act 2003 Sch 15 para 63D (as added: see note 67). As to this offence (ie an offence under the Terrorism Act 2006 s 9) see CRIMINAL LAW vol 25 (2010) PARA 375.

80   Criminal Justice Act 2003 Sch 15 para 63E (as added: see note 67). As to this offence (ie an offence under the Terrorism Act 2006 s 10) see CRIMINAL LAW vol 25 (2010) PARA 375.

81   Criminal Justice Act 2003 Sch 15 para 63F (as added: see note 67). As to this offence (ie an offence under the Terrorism Act 2006 s 11) see CRIMINAL LAW vol 25 (2010) PARA 376.

82   Criminal Justice Act 2003 Sch 15 para 63G (Sch 15 paras 63G, 63H added by the Modern Slavery Act 2015 s 6(1), (2)). As to this offence (ie an offence under the Modern Slavery Act 2015 s 1) see CRIMINAL LAW.

83   Criminal Justice Act 2003 Sch 15 para 63H (as added: see note 82). As to this offence (ie an offence under the Modern Slavery Act 2015 s 2 which is not within the Criminal Justice Act 2003 Sch 15 Pt 2) see CRIMINAL LAW.

84   Criminal Justice Act 2003 Sch 15 para 64(1) (Sch 15 paras 64, 65 substituted by the Criminal Justice and Courts Act 2015 s 2(3), (4)).

85   Criminal Justice Act 2003 Sch 15 paras 64(2), 65(1) (as substituted: see note 84). This does not, however, include an attempt to incite the commission of an offence: see *R v Parnell* [2004] EWCA Crim 2523, [2005] 1 WLR 853, (2004) Times, 8 November (case concerned with similar terminology in the Sex Offenders Act 1997 Sch 1 (repealed)).

86   Criminal Justice Act 2003 Sch 15 paras 64(3), 65(2) (as substituted: see note 84).

87   Criminal Justice Act 2003 Sch 15 paras 64(4), 65(3) (as substituted: see note 84).

88   Ie an offence under the Serious Crime Act 2007 Pt 2 (ss 44–67) (see CRIMINAL LAW vol 25 (2010) PARAS 65–72).

89   Criminal Justice Act 2003 Sch 15 paras 64(5), 65(4) (as substituted: see note 84).

90   See the Criminal Justice Act 2003 ss 325, 326, 327(1), (3), (4).

24. Specified sexual offences. The specified sexual offences for the purposes of the statutory provisions dealing with the sentencing of dangerous offenders[1] are:

(1)   rape[2];

(2)   assault by penetration[3];

(3) sexual assault[4];

(4) causing a person to engage in sexual activity without consent[5];

(5) rape of a child aged under 13[6];

(6) assault of a child aged under 13 by penetration[7];

(7) sexual assault of a child aged under 13[8];

(8) causing or inciting a child under 13 to engage in sexual activity[9];

(9) sexual activity with a child[10];

(10) causing or inciting a child to engage in sexual activity[11];

(11) engaging in sexual activity in the presence of a child[12];

(12) causing a child to watch a sexual act[13];

(13) child sex offences committed by children or young persons[14];

(14) arranging or facilitating the commission of a child sex offence[15];

(15) meeting a child following sexual grooming[16];

(16) any of the child sex offences involving abuse of a position of trust[17];

(17) any familial child sex offence[18];

(18) any sexual offences against mentally disordered persons (including offences by care workers)[19];

(19) paying for the sexual services of a child[20];

(20) causing or inciting sexual exploitation of a child[21];

(21) controlling a child in relation to sexual exploitation[22];

(22) arranging or facilitating sexual exploitation of a child[23];

(23) causing or inciting prostitution for gain[24];

(24) controlling prostitution for gain[25];

(25) trafficking into, out of or within the United Kingdom for sexual exploitation[26];

(26) the offences of administering a substance, committing an offence or trespassing with intent to commit a sexual offence[27];

(27) sex with an adult relative[28];

(28) exposure[29];

(29) voyeurism[30];

(30) intercourse with an animal[31];

(31) sexual penetration of a corpse[32];

(32) human trafficking with a view to exploitation[33];

(33) keeping a brothel used for prostitution[34];

(34) the offences relating to the taking, possession etc of indecent photographs of children[35];

(35) certain customs offences relating to the prohibited importation of indecent or obscene articles[36]; and

(36) as from a day to be appointed, sexual communication with a child[37].

Also specified for these purposes are a number of statutory offences which have been repealed[38]. Aiding, abetting, counselling or procuring the commission of any of these offences[39], an attempt[40], conspiracy[41] or incitement[42] to commit any such offence, is also a specified sexual offence for these purposes, as is an offence of encouraging or assisting the commission of an offence[43] in relation to which any such offence is the offence (or one of the offences) which the person intended or believed would be committed[44].

Provision is made for the assessment and management of the risks posed by persons who have been convicted and sentenced for, or (in certain circumstances) found to be not guilty and made the subject of a hospital or guardianship order in consequence of, a specified sexual offence, and other persons who, by reason of offences committed by them, are considered by the responsible authority to be persons who may cause serious harm to the public[45].

1 Ie for the purposes of the Criminal Justice Act 2003 Pt 12 Ch 5 (ss 224–236) (see PARAS 18–23, 33–34): see the Criminal Justice Act 2003 s 224(1), (2)(a), (3), Sch 15 Pt 2 (paras 66–153). For the specified violent offences see PARA 23.

2 Criminal Justice Act 2003 Sch 15 paras 66, 102. As to the offence of rape see the Sexual Offences Act 2003 s 1; and CRIMINAL LAW vol 25 (2010) PARA 178. The offence was formerly committed under the Sexual Offences Act 1956 s 1 (repealed) (see note 38).

3 Criminal Justice Act 2003 Sch 15 para 103. As to this offence (ie an offence under the Sexual Offences Act 2003 s 2) see CRIMINAL LAW vol 25 (2010) PARA 180.

4 Criminal Justice Act 2003 Sch 15 para 104. As to this offence (ie an offence under the Sexual Offences Act 2003 s 3) see CRIMINAL LAW vol 25 (2010) PARA 182.

5 Criminal Justice Act 2003 Sch 15 para 105. As to this offence (ie an offence under the Sexual Offences Act 2003 s 4) see CRIMINAL LAW vol 25 (2010) PARA 184.

6 Criminal Justice Act 2003 Sch 15 para 106. As to this offence (ie an offence under the Sexual Offences Act 2003 s 5) see CRIMINAL LAW vol 25 (2010) PARA 179. As to the determination of a person's age see the Children and Young Persons Act 1933 s 99; and CHILDREN AND YOUNG PERSONS vol 10 (2012) PARA 1206.

7 Criminal Justice Act 2003 Sch 15 para 107. As to this offence (ie an offence under the Sexual Offences Act 2003 s 6) see CRIMINAL LAW vol 25 (2010) PARA 181.

8 Criminal Justice Act 2003 Sch 15 para 108. As to this offence (ie an offence under the Sexual Offences Act 2003 s 7) see CRIMINAL LAW vol 25 (2010) PARA 183.

9 Criminal Justice Act 2003 Sch 15 para 109. As to this offence (ie an offence under the Sexual Offences Act 2003 s 8) see CRIMINAL LAW vol 25 (2010) PARA 185.

10 Criminal Justice Act 2003 Sch 15 para 110. As to this offence (ie an offence under the Sexual Offences Act 2003 s 9) see CRIMINAL LAW vol 25 (2010) PARA 186.

11 Criminal Justice Act 2003 Sch 15 para 111. As to this offence (ie an offence under the Sexual Offences Act 2003 s 10) see CRIMINAL LAW vol 25 (2010) PARA 187.

12 Criminal Justice Act 2003 Sch 15 para 112. As to this offence (ie an offence under the Sexual Offences Act 2003 s 11) see CRIMINAL LAW vol 25 (2010) PARA 188.

13 Criminal Justice Act 2003 Sch 15 para 113. As to this offence (ie an offence under the Sexual Offences Act 2003 s 12) see CRIMINAL LAW vol 25 (2010) PARA 189.

14 Criminal Justice Act 2003 Sch 15 para 114. As to this offence (ie an offence under the Sexual Offences Act 2003 s 13) see CRIMINAL LAW vol 25 (2010) PARA 190.

15 Criminal Justice Act 2003 Sch 15 para 115. As to this offence (ie an offence under the Sexual Offences Act 2003 s 14) see CRIMINAL LAW vol 25 (2010) PARA 191.

16 Criminal Justice Act 2003 Sch 15 para 116. As to this offence (ie an offence under the Sexual Offences Act 2003 s 15) see CRIMINAL LAW vol 25 (2010) PARA 192.

17 Criminal Justice Act 2003 Sch 15 paras 117–120. As to these offences (ie offences under the Sexual Offences Act 2003 ss 16–19) see CRIMINAL LAW vol 25 (2010) PARAS 193–198.

18 Criminal Justice Act 2003 Sch 15 paras 121, 122. As to these offences (ie offences under the Sexual Offences Act 2003 ss 25, 26) see CRIMINAL LAW vol 25 (2010) PARAS 204, 206.

19 Criminal Justice Act 2003 Sch 15 paras 123–134. As to these offences (ie offences under the Sexual Offences Act 2003 ss 30–41) see CRIMINAL LAW vol 25 (2010) PARAS 209–227.

20 Criminal Justice Act 2003 Sch 15 para 135. As to this offence (ie an offence under the Sexual Offences Act 2003 s 47) see CRIMINAL LAW vol 25 (2010) PARA 228.

21 Criminal Justice Act 2003 Sch 15 para 136 (Sch 15 paras 136–138 amended, Sch 15 para 116A prospectively added, by the Serious Crime Act 2007 Sch 4 para 68). As to this offence (ie an offence under the Sexual Offences Act 2003 s 48) see CRIMINAL LAW vol 25 (2010) PARA 229. At the date at which this volume states the law no day had been appointed for the coming onto force of the Serious Crime Act 2007 Sch 4 para 68 so far as relating to the addition of Sch 15 para 116A.

22 Criminal Justice Act 2003 Sch 15 para 137 (as amended: see note 21). As to this offence (ie an offence under the Sexual Offences Act 2003 s 49) see CRIMINAL LAW vol 25 (2010) PARA 229.

23 Criminal Justice Act 2003 Sch 15 para 138 (as amended: see note 21). As to this offence (ie an offence under the Sexual Offences Act 2003 s 50) see CRIMINAL LAW vol 25 (2010) PARA 229.

24 Criminal Justice Act 2003 Sch 15 para 139. As to this offence (ie an offence under the Sexual Offences Act 2003 s 52) see CRIMINAL LAW vol 25 (2010) PARA 230.

25 Criminal Justice Act 2003 Sch 15 para 140. As to this offence (ie an offence under the Sexual Offences Act 2003 s 53) see CRIMINAL LAW vol 25 (2010) PARA 230.

26 Criminal Justice Act 2003 Sch 15 paras 141–143, 143A(Sch 15 para 143A added by the Protection of Freedoms Act 2012 Sch 9 para 139). As to these offences (ie an offence under the Sexual Offences Act 2003 s 57, s 58, s 59 or s 59A) see CRIMINAL LAW vol 25 (2010) PARA 254. As to the meaning of 'United Kingdom' see PARA 4 note 3.

27 Criminal Justice Act 2003 Sch 15 paras 144–146. As to these offences (ie an offence under the Sexual Offences Act 2003 ss 61–63) see CRIMINAL LAW vol 25 (2010) PARAS 257–259.

28 Criminal Justice Act 2003 Sch 15 paras 147, 148. As to these offences (ie an offence under the Sexual Offences Act 2003 ss 64, 65) see CRIMINAL LAW vol 25 (2010) PARAS 201–203.

29 Criminal Justice Act 2003 Sch 15 para 149. As to this offence (ie an offence under the Sexual Offences Act 2003 s 66) see CRIMINAL LAW vol 25 (2010) PARA 265.

30 Criminal Justice Act 2003 Sch 15 para 150. As to this offence (ie an offence under the Sexual Offences Act 2003 s 67) see CRIMINAL LAW vol 25 (2010) PARA 266.

31 Criminal Justice Act 2003 Sch 15 para 151. As to this offence (ie an offence under the Sexual Offences Act 2003 s 69) see CRIMINAL LAW vol 25 (2010) PARA 267.

32 Criminal Justice Act 2003 Sch 15 para 152. As to this offence (ie an offence under the Sexual Offences Act 2003 s 70) see CRIMINAL LAW vol 25 (2010) PARA 268.

33 Criminal Justice Act 2003 Sch 15 para 152A (added by the Modern Slavery Act 2015 s 6(3)). As to this offence (ie an offence under the Modern Slavery Act 2015 s 2 committed with a view to exploitation that consists of or includes behaviour within s 3(3) (sexual exploitation) see CRIMINAL LAW.

34 Criminal Justice Act 2003 Sch 15 para 92A (added by the Criminal Justice and Courts Act 2015 s 2(6)). As to this offence (ie an offence under the Sexual Offences Act 1956 s 33) see CRIMINAL LAW vol 25 (2010) PARA 244.

35 Criminal Justice Act 2003 Sch 15 paras 99, 101. As to these offences (ie offences under the Protection of Children Act 1978 s 1 and the Criminal Justice Act 1988 s 160 see CRIMINAL LAW vol 25 (2010) PARAS 260–261.

36 Criminal Justice Act 2003 Sch 15 para 100. As to these offences (ie offences under the Customs and Excise Management Act 1979 s 170 (penalty for fraudulent evasion of duty etc) in relation to goods prohibited to be imported under the Customs Consolidation Act 1876 s 42 (indecent or obscene articles) (repealed), if the prohibited goods included indecent photographs of persons under 16) see CUSTOMS AND EXCISE vol 31 (2012) PARA 1175.

37 Criminal Justice Act 2003 Sch 15 para 116A (prospectively added: see note 21). As to this offence (ie an offence under the Sexual Offences Act 2003 s 15A) see CRIMINAL LAW.

38 Ie, in addition to the offence of rape under the Sexual Offences Act 1956 s 1 (repealed) (see the text and note 2), the offences of procurement of a woman by threats (see s 2 (repealed)) or false pretences (see s 3 (repealed)), administering drugs to obtain or facilitate intercourse (see s 4 (repealed)), intercourse with a girl aged under 13 (see s 5 (repealed)) or, where the offender is aged 20 or over, under 16 (see s 6 (repealed)), intercourse with or procurement of a defective (see ss 7, 9 (repealed)), incest by a man (see s 10 (repealed)) or a woman (see s 11 (repealed)), indecent assault on a woman or man (see ss 14, 15 (both repealed)), assault with intent to commit buggery (if the victim or (as the case may be) other party was under 18) (see s 16 (repealed)), abduction of a woman by force or for the sake of her property (see s 17 (repealed)), abduction of an unmarried girl from her parent or guardian (see ss 18–20 (repealed)), abduction of a defective from his parent or guardian (see s 21 (repealed)), causing prostitution of women (see s 22 (repealed)), procuration of a girl aged under 21 (see s 23 (repealed)), detention of women in a brothel (see s 24 (repealed)), permitting a girl under 16 to use premises for intercourse (see ss 25, 26 (repealed)), permitting a defective to use premises for intercourse (see s 27 (repealed)), causing or encouraging the prostitution of, intercourse with or indecent assault on a girl under 16 (see s 28 (repealed)), causing or encouraging the prostitution of a defective (see s 29 (repealed)), soliciting by men (see s 32 (repealed)), sexual intercourse with mental patients (see the Mental Health Act 1959 (repealed)), indecent conduct towards a young child (see the Indecency with Children Act 1960 s 1 (repealed)), procuring others to commit homosexual acts (see the Sexual Offences Act 1967 s 4 (repealed)), living on the earnings of male prostitution (see s 5 (repealed)), burglary with intent to commit rape (see the Theft Act 1968 s 9 (no longer in effect with regard to this offence)), and inciting a girl under 16 to have incestuous sexual intercourse (see the Criminal Law Act 1977 s 54 (repealed)): see the Criminal Justice Act 2003 Sch 15 paras 66–91, 93–98.

39 Criminal Justice Act 2003 Sch 15 para 153(1) (Sch 15 para 153 substituted by the Criminal Justice and Courts Act 2015 s 2(7)).

40 Criminal Justice Act 2003 Sch 15 para 153(2) (as substituted: see note 39). This does not, however, include an attempt to incite the commission of an offence: see *R v Parnell* [2004] EWCA Crim 2523, [2005] 1 WLR 853, (2004) Times, 8 November (case concerned with similar terminology in the Sex Offenders Act 1997 Sch 1 (repealed)).

41 Criminal Justice Act 2003 Sch 15 para 153(3) (as substituted: see note 39).
42 Criminal Justice Act 2003 Sch 15 para 153(4) (as substituted: see note 39).
43 Ie an offence under the Serious Crime Act 2007 Pt 2 (ss 44–67) (see CRIMINAL LAW vol 25 (2010) PARAS 65–72).
44 Criminal Justice Act 2003 Sch 15 para 153(5) (as substituted: see note 39).
45 See the Criminal Justice Act 2003 ss 325, 326, 327(1), (3), (4).

25. Offences an existing conviction for which qualify an offender for a life sentence or an extended sentence of imprisonment ('second listed offences'). The offences an existing conviction for which may trigger an automatic life sentence[1] or an extended sentence of imprisonment[2] are:

    (1)   murder[3];
    (2)   manslaughter[4];
    (3)   soliciting murder[5];
    (4)   wounding with intent to cause grievous bodily harm[6];
    (5)   causing bodily injury by explosives[7];
    (6)   using explosives etc with intent to do grievous bodily harm[8];
    (7)   causing an explosion likely to endanger life or property[9];
    (8)   attempting to cause an explosion, or making or keeping explosive with intent to endanger life or property[10];
    (9)   making or possession of explosive under suspicious circumstances[11];
    (10)   possession of a firearm with intent to endanger life[12];
    (11)   using a forearm to resist arrest[13];
    (12)   carrying a firearm with criminal intent[14];
    (13)   robbery[15] involving possession of a firearm[16];
    (14)   offences relating to the taking, making and distribution of indecent photographs of children[17];
    (15)   directing terrorist organisations[18];
    (16)   weapons training[19];
    (17)   possessing articles for terrorist purposes[20];
    (18)   inciting terrorism overseas[21];
    (19)   use of nuclear weapons[22];
    (20)   assisting or inducing certain weapons-related acts overseas[23];
    (21)   use of noxious substances or things to cause harm or intimidate[24];
    (22)   rape[25];
    (23)   assault by penetration[26];
    (24)   causing a person to engage in sexual activity without consent[27];
    (25)   rape of a child aged under 13[28];
    (26)   assault of a child aged under 13 by penetration[29];
    (27)   sexual assault of a child aged under 13[30];
    (28)   causing or inciting a child under 13 to engage in sexual activity[31];
    (29)   sexual activity with a child[32];
    (30)   causing or inciting a child to engage in sexual activity[33];
    (31)   engaging in sexual activity in the presence of a child[34];
    (32)   causing a child to watch a sexual act[35];
    (33)   arranging or facilitating the commission of a child sex offence[36];
    (34)   meeting a child following sexual grooming[37];
    (35)   sexual activity with a child family member[38];
    (36)   inciting a child family member to engage in sexual activity[39];
    (37)   sexual activity with a person with a mental disorder impeding choice[40];
    (38)   causing or inciting a person with a mental disorder to engage in sexual activity[41];

(39) inducement, threat or deception to procure sexual activity with a person with a mental disorder[42];

(40) causing a person with a mental disorder to engage in or agree to engage in sexual activity by inducement[43];

(41) paying for the sexual services of a child[44];

(42) causing or inciting child prostitution or pornography[45];

(43) controlling a child prostitute or a child involved in pornography[46];

(44) arranging or facilitating child prostitution or pornography[47];

(45) committing an offence with intent to commit a sexual offence)[48];

(46) causing or allowing a child or vulnerable adult to die or suffer serious physical harm[49];

(47) preparation of terrorist acts[50];

(48) training for terrorism[51];

(49) making or possession of radioactive device or material[52];

(50) use of radioactive device or material for terrorist purposes[53];

(51) terrorist threats relating to radioactive devices[54];

(52) slavery, servitude and forced or compulsory labour[55];

(53) human trafficking[56]; and

(52) any offence that was abolished (with or without savings) before 3 December 2012[57] and would, if committed on the relevant day[58], have constituted an offence listed above (other than murder)[59].

An attempt, conspiracy or incitement to commit any of these offences, other than the abolished offences, or aiding, abetting, counselling or procuring the commission of any such offence, is also a specified offence for these purposes[60], as is an offence of encouraging or assisting the commission of an offence[61] in relation to which one of the offences listed above is the offence (or one of the offences) which the person intended or believed would be committed[62]. Corresponding offences under service law[63] and convictions elsewhere in the United Kingdom or in other member states[64] also apply for these purposes[65].

1   Ie pursuant to the Criminal Justice Act 2003 s 224A (see PARA 35).

2   Ie pursuant to the Criminal Justice Act 2003 s 226A (see PARAS 18–20). These provisions also apply in connection with s 246A (release on licence of prisoners serving extended sentences: see PARA 716).

3   Criminal Justice Act 2003 Sch 15B para 45 (Sch 15B added by the Legal Aid, Sentencing and Punishment of Offenders Act 2012 Sch 18).

4   Criminal Justice Act 2003 Sch 15B para 1 (Sch 15B added by the Legal Aid, Sentencing and Punishment of Offenders Act 2012 Sch 18).

5   Criminal Justice Act 2003 Sch 15B para 2 (as added: see note 3). As to the offence of soliciting murder (ie an offence under the Offences Against the Person Act 1861 s 4) see CRIMINAL LAW vol 25 (2010) PARA 114.

6   Criminal Justice Act 2003 Sch 15B para 3 (as added: see note 3). As to the offence of wounding with intent to cause grievous bodily harm (ie an offence under the Offences Against the Person Act 1861 s 18) see CRIMINAL LAW vol 25 (2010) PARA 128.

7   Criminal Justice Act 2003 Sch 15B para 3A (as added (see note 3); Sch 15B paras (3A)–(3E) further added by the Criminal Justice and Courts Act 2015 s 3(2)). As to the offence of causing bodily injury by explosives (ie an offence under the Offences Against the Person Act 1861 s 28) see CRIMINAL LAW vol 25 (2010) PARA 135.

8   Criminal Justice Act 2003 Sch 15B para 3B (as added: see notes 3, 7). As to the offence of using explosives etc with intent to do grievous bodily harm (ie an offence under the Offences Against the Person Act 1861 s 29) see CRIMINAL LAW vol 25 (2010) PARA 136.

9   Criminal Justice Act 2003 Sch 15B para 3C (as added: see notes 3, 7). As to the offence of causing an explosion likely to endanger life or property (ie an offence under the Explosive Substances Act 1883 s 2) see CRIMINAL LAW vol 25 (2010) PARA 137.

10 Criminal Justice Act 2003 Sch 15B para 3D (as added: see notes 3, 7). As to the offence of attempting to cause an explosion, or making or keeping explosive with intent to endanger life or property (ie an offence under the Explosive Substances Act 1883 s 3) see CRIMINAL LAW vol 25 (2010) PARA 138.

11 Criminal Justice Act 2003 Sch 15B para 3E (as added: see notes 3, 7). As to the offence of making or possession of explosive under suspicious circumstances (ie an offence under the Explosive Substances Act 1883 s 4) see CRIMINAL LAW vol 26 (2010) PARA 666.

12 Criminal Justice Act 2003 Sch 15B para 4 (as added: see note 3). As to this offence (ie an offence under the Firearms Act 1968 s 16) see CRIMINAL LAW vol 26 (2010) PARA 628.

13 Criminal Justice Act 2003 Sch 15B para 5 (as added: see note 3). As to this offence (ie an offence under the Firearms Act 1968 s 17(1)) see CRIMINAL LAW vol 26 (2010) PARA 630.

14 Criminal Justice Act 2003 Sch 15B para 6 (as added: see note 3). As to this offence (ie an offence under the Firearms Act 1968 s 18) see CRIMINAL LAW vol 26 (2010) PARA 633.

15 Ie an offence under the Theft Act 1968 s 8 (see CRIMINAL LAW vol 25 (2010) PARA 289).

16 Criminal Justice Act 2003 Sch 15B para 7 (as added: see note 3). This offence is committed where at some time during the commission of the offence the offender has in his possession a firearms or imitation firearm within the meaning of the Firearms Act 1968 (see CRIMINAL LAW vol 26 (2010) PARAS 578, 581): Criminal Justice Act 2003 Sch 15B para 7 (as so added). As to the use of a firearm in the commission of a second serious offence see further *R v Buckland* [2000] 1 All ER 907, [2000] 1 Cr App Rep 471, CA; *R v Benfield* [2003] EWCA Crim 2223, [2004] 1 Cr App Rep (S) 307, [2003] Crim LR 811 (explained in *R v Hylands* [2004] EWCA Crim 2999, [2005] 2 Cr App Rep (S) 135, [2005] Crim LR 154).

17 Criminal Justice Act 2003 Sch 15B para 8 (as added: see note 3). As to this offence (ie an offence under the Protection of Children Act 1978 s 1) see CRIMINAL LAW vol 25 (2010) PARA 260.

18 Criminal Justice Act 2003 Sch 15B para 8A (as added (see note 3); Sch 15B para 8A further added, Sch 15B para 9 amended, by the Criminal Justice and Courts Act 2015 s 3(3), (4)). As to this offence (ie an offence under the Terrorism Act 2000 s 54) see CRIMINAL LAW vol 25 (2010) PARA 401.

19 Criminal Justice Act 2003 Sch 15B para 9 (as added and amended: see notes 3, 18). As to this offence (ie an offence under the Terrorism Act 2000 s 56) see CRIMINAL LAW vol 25 (2010) PARA 403.

20 Criminal Justice Act 2003 Sch 15B para 10 (as added: see note 3). As to this offence (ie an offence under the Terrorism Act 2000 s 57) see CRIMINAL LAW vol 25 (2010) PARA 404.

21 Criminal Justice Act 2003 Sch 15B para 11 (as added: see note 3). As to this offence (ie an offence under the Terrorism Act 2000 s 59) see CRIMINAL LAW vol 25 (2010) PARA 415. This offence is applicable for these purposes only if the offender is liable on conviction on indictment to imprisonment for life: Criminal Justice Act 2003 Sch 15B para 11 (as so added). In Sch 15B 'imprisonment for life' includes custody for life (see PARAS 36–37) and detention for life (see PARAS 16–17): Sch 15B para 50 (as so added).

22 Criminal Justice Act 2003 Sch 15B para 12 (as added: see note 3). As to this offence (ie an offence under the Anti-terrorism, Crime and Security Act 2001 s 47) see ARMED CONFLICT AND EMERGENCY vol 3 (2011) PARA 92.

23 Criminal Justice Act 2003 Sch 15B para 13 (as added: see note 3). As to this offence (ie an offence under the Anti-terrorism, Crime and Security Act 2001 s 50) see ARMED CONFLICT AND EMERGENCY vol 3 (2011) PARA 97.

24 Criminal Justice Act 2003 Sch 15B para 14 (as added: see note 3). As to this offence (ie an offence under the Anti-terrorism, Crime and Security Act 2001 s 113) see CRIMINAL LAW vol 25 (2010) PARA 134.

25 Criminal Justice Act 2003 Sch 15B para 15 (as added: see note 3). As to the offence of rape see the Sexual Offences Act 2003 s 1; and CRIMINAL LAW vol 25 (2010) PARA 178.

26 Criminal Justice Act 2003 Sch 15B para 16 (as added: see note 3). As to this offence (ie an offence under the Sexual Offences Act 2003 s 2) see CRIMINAL LAW vol 25 (2010) PARA 180.

27 Criminal Justice Act 2003 Sch 15B para 17 (as added: see note 3). As to this offence (ie an offence under the Sexual Offences Act 2003 s 4) see CRIMINAL LAW vol 25 (2010) PARA 184. This offence is applicable for these purposes only if the offender is liable on conviction on indictment to imprisonment for life: Criminal Justice Act 2003 Sch 15B para 17 (as so added).

28 Criminal Justice Act 2003 Sch 15B para 18 (as added: see note 3). As to this offence (ie an offence under the Sexual Offences Act 2003 s 5) see CRIMINAL LAW vol 25 (2010) PARA 179. As to the determination of a person's age see the Children and Young Persons Act 1933 s 99; and CHILDREN AND YOUNG PERSONS vol 10 (2012) PARA 1206.

29 Criminal Justice Act 2003 Sch 15B para 19 (as added: see note 3). As to this offence (ie an offence under the Sexual Offences Act 2003 s 6) see CRIMINAL LAW vol 25 (2010) PARA 181.

30 Criminal Justice Act 2003 Sch 15B para 20 (as added: see note 3). As to this offence (ie an offence under the Sexual Offences Act 2003 s 7) see CRIMINAL LAW vol 25 (2010) PARA 183.

31 Criminal Justice Act 2003 Sch 15B para 21 (as added: see note 3). As to this offence (ie an offence under the Sexual Offences Act 2003 s 8) see CRIMINAL LAW vol 25 (2010) PARA 185.

32 Criminal Justice Act 2003 Sch 15B para 22 (as added: see note 3). As to this offence (ie an offence under the Sexual Offences Act 2003 s 9) see CRIMINAL LAW vol 25 (2010) PARA 186.

33 Criminal Justice Act 2003 Sch 15B para 23 (as added: see note 3). As to this offence (ie an offence under the Sexual Offences Act 2003 s 10) see CRIMINAL LAW vol 25 (2010) PARA 187.

34 Criminal Justice Act 2003 Sch 15B para 24 (as added: see note 3). As to this offence (ie an offence under the Sexual Offences Act 2003 s 11) see CRIMINAL LAW vol 25 (2010) PARA 188.

35 Criminal Justice Act 2003 Sch 15B para 25 (as added: see note 3). As to this offence (ie an offence under the Sexual Offences Act 2003 s 12) see CRIMINAL LAW vol 25 (2010) PARA 189.

36 Criminal Justice Act 2003 Sch 15B para 26 (as added: see note 3). As to this offence (ie an offence under the Sexual Offences Act 2003 s 14) see CRIMINAL LAW vol 25 (2010) PARA 191.

37 Criminal Justice Act 2003 Sch 15B para 27 (as added: see note 3). As to this offence (ie an offence under the Sexual Offences Act 2003 s 15) see CRIMINAL LAW vol 25 (2010) PARA 192.

38 Criminal Justice Act 2003 Sch 15B para 28 (as added: see note 3). As to this offence (ie an offence under the Sexual Offences Act 2003 s 25) see CRIMINAL LAW vol 25 (2010) PARAS 204, 206.

39 Criminal Justice Act 2003 Sch 15B para 29 (as added: see note 3). As to this offence (ie an offence under the Sexual Offences Act 2003 s 26) see CRIMINAL LAW vol 25 (2010) PARAS 204, 206.

40 Criminal Justice Act 2003 Sch 15B para 30 (as added: see note 3). As to this offence (ie an offence under the Sexual Offences Act 2003 s 30) see CRIMINAL LAW vol 25 (2010) PARAS 210, 214. This offence is applicable for these purposes only if the offender is liable on conviction on indictment to imprisonment for life: Criminal Justice Act 2003 Sch 15B para 30 (as so added).

41 Criminal Justice Act 2003 Sch 15B para 31 (as added: see note 3). As to this offence (ie an offence under the Sexual Offences Act 2003 s 31) see CRIMINAL LAW vol 25 (2010) PARAS 211, 214. This offence is applicable for these purposes only if the offender is liable on conviction on indictment to imprisonment for life: Criminal Justice Act 2003 Sch 15B para 31 (as so added).

42 Criminal Justice Act 2003 Sch 15B para 32 (as added: see note 3). As to this offence (ie an offence under the Sexual Offences Act 2003 s 34) see CRIMINAL LAW vol 25 (2010) PARAS 215, 219. This offence is applicable for these purposes only if the offender is liable on conviction on indictment to imprisonment for life: Criminal Justice Act 2003 Sch 15B para 32 (as so added).

43 Criminal Justice Act 2003 Sch 15B para 33 (as added: see note 3). As to this offence (ie an offence under the Sexual Offences Act 2003 s 35) see CRIMINAL LAW vol 25 (2010) PARAS 216, 219. This offence is applicable for these purposes only if the offender is liable on conviction on indictment to imprisonment for life: Criminal Justice Act 2003 Sch 15B para 33 (as so added).

44 Criminal Justice Act 2003 Sch 15B para 34 (as added: see note 3). As to this offence (ie an offence under the Sexual Offences Act 2003 s 47) see CRIMINAL LAW vol 25 (2010) PARA 228. This offence is applicable for these purposes only if person against whom it is committed is aged under 16: Criminal Justice Act 2003 Sch 15B para 34 (as so added).

45 Criminal Justice Act 2003 Sch 15B para 35 (as added: see note 3). As to this offence (ie an offence under the Sexual Offences Act 2003 s 48) see CRIMINAL LAW vol 25 (2010) PARA 229.

46 Criminal Justice Act 2003 Sch 15B para 36 (as added: see note 3). As to this offence (ie an offence under the Sexual Offences Act 2003 s 49) see CRIMINAL LAW vol 25 (2010) PARA 229.

47 Criminal Justice Act 2003 Sch 15B para 37 (as added: see note 3). As to this offence (ie an offence under the Sexual Offences Act 2003 s 50) see CRIMINAL LAW vol 25 (2010) PARA 229.

48 Criminal Justice Act 2003 Sch 15B para 38 (as added: see note 3). As to this offence (ie an offence under the Sexual Offences Act 2003 s 62) see CRIMINAL LAW vol 25 (2010) PARA 258. This offence is applicable for these purposes only if the offender is liable on conviction on indictment to imprisonment for life: Criminal Justice Act 2003 Sch 15B para 38 (as so added).

49 Criminal Justice Act 2003 Sch 15B para 39 (as added: see note 3). As to this offence (ie an offence under the Domestic Violence, Crime and Victims Act 2004 s 5) see CRIMINAL LAW vol 25 (2010) PARA 117.

50 Criminal Justice Act 2003 Sch 15B para 40 (as added: see note 3). As to this offence (ie an offence under the Terrorism Act 2006 s 5) see CRIMINAL LAW vol 25 (2010) PARA 375.

51 Criminal Justice Act 2003 Sch 15B para 40A (as added (see note 3); further added by the Criminal Justice and Courts Act 2015 s 3(5)). As to this offence (ie an offence under the Terrorism Act 2006 s 6) see CRIMINAL LAW vol 25 (2010) PARA 375.

52 Criminal Justice Act 2003 Sch 15B para 41 (as added: see note 3). As to this offence (ie an offence under the Terrorism Act 2006 s 9) see CRIMINAL LAW vol 25 (2010) PARA 375.

53 Criminal Justice Act 2003 Sch 15B para 42 (as added: see note 3). As to this offence (ie an offence under the Terrorism Act 2006 s 10) see CRIMINAL LAW vol 25 (2010) PARA 375.
54 Criminal Justice Act 2003 Sch 15B para 43 (as added: see note 3). As to this offence (ie an offence under the Terrorism Act 2006 s 11) see CRIMINAL LAW vol 25 (2010) PARA 376.
55 Criminal Justice Act 2003 Sch 15B para 43A (Sch 15B paras 43A, 43B added by the Modern Slavery Act 2015 s 6(4)). As to this offence (ie an offence under the Modern Slavery Act 2015 s 1) see CRIMINAL LAW.
56 Criminal Justice Act 2003 Sch 15B para 43B (as added: see note 55). As to this offence (ie an offence under the Modern Slavery Act 2015 s 2) see CRIMINAL LAW.
57 Criminal Justice Act 2003 Sch 15B para 46(1)(a) (as added: see note 3). 3 December 2012 is the date on which the Criminal Justice Act 2003 Sch 15B was brought into force by virtue of the Legal Aid, Sentencing and Punishment of Offenders Act 2012 (Commencement No 4 and Saving Provisions) Order 2012, SI 2012/2906.
58 'Relevant day', in relation to an offence, means: (1) for the purposes of the Criminal Justice Act 2003 Sch 15B para 46 as it applies for the purposes of s 246A(2) (see PARA 716), the day on which the offender was convicted of that offence (Sch 15B para 46(2)(a) (as added: see note 3)); and (2) for the purposes of Sch 15B para 46 as it applies for the purposes of ss 224A(4), 226A(2) (see PARAS 18–20, 35), the day on which the offender was convicted of the offence referred to in s 224A(1)(a) or s 226A(1)(a) (as appropriate) (Sch 15B para 46(2)(a) (as so added)).
59 Criminal Justice Act 2003 Sch 15B para 46(1)(b) (as added: see note 3).
60 Criminal Justice Act 2003 Sch 15B para 44(1)–(3), (5) (as added: see note 3).
61 Ie an offence under the Serious Crime Act 2007 Pt 2 (ss 44–67) (see CRIMINAL LAW vol 25 (2010) PARAS 65–72).
62 Criminal Justice Act 2003 Sch 15B para 44(4) (as added: see note 3).
63 Ie an offence under the Armed Forces Act 2006 s 42 (criminal conduct: see ARMED FORCES vol 3 (2011) PARA 587) as respects which the corresponding offence under the law of England and Wales (within the meaning given by s 42) is an offence specified in the Criminal Justice Act 2003 Sch 15B paras 1–46 (see the text and notes 1–59) (Sch 15B para 48(1) (as added: see note 3)) and an offence under the Army Act 1955 s 70, the Air Force Act 1955 s 70 or the Naval Discipline Act 1957 s 42 (all repealed) as respects which the corresponding civil offence (within the meaning of the Act in question) is an offence specified in the Criminal Justice Act 2003 Sch 15B paras 1–46 (Sch 15B para 47(1) (as so added)).
64 Ie an offence for which the person was convicted in Scotland, Northern Ireland or a member State other than the United Kingdom and which, if committed in England and Wales at the time of the conviction, would have constituted an offence specified in the Criminal Justice Act 2003 Sch 15B paras 1–46: Sch 15B para 49 (as added: see note 3).
65 Criminal Justice Act 2003 Sch 15B paras 47(1), 48(1), 49, 49A, 49B (as added (see note 3); Sch 15B para 49 amended, Sch 15B paras 49A, 49B further added, by the Criminal Justice and Courts Act 2015 s 3(6)–(8)). So far as offences under the Armed Forces Act 2006 are concerned, s 48 (attempts, conspiracy etc: see ARMED FORCES vol 3 (2011) PARA 587) applies with specified modifications for the purposes of the Criminal Justice Act 2003 Sch 15B para 48: Sch 15B para 48(2) (as so added).

(4) TERMS, TARIFF AND COMMENCEMENT OF SENTENCE

(i) Imprisonment Generally

26. Tariff. In the majority of custodial sentences the tariff will be determined in accordance with sentencing guidelines issued by the Sentencing Council for England and Wales[1]. There is also a type of 'tariff' system which has been developed on a non-statutory basis through guideline judgments delivered by the Court of Appeal (in which, having considered the existing practice in sentencing for the offence in question, and identified mitigating and aggravating features, the Court of Appeal has set out a 'tariff' or starting point for passing sentence)[2]. The Court of Appeal has occasionally also given guideline decisions on particular types of sentence[3]. Guideline cases provide guidelines only and should not be applied rigidly to every case[4].

1   See PARA 557 et seq.
2   For examples of guideline cases see *R v Aramah* (1982) 76 Cr App Rep 190, 4 Cr App Rep (S)
    407, CA (guidelines on appropriate sentences for possession of controlled drugs); *R v Millberry*
    [2002] EWCA Crim 2891, [2003] 2 All ER 939, [2003] 1 Cr App Rep 396 (guidelines on
    appropriate sentences for rape); *R v Saw* [2009] EWCA Crim 1, [2009] 2 All ER 1138, [2009]
    2 Cr App Rep (S) 367 (guidelines on appropriate sentences for domestic burglary). As to
    sentencing authorities generally see *R v De Havilland* (1983) 5 Cr App Rep (S) 109 at 114, CA;
    R v Morris (1987) 9 Cr App Rep (S) 528 at 530, CA; *R v Lyon* [2005] EWCA Crim 1365,
    (2005) Times, 19 May, [2005] All ER (D) 179 (May). Contrast *R v Johnson* (1994) 15 Cr App
    Rep (S) 827, [1994] Crim LR 537, CA; *A-G's Reference (No 7 of 1997), R v Fearon* [1998] 1 Cr
    App Rep (S) 268, [1997] Crim LR 908, CA; *A-G's Reference (No 52 of 2003), R v Webb* [2003]
    EWCA Crim 3731, [2004] Crim LR 306.
3   See eg *R v George* [1984] 3 All ER 13, 79 Cr App Rep 26, CA (deferment of sentence).
4   See *R v Nicholas* (1986) Times, 23 April, CA; *R v Attuh-Benson* [2004] EWCA Crim 3032,
    [2005] 2 Cr App Rep (S) 52; *A-G's Reference (No 4 of 1989)* [1990] 1 WLR 41, 90 Cr App Rep
    366, CA (task of sentencing judge should not involve a rigid arithmetical approach); *A-G's*
    References (Nos 31, 45, 43, 42, 50 and 51 of 2004) [2004] EWCA Crim 1934, [2005] 1 Cr App
    Rep (S) 377 (judge can choose whether or not to apply a Court of Appeal guideline depending
    on whether it is appropriate to do so; if the guidelines are not followed, an explanation should
    be given). It is not open to a judge to disregard a Court of Appeal guideline because he does not
    agree with it: *R v Chambers* [2005] EWCA Crim 1160, [2006] 1 Cr App Rep (S) 135.

27.   Commencement of a Crown Court sentence.   A sentence[1] imposed, or
other order[2] made, by the Crown Court when dealing with an offender takes
effect from the beginning of the day on which it is imposed, unless the court
otherwise directs[3]. This power to direct, however, has effect subject to the
requirement that a court sentencing a person to a term of imprisonment may not
order or direct that the term is to commence on the expiry of any other sentence
of imprisonment[4] from which he has been[5] released early[6].

1   For this purpose 'sentence' includes a recommendation for deportation made when dealing with
    an offender: Powers of Criminal Courts (Sentencing) Act 2000 ss 154(3), 155(8).
2   For this purpose 'order' does not include an order relating to a requirement to make a payment
    under regulations under the Legal Aid, Sentencing and Punishment of Offenders Act 2012 s 23
    or s 24 (see LEGAL AID vol 65 (2014) PARAS 46, 47, 143): Powers of Criminal Courts
    (Sentencing) Act 2000 s 155(8) (amended by the Legal Aid, Sentencing and Punishment of
    Offenders Act 2012 Sch 5 paras 52, 54).
3   Powers of Criminal Courts (Sentencing) Act 2000 s 154(1). This does not empower the court to
    antedate a sentence: *R v Gilbert* [1975] 1 All ER 742, 60 Cr App Rep 220, CA; *R v Whitfield*
    [2001] EWCA Crim 3043, [2002] 2 Cr App Rep (S) 44, CA; *R v Salmon* [2002] EWCA Crim
    2088, [2003] 1 Cr App Rep (S) 441. See, however, the text and notes 4–6. Where a sentence or
    order is varied by the Crown Court (see CRIMINAL PROCEDURE vol 27 (2015) PARA 433), the
    sentence or order as so varied takes effect from the beginning of the day on which it was
    originally imposed or made unless the court otherwise directs (Powers of Criminal Courts
    (Sentencing) Act 2000 s 155(5)); although for the purposes of time running in respect of a notice
    of appeal or of application for leave to appeal under the Criminal Appeal Act 1968 s 18(2) (see
    CRIMINAL PROCEDURE vol 28 (2015) PARA 749) or of an application for leave to refer a case
    under the Criminal Justice Act 1988 Sch 3 para 1 it is to be regarded as imposed on the day on
    which it is varied (Powers of Criminal Courts (Sentencing) Act 2000 s 155(6)).
4   'Sentence of imprisonment' does not include a committal in default of payment of any sum of
    money, for want of sufficient distress to satisfy any sum of money, or for failure to do or abstain
    from doing anything required to be done or left undone (including, as from a day to be
    appointed, contempt of court or any kindred offence); and references to 'sentencing an offender
    to imprisonment' are to be read accordingly: Criminal Justice Act 2003 s 305(1) (prospectively
    amended by the Police and Justice Act 2006 s 34(1), (6)). At the date at which this volume states
    the law no day had been appointed for this purpose. For this purpose 'sentence of
    imprisonment' also includes a sentence of detention under the Powers of Criminal Courts
    (Sentencing) Act 2000 s 91 (see PARA 8) or s 96 (see PARA 16) or under the Criminal Justice
    Act 2003 s 226A or s 226B (extended sentence for violent and sexual offence: see PARAS 18–20)
    or the repealed provisions which formerly made provision for extended sentences (ie ss 227,
    228) or s 236A (offenders of particular concern: see PARA 32): Criminal Justice Act 2003

s 265(2) (amended by the Legal Aid, Sentencing and Punishment of Offenders Act 2012 s 117(1), (9), Sch 20 paras 1, 13; by the Criminal Justice and Courts Act 2015 Sch 1 para 24; and by SI 2005/643).

5   Ie under the early release provisions of the Criminal Justice Act 2003 Pt 12 Ch 6 (ss 237–268) (see PARAS 688–745) or the Criminal Justice Act 1991 Pt 2 (ss 32–51) (repealed other than in relation to sentences of imprisonment of less than 12 months or imposed in respect of offences committed before 4 April 2005: see the Criminal Justice Act 2003 (Commencement No 8 and Transitional and Saving Provisions) Order 2005, SI 2005/950, Sch 2 paras 14, 19(c), 20): Criminal Justice Act 2003 s 265(1) (amended by the Criminal Justice and Immigration Act 2008 s 20(1), (4)). In connection with the sentencing of dangerous offenders for offences committed pre- and post-4 April 2005 see PARA 18 note 3.

6   Powers of Criminal Courts (Sentencing) Act 2000 s 154(2) (amended by the Criminal Justice Act 2003 Sch 32 paras 90, 121); Criminal Justice Act 2003 s 265(1) (as amended: see note 5). See *R v Costello* [2010] EWCA Crim 371, [2010] 3 All ER 490, [2011] 1 WLR 638.

28.   Imprisonment in cases where no term is fixed.   Where a person is convicted on indictment of an offence against any enactment and is for that offence liable to be sentenced to imprisonment, but the sentence is not by any enactment either limited to a specified term or expressed to extend to imprisonment for life, he is liable to imprisonment for not more than two years[1].

An indictable offence at common law for which no maximum is provided by statute is punishable by fine and imprisonment, and in such a case there is no limit fixed for the period of imprisonment provided that it is not inordinate[2].

A magistrates' court may not impose imprisonment for less than five days[3], but in certain cases detention within the precincts of the court or in police custody or in a police station may be ordered[4]. There are also restrictions on the passing of custodial sentences on defendants who are not legally represented[5].

1   Powers of Criminal Courts (Sentencing) Act 2000 s 77. For restrictions on passing a custodial sentence see PARA 536.

2   *R v Castro* (1880) 5 QBD 490 at 509, CA, per Bramwell LJ; affd sub nom *Castro v R* (1881) 6 App Cas 229, HL. As to fines see PARAS 174–184.

3   Magistrates' Courts Act 1980 s 132. 'Impose imprisonment' in this context means pass a sentence of imprisonment or fix a term of imprisonment for failure to pay any sum of money, or for want of sufficient goods to satisfy any sum of money, or for failure to do or abstain from doing anything required to be done or left undone: s 150(1) (amended by the Tribunals, Courts and Enforcement Act 2007 Sch 13 paras 45, 63). Justices who activate a suspended sentence are not 'imposing' a sentence (*R v Chamberlain* (1991) 13 Cr App Rep (S) 525, 156 JP 440, CA), and therefore the restrictions on imposing consecutive terms in the Magistrates' Courts Act 1980 (see PARA 555) do not apply.

4   See the Magistrates' Courts Act 1980 ss 135, 136; and PARA 3. Note also s 34 (magistrates' power to mitigate sentences, which is in practice never used).

5   See PARA 537.

29.   Term must be shortest available.   Where a court passes a custodial sentence[1] in relation to an offence committed after 4 April 2005[2] it must in general[3] be for the shortest term (not exceeding the permitted maximum) that in the opinion of the court is commensurate[4] with the seriousness[5] of the offence, or the combination of the offence and one or more offences associated[6] with it[7].

This requirement does not apply in the case of a custodial sentence fixed by law or a life sentence for serious or second listed offences[8] and is subject to the statutory provisions specifying:

(1)   the required minimum sentences for threatening with an offensive weapon or an article with a blade or point in public in public[9];

(2)   the required custodial sentence for possession of a firearm or using a person to mind a weapon[10];

(3) the specified minimum term for a third class A drug trafficking offence[11];

(4) the specified minimum term for a third domestic burglary[12]; or

(5) extended sentences for violent or sexual offences[13].

1   As to the meaning of 'custodial sentence' see PARA 9 note 15.

2   4 April 2005 is the date on which the Criminal Justice Act 2003 s 153 (see the text and notes 3–13) was brought into force by the Criminal Justice Act 2003 (Commencement No 8 and Transitional and Saving Provisions) Order 2005, SI 2005/950, Sch 2 para 5(1), (2) of which provides that the coming into effect of the Criminal Justice Act 2003 s 153 on that date is of no effect in relation to offences committed before that date.

3   For the exceptions to this rule see the text and notes 8–13.

4   Where an offender who is already serving a sentence of life imprisonment is convicted of a subsequent offence for which a term of imprisonment is appropriate, a sentence longer than is commensurate with the seriousness of that offence may not be imposed solely to ensure that he will remain in prison after the date on which he would be eligible for release on licence in respect of the life sentence: *R v Black (Craig)* [2000] 2 Cr App Rep (S) 41, [2000] Crim LR 317, CA.

5   As to determining the seriousness of an offence see PARA 586.

6   As to an 'associated offence' see PARA 9 note 7.

7   Criminal Justice Act 2003 s 153(2). As to pre-sentence reports and other requirements see s 156; and PARA 579.

8   Criminal Justice Act 2003 s 153(1) (amended by the Criminal Justice and Immigration Act 2008 Sch 26 paras 59, 67, Sch 28 Pt 2; and by the Legal Aid, Sentencing and Punishment of Offenders Act 2012 Sch 19 paras 8, 12). As to the sentences referred to see the Criminal Justice Act 2003 ss 224A, 225, 226; and PARAS 34, 35, 37. As to when those sentences fall to be imposed see PARA 536 note 2.

9   Criminal Justice Act 2003 s 153(2), (2A)(a), (c) (s 153(2) amended by the Violent Crime Reduction Act 2006 Sch 1 para 9; and by the Legal Aid, Sentencing and Punishment of Offenders Act 2012 Sch 26 paras 15, 20, 21; Criminal Justice Act 2003 s 153(2) further amended, s 153(3) added, by the Criminal Justice and Courts Act 2015 Sch 5 para 15). As to the sentences referred to see the Prevention of Crime Act 1953 ss 1(2B), 1A(5); the Criminal Justice Act 1988 ss 139(6B), 139A(5B), 139AA(7); and CRIMINAL LAW. As to when such a sentence falls to be imposed see PARA 536 note 2.

10 Criminal Justice Act 2003 s 153(2), (2A)(b), (f) (as amended and added: see note 9). As to the sentences referred to see the Firearms Act 1968 s 51A(2); the Violent Crime Reduction Act 2006 s 29(4), (6); and CRIMINAL LAW vol 26 (2010) PARAS 614, 656. As to when such a sentence falls to be imposed see PARA 536 note 2.

11 Criminal Justice Act 2003 s 153(2), (2A)(d) (as amended and added: see note 9). As to the sentence referred to see the Powers of Criminal Courts (Sentencing) Act 2000 s 110(2); and CRIMINAL LAW vol 26 (2010) PARA 725. As to when such a sentence falls to be imposed see PARA 536 note 2.

12 Criminal Justice Act 2003 s 153(2), (2A)(d) (as amended and added: see note 9). As to the sentence referred to see the Powers of Criminal Courts (Sentencing) Act 2000 s 111(2); and CRIMINAL LAW vol 25 (2010) PARA 290. As to when such a sentence falls to be imposed see PARA 536 note 2.

13 Criminal Justice Act 2003 s 153(2), (2A)(e) (as amended and added: see note 9). As to the sentence referred to see ss 226A(4), 226B(2); and PARAS 19, 20.

30.   Crediting of periods of remand in custody. Where an offender is serving a term of imprisonment[1] or detention[2] in respect of an offence[3] and has been remanded in custody[4] in connection with the offence or a related offence[5]:

(1) it is immaterial for that purpose whether, for all or part of the period during which the offender was remanded in custody, he was also remanded in custody in connection with other offences[6]; and

(2) the number of days for which the offender was remanded in custody in connection with the offence or a related offence is to count as time served by him as part of the sentence[7].

1   For these purposes a suspended sentence is to be treated as a sentence of imprisonment when it takes effect under the Criminal Justice Act 2003 Sch 12 para 8(2)(a) or (b) (see PARA 117) and is to be treated as being imposed by the order under which it takes effect: s 240ZA(7) (ss 240ZA, 243(2A) added, ss 240ZA(11), 242(1) amended, s 243(2) substituted, by the Legal Aid, Sentencing and Punishment of Offenders Act 2012 ss 108(2), 110(1), (7), (8), Sch 12 paras 50, 51(a), Sch 20 paras 1, 4).

As to the meaning of 'sentence of imprisonment' see PARA 27 note 4: for the purposes of the Criminal Justice Act 2003 ss 240ZA (see the text and notes 2–7), s 240A (see PARA 31), and s 241 (see note 709), 'sentence of imprisonment' does not include a committal in default of payment of any sum of money other than one adjudged to be paid on a conviction, and references to 'sentencing an offender to imprisonment', and to an offender's sentence, are to be read accordingly: s 242(1) (as so amended; s 242(1), (2) amended by the Criminal Justice and Immigration Act 2008 s 21(1), (6)).

2   These provisions (ie the Criminal Justice Act 2003 s 240ZA: see the text and notes 3–7) apply to a determinate sentence of detention under the Powers of Criminal Courts (Sentencing) Act 2000 s 91 (see PARA 8) or s 96 (see PARA 16) or under the Criminal Justice Act 2003 s 226A (see PARAS 18–20), s 226B (see PARAS 18–20), s 227 (repealed), s 228 (repealed) or s 236A (see PARA 32) as they apply to an equivalent sentence of imprisonment: s 240ZA(11) (as added and amended (see note 1); amended by the Criminal Justice and Courts Act 2015 Sch 1 para 16).

3   Criminal Justice Act 2003 s 240ZA(1)(a) (as added: see note 1).

4   References in the Criminal Justice Act 2003 ss 240ZA, 240A, 241 to an offender's being remanded in custody are references to his being:

(1)   remanded in or committed to custody by order of a court (s 242(2)(a) (s 242(2) as amended: see note 1));

(2)   remanded to youth detention accommodation under the Legal Aid, Sentencing and Punishment of Offenders Act 2021 s 91(4) (see PARA 8) (Criminal Justice Act 2003 s 242(2)(b)); or

(3)   remanded, admitted or removed to hospital under the Mental Health Act 1983 s 35, s 36 or s 38 (see PARAS 474–476) or s 48 (see **MENTAL HEALTH AND CAPACITY** vol 75 (2013) PARA 893) (Criminal Justice Act 2003 s 242(2)(c)).

5   Criminal Justice Act 2003 s 240ZA(1)(b) (as added: see note 1).

6   Criminal Justice Act 2003 s 240ZA(2) (as added: see note 1). A day counts as time served in relation to only one sentence and only once in relation to that sentence: s 240ZA(5) (as so added).

For the purposes of the references in s 240ZA(3), (5) to the term of imprisonment to which a person has been sentenced (that is to say, the reference to the offender's 'sentence'), consecutive terms and terms which are wholly or partly concurrent are to be treated as a single term if the sentences were passed on the same occasion or where they were passed on different occasions, the person has not been released at any time during the period beginning with the first and ending with the last of those occasions: s 240ZA(9) (as so added).

7   Criminal Justice Act 2003 s 240ZA(3) (as added: see note 1). If, on any day on which the offender was remanded in custody, he was also detained in connection with any other matter, that day is not to count as time served: s 240ZA(4) (as so added). The reference in s 240ZA(4) to detention in connection with any other matter does not include remand in custody in connection with another offence but includes:

(1)   detention pursuant to any custodial sentence (s 240ZA(10)(a) (as so added));

(2)   committal in default of payment of any sum of money (s 240ZA(10)(b) (as so added));

(3)   committal for want of sufficient distress to satisfy any sum of money (s 240ZA(10)(c) (as so added));

(4)   committal for failure to do or abstain from doing anything required to be done or left undone (s 240ZA(10)(d) (as so added)).

A day is not to count as time served as part of any automatic release period served by the offender: s 240ZA(6) (as so added; amended by the Offender Rehabilitation Act 2014 s 9(1), (6)). See further the Criminal Justice Act 2003 s 255B(1); and PARA 719.

In the case of an extradited prisoner, the court must specify in open court the number of days for which the prisoner was kept in custody while awaiting extradition: s 243(2) (as so substituted). Section 240ZA applies to days so specified as if they were days for which the prisoner was remanded in custody in connection with the offence or a related offence: s 243(2A) (as so added). A fixed-term prisoner is an 'extradited prisoner' for this purpose if he was tried for the offence in respect of which his sentence was imposed or he received that sentence after having been extradited to the United Kingdom and without having first been restored or had an opportunity of leaving the United Kingdom, and he was for any period kept in custody while awaiting such extradition: s 243(1) (amended by the Police and Justice Act 2006 Sch 13 para 31). Section 243 does not apply in the case of an extradited prisoner where the offence referred to in s 243(1) was committed before 4 April 2005: Criminal Justice Act 2003 (Commencement No 8 and Transitional and Saving Provisions) Order 2005, SI 2005/950, Sch 2 para 17.

In connection with the interpretation of the Powers of Criminal Courts (Sentencing) Act 2000 s 240ZA(3) see *Galiazia v Governor of HMP Hewell* [2014] EWHC 3427 (Admin), [2015] 1 WLR 2767, [2015] 1 Cr App Rep (S) 100 (time on remand may be counted only against time spent in custody; it cannot be credited to reduce time spent on licence). Guidelines relating to the Criminal Justice Act 2003 s 240 (repealed), which formerly made provision in this regard, were set out in *R v Norman* [2006] EWCA Crim 1792, [2007] 1 Cr App Rep (S) 509, [2006] All ER (D) 278 (Jul).

Regarding 'open court', in *R v Denbigh Justices, ex p Williams* [1974] QB 759, [1974] 2 All ER 1052, DC, Lord Widgery CJ stated, in the context of a submission that a hearing had not been in open court: 'The trial should be 'public' in the ordinary common-sense acceptation of that term. The doors of the courtroom are expected to be kept open, the public are entitled to be admitted, and the trial is to be public in all respects ... with due regard to the size of the courtroom, the convenience of the court, the right to exclude objectionable characters and youth of tender years, and to do other things which may facilitate the proper conduct of the trial.'

31.   Crediting of periods of remand on bail. Where a court[1] sentences an offender to imprisonment[2] or detention[3] for a term in respect of an offence[4], the offender was remanded on bail by a court in course of or in connection with proceedings for the offence, or any related offence[5], after 3 November 2008[6], and the offender's bail was subject to a qualifying curfew condition[7] and an electronic monitoring condition[8] (the 'relevant conditions')[9], the court must direct that the 'credit period' is to count as time served by him as part of the sentence[10].

The credit period is calculated by taking the following steps[11]:

Step 1: add:

(1)   the day on which the offender's bail was first subject to the relevant conditions (and for this purpose a condition is not prevented from being a relevant condition by the fact that it does not apply for the whole of the day in question); and

(2)   the number of other days on which the offender's bail was subject to those conditions (but exclude the last of those days if the offender spends the last part of it in custody);

Step 2: deduct the number of days on which the offender, whilst on bail subject to the relevant conditions, was also:

(a)   subject to any requirement imposed for the purpose of securing the electronic monitoring of the offender's compliance with a curfew requirement[12]; or

(b)   on temporary release[13];

Step 3: from the remainder, deduct the number of days during that remainder on which the offender has broken either or both of the relevant conditions;

Step 4: divide the result by two; and

Step 5: if necessary, round up to the nearest whole number.

Where the court gives such a direction[14] it must state in open court[15]:

(i)   the number of days for which the offender was subject to the relevant conditions[16]; and

(ii)   the number of days in relation to which the direction is given[17].

1   As to the meaning of 'court' see PARA 1 note 1.

2   For these purposes a suspended sentence and an order under the Powers of Criminal Courts (Sentencing) Act 2000 s 118(1) (repealed) is to be treated as a sentence of imprisonment when it takes effect under the Criminal Justice Act 2003 Sch 12 para 8(2)(a) or (b) (see PARA 117) or under the Powers of Criminal Courts (Sentencing) Act 2000 s 119(1)(a) or (b) (repealed) and is

to be treated as being imposed by the order under which it takes effect: Criminal Justice Act 2003 ss 240ZA(7), 240A(11)(a) (Criminal Justice Act 2003 s 240A added by the Criminal Justice and Immigration Act 2008 s 21(1), (4); Criminal Justice Act 2003 ss 240ZA, 240A(3A), (3B) added, ss 240A(1)(a), (2), (8), (11), (12), 240ZA(11) amended, s 240A(3), (8)(b) substituted, by the Legal Aid, Sentencing and Punishment of Offenders Act 2012 ss 108(2), 109, Sch 16 paras 13, 14, Sch 20 paras 1, 4).

As to the meaning of 'sentence of imprisonment' see PARAS 27 note 4, 30 note 1.

3 These provisions (ie the Criminal Justice Act 2003 s 240A: see the text and notes 4–17) apply to a determinate sentence of detention under the Powers of Criminal Courts (Sentencing) Act 2000 s 91 (see PARA 8) or s 96 (see PARA 16) or under the Criminal Justice Act 2003 s 226A (see PARAS 18–20), s 226B (see PARAS 18–20), s 227 (repealed) or s 228 (repealed) as they apply to an equivalent sentence of imprisonment: s 240ZA(11) (as added and amended: see note 2).

4 Criminal Justice Act 2003 s 240A(1)(a) (as added and amended: see note 2). For the purposes of references to the term of imprisonment to which a person has been sentenced (that is to say, the reference to the offender's 'sentence'), consecutive terms and terms which are wholly or partly concurrent are to be treated as a single term if the sentences were passed on the same occasion or where they were passed on different occasions, the person has not been released at any time during the period beginning with the first and ending with the last of those occasions: ss 240A(11)(b), 240ZA(9) (as so added and amended).

5 In the Criminal Justice Act 2003 s 240A 'related offence' means an offence, other than the offence for which the sentence is imposed ('offence A'), with which the offender was charged and the charge for which was founded on the same facts or evidence as offence A: s 240ZA(8) (as added: see note 2).

6 Criminal Justice Act 2003 s 240A(1)(b) (as added: see note 2). 3 November 2008 is the date on which the Criminal Justice and Immigration Act 2008 s 21 (see note 2) was brought into force by virtue of the Criminal Justice and Immigration Act 2008 (Commencement No 3 and Transitional Provisions) Order 2008, SI 2008/2712. It has been held that the Criminal Justice Act 2003 s 240A does not apply to a period on bail prior to 3 November 2008; but if a defendant was remanded on bail before 3 November 2008 subject to what were to become the relevant conditions on 3 November 2008 and continued to be on bail for a period on or after that date subject to those conditions without a further court order, s 240A does apply to the period on or after that date: see *R v Monaghan* [2009] EWCA Crim 2699, [2010] 2 Cr App Rep (S) 343, [2009] All ER (D) 225 (Dec).

7 'Qualifying curfew condition' means a condition of bail which requires the person granted bail to remain at one or more specified places for a total of not less than 9 hours in any given day: Criminal Justice Act 2003 s 240A(12) (as added: see note 2). See *R v Barrett* [2009] EWCA Crim 2213, [2009] 1 Cr App Rep (S) 572, [2009] All ER (D) 40 (Sep).

8 'Electronic monitoring condition' means any electronic monitoring requirements imposed under the Bail Act 1976 s 3(6ZAA) (see CRIMINAL PROCEDURE vol 27 (2015) PARA 73) for the purpose of securing the electronic monitoring of a person's compliance with a qualifying curfew condition: Criminal Justice Act 2003 s 240A(12) (as added: see note 2).

9 Criminal Justice Act 2003 s 240A(1)(c) (as added: see note 2). In connection with the conditions see *R v Barrett* [2009] EWCA Crim 2213, [2009] 1 Cr App Rep (S) 572, [2009] All ER (D) 40 (Sep).

10 Criminal Justice Act 2003 s 240A(2) (as added and amended: see note 2). This is subject to s 240A(3A) (as so added) (which provides that a day of the credit period counts as time served in relation to only one sentence and only once in relation to that sentence) and s 240A(3B) (as so added; amended by the Offender Management Act 2014 s 9(1), (7)) (which provides that a day of the credit period is not to count as time served as part of any automatic release period served by the offender (see s 255B(1); and PARA 719)).

11 See the Criminal Justice Act 2003 s 240A(3) (as added and substituted: see note 2). For the formula for calculating the credit period see further *R v Gordon* [2007] EWCA Crim 165, [2007] 2 All ER 768, [2007] 1 WLR 2117; *R v Irving* [2010] EWCA Crim 189, [2010] 2 Cr App Rep (S) 492; *R v Hoggard* [2013] EWCA Crim 1024, [2014] 1 Cr App Rep (S) 239, [2013] Crim LR 782.

12 'Curfew requirement' means a requirement (however described) to remain at one or more specified places for a specified number of hours in any given day, provided that the requirement is imposed by a court or the Secretary of State and arises as a result of a conviction: Criminal Justice Act 2003 s 240A(12) (as so amended).

13 Ie under rules made under the Prison Act 1952 s 47 (see PRISONS AND PRISONERS vol 85 (2012) PARAS 403–405).

14 Ie a direction under the Criminal Justice Act 2003 s 240A(2): see the text and notes 1–10.

15 As to the meaning of 'open court' see PARA 30 note 7.

16 Criminal Justice Act 2003 s 240A(8)(a) (as added and amended: see note 2).
17 Criminal Justice Act 2003 s 240A(8)(b) (as added: see note 2).

(ii) Offenders of Particular Concern Order

32.   Power to make order. Where a person aged 18 or over[1] is convicted of a specified terrorism[2] or sexual offence[3], a relevant inchoate offence[4], or a corresponding abolished offence[5], whenever committed[6], and the court imposes a sentence of imprisonment (or, until a day to be appointed[7], detention in a young offender institution[8]) for the offence which is not a sentence of imprisonment for life[9] or an extended sentence[10], the term of the sentence must be equal to the aggregate of the appropriate custodial term[11] and a further period of 1 year for which the offender is to be subject to a licence[12]. The term of a sentence of imprisonment (or detention) so imposed for an offence must not exceed the term that, at the time the offence was committed, was the maximum term permitted for the offence[13].

1   These provisions apply only in relation to a person who was aged 18 or over when the offence in question was committed: Criminal Justice Act 2003 s 236A(1)(b) (s 236A, Sch 18A added by the Criminal Justice and Courts Act 2015 Sch 1 paras 2, 4). As to the determination of a person's age see the Children and Young Persons Act 1933 s 99; and CHILDREN AND YOUNG PERSONS vol 10 (2012) PARA 1206.
2   The specified terrorism offences are:
    (1)   soliciting murder (ie an offence under the Offences Against the Person Act 1861 s 4: see CRIMINAL LAW vol 25 (2010) PARA 114) (as added: see note 1).
    (2)   causing bodily injury by explosives (ie an offence under the Offences Against the Person Act 1861 s 28: see CRIMINAL LAW vol 25 (2010) PARA 135) (Criminal Justice Act 2003 Sch 18A para 2 (as so added));
    (3)   using explosives, etc, with intent to do grievous bodily harm (ie an offence under the Offences Against the Person Act 1861 s 29: see CRIMINAL LAW vol 25 (2010) PARA 136) (Criminal Justice Act 2003 Sch 18A para 3 (as so added));
    (4)   causing an explosion likely to endanger life or property (ie an offence under the Explosive Substances Act 1883 s 2: see CRIMINAL LAW vol 25 (2010) PARA 137) (Criminal Justice Act 2003 Sch 18A para 4 (as so added));
    (5)   attempting to cause explosion, or making or keeping explosives, with intent to endanger life or property (ie an offence under the Explosive Substances Act 1883 s 3: see CRIMINAL LAW vol 25 (2010) PARA 138) (Criminal Justice Act 2003 Sch 18A para 5 (as so added));
    (6)   making or possession of explosive under suspicious circumstances (ie an offence under the Explosive Substances Act 1883 s 4: see CRIMINAL LAW vol 26 (2010) PARA 666) (Criminal Justice Act 2003 Sch 18A para 6 (as so added));
    (7)   weapons training (ie an offence under the Terrorism Act 2000 s 54: see CRIMINAL LAW vol 25 (2010) PARA 401) (Criminal Justice Act 2003 Sch 18A para 7 (as so added));
    (8)   directing terrorist organisations (ie an offence under the Terrorism Act 2000 s 56: see CRIMINAL LAW vol 25 (2010) PARA 403) (Criminal Justice Act 2003 Sch 18A para 8 (as so added));
    (9)   possessing articles for terrorist purposes (ie an offence under the Terrorism Act 2000 s 57: see CRIMINAL LAW vol 25 (2010) PARA 404) (Criminal Justice Act 2003 Sch 18A para 9 (as so added));
    (10) inciting terrorism overseas (ie an offence under the Terrorism Act 2000 s 59: see CRIMINAL LAW vol 25 (2010) PARA 415) (Criminal Justice Act 2003 Sch 18A para 10 (as so added));
    (11) use of nuclear weapons (ie an offence under the Anti-terrorism, Crime and Security Act 2001 s 47: see ARMED CONFLICT AND EMERGENCY vol 3 (2011) PARA 92) (Criminal Justice Act 2003 Sch 18A para 11 (as so added));
    (12) assisting or inducing certain weapons-related acts overseas (ie an offence under the Anti-terrorism, Crime and Security Act 2001 s 50: see ARMED CONFLICT AND EMERGENCY vol 3 (2011) PARA 97) (Criminal Justice Act 2003 Sch 18A para 12 (as so added));
    (13) use of noxious substances or things to cause harm or intimidate (ie an offence under the

Anti-terrorism, Crime and Security Act 2001 s 113: see CRIMINAL LAW vol 25 (2010) PARA 134) (Criminal Justice Act 2003 Sch 18A para 13 (as so added));

(14) preparation of terrorist acts (ie an offence under the Terrorism Act 2006 s 5: see CRIMINAL LAW vol 25 (2010) PARA 375) (Criminal Justice Act 2003 Sch 18A para 14 (as so added));

(15) training for terrorism (ie an offence under the Terrorism Act 2006 s 6: see CRIMINAL LAW vol 25 (2010) PARA 375) (Criminal Justice Act 2003 Sch 18A para 15 (as so added));

(16) making or possession of radioactive device or material (ie an offence under the Terrorism Act 2006 s 9: see CRIMINAL LAW vol 25 (2010) PARA 375) (Criminal Justice Act 2003 Sch 18A para 16 (as so added));

(17) use of radioactive device or material for terrorist purposes (ie an offence under the Terrorism Act 2006 s 10: see CRIMINAL LAW vol 25 (2010) PARA 375) (Criminal Justice Act 2003 Sch 18A para 17 (as so added)); and

(18) terrorist threats relating to radioactive devices (ie an offence under the Terrorism Act 2006 s 11: see CRIMINAL LAW vol 25 (2010) PARA 376) (Criminal Justice Act 2003 Sch 18A para 18 (as so added)).

The Secretary of State may by order amend Sch 18A by adding offences or varying or omitting offences listed therein: s 236A(6) (as so added). An order under s 236A(6) may, in particular, make provision that applies in relation to the sentencing of a person for an offence committed before the provision comes into force: s 236A(7) (as so added).

3   The specified sexual offences are an offence under the Sexual Offences Act 2003 s 5 (rape of a child under 13: see CRIMINAL LAW vol 25 (2010) PARA 179) or s 6 (assault of a child under 13 by penetration: see CRIMINAL LAW vol 25 (2010) PARA 181): Criminal Justice Act 2003 Sch 18A paras 19, 20 (as added: see note 1).

4   Ie aiding, abetting, counselling or procuring the commission of an offence specified in note 2 or 3 above (a 'relevant offence'), an attempt to commit a relevant offence, conspiracy to commit a relevant offence, or an offence under the Serious Crime Act 2007 Pt 2 (ss 44–67) (see CRIMINAL LAW vol 25 (2010) PARAS 65–72) in relation to which a relevant offence is the offence (or one of the offences) which the person intended or believed would be committed: Criminal Justice Act 2003 Sch 18A para 21 (as added: see note 1). These provisions also apply to an attempt to commit murder, conspiracy to commit murder, and an offence under the Serious Crime Act 2007 Pt 2 in relation to which murder is the offence (or one of the offences) which the person intended or believed would be committed, where that offence has a terrorist connection (Criminal Justice Act 2003 Sch 18A para 22 (as so added)): for these purposes, an offence has a terrorist connection if a court has determined under the Counter-Terrorism Act 2008 s 30 (see PARA 590) that the offence has such a connection (Criminal Justice Act 2003 Sch 18A para 24 (as so added)).

5   These provisions also apply to an offence that was abolished before 13 April 2015 (ie the date on which the Criminal Justice Act 2003 s 236A was brought into force by the Criminal Justice and Courts Act 2015 (Commencement No 1, Saving and Transitional Provisions) Order 2015, SI 2015/778), and if committed on the day on which the offender was convicted of the offence, would have constituted an offence specified in notes 2–4 above: Criminal Justice Act 2003 Sch 18A para 23 (as added: see note 1).

6   Criminal Justice Act 2003 s 236A(1)(a) (as added: see note 1). Section 236A applies in relation to the sentencing of a person for an offence after 13 April 2015 (see note 5), whether the person was convicted of the offence before or after that date: Criminal Justice and Courts Act 2015 Sch 1 para 9(1).

7   Ie until the coming into force of the Criminal Justice and Court Services Act 2000 s 61 (see PARA 36).

8   Criminal Justice and Courts Act 2015 Sch 1 para 10(1), (2).

9   Criminal Justice Act 2003 s 236A(1)(c)(i) (as added: see note 1). As to sentences of imprisonment for life see PARAS 33–41. The references in s 236A(1)(c), (2) to a sentence imposed for the offence include a sentence imposed for the offence and one or more offences associated with it: s 236A(5) (as so added).

10 Criminal Justice Act 2003 s 236A(1)(c)(ii) (as added: see note 1). As to extended sentences see s 226A; and PARAS 18–20. See note 9.

11 Criminal Justice Act 2003 s 236A(2)(a) (as added: see note 1). The 'appropriate custodial term' is the term that, in the opinion of the court, ensures that the sentence is appropriate: s 236A(3) (as so added). See note 9.

12 Criminal Justice Act 2003 s 236A(2)(b) (as added: see note 1). See note 9.

13 Criminal Justice Act 2003 s 236A(4) (as added: see note 1).

(5) LIFE SENTENCES UNDER THE 'DANGEROUSNESS' PROVISIONS

33. Life sentence for serious offences where there is a significant risk of serious harm. Where:

(1)   a person aged 18 or over[1] is convicted of a serious offence[2] committed on or after 4 April 2005[3]; and

(2)   the court[4] is of the opinion that there is a significant risk to members of the public of serious harm occasioned by the commission by him of further serious offences[5],

the court must impose a sentence[6] of imprisonment for life or[7], in the case of a person aged at least 18 but under 21, a sentence of custody for life[8] if:

(a)   the offence is one in respect of which the offender would otherwise[9] be liable to imprisonment for life[10]; and

(b)   the court considers that the seriousness[11] of the offence, or of the offence and one or more offences associated[12] with it, is such as to justify the imposition of a sentence of imprisonment for life[13].

1   As to the determination of a person's age see the Children and Young Persons Act 1933 s 99; and CHILDREN AND YOUNG PERSONS vol 10 (2012) PARA 1206. As to the position where a dangerous offender was under 18 at the time of conviction see the Criminal Justice Act 2003 s 226; and PARA 34.

2   As to the meaning of 'serious offence' see PARA 21; and as to the violent and sexual offences specified for these purposes see the Criminal Justice Act 2003 Schs 15, 15A, 15B; and PARAS 23–25.

3   Criminal Justice Act 2003 s 225(1)(a). As to 4 April 2005 see PARA 18 note 3.

4   As to the meaning of 'court' see PARA 1 note 1.

5   Criminal Justice Act 2003 s 225(1)(b). As to when there is a significant risk of serious harm to members of the public see PARA 22.

6   An offence the sentence for which is imposed under the Criminal Justice Act 2003 s 225 is not to be regarded as an offence the sentence for which is fixed by law: s 225(5).

7   Ie until the date on which the Criminal Justice and Court Services Act 2000 s 61 (see PARA 36) comes into force: Criminal Justice Act 2003 (Sentencing) (Transitory Provisions) Order 2005, SI 2005/643, art 3(4)(a).

8   Criminal Justice Act 2003 s 225(2) (amended by SI 2005/643).

9   Ie apart from the Criminal Justice Act 2003 s 225.

10   Criminal Justice Act 2003 s 225(2)(a). In the course of an inquiry pursuant to s 225(2)(a) it is not appropriate to consider whether, applying particular guidelines, a sentence of life imprisonment would in fact have been imposed, but rather the question was whether the defendant was liable to such a sentence: see *R v Beazley* [2006] EWCA Crim 3376, [2006] All ER (D) 175 (Oct); *R v Wood (Clive)* [2009] EWCA Crim 651, [2009] Crim LR 543, [2009] All ER (D) 49 (Apr). Where the criteria of dangerousness is satisfied, a life sentence should be imposed only for particularly serious offences: *R v Kehoe* [2008] EWCA Crim 819, [2009] 1 Cr App Rep (S) 41, [2008] All ER (D) 423 (Apr); *R v P* [2008] EWCA Crim 1228, [2008] All ER (D) 119 (Sep); and see also *R v Kiely* [2009] EWCA Crim 756, [2009] 2 Cr App Rep (S) 726; *R v Wilkinson* [2009] EWCA Crim 1925, [2010] 1 Cr App Rep (S) 628, [2010] Crim LR 69; *R v Saunders* [2013] EWCA Crim 1027, [2014] 1 Cr App Rep (S) 258, [2013] All ER (D) 17 (Jul).

11   See PARA 586.

12   As to an 'associated offence' see PARA 9 note 7.

13   Criminal Justice Act 2003 s 225(2)(b). As to where the court might consider that the seriousness of the offence justifies a sentence of imprisonment or detention for see *R v Terrell* [2007] EWCA Crim 3079, [2008] 2 All ER 1065, [2008] 2 Cr App Rep (S) 292 (indecent photographs of children); *R v Hicks* [2009] EWCA Crim 733, [2009] All ER (D) 141 (Apr) (same); *A-G's Reference (No 112 of 2006) (Glover)* [2006] EWCA Crim 3385, [2007] 2 Cr App Rep (S) 248 (serious case of wounding with intent); *A-G's Reference (No 27 of 2013)* [2014] EWCA Crim 334, [2015] 1 All ER 93, [2014] 1 WLR 4209.

34. Life sentence for offenders aged under 18 where there is a significant risk of serious harm. Where:

(1)   a person aged under 18[1] is convicted of a serious offence[2] committed on or after 4 April 2005[3]; and

(2)   the court[4] is of the opinion that there is a significant risk to members of the public of serious harm occasioned by the commission by him of further serious offences[5],

the court must impose a sentence[6] of detention for life[7] if:

(a)   the offence is one in respect of which the offender would otherwise[8] be liable[9] to a sentence of detention for life[10]; and

(b)   the court considers that the seriousness[11] of the offence, or of the offence and one or more offences associated[12] with it, is such as to justify the imposition of a sentence of detention for life[13].

1   As to the determination of a person's age see the Children and Young Persons Act 1933 s 99; and CHILDREN AND YOUNG PERSONS vol 10 (2012) PARA 1206. As to the position where a dangerous offender is aged 18 or over at the time of conviction see the Criminal Justice Act 2003 s 225; and PARA 33.
2   As to the meaning of 'serious offence' see PARA 21; and as to the violent and sexual offences specified for these purposes see PARAS 23–24.
3   Criminal Justice Act 2003 s 226(1)(a). As to 4 April 2005 see PARA 18 note 3.
4   As to the meaning of 'court' see PARA 1 note 1.
5   Criminal Justice Act 2003 s 226(1)(b). As to when there is a significant risk of serious harm to members of the public see PARA 22.
6   An offence the sentence for which is imposed under the Criminal Justice Act 2003 s 226 is not to be regarded as an offence the sentence for which is fixed by law: s 226(5).
7   Ie under the Powers of Criminal Courts (Sentencing) Act 2000 s 91 (see PARA 8).
8   Ie apart from the Criminal Justice Act 2003 s 226.
9   See note 7.
10   Criminal Justice Act 2003 s 226(2)(a).
11   See PARA 586.
12   As to an 'associated offence' see PARA 9 note 7.
13   Criminal Justice Act 2003 s 226(2)(b).

(6)   OTHER LIFE SENTENCES

(i) Automatic Life Sentences

35. Automatic life sentences. The court[1] must impose a sentence of imprisonment for life[2] where a person aged 18 or over[3] is convicted of a 'second listed offence'[4] committed after 3 December 2012[5] and:

(1)   the court would otherwise[6] impose a sentence of imprisonment for 10 years or more[7]; and

(2)   at the time the offence was committed, the offender had been convicted of a listed offence[8] ('the previous offence')[9] and a relevant life sentence[10] or a relevant sentence of imprisonment or detention for a determinate period[11] was imposed on him for that previous offence[12].

The court must impose a sentence of imprisonment for life in these circumstances unless it is of the opinion that there are particular circumstances which relate to the offence, to the previous offence[13] or to the offender[14], and would make it unjust to do so in all the circumstances[15].

1   As to the meaning of 'court' see PARA 1 note 1.
2   Criminal Justice Act 2003 s 224A(2) (ss 224A, 232A added by the Legal Aid, Sentencing and Punishment of Offenders Act 2012 s 122(1), Sch 19 para 21). There are exceptions to this

requirement: see the text and notes 13–15. An offence the sentence for which is imposed under this section is not to be regarded as an offence the sentence for which is fixed by law: Criminal Justice Act 2003 s 224A(11) (as so added).

3   As to the determination of a person's age see the Children and Young Persons Act 1933 s 99; and CHILDREN AND YOUNG PERSONS vol 10 (2012) PARA 1206.

4   Criminal Justice Act 2003 s 224A(1)(a) (as added: see note 2). A 'second listed offence' is an offence listed in the Criminal Justice Act 2003 Sch 15B Pt 1 (see PARA 25). In unusual cases, these provisions allow for the possibility of a life sentence being imposed in respect of an offence which does not carry life as a maximum: see *A-G's Reference (No 27 of 2013)* [2014] EWCA Crim 334 at [8], [2015] 1 All ER 93, [2014] 1 WLR 4209.

    Where on any date after 3 December 2012 (ie the date on which the Criminal Justice Act 2003 s 224A, Sch 15B were brought into force by the Legal Aid, Sentencing and Punishment of Offenders Act 2012 (Commencement No 4 and Saving Provisions) Order 2012, SI 2012/2906) a person is convicted in England and Wales of an offence listed therein, the court by or before which the person is so convicted states in open court that the person has been convicted of such an offence on that date, and that court subsequently certifies that fact, that certificate is evidence, for the purposes of the Criminal Justice Act 2003 s 224A and s 226A (see PARAS 18–20), that the person was convicted of such an offence on that date: s 232A (as so added; amended by the Criminal Justice and Courts Act 2015 s 5(2)). As to the meaning of 'open court' see PARA 30 note 7.

5   Criminal Justice Act 2003 s 224A(1)(b) (as added: see note 2). Where an offence is found to have been committed over a period of two or more days, or at some time during a period of two or more days, it must be taken for the purposes of s 224A(1)(b), (4)(a) to have been committed on the last of those days: s 224A(12) (added by the Criminal Justice and Courts Act 2015 s 5(1)).

6   Ie but for the Criminal Justice Act 2003 s 224A and in compliance with ss 152(2), 153(2) (see PARAS 29, 536) and disregarding any extension period imposed under s 226A (see PARAS 18–20).

7   Criminal Justice Act 2003 s 224A(1)(c), (3) (as added: see note 2). This is referred to as 'the sentence condition'.

8   Ie an offence listed in the Criminal Justice Act 2003 Sch 15B (see PARA 25).

9   Criminal Justice Act 2003 s 224A(1)(c), (4)(a) (as added: see note 2). See s 224A(12); and note 5. The provisions contained in s 224A(4) are referred to as 'the previous offence condition'.

10   For these purposes 'life sentence' means a life sentence as defined in the Crime (Sentences) Act 1997 s 34 (see PARA 706) or an equivalent sentence imposed under the law of Scotland, Northern Ireland or a member state (other than the United Kingdom): Criminal Justice Act 2003 s 224A(10) (as added: see note 2). A life sentence is relevant for these purposes if the offender was not eligible for release during the first 5 years of the sentence (s 224A(5)(a) (as so added)) or would not have been eligible for release during that period but for the reduction of the period of ineligibility to take account of a relevant pre-sentence period (s 224A(5)(b) (as so added)). 'Relevant pre-sentence period', in relation to the previous offence referred to in s 224A(4), means any period which the offender spent in custody or on bail before the sentence for that offence was imposed: s 224A(10) (as so added).

11   'Sentence of imprisonment or detention' includes any sentence of a period in custody (however expressed): Criminal Justice Act 2003 s 224A(10) (as added: see note 2). An extended sentence imposed under the Criminal Justice Act 2003 (including one imposed as a result of the Armed Forces Act 2006) is relevant for these purposes if the appropriate custodial term imposed was 10 years or more (Criminal Justice Act 2003 s 224A(6) (as so added)), and any other extended sentence is relevant for these purposes if the custodial term imposed was 10 years or more (s 224A(7) (as so added)). 'Extended sentence' means a sentence imposed under the Powers of Criminal Courts (Sentencing) Act 2000 s 85 (repealed) or under the Criminal Justice Act 2003 s 226A (see PARAS 18–20), s 226B (see PARAS 18–20), s 227 (repealed) or s 228 (repealed) (including one imposed as a result of the Armed Forces Act 2006 s 219A, s 220, s 221A or s 222 (see ARMED FORCES vol 3 (2011) PARA 611), or an equivalent sentence imposed under the law of Scotland, Northern Ireland or a member State (other than the United Kingdom): Criminal Justice Act 2003 s 224A(10) (as so added). Any other sentence of imprisonment or detention for a determinate period is relevant for these purposes if it was for a period of 10 years or more (s 224A(8) (as so added)), and an extended sentence or other sentence of imprisonment or detention is also relevant if it would have been relevant under s 224A(7) or (8) but for the reduction of the sentence, or any part of the sentence, to take account of a relevant pre-sentence period (s 224A(9) (as so added)).

12   Criminal Justice Act 2003 s 224A(4)(b) (as added: see note 2).

13   Ie the offence referred to in the Criminal Justice Act 2003 s 224A(4) (see the text and notes 8–12).

14   Criminal Justice Act 2003 s 224A(2)(a) (as added: see note 2).
15   Criminal Justice Act 2003 s 224A(2)(b) (as added: see note 2).

(ii) Custody for Life

36.   Custody for life (murder cases).   Until a day to be appointed[1], where a person under the age of 21[2] is convicted of murder or any other offence the sentence for which is fixed by law as imprisonment for life, the court must sentence him to custody for life unless he is liable to be detained[3] during Her Majesty's pleasure[4].

As from a day to be appointed no court is to pass a sentence of custody for life[5].

1   As from a day to be appointed the Powers of Criminal Courts (Sentencing) Act 2000 s 93 (see the text and notes 2–5) is repealed by the Criminal Justice and Court Services Act 2000 Sch 7 paras 160, 182, Sch 8. At the date at which this volume states the law no such day had been appointed. See further the text and note 5.
2   As to the determination of a person's age see the Children and Young Persons Act 1933 s 99; and CHILDREN AND YOUNG PERSONS vol 10 (2012) PARA 1206.
3   Ie under the Powers of Criminal Courts (Sentencing) Act 2000 s 90 (see PARA 38).
4   Powers of Criminal Courts (Sentencing) Act 2000 s 93 (prospectively repealed: see note 1). See also PARA 537 (restrictions on custodial sentences on persons not legally represented). The provisions of the Criminal Justice Act 2003 Pt 12 Ch 7 (ss 269–277) (effect of life sentences) apply to a sentence under the Powers of Criminal Courts (Sentencing) Act 2000 s 93: see CRIMINAL LAW vol 25 (2010) PARA 97; PRISONS AND PRISONERS vol 85 (2012) PARA 463.
5   Criminal Justice and Court Services Act 2000 s 61(1) (not yet in force): see also PARAS 16, 551. At the date at which this volume states the law no day had been appointed for the commencement of s 61.

37.   Custody for life (non-murder cases).   Until a day to be appointed[1], where a person aged at least 18 but under 21[2] is convicted of an offence for which the sentence is not fixed by law[3], but for which a person aged 21 years or over would be liable to imprisonment for life[4], the court must, if it considers that a sentence for life would be appropriate, sentence him to custody for life[5].

Where:

(1)   a person aged at least 18 but under 21 is convicted of a serious offence[6] committed on or after 4 April 2005[7]; and

(2)   the court[8] is of the opinion that there is a significant risk to members of the public of serious harm occasioned by the commission by him of further serious offences[9],

the court must, until a day to be appointed[10], impose a sentence[11] of custody for life if:

(a)   the offence is one in respect of which the offender would otherwise[12] be liable to imprisonment for life[13]; and

(b)   the court considers that the seriousness[14] of the offence, or of the offence and one or more offences associated[15] with it, is such as to justify the imposition of a sentence of imprisonment for life[16].

1   As from a day to be appointed the Powers of Criminal Courts (Sentencing) Act 2000 s 94 (see the text and notes 2–5) is repealed by the Criminal Justice and Court Services Act 2000 Sch 7 paras 160, 182, Sch 8. At the date at which this volume states the law no such day had been appointed.
2   As to the determination of a person's age see the Children and Young Persons Act 1933 s 99; and CHILDREN AND YOUNG PERSONS vol 10 (2012) PARA 1206.
3   Powers of Criminal Courts (Sentencing) Act 2000 s 94(1)(a) (prospectively repealed: see note 1).
4   Powers of Criminal Courts (Sentencing) Act 2000 s 94(1)(b) (prospectively repealed: see note 1).
5   Powers of Criminal Courts (Sentencing) Act 2000 s 94(1) (prospectively repealed: see note 1).

6   As to the meaning of 'serious offence' see PARA 21; and as to the violent and sexual offences specified for these purposes see PARAS 23–24.

7   Criminal Justice Act 2003 s 225(1)(a). As to 4 April 2005 see PARA 18 note 3.

8   As to the meaning of 'court' see PARA 1 note 1.

9   Criminal Justice Act 2003 s 225(1)(b). As to when there is a significant risk of serious harm to members of the public see PARA 22.

10 Ie until the date on which the Criminal Justice and Court Services Act 2000 s 61 (see PARA 36) comes into force: Criminal Justice Act 2003 (Sentencing) (Transitory Provisions) Order 2005, SI 2005/643, art 3(4)(a).

11 An offence the sentence for which is imposed under the Criminal Justice Act 2003 s 225 is not to be regarded as an offence the sentence for which is fixed by law: s 225(5).

12 Ie apart from the Criminal Justice Act 2003 s 225.

13 Criminal Justice Act 2003 s 225(2)(a).

14 See PARA 586.

15 As to an 'associated offence' see PARA 9 note 7.

16 Criminal Justice Act 2003 s 225(2)(b).

(iii) Detention during Her Majesty's Pleasure

38.   Detention during Her Majesty's pleasure (murder only).   Where a person convicted of murder or any other offence the sentence for which is fixed by law as life imprisonment appears to the court to have been aged under 18[1] at the time the offence was committed, the court must[2] sentence him to be detained during Her Majesty's pleasure[3], and, if so sentenced, he is liable to be detained in such place and under such conditions as the Secretary of State may direct[4] or may arrange with any person[5].

1   As to the determination of a person's age see the Children and Young Persons Act 1933 s 99; and CHILDREN AND YOUNG PERSONS vol 10 (2012) PARA 1206.

2   Ie notwithstanding anything in the Powers of Criminal Courts (Sentencing) Act 2000 or any other Act, and irrespective of the offender's age at the date of conviction.

3   Powers of Criminal Courts (Sentencing) Act 2000 s 90 (amended by the Criminal Justice and Court Services Act 2000 s 60(2), (3)). See PARA 537 (restrictions on custodial sentences on persons not legally represented); and see further CHILDREN AND YOUNG PERSONS vol 10 (2012) PARA 1308. The provisions of the Criminal Justice Act 2003 Pt 12 Ch 7 (ss 269–277) (effect of life sentences) apply to a sentence of detention during Her Majesty's pleasure: see CRIMINAL LAW vol 25 (2010) PARA 97; PRISONS AND PRISONERS vol 85 (2012) PARA 463.

4   Powers of Criminal Courts (Sentencing) Act 2000 s 92(1)(a). A person detained pursuant to the directions or arrangements made by the Secretary of State under s 92 is deemed to be in legal custody: s 92(2).

5   Powers of Criminal Courts (Sentencing) Act 2000 s 92(1)(b). See further note 4; and CRIMINAL LAW vol 25 (2010) PARA 97.

(7) LIFE SENTENCE PROVISIONS

(i) Setting the Minimum Term: Non-Murder Cases

39.   Life sentences: minimum terms.   If a court[1] passes a life sentence[2] in circumstances where the sentence is not fixed by law[3], the court must, unless it orders[4] otherwise, order that the early release provisions[5] apply to the offender as soon as he has served the part of the sentence which is specified in the order[6]. The part of the sentence must be such as the court considers appropriate, taking into account specified matters[7].

If the offender was aged 21 or over when he committed the offence and the court is of the opinion that, because of the seriousness of the offence or of the combination of the offence and one or more offences associated with it, no such order[8] should be made, the court must order that the early release provisions are not to apply to the offender[9].

There is no reason why a sentence should not be imposed which requires an offender to commence to serve an additional period after the minimum period before he could be considered for parole[10].

1 For these purposes 'court' includes the Court Martial: Powers of Criminal Courts (Sentencing) Act 2000 s 82A(7) (s 82A added by the Criminal Justice and Courts Service Act 2000 s 60(1), (3); Powers of Criminal Courts (Sentencing) Act 2000 s 82A(7) (definition of 'court') amended by the Armed Forces Act 2006 Sch 16 para 163).

2 As to the meaning of 'life sentence' for these purposes see the Crime (Sentences) Act 1997 s 34(2)(a)–(c), (f), (g); and PARA 706 (definition partly applied by the Powers of Criminal Courts (Sentencing) Act 2000 s 82A(7) (as added (see note 1); definition 'life sentence' amended by the Legal Aid, Sentencing and Punishment of Offenders Act 2012 Sch 21 paras 7, 11).

3 Powers of Criminal Courts (Sentencing) Act 2000 s 82A(1) (as added (see note 1); s 82A(1), (3)(c), (4) amended by the Criminal Justice Act 2003 Sch 32 paras 90, 109(1)–(4), Sch 37 Pt 8).

4 Ie under the Powers of Criminal Courts (Sentencing) Act 2000 s 82A(4) (see the text and note 9).

5 Ie the Crime (Sentences) Act 1997 s 28(5)–(8) (see PARA 707).

6 Powers of Criminal Courts (Sentencing) Act 2000 s 82A(2) (as added: see note 1). Thus the life sentence falls into two parts: (1) the relevant part, which consists of the period of detention imposed for punishment and deterrence, taking into account the seriousness of the offence; and (2) the remaining part of the sentence, during which the prisoner's detention will be governed by consideration of risk to the public: see the *Criminal Practice Directions 2015* [2015] EWCA Crim 1567, [2015] All ER (D) 134 (Sep) CPD VII Sentencing L: Imposition of Life Sentences para L.2. The judge is not obliged by statute to make use of the provisions of the Powers of Criminal Courts (Sentencing) Act 2000 s 82A when passing a life sentence: however he should do so, save in the very exceptional case where he considers that the offence is so serious that detention for life is justified by the seriousness of the offence alone, irrespective of the risk to the public, and in such a case he should state this in open court when passing sentence: *Criminal Practice Directions 2015* [2015] EWCA Crim 1567, [2015] All ER (D) 134 (Sep) CPD VII Sentencing L: Imposition of Life Sentences para L.3.

An order under the Powers of Criminal Courts (Sentencing) Act 2000 s 82A is a 'sentence' for the purposes of the Criminal Appeal Act 1968 s 9 (see PARA 627) and is therefore subject to appeal (*R v McBean* [2001] EWCA Crim 1891, [2002] 1 Cr App Rep (S) 430, [2001] Crim LR 839) or a reference by the Attorney General (*A-G's Reference (No 49 of 2005)* [2006] 2 Cr App Rep (S) 92; *A-G's Reference (No 3 of 2004)* [2004] EWCA Crim 1532, [2005] 1 Cr App Rep (S) 230).

7 Powers of Criminal Courts (Sentencing) Act 2000 s 82A(3) (as added: see note 1). The specified matters are:
    (1) the seriousness of the offence, or the combination of the offence and one or more offences associated with it (s 82A(3)(a) (as so added));
    (2) the effect that the Criminal Justice Act 2003 s 240ZA (crediting periods of remand in custody: see PARA 30), the Armed Forces Act 2006 s 246 (equivalent provision for service courts: see ARMED FORCES vol 3 (2011) PARA 596), or any direction which the court would have given under the Criminal Justice Act 2003 s 240A (crediting periods of remand on bail subject to certain types of condition: see PARA 31) would have if the court had sentenced the offender to a term of imprisonment (Powers of Criminal Courts (Sentencing) Act 2000 s 82A(3)(b) (as added (see note 1); substituted by the Criminal Justice and Courts Act 2015 s 15(1))); and
    (3) the early release provisions as compared with the Criminal Justice Act 2003 s 244(1) (duty to release prisoners on licence: see PARA 713) (Powers of Criminal Courts (Sentencing) Act 2000 s 82A(3)(c) (as so added and amended)).

In relation to head (2) above, although the judge is required to take into account time spent in custody on remand when fixing the specified period for the purposes of reference to the Parole Board, circumstances may arise where it will not be appropriate to give credit for that time: *R v M, R v L* [1998] 2 All ER 939, [1999] 1 Cr App Rep 9, CA.

When imposing a discretionary life sentence, the judge should first decide the determinate part of the sentence which he would have imposed if the need to protect the public and the potential danger of the offender had not required him to pass a life sentence, before going on to consider the length of the specified period: *R v M, R v L* (applying *R v Secretary of State for the Home Department, ex p Furber* [1998] 1 All ER 23, [1998] 1 Cr App Rep (S) 208, DC). In the case of a young offender, save in exceptional circumstances, the specified period should be fixed at half of the notional determinate sentence as the part of the sentence to be served before the case is referred to the Parole Board for consideration of release; and in the case of an adult offender, half the determinate period will also usually be appropriate, although there may well be circumstances which will justify a period of more than a half and up to two-thirds: *R v M*, *R v L*. The specified period should be fixed at half the determinate term unless there are particular grounds for a greater proportion, which grounds must be stated by the court: *R v Szczerba* [2002] EWCA Crim 440, [2002] 2 Cr App Rep (S) 387.

However, as from a day to be appointed, it is provided that if the offender was aged 18 or over when he committed the offence and the court is of the opinion that the seriousness of the offence, or of the combination of the offence and one or more other offences associated with it, is exceptional (but not such that the court proposes to make an order under the Powers of Criminal Courts (Sentencing) Act 2000 s 82A(4)), and would not be adequately reflected by the period which the court would otherwise specify under s 82A(2), then in deciding the effect which the comparison required by s 82A(3)(c) is to have on reducing the period which the court determines for the purposes of s 82A(3)(a) (and before giving effect to s 82A(3)(b)), the court may, instead of reducing that period by one-half, reduce it by such lesser amount (including nil) as the court may consider appropriate according to the seriousness of the offence: s 82A(3A), (3C)(a) (s 82A as so added; s 82A(3A)–(3C) prospectively added by the Criminal Justice and Immigration Act 2008 s 19). At the date at which this volume states the law no day had been appointed for the coming into force of these provisions.

Also as from a day to be appointed, where the court is of the opinion that the period which it would otherwise specify under the Powers of Criminal Courts (Sentencing) Act 2000 s 82A(2) would have little or no effect on time spent in custody, taking into account all the circumstances of the particular offender, then in deciding the effect which the comparison required by s 82A(3)(c) is to have on reducing the period which the court determines for the purposes of s 82A(3)(a) (and before giving effect to s 82A(3)(b)), the court may, instead of reducing that period by one-half, reduce it by such lesser amount (but not by less than one-third) as the court may consider appropriate in the circumstances: s 82A(3B), (3C)(b) (s 82A as so added; and s 82A(3B) as so prospectively added). At the date at which this volume states the law no day had been appointed for the coming into force of these provisions.

When fixing the determinate term, the sentencing judge should discount from it the element reflecting the need to protect the public from the danger posed by the offender because that is already reflected in the imposition of a discretionary life sentence. The fixing of a notional determinate sentence is not a precise calculation but requires a balancing exercise to take account of the risk of double punishment and ensure that the public risk element is not included; however, it is appropriate to reflect an element of deterrence as necessary: *R v Wheaton* [2004] EWCA Crim 2270, [2005] 1 Cr App Rep (S) 425; *R v Maguire* [2004] EWCA Crim 2220, [2005] 1 Cr App Rep (S) 435 (*R v M*, *R v L* applied).

As to an 'associated offence' see PARA 9 note 7.

8   Ie under the Powers of Criminal Courts (Sentencing) Act 2000 s 82A(2) (see the text and notes 1–6). As to the determination of a person's age see the Children and Young Persons Act 1933 s 99; and **CHILDREN AND YOUNG PERSONS** vol 10 (2012) PARA 1206.

9   Powers of Criminal Courts (Sentencing) Act 2000 s 82A(4) (as added and amended: see notes 1, 3). See further PARA 41.

10   See *R v Hills* [2008] EWCA Crim 1871, [2012] 1 WLR 2121, [2009] 1 Cr App Rep (S) 441. See also *R v Foy* [1962] 2 All ER 246, 46 Cr App Rep 290, CCA (a fixed-term of imprisonment may not be imposed to run consecutively to a sentence of life imprisonment), *R v Jones* [1962] AC 635 at 647 (affd on appeal on another point sub nom *Jones v DDP* [1962] AC 635, 46 Cr App Rep 129, HL) (although it is undesirable, a life sentence may be made consecutive to a fixed term of imprisonment) and *R v Bird* (2004) Times, 10 December, CA (there is no objection to imposing an extended sentence to run consecutively to a fixed-term one).

(ii) Licence Conditions

40.   Judge's power to recommend licence conditions.   A court[1] which, in respect of any offence[2] (other than an offence committed before 4 April 2005[3]), sentences an offender to a term of imprisonment of 12 months or more or, until a day to be appointed[4], a sentence of detention in a young offender institution may, when passing sentence, recommend to the Secretary of State particular conditions which in its view should be included in any licence granted[5] to the offender on his release from prison[6].

1 As to the meaning of 'court' see PARA 1 note 1.
2 These provisions do not apply in relation to a sentence of detention under the Powers of Criminal Courts (Sentencing) Act 2000 s 91 (see PARA 8) or the Criminal Justice Act 2003 s 226B (see PARAS 18–20): s 238(4) (amended by the Legal Aid, Sentencing and Punishment of Offenders Act 2012 Sch 20 paras 1, 3).
3 4 April 2005 is the date on which the Criminal Justice Act 2003 s 238 (see the text and notes 1, 2, 4–6) was brought into force by the Criminal Justice Act 2003 (Commencement No 8 and Transitional and Saving Provisions) Order 2005, SI 2005/950, Sch 2 para 15 which provides that such commencement is of no effect in a case in which a court sentences an offender in respect of an offence committed before that date.
4 These provisions apply to a court which sentences an offender to a sentence of detention in a young offender institution until the date on which the Criminal Justice and Court Services Act 2000 s 61 (see PARA 36) comes into force: Criminal Justice Act 2003 s 238(1) (amended by SI 2005/643). As to a sentence of detention in a young offender institution see PARA 16.
5 Ie granted under the Criminal Justice Act 2003 Pt 12 Ch 6 (ss 237–268) (see PARAS 688–745).
6 Criminal Justice Act 2003 s 238(1) (as amended: see note 4). A recommendation under s 238(1) is not to be treated for any purpose as part of the sentence passed on the offender: s 238(3). In exercising his powers under s 250(4)(b) (see PARA 736) in respect of an offender, the Secretary of State must have regard to any recommendation under s 238(1): s 238(2).

(iii) Whole Life Orders

41. Whole life orders. As a rule, where a court passes a life sentence[1] it must order that the early release provisions[2] apply to the offender as soon as he has served the part of the sentence which is specified in the order[3]. However, if the court is of the opinion that, because of the seriousness of the offence or of the combination of the offence and one or more offences associated with it, no such order should be made, it must instead order that the early release provisions are not to apply to the offender: this is referred to as a 'whole life order'[4]. A whole life order may be made only in respect of an offender who was aged 21 or over when he committed the offence[5] and should be made only where the seriousness of the offending is so exceptionally high that the just punishment requires the offender to be kept in prison for the rest of his life[6]. In the case of a life sentence which is fixed by law a whole life order is the appropriate starting point, and the court's judgment is subject to statutory guidance[7].

1 Ie whether the sentence is fixed by law (see the Criminal Justice Act 2003 s 269(1); and CRIMINAL LAW vol 25 (2010) PARA 97) or not (see the Powers of Criminal Courts (Sentencing) Act 2000 s 82A(4); and PARA 39).
2 Ie the Crime (Sentences) Act 1997 s 28(5)–(8) (see PARA 707).
3 See the Criminal Justice Act 2003 s 269(2); and CRIMINAL LAW vol 25 (2010) PARA 97; and the Powers of Criminal Courts (Sentencing) Act 2000 s 82A(2); and PARA 39.
4 See the Criminal Justice Act 2003 s 269(4); and CRIMINAL LAW vol 25 (2010) PARA 97; and the Powers of Criminal Courts (Sentencing) Act 2000 s 82A(4); and PARA 39.
5 See the Criminal Justice Act 2003 s 269(4); and CRIMINAL LAW vol 25 (2010) PARA 97; and the Powers of Criminal Courts (Sentencing) Act 2000 s 82A(4); and PARA 39. As to the determination of a person's age see the Children and Young Persons Act 1933 s 99; and CHILDREN AND YOUNG PERSONS vol 10 (2012) PARA 1206.
6 See *R v Jones (Neil)* [2005] EWCA Crim 3115 at [10], [2006] 2 Cr App Rep (S) 121 at [10]; *R v Oakes* [2012] EWCA Crim 2435 at [87], [2013] QB 979, [2013] 2 All ER 30.
7 See the Criminal Justice Act 2003 Sch 21; and CRIMINAL LAW vol 25 (2010) PARA 97.

3. COMMUNITY DISPOSALS

(1) COMMUNITY ORDERS AND YOUTH REHABILITATION ORDERS

(i) Imposition of Community Sentences

42. Restrictions on imposing community sentences. A court[1] must not pass a community order[2] or (in respect of a person aged under 18[3]) a youth rehabilitation order[4] — ie a 'community sentence'[5] — on an offender unless it is of the opinion that the offence, or the combination of the offence and one or more offences associated[6] with it, was serious enough to warrant such a sentence[7].

Where a court passes a community sentence:

(1) the particular requirement or requirements forming part of the community order or youth rehabilitation order comprised in the sentence must be such as, in the opinion of the court, is, or taken together are, the most suitable for the offender[8]; and

(2) the restrictions on liberty imposed by the order must be such as in the opinion of the court are commensurate with the seriousness of the offence, or the combination of the offence and one or more offences associated with it[9].

The fact that by virtue of any of these provisions[10] a community sentence may be passed in relation to an offence or particular restrictions on liberty may be imposed by a community order or youth rehabilitation order does not require a court to pass such a sentence or to impose those restrictions[11].

1   As to the meaning of 'court' see PARA 1 note 1.
2   As to community orders see the Criminal Justice Act 2003 s 177; and PARA 45 et seq.
3   As to the determination of a person's age see the Children and Young Persons Act 1933 s 99; and CHILDREN AND YOUNG PERSONS vol 10 (2012) PARA 1206.
4   As to youth rehabilitation orders see the Criminal Justice and Immigration Act 2008 Pt 1 (ss 1–8), Sch 27 para 1; and PARA 73 et seq. Youth rehabilitation orders may be passed in respect of offences committed on or after 30 November 2009: see the Criminal Justice and Immigration Act 2008 (Commencement No 13 and Transitory Provision) Order 2009, SI 2009/3074, art 2(a)–(h), (m)–(o). In respect of offences committed before 30 November 2009 by persons aged under 18, provision was made for the passing of youth community orders: see the Powers of Criminal Courts (Sentencing) Act 2000 s 33(2) (s 33 substituted by the Criminal Justice Act 2003 Sch 32 paras 90, 95; repealed as from 30 November 2009 by the Criminal Justice and Immigration Act 2008 Sch 28 Pt 1).
5   Criminal Justice Act 2003 s 147(1) (amended by the Criminal Justice and Immigration Act 2008 Sch 4 Pt 1 paras 71, 72, Sch 28 Pt 1). The Criminal Justice Act 2003 ss 147, 148 came into force on 4 April 2005 and do not apply to an offence committed before that date: see the Criminal Justice Act 2003 (Commencement No 8 and Transitional and Saving Provisions) Order 2005, SI 2005/950, art 2, Sch 1 para 7, Sch 2 para 5(1), (2).
6   As to an 'associated offence' see PARA 9 note 7.
7   Criminal Justice Act 2003 s 148(1). Section 148(1) has effect subject to s 151(2) (see PARA 47): s 148(4). As to pre-sentence and other reports see the Criminal Justice Act 2003 s 156; and PARA 580.
8   Criminal Justice Act 2003 s 148(2)(a) (s 148(2) amended, s 148(2A), (5) added, by the Criminal Justice and Immigration Act 2008 s 10, Sch 4 Pt 1 paras 71, 73, Sch 28 Pt 1). The Criminal Justice Act 2003 s 148(2) is subject to s 177(2A) (community orders: punitive elements: see PARA 48) and to the Criminal Justice and Immigration Act 2008 Sch 1 para 3(4) (youth rehabilitation order with intensive supervision and surveillance: see PARA 75): Criminal Justice Act 2003 s 148(2A) (as so added; amended by the Crime and Courts Act 2013 Sch 16 paras 1, 3).
9   Criminal Justice Act 2003 s 148(2)(b). Section 148(2)(b) has effect subject to s 151(2) (see PARA 47): s 148(4); see also note 8.

10 Ie by virtue of any provision of the Criminal Justice Act 2003 s 148 (see the text and notes 1–9).
11 Criminal Justice Act 2003 s 148(5) (as added: see note 8).

43. Passing of community sentence on offender remanded in custody. In determining the restrictions on liberty to be imposed in respect of an offence by a community order[1] or a youth rehabilitation order[2], the court[3] may have regard to any period for which the offender has been remanded in custody[4] in connection with the offence or any other offence the charge for which was founded on the same facts or evidence[5].

1 See PARA 45 et seq.
2 See PARA 73 et seq.
3 As to the meaning of 'court' see PARA 1 note 1.
4 For these purposes 'remanded in custody' has the same meaning as in the Criminal Justice Act 2003 s 242(2) (see PARA 30 note 4): s 149(2). In connection with this requirement see *R v Rakib* [2011] EWCA Crim 870, [2012] 1 Cr App Rep (S) 1, [2011] Crim LR570.
5 Criminal Justice Act 2003 s 149(1) (amended by the Criminal Justice and Immigration Act 2008 Sch 4 paras 71, 74). The Criminal Justice Act 2003 s 149 came into force on 4 April 2005, and is of no effect in relation to an offence committed before that date: Criminal Justice Act 2003 (Commencement No 8 and Transitional and Saving Provisions) Order 2005, SI 2005/950, art 2(1), Sch 1 para 7, Sch 2 para 5(1), (2)(a). See *R v Rakib* [2011] EWCA Crim 870, [2012] 1 Cr App Rep (S) 1, [2011] Crim LR570 (court considering non-custodial order where the offender had already served a period of custody on remand had to consider not only the punishment of the offender but also his rehabilitation and the protection of the public).

44. Community sentence not available where sentence fixed by law etc. The power to make a community order[1] or a youth rehabilitation order[2] is not exercisable in respect of an offence the sentence for which is:

(1) a sentence fixed by law[3];
(2) the required custodial sentence for possession of a firearm or using a person to mind a weapon[4];
(3) the specified minimum term for a third class A drug trafficking offence[5];
(4) the specified minimum term for a third domestic burglary[6];
(5) life sentence for serious or second listed offences[7]; or
(6) sentences of imprisonment for life or detention for life for public protection[8].

The power to make a community order is not exercisable in respect of an offence for which the sentence is the required minimum sentence for threatening with an offensive weapon or an article with a blade or point in public in public[9].

1 See PARA 45 et seq.
2 See PARA 73 et seq.
3 Criminal Justice Act 2003 s 150(1)(a) (s 150(1) renumbered, s 150(2) added, the Crime and Courts Act 2013 Sch 16 para 23(1); Criminal Justice Act 2003 s 150(1) amended by the Criminal Justice and Immigration Act 2008 Sch 4 paras 71, 75). The Criminal Justice Act 2003 s 150 came into force on 4 April 2005, and is of no effect in relation to an offence committed before that date: Criminal Justice Act 2003 (Commencement No 8 and Transitional and Saving Provisions) Order 2005, SI 2005/950, art 2(1), Sch 1 para 7, Sch 2 para 5(1), (2)(a).
4 Criminal Justice Act 2003 s 150(1)(b), (ca) (s 150(1)(ca) added by the Violent Crime Reduction Act 2006 Sch 1 para 9(1), (3)). As to the sentences referred to see the Firearms Act 1968 s 51A(2); the Violent Crime Reduction Act 2006 s 29(4), (6); and CRIMINAL LAW vol 26 (2010) PARAS 614, 656. As to when such a sentence falls to be imposed see PARA 536 note 2.
5 Criminal Justice Act 2003 s 150(1)(c). As to the sentence referred to see the Powers of Criminal Courts (Sentencing) Act 2000 s 110(2); and CRIMINAL LAW vol 26 (2010) PARA 725. As to when such a sentence falls to be imposed see PARA 536 note 2.
6 Criminal Justice Act 2003 s 150(1)(c). As to the sentence referred to see the Powers of Criminal Courts (Sentencing) Act 2000 s 111(2); and CRIMINAL LAW vol 25 (2010) PARA 290. As to when such a sentence falls to be imposed see PARA 536 note 2.

7   Criminal Justice Act 2003 s 150(1)(cb) (added by the Legal Aid, Sentencing and Punishment of
     Offenders Act 2012 Sch 19 paras 8, 10). As to the sentences referred to see the Criminal Justice
     Act 2003 s 224A; and PARA 35. As to when such a sentence falls to be imposed see PARA 536
     note 2.
8   Criminal Justice Act 2003 s 150(1)(d) (amended by the Criminal Justice and Immigration
     Act 2008 Sch 26 paras 59, 65). As to the sentences referred to see the Criminal Justice Act 2003
     ss 225(2), 226(2); and PARAS 34, 37. As to when such a sentence falls to be imposed see PARA
     536 note 2.
9   Criminal Justice Act 2003 s 150(2)(a), (b) (as added (see note 3); amended by the Criminal
     Justice and Courts Act 2015 Sch 3 para 13). As to the sentences referred to see the Prevention of
     Crime Act 1953 ss s 1(2B), 1A(5); the Criminal Justice Act 1988 s ss 139(6B), 139A(5B),
     139AA(7); and CRIMINAL LAW. As to when these sentences fall to be imposed see PARA 536
     note 2.

(ii) Community Orders

A. MAKING OF COMMUNITY ORDER

45.   Power to make community orders.   The power to make a community
order is exercisable in relation to offences punishable with imprisonment[1] and, in
certain other circumstances[2], in respect of persistent offenders[3]. The effect of a
community order is to impose on the offender one or more requirements with
which he must comply for the duration of the order[4].

1   Criminal Justice Act 2003 s 150A(1)(a) (s 150A added by the Criminal Justice and Immigration
     Act 2008 s 11(1)). For the purposes of the Criminal Justice Act 2003 ss 150A, 151 (see the text
     and notes 2–4; and PARA 47) an offence triable either way that was tried summarily is to be
     regarded as punishable with imprisonment only if it is so punishable by the sentencing court
     (and for this purpose s 148(1) (see PARA 42) is to be disregarded): s 150A(2) (as so added).
2   Ie where the Criminal Justice Act 2003 s 151(2) confers power to make such order: see PARA 47.
3   Criminal Justice Act 2003 s 150A(1)(b) (as added: see note 1). In connection with the sentencing
     of persistent offenders see PARA 47.
4   See PARA 48. The court by which a community order is made must forthwith provide copies of
     the order:
     (1)   to the offender (Criminal Justice Act 2003 s 219(1)(a) (s 219(1) substituted, s 219(4)
            added, by the Offender Management Act 2014 Sch 4 para 12));
     (2)   to the responsible officer (Criminal Justice Act 2003 s 219(1)(b) (as so substituted));
     (3)   to an officer who is acting at the court and is an officer of a provider of probation
            services that is a public sector provider (s 219(1)(c) (as so substituted)); and
     (4)   where the court specifies a local justice area in which the court making the order does
            not act, to a provider of probation services that is a public sector provider and is acting
            in that area (s 219(1)(d) (as so substituted)).
     In connection with the notification requirements see the Criminal Procedure Rules 2015,
     SI 2015/1490, r 28.2. For this purpose 'public sector provider' means a probation trust or other
     public body or the Secretary of State: Criminal Justice Act 2003 s 219(4) (as so added). As to
     provider of probation services see PARAS 666–687. As to youth offending teams see CHILDREN
     AND YOUNG PERSONS vol 10 (2012) PARA 1206.

46.   Age limits for community orders.   Where a person is convicted of an
offence committed on or after 30 November 2009 the court[1] by or before which
he is convicted may make a community order[2] in relation to him if he is aged 18
or over[3]. In certain circumstances a community order may be made in respect of
a persistent offender who is under the specified age[4].

1   As to the meaning of 'court' see PARA 1 note 1.
2   As to the power to make community orders see PARA 45.
3   Criminal Justice Act 2003 s 177(1) (amended by the Criminal Justice and Immigration Act 2008
     Sch 4 paras 71, 82). Where the offence was committed before 30 November 2009 the court may
     make a community order in relation to the person if he is aged 16 or over: Criminal Justice

Act 2003 s 177(1), Sch 27 para 1). As to the determination of a person's age see the Children and Young Persons Act 1933 s 99; and CHILDREN AND YOUNG PERSONS vol 10 (2012) PARA 1206.

4   See PARA 47.

47.   Persistent offenders.   As from a day to be appointed, provision is made for a community order to be made in respect of a persistent offender[1].

Where a court[2] convicts a person of an offence (the 'current offence') and the person is aged 18 or over[3] the court may make a community order in respect of that offence instead of imposing a fine[4] if:

(1)   until a day to be appointed[5], on three or more previous occasions he has, on conviction by a court in the United Kingdom[6] of any offence committed by him after attaining the age of 16, had passed on him a sentence consisting only of a fine, or, as from that day, on three or more previous occasions a sentence consisting only of a fine has been passed on the offender on conviction by a court in the United Kingdom of an offence committed by the offender after attaining the age of 16 or by a court in another member state of a relevant offence so committed[7];

(2)   the court would not[8] otherwise regard the current offence, or the combination of the current offence and one or more offences associated[9] with it, as being serious enough to warrant a community sentence[10]; and

(3)   the court considers that, having regard to all the circumstances[11], it would be in the interests of justice to make such an order[12].

As from day to be appointed, the provisions described above[13] continue to apply in respect of a person aged 16 or over who is convicted in respect of an offence which is punishable by imprisonment[14], and it is also provided that a court which convicts a person aged 18 or over[15] of an offence which is not punishable with imprisonment[16] may make a community order in respect of that offence instead of imposing a fine if (until a day to be appointed[17]) on three or more previous occasions the offender has, on conviction by a court in the United Kingdom[18] of any offence committed by him after attaining the applicable age[19], had passed on him a sentence consisting only of a fine or (as from that day) on three or more previous occasions a sentence consisting only of a fine has been passed on the offender on conviction by a court in the United Kingdom of an offence committed by the offender after attaining the age of 16 or by a court in another member state of a relevant offence so committed[20] and the court considers that, having regard to all the circumstances[21], it would be in the interests of justice to make such an order[22].

1   See the Criminal Justice Act 2003 s 151; and the text and notes 2–22. At the date at which this volume states the law no day had been appointed for the commencement of s 151. As to the making of community orders see PARA 45.

2   As to the meaning of 'court' see PARA 1 note 1.

3   As to the determination of a person's age see the Children and Young Persons Act 1933 s 99; and CHILDREN AND YOUNG PERSONS vol 10 (2012) PARA 1206. Where the offence was committed before 30 November 2009 these provisions apply in relation to a person if he is aged 16 or over: Criminal Justice Act 2003 s 151(1)(a), Sch 27 para 1).

4   Criminal Justice Act 2003 s 151(1)(a), (2) (s 151(1) amended by the Criminal Justice and Immigration Act 2008 Sch 4 para 76; prospectively amended by the Criminal Justice and Immigration Act 2008 s 11; and also prospectively amended by the Coroners and Justice Act 2009 Sch 17 para 8). At the date at which this volume states the law no day had been appointed for the coming into force of the amendments referred to above as prospective.

5   See note 6.

6   The reference in the Criminal Justice Act 2003 s 151(1)(b) (and s 151(2A)(b): see PARA 77) to conviction by a court in the United Kingdom includes a reference to a conviction in service disciplinary proceedings: s 151(4) (s 151(4), (5) amended, and s 151(8) added, by the Armed

Forces Act 2006 Sch 16 para 217). An order under the Prosecution of Offences Act 1985 s 21A (criminal courts charge: see CRIMINAL PROCEDURE), a compensation order, a service compensation order awarded in service disciplinary proceedings, a surcharge order under the Criminal Justice Act 2003 s 161A (see PARA 185), an unlawful profit under the Prevention of Social Housing Fraud Act 2013 s 4 (see LANDLORD AND TENANT) or a slavery and trafficking reparation order under the Modern Slavery Act 2015 s 8 (see CRIMINAL LAW) does not, for these purposes, form part of an offender's sentence: Criminal Justice Act 2003 s 151(5) (as so amended; also amended by the Domestic Violence, Crime and Victims Act 2004 Sch 10 para 63; the Prevention of Social Housing Fraud Act 2013 Schedule paras 28, 29; the Criminal Justice and Courts Act 2015 Sch 12 para 13; and the Modern Slavery Act 2015 Sch 5 para 24).

For these purposes 'service disciplinary proceedings' means:

(1) until a day to be appointed, proceedings (whether or not before a court) in respect of a service offence within the meaning of the Armed Forces Act 2006 (see s 50(2); and ARMED FORCES vol 3 (2011) PARA 569), and as from that day, proceedings (whether or not before a court) in respect of a service offence or a member state service offence (Criminal Justice Act 2003 s 151(8)(a) (as so added; and s 151(8)(a), (b) prospectively amended by the Coroners and Justice Act 2009 Sch 17 para 8)); and

(2) any reference to conviction or sentence, in the context of service disciplinary proceedings (ie, as from a day to be appointed, other than proceedings for a member state service offence), includes anything that under the Armed Forces Act 2006 s 376(1)–(3) (see ARMED FORCES vol 3 (2011) PARA 508) is to be treated as a conviction or sentence: Criminal Justice Act 2003 s 151(8)(b) (as so added and prospectively amended).

As from a day to be appointed:

(a) 'member state service offence' means an offence which was the subject of proceedings under the service law of a member state other than the United Kingdom and would constitute an offence under the law of any part of the United Kingdom, or a service offence, if it were done in any part of the United Kingdom, by a member of Her Majesty's forces, at the time of the conviction of the defendant for the current offence (s 151(8)(c) (s 151(8)(c)–(f) prospectively added by the Coroners and Justice Act 2009 Sch 17 para 8));

(b) 'Her Majesty's forces' has the same meaning as in the Armed Forces Act 2006 (see s 374; and ARMED FORCES vol 3 (2011) PARA 311) (Criminal Justice Act 2003 s 151(8)(d) (as so prospectively added));

(c) 'service law', in relation to a member state other than the United Kingdom, means the law governing all or any of the naval, military or air forces of that State (s 151(8)(e) (as so prospectively added)); and

(d) 'service offence' has the same meaning as in the Armed Forces Act 2006 (see s 50(2); and ARMED FORCES vol 3 (2011) PARA 569) (Criminal Justice Act 2003 s 151(8)(f) (as so prospectively added)).

At the date at which this volume states the law no day had been appointed for the coming into force of these prospective amendments.

7   Criminal Justice Act 2003 s 151(1)(b) (as amended and prospectively amended: see note 4). For these purposes, it is immaterial whether on other previous occasions a court has passed on the offender a sentence not consisting only of a fine: s 151(6). As from a day to be appointed, for the purposes of s 151(1)(b), (1A)(c), (2A)(b), an offence is 'relevant' if the offence would constitute an offence under the law of any part of the United Kingdom if it were done there at the time of the conviction of the defendant for the current offence: s 151(4A) (prospectively added by the Coroners and Justice Act 2009 Sch 17 para 8). At the date at which this volume states the law, no such day had been appointed.

8   Ie despite the effect of the Criminal Justice Act 2003 s 143(2) (see PARA 586). Section 151 does not limit the extent to which a court may, in accordance with s 143(2), treat any previous convictions of the offender as increasing the seriousness of an offence: s 151(7).

9   As to an 'associated offence' see PARA 9 note 7.

10 Criminal Justice Act 2003 s 151(1)(c).

11 Ie including the nature of the offences to which the previous convictions mentioned in the Criminal Justice Act 2003 s 151(1)(b) (see the text and notes 5–7) relate and their relevance to the current offence and the time that has elapsed since the offender's conviction of each of those offences: s 151(3).

12 Criminal Justice Act 2003 s 151(2).

13 Ie the Criminal Justice Act 2003 s 151(1)(a)–(c), (2): see the text and notes 1–12.

14 Criminal Justice Act 2003 s 151(A1), (1)(za), (a)–(c), (2) (s 151(A1) prospectively added by the Criminal Justice and Immigration Act 2008 s 11; Criminal Justice Act 2003 s 151(1) as

amended and prospectively amended (see note 4)). At the date at which this volume states the law no day had been appointed for the coming into force of the amendments referred to as prospective.

15 See note 3.

16 Criminal Justice Act 2003 s 151(1A)(a), (b) (s 151(1A) prospectively added by the Criminal Justice and Immigration Act 2008 s 11; and amended by the Criminal Justice and Immigration Act 2008 Sch 4 para 76). At the date at which this volume states the law no day had been appointed for the coming into force of the amendments referred to as prospective.

17 See note 20.

18 The reference in the Criminal Justice Act 2003 s 151(1A)(c) to conviction by a court in the United Kingdom includes a reference to a conviction in service disciplinary proceedings: s 151(4) (amended with savings by the Criminal Justice and Immigration Act 2008 Sch 4 para 76). A compensation order, a service compensation order awarded in service disciplinary proceedings, a surcharge order under the Criminal Justice Act 2003 s 161A (see PARA 185) or an unlawful profit under the Prevention of Social Housing Fraud Act 2013 s 4 does not, for these purposes, form part of an offender's sentence: Criminal Justice Act 2003 s 151(5) (amended by the Domestic Violence, Crime and Victims Act 2004 Sch 10 para 63; and by the Prevention of Social Housing Fraud Act 2013 Schedule paras 28, 29; and amended with savings by the Criminal Justice and Immigration Act 2008 Sch 4 para 76). As to 'service disciplinary proceedings' and references to conviction or sentence in the context of service disciplinary proceedings see note 6.

19 See note 15.

20 Criminal Justice Act 2003 s 151(1A)(c) (prospectively added (see note 16); prospectively substituted by the Coroners and Justice Act 2009 Sch 17 para 8; and amended with savings by the Criminal Justice and Immigration Act 2008 Sch 4 para 76). For these purposes, it is immaterial whether on other previous occasions a court has passed on the offender a sentence not consisting only of a fine: Criminal Justice Act 2003 s 151(6) (prospectively amended by the Criminal Justice and Immigration Act 2008 s 11; and amended with savings by the Criminal Justice and Immigration Act 2008 Sch 4 para 76). At the date at which this volume states the law no day had been appointed for the coming into force of the amendments referred to as prospective.

21 Ie including the nature of the offences to which the previous convictions mentioned in the Criminal Justice Act 2003 s 151(1A)(c) (see the text and notes 17–20) relate and their relevance to the current offence and the time that has elapsed since the offender's conviction of each of those offences: s 151(3) (amended with savings by the Criminal Justice and Immigration Act 2008 Sch 4 para 76).

22 Criminal Justice Act 2003 s 151(2).

48. Requirements which may be imposed. A community order[1] may impose on the offender any one or more[2] of the following requirements[3]:

(1)   an unpaid work requirement[4];

(2)   a rehabilitation activity requirement[5]; and

(3)   a programme requirement[6];

(4)   a prohibited activity requirement[7];

(5)   a curfew requirement[8];

(6)   an exclusion requirement[9];

(7)   a residence requirement[10];

(8)   a foreign travel prohibition requirement[11];

(9)   a mental health treatment requirement[12];

(10) a drug rehabilitation requirement[13];

(11) an alcohol treatment requirement[14];

(12) in a case where the offender is aged under 25[15], an attendance centre requirement[16];

(13) as from a day to be appointed, an alcohol abstinence and monitoring requirement[17];

(14) as from a day to be appointed, an electronic monitoring requirement[18].

Where the court[19] makes a community order it must, absent exceptional circumstances[20], either include in the order at least one requirement imposed for the purpose of punishment[21], impose a fine for the offence in respect of which the community order is made[22], or do both of those things[23]. Where the court makes a community order imposing a curfew requirement or an exclusion requirement, the court must also impose an electronic monitoring requirement[24] unless it is prevented[25] from doing so or, in the particular circumstances of the case, it considers it inappropriate to do so[26]. Until a day to be appointed where the court makes a community order imposing an unpaid work requirement, a rehabilitation activity requirement, a programme requirement, a prohibited activity requirement, a residence requirement, a foreign travel prohibition requirement, a mental health treatment requirement, a drug rehabilitation requirement, an alcohol treatment requirement or an attendance centre requirement, it may also impose an electronic monitoring requirement unless prevented[27] from doing so[28].

A community order must specify the local justice area in which the offender resides or will reside[29].

1   For the power to make community orders see PARAS 45, 47.
2   Before making a community order imposing two or more different requirements the court must consider whether, in the circumstances of the case, the requirements are compatible with each other: Criminal Justice Act 2003 s 177(6).
3   The Criminal Justice Act 2003 s 177(1) (see the text and notes 4–18) has effect subject to s 150 (see PARA 44) and s 218 (see PARAS 133, 134, 136), and, in connection with particular requirements, to s 199(3) (unpaid work requirement: see PARA 133), s 203(2) (prohibited activity requirement: see PARA 130), s 207(3) (mental health treatment requirement: see PARA 128), s 209(2) (drug rehabilitation requirement: see PARA 124) and s 212(2), (3) (alcohol treatment requirement: see PARA 122) (s 177(2)(a), (d)–(g)): as from a day to be appointed s 177(1) is also subject to s 212A(8)–(12) (alcohol abstinence and monitoring requirement: see PARA 135) and s 215(2) (electronic monitoring requirement: see PARA 136) (s 177(2)(h), (i) (prospectively added by the Legal Aid, Sentencing and Punishment of Offenders Act 2012 s 76(3)(b) and by the Crime and Courts Act 2013 Sch 16 paras 11, 12). At the date at which this volume states the law no day had been appointed for the coming into force of the amendments noted as prospective.
4   Ie as defined by the Criminal Justice Act 2003 s 199 (see PARA 133): s 177(1)(a).
5   Ie as defined by the Criminal Justice Act 2003 s 200A (see PARA 131): s 177(1)(aa) (s 177(1)(aa) added, s 177(4) amended, by the Offender Rehabilitation Act 2014 s 15(2), Sch 5 para 2)). Rehabilitation activity requirements replaced activity requirements under the Criminal Justice Act 2003 s 201 and supervision requirements under s 213, which have been abolished, as from 1 February 2015: see the Offender Rehabilitation Act 2014 s 15 and the Offender Rehabilitation Act 2014 (Commencement No 2) Order 2015), SI 2015/40.
6   Ie as defined by the Criminal Justice Act 2003 s 202 (see PARA 129): s 177(1)(c).
7   Ie as defined by the Criminal Justice Act 2003 s 203 (see PARA 130): s 177(1)(d).
8   Ie as defined by the Criminal Justice Act 2003 s 204 (see PARA 123): s 177(1)(e).
9   Ie as defined by the Criminal Justice Act 2003 s 205 (see PARA 126): s 177(1)(f).
10 Ie as defined by the Criminal Justice Act 2003 s 206 (see PARA 132): s 177(1)(g).
11 Ie as defined by the Criminal Justice Act 2003 s 206A (see PARA 127): s 177(1)(ga) (added by the Legal Aid, Sentencing and Punishment of Offenders Act 2012 s 72(1)).
12 Ie as defined by the Criminal Justice Act 2003 s 207 (see PARA 128): s 177(1)(h).
13 Ie as defined by the Criminal Justice Act 2003 s 209 (see PARA 124): s 177(1)(i).
14 Ie as defined by the Criminal Justice Act 2003 s 212 (see PARA 122): s 177(1)(j).
15 As to the determination of a person's age see the Children and Young Persons Act 1933 s 99; and CHILDREN AND YOUNG PERSONS vol 10 (2012) PARA 1206.
16 Ie as defined by the Criminal Justice Act 2003 s 214 (see PARA 134): s 177(1)(l).
17 Ie as defined by the Criminal Justice Act 2003 s 212A (see PARA 135): s 177(1)(ja) (prospectively added by the Legal Aid, Sentencing and Punishment of Offenders Act 2012 s 76(2)).
18 Ie as defined by the Criminal Justice Act 2003 s 215 (see PARA 136): s 177(1)(m) (prospectively added by the Crime and Courts Act 2013 Sch 16 para 12).
19 As to the meaning of 'court' see PARA 1 note 1.
20 Ie unless there are exceptional circumstances which relate to the offence or to the offender (Criminal Justice Act 2003 s 177(2B)(a) (s 177(2A), (2B) added by the Crime and Courts Act 2013 Sch 16 paras 1, 2), would make it unjust in all the circumstances for the court to comply with the Criminal Justice Act 2003 s 177(2A)(a) (see the text and note 21) in the

particular case (s 177(2B)(b) (as so added)), and would make it unjust in all the circumstances for the court to impose a fine for the offence concerned (s 177(2B)(c) (as so added)).

21 Criminal Justice Act 2003 s 177(2A)(a) (as added: see note 20).
22 Criminal Justice Act 2003 s 177(2A)(b) (as added: see note 20).
23 Criminal Justice Act 2003 s 177(2A)(c) (as added: see note 20).
24 Ie: (1) until a day to be appointed, an electronic monitoring requirement as defined by the Criminal Justice Act 2003 s 215 (see PARA 136); or (2) as from that day, an electronic monitoring requirement within s 215(1)(a) for securing the electronic monitoring of the curfew or exclusion requirement: s 177(3) (prospectively amended by the Crime and Courts Act 2013 Sch 16 paras 11, 12). At the date at which this volume states the law no day had been appointed for the coming into force of these amendments.
25 Ie by the Criminal Justice Act 2003 s 215(2) (see PARA 136) or s 218(4) (see PARA 136).
26 Criminal Justice Act 2003 s 177(3) (prospectively amended: see note 24).
27 See note 25.
28 Criminal Justice Act 2003 s 177(4) (as amended (see note 5); amended by the Legal Aid, Sentencing and Punishment of Offenders Act 2012 s 72(2); prospectively repealed by the Crime and Courts Act 2013 Sch 16 paras 11, 12). At the date at which this volume states the law no day had been appointed for the coming into force of this prospective repeal.
29 Criminal Justice Act 2003 s 216(1) (amended by SI 2005/886). Where an order specifies a local justice area in which the court making the order does not act, the court making the order must provide to the magistrates' court acting in that area a copy of the order and documents and information relating to the case likely to be of assistance to a court acting in that area in the exercise of its functions in relation to the order: Criminal Justice Act 2003 s 219(3) (amended by SI 2005/886).

49. Requirement to avoid conflict with religious beliefs and education. The court must ensure, as far as practicable, that any requirement imposed by a community order[1] is such as to avoid:

(1) any conflict with the offender's religious beliefs or with the requirements of any other relevant order[2] to which he may be subject[3]; and

(2) any interference with the times, if any, at which he normally works or attends any educational establishment[4].

It is the duty of the responsible officer[5] to ensure that these requirements are complied with[6].

1 For the power to make community orders see PARAS 45, 47.
2 Ie a suspended sentence order (see PARAS 100–120) or a community order.
3 Criminal Justice Act 2003 s 217(1)(a). The Secretary of State may by order provide that the Criminal Justice Act 2003 s 217(1) is to have effect with such additional restrictions as may be specified in the order: s 217(3). At the date at which this volume states the law no such order had been made.
4 Criminal Justice Act 2003 s 217(1)(b) (amended by the Criminal Justice and Immigration Act 2008 s 6(2), Sch 4 paras 71, 91).
5 As to the responsible officer see PARA 51 note 2.
6 See the Criminal Justice Act 2003 s 217(2); and PARA 51.

50. Time limits for compliance with requirements. A community order[1] must specify a date ('the end date'), not more than three years after the date of the order, by which all requirements[2] in it must have been complied with[3]; and a community order which imposes two or more different requirements must also specify a date by which each of those requirements must be complied with[4]. A community order ceases to be in force on the end date[5].

1 For the power to make community orders see PARAS 45, 47.
2 As to the requirements see PARA 48.
3 Criminal Justice Act 2003 s 177(5) (s 177(5) amended, s 177(5A), (5B) added, by the Legal Aid, Sentencing and Punishment of Offenders Act 2012 s 66). The period specified by the court when imposing the order is the relevant period for determining the order's duration, however long it takes for the offender to carry out the requirements: see *R v Davison* [2008] EWCA Crim 2795, [2009] 2 Cr App Rep (S) 76.

4   Criminal Justice Act 2003 s 177(5A) (as added: see note 3). The last of those dates must be the same as the end date: s 177(5A) (as so added).
5   Criminal Justice Act 2003 s 177(5B) (as added: see note 3). This is subject to s 200(3) (duration of community order imposing unpaid work requirement: see PARA 133): s 177(5B) (as so added).

51.   Duty of offender to keep in touch with responsible officer and to obtain permission before changing residence. An offender in respect of whom a community order[1] is in force must keep in touch with the responsible officer[2] in accordance with such instructions as he may from time to time be given by that officer[3]. He is also prohibited (unless there is a residence requirement in place[4]) from changing residence without the permission of either the responsible officer or the court[5], and it is provided that the officer or court may refuse an application for permission[6] if, in the opinion of the officer or court, the change in residence is likely to prevent the offender complying with a requirement imposed by the order[7] or would hinder the offender's rehabilitation[8]. A court may also give permission for a change of residence in certain proceedings[9] involving the breach or amendment of orders[10].

1   For the power to make community orders see PARAS 45, 47.
2   For the purposes of the Criminal Justice Act 2003 Pt 12 (ss 142–305) the 'responsible officer' in relation to an offender to whom a relevant order (ie a community order or a suspended sentence order: see PARAS 100–120) relates, means, the person who is for the time being responsible for discharging the functions conferred by Pt 12 on the responsible officer in accordance with arrangements made by the Secretary of State: s 197(1) (s 197 substituted by the Offender Rehabilitation Act 2014 s 14). The responsible officer must be an officer of a provider of probation services (Criminal Justice Act 2003 s 197(2)(a) (as so substituted)) or a person responsible for monitoring the offender in accordance with an electronic monitoring requirement imposed by the relevant order (s 197(2)(b) (as so substituted)). As to providers of probation services see PARAS 666–687.
     Where a relevant order has effect, it is the duty of the responsible officer:
    (1)   to make any arrangements that are necessary in connection with the requirements imposed by the order (s 198(1)(a)); and
    (2)   to promote the offender's compliance with those requirements (s 198(1)(b)).
     The responsible officer in relation to an offender to whom a relevant order relates must ensure, as far as practicable, that any instruction given or requirement imposed by him in pursuance of the order is such as to avoid any conflict with the offender's religious beliefs or with the requirements of any other relevant order to which he may be subject (s 217(1)(a), (2)) and any interference with the times, if any, at which he normally works or attends any educational establishment (s 217(1)(b) (amended by the Criminal Justice and Immigration Act 2008 Sch 4 paras 71, 91)). The Secretary of State may by order provide that the Criminal Justice Act 2003 s 217(2) is to have effect with such additional restrictions as may be specified in the order: s 217(3). At the date at which this volume states the law no such order had been made.
3   Criminal Justice Act 2003 s 220(1)(a). The obligation imposed by s 220(1) is enforceable as if it were a requirement imposed by the order: s 220(2). In connection with the requirement to 'keep in touch' see *Richards v National Probation Service* [2007] EWHC 3108 (Admin), 172 JP 100, 172 JPN 293.
4   The Criminal Justice Act 2003 s 220A (see the text and notes 5–10) does not apply if the relevant order includes a residence requirement imposed under s 206 (see PARA 132): s 220A(6) (s 220A added by the Offender Rehabilitation Act 2014 s 18(1), (2)).
5   Criminal Justice Act 2003 s 220A(1) (as added: see note 4). The obligation imposed by s 220A(1) is enforceable as if it were a requirement imposed by the relevant order: s 220A(5) (as so added). In connection with circumstances in which a relevant order has to be amended because of permission given under s 220A see Sch 8 para 16, Sch 12 para 14; and PARAS 59, 107.
6   The appropriate court (as defined: see Sch 8 para 16, Sch 12 para 14; and PARAS 59, 107) may, on an application by the offender, give permission in a case in which the responsible officer has refused: Criminal Justice Act 2003 s 220A(2), (8) (as added: see note 4).
7   Criminal Justice Act 2003 s 220A(4)(a) (as added: see note 4).
8   Criminal Justice Act 2003 s 220A(4)(b) (as added: see note 4).

9   Ie proceedings under the Criminal Justice Act 2003 Sch 8 (see PARA 57 et seq) or Sch 12 (see PARA 105 et seq).
10 Criminal Justice Act 2003 s 220A(3) (as added: see note 4).

52. Periodical review of orders. The Secretary of State may by order:
  (1)   enable or require a court[1] making a community order[2] to provide for the order to be reviewed periodically by that or another court[3];
  (2)   enable a court to amend a community order so as to include or remove a provision for review by a court[4]; and
  (3)   make provision as to the timing and conduct of reviews and as to the powers of the court on a review[5].

1   As to the meaning of 'court' see PARA 1 note 1.
2   For the power to make community orders see PARAS 45, 47.
3   Criminal Justice Act 2003 s 178(1)(a). At the date at which this volume states the law one such order had been made: see the Community Order (Review by Specified Courts) Order 2007, SI 2007/2162. Such an order may, in particular, make provision in relation to community orders corresponding to any provision made by the Criminal Justice Act 2003 ss 191, 192 (see PARA 104) in relation to suspended sentence orders (s 178(2)) and may repeal or amend any provision of Pt 12 (ss 142–305) (s 178(3)).
4   Criminal Justice Act 2003 s 178(1)(b). See note 3.
5   Criminal Justice Act 2003 s 178(1)(c). See note 3.

B. BREACH OF REQUIREMENT OF COMMUNITY ORDER

53. Duty to give warning and subsequent breach. If the responsible officer[1] is of the opinion that the offender[2] has failed without reasonable excuse to comply with any of the requirements of a community order[3], the officer must give him a warning unless:
  (1)   the offender has within the previous 12 months been given such a warning in relation to a failure to comply with any of the requirements of the order[4]; or
  (2)   the officer relates the matter to an enforcement officer[5].
The warning must:
  (a)   describe the circumstances of the failure[6];
  (b)   state that the failure is unacceptable[7]; and
  (c)   inform the offender that, if within the next 12 months he again fails to comply with any requirement of the order, he will be liable to be brought before a court[8].
The responsible officer must, as soon as practicable after the warning has been given, record that fact[9].
  If:
  (i)   the responsible officer has given such a warning to the offender in respect of a community order[10]; and
  (ii) at any time within the 12 months beginning with the date on which the warning was given, the responsible officer is of the opinion that the offender has since that date failed without reasonable excuse to comply with any of the requirements of the order[11],
the officer must refer the matter to an enforcement officer[12].

1   As to the meaning of 'responsible officer' see PARA 51 note 2.
2   The 'offender', in relation to a community order, is the person in respect of whom a community order is made: Criminal Justice Act 2003 Sch 8 para 1.
3   For the power to make community orders see PARAS 45, 47. The fact that a conviction is being appealed does not excuse non-compliance with the requirements of a community order: see *West Midlands Probation Board v Sadler* [2008] EWHC 15 (Admin), [2008] 1 WLR 918. For the

purposes of the Criminal Justice Act 2003 Sch 8 a requirement falling within any of s 177(1)(a)–(m) (see PARA 48) is of the same kind as any other requirement falling within those provisions and an electronic monitoring requirement (as from a day to be appointed, an electronic monitoring requirement within s 215(1)(a)) (see PARA 136), is a requirement of the same kind as any requirement falling within s 177(1) (as from a day to be appointed, s 177(1)(a)–(l)) to which it relates: Sch 8 para 3 (prospectively amended by the Crime and Courts Act 2013 Sch 16 paras 11, 19)). Where a community order has been made on appeal, it is to be taken for the purposes of the Criminal Justice Act 2003 Sch 8 to have been made by the Crown Court: Sch 8 para 4.

4 Criminal Justice Act 2003 Sch 8 para 5(1)(a).

5 Criminal Justice Act 2003 Sch 8 para 5(1)(b) (Sch 8 paras 1A, 6A added Sch 8 para 5(1)(b) substituted, Sch 8 para 6(1) amended, by the Offender Rehabilitation Act 2014 Sch 4 paras 1, 6). In the Criminal Justice Act 2003 Sch 8 'enforcement officer' means a person who is for the time being responsible for discharging the functions conferred by Sch 8 on an enforcement officer in accordance with arrangements made by the Secretary of State: Sch 8 para 1A(1) (as so added). An enforcement officer must be an officer of a provider of probation services that is a public sector provider: Sch 8 para 1A(2) (as so added). In Sch 8 para 1A(2) 'public sector provider' means a probation trust or other public body or the Secretary of State: Sch 8 para 1A(3) (as so added).

Where a matter is referred to an enforcement officer under the Criminal Justice Act 2003 Sch 8 para 5(1)(b) or Sch 8 para 6(1), it is the duty of the enforcement officer to consider the case and, where appropriate, to cause an information to be laid before a justice of the peace in respect of the offender's failure to comply with the requirement: Sch 8 para 6A(1) (as so added). In relation to any community order which was made by the Crown Court and does not include a direction that any failure to comply with the requirements of the order is to be dealt with by a magistrates' court, the reference in Sch 8 para 6A(1) to a justice of the peace is to be read as a reference to the Crown Court: Sch 8 para 6A(2) (as so added).

6 Criminal Justice Act 2003 Sch 8 para 5(2)(a).

7 Criminal Justice Act 2003 Sch 8 para 5(2)(b).

8 Criminal Justice Act 2003 Sch 8 para 5(2)(c).

9 Criminal Justice Act 2003 Sch 8 para 5(3).

10 Criminal Justice Act 2003 Sch 8 para 6(1)(a).

11 Criminal Justice Act 2003 Sch 8 para 6(1)(b).

12 Criminal Justice Act 2003 Sch 8 para 6(1) (as amended: see note 5). See Sch 8 para 6A; and note 5.

54. Issue of summons or warrant.
If at any time while:

(1) a community order[1] made by a magistrates' court[2]; or

(2) any community order which was made by the Crown Court and includes a direction that any failure to comply with the requirements of the order is to be dealt with by a magistrates' court[3],

is in force it appears on information to a justice of the peace that the offender[4] has failed to comply with any of the requirements of the order, the justice may issue a summons requiring the offender to appear at the place and time specified in it[5] or, if the information is in writing and on oath, issue a warrant for his arrest[6]. Any such summons or warrant must direct the offender to appear or be brought:

(a) in the case of a community order imposing a drug rehabilitation requirement which is subject to review[7], before the magistrates' court responsible for the order[8]; or

(b) in any other case, before a magistrates' court acting in the local justice area[9] in which the offender resides or, if it is not known where he resides, before a magistrates' court acting in the local justice area concerned[10].

If at any time while a community order made by the Crown Court, which does not include a direction that any failure to comply with the requirements of the order is to be dealt with by a magistrates' court, is in force it appears on information to the Crown Court that the offender has failed to comply with any of the requirements of the order, the Crown Court may issue a summons requiring the offender to appear at the place and time specified in it[11] or, if the information is in writing and on oath, issue a warrant for his arrest[12]. Any such summons or warrant must direct the offender to appear or be brought before the Crown Court[13].

1   For the power to make community orders see PARAS 45, 47.
2   Criminal Justice Act 2003 Sch 8 para 7(1)(a).
3   Criminal Justice Act 2003 Sch 8 para 7(1)(b). Where a community order has been made on appeal, it is to be taken for the purposes of Sch 8 to have been made by the Crown Court: Sch 8 para 4.
4   As to the meaning of 'offender' see PARA 53 note 2.
5   Criminal Justice Act 2003 Sch 8 para 7(2)(a) (Sch 8 para 7(2) amended by the Domestic Violence, Crime and Victims Act 2004 Sch 5 para 7(1), (2); and by SI 2005/886). Where such a summons requires the offender to appear before a magistrates' court and the offender does not appear in answer to the summons, the magistrates' court may issue a warrant for the arrest of the offender: Criminal Justice Act 2003 Sch 8 para 7(4).
6   Criminal Justice Act 2003 Sch 8 para 7(2)(b) (as amended: see note 5).
7   References to a drug rehabilitation requirement of a community order being subject to review are references to that requirement being subject to review in accordance with the Criminal Justice Act 2003 s 210(1)(b) (see PARA 125): Sch 8 para 2(a).
8   Criminal Justice Act 2003 Sch 8 para 7(3)(a). References to the court responsible for a community order imposing a drug rehabilitation requirement which is subject to review are to be construed in accordance with s 210(2) (see PARA 125): Sch 8 para 2(b).
9   Ie the local justice area for the time being specified in the order: Criminal Justice Act 2003 Sch 8 para 1 (amended by SI 2005/886).
10 Criminal Justice Act 2003 Sch 8 para 7(3)(b) (substituted by the Domestic Violence, Crime and Victims Act 2004 Sch 5 para 7(1), (3); and amended by SI 2005/886). In the Criminal Justice Act 2003 Sch 8 'the local justice area concerned', in relation to a community order, means the local justice area for the time being specified in the order: Sch 8 para 1 (amended by SI 2005/886).
11 Criminal Justice Act 2003 Sch 8 para 8(1), (2)(a). Where such a summons requires the offender to appear before the Crown Court and the offender does not appear in answer to the summons, the Crown Court may issue a warrant for the arrest of the offender: Sch 8 para 8(4).
12 Criminal Justice Act 2003 Sch 8 para 8(2).
13 Criminal Justice Act 2003 Sch 8 para 8(3).

55.   Powers of magistrates' court. If it is proved[1] to the satisfaction of a magistrates' court before which an offender[2] appears or is brought[3] that he has failed without reasonable excuse[4] to comply with any of the requirements of a community order[5], the court must (or, as from a day to be appointed, may) deal with him in respect of the failure in any one of the following ways:

(1)   by amending the terms of the community order so as to impose more onerous requirements which the court could include if it were then making the order[6];

(2)   by ordering the offender to pay a fine not exceeding £2,500[7];

(3)   where the community order was made by a magistrates' court, by dealing with him, for the offence in respect of which the order was made, in any way in which the court could deal with him if he had just been convicted by it of the offence[8]; or

(4)   where:

(a)   the community order was made by a magistrates' court[9];

(b)   the offence in respect of which the order was made was not an offence punishable by imprisonment[10];

(c)   the offender is aged 18[11] or over[12]; and

(d)   the offender has wilfully and persistently failed to comply with the requirements of the order[13], by dealing with him, in respect of that offence, by imposing a sentence of imprisonment or, until a day to be appointed[14], a sentence of detention in a young offender institution[15] for a term not exceeding six months (or, as from a day to be appointed[16], 51 weeks)[17].

In so dealing with an offender, a magistrates' court must take into account the extent to which the offender has complied with the requirements of the community order[18].

Where a magistrates' court deals with an offender under head (2) or head (3) above, it must revoke the community order if it is still in force[19]. Where a community order was made by the Crown Court and a magistrates' court would otherwise[20] be required to deal with the offender under heads (1) to (4) above, it may instead commit him to custody or release him on bail until he can be brought or appear before the Crown Court[21]. A person sentenced under head (3) or head (4) above for an offence may appeal to the Crown Court against the sentence[22].

1   The prosecution must prove each element of the breach beyond reasonable doubt, including proving that the defendant was the person named in the order: *West Yorkshire Probation Board v Boulter* [2005] EWHC 2342 (Admin), [2006] 1 WLR 232, 169 JP 601.

2   As to the meaning of 'offender' see PARA 53 note 2.

3   Ie under the Criminal Justice Act 2003 Sch 8 para 7 (see PARA 54). A magistrates' court may adjourn any hearing relating to an offender in any proceedings under Sch 8, and where it does so the court may direct that the offender be released forthwith or remand the offender: Sch 8 para 25A(1), (2) (Sch 8 para 25A added by the Criminal Justice and Immigration Act 2008 Sch 4 para 109). Where the court so remands the offender it must fix the time and place at which the hearing is to be resumed and that time and place must be the time and place at which the offender is required to appear or be brought before the court by virtue of the remand (Criminal Justice Act 2003 Sch 8 para 25A(3) (as so added)), and where the court so adjourns the hearing but does not remand the offender it may fix the time and place at which the hearing is to be resumed but, if it does not do so, it must not resume the hearing unless it is satisfied that the offender and any officer of a provider of probation services who the court thinks has an interest in the proceedings have had adequate notice of the time and place for the resumed hearing (Sch 8 para 25A(3), (4) (as so added; amended by the Offender Rehabilitation Act 2014 Sch 4 paras 10, 14)). These powers may be exercised by a single justice of the peace, notwithstanding anything in the Magistrates' Courts Act 1980: Criminal Justice Act 2003 Sch 8 para 25A(5) (as so added). These provisions apply to any hearing in any proceedings under Sch 8 in place of the Magistrates' Courts Act 1980 s 10 (adjournment of trial: see CRIMINAL PROCEDURE vol 27 (2015) PARAS 287, 290) where s 10 would otherwise apply, but do not affect the application of s 10 to hearings of any other description: Criminal Justice Act 2003 Sch 8 para 25A(6) (as so added).

4   The fact that an appeal against sentence had been lodged could not afford a reasonable excuse to a defendant for failing to comply with the requirements of a community order: see *West Midlands Probation Board v Sutton Coldfield Magistrates' Court* [2008] EWHC 15 (Admin), [2008] 3 All ER 1193, sub nom *West Midlands Probation Board v Sadler* [2008] 1 WLR 918.

5   For the power to make community orders see PARAS 45, 47. An offender who is required by a mental health treatment requirement (see PARA 128), a drug rehabilitation requirement (see PARA 124) or an alcohol treatment requirement (see PARA 122) to submit to treatment for his mental condition, or his dependency on or propensity to misuse drugs or alcohol, is not to be treated for these purposes as having failed to comply with that requirement on the ground only that he had refused to undergo any surgical, electrical or other treatment if, in the opinion of the court, his refusal was reasonable having regard to all the circumstances: Criminal Justice Act 2003 Sch 8 para 11(1).

6   Criminal Justice Act 2003 Sch 8 para 9(1)(a) (Sch 8 para 9(1) prospectively amended, Sch 8 paras 9(1)(aa), (3ZA)–(3ZC), (3B), 11A added, Sch 8 para 9(3), (6) amended, by the Legal Aid, Sentencing and Punishment of Offenders Act 2012 ss 66(3), 67(1)–(4)). At the date at which this volume states the law no day had been appointed for the coming into force of the amendment cited as prospective. In so dealing with an offender the court may extend the duration of particular requirements (subject to any limit imposed by the Criminal Justice Act 2003 Pt 12 Ch 4 (ss 196–223) (see PARA 121 et seq)) but may only amend the order to substitute a later date for that specified under s 177(5) (see PARA 50) in accordance with the following:

(1)　a date so substituted may not fall outside the period of six months beginning with the date previously specified under s 177(5) and, subject to that, may fall more than three years after the date of the order (Sch 8 para 9(3), (3ZA) (as so amended and added); and

(2)　the power under the Criminal Justice Act 2003 Sch 8 para 9(3) to substitute a date may not be exercised in relation to an order if that power or the power in Sch 8 para 10(3) (see PARA 56) to substitute a date has previously been exercised in relation to that order (Sch 8 para 9(3ZB) (as so added)).

A date substituted under Sch 8 para 9(3) is to be treated as having been specified in relation to the order under s 177(5): Sch 8 para 9(3ZC) (as so added).

Where the court is dealing with the offender under Sch 8 para 9(1)(a) and the community order does not contain an unpaid work requirement, the number of hours which a person may be required to work under an unpaid work requirement must be in the aggregate not less than 20 and not more than 300: s 199(2)(a), Sch 8 para 9(3A) (Sch 8 para 9(3A) added by the Criminal Justice and Immigration Act 2008 s 38(1), (2)).

Head (1) in the text has effect subject to the provisions mentioned in the Criminal Justice Act 2003 s 177(2), and to s 177(3), (6) (see PARA 48): Sch 8 para 26.

A court may not amend a mental health treatment requirement, a drug rehabilitation requirement or an alcohol treatment requirement under this provision unless the offender expresses his willingness to comply with the requirement as amended: Sch 8 para 11(2).

7　Criminal Justice Act 2003 Sch 8 para 9(1)(aa) (as added: see note 6). A fine imposed under Sch 8 para 9(1)(aa) is to be treated, for the purposes of any enactment, as being a sum adjudged to be paid by a conviction: Sch 8 para 9(3B) (as so added).

The Secretary of State may by order amend any sum for the time being specified in Sch 8 para 9(1)(aa) or Sch 8 para 10(1)(aa) (see PARA 56): Sch 8 para 11A(1) (as so added). This power may be exercised only if it appears to the Secretary of State that there has been a change in the value of money since the relevant date which justifies the change: Sch 8 para 11A(2) (as so added). In Sch 8 para 11A(2) 'the relevant date' means: (1) if the sum specified in Sch 8 para 9(1)(aa) or Sch 8 para 10(1)(aa) (as the case may be) has been substituted by an order under Sch 8 para 11A(1), the date on which the sum was last so substituted; and (2) otherwise, 3 December 2012 (ie the date on which the Legal Aid, Sentencing and Punishment of Offenders Act 2012 s 67 was brought into force by the Legal Aid, Sentencing and Punishment of Offenders Act 2012 (Commencement No 4 and Saving Provisions) Order 2012, SI 2012/2906): Criminal Justice Act 2003 Sch 8 para 11A(3) (as so added). An order under Sch 8 para 11A(1) (a 'fine amendment order') must not have effect in relation to any community order made in respect of an offence committed before the fine amendment order comes into force: Sch 8 para 11A(4) (as so added).

8　Criminal Justice Act 2003 Sch 8 para 9(1)(b). In so dealing with an offender, the court may, in the case of an offender who has wilfully and persistently failed to comply with the requirements of the community order, impose a custodial sentence (where the order was made in respect of an offence punishable with such a sentence) notwithstanding anything in 152(2) (see PARA 536): Sch 8 para 9(4).

9　Criminal Justice Act 2003 Sch 8 para 9(1)(c)(i).

10　Criminal Justice Act 2003 Sch 8 para 9(1)(c)(ii).

11　As to the determination of a person's age see the Children and Young Persons Act 1933 s 99; and CHILDREN AND YOUNG PERSONS vol 10 (2012) PARA 1206.

12　Criminal Justice Act 2003 Sch 8 para 9(1)(c)(iii).

13　Criminal Justice Act 2003 Sch 8 para 9(1)(c)(iv).

14　Ie until the date on which the Criminal Justice and Court Services Act 2000 s 61 (abolition of sentences of detention in a young offender institution, custody for life etc: PARA 36) comes into force. At the date at which this volume states the law no day had been appointed for the commencement of s 61.

15　For these purposes a sentence of detention in a young offender institution may be passed on a person aged at least 18 but under 21: Criminal Justice Act 2003 Sch 8 para 9(1)(c) (amended by SI 2005/643). As to a sentence of detention in a young offender institution see PARA 16.

16　Ie as from the date on which the repeal of the Powers of Criminal Courts (Sentencing) Act 2000 s 78 (general limits on magistrates' powers: see PARA 2) by the Criminal Justice Act 2003 Sch 37 Pt 7 comes into force. At the date at which this volume states the law no day had been appointed for that purpose.

17　Criminal Justice Act 2003 Sch 8 para 9(1)(c) (amended by SI 2005/643).

18　Criminal Justice Act 2003 Sch 8 para 9(2).

19　Criminal Justice Act 2003 Sch 8 para 9(5).

20　Ie apart from the Criminal Justice Act 2003 Sch 8 para 9(6).

21 Criminal Justice Act 2003 Sch 8 para 9(6) (as amended (see note 6); amended by the Crime and Courts Act 2013 Sch 16 para 22(2)). A magistrates' court which deals with an offender's case under the Criminal Justice Act 2003 Sch 8 para 9(6) must send to the Crown Court: (1) a certificate signed by a justice of the peace certifying that the offender has failed to comply with the requirements of the community order in the respect specified in the certificate (Sch 8 para 9(7)(a)); and (2) such other particulars of the case as may be desirable; and a certificate purporting to be so signed is admissible as evidence of the failure before the Crown Court (Sch 8 para 9(7)(b)).

Where a community order has been made on appeal, it is to be taken for the purposes of Sch 8 to have been made by the Crown Court: Sch 8 para 4.

22 Criminal Justice Act 2003 Sch 8 para 9(8) (amended by the Criminal Justice and Courts Act 2015 Sch 12 para 15). Appeal may also be brought against an order made by the court under the Prosecution of Offences Act 1985 s 21A (criminal courts charge: see CRIMINAL PROCEDURE) when imposing that sentence: Criminal Justice Act 2003 Sch 8 para 9(8) (as so amended).

56. Powers of Crown Court. Where[1] an offender[2] appears or is brought before the Crown Court and it is proved to the satisfaction of that court that he has failed without reasonable excuse[3] to comply with any of the requirements of the community order[4], the Crown Court must (or, as from a day to be appointed, may) deal with him in respect of the failure in any one of the following ways:

(1)   by amending the terms of the community order so as to impose more onerous requirements which the Crown Court could impose if it were then making the order[5];

(2)   by ordering the offender to pay a fine not exceeding £2,500[6];

(3)   by dealing with him, for the offence in respect of which the order was made, in any way in which he could have been dealt with for that offence by the court which made the order if the order had not been made[7];

(4)   where:

(a)   the offence in respect of which the order was made was not an offence punishable by imprisonment[8];

(b)   the offender is aged 18 or over[9]; and

(c)   the offender has wilfully and persistently failed to comply with the requirements of the order[10],

by dealing with him, in respect of that offence, by imposing a sentence of imprisonment or, until a day to be appointed[11], a sentence of detention in a young offender institution[12] for a term not exceeding six months (or, as from a day to be appointed[13], 51 weeks)[14].

In so dealing with an offender, the Crown Court must take into account the extent to which the offender has complied with the requirements of the community order[15].

Where the Crown Court deals with an offender under head (1) or head (3) above, it must revoke the community order if it is still in force[16].

1   Ie under the Criminal Justice Act 2003 Sch 8 para 8 (see PARA 54) or by virtue of Sch 8 para 9(6) (see PARA 55).

2   As to the meaning of 'offender' see PARA 53 note 2.

3   Cf, in connection with orders enforceable by magistrates' courts, *West Midlands Probation Board v Sutton Coldfield Magistrates' Court* [2008] EWHC 15 (Admin), [2008] 3 All ER 1193, sub nom *West Midlands Probation Board v Sadler* [2008] 1 WLR 918 (the fact that an appeal against sentence had been lodged could not afford a reasonable excuse to a defendant for failing to comply with the requirements of a community order).

4   For the power to make community orders see PARAS 45, 47. An offender who is required by a mental health treatment requirement (see PARA 128), a drug rehabilitation requirement (see PARA 124) or an alcohol treatment requirement (see PARA 122) to submit to treatment for his mental condition, or his dependency on or propensity to misuse drugs or alcohol, is not to be treated for

these purposes as having failed to comply with that requirement on the ground only that he had refused to undergo any surgical, electrical or other treatment if, in the opinion of the court, his refusal was reasonable having regard to all the circumstances: Criminal Justice Act 2003 Sch 8 para 11(1). Any question whether the offender has failed to comply with the requirements of the community order is to be determined by the court and not by the verdict of a jury: Sch 8 para 10(6).

5   Criminal Justice Act 2003 Sch 8 para 10(1)(a) (Sch 8 para 10(1) prospectively amended, Sch 8 para 10(1)(aa), (3ZA)–(3ZC), (3B) added, by the Legal Aid, Sentencing and Punishment of Offenders Act 2012 ss 66(4), 67(1), (5), (6)). At the date at which this volume states the law no day had been appointed for the coming into force of the amendment cited as prospective. In so dealing with an offender the court may extend the duration of particular requirements (subject to any limit imposed by the Criminal Justice Act 2003 Pt 12 Ch 4 (ss 196–223) (see PARA 121 et seq)) but may only amend the order to substitute a later date for that specified under s 177(5) (see PARA 50) in accordance with the following:

(1)   a date so substituted may not fall outside the period of six months beginning with the date previously specified under s 177(5) and, subject to that, may fall more than three years after the date of the order (Sch 8 para 10(3), (3ZA) (as so amended and added)); and

(2)   the power under the Criminal Justice Act 2003 Sch 8 para 9(3) to substitute a date may not be exercised in relation to an order if that power or the power in Sch 8 para 9(3) (see PARA 55) to substitute a date has previously been exercised in relation to that order (Sch 8 para 10(3ZB) (as so added).

A date substituted under Sch 8 para 10(3) is to be treated as having been specified in relation to the order under s 177(5): Sch 8 para 9(3ZC) (as so added).

Where the court is dealing with the offender under Sch 8 para 10(1)(a) and the community order does not contain an unpaid work requirement, the number of hours which a person may be required to work under an unpaid work requirement must be in the aggregate not less than 20 and not more than 300: s 199(2)(a), Sch 8 para 10(3A) (Sch 8 para 9(3A) added by the Criminal Justice and Immigration Act 2008 s 38(1), (3)).

Head (1) in the text has effect subject to the provisions mentioned in the Criminal Justice Act 2003 s 177(2), and to s 177(3), (6) (see PARA 48): Sch 8 para 26.

A court may not amend a mental health treatment requirement, a drug rehabilitation requirement or an alcohol treatment requirement under this provision unless the offender expresses his willingness to comply with the requirement as amended: Sch 8 para 11(2).

6   Criminal Justice Act 2003 Sch 8 para 10(1)(aa) (as added: see note 5). A fine imposed under Sch 8 para 10(1)(aa) is to be treated, for the purposes of any enactment, as being a sum adjudged to be paid by a conviction: Sch 8 para 10(3B) (as so added). See further Sch 8 para 11A; and PARA 55 note 7.

7   Criminal Justice Act 2003 Sch 8 para 10(1)(b). In so dealing with an offender, the Crown Court may, in the case of an offender who has wilfully and persistently failed to comply with the requirements of the community order, impose a custodial sentence (where the order was made in respect of an offence punishable with such a sentence) notwithstanding anything in s 152(2) (see PARA 536): Sch 8 para 10(4).

8   Criminal Justice Act 2003 Sch 8 para 10(1)(c)(i).

9   Criminal Justice Act 2003 Sch 8 para 10(1)(c)(ii). As to the determination of a person's age see the Children and Young Persons Act 1933 s 99; and CHILDREN AND YOUNG PERSONS vol 10 (2012) PARA 1206.

10   Criminal Justice Act 2003 Sch 8 para 10(1)(c)(iii).

11   Ie until the date on which the Criminal Justice and Court Services Act 2000 s 61 (abolition of sentences of detention in a young offender institution, custody for life etc: PARA 36) comes into force. At the date at which this volume states the law no day had been appointed for the commencement of s 61.

12   For these purposes a sentence of detention in a young offender institution may be passed on a person aged at least 18 but under 21: Criminal Justice Act 2003 Sch 8 para 10(1)(c) (amended by SI 2005/643). As to a sentence of detention in a young offender institution see PARA 16.

13   Ie as from the date on which the repeal of the Powers of Criminal Courts (Sentencing) Act 2000 s 78 (general limits on magistrates' powers: see PARA 2) by the Criminal Justice Act 2003 Sch 37 Pt 7 comes into force.

14   Criminal Justice Act 2003 Sch 8 para 10(1)(c) (amended by SI 2005/643).

15   Criminal Justice Act 2003 Sch 8 para 10(2).

16   Criminal Justice Act 2003 Sch 8 para 10(5).

C. REVOCATION AND AMENDMENT OF COMMUNITY ORDER

57. Revocation of order by magistrates' court. Where a community order[1] (other than one made by the Crown Court which does not include a direction that any failure to comply with its requirements is to be dealt with by a magistrates' court) is in force and, on the application of the offender or an officer of a provider of probation services[2], it appears to the appropriate magistrates' court[3] that, having regard to circumstances which have arisen subsequent to the order, it would be in the interests of justice for the order to be revoked[4] or for the offender to be dealt with in some other way for the offence in respect of which the order was made[5], the appropriate magistrates' court may:

(1) revoke the order[6]; or

(2) both revoke the order[7] and deal with the offender, for that offence[8], in any way in which it could deal with him if he had just been convicted by the court of the offence[9].

The circumstances in which a community order may be so revoked include the offender's making good progress or his responding satisfactorily to supervision or treatment[10].

Where a magistrates' court proposes to exercise its powers under these provisions otherwise than on the application of the offender it must summon him to appear before the court and, if he does not appear in answer to the summons, may issue a warrant for his arrest[11].

1   For the power to make community orders see PARAS 45, 47.
2   In connection with applications to the court see the Criminal Procedure Rules 2015, SI 2015/1490, rr 32.1–32.4. As to the meaning of 'offender' see PARA 53 note 2. No application may be made under the Criminal Justice Act 2003 Sch 8 para 13 (see the text and notes 3–11) while an appeal against the community order is pending: Sch 8 para 24(1).
3   In the Criminal Justice Act 2003 Sch 8 para 13 'appropriate magistrates' court' means:
    (1) in the case of an order imposing a drug rehabilitation requirement (see PARA 124) which is subject to review, the magistrates' court responsible for the order (Sch 8 para 13(7)(a)); and
    (2) in the case of any other community order, a magistrates' court acting in the local justice area concerned (Sch 8 para 13(7)(b) (amended by SI 2005/886)).
    As to the meaning of 'the local justice area concerned' see PARA 54 note 10. As to the adjournment of hearings by magistrates' courts and the remanding of offenders see PARA 55 note 3.
4   Criminal Justice Act 2003 Sch 8 para 13(1)(a) (amended by the Offender Rehabilitation Act 2014 Sch 4 paras 1, 6).
5   Criminal Justice Act 2003 Sch 8 para 13(1)(b).
6   Criminal Justice Act 2003 Sch 8 para 13(2)(a).
7   Criminal Justice Act 2003 Sch 8 para 13(2)(b)(i). In dealing with an offender under Sch 8 para 13(2)(b) a magistrates' court must take into account the extent to which the offender has complied with the requirements of the community order: Sch 8 para 13(4). A person sentenced under Sch 8 para 13(2)(b) for an offence may appeal to the Crown Court against the sentence: Sch 8 para 13(5).
8   Ie the offence in respect of which the order was made.
9   Criminal Justice Act 2003 Sch 8 para 13(2)(b)(ii). See note 7.
10 Criminal Justice Act 2003 Sch 8 para 13(3).
11 Criminal Justice Act 2003 Sch 8 para 13(6).

58. Revocation of order by Crown Court. Where there is in force a community order[1] made by the Crown Court[2] which does not include a direction that any failure to comply with its requirements is to be dealt with by a magistrates' court[3], and the offender[4] or an officer of a provider of probation services applies to the Crown Court for the order to be revoked or for the offender to be dealt with in some other way for the offence in respect of which the order was made[5], and it appears to the Crown Court to be in the interests of justice to do so, having regard to circumstances which have arisen subsequent to the order, the Crown Court may:

(1) revoke the order[6]; or

(2) both revoke the order[7] and deal with the offender, for that offence[8], in any way in which it could deal with him if he had just been convicted by the court of the offence[9].

The circumstances in which a community order may be so revoked include the offender's making good progress or his responding satisfactorily to supervision or treatment (as the case requires)[10].

Where the Crown Court proposes to exercise its powers under these provisions otherwise than on the application of the offender it must summon him to appear before the court and, if he does not appear in answer to the summons, may issue a warrant for his arrest[11].

1 For the power to make community orders see PARAS 45, 47.
2 Where a community order has been made on appeal, it is to be taken for the purposes of Sch 8 to have been made by the Crown Court: Criminal Justice Act 2003 Sch 8 para 4.
3 Criminal Justice Act 2003 Sch 8 para 14(1)(a).
4 As to the meaning of 'offender' see PARA 53 note 2.
5 Criminal Justice Act 2003 Sch 8 para 14(1)(b). In connection with applications to the court see the Criminal Procedure Rules 2015, SI 2015/1490, rr 32.1–32.4.
6 Criminal Justice Act 2003 Sch 8 para 14(2)(a).
7 Criminal Justice Act 2003 Sch 8 para 14(2)(b)(i). In dealing with an offender under Sch 8 para 14(2)(b) a magistrates' court must take into account the extent to which the offender has complied with the requirements of the community order: Sch 8 para 14(4).
8 Ie the offence in respect of which the order was made.
9 Criminal Justice Act 2003 Sch 8 para 14(2)(b)(ii). See note 7.
10 Criminal Justice Act 2003 Sch 8 para 14(3).
11 Criminal Justice Act 2003 Sch 8 para 14(5).

59. Amendment by reason of change of residence. Where at any time while a community order[1] is in force in respect of an offender[2] the offender is given permission[3] to change residence[4] and the local justice area in which the new residence is situated ('the new local justice area') is different from the local justice area specified in the order[5], then:

(1) if the permission is given by a court, the court must amend the order to specify the new local justice area[6]; and

(2) as from a day to be appointed, if the permission is given by the responsible officer[7], the officer must apply to the appropriate court[8] to amend the order to specify the new local justice area[9] and the court must make that amendment[10].

Where at any time while a community order is in force in respect of an offender:

(a) a court amends the order[11];

(b) the order as amended includes a residence requirement[12] requiring the offender to reside at a specified place[13]; and

(c) the local justice area in which that place is situated ('the new local justice area') is different from the local justice area specified in the order[14],

the court must amend the order to specify the new local justice area[15].

1 For the power to make community orders see PARAS 45, 47.
2 As to the meaning of 'offender' see PARA 53 note 2.
3 Ie under the Criminal Justice Act 2003 s 220A (see PARA 103).

4   Criminal Justice Act 2003 Sch 8 para 16(1)(a) (Sch 8 para 16 substituted, Sch 8 para 16A added, by the Offender Rehabilitation Act 2014 s 18(1), (5)). At the date at which this volume states the law the substituted Criminal Justice Act 2003 Sch 8 para 16(3) had yet to be brought into force: see the Offender Rehabilitation Act 2014 (Commencement No 2) Order 2015, SI 2015/40, art 2(p)(i).

5   Criminal Justice Act 2003 Sch 8 para 16(1)(b) (as substituted: see note 4).

6   Criminal Justice Act 2003 Sch 8 para 16(2) (as substituted: see note 4).

7   As to the meaning of 'responsible officer' see PARA 51 note 2.

8   For these purposes 'appropriate court' means:

    (1)   in relation to any community order imposing a drug rehabilitation requirement (see PARA 124) which is subject to review, the court responsible for the order (Criminal Justice Act 2003 Sch 8 paras 16(4)(a), 17(6), 18(4), 19A(5), 20(2) (Sch 8 para 16 as substituted (see note 4); Sch 8 para 19A added by the Legal Aid, Sentencing and Punishment of Offenders Act 2012 s 66(5));

    (2)   in relation to any community order which was made by the Crown Court and does not include any direction that any failure to comply with the requirements of the order is to be dealt with by a magistrates' court, the Crown Court (Criminal Justice Act 2003 Sch 8 para 16(4)(b) (as so substituted)); and

    (3)   in relation to any other community order, a magistrates' court acting in the local justice area specified in the order (Sch 8 para 16(4)(c) (as so substituted)).

    In connection with applications to the court see the Criminal Procedure Rules 2015, SI 2015/1490, rr 32.1–32.4. As to references to a drug rehabilitation requirement of a community order being subject to review and to the court responsible for a community order imposing a drug rehabilitation requirement which is subject to review see PARA 54 notes 7, 8. Where a community order has been made on appeal, it is to be taken for the purposes of the Criminal Justice Act 2003 Sch 8 to have been made by the Crown Court: Sch 8 para 4.

9   Criminal Justice Act 2003 Sch 8 para 16(3)(a) (prospectively substituted: see note 4).

10   Criminal Justice Act 2003 Sch 8 para 16(3)(b) (prospectively substituted: see note 4). Where a court proposes to exercise its powers of amendment under Sch 8 paras 16–21, otherwise than on the application of the offender, the court must summon him to appear before it (Sch 8 para 25(1)(a)); and, if he does not appear in answer to the summons, it may issue a warrant for his arrest (Sch 8 para 25(1)(b)). However, this does not apply to an order cancelling a requirement of a community order or reducing the period of a requirement, or substituting a new local justice area or a new place for the one specified in the order: Sch 8 para 25(2) (amended by SI 2005/886).

11   Criminal Justice Act 2003 Sch 8 para 16A(1)(a) (as added: see note 4).

12   See PARA 132.

13   Criminal Justice Act 2003 Sch 8 para 16A(1)(b) (as added: see note 4).

14   Criminal Justice Act 2003 Sch 8 para 16A(1)(c) (as added: see note 4).

15   Criminal Justice Act 2003 Sch 8 para 16A(2) (as added: see note 4).

60.   Amendment of requirements of community order.

The appropriate court[1] may, on the application[2] of the offender or an officer of a provider of probation services, by order amend a community order:

    (1)   by cancelling any of the requirements of the order[3]; or

    (2)   by replacing any of those requirements with a requirement of the same kind, which the court could include if it were then making the order[4].

The court may not so amend a mental health treatment requirement, a drug rehabilitation requirement or an alcohol treatment requirement unless the offender expresses his willingness to comply with the requirement as amended[5]. If the offender fails to express his willingness to comply with a mental health treatment requirement, drug rehabilitation requirement or alcohol treatment requirement as proposed to be so amended by the court, the court may:

    (a)   revoke the community order[6]; and

    (b)   deal with him, for the offence in respect of which the order was made, in any way in which he could have been dealt with for that offence by the court which made the order if the order had not been made[7].

1   As to the meaning of 'appropriate court' see PARA 59 note 8.

2 In connection with applications to the court see the Criminal Procedure Rules 2015, SI 2015/1490, rr 32.1–32.4. No application may be made under the Criminal Justice Act 2003 Sch 8 para 17 while an appeal against the community order is pending: Sch 8 para 24(1). However, this does not apply to an application under Sch 8 para 17 which relates to a mental health treatment requirement (see PARA 128), a drug rehabilitation requirement (see PARA 124) or an alcohol treatment requirement (see PARA 122) (Sch 8 para 24(2)(a)) and which is made by an officer of a provider of probation services with the consent of the offender (Sch 8 para 24(2)(b) (Sch 8 paras 17(1), 24(2)(b) amended by the Offender Rehabilitation Act 2014 Sch 4 paras 1, 6).

   For the power to make community orders see PARAS 45, 47. As to the meaning of 'offender' see PARA 53 note 2.

3 Criminal Justice Act 2003 Sch 8 para 17(1)(a) (as amended: see note 2). See also Sch 8 para 25; and PARA 59 note 10.

4 Criminal Justice Act 2003 Sch 8 para 17(1)(b). See note 3. Head (2) in the text has effect subject to the provisions mentioned in s 177(2), and to s 177(3), (6) (see PARA 48): Sch 8 para 26.

5 Criminal Justice Act 2003 Sch 8 para 17(2).

6 Criminal Justice Act 2003 Sch 8 para 17(3)(a).

7 Criminal Justice Act 2003 Sch 8 para 17(3)(b). In dealing with the offender under Sch 8 para 17(3)(b) the court must take into account the extent to which the offender has complied with the requirements of the order (Sch 8 para 17(4)(a)) and may impose a custodial sentence (where the order was made in respect of an offence punishable with such a sentence) notwithstanding anything in s 152(2) (see PARA 536) (Sch 8 para 17(4)(b)).

61.   Amendment of treatment requirements of community order on report of practitioner.   Where the medical practitioner or other person by whom or under whose direction an offender[1] is, in pursuance of a mental health treatment requirement[2], a drug rehabilitation requirement[3] or an alcohol treatment requirement[4], being treated for his mental condition or his dependency on or propensity to misuse drugs or alcohol:

   (1)   is of the opinion:
      (a)   that the treatment of the offender should be continued beyond the period specified in that behalf in the order[5];
      (b)   that the offender needs different treatment[6];
      (c)   that the offender is not susceptible to treatment[7]; or
      (d)   that the offender does not require further treatment[8]; or
   (2)   is for any reason unwilling to continue to treat or direct the treatment of the offender[9],

he must make a report in writing to that effect to the responsible officer[10] and that officer must cause an application to be made[11] to the appropriate court[12] for the variation or cancellation of the requirement[13].

1   As to the meaning of 'offender' see PARA 53 note 2.

2   Criminal Justice Act 2003 Sch 8 para 18(2)(a). As to a mental health treatment requirement see PARA 128.

3   Criminal Justice Act 2003 Sch 8 para 18(2)(b). As to a drug rehabilitation requirement see PARA 124.

4   Criminal Justice Act 2003 Sch 8 para 18(2)(c). As to an alcohol treatment requirement see PARA 122.

5   Criminal Justice Act 2003 Sch 8 para 18(1)(a), (3)(a).

6   Criminal Justice Act 2003 Sch 8 para 18(3)(b).

7   Criminal Justice Act 2003 Sch 8 para 18(3)(c).

8   Criminal Justice Act 2003 Sch 8 para 18(3)(d).

9   Criminal Justice Act 2003 Sch 8 para 18(1)(b).

10 As to the meaning of 'responsible officer' see PARA 51 note 2.

11 Ie under the Criminal Justice Act 2003 Sch 8 para 17 (see PARA 60).

12 As to the meaning of 'appropriate court' see PARA 59 note 8.

13 Criminal Justice Act 2003 Sch 8 para 18(1) (amended by the Offender Rehabilitation Act 2014 Sch 4 paras 1, 6). See also the Criminal Justice Act 2003 Sch 8 para 25; and PARA 59 note 10.

62.   Amendment in relation to review of drug rehabilitation requirement. Where an officer of a provider of probation services is of the opinion that a community order[1] imposing a drug rehabilitation requirement[2] which is subject to review[3] should be so amended as to provide for each subsequent periodic review[4] to be made without a hearing instead of at a review hearing, or vice versa, he must apply[5] to the court responsible for the order[6] for the variation of the order[7].

1   For the power to make community orders see PARAS 45, 47.
2   As to a drug rehabilitation requirement see PARA 124.
3   As to references to a drug rehabilitation requirement of a community order being subject to review see PARA 54.
4   Ie each periodic review required by the Criminal Justice Act 2003 s 211 (see PARA 125).
5   Ie under Criminal Justice Act 2003 Sch 8 para 17 (see PARA 60). In connection with applications to the court see the Criminal Procedure Rules 2015, SI 2015/1490, rr 32.1–32.4.
6   As to references to the court responsible for a community order imposing a drug rehabilitation requirement which is subject to review see PARA 54.
7   Criminal Justice Act 2003 Sch 8 para 19 (amended by the Offender Rehabilitation Act 2014 Sch 4 paras 1, 6). See also the Criminal Justice Act 2003 Sch 8 para 25; and PARA 59 note 10.

63.   Change of end date. The appropriate court[1] may, on the application of the offender or an officer of a provider of probation services[2], amend a community order[3] by substituting a later date for that specified[4] as the 'end date'[5]. A date so substituted may not fall outside the period of six months beginning with the date previously[6] specified[7] but subject to that, may fall more than three years after the date of the order[8]. This power may not be exercised in relation to an order if it has previously been exercised in relation to that order[9].

1   As to the meaning of 'appropriate court' see PARA 59 note 8.
2   In connection with applications to the court see the Criminal Procedure Rules 2015, SI 2015/1490, rr 32.1–32.4. As to the meaning of 'offender' see PARA 53 note 2.
3   For the power to make community orders see PARAS 45, 47.
4   Ie under the Criminal Justice Act 2003 s 177(5) (see PARA 50).
5   Criminal Justice Act 2003 Sch 8 para 19A(1) (Sch 8 para 19A added by the Legal Aid, Sentencing and Punishment of Offenders Act 2012 s 66(5); Criminal Justice Act 2003 Sch 8 para 19A(1) amended by the Offender Rehabilitation Act 2014 Sch 4 paras 1, 6). A date so substituted is to be treated as having been specified in relation to the order under the Criminal Justice Act 2003 s 177(5): Sch 8 para 19A(4) (as so added).
6   See note 4.
7   Criminal Justice Act 2003 Sch 8 para 19A(2)(a) (as added: see note 5).
8   Criminal Justice Act 2003 Sch 8 para 19A(2)(b) (as added: see note 5).
9   Criminal Justice Act 2003 Sch 8 para 19A(3) (as added: see note 5).

64.   Extension of unpaid work requirement. Where:

(1)   a community order[1] imposing an unpaid work requirement[2] is in force in respect of any offender[3]; and

(2)   on the application[4] of the offender[5] or an officer of a provider of probation services it appears to the appropriate court[6] that it would be in the interests of justice to do so having regard to circumstances which have arisen since the order was made[7],

the court may, in relation to the order, extend the specified[8] period of 12 months[9].

1   For the power to make community orders see PARAS 45, 47.
2   See PARA 133.
3   Criminal Justice Act 2003 Sch 8 para 20(1)(a).

4 In connection with applications to the court see the Criminal Procedure Rules 2015, SI 2015/1490, rr 32.1–32.4. No application may be made under the Criminal Justice Act 2003 Sch 8 para 20 while an appeal against the community order is pending: Sch 8 para 24(1).
5 As to the meaning of 'offender' see PARA 53 note 2.
6 As to the meaning of 'appropriate court' see PARA 59 note 8.
7 Criminal Justice Act 2003 Sch 8 para 20(1)(b).
8 Ie specified by the Criminal Justice Act 2003 s 200(2) (see PARA 133).
9 Criminal Justice Act 2003 Sch 8 para 20(1). See also Sch 8 para 25; and PARA 59 note 10.

65. Supplementary. On the making[1] of an order revoking or amending a community order[2], the proper officer[3] of the court must:

(1) provide copies of the revoking or amending order to the offender[4] and the responsible officer[5];

(2) in the case of an amending order which substitutes a new local justice area, provide a copy of the amending order to:
  (a) a provider of probation services that is a public sector provider[6] operating in that area[7]; and
  (b) the magistrates' court acting in that area[8]; and

(3) in the case of an amending order which imposes or amends a specified requirement[9], provide a copy of so much of the amending order as relates to that requirement to the person specified[10] in relation to that requirement[11]; and

(4) where the court acts in a local justice area other than the one specified in the order prior to the revocation or amendment, provide a copy of the revoking or amending order to a magistrates' court acting in the area so specified[12].

1 Ie under the Criminal Justice Act 2003 Sch 8.
2 For the power to make community orders see PARAS 45, 47.
3 Ie in relation to a magistrates' court, the designated officer for the court (Criminal Justice Act 2003 Sch 8 para 27(3)(a) (s 27(1)(b), (2), (3)(a) amended by SI 2005/886)); and in relation to the Crown Court, the appropriate officer (Criminal Justice act 2003 Sch 8 para 27(3)(b)).
4 As to the meaning of 'offender' see PARA 53 note 2.
5 Criminal Justice Act 2003 Sch 8 para 27(1)(a). As to the meaning of 'responsible officer' see PARA 51 note 2. In connection with the notification requirements see the Criminal Procedure Rules 2015, SI 2015/1490, r 28.2.
6 For these purposes 'public sector provider' means a probation trust or other public body or the Secretary of State: Criminal Justice Act 2003 Sch 8 para 27(4) (Sch 8 para 27(1)(b)(i) substituted, Sch 8 para 27(4) added, by the Offender Rehabilitation Act 2014 Sch 4 paras 10, 14).
7 Criminal Justice Act 2003 Sch 8 para 27(1)(b)(i) (as amended and substituted: see notes 3, 6). As to providers of probation services see PARAS 666–687.
8 Criminal Justice Act 2003 Sch 8 para 27(1)(b)(ii) (as amended: see note 3). Where the proper officer of the court so provides a copy of an amending order to a magistrates' court acting in a different area, the officer must also provide to that court documents and information relating to the case likely to be of assistance to a court acting in that area in the exercise of its functions in relation to the order: Sch 8 para 27(2) (as so amended).
9 Ie specified in the first column of the Criminal Justice Act 2003 Sch 14: see PARA 122 et seq.
10 Ie specified in the second column of the Criminal Justice Act 2003 Sch 14: see PARA 122 et seq.
11 Criminal Justice Act 2003 Sch 8 para 27(1)(c).
12 Criminal Justice Act 2003 Sch 8 para 27(1)(d) (added by the Domestic Violence, Crime and Victims Act 2004 Sch 5 para 7(1), (5)).

D. SUBSEQUENT CONVICTIONS

66. Powers of magistrates' courts. Where an offender[1] in respect of whom a community order[2] made by a magistrates' court is in force is convicted of an offence by a magistrates' court[3], and it appears to the court that it would be in the interests of justice so to act, having regard to circumstances which have arisen subsequent to the order[4], the magistrates' court may:

(1)   revoke the order[5]; or

(2)   both revoke the order[6] and deal with the offender, for the offence in respect of which the order was made, in any way in which he could have been dealt with for that offence by the court which made the order if the order had not been made[7].

Where an offender in respect of whom a community order made by the Crown Court is in force is convicted of an offence by a magistrates' court, the magistrates' court may commit the offender in custody or release him on bail until he can be brought before the Crown Court[8].

1   As to the meaning of 'offender' see PARA 53 note 2.
2   For the power to make community orders see PARAS 45, 47.
3   Criminal Justice Act 2003 Sch 8 para 21(1)(a). As to the adjournment of hearings by magistrates' courts and the remanding of offenders see PARA 55 note 3.
4   Criminal Justice Act 2003 Sch 8 para 21(1)(b).
5   Criminal Justice Act 2003 Sch 8 para 21(2)(a). Where a court proposes to exercise its powers of amendment under Sch 8 paras 21–23 (see the text and notes 6–8; and PARA 67), otherwise than on the application of the offender, the court must summon him to appear before it (Sch 8 para 25(1)(a)); and, if he does not appear in answer to the summons, it may issue a warrant for his arrest (Sch 8 para 25(1)(b)). However, this does not apply to an order cancelling a requirement of a community order or reducing the period of a requirement, or substituting a new local justice area or a new place for the one specified in the order: Sch 8 para 25(2) (amended by SI 2005/886).
6   Criminal Justice Act 2003 Sch 8 para 21(2)(b)(i). See note 5. In dealing with an offender under Sch 8 para 21(2)(b), a magistrates' court must take into account the extent to which the offender has complied with the requirements of the community order: Sch 8 para 21(3).
7   Criminal Justice Act 2003 Sch 8 para 21(2)(b)(ii). See notes 5, 6. A person sentenced under Sch 8 para 21(2)(b) for an offence may appeal to the Crown Court against the sentence: Sch 8 para 21(4).
8   Criminal Justice Act 2003 Sch 8 para 22(1). Where the magistrates' court so deals with an offender's case, it must send to the Crown Court such particulars of the case as may be desirable: Sch 8 para 22(2). See also Sch 8 para 25; and note 5. Where a community order has been made on appeal, it is to be taken for the purposes of Sch 8 to have been made by the Crown Court: Sch 8 para 4.

67. Powers of Crown Court. Where:

(1)   an offender[1] in respect of whom a community order[2] is in force is convicted of an offence by the Crown Court[3] or is brought or appears before the Crown Court[4] having been committed by the magistrates' court to the Crown Court for sentence[5]; and

(2)   it appears to the Crown Court that it would be in the interests of justice so to act, having regard to circumstances which have arisen since the community order was made[6],

the Crown Court may:

(a)   revoke the order[7]; or

(b)   both revoke the order[8] and deal with the offender, for the offence in respect of which the order was made, in any way in which he could have been dealt with for that offence by the court which made the order if the order had not been made[9].

1   As to the meaning of 'offender' see PARA 53 note 2.
2   For the power to make community orders see PARAS 45, 47.
3   Criminal Justice Act 2003 Sch 8 para 23(1)(a)(i).
4   Ie by virtue of the Criminal Justice Act 2003 Sch 8 para 22 (see PARA 66).
5   Criminal Justice Act 2003 Sch 8 para 23(1)(a)(ii).
6   Criminal Justice Act 2003 Sch 8 para 23(1)(b).

7   Criminal Justice Act 2003 Sch 8 para 23(2)(a). See PARA 66 note 5.
8   Criminal Justice Act 2003 Sch 8 para 23(2)(b)(i). In dealing with an offender under Sch 8
    para 23(2)(b), the Crown Court must take into account the extent to which the offender has
    complied with the requirements of the community order: Sch 8 para 23(3).
9   Criminal Justice Act 2003 Sch 8 para 23(2)(b)(ii). See note 8. Note that where the Crown Court
    imposes a custodial sentence in respect of an offence for which the magistrates' court has made
    a community order the Crown Court must observe all limitations on the powers of magistrates'
    courts including the restrictions on consecutive sentences: see the Magistrates' Courts Act 1980
    s 133; and PARA 555.

E.   ORDERS OPERATING IN SCOTLAND AND NORTHERN IRELAND

68.   Supervision arrangements. Where the court considering the making of a
community order[1] is satisfied that the offender resides in Scotland or Northern
Ireland, or will reside there when the order comes into force, it may not so make
an order in respect of the offender unless it appears to the court that suitable
arrangements for the offender's supervision can be made by the council in
Scotland[2] in whose area he resides, or will be residing when the order comes into
force, or by the Probation Board for Northern Ireland, as the case may be[3].

1   For the power to make community orders see PARAS 45, 47.
2   Ie the council constituted under the Local Government etc (Scotland) Act 1994 s 2: Criminal
    Justice Act 2003 Sch 9 para 1(1)(b).
3   Criminal Justice Act 2003 Sch 9 paras 1(1)(b), 3(1)(b). A community order made in accordance
    with Sch 9 para 1 or Sch 9 para 3 must:
    (1)   specify the locality in Scotland, or the local justice area in Northern Ireland, as the case
          may be, in which the offender resides or will be residing when the order or amendment
          comes into force (Sch 9 paras 1(6)(a), 3(5) (Sch 9 para 3(5) amended by SI 2005/886));
    (2)   specify as the corresponding order for these purposes an order that may be made by a
          court in Scotland or, as the case may be, Northern Ireland (Criminal Justice Act 2003
          Sch 9 paras 1(6)(b), 3(6)); and
    (3)   in relation to Scotland, specify as the appropriate court (ie for the purposes of the
          Criminal Procedure (Scotland) Act 1995 ss 227A–227ZK) a court of summary
          jurisdiction (which, in the case of an offender convicted on indictment, must be the
          sheriff court) having jurisdiction in the specified locality (Criminal Justice Act 2003
          Sch 9 para 1(6)(c) (amended by SI 2011/2298)).
    The Criminal Justice Act 2003 s 216 (local justice area to be specified: see PARA 48) does not
    apply to an order so made or amended: Sch 9 paras 1(6), 3(5) (amended by SI 2005/886).
    Where a community order is made or amended in accordance with the Criminal Justice
    Act 2003 Sch 9 para 1 or Sch 9 para 3, the court which makes or amends the order must provide
    the home court with a copy of the order as made or amended, together with such other
    documents and information relating to the case as it considers likely to be of assistance to that
    court: Sch 9 para 6. Section 219(1)(b)–(d) (provision of copies of relevant orders: see PARA 100)
    do not apply in these circumstances: Sch 9 para 6. For these purposes 'home court' means:
    (1)   if the offender resides in Scotland, or will be residing there at the relevant time, the
          sheriff court having jurisdiction in the locality in which the offender resides or proposes
          to reside (Sch 9 para 5); and
    (2)   if he resides in Northern Ireland, or will be residing there at the relevant time, the court
          of summary jurisdiction acting for the petty sessions district in which he resides or
          proposes to reside (Sch 9 para 5).
    'Relevant time' means the time when the order or the amendment to it comes into force:
    Sch 9 para 5.
    Before making or amending a community order in these circumstances the court must
    explain to the offender in ordinary language:
    (a)   the requirements of the legislation relating to corresponding orders which has effect in
          the part of the United Kingdom in which he resides or will be residing at the relevant
          time (Sch 9 para 9(a));
    (b)   the powers of the home court under that legislation (as modified by Sch 9 paras 5–15)
          (Sch 9 para 9(b)); and
    (c)   its own powers under Sch 9 paras 5–15 (Sch 9 para 9(c)).

69.   Compliance with requirements. Where the court considering the making of a community order[1] imposing:

    (1)   an unpaid work requirement[2];

    (2)   a rehabilitation activity requirement[3];

    (3)   a programme requirement[4];

    (4)   a mental health treatment requirement[5];

    (5)   a drug rehabilitation requirement[6];

    (6)   an alcohol treatment requirement[7];

    (7)   (in Northern Ireland only) an attendance centre requirement[8]; or

    (8)   an electronic monitoring requirement[9],

is satisfied that the offender resides in Scotland or Northern Ireland, or will reside there when the order comes into force, the court may not make an order in respect of the offender unless it appears to the court that arrangements exist for persons to comply with such a requirement in the locality in Scotland or petty sessions district in Northern Ireland, as the case may be, in which the offender resides, or will be residing when the order comes into force, and that provision can be made for him to comply with the requirement under those arrangements[10].

1   For the power to make community orders see PARAS 45, 47.
2   Criminal Justice Act 2003 Sch 9 paras 1(2)(a), 3(2)(a). As to unpaid work requirements see s 199; and PARA 133.
3   Criminal Justice Act 2003 Sch 9 paras 1(2)(b), 3(2)(b) (substituted by the Offender Rehabilitation Act 2014 Sch 5 paras 1, 7). As to rehabilitation activity requirements see the Criminal Justice Act 2003 s 200A; and PARA 131.
4   Criminal Justice Act 2003 Sch 9 paras 1(2)(c), 3(2)(c). As to programme requirements see s 202; and PARA 129.
5   Criminal Justice Act 2003 Sch 9 paras 1(2)(d), 3(2)(d). As to mental health treatment requirements see s 207; and PARA 128.
6   Criminal Justice Act 2003 Sch 9 paras 1(2)(e), 3(2)(e). As to drug rehabilitation requirements see s 209; and PARA 124.
7   Criminal Justice Act 2003 Sch 9 paras 1(2)(f), 3(2)(f). As to alcohol treatment requirements see s 212; and PARA 122.
8   Criminal Justice Act 2003 Sch 9 para 3(2)(g). As to attendance centre requirements in Northern Ireland see s 214; and PARA 134. The court may not by virtue of these provisions require an alcohol abstinence and monitoring requirement, an attendance centre requirement or an electronic monitoring requirement (as from a day to be appointed, an electronic monitoring requirement within s 215(1)(b) (see PARA 136)) to be complied with in Scotland: Sch 9 para 1(5) (amended by the Legal Aid, Sentencing and Punishment of Offenders Act 2012 s 76(9)(a); Criminal Justice Act 2003 Sch 9 para 3(1)(aa) prospectively added, Sch 9 paras 1(2)(g), (5), 3(2)(h) prospectively amended, by the Crime and Courts Act 2013 Sch 16 paras 11, 20). At the date at which this volume states the law no day had been appointed for the coming into force of the amendments made by the Crime and Courts Act 2013.
9   Criminal Justice Act 2003 Sch 9 paras 1(2)(g), 3(2)(h) (prospectively amended so as to refer to an electronic monitoring requirement within s 215(1)(b): see note 8). So far as relating to residence in Northern Ireland, as from the day on which said prospective amendment is brought into force the court may make an order imposing an electronic monitoring requirement within 215(1)(b) only if it appears to the court that any necessary provision can be made in the offender's case under arrangements that exist for persons resident in that locality (Sch 9 para 3(1)(aa)(i) (as so prospectively added)) and that arrangements are generally operational throughout Northern Ireland (even if not always operational everywhere there) under which the offender's whereabouts can be electronically monitored (Sch 9 para 3(1)(aa)(ii) (as so prospectively added)).
10   Criminal Justice Act 2003 Sch 9 paras 1(1)(a), 3(1)(a). See further PARA 68 note 3.

70.   Change of residence. Where:

    (1)   the appropriate court in connection with the provisions concerned with the amendment of a community order[1] by reason of change of

residence[2] is satisfied that an offender in respect of whom a community order is in force proposes to reside or is residing in Scotland or Northern Ireland, as the case may be[3]; and

(2)   it appears to the court that the conditions which determine whether a transfer order may be made[4] are satisfied[5],

the power of the court to amend the order[6] includes power to amend it by requiring it to be complied with in Scotland or Northern Ireland, as the case may be, and the offender to be supervised in accordance with the appropriate arrangements[7].

1   For the power to make community orders see PARAS 45, 47.
2   As to these powers see Criminal Justice Act 2003 Sch 8 para 16; and PARA 59.
3   Criminal Justice Act 2003 Sch 9 paras 1(3)(a), 3(3)(a).
4   Ie the conditions set out in the Criminal Justice Act 2003 Sch 9 paras 1(1), 3(1) (see PARAS 68, 69).
5   Criminal Justice Act 2003 Sch 9 paras 1(3)(b), 3(3)(b) (Sch 9 para 3(3)(b), (4) prospectively amended, but not so as to effect the sense of the text, by the Crime and Courts Act 2013 Sch 16 paras 11, 20). At the date at which this volume states the law no day had been appointed for the coming into force of the amendments made by the Crime and Courts Act 2013.
6   Ie under the Criminal Justice Act 2003 Sch 8 (see PARA 53 et seq).
7   Criminal Justice Act 2003 Sch 9 paras 1(3), 3(3). For the appropriate arrangements see Sch 9 paras 1(1)(b), 3(1)(b); and PARA 68. For these purposes, any reference in Sch 9 paras 1(1), 3(1) (see PARAS 68, 69) to the time when the order comes into force is treated as a reference to the time when the amendment comes into force: Sch 9 paras 1(4), 3(4) (Sch 9 para 3(4) prospectively amended: see note 5). The court may not by virtue of these provisions require an alcohol abstinence and monitoring requirement, an attendance centre requirement or (as from a day to be appointed) an electronic monitoring requirement within s 215(1)(b) (see PARA 136) to be complied with in Scotland: see Sch 9 para 1(5); and PARA 69 note 8. See further PARA 68 note 3.

71.   Status of transferred order.   Where a community order[1] is made or amended[2] so as to take effect in Scotland or Northern Ireland:

(1)   the order is to be treated as if it were a corresponding order[3] made in the part of the United Kingdom[4] in which the offender resides, or will be residing at the relevant time[5]; and

(2)   the legislation relating to such orders which has effect in that part of the United Kingdom applies accordingly[6].

1   For the power to make community orders see PARAS 45, 47.
2   Ie in accordance with the Criminal Justice Act 2003 Sch 9 para 1 or Sch 9 para 3 (see PARAS 68, 69). These provisions are subject to Sch 9 paras 9–15 (see PARAS 68, 72).
3   'Corresponding order' means the order specified under the Criminal Justice Act 2003 Sch 9 para 1(6)(b) or Sch 9 para 3(6) (see PARA 68 note 3): Sch 9 para 5.
4   As to the meaning of 'United Kingdom' see PARA 4 note 3.
5   Criminal Justice Act 2003 Sch 9 para 8(a).
6   Criminal Justice Act 2003 Sch 9 para 8(b). See further PARA 72.

72.   Powers of home courts.   Where a community order[1] is made or amended[2] so as to take effect in Scotland or Northern Ireland the home court[3] may exercise in relation to the order any power which it could exercise in relation to the corresponding order[4] made by a court in the part of the United Kingdom[5] in which the home court exercises jurisdiction, by virtue of the legislation relating to such orders which has effect in that part, except the following:

(1)   any power to discharge or revoke the order (other than a power to revoke the order where the offender has been convicted of a further offence and the court has imposed a custodial sentence)[6];

(2) any power to deal with the offender for the offence in respect of which the order was made[7];

(3) in the case of a community order imposing an unpaid work requirement[8], any power to vary the order by substituting for the number of hours of work specified in it any greater number than the court which made the order could have specified[9]; and

(4) in the case of a community order imposing a curfew requirement[10], any power to vary the order by substituting for the period specified in it any longer period than the court which made the order could have specified[11].

If at any time while legislation relating to corresponding orders which has effect in Scotland or Northern Ireland applies to a community order made in England and Wales:

(a) it appears to the home court on information from the local authority officer concerned[12], if that court is in Scotland, or upon a complaint being made to a justice of the peace acting for the petty sessions district for the time being specified in the order, if that court is in Northern Ireland, that the offender has failed to comply with any of the requirements of the order[13]; or

(b) it appears to the home court on the application of the offender or of the local authority officer concerned, if that court is in Scotland, or on the application of the offender or of the probation officer concerned[14], if that court is in Northern Ireland, that it would be in the interests of justice for a power of revocation[15] with or without re-sentencing to be exercised[16],

the home court may require the offender to appear before the court which made the order or the court which last amended the order in England and Wales[17].

1 For the power to make community orders see PARAS 45, 47.
2 Ie in accordance with the Criminal Justice Act 2003 Sch 9 para 1 or Sch 9 para 3 (see PARAS 68, 69). These provisions are subject to Sch 9 paras 9–15 (see text and notes 3–17; and PARA 68).
3 As to the meaning of 'home court' see PARA 68 note 3.
4 As to the meaning of 'corresponding order' see PARA 71 note 3.
5 As to the meaning of 'United Kingdom' see PARA 4 note 3.
6 Criminal Justice Act 2003 Sch 9 para 10(a).
7 Criminal Justice Act 2003 Sch 9 para 10(b).
8 As to unpaid work requirements see the Criminal Justice Act 2003 s 199; and PARA 133.
9 Criminal Justice Act 2003 Sch 9 para 10(c).
10 As to curfew requirements see the Criminal Justice Act 2003 s 204; and PARA 123.
11 Criminal Justice Act 2003 Sch 9 para 10(d).
12 'Local authority officer concerned', in relation to an offender, means the officer of a council constituted under the Local Government etc (Scotland) Act 1994 s 2 responsible for his supervision or, as the case may be, discharging in relation to him the functions in respect of community service orders assigned by the Criminal Procedure (Scotland) Act 1995 ss 227A–227ZK: Criminal Justice Act 2003 Sch 9 para 5 (amended by SI 2011/2298).
13 Criminal Justice Act 2003 Sch 9 para 11(a). Where an offender is required by this provision to appear before a court in England and Wales, the home court must send to that court a certificate certifying that the offender has failed to comply with such of the requirements of the order as may be specified in the certificate, together with such other particulars of the case as may be desirable (Sch 9 para 15(a)); and a certificate purporting to be signed by the clerk of the home court is admissible as evidence of the failure before the court which made the order (Sch 9 para 15(b)).
14 'Probation officer concerned', in relation to an offender, means the probation officer responsible for his supervision or, as the case may be, discharging in relation to him the functions conferred by the Criminal Justice (Northern Ireland) Order 1996, SI 1996/3160 (NI 24), Pt 2: Criminal Justice Act 2003 Sch 9 para 5.

15 Ie a power conferred by the Criminal Justice Act 2003 Sch 8 para 13 (see PARA 57) or Sch 8
    para 14 (see PARA 58).
16 Criminal Justice Act 2003 Sch 9 para 11(b).
17 Criminal Justice Act 2003 Sch 9 para 11. Where an offender is required by virtue of Sch 9
    para 11 to appear before a court in England and Wales that court may issue a warrant for his
    arrest (Sch 9 para 12(a)) and may exercise any power which it could exercise in respect of the
    community order if the offender resided in England and Wales (Sch 9 para 12(b)). Any
    enactment relating to the exercise of such powers has effect accordingly, and with any reference
    to the responsible officer being read as a reference to the local authority officer or probation
    officer concerned: Sch 9 para 12. Schedule 9 para 12(b) does not enable the court to amend the
    community order unless: (1) where the offender resides in Scotland, it appears to the court that
    the conditions in Sch 9 para 1(1)(a), (b) (see PARAS 68, 69) are satisfied in relation to any
    requirement to be imposed (Sch 9 para 13(a)); or (2) where the offender resides in Northern
    Ireland, it appears to the court that the conditions in Sch 9 para 3(1)(a), (b) (or, as from a day to
    be appointed, Sch 9 para 3(1)(a), (aa), (ab) (see PARAS 68, 69) are satisfied in relation to any
    requirement to be imposed (Sch 9 para 13(b) prospectively amended by the Crime and Courts
    Act 2013 Sch 16 paras 11, 20). At the date at which this volume states the law no day had been
    appointed for the coming into force of this amendment. The Criminal Justice Act 2003 Sch 9
    paras 1–13 have effect in relation to the amendment of a community order by virtue of Sch 9
    para 12(b) as they have effect in relation to the amendment of such an order by virtue of Sch 9
    para 1(3) or Sch 9 para 3(3) (see PARAS 68, 69): Sch 9 para 14.

(iii) Youth Rehabilitation Orders

A. MAKING OF YOUTH REHABILITATION ORDER

73.   Youth rehabilitation orders and requirements. Where a person aged under
18[1] is convicted of an offence the court by or before which the person is
convicted may make an order (a 'youth rehabilitation order'[2]) imposing on the
person any one or more of:

(1)   an activity requirement[3];
(2)   a supervision requirement[4];
(3)   in a case where the offender is aged 16 or 17 at the time of the
        conviction, an unpaid work requirement[5];
(4)   a programme requirement[6];
(5)   an attendance centre requirement[7];
(6)   a prohibited activity requirement[8];
(7)   a curfew requirement[9];
(8)   an exclusion requirement[10];
(9)   a residence requirement[11];
(10)   a local authority residence requirement[12];
(11)   a mental health treatment requirement[13];
(12)   a drug treatment requirement[14];
(13)   a drug testing requirement[15];
(14)   an intoxicating substance treatment requirement[16];
(15)   an education requirement[17];
(16)   in certain circumstances, a fostering requirement[18]; and
(17)   in certain circumstances, an electronic monitoring requirement[19].

A youth rehabilitation order may also make provision for intensive
supervision and surveillance, which requires the imposition of a number of the
requirements listed above[20]. An order must specify the local justice area in which
the offender resides or will reside[21]. As a rule a youth rehabilitation order takes
effect the day on which it is made[22], although a court making a youth
rehabilitation order may order that it is to take effect instead on a later date[23].

1   As to the determination of a person's age see the Children and Young Persons Act 1933 s 99; and **CHILDREN AND YOUNG PERSONS** vol 10 (2012) PARA 1206. For the purposes of any provision of the Criminal Justice and Immigration Act 2008 Pt 1 (ss 1–8) (see the text and notes 2–23; and PARAS 74–82) which requires the determination of the age of a person by the court, the Secretary of State or a local authority, the person's age is to be taken to be that which it appears to the court or (as the case may be) the Secretary of State or a local authority to be after considering any available evidence: s 7(2).

2   In connection with the making of youth rehabilitation orders (which may be made only if the offence for which the offender has been convicted was committed on or after 30 November 2009) generally see PARA 42. The power to make a youth rehabilitation order is subject to the Criminal Justice Act 2003 ss 148, 150 (restrictions on community sentences etc: see PARAS 42, 44) and the provisions of the Criminal Justice and Immigration Act 2008 Sch 1 Pts 1, 3 (see PARA 74 et seq): s 1(6).

    Where the Crown Court makes a youth rehabilitation order it may include in the order a direction that further proceedings relating to the order be in a youth court or other magistrates' court (subject to Sch 2 para 7: see PARA 85): Sch 1 para 36(1). For this purpose 'further proceedings', in relation to a youth rehabilitation order, means proceedings for any failure to comply with the order within the meaning given by Sch 2 para 1(2)(b) or on any application for amendment or revocation of the order under Sch 2 Pt 3 (see PARAS 87–88) or Pt 4 (see PARAS 89–91): Sch 1 para 36(2). As to youth courts see **CHILDREN AND YOUNG PERSONS** vol 10 (2012) PARA 1225 et seq.

    The court by which any youth rehabilitation order is made must forthwith provide copies of the order:
    (1)   to the offender (Sch 1 para 34(1)(a));
    (2)   if the offender is aged under 14, to the offender's parent or guardian (Sch 1 para 34(1)(b)); and
    (3)   to a member of a youth offending team assigned to the court, to an officer of a local probation board assigned to the court or to an officer of a provider of probation services (Sch 1 para 34(1)(c)).

    In connection with the notification requirements see the Criminal Procedure Rules 2015, SI 2015/1490, r 28.2. Provision is also made as to the provision of copies to the persons concerned with the supervision of requirements imposed by the orders: see the Criminal Justice Act 2003 Sch 1 para 34(4) (amended by SI 2010/1158). See also the Criminal Justice and Immigration Act 2008 Sch 1 para 34(2); and note 21.

    If a local authority has parental responsibility for an offender who is in its care or provided with accommodation by it in the exercise of any social services functions, any reference in Pt 1 (except in Sch 1 paras 4, 25) to the offender's parent or guardian is to be read as a reference to that authority: s 7(4). 'Parental responsibility' has the same meaning as it has in the Children Act 1989 by virtue of s 3 (see **CHILDREN AND YOUNG PERSONS** vol 9 (2012) PARA 151); and 'social services functions' has the same meaning as it has in the Local Authority Social Services Act 1970 by virtue of s 1A (see **SOCIAL SERVICES AND COMMUNITY CARE** vol 95 (2013) PARA 1): Criminal Justice and Immigration Act 2008 s 7(5). As to the meaning of 'guardian' see the Children and Young Persons Act 1933 s 107(1); and **CHILDREN AND YOUNG PERSONS** vol 10 (2012) PARA 709 (definition applied by the Criminal Justice and Immigration Act 2008 s 7(1)).

    In relation to England 'local authority' means a county council, a district council whose district does not form part of an area that has a county council, a London borough council or the Common Council of the City of London in its capacity as a local authority; and in relation to Wales it means a county council or a county borough council: Criminal Justice and Immigration Act 2008 s 7(1). As to the counties in England and their councils see **LOCAL GOVERNMENT** vol 69 (2009) PARA 24 et seq. As to the counties and county boroughs in Wales and their councils see **LOCAL GOVERNMENT** vol 69 (2009) PARA 37 et seq. As to the London boroughs and their councils see **LONDON GOVERNMENT** vol 71 (2013) PARA 20 et seq. As to the Common Council of the City of London see **LONDON GOVERNMENT** vol 71 (2013) PARA 34.

    'Youth offending team' means a team established under the Crime and Disorder Act 1998 s 39: Criminal Justice and Immigration Act 2008 s 7(1). As to youth offending teams see **CHILDREN AND YOUNG PERSONS** vol 10 (2012) PARA 1193. 'Local probation board' means a local probation board established under the Criminal Justice and Court Services Act 2000 s 4 (repealed): Criminal Justice and Immigration Act 2008 s 7(1). As to local probation boards and providers of probation services see PARAS 666–687.

3   Criminal Justice and Immigration Act 2008 s 1(1)(a). See Sch 1 paras 6–8; and PARA 139 (noting that by virtue of Sch 1 para 1(1)(a), the power to include an activity requirement in a youth rehabilitation order is particularly subject to Sch 1 para 8(3), (4)). An activity requirement may form the basis of an order with intensive supervision and surveillance: see PARA 75.

4 Criminal Justice and Immigration Act 2008 s 1(1)(b). See Sch 1 para 9; and PARA 140. A supervision requirement may form part of an order with intensive supervision and surveillance and an order with fostering: see PARAS 75, 76.

5 Criminal Justice and Immigration Act 2008 s 1(1)(c). See Sch 1 para 10; and PARA 141 (noting that by virtue of Sch 1 para 1(1)(b), the power to include an unpaid work requirement in a youth rehabilitation order is particularly subject to Sch 1 para 10(3)).

6 Criminal Justice and Immigration Act 2008 s 1(1)(d). See Sch 1 para 11; and PARA 142 (noting that by virtue of Sch 1 para 1(1)(c), the power to include a programme work requirement in a youth rehabilitation order is particularly subject to Sch 1 para 11(3), (4)).

7 Criminal Justice and Immigration Act 2008 s 1(1)(e). See Sch 1 para 12; and PARA 143 (noting that by virtue of Sch 1 para 1(1)(d), the power to include an attendance centre requirement in a youth rehabilitation order is particularly subject to Sch 1 para 12(3)).

8 Criminal Justice and Immigration Act 2008 s 1(1)(f). See Sch 1 para 13; and PARA 144 (noting that by virtue of Sch 1 para 1(1)(e), the power to include a prohibited activity requirement in a youth rehabilitation order is particularly subject to Sch 1 para 13(2)).

9 Criminal Justice and Immigration Act 2008 s 1(1)(g). See Sch 1 para 14; and PARA 145. A curfew requirement may form part of an order with intensive supervision and surveillance: see PARA 75.

10 Criminal Justice and Immigration Act 2008 s 1(1)(h). See Sch 1 para 15; and PARA 146.

11 Criminal Justice and Immigration Act 2008 s 1(1)(i). See Sch 1 para 16; and PARA 147 (noting that by virtue of Sch 1 para 1(1)(f), the power to include a residence requirement in a youth rehabilitation order is particularly subject to Sch 1 para 16(2), (4), (7)).

12 Criminal Justice and Immigration Act 2008 s 1(1)(j). See Sch 1 para 17; and PARA 148 (noting that by virtue of Sch 1 para 1(1)(g), the power to include a local authority residence requirement in a youth rehabilitation order is particularly subject to Sch 1 paras 17(3), (4), 19).

13 Criminal Justice and Immigration Act 2008 s 1(1)(k). See Sch 1 para 20; and PARA 149 (noting that by virtue of Sch 1 para 1(1)(h), the power to include a mental health treatment requirement in a youth rehabilitation order is particularly subject to Sch 1 para 20(3)).

14 Criminal Justice and Immigration Act 2008 s 1(1)(l). See Sch 1 para 22; and PARA 150 (noting that by virtue of Sch 1 para 1(1)(i), the power to include a drug treatment requirement in a youth rehabilitation order is particularly subject to Sch 1 para 22(2), (4)).

15 Criminal Justice and Immigration Act 2008 s 1(1)(m). See Sch 1 para 23; and PARA 151 (noting that by virtue of Sch 1 para 1(1)(j), the power to include a drug testing requirement in a youth rehabilitation order is particularly subject to Sch 1 para 23(3)).

16 Criminal Justice and Immigration Act 2008 s 1(1)(n). See Sch 1 para 24; and PARA 152 (noting that by virtue of Sch 1 para 1(1)(k), the power to include an intoxicating substance treatment requirement in a youth rehabilitation order is particularly subject to Sch 1 para 24(2), (4)).

17 Criminal Justice and Immigration Act 2008 s 1(1)(o). See Sch 1 para 25; and PARA 153 (noting that by virtue of Sch 1 para 1(1)(l), the power to include an education requirement in a youth rehabilitation order is particularly subject to Sch 1 para 25(4)).

18 See the Criminal Justice and Immigration Act 2008 Sch 1 para 18; and PARA 154.

19 See the Criminal Justice and Immigration Act 2008 Sch 1 para 2; and PARA 74.

20 See the Criminal Justice and Immigration Act 2008 Sch 1 para 3; and PARA 75.

21 Criminal Justice and Immigration Act 2008 Sch 1 para 33. Where a youth rehabilitation order is made by the Crown Court or is made by a magistrates' court which does not act in the local justice area specified in the order, the court making the order must:
   (1) provide to the magistrates' court acting in the local justice area specified in the order a copy of the order and such documents and information relating to the case as it considers likely to be of assistance to a court acting in that area in the exercise of its functions in relation to the order (Sch 1 para 34(2), (3)(a)); and
   (2) provide a copy of the order to the local probation board acting for that area or (as the case may be) a provider of probation services operating in that area (Sch 1 para 34(3)(b)).

22 Criminal Justice and Immigration Act 2008 Sch 1 para 30(1) (Sch 1 para 30(1) amended, Sch 1 para 30(1A) added, by the Coroners and Justice Act 2009 Sch 21 para 98). This is subject to the Criminal Justice and Immigration Act 2008 Sch 1 para 30(2) (see PARA 79).

23 Criminal Justice and Immigration Act 2008 Sch 1 para 30(1A) (as added: see note 22).

74. Electronic monitoring requirements in youth rehabilitation orders. A youth rehabilitation order[1] may, in addition to the requirements which may generally be imposed[2], also impose an electronic monitoring requirement[3], and it must impose such a requirement if it imposes a curfew requirement[4] or an exclusion requirement[5] unless:

(1) in the particular circumstances of the case, the court considers it inappropriate for the order to do so[6]; or

(2) the court is prevented[7] from including such a requirement in the order[8].

1 As to the making of youth rehabilitation orders see PARAS 42, 73.
2 As to the requirements which may be imposed by a youth rehabilitation order see PARA 73.
3 Criminal Justice and Immigration Act 2008 s 1(2)(a). As to electronic monitoring requirements in youth rehabilitation orders see Sch 1 para 26; and PARA 155 (noting that by virtue of Sch 1 para 2(3), the power to include an electronic monitoring requirement in a youth rehabilitation order is particularly subject to Sch 1 para 26(3), (6)).
4 Criminal Justice and Immigration Act 2008 s 1(2)(b), Sch 1 para 2(1)(a). As to curfew requirements see PARA 145. The power to impose an electronic monitoring requirement in addition to a curfew requirement applies whether the curfew requirement is imposed by virtue of Sch 1 para 3(4)(b) (see PARA 75) or otherwise: Sch 1 para 2(1)(a).
5 Criminal Justice and Immigration Act 2008 Sch 1 para 2(1)(b). As to exclusion requirements see PARA 146.
6 Criminal Justice and Immigration Act 2008 Sch 1 para 2(2)(a).
7 Ie by the Criminal Justice and Immigration Act 2008 Sch 1 para 26(3) or (6) (see PARA 155).
8 Criminal Justice and Immigration Act 2008 Sch 1 para 2(2)(b).

75. Youth rehabilitation orders with intensive supervision and surveillance. If:

(1) the court is dealing with an offender for an offence which is punishable with imprisonment[1];

(2) the court is of the opinion that the offence, or the combination of the offence and one or more offences associated[2] with it, was so serious that[3] a custodial sentence[4] would be[5] appropriate[6]; and

(3) if the offender was aged under 15 at the time of conviction, the court is of the opinion that the offender is a persistent offender[7],

the court may, if it makes a youth rehabilitation order[8] which imposes an activity requirement[9], specify in relation to that requirement a specified number of days[10] (an 'extended activity requirement')[11] and where it does so must also impose a supervision requirement[12], a curfew requirement[13] and, if thereby applicable[14], an electronic monitoring requirement[15]. A youth rehabilitation order which imposes an extended activity requirement[16] is[17] known as a 'youth rehabilitation order with intensive supervision and surveillance'[18].

1 Criminal Justice and Immigration Act 2008 s 1(4)(a). Any reference in Pt 1 (ss 1–8) to an offence punishable with imprisonment is to be read without regard to any prohibition or restriction imposed by or under any Act on the imprisonment of young offenders: s 7(3).
2 'Associated', in relation to offences, is to be read in accordance with the Powers of Criminal Courts (Sentencing) Act 2000 s 161(1) (see PARA 9 note 7): Criminal Justice and Immigration Act 2008 s 7(1).
3 Ie but for the Criminal Justice and Immigration Act 2008 Sch 1 para 3 or 4 (see the text and notes 8–18; and PARA 76).
4 As to the meaning of 'custodial sentence' see the Powers of Criminal Courts (Sentencing) Act 2000 s 76; and PARA 9 note 15 (definition applied by the Criminal Justice and Immigration Act 2008 s 7(1)).
5 Or, if the offender was aged under 12 at the time of conviction, would be if the offender had been aged 12: Criminal Justice and Immigration Act 2008 s 1(4)(b).
6 Criminal Justice and Immigration Act 2008 s 1(4)(b).
7 Criminal Justice and Immigration Act 2008 s 1(4)(c). As to the determination of a person's age see the Children and Young Persons Act 1933 s 99; and CHILDREN AND YOUNG PERSONS vol 10 (2012) PARA 1206.
8 As to the making of youth rehabilitation orders see PARAS 42, 73. Nothing in the Criminal Justice and Immigration Act 2008 s 1(4)(b) (see the text and notes 2–6) or the Criminal Justice

Act 2003 s 148(1) or (2)(b) (see PARA 42) prevents a court from making a youth rehabilitation order with intensive supervision and surveillance in respect of an offender if the offender fails to comply with an order under the Criminal Justice Act 2003 s 161(2) (pre-sentence drug testing): Criminal Justice and Immigration Act 2008 Sch 1 para 5(2).

9   As to activity requirements see PARA 139.
10 Ie more than 90 but not more than 180.
11 Criminal Justice and Immigration Act 2008 Sch 1 para 3(1)–(3).
12 Criminal Justice and Immigration Act 2008 Sch 1 para 3(4)(a). As to supervision requirements see PARA 140.
13 As to curfew requirements see PARA 145.
14 Ie if required by the Criminal Justice and Immigration Act 2008 Sch 1 para 2 (see PARA 74).
15 Criminal Justice and Immigration Act 2008 Sch 1 para 3(4)(b). As to electronic monitoring requirements see PARAS 74, 155.
16 And other requirements in accordance with the Criminal Justice and Immigration Act 2008 Sch 1 para 3(4) (see the text and notes 12–15).
17 Ie whether or not the order also imposes any other requirement mentioned in the Criminal Justice and Immigration Act 2008 s 1(1) (see PARA 73).
18 Criminal Justice and Immigration Act 2008 s 1(3)(a), Sch 1 para 3(5). As a rule a youth rehabilitation order takes effect on the day on which the order is made (see Sch 1 para 30(1), (1A); and PARA 73), although if the court makes two or more youth rehabilitation orders with intensive supervision and surveillance both or all of the orders must take effect at the same time (in accordance with Sch 1 para 30(1) or (2)): Sch 1 para 31(3). As to concurrent and consecutive orders see PARA 80.

76.   Youth rehabilitation orders with fostering.   The court may make a youth rehabilitation order[1] which imposes a fostering requirement[2] if:

(1)   the court is dealing with an offender for an offence which is punishable with imprisonment[3];

(2)   the court is of the opinion that the offence, or the combination of the offence and one or more offences associated[4] with it, was so serious that[5] a custodial sentence[6] would be[7] appropriate[8];

(3)   the court is of the opinion, where the offender was aged under 15 at the time of conviction, that the offender is a persistent offender[9];

(4)   the court is satisfied that the behaviour which constituted the offence was due to a significant extent to the circumstances in which the offender was living[10]; and

(5)   the court is satisfied that the imposition of a fostering requirement would assist in the offender's rehabilitation[11].

A youth rehabilitation order which imposes a fostering requirement must also impose a supervision requirement[12]. However, a court may not impose a fostering requirement unless it has consulted the offender's parents or guardians[13] (where it is not impracticable to do so)[14] and the local authority[15] which is to place the offender with a local authority foster parent[16].

A youth rehabilitation order which imposes a fostering requirement is known as a 'youth rehabilitation order with fostering'[17].

1   Ie in accordance with the Criminal Justice and Immigration Act 2008 s 1 (see PARAS 73–75).
2   As to fostering requirements see the Criminal Justice and Immigration Act 2008 Sch 1 para 18; and PARA 154. A youth rehabilitation order with intensive supervision and surveillance (see PARA 75) may not impose a fostering requirement: Sch 1 para 5(1). These provisions have effect subject in particular to Sch 1 paras 18(7), 19 (pre-conditions to imposing fostering requirement: see PARA 154): Sch 1 para 4(5).
3   Criminal Justice and Immigration Act 2008 s 1(4)(a). As to offences punishable with imprisonment see PARA 75 note 1.
4   As to an 'associated' offence see PARA 75 note 2.
5   Ie but for the Criminal Justice and Immigration Act 2008 Sch 1 para 3 or 4 (see the text and notes 10–17; and PARA 75).
6   As to custodial sentences see PARA 75 note 4.

7   Or, if the offender was aged under 12 at the time of conviction, would be if the offender had
     been aged 12: Criminal Justice and Immigration Act 2008 s 1(4)(b).
8   Criminal Justice and Immigration Act 2008 s 1(4)(b).
9   Criminal Justice and Immigration Act 2008 s 1(4)(c). As to the determination of a person's age
     see the Children and Young Persons Act 1933 s 99; and CHILDREN AND YOUNG PERSONS vol 10
     (2012) PARA 1206.
10   Criminal Justice and Immigration Act 2008 Sch 1 para 4(1), (2)(a).
11   Criminal Justice and Immigration Act 2008 Sch 1 para 4(2)(b).
12   Criminal Justice and Immigration Act 2008 Sch 1 para 4(4). As to supervision requirements see
     PARA 140.
13   As to an offender's parent or guardian see PARA 73 note 2.
14   Criminal Justice and Immigration Act 2008 Sch 1 para 4(3)(a).
15   As to local authorities see PARA 73 note 2.
16   Criminal Justice and Immigration Act 2008 Sch 1 para 4(3)(b).
17   Ie whatever other requirements mentioned in the Criminal Justice and Immigration Act 2008
     s 1(1) or (2) (see PARAS 73, 74) it imposes: s 1(3)(b), Sch 1 para 4(6). As a rule a youth
     rehabilitation order takes effect on the day on which the order is made (see Sch 1
     para 30(1), (1A); and PARA 73), although if the court makes two or more youth rehabilitation
     orders with fostering both or all of the orders must take effect at the same time (in accordance
     with Sch 1 para 30(1) or (2)): Sch 1 para 31(3). As to concurrent and consecutive orders see
     PARA 80.

77.   Persistent offenders.   Provision is made for a youth rehabilitation order to
be made in respect of a persistent offender[1].

Where:

(1)   a person aged 16 or 17 is convicted of an offence (the 'current
       offence')[2];

(2)   until a day to be appointed[3], on three or more previous occasions he
       has, on conviction by a court in the United Kingdom[4] of any offence
       committed by him after attaining the age of 16, had passed on him a
       sentence consisting only of a fine, or, as from that day, on three or more
       previous occasions a sentence consisting only of a fine has been passed
       on the offender on conviction by a court in the United Kingdom of an
       offence committed by the offender after attaining the age of 16 or by a
       court in another member state of a relevant offence so committed[5];

(3)   the court would not[6] otherwise regard the current offence, or the
       combination of the current offence and one or more offences associated[7]
       with it, as being serious enough to warrant a youth rehabilitation
       order[8],

the court may make a youth rehabilitation order in respect of the current offence
instead of imposing a fine if it considers that, having regard to all the
circumstances[9], it would be in the interests of justice to make such an order[10].

1   See the Criminal Justice Act 2003 s 151; and the text and notes 2–10. As to the making of youth
     rehabilitation orders see PARAS 42, 73.
2   Criminal Justice Act 2003 s 151(2A)(a) (s 151(2A), (2B) added, s 151(3)–(6) amended, by the
     Criminal Justice and Immigration Act 2008 Sch 4 paras 71, 76). As to the determination of a
     person's age see the Children and Young Persons Act 1933 s 99; and CHILDREN AND YOUNG
     PERSONS vol 10 (2012) PARA 1206.
3   See note 5.
4   As to the meaning of 'United Kingdom' see PARA 4 note 3. References to a conviction by a court
     in the United Kingdom include references to the finding of guilt in service disciplinary
     proceedings: see the Criminal Justice Act 2003 s 151(4), (5), (8); and PARA 47.
5   Criminal Justice Act 2003 s 151(2A)(b) (as added (see note 2)); prospectively substituted by the
     Coroners and Justice Act 2009 Sch 17 para 8(1), (4)). At the date at which this volume states the
     law no day had been appointed for the coming into force of the amendments made by the
     Coroners and Justice Act 2009. For these purposes, it is immaterial whether on other previous

occasions a court has passed on the offender a sentence not consisting only of a fine: Criminal Justice Act 2003 s 151(6) (as so amended). As to a 'relevant' offence for these purposes see s 151(4A); and PARA 47 note 7.

6   Ie despite the effect of the Criminal Justice Act 2003 s 143(2) (see PARA 586). Section 151 does not limit the extent to which a court may, in accordance with s 143(2), treat any previous convictions of the offender as increasing the seriousness of an offence: s 151(7).
7   As to an 'associated offence' see PARA 9 note 7.
8   Criminal Justice Act 2003 s 151(2A)(c) (as added: see note 2).
9   Ie including the nature of the offences to which the previous convictions mentioned in the Criminal Justice Act 2003 s 151(2A)(b) (see the text and note 5) relate and their relevance to the current offence and the time that has elapsed since the offender's conviction of each of those offences: s 151(3) (as amended: see note 2).
10 Criminal Justice Act 2003 s 151(2B) (as added: see note 2).

78.   Matters which the court must consider. Before making a youth rehabilitation order[1] the court must obtain and consider information about the offender's family circumstances and the likely effect of such an order on those circumstances[2].

Before making a youth rehabilitation order imposing two or more requirements[3] or two or more youth rehabilitation orders in respect of associated offences[4], the court must[5] consider whether, in the circumstances of the case, the requirements to be imposed by the order or orders are compatible with each other[6]. The court must also ensure, as far as practicable, that any requirement imposed by a youth rehabilitation order is such as to avoid:

(1)   any conflict with the offender's religious beliefs[7];

(2)   any interference with the times, if any, at which the offender normally works or attends school or any other educational establishment[8]; and

(3)   any conflict with the requirements of any other youth rehabilitation order to which the offender may be subject[9].

The Secretary of State may by order make provision for additional restrictions on the making of a youth rehabilitation order[10].

1   As to the making of youth rehabilitation orders see PARAS 42, 73.
2   Criminal Justice and Immigration Act 2008 Sch 1 para 28.
3   Criminal Justice and Immigration Act 2008 Sch 1 para 29(1)(a). As to the requirements which may be imposed by a youth rehabilitation order see PARA 73 et seq.
4   Criminal Justice and Immigration Act 2008 Sch 1 para 29(1)(b). As to an 'associated' offence see PARA 75 note 2.
5   Ie subject to the Criminal Justice and Immigration Act 2008 Sch 1 paras 2, 3(4), 4(4) (see PARAS 74–76): Criminal Justice and Immigration Act 2008 Sch 1 para 29(2).
6   Criminal Justice and Immigration Act 2008 Sch 1 para 29(1).
7   Criminal Justice and Immigration Act 2008 Sch 1 para 29(3)(a).
8   Criminal Justice and Immigration Act 2008 Sch 1 para 29(3)(b).
9   Criminal Justice and Immigration Act 2008 Sch 1 para 29(3)(c).
10   Criminal Justice and Immigration Act 2008 Sch 1 para 29(4). At the date at which this volume states the law no such order had been made.

79.   Operation in conjunction with other orders. If a detention and training order[1] is in force in respect of an offender a court making a youth rehabilitation order[2] in respect of that offender may order that it is to take effect[3]:

(1)   when the period of supervision begins[4] in relation to the detention and training order[5]; or

(2)   on the expiry of the term of the detention and training order[6].

A court must not make a youth rehabilitation order in respect of an offender at a time when another youth rehabilitation order[7] or a reparation order[8] is in force in respect of the offender, unless when it makes the order it revokes the earlier order[9].

1   References to a detention and training order include an order made under the Armed Forces
     Act 2006 s 211 (detention and training orders made by service courts: see ARMED FORCES vol 3
     (2011) PARA 611): Criminal Justice and Immigration Act 2008 Sch 1 para 30(3)(a).
2   As to the making of youth rehabilitation orders see PARAS 42, 73.
3   Ie instead of taking effect on the day on which the order was made: see the Criminal Justice and
     Immigration Act 2008 Sch 1 para 30(1); and PARA 73.
4   Ie in accordance with the Powers of Criminal Courts (Sentencing) Act 2000 s 103(1)(a) (see
     PARA 12). The reference to s 103(1)(a) includes that provision as applied by the Armed Forces
     Act 2006 s 213(1) (see ARMED FORCES vol 3 (2011) PARA 611): Criminal Justice and
     Immigration Act 2008 Sch 1 para 30(3)(b).
5   Criminal Justice and Immigration Act 2008 Sch 1 para 30(2)(a) (Sch 1 para 30(2) amended by
     the Coroners and Justice Act 2009 Sch 21 para 98).
6   Criminal Justice and Immigration Act 2008 Sch 1 para 30(2)(b).
7   Criminal Justice and Immigration Act 2008 Sch 1 para 30(4)(a).
8   Criminal Justice and Immigration Act 2008 Sch 1 para 30(4)(b). A 'reparation order' is an order
     made under the Powers of Criminal Courts (Sentencing) Act 2000 a 73(1) (see PARA 293).
9   Criminal Justice and Immigration Act 2008 Sch 1 para 30(4). Where the earlier order is revoked
     under Sch 1 para 30(4), Sch 2 para 24 (provision of copies of orders: see PARA 293) applies to
     the revocation as it applies to the revocation of a youth rehabilitation order: Sch 1 para 30(5).

80.   Concurrent and consecutive orders.   Where the court is dealing with an
offender who has been convicted of two or more associated[1] offences and in
respect of one of the offences makes:

(1)   a youth rehabilitation order[2] with intensive supervision and
       surveillance[3];

(2)   a youth rehabilitation order with fostering[4]; or

(3)   any other youth rehabilitation order[5],

it may not make an order of any other of those kinds in respect of the other
offence, or any of the other offences[6].

Where the court includes requirements of the same kind[7] in two or more
youth rehabilitation orders it must direct, in relation to each requirement of that
kind, whether:

(a)   it is to be concurrent with the other requirement or requirements of that
       kind, or any of them[8]; or

(b)   it and the other requirement or requirements of that kind, or any of
       them, are to be consecutive[9].

1   As to associated offences see PARA 75 note 2.
2   As to the making of youth rehabilitation orders see PARAS 42, 73.
3   Criminal Justice and Immigration Act 2008 Sch 1 para 31(1), (2)(a). As to the meaning of 'youth
     rehabilitation order with intensive supervision and surveillance' see PARA 75.
4   Criminal Justice and Immigration Act 2008 Sch 1 para 31(2)(b). As to the meaning of 'youth
     rehabilitation order with fostering' see PARA 76.
5   Criminal Justice and Immigration Act 2008 Sch 1 para 31(2)(c).
6   Criminal Justice and Immigration Act 2008 Sch 1 para 31(2).
7   As to the requirements which may be imposed by a youth rehabilitation order see PARA 73 et
     seq. For the purposes of the Criminal Justice and Immigration Act 2008 Sch 1 para 31(4), (6),
     requirements are of the same kind if they fall within the same provision of Sch 1 Pt 2 (see PARA
     73): Sch 1 para 31(7).
8   Criminal Justice and Immigration Act 2008 Sch 1 para 31(4)(a).
9   Criminal Justice and Immigration Act 2008 Sch 1 para 31(4)(b). The court may not direct that
     two or more fostering requirements are to be consecutive: Sch 1 para 31(5). As to fostering
     requirements see Sch 1 para 18; and PARA 154. Where the court directs that two or more
     requirements of the same kind (see note 7) are to be consecutive:
     (1)   the number of hours, days or months specified in relation to one of them is additional
            to the number of hours, days, or months specified in relation to the other or others
            (Sch 1 para 31(6)(a)); but

(2) the aggregate number of hours, days or months specified in relation to both or all of them must not exceed the maximum number which may be specified in relation to any one of them (Sch 1 para 31(6)(b)).

81. Time limits for compliance with requirements. A youth rehabilitation order[1] must specify a date ('the end date'), not more than three years after the date on which the order takes effect, by which all the requirements[2] in it must have been complied with[3]. A youth rehabilitation order which imposes two or more different requirements[4] may also specify a date by which each of those requirements must have been complied with[5]. A youth rehabilitation order ceases to be in force on the end date[6].

The appropriate court[7] may, on the application of the offender[8] or the responsible officer[9], amend a youth rehabilitation order by substituting a later date for that specified[10] under these provisions[11]. A date so substituted may not fall outside the period of six months beginning with the date previously specified[12] but subject to that, may fall more than three years after the date on which the order took effect[13].

1 As to the making of youth rehabilitation orders see PARAS 42, 73.

2 As to the requirements which may be imposed by a youth rehabilitation order see PARA 73 et seq.

3 Criminal Justice and Immigration Act 2008 Sch 1 para 32(1) (Sch 1 para 32(1) amended, Sch 1 para 32(2) substituted, Sch 1 paras 16A, 32(4) added, by the Legal Aid, Sentencing and Punishment of Offenders Act 2012 ss 83(1), (5)). In the case of a youth rehabilitation order with intensive supervision and surveillance (see PARA 75), the date specified for these purposes must not be earlier than six months after the date on which the order takes effect: Criminal Justice and Immigration Act 2008 Sch 1 para 32(3). In connection with the duration of an order see (by analogy) *R v Davison* [2008] EWCA Crim 2795, [2009] 2 Cr App Rep (S) 76; and PARA 50 note 3.

4 Ie two or more different requirements falling within the Criminal Justice and Immigration Act 2008 Sch 1 Pt 2 (see PARA 73 et seq).

5 Criminal Justice and Immigration Act 2008 Sch 1 para 32(2) (as substituted: see note 3). The last of those dates must be the same as the end date: Sch 1 para 32(2) (as so substituted).

6 Criminal Justice and Immigration Act 2008 Sch 1 para 32(4) (as added: see note 3). This is subject to Sch 1 para 10(7) (duration of youth rehabilitation order imposing unpaid work requirement: see PARA 141).

7 For these purposes 'appropriate court' means:
   (1) if the order was made by a youth court or other magistrates' court, or was made by the Crown Court and contains a direction under the Criminal Justice and Immigration Act 2008 Sch 1 para 36 (see PARA 73), either:
      (a) if the offender is aged under 18 when the application is made, a youth court acting in the local justice area specified in the youth rehabilitation order (Sch 1 para 16A(5)(a), (6)(a) (as added: see note 3)); or
      (b) if the offender is aged 18 or over at that time, a magistrates' court (other than a youth court) acting in that local justice area (Sch 1 para 16A(6)(b) (as so added)); and
   (2) if the order was made by the Crown Court and does not contain a direction under Sch 1 para 36, the Crown Court (Sch 1 para 16A(5)(b) (as so added)).
   In connection with applications to the court see the Criminal Procedure Rules 2015, SI 2015/1490, rr 32.1–32.4. As to youth courts see CHILDREN AND YOUNG PERSONS vol 10 (2012) PARA 1225 et seq. As to the determination of a person's age see the Children and Young Persons Act 1933 s 99; and CHILDREN AND YOUNG PERSONS vol 10 (2012) PARA 1206.

8 The 'offender' is the person in respect of whom a youth rehabilitation order is made: Criminal Justice and Immigration Act 2008 Sch 2 para 1(1).

9 For the purposes of the Criminal Justice and Immigration Act 2008 Pt 1 (ss 1–8) 'responsible officer', in relation to an offender to whom a youth rehabilitation order relates, means:
   (1) in a case where the order imposes a curfew requirement (see PARA 145) or an exclusion requirement (see PARA 146) but no other requirement mentioned in s 1(1) (see PARA 73),

and imposes an electronic monitoring requirement (see PARAS 74, 155), the person who under Sch 1 para 26(4) (see PARA 155) is responsible for the electronic monitoring required by the order (s 4(1)(a));

(2)   in a case where the only requirement imposed by the order is an attendance centre requirement (see PARA 143), the officer in charge of the attendance centre in question (s 4(1)(b)); and

(3)   in any other case, the qualifying officer who, as respects the offender, is for the time being responsible for discharging the functions conferred by Pt 1 on the responsible officer (s 4(1)(c)).

For this purpose 'qualifying officer', in relation to a youth rehabilitation order, means:

(a)   a member of a youth offending team established by a local authority for the time being specified in the order for these purposes (s 4(2)(a)); or

(b)   an officer of a local probation board appointed for or assigned to the local justice area for the time being so specified or (as the case may be) an officer of a provider of probation services acting in the local justice area for the time being so specified (s 4(2)(b)).

The Secretary of State may by order amend s 4(1), (2), and make any other amendments of Pt 1 or the Criminal Justice Act 2003 Pt 12 Ch 1 (ss 142–176) (general provisions about sentencing) that appear to be necessary or expedient in consequence of any amendment of the Criminal Justice and Immigration Act 2008 s 4(1), (2): s 4(3). Such an order may, in particular, provide for the court to determine which of two or more descriptions of responsible officer is to apply in relation to any youth rehabilitation order: s 4(4). At the date at which this volume states the law no such order had been made.

As to the making of youth rehabilitation orders see PARAS 42, 73. As to youth offending teams see **CHILDREN AND YOUNG PERSONS** vol 10 (2012) PARA 1193. As to the meanings of 'local authority' and 'local probation board' see PARA 73 note 2. As to local probation boards and providers of probation services see PARAS 666–687.

10   Ie specified under the Criminal Justice and Immigration Act 2008 Sch 1 para 32(1) (see the text and notes 1–3).
11   Criminal Justice and Immigration Act 2008 Sch 1 para 16A(1) (as added: see note 3). This power may not be exercised in relation to an order if it has previously been exercised in relation to that order: Sch 1 para 16A(3) (as so added). A date so substituted is to be treated as having been specified in relation to the order under Sch 1 para 32(1): Sch 1 para 16A(4) (as so added).
12   Criminal Justice and Immigration Act 2008 Sch 1 para 16A(2)(a) (as added: see note 3).
13   Criminal Justice and Immigration Act 2008 Sch 1 para 16A(2)(b) (as added: see note 3).

82. Periodical review of orders. The Secretary of State may by order:

(1)   enable or require a court making a youth rehabilitation order[1] to provide for the order to be reviewed periodically by that or another court[2];

(2)   enable a court to amend a youth rehabilitation order so as to include or remove a provision for review by a court[3]; and

(3)   make provision as to the timing and conduct of reviews and as to the powers of the court on a review[4].

1   As to the making of youth rehabilitation orders see PARAS 42, 73.
2   Criminal Justice and Immigration Act 2008 Sch 1 para 35(1)(a). At the date at which this volume states the law no such order had been made. Such an order may, in particular, make provision in relation to community orders corresponding to any provision made by the Criminal Justice Act 2003 ss 191, 192 (see PARA 104) in relation to suspended sentence orders (Criminal Justice and Immigration Act 2008 Sch 1 para 35(2)) and may repeal or amend any provision of the Criminal Justice and Immigration Act 2008 Pt 1 (ss 1–8) or the Criminal Justice Act 2003 Pt 12 Ch 1 (ss 142–176) (Criminal Justice and Immigration Act 2008 Sch 1 para 35(3)).
3   Criminal Justice and Immigration Act 2008 Sch 1 para 35(1)(b). See note 2.
4   Criminal Justice and Immigration Act 2008 Sch 1 para 35(1)(c). See note 2.

B. BREACH OF REQUIREMENT OF YOUTH REHABILITATION ORDER

83. Duty to give warning and subsequent breach. If the responsible officer[1] is of the opinion that the offender[2] has failed without reasonable excuse to comply with a youth rehabilitation order[3], the officer must give him a warning unless[4] the officer causes an information to be laid before a justice of the peace in respect of the failure[5]. The warning must:

(1)　describe the circumstances of the failure[6];

(2)　state that the failure is unacceptable[7]; and

(3)　state that the offender will be liable to be brought before a court:

(a)　in a case where the warning is given during the warned period[8] relating to a previous warning[9], if during that period the offender again fails to comply with the order[10]; or

(b)　in any other case, if during the warned period relating to the warning, the offender fails on more than one occasion to comply with the order[11].

The responsible officer must, as soon as practicable after the warning has been given, record that fact[12].

If:

(i)　the responsible officer has given such a warning (the 'first warning') to the offender in respect of a youth rehabilitation order[13];

(ii)　during the warned period relating to the first warning, has given another warning[14] to the offender in respect of a failure to comply with the order[15]; and

(iii)　is of the opinion that during the warned period relating to the first warning the offender has again failed without reasonable excuse to comply with the order[16],

the officer must cause an information to be laid before a justice of the peace in respect of the failure in question[17] unless he is of the opinion that there are exceptional circumstances which justify not causing an information to be so laid[18].

If the responsible officer is of the opinion that the offender has failed without reasonable excuse to comply with a youth rehabilitation order[19] and the above provisions[20] do not apply[21], the responsible officer may cause an information to be laid before a justice of the peace in respect of that failure[22].

1　As to the meaning of 'responsible officer' see PARA 81 note 9.

2　As to the meaning of 'offender' see PARA 81 note 8.

3　Any reference in the Criminal Justice and Immigration Act 2008 Sch 2 (however expressed) to an offender's compliance with a youth rehabilitation order is a reference to the offender's compliance with the requirement or requirements imposed by the order and, if the order imposes an attendance centre requirement (see PARA 143), rules made under the Criminal Justice Act 2003 s 222(1)(d) or (e) (attendance centre rules: see PARA 137): Criminal Justice and Immigration Act 2008 Sch 2 para 1(2)(a). Any reference (however expressed) to the offender's failure to comply with the order is a reference to any failure of the offender to comply with a requirement imposed by the order or, if the order imposes an attendance centre requirement, with attendance centre rules: Sch 2 para 1(2)(b).

4　Ie under the Criminal Justice and Immigration Act 2008 Sch 2 para 4(1), (3) (see the text and notes 13–22).

5　Criminal Justice and Immigration Act 2008 Sch 2 para 3(1).

6　Criminal Justice and Immigration Act 2008 Sch 2 para 3(2)(a).

7　Criminal Justice and Immigration Act 2008 Sch 2 para 3(2)(b).

8　'Warned period', in relation to a warning under the Criminal Justice and Immigration Act 2008 Sch 2 para 3, means the period of 12 months beginning with the date on which the warning was given: Sch 2 paras 3(3), 4(4).

9　Ie a previous warning under the Criminal Justice and Immigration Act 2008 Sch 2 para 3.

10　Criminal Justice and Immigration Act 2008 Sch 2 para 3(2)(c)(i).

11　Criminal Justice and Immigration Act 2008 Sch 2 para 3(2)(c)(ii).

12　Criminal Justice and Immigration Act 2008 Sch 2 para 3(3).

13　Criminal Justice and Immigration Act 2008 Sch 2 para 4(1)(a).

14 Ie under the Criminal Justice and Immigration Act 2008 Sch 2 para 3.
15 Criminal Justice and Immigration Act 2008 Sch 2 para 4(1)(b).
16 Criminal Justice and Immigration Act 2008 Sch 2 para 4(1)(c).
17 Criminal Justice and Immigration Act 2008 Sch 2 para 4(1).
18 Criminal Justice and Immigration Act 2008 Sch 2 para 4(2).
19 Criminal Justice and Immigration Act 2008 Sch 2 para 4(3)(a).
20 Ie the Criminal Justice and Immigration Act 2008 Sch 2 para 4(1) (see the text and notes 13–17), in a case not within Sch 2 para 4(2) (see the text and note 18).
21 Criminal Justice and Immigration Act 2008 Sch 2 para 4(3)(b).
22 Criminal Justice and Immigration Act 2008 Sch 2 para 4(3).

84. Issue of summons or warrant.   If at any time while a youth rehabilitation order[1] is in force it appears on information to a justice of the peace that the offender[2] has failed to comply with such an order, the justice may issue a summons requiring the offender to appear at the place and time specified in it[3] or, if the information is in writing and on oath, issue a warrant for his arrest[4]. Any such summons or warrant must direct the offender to appear or be brought:

(1)   if the youth rehabilitation order was made by the Crown Court and does not include a direction[5] in relation to further proceedings, before the Crown Court[6]; and

(2)   in any other case, before the appropriate court[7].

If the offender does not appear in answer to a summons so issued which required the offender to appear before the Crown Court, the Crown Court may[8] issue a further summons requiring the offender to appear at the place and time specified in it[9] or (in any case) issue a warrant for the arrest of the offender[10]. If the offender does not appear in answer to a summons so issued which required the offender to appear before a magistrates' court, the magistrates' court may issue a warrant for the arrest of the offender[11].

1   As to the making of youth rehabilitation orders see PARAS 42, 73.
2   As to the meaning of 'offender' see PARA 81 note 8.
3   Criminal Justice and Immigration Act 2008 Sch 2 para 5(1)(a).
4   Criminal Justice and Immigration Act 2008 Sch 2 para 5(1)(b).
    Where an offender is arrested in pursuance of a warrant issued by virtue of Sch 2 and cannot be brought immediately before the court before which the warrant directs the offender to be brought (the 'relevant court'), the person in whose custody the offender is:
    (1)   may make arrangements for the offender's detention in a place of safety for a period of not more than 72 hours from the time of the arrest (Sch 2 para 21(1), (2)(a)); and
    (2)   must within that period bring the offender before a magistrates' court (Sch 2 para 21(2)(b)).
    A person who is detained under arrangements made under Sch 2 para 21(2)(a) is deemed to be in legal custody: Sch 2 para 21(4). As to the meaning of 'place of safety' see the Children and Young Persons Act 1933 s 107(1); and CHILDREN AND YOUNG PERSONS vol 9 (2012) PARA 632 (definition applied by the Criminal Justice and Immigration Act 2008 Sch 2 para 21(5)). In the case of a warrant issued by the Crown Court, the Senior Courts Act 1981 s 81(5) (duty to bring person before magistrates' court: see CRIMINAL PROCEDURE vol 27 (2015) PARA 349) does not apply: Criminal Justice and Immigration Act 2008 Sch 2 para 21(3).
    Provision is made where under Sch 2 para 21(2) the offender is brought before a court (the 'alternative court') which is not the relevant court: Sch 2 para 21(6). If the relevant court is a magistrates' court the alternative court may direct that the offender be released forthwith (Sch 2 para 21(7)(a)(i)) or remand the offender (Sch 2 para 21(7)(a)(ii)), and the Magistrates' Courts Act 1980 s 128 (remand in custody or on bail: see MAGISTRATES vol 71 (2013) PARA 554) is applied with specified modifications: see the Criminal Justice and Immigration Act 2008 Sch 2 para 21(7). If the relevant court is the Crown Court, the Magistrates' Courts Act 1980 s 43A (functions of magistrates' court where a person in custody is brought before it with a view to appearance before the Crown Court: see CRIMINAL PROCEDURE vol 27 (2015) PARA 349) is applied with specified modifications: see the Criminal Justice and Immigration Act 2008 Sch 2 para 21(8) (amended by the Constitutional Reform Act 2005 Sch 11 para 1). Any power to remand the offender in custody which is conferred by the Magistrates' Courts Act 1980 s 43A or

s 128 is to be taken to be a power to remand the offender to accommodation provided by or on behalf of a local authority (if the offender is aged under 18) (Criminal Justice and Immigration Act 2008 Sch 2 para 21(9)(a)) and to remand the offender to a prison (in any other case) (Sch 2 para 21(9)(b)). Where the court remands the offender to accommodation provided by or on behalf of a local authority, the court must designate, as the authority which is to receive the offender, the local authority for the area in which it appears to the court that the offender resides: Sch 2 para 21(10).

'Accommodation provided by or on behalf of a local authority' has the same meaning as it has for the purposes of the Children Act 1989 by virtue of s 105(5) (see CHILDREN AND YOUNG PERSONS vol 10 (2012) PARA 839): Criminal Justice and Immigration Act 2008 s 7(1). As to the determination of a person's age see the Children and Young Persons Act 1933 s 99; and CHILDREN AND YOUNG PERSONS vol 10 (2012) PARA 1206.

5   Ie a direction under the Criminal Justice and Immigration Act 2008 Sch 1 para 36 (see PARA 73).
6   Criminal Justice and Immigration Act 2008 Sch 2 para 5(2)(a).
7   Criminal Justice and Immigration Act 2008 Sch 2 para 5(2)(b). For this purpose 'appropriate court' means:
    (1)   if the offender is aged under 18, a youth court acting in the relevant local justice area (Sch 2 para 5(3)(a)); and
    (2)   if the offender is aged 18 or over, a magistrates' court (other than a youth court) acting in that local justice area (Sch 2 para 5(3)(b)).
    'Relevant local justice area' means the local justice area in which the offender resides or if it is not known where the offender resides, the local justice area specified in the youth rehabilitation order: Sch 2 para 5(4). As to youth courts see CHILDREN AND YOUNG PERSONS vol 10 (2012) PARA 1225 et seq.
8   Ie unless the summons was issued under the Criminal Justice and Immigration Act 2008 Sch 2 para 5(6).
9   Criminal Justice and Immigration Act 2008 Sch 2 para 5(5), (6)(a).
10 Criminal Justice and Immigration Act 2008 Sch 2 para 5(6)(b).
11 Criminal Justice and Immigration Act 2008 Sch 2 para 5(7).

85.   Powers of magistrates' court.   If an offender[1] appears or is brought[2] before a youth court or other magistrates' court[3] and it is proved[4] to the satisfaction of the court that the offender has failed without reasonable excuse[5] to comply with a youth rehabilitation order[6], the court may deal with him in respect of the failure in any one of the following ways[7]:

(1)   by ordering him to pay a fine[8];

(2)   by amending the terms of the youth rehabilitation order so as to impose any requirement which could have been included in the order when it was made in addition to, or in substitution for, any requirement or requirements already imposed by the order[9]; or

(3)   by dealing with the offender, for the offence in respect of which the order was made, in any way in which the court could have dealt with the offender for that offence (had the offender been before that court to be dealt with for it)[10].

Where a youth rehabilitation order was made by the Crown Court[11] and contains a direction in relation to further proceedings[12] and a youth court or other magistrates' court would otherwise[13] be required, or has the power, to deal with the offender[14], the court may instead commit him to custody or release him on bail until he can be brought or appear before the Crown Court[15].

1   As to the meaning of 'offender' see PARA 81 note 8.
2   Ie under the Criminal Justice and Immigration Act 2008 Sch 2 para 5 (see PARA 84). A youth court or a magistrates' court may adjourn any hearing relating to an offender in any proceedings under Sch 2, and where it does so the court may direct that the offender be released forthwith or remand the offender: Sch 2 para 22(1), (2). Where the court so remands the offender it must fix the time and place at which the hearing is to be resumed and that time and place must be the time and place at which the offender is required to appear or be brought before the court by virtue of the remand, and where the court so adjourns the hearing but does not remand the offender it may fix the time and place at which the hearing is to be resumed but, if it does not do

so, it must not resume the hearing unless it is satisfied that the offender, the responsible officer and, if the offender is aged under 14, a parent or guardian of the offender, have had adequate notice of the time and place for the resumed hearing: Sch 2 para 22(3), (4). These powers may be exercised by a single justice of the peace, notwithstanding anything in the Magistrates' Courts Act 1980: Criminal Justice and Immigration Act 2008 Sch 2 para 22(5). These provisions apply to any hearing in any proceedings under Sch 2 in place of the Magistrates' Courts Act 1980 s 10 (adjournment of trial: see CRIMINAL PROCEDURE vol 27 (2015) PARAS 287, 290) where s 10 would otherwise apply, but do not affect the application of s 10 to hearings of any other description: Criminal Justice and Immigration Act 2008 Sch 2 para 22(6). As to the responsible officer see PARA 81 note 9. As to an offender's parent or guardian see PARA 73 note 2. As to youth courts see CHILDREN AND YOUNG PERSONS vol 10 (2012) PARA 1225 et seq. As to the determination of a person's age see the Children and Young Persons Act 1933 s 99; and CHILDREN AND YOUNG PERSONS vol 10 (2012) PARA 1206.

3   Criminal Justice and Immigration Act 2008 Sch 2 para 6(1)(a).

4   The prosecution must prove each element of the breach beyond reasonable doubt, including proving that the offender was the person named in the order: see *West Yorkshire Probation Board v Boulter* [2005] EWHC 2342 (Admin), 169 JP 601, [2006] 1 WLR 232 (decided in connection with the breach of a community order under the Criminal Justice Act 2003).

5   The fact that an appeal against sentence had been lodged could not afford a reasonable excuse to a defendant for failing to comply with the requirements of a community order: see *West Midlands Probation Board v Sutton Coldfield Magistrates' Court* [2008] EWHC 15 (Admin), [2008] 3 All ER 1193, sub nom *West Midlands Probation Board v Sadler* [2008] 1 WLR 918 (decided in connection with the breach of a community order under the Criminal Justice Act 2003).

6   Criminal Justice and Immigration Act 2008 Sch 2 para 6(1)(b). As to the making of youth rehabilitation orders see PARAS 42, 73. Where a youth rehabilitation order imposes a mental health treatment requirement (see PARA 149), a drug treatment requirement (see PARA 150) or an intoxicating substance treatment requirement (see PARA 152) in respect of an offender the offender is not to be treated for these purposes as having failed to comply with an order on the ground only that he had refused to undergo any surgical, electrical or other treatment if, in the opinion of the court, his refusal was reasonable having regard to all the circumstances: Sch 2 para 9.

7   In dealing with the offender under these provisions the court must take into account the extent to which the offender has complied with the youth rehabilitation order: Criminal Justice and Immigration Act 2008 Sch 2 para 6(4).

8   Criminal Justice and Immigration Act 2008 Sch 2 para 6(2)(a). The fine must not exceed £2,500: Sch 2 para 6(2)(a) (Sch 2 paras 6(2)(a), (6), 10(1), (3)(a), (b) amended, Sch 2 para 6(6A)–(6D) added, by the Legal Aid, Sentencing and Punishment of Offenders Act 2012 ss 83(2), 84(1), (2), (4)). A fine so imposed is to be treated, for the purposes of any enactment, as being a sum adjudged to be paid by a conviction: Criminal Justice and Immigration Act 2008 Sch 2 para 6(5). The Secretary of State may by order amend any sum for the time being specified in Sch 2 para 6(2)(a) or Sch 2 para 8(2)(a) (see PARA 86) if it appears to him that there has been a change in the value of money since the relevant date which justifies the change: Sch 2 para 10(1), (2) (Sch 2 para 10(1) as so amended). At the date at which this volume states the law no such order had been made. 'Relevant date' means:

    (1)   if the sum specified in Sch 2 para 6(2)(a) or Sch 2 para 8(2)(a) (as the case may be) has been substituted by an order under Sch 2 para 10(1), the date on which the sum was last so substituted (Sch 2 para 10(3)(a) (as so amended)); and

    (2)   otherwise, 3 December 2012 (ie the date on which the Legal Aid, Sentencing and Punishment of Offenders Act 2012 s 84 was brought into force by the Legal Aid, Sentencing and Punishment of Offenders Act 2012 (Commencement No 4 and Saving Provisions) Order 2012, SI 2012/2906) (Criminal Justice and Immigration Act 2008 Sch 2 para 10(3)(b) (as so amended)).

   An order under Sch 2 para 10(1) (a 'fine amendment order') must not have effect in relation to any youth rehabilitation order made in respect of an offence committed before the fine amendment order comes into force: Sch 2 para 10(4).

9   Criminal Justice and Immigration Act 2008 Sch 2 para 6(2)(b). When imposing a requirement under Sch 2 para 6(2)(b) the court may amend the order to substitute a later date for that specified under Sch 1 para 32(1) (see PARA 81): Sch 2 para 6(6A) (as added: see note 8). A date so substituted may not fall outside the period of six months beginning with the date previously specified under Sch 1 para 32(1) but, subject to that, may fall more than three years after the date on which the order took effect: Sch 2 para 6(6B) (as so added). The power under Sch 2 para 6(6A) may not be exercised in relation to an order if that power or the power in Sch 2

para 8(6A) (see PARA 86) has previously been exercised in relation to that order: Sch 2 para 6(6C) (as so added). A date substituted under Sch 2 para 6(6A) is to be treated as having been specified in relation to the order under Sch 1 para 32(1): Sch 2 para 6(6D) (as so added).

Section 1(4), and the provisions mentioned in s 1(6) (see PARA 73 note 2), apply in relation to a power conferred by Sch 2 para 6(2)(b) to impose a requirement as they apply in relation to any power conferred by s 1 or Sch 1 paras 1–5 (see PARA 73 et seq) to make a youth rehabilitation order which includes such a requirement: Sch 2 para 23. As to the requirements which may be imposed by a youth rehabilitation order see PARA 73 et seq. Any requirement imposed under Sch 2 para 6(2)(b) must be capable of being complied with before the date specified under Sch 1 para 32(1), although this is subject to Sch 2 para 6(6A) (see above): Sch 2 para 6(3), (6) (as so amended). The court may not under Sch 2 para 6(2)(b) impose an extended activity requirement (see PARA 75) or a fostering requirement (see PARA 154) if the order does not already impose such a requirement: Sch 2 para 6(8). See also Sch 2 para 6(7), (9), (10); and PARAS 89, 141, 154.

10 Criminal Justice and Immigration Act 2008 Sch 2 para 6(2)(c). Where the court deals with the offender under Sch 2 para 6(2)(c) it must revoke the youth rehabilitation order if it is still in force: Sch 2 para 6(11). An offender may appeal to the Crown Court against a sentence imposed under Sch 2 para 6(2)(c): Sch 2 para 6(16).

Where the court is dealing with the offender under Sch 2 para 6(2)(c) and the offender has wilfully and persistently failed to comply with a youth rehabilitation order (Sch 2 para 6(12)), the court may impose a youth rehabilitation order with intensive supervision and surveillance notwithstanding anything in s 1(4)(a) or (b) (see PARA 75) (Sch 2 para 6(13)), and if the order is a youth rehabilitation order with intensive supervision and surveillance (see PARA 75) and the offence mentioned in Sch 2 para 6(2)(c) was punishable with imprisonment, the court may impose a custodial sentence notwithstanding anything in the Criminal Justice Act 2003 s 152(2) (general restrictions on imposing discretionary custodial sentences: see PARA 536) (Criminal Justice and Immigration Act 2008 Sch 2 para 6(14)).

If the order is a youth rehabilitation order with intensive supervision and surveillance which was imposed by virtue of Sch 2 para 6(13) and the offence mentioned in Sch 2 para 6(2)(c) was not punishable with imprisonment, for the purposes of dealing with the offender under Sch 2 para 6(2)(c) the court is to be taken to have had power to deal with the offender for that offence by making a detention and training order (see PARA 9) for a term not exceeding four months: Sch 2 para 6(15).

11 Where a youth rehabilitation order has been made on appeal it is to be treated:

(1) if it was made on an appeal from a magistrates' court, as having been made by a magistrates' court (Criminal Justice and Immigration Act 2008 Sch 2 para 2(a)); and

(2) if it was made on an appeal brought from the Crown Court or from the criminal division of the Court of Appeal, as having been made by the Crown Court (Sch 2 para 2(b)).

12 Ie a direction under the Criminal Justice and Immigration Act 2008 Sch 1 para 36 (see PARA 73).

13 Ie apart from the Criminal Justice and Immigration Act 2008 Sch 2 para 7(1).

14 Ie in one of the ways mentioned in the Criminal Justice and Immigration Act 2008 Sch 2 para 6(2) (see the text and notes 7–10).

15 Criminal Justice and Immigration Act 2008 Sch 2 para 7(1), (2). A court which deals with an offender's case under these provisions must send to the Crown Court: (1) a certificate signed by a justice of the peace certifying that the offender has failed to comply with the youth rehabilitation order in the respect specified in the certificate (Sch 2 para 7(3)(a)); and (2) such other particulars of the case as may be desirable (Sch 2 para 7(3)(b)); and a certificate purporting to be so signed is admissible as evidence of the failure before the Crown Court (Sch 2 para 7(3)).

86. Powers of Crown Court. If an offender[1] appears or is brought[2] before the Crown Court[3] and it is proved[4] to the satisfaction of the court that the offender has failed without reasonable excuse[5] to comply with a youth rehabilitation order[6], the Crown Court may deal with him in respect of the failure in any one of the following ways[7]:

(1) by ordering him to pay a fine[8];

(2) by amending the terms of the youth rehabilitation order so as to impose any requirement which could have been included in the order when it was made in addition to, or in substitution for, any requirement or requirements already imposed by the order[9]; or

(3)   by dealing with the offender, for the offence in respect of which the order was made, in any way in which the Crown Court could have dealt with the offender for that offence[10].

1   As to the meaning of 'offender' see PARA 81 note 8.

2   Ie under the Criminal Justice and Immigration Act 2008 Sch 2 para 5 (see PARA 84) or by virtue of Sch 2 para 7(2) (see PARA 85).

3   Criminal Justice and Immigration Act 2008 Sch 2 para 8(1)(a).

4   See PARA 85 note 4.

5   See PARA 85 note 5.

6   Criminal Justice and Immigration Act 2008 Sch 2 para 8(1)(b). As to the making of youth rehabilitation orders see PARAS 42, 73. Where a youth rehabilitation order imposes a mental health treatment requirement (see PARA 149), a drug treatment requirement (see PARA 150) or an intoxicating substance treatment requirement (see PARA 152) in respect of an offender the offender is not to be treated for these purposes as having failed to comply with an order on the ground only that he had refused to undergo any surgical, electrical or other treatment if, in the opinion of the court, his refusal was reasonable having regard to all the circumstances: Sch 2 para 9.

7   In proceedings before the Crown Court under these provisions any question whether the offender has failed to comply with the youth rehabilitation order is to be determined by the court and not by the verdict of a jury: Criminal Justice and Immigration Act 2008 Sch 2 para 8(15). In dealing with the offender under these provisions the Crown Court must take into account the extent to which the offender has complied with the youth rehabilitation order: Sch 2 para 8(4).

8   Criminal Justice and Immigration Act 2008 Sch 2 para 8(2)(a). The fine must not exceed £2,500: Sch 2 para 8(2)(a) (Sch 2 paras 8(2)(a), (6) amended, Sch 2 para 8(6A)–(6D) added, by the Legal Aid, Sentencing and Punishment of Offenders Act 2012 ss 83(3), 84(3)). As to the amendment of this sum see PARA 85 note 8. A fine so imposed is to be treated, for the purposes of any enactment, as being a sum adjudged to be paid by a conviction: Criminal Justice and Immigration Act 2008 Sch 2 para 8(5).

9   Criminal Justice and Immigration Act 2008 Sch 2 para 8(2)(b). When imposing a requirement under Sch 2 para 8(2)(b) the court may amend the order to substitute a later date for that specified under Sch 1 para 32(1) (see PARA 81): Sch 2 para 8(6A) (as added: see note 8). A date so substituted may not fall outside the period of six months beginning with the date previously specified under Sch 1 para 32(1) but, subject to that, may fall more than three years after the date on which the order took effect: Sch 2 para 8(6B) (as so added). The power under Sch 2 para 8(6A) may not be exercised in relation to an order if that power or the power in Sch 2 para 6(6A) (see PARA 85) has previously been exercised in relation to that order: Sch 2 para 8(6C) (as so added). A date substituted under Sch 2 para 8(6A) is to be treated as having been specified in relation to the order under Sch 1 para 32(1): Sch 2 para 8(6D) (as so added).

Section 1(4), and the provisions mentioned in s 1(6) (see PARA 73 note 2), apply in relation to a power conferred by Sch 2 para 8(2)(b) to impose a requirement as they apply in relation to any power conferred by s 1 or Sch 1 paras 1–5 (see PARA 73 et seq) to make a youth rehabilitation order which includes such a requirement: Sch 2 para 23. As to the requirements which may be imposed by a youth rehabilitation order see PARA 73 et seq. Any requirement imposed under Sch 2 para 8(2)(b) must be capable of being complied with before the date specified under Sch 1 para 32(1), although this is subject to Sch 2 para 8(6A) (see above): Sch 2 para 8(3), (6) (as so amended). The court may not under Sch 2 para 8(2)(b) impose an extended activity requirement (see PARA 75) or a fostering requirement (see PARA 154) if the order does not already impose such a requirement: Sch 2 para 8(8).

10   Criminal Justice and Immigration Act 2008 Sch 2 para 8(2)(c). Where the court deals with the offender under Sch 2 para 8(2)(c) it must revoke the youth rehabilitation order if it is still in force: Sch 2 para 8(10).

Where the Crown Court is dealing with the offender under Sch 2 para 8(2)(c) and the offender has wilfully and persistently failed to comply with a youth rehabilitation order (Sch 2 para 8(11)), the court may impose a youth rehabilitation order with intensive supervision and surveillance notwithstanding anything in s 1(4)(a) or (b) (see PARA 75) (Sch 2 para 8(12)), and if the order is a youth rehabilitation order with intensive supervision and surveillance (see PARA 75) and the offence mentioned in Sch 2 para 8(2)(c) was punishable with imprisonment, the court may impose a custodial sentence notwithstanding anything in the Criminal Justice Act 2003 s 152(2) (general restrictions on imposing discretionary custodial sentences: see PARA 536) (Criminal Justice and Immigration Act 2008 Sch 2 para 8(13)).

If the order is a youth rehabilitation order with intensive supervision and surveillance which was imposed by virtue of Sch 2 para 6(13) (see PARA 85) or Sch 2 para 8(12) and the offence mentioned in Sch 2 para 8(2)(c) was not punishable with imprisonment, for the purposes of dealing with the offender under Sch 2 para 8(2)(c) the court is to be taken to have had power to deal with the offender for that offence by making a detention and training order (see PARA 9) for a term not exceeding four months: Sch 2 para 8(14).

C. REVOCATION AND AMENDMENT OF YOUTH REHABILITATION ORDER

87. Revocation of order by magistrates' court or youth court. Where a youth rehabilitation order[1] is in force in respect of an offender[2] and, on the application of the offender or the responsible officer[3], it appears to the appropriate court[4] that, having regard to circumstances which have arisen subsequent to the order, it would be in the interests of justice for the order to be revoked or for the offender to be dealt with in some other way for the offence in respect of which the order was made, the appropriate court may:

(1) revoke the order[5]; or

(2) both revoke the order[6] and deal with the offender, for that offence[7], in any way in which the appropriate court could have dealt with the offender for that offence (had the offender been before that court to be dealt with for it)[8].

The circumstances in which a youth rehabilitation order may be so revoked include the offender's making good progress or his responding satisfactorily to supervision or treatment[9].

1   Ie a youth rehabilitation order made by a youth court or other magistrates' court, or made by the Crown Court and containing a direction under the Criminal Justice and Immigration Act 2008 Sch 1 para 36 (see PARA 202 note 3): Sch 2 para 11(1)(b). As to the making of youth rehabilitation orders see PARAS 42, 73. As to youth courts see CHILDREN AND YOUNG PERSONS vol 10 (2012) PARA 1225 et seq.

2   Criminal Justice and Immigration Act 2008 Sch 2 para 11(1)(a). As to the meaning of 'offender' see PARA 81 note 8.

3   Criminal Justice and Immigration Act 2008 Sch 2 para 11(1)(c). In connection with applications to the court see the Criminal Procedure Rules 2015, SI 2015/1490, rr 32.1–32.4. As to the meaning of 'responsible officer' see PARA 81 note 9. Where, otherwise than on the application of the offender, a court proposes to exercise its powers under any of the Criminal Justice and Immigration Act 2008 Sch 2 paras 11–19, the court must summon the offender to appear before the court (Sch 2 para 20(1)(a)) and if the offender does not appear in answer to the summons, may issue a warrant for the offender's arrest (Sch 2 para 20(1)(b)). These provisions do not, however, apply where a court proposes to make an order revoking a youth rehabilitation order (Sch 2 para 20(2)(a)), cancelling, or reducing the duration of, a requirement of a youth rehabilitation order (Sch 2 para 20(2)(b)), or substituting a new local justice area or place for one specified in a youth rehabilitation order (Sch 2 para 20(2)(c)). See further Sch 2 para 21; and PARA 84 note 4.

 If an application under these provisions relating to a youth rehabilitation order is dismissed, then during the period of three months beginning with the date on which it was dismissed no further such application may be made in relation to the order by any person except with the consent of the appropriate court: Sch 2 para 11(7). No application may be made under these provisions while an appeal against the community order is pending: Sch 2 para 11(6).

4   For these purposes 'appropriate court' means:

 (1)   if the offender is aged under 18 when the application under the Criminal Justice and Immigration Act 2008 Sch 2 para 11(1) was made, a youth court acting in the local justice area specified in the youth rehabilitation order (Sch 2 para 11(8)(a)); and

 (2)   if the offender is aged 18 or over at that time, a magistrates' court (other than a youth court) acting in that local justice area (Sch 2 para 11(8)(b)).

 As to the determination of a person's age see the Children and Young Persons Act 1933 s 99; and CHILDREN AND YOUNG PERSONS vol 10 (2012) PARA 1206.

5   Criminal Justice and Immigration Act 2008 Sch 2 para 11(2)(a).

6   Criminal Justice and Immigration Act 2008 Sch 2 para 11(2)(b)(i). In dealing with an offender
     under Sch 2 para 11(2)(b) the court must take into account the extent to which the offender has
     complied with the youth rehabilitation order: Sch 2 para 11(4). A person sentenced under Sch 2
     para 11(2)(b) for an offence may appeal to the Crown Court against the sentence: Sch 2
     para 11(5).
7   Ie the offence in respect of which the order was made.
8   Criminal Justice and Immigration Act 2008 Sch 2 para 11(2)(b)(ii). See note 6.
9   Criminal Justice and Immigration Act 2008 Sch 2 para 11(3).

88.   Revocation of order by Crown Court.   Where a youth rehabilitation
order[1] is in force in respect of an offender[2] and, on the application of the
offender or the responsible officer[3], it appears to the Crown Court that, having
regard to circumstances which have arisen subsequent to the order, it would be in
the interests of justice for the order to be revoked or for the offender to be dealt
with in some other way for the offence in respect of which the order was made,
the Crown Court may:

(1)   revoke the order[4]; or
(2)   both revoke the order[5] and deal with the offender, for that offence[6], in
       any way in which the Crown Court could have dealt with the offender
       for that offence[7].

The circumstances in which a youth rehabilitation order may be so revoked
include the offender's making good progress or his responding satisfactorily to
supervision or treatment[8].

1   Ie a youth rehabilitation order made by a Crown Court and not containing a direction under the
     Criminal Justice and Immigration Act 2008 Sch 1 para 36 (see PARA 73 note 2): Sch 2
     para 12(1)(b). As to the making of youth rehabilitation orders see PARAS 42, 73.
2   Criminal Justice and Immigration Act 2008 Sch 2 para 12(1)(a). As to the meaning of 'offender'
     see PARA 81 note 8.
3   Criminal Justice and Immigration Act 2008 Sch 2 para 12(1)(c). See further Sch 2 para 20; and
     PARA 87 note 3. In connection with applications to the court see the Criminal Procedure
     Rules 2015, SI 2015/1490, rr 32.1–32.4. As to the meaning of 'responsible officer' see PARA 81
     note 9. If an application under these provisions relating to a youth rehabilitation order is
     dismissed, then during the period of three months beginning with the date on which it was
     dismissed no further such application may be made in relation to the order by any person except
     with the consent of the Crown Court: Criminal Justice and Immigration Act 2008 Sch 2
     para 12(6). No application may be made under these provisions while an appeal against the
     community order is pending: Sch 2 para 12(5).
4   Criminal Justice and Immigration Act 2008 Sch 2 para 12(2)(a).
5   Criminal Justice and Immigration Act 2008 Sch 2 para 12(2)(b)(i). In dealing with an offender
     under Sch 2 para 12(2)(b) the court must take into account the extent to which the offender has
     complied with the youth rehabilitation order: Sch 2 para 12(4).
6   Ie the offence in respect of which the order was made.
7   Criminal Justice and Immigration Act 2008 Sch 2 para 12(2)(b)(ii). See note 5.
8   Criminal Justice and Immigration Act 2008 Sch 2 para 12(3).

**89.   Amendment by magistrates' court or youth court by reason of change of
residence.**   If a youth rehabilitation order[1] is in force in respect of an offender[2]
and the appropriate court[3] is satisfied that the offender proposes to reside, or is
residing, in a local justice area (the 'new local justice area') other than the local
justice area for the time being specified in the order, the appropriate court may,
and on the application of the offender or the responsible officer[4] must, amend
the order by substituting the new local justice area for the area specified in the
order[5]. The court may also by order amend the youth rehabilitation order by
cancelling any of the requirements of the order[6] or by replacing any of those
requirements with a requirement of the same kind[7] which could have been
included in the order when it was made[8].

1 Ie a youth rehabilitation order made by a youth court or other magistrates' court, or made by the Crown Court and containing a direction under the Criminal Justice and Immigration Act 2008 Sch 1 para 36 (see PARA 73 note 3): Sch 2 para 13(1)(b). As to the making of youth rehabilitation orders see PARAS 42, 73. As to youth courts see CHILDREN AND YOUNG PERSONS vol 10 (2012) PARA 1225 et seq.

2 Criminal Justice and Immigration Act 2008 Sch 2 para 13(1)(a). As to the meaning of 'offender' see PARA 81 note 8.

3 For these purposes 'appropriate court' means:

   (1) if the offender is aged under 18 when the application under the Criminal Justice and Immigration Act 2008 Sch 2 para 13(1) was made, a youth court acting in the local justice area specified in the youth rehabilitation order (Sch 2 para 13(6)(a)); and

   (2) if the offender is aged 18 or over at that time, a magistrates' court (other than a youth court) acting in that local justice area (Sch 2 para 13(6)(b)).

   Where the court deals with the offender under Sch 2 para 6(2)(b) (see PARA 85) and it would not otherwise have the power to amend the youth rehabilitation order under Sch 2 para 13, Sch 2 para 13 has effect as if references in it to the appropriate court were references to the court which is dealing with the offender: Sch 2 para 6(10). As to the determination of a person's age see the Children and Young Persons Act 1933 s 99; and CHILDREN AND YOUNG PERSONS vol 10 (2012) PARA 1206.

4 Criminal Justice and Immigration Act 2008 Sch 2 para 13(1)(c). See further Sch 2 para 20; and PARA 87 note 3. In connection with applications to the court see the Criminal Procedure Rules 2015, SI 2015/1490, rr 32.1–32.4. As to the meaning of 'responsible officer' see PARA 81 note 9.

5 Criminal Justice and Immigration Act 2008 Sch 2 para 13(2). A court may not under Sch 2 para 13(2) or Sch 2 para 14(2) (see PARA 90) amend a youth rehabilitation order which contains specific area requirements (ie a requirement contained in the order which, in the opinion of the court, cannot be complied with unless the offender continues to reside in the local justice area specified in the order: Sch 2 paras 13(3), 14(3), 15(1)) unless, in accordance with Sch 2 para 13(4) or, as the case may be, Sch 2 para 14(4) (see PARA 90), it either cancels those requirements or substitutes for those requirements other requirements which can be complied with if the offender resides in the new local justice area mentioned in Sch 2 para 13(2) or (as the case may be) Sch 2 para 14(2): Sch 2 para 15(2). If the application under Sch 2 para 13(1)(c) or Sch 2 para 14(1)(c) was made by the responsible officer and the youth rehabilitation order contains specific area requirements the court must, unless it considers it inappropriate to do so, so exercise its powers under Sch 2 para 13(4) or, as the case may be, Sch 2 para 14(4) that it is not prevented by Sch 2 para 15(2) from amending the order under Sch 2 para 13(2) or, as the case may be, Sch 2 para 14(2): Sch 2 para 15(3). The court may not under Sch 2 para 13(2) or, as the case may be, Sch 2 para 14(2) amend a youth rehabilitation order imposing a programme requirement (see PARA 142) unless the court is satisfied that a programme which corresponds as nearly as practicable to the programme specified in the order for the purposes of that requirement and is suitable for the offender is available in the new local justice area: Sch 2 para 15(4).

6 Criminal Justice and Immigration Act 2008 Sch 2 para 13(4)(a).

7 For the purposes of the Criminal Justice and Immigration Act 2008 Sch 2 a requirement falling within any of Sch 1 paras 6–27 (see PARA 73 et seq) is of the same kind as any other requirement falling within those provisions and an electronic monitoring requirement (see PARAS 74, 155) is a requirement of the same kind as any requirement falling within those provisions to which it relates: Sch 2 para 1(3).

8 Criminal Justice and Immigration Act 2008 Sch 2 para 13(4)(b). Section 1(4), and the provisions mentioned in s 1(6) (see PARA 73 note 2), apply in relation to a power conferred by Sch 2 para 13(4)(b) or Sch 2 para 14(4)(b) to impose a requirement as they apply in relation to any power conferred by s 1 or Sch 1 paras 1–5 (see PARA 73 et seq) to make a youth rehabilitation order which includes such a requirement: Sch 2 para 23. Subject to Sch 2 para 16A, any requirement imposed under Sch 2 para 13(4)(b) or Sch 2 para 14(4)(b) must be capable of being complied with before the date specified under Sch 1 para 32(1) (see PARA 81): Sch 2 para 16(1) (amended by the Legal Aid, Sentencing and Punishment of Offenders Act 2012 s 83(4)). Where a youth rehabilitation order imposes a fostering requirement (see PARAS 76, 154) (the 'original requirement'), and under the Criminal Justice and Immigration Act 2008 Sch 2 para 13(4)(b) or Sch 2 para 14(4)(b) a court proposes to substitute a new fostering requirement (the 'substitute requirement') for the original requirement, Sch 1 para 18(2) (see PARA 154) applies in relation to the substitute requirement as if the reference to the period of 12 months beginning with the date on which the original requirement first had effect were a reference to the period of 18 months beginning with that date: Sch 2 para 16(2). The Secretary of State may by order amend Sch 2

para 16(2) by substituting for the specified period of 18 months or any other period which may be so specified by virtue of a previous order such other period as may be specified in the order: Sch 2 para 25. At the date at which this volume states the law no such order had been made.

The court may not under Sch 2 para 13(4) or Sch 2 para 14(4) impose a mental health treatment requirement (see PARA 149), a drug treatment requirement (see PARA 150) or a drug testing requirement (see PARA 151) unless the offender has expressed willingness to comply with the requirement: Sch 2 para 16(3). If an offender fails to express willingness to comply with a mental health treatment requirement, a drug treatment requirement or a drug testing requirement which the court proposes to impose under Sch 2 para 13(4) or Sch 2 para 14(4) the court may revoke the youth rehabilitation order (Sch 2 para 16(4)(a)) and deal with the offender, for the offence in respect of which the order was made, in any way in which that court could have dealt with the offender for that offence (had the offender been before that court to be dealt with for it) (Sch 2 para 16(4)(b)). In dealing with the offender under Sch 2 para 16(4)(b) the court must take into account the extent to which the offender has complied with the order: Sch 2 para 16(5).

90.   Amendment by Crown Court by reason of change of residence.   If a youth rehabilitation order[1] is in force in respect of an offender[2] and the Crown Court is satisfied that the offender proposes to reside, or is residing, in a local justice area (the 'new local justice area') other than the local justice area for the time being specified in the order, the Crown Court may, and on the application of the offender or the responsible officer[3] must, amend the order by substituting the new local justice area for the area specified in the order[4]. The Crown Court may also by order amend the youth rehabilitation order by cancelling any of the requirements of the order[5] or by replacing any of those requirements with a requirement of the same kind[6] which could have been included in the order when it was made[7].

1   Ie a youth rehabilitation order made by a Crown Court and not containing a direction under the Criminal Justice and Immigration Act 2008 Sch 1 para 36 (see PARA 73 note 2): Sch 2 para 14(1)(b). As to the making of youth rehabilitation orders see PARAS 42, 73.
2   Criminal Justice and Immigration Act 2008 Sch 2 para 14(1)(a). As to the meaning of 'offender' see PARA 81 note 8.
3   Criminal Justice and Immigration Act 2008 Sch 2 para 14(1)(c). See further Sch 2 para 20; and PARA 87 note 3. In connection with applications to the court see the Criminal Procedure Rules 2015, SI 2015/1490, rr 32.1–32.4. As to the meaning of 'responsible officer' see PARA 81 note 9.
4   Criminal Justice and Immigration Act 2008 Sch 2 para 14(2). In connection with this power to amend the order see Sch 2 para 15; and PARA 89 note 5.
5   Criminal Justice and Immigration Act 2008 Sch 2 para 14(4)(a).
6   As to when a requirement is of the same kind as another requirement see PARA 89 note 7.
7   Criminal Justice and Immigration Act 2008 Sch 2 para 14(4)(b). In connection with this power to amend the order see Sch 2 para 16; and PARA 89 note 8.

91.   Extension of unpaid work requirement.   Where:

(1)   a youth rehabilitation order[1] imposing an unpaid work requirement[2] is in force in respect of any offender[3]; and

(2)   on the application of the offender or the responsible officer[4], it appears to the appropriate court that it would be in the interests of justice to do so having regard to circumstances which have arisen since the order was made[5],

the court may, in relation to the order, extend the specified[6] period of 12 months[7].

1   As to the making of youth rehabilitation orders see PARAS 42, 73.
2   See PARA 141.
3   Criminal Justice and Immigration Act 2008 Sch 2 para 17(a). As to the meaning of 'offender' see PARA 81 note 8.

4 As to the meaning of 'responsible officer' see PARA 81 note 9. See further Sch 2 para 20; and PARA 87 note 3. In connection with applications to the court see the Criminal Procedure Rules 2015, SI 2015/1490, rr 32.1–32.4.
5 Criminal Justice and Immigration Act 2008 Sch 2 para 17(b).
6 Ie specified by the Criminal Justice and Immigration Act 2008 Sch 1 para 10(6) (see PARA 141).
7 Criminal Justice and Immigration Act 2008 Sch 2 para 17.

92. Supplementary. On the making[1] of an order revoking or amending a youth rehabilitation order[2], the proper officer[3] of the court must:

(1) provide copies of the revoking or amending order to the offender[4] and, if the offender is aged under 14[5], to the offender's parent or guardian[6];

(2) provide a copy of the revoking or amending order to the responsible officer[7];

(3) in the case of an amending order which substitutes a new local justice area, provide a copy of the amending order to:

(a) the local probation board acting for that area (or, as the case may be, a provider of probation services operating in that area)[8]; and

(b) the magistrates' court acting in that area[9]; and

(4) in the case of an amending order which imposes or cancels a specified requirement[10], provide a copy of so much of the amending order as relates to that requirement to the person specified[11] in relation to that requirement[12];

(5) in the case of an order which revokes a specified requirement[13], provide a copy of the revoking order as relates to that requirement to the person specified[14] in relation to that requirement[15]; and

(6) where the court is a magistrates' court acting in a local justice area other than the one specified in the youth rehabilitation order, provide a copy of the revoking or amending order to a magistrates' court acting in the area so specified[16].

1 Ie under the Criminal Justice and Immigration Act 2008 Sch 2.
2 As to the making of youth rehabilitation orders see PARAS 42, 73.
3 Ie in relation to a magistrates' court, the designated officer for the court (Criminal Justice and Immigration Act 2008 Sch 2 para 24(3)(a)); and in relation to the Crown Court, the appropriate officer (Sch 2 para 24(3)(b)).
4 As to the meaning of 'offender' see PARA 81 note 8.
5 As to the determination of a person's age see the Children and Young Persons Act 1933 s 99; and CHILDREN AND YOUNG PERSONS vol 10 (2012) PARA 1206.
6 Criminal Justice and Immigration Act 2008 Sch 2 para 24(1)(a). As to an offender's parent or guardian see PARA 73 note 2. In connection with the notification requirements see the Criminal Procedure Rules 2015, SI 2015/1490, r 28.2.
7 Criminal Justice and Immigration Act 2008 Sch 2 para 24(1)(b). As to the meaning of 'responsible officer' see PARA 81 note 9.
8 Criminal Justice and Immigration Act 2008 Sch 2 para 24(1)(c)(i). As to local probation boards and providers of probation services see PARAS 666–687.
9 Criminal Justice and Immigration Act 2008 Sch 2 para 24(1)(c)(ii). Where the proper officer of the court so provides a copy of an amending order to a magistrates' court acting in a different area, the officer must also provide to that court documents and information relating to the case likely to be of assistance to a court acting in that area in the exercise of its functions in relation to the order: Sch 2 para 24(2).
10 Ie specified in the first column of the Criminal Justice and Immigration Act 2008 Sch 1 para 34(4): see PARA 73.
11 Ie specified in the second column of the Criminal Justice and Immigration Act 2008 Sch 1 para 34(4).
12 Criminal Justice and Immigration Act 2008 Sch 2 para 24(1)(d).
13 See note 10.
14 See note 11.

15 Criminal Justice and Immigration Act 2008 Sch 2 para 24(1)(e).
16 Criminal Justice and Immigration Act 2008 Sch 2 para 24(1)(f).

D. SUBSEQUENT CONVICTIONS

93.   Powers of magistrates' courts.   Where a youth rehabilitation order[1] is in force in respect of an offender[2], the offender is convicted of an offence (the 'further offence') by a youth court or other magistrates' court (the 'convicting court')[3], and the convicting court is dealing with the offender for the further offence[4], the convicting court may, if it considers that it would be in the interests of justice to do so having regard to circumstances which have arisen since the youth rehabilitation order was made[5], revoke the order[6] and deal with the offender, for the offence in respect of which the order was made, in any way in which it could have dealt with the offender for that offence had the offender been before that court to be dealt with for the offence[7]. In so dealing with an offender the sentencing court must take into account the extent to which the offender has complied with the order[8].

If the order was made by the Crown Court and contains a direction[9] in relation to further proceedings[10], and the convicting court would otherwise[11] deal with the offender for the further offence[12], the convicting court may, instead of revoking the order[13], commit the offender in custody or release him on bail until he can be brought before the Crown Court[14]. If the order was made by the Crown Court and does not contain a direction[15] in relation to further proceedings[16] the convicting court may commit the offender in custody or release him on bail until he can be brought before the Crown Court[17].

1   Ie a youth rehabilitation order made by a youth court or other magistrates' court, or made by the Crown Court and containing a direction in relation to further proceedings under the Criminal Justice and Immigration Act 2008 Sch 1 para 36 (see PARA 73 note 2): Sch 2 para 18(2)(a). As to the making of youth rehabilitation orders see PARAS 42, 73. As to youth courts see CHILDREN AND YOUNG PERSONS vol 10 (2012) PARA 1225 et seq.
2   As to the meaning of 'offender' see PARA 81 note 8.
3   Criminal Justice and Immigration Act 2008 Sch 2 para 18(1).
4   Criminal Justice and Immigration Act 2008 Sch 2 para 18(2)(b).
5   Criminal Justice and Immigration Act 2008 Sch 2 para 18(5).
6   Criminal Justice and Immigration Act 2008 Sch 2 para 18(3).
7   Criminal Justice and Immigration Act 2008 Sch 2 para 18(4). A person sentenced under Sch 2 para 18(4) for an offence may appeal to the Crown Court against the sentence: Sch 2 para 18(7).
8   Criminal Justice and Immigration Act 2008 Sch 2 para 18(6).
9   Ie a direction in relation to further proceedings under the Criminal Justice and Immigration Act 2008 Sch 1 para 36 (see PARA 73 note 3).
10 Criminal Justice and Immigration Act 2008 Sch 2 para 18(8)(a).
11 Ie but for the Criminal Justice and Immigration Act 2008 Sch 2 para 18(9) (see the text and notes 13–14).
12 Criminal Justice and Immigration Act 2008 Sch 2 para 18(8)(b).
13 Ie instead of proceeding under the Criminal Justice and Immigration Act 2008 Sch 2 para 18(3) (see the text and note 6).
14 Criminal Justice and Immigration Act 2008 Sch 2 para 18(9). See further PARA 94 (powers of Crown Court). Where the convicting court deals with an offender's case under Sch 2 para 18(9) or Sch 2 para 18(11) it must send to the Crown Court such particulars of the case as may be desirable: Sch 2 para 18(12).
15 See note 9.
16 Criminal Justice and Immigration Act 2008 Sch 2 para 18(10).
17 Criminal Justice and Immigration Act 2008 Sch 2 para 18(11). See note 14.

94.   Powers of Crown Court.   If:

(1)   a youth rehabilitation order[1] is in force in respect of an offender[2]; and

(2)   the offender is convicted by the Crown Court of an offence[3] or is
        brought or appears[4] before the Crown Court[5],

the Crown Court may, if it considers that it would be in the interests of justice to
do so having regard to circumstances which have arisen since the youth
rehabilitation order was made[6], revoke the order[7] and deal with the offender, for
the offence in respect of which the order was made, in any way in which the
court which made the order could have dealt with the offender for that offence[8].

1   As to the making of youth rehabilitation orders see PARAS 42, 73. As to youth courts see
    CHILDREN AND YOUNG PERSONS vol 10 (2012) PARA 1225 et seq.
2   Criminal Justice and Immigration Act 2008 Sch 2 para 19(1)(a). As to the meaning of 'offender'
    see PARA 81 note 8.
3   Criminal Justice and Immigration Act 2008 Sch 2 para 19(1)(b)(i).
4   Ie by virtue of Criminal Justice and Immigration Act 2008 Sch 2 para 18(9) or (11) (see PARA
    93) or having been committed by the magistrates' court to the Crown Court for sentence: Sch 2
    para 19(1)(b)(ii). If the offender is brought or appears before the Crown Court by virtue of
    Sch 2 para 18(9) or (11) the Crown Court may deal with the offender for the further offence in
    any way which the convicting court could have dealt with the offender for that offence: Sch 2
    para 19(6). As to the meanings of 'further offence' and 'convicting court' see Sch 2 para 18; and
    PARA 93 (definitions applied by Sch 2 para 19(7)).
5   Criminal Justice and Immigration Act 2008 Sch 2 para 19(1)(b)(ii).
6   Criminal Justice and Immigration Act 2008 Sch 2 para 19(4).
7   Criminal Justice and Immigration Act 2008 Sch 2 para 19(2).
8   Criminal Justice and Immigration Act 2008 Sch 2 para 19(3). In so dealing with an offender the
    Crown Court must take into account the extent to which the offender has complied with the
    order: Sch 2 para 19(5).

E.   ORDERS OPERATING IN NORTHERN IRELAND

95.   Supervision arrangements.   Where the court considering the making of a
youth rehabilitation order[1] is satisfied that the offender[2] resides in Northern
Ireland, or will reside there when the order takes effect[3], it may not so make an
order in respect of the offender unless it appears to the court that the conditions
imposed by the order are compliant with similar requirements which may be
imposed in Northern Ireland and that suitable arrangements for the offender's
supervision can be made by the Probation Board for Northern Ireland[4].

1   As to the making of youth rehabilitation orders see PARAS 42, 73.
2   As to the meaning of 'offender' see PARA 81 note 8.
3   Criminal Justice and Immigration Act 2008 Sch 3 para 1(1).
        Where a change is made to the law in Northern Ireland adding further descriptions of orders
    to the kinds of orders which a court in that jurisdiction may impose in dealing with an offender
    aged under 18 at the time of conviction the Secretary of State may by order make such
    amendments to Sch 3 (see the text and note 4; and PARAS 96–99) as appear expedient in
    consequence of the change: Sch 3 para 17. At the date at which this volume states the law no
    such order had been made. As to the determination of a person's age see the Children and Young
    Persons Act 1933 s 99; and CHILDREN AND YOUNG PERSONS vol 10 (2012) PARA 1206.
4   See the Criminal Justice and Immigration Act 2008 Sch 3 para 1(2); and PARA 96.
        A youth rehabilitation order made in accordance with Sch 3 para 1 must specify the petty
    sessions district in Northern Ireland in which the offender resides or will be residing when the
    order or amendment takes effect (Sch 3 para 3(a)) and specify as the corresponding order for
    these purposes an order that may be made by a court in Northern Ireland (Sch 3 para 3(b)).
    Schedule 1 para 33 (local justice area to be specified: see PARA 73) does not apply to an order so
    made or amended: Sch 3 para 3.
        Where a youth rehabilitation order is made or amended in accordance with these provisions
    the court which makes or amends the order must provide the following persons with a copy of
    the order as made or amended:
    (1)   the offender (Sch 3 para 4(2)(a), (3)(a));
    (2)   where the offender is aged under 14, the offender's parent or guardian or, if an

authority in Northern Ireland has parental responsibility for, and is looking after, the offender, the authority (Sch 3 para 4(3)(b));

(3)   the body which is to make suitable arrangements for the offender's supervision under the order (Sch 3 para 4(3)(c)); and

(4)   the home court (Sch 3 para 4(3)(d)),

and must provide the home court with such other documents and information relating to the case as it considers likely to be of assistance to that court (Sch 3 para 4(2)(b)). The provisions of Sch 1 para 34(1)–(3) (provision of copies of relevant orders: see PARA 73) do not apply in these circumstances: Sch 3 para 4(2).

For these purposes 'home court' means the court of summary jurisdiction acting for the petty sessions district in Northern Ireland in which the offender resides or proposes to reside or, where the youth rehabilitation order was made or amended by the Crown Court and the Crown Court in Northern Ireland has not made a direction under Sch 3 para 11 (see PARA 97), the Crown Court in Northern Ireland: Sch 3 paras 4(5), 8). As to the meanings of 'authority' and 'parental responsibility' for these purposes, and as to references to an offender who is looked after by an authority, see the Children (Northern Ireland) Order 1995, SI 1995/755 (NI 2), arts 2, 25 (definitions applied by the Criminal Justice and Immigration Act 2008 Sch 3 para 4(4)).

Before making or amending a youth rehabilitation order in these circumstances the court must explain to the offender in ordinary language:

(a)   the requirements of the legislation in Northern Ireland relating to the order to be specified under Sch 3 para 3(b) (Sch 3 para 4(1)(a));

(b)   the powers of the home court under that legislation (as modified by Sch 3 paras 7–17) (Sch 3 para 4(1)(b)); and

(c)   its own powers under Sch 3 paras 7–17 (Sch 3 para 4(1)(c)).

96.   Making of order in respect of offender residing in Northern Ireland.   A court may not make a youth rehabilitation order[1] in respect of an offender[2] who resides or will reside in Northern Ireland[3] unless:

(1)   the number of hours, days or months in respect of which any requirement of the order[4] is imposed is no greater than the number of hours, days or months which may be imposed by a court in Northern Ireland in respect of a similar requirement in the order which the court proposes to specify[5] as the corresponding order[6]; and

(2)   suitable arrangements for the offender's supervision[7] can be made by the Probation Board for Northern Ireland or any other body designated by the Secretary of State by order[8].

In addition, a court may not make in respect of such an offender a youth rehabilitation order imposing one or more specified requirements[9] unless:

(a)   arrangements exist for persons to comply with such a requirement in the petty sessions district in Northern Ireland in which the offender resides, or will be residing when the order takes effect[10]; and

(b)   provision can be made for the offender to comply with the requirement under those arrangements[11].

1   As to the making of youth rehabilitation orders see PARAS 42, 73.
2   As to the meaning of 'offender' see PARA 81 note 8.
3   See PARAS 95, 97–99.
4   As to the requirements which may be imposed by a youth rehabilitation order see PARA 73 et seq. The court may not by virtue of these provisions require a local authority residence requirement (see PARA 148) or a fostering requirement (see PARA 154) to be complied with in Northern Ireland: Criminal Justice and Immigration Act 2008 Sch 3 para 1(7).
5   Ie under the Criminal Justice and Immigration Act 2008 Sch 3 para 3(b) (see PARA 95).
6   Criminal Justice and Immigration Act 2008 Sch 3 para 1(2)(b), (3).
7   'Supervision', in relation to a youth rehabilitation order which a court is considering making or amending in accordance with the Criminal Justice and Immigration Act 2008 Sch 3 para 1 or Sch 3 para 2 (see PARAS 95, 97), means the performance of supervisory, enforcement and other related functions conferred by the legislation which has effect in Northern Ireland relating to corresponding orders of the kind which the court proposes to specify under Sch 3 para 3(b) (see PARA 95): Criminal Justice and Immigration Act 2008 Sch 3 para 6.

8 Criminal Justice and Immigration Act 2008 Sch 3 para 1(4).
9 Ie an activity requirement (see PARA 139) (including an extended activity requirement (see PARA 75)), an unpaid work requirement (see PARA 141), a programme requirement (see PARA 142), an attendance centre requirement (see PARA 143), a mental health treatment requirement (see PARA 149), a drug treatment requirement (see PARA 150), a drug testing requirement (see PARA 151), an education requirement (see PARA 153) or an electronic monitoring requirement (see PARAS 74, 155): Criminal Justice and Immigration Act 2008 Sch 3 para 1(2)(a), (6).
10 Criminal Justice and Immigration Act 2008 Sch 3 para 1(5)(a).
11 Criminal Justice and Immigration Act 2008 Sch 3 para 1(5)(b).

97. Amendment of order in respect of offender residing in Northern Ireland.
Where the appropriate court[1] is satisfied that an offender[2] in respect of whom a youth rehabilitation order[3] is in force is residing or proposes to reside in Northern Ireland[4], the power of the court to amend the order[5] includes power to amend it by requiring it to be complied with in Northern Ireland if it appears to the court that:

(1)   the number of hours, days or months in respect of which any requirement of the order[6] is imposed is no greater than the number of hours, days or months which may be imposed by a court in Northern Ireland in respect of a similar requirement in the order which the court proposes to specify[7] as the corresponding order[8]; and

(2)   suitable arrangements for the offender's supervision[9] can be made by the Probation Board for Northern Ireland or any other body designated by the Secretary of State by order[10].

In addition, the power of the court to amend a youth rehabilitation order made in respect of such an offender which imposes one or more specified requirements[11] includes power to amend it by requiring it to be complied with in Northern Ireland if it appears to the court that:

(a)   arrangements exist for persons to comply with such a requirement in the petty sessions district in Northern Ireland in which the offender resides, or will be residing when the amendment to the order takes effect[12]; and

(b)   provision can be made for the offender to comply with the requirement under those arrangements[13].

1   For these purposes 'appropriate court' means either the Crown Court or:
    (1)   if the offender is aged under 18 when the application under the Criminal Justice and Immigration Act 2008 Sch 2 para 13(1) (see PARA 89) was made, a youth court acting in the local justice area specified in the youth rehabilitation order (Sch 2 para 13(6)(a), Sch 3 para 2(1)); and
    (2)   if the offender is aged 18 or over at that time, a magistrates' court (other than a youth court) acting in that local justice area (Sch 2 para 13(6)(b)).
    As to youth courts see CHILDREN AND YOUNG PERSONS vol 10 (2012) PARA 1225 et seq. As to the determination of a person's age see the Children and Young Persons Act 1933 s 99; and CHILDREN AND YOUNG PERSONS vol 10 (2012) PARA 1206. Where a youth rehabilitation order was made or amended by the Crown Court, the Crown Court in Northern Ireland may direct that any proceedings in Northern Ireland in relation to the order be before the court of summary jurisdiction acting for the petty sessions district in which the offender resides or proposes to reside: Sch 3 para 11.
2   As to the meaning of 'offender' see PARA 81 note 8.
3   As to the making of youth rehabilitation orders see PARAS 42, 73.
4   Criminal Justice and Immigration Act 2008 Sch 3 para 2(1).
5   Ie under the Criminal Justice and Immigration Act 2008 Sch 2 paras 13–17 (see PARAS 89–91).
6   As to the requirements which may be imposed by a youth rehabilitation order see PARA 73 et seq. The court may not by virtue of these provisions require a local authority residence requirement (see PARA 148) or a fostering requirement (see PARA 154) to be complied with in Northern Ireland: Criminal Justice and Immigration Act 2008 Sch 3 para 2(7).
7   Ie under the Criminal Justice and Immigration Act 2008 Sch 3 para 3(b) (see PARA 95).
8   Criminal Justice and Immigration Act 2008 Sch 3 para 2(2)(b), (3).

9 As to the meaning of 'supervision' see PARA 96 note 7.
10 Criminal Justice and Immigration Act 2008 Sch 3 para 2(4).
11 Ie an activity requirement (see PARA 139) (including an extended activity requirement (see PARA 75)), an unpaid work requirement (see PARA 141), a programme requirement (see PARA 142), an attendance centre requirement (see PARA 143), a mental health treatment requirement (see PARA 149), a drug treatment requirement (see PARA 150), a drug testing requirement (see PARA 151), an education requirement (see PARA 153) or an electronic monitoring requirement (see PARAS 74, 155): Criminal Justice and Immigration Act 2008 Sch 3 para 2(2)(a), (6).
12 Criminal Justice and Immigration Act 2008 Sch 3 para 2(5)(a).
13 Criminal Justice and Immigration Act 2008 Sch 3 para 2(5)(b).

98. Status of transferred order. Where a youth rehabilitation order[1] is made or amended[2] so as to take effect in Northern Ireland the order is to be treated in Northern Ireland as if it were a corresponding order[3] and the legislation which has effect in Northern Ireland in relation to such orders applies accordingly[4].

1 As to the making of youth rehabilitation orders see PARAS 42, 73.
2 Ie in accordance with the Criminal Justice and Immigration Act 2008 Sch 3 Pt 1 (paras 1–6: see PARAS 95–97). These provisions are subject to Sch 3 paras 12–16 (see PARA 99): Sch 3 paras 7, 9(2).
3 'Corresponding order' means the order specified under the Criminal Justice and Immigration Act 2008 Sch 3 para 3(b) (see PARA 95): Sch 3 para 8.
4 Criminal Justice and Immigration Act 2008 Sch 3 para 9(1).

99. Powers of home courts. Where a youth rehabilitation order[1] is made or amended[2] so as to take effect in Northern Ireland the home court[3] may exercise in relation to the order any power which it could exercise in relation to a corresponding order[4] made by a court in Northern Ireland, by virtue of the legislation relating to such orders which has effect there, except the following:

(1) any power to discharge or revoke the order (other than a power to revoke the order where the offender[5] has been convicted of a further offence and the court has imposed a custodial sentence)[6];

(2) any power to deal with the offender for the offence in respect of which the order was made[7];

(3) in the case of a youth rehabilitation order imposing a curfew requirement[8], any power to vary the order by substituting for the period specified in it any longer period than the court which made the order could have specified[9].

If it appears to the home court:

(a) upon a complaint being made to a lay magistrate acting for the petty sessions district for the time being specified in the order that the offender has failed to comply with one or more requirements of the order[10]; or

(b) on the application of the offender or the relevant officer[11], that it would be in the interests of justice for a power of revocation or amendment[12] to be exercised[13],

the home court may require the offender to appear before the relevant court in England and Wales[14].

1 As to the making of youth rehabilitation orders see PARAS 42, 73.
2 Ie in accordance with the Criminal Justice and Immigration Act 2008 Sch 3 Pt 1 (paras 1–6: see PARAS 95–97).
3 As to the meaning of 'home court' see PARA 95 note 4.
4 As to the meaning of 'corresponding order' see PARA 98 note 3.
5 As to the meaning of 'offender' see PARA 81 note 8.
6 Criminal Justice and Immigration Act 2008 Sch 3 para 12(a).
7 Criminal Justice and Immigration Act 2008 Sch 3 para 12(b).

8 As to curfew requirements see PARA 145.
9 Criminal Justice and Immigration Act 2008 Sch 3 para 12(c).
10 Criminal Justice and Immigration Act 2008 Sch 3 para 13(2).
11 Ie the person responsible for the offender's supervision under the order: Criminal Justice and Immigration Act 2008 Sch 3 para 8. 'Supervision' means the performance of supervisory, enforcement and other related functions conferred by the legislation which has effect in Northern Ireland relating to the corresponding order: Sch 3 para 8.
12 Ie a power conferred by the Criminal Justice and Immigration Act 2008 Sch 2 paras 11–14 (see PARAS 87–89).
13 Criminal Justice and Immigration Act 2008 Sch 3 para 13(3).
14 Criminal Justice and Immigration Act 2008 Sch 3 para 13(1). 'Relevant court in England or Wales' means:
  (1) the court in England and Wales which made or which last amended the order (Sch 3 para 8); or
  (2) if the order was made by the Crown Court and includes a direction under Sch 1 para 36 (see PARA 73), such youth court or other magistrates' court as may be specified in the order (Sch 3 para 8).
  As to youth courts see CHILDREN AND YOUNG PERSONS vol 10 (2012) PARA 1225 et seq.
  Where an offender is required by Sch 3 para 13 to appear before the relevant court in England and Wales, the home court must send to that court a certificate certifying that the offender has failed to comply with such of the requirements of the order as may be specified in the certificate, together with such other particulars of the case as may be desirable (Sch 3 para 14(a)); and a certificate purporting to be signed by the clerk of the home court (or, if the home court is the Crown Court in Northern Ireland, by the chief clerk) is admissible as evidence of the failure before the relevant court in England and Wales (Sch 3 para 14(b)).
  Where an offender is required by virtue of Sch 3 para 13 to appear before the relevant court in England and Wales that court may issue a warrant for his arrest (Sch 3 para 15(a)) and may exercise any power which it could exercise in respect of the youth rehabilitation order if the offender resided in England and Wales (Sch 3 para 15(b)). Any enactment relating to the exercise of such powers has effect accordingly, and with any reference to the responsible officer being read as a reference to the relevant officer: Sch 3 para 15. Schedule 3 para 15(b) does not enable the court to amend the youth rehabilitation order unless it appears to the court that the conditions in Sch 3 para 2(2)(a), (b) (see PARA 97) are satisfied in relation to any requirement to be imposed: Sch 3 para 16(1). Schedule 3 paras 1–16 have effect in relation to the amendment of a youth rehabilitation order by virtue of Sch 3 para 15(b) as they have effect in relation to the amendment of such an order by virtue of Sch 3 para 2(2): Sch 3 para 16(2). See further Sch 2 para 21; and PARA 84 note 4.

(2) SUSPENDED SENTENCE ORDERS

(i) Making a Suspended Sentence Order

100. Powers of court. If a court[1] passes a sentence of imprisonment for a term of least 14 days but not more than two years[2], it may make an order providing that the sentence of imprisonment is not to take effect unless:

  (1) during a period specified in the order[3] ('the operational period') the offender commits another offence in the United Kingdom[4] (whether or not punishable with imprisonment)[5]; and

  (2) a court having power to do so subsequently orders[6] that the original sentence is to take effect[7].

Such an order may also provide that the offender must comply during a period specified[8] in the order ('the supervision period') with one or more requirements[9] (referred to as 'community requirements'[10]) specified in the order[11].

Such an order is known as a 'suspended sentence order' and the sentence under it as a 'suspended sentence'[12]. The supervision period (if any) and the operational period must each be a period of not less than six months and not more than two years beginning with the date of the order[13]. Where an order[14] imposes one or more community requirements, the supervision period must not end later than the operational period[15]. A court which passes a suspended sentence on any person for an offence may not impose a community sentence[16] in his case in respect of that offence or any other offence of which he is convicted by or before the court or for which he is dealt with by the court[17].

1   As to the meaning of 'court' see PARA 1 note 1.
2   As to the meaning of 'sentence of imprisonment' see PARA 27 note 4. For the purposes of the making of a suspended sentence order under these provisions, until a day to be appointed 'sentence of imprisonment' does not include a committal for contempt of court or any kindred offence, and as from that day does not include a sentence of imprisonment passed in respect of a summary conviction for an offence under the Bail Act 1976 s 6(1), (2) (see CRIMINAL PROCEDURE vol 27 (2015) PARA 121): Criminal Justice Act 2003 s 195(1) (definition prospectively substituted by the Police and Justice Act 2006 s 34(1), (2)). At the date at which this volume states the law no day had been appointed for the coming into force of this amendment. Where two or more sentences imposed on the same occasion are to be served consecutively, the power conferred by these provisions is not exercisable in relation to any of them unless the aggregate of the terms of the sentences does not exceed 2 years: Criminal Justice Act 2003 s 189(2) (s 189(1) substituted, s 189(1A), (1B) added, ss 189(2)–(4), (7)(c), 190(2) amended, s 190(2)(h) prospectively added, by the Legal Aid, Sentencing and Punishment of Offenders Act 2012 ss 68(1), (2), (5), 76(5)(b), Sch 9 paras 2, 4). At the date at which this volume states the law no day had been appointed for the coming into force of the amendment noted as prospective.
    The Criminal Justice Act 2003 ss 189–194 (see the text and notes 3–17; and PARA 101 et seq) were brought into force on 4 April 2005 by the Criminal Justice Act 2003 (Commencement No 8 and Transitional and Saving Provisions) Order 2005, SI 2005/950, Sch 2 para 5(1), (2), and apply only in respect of offences committed on or after that date. The amendments effected by the Legal Aid, Sentencing and Punishment of Offenders Act 2012 were brought into force on 3 December 2012 by the Legal Aid, Sentencing and Punishment of Offenders Act 2012 (Commencement No 4 and Saving Provisions) Order 2012, SI 2012/2906.
3   Ie for the purposes of the Criminal Justice Act 2003 s 189(1)(a).
4   As to the meaning of 'United Kingdom' see PARA 4 note 3.
5   Criminal Justice Act 2003 s 189(1)(a) (as substituted: see note 2).
6   Ie under the Criminal Justice Act 2003 Sch 12 para 8 (see PARA 117). Subject to any provision to the contrary contained in the Criminal Justice Act 1967, the Powers of Criminal Courts (Sentencing) Act 2000 or any other enactment passed or instrument made under any enactment after 31 December 1967, a suspended sentence which has not taken effect under the Criminal Justice Act 2003 Sch 12 para 8 is to be treated as a sentence of imprisonment (or, until the date on which the Criminal Justice and Court Services Act 2000 s 61 (abolition of sentences of detention in a young offender institution, custody for life etc: PARA 36) comes into force, in the case of a person aged at least 18 but under 21, a sentence of detention in a young offender institution) for the purposes of all enactments and instruments made under enactments: Criminal Justice Act 2003 s 189(6) (amended by SI 2005/643). At the date at which this volume states the law no day had been appointed for the commencement of s 61. As to the determination of a person's age see the Children and Young Persons Act 1933 s 99; and CHILDREN AND YOUNG PERSONS vol 10 (2012) PARA 1206.
7   Criminal Justice Act 2003 s 189(1)(b) (as substituted: see note 2). As to the information to be supplied see the Criminal Procedure Rules 2015, SI 2015/1490, r 28.10.
8   Ie specified for the purposes of the Criminal Justice Act 2003 s 189(2).
9   Ie one or more requirements falling within the Criminal Justice Act 2003 s 190(1): see PARA 101.
10 Criminal Justice Act 2003 s 189(7)(c) (as amended: see note 2).
11 Criminal Justice Act 2003 s 189(1A) (as added: see note 2). Where an order under s 189(1) contains provision under s 189(1A), it must provide that the sentence of imprisonment will also take effect if: (1) during the supervision period the offender fails to comply with a requirement imposed under s 189(1A) (s 189(1B)(a) (as so added)); and (2) a court having power to do so subsequently orders under Sch 12 para 8 that the original sentence is to take effect (s 189(1B)(b) (as so added)). Section 189(1A) has effect subject to s 218 (availability of arrangements in local area: see PARAS 133, 134–136) (s 190(2) (as so amended)) and, in connection with particular requirements:
    (1)   s 199(3) (unpaid work requirement: see PARA 133) (s 190(2)(a));
    (2)   s 203(2) (prohibited activity requirement: see PARA 130) (s 190(2)(d));
    (3)   s 207(3) (mental health treatment requirement: see PARA 128) (s 190(2)(e));

(4)   s 209(2) (drug rehabilitation requirement: see PARA 124) (s 190(2)(f));
(5)   s 212(2), (3) (alcohol treatment requirement: see PARA 122) (s 190(2)(g));
(6)   as from a day to be appointed, s 212A(8)–(12) (alcohol abstinence and monitoring requirement: see PARA 135) (s 190(2)(h) (prospectively added: see note 2)); and
(7)   as from a day to be appointed, s 215(2) (electronic monitoring requirement: see PARA 136) (s 190(2)(i) (prospectively added by the Crime and Courts Act 2013 Sch 16 paras 11, 13)).
At the date at which this volume states the law no day had been appointed for the coming into force of the amendments noted as prospective.

12 A 'suspended sentence' means a sentence to which a suspended sentence order relates and a 'suspended sentence order' means an order under the Criminal Justice Act 2003 s 189(1): s 189(7)(a), (b). The court by which a suspended sentence order is made must forthwith provide copies of the order:

(1)   to the offender (Criminal Justice Act 2003 s 219(1)(a) (s 219(1) substituted, s 219(4) added, by the Offender Management Act 2014 Sch 4 para 12));
(2)   to the responsible officer (Criminal Justice Act 2003 s 219(1)(b) (as so substituted));
(3)   to an officer who is acting at the court and is an officer of a provider of probation services that is a public sector provider (s 219(1)(c) (as so substituted)); and
(4)   where the court specifies a local justice area in which the court making the order does not act, to a provider of probation services that is a public sector provider and is acting in that area (s 219(1)(d) (as so substituted)).

In connection with the notification requirements see the Criminal Procedure Rules 2015, SI 2015/1490, r 28.2. For this purpose 'public sector provider' means a probation trust or other public body or the Secretary of State: Criminal Justice Act 2003 s 219(4) (as so added). As to the provision of probation services see PARAS 666–687. Provision is also made as to the provision of copies to the persons concerned with the supervision of requirements imposed by an order: see the Criminal Justice Act 2003 s 219(2), Sch 14; and PARA 122 et seq. See also s 219(3); and PARA 48. 'Local probation board' means a local probation board established under the Criminal Justice and Court Services Act 2000 s 4 (repealed); and 'youth offending team' means a team established under the Crime and Disorder Act 1998 s 39: Criminal Justice Act 2003 s 305(1). As to local probation boards and providers of probation services see PARAS 666–687. As to youth offending teams see CHILDREN AND YOUNG PERSONS vol 10 (2012) PARA 1193. As to the determination of a person's age see the Children and Young Persons Act 1933 s 99; and CHILDREN AND YOUNG PERSONS vol 10 (2012) PARA 1206.

13 Criminal Justice Act 2003 s 189(3) (as amended: see note 2).
14 Ie an order under the Criminal Justice Act 2003 s 189(1).
15 Criminal Justice Act 2003 s 189(4) (as amended: see note 2).
16 As to the meaning of 'community sentence' see the Criminal Justice Act 2003 s 147(1); and PARA 42 (definition applied by virtue of s 305(1)).
17 Criminal Justice Act 2003 s 189(5).

101.   Community requirements.   The community requirements required to be specified for the purposes of a suspended sentence order[1] are:

(1)   an alcohol treatment requirement[2];
(2)   a curfew requirement[3];
(3)   a drug rehabilitation requirement[4];
(4)   an exclusion requirement[5];
(5)   a foreign travel prohibition requirement[6];
(6)   a mental health treatment requirement[7];
(7)   a programme requirement[8];
(8)   a prohibited activity requirement[9];
(9)   a rehabilitation activity requirement[10];
(10)   a residence requirement[11];
(11)   an unpaid work requirement[12];
(12)   (in a case where the offender is aged under 25[13] only), an attendance centre requirement[14];
(13)   as from a day to be appointed, an alcohol abstinence and monitoring requirement[15]; and
(14)   as from a day to be appointed, an electronic monitoring requirement[16].

Where the court makes a suspended sentence order imposing a curfew requirement or an exclusion requirement, it must also impose an electronic monitoring requirement[17] unless it is prevented[18] from doing so or unless, in the particular circumstances of the case, it considers it inappropriate to do so[19]. Until a day to be appointed, where the court makes a suspended sentence order imposing an unpaid work requirement, a rehabilitation activity requirement, a programme requirement, a prohibited activity requirement, a residence requirement, a foreign travel prohibition requirement, a mental health treatment requirement, a drug rehabilitation requirement, an alcohol treatment requirement or an attendance centre requirement, the court may also impose an electronic monitoring requirement unless it is prevented[20] from doing so[21].

A suspended sentence order must specify the local justice area in which the offender resides or will reside[22].

1   As to the meanings of 'suspended sentence' and 'suspended sentence order', and as to the making of suspended sentence orders, see PARA 100. Before making a suspended sentence order imposing two or more different requirements falling within heads (1) to (15) in the text, the court must consider whether, in the circumstances of the case, the requirements are compatible with each other: Criminal Justice Act 2003 s 190(5).
2   Criminal Justice Act 2003 s 190(1)(j). See s 212; and PARA 122.
3   Criminal Justice Act 2003 s 190(1)(e). See s 204; and PARA 123.
4   Criminal Justice Act 2003 s 190(1)(i). See s 209; and PARA 124.
5   Criminal Justice Act 2003 s 190(1)(f). See s 205; and PARA 126.
6   Criminal Justice Act 2003 s 190(1)(ga) (s 190(1)(ga) added, s 190(1)(ja) prospectively added, s 190(4) amended, by the Legal Aid, Sentencing and Punishment of Offenders Act 2012 ss 72(3), (4), 76(4)). At the date at which this volume states the law no day had been appointed for the coming into force of the amendment noted as prospective. As to foreign travel prohibition requirements see the Criminal Justice Act 2003 s 206A; and PARA 127.
7   Criminal Justice Act 2003 s 190(1)(h). See s 207; and PARA 128.
8   Criminal Justice Act 2003 s 190(1)(c). See s 202; and PARA 129.
9   Criminal Justice Act 2003 s 190(1)(d). See s 203; and PARA 130.
10 Ie as defined by the Criminal Justice Act 2003 s 212A (see PARA 131): s 190(1)(aa) (s 190(1)(aa) added, s 190(4) amended, by the Offender Rehabilitation Act 2014 s 15(2), Sch 5 para 3(1), (4)). Rehabilitation activity requirements replaced activity requirements under the Criminal Justice Act 2003 s 201 and supervision requirements under s 213, which have been abolished, as from 1 February 2015: see the Offender Rehabilitation Act 2014 s 15 and the Offender Rehabilitation Act 2014 (Commencement No 2) Order 2015), SI 2015/40.
11 Criminal Justice Act 2003 s 190(1)(g). See s 206; and PARA 132.
12 Criminal Justice Act 2003 s 190(1)(a). See s 199; and PARA 133.
13 As to the determination of a person's age see the Children and Young Persons Act 1933 s 99; and CHILDREN AND YOUNG PERSONS vol 10 (2012) PARA 1206.
14 Criminal Justice Act 2003 s 190(1)(l). See s 214; and PARA 134.
15 Criminal Justice Act 2003 s 190(1)(ja) (prospectively added: see note 6). As to an alcohol abstinence and monitoring requirement see s 212A; and PARA 135.
16 Criminal Justice Act 2003 s 190(1)(m) (s 190(1)(m) prospectively added, s 190(3) prospectively amended, s 190(4) prospectively repealed, by the Crime and Courts Act 2013 Sch 16 paras 11–13). At the date at which this volume states the law no day had been appointed for the coming into force of these amendments. As to an electronic monitoring requirement (which the Criminal Justice Act 2003 s 190(1)(m) specifies as being an electronic monitoring requirement as defined by s 215) see PARA 136.
17 Ie: (1) until a day to be appointed, an electronic monitoring requirement as defined by the Criminal Justice Act 2003 s 215; or (2) as from that day, an electronic monitoring requirement within s 215(1)(a) for securing the electronic monitoring of the curfew or exclusion requirement: s 190(3) (prospectively amended: see note 16).
18 Ie by the Criminal Justice Act 2003 s 215(2) (see PARA 136) or s 218(4) (see PARA 136).
19 Criminal Justice Act 2003 s 190(3) (prospectively amended: see note 16).
20 See note 18.
21 Criminal Justice Act 2003 s 190(4) (as amended and prospectively repealed: see notes 6, 10, 16).
22 Criminal Justice Act 2003 s 216(1) (amended by SI 2005/886). Where an order specifies a local justice area in which the court making the order does not act, the court making the order must

provide to the magistrates' court acting in that area a copy of the order and documents and information relating to the case likely to be of assistance to a court acting in that area in the exercise of its functions in relation to the order: Criminal Justice Act 2003 s 219(3) (amended by SI 2005/886).

102. Requirement to avoid conflict with religious beliefs and education. The court must ensure, as far as practicable, that any requirement imposed by a suspended sentence order[1] is such as to avoid:

(1)   any conflict with the offender's religious beliefs or with the requirements of any other relevant order[2] to which he may be subject[3]; and

(2)   any interference with the times, if any, at which he normally works or attends any educational establishment[4].

It is the duty of the responsible officer[5] to ensure that these requirements are complied with[6].

1   As to the meanings of 'suspended sentence' and 'suspended sentence order', and as to the making of suspended sentence orders, see PARA 100.
2   Ie a suspended sentence order (see PARA 100) or a community order (see PARA 45).
3   Criminal Justice Act 2003 s 217(1)(a). The Secretary of State may by order provide that s 217(1) is to have effect with such additional restrictions as may be specified in the order: s 217(3). At the date at which this volume states the law no such order had been made.
4   Criminal Justice Act 2003 s 217(1)(b) (amended by the Criminal Justice and Immigration Act 2008 s 6(2), Sch 4 paras 71, 91).
5   As to the responsible officer see PARA 51 note 2.
6   See the Criminal Justice Act 2003 s 217(2); and PARA 51.

103. Duty of offender to keep in touch with responsible officer and to obtain permission before changing residence. An offender in respect of whom a suspended sentence order[1] is in force must keep in touch with the responsible officer[2] in accordance with such instructions as he may from time to time be given by that officer[3]. The offender is also prohibited (unless there is a residence requirement in place[4]) from changing residence without the permission of either the responsible officer or the court[5], and it is provided that the officer or court may refuse an application for permission[6] if, in the opinion of the officer or court, the change in residence is likely to prevent the offender complying with a requirement imposed by the order[7] or would hinder the offender's rehabilitation[8]. A court may also give permission for a change of residence in certain proceedings[9] involving the breach or amendment of orders[10].

1   As to the meanings of 'suspended sentence' and 'suspended sentence order', and as to the making of suspended sentence orders, see PARA 100.
2   As to the meaning of 'responsible officer' see the Criminal Justice Act 2003 s 197; and PARA 51 note 2. In connection with the requirement to 'keep in touch' see *Richards v National Probation Service* [2007] EWHC 3108 (Admin), 172 JP 100, 172 JPN 293. The responsible officer in relation to an offender to whom a relevant order relates must ensure, as far as practicable, that any instruction given or requirement imposed by him in pursuance of the order is such as to avoid any conflict with the offender's religious beliefs or with the requirements of any other relevant order to which he may be subject (Criminal Justice Act 2003 s 217(1)(a), (2)) and any interference with the times, if any, at which he normally works or attends any educational establishment (s 217(1)(b) (amended by the Criminal Justice and Immigration Act 2008 Sch 4 paras 71, 91)). The Secretary of State may by order provide that the Criminal Justice Act 2003 s 217(2) is to have effect with such additional restrictions as may be specified in the order: s 217(3). At the date at which this volume states the law no such order had been made.
3   Criminal Justice Act 2003 s 220(1)(a). The obligation imposed by s 220(1) is enforceable as if it were a requirement imposed by the order: s 220(2). As to the community requirements see s 190(1); and PARA 101.
4   The Criminal Justice Act 2003 s 220A (see the text and notes 5–10) does not apply if the relevant order includes a residence requirement imposed under s 206 (see PARA 132): s 220A(6) (s 220A added by the Offender Rehabilitation Act 2014 s 18(1), (2)).

5   Criminal Justice Act 2003 s 220A(1) (as added: see note 4). See note 3. The obligation imposed
    by s 220A(1) is enforceable as if it were a requirement imposed by the relevant order: s 220A(5)
    (as so added). In connection with circumstances in which a relevant order has to be amended
    because of permission given under s 220A, see Sch 8 para 16, Sch 12 para 14; and PARA 132 et
    seq.
6   The appropriate court (as defined: see the Criminal Justice Act 2003 Sch 8 para 16, Sch 12
    para 14) may, on an application by the offender, give permission in a case in which the
    responsible officer has refused: Criminal Justice Act 2003 s 220A(2), (8) (as added: see note 4).
7   Criminal Justice Act 2003 s 220A(4)(a) (as added: see note 4).
8   Criminal Justice Act 2003 s 220A(4)(b) (as added: see note 4).
9   Ie proceedings under the Criminal Justice Act 2003 Sch 8 (see PARA 53 et seq) or Sch 12 (see
    PARA 114 et seq).
10 Criminal Justice Act 2003 s 220A(3) (as added: see note 4).

104.   Provision for review of order. A suspended sentence order[1] that imposes
one or more community requirements[2] may (except in the case of an order
imposing a drug rehabilitation requirement)[3]:

(1)   provide for the order to be reviewed periodically at specified intervals[4];
(2)   provide for each review to be made[5] at a hearing held for the purpose by
        the court responsible for the order[6] (a 'review hearing')[7];
(3)   require the offender to attend each review hearing[8]; and
(4)   provide for the an officer of a provider of probation services[9] to make to
        the court responsible for the order, before each review, a report on the
        offender's progress in complying with the community requirements[10] of
        the order[11].

If at a review held without a hearing the court[12], after considering the review
officer's report, is of the opinion that the offender's progress under the order is
no longer satisfactory, it may require the offender to attend a hearing of the court
at a specified time and place[13]. If at a review hearing the court is of the opinion
that the offender has without reasonable excuse failed to comply with any of the
community requirements of the order, it may adjourn the hearing for the purpose
of dealing with the case under its powers[14] to deal with a breach of a community
requirement[15].

1   As to the meanings of 'suspended sentence' and 'suspended sentence order', and as to the
    making of suspended sentence orders, see PARA 100.
2   As to the community requirements which may be specified for the purposes of a suspended
    sentence order see PARA 101.
3   Criminal Justice Act 2003 s 191(1) (amended by the Legal Aid, Sentencing and Punishment of
    Offenders Act 2012 Sch 9 paras 2, 5). As to drug rehabilitation requirements see the Criminal
    Justice Act 2003 s 209; and PARA 124. Section 191(1) (see the text and notes 4–11) does not
    apply in the case of an order imposing such a requirement, provision for the review of which is
    made by s 210 (see PARA 125): s 191(2).
4   Criminal Justice Act 2003 s 191(1)(a).
5   Ie subject to the Criminal Justice Act 2003 s 192(4) (see PARA 106).
6   In the Criminal Justice Act 2003 s 191 references to the court responsible for a suspended
    sentence order are references: (1) where a court is specified in the order in accordance with
    s 192(4), to that court (s 191(3)(a)); and (2) in any other case, to the court by which the order
    is made (s 191(3)(b)). Where the area specified in a suspended sentence order made by a
    magistrates' court is not the area for which the court acts, the court may, if it thinks fit, include
    in the order provision specifying for this purpose a magistrates' court which acts for the area
    specified in the order: s 191(4). Where a suspended sentence order has been made on an appeal
    brought from the Crown Court or from the criminal division of the Court of Appeal, it is to be
    taken for the purposes of s 191(3)(b) to have been made by the Crown Court: s 191(5).
7   Criminal Justice Act 2003 s 191(1)(b).
8   Criminal Justice Act 2003 s 191(1)(c).
9   As to the provision of probation services see PARAS 666–687.
10 As to the meaning of 'community requirements' see the Criminal Justice Act 2003 s 189(7)(c);
    and PARAS 100, 101.

11 Criminal Justice Act 2003 s 191(1)(d) (amended by the Offender Rehabilitation Act 2014 Sch 4 para 2).

12 In the Criminal Justice Act 2003 s 192, any reference to the court, in relation to a review without a hearing, is to be read: (1) in the case of the Crown Court, as a reference to a judge of the court (s 192(8)(a)); and (2) in the case of a magistrates' court, as a reference to a justice of the peace (s 192(8)(b) (amended by SI 2005/886)).

13 Criminal Justice Act 2003 s 192(5) (amended by the Offender Rehabilitation Act 2014 Sch 4 para 3(3)).

14 Ie under the Criminal Justice Act 2003 Sch 12 para 8 (see PARA 117).

15 Criminal Justice Act 2003 s 192(6).

(ii) Amending the Order

105. Amendment of substantive provisions following review. At a review hearing[1] of a suspended sentence order[2] the court[3] may, after considering the review officer's report[4], amend the community requirements[5] of the order, or any provision of the order which relates to those requirements[6]. However the court:

(1)   may not amend the community requirements of the order so as to impose a requirement of a different kind unless the offender expresses his willingness to comply with that requirement[7];

(2)   may not amend a mental health treatment requirement[8], a drug rehabilitation requirement[9] or an alcohol treatment requirement[10] unless the offender expresses his willingness to comply with the requirement as amended[11];

(3)   may amend the supervision period[12] only if the period as amended complies with specified provisions[13];

(4)   may not amend the operational period[14] of the suspended sentence[15]; and

(5)   except with the consent of the offender, may not amend the order while an appeal against it is pending[16].

1 Ie within the meaning of the Criminal Justice Act 2003 s 191(1) (see PARA 104).

2 As to the meanings of 'suspended sentence' and 'suspended sentence order', and as to the making of suspended sentence orders, see PARA 100.

3 As to the meaning of 'court' see PARAS 1 note 1, 104 note 12.

4 Ie the report referred to in the Criminal Justice Act 2003 s 191(1).

5 As to the community requirements which may be specified for the purposes of a suspended sentence order see PARA 101.

6 Criminal Justice Act 2003 s 192(1) (amended by the Offender Rehabilitation Act 2014 Sch 4 para 3(2)).

7 Criminal Justice Act 2003 s 192(2)(a). For these purposes, a community requirement falling within any of s 190(1) (see PARA 101) is of the same kind as any other community requirement falling within those provisions (s 192(3)(a)); and an electronic monitoring requirement (as from a day to be appointed, an electronic monitoring requirement within s 215(1)(a)) (see PARA 136) is a community requirement of the same kind as any requirement falling within s 190(1) (as from a day to be appointed, s 190(1)(a)–(l)) to which it relates (s 192(3)(b) prospectively amended by the Crime and Courts Act 2013 Sch 16 paras 11, 14)). At the date at which this volume states the law no day had been appointed for the coming into force of these amendments.

8 See the Criminal Justice Act 2003 s 207; and PARA 128.

9 See the Criminal Justice Act 2003 s 209; and PARA 124.

10 See the Criminal Justice Act 2003 s 212; and PARA 122.

11 Criminal Justice Act 2003 s 192(2)(b).

12 As to the supervision period see PARA 100.

13 Criminal Justice Act 2003 s 192(2)(c). The specified provisions are s 189(3), (4) (see PARA 100).

14 As to the operational period see PARA 100.

15 Criminal Justice Act 2003 s 192(2)(d).

16 Criminal Justice Act 2003 s 192(2)(e).

106. Amendment of review provisions following review. If at any review of a suspended sentence order[1] the court[2], after considering the review officer's report[3] but before the review hearing is held, is of the opinion that the offender's progress in complying with the community requirements[4] of the order is satisfactory, it may order that no review hearing is to be held at that review; and if at any review, before a review hearing is held or at a review hearing, the court, after considering that report, is of that opinion, it may amend the suspended sentence order so as to provide for each subsequent review to be held without a hearing[5].

At a review hearing the court may amend the suspended sentence order so as to vary the intervals for periodic review specified[6] in it[7].

1   As to the meanings of 'suspended sentence' and 'suspended sentence order', and as to the making of suspended sentence orders, see PARA 100.
2   As to the meaning of 'court' see PARAS 1 note 1, 104 note 12.
3   See PARA 105.
4   As to the community requirements which may be specified for the purposes of a suspended sentence order see PARA 101.
5   Criminal Justice Act 2003 s 192(4) (amended by the Offender Rehabilitation Act 2014 Sch 4 para 3(3)).
6   Ie specified under the Criminal Justice Act 2003 s 191(1) (see PARA 104).
7   Criminal Justice Act 2003 s 192(7).

107. Cancellation of community requirements. Where, at any time while a suspended sentence order[1] which imposes one or more community requirements[2] is in force, it appears to the appropriate court[3] on the application of the offender[4] or an officer of a provider of probation service that, having regard to the circumstances which have arisen since the order was made, it would be in the interests of justice to do so, the court may cancel the community requirements of the suspended sentence order[5]. The circumstances in which the appropriate court may exercise this power include the offender's making good progress or his responding satisfactorily to supervision[6].

1   As to the meanings of 'suspended sentence' and 'suspended sentence order', and as to the making of suspended sentence orders, see PARA 100.
2   As to the community requirements which may be specified for the purposes of a suspended sentence order see PARA 101.
3   For these purposes 'appropriate court' means: (1) in the case of a suspended sentence order which is subject to review, the court responsible for the order (Criminal Justice Act 2003 Sch 12 paras 13(3)(a), 14(4), 15(6), 16(4), 18(2) (Sch 12 para 14(4) substituted by the Offender Rehabilitation Act 2014 s 18(1), (8))); (2) in the case of a suspended sentence order which was made by the Crown Court and does not include any direction that any failure to comply with the community requirements of the order is to be dealt with by a magistrates' court, the Crown Court (Criminal Justice Act 2003 Sch 12 para 13(3)(b)); and (3) in any other case, a magistrates' court acting in the local justice area concerned (Sch 12 para 13(3)(c) (amended by SI 2005/886). In the Criminal Justice Act 2003 Sch 12 any reference to a suspended sentence order being subject to review is a reference to such an order being subject to review in accordance with s 191(1)(b) (see PARA 104) or to a drug rehabilitation requirement of such an order being subject to review in accordance with s 210(1)(b) (see PARA 125) (Sch 12 para 2(a)) and any reference to the court responsible for a suspended sentence order which is subject to review is to be construed in accordance with s 191(3) (see PARA 104) or, as the case may be, s 210(2) (see PARA 125) (Sch 12 para 2(b)). Where a suspended sentence order made or amended in accordance with Sch 13 para 1 or Sch 13 para 6 (see PARA 119) is in force in respect of an offender, any reference to the appropriate court has effect as a reference to the original court: Sch 13 para 12(1), (4). As to the meaning of 'original court' for those purposes see PARA 120 note 10.

    'Local justice area concerned', in relation to a suspended sentence order, means the local justice area for the time being specified in the order: Criminal Justice Act 2003 Sch 12 para 1 (amended by SI 2005/886). Where a suspended sentence order made or amended in accordance with the Criminal Justice Act 2003 Sch 13 para 1 or Sch 13 para 6 is in force in respect of an offender, any reference to a magistrates' court acting in the local justice area concerned has effect as a reference to a magistrates' court acting in the same local justice area as the original court; and any reference to a justice of the peace acting in the local justice area concerned has effect as a reference to a justice of the peace acting in the same local justice area as that court: Sch 13 para 12(3) (amended by SI 2005/886).

4   In connection with applications to the court see the Criminal Procedure Rules 2015, SI 2015/1490, rr 32.1–32.4. For these purposes the 'offender' is the person in respect of whom a suspended sentence order is made: Criminal Justice Act 2003 Sch 12 para 1.

5   Criminal Justice Act 2003 Sch 12 paras 12B, 13(1) (Sch 12 para 12B added by the Legal Aid, Sentencing and Punishment of Offenders Act 2014 Sch 9 paras 2, 11; Criminal Justice Act 2003 Sch 12 para 13(1) amended by the Offender Rehabilitation Act 2014 Sch 4 paras 1, 7). No application may be made under the Criminal Justice Act 2003 Sch 12 para 13 while an appeal against the suspended sentence is pending: Sch 12 para 19(1).

6   Criminal Justice Act 2003 Sch 12 para 13(2).

108.   Amendment of community requirements. Where a suspended sentence order[1] which imposes one or more community requirements[2] is in force, the appropriate court[3] may, at any time during the supervision period[4] and on the application[5] of the offender or an officer of a provider of probation services, by order amend any community requirement of a suspended sentence order either by cancelling the requirement[6] or by replacing it with a requirement of the same kind[7] which the court could include if it were then making the order[8]. The court may not so amend a mental health treatment requirement, a drug rehabilitation requirement or an alcohol treatment requirement unless the offender expresses his willingness to comply with the requirement as amended[9]. If the offender fails to express his willingness to comply with a mental health treatment requirement, a drug rehabilitation requirement or an alcohol treatment requirement as proposed to be so amended by the court, the court may revoke the suspended sentence order and the suspended sentence to which it relates[10] and deal with him, for the offence in respect of which the suspended sentence was imposed, in any way in which it could have dealt with him if he had just been convicted by or before the court of the offence[11].

1   As to the meanings of 'suspended sentence' and 'suspended sentence order', and as to the making of suspended sentence orders, see PARA 100.

2   As to the community requirements which may be specified for the purposes of a suspended sentence order see PARA 101.

3   As to the meaning of 'appropriate court' see PARA 107 note 3.

4   As to the supervision period see PARA 100.

5   In connection with applications to the court see the Criminal Procedure Rules 2015, SI 2015/1490, rr 32.1–32.4. No application may be made under these provisions while an appeal against the suspended sentence is pending: Criminal Justice Act 2003 Sch 12 para 19(1). However, this does not apply to an application which relates to a mental health treatment requirement (see PARA 128), a drug rehabilitation requirement (see PARA 124) or an alcohol treatment requirement (see PARA 122) and which is made by an officer of a provider of probation services with the consent of the offender: Sch 12 para 19(2) (Sch 12 paras 15(1), 19(2) amended by the Offender Rehabilitation Act 2014 Sch 4 paras 1, 7). As to the meaning of 'offender' see PARA 107 note 4.

Where a court proposes to exercise its powers under these provisions otherwise than on the application of the offender, the court must summon him to appear before the court (Criminal Justice Act 2003 Sch 12 para 20(1)(a)) and, if he does not appear in answer to the summons, it may issue a warrant for his arrest (Sch 12 para 20(1)(b)). However, this does not apply to an order cancelling any community requirement of a suspended sentence order: Sch 12 para 20(2).

6   Criminal Justice Act 2003 Sch 12 paras 12B, 15(1)(a) (Sch 12 para 12B added by the Legal Aid, Sentencing and Punishment of Offenders Act 2014 Sch 9 paras 2, 11; Criminal Justice Act 2003 Sch 12 para 15(1) as amended (see note 5)).

7   For these purposes, a requirement falling within any of the Criminal Justice Act 2003 s 190(1)(a)–(m) (see PARA 101) is of the same kind as any other requirement falling within that provision (Sch 12 para 15(2)(a)); and an electronic monitoring requirement (as from a day to be

appointed, an electronic monitoring requirement within s 215(1)(a)) (see PARA 136) is a community requirement of the same kind as any requirement falling within s 190(1) (as from a day to be appointed, s 190(1)(a)–(l)) to which it relates (s 192(3)(b) prospectively amended by the Crime and Courts Act 2013 Sch 16 paras 11, 21)). At the date at which this volume states the law no day had been appointed for the coming into force of these amendments.

8   Criminal Justice Act 2003 Sch 12 para 15(1)(b). This provision has effect subject to the provisions referred to in s 190(2) (see PARA 100) and s 190(3)–(5) (see PARA 101): Sch 12 para 21.
9   Criminal Justice Act 2003 Sch 12 para 15(3).
10 Criminal Justice Act 2003 Sch 12 para 15(4)(a).
11 Criminal Justice Act 2003 Sch 12 para 15(4)(b). In so dealing with the offender the court must take into account the extent to which the offender has complied with the requirements of the order: Sch 12 para 15(5).

109.   Amendment by reason of change of residence. Where at any time while a suspended sentence order[1] which imposes one or more community requirements[2] is in force in respect of an offender[3] the offender is given permission[4] to change residence[5] and the local justice area in which the new residence is situated ('the new local justice area') is different from the local justice area specified in the order[6], then:

(1)   if the permission is given by a court, the court must amend the order to specify the new local justice area[7]; and

(2)   as from a day to be appointed, if the permission is given by the responsible officer[8], the officer must apply to the appropriate court[9] to amend the order to specify the new local justice area[10] and the court must make that amendment[11].

Where at any time while a suspended sentence order which imposes one or more community requirements is in force in respect of an offender:

(a)   a court amends the order[12];

(b)   the order as amended includes a residence requirement[13] requiring the offender to reside at a specified place[14]; and

(c)   the local justice area in which that place is situated ('the new local justice area') is different from the local justice area specified in the order[15],

the court must amend the order to specify the new local justice area[16].

1   As to the meanings of 'suspended sentence' and 'suspended sentence order', and as to the making of suspended sentence orders, see PARA 100.
2   As to the community requirements which may be specified for the purposes of a suspended sentence order see PARA 101.
3   As to the meaning of 'offender' see PARA 107 note 4.
4   Ie under the Criminal Justice Act 2003 s 220A (see PARA 103).
5   Criminal Justice Act 2003 Sch 12 paras 12B, 14(1)(a) (Sch 12 para 12B added by the Legal Aid, Sentencing and Punishment of Offenders Act 2014 Sch 9 paras 2, 11; Criminal Justice Act 2003 Sch 12 para 14 substituted, Sch 12 para 14A added, by the Offender Rehabilitation Act 2014 s 18(1), (8)). At the date at which this volume states the law the substituted Criminal Justice Act 2003 Sch 12 para 14(3) had yet to be brought into force: see the Offender Rehabilitation Act 2014 (Commencement No 2) Order 2015, SI 2015/40, art 2(p)(ii).
6   Criminal Justice Act 2003 Sch 12 para 14(1)(b) (as substituted: see note 5).
7   Criminal Justice Act 2003 Sch 12 para 14(2) (as substituted: see note 5).
8   As to the meaning of 'responsible officer' see the Criminal Justice Act 2003 s 197; and PARA 51 note 2. See also PARA 104 note 6.
9   In connection with applications to the court see the Criminal Procedure Rules 2015, SI 2015/1490, rr 32.1–32.4. As to the meaning of 'appropriate court' see PARA 107 note 3.
10 Criminal Justice Act 2003 Sch 12 para 14(3)(a) (prospectively substituted: see note 5).
11 Criminal Justice Act 2003 Sch 12 para 14(3)(b) (prospectively substituted: see note 5).
12 Criminal Justice Act 2003 Sch 12 para 14A(1)(a) (as added: see note 5).
13 See PARA 132.

14 Criminal Justice Act 2003 Sch 12 para 14A(1)(b) (as added: see note 5).
15 Criminal Justice Act 2003 Sch 12 para 14A(1)(c) (as added: see note 5).
16 Criminal Justice Act 2003 Sch 12 para 14A(2) (as added: see note 5).

110.   Amendment of treatment requirements of suspended sentence order on report of practitioner. Where a suspended sentence order[1] which imposes one or more community requirements[2] is in force and the medical practitioner or other person by whom or under whose direction an offender[3] is, in pursuance of a mental health treatment requirement[4], a drug rehabilitation requirement[5] or an alcohol treatment requirement[6], being treated for his mental condition or his dependency on or propensity to misuse drugs or alcohol:

(1) is of the opinion that the treatment of the offender should be continued beyond the period specified in that behalf in the order[7], that the offender needs different treatment[8], that the offender is not susceptible to treatment[9], or that the offender does not require further treatment[10]; or

(2) is for any reason unwilling to continue to treat or direct the treatment of the offender[11],

he must make a report in writing to that effect to the responsible officer[12] and that officer must cause an application to be made[13] to the appropriate court[14] for the variation or cancellation of the requirement[15].

1 As to the meanings of 'suspended sentence' and 'suspended sentence order', and as to the making of suspended sentence orders, see PARA 100.
2 As to the community requirements which may be specified for the purposes of a suspended sentence order see PARA 101.
3 As to the meaning of 'offender' see PARA 107 note 4.
4 Criminal Justice Act 2003 Sch 12 paras 12B, 16(1), (2)(a) (Sch 12 para 12B added by the Legal Aid, Sentencing and Punishment of Offenders Act 2014 Sch 9 paras 2, 11). As to a mental health treatment requirement see PARA 128.
5 Criminal Justice Act 2003 Sch 12 para 16(2)(b). As to a drug rehabilitation requirement see PARA 124.
6 Criminal Justice Act 2003 Sch 12 para 16(2)(c). As to an alcohol treatment requirement see PARA 122.
7 Criminal Justice Act 2003 Sch 12 para 16(1)(a), (3)(a).
8 Criminal Justice Act 2003 Sch 12 para 16(3)(b).
9 Criminal Justice Act 2003 Sch 12 para 16(3)(c).
10 Criminal Justice Act 2003 Sch 12 para 16(3)(d).
11 Criminal Justice Act 2003 Sch 12 para 16(1)(b).
12 As to the meaning of 'responsible officer' see the Criminal Justice Act 2003 s 197; and PARA 51 note 2. See also PARA 104 note 6.
13 Ie under the Criminal Justice Act 2003 Sch 12 para 15 (see PARA 108). In connection with applications to the court see the Criminal Procedure Rules 2015, SI 2015/1490, rr 32.1–32.4.
14 As to the meaning of 'appropriate court' see PARA 107 note 3.
15 Criminal Justice Act 2003 Sch 12 para 16(1) (amended by the Offender Rehabilitation Act 2014 Sch 4 paras 1, 7(1), (7)).

111.   Amendment in relation to review of drug rehabilitation requirement. Where an officer of a provider of probation services is of the opinion that a suspended sentence order[1] imposing a drug rehabilitation requirement[2] which is subject to review should be so amended as to provide for each periodic review[3] to be made without a hearing instead of at a review hearing, or vice versa, he must apply[4] to the court responsible for the order for the variation of the order[5].

1 As to the meanings of 'suspended sentence' and 'suspended sentence order', and as to the making of suspended sentence orders, see PARA 100.
2 As to a drug rehabilitation requirement see PARA 124.

3   Ie each periodic review required by the Criminal Justice Act 2003 s 211 (see PARA 125). As to 'subject to review' see PARA 107 note 3.
4   Ie under the Criminal Justice Act 2003 Sch 12 para 15 (see PARA 108). In connection with applications to the court see the Criminal Procedure Rules 2015, SI 2015/1490, rr 32.1–32.4.
5   Criminal Justice Act 2003 Sch 12 para 17 (amended by the Offender Rehabilitation Act 2014 Sch 4 paras 1, 7(1), (6)).

112. Extension of unpaid work requirement. Where:

(1)   a suspended sentence order[1] which imposes an unpaid work requirement[2] is in force in respect of an offender[3]; and

(2)   on the application[4] of the offender or an officer of a provider of probation services it appears to the appropriate court[5] that it would be in the interests of justice to do so having regard to circumstances which have arisen since the order was made[6],

the court may, in relation to the order, extend the specified[7] period of 12 months[8].

1   As to the meanings of 'suspended sentence' and 'suspended sentence order', and as to the making of suspended sentence orders, see PARA 100.
2   As to an unpaid work requirement see PARA 133.
3   Criminal Justice Act 2003 Sch 12 para 18(1)(a). As to the meaning of 'offender' see PARA 107 note 4.
4   In connection with applications to the court see the Criminal Procedure Rules 2015, SI 2015/1490, rr 32.1–32.4. No application may be made under these provisions while an appeal against the suspended sentence order is pending: Criminal Justice Act 2003 Sch 12 para 19(1).
5   As to the meaning of 'appropriate court' see PARA 107 note 3.
6   Criminal Justice Act 2003 Sch 12 para 18(1)(b).
7   Ie specified by the Criminal Justice Act 2003 s 200(2) (see PARA 133).
8   Criminal Justice Act 2003 Sch 12 para 18(1).

113. Administration of amendments. On the making of an order amending a suspended sentence order[1] the proper officer[2] of the court must:

(1)   provide copies of the amending order to the offender[3] and the responsible officer[4];

(2)   in the case of an amending order which substitutes a new local justice area, provide a copy of the amending order to a provider of probation services that is a public sector provider[5] operating in that area[6] and the magistrates' court acting in that area[7];

(3)   in the case of an amending order which imposes or amends a specified requirement[8], provide a copy of so much of the amending order as relates to that requirement to the person specified[9] in relation to that requirement[10]; and

(4)   where the court acts in a local justice area other than the one specified in the order prior to the revocation or amendment, provide a copy of the amending order to a magistrates' court acting in the area so specified[11].

1   As to the meanings of 'suspended sentence' and 'suspended sentence order', and as to the making of suspended sentence orders, see PARA 100.
2   Ie, in relation to a magistrates' court, the designated officer for the court (Criminal Justice Act 2003 Sch 12 para 22(3)(a) (Sch 12 para 22(2), (3)(a) amended by SI 2005/886)) and, in relation to the Crown Court, the appropriate officer (Criminal Justice Act 2003 Sch 12 para 22(3)(b)).
3   As to the meaning of 'offender' see PARA 107 note 4.

4   Criminal Justice Act 2003 Sch 12 para 22(1)(a). As to the meaning of 'responsible officer' see the Criminal Justice Act 2003 s 197; and PARA 51 note 2. See also PARA 104 note 6. In connection with the notification requirements see the Criminal Procedure Rules 2015, SI 2015/1490, r 28.2.

5   'Public sector provider' means a probation trust or other public body or the Secretary of State: Criminal Justice Act 2003 Sch 12 para 22(4) (Sch 12 para 22(1)(b) substituted, Sch 12 para 22(4) added, by the Offender Rehabilitation Act 2014 Sch 4 paras 10, 15(1)–(3)).

6   Criminal Justice Act 2003 Sch 12 para 22(1)(b)(i) (as substituted: see note 5). As to the provision of probation services see PARAS 666–687. Where the proper officer of the court so provides a copy of an amending order to a magistrates' court acting in a different area, the officer must also provide to that court documents and information relating to the case likely to be of assistance to a court acting in that area in the exercise of its functions in relation to the order: Sch 12 para 22(2) (as amended: see note 2).

7   Criminal Justice Act 2003 Sch 12 para 22(1)(b)(ii) (as substituted: see note 5).

8   Ie a requirement specified in the first column of the Criminal Justice Act 2003 Sch 14 (see PARA 122 et seq).

9   Ie specified in the second column of the Criminal Justice Act 2003 Sch 14.

10 Criminal Justice Act 2003 Sch 12 para 22(1)(c).

11 Criminal Justice Act 2003 Sch 12 para 22(1)(d) (added by the Domestic Violence, Crime and Victims Act 2004 Sch 5 para 8(1), (5)).

(iii) Breach of Order and Effect of Further Conviction

114. Warning and subsequent breach. Where a suspended sentence order[1] is in force and the responsible officer[2] is of the opinion that the offender[3] has failed without reasonable excuse to comply with any of the community requirements[4] of the order, he must give the offender a warning[5] unless either:

(1)   the offender has within the previous 12 months been given such a warning in relation to a failure to comply with any of the community requirements of the order[6]; or

(2)   the officer refers the matter to an enforcement officer[7].

If the responsible officer has given such a warning to the offender in respect of a suspended sentence order[8] and at any time within the 12 months beginning with the date on which the warning was given the responsible officer is of the opinion that the offender has since that date failed without reasonable excuse to comply with any of the community requirements of the order[9], the officer must refer the matter to an enforcement officer[10].

1   As to the meanings of 'suspended sentence' and 'suspended sentence order', and as to the making of suspended sentence orders, see PARA 100.

2   As to the meaning of 'responsible officer' see the Criminal Justice Act 2003 s 197; and PARA 51 note 2. See also PARA 104 note 6.

3   As to the meaning of 'offender' see PARA 107 note 4.

4   As to the community requirements which may be specified for the purposes of a suspended sentence order see PARA 101.

5   Such a warning must:
   (1)   describe the circumstances of the failure (Criminal Justice Act 2003 Sch 12 para 4(2)(a));
   (2)   state that the failure is unacceptable (Sch 12 para 4(2)(b)); and
   (3)   inform the offender that, if within the next 12 months he again fails to comply with any requirement of the order, he will be liable to be brought before a court (Sch 12 para 4(2)(c)),
   and the responsible officer must, as soon as practicable after the warning has been given, record that fact (Sch 12 para 4(3)).

6   Criminal Justice Act 2003 Sch 12 para 4(1)(a).

7   Criminal Justice Act 2003 Sch 12 para 4(1)(b) (Sch 12 paras 1A, 5A added, Sch 12 para 4(1)(b) substituted, Sch 12 para 5(1) amended, by the Offender Rehabilitation Act 2014 Sch 4 paras 1, 7)).

'Enforcement officer' means a person who is for the time being responsible for discharging the functions conferred by the Criminal Justice Act 2003 Sch 12 on an enforcement officer in accordance with arrangements made by the Secretary of State: Sch 12 para 1A(1) (as so added). An enforcement officer must be an officer of a provider of probation services that is a public sector provider: Sch 12 para 1A(2) (as so added). For this purpose 'public sector provider' means a probation trust or other public body or the Secretary of State: Sch 12 para 1A(3) (as so added).

Where a matter is referred to an enforcement officer under Sch 12 para 4(1)(b) or Sch 12 para 5(1) it is the duty of the enforcement officer to consider the case and, where appropriate, to cause an information to be laid before a justice of the peace in respect of the offender's failure to comply with the requirement: Sch 12 para 5A(1) (as so added). In relation to any suspended sentence order which was made by the Crown Court and does not include a direction that any failure to comply with the requirements of the order is to be dealt with by a magistrates' court, the reference in Sch 12 para 5A(1) to a justice of the peace is to be read as a reference to the Crown Court: Sch 12 para 5A(2) (as so added).

Where a suspended sentence order made or amended in accordance with Sch 13 para 1 or Sch 13 para 6 (see PARA 119) is in force in respect of an offender, any reference in Sch 12 para 4 or Sch 12 para 5 to causing an information to be laid before a justice of the peace has effect as a reference either to providing information to the home court with a view to it issuing a citation (if the home court is in Scotland) (Sch 13 para 12(1), (5)(a)) or to making a complaint to a justice of the peace in Northern Ireland (if the home court is in Northern Ireland) (Sch 13 para 12(5)(b)). As to the meaning of 'home court' for these purposes see PARA 120 note 2.

8   Criminal Justice Act 2003 Sch 12 para 5(1)(a).
9   Criminal Justice Act 2003 Sch 12 para 5(1)(b).
10   Criminal Justice Act 2003 Sch 12 para 5(1) (as amended: see note 8).

115. Failure to comply with order made or enforceable by magistrates' court.
If a suspended sentence order[1] is enforceable by a magistrates' court[2] and at any time while the order is in force it appears on information to a justice of the peace that the offender[3] has failed to comply with any of the community requirements of the order, the justice of the peace may either issue a summons requiring the offender to appear at the place and time specified in it[4] or, if the information is in writing and on oath, issue a warrant for the offender's arrest[5]. Any such summons or warrant must direct the offender to appear or be brought:

(1)   in the case of a suspended sentence order which is subject to review[6], before the court responsible for the order[7]; or

(2)   in any other case, before a magistrates' court acting in the local justice area in which the offender resides or, if it is not known where he resides, before a magistrates' court acting in the local justice area concerned[8].

1   As to the meanings of 'suspended sentence' and 'suspended sentence order', and as to the making of suspended sentence orders, see PARA 100.
2   Thus these provisions apply to:
    (1)   any suspended sentence order made by a magistrates' court (Criminal Justice Act 2003 Sch 12 para 6(1)(a)); and
    (2)   any suspended sentence order which was made by the Crown Court and includes a direction that any failure to comply with the community requirements of the order is to be dealt with by a magistrates' court (Sch 12 para 6(1)(b)).
    As to the community requirements which may be specified for the purposes of a suspended sentence order see PARA 101.
3   As to the meaning of 'offender' see PARA 107 note 4.
4   Criminal Justice Act 2003 Sch 12 para 6(2)(a) (Sch 12 para 6(2) amended, Sch 12 para 6(3)(b) substituted, Sch 13 para 12(5A) added, by the Domestic Violence, Crime and Victims Act 2004 Sch 5 para 8(1)–(3), 9). Where such a summons requires the offender to appear before a magistrates' court and the offender does not appear in answer to the summons, the magistrates' court may issue a warrant for the arrest of the offender: Criminal Justice Act 2003 Sch 12 para 6(4).
5   Criminal Justice Act 2003 Sch 12 para 6(2)(b).
6   As to 'subject to review' see PARA 107 note 3.
7   Criminal Justice Act 2003 Sch 12 para 6(3)(a).

8   Criminal Justice Act 2003 Sch 12 para 6(3)(b) (as substituted: see note 4). Where a suspended sentence order made or amended in accordance with Sch 13 para 1 or Sch 13 para 6 (see PARA 119) is in force in respect of an offender, the summons or warrant must direct the offender to appear or be brought, in any case other than that of a suspended sentence order which is subject to review, before a magistrates' court acting in the local justice area concerned: Sch 13 para 12(5A) (as so added).

116. Failure to comply with order enforceable by the Crown Court. If at any time while a suspended sentence order[1] made by the Crown Court, which does not include a direction that any failure to comply with the community requirements[2] of the order is to be dealt with by a magistrates' court[3], is in force it appears on information to the Crown Court that the offender has failed to comply with any of the community requirements of the order, the Crown Court may issue a summons requiring the offender to appear at the place and time specified in it[4] or, if the information is in writing and on oath, issue a warrant for his arrest[5]. Any such summons or warrant must direct the offender to appear or be brought before the Crown Court[6].

1   As to the meanings of 'suspended sentence' and 'suspended sentence order', and as to the making of suspended sentence orders, see PARA 100.
2   As to the community requirements which may be specified for the purposes of a suspended sentence order see PARA 101.
3   See PARA 115.
4   Criminal Justice Act 2003 Sch 12 para 7(1), (2)(a). Where such a summons requires the offender to appear before the Crown Court and the offender does not appear in answer to the summons, the Crown Court may issue a warrant for the arrest of the offender: Sch 12 para 7(4).
5   Criminal Justice Act 2003 Sch 12 para 7(2)(b).
6   Criminal Justice Act 2003 Sch 12 para 7(3).

117. Powers of courts on failure to comply or subsequent conviction. If a suspended sentence order[1] is in force and:

(1)   it is proved to the satisfaction of a court before which an offender[2] appears or is brought[3] that he has failed without reasonable excuse to comply with any of the community requirements[4] of the order[5]; and

(2)   an offender is convicted of an offence committed during the operational period[6] of a suspended sentence (other than one which has already taken effect) and either he is so convicted by or before a court having power[7] to deal with him in respect of the suspended sentence[8] or he subsequently appears or is brought before a court[9],

the court must consider his case[10] and may:

(a)   order that the suspended sentence is to take effect with its original term unaltered[11];

(b)   order that the sentence is to take effect with the substitution for the original term of a lesser term[12];

(c)   order the offender to pay a fine[13];

(d)   in the case of an order that imposes one or more community requirements, amend the order by imposing more onerous requirements which the court could include if it were then making the order[14], extending[15] the supervision period[16], or extending[17] the operational period[18]; or

(e)   in the case of an order that does not impose any community requirements, amend the order[19] by extending the operational period[20].

The court must make an order under head (a) or head (b) above unless it is of the opinion that it would be unjust to do so in view of all the circumstances[21]; and where it is of that opinion the court must state its reasons[22].

1   As to the meanings of 'suspended sentence' and 'suspended sentence order', and as to the making of suspended sentence orders, see PARA 100.
2   As to the meaning of 'offender' see PARA 107 note 4.
3   Ie under the Criminal Justice Act 2003 Sch 12 para 6 or Sch 12 para 7 (see PARAS 115–116) or by virtue of s 192(6) (see PARA 104).
4   As to the community requirements which may be specified for the purposes of a suspended sentence order see PARA 101.
5   Criminal Justice Act 2003 Sch 12 para 8(1)(a). In proceedings before the Crown Court under Sch 12 para 8 any question whether the offender has failed to comply with any community requirements of the suspended sentence order is to be determined by the court and not by the verdict of a jury: Sch 12 para 8(8) (Sch 12 paras 8(2)(b), (2)(c), (4)(a), (6), 9(1) amended, Sch 12 paras 8(2)(ba), (d), (4)(za), 12A added, by the Legal Aid, Sentencing and Punishment of Offenders Act 2012 s 69(1)–(3), Sch 9 paras 2, 10, Sch 10 paras 12, 38(1)–(3)). An offender who is required by a mental health treatment requirement (see PARA 128), a drug rehabilitation requirement (see PARA 124) or an alcohol treatment requirement (see PARA 122) to submit to treatment for his mental condition, or his dependency on or propensity to misuse drugs or alcohol, is not to be treated for these purposes as having failed to comply with that requirement on the ground only that he had refused to undergo any surgical, electrical or other treatment if, in the opinion of the court, his refusal was reasonable having regard to all the circumstances: Criminal Justice Act 2003 Sch 12 para 10(1).
6   As to the operational period see PARA 100.
7   Ie under the Criminal Justice Act 2003 Sch 12 para 11, which provides that:
     (1)   an offender may be dealt with under Sch 12 para 8(1)(b) in respect of a suspended sentence by the Crown Court or, where the sentence was passed by a magistrates' court, by any magistrates' court before which he appears or is brought (Sch 12 para 11(1)); and
     (2)   where an offender is convicted by a magistrates' court of any offence and the court is satisfied that the offence was committed during the operational period of a suspended sentence passed by the Crown Court, the court may, if it thinks fit, commit him in custody or on bail to the Crown Court and, if it does not, must give written notice of the conviction to the appropriate officer of the Crown Court (Sch 12 para 11(2)).
     In connection with the Crown Court's powers under Sch 12 para 11(2) see *R v Bateman* [2012] EWCA Crim 2518, [2013] 1 WLR 1710, [2013] 2 Cr App Rep (S) 174.
8   Criminal Justice Act 2003 Sch 12 para 8(1)(b)(i). See Sch 12 para 11; and note 7.
9   Criminal Justice Act 2003 Sch 12 para 8(1)(b)(ii). See Sch 12 para 11; and note 7. In proceedings before the Crown Court any question whether the offender has been convicted of an offence committed during the operational period of the suspended sentence is to be determined by the court and not by the verdict of a jury: Sch 12 para 8(8).
10   Where a suspended sentence order was made by the Crown Court and a magistrates' court would otherwise be required to deal with the offender under head (a), (b), (c) or (d) in the text, it may instead commit him to custody or release him on bail until he can be brought or appear before the Crown Court: Criminal Justice Act 2003 Sch 12 para 8(6) (as amended: see note 5). A magistrates' court which deals with an offender's case under Sch 12 para 8(6) must send to the Crown Court:
     (1)   a certificate signed by a justice of the peace certifying that the offender has failed to comply with the community requirements of the suspended sentence order in the respect specified in the certificate (Sch 12 para 8(7)(a)); and
     (2)   such other particulars of the case as may be desirable (Sch 12 para 8(7)(b)),
     and a certificate purporting to be so signed is admissible as evidence of the failure before the Crown Court (Sch 12 para 8(7)).
11   Criminal Justice Act 2003 Sch 12 para 8(2)(a) (as amended: see note 5). Time spent on remand is automatically deducted when a suspended sentence is activated: see s 240ZA; and PARA 30. The proper approach where a new offence has been committed during the period of suspension of an earlier sentence is that the court should first sentence the defendant in respect of the new offence and thereafter address itself to the question of the suspended sentence: see *R v Ithell* [1969] 2 All ER 449, 53 Cr App Rep 210, CA. In connection with the activation of the original term following failure to comply with community requirements see *R v Sheppard* [2008] EWCA Crim 799, [2008] 2 Cr App Rep (S) 524, [2008] All ER (D) 54 (May).
     When making an order under the Criminal Justice Act 2003 Sch 12 para 8(2)(a) or (b) that a sentence is to take effect (with or without any variation of the original term), the court may order that the sentence is to take effect immediately or that the term of the sentence is to commence on the expiry of another term of imprisonment passed on the offender by that or

another court: Sch 12 para 9(1)(b) (as so amended). The power to make such an order has effect subject to the restriction under s 265 (see PARA 27) on consecutive sentences for released prisoners: Sch 12 para 9(2).

Where a court deals with an offender under Sch 12 para 8(2), the appropriate officer of the court must notify the appropriate officer of the court which passed the sentence of the method adopted: Sch 12 para 8(5).

For the purpose of any enactment conferring rights of appeal in criminal cases, any order made by the court under head (a) or head (b) above, and an order made by the court under the Prosecution of Offences Act 1985 s 21A (criminal courts charge: see CRIMINAL PROCEDURE) when making an order under head (a) above, is to be treated as a sentence passed on the offender by that court for the offence for which the suspended sentence was passed: Criminal Justice Act 2003 Sch 12 para 9(3) (amended by the Criminal Justice and Courts Act 2015 Sch 12 para 16).

12 Criminal Justice Act 2003 Sch 12 para 8(2)(b) (as amended: see note 5).

13 Criminal Justice Act 2003 Sch 12 para 8(2)(ba) (as added: see note 5). The fine must not exceed £2,500: Sch 12 para 8(2)(ba) (as so added). A fine imposed under Sch 12 para 8(2)(ba) is treated, for the purposes of any enactment, as being a sum adjudged to be paid by a conviction: Sch 12 para 8(4ZA) (as so added).

The Secretary of State may by order amend the sum for the time being specified in Sch 12 para 8(2)(ba) (Sch 12 para 12A(1) (as so added)) if it appears to him that there has been a change in the value of money since 3 December 2012 which justifies the change (Sch 12 para 12A(2), (3) (as so added); Legal Aid, Sentencing and Punishment of Offenders Act 2012 (Commencement No 4 and Saving Provisions) Order 2012, SI 2012/2906). An order under the Criminal Justice Act 2003 Sch 12 para 12A(1) (a 'fine amendment order') must not have effect in relation to any suspended sentence order made in respect of an offence committed before the fine amendment order comes into force: Sch 12 para 12A(4) (as so added). At the date at which this volume states the law no such order had been made.

14 Criminal Justice Act 2003 Sch 12 para 8(2)(c)(i) (as amended: see note 5); and as to this power see eg *R v Jones* [2010] EWCA Crim 3298. The Criminal Justice Act 2003 Sch 12 para 8(2)(c) has effect subject to the provisions referred to in s 190(2) (see PARA 100) and s 190(3)–(5) (see PARA 101): Sch 12 para 21. A court may not under Sch 12 para 8(2)(c)(i) amend a mental health treatment requirement, a drug rehabilitation requirement or an alcohol treatment requirement unless the offender expresses his willingness to comply with the requirement as amended: Sch 12 para 10(2).

15 Ie subject to the Criminal Justice Act 2003 s 189(3), (4) (see PARA 100).

16 Criminal Justice Act 2003 Sch 12 para 8(2)(c)(ii). See note 14.

17 Ie subject to the Criminal Justice Act 2003 s 189(3).

18 Criminal Justice Act 2003 Sch 12 para 8(2)(c)(iii). See note 14.

19 Ie subject to the Criminal Justice Act 2003 s 189(3).

20 Criminal Justice Act 2003 Sch 12 para 8(2)(d) (as added: see note 5).

21 Ie including the extent to which the offender has complied with any community requirements of the suspended sentence order (Criminal Justice Act 2003 Sch 12 para 8(4)(a) (as amended: see note 5)) and, in a case falling within Sch 12 para 8(1)(b) (see head (2) in the text), the facts of the subsequent offence (Sch 12 para 8(4)(b)). In this regard see further *R v Sheppard* [2008] EWCA Crim 799, [2008] 2 Cr App Rep (S) 524, [2008] All ER (D) 54 (May); *R v Zeca* [2009] EWCA Crim 133, [2009] 2 Cr App Rep (S) 460, [2009] All ER (D) 163 (May).

22 Criminal Justice Act 2003 Sch 12 para 8(3). In connection with this requirement see the Criminal Procedure Rules 2015, SI 2015/1490, r 28.1.

118. Procedure where court convicting of further offence does not deal with suspended sentence. If it appears to the Crown Court, where that court has jurisdiction[1] or to a justice of the peace having jurisdiction[2]:

(1) that an offender[3] has been convicted in the United Kingdom[4] of an offence committed during the operational period[5] of a suspended sentence[6]; and

(2) that he has not been dealt with in respect of the suspended sentence[7],

that court or justice may issue a summons requiring the offender to appear at the place and time specified in it, or a warrant for his arrest[8].

Where:

(a) an offender is convicted in Scotland or Northern Ireland of an offence[9]; and

(b) the court is informed that the offence was committed during the operational period of a suspended sentence passed in England or Wales[10],

the court must give written notice of the conviction to the appropriate officer of the court by which the suspended sentence was passed[11].

1 Jurisdiction may be exercised for these purposes: (1) if the suspended sentence was passed by the Crown Court, by that court (Criminal Justice Act 2003 Sch 12 para 12(2)(a)); and (2) if it was passed by a magistrates' court, by a justice acting in the local justice area for which that court acted (Sch 12 para 12(2)(b) (amended by SI 2005/886)).

2 Ie in accordance with the Criminal Justice Act 2003 Sch 12 para 12(2) (see note 1).

3 As to the meaning of 'offender' see PARA 107 note 4.

4 As to the meaning of 'United Kingdom' see PARA 4 note 3.

5 As to the operational period see PARA 100.

6 Criminal Justice Act 2003 Sch 12 para 12(1)(a). As to the meanings of 'suspended sentence' and 'suspended sentence order', and as to the making of suspended sentence orders, see PARA 100.

7 Criminal Justice Act 2003 Sch 12 para 12(1)(b).

8 Criminal Justice Act 2003 Sch 12 para 12(1). Such a summons or warrant must direct the offender to appear or be brought before the court by which the suspended sentence was passed: Sch 12 para 12(5).

9 Criminal Justice Act 2003 Sch 12 para 12(3)(a).

10 Criminal Justice Act 2003 Sch 12 para 12(3)(b).

11 Criminal Justice Act 2003 Sch 12 para 12(3). Unless he is acting in consequence of such a notice, a justice of the peace may not issue a summons under Sch 12 para 12 except on information and may not issue a warrant under these provisions except on information in writing and on oath: Sch 12 para 12(4).

(iv) Transfer to Scotland or Northern Ireland

119. Powers to transfer. Where the court considering the making of a suspended sentence order[1] that imposes one or more community requirements[2] is satisfied that the offender resides in Scotland or Northern Ireland, or will reside there when the order comes into force, it may not make such an order unless it appears to the court that suitable arrangements for the offender's supervision can be made by the local authority in Scotland in whose area he resides, or will be residing when the order comes into force, or by the Probation Board for Northern Ireland, as the case may be[3], and that in the case of an order imposing:

(1) an unpaid work requirement[4];

(2) a rehabilitation activity requirement[5];

(3) a programme requirement[6];

(4) a mental health treatment requirement[7];

(5) a drug rehabilitation requirement[8];

(6) an alcohol treatment requirement[9];

(7) (in Northern Ireland only) an attendance centre requirement[10]; or

(8) an electronic monitoring requirement[11],

arrangements exist for persons to comply with such a requirement in the locality in Scotland or petty sessions district in Northern Ireland, as the case may be, in which the offender resides, or will be residing when the order comes into force, and that provision can be made for him to comply with the requirement under those arrangements[12]. As from a day to be appointed, for the purposes of Northern Ireland only, it is further provided that in the case of an order imposing an electronic monitoring requirement[13] the court may not make the order referred to unless it appears to the court that any necessary provision can be made in the offender's case under arrangements that exist for persons resident in that locality[14] and that arrangements are generally operational throughout Northern Ireland (even if not always operational everywhere there) under which the offender's whereabouts can be electronically monitored[15].

Where:

(a) the appropriate court for the purposes of its powers of amendment by reason of change of residence[16] is satisfied that an offender in respect of whom a suspended sentence order is in force proposes to reside or is residing in Scotland or Northern Ireland, as the case may be[17]; and

(b) it appears to the court that the conditions which determine whether a transfer order may be made[18] are satisfied[19],

the power of the court to amend the order[20] includes power to amend it by requiring it to be complied with in Scotland or Northern Ireland, as the case may be, and the offender to be supervised in accordance with such arrangements as can be made by the local authority in Scotland in whose area he resides, or will be residing when the order or amendment comes into force, or by the Probation Board for Northern Ireland, as the case may be[21].

A suspended sentence order so made[22] must:

(i) specify the local authority area in Scotland, or the petty sessions district in Northern Ireland, as the case may be, in which the offender resides or will be residing when the order or amendment comes into force[23]; and

(ii) require the local authority for that area in Scotland or the Probation Board for Northern Ireland, as the case may be, to appoint or assign an officer who will be responsible for discharging in relation to him the functions conferred[24] on responsible officers[25].

Where a court so makes or amends a suspended sentence order it must provide the relevant documents[26] to the local authority for the area in Scotland specified in the order or the Probation Board for Northern Ireland, as the case may be[27], and to the sheriff court in Scotland having jurisdiction in the locality, or the court of summary jurisdiction acting for the petty sessions district in Northern Ireland, as the case may be, in which the offender resides or proposes to reside[28].

1   As to the meanings of 'suspended sentence' and 'suspended sentence order', and as to the making of suspended sentence orders, see PARA 100.

2   As to the community requirements which may be specified for the purposes of a suspended sentence order see PARA 101.

3   Criminal Justice Act 2003 Sch 13 paras 1(1)(b), 6(1)(b) (Sch 13 paras 1(1), (5), 6(1) amended, Sch 13 para 6(4A) added, by the Legal Aid, Sentencing and Punishment of Offenders Act 2012 s 76(10)(b), Sch 9 paras 2, 12). In the Criminal Justice Act 2003 Sch 13 Pt 1 (paras 2–5), 'local authority' means a council constituted under the Local Government etc (Scotland) Act 1994; and any reference to the area of such an authority is a reference to the local government area within the meaning of that Act: Criminal Justice Act 2003 Sch 13 para 5.

   The court may not provide for an order relating to Scotland or Northern Ireland made in accordance with Sch 13 para 1 or Sch 13 para 6 (as the case may be) to be subject to review under s 191 (see PARA 104) or s 210 (see PARA 125); and where an order which is subject to review under either of those provisions is amended in accordance with Sch 13 para 1 or Sch 13 para 6 (as the case may be), it ceases to be so subject: Sch 13 paras 1(6), 6(5).

4   Criminal Justice Act 2003 Sch 13 paras 1(2)(a), 6(2)(a). As to unpaid work requirements see s 199; and PARA 133.

5   Criminal Justice Act 2003 Sch 13 paras 1(2)(b), 6(2)(b) (Sch 13 paras 1(2)(b), 6(2)(b) substituted by the Offender Rehabilitation Act 2014 Sch 5 paras 1, 8). As to rehabilitation activity requirements see s 200A; and PARA 131.

6   Criminal Justice Act 2003 Sch 13 paras 1(2)(c), 6(2)(c). As to programme requirements see s 202; and PARA 129.

7   Criminal Justice Act 2003 Sch 13 paras 1(2)(d), 6(2)(d). As to mental health treatment requirements see s 207; and PARA 128.
8   Criminal Justice Act 2003 Sch 13 paras 1(2)(e), 6(2)(e). As to drug rehabilitation requirements see s 209; and PARA 124.
9   Criminal Justice Act 2003 Sch 13 paras 1(2)(f), 6(2)(f). As to alcohol treatment requirements see s 212; and PARA 122.
10 Criminal Justice Act 2003 Sch 13 para 6(2)(g). As to attendance centre requirements in Northern Ireland see s 214; and PARA 134. The court may not by virtue of these provisions require an alcohol abstinence and monitoring requirement or an attendance centre requirement to be complied with in Scotland or Northern Ireland: Sch 13 paras 1(5), 6(4A) (as amended and added: see note 3).
11 Criminal Justice Act 2003 Sch 13 paras 1(2)(g), 6(2)(h). As from a day to be appointed this is expressed as an electronic monitoring requirement within s 215(1)(a) (Sch 13 paras 1(2)(g), 6(2)(h) (Sch 13 paras 1(2)(g), 6(2)(h), (3)(b), (4) prospectively amended, Sch 13 para 6(1)(aa) prospectively added, by the Crime and Courts Act 2013 Sch 16 paras 11, 20)) and the court may not by virtue of these provisions require an electronic monitoring requirement within the Criminal Justice Act 2003 s 215(1)(b) to be complied with in Scotland (Sch 13 para 1(5) (as so prospectively amended). At the date at which this volume states the law no such day had been appointed. As to electronic monitoring requirements see s 215; and PARA 136.
12 Criminal Justice Act 2003 Sch 13 paras 1(1)(a), 6(1)(a).
13 Ie an electronic monitoring requirement within the Criminal Justice Act 2003 s 215(1)(b).
14 Criminal Justice Act 2003 Sch 13 para 6(1)(aa)(i) (prospectively added: see note 11).
15 Criminal Justice Act 2003 Sch 13 para 6(1)(aa)(ii) (prospectively added: see note 11).
16 As to these powers see the Criminal Justice Act 2003 Sch 12 para 14; and PARA 109.
17 Criminal Justice Act 2003 Sch 13 paras 1(3)(a), 6(3)(a).
18 Ie the conditions set out in the Criminal Justice Act 2003 Sch 13 paras 1(1), 6(1) (see the text and notes 1–15).
19 Criminal Justice Act 2003 Sch 13 paras 1(3)(b), 6(3)(b) (Sch 13 para 6(3)(b) prospectively amended: see note 11).
20 Ie under the Criminal Justice Act 2003 Sch 12 (see PARA 107 et seq).
21 Criminal Justice Act 2003 Sch 13 paras 1(3), (4), 6(3), (4) (Sch 13 para 6(4) prospectively amended: see note 11). The arrangements referred to in the text are those set out in Sch 13 paras 1(1)(b), 6(1)(b) (see the text and note 3). The court may not by virtue of these provisions require an attendance centre requirement to be complied with in Scotland: Sch 13 para 1(5).
22 Ie made in accordance with the Criminal Justice Act 2003 Sch 13 para 1 or Sch 13 para 6 (see the text and notes 1–21).
23 Criminal Justice Act 2003 Sch 13 paras 2(a), 7(a).
24 Ie the functions conferred by the Criminal Justice Act 2003 Pt 12 (ss 142–305).
25 Criminal Justice Act 2003 Sch 13 paras 2(b), 7(b). Section 216 (local justice area to be specified: see PARA 48) does not apply to an order so made or amended: Sch 13 paras 2, 7 (amended by SI 2005/886).
26 For these purposes 'relevant document' means a copy of the order as made or amended (Criminal Justice Act 2003 Sch 13 paras 3(2)(a), 8(2)(a)) and such other documents and information relating to the case as the court making or amending the order considers likely to be of assistance (Sch 13 paras 3(2)(b), 8(2)(b)).
27 Criminal Justice Act 2003 Sch 13 paras 3(1)(a), 8(1)(a).
28 Criminal Justice Act 2003 Sch 13 paras 3(1)(b), 8(1)(b). The provisions of s 219(1)(b)–(d) (which relate to the provision of copies: see PARA 100 note 12) do not apply in relation to an order so made or amended: Sch 13 paras 3(1), 8(1).

120.   After transfer to Scotland or Northern Ireland.   If at any time while a suspended sentence order[1] is in force in respect of an offender residing in Scotland or Northern Ireland it appears to the home court[2], either on information from (if that court is in Scotland)[3] or upon a complaint made by (if that court is in Northern Ireland)[4] the relevant officer[5], that the offender has failed without reasonable excuse to comply with any of the community requirements of the order[6], the home court may issue a citation (if it is in Scotland) or summons (if it is in Northern Ireland) requiring the offender to appear before it at the time specified in the citation or summons[7], and if he does not appear in answer to the citation or summons it may issue a warrant for the offender's arrest[8]. The court before which an offender appears or is brought by virtue of these requirements must either determine whether the offender has failed without reasonable excuse to comply with any of the community requirements of the suspended sentence order[9] or require the offender to appear before the original court[10], and if the home court determines that the offender has failed without reasonable excuse to comply with any of the community requirements of the order[11] it must require the offender to appear before the original court[12]. The home court may also exercise any power of amendment of a suspended sentence order[13] as if it were the original court[14]. Where the home court proposes to exercise the power of amendment[15], otherwise than on the application of the offender, it must issue a citation (if it is in Scotland) or summons (if it is in Northern Ireland) requiring the offender to appear before it[16], and if he does not appear in answer to the citation or summons it may issue a warrant for the offender's arrest[17]. However, this does not apply to any order cancelling any community requirement of a suspended sentence order[18].

Where an application is made[19] to the home court for the amendment of a suspended sentence order the home court may (instead of dealing with the application) require the offender to appear before the original court[20].

No court may amend or further amend a suspended sentence order unless it appears to the court that the conditions which determine whether a transfer order may be made[21] are satisfied in relation to any requirement to be imposed[22].

On the making of an order amending a suspended sentence order the court must provide copies of the amending order to the offender and the relevant officer[23].

Where the home court is satisfied that the offender is residing or proposes to reside in England and Wales[24] it may, and on the application of the relevant officer must, amend the suspended sentence order by requiring it to be complied with in England and Wales[25].

1 Ie a suspended sentence order made or amended in accordance with the Criminal Justice Act 2003 Sch 13 para 1 or Sch 13 para 6 (see PARA 119). As to the meanings of 'suspended sentence' and 'suspended sentence order', and as to the making of suspended sentence orders, see PARA 100.

2 For these purposes, 'home court' means:
   (1)   if the offender resides in Scotland, or will be residing there at the relevant time, the sheriff court having jurisdiction in the locality in which the offender resides or proposes to reside (Criminal Justice Act 2003 Sch 13 para 11); and
   (2)   if he resides in Northern Ireland, or will be residing there at the relevant time, the court of summary jurisdiction acting for the petty sessions district in which he resides or proposes to reside (Sch 13 para 11).
   'Relevant time' means the time when the order or the amendment to it comes into force: Sch 13 para 11. As to the meanings of 'local authority' and 'local authority area' see PARA 119 note 3.

3 Criminal Justice Act 2003 Sch 13 para 13(1)(a).

4 Criminal Justice Act 2003 Sch 13 para 13(1)(b).

5 'Relevant officer' means:
   (1)   where the order specifies a local authority area in Scotland, the local authority officer appointed or assigned under the Criminal Justice Act 2003 Sch 13 para 2(b) (see PARA 119) (Sch 13 para 11); and
   (2)   where the order specifies a petty sessions district in Northern Ireland, the probation officer appointed or assigned under Sch 13 para 7(b) (see PARA 119) (Sch 13 para 11).

6 As to the community requirements of a suspended sentence order see PARA 101.

7 Criminal Justice Act 2003 Sch 13 para 13(2)(a)(i), (b)(i). The Summary Jurisdiction (Process) Act 1881 s 4 (which provides, among other things, for service in England and Wales of Scottish citations or warrants) applies to any citation or warrant issued under the Criminal Justice Act 2003 Sch 13 para 13(2)(a) or Sch 13 para 15(3)(a) (see the text and notes 15–17) as it applies to a citation or warrant granted under the Criminal Procedure (Scotland) Act 1995

s 134: Criminal Justice Act 2003 Sch 13 para 22(1). A summons issued by a court in Northern Ireland under Sch 13 para 13(2)(b) or Sch 13 para 15(3)(a) may, in such circumstances as may be prescribed by rules of court, be served in England, Wales or Scotland: Sch 13 para 22(2).

8 Criminal Justice Act 2003 Sch 13 para 13(2)(a)(ii), (b)(ii).

9 Criminal Justice Act 2003 Sch 13 para 14(1)(a).

10 Criminal Justice Act 2003 Sch 13 para 14(1)(b). 'Original court' means the court in England and Wales which made or last amended the order: Sch 13 para 11. Where a suspended sentence order made or amended in accordance with Sch 13 para 1 or Sch 13 para 6 (see PARA 119) is in force in respect of an offender, no court in England and Wales may exercise any power in relation to any failure by the offender to comply with any community requirement of the order unless the offender has been required in accordance with Sch 13 para 14(1)(b) or Sch 13 para 14(2)(a) (see the text and notes 11–12) to appear before that court: Sch 13 para 12(1), (8)(a).

11 An offender who is required by a mental health treatment requirement (see the Criminal Justice Act 2003 s 207; and PARA 128), a drug rehabilitation requirement (see s 209; and PARA 124) or an alcohol treatment requirement (see s 212; and PARA 122) to submit to treatment for his mental condition, or his dependency on or propensity to misuse drugs or alcohol, is not to be treated for these purposes as having failed to comply with that requirement on the ground only that he has refused to undergo any surgical, electrical or other treatment if, in the opinion of the court, his refusal was reasonable having regard to all the circumstances: Sch 13 para 14(3).

12 Criminal Justice Act 2003 Sch 13 para 14(2)(a). See note 9. Where an offender is required by virtue of this provision to appear before the original court, the home court must send to the original court a certificate certifying that the offender has failed without reasonable excuse to comply with the requirements of the order in the respect specified (Sch 13 para 14(6)(a)) and such a certificate signed by the clerk of the home court is admissible before the original court as conclusive evidence of the matters specified in it (Sch 13 para 14(6)(b)). When the offender appears before the original court, Sch 12 para 8 (see PARA 117) applies as if it had already been proved to the satisfaction of the original court that the offender failed without reasonable excuse to comply with such of the community requirements of the order as may have been determined: Sch 13 para 14(2)(b). The evidence of one witness is sufficient for these purposes: Sch 13 para 14(4).

13 Ie any power under the Criminal Justice Act 2003 Sch 12 Pt 3 (paras 13–22) (see PARAS 107–113), except that conferred by Sch 12 para 15(4) (see PARA 108): Sch 13 para 15(1). Where Sch 12 para 15(4) applies the home court must require the offender to appear before the original court: Sch 13 para 15(2). Where a suspended sentence order made or amended in accordance with Sch 13 para 1 or Sch 13 para 6 (see PARA 119) is in force in respect of an offender, no court in England and Wales may exercise any power under Sch 12 Pt 3 unless the offender has been required in accordance with Sch 13 para 15(2) or Sch 13 para 16 (see the text and notes 19–20) to appear before that court: Sch 13 para 12(8)(b).

14 Criminal Justice Act 2003 Sch 13 para 15(1).

15 Ie the power conferred by the Criminal Justice Act 2003 Sch 12 para 15(1) (see PARA 108).

16 Criminal Justice Act 2003 Sch 13 para 15(3)(a)(i), (b)(i). See note 7.

17 Criminal Justice Act 2003 Sch 13 para 15(3)(a)(ii), (b)(ii).

18 Criminal Justice Act 2003 Sch 13 para 15(4).

19 Ie by virtue of the Criminal Justice Act 2003 Sch 13 para 15 (see the text and notes 13–18).

20 Criminal Justice Act 2003 Sch 13 para 16.

21 Ie the conditions set out in the Criminal Justice Act 2003 Sch 13 para 1(1)(a) or Sch 13 para 6(1)(a) (see PARA 119).

22 Criminal Justice Act 2003 Sch 13 para 17 (prospectively amended by the Crime and Courts Act 2013 Sch 16 paras 11, 20). The Criminal Justice Act 2003 Sch 13 para 17 does not apply to any amendment made by Sch 13 para 20(2) (see the text and note 25): Sch 13 para 17 (as so prospectively amended). The provisions of Sch 13 paras 1–17 have effect in relation to any amendment of a suspended sentence order by any court as they have effect in relation to the amendment of such an order by virtue of Sch 13 para 1(3) or Sch 13 para 6(3) (see PARA 119): Sch 13 para 18.

23 Criminal Justice Act 2003 Sch 13 para 19(a). In the case of an amending order which substitutes a new local authority area or petty sessions district, Sch 13 paras 2, 3 (see PARA 119), or as the case may be Sch 13 paras 7, 8 (see PARA 119), have effect in relation to the order as they have effect in relation to an order made or amended in accordance with Sch 13 para 1 or Sch 13 para 6 (see PARA 119): Sch 13 para 19(b).

24 Criminal Justice Act 2003 Sch 13 para 20(1).

25 Criminal Justice Act 2003 Sch 13 para 20(2). The court may not amend under these provisions a suspended sentence order which contains requirements which, in the opinion of the court,

cannot be complied with in the local justice area in which the offender is residing or proposes to reside unless, in accordance with Sch 12 para 15 (see PARA 108), it either cancels those requirements or substitutes for them other requirements which can be complied with if the offender resides in that area: Sch 13 para 20(3) (Sch 13 para 20(3), (4), (6)(a), (b) amended by SI 2005/886). The court may not amend under these provisions any suspended sentence order imposing a programme requirement unless it appears to the court that the accredited programme specified in the requirement is available in the local justice area in England and Wales in which the offender is residing or proposes to reside: Criminal Justice Act 2003 Sch 13 para 20(4) (as so amended). As to programme requirements see s 202; and PARA 129.

The suspended sentence order as amended under Sch 13 para 20 must specify the local justice area in which the offender resides or proposes to reside: Sch 13 para 20(5).

On the making under Sch 13 para 20 of an order amending a suspended sentence order, the home court must:

(1) provide copies of the amending order to the offender, the relevant officer and the local probation board acting in the new local justice area (Sch 13 para 20(6)(a) (as so amended)); and

(2) provide the magistrates' court acting in that area with a copy of the amending order and such other documents and information relating to the case as the home court considers likely to be of assistance to the court acting in that area in the exercise of its functions in relation to the order (Sch 13 para 20(6)(b) (as so amended)).

Where an order has been amended under Sch 13 para 20, the provisions of Sch 13 paras 1–19 cease to apply to the order as amended: Sch 13 para 20(7). As to the meaning of 'local probation board' see PARA 100 note 12. As to the provision of probation services see PARAS 666–687.

(3) REQUIREMENTS FOR COMMUNITY ORDERS, SUSPENDED SENTENCE ORDERS AND YOUTH REHABILITATION ORDERS

(i) Requirements applicable to Community Orders and Suspended Sentence Orders

121. Requirements which may be imposed. Community orders and suspended sentence orders are required to specify one or more requirements with which the offender is required to comply for the duration of the order or (where applicable) during the non-custodial element of the term[1]. The requirements which may be specified for the purposes of these orders are:

(1) an alcohol treatment requirement[2];

(2) a curfew requirement[3];

(3) a drug rehabilitation requirement[4];

(4) an exclusion requirement[5];

(5) a foreign travel prohibition requirement[6];

(6) a mental health treatment requirement[7];

(7) a programme requirement[8];

(8) a prohibited activity requirement[9];

(9) a rehabilitation activity requirement[10];

(10) a residence requirement[11];

(11) an unpaid work requirement[12];

(12) in a case where the offender is aged under 25[13], an attendance centre requirement[14];

(13) as from a day to be appointed, an alcohol abstinence and monitoring requirement[15]; and

(14) as from a day to be appointed, an electronic monitoring requirement[16].

An electronic monitoring requirement may also be imposed for the purpose of securing the offender's compliance with any of the requirements listed above[17].

1 Community orders and suspended sentence orders are 'relevant orders' for the purposes of the Criminal Justice Act 2003 Pt 12 Ch 4 (ss 196–223): s 196(1)(a), (c) (s 196(1)(a) amended, s 196(1A) added, by the Legal Aid, Sentencing and Punishment of Offenders Act 2012 Sch 9 paras 2, 7). As to community orders see PARAS 45–72; as to the imposition of requirements pursuant to community orders see PARA 48. As to suspended sentence orders (which for these purposes means suspended sentence orders that impose one or more community requirements: Criminal Justice Act 2003 s 196(1A) (as so added)) see PARAS 100–120; as to the imposition of requirements pursuant to suspended sentence orders see PARA 101. As to community sentences generally see PARAS 42–44.

The Criminal Justice Act 2003 Pt 12 Ch 4 has effect, subject to specified modifications, in relation to an enforcement order (ie an order under the Children Act 1989 ss 11J–11M, Sch A1) as it has effect in relation to a community order: see Sch A1 para 1; and CHILDREN AND YOUNG PERSONS vol 9 (2012) PARA 296.

2 See the Criminal Justice Act 2003 ss 177(1)(j), 190(1)(j), 212; and PARA 122.
3 See the Criminal Justice Act 2003 ss 177(1)(e), 190(1)(e), 204; and PARA 123.
4 See the Criminal Justice Act 2003 ss 177(1)(i), 190(1)(i), 209; and PARA 124.
5 See the Criminal Justice Act 2003 ss 177(1)(f), 190(1)(f), 205; and PARA 126.
6 See the Criminal Justice Act 2003 ss 177(1)(ga), 190(1)(ga), 206A; and PARA 127.
7 See the Criminal Justice Act 2003 ss 177(1)(h), 190(1)(h), 207; and PARA 128.
8 See the Criminal Justice Act 2003 ss 177(1)(c), 190(1)(c), 202; and PARA 129.
9 See the Criminal Justice Act 2003 ss 177(1)(d), 190(1)(d), 203; and PARA 130.
10 See the Criminal Justice Act 2003 ss 177(1)(aa), 190(1)(aa), 200A; and PARA 131. Rehabilitation activity requirements replaced activity requirements under s 201 and supervision requirements under s 213, which have been abolished, as from 1 February 2015: see the Offender Rehabilitation Act 2014 s 15 and the Offender Rehabilitation Act 2014 (Commencement No 2) Order 2015), SI 2015/40.
11 See the Criminal Justice Act 2003 ss 177(1)(g), 190(1)(g), 206; and PARA 132.
12 See the Criminal Justice Act 2003 ss 177(1)(a), 190(1)(a), 199; and PARA 133.
13 As to the determination of a person's age see the Children and Young Persons Act 1933 s 99; and CHILDREN AND YOUNG PERSONS vol 10 (2012) PARA 1206.
14 See the Criminal Justice Act 2003 ss 177(1)(l), 190(1)(l), 214; and PARA 134.
15 See the Criminal Justice Act 2003 ss 177(1)(ja), 190(1)(ja), 212A; and PARA 135.
16 See the Criminal Justice Act 2003 ss 177(1)(m), 190(1)(m), 215; and PARA 136.
17 See the Criminal Justice Act 2003 ss 215, 218(4); and PARA 136.

122. Alcohol treatment requirement. 'Alcohol treatment requirement', in relation to a community order or suspended sentence order[1], means a requirement that the offender must submit during a period specified in the order to treatment by or under the direction of a specified person having the necessary qualifications or experience with a view to the reduction or elimination of the offender's dependency on alcohol[2].

A court may not impose an alcohol treatment requirement in respect of an offender unless:

(1)　it is satisfied that he is dependent on alcohol[3];

(2)　it is satisfied that his dependency is such as requires and may be susceptible to treatment[4];

(3)　it is satisfied that arrangements have been or can be made for the treatment intended to be specified in the order (including arrangements for the reception of the offender where he is to be required to submit to treatment as a resident)[5]; and

(4)　the offender expresses his willingness to comply with its requirements[6].

The treatment required by an alcohol treatment requirement for any particular period must be:

(a)　treatment as a resident in such institution or place as may be specified in the order[7];

(b)　treatment as a non-resident in or at such institution or place, and at such intervals, as may be so specified[8]; or

(c)   treatment by or under the direction of such person having the necessary qualification or experience as may be so specified[9],

but the nature of the treatment may not otherwise be specified in the order[10].

1   Ie a 'relevant order': see PARA 121.
2   Criminal Justice Act 2003 s 212(1).
3   Criminal Justice Act 2003 s 212(2)(a).
4   Criminal Justice Act 2003 s 212(2)(b).
5   Criminal Justice Act 2003 s 212(2)(c).
6   Criminal Justice Act 2003 s 212(3).
7   Criminal Justice Act 2003 s 212(5)(a). Where a relevant order imposes an alcohol treatment requirement the court by which the order is made must also forthwith provide the person specified under s 212(5)(c) or the person in charge of the institution or place specified under s 212(5)(a) or (b) with a copy of so much of the order as relates to that requirement: s 219(2), Sch 14.
8   Criminal Justice Act 2003 s 212(5)(b). See note 7.
9   Criminal Justice Act 2003 s 212(5)(c). See note 7.
10 Criminal Justice Act 2003 s 212(5).

123.   Curfew requirement. 'Curfew requirement', in relation to a community order or a suspended sentence order[1], means a requirement that the offender must remain, for periods specified in the order, at a place so specified[2]. Before making an order imposing a curfew requirement, the court must obtain and consider information about the place proposed to be specified in the order (including information as to the attitude of persons likely to be affected by the enforced presence there of the offender)[3].

1   Ie a 'relevant order': see PARA 121.
2   Criminal Justice Act 2003 s 204(1). An order imposing a curfew requirement may specify different places or different periods for different days, but may not specify periods which amount to less than two hours or more than 16 hours in any day (s 204(2) (s 204(2), (3) amended by the Legal Aid, Sentencing and Punishment of Offenders Act 2012 s 71)) and may not specify periods which fall outside the period of six months beginning with the day on which it is made (Criminal Justice Act 2003 s 204(3) (as so amended)). The Secretary of State may by order amend the Criminal Justice Act 2003 s 204(2) by substituting, for the maximum number of hours for the time being specified in that provision, such other number of hours as may be specified in the order (s 223(1)(b)) and may by order amend s 204(3) by substituting, for any period for the time being specified therein, such other period as may be specified in the order (s 223(2), (3)(a)). At the date at which this volume states the law no such order had been made. See *R v Ali (Saeed)* [2011] EWCA Crim 2747, 176 JP 1 (a previous six-month curfew requirement imposed pursuant to deferral of sentencing did not preclude the court from imposing a curfew order at sentencing).
     Where the court makes a community order imposing a curfew requirement the court must also impose an electronic monitoring requirement unless it is prevented from doing so or unless, in the particular circumstances of the case, it considers it inappropriate to do so: see the Criminal Justice Act 2003 s 177(3); and PARA 48.
3   Criminal Justice Act 2003 s 204(6).

124.   Drug rehabilitation requirement. 'Drug rehabilitation requirement', in relation to a community order or suspended sentence order[1], means a requirement that during a period specified in the order (the 'treatment and testing period') the offender:

(1)   must submit to treatment by or under the direction of a specified person having the necessary qualifications or experience with a view to the reduction or elimination of the offender's dependency on or propensity to misuse drugs[2]; and

(2)   for the purpose of ascertaining whether he has any drug in his body during that period, must provide samples of such description as may be

so determined, at such times or in such circumstances as may (subject to the provisions of the order) be determined by the responsible officer[3] or by the person specified as the person by or under whose direction the treatment is to be provided[4].

A court may not impose a drug rehabilitation requirement unless:

(a)   it is satisfied that the offender is dependent on, or has a propensity to misuse, drugs[5] and that his dependency or propensity is such as requires and may be susceptible to treatment[6];

(b)   it is also satisfied that arrangements have been or can be made for the treatment intended to be specified in the order (including arrangements for the reception of the offender where he is to be required to submit to treatment as a resident)[7];

(c)   the requirement has been recommended to the court by as being suitable for the offender by an officer of a local probation board or an officer of a provider of probation services[8]; and

(d)   the offender expresses his willingness to comply with the requirement[9].

The required treatment for any particular period must be treatment as a resident in such institution or place as may be specified in the order[10] or treatment as a non-resident in or at such institution or place, and at such intervals, as may be so specified[11]; but the nature of the treatment is not to be otherwise specified in the order[12].

1   Ie a 'relevant order': see PARA 121. For examples of circumstances in which a drug rehabilitation requirement would be suitable see *R v Woods* [2005] EWCA Crim 2065, [2006] 1 Cr App Rep (S) 477; *A-G's Reference (No 82 of 2005) (Toulson)* [2005] EWCA Crim 2692, [2006] 1 Cr App Rep (S) 679; *A-G's Reference (Nos 68 and 92 of 2007)* [2007] EWCA Crim 2634.
2   Criminal Justice Act 2003 s 209(1)(a). For these purposes 'drug' means a controlled drug as defined by the Misuse of Drugs Act 1971 s 2 (see CRIMINAL LAW vol 26 (2010) PARA 723): Criminal Justice Act 2003 s 209(7).
3   As to the meaning of 'responsible officer' see PARA 81 note 9. A community order or suspended sentence order imposing a drug rehabilitation requirement must provide that the results of tests carried out on any samples provided by the offender in pursuance of the requirement to a person other than the responsible officer are to be communicated to the responsible officer: Criminal Justice Act 2003 s 209(6).
4   Criminal Justice Act 2003 s 209(1)(b). The function of making a determination as to the provision of samples under provision included in the community order or suspended sentence order by virtue of s 209(1)(b) is to be exercised in accordance with guidance given from time to time by the Secretary of State: s 209(5).
5   Criminal Justice Act 2003 s 209(2)(a)(i).
6   Criminal Justice Act 2003 s 209(2)(a)(ii). In connection with the circumstances under which it is appropriate to pass a suspended sentence with a drug rehabilitation requirement see eg *A-G's Reference (No 101 of 2009), R v Matheson* [2010] EWCA Crim 238, [2010] 2 Cr App Rep (S) 524, [2010] All ER (D) 130 (Feb).
7   Criminal Justice Act 2003 s 209(2)(b).
8   Criminal Justice Act 2003 s 209(2)(c) (amended by the Criminal Justice and Immigration Act 2008 Sch 4 paras 71, 88). As to the meaning of 'local probation board' see PARA 100 note 12; as the provision of probation services see PARAS 666–786.
9   Criminal Justice Act 2003 s 209(2)(d).
10   Criminal Justice Act 2003 s 209(4)(a). Where a relevant order imposes a drug rehabilitation requirement the court by which the order is made must also forthwith provide the person in charge of the institution or place specified under s 209(4) with a copy of so much of the order as relates to that requirement: s 219(2), Sch 14.
11   Criminal Justice Act 2003 s 209(4)(b).
12   Criminal Justice Act 2003 s 209(4).

125.   Review of drug rehabilitation requirement. A community order or suspended sentence order[1] imposing a drug rehabilitation requirement[2] may (and must if the treatment and testing period is more than 12 months[3]):

(1) provide for the requirement to be reviewed periodically at intervals of not less than one month[4];

(2) provide for each review of the requirement to be made[5] at a hearing held for the purpose by the court responsible for the order (a 'review hearing')[6];

(3) require the offender to attend each review hearing[7];

(4) provide for an officer of a provider of probation services to make to the court responsible for the order[8], before each review, a report in writing on the offender's progress under the requirement[9]; and

(5) provide for each such report to include the test results communicated to the responsible officer[10] and the views of the treatment provider as to the treatment and testing of the offender[11].

At a review hearing[12] the court may, after considering the officer's report[13], amend the community order or suspended sentence order, so far as it relates to the drug rehabilitation requirement[14]. The court:

(a) may not amend the drug rehabilitation requirement unless the offender expresses his willingness to comply with the requirement as amended[15]; and

(b) except with the consent of the offender, may not amend any requirement or provision of the order while an appeal against the order is pending[16].

If the offender fails to express his willingness to comply with the drug rehabilitation requirement as proposed to be amended by the court, the court may revoke the community order, or the suspended sentence order and the suspended sentence to which it relates[17], and deal with him, for the offence in respect of which the order was made, in any way in which he could have been dealt with for that offence by the court which made the order if the order had not been made[18].

If at a review without a hearing the court, after considering the officer's report, is of the opinion that the offender's progress under the requirement is no longer satisfactory, the court may require the offender to attend a hearing of the court at a specified time and place[19]. At that hearing the court, after considering that report, may exercise its powers[20] as if the hearing were a review hearing[21] and so amend the order as to provide for each subsequent review to be made at a review hearing[22].

1 Ie a 'relevant order': see PARA 121.
2 See PARA 124.
3 As to the treatment and testing period see PARA 124.
4 Criminal Justice Act 2003 s 210(1)(a).
5 Ie subject to the Criminal Justice Act 2003 s 211(6) (see note 6).
6 Criminal Justice Act 2003 s 210(1)(b). If at a review hearing the court, after considering the officer's report, is of the opinion that the offender's progress under the requirement is satisfactory, the court may amend the order as to provide for each subsequent review to be made by the court without a hearing: s 211(6) (s 211(1), (6), (7) amended by the Offender Rehabilitation Act 2014 Sch 4 para 5(2)). For these purposes, reference to the court, in relation to a review without a hearing, is to be read: (1) in the case of the Crown Court, as a reference to a judge of the court (Criminal Justice Act 2003 s 211(9)(a)); (2) in the case of a magistrates' court, as a reference to a justice of the peace (s 211(9)(b) (amended by SI 2005/886)). As to the meaning of 'responsible officer' see PARA 81 note 9.
7 Criminal Justice Act 2003 s 210(1)(c).
8 In the Criminal Justice Act 2003 s 210 references to the court responsible for a community order or suspended sentence order imposing a drug rehabilitation requirement are references:
    (1) where a court is specified in the order in accordance with s 210(3), to that court (s 210(2)(a));

(2)   in any other case, to the court by which the order is made (s 210(2)(b)).

Where the area specified in a community order or suspended sentence order which is made by a magistrates' court and imposes a drug rehabilitation requirement is not the area for which the court acts, the court may, if it thinks fit, include in the order provision specifying for the purposes of s 210(2) a magistrates' court which acts for the area specified in the order: s 210(3).

Where a community order or suspended sentence order imposing a drug rehabilitation requirement has been made on an appeal brought from the Crown Court or from the criminal division of the Court of Appeal, for the purposes of s 210(1)(b) it is to be taken to have been made by the Crown Court: s 210(4).

9   Criminal Justice Act 2003 s 210(1)(d) (amended by the Offender Rehabilitation Act 2014 Sch 4 para 4).
10   Ie under the Criminal Justice Act 2003 s 209(6) (see PARA 124) or otherwise.
11   Criminal Justice Act 2003 s 210(1)(e).
12   Ie within the meaning given by the Criminal Justice Act 2003 s 210(1): see the text and notes 1–11.
13   Ie the report under the Criminal Justice Act 2003 s 210(1).
14   Criminal Justice Act 2003 s 211(1) (as amended: see note 6).
15   Criminal Justice Act 2003 s 211(2)(a).
16   Criminal Justice Act 2003 s 211(2)(c).
17   Criminal Justice Act 2003 s 211(3)(a).
18   Criminal Justice Act 2003 s 211(3)(b). In so dealing with the offender, the court must take into account the extent to which the offender has complied with the requirements of the order (s 211(4)(a)) and may impose a custodial sentence (where the order was made in respect of an offence punishable with such a sentence) notwithstanding anything in s 152(2) (see PARA 536) (s 211(4)(b)).
19   Criminal Justice Act 2003 s 211(7) (as amended: see note 6).
20   Ie the powers conferred by the Criminal Justice Act 2003 s 211.
21   Criminal Justice Act 2003 s 211(8)(a).
22   Criminal Justice Act 2003 s 211(8)(b).

126.   Exclusion requirement. 'Exclusion requirement', in relation to a community order or a suspended sentence order[1], means a provision prohibiting the offender from entering a place[2] specified in the order for a period so specified[3]. An exclusion requirement may provide for the prohibition to operate only during the periods specified in the order[4] and may specify different places for different periods or days[5].

1   Ie a 'relevant order': see PARA 121.
2   In the Criminal Justice Act 2003 s 205, 'place' includes an area: s 205(4).
3   Criminal Justice Act 2003 s 205(1). Where the relevant order is a community order the period specified must not be more than two years: s 205(2). The Secretary of State may by order amend s 205(2) by substituting, for any period for the time being specified therein, such other period as may be specified in the order: s 223(2), (3)(b). At the date at which this volume states the law no such order had been made. Where a relevant order imposes an exclusion requirement for the purpose (or partly for the purpose) of protecting a person from being approached by the offender, the court by which the order is made must also forthwith provide the person intended to be protected with a copy of so much of the order as relates to that requirement: s 219(2), Sch 14. Where the court makes a community order imposing an exclusion requirement the court must also impose an electronic monitoring requirement unless it is prevented from doing so or unless, in the particular circumstances of the case, it considers it inappropriate to do so: see s 177(3); and PARA 48. In connection with the circumstances in which an exclusion requirement would be appropriate see *R v Jacob* [2008] EWCA Crim 2002, 172 JP 513, 172 JPN 742 (exclusion from own home 'disproportionate'); *R (on the application of Dragoman) v Camberwell Green Magistrates' Court* [2012] EWHC 4105 (Admin), 177 JP 372 (exclusion from entering the United Kingdom amounting to expulsion).
4   Criminal Justice Act 2003 s 205(3)(a).
5   Criminal Justice Act 2003 s 205(3)(b).

127.   Foreign travel prohibition requirement. 'Foreign travel prohibition requirement', in relation to a community order or a suspended sentence order[1], means a requirement prohibiting the offender from travelling, on a day or days specified in the order[2], or for a period so specified:

(1) to any country or territory outside the British Islands[3] specified or described in the order[4];

(2) to any country or territory outside the British Islands other than a country or territory specified or described in the order[5]; or

(3) to any country or territory outside the British Islands[6].

1 Ie a 'relevant order': see PARA 121.
2 A day so specified may not fall outside the period of 12 months beginning with the day on which the relevant order is made (Criminal Justice Act 2003 s 206A(2) (s 206A added by the Legal Aid, Sentencing and Punishment of Offenders Act 2012 s 72(5))) and a period so specified may not exceed 12 months beginning with the day on which the relevant order is made (Criminal Justice Act 2003 s 206A(3) (as so added)).
3 As to the meaning of 'British Islands' see the Interpretation Act 1978 Sch1; and STATUTES AND LEGISLATIVE PROCESS vol 96 (2012) PARA 1208.
4 Criminal Justice Act 2003 s 206A(1)(a) (as added: see note 2).
5 Criminal Justice Act 2003 s 206A(1)(b) (as added: see note 2).
6 Criminal Justice Act 2003 s 206A(1)(c) (as added: see note 2).

128. Mental health treatment requirement. 'Mental health treatment requirement', in relation to a community order or a suspended sentence order[1], means a requirement that the offender must submit, during a period or periods specified in the order, to treatment[2] by or under the direction of a registered medical practitioner or a registered psychologist (or both, for different periods) with a view to the improvement of the offender's mental condition[3].

A court may not include a mental health treatment requirement unless:

(1) the court is satisfied that the mental condition of the offender is such as requires and may be susceptible to treatment[4] but is not such as to warrant the making of a hospital order or guardianship order[5];

(2) the court is also satisfied that arrangements have been or can be made for the treatment intended to be specified in the order (including arrangements for the reception of the offender where he is to be required to submit to treatment as a resident patient)[6]; and

(3) the offender has expressed his willingness to comply with such a requirement[7].

1 Ie a 'relevant order': see PARA 121.
2 The treatment required must be such one of the following kinds of treatment as may be specified in the relevant order:
   (1) treatment as a resident patient in a care home within the meaning of the Care Standards Act 2000 (see s 3; and CHILDREN AND YOUNG PERSONS vol 10 (2012) PARA 994), an independent hospital (ie, in England, a hospital as defined by the National Health Service Act 2006 s 275 that is not a health service hospital as so defined (see HEALTH SERVICES vol 54 (2008) PARA 748), or in relation to Wales, an independent hospital as defined in the Care Standards Act 2000 (see s 2; and HEALTH SERVICES vol 54 (2008) PARAS 748–750)) or a hospital within the meaning of the Mental Health Act 1983 (see s 145(1); and MENTAL HEALTH AND CAPACITY vol 75 (2013) PARAS 577, 578), but not in hospital premises where high security psychiatric services within the meaning of the Mental Health Act 1983 (see s 145(1); the National Health Service Act 2006 s 4(2); the National Health Service (Wales) Act 2006 s 4(2); HEALTH SERVICES vol 54 (2008) PARAS 12, 74; MENTAL HEALTH AND CAPACITY vol 75 (2013) PARA 569) are provided (see the Criminal Justice Act 2003 s 207(2)(a), (4A) (s 207(2)(a) amended, s 207(4A) added, by SI 2010/813; Criminal Justice Act 2003 s 207(2)(a) modified in relation to the transfer of suspended sentence orders or community orders to Scotland and in relation to the transfer of suspended sentence orders to Northern Ireland by Sch 9 paras 2(1), (4), 4(1), (4), Sch 13 para 4(1), (4)));

(2)   treatment as a non-resident patient at such institution or place as may be specified in the order (s 207(2)(b));

(3)   treatment by or under the direction of such registered medical practitioner or registered psychologist (or both) as may be so specified (s 207(2)(c) (amended by SI 2009/1182)),

but the nature of the treatment is not to be specified in the order except as mentioned in head (1), (2) or (3) above (Criminal Justice Act 2003 s 207(2)). Where a relevant order imposes a mental health treatment requirement the court by which the order is made must also forthwith provide the person specified under s 207(2)(c) or the person in charge of the institution or place specified under s 207(2)(a) or (b) with a copy of so much of the order as relates to that requirement: s 219(2), Sch 14.

Where the medical practitioner or registered psychologist by whom or under whose direction an offender is being treated for his mental condition in pursuance of a mental health treatment requirement is of the opinion that part of the treatment can be better or more conveniently given in or at an institution or place which (s 208(1) (amended by SI 2009/1182)):

(a)   is not specified in the order (Criminal Justice Act 2003 s 208(1)(a)); and

(b)   is one in or at which the treatment of the offender will be given by or under the direction of a registered medical practitioner or registered psychologist (s 208(1)(b) (as so amended)),

he may, with the consent of the offender, make arrangements for him to be treated accordingly: s 208(1). Such arrangements as are mentioned in s 208(1) may provide for the offender to receive part of his treatment as a resident patient in an institution or place notwithstanding that the institution or place is not one which could have been specified for that purpose in the relevant order: s 208(2). Where any such arrangements are made for the treatment of an offender:

(i)   the medical practitioner or registered psychologist by whom the arrangements are made must give notice in writing to the offender's responsible officer, specifying the institution or place in or at which the treatment is to be carried out (s 208(3)(a) (amended by SI 2009/1182)); and

(ii)   the treatment provided for by the arrangements is deemed to be treatment to which he is required to submit in pursuance of the relevant order (Criminal Justice Act 2003 s 208(3)(b)).

In ss 207, 208, 'registered psychologist' means a person registered in the part of the register maintained under the Health and Social Work Professions Order 2001, SI 2002/254, which relates to practitioner psychologists: s 207(6) (substituted by SI 2009/1182; amended by the Health and Social Care Act 2012 s 218(3)(b)). As to the meaning of 'responsible officer' see PARA 81 note 9.

3   Criminal Justice Act 2003 s 207(1) (amended by SI 2009/1182).

4   Criminal Justice Act 2003 s 207(3)(a)(i) (s 207(3)(a) amended by the Legal Aid, Sentencing and Punishment of Offenders Act 2012 s 73(1), (2)). In connection with requests for medical reports see the Criminal Procedure Rules 2015, SI 2015/1490, r 28.8.

5   Criminal Justice Act 2003 s 207(3)(a)(ii) (as amended: see note 4). The reference in the text to a hospital order and a guardianship order is a reference to a hospital order and a guardianship order within the meaning of the Mental Health Act 1983: see s 37; and PARA 472 et seq.

6   Criminal Justice Act 2003 s 207(3)(b). While the offender is under treatment as a resident patient in pursuance of a mental health treatment requirement, his responsible officer must carry out the supervision of the offender to such extent only as may be necessary for the purpose of the revocation or amendment of the order: s 207(4).

7   Criminal Justice Act 2003 s 207(3)(c).

129. Programme requirement. 'Programme requirement', in relation to a community order or a suspended sentence order[1], means a requirement that the offender must participate[2] in an accredited programme[3] on the number of days specified in the order[4]. A programme requirement operates to require the offender:

(1)   in accordance with instructions given by the responsible officer[5], to participate in the accredited programme that is from time to time specified by the responsible officer at the place that is so specified on the number of days specified in the order[6]; and

(2)   while at that place, to comply with instructions given by, or under the authority of, the person in charge of the programme[7].

1   Ie a 'relevant order': see PARA 121.
2   Ie in accordance with the Criminal Justice Act 2003 s 202 (see the text and notes 3–7): s 202(1) (s 202(1), (6), (7) amended by the Legal Aid, Sentencing and Punishment of Offenders Act 2012 s 70(3), (4), (6), (7)).
3   In the Criminal Justice Act 2003 Pt 12 (ss 142–305), 'accredited programme' means a systematic set of activities (a 'programme') that is for the time being accredited by the Secretary of State for the purposes of s 202: s 202(2), (3)(a) (s 202(2) amended by the Offender Management Act 2007 s 31(1)(a)). The programme must be specified in the order: see *R v Price* [2013] EWCA Crim 1283, [2014] 1 Cr App Rep (S) 216.
4   Criminal Justice Act 2003 s 202(1) (as amended: see note 2).
5   As to the meaning of 'responsible officer' see PARA 81 note 9.
6   Criminal Justice Act 2003 s 202(6)(a) (as amended: see note 2).
7   Criminal Justice Act 2003 s 202(6)(b).

130.   Prohibited activity requirement. 'Prohibited activity requirement', in relation to a community order or a suspended sentence order[1], means a requirement that the offender must refrain from participating in activities specified in the order on a day or days so specified[2] or during a period so specified[3]. A court may not include a prohibited activity requirement in a relevant order unless it has consulted an officer of a local probation board or an officer of a provider of probation services[4]. The requirements that may be included in a relevant order include a requirement that the offender must not possess, use or carry a firearm[5].

1   Ie a 'relevant order': see PARA 121.
2   Criminal Justice Act 2003 s 203(1)(a).
3   Criminal Justice Act 2003 s 203(1)(b). The primary purpose of a prohibited activity requirement is not punishment, but the prevention of reoffending: see *R v Jacob* [2008] EWCA Crim 2002, 172 JP 513, 172 JPN 742.
4   Criminal Justice Act 2003 s 203(2) (amended by the Criminal Justice and Immigration Act 2008 Sch 4 paras 71, 87). As to the meaning of 'local probation board' see PARA 100 note 12; as the provision of probation services see PARAS 666–786.
5   Criminal Justice Act 2003 s 203(3). For these purposes 'firearm' means a firearm within the meaning of the Firearms Act 1968: see CRIMINAL LAW vol 26 (2010) PARA 578.

131.   Rehabilitation activity requirement. 'Rehabilitation activity requirement', in relation to a community order or suspended sentence order[1], means a requirement that, during the relevant period[2], the offender must comply with any instructions given by the responsible officer[3] to attend appointments[4] or participate in activities[5] or both[6]. The activities that responsible officers may instruct offenders to participate in include activities forming an accredited programme[7] and activities whose purpose is reparative, such as restorative justice activities[8], and any instructions given by the responsible officer must be given with a view to promoting the offender's rehabilitation[9].

A relevant order imposing a rehabilitation activity requirement must specify the maximum number of days for which the offender may be instructed to participate in activities[10].

1   Ie a 'relevant order': see PARA 121.
2   For these purposes 'the relevant period' means: (1) in relation to a community order, the period for which the community order remains in force (Criminal Justice Act 2003 s 200A(11)(a) (s 200A added by the Offender Rehabilitation Act 2014 s 15(1), (3)); and (2) in relation to a suspended sentence order, the supervision period as defined by the Criminal Justice Act 2003 s 189(1A) (see PARA 100) (s 200A(11)(b) (as so added)).
3   As to the meaning of 'responsible officer' see PARA 81 note 9. Where compliance with an instruction would require the co-operation of a person other than the offender, the responsible officer may give the instruction only if that person agrees: Criminal Justice Act 2003 s 200A(10) (as added: see note 2).

4   The responsible officer may instruct the offender to attend appointments with the responsible
     officer or with someone else: Criminal Justice Act 2003 s 200A(4) (as added: see note 2).
5   When instructing the offender to participate in activities, the responsible officer may require the
     offender to participate in specified activities and, while doing so, comply with instructions given
     by the person in charge of the activities (Criminal Justice Act 2003 s 200A(5)(a) (as added: see
     note 2)), or go to a specified place and, while there, comply with any instructions given by the
     person in charge of the place (s 200A(5)(b) (as so added)). The references in s 200A(5)(a), (b) to
     instructions given by a person include instructions given by anyone acting under the person's
     authority: s 200A(6) (as so added).
6   Criminal Justice Act 2003 s 200A(1) (as added: see note 2). Rehabilitation activity requirements
     replaced activity requirements under s 201 and supervision requirements under s 213, which
     have been abolished, as from 1 February 2015: see the Offender Rehabilitation Act 2014 s 15
     and the Offender Rehabilitation Act 2014 (Commencement No 2) Order 2015), SI 2015/40.
7   Criminal Justice Act 2003 s 200A(7)(a) (as added: see note 2). As to an 'accredited programme'
     see s 202(2); and PARA 129.
8   Criminal Justice Act 2003 s 200A(7)(b) (as added: see note 2). For these purposes an activity is
     a 'restorative justice activity' if the participants consist of, or include, the offender and one or
     more of the victims (s 200A(8)(a) (as so added)), the aim of the activity is to maximise the
     offender's awareness of the impact of the offending concerned on the victims (s 200A(8)(b) (as
     so added)), and the activity gives a victim or victims an opportunity to talk about, or by other
     means express experience of, the offending and its impact (s 200A(8)(c) (as so added)). In
     s 200A(8) 'victim' means a victim of, or other person affected by, the offending concerned:
     s 200A(9) (as so added).
9   Criminal Justice Act 2003 s 200A(3) (as added: see note 2). This requirement does not prevent
     the responsible officer giving instructions with a view to other purposes in addition to
     rehabilitation: s 200A(3) (as so added).
10   Criminal Justice Act 2003 s 200A(2) (as added: see note 2).

132.   Residence requirement. 'Residence requirement', in relation to a
community order or a suspended sentence order[1], means a requirement that,
during a period specified in the relevant order, the offender must reside at a place
specified in the order[2]. If the order so provides, a residence requirement does not
prohibit the offender from residing, with the prior approval of the responsible
officer[3], at a place other than that specified in the order[4]. Before making an order
containing a residence requirement, the court must consider the home
surroundings of the offender[5].

1   Ie a 'relevant order': see PARA 121.
2   Criminal Justice Act 2003 s 206(1). A court may not specify a hostel or other institution as the
     place where an offender must reside, except on the recommendation of an officer of a local
     probation board or an officer of a provider of probation services: s 206(4) (amended by
     SI 2008/912). As to the meaning of 'local probation board' see PARA 100 note 12; as the
     provision of probation services see PARAS 666–786. Where a relevant order imposes a residence
     requirement relating to residence in an institution, the court by which the order is made must
     also forthwith provide the person in charge of the institution with a copy of so much of the
     order as relates to that requirement: Criminal Justice Act 2003 s 219(2), Sch 14.
        Note that this provision does not apply in relation to the transfer of suspended sentence
     orders or community orders to Scotland or Northern Ireland (as to which see PARAS 68–72,
     119–120): see Sch 9 paras 2(1), (3)(c), 4(1), (3)(c), Sch 13 paras 4(1), (3)(c), 9(1), (3)(c).
3   As to the meaning of 'responsible officer' see PARA 81 note 9.
4   Criminal Justice Act 2003 s 206(2).
5   Criminal Justice Act 2003 s 206(3).

133.   Unpaid work requirement. 'Unpaid work requirement', in relation to a
community order or a suspended sentence order[1], means a requirement that the
offender must perform unpaid work for a specified number of hours[2]. A court
may not impose an unpaid work requirement unless the court is satisfied:

   (1)   that provision for the offender to work under such a requirement can be

made under the arrangements for persons to perform work under such a requirement which exist in the local justice area in which he resides or will reside[3]; and

(2)   that the offender is a suitable person to perform work under such a requirement[4].

An offender in respect of whom an unpaid work requirement of a relevant order is in force must perform for the number of hours specified in the order such work at such times as he may be instructed by the responsible officer[5]. The work required to be performed under an unpaid work requirement must[6] be performed during a period of 12 months[7]. Unless revoked, a community order imposing an unpaid work requirement remains in force until the offender has worked under it for the number of hours specified in it[8]. Where an unpaid work requirement is imposed by a suspended sentence order, the supervision period[9] continues until the offender has worked under the order for the number of hours specified in the order, but does not continue beyond the end of the operational period[10].

1   Ie a 'relevant order': see PARA 121.
2   Criminal Justice Act 2003 s 199(1), (2). The number of hours must be specified in the order and must be in the aggregate not less than 40 and not more than 300 (s 199(2)(a), (b)), although where the court is amending a community order so as to impose more onerous requirements under Sch 8 para 9(1)(a) (see PARA 55) or Sch 8 para 10(1)(a) (see PARA 56) and the community order does not contain an unpaid work requirement, the minimum aggregate number of hours which may be specified in the order is 20 rather than 40: Sch 8 paras 9(3A), 10(3A) (added by the Criminal Justice and Immigration Act 2008 s 38). As a general policy it is appropriate to keep some hours in reserve to be added to the term in the event of a breach: see *R v Fergie* [2007] EWCA Crim 1883, [2007] All ER (D) 139 (Sep). The Secretary of State may by order amend the Criminal Justice Act 2003 s 199(2) by substituting, for the maximum number of hours for the time being specified in that provision, such other number of hours as may be specified in the order: s 223(1)(a). At the date at which this volume states the law no such order had been made.
     Where the court makes relevant orders in respect of two or more offences of which the offender has been convicted on the same occasion and includes unpaid work requirements in each of them, the court may direct that the hours of work specified in any of those requirements is to be concurrent with or additional to those specified in any other of those orders, but so that the total number of hours which are not concurrent does not exceed the 300 hours: Criminal Justice Act 2003 s 199(5).
3   Criminal Justice Act 2003 s 218(1) (amended by SI 2005/886).
4   Criminal Justice Act 2003 s 199(3). The court may, if it thinks necessary, hear an officer of a local probation board or an officer of a provider of probation services before arriving at a conclusion on this matter: s 199(3) (amended by the Criminal Justice and Immigration Act 2008 Sch 4 paras 71, 84). As to the meaning of 'local probation board' see PARA 100 note 12; as the provision of probation services see PARAS 666–786.
5   Criminal Justice Act 2003 s 200(1). As to the meaning of 'responsible officer' see PARA 81 note 9.
6   This duty is subject to the Criminal Justice Act 2003 Sch 8 para 20, Sch 12 para 18 (extension of unpaid work requirement): see PARAS 64, 112.
7   Criminal Justice Act 2003 s 200(2).
8   Criminal Justice Act 2003 s 200(3).
9   Ie as defined by the Criminal Justice Act 2003 s 189(1A) (see PARA 100): s 200(4) (amended by the Legal Aid, Sentencing and Punishment of Offenders Act 2012 Sch 9 paras 2, 8).
10   Criminal Justice Act 2003 s 200(4) (as amended: see note 9). 'The operational period' is to be read in accordance with s 189(1)(a): s 200(4) (as so amended).

134.   Attendance centre requirement. 'Attendance centre requirement', in relation to a community order or suspended sentence order[1] made in respect of an offender aged under 25[2], means a requirement that the offender must attend at an attendance centre[3] for such number of hours as may be specified in the order[4]. The court may not impose an attendance centre requirement unless it has been notified by the Secretary of State that an attendance centre is available for persons of the offender's description[5]: additionally, the court may not impose the requirement unless it is satisfied that an attendance centre which is available for persons of the offender's description is reasonably accessible[6] to the offender concerned[7].

A requirement to attend at an attendance centre for any period on any occasion operates as a requirement, during that period, to engage in occupation, or receive instruction, under the supervision of and in accordance with instructions given by, or under the authority of, the officer in charge of the centre, whether at the centre or elsewhere[8].

1   Ie a 'relevant order': see PARA 121.

2   Attendance centre requirements may be imposed only in respect of offenders aged under 25: see the Criminal Justice Act 2003 ss 177(1)(l), 190(1)(l); and PARAS 46, 101. As to the determination of a person's age see the Children and Young Persons Act 1933 s 99; and CHILDREN AND YOUNG PERSONS vol 10 (2012) PARA 1206.

3   In connection with the provision of attendance centres by the Secretary of State see the Criminal Justice Act 2003 s 221; and PRISONS AND PRISONERS vol 85 (2012) PARA 515. The centre at which the offender is required to attend is to be notified to the offender by the responsible officer from time to time: s 214(3A) (s 214(1), (3) amended, s 214(3A), (3B) added, by the Offender Rehabilitation Act 2014 s 17(1)–(5)). In relation to the transfer of suspended sentence orders or community orders to Northern Ireland (as to which see PARAS 68–72, 119–120) any reference in Criminal Justice Act 2003 s 214 to an attendance centre has effect as a reference to a day centre, as defined by the Criminal Justice (Northern Ireland) Order 1996, SI 1996/3160 (NI 24), Sch 1 para 36: see the Criminal Justice Act 2003 Sch 9 para 4(1), (5), Sch 13 para 9(1), (5).

4   Criminal Justice Act 2003 s 214(1) (as amended: see note 3). The aggregate number of hours for which the offender may be required to attend at an attendance centre must not be less than 12 or more than 36: s 214(2). The first time at which the offender is required to attend at the attendance centre is a time notified to the offender by the responsible officer (s 214(4)), and the subsequent hours are to be fixed by the officer in charge of the centre, having regard to the offender's circumstances (s 214(5)). An offender may not be required under these provisions to attend at an attendance centre on more than one occasion on any day, or for more than three hours on any occasion: s 214(6). As to the meaning of 'responsible officer' see PARA 81 note 9.

5   Criminal Justice Act 2003 s 218(3).

6   Ie having regard to the means of access available to the offender and any other circumstances: Criminal Justice Act 2003 s 214(3).

7   Criminal Justice Act 2003 s 214(3) (as amended: see note 3). When choosing an attendance centre, the responsible officer must consider the accessibility of the attendance centre to the offender, having regard to the means of access available to the offender and any other circumstances, and the description of persons for whom it is available: Criminal Justice Act 2003 s 214(3B) (as so added).

8   Criminal Justice Act 2003 s 214(7) (added by the Criminal Justice and Immigration Act 2008 Sch 4 paras 71, 90).

135. Alcohol abstinence and monitoring requirement. Partly as from a day to be appointed[1] 'alcohol abstinence and monitoring requirement', in relation to a community order or suspended sentence order[2], means a requirement:

(1)   that the offender must[3] abstain from consuming alcohol[4] throughout a specified period[5] or must not consume alcohol so that at any time during a specified period there is more than a specified level of alcohol in his body[6]; and

(2)   that the offender must, for the purpose of ascertaining whether the offender is complying with provision under head (1) above, submit during the specified period to monitoring in accordance with specified arrangements[7].

A court may not include an alcohol abstinence and monitoring requirement in a relevant order unless:

(a) either the consumption of alcohol by the offender is an element of the offence for which the order is to be imposed or an associated offence[8] or the court is satisfied that the consumption of alcohol by the offender was a factor that contributed to the commission of that offence or an associated offence[9];

(b) the court is satisfied that the offender is not dependent on alcohol[10];

(c) the court does not include an alcohol treatment requirement[11] in the order[12]; and

(d) the court has been notified by the Secretary of State that arrangements for monitoring of the kind to be specified are available in the local justice area to be specified[13].

1 The Criminal Justice Act 2003 ss 212A, 223(3)(ba) (see the text and notes 2–13) are added by the Legal Aid, Sentencing and Punishment of Offenders Act 2012 s 76(1), (7): at the date at which this volume states the law s 76 had been brought into force (for all purposes other than application by the Armed Forces Act 2006) only in relation to the South London local justice area and ceases to have effect at the end of the period of 18 months beginning with 31 July 2014: see the Legal Aid, Sentencing and Punishment of Offenders Act 2012 (Alcohol Abstinence and Monitoring Requirements) Piloting Order 2014, SI 2014/1777 (amended by SI 2015/1480).

2 Ie a 'relevant order': see PARA 121.

3 Ie subject to such exceptions (if any) as are specified: Criminal Justice Act 2003 s 212A(1)(a) (as added: see note 1).

4 'Alcohol' includes anything containing alcohol: Criminal Justice Act 2003 s 212A(13) (as added: see note 1).

5 Criminal Justice Act 2003 s 212A(1)(a)(i) (as added: see note 1). 'Specified', in relation to a relevant order, means specified in the order: s 212A(13) (as so added). A period specified under s 212A(1)(a) must not exceed 120 days: s 212A(2) (as so added). If the Secretary of State by order prescribes a minimum period for the purposes of s 212(1)(a), a period specified thereunder must be at least as long as the period prescribed: s 212A(3) (as so added). At the date at which this volume states the law no such order had been made.

The Secretary of State may by order amend s 212A(2) by substituting, for any period for the time being specified therein, such other period as may be specified in the order: s 223(2), (3)(ba) (as so added). At the date at which this volume states the law no such order had been made.

6 Criminal Justice Act 2003 s 212A(1)(a)(ii) (as added: see note 1). The level of alcohol specified under s 212A(1)(a)(ii) must be that prescribed by the Secretary of State by order for the purposes thereof (and a requirement under that provision may not be imposed unless such an order is in force): s 212A(4) (as so added). An order under s 212A(4) may prescribe a level by reference to the proportion of alcohol in any one or more of an offender's breath, blood, urine or sweat, or by some other means): s 212A(5) (as so added). At the date at which this volume states the law no such order had been made.

7 Criminal Justice Act 2003 s 212A(1)(b) (as added: see note 1). The arrangements for monitoring specified under s 212A(1)(b) must be consistent with those prescribed by the Secretary of State under the Criminal Justice Act 2003 (Alcohol Abstinence and Monitoring Requirement) (Prescription of Arrangement for Monitoring) Order 2014, SI 2014/1787 (amended by SI 2015/1482) (and an alcohol abstinence and monitoring requirement may not be imposed unless such an order is in force) (Criminal Justice Act 2003 s 212A(6), (7) (as so added)).

8 Criminal Justice Act 2003 s 212A(8), (9)(a) (as added: see note 1). As to an 'associated' offence see PARA 9 note 7.

9 Criminal Justice Act 2003 s 212A(9)(b) (as added: see note 1).

10 Criminal Justice Act 2003 s 212A(10) (as added: see note 1).

11 As to alcohol treatment requirements see PARA 122.

12 Criminal Justice Act 2003 s 212A(11) (as added: see note 1).

13 Criminal Justice Act 2003 s 212A(12) (as added: see note 1).

136. Electronic monitoring requirement. Until a day to be appointed[1] 'electronic monitoring requirement', in relation to a community order or suspended sentence order[2], means a requirement for securing the electronic monitoring of the offender's compliance with other requirements imposed by the order during a period specified in the order, or determined by the responsible officer[3] in accordance with the relevant order[4]. As from that day, it means a requirement to submit to either or both of:

(1)   electronic monitoring of compliance with requirements as described above[5]; and

(2)   electronic monitoring of the offender's whereabouts (otherwise than for the purpose of monitoring the offender's compliance with any other requirements included in the order) during a period specified in the order[6].

Where:

(a)   it is proposed to include in a relevant order a requirement for securing[7] electronic monitoring[8]; but

(b)   there is a person (other than the offender) without whose co-operation it will not be practicable to secure the monitoring[9],

the requirement may not be included in the order without that person's consent[10].

A relevant order which includes an electronic monitoring requirement must include provision for making a person responsible for the monitoring; and[11] a person who is made so responsible must be of a description specified in an order[12] made by the Secretary of State[13].

Where an electronic monitoring requirement is required to take effect during a period determined by the responsible officer in accordance with the relevant order, the responsible officer must, before the beginning of that period, notify:

(i)   the offender[14];

(ii)   the person responsible for the monitoring[15]; and

(iii)   any person falling within head (2) above[16],

of the time when the period is to begin[17].

As from a day to be appointed where a relevant order imposes an electronic monitoring requirement the offender must (in particular):

(A)   submit, as required from time to time by the responsible officer or the person responsible for the monitoring, to being fitted with, or installation of, any necessary apparatus[18] and inspection or repair of any apparatus fitted or installed for the purposes of the monitoring[19];

(B)   not interfere with, or with the working of, any apparatus fitted or installed for the purposes of the monitoring[20]; and

(C)   take any steps required by the responsible officer, or the person responsible for the monitoring, for the purpose of keeping in working order any apparatus fitted or installed for the purposes of the monitoring[21].

1   The Criminal Justice Act 2003 ss 215(1), (5), (6), 218(4), Sch 9 para 4(3)(d), Sch 13 para 9(3)(d) are prospectively amended, and ss 215(1)(b), (4A), 218(9) are prospectively added, by the Crime and Courts Act 2013 Sch 16 paras 11, 16, 20, as from a day to be appointed: at the date at which this volume states the law no day had been appointed for these purposes.

2   Ie a 'relevant order': see PARA 121.

3   As to the meaning of 'responsible officer' see PARA 81 note 9.

4   Criminal Justice Act 2003 s 215(1). A court may not include an electronic monitoring requirement (or, as from the appointed day, an electronic monitoring requirement as described in s 215(1)(a) (see the text and note 5)) in a relevant order in respect of an offender unless the court has been notified by the Secretary of State that electronic monitoring arrangements are available in the specified relevant areas (as to which see s 218(5)–(7) below) (s 218(4)(a) (s 218(4)(a), (6) amended by the Offender Rehabilitation Act 2014 s 17(6)–(8); Criminal Justice Act 2003 s 218(4) prospectively further amended (see note 1))) and it is satisfied that the

necessary provision can be made under electronic monitoring arrangements (or, as from the appointed day, under the electronic monitoring arrangements currently available) (Criminal Justice Act 2003 s 218(4)(b) (as so prospectively further amended)).

In the case of a relevant order containing a curfew requirement (see PARA 123) or an exclusion requirement (see PARA 126), the relevant area for the purposes of s 218(4) is the area in which the place proposed to be specified in the order is situated: s 218(5). In relation to an exclusion requirement, 'place' has the same meaning as in s 205 (see PARA 126): s 218(8). In the case of a relevant order containing an attendance centre requirement (see PARA 134) the relevant area for the purposes of s 218(4) is an area in which there is an attendance centre which is available for persons of the offender's description and which the court is satisfied is reasonably accessible to the offender: s 218(6) (as so amended). In the case of any other relevant order, the relevant area for the purposes of s 218(4) is the local justice area proposed to be specified in the order: s 218(7) (amended by SI 2005/886).

The Criminal Justice Act 2003 218(4) does not apply in relation to the transfer of suspended sentence orders or community orders to Scotland or Northern Ireland (as to which see PARAS 68–72, 119–120): see Sch 9 paras 2(1), (3)(d), 4(1), (3)(d), Sch 13 paras 4(1), (3)(d), 9(1), (3)(d).

As from a day to be appointed an electronic monitoring requirement (or, as from the appointed day for the purposes of the amendments made by the Crime and Courts Act 2013 (see note 1), an electronic monitoring requirement as described in the Criminal Justice Act 2003 s 215(1)(a)) may not be included in a relevant order for the purposes of securing the electronic monitoring of the offender's compliance with an alcohol abstinence and monitoring requirement (see PARA 135): s 215(5) (s 215(5), (6) prospectively added by the Legal Aid, Sentencing and Punishment of Offenders Act 2012 s 76(6); prospectively amended (see note 1)). The Criminal Justice Act 2003 s 215(5) does not prevent the inclusion of an electronic monitoring requirement in a relevant order which includes an alcohol abstinence and monitoring requirement where this is included (or, as from the appointed day for the purposes of the amendments made by the Crime and Courts Act 2013, the electronic monitoring requirement is within the Criminal Justice Act 2003 s 215(1)(b) or is included) for the purpose of securing the electronic monitoring of an offender's compliance with a requirement other than the alcohol abstinence and monitoring requirement: s 215(6) (as so prospectively added and amended).

5   Criminal Justice Act 2003 s 215(1)(a) (s 215(1) prospectively amended: see note 1). See note 4.
6   Criminal Justice Act 2003 s 215(1)(b) (prospectively added: see note 1). A court may not include an electronic monitoring requirement within s 215(1)(b) in a relevant order in respect of an offender unless the court: (1) has been notified by the Secretary of State that electronic monitoring arrangements are available in the local justice area proposed to be specified in the order (s 218(9)(a) (as so prospectively added)); (2) is satisfied that the offender can be fitted with any necessary apparatus under the arrangements currently available and that any other necessary provision can be made under those arrangements (s 218(9)(b) (as so prospectively added)); and (3) is satisfied that arrangements are generally operational throughout England and Wales (even if not always operational everywhere there) under which the offender's whereabouts can be electronically monitored (s 218(9)(c) (as so prospectively added)). Section 218(9) does not apply in relation to the transfer of suspended sentence orders or community orders to Northern Ireland (as to which see PARAS 68–72, 119–120): see Sch 9 para 4(1), (3)(d), Sch 13 para 9(1), (3)(d) (as so prospectively amended).
7   Ie in accordance with the Criminal Justice Act 2003 s 215.
8   Criminal Justice Act 2003 s 215(2)(a).
9   Criminal Justice Act 2003 s 215(2)(b).
10 Criminal Justice Act 2003 s 215(2).
11 Ie except in relation to the transfer of suspended sentence orders or community orders to Scotland or Northern Ireland: see the Criminal Justice Act 2003 Sch 9 paras 2(1), (4), 4(1), (5), Sch 13 paras 4(1), (5), 9(1), (6).
12 As to the person responsible for the monitoring of an electronic monitoring requirement for these purposes see the Criminal Justice (Electronic Monitoring) (Responsible Person) (No 2) Order 2014, SI 2014/669.
13 Criminal Justice Act 2003 s 215(3). Where a relevant order imposes an electronic monitoring requirement the court by which the order is made must also forthwith provide any person who by virtue of s 215(3) will be responsible for the electronic monitoring and any person by virtue of whose consent the requirement is included in the order with a copy of so much of the order as relates to that requirement: s 219(2), Sch 14.
14 Criminal Justice Act 2003 s 215(4)(a).
15 Criminal Justice Act 2003 s 215(4)(b).
16 Criminal Justice Act 2003 s 215(4)(c).
17 Criminal Justice Act 2003 s 215(4).

18 Criminal Justice Act 2003 s 215(4A)(a)(i) (prospectively added: see note 1).
19 Criminal Justice Act 2003 s 215(4A)(a)(ii) (prospectively added: see note 1).
20 Criminal Justice Act 2003 s 215(4A)(b) (prospectively added: see note 1).
21 Criminal Justice Act 2003 s 215(4A)(c) (prospectively added: see note 1).

137. Rules. The Secretary of State may make rules for regulating:
(1)   the supervision of persons who are subject to relevant orders[1];
(2)   without prejudice to the generality of head (1) above, the functions of responsible officers[2] in relation to offenders subject to relevant orders[3];
(3)   the arrangements to be made by local probation boards or providers of probation services[4] for persons subject to unpaid work requirements[5] to perform work and the performance of such work[6];
(4)   the provision and carrying on of attendance centres[7];
(5)   the attendance of persons subject to rehabilitation activity requirements[8] or attendance centre requirements[9] at the places at which they are required to attend, including hours of attendance, reckoning days of attendance and the keeping of attendance records[10];
(6)   electronic monitoring in pursuance of an electronic monitoring requirement[11]; and
(7)   without prejudice to the generality of head (6) above, the functions of persons made responsible for securing electronic monitoring in pursuance of such a requirement[12].

At the date at which this volume states the law no rules had been made for these purposes.

1   Criminal Justice Act 2003 s 222(1)(a). As to relevant orders see PARA 121.
2   As to the meaning of 'responsible officer' see PARA 81 note 9.
3   Criminal Justice Act 2003 s 222(1)(b).
4   As to the meaning of 'local probation board' see PARA 100 note 12; as to the provision of probation services see PARAS 666–687.
5   See PARA 133.
6   Criminal Justice Act 2003 s 222(1)(c) (amended by SI 2008/912). Rules under the Criminal Justice Act 2003 s 222(1)(c) may, in particular, make provision:
    (1)   limiting the number of hours of work to be done by a person on any one day (s 222(2)(a));
    (2)   as to the reckoning of hours worked and the keeping of work records (s 222(2)(b)); and
    (3)   for the payment of travelling and other expenses in connection with the performance of work (s 222(2)(c)).
7   Criminal Justice Act 2003 s 222(1)(d) (s 221(d), (e) amended by the Offender Rehabilitation Act 2014 Sch 5 paras 1, 5). In connection with the provision of attendance centres by the Secretary of State see the Criminal Justice Act 2003 s 221; and PRISONS AND PRISONERS vol 85 (2012) PARA 515.
8   As to rehabilitation activity requirements see PARA 131.
9   See PARA 134. The reference to attendance centre requirements includes a reference to attendance centre requirements imposed by youth rehabilitation orders under the Criminal Justice and Immigration Act 2008 Pt 1 (ss 1–8) (see PARA 73 et seq): Criminal Justice Act 2003 s 222(1)(e) (as amended (see note 7); amended by the Criminal Justice and Immigration Act 2008 s 6(2), Sch 4 paras 71, 93).
10   Criminal Justice Act 2003 s 222(1)(e) (as amended: see note 9).
11   Criminal Justice Act 2003 s 222(1)(e). As to electronic monitoring requirements see PARA 136.
12   Criminal Justice Act 2003 s 222(1)(f).

(ii) Requirements applicable to Youth Rehabilitation Orders

138. Requirements which may be imposed. The following requirements may be imposed by a youth rehabilitation order[1]:
(1)   an activity requirement[2];

(2)   a supervision requirement[3];

(3)   in a case where the offender is aged 16 or 17 at the time of the conviction, an unpaid work requirement[4];

(4)   a programme requirement[5];

(5)   an attendance centre requirement[6];

(6)   a prohibited activity requirement[7];

(7)   a curfew requirement[8];

(8)   an exclusion requirement[9];

(9)   a residence requirement[10];

(10)   a local authority residence requirement[11];

(11)   a mental health treatment requirement[12];

(12)   a drug treatment requirement[13];

(13)   a drug testing requirement[14];

(14)   an intoxicating substance treatment requirement[15];

(15)   an education requirement[16];

(16)   in certain circumstances, a fostering requirement[17]; and

(17)   in certain circumstances, an electronic monitoring requirement[18].

A youth rehabilitation order may also be made with intensive supervision and surveillance[19].

Where a youth rehabilitation order has effect, it is the duty of the responsible officer[20] to make any arrangements that are necessary in connection with the requirements imposed by the order, to promote the offender's compliance with those requirements, and where appropriate, to take steps to enforce those requirements[21]. In giving instructions in pursuance of a youth rehabilitation order relating to an offender, the responsible officer must ensure, as far as practicable, that any instruction is such as to avoid any conflict with the offender's religious beliefs, any interference with the times, if any, at which the offender normally works or attends school or any other educational establishment and any conflict with the requirements of any other youth rehabilitation order to which the offender may be subject[22].

An offender in respect of whom a youth rehabilitation order is in force must keep in touch with the responsible officer in accordance with such instructions as the offender may from time to time be given by that officer and must notify the responsible officer of any change of address[23].

1   As to the making of youth rehabilitation orders see PARAS 42, 73 et seq.
2   See the Criminal Justice and Immigration Act 2008 s 1(1)(a), Sch 1 para 6; and PARA 139.
3   See the Criminal Justice and Immigration Act 2008 s 1(1)(b), Sch 1 para 9; and PARA 140.
4   See the Criminal Justice and Immigration Act 2008 s 1(1)(c), Sch 1 para 10; and PARA 141.
5   See the Criminal Justice and Immigration Act 2008 s 1(1)(d), Sch 1 para 11; and PARA 142. As to the determination of a person's age see the Children and Young Persons Act 1933 s 99; and CHILDREN AND YOUNG PERSONS vol 10 (2012) PARA 1206.
6   See the Criminal Justice and Immigration Act 2008 s 1(1)(e), Sch 1 para 12; and PARA 143.
7   See the Criminal Justice and Immigration Act 2008 s 1(1)(f), Sch 1 para 13; and PARA 144.
8   See the Criminal Justice and Immigration Act 2008 s 1(1)(g), Sch 1 para 14; and PARA 145.
9   See the Criminal Justice and Immigration Act 2008 s 1(1)(h), Sch 1 para 15; and PARA 146.
10 See the Criminal Justice and Immigration Act 2008 s 1(1)(i), Sch 1 para 16; and PARA 147.
11 See the Criminal Justice and Immigration Act 2008 s 1(1)(j), Sch 1 para 17; and PARA 148.
12 See the Criminal Justice and Immigration Act 2008 s 1(1)(k), Sch 1 para 20; and PARA 149.
13 See the Criminal Justice and Immigration Act 2008 s 1(1)(l), Sch 1 para 22; and PARA 150.
14 See the Criminal Justice and Immigration Act 2008 s 1(1)(m), Sch 1 para 23; and PARA 151.
15 See the Criminal Justice and Immigration Act 2008 s 1(1)(n), Sch 1 para 24; and PARA 152.
16 See the Criminal Justice and Immigration Act 2008 s 1(1)(o), Sch 1 para 25; and PARA 153.
17 See the Criminal Justice and Immigration Act 2008 s 1(3)(b), Sch 1 paras 4, 18; and PARA 154.
18 See the Criminal Justice and Immigration Act 2008 s 1(2), Sch 1 paras 2, 26; and PARA 155.

19 See, in particular, the Criminal Justice and Immigration Act 2008 s 1(3)(a), (4); and PARAS 73, 75.

20 As to the meaning of 'responsible officer' see PARA 81 note 9. However for the purposes of the Criminal Justice and Immigration Act 2008 s 5(1) 'responsible officer' does not include a person falling within s 4(1)(a): s 5(2).

21 Criminal Justice and Immigration Act 2008 s 5(1).

22 Criminal Justice and Immigration Act 2008 s 5(3). The Secretary of State may by order provide that s 5(3) is to have effect with such additional restrictions as may be specified in the order: s 5(4). At the date at which this volume states the law no such order had been made.

23 Criminal Justice and Immigration Act 2008 s 5(5). The obligation imposed by s 5(5) is enforceable as if it were a requirement imposed by the order: s 5(6).

139.   Activity requirement.   'Activity requirement', in relation to a youth rehabilitation order[1] means a requirement that the offender must do any or all of the following:

(1)   participate, on such number of days as may be specified in the order, in activities at a place, or places, so specified[2];

(2)   participate in an activity, or activities, specified in the order on such number of days as may be so specified[3];

(3)   participate in one or more residential exercises for a continuous period or periods comprising such number or numbers of days as may be specified in the order[4];

(4)   engage in activities in accordance with instructions of the responsible officer[5] on such days as may be specified in the order[6].

A requirement, such as is mentioned in head (1) or (2), operates to require the offender, in accordance with instructions given by the responsible officer, on the number of days specified in the order in relation to the requirement:

(a)   in the case of a requirement such as is mentioned in head (1) to present himself or herself at a place specified in the order to a person of a description so specified[7];

(b)   in the case of a requirement such as is mentioned in head (2) to participate in an activity specified in the order[8].

Where the order requires the offender to participate in a residential exercise, it must specify, in relation to the exercise a place[9] or an activity[10].

An activity specified in head (2) above, or in instructions given under head (4) above, may consist of or include an activity whose purpose is that of reparation, such as an activity involving contact between an offender and persons affected by the offences in respect of which the order was made[11].

A court may not include an activity requirement in a youth rehabilitation order unless it has consulted a member of a youth offending team, an officer of a local probation board[12] or an officer of a provider of probation services[13]. Nor may the court include an activity requirement in a youth rehabilitation order unless it is satisfied that it is feasible to secure compliance with the requirement and that provision for the offender to participate in the activities proposed to be specified in the order can be made under the arrangements for persons to participate in such activities which exist in the local justice area in which the offender resides or is to reside[14].

A court may not include an activity requirement in a youth rehabilitation order if compliance with that requirement would involve the co-operation of a person other than the offender and the responsible officer, unless that other person consents to its inclusion[15].

1 As to the making of youth rehabilitation orders see PARAS 42, 73 et seq. A youth rehabilitation order may impose an extended activity requirement known as a youth rehabilitation order with intensive supervision and surveillance: see PARA 75.

2 Criminal Justice and Immigration Act 2008 Sch 1 para 6(1)(a). Subject to Sch 1 para 3(2) the number of days specified in the order under Sch 1 para 6(1)(a) must not in aggregate be more than 90: Sch 1 para 6(2).

3 Criminal Justice and Immigration Act 2008 Sch 1 para 6(1)(b).

4 Criminal Justice and Immigration Act 2008 Sch 1 para 6(1)(c).

5 As to the meaning of 'responsible officer' see PARA 81 note 9; and as to the duties of the responsible officer in respect of a youth rehabilitation order see PARA 138.

6 Criminal Justice and Immigration Act 2008 Sch 1 para 6(1)(d). This requirement is in accordance with Sch 1 para 7 whereby instructions under Sch 1 para 6(1)(d) relating to any day must require the offender to either present himself or herself to a person or persons of a description specified in the instructions at a place so specified or to participate in an activity specified in the instructions: Sch 1 para 7(1). Any such instructions operate to require the offender, on that day, or while participating in that activity, to comply with instructions given by, or under the authority of, the person in charge of the place or, as the case may be, the activity: Sch 1 para 7(2). If the order so provides, instructions under Sch 1 para 6(1)(d) may require the offender to participate in a residential exercise for a period comprising not more than seven days, and, for that purpose to present himself or herself at the beginning of that period to a person of a description specified in the instructions at a place so specified and to reside there for that period or to participate for that period in an activity specified in the instructions: Sch 1 para 7(3). Such instructions operate to require the offender, during the period specified under Sch 1 para 7(3), to comply with instructions given by, or under the authority of, the person in charge of the specified place or activity (as the case may be): Sch 1 para 7(4)(b). However instructions under Sch 1 para 7(3) may not be given except with the consent of a parent or guardian of the offender: Sch 1 para 7(4)(a). As to the parent or guardian of the offender see PARA 73 note 2. Instructions given by, or under the authority of, a person in charge of any place under Sch 1 para 7(2) or Sch 1 para 7(4)(b) may require the offender to engage in activities otherwise than at that place: Sch 1 para 8(1)(c), (d).

7 Criminal Justice and Immigration Act 2008 Sch 1 para 6(3)(a). Instructions given by, or under the authority of, a person in charge or any place under Sch 1 para 6(3) may require the offender to engage in activities otherwise than at that place: Sch 1 para 8(1)(a).

8 Criminal Justice and Immigration Act 2008 Sch 1 para 6(3)(b).

9 Criminal Justice and Immigration Act 2008 Sch 1 para 6(4)(a). If a place is so specified a requirement to participate in a residential exercise operates to require himself or herself, in accordance with instructions given by the responsible officer, to present himself or herself at the beginning of the period specified in the order in relation to the exercise, at the place so specified to a person of a description specified in the instructions and to reside there for that period (Sch 1 para 6(5)(a)), and during that period, to comply with instructions given by, or under the authority of the person in charge of the place or the activity (as the case may be) (Sch 1 para 6(5)).

10 Criminal Justice and Immigration Act 2008 Sch 1 para 6(4)(b). If an activity is specified a requirement to participate in a residential exercise operates to require the offender, in accordance with instructions given by the responsible officer, to participate, for the period specified in the order in relation to the exercise, in the activity so specified (Sch 1 para 6(5)(b)) and, during that period, to comply with instructions given by, or under the authority of, the person in charge of the place or the activity (as the case may be) (Sch 1 para 6(5)). Instructions given by, or under the authority of, a person in charge or any place under Sch 1 para 6(5) may require the offender to engage in activities otherwise than at that place: Sch 1 para 8(1)(b).

11 Criminal Justice and Immigration Act 2008 Sch 1 para 8(2).

12 As to the meaning of 'local probation board' see PARA 73 note 2.

13 Criminal Justice and Immigration Act 2008 Sch 1 para 8(3)(a). As to the provision of probation services see PARAS 666–687.

14 Criminal Justice and Immigration Act 2008 Sch 1 para 8(3)(b), (c).

15 Criminal Justice and Immigration Act 2008 Sch 1 para 8(4).

140. Supervision requirement. 'Supervision requirement', in relation to a youth rehabilitation order[1], means a requirement that during the period for which the order remains in force, the offender must attend appointments with the responsible officer[2], or another person determined by the responsible officer, at such times and places as may be determined by the responsible officer[3].

1 As to the making of youth rehabilitation orders see PARAS 42, 73 et seq.
2 As to the meaning of 'responsible officer' see PARA 81 note 9; and as to the duties of the responsible officer in respect of a youth rehabilitation order see PARA 138.
3 Criminal Justice and Immigration Act 2008 Sch 1 para 9.

141. Unpaid work requirement. 'Unpaid work requirement', in relation to a youth rehabilitation order[1], means a requirement that the offender must perform unpaid work for a specified number of hours[2]. A court may not impose an unpaid work requirement in respect of an offender unless:

(1) after hearing (if the court thinks necessary) an appropriate officer[3], the court is satisfied that the offender is a suitable person to perform work under such a requirement[4]; and

(2) the court is satisfied that provision for the offender to work under such a requirement can be made under the arrangements for persons to perform work under such a requirement which exist in the local justice area in which the offender resides or is to reside[5].

An offender in respect of whom an unpaid work requirement of a youth rehabilitation order is in force must perform for the number of hours specified in the order such work at such times as the responsible officer may specify in instructions[6]. The work required to be performed under an unpaid work requirement of a youth rehabilitation order must[7] be performed during the period of 12 months beginning with the day on which the order takes effect[8]. Unless revoked, a youth rehabilitation order imposing an unpaid work requirement remains in force until the offender has worked under it for the number of hours specified in it[9].

1 As to the making of youth rehabilitation orders see PARAS 42, 73 et seq.
2 See the Criminal Justice and Immigration Act 2008 Sch 1 para 10(1). The number of hours which a person may be required to work under an unpaid work requirement must be specified in the youth rehabilitation order and must be, in aggregate not less than 40 and not more than 240: Sch 1 para 10(2). Where the court is dealing with the offender under Sch 2 para 6(2)(b) (see PARA 85) or Sch 2 para 8(2)(b) (see PARA 86) and the youth rehabilitation order does not contain an unpaid work requirement, Sch 1 para 10(2) applies in relation to the inclusion of such a requirement as if for '40' there were substituted '20': see Sch 2 paras 6(7), 8(7). The Secretary of State may by order amend Sch 1 para 10(2) by substituting, for the maximum number of hours for the time being specified in that provision, such other number of hours as may be specified in the order: Sch 1 para 27(1). At the date at which this volume states the law no such order had been made.
3 For this purpose 'appropriate officer' means a member of a youth offending team, an officer of a local probation board or an officer of a provider of probation services: Criminal Justice and Immigration Act 2008 Sch 1 para 10(4). As to the meanings of 'local probation board' and 'youth offending team' see PARA 73 note 2; as to the provision of probation services see PARAS 666–687.
4 Criminal Justice and Immigration Act 2008 Sch 1 para 10(3)(a).
5 Criminal Justice and Immigration Act 2008 Sch 1 para 10(3)(b).
6 Criminal Justice and Immigration Act 2008 Sch 1 para 10(5). As to the meaning of 'responsible officer' see PARA 81 note 9; and as to the duties of the responsible officer in respect of a youth rehabilitation order see PARA 138.
7 This duty is subject to the Criminal Justice and Immigration Act 2008 Sch 2 para 17 (extension of unpaid work requirement: see PARA 91).
8 Criminal Justice and Immigration Act 2008 Sch 1 para 10(6).
9 Criminal Justice and Immigration Act 2008 Sch 1 para 10(7).

142. Programme requirement. 'Programme requirement', in relation to a youth rehabilitation order[1], means a requirement that the offender must participate in a systematic set of activities (a 'programme') specified in the order at a place or places so specified on such number of days as may be so specified[2]. A programme requirement may require the offender to reside at any place so specified in the order or any period so specified if it is necessary for the offender to reside there for that period in order to participate in the programme[3].

A court may not include a programme requirement in a youth rehabilitation order unless:

(1)   the programme which the court proposes to specify in the order has been recommended to the court by a member of a youth offending team, an officer of a local probation board or an officer of a provider of probation services, as being suitable for the offender[4]; and

(2)   the court is satisfied that the programme is available at the place or places proposed to be specified[5].

A court may not include a programme requirement in a youth rehabilitation order if compliance with that requirement would involve the co-operation of a person other than the offender and the offender's responsible officer[6], unless that other person consents to its inclusion[7].

1   As to the making of youth rehabilitation orders see PARAS 42, 73 et seq.
2   Criminal Justice and Immigration Act 2008 Sch 1 para 11(1). A requirement to participate in a programme operates to require the offender:
     (1)   in accordance with instructions given by the responsible officer to participate in the programme at the place or places specified in the order on the number of days so specified (Sch 1 para 11(5)(a)); and
     (2)   while at any of those places, to comply with instructions given by, or under the authority of, the person in charge of the programme (Sch 1 para 11(5)(b)).
     The programme must be specified in the order: see *R v Price* [2013] EWCA Crim 1283, [2014] 1 Cr App Rep (S) 216.
3   Criminal Justice and Immigration Act 2008 Sch 1 para 11(2).
4   Criminal Justice and Immigration Act 2008 Sch 1 para 11(3)(a). As to the meanings of 'local probation board' and 'youth offending team' see PARA 73 note 2; as to the provision of probation services see PARAS 666–687.
5   Criminal Justice and Immigration Act 2008 Sch 1 para 11(3)(b).
6   As to the meaning of 'responsible officer' see PARA 81 note 9; and as to the duties of the responsible officer in respect of a youth rehabilitation order see PARA 138.
7   Criminal Justice and Immigration Act 2008 Sch 1 para 11(4).

143.   Attendance centre requirement. 'Attendance centre requirement', in relation to a youth rehabilitation order[1], means a requirement that the offender must attend at an attendance centre specified in the order for such number of hours[2] as may be so specified[3]. A court may not include an attendance centre requirement in a youth rehabilitation order unless it:

(1)   has been notified by the Secretary of State that an attendance centre is available for persons of the offender's description and provision can be made at the centre for the offender[4]; and

(2)   is satisfied that the attendance centre proposed to be specified is reasonably accessible to the offender, having regard to the means of access available to the offender and any other circumstances[5].

A requirement to attend at an attendance centre for any period on any occasion operates as a requirement to attend at the centre at the beginning of the period and, during that period, to engage in occupation, or receive instruction, under the supervision of and in accordance with instructions given by, or under the authority of, the officer in charge of the centre, whether at the centre or elsewhere[6].

1   As to the making of youth rehabilitation orders see PARAS 42, 73 et seq.

2   The aggregate number of hours for which the offender may be required to attend at an
     attendance centre:
     (1)   if the offender is aged 16 or over at the time of conviction, must be not less than 12 and
            not more than 36 (Criminal Justice and Immigration Act 2008 Sch 1 para 12(2)(a));
     (2)   if the offender is aged 14 or over but under 16 at the time of conviction, must be not
            less than 12 and not more than 24 (Sch 1 para 12(2)(b));
     (3)   if the offender is aged under 14 at the time of conviction, must not be more than 12
            (Sch 1 para 12(2)(c)).
     The first time at which the offender is required to attend at the attendance centre is a time
     notified to the offender by the responsible officer: Sch 1 para 12(4). The subsequent hours are to
     be fixed by the officer in charge of the centre in accordance with arrangements made by the
     responsible officer and having regard to the offender's circumstances: Sch 1 para 12(5). An
     offender may not be required under Sch 1 para 12 to attend at an attendance centre on more
     than one occasion on any day or for more than three hours on any occasion: Sch 1 para 12(6).
     As to the power of the Secretary of State to may make rules for regulating the attendance of
     persons subject to attendance centre requirements imposed by youth rehabilitation orders see the
     Criminal Justice Act 2003 s 222(1)(e); and PARA 137. As to the meaning of 'responsible officer'
     see PARA 81 note 9; and as to the duties of the responsible officer in respect of a youth
     rehabilitation order see PARA 138. In connection with the provision of attendance centres by the
     Secretary of State see the Criminal Justice Act 2003 s 221; and PRISONS AND PRISONERS vol 85
     (2012) PARA 515. As to the determination of a person's age see the Children and Young Persons
     Act 1933 s 99; and CHILDREN AND YOUNG PERSONS vol 10 (2012) PARA 1206.
3   Criminal Justice and Immigration Act 2008 Sch 1 para 12(1).
4   Criminal Justice and Immigration Act 2008 Sch 1 para 12(3)(a).
5   Criminal Justice and Immigration Act 2008 Sch 1 para 12(3)(b).
6   Criminal Justice and Immigration Act 2008 Sch 1 para 12(7).

144.   Prohibited activity requirement.   'Prohibited activity requirement', in
relation to a youth rehabilitation order[1], means a requirement that the offender
must refrain from participating in activities specified in the order on a day or
days so specified or during a period so specified[2].

A court may not include a prohibited activity requirement in a youth
rehabilitation order unless it has consulted a member of a youth offending team,
an officer of a local probation board or an officer of a provider of probation
services[3].

1   As to the making of youth rehabilitation orders see PARAS 42, 73 et seq.
2   Criminal Justice and Immigration Act 2008 Sch 1 para 13(1). The requirements that may by
     virtue of Sch 1 para 13 be included in a youth rehabilitation order include a requirement that the
     offender does not possess, use or carry a firearm within the meaning of the Firearms Act 1968
     (see CRIMINAL LAW vol 26 (2010) PARA 578): Criminal Justice and Immigration Act 2008 Sch 1
     para 13(3). The primary purpose of a prohibited activity requirement is not punishment, but the
     prevention of reoffending: see *R v Jacob* [2008] EWCA Crim 2002, 172 JP 513, 172 JPN 742.
3   Criminal Justice and Immigration Act 2008 Sch 1 para 13(2). As to the meanings of 'local
     probation board' and 'youth offending team' see PARA 73 note 2; as to the provision of
     probation services see PARAS 666–687.

145.   Curfew requirement.   'Curfew requirement', in relation to a youth
rehabilitation order[1], means a requirement that the offender must remain, for
periods specified in the order, at a place so specified[2].

Before making a youth rehabilitation order imposing a curfew requirement,
the court must obtain and consider information about the place proposed to be
specified in the order (including information as to the attitude of persons likely
to be affected by the enforced presence there of the offender)[3].

1   As to the making of youth rehabilitation orders see PARAS 42, 73 et seq.
2   Criminal Justice and Immigration Act 2008 Sch 1 para 14(1). A youth rehabilitation order
     imposing a curfew requirement may specify different places or different periods for different
     days, but may not specify periods which amount to less than two hours or more than 16 hours
     in any day: Sch 1 para 14(2) (Sch 1 para 14(2), (3) amended by the Legal Aid, Sentencing and

Punishment of Offenders Act 2012 s 81). A youth rehabilitation order imposing a curfew requirement may not specify periods which fall outside the period of 12 months beginning with the day on which the requirement first takes effect: Criminal Justice and Immigration Act 2008 Sch 1 para 14(1) (as so amended). The Secretary of State may by order amend Sch 1 para 14(2) by substituting, for the maximum number of hours for the time being specified in that provision, such other number of hours as may be specified in the order: Sch 1 para 27(1). The Secretary of State may by order amend Sch 1 para 14(3) by substituting, for any period for the time being specified in that provision, such other period as may be specified in the order: Sch 1 para 27(2), (3)(a). At the date at which this volume states the law no such order had been made.

3   Criminal Justice and Immigration Act 2008 Sch 1 para 14(4).

146.   Exclusion requirement. 'Exclusion requirement', in relation to a youth rehabilitation order[1], means a provision prohibiting the offender from entering a place[2] specified in the order for a period so specified[3].

1   As to the making of youth rehabilitation orders see PARAS 42, 73 et seq.

2   For this purpose 'place' includes an area: Criminal Justice and Immigration Act 2008 Sch 1 para 15(4).

3   Criminal Justice and Immigration Act 2008 Sch 1 para 15(1). The period must not be more than three months: Sch 1 para 15(2). The Secretary of State may by order amend Sch 1 para 15(2) by substituting, for any period for the time being specified in that provision, such other period as may be specified in the order: Sch 1 para 27(2), (3)(b). At the date at which this volume states the law no such order had been made. An exclusion requirement may provide for the prohibition to operate only during the periods specified in the order and may specify different places for different periods or days: Sch 1 para 15(3). In connection with the circumstances in which an exclusion requirement would be appropriate see *R v Jacob* [2008] EWCA Crim 2002, 172 JP 513, 172 JPN 742 (exclusion from own home 'disproportionate'); *R (on the application of Dragoman) v Camberwell Green Magistrates' Court* [2012] EWHC 4105 (Admin), 177 JP 372 (exclusion from entering the United Kingdom amounting to expulsion).

147.   Residence requirement. 'Residence requirement', in relation to a youth rehabilitation order[1], means a requirement that, during the period specified in the order, the offender must reside with an individual specified in the order[2] or at a place specified in the order[3]. Before making a youth rehabilitation order containing a place of residence requirement, the court must consider the home surroundings of the offender[4].

A court may not include a place of residence requirement in a youth rehabilitation order unless the offender was aged 16 or over at the time of conviction[5].

If the order so provides, a place of residence requirement does not prohibit the offender from residing, with the prior approval of the responsible officer[6], at a place other than that specified in the order[7].

1   As to the making of youth rehabilitation orders see PARAS 42, 73 et seq.

2   Criminal Justice and Immigration Act 2008 Sch 1 para 16(1)(a). A court may not by virtue of Sch 1 para 16(1)(a) include in a youth rehabilitation order a requirement that the offender reside with an individual unless that individual has consented to the requirement: Sch 1 para 16(2).

3   Criminal Justice and Immigration Act 2008 Sch 1 para 16(1)(b). A residence requirement falling within Sch 1 para 16(1)(b) is referred to as a 'place of residence requirement': Sch 1 para 16(3). A court may not specify a hostel or other institution as the place where an offender must reside for the purposes of a place of residence requirement except on the recommendation of a member of a youth offending team, an officer of a local probation board, an officer of a provider of probation services or a social worker of a local authority: Sch 1 para 16(7). As to the meanings of 'local probation board' and 'youth offending team' see PARA 73 note 2; as to the provision of probation services see PARAS 666–687.

4   Criminal Justice and Immigration Act 2008 Sch 1 para 16(6).

5   Criminal Justice and Immigration Act 2008 Sch 1 para 16(4). As to the determination of a person's age see the Children and Young Persons Act 1933 s 99; and CHILDREN AND YOUNG PERSONS vol 10 (2012) PARA 1206.

6   As to the meaning of 'responsible officer' see PARA 81 note 9; and as to the duties of the responsible officer in respect of a youth rehabilitation order see PARA 138.

7   Criminal Justice and Immigration Act 2008 Sch 1 para 16(5).

148. Local authority residence requirement. 'Local authority residence requirement', in relation to a youth rehabilitation order[1], means a requirement that, during the period specified in the order[2], the offender must reside in accommodation provided by or on behalf of a local authority specified in the order for the purposes of the requirement[3]. A youth rehabilitation order which imposes a local authority residence requirement may also stipulate that the offender is not to reside with a person specified in the order[4].

A youth rehabilitation order which imposes a local authority residence requirement must specify, as the local authority which is to receive the offender, the local authority in whose area the offender resides or is to reside[5].

A court may not include a local authority residence requirement in a youth rehabilitation order made in respect of an offence unless it is satisfied that the behaviour which constituted the offence was due to a significant extent to the circumstances in which the offender was living and that the imposition of that requirement will assist in the offender's rehabilitation[6].

A court may not include a local authority residence requirement in a youth rehabilitation order unless it has consulted a parent or guardian[7] of the offender (unless it is impracticable to consult such a person) and the local authority[8] which is to receive the offender[9].

A court may not include a local authority residence requirement in a youth rehabilitation order in respect of an offender unless the offender was legally represented at the relevant time[10] in court[11] or either of the following conditions is satisfied:

(1)   that representation was made available to the offender[12] for the purposes of the proceedings but right was withdrawn because of his conduct[13]; or

(2)   that the offender has been informed of the right to apply for such representation for the purposes of the proceedings and has had the opportunity to do so, but nevertheless refused or failed to apply[14].

1   As to the making of youth rehabilitation orders see PARAS 42, 73 et seq.

2   Any period specified in a youth rehabilitation order as a period for which the offender must reside in accommodation provided by or on behalf of a local authority must not be longer than six months and not include any period after the offender has reached the age of 18: Criminal Justice and Immigration Act 2008 Sch 1 para 17(6). The Secretary of State may by order amend Sch 1 para 17(6) by substituting, for any period for the time being specified in that provision, such other period as may be specified in the order: Sch 1 para 27(2), (3)(c). At the date at which this volume states the law no such order had been made. As to the meaning of 'local authority' see PARA 73 note 2. As to the determination of a person's age see the Children and Young Persons Act 1933 s 99; and CHILDREN AND YOUNG PERSONS vol 10 (2012) PARA 1206.

3   Criminal Justice and Immigration Act 2008 Sch 1 para 17(1). As to the meaning of 'accommodation provided by or on behalf of a local authority' see PARA 84 note 4.

4   Criminal Justice and Immigration Act 2008 Sch 1 para 17(2).

5   Criminal Justice and Immigration Act 2008 Sch 1 para 17(5).

6   Criminal Justice and Immigration Act 2008 Sch 1 para 17(3).

7   As to the parent or guardian of the offender see PARA 73 note 2.

8   As to the meaning of 'local authority' see PARA 73 note 2.

9   Criminal Justice and Immigration Act 2008 Sch 1 para 17(4).

10   For this purpose 'relevant time' means the time when the court is considering whether to impose that requirement: Criminal Justice and Immigration Act 2008 Sch 1 para 19(3).

11   Criminal Justice and Immigration Act 2008 Sch 1 para 19(1)(a).

12 Ie under the Legal Aid, Sentencing and Punishment of Offenders Act 2012 Pt 1 (ss 1–43) (see LEGAL AID vol 65 (2015) PARA 31 et seq).

13 Criminal Justice and Immigration Act 2008 Sch 1 para 19(1)(b), (2)(a) (Sch 1 para 19(2)(a) amended by the Legal Aid, Sentencing and Punishment of Offenders Act 2012 Sch 5 para 69). For this purpose 'proceedings' means the whole proceedings or the part of the proceedings relating to the imposition of the local authority residence requirement: Criminal Justice and Immigration Act 2008 Sch 1 para 19(3).

14 Criminal Justice and Immigration Act 2008 Sch 1 para 19(2)(b).

149.   Mental health treatment requirement. 'Mental health treatment requirement', in relation to a youth rehabilitation order[1], means a requirement that the offender must submit, during a period or periods specified in the order, to treatment[2] by or under the direction of a registered medical practitioner or a registered psychologist (or both, for different periods) with a view to the improvement of the offender's mental condition[3].

A court may not include a mental health treatment requirement in a youth rehabilitation order unless:

(1) the court is satisfied, on the evidence of an approved[4] registered medical practitioner, that the mental condition of the offender is such as requires and may be susceptible to treatment[5] but is not such as to warrant the making of a hospital order or guardianship order[6];

(2) the court is also satisfied that arrangements have been or can be made for the treatment intended to be specified in the order (including, where the offender is to be required to submit to treatment as a resident patient, arrangements for the reception of the offender)[7]; and

(3) the offender has expressed willingness to comply with the requirement[8].

1 As to the making of youth rehabilitation orders see PARAS 42, 73 et seq.

2 The treatment required during a period specified under the Criminal Justice and Immigration Act 2008 Sch 1 para 20(1) must be such one of the following kinds of treatment as may be specified in the youth rehabilitation order:

(1) treatment as a resident patient in a care home within the meaning of the Care Standards Act 2000 (see s 3; and CHILDREN AND YOUNG PERSONS vol 10 (2012) PARA 994), an independent hospital (ie, in England, a hospital as defined by the National Health Service Act 2006 s 275 that is not a health service hospital as so defined (see HEALTH SERVICES vol 54 (2008) PARA 748), or in relation to Wales, an independent hospital as defined in the Care Standards Act 2000 (see s 2; and HEALTH SERVICES vol 54 (2008) PARAS 748–750)) or a hospital within the meaning of the Mental Health Act 1983 (see s 145(1); and MENTAL HEALTH AND CAPACITY vol 75 (2013) PARAS 577, 578), but not in hospital premises where high security psychiatric services within the meaning of the Mental Health Act 1983 (see s 145(1); the National Health Service Act 2006 s 4(2); the National Health Service (Wales) Act 2006 s 4(2); HEALTH SERVICES vol 54 (2008) PARAS 12, 74; MENTAL HEALTH AND CAPACITY vol 75 (2013) PARA 569) are provided (see the Criminal Justice and Immigration Act 2008 Sch 1 para 20(2)(a), (4A) (Sch 1 para 20(2)(a) amended, s 207(4A) added, by SI 2010/813));

(2) treatment as a non-resident patient at such institution or place as may be specified in the order (Criminal Justice and Immigration Act 2008 Sch 1 para 20(2)(b));

(3) treatment by or under the direction of such registered medical practitioner or registered psychologist (or both) as may be so specified (Sch 1 para 20(2)(c) (amended by SI 2009/1182));

but the order must not otherwise specify the nature of the treatment: Criminal Justice and Immigration Act 2008 Sch 1 para 20(2).

For the purposes of Sch 1 paras 20, 21, 'registered psychologist' means a person for the time being registered in the part of the register maintained under the Health Professions Order 2001, SI 2002/254 (see MEDICAL PROFESSIONS vol 74 (2011) PARA 916 et seq) which relates to practitioner psychologists: Criminal Justice and Immigration Act 2008 Sch 1 para 20(6) (substituted by SI 2009/1182).

Where the registered medical practitioner or registered psychologist by whom or under whose direction an offender is being treated in pursuance of a mental health treatment requirement is of the opinion that part of the treatment can be better or more conveniently given in or at an institution or place which (Criminal Justice and Immigration Act 2008 Sch 1 para 21(1) (amended by SI 2009/1182)):

(a)   is not specified in the youth rehabilitation order (Criminal Justice and Immigration Act 2008 Sch 1 para 21(1)(a)); and

(b)   is one in or at which the treatment of the offender will be given by or under the direction of a registered medical practitioner or registered psychologist (Sch 1 para 21(1)(b) (amended by SI 2009/1182)),

the medical practitioner or psychologist may make arrangements for the offender to be treated accordingly (Criminal Justice and Immigration Act 2008 Sch 1 para 21(1)). Such arrangements may only be made if the offender has expressed willingness for the treatment to be given: Sch 1 para 21(2). Such arrangements may provide for part of the treatment to be provided to the offender as a resident patient in an institution or place notwithstanding that the institution or place is not one which could have been specified for that purpose in the youth rehabilitation order: Sch 1 para 21(3). Where any such arrangements are made for the treatment of an offender:

(i)   the registered medical practitioner or registered psychologist by whom the arrangements are made must give notice in writing to the offender's responsible officer, specifying the institution or place in or at which the treatment is to be carried out (Sch 1 para 21(4)(a) (amended by SI 2009/1182)); and

(ii)   the treatment provided for by the arrangements is deemed to be treatment to which the offender is required to submit in pursuance of the youth rehabilitation order (Criminal Justice and Immigration Act 2008 Sch 1 para 21(4)(b)).

As to the meaning of 'responsible officer' see PARA 81 note 9; and as to the duties of the responsible officer in respect of a youth rehabilitation order see PARA 138.

3   Criminal Justice and Immigration Act 2008 Sch 1 para 20(1) (amended by SI 2009/1182).
4   Ie approved for the purposes of the Mental Health Act 1983 s 12 (see MENTAL HEALTH AND CAPACITY vol 75 (2013) PARA 849).
5   Criminal Justice and Immigration Act 2008 Sch 1 para 20(3)(a)(i) (Sch 1 para 20(3)(a) amended by the Legal Aid, Sentencing and Punishment of Offenders Act 2012 s 82).
6   Criminal Justice and Immigration Act 2008 Sch 1 para 20(3)(a)(ii) (as amended: see note 5). As to the meanings of 'hospital order' and 'guardianship order' see the Mental Health Act 1983; and MENTAL HEALTH AND CAPACITY vol 75 (2013) PARAS 864, 877.
7   Criminal Justice and Immigration Act 2008 Sch 1 para 20(3)(b). While the offender is under treatment as a resident patient in pursuance of a mental health treatment requirement of a youth rehabilitation order, the responsible officer is to carry out the supervision of the offender to such extent only as may be necessary for the purpose of the revocation or amendment of the order: Sch 1 para 20(4).
8   Criminal Justice and Immigration Act 2008 Sch 1 para 20(3)(c).

150. Drug treatment requirement. 'Drug treatment requirement', in relation to a youth rehabilitation order[1], means a requirement that the offender must submit, during a period or periods specified in the order, to treatment, by or under the direction of a person so specified having the necessary qualifications or experience (the 'treatment provider'), with a view to the reduction or elimination of the offender's dependency on, or propensity to misuse, drugs[2].

A court may not include a drug treatment requirement in a youth rehabilitation order unless it is satisfied that the offender is dependent on, or has a propensity to misuse, drugs and that the offender's dependency or propensity is such as requires and may be susceptible to treatment[3].

The treatment required during the period specified must be such one of the following kinds of treatment as may be specified in the youth rehabilitation order:

(1)   treatment as a resident in such institution or place as may be specified in the order[4]; or

(2)   treatment as a non-resident at such institution or place, and at such intervals, as may be so specified[5],

but the order must not otherwise specify the nature of the treatment[6].

A court may not include a drug treatment requirement in a youth rehabilitation order unless:

(a)   the court has been notified by the Secretary of State that arrangements for implementing drug treatment requirements are in force in the local justice area in which the offender resides or is to reside[7];

(b)   the court is satisfied that arrangements have been or can be made for the treatment intended to be specified in the order (including, where the offender is to be required to submit to treatment as a resident, arrangements for the reception of the offender)[8];

(c)   the requirement has been recommended to the court as suitable for the offender by a member of a youth offending team, an officer of a local probation board or an officer of a provider of probation services[9]; and

(d)   the offender has expressed willingness to comply with the requirement[10].

1   As to the making of youth rehabilitation orders see PARAS 42, 73 et seq.
2   Criminal Justice and Immigration Act 2008 Sch 1 para 22(1). For these purposes 'drug' means a controlled drug as defined by the Misuse of Drugs Act 1971 s 2 (see CRIMINAL LAW vol 26 (2010) PARA 723): Criminal Justice and Immigration Act 2008 Sch 1 para 22(5).
3   Criminal Justice and Immigration Act 2008 Sch 1 para 22(2).
4   Criminal Justice and Immigration Act 2008 Sch 1 para 22(3)(a).
5   Criminal Justice and Immigration Act 2008 Sch 1 para 22(3)(b).
6   Criminal Justice and Immigration Act 2008 Sch 1 para 22(3).
7   Criminal Justice and Immigration Act 2008 Sch 1 para 22(4)(a).
8   Criminal Justice and Immigration Act 2008 Sch 1 para 22(4)(b).
9   Criminal Justice and Immigration Act 2008 Sch 1 para 22(4)(c). As to the meanings of 'local probation board' and 'youth offending team' see PARA 73 note 2; as to the provision of probation services see PARAS 666–687.
10   Criminal Justice and Immigration Act 2008 Sch 1 para 22(4)(d).

151.   Drug testing requirement. 'Drug testing requirement', in relation to a youth rehabilitation order[1], means a requirement that, for the purpose of ascertaining whether there is any drug[2] in the offender's body during any treatment period[3], the offender must, during that period[4], provide samples in accordance with instructions given by the responsible officer or the treatment provider[5].

A court may not include a drug testing requirement in a youth rehabilitation order unless:

(1)   the court has been notified by the Secretary of State that arrangements for implementing drug testing requirements are in force in the local justice area in which the offender resides or is to reside[6];

(2)   the order also imposes a drug treatment requirement[7]; and

(3)   the offender has expressed willingness to comply with the requirement[8].

A youth rehabilitation order which imposes a drug testing requirement must provide for the results of tests carried out otherwise than by the responsible officer on samples provided by the offender in pursuance of the requirement to be communicated to the responsible officer[9].

1   As to the making of youth rehabilitation orders see PARAS 42, 73 et seq.
2   As to the meaning of 'drug' see Criminal Justice and Immigration Act 2008 Sch 1 para 22; and PARA 150 note 2 (definition applied by Sch 1 para 23(2)).
3   For these purposes 'treatment period' means a period specified in the youth rehabilitation order as a period during which the offender must submit to treatment as mentioned in the Criminal Justice and Immigration Act 2008 Sch 1 para 22(1) (see PARA 150): Sch 1 para 23(2).
4   A youth rehabilitation order which imposes a drug testing requirement must (1) specify for each month the minimum number of occasions on which samples are to be provided; and (2) the

times at which and circumstances in which the responsible officer or treatment provider may require samples to be provided and descriptions of the samples which may be so required: Criminal Justice and Immigration Act 2008 Sch 1 para 23(4).

5   Criminal Justice and Immigration Act 2008 Sch 1 para 23(1). As to the meaning of 'treatment provider' see PARA 150 (definition applied by Sch 1 para 23(2)). As to the meaning of 'responsible officer' see PARA 81 note 9; and as to the duties of the responsible officer in respect of a youth rehabilitation order see PARA 138.
6   Criminal Justice and Immigration Act 2008 Sch 1 para 23(3)(a).
7   Criminal Justice and Immigration Act 2008 Sch 1 para 23(3)(b).
8   Criminal Justice and Immigration Act 2008 Sch 1 para 23(3)(c).
9   Criminal Justice and Immigration Act 2008 Sch 1 para 23(5).

152.   Intoxicating substance treatment requirement. 'Intoxicating substance treatment requirement', in relation to a youth rehabilitation order[1], means a requirement that the offender must submit, during a period or periods specified in the order, to treatment, by or under the direction of a person so specified having the necessary qualifications or experience, with a view to the reduction or elimination of the offender's dependency on or propensity to misuse intoxicating substances[2].

The treatment required during the period so specified must be such one of the following kinds of treatment as may be specified in the youth rehabilitation order:

(1)   treatment as a resident in such institution or place as may be specified in the order[3]; or

(2)   treatment as a non-resident at such institution or place, and at such intervals, as may be so specified[4],

but the order must not otherwise specify the nature of the treatment[5].

A court may not include an intoxicating substance treatment requirement in a youth rehabilitation order unless it is satisfied that the offender is dependent on, or has a propensity to misuse, intoxicating substances and that the offender's dependency or propensity is such as requires and may be susceptible to treatment[6].

A court may not include an intoxicating substance treatment requirement in a youth rehabilitation order unless:

(a)   the court is satisfied that arrangements have been or can be made for the treatment intended to be specified in the order (including, where the offender is to be required to submit to treatment as a resident, arrangements for the reception of the offender)[7];

(b)   the requirement has been recommended to the court as suitable for the offender by a member of a youth offending team, an officer of a local probation board[8] or an officer of a provider of probation services[9]; and

(c)   the offender has expressed willingness to comply with the requirement[10].

1   As to the making of youth rehabilitation orders see PARAS 42, 73 et seq.
2   Criminal Justice and Immigration Act 2008 Sch 1 para 24(1). For these purposes 'intoxicating substance' means alcohol or any other substance or product (other than a drug) which is, or the fumes of which are, capable of being inhaled or otherwise used for the purpose of causing intoxication: Sch 1 para 24(5). For this purpose 'drug' means a controlled drug as defined by the Misuse of Drugs Act 1791 s 2 (see CRIMINAL LAW vol 26 (2010) PARA 723): Criminal Justice and Immigration Act 2008 Sch 1 para 24(6).
3   Criminal Justice and Immigration Act 2008 Sch 1 para 24(3)(a).
4   Criminal Justice and Immigration Act 2008 Sch 1 para 24(3)(b).
5   Criminal Justice and Immigration Act 2008 Sch 1 para 24(3).
6   Criminal Justice and Immigration Act 2008 Sch 1 para 24(2).
7   Criminal Justice and Immigration Act 2008 Sch 1 para 24(4)(a).

8   As to the meanings of 'local probation board' and 'youth offending team' see PARA 73 note 2; as to the provision of probation services see PARAS 666–687.
9   Criminal Justice and Immigration Act 2008 Sch 1 para 24(4)(b).
10 Criminal Justice and Immigration Act 2008 Sch 1 para 24(4)(c).

153. Education requirement. 'Education requirement', in relation to a youth rehabilitation order[1], means a requirement that the offender must comply, during a period or periods[2] specified in the order, with approved education arrangements[3].

A court may not include an education requirement in a youth rehabilitation order unless it has consulted the local authority proposed to be specified in the order with regard to the proposal to include the requirement[4] and it is satisfied:

(1)   that, in the view of that local authority, arrangements exist for the offender to receive efficient full-time education suitable to the offender's age, ability, aptitude and special educational needs (if any)[5]; and

(2)   that, having regard to the circumstances of the case, the inclusion of the education requirement is necessary for securing the good conduct of the offender or for preventing the commission of further offences[6].

1   As to the making of youth rehabilitation orders see PARAS 42, 73 et seq.
2   Any period specified in a youth rehabilitation order as a period during which an offender must comply with approved education arrangements must not include any period after the offender has ceased to be of compulsory school age: Criminal Justice and Immigration Act 2008 Sch 1 para 25(5). As to compulsory school age see EDUCATION vol 35 (2011) PARA 18. As to the determination of a person's age see the Children and Young Persons Act 1933 s 99; and CHILDREN AND YOUNG PERSONS vol 10 (2012) PARA 1206.
3   Criminal Justice and Immigration Act 2008 Sch 1 para 25(1). For this purpose, 'approved education arrangements' means arrangements for the offender's education made for the time being by the offender's parent or guardian and approved by the local authority specified in the order: Sch 1 para 25(2) (Sch 1 para 25(2), (3), (4), (6) amended by SI 2010/1158). The local authority so specified must be the local authority for the area in which the offender resides or is to reside: Criminal Justice and Immigration Act 2008 Sch 1 para 25(3) (as so amended). As to the meanings of 'parent' and 'local authority' see the Education Act 1996 ss 576(1), 579(1); and EDUCATION vol 35 (2011) PARAS 7, 24 (definition applied by the Criminal Justice and Immigration Act 2008 Sch 1 para 25(6) (as so amended)).
4   Criminal Justice and Immigration Act 2008 Sch 1 para 25(4)(a) (as amended: see note 3).
5   Criminal Justice and Immigration Act 2008 Sch 1 para 25(4)(b)(i) (as amended: see note 3).
6   Criminal Justice and Immigration Act 2008 Sch 1 para 25(4)(b)(ii) (as amended: see note 3).

154. Fostering requirement. 'Fostering requirement', in relation to a youth rehabilitation order[1], means a requirement that the offender must reside with a local authority foster parent[2] for a period specified in the order[3]. If at any time during the period so specified, the responsible officer[4] notifies the offender that no suitable local authority foster parent is available and that the responsible officer has applied or proposes to apply for the revocation or amendment of the order[5], the fostering requirement is, until the determination of the application, to be taken to require the offender to reside in accommodation provided by or on behalf of a local authority[6].

A court may not include a fostering requirement in a youth rehabilitation order unless the court has been notified by the Secretary of State that arrangements for implementing such a requirement are available in the area of the local authority which is to place the offender with a local authority foster parent[7].

A court may not include a fostering requirement in a youth rehabilitation order in respect of an offender unless the offender was legally represented at the relevant time[8] in court[9] or either of the following conditions are satisfied:

(1)   that representation was made available to the offender[10] for the purposes of the proceedings[11] but right was withdrawn because of his conduct[12]; or

(2)   that the offender has been informed of the right to apply for such representation for the purposes of the proceedings[13] and has had the opportunity to do so, but nevertheless refused or failed to apply[14].

1   As to the making of youth rehabilitation orders see PARAS 42, 73 et seq. A fostering requirement may be made only if the offence is punishable with imprisonment and would otherwise justify a custodial sentence: see the Criminal Justice and Immigration Act 2008 s 1(4); and PARA 75.

2   As to the meaning of 'local authority foster parent' see the Children Act 1989 s 22C(12); and CHILDREN AND YOUNG PERSONS vol 10 (2012) PARA 845 (definition applied by the Criminal Justice and Immigration Act 2008 Sch 1 para 18(8)). As to the meaning of 'local authority' see PARA 73 note 2. A youth rehabilitation order which imposes a fostering requirement must specify the local authority which is to place the offender with a local authority foster parent under the Children Act 1989 s 22C (in England: see CHILDREN AND YOUNG PERSONS vol 10 (2012) PARA 858) or s 23(2)(a) (in Wales: see CHILDREN AND YOUNG PERSONS vol 10 (2012) PARA 859): Criminal Justice and Immigration Act 2008 Sch 1 para 18(3) (amended, as from a day to be appointed in relation to Wales, by the Children and Young Persons Act 2008 Sch 1 para 21). The authority so specified must be the local authority in whose area the offender resides or is to reside: Criminal Justice and Immigration Act 2008 Sch 1 para 18(4).

3   Criminal Justice and Immigration Act 2008 Sch 1 para 18(1). Schedule 1 para 18 does not affect the power of a local authority to place with a local authority foster parent an offender in respect of whom a local authority residence requirement (see PARA 148) is imposed: Sch 1 para 18(6).

    A period specified in a youth rehabilitation order as a period for which the offender must reside with a local authority foster parent must:

(1)   end no later than the end of the period of 12 months beginning with the date on which the requirement first has effect (but subject to the Criminal Justice and Immigration Act 2008 Sch 2 paras 6(9), 8(9) and 16(2)) (Sch 1 para 18(2)(a)); and

(2)   not include any period after the offender has reached the age of 18 (Sch 1 para 18(2)(b)).

    The Secretary of State may by order amend Sch 1 para 18(2) by substituting, for any period for the time being specified in that provision, such other period as may be specified in the order: Sch 1 para 27(2), (3)(d). Such an order may also make consequential amendments to Sch 2 paras 6(2), 8(9), 16(2) (see PARAS 85, 89): Sch 1 para 27(4). At the date at which this volume states the law no such order had been made. As to the determination of a person's age see the Children and Young Persons Act 1933 s 99; and CHILDREN AND YOUNG PERSONS vol 10 (2012) PARA 1206.

    Where a youth rehabilitation order imposes a fostering requirement (the 'original requirement'), and under the Criminal Justice and Immigration Act 2008 Sch 2 para 6(2)(b) (see PARA 85) or Sch 2 para 8(2)(b) (see PARA 86) the court proposes to substitute a new fostering requirement (the 'substitute requirement') for the original requirement, Sch 1 para 18(2) applies in relation to the substitute requirement as if the reference to the period of 12 months beginning with the date on which the original requirement first had effect were a reference to the period of 18 months beginning with that date: Sch 2 paras 6(9), 8(9). The Secretary of State may by order amend Sch 2 paras 6(9), 8(9) by substituting for the period of 18 months specified therein the provision or any other period which may be so specified by virtue of a previous order such other period as may be specified in the order: Sch 2 para 25. At the date at which this volume states the law no such order had been made.

    The provisions of Sch 1 para 18 also apply where a youth rehabilitation order imposes a fostering requirement and the court intends to substitute a new fostering requirement: see Sch 2 para 16; and PARA 89.

4   As to the meaning of 'responsible officer' see PARA 81 note 9; and as to the duties of the responsible officer in respect of a youth rehabilitation order see PARA 138.

5   Ie apply for an order under the Criminal Justice and Immigration Act 2008 Pt 3 or Pt 4.

6   Criminal Justice and Immigration Act 2008 Sch 1 para 18(5). As to the meaning of 'accommodation provided by or on behalf of a local authority' see PARA 84 note 4.

7   Criminal Justice and Immigration Act 2008 Sch 1 para 18(7).

8   As to the meaning of 'relevant time' see PARA 148 note 10.

9   Criminal Justice and Immigration Act 2008 Sch 1 para 19(1)(a).

10   Ie under the Legal Aid, Sentencing and Punishment of Offenders Act 2012 Pt 1 (ss 1–43) (see LEGAL AID vol 65 (2015) PARA 31 et seq).

11 For this purpose 'proceedings' means the whole proceedings or the part of the proceedings relating to the imposition of the local authority residence requirement: Criminal Justice and Immigration Act 2008 Sch 1 para 19(3).
12 Criminal Justice and Immigration Act 2008 Sch 1 para 19(1)(b), (2)(a) (Sch 1 para 19(2)(a) amended by the Legal Aid, Sentencing and Punishment of Offenders Act 2012 Sch 5 para 69).
13 Criminal Justice and Immigration Act 2008 Sch 1 para 19(1)(b), (2)(a).
14 Criminal Justice and Immigration Act 2008 Sch 1 para 19(2)(b).

155. Electronic monitoring requirement. 'Electronic monitoring requirement', in relation to a youth rehabilitation order[1], means a requirement for securing the electronic monitoring of the offender's compliance with other requirements imposed by the order during a period specified in the order[2] or determined by the responsible officer in accordance with the order[3].

Where:

(1)   it is proposed to include an electronic monitoring requirement in a youth rehabilitation order[4]; but

(2)   there is a person (other than the offender) without whose co-operation it will not be practicable to secure that the monitoring takes place[5],

the requirement may not be included in the order without that person's consent[6].

A youth rehabilitation order which imposes an electronic monitoring requirement must include provision for making a person responsible for the monitoring[7] and the person who is made responsible for the monitoring must be of a description specified in an order made by the Secretary of State[8].

A court may not include an electronic monitoring requirement in a youth rehabilitation order unless the court:

(a)   has been notified by the Secretary of State that arrangements for electronic monitoring of offenders are available in the local justice area proposed to be specified in the order and for each a curfew requirement, an exclusion requirement and an attendance centre requirement which the court proposes to include in the order, in the area in which the relevant place[9] is situated[10]; and

(b)   is satisfied that the necessary provision can be made under the arrangements currently available[11].

1 As to the making of youth rehabilitation orders see PARAS 42, 73 et seq.
2 Where an electronic monitoring requirement is required to take effect during a period determined by the responsible officer in accordance with the youth rehabilitation order, the responsible officer must, before the beginning of that period, notify the offender, the person responsible for the monitoring and any person falling within the Criminal Justice and Immigration Act 2008 Sch 1 para 26(3)(b), of the time when the period is to begin: Sch 1 para 26(2). As to the meaning of 'responsible officer' see PARA 81 note 9; and as to the duties of the responsible officer in respect of a youth rehabilitation order see PARA 138.
3 Criminal Justice and Immigration Act 2008 Sch 1 para 26(1).
4 Criminal Justice and Immigration Act 2008 Sch 1 para 26(3)(a).
5 Criminal Justice and Immigration Act 2008 Sch 1 para 26(3)(b).
6 Criminal Justice and Immigration Act 2008 Sch 1 para 26(3).
7 Criminal Justice and Immigration Act 2008 Sch 1 para 26(4).
8 Criminal Justice and Immigration Act 2008 Sch 1 para 26(5). See the Criminal Justice (Electronic Monitoring) (Responsible Person) (No 2) Order 2014, SI 2014/669.
9 The relevant places are: (1) in relation to a curfew requirement, the place which the court proposes to specify in the order for the purposes of that requirement; (2) in relation to an exclusion requirement, the place (within the meaning of the Criminal Justice and Immigration Act 2008 Sch 1 para 15 (see PARA 146)) which the court proposes to specify in the order; (3) in relation to an attendance centre requirement, the attendance centre which the court proposes to specify in the order: Sch 1 para 26(7). As to a curfew requirement see PARA 145. As to an attendance centre requirement see PARA 143. As to an exclusion requirement see PARA 146. In

connection with the provision of attendance centres by the Secretary of State see the Criminal Justice Act 2003 s 221; and PRISONS AND PRISONERS vol 85 (2012) PARA 515.

10 Criminal Justice and Immigration Act 2008 Sch 1 para 26(6)(a).

11 Criminal Justice and Immigration Act 2008 Sch 1 para 26(6)(b).

(4) REFERRAL ORDERS

156. Duty and power to refer to youth offender panels. The following provisions[1] apply where a youth court[2] or other magistrates' court is dealing with a person aged under 18[3] for an offence and:

(1) neither the offence nor any connected offence[4] is one for which the sentence is fixed by law[5];

(2) the court is not, in respect of the offence or any connected offence, proposing to impose a custodial sentence on the offender or make a hospital order[6] in his case[7]; and

(3) the court is not proposing to discharge him, whether absolutely or conditionally, in respect of the offence[8].

If the compulsory referral conditions are satisfied[9], and referral is available to the court[10], the court must sentence the offender for the offence by ordering him to be referred to a youth offender panel[11]. If the discretionary referral conditions are satisfied[12], and referral is available to the court, the court may sentence the offender for the offence by ordering him to be referred to a youth offender panel[13]. Both such orders are termed referral orders[14].

1 Ie the Powers of Criminal Courts (Sentencing) Act 2000 s 16: see the text and notes 2–14.

2 As to youth courts see CHILDREN AND YOUNG PERSONS vol 10 (2012) PARA 1225 et seq.

3 As to the determination of a person's age see the Children and Young Persons Act 1933 s 99; and CHILDREN AND YOUNG PERSONS vol 10 (2012) PARA 1206.

4 For the purposes of the Powers of Criminal Courts (Sentencing) Act 2000 Pt III (ss 16–32) an offence is connected with another if the offender falls to be dealt with for it at the same time as he is dealt with for the other offence (whether or not he is convicted of the offences at the same time or by or before the same court): s 16(4).

5 Powers of Criminal Courts (Sentencing) Act 2000 s 16(1)(a).

6 Ie within the meaning of the Mental Health Act 1983: see s 37; and PARA 472 et seq.

7 Powers of Criminal Courts (Sentencing) Act 2000 s 16(1)(b).

8 Powers of Criminal Courts (Sentencing) Act 2000 s 16(1)(c) (amended by the Legal Aid, Sentencing and Punishment of Offenders Act 2012 s 79(1)). As to discharge see PARA 443.

9 As to compulsory referral conditions see the Powers of Criminal Courts (Sentencing) Act 2000 s 17; and PARA 157.

10 For these purposes, referral is available to a court if the court has been notified by the Secretary of State that arrangements for the implementation of referral orders are available in the area in which it appears to the court that the offender resides or will reside; and the notice has not been withdrawn: Powers of Criminal Courts (Sentencing) Act 2000 s 16(5).

11 Powers of Criminal Courts (Sentencing) Act 2000 s 16(2). As to the establishment of youth offender panels, and attendance at youth offender panel meetings, see ss 21–27; and PARAS 161–167. Where s 16(2) requires a court to make a referral order, the court may not under s 1 (see PARA 457) defer passing sentence on him, but s 16(2) does not affect any power or duty of a magistrates' court under:

(1) s 8 (remission to youth court, or another such court, for sentence) (see PARA 1; and CHILDREN AND YOUNG PERSONS vol 10 (2012) PARA 1221) (s 19(7)(a));

(2) the Magistrates' Courts Act 1980 s 10(3) (adjournment for inquiries) (see CRIMINAL PROCEDURE vol 27 (2015) PARA 290) (Powers of Criminal Courts (Sentencing) Act 2000 s 19(7)(b)); or

(3) the Mental Health Act 1983 s 35, s 38, s 43 or s 44 (remand for reports, interim hospital orders and committal to Crown Court for restriction order) (see MENTAL HEALTH AND CAPACITY vol 75 (2013) PARAS 862, 864, 873) (Powers of Criminal Courts (Sentencing) Act 2000 s 19(7)(c)).

12 As to the discretionary referral conditions see the Powers of Criminal Courts (Sentencing) Act 2000 s 17; and PARA 157.

13 Powers of Criminal Courts (Sentencing) Act 2000 s 16(3).
14 Powers of Criminal Courts (Sentencing) Act 2000 s 16(6). No referral order may be made in respect of any offence committed before 25 August 2000 (ie the commencement of the Youth Justice and Criminal Evidence Act 1999 s 1 (repealed), from which these provisions derive): Powers of Criminal Courts (Sentencing) Act 2000 s 16(7).

157. The referral conditions. The compulsory referral conditions[1] are satisfied in relation to an offence if the offence is punishable with imprisonment and the offender[2]:

(1)   pleaded guilty to the offence and to any connected offence[3]; and

(2)   has never been convicted by or before a court in the United Kingdom[4] of any offence other than the offence and any connected offence or convicted by or before a court in another member state of any offence[5].

The discretionary referral conditions are satisfied[6] in relation to an offence if the compulsory referral conditions are not satisfied in relation to the offence[7] and the offender pleaded guilty to the offence or, if the offender is being dealt with by the court for the offence and any connected offence, to at least one of those offences[8].

1 Ie in relation to the Powers of Criminal Courts (Sentencing) Act 2000 s 16(2) (see PARA 156) and s 17(2) (see the text and notes 6–8).
2 Powers of Criminal Courts (Sentencing) Act 2000 s 17(1) (s 17(1) amended, s 17(2) substituted, by the Criminal Justice and Immigration Act 2008 s 35(1)–(3); Powers of Criminal Courts (Sentencing) Act 2000 s 17(1) also amended by SI 2003/1605). The Referral Orders (Amendment of Referral Conditions) Regulations 2003, SI 2003/1605, were made pursuant to the Powers of Criminal Courts (Sentencing) Act 2000 s 17(3), which empowers the Secretary of State by regulations to make such amendments of s 17 as he considers appropriate for altering in any way the descriptions of offenders in the case of which the compulsory referral conditions or the discretionary referral conditions fall to be satisfied for the purposes of s 16(2) or (3) (see PARA 156). Any description of offender having effect for those purposes by virtue of the Referral Orders (Amendment of Referral Conditions) Regulations 2003, SI 2003/1605, may be framed by reference to such matters as the Secretary of State considers appropriate, including, in particular, one or more of:
    (1)   the offender's age (Powers of Criminal Courts (Sentencing) Act 2000 s 17(4)(a));
    (2)   how the offender has pleaded (s 17(4)(b));
    (3)   the offence (or offences) of which the offender has been convicted (s 17(4)(c));
    (4)   the offender's previous convictions, if any (s 17(4)(d));
    (5)   how, if at all, the offender has been previously punished or otherwise dealt with by any court (s 17(4)(e)); and
    (6)   any characteristics or behaviour of, or circumstances relating to, any person who has at any time been charged in the same proceedings as the offender (whether or not in respect of the same offence) (s 17(4)(f)).
    As to the determination of a person's age see the Children and Young Persons Act 1933 s 99; and CHILDREN AND YOUNG PERSONS vol 10 (2012) PARA 1206.
3 Powers of Criminal Courts (Sentencing) Act 2000 s 17(1)(a) (as amended: see note 2). As to the meaning of 'connected offence' see PARA 156 note 4.
4 As to the meaning of 'United Kingdom' see PARA 4 note 3.
5 Powers of Criminal Courts (Sentencing) Act 2000 s 17(1)(b) (substituted by the Coroners and Justice Act 2009 Sch 17 para 12(1), (2)).
6 Ie for the purposes of the Powers of Criminal Courts (Sentencing) Act 2000 s 16(3): see PARA 156.
7 Powers of Criminal Courts (Sentencing) Act 2000 s 17(2)(a) (as substituted: see note 2).
8 Powers of Criminal Courts (Sentencing) Act 2000 s 17(2)(b) (as substituted: see note 2).

158. Making of referral orders. A referral order must:

(1)   specify the youth offending team[1] responsible for implementing the order[2];

(2)   require the offender to attend each of the meetings of a youth offender panel[3] to be established by the team for the offender[4]; and

(3)   specify the period for which any youth offender contract taking effect between the offender and the panel[5] is to have effect[6].

The youth offending team specified under head (1) above is the team having the function of implementing referral orders in the area in which it appears to the court that the offender resides or will reside[7].

On making a referral order the court must explain to the offender in ordinary language the effect of the order, and the consequences which may follow if no youth offender contract takes effect between the offender and the panel[8], or if the offender breaches any of the terms of any such contract[9].

Where, in dealing with an offender for two or more connected offences[10], a court makes a referral order in respect of each, or each of two or more, of the offences[11]:

(a)   the orders have the effect of referring the offender to a single youth offender panel[12];

(b)   the court may direct that the period so specified in either or any of the orders is to run concurrently with or to be additional to that specified in the other or any of the others[13]; and

(c)   each of the orders[14] must, for these purposes[15], be treated as associated with the other or each of the others[16].

1   As to youth offending teams see **CHILDREN AND YOUNG PERSONS** vol 10 (2012) PARA 1193.
2   Powers of the Criminal Courts (Sentencing) Act 2000 s 18(1)(a).
3   As to the establishment of youth offender panels, and attendance at youth offender panel meetings, see the Powers of the Criminal Courts (Sentencing) Act 2000 ss 21–27; and PARAS 161–167 (for these purposes, 'meeting', in relation to a youth offender panel, is to be construed in accordance with the Powers of the Criminal Courts (Sentencing) Act 2000 s 21(7)): s 32.
4   Powers of the Criminal Courts (Sentencing) Act 2000 s 18(1)(b).
5   Ie under the Powers of the Criminal Courts (Sentencing) Act 2000 s 23: see PARA 163.
6   Powers of the Criminal Courts (Sentencing) Act 2000 s 18(1)(c). The specified period must not be less than three nor more than 12 months: s 18(1)(c).
7   Powers of the Criminal Courts (Sentencing) Act 2000 s 18(2).
8   See note 3.
9   Powers of the Criminal Courts (Sentencing) Act 2000 s 18(3).
10   As to the meaning of 'connected offence' see PARA 156 note 4.
11   Powers of the Criminal Courts (Sentencing) Act 2000 s 18(4).
12   Powers of the Criminal Courts (Sentencing) Act 2000 s 18(5). The provision made under heads (1)–(3) in the text must accordingly be the same in each case, except that the periods specified under head (3) in the text may be different: s 18(5).
13   Powers of the Criminal Courts (Sentencing) Act 2000 s 18(6). However, in exercising its power under s 18(6), the court must ensure that the total period for which such a contract as is mentioned in head (3) in the text is to have effect does not exceed 12 months: s 18(6).
14   Ie the orders mentioned in the Powers of the Criminal Courts (Sentencing) Act 2000 s 18(4): see the text to notes 10–11.
15   Ie for the purposes of the Powers of the Criminal Courts (Sentencing) Act 2000 Pt III (ss 16–32).
16   Powers of the Criminal Courts (Sentencing) Act 2000 s 18(7).

159.   The effect of referral orders on the court's other sentencing powers.
Where a court makes a referral order in respect of an offence[1]:

(1)   the court may not deal with the offender for the offence by[2]:

(a)   imposing a sentence which consists of or includes a youth rehabilitation order[3] on the offender[4];

(b)   ordering him to pay a fine[5];

(c)   making an order[6] requiring the offender to attend meetings in connection with a prostitution offence[7];

(d)   making a reparation order[8] in respect of him[9]; or

(e)   making an order discharging him conditionally[10];

(2) the court:

    (a) must, in respect of any connected offence[11], either sentence the offender by making a referral order or make an order discharging him absolutely[12]; and

    (b) may not deal with the offender for any such offence in any of the prohibited ways listed in heads (1)(a) to (d) above[13]; and

(3) the court may not make, in connection with the conviction of the offender for the offence or any connected offence:

    (a) an order binding him over to keep the peace or to be of good behaviour[14]; or

    (b) an order binding over an offender's parent or guardian[15].

Where a court is required to make a referral order[16], the court may not[17] defer passing sentence on him[18].

1   Powers of Criminal Courts (Sentencing) Act 2000 s 19(1).

2   Powers of Criminal Courts (Sentencing) Act 2000 s 19(2). The provisions of s 19(2), (3), (5) do not affect the exercise of any power to deal with the offender conferred by Sch 1 Pt I para 5 (offender referred back to court by panel: see PARA 169) or Sch 1 Pt II para 14 (powers of a court where offender convicted while subject to referral: see PARA 172): s 19(6).

3   As to the making of youth rehabilitation orders see PARA 73.

4   Powers of Criminal Courts (Sentencing) Act 2000 s 19(4)(a) (amended by the Criminal Justice and Immigration Act 2008 Sch 4 paras 51, 52).

5   Powers of Criminal Courts (Sentencing) Act 2000 s 19(4)(b). As to fines and surcharges see PARA 174 et seq.

6   Ie an order under the Street Offences Act 1959 s 1(2A) (see CRIMINAL LAW vol 25 (2010) PARA 251).

7   Powers of Criminal Courts (Sentencing) Act 2000 s 19(4)(ba) (added by the Policing and Crime Act 2009 Sch 7 para 22).

8   As to reparation orders see PARA 293 et seq.

9   Powers of Criminal Courts (Sentencing) Act 2000 s 19(4)(c).

10 Powers of Criminal Courts (Sentencing) Act 2000 s 19(4)(d). As to discharge see PARA 443 et seq.

11 As to the meaning of 'connected offence' see PARA 156 note 4.

12 Powers of Criminal Courts (Sentencing) Act 2000 s 19(3)(a). See note 2. Where s 16(2) (see PARA 156) requires a court to make a referral order, the court may not under s 1 (see PARA 457) defer passing sentence on him, but s 19(3)(a) does not affect any power or duty of a magistrates' court under:

    (1) s 8 (remission to youth court, or another such court, for sentence) (see PARA 1; and CHILDREN AND YOUNG PERSONS vol 10 (2012) PARA 1221) (s 19(7)(a));

    (2) the Magistrates' Courts Act 1980 s 10(3) (adjournment for inquiries) (see CRIMINAL PROCEDURE vol 27 (2015) PARA 290) (Powers of Criminal Courts (Sentencing) Act 2000 s 19(7)(b)); or

    (3) the Mental Health Act 1983 s 35, s 38, s 43 or s 44 (remand for reports, interim hospital orders and committal to Crown Court for restriction order) (see MENTAL HEALTH AND CAPACITY vol 75 (2013) PARAS 862, 864, 873) (Powers of Criminal Courts (Sentencing) Act 2000 s 19(7)(c)).

13 Powers of Criminal Courts (Sentencing) Act 2000 s 19(3)(b). See note 2.

14 Powers of Criminal Courts (Sentencing) Act 2000 s 19(5)(a). See note 2. As to binding over see PARAS 447–448.

15 Powers of Criminal Courts (Sentencing) Act 2000 s 19(5)(b). As to such an order see s 150; and CHILDREN AND YOUNG PERSONS vol 10 (2012) PARA 1299. See note 2.

16 Ie under the Powers of Criminal Courts (Sentencing) Act 2000 s 16(2): see PARA 156.

17 Ie under the Powers of Criminal Courts (Sentencing) Act 2000 s 1: see PARA 457.

18 Powers of Criminal Courts (Sentencing) Act 2000 s 19(7).

160. Attendance of parents at the making of referral orders. A court making a referral order[1] may make an order requiring the guardian or parent of the offender (the 'appropriate person')[2], or, in a case where there are two or more appropriate persons, any one or more of them, to attend the meetings of the youth offender panel[3]. Where an offender is aged under 16 when a court makes a referral order in his case the court must exercise this power so as to require at least one appropriate person to attend meetings of the youth offender panel[4]. If the offender is a child who is looked after by the local authority[5], the person or persons so required to attend those meetings must be or include a representative of the relevant local authority[6]. The court must not[7] make an order requiring a person to attend meetings of the youth offender panel if the court is satisfied that it would be unreasonable to do so, or to an extent which the court is satisfied would be unreasonable[8].

If, at the time when a court makes such an order[9]:

(1)   a person who is required by the order to attend meetings of a youth offender panel is not present in court[10]; or

(2)   a local authority whose representative is so required to attend such meetings is not represented in court[11],

the court must send him or (as the case may be) the authority a copy of the order immediately[12].

1   As to the making of referral orders see PARA 156.
2   Except where the offender falls within the Powers of Criminal Courts (Sentencing) Act 2000 s 20(6) (see the text and note 5), each person who is a parent or guardian of the offender is an 'appropriate person' for the purposes of s 20: s 20(4).
3   Powers of Criminal Courts (Sentencing) Act 2000 s 20(1). As to the establishment of youth offender panels, and attendance at youth offender panel meetings, see ss 21–27; and PARAS 161–167.
4   Powers of Criminal Courts (Sentencing) Act 2000 s 20(2)(a). As to the determination of a person's age see the Children and Young Persons Act 1933 s 99; and CHILDREN AND YOUNG PERSONS vol 10 (2012) PARA 1206.
5   Ie within the meaning of the Children Act 1989: see the Powers of Criminal Courts (Sentencing) Act 2000 s 20(6); and CHILDREN AND YOUNG PERSONS vol 10 (2012) PARA 843. Where the offender falls within s 20(6), each of the following is an 'appropriate person' for the purposes of s 20:
    (1)   a representative of the local authority mentioned in s 20(6) (s 20(5)(a)); and
    (2)   each person who is a parent or guardian of the offender with whom the offender is allowed to live (s 20(5)(b)).
6   Powers of Criminal Courts (Sentencing) Act 2000 s 20(2)(b).
7   Ie under the Powers of Criminal Courts (Sentencing) Act 2000 s 20.
8   Powers of Criminal Courts (Sentencing) Act 2000 s 20(3).
9   See note 7.
10 Powers of Criminal Courts (Sentencing) Act 2000 s 20(7)(a).
11 Powers of Criminal Courts (Sentencing) Act 2000 s 20(7)(b).
12 Powers of Criminal Courts (Sentencing) Act 2000 s 20(7).

161. Establishment of youth offender panels. Where a referral order has been made[1] in respect of an offender (or two or more associated[2] referral orders have been so made), it is the duty of the youth offending team specified in the order (or orders):

(1)   to establish a youth offender panel for the offender[3];

(2)   to arrange for the first meeting of the panel to be held[4]; and

(3)   subsequently to arrange for the holding of any further meetings of the panel required[5].

A youth offender panel must be constituted, conduct its proceedings, and discharge its functions[6] in accordance with guidance given from time to time by the Secretary of State[7]. At each of its meetings a panel must, however, consist of at least one member appointed by the youth offending team from among its members, and two members so appointed who are not members of the team[8]. The Secretary of State may by regulations make provision requiring persons appointed as members of a youth offender panel to have such qualifications, or satisfy such other criteria, as are specified in the regulations[9].

Where it appears to the court which made a referral order that, by reason of either a change or a prospective change in the offender's place or intended place of residence, the youth offending team for the time being specified in the order ('the current team') either does not or will not have the function of implementing referral orders in the area in which the offender resides or will reside, the court may amend the order so that it instead specifies the team which has the function of implementing such orders in that area ('the new team')[10]. Where a court so amends a referral order:

(a)   the new youth offending team must establish a youth offender panel for the offender[11];

(b)   the new youth offending team must arrange for the first meeting of the panel to be held if no youth offender contract has taken effect[12] between the offender and a youth offender panel established by the current team[13]; and

(c)   if such a contract has so taken effect[14], it must (after the amendment) be treated as if it were a contract which had taken effect[15] between the offender and the panel being established for the offender by the new team[16].

1   As to the making of referral orders see PARAS 156–158.
2   As to when orders are to be treated as associated see the Powers of Criminal Courts (Sentencing) Act 2000 s 18(7); and PARA 158.
3   Powers of Criminal Courts (Sentencing) Act 2000 s 21(1)(a). As to youth offending teams see **CHILDREN AND YOUNG PERSONS** vol 10 (2012) PARA 1193.
4   Powers of Criminal Courts (Sentencing) Act 2000 s 21(1)(b). The first meeting of the panel has as its aim to reach agreement with the offender on a programme of behaviour the aim (or principal aim) of which is the prevention of re-offending by the offender: see s 23; and PARA 163. References in Pt III (ss 16–32) to the meetings of a youth offender panel (or any such meeting) are to the following meetings of the panel (or any of them):
      (1)   the first meeting held in pursuance of s 21(1)(b) (s 21(7)(a));
      (2)   any further meetings held in pursuance of s 25 (see PARA 165) (s 21(7)(b));
      (3)   any progress meeting held under s 26 (see PARA 166) (s 21(7)(c)); and
      (4)   the final meeting held under s 27 (see PARA 167) (s 21(7)(d)).
      As to meetings in relation to youth offender panels see PARA 158.
5   Powers of Criminal Courts (Sentencing) Act 2000 s 21(1)(c). Such further meetings of the panel may be required by virtue of s 25, in addition to those required by virtue of any other provisions of Pt III: see PARA 165.
6   Ie its functions under the Powers of Criminal Courts (Sentencing) Act 2000 Pt III. Particular attention must be given to those functions arising under s 23: see PARA 163.
7   Powers of Criminal Courts (Sentencing) Act 2000 s 21(2).
8   Powers of Criminal Courts (Sentencing) Act 2000 s 21(3).
9   Powers of Criminal Courts (Sentencing) Act 2000 s 21(4). At the date at which this volume states the law no such regulations had been made.
10   Powers of Criminal Courts (Sentencing) Act 2000 s 21(5).
11   Powers of Criminal Courts (Sentencing) Act 2000 s 21(6)(a); and see s 21(1)(a).
12   Or has been treated as having taken effect: Powers of Criminal Courts (Sentencing) Act 2000 s 21(6)(b).
13   Powers of Criminal Courts (Sentencing) Act 2000 s 21(6)(b); and see s 21(1)(b).
14   Or has previously under Powers of Criminal Courts (Sentencing) Act 2000 s 21(6) been treated as having so taken effect: s 21(6)(c).
15   Ie under the Powers of Criminal Courts (Sentencing) Act 2000 s 23.
16   Powers of Criminal Courts (Sentencing) Act 2000 s 21(6)(c).

162.   Attendance at youth offender panel meetings. The specified youth offending team must, in the case of each meeting of the youth offender panel established for the offender[1], notify the offender, and any person who is required by order to attend the meeting of the youth offender panel[2], of the time and place at which he is required to attend that meeting[3]. If the offender fails to attend any part of such a meeting the panel may adjourn the meeting[4] to such time and place as it may specify, or end the meeting and refer the offender back to the appropriate court[5]. If a parent or guardian of the offender fails to comply with an order requiring attendance at meetings and the offender is aged under 18 at the time of the failure, the panel may refer that parent or guardian to a youth court acting in the local justice area[6]. One person aged 18 or over chosen by the offender, with the agreement of the panel, is entitled to accompany the offender to any meeting of the panel (and it need not be the same person who accompanies him to every meeting)[7].

The panel may allow to attend any such meeting:

(1) any person who appears to the panel to be a victim of, or otherwise affected by, the offence, or any of the offences, in respect of which the offender was referred to the panel[8]; and

(2) any person who appears to the panel to be someone capable of having a good influence on the offender[9].

Where the panel allows any such person as is mentioned in head (1) above ('the victim') to attend a meeting of the panel, the panel may allow the victim to be accompanied to the meeting by one person chosen by the victim with the agreement of the panel[10].

1 See PARA 161. As to meetings in relation to youth offender panels see PARA 158.

2 Ie the appropriate person or persons to whom an order under the Powers of Criminal Courts (Sentencing) Act 2000 s 20 applies: see PARA 160.

3 Powers of Criminal Courts (Sentencing) Act 2000 s 22(1).

4 Powers of Criminal Courts (Sentencing) Act 2000 s 22(1) applies in relation to any such adjourned meeting: s 22(2).

5 Powers of Criminal Courts (Sentencing) Act 2000 s 22(2). As to the meaning of 'appropriate court' see Sch 1 para 1(2); and PARA 169 note 2 (definition applied by s 32). Nothing in s 22(2) prevents the panel from making the decision mentioned in s 27(3) (where the panel decides that the offender's compliance with the terms of the youth offender contract has been such as to justify the conclusion that, by the time the compliance period expires, the young offender will have satisfactorily completed that contract, that decision has the effect of discharging the referral order (or orders) as from the end of the compliance period: see PARA 167) in the offender's absence if it appears to the panel to be appropriate to do that instead of exercising either of its powers under s 22(2): s 27(5). See also the Home Office, Lord Chancellor's Department and Youth Justice Board publication *Referral Orders and Youth Offender Panels—Guidance for Courts, Youth Offending Teams and Youth Offender Panels* (May 2009).

6 Powers of Criminal Courts (Sentencing) Act 2000 s 22(2A) (added by the Criminal Justice Act 2003 s 324, Sch 34 para 4). As to what happens on a such a referral see the Powers of Criminal Courts (Sentencing) Act 2000 Sch 1 Pt 1A; and PARA 170. As to the determination of a person's age see the Children and Young Persons Act 1933 s 99; and CHILDREN AND YOUNG PERSONS vol 10 (2012) PARA 1206.

7 Powers of Criminal Courts (Sentencing) Act 2000 s 22(3).

8 Powers of Criminal Courts (Sentencing) Act 2000 s 22(4)(a).

9 Powers of Criminal Courts (Sentencing) Act 2000 s 22(4)(b).

10 Powers of Criminal Courts (Sentencing) Act 2000 s 22(5).

163. Agreement of youth offender contract with offender. At the first meeting of the youth offender panel established for an offender[1], the panel must seek to reach agreement with the offender on a programme of behaviour the aim (or principal aim) of which is the prevention of re-offending by the offender[2]. The terms of the programme may, in particular, include provision for[3]:

(1) the offender to make financial or other reparation to any person who

appears to the panel to be a victim of, or otherwise affected by, the offence, or any of the offences, for which the offender was referred to the panel[4];

(2) the offender to attend mediation sessions with any such victim or other person[5];

(3) the offender to carry out unpaid work or service in or for the community[6];

(4) the offender to be at home at times specified in or determined under the programme[7];

(5) attendance by the offender at a school or other educational establishment or at a place of work[8];

(6) the offender to participate in specified activities (such as those designed to address offending behaviour, those offering education or training or those assisting with the rehabilitation of persons dependent on, or having a propensity to misuse, alcohol or drugs)[9];

(7) the offender to present himself to specified persons at times and places specified in or determined under the programme[10];

(8) the offender to stay away from specified places or persons (or both)[11];

(9) enabling the offender's compliance with the programme to be supervised and recorded[12].

The programme may not, however, provide for the electronic monitoring of the offender's whereabouts, or for the offender to have imposed on him any physical restriction on his movements[13]. Where a programme is agreed between the offender and the panel, the panel must cause a written record of the programme to be produced immediately in language capable of being readily understood by, or explained to, the offender, and for signature by him[14]. Once the record has been signed by the offender, and by a member of the panel on behalf of the panel, the terms of the programme, as set out in the record, take effect as the terms of a 'youth offender contract' between the offender and the panel; and the panel must cause a copy of the record to be given or sent to the offender[15].

1 As to the establishment of youth offender panels see PARA 161. As to meetings in relation to youth offender panels see PARA 158.
2 Powers of Criminal Courts (Sentencing) Act 2000 s 23(1).
3 Powers of Criminal Courts (Sentencing) Act 2000 s 23(2).
4 Powers of Criminal Courts (Sentencing) Act 2000 s 23(2)(a). No term which provides for anything to be done to or with any such victim or other affected person as is mentioned in s 23(2)(a) may be included in the programme without the consent of that person: s 23(4).
5 Powers of Criminal Courts (Sentencing) Act 2000 s 23(2)(b).
6 Powers of Criminal Courts (Sentencing) Act 2000 s 23(2)(c).
7 Powers of Criminal Courts (Sentencing) Act 2000 s 23(2)(d).
8 Powers of Criminal Courts (Sentencing) Act 2000 s 23(2)(e).
9 Powers of Criminal Courts (Sentencing) Act 2000 s 23(2)(f).
10 Powers of Criminal Courts (Sentencing) Act 2000 s 23(2)(g).
11 Powers of Criminal Courts (Sentencing) Act 2000 s 23(2)(h).
12 Powers of Criminal Courts (Sentencing) Act 2000 s 23(2)(i).
13 Powers of Criminal Courts (Sentencing) Act 2000 s 23(3).
14 Powers of Criminal Courts (Sentencing) Act 2000 s 23(5).
15 Powers of Criminal Courts (Sentencing) Act 2000 s 23(6). A copy should be given to the parent or guardian as well as anyone else who will be assisting the offender: see the Home Office, Lord Chancellor's Department and Youth Justice Board publication *Referral Orders and Youth Offender Panels—Guidance for Courts, Youth Offending Teams and Youth Offender Panels* (May 2009) para 8.39.

164.   Duration of youth offender contracts. The following provisions[1] apply where a youth offender contract has taken effect[2] between an offender and a youth offender panel[3]. The day on which the youth offender contract so takes effect is the first day of the period for which it has effect[4].

Where the panel was established in pursuance of a single referral order, the length of the period for which the contract has effect is that of the period specified[5] in the referral order[6]. Where the panel was established in pursuance of two or more associated[7] referral orders, the length of the period for which the contract has effect is that resulting from the court's directions[8].

If the referral order, or each of the associated referral orders, is revoked[9], the period for which the contract has effect expires at the time when the order or orders is or are revoked unless it has already expired[10].

1   Ie the Powers of Criminal Courts (Sentencing) Act 2000 s 24.
2   Ie under the Powers of Criminal Courts (Sentencing) Act 2000 s 23: see PARA 163.
3   Powers of Criminal Courts (Sentencing) Act 2000 s 24(1). As to the establishment of youth offender panels see PARA 161.
4   Powers of Criminal Courts (Sentencing) Act 2000 s 24(2).
5   Ie the period specified under the Powers of Criminal Courts (Sentencing) Act 2000 s 18(1)(c): see PARA 158.
6   Powers of Criminal Courts (Sentencing) Act 2000 s 24(3). Section 24(3), (4) have effect subject to: (1) any order under s 28, Sch 1 Pt 1ZA para 9ZD or Pt II para 11 or 12 extending the length of the period for which the contract has effect (s 24(5)(a) (amended by the Criminal Justice and Immigration Act 2008 Sch 26 Pt 2 paras 40, 42)); and (2) the Powers of Criminal Courts (Sentencing) Act 2000 s 24(6) (see the text and notes 9–10) (s 24(5)(b)). As to the making of referral orders see PARAS 156–158.
7   As to when orders are to be treated as associated see the Powers of Criminal Courts (Sentencing) Act 2000 s 18(7); and PARA 158 (definition applied by s 32).
8   Powers of Criminal Courts (Sentencing) Act 2000 s 24(4). See note 6.
9   Ie whether under the Powers of Criminal Courts (Sentencing) Act 2000 Sch 1 Pt I para 5(2) or by virtue of Sch 1 Pt II para 14(2): see PARA 172.
10 Powers of Criminal Courts (Sentencing) Act 2000 s 24(6).

165.   Failure to agree a youth offender contract. Where it appears to a youth offender panel to be appropriate to do so, the panel may:

(1)   end the first meeting[1] (or any further meeting held in pursuance of head (2) below) without having reached agreement with the offender on a programme of behaviour[2]; and

(2)   resume consideration of the offender's case at a further meeting of the panel[3].

If, however, it appears to the panel at the first meeting or any such further meeting that there is no prospect of agreement being reached with the offender within a reasonable period after the making of the referral order (or orders), head (2) above does not apply and instead the panel must refer the offender back to the appropriate court[4].

If, at a meeting of the panel, agreement is reached with the offender but he does not sign the record produced[5], and his failure to do so appears to the panel to be unreasonable, the panel must end the meeting and refer the offender back to the appropriate court[6].

1   As to meetings in relation to youth offender panels see PARA 158. As to the establishment of youth offender panels see PARA 161.
2   Ie a programme of behaviour of the kind mentioned in the Powers of Criminal Courts (Sentencing) Act 2000 s 23(1): see PARA 163.
3   Powers of Criminal Courts (Sentencing) Act 2000 s 25(1).
4   Powers of Criminal Courts (Sentencing) Act 2000 s 25(2). As to the appropriate court see PARA 169 note 2.

5 Ie in pursuance of the Powers of Criminal Courts (Sentencing) Act 2000 s 23(5): see PARA 163.
6 Powers of Criminal Courts (Sentencing) Act 2000 s 25(3).

166. Progress meetings. At any time after a youth offender contract has taken effect[1], but before the end of the period for which the contract has effect[2], the specified youth offending team[3] must, if so requested by the panel, arrange for the holding of a meeting of the panel ('a progress meeting')[4]. Such meetings should take place at least every three months[5]. The panel may make such a request if it appears to it to be expedient to review the offender's progress in implementing the programme of behaviour contained in the contract, or any other matter arising in connection with the contract[6]. However, the panel must make such a request if:

(1) the offender has notified the panel that:
 (a) he wishes to seek the panel's agreement to a variation in the terms of the contract[7]; or
 (b) he wishes the panel to refer him back to the appropriate court with a view to the referral order (or orders)[8] being revoked on account of a significant change in his circumstances (such as his being taken to live abroad) making compliance with any youth offender contract impractical[9]; or
(2) it appears to the panel that the offender is in breach of any of the terms of the contract[10].

At a progress meeting the panel must do such one or more of the following things as it considers appropriate in the circumstances, namely[11]:

(i) review the offender's progress or any such other matter as is mentioned in heads (1) and (2) above[12];
(ii) discuss with the offender any breach of the terms of the contract which it appears to the panel that he has committed[13];
(iii) consider any variation in the terms of the contract sought by the offender or which it appears to the panel to be expedient to make in the light of any such review or discussion[14]; and
(iv) consider whether to accede to any request by the offender that he be referred back to the appropriate court[15].

Where the panel has discussed with the offender such a breach as is mentioned in head (ii) above:

(A) the panel and the offender may agree that the offender is to continue to be required to comply with the contract (either in its original form or with any agreed variation in its terms) without being referred back to the appropriate court[16]; or
(B) the panel may decide to end the meeting and refer the offender back to that court[17].

Where a variation in the terms of the contract is agreed between the offender and the panel, the panel must cause a written record of the variation to be produced immediately in language capable of being readily understood by, or explained to, the offender, and for signature by him[18]. Any such variation takes effect once the record has been signed by the offender, and by a member of the panel on behalf of the panel[19]. The panel must cause a copy of the record to be given or sent to the offender[20]. If at a progress meeting any such variation is agreed but the offender does not sign the record produced[21], and his failure to do so appears to the panel to be unreasonable, the panel may end the meeting and refer the offender back to the appropriate court[22].

Certain of the provisions relating to the agreement of the youth offender contract with the offender[23] apply in connection with what may be provided for by the terms of the contract as varied[24] as they apply in connection with what may be provided for by the terms of a programme of behaviour[25].

1   Ie under the Powers of Criminal Courts (Sentencing) Act 2000 s 23: see PARA 163.
2   As to the duration of youth offender contracts see PARA 164.
3   See PARA 158. 'The specified team', in relation to an offender to whom a referral order applies (or two or more associated referral orders apply), means the youth offending team for the time being specified in the order (or orders): Powers of Criminal Courts (Sentencing) Act 2000 s 32.
4   Powers of Criminal Courts (Sentencing) Act 2000 s 26(1). As to meetings in relation to youth offender panels see PARA 158.
5   See the Home Office, Lord Chancellor's Department and Youth Justice Board publication *Referral Orders and Youth Offender Panels—Guidance for Courts, Youth Offending Teams and Youth Offender Panels* (May 2009) para 9.2.
6   Powers of Criminal Courts (Sentencing) Act 2000 s 26(2).
7   Powers of Criminal Courts (Sentencing) Act 2000 s 26(3)(a)(i).
8   As to referral orders see PARA 156 et seq.
9   Powers of Criminal Courts (Sentencing) Act 2000 s 26(3)(a)(ii). As to the appropriate court see PARA 169 note 2.
10 Powers of Criminal Courts (Sentencing) Act 2000 s 26(3)(b).
11 Powers of Criminal Courts (Sentencing) Act 2000 s 26(4).
12 Powers of Criminal Courts (Sentencing) Act 2000 s 26(4)(a).
13 Powers of Criminal Courts (Sentencing) Act 2000 s 26(4)(b).
14 Powers of Criminal Courts (Sentencing) Act 2000 s 26(4)(c). See the Home Office, Lord Chancellor's Department and Youth Justice Board publication *Referral Orders and Youth Offender Panels—Guidance for Courts, Youth Offending Teams and Youth Offender Panels* (May 2009) para 9.14.
15 Powers of Criminal Courts (Sentencing) Act 2000 s 26(4)(d). Where the panel has discussed with the offender such a request as is mentioned in s 26(4)(d), the panel may, if it is satisfied that there is (or is soon to be) such a change in circumstances as is mentioned in s 26(3)(a)(ii), decide to end the meeting and refer the offender back to the appropriate court: s 26(10).
16 Powers of Criminal Courts (Sentencing) Act 2000 s 26(5)(a).
17 Powers of Criminal Courts (Sentencing) Act 2000 s 26(5)(b).
18 Powers of Criminal Courts (Sentencing) Act 2000 s 26(6).
19 Powers of Criminal Courts (Sentencing) Act 2000 s 26(7).
20 Powers of Criminal Courts (Sentencing) Act 2000 s 26(7).
21 Ie produced in pursuance of the Powers of Criminal Courts (Sentencing) Act 2000 s 26(6): see the text and note 18.
22 Powers of Criminal Courts (Sentencing) Act 2000 s 26(8).
23 Ie the Powers of Criminal Courts (Sentencing) Act 2000 s 23(2), (3), (4): see PARA 163.
24 Ie as varied under the Powers of Criminal Courts (Sentencing) Act 2000 s 26.
25 Powers of Criminal Courts (Sentencing) Act 2000 s 26(9). The text refers to a programme of behaviour, the aim (or principal aim) of which is the prevention of re-offending by the offender: see s 23(1); and PARA 163.

167.   Final meeting of youth offender panel.   Where the compliance period[1] in the case of a youth offender contract is due to expire, the specified youth offending team[2] must arrange for the holding, before the end of that period, of a meeting of the youth offender panel ('the final meeting')[3]. At the final meeting the panel must:

(1)   review the extent of the offender's compliance to date with the terms of the contract[4]; and

(2)   decide, in the light of that review, whether his compliance with those terms has been such as to justify the conclusion that, by the time the compliance period expires, he will have satisfactorily completed the contract[5],

and the panel must give the offender written confirmation of its decision[6].

Where the panel decides that the offender's compliance with the terms of the contract has been such as to justify that conclusion, the panel's decision has the effect of discharging the referral order (or orders) as from the end of the compliance period[7]. Otherwise the panel must refer the offender back to the appropriate court[8].

It is not permitted[9] for the final meeting to be adjourned (or re-adjourned) to a time falling after the end of the compliance period[10].

1   For the purposes of the Powers of Criminal Courts (Sentencing) Act 2000, 'the compliance period', in relation to a youth offender contract, means the period for which the contract has effect in accordance with s 24 (see PARA 164): s 27(7). As to the offender's compliance with the programme agreed between the offender and the youth offender panel see PARA 163.
2   Ie the specified youth offending team: see PARA 158. As to the meaning of 'the specified team' see PARA 166 note 3.
3   Powers of Criminal Courts (Sentencing) Act 2000 s 27(1). As to meetings in relation to youth offender panels see PARA 158.
4   Powers of Criminal Courts (Sentencing) Act 2000 s 27(2)(a).
5   Powers of Criminal Courts (Sentencing) Act 2000 s 27(2)(b).
6   Powers of Criminal Courts (Sentencing) Act 2000 s 27(2).
7   Powers of Criminal Courts (Sentencing) Act 2000 s 27(3). Nothing in s 22(2) (power of the youth offender panel to adjourn or end the meeting if the young offender fails to attend any part of that meeting) prevents the panel from making the decision mentioned in s 27(3) in the offender's absence if it appears to the panel to be appropriate to do that instead of exercising either of its powers under s 22(2) (see PARA 162): s 27(5).
8   Powers of Criminal Courts (Sentencing) Act 2000 s 27(4). See also PARA 169. As to the appropriate court see PARA 169 note 2.
9   Ie under the provisions of the Powers of Criminal Courts (Sentencing) Act 2000 s 22(2)(a): see PARA 162.
10   Powers of Criminal Courts (Sentencing) Act 2000 s 27(6).

168.   Revocation and extension.   Where, having regard to circumstances which have arisen since a youth offender contract took effect[1], it appears to the youth offender panel[2] to be in the interests of justice for the referral order[3] (or each of the referral orders) to be revoked, the panel may refer the offender back to the appropriate court[4] requesting it:

(1)   to exercise only the power[5] to revoke the order (or each of the orders)[6]; or

(2)   to exercise both the power to revoke the order (or each of the orders) and the power[7] to deal with the offender for the offence in respect of which the revoked order was made[8].

The circumstances in which the panel may make such a referral include the offender's making good progress under the contract[9].

Where the panel makes such a referral in relation to any offender and any youth offender contract, and the appropriate court decides not to revoke the referral order (or each of the referral orders) in consequence of that referral, the panel may not make a further such referral in relation to that offender and contract during the relevant period[10] except with the consent of the appropriate court[11].

Where at any time a youth offender contract has taken effect[12] for a period which is less than 12 months, and that period has not ended, and having regard to circumstances which have arisen since the contract took effect, it appears to the youth offender panel to be in the interests of justice for the length of that period to be extended[13] the panel may refer the offender back to the appropriate court[14] requesting it to extend the length of that period[15]. If it appears to the appropriate court that it would be in the interests of justice to do so having regard to circumstances which have arisen since the contract took effect, the court may make an order extending the length of the period for which the contract has effect[16].

1   Ie under the Powers of Criminal Courts (Sentencing) Act 2000 s 23: see PARA 163.
2   As to the establishment of youth offender panels see PARA 161.
3   Ie an order pursuant to the Powers of Criminal Courts (Sentencing) Act 2000 s 16(2), (3): see PARA 158. As to referral orders generally see PARA 156 et seq.
4   Powers of Criminal Courts (Sentencing) Act 2000 s 27A(1), (2) (ss 27A, 27B, Sch 1 Pt 1ZA added, Sch 1 para 1 amended, by the Criminal Justice and Immigration Act 2008 ss 36(1)–(3), 37(1)–(3)). The appropriate court is, in the case of an offender aged under 18 at the time when (in pursuance of the referral back) he first appears before the court, a youth court acting in the local justice area in which it appears to the youth offender panel that the offender resides or will reside and otherwise, a magistrates' court (other than a youth court) acting in that area: Sch 1 para 1(1), (2) (as so amended; amended by SI 2005/886). As to the determination of a person's age see the Children and Young Persons Act 1933 s 99; and CHILDREN AND YOUNG PERSONS vol 10 (2012) PARA 1206.
5   Ie the power conferred by the Powers of Criminal Courts (Sentencing) Act 2000 Sch 1 para 5(2) (see PARA 169).
6   Powers of Criminal Courts (Sentencing) Act 2000 s 27A(2)(a) (as added: see note 4).
7   Ie the power conferred by the Powers of Criminal Courts (Sentencing) Act 2000 Sch 1 para 5(4) (see PARA 169).
8   Powers of Criminal Courts (Sentencing) Act 2000 s 27A(2)(b) (as added: see note 4).
9   Powers of Criminal Courts (Sentencing) Act 2000 s 27A(3) (as added: see note 4).
10 'The relevant period' means the period of three months beginning with the date on which the appropriate court made the decision not to revoke the referral order: Powers of Criminal Courts (Sentencing) Act 2000 s 27A(5) (as added: see note 4).
11 Powers of Criminal Courts (Sentencing) Act 2000 s 27A(4) (as added: see note 4).
12 See note 1.
13 Powers of Criminal Courts (Sentencing) Act 2000 s 27B(1) (as added: see note 4).
14 The 'appropriate court', in the case of an offender aged under 18 at the time when (in pursuance of the referral back) he first appears before the court, a youth court acting in the local justice area in which it appears to the youth offender panel that the offender resides or will reside and otherwise, a magistrates' court (other than a youth court) acting in that area: Powers of Criminal Courts (Sentencing) Act 2000 Sch 1 para 9ZB(1), (2) (as added: see note 4).
15 Powers of Criminal Courts (Sentencing) Act 2000 s 27B(2) (as added: see note 4). The requested period of extension must not exceed three months: s 27B(3) (as so added). The panel must make the referral by sending a report to the appropriate court explaining why the offender is being referred back to it: Sch 1 para 9ZC (as so added).
16 Powers of Criminal Courts (Sentencing) Act 2000 Sch 1 para 9ZD(1) (as added: see note 4). Such an order must not extend that period by more than three months and must not so extend that period as to cause it to exceed 12 months: Sch 1 para 9ZD(2) (as so added). In deciding whether to make an order extending the term the court must have regard to the extent of the offender's compliance with the terms of the contract: Sch 1 para 9ZD(3) (as so added). The court may not make an order extending the term unless the offender is present before it and the contract has effect at the time of the order: Sch 1 para 9ZD(4) (as so added). The provisions of Sch 1 para 3 (bringing the offender before the court), para 4 (detention and remand of arrested offender) and Sch 1 para 9ZA (power to adjourn hearing and remand offender) apply for the purposes of Sch 1 Pt 1ZA as they apply for the purposes of Sch 1 Pt 1 (see PARA 169): Sch 1 para 9ZE (as so added).

169.   Referral back to appropriate court. Provision is made for what is to happen when a youth offender panel[1] refers an offender back to the appropriate court[2]. The panel makes the referral by sending a report to the appropriate court explaining why the offender is being referred back to it[3]. Where the appropriate court receives such a report, the court must cause the offender to appear before it[4]. For the purpose of securing the attendance of the offender before the court, a justice acting in the local justice area in which the court acts may issue a summons requiring the offender to appear at the place and time specified in it, or if the report is substantiated on oath, issue a warrant for the offender's arrest[5].

Where the offender is arrested in pursuance of a warrant[6] and cannot be brought immediately before the appropriate court:

(1) the person in whose custody he is may make arrangements for his detention in a place of safety[7] for a period of not more than 72 hours from the time of the arrest (and it is lawful for him to be detained in pursuance of those arrangements)[8]; and

(2) that person must within that period bring him before a court which[9], if he is under the age of 18 when he is brought before the court, must be a youth court[10], and if he has then attained that age, must be a magistrate's court other than a youth court[11].

If it is proved to the satisfaction of the appropriate court as regards any decision of the panel which resulted in the offender being referred back to the court that[12]:

(a) so far as the decision relied on any finding of fact by the panel, the panel was entitled to make that finding in the circumstances[13]; and

(b) that, so far as the decision involved any exercise of discretion by the panel, the panel reasonably exercised that discretion in the circumstances[14],

the court may exercise the power to revoke a referral order[15].

The court may then deal with the offender for the offence for which the revoked order was originally made[16]. The offender may appeal to the Crown Court against that sentence[17].

The following provisions[18] apply where the appropriate court decides that the matters mentioned in heads (a) and (b) above have not been proved to its satisfaction, or where, although by virtue of head (a) above the appropriate court is able to exercise the power to revoke the referral order[19], or would be able to do so if the offender were present before it, the court (for any reason) decides not to exercise that power[20]. If either no contract has taken effect[21] between the offender and the panel, or a contract has so taken effect but the period for which it has effect has not expired, the offender must continue to remain subject to the referral order (or orders) in all respects as if he had not been referred back to the court[22]; and if a contract had taken effect[23], but the period for which it has effect has expired[24], the court must make an order declaring that the referral order (or each of the referral orders) is discharged[25].

If, in a case where the offender is referred back to the court[26], the court decides (contrary to the decision of the panel) that the offender's compliance with the terms of the contract has, or will have, been such as to justify the conclusion that he has satisfactorily completed the contract, the court must make an order declaring that the referral order (or each of the referral orders) is discharged[27].

1 As to the establishment of youth offender panels see PARA 161.

2 See the Powers of Criminal Courts (Sentencing) Act 2000 Sch 1 Pt I, which applies where a youth offender panel refers an offender back to the appropriate court under s 22(2) (see PARA 162), s 25(2) or (3) (see PARA 165), s 26(5), (8) or (10) (see PARA 166), s 27(4) (see PARA 167) or s 27A(2) (see PARA 168): s 28(a), Sch 1 para 1(1) (s 28(a), Sch 1 paras 1(1), 5(3), 9 amended by the Criminal Justice and Immigration Act 2008 s 36(1), (3), Sch 26 paras 43, 49(1), (3)). For these purposes, the appropriate court is:

(1) in the case of an offender aged under 18 at the time when (in pursuance of the referral back) he first appears before the court, a youth court acting in the local justice area in which it appears to the youth offender panel that the offender resides or will reside (Powers of Criminal Courts (Sentencing) Act 2000 Sch 1 para 1(2)(a) (Sch 1 para 1(2) amended by SI 2005/886)); and

(2)　otherwise, a magistrates' court (other than a youth court) acting in that area (Powers of Criminal Courts (Sentencing) Act 2000 Sch 1 para 1(2)(b) (as so amended)).

3　Powers of Criminal Courts (Sentencing) Act 2000 Sch 1 para 2.

4　Powers of Criminal Courts (Sentencing) Act 2000 Sch 1 para 3(1).

5　Powers of Criminal Courts (Sentencing) Act 2000 Sch 1 para 3(2) (amended by SI 2005/886). Any summons or warrant issued under the Powers of Criminal Courts (Sentencing) Act 2000 Sch 1 para 3(2) must direct the offender to appear or be brought before the appropriate court: Sch 1 para 3(3).

6　Ie under the Powers of Criminal Courts (Sentencing) Act 2000 Sch 1 para 3(2): see the text and note 5.

7　As to the meaning of 'place of safety' see the Children and Young Persons Act 1933 s 107(1); and CHILDREN AND YOUNG PERSONS vol 10 (2012) PARA 632.

8　Powers of Criminal Courts (Sentencing) Act 2000 Sch 1 para 4(1)(a).

9　Powers of Criminal Courts (Sentencing) Act 2000 Sch 1 para 4(1)(b). Where the court before which the offender is brought under Sch 1 para 4(1)(b) ('the alternative court') is not the appropriate court (Sch 1 para 4(2)):

(1)　the alternative court may direct that he is to be released immediately or remand him (Sch 1 para 4(3));

(2)　the Magistrates' Courts Act 1980 s 128 (remand in custody or on bail) (see CRIMINAL PROCEDURE vol 27 (2015) PARA 91 et seq) has effect where the alternative court has power under the Powers of Criminal Court (Sentencing) Act 2000 Sch 1 para 4(3) to remand the offender as if the court referred to in the Magistrates' Courts Act 1980 s 128(1)(a), (3), (4)(a), (5) were the appropriate court (Powers of Criminal Courts (Sentencing) Act 2000 Sch 1 para 4(4));

(3)　the Magistrates' Courts Act 1980 s 128 has effect where the alternative court has power so to remand him, or the appropriate court has (by virtue of the Powers of Criminal Courts (Sentencing) Act 2000 Sch 1 para 4(4)) power to further remand him, as if in the Magistrates' Courts Act 1980 s 128(1) there were inserted after s 128(1)(c) 'or (d) if he is aged under 18, remand him to accommodation provided by or on behalf of a local authority (within the meaning of the Children Act 1989) (see CHILDREN AND YOUNG PERSONS vol 10 (2012) PARA 839) and, if it does so, must designate as the authority who are to receive him the local authority for the area in which it appears to the court that he resides or will reside' (Powers of Criminal Courts (Sentencing) Act 2000 Sch 1 para 4(5)).

10　Powers of Criminal Courts (Sentencing) Act 2000 Sch 1 para 4(1)(b)(i). As to youth courts see CHILDREN AND YOUNG PERSONS vol 10 (2012) PARA 1225 et seq. As to the determination of a person's age see the Children and Young Persons Act 1933 s 99; and CHILDREN AND YOUNG PERSONS vol 10 (2012) PARA 1206.

11　Powers of Criminal Courts (Sentencing) Act 2000 Sch 1 para 4(1)(b)(ii).

12　Powers of Criminal Courts (Sentencing) Act 2000 Sch 1 para 5(1).

13　Powers of Criminal Courts (Sentencing) Act 2000 Sch 1 para 5(1)(a).

14　Powers of Criminal Courts (Sentencing) Act 2000 Sch 1 para 5(1)(b).

15　Powers of Criminal Courts (Sentencing) Act 2000 Sch 1 para 5(2). As to the power to revoke the referral order (or each of the referral orders) see Sch 1 para 5(2). The revocation under Sch 1 para 5(2) of a referral order has the effect of revoking any related order under Sch 1 para 9ZD (see PARA 168) or Sch 1 para 11 or Sch 1 para 12 (see PARA 171): Sch 1 para 5(3) (as amended: see note 2). Where any order is revoked under Sch 1 para 5(2) or by virtue of Sch 1 para 5(3), the appropriate court may deal with the offender in accordance with Sch 1 para 5(5) for the offence in respect of which the revoked order was made: Sch 1 para 5(4). In so dealing with the offender for such an offence, the appropriate court:

(1)　may deal with him in any way in which (assuming s 16 (see PARA 156) had not applied) he could have been dealt with for that offence by the court which made the order (Sch 1 para 5(5)(a)); and

(2)　must have regard to the circumstances of his referral back to the court, and where a contract has taken effect under s 23 (see PARA 163) between the offender and the panel, the extent of his compliance with the terms of the contract (Sch 1 para 5(5)(b)).

　　The appropriate court may not exercise the powers conferred by Sch 1 para 5(2) or Sch 1 para 5(4) unless the offender is present before it; but those powers are exercisable even if, in a case where a contract has taken effect under s 23, the period for which the contract has effect has expired (whether before or after the referral of the offender back to the court): Sch 1 para 5(6).

16　Ie in exercise of the power conferred by the Powers of Criminal Courts (Sentencing) Act 2000 Sch 1 para 5(4): see note 15.

17 Powers of Criminal Courts (Sentencing) Act 2000 Sch 1 para 6.
18 Ie the Powers of Criminal Courts (Sentencing) Act 2000 Sch 1 para 7: see the text and notes 19–25.
19 Ie the power conferred by the Powers of Criminal Courts (Sentencing) Act 2000 Sch 1 para 5(2): see the text and note 15.
20 Powers of Criminal Courts (Sentencing) Act 2000 Sch 1 para 7(1).
21 Ie under the Powers of Criminal Courts (Sentencing) Act 2000 s 23: see PARA 163.
22 Powers of Criminal Courts (Sentencing) Act 2000 Sch 1 para 7(2).
23 See note 21.
24 Ie expired otherwise than by virtue of the Powers of Criminal Courts (Sentencing) Act 2000 s 24(6): see PARA 164.
25 Powers of Criminal Courts (Sentencing) Act 2000 Sch 1 para 7(3). The discharge under Sch 1 para 7(3) of a referral order has the effect of discharging any related order under Sch 1 para 9ZD (see PARA 168) or Sch 1 para 11 or Sch 1 para 12 (see PARA 171): Sch 1 para 9 (as amended: see note 2).
26 Ie under the Powers of Criminal Courts (Sentencing) Act 2000 s 27(4): see PARA 167.
27 Powers of Criminal Courts (Sentencing) Act 2000 Sch 1 para 8. The discharge under Sch 1 para 8 of a referral order has the effect of discharging any related order under Sch 1 para 9ZD (see PARA 168) or Sch 1 para 11 or Sch 1 para 12 (see PARA 171): Sch 1 para 9 (as amended: see note 2).

170. Referral of parent or guardian. Provision is made for what is to happen when a youth offender panel[1] refers an offender's[2] parent or guardian to a youth court[3]. The panel makes the referral by sending a report to the youth court explaining why the parent is being referred to it[4]. Where the youth court receives such a report it must cause the parent to appear before it[5]. For the purpose of securing the attendance of the parent before the court, a justice acting in the local justice area in which the court acts may issue a summons requiring the parent to appear at the place and time specified in it or, if the report is substantiated on oath, issue a warrant for the parent's arrest[6]. Where the parent appears or is so brought before the youth court[7], the court may make a parenting order in respect of the parent if:

(1) it is proved to the satisfaction of the court that the parent has failed without reasonable excuse to comply with the order[8]; and

(2) the court is satisfied that the parenting order would be desirable in the interests of preventing the commission of any further offence by the offender[9].

A 'parenting order'[10] is an order which requires the parent: (a) to comply, for a period not exceeding 12 months, with such requirements as are specified in the order[11]; and (b) to attend[12], for a concurrent period not exceeding three months, such counselling or guidance programme[13] as may be specified in directions given by the responsible officer[14].

Before making such a parenting order where the offender is aged under 16, the court must obtain and consider information about his family circumstances and the likely effect of the order on those circumstances[15].

1 As to the establishment of youth offender panels see PARA 161.
2 'The offender' means the offender whose parent or guardian is referred under the Powers of Criminal Courts (Sentencing) Act 2000 s 22(2A) (see PARA 162): Sch 1 para 9A(2)(a) (Sch 1 Pt 1A (paras 9A–9F) added by the Criminal Justice Act 2003 Sch 34 para 6). 'The parent' means the parent or guardian so referred: Powers of Criminal Courts (Sentencing) Act 2000 Sch 1 para 9A(2)(b) (as so added).
3 See the Powers of Criminal Courts (Sentencing) Act 2000 Sch 1 para 9A(1) (as added: see note 2). 'The youth court' means a youth court as mentioned in s 22(2A) (see PARA 1253): Sch 1 Pt 1A para 9A(2)(c) (as so added).
4 Powers of Criminal Courts (Sentencing) Act 2000 Sch 1 para 9B (as added: see note 2).
5 Powers of Criminal Courts (Sentencing) Act 2000 Sch 1 para 9C(1) (as added: see note 2).

6   Powers of Criminal Courts (Sentencing) Act 2000 Sch 1 para 9C(2) (as added (see note 2); and amended by SI 2005/886). Any summons or warrant so issued must direct the parent to appear or be brought before the youth court: Powers of Criminal Courts (Sentencing) Act 2000 Sch 1 para 9C(3) (as so added).

7   Ie under the Powers of Criminal Courts (Sentencing) Act 2000 Sch 1 para 9C.

8   Powers of Criminal Courts (Sentencing) Act 2000 Sch 1 para 9D(1)(a) (as added: see note 2).

9   Powers of Criminal Courts (Sentencing) Act 2000 Sch 1 para 9D(1)(b) (as added: see note 2).

10 The Crime and Disorder Act 1998 ss 8(3), (8), s 9(3)–(7), 18(3), (4) (see CHILDREN AND YOUNG PERSONS vol 10 (2012) PARA 1279) apply in relation to a parenting order made under the Powers of Criminal Courts (Sentencing) Act 2000 Sch 1 para 9D as they apply in relation to any other parenting order: Sch 1 para 9D(7) (as added: see note 2). An appeal lies to the Crown Court against the making of a parenting order under Sch 1 para 9D: Sch 1 para 9E(1) (as so added). The provisions of the Crime and Disorder Act 1998 s 10(2), (3) (see CHILDREN AND YOUNG PERSONS vol 10 (2012) PARA 1282) apply in relation to an appeal under the Powers of Criminal Courts (Sentencing) Act 2000 Sch 1 para 9E as they apply in relation to an appeal under the Crime and Disorder Act 1998 s 10(1)(b): Powers of Criminal Courts (Sentencing) Act 2000 Sch 1 Pt 1A para 9E(2) (as so added).

11 Powers of Criminal Courts (Sentencing) Act 2000 Sch 1 para 9D(2)(a) (as added: see note 2). The order referred to in the text is one under s 20 (see PARA 160). The making of a parenting order under Sch 1 para 9D is without prejudice to the continuance of the order under s 20: Sch 1 para 9F(1) (as so added). The provisions of the Magistrates' Courts Act 1980 s 63(1)–(4) (power of magistrates' court to deal with person for breach of order, etc) apply (as well as the Powers of Criminal Courts (Sentencing) Act 2000 s 22(2A) and Sch 1 Pt 1A) in relation to an order under s 20: Sch 1 para 9F(2).
    The requirements that may be specified under head (a) in the text are those which the court considers desirable in the interests of preventing the commission of any further offence by the offender: Sch 1 para 9D(3) (as so added).

12 A parenting order may, but need not, include a requirement mentioned in head (b) in the text in any case where a parenting order under the Powers of Criminal Courts (Sentencing) Act 2000 Sch para 9D or any other enactment has been made in respect of the parent on a previous occasion: Sch 1 para 9D(4) (as added: see note 2).

13 A counselling or guidance programme which a parent is required to attend by virtue of head (b) in the text may be or include a residential course but only if the court is satisfied:
    (1)   that the attendance of the parent at a residential course is likely to be more effective than his attendance at a non-residential course in preventing the commission of any further offence by the offender (Powers of Criminal Courts (Sentencing) Act 2000 Sch 1 para 9D(5)(a) (as added: see note 2)); and
    (2)   that any interference with family life which is likely to result from the attendance of the parent at a residential course is proportionate in all the circumstances (Sch 1 para 9D(5)(b) (as so added)).

14 Powers of Criminal Courts (Sentencing) Act 2000 Sch 1 para 9D(2)(b) (as added: see note 2).

15 Powers of Criminal Courts (Sentencing) Act 2000 Sch 1 para 9D(6) (as added: see note 2). As to the determination of a person's age see the Children and Young Persons Act 1933 s 99; and CHILDREN AND YOUNG PERSONS vol 10 (2012) PARA 1206.

171.   Extension of referral. Provision is made for what is to happen when an offender is convicted of further offences while for the time being subject to a referral order[1]. If:

(1)   the occasion on which the offender was referred to the youth offender panel[2] is the only other occasion on which it has fallen to a court in the United Kingdom[3] to deal with the offender for any offence or offences[4], and the offender committed the relevant offence[5], and any connected offence, before he was referred to the panel[6], the relevant court may sentence the offender for the offence by making an order extending his compliance period[7]; and

(2)   if head (1) above applies, but the offender committed the relevant offence[8], or any connected offence, after he was referred to the panel,

the relevant court may sentence the offender for the offence by making an order extending his compliance period, but only if the relevant requirements[9] are complied with[10].

An order under head (1) or head (2) above, or two or more orders under one or other of those heads made in respect of connected offences, must not so extend the offender's compliance period as to cause it to exceed 12 months[11].

Where the relevant court makes an order[12] in respect of the relevant offence[13], it:

(a)   may not deal with the offender for that offence in any of the specified prohibited ways[14];

(b)   must, in respect of any connected offence, either sentence the offender by making an order under the same provision as the original order[15], or make an order discharging him absolutely[16];

(c)   may not deal with the offender for any connected offence in any of those prohibited ways[17]; and

(d)   may not, in connection with the conviction of the offender for the offence or any connected offence, make:

(i)   an order binding him over to keep the peace or to be of good behaviour;

(ii)   an order binding over the offender's parent or guardian[18].

For the purposes of heads (1) and (2) above, any occasion on which the offender was discharged absolutely[19] in respect of the offence, or each of the offences, for which he was being dealt with must be disregarded[20]. Any occasion on which, in criminal proceedings in England, Wales or Northern Ireland, the offender was bound over[21] to keep the peace or to be of good behaviour must be regarded for those purposes as an occasion on which it fell to a court in the United Kingdom to deal with the offender for an offence[22].

The Secretary of State[23] may by regulations make such amendments of the above provisions[24] as he considers appropriate for altering in any way the descriptions of offenders in the case of which an order extending the compliance period may be made[25].

1   See the Powers of Criminal Courts (Sentencing) Act 2000 Sch 1 Pt II (paras 10–15); the text and notes 2–25; and PARA 172. For the purposes of Sch 1 Pt II, an offender is for the time being subject to referral if:

(1)   a referral order has been made in respect of him and that order has not been discharged (whether by virtue of s 27(3) (see PARA 167) or under Sch 1 paras 7(3) or 8 (see PARA 169)) or revoked (whether under Sch 1 para 5(2) (see PARA 169) or by virtue of Sch 1 para 14(2) (see PARA 172)) (Sch 1 para 15(1)(a)); or

(2)   two or more referral orders have been made in respect of him and any of those orders has not been discharged (whether by virtue of s 27(3) or under Sch 1 paras 7(3) or 8) or revoked (whether under Sch 1 para 5(2) or by virtue of Sch 1 para 14(2)) (Sch 1 para 15(1)(b)).

2   As to the establishment of youth offender panels see PARA 161.

3   As to the meaning of 'United Kingdom' see PARA 4 note 3.

4   Powers of Criminal Courts (Sentencing) Act 2000 Sch 1 para 11(a). Schedule 1 paras 11, 12 apply where, at a time when an offender aged under 18 is subject to referral, a youth court or other magistrates' court ('the relevant court') is dealing with him for an offence in relation to which the provisions of s 16(1)(a)–(c) (see PARA 156) are applicable: Sch 1 para 10(1). However, Sch 1 paras 11, 12 do not apply unless the offender's compliance period is less than 12 months: Sch 1 para 10(2). As to youth courts see CHILDREN AND YOUNG PERSONS vol 10 (2012) PARA 1225 et seq. As to the determination of a person's age see the Children and Young Persons Act 1933 s 99; and CHILDREN AND YOUNG PERSONS vol 10 (2012) PARA 1206.

5   Ie the offence mentioned in the Powers of Criminal Courts (Sentencing) Act 2000 Sch 1 para 10: see note 4.

6   Powers of Criminal Courts (Sentencing) Act 2000 Sch 1 para 11(b). As to the application of Sch 1 para 11 see note 4.

7   Powers of Criminal Courts (Sentencing) Act 2000 Sch 1 para 11. For the purposes of Sch 1 Pt II, 'compliance period', in relation to an offender who is for the time being subject to referral, means the period for which (in accordance with s 24 (see PARA 164)) any youth offender contract taking effect in his case under s 23 (see PARA 163) has (or would have) effect: Sch 1 para 15(2).

8   See note 5.

9   The relevant requirements are that the court must:
    (1)   be satisfied, on the basis of a report made to it by the relevant body, that there are exceptional circumstances which indicate that, even though the offender has re-offended since being referred to the panel, extending his compliance period is likely to help prevent further re-offending by him (Powers of Criminal Courts (Sentencing) Act 2000 Sch 1 para 12(2)(a)); and
    (2)   state in open court that it is so satisfied and why it is (Sch 1 para 12(2)(b)).
    For these purposes 'the relevant body' means the panel to which the offender has been referred or, if no contract has yet taken effect between the offender and the panel under s 23, the specified youth offending team: Sch 1 para 12(3). As to the meaning of 'the specified team' see PARA 166 note 3.

10   Powers of Criminal Courts (Sentencing) Act 2000 Sch 1 para 12(1). As to the application of Sch 1 para 12 see note 4.

11   Powers of Criminal Courts (Sentencing) Act 2000 Sch 1 para 13(1).

12   Ie an order under the Powers of Criminal Courts (Sentencing) Act 2000 Sch 1 para 11 or Sch 1 para 12: see the text and notes 7–10.

13   Powers of Criminal Courts (Sentencing) Act 2000 Sch 1 para 13(2). The relevant offence is that which is mentioned in Sch 1 para 10: see note 4. However, heads (a)–(d) in the text do not affect the exercise of any power to deal with the offender conferred by Sch 1 para 5 or Sch 1 para 14: Sch 1 para 13(2).

14   Powers of Criminal Courts (Sentencing) Act 2000 Sch 1 para 13(3). The prohibited ways are those specified in s 19(4): see PARA 159.

15   Ie under the Powers of Criminal Courts (Sentencing) Act 2000 Sch 1 para 11 or Sch 1 para 12, as the case may be: see the text and notes 1–10.

16   Powers of Criminal Courts (Sentencing) Act 2000 Sch 1 para 13(4)(a).

17   Powers of Criminal Courts (Sentencing) Act 2000 Sch 1 para 13(4)(b).

18   Powers of Criminal Courts (Sentencing) Act 2000 Sch 1 para 13(5). The orders that are described in the text are those mentioned in s 19(5): see PARA 159.

19   As to absolute discharge see PARA 443.

20   Powers of Criminal Courts (Sentencing) Act 2000 Sch 1 para 13(6).

21   As to binding over see PARA 447 et seq.

22   Powers of Criminal Courts (Sentencing) Act 2000 Sch 1 para 13(7).

23   As to the Secretary of State see PARA 5 note 7.

24   Ie the Powers of Criminal Courts (Sentencing) Act 2000 Sch 1 paras 10, 11, 12: see the text and notes 1–10.

25   Powers of Criminal Courts (Sentencing) Act 2000 Sch 1 para 13(8). The Secretary of State may also by regulations make such amendments of Sch 1 para 13 as he considers appropriate: Sch 1 para 13(8). At the date at which this volume states the law no such regulations have been made. Any description of offender having effect by virtue of regulations under Sch 1 para 13(8) may be framed by reference to such matters as the Secretary of State considers appropriate, including, in particular, one or more of the following:
    (1)   the offender's age (s 17(4)(a), Sch 1 para 13(8));
    (2)   how the offender has pleaded (s 17(4)(b));
    (3)   the offence (or offences) of which the offender has been convicted (s 17(4)(c));
    (4)   the offender's previous convictions, if any (s 17(4)(d));
    (5)   how, if at all, the offender has been previously punished or otherwise dealt with by any court (s 17(4)(e)); and
    (6)   any characteristics or behaviour of, or circumstances relating to, any person who has at any time been charged in the same proceedings as the offender (whether or not in respect of the same offence) (s 17(4)(f)).

172.   Further convictions which lead to revocation of referral. The following provisions[1] apply where, at a time when an offender is subject to referral[2], a court in England and Wales deals with him for an offence (whether committed before or after he was referred to the youth offender panel[3]) by making an order other than an order for extension of referral[4], or an order discharging him absolutely[5]. In such a case the order of the court has the effect of revoking the referral order (or orders), and any related order or orders[6]. Where any order is so revoked[7], the court may, if it appears to the court that it would be in the interests of justice to do so, deal with the offender for the offence in respect of which the revoked order was made in any way in which[8] he could have been dealt with for that offence by the court which made the order[9].

1   Ie the Powers of Criminal Courts (Sentencing) Act 2000 Sch 1 para 14: see the text and notes 2–9.
2   As to when an offender is subject to referral for these purposes see PARA 171.
3   As to the establishment of youth offender panels see PARA 161.
4   Ie an order under the Powers of Criminal Courts (Sentencing) Act 2000 Sch 1 para 11 or Sch 1 para 12: see PARA 171.
5   Powers of Criminal Courts (Sentencing) Act 2000 Sch 1 para 14(1). As to absolute discharge see PARA 443.
6   Powers of Criminal Courts (Sentencing) Act 2000 Sch 1 para 14(2) (amended by the Criminal Justice and Immigration Act 2008 Sch 26 Pt 2 paras 40, 49(1), (3)). The related order or orders mentioned in the text are those under Sch 1 para 9ZD (see PARA 168) or Sch 1 para 11 or Sch 1 para 12 (see PARA 171).
7   Ie by virtue of the Powers of Criminal Courts (Sentencing) Act 2000 Sch 1 para 14(2): see the text and note 6.
8   Ie assuming the Powers of Criminal Courts (Sentencing) Act 2000 s 16 (see PARA 160) had not applied.
9   Powers of Criminal Courts (Sentencing) Act 2000 Sch 1 para 14(3). When dealing with the offender under Sch 1 para 14(3), the court must, where a contract has taken effect between the offender and the panel under s 23 (see PARA 163), have regard to the extent of his compliance with the terms of the contract: Sch 1 para 14(4).

173.   Functions of youth offending teams.   The functions of a youth offending team responsible for implementing a referral order[1] include, in particular, arranging for the provision of such administrative staff, accommodation or other facilities as are required by the youth offender panel[2] established in pursuance of the order[3].

During the period for which a youth offender contract[4] between a youth offender panel and an offender has effect:

(1)   the specified youth offending team[5] must make arrangements for supervising the offender's compliance with the terms of the contract[6]; and

(2)   the person who is the member of the panel appointed by the youth offending team from among its members[7] must ensure that records are kept of the offender's compliance (or non-compliance) with those terms[8].

1   As to referral orders see PARA 156 et seq. In implementing referral orders a youth offending team must have regard to any guidance given from time to time by the Secretary of State: Powers of Criminal Courts (Sentencing) Act 2000 s 29(3). As to the establishment of youth offending teams see CHILDREN AND YOUNG PERSONS vol 10 (2012) PARA 1193.
2   As to the establishment of youth offender panels see PARA 161.
3   Powers of Criminal Courts (Sentencing) Act 2000 s 29(1).
4   As to the duration of youth offender contracts see PARA 164.
5   See PARA 166 note 3.
6   Powers of Criminal Courts (Sentencing) Act 2000 s 29(2)(a).
7   Ie appointed under the Powers of Criminal Courts (Sentencing) Act 2000 s 21(3)(a): see PARA 161.
8   Powers of Criminal Courts (Sentencing) Act 2000 s 29(2)(b).

4. FINANCIAL ORDERS

(1) FINES AND SURCHARGES

(i) Fines

174. Fines at common law and under statute. At common law a fine, either with or without imprisonment, is a penalty at the discretion of the court[1]. By statute, the Crown Court has power to pass an unlimited fine except in murder cases or where a minimum sentence applies[2], and a magistrates' court[3] has power under statute to punish offences by the imposition of fines[4] (which in certain cases may be unlimited[5]) as an alternative, or in addition, to imprisonment[6]. Where a magistrates' court tries a person under 18 years for an indictable offence[7] and finds him guilty, it may in general impose a fine or may exercise the same powers as it could have exercised if he had been found guilty of an offence for which, but for the provisions relating to the restrictions on the imprisonment of young offenders[8], it could have sentenced him to imprisonment for a term not exceeding the maximum term of imprisonment for the offence on conviction on indictment, or six months, whichever is the less[9]. Where a child or young person is convicted of any offence for the commission of which a fine or costs may be imposed or a compensation order[10] may be made, a magistrates' court may order that the fine, compensation or costs awarded be paid by the parent or guardian of the child or young person instead of by the child or young person himself[11].

Where under any enactment[12] a magistrates' court has power to sentence an offender to imprisonment or other detention but not to a fine, then, except where an Act passed after 31 December 1879 expressly provides to the contrary, the court may, instead of sentencing him to imprisonment or other detention, impose a fine which for an offence triable either way[13] must not exceed the prescribed sum[14], and for a summary offence[15] must not exceed level 3 on the standard scale[16], and not be of such amount as would subject the offender, in default of payment of the fine, to a longer term of imprisonment or detention[17] than the term to which he is liable on conviction of the offence[18].

1   *R v Castro* (1880) 5 QBD 490, CA; affd sub nom *Castro v R* (1881) 6 App Cas 229, HL. As to the history of the common law power to fine see *R v Morris* [1951] 1 KB 394 at 396, 34 Cr App Rep 210 at 212, CCA, per Lord Goddard CJ. As to fines generally see *R v Olliver (Richard), R v Olliver (Michael)* (1989) 11 Cr App Rep (S) 10, CA; *R v Crown Court at Chelmsford, ex p Birchall* [1990] RTR 80, (1989) 11 Cr App Rep (S) 510, DC; and PARA 175.

    As to combining custodial sentences with fines for offenders believed to be in possession of substantial sums representing the proceeds of their offences see generally *R v Garner, R v Breeze* [1986] 1 All ER 78, 82 Cr App Rep 27, CA (where the authorities are reviewed).

2   See the Criminal Justice Act 2003 s 163 (amended by the Criminal Justice and Immigration Act 2008 Sch 26 paras 59, 68; and by the Legal Aid, Sentencing and Punishment of Offenders Act 2012 Sch 19 paras 8, 14), which provides that where a person is convicted on indictment of any offence, other than an offence for which the sentence is fixed by law or falls to be imposed under the Powers of Criminal Courts (Sentencing) Act 2000 s 110(2) (see CRIMINAL LAW vol 26 (2010) PARA 725) or s 111(2) (see CRIMINAL LAW vol 25 (2010) PARA 290) or under the Criminal Justice Act 2003 s 224A (see PARA 35), s 225(2) (see PARA 37) or s 226(2) (see PARA 34), the court, if not precluded from sentencing an offender by its exercise of some other power, may impose a fine instead of or in addition to dealing with him in any other way in which the court has power to deal with him, subject however to any enactment requiring the offender to be dealt with in a particular way. As to when such sentences fall to be imposed see PARA 536 note 2.

    Where a person convicted on indictment of any offence (whether triable only on indictment or either way) would otherwise be liable to a fine not exceeding a specified amount, he is liable to a fine of any amount: Criminal Law Act 1977 s 32(1). As to the application of this provision to Guernsey see the Criminal Justice Act 1982 (Guernsey) Order 1986, SI 1986/1884.

3   As to the meaning of 'magistrates' court' see MAGISTRATES vol 71 (2013) PARA 470.

4   In the Magistrates' Courts Act 1980 'fine', except for the purposes of any enactment imposing a limit on the amount of any fine, includes any pecuniary penalty, forfeiture or compensation payable under a conviction: s 150(1); cf *Leach v Litchfield* [1960] 3 All ER 739, [1960] 1 WLR 1392, DC (arrears of national insurance contributions recoverable as a penalty are not a fine).

5   See PARA 176.

6   As to justices' power of mitigating the fine see PARA 182. As to fixing the amount of the fine see PARA 178. If the fine imposed is in excess of the maximum prescribed by statute, the conviction may be quashed by order: *R v Willesden Justices, ex p Utley* [1948] 1 KB 397, [1947] 2 All ER 838, DC. As to enforcement of the fine in default of payment see MAGISTRATES vol 71 (2013) PARA 667 et seq. As to means inquiry see MAGISTRATES vol 71 (2013) PARA 677. A magistrates' court may not remit the whole or part of a fine imposed by, or sum due under a recognisance forfeited by the Crown Court, the criminal division of the Court of Appeal, or the Supreme Court, on appeal from that division without the consent of the Crown Court: Powers of Criminal Courts (Sentencing) Act 2000 s 140(5) (amended by the Constitutional Reform Act 2005 Sch 9 para 69).

7   As to indictments generally see CRIMINAL PROCEDURE vol 27 (2015) PARA 311 et seq.

8   Ie under the Powers of Criminal Courts (Sentencing) Act 2000 s 89(1): see PARA 551.

9   See the Magistrates' Courts Act 1980 s 24; and CRIMINAL PROCEDURE vol 27 (2015) PARA 226.

10   As to compensation orders see PARA 281 et seq.

11   See the Powers of Criminal Courts (Sentencing) Act 2000 s 137; and CHILDREN AND YOUNG PERSONS vol 10 (2012) PARAS 1249–1250.

12   Ie any enactment whether passed before or after 6 July 1981 (ie the commencement of the Magistrates' Courts Act 1980: see the Magistrates' Courts Act 1980 (Commencement) Order 1981, SI 1981/457).

13   As to offences triable either way see MAGISTRATES vol 71 (2013) PARA 511.

14   Magistrates' Courts Act 1980 s 34(3)(a). As to the standard scale, the statutory maximum, the prescribed sum, and magistrates' powers to levy unlimited fines see PARA 176.

15   As to summary offences see MAGISTRATES vol 71 (2013) PARA 511.

16   Magistrates' Courts Act 1980 s 34(3)(b)(i) (amended by virtue of the Criminal Justice Act 1991 Sch 4 Pt II). As to the standard scale, the statutory maximum, the prescribed sum, and magistrates' powers to levy unlimited fines see PARA 176.

17   As to imprisonment in default of payment of fine see MAGISTRATES vol 71 (2013) PARA 667 et seq.

18   Magistrates' Courts Act 1980 s 34(3)(b)(ii).

175. Principles. Fines are in the lowest range of sentences: there is no threshold for their imposition, and once a court has decided that a fine is the appropriate penalty, the amount should be determined in relation to the justice of the case[1]. The offender's means should then be considered to decide whether he has the capacity to pay such an amount[2]. An affluent defendant should not be fined where the offence merits custody and a less affluent defendant would have been given a custodial sentence[3]. It is wrong to impose a sentence of imprisonment, immediate or suspended, where an offender lacks the means to pay a fine[4] and it is wrong to impose a fine on the assumption that others will pay it[5]. It is normally appropriate to make an allowance before fixing a fine for any time spent by the offender in custody on remand[6].

1   *R v Fairbairn* (1980) 2 Cr App Rep (S) 315, CA; *R v Messana* (1981) 3 Cr App Rep (S) 88, CA; *R v Cleminson* (1985) 7 Cr App Rep (S) 128, CA.

2   *R v Fairbairn*; *R v Cleminson*; *R v Phillips* (1989) Times, 9 June, CA.

3   *R v Markwick* (1953) 37 Cr App Rep 125, CCA.

4   *R v Reeves* (1972) 56 Cr App Rep 366, [1972] Crim LR 194, CA; *R v Crown Court at Liverpool, ex p Baird* [1986] RTR 346, (1985) 7 Cr App Rep (S) 437, CA.

5   *R v Baxter* [1974] Crim LR 611, CA; *R v Curtis* (1984) 6 Cr App Rep (S) 250, [1984] Crim LR 692, CA; *R v Charalambous* (1984) 6 Cr App Rep (S) 389, [1985] Crim LR 328, CA). See also *R v Barnet Magistrates' Court, ex p Cantor* [1998] 2 All ER 333, [1999] 1 WLR 334, DC.

6   *R v Warden* [1996] 2 Cr App Rep (S) 269, 160 JP 363, CA.

176. Powers of magistrates' courts to issue fines on summary conviction. An enactment may provide that an offence is punishable on summary conviction by a fine or maximum fine not exceeding a specified level on the 'standard scale'[1]. There are five levels on the standard scale, the highest being £5,000[2]. An enactment may also provide that a fine or penalty on summary conviction for an offence triable either way may not exceed the 'statutory maximum' of £5,000[3]. However:

(1) where a common law or statutory offence[4] would[5] be punishable on summary conviction by a fine or maximum fine of £5,000 or more (however expressed), the offence is punishable on summary conviction by a fine of any amount[6];

(2) where a common law or statutory offence[7] is punishable on summary conviction by a fine or maximum fine of a fixed amount of less than £5,000, the Secretary of State may by regulations make provision for the offence to be punishable on summary conviction by a fine or maximum fine of an amount (not exceeding £5,000[8]) specified or described in the regulations[9];

(3) where a statutory power[10] could[11] be exercised to create an offence punishable on summary conviction by a fine or maximum fine of £5,000 or more (however expressed), the power may be exercised to create an offence punishable on summary conviction by a fine of any amount[12]; and

(4) where a statutory power[13] can be exercised to create an offence punishable on summary conviction by a fine or maximum fine of a fixed amount of less than £5,000 but not to create an offence so punishable by a fine or maximum fine of a fixed amount of £5,000 or more, the Secretary of State may by regulations make provision for the power to be exercisable to create an offence punishable on summary conviction by a fine or maximum fine of an amount (not exceeding £5,000[14]) specified or described in the regulations[15].

Note that the provisions set out in heads (1) to (4) above do not affect the operation of restrictions on fines that may be imposed on a person aged under 18[16].

The court's power to impose unlimited fines on summary conviction[17], and the power to create summary offences punishable on summary conviction by an unlimited fine[18], may be excluded in relation to specified offences and fines of other amounts, or powers to create offences punishable by fines of other amounts, may be specified instead[19]. This power has been exercised in relation to a number of specified offences involving the evasion of VAT, excise and other duties[20]. At the date at which this volume states the law the powers relating to increasing fines of less than £5,000 to a maximum of 5,000[21] had not been exercised.

1 Criminal Justice Act 1982 s 37(1). This applies in relation to all enactments, whether passed before or after the Criminal Justice Act 1982: s 37(3). The Interpretation Act 1978 Sch 1 (amended by the Criminal Justice Act 1988 Sch 15 para 58(a)) provides that with reference to a fine or penalty for an offence triable only summarily, 'standard scale' has the meaning given by the Criminal Justice Act 1982 s 37.

2 The levels are: level 1 — £200; level 2 — £500; level 3 — £1,000; level 4 — £2,500; level 5 — £5,000: Criminal Justice Act 1982 s 37(2) (substituted by the Criminal Justice Act 1991 s 17(1)). The Secretary of State may by order substitute for the sums for the time being specified as levels 1 to 4 on the standard scale such other sums as the Secretary of State considers appropriate: Legal Aid, Sentencing and Punishment of Offenders Act 2012 s 87(1), (5)–(7). This power may not be exercised so as to alter the ratio of one of those levels to another: s 87(2). At

the date at which this volume states the law this power had not been exercised. Where any enactment provides that a person convicted of a summary offence is to be liable on conviction to a fine or a maximum fine by reference to a specified level on the standard scale, it is to be construed as referring to this scale as it has effect by virtue of either of the Criminal Justice Act 1982 s 37 or an order under the Magistrates' Courts Act 1980 s 143 (see note 3) or the Legal Aid, Sentencing and Punishment of Offenders Act 2012 s 87 (see note 1) from time to time (Criminal Justice Act 1982 s 37(3) (amended by the Legal Aid, Sentencing and Punishment of Offenders Act 2012 s 87(4)). As to the application of these provisions to Guernsey see the Criminal Justice Act 1982 (Guernsey) Order 1992, SI 1992/3202.

By virtue of the Criminal Justice Act 1988 s 59(1), (2), the Secretary of State may by order amend any enactment or subordinate instrument specifying a sum which:

(1)   is specified as the maximum fine which may be imposed on conviction of a summary offence; and

(2)   is higher than level 5 on the standard scale,

so as to substitute for that sum such other sum as appears to him:

(a)   to be justified by a change in the value of money appearing to him to have taken place since the last occasion on which the sum in question was fixed; or

(b)   to be appropriate to take account of an order made or proposed to be made altering the standard scale.

For the purposes of s 59 'enactment' includes an enactment passed after the Criminal Justice Act 1988; and 'subordinate instrument' includes an instrument made after 29 July 1988 (ie the date on which the Criminal Justice Act 1988 received Royal Assent): s 59(6). Any such order does not affect the punishment for an offence committed before it comes into force: s 59(5). At the date at which this volume states the law no such order had been made.

3   Interpretation Act 1978 Sch 1 (amended by the Criminal Justice Act 1988 Sch 15 para 58(b)). £5,000 is the sum prescribed for the purposes of the Magistrates' Courts Act 1980 s 32 ('the prescribed sum'): see s 32(9) (amended by the Criminal Justice Act 1991 s 17(2)(c)). A different sum may be prescribed by order if it appears to the Secretary to State that there has been a change in the value of money since the relevant date: see the Magistrates' Courts Act 1980 s 143(1), (2)(b) (s 143(1) substituted by the Criminal Justice Act 1982 s 48(1)).

By virtue of the Criminal Justice Act 1988 s 59(3), (4) the Secretary of State may by order amend any enactment or subordinate instrument specifying a sum which:

(1)   is specified as the maximum fine which may be imposed on summary conviction of an offence triable either way; and

(2)   is higher than the statutory maximum,

so as to substitute for that sum such other sum as appears to him:

(a)   to be justified by a change in the value of money appearing to him to have taken place since the last occasion on which the sum in question was fixed; or

(b)   to be appropriate to take account of an order made or proposed to be made altering the statutory maximum.

At the date at which this volume states the law no such order had been made.

4   Ie an offence which, immediately before 12 March 2015, is a common law offence or is contained in an Act or an instrument made under an Act (whether or not the offence is in force at that time) (a 'relevant offence'): Legal Aid, Sentencing and Punishment of Offenders Act 2012 ss 85(3)(a), 86(13). 'Act' includes an Act or Measure of the National Assembly for Wales; and references to an offence contained in an Act or instrument include an offence applied by, or extending to England and Wales by virtue of, an Act or instrument: ss 85(17), 86(13).

12 March 2015 is the day on which the Legal Aid, Sentencing and Punishment of Offenders Act 2012 s 85(1) was brought into force by the Legal Aid, Sentencing and Punishment of Offenders Act 2012 (Commencement No 11) Order 2015, SI 2015/504 (referred to as 'the commencement day'): Legal Aid, Sentencing and Punishment of Offenders Act 2012 ss 85(17), 86(13).

5   Ie apart from the Legal Aid, Sentencing and Punishment of Offenders Act 2012 s 85(1).

6   Legal Aid, Sentencing and Punishment of Offenders Act 2012 s 85(1). This provision applies only to offences which would otherwise have been punishable on summary conviction by a fine or maximum fine of £5,000 or more on 12 March 2015 (see note 4), and applies only to offences being punished on or after that date: s 85(1). Nothing in s 85(1) affects fines for offences committed before the commencement day (s 85(3)(a)), the operation of restrictions on fines that may be imposed on a person aged under 18 (s 85(3)(b)), or fines that may be imposed on a person convicted by a magistrates' court who is to be sentenced as if convicted on indictment (s 85(3)(c)).

The Criminal Justice Act 1982 s 37(4) (added by SI 2015/664) provides that the Criminal Justice Act 1982 s 37 (see the text and notes 1–2) has effect subject to provision made by the Legal Aid, Sentencing and Punishment of Offenders Act 2012 s 85.

7   Ie a 'relevant offence': see note 4.

8   Ie the regulations may not specify or describe an amount exceeding whichever is the greater of £5,000 or the sum specified for the time being as level 4 on the standard scale (see note 2): Legal Aid, Sentencing and Punishment of Offenders Act 2012 s 86(3).

9   Legal Aid, Sentencing and Punishment of Offenders Act 2012 s 86(1), (2). This provision applies only to an offence which was so punishable immediately before 12 March 2015: s 86(1). Regulations under s 86 may not include provision affecting fines for offences committed before the regulations come into force (s 86(6)(a)), the operation of restrictions on fines that may be imposed on a person aged under 18 (s 86(6)(b)), or fines that may be imposed on a person convicted by a magistrates' court who is to be sentenced as if convicted on indictment (s 86(6)(c)). In connection with the making of regulations see s 86(7)–(10). Powers under s 86 may be exercised from time to time and are without prejudice to other powers to modify fines for relevant offences or fines that may be specified or described when exercising a relevant power: s 86(12).

10 Ie a power which, immediately before 12 March 2015, is contained in an Act or an instrument made under an Act (whether or not the power is in force at that time) (a 'relevant power'): Legal Aid, Sentencing and Punishment of Offenders Act 2012 ss 85(3)(b), 86(13). References to a power or provision contained in an Act or instrument include a power or provision applied by, or extending to England and Wales by virtue of, an Act or instrument: s 85(17),

11 Ie apart from the Legal Aid, Sentencing and Punishment of Offenders Act 2012 s 85(2).

12 Legal Aid, Sentencing and Punishment of Offenders Act 2012 s 85(2). This provision applies only to powers which would otherwise have been exercisable on 12 March 2015, and applies only to the exercise of such powers on or after that date: s 85(2). Provision made in exercise of a relevant power in reliance on s 85(2) does not affect fines for offences committed before the commencement day (s 85(3)(a)), the operation of restrictions on fines that may be imposed on a person aged under 18 (s 85(3)(b)), or fines that may be imposed on a person convicted by a magistrates' court who is to be sentenced as if convicted on indictment (s 85(3)(c)).

13 Ie a 'relevant power': see note 10.

14 See note 8.

15 Legal Aid, Sentencing and Punishment of Offenders Act 2012 s 86(3), (4). This provision applies only to powers which were so exercisable immediately before 12 March 2015: s 86(3). Provision made in exercise of a relevant power in reliance on regulations under s 86(4) may not include provision affecting fines for offences committed before the regulations come into force (s 86(6)(a)), the operation of restrictions on fines that may be imposed on a person aged under 18 (s 86(6)(b)), or fines that may be imposed on a person convicted by a magistrates' court who is to be sentenced as if convicted on indictment (s 86(6)(c)).

16 See the Legal Aid, Sentencing and Punishment of Offenders Act 2012 ss 85(3)(b), 86(6)(b); and notes 6, 9, 12, 15. As to the determination of a person's age see the Children and Young Persons Act 1933 s 99; and CHILDREN AND YOUNG PERSONS vol 10 (2012) PARA 1206.

17 Ie the power conferred by the Legal Aid, Sentencing and Punishment of Offenders Act 2012 s 85(1): see the text and notes 4–6.

18 Ie the power conferred by the Legal Aid, Sentencing and Punishment of Offenders Act 2012 s 85(2): see the text and notes 10–12.

19 Ie by regulations made by the Secretary of State: see the Legal Aid, Sentencing and Punishment of Offenders Act 2012 s 85(5)–(13). These powers may be exercised from time to time and are without prejudice to other powers to modify fines for relevant offences or fines that may be specified or described when exercising a relevant power: s 85(15).

20 See the Legal Aid, Sentencing and Punishment of Offenders Act 2012 (Fines on Summary Conviction) Regulations 2015, SI 2015/664.

21 Ie the power conferred by the Legal Aid, Sentencing and Punishment of Offenders Act 2012 s 86(1)–(4): see the text and notes 7–9, 13–15.

177.   Young offenders.   Where a person aged under 18[1] is found guilty by a magistrates' court of an offence for which[2] the court would have power to impose a fine of an amount exceeding £1,000, the amount of any fine imposed by the court must not exceed £1,000[3], and where a person aged under 14 is found guilty by a magistrates' court of an offence for which[4] the court would have power to impose a fine of an amount exceeding £250, the amount of any fine imposed by the court must not exceed £250[5].

A magistrates' court may order the parent or guardian of a young person to pay a fine incurred by that person[6].

1 As to the determination of a person's age see the Children and Young Persons Act 1933 s 99; and CHILDREN AND YOUNG PERSONS vol 10 (2012) PARA 1206.
2 Ie apart from the Powers of Criminal Courts (Sentencing) Act 2000 s 135: see the text and notes 3–5.
3 Powers of Criminal Courts (Sentencing) Act 2000 s 135(1).
4 See note 2.
5 Powers of Criminal Courts (Sentencing) Act 2000 s 135(2).
6 See the Powers of Criminal Courts (Sentencing) Act 2000 ss 136, 137; and CHILDREN AND YOUNG PERSONS vol 10 (2012) PARAS 1249–1250.

178. Fixing of fines. The amount of any fine fixed by a court must be such as, in the opinion of the court, reflects the seriousness of the offence[1], and in fixing the amount of any fine to be imposed on an offender (whether an individual or other person), a court must take into account the circumstances of the case including, among other things, the financial circumstances of the offender so far as they are known, or appear, to the court[2].

Where an offender:

(1) has been convicted[3] in his absence[4];

(2) has been convicted in his absence[5] in a trial by a single justice on the papers[6];

(3) has failed to furnish a statement of his financial circumstances in response to a request which is an official request[7];

(4) has failed to comply with a financial circumstances order[8]; or

(5) has otherwise failed to co-operate with the court in its inquiry into his financial circumstances[9],

and the court considers that it has insufficient information to make a proper determination of the financial circumstances of the offender, it may make such determination as it thinks fit[10].

1 Criminal Justice Act 2003 s 164(2).
2 Criminal Justice Act 2003 s 164(3). Before fixing the amount of any fine to be imposed on an offender who is an individual, a court must inquire into his financial circumstances: s 164(1). Section 164(3) applies whether taking into account the financial circumstances of the offender has the effect of increasing or reducing the amount of the fine (s 164(4)), and in applying s 164(3) a court must not reduce the amount of a fine on account of any surcharge it orders the offender to pay under s 161A (see PARA 185), except to the extent that he has insufficient means to pay both: s 164(4A) (added by the Domestic Violence, Crime and Victims Act 2004 s 14(2)). See *R v Guy's and St Thomas' NHS Trust* [2008] EWCA Crim 2187, [2008] 4 All ER 1174, [2009] 1 Cr App Rep (S) 585 (public benefit considerations in fining not-for-profit body); *R v Cotswold Geotechnical (Holdings) Ltd* [2011] EWCA Crim 1337, [2012] 1 Cr App Rep (S) 153 (fine imposed for corporate manslaughter was beyond company's means and caused it to be put into liquidation, but this was inevitable and unavoidable in the circumstances and was not a reason to reduce the fine).
3 Ie in pursuance of the Magistrates' Courts Act 1980 s 11 or s 12 (non-appearance of defendant: see CRIMINAL PROCEDURE vol 27 (2015) PARA 248 et seq).
4 Criminal Justice Act 2003 s 164(5)(a).
5 Ie in proceedings conducted in accordance with the Magistrates' Courts Act 1980 s 16A (see CRIMINAL PROCEDURE).
6 Criminal Justice Act 2003 s 164(5)(aa) (added by the Criminal Justice and Courts Act 2015 Sch 11 para 23).
7 Criminal Justice Act 2003 s 164(5)(b)(i). The reference in the text to a request which is an official request is a reference to an official request for the purposes of the Criminal Justice Act 1991 s 20A (offences of making false statement as to financial circumstances: see PARA 179).

8   Criminal Justice Act 2003 s 164(5)(b)(ii). A financial circumstances order is an order under s 162(1): see PARA 180.
9   Criminal Justice Act 2003 s 164(5)(b)(iii).
10 Criminal Justice Act 2003 s 164(5).

179. Statement as to offender's financial circumstances before conviction. The designated officer for a magistrates' court and the appropriate officer of the Crown Court may request a person who is charged with an offence to furnish a statement of financial circumstances (whether a statement of assets, of other financial circumstances or of both) in order to inform the court, in the event of that person being convicted, of his financial circumstances for the purpose of determining the amount of any fine the court may impose and how it should be paid[1], and it is an offence[2] for such a person:

(1) to fail to furnish such a statement[3]; or
(2) in furnishing such a statement:
(a)   to make a statement which he knows to be false in a material particular[4];
(b)   recklessly to furnish a statement which is false in a material particular[5]; or
(c)   knowingly to fail to disclose any material fact[6].

1   See the Criminal Justice Act 1991 s 20A(1), (2) (s 20A added by the Criminal Justice and Public Order Act 1994 Sch 9 para 43; Criminal Justice Act 1991 s 20A(1A) added, s 20A(2) amended, by the Courts Act 2003 Sch 8 para 350; Criminal Justice Act 1991 s 20A(1), (1A) amended by the Crime and Courts Act 2013 Sch 16 para 26). Such a request is referred to as an 'official request': Criminal Justice Act 1991 s 20A(2) (as so added and amended).
2   Proceedings in respect of an offence under the Criminal Justice Act 1991 s 20A may, notwithstanding anything in the Magistrates' Courts Act 1980 s 127(1) (limitation of time: see MAGISTRATES vol 71 (2013) PARA 526), be commenced at any time within two years from the date of the commission of the offence or within six months from its first discovery by the prosecutor, whichever period expires the earlier: Criminal Justice Act 1991 s 20A(3) (as added: see note 1).
3   Criminal Justice Act 1991 s 20A(1A) (as added and amended: see note 1). This offence is punishable on summary conviction by a fine not exceeding level 2 on the standard scale: s 20A(1A) (as so added and amended). As to the standard scale, the statutory maximum, the prescribed sum, and magistrates' powers to levy unlimited fines see PARA 176.
4   Criminal Justice Act 1991 s 20A(1)(a) (as added: see note 1). An offence under s 20A(1) is punishable on summary conviction by imprisonment for a term not exceeding three months or a fine not exceeding level 4 on the standard scale or both: s 20A(1) (as so added).
5   Criminal Justice Act 1991 s 20A(1)(b) (as added: see note 1). See note 3.
6   Criminal Justice Act 1991 s 20A(1)(c) (as added: see note 1). See note 3.

180. Statement as to offender's financial circumstances after conviction. Where an individual has been convicted of an offence the court may, before sentencing him, make a financial circumstances order with respect to him[1]. A 'financial circumstances order' means, in relation to any individual, an order requiring him to give to the court, within such period as may be specified in the order, such a statement of his assets and other financial circumstances as the court may require[2].

It is an offence for an individual:
(1)   without reasonable excuse to fail to comply with a financial circumstances order[3]; or
(2)   in furnishing any statement in pursuance of a financial circumstances order:
(a)   to make a statement which he knows to be false in a material particular[4];

(b) recklessly to furnish a statement which is false in a material particular[5]; or

(c) knowingly to fail to disclose any material fact[6].

1 Criminal Justice Act 2003 s 162(1). A court may also make a financial circumstances order where a magistrates' court has been notified in accordance with the Magistrates' Courts Act 1980 s 12(4) (see CRIMINAL PROCEDURE vol 27 (2015) PARA 253) that an individual desires to plead guilty without appearing before the court: Criminal Justice Act 2003 s 162(2).

2 Criminal Justice Act 2003 s 162(3) (amended by the Crime and Courts Act 2013 Sch 16 para 24).

3 Criminal Justice Act 2003 s 162(4). This offence is punishable on summary conviction by a fine not exceeding level 3 on the standard scale: s 162(4). As to the standard scale, the statutory maximum, the prescribed sum, and magistrates' powers to levy unlimited fines see PARA 176.

4 Criminal Justice Act 2003 s 162(5)(a). An offence under s 162(5) is punishable on summary conviction by a fine not exceeding level 4 on the standard scale: s 162(5). Proceedings in respect of an offence under s 162(5) may, notwithstanding anything in the Magistrates' Courts Act 1980 s 127(1) (limitation of time: see MAGISTRATES vol 71 (2013) PARA 526), be commenced at any time within two years from the date of the commission of the offence or within six months from its first discovery by the prosecutor, whichever period expires the earlier: Criminal Justice Act 2003 s 162(6).

5 Criminal Justice Act 2003 s 162(5)(b). See note 4.

6 Criminal Justice Act 2003 s 162(5)(c). See note 4.

181. Remission of fines. Where, in fixing the amount of a fine, a court has determined the offender's financial circumstances[1] and, on subsequently inquiring into the offender's financial circumstances, is satisfied that had it had the results of that inquiry when sentencing the offender it would:

(1) have fixed a smaller amount[2]; or

(2) not have fined him[3],

it may remit the whole or part of the fine[4]. Where the court so remits the whole or part of a fine after a term of imprisonment in default has been fixed[5], it must reduce the term by the corresponding proportion[6]. Where the court remits the whole or part of a fine pursuant to these provisions[7] and the offender was ordered[8] to pay a surcharge the amount of which was set by reference to the amount of the fine[9], the court must determine how much the surcharge would have been if the fine had not included the amount remitted, and remit the balance of the surcharge[10].

1 Ie in accordance with the Criminal Justice Act 2003 s 164(5); and PARA 178.

2 Criminal Justice Act 2003 s 165(1), (2)(a).

3 Criminal Justice Act 2003 s 165(2)(b).

4 Criminal Justice Act 2003 s 165(2). In connection with remission see the Criminal Procedure Rules 2015, SI 2015/1490, r 52.5.

5 Ie under the Powers of Criminal Courts (Sentencing) Act 2000 s 139 (see PARA 186) or the Magistrates' Courts Act 1980 s 82(5) (magistrates' powers in relation to default: see MAGISTRATES vol 71 (2013) PARA 674).

6 Criminal Justice Act 2003 s 165(3). In calculating any reduction so required, any fraction of a day is to be ignored: s 165(4).

7 Criminal Justice Act 2003 s 165(5)(a) (s 165(5) added by the Anti-social Behaviour, Crime and Policing Act 2014 s 179(3)).

8 Ie under the Criminal Justice Act 2003 s 161A; and PARA 185.

9 Criminal Justice Act 2003 s 165(5)(b) (as added: see note 7).

10 Criminal Justice Act 2003 s 165(5) (as added: see note 7).

182. Mitigation of fine. Where under any enactment[1] a magistrates' court[2] has power to sentence an offender to a fine[3] of an amount specified in the enactment, then, except where an Act passed after 31 December 1879[4] expressly provides to the contrary, the court may sentence him to a fine of less than that amount[5]. Where under any such enactment an offender sentenced on summary conviction to a fine is required to enter into a recognisance[6] with or without sureties to keep the peace or observe any other condition, the court convicting him may dispense with or modify the requirement[7].

1 Ie any enactment whether passed before or after 6 July 1981 (ie the commencement of the Magistrates' Courts Act 1980: see the Magistrates' Courts Act 1980 (Commencement) Order 1981, SI 1981/457).
2 As to the meaning of 'magistrates' court' see MAGISTRATES vol 71 (2013) PARA 470.
3 As to the power to impose fines see PARA 174 et seq.
4 Where by a statute passed since 31 December 1879 (the date of the passing of the Summary Jurisdiction Act 1879), it is provided that not less than a minimum sum is to be imposed for a first offence, the justices have no power to reduce the penalty below that amount: *Osborn v Wood Bros* [1897] 1 QB 197, DC.
5 Magistrates' Courts Act 1980 s 34(1). Arrears of national insurance contributions, although recoverable as a penalty, may not be reduced under this provision: *Leach v Litchfield* [1960] 3 All ER 739, [1960] 1 WLR 1392, DC.
6 As to recognisances see PARAS 447–453.
7 Magistrates' Courts Act 1980 s 34(2).

183. On the spot penalties and fixed penalties. On the spot penalties may be given in respect of a number of specified public order offences[1], and a number of road traffic offences may be dealt with by way of fixed penalty[2]. On the spot penalties and fixed penalties are administered by means of the giving of penalty notices in respect of the offence, which give the offender the opportunity to discharge his liability to be convicted of the offence in return for the payment of a penalty which is significantly lower than the maximum fine for which the person might be liable on conviction[3].

1 As to these offences see the Criminal Justice and Police Act 2001 s 1; and CRIMINAL LAW vol 26 (2010) PARA 541.
2 As to these offences see the Road Traffic Offenders Act 1988 Sch 3; and ROAD TRAFFIC vol 90 (2011) PARA 851.
3 See the Criminal Justice and Police Act 2001 ss 2, 3; the Road Traffic Offenders Act 1988 ss 52, 53; CRIMINAL LAW vol 26 (2010) PARAS 542, 544; ROAD TRAFFIC vol 90 (2011) PARAS 852–853.

184. Financial penalty deposits. A 'financial penalty deposit requirement' is a requirement to make a payment to the Secretary of State or the Welsh Ministers (as the case may be)[1] where:
(1) a constable or vehicle examiner has reason to believe that a person is committing or has on that occasion committed an offence relating to a motor vehicle and the offence and the circumstances in which the offence is committed are of a specified description[2];
(2) the person must has been given written notification that it appears likely that proceedings will be brought against him in respect of the offence or (if the offence is a fixed penalty offence) either given such notification or given a fixed penalty notice in respect of the offence[3]; and
(3) the person has failed to provide a satisfactory address[4].
A person who fails to make a payment in accordance with a financial penalty deposit requirement may be prohibited from driving[5].

1 See the Road Traffic Offenders Act 1988 s 90B(1); and ROAD TRAFFIC vol 90 (2011) PARA 883. In connection with the making of payments see s 90C; and ROAD TRAFFIC vol 90 (2011) PARA 884.
2 See the Road Traffic Offenders Act 1988 s 90A(2); and ROAD TRAFFIC vol 90 (2011) PARA 883.
3 See the Road Traffic Offenders Act 1988 s 90A(3); and ROAD TRAFFIC vol 90 (2011) PARA 883. As to fixed penalties see PARA 183.
4 See the Road Traffic Offenders Act 1988 s 90A(4); and ROAD TRAFFIC vol 90 (2011) PARA 883.
5 See the Road Traffic Offenders Act 1988 s 90D; and ROAD TRAFFIC vol 90 (2011) PARA 885.

(ii) Surcharges

185. Victim surcharge. If when dealing with a person[1] for one or more offences the court:

(1)   imposes a custodial sentence[2];

(2)   imposes a suspended sentence of imprisonment[3];

(3)   imposes a fine[4];

(4)   makes a youth rehabilitation order[5];

(5)   makes a referral order[6];

(6)   makes a community order[7]; or

(7)   conditionally discharges[8] the person[9],

the court must also order the person to pay a victim surcharge of an amount ranging from £10 to £120[10]. Where a court dealing with an offender considers that it would be appropriate to make a compensation order[11], an unlawful profit order[12] or a slavery and trafficking reparation order[13] but that he has insufficient means to pay both the surcharge and the appropriate amounts under such of those orders as it would have been appropriate to make, the court must reduce the surcharge accordingly (if necessary to nil)[14].

1   For these purposes, a court does not 'deal with' a person if it discharges him absolutely or makes an order under the Mental Health Act 1983 in respect of him: Criminal Justice Act 2003 s 161A(4) (ss 161A, 161B added by the Domestic Violence, Crime and Victims Act 2004 s 14(1)).

2   Criminal Justice Act 2003 (Surcharge) Order 2012, SI 2012/1696, art 2, Schedule (amended by SI 2012/2824; SI 2014/2120). The reference to a custodial sentence is a reference to a custodial sentence within the meaning of the Criminal Justice Act 2003 s 76 (see PARA 9 note 15).

3   Criminal Justice Act 2003 (Surcharge) Order 2012, SI 2012/1696, Schedule. Suspended sentences are imposed under the Criminal Justice Act 2003 s 189(1) (see PARA 100).

4   Criminal Justice Act 2003 (Surcharge) Order 2012, SI 2012/1696, Schedule.

5   Criminal Justice Act 2003 (Surcharge) Order 2012, SI 2012/1696, Schedule. A youth rehabilitation order is an order under the Criminal Justice and Immigration Act 2008 s 1: see PARA 73 et seq.

6   Criminal Justice Act 2003 (Surcharge) Order 2012, SI 2012/1696, Schedule. A referral order is an order under the Powers of Criminal Courts (Sentencing) Act 2000 s 16(2) or (3) (see PARA 156).

7   Criminal Justice Act 2003 (Surcharge) Order 2012, SI 2012/1696, Schedule. A community order is an order under the Criminal Justice Act 2003 s 177(1) (see PARA 48).

8   Ie makes an order under the Powers of Criminal Courts (Sentencing) Act 2000 s 12(1)(b) (see PARA 454).

9   Criminal Justice Act 2003 s 161A(2) (as added: see note 1); Criminal Justice Act 2003 (Surcharge) Order 2012, SI 2012/1696, Schedule.

10   Criminal Justice Act 2003 ss 161A(1), 161B(1) (as added: see note 1). The amount of the surcharge is specified in the Criminal Justice Act 2003 (Surcharge) Order 2012, SI 2012/1696, arts 3–6, Schedule. The amount of the surcharge as specified by order may depend on the offence or offences committed, how the offender is otherwise dealt with (including, where the offender is fined, the amount of the fine), and the age of the offender: Criminal Justice Act 2003 s 161B(2)(a)–(c) (as so added). Section 161B is not to be read as limiting s 330(3) (orders and rules: power to make different provision for different purposes etc): s 161B(2).

     Where the Crown Court orders a person to pay a surcharge under s 161A then, if that person is before it, the Crown Court may order him to be searched: Powers of Criminal Courts (Sentencing) Act 2000 s 142(1)(za) (added by the Domestic Violence, Crime and Victims Act 2004 Sch 10 para 53(a)). See also PARA 186 note 2.

     As to the determination of a person's age see the Children and Young Persons Act 1933 s 99; and CHILDREN AND YOUNG PERSONS vol 10 (2012) PARA 1206.

11   See PARA 281 et seq.

12   Ie an unlawful profit order under the Prevention of Social Housing Fraud Act 2013 s 4 (see LANDLORD AND TENANT): Criminal Justice Act 2003 s 161A(5) (as added (see note 1); s 161A(5) further added by the Prevention of Social Housing Fraud Act 2013 Schedule paras 28, 30).

13 Ie a slavery and trafficking reparation order under the Modern Slavery Act 2015 s 8 (see CRIMINAL LAW): Criminal Justice Act 2003 s 161A(5) (as added (see notes 1, 12); s 161A(3), (5) amended by the Modern Slavery Act 2015 Sch 5 para 25).
14 Criminal Justice Act 2003 s 161A(3) (as added and amended: see notes 1, 13).

(iii) Payment and Collection

186. Time to pay. Except in the case of a fine imposed on appeal from a magistrates' court[1], if the Crown Court imposes a fine on any person or forfeits his recognisance[2], the court may make an order:

(1) allowing time for payment of the amount of the fine or the amount due under the recognisance[3];

(2) directing payment of that amount by instalments of such amounts and on such dates respectively as may be specified in the order[4];

(3) in the case of a recognisance, discharging the recognisance or reducing the amount due thereunder[5].

If the Crown Court imposes a fine on any person or forfeits his recognisance, the court must make an order fixing a term of imprisonment[6] which he is to undergo if any sum which he is liable to pay is not duly paid or recovered[7]. No person may on the occasion when the fine is imposed on him or his recognisance is forfeited by the Crown Court be committed to prison[8] in pursuance of such an order unless:

(a) in the case of an offence punishable with imprisonment, he appears to the court to have sufficient means to pay the sum forthwith[9];

(b) it appears to the court that he is unlikely to remain long enough at a place of abode in the United Kingdom[10] to enable payment of the sum to be enforced by other methods[11]; or

(c) on the occasion when the order is made, the court sentences him to immediate imprisonment[12] for that or another offence, or so sentences him for an offence in addition to forfeiting his recognisance, or he is already serving a sentence of custody for life or a term of imprisonment[13], or of detention[14].

These provisions[15] do not apply to a fine imposed by the Crown Court on appeal against a decision of the magistrates' court, but the requirement that the court must make an order fixing a term of imprisonment and the provisions limiting the circumstances in which a person may be committed to prison or detained in pursuance of such an order[16] do apply in relation to a fine imposed or recognisance forfeited by the criminal division of the Court of Appeal or by the Supreme Court on appeal from that division as they apply in relation to a fine imposed or recognisance forfeited by the Crown Court[17].

Where a person has been sentenced by a magistrates' court to imprisonment and a fine for the same offence, a period of imprisonment imposed for non-payment of the fine, or for want of sufficient goods to satisfy the fine, must not be subject to these limitations[18].

1 Powers of Criminal Courts (Sentencing) Act 2000 s 139(9).
2 Where the Crown Court imposes a fine on a person or makes a surcharge order (see PARA 185) or forfeits his recognisance, then, if the person is before it, the Crown Court may order him to be searched: Powers of Criminal Courts (Sentencing) Act 2000 s 142(1)(za), (a) (s 142(1)(za) added by the Domestic Violence, Crime and Victims Act 2004 Sch 10 para 53(a)). Any money found on a person in such a search may be applied, unless the court otherwise directs, towards payment of the fine or other sum payable by him; and the balance, if any, must be returned to him: Powers of Criminal Courts (Sentencing) Act 2000 s 142(2). Where payment of a fine imposed by any court falls to be enforced as mentioned in the Contempt of Court Act 1981

s 16(1)(b), the provisions of the Powers of Criminal Courts (Sentencing) Act 2000 ss 139, 140 apply as they apply to a fine imposed by the Crown Court: see the Contempt of Court Act 1981 s 16(3); and CONTEMPT OF COURT vol 22 (2012) PARA 108. Provision for the recovery and application of fines imposed and recognisances forfeited by the Crown Court and appellate courts is made by the Powers of Criminal Courts (Sentencing) Act 2000 s 140 (amended by the Criminal Justice Act 2003 Sch 3 para 74(1), (4)(a), Sch 37 Pt 4; and by the Constitutional Reform Act 2005 Sch 9 para 69; prospectively amended by the Criminal Justice and Court Services Act 2000 Sch 7 paras 160, 194, Sch 8).

3   Powers of Criminal Courts (Sentencing) Act 2000 s 139(1)(a).

4   Powers of Criminal Courts (Sentencing) Act 2000 s 139(1)(b). As to the length of time for payment by instalments see *R v Olliver, R v Olliver* (1989) 11 Cr App Rep (S) 10, CA (two years would seldom seem to be too long, and in an appropriate case three years would be unassailable), explaining *R v Hewitt* (1971) 55 Cr App Rep 433, CA (a large fine payable by small instalments over a long period is undesirable). Where a fine is imposed on a company a longer period may be appropriate (*R v Rollco Screw and Rivet Co Ltd* [1999] 2 Cr App Rep (S) 436, [1999] IRLR 439, CA).

5   Powers of Criminal Courts (Sentencing) Act 2000 s 139(1)(c). The power conferred by these provisions to discharge a recognisance or reduce the amount due thereunder is in addition to the powers conferred by any other Act relating to the discharge, cancellation, mitigation or reduction of recognisances or sums forfeited thereunder: s 139(6).

There is no right to make more than one application under s 139(1): *R v Crown Court at Wood Green, ex p Howe* [1992] 3 All ER 366, (1991) 93 Cr App Rep 213, DC.

6   Or, until a day to be appointed, of detention under the Powers of Criminal Courts (Sentencing) Act 2000 s 108 (see PARA 551): s 139(2) (s 139(2)–(5) prospectively amended by the Criminal Justice and Court Services Act 2000 ss 74, 75, Sch 7 paras 160, 193, Sch 8). At the date at which this volume states the law no day had been appointed for these amendments to come into force.

For the purposes of any reference in the Powers of Criminal Courts (Sentencing) Act 2000 s 139, however expressed, to the term of imprisonment or other detention to which a person has been sentenced or which, or part of which, he has served, consecutive terms and terms which are wholly or partly concurrent must, unless the context otherwise requires, be treated as a single term: s 139(10). Any reference in s 139, however expressed, to a previous sentence is to be construed as a reference to a previous sentence passed by a court in Great Britain: s 139(11).

7   Powers of Criminal Courts (Sentencing) Act 2000 s 139(2) (prospectively amended: see note 6). By virtue of s 139(4) (as so prospectively amended) the following periods are the maximum periods of imprisonment (or, until a day to be appointed, detention (see note 6)) applicable:

(1)   in relation to an amount not exceeding £200, seven days;
(2)   in relation to an amount exceeding £200 but not exceeding £500, 14 days;
(3)   in relation to an amount exceeding £500 but not exceeding £1,000, 28 days;
(4)   in relation to an amount exceeding £1,000 but not exceeding £2,500, 45 days;
(5)   in relation to an amount exceeding £2,500 but not exceeding £5,000, three months;
(6)   in relation to an amount exceeding £5,000 but not exceeding £10,000, six months;
(7)   in relation to an amount exceeding £10,000 but not exceeding £20,000, 12 months;
(8)   in relation to an amount exceeding £20,000 but not exceeding £50,000, 18 months;
(9)   in relation to an amount exceeding £50,000 but not exceeding £100,000, two years;
(10)   in relation to an amount exceeding £100,000 but not exceeding £250,000, three years;
(11)   in relation to an amount exceeding £250,000 but not exceeding £1,000,000, five years; and
(12)   in relation to an amount exceeding £1,000,000, ten years.

The court should select an appropriate default term rather than simply impose the maximum term: *R v Szrabjer* (1994) 15 Cr App Rep (S) 821, CA. In determining the default term the judge is entitled to take account of what has been learned about the defendant during the trial: see *R v Piggott* [2009] EWCA Crim 2292, [2010] 2 Cr App Rep (S) 91.

Where any person liable for the payment of a fine or a sum due under a recognisance is sentenced by the court to, or is serving or otherwise liable to serve, a term of imprisonment or detention in a young offender institution (see PARA 16) or a term of detention under the Powers of Criminal Courts (Sentencing) Act 2000 s 108, the court may order that any term of imprisonment (or, until a day to be appointed, detention (see note 6)) fixed under s 139(2) is not to begin until after the end of the first-mentioned term: s 139(5) (as so prospectively amended).

The powers conferred by s 139 are not to be taken as restricted by any enactment about committal by a magistrates' court to the Crown Court which authorises the Crown Court to deal with an offender in any way in which the magistrates' court might have dealt with him or could deal with him: s 139(7). However, any term fixed under s 139(2) as respects a fine imposed in pursuance of such an enactment, that is to say a fine which the magistrates' court could have imposed, may not exceed the period applicable to that fine (if imposed by the magistrates' court) under the Customs and Excise Management Act 1979 s 149(1) (see CUSTOMS AND EXCISE vol 31 (2012) PARA 1187): Powers of Criminal Courts (Sentencing) Act 2000 s 139(8).

If the Crown Court fails to fix a term of imprisonment to be served in default of payment of a fine, the validity of the fine is not affected but the power of the magistrates' court to commit to prison in the event of default is open to question: *R v Hamilton* (1980) 2 Cr App Rep (S) 1, [1980] Crim LR 441, CA.

Where fines are imposed on more than one count, the terms of imprisonment imposed in default of payment may be ordered to run consecutively to each other and consecutively to any term or terms of imprisonment imposed on the same or other counts: *R v Savundranayagan and Walker* [1968] 3 All ER 439n, 52 Cr App Rep 637, CA.

Where payment by instalments is ordered, the default term should be expressed in default of the whole fine, not in default of each and every instalment: *R v Aitchison and Bentley* (1982) 4 Cr App Rep (S) 404, CA; *R v Power* (1986) 8 Cr App Rep (S) 8, CA.

8   Or, until a day to be appointed, detained (see note 6): see the Powers of Criminal Courts (Sentencing) Act 2000 s 139(3) (prospectively amended: see note 6).

9   Powers of Criminal Courts (Sentencing) Act 2000 s 139(3)(a).

10 As to the meaning of 'United Kingdom' see PARA 4 note 3.

11 Powers of Criminal Courts (Sentencing) Act 2000 s 139(3)(b).

12 Or, until a day to be appointed, custody for life or detention in a young offender institution: Powers of Criminal Courts (Sentencing) Act 2000 s 139(3)(c) (prospectively amended: see note 6).

13 Powers of Criminal Courts (Sentencing) Act 2000 s 139(3)(c)(i).

14 Powers of Criminal Courts (Sentencing) Act 2000 s 139(3)(c)(ii), (iii). The reference to 'detention' is to detention in a young offender institution or detention under s 108.

15 Ie the Powers of Criminal Courts (Sentencing) Act 2000 s 139.

16 Ie the Powers of Criminal Courts (Sentencing) Act 2000 s 139(2)–(4) (see the text and notes 6–14).

17 Powers of Criminal Courts (Sentencing) Act 2000 s 139(9) (amended by the Constitutional Reform Act 2005 Sch 9 para 69).

18 Magistrates' Courts Act 1980 s 133(4) (amended by the Tribunals, Courts and Enforcement Act 2007 Sch 13 paras 45, 62).

187.   Supervision orders. Where any person is adjudged to pay a sum by a summary conviction and the convicting magistrates' court[1] does not commit him to prison forthwith in default of payment, the court may order him to be placed under the supervision of an appointed person for so long as he remains liable to pay the sum or any part of it[2].

1   As to the meaning of 'magistrates' court' see MAGISTRATES vol 71 (2013) PARA 470.
2   See the Magistrates' Courts Act 1980 s 88; and MAGISTRATES vol 71 (2013) PARAS 687–689.

188.   Attachment of earnings orders. Where any sum is payable under a judgment or order enforceable by a court in England and Wales (not being a magistrates' court) the county court may, on an application for the purpose, make an attachment of earnings order to secure the payment of that sum[1]. Such an order operates as an instruction to the judgment debtor's employer to make periodical deductions from the debtor's earnings and pay the amounts deducted to the court[2].

1   See the Attachment of Earnings Act 1971 ss 1(2)(b), 2, 3; and CIVIL PROCEDURE vol 12 (2009) PARAS 1431–1433.
2   See the Attachment of Earnings Act 1971 s 6; and CIVIL PROCEDURE vol 12 (2009) PARA 1441.

(2) CONFISCATION ORDERS

(i) Pre-Hearing Matters

A. INTRODUCTORY

189. The different confiscation regimes. The power to make a confiscation order under the Proceeds of Crime Act 2002[1] applies only in respect of an offence committed on or after 24 March 2003[2]. The making of confiscation orders in relation to offences committed before that date continues to be governed by repealed provisions of the Criminal Justice Act 1988[3] or, where applicable, the Drug Trafficking Act 1994[4], which are specifically saved for the purpose[5].

1   See the Proceeds of Crime Act 2002 Pt 2 (ss 6–91); the Criminal Procedure Rules 2015, SI 2015/1490, Pt 33;and PARA 190 et seq.

2   Ie the date on which the Proceeds of Crime Act 2002 Pt 2 was brought into force by the Proceeds of Crime Act 2002 (Commencement No 5, Transitional Provisions, Savings and Amendment) Order 2003, SI 2003/333, art 2, Schedule. Thus the Proceeds of Crime Act 2002 applies only if all the offences on an indictment were committed on or after 24 March 2003 (the corollary of this being that the Proceeds of Crime Act 2002 does not apply, but the Criminal Justice Act 1988 (see the text and note 3) does, if any of the offences on the indictment were committed before 24 March 2003), and an offence committed over a period of time commencing before 24 March 2003 is treated as having been committed before that date: see the Proceeds of Crime Act 2002 (Commencement No 5, Transitional Provisions, Savings and Amendment) Order 2003, SI 2003/333, arts 3, 7 (art 7 substituted by SI 2003/531); and see also (in connection with continuing offences or a sequence of offences commenced before 24 March 2003) *R v Simpson* [2003] EWCA Crim 1499, [2004] QB 118, [2003] 2 Cr App Rep 545; *R v Aslam* [2004] EWCA Crim 2801, [2005] 1 Cr App Rep (S) 660, [2005] Crim LR 145; *R v Stapleton* [2008] EWCA Crim 1308, [2009] 1 Cr App Rep (S) 209, [2008] Crim LR 813; *R v Moulden* [2008] EWCA Crim 2561, [2009] 2 All ER 912, [2009] 1 Cr App Rep 362 (if offences are charged in separate indictments each is a separate proceedings for the purposes of confiscation); *R v Evwierhowa* [2011] EWCA Crim 572 at [28]–[29], [2011] 2 Cr App Rep (S) 442, [2011] Crim LR 498 (where a conspiracy continued either side of 24 March 2003 it will be taken to have been completed on the earliest date, i e when the agreement was made or the defendant joined the conspiracy).

3   Ie the Criminal Justice Act 1988 Pt VI (ss 71–103) (repealed by the Proceeds of Crime Act 2002 Sch 11 paras 1, 17, Sch 12, and replaced by Pt 2).

4   Ie the Drug Trafficking Act 1994 Pt 1 (ss 1–41) (repealed by the Proceeds of Crime Act 2002 Sch 11 para 25, Sch 12, and replaced by Pt 2).

5   See the Proceeds of Crime Act 2002 (Commencement No 5, Transitional Provisions, Savings and Amendment) Order 2003, SI 2003/333, art 10(1)(a), (e). For a history of confiscation orders and in connection with the purpose of confiscation see *R v May* [2008] UKHL 28, [2008] 1 AC 1028, [2008] 4 All ER 97; in connection with the purpose of confiscation see also eg *R v Modjiri* [2010] EWCA Crim 829, [2010] 4 All ER 837, [2010] 1 WLR 2096; *R v Waya* [2012] UKSC 51, [2013] 1 AC 294, [2013] 1 All ER 889.

190. Committal by magistrates' court. Where a defendant[1] is convicted of an offence by a magistrates' court[2], and the prosecutor asks the court to commit the defendant to the Crown Court with a view to a confiscation order[3] being considered[4], the magistrates' court:

(1)   must commit the defendant to the Crown Court in respect of the offence[5]; and

(2)   may commit him to the Crown Court in respect of any other offence of a specified[6] type[7].

If such a committal is made in respect of an offence or offences, the provisions[8] relating to the making of a confiscation order apply accordingly[9] and the committal operates as a committal of the defendant to be dealt with[10] by the Crown Court[11].

1   As to the meaning of 'defendant' for these purposes see PARA 221 note 1.
2   Proceeds of Crime Act 2002 s 70(1)(a). Section 70(1) is not limited to either-way offences: see *R v Sumal & Sons (Properties) Ltd* [2012] EWCA Crim 1840, [2013] 1 WLR 2078, [2012] HLR 700.
3   Ie an order under the Proceeds of Crime Act 2002 s 6: see PARA 221.
4   Proceeds of Crime Act 2002 s 70(1)(b). The reference in the text to a confiscation order being considered is a reference to an order being considered under s 6 (see PARA 221).
5   Proceeds of Crime Act 2002 s 70(2)(a). A committal under s 70 may be in custody or on bail: s 70(6).
6   Ie an offence falling within the Proceeds of Crime Act 2002 s 70(3). An offence falls within s 70(3) if: (1) the defendant has been convicted of it by the magistrates' court or any other court (s 70(3)(a)); and (2) the magistrates' court has power to deal with him in respect of it (s 70(3)(b)).
7   Proceeds of Crime Act 2002 s 70(2)(b).
8   Ie the Proceeds of Crime Act 2002 s 6 (see PARA 221).
9   Proceeds of Crime Act 2002 s 70(4)(a).
10 Ie in accordance with the Proceeds of Crime Act 2002 s 71 (see PARA 191).
11 Proceeds of Crime Act 2002 s 70(4)(b). If a committal is made under s 70 in respect of an offence for which (apart from s 70) the magistrates' court could have committed the defendant for sentence under the Powers of Criminal Courts (Sentencing) Act 2000 s 3(2) (offences triable
·   either way: see CRIMINAL PROCEDURE vol 27 (2015) PARA 292) or under s 3B(2) (committal of a child or young person: see CRIMINAL PROCEDURE vol 27 (2015) PARA 234) the court must state whether it would have done so: Proceeds of Crime Act 2002 s 70(5) (amended by the Criminal Justice Act 2003 s 41, Sch 3 para 75(1), (4)).

191.   Sentencing powers after a committal for a confiscation order. If a defendant[1] is committed to the Crown Court[2] in respect of an offence or offences with a view to a confiscation order[3] being made, the following provisions apply (whether or not the court proceeds under the provisions[4] relating to making a confiscation order)[5].

In the case of an offence in respect of which the magistrates' court has stated[6] that it would have committed the defendant for sentence, the Crown Court must inquire into the circumstances of the case[7] and may deal with the defendant in any way in which it could deal with him if he had just been convicted of the offence on indictment before it[8]. In the case of any other offence the Crown Court must inquire into the circumstances of the case[9] and may deal with the case in any way in which the magistrates' court could deal with him if it had just convicted him of the offence[10].

1   As to the meaning of 'defendant' for these purposes see PARA 221 note 1.
2   Ie under the Proceeds of Crime Act 2002 s 70 (see PARA 190).
3   Ie an order under the Proceeds of Crime Act 2002 s 6: see PARA 221.
4   Ie under the Proceeds of Crime Act 2002 s 6.
5   Proceeds of Crime Act 2002 s 71(1).
6   Ie under the Proceeds of Crime Act 2002 s 70(5) (see PARA 190).
7   Proceeds of Crime Act 2002 s 71(2)(a).
8   Proceeds of Crime Act 2002 s 71(2)(b).
9   Proceeds of Crime Act 2002 s 71(3)(a).
10 Proceeds of Crime Act 2002 s 71(3)(b).

192.   Postponement of confiscation proceedings. The court may:
  (1)   proceed[1] to make a confiscation order[2] before it sentences the defendant[3] for the offence (or any of the offences) concerned[4]; or

(2)   postpone proceedings[5] for a confiscation order for a specified period[6].

A period of postponement may be extended[7]. Unless there are exceptional circumstances[8], a period of postponement (including one as extended) must not end after the permitted period ends[9]. The permitted period is two years starting with the date of conviction[10]; except that if the defendant appeals[11] against his conviction for the offence (or any of the offences) concerned[12], and the period of three months (starting with the day when the appeal is determined or otherwise disposed of) ends after such period of two years[13], the permitted period is that period of three months[14].

A postponement or extension may be made[15]:

(a)   on application by the defendant[16];

(b)   on application by the prosecutor[17];

(c)   by the court of its own motion[18].

1   Ie under the Proceeds of Crime Act 2002 s 6 (see PARA 221).
2   As to the meaning of 'confiscation order' see PARA 234 note 1.
3   As to the meaning of 'defendant' for these purposes see PARA 221 note 1.
4   Proceeds of Crime Act 2002 s 14(1)(a). As to references to the 'offence or offences concerned' see PARA 229 note 2. A power to sentence in advance of the completion of s 6 proceedings can be read into s 14(1)(a): see *Crown Prosecution Service v Gilleeney* [2009] EWCA Crim 193, [2009] Crim LR 455, [2009] All ER (D) 168 (Feb).
5   Ie under the Proceeds of Crime Act 2002 s 6 (see PARA 221). A lengthy postponement may be a breach of the defendant's right a to hearing 'within a reasonable time' under the Convention for the Protection of Human Rights and Fundamental Freedoms (Rome, 4 November 1950; TS 71 (1953; Cmd 8969) (the European Convention on Human Rights) art 6 (the right to a fair hearing: see RIGHTS AND FREEDOMS vol 88A (2013) PARAS 243–300): see *Minshall v United Kingdom* [2012] STC 731, ECtHR; *Bullen v United Kingdom* (2009) Times, 2 February, [2009] All ER (D) 90 (Jan), ECtHR. Procedural errors relating to the postponement of confiscation proceedings are not fatal to making an order: see *R v Soneji* [2005] UKHL 49, [2006] 1 AC 340, [2006] 2 Cr App Rep 298 (decided under corresponding provisions of the Criminal Justice Act 1988 and reviewing the case law in this area). In connection with confiscation proceedings and the European Convention on Human Rights see also PARA 222.
6   Proceeds of Crime Act 2002 s 14(1)(b).
7   Proceeds of Crime Act 2002 s 14(2). If proceedings are postponed for a period (s 14(8)(a)), and an application to extend the period is made before it ends (s 14(8)(b)), the application may be granted even after the period ends (s 14(8)).
8   Proceeds of Crime Act 2002 s 14(4).
9   Proceeds of Crime Act 2002 s 14(3). See eg *R v Iqbal* [2010] EWCA Crim 376, [2010] 1 WLR 1985.
10 Proceeds of Crime Act 2002 s 14(5). The date of conviction is: (1) the date on which the defendant was convicted of the offence concerned (s 14(9)(a)); or (2) if there are two or more offences and the convictions were on different dates, the date of the latest (s 14(9)(b)).
11 'Appealing' includes applying to a magistrates' court to state a case for the opinion of the High Court under the Magistrates' Courts Act 1980 s 111 (see CRIMINAL PROCEDURE vol 28 (2015) PARA 654): Proceeds of Crime Act 2002 s 14(10).
12 Proceeds of Crime Act 2002 s 14(6)(a).
13 Proceeds of Crime Act 2002 s 14(6)(b).
14 Proceeds of Crime Act 2002 s 14(6).
15 A confiscation order may not be quashed only on the ground that there was a defect or omission in the procedure connected with the application for or the granting of a postponement: Proceeds of Crime Act 2002 s 14(11). However, s 14(11) does not apply if before it made the confiscation order, the court: (1) imposed a fine on the defendant (s 14(12)(a)); (2) made an order falling within s 13(3) (see PARA 237) (s 14(12)(b)); (3) made a compensation order under the Powers of Criminal Courts (Sentencing) Act 2000 s 130 (see PARA 281) (Proceeds of Crime Act 2002 s 14(12)(c)); (4) made an order under the Criminal Justice Act 2003 s 161A (orders requiring payment of surcharge: see PARA 185) (Proceeds of Crime Act 2002 s 14(12)(ca (added by the Serious Crime Act 2015 Sch 4 para 21)); or (5) made an order under the Prevention of Social Housing Fraud Act 2013 s 4 (unlawful profit orders: see LANDLORD AND TENANT) (Proceeds of Crime Act 2002 s 14(12)(d) (added by the Prevention of Social Housing Fraud Act 2013 Schedule paras 11, 15)). These provisions do not deprive the court of its jurisdiction to make a

confiscation order where there has been an error in making an order for forfeiture: see *R v Donahoe* [2006] EWCA Crim 2200, [2006] All ER (D) 440 (Jul), sub nom *R v Donohoe* [2007] 1 Cr App Rep (S) 548. See also *R v Neish* [2010] EWCA Crim 1011, [2010] 1 WLR 2395, [2010] All ER (D) 39 (May); *R v Guraj* [2015] EWCA Crim 305, [2015] 2 Cr App Rep (S) 202, [2015[All ER (D) 83 (Mar).

16   Proceeds of Crime Act 2002 s 14(7)(a).
17   Proceeds of Crime Act 2002 s 14(7)(b).
18   Proceeds of Crime Act 2002 s 14(7)(c).

193.   Effect of postponement.   If the court postpones proceedings for a confiscation order[1] it may proceed to sentence the defendant for the offence (or any of the offences)[2] concerned[3]. If the court sentences the defendant for the offence (or any of the offences) concerned in the postponement period[4], it may vary the sentence[5] but it may do so only within the period of 28 days which starts with the last day of the postponement period[6].

If the court postpones proceedings for a confiscation order but proceeds to sentence the defendant for the offence (or any of the offences) concerned, the provisions[7] relating to the making of a confiscation order have effect as if the defendant's particular conduct[8] included conduct which constitutes offences which the court has taken into consideration in deciding his sentence for the offence or offences concerned[9].

1   Ie under the Proceeds of Crime Act 2002 s 6: see PARA 221.
2   As to the meaning of 'defendant' for these purposes see PARA 221 note 1. References to 'sentencing the defendant for an offence' include references to dealing with him otherwise in respect of the offence: Proceeds of Crime Act 2002 s 88(4).
3   Proceeds of Crime Act 2002 s 15(1). As to references to the 'offence or offences concerned' see PARA 229 note 2. In sentencing the defendant for the offence (or any of the offences) concerned in the postponement period, the court must not:
    (1)   impose a fine on him (s 15(2)(a));
    (2)   make an order falling within s 13(3) (see PARA 237) (s 15(2)(b));
    (3)   make a compensation order under the Powers of Criminal Courts (Sentencing) Act 2000 s 130 (see PARA 281) (Proceeds of Crime Act 2002 s 15(2)(c));
    (4)   make an order requiring the payment of a surcharge under the Criminal Justice Act 2003 s 161A (see PARA 185) (Proceeds of Crime Act 2002 s 15(2)(ca) (s 15(2)(ca), (3)(ca) added by the Serious Crime Act 2015 Sch 4 para 22)); or
    (5)   make an unlawful profit order under the Prevention of Social Housing Fraud Act 2013 s 4 (see LANDLORD AND TENANT) (Proceeds of Crime Act 2002 s 15(2)(d) (s 15(2)(d), (3)(d) added by the Prevention of Social Housing Fraud Act 2013 Schedule para 16)).
4   The postponement period is the period for which proceedings under the Proceeds of Crime Act 2002 s 6 are postponed: s 15(7).
5   Ie by imposing a fine on him or making an order note 3 above: Proceeds of Crime Act 2002 s 15(3)(a)–(c), (ca), (d) (s 15(3)(ca), (d) as added: see note 3). For the purposes of the Criminal Appeal Act 1968 s 18(2) (time limit for notice of appeal or of application for leave to appeal: see CRIMINAL PROCEDURE vol 28 (2015) PARA 749) and the Criminal Justice Act 1988 s 36, Sch 3 para 1 (time limit for notice of application for leave to refer a case under s 36: see PARA 546), the sentence must be regarded as imposed or made on the day on which it is varied under the Proceeds of Crime Act 2002 s 15(3): s 15(5).
6   Proceeds of Crime Act 2002 s 15(4).
7   Ie the Proceeds of Crime Act 2002 s 6.
8   As to 'conduct' see PARA 225.
9   Proceeds of Crime Act 2002 s 15(6).

194.   Statement of information, and defendant's response.   If the court is proceeding under the provisions relating to the making of a confiscation order[1] in a case where the prosecutor asks the court so to proceed[2], the prosecutor must give the court a statement of information within the period the court orders[3].

If the court is proceeding under the provisions relating to the making of a confiscation order in a case where it believes it appropriate to do so[4], and it orders the prosecutor to give it a statement of information, the prosecutor must give it such a statement within the period the court orders[5].

If the prosecutor believes the defendant[6] has a criminal lifestyle[7] the statement of information is a statement of matters the prosecutor believes are relevant in connection with deciding these issues[8]:

(1) whether the defendant has a criminal lifestyle[9];

(2) whether he has benefited from his general criminal conduct[10];

(3) his benefit from the conduct[11].

Such a statement must include information the prosecutor believes is relevant[12]:

(a) in connection with the making by the court of a required assumption[13]; and

(b) for the purpose of enabling the court to decide if the circumstances are such that it must not make such an assumption[14].

If the prosecutor does not believe the defendant has a criminal lifestyle the statement of information is a statement of matters the prosecutor believes are relevant in connection with deciding these issues[15]:

(i) whether the defendant has benefited from his particular criminal conduct[16]; and

(ii) his benefit from the conduct[17].

A statement of information[18] must include any information known to the prosecutor which the prosecutor believes is or would be relevant for the purpose of enabling the court to decide whether to make a determination[19] of the extent of the defendant's interest in property[20] or what determination to make (if the court decides to make one)[21].

If the prosecutor gives the court a statement of information he may at any time give the court a further statement of information[22] and he must give the court a further statement of information if it orders him to do so, and he must give it within the period the court orders[23].

If the court makes an order under the above provisions[24] it may at any time vary it by making another one[25].

If the prosecutor gives the court a statement of information and a copy is served on the defendant, the court may order the defendant to indicate (within the period it orders) the extent to which he accepts each allegation in the statement[26], and so far as he does not accept such an allegation, to give particulars of any matters he proposes to rely on[27]. If the defendant accepts to any extent an allegation in a statement of information, the court may treat his acceptance as conclusive of the matters to which it relates for the purpose of deciding the issues referred to in heads (1) to (3) or (i) to (ii)[28] (as the case may be) above[29]. If the defendant fails in any respect to comply with such an order[30], he may be treated[31] as accepting every allegation in the statement of information, apart from any allegation in respect of which he has complied with the requirement[32] or any allegation that he has benefited from his general or particular criminal conduct[33]. An order made under these provisions may be varied at any time by the court by making another one[34].

1 Ie under the Proceeds of Crime Act 2002 s 6: see PARA 221.

2 Ie a case where the Proceeds of Crime Act 2002 s 6(3)(a) (see PARA 221) applies.

3 Proceeds of Crime Act 2002 s 16(1) (ss 16(1), (3)–(6), 17(1) amended by the Serious Crime Act 2007 Sch 8 para 5(2), 6, Sch 14). In connection with the giving of statements see the Criminal Procedure Rules 2015, SI 2015/1490, r 33.13.

4 Ie a case where the Proceeds of Crime Act 2002 s 6(3)(b) (see PARA 221) applies.

5 Proceeds of Crime Act 2002 s 16(2).

6   As to the meaning of 'defendant' for these purposes see PARA 221 note 1.
7   As to the circumstances under which the defendant may be judged to have a criminal lifestyle see PARA 229.
8   Proceeds of Crime Act 2002 s 16(3) (as amended: see note 3).
9   Proceeds of Crime Act 2002 s 16(3)(a).
10 Proceeds of Crime Act 2002 s 16(3)(b). As to the meanings of 'criminal conduct' and 'general criminal conduct' see PARA 225. As to when a person benefits from conduct see PARA 223.
11 Proceeds of Crime Act 2002 s 16(3)(c).
12 Proceeds of Crime Act 2002 s 16(4) (as amended: see note 3).
13 Proceeds of Crime Act 2002 s 16(4)(a). The 'required assumption' is the assumption under s 10 (see PARA 231).
14 Proceeds of Crime Act 2002 s 16(4)(b).
15 Proceeds of Crime Act 2002 s 16(5) (as amended: see note 3).
16 Proceeds of Crime Act 2002 s 16(5)(a).
17 Proceeds of Crime Act 2002 s 16(5)(b).
18 Ie other than a statement of information to which the Proceeds of Crime Act 2002 s 16(6B) (see note 23) applies: s 16(6A) (s 16(6A), (6B) added by the Serious Crime Act 2015 s 2(1)).
19 Ie a determination under the Proceeds of Crime Act 2002 s 10A (see PARA 226).
20 Proceeds of Crime Act 2002 s 16(6A)(a) (as added: see note 18).
21 Proceeds of Crime Act 2002 s 16(6A)(b) (as added: see note 18).
22 Proceeds of Crime Act 2002 s 16(6)(a) (as amended: see note 3)
23 Proceeds of Crime Act 2002 s 16(6)(b) (as amended: see note 3). If the court has decided to make a determination under s 10A, a further statement of information under s 16(6)(b) must, if the court so orders, include specified information that is relevant to the determination: s 16(6B) (as added: see note 18).
24 Ie under the Proceeds of Crime Act 2002 s 16 (see the text and notes 1–23).
25 Proceeds of Crime Act 2002 s 16(7).
26 Proceeds of Crime Act 2002 s 17(1)(a) (as amended: see note 3). For the purposes of s 17 an allegation may be accepted or particulars may be given in a manner ordered by the court: s 17(4).
27 Proceeds of Crime Act 2002 s 17(1)(b). See note 26.
28 Ie the issues referred to in the Proceeds of Crime Act 2002 s 16(3) (see heads (1)–(3) in the text) or s 16(5) (see heads (i)–(ii) in the text).
29 Proceeds of Crime Act 2002 s 17(2). No acceptance under s 17 that the defendant benefited from conduct is admissible in evidence in proceedings for an offence: s 17(6).
30 Ie under the Proceeds of Crime Act 2002 s 17(1) (see the text and notes 26–27).
31 Ie for the purposes of the Proceeds of Crime Act 2002 s 17(2) (see the text and notes 28–29).
32 Proceeds of Crime Act 2002 s 17(3)(a).
33 Proceeds of Crime Act 2002 s 17(3)(b). As to the meaning of 'particular criminal conduct' see PARA 225.
34 Proceeds of Crime Act 2002 s 17(5).

195. Provision of information by defendant or other interested person. Where the court is proceeding under the provisions relating to the making of a confiscation order[1] in a case where the prosecutor asks the court so to proceed[2], or is so proceeding in a case where it believes it appropriate to do[3] so, or it is considering whether to proceed[4], the following provisions apply.

For the purpose of obtaining information to help it in carrying out its functions[5] the court may at any time order the defendant[6] and, where applicable[7], another interested person[8], to give it information specified in the order[9]. If the defendant or interested person fails without reasonable excuse to comply with such an order the court may draw such inference as it believes is appropriate[10].

If the prosecutor accepts to any extent an allegation made by the defendant or an interested person[11]:

(1)   in giving information required by an order[12] for the provision of information[13]; or

(2)   in any other statement given to the court in relation to any matter relevant to deciding the available amount[14] or to a determination of the

extent of the defendant's interest in property[15], or whether to make a determination as to the extent of the defendant's interest in property or what determination to make (if the court decides to make one)[16], the court may treat the acceptance as conclusive of the matters to which it relates[17].

If the court makes an order for the provision of information it may at any time vary it by making another one[18].

1   As to the meaning of 'confiscation order' see the Proceeds of Crime Act 2002 s 6; and PARA 221.
2   Proceeds of Crime Act 2002 s 18(1)(a). The text refers to a case where s 6(3)(a) (see PARA 221) applies.
3   Ie a case where the Proceeds of Crime Act 2002 s 6(3)(b) (see PARA 221) applies.
4   Proceeds of Crime Act 2002 s 18(1)(b).
5   The functions referred to in this provision include functions under the Proceeds of Crime Act 2002 s 10A (determination of extent of defendant's interest in property: see PARA 226): s 18(2) (s 18(2), (6)(b) amended, s 18A added, by the Serious Crime Act 2015 s 2(2), (3))).
6   As to the meaning of 'defendant' for these purposes see PARA 221 note 1.
7   Ie where the court is considering whether to make a determination under the Proceeds of Crime Act 2002 s 10A (see PARA 226) of the extent of the defendant's interest in any property (s 18A(1)(a) (as added: see note 5)) or is deciding what determination to make (if the court has decided to make a determination thereunder) (s 18A(1)(b) (as so added)).
8   In the Proceeds of Crime Act 2002 s 18A 'interested person' means a person (other than the defendant) who the court thinks is or may be a person holding an interest in the property: s 18A(1) (as so added).
9   Proceeds of Crime Act 2002 ss 18(2), 18A(2) (as amended and added: see note 5). An order requiring the provision of information may require all or a specified part of the information to be given in a specified manner and before a specified date: ss 18(3), 18A(3) (s 18A(3) as so added). No information given under s 18 or s 18A which amounts to an admission by the defendant that he has benefited from criminal conduct is admissible in evidence in proceedings for an offence: ss 18(9), 18A(9) (s 18A(9) as so added). As to 'conduct' and 'criminal conduct' see PARA 225; as to when a person 'benefit's from conduct see PARA 223.
10 Proceeds of Crime Act 2002 ss 18(4), 18A(4) (s 18A as added: see note 5). Sections 18(4), 18A(4) do not affect any power of the court to deal with the defendant in respect of a failure to comply with an order under s 18 or s 18A: ss 18(5), 18A(5) (s 18A(5) as so added).
11 Proceeds of Crime Act 2002 ss 18(6), 18A(6) (s 18(6) amended by the Serious Crime Act 2007 Sch 8 para 7, Sch 14; Proceeds of Crime Act 2002 s 18A as added (see note 5)). For these purposes, an allegation may be accepted in a manner ordered by the court: Proceeds of Crime Act 2002 s 18(7).
12 Ie an order under the Proceeds of Crime Act 2002 s 18 or s 18A.
13 Proceeds of Crime Act 2002 ss 18(6)(a), 18A(6)(a) (s 18A as added: see note 5).
14 Ie deciding the available amount under the Proceeds of Crime Act 2002 s 9: see PARA 233.
15 Ie a determination under the Proceeds of Crime Act 2002 s 10A: see PARA 226.
16 Proceeds of Crime Act 2002 ss 18(6)(b), 18A(6)(b) (as amended and added: see note 5).
17 Proceeds of Crime Act 2002 ss 18(6), 18A(6) (as amended and added: see note 5).
18 Proceeds of Crime Act 2002 ss 18(8), 18A(8) (s 18A as added: see note 5).

B. DEFINITIONS

(A) Seized Money and Property

196. Seized money. The provisions relating to seized money[1] apply to money which:

(1)   is held by a person[2] in an account maintained by him with a bank or a building society[3];

(2)   is held by a person and has been seized by a constable under his general power[4] of seizure[5], and is held in an account maintained by a police force with a bank or building society[6];

(3)   is held by a person and has been seized by an officer of Revenue and Customs under his general power[7] of seizure[8], and is held in an account

maintained by the Commissioners for Her Majesty's Revenue and Customs with a bank or building society[9].

If a confiscation order[10] is made against a person holding money to which these provisions apply[11] and a receiver has not been appointed[12] in relation to the money[13], a magistrates' court may order the bank or building society to pay the money to the designated officer for the court on account of the amount payable under the confiscation order[14]. If a bank or building society fails to comply with such an order the magistrates' court may order it to pay an amount not exceeding £5,000[15] and the sum is to be treated[16] as adjudged to be paid by a conviction of the court[17].

1   Ie the Proceeds of Crime Act 2002 s 67 (see the text and notes 2–17).
2   Proceeds of Crime Act 2002 s 67(1)(a).
3   Proceeds of Crime Act 2002 s 67(1)(b). For these purposes, a 'bank' is a deposit-taking business within the meaning of the Banking Act 1987 (see s 6 (repealed)); and 'building society' has the same meaning as in the Building Societies Act 1986 (see ss 5(3), 119(1), 125; and FINANCIAL SERVICES AND INSTITUTIONS vol 50 (2008) PARA 1856): Proceeds of Crime Act 2002 s 67(8)(a), (b).
    The Secretary of State may by order amend s 67 so that it applies not only to money held in an account maintained with a bank or building society but also to money held in an account maintained with a financial institution of a specified kind (s 67(7A)(a) (s 67(5) substituted, s 67(5A), (5B), (7A), (7B) added, by the Serious Crime Act 2015 s 14(1)–(3))) or money that is represented by, or may be obtained from, a financial instrument or product of a specified kind (Proceeds of Crime Act 2002 s 67(7A)(b) (as so substituted)). An order under s 67(7A) may amend s 67 so that it makes provision about realising an instrument or product within s 67(7A)(b) or otherwise obtaining money from it: s 67(7B) (as so substituted).
4   Ie under the Police and Criminal Evidence Act 1984 s 19 (see POLICE AND INVESTIGATORY POWERS vol 84 (2013) PARA 465).
5   Proceeds of Crime Act 2002 s 67(2)(a).
6   Proceeds of Crime Act 2002 s 67(2)(b).
7   Ie under the Police and Criminal Evidence Act 1984 s 19 as applied by the Police and Criminal Evidence Act 1984 (Application to Customs and Excise) Order 2007, SI 2007/3175, art 3(1), Sch 1 (see POLICE AND INVESTIGATORY POWERS vol 84A (2013) PARAS 463–468).
8   Proceeds of Crime Act 2002 s 67(3)(a) (s 67(3) amended by virtue of the Commissioners for Revenue and Customs Act 2005 s 50(1), (2), (7)).
9   Proceeds of Crime Act 2002 s 67(3)(b) (as amended: see note 8).
10 As to a 'confiscation order' (ie an order under the Proceeds of Crime Act 2002 s 6) see PARA 221.
11 Proceeds of Crime Act 2002 s 67(5)(a) (as substituted: see note 3).
12 Ie under the Proceeds of Crime Act 2002 s 50 (see PARA 249).
13 Proceeds of Crime Act 2002 s 67(5)(b) (as substituted: see note 3).
14 Proceeds of Crime Act 2002 s 67(5) (as substituted: see note 3). As to the 'amount payable' under a confiscation order see PARA 258 note 10. This power must be exercised with regard to the matters specified in s 69 (see PARA 251): s 69(1). In connection with orders under s 67 see the Criminal Procedure Rules 2015, SI 2015/1490, r 33.24. A person applying for an order under the Proceeds of Crime Act 2002 s 67(5) must give notice of the application to the bank or building society with which the account is held: s 67(5A) (as so substituted). In the case of money held in an account not maintained by the person against whom the confiscation order is made, a magistrates' court may make an order under s 67(5) only if the extent of the person's interest in the money has been determined under s 10A (see PARA 226) (s 67(5B)(a) (as so substituted)) and must have regard to that determination in deciding what is the appropriate order to make (s 67(5B)(b) (as so substituted)).
15 Proceeds of Crime Act 2002 s 67(6)(a). In order to take account of changes in the value of money the Secretary of State may by order substitute another sum for the sum for the time being specified in this provision: s 67(7). At the date at which this volume states the law no such order had been made.
16 Ie for the purposes of the Magistrates' Courts Act 1980 (see MAGISTRATES).
17 Proceeds of Crime Act 2002 s 67(6)(b).

197.   Seized personal property. A magistrates' court may by order authorise an appropriate officer[1] to realise personal property which is held by a person and which either has been seized by an appropriate officer under a relevant seizure power[2] or has been produced[3] to an appropriate officer[4] if:

(1)   a confiscation order[5] is made against the person by whom the property is held[6]; and

(2)   a receiver has not been appointed[7] in relation to the property[8].

If a magistrates' court makes such an order[9] a person affected by the order may appeal against the decision; and if the court decides not to make an order an appropriate officer may appeal against that decision[10]. Provision is made for the application of the proceeds of any realisation of property under these provisions[11] and for the determination of amounts payable in respect of the costs of storage etc[12].

1   As to the meaning of 'appropriate officer' see the Proceeds of Crime Act 2002 s 41A(3); and PARA 201 note 7 (definition applied by ss 67A(4), 67B(5), 67C(5), 67D(6) (ss 67A–67D added by the Policing and Crime Act 2009 s 58(1), (2))).
2   Proceeds of Crime Act 2002 s 67A(1)(a) (as added: see note 1). As to the meaning of 'relevant seizure power' see s 41A(4); and PARA 201 note 8 (definition applied by s 67A(4) (as so added)).
3   Ie in compliance with a production order under the Proceeds of Crime Act 2002 s 345 (see POLICE AND INVESTIGATORY POWERS vol 84A (2013) PARAS 780–781).
4   Proceeds of Crime Act 2002 s 67A(1)(b) (as added: see note 1).
5   As to a 'confiscation order' (ie an order under the Proceeds of Crime Act 2002 s 6) see PARA 221.
6   Proceeds of Crime Act 2002 s 67A(3)(a) (as added (see note 1); s 67A(3) substituted by the Serious Crime Act 2015 s 14(4)).
7   Ie under the Proceeds of Crime Act 2002 s 50 (see PARA 249).
8   Proceeds of Crime Act 2002 s 67A(3)(b) (as added and substituted: see notes 1, 6).
9   Ie an order under the Proceeds of Crime Act 2002 s 67A (see the text and notes 1–8).
10 Proceeds of Crime Act 2002 s 67C(1), (2) (as added: see note 1). The person by whom the property is held (ie the person mentioned in s 67A(3)(a): see the text and notes 5–6) may not appeal: s 67C(3) (as so added). All such appeals are to the Crown Court: s 67C(1), (2) (as so added).
11 Sums which are in the hands of an appropriate officer and are the proceeds of the realisation of property under the Proceeds of Crime Act 2002 s 67A must be applied as follows:
    (1)   first, they must be applied in payment of such expenses incurred by a person acting as an insolvency practitioner as are payable under s 67D(2) by virtue of s 432 (see PARA 270) (s 67D(1), (2)(a) (as added: see note 1));
    (2)   second, they must be applied in making any payments directed by the magistrates' court or the Crown Court (s 67D(2)(b) (as so added)); and
    (3)   third, they must be paid to the appropriate designated officer (ie the designated officer for the magistrates' court which, by virtue of s 35 (see PARA 238), is responsible for enforcing the confiscation order as if it were a fine) on account of the amount payable under the confiscation order (s 67D(2)(c), (6) (as so added)).
    As to the 'amount payable' under a confiscation order see PARA 258 note 10. If the amount payable under the confiscation order has been fully paid and any sums remain in the appropriate officer's hands, the appropriate officer must distribute them:
    (a)   among such persons who held (or hold) interests in the property represented by the proceeds as the magistrates' court or the Crown Court directs (s 67D(3)(a) (as so added)); and
    (b)   in such proportions as it directs (s 67D(3)(b) (as so added)).
    Before making a direction under s 67D(3) the court must give persons who held (or hold) interests in the property a reasonable opportunity to make representations to it: s 67D(4) (as so added). If the magistrates' court has made a direction under s 67D(2)(b) or (3) in respect of the proceeds of realisation of any property, the Crown Court may not make a direction under either of those provisions in respect of the proceeds of realisation of that property; and vice versa: s 67D(5) (as so added).
12 If a magistrates' court makes an order under the Proceeds of Crime Act 2002 s 67A the court may determine an amount which may be recovered by the appropriate officer in respect of reasonable costs incurred in storing or insuring the property since it was seized or produced as mentioned in s 67A(1) (see the text and notes 1–4) or in realising the property: s 67B(1), (2) (as added: see note 1). If the court makes such a determination the appropriate officer is entitled to

payment of the amount under 55(4) (see PARA 259): s 67B(3) (as so added). A determination under s 67B may be made on the same occasion as the section 67A order or on any later occasion; and more than one determination may be made in relation to any case: s 67B(4) (as so added). An appropriate officer may appeal against a determination made by a magistrates' court under s 67B and a decision by a magistrates' court not to make such a determination: s 67C(4) (as so added). All such appeals are to the Crown Court: s 67C(4) (as so added).

(B) Financial Investigators

198. Qualifications required. An accredited financial investigator:
(1) must not make an application under the provisions relating to: the making, discharge and variation of restraint orders[1]; the appointment and powers of management receivers[2]; or the discharge and variation of an order conferring a power on a receiver[3];
(2) must not bring an appeal (or further appeal) in respect of the making or refusal of a restraint order[4], or of the making or refusal of an order for the appointment of a management receiver or an enforcement receiver or of an order conferring a power on such a receiver[5],

unless he is one of the following or is authorised for these purposes by one of the following:
(a) a police officer who is not below the rank of superintendent[6];
(b) an officer of Revenue and Customs who is not below such grade as is designated by the Commissioners for Her Majesty's Revenue and Customs as equivalent to that rank[7];
(c) an accredited financial investigator who falls within a specified description[8].

If such an application is made or appeal brought by an accredited financial investigator, any subsequent step in the application or appeal or any further application or appeal relating to the same matter may be taken, made or brought by a different accredited financial investigator who falls within, or is authorised by someone within, heads (a) to (c) above[9].

1 Ie under the Proceeds of Crime Act 2002 ss 41, 42 (see PARAS 201–204).
2 Ie under the Proceeds of Crime Act 2002 ss 48, 49 (see PARAS 247–248).
3 Proceeds of Crime Act 2002 s 68(1)(a). The reference in the text to the discharge and variation of an order conferring a power on a receiver is a reference to the discharge and variation of such an order under s 63 (see PARA 254).
4 Ie under the Proceeds of Crime Act 2002 ss 43, 44 (see PARA 205).
5 Proceeds of Crime Act 2002 s 68(1)(b). The reference in the text to the making or refusal of an order for the appointment of a management receiver or an enforcement receiver or of an order conferring a power on such a receiver or a Director's receiver is a reference to the making or refusal of such an order under ss 65, 66 (see PARA 257).
6 Proceeds of Crime Act 2002 s 68(2), (3)(a).
7 Proceeds of Crime Act 2002 s 68(3)(b) (amended by virtue of the Commissioners for Revenue and Customs Act 2005 s 50(1), (2), (7)).
8 Proceeds of Crime Act 2002 s 68(3)(c). The description referred to in the text is a description specified in an order made for these purposes by the Secretary of State under s 453 (see POLICE AND INVESTIGATORY POWERS vol 84A (2013) PARA 780).
9 Proceeds of Crime Act 2002 s 68(4). If: (1) an application for a restraint order is made by an accredited financial investigator; and (2) a court is required under s 58(6) (see PARA 207) to give the applicant for the order an opportunity to be heard, the court may give the opportunity to a different accredited financial investigator who falls within heads (a)–(c) in the text: s 68(5).

(C) Proceedings

199. When proceedings are 'started' and 'concluded'. Proceedings for an offence are 'started' when a justice of the peace issues[1] a summons or warrant[2], when a relevant prosecutor issues a written charge and requisition or single justice procedure notice in respect of the offence[3], when a person is charged with the offence after being taken into custody without a warrant[4], or when a bill of indictment is[5] preferred[6]. If more than one time is so found in relation to proceedings they are started at the earliest of them[7].

If the defendant is acquitted on all counts in proceedings for an offence, the proceedings are concluded when he is acquitted[8]; and if the defendant is convicted in proceedings for an offence and the conviction is quashed or the defendant is pardoned before a confiscation order is made, the proceedings are concluded when the conviction is quashed or the defendant is pardoned[9].

If a confiscation order is made against the defendant in proceedings for an offence[10] the proceedings are concluded when the order is satisfied or discharged[11] or when the order is quashed and there is no further possibility of an appeal against the decision to quash the order[12]. If the defendant is convicted in proceedings for an offence but the Crown Court decides not to make a confiscation order against him, the following rules apply:

(1) if an application for leave to appeal by the prosecutor[13] is refused, the proceedings are concluded when the decision to refuse is made[14];

(2) if the time for applying for leave to appeal by the prosecutor expires without an application being made, the proceedings are concluded when the time expires[15];

(3) if on appeal by the prosecutor the Court of Appeal confirms the Crown Court's decision, and an application for leave to appeal to the Supreme Court[16] is refused, the proceedings are concluded when the decision to refuse is made[17];

(4) if on appeal by the prosecutor the Court of Appeal confirms the Crown Court's decision, and the time for applying for leave to appeal to the Supreme Court expires without an application being made, the proceedings are concluded when the time expires[18];

(5) if on appeal by the prosecutor the Court of Appeal confirms the Crown Court's decision, and on appeal to the Supreme Court the Court confirms the Court of Appeal's decision, the proceedings are concluded when the Supreme Court confirms the decision[19];

(6) if on appeal by the prosecutor the Court of Appeal directs the Crown Court to reconsider the case, and on reconsideration the Crown Court decides not to make a confiscation order against the defendant, the proceedings are concluded when the Crown Court makes that decision[20]; and

(7) if on appeal to the Supreme Court the Court directs the Crown Court to reconsider the case, and on reconsideration the Crown Court decides not to make a confiscation order against the defendant, the proceedings are concluded when the Crown Court makes that decision[21].

1   Ie under the Magistrates' Courts Act 1980 s 1 (see CRIMINAL PROCEDURE vol 27 (2015) PARA 144).

2   Proceeds of Crime Act 2002 s 85(1)(a).

3   Proceeds of Crime Act 2002 85(1)(aa) (s 85(1)(aa), (9) added by the Criminal Justice Act 2003 Sch 36 para 15; amended by the Criminal Justice and Courts Act 2015 Sch 11 para 18). As to the meanings of 'relevant prosecutor', 'requisition', 'single justice procedure notice' and 'written charge' see the Criminal Justice Act 2003 s 29; and CRIMINAL PROCEDURE vol 27 (2015) PARA 139 (definitions applied by the Proceeds of Crime Act 2002 s 85(9) (as so added and amended)).

4   Proceeds of Crime Act 2002 s 85(1)(b).

5 Ie under the Administration of Justice (Miscellaneous Provisions) Act 1933 s 2 in a case falling within s 2(2)(b) (preferment by Court of Appeal or High Court judge) or s 2(2)(ba) (preferment by Crown Court judge following approval of deferred prosecution agreement) (see CRIMINAL PROCEDURE vol 27 (2015) PARAS 316–317).
6 Proceeds of Crime Act 2002 s 85(1)(c) (amended by the Crime and Courts Act 2013 Sch 17 para 38).
7 Proceeds of Crime Act 2002 s 85(2).
8 Proceeds of Crime Act 2002 s 85(3). As to the meaning of 'defendant' for these purposes see PARA 221 note 1.
9 Proceeds of Crime Act 2002 s 85(4).
10 Ie whether the order is made by the Crown Court or the Court of Appeal.
11 Proceeds of Crime Act 2002 s 85(5)(a). A confiscation order is 'satisfied' when no amount is due under it: s 87(1).
12 Proceeds of Crime Act 2002 s 85(5)(b). A confiscation order is subject to appeal until there is no further possibility of an appeal on which the order could be varied or quashed: s 87(2) (s 85(7) substituted, s 87(2) amended, s 87A added, by the Policing and Crime Act 2009 Sch 7 paras 66–70, Sch 8 Pt 4). Where any provision of the Proceeds of Crime Act 2002 Pt 2 (ss 6–91) refers to there being no further possibility of an appeal against a decision of a court or an appeal on which an order of a court could be varied or quashed any power to extend the time for giving notice of application for leave to appeal, or for applying for leave to appeal, must be ignored: s 87A (as so added).
13 Ie under the Proceeds of Crime Act 2002 s 31(2) (see PARA 243).
14 Proceeds of Crime Act 2002 s 85(6)(a). Any power to extend the time for giving notice of application for leave to appeal, or for applying for leave to appeal, must be ignored for the purposes of s 85(6): s 85(7) (as substituted: see note 12). In applying s 85(6), the fact that a court may decide on a later occasion to make a confiscation order against the defendant must be ignored: s 85(8).
15 Proceeds of Crime Act 2002 s 85(6)(b).
16 Ie under the Proceeds of Crime Act 2002 s 33 (see PARA 245).
17 Proceeds of Crime Act 2002 s 85(6)(c).
18 Proceeds of Crime Act 2002 s 85(6)(d).
19 Proceeds of Crime Act 2002 s 85(6)(e) (s 85(6)(e), (g) amended by the Constitutional Reform Act 2005 Sch 9 para 77(4)).
20 Proceeds of Crime Act 2002 s 85(6)(f).
21 Proceeds of Crime Act 2002 s 85(6)(g) (as amended: see note 19).

C. RESTRAINT ORDERS

200. Conditions for exercise of powers etc to make a restraint order. The Crown Court has powers[1] to make restraint orders, which it may exercise if[2]:

(1) a criminal investigation[3] has been started in England and Wales with regard to an offence[4], and there are reasonable grounds to suspect that the alleged offender has benefited from his criminal conduct[5];

(2) proceedings for an offence have been started[6] in England and Wales and not concluded[7], and there is reasonable cause to believe that the defendant[8] has benefited from his criminal conduct[9];

(3) either an application has been made by the prosecutor relating to the reconsideration of the case[10] or in connection with the defendant absconding[11] and has not been concluded[12], court believes that such an application is to be made[13], and there is reasonable cause to believe that the defendant has benefited from his criminal conduct[14];

(4) an application by the prosecutor has been made under the provisions[15] relating to reconsideration of benefit (where a confiscation order has been made) and not concluded[16], or the court believes that such an application is to be made[17], and there is reasonable cause to believe that the court will decide under those provisions that the amount found under the new calculation of the defendant's benefit exceeds the relevant amount (as defined in those provisions)[18]; or

(5) an application by the prosecutor has been made under the provisions[19] relating to reconsideration of the available amount (where a confiscation order has been made) and not concluded, or the court believes that such an application is to be made[20], and there is reasonable cause to believe that the court will decide under those provisions that the amount found under the new calculation of the available amount exceeds the relevant amount (as defined in those provisions)[21].

The Crown Court has inherent power to punish for contempt of court any order it makes[22].

1　Ie under the Proceeds of Crime Act 2002 s 41 (see PARA 201). The powers conferred on a court by s 41 must be exercised with regard to the matter specified in s 69 (see PARA 251): s 69(1).

2　Proceeds of Crime Act 2002 s 40(1).

3　A 'criminal investigation' is an investigation which police officers or other persons have a duty to conduct with a view to it being ascertained whether a person should be charged with an offence: Proceeds of Crime Act 2002 s 88(2).

4　Proceeds of Crime Act 2002 s 40(2)(a). See *Revenue and Customs Prosecutions Office v Hill* [2005] EWCA Crim 3271, [2005] All ER (D) 296 (Dec). If this condition is satisfied:

    (1)　references in the Proceeds of Crime Act 2002 Pt 2 (ss 6–91) to the defendant are references to the alleged offender (s 40(9)(a));

    (2)　references in Pt 2 to the prosecutor are references to the person the court believes is to have conduct of any proceedings for the offence (s 40(9)(b)); and

    (3)　s 77(9) (see PARA 228) has effect as if proceedings for the offence had been started against the defendant when the investigation was started (s 40(9)(c)).

5　Proceeds of Crime Act 2002 s 40(2)(b) (amended by the Serious Crime Act 2015 s 11(1)). See note 4. As to 'conduct' and 'criminal conduct' see PARA 225. As to when a person benefits from conduct see PARA 223.

6　As to when proceedings for an offence are 'started' and 'concluded' see PARA 199.

7　Proceeds of Crime Act 2002 s 40(3)(a). This condition is not satisfied if the court believes that there has been undue delay in continuing the proceedings (s 40(7)(a)) or that the prosecutor does not intend to proceed (s 40(7)(b)).

8　As to the meaning of 'defendant' for these purposes see PARA 221 note 1.

9　Proceeds of Crime Act 2002 s 40(3)(b). See note 7.

10　Ie an application under the Proceeds of Crime Act 2002 s 19 (see PARA 273) or s 20 (see PARA 274).

11　Ie an application under the Proceeds of Crime Act 2002 s 27 (see PARA 216) or s 28 (see PARA 217).

12　An application under the Proceeds of Crime Act 2002 s 19, s 20, s 27 or s 28 is concluded:

    (1)　in a case where the court decides not to make a confiscation order against the defendant, when it makes the decision (s 86(1)(a));

    (2)　in a case where a confiscation order is made against him as a result of the application, when the order is satisfied or discharged, or when the order is quashed and there is no further possibility of appeal against the decision to quash the order (s 86(1)(b));

    (3)　in a case where the application is withdrawn, when the person who made the application notifies the withdrawal to the court to which the application was made (s 86(1)(c)).

As to the making of confiscation orders see s 6; and PARA 221. As to references to there being no further possibility of an appeal see s 87A; and PARA 199.

13　Proceeds of Crime Act 2002 s 40(4)(a) (s 40(4)(a), (5)(a), (6)(a), (8)(b) amended by the Serious Crime Act 2007 Sch 8 para 22(2), Sch 14). If an application mentioned in the Proceeds of Crime Act 2002 s 40(4), (5) or (6) has been made, the condition is not satisfied if the court believes that: (1) there has been undue delay in continuing the application (s 40(8)(a)); or (2) the prosecutor does not intend to proceed (s 40(8)(b) (as so amended).

14　Proceeds of Crime Act 2002 s 40(4)(b). See note 13.

15　Ie the Proceeds of Crime Act 2002 s 21 (see PARA 275).

16　An application under the Proceeds of Crime Act 2002 s 21 or s 22 (see PARA 276) is concluded:

    (1)　in a case where the court decides not to vary the confiscation order concerned, when it makes the decision (s 86(2)(a));

    (2)　in a case where the court varies the confiscation order as a result of the application, when the order is satisfied or discharged, or when the order is quashed and there is no further possibility of an appeal against the decision to quash the order (s 86(2)(b));

(3)   in a case where the application is withdrawn, when the person who made the application notifies the withdrawal to the court to which the application was made (s 86(2)(c)).

17 Proceeds of Crime Act 2002 s 40(5)(a) (as amended: see note 13).
18 Proceeds of Crime Act 2002 s 40(5)(b). See note 13.
19 Ie the Proceeds of Crime Act 2002 s 22 (see PARA 276).
20 Proceeds of Crime Act 2002 s 40(6)(a) (as amended: see note 13).
21 Proceeds of Crime Act 2002 s 40(6)(b). See note 13.
22 See the Senior Courts Act 1981 s 45; and COURTS AND TRIBUNALS vol 24 (2010) PARA 721. In connection with restraint proceedings see the Criminal Procedure Rules 2015, SI 2015/1490, rr 33.51–33.55.

201. Restraint orders. If any of the requisite conditions[1] is satisfied, the Crown Court may make an order (a 'restraint order') prohibiting any specified person from dealing with[2] any realisable property[3] held by him[4]. A restraint order may provide that it applies:

(1)   to all realisable property held by the specified person whether or not the property is described in the order[5];

(2)   to realisable property transferred to the specified person after the order is made[6],

and may include provision authorising the detention of any property to which it applies if the property is seized by an appropriate officer[7] under a relevant seizure power[8] or is produced[9] to an appropriate officer[10].

Where a court makes a restraint order[11], and the applicant for the order applies to the court so to proceed[12] (whether as part of the application for the restraint order or at any time afterwards)[13], the court may make such order as it believes is appropriate for the purpose of ensuring that the restraint order is effective[14].

The registration and charges Acts[15]:

(a)   apply in relation to restraint orders as they apply in relation to orders which affect land and are made by the court for the purpose of enforcing judgments or recognisances[16]; and

(b)   apply in relation to applications for restraint orders as they apply in relation to other pending land actions[17].

However, no notice may be entered in the register of title[18] in respect of a restraint order[19].

1 Ie any of the five conditions under the Proceeds of Crime Act 2002 s 40 (see PARA 200).
2 'Dealing with property' includes removing it from England and Wales: Proceeds of Crime Act 2002 s 41(9).
3 As to the meanings of 'property' and 'realisable property' see PARA 226.
4 Proceeds of Crime Act 2002 ss 41(1), 88(6)(b). The powers conferred on a court by s 41 must be exercised with regard to the matters specified in s 69 (see PARA 251): s 69(1).
      An order made under or for the purposes of s 41(1), s 41(7) (see the text and note 14), s 42(5) (see PARA 204), s 43(3) (see PARA 205) or s 44(3) (see PARA 205) has effect in Scotland or Northern Ireland: see s 443(1)(a)–(c), (3), (4); the Proceeds of Crime Act 2002 (Enforcement in different parts of the United Kingdom) Order 2002, SI 2002/3133 (which also makes provision for a corresponding order made in Scotland or Northern Ireland to be enforced in England and Wales).
      In making a restraint order against a prospective defendant to criminal proceedings, a judge is entitled to take into account the statutory assumptions in the Proceeds of Crime Act 2002 s 10 (see PARA 231) in relation to criminal lifestyle and to make an order unlimited in amount: *Re K* [2005] EWCA Crim 619, (2005) Times, 15 March, [2005] All ER (D) 23 (Mar). A restraint order does not affect property for the time being subject to a charge under any of the following repealed or revoked provisions: the Drug Trafficking Offences Act 1986 s 9; the Criminal Justice Act 1988 s 78; the Criminal Justice (Confiscation) (Northern Ireland) Order 1990, SI 1990/2588

(NI 17), art 14; the Drug Trafficking Act 1994 s 27; and the Proceeds of Crime Act 2002 (Northern Ireland) Order 1996, SI 1996/1299 (NI 9), art 32: see the Proceeds of Crime Act 2002 s 41(8).

Whereas a confiscation order constitutes a final payment, subject to appeal, of what should be taken from the defendant as representing the proceeds of his crime, a restraint order is in contrast pre-emptive and provisional: see *Re Peters* [1988] QB 871, [1988] 3 All ER 46, CA; *Jennings v Crown Prosecution Service* [2005] EWCA Civ 746 at [43], [2005] 4 All ER 391 at [43], [2006] 1 WLR 182 at [43] per Laws LJ (affirmed on other grounds [2008] UKHL 29, [2008] 1 AC 1046, [2008] 4 All ER 113). As to the duty of an applicant for a restraint order to set out his reasons for fearing a risk of dissipation of the respondent's assets (ie the reason for seeking the order) and to make a full and frank disclosure see *Jennings v Crown Prosecution Service* at [61]–[64] per Longmore LJ.

Provision is also made by Order in Council for prohibitions to be imposed on dealing with property which is the subject of an external request (ie a request by an overseas authority to prohibit dealing with relevant property which is identified in the request) and for the realisation of property for the purpose of giving effect to an external order (ie an order which is made by an overseas court where property is found or believed to have been obtained as a result of or in connection with criminal conduct and is for the recovery of specified property or a specified sum of money): see the Proceeds of Crime Act 2002 ss 444, 447(1); the Proceeds of Crime Act 2002 (External Requests and Orders) Order 2005, SI 2005/3181 (amended by SI 2006/594; SI 2008/302; SI 2009/2054; SI 2011/1242; SI 2013/472; SI 2013/534; SI 2013/2604); the Proceeds of Crime Act 2002 (External Requests and Orders) Order 2005 (England and Wales) (Appeals under Part 2) Order 2012, SI 2012/138. See also the Criminal Procedure Rules 2015, SI 2015/1490, r 33.12.

5 Proceeds of Crime Act 2002 s 41(2)(a).
6 Proceeds of Crime Act 2002 s 41(2)(b).
7 'Appropriate officer' means an accredited financial investigator (cf PARA 208), a constable, an officer of Revenue and Customs, an immigration officer, a national crime agency officer, and a member of staff of the relevant director (within the meaning of the Proceeds of Crime Act 2002 s 352(5A) (see POLICE AND INVESTIGATORY POWERS vol 84A (2013) PARA 785)): s 41A(3) (s 41A added by the Policing and Crime Act 2009 s 52(1), (2); Proceeds of Crime Act 2002 s 41A(3) amended by the Crime and Courts Act 2013 Sch 8 para 112, Sch 21 para 15).
8 'Relevant seizure power' means a power to seize property which is conferred by or by virtue of the Proceeds of Crime Act 2002 s 47C (see PARAS 208, 210) or s 352 (see POLICE AND INVESTIGATORY POWERS vol 84A (2013) PARA 785) or under the Police and Criminal Evidence Act 1984 Pt 2 (ss 8–23) (see POLICE AND INVESTIGATORY POWERS vol 84A (2013) PARA 452 et seq) or Pt 3 (ss 24–32) (see POLICE AND INVESTIGATORY POWERS vol 84A (2013) PARA 487 et seq) (including as applied by order under s 114(2) (see POLICE AND INVESTIGATORY POWERS vol 84A (2013) PARA 453): Proceeds of Crime Act 2002 s 41A(4) (as added: see note 7). The Secretary of State may by order amend the definition of 'relevant seizure power': s 41A(5) (as so added). At the date at which this volume states the law no such order had been made.
9 Ie in compliance with a production order under the Proceeds of Crime Act 2002 s 345 (see POLICE AND INVESTIGATORY POWERS vol 84A (2013) PARAS 780–781).
10 Proceeds of Crime Act 2002 s 41A(1) (as added: see note 7). Such provision may, in particular, relate to specified property, to property of a specified description or to all property to which the restraint order applies, or may relate to property that has already been seized or produced or to property that may be seized or produced in future: s 41A(2) (as so added).
11 Proceeds of Crime Act 2002 s 41(6)(a).
12 Ie under the Proceeds of Crime Act 2002 s 41(7) (see the text and note 14).
13 Proceeds of Crime Act 2002 s 41(6)(b).
14 Proceeds of Crime Act 2002 s 41(7). In considering whether to make an order under s 41(7), the court must, in particular, consider whether any restriction or prohibition on the defendant's travel outside the United Kingdom ought to be imposed for the purpose mentioned in that subsection: s 41(7D) (added by the Serious Crime Act 2015 Sch 4 para 31). As to the enforcement in Scotland or Northern Ireland of an order made under or for the purposes of the Proceeds of Crime Act 2002 s 41(7), or the enforcement in England and Wales of a corresponding Scottish or Northern Ireland order, see note 4.
15 Ie the Land Registration Act 2002 (see REAL PROPERTY AND REGISTRATION vol 87 (2012) PARA 328 et seq) and the Land Charges Act 1972 (see REAL PROPERTY AND REGISTRATION vol 87 (2012) PARA 693 et seq): Proceeds of Crime Act 2002 s 47(2) (which also refers to the Land Registration Act 1925 (repealed)).
16 Proceeds of Crime Act 2002 s 47(1)(a).
17 Proceeds of Crime Act 2002 s 47(1)(b).

18 Ie under the Land Registration Act 2002: see REAL PROPERTY AND REGISTRATION vol 87 (2012) PARA 328 et seq.
19 Proceeds of Crime Act 2002 s 47(3).

202. Restraint orders deriving from criminal investigations. Where the Crown Court makes a restraint order[1] as a result of a criminal investigation having been started in England and Wales with regard to an offence the court:

(1) must include in the order a requirement for the applicant for the order to report to the court on the progress of the investigation at such times and in such manner as the order may specify (a 'reporting requirement')[2]; and

(2) must discharge the order if proceedings for the offence are not started within a reasonable time[3].

The duty to impose a reporting requirement[4] does not apply if the court decides that, in the circumstances of the case, a reporting requirement should not be imposed[5].

1 Ie by virtue of the first condition in the Proceeds of Crime Act 2002 s 40 (see PARA 200): s 41(7A) (s 40(7A)–(7C) added by the Proceeds of Crime Act 2015 s 11(2)). As to restraint orders see PARA 201.
2 Proceeds of Crime Act 2002 s 41(7B)(a) (as added: see note 1).
3 Proceeds of Crime Act 2002 s 41(7B)(b) (as added: see note 1). This duty applies whether or not an application to discharge the order is made under s 42(3) (see PARA 204): s 41(7B)(b) (as so added).
4 Ie the duty under the Proceeds of Crime Act 2002 s 41(7B)(a) (see the text and notes 1–2).
5 Proceeds of Crime Act 2002 s 41(7C) (as added: see note 1). The court must give reasons for its decision (s 41(7C)(a) (as so added)) and may at any time vary the order so as to include a reporting requirement (and this power applies whether or not an application to vary the order is made under s 42(3) (s 41(7C)(b) (as so added)).

203. Exceptions for legal aid and other payments. A restraint order[1] must be made subject to an exception enabling relevant legal aid payments[2] to be made[3] and may be made subject to other exceptions, which may in particular:

(1) make provision for reasonable living expenses[4] and reasonable legal expenses[5]; and

(2) make provision for the purpose of enabling any person to carry on any trade, business, profession or occupation[6],

and which may be subject to conditions[7].

Restraint orders may also be made subject to exceptions for reasonable living and legal expenses[8].

1 As to restraint orders see PARA 201.
2 A 'relevant legal aid payment' is a payment that the specified person is obliged to make:
(1) pursuant to any of the Criminal Legal Aid (Financial Resources) Regulations 2013, SI 2013/471, the Criminal Legal Aid (Contribution Orders) Regulations 2013, SI 2013/483, the Criminal Legal Aid (Recovery of Defence Costs Orders) Regulations 2013, SI 2013/511, the Civil Legal Aid (Financial Resources and Payment for Services) Regulations 2013, SI 2013/480, or the Legal Aid (Financial Resources and Payment for Services) (Legal Persons) Regulations 2013, SI 2013/512 (ie regulations under the Legal Aid, Sentencing and Punishment of Offenders Act 2012 s 23 or s 24: see LEGAL AID vol 65 (2015) PARAS 46, 47, 143) (Proceeds of Crime Act 2002 s 41(2B)(a) (s 41(2A), (2B), (5A), (5B), (10) added, s 41(3), (4) amended, by the Crime and Courts Act 2013 s 46)); and
(2) in connection with services provided in relation to an offence which is either: (a) the offence mentioned in the Proceeds of Crime Act 2002 s 40(2) or (3) (see PARA 200), if the first or second condition (as the case may be) is satisfied (s 41(2B)(a), (5)(a) (s 41(2B)(a) as so added)); or (b) the offence (or any of the offences) concerned, if the third, fourth or fifth condition is satisfied (s 41(5)(b)),

whether the obligation to make the payment arises before or after the restraint order is made (s 41(2B) (as so added)).

3   Proceeds of Crime Act 2002 s 41(2A) (as added: see note 2). This is referred to as a 'legal aid exception': s 41(2A) (as so added). A legal aid exception:
     (1)   must be made subject to prescribed restrictions (if any) on the circumstances in which payments may be made in reliance on the exception (s 41(5A)(a)(i) (as so added)) or the amount of the payments that may be made in reliance on the exception (s 41(5A)(a)(ii) (as so added));
     (2)   must be made subject to other prescribed conditions (if any) (s 41(5A)(b) (as so added)); and
     (3)   may be made subject to other conditions (s 41(5A)(c) (as so added)).
     'Prescribed' means prescribed by regulations made by the Secretary of State: s 41(10) (as so added). See the Restraint Orders (Legal Aid Exception and Relevant Legal Aid Payments) Regulations 2015, SI 2015/868.
4   'Living expenses' are 'ordinary, recurrent expenses involved in maintaining the subject … in the style of life to which he is reasonably accustomed': see *FSA v M* [2009] EWCA Crim 997, [2009] All ER (D) 204 (May) (a contribution to the Legal Services Commission could not on any reasonable construction be treated as a 'living expense', although a contribution to the Commission to institute judicial review proceedings in connection with the offence in which the restraint order was made was a 'legal expense').
5   Proceeds of Crime Act 2002 s 41(3)(a). Where an exception to a restraint order is made under s 41(3) it must not make provision for any legal expenses which: (1) relate to either the offence mentioned in s 40(2) or (3) (see PARA 200), if the first or second condition (as the case may be) is satisfied (s 41(4)(a), (5)(a) (s 41(4) as amended: see note 2)), or the offence (or any of the offences) concerned, if the third, fourth or fifth condition is satisfied (s 41(5)(b)); and (2) are incurred by the defendant or by a recipient of a tainted gift (s 41(4)(b)). As to references to the 'offence or offences concerned' see PARA 229 note 2. As to the meaning of 'defendant' for these purposes see PARA 221 note 1. Section 41(4) prevents an exception being made under s 41(3) for legal expenses for proceedings in connection with a restraint order: *Re S (restraint order: release of assets)* [2004] EWCA Crim 2374, [2005] 1 WLR 1338, [2005] 1 Cr App Rep 239. See also *R v AP; R v U Ltd* [2007] EWCA Crim 3128, [2008] 1 Cr App Rep 497, sub nom *R v P (the Ministry of Justice and the Home Office intervening) R v A Company* [2007] All ER (D) 333 (Dec); *Revenue and Customs Prosecutions Office v Allad* [2008] EWCA Crim 1741, [2009] 3 All ER 530, sub nom *Irwin Mitchell (a firm) v Revenue and Customs Prosecutions Office* [2009] 1 WLR 1079.
6   Proceeds of Crime Act 2002 s 41(3)(b).
7   Proceeds of Crime Act 2002 s 41(5B) (as added: see note 2).
8   See the Criminal Procedure Rules 2015, SI 2015/1490, r 33.52.

204.   Application, discharge and variation. A restraint order[1] may be made only on application[2] by the prosecutor[3] or by an accredited financial investigator[4]. An order may be made on an ex parte application to a judge in chambers[5].

An application to discharge or vary a restraint order or an order[6] made to ensure that a restraint order is effective may be made to the Crown Court by the person who applied for the order[7] or by any person affected by the order[8]. On such an application, the court may discharge the order[9] or may vary it[10]. If the prerequisite condition[11] for a restraint order which was satisfied was that proceedings were started[12] or an application was made, the court must discharge the order on the conclusion of the proceedings or of the application (as the case may be)[13]. If the prerequisite condition which was satisfied was that an investigation was started the court must discharge the order if within a reasonable time proceedings for the offence are not started[14] and otherwise, the court must discharge the order on the conclusion of the proceedings[15]. If the prerequisite condition which was satisfied was that an application was to be made the court must discharge the order if within a reasonable time the application is not made[16] and otherwise, the court must discharge the order on the conclusion of the application[17].

1   As to restraint orders see PARA 201.

2   In connection with applications under the Proceeds of Crime Act 2002 s 42 see the Criminal Procedure Rules 2015, SI 2015/1490, r 33.51.

3   Proceeds of Crime Act 2002 s 42(1)(a), (2)(a).

4   Proceeds of Crime Act 2002 s 42(2)(c). See s 69; and PARA 251.

5   Proceeds of Crime Act 2002 s 42(1)(b). In connection with restraint proceedings see the Criminal Procedure Rules 2015, SI 2015/1490, rr 33.51–33.63.

6   Ie an order made under the Proceeds of Crime Act 2002 s 41(7) (see PARA 201).

7   Proceeds of Crime Act 2002 s 42(3)(a). In connection with applications under s 42(3) see the Criminal Procedure Rules 2015, SI 2015/1490, rr 33.53–33.55.

8   Proceeds of Crime Act 2002 s 42(3)(b). See note 7.

9   Proceeds of Crime Act 2002 s 42(4), (5)(a) (s 42(4) amended, s 42(7) substituted, s 42(8) added, by the Serious Crime Act 2015 Sch 4 para 32). If a restraint order includes provision under the Proceeds of Crime Act 2002 s 41A (see PARA 201) authorising the detention of property and the restraint order is discharged under s 42(5) the property may be detained until there is no further possibility of an appeal against the decision to discharge the restraint order or any decision made on an appeal against that decision: s 44A(1), (3) (s 44A added by the Policing and Crime Act 2009 s 52(1), (3)). As to references to there being no further possibility of an appeal see the Proceeds of Crime Act 2002 s 87A; and PARA 199.

    As to the enforcement in Scotland or Northern Ireland of an order made under or for the purposes of s 42(5), or the enforcement in England and Wales of a corresponding Scottish or Northern Ireland order, see PARA 201 note 4.

10 Proceeds of Crime Act 2002 s 42(5)(b). If a restraint order includes provision under s 41A (see PARA 201) authorising the detention of property and the restraint order is varied under s 42(5) so as to omit any such provision, the property may be detained until there is no further possibility of an appeal against the decision to vary the restraint order or any decision made on an appeal against that decision: s 44A(2), (3) (as added: see note 9).

11 Ie under the Proceeds of Crime Act 2002 s 40 (see PARA 200).

12 As to when proceedings for an offence are 'started' and 'concluded' see PARA 199.

13 Proceeds of Crime Act 2002 s 42(6). The duty in s 42(6) to discharge a restraint order on the conclusion of proceedings does not apply where the proceedings are concluded by reason of a defendant's conviction for an offence being quashed (s 42(6A)(a) (s 42(6A), (6B) added by the Serious Crime Act 2007 s 12)), the order is in force at the time when the conviction is quashed (Proceeds of Crime Act 2002 s 42(6A)(b) (as so added)), and the Court of Appeal has ordered the defendant to be retried for the offence or the prosecutor has applied for such an order to be made (s 42(6A)(c) (as so added)). However the court must discharge the restraint order if the Court of Appeal declines to make an order for the defendant to be retried (s 42(6B)(a) (as so added)), if the Court of Appeal orders the defendant to be retried but proceedings for the retrial are not started within a reasonable time (s 42(6B)(b) (as so added)), or otherwise, on the conclusion of proceedings for the retrial of the defendant (s 42(6B)(c) (as so added)).

14 Proceeds of Crime Act 2002 s 42(7)(a) (as substituted: see note 9).

15 Proceeds of Crime Act 2002 s 42(7)(b) (as substituted: see note 9).

16 Proceeds of Crime Act 2002 s 42(8)(a) (as added: see note 9).

17 Proceeds of Crime Act 2002 s 42(8)(b) (as added: see note 9).

205.   Appeal to the Court of Appeal and to the Supreme Court.   If on an application for a restraint order[1] the court decides not to make one, the person who applied for the order may appeal to the Court of Appeal against the decision[2].

If an application is made[3] to the Crown Court for the discharge or variation of a restraint order or an order[4] made to ensure that a restraint order is effective, the person who applied for the order[5], or any person affected by the order[6], may appeal to the Court of Appeal in respect of the Crown Court's decision on the application[7]. On such an appeal[8] the Court of Appeal may confirm the decision[9] or make such order as it believes is appropriate[10].

At the instance of any person who was a party to the proceedings before the Court of Appeal[11], an appeal lies to the Supreme Court[12] from a decision of the

Court of Appeal on such an appeal[13]. The Supreme Court may either confirm the decision of the Court of Appeal[14] or make such order as it believes is appropriate[15].

1 As to restraint orders see PARA 201.
2 Proceeds of Crime Act 2002 s 43(1). As to appeals to the Court of Appeal see s 89(1)–(3); and PARA 242. Subject to any rules made under s 91 (see PARAS 221, 247), the costs of, and incidental to, all proceedings on an appeal to the criminal division of the Court of Appeal under s 31(4) (appeals against determinations under s 10A: see PARA 226), s 43(1) or (2) (appeals against orders made in restraint proceedings: see the text and notes 3–7) or s 65 (appeals against, or relating to, the making of receivership orders: see PARA 257) are in the discretion of the court: s 89(4) (s 89(4)–(9) added by the Courts Act 2003 s 94; Proceeds of Crime Act 2002 s 89(4) amended by the Serious Crime Act 2007 Sch 4 para 34). Such rules may in particular make provision for regulating matters relating to the costs of those proceedings, including prescribing scales of costs to be paid to legal or other representatives: Proceeds of Crime Act 2002 s 89(5) (as so added).
   The court has full power to determine by whom and to what extent the costs are to be paid: s 89(6) (as so added). In any proceedings mentioned in s 89(4), the court may disallow or (as the case may be) order the legal or other representative concerned to meet the whole of any wasted costs or such part of them as may be determined in accordance with any rules under s 91: see s 89(7) (as so added). In s 89(7) 'wasted costs' means any costs incurred by a party: (1) as a result of any improper, unreasonable or negligent act or omission on the part of any legal or other representative or any employee of such a representative (s 89(8)(a) (as so added)); or (2) which, in the light of any such act or omission occurring after they were incurred, the court considers it is unreasonable to expect that party to pay (s 89(8)(b) (as so added)). 'Legal or other representative', in relation to a party to proceedings means any person exercising a right of audience or right to conduct litigation on his behalf: s 89(9) (as so added).
3 Ie under the Proceeds of Crime Act 2002 s 42(3) (see PARA 204).
4 Ie under the Proceeds of Crime Act 2002 s 41(7) (see PARA 201).
5 Proceeds of Crime Act 2002 s 43(2)(a).
6 Proceeds of Crime Act 2002 s 43(2)(b).
7 Proceeds of Crime Act 2002 s 43(2). See note 2.
8 Ie under the Proceeds of Crime Act 2002 s 43(1) or (2).
9 Proceeds of Crime Act 2002 s 43(3)(a). See PARA 251. As to the enforcement in Scotland or Northern Ireland of an order made under or for the purposes of s 43(3), or the enforcement in England and Wales of a corresponding Scottish or Northern Ireland order, see PARA 201 note 4.
10 Proceeds of Crime Act 2002 s 43(3)(b). If a restraint order includes provision under s 41A (see PARA 201) authorising the detention of property and the restraint order is discharged under s 43(3)(b), or is varied under s 43(3)(b) so as to omit any such provision, the property may be detained until there is no further possibility of an appeal against the decision to discharge the restraint order or any decision made on an appeal against that decision: s 44A (added by the Policing and Crime Act 2009 s 52(1), (3)). As to references to there being no further possibility of an appeal see the Proceeds of Crime Act 2002 s 87A; and PARA 199.
   As to the enforcement in Scotland or Northern Ireland of an order made under or for the purposes of s 42(5), or the enforcement in England and Wales of a corresponding Scottish or Northern Ireland order, see PARA 201 note 4.
11 Proceeds of Crime Act 2002 s 44(2).
12 As to the procedure on such an appeal see PARA 245.
13 Proceeds of Crime Act 2002 s 44(1) (s 44(1), (3) amended by the Constitutional Reform Act 2005 Sch 9 para 77(1), (3)).
14 Proceeds of Crime Act 2002 s 44(3)(a) (as amended: see note 13). As to the enforcement in Scotland or Northern Ireland of an order made under or for the purposes of s 44(3) or the enforcement in England and Wales of a corresponding Scottish or Northern Ireland order, see PARA 201 note 4.
15 Proceeds of Crime Act 2002 s 44(3)(b) (as amended: see note 13). See note 14.

206. Hearsay evidence. Evidence must not be excluded in restraint proceedings[1] on the ground that it is hearsay[2] (of whatever degree)[3]. However, the safeguards[4] which apply under the law of evidence to the admission of hearsay evidence in civil proceedings apply in relation to restraint proceedings as they apply in relation to civil proceedings[5].

1 Restraint proceedings are proceedings: (1) for a restraint order (see PARA 201) (Proceeds of Crime Act 2002 s 46(3)(a)); (2) for the discharge or variation of a restraint order (see PARA 204) (s 46(3)(b)); and (3) on an appeal under s 43 or s 44 (see PARA 205) (s 46(3)(c)).

2 Hearsay is a statement which is made otherwise than by a person while giving oral evidence in the proceedings and which is tendered as evidence of the matters stated: Proceeds of Crime Act 2002 s 46(4). As to hearsay evidence in criminal proceedings generally see CRIMINAL PROCEDURE vol 28 (2015) PARA 608 et seq.

3 Proceeds of Crime Act 2002 s 46(1). Nothing in s 46 affects the admissibility of evidence which is admissible apart from s 46: s 46(5). See also s 69; and PARA 251.

4 Ie under the Civil Evidence Act 1995 ss 2–4 (see CIVIL PROCEDURE vol 11 (2009) PARAS 811–815).

5 Proceeds of Crime Act 2002 s 46(2).

207. Restrictions. Where a court makes a restraint order[1]:

(1) no distress may be levied, and the statutory procedure for taking control of goods[2] cannot be exercised, against any realisable property[3] to which the order applies, except with the leave of the Crown Court and subject to any terms the Crown Court may impose[4]; and

(2) if the order applies to a tenancy of any premises, no landlord or other person to whom rent is payable may exercise a right of forfeiture by peaceable re-entry in relation to the premises in respect of any failure by the tenant to comply with any term or condition of the tenancy, except with the leave of the Crown Court and subject to any terms the Crown Court may impose[5].

If a court in which proceedings are pending in respect of any property is satisfied that a restraint order has been applied for or made in respect of the property, the court may either stay the proceedings or allow them to continue on any terms it thinks fit[6].

1 Proceeds of Crime Act 2002 s 58(1). As to restraint orders see PARA 201.

2 Ie the procedure in the Tribunals, Courts and Enforcement Act 2007 Sch 12 (taking control of goods): see CIVIL PROCEDURE vol 11 (2009) PARA 1386 et seq.

3 As to 'property' and 'realisable property' see PARA 226.

4 Proceeds of Crime Act 2002 s 58(2) (amended by the Tribunals, Courts and Enforcement Act 2007 Sch 13 para 143). In connection with applications under the Proceeds of Crime Act 2002 s 58(2), (3) see the Criminal Procedure Rules 2015, SI 2015/1490, r 33.51–33.63.

5 Proceeds of Crime Act 2002 s 58(3), (4).

6 Proceeds of Crime Act 2002 s 58(5). Before exercising any power conferred by s 58(5), the court must give an opportunity to be heard to: (1) the applicant for the restraint order (s 58(6)(a)); and (2) any receiver appointed in respect of the property under s 48 (see PARA 247) or s 50 (see PARA 249) (s 58(6)(b) (amended by the Serious Crime Act 2007 Sch 8 para 26)).

D. SEARCH AND SEIZURE OF PROPERTY

208. Power to seize property. An appropriate officer[1] may seize any realisable property[2] if he has reasonable grounds for suspecting that the property may otherwise be made unavailable for satisfying any confiscation order[3] that has been or may be made against the defendant[4] or the value of the property may otherwise be diminished as a result of conduct by the defendant or any other person[5], provided he is satisfied that:

(1) a criminal investigation[6] has been started in England and Wales with regard to an indictable offence, a person has been arrested for the offence, proceedings for the offence have not yet been started against the person in England and Wales, there are reasonable grounds to

suspect that the person has benefited from conduct constituting the offence, and a restraint order is not in force in respect of any realisable property[7];

(2)   a criminal investigation has been started in England and Wales with regard to an indictable offence, a person has been arrested for the offence, proceedings for the offence have not yet been started against the person in England and Wales and a restraint order is in force in respect of any realisable property[8];

(3)   proceedings for an indictable offence have been started in England and Wales and have not been concluded, there is reasonable cause to believe that the defendant has benefited from conduct constituting the offence and a restraint order is not in force in respect of any realisable property[9];

(4)   proceedings for an indictable offence have been started in England and Wales and have not been concluded, and a restraint order is in force in respect of any realisable property[10];

(5)   an application by the prosecutor has been made[11] and not concluded, or the officer believes that such an application is to be made, and there is reasonable cause to believe that the defendant has benefited from criminal conduct[12];

(6)   an application by the prosecutor has been made[13] and not concluded, or the officer believes that such an application is to be made, and there is reasonable cause to believe that the court will decide that the amount found under the new calculation of the defendant's benefit exceeds the relevant amount[14]; or

(7)   an application by the prosecutor has been made[15] and not concluded, or the officer believes that such an application is to be made, and there is reasonable cause to believe that the court will decide that the amount found under the new calculation of the available amount exceeds the relevant amount[16].

The power to seize property[17] may be exercised only with the appropriate approval[18] unless in the circumstances it is not practicable to obtain that approval before exercising the power[19]. Particular provision is also made in connection with the exercise of the power of seizure by an officer of Revenue and Customs[20] or an immigration officer[21]. If an appropriate officer seizes property under these provisions the property may be detained initially for a period of 48 hours[22], although provision is made for the further detention of seized property in specified circumstances[23].

1   In the Proceeds of Crime Act 2002 ss 47B–47S (see the text and notes 2–23; and PARAS 209–215) 'appropriate officer' means an officer of Revenue and Customs, an immigration officer, a constable or an accredited financial investigator (i e an accredited financial investigator who falls within a description specified in an order made for the purposes of that provision by the Secretary of State under s 453: s 47A (ss 47A–47S added by the Policing and Crime Act 2009 s 55(1)–(3), Sch 8 Pt 4; Proceeds of Crime Act 2002 ss 47A, 47B(6)(b), 47G(3) amended, s 47B(6)(aa), (6A), (6B), (8) added, by the Crime and Courts Act 2103 s 55(3), (4)(a), Sch 21 paras 16, 17). As to the accreditation and training of an accredited financial investigator see the Proceeds of Crime Act 2002 (References to Financial Investigators) Order 2009, SI 2009/975 (amended by SI 2009/2707; SI 2011/2085; SI 2013/472; SI 2013/755; SI 2013/2318; SI 2014/549; SI 2014/467).

2   As to 'property' and 'realisable property' see PARA 226.

3   Ie an order under the Proceeds of Crime Act 2002 s 6: see PARA 221.

4   Proceeds of Crime Act 2002 s 47C(1)(a) (as added: see note 1).

5   Proceeds of Crime Act 2002 s 47C(1)(b) (as added: see note 1).

6   As to the meaning of 'criminal investigation' see PARA 200 note 3.

7   Proceeds of Crime Act 2002 s 47B(1), (2) (as added (see note 1); s 47B(2) amended by the Serious Crime Act 2015 s 13(1)). In relation to this condition and the condition set out in the Proceeds of Crime Act 2002 s 47B(3) (see the text and note 8) references in ss 47C–47S to the defendant are to the person mentioned in the applicable condition (s 47B(11) (as so added)) and s 77(9) (see PARA 228) has effect as if proceedings for the offence had been started against the defendant when the investigation was started (s 47B(12) (as so added)). Section 47B(11) is subject to s 47C(5) (see PARA 210): s 47C(5) (as so added).

8   Proceeds of Crime Act 2002 s 47B(3) (as added: see note 1). As to this condition see note 7. As to when proceedings for an offence are 'started' and 'concluded' see PARA 199.

9   Proceeds of Crime Act 2002 s 47B(4) (as added: see note 1). This condition and the condition set out in s 47B(5) (see the text and note 10) are not met if the officer believes that there has been undue delay in continuing the proceedings or the prosecutor does not intend to proceed: s 47B(9) (as so added).

10   Proceeds of Crime Act 2002 s 47B(5) (as added: see note 1). As to this condition see note 9.

11   Ie under the Proceeds of Crime Act 2002 s 19, s 20, s 27 or s 28 (see PARAS 273, 274, 216, 217).

12   Proceeds of Crime Act 2002 s 47B(6) (as added: see note 1). If an application mentioned in this condition or the condition set out in s 47B(7) (see the text and notes 13–14) or s 47B(8) (see the text and notes 15–16) has been made the condition is not met if the officer believes that there has been undue delay in continuing the application or the prosecutor does not intend to proceed: s 47B(10) (as so added). As to 'conduct' see PARA 225; as to when a person 'benefits' from conduct see PARA 223.

13   Ie under the Proceeds of Crime Act 2002 s 21 (see PARA 275).

14   Proceeds of Crime Act 2002 s 47B(7) (as added: see note 1). As to this condition see note 12.

15   Ie under the Proceeds of Crime Act 2002 s 22 (see PARA 276).

16   Proceeds of Crime Act 2002 s 47B(8) (as added: see note 1). As to this condition see note 12.

17   Ie the power conferred by the Proceeds of Crime Act 2002 s 47C.

18   Ie approval under the Proceeds of Crime Act 2002 s 47G (as added: see note 1), which provides that for the purposes of s 47C and ss 47D–47F (see PARA 209), in relation to the exercise of a power by an appropriate officer, means the approval of a justice of the peace or (if that is not practicable in any case) the approval of a senior officer: s 47G(1), (2) (as so added). By virtue of s 47G(3) (as so added and amended; further amended by the Serious Crime Act 2015 s 13(2)) 'senior officer' means: (1) in relation to the exercise of a power by an officer of Revenue and Customs, an officer of Revenue and Customs of a rank designated by the Commissioners for Her Majesty's Revenue and Customs as equivalent to that of a senior police officer; (2) in relation to the exercise of a power by an immigration officer, an immigration officer of a rank designated by the Secretary of State as equivalent to that of a senior police officer; (3) in relation to the exercise of a power by a National Crime Agency officer, the Director General of the National Crime Agency or any other National Crime Agency officer authorised by the Director General (whether generally or specifically) for this purpose; (4) in relation to the exercise of a power by a constable, a senior police officer; and (5) in relation to the exercise of a power by an accredited financial investigator, an accredited financial investigator who falls within a description specified in an order made for this purpose by the Secretary of State under the Proceeds of Crime Act 2002 s 453. A 'senior police officer' means a police officer of at least the rank of inspector: s 47G(4) (as so added). As to the National Crime Agency see POLICE AND INVESTIGATORY POWERS vol 84 (2013) PARA 424. As to Her Majesty's Revenue and Customs see CUSTOMS AND EXCISE vol 31 (2012) PARA 921 et seq.

19   Proceeds of Crime Act 2002 s 47C(6)(a) (as added: see note 1).

20   The power conferred by the Proceeds of Crime Act 2002 s 47C is exercisable by an officer of Revenue and Customs only if the officer has reasonable grounds for suspecting that conduct constituting the relevant offence relates to an assigned matter: Proceeds of Crime Act 2002 s 47C(6)(aa), (b), (6A) (as added and amended: see note 1). 'Relevant offence' means: (1) in a case where the officer is satisfied that the condition set out in s 47B(2), (3), (4) or (5) (see the text and notes 6–10) is met, the offence mentioned in that condition (s 47C(7)(a) (as so added)); and (2) in a case where the officer is satisfied that any of the other conditions in s 47B (see the text and notes 6–16) is met, the offence (or any of the offences) concerned (s 47C(7)(b) (as so added)).

21   The power conferred by the Proceeds of Crime Act 2002 s 47C is exercisable by an immigration officer only if he has reasonable grounds for suspecting that conduct constituting the relevant offence relates to the entitlement of one or more persons who are not nationals of the United Kingdom to enter, transit across, or be in, the United Kingdom (including conduct which relates to conditions or other controls on any such entitlement) (s 47C(6B)(a) (as added: see note 1), or is undertaken for the purposes of, or otherwise in relation to, a relevant nationality enactment (s 47C(6B)(b) (as so added). For this purpose 'relevant nationality enactment' means any

enactment in the British Nationality Act 1981, the Hong Kong Act 1985, the Hong Kong (War Wives and Widows) Act 1996, the British Nationality (Hong Kong) Act 1997, the British Overseas Territories Act 2002, or an instrument made under any of those Acts: see the Proceeds of Crime Act 2002 s 47C(8) (as so added); and BRITISH NATIONALITY.

22 Proceeds of Crime Act 2002 s 47J(1), (2) (as added: see note 1). In calculating a period of 48 hours for this purpose no account is to be taken of any Saturday or Sunday, Christmas Day, Good Friday or any day that is a bank holiday under the Banking and Financial Dealings Act 1971 (see FINANCIAL SERVICES AND INSTITUTIONS vol 49 (2008) PARA 1437) in England and Wales: Proceeds of Crime Act 2002 ss 47H(7), 47J(3) (as so added).

23 See the Proceeds of Crime Act 2002 ss 47K–47Q; and PARAS 212–213.

209. Powers of search. If an appropriate officer[1] is lawfully on any premises[2] he may search the premises for the purpose of finding any property[3] which he has reasonable grounds for suspecting may be found there[4] and, if found there, he intends[5] to seize[6]. An appropriate officer may also:

(1) if he has reasonable grounds for suspecting that a person is carrying property that may be so seized and so far as he thinks it necessary or expedient for the purpose of seizing the property, require the person to permit a search of any article with the person[7] and to permit a search of the person[8]; and

(2) if he has reasonable grounds for suspecting that a vehicle contains property that may be so seized and it appears to him that the vehicle is under the control of a person who is in or in the vicinity of the vehicle, and so far as he thinks it necessary or expedient for the purpose of seizing the property, require the person to permit entry to the vehicle[9] and to permit a search of the vehicle[10].

These powers[11] may be exercised only with the appropriate approval[12] unless, in the circumstances, it is not practicable to obtain that approval before exercising the power[13], and the powers relating to the searching of vehicles[14] are exercisable only if the vehicle is in any place to which, at the time of the proposed exercise of the powers, the public or any section of the public has access, on payment or otherwise, as of right or by virtue of express or implied permission, or in any other place to which at that time people have ready access but which is not a dwelling[15].

1   As to the meaning of 'appropriate officer' see PARA 208 note 1.
2   As to the meaning of 'premises' see the Police and Criminal Evidence Act 1984 s 23; and POLICE AND INVESTIGATORY POWERS vol 84A (2013) PARA 433 (definition applied by the Proceeds of Crime Act 2002 s 47D(3) (ss 47A–47S (see the text and notes 3–15; and PARAS 208, 210–215) added by the Policing and Crime Act 2009 s 55(1), (2)).
3   As to 'property' and related expressions see PARA 226; and see also the Proceeds of Crime Act 2002 s 47C(2)–(5); and PARA 210.
4   Proceeds of Crime Act 2002 s 47D(1)(a) (as added: see note 2).
5   Ie under the Proceeds of Crime Act 2002 s 47C (see PARA 208).
6   Proceeds of Crime Act 2002 s 47D(1)(b) (as added: see note 2).
7   Proceeds of Crime Act 2002 s 47E(1), (2)(a) (as added: see note 2). An officer exercising a power under s 47E(2) may detain the person for so long as is necessary for its exercise: s 47E(3) (as so added).
8   Proceeds of Crime Act 2002 s 47E(2)(b) (as added: see note 2). See note 7. These provisions do not require a person to submit to an intimate search or strip search (within the meaning of the Customs and Excise Management Act 1979 s 164: see CUSTOMS AND EXCISE vol 31 (2012) PARA 1147): Proceeds of Crime Act 2002 s 47E(5) (as so added).
9   Proceeds of Crime Act 2002 s 47F(1), (4)(a) (as added: see note 2). An officer exercising a power under s 47F(4) may detain the vehicle for so long as is necessary for its exercise: s 47F(5) (as so added).
10 Proceeds of Crime Act 2002 s 47F(4)(b) (as added: see note 2). See note 9.
11 Ie the powers conferred by the Proceeds of Crime Act 2002 ss 47D–47F (see the text and notes 1–10).

12 Ie the appropriate approval under the Proceeds of Crime Act 2002 s 47G (see PARA 208 note 18).

13 Proceeds of Crime Act 2002 ss 47D(2), 47E(4), 47F(6) (as added: see note 2).

14 Ie the powers conferred by the Proceeds of Crime Act 2002 s 47F (see the text and notes 9–13, 15).

15 Proceeds of Crime Act 2002 s 47F(2) (as added: see note 2). If the vehicle is in a garden or yard or other land occupied with and used for the purposes of a dwelling, the officer may exercise the powers under s 47F(4) only if the officer has reasonable grounds for believing that the person does not reside in the dwelling and that the vehicle is not in the place in question with the express or implied permission of another who resides in the dwelling: s 47F(3) (as so added).

210. Exempt property. An appropriate officer[1] may not seize cash[2] or exempt property[3] (ie such tools, books, vehicles and other items of equipment as are necessary to the defendant[4] for use personally in the defendant's employment, business or vocation and such clothing, bedding, furniture, household equipment, provisions or other things as are necessary for satisfying the basic domestic needs of the defendant and the defendant's family[5]) under the provisions relating to the power to seize property[6].

1 As to the meaning of 'appropriate officer' see PARA 208 note 1.

2 'Cash means notes and coins in any currency, postal orders, cheques of any kind (including travellers' cheques), bankers' drafts, bearer bonds and bearer shares, found at any place in the United Kingdom; and also includes any kind of monetary instrument which is found at any place in the United Kingdom if the instrument is specified by the Secretary of State by order: Proceeds of Crime Act 2002 ss 47C(3), 289(6), (7) (ss 47A–47S (see the text and notes 3–6; and PARAS 208–209, 211–215) added by the Policing and Crime Act 2009 s 55(1), (2); Proceeds of Crime Act 2002 s 289(7) amended by SI 2010/976).

3 As to 'property' and related expressions see PARA 226.

4 In relation to realisable property which is free property (see PARA 226) held by the recipient of a tainted gift (see PARA 228), references in the Proceeds of Crime Act 2002 s 47C(4) to the defendant are to be read as references to the recipient of that gift: s 47C(5) (as added: see note 2).

5 Proceeds of Crime Act 2002 s 47C(4) (prospectively added: see note 2).

6 Ie under the Proceeds of Crime Act 2002 s 47C (see PARA 208): s 47C(2)–(5) (as added: see note 2).

211. Exercise of powers without judicial approval. An appropriate officer[1] must give a written report to the appointed person[2] in any case where:

(1) the officer seizes property[3] without the approval of a justice of the peace[4] and any of the property seized is not detained for more than 48 hours[5]; or

(2) the officer exercises any of the search powers[6] without the approval of a justice of the peace[7] and no property is[8] seized[9].

A report under these provisions must give particulars of the circumstances which led the officer to believe that the powers were exercisable[10] and it was not practicable to obtain the approval of a justice of the peace[11].

1 As to the meaning of 'appropriate officer' see PARA 208 note 1.

2 Ie a person appointed for these purposes by the Secretary of State: Proceeds of Crime Act 2002 s 47H(4) (ss 47A–47S (see the text and notes 3–11; and PARAS 208–210, 212–215) added by the Policing and Crime Act 2009 s 55(1), (2)). The appointed person must not be a person employed under or for the purposes of a government department; and the terms and conditions of appointment, including any remuneration or expenses to be paid, are to be determined by the Secretary of State: Proceeds of Crime Act 2002 s 47H(5) (as so added). At the date at which this volume states the law no person had been appointed for this purpose.

As soon as possible after the end of each financial year the appointed person must prepare a report for that year (s 47I(1) (as so added)), which must give the appointed person's opinion as to the circumstances and manner in which the powers conferred by ss 47C–47F (see PARAS 208–210) are being exercised in cases where the officer who exercised them is required to give a report under s 47H (s 47I(3) (as so added)) and may make any recommendations the appointed person considers appropriate (s 47I(4) (as so added)). The appointed person must send a copy of the report to the Secretary of State who must publish any report so received and lay a copy before Parliament, although before so acting the Secretary of State must exclude from the report any matter which the Secretary of State thinks is likely to prejudice any criminal investigation or criminal proceedings: s 47I(5)–(7) (as so added). If the Secretary of State excludes any matter from the report the Secretary of State must publish and lay before Parliament the whole of the report as soon as he thinks that the excluded matter is no longer likely to prejudice any criminal investigation or criminal proceedings: s 47I(8) (as so added).

For this purpose 'financial year' means the period beginning with the day on which the Policing and Crime Act 2009 s 55 (see note 1) comes into force and ending with the next 31 March (which is the first financial year), and each subsequent period of 12 months beginning with 1 April: s 47I(2) (as so added). At the date at which this volume states the law no such day had been appointed.

3 Ie under the Proceeds of Crime Act 2002 s 47C: see PARA 208. As to 'property' and related expressions see PARA 226; and see also the Proceeds of Crime Act 2002 s 47C(2)–(5); and PARA 210.
4 Proceeds of Crime Act 2002 ss 47H(1)(a) (as added: see note 2).
5 Proceeds of Crime Act 2002 ss 47H(1)(b) (as added: see note 2). In calculating a period of 48 hours for this purpose no account is to be taken of any Saturday or Sunday, Christmas Day, Good Friday or any day that is a bank holiday under the Banking and Financial Dealings Act 1971 (see FINANCIAL SERVICES AND INSTITUTIONS vol 49 (2008) PARA 1437) in England and Wales: Proceeds of Crime Act 2002 s 47H(6), (7) (as so added).
6 Ie the powers conferred by the Proceeds of Crime Act 2002 ss 47D–47F: see PARA 430.
7 Proceeds of Crime Act 2002 ss 47H(2)(a) (as added: see note 2).
8 See note 3.
9 Proceeds of Crime Act 2002 ss 47H(2)(b) (as added: see note 2).
10 Proceeds of Crime Act 2002 ss 47H(3)(a) (as added: see note 2).
11 Proceeds of Crime Act 2002 ss 47H(3)(b) (as added: see note 2).

212. Further detention of seized property pending the making or variation of a restraint order. Detained property[1] may be detained until the following applications are determined or otherwise disposed of[2]:

(1) an application[3] for a restraint order[4] which includes provision[5] authorising detention of the property[6], where the property is detained and no restraint order is in force in respect of it[7]; and

(2) an application for the order to be varied so as to include provision authorising detention of the property[8], where the property is detained, a restraint order is in force in respect of it, and the order does not include provision authorising the detention of the property[9].

If either such application is made[10] and is refused, the property may be detained until there is no further possibility of an appeal against the decision to refuse the application[11] or any decision made on an appeal against that decision[12].

1 Ie property detained under the Proceeds of Crime Act 2002 s 47J: see PARA 208. As to 'property' and related expressions see PARA 226; and see also s 47C(2)–(5); and PARA 210.
2 Proceeds of Crime Act 2002 ss 47K(2), 47L(2) (ss 47A–47S (see the text and notes 3–12; and PARAS 208–211, 213–215) added by the Policing and Crime Act 2009 s 55(1), (2)).
3 Ie an application made within the period mentioned in the Proceeds of Crime Act 2002 s 47J (see PARA 208). For the purposes of the Proceeds of Crime Act 2002 ss 47K(2) the reference to the period mentioned in s 47J includes that period as extended by any order under s 47M (see PARA 213): s 47K(4) (as added: see note 2).
4 Ie an order under the Proceeds of Crime Act 2002 s 41: see PARA 201.
5 Ie under the Proceeds of Crime Act 2002 s 41A: see PARA 201.
6 Proceeds of Crime Act 2002 s 47K(2) (as added: see note 2).
7 Proceeds of Crime Act 2002 s 47K(1) (as added: see note 2).
8 Proceeds of Crime Act 2002 s 47L(2) (as added: see note 2).
9 Proceeds of Crime Act 2002 s 47L(1) (as added: see note 2).

10 Ie within the period mentioned in the Proceeds of Crime Act 2002 s 47J (see PARA 208); and see note 3.
11 Proceeds of Crime Act 2002 ss 47K(4)(a), 47L(3)(a) (as added: see note 2). As to references to there being no further possibility of an appeal see s 87A; and PARA 199.
12 Proceeds of Crime Act 2002 ss 47K(4)(b), 47L(3)(b) (as added: see note 2).

213. Further detention of seized property in other cases. If property[1] is detained[2], no restraint order[3] is in force in respect of the property, and no application has been made for a restraint order which includes provision[4] authorising detention of the property[5], a magistrates' court may by order[6] extend the period for which the property or any part[7] of it may be so detained if satisfied that:

(1) any of the conditions for exercising the power to seize property[8] is met[9];
(2) the property or part is realisable property[10] other than exempt property[11]; and
(3) there are reasonable grounds for suspecting that the property may otherwise be made unavailable for satisfying any confiscation order[12] that has been or may be made against the defendant[13] or the value of the property may otherwise be diminished as a result of conduct by the defendant or any other person[14].

An application for such an order may be made by the Commissioners for Her Majesty's Revenue and Customs, an immigration officer, a constable, an accredited financial investigator or the prosecutor[15]. Those persons may also apply for variation or discharge of such an order[16], as may any person affected by it[17], and on such an application the court must discharge the order if an applicable condition is met[18]. Such an order will lapse if a restraint order is made in respect of the property to which it relates[19]. The persons who may apply for an order[20] may appeal to the Crown Court against a decision not to make an order, and the persons who may apply for the variation or discharge of an order[21] may appeal to the Crown Court in respect of a decision not to discharge or vary an order[22], and provision is made for the continuing detention of property pending such an appeal[23].

Evidence must not be excluded in detention order proceedings[24] on the ground that it is hearsay (of whatever degree)[25].

1 As to 'property' and related expressions see PARA 226; and see also the Proceeds of Crime Act 2002 s 47C(2)–(5); and PARA 210.
2 Ie detained under the Proceeds of Crime Act 2002 s 47J: see PARA 208.
3 Ie an order under the Proceeds of Crime Act 2002 s 41: see PARA 201.
4 Ie under the Proceeds of Crime Act 2002 s 41A: see PARA 201.
5 Proceeds of Crime Act 2002 s 47M(1) (ss 47A–47S (see the text and notes 6–25; and PARAS 208–212, 214–215) added by the Policing and Crime Act 2009 s 55(1), (2)).
6 An order under these provisions must provide for notice to be given to persons affected by it: Proceeds of Crime Act 2002 s 47M(5) (as added: see note 5).
7 In the Proceeds of Crime Act 2002 s 47M 'part' includes portion: s 47M(6) (as added: see note 5).
8 Ie the conditions set out in the Proceeds of Crime Act 2002 s 47B: see PARA 208. For this purpose references in s 47B to the officer are to be read as references to the court: s 47M(2)(a) (as added: see note 5).
9 Proceeds of Crime Act 2002 s 47M(2)(a) (as added: see note 5).
10 As to the meaning of 'realisable property' see PARA 226.
11 Proceeds of Crime Act 2002 s 47M(2)(b) (as added: see note 5). 'Exempt property' means exempt property within the meaning of s 47C(4) (see PARA 210): s 47M(2)(b) (as so added).
12 Ie an order under the Proceeds of Crime Act 2002 s 6: see PARA 221.
13 Proceeds of Crime Act 2002 s 47M(2)(c)(i) (as added: see note 5).
14 Proceeds of Crime Act 2002 s 47M(2)(c)(ii) (as added: see note 5).

15 Proceeds of Crime Act 2002 s 47M(3) (as added (see note 5); amended by the Crime and Courts Act 2013 Sch 21 para 18). If the property was seized in reliance on the first or second condition in the Proceeds of Crime Act 2002 s 47B the 'prosecutor' means a person who is to have conduct of any proceedings for the offence: s 47M(4) (as so added).

16 Proceeds of Crime Act 2002 s 47N(2)(a) (as added: see note 5).

17 Proceeds of Crime Act 2002 s 47N(2)(b) (as added: see note 5).

18 Proceeds of Crime Act 2002 s 47N(1), (3) (as added: see note 5). The applicable conditions are:

    (1)   that the order was made on the ground that the first or second condition in s 47B (see s 47B(2), (3); and PARA 208) was met but proceedings for the offence mentioned in that condition have not been started within a reasonable time (s 47N(3)(a) (as so added));

    (2)   that the order was made on the ground that the third or fourth condition in s 47B (see s 47B(4), (5); and PARA 208) was met but proceedings for the offence mentioned in that condition have now been concluded (s 47N(3)(b) (as so added)); and

    (3)   that the order was made on the ground that the fifth, sixth or seventh condition in s 47B (see s 47B(6)–(8); and PARA 208) was met but the application mentioned in that condition has now been concluded or, as the case may be, has not been made within a reasonable time (s 47N(3)(c) (as so added)).

19 Proceeds of Crime Act 2002 s 47N(4) (as added: see note 5). Provision authorising detention of the property may have been included in the restraint order by virtue of s 41A: s 47N(4) (as so added).

20 See the text and note 15.

21 See the text and notes 16–17.

22 Proceeds of Crime Act 2002 s 47O (as added: see note 5).

23 See the Proceeds of Crime Act 2002 s 47P (as added: see note 5), which provides that where an application for an order under s 47M (see the text and notes 1–15) is made within the period mentioned in s 47J (see PARA 208) and the application is refused, or where an order is made under s 47M extending the period for which property may be detained under s 47J and the order is discharged or varied so that detention of the property is no longer authorised by virtue of the order, the property may be detained until there is no further possibility of an appeal against the decision to refuse the application or discharge or vary the order (as the case may be). As to references to there being no further possibility of an appeal see s 87A; and PARA 199.

24 Detention order proceedings are proceedings for an order under the Proceeds of Crime Act 2002 s 47M, for the discharge or variation of such an order (see the text and notes 16–18) or on an appeal under s 47O (see the text and notes 19–22): s 47Q(3) (as added: see note 5). The Civil Evidence Act 1995 ss 2–4 (see CIVIL PROCEDURE vol 11 (2009) PARAS 811–815) apply in relation to detention order proceedings as they apply in relation to civil proceedings: Proceeds of Crime Act 2002 s 47Q(2) (as so added).

25 Proceeds of Crime Act 2002 s 47Q(1) (as added: see note 5). For this purpose hearsay is a statement which is made otherwise than by a person while giving oral evidence in the proceedings and which is tendered as evidence of the matters stated: s 47Q(4) (as so added). Nothing in s 47Q affects the admissibility of evidence which is admissible apart from s 47Q: s 47Q(5) (as so added).

214. Release of property. Any property[1] which has been seized[2] by an appropriate officer[3] and is detained[4] must be released if at any time an appropriate officer decides that the detention condition is no longer met[5], although property is not hereby required to be released if there is a power to detain it otherwise[6] and these provisions do not affect the operation of any power or duty to release property that arises apart therefrom[7].

1 As to 'property' and related expressions see PARA 226; and see also the Proceeds of Crime Act 2002 s 47C(2)–(5); and PARA 210.

2 Ie under the Proceeds of Crime Act 2002 s 47C: see PARA 208.

3 As to the meaning of 'appropriate officer' see PARA 208 note 1.

4 Ie under or by virtue of any of the Proceeds of Crime Act 2002 ss 47J–47M, 47P: see PARAS 208, 212, 213.

5 Proceeds of Crime Act 2002 s 47R(1), (2) (ss 47A–47S (see the text and notes 6–7; and PARAS 208–213, 215) added by the Policing and Crime Act 2009 s 55(1), (2)). The detention condition is met for so long as any of the conditions in the Proceeds of Crime Act 2002 s 47B (see PARA 208) is met and there are reasonable grounds for the suspicion mentioned in s 47C(1) (see PARA 208): s 47R(3) (as so added).

6 Proceeds of Crime Act 2002 s 47R(4) (as added: see note 5), providing that nothing in s 47R requires property to be released if there is a power to detain it otherwise than under or by virtue of ss 47J–47M, 47P.

7 Proceeds of Crime Act 2002 s 47R(5) (as added: see note 5).

215. Codes of practice. The Secretary of State must make a code of practice in connection with the carrying out by appropriate officers[1] of their functions[2] relating to the seizure of property and the searching of persons and premises[3], the carrying out by senior officers[4] of their functions[5] relating to the approval of seizures and searches[6], and the detention of property[7] generally[8]. Where the Secretary of State proposes to issue a code of practice he must publish a draft[9] and consider any representations made about it[10], and if he thinks it appropriate must modify the draft in the light of any such representations[11]. The Secretary of State must lay a draft of the code before Parliament[12] and when he has done so may bring it into operation by order[13]. He may also revise the whole or any part of the code and issue the code as revised[14].

A failure by a person to comply with a provision of the code does not of itself make the person liable to criminal or civil proceedings[15]; however the code is admissible in evidence in criminal or civil proceedings and is to be taken into account by a court or tribunal in any case in which it appears to the court or tribunal to be relevant[16].

1 As to the meaning of 'appropriate officer' see PARA 208 note 1.
2 Ie the functions conferred by the Proceeds of Crime Act 2002 ss 47C–47H: see PARAS 208–211.
3 Proceeds of Crime Act 2002 s 47S(1)(a) (ss 47A–47S (see the text and notes 4–16; and PARAS 208–214) added by the Policing and Crime Act 2009 s 55(1), (2)).
4 As to the meaning of 'senior officer' see PARA 208 note 18.
5 Ie the functions conferred by the Proceeds of Crime Act 2002 s 47G: see PARA 208.
6 Proceeds of Crime Act 2002 s 47S(1)(b) (as added: see note 3).
7 Ie under or by virtue of the Proceeds of Crime Act 2002 ss 41A, 44A, 47J–47P: see PARAS 201, 208, 212, 213.
8 Proceeds of Crime Act 2002 s 47S(1)(c) (as added: see note 3). As to the Code see note 13.
9 Proceeds of Crime Act 2002 s 47S(2)(a) (as added: see note 3).
10 Proceeds of Crime Act 2002 s 47S(2)(b) (as added: see note 3).
11 Proceeds of Crime Act 2002 s 47S(2)(c) (as added: see note 3).
12 Proceeds of Crime Act 2002 s 47S(3) (as added: see note 3).
13 Proceeds of Crime Act 2002 s 47S(4) (as added: see note 3). See the Proceeds of Crime Act 2002 (Search, Seizure and Detention of Property: Code of Practice) (England and Wales) Order 2015, SI 2015/730.
14 Proceeds of Crime Act 2002 s 47S(5) (as added: see note 3). Where the Secretary of State proposes to issue a revised code and s 47S(2)–(4) (see the text and notes 9–13) apply to such a revised code as they apply to the original code: s 47S(5) (as so added).
15 Proceeds of Crime Act 2002 s 47S(6) (as added: see note 3).
16 Proceeds of Crime Act 2002 s 47S(7) (as added: see note 3).

E. DEFENDANT ABSCONDS

216. Defendant convicted or committed. Where a defendant absconds[1]:

(1) and either before or after doing so, he is convicted of an offence or offences in proceedings before the Crown Court[2];

(2) after being committed[3] to the Crown Court for sentence in respect of an offence or offences[4]; or

(3) after being committed[5] to the Crown Court in respect of an offence or offences with a view to a confiscation order being considered[6],

and:

(a) the prosecutor applies to the Crown Court to proceed as described below[7]; and

(b) the court believes it is appropriate for it to do so[8],

the court must, subject to certain modifications[9], proceed under the provisions relating to the making of a confiscation order in the same way as it must proceed if the two conditions mentioned in them are satisfied[10].

1 As to the meaning of 'defendant' for these purposes see PARA 221 note 1; as to what amounts to 'absconding' see *R v Bestel* [2013] EWCA Crim 1305, [2014] 1 WLR 457, [2013] 2 Cr App Rep 317.
2 Proceeds of Crime Act 2002 s 27(1), (2)(a) (s 27(2) substituted by the Serious Crime Act 2015 s 9(1)).
3 Ie under the Powers of Criminal Courts (Sentencing) Act 2000 s 3, s 3A, s 3B, s 3C, s 4, s 4A or s 6 (see CRIMINAL PROCEDURE vol 27 (2015) PARAS 234–236, 292–296): Proceeds of Crime Act 2002 s 27(2)(b) (as substituted: see note 2).
4 Proceeds of Crime Act 2002 s 27(2)(b) (as substituted: see note 2).
5 Ie under the Proceeds of Crime Act 2002 s 70 (see PARA 190).
6 Proceeds of Crime Act 2002 s 27(2)(c) (as substituted: see note 2).
7 Proceeds of Crime Act 2002 s 27(3)(a) (s 27(3)(a), (5)(b) amended by the Serious Crime Act 2007 Sch 8 para 14(2)–(4), Sch 14).
8 Proceeds of Crime Act 2002 s 27(3)(b).
9 If the court proceeds under the Proceeds of Crime Act 2002 s 6 (ie the provisions relating to the making of a confiscation order: see PARA 221) as applied by s 27, then Pt 2 (ss 6–91) has effect with these modifications:
   (1) any person the court believes is likely to be affected by an order under s 6 is entitled to appear before the court and make representations (s 27(5)(a));
   (2) the court must not make an order under s 6 unless the prosecutor has taken reasonable steps to contact the defendant (s 27(5)(b) (as amended: see note 7));
   (3) s 6(9) (see PARA 229) applies as if the reference to offences mentioned in s 6(2) were a reference to those mentioned in s 27(2) (see the text and notes 1–6) (s 27(5)(c));
   (4) s 10 (see PARA 231), s 16(4) (see PARA 194), s 17 (see PARA 194) and s 18 (see PARA 195) must be ignored (s 27(5)(d)); and
   (5) s 19 (see PARA 273), s 20 (see PARA 274) and s 21 (see PARA 275) must be ignored while the defendant is still an absconder (s 27(5)(e)).
   Where a defendant has ceased to be an absconder the modifications set out in s 27(5)(a)–(d) do not apply to proceedings that take place by virtue of s 19, s 20 or s 21 (as applied by s 27(5)): s 27(6)(d) (s 27(6) substituted by the Serious Crime Act 2007 s 9(2)).
10 Proceeds of crime Act 2002 s 27(4). A discretion to continue confiscation proceedings in a defendant's absence should never be exercised when it is the action of the state that causes the absence: see *R v Gavin* [2010] EWCA Crim 2727, [2011] 1 Cr App Rep (S) 731.

217. Defendant neither convicted nor acquitted. Where:

(1) proceedings for an offence or offences are started[1] against a defendant[2] but are not concluded[3];

(2) he absconds[4]; and

(3) the period of three months (starting with the day the court believes he absconded) has ended[5],

and

(a) the prosecutor applies to the Crown Court to proceed[6]; and

(b) the court believes it is appropriate for it to do so[7],

the court must proceed under the provisions relating to the making of confiscation orders[8] in the same way as it must proceed if the two conditions there mentioned[9] are satisfied[10], subject to a number of modifications[11].

1 As to when proceedings for an offence are started and concluded see PARA 199.
2 As to the meaning of 'defendant' for these purposes see PARA 221 note 1.
3 Proceeds of Crime Act 2002 s 28(1), (2)(a).
4 Proceeds of Crime Act 2002 s 28(2)(b).

5 Proceeds of Crime Act 2002 s 28(2)(c) (ss 27(6), 28(6) substituted, s 28(2)(c), (3)(a), (5)(b) amended, by the Serious Crime Act 2007 s 9(2)–(4), Sch 8 para 15(1)–(3), Sch 14).
6 Proceeds of Crime Act 2002 s 28(3)(a) (as amended: see note 5). The text refers to an application to proceed under the Proceeds of Crime Act 2002 s 28.
7 Proceeds of Crime Act 2002 s 28(3)(b).
8 As to the making of confiscation orders see the Proceeds of Crime Act 2002 s 6; and PARA 221.
9 See PARA 221.
10 Proceeds of Crime Act 2002 s 28(4).
11 Proceeds of Crime Act 2002 s 28(4). If the court proceeds under s 6 as applied by s 28, then Pt 2 (ss 6–91) has effect with the following modifications:
    (1) any person the court believes is likely to be affected by an order under s 6 is entitled to appear before the court and make representations (s 28(5)(a));
    (2) the court must not make an order under s 6 unless the prosecutor has taken reasonable steps to contact the defendant (s 28(5)(b) (as amended: see note 5));
    (3) s 6(9) (see PARA 229) applies as if the reference to offences mentioned in s 6(2) were a reference to those mentioned in s 28(2) (see the text and notes 1–5) (s 28(5)(c));
    (4) s 10 (see PARA 231), s 16(4) (see PARA 194) and ss 17–20 (see PARAS 194–195, 273–274) must be ignored (s 28(5)(d)); and
    (5) s 21 (see PARA 275) must be ignored while the defendant is still an absconder (s 28(5)(e)).
Where a defendant has ceased to be an absconder the modifications set out in s 28(5)(a)–(d) do not apply to proceedings that take place by virtue of s 19, s 20 or s 21 (as applied by s 28(5)) (s 27(6)(b) (as so substituted)) and s 21 has effect as if it applied where a court has made a confiscation order, the prosecutor believes that if the court were to find the amount of the defendant's benefit in pursuance of this section it would exceed the relevant amount, and before the end of the period of six years starting with the day when the defendant ceased to be an absconder, the prosecutor applies to the Crown Court to proceed under s 21 and the court believes it is appropriate for it to do so (s 28(6)(b) (as so substituted)).
If: (i) the court makes an order under s 6 as applied by s 28 (s 28(7)(a)); and (ii) the defendant is later convicted in proceedings before the Crown Court of the offence (or any of the offences) concerned (s 28(7)(b)), then s 6 does not apply so far as that conviction is concerned (s 28(7)).
As to references to the 'offence or offences concerned' see PARA 229 note 2.

218. Variation of order.   Where:

(1) the court makes a confiscation order under the provisions relating to the making of such an order[1] as applied by the provisions for the making of an order where the defendant[2] has been neither convicted nor acquitted[3];
(2) the defendant ceases to be an absconder[4];
(3) he is convicted of an offence (or any of the offences) in respect of which proceedings were not cancelled[5];
(4) he believes that the amount required to be paid was too large (taking the circumstances prevailing when the amount was found for the purposes of the order)[6]; and
(5) before the end of the relevant period[7] he applies[8] to the Crown Court to consider the evidence on which his belief is based[9],

and (after considering the evidence) the court concludes that the defendant's belief is well founded then:
(a) it must find the amount which should have been the amount required to be paid (taking the circumstances prevailing when the amount was found for the purposes of the order)[10]; and
(b) it may vary the order by substituting for the amount required to be paid such amount as it believes is just[11].

1 As to the making of confiscation orders see the Proceeds of Crime Act 2002 s 6; and PARA 221.
2 As to the meaning of 'defendant' for these purposes see PARA 221 note 1.

3   Proceeds of Crime Act 2002 s 29(1)(a). The provisions for the making of a confiscation order where the defendant has been neither convicted nor acquitted are those set out in s 28 (see PARA 217).

4   Proceeds of Crime Act 2002 s 29(1)(b).

5   Proceeds of Crime Act 2002 s 29(1)(c). The reference in the text to a conviction for an offence (or any offence) in respect of which proceedings were not cancelled is a reference to a conviction under s 28(2)(a) (see PARA 217).

6   Proceeds of Crime Act 2002 s 29(1)(d).

7   The 'relevant period' is the period of 28 days starting with: (1) the date on which the defendant was convicted of the offence mentioned in the Proceeds of Crime Act 2002 s 28(2)(a) (s 29(3)(a)); or (2) if there are two or more offences and the convictions were on different dates, the date of the latest (s 29(3)(b)). However, in a case where s 28(2)(a) applies to more than one offence the court must not make an order under these provisions unless it is satisfied that there is no possibility of any further proceedings being taken or continued in relation to any such offence in respect of which the defendant has not been convicted: s 29(4).

8   In connection with applications under the Proceeds of Crime Act 2002 s 29 see the Criminal Procedure Rules 2015, SI 2015/1490, r 33.19.

9   Proceeds of Crime Act 2002 s 29(1)(e).

10 Proceeds of Crime Act 2002 s 29(2)(a).

11 Proceeds of Crime Act 2002 s 29(2)(b). An order varying a confiscation order under s 29 is a 'sentence' for the purposes of an appeal against sentence under the Criminal Appeal Act 1968: see s 50(1)(cb); and PARA 626.

219. Discharge of order. If:

(1)   the court makes a confiscation order[1] in respect of a defendant[2] who has neither been convicted nor acquitted[3];

(2)   the defendant is later tried for the offence or offences concerned and acquitted on all counts[4]; and

(3)   he applies[5] to the Crown Court to discharge the confiscation order[6],

the court must discharge the order[7].

If:

(a)   the court makes a confiscation order in respect of a defendant who has neither been convicted nor acquitted[8];

(b)   the defendant ceases to be an absconder[9];

(c)   the defendant is not later tried for the offence or offences concerned and acquitted on all counts[10]; and

(d)   the defendant applies to the Crown Court to discharge the confiscation order[11],

the court may discharge the order if it finds that: (i) there has been undue delay in continuing the proceedings[12] in respect of which he absconded[13]; or (ii) the prosecutor does not intend to proceed with the prosecution[14].

If the court discharges a confiscation order under these provisions it may make such a consequential or incidental order as it believes appropriate[15].

1   As to the making of confiscation orders see the Proceeds of Crime Act 2002 s 6; and PARA 221.

2   As to the meaning of 'defendant' for these purposes see PARA 221 note 1.

3   Proceeds of Crime Act 2002 s 30(1)(a). The provisions for the making of a confiscation order where the defendant has been neither convicted nor acquitted are those set out in s 28 (see PARA 217).

4   Proceeds of Crime Act 2002 s 30(1)(b).

5   In connection with applications under the Proceeds of Crime Act 2002 s 30 see the Criminal Procedure Rules 2015, SI 2015/1490, r 33.20.

6   Proceeds of Crime Act 2002 s 30(1)(c).

7   Proceeds of Crime Act 2002 s 30(2).

8   Proceeds of Crime Act 2002 s 30(3)(a).

9   Proceeds of Crime Act 2002 s 30(3)(b).

10 Proceeds of Crime Act 2002 s 30(3)(c).

11 Proceeds of Crime Act 2002 s 30(3)(d).

12 Ie the proceedings mentioned in the Proceeds of Crime Act 2002 s 28(2) (see PARA 217).
13 Proceeds of Crime Act 2002 s 30(4)(a).
14 Proceeds of Crime Act 2002 s 30(4)(b).
15 Proceeds of Crime Act 2002 s 30(5).

(ii) Making of Confiscation Orders under the Proceeds of Crime Act 2002

A. INTRODUCTORY PROVISIONS

220. Evidence. When assessing matters relating to the confiscation of criminal proceeds the court is not limited to considering the facts on which the jury based their decision to convict, but may consider additional evidence[1]. All evidence to be relied on in confiscation proceedings must be given clearly and cogently[2]. Hearsay evidence is admissible, subject to safeguards[3]. Provision is made in connection with the adducing of expert evidence[4].

A defendant who pleaded guilty and did not challenge the evidence against him at the trial is not thereby barred from challenging that evidence at the confiscation hearing[5].

1 See *R v Sangha* [2008] EWCA Crim 2562, [2009] STC 570, [2009] 2 Cr App Rep (S) 94; and see also *R v Threapleton* [2001] EWCA Crim 2892, [2003] 3 All ER 458; *R v Olubitan* [2003] EWCA Crim 2940, [2004] 2 Cr App Rep (S) 70, [2004] Crim LR 155; *R v Silcock* [2004] EWCA Crim 408, [2004] 2 Cr App Rep (S) 323.
2 See *R v Walbrook* [1994] 15 Cr App Rep (S) 783.
3 See *R v Clipston* [2011] EWCA Crim 446, [2011] 2 Cr App Rep (S) 569 (hearsay evidence is admissible within the framework established under the Criminal Justice Act 2003 s 114 (see CRIMINAL PROCEDURE vol 28 (2015) PARA 608 et seq)). Provision is also made for the admissibility of hearsay evidence in in restraint proceedings: see PARA 206.
4 See the Criminal Procedure Rules 2015, SI 2015/1490, rr 33.36–33.37.
5 See *R v Knaggs* [2009] EWCA Crim 1363, [2010] 1 WLR 435, [2010] 1 Cr App Rep (S) 495.

221. Making a confiscation order. Provision is made for the making of a confiscation order where the defendant[1] is either:
  (1) convicted of an offence or offences in proceedings before the Crown Court[2];
  (2) committed[3] to the Crown Court for sentence in respect of an offence or offences[4]; or
  (3) committed[5] to the Crown Court in respect of an offence or offences with a view to a confiscation order being considered[6].

If the prosecutor asks the court to proceed under these provisions[7] or the court believes it is appropriate for it to do so[8], the Crown Court must[9]:
  (a) decide[10] whether the defendant has a criminal lifestyle[11];
  (b) if it decides that he has a criminal lifestyle it must decide whether he has benefited[12] from his general criminal conduct[13];
  (c) if it decides that he does not have a criminal lifestyle it must decide whether he has benefited from his particular criminal conduct[14].

If the Crown Court decides under head (a) or head (c) above that the defendant has benefited from the conduct referred to it must decide[15] the recoverable amount[16], and must make an order (a 'confiscation order') requiring him to pay that amount[17].

The Secretary of State may by order make such provision as he considers appropriate for or in connection with enabling confiscation orders[18] to be made by magistrates' courts in England and Wales[19]. However, such an order by the Secretary of State may not enable such a confiscation order to be made by any magistrates' court in respect of an amount exceeding £10,000[20].

1 A defendant is a person against whom proceedings for an offence have been started (whether or not he has been convicted): Proceeds of Crime Act 2002 s 88(3). As to when proceedings for an offence are started and concluded see PARA 199.

2 See the Proceeds of Crime Act 2002 s 6(1), (2)(a). The defendant having been conditionally or absolutely discharged does not prevent the court from having to make a confiscation order under these provisions: see *R v Varma* [2012] UKSC 42, [2013] 1 AC 463, [2013] 1 All ER 129. 'Proceedings' under the Proceeds of Crime Act 2002 s 6(2)(a) means proceedings under a single indictment: *R v Moulden* [2008] EWCA Crim 2561, [2009] 2 All ER 912, [2009] 1 Cr App Rep 362. The condition set out in the Proceeds of Crime Act 2002 s 6(2) is not satisfied if the defendant absconds (although s 27 (see PARA 216) may apply): s 6(8). Section 6 does not have effect where the offence, or any of the offences, mentioned in s 6(2) (see the text and notes 3–6) was committed before 24 March 2003: see PARA 189.

3 The text refers to committal under the Powers of Criminal Courts (Sentencing) Act 2000 s 3, s 3A, s 3B, s 3C, s 4, s 4A or s 6 (see CRIMINAL PROCEDURE vol 27 (2015) PARAS 234–236, 292–296): Proceeds of Crime Act 2002 s 6(2)(b) (amended by the Criminal Justice Act 2003 s 41, Sch 3 para 75(1), (2)).

4 Proceeds of Crime Act 2002 s 6(2)(b) (as amended: see note 3). See note 2.

5 Ie under the Proceeds of Crime Act 2002 s 70 (see PARA 190).

6 Proceeds of Crime Act 2002 s 6(2)(c). See note 2.

7 Proceeds of Crime Act 2002 s 6(3)(a) (amended by the Serious Crime Act 2007 Sch 8 para 2, Sch 14). In connection with the precondition under the Proceeds of Crime Act 2002 s 6(3) see *R v Meader* [2011] EWCA Crim 2018.

8 Proceeds of Crime Act 2002 s 6(3)(b).

9 In connection with judicial attempts at acquiring a discretion in this matter see *R v Jones* [2006] EWCA Crim 2061, [2007] 1 WLR 7, [2007] 1 Cr App Rep (S) 414; *R v Hockey* [2007] EWCA Crim 1577, [2008] 1 Cr App Rep (S) 279, [2008] Crim LR 59. See also *R v Mahmood* [2005] EWCA Crim 2168, [2006] 1 Cr App Rep (S) 570, [2006] Crim LR 75; *R v Shabir* [2008] EWCA Crim 1809, [2009] 1 Cr App Rep (S) 497, [2008] All ER (D) 414 (Jul); *R v Lowe* [2009] EWCA Crim 194, [2009] 2 Cr App Rep (S) 544, [2009] Crim LR 452; *R v Nelson (Prosecution Appeal under section 31 of the Proceeds of Crime Act 2002)* [2009] EWCA Crim 1573, [2010] QB 678, [2009] All ER (D) 283 (Jul); *R v Silvester* [2009] EWCA Crim 2182, [2009] All ER (D) 103 (Nov).

10 The court must decide any questions arising under the Proceeds of Crime Act 2002 s 6(4) (see the text and notes 11–14) on the balance of probabilities: s 6(7).

11 Proceeds of Crime Act 2002 s 6(4)(a). As to whether a defendant has a criminal lifestyle see PARA 229.

12 As to when the defendant benefits from criminal conduct see PARAS 223–224.

13 Proceeds of Crime Act 2002 s 6(4)(b). As to 'criminal conduct' and 'general criminal conduct' see PARA 225.

14 Proceeds of Crime Act 2002 s 6(4)(c). In relation to proceedings under the Proceeds of Crime Act 2002 Pt 2, Criminal Procedure Rules may make provision corresponding to provision in Civil Procedure Rules: Proceeds of Crime Act 2002 s 91(a) (amended by the Courts Act 2003 s 109(1), Sch 8 para 410).

15 The court must decide any questions arising under the Proceeds of Crime Act 2002 s 6(5) on the balance of probabilities: s 6(7). As to an appeal by the prosecutor in respect of a confiscation order or against a refusal to make a confiscation order see PARA 243.

16 Proceeds of Crime Act 2002 s 6(5)(a). As to the 'recoverable amount' see PARA 233.

17 Proceeds of Crime Act 2002 ss 6(5)(b), 88(6)(a). See s 6(6), (6A); and PARAS 235–236. Section 6(5)(b) applies only if, or to the extent that, it would not be disproportionate to require the defendant to pay the recoverable amount: s 6(5) (ss 6(5), 97(2) amended, s 97(1ZA), (1ZB) added, by the Serious Crime Act 2015 s 40(1)–(3), Sch 4 para 19). In making a confiscation order a judge is entitled to take into account all evidence heard and to make his own relevant findings of fact, provided that he acts consistently with the verdict and its factual basis: *R v Sangha* [2008] EWCA Crim 2562, [2009] STC 570, [2008] All ER (D) 161 (Nov). Provision is also made by Order in Council for prohibitions to be imposed on dealing with property which is the subject of an external request (ie a request by an overseas authority to prohibit dealing with relevant property which is identified in the request) and for the realisation of property for the purpose of giving effect to an external order (ie an order which is made by an overseas court where property is found or believed to have been obtained as a result of or in connection with criminal conduct and is for the recovery of specified property or a specified sum of money): see the Proceeds of Crime Act 2002 (External Requests and Orders) Order 2005, SI 2005/3181 (amended by SI 2006/594; SI 2008/302; SI 2009/2054; SI 2011/1242; SI 2013/472; SI 2013/534; SI 2013/2604); and the Proceeds of Crime Act 2002 (External Requests and Orders) Order 2005

(England and Wales) (Appeals under Part 2) Order 2012, SI 2012/138. See also the Criminal Procedure Rules 2015, SI 2015/1490, r 33.14. Before the enactment of the Proceeds of Crime Act 2002, provision in this regard was made by the Criminal Justice Act 1988 ss 96, 97 (amended by the Criminal Justice Act 1993 s 21(2), (3)(g); prospectively repealed by the Proceeds of Crime Act 2002 ss 456, 457, Sch 11 paras 1, 17(1), (2)(a), Sch 12); and the Criminal Justice Act 1988 (Designated Countries and Territories) (Amendment) Order 1991, SI 1991/2873 (amended by SI 1993/1790; SI 1993/3147; SI 1994/1639; SI 1996/278; SI 1996/2877; SI 1997/1316; SI 1997/2976; SI 1999/282; SI 2001/960; SI 2002/256; SI 2002/2844; SI 2004/1981); and by the Drug Trafficking Act 1994 ss 39, 40 (prospectively repealed by the Proceeds of Crime Act 2002 Sch 11 para 25(1), (2)(a), Sch 12); and the Drug Trafficking Act 1994 (Designated Countries and Territories) Order 1996, SI 1996/2880 (amended by SI 1997/1318; SI 1997/2980; SI 2001/956; SI 2002/257; SI 2002/2846).

    A confiscation order under the Proceeds of Crime Act 2002 Pt 2 is a 'sentence' for the purposes of an appeal against sentence under the Criminal Appeal Act 1968: see s 50(1)(ca); and PARA 626.
18 Ie orders under the Proceeds of Crime Act 2002 Pt 2.
19 Serious Organised Crime and Police Act 2005 s 97(1)(a). At the date at which this volume states the law no such order had been made.
20 Serious Organised Crime and Police Act 2005 s 97(1ZA), (2) (as added and amended: see note 17). The Secretary of State may by order amend the Proceeds of Crime Act 2002 s 97(1ZA) so as to substitute a different amount: s 97(1ZB) (as so added).

222. European Convention on Human Rights.

A confiscation order may not be made[1] where it would be wholly disproportionate so as to amount to a breach of the defendant's rights to peaceful enjoyment of property and possessions under the European Convention on Human Rights[2]: there must be a reasonable relationship of proportionality between the means employed and the aim sought to be realised by any measure depriving a person of his possessions[3].

    Confiscation proceedings are 'criminal proceedings' within the scope of the Convention right to a fair hearing[4] because they are part of the sentencing process following conviction[5]. Thus proceedings must, for example, be determined within a reasonable time[6] and proper process must be followed[7].

1 Ie under the Proceeds of Crime Act 2002 s 6(5)(b) (see PARA 221).
2 Ie the Convention for the Protection of Human Rights and Fundamental Freedoms (Rome, 4 November 1950; TS 71 (1953; Cmd 8969) Protocol 1 (Paris, 20 March 1952; TS 46; Cmnd 9221) art 1 (see RIGHTS AND FREEDOMS vol 88A (2013) PARAS 534–547): see *R v Waya* [2012] UKSC 51, [2013] 1 AC 294, [2013] 1 All ER 889 (applied in *R v Morgan* [2013] EWCA Crim 1307, [2014] 1 All ER 1208, [2014] 1 WLR 3450; *R v Jawad* [2013] EWCA Crim 644, [2014] 1 Cr App Rep (S) 85, [2013] Crim LR 698 (a confiscation order would generally be disproportionate if it would require the defendant to pay for a second time money which he had previously restored to the loser); *R v Sale* [2013] EWCA Crim 1306, [2014] 1 WLR 663).
3 See eg *Jahn v Germany* (2005) 42 EHRR 1084, [2005] ECHR 46720/99, ECtHR.
4 Ie under the European Convention on Human Rights art 6 (see RIGHTS AND FREEDOMS vol 88A (2013) PARAS 243–300).
5 See *R v Briggs-Price* [2009] UKHL 19, [2009] AC 1026, [2009] 4 All ER 594. Note however that the right to be presumed innocent under the European Convention on Human Rights art 6.2 (see RIGHTS AND FREEDOMS vol 88A (2013) PARAS 284–285) and many (though not all) of the procedural protections listed in art 6.3 (see RIGHTS AND FREEDOMS vol 88A (2013) PARAS 287–290) will be inapplicable in confiscation proceedings because the defendant has already been convicted: *R v Briggs-Price*; *R v Gavin* [2010] EWCA Crim 2727, [2011] 1 Cr App Rep (S) 731.
6 See *Minshall v United Kingdom* [2012] STC 731, ECtHR; *Bullen v United Kingdom* (2009) Times, 2 February, [2009] All ER (D) 90 (Jan), ECtHR; and PARA 192.
7 See *R v Waya* [2012] UKSC 51, [2013] 1 AC 294, [2013] 1 All ER 889, in which it was held that matters of abuse of process should be brought on proportionality grounds under the European Convention on Human Rights Protocol 1 art 1 (see note 2) and not under the Human Rights Act 1998 s 3 (the interpretative obligation: see RIGHTS AND FREEDOMS vol 88A (2013) PARA 16). For examples of abuse of process applications prior to *R v Waya* see *R v Mahmood* [2005] EWCA Crim 2168, [2006] 1 Cr App Rep (S) 570; *R v Shabir* [2008] EWCA Crim 1809, [2009] 1 Cr App Rep (S) 497; *R (on the application of the Secretary of State for Work and*

Pensions) v Croydon Crown Court [2010] EWHC 805 (Admin), [2011] 1 Cr App Rep (S) 1; *R v Nelson* [2009] EWCA Crim 1573, [2010] QB 678, [2010] 4 All ER 666.

B. DETERMINING THE BENEFIT

223.   Defendant's benefit.   A person benefits from conduct if he obtains property[1] as a result of, or in connection with, the conduct[2] and, if a person benefits from conduct, his benefit is the value of the property obtained[3]. If a person obtains a pecuniary advantage as a result of or in connection with conduct, he is to be taken to obtain as a result of or in connection with the conduct a sum of money equal to the value of the pecuniary advantage[4].

The benefit obtained may exceed the profit derived from the activity[5]. To determine whether a defendant has benefited the prosecution must prove, to the civil standard, that expenditure has been incurred by the defendant, prima facie evidence is not sufficient[6]. The question of whether there has been a 'benefit' cannot depend on what the defendant intended would be the outcome of his criminal conduct, but has to depend on what, in fact, actually happened[7]. Similarly, it is unimportant what happened to the property subsequent to the defendant obtaining it[8].

The benefit gained is the total value of the property or pecuniary advantage gained, not the particular defendant's net profit; and where two or more defendants obtain property jointly, each is regarded as obtaining the whole of it[9]. The burden of proving the benefit is on the prosecution[10].

1   As to the meaning of 'property' and as to when property is 'obtained' see PARA 226. References to property or a pecuniary advantage obtained in connection with conduct include references to property or a pecuniary advantage obtained both in that connection and some other: Proceeds of Crime Act 2002 s 76(6).

2   Proceeds of Crime Act 2002 s 76(4). As to the meaning of 'in connection with the conduct' see *R v Ahmad* [2012] EWCA Crim 391, [2012] 2 All ER 1137, [2012] 1 WLR 2335 (affd [2014] UKSC 36, [2015] AC 299, [2014] 4 All ER 767); *R v Hussain* [2014] EWCA Crim 2344, [2015] PTSR D7, [2014] All ER (D) 217 (Nov). As to calculating the defendant's benefit see PARA 224.

3   Proceeds of Crime Act 2002 s 76(7).

4   Proceeds of Crime Act 2002 s 76(5). A person obtains a pecuniary advantage if (among other things) he evades a liability to which he is personally subject: see *R v May* [2008] UKHL 28, [2008] 1 AC 1028, [2008] 4 All ER 97 (cited in *R v Sivaraman* [2008] EWCA Crim 1736, [2009] 1 Cr App Rep (S) 469, [2008] All ER (D) 447 (Jul)); reviewed in *R v Allpress* [2009] EWCA Crim 8, [2009] 2 Cr App Rep (S) 399, [2009] All ER (D) 126 (Jan)). See also *R v Bakewell* [2006] EWCA Crim 2, [2006] 2 Cr App Rep (S) 277, [2006] Crim LR 453; *R v Rowbotham* [2006] EWCA Crim 747, [2006] 2 Cr App Rep (S) 642, [2006] All ER (D) 165 (Mar); and cf *R v Rigby* [2006] EWCA Crim 1653, [2006] 1 WLR 3067, [2007] 1 Cr App Rep (S) 428 (decided under corresponding provisions in the Criminal Justice Act 1988 s 71 (repealed)).

5   *R v May* [2008] UKHL 28, [2008] 1 AC 1028, [2008] 4 All ER 97; *R v Shabir* [2008] EWCA Crim 1809, [2009] 1 Cr App Rep (S) 497, [2008] All ER (D) 414 (Jul). A confiscation order should not include provision enabling the defendant to 'set off' the expenses of committing the crime: *R v May*.

6   *A-G's Reference (No 2 of 2008), R v Winters* [2008] EWCA Crim 2953, (2009) Times, 12 January, [2008] All ER (D) 112 (Dec).

7   See *R v Morgan* [2013] EWCA Crim 1307, [2014] 1 All ER 1208, [2014] 1 WLR 3450; and see also *R v Mackle (Northern Ireland)* [2014] UKSC 5, [2014] AC 678, [2014] 2 All ER 170.

8   See *R v Waya* [2012] UKSC 51, [2013] 1 AC 294, [2013] 1 All ER 889 (pecuniary advantage gained by evasion of duty on imported goods was not undone by seizure of the goods in question); *R v Del Basso* [2010] EWCA Crim 1119, [2011] 1 Cr App Rep (S) 268, [2010] All ER (D) 176 (May); *R v Nelson* [2009] EWCA Crim 1573, [2010] QB 678, [2010] 4 All ER 666.

9   See *R v May* [2008] UKHL 28, [2008] 1 AC 1028, [2008] 4 All ER 97 (no-one is to be penalised for not paying what he has not got); *R v Green* [2008] UKHL 30, [2008] 1 AC 1053, [2008] 4 All ER 119 (cited in *R v Sivaraman* [2008] EWCA Crim 1736, [2009] 1 Cr App Rep (S) 469,

[2008] All ER (D) 447 (Jul); reviewed in *R v Allpress* [2009] EWCA Crim 8, [2009] 2 Cr App Rep (S) 399, [2009] All ER (D) 126 (Jan)); *R v Briggs-Price* [2009] UKHL 19, [2009] 1 AC 1026, [2009] 4 All ER 594; *R v Farquhar* [2008] EWCA Crim 806, [2008] 2 Cr App Rep (S) 601, [2008] All ER (D) 140 (Mar); *R v Gangar* [2012] EWCA Crim 1378, [2012] 4 All ER 972, [2013] 1 WLR 147; *R v Lambert* [2012] EWCA Crim 421, [2012] 2 Cr App Rep (S) 535, [2012] All ER (D) 59 (Mar); *R v Ahmad* [2014] UKSC 36, [2015] AC 299, [2014] 4 All ER 767. As to the calculation of the value of benefit to an individual where the criminal conduct was undertaken via a company see *R v Seager* [2009] EWCA Crim 1303, [2010] 1 WLR 815, [2009] Crim LR 816 (reviewing *R v May*; *R v Green*; *Jennings v Crown Prosecution Service* [2008] UKHL 29, [2008] 1 AC 1046, [2008] 4 All ER 113). The proposition that a person acting purely in capacity of employee who has received only an enhanced wage has necessarily, as a matter of law, to be taken to profit to the same extent as his employer is unsound: *R v Sivaraman*.

10 See e g *R v Whittington* [2009] EWCA Crim 1641, [2010] Crim LR 65; *A-G's Reference (No 2 of 2008)* [2008] EWCA Crim 2953, [2008] All ER (S) 112 (Dec).

224. Calculating the defendant's benefit.

224. Calculating the defendant's benefit. If the court is proceeding in relation to a confiscation order[1], then the following applies for the purpose of deciding whether the defendant has benefited from conduct[2], and deciding his benefit from the conduct[3]. The court must take account of conduct occurring up to the time it makes its decision[4] and take account of property obtained up to that time[5]. Where:

(1)   the conduct concerned is general criminal conduct[6];

(2)   a confiscation order[7] has at an earlier time been made against the defendant[8]; and

(3)   his benefit for the purposes of that order was benefit from his general criminal conduct[9],

the defendant's benefit found at the time the last confiscation order mentioned in head (3) was made against him must be taken to be his benefit from his general criminal conduct at that time[10]. If the conduct concerned is general criminal conduct, the court must deduct the aggregate of the following amounts: (a) the amount ordered to be paid under each confiscation order previously made against the defendant[11]; (b) the amount ordered to be paid under each confiscation order previously made[12] against him[13].

1   Ie if the court is proceeding under the Proceeds of Crime Act 2002 s 6 (see PARA 221).
2   Proceeds of Crime Act 2002 s 8(1)(a). As to 'conduct' see PARA 225; as to the defendant's benefit see PARA 223.
3   Proceeds of Crime Act 2002 s 8(1)(b). As to assumptions that may be made see s 10; and PARA 231.
4   Proceeds of Crime Act 2002 s 8(2)(a).
5   Proceeds of Crime Act 2002 s 8(2)(b). As to the meaning of 'property' and as to when property is 'obtained' see PARAS 226, 223 note 1.
6   Proceeds of Crime Act 2002 s 8(3)(a). As to 'criminal conduct' and 'general criminal conduct' see PARA 225.
7   Ie a confiscation order under the Proceeds of Crime Act 2002 s 8(5).
8   Proceeds of Crime Act 2002 s 8(3)(b).
9   Proceeds of Crime Act 2002 s 8(3)(c).
10 Proceeds of Crime Act 2002 s 8(4).
11 Proceeds of Crime Act 2002 s 8(5)(a). However, s 8(5) does not apply to an amount which has been taken into account for the purposes of a deduction under s 8(5) on any earlier occasion: s 8(6).
12 Ie (by virtue of the Proceeds of Crime Act 2002 s 8(7)(a)–(h)) made under:
    (1)   the Drug Trafficking Offences Act 1986 (repealed);
    (2)   the Criminal Justice (Scotland) Act 1987 Pt 1 (repealed);
    (3)   the Criminal Justice Act 1988 Pt 6 (repealed);
    (4)   the Criminal Justice (Confiscation) (Northern Ireland) Order 1990, SI 1990/2588 (NI 17) (repealed);
    (5)   the Drug Trafficking Act 1994 Pt 1 (repealed);

(6) the Proceeds of Crime (Scotland) Act 1995 Pt 1 (repealed);
(7) the Proceeds of Crime (Northern Ireland) Order 1996, SI 1996/1299 (NI 9) (repealed); and
(8) the Proceeds of Crime Act 2002 Pt 3 or Pt 4 (confiscation orders: Scotland and Northern Ireland).

The reference to general criminal conduct in the case of a confiscation order made under any of the provisions listed in the Proceeds of Crime Act 2002 s 8(7) is a reference to conduct in respect of which a court is required or entitled to make one or more assumptions for the purpose of assessing a person's benefit from the conduct: s 8(8).

13 Proceeds of Crime Act 2002 s 8(5)(b).

225. 'Criminal conduct'. 'Criminal conduct' is conduct which constitutes an offence in England and Wales[1] or would constitute such an offence if it occurred in England and Wales[2]. 'General criminal conduct' of the defendant is all his criminal conduct, and it is immaterial when[3] the conduct occurred[4] or when[5] property constituting a benefit from conduct was obtained[6]. 'Particular criminal conduct' of the defendant is all his criminal conduct which falls within the following:

(1) conduct which constitutes the offence or offences concerned[7];
(2) conduct which constitutes offences of which he was convicted in the same proceedings as those in which he was convicted of the offence or offences concerned[8]; and
(3) conduct which constitutes offences which the court will be taking into consideration in deciding his sentence for the offence or offences concerned[9].

Conduct which constitutes an offence which was committed before 24 March 2003[10] is not 'particular criminal conduct' for these purposes[11].

1 Proceeds of Crime Act 2002 s 76(1)(a).
2 Proceeds of Crime Act 2002 s 76(1)(b).
3 Ie whether the conduct occurred before or after the passing of the Proceeds of Crime Act 2002: s 76(2)(a). The Act was passed, ie received the Royal Assent, on 24 July 2002.
4 Proceeds of Crime ACT 2002 s 76(2)(a).
5 Ie whether the property was obtained before or after 24 July 2002 (see note 3): Proceeds of Crime Act 2002 s 76(2)(b).
6 Proceeds of Crime Act 2002 s 76(2)(b). As to 'property', and property being 'obtained', see PARA 226. As to when a person benefits from conduct see PARAS 223–224.
7 Proceeds of Crime Act 2002 s 76(3)(a).
8 Proceeds of Crime Act 2002 s 76(3)(b).
9 Proceeds of Crime Act 2002 s 76(3)(c).
10 Ie the date on which the Proceeds of Crime Act 2002 Pt 2 was brought into force: see PARA 189.
11 Proceeds of Crime Act 2002 (Commencement No 5, Transitional Provisions, Savings and Amendment) Order 2003, art 9.

226. 'Property', 'holding' property and cognate expressions. 'Property' is all property wherever situated and includes money, all forms of real or personal property, and things in action and other intangible or incorporeal property[1]. Property is 'obtained' by a person if he obtains an interest in it[2] (that is to say, if he 'owns' it, which connotes a power of disposition or control[3]), and is 'held' by a person if he holds an interest in it[4]; and references to property 'held' by a person also include references to property vested in his trustee in bankruptcy, permanent or interim trustee[5] or liquidator[6]. Provision is made for determining the extent of a person's interest in property in which another persons holds or may hold an interest[7].

References to an interest held by a person beneficially in property include references to an interest which would be held by him beneficially if the property were not so vested[8]. References to an 'interest' in relation to land are references to any legal estate or equitable interest or power (in relation to land in England and Wales or Northern Ireland)[9] or to any estate, interest, servitude or other heritable right in or over land, including a heritable security (in relation to land in Scotland)[10]; and, in relation to property other than land, references to an 'interest' include references to a right (including a right to possession)[11]. Property is 'transferred' by one person to another if the first one transfers or grants an interest in it to the second[12]. Debts and contingent interests under a will fall within the definition of 'property' for these purposes, as do interests in unadministered estates and choses in action of a personal nature such as a right of action in damages[13].

'Realisable property' is any free property held by the defendant[14] and any free property held by the recipient of a tainted gift[15]. Property is 'free'[16] unless there is in force in respect of it a forfeiture order relating to drugs[17] or terrorism offences[18] or a specified order relating to the confiscation of criminal proceeds[19], or it has been forfeited or detained in pursuance of a forfeiture notice[20].

Once property has been identified as 'realisable' it may be recovered from any trust or company irrespective of any legal obstacles or protection for the benefit of the defendant which would otherwise arise under the relevant law[21].

1   Proceeds of Crime Act 2002 s 84(1). In connection with gifts (and tainted gifts) as property see PARAS 227–228. A pension policy is 'property' for these purposes, although the valuation of such policies for confiscation purposes is problematic: see *R v Chen* [2009] EWCA Crim 2669, [2010] 2 Cr App Rep (S) 221.

2   Proceeds of Crime Act 2002 s 84(2)(b). An offender 'obtains' property (ie within the meaning of s 76(4): see PARA 223) if he takes possession of it, even if only on a temporary basis: see *R v Stanley* [2007] EWCA Crim 2857, [2008] 2 Cr App Rep (S) 107.

3   See *R v May* [2008] UKHL 28, [2008] 1 AC 1028, [2008] 4 All ER 97 (a mere courier or custodian, rewarded by a specific fee and having no interest in the property or the proceeds of sale, is unlikely to be found to have 'obtained' the property). See also *R v Clark* [2011] EWCA Crim 15, [2011] 2 Cr App Rep (S) 319, [2011] All ER (D) 199 (Jan) (bailee who played an important role in a handling conspiracy did not necessarily 'obtain' property).

4   Proceeds of Crime Act 2002 s 84(2)(a).

5   Ie within the meaning of the Bankruptcy (Scotland) Act 1985.

6   Proceeds of Crime Act 2002 s 84(2)(d).

7   In the Proceeds of Crime Act 2002 Pt 2 (ss 6–91) the 'extent' of the defendant's interest in property means the proportion that the value of the defendant's interest in it bears to the value of the property itself: Proceeds of Crime Act 2002 s 10A(5) (s 10A added by the Serious Crime Act 2015 s 1). Where it appears to a court making a confiscation order that there is property held by the defendant that is likely to be realised or otherwise used to satisfy the order and a person other than the defendant holds, or may hold, an interest in the property, the court may, if it thinks it appropriate to do so, determine the extent (at the time the confiscation order is made) of the defendant's interest in the property: Proceeds of Crime Act 2002 s 10A(1) (as so added). The court must not exercise this power unless it gives to anyone who the court thinks is or may be a person holding an interest in the property a reasonable opportunity to make representations to it: s 10A(2) (as so added). A determination under s 10A is conclusive in relation to any question as to the extent of the defendant's interest in the property that arises in connection with the realisation of the property, or the transfer of an interest in the property, with a view to satisfying the confiscation order, or any action or proceedings taken for the purposes of any such realisation or transfer (s 10A(3) (as so added)), although this is subject to s 51(8B) (see PARA 250) and does not apply in relation to a question that arises in proceedings before the Court of Appeal or the Supreme Court (s 10A(4) (as so added)).

8   Proceeds of Crime Act 2002 s 84(2)(e).

9   Proceeds of Crime Act 2002 s 84(2)(f).

10 Proceeds of Crime Act 2002 s 84(2)(g).

11 Proceeds of Crime Act 2002 s 84(2)(h).

12 Proceeds of Crime Act 2002 s 84(2)(c).

13 See *R v Walbrook* (1994) 15 Cr App Rep (S) 783, [1994] Crim LR 613, CA.

14 Proceeds of Crime Act 2002 s 83(a). Debts and loans are 'property held by the defendant' and are therefore realisable property for these purposes: see *R v McQueen* [2001] EWCA Crim 2460.

15 Proceeds of Crime Act 2002 s 83(b).

16 Ie by virtue of the Proceeds of Crime Act 2002 s 82(a)–(f) (s 82(e) amended by the Counter-Terrorism Act 2008 Sch 9 para 7(3); Proceeds of Crime Act 2002 s 82(f) amended by the Serious Organised Crime and Police Act 2005 Sch 6 paras 4, 5)).

17 Ie an order under the Misuse of Drugs Act 1971 s 27 (see MEDICAL PRODUCTS AND DRUGS vol 75 (2013) PARA 526).

18 Ie an order under the Terrorism Act 2000 s 23, s 23A (see PARA 301) or s 111 (Northern Ireland only).

19 Ie an order under the Powers of Criminal Courts (Sentencing) Act 2000 s 143 (deprivation orders: see PARA 470); the Proceeds of Crime Act 2002 s 245A (property freezing order: see CRIMINAL PROCEDURE vol 28 (2015) PARA 914), s 246 (application for interim receiving order: see CRIMINAL PROCEDURE vol 28 (2015) PARA 917), s 255A (application for prohibitory property order: applies in Scotland only), s 256 (application for interim administration order: applies in Scotland only), s 266 (civil recovery order: see CRIMINAL PROCEDURE vol 28 (2015) PARA 921), s 295(2) (order for detention of seized cash: see CRIMINAL PROCEDURE vol 28 (2015) PARA 936) or s 298(2) (order for forfeiture of detained cash: see CRIMINAL PROCEDURE vol 28 (2015) PARA 940); the Criminal Justice (Northern Ireland) Order 1994, SI 1994/2795 (NI 15) art 11; or the Proceeds of Crime (Scotland) Act 1995 Pt 2.

20 Proceeds of Crime Act 2002 s 82(1)–(3) (s 82(1), (3) added, s 82(2) numbered and amended, by the Policing and Crime Act 2009 Sch 7 para 101). The reference to forfeiture under a forfeiture notice is a reference to forfeiture under a notice under the Proceeds of Crime Act 2002 s 297A, s 297C or s 297D (see CRIMINAL PROCEDURE vol 28 (2015) PARA 938).

21 See *Revenue and Customs Prosecutions Office v May* [2009] EWHC 1826 (QB), [2009] STC 2466 (revsd, but not so as to challenge the stated principle [2010] EWCA Civ 521, [2010] 3 All ER 1173, [2010] STC 1506).

227. 'Gifts'. If the defendant[1] transfers property[2] to another person for a consideration whose value is significantly less than the value of the property at the time of the transfer, he is to be treated as making a gift[3], and if this provision applies the property given is to be treated as such share in the property transferred as is represented by the fraction whose numerator is the difference between those two values[4] and whose denominator is the value of the property at the time of the transfer[5].

1 As to the meaning of 'defendant' see PARA 221 note 1.
2 As to the meaning of 'property' see PARA 227.
3 Proceeds of Crime Act 2002 s 78(1).
4 Ie the two values mentioned in the Proceeds of Crime Act 2002 s 78(1) (see the text and notes 1–3).
5 Proceeds of Crime Act 2002 s 78(2).

228. 'Tainted gifts'. Where no court has made a decision as to whether the defendant[1] has a criminal lifestyle[2], or a court has decided that the defendant has a criminal lifestyle[3], a gift is 'tainted'[4] if:

(1) it was made by the defendant at any time after the first day of the period of six years ending with the day when proceedings for the offence concerned were started[5] against the defendant ('the relevant day')[6]; or

(2) if it was made by the defendant at any time and was of property which was obtained[7] by the defendant as a result of or in connection with his general criminal conduct[8] or which (in whole or part and whether directly or indirectly) represented in the defendant's hands property obtained by him as a result of or in connection with his general criminal conduct[9].

Where a court has decided that the defendant does not have a criminal lifestyle, a gift is tainted if it was made by the defendant at any time after the date on which the offence concerned was committed[10] or, if his particular criminal conduct consists of two or more offences and they were committed on different dates, the date of the earliest[11].

1   As to the meaning of 'defendant' see PARA 221 note 1.
2   Proceeds of Crime Act 2002 s 77(1)(a). As to when a defendant has a criminal lifestyle see PARA 229.
3   Proceeds of Crime Act 2002 s 77(1)(b).
4   As to the meaning of 'gift' see PARA 227. A gift may be a tainted gift under these provisions whether it was made before or after 24 July 2002 (that is, the date on which the Proceeds of Crime Act 2002 was passed (ie received Royal Assent)): s 77(8). In connection with tainted gifts see eg *Revenue and Customs Prosecution Office v Backhouse* [2012] EWCA Civ 1000, [2012] All ER (D) 227 (Jul).
5   As to when proceedings for an offence are started and concluded see PARA 199.
6   Proceeds of Crime Act 2002 s 77(2), (9)(a). If there are two or more offences and proceedings for them were started on different days, the relevant day is the earliest of those days: s 77(9)(b).
7   As to 'property' and when property is 'obtained' see PARA 226.
8   Proceeds of Crime Act 2002 s 77(3)(a). As to the meanings of 'criminal conduct' and 'general criminal conduct' see PARA 225.
9   Proceeds of Crime Act 2002 s 77(3)(b).
10 Proceeds of Crime Act 2002 s 77(4), (5)(a).
11 Proceeds of Crime Act 2002 s 77(5)(b). For these purposes, an offence which is a continuing offence is committed on the first occasion when it is committed (s 77(6)); and the defendant's particular criminal conduct includes any conduct which constitutes offences which the court has taken into consideration in deciding his sentence for the offence or offences concerned (s 77(7)). As to 'particular criminal conduct' see PARA 225.

229.   'Criminal lifestyle'. A defendant[1] has a criminal lifestyle if, and only if, the offence (or any of the offences) concerned[2] satisfies any of the following tests:

(1)   it is a lifestyle offence[3];
(2)   it constitutes conduct forming part of a course of criminal activity[4];
(3)   it is an offence committed over a period of at least six months and the defendant has benefited from the conduct which constitutes the offence[5].

Conduct forms part of a course of criminal activity if the defendant has benefited from the conduct and (a) in the proceedings in which he was convicted he was convicted of three or more other offences, each of three or more of them constituting conduct from which he has benefited[6]; or (b) in the period of six years ending with the day when those proceedings were started (or, if there is more than one such day, the earliest day) he was convicted on at least two separate occasions of an offence constituting conduct from which he has benefited[7].

1   As to the meaning of 'defendant' see PARA 221 note 1.
2   References to the offence (or offences) concerned are references to the offence (or offences) mentioned in the Proceeds of Crime Act 2002 s 6(2) (see PARA 221): ss 6(9), 88(1).
3   See the Proceeds of Crime Act 2002 s 75(1), (2)(a). As to lifestyle offences see PARA 230.
4   Proceeds of Crime Act 2002 s 75(2)(b). An offence does not satisfy the test in s 75(2)(b) unless the defendant obtains relevant benefit of not less than £5,000: s 75(4). The Secretary of State may by order vary the amount for the time being specified in s 75(4): s 75(8). At the date at which this volume states the law no such order had been made. 'Relevant benefit' for the purposes of s 75(2)(b) is: (1) benefit from conduct which constitutes the offence (s 75(5)(a)); (2) benefit from any other conduct which forms part of the course of criminal activity and which constitutes an offence of which the defendant has been convicted (s 75(5)(b)); and (3) benefit from conduct which constitutes an offence which has been or will be taken into consideration by the court in sentencing the defendant for an offence mentioned in head (1) or head (2) (s 75(5)(c)). Where the court is applying the rule in s 75(5) on the calculation of relevant benefit for the purposes of determining whether or not the test in s 75(2)(b) is satisfied by virtue of conduct forming part of a course of criminal activity under s 75(3)(a), the court must not take

into account benefit from conduct constituting an offence mentioned in s 75(5)(c) which was committed before 24 March 2003: Proceeds of Crime Act 2002 (Commencement No 5, Transitional Provisions, Savings and Amendment) Order 2003, SI 2003/333, art 7(3) (art 7 substituted by SI 2003/531). Where the court is applying the rule in the Proceeds of Crime Act 2002 s 75(5) on the calculation of relevant benefit for the purposes of determining whether or not the test in s 75(2)(b) is satisfied by virtue of conduct forming part of a course of criminal activity under s 75(3)(b), the court may take into account benefit from conduct constituting an offence committed before 24 March 2003: Proceeds of Crime Act 2002 (Commencement No 5, Transitional Provisions, Savings and Amendment) Order 2003, SI 2003/333, art 7(5) (as so substituted). As to the scope of the legislation governing confiscation orders see PARA 189.

5   Proceeds of Crime Act 2002 s 75(2)(c). See *R v Takkar* [2011] EWCA Crim 646, [2011] 3 All ER 340, [2011] 1 WLR 3062 (several separate offences involving non-payment of tax); *R v Bajwa* [2011] EWCA Crim 1093, [2012] 1 All ER 348, [2012] 1 WLR 601 (concerning the six-month period referred to in the text). An offence does not satisfy the test in the Proceeds of Crime Act 2002 s 75(2)(c) unless the defendant obtains relevant benefit of not less than £5,000: s 75(4). The Secretary of State may by order vary the amount for the time being specified in s 75(4): s 75(8). At the date at which this volume states the law no such order had been made. 'Relevant benefit' for the purposes of s 75(2)(c) is: (1) benefit from conduct which constitutes the offence (s 75(6)(a)); and (2) benefit from conduct which constitutes an offence which has been or will be taken into consideration by the court in sentencing the defendant for the offence mentioned in head (1) (s 75(6)(b)). Where the court is applying the rule in s 75(6) on the calculation of relevant benefit for the purposes of determining whether or not the test in s 75(2)(c) is satisfied, the court must not take into account benefit from conduct constituting an offence mentioned in s 75(6)(b) which was committed before 24 March 2003: Proceeds of Crime Act 2002 (Commencement No 5, Transitional Provisions, Savings and Amendment) Order 2003, SI 2003/333, art 7(6) (as substituted: see note 4).

6   Proceeds of Crime Act 2002 s 75(3)(a). Where the court is determining whether the defendant has a criminal lifestyle conduct does not form part of a course of criminal activity under s 75(3)(a) where any of the three or more offences mentioned in s 75(3)(a) was committed before 24 March 2003: Proceeds of Crime Act 2002 (Commencement No 5, Transitional Provisions, Savings and Amendment) Order 2003, SI 2003/333, art 7(1), (2) (as substituted: see note 4).

7   Proceeds of Crime Act 2002 s 75(3)(b). Conduct forms part of a course of criminal activity under s 75(3)(b), notwithstanding that any of the offences of which the defendant was convicted on at least two separate occasions in the period mentioned in s 75(3)(b) was committed before 24 March 2003: Proceeds of Crime Act 2002 (Commencement No 5, Transitional Provisions, Savings and Amendment) Order 2003, SI 2003/333, art 7(4) (as substituted: see note 4). As to when proceedings for an offence are started and concluded see PARA 199.

230.   Lifestyle offences.   The following are 'lifestyle offences' under the Proceeds of Crime Act 2002:

(1)   a specified drug trafficking offence[1];
(2)   a money laundering offence in relation to concealing criminal property[2] or assisting another to retain criminal property[3];
(3)   an offence of directing the activities of a terrorist organisation[4];
(4)   a specified offence involving slavery, servitude and forced or compulsory labour[5];
(5)   a specified people trafficking offence[6];
(6)   a specified arms trafficking offence[7];
(7)   a specified counterfeiting offence[8];
(8)   a specified offence relating to intellectual property[9];
(9)   a specified offence relating to prostitution and child sex[10];
(10)   the offence of blackmail[11];
(11)   an offence[12] of acting as a gangmaster other than under the authority of a licence and of being in possession of false documents etc[13];
(12)   a specified inchoate offence[14].

1   Proceeds of Crime Act 2002 Sch 2 para 1(1)–(3). The offences referred to are: (1) an offence under the Misuse of Drugs Act 1971 s 4(2) or (3) (unlawful production or supply of controlled

drugs), s 5(3) (possession of controlled drug with intent to supply), s 8 (permitting certain activities relating to controlled drugs), or s 20 (assisting in or inducing the commission outside the United Kingdom of an offence punishable under a corresponding law (see CRIMINAL LAW vol 26 (2010) PARAS 725, 730, 732); (2) an offence under the Customs and Excise Management Act 1979 s 50(2) or (3) (improper importation of goods), s 68(2) (exportation of prohibited or restricted goods), or s 170 (fraudulent evasion) (see CUSTOMS AND EXCISE vol 31 (2012) PARAS 992, 1027, 1175) (in each case, if it is committed in connection with a prohibition or restriction on importation or exportation which has effect by virtue of the Misuse of Drugs Act 1971 s 3 (see MEDICAL PRODUCTS AND DRUGS vol 75 (2013) PARA 491)); or (3) an offence under the Criminal Justice (International Co-operation) Act 1990 s 12 (manufacture or supply of controlled substances) or s 19 (using a ship for illicit traffic in controlled drugs) (see CRIMINAL LAW vol 26 (2010) PARAS 726, 733).

2   Ie an offence under the Proceeds of Crime Act 2002 s 327 (see CRIMINAL LAW vol 26 (2010) PARA 744).

3   Proceeds of Crime Act 2002 Sch 2 para 2. As to 'property' see PARA 226. An offence of assisting another to retain criminal property mentioned in the text is an offence under the Proceeds of Crime Act 2002 s 328 (see CRIMINAL LAW vol 26 (2010) PARA 745). Money laundering offences do not constitute a special category of offence to which a separate approach to confiscation orders should apply: *R v Allpress* [2009] EWCA Crim 8, [2009] 2 Cr App Rep (S) 399, [2009] All ER (D) 126 (Jan).

4   Proceeds of Crime Act 2002 Sch 2 para 3. An offence of directing the activities of a terrorist organisation is an offence under the Terrorism Act 2000 s 56 (see CRIMINAL LAW vol 25 (2010) PARA 403).

5   Proceeds of Crime Act 2002 Sch 2 para 3A (added by the Modern Slavery Act 2015 s 7(1), (2)). This is an offence under the Modern Slavery Act 2015 s 1: see CRIMINAL LAW.

6   Proceeds of Crime Act 2002 Sch 2 para 4(1), (4) (Sch 2 para 4 substituted by the Nationality, Immigration and Asylum Act 2002 Sch 7 para 31; Proceeds of Crime Act 2002 Sch 2 para 4(4) added by the Modern Slavery Act 2015 s 7(3)). The offences referred to are assisting unlawful immigration under the Immigration Act 1971 s 25, s 25A or s 25B (see IMMIGRATION AND ASYLUM vol 57 (2012) PARAS 213–215, 235) and human trafficking under the Modern Slavery Act 2015 s 2 (see CRIMINAL LAW).

7   Proceeds of Crime Act 2002 Sch 2 para 5(1), (2). The offences referred to are: (1) an offence under the Customs and Excise Management Act 1979 s 68(2) (exportation of prohibited goods) or s 170 (fraudulent evasion: see CUSTOMS AND EXCISE vol 31 (2012) PARAS 1027, 1175) if it is committed in connection with a firearm or ammunition; and (2) an offence under the Firearms Act 1968 s 3(1) (dealing in firearms or ammunition by way of trade or business: see CRIMINAL LAW vol 26 (2010) PARA 584). As to the meanings of 'firearm' and 'ammunition' see the Firearms Act 1968 s 57; and CRIMINAL LAW vol 26 (2010) PARAS 578, 582 (definitions applied by the Proceeds of Crime Act 2002 Sch 2 para 5(3)).

8   Proceeds of Crime Act 2002 Sch 2 para 6(a)–(d). The offences referred to are offences under the Forgery and Counterfeiting Act 1981 s 14 (making counterfeit notes or coins), s 15 (passing etc counterfeit notes or coins), s 16 (having counterfeit notes or coins), and s 17 (making or possessing materials or equipment for counterfeiting) (see CRIMINAL LAW vol 26 (2010) PARAS 476–479).

9   Proceeds of Crime Act 2002 Sch 2 para 7(1), (2). The offences referred to are: (1) an offence under the Copyright, Designs and Patents Act 1988 s 107(1) (making or dealing in an article which infringes copyright), s 107(2) (making or possessing an article designed or adapted for making a copy of a copyright work), s 198(1) (making or dealing in an illicit recording); and s 297A (making or dealing in unauthorised decoders) (see COPYRIGHT vol 23 (2013) PARAS 984, 1261); and (2) an offence under the Trade Marks Act 1994 s 92(1), (2) or (3) (unauthorised use etc of trade mark: see TRADE MARKS AND TRADE NAMES vol 97A (2014) PARAS 124–126).

10   Proceeds of Crime Act 2002 Sch 2 para 8(1), (2) (Sch 2 para 8 substituted by the Sexual Offences Act 2003 Sch 6 para 46(1), (3); and amended by the Serious Crime Act 2015 Sch 4 para 58). The offences referred to are: (1) an offence under the Sexual Offences Act 1956 s 33 or s 34 (keeping or letting premises for use as a brothel: see CRIMINAL LAW vol 25 (2010) PARAS 244, 246); and (2) an offence under the Sexual Offences Act 2003 s 14 (arranging or facilitating commission of a child sex offence), s 48 (causing or inciting sexual exploitation of a child), s 49 (controlling a child in relation to sexual exploitation), s 50 (arranging or facilitating sexual exploitation of a child), s 52 (causing or inciting prostitution for gain) and s 53 (controlling prostitution for gain) (see CRIMINAL LAW vol 25 (2010) PARAS 191, 229, 230).

11   Proceeds of Crime Act 2002 Sch 2 para 9. The offence of blackmail mentioned in the text is an offence under the Theft Act 1968 s 21 (see CRIMINAL LAW vol 25 (2010) PARA 304).

12 Ie an offence under the Gangmasters (Licensing) Act 2004 s 12(1) or (2) (see AGRICULTURAL
    PRODUCTION AND MARKETING vol 1 (2008) PARA 1253).
13 Proceeds of Crime Act 2002 Sch 2 para 9A (added by the Gangmasters (Licensing) Act 2004
    s 14(4)).
14 Proceeds of Crime Act 2002 Sch 2 para 10(1), (1A), (2) (Sch 2 para 10(1A) added by the Serious
    Crime Act 2007 Sch 6 para 62). The offences referred to are: (1) an offence of attempting,
    conspiring or inciting the commission of a lifestyle offence; (2) an offence under the Serious
    Crime Act 2007 s 44 (doing an act capable of encouraging or assisting in the commission of a
    specified offence: see CRIMINAL LAW vol 25 (2010) PARA 65); or (3) an offence of aiding,
    abetting, counselling or procuring the commission of such an offence.

231.   Assumptions to made in case of criminal lifestyle. If the court decides[1]
that the defendant[2] has a criminal lifestyle[3], it must make the following four
assumptions for the purpose of deciding whether he has benefited from his
general criminal conduct[4] and deciding his benefit from the conduct[5]. The first
assumption is that any property transferred to the defendant at any time after the
relevant day[6] was obtained by him as a result of his general criminal conduct[7]
and at the earliest time he appears to have held it[8]. The second assumption is
that any property held by the defendant at any time after the date of conviction[9]
was obtained by him as a result of his general criminal conduct[10] and at the
earliest time he appears to have held it[11]. The third assumption is that any
expenditure incurred by the defendant at any time after the relevant day was met
from property obtained by him as a result of his general criminal conduct[12]. The
fourth assumption is that, for the purpose of valuing any property obtained[13] (or
assumed to have been obtained) by the defendant, he obtained it free of any
other interests in it[14]. The court must not, however, make a required assumption
in relation to particular property or expenditure if the assumption is shown to be
incorrect[15] or if there would be a serious risk of injustice[16] if the assumption
were made[17]. If the court does not make one or more of the required
assumptions it must state its reasons[18].

1   Ie if the court decides under the Proceeds of Crime Act 2002 s 6 (see PARA 221).
2   As to the meaning of 'defendant' see PARA 221 note 1.
3   As to when a defendant has a criminal lifestyle see PARA 229.
4   Proceeds of Crime Act 2002 s 10(1)(a). As to the meanings of 'criminal conduct' and 'general
    criminal conduct' see PARA 225.
5   Proceeds of Crime Act 2002 s 10(1)(b).
6   For the purposes of the Proceeds of Crime Act 2002 s 10, the 'relevant day' is the first day of the
    period of six years ending with the day when proceedings for the offence concerned were started
    against the defendant (s 10(8)(a)) or if there are two or more offences and proceedings for them
    were started on different days, the earliest of those days (s 10(8)(b)); however, if a confiscation
    order mentioned in s 8(3)(c) has been made against the defendant at any time during the period
    mentioned in s 10(8), then the relevant day is the day when the defendant's benefit was
    calculated for the purposes of the last such confiscation order (s 10(9)(a)) and the second
    assumption does not apply to any property which was held by him on or before the relevant day
    (s 10(9)(b)). As to when proceedings for an offence are started and concluded see PARA 199.
7   Proceeds of Crime Act 2002 s 10(2)(a). In connection with the assumption under s 10(2) see *R v
    Ernest* [2014] EWCA Crim 1312, 178 CL & J 429, [2014] All ER (D) 65 (Jul).
8   Proceeds of Crime Act 2002 s 10(2)(b).
9   The date of conviction is the date on which the defendant was convicted of the offence
    concerned (Proceeds of Crime Act 2002 s 10(10)(a)) or if there are two or more offences and the
    convictions were on different dates, the date of the latest (s 10(10)(b)).
10 Proceeds of Crime Act 2002 s 10(3)(a).
11 Proceeds of Crime Act 2002 s 10(3)(b).
12 Proceeds of Crime Act 2002 s 10(4).
13 As to deciding the value of property see PARA 232.
14 Proceeds of Crime Act 2002 s 10(5).
15 Proceeds of Crime Act 2002 s 10(6)(a).

16 'Serious risk of injustice' does not mean hardship to the defendant by virtue of the order: see *R v Jones* [2006] EWCA Crim 2061, [2007] 1 WLR 7, [2007] 1 Cr App Rep (S) 414 (the purpose of the Proceeds of Crime Act 2002 s 10(6) is not to provide for the exercise of discretion by the judge to determine whether it is fair to make the order against a particular defendant, but rather to ensure a sensible calculation of the benefit and to ensure that the assumptions are not so unreasonable or unjust in respect of the particular defendant that they should not be made); and see also *R v Singh* [2008] EWCA Crim 243, [2008] 2 Cr App Rep (S) 387. The risk of injustice must arise from the operation of the assumption in the calculation of benefit and not from eventual hardship in the making of the confiscation order: see *R v Dore* [1997] 2 Cr App Rep (S) 152, [1997] Crim LR 299, CA; *R v Ahmed* [2004] EWCA Crim 2599, [2005] 1 All ER 128, [2005] 1 WLR 122.

17 Proceeds of Crime Act 2002 s 10(6)(b).

18 Proceeds of Crime Act 2002 s 10(7).

232. Value of property. The basic rule for the purpose of deciding the value at any time of property then held[1] by a person[2] is that its value is the market value[3] of the property at that time[4].

For the purpose of deciding the value of property obtained by a person as a result of, or in connection with, his criminal conduct[5], and for the purposes of determining the value of tainted gifts[6], the value of the property at the material time[7] and the value at any time of a tainted gift is the greater of[8]:

(1)   the value[9] of the property (at the time the person obtained it), or the value[10] (at the time of the gift) of the property given, adjusted to take account of later changes in the value of money[11];

(2)   the value (at the material time) of the property found:

(a)   if the person holds the property obtained, or if the recipient holds the property given, the property found is that property[12];

(b)   if he holds no part of the property obtained, or the recipient holds no part of the property given, the property found is any property which directly or indirectly represents it in his hands[13]; and

(c)   if he holds part of the property obtained, or if the recipient holds part of the property given, the property found is that part and any property which directly or indirectly represents the other part in his hands[14].

1   As to the meaning of 'property' and as to when property is 'held' by a person see PARA 226.

2   Proceeds of Crime Act 2002 s 79(1). It is not a pre-requisite in establishing the market value of goods that the market in question is a lawful one, and hence the black market value of goods can be taken into account when valuing the benefit obtained by the defendant from their illegal importation, pursuant to ss 76(4), (7), 79(2), 80(2): see *R v Islam* [2009] UKHL 30, [2009] AC 1076, [2010] 1 All ER 493 (overruling *R v Hussain* [2006] EWCA Crim 621, [2006] All ER (D) 395 (Feb)). It is also consistent with both the language and the spirit of the Proceeds of Crime Act 2002 to take account of the black market value of goods when valuing the benefit obtained by the defendant from their illegal importation, even if such goods had a nil market value after seizure for the purposes of assessing the amount available for confiscation: *R v Islam*. The Proceeds of Crime Act 2002 s 79 has effect subject to ss 80, 81: s 79(5).

3   The market value of property is the amount it would have cost the defendant to obtain the property legitimately, or the economic value to the loser, rather than the value the defendant could obtain if he sold it: *R v Rose, R v Whitwam* [2008] EWCA Crim 239, [2008] 3 All ER 315, [2008] 2 Cr App Rep 202. 'Market value' includes 'black market' value, in the context of unlawful products: see *R v Islam* [2009] UKHL 30, [2009] AC 1076, [2010] 1 All ER 493.

4   Proceeds of Crime Act 2002 s 79(2). However, if at that time another person holds an interest in the property, its value, in relation to the person mentioned in s 79(1), is the market value of his interest at that time: s 79(3). Section 79(3) is concerned with the valuation of property, not with its realisation, and does not require the court to assume that a beneficial interest has to be sold separately as such: see *R v Modjiri* [2010] EWCA Crim 829, [2010] 4 All ER 837, [2011] 1 Cr App Rep (S) 137. For the purposes of calculating market value under the Proceeds of Crime Act 2002 s 79(3), ignoring any charging order under the Drug Trafficking Offences Act 1986 s 9 (repealed), the Criminal Justice Act 1988 s 78 (repealed), the Criminal Justice (Confiscation)

(Northern Ireland) Order 1990, SI 1990/2588 (NI 17), art 14 (revoked), the Drug Trafficking Act 1994 s 27 (repealed), or the Proceeds of Crime (Northern Ireland) Order 1996, SI 1996/1299 (NI 9), art 32 (revoked), is to be ignored: see the Proceeds of Crime Act 2002 s 79(4)(a)–(e).

5   Proceeds of Crime Act 2002 s 80(1). As to the meaning of 'criminal conduct' see PARA 225.

6   As to 'gifts' see PARA 227; as to 'tainted gifts' see PARA 228. In connection with the valuation of tainted gifts see e g *R v Richards* [2008] EWCA Crim 1841; *R v Smith* [2013] EWCA Crim 502, [2014] 1 WLR 898, [2013] 2 Cr App Rep (S) 506.

7   Ie the time the court makes its decision: s 80(1).

8   See the Proceeds of Crime Act 2002 ss 80(2), 81(1).

9   References in the Proceeds of Crime Act 2002 s 80(2)(a) and (b) and s 81(1)(a), (b) to value are to the value found in accordance with s 79: ss 80(4), 81(3).

10   See note 7.

11   Proceeds of Crime Act 2002 ss 80(2)(a), 81(2)(a).

12   Proceeds of Crime Act 2002 ss 80(2)(b), (3)(a), 81(2)(b), (3)(a).

13   Proceeds of Crime Act 2002 ss 80(2)(b), (3)(b), 81(2)(b), (3)(b).

14   Proceeds of Crime Act 2002 ss 80(2)(b), (3)(c), 81(2)(b), (3)(b).

C. DETERMINING THE RECOVERABLE AMOUNT

233. Recoverable and available amounts. For the purposes of making a confiscation order[1] the 'recoverable amount' is an amount equal to the defendant's benefit from the conduct[2] concerned[3]. But if the defendant shows that the available amount is less than that benefit the recoverable amount is the available amount[4] or a nominal amount, if the available amount is nil[5]. If the court decides the available amount, it must include in the confiscation order a statement of its findings as to the matters relevant for deciding that amount[6].

For the purposes of deciding the recoverable amount, the 'available amount' is the aggregate of: (1) the total of the values, at the time the confiscation order is made, of all the free property[7] then held by the defendant minus the total amount payable in pursuance of obligations which then have priority[8]; and (2) the total of the values (at that time) of all tainted gifts[9].

1   Ie for the purposes of the Proceeds of Crime Act 2002 s 6 (see PARA 221).

2   As to the meaning of 'defendant' see PARA 221 note 1. As to when a defendant has benefited see PARAS 223–224. As to 'conduct' see PARA 225.

3   Proceeds of Crime Act 2002 s 7(1). However if s 6(6) or s 6(6A) (see PARA 221) applies the recoverable amount is such amount as the court thinks just but does not exceed the amount found under s 7(1) or (2) as the case may be: s 7(3) (amended by the Prevention of Social Housing Fraud Act 2013 Schedule para 13). In calculating the defendant's benefit from the conduct concerned for the purposes of the Proceeds of Crime Act 2002 s 7(1) there must be ignored any property in respect of which a recovery order is in force under s 266 (see CRIMINAL PROCEDURE vol 28 (2015) PARA 921), any property in respect of which a forfeiture order is in force under s 298(2) (see CRIMINAL PROCEDURE vol 28 (2015) PARA 940), and any property which has been forfeited in pursuance of a forfeiture notice under s 297A (see CRIMINAL PROCEDURE vol 28 (2015) PARA 938): s 7(4) (amended by the Policing and Crime Act 2009 Sch 7 para 100).

4   Proceeds of Crime Act 2002 s 7(2)(a). Placing the onus of proving that the available amount is less than the recoverable amount on the defendant is not incompatible with the concept of a fair hearing under the Convention for the Protection of Human Rights and Fundamental Freedoms (Rome, 4 November 1950; TS 71 (1953; Cmd 8969) (the European Convention on Human Rights) art 6 (the right to a fair hearing) and Protocol 1 (Paris, 20 March 1952; TS 46; Cmnd 9221) art 1 (the right to peaceful enjoyment of property and possessions): see *Grayson v United Kingdom* (2008) 48 EHRR 722, [2009] Crim LR 200, [2008] All ER (D) 110 (Sep), ECtHR; and RIGHTS AND FREEDOMS vol 88A (2013) PARAS 243–300, 534–547. In connection with the defendant's duty in this matter see *R v Summers* [2008] EWCA Crim 872, [2008] 2 Cr App Rep (S) 569 (decided under corresponding provisions of the Criminal Justice Act 1988), and considering in particular *R v Barwick* [2001] 1 Cr App Rep (S) 129, [2001] Crim LR 52, [2000] All ER (D) 1398, CA; *R v Barnham* [2005] EWCA Crim 1049, [2006] 1 Cr App Rep (S) 83, [2005] Crim LR 657). The Crown Court must have regard to a property adjustment order

which has been made in favour of a third party, such as a spouse, in determining the 'available amount': *Webber v Webber* [2006] EWHC 2893 (Fam), [2007] 1 WLR 1052. See also *Gibson v Revenue and Customs Prosecution Office* [2008] EWCA Civ 645, [2009] QB 348, [2009] 2 WLR 471 (court had no power to supplement provisions of confiscation order legislation to bring wife's share of matrimonial home within confiscation order despite finding she had guilty knowledge of source of husband's wealth); and for a detailed exposition concerning jointly-held matrimonial property see *Jones v Kernott* [2011] UKSC 53, [2012] 1 AC 776, [2012] 1 All ER 1265. In connection with confiscation proceedings and the European Convention on Human Rights see also PARA 222.

5 Proceeds of Crime Act 2002 s 7(2)(b). See, however, s 6(6); and PARA 221.

6 Proceeds of Crime Act 2002 s 7(5).

7 As to when property is 'free' and PARA 226.

8 Proceeds of Crime Act 2002 s 9(1)(a). An obligation has priority if it is an obligation of the defendant: (1) to pay an amount due in respect of a fine or other order of a court which was imposed or made on conviction of an offence and at any time before the time the confiscation order is made (s 9(2)(a)); or (2) to pay a sum which would be included among the preferential debts if the defendant's bankruptcy had commenced on the date of the confiscation order or his winding up had been ordered on that date (s 9(2)(b)). For these purposes, 'preferential debts' has the meaning given by the Insolvency Act 1986 s 386 (see BANKRUPTCY AND INDIVIDUAL INSOLVENCY vol 5 (2013) PARA 591): Proceeds of Crime Act 2002 s 9(3). Irrecoverable debts (even if arising out of an illegal contract) should not be counted against the defendant: see *R v Najafpour* [2009] EWCA Crim 2723, [2010] 2 Cr App Rep (S) 245.

9 Proceeds of Crime Act 2002 s 9(1)(b). As to the value of tainted gifts see s 81; and PARA 232.

234. Time for payment; interest on unpaid sums.

The full amount ordered to be paid under a confiscation order[1] must be paid on the day on which the order is made[2] unless the court making the order is satisfied that the defendant[3] is unable to pay the full amount on that day, in which case it may make an order requiring whatever cannot be paid on that day to be paid in a specified period[4] or in specified periods each of which relates to a specified amount[5]. If within any specified period the defendant applies to the Crown Court for that period to be extended[6] and the court is satisfied that, despite having made all reasonable efforts, the defendant is unable to pay the amount to which the specified period relates within that period[7], the court may make an order extending the period (for all or any part or parts of the amount in question)[8]. Periods specified or extended under these provisions must be such that, where the court believes that a defendant will by a particular day be able to pay the amount remaining to be paid[9], or to pay an amount towards what remains to be paid[10], that amount is required to be paid no later than that day.

If any amount required to be paid by a person under a confiscation order is not paid when it is required to be paid, the person must pay interest on that amount for the period for which it remains unpaid[11]. If an application has been made[12] for a specified period to be extended[13], the application has not been determined by the court[14], and the period of six months starting with the day on which the confiscation order was made has not ended[15], the amount on which interest is payable under these provisions does not include the amount to which the specified period relates[16].

1 Ie an order under the Proceeds of Crime Act 2002 s 6: see PARA 221. As to the 'amount payable' under a confiscation order see PARA 258 note 10.

2 Proceeds of Crime Act 2002 s 11(1) (ss 11, 12(3) substituted by the Serious Crime Act 2007 s 5(1), (2)).

3 As to the meaning of 'defendant' for these purposes see PARA 221 note 1.

4 Proceeds of Crime Act 2002 s 11(2)(a) (as substituted: see note 2). The specified period must start with the day on which the confiscation order is made (s 11(3)(a) (as so substituted)) and must not exceed three months (s 11(3)(b) (as so substituted)). The court should normally set a specific date by which the sum is to be paid: see *R v City of London Justices, ex p Chapman*

(1998) 162 JP 359. The court must not make an order under the Proceeds of Crime Act 2002 s 11(2) unless it gives the prosecutor an opportunity to make representations: s 11(8) (as so substituted).

5   Proceeds of Crime Act 2002 s 11(2)(b) (as substituted: see note 2).
6   Proceeds of Crime Act 2002 s 11(4)(a) (as substituted: see note 2). The court must not make an order under the Proceeds of Crime Act 2002 s 11(4) unless it gives the prosecutor an opportunity to make representations: s 11(8) (as so substituted).
7   Proceeds of Crime Act 2002 s 11(4)(b) (as substituted: see note 2).
8   Such an order may be made after the end of the specified period to which it relates (Proceeds of Crime Act 2002 s 11(6)(a) (as substituted: see note 2)) but must not be made after the end of the period of six months starting with the day on which the confiscation order is made (s 11(6)(b) (as so substituted)). An extended period must start with the day on which the confiscation order is made (s 11(5)(a) (as so substituted)) and must not exceed six months (s 11(5)(b) (as so substituted)).
9   Proceeds of Crime Act 2002 s 11(7)(a) (as substituted: see note 2).
10 Proceeds of Crime Act 2002 s 11(7)(b) (as substituted: see note 2).
11 Proceeds of Crime Act 2002 s 12(1) (amended by the Serious Crime Act 2015 Sch 4 para 20). The rate of interest is the same rate as that for the time being specified in the Judgments Act 1838 s 17 (ie 8% per annum): Proceeds of Crime Act 2002 s 12(2); and see the Judgments Act 1838 s 17 (amended by SI 1993/564). The amount of the interest must be treated as part of the amount to be paid under the confiscation order: Proceeds of Crime Act 2002 s 12(4).
12 Ie under the Proceeds of Crime Act 2002 s 11(4) (see the text and notes 6–7).
13 Proceeds of Crime Act 2002 s 12(3)(a) (as substituted: see note 2).
14 Proceeds of Crime Act 2002 s 12(3)(b) (as substituted: see note 2).
15 Proceeds of Crime Act 2002 s 12(3)(c) (as substituted: see note 2).
16 Proceeds of Crime Act 2002 s 12(3) (as substituted: see note 2).

D. MATTERS WHICH MAKE AMOUNT OF ORDER DISCRETIONARY

235. Victim intends to start proceedings. If the Crown Court decides[1] that the defendant has benefited from criminal conduct it must decide the recoverable amount[2] and make a confiscation order requiring him to pay that amount[3]. The court is, however, required to treat this duty as a power if it believes that any victim of the conduct has at any time started or intends to start proceedings against the defendant in respect of loss, injury or damage sustained in connection with the conduct[4], although nothing in these provisions gives the court power to decline to discharge its duty to make a confiscation order[5].

1   Ie under the Proceeds of Crime Act 2002 s 6(4)(a) or (c): see PARA 221.
2   As to the 'recoverable amount' see PARA 233.
3   See the Proceeds of Crime Act 2002 s 6(5)(b); and PARA 221.
4   Proceeds of Crime Act 2002 s 6(6). If s 6(6) applies, the recoverable amount is such amount as the court believes is just (s 7(3)(a) (s 7(3) amended by the Prevention of Social Housing Fraud Act 2013 Schedule paras 12, 13)) but does not exceed the amount found under the Proceeds of Crime Act 2002 s 7(1) or (2) (as the case may be) (see PARA 233) (s 7(3)(b)). It appears that s 6(6) does not apply where a defendant has voluntarily repaid a victim for loss or damage before the victim has started or expressed an intention to start civil proceedings against him: see *R v Nelson* [2009] EWCA Crim 1573, [2010] QB 678, [2010] 4 All ER 666; and as to civil recovery see the Proceeds of Crime Act 2002 Pt 5 (ss 240–316); and CRIMINAL PROCEDURE vol 28 (2015) PARA 906 et seq.
5   *R v Varma* [2012] UKSC 42, [2013] 1 AC 463, [2013] 1 All ER 129.

236. Criminal unlawful profits order made. If the Crown Court decides[1] that the defendant has benefited from criminal conduct it must decide the recoverable amount[2] and make a confiscation order requiring him to pay that amount[3]. The court is, however, required to treat this duty as a power if either a criminal unlawful profit order[4] has been made, or the court believes such an order may be made, against the defendant in respect of profit made by the defendant in connection with the conduct[5], or the court believes that a person has at any time started or intends to start proceedings against the defendant[6] in respect of such profit[7], although nothing in these provisions gives the court power to decline to discharge its duty to make a confiscation order[8].

1   Ie under the Proceeds of Crime Act 2002 s 6(4)(a) or (c): see PARA 221.
2   As to the 'recoverable amount' see PARA 233.
3   See the Proceeds of Crime Act 2002 s 6(5)(b); and PARA 221.
4   Ie an order under the Prevention of Social Housing Fraud Act 2013 s 4 (see LANDLORD AND TENANT).
5   Proceeds of Crime Act 2002 s 6(6A)(a) (s 6(6A) added, s 7(3) amended, by the Prevention of Social Housing Fraud Act 2013 Schedule paras 12, 13)). If the Proceeds of Crime Act 2002 s 6(6A) applies, the recoverable amount is such amount as the court believes is just (s 7(3)(a) (as so amended)) but does not exceed the amount found under s 7(1) or (2) (as the case may be) (see PARA 233) (s 7(3)(b)).
6   Ie under the Prevention of Social Housing Fraud Act 2013 s 5 (see LANDLORD AND TENANT).
7   Proceeds of Crime Act 2002 s 6(6A)(b) (as added: see note 5).
8   *R v Varma* [2012] UKSC 42, [2013] 1 AC 463, [2013] 1 All ER 129.

E. COMBINED WITH OTHER ORDERS

237.   Effect of confiscation order on court's other powers.   If the court makes a confiscation order[1] it must, in respect of the offence or offences concerned[2]:
  (1)   take account of the confiscation order before it imposes a fine on the defendant[3] or makes another specified financial order[4]; and
  (2)   subject to this, leave the confiscation order out of account in deciding the appropriate sentence for the defendant[5].
Where the Crown Court makes both a confiscation order and one or more priority orders against the same person in the same proceedings[6], and the court believes he will not have sufficient means to satisfy all of those orders in full[7], the court must direct that a specified sum[8] is to be paid out of any sums recovered under the confiscation order[9].

1   Ie an order under the Proceeds of Crime Act 2002 s 6: see PARA 221.
2   As to references to the 'offence or offences concerned' see PARA 229 note 2.
3   Proceeds of Crime Act 2002 s 13(1), (2)(a). As to the meaning of 'defendant' for these purposes see PARA 221 note 1.
4   Proceeds of Crime Act 2002 s 13(2)(b). The orders specified for this purpose are:
    (1)   an order involving payment by the defendant other than an order under the Prosecution of Offences Act 1985 s 21A (criminal courts charge: see CRIMINAL PROCEDURE) or a 'priority order' (ie an order under the Powers of Criminal Courts (Sentencing) Act 2000 s 130 (compensation orders: see PARA 281), an order requiring the payment of a surcharge under the Criminal Justice Act 2003 s 161A, an order under the Prevention of Social Housing Fraud Act 2013 s 4 (unlawful profit orders: see LANDLORD AND TENANT) or (as from a day to be appointed) an order under the Modern Slavery Act 2015 s 8 (slavery and trafficking reparation orders: see CRIMINAL LAW) (Proceeds of Crime Act 2002 s 13(3)(a), (3A) (s 13(3)(a), (6) amended, s 13(3A) added, s 13(5) substituted, by the Serious Crime Act 2015 s 6); Proceeds of Crime Act 2002 s 13(3)(a) further amended by the Criminal Justice and Courts Act 2015 Sch 12 para 11); Proceeds of Crime Act 2002 s 13(3), (5), (6) prospectively further amended by the Modern Slavery Act 2015 Sch 5 para 15));
    (2)   an order under the Misuse of Drugs Act 1971 s 27 (forfeiture orders: see MEDICAL PRODUCTS AND DRUGS vol 75 (2013) PARA 526) (Proceeds of Crime Act 2002 s 13(3)(b));
    (3)   an order under the Powers of Criminal Courts (Sentencing) Act 2000 s 143 (deprivation orders: see PARA 470) (Proceeds of Crime Act 2002 s 13(3)(c)); and
    (4)   an order under the Terrorism Act 2000 ss 23, 23A (forfeiture orders: see PARA 301). (Proceeds of Crime Act 2002 s 13(3)(d) (amended by the Counter-Terrorism Act 2008 Sch 3 para 7(2)).
    The reference in the Proceeds of Crime Act 2002 s 13(2) to 'an order involving payment by the defendant' covers both an order that a defendant pays costs and one under which he does

not: see *R v Constantine* [2010] EWCA Crim 2406, [2011] 3 All ER 767, [2011] 1 WLR 1086. At the date at which this volume states the law no day had been appointed for the coming into force of the amendments made by the Modern Slavery Act 2015.

5   Proceeds of Crime Act 2002 s 13(4).
6   Proceeds of Crime Act 2002 s 13(5)(a) (as substituted and prospectively amended: see note 4).
7   Proceeds of Crime Act 2002 s 13(5)(b) (as substituted and prospectively amended: see note 4).
8   Ie so much of the amount payable under the priority order (or orders) as the court specifies: Proceeds of Crime Act 2002 s 13(6) (as substituted and prospectively amended: see note 4). The amount it specifies must be the amount it believes will not be recoverable because of the insufficiency of the person's means: s 13(6) (as so amended).
9   Proceeds of Crime Act 2002 s 13(6) (as substituted and prospectively amended: see note 4).

(iii) Post-Hearing Matters

238. Enforcement of confiscation orders as fines. Where a court makes a confiscation order[1] the statutory provisions relating to the functions of courts as to fines and enforcing fines[2] apply as if the amount ordered to be paid were a fine imposed on the defendant[3] by the court making the confiscation order[4].

1   Proceeds of Crime Act 2002 s 35(1)(a) (amended by the Serious Crime Act 2007 Sch 8 para 19(2), Sch 14). As to the making of confiscation orders see the Proceeds of Crime Act 2002 s 6; and PARA 221.
2   Ie the Powers of Criminal Courts (Sentencing) Act 2000 ss 139(2), (3), (9), 140(1)–(4) (see PARA 186). See also the modifications set out in the Proceeds of Crime Act 2002 s 35(2A)–(2C) (s 35(2) amended, s 35(2A)–(2C) added, by the Serious Crime Act 2015 s 10(1), Sch 4 para 30).
3   As to the meaning of 'defendant' for these purposes see PARA 221 note 1.
4   Proceeds of Crime Act 2002 s 35(2) (as amended: see note 2). In the application of the Magistrates' Courts Act 1980 Pt 3 (ss 75–96A) (see MAGISTRATES vol 71 (2013) PARA 627 et seq) to an amount payable under a confiscation order: (1) s 75 (power to dispense with immediate payment: see MAGISTRATES vol 71 (2013) PARAS 627, 635, 649) is for these purposes ignored (Proceeds of Crime Act 2002 s 35(3)(a)); (2) such an amount is not a sum adjudged to be paid by a conviction for the purposes of the Magistrates' Courts Act 1980 s 81 (enforcement of fines imposed on young offenders: see MAGISTRATES vol 71 (2013) PARA 683) or a fine for the purposes of s 85 (remission of fines: see MAGISTRATES vol 71 (2013) PARA 675) (Proceeds of Crime Act 2002 s 35(3)(b)); and (3) the Magistrates' Courts Act 1980 s 87(3) (inquiry into means: see MAGISTRATES vol 71 (2013) PARA 682) is for these purposes ignored (Proceeds of Crime Act 2002 s 35(3)(c)).

239. Provisions about imprisonment or detention. Where:

(1)   a warrant committing the defendant[1] to prison or detention is issued for a default in payment of an amount ordered to be paid under a confiscation order[2] in respect of an offence or offences[3]; and

(2)   at the time the warrant is issued the defendant is liable to serve a term of custody in respect of the offence (or any of the offences)[4],

the term of imprisonment or of detention[5] to be served in default of payment of the amount does not begin to run until after the term mentioned in head (2) above[6].

If the defendant serves a term of imprisonment or detention in default of paying any amount due under a confiscation order, his serving that term does not prevent the confiscation order from continuing to have effect so far as any other method of enforcement is concerned[7].

1   As to the meaning of 'defendant' for these purposes see PARA 221 note 1.
2   As to the making of confiscation orders see the Proceeds of Crime Act 2002 s 6; and PARA 221.
3   Proceeds of Crime Act 2002 s 38(1)(a).
4   Proceeds of Crime Act 2002 s 38(1)(b). Where a defendant is sentenced to a period of imprisonment with a confiscation order with a period of imprisonment in default; the principle of totality (see PARA 555) does not apply as between the sentence of imprisonment and the term

in default: see *R v Price* [2009] EWCA Crim 2918, [2010] 2 Cr App Rep (S) 283, [2010] Crim
LR 522. See also *R v Aspinwell* [2010] EWCA Crim 1294, [2011] 1 Cr App Rep (S) 346.
5   Ie detention under the Powers of Criminal Courts (Sentencing) Act 2000 s 108 (prospectively
     repealed) (detention of persons aged 18–20 for default: see PARA 551).
6   Proceeds of Crime Act 2002 s 38(2). The reference in s 38(2) to the term of custody the
     defendant is liable to serve in respect of the offence (or any of the offences) is a reference to the
     term of imprisonment, or detention in a young offender institution, which he is liable to serve in
     respect of the offence (or any of the offences): s 38(3). For these purposes, consecutive terms and
     terms which are wholly or partly concurrent must be treated as a single term and the following
     must be ignored:
     (1)   any sentence suspended under the Criminal Justice Act 2003 s 189(1) (see PARA 100)
            which has not taken effect at the time the warrant is issued (Proceeds of Crime
            Act 2002 s 38(4)(a) (amended by the Criminal Justice Act 2003 s 304, Sch 32
            para 141));
     (2)   in the case of a sentence of imprisonment passed with an order under the Criminal Law
            Act 1977 s 47(1) (repealed) any part of the sentence which the defendant has not at that
            time been required to serve in prison (Proceeds of Crime Act 2002 s 38(4)(b)); and
     (3)   any term of imprisonment or detention fixed under the Powers of Criminal Courts
            (Sentencing) Act 2000 s 139(2) (term to be served in default of payment of fine etc: see
            PARA 186) for which a warrant committing the defendant to prison or detention has not
            been issued at that time (Proceeds of Crime Act 2002 s 38(4)(c)).
7   Proceeds of Crime Act 2002 s 38(5).

240.   Reconsideration etc: variation of prison term.   Where:

(1)   a court varies[1] a confiscation order[2];
(2)   the effect of the variation is to vary the maximum period applicable[3] in
       relation to the order[4]; and
(3)   the result is that that maximum period is less than the term of
       imprisonment or detention fixed[5] in respect of the order[6],

the court must fix[7] a reduced term of imprisonment or detention in respect of the
confiscation order in place of the term previously fixed[8].

Where heads (1) and (2) above apply but head (3) above does not[9], the court
may amend the term of imprisonment or detention fixed[10] in respect of the
confiscation order[11].

If the effect of the provisions[12] on unpaid interest sums is to increase the
maximum period applicable[13] in relation to a confiscation order, the Crown
Court (on the application of the prosecutor[14]) may amend the term of
imprisonment or detention fixed[15] in respect of the order[16].

1   Ie under the Proceeds of Crime Act 2002 s 21 (see PARA 275), s 22 (see PARA 276), s 23 (see PARA
     277), s 29 (see PARA 218), s 32 (see PARA 244) or s 33 (see PARA 245).
2   Proceeds of Crime Act 2002 s 39(1)(a). As to the making of confiscation orders see the Proceeds
     of Crime Act 2002 s 6; and PARA 221.
3   Ie the period applicable under the Powers of Criminal Courts (Sentencing) Act 2000 s 139(4)
     (see PARA 186).
4   Proceeds of Crime Act 2002 s 39(1)(b).
5   Ie under the Powers of Criminal Courts (Sentencing) Act 2000 s 139(2) (see PARA 186).
6   Proceeds of Crime Act 2002 s 39(1)(c).
7   Ie under the Powers of Criminal Courts (Sentencing) Act 2000 s 139(2).
8   Proceeds of Crime Act 2002 s 39(2).
9   Proceeds of Crime Act 2002 s 39(3).
10   Ie under the Powers of Criminal Courts (Sentencing) Act 2000 s 139(2).
11   Proceeds of Crime Act 2002 s 39(4).
12   Ie the Proceeds of Crime Act 2002 s 12 (see PARA 234).
13   Ie under the Powers of Criminal Courts (Sentencing) Act 2000 s 139(4).
14   In connection with applications under the Proceeds of Crime Act 2002 s 39(5) see the Criminal
     Procedure Rules 2015, SI 2015/1490, r 33.21.
15   Ie under the Powers of Criminal Courts (Sentencing) Act 2000 s 139(2).
16   Proceeds of Crime Act 2002 s 39(5).

(iv) Appeals

A. APPEALS BY DEFENDANT

241. Right to appeal. Confiscation orders and orders varying confiscation orders are 'sentences' for the purposes of the Criminal Appeal Act 1968, and accordingly appeals against such orders are governed by the provisions of that Act[1].

1 See the Criminal Appeal Act 1968 s 50(1)(ca), (cb); and PARA 625 et seq.

B. APPEALS BY PROSECUTOR

242. Appeals procedure. An appeal to the Court of Appeal under the provisions relating to confiscation orders[1] lies only with the leave of that court[2]. Subject to rules of court[3], the criminal division of the Court of Appeal is the division to which an appeal to that court under these provisions is to lie[4] and which is to exercise that court's jurisdiction under these provisions[5]. Detailed procedural provision about the bringing of appeals is contained in regulations[6].

1 Ie under the Proceeds of Crime Act 2002 Pt 2 (ss 6–91).
2 Proceeds of Crime Act 2002 s 89(1).
3 Ie rules made under the Senior Courts Act 1981 s 53(1) (distribution of business between civil and criminal divisions: see COURTS AND TRIBUNALS vol 24 (2010) PARAS 693–694).
4 Proceeds of Crime Act 2002 s 89(2)(a) (amended by the Constitutional Reform Act 2005 Sch 11 para 1).
5 Proceeds of Crime Act 2002 s 89(2)(b).
6 See the Proceeds of Crime Act 2002 (Appeals under Part 2) Order 2003, SI 2003/82 (amended by SI 2011/1242; SI 2013/24) (made under the Proceeds of Crime Act 2002 s 89(3)).

243. Appeals by the prosecutor. With specified exceptions[1], if the Crown Court makes a confiscation order[2] the prosecutor may appeal to the Court of Appeal in respect of the order[3].

With specified exceptions[4], if the Crown Court decides not to make a confiscation order the prosecutor may appeal to the Court of Appeal against the decision[5].

An appeal lies to the Court of Appeal against a determination[6] of the extent of the defendant's interest in property[7]. Such an appeal lies at the instance of the prosecutor[8] or[9] a person who the Court of Appeal thinks is or may be a person holding an interest in the property[10], but does not lie where the Court of Appeal believes that an application for the appointment of an enforcement receiver[11] is to be made by the prosecutor[12], such an application has been made but has not yet been determined[13], or a receiver has been[14] appointed[15].

1 The provisions of the Proceeds of Crime Act 2002 s 31(1), (2) (see the text and notes 2–5) do not apply to an order or decision under s 10A (see PARA 226), s 19 (see PARA 273), s 20 (see PARA 274), s 27 (see PARA 216) or s 28 (see PARA 217): Proceeds of Crime Act 2002 s 31(3) (s 31(3) amended, s 31(4)–(8) added, by the Serious Crime Act 2015 s 3(1), Sch 4 para 27(1), (3)).
2 As to the making of confiscation orders see the Proceeds of Crime Act 2002 s 6; and PARA 221.
3 Proceeds of Crime Act 2002 s 31(1). As to appeal by a defendant against the making of a confiscation order see PARA 245.
4 See note 1.
5 Proceeds of Crime Act 2002 s 31(2).
6 Ie a determination under the Proceeds of Crime Act 2002 s 10A (see PARA 226).
7 Proceeds of Crime Act 2002 s 31(4) (as added: see note 1).

8 Proceeds of Crime Act 2002 s 31(5)(a) (as added: see note 1).
9 Ie if either:
    (1)   the person was not given a reasonable opportunity to make representations when the determination was made (Proceeds of Crime Act 2002 s 31(6) (as added: see note 1)); or
    (2)   it appears to the Court of Appeal to be arguable that giving effect to the determination would result in a serious risk of injustice to the person (Proceeds of Crime Act 2002 s 31(7) (as so added)).
10 Proceeds of Crime Act 2002 s 31(5)(b) (as added: see note 1).
11 Ie an application under the Proceeds of Crime Act 2002 s 50 (see PARA 249).
12 Proceeds of Crime Act 2002 s 31(8)(a) (as added: see note 1).
13 Proceeds of Crime Act 2002 s 31(8)(b) (as added: see note 1).
14 Ie under the Proceeds of Crime Act 2002 s 50.
15 Proceeds of Crime Act 2002 s 31(8)(c) (as added: see note 1).

244. Court of Appeal's powers on appeal by the prosecutor. On an appeal by the prosecutor in respect of a confiscation order[1] the Court of Appeal may confirm, quash or vary the order[2].

On an appeal by the prosecutor against a decision not to make a confiscation order[3] the Court of Appeal may confirm the decision, or if it believes that the decision was wrong it may:

    (1)   itself proceed under the provisions relating to the making of a confiscation order[4]; or

    (2)   direct the Crown Court to proceed afresh under those provisions[5].

On an appeal by the prosecutor or another interested person against a determination of the extent of a defendant's interest in property[6] the Court of Appeal may confirm the determination[7] or make such order as it believes is appropriate[8].

If a court so makes or varies a confiscation order or makes or varies a confiscation order in pursuance of such a direction, it must:

    (a)   have regard to any fine imposed on the defendant in respect of the offence (or any of the offences) concerned[9];

    (b)   have regard to any specified order involving the making of a payment by the defendant or another interference with the defendant's property[10] which has been made against the defendant in respect of the offence (or any of the offences) concerned, unless the order has already been taken into account by a court in deciding what is the free property[11] held[12] by the defendant[13].

If the Court of Appeal proceeds under the provisions relating to the making of a confiscation order or the Crown Court proceeds afresh under them in pursuance of a direction, the relevant provisions apply with modifications[14].

1 Ie an appeal under the Proceeds of Crime Act 2002 s 31(1) (see PARA 243). As to the making of confiscation orders see the Proceeds of Crime Act 2002 s 6; and PARA 221.
2 Proceeds of Crime Act 2002 s 32(1).
3 Ie an appeal under the Proceeds of Crime Act 2002 s 31(2) (see PARA 243).
4 Proceeds of Crime Act 2002 s 32(2)(a). As to the provisions relating to the making of a confiscation order see s 6; and PARA 221. In proceeding, the court must ignore the two conditions set out in s 6: s 32(2)(a).
5 Proceeds of Crime Act 2002 s 32(2)(b). In proceeding afresh pursuant to these provisions the Crown Court must comply with any directions the Court of Appeal may make: s 32(3).
6 Ie an appeal under the Proceeds of Crime Act 2002 s 31(4) (see PARA 243). As to the meaning of 'defendant' for these purposes see PARA 221 note 1.
7 Proceeds of Crime Act 2002 s 32(2A)(a) (s 32(2A) added, s 32(7) amended, by the Serious Crime Act 2015 s 3(2), Schedule paras 20, 28).
8 Proceeds of Crime Act 2002 s 32(2A)(b) (as added: see note 7).

9   Proceeds of Crime Act 2002 s 32(4)(a). As to references to the 'offence or offences concerned' see PARA 229 note 2.

10 Ie an order falling within the Proceeds of Crime Act 2002 s 13(3) (see PARA 237).

11 As to when property is 'free' see PARA 226.

12 Ie held for the purposes of the Proceeds of Crime Act 2002 s 9 (see PARA 233). As to when property is 'held' or 'obtained' see PARA 226.

13 Proceeds of Crime Act 2002 s 32(4)(b).

14 See the Proceeds of Crime Act 2002 s 32(5). If the court has already sentenced the defendant for the offence (or any of the offences) concerned, s 6 has effect as if his particular criminal conduct included conduct which constitutes offences which the court has taken into consideration in deciding his sentence for the offence or offences concerned: s 32(6). As to 'conduct', 'criminal conduct' and 'particular criminal conduct' see PARA 225.

   If a compensation order under the Powers of Criminal Courts (Sentencing) Act 2000 s 130 (see PARA 281), an order requiring the payment of surcharge under the Criminal Justice Act 2003 s 161A (see PARA 185), or an order requiring the payment of a surcharge under the Criminal Justice Act 2003 s 161A, or an unlawful profits order under the Prevention of Social Housing Fraud Act 2013 s 4 (see LANDLORD AND TENANT), has been made against the defendant in respect of the offence (or any of the offences) concerned, the court must have regard to it (Proceeds of Crime Act 2002 s 32(7)(a) (s 32(7) as amended (see note 7); further amended by the Prevention of Social Housing Fraud Act 2013 Schedule paras 11, 20)) and the provisions of the Proceeds of Crime Act 2002 s 13(5), (6) (see PARA 237) do not apply in relation to it (s 32(7)(b) (amended by the Modern Slavery Act 2015 Sch 5 para 18)).

   The Proceeds of Crime Act 2002 s 8(2) (see PARA 224) does not apply, and the rules applying instead are that the court must:

   (1)   take account of conduct occurring before the relevant date (s 32(8)(a));

   (2)   take account of property obtained before that date (s 32(8)(b));

   (3)   take account of property obtained on or after that date if it was obtained as a result of or in connection with conduct occurring before that date (s 32(8)(c)).

   The relevant date is the date on which the Crown Court decided not to make a confiscation order: s 32(11).

   In s 10 (see PARA 231):

   (a)   the first and second assumptions do not apply with regard to property first held by the defendant on or after the relevant date (s 32(9)(a));

   (b)   the third assumption does not apply with regard to expenditure incurred by him on or after that date (s 32(9)(b));

   (c)   the fourth assumption does not apply with regard to property obtained (or assumed to have been obtained) by him on or after that date (s 32(9)(c)).

   Section 26 (see PARA 272) applies as it applies in the circumstances mentioned in s 26(1): s 32(10).

245. Appeal to the Supreme Court. An appeal lies to the Supreme Court[1] from a decision of the Court of Appeal on an appeal by the prosecutor in respect of a confiscation order[2]. As a rule, such an appeal[3] lies at the instance of the defendant[4] or the prosecutor[5].

On an appeal from a decision of the Court of Appeal to confirm, vary or make a confiscation order the Supreme Court may confirm, quash or vary the order[6].

On an appeal from a decision of the Court of Appeal to confirm the decision of the Crown Court not to make a confiscation order or from a decision of the Court of Appeal to quash a confiscation order the Supreme Court may confirm the decision[7] or direct the Crown Court to proceed afresh under the provisions relating to the making of a confiscation order[8] if it believes the decision was wrong[9].

If a court varies a confiscation order under these provisions or makes a confiscation order in pursuance of a direction under them it must:

(1)   have regard to any fine imposed on the defendant in respect of the offence (or any of the offences) concerned[10];

(2)   have regard to any specified order involving the making of a payment by

the defendant or another interference with the defendant's property[11] which has been made against the defendant in respect of the offence (or any of the offences) concerned, unless the order has already been taken into account by a court in deciding what is the free property[12] held[13] by the defendant[14].

If the Crown Court proceeds afresh under the provisions relating to the making of a confiscation order in pursuance of a direction by the Supreme Court, the relevant provisions apply with modifications[15].

1   The Criminal Appeal Act 1968 s 33(3) (see CRIMINAL PROCEDURE vol 28 (2015) PARA 812) does not prevent an appeal to the Supreme Court under the Proceeds of Crime Act 2002 Pt 2 (ss 6–91): s 90(1).

2   Proceeds of Crime Act 2002 s 33(1) (s 33(1), (3)–(5), amended by the Constitutional Reform Act 2005 Sch 9 para 77(2)). The appeal referred to in the text is an appeal under the Proceeds of Crime Act 2002 s 31 (see PARA 243). As to the making of confiscation orders see s 6; and PARA 221.

3   Ie under the Proceeds of Crime Act 2002 s 33.

4   As to the meaning of 'defendant' for these purposes see PARA 221 note 1. A defendant is not precluded from appealing against a confiscation order to which he has consented when that consent was based a mistake of law or erroneous legal advice: see *R v Mackle (Northern Ireland)* [2014] UKSC 5, [2014] AC 678, [2014] 2 All ER 170.

5   Proceeds of Crime Act 2002 s 33(2)(a) (s 33(2) substituted, s 33(3A) added, by the Serious Crime Act 2015 s 3(3)). If the proceedings in the Court of Appeal were proceedings on an appeal under the Proceeds of Crime Act 2002 s 31(4) (see PARA 243), the appeal lies at the instance of any person who was a party to those proceedings: s 33(2)(a) (as so substituted).

6   Proceeds of Crime Act 2002 s 33(3) (as amended: see note 2). On an appeal under s 33 from a decision under s 32(2A) (see PARA 244) the Supreme Court may confirm the decision of the Court of Appeal or make such order as it believes is appropriate: s 33(3A) (as added: see note 5).

7   Proceeds of Crime Act 2002 s 33(4)(a) (as amended: see note 2).

8   Ie under the Proceeds of Crime Act 2002 s 6 (see PARA 221).

9   Proceeds of Crime Act 2002 s 33(4)(b) (as amended: see note 2). In proceeding afresh in pursuance of these provisions the Crown Court must comply with any directions the Supreme Courts may make: s 33(5) (as so amended).

10 Proceeds of Crime Act 2002 s 33(6)(a). As to references to the 'offence or offences concerned' see PARA 229 note 2.

11 Ie an order falling within the Proceeds of Crime Act 2002 s 13(3) (see PARA 237).

12 As to when property is 'free' see PARA 226.

13 Ie held for the purposes of the Proceeds of Crime Act 2002 s 9 (see PARA 233). As to when property is 'held' or 'obtained' see PARA 226.

14 Proceeds of Crime Act 2002 s 33(6)(b).

15 Proceeds of Crime Act 2002 s 33(7). If a court has already sentenced the defendant for the offence (or any of the offences) concerned, s 6 (see PARA 221) has effect as if his particular criminal conduct included conduct which constitutes offences which the court has taken into consideration in deciding his sentence for the offence or offences concerned: s 33(8). As to 'conduct', 'criminal conduct' and 'particular criminal conduct' see PARA 225.

    If a compensation order under the Powers of Criminal Courts (Sentencing) Act 2000 s 130 (see PARA 281), an order requiring the payment of surcharge under the Criminal Justice Act 2003 s 161A (see PARA 185), or an unlawful profits order under the Prevention of Social Housing Fraud Act 2013 s 4 (see LANDLORD AND TENANT) has been made against the defendant in respect of the offence (or any of the offences) concerned, the court must have regard to it (Proceeds of Crime Act 2002 s 33(9)(a) (s 33(9) amended by the Prevention of Social Housing Fraud Act 2013 Schedule paras 11, 21; and by the Serious Crime Act 2015 Sch 4 para 29)) and the provisions of the Proceeds of Crime Act 2002 s 13(5), (6) (see PARA 237) do not apply in relation to it (s 33(9)(b) (amended by the Modern Slavery Act 2015 Sch 5 para 19)).

    The Proceeds of Crime Act 2002 s 8(2) (see PARA 224) does not apply, and the rules applying instead are that the court must:

    (1)   take account of conduct occurring before the relevant date (s 33(10)(a));
    (2)   take account of property obtained before that date (s 33(10)(b));
    (3)   take account of property obtained on or after that date if it was obtained as a result of or in connection with conduct occurring before that date (s 33(10)(c)).

The relevant date is either the date on which the Crown Court made a confiscation order (in the case where the Crown Court made a confiscation order which was quashed by the Court of Appeal) (s 33(13)(a)) or the date on which the Crown Court decided not to make a confiscation order (in any other case) (s 33(13)(b)).

In s 10 (see PARA 231):

(a)   the first and second assumptions do not apply with regard to property first held by the defendant on or after the relevant date (s 33(11)(a));

(b)   the third assumption does not apply with regard to expenditure incurred by him on or after that date (s 33(11)(b));

(c)   the fourth assumption does not apply with regard to property obtained (or assumed to have been obtained) by him on or after that date (s 33(11)(c)).

Section 26 (see PARA 272) applies as it applies in the circumstances mentioned in s 26(1): s 33(12).

(v) Enforcement

A. IN GENERAL

246. Orders for securing compliance. Where the court makes a confiscation order[1] it may make such order as it believes is appropriate for the purpose of ensuring that the order is effective (a 'compliance order')[2]. The court must consider whether to make a compliance order on the making of the confiscation order[3] and if it does not make a compliance order then, at any later time (while the confiscation order is still in effect) on the application of the prosecutor[4]. The court may discharge or vary a compliance order on an application made by the prosecutor[5] or any person affected by the order[6].

1   As to the making of confiscation orders see the Proceeds of Crime Act 2002 s 6; and PARA 221.

2   Proceeds of Crime Act 2002 ss 13A(1), (2), 13B(7) (ss 13A, 13B added by the Serious Crime Act 2015 s 7). In considering whether to make a compliance order, the court must, in particular, consider whether any restriction or prohibition on the defendant's travel outside the United Kingdom ought to be imposed for the purpose mentioned in the Proceeds of Crime Act 2002 s 13A(2): s 13A(4) (as so added).

3   Proceeds of Crime Act 2002 s 13A(3)(a) (as added: see note 2).

4   Proceeds of Crime Act 2002 s 13A(3)(b) (as added: see note 2). If on an application under s 13A(3)(b) the Crown Court decides not to make a compliance order, the prosecutor may appeal to the Court of Appeal against the decision: s 13B(1) (as so added). On an appeal under s 13B(1) or (2) the Court of Appeal may confirm the decision (s 13B(3)(a) (as so added)) or make such order as it believes is appropriate (s 13B(3)(b) (as so added)). An appeal lies to the Supreme Court against a decision of the Court of Appeal under s 13B(3): s 13B(4) (as so added). An appeal under s 13B(4) lies at the instance of any person who was a party to the proceedings before the Court of Appeal: s 13B(5) (as so added). On an appeal under s 13B(4) the Supreme Court may confirm the decision of the Court of Appeal (s 13B(6)(a) (as so added)) or make such order as it believes is appropriate (s 13B(6)(b) (as so added)).

5   Proceeds of Crime Act 2002 s 13A(5)(a) (as added: see note 2). The prosecutor may appeal to the Court of Appeal in respect of the Crown Court's decision to make, discharge or vary a compliance order: s 13B(2)(a) (as so added). As to appeals see note 4.

6   Proceeds of Crime Act 2002 s 13A(5)(b) (as added: see note 2). Any person affected by a compliance order may appeal to the Court of Appeal in respect of the Crown Court's decision to make, discharge or vary it: s 13B(2)(b) (as so added). As to appeals see note 4.

B. MANAGEMENT RECEIVERS AND ENFORCEMENT RECEIVERS

247. Appointment of management receivers. Where the Crown Court makes a restraint order[1], and the applicant for the order applies to the court to appoint a receiver in respect of any realisable property[2] (whether as part of the application for the restraint order or at any time afterwards)[3], the Crown Court may appoint a receiver in respect of any realisable property to which the restraint order applies[4].

1   Proceeds of Crime Act 2002 s 48(1)(a). As to restraint orders see PARA 201.
2   As to 'property', 'realisable property' and related expressions see PARA 226.
3   Proceeds of Crime Act 2002 s 48(1)(b).
4   Proceeds of Crime Act 2002 s 48(2). The receiver may be required to give security: see the Criminal Procedure Rules 2015, SI 2015/1490, r 33.60. As to an appeal against the making of, or refusal to make, an order under the Proceeds of Crime Act 2002 s 48, see PARA 257. An order made under or for the purposes of s 48(2), s 49 (see PARA 248), s 50(2) (see PARA 249), s 51 (see PARA 250), s 54(3) (see PARA 258), s 62(4) (see PARA 253), s 63(2) (see PARA 254), s 64(2), (6) (see PARA 255), s 65(6) (see PARA 257) or s 66(3) (see PARA 257) has effect, and functions of a receiver under Pt 2 (ss 6–91) are exercisable, in Scotland or Northern Ireland: see s 443(2)–(4) (amended by the Serious Crime Act 2007 Sch 8 para 137; and by the Crime and Courts Act 2013 Sch 8 para 148) and see the Proceeds of Crime Act 2002 (Enforcement in different parts of the United Kingdom) Order 2002, SI 2002/3133 (amended by SI 2003/425; SI 2008/298); and the Criminal Procedure Rules 2015, SI 2015/1490, rr 33.4–33.6.
     In relation to receivers appointed under the Proceeds of Crime Act 2002 Pt 2, Criminal Procedure Rules may make provision corresponding to provision in Civil Procedure Rules: s 91(b) (amended by the Courts Act 2003 s 109(1), Sch 8 para 410). In connection with an application for the appointment of a management receiver see the Criminal Procedure Rules 2015, SI 2015/1490, rr 33.56, 33.57. The receiver may be required to give security (see r 33.60) and provision is made for the receiver's remuneration (see r 33.61), the preparation and service of accounts (see r 33.62), and non-compliance (see r 33.63).

248.   Powers of management receivers.   If the court appoints a receiver[1] it may act under the following provisions on the application of the person who applied for the restraint order[2].

The court may by order confer on the receiver the following powers in relation to any realisable property to which the restraint order applies:

(1)   power to take possession of the property[3];
(2)   power to manage or otherwise deal with[4] the property[5];
(3)   power to start, carry on or defend any legal proceedings in respect of the property[6];
(4)   power to realise so much of the property as is necessary to meet the receiver's remuneration and expenses[7].

The court may also by order confer on the receiver power to enter any premises in England and Wales and to do any of the following:

(a)   search for or inspect anything authorised by the court[8];
(b)   make or obtain a copy, photograph or other record of anything so authorised[9];
(c)   remove anything which the receiver is required or authorised to take possession of in pursuance of an order of the court[10].

The court may by order authorise the receiver to do any of the following for the purpose of the exercise of his functions:

(i)   hold property[11];
(ii)   enter into contracts[12];
(iii)   sue and be sued[13];
(iv)   employ agents[14];
(v)   execute powers of attorney, deeds or other instruments[15];
(vi)   take any other steps the court thinks appropriate[16].

The court may order any person who has possession of realisable property to which the restraint order applies to give possession of it to the receiver[17].

The court:

(A)   may order a person holding an interest in realisable property to which the restraint order applies to make to the receiver such payment as the court specifies in respect of a beneficial interest held by the defendant or the recipient of a tainted gift[18];

(B)   may (on the payment being made) by order transfer[19], grant or extinguish any interest in the property[20].

The court may order that a power conferred by an order under these provisions is to be subject to such conditions and exceptions as it specifies[21].

1 Ie under the Proceeds of Crime Act 2002 s 48 (see PARA 247).
2 Proceeds of Crime Act 2002 s 49(1). As to restraint orders see PARA 201. As to an appeal against the making of, or refusal to make an order under s 49, see PARA 257. As to the enforcement in Scotland or Northern Ireland of an order made under or for the purposes of s 49, or the enforcement in England and Wales of a corresponding Scottish or Northern Ireland order, see PARA 247 note 4. In connection with an application for the conferral of powers on a management receiver see the Criminal Procedure Rules 2015, SI 2015/1490, r 33.57.
3 Proceeds of Crime Act 2002 s 49(2)(a). Section 49(2), s 49(5) (see the text and notes 4–7, 17) and s 49(6) (see the text and notes 18–20) do not apply to property for the time being subject to a charge under any of the following repealed or revoked provisions: the Drug Trafficking Offences Act 1986 s 9; the Criminal Justice Act 1988 s 78; the Criminal Justice (Confiscation) (Northern Ireland) Order 1990, SI 1990/2588 (NI 17), art 14; the Drug Trafficking Act 1994 s 27; and the Proceeds of Crime (Northern Ireland) Order 1996, SI 1996/1299 (NI 9), art 32: see the Proceeds of Crime Act 2002 s 49(7).
4 Managing or otherwise dealing with property includes: (1) selling the property or any part of it or interest in it (Proceeds of Crime Act 2002 s 49(10)(a)); (2) carrying on or arranging for another person to carry on any trade or business the assets of which are or are part of the property (s 49(10)(b)); (3) incurring capital expenditure in respect of the property (s 49(10)(c)).
5 Proceeds of Crime Act 2002 s 49(2)(b). See note 3. The court must not confer the power mentioned in s 49(2)(b) or (d) in respect of property unless it gives persons holding interests in the property a reasonable opportunity to make representations to it: s 49(8)(a). Section 49(8), so far as relating to the power mentioned in s 49(2)(b), does not apply to property which is perishable or ought to be disposed of before its value diminishes: s 49(8A) (added by the Serious Crime Act 2007 s 82(1)).
6 Proceeds of Crime Act 2002 s 49(2)(c). See note 3.
7 Proceeds of Crime Act 2002 s 49(2)(d). See notes 3, 5.
8 Proceeds of Crime Act 2002 s 49(3)(a).
9 Proceeds of Crime Act 2002 s 49(3)(b).
10 Proceeds of Crime Act 2002 s 49(3)(c).
11 Proceeds of Crime Act 2002 s 49(4)(a).
12 Proceeds of Crime Act 2002 s 49(4)(b).
13 Proceeds of Crime Act 2002 s 49(4)(c).
14 Proceeds of Crime Act 2002 s 49(4)(d).
15 Proceeds of Crime Act 2002 s 49(4)(e).
16 Proceeds of Crime Act 2002 s 49(4)(f).
17 Proceeds of Crime Act 2002 s 49(5). See note 3.
18 Proceeds of Crime Act 2002 s 49(6)(a). See note 3. As to tainted gifts see PARA 228. The court must not exercise the power conferred on it by s 49(6) in respect of property unless it gives persons holding interests in the property a reasonable opportunity to make representations to it: s 49(8)(b).
19 As to when property is 'transferred' see PARA 226.
20 Proceeds of Crime Act 2002 s 49(6)(b).
21 Proceeds of Crime Act 2002 s 49(9). See also PARA 253.

249. Appointment of enforcement receivers. Where:

(1)   a confiscation order[1] is made[2];
(2)   it is not satisfied[3]; and
(3)   it is not subject to appeal[4],

the Crown Court, on the application of the prosecutor, may by order appoint a receiver in respect of realisable property[5].

1 Ie an order under the Proceeds of Crime Act 2002 s 6: see PARA 221.

2   Proceeds of Crime Act 2002 s 50(1)(a).
3   Proceeds of Crime Act 2002 s 50(1)(b). As to when a confiscation order is 'satisfied' see PARA
     199 note 11.
4   Proceeds of Crime Act 2002 s 50(1)(c).
5   Proceeds of Crime Act 2002 s 50(2). As to 'property' and 'realisable property' see PARA 226. As
     to an appeal against the making of, or refusal to make, an order under s 50 see PARA 257. As to
     the enforcement in Scotland or Northern Ireland of an order made under or for the purposes of
     s 50(2), or the enforcement in England and Wales of a corresponding Scottish or Northern
     Ireland order, see PARA 247 note 4. In connection with an application for the appointment of a
     management receiver see the Criminal Procedure Rules 2015, SI 2015/1490, rr 33.56, 33.57.
     The receiver may be required to give security (see r 33.60) and provision is made for the
     receiver's remuneration (see r 33.61), the preparation and service of accounts (see r 33.62), and
     non-compliance (see r 33.63).

250. Powers of enforcement receivers. If the court appoints a receiver[1] the
court may act under the following provisions on the application of the
prosecutor[2].
The court may by order confer on the receiver the following powers in
relation to the realisable property[3]:

(1)   power to take possession of the property[4];
(2)   power to manage or otherwise deal with[5] the property[6];
(3)   power to realise the property, in such manner as the court may specify[7];
(4)   power to start, carry on or defend any legal proceedings in respect of the
       property[8].

The court may also by order confer on the receiver power to enter any premises
in England and Wales and to do any of the following:

(a)   search for or inspect anything authorised by the court[9];
(b)   make or obtain a copy, photograph or other record of anything so
       authorised[10];
(c)   remove anything which the receiver is required or authorised to take
       possession of in pursuance of an order of the court[11].

The court may by order authorise the receiver to do any of the following for the
purpose of the exercise of his functions:

(i)   hold property[12];
(ii)   enter into contracts[13];
(iii)   sue and be sued[14];
(iv)   employ agents[15];
(v)   execute powers of attorney, deeds or other instruments[16];
(vi)   take any other steps the court thinks appropriate[17].

The court may order any person who has possession of realisable property to
give possession of it to the receiver[18].
The court:

(A)   may order a person holding an interest in realisable property to make to
       the receiver such payment as the court specifies in respect of a beneficial
       interest held by the defendant[19] or the recipient of a tainted gift[20];
(B)   may (on the payment being made) by order transfer, grant or extinguish
       any interest in the property[21].

The court may order that a power conferred by an order under these
provisions is to be subject to such conditions and exceptions as it specifies[22].

1   Ie under the Proceeds of Crime Act 2002 s 50 (see PARA 249).
2   Proceeds of Crime Act 2002 s 51(1). As to an appeal against the making of, or refusal to make,
     an order under s 51 see PARA 257. As to the enforcement in Scotland or Northern Ireland of an
     order made under or for the purposes of s 51, or the enforcement in England and Wales of a
     corresponding Scottish or Northern Ireland order, see PARA 247 note 4. In connection with an

application for the conferral of powers on a management receiver see the Criminal Procedure Rules 2015, SI 2015/1490, r 33.57. See also the Proceeds of Crime Act 2002 s 69; and PARA 251.

3   As to 'property' and 'realisable property' see PARA 226.

4   Proceeds of Crime Act 2002 s 51(2)(a). Section 51(2) (see the text and notes 1–3, 5–8), s 51(5) (see the text and note 18) and s 51(6) (see the text and notes 19–21) do not apply to property for the time being subject to a charge under any of the following repealed or revoked provisions: the Drug Trafficking Offences Act 1986 s 9; the Criminal Justice Act 1988 s 78; the Criminal Justice (Confiscation) (Northern Ireland) Order 1990, SI 1990/2588 (NI 17), art 14; the Drug Trafficking Act 1994 s 27; and the Proceeds of Crime (Northern Ireland) Order 1996, SI 1996/1299 (NI 9), art 32: see the Proceeds of Crime Act 2002 s 51(7).

5   Managing or otherwise dealing with property includes: (1) selling the property or any part of it or interest in it (Proceeds of Crime Act 2002 s 51(10)(a)); (2) carrying on or arranging for another person to carry on any trade or business the assets of which are or are part of the property (s 51(10)(b)); (3) incurring capital expenditure in respect of the property (s 51(10)(c)).

6   Proceeds of Crime Act 2002 s 51(2)(b). See note 4. The court must not confer the power mentioned in s 51(2)(b) or (c) in respect of property unless it gives persons holding interests in the property a reasonable opportunity to make representations to it: s 51(8)(a). Representations that a person is entitled to make by virtue of s 51(8) do not include representations that are inconsistent with a determination made under s 10A (see PARA 226) unless the person was not given a reasonable opportunity to make representations when the determination was made and has not appealed against the determination (s 51(8B)(a) (s 51(8B) added by the Serious Crime Act 2007 s 4)) or it appears to the court that there would be a serious risk of injustice to the person if the court was bound by the determination (Proceeds of Crime Act 2002 s 51(8B)(b) (as so added)), and the determination does not bind the court if s 51(8B)(a) or (b) applies. Section 51(8), so far as relating to the power mentioned in subsection (2)(b), does not apply to property which is perishable or ought to be disposed of before its value diminishes: s 51(8A) (added by the Serious Crime Act 2007 s 82(2)).

7   Proceeds of Crime Act 2002 s 51(2)(c). See notes 4, 6.

8   Proceeds of Crime Act 2002 s 51(2)(d). See note 4.

9   Proceeds of Crime Act 2002 s 51(3)(a).

10 Proceeds of Crime Act 2002 s 51(3)(b).

11 Proceeds of Crime Act 2002 s 51(3)(c).

12 Proceeds of Crime Act 2002 s 51(4)(a). As to when property is 'held' by a person see PARA 226.

13 Proceeds of Crime Act 2002 s 51(4)(b).

14 Proceeds of Crime Act 2002 s 51(4)(c).

15 Proceeds of Crime Act 2002 s 51(4)(d).

16 Proceeds of Crime Act 2002 s 51(4)(e).

17 Proceeds of Crime Act 2002 s 51(4)(f).

18 Proceeds of Crime Act 2002 s 51(5). See note 4. In s 51(5) 'any person' does not include tenants protected by contract and/or statute who were living in a property classified as a realisable asset belonging to the person who is the subject of a confiscation order: see *Brittain (in her capacity as receiver) v N* [2009] EWHC 2884 (Admin), [2009] 46 EG 143 (CS), [2009] All ER (D) 173 (Nov) (decided under the corresponding provisions of the Criminal Justice Act 1988 (ie s 80(4) (repealed)).

19 As to the meaning of 'defendant' for these purposes see PARA 221 note 1.

20 Proceeds of Crime Act 2002 s 51(6)(a). See note 4. As to tainted gifts see PARA 228. The court must not exercise the power conferred on it by s 51(6) in respect of property unless it gives persons holding interests in the property a reasonable opportunity to make representations to it: s 51(8)(b).

21 Proceeds of Crime Act 2002 s 51(6)(b). See notes 4, 20.

22 Proceeds of Crime Act 2002 s 51(9). See also PARA 253.

251.   Powers of court and receiver.   Certain powers conferred on a court[1], the powers of a management receiver[2] or an enforcement receiver[3], and the powers of an appropriate officer and a senior officer in connection with the seizure of property[4]:

(1)   must be exercised with a view to the value for the time being of realisable property[5] being made available (by the property's realisation) for satisfying any confiscation order[6] that has been or may be made against the defendant[7];

(2)   must be exercised, in a case where a confiscation order has not been
        made, with a view to securing that there is no diminution in the value of
        realisable property[8];

(3)   must be exercised without taking account of any obligation of the
        defendant or a recipient of a tainted gift[9] if the obligation conflicts with
        the object of satisfying any confiscation order that has been or may be
        made against the defendant[10]; and

(4)   may be exercised in respect of a debt owed by the Crown[11].

However, heads (1) to (4) above have effect subject to the following rules:

(a)   the powers must be exercised with a view to allowing a person other
        than the defendant or a recipient of a tainted gift to retain or recover the
        value of any interest[12] held by him[13];

(b)   in the case of realisable property held by a recipient of a tainted gift, the
        powers must be exercised with a view to realising no more than the
        value for the time being of the gift[14]; and

(c)   in a case where a confiscation order has not been made against the
        defendant, property must not be sold if the court so orders under the
        provision[15] described below[16].

If on an application by the defendant, or by the recipient of a tainted gift, the
court decides that property cannot be replaced it may order that it must not be
sold[17].

1   Ie the powers conferred by the Proceeds of Crime Act 2002 ss 41–59 (see PARAS 201–215,
    247–256), ss 62–67 (see PARAS 196, 253–255, 257) and ss 67A–67D (see PARA 197): Proceeds of
    Crime Act 2002 s 69(1)(a) (s 69(1)(a), (b) amended by the Serious Crime Act 2007 Sch 8
    para 34; Proceeds of Crime Act 2002 s 69(1)(a) amended, s 69(1)(c), (d) added, by the Policing
    and Crime Act 2009 Sch 7 paras 66, 67).
2   Ie a receiver appointed under the Proceeds of Crime Act 2002 s 48 (see PARA 247).
3   Proceeds of Crime Act 2002 s 69(1)(b) (as amended: see note 1). An enforcement receiver is a
    receiver appointed under the Proceeds of Crime Act 2002 s 50 (see PARA 249).
4   Proceeds of Crime Act 2002 s 69(1)(c), (d) (as added: see note 1). As to the powers referred to
    see the Proceeds of Crime Act 2002 ss 47C–47L (appropriate officers) and s 47G (senior
    officers); and PARAS 208–212.
5   As to the meanings of 'property' and 'realisable property' see PARA 226.
6   Ie an order under the Proceeds of Crime Act 2002 s 6: see PARA 221. As to when a confiscation
    order is 'satisfied' see PARA 199 note 11.
7   Proceeds of Crime Act 2002 s 69(2)(a). As to the meaning of 'defendant' for these purposes see
    PARA 221 note 1.
8   Proceeds of Crime Act 2002 s 69(2)(b).
9   As to tainted gifts see PARA 228.
10 Proceeds of Crime Act 2002 s 69(2)(c).
11 Proceeds of Crime Act 2002 s 69(2)(d). See further *Serious Fraud Office v Lexi Holdings plc*
    [2008] EWCA Crim 1443, [2009] QB 376, [2009] 1 All ER 586.
12 As to an 'interest' in property see PARA 221. As to when property is 'held' by a person see PARA
    226.
13 Proceeds of Crime Act 2002 s 69(3)(a).
14 Proceeds of Crime Act 2002 s 69(3)(b).
15 Ie the Proceeds of Crime Act 2002 s 69(4) (see the text and note 17).
16 Proceeds of Crime Act 2002 s 69(3)(c).
17 Proceeds of Crime Act 2002 s 69(4). An order under s 69(4) may be revoked or varied: s 69(5).

252. Protection. If a management receiver[1] or an enforcement receiver[2]:

(1)   takes action in relation to property which is not realisable property[3];

(2)   would be entitled to take the action if it were realisable property[4]; and

(3)   believes on reasonable grounds that he is entitled to take the action[5],

he is not liable to any person in respect of any loss or damage resulting from the
action, except so far as the loss or damage is caused by his negligence[6].

1 Ie a receiver appointed under the Proceeds of Crime Act 2002 s 48 (see PARA 247).
2 Proceeds of Crime Act 2002 s 61 (amended by the Serious Crime Act 2007 Sch 8 para 28). An enforcement receiver mentioned in the text refers to a receiver appointed under the Proceeds of Crime Act 2002 s 50 (see PARA 249).
3 Proceeds of Crime Act 2002 s 61(a). As to the meanings of 'property' and 'realisable property' see PARA 226.
4 Proceeds of Crime Act 2002 s 61(b).
5 Proceeds of Crime Act 2002 s 61(c).
6 Proceeds of Crime Act 2002 s 61.

253. Further applications. A management receiver[1] or an enforcement receiver[2] may apply to the Crown Court for an order giving directions as to the exercise of his powers[3].

Any person affected by action taken by such a receiver[4], or who may be affected by action such a receiver proposes to take[5], may apply to the Crown Court[6].

On an application under these provisions the court may make such order as it believes is appropriate[7].

1 Ie a receiver appointed under the Proceeds of Crime Act 2002 s 48 (see PARA 247).
2 Ie a receiver appointed under the Proceeds of Crime Act 2002 s 50 (see PARA 249).
3 Proceeds of Crime Act 2002 s 62(1), (2) (s 62(1) amended by the Serious Crime Act 2007 Sch 8 para 29).
4 Proceeds of Crime Act 2002 s 62(3)(a).
5 Proceeds of Crime Act 2002 s 62(3)(b).
6 Proceeds of Crime Act 2002 s 62(3). In connection with an application under s 62(3) see the Criminal Procedure Rules 2015, SI 2015/1490, r 33.58.
7 Proceeds of Crime Act 2002 s 62(4). The power under s 62(4) must be exercised with regard to the matters listed in s 69 (see PARA 251): see s 69(1), (2); and PARA 251. As to an appeal against the making of, or refusal to make, an order under s 62 see PARA 257. As to the enforcement in Scotland or Northern Ireland of an order made under or for the purposes of s 62(4), or the enforcement in England and Wales of a corresponding Scottish or Northern Ireland order, see PARA 247 note 4.

254. Discharge and variation. The following persons may apply to the Crown Court to vary or discharge an order made under any of the provisions relating to the appointment and powers of management receivers, enforcement receivers[1]:

(1) the receiver[2];
(2) the person who applied for the order[3];
(3) any person affected by the order[4].

On such an application the court: (a) may discharge the order[5]; (b) may vary the order[6].

1 Ie the Proceeds of Crime Act 2002 ss 48–51 (see PARAS 247–250): see s 63(1) (amended by the Serious Crime Act 2007 Sch 8 para 30(a)). In connection with an application under the Proceeds of Crime Act 2002 s 63(1) see the Criminal Procedure Rules 2015, SI 2015/1490, r 33.58.
2 Proceeds of Crime Act 2002 s 63(1)(a).
3 Proceeds of Crime Act 2002 s 63(1)(b) (amended by the Serious Crime Act 2007 Sch 8 para 30(b), Sch 14).
4 Proceeds of Crime Act 2002 s 63(1)(c). For procedural provisions see PARA 253 note 6.
5 Proceeds of Crime Act 2002 s 63(2)(a). However, in the case of an order under s 48 or s 49 (see PARAS 247–248):
    (1) if the condition in s 40 (see PARA 200) which was satisfied was that proceedings were started or an application was made, the court must discharge the order on the conclusion of the proceedings or of the application (as the case may be) (s 63(3)(a));
    (2) if the condition which was satisfied was that an investigation was started or an application was to be made, the court must discharge the order if within a reasonable time proceedings for the offence are not started or the application is not made (as the case may be) (s 63(3)(b)).

As to when proceedings for an offence are 'started' and 'concluded' see PARA 199.

The powers given by s 63(2) must be exercised with regard to the matters specified in s 69 (see PARA 251): s 69(1).

As to an appeal against the making of, or a refusal to make, an order under the Proceeds of Crime Act 2002 s 63(2) see PARA 257. As to the enforcement in Scotland or Northern Ireland of an order made under or for the purposes of s 63(2), or the enforcement in England and Wales of a corresponding Scottish or Northern Ireland order, see PARA 247 note 4.

6   Proceeds of Crime Act 2002 s 63(2)(b). See note 5.

255.   Management receivers: discharge. Where a management receiver stands appointed[1] in respect of realisable property[2], and the court appoints[3] an enforcement receiver[4], the court must order the management receiver to transfer to the other receiver all the property held by the management receiver by virtue of the powers conferred[5] on him as such[6]. If the management receiver complies with such an order, he is discharged: (1) from his appointment as management receiver[7]; (2) from any obligation[8] arising from his appointment[9].

1   Ie under the Proceeds of Crime Act 2002 s 48 (see PARA 247).
2   Proceeds of Crime Act 2002 s 64(1)(a). As to the meanings of 'property' and 'realisable property' see PARA 226.
3   Ie under the Proceeds of Crime Act 2002 s 50 (see PARA 249).
4   Proceeds of Crime Act 2002 s 64(1)(b) (amended by the Serious Crime Act 2007 Sch 8 para 31(2), Sch 14).
5   Ie by the Proceeds of Crime Act 2002 s 49 (see PARA 248).
6   Proceeds of Crime Act 2002 s 64(2). Section 64(2) does not apply to property which the management receiver holds by virtue of the exercise by him of his power under s 49(2)(d) (see PARA 248): s 64(4). See also s 69; and PARA 251. As to the enforcement in Scotland or Northern Ireland of an order made under or for the purposes of s 64(2), (6), or the enforcement in England and Wales of a corresponding Scottish or Northern Ireland order, see PARA 247 note 4.
7   Proceeds of Crime Act 2002 s 64(5)(a).
8   Ie under the Proceeds of Crime Act 2002.
9   Proceeds of Crime Act 2002 s 64(5)(b).

256.   Restrictions. Where a court makes an order[1] appointing an enforcement receiver in respect of any realisable property[2]:

(1)   no distress may be levied against the property, and the statutory procedure for taking control of goods[3] may not be exercised, except with the leave of the Crown Court and subject to any terms the Crown Court may impose[4]; and

(2)   if the receiver is appointed in respect of a tenancy of any premises, no landlord or other person to whom rent is payable may exercise a right of forfeiture by peaceable re-entry in relation to the premises in respect of any failure by the tenant to comply with any term or condition of the tenancy, except with the leave of the Crown Court and subject to any terms the Crown Court may impose[5].

If a court in which proceedings are pending in respect of any property is satisfied that an order appointing an enforcement receiver in respect of the property has been applied for or made, the court may either stay the proceedings or allow them to continue on any terms it thinks fit[6].

1   Ie under the Proceeds of Crime Act 2002 s 50 (see PARA 249).
2   Proceeds of Crime Act 2002 s 59(1). As to the meanings of 'property' and 'realisable property' see PARA 226.
3   Ie the procedure in the Tribunals, Courts and Enforcement Act 2007 Sch 12 (taking control of goods): see CIVIL PROCEDURE vol 11 (2009) PARA 1386 et seq.
4   Proceeds of Crime Act 2002 s 59(2) (amended by the Tribunals, Courts and Enforcement Act 2007 Sch 13 para 144). In connection with applications under the Proceeds of Crime Act 2002 s 59(2), (3) see the Criminal Procedure Rules 2015, SI 2015/1490, r 33.32.

5　Proceeds of Crime Act 2002 s 59(3), (4).
6　Proceeds of Crime Act 2002 s 59(5). Before exercising any power conferred by s 59(5), the court must give an opportunity to be heard to the prosecutor (s 59(6)(a)) and to the receiver (if the order appointing an enforcement receiver has been made) (s 59(6)(b)). See also s 69; and PARA 251.

257. Appeal. If, on an application for an order[1] for the appointment of a management receiver or enforcement receiver or an order authorising such a receiver to act with respect to realisable property[2], the court decides not to make an order, the person who applied for the order may appeal to the Court of Appeal against the decision[3].

If the court makes an order[4] appointing a management receiver or enforcement receiver or an order authorising such a receiver to act with respect to realisable property[5], any person who applied for the order[6], or any other person affected by the order[7], may appeal to the Court of Appeal[8] in respect of the court's decision[9].

If, on a further application[10], the court decides not to make the order sought, the person who applied for the order may appeal to the Court of Appeal against the decision[11]. If the court makes an order on a further application, the following persons may appeal to the Court of Appeal in respect of the court's decision:

(1)　the person who applied for the order[12];
(2)　any person affected by the order[13];
(3)　the receiver[14].

The following persons may appeal to the Court of Appeal against a decision of the court on an application[15] for the discharge or variation of an order relating to the appointment of or powers of a receiver:

(a)　the person who applied for the order in respect of which the application was made[16];
(b)　any person affected by the court's decision[17];
(c)　the receiver[18].

On any of these appeals, the Court of Appeal may:

(i)　confirm the decision[19]; or
(ii)　make such order as it believes is appropriate[20].

An appeal lies to the Supreme Court[21] from a decision of the Court of Appeal on such an appeal[22] at the instance of any person who was a party to the proceedings before the Court of Appeal[23]. In such a case the Supreme Court may: (A) confirm the decision of the Court of Appeal[24]; or (B) make such order as it believes is appropriate[25].

1　Ie an order under any of the following provisions in the Proceeds of Crime Act 2002: s 48 (see PARA 247), s 49 (see PARA 248), s 50 (see PARA 249), s 51 (see PARA 250).
2　As to 'property' and 'realisable property' see PARA 226.
3　Proceeds of Crime Act 2002 s 65(1) (s 65(1), (2) amended by the Serious Crime Act 2007 Sch 8 para 32(1)–(3), Sch 14). In connection with receivership proceedings see the Criminal Procedure Rules 2015, SI 2015/1490, rr 33.32–33.63.
4　See note 1.
5　Proceeds of Crime Act 2002 s 65(2) (as amended: see note 3).
6　Proceeds of Crime Act 2002 s 65(2)(a).
7　Proceeds of Crime Act 2002 s 65(2)(b).
8　See PARA 205 note 2.
9　Proceeds of Crime Act 2002 s 65(2).
10　Ie an application for an order under the Proceeds of Crime Act 2002 s 62 (see PARA 253).
11　Proceeds of Crime Act 2002 s 65(3).
12　Proceeds of Crime Act 2002 s 65(4)(a).
13　Proceeds of Crime Act 2002 s 65(4)(b).
14　Proceeds of Crime Act 2002 s 65(4)(c).

15   Ie under the Proceeds of Crime Act 2002 s 63 (see PARA 254).
16   Proceeds of Crime Act 2002 s 65(5)(a) (Serious Crime Act 2007 Sch 8 para 32(4), Sch 14).
17   Proceeds of Crime Act 2002 s 65(5)(b).
18   Proceeds of Crime Act 2002 s 65(5)(c).
19   Proceeds of Crime Act 2002 s 65(6)(a). In exercising its powers under s 65(6), the Court of Appeal must have regard to matters listed in s 69 (see PARA 251): s 69(1). As to the enforcement in Scotland or Northern Ireland of an order made under or for the purposes of s 65(6), or the enforcement in England and Wales of a corresponding Scottish or Northern Ireland order, see PARA 247 note 4.
20   Proceeds of Crime Act 2002 s 65(6)(b). See note 19.
21   As to the procedure on such an appeal see PARA 245.
22   Proceeds of Crime Act 2002 s 66(1) (s 66(1), (3) amended by the Constitutional Reform Act 2005 Sch 9 para 77(1), (3)).
23   Proceeds of Crime Act 2002 s 66(2).
24   Proceeds of Crime Act 2002 s 66(3)(a) (as amended: see note 22). In exercising powers under the Proceeds of Crime Act 2002 s 66(3), regard must be had to the matters specified in s 69 (see PARA 251): s 69(1). As to the enforcement in Scotland or Northern Ireland of an order made under or for the purposes of s 66(3), or the enforcement in England and Wales of a corresponding Scottish or Northern Ireland order, see PARA 247 note 4.
25   Proceeds of Crime Act 2002 s 66(3)(b) (as amended: see note 22). See note 24.

C. APPLICATION OF SUMS

258. Enforcement receivers. Where sums which are in the hands of an enforcement receiver[1] are:

(1)   the proceeds of the realisation of property[2] by the receiver[3];
(2)   sums (other than those mentioned in head (1) above) in which the defendant[4] holds an interest[5],

the sums must be applied as follows:

(a)   first, they must be applied in payment of such expenses incurred by a person acting as an insolvency practitioner as are payable[6];
(b)   second, they must be applied in making any payments directed by the Crown Court[7];
(c)   third, they must be applied[8] on the defendant's behalf towards satisfaction of the confiscation order[9].

If the amount payable under the confiscation order[10] has been fully paid and any sums remain in the receiver's hands, he must distribute them:

(i)   among such persons who held (or hold) interests in the property concerned[11] as the Crown Court directs[12]; and
(ii)   in such proportions as it directs[13].

Before making such a direction the court must give persons who held (or hold) interests in the property concerned a reasonable opportunity to make representations to it[14].

1   Ie a receiver appointed under the Proceeds of Crime Act 2002 s 50 (see PARA 249).
2   Ie the realisation of property under the Proceeds of Crime Act 2002 s 51 (see PARA 250). As to 'property' and related expressions see PARA 226.
3   Proceeds of Crime Act 2002 s 54(1)(a).
4   As to the meaning of 'defendant' for these purposes see PARA 221 note 1.
5   Proceeds of Crime Act 2002 s 54(1)(b). As to an 'interest' see PARA 226.
6   Proceeds of Crime Act 2002 s 54(2)(a). The reference in the text to sums being payable is a reference to sums being payable by virtue of s 432. If property is subject to a restraint order made under s 41 (see PARA 201) (or corresponding Scottish or Northern Ireland provisions) (s 432(5)(a), (6)(a)) and either a person acting as an insolvency practitioner incurs expenses in respect of property subject to the order in circumstances where he does not know (and has no reasonable grounds to believe) that the property is subject to the restraint order (s 432(5)(b), (c)), or a person acting as an insolvency practitioner incurs expenses which are not ones in respect of property subject to the order in circumstances where the expenses are ones which (but

for the effect of the order) might have been met by taking possession of and realising property subject to it (s 432(6)(b), (c)), or property is detained under or by virtue of s 44A (see PARAS 204, 205), s 47J (see PARA 208), s 47K (see PARA 212), s 47M (see PARA 213), s 47P (see PARA 213) (or corresponding Scotland or Northern Ireland provisions), a person acting as an insolvency practitioner incurs expenses which are not ones in respect of the detained property and the expenses are ones which (but for the effect of the detention of the property) might have been met by taking possession of and realising the property (s 432(6A) (s 432(6A) added, s 432(7) substituted, by the Policing and Crime Act 2009 Sch 7 para 93 (subject to limited savings: see the Policing and Crime Act 2009 (Commencement No 10, Transitional Provision and Savings) Order 2015, SI 2015/983))), then whether or not the insolvency practitioner has seized or disposed of any property, the insolvency practitioner is entitled to payment of the expenses under the Proceeds of Crime Act 2002 s 54(2), s 55(3) (see PARA 259) or s 67D(2) (see PARA 197) if the restraint order was made under s 41 or (as the case may be) the property was detained under or by virtue of s 44A, s 47J, s 47K, s 47M or s 47P (s 432(7)(a) (as so substituted)).

7   Proceeds of Crime Act 2002 s 54(2)(b).

8   For these purposes, the receiver applies such sums by paying them to the appropriate designated officer on account of the amount payable under the order: Proceeds of Crime Act 2002 s 54(6) (s 54(6), (7) amended by the Courts Act 2003 Sch 8 para 407). The appropriate designated officer is the one for the magistrates' court responsible for enforcing the confiscation order as if the amount ordered to be paid were a fine: Proceeds of Crime Act 2002 s 54(7) (as so amended).

9   Proceeds of Crime Act 2002 s 54(2)(c). As to a 'confiscation order' (ie an order under the Proceeds of Crime Act 2002 s 6) see PARA 221.

10 The 'amount payable' under a confiscation order, where part of that amount has been paid, means the amount that remains to be paid: Proceeds of Crime Act 2002 s 87(1A) (added by the Serious Crime Act 2007 s 5(3)).

11 For the purposes of the Proceeds of Crime Act 2002 s 54(3), (4) (see the text and notes 12–14), the 'property concerned' is: (1) the property represented by the proceeds mentioned in s 54(1)(a) (see head (1) in the text) (s 54(5)(a)); and (2) the sums mentioned in s 54(1)(b) (see head (2) in the text) (s 54(5)(b)). The receiver must apply for and act in accordance with directions: see the Criminal Procedure Rules 2015, SI 2015/1490, r 33.59.

12 Proceeds of Crime Act 2002 s 54(3)(a). See note 11. As to the enforcement in Scotland or Northern Ireland of an order made under or for the purposes of s 54(3), or the enforcement in England and Wales of a corresponding Scottish or Northern Ireland order, see PARA 247 note 4.
    See also the Proceeds of Crime Act 2002 s 69; and PARA 251.

13 Proceeds of Crime Act 2002 s 54(3)(b). See notes 11, 12.

14 Proceeds of Crime Act 2002 s 54(4).

259. Sums received by designated officer. Where a designated officer receives sums[1] on account of the amount payable under a confiscation order[2], the designated officer's receipt of the sum reduces the amount payable under the order, but he must apply the sums received as follows[3].

First he must apply them in payment of such expenses incurred by a person acting as an insolvency practitioner as: (1) are payable[4]; but (2) are not already[5] paid[6].

If the designated officer received the sums under the provisions relating to enforcement receivers[7] or, as from a day to be appointed, the provisions relating to the seizure of personal property[8], he must next apply them:

(a)   first, in payment of the remuneration and expenses of a management receiver[9], to the extent that they have not been met by virtue of the exercise by that receiver of a power[10] to realise so much of the proportion as is necessary to meet the receiver's remuneration and expenses[11];

(b)   second, in payment of the remuneration and expenses of any receiver[12]; and

(c)   third, in payment to an appropriate officer of any amount to which the officer is[13] entitled[14].

If a direction was made[15] for an amount payable under a priority order (or orders), to be paid out of any sums recovered under the confiscation order, the designated officer must next apply the sums in payment of that amount[16].

If any amount remains after the designated officer makes any payments required by these provisions, the amount must be treated[17] as if it were a fine imposed by a magistrates' court[18].

1   Ie whether under the Proceeds of Crime Act 2002 s 54 (see PARA 258) or otherwise.
2   Proceeds of Crime Act 2002 s 55(1) (s 55(1), (2), (4)–(6) amended by the Courts Act 2003 Sch 8 para 408). As to a 'confiscation order' (ie an order under the Proceeds of Crime Act 2002 s 6) see PARA 221. As to the 'amount payable' under a confiscation order see PARA 258 note 10.
3   Proceeds of Crime Act 2002 s 55(2) (as amended: see note 2).
4   Proceeds of Crime Act 2002 s 55(3)(a). The reference in the text to sums being 'payable' is a reference to sums being payable under s 55(2) (see the text and note 3) by virtue of s 432: s 55(3)(a).
5   Ie under the Proceeds of Crime Act 2002 s 54(2)(a) (see PARA 258) or under s 67D(2)(a) (see PARA 197). As to the payment of expenses see further PARA 258 note 6.
6   Proceeds of Crime Act 2002 s 55(3)(b) (s 55(3), (4) amended, s 55(4)(c) added, by the Policing and Crime Act 2009 s 58(1), (4), (5)).
7   Ie the Proceeds of Crime Act 2002 s 54 (see PARA 258).
8   Ie the Proceeds of Crime Act 2002 s 67D.
9   Ie a receiver appointed under the Proceeds of Crime Act 2002 s 48 (see PARA 247).
10   Ie a power conferred by the Proceeds of Crime Act 2002 s 49(2)(d) (see PARA 248).
11   Proceeds of Crime Act 2002 s 55(4)(a) (as amended: see note 2). Section 55(4) does not apply if the receiver is:
      (1)   a constable (Proceeds of Crime Act 2002 s 55(7), (8)(a) (s 55(7) substituted, s 55(8)–(10) added, by the Policing and Crime Act 2009 s 51(1), (2)));
      (2)   a member of a Police and Crime Commissioner's staff (Proceeds of Crime Act 2002 s 55(8)(aa) (as so added; s 55(8)(aa), (ab), (ac) added, s 55(8)(b) amended, by the Police Reform and Social Responsibility Act 2011 Sch 16 paras 205, 206));
      (3)   a member of staff of the Mayor's Office for Policing and Crime (s 55(8)(ab) (as so added));
      (4)   a member of the civilian staff of a police force, including the metropolitan police force (s 55(8)(ac) (as so added));
      (5)   a member of staff of the City of London police force (s 55(8)(b) (as so added));
      (6)   an accredited financial investigator (s 55(8)(c) (as so added));
      (7)   a member of staff of the Crown Prosecution Service (s 55(8)(d) (as so added));
      (8)   a member of staff of the Serious Fraud Office (s 55(8)(e) (as so added));
      (9)   a member of the staff of the Commissioners for Her Majesty's Revenue and Customs (s 55(8)(g) (as so added));
    (10)   a National Crime Agency officer (s 55(8)(h) (as so added; substituted by the Crime and Courts Act 2013 Sch 8 para 113)); or
    (11)   a member of staff of any government department not mentioned above (Proceeds of Crime Act 2002 s 55(8)(i) (as so added)).
    It is immaterial for these purposes whether a person falls within any of the listed categories by virtue of a permanent or temporary appointment or a secondment from elsewhere (s 55(9) (as so added)). The references to a member of a Police and Crime Commissioner's staff, a member of staff of the Mayor's Office for Policing and Crime and a member of the civilian staff of a police force, including the metropolitan police force are reference to such persons within the meaning of the Police Reform and Social Responsibility Act 2011 Pt 1 (ss 1–102) (see POLICE AND INVESTIGATORY POWERS vol 84 (2013) PARA 85 et seq): Proceeds of Crime Act 2002 s 55(8)(aa)–(ac) (as so substituted and added). An 'accredited financial investigator' is an accredited financial investigator who falls within a description specified in an order made for the purposes of the Proceeds of Crime Act 2002 s 55(4) by the Secretary of State under s 453: s 55(10) (as so added). At the date at which this volume states the law no such order had been made. As to the City of London police force see POLICE AND INVESTIGATORY POWERS vol 84 (2013) PARA 54. As to the Commissioners for Her Majesty's Revenue and Customs see CUSTOMS AND EXCISE vol 31 (2012) PARA 921 et seq. As to the National Crime Agency see POLICE AND INVESTIGATORY POWERS vol 84 (2013) PARA 424.
12   Proceeds of Crime Act 2002 s 55(4)(b) (as amended and: see notes 2, 6). See also note 11. As to enforcement receivers see PARAS 249–250.
13   Ie by virtue of the Proceeds of Crime Act 2002 s 67B (see PARA 197).

14 Proceeds of Crime Act 2002 s 55(4)(c) (as added: see note 6).
15 Ie under the Proceeds of Crime Act 2002 s 13(6) (see PARA 237).
16 Proceeds of Crime Act 2002 s 55(5) (as amended (see note 2); amended by the Serious Crime Act 2015 Sch 4 para 33). As to 'priority orders' see PARA 237 note 4.
17 Ie for the purposes of the Courts Act 2003 s 38 (application of fines etc: see MAGISTRATES vol 71 (2013) PARA 696).
18 Proceeds of Crime Act 2002 s 55(6) (as amended: see note 2).

D. COMPENSATION DURING ENFORCEMENT

260. Serious default. If either of two sets of three conditions is satisfied the Crown Court may order the payment of such compensation as it believes is just[1].
The first set of conditions is that:

(1)   a criminal investigation[2] has been started with regard to an offence, and proceedings are not started[3] for the offence[4];

(2)   in the criminal investigation there has been serious default by a specified[5] person[6], and the investigation would not have continued if the default had not occurred[7];

(3)   an application is made[8] by a person who held realisable property[9] and has suffered loss in consequence of anything done in relation to it by or in pursuance of an order[10].

The second set of conditions is that:

(a)   proceedings for an offence are started against a person and either they do not result in his conviction for the offence[11] or he is convicted of the offence but the conviction is quashed or he is pardoned in respect of it[12];

(b)   in the criminal investigation with regard to the offence or in its prosecution there has been a serious default by a specified person[13] and the proceedings would not have been started or continued if the default had not occurred[14]; and

(c)   an application is made by a person who held realisable property and has suffered loss in consequence of anything done in relation to it by or in pursuance of an order[15].

Compensation[16] is payable to the applicant[17]. It is payable only by specified bodies[18].

1   Proceeds of Crime Act 2002 s 72(1).
2   As to the meaning of 'criminal investigation' see PARA 200 note 3.
3   As to when proceedings for an offence are 'started' and 'concluded' see PARA 199.
4   Proceeds of Crime Act 2002 s 72(2). The offence referred to in s 72(2) may be one of a number of offences with regard to which the investigation is started: s 72(7).
5   Ie a person mentioned in the Proceeds of Crime Act 2002 s 72(9) (see note 18).
6   Proceeds of Crime Act 2002 s 72(4)(a).
7   Proceeds of Crime Act 2002 s 72(4)(b).
8   Ie under the Proceeds of Crime Act 2002 s 72. In connection with applications under s 72 see the Criminal Procedure Rules 2015, SI 2015/1490, r 33.22.
9   As to 'property' and 'realisable property' see PARA 226.
10 Proceeds of Crime Act 2002 s 72(6). The reference in the text to an order is a reference to an order under Pt 2 (ss 6–91).
11 Proceeds of Crime Act 2002 s 72(3)(a). The offence referred to in s 72(3) may be one of a number of offences for which the proceedings are started: s 72(8).
12 Proceeds of Crime Act 2002 s 72(3)(b).
13 Proceeds of Crime Act 2002 s 72(5)(a). As to the specified person see note 18.
14 Proceeds of Crime Act 2002 s 72(5)(b).
15 Proceeds of Crime Act 2002 s 72(6). The reference in the text to an order is a reference to an order under Pt 2.
16 Ie under the Proceeds of Crime Act 2002 s 72.

17 See the Proceeds of Crime Act 2002 s 72(9); and note 18.

18 Ie:
- (1) if the person in default was or was acting as a member of a police force, the compensation is payable out of the police fund from which the expenses of that force are met (Proceeds of Crime Act 2002 s 72(9)(a));
- (2) if the person in default was a member of the Crown Prosecution Service or was acting on its behalf, the compensation is payable by the Director of Public Prosecutions (s 72(9)(b));
- (3) if the person in default was a National Crime Agency officer, the compensation is payable by the National Crime Agency (s 72(9)(ba) (s 72(9)(ba), (f) added by the Policing and Crime Act 2009 s 61(1), (2); Proceeds of Crime Act 2002 s 72(9)(ba) amended, s 72(9)(ea) added, by the Crime and Courts Act 2013 Sch 8 para 114, Sch 21 para 19));
- (4) if the person in default was a member of the Serious Fraud Office, the compensation is payable by the Director of that Office (Proceeds of Crime Act 2002 s 72(9)(c));
- (5) if the person in default was an officer of Revenue and Customs, the compensation is payable by the Commissioners for Her Majesty's Revenue and Customs (Proceeds of Crime Act 2002 s 72(9)(e) (amended by virtue of the Commissioners for Revenue and Customs Act 2005 s 50(1), (7)));
- (6) if the person in default was an immigration officer, the compensation is payable by the Secretary of State (Proceeds of Crime Act 2002 s 72(9)(ea) (as so added)); and
- (7) if the person in default was an accredited financial investigator and none of the above applies, the compensation is payable in accordance with the Proceeds of Crime Act 2002 s 302(7A)(a), (c) or (e) (see CRIMINAL PROCEDURE vol 28 (2015) PARA 943) as the case may be (s 72(9)(f) (as so added)).

As to the National Crime Agency see POLICE AND INVESTIGATORY POWERS vol 84 (2013) PARA 424. As to the Commissioners for Her Majesty's Revenue and Customs see CUSTOMS AND EXCISE vol 31 (2012) PARA 921 et seq.

261.   Order varied or discharged.   Where the court varies[1] a confiscation order[2] or discharges[3] one[4], and an application[5] is made to the Crown Court by a person who held realisable property[6] and has suffered loss as a result of the making of the order[7], the court may order the payment of such compensation as it believes is just[8]. Such compensation is payable to the applicant[9] by the Lord Chancellor[10].

1 Ie under the Proceeds of Crime Act 2002 s 29 (see PARA 218).
2 Ie an order under the Proceeds of Crime Act 2002 s 6: see PARA 221.
3 Ie under the Proceeds of Crime Act 2002 s 30 (see PARA 219).
4 Proceeds of Crime Act 2002 s 73(1)(a).
5 In connection with applications under the Proceeds of Crime Act 2002 s 73 see the Criminal Procedure Rules 2015, SI 2015/1490, r 33.23.
6 As to when property is 'held' by a person see PARA 226.
7 Proceeds of Crime Act 2002 s 73(1)(b).
8 Proceeds of Crime Act 2002 s 73(2).
9 Proceeds of Crime Act 2002 s 73(3)(a).
10 Proceeds of Crime Act 2002 s 73(3)(b).

E. ENFORCEMENT ABROAD

262.   Enforcement abroad.   The following provisions apply if:
- (1)   any of the conditions[1] for the making of a restraint order[2] is satisfied[3];
- (2)   the prosecutor believes that realisable property[4] is situated in a country or territory outside the United Kingdom[5] (the receiving country)[6]; and
- (3)   the prosecutor sends a request for assistance to the Secretary of State with a view to it being forwarded to the government of the receiving country[7].

In a case where no confiscation order[8] has been made, a request for assistance is a request to the government of the receiving country to secure that any person is prohibited from dealing with realisable property[9].

In a case where a confiscation order has been made and has not been satisfied[10], discharged or quashed, a request for assistance is a request to the government of the receiving country to secure that:

(a)   any person is prohibited from dealing with realisable property[11]; and

(b)   realisable property is realised and the proceeds are applied in accordance with the law of the receiving country[12].

No request for assistance may be made for these purposes in a case where a confiscation order has been made and has been satisfied, discharged or quashed[13].

If the Secretary of State believes it is appropriate to do so, he may forward the request for assistance to the government of the receiving country[14].

1   Ie any of the conditions in the Proceeds of Crime Act 2002 s 40 (see PARA 200).
2   As to restraint orders see PARA 201.

3   Proceeds of Crime Act 2002 s 74(1)(a).
4   As to 'property' and 'realisable property' see PARA 226.
5   As to the meaning of 'United Kingdom' see PARA 4 note 3.
6   Proceeds of Crime Act 2002 s 74(1)(b) (s 74(1)(b), (c) amended by the Serious Crime Act 2007 Sch 8 para 35, Sch 14).

7   Proceeds of Crime Act 2002 s 74(1)(c) (as amended: see note 6).
8   Ie an order under the Proceeds of Crime Act 2002 s 6: see PARA 221.

9   Proceeds of Crime Act 2002 s 74(2).
10   As to when a confiscation order is 'satisfied' see PARA 199 note 11.

11   Proceeds of Crime Act 2002 s 74(3)(a).

12   Proceeds of Crime Act 2002 s 74(3)(b). If property is realised in pursuance of a request under s 74(3), the amount ordered to be paid under the confiscation order must be taken to be reduced by an amount equal to the proceeds of realisation: s 74(6). A certificate purporting to be issued by or on behalf of the requested government is admissible as evidence of the facts it states if it states: (1) that property has been realised in pursuance of a request under s 74(3) (s 74(7)(a)); (2) the date of realisation (s 74(7)(b)); and (3) the proceeds of realisation (s 74(7)(c)).

       If the proceeds of realisation made in pursuance of a request under s 74(3) are expressed in a currency other than sterling, they must be taken to be the sterling equivalent calculated in accordance with the rate of exchange prevailing at the end of the day of realisation: s 74(8).

13   Proceeds of Crime Act 2002 s 74(4).

14   Proceeds of Crime Act 2002 s 74(5).

F. EXTERNAL REQUESTS AND ORDERS

263.   External requests and orders. Provision broadly corresponding with the provisions relating to restraint orders[1] and management receivers[2] has been made in relation to an external request[3], and provision broadly corresponding with the provisions relating to enforcement receivers[4] has been made in relation to an external order[5].

1   See PARA 200 et seq.
2   See PARA 247 et seq.
3   As to the meaning of 'external request' see PARA 221 note 17.
4   See PARAS 249–250.

5   See the Proceeds of Crime Act 2002 (External Requests and Orders) Order 2005, SI 2005/3181; and PARAS 221 note 17, 201 note 4. As to the meaning of 'external order' see PARA 221 note 17. See *King v Director of Serious Fraud Office* [2009] UKHL 17, [2009] 2 All ER 223, [2009] 2 Cr App Rep 43.

G. PROVISIONS RELATING TO BANKRUPTCY AND INSOLVENCY

(A) *Individuals*

264. Excluded property. If a person is adjudged bankrupt in England and Wales the following property is excluded from his estate for the purposes of the provisions relating to applications for individual bankruptcy[1]:

(1) property for the time being subject to a restraint order[2] before the order adjudging him bankrupt[3];

(2) any property in respect of which an order appointing a receiver[4] is in force[5];

(3) property which is for the time being detained[6] in connection with restraint orders and search and seizure powers[7]; and

(4) personal property an order for the realisation of which[8] has been made[9].

1 Ie for the purposes of the Insolvency Act 1986 Pt 9 (ss 264–371) (see BANKRUPTCY AND INDIVIDUAL INSOLVENCY vol 5 (2013) PARA 129 et seq). Corresponding provision for a sequestration order made in Scotland and a bankruptcy adjudication made in Northern Ireland is made by the Proceeds of Crime Act 2002 ss 420, 423.
2 Ie an order which was made under the Proceeds of Crime Act 2002 s 41 (see PARA 201) (or corresponding Scottish or Northern Ireland provisions). If in the case of a debtor an interim receiver stands at any time appointed under the Insolvency Act 1986 s 286 (see BANKRUPTCY AND INDIVIDUAL INSOLVENCY vol 5 (2013) PARA 842) and any property of the debtor is then subject to a restraint order, the powers conferred on the receiver by virtue of the Insolvency Act 1986 do not apply to property then subject to the restraint order: Proceeds of Crime Act 2002 s 417(4).
3 Proceeds of Crime Act 2002 s 417(1), (2)(a) (s 417(2) substituted by the Policing and Crime Act 2009 Sch 7 para 79 (subject to limited savings: see the Policing and Crime Act 2009 (Commencement No 10, Transitional Provision and Savings) Order 2015, SI 2015/983)). The Proceeds of Crime Act 2002 s 417(2)(a) applies to heritable property in Scotland only if the restraint order is recorded in the General Register of Sasines or registered in the Land Register of Scotland before the order adjudging the person bankrupt: s 417(3).
4 Ie an order under the Proceeds of Crime Act 2002 s 50 (see PARA 249) (or corresponding Scottish or Northern Ireland provisions).
5 Proceeds of Crime Act 2002 s 417(2)(b), (c) (as substituted: see note 3).
6 Ie under or by virtue of the Proceeds of Crime Act 2002 s 44A (see PARAS 204, 205), s 47J (see PARA 208), s 47K (see PARA 212), s 47M (see PARA 213) or s 47P (see PARA 213) (or corresponding Scottish or Northern Ireland provisions).
7 Proceeds of Crime Act 2002 s 417(2)(b) (as substituted: see note 3).
8 Ie any property in respect of which an order under the Proceeds of Crime Act 2002 s 67A (see PARA 197) (or corresponding Scottish or Northern Ireland provisions) is in force.
9 Proceeds of Crime Act 2002 s 417(2)(d) (as substituted: see note 3).

265. Excluded powers. If a person is adjudged bankrupt, the powers conferred on a court by the provisions relating to restraint orders and the search and seizure of property[1], the powers conferred on management and enforcement receivers by such provisions[2] and the powers conferred on an 'appropriate officer' in relation to the seizure of property[3], must not be exercised in relation to:

(1) property which is for the time being comprised[4] in the bankrupt's estate[5];

(2) property in respect of which his trustee in bankruptcy may (without leave of the court) serve a notice[6] relating to after-acquired property, items of excess value and certain tenancies[7];

(3) property which is[8] to be applied for the benefit of creditors of the bankrupt[9];

(4) in a case where a confiscation order[10] has been made, any sums

remaining in the hands of a receiver[11] after the amount required to be paid under the confiscation order has been fully paid[12]; and

(5) in a case where a confiscation order has been made, any sums remaining in the hands of an appropriate officer after the amount required to be paid under the confiscation order has been[13] fully paid[14].

1 Ie the powers conferred on a court by the Proceeds of Crime Act 2002 ss 41–67 (see PARA 201 et seq) and ss 67A, 67B (see PARA 197). Nothing in the Insolvency Act 1986 must be taken to restrict (or enable the restriction of) the powers conferred on a court by the Proceeds of Crime Act 2002 ss 41–67: s 418(4).

2 Ie the powers conferred on management and enforcement receivers by the Proceeds of Crime Act 2002 ss 48, 50 (see PARAS 247, 249).

3 Ie the powers conferred by the Proceeds of Crime Act 2002 s 47C (see PARAS 208, 210).

4 Ie for the purposes of the Insolvency Act 1986 Pt 9 (ss 264–371) (see BANKRUPTCY AND INDIVIDUAL INSOLVENCY vol 5 (2013) PARA 129 et seq).

5 Proceeds of Crime Act 2002 s 418(1), (2)(a), (3)(a) (s 418(2)(a), (3)(d) amended by the Serious Crime Act 2007 Sch 8 para 70; Proceeds of Crime Act 2002 s 418(2)(a) amended, s 418(3)(f) added, by the Policing and Crime Act 2009 Sch 7 para 80 (subject to limited savings: see the Policing and Crime Act 2009 (Commencement No 10, Transitional Provision and Savings) Order 2015, SI 2015/983)). Corresponding provision for a sequestration order made in Scotland and a bankruptcy adjudication made in Northern Ireland is made by the Proceeds of Crime Act 2002 ss 421, 424.

6 Ie a notice under the Insolvency Act 1986 s 307, s 308 or s 308A: see BANKRUPTCY AND INDIVIDUAL INSOLVENCY vol 5 (2013) PARAS 404, 405, 458–459.

7 Proceeds of Crime Act 2002 s 418(3)(b).

8 Ie by virtue of a condition imposed under the Insolvency Act 1986 s 280(2)(c) (see BANKRUPTCY AND INDIVIDUAL INSOLVENCY vol 5 (2013) PARA 638.

9 Proceeds of Crime Act 2002 s 418(3)(c).

10 Ie an order under the Proceeds of Crime Act 2002 s 6: see PARA 221.

11 Ie a receiver appointed under the Proceeds of Crime Act 2002 s 50 (see PARA 249) (or corresponding Scottish or Northern Ireland provisions).

12 Proceeds of Crime Act 2002 s 418(3)(d) (as amended: see note 5).

13 Ie under the Proceeds of Crime Act 2002 s 67D(2)(c) (see PARA 197) (or corresponding Scottish or Northern Ireland provisions).

14 Proceeds of Crime Act 2002 s 418(3)(f) (as added: see note 5).

266. Provision relating to tainted gifts. If a person who is adjudged bankrupt has made a tainted gift[1] (whether directly or indirectly) no order correcting an undervalued, preferential or fraudulent transaction[2] may be made in respect of the making of the gift at any time when:

(1) any property of the recipient of the tainted gift is[3] subject to a restraint order[4];

(2) there is in respect of such property an order[5] appointing a receiver[6];

(3) there is in respect of such property an order[7] for the realisation of that property[8]; or

(4) such property is detained[9] in connection with restraint orders and search and seizure powers[10],

and any correcting an undervalued, preferential or fraudulent transaction[11] made after such an order (other than an order referred to in head (4) above) is discharged must take into account any realisation[12] of property held by the recipient of the tainted gift[13].

1 As to gifts see PARA 227; as to 'tainted' gifts see PARA 228.

2 Ie an order under the Insolvency Act 1986 s 339, s 340 or s 423 (avoidance of certain transactions: see BANKRUPTCY AND INDIVIDUAL INSOLVENCY vol 5 (2013) PARAS 678–683, 689).

3 Ie under the Proceeds of Crime Act 2002 s 41 (see PARA 201) (or corresponding Scottish or Northern Ireland provisions).

4 Proceeds of Crime Act 2002 s 419(1), (2)(a), (4).

5   Ie an order under the Proceeds of Crime Act 2002 s 50 (see PARA 249) (or corresponding Scottish or Northern Ireland provisions).
6   Proceeds of Crime Act 2002 s 419(2)(b) (amended by the Serious Crime Act 2007 Sch 8 para 71, Sch 14).
7   Ie an order under the Proceeds of Crime Act 2002 s 67A (see PARA 197) (or corresponding Scottish or Northern Ireland provisions).
8   Proceeds of Crime Act 2002 s 419(2)(c) (s 419(2)(aa), (c) added, s 419(3) amended, by the Policing and Crime Act 2009 Sch 7 para 81 (subject to limited savings: see the Policing and Crime Act 2009 (Commencement No 10, Transitional Provision and Savings) Order 2015, SI 2015/983)).
9   Ie under or by virtue of the Proceeds of Crime Act 2002 s 44A (see PARAS 204, 205), s 47J (see PARA 208), s 47K (see PARA 212), s 47M (see PARA 213) or s 47P (see PARA 213) (or corresponding Scottish or Northern Ireland provisions).
10 Proceeds of Crime Act 2002 s 419(2)(aa) (as added: see note 8).
11 See note 2.
12 Ie under the Proceeds of Crime Act 2002 Pt 2 (ss 6–91) (or corresponding Scottish or Northern Ireland provisions).
13 Proceeds of Crime Act 2002 s 419(3) (as amended: see note 8). Corresponding provision for a sequestration order made in Scotland and a bankruptcy adjudication made in Northern Ireland is made by the Proceeds of Crime Act 2002 ss 422, 425.

(B) Companies and Limited Liability Partnerships

267.   Winding up.   If an order for the winding up of a company or limited liability partnership[1] is made, or such a company or partnership passes a resolution or (as the case may be) makes a determination for its voluntary winding up[2], the functions of the liquidator (or any provisional liquidator) are not exercisable in relation to:

(1)   property for the time being subject to a restraint order[3] before the relevant time[4];

(2)   any property in respect of which an order appointing a receiver[5] is in force[6];

(3)   property which is for the time being detained[7] in connection with restraint orders and search and seizure powers[8]; and

(4)   personal property an order for the realisation of which[9] has been made[10],

and the powers[11] conferred on a court by the provisions relating to restraint orders and the search and seizure of property[12] must not be exercised, in relation to any property which is held by the company or partnership[13] and in relation to which the functions of the liquidator are exercisable[14], either so as to inhibit the liquidator from exercising his functions for the purpose of distributing property to the company or partnership's creditors[15] or so as to prevent the payment out of any property of expenses (including the remuneration of the liquidator or any provisional liquidator) properly incurred in the winding up in respect of the property[16].

1   Ie a company or limited liability partnership which may be wound up under the Insolvency Act 1986: see COMPANY AND PARTNERSHIP INSOLVENCY vol 16 (2011) PARA 383; COMPANY AND PARTNERSHIP INSOLVENCY vol 17 (2011) PARA 1368. Corresponding provision for company or limited liability partnership being wound up in Northern Ireland is made by the Proceeds of Crime Act 2002 s 428.
2   See COMPANY AND PARTNERSHIP INSOLVENCY vol 17 (2011) PARA 902 et seq.
3   Ie an order which was made under the Proceeds of Crime Act 2002 s 41 (see PARA 201) (or corresponding Scottish or Northern Ireland provisions).
4   Proceeds of Crime Act 2002 ss 426(1), (2)(a), 431(1), (2) (s 426(2) substituted, s 426(5)(a) amended, by the Policing and Crime Act 2009 Sch 7 para 88 (subject to limited savings: see the Policing and Crime Act 2009 (Commencement No 10, Transitional Provision and Savings) Order 2015, SI 2015/983)). The 'relevant time' for these purposes is:

(1) if no order for the winding up of the company has been made, the time of the passing of the resolution or the making of the determination for voluntary winding up (Proceeds of Crime Act 2002 s 426(9)(a));

(2) if such an order has been made, but before the presentation of the petition for the winding up of the company by the court such a resolution has been passed by the company or such a determination has been made by the partnership, the time of the passing of the resolution or the making of the determination (s 426(9)(b)); or

(3) if such an order has been made, but head (2) above does not apply, the time of the making of the order (s 426(9)(c)).

Section 426(2)(a) applies to heritable property in Scotland only if the restraint order is recorded in the General Register of Sasines or registered in the Land Register of Scotland before the order adjudging the person bankrupt: s 426(3).

5 Ie an order under the Proceeds of Crime Act 2002 s 50 (see PARA 249) (or corresponding Scottish or Northern Ireland provisions).

6 Proceeds of Crime Act 2002 s 426(2)(b), (c) (as substituted (see note 4); s 426(2)(b), (5)(a) amended by the Serious Crime Act 2007 Sch 8 para 78, Sch 14).

7 Ie under or by virtue of the Proceeds of Crime Act 2002 s 44A (see PARAS 204, 205), s 47J (see PARA 208), s 47K (see PARA 212), s 47M (see PARA 213) or s 47P (see PARA 213) (or corresponding Scottish or Northern Ireland provisions).

8 Proceeds of Crime Act 2002 s 426(2)(b) (as substituted: see note 4).

9 Ie any property in respect of which an order under the Proceeds of Crime Act 2002 s 67A (see PARA 197) (or corresponding Scottish or Northern Ireland provisions) is in force.

10 Proceeds of Crime Act 2002 s 426(2)(d) (as substituted: see note 4).

11 Ie the powers conferred on a court by the Proceeds of Crime Act 2002 ss 41–67 (see PARA 201 et seq) and ss 67A, 67B (see PARA 197). Nothing in the Insolvency Act 1986 must be taken to restrict (or enable the restriction of) the powers conferred on a court by the Proceeds of Crime Act 2002 ss 41–67: s 426(7).

12 Proceeds of Crime Act 2002 s 426(5)(a) (as amended and amended: see notes 4, 6).

13 Proceeds of Crime Act 2002 s 426(4)(a).

14 Proceeds of Crime Act 2002 s 426(4)(b).

15 Proceeds of Crime Act 2002 s 426(6)(a).

16 Proceeds of Crime Act 2002 s 426(6)(b).

268. Provision relating to tainted gifts. If an order for the winding up of a company or limited liability partnership[1] is made, or such a company or partnership passes a resolution or (as the case may be) makes a determination for its voluntary winding up[2], and the company or partnership has made a tainted gift[3] (whether directly or indirectly)[4], no order correcting an undervalued, preferential or fraudulent transaction[5] may be made in respect of the making of the gift at any time when:

(1) any property of the recipient of the tainted gift is[6] subject to a restraint order[7];

(2) there is in respect of such property an order[8] appointing a receiver[9];

(3) there is in respect of such property an order[10] for the realisation of that property[11]; or

(4) such property is detained[12] in connection with restraint orders and search and seizure powers[13],

and any correcting an undervalued, preferential or fraudulent transaction[14] made after such an order (other than an order referred to in head (4) above) is discharged must take into account any realisation[15] of property held by the recipient of the tainted gift[16].

1 Ie a company or limited liability partnership which may be wound up under the Insolvency Act 1986: see COMPANY AND PARTNERSHIP INSOLVENCY vol 16 (2011) PARA 383; COMPANY AND PARTNERSHIP INSOLVENCY vol 17 (2011) PARA 1368. Corresponding provision for company or limited liability partnership being wound up in Northern Ireland is made by the Proceeds of Crime Act 2002 s 428.

2 Proceeds of Crime Act 2002 ss 427(1), (2)(a), 431(1), (2). In connection with voluntary winding up see COMPANY AND PARTNERSHIP INSOLVENCY vol 17 (2011) PARA 902 et seq.

3   As to gifts see PARA 227; as to 'tainted' gifts see PARA 228.
4   Proceeds of Crime Act 2002 ss 427(2)(b).
5   Ie an order under the Insolvency Act 1986 s 339, s 340 or s 423 (avoidance of certain
     transactions: see BANKRUPTCY AND INDIVIDUAL INSOLVENCY vol 5 (2013) PARAS 678–683, 689).
6   Ie under the Proceeds of Crime Act 2002 s 41 (see PARA 201) (or corresponding Scottish or
     Northern Ireland provisions).
7   Proceeds of Crime Act 2002 s 427(3)(a), (5).
8   Ie an order under the Proceeds of Crime Act 2002 s 50 (see PARA 249) (or corresponding
     Scottish or Northern Ireland provisions).
9   Proceeds of Crime Act 2002 s 427(3)(b) (amended by the Serious Crime Act 2007 Sch 8 para 79,
     Sch 14).
10   Ie an order under the Proceeds of Crime Act 2002 s 67A (see PARA 197) (or corresponding
     Scottish or Northern Ireland provisions).
11   Proceeds of Crime Act 2002 s 427(3)(c) (s 427(3)(aa), (c) added, s 427(4) amended, by the
     Policing and Crime Act 2009 Sch 7 para 89 (subject to limited savings: see the Policing and
     Crime Act 2009 (Commencement No 10, Transitional Provision and Savings) Order 2015,
     SI 2015/983)).
12   Ie under or by virtue of the Proceeds of Crime Act 2002 s 44A (see PARAS 204, 205), s 47J (see
     PARA 208), s 47K (see PARA 212), s 47M (see PARA 213) or s 47P (see PARA 213) (or
     corresponding Scottish or Northern Ireland provisions).
13   Proceeds of Crime Act 2002 s 427(3)(aa) (as added: see note 11).
14   See note 5.
15   Ie under the Proceeds of Crime Act 2002 Pt 2 (ss 6–91) (or corresponding Scottish or Northern
     Ireland provisions).
16   Proceeds of Crime Act 2002 s 427(4) (as amended: see note 11). Corresponding provision in
     connection with a company being wound up in Northern Ireland is made by the Proceeds of
     Crime Act 2002 s 429.

269. Floating charges. If a company or a limited liability partnership[1] holds
property which is subject to a floating charge[2], and a receiver has been appointed
by or on the application of the holder of the charge, the functions of the receiver
are not exercisable in relation to:

(1)   property for the time being subject to a restraint order[3] which was made
       before the appointment of the receiver[4];

(2)   any property in respect of which an order appointing a receiver[5] is in
       force[6];

(3)   property which is for the time being detained[7] in connection with
       restraint orders and search and seizure powers[8]; and

(4)   personal property an order for the realisation of which[9] has been
       made[10].

and the powers[11] conferred on a court by the provisions relating to restraint
orders and the search and seizure of property[12] must not be exercised, in relation
to any property which is held by the company or partnership[13] and in relation to
which the functions of the liquidator are exercisable[14], either so as to inhibit the
liquidator from exercising his functions for the purpose of distributing property
to the company or partnership's creditors[15] or so as to prevent the payment out
of any property of expenses (including the remuneration of the liquidator or any
provisional liquidator) properly incurred in the winding up in respect of the
property[16].

1   Ie a company or limited liability partnership which may be wound up under the Insolvency
     Act 1986 or corresponding Northern Ireland legislation: see COMPANY AND PARTNERSHIP
     INSOLVENCY vol 16 (2011) PARA 383; COMPANY AND PARTNERSHIP INSOLVENCY vol 17 (2011)
     PARA 1368.
2   As to floating charges generally see COMPANIES vol 15 (2009) PARA 1269.
3   Ie an order which was made under the Proceeds of Crime Act 2002 s 41 (see PARA 201) (or
     corresponding Scottish or Northern Ireland provisions). If in the case of a debtor an interim
     receiver stands at any time appointed under the Insolvency Act 1986 s 286 (see BANKRUPTCY

AND INDIVIDUAL INSOLVENCY vol 5 (2013) PARA 842) and any property of the debtor is then subject to a restraint order, the powers conferred on the receiver by virtue of the Insolvency Act 1986 do not apply to property then subject to the restraint order: Proceeds of Crime Act 2002 s 417(4).

4 Proceeds of Crime Act 2002 s 430(1), (2)(a) (s 430(2) substituted, s 430(5)(a) amended, by the Policing and Crime Act 2009 Sch 7 para 92 (subject to limited savings: see the Policing and Crime Act 2009 (Commencement No 10, Transitional Provision and Savings) Order 2015, SI 2015/983)). The Proceeds of Crime Act 2002 s 430(2)(a) as originally drafted refers to a restraint order that was made 'before the appointment of the receiver'; that provision as substituted refers to a restraint order that was made 'before the relevant time', but 'relevant time' is not defined for the purposes of s 430. Section 430(2)(a) applies to heritable property in Scotland only if the restraint order is recorded in the General Register of Sasines or registered in the Land Register of Scotland before the order adjudging the person bankrupt: s 430(3).

5 Ie an order under the Proceeds of Crime Act 2002 s 50 (see PARA 249) (or corresponding Scottish or Northern Ireland provisions).

6 Proceeds of Crime Act 2002 s 430(2)(b), (c) (s 430(2)(b), (d), (5)(a) amended by the Serious Crime Act 2007 Sch 8 para 82, Sch 14; Proceeds of Crime Act 2002 s 430(2) as substituted (see note 4)).

7 Ie under or by virtue of the Proceeds of Crime Act 2002 s 44A (see PARAS 204, 205), s 47J (see PARA 208), s 47K (see PARA 212), s 47M (see PARA 213) or s 47P (see PARA 213) (or corresponding Scottish or Northern Ireland provisions).

8 Proceeds of Crime Act 2002 s 430(2)(b) (as substituted: see note 4).

9 Ie any property in respect of which an order under the Proceeds of Crime Act 2002 s 67A (see PARA 197) (or corresponding Scottish or Northern Ireland provisions) is in force.

10 Proceeds of Crime Act 2002 s 430(2)(d) (as substituted: see note 4).

11 Ie the powers conferred on a court by the Proceeds of Crime Act 2002 ss 41–67 (see PARA 201 et seq) and ss 67A, 67B (see PARA 197). Nothing in the Insolvency Act 1986 must be taken to restrict (or enable the restriction of) the powers conferred on a court by the Proceeds of Crime Act 2002 ss 41–67: s 430(7).

12 Proceeds of Crime Act 2002 s 430(5)(a) (as amended: see notes 4, 6).

13 Proceeds of Crime Act 2002 s 430(4)(a).

14 Proceeds of Crime Act 2002 s 430(4)(b).

15 Proceeds of Crime Act 2002 s 430(6)(a).

16 Proceeds of Crime Act 2002 s 430(6)(b).

(C) Insolvency Practitioners

270. Liability and lien. If a person acting as an insolvency practitioner[1] seizes or disposes of any property in relation to which his functions are not exercisable because it is for the time being subject to a restraint order[2] and at the time of the seizure or disposal he believes on reasonable grounds that he is entitled (whether in pursuance of an order of a court or otherwise) to seize or dispose of the property:

(1) he is not liable to any person in respect of any loss or damage resulting from the seizure or disposal, except so far as the loss or damage is caused by his negligence[3]; and

(2) he has a lien on the property or the proceeds of its sale for such of his expenses as were incurred in connection with the liquidation, bankruptcy, sequestration or other proceedings in relation to which he purported to make the seizure or disposal[4] and for so much of his remuneration as may reasonably be assigned to his acting in connection with those proceedings[5].

1 For the purposes of the Proceeds of Crime Act 2002 s 432, a person 'acts as an insolvency practitioner' if he so acts within the meaning given by the Insolvency Act 1986 s 388 (see BANKRUPTCY AND INDIVIDUAL INSOLVENCY vol 5 (2013) PARA 40) (Proceeds of Crime Act 2002 s 433(1), (2)), subject to the following: (1) the expression 'person acting as an insolvency practitioner' includes the official receiver acting as receiver or manager of the property concerned (s 433(3)); and (2) in applying the Insolvency Act 1986 s 388, the reference in

s 388(2)(a) to a permanent or interim trustee in sequestration must be taken to include a reference to a trustee in sequestration and s 388(5) (which includes provision that nothing in s 388 applies to anything done by the official receiver or the Accountant in Bankruptcy) must be ignored (Proceeds of Crime Act 2002 s 433(4)).

2   Proceeds of Crime Act 2002 s 432(1)(a). A restraint order is an order which was made under the Proceeds of Crime Act 2002 s 41 (see PARA 201).
3   Proceeds of Crime Act 2002 s 432(2). This is without prejudice to the generality of any provision of the Insolvency Act 1986 or any other Act or Order which confers protection from liability on him: Proceeds of Crime Act 2002 s 432(4).
4   Proceeds of Crime Act 2002 s 432(3)(a).
5   Proceeds of Crime Act 2002 s 432(3)(b).

271. Expenses. If:

(1)   property is subject to a restraint order[1], a person acting as an insolvency practitioner incurs expenses in respect of property subject to the order[2], and he does not know (and has no reasonable grounds to believe) that the property is subject to the order[3];

(2)   property is subject to a restraint order[4], a person acting as an insolvency practitioner incurs expenses which are not ones in respect of property subject to the order[5], and the expenses are ones which (but for the effect of the restraint order) might have been met by taking possession of and realising property subject to it[6]; or

(3)   property is detained[7] in connection with restraint orders and search and seizure powers[8], a person acting as an insolvency practitioner incurs expenses which are not ones in respect of the detained property[9], and the expenses are ones which (but for the effect of the detention of the property) might have been met by taking possession of and realising the property[10],

the person acting as the insolvency practitioner is entitled, whether or not he has seized or disposed of any property, to payment[11] of the expenses[12].

1   Proceeds of Crime Act 2002 s 432(5)(a). A restraint order is an order which was made under the Proceeds of Crime Act 2002 s 41 (see PARA 201).
2   Proceeds of Crime Act 2002 s 432(5)(b).
3   Proceeds of Crime Act 2002 s 432(5)(c).
4   Proceeds of Crime Act 2002 s 432(6)(a).
5   Proceeds of Crime Act 2002 s 432(6)(b).
6   Proceeds of Crime Act 2002 s 432(6)(c).
7   Ie under or by virtue of the Proceeds of Crime Act 2002 s 44A (see PARAS 204, 205), s 47J (see PARA 208), s 47K (see PARA 212), s 47M (see PARA 213) or s 47P (see PARA 213) (or corresponding Scottish or Northern Ireland provisions).
8   Proceeds of Crime Act 2002 s 432(6A)(a) (s 432(6A) added, s 432(7) substituted, by the Policing and Crime Act 2009 Sch 7 para 93 (subject to limited savings: see the Policing and Crime Act 2009 (Commencement No 10, Transitional Provision and Savings) Order 2015, SI 2015/983)).
9   Proceeds of Crime Act 2002 s 432(6A)(b) (as added: see note 8).
10   Proceeds of Crime Act 2002 s 432(6A)(c) (as added: see note 8).
11   Ie under the Proceeds of Crime Act 2002 s 54(2) (see PARA 258), s 55(3) (see PARA 259) or s 67D(2) (see PARA 197).
12   Proceeds of Crime Act 2002 s 432(7)(a) (amended by the Serious Crime Act 2007 Sch 8 para 83; as substituted (see note 8)).

(vi) Variation and Reconsideration

A. PROCEDURE

272. Duty of prosecutor to provide information. Where:

(1)   the court proceeds under the provisions relating to the making of a confiscation order[1] in a case[2] where, no order having been made, there is a reconsideration of the case or of the decision that there was no benefit to the defendant from the offence or offences concerned[3]; or

(2)   an order having been made, the prosecutor applies[4] for a reconsideration of the benefit to the defendant from such offence or offences[5],

the prosecutor must give the court a statement of information within the period which the court orders[6].

1   As to the making of confiscation orders see the Proceeds of Crime Act 2002 s 6; and PARA 221.
2   Ie where the court proceeds in pursuance of the Proceeds of Crime Act 2002 s 19 (see PARA 273) or s 20 (see PARA 274).
3   Proceeds of Crime Act 2002 s 26(1)(a).
4   Ie under the Proceeds of Crime Act 2002 s 21 (see PARA 275).
5   Proceeds of Crime Act 2002 s 26(1)(b) (s 26(1)(b), (2)(a) amended by the Serious Crime Act 2007 Sch 8 para 13(2), Sch 14).
6   Proceeds of Crime Act 2002 s 26(2)(a) (as amended: see note 5). In such a case:
    (1)   s 16 (see PARA 194) applies accordingly (with appropriate modifications where the prosecutor or the Director applies under s 21 (see PARA 275)) (s 26(2)(b));
    (2)   s 17 (see PARA 194) applies accordingly (s 26(2)(c)); and
    (3)   s 18 (see PARA 195) applies as it applies in the circumstances mentioned in s 18(1) (see PARA 195) (s 26(2)(d)).

B.   RECONSIDERATION

(A)   Prosecution Applications

273.   No order made: reconsideration of case.   Where:
   (1)   the defendant[1] is convicted of an offence or offences in proceedings before the Crown Court[2], is committed[3] to the Crown Court for sentence in respect of an offence or offences[4], or is committed[5] to the Crown Court in respect of an offence or offences with a view to a confiscation order being considered[6], but no court has proceeded under the provisions relating to the making of a confiscation order[7];
   (2)   there is evidence which was not available to the prosecutor on the relevant date[8];
   (3)   before the end of the period of six years starting with the date of conviction the prosecutor applies[9] to the Crown Court to consider the evidence[10]; and
   (4)   after considering the evidence, the court believes it is appropriate for it to proceed under the provisions relating to the making of confiscation orders[11],
or, where a defendant ceases to be an absconder:
   (a)   at a time when the first condition for the making of a confiscation order in relation to an absconding offender[12] was satisfied the court did not proceed[13] to make a confiscation order[14];
   (b)   before the end of the period of six years starting with the day when the defendant ceased to be an absconder, the prosecutor applies to the Crown Court to proceed[15] to make a confiscation order[16]; and
   (c)   the court believes it is appropriate for it to do so[17],
the court must proceed under the provisions relating to the making of confiscation orders, and when it does so the following provisions[18] apply[19].

If the court has already sentenced the defendant for the offence (or any of the offences) concerned[20], the provisions relating to the making of confiscation orders have effect as if his particular criminal conduct[21] included conduct which constitutes offences which the court has taken into consideration in deciding his sentence for the offence or offences concerned[22].

The court must take account of conduct occurring before the relevant date[23]; of property obtained before that date[24]; and of property obtained on or after that date if it was obtained as a result of or in connection with conduct occurring before that date[25].

In relation to the assumptions to be made in the case of a criminal lifestyle[26]:

(i) the first and second assumptions do not apply with regard to property first held by the defendant on or after the relevant date[27];

(ii) the third assumption does not apply with regard to expenditure incurred by him on or after that date[28]; and

(iii) the fourth assumption does not apply with regard to property obtained (or assumed to have been obtained) by him on or after that date[29].

The recoverable amount for the purposes of the provisions relating to the making of a confiscation order is such amount as the court believes is just[30], but does not exceed the amount found by the court under the provisions[31] relating to the recoverable amount[32].

In arriving at the just amount the court must have regard in particular to:

(A) the amount found under the provisions relating to the recoverable amount[33];

(B) any fine imposed on the defendant in respect of the offence (or any of the offences) concerned[34];

(C) any order involving payment, other than a compensation order[35], a forfeiture order[36] or a deprivation order[37] which has been made against the defendant in respect of the offence (or any of the offences) concerned and has not already been taken into account by the court in deciding what is the free property[38] held by him for the purposes of the provisions[39] relating to the available amount[40];

(D) any order which has been made against the defendant in respect of the offence (or any of the offences) concerned[41] under the provisions relating to compensation orders[42];

(E) any order which has been made requiring the payment of a surcharge[43] against the defendant in respect of the offence (or any of the offences) concerned[44]; and

(F) any order which has been made against the defendant in respect of the offence (or any of the offences) concerned[45] under the provisions relating to unlawful profit orders[46].

If a compensation order, an order for the payment of a surcharge or an unlawful profit order has been made against the defendant in respect of the offence or offences concerned, the provisions dealing with the case where the court believes that the defendant has insufficient means to satisfy a confiscation order and a compensation order or an unlawful profit order[47] do not apply in relation to it[48].

1 As to the meaning of 'defendant' for these purposes see PARA 221 note 1.
2 Proceeds of Crime Act 2002 ss 6(1), (2)(a), 19(1)(a). See further PARA 221 note 2.
3 The text refers to committal under the Powers of Criminal Courts (Sentencing) Act 2000 s 3, s 3A, s 3B, s 3C, s 4, s 4A or s 6 (see CRIMINAL PROCEDURE vol 27 (2015) PARAS 234–236, 292–296): Proceeds of Crime Act 2002 s 6(2)(b) (amended by the Criminal Justice Act 2003 s 41, Sch 3 para 75(1), (2)).

4   Proceeds of Crime Act 2002 ss 6(2)(b) (as amended: see note 3), 19(1)(a).

5   Ie under the Proceeds of Crime Act 2002 s 70 (see PARA 190).

6   Proceeds of Crime Act 2002 ss 6(2)(c), 19(1)(a).

7   Proceeds of Crime Act 2002 s 19(1)(a). The provisions relating to the making of a confiscation order are the provisions of s 6 (see PARA 221).

8   Proceeds of Crime Act 2002 s 19(1)(b). The 'relevant date' is: (1) if the court made a decision not to proceed under s 6, the date of the decision (s 19(9)(a)); and (2) if the court did not make such a decision, the date of conviction (s 19(9)(b)). The date of conviction is the date on which the defendant was convicted of the offence concerned (s 19(10)(a)) or if there are two or more offences and the convictions were on different dates, the date of the latest (s 19(10)(b)).

9   In connection with applications under the Proceeds of Crime Act 2002 s 19 see the Criminal Procedure Rules 2015, SI 2015/1490, r 33.15.

10 Proceeds of Crime Act 2002 s 19(1)(c) (amended by the Serious Crime Act 2007 Sch 8 para 8, Sch 14).

11 Proceeds of Crime Act 2002 s 19(1)(d).

12 Ie the first condition in the Proceeds of Crime Act 2002 s 27: see s 27(1); and PARA 216.

13 Ie under the Proceeds of Crime Act 2002 s 6.

14 Proceeds of Crime Act 2002 ss 19(1)(a), 27(6)(a) (s 19(7)(da) added, s 19(8) amended, s 27(6) substituted, by the Serious Crime Act 2015 s 9(2), Sch 4 para 23).

15 See note 13.

16 Proceeds of Crime Act 2002 s 19(1)(b).

17 Proceeds of Crime Act 2002 s 19(1)(c).

18 Ie the Proceeds of Crime Act 2002 s 19(3)–(8) (see the text and notes 20–46).

19 Proceeds of Crime Act 2002 s 19(2).

20 As to references to 'sentencing the defendant for an offence' see PARA 193 note 2. As to references to the 'offence or offences concerned' see PARA 229 note 2.

21 As to 'conduct', 'criminal conduct' and 'particular criminal conduct' see PARA 225.

22 Proceeds of Crime Act 2002 s 19(3).

23 Proceeds of Crime Act 2002 s 19(4)(a). Section 19 applies instead of s 8(2) (see PARA 223).

24 Proceeds of Crime Act 2002 s 19(4)(b). See note 23. As to 'property' and when property is 'obtained' see PARA 226.

25 Proceeds of Crime Act 2002 s 19(4)(c). See note 23. As to references to property obtained in connection with conduct see PARA 226.

26 Ie the assumptions made under the Proceeds of Crime Act 2002 s 10 (see PARA 231).

27 Proceeds of Crime Act 2002 s 19(5)(a).

28 Proceeds of Crime Act 2002 s 19(5)(b).

29 Proceeds of Crime Act 2002 s 19(5)(c).

30 Proceeds of Crime Act 2002 s 19(6)(a).

31 Ie the Proceeds of Crime Act 2002 s 7 (see PARA 233).

32 Proceeds of Crime Act 2002 s 19(6)(b).

33 Proceeds of Crime Act 2002 s 19(7)(a).

34 Proceeds of Crime Act 2002 s 19(7)(b).

35 Ie an order under the Powers of Criminal Courts (Sentencing) Act 2000 s 130 (see PARA 281).

36 Ie an order under the Misuse of Drugs Act 1971 s 27 (see MEDICAL PRODUCTS AND DRUGS vol 75 (2013) PARA 526) or the Terrorism Act 2000 s 23 (see PARA 301).

37 Ie an order under the Powers of Criminal Courts (Sentencing) Act 2000 s 143 (see PARA 470).

38 As to when property is 'free' see PARA 226.

39 Ie the Proceeds of Crime Act 2002 s 9 (see PARA 233).

40 Proceeds of Crime Act 2002 s 19(7)(c).

41 Ie under the Powers of Criminal Courts (Sentencing) Act 2000 s 130.

42 Proceeds of Crime Act 2002 s 19(7)(d).

43 Ie under the Criminal Justice Act 2003 s 161A (orders requiring payment of surcharge: see PARA 185).

44 Proceeds of Crime Act 2002 s 19(7)(da) (as added: see note 14).

45 Ie under the Prevention of Social Housing Fraud Act 2013 s 4 (see LANDLORD AND TENANT).

46 Proceeds of Crime Act 2002 s 19(7)(e) (s 19(7)(e) added, s 19(8) amended, by the Prevention of Social Housing Fraud Act 2013 Schedule paras 11, 17).

47 Ie the Proceeds of Crime Act 2002 s 13(5), (6) (see PARA 237).

48 Proceeds of Crime Act 2002 s 19(8) (as amended (see notes 14, 46); amended by the Modern Slavery Act 2015 Sch 5 para 16).

274.   No order made: reconsideration of benefit. If in proceeding under the provisions relating to the making of a confiscation order[1] the court has decided that the defendant[2] has a criminal lifestyle[3] but has not benefited from his general criminal conduct[4], or that the defendant does not have a criminal lifestyle and has not benefited from his particular criminal conduct[5], and:

(1)   there is evidence which was not available to the prosecutor when the court decided that the defendant had not benefited from his general or particular criminal conduct[6], before the end of the period of six years starting with the date of conviction the prosecutor applies to the Crown Court to consider the evidence[7], and after considering the evidence, the court concludes that it would have decided that the defendant had benefited from his general or particular criminal conduct (as the case may be) if the evidence had been available to it[8]; or

(2)   where a defendant ceases to be an absconder, before the end of the period of six years starting with the day when the defendant ceased to be an absconder, the prosecutor applies to the Crown Court to reconsider whether the defendant has benefited from his general or particular criminal conduct (as the case may be)[9] and the court believes it is appropriate for it to do so[10],

the court must make a fresh decision[11] whether the defendant has benefited from his general or particular conduct (as the case may be)[12] and may make[13] a confiscation order[14].

If the court proceeds under the provisions relating to the making of a confiscation order by virtue of the above provisions, the provisions apply with modifications[15].

1   Ie the Proceeds of Crime Act 2002 s 6 (see PARA 221).
2   As to the meaning of 'defendant' for these purposes see PARA 221 note 1.
3   As to the circumstances under which the defendant may be judged to have a 'criminal lifestyle' see PARA 229.
4   Proceeds of Crime Act 2002 s 20(1), (2)(a). As to 'conduct', 'criminal conduct' and 'general' and 'particular' criminal conduct, see PARA 225; as to when a person benefits from conduct see PARA 223.
5   Proceeds of Crime Act 2002 s 20(2)(b).
6   Proceeds of Crime Act 2002 s 20(4)(a).
7   Proceeds of Crime Act 2002 s 20(4)(b) (amended by the Serious Crime Act 2007 Sch 8 para 9(3), Sch 14). In connection with applications under the Proceeds of Crime Act 2002 s 20 see the Criminal Procedure Rules 2015, SI 2015/1490, r 33.15.
8   Proceeds of Crime Act 2002 s 20(4)(c).
9   Proceeds of Crime Act 2002 ss 20(4)(a), 27(6)(b) (s 20(11)(da) added, s 20(8) amended, s 27(6) substituted, by the Serious Crime Act 2015 s 9(2), Sch 4 para 24).
10   Proceeds of Crime Act 2002 s 20(4)(b).
11   Ie under the Proceeds of Crime Act 2002 s 6(4)(b) or (c) (see PARA 221).
12   Proceeds of Crime Act 2002 s 20(5)(a).
13   Ie under the Proceeds of Crime Act 2002 s 6 (see PARA 221).
14   Proceeds of Crime Act 2002 s 20(5)(b).
15   Proceeds of Crime Act 2002 s 20(6). If the court has already sentenced the defendant for the offence (or any of the offences) concerned, s 6 has effect as if his particular criminal conduct included conduct which constitutes offences which the court has taken into consideration in deciding his sentence for the offence or offences concerned: s 20(7). As to references to the 'offence or offences concerned' see PARA 229 note 2. As to references to 'sentencing the defendant for an offence' see PARA 193 note 2.

    Section 8(2) (see PARA 224) does not apply, and the rules applying instead are that the court must:
(1)   take account of conduct occurring before the date of the original decision that the defendant had not benefited from his general or particular criminal conduct (s 20(8)(a));

(2) take account of property obtained before that date (s 20(8)(b));

(3) take account of property obtained on or after that date if it was obtained as a result of or in connection with conduct occurring before that date (s 20(8)(c)).

As to 'property' and when property is 'obtained' see PARA 226.

In s 10 (see PARA 231):

(a) the first and second assumptions do not apply with regard to property first held by the defendant on or after the date of the original decision that the defendant had not benefited from his general or particular criminal conduct (s 20(9)(a));

(b) the third assumption does not apply with regard to expenditure incurred by him on or after that date (s 20(9)(b));

(c) the fourth assumption does not apply with regard to property obtained (or assumed to have been obtained) by him on or after that date (s 20(9)(c)).

The recoverable amount (see PARA 233) for the purposes of s 6 is such amount as the court believes is just but does not exceed the amount found under s 7 (s 20(10)). In arriving at the just amount the court must have regard in particular to:

(i) the amount found under s 7 (s 20(11)(a));

(ii) any fine imposed on the defendant in respect of the offence (or any of the offences) concerned (s 20(11)(b));

(iii) any order which falls within s 13(3) (see PARA 237) and has been made against him in respect of the offence (or any of the offences) concerned and has not already been taken into account by the court in deciding what is the free property held by him for the purposes of s 9 (see PARA 233) (s 20(11)(c));

(iv) any order which has been made against him in respect of the offence (or any of the offences) concerned under the Powers of Criminal Courts (Sentencing) Act 2000 s 130 (compensation orders: see PARA 281) (Proceeds of Crime Act 2002 s 20(11)(d));

(v) any order which has been made against him in respect of the offence (or any of the offences) concerned under the Criminal Justice Act 2003 s 161A (orders requiring payment of surcharge: see PARA 185) (Proceeds of Crime Act 2002 s 20(11)(da) (as added: see note 9)); and

(vi) any order which has been made against him in respect of the offence (or any of the offences) concerned under the Prevention of Social Housing Fraud Act 2013 s 4 (unlawful profit orders: see LANDLORD AND TENANT) (Proceeds of Crime Act 2002 s 20(11)(e) (s 20(11)(e) added, s 20(12) amended, by the Prevention of Social Housing Fraud Act 2013 Schedule paras 11, 18)).

As to when property is 'free' see PARA 226.

If an order for the payment of compensation under the Powers of Criminal Courts (Sentencing) Act 2000 s 130, an order for the payment of a surcharge under the Criminal Justice Act 2003 s 161A or an unlawful profit order under the Prevention of Social Housing Fraud Act 2013 s 4 has been made against the defendant in respect of the offence or offences concerned, the provisions of the Proceeds of Crime Act 2002 s 13(5), (6) (see PARA 237) do not apply in relation to it: s 20(12) (as so amended; amended by the Modern Slavery Act 2015 Sch 5 para 17).

The date of conviction is the date found by applying the Proceeds of Crime Act 2002 s 19(10) (see PARA 273): s 20(13).

275. Order made: reconsideration of benefit. If:

(1) a court has made a confiscation order[1];

(2) there is evidence which was not available to the prosecutor at the relevant time[2];

(3) the prosecutor believes that if the court were to find the amount of the defendant's benefit[3] it would exceed the relevant amount[4];

(4) before the end of the period of six years starting with the date of conviction[5] the prosecutor applies[6] to the Crown Court to consider the evidence[7]; and

(5) after considering the evidence, the court believes it is appropriate for it to proceed to reconsider the benefit[8],

or, where a defendant ceases to be an absconder:

(a) a court has made a confiscation order[9];

(b)   the prosecutor believes that if the court were to find the amount of the defendant's[10] benefit in pursuance of this provision it would exceed the relevant amount[11];

(c)   before the end of the period of six years starting with the day when the defendant ceased to be an absconder, the prosecutor applies to the Crown Court[12] to proceed to recalculate the defendant's benefit[13]; and

(d)   the court believes it is appropriate for it to do so[14],

the court must make a new calculation of the defendant's benefit from the conduct concerned[15], and when it does so there are a number of modifications to the material part of the provisions[16] relating to the making of a confiscation order[17].

If the amount found under the new calculation of the defendant's benefit exceeds the relevant amount, the court:

(i)   must make a new calculation of the recoverable amount[18] for the purposes of the provisions relating to the making of a confiscation order[19]; and

(ii)   if it exceeds[20] the amount required to be paid under the confiscation order, may vary the order by substituting for the amount required to be paid such amount as it believes is just[21].

1   Proceeds of Crime Act 2002 s 21(1)(a). As to the making of confiscation orders see s 6; and PARA 221.
2   Proceeds of Crime Act 2002 s 21(1)(b) (s 21(1)(b)–(d) amended by the Serious Crime Act 2007 Sch 8 para 10, Sch 14). The 'relevant time' is:
    (1)   when the court calculated the defendant's benefit for the purposes of the confiscation order, if the Proceeds of Crime Act 2002 s 21 (see the text and notes 3–21) has not applied previously (s 21(12)(a));
    (2)   when the court last calculated the defendant's benefit in pursuance of s 21, if s 21 has applied previously (s 21(12)(b)).
3   Ie in pursuance of the Proceeds of Crime Act 2002 s 21. As to when a person benefits from conduct see PARA 223.
4   Proceeds of Crime Act 2002 s 21(1)(c) (as amended: see note 2). The 'relevant amount' is:
    (1)   the amount found as the defendant's benefit for the purposes of the confiscation order, if s 21 has not applied previously (s 21(13)(a));
    (2)   the amount last found as the defendant's benefit in pursuance of s 21, if s 21 has applied previously (s 21(13)(b)).
5   The date of conviction is the date found by applying the Proceeds of Crime Act 2002 s 19(10) (see PARA 273): s 21(14).
6   See PARA 273. In connection with applications under the Proceeds of Crime Act 2002 s 21 see the Criminal Procedure Rules 2015, SI 2015/1490, r 33.15.
7   Proceeds of Crime Act 2002 s 21(1)(d) (as amended: see note 2).
8   Proceeds of Crime Act 2002 s 21(1)(e).
9   Proceeds of Crime Act 2002 ss 21(1)(a), 27(6)(c), 28(6)(a) (ss 27(6), 28(6) substituted by the Serious Crime Act 2007 s 9(2), (4)).
10 As to the meaning of 'defendant' for these purposes see PARA 221 note 1.
11 Proceeds of Crime Act 2002 s 21(1)(b).
12 Ie applies to proceed under the Proceeds of Crime Act 2002 s 21.
13 Proceeds of Crime Act 2002 s 21(1)(c).
14 Proceeds of Crime Act 2002 s 21(1)(c).
15 Proceeds of Crime Act 2002 s 21(2). As to 'conduct', 'criminal conduct' and 'general' and 'particular' criminal conduct, see PARA 225.
16 Ie the Proceeds of Crime Act 2002 s 6.
17 Proceeds of Crime Act 2002 s 21(2). If a court has already sentenced the defendant for the offence (or any of the offences) concerned, s 6 has effect as if his particular criminal conduct included conduct which constitutes offences which the court has taken into consideration in deciding his sentence for the offence or offences concerned: s 21(3). As to references to the 'offence or offences concerned' see PARA 229 note 2. As to references to 'sentencing the defendant for an offence' see PARA 193 note 2.

Section 8(2) (see PARA 224) does not apply, and the rules applying instead are that the court must:

(1) take account of conduct occurring up to the time it decided the defendant's benefit for the purposes of the confiscation order (s 21(4)(a));

(2) take account of property obtained up to that time (s 21(4)(b)); and

(3) take account of property obtained after that time if it was obtained as a result of or in connection with conduct occurring before that time (s 21(4)(c)).

As to 'property' and when property is 'obtained' see PARA 226.

In applying s 8(5) (see PARA 224), the confiscation order must be ignored: s 21(5).

In s 10 (see PARA 231):

(a) the first and second assumptions do not apply with regard to property first held by the defendant after the time the court decided his benefit for the purposes of the confiscation order (s 21(6)(a));

(b) the third assumption does not apply with regard to expenditure incurred by him after that time (s 21(6)(b)); and

(c) the fourth assumption does not apply with regard to property obtained (or assumed to have been obtained) by him after that time (s 21(6)(c)).

18 As to the meaning of 'recoverable amount' see PARA 233.

19 Proceeds of Crime Act 2002 s 21(7)(a). In applying s 21(7)(a) the court must:

(1) take the new calculation of the defendant's benefit (s 21(8)(a)); and

(2) apply s 9 (see PARA 233) as if references to the time the confiscation order is made were references to the time of the new calculation of the recoverable amount and as if references to the date of the confiscation order were references to the date of that new calculation (s 21(8)(b)).

20 In deciding under the Proceeds of Crime Act 2002 s 21 whether one amount exceeds another the court must take account of any change in the value of money: s 21(11).

21 Proceeds of Crime Act 2002 s 21(7)(b). In applying s 21(7)(b) the court must have regard in particular to:

(1) any fine imposed on the defendant for the offence (or any of the offences) concerned (s 21(9)(a));

(2) any order which falls within s 13(3) (see PARA 237) and has been made against him in respect of the offence (or any of the offences) concerned and has not already been taken into account by the court in deciding what is the free property (see PARA 226) held by him for the purposes of s 9 (s 21(9)(b));

(3) any order which has been made against him in respect of the offence (or any of the offences) concerned under the Powers of Criminal Courts (Sentencing) Act 2000 s 130 (see PARA 281) (Proceeds of Crime Act 2002 s 21(9)(c));

(4) any order which has been made against him in respect of the offence (or any of the offences) concerned under the Criminal Justice Act 2003 s 161A (orders requiring payment of surcharge: see PARA 185) (Proceeds of Crime Act 2002 s 21(9)(ca) (s 21(9)(ca) added, s 21(10) amended, by the Serious Crime Act 2015 Sch 4 para 21)); and

(5) any order which has been made against him in respect of the offence (or any of the offences) concerned under the Prevention of Social Housing Fraud Act 2013 s 4 (unlawful profit orders: see LANDLORD AND TENANT) (Proceeds of Crime Act 2002 s 21(9)(d) (s 21(9)(d) added, s 21(10) amended, by the Prevention of Social Housing Fraud Act 2013 Schedule paras 11, 19)).

However, in applying the Proceeds of Crime Act 2002 s 21(7)(b) the court must not have regard to an order falling within s 21(9)(c), (ca) or (d) (see heads (3)–(5) above) if a court has made a direction under s 13(6): s 21(10) (as so amended).

An order varying a confiscation order under s 21 is a 'sentence' for the purposes of an appeal against sentence under the Criminal Appeal Act 1968: see s 50(1)(cb); and PARA 626.

276. Order made: reconsideration of available amount. If:

(1) a court has made a confiscation order[1];

(2) the amount required to be paid was less than the defendant's benefit[2]; and

(3) the prosecutor[3], or an appointed[4] receiver[5] applies to the Crown Court to make a new calculation of the available amount[6],

the court must make the new calculation, and in doing so it must apply the provisions[7] relating to the determination of the available amount as if references to the time the confiscation order is made were references to the time of the new calculation and as if references to the date of the confiscation order were references to the date of the new calculation[8].

If the amount found under the new calculation exceeds the relevant amount[9], the court may vary the order by substituting for the amount required to be paid such amount as:

(a)   it believes is just[10]; but

(b)   does not exceed the amount found as the defendant's benefit from the conduct concerned[11].

In deciding what is just the court must have regard in particular to:

(i)   any fine imposed on the defendant for the offence (or any of the offences) concerned[12];

(ii)   any specified order involving the making of a payment by the defendant or another interference with the defendant's property[13] which has been made against him in respect of the offence (or any of the offences) concerned and has not already been taken into account by the court in deciding what is the free property[14] held by him for the purposes of the provisions relating to the determination of the available amount[15];

(iii)   any compensation order which has been made against him in respect of the offence (or any of the offences) concerned[16]; and

(iv)   any order for the payment of a surcharge[17] which has been made against the defendant in respect of the offence (or any of the offences) concerned[18].

1   Proceeds of Crime Act 2002 s 22(1)(a). As to the making of confiscation orders see s 6; and PARA 221.
2   Proceeds of Crime Act 2002 s 22(1)(b). As to when a person benefits from conduct see PARA 223. As to the meaning of 'defendant' for these purposes see PARA 221 note 1.
3   Proceeds of Crime Act 2002 s 22(2)(a).
4   Ie appointed under the Proceeds of Crime Act 2002 s 50 (see PARA 249).
5   Proceeds of Crime Act 2002 s 22(2)(c) (amended by the Serious Crime Act 2007 Sch 8 para 11, Sch 14).
6   Proceeds of Crime Act 2002 s 22(1)(c). As to the meaning of 'available amount' see PARA 233. In connection with applications under s 22 see the Criminal Procedure Rules 2015, SI 2015/1490, r 33.16.
7   Ie the Proceeds of Crime Act 2002 s 9 (see PARA 233).
8   Proceeds of Crime Act 2002 s 22(3). Thus, assets lawfully acquired after the confiscation order was made can be treated as part of the new available amount: see *R v Bates* [2006] EWCA Crim 1015, [2007] 1 Cr App Rep (S) 9, [2006] All ER (D) 59 (Apr) (decided under corresponding provisions of the Drug Trafficking Act 1994).
9   The relevant amount is:
    (1)   the amount found as the available amount for the purposes of the confiscation order, if the Proceeds of Crime Act 2002 s 22 has not applied previously (s 22(8)(a));
    (2)   the amount last found as the available amount in pursuance of s 22, if s 22 has applied previously (s 22(8)(b)).
10 Proceeds of Crime Act 2002 s 22(4)(a). An order varying a confiscation order under s 22 is a 'sentence' for the purposes of an appeal against sentence under the Criminal Appeal Act 1968: see s 50(1)(cb); and PARA 626.
11 Proceeds of Crime Act 2002 s 22(4)(b). In deciding under s 22 whether one amount exceeds another, the court must take account of any change in the value of money: s 22(7). The amount found as the defendant's benefit from the conduct concerned is:
    (1)   the amount so found when the confiscation order was made (s 22(9)(a)); or
    (2)   if one or more new calculations of the defendant's benefit have been made under s 21 (see PARA 275), the amount found on the occasion of the last such calculation (s 22(9)(b)).
12 Proceeds of Crime Act 2002 s 22(5)(a). As to references to the 'offence or offences concerned' see PARA 229 note 2.
13 Ie an order falling within the Proceeds of Crime Act 2002 s 13(3) (see PARA 237).

14 As to when property is 'free' see PARA 226.

15 Proceeds of Crime Act 2002 s 22(5)(b).

16 Proceeds of Crime Act 2002 s 22(5)(c). However, in deciding what is just the court must not have regard to an order falling within s 22(5)(c) or (d) if a court has made a direction under s 13(6) (see PARA 237): s 22(6) (s 22(5)(d) added, s 22(6) amended, by the Serious Crime Act 2007 Sch 4 para 26).

17 Ie under Criminal Justice Act 2003 s 161A (orders requiring payment of surcharge: see PARA 185).

18 Proceeds of Crime Act 2002 s 22(5)(d) (as added: see note 16).

(B) Defence or Receiver Applications

277. Inadequacy of available amount: variation of order. Where a court has made a confiscation order[1], and the defendant[2] or the prosecutor or an appointed receiver[3] applies[4] to the Crown Court to vary[5] the order[6], the court must calculate the available amount[7], and in doing so must apply the provisions[8] relating to the determination of the available amount as if references to the time the confiscation order is made were references to the time of the calculation and as if the reference to the date of the confiscation were references to the date of the calculation[9].

If the court finds that the available amount (as so calculated) is inadequate for the payment of any amount remaining to be paid under the confiscation order, it may vary the order by substituting for the amount required to be paid such smaller amount as the court believes is just[10].

If a person has been adjudged bankrupt or his estate has been sequestrated, or if an order for the winding up of a company[11] has been made, the court must take into account the extent to which realisable property[12] held by that person or that company may be distributed among creditors[13].

The court may disregard any inadequacy which it believes is attributable (wholly or partly) to anything done by the defendant for the purpose of preserving property held by the recipient of a tainted gift from any risk[14] of realisation[15].

1   Proceeds of Crime Act 2002 s 23(1)(a). As to the making of confiscation orders see s 6; and PARA 221.

2   As to the meaning of 'defendant' for these purposes see PARA 221 note 1.

3   Ie under the Proceeds of Crime Act 2002 s 50 (see PARA 249).

4   In connection with applications under the Proceeds of Crime Act 2002 s 23 see the Criminal Procedure Rules 2015, SI 2015/1490, r 33.17.

5   Ie under the Proceeds of Crime Act 2002 s 23.

6   Proceeds of Crime Act 2002 s 23(1)(b) (amended by the Serious Crime Act 2007 Sch 8 para 12, Sch 14; and by the Serious Crime Act 2015 s 8(1)).

7   As to the meaning of 'available amount' see PARA 233.

8   Ie the Proceeds of Crime Act 2002 s 9 (see PARA 233).

9   Proceeds of Crime Act 2002 s 23(2). See *R v Rooney (appeal under s 31 of the Proceeds of Crime Act 2002)* [2007] EWCA Crim 236, [2007] All ER (D) 238 (Jan) (it is inappropriate to proceed under the Proceeds of Crime Act 2002 s 23 after cash has been seized and an order for forfeiture has been made).

10 Proceeds of Crime Act 2002 s 23(3). If a property adjustment order has been made after the confiscation order but before enforcement, the Crown Court must have regard to it in varying the available amount: *Webber v Webber* [2006] EWHC 2893 (Fam), [2007] 1 WLR 1052. Where realisable assets at the time a confiscation order is made include unidentified assets, the fact that a particular asset is no longer available for realisation does not demonstrate the inadequacy of the current value of realisable assets: *Telli v Revenue and Customs Prosecution Office* [2007] EWCA Civ 1385, [2008] 3 All ER 405, [2008] 2 Cr App Rep (S) 278.

Where the Crown Court has determined in confiscation proceedings that the defendant has hidden assets, it is not open to the defendant to challenge that finding on an application under the Proceeds of Crime Act 2002 s 23, for variation of the confiscation order on the grounds of the inadequacy of the available amount: see *R v Younis* [2008] EWCA Crim 2950, [2009] 2 Cr App Rep (S) 247, [2009] Crim LR 372.

11 For these purposes, 'company' means any company which may be wound up under the Insolvency Act 1986 (see COMPANY AND PARTNERSHIP INSOLVENCY) or the Insolvency (Northern Ireland) Order 1989, SI 1989/2405 (NI 19): Proceeds of Crime Act 2002 s 23(6).

12 As to 'property' and 'realisable property' see PARA 226.

13 Proceeds of Crime Act 2002 s 23(4).

14 Ie under the Proceeds of Crime Act 2002 Pt 2 (ss 6–91). References to a recipient of a tainted gift are references to a person to whom the defendant has made the gift: s 78(3).

15 Proceeds of Crime Act 2002 s 23(5).

278. Inadequacy of available amount: discharge of order. Where:

(1) a court has made a confiscation order[1];

(2) the designated officer for the magistrates' court applies[2] to the Crown Court for the discharge of the order[3]; and

(3) the amount remaining to be paid under the order is less than £1,000[4],

the court must calculate the available amount[5], and in doing so it must apply the provisions[6] relating to the determination of the available amount as if references to the time the confiscation order is made were references to the time of the calculation and as if references to the date of the confiscation order were references to the date of the calculation[7].

If the court:

(a) finds that the available amount (as so calculated) is inadequate to meet the amount remaining to be paid[8]; and

(b) is satisfied that the inadequacy is due wholly to a specified reason or a combination of specified reasons[9],

it may discharge the confiscation order[10]. The specified reasons are:

(i) in a case where any of the realisable property[11] consists of money in a currency other than sterling, that fluctuations in currency exchange rates have occurred[12]; and

(ii) any reason specified by the Secretary of State by order[13].

1 Proceeds of Crime Act 2002 s 24(1)(a). As to the making of confiscation orders see s 6; and PARA 221.

2 In connection with applications under the Proceeds of Crime Act 2002 s 24 see the Criminal Procedure Rules 2015, SI 2015/1490, r 33.18.

3 Proceeds of Crime Act 2002 s 24(1)(b) (amended by the Courts Act 2003 s 109(1), Sch 8 para 406(a)).

4 Proceeds of Crime Act 2002 s 24(1)(c). The Secretary of State may by order vary the amount for the time being specified in head (3) in the text: s 24(5). At the date at which this volume states the law no such order had been made.

5 As to the meaning of 'available amount' see PARA 233.

6 Ie the Proceeds of Crime Act 2002 s 9 (see PARA 233).

7 Proceeds of Crime Act 2002 s 24(2).

8 Proceeds of Crime Act 2002 s 24(3)(a).

9 Proceeds of Crime Act 2002 s 24(3)(b).

10 Proceeds of Crime Act 2002 s 24(3).

11 As to the meaning of 'realisable property' see PARA 226.

12 Proceeds of Crime Act 2002 s 24(4)(a).

13 Proceeds of Crime Act 2002 s 24(4)(b). At the date at which this volume states the law no such order had been made.

279. Death of defendant: discharge of order. If a court has made a confiscation order[1], the defendant[2] dies while the order is not satisfied[3], and the designated officer for a magistrates' court applies to the Crown Court for the discharge of the order[4], the court may discharge the order if it appears to the court that it is not possible to recover anything from the estate of the deceased for the purpose of satisfying the order to any extent[5] or it would not be reasonable to make any attempt, or further attempt, to recover anything from the estate of the deceased for that purpose[6].

1 Proceeds of Crime Act 2002 s 25A(1)(a) (s 25A added by the Serious Crime Act 2015 s 8(2)). As to the making of confiscation orders see the Proceeds of Crime Act 2002 s 6; and PARA 221.
2 As to the meaning of 'defendant' for these purposes see PARA 221 note 1.
3 Proceeds of Crime Act 2002 s 25A(1)(b) (as added: see note 1).
4 Proceeds of Crime Act 2002 s 25A(1)(c) (as added: see note 1).
5 Proceeds of Crime Act 2002 s 25A(2)(a) (as added: see note 1).
6 Proceeds of Crime Act 2002 s 25A(2)(b) (as added: see note 1).

280. Small amount outstanding: discharge of debt. Where:

(1)   a court has made a confiscation order[1];

(2)   the designated officer for a magistrates' court applies[2] to the Crown Court for the discharge of the order[3]; and

(3)   the amount remaining to be paid under the order is £50 or less[4],

the court may discharge the order[5].

1 Proceeds of Crime Act 2002 s 25(1)(a). As to the making of confiscation orders see s 6; and PARA 221.
2 In connection with applications under the Proceeds of Crime Act 2002 s 25 see the Criminal Procedure Rules 2015, SI 2015/1490, r 33.18.
3 Proceeds of Crime Act 2002 s 25(1)(b) (amended by the Courts Act 2003 s 109(1), Sch 8 para 406(b)).
4 Proceeds of Crime Act 2002 s 25(1)(c). The Secretary of State may by order vary the amount for the time being specified in head (3) in the text: s 25(3). At the date at which this volume states the law no such order had been made.
5 Proceeds of Crime Act 2002 s 25(2).

(3) COMPENSATION ORDERS

281. Compensation orders. A compensation order is an order which may be made in respect of an offender requiring him to pay compensation for any personal injury[1], loss or damage[2] resulting from that offence[3]or any other offence which is taken into consideration by the court in determining sentence[4], or to make payments for funeral expenses[5] or bereavement[6] in respect of a death resulting from any such offence, other than a death due to an accident arising out of the presence of a motor vehicle on a road[7].

1 Where a substantial sum of compensation for personal injury is contemplated, there should be up to date and detailed information as to the extent of the injury: *R v Cooper* (1982) 4 Cr App Rep (S) 55, [1982] Crim LR 308, CA; *R v Welch* (1984) 6 Cr App Rep (S) 13, [1984] Crim LR 242, CA. The starting point on making a compensation order for personal injury is the extent and severity of those injuries: see *R v Smith* [1998] 2 Cr App Rep (S) 400, CA.
2 As to 'loss' and 'damage' see PARA 282.
3 As to when loss and damage 'result' from an offence see PARA 283.
4 Powers of Criminal Courts (Sentencing) Act 2000 s 130(1)(a). As to the making of compensation orders generally see PARA 285; as to appeals against compensation orders see PARA 292; and as to review of such orders see PARA 289. As to the making of an order for payment to a person for personal injury, loss or damage out of the proceeds of disposal of property upon the making of a deprivation order under the Powers of Criminal Courts (Sentencing) Act 2000 when the offender does not have the means to permit the making of a compensation order see PARA 470. Where a compensation order has been made against any person in respect of an offence taken into consideration in determining his sentence: (1) the order ceases to have effect if he successfully appeals against his conviction of the offence or, if more than one, all the offences, of which he was convicted in the proceedings in which the order

was made (s 132(5)(a)); and (2) he may appeal against the order as if it were part of the sentence imposed in respect of the offence or, if more than one, any of the offences, of which he was so convicted (s 132(5)(b)).

Where the Crown Court makes a compensation order against a person, then, if that person is before it, the Crown Court may order him to be searched: s 142(1)(c). Any money found on a person in such a search may be applied, unless the court otherwise directs, towards payment of the sum payable by him; and the balance, if any, must be returned to him: s 142(2).

5   A compensation order in respect of funeral expenses may be made for the benefit of anyone who incurred the expenses: Powers of Criminal Courts (Sentencing) Act 2000 s 130(9).

6   A compensation order in respect of bereavement may be made only for the benefit of a person for whose benefit a claim for damages for bereavement could be made under the Fatal Accidents Act 1976 s 1A (see NEGLIGENCE vol 78 (2010) PARA 25): Powers of Criminal Courts (Sentencing) Act 2000 s 130(10). The amount of compensation in respect of bereavement may not exceed the amount for the time being specified in the Fatal Accidents Act 1976 s 1A(3): Powers of Criminal Courts (Sentencing) Act 2000 s 130(10).

7   Powers of Criminal Courts (Sentencing) Act 2000 s 130(1)(b). For particular provision relating to road traffic accidents see PARA 284.

282. 'Loss' and 'damage'. Where a compensation order is contemplated[1], the 'loss' is the loss which the victim has actually suffered[2]; and this may include a sum by way of interest[3]. If property is stolen and recovered, the court is not entitled thereby to make a compensation order unless the victim can show a loss that has arisen from his having been without the property for a period of time[4]. 'General inconvenience' is not loss[5]. Where specimen counts are charged, the court cannot make an order in respect of the other offences which have not been taken into consideration[6]. The death of the person who has suffered the loss does not mean a compensation order cannot be made[7].

'Damage' may include compensation for fear and anxiety[8] or emotional distress[9]. There must be some evidence that the distress was experienced[10].

1   See PARA 281.

2   The court has no jurisdiction to make a compensation order where there are real issues as to whether those to benefit have suffered any, and if so what, loss: see *R v Horsham Justices, ex p Richards* [1985] 2 All ER 1114, 82 Cr App Rep 254, DC; *R v Stapylton* [2012] EWCA Crim 728, [2013] 1 Cr App Rep (S) 68. The fact that the victim is insured against the loss is irrelevant, since insurance doesn't negate loss, it merely shifts the burden onto the insurer: *R v Townsend* (1980) 2 Cr App Rep (S) 328, CA. Quaere whether an obligation to pay costs in independent civil proceedings can ever come within the phrase 'loss or damage': see *Hammerton Cars Ltd v London Borough of Redbridge* [1974] 2 All ER 216, [1974] 1 WLR 484, DC.

3   *R v Schofield* [1978] 2 All ER 705, 67 Cr App Rep 282, CA; and see also *R v Vivian* [1979] 1 All ER 48, 68 Cr App Rep 53, CA (order should not be made unless figure either agreed or approved).

4   *R v Hier* (1976) 62 Cr App Rep 233, [1969] Crim LR 304, CA; *R v Boardman* (1987) 9 Cr App Rep (S) 74, [1987] Crim LR 430, CA; *R v Tyce* (1994) 15 Cr App Rep (S) 415, [1994] Crim LR 71, CA; *R v Sharkey* [1976] Crim LR 388, CA. See also *R v Cadamarteris* [1977] Crim LR 236, CA (stolen car dismantled and returned in pieces; no basis for compensation order as no assessable sum in loss or damage suffered as result of defendant's dishonesty and no evidence of difference in value).

5   *R v Stapylton* [2012] EWCA Crim 728, [2013] 1 Cr App Rep (S) 68.

6   *R v Crutchley, R v Tonks* (1993) 15 Cr App Rep (S) 627, [1994] Crim LR 309, CA; followed in *R v Hose* (1994) 16 Cr App Rep (S) 682, [1995] Crim LR 259, CA.

7   See *Holt v DPP* [1996] 2 Cr App Rep (S) 314, DC.

8   *Bond v Chief Constable of Kent* [1983] 1 All ER 456, 76 Cr App Rep 56, DC (award made to compensate owner of house for damage caused when accused threw stone through owner's window).

9   *R v Thomson Holidays Ltd* [1974] QB 592, 58 Cr App Rep 429, CA; and see also see PARA 283 (loss or damage 'resulting' from an offence).

10   *R v Vaughan* (1990) 12 Cr App Rep (S) 46, [1990] Crim LR 443, CA.

283.   'Resulting from an offence'.   Where a compensation order is contemplated[1] the injury, loss or damage need not be inflicted intentionally[2], although it must result from the offence for which the order is made[3]. If the offender is acquitted of an offence alleged to have resulted in personal injury, loss or damage, but convicted of some other offence, a compensation order may not be made[4]. In determining whether loss or damage resulted from an offence, the principles of causation are not to be adopted; but the court must ask itself whether the loss or damage can fairly be said to have resulted to anyone from the relevant offence[5]. The amount payable under a compensation order may be reduced where the victim has provoked the offence[6].

In certain property offences[7] where the property in question is recovered, any damage to the property occurring while it was out of the owner's possession is to be treated for these purposes as having resulted from the offence, however and by whomsoever the damage was caused[8].

1   See PARA 281.
2   See *R v Corbett* (1993) 14 Cr App Rep (S) 101, [1992] Crim LR 833, CA.
3   *R v Oddy* [1974] 2 All ER 666, 59 Cr App Rep 66, CA; *Berkeley v Orchard* [1975] Crim LR 225, DC (injury from taking controlled drugs not injury resulting from offence of unlawful possession of drug); *R v Boardman* (1987) 9 Cr App Rep (S) 74, [1987] Crim LR 430, CA (no loss resulting from theft; compensation order quashed); *R v Bateman, R v Blackwell* (1988) 10 Cr App Rep (S) 240, CA (no evidence of loss before judge; compensation order quashed); *Revenue and Customs Comrs v Duffy* [2008] EWHC 848 (Admin), [2008] 2 Cr App Rep (S) 593, [2008] Crim LR 734 (loss arising from fraudulent claims for tax credits). As to whether injury, loss or damage caused by others in the course of a violent disorder or affray of which the offender has been convicted can be said to have resulted from his offence see *R v Derby* (1990) 12 Cr App Rep (S) 502, CA; *R v Taylor* (1993) 14 Cr App Rep (S) 276, [1993] Crim LR 317; *R v Geurtjens* (1993) 14 Cr App Rep (S) 280, [1993] Crim LR 317, CA; *R v Deary* (1993) 14 Cr App Rep (S) 648, [1993] Crim LR 750, CA; cf *R v Denness* [1996] 1 Cr App Rep (S) 159, [1995] Crim LR 750, CA.
4   *R v Halliwell* (1991) 12 Cr App Rep (S) 692, CA; *R v Graves* (1993) 14 Cr App Rep (S) 790, CA.
5   *R v Thomson Holidays Ltd* [1974] QB 592, 58 Cr App Rep 429, CA (compensation order for modest amount in respect of emotional distress); and see also *Rowlston v Kenny* (1982) 4 Cr App Rep (S) 85, CA (the test in deciding whether a particular loss resulted from an offence is not whether the loss resulted solely from that offence, but whether it can fairly be said to have resulted from that offence; the fact that the defendant could have been charged with another offence provides no reason for refusing compensation if the loss can fairly be said to have resulted from the offence in respect of which he is convicted); and *Revenue and Customs Comrs v Duffy* (test is whether the loss could fairly be said to have resulted from the offences in question). In connection with the attribution of loss arising from a single incident involving multiple offences and offenders see eg *R v Taylor* (1993) 14 Cr App Rep (S) 276, [1993] Crim LR 317, CA.
6   See eg *R v Flinton* [2007] EWCA Crim 2322, [2008] 1 Cr App Rep (S) 575.
7   Ie the case of an offence under the Theft Act 1968 or the Fraud Act 2006.
8   Powers of Criminal Courts (Sentencing) Act 2000 s 130(5) (amended by the Fraud Act 2006 Sch 1 para 29).

284.   Particular provision for road traffic accidents.   A compensation order[1] may be made in respect of injury, loss or damage (other than loss suffered by a person's dependants in consequences of his death) which was due to an accident[2] arising out of the presence of a motor vehicle on a road only if:

(1)   it is in respect of damage which is treated[3] as resulting from an offence under the Theft Act 1968 or the Fraud Act 2006[4]; or

(2)   it is in respect of injury, loss or damage as respects which the offender is uninsured in relation to the use of the vehicle[5] and compensation is not payable under any arrangements to which the Secretary of State is a party[6].

Thus although a compensation order may validly be made in respect of a vehicle taken without lawful authority by the defendant, which is damaged in an accident while being driven by him, such an order cannot validly be made in respect of any other vehicle (or property) damaged in the accident[7]. Where a compensation order is made in respect of injury, loss or damage due to such an accident, the amount to be paid may include an amount representing the whole or part of any loss of or reduction in preferential rates of insurance attributable to the accident[8].

1 See PARA 281.
2 As to when damage is attributable to an 'accident' see *Mayor v Oxford* [1980] 2 Cr App Rep (S) 280, DC (stolen lorry crashed by drunk drivers); *R v Stapylton* [2012] EWCA Crim 728, [2013] 1 Cr App Rep (S) 68 (dangerous driving: car crashing into garage); *Chief Constable of Staffordshire v Rees* [1981] RTR 506, DC (driving deliberately at a gate); *Bremner v Westwater* 1994 SLT 707 (forcing police car of the road).
3 Ie by virtue of the Powers of Criminal Courts (Sentencing) Act 2000 s 130(5) (see PARA 283).
4 Powers of Criminal Courts (Sentencing) Act 2000 s 130(6)(a) (amended by the Fraud Act 2006 Sch 1 para 29).
5 Powers of Criminal Courts (Sentencing) Act 2000 s 130(6)(b)(i). For the purposes of s 130(6), (7), an offender will not be regarded as uninsured merely because he does not disclose details of his insurance at the scene of the accident (*McDermott v DPP* [1997] RTR 474, (1996) 161 JP 244, DC), and a vehicle the use of which is exempted from insurance by the Road Traffic Act 1988 s 144 (see ROAD TRAFFIC vol 90 (2011) PARA 695) is not uninsured for these purposes (Powers of Criminal Courts (Sentencing) Act 2000 s 130(8)).
6 Powers of Criminal Courts (Sentencing) Act 2000 s 130(6)(b)(ii). The 'arrangements' referred to are the Secretary of State's arrangements with the Motor Insurers' Bureau; and 'payable' means payable now or in the future (and not 'immediately payable'): see *DPP v Scott* (1995) 16 Cr App Rep (S) 292, 159 JP 261, DC; *R v Austin* [1996] 2 Cr App Rep (S) 191, [1996] Crim LR 446, CA.
7 *Quigley v Stokes* [1977] 2 All ER 317, 64 Cr App Rep 198, DC; *Mayor v Oxford* (1980) 2 Cr App Rep (S) 280, DC; *R v Divers* [2006] EWCA Crim 169, [2006] All ER (D) 210 (Jan).
8 Powers of Criminal Courts (Sentencing) Act 2000 s 130(7).

285. Making of compensation orders. A compensation order[1] may be made by a court by or before which a person is convicted of an offence[2]. Where the person in question is convicted of an offence the sentence for which is:
  (1)   a sentence fixed by law[3];
  (2)   a life sentence for serious or second listed offences[4];
  (3)   the required minimum sentences for threatening with an offensive weapon or an article with a blade or point in public in public[5];
  (4)   the required custodial sentence for possession of a firearm or using a person to mind a weapon[6];
  (5)   the specified minimum term for a third class A drug trafficking offence[7]; or
  (6)   the specified minimum term for a third domestic burglary[8],
the court by or before which he is convicted may make the compensation order in addition to dealing with him in any other way[9]. Where a court convicts a person of any other offence, it may exercise this power either as an alternative or in addition to dealing with the offender in any other way[10]. A court has power to make a joint and several order against joint offenders, but such an order should not be made if substantial justice can be achieved by orders made severally[11]. A court must consider making a compensation order in any case where it is empowered[12] so to do[13], and must give reasons, on passing sentence, if it does not make a compensation order in a case where it is empowered so to do[14].

It is not right, at least not in every case, to regard the imposition of a compensation order as being additional punishment[15]. The making of a compensation order is not conditional on the existence of a civil cause of action[16]. It must be remembered by courts considering compensation orders that the civil remedy for damages still exists; the order is a quick and simple way of dealing with the claim in simple cases[17].

1 See PARA 281.

2 Powers of Criminal Courts (Sentencing) Act 2000 s 130(1). The order may be made on an application or otherwise (s 130(1)), and the victim does not have to make an application for a compensation order: *Holt v DPP* [1996] 2 Cr App Rep (S) 314, [1996] Crim LR 524, DC (victim of theft had died before sentence). If it has not been raised by counsel, a judge who has a compensation order in mind must raise the matter so that it can be ventilated: *R v Stanley* (1989) 11 Cr App Rep (S) 446, [1990] Crim LR 208, CA. Where the offender has denied the particular items were stolen, the court should not make an order unless an application is made and the applicant prepared to adduce evidence that the items had been stolen: *R v Kneeshaw* [1975] QB 57, 58 Cr App Rep 439, CA. Where compensation is awarded in respect of numerous offences, there should be a separate order for each sum in respect of each offence: *R v Inwood* (1974) 60 Cr App Rep 70, CA. Excessively long periods of payment must not be ordered: see *R v Daly* [1974] 1 All ER 290, 58 Cr App Rep 333, CA (payment period initially six years; period substantially reduced on appeal; held that the machinery of the compensation order should not be used where recompense involves a weekly payment over too long a period); *R v McCullough* (1982) 4 Cr App Rep (S) 98, [1982] Crim LR 461, CA; *R v Makin* (1982) 4 Cr App Rep (S) 180, CA; *R v Holden* (1985) 7 Cr App Rep (S) 7, [1985] Crim LR 397, CA; *R v Hills* (1986) 8 Cr App Rep (S) 199, [1986] Crim LR 756, CA. The previous principle was confirmed in *R v Broughton* (1986) 8 Cr App Rep (S) 379, [1987] Crim LR 140, CA (as a general guideline with regard to compensation orders a period of 12 months or thereabouts should normally be considered for instalment payments; a margin of three months would seem to be the maximum); and see also *R v Ramsey* (1987) 9 Cr App Rep (S) 251, [1987] Crim LR 714, CA; *R v Roberts* (1987) 9 Cr App Rep (S) 275, [1987] Crim LR 712, CA; *R v Diggles* [1988] Crim LR 851, CA (improper to make order which could only be activated when the defendant has sufficient means); *R v Holah* (1989) 11 Cr App Rep (S) 282, [1989] Crim LR 751, CA. A period of two years, or exceptionally three years, for payment would not be too long: *R v Olliver (Richard), R v Olliver (Michael)* (1989) 11 Cr App Rep (S) 10, [1989] Crim LR 387, CA; *R v Yehou* [1997] 2 Cr App Rep (S) 48, CA.

3 Powers of Criminal Courts (Sentencing) Act 2000 s 130(2) (amended by the Criminal Justice Act 2003 Sch 32 paras 90, 117; the Violent Crime Reduction Act 2006 Sch 1 para 6; the Criminal Justice and Immigration Act 2008 Sch 26 paras 40, 46; and the Legal Aid, Sentencing and Punishment of Offenders Act 2012 Sch 19 para 5, Sch 26 para 12; Powers of Criminal Courts (Sentencing) Act 2000 s 130(2) further amended by the Criminal Justice and Courts Act 2015 Sch 5 para 6; Powers of Criminal Courts (Sentencing) Act 2000 s 130(2A) added by the Legal Aid, Sentencing and Punishment of Offenders Act 2012 s 63(1)).

4 Powers of Criminal Courts (Sentencing) Act 2000 s 130(2), (2A)(e) (as amended and added: see note 3). As to the sentences referred to see the Criminal Justice Act 2003 ss 224A, 225(2), 226(2); and PARAS 34, 35, 37. As to when such sentences fall to be imposed see PARA 536 note 2.

5 Powers of Criminal Courts (Sentencing) Act 2000 s 130(2), (2A)(a), (c) (as amended and added: see note 3). As to the sentences referred to see the Prevention of Crime Act 1953 ss 1(2B), 1A(5); the Criminal Justice Act 1988 ss 139(6B), 139A(5B), 139AA(7); and CRIMINAL LAW. As to when such sentences fall to be imposed see PARA 536 note 2.

6 Powers of Criminal Courts (Sentencing) Act 2000 s 130(2), (2A)(b), (f) (as amended and added: see note 3). As to the sentences referred to see the Firearms Act 1968 s 51A(2); the Violent Crime Reduction Act 2006 s 29(4), (6); and CRIMINAL LAW vol 26 (2010) PARAS 614, 656. As to when such a sentence falls to be imposed see PARA 536 note 2.

7 Powers of Criminal Courts (Sentencing) Act 2000 s 130(2), (2A)(d) (as amended and added: see note 3). As to the sentence referred to see the Powers of Criminal Courts (Sentencing) Act 2000 s 110(2); and CRIMINAL LAW vol 26 (2010) PARA 725. As to when such a sentence falls to be imposed see PARA 536 note 2.

8 Powers of Criminal Courts (Sentencing) Act 2000 s 130(2), (2A)(d) (as amended and added: see note 3). As to the sentence referred to see the Powers of Criminal Courts (Sentencing) Act 2000 s 111(2); and CRIMINAL LAW vol 25 (2010) PARA 290. As to when such a sentence falls to be imposed see PARA 536 note 2.

9 Powers of Criminal Courts (Sentencing) Act 2000 s 130(2) (as amended: see note 3). See eg *R v Holmes* (1992) 13 Cr App Rep (S) 29, CA (where a compensation order is made it is wrong in principle also to make an order, for example a disqualification order, which restricts the

defendant's ability to pay the compensation). Where the court considers that it would be appropriate both to impose a fine and to make a compensation order (Powers of Criminal Courts (Sentencing) Act 2000 s 130(12)(a)), but that the offender has insufficient means to pay both an appropriate fine and appropriate compensation (s 130(12)(b)), the court must give preference to compensation (though it may impose a fine as well) (s 130(12)). When committing an offender for sentence, a magistrates' court should not make an order but should leave questions associated with sentence to be dealt with by the Crown Court: *R v Brogan* [1975] 1 All ER 879, 60 Cr App Rep 279, CA.

10 Powers of Criminal Courts (Sentencing) Act 2000 s 130(1), (2). See note 9.

11 *R v Grundy, R v Moorhouse* [1974] 1 All ER 292, [1974] 1 WLR 139, CA.

12 Ie by the Powers of Criminal Courts (Sentencing) Act 2000 s 130: see the text and notes 1–11.

13 Powers of Criminal Courts (Sentencing) Act 2000 s 130(2A) (added by the Legal Aid, Sentencing and Punishment of Offenders Act 2012 s 63(1)).

14 Powers of Criminal Courts (Sentencing) Act 2000 s 130(3). In connection with this requirement see the Criminal Procedure Rules 2015, SI 2015/1490, r 28.1. The court does not have jurisdiction to hear an application for judicial review of a decision of the Crown Court not to make a compensation order (see *R (on the application of Faithfull) v Ipswich Crown Court* [2007] EWHC 2763 (Admin), [2008] 3 All ER 749, [2008] 1 WLR 1636); where a magistrates' court fails to make a compensation order as a result of an error of law the prosecution may appeal to the High Court by way of case stated (*Revenue and Customs Comrs v Duffy* [2008] EWHC 848 (Admin), [2008] 2 Cr App Rep (S) 593, [2008] Crim LR 734).

15 Thus a compensation order was upheld in addition to an immediate sentence of imprisonment: see *R v Dorton* (1987) 9 Cr App Rep (S) 514, [1988] Crim LR 254, CA; and see also *R v Love* [1999] 1 Cr App Rep (S) 484, [1999] Crim LR 171, CA.

16 *R v Chappell* (1984) 80 Cr App Rep 31, 6 Cr App Rep (S) 342, CA.

17 *R v Daly* [1974] 1 All ER 290, [1974] 1 WLR 133, CA; *R v Inwood* (1974) 60 Cr App Rep 70 at 73, CA; *R v Donovan* (1981) 3 Cr App Rep (S) 192, [1981] Crim LR 723, CA (case in question too complex for a type of case for which compensation order was designed); *R v Ramsey* (1987) 9 Cr App Rep (S) 251, [1987] Crim LR 714, CA (compensation orders are not intended to be straight alternatives to civil process; they are useful where the amounts involved are not substantial and the means to pay are established; but the courts must understand the limits of a compensation order); *R v Barney* (1989) 11 Cr App Rep (S) 448, [1990] Crim LR 209, CA (compensation order some token of remorse on offender's behalf as well as redressing private loss of victim, but otherwise wholly independent of sentencing exercise); *R v Bewick* [2007] EWCA Crim 3297, [2008] 2 Cr App Rep (S) 184 (complex compensation proceedings should not be dealt with by the Crown Court and there should be no 'cheap and convenient' short cut where there were difficult issues of fact and law to be decided).

286. Requirement to take account of defendant's means. In determining whether to make a compensation order[1] against any person, and in determining the amount to be paid by any person under such an order, the court must have regard to his means[2] so far as they appear or are known to the court[3]. It is no use making a compensation order if there is no realistic possibility of it being complied with[4]. In particular, a compensation order should not be made in conjunction with a custodial sentence if its effect would be to subject the offender on discharge from custody to a financial burden which he might not be able to meet and which might induce him to re-offend to satisfy the order[5].

Defendants with means cannot 'buy' their way out of prison, or 'buy' a shorter sentence, by offering or being ordered to pay compensation[6].

1 See PARA 281.

2 See PARA 287.

3 Powers of Criminal Courts (Sentencing) Act 2000 s 130(11).

4 *R v Webb, R v Davies* (1979) 1 Cr App Rep (S) 16, [1979] Crim LR 466, CA; *R v Grafton* (1979) 1 Cr App Rep (S) 305, CA (realistic sum to be paid after release; compensation order quashed because no immediate prospect of work and little chance of reconciliation with husband; appellant should start her life again with a clean sheet after imprisonment); *R v Parker* (1981) 3 Cr App Rep (S) 278, [1982] Crim LR 130, CA (appellant had neither means nor any immediate prospect of obtaining means).

5   See *R v Panayioutou* (1989) 11 Cr App Rep (S) 535, [1990] Crim LR 349, CA; *R v Inwood*
     (1974) 60 Cr App Rep 70, CA (compensation orders, which may appear at the trial to the
     convicted person to be a lifeline, may, however, become a millstone round his neck, when he is
     released from prison; they may be counterproductive, and force him back into crime to find the
     money); *R v Clark* (1991) 13 Cr App Rep (S) 124, CA; *R v Love* [1999] 1 Cr App Rep (S) 484,
     [1999] Crim LR 171, CA; *R v Jorge* [1999] 2 Cr App Rep (S) 1, CA.
6   *R v Copley* (1979) 1 Cr App Rep (S) 55, CA; *R v Barney* (1989) 11 Cr App Rep (S) 448, CA.

287.   Consideration of financial resources and assessment of means.   Where
the court is contemplating making a compensation order[1] it must be satisfied
after sufficient inquiry that the defendant has the financial resources to pay the
order[2]. A compensation order is wrong in principle when coupled with an
immediate sentence of imprisonment on a person who has many debts and in
respect of whom there is no evidence of resources[3], although this principle does
not apply where a person has good prospects so that the compensation order
appears to be a reasonable addition to a modest prison sentence for a serious
crime[4]. Compensation orders should not be made where there is any doubt as to
the liability to compensate or where there is a real doubt as to whether the
convicted person can find the compensation[5].

In assessing means, the court is not required to make a precise calculation of
the defendant's means: a broad picture is sufficient[6]. The court is not limited to
considering the proceeds of the relevant offence[7]. An apparently onerous burden
imposed by a compensation order may be justifiable when its impact can to some
extent be ameliorated, since, for example, allowing someone to continue to live
in a house bought with the proceeds of the theft is not only unacceptable, but
contrary to propriety and justice[8]. However, if the only asset available to satisfy
a compensation order is the matrimonial home which is still in occupation of
other members of the family, such an order will be inappropriate[9] (although
there can be exceptions[10]).

If the court cannot properly value an article out of the sale of which a
compensation order is to be paid, the order should not be made[11].

Where an offender is unable to make compensation this should not affect the
length of his sentence; he must not be given the impression by the sentencing
judge that he has therefore received a longer custodial sentence than would
otherwise be regarded as proper[12].

1   See PARA 281.
2   *R v Phillips* (1988) 10 Cr App Rep (S) 419, [1989] Crim LR 160, CA. No burden is laid on the
     prosecution to establish the defendant's means and the prosecution has no duty to conduct a
     detailed inquiry into the defendant's means: *R v Johnstone* (1982) 4 Cr App Rep (S) 141, [1982]
     Crim LR 537, CA. Counsel and solicitors for the defendant must, however, make the most
     careful examination as to means; documents should be obtained and evidence on affidavit or
     orally should be given; and proceedings may be adjourned for this purpose: *R v Huish* (1985) 7
     Cr App Rep (S) 272, [1985] Crim LR 800, CA; and see also *R v Coughlin* (1984) 6 Cr App Rep
     (S) 102, [1984] Crim LR 432, CA (counsel must not merely utter without examination all that
     he is told by his client); *R v Bond* (1986) 8 Cr App Rep (S) 11, [1986] Crim LR 413, CA; *R v
     Slack* (1987) 9 Cr App Rep (S) 65, [1987] Crim LR 428, CA; *R v Roberts (William)* (1987) 9 Cr
     App Rep (S) 275, [1987] Crim LR 712, CA. It is not right to make a compensation order
     without some inquiry about the offender's means; if information about his means is not
     available from evidence heard at the trial, an inquiry should be made first to see if there are any
     assets which could properly be made the subject of a compensation order, and then to decide the
     period over which the order should be paid: *R v Holah* (1989) 11 Cr App Rep (S) 282, [1989]
     Crim LR 751, CA.
3   *R v Shenton* (1979) 1 Cr App Rep (S) 81, CA; *R v Morgan* (1982) 4 Cr App Rep (S) 358, CA.
4   *R v Townsend* (1980) 2 Cr App Rep (S) 328, CA.
5   *R v Inwood* (1974) 60 Cr App Rep 70, CA.
6   *R v Howell* (1978) 66 Cr App Rep 179, CA.

7   *R v Copley* (1979) 1 Cr App Rep (S) 55, CA.
8   *R v Workman* (1979) 1 Cr App Rep (S) 335, [1980] Crim LR 189, CA. See also *R v Harrison* (1980) 2 Cr App Rep (S) 313, CA (compensation order quashed which expected sale of matrimonial home; garage business defrauded could have sought judgment for full sum in civil action which would be able to deal with the complex issues involved); *R v Blackmore* (1984) 6 Cr App Rep (S) 244, CA; *R v Heath* (1984) 6 Cr App Rep (S) 397, [1985] Crim LR 247, DC.
9   *R v Butt* (1986) 8 Cr App Rep (S) 216, [1986] Crim LR 755, CA; and see also *R v Hackett* (1988) 10 Cr App Rep (S) 388, [1989] Crim LR 230, CA; *R v Holah* (1989) 11 Cr App Rep (S) 282, [1989] Crim LR 751, CA.
10   See *R v McGuire* (1991) 13 Cr App Rep (S) 332, CA (no general principle that compensation order should not be made if it would force offender to sell matrimonial home; the appellant would have enough left to buy cheaper home and the compensation order was upheld). See also *R v Griffiths (James Mervin), R v Griffiths (Susan Lindsey)* [2001] EWCA Crim 2093, (2001) Times, 17 October (a matrimonial home may be sold in order to satisfy a compensation order, even if it renders a wife and children homeless, if the wife, as well as the husband, is implicated in the offence in respect of which the order is made).
11   *R v Chambers* (1981) 3 Cr App Rep (S) 318, [1982] Crim LR 189, DC; and see also *R v Heads and Redfern* (1981) 3 Cr App Rep (S) 322, [1982] Crim LR 189, DC (compensation order with regard to H was not interfered with because of the ample evidence before the court with regard to the value of his assets; but in the case of R the estimate was vague and subsequently proved wrong, and that compensation order was reduced in amount); *R v Stewart* (1983) 5 Cr App Rep (S) 320, [1983] Crim LR 830, CA (appeal dismissed in respect of compensation order; appellant went to the Court of Appeal without any evidence at all to show that the value which the judge put on his car was in any way erroneous).
12   *R v Barney* (1989) 11 Cr App Rep (S) 448, [1990] Crim LR 209, CA.

288.   Amount of compensation order and limit on amount payable by young offenders.   Where a court makes a compensation order[1] it must generally be of such amount as the court considers appropriate, having regard to any evidence and to any representations that are made by or on behalf of the defendant or the prosecutor[2]. However if (and only if) a magistrates' court has convicted a person aged under 18[3] of an offence or offences, then:

(1)   the compensation to be paid under a compensation order made by the court in respect of the offence or any one of the offences may not exceed £5,000[4]; and

(2)   the compensation or total compensation to be paid under a compensation order or compensation orders made by the court in respect of any offence or offences taken into consideration in determining sentence may not exceed the difference (if any) between the amount or total amount which under head (1) above is the maximum for the offence or offences of which the offender has been convicted[5] and the amount or total amounts (if any) which are in fact ordered to be paid in respect of that offence or those offences[6].

Where there are a number of claimants and the defendant's means are insufficient to satisfy each of them, the amounts payable may be scaled down appropriately[7]. The amount payable under a compensation order also may be reduced where the victim has provoked the offence[8].

1   See PARA 281.
2   Powers of Criminal Courts (Sentencing) Act 2000 s 130(4). The effect of s 130(4) is to reduce the burden of proof required (which had been laid down in *R v Vivian* [1979] 1 All ER 48, 68 Cr App Rep 53, CA; *R v Amey, R v James* [1983] 1 All ER 865, 76 Cr App Rep 206, CA) for establishing the criteria for a compensation order, but a trial judge may not pluck a figure out of the air and have no regard to whether the offender can meet it; there must be some evidence of means (*R v Swann, R v Webster* (1984) 6 Cr App Rep (S) 22, [1984] Crim LR 300, CA). The court may make assessments and approximations where the evidence is scanty or incomplete, and it may then make an order which is appropriate. However, where the defendant is challenging the basis on which any compensation can be paid, justice requires that he should

have a proper opportunity to test the grounds on which the order is to be made against him; it is for the prosecution to place evidence before the court (*R v Horsham Justices, ex p Richards* [1985] 2 All ER 1114, 82 Cr App Rep 254, DC: see also *R v Watson* (1990) 12 Cr App Rep (S) 508, CA; *R v Clelland* (1991) 12 Cr App Rep (S) 697, CA), and criminal courts should not become involved in complicated investigations as to the fact, or amount, of loss: *R v Kneeshaw* [1975] QB 57, 58 Cr App Rep 439, CA; *Hyde v Emery* (1984) 6 Cr App Rep (S) 206, DC; *R v Briscoe* (1994) 15 Cr App Rep (S) 699, CA; *R v White* [1996] 2 Cr App Rep (S) 58, CA.

3 As to the determination of a person's age see the Children and Young Persons Act 1933 s 99; and CHILDREN AND YOUNG PERSONS vol 10 (2012) PARA 1206.

4 Powers of Criminal Courts (Sentencing) Act 2000 s 131(A1), (1) (s 131(A1) added, s 131(1), (2) amended, by the Crime and Courts Act 2013 Sch 16 para 8).

5 Powers of Criminal Courts (Sentencing) Act 2000 s 131(2)(a) (as amended: see note 4).

6 Powers of Criminal Courts (Sentencing) Act 2000 s 131(2)(b) (as amended: see note 4).

7 See eg *R v Amey* (1982) 4 Cr App Rep (S) 410.

8 See eg *R v Flinton* [2007] EWCA Crim 2322, [2008] 1 Cr App Rep (S) 575.

289. Review of compensation orders. At any time before the person against whom a compensation order has been made has paid into court the whole of the compensation which the order requires him to pay[1], but at a time when (disregarding any power of a court to grant leave to appeal out of time) there is no further possibility of an appeal[2] on which the order could be varied or set aside[3], the magistrates' court for the time being having functions in relation to the enforcement[4] of the order may, on the application of the person against whom it was made[5], discharge the order, or reduce the amount which remains to be paid[6], if it appears to the court:

(1) that the injury, loss or damage in respect of which the order was made has been held in civil proceedings to be less than it was taken to be for the purposes of the order[7];

(2) in the case of an order in respect of the loss of any property, that the property has been recovered by the person in whose favour the order was made[8];

(3) that the means of the person against whom the order was made are insufficient to satisfy in full both the order and a confiscation order[9], an unlawful profit order[10] or a slavery and trafficking reparation order[11] made against him in the same proceedings[12]; or

(4) that the person against whom the order was made has suffered a substantial reduction in his means which was unexpected at the time when the compensation order was made, and that his means seem unlikely to increase for a considerable period[13].

However, where the order was made by the Crown Court, a magistrates' court may not exercise any of the above powers in a case where it is satisfied as mentioned in head (3) or head (4) above unless it has first obtained the consent of the Crown Court[14].

1 Powers of Criminal Courts (Sentencing) Act 2000 s 133(2)(b). As to the making of compensation orders see PARAS 281, 285; as to the amount of compensation and the defendant's means see PARA 288.

2 As to appeals against compensation orders see PARA 292.

3 Powers of Criminal Courts (Sentencing) Act 2000 s 133(2)(a).

4 As to enforcement see PARA 290.

5 In connection with applications for variation or discharge see the Criminal Procedure Rules 2015, SI 2015/1490, r 28.5.

6 Powers of Criminal Courts (Sentencing) Act 2000 s 133(1).

7 Powers of Criminal Courts (Sentencing) Act 2000 s 133(3)(a).

8 Powers of Criminal Courts (Sentencing) Act 2000 s 133(3)(b).

9   Ie a confiscation order under the Proceeds of Crime Act 2002 Pt 2 (ss 6–91) (see PARA 221 et seq) or the Criminal Justice Act 1988 Pt VI (ss 71–103) (largely repealed): Powers of Criminal Courts (Sentencing) Act 2000 s 133(3)(c)(i) (s 133(3)(c)(i)–(iii) added by Modern Slavery Act 2015 Sch 5 para 14).

10 Ie an unlawful profit order under the Prevention of Social Housing Fraud Act 2013 s 4 (see LANDLORD AND TENANT): Powers of Criminal Courts (Sentencing) Act 2000 s 133(3)(c)(ii) (as added: see note 9).

11 Ie an order under the Modern Slavery Act 2015 s 8 (see CRIMINAL LAW): Powers of Criminal Courts (Sentencing) Act 2000 s 133(3)(c)(iii) (as added: see note 9).

12 Powers of Criminal Courts (Sentencing) Act 2000 s 133(3)(c) (as amended: see note 9).

13 Powers of Criminal Courts (Sentencing) Act 2000 s 133(3)(d).

14 Powers of Criminal Courts (Sentencing) Act 2000 s 133(4). Where a compensation order has been made on appeal, for the purposes of s 133(4) it is deemed: (1) if it was made on an appeal brought from a magistrates' court, to have been made by that magistrates' court (s 133(5)(a)); and (2) if it was made on an appeal brought from the Crown Court or from the criminal division of the Court of Appeal, to have been made by the Crown Court (s 133(5)(b)).

290.   Enforcement of compensation orders.   A person in whose favour a compensation order is made[1] is not entitled to receive the amount due to him until (disregarding any power of a court to grant leave to appeal out of time) there is no further possibility of an appeal[2] on which the order could be varied or set aside[3]. Where more than one person is entitled to compensation, as a general rule apportionment, and not selection, should be the adopted course where there are insufficient means to meet every established claim, although the court may depart from that basis where there are strong grounds for doing so, and in such cases the court may select some of the claimants and order that compensation be paid to them to the exclusion of the others[4].

1 As to the making of compensation orders see PARAS 281, 285; as to the amount of compensation and the defendant's means see PARA 288.

2 As to appeals against compensation orders see PARA 292.

3 Powers of Criminal Courts (Sentencing) Act 2000 s 132(1). A magistrates' clerk may not issue third party debt order proceedings in respect of a compensation order suspended pending appeal: *Gooch v Ewing (Allied Irish Bank Ltd, garnishee)* [1986] QB 791, [1985] 3 All ER 654, CA (decided under the Criminal Appeal Act 1968 s 42 (repealed)). Criminal Procedure Rules may make provision regarding the way in which the magistrates' court for the time being having functions, by virtue of the Administration of Justice Act 1970 s 41(1) (see MAGISTRATES vol 71 (2013) PARA 693), in relation to the enforcement of a compensation order is to deal with money paid in satisfaction of the order where the entitlement of the person in whose favour it was made is suspended: Powers of Criminal Courts (Sentencing) Act 2000 s 132(2) (amended by SI 2004/2035). At the date at which this volume states the law no such rules had been made.

    Where in the case specified in the Administration of Justice Act 1970 Sch 9 para 10 or 13A (see CRIMINAL PROCEDURE vol 28 (2015) PARA 875) the Crown Court thinks that the period for which the person subject to the order is otherwise liable to be committed to prison for default under the order is insufficient, it may specify a longer period for that purpose; and then in the case of default: (1) the specified period is to be substituted as the maximum for which the person may be imprisoned under the Magistrates' Courts Act 1980 s 76 (see MAGISTRATES vol 71 (2013) PARA 627) (Administration of Justice Act 1970 s 41(8)(a) (s 41(8) substituted, and s 41(8A) added, by the Criminal Justice Act 1988 s 106; repealed by the Criminal Justice Act 1991 s 170(2), Sch 16; re-enacted by virtue of the Criminal Justice Act 1991 s 23(3); Administration of Justice Act 1970 s 41(8)(a) amended by the Prevention of Social Housing Fraud Act 2013 Schedule para 2)); and (2) the Administration of Justice Act 1970 Sch 4 para 2 applies, with any necessary modifications, for the reduction of the specified period where, at the time of the person's imprisonment, he has made part payment under the order (Administration of Justice Act 1970 s 41(8)(b) (as so substituted)). However, the Crown Court may not so specify a period of imprisonment longer than that which it could order a person to undergo on imposing on him a fine equal in amount to the sum required to be paid by the order: s 41(8A) (as so added).

4 *R v Amey, R v James* [1983] 1 All ER 865, 76 Cr App Rep 206, CA.

291. Effect of compensation order on subsequent award of damages in civil proceedings. Where a compensation order has been made[1] in favour of any person in respect of any injury, loss or damage and a claim by him in civil proceedings for damages in respect of the injury, loss or damage subsequently falls to be determined[2], the damages in the civil proceedings must be assessed without regard to the order; but the claimant may recover only an amount equal to the aggregate of:

(1) any amount by which they exceed the compensation[3]; and

(2) a sum equal to any portion of the compensation which he fails to recover[4],

and may not enforce the judgment, so far as it relates to a sum such as is mentioned in head (2) above, without the leave of the court[5].

1 As to the making of compensation orders see PARAS 281, 285; as to the amount of compensation and the defendant's means see PARA 288.
2 Powers of Criminal Courts (Sentencing) Act 2000 s 134(1).
3 Powers of Criminal Courts (Sentencing) Act 2000 s 134(2)(a).
4 Powers of Criminal Courts (Sentencing) Act 2000 s 134(2)(b).
5 Powers of Criminal Courts (Sentencing) Act 2000 s 134(2).

292. Suspension of compensation orders. A person in whose favour a compensation order is made[1] is not entitled to receive the amount due to him until (disregarding any power of a court to grant leave to appeal out of time) there is no further possibility of an appeal on which the order could be varied or set aside[2]; and provision may be made[3] regarding the way in which the magistrates' court for the time being having functions[4] in relation to the enforcement of a compensation order is to deal with money paid in satisfaction of the order where the entitlement of the person in whose favour it was made is suspended[5].

The Court of Appeal may by order annul or vary any compensation order made by the court of trial, although the conviction is not quashed; and the order, if annulled, does not take effect and, if varied, takes effect as varied[6]. Where the Supreme Court restores a conviction, it may make any compensation order which the court of trial could have made[7].

1 As to the making of compensation orders see PARAS 281, 285; as to the amount of compensation and the defendant's means see PARA 288.
2 See the Powers of Criminal Courts (Sentencing) Act 2000 s 132(1); and PARA 290.
3 Ie by virtue of the Criminal Procedure Rules.
4 Ie by virtue of the Administration of Justice Act 1970 s 41(1): see CRIMINAL PROCEDURE vol 28 (2015) PARA 875.
5 See the Powers of Criminal Courts (Sentencing) Act 2000 s 132(2); and PARA 290.
6 Powers of Criminal Courts (Sentencing) Act 2000 s 132(3). Where there is a subsequent material change to the offender's financial circumstances, an application should be made for review rather than an appeal: see *R v Palmer* (1993) 15 Cr App Rep (S) 550, [1994] Crim LR 228, CA; and PARA 289.
7 Powers of Criminal Courts (Sentencing) Act 2000 s 132(4) (amended by the Constitutional Reform Act 2005 Sch 9 para 9). Where an order is made under the Powers of Criminal Courts (Sentencing) Act 2000 s 132(3) or (4), the Court of Appeal or the Supreme Court must make such order for the payment of a surcharge under the Criminal Justice Act 2003 s 161A (see PARA 185), or such variation of the order of the Crown Court under that provision, as is necessary to secure that the person's liability under that provision is the same as it would be if he were being dealt with by the Crown Court: Powers of Criminal Courts (Sentencing) Act 2000 s 132(4A) (added by the Domestic Violence, Crime and Victims Act 2004 Sch 10 para 49; amended by the Criminal Justice and Courts Act 2015 s 83(1)).

(4) REPARATION ORDERS

293. Reparation orders. Where a child or young person (that is to say, any person aged under 18)[1] is convicted of an offence other than one for which the sentence is fixed by law, the court by or before which he is convicted may make an order (a 'reparation order'[2]) requiring him to make reparation[3] specified in the order to a person or persons so specified[4] or to the community at large[5]. Any person so specified must be a person identified by the court as a victim of the offence or a person otherwise affected by it[6]. The court must not make a reparation order unless it has been notified by the Secretary of State that arrangements for implementing such orders are available in the area proposed to be named in the order[7] and the notice has not been withdrawn[8]. The court must also not make a reparation order in respect of the offender if it proposes to pass on him a custodial sentence[9] or to make in respect of him a youth rehabilitation order[10] or a referral order[11].

A reparation order must not require the offender to work for more than 24 hours in aggregate[12] or to make reparation to any person without the consent of that person[13]. Subject to this, requirements specified in a reparation order must be such as in the opinion of the court are commensurate with the seriousness of the offence, or the combination of the offence and one or more offences associated with it[14]. Requirements so specified must, as far as practicable, be such as to avoid any conflict with the offender's religious beliefs or (until a day to be appointed) with the requirements of any youth community order to which he may be subject[15], and any interference with the times, if any, at which the offender normally works or attends school or any other educational establishment[16]. Any reparation required by a reparation order must be made under the supervision of the responsible officer[17], and must be made within a period of three months from the date of the making of the order[18]. The court must give reasons if it does not make a reparation order in a case where it has power to do so[19].

Before making a reparation order, a court must obtain and consider a written report by an officer of a local probation board, an officer of a provider of probation services, a social worker of a local authority or a member of a youth offending team, indicating the type of work that is suitable for the offender[20] and the attitude of the victim or victims to the requirements proposed to be included in the order[21].

Provision is made in connection with a breach of a reparation order[22] and in connection with the revocation and amendment of such an order[23].

1   As to the determination of a person's age see the Children and Young Persons Act 1933 s 99; and CHILDREN AND YOUNG PERSONS vol 10 (2012) PARA 1206.
2   Powers of Criminal Courts (Sentencing) Act 2000 s 73(2). A reparation order must name the local justice area in which it appears to the court making the order, or to the court varying any provision included in it, that the offender resides or will reside: s 74(4) (amended by SI 2005/886).
3   'Make reparation', in relation to an offender, means make reparation for the offence otherwise than by the payment of compensation and the requirements that may be specified in a reparation order are subject to the Powers of Criminal Courts (Sentencing) Act 2000 s 74(1)–(3) (see the text and notes 12–16): s 73(3).
4   Powers of Criminal Courts (Sentencing) Act 2000 s 73(1)(a).
5   Powers of Criminal Courts (Sentencing) Act 2000 s 73(1)(b).
6   Powers of Criminal Courts (Sentencing) Act 2000 s 73(1).
7   Ie under the Powers of Criminal Courts (Sentencing) Act 2000 s 74(4) (see note 2).
8   Powers of Criminal Courts (Sentencing) Act 2000 s 73(6).

9 Powers of Criminal Courts (Sentencing) Act 2000 s 73(4)(a).

10 See PARA 73 et seq.

11 Powers of Criminal Courts (Sentencing) Act 2000 s 73(4)(b) (s 73(4)(b) substituted, s 73(4A), (4B) added, by the Criminal Justice and Immigration Act 2008 Sch 4 paras 51, 53). As to referral orders see PARA 156 et seq). The court may not make a reparation order in respect of the offender at a time when a youth rehabilitation order is in force in respect of him unless when it makes the reparation order it revokes the youth rehabilitation order (s 73(4A) (as so added)), and where a youth rehabilitation order is so revoked, the Criminal Justice and Immigration Act 2008 Sch 2 para 24 (breach, revocation or amendment of youth rehabilitation order: see PARA 92) applies to the revocation (Powers of Criminal Courts (Sentencing) Act 2000 s 73(4B) (as so added))

12 Powers of Criminal Courts (Sentencing) Act 2000 s 74(1)(a).

13 Powers of Criminal Courts (Sentencing) Act 2000 s 74(1)(b).

14 Powers of Criminal Courts (Sentencing) Act 2000 s 74(2). As to an 'associated offence' see PARA 9 note 7.

15 Powers of Criminal Courts (Sentencing) Act 2000 s 74(3)(a) (amended by the Criminal Justice Act 2003 Sch 32 paras 90, 106(1), (2), 107; and prospectively amended by the Criminal Justice and Immigration Act 2008 Sch 4 paras 51, 54). The amendment made by the Criminal Justice and Immigration Act 2008 has been brought into force in so far as it repeals the reference to community orders: see the Criminal Justice and Immigration Act 2008 (Commencement No 13 and Transitory Provision) Order 2009, SI 2009/3074.

16 Powers of Criminal Courts (Sentencing) Act 2000 s 74(3)(b).

17 Powers of Criminal Courts (Sentencing) Act 2000 s 74(8)(a). 'Responsible officer', in relation to an offender subject to a reparation order, means one of:

    (1)   an officer of a local probation board or, as the case may be, an officer of a provider of probation services (s 74(5)(a) (ss 73(5), 74(5)(a), (6) amended by the Criminal Justice and Courts Services Act 2000 Sch 7 para 4(1)(a), (2); Powers of Criminal Courts (Sentencing) Act 2000 ss 73(5), 74(5)(a) amended, s 74(6A) added by SI 2008/912));

    (2)   a social worker of a local authority (Powers of Criminal Courts (Sentencing) Act 2000 s 74(5)(b) (ss 73(5), 74(5)(b), (7) amended by the Children Act 2004 Sch 5 Pt 4)); or

    (3)   a member of a youth offending team (Powers of Criminal Courts (Sentencing) Act 2000 s 74(5)(c)).

As to local probation boards and the provision of probation services see PARAS 666–687. As to youth offending teams see CHILDREN AND YOUNG PERSONS vol 10 (2012) PARA 1193. Where a reparation order specifies an officer of the local probation board under s 74(5)(a) the officer so specified must be an officer appointed for or assigned to the local justice area named in the order (s 74(6) (as so amended; and amended by SI 2005/886)). Where a reparation order specifies an officer of a provider of probation services under the Powers of Criminal Courts (Sentencing) Act 2000 s 74(5), the officer specified must be an officer acting in the local justice area named in the order (s 74(6A) (as so added)). Where a reparation order specifies under s 74(5)(b) or s 74(5)(c) a social worker of a local authority or a member of a youth offending team, the social worker or member specified must be a social worker of, or a member of a youth offending team established by, the local authority within whose area it appears to the court that the child or young person resides or will reside: s 74(7) (as so amended).

18 Powers of Criminal Courts (Sentencing) Act 2000 s 74(8)(b).

19 Powers of Criminal Courts (Sentencing) Act 2000 s 73(8). In connection with this requirement see the Criminal Procedure Rules 2015, SI 2015/1490, r 28.1.

20 Powers of Criminal Courts (Sentencing) Act 2000 s 73(5)(a) (as amended: see note 17).

21 Powers of Criminal Courts (Sentencing) Act 2000 s 73(5)(b).

22 See the Powers of Criminal Courts (Sentencing) Act 2000 Sch 8 paras 1–4, 6, 7; and PARAS 294, 296.

23 See the Powers of Criminal Courts (Sentencing) Act 2000 Sch 8 paras 5–7; and PARAS 295–296.

294. Breach of requirement of reparation order. If while a reparation order[1] is in force in respect of an offender it is proved to the satisfaction of the court[2], on the application of the responsible officer, that the offender has failed to comply with any requirement included in the order[3], the court:

    (1)   whether or not it also makes an order[4] revoking or amending the reparation order, may order the offender to pay a fine[5];

    (2)   if the reparation order was made by a magistrates' court, may revoke the order and deal with the offender, for the offence in respect of which

the order was made, in any way in which he could have been dealt with for that offence by the court which made the order[6]; or

(3)　if the reparation order was made by the Crown Court, may commit him in custody or release him on bail until he can be brought or appear before the Crown Court[7].

In dealing with an offender under these provisions a court must take into account the extent to which the offender has complied with the requirements of the reparation order[8].

These provisions have effect subject to the provision[9] relating to the presence of the offender in court when an application[10] is made by the appropriate officer[11].

1　As to the meaning of 'reparation order' see PARA 293.

2　Ie, a youth court acting in the local justice area in which the offender resides or, if it is not known where the offender resides, a youth court acting in the local justice area for the time being named in the order in pursuance of the Powers of Criminal Courts (Sentencing) Act 2000 s 74(4) (see PARA 293) (Sch 8 para 2(1) (Sch 8 para 2 amended, Sch 8 para 6A added, by the Criminal Justice and Immigration Act 2008 s 6(3), Sch 4 paras 51, 62, 106, 108, Sch 28 Pt 1)). As to youth courts see CHILDREN AND YOUNG PERSONS vol 10 (2012) PARA 1225 et seq.

　　It is provided that a youth court may adjourn any hearing relating to an offender in any proceedings under the Powers of Criminal Courts (Sentencing) Act 2000 Sch 8, and that where it does so the court may direct that the offender be released forthwith or remand the offender: Sch 8 para 6A(1), (2) (as so added). Where the court so remands the offender it must fix the time and place at which the hearing is to be resumed and that time and place must be the time and place at which the offender is required to appear or be brought before the court by virtue of the remand, and where the court so adjourns the hearing but does not remand the offender it may fix the time and place at which the hearing is to be resumed but, if it does not do so, it must not resume the hearing unless it is satisfied that the offender, the responsible officer and (if the offender is aged under 14) either a parent or guardian of the offender or, if a local authority has parental responsibility for an offender who is in its care or provided with accommodation by it in the exercise of any social services functions, that authority, have had adequate notice of the time and place for the resumed hearing: Sch 8 para 6A(3)–(6) (as so added). These powers may be exercised by a single justice of the peace, notwithstanding anything in the Magistrates' Courts Act 1980: Powers of Criminal Courts (Sentencing) Act 2000 Sch 8 para 6A(8) (as so added). These provisions apply to any hearing in any proceedings under Sch 8 in place of the Magistrates' Courts Act 1980 s 10 (adjournment of trial: see CRIMINAL PROCEDURE vol 27 (2015) PARAS 287, 290) where s 10 would otherwise apply, but do not affect the application of s 10 to hearings of any other description: Powers of Criminal Courts (Sentencing) Act 2000 Sch 8 para 6A(9) (as so added).

　　For these purposes 'local authority' has the same meaning as it has in the Criminal Justice and Immigration Act 2008 Pt 1 (ss 1–8) by virtue of s 7 (see PARA 73); 'parental responsibility' has the same meaning as it has in the Children Act 1989 by virtue of s 3 (see CHILDREN AND YOUNG PERSONS vol 9 (2012) PARA 151); and 'social services functions' has the same meaning as it has in the Local Authority Social Services Act 1970 by virtue of s 1A (see SOCIAL SERVICES AND COMMUNITY CARE vol 95 (2013) PARA 1): Powers of Criminal Courts (Sentencing) Act 2000 Sch 8 para 6A(7) (as so added). As to the meaning of 'responsible officer' see PARA 293 note 17. As to the determination of a person's age see the Children and Young Persons Act 1933 s 99; and CHILDREN AND YOUNG PERSONS vol 10 (2012) PARA 1206.

3　Powers of Criminal Courts (Sentencing) Act 2000 Sch 8 para 2(1) (as amended: see note 2). In connection with applications to the court see the Criminal Procedure Rules 2015, SI 2015/1490, rr 32.1–32.4.

4　Ie under the Powers of Criminal Courts (Sentencing) Act 2000 Sch 8 para 5(1) (see PARA 295).

5　Powers of Criminal Courts (Sentencing) Act 2000 Sch 8 para 2(2)(a)(i). The amount of the fine must not exceed £1,000: Sch 8 para 2(2)(a)(i). A fine imposed under Sch 8 para 2 is deemed, for the purposes of any enactment, to be a sum adjudged to be paid by a conviction: Sch 8 para 2(6).

　　The offender may appeal to the Crown Court against any order under Sch 8 para 2(2) except an order made or which could have been made in his absence by virtue of Sch 8 para 6(9) (see PARA 296): Sch 8 para 7(a).

6　Powers of Criminal Courts (Sentencing) Act 2000 Sch 8 para 2(2)(b) (as amended: see note 2). See note 5. Unless the order in question was made on appeal, the proviso to the court's powers to deal with the offender under this provision is that it may deal with the offender in any way in which he could have been dealt with by the court which made the order if the order had not been made: Sch 8 para 2(2)(b), (8) (as so amended).

Where a reparation order has been made on appeal it is deemed:

(1) if it was made on an appeal brought from a magistrates' court, to have been made by that magistrates' court (Sch 8 para 2(8)(a) (as so amended)); and

(2) if it was made on an appeal brought from the Crown Court or from the criminal division of the Court of Appeal, to have been made by the Crown Court (Sch 8 para 2(8)(b) (as so amended)).

7   Powers of Criminal Courts (Sentencing) Act 2000 Sch 8 para 2(2)(c) (as amended: see note 2). See note 5. As to bail generally see CRIMINAL PROCEDURE vol 27 (2015) PARA 67 et seq. Where a court deals with an offender under Sch 8 para 2(2)(c) it must send to the Crown Court a certificate signed by a justice of the peace giving particulars of the offender's failure to comply with the requirement in question (Sch 8 para 2(3)(a)) and such other particulars of the case as may be desirable (Sch 8 para 2(3)(b)). A certificate purporting to be so signed is admissible as evidence of the failure before the Crown Court: Sch 8 para 2(3). Where by virtue of Sch 8 para 2(2)(c) the offender is brought or appears before the Crown Court (Sch 8 para 2(4)(a)) and it is proved to the satisfaction of the court that he has failed to comply with the requirement in question (Sch 8 para 2(4)(b)), that court may deal with him, for the offence in respect of which the order was made, in any way in which it could have dealt with him for that offence (Sch 8 para 2(4)). Unless the order in question was made on appeal, the proviso to the court's powers to deal with the offender under Sch 8 para 2(4) is that the court may deal with the offender in any way in which it could have dealt with him if it had not made the order: Sch 8 para 2(8) (as so amended). Where the Crown Court deals with an offender under Sch 8 para 2(4), it must revoke the action plan order or reparation order if it is still in force: Sch 8 para 2(5) (as so amended).

8   Powers of Criminal Courts (Sentencing) Act 2000 Sch 8 para 2(7) (as amended: see note 2).

9   Ie the Powers of Criminal Courts (Sentencing) Act 2000 Sch 8 para 6 (see PARA 296).

10   Ie an application under the Powers of Criminal Courts (Sentencing) Act 2000 Sch 8 para 2(1) (see the text and notes 1–3) or Sch 8 para 5(1) (see PARA 295).

11   Powers of Criminal Courts (Sentencing) Act 2000 Sch 8 para 2(9).

295.   Revocation and amendment of reparation orders. If while a reparation order[1] is in force in respect of an offender it appears to the court[2], on the application of the responsible officer or the offender[3], that it is appropriate to make an order revoking or amending the order, the court may:

(1)   make an order revoking the order[4]; or

(2)   make an order amending it by cancelling any provision included in it[5], or by inserting in it (either in addition to or in substitution for any of its provisions) any provision which could have been included in the order if the court had then had power to make it and were exercising the power[6].

1   As to the meaning of 'reparation order' see PARA 293.

2   Ie the 'relevant court' (ie a youth court acting in the local justice area for the time being named in the order in pursuance of the Powers of Criminal Courts (Sentencing) Act 2000 s 74(4) (see PARA 293) (Sch 8 para 5(4)(a) (Sch 8 paras 5(1), (3), 7(b) amended, Sch 8 para 5(4) added, by the Criminal Justice and Immigration Act 2008 s 6(3), Sch 4 paras 51, 52, 62, 106, 108, Sch 28 Pt 1)) or, in the case of an application made both under the Powers of Criminal Courts (Sentencing) Act 2000 Sch 8 para 5 (see the text and notes 3–6) and under Sch 8 para 2(1) (see PARA 294), the court mentioned in Sch 8 para 2(1) (Sch 8 para 5(4)(b) (as so added))). As to youth courts see CHILDREN AND YOUNG PERSONS vol 10 (2012) PARA 1225 et seq.

3   In connection with applications to the court see the Criminal Procedure Rules 2015, SI 2015/1490, rr 32.1–32.4. As to the meaning of 'responsible officer' see PARA 293 note 17.

4   Powers of Criminal Courts (Sentencing) Act 2000 Sch 8 para 5(1)(a) (as amended: see note 2). Schedule 8 para 5(1) has effect subject to Sch 8 para 6 (see PARA 296): Sch 8 para 5(2). Where an application under Sch 8 para 5(1) for the revocation of a reparation order is dismissed, no further application for its revocation may be made thereunder by any person except with the consent of the appropriate court: Sch 8 para 5(3) (as so amended).

The offender may appeal to the Crown Court against:

(1) any order under Sch 8 para 5(1) except an order made or which could have been made in his absence by virtue of Sch 8 para 6(9) (see PARA 296) (Sch 8 para 7(a)); and

(2) the dismissal of an application under Sch 8 para 5(1) to revoke an action plan order (Sch 8 para 7(b) (as so amended)).

5 Powers of Criminal Courts (Sentencing) Act 2000 Sch 8 para 5(1)(b)(i) (as amended: see note 2). See note 4.

6 Powers of Criminal Courts (Sentencing) Act 2000 Sch 8 para 5(1)(b)(ii) (as amended: see note 2). See note 4.

296. Presence of offender in court. Where the responsible officer[1] makes an application[2] to a court that the offender has failed to comply with any requirement included in a reparation order[3], or makes an application[4] that it is appropriate for the court to make an order revoking or amending the order, he may bring the offender before the court[5]. Without prejudice to any other power to issue a summons or warrant[6], the court to which such an application is made may issue a summons or warrant for the purpose of securing the attendance of the offender before it[7]. Where the offender is arrested in pursuance of such a warrant[8] and cannot be brought immediately before the court[9], the person in whose custody he is may make arrangements for his detention in a place of safety[10] for a period of not more than 72 hours from the time of the arrest (and it is lawful for him to be detained in pursuance of the arrangements)[11], and must within that period bring him before a youth court[12].

Where an application is made to a court that it is appropriate for the court to make an order revoking or amending a revocation order[13], the court may remand (or further remand) the offender to local authority accommodation if a warrant has been issued[14] for the purpose of securing the attendance of the offender before the court[15], or the court considers that remanding (or further remanding) him will enable information to be obtained which is likely to assist the court in deciding whether, and, if so, how, to exercise its powers to revoke or amend the action plan order[16].

A court remanding an offender to local authority accommodation[17] must designate, as the authority which is to receive him, the local authority for the area in which the offender resides or, where it appears to the court that he does not reside in the area of a local authority, the local authority specified by the court[18], and in whose area the offence or an offence associated with it was committed[19].

1 As to the meaning of 'responsible officer' see PARA 293 note 17.

2 Ie an application under the Powers of Criminal Courts (Sentencing) Act 2000 Sch 8 para 2(1) (see PARA 294) or Sch 8 para 5(1) (see PARA 295).

3 As to reparation orders see PARA 293.

4 Ie an application under the Powers of Criminal Courts (Sentencing) Act 2000 Sch 8 para 5(1).

5 Powers of Criminal Courts (Sentencing) Act 2000 Sch 8 para 6(1) (Sch 8 para 6(1), (4), (5), (7), (9) amended by the Criminal Justice and Immigration Act 2008 s 6(2), (3), Sch 4 paras 106, 108(1), (5), Sch 28 Pt 1). A court must not in general make an order under the Powers of Criminal Courts (Sentencing) Act 2000 Sch 8 para 2(1) or Sch 8 para 5(1) unless the offender is present before the court (Sch 8 para 6(1) (as so amended)), although a court may make an order under Sch 8 para 5(1) in the absence of the offender if the effect of the order is confined to one or more of the following, that is to say:

(1) revoking the reparation order (Sch 8 para 6(9)(a) (as so amended));

(2) cancelling a requirement included in the order (Sch 8 para 6(9)(b) (as so amended));

(3) altering in the order the name of any area (Sch 8 para 6(9)(c) (as so amended)); or

(4) changing the responsible officer (Sch 8 para 6(9)(d)).

6 Ie apart from the power under the Powers of Criminal Courts (Sentencing) Act 2000 Sch 8 para 6(2) (see the text and note 7). As to the issue of summonses and warrants see MAGISTRATES vol 71 (2013) PARAS 527, 535.

7 Powers of Criminal Courts (Sentencing) Act 2000 Sch 8 para 6(2). The court must not begin to hear the complaint in the absence of the defendant or issue a warrant under the Magistrates' Courts Act 1980 s 55 unless either it is proved to the satisfaction of the court, on oath or in such other manner as may be prescribed, that the summons cannot be served or was served on him within what appears to the court to be a reasonable time before the hearing or adjourned hearing or the defendant has appeared on a previous occasion to answer to the complaint: see s 55(3); the Powers of Criminal Courts (Sentencing) Act 2000 Sch 8 para 6(3); and MAGISTRATES vol 71 (2013) PARA 533. Where the defendant fails to appear at an adjourned hearing, the court must not issue a warrant under the Magistrates' Courts Act 1980 s 55 unless it is satisfied that he has had adequate notice of the time and place of the adjourned hearing: see s 55(4); the Powers of Criminal Courts (Sentencing) Act 2000 Sch 8 para 6(3); and MAGISTRATES vol 71 (2013) PARA 533.

8 Ie a warrant issued by virtue of the Powers of Criminal Courts (Sentencing) Act 2000 Sch 8 para 6(2) (see the text and notes 6–7).

9 Ie the court before which the warrant directs the offender to be brought (the 'relevant court'): Powers of Criminal Courts (Sentencing) Act 2000 Sch 8 para 6(4) (as amended: see note 5).

10 As to the meaning of 'place of safety' see the Children and Young Persons Act 1933 s 107(1); and CHILDREN AND YOUNG PERSONS vol 9 (2012) PARA 632 (definition applied by the Powers of Criminal Courts (Sentencing) Act 2000 Sch 8 para 6(4) (as amended: see note 5)).

11 Powers of Criminal Courts (Sentencing) Act 2000 Sch 8 para 6(4)(a) (s 6(4) as amended: see note 5).

12 Powers of Criminal Courts (Sentencing) Act 2000 Sch 8 para 6(4)(b) (s 6(4) as amended: see note 5). As to youth courts see CHILDREN AND YOUNG PERSONS vol 10 (2012) PARA 1225 et seq. Where an offender is so brought before a youth court other than the appropriate or relevant court, as the case may be (see note 9), the youth court may direct that he be released forthwith or remand him to local authority accommodation: Sch 8 para 6(5) (as so amended).

Until a day to be appointed where the offender is aged 18 or over at the time when he is brought before a youth court other than the relevant court under Sch 8 para 6(4), or is aged 18 or over at a time when (apart from these provisions) the relevant court could exercise its powers under Sch 8 para 6(6) (see the text and notes 13–16) in respect of him, he must not be remanded to local authority accommodation but may instead be remanded either to a remand centre (if the court has been notified that such a centre is available for the reception of persons under this provision) or to a prison (if it has not been so notified): Sch 8 para 6(7) (as so amended; prospectively further amended by the Criminal Justice and Courts Services Act 2000 Sch 7 paras 160, 202(1), (3), Sch 8). As from the appointed day it is instead provided that such an offender may in such circumstances only be remanded to a prison: see the Powers of Criminal Courts (Sentencing) Act 2000 Sch 8 para 6(7) (as so prospectively amended). At the date at which this volume states the law no such day had been appointed.

For these purposes 'local authority accommodation' means accommodation provided by or on behalf of a local authority; and 'accommodation provided by or on behalf of a local authority' has the same meaning as it has for the purposes of the Children Act 1989 by virtue of s 105 (see CHILDREN AND YOUNG PERSONS vol 10 (2012) PARA 839): Powers of Criminal Courts (Sentencing) Act 2000 s 163. As to the determination of a person's age see the Children and Young Persons Act 1933 s 99; and CHILDREN AND YOUNG PERSONS vol 10 (2012) PARA 1206.

13 Ie an application under the Powers of Criminal Courts (Sentencing) Act 2000 Sch 8 para 5(1) (see PARA 295).

14 Ie under the Powers of Criminal Courts (Sentencing) Act 2000 Sch 8 para 6(2) (see the text and notes 6–7).

15 Powers of Criminal Courts (Sentencing) Act 2000 Sch 8 para 6(6)(a).

16 Powers of Criminal Courts (Sentencing) Act 2000 Sch 8 para 6(6)(b).

17 Ie under the Powers of Criminal Courts (Sentencing) Act 2000 Sch 8 para 6.

18 Powers of Criminal Courts (Sentencing) Act 2000 Sch 8 para 6(8)(a).

19 Powers of Criminal Courts (Sentencing) Act 2000 Sch 8 para 6(8)(b).

(5) UNLAWFUL PROFIT ORDERS

297. Making an unlawful profit order. An 'unlawful profit order' is an order requiring a person who has been convicted of an offence of unlawfully sub-letting a dwelling house[1], or an associated offence, to pay to his landlord[2] an amount representing the profit made by him as a result of his conduct[3]. Orders may be made, on application or otherwise, by the court by or before which the offender is convicted[4], and the court may, if it considers it appropriate to do so, make the order instead of or in addition to dealing with the offender in any other way[5].

1 Ie an offence under the Prevention of Social Housing Fraud Act 2013 s 1 (unlawful sub-letting of a dwelling house let under a secure tenancy) or s 2 (unlawful sub-letting of a dwelling house let under an assured tenancy): see LANDLORD AND TENANT. Provision is also made for the creation of related offences: see ss 7–9; and LANDLORD AND TENANT. Unlawful profit orders may also be made in civil proceedings: see s 5; and LANDLORD AND TENANT.

2 In the context of an unlawful profit order 'the landlord' means the landlord under the tenancy in respect of which the offence was committed: Prevention of Social Housing Fraud Act 2013 s 4(13).

3 Prevention of Social Housing Fraud Act 2013 s 4(1), (3). Where an unlawful profit order has been made against any person in respect of an offence taken into consideration in determining his sentence: (1) the order ceases to have effect if he successfully appeals against his conviction of the offence or, if more than one, all the offences, of which he was convicted in the proceedings in which the order was made (Powers of Criminal Courts (Sentencing) Act 2000 s 132(5)(a); Prevention of Social Housing Fraud Act 2013 s 4(12)(a), (b)); and (2) he may appeal against the order as if it were part of the sentence imposed in respect of the offence or, if more than one, any of the offences, of which he was so convicted (Powers of Criminal Courts (Sentencing) Act 2000 s 132(5)(b)).

4 Prevention of Social Housing Fraud Act 2013 s 4(2)(a). If the court decides not to make an unlawful profits order it must give reasons for that decision on passing sentence on the offender: s 4(4).

5 Prevention of Social Housing Fraud Act 2013 s 4(2)(b). In connection with the amount payable under an unlawful profit order see PARA 298 (noting in particular that the amount payable under an order will take precedence over an amount payable pursuant to a fine if the offender is of insufficient means to satisfy both).

298.   Amount payable under an unlawful profit order.   The amount payable under an unlawful profit order made in criminal proceedings[1] must be such amount as the court considers appropriate, having regard to any evidence and to any representations that are made by or on behalf of the offender or the prosecutor[2]. However if (and only if) a magistrates' court has convicted a person aged under 18[3] of an offence or offences, then:

(1)   the amount to be paid under an unlawful profit order made by the court in respect of the offence or any one of the offences may not exceed £5,000[4]; and

(2)   the amount or total amount to be paid under an unlawful profit order or unlawful profit orders made by the court in respect of any offence or offences taken into consideration in determining sentence may not exceed the difference (if any) between the amount or total amount which under head (1) above is the maximum for the offence or offences of which the offender has been convicted[5] and the amount or total amounts (if any) which are in fact ordered to be paid in respect of that offence or those offences[6].

Subject to this, provision is made for the calculation of the maximum amount which may be payable under the order[7]. The amount which may be recoverable under an unlawful profit order made in criminal proceedings will also be limited where a civil order[8] has also been made[9]. Where the court also wishes to fine the offender but he has insufficient means both to pay the fine and satisfy the order, the order takes precedence[10].

If the amount required to be paid by a person under an unlawful profit order is not paid when it is required to be paid, that person must pay interest on the amount for the period for which it remains unpaid[11].

1 See PARA 297.

2 Prevention of Social Housing Fraud Act 2013 s 4(5).

3 As to the determination of a person's age see the Children and Young Persons Act 1933 s 99; and CHILDREN AND YOUNG PERSONS vol 10 (2012) PARA 1206.

4 Powers of Criminal Courts (Sentencing) Act 2000 s 131(A1), (1) (s 131(A1) added, s 131(1), (2) amended, by the Crime and Courts Act 2013 Sch 16 para 8); Prevention of Social Housing Fraud Act 2013 s 4(12)(a), (b).

5 Powers of Criminal Courts (Sentencing) Act 2000 s 131(2)(a) (as amended: see note 4).

6 Powers of Criminal Courts (Sentencing) Act 2000 s 131(2)(b) (as amended: see note 4).

7 The Prevention of Social Housing Fraud Act 2013 s 4(5) is subject to s 4(6), which provides that the maximum amount payable under an unlawful profit order is calculated as follows:
  (1)   determine the total amount the offender received as a result of the conduct constituting the offence (or the best estimate of that amount); and
  (2)   deduct from the amount determined under step 1 above the total amount, if any, paid by the offender as rent to the landlord (including service charges) over the period during which the offence was committed.
  As to the meaning of 'the landlord' see PARA 297 note 2.

8 As to the making of unlawful profit orders in civil proceedings see the Prevention of Social Housing Fraud Act 2013 s 5; and LANDLORD AND TENANT.

9 The Prevention of Social Housing Fraud Act 2013 s 4(5) is subject to s 4(7), which provides that were an unlawful profit order has been made against the offender under s 5, an order under s 4 may only provide for the landlord to recover an amount equal to the aggregate of:
  (1)   any amount by which the amount of the offender's profit found under s 4 exceeds the amount payable under the order made under s 5 (s 4(7)(a)); and
  (2)   a sum equal to any portion of the amount payable under the order made under s 5 that the landlord fails to recover (s 4(7)(b)),
  and the landlord may not enforce the order under s 4, so far as it relates to a sum mentioned in s 4(7)(b), without the leave of the court.

10 See the Prevention of Social Housing Fraud Act 2013 s 4(8), (9), which provide that where the court considers:
  (1)   that, as well as being appropriate to make an unlawful profit order, it would be appropriate to impose a fine (s 4(8)(a)); and
  (2)   that the offender has insufficient means to pay both an appropriate sum under an unlawful profit order and an appropriate sum under a fine (s 4(8)(b)),
  the court must give preference to making an unlawful profit order (though it may impose a fine as well) (s 4(9)).

11 Prevention of Social Housing Fraud Act 2013 s 4(10). The rate of interest is the same rate as that for the time being specified in the Judgments Act 1838 s 17 (ie 8% per annum): Prevention of Social Housing Fraud Act 2013 s 4(11); and see the Judgments Act 1838 s 17 (amended by SI 1993/564).

299.   Review of unlawful profit orders. At any time before the person against whom an unlawful profit order[1] has been made has paid into court the whole of the amount which the order requires him to pay[2], but at a time when (disregarding any power of a court to grant leave to appeal out of time) there is no further possibility of an appeal[3] on which the order could be varied or set aside[4], the magistrates' court for the time being having functions in relation to the enforcement[5] of the order may, on the application of the person against whom it was made, discharge the order, or reduce the amount which remains to be paid[6], if it appears to the court:

  (1)   that the means of the person against whom the order was made are insufficient to satisfy in full both the order and a confiscation order[7], a compensation order[8] or a slavery and trafficking reparation order[9] made against him in the same proceedings[10]; or

  (2)   that the person against whom the order was made has suffered a substantial reduction in his means which was unexpected at the time when the order was made, and that his means seem unlikely to increase for a considerable period[11].

However, where the order was made by the Crown Court, a magistrates' court may not exercise any of the above powers in a case where it is satisfied as mentioned in head (1) or head (2) above unless it has first obtained the consent of the Crown Court[12].

1 See PARA 297.
2 Powers of Criminal Courts (Sentencing) Act 2000 s 133(2)(b); Prevention of Social Housing Fraud Act 2013 s 4(12)(a)–(c). As to the amount of an unlawful profit order see PARA 298.
3 As to appeals against unlawful profit orders see PARA 299.
4 Powers of Criminal Courts (Sentencing) Act 2000 s 133(2)(a).
5 As to enforcement see PARA 300.
6 Powers of Criminal Courts (Sentencing) Act 2000 s 133(1). In connection with applications for variation or discharge see the Criminal Procedure Rules 2015, SI 2015/1490, r 28.5.
7 Ie under the Proceeds of Crime Act 2002 Pt 2 (ss 6–91) or the Criminal Justice Act 1988 Pt VI (ss 71–103) (largely repealed): Powers of Criminal Courts (Sentencing) Act 2000 s 133(3)(c)(i) (s 133(3)(c)(i)–(iii) added, Prevention of Social Housing Fraud Act 2013 s 4(12)(d) amended, by Modern Slavery Act 2015 Sch 5 paras 14, 27(1), (2)).
8 Ie a compensation order under the Powers of Criminal Courts (Sentencing) Act 2000 s 130 (see PARA 281): s 133(3)(c)(ii) (as added: see note 7).
9 Ie an order under the Modern Slavery Act 2015 s 8 (see CRIMINAL LAW): Powers of Criminal Courts (Sentencing) Act 2000 s 133(3)(c)(iii) (as added: see note 7).
10 Powers of Criminal Courts (Sentencing) Act 2000 s 133(3)(c) (as amended: see note 7); Prevention of Social Housing Fraud Act 2013 s 4(12)(d) (as so amended).
11 Powers of Criminal Courts (Sentencing) Act 2000 s 133(3)(d).
12 Powers of Criminal Courts (Sentencing) Act 2000 s 133(4). Where an unlawful profit order has been made on appeal, for the purposes of s 133(4) it is deemed: (1) if it was made on an appeal brought from a magistrates' court, to have been made by that magistrates' court (s 133(5)(a)); and (2) if it was made on an appeal brought from the Crown Court or from the criminal division of the Court of Appeal, to have been made by the Crown Court (s 133(5)(b)).

300. Enforcement and suspension of orders. A person in whose favour an unlawful profit order is made[1] is not entitled to receive the amount due to him until (disregarding any power of a court to grant leave to appeal out of time) there is no further possibility of an appeal on which the order could be varied or set aside[2].

The Court of Appeal may by order annul or vary any unlawful profit order made by the court of trial, although the conviction is not quashed; and the order, if annulled, does not take effect and, if varied, takes effect as varied[3]. Where the Supreme Court restores a conviction, it may make any unlawful profit order which the court of trial could have made[4].

1 See PARA 297.
2 Powers of Criminal Courts (Sentencing) Act 2000 s 132(1); Prevention of Social Housing Fraud Act 2013 s 4(12)(a), (b). As to appeals against unlawful profit orders see PARA 299. Criminal Procedure Rules may make provision regarding the way in which the magistrates' court for the time being having functions, by virtue of the Administration of Justice Act 1970 s 41(1) (see MAGISTRATES vol 71 (2013) PARA 693), in relation to the enforcement of an unlawful profit order is to deal with money paid in satisfaction of the order where the entitlement of the person in whose favour it was made is suspended: Powers of Criminal Courts (Sentencing) Act 2000 s 132(2) (amended by SI 2004/2035). At the date at which this volume states the law no such rules had been made.
    Where in the case specified in the Administration of Justice Act 1970 Sch 9 para 10 or 13A (see CRIMINAL PROCEDURE vol 28 (2015) PARA 875) the Crown Court thinks that the period for which the person subject to the order is otherwise liable to be committed to prison for default under the order is insufficient, it may specify a longer period for that purpose; and then in the case of default: (1) the specified period is to be substituted as the maximum for which the person may be imprisoned under the Magistrates' Courts Act 1980 s 76 (see MAGISTRATES vol 71 (2013) PARA 627) (Administration of Justice Act 1970 s 41(8)(a) (s 41(8) substituted, and s 41(8A) added, by the Criminal Justice Act 1988 s 106; repealed by the Criminal Justice Act 1991 s 170(2), Sch 16; re-enacted by virtue of the Criminal Justice Act 1991 s 23(3);

Administration of Justice Act 1970 s 41(8)(a) amended by the Prevention of Social Housing Fraud Act 2013 Schedule para 2)); and (2) the Administration of Justice Act 1970 Sch 4 para 2 applies, with any necessary modifications, for the reduction of the specified period where, at the time of the person's imprisonment, he has made part payment under the order (Administration of Justice Act 1970 s 41(8)(b) (as so substituted)). However, the Crown Court may not so specify a period of imprisonment longer than that which it could order a person to undergo on imposing on him a fine equal in amount to the sum required to be paid by the order: s 41(8A) (as so added).

3   Powers of Criminal Courts (Sentencing) Act 2000 s 132(3).
4   Powers of Criminal Courts (Sentencing) Act 2000 s 132(4) (amended by the Constitutional Reform Act 2005 Sch 9 para 9). Where an order is made under the Powers of Criminal Courts (Sentencing) Act 2000 s 132(3) or (4), the Court of Appeal or the Supreme Court must make such order for the payment of a surcharge under the Criminal Justice Act 2003 s 161A (see PARA 185), or such variation of the order of the Crown Court under that provision, as is necessary to secure that the person's liability under that provision is the same as it would be if he were being dealt with by the Crown Court: Powers of Criminal Courts (Sentencing) Act 2000 s 132(4A) (added by the Domestic Violence, Crime and Victims Act 2004 Sch 10 para 49).

(6) FORFEITURE OF TERRORIST PROPERTY

(i) Forfeiture Orders under the Terrorism Act 2000

301. Forfeiture on conviction for an offence relating to terrorist property. The court by or before which a person is convicted of an offence of fund-raising or entering into funding arrangements for terrorist purposes[1], the use and possession of money or other property for the purposes of terrorism[2], providing insurance against payments made in response to terrorist demands[3], or money laundering in connection with terrorist property[4], may[5] make an order (a 'forfeiture order'[6]) for the forfeiture of any money or other property which wholly or partly, and directly or indirectly, is received by any person as a payment or other reward in connection with the commission of the offence[7].

The court by or before which a person is convicted of an offence of weapons training[8], possessing things and collecting information for the purposes of terrorism[9], inciting terrorism outside the United Kingdom[10], the dissemination of terrorist publications[11], the preparation of terrorist acts[12] or training for terrorism[13], or an offence involving radioactive devices or materials[14], may order the forfeiture of any money or other property which was, at the time of the offence, in the possession or control of the person convicted[15], provided that:

(1)   it had been used for the purposes of terrorism[16];
(2)   it was intended by that person that it should be used for the purposes of terrorism[17]; or
(3)   the court believes that it will be used for the purposes of terrorism unless forfeited[18].

Forfeiture orders may also be made in respect of ancillary offences[19] and certain offences in relation to which a terrorist connection is to be considered[20].

1   Ie an offence under the Terrorism Act 2000 s 15 or s 17: see CRIMINAL LAW vol 25 (2010) PARAS 375, 381.
2   Ie an offence under the Terrorism Act 2000 s 16: see CRIMINAL LAW vol 25 (2010) PARA 380.
3   Ie an offence under the Terrorism Act 2000 s 17A: see CRIMINAL LAW.
4   Ie an offence under the Terrorism Act 2000 s 18: see CRIMINAL LAW vol 25 (2010) PARA 382.
5   Ie in accordance with the Terrorism Act 2000 s 23 (see the text and note 7).
6   A forfeiture order does not come into force until there is no further possibility of it being varied, or set aside, on appeal (disregarding any power of a court to grant leave to appeal out of time): Terrorism Act 2000 Sch 4 para 2(2).
7   Terrorism Act 2000 s 23(1), (7) (s 23 substituted, s 23A added, by the Counter-Terrorism Act 2008 ss 34, 35). Specific provision is made for the content of a forfeiture order as follows:

(1)   where a person is convicted of an offence under the Terrorism Act 2000 s 15(1), s 15(2) or s 16, the court may order the forfeiture of any money or other property which, at the time of the offence, the person had in their possession or under their control and which had been used for the purposes of terrorism or they intended should be used, or had reasonable cause to suspect might be used, for those purposes (s 23(2) (as so substituted));

(2)   where a person is convicted of an offence under s 15(3) the court may order the forfeiture of any money or other property which, at the time of the offence, the person had in their possession or under their control and which had been used for the purposes of terrorism or which, at that time, they knew or had reasonable cause to suspect would or might be used for those purposes (s 23(3) (as so substituted));

(3)   where a person is convicted of an offence under s 17 or s 18 the court may order the forfeiture of any money or other property which, at the time of the offence, the person had in their possession or under their control and which had been used for the purposes of terrorism or was, at that time, intended by them to be used for those purposes (s 23(4) (as so substituted));

(4)   where a person is convicted of an offence under s 17 the court may order the forfeiture of the money or other property to which the arrangement in question related, and which had been used for the purposes of terrorism or at the time of the offence, the person knew or had reasonable cause to suspect would or might be used for those purposes (s 23(5) (as so substituted));

(5)   where a person is convicted of an offence under s 17A the court may order the forfeiture of the amount paid under, or purportedly under, the insurance contract (s 23(5A) (as so substituted; added by the Counter-Terrorism and Security Act 2015 s 42(2))); and

(6)   where a person is convicted of an offence under the Terrorism Act 2000 s 18, the court may order the forfeiture of the money or other property to which the arrangement in question related (s 23(6) (as so substituted)).

As to the meanings of 'terrorism' and 'property' for these purposes see CRIMINAL LAW vol 25 (2010) PARAS 372, 377. The Magistrates' Courts Act 1980 s 140 (disposal of non-pecuniary forfeitures: see PARA 471), does not apply to a forfeiture under the Terrorism Act 2000: Sch 4 para 2(4).

8   Ie an offence under the Terrorism Act 2000 s 54: see CRIMINAL LAW vol 25 (2010) PARA 401.
9   Ie an offence under the Terrorism Act 2000 s 57, s 58 or s 58A: see CRIMINAL LAW vol 25 (2010) PARAS 404, 409–410.
10   Ie an offence under the Terrorism Act 2000 s 59, s 60 or s 61: see CRIMINAL LAW vol 25 (2010) PARA 415.
11   Ie an offence under the Terrorism Act 2006 s 2: see CRIMINAL LAW vol 25 (2010) PARA 412.
12   Ie an offence under the Terrorism Act 2006 s 5: see CRIMINAL LAW vol 25 (2010) PARA 405.
13   Ie an offence under the Terrorism Act 2006 s 6: see CRIMINAL LAW vol 25 (2010) PARA 401.
14   Ie an offence under the Terrorism Act 2006 ss 9–11: see CRIMINAL LAW vol 25 (2010) PARAS 406–408.
15   Terrorism Act 2000 s 23A(1)(a), (2) (as added: see note 7). The Secretary of State may by order amend s 23A(2), but an order adding an offence to s 23A(2) applies only in relation to offences committed after the order comes into force: s 23A(5), (6) (as so added). At the date at which this volume states the law no such order had been made.
16   Terrorism Act 2000 s 23A(1)(b)(i) (as added: see note 7).
17   Terrorism Act 2000 s 23A(1)(b)(ii) (as added: see note 7).
18   Terrorism Act 2000 s 23A(1)(b)(iii) (as added: see note 7).
19   See the Terrorism Act 2000 s 23A(3) (as added: see note 7), which provides that s 23A applies to any ancillary offence (as defined in the Counter-Terrorism Act 2008 s 94: see PARA 519) in relation to an offence listed in the Terrorism Act 2000 s 23A(2) (see the text and notes 7–15).
20   See the Terrorism Act 2000 s 23A(4) (as added: see note 7), which provides that s 23A also applies to an offence specified in the Counter-Terrorism Act 2008 Sch 2 (offences where terrorist connection to be considered) as to which the court dealing with the offence has determined, in accordance with s 30 (see PARA 590) that the offence has a terrorist connection.

302.   Additional provisions in forfeiture orders. Before making a forfeiture order[1] a court must give an opportunity to be heard to any person, other than the convicted person, who claims to be the owner or otherwise interested in anything which can be[2] forfeited[3]. In considering whether to make such an order in respect of any property a court must have regard to the value of the property and the likely financial and other effects on the convicted person of the making of the order (taken together with any other order that the court contemplates making)[4].

Where a court makes a forfeiture order it may make such other provision as appears to it to be necessary for giving effect to the order, and in particular it may:

(1)   require any of the forfeited property[5] to be paid or handed over to the proper officer[6] or to a constable designated for the purpose by the chief officer of police of a police force specified in the order[7];

(2)   direct any of the forfeited property other than money or land to be sold or otherwise disposed of in such manner as the court may direct and the proceeds[8] (if any) to be paid to the proper officer[9];

(3)   appoint a receiver[10] to take possession, subject to such conditions and exceptions as may be specified by the court, of any of the forfeited property, to realise it in such manner as the court may direct and to pay the proceeds to the proper officer[11];

(4)   direct a specified part of any forfeited money, or of the proceeds of the sale, disposal or realisation of any forfeited property[12], to be paid by the proper officer to a specified person claiming to be the owner or otherwise interested in that money or property[13].

The proper officer must issue a certificate in respect of a forfeiture order if an application is made by the prosecutor in the proceedings in which the forfeiture order was made[14], the defendant in those proceedings[15], or a person whom the court heard[16] before making the order[17]. The certificate must state the extent (if any) to which, at the date of the certificate, effect has been given to the forfeiture order[18].

Where a court makes a forfeiture order in a case where the offender has been convicted of an offence that has resulted in a person suffering personal injury, loss or damage[19] or any such offence is taken into consideration by the court in determining sentence[20], the court may also order that an amount not exceeding a sum specified by the court is to be paid to that person out of the proceeds of the forfeiture[21].

1   Ie an order under the Terrorism Act 2000 s 23 or s 23A (see Sch 4 para 1 (s 23B, Sch 4 para 4A added, Sch 4 paras 1, 2(1)(d), 4(2)(c) amended, by the Counter-Terrorism Act 2008 ss 36, 37(1), Sch 3 para 5); and PARA 301).

2   Ie under the Terrorism Act 2000 s 23 or s 23A (see PARA 301).

3   Terrorism Act 2000 s 23B(1) (as added: see note 1).

4   Terrorism Act 2000 s 23B(2) (as added: see note 1).

5   'Forfeited property' means the money or other property to which a forfeiture order applies: Terrorism Act 2000 Sch 4 para 1.

6   'Proper officer' means:
    (1)   where the forfeiture order is made by a magistrates' court, the designated officer for that court (Terrorism Act 2000 Sch 4 para 4(1)(a) (Sch 4 para 4(1) amended by the Courts Act 2003 Sch 8 para 388));
    (2)   where the forfeiture order is made by the Crown Court and the defendant was committed to the Crown Court by a magistrates' court, the designated officer for the magistrates' court (Terrorism Act 2000 Sch 4 para 4(1)(b) (as so amended)); and
    (3)   where the forfeiture order is made by the Crown Court and the proceedings were instituted by a bill of indictment preferred by virtue of the Administration of Justice (Miscellaneous Provisions) Act 1933 s 2(2)(b) (see CRIMINAL PROCEDURE vol 27 (2015) PARA 317), the designated officer for the magistrates' court for the place where the trial took place (Terrorism Act 2000 Sch 4 para 4(1)(c) (as so amended)).

7   Terrorism Act 2000 Sch 4 para 2(1)(a).

8   The reference in heads (2) and (4) in the text to the proceeds of the sale, disposal or realisation of property is a reference to the proceeds after deduction of the costs of sale, disposal or realisation: Terrorism Act 2000 Sch 4 para 2(3).

9   Terrorism Act 2000 Sch 4 para 2(1)(b).

10 As to the remuneration and liability of such a receiver see the Terrorism Act 2000 Sch 4 para 3.

11 Terrorism Act 2000 Sch 4 para 2(1)(c).

12 See note 5.

13 Terrorism Act 2000 Sch 4 para 2(1)(d) (as amended: see note 1). The specified person must fall within s 23B(1) (see the text and notes 1–3).

14 Terrorism Act 2000 Sch 4 para 4(2)(a).

15 Terrorism Act 2000 Sch 4 para 4(2)(b).

16 Ie under the Terrorism Act 2000 s 23B(1).

17 Terrorism Act 2000 Sch 4 para 4(2)(c) (as amended: see note 1).

18 Terrorism Act 2000 Sch 4 para 4(3).

19 Terrorism Act 2000 Sch 4 para 4A(1)(a) (as added: see note 1).

20 Terrorism Act 2000 Sch 4 para 4A(1)(b) (as added: see note 1).

21 Terrorism Act 2000 Sch 4 para 4A(1) (as added: see note 1). For this purpose the 'proceeds of the forfeiture' means the aggregate amount of any forfeited money and the proceeds of the sale, disposal or realisation of any forfeited property, after deduction of the costs of the sale, disposal or realisation, reduced by the amount of any payment under Sch 4 para 2(1)(d) (see the text and notes 12–13) or Sch 4 para 3(1) (see the text and note 10): Sch 4 para 4A(2) (as so added). The court may make an order under Sch 4 para 4A only if it is satisfied that but for the inadequacy of the offender's means it would have made a compensation order under the Powers of Criminal Courts (Sentencing) Act 2000 s 130 (see PARAS 281–292) under which the offender would have been required to pay compensation of an amount not less than the specified amount: Terrorism Act 2000 Sch 4 para 4A(3) (as so added).

303.   Restraint orders. The High Court may make a restraint order in two situations[1]. First, it may make a restraint order where:

(1)   proceedings have been instituted in England and Wales for a relevant offence[2];

(2)   the proceedings have not been concluded[3];

(3)   an application for a restraint order is made to the High Court by the prosecutor[4]; and

(4)   a forfeiture order[5] has been made, or it appears to the High Court that a forfeiture order may be made, in the proceedings for the offence[6].

Secondly, the High Court may make a restraint order where:

(a)   a criminal investigation has been started in England and Wales with regard to a relevant offence[7];

(b)   an application for a restraint order is made to the High Court by the person who the High Court is satisfied will have the conduct of any proceedings for the offence[8]; and

(c)   it appears to the High Court that a forfeiture order may be made in any proceedings for the offence[9].

A restraint order prohibits a person to whom notice of it is given, subject to any conditions and exceptions specified in the order, from dealing with[10] property in respect of which a forfeiture order has been or could be made in any proceedings referred to above[11]. It may be discharged or varied by the High Court on the application of the person affected by it[12]. A restraint order made under heads (1) to (4) above[13] must be discharged on an application if the proceedings for the offence have been concluded[14]. A restraint order made under heads (a) to (c) above[15] must be discharged on an application if no proceedings in respect of relevant offences are instituted[16] within such time as the High Court considers reasonable[17] and all proceedings in respect of such offences have been concluded[18].

A constable may seize any property subject to a restraint order for the purpose of preventing it being removed from Great Britain[19]. Property so seized must be dealt with in accordance with the High Court's directions[20].

1   An application for a restraint order may be made to a judge in chambers without notice: Terrorism Act 2000 Sch 4 para 5(4). A restraint order must provide for notice of it to be given to any person affected by the order: Sch 4 para 6(1).

      The Land Charges Act 1972 (see REAL PROPERTY AND REGISTRATION) and the Land Registration Act 2002 (see REAL PROPERTY AND REGISTRATION) apply:

    (1)   in relation to restraint orders as they apply in relation to orders affecting land made by the court for the purpose of enforcing judgments or recognisances, except that no notice may be entered in the register of title under the Land Registration Act 2002 in respect of such orders (Terrorism Act 2000 Sch 4 para 8(1)(a) (Sch 4 para 8(1) amended by the Land Registration Act 2002 Sch 11 para 38)); and

    (2)   in relation to applications for restraint orders as they apply in relation to other pending land actions (Terrorism Act 2000 Sch 4 para 8(1)(b)).

      See also the Land Registration Rules 2003, SI 2003/1417, r 93; and REAL PROPERTY AND REGISTRATION vol 87 (2012) PARA 526.

2   Terrorism Act 2000 Sch 4 para 5(1)(a) (Sch 4 paras 1, 5(1)(a), (2)(a), 6(4) amended by the Counter-Terrorism Act 2008 Sch 3 para 5). 'Relevant offence' means an offence under any of the Terrorism Act 2000 ss 15–18 (see CRIMINAL LAW vol 25 (2010) PARAS 379–382), an offence to which s 23A (see PARA 301) applies, or, in relation to a restraint order, any offence specified in the Counter-Terrorism Act 2008 Sch 2 (offences where terrorist connection to be considered: see PARA 590): Terrorism Act 2000 Sch 4 para 1 (as so amended).

3   Terrorism Act 2000 Sch 4 para 5(1)(b). As to when proceedings are concluded see note 14.

4   Terrorism Act 2000 Sch 4 para 5(1)(c).

5   Ie an order under the Terrorism Act 2000 s 23 or s 23A: see Sch 4 para 1; and PARA 301.

6   Terrorism Act 2000 Sch 4 para 5(1)(d).

7   Terrorism Act 2000 Sch 4 para 5(2)(a) (Sch 4 paras 5(2), 6(3) substituted, Sch 4 para 5(3) amended, Sch 4 paras 5(6), 6(4) added, by the Anti-terrorism, Crime and Security Act 2001 Sch 2 para 2; Terrorism Act 2000 Sch 4 para 5(2)(a) as amended (see note 2)). 'Criminal investigation' means an investigation which police officers or other persons have a duty to conduct with a view to it being ascertained whether a person should be charged with an offence: Terrorism Act 2000 Sch 4 para 5(6) (as so added).

8   Terrorism Act 2000 Sch 4 para 5(2)(b) (as substituted: see note 7).

9   Terrorism Act 2000 Sch 4 para 5(2)(c) (as substituted: see note 7).

10   'Dealing with' includes a reference to removing the property from Great Britain: Terrorism Act 2000 Sch 4 para 5(5). As to the meaning of 'Great Britain' see PARA 4 note 3.

11   Terrorism Act 2000 Sch 4 para 5(3) (as amended: see note 7). The proceedings referred to in the text are those referred to in the Terrorism Act 2000 Sch 4 para 5(1) or (2): see heads (1)–(4) and heads (a)–(c) in the text.

12   Terrorism Act 2000 Sch 4 para 6(2).

13   Ie under the Terrorism Act 2000 Sch 4 para 5(1).

14   Terrorism Act 2000 Sch 4 para 6(3) (as substituted: see note 7). Proceedings are concluded: (1) when a forfeiture order has been made in those proceedings and effect has been given to it in respect of all the forfeited property (Sch 4 para 11(3)(a)); or (2) when no further forfeiture order has been made in those proceedings and there is no further possibility of one being made as a result of an appeal (disregarding any power of a court to grant leave to appeal out of time) (Sch 4 para 11(3)(b)).

15   Ie under the Terrorism Act 2000 Sch 4 para 5(2).

16   For the purposes of Sch 4, proceedings for an offence are instituted:

    (1)   when a justice of the peace issues a summons or warrant under the Magistrates' Courts Act 1980 s 1 in respect of the offence (see MAGISTRATES vol 71 (2013) PARA 429) (Terrorism Act 2000 Sch 4 para 11(1)(a));

    (2)   when a person is charged with the offence after being taken into custody without a warrant (see POLICE AND INVESTIGATORY POWERS vol 84A (2013) PARAS 487–493) (Sch 4 para 11(1)(b));

    (3)   when a voluntary bill of indictment charging a person with the offence is preferred by virtue of the Administration of Justice (Miscellaneous Provisions) Act 1933 s 2(2)(b) (see CRIMINAL PROCEDURE vol 27 (2015) PARA 317) (Terrorism Act 2000 Sch 4 para 11(1)(c)); and

    (4)   as from a day to be appointed, when a relevant prosecutor issues a written charge and

requisition in respect of the offence (Sch 4 para 11(1)(aa) (Sch 4 para 11(1)(aa), (2A) prospectively added by the Criminal Justice Act 2003 Sch 36 para 14(1), (2)); amended by the Crime and Courts Act 2015 Sch 11 para 17)).

For this purpose 'relevant prosecutor', 'requisition' and 'written charge' have the same meanings as in the Criminal Justice Act 2003 s 29 (see CRIMINAL PROCEDURE vol 27 (2015) PARA 139): Terrorism Act 2000 Sch 4 para 11(2A) (as so prospectively added; as so amended). At the date at which this volume states the law no day had been appointed for the purposes of the amendments made by the Criminal Justice Act 2003.

Where the application of these provisions would result in there being more than one time for the institution of proceedings they are to be taken to be instituted at the earliest of those times: Terrorism Act 2000 Sch 4 para 11(2).

17 Terrorism Act 2000 Sch 4 para 6(4)(a) (as added and amended: see notes 2, 7).
18 Terrorism Act 2000 Sch 4 para 6(4)(b) (as added and amended: see notes 2, 7).
19 Terrorism Act 2000 Sch 4 para 7(1).
20 Terrorism Act 2000 Sch 4 para 7(2).

304. Compensation orders. Where a restraint order[1] is discharged on the ground that no proceedings in respect of relevant offences[2] are instituted within a reasonable time[3], compensation may be ordered to be paid[4].

Compensation may be ordered to be paid where a forfeiture order[5] or a restraint order is made in relation to proceedings for a relevant offence which:

(1) do not result in conviction for a relevant offence[6];
(2) result in conviction for such a relevant offence in respect of which the person convicted is subsequently pardoned[7]; or
(3) result in conviction for such a relevant offence which is subsequently quashed[8].

A person who had an interest in any property subject to the restraint order may apply to the High Court for compensation[9]. The High Court may order compensation to be paid to the applicant if satisfied:

(a) that there was a serious default on the part of a person concerned in the investigation or prosecution of the offence[10];
(b) that the person in default was or was acting as a member of a police force, or was a member of the Crown Prosecution Service or was acting on behalf of the Service[11];
(c) that the applicant has suffered loss in consequence of anything done in relation to the property by or in pursuance of the forfeiture order or restraint order[12]; and
(d) that, having regard to all the circumstances, it is appropriate to order compensation to be paid[13].

The High Court may not order compensation to be paid where it appears that proceedings would have been instituted even if the serious default had not occurred[14].

Where a forfeiture order or a restraint order is made in or in relation to proceedings for a relevant offence[15], and the proceedings result in a conviction which is subsequently quashed on appeal[16] following the deproscription of a proscribed organisation[17], a person who had an interest in any property which was subject to the order may apply to the High Court for compensation[18]. The High Court may order compensation to be paid to the applicant if satisfied that the applicant has suffered loss in consequence of anything done in relation to the property by or in pursuance of the forfeiture order or restraint order[19] and that, having regard to all the circumstances, it is appropriate to order compensation to be paid[20].

1 See PARA 303.
2 As to the meaning of 'relevant offence' see PARA 303 note 2.

3   Ie where a restraint order is discharged under the Terrorism Act 2000 Sch 4 para 6(4)(a) (see
    PARA 303).
4   Terrorism Act 2000 Sch 4 para 9(1) (amended by the Anti-terrorism, Crime and Security
    Act 2001 Sch 2 para 2).
5   Ie an order under the Terrorism Act 2000 s 23 or s 23A: see Sch 4 para 1; and PARA 301.
6   Terrorism Act 2000 Sch 4 para 9(2)(a) (Sch 4 paras 9(2), 10(1)(a) amended by the
    Counter-Terrorism Act 2008 Sch 3 para 5).
7   Terrorism Act 2000 Sch 4 para 9(2)(b) (as amended: see note 6).
8   Terrorism Act 2000 Sch 4 para 9(2)(c) (as amended: see note 6).
9   Terrorism Act 2000 Sch 4 para 9(3).
10 Terrorism Act 2000 Sch 4 para 9(4)(a).
11 Terrorism Act 2000 Sch 4 para 9(4)(b). If compensation is ordered, it is to be paid out of the
    police fund of the police force in question where the person in default was or was acting as a
    member of a police force, and by the Director of Public Prosecutions where the person in default
    was a member of the Crown Prosecution Service or was acting on behalf of it: Sch 4 para 9(6).
12 Terrorism Act 2000 Sch 4 para 9(4)(c).
13 Terrorism Act 2000 Sch 4 para 9(4)(d).
14 Terrorism Act 2000 Sch 4 para 9(5).
15 Terrorism Act 2000 Sch 4 para 10(1)(a) (as amended: see note 6).
16 Ie under the Terrorism Act 2000 s 7(2), (5): see CRIMINAL LAW vol 25 (2010) PARA 375.
17 Terrorism Act 2000 Sch 4 para 10(1)(b).
18 Terrorism Act 2000 Sch 4 para 10(2).
19 Terrorism Act 2000 Sch 4 para 10(3)(a). If compensation is ordered to be paid, it is to be paid
    by the Secretary of State: Sch 4 para 10(4). As to the meaning of 'property' see CRIMINAL LAW
    vol 25 (2010) PARA 377.
20 Terrorism Act 2000 Sch 4 para 10(3)(b).

305.   Freezing orders. If any of the property to which an application for a restraint order[1] relates is property in a participating country[2], the applicant may ask the High Court to make a certificate which is made for the purposes of the relevant Framework Decision[3] on the execution in the European Union of orders freezing property, and gives specified information[4].

The High Court may make such a certificate if it makes a restraint order in relation to property in the participating country and it is satisfied that there is a good arguable case[5] that the property is likely to be used for the purposes of a listed offence[5] or is the proceeds of the commission of a listed offence[6].

If the High Court makes a certificate the restraint order must provide for notice of the certificate to be given to the person affected by it, and specified provisions[7] apply to the certificate as they apply to the restraint order[8].

If a certificate is made, the restraint order and the certificate are to be sent to the Secretary of State for forwarding to a court exercising jurisdiction in the place where the property is situated, or any authority recognised by the government of the participating country as the appropriate authority for receiving orders of that kind[9].

An overseas freezing order[10] is an order prohibiting dealing with property:

(1)   which is in the United Kingdom[11];

(2)   which the appropriate court or authority[12] considers is likely to be used for the purposes of a listed offence or is the proceeds of the commission of such an offence[13]; and

(3)   in respect of which an order has been or may be made by a court exercising criminal jurisdiction in the participating country for the forfeiture of the property[14],

and in respect of which specified requirements[15] are met[16].

Where an overseas freezing order made by an appropriate court or authority in a participating country is received by the Secretary of State from the court or authority which made or confirmed the order, the Secretary of State must send a copy of the overseas freezing order to the High Court and to the Director of Public Prosecutions[17]. The court may decide not to give effect to the overseas freezing order only if, in its opinion, giving effect to it would be incompatible with any of the Convention rights[18]. Where the High Court decides to give effect to an overseas freezing order, it must register the order in that court, and provide for notice of the registration to be given to any person affected by it[19].

1   As to restraint orders see PARA 303.
2   A 'participating country' means: (1) a country other than the United Kingdom which is a member state on 3 December 2014 (ie the day appointed for the commencement of the Crime (International Co-operation) Act 2003 Sch 4 by the Crime (International Co-operation) Act 2003 (Commencement No 6) Order 2014, SI 2014/3192); and (2) any other member state designated by an order made by the Secretary of State: Terrorism Act 2000 Sch 4 para 11A(1), (7) (Sch 4 paras 11A–11G added by the Crime (International Co-operation) Act 2003 Sch 4 paras 1, 3). 'Country' includes territory: Terrorism Act 2000 Sch 4 para 11A(8) (as so added). As to the meaning of 'United Kingdom' see PARA 4 note 3.
3   Ie the Framework Decision on the execution in the European Union of orders freezing property or evidence adopted by the Council of the European Union on 22 July 2003: Terrorism Act 2000 Sch 4 para 11A(2) (as added: see note 2).
4   Terrorism Act 2000 Sch 4 para 11B(1), (3) (as added: see note 2). 'Specified information', in relation to a certificate under Sch 4 para 11B or Sch 4 para 11D means any information required to be given by the form of certificate annexed to the relevant Framework Decision, or any information prescribed by an order made by the Secretary of State: Sch 4 para 11A(5), (6) (as so added).
5   A listed offence means an offence described in art 3(2) of the relevant Framework Decision, or a prescribed offence or an offence of a prescribed description: Terrorism Act 2000 Sch 4 para 11A(3) (as added: see note 2). An order relating to a prescribed offence or an offence of a prescribed description which, for the purposes of Sch 4 para 11D prescribes an offence or a description of offences may require that the conduct which constitutes the offence or offences would, if it occurred in a part of the United Kingdom, constitute an offence in that part: Sch 4 para 11A(4) (as so added).
6   Terrorism Act 2000 Sch 4 para 11B(2) (as added: see note 2). Section 14(2)(a) (see CRIMINAL LAW vol 25 (2010) PARA 382) applies for the purposes of determining what are the proceeds of the commission of an offence: Sch 4 para 11A(9) (as so added).
7   Ie the Terrorism Act 2000 Sch 4 para 6(2)–(4): see PARA 303.
8   Terrorism Act 2000 Sch 4 para 11B(4) (as added: see note 2).
9   Terrorism Act 2000 Sch 4 para 11C(1) (as added: see note 2). The restraint order and the certificate must be accompanied by a forfeiture order (see PARA 301), unless the certificate indicates when the court expects a forfeiture order to be sent: Sch 4 para 11C(2) (as so added). The certificate must include a translation of it into an appropriate language of the participating country (if that language is not English): Sch 4 para 11C(3) (as so added). The certificate must be signed by or on behalf of the court and must include a statement as to the accuracy of the information given in it; and the signature may be an electronic signature: Sch 4 para 11C(4) (as so added). If the restraint order and the certificate are not accompanied by a forfeiture order, but a forfeiture order is subsequently made, it is to be sent to the Secretary of State for forwarding to a court exercising jurisdiction in the place where the property is situated, or any authority recognised by the government of the participating country as the appropriate authority for receiving orders of that kind: Sch 4 para 11C(1), (5) (as so added).
10   References in the Terrorism Act 2000 Sch 4 paras 11E–11G to an overseas freezing order include its accompanying certificate: Sch 4 para 11D(9) (as added: see note 2).
11   Terrorism Act 2000 Sch 4 para 11D(2)(a) (as added: see note 2).
12   An appropriate court or authority in a participating country in relation to an overseas freezing order is a court exercising criminal jurisdiction in the country, a prosecuting authority in the country, any other authority in the country which appears to the Secretary of State to have the function of making such orders: Terrorism Act 2000 Sch 4 para 11D(8) (as added: see note 2).
13   Terrorism Act 2000 Sch 4 para 11D(2)(b) (as added: see note 2).
14   Terrorism Act 2000 Sch 4 para 11D(2)(c) (as added: see note 2).
15   The specified requirements are that:
      (1)   the action which the appropriate court or authority considered would constitute or, as the case may be, constituted the listed offence is action done as an act of terrorism or for the purposes of terrorism (Terrorism Act 2000 Sch 4 para 11D(3) (as added: see note 2));

(2) the order must relate to criminal proceedings instituted in the participating country, or a criminal investigation being carried on there (Sch 4 para 11D(4) (as so added));

(3) the order must be accompanied by a certificate which gives the specified information; but a certificate may be treated as giving any specified information which is not given in it if the Secretary of State has the information in question (Sch 4 para 11D(5) (as so added));

(4) the certificate must: (a) be signed by or on behalf of the court or authority which made or confirmed the order (and the signature may be an electronic signature); (b) include a statement as to the accuracy of the information given in it; (c) if it is not in English, include a translation of it into English (or, if appropriate, Welsh) (Sch 4 para 11D(6) (as so added));

(5) the order must be accompanied by an order made by a court exercising criminal jurisdiction in that country for the forfeiture of the property, unless the certificate indicates when such an order is expected to be sent (Sch 4 para 11D(7) (as so added)).

16 Terrorism Act 2000 Sch 4 para 11D(2) (as added: see note 2).

17 Terrorism Act 2000 Sch 4 paras 11D(1), 11E(1) (as added: see note 2). The court must consider the overseas freezing order on its own initiative within a period prescribed by rules of court: Sch 4 para 11E(2) (as so added). The High Court may postpone giving effect to an overseas freezing order in respect of any property: (1) in order to avoid prejudicing a criminal investigation which is taking place in the United Kingdom; or (2) if, under an order made by a court in criminal proceedings in the United Kingdom, the property may not be dealt with: Sch 4 para 11F (as so added). Before giving effect to the overseas freezing order the court must give the Director of Public Prosecutions an opportunity to be heard: Sch 4 paras 11D(1), 11E(3) (as so added).

18 Terrorism Act 2000 Sch 4 para 11E(4) (as added: see note 2). As to the Convention rights (ie within the meaning of the Human Rights Act 1998) see s 1; and RIGHTS AND FREEDOMS vol 88A (2013) PARA 14.

19 Terrorism Act 2000 Sch 4 para 11G(1) (as added: see note 2). For the purpose of enforcing an overseas freezing order registered in the High Court, the order is to have effect as if it were an order made by that court: Sch 4 para 11G(2) (as so added). A constable may seize property subject to an overseas freezing order for the purpose of preventing it from being removed from Great Britain: Sch 4 para 11G(3) (as so added). The High Court may cancel the registration of the order, or vary the property to which the order applies, on an application by the Director of Public Prosecutions or any other person affected by it, if or to the extent that the court is of the opinion that giving effect to the order would be incompatible with any of the Convention rights under the Human Rights Act 1998, or that the order has ceased to have effect in the participating country: Terrorism Act 2000 Sch 4 paras 11E(4), 11G(4) (as so added). Her Majesty may by Order in Council make further provision for the enforcement in England and Wales of registered overseas freezing orders: Sch 4 para 11G(5) (as so added).

306. Enforcement of forfeiture or restraint orders made outside England and Wales. A forfeiture order[1] or restraint order[2] made in Scotland, Northern Ireland, the Channel Islands or the Isle of Man, or an order relating to its discharge or variation, has effect in the law of England and Wales[3].

Her Majesty may by Order in Council make provision for the purpose of enabling the enforcement in England and Wales of an 'external order' (that is, an order other than an overseas freezing order[4] which is made in a country or territory designated for this purpose by the Order in Council, and which makes relevant provision)[5].

1 As to forfeiture orders see PARA 301.

2 As to restraint orders see PARA 303.

3 Terrorism Act 2000 Sch 4 paras 12, 13(1). As to the provisions relating to Scottish and Northern Ireland orders see Sch 4 paras 12, 15–44. Such orders can be enforced only in accordance with the Terrorism Act 2000 Sch 4 para 13 and any provision made by rules of court: Sch 4 para 13(2). Rules of court govern the registration of such orders: see Sch 4 para 13(3), (4). As to the registration of forfeiture orders see Sch 4 para 13(5) (amended by the Courts Act 2003 Sch 8 para 388) and as to the registration of restraint orders see the Terrorism Act 2000 Sch 4 para 13(6) (amended by the Constitutional Reform Act 2005 Sch 11 para 1(2)). The High Court has the same power in relation to the order's enforcement as if the order had

originally been made in the High Court: see the Terrorism Act 2000 Sch 4 para 13(7), (8). As to the documents to be received in evidence see Sch 4 para 13(9).

4   Ie an order other than an overseas freezing order within the meaning of the Terrorism Act 2000 Sch 4 para 11D (PARA 305).

5   See the Terrorism Act 2000 Sch 4 para 14(1), (2) (amended by the Crime (International Co-operation) Act 2003 Sch 4 paras 1, 4). 'Relevant provision' means: (1) provision for the forfeiture of terrorist property (an 'external forfeiture order'); or (2) provision prohibiting dealing with property which is subject to an external forfeiture order or in respect of which such an order could be made in proceedings which have been or are to be instituted in the designated country or territory (an 'external restraint order'): Terrorism Act 2000 Sch 4 para 14(3). As to the meaning of 'terrorist property' see s 14(1); and CRIMINAL LAW vol 25 (2010) PARA 382.

An Order in Council under Sch 4 para 14 may, in particular, include provision:

(a)   which for the purpose of facilitating the enforcement of any external order that may be made, has effect at times before there is an external order to be enforced (Sch 4 para 14(4)(a));

(b)   for matters corresponding to those for which provision is made by, or can be made under, Sch 4 para 13(1)–(8) in relation to the orders to which Sch 4 para 13 applies (Sch 4 para 14(4)(b));

(c)   for the proof of any matter relevant for the purposes of anything falling to be done in pursuance of the Order in Council (Sch 4 para 14(4)(c)).

Such an Order in Council may also make provision with respect to anything falling to be done on behalf of the United Kingdom in a designated country or territory in relation to proceedings in that country or territory for or in connection with the making of an external order: Sch 4 para 14(5). The Terrorism Act 2000 (Enforcement of External Orders) Order 2001, SI 2001/3927, makes provision for the purpose of enabling the enforcement in England and Wales (and the rest of the United Kingdom) of an external order made by a court in Austria, Belgium, Canada, Denmark, Finland, France, Germany, Greece, India, Ireland, Italy, Japan, Luxembourg, the Netherlands, Portugal, Spain, Sweden and the United States of America.

307. Protection of creditors against forfeiture. During the six-month period beginning with the making of a forfeiture order[1], neither the money to which the order applies nor the money which represents any property to which the order applies may be finally disposed of[2].

Where:

(1)   before or after a forfeiture order is made, the commencement of an insolvency[3] occurs in qualifying insolvency proceedings[4];

(2)   an insolvency practitioner[5] would, but for the forfeiture order, exercise a function in those proceedings in relation to property to which the forfeiture order applies[6]; and

(3)   he gives written[7] notice to the relevant officer[8] of the matters referred to in head (1) and (2) above before the end of the period of six months beginning with the making of the forfeiture order[9],

the property in relation to which the insolvency practitioner would, but for the forfeiture order, exercise a function in those proceedings, and the proceeds of sale[10] of that property, cease to be subject to the forfeiture order and any ancillary order[11], and must be dealt with in the insolvency proceedings as if the forfeiture order had never been made[12].

Where by virtue of this provision property falls to be dealt with in insolvency proceedings, the Secretary of State is taken to be a creditor in those proceedings to the amount or value of the property[13]. Except in a sequestration, his debt ranks after the debts of all other creditors, and must not be paid until they have been paid in full with interest under the relevant provision[14].

Property which has ceased to be subject to a forfeiture order by virtue of the provisions described above in consequence of the making of a bankruptcy order or an award of sequestration becomes again subject to the forfeiture order and, if applicable, any ancillary order if the bankruptcy order is annulled or the award of sequestration is recalled or reduced[15].

Where under the provisions described above money or other property falls to be dealt with in insolvency proceedings as if the forfeiture order had never been made, the relevant officer may deduct allowable forfeiture expenses[16] from that money and retain so much of that property as he considers necessary for the purpose of realising it and deducting allowable forfeiture expenses from the proceeds of realisation[17].

1   Ie an order under the Terrorism Act 2000 s 23 or s 23A (see PARA 301), a forfeiture order of the Channel Islands or Isle of Man within the meaning of Sch 4 (see PARAS 303, 306), or an external forfeiture order enforceable in England and Wales or Scotland or Northern Ireland by virtue of an Order in Council made under Sch 4 para 14 (see PARA 306): Sch 4 para 45 (Sch 4 para 45 amended by the Counter-Terrorism Act 2000 Sch 3 para 5).

2   Terrorism Act 2000 Sch 4 para 46(1). In England and Wales, money is finally disposed of when it is paid to the Lord Chancellor in accordance with the Courts Act 2003 s 38 (see MAGISTRATES vol 71 (2013) PARA 696) or to the Secretary of State in accordance with the provisions relating to the payment of the balance remaining, after the required payments, under a registered forfeiture order made in another part of the British Isles: Terrorism Act 2000 Sch 4 para 46(2)(a) (s 46(2) amended by the Courts Act 2003 Sch 8 para 388(1), (4)(a)). As to provision for Scotland and Northern Ireland see the Terrorism Act 2000 Sch 4 para 46(2)(b), (c).

3   'Commencement of an insolvency' means:
    (1)   the making of a bankruptcy order (Terrorism Act 2000 Sch 4 para 47(5)(a));
    (2)   the award of sequestration (s 47(5)(b));
    (3)   in the case of an insolvent estate of a deceased person, the making of an insolvency administration order (s 47(5)(c)); or
    (4)   in the case of a company, the passing of a resolution for its winding up, or where no such resolution has been passed, the making of an order by the court for the winding up of the company (s 47(5)(d)).

4   Terrorism Act 2000 Sch 4 para 47(1)(a). 'Qualifying insolvency proceedings' means:
    (1)   any proceedings under the Insolvency Act 1986 or the Insolvency (Northern Ireland) Order 1989, SI 1989/2405 (NI 19)) for the winding up of a company or an unregistered company and includes any voluntary winding up of a company under the Insolvency Act 1986 Pt IV (ss 73–219) or the Insolvency (Northern Ireland) Order 1989, SI 1989/2405, Pt V (Terrorism Act 2000 Sch 4 para 53(2)(a));
    (2)   any proceedings in England and Wales or Northern Ireland under or by virtue of the Insolvency Act 1986 s 420 or the Insolvency (Northern Ireland) Order 1989, SI 1989/2405, art 364 for the winding up of an insolvent partnership (Terrorism Act 2000 Sch 4 para 53(2)(b));
    (3)   any proceedings in bankruptcy or, in Scotland, any sequestration of a debtor's estate (Sch 4 para 53(2)(c)); or
    (4)   any proceedings in England and Wales or in Northern Ireland under or by virtue of the Insolvency Act 1986 s 421 (see BANKRUPTCY AND INDIVIDUAL INSOLVENCY vol 5 (2013) PARA 830) or the Insolvency (Northern Ireland) Order 1989, SI 1989/2405, art 365 in relation to the insolvent estate of a deceased person (Terrorism Act 2000 Sch 4 para 53(2)(d)).

5   'Insolvency practitioner' means a person acting in any qualifying insolvency proceedings in any part of the United Kingdom as:
    (1)   a liquidator of a company or partnership (Terrorism Act 2000 Sch 4 para 53(1)(a));
    (2)   a trustee in bankruptcy (Sch 4 para 53(1)(b));
    (3)   the permanent or interim trustee on the debtor's estate (Sch 4 para 53(1)(c));
    (4)   an administrator of the insolvent estate of a deceased person (Sch 4 para 53(1)(d)); or
    (5)   a receiver or manager of any property (Sch 4 para 53(1)(e)).
    This definition does not apply to Sch 4 para 51 (see PARA 308): Sch 4 para 53(1).

6   Terrorism Act 2000 Sch 4 para 47(1)(b).

7   See POLICE AND INVESTIGATORY POWERS vol 84A (2013) PARA 732.

8   Where the forfeiture order in question is made in England and Wales, the 'relevant officer' is the proper officer within the meaning given in the Terrorism Act 2000 Sch 4 para 4 (see PARA 302): see Sch 4 para 53(3). In any case where the forfeiture order is made outside England, Wales, Scotland or Northern Ireland, the relevant officer is the appropriate officer of the High Court: Sch 4 para 53(3)(a), (c). As to Northern Ireland and Scotland see Sch 4 para 53(3)(b), (4).

9 Terrorism Act 2000 Sch 4 para 47(1)(c).

10 The reference to the 'proceeds of sale' is a reference to proceeds after deduction of the costs of sale: Terrorism Act 2000 Sch 4 para 53(5).

11 Ie an order made in connection with a forfeiture, other than the forfeiture order: Terrorism Act 2000 Sch 4 para 45.

12 Terrorism Act 2000 Sch 4 para 47(1), (2), (3). The property which ceases to be subject to the forfeiture order and any ancillary order, and which must be dealt with in the insolvency proceedings as if the forfeiture order had never been made, is the balance remaining after the relevant officer has exercised his powers under Sch 4 para 50(1) (see the text and note 17): Sch 4 para 47(4)(a). Where the relevant officer, or any person acting in pursuance of an ancillary order, has incurred obligations in relation to property, the provision that property ceases to be subject to the forfeiture order and any ancillary order, and must be dealt with in the insolvency proceedings as if the forfeiture order had never been made, does not take effect until those obligations have been discharged: Sch 4 para 47(4)(b).

13 Terrorism Act 2000 Sch 4 para 48(1).

14 Terrorism Act 2000 Sch 4 para 48(2). 'Relevant provision' means, in relation to the winding up of a company in England, Wales or Scotland, the Insolvency Act 1986 s 189(2) (see COMPANY AND PARTNERSHIP INSOLVENCY vol 17 (2011) PARA 785), and, in relation to a bankruptcy, s 328(4) (see BANKRUPTCY AND INDIVIDUAL INSOLVENCY vol 5 (2013) PARA 596): see the Terrorism Act 2000 Sch 4 para 48(3)(a), (b). As to the relevant provision in relation to Scotland and Northern Ireland see Sch 4 para 48(3)(c), (d). Note that the provisions of Sch 4 para 48(2), (3) apply notwithstanding any provision in or made under any other enactment: Sch 4 para 48(5). As to sequestration in Scotland see Sch 4 para 48(4).

15 Terrorism Act 2000 Sch 4 para 49(1), (2). Where the property is money or has been converted into money the relevant court must make an order specifying property comprised in the estate of the bankrupt or debtor to the amount or value of the property and the specified property becomes subject to the forfeiture order, and any applicable ancillary order, in place of the property: Sch 4 para 49(3). The 'relevant court' means the court which ordered the annulment of the bankruptcy, or recalled or reduced the award of sequestration: Sch 4 para 49(4).

16 'Allowable forfeiture expenses':
    (1)   means expenses incurred in relation to the forfeited property by the relevant officer (Terrorism Act 2000 Sch 4 para 50(3)(a));
    (2)   means expenses incurred in relation to the forfeited property by a receiver, administrator or other person appointed by the relevant officer (Sch 4 para 50(3)(b));
    (3)   means expenses incurred in relation to the forfeited property by any person appointed or directed to deal with any property under Terrorism Act 2000 Sch 4 para 16 (provisions applying to Scotland) (Sch 4 para 50(3)(c)); and
    (4)   includes sums paid or required to be paid under Sch 4 para 2(1)(d) (see PARA 302), Sch 4 para 16(1)(c) (Scotland) or Sch 4 para 30(1)(d) (Northern Ireland) (Sch 4 para 50(3)(d)).

17 Terrorism Act 2000 Sch 4 para 50(1). Where property is delivered up and the relevant officer has not made provision under Sch 4 para 50(1) for all the allowable forfeiture expenses then a person who has incurred allowable forfeiture expenses for which provision has not been made has a claim to their value in the insolvency proceedings and the expenses in question are to be treated for the purposes of the insolvency proceedings as if they were expenses of those proceedings: Sch 4 para 50(2).

308. Protection of insolvency practitioners. An insolvency practitioner[1] who seizes or disposes of property which is subject to a forfeiture order[2] or a restraint order[3] is not liable to any person in respect of any loss or damage resulting from the seizure or disposal, except in so far as the loss or damage is caused by his negligence, if he reasonably believes that he is entitled to do so in the exercise of his functions and he would be so entitled if the property were not subject to a forfeiture order or a restraint order[4].

The insolvency practitioner has a lien on the property seized or the proceeds or its sale for such of his expenses as were incurred in connection with the insolvency proceedings in relation to which the seizure or disposal purported to take place, and for so much of his remuneration as may be reasonably assigned for his acting in connection with those proceedings[5].

1   For these purposes, 'insolvency practitioner' in any part of the United Kingdom, means a person acting as an insolvency practitioner in that or any other part of the United Kingdom: Terrorism Act 2000 Sch 4 para 51(5). For the purpose of Sch 4 para 51(5), any question whether a person is acting as an insolvency practitioner in England and Wales or in Scotland is to be determined in accordance with the Insolvency Act 1986 s 388 (see BANKRUPTCY AND INDIVIDUAL INSOLVENCY vol 5 (2013) PARA 40), subject to specified modifications: Terrorism Act 2000 Sch 4 para 51(6). For the purpose of Sch 4 para 51(5), any question whether a person is acting as an insolvency practitioner in Northern Ireland is to be determined in accordance with the Insolvency (Northern Ireland) Order 1989, SI 1989/2405 (NI 19), art 3, subject to specified modifications: Terrorism Act 2000 Sch 4 para 51(7).

2   As to the meaning of 'forfeiture order' for these purposes see PARA 307 note 1.

3   Ie an order under the Terrorism Act 2000 Sch 4 para 5 (or the corresponding order in Scotland or Northern Ireland under Sch 4 para 18 or Sch 4 para 33), a restraint order of the Channel Islands or Isle of Man, or an external restraint order enforceable in England and Wales or Scotland or Northern Ireland by virtue of an Order in Council: Sch 4 para 45 (amended by the Crime (International Co-operation) Act 2003 Sch 4 para 9).

4   Terrorism Act 2000 Sch 4 para 51(1), (2). Provision is made to ensure that an Islands or external insolvency practitioner (ie a person exercising under the insolvency law of a relevant country or territory functions corresponding to those exercised by insolvency practitioners under the insolvency law of any part of the United Kingdom) has the same rights in relation to property situated in England, Wales, Scotland or Northern Ireland as he would have if he were an insolvency practitioner in that part of the United Kingdom: see Sch 4 para 52.

5   Terrorism Act 2000 Sch 4 para 51(3). As to lien see generally LIEN. See also note 4.

(ii) Additional Powers of Forfeiture under the Terrorism Act 2000

309. Forfeiture of property associated with terrorist activity. In addition to the power to make forfeiture orders[1]:

(1)   a court by or before which a person is convicted of an offence of weapons training[2] may order the forfeiture of anything that the court considers to have been in the possession of the person for purposes connected with the offence[3];

(2)   a court by or before which a person is convicted of an offence of possessing things for the purposes of terrorism[4] may order the forfeiture of any article that is the subject-matter of the offence[5]; and

(3)   a court by or before which a person is convicted of an offence of collecting information for the purposes of terrorism[6] may order the forfeiture of any document or record[7] relevant to the offence[8].

Before making such an order a court must give an opportunity to be heard to any person, other than the convicted person, who claims to be the owner or otherwise interested in anything which can be forfeited under these provisions[9]; and such an order does not come into force until there is no further possibility of it being varied, or set aside, on appeal (disregarding any power of a court to grant leave to appeal out of time)[10]. Where a court makes such an order it may also make such other provision as appears to it to be necessary for giving effect to the forfeiture, including, in particular, provision relating to the retention, handling, disposal or destruction of what is forfeited[11].

1   Ie in addition to the powers conferred by the Terrorism Act 2000 s 23A (see PARA 301): s 120A(6) (s 120A added by the Counter-Terrorism Act 2000 s 38(1)).

2   Ie an offence under the Terrorism Act 2000 s 54: see CRIMINAL LAW vol 25 (2010) PARA 401.

3   Terrorism Act 2000 s 120A(1) (as added: see note 1).

4   Ie an offence under the Terrorism Act 2000 s 57: see CRIMINAL LAW vol 25 (2010) PARA 404.

5   Terrorism Act 2000 s 120A(1) (as added: see note 1).

6   Ie an offence under the Terrorism Act 2000 s 58 or s 58A: see CRIMINAL LAW vol 25 (2010) PARAS 409–410.

7 Ie any document or record containing information of the kind mentioned in s 58(1)(a) or s 58A(1)(a) (see CRIMINAL LAW vol 25 (2010) PARAS 409–410): Terrorism Act 2000 s 120A(1) (as added: see note 1).
8 Terrorism Act 2000 s 120A(1) (as added: see note 1).
9 Terrorism Act 2000 s 120A(2) (as added: see note 1).
10 Terrorism Act 2000 s 120A(3) (as added: see note 1).
11 Terrorism Act 2000 s 120A(4) (as added: see note 1). Provision made by virtue of s 120A(4) may be varied at any time by the court that made it: s 120A(5) (as so added).

(iii) Forfeiture Orders under the Terrorism Act 2006

310. Making of forfeiture orders. A court before which a person is convicted of an offence[1] relating to the giving or receiving of instruction or training in:

(1)   the making, handling or use of a noxious substance[2], or of substances of a description of such substances[3];

(2)   the use of any method or technique for doing anything else that is capable of being done for the purposes of terrorism[4], in connection with the commission or preparation of an act of terrorism[5] or Convention offence[6] or in connection with assisting the commission or preparation by another of such an act or offence[7]; or

(3)   the design or adaptation for the purposes of terrorism, or in connection with the commission or preparation of an act of terrorism or Convention offence, of any method or technique for doing anything[8],

may order the forfeiture of anything the court considers to have been in the person's possession for purposes connected with the offence[9].

1 Ie an offence under the Terrorism Act 2006 s 6 (see CRIMINAL LAW vol 25 (2010) PARA 401).
2 As to the meaning of 'noxious substance' see the Terrorism Act 2006 s 6(7); and CRIMINAL LAW vol 25 (2010) PARA 401.
3 See the Terrorism Act 2006 s 6(1), (2), (3)(a); and CRIMINAL LAW vol 25 (2010) PARA 401.
4 As to the meaning of 'terrorism' see the Terrorism Act 2000 s 1; the Terrorism Act 2006 s 20(1); and CRIMINAL LAW vol 25 (2010) PARA 401.
5 As to the meaning of 'act of terrorism' see the Terrorism Act 2006 s 20(2); and CRIMINAL LAW vol 25 (2010) PARA 401.
6 As to the meaning of 'Convention offence' see the Terrorism Act 2006 Sch 1; and CRIMINAL LAW vol 25 (2010) PARA 373.
7 See the Terrorism Act 2006 s 6(1), (2), (3)(b); and CRIMINAL LAW vol 25 (2010) PARA 401.
8 See the Terrorism Act 2006 s 6(1), (2), (3)(c); and CRIMINAL LAW vol 25 (2010) PARA 401.
9 Terrorism Act 2006 s 7(1). The power of forfeiture under s 7 is in addition to any power of forfeiture under the Terrorism Act 2000 s 23A (see PARA 301): Terrorism Act 2006 s 7(7) (added by the Counter-Terrorism Act 2008 s 38(2)). Such an order may not be made so as to come into force at any time before there is no further possibility (disregarding any power to grant permission for the bringing of an appeal out of time) of the order's being varied or set aside on appeal: Terrorism Act 2006 s 7(3). Where a court makes such an order it may also make such other provision as appears to it to be necessary for giving effect to the forfeiture (s 7(4)); and that provision may include, in particular, provision relating to the retention, handling, destruction or other disposal of what is forfeited (s 7(5)). Provision made by virtue of these provisions may be varied at any time by the court that made it: s 7(6).
   Before making such an order in relation to anything the court must give an opportunity of being heard to any person (in addition to the convicted person) who claims to be the owner of that thing or otherwise to have an interest in it: s 7(2).

(iv) Financial Information Orders and Account Monitoring Orders

311. Financial information orders. A financial information order[1] made in relation to a terrorist investigation[2] authorises a constable named in the order to require a financial institution[3] to which the order applies to provide customer information[4] for the purposes of the investigation[5]. The information must be provided in such manner and within such time as the constable may specify, and notwithstanding any restriction on the disclosure of information imposed by statute or otherwise[6]. An institution which fails to comply with a financial information order is guilty of an offence[7]. It is, however, a defence for the institution to prove[8] that the information required was not in the institution's possession, or that it was not reasonably practicable for the institution to comply with the requirement[9].

1   Ie an order under the Terrorism Act 2000 Sch 6 para 1(1).
2   As to the meaning of 'terrorist investigation' see the Terrorism Act 2000 s 32; and POLICE AND INVESTIGATORY POWERS vol 84A (2013) PARA 726.
3   'Financial institution' means:
    (1) a person who has permission under the Financial Services and Markets Act 2000 Pt 4A (ss 55A–55Z4) (see FINANCIAL SERVICES AND INSTITUTIONS) to accept deposits (Terrorism Act 2000 Sch 6 para 6(1)(a) (substituted by SI 2001/3649; amended by the Financial Services and Markets Act 2012 Sch 18 para 87)); .
    (2) a credit union (within the meaning of the Credit Unions Act 1979 (see FINANCIAL SERVICES AND INSTITUTIONS vol 50 (2008) PARA 2402 et seq) or the Credit Unions (Northern Ireland) Order 1985, SI 1985/1205 (NI 12)) (Terrorism Act 2000 Sch 6 para 6(1)(c));
    (3) a person carrying on a 'relevant regulated activity' (ie dealing in investments as principal or as agent, arranging deals in investments, operating a multilateral trading facility, managing investments, safeguarding and administering investments, sending dematerialised instructions, managing a UCITS, acting as trustee or depositary of a UCITS, managing an AIF, acting as trustee or depositary of an AIF, establishing etc collective investment schemes, advising on investments) (Sch 6 para 6(1)(d), (1A) (Sch 6 para 6(1)(d) substituted, and Sch 6 para 6(1A) added, by SI 2001/3649; Terrorism Act 2000 Sch 6 para 6(1A) amended by SI 2006/3384; SI 2013/1773));
    (4) the National Savings Bank (Terrorism Act 2000 Sch 6 para 6(1)(e));
    (5) a person who carries out an activity for the purposes of raising money authorised to be raised under the National Loans Act 1968 under the auspices of the Director of National Savings (Terrorism Act 2000 Sch 6 para 6(1)(f));
    (6) a European institution carrying on a home member state regulated activity (within the meaning of Parliament and Council Regulation (EU) 575/2013 (OJ L176, 27.6.2013, p 1) on prudential requirements for credit institutions and investment firms) (Terrorism Act 2000 Sch 6 para 6(1)(g) (substituted by SI 2013/3115));
    (7) a person carrying out an activity specified in any of Parliament and Council Directive (EU) 2013/36 (OJ L176, 27.6.2013, p 338) on access to the activity of credit institutions and the prudential supervision of credit institutions and investment firms, Annex 1 points 1–12, 14, 15 (Terrorism Act 2000 Sch 6 para 6(1)(h) (amended by SI 2000/2952; SI 2011/99; SI 2013/3115));
    (8) an electronic money institution within the meaning of Parliament and Council Directive (EU) 2009/110 (OJ L267, 10.10.2009, p 7) on the taking up, pursuit of and prudential supervision of the business of electronic money institutions (Terrorism Act 2000 Sch 6 para 6(1)(ha) (added by SI 2011/99)); and
    (9) a person who carries on an insurance business in accordance with: (a) until 1 January 2016, an authorisation pursuant to Council Directive (EC) 2002/83 (OJ L345, 19.12.2002, p 1) concerning life insurance, art 4 or art 51; or (b) as from that date, an authorisation pursuant to Parliament and Council Directive (EC) 2009/138 (OJ L335, 17.12.99, p 1) on the taking-up and pursuit of the business of insurance and reinsurance, art 14 or 162 (Terrorism Act 2000 Sch 6 para 6(1)(i) (amended by SI 2004/3379; SI 2015/575)).
    Head (1) of this definition and the definition of 'relevant regulated activity' in the Terrorism Act 2000 Sch 6 para 6(1A) must be read with the Financial Services and Markets Act 2000 s 22 (see FINANCIAL SERVICES AND INSTITUTIONS vol 48 (2008) PARA 84), any relevant order under that provision, and Sch 2 (see FINANCIAL SERVICES AND INSTITUTIONS vol 48 (2008) PARAS 84–85): Terrorism Act 2000 Sch 6 para 6(1B) (added by SI 2001/3649).
    The Secretary of State may by order provide for a class of person to be a financial institution, or to cease to be a financial institution, for the purposes of Sch 6 (Sch 6 para 6(2)): such orders as have been made are recorded above.

An institution which ceases to be a financial institution for the purposes of Sch 6 continues to be treated as a financial institution for the purposes of any requirement under Sch 6 para 1 to provide customer information (see note 5) which relates to a time when the institution was a financial institution: Sch 6 para 6(3).

4 'Customer information' means:

(1) information whether a business relationship exists or existed between a financial institution and a particular person (a 'customer') (Terrorism Act 2000 Sch 6 para 7(1)(a));

(2) a customer's account number (Sch 6 para 7(1)(b));

(3) a customer's full name (Sch 6 para 7(1)(c));

(4) a customer's date of birth (Sch 6 para 7(1)(d));

(5) a customer's address or former address (Sch 6 para 7(1)(e));

(6) the date on which a business relationship between a financial institution and a customer begins or ends (Sch 6 para 7(1)(f));

(7) any evidence of a customer's identity obtained by a financial institution in pursuance of or for the purposes of any legislation relating to money laundering (Sch 6 para 7(1)(g)); and

(8) the identity of a person sharing an account with a customer (Sch 6 para 7(1)(h)).

For the purposes of Sch 6 there is a business relationship between a financial institution and a person if (and only if) there is an arrangement between them designed to facilitate the carrying out of frequent or regular transactions between them, and the total amount of payments to be made in the course of the arrangement is neither known nor capable of being ascertained when the arrangement is made: Sch 6 para 7(2). The Secretary of State may by order provide for a class of information to be customer information for the purposes of Sch 6 or to cease to be customer information for the purposes of Sch 6: Sch 6 para 7(3).

5 Terrorism Act 2000 Sch 6 para 1(1) (Sch 6 para 1(1) amended, Sch 6 para 1(1A) added, by the Anti-terrorism, Crime and Security Act 2001 Sch 2 para 6). The order may provide that it applies to all financial institutions, a particular description (or particular descriptions) of financial institution, or a particular institution or particular institutions: Terrorism Act 2000 Sch 6 para 1(1A) (as so added). Customer information provided by a financial institution under Sch 6 is not admissible in evidence in criminal proceedings against the institution or any of its officers or employees (Sch 6 para 9(1)), except in relation to proceedings for an offence under Sch 6 para 1(3) (see the text and note 7) (including proceedings brought by virtue of Sch 6 para 8 (see note 7)) (Sch 6 para 9(2)).

6 Terrorism Act 2000 Sch 6 para 1(2).

7 Terrorism Act 2000 Sch 6 para 1(3). The offence is punishable on summary conviction with a fine not exceeding level 5 on the standard scale: Sch 6 para 1(5). As to the standard scale, the statutory maximum, the prescribed sum, and magistrates' powers to levy unlimited fines see PARA 176. Where an offence is committed by an institution and it is proved that the offence was committed with the consent or connivance of an officer of the institution or was attributable to neglect on the part of an officer of the institution, the officer, as well as the institution, is guilty of the offence (see Sch 6 para 8(1), (2); and CRIMINAL LAW vol 25 (2010) PARA 37), and is liable on summary conviction to imprisonment for a term not exceeding six months or to a fine not exceeding level 5 on the standard scale or to both (Sch 6 para 8(3)). In the case of an institution which is a body corporate, 'officer' includes a director, manager or secretary, a person purporting to act as a director, manager or secretary, and, if the affairs of the body are managed by its members, a member: Sch 6 para 8(4). In the case of an institution which is a partnership, 'officer' means a partner: Sch 6 para 8(5). In the case of an institution which is an unincorporated association (other than a partnership), 'officer' means a person concerned in the management or control of the association: Sch 6 para 8(6).

Proceedings for this offence require the consent of the Director of Public Prosecutions: s 117(1), (2)(a). Where, however, it appears to the Director of Public Prosecutions that an offence to which s 117 applies has been committed outside the United Kingdom or for a purpose wholly or partly connected with the affairs of a country other than the United Kingdom, his consent for these purposes may be given only with the permission of the Attorney General: s 117(2A) (added by the Terrorism Act 2006 s 37(2); amended by the Counter-Terrorism Act 2008 s 29). As to the effect of these restrictions see CRIMINAL PROCEDURE vol 27 (2015) PARA 51.

8 Note that this is not one of the defences to be proved by the defendant to which the Terrorism Act 2000 s 118 (which states that in relation to certain provisions of the Act where the defendant has the burden of proof that burden is only an evidential one: see CRIMINAL LAW vol 25 (2010) PARA 377) applies: see s 118. It may therefore be inferred that the burden imposed on the defendant of proving the present defence is a legal (or persuasive) one, but that

implication was not drawn in respect of the corresponding issue in the context of s 11 (see CRIMINAL LAW vol 25 (2010) PARA 376): see *Sheldrake v DPP, A-G's Reference (No 4 of 2002)* [2004] UKHL 43, [2005] 1 AC 264, [2005] 1 Cr App Rep 450. See further CRIMINAL PROCEDURE vol 28 (2015) PARA 447 et seq.

9 Terrorism Act 2000 Sch 6 para 1(4).

312. Procedure and criteria for making financial information orders. A financial information order[1] may be made in England and Wales only on the application of a police officer of at least the rank of superintendent[2] and only if the person making it is satisfied that:

(1) the order is sought for the purposes of a terrorist investigation[3];

(2) the tracing of terrorist property[4] is desirable for the purposes of the investigation[5]; and

(3) the order will enhance the effectiveness of the investigation[6].

1 Ie an order under the Terrorism Act 2000 Sch 6 para 1(1): see PARA 311.
2 Terrorism Act 2000 Sch 6 para 2(a). The order is made by a circuit judge or a District Judge (Magistrates' Courts): see Sch 6 para 3 (amended by the Courts Act 2003 Sch 4 para 10). Criminal Procedure Rules may make provision about the procedure for an application for a financial information order: Terrorism Act 2000 Sch 6 para 4(1) (amended by Courts Act 2003 Sch 8 para 390).
3 Terrorism Act 2000 Sch 6 para 5(a). As to the meaning of 'terrorist investigation' see s 32; and POLICE AND INVESTIGATORY POWERS vol 84A (2013) PARA 726.
4 As to the meaning of 'terrorist property' see the Terrorism Act 2000 s 14(1); and CRIMINAL LAW vol 25 (2010) PARA 382.
5 Terrorism Act 2000 Sch 6 para 5(b).
6 Terrorism Act 2000 Sch 6 para 5(c).

313. Account monitoring orders. An account monitoring order is an order that the financial institution[1] specified in the application for the order must:

(1) for the period specified in the order[2];

(2) in the manner so specified[3];

(3) at or by the time or times so specified[4]; and

(4) at the place or places so specified[5],

provide information of the description specified in the application to an appropriate officer[6].

An account monitoring order has effect as if it were an order of the Crown Court[7]. It has effect in spite of any restrictions on disclosure of information (however imposed)[8].

1 As to the meaning of 'financial institution' see PARA 311 note 3 (definition applied by the Terrorism Act 2000 Sch 6A para 1(1), (5) (Sch 6A added by the Anti-terrorism, Crime and Security Act 2001 Sch 2 para 1)).
2 Terrorism Act 2000 Sch 6A para 2(4)(a) (as added: see note 1). The period stated in an account monitoring order must not exceed the period of 90 days beginning with the day on which the order is made: Sch 6A para 2(5) (as so added).
3 Terrorism Act 2000 Sch 6A para 2(4)(b) (as added: see note 1).
4 Terrorism Act 2000 Sch 6A para 2(4)(c) (as added: see note 1).
5 Terrorism Act 2000 Sch 6A para 2(4)(d) (as added: see note 1).
6 Terrorism Act 2000 Sch 6A para 2(4) (as added: see note 1). In England and Wales, an 'appropriate officer' is a constable: Sch 6A para 1(4) (as so added). A statement made by a financial institution in response to an account monitoring order may not be used in evidence against it in criminal proceedings (Sch 6A para 7(1) (as so added)), except:
　(1) in the case of proceedings for contempt of court (Sch 6A para 7(2)(a) (as so added));
　(2) in the case of proceedings under s 23 (see PARA 301) where the financial institution has been convicted of an offence under any of ss 15–18 (see CRIMINAL LAW vol 25 (2010) PARAS 379–382) (Sch 6A para 7(2)(b) (as so added)); or
　(3) on a prosecution for an offence where, in giving evidence, the financial institution makes a statement inconsistent with it (Sch 6A para 7(2)(c) (as so added)).

A statement may not be used by virtue of head (3) above against a financial institution unless evidence relating to it is adduced, or a question relating to it is asked, by or on behalf of the financial institution in the proceedings arising out of the prosecution: Sch 6A para 7(3) (as so added).

7   Terrorism Act 2000 Sch 6A paras 1(3), 6(1) (as added: see note 1).
8   Terrorism Act 2000 Sch 6A para 6(2) (as added: see note 1).

314.   Procedure and criteria for making, discharging and varying account monitoring orders.   A circuit judge or a District Judge (Magistrates' Courts)[1] may make an account monitoring order[2] on an application by an appropriate officer[3] if he is satisfied that:

(1)   the order is sought for the purposes of a terrorist investigation[4];
(2)   the tracing of terrorist property[5] is desirable for the purposes of the investigation[6]; and
(3)   the order will enhance the effectiveness of the investigation[7].

An application for an account monitoring order may be made without notice to a judge in chambers[8]. The application must state that the order is sought against the financial institution[9] specified in the application in relation to information which relates to an account or accounts held at the institution by the person specified in the application (whether solely or jointly with another), and is of the description so specified[10].

The Crown Court has power to discharge or vary an account monitoring order[11]. An application to discharge or vary an account monitoring order may be made to the Crown Court by the person who applied for it (or another police officer) or any person affected by it[12].

1   Terrorism Act 2000 Sch 6A para 1(2) (Sch 6A added by the Anti-terrorism, Crime and Security Act 2001 Sch 2 para 1).
2   As to account monitoring orders see PARA 313.
3   As to the meaning of 'appropriate officer' see PARA 313 note 6.
4   Terrorism Act 2000 Sch 6A para 2(1)(a) (as added: see note 1). As to the meaning of 'terrorist investigation' see s 32; and POLICE AND INVESTIGATORY POWERS vol 84A (2013) PARA 726.
5   As to the meaning of 'terrorist property' see s 14(1); and CRIMINAL LAW vol 25 (2010) PARA 382.
6   Terrorism Act 2000 Sch 6A para 2(1)(b) (as added: see note 1).
7   Terrorism Act 2000 Sch 6A para 2(1)(c) (as added: see note 1).
8   Terrorism Act 2000 Sch 6A para 3(1) (as added: see note 1). The description of information specified in an application for an account monitoring order may be varied by the person who made the application: Sch 6A para 3(2) (as so added). If the application was made by a police officer, the description of information specified in it may be varied by a different police officer: Sch 6A para 3(3) (as so added). Rules of court may make provision as to the practice and procedure to be followed in connection with proceedings relating to account monitoring orders: Sch 6A para 5(1) (as so added).
9   As to the meaning of 'financial institution' see PARA 311 note 3.
10 Terrorism Act 2000 Sch 6A para 2(2) (as added: see note 1). The application may specify information relating to all accounts held by the person specified in the application for the order at the financial institution so specified, a particular description, or particular descriptions of accounts so held, or a particular account, or particular accounts, so held: Sch 6A para 2(3) (as so added).
11 Terrorism Act 2000 Sch 6A para 4(3) (as added: see note 1).
12 Terrorism Act 2000 Sch 6A para 4(1), (2) (as added: see note 1).

5. ROAD TRAFFIC ORDERS

315. Disqualification for road traffic offences. Some road traffic offences, including causing death, vehicle taking, and driving while unfit, carry obligatory disqualification; other, less serious, offences carry disqualification at the discretion of the court[1]. The obligatory minimum disqualification period is six, twelve, 24 or 36 months depending on the offence and, for certain offences, whether the offender is a repeat offender, and the discretionary disqualification period is at the discretion of the court, although the disqualification period actually imposed will also depend on the offender's previous convictions and any mitigating circumstances[2], and may also be influenced by the imposition of a custodial sentence for the offence[3].

The period of disqualification may be reduced if an approved course is attended: at the date at which this volume states the law this option is available only to persons convicted of specified serious offences involving driving under the influence, although as from a day to be appointed it is extended to cover other offences involving careless and inconsiderate driving[4]. The period of disqualification for offences involving driving under the influence may also be reduced if the offender participates in an alcohol ignition interlock programme[5].

A disqualified person may appeal to the Crown Court or the Court of Appeal against disqualification, and the appellate court may suspend disqualification[6]. A disqualified person may also (after a time period determined by the length of his disqualification) apply to the court which disqualified him for disqualification to be removed on grounds relating to his character or conduct, the nature of the offence or other circumstances of the case[7].

1   The offences involving obligatory and discretionary disqualification are listed in the Road Traffic Offenders Act 1988 Sch 2: see ss 34(1), 97; and ROAD TRAFFIC vol 90 (2011) PARAS 815, 817, 818. Disqualification may also be imposed in relation to inchoate offences: see s 34(5); and ROAD TRAFFIC vol 90 (2011) PARAS 815, 817. Where a person is disqualified his licence is treated as having been revoked: see s 37; and ROAD TRAFFIC vol 90 (2011) PARA 830. A disqualified person will also have his licence or driving record endorsed: see PARA 318.
2   See the Road Traffic Offenders Act 1988 ss 34(1)–(4), (4A), 35, 43; and ROAD TRAFFIC vol 90 (2011) PARAS 815, 817, 818, 827, 837.
3   See the Road Traffic Offenders Act 1988 ss 35A, 35B; and ROAD TRAFFIC vol 90 (2011) PARA 828.
4   See the Road Traffic Offenders Act 1988 ss 34A, 34B, 34BA, 34C, 41A; and ROAD TRAFFIC vol 90 (2011) PARAS 819–822, 834.
5   See the Road Traffic Offenders Act 1988 ss 34D–34G, 41B; and ROAD TRAFFIC vol 90 (2011) PARAS 823–826, 835.
6   See the Road Traffic Offenders Act 1988 ss 38, 40; and ROAD TRAFFIC vol 90 (2011) PARAS 831, 833. Disqualification is suspended pending the outcome of any such appeal: see s 39; and ROAD TRAFFIC vol 90 (2011) PARA 832.
7   See the Road Traffic Offenders Act 1988 s 42; and ROAD TRAFFIC vol 90 (2011) PARA 836.

316. Disqualification for non-road traffic offences. Where a person is convicted of an offence[1] the court by or before which he is convicted may order him to be disqualified, for such period as it thinks fit, for holding or obtaining a driving licence[2]. Where the offence is an offence the sentence for which is:

(1)   a sentence fixed by law[3];
(2)   a life sentence for a serious or second listed offence[4];
(3)   the required minimum sentences for threatening with an offensive weapon or an article with a blade or point in public in public[5];
(4)   the required custodial sentence for possession of a firearm or using a person to mind a weapon[6];

(5)   the specified minimum term for a third class A drug trafficking offence[7]; or

(6)   the specified minimum term for a third domestic burglary[8],

disqualification can be ordered only in addition to the court dealing with the offender in another way[9]. For other offences the court may order disqualification either instead of, or in addition to, dealing with the offender in any other way[10].

1   For these purposes the offence need not be connected in any way with the use of a motor vehicle: *R v Cliff* [2004] EWCA Crim 3139, [2005] Crim LR 250, CA.

2   Powers of Criminal Courts (Sentencing) Act 2000 s 146(1). Section 147 (amended by the Crime (International Co-operation) Act 1990 Sch 5 para 74, Sch 6; and by the Road Safety Act 2006 Sch 3 para 73) makes provision in connection with the disqualification of a person where a vehicle is used for purposes of crime, but these provisions (ie the Powers of Criminal Courts (Sentencing) Act 2000 s 146: see the text and notes 3–10) are wider than s 147 and effectively render that provision redundant. A court may not make an order under s 146 unless it has been notified by the Secretary of State that the power to make such orders is exercisable by the court and the notice has not been withdrawn: s 146(3). A court which makes an order under s 146 disqualifying a person for holding or obtaining a driving licence must require him to produce:

     (1)   any such licence held by him (s 146(4)(a) (Powers of Criminal Courts (Sentencing) Act 2000 s 146(4)(a), (aa), (b) amended by the Road Safety Act 2006 Sch 3 para 72; Powers of Criminal Courts (Sentencing) Act 2000 s 146(4)(a) further amended, s 146(4)(aa) added, by the Crime (International Co-operation) Act 2003 Sch 5 paras 72, 73));

     (2)   in the case where he holds a Northern Ireland licence (within the meaning of the Road Traffic Act 1988 Pt III (ss 87–109C): see ROAD TRAFFIC vol 89 (2011) PARA 247 et seq), his Northern Ireland licence and its counterpart (if any) (Powers of Criminal Courts (Sentencing) Act 2000 s 146(4)(aa) (as so added)); or

     (3)   in the case where he holds a Community licence (within the meaning of the Road Traffic Act 1988 Pt III), his Community licence and its counterpart (if any) (Powers of Criminal Courts (Sentencing) Act 2000 s 146(4)(b)).

     For these purposes 'driving licence' means a licence to drive a motor vehicle granted under the Road Traffic Act 1988: Powers of Criminal Courts (Sentencing) Act 2000 s 146(5).

3   Powers of Criminal Courts (Sentencing) Act 2000 s 146(2) (s 146(2) amended, s 146(2A) added, by the Criminal Justice and Courts Act 2015 Sch 5 para 7).

4   Powers of Criminal Courts (Sentencing) Act 2000 s 146(2), (2A)(e) (as amended and added: see note 3). As to the sentences referred to and when those sentences fall to be imposed see the Criminal Justice Act 2003 ss 224A, 225(2), 226(2); and PARAS 34, 35, 37.

5   Powers of Criminal Courts (Sentencing) Act 2000 s 146(2), (2A)(a), (c) (as amended and added: see note 3). As to the sentences referred to see the Prevention of Crime Act 1953 ss 1(2B), 1A(5); the Criminal Justice Act 1988 ss 139(6B), 139A(5B), 139AA(7); and CRIMINAL LAW. As to when such a sentence falls to be imposed see PARA 536 note 2.

6   Powers of Criminal Courts (Sentencing) Act 2000 s 146(2), (2A)(b), (f) (as amended and added: see note 3). As to the sentences referred to see the Firearms Act 1968 s 51A(2); the Violent Crime Reduction Act 2006 s 29(4), (6); and CRIMINAL LAW vol 26 (2010) PARAS 614, 656. As to when such a sentence falls to be imposed see PARA 536 note 2.

7   Powers of Criminal Courts (Sentencing) Act 2000 s 146(2), (2A)(d) (as amended and added: see note 3). As to the sentence referred to see the Powers of Criminal Courts (Sentencing) Act 2000 s 110(2); and CRIMINAL LAW vol 26 (2010) PARA 725. As to when such a sentence falls to be imposed see PARA 536 note 2.

8   Powers of Criminal Courts (Sentencing) Act 2000 s 146(2), (2A)(d) (as amended and added: see note 3). As to the sentence referred to see the Powers of Criminal Courts (Sentencing) Act 2000 s 111(2); and CRIMINAL LAW vol 25 (2010) PARA 290. As to when such a sentence falls to be imposed see PARA 536 note 2.

9   Powers of Criminal Courts (Sentencing) Act 2000 s 146(2), (2A) (as amended and added: see note 3).

10   Powers of Criminal Courts (Sentencing) Act 2000 s 146(2), (2A) (as amended and added: see note 3).

317. Extension of disqualification where custodial sentence also imposed.
Where a person is convicted of an offence for which the court imposes a custodial sentence[1] and orders the person to be disqualified[2] for holding or

obtaining a driving licence[3] the disqualification order[4] must provide for the person to be disqualified for the appropriate extension period[5] in addition to the discretionary disqualification period[6]. These provisions do not apply where the custodial sentence was a suspended sentence[7], where the court has made an order[8] for determining the minimum term in relation to a mandatory life sentence in relation to the custodial sentence[9], or where the court has made an order[10] for determining the minimum term in relation to a discretionary life sentence in relation to the custodial sentence[11].

Where a person is convicted of an offence for which a court proposes[12] to order the person to be disqualified for holding or obtaining a driving licence and the court proposes to impose on the person a custodial sentence (other than a suspended sentence[13]) for another offence[14] or at the time of sentencing for the offence, a custodial sentence imposed on the person on an earlier occasion has not expired[15], then in determining the period for which the person is to be disqualified, the court must have regard, if and to the extent that it is appropriate to do so to, the consideration of the diminished effect of disqualification as a distinct punishment if the person who is disqualified is also detained in pursuance of a custodial sentence[16]. If the court proposes to order the person to be disqualified and to impose a custodial sentence for the same offence, the court may not in relation to that disqualification take that custodial sentence into account for these purposes[17].

1 Powers of Criminal Courts (Sentencing) Act 2000 s 147A(1)(a) (ss 147A, 147B added by the Coroners and Justice Act 2009 Sch 16 para 5).

2 Ie under the Powers of Criminal Courts (Sentencing) Act 2000 s 146 or s 147 (see PARA 316).

3 Powers of Criminal Courts (Sentencing) Act 2000 s 147A(1)(b) (as added: see note 1). 'Driving licence' means a licence to drive a motor vehicle granted under the Road Traffic Act 1988 Pt 3 (ss 87–109C) (see ROAD TRAFFIC vol 89 (2011) PARA 247 et seq): Powers of Criminal Courts (Sentencing) Act 2000 s 147A(10) (as so added).

4 Ie the order under the Powers of Criminal Courts (Sentencing) Act 2000 s 146 or s 147.

5 The 'appropriate extension period is:
   (1) where an order under the Powers of Criminal Courts (Sentencing) Act 2000 s 82A(2) (determination of tariffs: see PARA 39) is made in relation to the custodial sentence, a period equal to the part of the sentence specified in that order (s 147A(4)(a) (as added: see note 1));
   (2) in the case of a detention and training order under s 100 (offenders under 18: detention and training orders: see PARA 9), a period equal to half the term of that order (s 147A(4)(b) (as so added));
   (3) where the Criminal Justice Act 2003 s 226A (extended sentence for certain violent or sexual offences: persons 18 or over: see PARAS 18–20) applies in relation to the custodial sentence, a period equal to two thirds of the term imposed pursuant to s 226A(5)(a) (Powers of Criminal Courts (Sentencing) Act 2000 s 147A(4)(e) (as so added; s 147A(4)(e), (f), (6)(a), (b), (8), (9)(a) amended by the Legal Aid, Sentencing and Punishment of Offenders Act 2012 Sch 21 para 15; Powers of Criminal Courts (Sentencing) Act 2000 s 147A(4)(e), (f), (h) amended, s 147A(4)(fa) added, by the Criminal Justice and Courts Act 2015 s 30(2), Sch 1 para 13));
   (4) where the Criminal Justice Act 2003 s 226B (extended sentence for certain violent or sexual offences: persons under 18: see PARAS 18–20) applies in relation to the custodial sentence, a period equal to two thirds of the term imposed pursuant to s 226B(3)(a) (Powers of Criminal Courts (Sentencing) Act 2000 s 147A(4)(f) (as so added and amended));
   (5) in the case of a sentence under the Criminal Justice Act 2003 s 236A (special custodial sentence for certain offenders of particular concern: see PARA 32), a period equal to half of the term imposed pursuant to s 236A(2)(a) (Powers of Criminal Courts (Sentencing) Act 2000 s 147A(4)(fa) (as so added));
   (6) where an order under the Criminal Justice Act 2003 s 269(2) (determination of minimum term in relation to mandatory life sentence: early release: see CRIMINAL LAW

vol 25 (2010) PARA 97) is made in relation to the custodial sentence, a period equal to the part of the sentence specified in that order (Powers of Criminal Courts (Sentencing) Act 2000 s 147A(4)(g) (as so added)); and

(7)   in any other case, a period equal to half the custodial sentence imposed (s 147A(4)(h) (as so added and amended)).

Where an amending order (ie an order under the Criminal Justice Act 2003 s 267 (alteration by order of relevant proportion of sentence: see PARAS 713, 716) provides that the proportion of a prisoner's sentence referred to in s 243A(3)(a) or s 244(3)(a) (release of prisoners in certain circumstances: see PARAS 712, 713) is to be read as a reference to another proportion (the 'new proportion') the Secretary of State may by order: (a) if the amending order makes provision in respect of s 243A(3)(a) or s 244(3)(a), provide that the proportion specified in the Powers of Criminal Courts (Sentencing) Act 2000 s 147A(4)(h) (see head (6) above) is to be read, in the case of a custodial sentence to which the amending order applies, as a reference to the new proportion: s 147A(8), (9)(a) (as so added and amended).

If a period determined under s 147A(4) includes a fraction of a day, that period is to be rounded up to the nearest number of whole days: s 147A(5) (as so added).

6   Powers of Criminal Courts (Sentencing) Act 2000 s 147A(2) (as added: see note 1). The discretionary disqualification period is the period for which, in the absence of s 147A, the court would have disqualified the person under s 146 or s 147: s 147A(3) (as so added).

7   Powers of Criminal Courts (Sentencing) Act 2000 s 147A(7)(a) (as added: see note 1). For these purposes 'suspended sentence' means a suspended sentence within the meaning given by the Criminal Justice Act 2003 s 189 (see PARA 100): Powers of Criminal Courts (Sentencing) Act 2000 ss 147A(10), 147B(5) (as added: see note 1).

8   Ie under the Criminal Justice Act 2003 s 269(4): see CRIMINAL LAW vol 25 (2010) PARA 97.

9   Powers of Criminal Courts (Sentencing) Act 2000 s 147A(7)(b) (as added: see note 1).

10   Ie under the Powers of Criminal Courts (Sentencing) Act 2000 s 82A(4): see PARA 39.

11   Powers of Criminal Courts (Sentencing) Act 2000 s 147A(7)(c) (as added: see note 1).

12   See note 2.

13   See note 7.

14   Powers of Criminal Courts (Sentencing) Act 2000 s 147B(1)(a) (as added: see note 1).

15   Powers of Criminal Courts (Sentencing) Act 2000 s 147B(1)(b) (as added: see note 1).

16   Powers of Criminal Courts (Sentencing) Act 2000 s 147B(2), (3) (as added: see note 1).

17   Powers of Criminal Courts (Sentencing) Act 2000 s 147B(4) (as added: see note 1).

318.   Endorsement. Most road traffic offences attract obligatory endorsement[1]. This involves the court ordering that there be endorsed on the licence of the convicted person particulars of the conviction and of either the disqualification or, if disqualification has not been ordered, particulars of the offence and the penalty points to be attributed to it[2]. Endorsement may be taken into account in sentencing for a subsequent offence[3].

1   The offences involving obligatory endorsement are listed in the Road Traffic Offenders Act 1988 Sch 2: see s 96; and ROAD TRAFFIC vol 90 (2011) PARA 838 (noting also s 48, which provides for exemptions from endorsement for specified offences involving a vehicle being in a dangerous condition where the person did not know that the vehicle was dangerous: see ROAD TRAFFIC vol 90 (2011) PARA 845). The court may order endorsement even where the offender is discharged: see s 46(1); and ROAD TRAFFIC vol 90 (2011) PARA 843,

2   See the Road Traffic Offenders Act 1988 ss 44, 45A; and ROAD TRAFFIC vol 90 (2011) PARAS 839, 841. As to disqualification see PARAS 315–317. Endorsement must be notified to the Secretary of State or, in Wales, the Welsh Ministers: see s 44A; and ROAD TRAFFIC vol 90 (2011) PARA 840. In connection with administration see also s 47; and ROAD TRAFFIC vol 90 (2011) PARA 844.

3   See the Road Traffic Offenders Act 1988 s 46(2); and ROAD TRAFFIC vol 90 (2011) PARA 843.

6. PREVENTIVE ORDERS

(1) CRIMINAL ORDERS

(i) Criminal Behaviour Orders

319. Purpose of criminal behaviour orders. A 'criminal behaviour order' is an order which, for the purpose of preventing an offender from engaging in behaviour causing or likely to cause harassment, alarm or distress[1] to any person[2]:

(1) prohibits the offender from doing anything described in the order[3]; and

(2) requires the offender to do anything described in the order[4].

A criminal behaviour order may be made only in respect of a person who has been convicted of an offence[5] and only on the application of the prosecution[6]. The court may make the order only if it is satisfied beyond reasonable doubt[7] that the offender has engaged in such behaviour[8] and considers that making the order will help in preventing the offender from engaging in such behaviour[9].

The power to make criminal behaviour orders has effect as from 20 October 2014[10], replacing the powers to make anti-social behaviour orders on conviction, which were abolished as from that date[11].

1 In the context of the former powers to make anti-social behaviour orders (which have been abolished: see PARA 439) it was held that the powers to make the orders were concerned simply with a defendant's conduct and its effect on the victim's mind, and that there was no requirement for proof of intent to cause harassment, alarm or distress: see *Chief Constable of Lancashire v Potter* [2003] EWHC 2272 (Admin), [2003] 42 LS Gaz R 31.

2 Anti-social Behaviour, Crime and Policing Act 2014 s 22(3), (5).

3 Anti-social Behaviour, Crime and Policing Act 2014 s 22(5)(a). As to prohibitions see PARA 322.

4 Anti-social Behaviour, Crime and Policing Act 2014 s 22(5)(b). As to requirements see PARA 322.

5 Anti-social Behaviour, Crime and Policing Act 2014 s 22(1). An order may be made against an offender only if it is made in addition to a sentence imposed in respect of the offence (s 22(6)(a)) or an order discharging the offender conditionally (s 22(6)(b)). The prosecution must find out the views of the local youth offending team before applying for a criminal behaviour order to be made if the offender will be under the age of 18 when the application is made: s 22(8). 'Local youth offending team' means the youth offending team in whose area it appears to the prosecution that the offender lives or, if it appears to the prosecution that the offender lives in more than one such area, whichever one or more of the relevant youth offending teams the prosecution thinks appropriate: s 22(10). As to youth offending teams see CHILDREN AND YOUNG PERSONS vol 10 (2012) PARA 1193. As to the determination of a person's age see the Children and Young Persons Act 1933 s 99; and CHILDREN AND YOUNG PERSONS vol 10 (2012) PARA 1206.

6 Anti-social Behaviour, Crime and Policing Act 2014 s 22(7). For procedural rules in connection with the making of criminal behaviour orders see the Criminal Procedure Rules 2015, SI 2015/1490, Pt 31. The court may adjourn any proceedings on an application for a criminal behaviour order even after sentencing the offender: Anti-social Behaviour, Crime and Policing Act 2014 s 23(3). If the offender does not appear for any adjourned proceedings the court may further adjourn the proceedings (s 23(4)(a)), issue a warrant for the offender's arrest (provided it is satisfied that the offender has had adequate notice of the time and place of the adjourned proceedings) (s 23(4)(b), (5)), or hear the proceedings in the offender's absence (provided it is satisfied that the offender has had adequate notice of the time and place of the adjourned proceedings and has been informed that if the offender does not appear for those proceedings the court may hear the proceedings in his or her absence (s 23(4)(c), (6)). Where the court adjourns proceedings it may make an interim order: see s 26; and PARA 320.

The statutory provisions providing for the giving of special measures directions in the case of vulnerable and intimidated witnesses (ie the Youth Justice and Criminal Evidence Act 1999 Pt 2 Ch 1 (ss 16–33): see CRIMINAL PROCEDURE vol 28 (2015) PARA 501 et seq) apply with modifications to proceedings in a magistrates' court of the Crown Court so far as relating to the issue of whether to make a criminal behaviour order: see the Anti-social Behaviour, Crime and Policing Act 2014 s 31. The Children and Young Persons Act 1933 s 49 (restrictions on reports of proceedings in which children and young persons are concerned: see CHILDREN AND YOUNG PERSONS vol 10 (2012) PARAS 1234–1236) does not apply in relation to proceedings in which a criminal behaviour order is made against an offender who is under the age of 18 (Anti-social Behaviour, Crime and Policing Act 2014 s 23(7), (8)(a)): however the Children and Young Persons Act 1933 s 39 (power to prohibit publication of certain matters: see CHILDREN AND YOUNG PERSONS vol 10 (2012) PARA 1233) does so apply (Anti-social Behaviour, Crime and Policing Act 2014 s 23(8)(b)).

7 For the purpose of deciding whether to make a criminal behaviour order the court may consider evidence led by the prosecution and evidence led by the offender: Anti-social Behaviour, Crime and Policing Act 2014 s 23(1). It does not matter whether the evidence would have been admissible in the proceedings in which the offender was convicted: s 23(2).

8 Anti-social Behaviour, Crime and Policing Act 2014 s 22(2), (3). See the text and note 1. In deciding whether to make a criminal behaviour order a court may take account of conduct occurring up to one year before 20 October 2014 (as to which see note 10): s 33(5), (6).

9 Anti-social Behaviour, Crime and Policing Act 2014 s 22(4).

10 Ie the date on which the Anti-social Behaviour, Crime and Policing Act 2014 Pt 2 (ss 22–33) was brought into force by the Anti-social Behaviour, Crime and Policing Act 2014 (Commencement No 7, Saving and Transitional Provisions) Order 2014, SI 2014/2590, art 3(a).

11 See PARA 439.

320. Interim orders. Where a court adjourns the hearing of an application for a criminal behaviour order[1] it may make a criminal behaviour order that lasts until the final hearing of the application or until further order ('an interim order') if it thinks it just to do so[2].

1 As to criminal behaviour orders see PARA 319.

2 Anti-social Behaviour, Crime and Policing Act 2014 s 26(1), (2). Sections 22(6)–(8), 25(3)–(5) (see PARAS 319, 323) do not apply in relation to the making of an interim order: s 26(3). Subject to that, the court has the same powers whether or not the criminal behaviour order is an interim order: s 26(4).

321. Supervision. A criminal behaviour order that includes a requirement[1] must specify the person[2] who is to be responsible for supervising compliance with the requirement[3]. It is the duty of such a person to make any necessary arrangements in connection with the requirements for which the person has responsibility[4], to promote the offender's compliance with those requirements[5], and, if he considers that the offender has complied with all such requirements[6] or has failed to comply with a requirement[7], to inform the prosecution and the appropriate chief officer of police[8].

An offender subject to a requirement in a criminal behaviour order must[9] keep in touch with the specified person[10] in relation to that requirement, in accordance with any instructions given by that person from time to time[11], and notify the person of any change of address[12].

1 As to criminal behaviour orders see PARA 319; as to requirements see PARA 322.

2 The person may be an individual or an organisation: Anti-social Behaviour, Crime and Policing Act 2014 s 24(1).

3 Anti-social Behaviour, Crime and Policing Act 2014 s 24(1).

4 Anti-social Behaviour, Crime and Policing Act 2014 s 24(4)(a).

5 Anti-social Behaviour, Crime and Policing Act 2014 s 24(4)(b).

6 Anti-social Behaviour, Crime and Policing Act 2014 s 24(4)(c)(i).

7 Anti-social Behaviour, Crime and Policing Act 2014 s 24(4)(c)(ii).

8 Anti-social Behaviour, Crime and Policing Act 2014 s 24(4)(c). In s 24(4)(c) 'the appropriate chief officer of police' means the chief officer of police for the police area in which it appears to the person specified under s 24(1) that the offender lives (s 24(5)(a)) or, if it appears to that person that the offender lives in more than one police area, whichever of the relevant chief

officers of police that person thinks it most appropriate to inform (s 24(5)(b)). As to police forces, police areas and chief officers of police see POLICE AND INVESTIGATORY POWERS vol 84 (2013) PARAS 52 et seq, 123 et seq.

9 These obligations have effect as requirements of the order: Anti-social Behaviour, Crime and Policing Act 2014 s 24(6).

10 Ie the person specified under the Anti-social Behaviour, Crime and Policing Act 2014 s 24(1).

11 Anti-social Behaviour, Crime and Policing Act 2014 s 24(6)(a).

12 Anti-social Behaviour, Crime and Policing Act 2014 s 24(6)(b).

322. Requirements and prohibitions. Before including a requirement in a criminal behaviour order[1] the court must receive evidence about its suitability and enforceability from the supervisor[2]. Before including two or more requirements, the court must consider their compatibility with each other[3].

Prohibitions and requirements in a criminal behaviour order must, so far as practicable, be such as to avoid any interference with the times, if any, at which the offender normally works or attends school or any other educational establishment[4] and any conflict with the requirements of any other court order or injunction to which the offender may be subject[5].

1 As to criminal behaviour orders see PARA 319.

2 Anti-social Behaviour, Crime and Policing Act 2014 s 24(2). The reference to 'the supervisor' is a reference to the individual to be specified under s 24(1) (see PARA 321), if an individual is to be specified (s 24(2)(a)) or an individual representing the organisation to be so specified, if an organisation is to be specified (s 24(2)(b)).

3 Anti-social Behaviour, Crime and Policing Act 2014 s 24(3).

4 Anti-social Behaviour, Crime and Policing Act 2014 s 22(9)(a).

5 Anti-social Behaviour, Crime and Policing Act 2014 s 22(9)(b).

323. Duration. A criminal behaviour order[1] takes effect on the day it is made[2]. The order must specify the period for which it has effect[3], which:

(1)   in the case of an order made before the offender has reached the age of 18, must be a fixed period of not less than one year[4] and not more than three years[5]; and

(2)   in the case of an order made after the offender has reached the age of 18, must be a fixed period of not less than two years[6] or an indefinite period (so that the order has effect until further order)[7].

The order may also specify periods for which particular prohibitions or requirements[8] have effect[9].

1 As to criminal behaviour orders see PARA 319.

2 Anti-social Behaviour, Crime and Policing Act 2014 s 25(1). If on the day a criminal behaviour order is made the offender is subject to another criminal behaviour order, the new order may be made so as to take effect on the day on which the previous order ceases to have effect: s 25(2).

3 Anti-social Behaviour, Crime and Policing Act 2014 s 25(3).

4 Anti-social Behaviour, Crime and Policing Act 2014 s 25(4)(a). As to the determination of a person's age see the Children and Young Persons Act 1933 s 99; and CHILDREN AND YOUNG PERSONS vol 10 (2012) PARA 1206.

5 Anti-social Behaviour, Crime and Policing Act 2014 s 25(4)(b).

6 Anti-social Behaviour, Crime and Policing Act 2014 s 25(5)(a).

7 Anti-social Behaviour, Crime and Policing Act 2014 s 25(5)(b).

8 As to prohibitions and requirements see PARA 322.

9 Anti-social Behaviour, Crime and Policing Act 2014 s 25(6).

324. Variation and discharge. A criminal behaviour order[1] may be varied or discharged by the court which made it[2] on the application of the offender[3] or the prosecution[4]. The power to vary an order includes power to include an additional prohibition or requirement in the order[5] or to extend the period for which a prohibition or requirement has effect[6].

If an application by the offender is dismissed, he may make no further application without the consent of the court which made the order[7] or the agreement of the prosecution[8]; if an application by the prosecution is dismissed, it may make no further application without the consent of the court which made the order[9] or the agreement of the offender[10].

1   As to criminal behaviour orders see PARA 319.
2   In the case of a criminal behaviour order made by a magistrates' court, the references in these provisions to the court which made the order include a reference to any magistrates' court acting in the same local justice area as that court: Anti-social Behaviour, Crime and Policing Act 2014 s 27(6).
3   Anti-social Behaviour, Crime and Policing Act 2014 s 27(1)(a).
4   Anti-social Behaviour, Crime and Policing Act 2014 s 27(1)(b).
5   The Anti-social Behaviour, Crime and Policing Act 2014 s 24 (see PARAS 321, 322) applies to additional requirements included under s 27(4) as it applies to requirements included in a new order: s 27(5).
6   Anti-social Behaviour, Crime and Policing Act 2014 s 27(4).
7   Anti-social Behaviour, Crime and Policing Act 2014 s 27(2)(a).
8   Anti-social Behaviour, Crime and Policing Act 2014 s 27(2)(b).
9   Anti-social Behaviour, Crime and Policing Act 2014 s 27(3)(a).
10   Anti-social Behaviour, Crime and Policing Act 2014 s 27(3)(b).

325. Review of orders where offender is aged under 18. If:
    (1)   a person subject to a criminal behaviour order[1] will be under the age of 18 at the end of a review period[2];
    (2)   the term of the order runs until the end of that period or beyond[3]; and
    (3)   the order is not discharged before the end of that period[4],
a review of the operation of the order must be carried out before the end of that period[5]. The review must be carried out by the chief officer of police of the police force maintained for the police area in which the offender lives or appears to be living[6], and must include consideration of:
    (a)   the extent to which the offender has complied with the order[7];
    (b)   the adequacy of any support available to the offender to help him or her comply with it[8]; and
    (c)   any matters relevant to the question whether an application should be made for the order to be varied or discharged[9].

1   As to criminal behaviour orders see PARA 319.
2   Anti-social Behaviour, Crime and Policing Act 2014 s 28(1)(a). The 'review periods' are:
    (1)   the period of 12 months beginning with the day on which the criminal behaviour order takes effect (s 28(2)(a)(i)) or, if during that period the order is varied under s 27 (see PARA 324), the day on which it is varied (or most recently varied, if the order is varied more than once) (s 28(2)(a)(ii));
    (2)   a period of 12 months beginning with the day after the end of the previous review period (s 28(2)(b)(i)) or, if during that period of 12 months the order is varied under s 27, the day on which it is varied (or most recently varied, if the order is varied more than once) (s 28(2)(b)(ii)).
    As to the determination of a person's age see the Children and Young Persons Act 1933 s 99; and **CHILDREN AND YOUNG PERSONS** vol 10 (2012) PARA 1206.
3   Anti-social Behaviour, Crime and Policing Act 2014 s 28(1)(b).
4   Anti-social Behaviour, Crime and Policing Act 2014 s 28(1)(c).
5   Anti-social Behaviour, Crime and Policing Act 2014 s 28(1). Those carrying out or participating in a review under s 28 must have regard to any relevant guidance issued by the Secretary of State under s 32 when considering how the review should be carried out (s 28(4)(a)), what particular matters the review should deal with (s 28(4)(b)), and what action (if any) it would be appropriate to take as a result of the findings of the review (s 28(4)(c)).
6   Anti-social Behaviour, Crime and Policing Act 2014 s 29(1). As to police forces, police areas and chief officers of police see **POLICE AND INVESTIGATORY POWERS** vol 84 (2013) PARAS 52 et seq, 123 et seq. The chief officer, in carrying out a review under s 28, must act in co-operation with

the council for the local government area in which the offender lives or appears to be living; and the council must co-operate in the carrying out of the review: s 29(2). The chief officer may invite the participation in the review of any other person or body: s 29(3). For these purposes 'local government area' means:

(1) in relation to England, a district or London borough, the City of London, the Isle of Wight and the Isles of Scilly (s 29(4)(a)); and

(2) in relation to Wales, a county or a county borough (s 29(4)(b)).

The Secretary of State may issue guidance to chief officers of police (s 32(1)(a)) and the councils mentioned in s 29(2) (s 32(1)(b)) about the exercise of their functions under Pt 2 (ss 22–33). The Secretary of State may revise any guidance so issued (s 32(2)) and must arrange for any guidance issued or revised under this section to be published (s 32(3)). See *Anti-social Behaviour, Crime and Policing Act 2014: Reform of anti-social behaviour powers: Statutory guidance for frontline professionals* (July 2014), published by the Home Office.

As to local government areas and authorities in England and Wales see LOCAL GOVERNMENT vol 69 (2009) PARA 22 et seq. As to the London boroughs and the City of London see LONDON GOVERNMENT vol 71 (2013) PARAS 15, 16. For these purposes the council for the Inner and Middle Temples is the Common Council of the City of London: s 29(4).

7 Anti-social Behaviour, Crime and Policing Act 2014 s 28(3)(a).

8 Anti-social Behaviour, Crime and Policing Act 2014 s 28(3)(b).

9 Anti-social Behaviour, Crime and Policing Act 2014 s 28(3)(c).

326. Breach. A person commits an offence if without reasonable excuse he does anything he is prohibited from doing by a criminal behaviour order[1] or fails to do anything he is required to do by a criminal behaviour order[2]. A person guilty of this offence is liable on summary conviction, to imprisonment for a period not exceeding 6 months or to a fine, or to both[3], or on conviction on indictment, to imprisonment for a period not exceeding 5 years or to a fine, or to both[4], and may not be conditionally discharged[5].

In proceedings for this offence a copy of the original criminal behaviour order, certified by the proper officer of the court which made it, is admissible as evidence of its having been made and of its contents to the same extent that oral evidence of those things is admissible in those proceedings[6]. Special provision is made in respect of proceedings involving young persons[7].

1 Anti-social Behaviour, Crime and Policing Act 2014 s 30(1)(a). As to criminal behaviour orders see PARA 319.

2 Anti-social Behaviour, Crime and Policing Act 2014 s 30(1)(b).

3 Anti-social Behaviour, Crime and Policing Act 2014 s 30(2)(a). As to the standard scale, the statutory maximum, the prescribed sum, and magistrates' powers to levy unlimited fines see PARA 176.

4 Anti-social Behaviour, Crime and Policing Act 2014 s 30(2)(b). As to fines generally see PARA 174 et seq.

5 If a person is convicted of an offence under these provisions it is not open to the court by or before which the person is convicted to make an order under the Powers of Criminal Courts (Sentencing) Act 2000 s 12(1)(b) (conditional discharge: see PARA 443): s 30(3).

6 Anti-social Behaviour, Crime and Policing Act 2014 s 30(4).

7 In relation to any proceedings for an offence under the Anti-social Behaviour, Crime and Policing Act 2014 s 30 that are brought against a person under the age of 18:

(1) the Children and Young Persons Act 1933 s 49 (restrictions on reports of proceedings in which children and young persons are concerned: see CHILDREN AND YOUNG PERSONS vol 10 (2012) PARAS 1234–1236) does not apply in respect of the person (Anti-social Behaviour, Crime and Policing Act 2014 s 30(5)(a));

(2) the Youth Justice and Criminal Evidence Act 1999 s 45 (power to restrict reporting of criminal proceedings involving persons under 18: see CHILDREN AND YOUNG PERSONS vol 10 (2012) PARAS 1238) does so apply (Anti-social Behaviour, Crime and Policing Act 2014 s 30(5)(b)).

If, in relation to any proceedings mentioned in s 30(5), the court does exercise its power to give a direction under the Youth Justice and Criminal Evidence Act 1999 s 45, it must give its reasons for doing so: Anti-social Behaviour, Crime and Policing Act 2014 s 30(6). As to the determination of a person's age see the Children and Young Persons Act 1933 s 99; and CHILDREN AND YOUNG PERSONS vol 10 (2012) PARA 1206.

(ii) Sexual Harm Prevention Orders

327. Purpose of sexual harm prevention orders. A 'sexual harm prevention order' is an order which, for the purpose of:

(1) protecting the public[1] or any particular members of the public from sexual harm[2] from the defendant[3]; or

(2) protecting children[4] or vulnerable adults[5] generally, or any particular children or vulnerable adults, from sexual harm from the defendant outside the United Kingdom[6],

prohibits the offender from doing anything described in the order[7]. A sexual harm prevention order may be made in respect of a person either where the court is dealing with him in relation to an applicable offence[8] or on the application of the police[9]. The court may make the order only if it is satisfied that it is necessary[10] to make it for the purpose described above[11]. Where a court makes a sexual harm prevention order in relation to a person who is already subject to such an order (whether made by that court or another), the earlier order ceases to have effect[12]. Failure to comply with an order is an offence[13] punishable by imprisonment[14].

The power to make sexual harm prevention orders has effect as from 8 March 2015[15], replacing the powers to make foreign travel orders and sexual offences prevention orders, which were abolished as from that date[16].

1 Ie the public in the United Kingdom: Sexual Offences Act 2003 ss 103B(1), 103C(5) (ss 103A–103K added by the Anti-social Behaviour, Crime and Policing Act 2014 Sch 5 para 2).

2 'Sexual harm' from a person means physical or psychological harm caused by the person committing one or more of the sexual offences listed in the Sexual Offences Act 2003 Sch 3 (see PARA 329) or (in the context of harm outside the United Kingdom) by the person doing, outside the United Kingdom, anything which would constitute such an offence if done in any part of the United Kingdom: Sexual Offences Act 2003 s 103B(1) (as added: see note 1).

For the purposes of ss 103A, 103B, in construing any reference to an offence listed in Sch 3 any condition subject to which an offence is so listed that relates to the way in which the defendant is dealt with in respect of an offence so listed or a relevant finding (as defined by s 132(9): see PARA 329) (s 103B(8), (9)(a) (as so added)), or to the age of any person (s 103B(9)(b) (as so added)), is to be disregarded.

3 Sexual Offences Act 2003 ss 103A(2)(b)(i), (3)(b)(i), 103C(4)(a), 103E(5)(a) (as added: see note 1).

4 'Child' means a person under 18: Sexual Offences Act 2003 s 103B(1) (as added: see note 1).

5 'Vulnerable adult' means a person aged 18 or over whose ability to protect himself or herself from physical or psychological harm is significantly impaired through physical or mental disability or illness, through old age or otherwise: Sexual Offences Act 2003 s 103B(1) (as added: see note 1). For the purposes of ss 103A–103K a person's age is treated as being that which it appears to the court to be after considering any available evidence: s 103K(2) (as so added). As to the determination of a person's age see the Children and Young Persons Act 1933 s 99; and CHILDREN AND YOUNG PERSONS vol 10 (2012) PARA 1206.

6 Sexual Offences Act 2003 ss 103A(2)(b)(ii), (3)(b)(ii), 103C(4)(b), 103E(5)(b) (as added: see note 1). As to the United Kingdom see PARA 4 note 3.

7 Sexual Offences Act 2003 s 103C(1) (as added: see note 1). As to prohibitions see PARA 331.

8 Sexual Offences Act 2003 s 103A(1) (as added: see note 1). An order may be made against a person ('the defendant') where the court deals with him in respect of any of the sexual offences listed in Sch 3 or any of the non-sexual offences listed in Sch 5 (see PARA 330) (s 103A(2)(a)(i) (as so added)), a finding that the defendant is not guilty of such an offence by reason of insanity(s 103A(2)(a)(ii) (as so added)), or a finding that the defendant is under a disability and has done the act charged against the defendant in respect of such an offence (s 103A(2)(a)(iii) (as so added)).

9   Sexual Offences Act 2003 s 103A(1) (as added: see note 1). A chief officer of police or the
     Director General of the National Crime Agency ('the Director General') may by complaint to a
     magistrates' court (or, where the defendant is a child, a youth court) apply for a sexual harm
     prevention order in respect of a person if it appears to the chief officer or the Director General
     that the person is a qualifying offender (see PARA 328) (s 103A(4)(a), (8) (as so added)) and has
     since the appropriate date (ie the date or (as the case may be) the first date on which the
     offender was convicted, found or cautioned as mentioned in s 103A(2) or (3) acted in such a
     way as to give reasonable cause to believe that it is necessary for such an order to be made
     (s 103A(4)(b) (as so added)). Before a sexual harm prevention order can be made against a
     person who is the subject of such an application it must be proved on the application that the
     defendant is a qualifying offender: s 103A(3)(a) (as so added). For the purposes of s 103A, acts,
     behaviour, convictions and findings include those occurring before 1 May 2004 (ie the date on
     which Pt 2 (ss 80–136ZD) was brought into force by the Sexual Offences Act 2003
     (Commencement) Order 2004, SI 2004/874): Sexual Offences Act 2003 s 103B(5) (as so added).
          A chief officer of police may make an application under s 103A(4) only in respect of a person
     who resides in the chief officer's police area (s 103A(3)(a) (as so added)) or who the chief officer
     believes is in that area or is intending to come to it (s 103A(5)(b) (as so added)). An application
     under s 103A(4) may be made to any magistrates' court (or youth court) acting for a local
     justice area that includes any part of a relevant police area (s 103A(6)(a) (as so added)) or any
     place where it is alleged that the person acted in a way mentioned in s 103A(4)(b) (s 103A(6)(b)
     (as so added)). The Director General must as soon as practicable notify the chief officer of police
     for a relevant police area of any application that the Director has made under s 103A(4):
     s 103A(7) (as so added). 'Relevant police area' means: where the applicant is a chief officer of
     police, the officer's police area (s 103A(9)(a) (as so added)) and where the applicant is the
     Director General, the police area where the person in question resides or a police area which the
     Director General believes the person is in or is intending to come to (s 103A(9)(b) (as so added)).
     As to the making of interim orders where a police application has been made see PARA 332. As
     to police forces, police areas and chief officers of police see POLICE AND INVESTIGATORY POWERS
     vol 84 (2013) PARAS 52 et seq, 123 et seq. As to youth courts see CHILDREN AND YOUNG
     PERSONS vol 10 (2012) PARA 1225 et seq. Rules of court may provide for a youth court to give
     permission for an application under s 103A(4) against a person aged 18 or over to be made to
     the youth court if an application to the youth court has been made, or is to be made, under
     s 103A against a person aged under 18 (s 103K(1)(a)(i) (as so added)) and the youth court
     thinks that it would be in the interests of justice for the applications to be heard together
     (s 103K(1)(a)(ii) (as so added)), and may, in relation to a person attaining the age of 18 after
     proceedings against that person by virtue of s 103A, s 103E, s 103F or s 103G(6) or (7) have
     begun, prescribe circumstances in which the proceedings may or must remain in the youth court
     (s 103K(2)(a)(i) (as so added)) and make provision for the transfer of the proceedings from the
     youth court to a magistrates' court that is not a youth court (including provision applying
     s 103F (see PARA 332) with modifications) (s 103K(1)(b)(ii) (as so added)).
          The Secretary of State must issue guidance to chief officers of police and to the Director
     General of the National Crime Agency in relation to the exercise by them of their powers with
     regard to sexual harm prevention orders and interim sexual harm prevention orders (s 103J(1)
     (as so added)), may from time to time, revise the guidance so issued (s 103J(2) (as so added)),
     and must arrange for any guidance so issued or revised to be published in such manner as he
     considers appropriate (s 103J(3) (as so added)). At the date at which this volume states the law
     no such guidance had been issued.
10   Where the order is sought on police application under the Sexual Offences Act 2003 s 103A(3)
     the court must be satisfied that the defendant's behaviour since the appropriate date (see note 9)
     makes it necessary to make the order for the purpose specified in the text: Sexual Offences
     Act 2003 s 103A(3)(b) (as added: see note 1).
11   Sexual Offences Act 2003 s 103A(2)(b), (3)(b) (as added: see note 1). For procedural rules in
     connection with the making of sexual harm prevention orders see the Criminal Procedure
     Rules 2015, SI 2015/1490, Pt 31. As to appeals against an order see PARA 334. In connection
     with the variation, renewal and discharge of an order see PARA 335.
12   Sexual Offences Act 2003 s 103C(6) (as added: see note 1).
13   A person commits an offence if, without reasonable excuse, he does anything that he is
     prohibited from doing by a sexual harm prevention order: Sexual Offences Act 2003
     s 103I(1)(a) (as added: see note 1).
14   A person guilty of an offence under the Sexual Offences Act 2003 s 103I is liable on summary
     conviction, to imprisonment for a term not exceeding 6 months or a fine or both (s 103I(3)(a)
     (as added: see note 1)) and on conviction on indictment, to imprisonment for a term not
     exceeding 5 years (s 103I(3)(b) (as so added)). Where a person is convicted of an offence under

s 103I it is not open to the court by or before which the person is convicted to make, in respect of the offence, an order for conditional discharge: s 103I(4) (as so added)).

15   Ie the date on which the Anti-social Behaviour, Crime and Policing Act 2014 ss 103A–103K were brought into force by the Anti-social Behaviour, Crime and Policing Act 2014 (Commencement No 8, Saving and Transitional Provisions) Order 2015, SI 2015/373, art 2(a), (e).

16   See PARAS 441, 442.

328.   Qualifying offenders.   For the purposes of the power to make sexual harm prevention orders[1] a person is a 'qualifying offender' if he[2]:

> (1)   has been convicted of an applicable offence[3];
>
> (2)   has been found not guilty of such an offence by reason of insanity[4];
>
> (3)   has been found to be under a disability and to have done the act charged against him in respect of such an offence[5]; or
>
> (4)   has been cautioned in respect of such an offence[6].

A person is also a 'qualifying offender' if[7], under the law in force in a country outside the United Kingdom[8]:

> (a)   he has been convicted of a relevant offence[9] (whether or not he has been punished for it)[10];
>
> (b)   a court exercising jurisdiction under that law has made in respect of a relevant offence a finding equivalent to a finding that he is not guilty by reason of insanity[11];
>
> (c)   such a court has made in respect of a relevant offence a finding equivalent to a finding that he is under a disability and did the act charged against the person in respect of the offence[12]; or
>
> (d)   he has been cautioned in respect of a relevant offence[13].

1   See PARA 327.
2   Ie whether before or after 1 May 2004 (the date on which the Sexual Offences Act 2003 Pt 2 (ss 80–136ZD) was brought into force by the Sexual Offences Act 2003 (Commencement) Order 2004, SI 2004/874): Sexual Offences Act 2003 ss 103B(2), (3) (ss 103A–103K added by the Anti-social Behaviour, Crime and Policing Act 2014 Sch 5 para 2).
3   Sexual Offences Act 2003 s 103B(2)(a) (as added: see note 2). An 'applicable offence' is any of the sexual offences listed in Sch 3 (see PARA 329) (other than Sch 3 para 60) or a non-sexual offence listed in Sch 5 (see PARA 330). In connection with the offences listed in Sch 3 see s 103B(8), (9); and PARA 327 note 2.
4   Sexual Offences Act 2003 s 103B(2)(b) (as added: see note 2).
5   Sexual Offences Act 2003 s 103B(2)(c) (as added: see note 2).
6   Sexual Offences Act 2003 s 103B(2)(d) (as added: see note 2).
7   See note 2.
8   As to the meaning of 'United Kingdom' see PARA 4 note 3.
9   In the Sexual Offences Act 2003 s 103B(3) 'relevant offence' means an act which constituted an offence under the law in force in the country concerned (s 103B(4)(a) (as added: see note 2)) and would have constituted an offence listed in Sch 3 (other than at Sch 3 para 60) or in Sch 5 if it had been done in any part of the United Kingdom (s 103B(4)(b) (as so added). For this purpose an act punishable under the law in force in a country outside the United Kingdom constitutes an offence under that law, however it is described in that law: s 103B(4) (as so added). On an application under s 103A(4) the condition in s 103B(4)(b) (where relevant) is to be taken as met unless, not later than rules of court may provide, the defendant serves on the applicant a notice stating that, on the facts as alleged with respect to the act concerned, the condition is not in the defendant's opinion met (s 103B(6)(a) (as so added), showing the grounds for that opinion (s 103B(6)(b) (as so added), and requiring the applicant to prove that the condition is met (s 103B(6)(c) (as so added). This is subject to s 103B(7) (as so added), which provides that the court, if it thinks fit, may permit the defendant to require the applicant to prove that the condition is met without service of a notice under s 103B(6).
10 Sexual Offences Act 2003 s 103B(3)(a) (as added: see note 2).
11 Sexual Offences Act 2003 s 103B(3)(b) (as added: see note 2).
12 Sexual Offences Act 2003 s 103B(3)(c) (as added: see note 2).
13 Sexual Offences Act 2003 s 103B(3)(d) (as added: see note 2).

329.   Relevant sexual offences.   The sexual offences in respect of which a sexual harm prevention order may be made[1], and in respect of which the notification requirements may arise[2], are:

(1)   rape[3];

(2)   assault by penetration[4];

(3)   sexual assault[5];

(4)   causing a person to engage in sexual activity without consent[6];

(5)   rape of a child aged under 13[7];

(6)   assault of a child aged under 13 by penetration[8];

(7)   sexual assault of a child aged under 13[9];

(8)   causing or inciting a child under 13 to engage in sexual activity[10];

(9)   sexual activity with a child[11];

(10)   causing or inciting a child to engage in sexual activity[12];

(11)   engaging in sexual activity in the presence of a child[13];

(12)   causing a child to watch a sexual act[14];

(13)   child sex offences committed by children or young persons[15];

(14)   arranging or facilitating the commission of a child sex offence[16];

(15)   meeting a child following sexual grooming[17];

(16)   sexual communication with a child[18];

(17)   any of the offences involving abuse of a position of trust[19];

(18)   any familial child sex offence[20];

(19)   any sexual offences against mentally disordered persons (including offences by care workers)[21];

(20)   paying for the sexual services of a child[22];

(21)   causing or inciting child prostitution or pornography[23];

(22)   controlling a child prostitute or a child involved in pornography[24];

(23)   arranging or facilitating child prostitution or pornography[25];

(24)   administering a substance, committing an offence or trespassing with intent to commit a sexual offence[26];

(25)   sex with an adult relative[27];

(26)   exposure[28];

(27)   voyeurism[29];

(28)   intercourse with an animal[30];

(29)   sexual penetration of a corpse[31];

(30)   possession of extreme pornographic images[32];

(31)   the offences relating to the taking, possession etc of indecent photographs of children[33];

(32)   possession of a paedophile manual[34]; and

(33)   certain customs offences relating to the prohibited importation of indecent or obscene articles[35].

A sexual harm prevention order may also be made, and the notification requirements may also arise, in respect of a number of statutory offences which no longer have effect[36].

A reference in this list to an offence includes a reference to any attempt, conspiracy or incitement of another to commit[37], and to aiding, abetting, counselling or procuring the commission of[38], any of the offences in respect of which a sexual harm prevention order may be made or the notification requirements arise, and also includes a reference to an offence under the statutory provisions relating to the encouragement or assistance of crime[39] in relation to which the listed offence is the offence (or one of the offences) which the person intended or believed would be committed[40]. Provision is also made in respect of corresponding service offences[41] and Scottish[42] and Northern Ireland[43] offences.

If the court[44] by or before which a person is convicted of a listed offence[45] or is the subject of a finding of not guilty by reason of insanity[46] or of being under a disability and to have done the act charged against him in respect of an offence[47] states in open court[48] that on that date he has been convicted, found not guilty by reason of insanity or found to be under a disability and to have done the act charged against him[49], and that the offence in question is a listed offence[50], and certifies those facts, whether at the time or subsequently[51], the certificate is evidence of those facts[52] for these purposes[53]. Where a person is cautioned in respect of a listed offence, and the constable informs the person that he has been cautioned on that date and that the offence in question is a listed offence[54] and certifies those facts, whether at the time or subsequently, in such form as the Secretary of State by order prescribes[55], the certificate is evidence of those facts for these purposes[56].

1   Ie the offences referred to in the Sexual Offences Act 2003 s 103A(2)(a), 103B(1) (see PARA 327) and listed in Sch 3 (see the text and notes 2–43). Where an offence is listed in Sch 3 subject to a condition relating to the way in which the defendant is dealt with in respect of the offence or (where a relevant finding has been made in respect of him) in respect of the finding (a 'sentencing condition') (s 132(1)), a person is to be regarded as convicted of such an offence (s 132(3)(a)) or (as the case may be) a relevant finding in relation to such an offence is regarded as made (s 132(3)(b)) at the time when the sentencing condition is met (s 132(3)). A 'relevant finding' is a finding that a person is not guilty of the offence by reason of insanity (see s 132(9)(a); and CRIMINAL LAW vol 25 (2010) PARA 30) or a finding that a person is under a disability and did the act charged against him in respect of the offence (s 132(9)(b)). A reference to a person being or having been found to be under a disability and to have done the act charged against him in respect of an offence includes a reference to his being or having been found unfit to be tried and to have done the act charged against him in respect of the offence (see the Criminal Procedure (Insanity) Act 1964 s 4, s 4A; and CRIMINAL PROCEDURE vol 27 (2015) PARA 357) (Sexual Offences Act 2003 s 135(3)(c)), unfit to be tried for the offence (s 135(3)(a)), or to be insane so that his trial for the offence cannot or could not proceed (s 135(3)(b)). Where an offence is listed if either a sentencing condition or a condition of another description is met, this requirement applies only to the offence as listed subject to the sentencing condition: s 132(2). Where the offence in question is a foreign offence (ie an act which constituted an offence under the law in force in a country outside the United Kingdom (the 'relevant foreign law') (s 132(4)(a)) and would have constituted an offence subject to a sentencing condition (but not any other offence listed in Sch 3) if it had been done in any part of the United Kingdom (s 132(4)(b)), a person is regarded as convicted under the relevant foreign law of a foreign offence at the time when he is, in respect of the offence, dealt with under that law in a way equivalent to that mentioned in Sch 3 as it applies to the corresponding United Kingdom offence (s 132(6)). In relation to a foreign offence, references to the corresponding United Kingdom offence are references to the offence (or any offence) to which s 132(4)(b) applies in the case of that foreign offence: s 132(5). Where in the case of any person a court exercising jurisdiction under the relevant foreign law makes in respect of a foreign offence a finding equivalent to a relevant finding, the court's finding is for these purposes to be regarded as made at the time when the person is, in respect of the finding, dealt with under that law in a way equivalent to that mentioned in Sch 3 as it applies to the corresponding United Kingdom offence: s 132(7). 'Country' includes territory: s 133(1). As to the meaning of 'United Kingdom' see PARA 4 note 3. The Magistrates' Courts Act 1980 s 127 (time limits: see MAGISTRATES vol 71 (2013) PARA 526) does not apply to a complaint under any provision of the Sexual Offences Act 2003 (ss 80–136): s 132A (added by the Policing and Crime Act 2009 s 22(1), (2)).

2   As to the circumstances in which the notification requirements arise in respect of an offender see PARAS 499–500. For the matters required to be notified and the means of notification see PARA 503 et seq.

3   Ie an offence under the Sexual Offences Act 2003 s 1 (see CRIMINAL LAW vol 25 (2010) PARA 178) (Sch 3 para 17) or under the Sexual Offences Act 1956 s 1 (repealed) (Sexual Offences Act 2003 Sch 3 para 1).

4   Ie an offence under the Sexual Offences Act 2003 s 2 (see CRIMINAL LAW vol 25 (2010) PARA 180): Sch 3 para 17.

5   Ie under the Sexual Offences Act 2003 s 3 (see CRIMINAL LAW vol 25 (2010) PARA 182): Sch 3 para 18. A sexual harm prevention order may be made, and the notification requirements may arise, in respect of this offence and the offences under ss 62, 63, 66, 67 (see the text and notes 26, 28, 29) if:

    (1)   where the offender was under 18, he is or has been sentenced, in respect of the offence, to imprisonment for a term of at least 12 months (Sch 3 paras 18(a), 31(a), 33(a), 34(a)); or

    (2)   in any other case, the victim was under 18 (Sch 3 paras 18(b)(i), 33(b)(i), 34(b)(i)) (or, in the case of an offence under s 62 or s 63, the intended offence was an offence against a person aged under 18 (Sch 3 para 31(b)(i))) or the offender, in respect of the offence or finding, is or has been sentenced to a term of imprisonment (Sch 3 paras 18(b)(ii)(a), 31(b)(ii)(a), 33(b)(ii)(a), 34(b)(ii)(a)), detained in a hospital (Sch 3 paras 18(b)(ii)(b), 31(b)(ii)(b), 33(b)(ii)(b), 34(b)(ii)(b)), or made the subject of a community sentence of at least 12 months (Sch 3 paras 18(b)(ii)(c), 31(b)(ii)(c), 33(b)(ii)(c), 34(b)(ii)(c)).

For this purpose 'imprisonment' is to be construed in accordance with the provisions applying the notification requirements to young offenders serving periods of detention: see s 131; and PARA 502. In general, a reference to a person's age is a reference to his age at the time of the offence: Sch 3 para 95(b). See the Children and Young Persons Act 1933 s 99(2) (which provides that where a charge or indictment alleges that a person in respect of whom an offence has been committed is under a specified age, there is a rebuttable presumption that the person is under that age); and CHILDREN AND YOUNG PERSONS vol 10 (2012) PARA 1206. As to the meaning of 'detained in a hospital' see PARA 500 note 6. As to the meaning of 'community sentence' see the Powers of Criminal Courts (Sentencing) Act 2000 s 33(2); and PARA 42 (definition applied by the Sexual Offences Act 2003 Sch 3 para 96(a)). The former offences involving indecent assaults on men and women are also offences in respect of which a sexual harm prevention order may be made and the notification requirements may arise: see note 36.

6   Ie an offence under the Sexual Offences Act 2003 s 4 (see CRIMINAL LAW vol 25 (2010) PARA 184): Sch 3 para 19.

7   Ie an offence under the Sexual Offences Act 2003 s 5 (see CRIMINAL LAW vol 25 (2010) PARA 179): Sch 3 para 19. The former offences involving intercourse with girls under 16 are also offences in respect of which a sexual harm prevention order may be made and the notification requirements may arise: see note 36. As to the determination of a person's age see the Children and Young Persons Act 1933 s 99; and CHILDREN AND YOUNG PERSONS vol 10 (2012) PARA 1206.

8   Ie an offence under the Sexual Offences Act 2003 s 6 (see CRIMINAL LAW vol 25 (2010) PARA 181): Sch 3 para 19. See note 7.

9   Ie an offence under the Sexual Offences Act 2003 s 7 (see CRIMINAL LAW vol 25 (2010) PARA 183): Sch 3 para 20. This offence and the offences under ss 14, 25, 26, 47–50 (see the text and notes 16, 17, 21–24) are applicable only if the offender either was 18 or over (Sch 3 paras 20(a), 23(a), 26(a), 29(a), 29A(a), 29B(a), 29C(a) (Sch 3 paras 29A–29C added by SI 2007/296)) or is or has been sentenced, in respect of the offence, to imprisonment for a term of at least 12 months (Sexual Offences Act 2003 Sch 3 para 20(b), 23(b), 26(b), 29(b), 29A(b), 29B(b), 29C(b) (as so added)). The former offences involving indecent conduct towards a young child are also offences in respect of which a sexual harm prevention order may be made and the notification requirements may arise: see note 36.

The Sexual Offences Act 2003 (Amendment of Schedules 3 and 5) Order 2007, SI 2007/296, was made under the Sexual Offences Act 2003 s 130, pursuant to which the Secretary of State may by order amend Sch 3 (see the text and notes 1–9, 11–43) and Sch 5 (see PARA 330): s 130(1). Any such amendment which either adds an offence (s 130(4)(a)), removes a threshold relating to an offence (s 130(4)(b)) or changes a threshold in such a way as to cause an offence committed by or against a person of a particular age or in certain circumstances, or resulting in a particular disposal, to be within Sch 3 or Sch 5 when it would not otherwise be (s 130(4)(c)) does not apply to convictions, findings and cautions before the amendment takes effect (s 130(2)).

10   Ie an offence under the Sexual Offences Act 2003 s 8 (see CRIMINAL LAW vol 25 (2010) PARA 185): Sch 3 para 21.

11   Ie an offence under the Sexual Offences Act 2003 s 9 (see CRIMINAL LAW vol 25 (2010) PARA 186): Sch 3 para 21.

12   Ie an offence under the Sexual Offences Act 2003 s 10 (see CRIMINAL LAW vol 25 (2010) PARA 187): Sch 3 para 21.

13 Ie an offence under the Sexual Offences Act 2003 s 11 (see CRIMINAL LAW vol 25 (2010) PARA 188): Sch 3 para 21.

14 Ie an offence under the Sexual Offences Act 2003 s 12 (see CRIMINAL LAW vol 25 (2010) PARA 189): Sch 3 para 21.

15 Ie an offence under the Sexual Offences Act 2003 s 13 (see CRIMINAL LAW vol 25 (2010) PARA 190): Sch 3 para 22. This offence is applicable only if the offender is or has been sentenced, in respect of the offence, to imprisonment for a term of at least 12 months: Sch 3 para 22.

16 Ie an offence under the Sexual Offences Act 2003 s 14 (see CRIMINAL LAW vol 25 (2010) PARA 191): Sch 3 para 23. As to the circumstances under which this offence is applicable see note 9. The former offences involving causing or encouraging the prostitution of, intercourse with, or indecent assault on, a girl under 16 are also offences in respect of which a sexual harm prevention order may be made and the notification requirements may arise: see note 36.

17 Ie an offence under the Sexual Offences Act 2003 s 15 (see CRIMINAL LAW vol 25 (2010) PARA 192): Sch 3 para 24.

18 Ie an offence under the Sexual Offences Act 2003 s 15A (see CRIMINAL LAW): Sch 3 para 24A (Sch 3 paras 24A, 35C added by the Serious Crime Act 2007 Sch 4 para 66).

19 Ie an offence under the Sexual Offences Act 2003 ss 16–19 (see CRIMINAL LAW vol 25 (2010) PARAS 193–196): Sch 3 para 25. The notification requirements arise in respect of these offences if the offender, in respect of the offence, is or has been sentenced to a term of imprisonment (Sch 3 para 25(a)), detained in a hospital (Sch 3 para 25(b)), or made the subject of a community sentence of at least 12 months (Sch 3 para 25(c)).

20 Ie an offence under the Sexual Offences Act 2003 ss 25, 26 (see CRIMINAL LAW vol 25 (2010) PARAS 204, 206): Sch 3 para 26. As to the circumstances under which this offence is applicable see note 9. The former offences involving incest by a man and inciting a girl under 16 to have incestuous sexual intercourse are also offences in respect of which a sexual harm prevention order may be made and the notification requirements may arise: see note 36.

21 Ie an offence under the Sexual Offences Act 2003 ss 30–41 (see CRIMINAL LAW vol 25 (2010) PARAS 209–227): Sch 3 paras 27, 28. The offences under ss 38–41 (ie the offences which may be committed by care workers) are applicable for these purposes if: (1) where the offender was under 18, he is or has been sentenced, in respect of the offence, to imprisonment for a term of at least 12 months (Sch 3 para 28(a)); or (2) in any other case, either the victim was under 18 (or the offender, in respect of the offence or finding, is or has been sentenced to a term of imprisonment (Sch 3 para 28(b)(i)), detained in a hospital (Sch 3 para 28(b)(ii)), or made the subject of a community sentence of at least 12 months (Sch 3 para 28(b)(iii)).

22 Ie an offence under the Sexual Offences Act 2003 s 47 (see CRIMINAL LAW vol 25 (2010) PARA 228): Sch 3 para 29. As to the circumstances under which this offence is applicable see note 9.

23 Ie an offence under the Sexual Offences Act 2003 s 48 (see CRIMINAL LAW vol 25 (2010) PARA 229): Sch 3 para 29A (as added: see note 9).

24 Ie an offence under the Sexual Offences Act 2003 s 49 (see CRIMINAL LAW vol 25 (2010) PARA 229): Sch 3 para 29B (as added: see note 9).

25 Ie an offence under the Sexual Offences Act 2003 s 50 (see CRIMINAL LAW vol 25 (2010) PARA 229): Sch 3 para 29C (as added: see note 9).

26 Ie an offence under the Sexual Offences Act 2003 ss 61–63 (see CRIMINAL LAW vol 25 (2010) PARAS 257–259): Sch 3 paras 30, 31. As to the circumstances in which a sexual harm prevention order may be made, and the notification requirements may arise, in respect of offences under ss 62, 63 (ie the offences of committing an offence or trespassing with intent to commit a sexual offence) see note 5.

27 Ie an offence under the Sexual Offences Act 2003 ss 64, 65 (see CRIMINAL LAW vol 25 (2010) PARAS 201–203): Sch 3 para 32. A sexual harm prevention order may be made, and the notification requirements may arise, in respect of these offences and the offence under ss 69, 70 (see the text and notes 30, 31) if: (1) where the offender was under 18, he is or has been sentenced, in respect of the offence, to imprisonment for a term of at least 12 months (Sch 3 paras 32(a), 35(a)); or (2) in any other case, in respect of the offence or finding, the offender is or has been sentenced to a term of imprisonment (Sch 3 paras 32(b)(i), 35(b)(i)) or detained in a hospital (Sch 3 paras 32(b)(ii), 35(b)(ii)).

28 Ie an offence under the Sexual Offences Act 2003 s 66 (see CRIMINAL LAW vol 25 (2010) PARA 265): Sch 3 para 33. As to the circumstances in which a sexual harm prevention order may be made, and the notification requirements may arise, in respect of this offence see note 5.

29 Ie an offence under the Sexual Offences Act 2003 s 67 (see CRIMINAL LAW vol 25 (2010) PARA 266): Sch 3 para 34. As to the circumstances in which a sexual harm prevention order may be made, and the notification requirements may arise, in respect of this offence see note 5.

30 Ie an offence under the Sexual Offences Act 2003 s 69 (see CRIMINAL LAW vol 25 (2010) PARA 267): Sch 3 para 35. As to the circumstances in which a sexual harm prevention order may be made, and the notification requirements may arise, in respect of this offence see note 27.

31 Ie an offence under the Sexual Offences Act 2003 s 70 (see CRIMINAL LAW vol 25 (2010) PARA 268): Sch 3 para 35. As to the circumstances in which a sexual harm prevention order may be made, and the notification requirements may arise, in respect of this offence see note 27.

32 Ie an offence under the Criminal Justice and Immigration Act 2008 s 63 (see CRIMINAL LAW vol 26 (2010) PARA 716): Sexual Offences Act 2003 Sch 3 para 35A (added by the Criminal Justice and Immigration Act 2008 Sch 26 paras 53, 58). A sexual harm prevention order may be made, and the notification requirements may arise, in respect of this offence if the offender was 18 or over and is sentenced in respect of the offence to imprisonment for a term of at least two years: Sexual Offences Act 2003 Sch 3 para 35A (as so added).

33 Ie an offence under the Protection of Children Act 1978 s 1 (see CRIMINAL LAW vol 25 (2010) PARA 260), the Criminal Justice Act 1988 s 160 (see CRIMINAL LAW vol 25 (2010) PARA 261) or the Coroners and Justice Act 2009 s 62(1) (see CRIMINAL LAW vol 25 (2010) PARA 262): Sexual Offences Act 2003 Sch 3 paras 13, 15, 35B (Sch 3 para 35B added by the Coroners and Justice Act 2009 Sch 21 para 62(1), (2)). A sexual harm prevention order may be made, and the notification requirements may arise, in respect of the offences under the Protection of Children Act 1978 s 1, the Criminal Justice Act 1988 s 160 and the offence under the Customs and Excise Management Act 1979 s 170 (see the text and note 35) if (in the case of the offences specifically relating to photography and pseudo-photography) the indecent photographs or pseudo-photographs showed persons under 16 (Sexual Offences Act 2003 Sch 3 paras 13, 15) and either the conviction, finding or caution was before 1 May 2004 (ie the date on which Pt 2 (ss 80–136) was brought into force by the Sexual Offences Act 2003 (Commencement) Order 2004, SI 2004/874) (Sexual Offences Act 2003 Sch 3 paras 13(a), 14(a), 15(a)) or the offender was aged 18 or over (Sch 3 paras 13(b)(i), 14(b)(i), 15(b)(i)) or is sentenced in respect of the offence to imprisonment for a term of at least 12 months (Sch 3 paras 13(b)(ii), 14(b)(ii), 15(b)(i)), and a sexual harm prevention order may be made, and the notification requirements may arise, in respect of the offence under the Coroners and Justice Act 2009 s 62(1) if the offender was 18 or over and is sentenced in respect of the offence to imprisonment for a term of at least two years (Sexual Offences Act 2003 Sch 3 para 35B (as so added)). In the case of an indecent photograph, a reference to a person's age is a reference to his age when the photograph was taken (Sch 3 para 95(a)); and, for the purposes of Sch 3 para 14, a person is to be taken to have been under 16 at any time if it appears from the evidence as a whole that he was under that age at that time (Sch 3 para 97(a)). As to the meanings of 'photograph', 'indecent photograph' and 'pseudo-photograph' see the Protection of Children Act 1978 s 7; and CRIMINAL LAW vol 25 (2010) PARA 260 (definitions applied for these purposes by the Sexual Offences Act 2003 Sch 3 para 97(b)).

34 Ie an offence under the Serious Crime Act 2015 s 69 (see CRIMINAL LAW): Sexual Offences Act 2003 Sch 3 para 35C (as added: see note 18). A sexual harm prevention order may be made, and the notification requirements may arise, in respect of this offence if the offender was 18 or over and is sentenced in respect of the offence to imprisonment for a term of at least 12 months: Sch 3 para 35C (as so added).

35 Ie an offence under the Customs and Excise Management Act 1979 s 170 (penalty for fraudulent evasion of duty etc: see CUSTOMS AND EXCISE vol 31 (2012) PARA 1175) in relation to goods prohibited from importation under the Customs Consolidation Act 1876 s 42 (repealed) (indecent or obscene articles), if the prohibited goods included indecent photographs of persons under 16: Sexual Offences Act 2003 Sch 3 para 14(a). As to the circumstances in which a sexual harm prevention order may be made, and the notification requirements may arise, in respect of this offence see note 33.

36 Ie, in addition to the offence of rape under the Sexual Offences Act 1956 s 1 (repealed) (see the text and note 3), the offences of intercourse with a girl aged under 13 (see s 5 (repealed)) or, where the offender is aged 20 or over, under 16 (see s 6 (repealed)), incest by a man (if the victim or (as the case may be) other party was under 18) (see s 10 (repealed)), buggery or indecency between men (if the offender was aged 20 or over and the victim or (as the case may be) other party was under 18) (see ss 12, 13 (both repealed)), indecent assault on a woman or man (if the victim or (as the case may be) other party was under 18, or if the offender, in respect of the offence or finding, is or has been either sentenced to imprisonment for a term of at least 30 months or admitted to hospital subject to a restriction order) (see ss 14, 15 (both repealed)), assault with intent to commit buggery (if the victim or (as the case may be) other party was under 18) (see s 16 (repealed)), causing or encouraging the prostitution of, intercourse with, or indecent assault on, a girl under 16 (see s 28 (repealed)), indecent conduct towards a young child (see the Indecency with Children Act 1960 s 1 (repealed)), and inciting a girl under 16 to

have incestuous sexual intercourse (see the Criminal Law Act 1977 s 54 (repealed)): see the Sexual Offences Act 2003 Sch 3 paras 1–12. Note that men who are subject to the notification requirements as a result of a conviction, finding or caution for buggery or gross indecency contrary to the Sexual Offences Act 1956 ss 12, 13 (repealed) can apply for exemption from those requirements on the basis of the abolition of criminal liability for consensual homosexual acts with 16- or 17-year olds: see the Sexual Offences Act 2003 Sch 4; and PARA 500 note 6.

37 Sexual Offences Act 2003 Sch 3 para 94(a). This does not, however, include an attempt to incite the commission of an offence: see *R v Parnell* [2004] EWCA Crim 2523, [2005] 1 WLR 853 (case concerned with identical terminology in the Sex Offenders Act 1997 Sch 1 para 5(1) (repealed)).

38 Sexual Offences Act 2003 Sch 3 para 94(b).

39 Ie the Serious Crime Act 2007 Pt 2 (ss 44–67) (see CRIMINAL LAW vol 25 (2010) PARAS 65–72).

40 Sexual Offences Act 2003 Sch 3 para 94A (added by the Serious Crime Act 2007 Sch 6 para 63(1), (2)).

41 Ie an offence against the Army Act 1955 s 70, the Air Force Act 1955 s 70 or the Naval Discipline Act 1957 s 42 (all repealed) of which the corresponding civil offence is an offence listed in any of heads (1)–(33) in the text (Sexual Offences Act 2003 Sch 3 para 93(1) (amended by the Coroners and Justice Act 2009 Sch 21 para 62(5))), and an offence under the Armed Forces Act 2006 s 42 (see ARMED FORCES vol 3 (2011) PARA 587) as respects which the corresponding offence under the law of England and Wales (within the meaning given by s 42) is an offence listed in any of heads (1)–(33) in the text (Sexual Offences Act 2003 Sch 3 para 93A(1) (Sch 3 para 93A added by the Armed Forces Act 2006 Sch 16 para 212; amended by the Coroners and Justice Act 2009 Sch 21 para 62(5))). The Armed Forces Act 2006 s 48 (attempts, conspiracy, encouragement and assistance and aiding and abetting outside England and Wales: see ARMED FORCES vol 3 (2011) PARA 587) applies with modifications for the purposes of the Sexual Offences Act 2003 Sch 3 para 93A: Sch 3 para 93A(3) (as so added and amended).

In the context of offences against the Army Act 1955 s 70, the Air Force Act 1955 s 70 or the Naval Discipline Act 1957 s 42 (all repealed), a reference in the text and notes to being made the subject of a community sentence of at least 12 months is to be read as a reference to being sentenced to a term of detention of at least 112 days (Sexual Offences Act 2003 Sch 3 para 93(2) (amended by the Armed Forces Act 2006 Sch 16 para 212, Sch 17)), and in the context of offences under the Armed Forces Act 2006 s 42, such a reference is to be read as a reference to being made the subject of a service community order or overseas community order under the Armed Forces Act 2006 of at least 12 months or being sentenced to a term of service detention of at least 112 days (Sexual Offences Act 2003 Sch 3 para 93A(2) (as so added)). In the context of offences against the Army Act 1955 s 70, the Air Force Act 1955 s 70 or the Naval Discipline Act 1957 s 42 (all repealed), the reference to detention is to detention awarded under the Army Act 1955 s 71(1)(e), the Air Force Act 1955 s 71(1)(e) or the Naval Discipline Act 1957 43(1)(e) (all repealed): Sexual Offences Act 2003 Sch 3 para 93(3) (added by the Armed Forces Act 2006 Sch 16 para 212).

In the Sexual Offences Act 2003 a reference to a court order or a conviction or finding includes a reference to an order of or a conviction or finding by a service court (ie the Court-Martial or the Service Civilian Court) (s 137(1)(a), (4) (s 137(1)(d), (4) amended by the Armed Forces Act 2006 Sch 16 para 211)), a reference to an 'offence' includes a reference to an offence triable by a service court (Sexual Offences Act 2003 s 137(1)(b)), 'proceedings' includes proceedings before a service court (s 137(1)(c)), and a reference to proceedings for an offence under the Sexual Offences Act 2003 includes a reference to proceedings for a corresponding offence under the Armed Forces Act 2006 s 42 (see the Sexual Offences Act 2003 s 137(1)(d) (as so amended)).

42 See the Sexual Offences Act 2003 Sch 3 paras 36–60 (amended by the Protection of Children and Prevention of Sexual Offences (Scotland) Act 2005 Schedule para 3; the Sexual Offences (Scotland) Act 2009 Sch 5 para 5, Sch 6; the Criminal Justice and Licensing (Scotland) Act 2010 ss 41(3), 42(3); and by SSI 2010/421).

43 See the Sexual Offences Act 2003 Sch 3 paras 61–92Y (amended by the Criminal Justice and Immigration Act 2008 Sch 26 para 58; the Coroners and Justice Act 2009 Sch 21 para 62; the Serious Crime Act 2015 Sch 4 para 66; SI 2007/296; and SI 2008/1779).

44 For these purposes, 'court' includes a 'service court' (ie the Court Martial and the Service Civilian Court): Sexual Offences Act 2003 s 137(2), (4) (amended by the Anti-social Behaviour, Crime and Policing Act 2014 Sch 5 para 7; and by the Armed Forces Act 2006 Sch 16 para 211).

45 Sexual Offences Act 2003 s 92(1)(a).

46 Sexual Offences Act 2003 s 92(1)(b). As to verdicts of not guilty by reason of insanity see CRIMINAL LAW vol 25 (2010) PARA 30.
47 Sexual Offences Act 2003 s 92(1)(c).
48 As to the meaning of 'open court' see PARA 30 note 7.
49 Sexual Offences Act 2003 s 92(2)(a)(i).
50 Sexual Offences Act 2003 s 92(2)(a)(ii).
51 Sexual Offences Act 2003 s 92(2)(b).
52 Sexual Offences Act 2003 s 92(2).
53 Ie for the purposes of the Sexual Offences Act 2003 Pt 2.
54 Sexual Offences Act 2003 s 92(3), (4)(a).
55 Sexual Offences Act 2003 s 92(4)(b). At the date at which this volume states the law no such order had been made.
56 Sexual Offences Act 2003 s 92(4). See note 55.

330.   Relevant non-sexual offences.   The non-sexual offences in respect of which a sexual harm prevention order may be made[1] are[2]:

(1)   murder[3];
(2)   manslaughter[4];
(3)   kidnapping[5];
(4)   false imprisonment[6];
(5)   outraging public decency[7];
(6)   soliciting murder[8];
(7)   threats to kill[9];
(8)   wounding with intent to cause grievous bodily harm[10];
(9)   malicious wounding[11];
(10) attempting to choke, suffocate or strangle in order to commit or assist in committing an indictable offence[12];
(11) using chloroform, etc, to commit or assist in the committing of any indictable offence[13];
(12) maliciously administering poison, etc, so as to endanger life or inflict grievous bodily harm[14];
(13) abandoning children[15];
(14) causing bodily injury by explosives[16];
(15) using explosives, etc, with intent to do grievous bodily harm[17];
(16) placing explosives with intent to do bodily injury[18];
(17) setting spring guns, etc, with intent to do grievous bodily harm[19];
(18) endangering the safety of railway passengers[20];
(19) injuring persons by furious driving[21];
(20) assaulting an officer preserving a wreck[22];
(21) assault with intent to resist arrest[23];
(22) assault occasioning actual bodily harm[24];
(23) causing an explosion likely to endanger life or property[25];
(24) attempting to cause explosion, or making or keeping explosives, with intent to endanger life or property[26];
(25) child destruction[27];
(26) cruelty to children[28];
(27) infanticide[29];
(28) possession of a firearm with intent to endanger life[30];
(29) possession of a firearm with intent to cause fear of violence[31];
(30) use of a firearm to resist arrest[32];
(31) possession of a firearm when committing or being arrested for a violent offence[33];
(32) carrying a firearm with criminal intent[34];
(33) theft[35];

(34) robbery or assault with intent to rob[36];
(35) burglary with intent to steal, inflict grievous bodily harm or do unlawful damage[37];
(36) aggravated burglary[38];
(37) aggravated vehicle-taking[39] involving an accident which caused the death of any person[40];
(38) arson[41];
(39) destroying or damaging property[42] other than an offence of arson[43];
(40) hostage-taking[44];
(41) hijacking of ships or aircraft[45];
(42) destroying, damaging or endangering the safety of aircraft[46];
(43) other acts endangering or likely to endanger the safety of aircraft[47];
(44) offences in relation to the carrying of certain dangerous articles on aircraft or in aviation installations[48];
(45) ill-treatment of mentally-disordered persons[49];
(46) child abduction[50];
(47) female genital mutilation[51];
(48) riot[52];
(49) violent disorder[53];
(50) affray[54];
(51) torture[55];
(52) causing death by dangerous driving[56];
(53) causing death by careless driving when under the influence of drink or drugs[57];
(54) endangering safety at aerodromes[58];
(55) seizing or exercising control of fixed platforms[59];
(56) destroying fixed platforms or endangering their safety[60];
(57) other acts endangering or likely to endanger safe navigation[61];
(58) offences involving threats to ships or fixed platforms[62];
(59) harassment and stalking[63];
(60) putting people in fear of violence and stalking involving fear of violence or serious harm or distress[64];
(61) racially or religiously aggravated assaults[65];
(62) racially or religiously aggravated public order offences[66];
(63) offences relating to Channel Tunnel trains and the tunnel system[67];
(64) contravention of a notice relating to encrypted information or tipping off in connection with such a notice[68];
(65) sending certain articles by post[69];
(66) genocide, crimes against humanity, war crimes and related offences[70], other than an offence involving murder[71];
(67) improper use of public telecommunications network[72];
(68) paying for the sexual services of a child[73] where the victim or (as the case may be) other party was aged 16 or over[74];
(69) causing or inciting prostitution for gain[75];
(70) controlling prostitution for gain[76];
(71) trafficking people for sexual exploitation[77];
(72) causing or allowing a child or vulnerable adult to die or suffer serious physical harm[78]; and
(73) human trafficking[79].

A reference in this list to an offence includes a reference to any attempt, conspiracy or incitement of another to commit[80], and to aiding, abetting, counselling or procuring the commission of[81], any of the offences in respect of which such an order may be made, and also includes a reference to an offence under the statutory provisions relating to the encouragement or assistance of crime[82] in relation to which the listed offence is the offence (or one of the offences) which the person intended or believed would be committed[83]. Provision is also made in respect of corresponding service offences[84], and Scottish[85] and Northern Ireland[86] offences.

1 Ie the offences referred to in the Sexual Offences Act 2003 s 103A(2)(a), 103B(1): see PARA 327.

2 The Secretary of State may by order amend the Sexual Offences Act 2003 Sch 5 (see the text and notes 3–86): see s 130(1); and PARA 329 note 9. Where (by virtue of an order under s 130 or otherwise) an offence is listed in Sch 5 subject to a sentencing condition, s 132 (see PARA 329 note 1) applies to that offence as if references to Sch 3 were references to Sch 5: s 132(8).

3 Sexual Offences Act 2003 Sch 5 para 1. As to the offence of murder see CRIMINAL LAW vol 25 (2010) PARAS 96–97.

4 Sexual Offences Act 2003 Sch 5 para 2. As to the offence of manslaughter see CRIMINAL LAW vol 25 (2010) PARA 98 et seq.

5 Sexual Offences Act 2003 Sch 5 para 3. As to the offence of kidnapping see CRIMINAL LAW vol 25 (2010) PARA 146.

6 Sexual Offences Act 2003 Sch 5 para 4. As to the offence of false imprisonment see CRIMINAL LAW vol 25 (2010) PARA 145.

7 Sexual Offences Act 2003 Sch 5 para 4A (Sch 5 paras 4A, 31A, 43A, 43B, 56A, 60A, 61A, 117A, 138A, 139A, 154A, 154B, 165A, 168A, 169A added, Sch 5 paras 32, 57, 140, 166 amended, Sch 5 paras 33, 63, 141, 171 substituted, by SI 2007/296). The Sexual Offences Act 2003 (Amendment of Schedules 3 and 5) Order 2007, SI 2007/296, was made under the Sexual Offences Act 2003 s 130: see PARA 329 note 9. As to the offence of outraging public decency see CRIMINAL LAW vol 26 (2010) PARA 717.

8 Sexual Offences Act 2003 Sch 5 para 5. As to the offence of soliciting murder (ie an offence under the Offences Against the Person Act 1861 s 4) see CRIMINAL LAW vol 25 (2010) PARA 114.

9 Sexual Offences Act 2003 Sch 5 para 6. As to this offence (ie an offence under the Offences Against the Person Act 1861 s 16) see CRIMINAL LAW vol 25 (2010) PARA 115.

10 Sexual Offences Act 2003 Sch 5 para 7. As to the offence of wounding with intent to cause grievous bodily harm (ie an offence under the Offences Against the Person Act 1861 s 18) see CRIMINAL LAW vol 25 (2010) PARA 128.

11 Sexual Offences Act 2003 Sch 5 para 8. As to the offence of malicious wounding (ie an offence under the Offences Against the Person Act 1861 s 20) see CRIMINAL LAW vol 25 (2010) PARA 130.

12 Sexual Offences Act 2003 Sch 5 para 9. As to this offence (ie an offence under the Offences Against the Person Act 1861 s 21) see CRIMINAL LAW vol 25 (2010) PARA 131.

13 Sexual Offences Act 2003 Sch 5 para 10. As to this offence (ie an offence under the Offences Against the Person Act 1861 s 22) see CRIMINAL LAW vol 25 (2010) PARA 132.

14 Sexual Offences Act 2003 Sch 5 para 11. As to this offence (ie an offence under the Offences Against the Person Act 1861 s 23) see CRIMINAL LAW vol 25 (2010) PARA 133.

15 Sexual Offences Act 2003 Sch 5 para 12. As to this offence (ie an offence under the Offences Against the Person Act 1861 s 27) see CRIMINAL LAW vol 25 (2010) PARA 153.

16 Sexual Offences Act 2003 Sch 5 para 13. As to this offence (ie an offence under the Offences Against the Person Act 1861 s 28) see CRIMINAL LAW vol 25 (2010) PARA 135.

17 Sexual Offences Act 2003 Sch 5 para 14. As to this offence (ie an offence under the Offences Against the Person Act 1861 s 29) see CRIMINAL LAW vol 25 (2010) PARA 136.

18 Sexual Offences Act 2003 Sch 5 para 15. As to this offence (ie an offence under the Offences Against the Person Act 1861 s 30) see CRIMINAL LAW vol 25 (2010) PARA 140.

19 Sexual Offences Act 2003 Sch 5 para 16. As to this offence (ie an offence under the Offences Against the Person Act 1861 s 31) see CRIMINAL LAW vol 25 (2010) PARA 141.

20 Sexual Offences Act 2003 Sch 5 para 17. As to this offence (ie an offence under the Offences Against the Person Act 1861 s 32) see CRIMINAL LAW vol 25 (2010) PARA 142.

21 Sexual Offences Act 2003 Sch 5 para 18. As to this offence (ie an offence under the Offences Against the Person Act 1861 s 35) see ROAD TRAFFIC vol 90 (2011) PARA 775.

22 Sexual Offences Act 2003 Sch 5 para 19. As to this offence (ie an offence under the Offences Against the Person Act 1861 s 37) see SHIPPING AND MARITIME LAW vol 94 (2008) PARA 1228.

23 Sexual Offences Act 2003 Sch 5 para 20. As to this offence (ie an offence under the Offences Against the Person Act 1861 s 38) see CRIMINAL LAW vol 25 (2010) PARA 717.

24 Sexual Offences Act 2003 Sch 5 para 21. As to this offence (ie an offence under the Offences Against the Person Act 1861 s 47) see CRIMINAL LAW vol 25 (2010) PARA 717.

25 Sexual Offences Act 2003 Sch 5 para 22. As to this offence (ie an offence under the Explosive Substances Act 1883 s 2) see CRIMINAL LAW vol 25 (2010) PARA 137.

26 Sexual Offences Act 2003 Sch 5 para 23. As to this offence (ie an offence under the Explosive Substances Act 1883 s 3) see CRIMINAL LAW vol 25 (2010) PARA 138.

27 Sexual Offences Act 2003 Sch 5 para 24. As to this offence (ie an offence under the Infant Life (Preservation) Act 1929 s 1) see CRIMINAL LAW vol 25 (2010) PARA 118.

28 Sexual Offences Act 2003 Sch 5 para 25. As to this offence (ie an offence under the Children and Young Persons Act 1933 s 1) see CRIMINAL LAW vol 25 (2010) PARA 153.

29 Sexual Offences Act 2003 Sch 5 para 26. As to this offence (ie an offence under the Infanticide Act 1938 s 1) see CRIMINAL LAW vol 25 (2010) PARA 113.

30 Sexual Offences Act 2003 Sch 5 para 27. As to this offence (ie an offence under the Firearms Act 1968 s 16) see CRIMINAL LAW vol 26 (2010) PARA 628.

31 Sexual Offences Act 2003 Sch 5 para 28. As to this offence (ie an offence under the Firearms Act 1968 s 16A) see CRIMINAL LAW vol 26 (2010) PARA 629.

32 Sexual Offences Act 2003 Sch 5 para 29. As to this offence (ie an offence under the Firearms Act 1968 s 17(1)) see CRIMINAL LAW vol 25 (2010) PARA 630.

33 Sexual Offences Act 2003 Sch 5 para 30. As to this offence (ie an offence under the Firearms Act 1968 s 17(2), Sch 1) see CRIMINAL LAW vol 26 (2010) PARA 631.

34 Sexual Offences Act 2003 Sch 5 para 31. As to this offence (ie an offence under the Firearms Act 1968 s 18) see CRIMINAL LAW vol 26 (2010) PARA 633.

35 Sexual Offences Act 2003 Sch 5 para 31A (as added: see note 7). As to this offence (ie an offence under the Theft Act 1968 s 1) see CRIMINAL LAW vol 25 (2010) PARA 278.

36 Sexual Offences Act 2003 Sch 5 para 32 (as amended: see note 7). As to this offence (ie an offence under the Theft Act 1968 s 8) see CRIMINAL LAW vol 25 (2010) PARA 289.

37 Sexual Offences Act 2003 Sch 5 para 33 (as substituted: see note 7). As to this offence (ie an offence under the Theft Act 1968 s 9(1)(a)) see CRIMINAL LAW vol 25 (2010) PARA 290.

38 Sexual Offences Act 2003 Sch 5 para 34. As to the offence of aggravated burglary (ie an offence under the Theft Act 1968 s 10) see CRIMINAL LAW vol 25 (2010) PARA 291.

39 As to the offence of aggravated vehicle-taking (ie an offence under the Theft Act 1968 s 12A) see CRIMINAL LAW vol 25 (2010) PARA 295.

40 Sexual Offences Act 2003 Sch 5 para 35.

41 Sexual Offences Act 2003 Sch 5 para 36. As to the offence of arson (ie an offence under the Criminal Damage Act 1971 s 1) see CRIMINAL LAW vol 25 (2010) PARA 327.

42 Ie an offence under the Criminal Damage Act 1971 s 1(2) (see CRIMINAL LAW vol 25 (2010) PARA 327).

43 Sexual Offences Act 2003 Sch 5 para 37.

44 Sexual Offences Act 2003 Sch 5 para 38. As to the offence of hostage-taking (ie an offence under the Taking of Hostages Act 1982 s 1) see CRIMINAL LAW vol 25 (2010) PARA 416.

45 Sexual Offences Act 2003 Sch 5 paras 39, 52. As to the offence of hijacking (ie an offence under the Aviation Security Act 1982 s 1 in relation to aircraft or under the Aviation and Maritime Security Act 1990 s 9 in relation to ships) see AIR LAW vol 2 (2008) PARA 624; SHIPPING AND MARITIME LAW vol 94 (2008) PARA 1210.

46 Sexual Offences Act 2003 Sch 5 para 40. As to this offence (ie an offence under the Aviation Security Act 1982 s 2) see AIR LAW vol 2 (2008) PARA 628.

47 Sexual Offences Act 2003 Sch 5 para 41. As to this offence (ie an offence under the Aviation Security Act 1982 s 3) see AIR LAW vol 2 (2008) PARA 629.

48 Sexual Offences Act 2003 Sch 5 para 42. As to this offence (ie an offence under the Aviation Security Act 1982 s 4) see AIR LAW vol 2 (2008) PARA 630.

49 Sexual Offences Act 2003 Sch 5 para 43. As to this offence (ie an offence under the Mental Health Act 1983 s 127) see MENTAL HEALTH AND CAPACITY vol 75 (2013) PARA 1010.

50 Sexual Offences Act 2003 Sch 5 paras 43A, 43B (as added: see note 7). As to this offence (ie an offence under the Child Abduction Act 1984 ss 1, 2) see CRIMINAL LAW vol 25 (2010) PARAS 147–151.

51 Sexual Offences Act 2003 Sch 5 para 44. This provision refers to this offence as being committed under the Prohibition of Female Circumcision Act 1985 s 1 (repealed): the offence of female genital mutilation is now committed under the Female Genital Mutilation Act 2003 s 1 (see CRIMINAL LAW vol 25 (2010) PARA 168).

52 Sexual Offences Act 2003 Sch 5 para 45. As to the offence of riot (ie an offence under the Public Order Act 1986 s 1) see CRIMINAL LAW vol 26 (2010) PARA 487.

53 Sexual Offences Act 2003 Sch 5 para 46. As to the offence of violent disorder (ie an offence under the Public Order Act 1986 s 2) see CRIMINAL LAW vol 26 (2010) PARA 488.

54 Sexual Offences Act 2003 Sch 5 para 47. As to the offence of affray (ie an offence under the Public Order Act 1986 s 3) see CRIMINAL LAW vol 26 (2010) PARA 489.

55 Sexual Offences Act 2003 Sch 5 para 48. As to the offence of torture (ie an offence under the Criminal Justice Act 1988 s 134) see CRIMINAL LAW vol 25 (2010) PARA 172.

56 Sexual Offences Act 2003 Sch 5 para 49. As to this offence (ie an offence under the Road Traffic Act 1988 s 1) see ROAD TRAFFIC vol 90 (2011) PARA 720.

57 Sexual Offences Act 2003 Sch 5 para 50. As to this offence (ie an offence under the Road Traffic Act 1988 s 3A) see ROAD TRAFFIC vol 90 (2011) PARA 731.

58 Sexual Offences Act 2003 Sch 5 para 51. As to this offence (ie an offence under the Aviation and Maritime Security Act 1990 s 1) see AIR LAW vol 2 (2008) PARA 631.

59 Sexual Offences Act 2003 Sch 5 para 53. As to this offence (ie an offence under the Aviation and Maritime Security Act 1990 s 10) see SHIPPING AND MARITIME LAW vol 94 (2008) PARA 1211. As to the meaning of 'fixed platform' see SHIPPING AND MARITIME LAW vol 94 (2008) PARA 1211.

60 Sexual Offences Act 2003 Sch 5 para 54. As to this offence (ie an offence under the Aviation and Maritime Security Act 1990 s 11) see SHIPPING AND MARITIME LAW vol 94 (2008) PARA 1212.

61 Sexual Offences Act 2003 Sch 5 para 55. As to this offence (ie an offence under the Aviation and Maritime Security Act 1990 s 12) see SHIPPING AND MARITIME LAW vol 94 (2008) PARA 1213.

62 Sexual Offences Act 2003 Sch 5 para 56. As to this offence (ie an offence under the Aviation and Maritime Security Act 1990 s 13) see SHIPPING AND MARITIME LAW vol 94 (2008) PARA 1214.

63 Sexual Offences Act 2003 Sch 5 para 56A (as added (see note 7); Sch 5 paras 56A, 57, 63 amended by the Protection of Freedoms Act 2012 Sch 9 paras 140, 146). As to these offences (ie offences under the Protection from Harassment Act 1997 ss 2, 2A) see CRIMINAL LAW vol 25 (2010) PARA 163.

64 Sexual Offences Act 2003 Sch 5 para 57 (as amended: see note 7). As to these offences (ie offences under the Protection from Harassment Act 1997 ss 4, 4A) see CRIMINAL LAW vol 25 (2010) PARA 164.

65 Sexual Offences Act 2003 Sch 5 para 58. As to this offence (ie an offence under the Crime and Disorder Act 1998 s 29) see CRIMINAL LAW vol 25 (2010) PARA 166.

66 Sexual Offences Act 2003 Sch 5 para 59. The offences referred to in the text are offences under the Public Order Act 1986 s 4 or s 4A (see CRIMINAL LAW vol 26 (2010) PARAS 490–491) which fall within the Crime and Disorder Act 1998 s 31(1)(a) or (b) (see CRIMINAL LAW vol 26 (2010) PARA 493): Sexual Offences Act 2003 Sch 5 para 59.

67 Sexual Offences Act 2003 Sch 5 para 60. The offences referred to in the text are offences under the Channel Tunnel (Security) Order 1994, SI 1994/570, Pt II.

68 Sexual Offences Act 2003 Sch 5 para 60ZA (Sch 5 paras 60ZA, 106A, 168ZA added by the Policing and Crime Act 2009 Sch 7 para 25). As to these offences (ie offences under the Regulation of Investigatory Powers Act 2000 ss 53, 54) see POLICE AND INVESTIGATORY POWERS vol 84A (2013) PARAS 713, 714).

69 Sexual Offences Act 2003 Sch 5 para 60A (as added: see note 7). The offence referred to in the text is an offence under the Postal Services Act 2000 s 85(3) or (4): CRIMINAL LAW vol 26 (2010) PARA 718.

70 Ie an offence under the International Criminal Court Act 2001 s 51 or s 52 (see INTERNATIONAL RELATIONS LAW vol 6 (2010) PARAS 454, 455).

71 Sexual Offences Act 2003 Sch 5 para 61.

72 Sexual Offences Act 2003 Sch 5 para 61A (as added: see note 7). As to this offence (ie an offence under the Communications Act 2003 s 127(1)) see CRIMINAL LAW vol 26 (2010) PARA 719.

73 Ie an offence under the Sexual Offences Act 2003 s 47 (see CRIMINAL LAW vol 25 (2010) PARA 228).

74 Sexual Offences Act 2003 Sch 5 para 62. A reference to a person's age is a reference to his age at the time of the offence: Sch 5 para 174. As to the determination of a person's age see the Children and Young Persons Act 1933 s 99; and CHILDREN AND YOUNG PERSONS vol 10 (2012) PARA 1206.

75 Sexual Offences Act 2003 Sch 5 para 63 (as substituted and amended: see notes 7, 63). As to this offence (ie an offence under the Sexual Offences Act 2003 ss 51, 52) see CRIMINAL LAW vol 25 (2010) PARAS 229, 230.

76 Sexual Offences Act 2003 Sch 5 para 63 (as substituted and amended: see notes 7, 63). As to this offence (ie an offence under the Sexual Offences Act 2003 ss 51, 53) see CRIMINAL LAW vol 25 (2010) PARAS 229, 230.

77   Sexual Offences Act 2003 Sch 5 para 63 (as substituted and amended: see notes 7, 63). As to these offences (ie an offence under the Sexual Offences Act 2003 s 57, s 58, s 59 or s 59A) see CRIMINAL LAW vol 25 (2010) PARA 254.

78   Sexual Offences Act 2003 Sch 5 para 63A (Sch 5 paras 63A, 171A added by the Domestic Violence, Crime and Victims Act 2004 Sch 10 para 59(1), (2); amended by the Domestic Violence, Crime and Victims (Amendment) Act 2012 Schedule para 5). As to this offence (ie an offence under the Domestic Violence, Crime and Victims Act 2004 s 5) see CRIMINAL LAW vol 25 (2010) PARA 117.

79   Sexual Offences Act 2003 Sch 5 para 63B (added by the Modern Slavery Act 2015 Sch 5 para 5(1), (3)). As to this offence (ie an offence under the Modern Slavery Act 2015 s 2) see CRIMINAL LAW.

80   Sexual Offences Act 2003 Sch 5 para 173(a). This does not, however, include an attempt to incite the commission of an offence: see *R v Parnell* [2004] EWCA Crim 2523, [2005] 1 WLR 853, (2004) Times, 8 November (case concerned with similar terminology in the Sex Offenders Act 1997 Sch 1 para 5(1) (repealed)).

81   Sexual Offences Act 2003 Sch 5 para 173(b).

82   Ie the Serious Crime Act 2007 Pt 2 (ss 44–67) (see CRIMINAL LAW vol 25 (2010) PARAS 65–72).

83   Sexual Offences Act 2003 Sch 5 para 173A (added by the Serious Crime Act 2007 Sch 6 para 63(1), (3)).

84   Ie an offence against the Army Act 1955 s 70, the Air Force Act 1955 s 70 or the Naval Discipline Act 1957 s 42 (all repealed) of which the corresponding civil offence is an offence listed in any of heads (1)–(72) in the text (Sexual Offences Act 2003 Sch 5 para 172 (amended by the Domestic Violence, Crime and Victims Act 2004 Sch 10 para 59(4))), and an offence under the Armed Forces Act 2006 s 42 (see ARMED FORCES vol 3 (2011) PARA 587) as respects which the corresponding offence under the law of England and Wales (within the meaning given by s 42) is an offence listed in any of heads (1)–(72) in the text (Sexual Offences Act 2003 Sch 5 para 172A(1) (Sch 5 para 172A added by the Armed Forces Act 2006 Sch 16 para 213; and amended by the Serious Crime Act 2007 Sch 5 para 4(1), (3))). The Armed Forces Act 2006 s 48 (attempts, conspiracy, encouragement and assistance and aiding and abetting outside England and Wales: see ARMED FORCES vol 3 (2011) PARA 587) applies with modifications for the purposes of the Sexual Offences Act 2003 Sch 5 para 172A: Sch 5 para 172A(2) (as so added and amended).

85   See the Sexual Offences Act 2003 Sch 5 paras 64–111 (as amended: see note 68).

86   See the Sexual Offences Act 2003 Sch 5 paras 112–171B (as amended (see notes 7, 78); amended by SI 2004/702; SI 2008/1779).

331. Prohibitions. The only prohibitions that may be included in a sexual harm prevention order[1] are those that are necessary for the stated purpose[2]. Prohibitions have effect either for a fixed period, specified in the order, of at least five years[3] or until further order[4]: the order may specify that some of its prohibitions have effect until further order and some for a fixed period[5] and may specify different periods for different prohibitions[6].

An order may contain a 'prohibition on foreign travel', that is to say:

(1)   a prohibition on travelling to any country outside the United Kingdom[7] named or described in the order[8];

(2)   a prohibition on travelling to any country outside the United Kingdom other than a country named or described in the order[9]; or

(3)   a prohibition on travelling to any country outside the United Kingdom[10].

A prohibition on foreign travel contained in a sexual harm prevention order must be for a fixed period of not more than five years[11].

1   See PARA 327.

2   Sexual Offences Act 2003 ss 103C(4) (ss 103A–103K added by the Anti-social Behaviour, Crime and Policing Act 2014 Sch 5 para 2). As to the stated purpose see the Sexual Offences Act 2003 ss 103C(4)(a), (b); and PARA 327.

3   Sexual Offences Act 2003 s 103C(2)(a) (as added: see note 2).

4   Sexual Offences Act 2003 s 103C(2)(b) (as added: see note 2).

5   Sexual Offences Act 2003 s 103C(3)(a) (as added: see note 2).

6 Sexual Offences Act 2003 s 103C(3)(b) (as added: see note 2).

7 As to the meaning of 'United Kingdom' see PARA 4 note 3.

8 Sexual Offences Act 2003 s 103D(2)(a) (as added: see note 2).

9 Sexual Offences Act 2003 s 103D(2)(b) (as added: see note 2).

10 Sexual Offences Act 2003 s 103D(2)(c) (as added: see note 2). A sexual harm prevention order that contains a prohibition within s 103D(2)(c) must require the defendant to surrender all of his passports at a police station specified in the order on or before the date when the prohibition takes effect (s 103D(4)(a) (as so added)) or within a period specified in the order (s 103D(4)(b) (as so added)). For these purposes 'passport' means a United Kingdom passport within the meaning of the Immigration Act 1971 (see IMMIGRATION AND ASYLUM vol 57 (2012) PARA 33) (s 103D(7)(a) (as so added)), a passport issued by or on behalf of the authorities of a country outside the United Kingdom, or by or on behalf of an international organisation (s 103D(7)(b) (as so added)), or a document that can be used (in some or all circumstances) instead of a passport (s 103D(7)(c) (as so added)). Any passports so surrendered must be returned as soon as reasonably practicable after the person ceases to be subject to a sexual harm prevention order containing a prohibition within s 103D(2)(c) (unless the person is subject to an equivalent prohibition under another order): s 103D(5) (as so added). Section 103D (5) does not apply in relation to a passport issued by or on behalf of the authorities of a country outside the United Kingdom if the passport has been returned to those authorities (s 103D(6)(a) (as so added)) or a passport issued by or on behalf of an international organisation if the passport has been returned to that organisation (s 103D(6)(b) (as so added)). A person commits an offence if, without reasonable excuse, he fails to comply with a requirement imposed under s 103D(4): s 103I(2) (as so added). A person guilty of an offence under s 103I is liable on summary conviction, to imprisonment for a term not exceeding 6 months or a fine or both (s 103I(3)(a) (as so added)) and on conviction on indictment, to imprisonment for a term not exceeding 5 years (s 103I(3)(b) (as so added)). Where a person is convicted of an offence under s 103I it is not open to the court by or before which the person is convicted to make, in respect of the offence, an order for conditional discharge: s 103I(4) (as so added).

11 Sexual Offences Act 2003 s 103D(1) (as added: see note 2). This does not prevent a prohibition on foreign travel from being extended for a further period (of no more than 5 years each time) under s 103E (see PARA 335) (s 103D(3) (as so added)).

332. Interim orders. Where a police application for a sexual harm prevention order[1] ('the main application') has not been determined[2] an application for an interim sexual harm prevention order may be made by the complaint by which the main application is made[3] or, if the main application has been made, may be made by the person who has made that application, by complaint to the court to which that application has been made[4]. The court may, if it considers it just to do so, make an interim sexual harm prevention order, prohibiting the defendant from doing anything described in the order[5]. An interim order has effect only for a fixed period, specified in the order[6], and ceases to have effect, if it has not already done so, on the determination of the main application[7]. Failure to comply with an interim order is an offence[8] punishable by imprisonment[9].

1 Ie an application under the Sexual Offences Act 2003 s 103A(4) (see PARA 327).

2 Sexual Offences Act 2003 ss 103F(1) (ss 103A–103K added by the Anti-social Behaviour, Crime and Policing Act 2014 Sch 5 para 2).

3 Sexual Offences Act 2003 ss 103F(2)(a) (as added: see note 2).

4 Sexual Offences Act 2003 ss 103F(2)(b) (as added: see note 2).

5 Sexual Offences Act 2003 ss 103F(3) (as added: see note 2). As to prohibitions see PARA 331. As to appeals against an interim order see PARA 334. In connection with the variation, renewal and discharge of an order see PARA 335.

6 Sexual Offences Act 2003 ss 103F(4)(a) (as added: see note 2).

7 Sexual Offences Act 2003 ss 103F(4)(b) (as added: see note 2).

8 A person commits an offence if, without reasonable excuse, he does anything that he is prohibited from doing by an interim sexual harm prevention order: Sexual Offences Act 2003 s 103I(1)(b) (as added: see note 2).

9 A person guilty of an offence under the Sexual Offences Act 2003 s 103I is liable on summary conviction, to imprisonment for a term not exceeding 6 months or a fine or both (s 103I(3)(a) (as added: see note 2)) and on conviction on indictment, to imprisonment for a term not

exceeding 5 years (s 103I(3)(b) (as so added)). Where a person is convicted of an offence under s 103I it is not open to the court by or before which the person is convicted to make, in respect of the offence, an order for conditional discharge: s 103I(4) (as so added)).

333. Coordination with notification requirements and notification orders. Persons convicted of or cautioned for sexual offences against children may be required to provide the police with specified information about themselves: these are referred to as 'notification requirements'[1]. Where a person's convictions relate to overseas offences, the notification requirements are imposed via 'notification orders'[2]. Provision is made for imposing notification requirements on persons who are made subject to sexual harm prevention orders and interim orders[3], for coordinating the terms of sexual harm prevention orders and interim orders with those of any existing notification requirements[4], and for making a notification order, either instead of or in addition to a sexual harm prevention order or an interim order, in appropriate circumstances[5].

1   As to the notification requirements see PARAS 498–514.
2   As to notification orders see PARAS 515–517.
3   See the Sexual Offences Act 2003 s 103G(2)–(4); and PARA 499.
4   See the Sexual Offences Act 2003 s 103G(1), (3), (4); and PARA 499. See also s 103G(5); and PARA 335.
5   See the Sexual Offences Act 2003 s 103G(6), (7); and PARA 499.

334. Appeals. A defendant may appeal against the making of a sexual harm prevention order[1]. Where the order was made by a court dealing with the defendant in respect of an offence[2], the appeal is brought as if the order were a sentence passed on the defendant for the offence[3]; where the order is made in respect of a finding that the defendant is not guilty of an offence by reason of insanity[4] or a finding that the defendant is under a disability and has done the act charged against the defendant in respect of such an offence[5], the appeal is brought as if the defendant had been convicted of the offence and the order were a sentence passed on the defendant for that offence[6]; and where the order was made on an application[7], the appeal is brought to the Crown Court[8]. A defendant may also appeal to the Crown Court against the making of an interim sexual harm prevention order[9].

On an appeal against an order made on application[10] or an interim order[11] the Crown Court may make such orders as may be necessary to give effect to its determination of the appeal, and may also make such incidental or consequential orders as appear to it to be just[12].

1   As to the making of sexual harm prevention orders see PARA 327.
2   Ie where the order was made by virtue of the Sexual Offences Act 2003 s 103A(2)(a)(i) (see PARA 327).
3   Sexual Offences Act 2003 ss 103H(1)(a) (ss 103A–103K added by the Anti-social Behaviour, Crime and Policing Act 2014 Sch 5 para 2).
4   Ie where the order was made by virtue of the Sexual Offences Act 2003 s 103A(2)(a)(ii) (see PARA 327).
5   Ie where the order was made by virtue of the Sexual Offences Act 2003 s 103A(2)(a)(iii) (see PARA 327).
6   Sexual Offences Act 2003 s 103H(1)(b) (as added: see note 3).
7   Ie where the order was made on police application under the Sexual Offences Act 2003 s 103A(4) (see PARA 327).
8   Sexual Offences Act 2003 s 103H(1)(c) (as added: see note 3).
9   Sexual Offences Act 2003 s 103H(2) (as added: see note 3). As to the making of interim orders see PARA 332.
10   Ie an appeal under the Sexual Offences Act 2003 s 103H(1)(c) (see the text and notes 7–8).
11   Ie an appeal under the Sexual Offences Act 2003 s 103H(2) (see the text and note 9).

12 Sexual Offences Act 2003 s 103H(4) (as added: see note 3). Any order made by the Crown Court on an appeal under s 103H(1)(c) or (2) (other than an order directing that an application be re-heard by a magistrates' court) is for the purposes of s 103E(9) (see PARA 335) or s 103F(5) (see PARA 327) (respectively) to be treated as if it were an order of the court from which the appeal was brought (and not an order of the Crown Court): s 103H(5) (as so added).

335. Variation, renewal and discharge. An application for an order varying, renewing or discharging a sexual harm prevention order[1] may be made by the defendant[2], the chief officer of police for the area in which the defendant resides[3], a chief officer of police who believes that the defendant is in, or is intending to come to, that officer's police area[4] and (where applicable[5]), the chief officer of police who made the original application[6]. The application must be made to the appropriate court[7] and the court may[8] make any order, varying, renewing or discharging the sexual harm prevention order that the court considers appropriate[9]. An order may be renewed, or varied so as to impose additional prohibitions on the defendant[10], only if it is necessary to do so for the stated purpose[11], and the court must not without consent[12] discharge an order before the end of five years beginning with the day on which the order was made[13]. A defendant may appeal against the making of an order for variation, renewal or discharge[14], or the refusal to make such an order[15].

Where an interim sexual harm prevention order is in effect[16], the applicant or the defendant may by complaint apply to the court that made the order for it to be varied, renewed or discharged[17].

Where a sexual harm prevention order is in effect in relation to a relevant sex offender[18] and the relevant sex offender ceases[19] to be subject to the notification requirements[20], the sexual harm prevention order ceases to have effect[21].

1 As to the making of sexual harm prevention orders see PARA 327.
2 Sexual Offences Act 2003 s 103E(1), (2)(a) (ss 103A–103K added by the Anti-social Behaviour, Crime and Policing Act 2014 Sch 5 para 2).
3 Sexual Offences Act 2003 s 103E(2)(b) (as added: see note 2). As to police forces, police areas and chief officers of police see POLICE AND INVESTIGATORY POWERS vol 84 (2013) PARAS 52 et seq, 123 et seq.
4 Sexual Offences Act 2003 s 103E(2)(c) (as added: see note 2).
5 Ie where the order was made on an application by a chief officer of police under the Sexual Offences Act 2003 s 103A(4) (see PARA 327).
6 Sexual Offences Act 2003 s 103E(2)(d) (as added: see note 2).
7 Sexual Offences Act 2003 s 103E(1) (as added: see note 2). For the purposes of s 103E 'the appropriate court' means:
  (1) where the Crown Court or the Court of Appeal made the sexual harm prevention order, the Crown Court (s 103E(9)(a) (as so added));
  (2) where an adult magistrates' court made the order, that court, an adult magistrates' court for the area in which the defendant resides or, where the application is made by a chief officer of police, any adult magistrates' court acting for a local justice area that includes any part of the chief officer's police area (s 103E(9)(b) (as so added));
  (3) where a youth court made the order and the defendant is under the age of 18, that court, a youth court for the area in which the defendant resides or, where the application is made by a chief officer of police, any youth court acting for a local justice area that includes any part of the chief officer's police area (s 103E(9)(c) (as so added));
  (4) where a youth court made the order and the defendant is aged 18 or over, an adult magistrates' court for the area in which the defendant resides or, where the application is made by a chief officer of police, any adult magistrates' court acting for a local justice area that includes any part of the chief officer's police area (s 103E(9)(d) (as so added)).
  Where the appropriate court is the Crown Court, the application must be made in accordance with rules of court (s 103E(3)(a) (as so added)); in any other case it must be made by complaint (s 103E(3)(b) (as so added)). For these purposes 'adult magistrates' court' means a magistrates' court that is not a youth court: s 103E(9) (as so added). As to youth courts see

CHILDREN AND YOUNG PERSONS vol 10 (2012) PARA 1225 et seq. As to the determination of a person's age see the Children and Young Persons Act 1933 s 99; and CHILDREN AND YOUNG PERSONS vol 10 (2012) PARA 1206.

8   Ie after hearing the person making the application and (if they wish to be heard) the other persons mentioned in the Sexual Offences Act 2003 s 103E(2) (see the text and notes 1–6): s 103E(4) (as so added).

9   Sexual Offences Act 2003 s 103E(4) (as added: see note 2).

10 As to prohibitions see PARA 331.

11 Sexual Offences Act 2003 s 103E(5), (6) (as added: see note 2). As to the stated purpose see s 103E(5)(a), (b); and PARA 327.

12 Ie without the consent of the defendant and either:
    (1)   where the application is made by a chief officer of police, that chief officer (Sexual Offences Act 2003 s 103E(7)(a) (as added: see note 2)); or
    (2)   in any other case, the chief officer of police for the area in which the defendant resides (s 103E(7)(b) (as so added)).

13 Sexual Offences Act 2003 s 103E(7) (as added: see note 2). This does not apply to an order containing a prohibition on foreign travel (see PARA 331) and no other prohibitions: s 103E(8) (as so added).

14 Ie an order under the Sexual Offences Act 2003 s 103E (see the text and notes 1–13).

15 Sexual Offences Act 2003 s 103H(3) (as added: see note 2). Where the application for the order was made to the Crown Court, appeal is to the Court of Appeal (s 103H(3)(a) (as so added)); in any other case, appeal is to the Crown Court (s 103H(3)(b) (as so added)). On an appeal under s 103H(3)(b) the Crown Court may make such orders as may be necessary to give effect to its determination of the appeal, and may also make such incidental or consequential orders as appear to it to be just: s 103H(4) (as so added).

16 As to the making of interim orders see PARA 332.

17 Sexual Offences Act 2003 s 103F(5) (as added: see note 2).

18 Ie within the meaning of the Sexual Offences Act 2003 s 88A (applies to Scotland only).

19 Ie by virtue of the Sexual Offences Act 2003 s 88F (applies to Scotland only) or s 88G (applies to Scotland only).

20 As to the notification requirements see PARAS 498–514.

21 Sexual Offences Act 2003 s 103G(5) (as added: see note 2).

(iii) Financial Reporting Orders

336.   Making of financial reporting orders.   Until a day to be appointed[1] a court sentencing or otherwise dealing with a person convicted of a specified offence[2] may also make a financial reporting order in respect of him[3]. However, it may do so only if it is satisfied that the risk of the person's committing another specified offence is sufficiently high to justify the making of a financial reporting order[4].

A financial reporting order:

(1)   comes into force when it is made[5]; and

(2)   has effect for the period specified in the order, beginning with the date on which it is made[6].

If the order is made by a magistrates' court, the period referred to in head (2) above must not exceed five years[7]. Otherwise, that period must not exceed:

(a)   if the person is sentenced to imprisonment for life, 20 years[8]; or

(b)   otherwise, 15 years[9].

A financial reporting order is not a 'penalty' for the purposes of the prohibition[10] against retrospective laws[11].

1   The Serious Organised Crime and Police Act 2005 ss 79–81 (see the text and notes 2–11; and PARAS 338–340) are repealed, as from a day to be appointed, by the Serious Crime Act 2015 Sch 4 para 71. At the date at which this volume states the law no day had been appointed for this purpose.

2   As to the offences in relation to which financial reporting orders may be made see PARA 337.

3   Serious Organised Crime and Police Act 2005 s 76(1) (prospectively repealed: see note 1). As to the effect of financial reporting orders see PARA 338. A financial reporting order is a preventative

measure and not a penalty for the purposes of the Convention for the Protection of Human Rights and Fundamental Freedoms (Rome, 4 November 1950; TS 71 (1953); Cmd 8969) art 7 (prohibition of retrospective laws: see RIGHTS AND FREEDOMS vol 88A (2013) PARAS 301–316): see *R v Adams* [2008] EWCA Crim 914, [2008] 4 All ER 574, [2009] 1 WLR 310, obiter per Latham LJ; *R v Wright* [2008] EWCA Crim 3207, [2009] 2 Cr App Rep (S) 313, [2009] Crim LR 373.

4 Serious Organised Crime and Police Act 2005 s 76(2) (prospectively repealed: see note 1). In connection with the assessment of this risk see *R v Wright* [2008] EWCA Crim 3207, [2009] 2 Cr App Rep (S) 313, [2009] Crim LR 373.

5 Serious Organised Crime and Police Act 2005 s 76(5)(a) (prospectively repealed: see note 1).

6 Serious Organised Crime and Police Act 2005 s 76(5)(b) (prospectively repealed: see note 1).

7 Serious Organised Crime and Police Act 2005 s 76(6) (prospectively repealed: see note 1).

8 Serious Organised Crime and Police Act 2005 s 76(7)(a) (prospectively repealed: see note 1).

9 Serious Organised Crime and Police Act 2005 s 76(7)(b) (prospectively repealed: see note 1).

10 Ie under the Convention for the Protection of Human Rights and Fundamental Freedoms (Rome, 4 November 1950; TS 71 (1953); Cmd 8969), art 7.1 (see RIGHTS AND FREEDOMS vol 88A (2013) PARA 301).

11 See *R v Adams* [2008] EWCA Crim 914, [2008] 4 All ER 574.

337. Offences in relation to which financial reporting orders may be made. Until a day to be appointed[1] the offences in relation to which financial reporting orders[2] may be made are:

(1) fraud[3];

(2) obtaining services dishonestly[4];

(3) a common law offence of conspiracy to defraud[5];

(4) false accounting[6];

(5) 'lifestyle offences' under proceeds of crime legislation[7];

(6) bribing another person[8];

(7) offences relating to being bribed[9];

(8) bribery of foreign public officials[10];

(9) assisting another to retain the benefit of criminal conduct[11];

(10) acquisition, possession or use of proceeds of criminal conduct[12];

(11) concealing or transferring proceeds of criminal conduct[13];

(12) concealing or transferring proceeds of drug trafficking[14];

(13) assisting another person to retain the benefit of drug trafficking[15];

(14) acquisition, possession or use of proceeds of drug trafficking[16];

(15) fund-raising for purposes of terrorism[17];

(16) use and possession of money etc for purposes of terrorism[18];

(17) funding arrangements for purposes of terrorism[19];

(18) money laundering in connection with terrorism[20];

(19) acquisition, use and possession of criminal property[21];

(20) a common law offence of cheating in relation to the public revenue[22];

(21) fraudulent evasion of duty[23];

(22) offences relating to value added tax[24];

(23) fraudulent evasion of income tax[25];

(24) tax credit fraud[26];

(25) attempting, conspiring in or inciting, or aiding, abetting, counselling or procuring, the commission of an offence mentioned in heads (1), (4) or (6) to (25)[27].

1 The Serious Organised Crime and Police Act 2005 ss 79–81 (see the text and notes 2–27; and PARAS 336, 338–340) are repealed, as from a day to be appointed, by the Serious Crime Act 2015 Sch 4 para 71. At the date at which this volume states the law no day had been appointed for this purpose.

2 See PARA 336.

3 Serious Organised Crime and Police Act 2005 s 76(3)(aa)(i) (s 76(3)(aa) added by the Fraud Act 2006 Sch 1 para 36). As to this offence see the Fraud Act 2006 s 1; and CRIMINAL LAW vol 25 (2010) PARA 305.

4 Serious Organised Crime and Police Act 2005 s 76(3)(aa)(ii) (as added and prospectively repealed: see notes 1, 3). As to this offence see the Fraud Act 2006 s 11; and CRIMINAL LAW vol 25 (2010) PARA 309.

5 Serious Organised Crime and Police Act 2005 s 76(3)(ab) (s 76(3)(ab), (ac), (d)–(q) added by SI 2007/1392; prospectively repealed (see note 1)). As to this offence see CRIMINAL LAW vol 25 (2010) PARA 80.
The Serious Organised Crime and Police Act 2005 (Amendment of Section 76(3)) Order 2007, SI 2007/1392, is made under the Serious Organised Crime and Police Act 2005 s 76(4) (as so prospectively repealed), which provides that the Secretary of State may by order amend s 76(3) so as to remove an offence from it or add an offence to it.

6 Serious Organised Crime and Police Act 2005 s 76(3)(ac) (as added and prospectively repealed: see notes 1, 3). As to this offence see CRIMINAL LAW vol 25 (2010) PARA 311.

7 Serious Organised Crime and Police Act 2005 s 76(3)(c) (prospectively repealed: see note 1). As to these offences see the Proceeds of Crime Act 2002 Sch 2; and PARA 230.

8 Serious Organised Crime and Police Act 2005 s 76(3)(da)(i) (s 76(3)(da) added by the Bribery Act 2010 Sch 1 para 9; prospectively repealed (see note 1)). As to this offence see s 1; and CRIMINAL LAW vol 26 (2010) PARA 459.

9 Serious Organised Crime and Police Act 2005 s 76(3)(da)(ii) (as added and prospectively repealed: see notes 1, 8). As to this offence see the Bribery Act 2010 s 2; and CRIMINAL LAW vol 26 (2010) PARA 459.

10 Serious Organised Crime and Police Act 2005 s 76(3)(da)(iii) (as added and prospectively repealed: see notes 1, 8). As to this offence see the Bribery Act 2010 s 6; and CRIMINAL LAW vol 26 (2010) PARA 460.

11 Serious Organised Crime and Police Act 2005 s 76(3)(g) (as added and prospectively repealed: see notes 1, 5). This offence was previously enacted under the Criminal Justice Act 1988 s 93A (repealed).

12 Serious Organised Crime and Police Act 2005 s 76(3)(g) (as added and prospectively repealed: see notes 1, 5). This offence was previously enacted under the Criminal Justice Act 1988 s 93B (repealed).

13 Serious Organised Crime and Police Act 2005 s 76(3)(g) (as added and prospectively repealed: see notes 1, 5). This offence was previously enacted under the Criminal Justice Act 1988 s 93C (repealed).

14 Serious Organised Crime and Police Act 2005 s 76(3)(h) (as added and prospectively repealed: see notes 1, 5). This offence was previously enacted under the Drug Trafficking Act 1994 s 49 (repealed).

15 Serious Organised Crime and Police Act 2005 s 76(3)(h) (as added and prospectively repealed: see notes 1, 5). This offence was previously enacted under the Drug Trafficking Act 1994 s 50 (repealed).

16 Serious Organised Crime and Police Act 2005 s 76(3)(h) (as added and prospectively repealed: see notes 1, 5). This offence was previously enacted under the Drug Trafficking Act 1994 s 51 (repealed).

17 Serious Organised Crime and Police Act 2005 s 76(3)(i) (as added and prospectively repealed: see notes 1, 5). As to this offence see the Terrorism Act 2000 s 15; and CRIMINAL LAW vol 25 (2010) PARA 379.

18 Serious Organised Crime and Police Act 2005 s 76(3)(i) (as added and prospectively repealed: see notes 1, 5). As to this offence see the Terrorism Act 2000 s 16; and CRIMINAL LAW vol 25 (2010) PARA 380.

19 Serious Organised Crime and Police Act 2005 s 76(3)(i) (as added and prospectively repealed: see notes 1, 5). As to this offence see the Terrorism Act 2000 s 17; and CRIMINAL LAW vol 25 (2010) PARA 381.

20 Serious Organised Crime and Police Act 2005 s 76(3)(i) (as added and prospectively repealed: see notes 1, 5). As to this offence see the Terrorism Act 2000 s 18; and CRIMINAL LAW vol 25 (2010) PARA 382.

21 Serious Organised Crime and Police Act 2005 s 76(3)(j) (as added and prospectively repealed: see notes 1, 5). As to these offences see the Proceeds of Crime Act 2002 s 329; and CRIMINAL LAW vol 26 (2010) PARA 746.

22 Serious Organised Crime and Police Act 2005 s 76(3)(k) (as added and prospectively repealed: see notes 1, 5).

23 Serious Organised Crime and Police Act 2005 s 76(3)(l) (as added and prospectively repealed: see notes 1, 5). As to these offences see the Customs and Excise Management Act 1979 s 170; and CUSTOMS AND EXCISE vol 31 (2012) PARA 1175.

24 Serious Organised Crime and Police Act 2005 s 76(3)(m) (as added and prospectively repealed: see notes 1, 5). As to these offences see the Value Added Tax Act 1994 s 72; and VALUE ADDED TAX vol 99 (2012) PARAS 403–405.

25 Serious Organised Crime and Police Act 2005 s 76(3)(n) (as added and prospectively repealed (see notes 1, 5)); amended by the Taxation (International and Other Provisions) Act 2010 Sch 7 para 99). As to these offences see the Taxes Management Act 1970 s 106A; and INCOME TAXATION vol 59 (2014) PARA 2316.

26 Serious Organised Crime and Police Act 2005 s 76(3)(o) (as added and prospectively repealed: see notes 1, 5). As to these offences see the Tax Credits Act 2002 s 35; and WELFARE BENEFITS AND STATE PENSIONS vol 104 (2014) PARA 367.

27 Serious Organised Crime and Police Act 2005 s 76(3)(p), (q) (as added and prospectively repealed: see notes 1, 5).

338. Effect of financial reporting orders. Until a day to be appointed[1] a person in relation to whom a financial reporting order[2] has effect must:

(1) make a report in respect of:

    (a) the period of a length specified[3] in the order beginning with the date on which the order comes into force[4]; and

    (b) subsequent periods of specified lengths, each period beginning immediately after the end of the previous one[5];

(2) set out in each report, in the specified manner, such particulars of his financial affairs relating to the period in question as may be specified[6];

(3) include any specified documents with each report[7];

(4) make each report within the specified number of days after the end of the period in question[8]; and

(5) make each report to the specified person[9].

A person who without reasonable excuse includes false or misleading information in a report, or otherwise fails to comply with any of these requirements, is guilty of an offence[10].

1 The Serious Organised Crime and Police Act 2005 ss 79–81 (see the text and notes 2–10; and PARAS 336–337, 339–340) are repealed, as from a day to be appointed, by the Serious Crime Act 2015 Sch 4 para 71. At the date at which this volume states the law no day had been appointed for this purpose.

2 See PARA 336; and as to the offences in relation to which a financial reporting order may be made see PARA 337. Where a court makes a financial reporting order it must state precisely what is required in terms of reporting and must demonstrate why such conditions are necessary: see *R v Mullen* [2012] EWCA Crim 606.

3 In the Serious Organised Crime and Police Act 2005 s 79, 'specified' means specified by the court in the order: s 79(8) (prospectively repealed: see note 1).

4 Serious Organised Crime and Police Act 2005 s 79(1), (2)(a) (prospectively repealed: see note 1). Rules of court may provide for the maximum length of the periods which may be specified under s 79(2): s 79(7) (as so prospectively repealed).

5 Serious Organised Crime and Police Act 2005 s 79(2)(b) (prospectively repealed: see note 1). See note 3.

6 Serious Organised Crime and Police Act 2005 s 79(3) (prospectively repealed: see note 1).

7 Serious Organised Crime and Police Act 2005 s 79(4) (prospectively repealed: see note 1).

8 Serious Organised Crime and Police Act 2005 s 79(5) (prospectively repealed: see note 1).

9 Serious Organised Crime and Police Act 2005 s 79(6) (prospectively repealed: see note 1).

10 Serious Organised Crime and Police Act 2005 s 79(10)(a)(i), (b) (prospectively repealed: see note 1). A person who commits this offence is liable on summary conviction to imprisonment for a term not exceeding 51 weeks or to a fine not exceeding level 5 on the standard scale or to both: s 79(10) (as so prospectively repealed). As to the standard scale, the statutory maximum, the prescribed sum, and magistrates' powers to levy unlimited fines see PARA 176.

339.   Variation and revocation of financial reporting orders.   Until a day to be appointed[1] an application for the variation or revocation of a financial reporting order[2] may be made by:

(1)   the person in respect of whom it has been made[3]; and

(2)   the person[4] to whom reports are to be made under it[5].

The application must be made to the court which made the order[6]. However, if the order was made on appeal, the application must be made to the court which originally sentenced the person in respect of whom the order was made[7]. If (in either case) that court was a magistrates' court, the application may be made to any magistrates' court acting in the same local justice area as that court[8].

1   The Serious Organised Crime and Police Act 2005 ss 79–81 (see the text and notes 2–8; and PARAS 336–338, 340) are repealed, as from a day to be appointed, by the Serious Crime Act 2015 Sch 4 para 71. At the date at which this volume states the law no day had been appointed for this purpose.

2   See PARA 336; and as to the offences in relation to which a financial reporting order may be made see PARA 337. As to the effect of financial reporting orders see PARA 338.

3   Serious Organised Crime and Police Act 2005 s 80(1)(a) (prospectively repealed: see note 1).

4   Ie the person to whom reports are to be made under the Serious Organised Crime and Police Act 2005 s 79(6) (see PARA 338).

5   Serious Organised Crime and Police Act 2005 s 80(1)(b) (prospectively repealed: see note 1).

6   Serious Organised Crime and Police Act 2005 s 80(2) (prospectively repealed: see note 1).

7   Serious Organised Crime and Police Act 2005 s 80(3) (prospectively repealed: see note 1).

8   Serious Organised Crime and Police Act 2005 s 80(4) (prospectively repealed: see note 1).

340.   Verification and disclosure.   Until a day to be appointed[1], the specified person[2] may, for the purpose of:

(1)   checking the accuracy of a report[3] or of any other report made pursuant to the same financial reporting order[4]; or

(2)   discovering the true position[5],

disclose a report to any person who he reasonably believes may be able to contribute to doing either of those things[6].

Any other person may disclose information to:

(a)   the specified person[7]; or

(b)   a person to whom the specified person has disclosed a report[8],

for the purpose of contributing to doing either of the things mentioned in head (1) or head (2) above[9].

The specified person may also disclose a report for the purposes of:

(i)   the prevention, detection, investigation or prosecution of criminal offences, whether in the United Kingdom[10] or elsewhere[11];

(ii)   the prevention, detection or investigation of conduct for which penalties other than criminal penalties are provided under the law of any part of the United Kingdom or of any country or territory outside the United Kingdom[12].

1   The Serious Organised Crime and Police Act 2005 ss 79–81 (see the text and notes 2–12; and PARAS 336–339) are repealed, as from a day to be appointed, by the Serious Crime Act 2015 Sch 4 para 71. At the date at which this volume states the law no day had been appointed for this purpose.

2   In the Serious Organised Crime and Police Act 2005 s 81, 'specified person' means the person to whom reports under a financial reporting order (see PARA 336) are to be made: s 81(1) (prospectively repealed: see note 1).

3   In the Serious Organised Crime and Police Act 2005 s 81, references to a report include any of its contents, any document included with the report, or any of the contents of such a document: s 81(8) (prospectively repealed: see note 1).

4   Serious Organised Crime and Police Act 2005 s 81(4)(a) (prospectively repealed: see note 1).
5   Serious Organised Crime and Police Act 2005 s 81(4)(b) (prospectively repealed: see note 1).
6   Serious Organised Crime and Police Act 2005 s 81(2) (prospectively repealed: see note 1). A disclosure under s 81 does not breach any obligation of confidence owed by the person making the disclosure (s 81(6)(a) (as so prospectively repealed)) or any other restriction on the disclosure of information (however imposed) (s 81(6)(b) (as so prospectively repealed)). However, nothing in s 81 authorises a disclosure, in contravention of any provisions of the Data Protection Act 1998, of personal data which are not exempt from those provisions: Serious Organised Crime and Police Act 2005 s 81(7) (as so prospectively repealed). As to the Data Protection Act 1998 see CONFIDENCE AND INFORMATIONAL PRIVACY vol 19 (2011) PARA 95 et seq.
7   Serious Organised Crime and Police Act 2005 s 81(3)(a) (prospectively repealed: see note 1).
8   Serious Organised Crime and Police Act 2005 s 81(3)(b) (prospectively repealed: see note 1).
9   Serious Organised Crime and Police Act 2005 s 81(3) (prospectively repealed: see note 1).
10   As to the meaning of 'United Kingdom' see PARA 4 note 3.
11   Serious Organised Crime and Police Act 2005 s 81(5)(a) (prospectively repealed: see note 1).
12   Serious Organised Crime and Police Act 2005 s 81(5)(b) (prospectively repealed: see note 1).

(iv)   Football Banning Orders made on Conviction

341.   Football banning orders and regulated football matches. A football banning order (or banning order) is an order made by the court[1] which:

(1)   in relation to regulated football matches in the United Kingdom[2], prohibits the person who is subject to the order from entering any premises for the purpose of attending such matches[3]; and

(2)   in relation to regulated football matches outside the United Kingdom, requires that person to report[4] at a police station[5].

'Regulated football match' means an association football match[6] (whether in the United Kingdom or elsewhere) in which one or both of the participating teams represents:

(a)   a club which is for the time being a member (whether a full or associate member) of the Football League, the Football Association Premier League, the Football Conference, the Welsh Premier League or the Scottish Professional Football League[7];

(b)   a club whose home ground is situated outside England and Wales[8]; or

(c)   a country or territory[9],

and an association football match outside the United Kingdom involving:

(i)   a national team appointed by the Football Association to represent England or appointed by the Football Association of Wales to represent Wales[10];

(ii)   a team representing a club which is for the time being a full or associate member of the Football League, the Football Association Premier League, the Football Conference, the Welsh Premier League or the Scottish Professional Football League[11];

(iii)   a team representing any country or territory whose football association is for the time being a member of FIFA[12] where the match is part of a competition or tournament organised by, or under the authority of, FIFA or UEFA[13] and the competition or tournament is one in which a national team appointed by the Football Association to represent England or appointed by the Football Association of Wales to represent Wales is eligible to participate or has participated[14]; or

(iv)   a team representing a club which is for the time being a full or associate member of, or affiliated to, a national football association which is a member of FIFA, where the match is part of a competition or tournament organised by, or under the authority of, FIFA or UEFA, and the competition or tournament is one in which a team representing a club which is for the time being a full or associate member of the Football League, the Football Association Premier League, the Football Conference, the Welsh Premier League or the Scottish Professional Football League is eligible to participate or has participated[15].

1   Ie under the Football Spectators Act 1989 Pt II (ss 14–22A). A football banning order may be made on conviction in criminal proceedings (see s 14A; and PARA 344) and following convictions for offences committed outside England and Wales (see s 22; and PARA 346), and may also be made without a conviction on a complaint (see s 14B; and PARA 398) or on the application of a constable (see s 21A; and PARA 399). A football banning order is a preventative, not a punitive, measure: see *R v Doyle* [2012] EWCA Crim 995, [2013] 1 Cr App Rep (S) 197. For procedural rules in connection with the making of football banning orders see the Criminal Procedure Rules 2015, SI 2015/1490, Pt 31.
2   As to the meaning of 'United Kingdom' see PARA 4 note 3.
3   Football Spectators Act 1989 s 14(1), (4)(a) (s 14 substituted by the Football (Disorder) Act 2000 Sch 1 paras 1, 2; Football Spectators Act 1989 s 14(2), (4) amended by the Policing and Crime Act 2009 s 103(1), (2)(a)).
4   Ie in accordance with the Football Spectators Act 1989 Pt II.
5   Football Spectators Act 1989 s 14(4)(b) (as substituted and amended: see note 3).
6   References to 'football matches' are to football matches played or intended to be played: Football Spectators Act 1989 s 14(7) (as substituted: see note 3). A 'regulated football match' includes an association football match played in the Football Association Cup (other than in a preliminary or qualifying round): s 14(2) (as so substituted and amended); Football Spectators (Prescription) Order 2004, SI 2004/2409, art 3(3) (art 3(1) amended, art 3(3) added, by SI 2010/584).
7   Football Spectators (Prescription) Order 2004, SI 2004/2409, art 3(1), (2)(a) (as amended (see note 6); arts 1(2), 3(2), 4(2) substituted by SI 2006/761; Football Spectators (Prescription) Order 2004, SI 2004/2409, arts 3(2)(a), (b), 4(2)(b), (e) amended by SI 2010/584, SI 2013/1709).
8   Football Spectators (Prescription) Order 2004, SI 2004/2409, art 3(2)(b) (as substituted and amended: see note 7).
9   Football Spectators (Prescription) Order 2004, SI 2004/2409, art 3(2)(c) (as substituted: see note 7).
10 Football Spectators (Prescription) Order 2004, SI 2004/2409, art 4(1), (2)(a) (as substituted: see note 7).
11 Football Spectators (Prescription) Order 2004, SI 2004/2409, art 4(2)(b) (as substituted and amended: see note 7).
12 'FIFA' means the Federation Internationale de Football Associations: Football Spectators (Prescription) Order 2004, SI 2004/2409, art 1(2) (as substituted: see note 7).
13 'UEFA' means the Union des Associations Europeennes de Football: Football Spectators (Prescription) Order 2004, SI 2004/2409, art 1(2) (as substituted: see note 7)
14 Football Spectators (Prescription) Order 2004, SI 2004/2409, art 4(2)(c) (as substituted: see note 7).
15 Football Spectators (Prescription) Order 2004, SI 2004/2409, art 4(2)(d) (as substituted: see note 7).

342.   Offences in connection with which football banning orders may be made. An offence in connection with which a football banning order[1] may be made (ie a 'relevant offence') is:

(1)   an offence[2] of failure to comply with a football banning order[3];
(2)   an offence of failure to comply with a requirement imposed by the enforcing authority[4];
(3)   an offence of making a false or misleading statement in an application to be exempt from reporting requirements[5];
(4)   an offence of failure to comply with a notice given in connection with the prevention of violence or disorder[6] at or in connection with a regulated football match[7];
(5)   an offence relating to the control of alcohol at sporting events[8];

(6)   an offence of harassment, alarm or distress or hatred by reference to race etc[9];

(7)   an offence involving the use or threat of violence by the accused towards another person or property[10];

(8)   an offence involving the use, carrying or possession of an offensive weapon or a firearm[11];

(9)   an offence of being found drunk in a highway or other public place[12];

(10)   an offence of disorderly behaviour while drunk in a public place[13];

(11)   an offence relating to the possession of alcohol on coaches or trains to or from sporting events[14];

(12)   an offence of driving when under the influence of drink or drugs or with an alcohol concentration above the prescribed limit[15];

(13)   any offence under the Football (Offences) Act 1991[16]; or

(14)   an offence involving the sale of tickets by unauthorised persons which relates to tickets for a football match[17].

Her Majesty may by Order in Council specify offences ('corresponding offences') under the law of any country outside England and Wales which appear to Her to correspond to any of the offences described above[18].

1   As to the meaning of 'football banning order' see PARA 341; as to the making of a football banning order on conviction see PARA 344.

2   Any reference to an 'offence' in the Football Spectators Act 1989 Sch 1 para 1 includes a reference to any attempt, conspiracy or incitement to commit that offence and a reference to aiding and abetting, counselling or procuring the commission of that offence: s 14(8), Sch 1 para 2 (s 14, Sch 1 substituted, s 14C added, by the Football (Disorder) Act 2000 Sch 1 paras 1, 2, 5).

3   Football Spectators Act 1989 Sch 1 para 1(a) (as substituted: see note 2). The offence referred to in the text is an offence under s 14J(1) (see PARA 347).

4   Football Spectators Act 1989 Sch 1 para 1(a) (as substituted (see note 2); amended by the Policing and Crime Act 2009 s 107). The offence referred to in the text is an offence under the Football Spectators Act 1989 s 19(6) (see SPORTS LAW vol 96 (2012) PARA 125).

5   Football Spectators Act 1989 Sch 1 para 1(a) (as substituted and amended: see notes 2, 4). The offence referred to in the text is an offence under the Football Spectators Act 1989 s 20(10) (see SPORTS LAW vol 96 (2012) PARA 125).

6   For these purposes 'violence' means violence against persons or property and includes threatening violence and doing anything which endangers the life of any person; and 'disorder' includes:

      (1)   stirring up hatred against a group of persons defined by reference to colour, race, nationality (including citizenship) or ethnic or national origins, or against an individual as a member of such a group (Football Spectators Act 1989 s 14C(1), (2)(a) (as added: see note 2));

      (2)   using threatening, abusive or insulting words or behaviour or disorderly behaviour (s 14C(2)(b) (as so added)); and

      (3)   displaying any writing or other thing which is threatening, abusive or insulting (s 14C(2)(c) (as so added)).

    'Violence' and 'disorder' are not limited to violence or disorder in connection with football: s 14C(3) (as so added).

7   Football Spectators Act 1989 Sch 1 para 1(a) (as substituted: see note 2). The offence referred to in the text is an offence under s 21C(2) (see PARA 399). For the purposes of Sch 1 'football match' means a match which is a regulated football match for the purposes of Pt II (ss 14–22A: see PARA 341 et seq): Sch 1 para 4(1) (as so substituted). As to the meaning of 'regulated football match' see PARA 341.

8   Football Spectators Act 1989 Sch 1 para 1(b) (as substituted: see note 2). The offence referred to in the text is an offence under the Sporting Events (Control of Alcohol etc) Act 1985 s 2 or s 2A (alcohol, containers and fireworks: see SPORTS LAW vol 96 (2012) PARAS 131, 132) committed by the accused at any football match to which the Football Spectators Act 1989 Sch 1 applies or while entering or trying to enter the ground: Sch 1 para 1(b) (as so substituted).

9   Football Spectators Act 1989 Sch 1 para 1(c), (k), (q) (as substituted (see note 2); and amended by the Violent Crime Reduction Act 2006 Sch 3 paras 1, 9; and by the Criminal Justice and

Immigration Act 2008 Sch 26 para 26). The offences referred to in the text is an offence under the Public Order Act 1986 s 4A or s 5 or any provision of Pt 3 (ss 17–29) or Pt 3A (ss 29A–29N) (see CRIMINAL LAW vol 26 (2010) PARAS 491–519):

(1) committed during a period relevant to a football match to which the Football Spectators Act 1989 Sch 1 applies at any premises while the accused was at, or was entering or leaving or trying to enter or leave, the premises (Sch 1 para 1(c) (as so substituted and amended));

(2) committed while the accused was on a journey to or from a football match to which to which Sch 1 applies, being an offence as respects which the court makes a declaration that the offence related to football matches (a 'declaration of relevance': see PARA 343) (Sch 1 para 1(k) (as so substituted and amended)); or

(3) any such offence not falling within Sch 1 para 1(c) or (k) which was committed during a period relevant to a football match to which Sch 1 applies and as respects which the court makes a declaration that the offence related to that match or to that match and any other football match which took place during that period (Sch 1 para 1(q) (as so substituted and amended)).

For the purposes of Sch 1 each of the following periods is 'relevant to' a football match to which Sch 1 applies:

(a) in the case of a match which takes place on the day on which it is advertised to take place, the period beginning 24 hours before whichever is the earlier of the start of the match and the time at which it was advertised to start and ending 24 hours after it ends (Sch 1 para 4(2)(a) (as so substituted; Sch 1 para 4(2) further substituted by the Violent Crime Reduction Act 2006 Sch 3 para 13)); and

(b) in the case of a match which does not take place on the day on which it was advertised to take place, the period beginning 24 hours before the time at which it was advertised to start on that day and ending 24 hours after that time (Football Spectators Act 1989 Sch 1 para 4(2)(b) (as so substituted)).

For the purposes of Sch 1 para 1(g)–(o) a person may be regarded as having been on a journey to or from a football match to which Sch 1 applies whether or not he attended or intended to attend the match, and a person's journey includes breaks (including overnight breaks): Sch 1 para 3 (as so substituted). Where the person's being on a 'journey' to a football match is stipulated, it is insufficient to show that he was on such a journey: his behaviour must also be 'related to football matches' (see PARA 343): *R v Doyle* [2012] EWCA Crim 995, [2013] 1 Cr App Rep (S) 197.

10 Football Spectators Act 1989 Sch 1 para 1(d), (e), (m), (n), (r), (s) (as substituted: see note 2). The offence must be:

(1) committed during a period relevant to a football match to which Sch 1 applies at any premises while the accused was at, or was entering or leaving or trying to enter or leave, the premises (Sch 1 para 1(d), (e) (as so substituted));

(2) committed while the accused (or one or each of the accused or the victim) was on a journey (see note 9) to or from a football match to which Sch 1 applies being an offence as respects which the court makes a declaration of relevance (Sch 1 para 1(m), (n) (as so substituted)); or

(3) any such offence not falling within Sch 1 para 1(d), (e), (m) or (n) which was committed during a period relevant to a football match to which Sch 1 applies and as respects which the court makes a declaration that the offence related to that match or to that match and any other football match which took place during that period (Sch 1 para 1(r), (s) (as so substituted and amended)).

Although not specifically referred to in Sch 1, an offence under the Public Order Act 1986 s 4 (fear or provocation of violence: see CRIMINAL LAW vol 26 (2010) PARA 490) would clearly fall within this provision: see *R v O'Keefe* [2003] EWCA Crim 2629, [2004] 1 Cr App Rep (S) 402.

11 Football Spectators Act 1989 Sch 1 para 1(f), (o), (t) (as substituted: see note 2). The offence must be:

(1) committed during a period relevant to a football match to which Sch 1 applies at any premises while the accused was at, or was entering or leaving or trying to enter or leave, the premises (Sch 1 para 1(f) (as so substituted));

(2) committed while the accused was on a journey (see note 9) to or from a football match to which Sch 1 applies being an offence as respects which the court makes a declaration of relevance: see PARA 343) (Sch 1 para 1(o) (as so substituted)); or

(3) any such offence not falling within Sch 1 para 1(f) or (o) which was committed during a period relevant to a football match to which Sch 1 applies and as respects which the

court makes a declaration that the offence related to that match or to that match and any other football match which took place during that period (Sch 1 para 1(t) (as so substituted and amended)).

12 Football Spectators Act 1989 Sch 1 para 1(g) (as substituted: see note 2). The offence referred to in the text is an offence under the Licensing Act 1872 s 12 (see ROAD TRAFFIC vol 90 (2011) PARA 734) committed while the accused was on a journey (see note 9) to or from a football match to which the Football Spectators Act 1989 Sch 1 applies being an offence as respects which the court makes a declaration of relevance: Sch 1 para 1(g) (as so substituted).

13 Football Spectators Act 1989 Sch 1 para 1(h) (as substituted: see note 2). The offence referred to in the text is an offence under the Criminal Justice Act 1967 s 91(1) (see CRIMINAL LAW vol 26 (2010) PARA 521) committed in a highway or other public place while the accused was on a journey (see note 9) to or from a football match to which the Football Spectators Act 1989 Sch 1 applies being an offence as respects which the court makes a declaration of relevance: Sch 1 para 1(h) (as so substituted).

14 Football Spectators Act 1989 Sch 1 para 1(j) (as substituted: see note 2). The offence referred to in the text is an offence under the Sporting Events (Control of Alcohol etc) Act 1985 s 1 (see SPORTS LAW vol 96 (2012) PARA 129) committed while the accused was on a journey (see note 9) to or from a football match to which the Football Spectators Act 1989 Sch 1 applies being an offence as respects which the court makes a declaration of relevance: Sch 1 para 1(j) (as so substituted).

15 Football Spectators Act 1989 Sch 1 para 1(l) (as substituted (see note 2); amended by the Crime and Courts Act 2013 Sch 22 para 15). The offence referred to in the text is an offence under the Road Traffic Act 1988 s 4, 5 or 5A (see ROAD TRAFFIC vol 90 (2011) PARAS 732, 735) committed while the accused was on a journey (see note 9) to or from a football match to which the Football Spectators Act 1989 Sch 1 applies being an offence as respects which the court makes a declaration of relevance: Sch 1 para 1(l) (as so substituted and amended).

16 Football Spectators Act 1989 Sch 1 para 1(p) (as substituted: see note 2). As to the Football Offences Act 1991 see CRIMINAL LAW vol 26 (2010) PARA 552.

17 Football Spectators Act 1989 Sch 1 para 1(u) (as substituted: see note 2). As to this offence see the Criminal Justice and Public Order Act 1994 s 166; and SPORTS LAW vol 96 (2012) PARA 126.

18 Football Spectators Act 1989 s 22(1) (s 22(1), (1A) amended by the Football (Disorder) Act 2000 Sch 2 paras 9, 17). For this purpose an offence specified in an Order in Council under the Football Spectators Act 1989 s 22(1) will be regarded as corresponding to an offence to which Sch 1 (see the text and notes 1–17) applies notwithstanding that any period specified in the Order is longer than any corresponding period specified in Sch 1: s 22(1A) (s 22(1A) added, s 22(9)–(11) substituted, by the Football (Offences and Disorder) Act 1999s 5(1), (2), (5); as so amended). 'Country' includes territory: Football Spectators Act 1989 s 22A(1) (s 22A added by the Football (Disorder) Act 2000 Sch 2 paras 9, 18). An Order in Council under the Football Spectators Act 1989 s 22(1) relating to any country may include provision specifying the documentary form in which details are to be given of the conviction of a person in that country of a corresponding offence, the nature and circumstances of the offence, and whether or not the conviction is the subject of proceedings in that country questioning it: s 22(9) (as so substituted). A document in the form so specified is admissible in any proceedings under the Football Spectators Act 1989 Pt II as evidence of the facts stated in it unless the contrary is proved, and must be taken as such a document unless the contrary is proved: s 22(10) (as so substituted). In proceedings against a person under s 22 the facts stated in a document in the form so specified must, on production of the document and proof that that person is the person whose conviction is set out in the document, be taken to be proved unless the contrary is proved: s 22(11) (as so substituted). At the date at which this volume states the law no corresponding offence were specified for the purposes of these provisions.

343. Declarations of relevance. In relation to certain offences for which a football banning order may be made[1] the court is required to make a 'declaration of relevance', ie a declaration that the offence related to football matches or to one or more particular football matches[2]. The requirement that an offence be 'related to football matches' means that what falls to be determined is not the legal character of the offence, but whether it was related to the match or matches, which is left to the discretion of the judge, on the particular facts before him[3].

A court may not in general make a declaration of relevance as respects any offence unless it is satisfied that the prosecutor gave notice to the defendant, at least five days before the first day of the trial, that it was proposed to show that the offence related to football matches, to a particular football match or to particular football matches (as the case may be)[4], although the court may, in any particular case, make a declaration of relevance notwithstanding that such notice has not been given if the defendant consents to waive the giving of full notice or the court is satisfied that the interests of justice do not require more notice to be given[5]. A person convicted of an offence as respects which the court makes a declaration of relevance may appeal against the making of the declaration of relevance as if the declaration were included in any sentence passed on him for the offence[6], and a banning order made upon a person's conviction of a relevant offence must be quashed if the making of a declaration of relevance as respects that offence is reversed on appeal[7].

1 As to the meaning of 'football banning order' see PARA 341. As to the offences in connection with which football banning orders may be made see PARA 342. As to the making of football banning orders on conviction see PARA 344.

2 Football Spectators Act 1989 s 23(5) (amended by the Violent Crime Reduction Act 2006 Sch 3 para 12). See the Football Spectators Act 1989 Sch 1 paras (g), (h), (j)–(o), (q)–(t); and PARA 342.

3 See *R v Doyle* [2012] EWCA Crim 995, [2013] 1 Cr App Rep (S) 197; see also *R v Smith* [2003] EWCA Crim 2480, [2004] 1 Cr App Rep (S) 341; *R v Eliot* [2007] EWCA Crim 1002, [2007] 2 Cr App Rep (S) 430; *R v Mabee* [2007] EWCA Crim 3230, [2008] 2 Cr App Rep (S) 143; *R v Parkes* [2010] EWCA Crim 2803, [2011] 2 Cr App Rep (S) 54 (irrelevant that no match was actually played); *R v Boggild* [2011] EWCA Crim 1928, [2011] 4 All ER 1285, [2012] 1 WLR 1298.

4 Football Spectators Act 1989 s 23(1) (amended by the Football (Offences and Disorder) Act 1999 s 12(2), (3)).

5 Football Spectators Act 1989 s 23(2).

6 Football Spectators Act 1989 s 23(3).

7 Football Spectators Act 1989 s 23(4) (amended by the Football (Disorder) Act 2000 Sch 2 para 10).

344. Making of football banning orders on conviction. Where a person (the 'offender') is convicted of a relevant offence[1] the court[2] must make a football banning order[3] in relation to him if satisfied that there are reasonable grounds for believing that making such an order in relation to the offender would help to prevent violence or disorder[4] at or in connection with any regulated football matches[5]. This condition clearly contemplates that there must be a risk of repetition of violence or disorder at a football match before it is met, although it is not automatically satisfied merely because the instant offence is football-related[6]. There is no necessity for either repetition or propensity before the court is able to make a football banning order[7]. For the purpose of deciding whether to make a football banning order under these provisions the court may consider evidence led by the prosecution and evidence led by the defence[8], and it is immaterial whether the evidence would have been admissible in the proceedings in which the offender was convicted[9]. A court considering the making of a football banning order is entitled to take into account and give weight to the question of the deterrent effect of the order on other persons[10].

A banning order may only be made in addition to a sentence imposed in respect of the relevant offence or in addition to an order conditionally discharging an offender[11].

The prosecution has a right of appeal against a failure by the court to make a banning order under these provisions[12].

1 For the offences which are 'relevant' for these purposes see the Football Spectators Act 1989 Sch 1; and PARA 342. A football banning order is not an inevitable consequence of a football-related conviction: the judge is entitled to consider other appropriate sentences: see *R v Boggild* [2011] EWCA Crim 1928, [2011] 4 All ER 1285, [2012] 1 WLR 1298.

2 For this purpose the 'court' in relation to an offender means the court by or before which he is convicted of the relevant offence or, if he is committed to the Crown Court to be dealt with for that offence, the Crown Court: Football Spectators Act 1989 s 14A(6) (s 14 substituted, ss 14A, 22A added, s 18(1) amended, by the Football (Disorder) Act 2000 Sch 1 paras 1, 2, Sch 2 paras 9, 10, 14, 18).

3 As to the meaning of 'football banning order' see PARA 341. As to the making of football banning orders on conviction for an offence committed outside England and Wales see the Football Spectators Act 1989 s 22; and PARA 346. Where a court makes a banning order the designated officer for the court (in the case of a magistrates' court) or the appropriate officer (in the case of the Crown Court) must:

(1) give a copy of it to the person to whom it relates (s 18(1)(a) (as amended (see note 2); amended by the Courts Act 2003 Sch 8 para 333));

(2) (as soon as reasonably practicable) send a copy of it to the enforcing authority and to any prescribed person (Football Spectators Act 1989 s 18(1)(b) (as so amended));

(3) as soon as reasonably practicable send a copy of it to the police station (addressed to the officer responsible for the police station) at which the person subject to the order is to report initially (s 18(1)(c) (as so amended)); and

(4) in a case where the person subject to the order is detained in legal custody, as soon as reasonably practicable send a copy of it to the person in whose custody he is detained (s 18(1)(d) (as so amended)).

'Enforcing authority' means a prescribed organisation established by the Secretary of State under the Police Act 1996 s 57 (central police organisations: see POLICE AND INVESTIGATORY POWERS vol 84 (2013) PARA 152): Football Spectators Act 1989 s 22A(1) (as added: see note 2). As to the functions of the enforcing authority see ss 19, 21; and SPORTS LAW vol 96 (2012) PARA 125.

4 As to the meanings of 'violence' and 'disorder' see PARA 342 note 6.

5 Football Spectators Act 1989 s 14A(1), (2) (as added: see note 2). As to the meanings of 'regulated football match' and 'football match' see PARA 341. If the court is not so satisfied it must state that fact in open court and give its reasons: s 14A(3) (as so added). As to the meaning of 'open court' see PARA 30 note 7.

6 See *R v Doyle* [2012] EWCA Crim 995, [2013] 1 Cr App Rep (S) 197; *R v Boggild* [2011] EWCA Crim 1928, [2011] 4 All ER 1285, [2012] 1 WLR 1298.

7 See *R (on the application of White) v Crown Court at Blackfriars* [2008] EWHC 510 (Admin), [2008] 2 Cr App Rep (S) 542, [2008] Crim LR 575 (distinguishing the Football Spectators Act 1989 s 14A from s 14B (see PARA 398) in that where the offender has actually been involved in football-related violence constituting an offence, a football banning order would be considered appropriate without any need to evaluate the risk of repeat offending); *R v Hughes* [2005] EWCA Crim 2537, [2006] 1 Cr App Rep (S) 632.

8 Football Spectators Act 1989 s 14A(3A) (as added (see note 2); s 14A(3A), (3B) further added by the Anti-social Behaviour Act 2003 s 86(5)).

9 Football Spectators Act 1989 s 14A(3B) (as added: see notes 2, 8).

10 See *R (on the application of White) v Crown Court at Blackfriars* [2008] EWHC 510 (Admin), [2008] 2 Cr App Rep (S) 542, [2008] Crim LR 575; *R v Curtis* [2009] EWCA Crim 1225, [2010] 1 Cr App Rep (S) 193.

11 Football Spectators Act 1989 s 14A(4) (as added: see note 2). A banning order may be made in addition to a conditional discharge notwithstanding anything in the Powers of Criminal Courts (Sentencing) Act 2000 s 12 (see PARA 443) and s 14 (see PARA 445): Football Spectators Act 1989 s 14A(5) (as so added).

12 Football Spectators Act 1989 s 14A(5A) (as added (see note 2); s 14A(5A)–(5C) further added by the Violent Crime Reduction Act 2006 Sch 3 para 3). Where the failure is by a magistrates' court appeal is to the Crown Court (Football Spectators Act 1989 s 14A(5A)(a) (as so added)) and where the failure is by the Crown Court appeal is to the Court of Appeal (s 14A(5A)(b) (as so added)). Appeal is to the civil division of the Court of Appeal, the criminal division does not have jurisdiction: see *R v Boggild* [2011] EWCA Crim 1928, [2011] 4 All ER 1285, [2012] 1 WLR 1298. An appeal under the Football Spectators Act 1989 s 14A(5A)(b) may be brought only if the Court of Appeal gives permission or the judge who decided not to make an order grants a certificate that his decision is fit for appeal: s 14A(5B) (as so added). An order made on appeal under s 14A (other than one directing that an application be re-heard by the court from

which the appeal was brought) is to be treated for these purposes as if it were an order of the court from which the appeal was brought: s 14A(5C) (as so added).

345. Adjournments. The court may adjourn any proceedings in relation to a football banning order[1] even after sentencing the offender[2]. If the offender does not appear for any adjourned proceedings, the court may further adjourn the proceedings or may issue a warrant for his arrest[3]. The court may not, however, issue a warrant for the offender's arrest unless it is satisfied that he has had adequate notice of the time and place of the adjourned proceedings[4]. If the court adjourns or further adjourns any proceedings[5] the court may remand the offender[6], and a person so remanded may be required by the conditions of his bail not to leave England and Wales before his appearance before the court and, if the control period[7] relates to a regulated football match outside the United Kingdom or to an external tournament which includes such matches, to surrender his passport to a police constable, if he has not already done so[8].

1 Ie an order under the Football Spectators Act 1989 s 14A: see PARA 344.
2 Football Spectators Act 1989 s 14A(4A) (s 14 substituted, s 14A added, by the Football (Disorder) Act 2000 Sch 1 paras 1, 2,; Football Spectators Act 1989 s 14A(4A)–(4C) further added by the Serious Organised Crime and Police Act 2005 s 139(10)).
3 Football Spectators Act 1989 s 14A(4B) (as added: see note 2).
4 Football Spectators Act 1989 s 14A(4C) (as added (see note 2); s 14A(4BA), (4BB) further added, s 14A(4C) amended, by the Violent Crime Reduction Act 2006 Sch 3 paras 1–3, Sch 5).
5 Ie under the Football Spectators Act 1989 s 14A(4A) or (4B) (see the text and notes 1–4).
6 Football Spectators Act 1989 s 14A(4BA) (as added: see notes 2, 4).
7 In relation to a regulated football match outside the United Kingdom 'control period' means the period beginning five days before the day of the match and ending when the match is finished or cancelled: Football Spectators Act 1989 s 14(5) (as substituted (see note 2); s 14(3), (5), (6) amended by the Policing and Crime Act 2009 s 103(1), (2)(a)). In relation to an external tournament (ie a football competition which includes regulated football matches outside the United Kingdom) 'control period' means any period described in an order made by the Secretary of State beginning five days before the day of the first football match outside the United Kingdom which is included in the tournament (leaving out of account any football match included in the qualifying or pre-qualifying stages of the tournament) and ending when the last football match outside the United Kingdom which is included in the tournament is finished or cancelled: Football Spectators Act 1989 s 14(3), (6) (as so substituted and amended). The Secretary of State may, if he considers it necessary or expedient to do so in order to secure the effective enforcement of these provisions, by order provide for s 14(5), (6) to have effect in relation to any, or any description of, regulated football match or external tournament as if, for any reference to five days, there were substituted a reference to the number of days (not exceeding ten) specified in the order: s 22A(2) (as so added). In this regard see the Football Spectators (2014 World Cup Control Period) Order 2014, SI 2014/144.
8 Football Spectators Act 1989 s 14A(4BB) (as added: see notes 2, 4).

346. Football banning orders arising out of offences committed outside England and Wales. Upon an information being laid before a justice of the peace that a person has been convicted of a corresponding offence[1] in a country[2] outside England and Wales, the justice may:

(1) issue a summons directed to that person requiring him to appear before a magistrates' court to answer to the information[3]; or

(2) issue a warrant to arrest that person and bring him before a magistrates' court[4].

Where a person so appears or is so brought before a magistrates' court, the court, if satisfied that he is ordinarily resident in England and Wales, and has been convicted in the country outside England and Wales of the corresponding offence, may, unless it appears that the conviction is the subject of proceedings in a court of law in that country questioning the conviction, make a football banning order[5] in relation to him[6]. A magistrates' court which has power to make a banning order in relation to a person is under a duty to make the order in relation to him if it is satisfied that there are reasonable grounds to believe that making the order would help to prevent violence or disorder[7] at or in connection with regulated football matches[8].

1 Her Majesty may by Order in Council specify offences ('corresponding offences') under the law of any country outside England and Wales which appear to Her to correspond to any of the domestic offences described in the Football Spectators Act 1989 Sch 1: see s 22(1), (1A); and PARA 342.

2 As to the meaning of 'country' see PARA 342 note 18.

3 Football Spectators Act 1989 s 22(2)(a) (s 22(2) amended by the Courts Act 2003 Sch 8 para 335, Sch 10).

4 Football Spectators Act 1989 s 22(2)(b) (as amended: see note 3). Section 22(2)(b) is expressed to be subject to s 22(3), which provides that a warrant may not be issued unless the information is in writing and substantiated on oath.

5 As to the meaning of 'football banning order' see PARA 341.

6 Football Spectators Act 1989 s 22(4) (s 22(4) amended, s 22(5) substituted, s 22(5A) added, by the Football (Offences and Disorder) Act 1999 ss 1(2)(b), 5(1), (3)). In proceedings under the Football Spectators Act 1989 s 22(4) the court has the like powers, including power to adjourn the proceedings and meanwhile to remand the defendant on bail (but not in custody), and the proceedings must be conducted as nearly as may be in the like manner, as if the proceedings were the trial of an information for a summary offence: s 22(6).

7 As to the meanings of 'violence' and 'disorder' see PARA 342 note 6.

8 Football Spectators Act 1989 s 22(5) (as substituted (see note 6); s 22(5), (5A), (7) amended, s 22(8) substituted, by the Football (Disorder) Act 2000 Sch 2 paras 9–11, 17). As to the meanings of 'regulated football match' and 'football match' see PARA 341. Where a magistrates' court has power to make a banning order in relation to a person but does not do so, it must state in open court that it is not satisfied that there are such reasonable grounds and give reasons why it is not satisfied: Football Spectators Act 1989 s 22(5A) (as so added and amended). As to the meaning of 'open court' see PARA 30 note 7. Any person aggrieved by the decision of a magistrates' court making a banning order under these provisions may appeal to the Crown Court against the decision: s 22(7) (as so amended).

The Football Spectators Act 1989 ss 14E–14J (see PARAS 347–348), and ss 18–21 (see PARAS 344, 348; and SPORTS LAW vol 96 (2012) PARA 125) apply in relation to a person subject to a banning order under s 22 as they apply in relation to a person subject to a banning order made by a magistrates' court under s 14A (see PARA 344): s 22(8) (as so substituted).

347. Requirements of banning order. A football banning order[1] must:

(1) require the person subject to the order to report initially at a police station specified in the order within five days beginning with the day upon which the order is made[2];

(2) require the person subject to the order to give notification of specified events[3] to the enforcing authority[4]; and

(3) impose a requirement as to the surrender[5], in connection with regulated football matches[6] outside the United Kingdom, of the passport of the person subject to the order[7].

A banning order may also, if the court making the order thinks fit, impose additional requirements on the person subject to the order in relation to any regulated football matches[8] and the court by which a banning order was made may, on an application[9], vary the order so as to impose, replace or omit any such requirements[10].

A person subject to a banning order who fails to comply with any requirement imposed by the order is guilty of an offence[11], although there is provision for exemption from certain requirements to be granted in some circumstances[12].

1 As to the meaning of 'football banning order' see PARA 341; as to the making of football banning orders on conviction see PARA 344. The restraints imposed by a football banning order

under these provisions are not in themselves unlawful under Council Directive (EC) 2004/38 (OJ L158, 30.4.2004, p 77) on the right of citizens of the union and their family members to move and reside freely within the territory of the member states: see *Gough v Chief Constable of the Derbyshire Constabulary* [2002] EWCA Civ 351, [2002] QB 1213, [2002] 2 All ER 985 (decided under the Football Spectators Act 1989 s 14B (football banning orders made otherwise than on conviction: see PARA 398)). A court considering the making of a football banning order is entitled to take into account and give weight to the question of the deterrent effect of the order on other persons: see *R (on the application of White) v Crown Court at Blackfriars* [2008] EWHC 510 (Admin), [2008] 2 Cr App Rep (S) 542, [2008] Crim LR 575; *R v Curtis* [2009] EWCA Crim 1225, [2010] 1 Cr App Rep (S) 193.

2   Football Spectators Act 1989 s 14E(2) (ss 14E, 14G, 14J added, s 18(3) substituted, by the Football (Disorder) Act 2000 Sch 1 paras 1, 2, Sch 2 paras 9, 14; Football Spectators Act 1989 s 14E(2) amended by the Policing and Crime Act 2009 Sch 8 Pt 11). The police station may be in England, Wales, Scotland or Northern Ireland: Policing and Crime Act 2009 s 104(1), (2)(a). On making the order in relation to the offender the court must explain its effect to him in ordinary language: Football Spectators Act 1989 s 14E(1) (as so added). As to the functions of the officer responsible for the police station to which a person subject to a football banning order reports see ss 19, 21; and SPORTS LAW vol 96 (2012) PARA 125.

In the case of a person detained in legal custody the requirement under s 14E to report at a police station (and any reporting requirements imposed under s 19, as to which see SPORTS LAW vol 96 (2012) PARA 125) is suspended until his release from custody: s 14E(5) (as so added). If he is released from custody more than five days before the expiry of the period for which the order has effect and he was precluded by his being in custody from reporting initially, the order is to have effect as if it required him to report initially at the police station specified in the order within the period of five days beginning with the date of his release: s 14E(6) (as so added).

Where a person subject to a banning order is released from custody and, in the case of a person who has not reported initially to a police station, is released more than five days before the expiry of the banning order, the person in whose custody he is must (as soon as reasonably practicable) give notice of his release to the enforcing authority: s 18(3) (as so substituted). As to the meaning of 'enforcing authority' see PARA 344 note 3.

3   The specified events for the purposes of the Football Spectators Act 1989 s 14E(2A) are:
    (1)   a change of any of his names (Football Spectators Act 1989 s 14E(2B)(a) (s 14E as added (see note 2); s 14E(2A)–(2C), (8) added by the Violent Crime Reduction Act 2006 Sch 3 paras 1, 5));
    (2)   the first use by him after the making of the order of a name for himself that was not disclosed by him at the time of the making of the order (Football Spectators Act 1989 s 14E(2B)(b) (as so added));
    (3)   a change of his home address (s 14E(2B)(c) (as so added));
    (4)   his acquisition of a temporary address (s 14E(2B)(d) (as so added));
    (5)   a change of his temporary address or his ceasing to have one (s 14E(2B)(e) (as so added));
    (6)   his becoming aware of the loss of his passport (s 14E(2B)(f) (as so added; s 14E(2B)(f), (g), (2C)(c), (3) amended by the Identity Documents Act 2010 Schedule paras 3, 4));
    (7)   receipt by him of a new passport (Football Spectators Act 1989 s 14E(2B)(g) (as so added and amended));
    (8)   an appeal made by him in relation to the order (s 14E(2B)(h) (as so added));
    (9)   an application made by him under s 14H(2) (see PARA 348) for termination of the order (s 14E(2B)(i) (as so added)); and
    (10) an appeal made by him under s 23(3) against the making of a declaration of relevance (see PARA 343) in respect of an offence of which he has been convicted (s 14E(2B)(j) (as so added)).

'Home address', in relation to any person, means the address of his sole or main residence; 'temporary address', in relation to any person, means the address (other than his home address) of a place at which he intends to reside, or has resided, for a period of at least four weeks; 'loss' includes theft or destruction; and 'new' includes replacement: s 14E(8) (as so added). A notification required by a banning order by virtue of these provisions must be given before the end of the period of seven days beginning with the day on which the event in question occurs and:
    (a)   in the case of a change of a name or address or the acquisition of a temporary address, must specify the new name or address (s 14E(2C)(a) (as so added));
    (b)   in the case of a first use of a previously undisclosed name, must specify that name (s 14E(2C)(b) (as so added)); and

(c)   in the case of a receipt of a new passport, must give details of that passport
        (s 14E(2C)(c) (as so added and amended)).
4   Football Spectators Act 1989 s 14E(2A) (as added: see notes 2, 3).
5   Ie in accordance with the Football Spectators Act 1989 Pt II (ss 14–22A).
6   As to the meanings of 'regulated football match' and 'football match' see PARA 341.
7   Football Spectators Act 1989 s 14E(3) (as added and amended: see notes 2, 3).
8   Football Spectators Act 1989 s 14G(1) (as added: see note 2).
9   Ie an application by the person subject to the order or the person who applied for the order or
      who was the prosecutor in relation to the order: Football Spectators Act 1989 s 14G(2) (as
      added: see note 2). In the case of a banning order made by a magistrates' court, the reference in
      s 14G(2) to the court by which it was made includes a reference to any magistrates' court acting
      in the same local justice area as that court: s 14G(3) (as so added; amended by the Courts
      Act 2003 s 8).
10 Football Spectators Act 1989 s 14G(2) (as added: see note 2).
11 Football Spectators Act 1989 s 14J(1)(a) (as added: see note 2). A person guilty of this offence is
      liable on summary conviction to imprisonment for a term not exceeding six months, or a fine
      not exceeding level 5 on the standard scale, or both: s 14J(2) (as so added). As to the standard
      scale, the statutory maximum, the prescribed sum, and magistrates' powers to levy unlimited
      fines see PARA 176. As to the reciprocal enforcement of these provisions and corresponding
      provisions for Scotland and Northern Ireland see the Policing and Crime Act 2009 ss 105(1)(a),
      (2)–(5), 106(1)(a), (2)–(5).
12 See the Football Spectators Act 1989 ss 20, 21; and SPORTS LAW vol 96 (2012) PARA 125.

348.   Duration and termination of banning order.   A football banning order[1]
has effect[2] for a period beginning with the day on which the order is made[3], and
that period must not be longer than the maximum or shorter than the
minimum[4]. Where the order was made on conviction[5] in addition to a sentence
of imprisonment[6] taking immediate effect, the maximum is ten years and the
minimum is six years[7]; in any other case where an order is made on conviction
the maximum is five years and the minimum is three years[8].

If a banning order has had effect for at least two-thirds of the period
determined under these provisions[9] the person subject to the order may apply to
the court by which it was made[10] to terminate it[11], and on such an application
the court may by order terminate the banning order as from a specified date or
refuse the application[12]. Where such an application in respect of a banning order
is refused, no further application in respect of the order may be made within the
period of six months beginning with the day of the refusal[13].

1   As to the meaning of 'football banning order' see PARA 341.
2   Ie subject to the Football Spectators Act 1989 Pt II (ss 14–22A).
3   Football Spectators Act 1989 s 14F(1) (ss 14F, 14H added, s 18(2) amended, by the Football
      (Disorder) Act 2000 Sch 1 paras 1, 2, 9, 10, 14).
4   Football Spectators Act 1989 s 14F(2) (as added: see note 3).
5   As to the making of football banning orders on conviction see the Football Spectators Act 1989
      s 14A; and PARA 344.
6   'Imprisonment' includes any form of detention: Football Spectators Act 1989 s 14F(3) (as
      added: see note 3).
7   Football Spectators Act 1989 s 14F(3) (as added: see note 3).
8   Football Spectators Act 1989 s 14F(4) (as added: see note 3).
9   Ie under the Football Spectators Act 1989 s 14F: see the text and notes 1–8.
10 In the case of a banning order made by a magistrates' court, the reference in the Football
      Spectators Act 1989 s 14H(1) to the court by which it was made includes a reference to any
      magistrates' court acting in the same local justice area as that court: s 14H(6) (as added (see note
      3); amended by the Courts Act 2003 Sch 8 para 332). The court may order the applicant to pay
      all or any part of the costs of an application under the Football Spectators Act 1989 s 14H:
      s 14H(5) (as so added).
11 Football Spectators Act 1989 s 14H(1) (as added: see note 3).
12 Football Spectators Act 1989 s 14H(2) (as added: see note 3). In exercising its powers under
      s 14H(2) the court must have regard to the person's character, his conduct since the banning
      order was made, the nature of the offence or conduct which led to it and any other

circumstances which appear to it to be relevant: s 14H(3) (as so added). Where a court terminates a banning order under s 14H the designated officer for the court (in the case of a magistrates' court) or the appropriate officer (in the case of the Crown Court) must:

(1)   give a copy of the terminating order to the person to whom the banning order relates (s 18(2)(a) (as so amended; amended by the Courts Act 2003 Sch 8 para 333));

(2)   as soon as reasonably practicable send a copy of it to the enforcing authority and to any prescribed person (Football Spectators Act 1989 s 18(2)(b) (as so amended)); and

(3)   in a case where the person subject to the banning order is detained in legal custody, as soon as reasonably practicable send a copy of the terminating order to the person in whose custody he is detained (s 18(2)(c) (as so amended)).

As to the meaning of 'enforcing authority' see PARA 344 note 3.

13 Football Spectators Act 1989 s 14H(5) (as added: see note 3).

(v) Exclusion Orders

349.   Making of exclusion orders. Until a day to be appointed[1], where a court by or before which a person is convicted of an offence committed on licensed premises[2] is satisfied that in committing that offence he resorted to violence or offered or threatened to resort to violence, the court may make an order (an 'exclusion order') prohibiting him from entering those premises or any other specified premises[3], without the express consent of the licensee[4] of the premises or his servant or agent[5].

An exclusion order may be made either:

(1)   in addition to any sentence which is imposed in respect of the offence of which the person is convicted[6]; or

(2)   where the offence was committed in England or Wales[7], in addition to discharging him absolutely or conditionally[8],

but not otherwise.

An exclusion order has effect[9] for such period, not less than three months or more than two years, as is specified in the order[10].

1   The Licensed Premises (Exclusion of Certain Persons) Act 1980 (see the text and notes 2–10; and PARA 350) is repealed, as from a day to be appointed, by the Violent Crime Reduction Act 2006 Sch 5: at the date at which this volume states the law no date had been appointed for these purposes.

2   For these purposes 'licensed premises' means premises in respect of which there is in force a premises licence under the Licensing Act 2003 authorising the supply of alcohol (within the meaning of s 14: see LICENSING AND GAMBLING vol 67 (2008) PARA 53) for consumption on the premises: Licensed Premises (Exclusion of Certain Persons) Act 1980 s 4(1) (amended by the Licensing Act 2003 Sch 6 para 74; prospectively repealed (see note 1)).

3   For these purposes 'specified premises', in relation to an exclusion order, means any licensed premises which the court may specify by name and address in the order: Licensed Premises (Exclusion of Certain Persons) Act 1980 s 4(1) (prospectively repealed: see note 1).

4   For these purposes 'licensee', in relation to any licensed premises, means the holder of the licence granted in respect of those premises: Licensed Premises (Exclusion of Certain Persons) Act 1980 s 4(1) (prospectively repealed: see note 1).

5   Licensed Premises (Exclusion of Certain Persons) Act 1980 s 1(1) (prospectively repealed: see note 1). An exclusion order may be made by the court of its own motion: *R v Penn* [1996] 2 Cr App Rep (S) 214, [1996] Crim LR 360, CA. Persons who are neither a victim nor a party to the proceedings should not apply for such an order, but should make representations to the prosecuting authority: *R v Penn*. An exclusion order is designed for cases of offenders who make a nuisance of themselves in public houses: *R v Grady* (1990) 12 Cr App Rep (S) 152, [1990] Crim LR 608, CA. An order may specify all licensed premises in a particular area (any one of which the offender could readily visit) where the court is satisfied that the offender is prone to committing offences of violence on licensed premises generally: *R v Arrowsmith* [2003] 2 Cr App Rep (S) 301, [2003] Crim LR 412, CA (order applying to 165 public houses in metropolitan area justified). Where a court makes an exclusion order or an order terminating or varying an exclusion order, the designated officer for a magistrates' court or the proper officer of the Crown Court, as the case may be, must send a copy of the order to the licensee of the

premises to which the order relates: Licensed Premises (Exclusion of Certain Persons) Act 1980 s 4(3), (4) (s 4(3) amended, s 4(4) added, by the Access to Justice Act 1999 Sch 13 para 94; Licensed Premises (Exclusion of Certain Persons) Act 1980 s 4(4) amended by the Courts Act 2003 Sch 8; as so prospectively repealed). Consequently, the order must identify individually the licensed premises to which it relates: *R v Arrowsmith*.

6   Licensed Premises (Exclusion of Certain Persons) Act 1980 s 1(2)(a) (prospectively repealed: see note 1).

7   Ie notwithstanding the provisions of the Powers of Criminal Courts (Sentencing) Act 2000 s 12 (see PARA 443) and s 14 (see PARA 445).

8   Licensed Premises (Exclusion of Certain Persons) Act 1980 s 1(2)(b) (substituted by the Criminal Justice Act 1991 Sch 11 para 23; amended by the Powers of Criminal Courts (Sentencing) Act 2000 Sch 11 para 60; prospectively repealed (see note 1)).

9   Ie unless it is terminated under the Licensed Premises (Exclusion of Certain Persons) Act 1980 s 2(2) (see PARA 350).

10 Licensed Premises (Exclusion of Certain Persons) Act 1980 s 1(3) (prospectively repealed: see note 1).

350.   Penalty for non-compliance. Until a day to be appointed[1] a person who enters any premises in breach of an exclusion order[2] is guilty of an offence[3]. The court by which a person is convicted of such an offence must consider whether or not the exclusion order should continue in force, and may, if it thinks fit, by order terminate the exclusion order or vary it by deleting the name of any specified premises; but an exclusion order may not otherwise be affected by a person's conviction for such an offence[4].

Provision is also made for the expulsion from licensed premises of a person who enters such premises in breach of an exclusion order[5].

1   The Licensed Premises (Exclusion of Certain Persons) Act 1980 (see the text and notes 2–5; and PARA 349) is repealed, as from a day to be appointed, by the Violent Crime Reduction Act 2006 Sch 5: at the date at which this volume states the law no date had been appointed for these purposes.

2   As to the meaning of 'exclusion order' see PARA 349.

3   Licensed Premises (Exclusion of Certain Persons) Act 1980 s 2(1) (prospectively repealed: see note 1). A person who commits this offence is liable on summary conviction to imprisonment for a term not exceeding one month (or, as from a day to be appointed, 51 weeks: see s 2(1) (prospectively amended by the Criminal Justice Act 2003 Sch 26 para 27), noting that this increase does not apply to any offence committed before the appointed day (s 280(3)), or to a fine not exceeding level 3 on the standard scale or to both: Licensed Premises (Exclusion of Certain Persons) Act 1980 s 2(1) (amended by virtue of the Criminal Justice Act 1982 s 46; as so prospectively amended and prospectively repealed)). At the date at which this volume states the law no date had been appointed for the coming into force of the amendment made by the Criminal Justice Act 2003. As to the standard scale, the statutory maximum, the prescribed sum, and magistrates' powers to levy unlimited fines see PARA 176.

4   Licensed Premises (Exclusion of Certain Persons) Act 1980 s 2(2) (prospectively repealed: see note 1).

5   See the Licensed Premises (Exclusion of Certain Persons) Act 1980 s 3; and LICENSING AND GAMBLING vol 67 (2008) PARA 141.

(vi)   Serious Crime Prevention Orders

351.   Power to make orders on conviction. Where the Crown Court in England and Wales[1] is dealing with a person aged 18 or over[2] who:

(1)   has been convicted by or before a magistrates' court of having committed a serious offence[3] in England and Wales[4] and has been committed to the Crown Court to be dealt with[5]; or

(2)   has been convicted by or before the Crown Court of having committed a serious offence in England and Wales[6],

the court may, in addition to dealing with the person in relation to the offence, on application[7] make a serious crime prevention order if it has reasonable grounds to believe that the order would protect the public[8] by preventing, restricting or disrupting involvement by the person in serious crime[9] in England and Wales[10]. Although these provisions are not couched in terms of necessity, it is essential that an order is proportionate[11]. Such an order may be made only in addition to a sentence imposed in respect of the offence concerned[12] or in addition to an order discharging the person conditionally[13], and may contain such prohibitions, restrictions, requirements and other terms as the court considers appropriate[14]. A court that makes a serious crime prevention order[15] in the case of a person who is already the subject of a serious crime prevention order in England and Wales must discharge the existing order[16].

Orders may be made against bodies corporate, partnerships and unincorporated associations as well as against individuals[17]. Provision is made in connection with the duration of orders[18], and the variation and discharge of orders by the High Court[19].

Proceedings relating to serious crime prevention orders[20] are civil proceedings[21]. One consequence of this is that the standard of proof to be applied by the court in such proceedings is the civil standard of proof[22], and two other consequences of this are that the court is not restricted to considering evidence that would have been admissible in the criminal proceedings in which the person concerned was convicted[23] and may adjourn any proceedings in relation to a serious crime prevention order even after sentencing the person concerned[24]. The Crown Court, when exercising its jurisdiction[25] in England and Wales is[26] a criminal court[27].

Failure to comply with a serious crime prevention order is an offence[28] in respect of which a forfeiture order[29] or (where applicable) a winding-up order[30] may be made.

1   As to appeals from decisions of the Crown Court see PARA 360.
2   An individual under the age of 18 may not be the subject of a serious crime prevention order: Serious Crime Act 2007 ss 6, 19(6). A person also may not be the subject of a serious crime prevention order if he falls within a description specified by order of the Secretary of State (s 7(1) (substituted by SI 2010/976)): at the date at which this volume states the law no such order had been made. For the purposes of the Serious Crime Act 2007 Pt 1 references to the person who is the subject of a serious crime prevention order are references to the person against whom the public are to be protected: s 1(6). As to the determination of a person's age see the Children and Young Persons Act 1933 s 99; and CHILDREN AND YOUNG PERSONS vol 10 (2012) PARA 1206.
3   In considering for the purposes of the Serious Crime Act 2007 Pt 1 whether a person has committed a serious offence (see note 4):
    (1)   the court must decide that the person has committed the offence if he has been convicted of the offence and the conviction has not been quashed on appeal nor has the person been pardoned of the offence (s 4(1)(a)); but
    (2)   the court must not otherwise decide that the person has committed the offence (s 4(1)(b)).
4   As to a 'serious offence in England and Wales', and the offences in relation to which serious crime prevention orders may be made, see PARA 353.
5   Serious Crime Act 2007 s 19(1)(a).
6   Serious Crime Act 2007 s 19(1)(b).
7   A serious crime prevention order in England and Wales may be made only on an application by the Director of Public Prosecutions or the Director of the Serious Fraud Office: Serious Crime Act 2007 s 8(a) (amended by SI 2014/834). As to the functions of the Directors see PARA 362.
8   'The public' includes a section of the public or a particular member of the public: Serious Crime Act 2007 s 42.
9   As to involvement by a person in serious crime in England and Wales see PARA 354.
10 Serious Crime Act 2007 ss 1(5)(b), 19(2), (8). For procedural rules in connection with the making of serious crime prevention orders see the Criminal Procedure Rules 2015, SI 2015/1490, Pt 31. The requirements set out in the Serious Crime Act 2007 s 19(2) need not

be satisfied if the order proposed to be made contains terms requiring the subject of the order to pay the costs of monitoring compliance with the order (ie under s 39(4), (5)): see s 39(6); and PARA 361 note 7.

Serious crime prevention orders may also be made other than on conviction by the High Court (see s 1; and PARA 352), and a decision by the Crown Court not to make an order under s 19 does not prevent a subsequent application to the High Court for an order under s 1 in consequence of the same offence: s 22(3). Provision is also made in connection with the making of serious crime prevention orders in Northern Ireland: see s 19(3), (4).

11 See *R v Hancox* [2010] EWCA Crim 102, [2010] 4 All ER 537, [2010] 2 Cr App Rep (S) 484.
12 Serious Crime Act 2007 s 19(7)(a).
13 Serious Crime Act 2007 s 19(7)(b). A serious crime prevention order may be made as mentioned in s 19(7)(b) notwithstanding anything in the Powers of Criminal Courts (Sentencing) Act 2000 ss 12, 14 (which relate to orders discharging a person absolutely or conditionally and their effect: see PARAS 443, 445): Serious Crime Act 2007 s 36(5).
14 See the Serious Crime Act 2007 s 19(5); and PARA 355. The requirement set out in s 19(5) need not be satisfied if the order proposed to be made contains terms requiring the subject of the order to pay the costs of monitoring compliance with the order (ie under s 39(4), (5)): see s 39(6); and PARA 361 note 7.

The subject of a serious crime prevention order is bound by it (or a variation of it: see PARAS 357, 358) only if he is represented (whether in person or otherwise) at the proceedings at which the order or (as the case may be) variation is made or a notice setting out the terms of the order or (as the case may be) variation has been served on him: s 10(1). The notice may be served on him by delivering it to him in person or sending it by recorded delivery to him at his last-known address (whether residential or otherwise): s 10(2). For the purposes of delivering such a notice to him in person, a constable or a person authorised for the purpose by the relevant applicant authority may (if necessary by force) enter any premises where he has reasonable grounds for believing the person to be and search those premises for him: s 10(3). In Pt 1 the 'relevant applicant authority' means, in relation to a serious crime prevention order in England and Wales, either the Director of Public Prosecutions (where the order was applied for by the Director of Public Prosecutions) or the Director of the Serious Fraud Office (where the order was applied for by the Director of the Serious Fraud Office): s 10(4) (amended by SI 2014/834).

For the purposes of the Serious Crime Act 2007 s 10 in its application to a serious crime prevention order against a body corporate, a partnership or an unincorporated association, or to the variation of such an order, a notice setting out the terms of the order or variation is delivered to the body corporate, partnership or association in person if it is delivered to an officer of the body corporate or any of the partners or an officer of the association in person (ss 30(1)(a)(i), 31(4)(a)(i), 32(3)(a)(i)) and is sent by recorded delivery to the body corporate, partnership or association at its last-known address if it is so sent to an officer of the body corporate or any of the partners or a senior officer of the partnership or an officer of the association at the address of the registered office of that body or at the address of the body's, partnership's or association's principal office in the United Kingdom (ss 30(1)(a)(ii), 31(4)(a)(ii), 32(3)(a)(ii)), and the power conferred by s 10(3) is a power to enter any premises where the person exercising the power has reasonable grounds for believing an officer of the body corporate or association or a partner or senior officer of the partnership to be and to search those premises for the officer, partner or senior officer (ss 30(1)(b), 31(4)(b), 32(3)(b)). For this purpose 'body corporate' includes a limited liability partnership; 'officer of a body corporate' means any director, manager, secretary or other similar officer of the body corporate; 'director', in relation to a body corporate whose affairs are managed by its members, means a member of the body corporate; 'senior officer of a partnership' means any person who has the control or management of the business carried on by the partnership at the principal place where it is carried on; 'partnership' does not include a limited liability partnership; 'officer of an unincorporated association' means any officer of an unincorporated association or any member of its governing body; and 'unincorporated association' means any body of persons unincorporate but does not include a partnership: ss 30(4), 31(11), 32(10). Nothing in ss 30, 31, 32 prevents a serious crime prevention order from being made against an officer or employee of a body corporate, a particular partner or senior officer or employee of a partnership, a member, officer or employee of an unincorporated association, or any other person associated with a body corporate, partnership or unincorporated association: ss 30(3), 31(10), 32(9).

The Secretary of State may by order modify s 30, s 31 or s 32 in its application to a body of persons formed under law having effect outside the United Kingdom: s 33. At the date at which this volume states the law no such order had been made.

15 Ie an order under the Serious Crime Act 2007 s 19(2) (see the text and notes 1–10).
16 Serious Crime Act 2007 s 19(2A) (added by the Serious Crime Act 2015 Sch 4 para 78).

17 See notes 14, 18. A serious crime prevention order against a partnership or unincorporated association must be made in the name of the partnership or association (and not in that of any of the partners or members): Serious Crime Act 2007 ss 31(1), 32(1). An order made in the name of the partnership or association continues to have effect despite a change of partners or a change in the membership of the association provided that at least one of the persons who was a partner or a member of the association before the change remains a partner or member after it: ss 31(2), 32(2).

The Crown Court must, on an application by a person, give the person an opportunity to make representations in proceedings before it arising by virtue of s 19 if it considers that the making of the serious crime prevention order concerned would be likely to have a significant adverse effect on that person: s 9(4).

18 See the Serious Crime Act 2007 s 16; and PARA 356.

19 See the Serious Crime Act 2007 ss 17, 18; and PARA 357. The fact that a serious crime prevention order has been made or varied by the Crown Court does not prevent it from being varied or discharged by the High Court in accordance with Pt 1 (ss 1–43): s 22(2).

20 Ie proceedings relating to serious crime prevention orders before the Crown Court arising by virtue of the Serious Crime Act 2007 s 19 (see the text and notes 2–16), s 20 (see PARA 358), s 21 (see PARA 358) or s 22E (see PARA 359).

21 See the Serious Crime Act 2007 s 36(1) (amended by the Serious Crime Act 2007 Sch 4 para 80); and as to proceedings in connection with serious crime prevention orders see CPR Pt 77.

22 Serious Crime Act 2007 s 36(2).

23 Serious Crime Act 2007 s 36(3)(a).

24 Serious Crime Act 2007 s 36(3)(b).

25 Ie its jurisdiction under the Serious Crime Act 2007 Pt 1 (ss 1–43).

26 Ie for the purposes of the Courts Act 2003 Pt 7 (ss 68–85) (procedure rules and practice directions: see COURTS AND TRIBUNALS vol 24 (2010) PARA 861).

27 Serious Crime Act 2007 s 36(4).

28 See PARA 363.

29 See PARA 364.

30 See PARA 365.

352. Power of High Court to make orders.

The High Court in England and Wales may make a serious crime prevention order[1] if it is satisfied that a person aged 18 or over[2] has been involved in serious crime (whether in England and Wales or elsewhere)[3] and it has reasonable grounds to believe that the order would protect the public[4] by preventing, restricting or disrupting involvement by the person in serious crime in England and Wales[5]. Such an order may be made only on application[6], and may contain such prohibitions, restrictions or requirements and such other terms as the court considers appropriate for the purpose of protecting the public by preventing, restricting or disrupting involvement by the person concerned in serious crime[7]. Orders may be made against bodies corporate, partnerships and unincorporated associations as well as against individuals[8]. Provision is made in connection with the duration of orders[9], and the variation and discharge of orders by the High Court[10].

An appeal may be made to the Court of Appeal in relation to a decision of the High Court to make a serious crime prevention order[11]. Failure to comply with a serious crime prevention order is an offence in respect of which a forfeiture order or (where applicable) a winding-up order may be made[12].

1 Serious Crime Act 2007 s 1(1), (5)(a). Proceedings before the High Court in relation to serious crime prevention orders are civil proceedings (s 35(1)), one consequence of which is that the standard of proof to be applied by the court in such proceedings is the civil one (s 35(2)). Serious crime prevention orders may also be made by the Crown Court on conviction under s 19: see PARA 351. As to the extent to which a person is bound by an order see ss 10, 30–32; and PARA 351 note 14. Corresponding provision is made in connection with the making of serious crime prevention orders by the High Court in Northern Ireland: see s 1(2).

The High Court must, on an application by a person, give the person an opportunity to make representations in proceedings before it about the making of a serious crime prevention order if it considers that the making of the order would be likely to have a significant adverse effect on that person: s 9(1).

2 An individual under the age of 18 may not be the subject of a serious crime prevention order: Serious Crime Act 2007 ss 1(4), 6. A person also may not be the subject of a serious crime prevention order if he falls within a description specified by order of the Secretary of State (s 7) (substituted by SI 2010/976): at the date at which this volume states the law no such order had been made. As to the 'subject' of a serious crime prevention order see PARA 351 note 2. As to the determination of a person's age see the Children and Young Persons Act 1933 s 99; and CHILDREN AND YOUNG PERSONS vol 10 (2012) PARA 1206.

3 Serious Crime Act 2007 s 1(1)(a). As to involvement by a person in serious crime (which for these purposes may be in England and Wales or (as the case may be) Northern Ireland) see PARA 354. For the purposes of s 1(1)(a) a person has been involved in serious crime elsewhere than in England and Wales if he has committed a serious offence in a country outside England and Wales (s 2(4)(a)), has facilitated the commission by another person of a serious offence in a country outside England and Wales (s 2(4)(b)) or has conducted himself in a way that was likely to facilitate the commission by himself or another person of a serious offence in a country outside England and Wales (whether or not such an offence was committed) (s 2(4)(c)). For this purpose a 'serious offence in a country outside England and Wales' means an offence under the law of a country outside England and Wales which, at the time when the court is considering the application or matter in question, would be an offence under the law of England and Wales if committed in or as regards England and Wales (s 2(5)(a)) and either would be an offence which is specified, or falls within a description specified, in Sch 1 Pt 1 (see PARA 353) if committed in or as regards England and Wales (s 2(5)(b)(i)) or is conduct which, in the particular circumstances of the case, the court considers to be sufficiently serious to be treated for the purposes of the application or matter as if it meets the test in s 2(5)(b)(i) (s 2(5)(b)(ii)). An act punishable under the law of a country outside the United Kingdom constitutes an offence under that law for the purposes of s 2(5), however it is described in that law: s 2(7). Corresponding provision is made in connection with the making of serious crime prevention orders by the High Court in Northern Ireland: see ss 2(6), 3(4)–(7).

4 As to the meaning of 'the public' see PARA 351 note 8.

5 Serious Crime Act 2007 s 1(1)(b). This requirement need not be satisfied if the order proposed to be made contains terms requiring the subject of the order to pay the costs of monitoring compliance with the order (ie under s 39(4), (5)): see s 39(6); and PARA 361 note 7.

6 A serious crime prevention order in England and Wales may be made only on an application by the Director of Public Prosecutions or the Director of the Serious Fraud Office: Serious Crime Act 2007 s 8(a) (amended by SI 2014/834). As to the functions of the Directors see PARA 362.

7 See the Serious Crime Act 2007 ss 1(3), 5, 11–15, 34, 38; and PARA 355.

8 See the Serious Crime Act 2007 ss 10, 30–32; and PARA 351 note 14. As to compliance with orders made against corporations, partnerships and associations see ss 39, 40; and PARA 361.

9 See the Serious Crime Act 2007 s 16; and PARA 356.

10 See the Serious Crime Act 2007 ss 17, 18; and PARA 357. The fact that a serious crime prevention order has been made or varied by the Crown Court does not prevent it from being varied or discharged by the High Court in accordance with Pt 1 (ss 1–43): s 22(2).

11 Serious Crime Act 2007 s 23(1)(a). The appeal may be brought by any person who was given an opportunity to make representations in the proceedings concerned by virtue of s 9(1) (see note 1): s 23(1). This provision is without prejudice to the rights of other persons to make appeals, by virtue of the Senior Courts Act 1981 s 16 (see COURTS AND TRIBUNALS vol 24 (2010) PARA 693) in relation to any judgments or orders of the High Court about serious crime prevention orders: Serious Crime Act 2007 s 23(2).

12 See the Serious Crime Act 2007 s 25 (offences), s 26 (powers of forfeiture in respect of offences) and ss 27, 29 (powers to wind up companies); and PARAS 363–365.

353. Offences in relation to which serious crime prevention orders may be made. For the purposes of the making of a serious crime prevention order on conviction[1] the offender is required to have been convicted of having committed a serious offence[2] in England and Wales[3], that is to say, an offence under the law of England and Wales[4] which, at the time when the court is considering the application or matter in question, is an offence[5] of or involving:

(1) drug trafficking and cultivation[6];

(2)   slavery, servitude and forced or compulsory labour[7];
(3)   people trafficking[8];
(4)   firearms offences[9];
(5)   prostitution and child sex[10];
(6)   armed robbery[11];
(7)   money laundering[12];
(8)   fraud[13];
(9)   cheating the public revenue[14];
(10)   bribery[15];
(11)   counterfeiting[16];
(12)   blackmail[17];
(13)   computer misuse[18];
(14)   intellectual property[19];
(15)   environmental damage and control[20]; or
(16)   organised crime[21],

or an offence which, in the particular circumstances of the case, the court considers to be sufficiently serious to be treated for the purposes of the application or matter as if it were so specified[22]. Certain offences inchoate to the listed offences are also applicable for these purposes[23].

1   Ie for the purposes of the Serious Crime Act 2007 Pt 1 (ss 1–43). As to the making of a serious crime prevention order on conviction see PARA 351. Serious crime prevention orders may also be made other than on conviction by the High Court: see s 1; and PARA 352.
2   As to whether a person has committed a serious offence see PARA 351 note 3.
3   See the Serious Crime Act 2007 s 19(1); and PARA 351.
4   Where the Serious Crime Act 2007 Sch 1 Pt 1 (see the text and notes 6–21) refers to offences which are offences under the law of England and Wales and another country, the reference is to be read as limited to the offences so far as they are offences under the law of England and Wales: Sch 1 para 16.
        Sch 1 Pt 1 (apart from Sch 1 para 14(2): see the text and note 23) has effect, in its application to conduct before 30 October 2007 (ie the date on which the Serious Crime Act 2007 received the Royal Assent), as if the offences specified or described in Sch 1 Pt 1 included any corresponding offences under the law in force at the time of the conduct: Sch 1 para 15(1).
5   Ie an offence specified, or falling within a description specified, in the Serious Crime Act 2007 Sch 1 Pt 1: s 2(2)(a). The Secretary of State may by order amend Sch 1 Pt 1: s 4(4) (amended by SI 2010/976). At the date at which this volume states the law no such order had been made. Corresponding provision is made in connection with the making of serious crime prevention orders in Northern Ireland: see the Serious Crime Act 2007 s 3(2)(a), Sch 1 Pt 2.
6   Ie an offence under:
    (1)   the Misuse of Drugs Act 1971 4(2) or (3) (unlawful production or supply of controlled drugs: see CRIMINAL LAW vol 26 (2010) PARA 725) (Serious Crime Act 2007 Sch 1 para 1(1)(a));
    (2)   the Misuse of Drugs Act 1971 s 5(3) (possession of controlled drug with intent to supply: see CRIMINAL LAW vol 26 (2010) PARA 725) (Serious Crime Act 2007 Sch 1 para 1(1)(b));
    (3)   the Misuse of Drugs Act 1971 s 6 (restriction of cultivation of cannabis plant: see CRIMINAL LAW vol 26 (2010) PARA 730) (Serious Crime Act 2007 Sch 1 para 1(1)(ba) (Sch 1 paras 1(1)(ba), 11A, 13A added, Sch 1 para 3 substituted, Sch 1 para 4(2)(b)–(d) amended, by the Serious Crime Act 2015 s 47(1)–(4), Sch 4 para 81(1), (2)));
    (4)   the Misuse of Drugs Act 1971 s 8 (permitting etc certain activities relating to controlled drugs: see CRIMINAL LAW vol 26 (2010) PARA 730) (Serious Crime Act 2007 Sch 1 para 1(1)(c));
    (5)   the Misuse of Drugs Act 1971 s 20 (assisting in or inducing the commission outside the United Kingdom of an offence punishable under a corresponding law: see CRIMINAL LAW vol 26 (2010) PARA 732) (Serious Crime Act 2007 Sch 1 para 1(d));
    (6)   the Customs and Excise Management Act 1979 s 50(2) or (3) (improper importation of goods: see CUSTOMS AND EXCISE vol 31 (2012) PARA 992) (Serious Crime Act 2007 Sch 1 para 1(2)(a));

(7) the Customs and Excise Management Act 1979 s 68(2) (exportation of prohibited or restricted goods: see CUSTOMS AND EXCISE vol 31 (2012) PARA 1027) (Serious Crime Act 2007 Sch 1 para 1(2)(b));

(8) the Customs and Excise Management Act 1979 s 170 (fraudulent evasion of duty etc: see CUSTOMS AND EXCISE vol 31 (2012) PARA 1175) (Serious Crime Act 2007 Sch 1 para 1(2)(c)); or

(9) the Criminal Justice (International Co-operation) Act 1990 s 12 (manufacture or supply of a substance for the time being specified in Sch 2: see CRIMINAL LAW vol 26 (2010) PARA 726) or s 19 (using a ship for illicit traffic in controlled drugs: see CRIMINAL LAW vol 26 (2010) PARA 733) (Serious Crime Act 2007 Sch 1 para 1(3)).

Offences under the Customs and Excise Management Act 1979 are applicable for these purposes only if committed in connection with a prohibition or restriction on importation or exportation which has effect by virtue of the Misuse of Drugs Act 1971 s 3: Serious Crime Act 2007 Sch 1 para 1(2).

7 Ie an offence under the Modern Slavery Act 2015 s 1 (see CRIMINAL LAW): Serious Crime Act 2007 Sch 1 para 1A (added by the Modern Slavery Act 2015 Sch 5 para 7(1), (2)).

8 Ie an offence under:

(1) the Immigration Act 1971 s 25, 25A or 25B (assisting unlawful immigration etc: see IMMIGRATION AND ASYLUM vol 57 (2012) PARAS 213–215) (Serious Crime Act 2007 Sch 1 para 2(1));

(2) the Sexual Offences Act 2003 ss 57–59A (trafficking for sexual exploitation: see CRIMINAL LAW vol 25 (2010) PARA 254) (Serious Crime Act 2007 Sch 1 para 2(2) (amended by the Protection of Freedoms Act 2012 Sch 9 para 142));

(3) the Asylum and Immigration (Treatment of Claimants, etc) Act 2004 s 4 (trafficking people for exploitation: see IMMIGRATION AND ASYLUM vol 57 (2012) PARA 218) (Serious Crime Act 2007 Sch 1 para 2(3)); or

(4) the Modern Slavery Act 2015 s 2 (see CRIMINAL LAW) (Serious Crime Act 2007 Sch 1 para 2(4) (added by the Modern Slavery Act 2015 Sch 5 para 7(3))).

9 Ie an offence under:

(1) the Firearms Act 1968 s 1(1) (possession of firearms or ammunition without certificate: see CRIMINAL LAW vol 26 (2010) PARA 582) (Serious Crime Act 2007 Sch 1 para 3(1)(a) (as substituted: see note 6));

(2) the Firearms Act 1968 s 2(1) (possession of shot gun without certificate: see CRIMINAL LAW vol 26 (2010) PARA 583) (Serious Crime Act 2007 Sch 1 para 3(1)(b) (as so substituted));

(3) the Firearms Act 1968 s 3(1) (dealing etc in firearms or ammunition by way of trade or business without being registered: see CRIMINAL LAW vol 26 (2010) PARA 584) (Serious Crime Act 2007 Sch 1 para 3(1)(c) (as so substituted));

(4) the Firearms Act 1968 s 5(1), (1A) or (2A) (possession, manufacture etc of prohibited weapons: see CRIMINAL LAW vol 26 (2010) PARA 613) (Serious Crime Act 2007 Sch 1 para 3(1)(d) (as so substituted));

(5) either of the Customs and Excise Management Act 1979 s 68(2) (exportation of prohibited or restricted goods: see CUSTOMS AND EXCISE vol 31 (2012) PARA 1027) or s 170 (fraudulent evasion of duty etc: see CUSTOMS AND EXCISE vol 31 (2012) PARA 1175) if committed in connection with a firearm or ammunition (Serious Crime Act 2007 Sch 1 para 3(2) (as so substituted)).

As to the meanings of 'firearm' and 'ammunition' see the Firearms Act 1968 s 57; and CRIMINAL LAW vol 26 (2010) PARAS 578, 582 (definitions applied by the Serious Crime Act 2007 Sch 1 para 3(3) (as so substituted)).

10 Ie an offence under:

(1) the Sexual Offences Act 1956 s 33A (keeping a brothel used for prostitution: see CRIMINAL LAW vol 25 (2010) PARA 245) (Serious Crime Act 2007 Sch 1 para 4(1));

(2) the Sexual Offences Act 2003 s 14 (arranging or facilitating commission of a child sex offence: see CRIMINAL LAW vol 25 (2010) PARA 191) (Serious Crime Act 2007 Sch 1 para 4(2)(a));

(3) the Sexual Offences Act 2003 s 48 (causing or inciting sexual exploitation of a child: see CRIMINAL LAW vol 25 (2010) PARA 229) (Serious Crime Act 2007 Sch 1 para 4(2)(b) (as amended: see note 6));

(4) the Sexual Offences Act 2003 s 49 (controlling a child in relation to sexual exploitation: see CRIMINAL LAW vol 25 (2010) PARA 229) (Serious Crime Act 2007 Sch 1 para 4(2)(c) (as so amended));

(5)   the Sexual Offences Act 2003 s 50 (arranging or facilitating sexual exploitation of a child: see CRIMINAL LAW vol 25 (2010) PARA 229) (Serious Crime Act 2007 Sch 1 para 4(2)(d) (as so amended));

(6)   the Sexual Offences Act 2003 s 52 (causing or inciting prostitution for gain: see CRIMINAL LAW vol 25 (2010) PARA 230) (Serious Crime Act 2007 Sch 1 para 4(2)(e)); or

(7)   the Sexual Offences Act 2003 s 53 (controlling prostitution for gain: see CRIMINAL LAW vol 25 (2010) PARA 230) (Serious Crime Act 2007 Sch 1 para 4(2)(f)).

11   Ie an offence under the Theft Act 1968 s 8(1) (robbery: see CRIMINAL LAW vol 25 (2010) PARA 289) where the use or threat of force involves a firearm, an imitation firearm or an offensive weapon and an offence at common law of an assault with intent to rob where the assault involves a firearm, imitation firearm or an offensive weapon: Serious Crime Act 2007 Sch 1 para 5(1), (2)). As to the meanings of 'firearm' and 'imitation firearm' see the Firearms Act 1968 s 57(1), (4); and CRIMINAL LAW vol 26 (2010) PARAS 578, 581 (definitions applied by the Serious Crime Act 2007 Sch 1 para 5(3)). 'Offensive weapon' means any weapon to which the Criminal Justice Act 1988 s 141 (offensive weapons: see CRIMINAL LAW vol 26 (2010) PARA 657) applies: Serious Crime Act 2007 Sch 1 para 5(3). As to defendants charged with robbery but not with the possession of a firearm see *R v Benfield* [2003] EWCA Crim 2223, [2004] 1 Cr App Rep (S) 307, [2003] Crim LR 811 (explained in *R v Hylands* [2004] EWCA Crim 2999, [2005] 2 Cr App Rep (S) 135, [2005] Crim LR 154).

12   Ie an offence under the Proceeds of Crime Act 2002 s 327 (concealing etc criminal property: see CRIMINAL LAW vol 26 (2010) PARA 744), s 328 (facilitating the acquisition etc of criminal property by or on behalf of another: see CRIMINAL LAW vol 26 (2010) PARA 745) or s 329 (acquisition, use and possession of criminal property: see CRIMINAL LAW vol 26 (2010) PARA 746): Serious Crime Act 2007 Sch 1 para 6.

13   Ie an offence under:

(1)   the Theft Act 1968 s 17 (false accounting: see CRIMINAL LAW vol 25 (2010) PARA 311) (Serious Crime Act 2007 Sch 1 para 7(1));

(2)   the Fraud Act 2006 s 1 (fraud by false representation, failing to disclose information or abuse of position: see CRIMINAL LAW vol 25 (2010) PARA 305) (Serious Crime Act 2007 Sch 1 para 7(2)(a));

(3)   the Fraud Act 2006 s 6 (possession etc of articles for use in frauds: see CRIMINAL LAW vol 25 (2010) PARA 306) (Serious Crime Act 2007 Sch 1 para 7(2)(b));

(4)   the Fraud Act 2006 s 7 (making or supplying articles for use in frauds: see CRIMINAL LAW vol 25 (2010) PARA 307) (Serious Crime Act 2007 Sch 1 para 7(2)(c));

(5)   the Fraud Act 2006 s 9 (participating in fraudulent business carried on by sole trader etc: see CRIMINAL LAW vol 25 (2010) PARA 308) (Serious Crime Act 2007 Sch 1 para 7(2)(d));

(6)   the Fraud Act 2006 s 11 (obtaining services dishonestly: see CRIMINAL LAW vol 25 (2010) PARA 309) (Serious Crime Act 2007 Sch 1 para 7(2)(e)),

or an offence at common law of conspiracy to defraud (see CRIMINAL LAW vol 25 (2010) PARA 80) (Serious Crime Act 2007 Sch 1 para 7(3)).

14   Ie an offence under:

(1)   the Customs and Excise Management Act 1979 s 170 (fraudulent evasion of duty etc: see CUSTOMS AND EXCISE vol 31 (2012) PARA 1175) so far as not falling within the offences under s 170 referred to in notes 6, 9 (Serious Crime Act 2007 Sch 1 para 8(1));

(2)   the Value Added Tax Act 1994 s 72 (fraudulent evasion of VAT etc: see VALUE ADDED TAX vol 99 (2012) PARA 402 et seq) (Serious Crime Act 2007 Sch 1 para 8(2));

(3)   the Taxes Management Act 1970 s 106A (fraudulent evasion of income tax: see INCOME TAXATION vol 59 (2014) PARA 2316) (Serious Crime Act 2007 Sch 1 para 8(3) (amended by the Taxation (International and Other Provisions) Act 2010 Sch 17 para 101));

(4)   the Tax Credits Act 2002 s 35 (tax credit fraud: see WELFARE BENEFITS AND STATE PENSIONS vol 104 (2014) PARA 367) (Serious Crime Act 2007 Sch 1 para 8(4)),

or an offence at common law of cheating in relation to the public revenue (see CRIMINAL LAW vol 25 (2010) PARA 317) (Serious Crime Act 2007 Sch 1 para 8(5)).

15   Ie an offence under the Bribery Act 2010 s 1 (bribing another person: see CRIMINAL LAW vol 26 (2010) PARA 459) (Serious Crime Act 2007 Sch 1 para 9(a) (Sch 1 para 9 substituted by the Bribery Act 2010 Sch 1 para 14), the Bribery Act 2010 s 2 (offences relating to being bribed: see CRIMINAL LAW vol 26 (2010) PARA 459) (Serious Crime Act 2007 Sch 1 para 9(b) (as so substituted)), or the Bribery Act 2010 s 6 (bribery of foreign public officials: see CRIMINAL LAW vol 26 (2010) PARA 460) (Serious Crime Act 2007 Sch 1 para 9(c) (as so substituted)).

16   Ie an offence under the Forgery and Counterfeiting Act 1981 s 14 (making counterfeit notes or coins: see CRIMINAL LAW vol 26 (2010) PARA 476) (Serious Crime Act 2007 Sch 1 para 10(a)),

the Forgery and Counterfeiting Act 1981 s 15 (passing etc counterfeit notes or coins: see CRIMINAL LAW vol 26 (2010) PARA 477) (Serious Crime Act 2007 Sch 1 para 10(b)), the Forgery and Counterfeiting Act 1981 s 16 (having custody or control of counterfeit notes or coins: see CRIMINAL LAW vol 26 (2010) PARA 478) (Serious Crime Act 2007 Sch 1 para 10(c)) or the Forgery and Counterfeiting Act 1981 s 17 (making or having custody or control of counterfeiting materials or implements: see CRIMINAL LAW vol 26 (2010) PARA 479) (Serious Crime Act 2007 Sch 1 para 10(d)).

17 Ie an offence under the Theft Act 1968 s 21 (blackmail: see CRIMINAL LAW vol 25 (2010) PARA 304) (Serious Crime Act 2007 Sch 1 para 11(1)) or the Gangmasters (Licensing) Act 2004 s 12(1) or (2) (acting as a gangmaster other than under the authority of a licence, possession of false documents, etc: see AGRICULTURAL PRODUCTION AND MARKETING vol 1 (2008) PARA 1253) (see the Serious Crime Act 2007 Sch 1 para 11(2)).

18 An offence under the Computer Misuse Act 1990 s 1 (unauthorised access to computer material: see CRIMINAL LAW vol 25 (2010) PARA 350; INFORMATION TECHNOLOGY LAW vol 57 (2012) PARA 687) (Serious Crime Act 2007 Sch 1 para 11A(a) (as added: see note 6)), the Computer Misuse Act 1990 s 2 (unauthorised access with intent to commit or facilitate commission of further offences: see CRIMINAL LAW vol 25 (2010) PARA 351; INFORMATION TECHNOLOGY LAW vol 57 (2012) PARA 688) (Serious Crime Act 2007 Sch 1 para 11A(b) (as so added)), the Computer Misuse Act 1990 s 3 (unauthorised acts with intent to impair, or with recklessness as to impairing, operation of computer etc: see CRIMINAL LAW vol 25 (2010) PARA 352; INFORMATION TECHNOLOGY LAW vol 57 (2012) PARA 689) (Serious Crime Act 2007 Sch 1 para 11A(c) (as so added)), the Computer Misuse Act 1990 s 3ZA (unauthorised acts causing, or creating risk of, serious damage to human welfare etc: see CRIMINAL LAW; INFORMATION TECHNOLOGY LAW) (Serious Crime Act 2007 Sch 1 para 11A(d) (as so added)), or the Computer Misuse Act 1990 s 3A (making, supplying or obtaining articles for use in offence under s 1, s 3 or s 3ZA: see CRIMINAL LAW vol 25 (2010) PARA 354; INFORMATION TECHNOLOGY LAW vol 57 (2012) PARA 691) (Serious Crime Act 2007 Sch 1 para 11A(c) (as so added)).

19 Ie an offence under:
(1)   the Copyright, Designs and Patents Act 1988 s 107(1)(a), (b), (d)(iv) or (e) (making, importing or distributing an article which infringes copyright: see COPYRIGHT vol 23 (2013) PARA 984) (Serious Crime Act 2007 Sch 1 para 12(1)(a));
(2)   the Copyright, Designs and Patents Act 1988 s 198(1)(a), (b) or (d)(iii) (making, importing or distributing an illicit recording: see COPYRIGHT vol 23 (2013) PARAS 1261–1262) (Serious Crime Act 2007 Sch 1 para 12(1)(b));
(3)   the Copyright, Designs and Patents Act 1988 s 297A (making or dealing etc in unauthorised decoders: see COPYRIGHT vol 23 (2013) PARA 1039) (Serious Crime Act 2007 Sch 1 para 12(1)(c)); or
(4)   the Trade Marks Act 1994 s 92(1), (2) or (3) (unauthorised use of trade mark etc: see TRADE MARKS AND TRADE NAMES vol 97A (2014) PARAS 124–126) (Serious Crime Act 2007 Sch 1 para 12(2)).

20 Ie an offence under:
(1)   the Salmon and Freshwater Fisheries Act 1975 s 1 (fishing with prohibited implements etc: see FISHERIES AND AQUACULTURE vol 51 (2013) PARA 429) (Serious Crime Act 2007 Sch 1 para 13(1) (amended by the Marine and Coastal Access Act 2009 Sch 22 Pt 5(B)));
(2)   the Wildlife and Countryside Act 1981 s 14 (introduction of new species etc: see FISHERIES AND AQUACULTURE vol 51 (2013) PARA 463) (Serious Crime Act 2007 Sch 1 para 13(2));
(3)   the Environmental Protection Act 1990 s 33 (prohibition on unauthorised or harmful deposit, treatment or disposal etc of waste: see ENVIRONMENTAL QUALITY AND PUBLIC HEALTH vol 46 (2010) PARA 655) (Serious Crime Act 2007 Sch 1 para 13(3)); or
(4)   the Control of Trade in Endangered Species (Enforcement) Regulations 1997, SI 1997/1372, reg 8 (purchase and sale etc of endangered species and provision of false statements and certificates: see AGRICULTURAL PRODUCTION AND MARKETING vol 1 (2008) PARA 1169; ANIMALS vol 2 (2008) PARA 965) (Serious Crime Act 2007 Sch 1 para 13(4)).

21 Ie an offence under the Serious Crime Act 2015 s 45 (participating in activities of organised crime group see CRIMINAL LAW): Serious Crime Act 2007 Sch 1 para 13A (as added: see note 6)).

22 Serious Crime Act 2007 s 2(2)(b). Corresponding provision is made in connection with the making of serious crime prevention orders in Northern Ireland: see s 3(2)(b).

23 Ie an offence of attempting or conspiring the commission of an offence specified or described in the Serious Crime Act 2007 Sch 1 Pt 1 (Sch 1 para 14(1)), an offence under Pt 2 (ss 44–67) (encouraging or assisting: see CRIMINAL LAW vol 25 (2010) PARAS 65–72) where the offence (or

one of the offences) which the person in question intends or believes would be committed is an offence specified or described in Sch 1 Pt 1 (Sch 1 para 14(2)), or an offence of aiding, abetting, counselling or procuring the commission of an offence specified or described in Sch 1 Pt 1 (Sch 1 para 14(3)). Schedule 1 para 14(2) has effect, in its application to conduct before 30 October 2007 or before 1 October 2008 (i e the date on which s 59 was brought into force by the Serious Crime Act 2007 (Commencement No 3) Order 2008, SI 2008/2504), as if the offence specified or described in that provision were an offence of inciting the commission of an offence specified or described in the Serious Crime Act 2007 Sch 1 Pt 1: Sch 1 para 15(2). The references in Sch 1 para 14(1)–(3) to offences specified or described in Sch 1 Pt 1 do not include the offence at common law of conspiracy to defraud: Sch 1 para 14(4).

354.   Involvement in serious crime.   For the purposes of the making of a serious crime prevention order[1] a person has been involved in serious crime in England and Wales if he:

(1)   has committed a serious offence in England and Wales[2];

(2)   has facilitated the commission by another person of a serious offence in England and Wales[3]; or

(3)   has conducted himself in a way that was likely to facilitate the commission by himself or another person of a serious offence in England and Wales (whether or not such an offence was committed)[4].

'Involvement in serious crime in England and Wales' is any one or more of:

(a)   the commission of a serious offence in England and Wales[5];

(b)   conduct which facilitates the commission by another person of a serious offence in England and Wales[6];

(c)   conduct which is likely to facilitate the commission, by the person whose conduct it is or another person, of a serious offence in England and Wales (whether or not such an offence is committed)[7].

A partnership is involved in serious crime in England and Wales[8] if the partnership, or any of the partners, is so involved[9].

1   Ie for the purposes of the Serious Crime Act 2007 Pt 1 (ss 1–43). As to the making of a serious crime prevention order on conviction see PARA 351. These provisions are also applicable to a serious crime prevention order made other than on conviction by the High Court under the Serious Crime Act 2007 s 1 (see PARA 352).

2   Serious Crime Act 2007 s 2(1)(a). As to whether a person has committed a serious offence see PARA 351 note 3. Corresponding provision is made in connection with the making of serious crime prevention orders in Northern Ireland: see s 3(1)(a).

3   Serious Crime Act 2007 s 2(1)(b). In deciding for these purposes whether a person (the 'respondent') facilitates the commission by another person of a serious offence the court must ignore any act that the respondent can show to be reasonable in the circumstances (s 4(2)(a)) and, subject to this, his intentions, or any other aspect of his mental state, at the time (s 4(2)(b)). Corresponding provision is made in connection with the making of serious crime prevention orders in Northern Ireland: see s 3(1)(b).

4   Serious Crime Act 2007 s 2(1)(c). In deciding for these purposes whether a person (the 'respondent') conducts himself in a way that is likely to facilitate the commission by himself or another person of a serious offence (whether or not such an offence is committed), the court must ignore any act that the respondent can show to be reasonable in the circumstances (s 4(3)(a)) and, subject to this, his intentions, or any other aspect of his mental state, at the time (s 4(3)(b)). Corresponding provision is made in connection with the making of serious crime prevention orders in Northern Ireland: see s 3(1)(c).

5   Serious Crime Act 2007 s 2(3)(a). Corresponding provision is made in connection with the making of serious crime prevention orders in Northern Ireland: see s 3(3)(a).

6   Serious Crime Act 2007 s 2(3)(b). Corresponding provision is made in connection with the making of serious crime prevention orders in Northern Ireland: see s 3(3)(b).

7   Serious Crime Act 2007 s 2(3)(c). Corresponding provision is made in connection with the making of serious crime prevention orders in Northern Ireland: see s 3(3)(c).

8   Or Northern Ireland or elsewhere: Serious Crime Act 2007 s 31(3).

9   Serious Crime Act 2007 s 31(3). 'Involvement in serious crime in England and Wales' (or Northern Ireland) is to be read accordingly: s 31(3).

355.   Prohibitions, restrictions and requirements. A serious crime prevention order[1] may contain such prohibitions, restrictions or requirements[2] and such other terms[3] as the court considers appropriate for the purpose of protecting the public[4] by preventing, restricting or disrupting involvement by the person concerned in serious crime[5]. Examples of prohibitions, restrictions or requirements that may be imposed[6] on individuals (including partners in a partnership) by serious crime prevention orders include prohibitions or restrictions on, or requirements in relation to:

(1)   an individual's financial, property or business dealings or holdings[7];
(2)   an individual's working arrangements[8];
(3)   the means by which an individual communicates or associates with others, or the persons with whom he communicates or associates[9];
(4)   the premises[10] to which an individual has access[11];
(5)   the use of any premises or item by an individual[12];
(6)   an individual's travel (whether within the United Kingdom[13], between the United Kingdom and other places or otherwise)[14]; and
(7)   an individual's private dwelling[15].

Examples of prohibitions, restrictions or requirements that may be imposed[16] on bodies corporate, partnerships and unincorporated associations by serious crime prevention orders include prohibitions or restrictions on, or requirements in relation to:

(a)   financial, property or business dealings or holdings of such persons[17];
(b)   the types of agreements to which such persons may be a party[18];
(c)   the provision of goods or services by such persons[19];
(d)   the premises to which such persons have access[20];
(e)   the use of any premises or item by such persons[21]; and
(f)   the employment of staff by such persons[22].

Examples of requirements that may be imposed on any persons by serious crime prevention orders include a requirement on a person to answer specified or described questions, or provide specified or described information[23], and a requirement on a person to produce specified or described documents[24]. A serious crime prevention order may not include specified terms which restrict the freedom of a person providing information society services[25], terms which impose particular liabilities on service providers of intermediary services[26], or terms which impose certain monitoring obligations on service providers[27].

1   As to the making of a serious crime prevention order on conviction see PARA 351. These provisions are also applicable to a serious crime prevention order made other than on conviction by the High Court under the Serious Crime Act 2007 s 1 (see PARA 352).
2   Serious Crime Act 2007 ss 1(3)(a), 19(5)(a).
3   Serious Crime Act 2007 ss 1(3)(b), 19(5)(b). See also s 34; and the text and notes 25–27.
4   As to the meaning of 'the public' see PARA 351 note 8.
5   Serious Crime Act 2007 ss 1(3), 19(5). As to involvement by a person in serious crime (which for these purposes may be in England and Wales or (as the case may be) Northern Ireland) see PARA 354. This requirement need not be satisfied if the order proposed to be made or varied contains terms requiring the subject of the order to pay the costs of monitoring compliance with the order (ie under s 39(4), (5)): see s 39(6); and PARA 361 note 7.
6   The Serious Crime Act 2007 s 5 (see the text and notes 7–24) contains examples of the type of provision that may be made by a serious crime prevention order but it does not limit the type of provision that may be made by such an order: s 5(1). Examples of prohibitions, restrictions or requirements that may be imposed by serious crime prevention orders in England and Wales include prohibitions, restrictions or requirements in relation to places other than England and Wales: s 5(2). In connection with the compatibility of a serious crime prevention order with the Convention for the Protection of Human Rights and Fundamental Freedoms (Rome, 4 November 1950; TS 71 (1953; Cmd 8969) art 8 (right to family and private life: see RIGHTS

AND FREEDOMS vol 88A (2013) PARAS 317–367) see *R v Hancox* [2010] EWCA Crim 102, [2010] 4 All ER 537, [2010] 2 Cr App Rep (S) 484 (in which the Court of Appeal's judgment in *R v Boness, R v Bebbington* [2005] EWCA Crim 2395, 169 JP 621, [2006] Crim LR 160 on the matter of the proportionality, practicality, enforceability and precision of anti-social behaviour orders was applied in the context of serious crime prevention orders).

7   Serious Crime Act 2007 s 5(3)(a).
8   Serious Crime Act 2007 s 5(3)(b).
9   Serious Crime Act 2007 s 5(3)(c).
10 'Premises' includes any land, vehicle, vessel, aircraft or hovercraft: Serious Crime Act 2007 s 5(7).
11 Serious Crime Act 2007 s 5(3)(d).
12 Serious Crime Act 2007 s 5(3)(e).
13 As to the meaning of 'United Kingdom' see PARA 4 note 3.
14 Serious Crime Act 2007 s 5(3)(f).
15 Serious Crime Act 2007 s 5(6). These include, for example, prohibitions or restrictions on, or requirements in relation to, where an individual may reside: s 5(6).
16 See note 6.
17 Serious Crime Act 2007 s 5(4)(a).
18 Serious Crime Act 2007 s 5(4)(b).
19 Serious Crime Act 2007 s 5(4)(c).
20 Serious Crime Act 2007 s 5(4)(d).
21 Serious Crime Act 2007 s 5(4)(e).
22 Serious Crime Act 2007 s 5(4)(f).
23 Serious Crime Act 2007 s 5(5)(a). Where information is provided to a law enforcement officer in response to a requirement of the kind referred to in s 5(5)(a) or (b) (an 'information requirement') imposed by a serious crime prevention order the officer may, for the purpose of checking the accuracy of the information (s 5A(1), (2)(a) (s 5A added by the Serious Crime Act 2015 s 50(2)) or discovering the true position (Serious Crime Act 2007 s 5A(2)(b) (as so added)) disclose the information to any person who the officer reasonably believes may be able to contribute to doing either of those things, and any other person may disclose information to the law enforcement officer (s 5A(3)(a) (as so added)) or a person to whom the law enforcement officer has disclosed information under s 5A(2) (s 5A(3)(b) (as so added)), for the purpose of contributing to doing either of the things mentioned in s 5A(2)(a), (b). The law enforcement officer may also disclose the information referred to in s 5A(1) for the purposes of the prevention, detection, investigation or prosecution of criminal offences, whether in the United Kingdom or elsewhere (s 5A(4)(a) (as so added)) or the prevention, detection or investigation of conduct for which penalties other than criminal penalties are provided under the law of any part of the United Kingdom or of any country or territory outside the United Kingdom (s 5A(4)(b) (as so added)). A disclosure under s 5A does not breach any obligation of confidence owed by the person making the disclosure (s 5A(5)(a) (as so added)) or any other restriction on the disclosure of information (however imposed) (s 5A(5)(b) (as so added)). However, nothing in s 5A authorises a disclosure, in contravention of any provisions of the Data Protection Act 1998, of personal data which are not exempt from those provisions: s 5A(6) (as so added).

A person who complies with a requirement imposed by a serious crime prevention order to answer questions, provide information or produce documents (see note 24) does not breach any obligation of confidence or any other restriction on making the disclosure concerned (however imposed): s 38(1). A serious crime prevention order may not require a person to answer questions, or provide information, orally: ss 11, 38(2). The order may specify that these requirements are to be complied with at a time, within a period or at a frequency (s 5(5)(a)(i)), at a place (s 5(5)(a)(ii)), in a form and manner (s 5(5)(a)(iii)) and to a law enforcement officer or description of law enforcement officer (s 5(5)(a)(iv)), notified to the person by a law enforcement officer specified or described in the order. 'Law enforcement officer' means a constable, a National Crime Agency officer who is for the time being designated under the Crime and Courts Act 2013 s 9 or s 10 (see POLICE AND INVESTIGATORY POWERS), an officer of Revenue and Customs or a member of the Serious Fraud Office: Serious Crime Act 2007 s 5(7) (amended by the Crime and Courts Act 2013 Sch 8 para 177). A serious crime prevention order which provides for an authorised monitor (see s 39; and PARA 361) may, for the purpose of enabling the performance of monitoring services, impose requirements of the type mentioned in s 5(5) as if the references in s 5(5)(a)(iv) and s 5(5)(b)(iv) to a law enforcement officer included references to an authorised monitor: s 39(3).

A serious crime prevention order may not require a person to answer any privileged question (ie a question which the person would be entitled to refuse to answer on grounds of legal professional privilege in proceedings in the High Court), to provide any privileged information (ie information which the person would be entitled to refuse to provide on grounds of legal professional privilege in such proceedings) or to produce any privileged document (ie a document which the person would be entitled to refuse to produce on grounds of legal professional privilege in such proceedings) (s 12(1)–(4)), although this does not prevent an order from requiring a lawyer to provide the name and address of a client of his (s 12(5)). A person also may not be required to produce any excluded material as defined by the Police and Criminal Evidence Act 1984 s 11 (see POLICE AND INVESTIGATORY POWERS vol 84A (2013) PARA 454) (Serious Crime Act 2007 s 13(1)(a)) or to disclose any information or produce any document in respect of which he owes an obligation of confidence by virtue of carrying on a banking business (s 13(2)) unless (1) the person to whom the obligation of confidence is owed consents to the disclosure or production (s 13(3)); or (2) the order contains a requirement to disclose information, or produce documents, of this kind or to disclose specified information which is of this kind or to produce specified documents which are of this kind (s 13(4)). A person also may not be required to answer any question, to provide any information or to produce any document if the disclosure concerned is prohibited under any other enactment: s 14(1). For this purpose 'enactment' includes an Act of the Scottish Parliament, Northern Ireland legislation and an enactment comprised in subordinate legislation, and includes an enactment whenever passed or made; and 'subordinate legislation' has the same meaning as in the Interpretation Act 1978 (see STATUTES AND LEGISLATIVE PROCESS vol 96 (2012) PARAS 608, 1030) and also includes an instrument made under an Act of the Scottish Parliament or Northern Ireland legislation: Serious Crime Act 2007 s 14(2). A statement made by a person in response to a requirement imposed by a serious crime prevention order may not be used in evidence against him in any criminal proceedings unless:

(1)   the criminal proceedings relate to an offence under s 25 (see PARA 363) (s 15(1), (2)); or
(2)   (a) the criminal proceedings relate to another offence (s 15(3)(a)); (b) the person who made the statement gives evidence in the criminal proceedings (s 15(3)(b)); (c) in the course of that evidence, the person makes a statement which is inconsistent with the statement made in response to the requirement imposed by the order (s 15(3)(c)); and (d) in the criminal proceedings evidence relating to the statement made in response to the requirement imposed by the order is adduced, or a question about it is asked, by the person or on his behalf (s 15(3)(d)).

24 Serious Crime Act 2007 s 5(5)(b). In connection with the provision of information see note 23. 'Document' means anything in which information of any description is recorded (whether or not in legible form): s 5(7). Any reference in Pt 1 to the production of documents is, in the case of a document which contains information recorded otherwise than in legible form, a reference to the production of a copy of the information in legible form: s 5(8). The order may specify that these requirements are to be complied with at a time, within a period or at a frequency (s 5(5)(b)(i)), at a place (s 5(5)(b)(ii)), in a manner (s 5(5)(b)(iii)) and to a law enforcement officer or description of law enforcement officer (s 5(5)(b)(iv)), notified to the person by a law enforcement officer specified or described in the order. As to the excluded material see note 23.

A law enforcement officer may take and retain copies of, or extracts from, any document produced to a law enforcement officer in pursuance of a serious crime prevention order (s 41(1)(a)) and may retain any document so produced for as long as he considers that it is necessary to retain it (rather than any copy of it) for the purposes for which the document was obtained (s 41(1)(b)). A law enforcement officer may retain any document produced to a law enforcement officer in pursuance of a serious crime prevention order until the conclusion of any legal proceedings if he has reasonable grounds for believing that the document may have to be produced for the purposes of those proceedings (s 41(2)(a)) and might be unavailable unless retained (s 41(2)(b)).

25 See the Serious Crime Act 2007 s 34(1), which provides that a serious crime prevention order may not include terms which restrict the freedom of a service provider (ie a person providing an information society service) who is established in an EEA state other than the United Kingdom to provide information society services in relation to an EEA state unless:

(1)   the court concerned considers that the terms are necessary for the objective of protecting the public by preventing, restricting or disrupting involvement in serious crime in England and Wales (s 34(2)(a)(i)), relate to an information society service which prejudices that objective or presents a serious and grave risk of prejudice to it (s 34(2)(b)), and are proportionate to that objective (s 34(2)(c));
(2)   a law enforcement officer has requested the EEA state in which the service provider is established to take measures which the law enforcement officer considers to be of equivalent effect under the law of the EEA state to the terms and the EEA state has failed to take the measures (s 34(3)(a)); and

(3)   a law enforcement officer has notified the EU Commission and the EEA state of the intention to seek an order containing the terms and the terms (s 34(3)(b) (amended by SI 2011/1043)).

It does not matter for the purposes of the Serious Crime Act 2007 s 34(3) whether the request or notification is made before or after the making of the application for the order: s 34(4).

For the purposes of s 34 a service provider is established in a particular EEA state if he effectively pursues an economic activity using a fixed establishment in that EEA state for an indefinite period and he is a national of an EEA state or a company or firm mentioned in the Treaty on the Functioning of the European Union (Rome, 25 March 1957; TS 1 (1973); Cmnd 5179) ('TFEU') art 54 (see EUROPEAN UNION vol 47A (2014) PARA 303): Serious Crime Act 2007 s 34(7)(a) (amended by SI 2012/1809). The presence or use in a particular place of equipment or other technical means of providing an information society service does not, of itself, constitute the establishment of a service provider: Serious Crime Act 2007 s 34(7)(b). Where it cannot be determined from which of a number of establishments a given information society service is provided, that service is to be regarded as provided from the establishment where the service provider has the centre of his activities relating to the service: s 34(7)(c). References to a person being established in an EEA state are to be read accordingly: s 34(7).

For the purposes of s 34 'information society services' has the meaning given in Council Directive (EC) 2000/31 (OJ L178, 17.7.2000, p 1) on certain legal aspects of information society services, in particular electronic commerce, in the Internal Market (Directive on electronic commerce) (the 'E-Commerce Directive'), art 2(a) (which refers to Council Directive (EC) 98/34 (OJ L204, 21.7.98, p 37) laying down a procedure for the provision of information in the field of technical standards and regulations, art 1(2)) and is summarised in recital 17 of the E-Commerce Directive as covering 'any service normally provided for remuneration, at a distance, by means of electronic equipment for the processing (including digital compression) and storage of data, and at the individual request of a recipient of a service': Serious Crime Act 2007 s 34(8).

26 See the Serious Crime Act 2007 s 34(5), which provides that a serious crime prevention order may not include terms which impose liabilities on service providers of intermediary services so far as the imposition of those liabilities would result in a contravention of art 12, 13 or 14 of the E-Commerce Directive (see note 25) (various protections for service providers of intermediary services). For these purposes 'intermediary services' means (by virtue of the Serious Crime Act 2007 s 34(8)–(10)) an information society service which:
(1)   consists in the provision of access to a communication network or the transmission in a communication network of information provided by a recipient of the service (for which purpose the provision of access to a communication network and the transmission of information in a communication network includes the automatic, intermediate and transient storage of the information transmitted so far as the storage is for the sole purpose of carrying out the transmission in the network (although this does not apply if the information is stored for longer than is reasonably necessary for the transmission));
(2)   consists in the transmission in a communication network of information which is provided by a recipient of the service and is the subject of automatic, intermediate and temporary storage which is solely for the purpose of making the onward transmission of the information to other recipients of the service at their request more efficient; or
(3)   consists in the storage of information provided by a recipient of the service,
and 'recipient', in relation to a service, means any person who, for professional ends or otherwise, uses an information society service, in particular for the purposes of seeking information or making it accessible (s 34(8)).

27 See the Serious Crime Act 2007 s 34(6), which provides that a serious crime prevention order may not include terms which impose a general obligation on service providers of intermediary services covered by arts 12, 13, 14 of the E-Commerce Directive to monitor the information which they transmit or store when providing those services or actively to seek facts or circumstances indicating illegal activity when providing those services.

356. Duration of orders. A serious crime prevention order[1] must specify when it is to come into force and when it is to cease to be in force[2], although an order is not to be in force for more than five years beginning with the coming into force of the order[3]. An order can specify different times for the coming into force, or ceasing to be in force, of different provisions of the order[4].

The fact that an order, or any provision of an order, ceases to be in force does not prevent the court from making a new order to the same or similar effect[5]: a new order may be made in anticipation of an earlier order or provision ceasing to be in force[6].

1   As to the making of a serious crime prevention order on conviction see PARA 351. These provisions are also applicable to a serious crime prevention order made other than on conviction by the High Court under the Serious Crime Act 2007 s 1 (see PARA 352).
2   Serious Crime Act 2007 s 16(1).
3   Serious Crime Act 2007 s 16(2). Section 16(2), (4)(b) have effect subject to s 22E (see PARA 359): s 16(7) (added by the Serious Crime Act 2015 Sch 4 para 77).
4   Serious Crime Act 2007 s 16(3). Where it specifies different times in accordance with s 16(3) the order must specify when each provision is to come into force and cease to be in force (s 16(4)(a)) and is not to be in force for more than five years beginning with the coming into force of the first provision of the order to come into force (s 16(4)(b)). See note 3.
5   Serious Crime Act 2007 s 16(5).
6   Serious Crime Act 2007 s 16(6).

357.   Variation and discharge of orders by High Court.   The High Court in England and Wales may[1] vary a serious crime prevention order[2] if it has reasonable grounds to believe that the terms of the order as varied would protect the public[3] by preventing, restricting or disrupting involvement, by the person who is the subject of the order, in serious crime in England and Wales[4]. An application for variation may be made by the relevant applicant authority[5], the person who is the subject of the order[6] or any other person[7].

The High Court in England and Wales may also[8] discharge a serious crime prevention order in England and Wales[9], an application for which may be made by the relevant applicant authority[10], the person who is the subject of the order[11] or any other person[12].

Provision is made for the making of representations by affected parties[13]. An appeal may be made to the Court of Appeal in relation to a decision of the High Court to vary or discharge or not to vary or discharge a serious crime prevention order[14].

1   Ie on an application under the Serious Crime Act 2007 s 17 (see the text and notes 2–7). As to the conduct of proceedings see PARA 362.
2   As to the making of a serious crime prevention order on conviction see PARA 351. These provisions are also applicable to a serious crime prevention order made other than on conviction by the High Court under the Serious Crime Act 2007 s 1 (see PARA 352). As to the extent to which a person is bound by a variation see s 10; and PARA 351 note 14.
3   As to the meaning of 'the public' see PARA 351 note 8.
4   Serious Crime Act 2007 s 17(1). As to the 'subject' of a serious crime prevention order see PARA 351 note 2. Corresponding provision is made in connection with the making of serious crime prevention orders in Northern Ireland: see s 17(2). This requirement need not be satisfied if the order proposed to be varied contains terms requiring the subject of the order to pay the costs of monitoring compliance with the order (ie under s 39(4), (5)): see s 39(6); and PARA 361 note 7.
5   Serious Crime Act 2007 s 17(3)(a). As to the meaning of 'relevant applicant authority' see PARA 351 note 14. A variation on an application under s 17(3)(a) may include an extension of the period during which the order, or any provision of it, is in force (subject to the original limits imposed on the order by s 16(2), (4)(b) (see PARA 356)): s 17(8).
6   Serious Crime Act 2007 s 17(3)(b)(i). The court must not entertain an application by the person who is the subject of the order unless it considers that there has been a change of circumstances affecting the order: s 17(4).
7   Serious Crime Act 2007 s 17(3)(b)(ii). The court must not entertain an application by any person falling within s 17(3)(b)(ii) unless it considers that the person is significantly adversely affected by the order (s 17(5)(a)), condition A or B (see below) is met (s 17(5)(b)), and the application is not for the purpose of making the order more onerous on the person who is the subject of it (s 17(5)(c)). Condition A is that the person falling within s 17(3)(b)(ii) has, on an application under s 9 (see PARAS 352, 357, 358) been given an opportunity to make

representations (s 17(6)(a)(i)), or has made an application otherwise than under s 9 (s 17(6)(a)(ii)), in earlier proceedings in relation to the order (whether before the High Court or the Crown Court), and there has been a change of circumstances affecting the order (s 17(6)(b)). Condition B is that the person falling within s 17(3)(b)(ii) has not made an application of any kind in earlier proceedings in relation to the order (whether before the High Court or the Crown Court) (s 17(7)(a)) and it was reasonable in all the circumstances for the person not to have done so (s 17(7)(b)).

8   Ie on an application under the Serious Crime Act 2007 s 18 (see the text and notes 9–12).

9   Serious Crime Act 2007 s 18(1)(a). Corresponding provision is made in connection with the making of serious crime prevention orders in Northern Ireland: see s 18(1)(b).

10   Serious Crime Act 2007 s 18(2)(a).

11   Serious Crime Act 2007 s 18(2)(b)(i). The court must not entertain an application by the person who is the subject of the order unless it considers that there has been a change of circumstances affecting the order: s 18(3).

12   Serious Crime Act 2007 s 18(2)(b)(ii). The court must not entertain an application by any person falling within s 18(2)(b)(ii) unless it considers that the person is significantly adversely affected by the order (s 18(4)(a)) and condition A or B (see below) is met (s 18(4)(b)). Condition A is that the person has, on an application under s 9, been given an opportunity to make representations (s 18(5)(a)(i)), or has made an application otherwise than under s 9 (s 18(5)(a)(ii)), in earlier proceedings in relation to the order (whether before the High Court or the Crown Court), and there has been a change of circumstances affecting the order (s 18(5)(b)). Condition B is that the person has not made an application of any kind in earlier proceedings in relation to the order (whether before the High Court or the Crown Court) (s 18(6)(a)) and it was reasonable in all the circumstances for the person not to have done so (s 18(6)(b)).

13   The High Court must, on an application by a person, give the person an opportunity to make representations in proceedings before it about the variation or discharge of a serious crime prevention order if it considers that the variation or discharge of the order, or a decision not to vary or discharge it, would be likely to have a significant adverse effect on that person: Serious Crime Act 2007 s 9(2), (3).

14   Serious Crime Act 2007 s 23(1)(b), (c). The appeal may be brought by any person who was given an opportunity to make representations in the proceedings concerned by virtue of s 9(2) or s 9(3)) (see note 13): s 23(1). This provision is without prejudice to the rights of other persons to make appeals, by virtue of the Senior Courts Act 1981 s 16 (see COURTS AND TRIBUNALS vol 24 (2010) PARA 693) in relation to any judgments or orders of the High Court about serious crime prevention orders: Serious Crime Act 2007 s 23(2).

358.   Variation and replacement of orders on breach or conviction. The Crown Court may vary or replace a serious crime prevention order[1] where it is dealing with a person who is the subject of such an order[2] and who has been convicted of having committed a serious offence in England and Wales[3] or of having breached a serious crime prevention order[4]. An order may be varied or replaced only on an application by the relevant applicant authority[5] and only if the court has reasonable grounds to believe that the terms of the order as varied, or the new order, would protect the public[6] by preventing, restricting or disrupting involvement by the person in serious crime in England and Wales[7], and a variation or a new order must not be made except in addition to a sentence imposed in respect of the offence concerned[8] or in addition to an order discharging the person conditionally[9].

1   As to the making of a serious crime prevention order on conviction see PARA 351. These provisions are also applicable to a serious crime prevention order made other than on conviction by the High Court under the Serious Crime Act 2007 s 1 (see PARA 352). The fact that a serious crime prevention order has been made or varied by the High Court does not prevent it from being varied by the Crown Court in accordance with Pt 1 (ss 1–43) (s 22(1)). A decision by the Crown Court not to vary a serious crime prevention order under s 20 or s 21 (see the text and notes 2–9) does not prevent a subsequent application to the High Court (see PARA 357) for a variation of the order in consequence of the same offence (s 22(4)). As to the extent to which a person is bound by a variation see s 10; and PARA 351 note 14. As to appeals from decisions of the Crown Court see PARA 360.

2   Serious Crime Act 2007 ss 20(2)(a), 21(2)(a) (ss 9(4), 21(2), (5), (6) amended, s 21(8) added, by the Serious Crime Act 2015 s 48, Sch 4 para 76). As to the 'subject' of a serious crime prevention order see PARA 351 note 2. The requirements set out in the Serious Crime Act 2007 ss 20(2), 21(2) need not be satisfied if the order proposed to be varied contains terms requiring the subject of the order to pay the costs of monitoring compliance with the order (ie under s 39(4), (5)): see s 39(6); and PARA 361 note 7.

3   Serious Crime Act 2007 s 20(1). The Crown Court's powers under these provisions arise where the court is dealing with a person who has been convicted by or before a magistrates' court of having committed a serious offence in England and Wales and has been committed to the Crown Court to be dealt with (s 20(1)(a)), or who has been convicted by or before the Crown Court of having committed a serious offence in England and Wales (s 20(1)(b)), and the court may exercise these powers in addition to dealing with the person in relation to the offence (s 20(2)(b)). As to whether a person has committed a serious offence see PARA 351 note 3. Corresponding provision is made in connection with the making of serious crime prevention orders in Northern Ireland: see s 20(3), (4).

4   Serious Crime Act 2007 s 21(1). A reference to replacing a serious crime prevention order is to making a new serious crime prevention order and discharging the existing one: s 21(8) (as added: see note 2). The Crown Court's powers under these provisions arise where the court is dealing with a person who has been convicted by or before a magistrates' court of having committed an offence under s 25 (see PARA 363) in relation to a serious crime prevention order and has been committed to the Crown Court to be dealt with (s 21(1)(a)) or who has been convicted by or before the Crown Court of having committed an offence under s 25 in relation to a serious crime prevention order (s 21(1)(b)), and the court may exercise these powers in addition to dealing with the person in relation to the offence (s 21(2)(b)). Corresponding provision is made in connection with the making of serious crime prevention orders in Northern Ireland: see s 21(3), (4).

5   Serious Crime Act 2007 ss 20(5), 21(5) (s 21(5) as amended: see note 2). As to the meaning of 'relevant applicant authority' see PARA 351 note 14.

6   As to the meaning of 'the public' see PARA 351 note 8.

7   Serious Crime Act 2007 ss 20(2), 21(2) (s 21(2) as amended: see note 2). As to involvement by a person in serious crime (which for these purposes may be in England and Wales or (as the case may be) Northern Ireland) see PARA 354. A variation may include an extension of the period during which the order, or any provision of it, is in force (subject to the original limits imposed on the order by s 16(2), (4)(b) (see PARA 356)): ss 20(7), 21(7). The Crown Court must, on an application by a person, give the person an opportunity to make representations in proceedings before it arising by virtue of s 20, s 21 or s 22E (see PARA 359) if it considers that the variation of the serious crime prevention order concerned (or a decision not to vary it) would be likely to have a significant adverse effect on that person: s 9(4) (as so amended).

8   Serious Crime Act 2007 ss 20(6)(a), 21(6)(a) (s 21(6) as amended: see note 2).

9   Serious Crime Act 2007 ss 20(6)(b), 21(6)(b). A variation of a serious crime prevention order may be made as mentioned in s 20(6)(b) or s 21(6)(b) notwithstanding anything in the Powers of Criminal Courts (Sentencing) Act 2000 ss 12, 14 (which relate to orders discharging a person absolutely or conditionally and their effect: see PARAS 443, 445): Serious Crime Act 2007 s 36(6).

359. Extension of orders pending outcome of criminal proceedings. Where a person subject to a serious crime prevention order[1] is charged with a serious offence[2] or an offence[3] of failing to comply with the serious crime prevention order[4] the Crown Court may, on application by the relevant applicant authority[5], vary the serious crime prevention order so that it continues in effect until one of the following occurs (if the order would otherwise cease to have effect before then)[6]:

(1)   following the person's conviction of the offence[7] the order is varied[8] by reference to the offence[9], a new serious crime prevention order is made[10] by reference to the offence[11], or the court deals with the person for the offence without varying the order or making a new one[12];

(2)   the person is acquitted of the offence[13];

(3)   the charge is withdrawn[14]; or

(4)   proceedings in respect of the charge are discontinued[15] or an order is made for the charge to lie on the file[16].

An order may be made under these provisions only if the serious crime prevention order is still in force[17] and the court has reasonable grounds for believing that the order would protect the public by preventing, restricting or disrupting involvement by the person in serious crime[18].

1   As to the making of a serious crime prevention order on conviction see PARA 351. These provisions are also applicable to a serious crime prevention order made other than on conviction by the High Court under the Serious Crime Act 2007 s 1 (see PARA 352).
2   Serious Crime Act 2007 s 22E(1)(a) (s 22E added by the Serious Crime Act 2015 s 49). As to the 'serious offences' see PARA 353.
3   Ie an offence under the Serious Crime Act 2007 s 25: see PARA 363.
4   Serious Crime Act 2007 s 22E(1)(b) (as added: see note 2).
5   As to the meaning of 'relevant applicant authority' see PARA 351 note 14.
6   Serious Crime Act 2007 s 22E(2)(a), (3) (as added: see note 2).
7   Ie the offence mentioned in the text and notes 1–4.
8   Ie under the Serious Crime Act 2007 s 20 or s 21 (see PARA 358) or under corresponding Scottish provisions.
9   Serious Crime Act 2007 s 22E(4)(a)(i) (as added: see note 2).
10 Ie under the Serious Crime Act 2007 s 19 (see PARA 358) or s 21 or under corresponding Scottish provisions.
11 Serious Crime Act 2007 s 22E(4)(a)(ii) (as added: see note 2).
12 Serious Crime Act 2007 s 22E(4)(a)(iii) (as added: see note 2).
13 Serious Crime Act 2007 s 22E(4)(b) (as added: see note 2).
14 Serious Crime Act 2007 s 22E(4)(c) (as added: see note 2).
15 Serious Crime Act 2007 s 22E(4)(d)(i) (as added: see note 2).
16 Serious Crime Act 2007 s 22E(4)(d)(ii) (as added: see note 2).
17 Serious Crime Act 2007 s 22E(5)(a) (as added: see note 2).
18 Serious Crime Act 2007 s 22E(5)(b) (as added: see note 2). In s 22E(5)(b) 'serious crime' means, in the case of a serious crime prevention order in England and Wales, serious crime in England and Wales: s 22E(6)(a) (as so added).

360. Appeals from decisions of Crown Court.

An appeal against a decision of the Crown Court in relation to a serious crime prevention order[1] may be made to the Court of Appeal[2] by the person who is the subject of the order[3] or the relevant applicant authority[4]. An appeal may also be made to the Court of Appeal by an affected party[5] in relation to a decision of the Crown Court to make a serious crime prevention order[6] or to vary, or not to vary, such an order[7]. Any such appeal lies only with the leave of the Court of Appeal[8] unless the judge who made the decision grants a certificate that the decision is fit[9] for appeal[10]. An appeal against a decision of the Court of Appeal on an appeal to that court under these provisions[11] may be made to the Supreme Court by any person who was a party to the proceedings before the Court of Appeal[12]: any such an appeal lies only with the leave of the Court of Appeal or the Supreme Court[13].

Appeals under these provisions are governed by rules made by the Secretary of State[14].

1   As to the making of a serious crime prevention order by the Crown Court see PARA 351 et seq.
2   Subject to any rules of court made under the Senior Courts Act 1981 s 53(1) (distribution of business between civil and criminal divisions: see COURTS AND TRIBUNALS vol 24 (2010) PARAS 693–694), the criminal division of the Court of Appeal is the division which is to exercise jurisdiction in relation to an appeal under these provisions from a decision of the Crown Court in the exercise of its jurisdiction in England and Wales under the Serious Crime Act 2007 Pt 1 (ss 1–43): s 24(5).
3   Serious Crime Act 2007 s 24(1)(a). As to the 'subject' of a serious crime prevention order see PARA 351 note 2. The power to make an appeal to the Court of Appeal under s 24(1)(a) operates instead of any power for the person who is the subject of the order to make an appeal against a

decision of the Crown Court in relation to a serious crime prevention order by virtue of the Criminal Appeal Act 1968 s 9 or s 10 (see PARAS 627, 628): Serious Crime Act 2007 s 24(11)(a).

4   Serious Crime Act 2007 s 24(1)(b). As to the meaning of 'relevant applicant authority' see PARA 351 note 14.

5   Ie any person who was given an opportunity to make representations in the proceedings concerned by virtue of the Serious Crime Act 2007 s 9(4) (see PARA 358).

6   Serious Crime Act 2007 s 24(2)(a).

7   Serious Crime Act 2007 s 24(2)(b).

8   Serious Crime Act 2007 s 24(3).

9   Ie under the Serious Crime Act 2007 s 24.

10   Serious Crime Act 2007 s 24(4).

11   Ie under the Serious Crime Act 2007 s 24(1), (2) (see the text and notes 1–7).

12   Serious Crime Act 2007 s 24(6). The Criminal Appeal Act 1968 s 33(3) (limitation on appeal from criminal division of the Court of Appeal: England and Wales: see CRIMINAL PROCEDURE vol 28 (2015) PARA 812) does not prevent an appeal to the Supreme Court under the Serious Crime Act 2007 s 24(6): s 24(12).

13   Serious Crime Act 2007 s 24(7). Such leave must not be granted unless it is certified by the Court of Appeal that a point of law of general public importance is involved in the decision (s 24(8)(a)) and it appears to the Court of Appeal or (as the case may be) the Supreme Court that the point is one which ought to be considered by the Supreme Court (s 24(8)(b)).

14   See the Serious Crime Act 2007 (Appeals under Section 24) Order 2008, SI 2008/1863 (amended by SI 2013/534). That order was made under the Serious Crime Act 2007 s 24(9), (10), under which it is provided that the Secretary of State may for the purposes of s 24 by order make provision corresponding (subject to any specified modifications) to that made by or under an enactment and relating to appeals to the Court of Appeal under the Criminal Appeal Act 1968 Pt 1 (ss 1–32) (or corresponding Northern Ireland provision) (Serious Crime Act 2007 s 24(9)(a)), appeals from any decision of the Court of Appeal on appeals falling within s 24(9)(a) (s 24(9)(b)) or any matter connected with or arising out of appeals falling within s 24(9)(a) or (b) (s 24(9)(c)). Such an order under may, in particular, make provision about the payment of costs: s 24(10). Corresponding Northern Ireland provision is made by s 24(9A) (added by SI 2010/976).

361.   Monitoring of compliance with orders made against corporations, partnerships and associations. A serious crime prevention order[1] against a body corporate, partnership or unincorporated association[2] may authorise a law enforcement agency[3] to enter into arrangements with a specified person[4] or any person who falls within a specified description of persons[5] to perform specified monitoring services[6] or monitoring services of a specified description (an 'authorised monitor')[7]. A serious crime prevention order which provides for an authorised monitor may require any body corporate, partnership or unincorporated association which is the subject of the order[8] to pay to the law enforcement agency concerned some or all of the costs incurred by the agency under the arrangements with the authorised monitor[9].

1   As to the making of a serious crime prevention order on conviction see PARA 351. These provisions are also applicable to a serious crime prevention order made other than on conviction by the High Court under the Serious Crime Act 2007 s 1 (see PARA 352).

2   As to the making of serious crime prevention orders against bodies corporate, partnerships and unincorporated associations see the Serious Crime Act 2007 ss 10, 30–32; and PARA 351 note 14. As to compliance with orders made against corporations, partnerships and associations see ss 39, 40; and PARA 361.

3   Ie, in England and Wales (by virtue of the Serious Crime Act 2007 ss 39(10), 40(8) (s 39(10) amended by the Crime and Courts Act 2013 Sch 8 para 178; and by the Police Reform and Social Responsibility Act 2011 Sch 16 para 370):

   (1)   the chief constable of a police force maintained under the Police Act 1996 s 2 (see POLICE AND INVESTIGATORY POWERS vol 84 (2013) PARA 52);

   (2)   the Commissioner of Police of the Metropolis (see POLICE AND INVESTIGATORY POWERS vol 84 (2013) PARA 117);

   (3)   the Common Council of the City of London (see LONDON GOVERNMENT vol 71 (2013) PARA 34) in its capacity as police authority;

(a)   the Northern Ireland Policing Board;
(5)   the National Crime Agency (see POLICE AND INVESTIGATORY POWERS vol 84 (2013) PARA 424);
(6)   the Commissioners for Her Majesty's Revenue and Customs (see CUSTOMS AND EXCISE vol 31 (2012) PARA 921 et seq); or
(7)   the Director of the Serious Fraud Office (see POLICE AND INVESTIGATORY POWERS vol 84A (2013) PARA 796).

4   Serious Crime Act 2007 s 39(1)(a). 'Specified', in relation to a serious crime prevention order, means specified in the order: s 39(10).
5   Serious Crime Act 2007 s 39(1)(b).
6   'Monitoring services' means analysing some or all information received in accordance with a serious crime prevention order, reporting to a law enforcement officer as to whether, on the basis of the information and any other information analysed for this purpose, the subject of the order appears to be complying with the order or any part of it, and any related services: Serious Crime Act 2007 s 39(10). As to the meaning of 'law enforcement officer' see PARA 355 note 23.
7   Serious Crime Act 2007 s 39(1), (2). Nothing in s 39 affects the ability of law enforcement agencies to enter into arrangements otherwise than in accordance with an authorisation under s 39: s 39(9). A law enforcement agency must inform the subject of a serious crime prevention order which provides for an authorised monitor of the name of, and an address for, any person with whom the agency has entered into arrangements in accordance with the authorisation in the order: s 39(8). As to the role of authorised monitors see also s 39(3); and PARA 355 note 23. The statutory tests for making or varying a serious crime prevention order (see ss 1(1)(b), (3), 17(1), (2), 19(2), (5), 20(2), 21(2); and PARAS 351, 352, 355, 357, 358) do not operate in relation to an order so far as the order contains terms of the kind envisaged by s 39(4), (5) (or by s 39(1) for the purposes of s 39(4), (5)): s 39(6).
8   As to the 'subject' of a serious crime prevention order see PARA 351 note 2.
9   Serious Crime Act 2007 s 39(4). Any such order must specify the period, or periods, within which payments are to be made (s 39(5)(a)), may require the making of payments on account (s 39(5)(b)) and may include other terms about the calculation or payment of costs (s 39(5)(c)): however a court must not include in a serious crime prevention order (whether initially or on a variation) terms of the kind envisaged by s 39(4) or (5) unless it considers that it is appropriate to do so having regard to all the circumstances including, in particular the means of the body corporate, partnership or unincorporated association concerned (s 39(7)(a)), the expected size of the costs (s 39(7)(b)) and the effect of the terms on the ability of any body corporate, partnership or unincorporated association which is carrying on business to continue to do so (s 39(7)(c)).
     The appropriate authority (ie in relation to England and Wales, the Secretary of State) may by order make provision (which may, in particular, include provision about appeals) about the practice and procedure for determining the amount of any costs payable by virtue of s 39(4), (5) and any interest payable in respect of those costs: s 40(1), (2) (s 40(1), (4) amended, s 40(9) added, by SI 2010/976). Where any amounts required to be paid by virtue of the Serious Crime Act 2007 s 39(4), (5) have not been paid within a required period, the law enforcement agency concerned must take reasonable steps (as determined by the Secretary of State by order) to recover them and any interest payable in respect of them (s 40(3), (4) (s 40(4) as so amended)): any amounts which have not been recovered despite the taking of the reasonable steps are recoverable as if due to the law enforcement agency concerned by virtue of a civil order or judgment (s 40(5)).
     Where any amounts required to be paid by virtue of s 39(4), (5) are, in the case of an order of the Crown Court, not paid within a required period, the unpaid balance from time to time carries interest at the rate for the time being specified in the Judgments Act 1838 s 17 (interest on civil judgment debts: see FINANCIAL SERVICES AND INSTITUTIONS vol 49 (2008) PARA 1307): Serious Crime Act 2007 s 40(6).

362.   Functions of applicant authorities.   The functions[1] of the Director of Public Prosecutions[2] and the Director of the Serious Fraud Office are exercisable under the superintendence of the Attorney General[3] and may be delegated[4]. Those functions are:

(1)   to have the conduct of applications for serious crime prevention orders[5] in England and Wales or for their variation or discharge[6];

(2)   to appear on any application made[7] by another person for the variation or discharge of a serious crime prevention order in England and Wales[8];

(3)   to have the conduct of, or (as the case may be) appear in, any other proceedings[9] in connection with serious crime prevention orders[10];

(4)   to give advice in connection with any proceedings or possible proceedings in connection with serious crime prevention orders[11]; and

(5)   to do anything for the purposes of, or in connection with, the functions referred to above[12].

1   Ie under the Serious Crime Act 2007 Pt 1 (ss 1–43) (see PARA 351 et seq).

2   The Code for Crown Prosecutors issued under the Prosecution of Offences Act 1985 s 10 (guidelines for Crown Prosecutors: see CRIMINAL PROCEDURE vol 27 (2015) PARA 35) may include guidance by the Director on general principles to be applied by Crown Prosecutors in determining in any case:
    (1)   whether to make an application for a serious crime prevention order in England and Wales or for the variation or discharge of such an order (Serious Crime Act 2007 Sch 2 para 4(1)(a));
    (2)   whether to present a petition by virtue of s 27 (see PARA 365) (Sch 2 para 4(1)(b)); or
    (3)   where such an application has been made or petition presented, whether the proceedings concerned should be discontinued (Sch 2 para 4(1)(c)),
    and the Prosecution of Offences Act 1985 s 10(2), (3) (power to make alterations in the Code and duty to set out alterations in Director's report: see CRIMINAL PROCEDURE vol 27 (2015) PARA 35) are to be read accordingly (Serious Crime Act 2007 Sch 2 para 4(2)). As to the variation and discharge of serious crime prevention orders see PARAS 357, 358.
    The Prosecution of Offences Act 1985 s 14 (power of Attorney General to make regulations about fees of legal representatives and costs and expenses of witnesses: see CRIMINAL PROCEDURE vol 27 (2015) PARA 36) applies in relation to proceedings in connection with serious crime prevention orders and attendance for the purposes of such cases as it applies in relation to criminal proceedings and attendance for the purposes of such cases: Serious Crime Act 2007 Sch 2 para 5.
    The Commissioners for Revenue and Customs Act 2005 s 21 (disclosure to prosecuting authority: see CUSTOMS AND EXCISE vol 31 (2012) PARA 923) has effect as if the purpose mentioned in s 21(1)(b) included the purpose of enabling the Director to exercise the Director's functions under the Serious Crime Act 2007 Pt 1: Sch 2 para 5A (added by SI 2014/834).
    Corresponding provision is made in connection with the functions of the Director of Public Prosecutions for Northern Ireland: see Sch 2 para 16.
    In Sch 2 references to having the conduct of proceedings include references to starting or discontinuing proceedings: Sch 2 para 21.

3   Serious Crime Act 2007 Sch 2 paras 3, 14. The Criminal Justice Act 1987 Sch 1 para 8 (power of Attorney General to make regulations about fees of counsel and costs and expenses of witnesses: see CRIMINAL PROCEDURE vol 27 (2015) PARA 40) applies in relation to proceedings in connection with serious crime prevention orders and attendance for the purposes of such cases as it applies in relation to criminal proceedings and attendance for the purposes of such cases: Serious Crime Act 2007 Sch 2 para 15.

4   The Director of Public Prosecutions may, to such extent as he may decide, delegate the exercise of his functions under the Serious Crime Act 2007 Pt 1 to a Crown Prosecutor (Sch 2 para 2(1)) and references in Pt 1 to the Director are accordingly to be read, so far as necessary for this purpose, as references to the Director or any Crown Prosecutor (Sch 2 para 2(2)). The Director of the Serious Fraud Office may, to such extent as he may decide, delegate the exercise of his functions under Pt 1 to a member of the Serious Fraud Office designated under the Criminal Justice Act 1987 s 1(7) (see CRIMINAL PROCEDURE vol 27 (2015) PARA 39) (Serious Crime Act 2007 Sch 2 para 13(1)), and references in Pt 1 to the Director are accordingly to be read, so far as necessary for this purpose, as references to the Director or any member of the Serious Fraud Office so designated (Sch 2 para 13(2)).

5   As to the making of a serious crime prevention order on conviction see PARA 351. These provisions are also applicable to a serious crime prevention order made other than on conviction by the High Court under the Serious Crime Act 2007 s 1 (see PARA 352).

6   Serious Crime Act 2007 Sch 2 paras 1(a), 12(a). See notes 2–3.

7   Ie under the Serious Crime Act 2007 s 17 or s 18 (see PARA 357).

8   Serious Crime Act 2007 Sch 2 paras 1(b), 12(b). See notes 2–3.

9   Ie, whether proceedings on appeal, by virtue of the Serious Crime Act 2007 s 27 (see PARA 365), or otherwise.

10   Serious Crime Act 2007 Sch 2 paras 1(c), 12(c). See notes 2–3.

11   Serious Crime Act 2007 Sch 2 paras 1(d), 12(d). See notes 2–3.
12   Serious Crime Act 2007 Sch 2 paras 1(e), 12(e). See notes 2–3.

363.   Offences.   A person who without reasonable excuse fails to comply with a serious crime prevention order commits an offence and is liable on summary conviction to imprisonment for a term not exceeding 12 months or to a fine not exceeding the statutory maximum or to both, and on conviction on indictment, to imprisonment for a term not exceeding five years or to a fine or to both[1]. A fine imposed on a partnership or unincorporated association on its conviction for such an offence is to be paid out of the partnership assets or, as the case may be, the funds of the corporation[2].

In proceedings for an offence, a copy of the original order or any variation of it, certified as such by the proper officer of the court which made it, is admissible as evidence of its having been made and of its contents to the same extent that oral evidence of those things is admissible in those proceedings[3]. For these purposes a failure to comply with a requirement to make payments[4] occurs when the amounts become[5] recoverable (and not before)[6].

If an offence committed by a body corporate, partnership or unincorporated association is proved to have been committed with the consent or connivance of an officer of the body corporate, a partner or senior officer of the partnership, an officer of the association, or a person who was purporting to act in any such capacity, he (as well as the body corporate, partnership or association) is guilty of the offence and liable to be proceeded against and punished accordingly[7]. Proceedings for an offence alleged to have been committed by a partnership or unincorporated association must be brought in the name of the partnership or association (and not in that of any of the partners or members), although this is not to be read as prejudicing any liability[8] of a partner or officer[9].

1   Serious Crime Act 2007 s 25(1), (2).
2   Serious Crime Act 2007 ss 31(7), 32(6). As to the meanings of the terms used in ss 30–32 see PARA 351 note 14.
3   Serious Crime Act 2007 s 25(4).
4   Ie a requirement imposed by virtue of the Serious Crime Act 2007 s 39(4), (5) (see PARA 361).
5   Ie as mentioned in the Serious Crime Act 2007 s 40(5) (see PARA 361).
6   Serious Crime Act 2007 s 40(7).
7   Serious Crime Act 2007 ss 30(2), 31(8), (9)(a), 32(7), (8)(a).
8   Ie under the Serious Crime Act 2007 s 31(8) or s 32(7).
9   Serious Crime Act 2007 ss 31(5), (9)(b), 32(4), (8)(b). For the purposes of such proceedings rules of court relating to the service of documents have effect as if the partnership were a body corporate (see PARA 351 note 15) (ss 31(6)(a), 32(5)(a)) and the Criminal Justice Act 1925 s 33 and the Magistrates' Courts Act 1980 Sch 3 (proceedings against corporations etc: see CRIMINAL PROCEDURE vol 27 (2015) PARA 198) (and corresponding Scottish and Northern Ireland provisions) apply as they apply in relation to a body corporate (Serious Crime Act 2007 ss 31(6)(b), 32(5)(b)).

364.   Forfeiture orders.   The court before which a person is convicted of an offence[1] may order the forfeiture of anything in his possession at the time of the offence which the court considers to have been involved in the offence[2]. Before making such an order in relation to anything the court must give an opportunity to make representations to any person (in addition to the convicted person) who claims to be the owner of that thing or otherwise to have an interest in it[3]. Such an order may not be made so as to come into force at any time before there is no further possibility (ignoring any power to appeal out of time) of the order being varied or set aside on appeal[4]. Where the court makes a forfeiture order it may also make such other provision as it considers to be necessary for giving effect to the forfeiture[5]: such provision may, in particular, include provision relating to the retention, handling, destruction or other disposal of what is forfeited[6]. Provision made by virtue of these provisions may be varied at any time by the court that made it[7].

1 Ie under the Serious Crime Act 2007 s 25 (see PARA 363).
2 Serious Crime Act 2007 s 26(1).
3 Serious Crime Act 2007 s 26(2).
4 Serious Crime Act 2007 s 26(3).
5 Serious Crime Act 2007 s 26(4).
6 Serious Crime Act 2007 s 26(5).
7 Serious Crime Act 2007 s 26(6).

365. Winding up petitions. The Director of Public Prosecutions or the Director of the Serious Fraud Office may present a petition[1] to the court for the winding up of a company, partnership or relevant body if the company, partnership or relevant body has been convicted of an offence[2] in relation to a serious crime prevention order[3] and the Director concerned considers that it would be in the public interest for the company, partnership or (as the case may be) relevant body to be wound up[4]. No petition may be presented, or order to wind up made, by virtue of these provisions if an appeal against conviction for the offence concerned has been made and not finally determined[5] or the period during which such an appeal may be made has not expired[6]: in deciding for these purposes whether an appeal is finally determined or whether the period during which an appeal may be made has expired, any power to appeal out of time is to be ignored[7]. No petition may be presented, or order to wind up made, by virtue of these provisions if the company, partnership or relevant body is already being wound up by the court[8].

1 The Insolvency Act 1986 applies in relation to a petition under these provisions for the winding up of a company and the company's winding up as it applies in relation to a petition under the Insolvency Act 1986 s 124A (see COMPANY AND PARTNERSHIP INSOLVENCY vol 16 (2011) PARA 392) for the winding up of a company and the company's winding up (winding up on grounds of public interest), subject to specified modifications (see the Serious Crime Act 2007 s 27(2)–(4) (s 27(3) amended by SI 2014/834)): the Insolvency Act 1986 s 420 (power to make provision about insolvent partnerships: see COMPANY AND PARTNERSHIP INSOLVENCY vol 17 (2011) PARA 1209) also applies to a partnership to which these provisions apply (see the Serious Crime Act 2007 s 27(5), (7)), and the appropriate Minister may by order provide for the Insolvency Act 1986 to apply, with such modifications as that person considers appropriate, in relation to a petition under this section for the winding up of a relevant body and the relevant body's winding up (see the Serious Crime Act 2007 s 27(6), (7)). The Secretary of State may by order make such modifications as he considers appropriate to the application of the Insolvency Act 1986 by virtue of the Serious Crime Act 2007 s 27(2): s 29(1)(a). Any modifications so made are in addition to the modifications made by s 27(3), (4): s 29(2). The Secretary of State may by order make such consequential or supplementary provision, applying with or without modifications any provision made by or under an enactment, as he considers appropriate in connection with s 27(2)–(4): s 29(3). An order made by virtue of s 27(5) or (6) or s 29(1) may, in particular, contain consequential or supplementary provision applying, with or without modifications, any provision made by or under an enactment: s 29(4).
   For the purposes of s 27 (by virtue of s 27(12) (amended by the Co-operative and Community Benefit Societies Act 2014 Sch 4 para 116; and by SI 2009/1941)):
   (1)'relevant body' means:
       (a) a building society (within the meaning of the Building Societies Act 1986: see FINANCIAL SERVICES AND INSTITUTIONS vol 50 (2008) PARA 1856);
       (b) an incorporated friendly society (within the meaning of the Friendly Societies Act 1992: see FINANCIAL SERVICES AND INSTITUTIONS vol 50 (2008) PARA 2082);
       (c) a registered society within the meaning of the Co-operative and Community Benefit Societies Act 2014 (see FINANCIAL SERVICES AND INSTITUTIONS);
       (d) a limited liability partnership; or

(e)   such other description of person as may be specified by order made by the Secretary of State;

(2)   'appropriate Minister' means the Treasury (in relation to a relevant body falling within heads (a)–(c) of the definition of 'relevant body' above) and the Secretary of State (in relation to any other relevant body);

(3)   'company' means a company registered under the Companies Act 2006 in England and Wales (COMPANIES vol 14 (2009) PARA 24 et seq) or an unregistered company within the meaning of the Insolvency Act 1986 Pt 5 (see s 220; and COMPANY AND PARTNERSHIP INSOLVENCY vol 17 (2011) PARA 1109) but does not include a relevant body;

(4)   'the court', in relation to a company, means a court in England and Wales having jurisdiction to wind up the company;

(5)   'partnership' does not include a relevant body; and

(6)   the references to the Insolvency Act 1986 ss 124–125 include references to those sections as applied by s 221(1) (unregistered companies: see COMPANY AND PARTNERSHIP INSOLVENCY vol 17 (2011) PARA 1110).

Corresponding provision is made for Northern Ireland: see the Serious Crime Act 2007 ss 25(3), 28, 29(1A), (2), (3), (3A), (4) (s 28 amended by SI 2009/1941; SI 2010/976; Serious Crime Act 2007 s 29(1A), (3A) added, s 29(2), (3), (4) amended, by SI 2010/976).

2   Ie under the Serious Crime Act 2007 s 25 (see PARA 363).
3   Serious Crime Act 2007 s 27(1)(a) (s 27(1) amended by SI 2014/834).
4   Serious Crime Act 2007 s 27(1)(b).
5   Serious Crime Act 2007 s 27(9)(a).
6   Serious Crime Act 2007 s 27(9)(b).
7   Serious Crime Act 2007 s 27(11).
8   Serious Crime Act 2007 s 27(8).

(vii) Travel Restriction Orders

366. Nature and effect of orders. A 'travel restriction order' is an order which may be made in respect of a person who has been convicted of a drug-trafficking offence[1]. It prohibits the offender from leaving the United Kingdom[2] at any time in the period which begins with the offender's release from custody[3] and continues after that time for such period of not less than two years as may be specified in the order[4].

A travel restriction order may contain a direction to the offender to deliver up, or cause to be delivered up, to the court any UK passport[5] held by him; and where such a direction is given, the court must send any passport delivered up in pursuance of the direction to the Secretary of State at such address as the Secretary of State may determine[6]. Where the offender's passport is held by the Secretary of State by reason of the making of any direction contained in a travel restriction order, the Secretary of State (without prejudice to any other power or duty of his to retain the passport) may retain it for so long as the prohibition imposed by the order applies to the offender, and is not for the time being suspended[7]; and must not return the passport after the prohibition has ceased to apply, or when it is suspended, except where the passport has not expired and an application for its return is made to him by the offender[8].

A travel restriction order made in relation to any person does not prevent the exercise in relation to that person of any prescribed removal power[9].

1   See the Criminal Justice and Police Act 2001 s 33(1)(a); and PARA 367. For this purpose 'drug trafficking offence' means any of the following offences (including one committed by aiding, abetting, counselling or procuring):

(1)   an offence under the Misuse of Drugs Act 1971 s 4(2) or s 4(3) (see CRIMINAL LAW vol 26 (2010) PARA 725) (Criminal Justice and Police Act 2001 s 34(1)(a));

(2)   an offence under the Misuse of Drugs Act 1971 s 20 (see CRIMINAL LAW vol 26 (2010) PARA 732) (Criminal Justice and Police Act 2001 s 34(1)(b));

(3) any such other offence under the Misuse of Drugs Act 1971 as may be designated by order made by the Secretary of State (Criminal Justice and Police Act 2001 s 34(1)(c));

(4) an offence under the Customs and Excise Management Act 1979 s 50(2), (3) (improper importation: see CUSTOMS AND EXCISE vol 31 (2012) PARA 992), s 68(2) (exportation: see CUSTOMS AND EXCISE vol 31 (2012) PARA 1027) or s 170 (fraudulent evasion: see CUSTOMS AND EXCISE vol 31 (2012) PARA 1175), or in connection with a prohibition or restriction on importation or exportation having effect by virtue of the Misuse of Drugs Act 1971 s 3 (see MEDICAL PRODUCTS AND DRUGS vol 75 (2013) PARA 491) (Criminal Justice and Police Act 2001 s 34(1)(d));

(5) an offence under the Criminal Law Act 1977 s 1 (see CRIMINAL LAW vol 25 (2010) PARA 73) of conspiracy to commit any of the offences in heads (1)–(4) above (Criminal Justice and Police Act 2001 s 34(1)(e));

(6) an offence under the Criminal Attempts Act 1981 s 1 (see CRIMINAL LAW vol 25 (2010) PARA 86) of attempting to commit any of those offences (Criminal Justice and Police Act 2001 s 34(1)(f)); or

(7) an offence under the Misuse of Drugs Act 1971 s 19 (see CRIMINAL LAW vol 26 (2010) PARAS 723, 725, 727–730, 732) or at common law of inciting another person to commit any of those offences (see CRIMINAL LAW vol 25 (2010) PARA 64) (Criminal Justice and Police Act 2001 s 34(1)(g)).

At the date at which this volume states the law no order had been made under the Criminal Justice and Police Act 2001 s 34(1)(c).

2 As to the meaning of 'United Kingdom' see PARA 4 note 3.

3 Criminal Justice and Police Act 2001 s 33(3)(a). References to the offender's release from custody are references to his first release from custody after the imposition of the travel restriction order which is neither a release on bail (s 33(7)(a)) nor a temporary release for a fixed period (s 33(7)(b)).

4 Criminal Justice and Police Act 2001 s 33(3)(b). The travel restriction order is not intended to be a substitute for imprisonment; its purpose is to reduce the risk of re-offending after release from prison: *R v Mee* [2004] EWCA Crim 629, [2004] 2 Cr App Rep (S) 434, [2004] Crim LR 487.

5 'UK passport' means a United Kingdom passport within the meaning of the Immigration Act 1971 s 33(1) (see IMMIGRATION AND ASYLUM vol 57 (2012) PARA 33): Criminal Justice and Police Act 2001 s 33(8) (s 33(4), (5) amended, s 33(8) substituted, by the Identity Documents Act 2010 Schedule para 16).

6 Criminal Justice and Police Act 2001 s 33(4) (as amended: see note 5).

7 Criminal Justice and Police Act 2001 s 33(5)(a) (as amended: see note 5).

8 Criminal Justice and Police Act 2001 s 33(5)(b) (as amended: see note 5).

9 Criminal Justice and Police Act 2001 s 37(1). 'Prescribed removal power' means any such power conferred by or under any enactment as consists in a power to order or direct the removal of a person from the United Kingdom (s 37(4)(a)) and is designated for the purposes of s 37 by an order made by the Secretary of State (s 37(4)(b)). The following powers are prescribed by the Travel Restriction Order (Prescribed Removal Powers) Order 2002, SI 2002/313, art 2, Schedule (amended by SI 2006/1003):

(1) Colonial Prisoners Removal Act 1884 s 3(1) (see COMMONWEALTH vol 13 (2009) PARA 839);

(2) United Nations Act 1946 (powers to order or direct removal of a person from United Kingdom conferred by Orders in Council made in exercise of power contained in s 1(1): see CONSTITUTIONAL AND ADMINISTRATIVE LAW vol 20 (2014) PARA 558);

(3) Immigration Act 1971 s 5(1) (see IMMIGRATION AND ASYLUM vol 57 (2012) PARA 181), Sch 2 paras 8–10, 12–14 (see IMMIGRATION AND ASYLUM vol 57 (2012) PARAS 152, 177, 178), Sch 3 para 1 (see IMMIGRATION AND ASYLUM vol 57 (2012) PARA 186);

(4) Mental Health Act 1983 s 86(2)(a), (b) (see MENTAL HEALTH AND CAPACITY vol 75 (2013) PARA 907);

(5) Repatriation of Prisoners Act 1984 ss 1(1), 2, 4(1) (see PRISONS AND PRISONERS vol 85 (2012) PARAS 463, 464, 466);

(6) Criminal Justice (International Co-operation) Act 1990 s 5 (see CRIMINAL PROCEDURE vol 27 (2015) PARAS 483–484);

(7) Immigration and Asylum Act 1999 s 10 (see IMMIGRATION AND ASYLUM vol 57 (2012) PARA 179);

(8) Immigration (European Economic Area) Regulations 2006, SI 2006/1003, reg 19(3) (see IMMIGRATION AND ASYLUM vol 57 (2012) PARA 271); and

(9) International Criminal Court Act 2001 ss 5, 7, 15, 21, 32, 43 (see INTERNATIONAL RELATIONS LAW vol 61 (2010) PARAS 438–440, 445, 448, 451).

The Travel Restriction Order (Prescribed Removal Powers) Order 2002, SI 2002/313, Schedule also prescribes powers under the Backing of Warrants (Republic of Ireland) Act 1965 s 2(1) and the Extradition Act 1989 s 12(1), both of which have been repealed: in connection with removal from the United Kingdom under extradition powers see now EXTRADITION vol 47 (2014) PARA 601 et seq.

367.   Power to make travel restriction order.   Where:

(1)   a person (the 'offender') has been convicted by any court of a post-commencement[1] drug trafficking offence[2];

(2)   the court has determined that it would be appropriate to impose a sentence of imprisonment for that offence[3]; and

(3)   the term of imprisonment which the court considers appropriate is a term of four years or more[4],

it is the duty of the court, on sentencing the offender:

(a)   to consider whether it would be appropriate for the sentence for the offence to include the making of a travel restriction order[5] in relation to the offender[6];

(b)   if the court determines that it is so appropriate, to make such travel restriction order in relation to the offender as the court thinks suitable in all the circumstances (including any other convictions of the offender for post-commencement drug trafficking offences in respect of which the court is also passing sentence)[7]; and

(c)   if the court determines that it is not so appropriate, to state its reasons for not making a travel restriction order[8].

The court must consider the duration of the order in terms of how long it is necessary to protect the public from the risk posed by the offender, taking into account factors such as the offender's age, previous convictions, risk of re-offending and family connections[9]. The period of restriction should be tailored to an offender to such a degree as the court feels able when balanced against the risk[10].

The order runs from the date of the offender's release from custody and not from the date of the sentence[11]. A travel restriction order made in relation to any person remains in force, notwithstanding the exercise of any prescribed removal power[12] in relation to that person, except in so far as either the Secretary of State by order otherwise provides[13] or the travel restriction order is suspended or revoked[14].

1   In the Criminal Justice and Police Act 2001 s 33 'post-commencement': (1) except in relation to an offence that is a drug trafficking offence by virtue of an order under s 34(1)(c) (see PARA 366 note 1), means committed after 1 April 2002 (ie the date on which s 33 was brought into force by the Criminal Justice and Police Act 2001 (Commencement No 4 and Transitional Provisions) Order 2002, SI 2002/344) (Criminal Justice and Police Act 2001 s 33(6)(a)); and (2) in relation to an offence that is a drug trafficking offence by virtue of such an order, means committed after the coming into force of that order (s 33(6)(b)).

2   Criminal Justice and Police Act 2001 s 33(1)(a). As to the meaning of 'drug trafficking offence' see PARA 366 note 1.

3   Criminal Justice and Police Act 2001 s 33(1)(b).

4   Criminal Justice and Police Act 2001 s 33(1)(c). In *R v Alexander* [2011] EWCA Crim 89, [2011] 2 Cr App Rep (S) 297, it was held that the Act refers to a single sentence of four years or more: consecutive sentences adding up to or exceeding four years did not qualify.

5   As to travel restriction orders see PARA 366.

6   Criminal Justice and Police Act 2001 s 33(2)(a). As to the Court of Appeal's observations in relation to the exercise of the power to impose a travel restriction order see *R v Mee* [2004] EWCA Crim 629, [2004] 2 Cr App Rep (S) 434, [2004] Crim LR 487. In *R v Graham* [2011] EWCA Crim 1905, [2012] 1 Cr App Rep (S) 332, it was held that a travel restriction order was unnecessary because s sentence of 10 years' imprisonment was sufficient deterrent against reoffending.

7   Criminal Justice and Police Act 2001 s 33(2)(b). See note 6.

8   Criminal Justice and Police Act 2001 s 33(2)(c). See note 6.

9   *R v Campbell (Michael)* [2004] EWCA Crim 2333, [2005] 1 Cr App Rep (S) 520. As to the determination of a person's age see the Children and Young Persons Act 1933 s 99; and CHILDREN AND YOUNG PERSONS vol 10 (2012) PARA 1206.

10   *R v Mee* [2004] EWCA Crim 629, [2004] 2 Cr App Rep (S) 434. See also *R v Fuller (Ellinor Victoria)* [2005] EWCA Crim 1029, [2006] 1 Cr App Rep (S) 52.

11   *R v Campbell (Michael)* [2004] EWCA Crim 2333, [2005] 1 Cr App Rep (S) 520.

12   As to the meaning of 'prescribed removal power' see PARA 366 note 9.

13   Criminal Justice and Police Act 2001 s 37(2)(a). At the date at which this volume states the law no such order had been made.

14   Criminal Justice and Police Act 2001 s 37(2)(b). The reference in the text to the suspension or revocation of a travel restriction order is a reference to suspension or revocation under s 35 (see PARA 368).

368. Revocation and suspension of a travel restriction order. The court by which a travel restriction order[1] has been made in relation to any person may:

(1)   on an application made by that person at any time which is both after the end of the minimum period[2] and not within three months after the making of any previous application for the revocation of the prohibition[3], revoke the prohibition imposed by the order with effect from such date as the court may determine[4]; or

(2)   on an application made by that person at any time after the making of the order, suspend the prohibition imposed by the order for such period as the court may determine[5].

A court to which an application for the revocation of the prohibition imposed on any person by a travel restriction order is made must not revoke that prohibition unless it considers that it is appropriate to do so in all the circumstances of the case and having regard, in particular, to:

(a)   that person's character[6];

(b)   his conduct since the making of the order[7]; and

(c)   the offences of which he was convicted on the occasion on which the order was made[8].

A court must not suspend the prohibition imposed on any person by a travel restriction order for any period unless it is satisfied that there are exceptional circumstances, in that person's case, that justify the suspension on compassionate grounds of that prohibition for that period[9]. In making any determination on an application for the suspension of the prohibition imposed on any person by a travel restriction order, a court must have regard[10] to the matters mentioned in heads (a) to (c) above[11] and any other circumstances of the case that the court considers relevant[12].

Where the prohibition imposed on any person by a travel restriction order is suspended, it is the duty of that person:

(i)   to be in the United Kingdom[13] when the period of the suspension ends[14]; and

(ii)   if the order contains a direction[15] to surrender, before the end of that period, any passport[16] returned or issued to that person, in respect of the suspension, by the Secretary of State[17],

and a passport that is required to be so surrendered must be surrendered to the Secretary of State in such manner or by being sent to such address as the Secretary of State may direct at the time when he returns or issues it[18].

Where the prohibition imposed on any person by a travel restriction order is suspended for any period under these provisions, the end of the period of the prohibition imposed by the order is to be treated[19] as postponed (or, if there has been one or more previous suspensions, further postponed) by the length of the period of suspension[20].

1   As to travel restriction orders see PARA 366 et seq.
2   Criminal Justice and Police Act 2001 s 35(1)(a)(i). 'Minimum period': (1) in the case of a travel restriction order imposing a prohibition for a period of four years or less, means the period of two years beginning at the time when the period of the prohibition began (s 35(7)(a)); (2) in the case of a travel restriction order imposing a prohibition of more than four years but less than ten years, means the period of four years beginning at that time (s 35(7)(b)); and (3) in any other case, means the period of five years beginning at that time (s 35(7)(c)).
3   Criminal Justice and Police Act 2001 s 35(1)(a)(ii).
4   Criminal Justice and Police Act 2001 s 35(1)(a).
5   Criminal Justice and Police Act 2001 s 35(1)(b).
6   Criminal Justice and Police Act 2001 s 35(2)(a).
7   Criminal Justice and Police Act 2001 s 35(2)(b).
8   Criminal Justice and Police Act 2001 s 35(2)(c).
9   Criminal Justice and Police Act 2001 s 35(3).
10   Ie in addition to considering the matters mentioned in Criminal Justice and Police Act 2001 s 35(3) (see the text and note 9).
11   Criminal Justice and Police Act 2001 s 35(4)(a)–(c).
12   Criminal Justice and Police Act 2001 s 35(4)(d).
13   As to the meaning of 'United Kingdom' see PARA 4 note 3.
14   Criminal Justice and Police Act 2001 s 35(5)(a).
15   Ie under the Criminal Justice and Police Act 2001 s 33(4) (see PARA 366).
16   As to references to passports see PARA 366 note 5.
17   Criminal Justice and Police Act 2001 s 35(5)(b) (s 33(5) amended by the Identity Documents Act 2010 Schedule para 17).
18   Criminal Justice and Police Act 2001 s 35(5) (as amended: see note 17).
19   Ie except for the purposes of the Criminal Justice and Police Act 2001 s 35(7) (see note 2).
20   Criminal Justice and Police Act 2001 s 35(6).

369. Offences of contravening travel restriction orders. A person who leaves the United Kingdom[1] at a time when he is prohibited from leaving it by a travel restriction order[2], and a person who is not in the United Kingdom at the end of a period during which a prohibition imposed on him by a travel restriction order has been suspended[3], is guilty of an offence[4].

A person who fails to comply:

(1)   with a direction contained in a travel restriction order to deliver up a passport[5] to a court, or to cause such a passport to be delivered up[6]; or

(2)   with any duty imposed on him[7] to surrender a passport to the Secretary of State[8],

is also guilty of an offence[9].

No person is guilty of an offence under these provisions in respect of any act or omission required of him by an obligation imposed in the exercise of a prescribed removal power[10].

1   As to the meaning of 'United Kingdom' see PARA 4 note 3.
2   Criminal Justice and Police Act 2001 s 36(1). As to travel restriction orders see PARA 366 et seq.
3   Criminal Justice and Police Act 2001 s 36(2).
4   Criminal Justice and Police Act 2001 s 36(1), (2). A person who commits either offence is liable on conviction on indictment to imprisonment for a term not exceeding five years or to a fine or to both (s 36(1)(b), (2)(b)) and on summary conviction to imprisonment for a term not exceeding six months or to a fine not exceeding the statutory maximum or to both (s 36(1)(a), (2)(a)). As from a day to be appointed the maximum term of six months referred to in s 36(1)(a), (2)(a) is increased to a maximum term of 12 months (see the Criminal Justice Act 2003 ss 281(7), 282(2), (3) (not yet in force)), although this does not affect the penalty for any offence committed before that day (see s 282(4) (not yet in force)). At the date at which this

volume states the law no such day had been appointed. As to the standard scale, the statutory maximum, the prescribed sum, and magistrates' powers to levy unlimited fines see PARA 176.

5   As to references to UK passports see PARA 366 note 5.

6   Criminal Justice and Police Act 2001 s 36(3)(a) (s 36(3) amended by the Identity Documents Act 2010 Schedule para 17).

7   Ie by the Criminal Justice and Police Act 2001 s 35(5)(b) (see PARA 368).

8   Criminal Justice and Police Act 2001 s 36(3)(b) (as amended: see note 6).

9   Criminal Justice and Police Act 2001 s 36(3) (as amended: see note 6). A person who commits either offence is liable on summary conviction to imprisonment for a term not exceeding six months or to a fine not exceeding level 5 on the standard scale or to both: s 36(3) (as so amended). As from a day to be appointed the maximum term referred to in s 36(3) is increased to a maximum term of 51 weeks (see the Criminal Justice Act 2003 s 281(4), (5), (7) (not yet in force)), although this does not affect the penalty for any offence committed before that day (s 281(6)(b) (not yet in force)). At the date at which this volume states the law no such day had been appointed. As to the standard scale, the statutory maximum, the prescribed sum, and magistrates' powers to levy unlimited fines see PARA 176.

10 Criminal Justice and Police Act 2001 ss 36(4), 37(3). As to the prescribed removal powers see PARA 366 note 9.

(viii) Hygiene Prohibition Orders

370.   Making of orders. If a food business operator is convicted of an offence under the regulations with regard to food hygiene applying in England or Wales[1] and the court is satisfied that the health risk condition is fulfilled with respect to the food business concerned, the court must impose a hygiene prohibition order[2]. The health risk condition is fulfilled with respect to any food business if any of:

(1)   the use for the purposes of the business of any process or treatment[3];

(2)   the construction of any premises used for the purposes of the business, or the use for those purposes of any equipment[4]; and

(3)   the state or condition of any premises or equipment used for the purposes of the business, involves risk of injury to health, including any impairment, whether permanent or temporary[5].

The appropriate prohibition is:

(a)   in a case falling within head (1) above, a prohibition on the use of the process or treatment for the purposes of the business[6];

(b)   in a case falling within head (2) above, a prohibition on the use of the premises or equipment for the purposes of the business or any other food business of the same class or description[7]; and

(c)   in a case falling within head (3) above, a prohibition on the use of the premises or equipment for the purposes of any food business[8].

If a food business operator is convicted of such an offence and the court by or before which he is so convicted thinks it proper to do so in all the circumstances of the case, the court may, by a hygiene prohibition order, impose a prohibition on the food business operator participating in the management of any food business, or any food business of a class or description specified in the order[9]. Any person who knowingly contravenes a hygiene prohibition order is guilty of an offence[10].

Prohibitions corresponding to those described above may also be imposed where an authorised officer of an enforcement authority is satisfied that the health risk condition is fulfilled with respect to any food business[11].

1   Ie an offence under the Food Safety and Hygiene (England) Regulations 2013, SI 2013/2966 or the Food Hygiene (Wales) Regulations 2006, SI 2006/31 (see FOOD AND DRINK vol 51 (2013) PARA 698 et seq).

2   See the Food Safety and Hygiene (England) Regulations 2013, SI 2013/2966, reg 7(1); the Food Hygiene (Wales) Regulations 2006, SI 2006/31, reg 7(1); and FOOD AND DRINK vol 51 (2013) PARA 702.
3   See the Food Safety and Hygiene (England) Regulations 2013, SI 2013/2966, reg 7(2)(a); the Food Hygiene (Wales) Regulations 2006, SI 2006/31, reg 7(2)(a); and FOOD AND DRINK vol 51 (2013) PARA 702.
4   See the Food Safety and Hygiene (England) Regulations 2013, SI 2013/2966, reg 7(2)(b); the Food Hygiene (Wales) Regulations 2006, SI 2006/31, reg 7(2)(b); and FOOD AND DRINK vol 51 (2013) PARA 702.
5   See the Food Safety and Hygiene (England) Regulations 2013, SI 2013/2966, reg 7(2)(c); the Food Hygiene (Wales) Regulations 2006, SI 2006/31, reg 7(2)(c); and FOOD AND DRINK vol 51 (2013) PARA 702.
6   See the Food Safety and Hygiene (England) Regulations 2013, SI 2013/2966, reg 7(3)(a); the Food Hygiene (Wales) Regulations 2006, SI 2006/31, reg 7(3)(a); and FOOD AND DRINK vol 51 (2013) PARA 702.
7   See the Food Safety and Hygiene (England) Regulations 2013, SI 2013/2966, reg 7(3)(b); the Food Hygiene (Wales) Regulations 2006, SI 2006/31, reg 7(3)(b); and FOOD AND DRINK vol 51 (2013) PARA 702.
8   See the Food Safety and Hygiene (England) Regulations 2013, SI 2013/2966, reg 7(3)(c); the Food Hygiene (Wales) Regulations 2006, SI 2006/31, reg 7(3)(c); and FOOD AND DRINK vol 51 (2013) PARA 702.
9   See the Food Safety and Hygiene (England) Regulations 2013, SI 2013/2966, reg 7(4); the Food Hygiene (Wales) Regulations 2006, SI 2006/31, reg 7(4); and FOOD AND DRINK vol 51 (2013) PARA 702.
10 See the Food Safety and Hygiene (England) Regulations 2013, SI 2013/2966, reg 7(5); the Food Hygiene (Wales) Regulations 2006, SI 2006/31, reg 7(5); and FOOD AND DRINK vol 51 (2013) PARA 702. As to offences and penalties see FOOD AND DRINK vol 51 (2013) PARA 707.
11 See the Food Safety and Hygiene (England) Regulations 2013, SI 2013/2966, reg 8; the Food Hygiene (Wales) Regulations 2006, SI 2006/31, reg 8; and FOOD AND DRINK vol 51 (2013) PARA 703.

(2) CIVIL ORDERS

(i) Civil Injunctions

A. APPLICATION AND GRANT

371. Power to grant injunctions for preventing anti-social behaviour. A court[1] may, on an application of a specified authority[2], grant an injunction for the purpose of preventing the respondent from engaging in anti-social behaviour[3]. Injunctions may be granted against a person aged 10 or over[4] if:

(1)   the court is satisfied, on the balance of probabilities, that the respondent has engaged or threatens to engage in anti-social behaviour[5]; and

(2)   the court considers it just and convenient to grant the injunction for the purpose of preventing the respondent from engaging in anti-social behaviour[6].

The power to grant civil injunctions for the prevention of anti-social behaviour has effect as from 23 March 2015[7], replacing the powers to make anti-social behaviour orders on application to the magistrates' court, to make orders in county court proceedings prohibiting anti-social behaviour, and to make intervention orders, which were abolished as from that date[8].

1   An application for an injunction under these provisions must be made to the High Court or the county court (Anti-social Behaviour, Crime and Policing Act 2014 s 1(8)(b)) or (in the case of a respondent aged under 18) a youth court (Anti-social Behaviour, Crime and Policing Act 2014 s 1(8)(a)). Rules of court may provide for a youth court to give permission for an application for an injunction under s 1 against a person aged 18 or over to be made to the youth court if an application to the youth court has been made, or is to be made, for an injunction against a

person aged under 18 (s 18(2)(a)) and the youth court thinks that it would be in the interests of justice for the applications to be heard together (s 18(2)(b)). Section 1(8)(b) is subject to any such rules: s 1(8). In relation to a respondent attaining the age of 18 after proceedings under Pt 1 (ss 1–21) have begun, rules of court may provide for the transfer of the proceedings from the youth court to the High Court or the county court (s 18(3)(a)) and prescribe circumstances in which the proceedings may or must remain in the youth court (s 18(3)(b)). For the applicable rules see the Magistrates' Courts (Injunctions: Anti-Social Behaviour) Rules 2015, SI 2015/423. As to youth courts see CHILDREN AND YOUNG PERSONS vol 10 (2012) PARA 1225 et seq. As to the determination of a person's age see the Children and Young Persons Act 1933 s 99; and CHILDREN AND YOUNG PERSONS vol 10 (2012) PARA 1206.

The statutory provisions providing for the giving of special measures directions in the case of vulnerable and intimidated witnesses (ie the Youth Justice and Criminal Evidence Act 1999 Pt 2 Ch 1 (ss 16–33): see CRIMINAL PROCEDURE vol 28 (2015) PARA 501 et seq) apply with modifications to any proceedings under the Anti-social Behaviour, Crime and Policing Act 2014 Pt 1: see s 16. The Children and Young Persons Act 1933 s 49 (restrictions on reports of proceedings in which children and young persons are concerned: see CHILDREN AND YOUNG PERSONS vol 10 (2012) PARAS 1234–1236) does not apply to proceedings under these provisions: Anti-social Behaviour, Crime and Policing Act 2014 s 17.

An appeal lies to the Crown Court against a decision of a youth court made under Pt 1: s 15(1). On such an appeal the Crown Court may make whatever orders are necessary to give effect to its determination of the appeal (s 15(2)(a)) and whatever incidental or consequential orders appear to it to be just (s 15(2)(b)).

2 As to who may apply for injunctions see PARA 373; as to the making of applications without notice see PARA 376.

3 Anti-social Behaviour, Crime and Policing Act 2014 s 1(4). As to the meaning of 'anti-social behaviour' see PARA 372. As to the prohibitions and requirements that may be included in an injunction see PARAS 374, 375. As to interim injunctions see PARA 377. As to variation and discharge see PARA 378; as to breach see PARAS 379–391.

4 Ie 'the respondent': Anti-social Behaviour, Crime and Policing Act 2014 s 1(1). A person's age is treated for the purposes of Pt 1 (ss 1–21) as being that which it appears to the court to be after considering any available evidence: s 20(2). As to the determination of a person's age see the Children and Young Persons Act 1933 s 99; and CHILDREN AND YOUNG PERSONS vol 10 (2012) PARA 1206.

5 Anti-social Behaviour, Crime and Policing Act 2014 s 1(2). In deciding whether to grant an injunction under s 1 a court may take account of conduct occurring up to 6 months before 23 March 2015 (as to which see note 7): s 21(7), (8).

6 Anti-social Behaviour, Crime and Policing Act 2014 s 1(3).

7 Ie the date on which the Anti-social Behaviour, Crime and Policing Act 2014 Pt 1 was brought into force by the Anti-social Behaviour, Crime and Policing Act 2014 (Commencement No 8, Saving and Transitional Provisions) Order 2015, SI 2015/373, art 4(a).

8 See PARA 439.

372. Meaning of 'anti-social behaviour'. For these purposes[1] 'anti-social behaviour' means:

(1) conduct that has caused, or is likely to cause, harassment, alarm or distress to any person[2];

(2) conduct capable of causing housing-related[3] nuisance or annoyance to any person[4]; or

(3) (where an injunction[5] is applied for by a housing provider[6], a local authority[7] or a chief officer of police[8]), conduct capable of causing nuisance or annoyance to a person in relation to that person's occupation of residential premises[9].

1 Ie for the purposes of the Anti-social Behaviour, Crime and Policing Act 2014 Pt 1 (ss 1–21).

2 Anti-social Behaviour, Crime and Policing Act 2014 s 2(1)(a).

3 Ie directly or indirectly relating to the housing management functions of a housing provider (see note 6) or a local authority (see note 7): Anti-social Behaviour, Crime and Policing Act 2014 s 2(3). For these purposes the housing management functions of a housing provider or a local authority include functions conferred by or under an enactment and the powers and duties of the housing provider or local authority as the holder of an estate or interest in housing accommodation: s 2(4). 'Housing accommodation' includes flats, lodging-houses and hostels,

any yard, garden, outhouses and appurtenances belonging to the accommodation or usually enjoyed with it, and any common areas used in connection with the accommodation: s 20(1).

4 Anti-social Behaviour, Crime and Policing Act 2014 s 2(1)(c).

5 Ie an injunction under the Anti-social Behaviour, Crime and Policing Act 2014 s 1 (see PARA 371).

6 Anti-social Behaviour, Crime and Policing Act 2014 s 2(2)(a). For these purposes, by virtue of s 20(1), 'housing provider' means:
    (1) a housing trust, within the meaning given by the Housing Associations Act 1985 s 2 (see HOUSING vol 56 (2011) PARA 12), that is a charity;
    (2) a housing action trust established under the Housing Act 1988 s 62 (see HOUSING vol 56 (2011) PARA 328);
    (3) in relation to England, a non-profit private registered provider of social housing;
    (4) in relation to Wales, a Welsh body registered as a social landlord under the Housing Act 1996 s 3 (see HOUSING vol 56 (2011) PARA 126);
    (5) any body (other than a local authority or a body within heads (1) to (4)) that is a landlord under a secure tenancy within the meaning given by the Housing Act 1985 s 79 (see LANDLORD AND TENANT vol 64 (2012) PARA 1297);
    As to 'registered providers' of social housing see the Housing and Regeneration Act 2008 s 80; and HOUSING vol 56 (2011) PARA 32; as to when a provider is 'non-profit' see s 115; and HOUSING vol 56 (2011) PARA 42.

7 Anti-social Behaviour, Crime and Policing Act 2014 s 2(2)(b). For these purposes, by virtue of s 20(1), 'local authority' means: in relation to England, a district council, a county council, a London borough council, the Common Council of the City of London or the Council of the Isles of Scilly; and in relation to Wales, a county council or a county borough council. As to local government areas and authorities in England and Wales see LOCAL GOVERNMENT vol 69 (2009) PARA 22 et seq. As to the London boroughs and the City of London see LONDON GOVERNMENT vol 71 (2013) PARAS 15, 16.

8 Anti-social Behaviour, Crime and Policing Act 2014 s 2(2)(c). As to police forces, police areas and chief officers of police see POLICE AND INVESTIGATORY POWERS vol 84 (2013) PARAS 52 et seq, 123 et seq.

9 Anti-social Behaviour, Crime and Policing Act 2014 s 2(1)(b).

373. Who may apply for an injunction. An injunction[1] may be granted only on the application of[2]:

(1) a local authority[3];

(2) a housing provider[4];

(3) the chief officer of police for a police area[5];

(4) the chief constable of the British Transport Police Force[6];

(5) Transport for London[7];

(6) the Environment Agency[8];

(7) the Natural Resources Body for Wales[9];

(8) the Secretary of State exercising security management functions[10], or a Special Health Authority[11] exercising security management functions on the direction of the Secretary of State[12]; or

(9) the Welsh Ministers exercising security management functions[13], or a person or body exercising security management functions on the direction of the Welsh Ministers or under arrangements made between the Welsh Ministers and that person or body[14].

A person applying for an injunction must before doing so[15] consult the local youth offending team[16] about the application, if the respondent will be aged under 18[17] when the application is made[18], and must inform any other body or individual the applicant thinks appropriate of the application[19].

1 Ie an injunction under the Anti-social Behaviour, Crime and Policing Act 2014 s 1: see PARA 371.

2 The Secretary of State may by order amend the Anti-social Behaviour, Crime and Policing Act 2014 s 5 (see the text and notes 2–14) or s 20 in relation to expressions used in s 5: s 5(5). At the date at which this volume states the law no such order had been made. The Secretary of State may issue guidance to persons entitled to apply for injunctions about the exercise of their

functions under Pt 1 (ss 1–21): s 19(1). The Secretary of State may revise any guidance so issued (s 19(2)) and must arrange for any guidance so issued or revised to be published (s 19(3)). At the date at which this volume states the law no guidance had been issued.

3   Anti-social Behaviour, Crime and Policing Act 2014 s 5(1)(a). As to the meaning of 'local authority' see PARA 372 note 7.

4   Anti-social Behaviour, Crime and Policing Act 2014 s 5(1)(b). As to the meaning of 'housing provider' see PARA 372 note 6. A housing provider may make an application only if the application concerns anti-social behaviour that directly or indirectly relates to or affects its housing management functions: s 5(3). As to the meaning of 'anti-social behaviour' see PARA 372. For these purposes the housing management functions of a housing provider include functions conferred by or under an enactment and the powers and duties of the housing provider as the holder of an estate or interest in housing accommodation: s 5(4). As to the meaning of 'housing accommodation' see PARA 372 note 3.

5   Anti-social Behaviour, Crime and Policing Act 2014 s 5(1)(c). As to police forces, police areas and chief officers of police see POLICE AND INVESTIGATORY POWERS vol 84 (2013) PARAS 52 et seq, 123 et seq.

6   Anti-social Behaviour, Crime and Policing Act 2014 s 5(1)(d). As to the British Transport Police Force (ie the British Transport Police Force established under the Railways and Transport Safety Act 2003 Pt 3 (ss 18–77)) see RAILWAYS AND TRAMWAYS vol 86 (2013) PARA 285.

7   Anti-social Behaviour, Crime and Policing Act 2014 s 5(1)(e). As to Transport for London (ie the body established by the Greater London Authority Act 1999 s 154) see LONDON GOVERNMENT vol 71 (2013) PARA 164.

8   Anti-social Behaviour, Crime and Policing Act 2014 s 5(1)(f). As to the Environment Agency see generally ENVIRONMENTAL QUALITY AND PUBLIC HEALTH vol 45 (2010) PARA 68 et seq.

9   Anti-social Behaviour, Crime and Policing Act 2014 s 5(1)(g). As to the Natural Resources Body for Wales, and the Welsh Ministers' powers generally relating to environmental and other bodies, see CONSTITUTIONAL AND ADMINISTRATIVE LAW vol 20 (2010) PARA 323.

10 Ie the Secretary of State's security management functions within the meaning given by the National Health Service Act 2006 s 195(3) (see HEALTH SERVICES vol 54 (2008) PARA 41): Anti-social Behaviour, Crime and Policing Act 2014 s 5(2)(a).

11 As to Special Health Authorities see HEALTH SERVICES vol 54 (2008) PARA 136 et seq.

12 Anti-social Behaviour, Crime and Policing Act 2014 s 5(1)(h).

13 Ie the functions of the Welsh Ministers corresponding to the Secretary of State's security management functions within the meaning given by the National Health Service Act 2006 s 195(3): Anti-social Behaviour, Crime and Policing Act 2014 s 5(2)(b).

14 Anti-social Behaviour, Crime and Policing Act 2014 s 5(1)(i).

15 This requirement does not apply to a without-notice application: Anti-social Behaviour, Crime and Policing Act 2014 s 14(1).

16 'Local youth offending team' means the youth offending team in whose area it appears to the applicant that the respondent lives, or, if it appears to the applicant that the respondent lives in more than one such area, whichever one or more of the relevant youth offending teams the applicant thinks it appropriate to consult: Anti-social Behaviour, Crime and Policing Act 2014 s 14(4). As to the meaning of 'the respondent' see PARA 371. As to youth offending teams see CHILDREN AND YOUNG PERSONS vol 10 (2012) PARA 1193.

17 As to the respondent's age see PARA 371 note 4. As to the determination of a person's age see the Children and Young Persons Act 1933 s 99; and CHILDREN AND YOUNG PERSONS vol 10 (2012) PARA 1206.

18 Anti-social Behaviour, Crime and Policing Act 2014 s 14(1)(a).

19 Anti-social Behaviour, Crime and Policing Act 2014 s 14(1)(b).

374. Prohibitions and requirements which may be imposed. An injunction[1] may, for the purpose of preventing the respondent[2] from engaging in anti-social behaviour[3], prohibit the respondent from doing anything described in the injunction[4] and require the respondent to do anything described in the injunction[5]. An injunction must specify the period for which it has effect[6] or state that it has effect until further order[7], and may specify periods for which particular prohibitions or requirements have effect[8].

A court granting an injunction may attach a power of arrest[9] to a prohibition or requirement[10] of the injunction if it thinks that the anti-social behaviour in which the respondent has engaged or threatens to engage consists of or includes the use or threatened use of violence against other persons[11] or there is a significant risk of harm[12] to other persons from the respondent[13].

An injunction that includes a requirement must specify the person who is to be responsible for supervising compliance with the requirement[14]. A respondent who is subject to a requirement must keep in touch with the person so specified in relation to that requirement, in accordance with any instructions given by that person from time to time[15], and notify the person of any change of address[16].

1   Ie an injunction under the Anti-social Behaviour, Crime and Policing Act 2014 s 1: see PARA 371.
2   As to the meaning of 'the respondent' see PARA 371.
3   As to the meaning of 'anti-social behaviour' see PARA 372.
4   Anti-social Behaviour, Crime and Policing Act 2014 s 1(4)(a). Prohibitions and requirements must, so far as practicable, be such as to avoid any interference with the times, if any, at which the respondent normally works or attends school or any other educational establishment (s 1(5)(a)) or any conflict with the requirements of any other court order or injunction to which the respondent may be subject (s 1(5)(b)).
5   Anti-social Behaviour, Crime and Policing Act 2014 s 1(4)(b). See note 4. As to prohibitions and requirements which have the effect of excluding a person from his home see PARA 375. Before including a requirement, the court must receive evidence about its suitability and enforceability from the individual to be specified under s 3(1) (see the text and note 14) as the person who is to be responsible for supervising compliance with the requirement (if an individual is to be specified) (s 3(2)(a)) or an individual representing the organisation to be specified under s 3(1) (if an organisation is to be specified) (s 3(2)(b)). Before including two or more requirements, the court must consider their compatibility with each other: s 3(3).
6   Anti-social Behaviour, Crime and Policing Act 2014 s 1(6)(a).
7   Anti-social Behaviour, Crime and Policing Act 2014 s 1(6)(b). In the case of an injunction granted before the respondent has reached the age of 18, a period must be specified and it must be no more than 12 months: s 1(6). As to the respondent's age see PARA 371 note 4. As to the determination of a person's age see the Children and Young Persons Act 1933 s 99; and CHILDREN AND YOUNG PERSONS vol 10 (2012) PARA 1206.
8   Anti-social Behaviour, Crime and Policing Act 2014 s 1(7).
9   If the court attaches a power of arrest, the injunction may specify a period for which the power is to have effect which is shorter than that of the prohibition or requirement to which it relates: Anti-social Behaviour, Crime and Policing Act 2014 s 4(2).
10 'Requirement' in this context does not include one that has the effect of requiring the respondent to participate in particular activities: Anti-social Behaviour, Crime and Policing Act 2014 s 4(1).
11 Anti-social Behaviour, Crime and Policing Act 2014 s 4(1)(a).
12 'Harm' includes serious ill-treatment or abuse, whether physical or not: Anti-social Behaviour, Crime and Policing Act 2014 s 20(1).
13 Anti-social Behaviour, Crime and Policing Act 2014 s 4(1)(b).
14 Anti-social Behaviour, Crime and Policing Act 2014 s 3(1). The person may be an individual or an organisation: s 3(1). It is the duty of a person so specified:
    (1)   to make any necessary arrangements in connection with the requirements for which the person has responsibility (the 'relevant requirements') (s 3(4)(a));
    (2)   to promote the respondent's compliance with the relevant requirements (s 3(4)(b)); and
    (3)   if the person considers that the respondent has complied with all the relevant requirements, or has failed to comply with a relevant requirement, to inform the person who applied for the injunction and the appropriate chief officer of police (s 3(4)(c)).
    For this purpose 'the appropriate chief officer of police' means:
    (a)   the chief officer of police for the police area in which it appears to the person specified under s 3(1) that the respondent lives (s 3(5)(a)); or
    (b)   if it appears to that person that the respondent lives in more than one police area, whichever of the relevant chief officers of police that person thinks it most appropriate to inform (s 3(5)(b)).
    As to police forces, police areas and chief officers of police see POLICE AND INVESTIGATORY POWERS vol 84 (2013) PARAS 52 et seq, 123 et seq.
15 Anti-social Behaviour, Crime and Policing Act 2014 s 3(6)(a). The obligations imposed by s 3(6) have effect as requirements of the injunction: s 3(6).
16 Anti-social Behaviour, Crime and Policing Act 2014 s 3(6)(b). See note 15.

375.   Exclusion of person from his home.   An injunction[1] may have the effect of excluding the respondent[2] from the place where he normally lives ('the premises') only if:

(1)   the respondent is aged 18 or over[3];

(2)   the injunction is granted on the application of a local authority[4], the chief officer of police for the police area that the premises are in[5] or, if the premises are owned or managed by a housing provider[6], that housing provider[7]; and

(3)   the court thinks that the anti-social behaviour[8] in which the respondent has engaged or threatens to engage consists of or includes the use or threatened use of violence against other persons[9] or there is a significant risk of harm[10] to other persons from the respondent[11].

1   Ie an injunction under the Anti-social Behaviour, Crime and Policing Act 2014 s 1: see PARA 371. As to who may apply for an injunction see PARA 373; as to the requirements and prohibitions that may be included in an injunction see PARA 374.
2   As to the meaning of 'respondent' see PARA 371.
3   Anti-social Behaviour, Crime and Policing Act 2014 s 13(1)(a). As to the respondent's age see PARA 371 note 4. As to the determination of a person's age see the Children and Young Persons Act 1933 s 99; and CHILDREN AND YOUNG PERSONS vol 10 (2012) PARA 1206.
4   As to the meaning of 'local authority' see PARA 372 note 7.
5   As to police forces, police areas and chief officers of police see POLICE AND INVESTIGATORY POWERS vol 84 (2013) PARAS 52 et seq, 123 et seq.
6   As to the meaning of 'housing provider' see PARA 372 note 6. For these purposes a housing provider owns a place if the housing provider is a person (other than a mortgagee not in possession) entitled to dispose of the fee simple of the place, whether in possession or in reversion, or the housing provider is a person who holds or is entitled to the rents and profits of the place under a lease that (when granted) was for a term of not less than 3 years: Anti-social Behaviour, Crime and Policing Act 2014 s 13(2).
7   Anti-social Behaviour, Crime and Policing Act 2014 s 13(1)(b).
8   As to the meaning of 'anti-social behaviour' see PARA 372.
9   Anti-social Behaviour, Crime and Policing Act 2014 s 13(1)(c)(i).
10   As to the meaning of 'harm' see PARA 374 note 12.
11   Anti-social Behaviour, Crime and Policing Act 2014 s 13(1)(c)(ii).

376.   Making of applications without notice.   An application for an injunction[1] may be made without notice being given to the respondent[2], in which event the court must either adjourn the proceedings and grant an interim injunction[3], adjourn the proceedings without granting an interim injunction[4] or dismiss the application[5].

Where the court adjourns a without-notice application[6], before the date of the first on-notice hearing[7] the applicant must consult the local youth offending team[8] about the application, if the respondent will be aged under 18[9] on that date[10], and inform any other body or individual the applicant thinks appropriate of the application[11].

1   Ie an injunction under the Anti-social Behaviour, Crime and Policing Act 2014 s 1: see PARA 371. As to who may apply for an injunction see PARA 373. For procedural provision see PARA 371 note 1.
2   Anti-social Behaviour, Crime and Policing Act 2014 s 6(1). As to the meaning of 'the respondent' see PARA 371.
3   Anti-social Behaviour, Crime and Policing Act 2014 s 6(2)(a): see s 7; and PARA 377.
4   Anti-social Behaviour, Crime and Policing Act 2014 s 6(2)(b).
5   Anti-social Behaviour, Crime and Policing Act 2014 s 6(2)(c). Rules of court may provide that an appeal from a decision of the High Court, the county court or a youth court to dismiss an application for an injunction under s 1 made without notice being given to the respondent may be made without notice being given to the respondent: s 18(1)(a). For the applicable rules see the Magistrates' Courts (Injunctions: Anti-Social Behaviour) Rules 2015, SI 2015/423.

6   Ie an application under the Anti-social Behaviour, Crime and Policing Act 2014 s 6 (see the text
    and notes 1–5): s 14(4).
7   'On-notice hearing' means a hearing of which notice has been given to the applicant and the
    respondent in accordance with rules of court: Anti-social Behaviour, Crime and Policing
    Act 2014 s 14(4).
8   As to the meaning of 'local youth offending team' see PARA 373 note 16.
9   As to the respondent's age see PARA 371 note 4. As to the determination of a person's age see the
    Children and Young Persons Act 1933 s 99; and CHILDREN AND YOUNG PERSONS vol 10 (2012)
    PARA 1206.
10 Anti-social Behaviour, Crime and Policing Act 2014 s 14(2)(a).
11 Anti-social Behaviour, Crime and Policing Act 2014 s 14(2)(b).

377.   Interim injunctions.   Where the court adjourns the hearing of an
application (whether made with notice or without) for an injunction[1] it may
grant an injunction lasting until the final hearing of the application or until
further order (an 'interim injunction') if the court thinks it just to do so[2]. An
interim injunction made at a hearing of which the respondent was not given
notice may not have the effect of requiring the respondent to participate in
particular activities[3].

1   Ie an injunction under the Anti-social Behaviour, Crime and Policing Act 2014 s 1: see PARA 371.
    As to who may apply for an injunction see PARA 373. For procedural provision see PARA 371
    note 1. For illustrative proceedings see *Chief Constable of the Bedfordshire Police v Golding*
    [2015] EWHC 1875 (QB), [2015] All ER (D) 23 (Jul).
2   Anti-social Behaviour, Crime and Policing Act 2014 s 7(1), (2). Rules of court may provide that
    an appeal from a decision of the High Court, the county court or a youth court to refuse to
    grant an interim injunction when adjourning proceedings following an application for an
    injunction being made without notice, may be made without notice being given to the
    respondent: s 18(1)(b). For the applicable rules see the Magistrates' Courts (Injunctions:
    Anti-Social Behaviour) Rules 2015, SI 2015/423.
3   Anti-social Behaviour, Crime and Policing Act 2014 s 7(3). Subject to that, the court has the
    same powers (including powers under s 4 (powers of arrest: see PARA 374) whether or not the
    injunction is an interim injunction: s 7(4).

378.   Variation and discharge.   The court[1] may vary or discharge an
injunction[2] on the application of the person who applied for it[3] or the
respondent[4]. The power to vary an injunction includes power to include an
additional prohibition or requirement in the injunction[5], or to extend the period
for which a prohibition or requirement has effect[6], or to attach a power of arrest,
or to extend the period for which a power of arrest has effect[7]. If an application
for variation or discharge is dismissed, the party by which the dismissed
application was made may make no further application for variation or
discharge without the consent of the court[8] or the agreement of the other party[9].

1   For these purposes 'the court' means the court that granted the injunction, except where the
    injunction was granted by a youth court but the respondent is aged 18 or over, in which case it
    means the county court: Anti-social Behaviour, Crime and Policing Act 2014 s 8(2). As to the
    meaning of 'the respondent' see PARA 371. As to the respondent's age see PARA 371 note 4. As to
    the determination of a person's age see the Children and Young Persons Act 1933 s 99; and
    CHILDREN AND YOUNG PERSONS vol 10 (2012) PARA 1206. An order of the Crown Court made
    on an appeal under s 15 (see PARA 371 note 1) (other than one directing that an application be
    re-heard by the youth court) is to be treated for these purposes as an order of the youth court:
    s 15(3). As to youth courts see CHILDREN AND YOUNG PERSONS vol 10 (2012) PARA 1225 et seq.
2   Ie an injunction under the Anti-social Behaviour, Crime and Policing Act 2014 s 1: see PARA 371.
    As to who may apply for an injunction see PARA 373.
3   Anti-social Behaviour, Crime and Policing Act 2014 s 8(1)(a). A person applying for variation or
    discharge of an injunction under s 1 granted on that person's application must before doing so
    consult the local youth offending team about the application for variation or discharge, if the
    respondent will be aged under 18 when that application is made (s 14(3)(a)) and inform any

other body or individual the applicant thinks appropriate of that application (s 14(3)(b)). As to youth offending teams see CHILDREN AND YOUNG PERSONS vol 10 (2012) PARA 1193.

4   Anti-social Behaviour, Crime and Policing Act 2014 s 8(1)(b).
5   As to the prohibitions and requirements that may be included in an injunction see PARAS 374, 375.
6   Anti-social Behaviour, Crime and Policing Act 2014 s 8(3)(a). Section 3 (requirements to be included in injunctions: see PARA 374) applies to additional requirements included under s 8(3)(a) as it applies to requirements included in a new injunction: s 8(5).
7   Anti-social Behaviour, Crime and Policing Act 2014 s 8(3)(b).
8   Anti-social Behaviour, Crime and Policing Act 2014 s 8(4)(a).
9   Anti-social Behaviour, Crime and Policing Act 2014 s 8(4)(b).

B.   BREACH OF INJUNCTIONS

(A)   Procedure

379.   Arrest without warrant. Where a power of arrest is attached to a provision of an injunction[1] a constable may arrest the respondent[2] without warrant if he has reasonable cause to suspect that the respondent is in breach of the provision[3]. The arrested person must be brought before a judge or justice[4] within the period of 24 hours beginning with the time of the arrest[5]: where he is brought before a judge[6], that judge may remand the person if the matter is not disposed of straight away[7]; where he is brought before a justice of the peace[8], that justice must remand the person to appear before the youth court that granted the injunction[9].

1   Ie an injunction under the Anti-social Behaviour, Crime and Policing Act 2014 s 1: see PARA 371. As to the attaching of powers of arrest to an injunction see PARA 374.
2   As to the meaning of 'the respondent' see PARA 371.
3   Anti-social Behaviour, Crime and Policing Act 2014 s 9(1). A constable who arrests a person under s 9(1) must inform the person who applied for the injunction: s 9(2). As to who may apply for an injunction see PARA 373. As to the prohibitions and requirements that may be included in an injunction see PARAS 374, 375.
4   Ie:
    (1)   where the injunction was granted by the High Court, a judge of the High Court or a judge of the county court (Anti-social Behaviour, Crime and Policing Act 2014 s 9(3)(a));
    (2)   where the injunction was granted by the county court (s 9(3)(b)(i)) or the injunction was granted by a youth court but the respondent is aged 18 or over (s 9(3)(b)(ii)), a judge of the county court (s 9(3)(b)); or
    (3)   if neither head (1) or (2) above applies, a justice of the peace (s 9(3)(c)).
    For procedural provision see PARA 371 note 1. As to the respondent's age see PARA 371 note 4. As to the determination of a person's age see the Children and Young Persons Act 1933 s 99; and CHILDREN AND YOUNG PERSONS vol 10 (2012) PARA 1206.
5   Anti-social Behaviour, Crime and Policing Act 2014 s 9(3). In calculating when the period of 24 hours ends, Christmas Day, Good Friday and any Sunday are to be disregarded: s 9(4).
6   Ie under the Anti-social Behaviour, Crime and Policing Act 2014 s 9(3)(a) or (b) (see note 4).
7   Anti-social Behaviour, Crime and Policing Act 2014 s 9(4). As to remand see PARAS 381–382.
8   Ie under the Anti-social Behaviour, Crime and Policing Act 2014 s 9(3)(c) (see note 4).
9   Anti-social Behaviour, Crime and Policing Act 2014 s 9(5). As to youth courts see CHILDREN AND YOUNG PERSONS vol 10 (2012) PARA 1225 et seq.

380.   Issue of arrest warrant. If the person who applied for an injunction[1] thinks that the respondent[2] is in breach of any of its provisions[3], the person may apply to a judge or justice[4] for the issue of a warrant for the respondent's arrest[5], and the judge or justice may issue such a warrant if (and only if) he has reasonable grounds for believing that the respondent is in breach of a provision of the injunction[6].

If the respondent is brought before a court by virtue of a warrant under these provisions but the matter is not disposed of straight away, the court may remand the respondent[7].

1   Ie an injunction under the Anti-social Behaviour, Crime and Policing Act 2014 s 1: see PARA 371. As to who may apply for an injunction see PARA 373.
2   As to the meaning of 'the respondent' see PARA 371.
3   As to the prohibitions and requirements that may be included in an injunction see PARAS 374, 375.
4   The application must be made to:
    (1)   where the injunction was granted by the High Court, a judge of the High Court or a judge of the county court (Anti-social Behaviour, Crime and Policing Act 2014 s 10(2)(a));
    (2)   where the injunction was granted by the county court (s 10(2)(b)(i)) or the injunction was granted by a youth court but the respondent is aged 18 or over (s 10(2)(b)(ii)), a judge of the county court (s 10(2)(b)); or
    (3)   if neither head (1) or (2) above applies, a justice of the peace (s 10(2)(c)).
    A warrant issued by a judge of the High Court must require the respondent to be brought before that court (s 10(4)); a warrant issued by a judge of the county court must require the respondent to be brought before that court (s 10(5)); and a warrant issued by a justice of the peace must require the respondent to be brought before either the youth court that granted the injunction (if the person is aged under 18) or the county court (if the person is aged 18 or over) (s 10(6)). As to the respondent's age see PARA 371 note 4. As to the determination of a person's age see the Children and Young Persons Act 1933 s 99; and CHILDREN AND YOUNG PERSONS vol 10 (2012) PARA 1206. For procedural provision see PARA 371 note 1. As to youth courts see CHILDREN AND YOUNG PERSONS vol 10 (2012) PARA 1225 et seq.
5   Anti-social Behaviour, Crime and Policing Act 2014 s 10(1). A constable who arrests a person under a warrant issued under these provisions must inform the person who applied for the injunction: s 10(7).
6   Anti-social Behaviour, Crime and Policing Act 2014 s 10(3).
7   Anti-social Behaviour, Crime and Policing Act 2014 s 10(8). As to remand see PARAS 381–382.

381.   Remand.

Where a judge or a court has power[1], or a justice of the peace is required[2], to remand a person[3], the judge, justice or court may remand that person either in custody[4] or on bail[5] (although a person aged under 18 may not be remanded in custody unless the provisions relating to the remand of mentally disordered persons[6] apply[7]). Where a person is brought before the court after remand, the court may further remand the person[8].

The judge, justice or court may not as a rule remand a person for a period exceeding eight clear days[9], although that maximum may be exceeded if the provisions relating to medical examinations and mentally disordered persons[10] apply[11] or the person is remanded on bail and both that person and the person who applied for the injunction[12] consent to a longer period[13]. Also, if the court is satisfied that a person who has been remanded is unable by reason of illness or accident to appear or be brought before the court at the end of the period of remand, the court may further remand the person in his or her absence[14].

1   Ie under the Anti-social Behaviour, Crime and Policing Act 2014 s 9(5) (see PARA 379) or s 10(8) (see PARA 380). For procedural provision see PARA 371 note 1.
2   Ie under the Anti-social Behaviour, Crime and Policing Act 2014 s 9(6) (see PARA 379).
3   Anti-social Behaviour, Crime and Policing Act 2014 s 11, Sch 1 para 1(1).
4   A reference in the Anti-social Behaviour, Crime and Policing Act 2014 Sch 1 to remanding a person in custody is a reference to committing the person to custody to be brought before the court at the end of the period of remand or at whatever earlier time the court may require: Sch 1 para 2(2). Where the judge, justice or court has power to remand a person in custody, the person may be committed to the custody of a constable if the remand is for a period not exceeding 3 clear days: Sch 1 para 4(2).
5   Anti-social Behaviour, Crime and Policing Act 2014 Sch 1 paras 1(2), 2(1). The judge, justice or court may remand a person on bail by taking from him a recognisance, with or without sureties,

conditioned as provided in Sch 1 para 3 (see below) (Sch 1 para 2(3)(a)), or by fixing the amount of the recognisances with a view to their being taken subsequently and, in the meantime, committing the person to custody as mentioned in the Sch 1 para 2(2) (see PARA 381) (Sch 1 para 2(3)(b)). The judge, justice or court may direct that the person's recognisance be conditioned for his or her appearance before the court at the end of the period of remand (Sch 1 para 3(1)(a)) or at every time and place to which during the course of the proceedings the hearing may from time to time be adjourned (Sch 1 para 3(1)(b)). Where a recognisance is conditioned for a person's appearance as mentioned in Sch 1 para 3(1)(b), the fixing of a time for the person next to appear is to be treated as a remand: Sch 1 para 3(2). Nothing in Sch 1 para 3 affects the power of the court at any subsequent hearing to remand the person afresh: Sch 1 para 3(3). Where under Sch 1 para 2(3)(b) the court fixes the amount in which the principal and the sureties, if any, are to be bound, the recognisance may afterwards be taken by a person prescribed by rules of court, with the same consequences as if it had been entered into before the court: Sch 1 para 8.

The court may when remanding a person on bail under these provisions require the person to comply, before release on bail or later, with any requirements that appear to the court to be necessary to secure that the person does not interfere with witnesses or otherwise obstruct the course of justice: Sch 1 para 9.

6 Ie the Anti-social Behaviour, Crime and Policing Act 2014 Sch 1 para 6 (see PARA 382). As to the determination of a person's age see the Children and Young Persons Act 1933 s 99; and CHILDREN AND YOUNG PERSONS vol 10 (2012) PARA 1206.

7 Anti-social Behaviour, Crime and Policing Act 2014 Sch 1 para 2(1).

8 Anti-social Behaviour, Crime and Policing Act 2014 Sch 1 para 2(4).

9 Anti-social Behaviour, Crime and Policing Act 2014 Sch 1 para 4(1).

10 Ie the Anti-social Behaviour, Crime and Policing Act 2014 Sch 1 paras 5, 6 (see PARA 382).

11 Anti-social Behaviour, Crime and Policing Act 2014 Sch 1 para 4(1)(a).

12 As to who may apply for an injunction see PARA 373.

13 Anti-social Behaviour, Crime and Policing Act 2014 Sch 1 para 4(1)(a).

14 Anti-social Behaviour, Crime and Policing Act 2014 Sch 1 para 7(1). This power may, in the case of a person who was remanded on bail, be exercised by enlarging the person's recognisance and those of any sureties for the person to a later time: Sch 1 para 7(2). Where a person remanded on bail is bound to appear before the court at any time and the court has no power to remand the person under Sch 1 para 7(1), the court may (in the person's absence) enlarge the person's recognisance and those of any sureties for the person to a later time: Sch 1 para 7(3). The enlargement of the person's recognisance is to be treated as a further remand: Sch 1 para 7(4). Sch 1 para 4(1) (limit of remand: see the text and notes 9–13) does not apply to the exercise of the powers conferred by Sch 1 para 7: Sch 1 para 7(5).

382. Medical examinations and mentally disordered persons. The period of remand may exceed the specified eight-day maximum[1] if the judge, justice or court:

(1) has reason to think that a medical report will be needed[2] and remands the person in order to enable a medical examination to take place and a report to be made[3]; or

(2) is satisfied[4] that there is reason to suspect that the person is suffering from mental disorder[5] and is of the opinion that it would be impracticable for a report on the person's mental condition to be made if he or she were remanded on bail[6].

In the former case, if the person is remanded in custody, the adjournment may be for a maximum of three weeks at a time (provided the person is aged 18 or over)[7], and if the person is remanded on bail the adjournment may not be for more than four weeks at a time[8]. In the latter case, the judge, justice or court may remand the person to a hospital[9] or registered establishment[10] specified by the judge, justice or court for such a report to be made[11].

1 Ie the period specified in the Anti-social Behaviour, Crime and Policing Act 2014 Sch 1 para 4 (see PARA 381).

2 Anti-social Behaviour, Crime and Policing Act 2014 Sch 1 para 5(1)(a).

3 Anti-social Behaviour, Crime and Policing Act 2014 Sch 1 para 5(1)(b).

4   Ie on the written or oral evidence of a registered medical practitioner: Anti-social Behaviour,
     Crime and Policing Act 2014 Sch 1 para 6(1)(a).
5   Anti-social Behaviour, Crime and Policing Act 2014 Sch 1 para 6(1)(a). As to the meaning of
     'mental disorder' see the Mental Health Act 1983 s 1 (reading s 1(2B) as if it included a
     reference to the Anti-social Behaviour, Crime and Policing Act 2014 Sch 1 para 6(1)); and
     MENTAL HEALTH AND CAPACITY vol 75 (2013) PARA 761 (definition applied by the Anti-social
     Behaviour, Crime and Policing Act 2014 Sch 1 para 6(2)).
6   Anti-social Behaviour, Crime and Policing Act 2014 Sch 1 para 6(1)(b).
7   Anti-social Behaviour, Crime and Policing Act 2014 Sch 1 para 5(2). As to the respondent's age
     see PARA 371 note 4. As to the determination of a person's age see the Children and Young
     Persons Act 1933 s 99; and CHILDREN AND YOUNG PERSONS vol 10 (2012) PARA 1206.
8   Anti-social Behaviour, Crime and Policing Act 2014 Sch 1 para 5(3).
9   As to the meaning of 'hospital' see the Mental Health Act 1983 s 145(1); and MENTAL HEALTH
     AND CAPACITY vol 75 (2013) PARA 577 (definition applied by the Anti-social Behaviour, Crime
     and Policing Act 2014 Sch 1 para 6(2)).
10   As to the meaning of 'registered establishment' see the Mental Health Act 1983 s 34(1); and
     MENTAL HEALTH AND CAPACITY vol 75 (2013) PARA 578 (definition applied by the Anti-social
     Behaviour, Crime and Policing Act 2014 Sch 1 para 6(2)).
11   Anti-social Behaviour, Crime and Policing Act 2014 Sch 1 para 6(1). The Mental Health
     Act 1983 s 35(4)–(10) (provisions relating to remand and further remand: see and MENTAL
     HEALTH AND CAPACITY vol 75 (2013) PARA 862) apply for the purposes of the Anti-social
     Behaviour, Crime and Policing Act 2014 Sch 1 para 6(1) with any necessary modifications (in
     particular, with references to the accused person being read as references to the person
     mentioned in Sch 1 para 6(1), and references to the court being read as references to the judge,
     justice or court): Sch 1 para 6(3).

(B)   Powers in Respect of Persons Aged Under 18

(a)   Orders to Secure Compliance

383.   Compliance. If a youth court[1] is satisfied beyond reasonable doubt that
a defaulter has without reasonable excuse failed to comply with a requirement of
the supervision order[2] it may:

(1)   revoke the supervision order and make a new one[3]; or

(2)   revoke the order and make a detention order[4].

The court may exercise these powers only on the application of the person
who originally applied for the order[5], and these powers may not be exercised
after the defaulter reaches the age of 18[6] and are in addition to any other power
of the court in relation to the breach of the order[7].

1   As to youth courts see CHILDREN AND YOUNG PERSONS vol 10 (2012) PARA 1225 et seq. For
     procedural provision, and as to appeals from decision of youth courts, see PARA 371 note 1.
2   As to the making of supervision orders see PARA 384. As to the requirements of a supervision
     order see PARAS 385–388.
3   Anti-social Behaviour, Crime and Policing Act 2014 Sch 2 para 12(4)(a).
4   Anti-social Behaviour, Crime and Policing Act 2014 Sch 2 para 12(4)(b). As to detention orders
     see PARAS 390–391.
5   Anti-social Behaviour, Crime and Policing Act 2014 Sch 2 para 12(2). The responsible officer is
     required to inform the applicant where he considers that a defaulter has complied with all the
     requirements of a supervision order (Sch 2 para 11) or has failed to comply with a requirement
     of a supervision order (Sch 2 para 12(1)). As to 'the responsible officer' see PARA 385. Before
     making an application under Sch 2 para 12(2) the original applicant must consult the youth
     offending team for the time being specified in the order (Sch 2 para 12(3)(a)) and inform any
     other body or individual the original applicant thinks appropriate (Sch 2 para 12(3)(b)). The
     court must consider any representations made by the youth offending team for the time being
     specified in the order before exercising its powers under these powers: Sch 2 para 12(6). As to
     youth offending teams see CHILDREN AND YOUNG PERSONS vol 10 (2012) PARA 1193.

6   Anti-social Behaviour, Crime and Policing Act 2014 Sch 2 para 12(5)(a). As to a person's age for these purposes see PARA 371 note 4. As to the determination of a person's age see the Children and Young Persons Act 1933 s 99; and CHILDREN AND YOUNG PERSONS vol 10 (2012) PARA 1206.

7   Anti-social Behaviour, Crime and Policing Act 2014 Sch 2 para 12(5)(b).

384. Power to make a supervision order. A youth court[1] may make a supervision order in respect of a person aged under 18[2] whom it is satisfied beyond reasonable doubt is in breach of a provision of an injunction[3]. This is an order imposing on that person one or more of a supervision requirement[4], an activity requirement[5] and a curfew requirement[6], and such an order may be made only on the application of the person who applied for the injunction[7].

Before making a supervision order the court must obtain and consider information about the defaulter's family circumstances and the likely effect of a supervision order on those circumstances[8], and before making a supervision order imposing two or more requirements, the court must consider their compatibility with each other[9]. The court must ensure, as far as practicable, that requirements imposed by a supervision order are such as to avoid any interference with the times, if any, at which the defaulter normally works or attends school or any other educational establishment[10] and any conflict with the requirements of any other court order or injunction to which the defaulter may be subject[11]. A supervision order must specify a maximum period for the operation of any requirement contained in the order[12], and must specify the youth offending team responsible for supervising the defaulter[13].

Where on an application made in relation to a supervision order by the original applicant or the defaulter the court is satisfied that the defaulter proposes to live, or is living, in the area of a youth offending team other than the team for the time being specified in the order[14], the court may amend the order by substituting for the youth offending team specified in the order the youth offending team for that area (or, if there is more than one youth offending team for that area, whichever of them the court decides)[15]. Where a court so amends an order but the order contains a requirement that, in the opinion of the court, cannot reasonably be complied with if the defaulter lives in the relevant area[16], the court must also amend the order by removing that requirement[17] or substituting for that requirement a new requirement that can reasonably be complied with if the defaulter lives in that area[18], and if the application for amendment was made by the original applicant, the court is not required to amend the order if in its opinion these provisions[19] would produce an inappropriate result[20]. The original applicant must consult the youth offending team for the time being specified in the order before making an application for amendment under these provisions[21].

Provision is made for the amendment and revocation of supervision orders[22] and for the renewal of an order, or the making of a detention order, for non-compliance[23].

1   As to youth courts see CHILDREN AND YOUNG PERSONS vol 10 (2012) PARA 1225 et seq. For procedural provision, and as to appeals from decision of youth courts, see PARA 371 note 1.

2   As to a person's age for these purposes see PARA 371 note 4. As to the determination of a person's age see the Children and Young Persons Act 1933 s 99; and CHILDREN AND YOUNG PERSONS vol 10 (2012) PARA 1206.

3   Anti-social Behaviour, Crime and Policing Act 2014 s 12, Sch 2 para 1(1)(a). The injunction referred to is an injunction under s 1: see PARA 371. As to the prohibitions and requirements that

may be included in an injunction see PARAS 374, 375. A youth court may alternatively make a detention order in respect of the person in breach (unless that person is aged under 14): see Sch 2 para 1(1)(b); and PARAS 390–391.

A court that makes a supervision order must straight away provide a copy of the order to the defaulter (Sch 2 para 13(1)(a)) and the youth offending team for the time being specified in the order (Sch 2 para 13(1)(b)). Where a supervision order is made, the original applicant must straight away provide a copy of so much of the order as is relevant:

(1)   in a case where the order includes an activity requirement specifying a place under Sch 2 para 4(1)(a) (see PARA 386), to the person in charge of that place (Sch 2 para 13(2)(a));

(2)   in a case where the order includes an activity requirement specifying an activity under Sch 2 para 4(1)(b) (see PARA 386), to the person in charge of that activity (Sch 2 para 13(2)(b));

(3)   in a case where the order includes an activity requirement specifying a residential exercise under Sch 2 para 4(1)(c) (see PARA 386), to the person in charge of the place or activity specified under Sch 2 para 4(5) in relation to that residential exercise (Sch 2 para 13(2)(c));

(4)   in a case where the order contains an electronic monitoring requirement, to any person who by virtue of Sch 2 para 6(4) (see PARA 388) will be responsible for the electronic monitoring (Sch 2 para 13(2)(d)(i)) and any person without whose consent that requirement could not have been included in the order (Sch 2 para 13(2)(d)(ii)).

Where a copy of a supervision order (or part of a supervision order) has been given to a person under Sch 2 para 13(2) by virtue of a requirement contained in the order (Sch 2 para 13(4)(a)) and the order is revoked, or amended in respect of that requirement (Sch 2 para 13(4)(b)), the original applicant must straight away give a copy of the revoking order, or of so much of the order as amended as is relevant, to that person. As to youth offending teams see CHILDREN AND YOUNG PERSONS vol 10 (2012) PARA 1193.

4   Anti-social Behaviour, Crime and Policing Act 2014 Sch 2 para 2(1)(a). As to supervision requirements see Sch 2 para 3; and PARA 385.

5   Anti-social Behaviour, Crime and Policing Act 2014 Sch 2 para 2(1)(b). As to activity requirements see Sch 2 para 4; and PARA 386.

6   Anti-social Behaviour, Crime and Policing Act 2014 Sch 2 para 2(1)(c). As to curfew requirements see Sch 2 para 5; and PARA 387. A supervision order containing a curfew requirement may also contain an electronic monitoring requirement: see Sch 2 para 6; and PARA 388.

7   Anti-social Behaviour, Crime and Policing Act 2014 Sch 2 para 1(2). As to who may apply for an injunction see PARA 373. A person making an application for an order under Sch 2 para 1(1) must before doing so consult any youth offending team specified under s 3(1) (see PARA 374) or, if a youth offending team is not so specified under that subsection, the local youth offending team within the meaning of s 14 (see PARA 373) (Sch 2 para 1(3)(a)) and inform any other body or individual the applicant thinks appropriate (Sch 2 para 1(3)(b)). In considering whether and how to exercise its powers under Sch 2 para 1, the court must consider any representations made by the youth offending team referred to in Sch 2 para 1(3)(a): Sch 2 para 1(4).

8   Anti-social Behaviour, Crime and Policing Act 2014 Sch 2 para 2(2).

9   Anti-social Behaviour, Crime and Policing Act 2014 Sch 2 para 2(3).

10   Anti-social Behaviour, Crime and Policing Act 2014 Sch 2 para 2(4)(a).

11   Anti-social Behaviour, Crime and Policing Act 2014 Sch 2 para 2(4)(b).

12   Anti-social Behaviour, Crime and Policing Act 2014 Sch 2 para 2(5). The period specified under Sch 2 para 2(5) may not exceed 6 months (not counting the day on which the order is made): Sch 2 para 2(6). The court may, on the application of the original applicant, amend a supervision order by substituting a new period for the one specified in the order for the time being under Sch 2 para 2(5) (subject to Sch 2 para 2(6)): Sch 2 para 8(1). A court so amending a supervision order may make whatever other amendments to the order the court considers appropriate in relation to a requirement imposed by the order: Sch 2 para 8(2).

13   A supervision order must for the purposes of this Schedule specify the youth offending team in whose area it appears to the court that the respondent will live during the period specified under Sch 2 para 2(5) (see the text and note 12) (Anti-social Behaviour, Crime and Policing Act 2014 Sch 2 para 2(6)(a)) or if it appears to the court that the defaulter will live in more than one such area, whichever of the relevant youth offending teams the court decides (Sch 2 para 2(6)(b)).

14   Anti-social Behaviour, Crime and Policing Act 2014 Sch 2 para 9(1).

15   Anti-social Behaviour, Crime and Policing Act 2014 Sch 2 para 9(2), (3).

16   Ie the area referred to in the Anti-social Behaviour, Crime and Policing Act 2014 Sch 2 para 9(1) (see the text and note 14).

17 Anti-social Behaviour, Crime and Policing Act 2014 Sch 2 para 9(4)(a).
18 Anti-social Behaviour, Crime and Policing Act 2014 Sch 2 para 9(4)(b).
19 Ie the Anti-social Behaviour, Crime and Policing Act 2014 Sch 2 para 9(4) (see the text and notes 16–18).
20 Anti-social Behaviour, Crime and Policing Act 2014 Sch 2 para 9(5).
21 Anti-social Behaviour, Crime and Policing Act 2014 Sch 2 para 9(6).
22 See PARA 389.
23 See PARAS 383, 390–391.

385. Supervision requirements. A 'supervision requirement', in relation to a supervision order[1], means a requirement that the defaulter attend appointments[2] with the responsible officer[3] or another person decided by the responsible officer[4], at whatever times and places the responsible officer instructs[5]. The 'responsible officer', in relation to a supervision order, means:

(1) in general, the member of the youth offending team[6] for the time being specified in the order who is for the time being responsible for discharging the relevant functions[7] on the responsible officer[8]; and

(2) in a case where the order imposes a curfew requirement[9] and an electronic monitoring requirement[10], but does not impose an activity requirement[11] or a supervision requirement, the person who is responsible[12] for the electronic monitoring[13].

Where a supervision order has been made, it is the duty of the responsible officer to make any arrangements that are necessary in connection with the requirements contained in the order[14] and to promote the defaulter's compliance with those requirements[15]. The responsible officer must ensure, so far as practicable, that any instructions given by the officer under a supervision order are such as to avoid interference with his education or other court-ordered activities[16]. A defaulter in respect of whom a supervision order is made must keep in touch with the responsible officer, in accordance with any instructions given by the responsible officer from time to time[17] and must notify the responsible officer of any change of address[18]. These obligations have effect as requirements of the order[19].

1 As to the making of supervision orders see PARA 384. As to compliance see PARA 383.
2 The appointments must be within the period for the time being specified in the order under the Anti-social Behaviour, Crime and Policing Act 2014 Sch 2 para 2(5) (see PARA 384): Sch 2 para 3(2).
3 Anti-social Behaviour, Crime and Policing Act 2014 Sch 2 para 3(1)(a).
4 Anti-social Behaviour, Crime and Policing Act 2014 Sch 2 para 3(1)(b).
5 Anti-social Behaviour, Crime and Policing Act 2014 Sch 2 para 3(1). A supervision order may be amended to remove a requirement from it: see PARA 389.
6 As to youth offending teams see CHILDREN AND YOUNG PERSONS vol 10 (2012) PARA 1193.
7 Ie the functions conferred by the Anti-social Behaviour, Crime and Policing Act 2014 Sch 2.
8 Anti-social Behaviour, Crime and Policing Act 2014 Sch 2 para 7(1)(b).
9 See PARA 387.
10 See PARA 388.
11 See PARA 386.
12 Ie under the Anti-social Behaviour, Crime and Policing Act 2014 Sch 2 para 6(4) (see PARA 388).
13 Anti-social Behaviour, Crime and Policing Act 2014 Sch 2 para 7(1)(a).
14 Anti-social Behaviour, Crime and Policing Act 2014 Sch 2 para 7(2)(a).
15 Anti-social Behaviour, Crime and Policing Act 2014 Sch 2 para 7(2)(b).
16 Anti-social Behaviour, Crime and Policing Act 2014 Sch 2 para 7(3). The reference to the defaulter's education or other court-ordered activities is a reference to the things referred to in Sch 2 para 2(4) (see PARA 384).
17 Anti-social Behaviour, Crime and Policing Act 2014 Sch 2 para 7(4)(a).
18 Anti-social Behaviour, Crime and Policing Act 2014 Sch 2 para 7(4)(b).
19 Anti-social Behaviour, Crime and Policing Act 2014 Sch 2 para 7(4).

386.   Activity requirements. An 'activity requirement', in relation to a supervision order[1], is a requirement that the defaulter do any or all of the following[2]:

(1)   participate, on however many days are specified in the order[3], in activities at a place or places specified in it[4];

(2)   participate in an activity or activities specified in the order on however many days are specified in it[5];

(3)   participate in one or more residential exercises for a continuous period or periods comprising however many days are specified in the order[6]; and

(4)   engage in activities[7] in accordance with instructions of the responsible officer on however many days are specified in the order[8].

Instructions[9] relating to any particular day must require the defaulter to do either of the following: (a) to present himself or herself to a person of a description specified in the instructions at a place specified in them[10]; or (b) to participate in an activity specified in the instructions[11]. Instructions given by, or under the authority of, a person in charge of a place[12] may require the defaulter to engage in activities otherwise than at that place[13]. The instructions operate to require the defaulter, on that day or while participating in that activity, to comply with instructions given by, or under the authority of, the person in charge of the place or activity[14].

A court may include an activity requirement in a supervision order or vary an activity requirement[15] only if:

(i)   it has consulted the youth offending team[16] that is to be, or is, specified in the order[17];

(ii)   it is satisfied that it is feasible to secure compliance with the requirement, or the requirement as varied[18];

(iii) it is satisfied that provision for the defaulter to participate in the activities proposed can be made under the arrangements for persons to participate in those activities which exist in the area of the youth offending team that is to be, or is, specified in the order[19]; and

(iv)   in a case where the requirement, or the requirement as varied, would involve the co-operation of a person other than the defaulter and the responsible officer, that person consents to its inclusion or variation[20].

1   As to the making of supervision orders see PARA 384. As to compliance see PARA 383.
2   Ie within the period for the time being specified in the order under the Anti-social Behaviour, Crime and Policing Act 2014 Sch 2 para 2(5) (see PARA 384): Sch 2 para 4(1). Where a supervision order contains an activity requirement, the court may, on the application of the original applicant or the defaulter, amend the order by substituting for a number of days, place, activity, period or description of persons specified in the order a new number of days, place, activity, period or description (subject, in the case of a number of days, to Sch 2 para 4(2) (see note 3)): Sch 2 para 4(12). As to the notification of amendments see PARA 389 note 5. A supervision order may also be amended to remove a requirement from it: see PARA 389.
3   The aggregate number of days specified in a supervision order in relation to an activity requirement must not be less than 12 or more than 24: Anti-social Behaviour, Crime and Policing Act 2014 Sch 2 para 4(2).
4   Anti-social Behaviour, Crime and Policing Act 2014 Sch 2 para 4(1)(a). As to the notification of requirements see PARA 384 note 3. A requirement referred to in Sch 2 para 4(1)(a) operates to require the defaulter, in accordance with instructions given by the responsible officer, on the number of days specified in the order in relation to the requirement to present himself or herself at a place specified in the order to a person of a description specified in it (Sch 2 para 4(3)(a)) and on each day, to comply with instructions given by, or under the authority of, the person in charge of the place (Sch 2 para 4(3)(b)). As to 'the responsible officer' see PARA 385. Instructions

given by, or under the authority of, a person in charge of a place under Sch 2 para 4(3)(b) may require the defaulter to engage in activities otherwise than at that place: Sch 2 para 4(11).

5   Anti-social Behaviour, Crime and Policing Act 2014 Sch 2 para 4(1)(b). A requirement referred to in Sch 2 para 4(1)(b) operates to require the defaulter, in accordance with instructions given by the responsible officer, on the number of days specified in the order in relation to the requirement to participate in an activity specified in the order (Sch 2 para 4(4)(a)) and on each day, to comply with instructions given by, or under the authority of, the person in charge of the activity (Sch 2 para 4(4)(b)).

6   Anti-social Behaviour, Crime and Policing Act 2014 Sch 2 para 4(1)(c). Where the order includes a requirement referred to in Sch 2 para 4(1)(c) to participate in a residential exercise, it must specify either a place (Sch 2 para 4(5)(a)) or an activity (Sch 2 para 4(5)(b)) in relation to the exercise. A requirement under Sch 2 para 4(1)(c) to participate in a residential exercise in relation to which a place is specified under Sch 2 para 4(5) operates to require the defaulter, in accordance with instructions given by the responsible officer to present himself or herself at the beginning of the period specified in the order in relation to the exercise, at the place specified in it, to a person of a description specified in the instructions (Sch 2 para 4(6)(a)), to live there for that period (Sch 2 para 4(6)(b)) and during that period to comply with instructions given by, or under the authority of, the person in charge of the place (Sch 2 para 4(6)(c)). Instructions given by, or under the authority of, a person in charge of a place under Sch 2 para 4(6)(c) may require the defaulter to engage in activities otherwise than at that place: Sch 2 para 4(11). A requirement under Sch 2 para 4(1)(c) to participate in a residential exercise in relation to which an activity is specified under Sch 2 para 4(5) operates to require the defaulter, in accordance with instructions given by the responsible officer, to participate, for the period specified in the order in relation to the exercise, in the activity specified in it (Sch 2 para 4(7)(a)) and during that period to comply with instructions given by, or under the authority of, the person in charge of the activity (Sch 2 para 4(7)(b)).

7   Ie in accordance with the Anti-social Behaviour, Crime and Policing Act 2014 Sch 2 para 4(8)–(10) (see note 14).

8   Anti-social Behaviour, Crime and Policing Act 2014 Sch 2 para 4(1)(d).

9   Ie instructions under the Anti-social Behaviour, Crime and Policing Act 2014 Sch 2 para 4(1)(d) (see the text and notes 7–8).

10   Anti-social Behaviour, Crime and Policing Act 2014 Sch 2 para 4(8)(a).

11   Anti-social Behaviour, Crime and Policing Act 2014 Sch 2 para 4(8)(b).

12   Ie under the Anti-social Behaviour, Crime and Policing Act 2014 Sch 2 para 4(8) (see the text and notes 9–11, 14).

13   Anti-social Behaviour, Crime and Policing Act 2014 Sch 2 para 4(11).

14   Anti-social Behaviour, Crime and Policing Act 2014 Sch 2 para 4(8). Schedule 2 para 4(8) is subject to Sch 2 para 4(9), which provides that if the supervision order so provides, instructions under Sch 2 para 4(1)(d) may require the defaulter to participate in a residential exercise for a period comprising not more than seven days, and for that purpose to present himself or herself at the beginning of that period to a person of a description specified in the instructions at a place specified in them, and to live there for that period (Sch 2 para 4(9)(a)), or to participate for that period in an activity specified in the instructions (Sch 2 para 4(9)(b)). Instructions of the kind mentioned in Sch 2 para 4(9) may not be given except with the consent of a parent or guardian of the defaulter (Sch 2 para 4(10)(a)) and operate to require the defaulter, during the period specified under that Sch 2 para 4(9), to comply with instructions given by, or under the authority of, the person in charge of the place or activity specified under Sch 2 para 4(9)(a) or Sch 2 para 4(9)(b) (Sch 2 para 4(10)(b)). Instructions given by, or under the authority of, a person in charge of a place under Sch 2 para 4(10)(b) may require the defaulter to engage in activities otherwise than at that place: Sch 2 para 4(11). As to the meaning of 'guardian' in Sch 2 para 4(10) see the Children and Young Persons Act 1933 s 107(1); and CHILDREN AND YOUNG PERSONS vol 10 (2012) PARA 709 (definition applied by the Anti-social Behaviour, Crime and Policing Act 2014 Sch 2 para 4(14)), except where a local authority has parental responsibility (within the meaning given by the Children Act 1989 s 3: see CHILDREN AND YOUNG PERSONS vol 9 (2012) PARA 151) for a defaulter who is in the authority's care or is provided with accommodation by the authority in the exercise of social services functions (within the meaning given by the Local Authority Social Services Act 1970 s 1A (see SOCIAL SERVICES AND COMMUNITY CARE vol 95 (2013) PARA 1), in which case the reference to 'guardian' in the Anti-social Behaviour, Crime and Policing Act 2014 Sch 2 para 4(10) is to be read as a reference to that authority (Sch 2 para 4(14)).

15   Ie under the Anti-social Behaviour, Crime and Policing Act 2014 Sch 2 para 4(12) (see note 2).

16   As to youth offending teams see CHILDREN AND YOUNG PERSONS vol 10 (2012) PARA 1193.

17   Anti-social Behaviour, Crime and Policing Act 2014 Sch 2 para 4(13)(a).

18 Anti-social Behaviour, Crime and Policing Act 2014 Sch 2 para 4(13)(b).
19 Anti-social Behaviour, Crime and Policing Act 2014 Sch 2 para 4(13)(c).
20 Anti-social Behaviour, Crime and Policing Act 2014 Sch 2 para 4(13)(d).

387.   Curfew requirements.   A 'curfew requirement', in relation to a supervision order[1], is a requirement that the defaulter remain at a place specified in the order for the periods specified in it[2]. A supervision order imposing a curfew requirement may specify different places or different periods for different days[3]. Before specifying a place for these purposes, the court making the order must obtain and consider information about the place proposed to be specified, including information as to the attitude of persons likely to be affected by the enforced presence there of the defaulter[4].

A supervision order containing a curfew requirement may also contain an electronic monitoring requirement[5].

1   As to the making of supervision orders see PARA 384. As to compliance see PARA 383.
2   Anti-social Behaviour, Crime and Policing Act 2014 Sch 2 para 5(1). The periods so specified must be within the period for the time being specified in the order under Sch 2 para 2(5) (see PARA 384) (Sch 2 para 5(3)(a)) and may not amount to less than 2 or more than 8 hours in any day (Sch 2 para 5(3)(b)). Where a supervision order contains a curfew requirement, the court may, on the application of the original applicant or the defaulter, amend the order by substituting new periods for the periods specified in the order under Sch 2 para 5 (subject to Sch 2 para 5(3)) (Sch 2 para 5(5)(a)) or substituting a new place for the place specified in the order under Sch 2 para 5 (subject to Sch 2 para 5(4)) (Sch 2 para 5(5)(b)). As to the notification of amendments see PARA 389 note 5. A supervision order may also be amended to remove a requirement from it: see PARA 389.
3   Anti-social Behaviour, Crime and Policing Act 2014 Sch 2 para 5(2).
4   Anti-social Behaviour, Crime and Policing Act 2014 Sch 2 para 5(4).
5   See PARA 388.

388.   Electronic monitoring requirements.   A supervision order containing a curfew requirement[1] may also contain a requirement (an 'electronic monitoring requirement') for securing the electronic monitoring of compliance with the curfew requirement during a period specified in the order[2] or determined by the responsible officer[3] in accordance with the order[4]. A supervision order imposing an electronic monitoring requirement must include provision for making a person responsible for the monitoring[5], and an electronic monitoring requirement may not be included in a supervision order unless the court making the order has been notified by the youth offending team[6] for the time being specified in the order that arrangements for electronic monitoring are available in the area that includes the place the court proposes to specify in the order for the purposes of the curfew requirement[7], and is satisfied that the necessary provision can be made under the arrangements currently available[8].

Where it is proposed to include an electronic monitoring requirement in a supervision order[9] but there is a person (other than the defaulter) without whose co-operation it will not be practicable to secure that the monitoring takes place[10], the requirement may not be included in the order without that person's consent.

1   As to the making of supervision orders see PARA 384; as to supervision orders containing curfew requirements see PARA 387. As to compliance see PARA 383.
2   Anti-social Behaviour, Crime and Policing Act 2014 Sch 2 para 6(1)(a). Where a supervision order contains an electronic monitoring requirement, the court may, on the application of the original applicant or the defaulter, amend the order by substituting a new period for the period specified in the order under these provisions: Sch 2 para 6(6). Schedule 2 para 6(3) (see the text and notes 9–10) applies in relation to the variation of an electronic monitoring requirement

under Sch 2 para 6(6) as it applies in relation to the inclusion of a requirement: Sch 2 para 6(7). As to the notification of amendments see PARA 389 note 5.

3   As to 'the responsible officer' see PARA 385.

4   Anti-social Behaviour, Crime and Policing Act 2014 Sch 2 para 6(1)(b). As to the notification of requirements see PARA 384 note 3. In the case referred to in Sch 2 para 6(1)(b), the responsible officer must, before the beginning of the period when the electronic monitoring requirement is to take effect, notify the defaulter (Sch 2 para 6(2)(a)), the person responsible for the monitoring (Sch 2 para 6(2)(b)), and any person within Sch 2 para 6(3)(b) (see the text and note 10) (Sch 2 para 6(2)(c)), of the time when that period is to begin. A supervision order may be amended to remove a requirement from it: see PARA 389.

5   Anti-social Behaviour, Crime and Policing Act 2014 Sch 2 para 6(4).

6   As to youth offending teams see CHILDREN AND YOUNG PERSONS vol 10 (2012) PARA 1193.

7   Anti-social Behaviour, Crime and Policing Act 2014 Sch 2 para 6(5)(a).

8   Anti-social Behaviour, Crime and Policing Act 2014 Sch 2 para 6(5)(b).

9   Anti-social Behaviour, Crime and Policing Act 2014 Sch 2 para 6(3)(a).

10 Anti-social Behaviour, Crime and Policing Act 2014 Sch 2 para 6(3)(b).

389.   Revocation and amendment.   The original applicant or the defaulter may apply to a youth court[1] to revoke a supervision order[2] or to amend a supervision order by removing a requirement from it[3], and if it appears to the court to be in the interests of justice to do so, having regard to circumstances that have arisen since the supervision order was made[4], the court may grant such an application and revoke or amend the order accordingly[5]. If an application for revocation or amendment is dismissed, the party by which the dismissed application was made may make no further application under these provisions without the consent of the court[6] or the agreement of the other party[7].

1   As to youth courts see CHILDREN AND YOUNG PERSONS vol 10 (2012) PARA 1225 et seq. For procedural provision, and as to appeals from decision of youth courts, see PARA 371 note 1. The original applicant must consult the youth offending team for the time being specified in the supervision order before making an application under these provisions: Anti-social Behaviour, Crime and Policing Act 2014 Sch 2 para 10(6).

2   Anti-social Behaviour, Crime and Policing Act 2014 Sch 2 para 10(1)(a). As to the making of supervision orders see PARA 384. As to compliance see PARA 383.

3   Anti-social Behaviour, Crime and Policing Act 2014 Sch 2 para 10(1)(b). As to the requirements of a supervision order see PARAS 385–388. There are also powers to amend supervision orders for administrative reasons: see PARAS 384 notes 12, 13, 386 note 2, 387 note 2, 388 note 2.

4   These circumstances include the conduct of the defaulter: Anti-social Behaviour, Crime and Policing Act 2014 Sch 2 para 10(3).

5   Anti-social Behaviour, Crime and Policing Act 2014 Sch 2 para 10(2). A court that revokes or amends a supervision order must straight away provide a copy of the revoking order, or of the order as amended, to the defaulter (Sch 2 para 13(3)(a)) and the youth offending team for the time being specified in the order (Sch 2 para 13(3)(b)). As to youth offending teams see CHILDREN AND YOUNG PERSONS vol 10 (2012) PARA 1193.

6   Anti-social Behaviour, Crime and Policing Act 2014 Sch 2 para 10(4)(a).

7   Anti-social Behaviour, Crime and Policing Act 2014 Sch 2 para 10(4)(b).

(b) Detention Orders

390.   Power to make a detention order.   A detention order is an order that the person in respect of whom it is made ('the defaulter') be detained for a period specified in the order in whatever youth detention accommodation[1] the Secretary of State[2] decides[3]. A youth court[4] may make a detention order:

(1)   in respect of a person aged under 18 (but not under 14[5]) whom it is satisfied beyond reasonable doubt is in breach of a provision of an injunction[6]; and

(2)   where it is satisfied that a defaulter has failed to comply with the requirements of a supervision order[7].

The court may make the order only on the application of the person who applied for the injunction[8] or the supervision order[9], as the case may be, and where the application relates to the breach of an injunction, the court may not make the order unless it is satisfied that, in view of the severity or extent of the breach, no other power available to the court is appropriate[10].

1   For these purposes 'youth detention accommodation' means a secure training centre (see PRISONS AND PRISONERS vol 85 (2012) PARA 491), a young offender institution (see PRISONS AND PRISONERS vol 85 (2012) PARA 487), or secure accommodation as defined by the Children and Young Persons Act 1969 s 23(12) (see CHILDREN AND YOUNG PERSONS vol 10 (2012) PARA 1209 et seq): Anti-social Behaviour, Crime and Policing Act 2014 Sch 2 para 14(3).

2   The function of the Secretary of State under these provisions is exercisable concurrently with the Youth Justice Board: Anti-social Behaviour, Crime and Policing Act 2014 Sch 2 para 14(4). As to the Youth Justice Board see the Crime and Disorder Act 1998 ss 38–42; and CHILDREN AND YOUNG PERSONS vol 10 (2012) PARA 1192 et seq.

3   Anti-social Behaviour, Crime and Policing Act 2014 Sch 2 para 14(1). The period so specified may not exceed the period of 3 months (not counting the day on which the order is made): Sch 2 para 14(2). A person detained under a detention order is in legal custody: Sch 2 para 14(5).

4   As to youth courts see CHILDREN AND YOUNG PERSONS vol 10 (2012) PARA 1225 et seq. For procedural provision, and as to appeals from decision of youth courts, see PARA 371 note 1.

5   Anti-social Behaviour, Crime and Policing Act 2014 Sch 2 para 1(5). As to a person's age for these purposes see PARA 371 note 4. As to the determination of a person's age see the Children and Young Persons Act 1933 s 99; and CHILDREN AND YOUNG PERSONS vol 10 (2012) PARA 1206.

6   Anti-social Behaviour, Crime and Policing Act 2014 Sch 2 para 1(1)(b). The injunction referred to is an injunction under s 1: see PARA 371. As to the prohibitions and requirements that may be included in an injunction see PARAS 374, 375. In these circumstances a youth court may alternatively make a supervision order in respect of the person in breach: see Sch 2 para 1(1)(a); and PARA 384.

7   See the Anti-social Behaviour, Crime and Policing Act 2014 Sch 2 para 12(4)(b); and PARA 383. Before making such an application the original applicant must consult the youth offending team for the time being specified in the order (Sch 2 para 12(3)(a)) and inform any other body or individual the original applicant thinks appropriate (Sch 2 para 12(3)(b)). The court must consider any representations made by the youth offending team for the time being specified in the order before exercising its powers under Sch 2 para 12: Sch 2 para 12(6). As to youth offending teams see CHILDREN AND YOUNG PERSONS vol 10 (2012) PARA 1193.

8   Anti-social Behaviour, Crime and Policing Act 2014 Sch 2 para 1(2). As to who may apply for an injunction see PARA 373. A person making such an application must before doing so consult any youth offending team specified under s 3(1) (see PARA 374) or, if a youth offending team is not so specified under that subsection, the local youth offending team within the meaning of s 14 (see PARA 373) (Sch 2 para 1(3)(a)) and inform any other body or individual the applicant thinks appropriate (Sch 2 para 1(3)(b)). In considering whether and how to exercise its powers under Sch 2 para 1, the court must consider any representations made by the youth offending team referred to in Sch 2 para 1(3)(a): Sch 2 para 1(4). As to youth offending teams see CHILDREN AND YOUNG PERSONS vol 10 (2012) PARA 1193.

9   See the Anti-social Behaviour, Crime and Policing Act 2014 Sch 2 para 12(2); and PARA 383.

10   Anti-social Behaviour, Crime and Policing Act 2014 Sch 2 para 1(6).

391. Revocation. Where a detention order is made[1], the original applicant or the defaulter may apply to a youth court[2] to revoke it[3], and if it appears to the court to be in the interests of justice to do so, having regard to circumstances that have arisen since the detention order was made[4], the court may grant the application and revoke the order accordingly[5]. If an application for revocation is dismissed, the party by which the dismissed application was made may make no further application without the consent of the court[6] or the agreement of the other party[7].

1   As to the making of detention orders see PARA 390.

2   As to youth courts see CHILDREN AND YOUNG PERSONS vol 10 (2012) PARA 1225 et seq. For procedural provision, and as to appeals from decision of youth courts, see PARA 371 note 1.

3 Anti-social Behaviour, Crime and Policing Act 2014 Sch 2 para 15(1). A person making an application in relation to a detention order made under Sch 2 para 1 (ie in the context of the breach of an injunction) must before doing so consult any youth offending team specified in the injunction under s 3(1) (see PARA 374) or, if none is specified, the local youth offending team within the meaning of s 14 (see PARA 373): Sch 2 para 15(5). A person making an application in relation to a detention order made under Sch 2 para 12(4)(b) (ie in the context of non-compliance with a supervision order) must before doing so consult the youth offending team for the time being specified in the relevant supervision order: Sch 2 para 15(6). As to youth offending teams see CHILDREN AND YOUNG PERSONS vol 10 (2012) PARA 1193.

4 These circumstances include the conduct of the defaulter: Anti-social Behaviour, Crime and Policing Act 2014 Sch 2 para 15(3).

5 Anti-social Behaviour, Crime and Policing Act 2014 Sch 2 para 15(2).

6 Anti-social Behaviour, Crime and Policing Act 2014 Sch 2 para 15(4)(a).

7 Anti-social Behaviour, Crime and Policing Act 2014 Sch 2 para 15(4)(b).

(ii) Sexual Risk Orders

392. Purpose of sexual risk orders. A 'sexual risk order' is an order which, for the purpose of:

(1) protecting the public[1] or any particular members of the public from harm[2] from the defendant[3]; or

(2) protecting children[4] or vulnerable adults[5] generally, or any particular children or vulnerable adults, from harm from the defendant outside the United Kingdom[6],

prohibits the offender from doing anything described in the order[7]. A sexual risk order may be made only on the application of the police[8]. The court may make the order only if it is satisfied that the defendant has[9] done an act of a sexual nature as a result of which it is necessary for such an order to be made for the purpose described above[10]. Where a court makes a sexual risk order in relation to a person who is already subject to such an order (whether made by that court or another), the earlier order ceases to have effect[11]. Failure to comply with an order is an offence[12] punishable by imprisonment[13].

The power to make sexual risk orders has effect as from 8 March 2015[14], partly replacing the powers to make sexual offences prevention orders, which were abolished as from that date[15].

1 Ie the public in the United Kingdom: Sexual Offences Act 2003 ss 122B(1), 122D(6) (ss 122A–122K added by the Anti-social Behaviour, Crime and Policing Act 2014 Sch 5 para 4).

2 'Harm' from the defendant means physical or psychological harm caused by the defendant doing an act of a sexual nature: Sexual Offences Act 2003 s 122B(1) (as added: see note 1).

3 Sexual Offences Act 2003 ss 122A(6)(a), (9)(a), 122D(4)(a) (as added: see note 1).

4 'Child' means a person under 18: Sexual Offences Act 2003 s 122B(1) (as added: see note 1).

5 'Vulnerable adult' means a person aged 18 or over whose ability to protect himself or herself from physical or psychological harm is significantly impaired through physical or mental disability or illness, through old age or otherwise: Sexual Offences Act 2003 s 122B(1) (as added: see note 1). For the purposes of ss 122A–122K a person's age is treated as being that which it appears to the court to be after considering any available evidence: s 122K(2) (as so added). As to the determination of a person's age see the Children and Young Persons Act 1933 s 99; and CHILDREN AND YOUNG PERSONS vol 10 (2012) PARA 1206.

6 Sexual Offences Act 2003 ss 122A(6)(b), (9)(b), 122D(4)(b) (as added: see note 1). As to the United Kingdom see PARA 4 note 3.

7 Sexual Offences Act 2003 s 122A(7)(a) (as added: see note 1). As to prohibitions see PARA 393.

8 Sexual Offences Act 2003 s 122A(1) (as added: see note 1). A chief officer of police or the Director General of the National Crime Agency ('the Director General') may by complaint to a magistrates' court (or, where the defendant is a child, a youth court) apply for a sexual risk order in respect of a person ('the defendant') if it appears to the chief officer or the Director General that the defendant has, whether before or after 1 May 2004, done an act of a sexual nature as a result of which there is reasonable cause to believe that it is necessary for such an

order to be made (ss 122A(1), (2), 122B(2) (as so added)). 1 May 2004 is the date on which Pt 2 (ss 80–136ZD) was brought into force by the Sexual Offences Act 2003 (Commencement) Order 2004, SI 2004/874.

A chief officer of police may make an application under the Sexual Offences Act 2003 s 122A(1) only in respect of a person who resides in the chief officer's police area (s 122A(3)(a) (as so added)) or who the chief officer believes is in that area or is intending to come to it (s 122A(3)(b) (as so added)). An application under s 122A(4) may be made to any magistrates' court (or youth court) acting for a local justice area that includes any part of a relevant police area (s 122A(4)(a) (as so added)) or any place where it is alleged that the person acted in a way mentioned in s 122A(2) (s 122A(4)(b) (as so added)). The Director General must as soon as practicable notify the chief officer of police for a relevant police area of any application that the Director has made under s 122A(1): s 122A(5) (as so added). 'Relevant police area' means: where the applicant is a chief officer of police, the officer's police area (s 122B(3)(a) (as so added)); and where the applicant is the Director General, the police area where the person in question resides or a police area which the Director General believes the person is in or is intending to come to (s 122B(3)(b) (as so added)). As to the making of interim orders where a police application has been made see PARA 394. As to police forces, police areas and chief officers of police see **POLICE AND INVESTIGATORY POWERS** vol 84 (2013) PARAS 52 et seq, 123 et seq. As to youth courts see **CHILDREN AND YOUNG PERSONS** vol 10 (2012) PARA 1225 et seq. Rules of court may provide for a youth court to give permission for an application under s 122A against a person aged 18 or over to be made to the youth court if an application to the youth court has been made, or is to be made, under s 122A against a person aged under 18 (s 122K(1)(a)(i) (as so added)) and the youth court thinks that it would be in the interests of justice for the applications to be heard together (s 122K(1)(a)(ii) (as so added)), and may, in relation to a person attaining the age of 18 after proceedings against that person by virtue of s 122A, s 122D or s 122E have begun, prescribe circumstances in which the proceedings may or must remain in the youth court (s 122K(2)(a)(i) (as so added)) and make provision for the transfer of the proceedings from the youth court to a magistrates' court that is not a youth court (including provision applying s 122E (see PARA 394) with modifications) (s 122K(1)(b)(ii) (as so added)).

The Secretary of State must issue guidance to chief officers of police and to the Director General of the National Crime Agency in relation to the exercise by them of their powers with regard to sexual risk orders and interim sexual risk orders (s 122J(1) (as so added)), may from time to time, revise the guidance so issued (s 122J(2) (as so added)), and must arrange for any guidance so issued or revised to be published in such manner as he considers appropriate (s 122J(3) (as so added)). At the date at which this volume states the law no such guidance had been issued.

9   Ie whether before or after 1 May 2004: see note 8.

10   Sexual Offences Act 2003 s 122A(6) (as added: see note 1). For procedural rules in connection with the making of sexual risk orders see the Criminal Procedure Rules 2015, SI 2015/1490, Pt 31. As to appeals against an order see PARA 396. In connection with the variation, renewal and discharge of an order see PARA 397.

11   Sexual Offences Act 2003 s 122A(10) (as added: see note 1).

12   A person commits an offence if, without reasonable excuse, he does anything that he is prohibited from doing by a sexual risk order: Sexual Offences Act 2003 s 122H(1)(a) (as added: see note 1).

13   A person guilty of an offence under the Sexual Offences Act 2003 s 122H is liable on summary conviction, to imprisonment for a term not exceeding 6 months or a fine or both (s 122H(3)(a) (as added: see note 1)) and on conviction on indictment, to imprisonment for a term not exceeding 5 years (s 122H(3)(b) (as so added)). Where a person is convicted of an offence under s 122H it is not open to the court by or before which the person is convicted to make, in respect of the offence, an order for conditional discharge: s 122H(4) (as so added).

14   Ie the date on which the Anti-social Behaviour, Crime and Policing Act 2014 ss 122A–122K were brought into force by the Anti-social Behaviour, Crime and Policing Act 2014 (Commencement No 8, Saving and Transitional Provisions) Order 2015, SI 2015/373, art 2(a), (e).

15   See PARA 442.

393. Prohibitions. The only prohibitions that may be included in a sexual risk order[1] are those that are necessary for the stated purpose[2]. Prohibitions have effect either for a fixed period, specified in the order, of at least two years or until further order[3]: and the order may specify different periods for different prohibitions[4].

An order may contain a 'prohibition on foreign travel', that is to say:

(1) a prohibition on travelling to any country outside the United Kingdom[5] named or described in the order[6];

(2) a prohibition on travelling to any country outside the United Kingdom other than a country named or described in the order[7]; or

(3) a prohibition on travelling to any country outside the United Kingdom[8].

A prohibition on foreign travel contained in a sexual risk order must be for a fixed period of not more than five years[9].

1 See PARA 392.
2 Sexual Offences Act 2003 s 122A(6) (ss 122A–122K added by the Anti-social Behaviour, Crime and Policing Act 2014 Sch 5 para 4). As to the stated purpose see the Sexual Offences Act 2003 ss 122A(6)(a), (b); and PARA 392.
3 Sexual Offences Act 2003 s 122A(7)(b) (as added: see note 2).
4 Sexual Offences Act 2003 s 122A(8) (as added: see note 2).
5 As to the meaning of 'United Kingdom' see PARA 4 note 3.
6 Sexual Offences Act 2003 s 122C(2)(a) (as added: see note 2).
7 Sexual Offences Act 2003 s 122C(2)(b) (as added: see note 2).
8 Sexual Offences Act 2003 s 122C(2)(c) (as added: see note 2). A sexual risk order that contains a prohibition within s 122C(2)(c) must require the defendant to surrender all of his passports at a police station specified in the order on or before the date when the prohibition takes effect (s 122C(4)(a) (as so added)) or within a period specified in the order (s 122C(4)(b) (as so added)). For these purposes 'passport' means a United Kingdom passport within the meaning of the Immigration Act 1971 (see IMMIGRATION AND ASYLUM vol 57 (2012) PARA 33) (s 122C(7)(a) (as so added)), a passport issued by or on behalf of the authorities of a country outside the United Kingdom, or by or on behalf of an international organisation (s 122C(7)(b) (as so added)), or a document that can be used (in some or all circumstances) instead of a passport (s 122C(7)(c) (as so added)). Any passports so surrendered must be returned as soon as reasonably practicable after the person ceases to be subject to a sexual risk order containing a prohibition within s 122C(2)(c) (unless the person is subject to an equivalent prohibition under another order): s 122C(5) (as so added). Section 122C(5) does not apply in relation to a passport issued by or on behalf of the authorities of a country outside the United Kingdom if the passport has been returned to those authorities (s 122C(6)(a) (as so added)) or a passport issued by or on behalf of an international organisation if the passport has been returned to that organisation (s 122C(6)(b) (as so added)). A person commits an offence if, without reasonable excuse, he fails to comply with a requirement imposed under s 122C(4): s 122H(2) (as so added). A person guilty of an offence under s 122H is liable on summary conviction, to imprisonment for a term not exceeding 6 months or a fine or both (s 122H(3)(a) (as so added)) and on conviction on indictment, to imprisonment for a term not exceeding 5 years (s 122H(3)(b) (as so added)). Where a person is convicted of an offence under s 122H it is not open to the court by or before which the person is convicted to make, in respect of the offence, an order for conditional discharge: s 122H(4) (as so added).
9 Sexual Offences Act 2003 s 122C(1) (as added: see note 2). This does not prevent a prohibition on foreign travel from being extended for a further period (of no more than 5 years each time) under s 122D (see PARAS 392, 397) (s 122C(3) (as so added)).

394. Interim orders. Where an application for a sexual risk order[1] ('the main application') has not been determined[2] an application for an interim sexual risk order may be made by the complaint by which the main application is made[3] or, if the main application has been made, may be made by the person who has made that application, by complaint to the court to which that application has been made[4]. The court may, if it considers it just to do so, make an interim sexual risk order, prohibiting the defendant from doing anything described in the order[5]. An interim order has effect only for a fixed period, specified in the order[6], and ceases to have effect, if it has not already done so, on the determination of the main application[7]. Failure to comply with an interim order is an offence[8] punishable by imprisonment[9].

1 As to an application for a sexual risk order see PARA 392.
2 Sexual Offences Act 2003 s 122E(1) (ss 122A–122K added by the Anti-social Behaviour, Crime and Policing Act 2014 Sch 5 para 4).
3 Sexual Offences Act 2003 s 122E(2)(a) (as added: see note 2).
4 Sexual Offences Act 2003 s 122E(2)(b) (as added: see note 2).
5 Sexual Offences Act 2003 s 122E(3) (as added: see note 2). As to prohibitions see PARA 393. As to appeals against an interim order see PARA 396. In connection with the variation, renewal and discharge of an order see PARA 397.
6 Sexual Offences Act 2003 s 122E(4)(a) (as added: see note 2).
7 Sexual Offences Act 2003 s 122E(4)(b) (as added: see note 2).
8 A person commits an offence if, without reasonable excuse, he does anything that he is prohibited from doing by an interim sexual risk order: Sexual Offences Act 2003 s 122H(1)(b) (as added: see note 2).
9 A person guilty of an offence under the Sexual Offences Act 2003 s 122H is liable on summary conviction, to imprisonment for a term not exceeding 6 months or a fine or both (s 122H(3)(a) (as added: see note 2)) and on conviction on indictment, to imprisonment for a term not exceeding 5 years (s 122H(3)(b) (as so added)). Where a person is convicted of an offence under s 122H it is not open to the court by or before which the person is convicted to make, in respect of the offence, an order for conditional discharge: s 122H(4) (as so added)).

395.   Notification.   A person in respect of whom a court makes a sexual risk order[1] or an interim sexual risk order[2] must[3] (unless he is subject to the notification requirements[4] on the date of service of the order) notify to the police his name[5] and home address[6]. A person who is subject to a sexual risk order or an interim sexual risk order (but is not subject to the notification requirements)[7] and uses a name which has not been so notified[8] or changes home address[9], must[10] notify to the police that name or (as the case may be) the new home address[11].

1 As to sexual risk orders see PARA 392. These provisions do not apply where a sexual risk order replaces an interim sexual risk order: Sexual Offences Act 2003 s 122F(1)(a) (ss 122A–122K added by the Anti-social Behaviour, Crime and Policing Act 2014 Sch 5 para 4). As to interim orders see PARA 394.
2 Sexual Offences Act 2003 s 122F(1)(b) (as added: see note 1).
3 Ie within the period of 3 days beginning with the date of service of the order: Sexual Offences Act 2003 s 122F(1) (as added: see note 1).
4 As to the notification requirements see PARAS 498–514.
5 Sexual Offences Act 2003 s 122F(2)(a) (as added: see note 1). Where the person uses one or more other names, each of those names must be notified: s 122F(2)(a) (as so added).
6 Sexual Offences Act 2003 s 122F(2)(b) (as added: see note 1). Sections 87 (method of notification and related matters: see PARA 508) and 91 (offences relating to notification: see PARA 510) apply for these purposes, subject to modifications: s 122F(4) (as so added).
7 Sexual Offences Act 2003 s 122F(3)(a) (as added: see note 1).
8 Ie notified under the Sexual Offences Act 2003 s 122F (see the text and notes 1–7, 9–11) or under any other provision of Pt 2 (ss 80–136ZD).
9 Sexual Offences Act 2003 s 122F(3)(b) (as added: see note 1).
10 Ie within the period of 3 days beginning with the date on which the event in question happens: Sexual Offences Act 2003 s 122F(3) (as added: see note 1).
11 Sexual Offences Act 2003 s 122F(3) (as added: see note 1).

396.   Appeals.   A defendant may appeal to the Crown Court against the making of a sexual risk order[1] or an interim sexual risk order[2]. On any such appeal, the Court may make such orders as may be necessary to give effect to its determination of the appeal, and may also make such incidental or consequential orders as appear to it to be just[3].

1   Sexual Offences Act 2003 s 122G(1)(a) (ss 122A–122K added by the Anti-social Behaviour,
     Crime and Policing Act 2014 Sch 5 para 4). As to the making of sexual risk orders see PARA 392.
2   Sexual Offences Act 2003 s 122G(1)(b) (as added: see note 1). As to the making of interim
     sexual risk orders see PARA 394.
3   Sexual Offences Act 2003 s 122G(2) (as added: see note 1). Any order made by the Crown
     Court on an appeal under these provisions (other than an order directing that an application be
     re-heard by a magistrates' court) is for the purposes of s 122D(7) (see PARA 397) or 122E(5) (see
     PARA 397) (respectively) to be treated as if it were an order of the court from which the appeal
     was brought (and not an order of the Crown Court): s 122G(3) (as so added).

397.   Variation, renewal and discharge.   An application for an order varying,
renewing or discharging a sexual risk order[1] may be made by the defendant[2], the
chief officer of police for the area in which the defendant resides[3], a chief officer
of police who believes that the defendant is in, or is intending to come to, that
officer's police area[4] and (where applicable[5]), the chief officer of police who
made the original application[6]. The application must be made to the appropriate
court[7] and the court may[8] make any order, varying, renewing or discharging the
sexual risk order that the court considers appropriate[9]. An order may be
renewed, or varied so as to impose additional prohibitions on the defendant[10],
only if it is necessary to do so for the stated purpose[11], and the court must not
without consent[12] discharge an order before the end of two years beginning with
the day on which the order was made[13]. A defendant may appeal to the Crown
Court against the making of an order for variation, renewal or discharge[14], or
the refusal to make such an order[15].

Where an interim sexual risk order is in effect[16], the applicant or the
defendant may by complaint apply to the court that made the order for it to be
varied, renewed or discharged[17].

1   As to the making of sexual risk orders see PARA 392.
2   Sexual Offences Act 2003 s 122D(1), (2)(a) (ss 122A–122K added by the Anti-social Behaviour,
     Crime and Policing Act 2014 Sch 5 para 4).
3   Sexual Offences Act 2003 s 122D(2)(b) (as added: see note 2). As to police forces, police areas
     and chief officers of police see POLICE AND INVESTIGATORY POWERS vol 84 (2013) PARAS 52 et
     seq, 123 et seq.
4   Sexual Offences Act 2003 s 122D(2)(c) (as added: see note 2).
5   Ie where the order was made on an application by a chief officer of police.
6   Sexual Offences Act 2003 s 122D(2)(d) (as added: see note 2).
7   Sexual Offences Act 2003 s 122D(1) (as added: see note 2). For the purposes of s 122D 'the
     appropriate court' means:
     (1)   where an adult magistrates' court made the order, that court, an adult magistrates'
            court for the area in which the defendant resides or, where the application is made by a
            chief officer of police, any adult magistrates' court acting for a local justice area that
            includes any part of the chief officer's police area (s 122D(7)(a) (as so added));
     (2)   where a youth court made the order and the defendant is under the age of 18, that
            court, a youth court for the area in which the defendant resides or, where the
            application is made by a chief officer of police, any youth court acting for a local justice
            area that includes any part of the chief officer's police area (s 122D(7)(b) (as so added));
     (3)   where a youth court made the order and the defendant is aged 18 or over, an adult
            magistrates' court for the area in which the defendant resides or, where the application
            is made by a chief officer of police, any adult magistrates' court acting for a local justice
            area that includes any part of the chief officer's police area (s 122D(7)(c) (as so added)).
     For these purposes 'adult magistrates' court' means a magistrates' court that is not a youth
     court: s 122D(7) (as so added). As to youth courts see CHILDREN AND YOUNG PERSONS vol 10
     (2012) PARA 1225 et seq. As to the determination of a person's age see the Children and Young
     Persons Act 1933 s 99; and CHILDREN AND YOUNG PERSONS vol 10 (2012) PARA 1206.
8   Ie after hearing the person making the application and (if they wish to be heard) the other
     persons mentioned in the Sexual Offences Act 2003 s 122D(2) (see the text and notes 1–6):
     s 122D(3) (as so added).
9   Sexual Offences Act 2003 s 122D(3) (as added: see note 2).

10 As to prohibitions see PARA 393.
11 Sexual Offences Act 2003 s 122D(4) (as added: see note 2). As to the stated purpose see s 122D(4)(a), (b); and PARA 392.
12 Ie without the consent of the defendant and either:
    (1)   where the application is made by a chief officer of police, that chief officer (Sexual Offences Act 2003 s 122D(5)(a) (as added: see note 2)); or
    (2)   in any other case, the chief officer of police for the area in which the defendant resides (s 122D(5)(b) (as so added)).
13 Sexual Offences Act 2003 s 122B(5) (as added: see note 2).
14 Ie an order under the Sexual Offences Act 2003 s 122D (see the text and notes 1–11).
15 Sexual Offences Act 2003 s 122G(1)(c) (as added: see note 2). On an appeal under s 122G(1)(c) the Crown Court may make such orders as may be necessary to give effect to its determination of the appeal, and may also make such incidental or consequential orders as appear to it to be just: s 122G(2) (as so added).
16 As to the making of interim orders see PARA 394.
17 Sexual Offences Act 2003 s 122E(5) (as added: see note 2).

(iii) Football Banning Orders made Otherwise than on Conviction

398. Making of banning order on complaint. An application for a football banning order[1] in respect of any person may be made by complaint to a magistrates' court[2] by the relevant chief officer[3], the Director of Public Prosecutions[4] or, where applicable, a constable[5], if it appears to him that the respondent has at any time caused or contributed to any violence or disorder[6] in the United Kingdom or elsewhere[7], and the court must make a banning order in respect of the respondent if:

    (1)   it is proved on the application that that condition[8] is met[9]; and
    (2)   the court is satisfied that there are reasonable grounds to believe that making a banning order would help to prevent violence or disorder at or in connection with any regulated football matches[10].

An appeal lies to the Crown Court against the making by a magistrates' court of a banning order under these provisions[11] and against the dismissal by a magistrates' court of an application for the making of a banning order under these provisions[12].

1 As to the meaning of 'football banning order' see PARA 341. A football banning order may also be made on conviction in criminal proceedings (see the Football Spectators Act 1989 s 14A; and PARA 344). The restraints imposed by a football banning order under these provisions are not in themselves unlawful under Council Directive (EC) 2004/38 (OJ L158, 30.4.2004, p 77) on the right of citizens of the union and their family members to move and reside freely within the territory of the member states: see *Gough v Chief Constable of the Derbyshire Constabulary* [2002] EWCA Civ 351, [2002] QB 1213, [2002] 2 All ER 985.
2 Football Spectators Act 1989 s 14B(3) (ss 14B–14D, 21B added by the Football (Disorder) Act 2000 Sch 1 paras 1, 2, 4). If the magistrates' court adjourns proceedings on an application under the Football Spectators Act 1989 s 14B the court may remand the person in respect of whom the application is made: s 14B(5) (as so added; ss 14B(1) substituted, ss 14B(1A), (5), (6), 14D(1A) added, ss 14D(2), 21B(4) amended, by the Violent Crime Reduction Act 2006 Sch 3 paras 1–4). A person who, by virtue of the Football Spectators Act 1989 s 14B(5) is remanded on bail under the Magistrates' Courts Act 1980 s 128 (see **MAGISTRATES** vol 71 (2013) PARA 554) may be required by the conditions of his bail:
    (1)   not to leave England and Wales before his appearance before the court (Football Spectators Act 1989 s 14B(6)(a) (as so added)); and
    (2)   if the control period relates to a regulated football match outside the United Kingdom or to an external tournament which includes such matches, to surrender his passport to a police constable, if he has not already done so (s 14B(6)(b) (as so added)).
    As to the meanings of 'regulated football match' and 'football match' see PARA 341. As to the meaning of 'United Kingdom' see PARA 4 note 3.
3 Football Spectators Act 1989 s 14B(1)(a) (as added and substituted: see note 2)). 'Relevant chief officer' means the chief officer of police of any police force maintained for a police area or the

chief constable of the British Transport Police Force (s 14B(1A) (as so added)), although see note 5. As to police forces, police areas and chief officers of police see **POLICE AND INVESTIGATORY POWERS** vol 84 (2013) PARAS 52 et seq, 123 et seq. As to the British Transport Police Force (ie the British Transport Police Force established under the Railways and Transport Safety Act 2003 Pt 3 (ss 18–77)) see **RAILWAYS AND TRAMWAYS** vol 86 (2013) PARA 285.

4   Football Spectators Act 1989 s 14B(1)(b) (as added and substituted: see note 2).

5   A notice given in connection with a football banning orders by a constable under the Football Spectators Act 1989 s 21B (see PARA 399) is treated as an application for a banning order made by complaint by the constable to the court in question: s 21B(4) (as added and amended: see note 2).

6   As to the meanings of 'violence' and 'disorder' see PARA 342 note 6.

7   Football Spectators Act 1989 s 14B(2) (as added: see note 2).

8   Ie the condition referred to in the Football Spectators Act 1989 s 14B(2): see the text and notes 5–7.

9   Football Spectators Act 1989 s 14B(4)(a) (as added: see note 2). The magistrates' court may take into account the following matters (among others), so far as they consider it appropriate to do so, in determining whether to make an order under s 14B:

(1)   any decision of a court or tribunal outside the United Kingdom (s 14C(4)(a) (as so added));

(2)   deportation or exclusion from a country outside the United Kingdom (s 14C(4)(b) (as so added));

(3)   removal or exclusion from premises used for playing football matches, whether in the United Kingdom or elsewhere (s 14C(4)(c) (as so added)); and

(4)   conduct recorded on video or by any other means (s 14C(4)(d) (as so added)).

In determining whether to make such an order:

(a)   the magistrates' court may not take into account anything done by the respondent before the beginning of the period of ten years ending with the application under s 14B(1), except circumstances ancillary to a conviction (s 14C(5)(a) (as so added)); and

(b)   before taking into account any conviction for a relevant offence, where a court made a statement under s 14A(3) (see PARA 344) (or s 15(2A) (repealed) or the Public Order Act 1986 s 30(3) (repealed)), the magistrates' court must consider the reasons given in the statement (Football Spectators Act 1989 s 14C(5)(b) (as so added)).

As to the meaning of 'circumstances ancillary to a conviction' see the Rehabilitation of Offenders Act 1974 s 4 (effect of rehabilitation); and PARA 593 note 9 (definition applied by the Football Spectators Act 1989 s 14C(5) (as so added)). Section 14C(5) does not prejudice anything in the Rehabilitation of Offenders Act 1974: Football Spectators Act 1989 s 14C(6) (as so added).

Although proceedings under s 14B are civil proceedings rather than criminal proceedings, the serious nature of the restraints on individual freedoms imposed by banning orders requires the application of an exacting standard of proof comparable to the criminal standard: see *Gough v Chief Constable of the Derbyshire Constabulary* [2002] EWCA Civ 351, [2002] QB 1213, [2002] 2 All ER 985.

Where a court makes a banning order the designated officer for the court (in the case of a magistrates' court) or the appropriate officer (in the case of the Crown Court) must:

(i)   give a copy of it to the person to whom it relates (Football Spectators Act 1989 s 18(1)(a) (s 18(1) amended by the Football (Disorder) Act 2000 Sch 2 paras 9, 10, 14; and by the Courts Act 2003 Sch 8 para 333));

(ii)   (as soon as reasonably practicable) send a copy of it to the enforcing authority and to any prescribed person (Football Spectators Act 1989 s 18(1)(b) (as so amended));

(iii)   as soon as reasonably practicable send a copy of it to the police station (addressed to the officer responsible for the police station) at which the person subject to the order is to report initially (s 18(1)(c) (as so amended)); and

(iv)   in a case where the person subject to the order is detained in legal custody, as soon as reasonably practicable send a copy of it to the person in whose custody he is detained (s 18(1)(d) (as so amended)).

As to the meaning of 'enforcing authority' see PARA 344 note 3.

10   Football Spectators Act 1989 s 14B(4)(b) (as added: see note 2). See note 9. See also *R (on the application of White) v Crown Court at Blackfriars* [2008] EWHC 510 (Admin), [2008] 2 Cr App Rep (S) 542, [2008] Crim LR 575 (distinguishing the Football Spectators Act 1989 s 14B from s 14A).

11   Football Spectators Act 1989 s 14D(1) (as added: see note 2). On an appeal under s 14D the Crown Court may make any orders necessary to give effect to its determination of the appeal and may also make any incidental or consequential orders which appear to it to be just:

s 14D(2) (as so added and amended). An order of the Crown Court made on an appeal under the Football Spectators Act 1989 s 14D (other than one directing that an application be re-heard by a magistrates' court) is to be treated for the purposes of Pt II (ss 14–22A) as if it were an order of the magistrates' court from which the appeal was brought: s 14D(3) (as so added).

12 Football Spectators Act 1989 s 14D(1A) (as added: see note 2).

399. Making of banning order by constable. During any control period[1] in relation to a regulated football match outside the United Kingdom[2] or an external tournament[3], a constable in uniform who:

(1) has reasonable grounds for suspecting that a British citizen[4] present before him has at any time caused or contributed to any violence or disorder[5] in the United Kingdom or elsewhere[6]; and

(2) has reasonable grounds to believe that making a football banning order[7] in his case would help to prevent violence or disorder at or in connection with any regulated football matches[8],

may[9] give the person a notice in writing[10] requiring him:

(a) to appear before a magistrates' court at a time, or between the times, specified in the notice[11];

(b) not to leave England and Wales before that time (or the later of those times)[12]; and

(c) if the control period relates to a regulated football match outside the United Kingdom or to an external tournament which includes such matches, to surrender his passport to the constable[13],

and may detain the person in his custody (whether there or elsewhere) until he has decided whether or not to issue a notice[14]. Failure to comply with a notice is an offence[15].

Where a person to whom a notice has been given under these provisions appears before a magistrates' court and the court refuses the application for a banning order in respect of him, it may order compensation to be paid to him out of central funds[16].

1 As to the meaning of 'control period' in relation to a regulated football match outside the United Kingdom see PARA 4 note 3. As to the meanings of 'regulated football match' and 'football match' see PARA 341.

2 As to the meaning of 'United Kingdom' see PARA 4 note 3.

3 As to the meaning of 'external tournament' see PARA 345 note 7.

4 The powers conferred by the Football Spectators Act 1989 ss 21A, 21B (see the text and notes 5–14) may only be exercised in relation to a person who is a British citizen: s 21C(1) (ss 14B, 21A–21D added by the Football (Disorder) Act 2000 Sch 1 paras 1, 2, 4). As to British citizenship see BRITISH NATIONALITY vol 4 (2011) PARA 421 et seq.

5 As to the meanings of 'violence' and 'disorder' see PARA 342 note 6.

6 Football Spectators Act 1989 ss 14B(2), 21A(1)(a) (as added (see note 4)); s 21A(1) amended by the Policing and Crime Act 2009 s 103(1), (2)(c)).

7 As to the meaning of 'football banning order' see PARA 341.

8 Football Spectators Act 1989 s 21A(1)(b) (as added: see note 4).

9 Ie if authorised to do so by an officer of at least the rank of inspector: Football Spectators Act 1989 s 21B(1) (as added: see note 4).

10 The notice is treated for the purposes of the Football Spectators Act 1989 s 14B (see PARA 398) as an application for a banning order made by complaint by the constable to the court in question (s 21B(4) (as added: see note 3)) and must state the grounds referred to in s 21A(1) (see the text and notes 1–8) (s 21B(2) (as so added)). A constable may arrest a person to whom he is giving such a notice if he has reasonable grounds to believe that it is necessary to do so in order to secure that the person complies with the notice: s 21B(5) (as so added).

11 Football Spectators Act 1989 s 21B(2)(a) (as added: see note 4). The times for appearance before the magistrates' court must be within the period of 24 hours beginning with the giving of the notice or the person's detention under s 21A(2) (see the text and note 14), whichever is the earlier: s 21B(3) (as so added). Where a person to whom a notice has been given under s 21B

above appears before a magistrates' court as required by the notice (whether under arrest or not), the court may remand him: s 21C(3) (as so added). A person who, by virtue of s 21C(3), is remanded on bail under the Magistrates' Courts Act 1980 s 128 (see MAGISTRATES vol 71 (2013) PARA 554) may be required by the conditions of his bail not to leave England and Wales before his appearance before the court and, if the control period relates to a regulated football match outside the United Kingdom or to an external tournament which includes such matches, to surrender his passport to a police constable, if he has not already done so: Football Spectators Act 1989 s 21C(4) (as so added; ss 21B(2)(c), (6), 21C(4) amended by the Identity Documents Act 2010 Schedule paras 3, 4).

12 Football Spectators Act 1989 s 21B(2)(b) (as added: see note 4).

13 Football Spectators Act 1989 s 21B(2)(c) (as added and amended: see notes 4, 11). Any passport surrendered by a person under s 21B must be returned to him in accordance with directions given by the court: s 21B(6) (as so added and amended).

14 Football Spectators Act 1989 s 21A(2) (as added: see note 4). This power is without prejudice to any power of the constable apart from s 21A to arrest the person: s 21A(2) (as so added). The constable must give the person his reasons for detaining him in writing: s 21A(2) (as so added).

   A person may not be detained under s 21A(2) for more than four hours or, with the authority of an officer of at least the rank of inspector, six hours: s 21A(3) (as so added). A person who has been detained under s 21A(2) may only be further detained thereunder in the same control period in reliance on information which was not available to the constable who previously detained him; and a person on whom a notice has been served under s 21B(2) (see the text and notes 9–13) may not be detained under s 21A(2) in the same control period: s 21A(4) (as so added).

15 Football Spectators Act 1989 s 21C(2) (as added: see note 4). A person guilty of this offence is liable on summary conviction to imprisonment for a term not exceeding six months, or a fine not exceeding level 5 on the standard scale, or both: s 21C(2) (as so added). As to the standard scale, the statutory maximum, the prescribed sum, and magistrates' powers to levy unlimited fines see PARA 176.

16 Football Spectators Act 1989 s 21D(1) (as added: see note 4). 'Central funds' has the same meaning as in enactments providing for the payment of costs: s 21D(5) (as so added). Before ordering the payment of compensation the court must be satisfied:

   (1)   that the notice should not have been given (s 21D(1)(a) (as so added));
   (2)   that he has suffered loss as a result of the giving of the notice (s 21D(1)(b) (as so added)); and
   (3)   that, having regard to all the circumstances, it is appropriate to order the payment of compensation in respect of that loss (s 21D(1)(c) (as so added)).

   An appeal lies to the Crown Court against any refusal by a magistrates' court to order the payment of compensation under s 21D(1): s 21D(2) (as so added). The compensation to be paid by order of the magistrates' court under s 21D(1) or by order of the Crown Court on an appeal under s 21D(2) must not exceed £5,000 (but no appeal may be made under s 21D(2) in respect of the amount of compensation awarded): s 21D(3) (as so added). If it appears to the Secretary of State that there has been a change in the value of money since 28 August 2000 (ie the date on which these provisions were brought into force by the Football (Disorder) Act 2000 (Commencement) Order 2000, SI 2000/2125) or, as the case may be, the last occasion when the power conferred by the Football Spectators Act 1989 s 21D was exercised, he may by order substitute for the amount specified in s 21D(3) such other amount as appears to him to be justified by the change: s 21D(4) (as so added). At the date at which this volume states the law no such order had been made.

400. Requirements of banning order. A football banning order[1] must:

(1)   require the person subject to the order to report initially at a police station specified in the order within five days beginning with the day upon which the order is made[2];

(2)   require the person subject to the order to give notification of specified events[3] to the enforcing authority[4]; and

(3)   impose a requirement as to the surrender[5], in connection with regulated football matches[6] outside the United Kingdom, of the passport of the person subject to the order[7].

A banning order may also, if the court making the order thinks fit, impose additional requirements on the person subject to the order in relation to any regulated football matches[8] and the court by which a banning order was made may, on an application[9], vary the order so as to impose, replace or omit any such requirements[10].

A person subject to a banning order who fails to comply with any requirement imposed by the order is guilty of an offence[11], although there is provision for exemption from certain requirements to be granted in some circumstances[12].

1   As to the meaning of 'football banning order' see PARA 341; as to the making of football banning orders on complaint see PARA 398; as to the making of football banning orders by constables see PARA 399. The restraints imposed by a football banning order under these provisions are not in themselves unlawful under Council Directive (EC) 2004/38 (OJ L158, 30.4.2004, p 77) on the right of citizens of the union and their family members to move and reside freely within the territory of the member states: see *Gough v Chief Constable of the Derbyshire Constabulary* [2002] EWCA Civ 351, [2002] QB 1213, [2002] 2 All ER 985. A court considering the making of a football banning order is entitled to take into account and give weight to the question of the deterrent effect of the order on other persons: see *R (on the application of White) v Crown Court at Blackfriars* [2008] EWHC 510 (Admin), [2008] 2 Cr App Rep (S) 542, [2008] Crim LR 575; *R v Curtis* [2009] EWCA Crim 1225, [2010] 1 Cr App Rep (S) 193.

2   Football Spectators Act 1989 s 14E(2) (ss 14E, 14G, 14J added, s 18(3) substituted, by the Football (Disorder) Act 2000 Sch 1 paras 1, 2, Sch 2 paras 9, 14; Football Spectators Act 1989 s 14E(2) amended by the Policing and Crime Act 2009 Sch 8 Pt 11). The police station may be in England, Wales, Scotland or Northern Ireland: Policing and Crime Act 2009 s 104(1), (2)(a). On making the order in relation to the offender the court must explain its effect to him in ordinary language: Football Spectators Act 1989 s 14E(1) (as so added). As to the functions of the officer responsible for the police station to which a person subject to a football banning order reports see ss 19, 21; and SPORTS LAW vol 96 (2012) PARA 125.

     In the case of a person detained in legal custody the requirement under s 14E to report at a police station (and any reporting requirements imposed under s 19, as to which see SPORTS LAW vol 96 (2012) PARA 125) is suspended until his release from custody: s 14E(5) (as so added). If he is released from custody more than five days before the expiry of the period for which the order has effect and he was precluded by his being in custody from reporting initially, the order is to have effect as if it required him to report initially at the police station specified in the order within the period of five days beginning with the date of his release: s 14E(6) (as so added).

     Where a person subject to a banning order is released from custody and, in the case of a person who has not reported initially to a police station, is released more than five days before the expiry of the banning order, the person in whose custody he is must (as soon as reasonably practicable) give notice of his release to the enforcing authority: s 18(3) (as so substituted). As to the meaning of 'enforcing authority' see PARA 344 note 3.

3   The specified events for the purposes of the Football Spectators Act 1989 s 14E(2A) are:
   (1)   a change of any of his names (Football Spectators Act 1989 s 14E(2B)(a) (s 14E as added (see note 2); s 14E(2A)–(2C), (8) added by the Violent Crime Reduction Act 2006 Sch 3 paras 1, 5));
   (2)   the first use by him after the making of the order of a name for himself that was not disclosed by him at the time of the making of the order (Football Spectators Act 1989 s 14E(2B)(b) (as so added));
   (3)   a change of his home address (s 14E(2B)(c) (as so added));
   (4)   his acquisition of a temporary address (s 14E(2B)(d) (as so added));
   (5)   a change of his temporary address or his ceasing to have one (s 14E(2B)(e) (as so added));
   (6)   his becoming aware of the loss of his passport (s 14E(2B)(f) (as so added; s 14E(2B)(f), (g), (2C)(c), (3) amended by the Identity Documents Act 2010 Schedule paras 3, 4));
   (7)   receipt by him of a new passport (Football Spectators Act 1989 s 14E(2B)(g) (as so added and amended));
   (8)   an appeal made by him in relation to the order (s 14E(2B)(h) (as so added));
   (9)   an application made by him under s 14H(2) (see PARA 348) for termination of the order (s 14E(2B)(i) (as so added)); and
  (10)   an appeal made by him under s 23(3) against the making of a declaration of relevance (see PARA 343) in respect of an offence of which he has been convicted (s 14E(2B)(j) (as so added)).

     'Home address', in relation to any person, means the address of his sole or main residence; 'temporary address', in relation to any person, means the address (other than his home address) of a place at which he intends to reside, or has resided, for a period of at least four weeks; 'loss' includes theft or destruction; and 'new' includes replacement: s 14E(8) (as so added). A notification required by a banning order by virtue of these provisions must be given before the end of the period of seven days beginning with the day on which the event in question occurs and:

  (a)   in the case of a change of a name or address or the acquisition of a temporary address, must specify the new name or address (s 14E(2C)(a) (as so added));

  (b)   in the case of a first use of a previously undisclosed name, must specify that name (s 14E(2C)(b) (as so added)); and

  (c)   in the case of a receipt of a new passport, must give details of that passport (s 14E(2C)(c) (as so added and amended)).

4   Football Spectators Act 1989 s 14E(2A) (as added: see notes 2, 3).

5   Ie in accordance with the Football Spectators Act 1989 Pt II (ss 14–22A).

6   As to the meanings of 'regulated football match' and 'football match' see PARA 341.

7   Football Spectators Act 1989 s 14E(3) (as added and amended: see notes 2, 3).

8   Football Spectators Act 1989 s 14G(1) (as added: see note 2).

9   Ie an application by the person subject to the order or the person who applied for the order or who was the prosecutor in relation to the order: Football Spectators Act 1989 s 14G(2) (as added: see note 2). In the case of a banning order made by a magistrates' court, the reference in s 14G(2) to the court by which it was made includes a reference to any magistrates' court acting in the same local justice area as that court: s 14G(3) (as so added; amended by the Courts Act 2003 s 8).

10 Football Spectators Act 1989 s 14G(2) (as added: see note 2).

11 Football Spectators Act 1989 s 14J(1)(a) (as added: see note 2). A person guilty of this offence is liable on summary conviction to imprisonment for a term not exceeding six months, or a fine not exceeding level 5 on the standard scale, or both: s 14J(2) (as so added). As to the standard scale, the statutory maximum, the prescribed sum, and magistrates' powers to levy unlimited fines see PARA 176. As to the reciprocal enforcement of these provisions and corresponding provisions for Scotland and Northern Ireland see the Policing and Crime Act 2009 ss 105(1)(a), (2)–(5), 106(1)(a), (2)–(5).

12 See the Football Spectators Act 1989 ss 20, 21; and SPORTS LAW vol 96 (2012) PARA 125.

401.   Duration and termination of banning order. A football banning order[1] has effect[2] for a period beginning with the day on which the order is made[3], and that period must not be longer than the maximum or shorter than the minimum[4]. Where an order is made on complaint[5] the period for must not be longer than five years or shorter than three years[6].

If a banning order has had effect for at least two-thirds of the period determined under these provisions[7] the person subject to the order may apply to the court by which it was made[8] to terminate it[9], and on such an application the court may by order terminate the banning order as from a specified date or refuse the application[10]. Where such an application in respect of a banning order is refused, no further application in respect of the order may be made within the period of six months beginning with the day of the refusal[11].

1   As to the meaning of 'football banning order' see PARA 341.

2   Ie subject to the Football Spectators Act 1989 Pt II (ss 14–22A).

3   Football Spectators Act 1989 s 14F(1) (ss 14F, 14H added, s 18(2) amended, by the Football (Disorder) Act 2000 Sch 1 paras 1, 2, 9, 10, 14).

4   Football Spectators Act 1989 s 14F(2) (as added: see note 3).

5   As to the making of football banning orders on complaint see the Football Spectators Act 1989 s 14B; and PARA 398.

6   Football Spectators Act 1989 s 14F(5) (as added (see note 3); and amended by the Violent Crime Reduction Act 2006 Sch 3 paras 1, 6).

7   Ie under the Football Spectators Act 1989 s 14F: see the text and notes 1–6.

8   In the case of a banning order made by a magistrates' court, the reference in the Football Spectators Act 1989 s 14H(1) to the court by which it was made includes a reference to any magistrates' court acting in the same local justice area as that court: s 14H(6) (as added (see

note 3); amended by the Courts Act 2003 Sch 8 para 332). The court may order the applicant to pay all or any part of the costs of an application under the Football Spectators Act 1989 s 14H: s 14H(5) (as so added).

9   Football Spectators Act 1989 s 14H(1) (as added: see note 3).
10   Football Spectators Act 1989 s 14H(2) (as added: see note 3). In exercising its powers under s 14H(2) the court must have regard to the person's character, his conduct since the banning order was made, the nature of the offence or conduct which led to it and any other circumstances which appear to it to be relevant: s 14H(3) (as so added). Where a court terminates a banning order under s 14H the designated officer for the court (in the case of a magistrates' court) or the appropriate officer (in the case of the Crown Court) must:
   (1)   give a copy of the terminating order to the person to whom the banning order relates (s 18(2)(a) (as so amended; amended by the Courts Act 2003 Sch 8 para 333));
   (2)   as soon as reasonably practicable send a copy of it to the enforcing authority and to any prescribed person (Football Spectators Act 1989 s 18(2)(b) (as so amended)); and
   (3)   in a case where the person subject to the banning order is detained in legal custody, as soon as reasonably practicable send a copy of the terminating order to the person in whose custody he is detained (s 18(2)(c) (as so amended)).
   As to the meaning of 'enforcing authority' see PARA 344 note 3.
11   Football Spectators Act 1989 s 14H(5) (as added: see note 3).

(iv) Violent Offender Orders

A. FORM AND PURPOSE OF ORDERS

402.   Violent offender orders.   A violent offender order is an order which contains such prohibitions, restrictions or conditions[1] as the court making the order considers necessary for the purpose of protecting the public from the risk of serious violent harm caused by the offender[2]. Such prohibitions, restrictions or conditions may prevent the offender:

(1)   from going to any specified[3] premises or any other specified place (whether at all, or at or between any specified time or times)[4];

(2)   from attending any specified event[5]; and

(3)   from having any, or any specified description of, contact with any specified individual[6].

A violent offender order (and, where applicable, an interim violent offender order[7]) may not be made so as to come into force when the person who is the subject of the order is in custody[8] or on licence[9] or is otherwise detained[10]: subject to this a violent offender order has effect, unless renewed or discharged[11], for such period of not less than two, nor more than five, years as is specified in the order[12].

Failure without reasonable excuse to comply with any prohibition, restriction or condition contained in a violent offender order or an interim violent offender order is an offence[13].

1   Ie as authorised by the Criminal Justice and Immigration Act 2008 s 102: see the text and notes 3–6. Any of the prohibitions, restrictions or conditions contained in a violent offender order may relate to conduct in Scotland or Northern Ireland (as well as to conduct in England or Wales): s 102(2).
2   Criminal Justice and Immigration Act 2008 s 98(1)(a). For the purposes of Pt 7 (ss 98–117) any reference to protecting the public from the risk of serious violent harm caused by a person is a reference to protecting the public in the United Kingdom, or any particular members of the public in the United Kingdom, from a current risk of serious physical or psychological harm caused by that person committing one or more specified offences: ss 98(2), 117(3). As to the specified prohibitions for these purposes see the text and notes 3–8; as to the qualifying offenders see PARA 404. 'Offender', in relation to a violent offender order or an interim violent offender order, means the person in respect of whom the order is made: s 117(1).
3   'Specified' means specified in the violent offender order concerned: Criminal Justice and Immigration Act 2008 s 102(4).

4   Criminal Justice and Immigration Act 2008 s 102(1)(a). The Secretary of State may by order
     amend s 102(1) (s 102(3)): at the date at which this volume states the law no such order had
     been made.
5   Criminal Justice and Immigration Act 2008 s 102(1)(b).
6   Criminal Justice and Immigration Act 2008 s 102(1)(c).
7   As to interim violent offender orders see PARA 406.
8   Ie subject to a custodial sentence imposed in respect of any offence: Criminal Justice and
     Immigration Act 2008 ss 101(5)(a), 104(5)(a). 'Custodial sentence' means a sentence of
     imprisonment, any other sentence or order mentioned in the Powers of Criminal Courts
     (Sentencing) Act 2000 s 76(1) (see PARA 9 note 15) or any corresponding sentence or order
     imposed or made under any earlier enactment (Criminal Justice and Immigration Act 2008
     s 117(1)), or a relevant service sentence, that is to say: a sentence of imprisonment passed under
     the Army Act 1955, the Air Force Act 1955 or the Naval Discipline Act 1957 (all repealed); a
     sentence of custody for life, or detention, under the Army Act 1955 s 71A, the Air Force
     Act 1955 s 71A or the Naval Discipline Act 1957 s 43A (all repealed); a sentence under a
     custodial order within the meaning of the Army Act 1955 s 71AA or Sch 5A para 10(1), the Air
     Force Act 1955 s 71AA or Sch 5A para 10(1), or the Naval Discipline Act 1957 s 43AA or
     Sch 4A para 10(1) (all repealed); or a custodial sentence within the meaning of the Armed Forces
     Act 2006 (see s 374; and see ARMED FORCES vol 3 (2011) PARA 594): Criminal Justice and
     Immigration Act 2008 s 117(2).
9   Ie on licence for part of the term of a custodial sentence imposed in respect of any offence:
     Criminal Justice and Immigration Act 2008 ss 101(5)(b), 104(5)(b).
10   Ie subject to a hospital order or a supervision order made in respect of any offence: Criminal
     Justice and Immigration Act 2008 ss 101(5)(c), 104(5)(c). 'Hospital order' means an order under
     the Mental Health Act 1983 s 37 (see PARA 472; and see MENTAL HEALTH AND CAPACITY vol 75
     (2013) PARA 864) or the Mental Health Act 1959 s 60 (repealed) or any other order providing
     for the admission of a person to hospital following a finding of the kind mentioned in the
     Criminal Justice and Immigration Act 2008 s 99(2)(b) or (c) (see PARA 404): s 117(1).
     'Supervision order' means a supervision order within the meaning of the Criminal Procedure
     (Insanity) Act 1964 Sch 1A (see PARA 495 et seq) or a supervision and treatment order within
     the meaning of Sch 2 (repealed): Criminal Justice and Immigration Act 2008 s 117(1).
11   Ie under the Criminal Justice and Immigration Act 2008 s 103: see PARA 407.
12   Criminal Justice and Immigration Act 2008 s 98(1)(b).
13   Criminal Justice and Immigration Act 2008 s 113(1)(a), (b). A person guilty of an offence under
     s 113 is liable on summary conviction to imprisonment for a term not exceeding 12 months or
     a fine not exceeding the statutory maximum or both, or on conviction on indictment to
     imprisonment for a term not exceeding 5 years or a fine or both: s 113(6), (7)(a). Proceedings
     for an offence under s 113 may be commenced in any court having jurisdiction in any place
     where the person charged with the offence resides or is found: s 113(8).

403.   Offences in respect of which violent offender orders may be made. A
violent offender order[1] may be made in respect of a person who has been
convicted[2] of any of the following offences[3]:

(1)   manslaughter[4];
(2)   soliciting murder[5];
(3)   wounding with intent to cause grievous bodily harm[6];
(4)   malicious wounding[7];
(5)   attempting to commit murder or conspiracy to commit murder[8]; or
(6)   a corresponding service offence[9],

where the court considers that the prohibitions, restrictions and conditions
contained in the order are necessary for the purpose of protecting the public[10]
from serious harm[11] caused by that person committing one or more of those
offences[12].

Such offences are referred to as 'specified offences'[13].

1   See PARA 402.
2   Or found not guilty or under a disability in relation to the offence: see the Criminal Justice and
     Immigration Act 2008 s 99(2); and PARA 404. As to references to a person being or having been

found to be under a disability and to have done the act charged against him see the Sexual Offences Act 2003 s 135(3); and PARA 329 note 1 (definition applied by the Criminal Justice and Immigration Act 2008 s 117(6)).

3   The Secretary of State may by order amend the Criminal Justice and Immigration Act 2008 s 98(3) (see the text and notes 4–13), and make consequential amendments to s 98(4) (see note 9): s 98(6) (added by the Anti-social Behaviour, Crime and Policing Act 2014 s 119(1)). At the date at which this volume states the law no such order had been made.

4   Criminal Justice and Immigration Act 2008 s 98(3)(a). As to the offence of manslaughter see CRIMINAL LAW vol 25 (2010) PARA 98 et seq.

5   Criminal Justice and Immigration Act 2008 s 98(3)(b). As to the offence of soliciting murder (ie an offence under the Offences Against the Person Act 1861 s 4) see CRIMINAL LAW vol 25 (2010) PARA 14.

6   Criminal Justice and Immigration Act 2008 s 98(3)(c). As to the offence of wounding with intent to cause grievous bodily harm (ie an offence under the Offences Against the Person Act 1861 s 18) see CRIMINAL LAW vol 25 (2010) PARA 128.

7·   Criminal Justice and Immigration Act 2008 s 98(3)(d). As to the offence of malicious wounding (ie an offence under the Offences Against the Person Act 1861 s 20) see CRIMINAL LAW vol 25 (2010) PARA 130.

8   Criminal Justice and Immigration Act 2008 s 98(3)(e). As to inchoate offences see CRIMINAL LAW vol 25 (2010) PARA 64 et seq.

9   Criminal Justice and Immigration Act 2008 s 98(3)(f). For this purpose a corresponding service offence is an offence against the Army Act 1955 s 70, the Air Force Act 1955 s 70 or the Naval Discipline Act 1957 s 42 (all repealed) of which the corresponding civil offence (within the meaning of those Acts) is an offence listed in any of heads (1)–(5) in the text (Criminal Justice and Immigration Act 2008 s 98(4)(a)), and an offence under the Armed Forces Act 2006 s 42 (see ARMED FORCES vol 3 (2011) PARA 587) as respects which the corresponding offence under the law of England and Wales (within the meaning given by s 42) is an offence listed in any of heads (1)–(5) in the text (Criminal Justice and Immigration Act 2008 s 98(4)(b)). The Armed Forces Act 2006 s 48 (attempts, conspiracy, encouragement and assistance and aiding and abetting outside England and Wales: see ARMED FORCES vol 3 (2011) PARA 587) applies with modifications for the purposes of the Criminal Justice and Immigration Act 2008 s 99(4)(b): s 98(5).

10   Ie the public in the United Kingdom, or any particular members of the public in the United Kingdom: see PARA 402 note 2.

11   Ie a current risk of serious physical or psychological harm: see PARA 402 note 2.

12   Criminal Justice and Immigration Act 2008 s 98(2).

13   Criminal Justice and Immigration Act 2008 s 98(3).

404.   Persons in respect of whom violent offender orders may be made.   A violent offender order[1] may be made in respect of a person aged 18 or over who has been[2] convicted of a specified offence[3], found not guilty of a specified offence by reason of insanity[4] or found to be under a disability and to have done the act charged in respect of a specified offence[5]. Where the person has been convicted, it is further required that either a custodial sentence[6] of at least 12 months was imposed for the offence[7] or that a hospital order[8] (with or without a restriction order[9]) was made in respect of it[10], and where the person has been found not guilty by reason of insanity or has been found to be under a disability it is further required that a hospital order (with or without a restriction order)[11] or a supervision order[12] was made in respect of the offence[13].

A violent offender order may also be made in respect of a person if[14], under the law in force in a country[15] outside England and Wales, he has been convicted of a relevant offence[16] or a court exercising jurisdiction under that law has made in respect of a relevant offence a finding equivalent to a finding that he was not guilty by reason of insanity[17] or a finding equivalent to a finding that he was under a disability and did the act charged in respect of the offence[18]. Where the person has been convicted, it is further required that either a sentence of imprisonment or other detention for at least 12 months was imposed for the offence[19] or an order equivalent to a hospital order was made in respect of it[20], and where a finding equivalent to a finding that the person has been found not guilty by reason of insanity or has been found to be under a disability has been made, it is further required that an order equivalent to a hospital order (with or without a restriction order) or a supervision order was made in respect of the offence[21].

1   See PARA 402.
2   Ie whether before or after 3 August 2009 (the date on which the Criminal Justice and Immigration Act 2008 Pt 7 (ss 98–117) was brought into force by the Criminal Justice and Immigration Act 2008 (Commencement No 10) Order 2009, SI 2009/1842). As to the determination of a person's age see the Children and Young Persons Act 1933 s 99; and CHILDREN AND YOUNG PERSONS vol 10 (2012) PARA 1206.
3   Criminal Justice and Immigration Act 2008 s 99(1), (2)(a). As to the specified offences for these purposes see PARA 403.
4   Criminal Justice and Immigration Act 2008 s 99(2)(b). As to verdicts of not guilty by reason of insanity see CRIMINAL LAW vol 25 (2010) PARA 30. As to references to a person being or having been found to be under a disability and to have done the act charged against him see PARA 403 note 2. References in Pt 7 to a finding of the kind mentioned in s 99(2)(b) or (c) or (4)(b) or (c) include references to a case where a decision on appeal is to the effect that there should have been such a finding in the proceedings concerned: s 117(4).
5   Criminal Justice and Immigration Act 2008 s 99(2)(c). See note 4.
6   As to the meaning of 'custodial sentence' see PARA 402 note 8.
7   Criminal Justice and Immigration Act 2008 s 99(2)(a)(i).
8   As to the meaning of 'hospital order' see PARA 402 note 10.
9   'Restriction order' means an order under the Mental Health Act 1983 s 41 (see PARA 477) or the Mental Health Act 1959 s 65 (repealed): Criminal Justice and Immigration Act 2008 s 117(1).
10 Criminal Justice and Immigration Act 2008 s 99(2)(a)(ii).
11 Criminal Justice and Immigration Act 2008 s 99(3)(a).
12 Criminal Justice and Immigration Act 2008 s 99(3)(b). As to the meaning of 'supervision order' see PARA 402 note 10.
13 Criminal Justice and Immigration Act 2008 s 99(3).
14 See note 2.
15 'Country' includes territory: Criminal Justice and Immigration Act 2008 s 117(1).
16 Criminal Justice and Immigration Act 2008 s 99(4)(a). For this purpose a 'relevant offence' is an act which constituted an offence under the law in force in the country concerned (s 99(5)(a)) and would have constituted a specified offence (see PARA 403), or the offence of murder (see CRIMINAL LAW vol 25 (2010) PARA 93), if it had been done in England and Wales (s 99(5)(b) (amended by the Anti-social Behaviour, Crime and Policing Act 2014 s 119(3))). An act punishable under the law in force in a country outside England and Wales constitutes an offence under that law for the purposes of the Criminal Justice and Immigration Act 2008 s 99(5) however it is described in that law: s 99(6). On an application for a violent offender order (ie under s 100: see PARA 405) the condition in s 99(5)(b) (where relevant) is to be taken as met in relation to the person to whom the application relates (P) unless, not later than three days before the hearing date for the application under s 100, P serves on the applicant a notice denying that, on the facts as alleged with respect to the act in question, the condition is met (s 99(7)(a); Magistrates' Courts (Violent Offender Orders) Rules 2009, SI 2009/2197, r 4), giving the reasons for denying that it is met (Criminal Justice and Immigration Act 2008 s 99(7)(b)) and requiring the applicant to prove that it is met (s 99(7)(c)). If the court thinks fit, it may permit P to require the applicant to prove that the condition is met even though no notice has been served under s 99(7): s 99(8).
17 Criminal Justice and Immigration Act 2008 s 99(4)(b).
18 Criminal Justice and Immigration Act 2008 s 99(4)(c).
19 Criminal Justice and Immigration Act 2008 s 99(4)(a)(i).
20 Criminal Justice and Immigration Act 2008 s 99(3)(a), (4)(a)(ii).
21 Criminal Justice and Immigration Act 2008 s 99(3)(b), (c).

405. Applications for, and making of, violent offender orders. Violent offender orders[1] may only be made on application by complaint to a magistrates' court[2] by a chief officer of police[3] where it appears to that officer that the person is a qualifying offender[4] who has, since the appropriate date[5], acted in such a way as to give reasonable cause to believe that it is necessary for a violent offender order to be made in respect of him[6]. The Secretary of State may by order make provision for applications for violent offender orders[7] to be made by such additional persons or bodies as are specified or described in the order[8], but at the date at which this volume states the law no such order had been made.

Where an application for a violent offender order is made[9] in respect of a person the court may make the order if, after hearing the applicant[10] and, if he wishes to be heard, the person in respect of whom the application is made[11], the court is satisfied that the person is a qualifying offender[12] and has, since the appropriate date, acted in such a way as to make it necessary to make a violent offender order for the purpose of protecting the public from the risk of serious violent harm caused by him[13].

An order cannot be made so as to come into force at any time when the person to whom the order applies is in custody, on licence or otherwise detained[14], but an order may be applied for, and made, at such a time[15]. A person in respect of whom a violent offender order has been made may appeal to the Crown Court against the making of the order[16].

1 See PARA 402.
2 Criminal Justice and Immigration Act 2008 s 100(1). An application may be made to any magistrates' court whose commission area includes any part of the applicant's police area or any place where it is alleged that the person acted in such a way as is mentioned in s 100(2)(b) (see the text and notes 5–6): s 100(3). As to the form of applications see the Magistrates' Courts (Violent Offender Orders) Rules 2009, SI 2009/2197, r 2(1)(a), Sch 1.
3 Criminal Justice and Immigration Act 2008 s 100(1). An application may only be made if the person resides in the chief officer's police area (s 100(1)(a)) or the chief officer believes that the person is in, or is intending to come to, that area (s 100(1)(b)). As to police forces, police areas and chief officers of police see POLICE AND INVESTIGATORY POWERS vol 84 (2013) PARAS 52 et seq, 123 et seq.
4 Criminal Justice and Immigration Act 2008 s 100(2)(a). As to qualifying offenders see PARA 404.
5 Ie the date (or, as the case may be, the first date) on which the person became a person within any of the Criminal Justice and Immigration Act 2008 s 99(2) or (4) (see PARA 404), whether that date fell before or after 3 August 2009 (ie the date on which Pt 7 (ss 98–117) was brought into force by the Criminal Justice and Immigration Act 2008 (Commencement No 10) Order 2009, SI 2009/1842): Criminal Justice and Immigration Act 2008 s 100(5).
6 Criminal Justice and Immigration Act 2008 s 100(2)(b).
7 Ie applications under the Criminal Justice and Immigration Act 2008 s 100.
8 Criminal Justice and Immigration Act 2008 s 100(4)(a). Such an order may also make provision specifying cases or circumstances in which applications may be so made (s 100(4)(b)) and for provisions of Pt 7 to apply, in relation to the making of applications (or cases where applications are made) by any such persons or bodies, with such modifications as are specified in relation to them in the order (s 100(4)(c)).
9 Ie an application under the Criminal Justice and Immigration Act 2008 s 100. A magistrates' court may not begin hearing an application under s 100 for a violent offender order, an application under s 104 for an interim violent offender order (see PARA 406) or an application under s 103 for the variation, discharge or renewal of a violent offender order, or for the variation or discharge of an interim violent offender order (see PARA 406), unless it is satisfied that the relevant person (ie the person to whom the application under s 100 or s 104 relates or, as the case may be, the person in respect of whom the order proposed to be varied, discharged or renewed under s 103 has been made) has been given notice of the application and the time and place of the hearing a reasonable time before the hearing: s 105.
10 Criminal Justice and Immigration Act 2008 s 101(1), (2)(a).
11 Criminal Justice and Immigration Act 2008 s 101(2)(b).
12 Criminal Justice and Immigration Act 2008 s 101(3)(a).
13 Criminal Justice and Immigration Act 2008 s 101(3)(b). As to the form of orders see the Magistrates' Courts (Violent Offender Orders) Rules 2009, SI 2009/2197, r 2(2), Sch 2. As to references to protecting the public from the risk of serious violent harm caused by a person see PARA 402 note 2. When deciding whether it is necessary to make an order for the purpose of protecting the public from the risk of serious violent harm caused by a person, the court must have regard to whether that person would, at any time when such an order would be in force, be

subject under any other enactment to any measures that would operate to protect the public from the risk of such harm: Criminal Justice and Immigration Act 2008 s 101(4).

14 See the Criminal Justice and Immigration Act 2008 s 101(5); and PARA 402.

15 Criminal Justice and Immigration Act 2008 s 101(6).

16 Criminal Justice and Immigration Act 2008 s 106(1)(a). On an appeal under s 106 the Crown Court may make such orders as may be necessary to give effect to its determination of the appeal (s 106(3)(a)) and may also make such incidental or consequential orders as appear to it to be just (s 106(3)(b)).

406. Interim violent offender orders. Where an application for a violent offender order[1] (the 'main application') has not yet been determined an application[2] for an interim violent offender order may be made by the complaint by which the main application is made[3] or, if the main application has already been made to a court, by means of a further complaint made to that court by the person making the main application[4], and the court may make the interim order if it appears to it:

(1)   that the person to whom the main application relates is a qualifying offender[5];

(2)   that, if the court were determining that application, it would be likely to make a violent offender order in respect of that person[6]; and

(3)   that it is desirable to act before that application is determined, with a view to securing the immediate protection of the public from the risk of serious violent harm caused by that person[7].

An interim violent offender order may contain such prohibitions, restrictions or conditions[8] as the court considers necessary for the purpose of protecting the public from the risk of serious violent harm caused by the person in question[9]. It has effect only for such period as is specified in the order[10] and ceases to have effect (if it has not already done so) at the appropriate time[11]. An interim violent offender order cannot be made so as to come into force at any time when the person to whom the order applies is in custody, on licence or otherwise detained[12]. A person in respect of whom an interim violent offender order has been made may appeal to the Crown Court against the making of the order[13]. Provision is also made for the variation and discharge of an interim violent offender order[14]. Failure without reasonable excuse to comply with any prohibition, restriction or condition contained in an interim violent offender order is an offence[15].

1   Ie under the Criminal Justice and Immigration Act 2008 s 100 (see PARA 405).

2   Ie under the Criminal Justice and Immigration Act 2008 s 104 (see the text and notes 3–11). The court may not begin hearing such an application without notice having been given: see s 105; and PARA 405 note 9.

3   Criminal Justice and Immigration Act 2008 s 104(1), (2)(a). As to the form of applications and interim orders see the Magistrates' Courts (Violent Offender Orders) Rules 2009, SI 2009/2197, r 2(1)(b), (3), Schs 1, 3.

4   Criminal Justice and Immigration Act 2008 s 104(2)(b).

5   Criminal Justice and Immigration Act 2008 s 104(3)(a). As to qualifying offenders see PARA 404.

6   Criminal Justice and Immigration Act 2008 s 104(3)(b).

7   Criminal Justice and Immigration Act 2008 s 104(3)(c). As to references to protecting the public from the risk of serious violent harm caused by a person see PARA 402 note 2.

8   This reference to prohibitions, restrictions or conditions is to prohibitions, restrictions or conditions authorised by the Criminal Justice and Immigration Act 2008 s 102 (see PARA 402): s 104(4).

9   Criminal Justice and Immigration Act 2008 s 104(3).

10   Criminal Justice and Immigration Act 2008 s 104(6)(a).

11   Criminal Justice and Immigration Act 2008 s 104(6)(b). The 'appropriate time' is either the time when a violent offender order made in pursuance of the main application comes into force (if the

court grants the main application) or the time when the court decides not to grant the main application or it is withdrawn (if applicable): s 104(7).
12 See the Criminal Justice and Immigration Act 2008 s 104(5); and PARA 402.
13 Criminal Justice and Immigration Act 2008 s 106(1)(b). As to the powers of the Crown Court on an appeal under s 106 see PARA 405.
14 See PARA 407.
15 Criminal Justice and Immigration Act 2008 s 113(1)(b). As to the punishment of, and proceedings for, an offence under s 113 see PARA 402.

407. Variation, renewal and discharge of violent offender orders and interim violent offender orders. The offender[1] and the chief officer of police[2] may by complaint apply to the appropriate magistrates' court[3] for an order varying or discharging a violent offender order[4] or an interim violent offender order[5] or for an order (a 'renewal order') renewing a violent offender order for such period of not more than five years as is specified in the renewal order[6]. On such an application the court may, after hearing the applicant[7] and any other persons entitled to make such an application[8] who wish to be heard[9], make such order varying, renewing or discharging the violent offender order or the interim order as the court considers appropriate[10]; however:

(1) a violent offender order or an interim order may only be renewed, or varied so as to impose additional prohibitions, restrictions or conditions on the offender[11], if the court considers that it is necessary to do so for the purpose of protecting the public from the risk of serious violent harm caused by the offender[12]; and

(2) the court may not discharge a violent offender order before the end of the period of two years beginning with the date on which it comes into force[13] unless consent to its discharge is given by the offender and the chief officer of police[14].

A person in respect of whom a violent offender order or an interim violent offender order has been made may appeal to the Crown Court against the making of an order for variation, renewal or discharge and against any refusal to make such an order[15].

1 Criminal Justice and Immigration Act 2008 ss 103(1), (2)(a). As to the meaning of 'offender' see PARA 402 note 2.
2 Ie the chief officer of police who applied for the order (Criminal Justice and Immigration Act 2008 s 103(2)(b)), (if different) the chief officer of police for the area in which the offender resides (s 103(2)(c)) or (if different) a chief officer of police who believes that the offender is in, or is intending to come to, his police areas (s 103(2)(d)). As to police forces, police areas and chief officers of police see **POLICE AND INVESTIGATORY POWERS** vol 84 (2013) PARAS 52 et seq, 123 et seq.
3 Ie the magistrates' court that made the violent offender order (see PARA 405) or (if different) a magistrates' court for the area in which the offender resides (Criminal Justice and Immigration Act 2008 s 103(3)(a)) or, where the application for variation, renewal or discharge is made by a chief officer of police, any magistrates' court whose commission area includes any part of the chief officer's police area (s 103(3)(b)). For the purposes of s 103(3) an order made by the Crown Court on an appeal made by virtue of s 106(1) or (2) (see PARAS 405, 406; and the text and note 15) is to be treated as if made by the court from which the appeal was brought: s 106(4). An application must be made in writing and must specify the reason why the applicant believes the court should vary, discharge or renew the order, as the case may be: Magistrates' Courts (Violent Offender Orders) Rules 2009, SI 2009/2197, r 3. The court may not begin hearing such an application without notice having been given: see the Criminal Justice and Immigration Act 2008 s 105; and PARA 405 note 9.
4 Criminal Justice and Immigration Act 2008 s 103(1)(a). As to violent offender orders see PARA 402.
5 Criminal Justice and Immigration Act 2008 s 104(8). As to interim violent offender orders see PARA 406.
6 Criminal Justice and Immigration Act 2008 s 103(1)(b).

7   Criminal Justice and Immigration Act 2008 s 103(4)(a).
8   Ie the persons mentioned in the Criminal Justice and Immigration Act 2008 s 103(2) (see the text and notes 1–2).
9   Criminal Justice and Immigration Act 2008 s 103(4)(b).
10 Criminal Justice and Immigration Act 2008 s 103(4).
11 This reference to prohibitions, restrictions or conditions is to prohibitions, restrictions or conditions authorised by the Criminal Justice and Immigration Act 2008 s 102 (see PARA 402): s 103(6).
12 Criminal Justice and Immigration Act 2008 s 103(5). As to references to protecting the public from the risk of serious violent harm caused by a person see PARA 402 note 2. Any renewed or varied order may contain only such prohibitions, restrictions or conditions as the court considers necessary for the purpose of protecting the public from the risk of serious violent harm caused by the offender: s 103(5).
13 Ie under the Criminal Justice and Immigration Act 2008 s 101 (see PARA 405).
14 Criminal Justice and Immigration Act 2008 s 103(7). Where the application under s 103 is made by a chief officer of police, consent must be given by that chief officer; and where the application is made by the offender, consent must be given by the chief officer of police for the area in which the offender resides: s 103(7). Section 103(7) does not apply to interim orders: s 104(8).
15 Criminal Justice and Immigration Act 2008 s 106(2). As to the powers of the Crown Court on an appeal under s 106 see PARA 405 note 16.

B. NOTIFICATION REQUIREMENTS

408. Initial notification and annual renotification under the notification requirements. An offender[1] subject to notification requirements[2] must[3] notify to the police[4]:

(1)   date of birth[5];

(2)   national insurance number[6];

(3)   name on the relevant date or, if the offender used two or more names on that date, each of those names[7];

(4)   home address on the relevant date[8];

(5)   name on the date on which the notification is given or, if the offender used two or more names on that date, each of those names[9];

(6)   home address on the date on which the notification is given[10];

(7)   the address of any other premises in the United Kingdom at which on that date the offender regularly resides or stays[11]; and

(8)   any other information prescribed by regulations made by the Secretary of State[12].

This information must, subject to any intervening statutory notifications, be re-notified to the police annually[13] unless the offender is in custody, imprisoned or detained[14] or outside the United Kingdom[15], in which event he must notify the police of this information within three days of his ceasing to be in custody, imprisoned, detained or outside the United Kingdom[16]. Provision is made for the verification of information notified under these provisions[17].

Failure without reasonable excuse to comply, or the notification of information known to be false in purported compliance, with the notification requirements[18] is an offence[19].

1   As to the meaning of 'offender' see PARA 402 note 2.
2   References in the Criminal Justice and Immigration Act 2008 Pt 7 (ss 98–117) to an offender subject to notification requirements are references to an offender who is for the time being subject to a violent offender order (see PARA 402) or an interim violent offender order (see PARA 406) which is in force under Pt 7: s 107(1) (having effect subject to s 110(7), which excludes from s 110 an offender subject to an interim violent offender order: s 107(2)).
3   Ie within the period of three days beginning with the date on which the violent offender order or the interim violent offender order comes into force in relation to the offender (the 'relevant date'): Criminal Justice and Immigration Act 2008 s 108(1). When determining the period of

three days mentioned in s 108(1) or s 109(1) (see PARA 409) or the period of six days for the purposes of s 109(6) (see PARA 409) there is to be disregarded any time when the offender is remanded in or committed to custody by an order of a court or kept in service custody (ss 108(4)(a)), 109(7)) serving a sentence of imprisonment or a term of service detention (s 108(4)(b)), detained in a hospital (s 108(4)(c)) or outside the United Kingdom (s 108(4)(d)). 'Kept in service custody' means kept in service custody by virtue of an order under the Armed Forces Act 2006 s 105(2) (see **ARMED FORCES** vol 3 (2011) PARA 523): Criminal Justice and Immigration Act 2008 s 117(1). As to the meanings of 'imprisonment' and 'detained in a hospital' see the Sexual Offences Act 2003 ss 131, 133; and PARA 500 note 6 (definitions applied by the Criminal Justice and Immigration Act 2008 s 117(6)). As to the meaning of 'service detention' see the Armed Forces Act 2006 s 374; and **ARMED FORCES** vol 3 (2011) PARA 349 (definition applied by the Criminal Justice and Immigration Act 2008 s 117(1)).

4   Notification under the Criminal Justice and Immigration Act 2008 s 108(1) (see the text and note 3), s 109(1) (notification of change: see PARA 409) or s 110(1) (periodic re-notification: see the text and note 13) must be made by the offender attending at a police station in his local police area (s 112(1)(a)) and making an oral notification to a police officer or to a person authorised for the purpose by the officer in charge of the station (s 112(1)(b)). The notification must be acknowledged in writing (s 112(3)(a)) and in such form as the Secretary of State may direct (s 112(3)(b)). The offender must, for the purpose of verifying his identity and if requested to do so by the police officer or person to whom the notification is made, allow the officer or person to take his fingerprints (s 112(4)(a)), photograph (which includes any process by means of which an image may be produced) any part of him (ss 112(4)(b), (5)) or do both these things (s 112(4)(c)). Failure without reasonable excuse to comply with s 112(4) is an offence: s 113(2)(a). As to the punishment of violations of s 112(4) (ie an offence under s 113) see PARA 402.

For the purposes of s 112 a person's 'local police area' means (by virtue of s 112(5)):

(1)   the police area in which the offender's home address is situated;
(2)   in the absence of a home address in England and Wales, the police area in which the home address last notified is situated; or
(3)   in the absence of a home address and of any such notification, the police area in which the court that made the order or the interim order (as the case may be) was situated.

In Pt 7 'home address' means, in relation to the offender, the address of his sole or main residence in the United Kingdom (s 108(5)(a)) or, where he has no such residence, the address or location of a place in the United Kingdom where he can regularly be found and, if there is more than one such place, such one of those places as he may select (s 108(5)(b)). As to the meaning of 'United Kingdom' see PARA 4 note 3.

5   Criminal Justice and Immigration Act 2008 s 108(2)(a).
6   Criminal Justice and Immigration Act 2008 s 108(2)(b).
7   Criminal Justice and Immigration Act 2008 s 108(2)(c).
8   Criminal Justice and Immigration Act 2008 s 108(2)(d).
9   Criminal Justice and Immigration Act 2008 s 108(2)(e).
10   Criminal Justice and Immigration Act 2008 s 108(2)(f).
11   Criminal Justice and Immigration Act 2008 s 108(2)(g).
12   Criminal Justice and Immigration Act 2008 s 108(2)(h), (3). At the date at which this volume states the law no regulations had been made for these purposes.
13   See the Criminal Justice and Immigration Act 2008 s 110(1), which requires an offender subject to notification requirements, within the applicable period after each notification date, to notify to the police the information mentioned in s 108(2) (see the text and notes 5–12) unless the offender has already given a notification under s 109(1) (see PARA 409) within that period. For this purpose the 'applicable period' is one year (s 110(5)(b)) unless the last home address notified by the offender under s 108(1) or 109(1) or s 110(1) was the address or location of such a place as is mentioned in s 108(5)(b) (ie was not his sole or main residence: see note 4), in which case it is one week (s 110(5)(a), (6); Criminal Justice and Immigration Act 2008 (Violent Offender Orders) (Notification Requirements) Regulations 2009, SI 2009/2019, reg 11). A 'notification date' means, in relation to the offender, the date of any notification given by the offender under the Criminal Justice and Immigration Act 2008 s 108(1) or s 109(1) or s 110(1): s 110(2).
14   Ie unless the applicable period would otherwise end while the offender is remanded in or committed to custody by an order of a court or kept in service custody (Criminal Justice and Immigration Act 2008 s 110(3), (4)(a)) serving a sentence of imprisonment or a term of service detention (s 110(4)(b)) or detained in a hospital (s 110(4)(c)).
15   Ie unless the applicable period would otherwise end while the offender is outside the United Kingdom: Criminal Justice and Immigration Act 2008 s 110(4)(d).

16 Criminal Justice and Immigration Act 2008 s 110(3).

17 Where information is notified to the police under the Criminal Justice and Immigration Act 2008 s 108(1), s 109(1) or s 110(1) a chief officer of police may, for the purposes of the prevention, detection, investigation or prosecution of offences under Pt 7, supply any such information to the Secretary of State or a person providing services to the Secretary of State in connection with a relevant function (ie a function relating to social security, child support, employment or training, a function relating to passports or a function under the Road Traffic Act 1988 Pt 3 (ss 87–109C) (driver licensing: see ROAD TRAFFIC vol 89 (2011) PARA 245 et seq), for use for the purpose of verifying the information: Criminal Justice and Immigration Act 2008 s 114(1), (2), (7). In relation to information so supplied the reference to verifying the information is a reference to checking its accuracy by comparing it with information held by the Secretary of State in connection with the exercise of a relevant function (where the person is the Secretary of State) or, where the person is a person providing services to the Secretary of State in connection with a relevant function, by that person in connection with the provision of such services, and compiling a report of that comparison: s 114(3). As to police forces, police areas and chief officers of police see POLICE AND INVESTIGATORY POWERS vol 84 (2013) PARAS 52 et seq, 123 et seq.

A report compiled under s 114 may be supplied to a chief officer of police by the Secretary of State or, as the case may be, the person providing services to the Secretary of State in connection with a relevant function (s 115(1)), and may contain any information held by the Secretary of State in connection with the exercise of a relevant function or by the person providing services in connection with the provision of services as mentioned there (s 115(2)). Where such a report contains information within s 115(2), the chief officer to whom it is supplied may retain the information, whether or not used for the purposes of the prevention, detection, investigation or prosecution of offences under Pt 7, and may use the information for any purpose related to the prevention, detection, investigation or prosecution of offences (whether or not under this Pt 7), but for no other purpose: s 115(3).

The supply of information under ss 114, 115 is to be taken not to breach any restriction on the disclosure of information (however arising) (ss 114(4), 115(4)), although those provisions do not authorise the doing of anything that contravenes the Data Protection Act 1998 (Criminal Justice and Immigration Act 2008 s 114(5)). These provisions also do not affect any power to supply information that exists apart therefrom: s 114(6).

18 Ie, for these purposes, the Criminal Justice and Immigration Act 2008 ss 108(1), 110(1) (see the text and notes 1–13).

19 Criminal Justice and Immigration Act 2008 s 113(2)(a), (3)(a). As to the punishment of, and proceedings for, an offence under s 113 see PARA 402. A person commits an offence of non-compliance with s 108(1) or s 110(1) on the first day on which he first fails, without reasonable excuse, to comply with the said provision, and continues to commit it throughout any period during which the failure continues: s 113(4)(a). However a person must not be prosecuted under s 113(2) more than once in respect of the same failure: s 113(5).

409. Notification of changes. An offender[1] subject to notification requirements[2] must notify the police[3]:

(1)   of any name he uses that has not previously been notified to the police[4];

(2)   if there is a change of his home address, of the new home address[5];

(3)   if he resides or stays for specified minimum periods[6] at premises in the United Kingdom[7] the address of which has previously not been notified to the police[8], of the address of those premises[9];

(4)   if he is released from custody, imprisonment or detention[10]; and

(5)   the prescribed details of any other prescribed change of circumstances[11].

Where the required new information[12] is notified the information required to be notified in initial notification[13] must also be notified[14].

Notification of changes under these provisions affects the annual re-notification schedule[15]. Failure without reasonable excuse to comply, or the notification of information known to be false in purported compliance, with the notification requirements[16] is an offence[17].

1 As to the meaning of 'offender' see PARA 402 note 2.

2 As to references to an offender subject to notification requirements see PARA 408 note 2.

3   Ie before the event in question occurs (Criminal Justice and Immigration Act 2008 s 109(4)) or within the period of three days beginning with the day on which it occurs (s 109(1)). If a notification is given before the notifiable event occurs the offender must also specify the date when the event is expected to occur (s 109(4)), and if such a notification is given and the event to which it relates occurs more than two days before the date specified, the notification does not affect the duty imposed by s 109(1) to give notification within the period of three days beginning with the day on which the event occurs (s 109(5)). If a notification is given in accordance with s 109(4) and the event to which it relates has not occurred by the end of the period of three days beginning with the date specified the notification does not affect the duty imposed by s 109(1) (s 109(6)(a)) and the offender must, within the period of six days beginning with the date specified, notify to the police the fact that the event did not occur within the period of three days beginning with the date specified (s 109(6)(b)).

     As to the determination of the three and six day periods referred to above see PARA 408 note 3. As to the giving of notifications see PARA 408 note 4. An offender making a notification under s 109 in relation to a prospective change of home address (see the text and note 5) or in relation to premises referred to in s 109(2)(c) (see the text and notes 6–9) may make the notification at a police station that would be a police station in his local police area for the purposes of s 112(1)(a) (see PARA 408 note 4) if the address of those premises were the person's home address: s 112(2).

4   Criminal Justice and Immigration Act 2008 s 109(1)(a), (2)(a), (3)(a). The 'previous notification' referred to is a previous notification under s 108 (see PARA 408) or s 109 (see the text and notes 5–14).

5   Criminal Justice and Immigration Act 2008 s 109(2)(b), (3)(b). As to the meaning of 'home address' see PARA 408 note 4.

6   Ie for a period of seven days (Criminal Justice and Immigration Act 2008 s 109(9)(a)) or for two or more periods, in any period of 12 months, that taken together amount to seven days (s 109(9)(b)).

7   As to the meaning of 'United Kingdom' see PARA 4 note 3.

8   See note 4.

9   Criminal Justice and Immigration Act 2008 s 109(2)(c), (3)(c).

10   Criminal Justice and Immigration Act 2008 s 109(2)(e), (3)(e). The notification requirements arise under this provision if the offender is released from custody pursuant to an order of a court or from imprisonment, service detention or detention in a hospital: s 109(2)(a). As to the meanings of 'imprisonment', 'service detention' and 'detained in a hospital' see PARA 408 note 3.

11   Criminal Justice and Immigration Act 2008 s 109(2)(d), (3)(d). 'Prescribed change of circumstances' means any change occurring in relation to any matter in respect of which information is required to be notified by virtue of s 108(2)(h) (see PARA 408) and of a description prescribed by regulations made by the Secretary of State; and the 'prescribed details', in relation to a prescribed change of circumstances, means such details of the change as may be so prescribed: s 109(8). At the date at which this volume states the law no regulations had been made for these purposes.

12   Ie the information referred to in the Criminal Justice and Immigration Act 2008 s 109(3): see the text and notes 1–11.

13   Ie the information referred to in the Criminal Justice and Immigration Act 2008 s 108(2): see PARA 408.

14   Criminal Justice and Immigration Act 2008 s 109(1)(b).

15   See the Criminal Justice and Immigration Act 2008 s 110; and PARA 408.

16   Ie, for these purposes, the Criminal Justice and Immigration Act 2008 s 109(1), (6)(b) (see the text and notes 1–14).

17   Criminal Justice and Immigration Act 2008 s 113(2)(a), (3)(a). As to the punishment of, and proceedings for, an offence under s 113 see PARA 402. A person commits an offence of non-compliance with s 109(1) on the first day on which he first fails, without reasonable excuse, to comply with the said provision, and continues to commit it throughout any period during which the failure continues: s 113(4)(a). However a person must not be prosecuted under s 113(2) more than once in respect of the same failure: s 113(5).

410. Foreign travel: notification of departure. If an offender[1] who is subject to the notification requirements[2] and who intends to leave the United Kingdom[3] for a period of three days or longer[4] must notify the police[5] of:

    (1)   the date on which the offender proposes to leave the United Kingdom[6];

(2)   the country[7] (or, if there is more than one, the first country) to which the offender proposes to travel and the proposed point of arrival[8] in that country[9];

(3)   where the offender proposes to travel to more than one country outside the United Kingdom, the offender's proposed point of arrival in each such additional country[10];

(4)   the identity of any carrier or carriers the offender proposes to use for the purposes of the offender's departure from and return to the United Kingdom, and of travelling to any other point of arrival in a country[11];

(5)   details of the offender's accommodation arrangements for the offender's first night outside the United Kingdom[12];

(6)   where the offender proposes to return to the United Kingdom on a particular date, that date[13]; and

(7)   where the offender proposes to return to the United Kingdom at a particular point of arrival, that point of arrival[14].

Where a relevant offender is required[15] to give a notification and knows the date on which he proposes to leave the United Kingdom and the country (or first country) to which he proposes to travel and the proposed point of arrival in that country[16] more than seven days before the proposed departure date, he must give a notification which sets out that information and as much of the other required[17] information as he holds not less than seven days before that date[18] or, if he has a reasonable excuse for not complying with the seven day notification requirement, as soon as reasonably practicable but in any event not less than 24 hours before that date[19]. Provision is also made for notification where the relevant offender does not know his date of departure or destination[20], for notification where a person becomes a relevant offender not more than 24 hours before the time of his intended departure[21], and for the notification of changes in information previously disclosed[22].

Failure without reasonable excuse to comply, or the notification of information known to be false in purported compliance with, with the notification requirements[23] is an offence[24].

1   As to the meaning of 'offender' see PARA 402 note 2.
2   As to references to an offender subject to notification requirements see PARA 408 note 2.
3   As to the meaning of 'United Kingdom' see PARA 4 note 3.
4   Criminal Justice and Immigration Act 2008 (Violent Offender Orders) (Notification Requirements) Regulations 2009, SI 2009/2019, reg 4. These regulations were made under the Criminal Justice and Immigration Act 2008 s 111, pursuant to which the Secretary of State may by regulations make provision with respect to offenders subject to notification requirements, or any description of such offenders, requiring such persons, before they leave the United Kingdom, to give in accordance with the regulations a notification under s 111(2) (see the text and notes 5–10) (s 111(1)(a)) and requiring such persons, if they subsequently return to the United Kingdom, to give in accordance with the regulations a notification under s 111(3) (see PARA 411) (s 111(1)(b)).
5   Ie before leaving the United Kingdom: Criminal Justice and Immigration Act 2008 s 111(1)(a). A relevant offender gives a notification under s 111(2) or (3) by attending at any police station in the offender's local police area (within the meaning of s 112(5): see PARA 408 note 4), subject to the Criminal Justice and Immigration Act 2008 (Violent Offender Orders) (Notification Requirements) Regulations 2009, SI 2009/2019, reg 10(2) (see note 20), and giving an oral notification to any police officer, or to any person authorised for the purpose by the officer in charge of the station: reg 10(1). When giving a notification under the Criminal Justice and Immigration Act 2008 s 111(2) or (3), a relevant offender must also disclose his name (or if he used two or more names, each of those names), his home address and his date of birth: Criminal Justice and Immigration Act 2008 (Violent Offender Orders) (Notification Requirements) Regulations 2009, SI 2009/2019, reg 10(3).
6   Criminal Justice and Immigration Act 2008 s 111(2)(a).

7 As to the meaning of 'country' see PARA 404 note 15.
8 In a case in which a relevant offender proposes to arrive in a country by rail, sea or air, the proposed point of arrival is the first station, port or airport at which the offender proposes to disembark; in any other case, the proposed point of arrival is the first place at which the offender proposes to enter the country: Criminal Justice and Immigration Act 2008 (Violent Offender Orders) (Notification Requirements) Regulations 2009, SI 2009/2019, reg 3.
9 Criminal Justice and Immigration Act 2008 s 111(2)(b).
10 Criminal Justice and Immigration Act 2008 s 111(2)(c); Criminal Justice and Immigration Act 2008 (Violent Offender Orders) (Notification Requirements) Regulations 2009, SI 2009/2019, reg 5(1), (2)(a). The information required to be notified pursuant to reg 5(2)(a)–(e) (see the text and notes 11–14) is required to be notified only inasmuch as that information is held by the offender: reg 5(1).
11 Criminal Justice and Immigration Act 2008 (Violent Offender Orders) (Notification Requirements) Regulations 2009, SI 2009/2019, reg 5(2)(b). As to the extent of notification under this requirement see note 10.
12 Criminal Justice and Immigration Act 2008 (Violent Offender Orders) (Notification Requirements) Regulations 2009, SI 2009/2019, reg 5(2)(c). As to the extent of notification under this requirement see note 10.
13 Criminal Justice and Immigration Act 2008 (Violent Offender Orders) (Notification Requirements) Regulations 2009, SI 2009/2019, reg 5(2)(d). As to the extent of notification under this requirement see note 10.
14 Criminal Justice and Immigration Act 2008 (Violent Offender Orders) (Notification Requirements) Regulations 2009, SI 2009/2019, reg 5(2)(e). As to the extent of notification under this requirement see note 10.
15 Ie under the Criminal Justice and Immigration Act 2008 s 111(2) (see the text and notes 1–10).
16 Ie the information required to be disclosed by the Criminal Justice and Immigration Act 2008 s 111(2)(a), (b) (see the text and notes 1–9).
17 Ie required to be given by the Criminal Justice and Immigration Act 2008 (Violent Offender Orders) (Notification Requirements) Regulations 2009, SI 2009/2019, reg 5 (see the text and notes 1–14).
18 Criminal Justice and Immigration Act 2008 (Violent Offender Orders) (Notification Requirements) Regulations 2009, SI 2009/2019, reg 6(1), (2)(a). This is referred to as the 'seven day notification requirement': reg 6(2)(a).
19 Criminal Justice and Immigration Act 2008 (Violent Offender Orders) (Notification Requirements) Regulations 2009, SI 2009/2019, reg 6(2)(b).
20 Where the relevant offender does not know the date on which he proposes to leave the United Kingdom and the country (or first country) to which he proposes to travel and the proposed point of arrival in that country (ie the information required to be disclosed by the Criminal Justice and Immigration Act 2008 s 111(2)(a), (b)) more than seven days before the proposed departure date, he must, as soon as reasonably practicable but in any event before his proposed departure from the United Kingdom, give a notification which sets out that information and as much of the other information required to be disclosed by reg 5 as he holds: reg 6(3). As to the giving of notifications see note 5; a relevant offender may give a notification under the Criminal Justice and Immigration Act 2008 s 111(2) as required by the Criminal Justice and Immigration Act 2008 (Violent Offender Orders) (Notification Requirements) Regulations 2009, SI 2009/2019, reg 6(3), reg 6(5) or reg 7 by attending at any police station: reg 10(2).
21 Where a person becomes a relevant offender not more than 24 hours before the time of his intended departure from the United Kingdom (Criminal Justice and Immigration Act 2008 (Violent Offender Orders) (Notification Requirements) Regulations 2009, SI 2009/2019, reg 6(4)(a)) and already intended to leave the United Kingdom at that time prior to becoming a relevant offender (reg 6(4)(b)), he must give a notification which sets out the date on which he proposes to leave the United Kingdom and the country (or first country) to which he proposes to travel and the proposed point of arrival in that country (ie the information required to be disclosed by s 111(2)(a), (b)) and as much of the other information required to be disclosed by reg 5 as he holds before his proposed departure from the United Kingdom: reg 6(5). As to the giving of notifications see notes 5, 20.
22 Where a relevant offender has given a notification under the Criminal Justice and Immigration Act 2008 s 111(2) (Criminal Justice and Immigration Act 2008 (Violent Offender Orders) (Notification Requirements) Regulations 2009, SI 2009/2019, reg 7(1)(a)) and at any time prior to his proposed departure from the United Kingdom the information disclosed in that notification becomes inaccurate or, as a statement of all the information mentioned in reg 5 which the offender currently holds, incomplete (reg 7(1)(b)), he must give a further notification under the Criminal Justice and Immigration Act 2008 s 111(2) (Criminal Justice and

Immigration Act 2008 (Violent Offender Orders) (Notification Requirements) Regulations 2009, SI 2009/2019, reg 7(1)). Such further notification must be given not less than 24 hours before the offender's proposed departure from the United Kingdom (reg 7(2)), although where the requirement to give a further notification under reg 7(1) arises less than 24 hours before the offender's proposed departure from the United Kingdom, such further notification must be given before the offender's proposed departure from the United Kingdom (reg 7(3)). As to the giving of notifications see notes 5, 20; a relevant offender giving a further notification under the Criminal Justice and Immigration Act 2008 s 111(2) as required by the Criminal Justice and Immigration Act 2008 (Violent Offender Orders) (Notification Requirements) Regulations 2009, SI 2009/2019, reg 7 must inform the person to whom the notification is given of the police station at which the offender first gave a notification in respect of the journey in question under the Criminal Justice and Immigration Act 2008 s 111(2): Criminal Justice and Immigration Act 2008 (Violent Offender Orders) (Notification Requirements) Regulations 2009, SI 2009/2019, reg 10(4).

23 Ie, for these purposes, any requirement imposed by the Criminal Justice and Immigration Act 2008 (Violent Offender Orders) (Notification Requirements) Regulations 2009, SI 2009/2019 (see the text and notes 1–22).

24 Criminal Justice and Immigration Act 2008 s 113(2)(b), (3)(b). As to the punishment of, and proceedings for, an offence under s 113 see PARA 402. A person commits an offence of non-compliance with any requirement of the Criminal Justice and Immigration Act 2008 (Violent Offender Orders) (Notification Requirements) Regulations 2009, SI 2009/2019, on the first day on which he first fails, without reasonable excuse, to comply with the requirement in question, and continues to commit it throughout any period during which the failure continues: s 113(4)(b). However a person must not be prosecuted under s 113(2) more than once in respect of the same failure: s 113(5).

411. Foreign travel: notification of return. If an offender[1] who is subject to the notification requirements[2] returns to the United Kingdom[3] after leaving for a period of three days or longer[4] (and thereby becoming liable to notify the police[5] in connection with his departure) he must notify the police[6] of his date of return to the United Kingdom[7] and his point of arrival in the United Kingdom[8]. This requirement does not, however, apply, if the offender has previously given notification[9] of his date and point of arrival[10] and his return to the United Kingdom was on that date and at that point of arrival[11].

Failure without reasonable excuse to comply, or the notification of information known to be false in purported compliance with, with the notification requirements[12] is an offence[13].

1 As to the meaning of 'offender' see PARA 402 note 2.
2 As to references to an offender subject to notification requirements see PARA 408 note 2.
3 As to the meaning of 'United Kingdom' see PARA 4 note 3.
4 Criminal Justice and Immigration Act 2008 (Violent Offender Orders) (Notification Requirements) Regulations 2009, SI 2009/2019, reg 4. As to these regulations see PARA 410 note 4.
5 Ie under the Criminal Justice and Immigration Act 2008 s 111(2): see PARA 410. As to the giving of notifications see PARA 410 note 5.
6 Criminal Justice and Immigration Act 2008 (Violent Offender Orders) (Notification Requirements) Regulations 2009, SI 2009/2019, reg 8(1). Notification must be given within three days of the offender's return to the United Kingdom: reg 8(2).
7 Criminal Justice and Immigration Act 2008 s 111(3); Criminal Justice and Immigration Act 2008 (Violent Offender Orders) (Notification Requirements) Regulations 2009, SI 2009/2019, reg 9(a).
8 Criminal Justice and Immigration Act 2008 (Violent Offender Orders) (Notification Requirements) Regulations 2009, SI 2009/2019, reg 9(b). As to the point of arrival see PARA 410 note 8.
9 See note 5.
10 Ie as specified in the Criminal Justice and Immigration Act 2008 (Violent Offender Orders) (Notification Requirements) Regulations 2009, SI 2009/2019, reg 5(2)(d), (3) (see PARA 410).
11 Criminal Justice and Immigration Act 2008 (Violent Offender Orders) (Notification Requirements) Regulations 2009, SI 2009/2019, reg 8(3).

12 Ie, for these purposes, any requirement imposed by the Criminal Justice and Immigration Act 2008 (Violent Offender Orders) (Notification Requirements) Regulations 2009, SI 2009/2019 (see the text and notes 1–11).

13 Criminal Justice and Immigration Act 2008 s 113(2)(b), (3)(b). As to the punishment of, and proceedings for, an offence under s 113 see PARA 402. A person commits an offence of non-compliance with any requirement of the Criminal Justice and Immigration Act 2008 (Violent Offender Orders) (Notification Requirements) Regulations 2009, SI 2009/2019, on the first day on which he first fails, without reasonable excuse, to comply with the requirement in question, and continues to commit it throughout any period during which the failure continues: Criminal Justice and Immigration Act 2008 s 113(4)(b). However a person must not be prosecuted under s 113(2) more than once in respect of the same failure: s 113(5).

412.   Information about release or transfer. The Secretary of State may by regulations make provision requiring the person who is responsible for an offender[1] subject to notification requirements[2] who is serving a sentence of imprisonment or a term of service detention, or detained in a hospital[3], to give notice to specified persons[4] of the fact that that person has become responsible for the offender[5] and of any occasion when the offender is released[6] or a different person is to become responsible for the offender[7].

1   As to the meaning of 'offender' see PARA 402 note 2. The regulations described in the text and notes 2–7 may make provision for determining who is to be taken for these purposes as being responsible for an offender: Criminal Justice and Immigration Act 2008 s 116(4).
2   As to references to an offender subject to notification requirements see PARA 408 note 2.
3   Criminal Justice and Immigration Act 2008 s 116(1). As to the meanings of 'imprisonment', 'service detention' and 'detained in a hospital' see PARA 408 note 3.
4   Ie persons specified, or of a description specified, in the regulations: Criminal Justice and Immigration Act 2008 s 116(3).
5   Criminal Justice and Immigration Act 2008 s 116(2)(a).
6   Criminal Justice and Immigration Act 2008 s 116(2)(b)(i).
7   Criminal Justice and Immigration Act 2008 s 116(2)(b)(ii).

(v) Domestic Violence Protection Orders

413.   Domestic Violence Protection Orders (DVPO) and Domestic Violence Protection Notices (DVPN). A domestic violence protection notice (DVPN) is a notice containing provision to prohibit the person in respect of whom it is issued (P) from molesting the person for whose protection it is issued[1]. If P lives in premises which are also lived in by a person for whose protection the DVPN is issued, the DVPN may also contain provision to prohibit him from evicting or excluding from the premises the person for whose protection the DVPN is issued[2], to prohibit him from entering the premises[3], to require him to leave the premises[4] or to prohibit him from coming within such distance of the premises as may be specified in the DVPN[5]. DVPNs are issued by police officers[6]. A domestic violence protection order (DVPO) is an order made by a magistrates' court imposing the same prohibitions[7]. DVPOs may be made on the application of constables[8], and must be applied for when a DVPN has been issued[9].

1   Crime and Security Act 2010 s 24(6). Provision required to be included by virtue of ss 24(6), 28(6) may be expressed so as to refer to molestation in general, to particular acts of molestation, or to both: ss 24(7), 28(7). In connection with the issue of DVPNs see PARA 414.
2   Crime and Security Act 2010 s 24(8)(a).
3   Crime and Security Act 2010 s 24(8)(b).
4   Crime and Security Act 2010 s 24(8)(c).
5   Crime and Security Act 2010 s 24(8)(d).
6   See the Crime and Security Act 2010 s 24(1); and PARA 414.
7   Crime and Security Act 2010 s 28(6), (8)(a)–(d).

8 The Secretary of State may from time to time issue guidance relating to the exercise by a constable of functions under the Crime and Security Act 2010 ss 24–30 (see PARAS 414–417) (s 31(1)), and a constable must have regard to any guidance so issued when exercising a function to which the guidance relates (s 31(2)). Before issuing such guidance the Secretary of State must consult the Association of Chief Police Officers and such other persons as the Secretary of State thinks fit: s 31(3) (amended by the Crime and Courts Act 2013 Sch 8 para 179).

9 See the Crime and Security Act 2010 s 27(1), (2); and PARA 415.

414. Circumstances in which a DVPN will be issued. A DVPN[1] may be issued[2] to a person (P) aged 18 years or over if the authorising officer[3] has reasonable grounds for believing that he has been violent towards, or has threatened violence towards, an associated person[4] and the issue of the DVPN is necessary to protect that person from violence or a threat of violence by him[5]. A DVPN may be issued in circumstances where the person for whose protection it is issued does not consent to its issuing[6]. Before issuing a DVPN the authorising officer must, in particular, consider[7]:

(1) the welfare of any person under the age of 18 whose interests the officer considers relevant to the issuing of the DVPN (whether or not that person is an associated person)[8];

(2) the opinion of the person for whose protection the DVPN would be issued as to the issuing of the DVPN[9];

(3) any representations made by P as to the issuing of the DVPN[10]; and

(4) in the case of provision relating to shared premises[11], the opinion of any other associated person who lives in the premises to which the provision would relate[12].

Where a DVPN has been issued, an application must be made for a DVPO[13]. The DVPN continues in effect until that application has been determined[14].

1 Ie a domestic violence protection notice: see PARA 413. A DVPN must state:
    (1) the grounds on which it has been issued (Crime and Security Act 2010 s 25(1)(a): see the text and notes 1–5);
    (2) that a constable may arrest the person without warrant if he has reasonable grounds for believing that that person is in breach of the DVPN (s 25(1)(b): see PARA 417);
    (3) that an application for a domestic violence protection order under s 27 will be heard within 48 hours of the time of service of the DVPN and a notice of the hearing will be given to the person (s 25(1)(c): see PARAS 415–416);
    (4) that the DVPN continues in effect until that application has been determined (s 25(1)(d)); and
    (5) the provision that a magistrates' court may include in a domestic violence protection order (s 25(1)(e): see PARAS 413, 415).
    Where a DVPN includes provision in relation to premises by virtue of s 24(8)(b) or (8)(c) (see PARA 413) and the authorising officer believes that P is a person subject to service law in accordance with the Armed Forces Act 2006 ss 367–369 (see ARMED FORCES vol 3 (2011) PARA 313 et seq) and the premises fall within paragraph (a) of the definition of 'service living accommodation' in s 96(1) (see ARMED FORCES vol 3 (2011) PARA 529), the authorising officer must make reasonable efforts to inform P's commanding officer (within the meaning of s 360: see ARMED FORCES vol 3 (2011) PARA 426) of the issuing of the notice: Crime and Security Act 2010 s 24(10), (11).

2 Ie by a member of a police force not below the rank of superintendent ('the authorising officer') (Crime and Security Act 2010 s 24(1)) or, if either P or the associated person (see note 4) lives in premises which fall within paragraph (a) of the definition of 'service living accommodation' in the Armed Forces Act 2006 s 96(1), a member of the Ministry of Defence Police not below the rank of superintendent (s 32(1)). If a DVPN is issued by a member of the Ministry of Defence Police by virtue of s 32(1), provision may be included in the DVPN by virtue of s 24(8) (see PARA 413) in relation to any other premises in England or Wales lived in by P and the associated person: s 32(2).

A DVPN must be in writing and must be served on P personally by a constable: s 25(2). On serving a person with a DVPN the constable must ask him for an address for the purposes of being given the notice of the hearing of the application for the domestic violence protection order (see PARA 415): s 25(3).

3   Or military equivalent: see note 2.
4   Crime and Security Act 2010 s 24(2)(a). An 'associated person' means a person who is associated with P within the meaning of the Family Law Act 1996 s 62 (see MATRIMONIAL AND CIVIL PARTNERSHIP LAW vol 72 (2015) PARAS 309, 311): Crime and Security Act 2010 s 24(9).
5   Crime and Security Act 2010 s 24(2)(b). As to the determination of a person's age see the Children and Young Persons Act 1933 s 99; and CHILDREN AND YOUNG PERSONS vol 10 (2012) PARA 1206.
6   Crime and Security Act 2010 s 24(5).
7   The authorising officer must take reasonable steps to discover the opinions mentioned in the Crime and Security Act 2010 s 24(3): s 24(4).
8   Crime and Security Act 2010 s 24(3)(a).
9   Crime and Security Act 2010 s 24(3)(b).
10   Crime and Security Act 2010 s 24(3)(c).
11   Ie provisions included by virtue of the Crime and Security Act 2010 s 24(8) (see PARA 413).
12   Crime and Security Act 2010 s 24(3)(d).
13   Ie a domestic violence protection order: see PARA 413; and as to applications for DVPNs see PARA 414.
14   See the Crime and Security Act 2010 s 25(1)(d); and note 1.

415.   Application for DVPO following issue of DVPN. If a DVPN[1] has been issued[2] a constable must apply, by complaint to a magistrates' court, for a DVPO[3], and the application must be heard by the court not later than 48 hours[4] after the DVPN was[5] served[6].

1   Ie a domestic violence protection notice: see PARA 413.
2   As to the circumstances in which a DVPN will be issued see PARA 414.
3   Crime and Security Act 2010 s 27(1), (2). A DVPO is a domestic violence protection order: see PARA 413; and as to the circumstances in which a DVPO will be made see PARA 416.
4   In calculating when the period of 48 hours mentioned in the Crime and Security Act 2010 s 27(3) ends, Christmas Day, Good Friday, any Sunday and any day which is a bank holiday in England and Wales under the Banking and Financial Dealings Act 1971 (see FINANCIAL SERVICES AND INSTITUTIONS vol 49 (2008) PARA 1437) are to be disregarded: Crime and Security Act 2010 s 27(4).
5   Ie pursuant to the Crime and Security Act 2010 s 25(2) (see PARA 414).
6   Crime and Security Act 2010 s 27(3). This must be explained in the DVPN: see s 25(1)(c); and PARA 414 note 1. A notice of the hearing of the application must be given to the person in respect of whom it is applied for (s 27(5)) and is deemed given if it has been left at the address given by the person under s 25(3) (see PARA 414) (s 27(6)). However if the notice has not been given because no address was given under s 25(3), the court may hear the application for the DVPO if it is satisfied that the constable applying for the DVPO has made reasonable efforts to give the notice: s 27(7).

The magistrates' court may adjourn the hearing of the application (s 27(8)) (and, if the person has been arrested for breach of the DVPN, remand him: see s 26(3); and PARA 417). The DVPN continues in effect until the application has been determined: s 27(9). On the hearing of an application for a DVPO, the Magistrates' Courts Act 1980 s 97 (summons to witness and warrant for his arrest: see CRIMINAL PROCEDURE vol 27 (2015) PARA 272) does not apply in relation to a person for whose protection the DVPO would be made, except where the person has given oral or written evidence at the hearing: Crime and Security Act 2010 s 27(10).

If the court adjourns the hearing of the application by virtue of section 27(8), the court may remand the person.

416.   Circumstances in which a DVPO will be made. The court may[1] make a DVPO[2] if it is satisfied on the balance of probabilities that the grounds on which the DVPN was issued[3] exist[4], and may make a DVPO in circumstances where the person for whose protection it is made does not consent to its making[5]. Before making a DVPO, the court must, in particular, consider the welfare of any person under the age of 18 whose interests the court considers relevant to the making of the DVPO (whether or not that person is an associated person)[6], and any opinion of which the court is made aware of the person for whose protection the DVPO would be made[7] and, in the case of provision relating to shared premises[8], of any other associated person who lives in the premises to which the provision would relate[9].

A DVPO may be in force for no fewer than 14 days beginning with the day on which it is made[10] and no more than 28 days beginning with that day[11], and must state the period for which it is to be in force[12].

1 Ie on application following the issue of a domestic violence protection notice (DVPN): see PARAS 413–415.
2 Ie a domestic violence protection order: see PARA 413. A DVPO must state that the person in respect of whom it is made may be arrested without warrant by a constable who has reasonable grounds for believing that that person is in breach of the DVPO: see the Crime and Security Act 2010 s 28(9); and PARA 417.
3 Ie the grounds set out in the Crime and Security Act 2010 s 24(2)(a), (b) (see PARA 414).
4 Crime and Security Act 2010 s 28(1)–(3).
5 Crime and Security Act 2010 s 28(5).
6 Crime and Security Act 2010 s 28(4)(a). As to the meaning of 'associated person' see PARA 414 note 4. As to the determination of a person's age see the Children and Young Persons Act 1933 s 99; and CHILDREN AND YOUNG PERSONS vol 10 (2012) PARA 1206.
7 Crime and Security Act 2010 s 28(4)(b).
8 Ie provisions included by virtue of the Crime and Security Act 2010 s 28(8) (see PARA 413).
9 Crime and Security Act 2010 s 28(4)(c).
10 Crime and Security Act 2010 s 28(10)(a).
11 Crime and Security Act 2010 s 28(10)(b).
12 Crime and Security Act 2010 s 28(11).

417. Arrest for breach of DVPN or DVPO. When a DVPN[1] has been issued[2], or a DPVO[3] has been made[4], the person in respect of whom it was issued or made may be arrested without warrant by a constable who has reasonable grounds for believing that he is in breach of the DVPN or DVPO[5].

A person arrested[6] for a breach of a DVPN must be held in custody and brought before the magistrates' court which will hear the application for the DVPO[7] before the end of the period of 24 hours[8] beginning with the time of the arrest[9] or, if earlier, at the hearing of that application[10]. A person arrested for a breach of a DVPN may be remanded[11] when he is brought[12] before the court[13] or if the court adjourns[14] the hearing of the application for the DVPO[15].

A person arrested[16] for a breach of a DVPO must be held in custody and brought before a magistrates' court within the period of 24 hours beginning with the time of the arrest[17], and if the matter is not disposed of when the person is brought before the court, the court may remand the person[18].

1 Ie a domestic violence protection notice: see PARA 413.
2 As to the circumstances in which a DVPN will be issued see PARA 414.
3 Ie a domestic violence protection order: see PARA 413.
4 As to the circumstances in which a DVPO will be made see PARA 415.
5 Crime and Security Act 2010 ss 25(1)(b), 28(9). This fact must be stated in the DVPN and the DVPO: see ss 25(1)(b), 28(9); and PARAS 414, 415.
6 Ie by virtue of the Crime and Security Act 2010 s 25(1)(b) (see the text and note 1–5).
7 Ie under the Crime and Security Act 2010 s 27 (see PARA 415).
8 In calculating when the period of 24 hours mentioned in the Crime and Security Act 2010 ss 26(1)(a), 29(1) ends, Christmas Day, Good Friday, any Sunday and any day which is a bank holiday in England and Wales under the Banking and Financial Dealings Act 1971 (see FINANCIAL SERVICES AND INSTITUTIONS vol 49 (2008) PARA 1437) are to be disregarded: Crime and Security Act 2010 ss 26(4), 29(3).
9 Crime and Security Act 2010 s 26(1)(a).
10 Crime and Security Act 2010 s 26(1)(b).

11 Where a person is remanded under the Crime and Security Act 2010 s 26(2) or (3) or 29(2) (see the text and notes 12–18):

(1)   if the court has reason to suspect that a medical report will be required, the power to remand a person may be exercised for the purpose of enabling a medical examination to take place and a report to be made (s 30(1), (3));

(2)   if the person is remanded in custody for that purpose, the adjournment may not be for more than 3 weeks at a time (s 30(4));

(3)   if the person is remanded on bail for that purpose, the adjournment may not be for more than 4 weeks at a time (s 30(5));

(4)   if the court has reason to suspect that the person is suffering from a mental disorder within the meaning of the Mental Health Act 1983 (see s 1; and MENTAL HEALTH AND CAPACITY vol 75 (2013) PARA 761), the court has the same power to make an order under 35 (remand to hospital for medical report: see MENTAL HEALTH AND CAPACITY vol 75 (2013) PARA 862) as it has under s 35 in the case of an accused person (within the meaning of s 35: see MENTAL HEALTH AND CAPACITY vol 75 (2013) PARA 862) (Crime and Security Act 2010 s 30(6)); and

(5)   the court may, when remanding the person on bail, require the person to comply, before release on bail or later, with such requirements as appear to the court to be necessary to secure that the person does not interfere with witnesses or otherwise obstruct the course of justice (s 30(7)).

The Magistrates' Courts Act 1980 s 128(6) (see CRIMINAL PROCEDURE vol 27 (2015) PARA 98) is applied with modifications for those purposes: see the Crime and Security Act 2010 s 30(2).

12 Ie by virtue of the Crime and Security Act 2010 s 26(1)(a) (see the text and notes 6–9).

13 Crime and Security Act 2010 s 26(2).

14 Ie by virtue of the Crime and Security Act 2010 s 27(8) (see PARA 415).

15 Crime and Security Act 2010 s 26(3).

16 Ie by virtue of the Crime and Security Act 2010 s 28(9) (see the text and note 1–5).

17 Crime and Security Act 2010 s 29(1).

18 Crime and Security Act 2010 s 29(2).

(vi) Temporary Exclusion Orders

418. Temporary exclusion orders. A 'temporary exclusion order' is an order made by the Secretary of State which requires an individual who is outside the United Kingdom[1], but has the right of abode in the United Kingdom[2], not to return to the United Kingdom on grounds connected to terrorism[3], unless the return is in accordance with a permit to return issued by the Secretary of State before the individual began the return[4] or the return is the result of the individual's deportation to the United Kingdom[5]. References to an individual's 'return' to the United Kingdom include, in the case of an individual who has never been in the United Kingdom, a reference to the individual's coming to the United Kingdom for the first time[6].

A temporary exclusion order may be made only with the permission of the High Court, except in urgent cases where it may first be made then referred to the court for approval[7]. An order comes into force when notice of its imposition is given[8] and is in force for the period of two years (unless revoked or otherwise brought to an end earlier)[9]. The validity of a temporary exclusion order is not affected by the excluded individual returning to or departing from the United Kingdom[10]. The Secretary of State may revoke a temporary exclusion order at any time[11], and orders may be reviewed on application[12].

An individual subject to a temporary exclusion order[13] is guilty of an offence if, without reasonable excuse[14], he returns to the United Kingdom in contravention of the restriction on return[15] specified in the order[16]. There is a right of appeal against conviction if an order is later quashed on review[17].

1   See the Counter-Terrorism and Security Act 2015 s 2(5); and PARA 421.

2 See the Counter-Terrorism and Security Act 2015 s 2(6); and PARA 421. As to right of abode see BRITISH NATIONALITY vol 4 (2011) PARA 412.

3 See the Counter-Terrorism and Security Act 2015 s 2(3), (4); and PARA 421. As to the meaning of 'involvement in terrorism-related activity' see PARA 420. In connection with passports see PARA 424.

4 Counter-Terrorism and Security Act 2015 s 2(1)(a). As to permits to return see PARA 419.

5 Counter-Terrorism and Security Act 2015 s 2(1)(b). References to deportation include references to any other kind of expulsion: s 14(7).

6 Counter-Terrorism and Security Act 2015 s 14(6).

7 See the Counter-Terrorism and Security Act 2015 ss 2(7), 14(2); and PARAS 421–423.

8 Counter-Terrorism and Security Act 2015 s 4(3)(a). The Secretary of State must give notice of the imposition of a temporary exclusion order to the individual on whom it is imposed (the 'excluded individual') (s 4(1)), which must include an explanation of the procedure for making an application under s 6 (see PARA 426) for a permit to return (s 4(2)). As to the giving of notices see the Temporary Exclusion Orders (Notices) Regulations 2015, SI 2015/438 (made under the Counter-Terrorism and Security Act 2015 s 13).

9 Counter-Terrorism and Security Act 2015 s 4(3)(b).

10 Counter-Terrorism and Security Act 2015 s 4(7).

11 Counter-Terrorism and Security Act 2015 s 4(4). The Secretary of State must give notice of the revocation of a temporary exclusion order to the excluded individual: s 4(5). The order will cease to be in force when notice of its revocation is given: s 4(6).

12 See the Counter-Terrorism and Security Act 2015 s 11(1), (2)(a)–(c), (3)–(5), (9)(a), (10), (11); and PARA 425.

13 An individual is subject to a temporary exclusion order if a temporary exclusion order is in force in relation to him: Counter-Terrorism and Security Act 2015 s 14(3)(a).

14 In a case where notice of the imposition of a temporary exclusion order has not actually been given to an individual, the fact that such notice is deemed to have been given under the Temporary Exclusion Orders (Notices) Regulations 2015, SI 2015/438, art 3 (see note 8), does not (of itself) prevent the individual from showing that lack of knowledge of the temporary exclusion order was a reasonable excuse for these purposes: s 10(4).

15 'Restriction on return' means the requirement specified in a temporary exclusion order in accordance with the Counter-Terrorism and Security Act 2015 s 2(1): s 10(8).

16 Counter-Terrorism and Security Act 2015 s 10(1). It is irrelevant for this purpose whether or not the individual has a passport or other similar identity document: s 10(2). An individual guilty of an offence under s 10 is liable on conviction on indictment to imprisonment for a term not exceeding 5 years or to a fine, or to both (s 10(5)(a)), or on summary conviction in England and Wales, to imprisonment for a term not exceeding 12 months or to a fine, or to both (s 10(5)(b)). Where an individual is convicted by or before a court of an offence under s 10 it is not open to that court to make in respect of the offence an order under the Powers of Criminal Courts (Sentencing) Act 2000 s 12(1)(b) (conditional discharge: see PARA 454): s 10(6)(a).

17 See the Counter-Terrorism and Security Act 2015 Sch 4; and PARA 431.

419. Permits to return. A 'permit to return' is a document giving an individual who is subject to a temporary exclusion order[1] permission to return to the United Kingdom[2]. The permission may be made subject to a requirement that the individual comply with conditions specified in the permit to return[3]: the individual's failure to comply with a specified condition has the effect of invalidating the permit to return[4]. It is for the Secretary of State to decide the terms of a permit to return[5]. A permit to return must state:

(1) the time at which, or period of time during which, the individual is permitted to arrive on return to the United Kingdom[6];

(2) the manner in which the individual is permitted to return to the United Kingdom[7]; and

(3) the place where the individual is permitted to arrive on return to the United Kingdom[8].

A permit to return must be issued on the application of the individual who is subject to the temporary exclusion order[9], and may be issued without such an application where the Secretary of State considers the individual's return to be urgent[10]. The Secretary of State is also obliged to issue a permit to return in respect of an individual who is to be deported to the United Kingdom[11]. The Secretary of State may vary[12] or revoke a permit to return[13].

1 As to the meaning of 'temporary exclusion order' see PARA 418. As to when an individual is subject to a temporary exclusion order see PARA 418 note 13.
2 Counter-Terrorism and Security Act 2015 s 5(1).
3 Counter-Terrorism and Security Act 2015 s 5(2).
4 Counter-Terrorism and Security Act 2015 s 5(3).
5 Counter-Terrorism and Security Act 2015 s 5(8). This is subject to s 6(3) (see PARA 426): s 5(8).
6 Counter-Terrorism and Security Act 2015 s 5(4)(a). Provision made under s 5(4)(a) or (c) may, in particular, be framed by reference to the arrival in the United Kingdom of a specific flight, sailing or other transport service: s 5(5).
7 Counter-Terrorism and Security Act 2015 s 5(4)(b). Provision made under s 5(4)(b) may, in particular, state a route, a method of transport, an airline, shipping line or other passenger carrier, or a flight, sailing or other transport service, which the individual is permitted to use to return to the United Kingdom: s 5(6).
8 Counter-Terrorism and Security Act 2015 s 5(4)(c). See note 6.
9 See the Counter-Terrorism and Security Act 2015 ss 5(7), 6; and PARA 426.
10 See the Counter-Terrorism and Security Act 2015 s 7(2), (3); and PARA 427.
11 See the Counter-Terrorism and Security Act 2015 s 7(1), (3); and PARA 427.
12 Counter-Terrorism and Security Act 2015 s 8(1).
13 See the Counter-Terrorism and Security Act 2015 s 8(2); and PARA 430.

420. Involvement in terrorism-related activity. 'Involvement in terrorism-related activity' is[1] any one or more of the following:

(1) the commission, preparation or instigation of acts of terrorism[2];

(2) conduct which facilitates the commission, preparation or instigation of such acts, or which is intended to do so[3];

(3) conduct which gives encouragement to the commission, preparation or instigation of such acts, or which is intended to do so[4]; and

(4) conduct which gives support or assistance to individuals who are known or believed by the individual concerned to be involved in conduct falling within head (1) above[5].

1 Ie for the purposes of the Counter-Terrorism and Security Act 2015 Pt 1 Ch 2 (ss 2–15). It is immaterial whether an individual's involvement in terrorism-related activity occurs before or after 12 February 2015 (ie the date on which the Counter-Terrorism and Security Act 2015 s 2 (see PARA 418) was brought into force by virtue of s 52(5)): s 14(5).
2 Counter-Terrorism and Security Act 2015 s 14(4)(a). 'Act of terrorism' includes anything constituting an action taken for the purposes of terrorism, within the meaning of the Terrorism Act 2000 (see s 1(5); and CRIMINAL LAW vol 25 (2010) PARA 372): Counter-Terrorism and Security Act 2015 s 14(2). For these purposes it is immaterial whether the acts of terrorism in question are specific acts of terrorism or acts of terrorism in general: s 14(4). As to the meaning of 'terrorism' see the Terrorism Act 2000 s 1(1)–(4); and CRIMINAL LAW vol 25 (2010) PARA 372 (definition applied by the Counter-Terrorism and Security Act 2015 s 14(2)). 'Act' and 'conduct' include omissions and statements: s 14(1).
3 Counter-Terrorism and Security Act 2015 s 14(4)(b).
4 Counter-Terrorism and Security Act 2015 s 14(4)(c).
5 Counter-Terrorism and Security Act 2015 s 14(4)(d).

421. When a temporary exclusion order may be imposed. The Secretary of State may impose a temporary exclusion order[1] on an individual if:

(1) the Secretary of State reasonably suspects that the individual is, or has been, involved in terrorism-related activity outside the United Kingdom[2];

(2) the Secretary of State reasonably considers that it is necessary, for purposes connected with protecting members of the public in the United Kingdom from a risk of terrorism, for a temporary exclusion order to be imposed on the individual[3];

(3)   the Secretary of State reasonably considers that the individual is outside the United Kingdom[4]; and

(4)   the individual has the right of abode in the United Kingdom[5].

As a rule an order may not be imposed unless the High Court gives the Secretary of State permission[6] to impose it[7]: however if the Secretary of State reasonably considers that the urgency of the case requires the order to be imposed without obtaining the court's permission[8] he may impose the order and then refer the matter to the court[9].

The imposition of a temporary exclusion order does not prevent a further temporary exclusion order from being imposed on the excluded individual (including in a case where an order ceases to be in force at the expiry of its two year duration)[10].

1   As to the meaning of 'temporary exclusion order' see PARA 418.
2   Counter-Terrorism and Security Act 2015 s 2(2), (3). This is referred to as 'condition A': s 2(3).
3   Counter-Terrorism and Security Act 2015 s 2(4). This is referred to as 'condition B': s 2(4). During the period that a temporary exclusion order (see PARA 418) is in force, the Secretary of State must keep under review whether condition B is met: s 2(8).
4   Counter-Terrorism and Security Act 2015 s 2(5). This is referred to as 'condition C': s 2(5).
5   Counter-Terrorism and Security Act 2015 s 2(6). This is referred to as 'condition D': s 2(6). As to right of abode see BRITISH NATIONALITY vol 4 (2011) PARA 412.
6   Ie under the Counter-Terrorism and Security Act 2015 s 3 (see PARA 422).
7   Counter-Terrorism and Security Act 2015 s 2(7)(a). The court giving the Secretary of State permission under these provisions is the first alternative of what is referred to as 'condition E' being met: s 2(7). As to an application for permission see PARA 422.
8   Counter-Terrorism and Security Act 2015 s 2(7)(b). The Secretary of State reasonably considering that the urgency of the case requires the order to be imposed without obtaining the court's permission (ie the 'urgency condition' being met) is the second alternative of what is referred to as 'condition E' being met: s 2(7), Sch 2 para 6(1).
9   See the Counter-Terrorism and Security Act 2015 Sch 2; and PARA 423.
10   Counter-Terrorism and Security Act 2015 s 4(8).

422.   Application to High Court for permission to make order in non-urgent cases. If in a non-urgent case[1] the Secretary of State decides that a temporary exclusion order[2] should be made in relation to an individual[3] he must apply to the High Court for permission to impose the order[4]. The court must give permission for the making of the order if it does not determine that the relevant decisions of the Secretary of State are obviously flawed[5], and may not give such permission if it does so determine[6]. In determining the application, the court must apply the principles applicable on an application for judicial review[7].

The court may consider the application in the absence of the individual[8], without the individual having been notified of the application[9], and without the individual having been given an opportunity (if the individual was aware of the application) of making any representations to the court[10]. Only the Secretary of State may appeal against a determination of the court under these provisions and such an appeal may only be made on a question of law[11].

1   As to the procedure in urgent cases see PARA 423.
2   As to the meaning of 'temporary exclusion order' see PARA 418.
3   Ie if the Secretary of State decides that conditions A–D (see PARA 421) are met in relation to the said individual (makes the 'relevant decisions'): Counter-Terrorism and Security Act 2015 s 3(1)(a), (10).
4   Counter-Terrorism and Security Act 2015 s 3(1)(b). For the rules of court relating to applications under s 3(1)(b) see CPR Pt 88; and in connection with the content and scope of those rules see the Counter-Terrorism and Security Act 2015 s 12(1), Sch 3.
5   Counter-Terrorism and Security Act 2015 s 3(7). The function of the court on the application is to determine whether the relevant decisions of the Secretary of State are obviously flawed: s 3(2).

6   Counter-Terrorism and Security Act 2015 s 3(6).
7   Counter-Terrorism and Security Act 2015 s 3(5).
8   Counter-Terrorism and Security Act 2015 s 3(3)(a). Section 3(3) does not limit the matters about
     which rules of court may be made: s 3(4).
9   Counter-Terrorism and Security Act 2015 s 3(3)(b).
10   Counter-Terrorism and Security Act 2015 s 3(3)(c).
11   Counter-Terrorism and Security Act 2015 s 3(9)(a).

423.   Making of order and reference to High Court in urgent cases. If the
Secretary of State decides that a temporary exclusion order[1] should be made in
relation to an individual[2] and reasonably considers that the urgency of the case
requires the order to be imposed without obtaining the permission of the High
Court[3], he may impose the order on the individual[4] but must[5] refer such
imposition to the High Court[6]. The court must confirm the order if it does not
determine that any of the relevant decisions of the Secretary of State are
obviously flawed[7], and must quash the order if it does so determine[8]. If the court
determines that the decision of the Secretary of State that the urgency condition
is met is obviously flawed, it must[9] make a declaration of that determination[10].
In determining the reference, the court must apply the principles applicable on an
application for judicial review[11].

The court may consider the reference in the absence of the individual[12],
without the individual having been notified of the reference[13], and without the
individual having been given an opportunity (if the individual was aware of the
reference) of making any representations to the court[14]. The court must,
however, ensure that the individual is notified of the court's decision on the
reference[15]. Only the Secretary of State may appeal against a determination of
the court under these provisions and such an appeal may only be made on a
question of law[16].

1   As to the meaning of 'temporary exclusion order' see PARA 418.
2   Ie if the Secretary of State decides that conditions A–D (see PARA 421) are met in relation to the
     said individual (makes the 'relevant decisions'): Counter-Terrorism and Security Act 2015 s 2(8),
     Sch 2 para 6(3).
3   Ie where the Secretary of State makes the 'urgent case decisions', that is, the relevant decisions
     (see note 2) and the decision that the urgency condition (see PARA 421 note 8) is met:
     Counter-Terrorism and Security Act 2015 Sch 2 paras 1(a), 6(2). As to obtaining the permission
     of the court see obtaining the permission of the court see s 3; and PARA 422.
4   Counter-Terrorism and Security Act 2015 Sch 2 para 1(b). The order must include a statement
     that the Secretary of State reasonably considers that the urgency of the case requires the order to
     be imposed without obtaining the permission of the court under s 3: Sch 2 para 2.
5   Ie immediately after giving notice of the imposition of the order: Counter-Terrorism and Security
     Act 2015 Sch 2 para 3(1).
6   Counter-Terrorism and Security Act 2015 Sch 2 para 3(1). For the rules of court relating to
     references under Sch 2 para 3(1) see CPR Pt 88; and in connection with the content and scope of
     those rules see the Counter-Terrorism and Security Act 2015 Sch 3. The court's consideration of
     the reference must begin within the period of 7 days beginning with the day on which notice of
     the imposition of the temporary exclusion order is given to the individual: Sch 2 para 3(3).
7   Counter-Terrorism and Security Act 2015 Sch 2 para 4(2). The function of the court on the
     reference is to consider whether the urgent case decisions were obviously flawed: Sch 2
     para 3(2).
8   Counter-Terrorism and Security Act 2015 Sch 2 para 4(1).
9   Ie whether the court quashes or confirms the temporary exclusion order under the
     Counter-Terrorism and Security Act 2015 Sch 2 para 4(1), (2) (see the text and notes 7–8).
10   Counter-Terrorism and Security Act 2015 Sch 2 para 5(3).
11   Counter-Terrorism and Security Act 2015 Sch 2 para 5(1).
12   Counter-Terrorism and Security Act 2015 Sch 2 para 3(4)(a). Schedule 2 para 3(4) does not limit
     the matters about which rules of court may be made: Sch 2 para 3(5).
13   Counter-Terrorism and Security Act 2015 Sch 2 para 3(4)(b).

14 Counter-Terrorism and Security Act 2015 Sch 2 para 3(4)(c).
15 Counter-Terrorism and Security Act 2015 Sch 2 para 5(2).
16 Counter-Terrorism and Security Act 2015 s 3(9)(b).

424.   Passports.   At the time when a temporary exclusion order comes into force[1], any British passport[2] held by the excluded individual is invalidated[3], and during the period when a temporary exclusion order is in force, the issue of a British passport to the excluded individual while he or she is outside the United Kingdom is not valid[4].

1 As to temporary exclusion orders and as to when such orders come into force see PARA 418.
2 'British passport' means a passport, or other document which enables or facilitates travel from one state to another (except a permit to return), that has been issued by or for Her Majesty's Government in the United Kingdom and issued in respect of a person's status as a British citizen: Counter-Terrorism and Security Act 2015 s 4(11). As to British citizenship see BRITISH NATIONALITY vol 4 (2011) PARA 421 et seq. As to permits to return see PARA 419.
3 Counter-Terrorism and Security Act 2015 s 4(9).
4 Counter-Terrorism and Security Act 2015 s 4(10).

425.   Reviews of temporary exclusion orders.   Where an individual who is subject to a temporary exclusion order[1] is in the United Kingdom[2] he may apply to the High Court[3] to review:

(1)   a decision of the Secretary of State on any of the factors on which the order was based[4];

(2)   a decision to impose the order[5]; and

(3)   a decision that it continues to be necessary, for purposes connected with protecting members of the public in the United Kingdom from a risk of terrorism, for an order to be imposed on the individual[6].

On such a review the court may either quash the order[7] or give directions to the Secretary of State for, or in relation to, the revocation of the order[8]: if the court does not exercise either of these powers it court must decide that the order is to continue in force[9]. The court must apply the principles applicable on an application for judicial review[10].

There is a right of appeal against a conviction for returning to the United Kingdom in breach of a temporary exclusion order if the order is later quashed on review[11]. An appeal against a determination of the court on a review under these provisions may only be made on a question of law[12].

1 As to temporary exclusion orders see PARA 418. As to when an individual is subject to a temporary exclusion order see PARA 418 note 13.
2 Counter-Terrorism and Security Act 2015 s 11(1).
3 For the rules of court relating to references under the Counter-Terrorism and Security Act 2015 s 11 see CPR Pt 88; and in connection with the content and scope of those rules see the Counter-Terrorism and Security Act 2015 Sch 3.
4 Counter-Terrorism and Security Act 2015 s 11(2)(a). The reference in the text to a decision of the Secretary of State on any of the factors on which the order was based is a reference to a decision of the Secretary of State that any of Conditions A-D (see PARA 421) was met in relation to the imposition of the order: Counter-Terrorism and Security Act 2015 s 11(2)(a).
5 Counter-Terrorism and Security Act 2015 s 11(2)(b).
6 Counter-Terrorism and Security Act 2015 s 11(2)(c). This is a reference to condition B (see PARA 421) continuing to be met: s 11(2)(c). A failure by the Secretary of State to make a decision whether condition B continues to be met is treated as a decision that it continues to be met: s 11(11).
7 Counter-Terrorism and Security Act 2015 s 11(4)(b). The power to quash a temporary exclusion order includes power to stay the quashing for a specified time, or pending an appeal or further appeal against the decision to quash: s 11(9)(a).
8 Counter-Terrorism and Security Act 2015 s 11(4)(b).
9 Counter-Terrorism and Security Act 2015 s 11(5).

10 Counter-Terrorism and Security Act 2015 s 11(3).
11 See the Counter-Terrorism and Security Act 2015 Sch 4; and PARA 431.
12 Counter-Terrorism and Security Act 2015 s 11(10).

426. Applications for permits to return. If an individual[1] applies to the Secretary of State for a permit to return[2] the Secretary of State must issue a permit within a reasonable period after the application[3] is made[4], although he may refuse to issue the permit if he requires the individual to attend an interview with a constable or immigration officer at a time and a place specified by the Secretary of State[5] and the individual fails to attend the interview[6]. Where a permit to return is issued the relevant return time[7] must fall within a reasonable period after the application is made[8].

The making of an application for a permit to return to be issued under these provisions (whether or not resulting in a permit to return being issued) does not prevent a subsequent application from being made[9], and the issuing of a permit to return (whether or not resulting in the individual's return to the United Kingdom) does not prevent a subsequent permit to return from being issued (whether or not the earlier permit is still in force)[10].

1 Ie an individual who is subject to a temporary exclusion order: see PARA 418.
2 As to permits to return see PARA 419.
3 'Application' means an application made by an individual to the Secretary of State for a permit to return to be issued: Counter-Terrorism and Security Act 2015 s 6(5). An application is not valid unless it is made in accordance with the procedure for applications specified by the Secretary of State: s 6(4).
4 Counter-Terrorism and Security Act 2015 s 6(1).
5 Counter-Terrorism and Security Act 2015 s 6(1)(a.
6 Counter-Terrorism and Security Act 2015 s 6(1)(b).
7 'Relevant return time' means either the time at which the individual is permitted to arrive on return to the United Kingdom (in a case where the permit to return states such a time), or the start of the period of time during which the individual is permitted to arrive on return to the United Kingdom (in a case where the permit to return states such a period): Counter-Terrorism and Security Act 2015 s 6(5).
8 Counter-Terrorism and Security Act 2015 s 6(3).
9 Counter-Terrorism and Security Act 2015 s 8(3). See, however, in connection with revocation s 8(2)(a), (d); and PARA 430.
10 Counter-Terrorism and Security Act 2015 s 8(4).

427. Permits to return in urgent cases and in deportation cases. The Secretary of State may issue a permit to return[1] to an individual[2] if he considers that, because of the urgency of the situation, it is expedient to issue a permit to return even though no application has[3] been made[4]. The Secretary of State must issue a permit to return to an individual if he considers that the individual is to be deported to the United Kingdom[5]. The issuing of a permit to return (whether or not resulting in the individual's return to the United Kingdom) does not prevent a subsequent permit to return from being issued (whether or not the earlier permit is still in force)[6].

1 As to permits to return see PARA 419.
2 Ie an individual who is subject to a temporary exclusion order: see PARA 418.
3 Ie under the Counter-Terrorism and Security Act 2015 s 6 (see PARA 426).
4 Counter-Terrorism and Security Act 2015 s 7(2)(a). This power may be exercised provided there is no duty to issue a permit to return under s 7(1) (see the text and note 5): s 7(2)(b). Section 7(2) applies whether or not any request has been made to issue the permit to return: s 7(3). A permit to return issued in these circumstances may be revoked: see s 8(2)(c); and PARA 430.

5   Counter-Terrorism and Security Act 2015 s 7(1). Section 7(1) applies whether or not any request
     has been made to issue the permit to return: s 7(3). A permit to return issued in these
     circumstances may be revoked: see s 8(2)(b); and PARA 430.
6   Counter-Terrorism and Security Act 2015 s 8(4).

428. Obligations after return. Where an individual is subject to a temporary
exclusion order[1] and has returned to the United Kingdom[2] the Secretary of State
may by notice[3] impose any or all of:

(1)   a requirement for the individual to report to such a police station, at
      such times and in such manner, as the Secretary of State may by notice
      require, and to comply with any directions given by a constable in
      relation to such reporting (a 'reporting measure')[4];

(2)   a requirement for the individual to attend appointments with specified
      persons or persons of specified descriptions, and to comply with any
      reasonable directions given by the Secretary of State that relate to
      matters about which he is required to attend an appointment (an
      'appointments measure')[5]; and

(3)   an obligation to notify the police[6] of the individual's place (or places) of
      residence[7] and any change in the individual's place (or places) of
      residence[8].

Such a notice comes into force when given to the individual[9] and is in force
until the temporary exclusion order ends (unless the notice is revoked or
otherwise brought to an end earlier)[10]. The validity of such a notice is not
affected by the individual departing from[11], or returning to[12], the United
Kingdom. The Secretary of State may, by notice, vary or revoke any such
notice[13].

An individual subject to an obligation imposed under these provisions[14] is
guilty of an offence if, without reasonable excuse[15], he does not comply with the
obligation[16]. Obligations may be reviewed on application[17] and if they are
quashed, there is a right of appeal against a relevant conviction[18].

1   Counter-Terrorism and Security Act 2015 s 9(1)(a). As to temporary exclusion orders see PARA
     418. As to when an individual is subject to a temporary exclusion order see PARA 418 note 13.
2   Counter-Terrorism and Security Act 2015 s 9(1)(b). As to permits to return see PARA 419.
3   As to the giving of notices see the Temporary Exclusion Orders (Notices) Regulations 2015,
     SI 2015/438 (made under the Counter-Terrorism and Security Act 2015 s 13).
4   Counter-Terrorism and Security Act 2015 s 9(2)(a)(i). This is an obligation of a kind that may be
     imposed on an individual subject to a TPIM notice under the Terrorism Prevention and
     Investigation Measures Act 2011 Sch 1 para 10 (see PARA 434): Counter-Terrorism and Security
     Act 2015 s 9(2)(a)(i). The giving of any notice to an individual under s 9 does not prevent any
     further notice under this section from being given to that individual: s 9(7).
5   Counter-Terrorism and Security Act 2015 s 9(2)(a)(ii). This is an obligation of a kind that may
     be imposed on an individual subject to a TPIM notice under the Terrorism Prevention and
     Investigation Measures Act 2011 Sch 1 para 10A (see PARA 434): Counter-Terrorism and
     Security Act 2015 s 9(2)(a)(ii).
6   Ie in such manner as a notice under the Counter-Terrorism and Security Act 2015 s 9 may
     require: s 9(2)(b).
7   Counter-Terrorism and Security Act 2015 s 9(2)(b)(i).
8   Counter-Terrorism and Security Act 2015 s 9(2)(b)(ii).
9   Counter-Terrorism and Security Act 2015 s 9(3)(a).
10   Counter-Terrorism and Security Act 2015 s 9(3)(b).
11   Counter-Terrorism and Security Act 2015 s 9(6)(a).
12   Counter-Terrorism and Security Act 2015 s 9(6)(b).
13   Counter-Terrorism and Security Act 2015 s 9(4). The variation or revocation of a notice under
     this section takes effect when the notice of variation or revocation is given to the individual:
     s 9(5).

14 An individual is subject to an obligation imposed under the Counter-Terrorism and Security Act 2015 s 9 if an obligation is imposed on him by a notice in force under s 9: s 14(3)(b).

15 In a case where a notice imposing an obligation under the Counter-Terrorism and Security Act 2015 s 9 has not actually been given to an individual, the fact that the notice is deemed to have been given to him under regulations under the Temporary Exclusion Orders (Notices) Regulations 2015, SI 2015/438, art 3 (see note 3) does not (of itself) prevent the individual from showing that lack of knowledge of the obligation was a reasonable excuse for these purposes: Counter-Terrorism and Security Act 2015 s 10(4).

16 Counter-Terrorism and Security Act 2015 s 10(3). As to punishment see s 10(5), (6); and PARA 418 note 16.

17 See the Counter-Terrorism and Security Act 2015 s 11(1), (2)(d), (3), (6)–(8), (9)(a), (10); and PARA 429.

18 See the Counter-Terrorism and Security Act 2015 Sch 4; and PARA 431.

429. Reviews of obligations. Where an individual who is subject to a temporary exclusion order[1] is in the United Kingdom[2] he may apply to the High Court to review a decision to impose[3] any of the permitted obligations on the individual[4].

On such a review of a decision the court may either:

(1) quash the permitted obligation in question[5];

(2) if that is the only permitted obligation imposed by the notice, quash the notice[6]; or

(3) directions to the Secretary of State for, or in relation to, the variation of the notice so far as it relates to that permitted obligation[7] or, if that is the only permitted obligation imposed by the notice, the revocation of the notice[8].

If the court does not exercise any of these powers, it must decide that the notice is to continue in force[9]. If the court exercises a power to quash or vary the notice[10] it must decide that the notice is to continue in force subject to that exercise of that power[11]. The court must apply the principles applicable on an application for judicial review[12].

If a temporary exclusion order[13] or a permitted obligation or notice is quashed[14] there is a right of appeal against a conviction for failure to comply with an associated obligation[15]. An appeal against a determination of the court on a review under these provisions may only be made on a question of law[16].

1 As to temporary exclusion orders see PARA 418. As to when an individual is subject to a temporary exclusion order see PARA 418 note 13.

2 Counter-Terrorism and Security Act 2015 s 11(1).

3 Ie by a notice under the Counter-Terrorism and Security Act 2015 s 9 (see PARA 428).

4 Counter-Terrorism and Security Act 2015 s 11(2)(d).

5 Counter-Terrorism and Security Act 2015 s 11(6)(a). The power to quash a permitted obligation or notice includes power to stay the quashing for a specified time, or pending an appeal or further appeal against the decision to quash: s 11(9)(a).

6 Counter-Terrorism and Security Act 2015 s 11(6)(b).

7 Counter-Terrorism and Security Act 2015 s 11(6)(c)(i).

8 Counter-Terrorism and Security Act 2015 s 11(6)(c)(ii).

9 Counter-Terrorism and Security Act 2015 s 11(7).

10 Ie exercises a power under the Counter-Terrorism and Security Act 2015 s 11(6)(a) or (c)(i) (see the text and notes 5–7).

11 Counter-Terrorism and Security Act 2015 s 11(8).

12 Counter-Terrorism and Security Act 2015 s 11(3).

13 A temporary exclusion order may be quashed on review: see the Counter-Terrorism and Security Act 2015 s 11; and PARA 425.

14 See the text and notes 5–6.

15 See the Counter-Terrorism and Security Act 2015 Sch 4; and PARA 431.

16 Counter-Terrorism and Security Act 2015 s 11(10).

430.   Revocation of permits to return.   The Secretary of State may revoke a permit to return[1] issued to an individual[2] only if:

(1)   the permit to return has been issued on an application by the individual[3] and the individual asks the Secretary of State to revoke it[4];

(2)   the permit to return has been issued in a deportation case[5] and the Secretary of State no longer considers that the individual is to be deported to the United Kingdom[6];

(3)   the permit to return has been issued because of the urgency of the situation[7] and the Secretary of State no longer considers that, because of the urgency of the situation, the issue of the permit to return is expedient[8];

(4)   the Secretary of State issues a subsequent permit to return to the individual[9]; or

(5)   the Secretary of State considers that the permit to return has been obtained by misrepresentation[10].

1   As to permits to return see PARA 419.
2   Ie an individual who is subject to a temporary exclusion order: see PARA 418.
3   Ie under the Counter-Terrorism and Security Act 2015 s 6: see PARA 426.
4   Counter-Terrorism and Security Act 2015 s 8(2)(a).
5   Ie under the Counter-Terrorism and Security Act 2015 s 7(1): see PARA 427.
6   Counter-Terrorism and Security Act 2015 s 8(2)(b).
7   Ie under the Counter-Terrorism and Security Act 2015 s 7(2): see PARA 427.
8   Counter-Terrorism and Security Act 2015 s 8(2)(c).
9   Counter-Terrorism and Security Act 2015 s 8(2)(d).
10 Counter-Terrorism and Security Act 2015 s 8(2)(e).

431.   Appeals.   An individual who has been convicted of an offence of returning to the United Kingdom in breach of a temporary exclusion order[1] or of failing to comply with a post-return obligation[2] may appeal against the conviction[3] if the order is quashed[4] and the individual could not have been convicted had the quashing occurred before the proceedings for the offence were brought[5]. An individual who has been convicted of the offence of failing to comply with a post-return obligation[6] may appeal against the conviction if the notice imposing the obligation[7], or a permitted obligation imposed by such a notice, is quashed[8], and the individual could not have been convicted had the quashing occurred before the proceedings for the offence were brought[9]. The right of appeal does not arise until there is no further possibility of an appeal against the decision to quash the temporary exclusion order, notice or permitted obligation (as the case may be)[10] or any decision on an appeal made against that decision[11]. On an appeal under these provisions to any court, that court must allow the appeal and quash the conviction[12].

1   Ie under the Counter-Terrorism and Security Act 2015 s 10(1): see PARA 418.
2   Ie under the Counter-Terrorism and Security Act 2015 s 10(3): see PARA 428.
3   Appeals under the Counter-Terrorism and Security Act 2015 Sch 4 are to the Court of Appeal (where the person was convicted on indictment) or to the Crown Court (where the person was summarily convicted): Counter-Terrorism and Security Act 2015 Sch 4 para 2(a), (c). An appeal to the Court of Appeal against a conviction on indictment may be brought irrespective of whether the appellant has previously appealed against the conviction (Sch 4 para 4(2)(a)), may not be brought after the end of the period of 28 days beginning with the day on which the right of appeal arises by virtue of Sch 4 para 3 (Sch 4 para 4(2)(b)) and is to be treated as an appeal under the Criminal Appeal Act 1968 s 1 (see CRIMINAL PROCEDURE vol 28 (2015) PARA 734), but does not require leave (Counter-Terrorism and Security Act 2015 Sch 4 para 4(2)(c)). An appeal to the Crown Court against a summary conviction may be brought irrespective of whether the appellant pleaded guilty (Sch 4 para 4(5)(a)), may be brought irrespective of

whether the appellant has previously appealed against the conviction or made an application in respect of the conviction under the Magistrates' Courts Act 1980 s 111 (case stated: see CRIMINAL PROCEDURE vol 28 (2015) PARA 654 et seq) (Counter-Terrorism and Security Act 2015 Sch 4 para 4(5)(b)), may not be brought after the end of the period of 21 days beginning with the day on which the right of appeal arises by virtue of Sch 4 para 3 (Sch 4 para 4(5)(c)) and is to be treated as an appeal under the Magistrates' Courts Act 1980 s 108(1)(b) (see CRIMINAL PROCEDURE vol 28 (2015) PARA 665) (Counter-Terrorism and Security Act 2015 Sch 4 para 4(5)(d)).

4   Ie on review: see the Counter-Terrorism and Security Act 2015 s 11; and PARA 425.
5   Counter-Terrorism and Security Act 2015 Sch 4 para 1(1).
6   See note 2.
7   Ie the notice under the Counter-Terrorism and Security Act 2015 s 9: see PARA 428.
8   Counter-Terrorism and Security Act 2015 Sch 4 para 1(2)(a).
9   Counter-Terrorism and Security Act 2015 Sch 4 para 1(2)(b).
10   Counter-Terrorism and Security Act 2015 Sch 4 para 3(1)(a). In determining whether there is no further possibility of an appeal against a decision of the kind mentioned in Sch 4 para 3(1), any power to extend the time for giving notice of application for leave to appeal, or for applying for leave to appeal, must be ignored: Sch 4 para 3(2).
11   Counter-Terrorism and Security Act 2015 Sch 4 para 3(1)(b).
12   Counter-Terrorism and Security Act 2015 Sch 4 para 1(1).

(vii) Terrorism Prevention and Investigation Measures

432. TPIM notices and orders. A TPIM notice is a notice issued by the Secretary of State which imposes specified terrorism prevention and investigation measures[1] on an individual[2]. TPIM notices may be issued if:

(1)   the Secretary of State is satisfied, on the balance of probabilities, that the individual is, or has been, involved in terrorism-related activity (the 'relevant activity')[3];

(2)   some or all of the relevant activity is new terrorism-related activity[4];

(3)   the Secretary of State reasonably considers that it is necessary, for purposes connected with protecting members of the public from a risk of terrorism, for terrorism prevention and investigation measures to be imposed on the individual[5];

(4)   the Secretary of State reasonably considers that it is necessary, for purposes connected with preventing or restricting the individual's involvement in terrorism-related activity, for the specified terrorism prevention and investigation measures to be imposed on the individual[6]; and

(5)   either the court gives[7] the Secretary of State permission[8] or the Secretary of State reasonably considers that the urgency of the case requires terrorism prevention and investigation measures to be imposed without obtaining such permission[9].

A TPIM notice remains in force for a period of one year, although it may by notice be extended by a period of one year beginning when it would otherwise expire[10]. The Secretary of State also has power to vary measures specified in a notice[11], to revoke a notice[12], to revive a notice which has expired or been revoked[13], and to replace a notice that has been quashed in, or in compliance with a decision in, TPIM proceedings[14].

Unless otherwise provided[15], the Secretary of State's TPIM powers[16] expire at the end of 14 December 2016[17]. Provision is also made for the imposition of enhanced measures, where necessary, during Parliamentary recesses[18].

1   'Terrorism prevention and investigation measures' means requirements, restrictions and other measures which may be made in relation to an individual by virtue of Sch 1: see the Terrorism Prevention and Investigation Measures Act 2011 s 2(2); and PARA 434.

2 Terrorism Prevention and Investigation Measures Act 2011 s 2(1). TPIMs were introduced in 2011 as a replacement for control orders, provision for which was made by the Prevention of Terrorism Act 2005 (repealed by the Terrorism Prevention and Investigation Measures Act 2011 s 1). Provision is made for the service of notices (failure to follow which will mean the individual is not bound by the notice (see s 28) and for the purpose of taking fingerprints and samples from individuals who are subject to TPIMs (see s 25, Sch 6).

The Secretary of State must make reports to Parliament regarding the exercise of his powers under the Terrorism Prevention and Investigation Measures Act 2011 (see s 19) and must appoint a person to review the operation of the Act (see s 20 (ss 3(1), 20 amended by the Counter-Terrorism and Security Act 2015 ss 20(1), 45(3))).

3 Terrorism Prevention and Investigation Measures Act 2011 ss 2(1), 3(1) (s 3(1) as amended: see note 2). As to the meaning of 'involvement in terrorism-related activity' see PARA 433.

4 Terrorism Prevention and Investigation Measures Act 2011 s 3(2). 'New terrorism-related activity' means: (1) if no TPIM notice relating to the individual has ever been in force, terrorism-related activity occurring at any time (s 3(6)(a)); (2) if only one TPIM notice relating to the individual has ever been in force, terrorism-related activity occurring after that notice came into force (s 3(6)(b)); or (3) if two or more TPIM notices relating to the individual have been in force, terrorism-related activity occurring after such a notice came into force most recently (s 3(6)(c)).

5 Terrorism Prevention and Investigation Measures Act 2011 s 3(3). During the period that a TPIM notice is in force, the Secretary of State must keep under review whether this condition is are met: s 11.

6 Terrorism Prevention and Investigation Measures Act 2011 s 3(4). During the period that a TPIM notice is in force, the Secretary of State must keep under review whether this condition is are met: s 11.

7 Ie under the Terrorism Prevention and Investigation Measures Act 2011 s 6, supplemented by ss 8, 9 (court hearings relating to the imposition of measures).

8 Terrorism Prevention and Investigation Measures Act 2011 s 3(5)(a).

9 Terrorism Prevention and Investigation Measures Act 2011 s 3(5)(b). Provision in connection with urgent cases is made by s 7, Sch 2, supplemented by ss 8, 9.

10 See the Terrorism Prevention and Investigation Measures Act 2011 s 5(1), (2).

11 See the Terrorism Prevention and Investigation Measures Act 2011 s 12. Notices may be varied either on the application of the individual to whom the notice relates (s 12(2)) or of the Secretary of State's own volition (s 12(1)).

12 See the Terrorism Prevention and Investigation Measures Act 2011 s 13(1)–(5). Notices may be varied either on the application of the individual to whom the notice relates (s 13(2)) or of the Secretary of State's own volition (s 13(1)).

13 See the Terrorism Prevention and Investigation Measures Act 2011 s 13(6)–(9). A notice can be revived only if the conditions set out in s 3(1), (3), (4) are met: s 13(6).

14 See the Terrorism Prevention and Investigation Measures Act 2011 ss 14, 15. As to the meaning of 'TPIM proceedings' see PARA 436 note 6.

15 Ie under the Terrorism Prevention and Investigation Measures Act 2011 ss 21(2)–(7), 22, which provide for the making of orders repealing, reviving or extending these powers. At the date at which this volume states the law no such orders had been made.

16 'Secretary of State's TPIM powers' means the power to impose a TPIM notice under the Terrorism Prevention and Investigation Measures Act 2011 s 2 (see the text and notes 1–9), the power to extend a TPIM notice under s 5(2) (see the text and note 10), the power to vary a TPIM notice under s 12(1)(c) (see the text and note 11) and the power to revive a TPIM notice under s 13(6)–(9) (see the text and note 13): s 21(8).

17 Terrorism Prevention and Investigation Measures Act 2011 s 21(1). 14 December 2016 is five years beginning with the day on which the Act was passed (ie received Royal Assent).

18 See the Terrorism Prevention and Investigation Measures Act 2011 ss 26, 27.

433. Involvement in terrorism-related activity. 'Involvement in terrorism-related activity' is[1] any one or more of the following:

(1) the commission, preparation or instigation of acts of terrorism[2];

(2) conduct which facilitates the commission, preparation or instigation of such acts, or which is intended to do so[3];

(3) conduct which gives encouragement to the commission, preparation or instigation of such acts, or which is intended to do so[4]; and

(4) conduct which gives support or assistance to individuals who are known or believed by the individual concerned to be involved in conduct falling within head (1) above[5].

1 Ie for the purposes of the Terrorism Prevention and Investigation Measures Act 2011: see PARA 432. It is immaterial whether an individual's involvement in terrorism-related activity occurs before or after 15 December 2011 (ie the date on which the Terrorism Prevention and Investigation Measures Act 2011 was brought into force by virtue of s 31(2)): s 4(2).
2 Terrorism Prevention and Investigation Measures Act 2011 s 4(1)(a). 'Act of terrorism' includes anything constituting an action taken for the purposes of terrorism, within the meaning of the Terrorism Act 2000 (see s 1(5); and CRIMINAL LAW vol 25 (2010) PARA 372): Terrorism Prevention and Investigation Measures Act 2011 s 30(1). For these purposes it is immaterial whether the acts of terrorism in question are specific acts of terrorism or acts of terrorism in general: s 4(1).
3 Terrorism Prevention and Investigation Measures Act 2011 s 4(1)(b).
4 Terrorism Prevention and Investigation Measures Act 2011 s 4(1)(c).
5 Terrorism Prevention and Investigation Measures Act 2011 s 4(1)(d).

434. Requirements, restrictions and other measures which may be imposed.
Pursuant to a TPIM notice[1] the Secretary of State may impose:
(1) restrictions on the individual in relation to the residence in which he resides (an 'overnight residence measure')[2];
(2) restrictions on the individual leaving a specified area or travelling outside that area (a 'travel measure')[3];
(3) restrictions on the individual entering a specified area or place or a place or area of a specified description (an 'exclusion measure')[4];
(4) a requirement for the individual to comply with directions given by a constable in respect of his movements (which may, in particular, include a restriction on movements) (a 'movement directions measure')[5];
(5) restrictions on the individual's use of, or access to, such descriptions of financial services as are specified (a 'financial services measure')[6];
(6) restrictions on the individual in relation to the transfer of property to, or by, him and/or requirements on him in relation to the disclosure of property (a 'property measure')[7];
(7) a prohibition on the possession by the individual of offensive weapons, imitation firearms or explosives and a prohibition on making an application for a firearm certificate or a shot gun certificate (a 'weapons and explosives measure')[8];
(8) restrictions on the individual's possession or use of electronic communication devices and/or requirements on him in relation to the possession or use of electronic communication devices by other persons in his residence (an 'electronic communication device measure')[9];
(9) restrictions on the individual's association or communication with other persons (an 'association measure')[10];
(10) restrictions on the individual in relation to his work or studies (a 'work or studies measure')[11];
(11) a requirement for the individual to report to such a police station, at such times and in such manner, as the Secretary of State may by notice require, and to comply with any directions given by a constable in relation to such reporting (a 'reporting measure')[12];
(12) a requirement for the individual to attend appointments with specified persons or persons of specified descriptions, and to comply with any

reasonable directions given by the Secretary of State that relate to matters about which he is required to attend an appointment (an 'appointments measure')[13];

(13) a requirement for the individual to allow photographs to be taken of him at such locations and at such times as the Secretary of State may by notice require (a 'photography measure')[14]; and

(14) requirements for the individual to co-operate with specified arrangements for enabling his movements, communications or other activities to be monitored by electronic or other means (a 'monitoring measure')[15].

Pursuant to the imposition of measures on individuals, provision is made for powers of entry, search and seizure[16].

1 See PARA 432.
2 Terrorism Prevention and Investigation Measures Act 2011 Sch 1 para 1(1). In connection with the content and operation of such a restriction see Sch 1 para 1(2), (3), (3A), (5), (5A), (6)–(11) (Sch 1 para 1(3) amended, Sch 1 paras 1(3A), (5A), 6A, 10A added, Sch 1 para 2(2) substituted, by the Counter-Terrorism and Security Act 2015 ss 16–19).
3 Terrorism Prevention and Investigation Measures Act 2011 Sch 1 para 2(1). In connection with the content and operation of such a restriction see Sch 1 para 2(2)–(5) (as amended: see note 2).
4 Terrorism Prevention and Investigation Measures Act 2011 Sch 1 para 3(1). In connection with the content and operation of such a restriction see Sch 1 para 3(2), (3).
5 Terrorism Prevention and Investigation Measures Act 2011 Sch 1 para 4(1). In connection with the content and operation of such a restriction see Sch 1 para 4(2), (3).
6 Terrorism Prevention and Investigation Measures Act 2011 Sch 1 para 5(1). In connection with the content and operation of such a restriction see Sch 1 para 5(2)–(8) (as amended: see note 2).
7 Terrorism Prevention and Investigation Measures Act 2011 Sch 1 para 6(1). In connection with the content and operation of such a restriction see Sch 1 para 6(2)–(5).
8 Terrorism Prevention and Investigation Measures Act 2011 Sch 1 para 6A(1) (as added: see note 2). In connection with the content and operation of such a restriction see Sch 1 para 6A(2), (3) (as so added).
9 Terrorism Prevention and Investigation Measures Act 2011 Sch 1 para 7(1). In connection with the content and operation of such a restriction see Sch 1 para 7(2)–(6).
10 Terrorism Prevention and Investigation Measures Act 2011 Sch 1 para 8(1). In connection with the content and operation of such a restriction see Sch 1 para 8(2), (3).
11 Terrorism Prevention and Investigation Measures Act 2011 Sch 1 para 9(1). In connection with the content and operation of such a restriction see Sch 1 para 9(2), (3).
12 Terrorism Prevention and Investigation Measures Act 2011 Sch 1 para 10(1). In connection with the content and operation of such a restriction see Sch 1 para 10(2).
13 Terrorism Prevention and Investigation Measures Act 2011 Sch 1 para 10A(1) (as added: see note 2). In connection with the content and operation of such a restriction see Sch 1 para 10A(2) (as so added).
14 Terrorism Prevention and Investigation Measures Act 2011 Sch 1 para 11.
15 Terrorism Prevention and Investigation Measures Act 2011 Sch 1 para 12(1). In connection with the content and operation of such a restriction see Sch 1 para 12(2), (3).
16 See the Terrorism Prevention and Investigation Measures Act 2011 s 24, Sch 5.

435. Duty to investigate individual's conduct. Before applying for[1] or issuing[2] a TPIM[3] the Secretary of State must consult the chief officer[4] of the appropriate police force[5] about whether there is evidence available that could realistically be used for the purposes of prosecuting the individual for an offence relating to terrorism[6].

If the Secretary of State serves a TPIM notice on an individual the chief officer of the appropriate police force must[7] secure that the investigation of the individual's conduct, with a view to a prosecution of the individual for an offence relating to terrorism, is kept under review throughout the period the TPIM notice is in force[8], and report to the Secretary of State on the review so carried out[9].

1   Ie before making an application under the Terrorism Prevention and Investigation Measures Act 2011 s 6 for permission to impose measures on an individual: s 10(1)(a).

2   Ie before imposing measures on an individual in a case to which the Terrorism Prevention and Investigation Measures Act 2011 s 3(5)(b) (urgency of the case requires measures to be imposed without obtaining the permission of the court) applies: s 10(1)(b).

3   As to TPIMs see PARAS 432–434.

4   In relation to a police force maintained for a police area in England and Wales 'chief officer' means the chief officer of police of that force; and in relation to the National Crime Agency, it means the Director General of the National Crime Agency: Terrorism Prevention and Investigation Measures Act 2011 s 10(1) (amended by the Crime and Courts Act 2013 Sch 8 paras 186, 188). 'Police force' means a police force maintained for a police area in England and Wales or, as the case may be, the National Crime Agency: s 10(1) (as so amended). As to police forces, police areas and chief officers of police see POLICE AND INVESTIGATORY POWERS vol 84 (2013) PARAS 52 et seq, 123 et seq. As to the National Crime Agency see POLICE AND INVESTIGATORY POWERS vol 84 (2013) PARA 424.

      The chief officer must consult the Director of Public Prosecutions (the 'relevant prosecuting authority' in the case of offences that would be likely to be prosecuted in England and Wales) before responding to consultation under the Terrorism Prevention and Investigation Measures Act 2011 s 10(1): s 10(6), (8)(a), (9).

5   The 'appropriate police force' means the police force that is investigating the commission of any such offence by the individual (Terrorism Prevention and Investigation Measures Act 2011 s 10(3)(a)) or by which it appears to the Secretary of State that the commission of any such offence by the individual would fall to be investigated (s 10(3)(b)).

6   Terrorism Prevention and Investigation Measures Act 2011 s 10(2).

7   Ie after having been informed by the Secretary of State that the TPIM notice has been served (Terrorism Prevention and Investigation Measures Act 2011 s 10(4)(a), (5)) and that the chief officer must act in accordance with the duty under s 10(5) (s 10(4)(b)).

8   Terrorism Prevention and Investigation Measures Act 2011 s 10(5)(a). The chief officer must, to the extent that he considers it appropriate to do so, consult the relevant prosecuting authority in carrying out the duty under s 10(5)(a): s 10(7).

9   Terrorism Prevention and Investigation Measures Act 2011 s 10(5)(b).

436.   Jurisdiction and appeals. TPIM decisions[1] are not to be questioned in any legal proceedings other than proceedings in the High Court[2] or proceedings on appeal from such proceedings[3]. The High Court is the appropriate tribunal[4] in relation to proceedings all or any part of which call a TPIM decision into question on the grounds of incompatibility with the European Convention on Human Rights[5].

No appeal lies from any determination of the court in TPIM proceedings[6], except on a question of law[7], and no appeal by any person other than the Secretary of State lies from any determination on an application for permission[8] to impose, or a reference relating to the imposition in urgent cases of[9], terrorism prevention and investigation measures[10]. However, the individual concerned may in specified circumstances appeal against the extension or revival of a TPIM notice[11], the variation of measures contained in a TPIM notice[12], the revocation of a TPIM notice[13], or any decision of the Secretary of State on an application for permission[14], and the court may deal with the appeal accordingly[15].

1   Ie:
    (1)   a decision made by the Secretary of State in exercise or performance of any power or duty under any of the Terrorism Prevention and Investigation Measures Act 2011 ss 2–15 or under Sch 1 or 2 (s 17(3)(a));
    (2)   a decision made by the Secretary of State for the purposes of, or in connection with, the exercise or performance of any such power or duty (s 17(3)(b));
    (3)   a decision by a constable to give a direction by virtue of Sch 1 para 4 (movement directions measure) or Sch 1 para 10(1)(b) (reporting measure) (see PARA 435) (s 17(3)(c));
    (4)   a decision by a person to give a direction by virtue of Sch 1 para 12(2)(d) (monitoring measure) (s 17(3)(d)).

2   Terrorism Prevention and Investigation Measures Act 2011 s 17(1)(a).

3   Terrorism Prevention and Investigation Measures Act 2011 s 17(1)(b).
4   Ie for the purposes of the Human Rights Act 1998 s 7 (see RIGHTS AND FREEDOMS vol 88A (2013) PARAS 27, 28).
5   Terrorism Prevention and Investigation Measures Act 2011 s 17(2). As to the European Convention on Human Rights (ie the Convention for the Protection of Human Rights and Fundamental Freedoms (Rome, 4 November 1950; TS 71 (1953; Cmd 8969) see RIGHTS AND FREEDOMS vol 88A (2013) PARA 88.
6   'TPIM proceedings' means: proceedings on an application for permission under the Terrorism Prevention and Investigation Measures Act 2011 s 6 to impose terrorism prevention and investigation measures; proceedings on a reference under Sch 2 (urgent cases); proceedings on a directions hearing held in accordance with directions under s 8(2); proceedings on a review hearing held in accordance with directions under s 8(4); proceedings on an appeal under s 16; proceedings by virtue of s 17(2); proceedings on an application made by virtue of rules of court made under Sch 4 para 6 (application for order requiring anonymity); and any other proceedings for questioning a TPIM decision (including any claim for damages or other relief arising out of such a decision): s 30(1). Provision in connection with TPIM proceedings and appeal proceedings is made under s 18(3), Sch 4.
7   Terrorism Prevention and Investigation Measures Act 2011 s 18(1).
8   Ie under the Terrorism Prevention and Investigation Measures Act 2011 s 6.
9   Ie a reference under the Terrorism Prevention and Investigation Measures Act 2011 Sch 2.
10 Terrorism Prevention and Investigation Measures Act 2011 s 18(2).
11 See the Terrorism Prevention and Investigation Measures Act 2011 s 16(1). As to extension and revival see ss 5(2), 13(6); and PARA 432.
12 See the Terrorism Prevention and Investigation Measures Act 2011 s 16(2), (3). As to variation see s 12; and PARA 432.
13 See the Terrorism Prevention and Investigation Measures Act 2011 s 16(4). As to revocation see s 13; and PARA 432.
14 See the Terrorism Prevention and Investigation Measures Act 2011 s 16(5). 'Permission' means permission for the purposes of measures specified in a TPIM notice (see PARA 434): s 16(9).
15 See the Terrorism Prevention and Investigation Measures Act 2011 s 16(6)–(8).

437.   Enforcement.
An individual is guilty of an offence if a TPIM notice[1] is in force in relation to him[2] and he contravenes[3], without reasonable excuse[4], any measure specified in it[5]. An individual guilty of such an offence is liable on conviction on indictment, to imprisonment for a term not exceeding 5 years (10 years where a travel measure is contravened) or to a fine, or to both[6], and on summary conviction to imprisonment for a term not exceeding six months[7] or to a fine not exceeding the statutory maximum[8], or to both[9]. An offender may not be conditionally discharged for this offence[10].

1   As to the meaning of 'TPIM notice' see PARA 432.
2   Terrorism Prevention and Investigation Measures Act 2011 s 23(1)(a).
3   If the individual has the permission of the Secretary of State by virtue of the Terrorism Prevention and Investigation Measures Act 2011 Sch 1 for an act which would, without that permission, contravene such a measure, he contravenes that measure by virtue of that act if the act is not in accordance with the terms of the permission: s 23(2).
4   The requirement that the contravention be 'without reasonable excuse' does not apply where the individual is subject to a travel measure under Sch 1 para 2 and leaves the United Kingdom or travels outside the United Kingdom: Terrorism Prevention and Investigation Measures Act 2011 s 23(1A) (s 23(1A), (3A) added by the Counter-Terrorism and Security Act 2015 s 17).
5   Terrorism Prevention and Investigation Measures Act 2011 s 23(1)(b). As to the measures that may be contained in a TPIM notice see PARA 434.
6   Terrorism Prevention and Investigation Measures Act 2011 s 23(3)(a). (3A) (s 23(3A) as added: see note 4).
7   In relation to an offence committed after the commencement of the Criminal Justice Act 2003 s 154(1) (not yet in force) this period is increased to 12 months: Terrorism Prevention and Investigation Measures Act 2011 s 23(4).
8   As to the standard scale, the statutory maximum, the prescribed sum, and magistrates' powers to levy unlimited fines see PARA 176.
9   Terrorism Prevention and Investigation Measures Act 2011 s 23(3)(b).

10 See the Terrorism Prevention and Investigation Measures Act 2011 s 23(5)(a) (which provides that where an individual is convicted by or before a court of an offence under s 23(1), it is not open to that court to make in respect of the offence an order under the Powers of Criminal Courts (Sentencing) Act 2000 s 12(1)(b) (see PARA 454).

(3) AUTOMATIC ORDERS

438. Barring. The Disclosure and Barring Service (DBS)[1] is required to maintain two lists, referred to as the children's barred list and the adult's barred list[2], for the purpose of regulating access to children and vulnerable adults and controlling the activities of barred persons[3]. Where a person has been convicted of, or cautioned in relation to, a specified sexual or violent offence[4] the DBS must include him in the appropriate barred list[5]. Provision is made in connection with the criteria for inclusion in the barred lists and the procedure leading to inclusion[6], the procedure for challenging inclusions[7], the referral of persons for inclusion in the lists[8], the collection of barring information by DBS[9], the disclosure of information about barred persons and persons of concern[10], and the imposition of restrictions on the activities of barred persons[11],

1 As to the Disclosure and Barring Service see SOCIAL SERVICES AND COMMUNITY CARE vol 95 (2013) PARA 237.

2 The DBS is required to maintain these lists pursuant to the Safeguarding Vulnerable Groups Act 2006 s 2(1): see SOCIAL SERVICES AND COMMUNITY CARE vol 95 (2013) PARAS 159, 160.

3 Provision in this regard is made under the Safeguarding Vulnerable Groups Act 2006: see generally SOCIAL SERVICES AND COMMUNITY CARE vol 95 (2013) PARAS 135–208.

4 The offences are specified in the Safeguarding Vulnerable Groups Act 2006 (Prescribed Criteria and Miscellaneous Provisions) Regulations 2009, SI 2009/37, Schedule: see SOCIAL SERVICES AND COMMUNITY CARE vol 95 (2013) PARAS 159, 160.

5 See the Safeguarding Vulnerable Groups Act 2006 s 2(2), (3), Sch 3; and SOCIAL SERVICES AND COMMUNITY CARE vol 95 (2013) PARAS 159–173. The DBS must also include a person in the children's barred list if he had been made the subject of a disqualification order under the Criminal Justice and Court Services Act 2000 s 28, s 29 or s 29A before 20 January 2009: see the Safeguarding Vulnerable Groups Act 2006 (Prescribed Criteria and Miscellaneous Provisions) Regulations 2009, SI 2009/37, reg 3(2)(a); and SOCIAL SERVICES AND COMMUNITY CARE vol 95 (2013) PARA 159. 20 January 2009 is the operative date for the substantive provisions of the Safeguarding Vulnerable Groups Act 2006 and the Safeguarding Vulnerable Groups Act 2006 (Prescribed Criteria and Miscellaneous Provisions) Regulations 2009, SI 2009/37: see reg 1(1).

6 See SOCIAL SERVICES AND COMMUNITY CARE vol 95 (2013) PARAS 159–168.
7 See SOCIAL SERVICES AND COMMUNITY CARE vol 95 (2013) PARAS 169–173.
8 See SOCIAL SERVICES AND COMMUNITY CARE vol 95 (2013) PARAS 174–180.
9 See SOCIAL SERVICES AND COMMUNITY CARE vol 95 (2013) PARAS 181–187.
10 See SOCIAL SERVICES AND COMMUNITY CARE vol 95 (2013) PARAS 188–204.
11 See SOCIAL SERVICES AND COMMUNITY CARE vol 95 (2013) PARAS 205–208.

(4) ABOLISHED ORDERS

439. Anti-social behaviour orders. The power to make anti-social behaviour orders was introduced in 1998[1] and brought into force in 1999[2]. The purpose of anti-social behaviour orders was to protect specified persons from anti-social acts by specified individuals[3]. Orders could be made either following the conviction of such an individual for an offence[4], or on application to the magistrates' court[5]. There was also provision for an application to be made in county court proceedings for an order prohibiting anti-social behaviour (which was not referred to in the legislation as an 'anti-social behaviour order')[6], and provision for the making of intervention orders, imposing additional requirements in respect of a person subject to an anti-social behaviour order or an order prohibiting anti-social behaviour[7].

These orders have been abolished[8]. The power to make anti-social behaviour orders following conviction was removed as from 20 October 2014[9], and replaced as from that date by a new system of criminal behaviour orders[10]. The powers to make anti-social behaviour orders on application to the magistrates' court, to make orders in county court proceedings prohibiting anti-social behaviour, and to make intervention orders, was removed as from 23 March 2015[11] and replaced as from that date by a new system of civil injunctions for the prevention of anti-social behaviour[12].

1   See the Crime and Disorder Act 1998 ss 1–4 (as originally enacted).
2   See the Crime and Disorder Act 1998 (Commencement No 3 and Appointed Day) Order 1998, SI 1998/3263.
3   See the Crime and Disorder Act 1998 ss 1(1)(b), 1C(2)(b) (repealed).
4   See the Crime and Disorder Act 1998 s 1C (repealed).
5   See the Crime and Disorder Act 1998 s 1 (repealed).
6   See the Crime and Disorder Act 1998 s 1B (repealed).
7   See the Crime and Disorder Act 1998 ss 1G, 1H (repealed).
8   The Crime and Disorder Act 1998 ss 1–1K, 4, 8A, which make substantive provision in connection with the making of anti-social behaviour orders, orders prohibiting anti-social behaviour and intervention orders, have been repealed by the Anti-social Behaviour, Crime and Policing Act 2014 Sch 11 para 24(a). For savings relating to existing orders see the Anti-social Behaviour, Crime and Policing Act 2014 ss 21(1)(d)–(f), (2)–(4), (5)(a), (c), 33(1), (2)(a), (b), (3), (4).
9   The repeals referred to in note 8 were brought into force on 20 October 2014 insofar as relating to the power to make anti-social behaviour orders following conviction: see the Anti-social Behaviour, Crime and Policing Act 2014 (Commencement No 7, Saving and Transitional Provisions) Order 2014, SI 2014/2590.
10 As to criminal behaviour orders see the Anti-social Behaviour, Crime and Policing Act 2014 Pt 2 (ss 22–33); and PARAS 319–326.
11 The repeals referred to in note 8 were brought into force on 23 March 2015 insofar as relating to the power to make anti-social behaviour orders on application to the magistrates' court, to make orders in county court proceedings prohibiting anti-social behaviour, and to make intervention orders: see the Anti-social Behaviour, Crime and Policing Act 2014 (Commencement No 8, Saving and Transitional Provisions) Order 2015, SI 2015/373.
12 As to civil injunctions for the prevention of anti-social behaviour see the Anti-social Behaviour, Crime and Policing Act 2014 Pt 1 (ss 1–21); and PARAS 371–391.

440.   Risk of sexual harm orders. The power to make risk of sexual harm orders was introduced in 2003[1] and brought into force in 2004[2]. Their purposes was to protect children generally, or any child, from harm from an offender who has:

(1)   engaged in sexual activity involving a child or in the presence of a child[3];

(2)   caused or incited a child to watch a person engaging in sexual activity or to look at a moving or still image that is sexual[4];

(3)   given a child anything that relates to sexual activity or contains a reference to such activity[5]; or

(4)   communicated with a child, where any part of the communication is sexual[6].

Orders could be made by magistrates' courts, on police application, in respect of a person who had engaged in any of the behaviour described above on at least two occasions[7]. Risk of sexual harm orders were abolished as from 8 March 2015[8] and have been replaced as from that date by sexual risk orders[9], although provision is made for existing risk of sexual harm orders to continue in force and to be varied or discharged[10].

1   See the Sexual Offences Act 2003 ss 123–129 (as originally enacted).
2   See the Sexual Offences Act 2003 (Commencement) Order 2004, SI 2004/874 (bringing the Sexual Offences Act 2003 ss 123–129, inter alia, into force on 1 May 2004).
3   See the Sexual Offences Act 2003 s 123(1)(b), (3)(a) (repealed).
4   See the Sexual Offences Act 2003 s 123(3)(b) (repealed).
5   See the Sexual Offences Act 2003 s 123(3)(c) (repealed).
6   See the Sexual Offences Act 2003 s 123(3)(d) (repealed).
7   See the Sexual Offences Act 2003 s 123(1)(a) (repealed).
8   The Sexual Offences Act 2003 ss 123–129 were repealed by the Anti-social Behaviour, Crime and Policing Act 2014 Sch 5 para 5; the repeal was brought into force on 8 March 2015 by the Anti-social Behaviour, Crime and Policing Act 2014 (Commencement No 8, Saving and Transitional Provisions) Order 2015, SI 2015/373.
9   See the Sexual Offences Act 2003 ss 122A–122K; and PARAS 392–397.
10   See the Anti-social Behaviour, Crime and Policing Act 2014 s 114.

441.   Foreign travel orders.   The power to make foreign travel orders was introduced in 2003[1] and brought into force in 2004[2]. Their purpose was to protect children outside the United Kingdom from serious sexual harm inflicted by an offender who has been convicted of specified sexual offences in the United Kingdom[3], by prohibiting such a person from:

(1)   travelling to any country outside the United Kingdom named or described in the order[4];

(2)   travelling to any country outside the United Kingdom other than a country named or described in the order[5]; or

(3)   travelling to any country outside the United Kingdom[6].

Orders could be made by magistrates' courts, on police application[7]. Foreign travel orders were abolished as from 8 March 2015[8] and have been replaced as from that date by sexual harm prevention orders[9] and sexual risk orders[10], although provision is made for existing foreign travel orders to continue in force and to be varied or discharged[11].

1   See the Sexual Offences Act 2003 ss 114–122 (as originally enacted).
2   See the Sexual Offences Act 2003 (Commencement) Order 2004, SI 2004/874 (bringing the Sexual Offences Act 2003 ss 114–122, inter alia, into force on 1 May 2004).
3   See the Sexual Offences Act 2003 s 117(3) (repealed).
4   See the Sexual Offences Act 2003 s 117(2)(a) (repealed).
5   See the Sexual Offences Act 2003 s 117(2)(b) (repealed).
6   See the Sexual Offences Act 2003 s 117(2)(c) (repealed).
7   See the Sexual Offences Act 2003 s 114(1) (repealed).
8   The Sexual Offences Act 2003 ss 114–122 were repealed by the Anti-social Behaviour, Crime and Policing Act 2014 Sch 5 para 3; the repeal was brought into force on 8 March 2015 by the Anti-social Behaviour, Crime and Policing Act 2014 (Commencement No 8, Saving and Transitional Provisions) Order 2015, SI 2015/373.
9   See the Sexual Offences Act 2003 ss 103A–103K; and PARAS 327–335.
10   See the Sexual Offences Act 2003 ss 122A–122K; and PARAS 392–397.
11   See the Anti-social Behaviour, Crime and Policing Act 2014 s 114.

442.   Sexual offences prevention orders.   The power to make sexual offences prevention orders was introduced in 2003[1] and brought into force in 2004[2]. Their purpose was to protect the public, or any particular members of the public, from serious sexual harm from an offender who has been convicted of, or otherwise dealt with in respect of, a specified sexual or non-sexual offence[3]. The effect of the order was to prohibit the offender from doing anything described in it[4]. Orders could be made by the court on its own initiative when dealing with the offender[5], or on police application[6]. Sexual offences prevention orders were abolished as from 8 March 2015[7] and have been replaced as from that date by sexual harm prevention orders[8], although provision is made for existing sexual offences prevention orders to continue in force and to be varied or discharged[9].

1 See the Sexual Offences Act 2003 ss 104–112 (as originally enacted).
2 See the Sexual Offences Act 2003 (Commencement) Order 2004, SI 2004/874 (bringing the Sexual Offences Act 2003 ss 104–112, inter alia, into force on 1 May 2004).
3 See the Sexual Offences Act 2003 ss 104(2), (3), 107(2) (repealed). The offences are set out in Schs 3, 5 (see PARAS 329, 330).
4 See the Sexual Offences Act 2003 s 107(1)(a) (repealed).
5 See the Sexual Offences Act 2003 s 104(1) (repealed).
6 See the Sexual Offences Act 2003 s 104(5), (6) (repealed).
7 The Sexual Offences Act 2003 ss 104–112 were repealed by the Anti-social Behaviour, Crime and Policing Act 2014 Sch 5 para 3; the repeal was brought into force on 8 March 2015 by the Anti-social Behaviour, Crime and Policing Act 2014 (Commencement No 8, Saving and Transitional Provisions) Order 2015, SI 2015/373.
8 See the Sexual Offences Act 2003 ss 103A–103K; and PARAS 327–335.
9 See the Anti-social Behaviour, Crime and Policing Act 2014 s 114.

7. OTHER COURT ORDERS

(1) ABSOLUTE DISCHARGE

443. Absolute discharge where person is convicted. A court[1] by or before which a person is convicted of an offence may, if it is of the opinion, having regard to the circumstances, including the nature of the offence and character of the offender, that it is inexpedient to inflict punishment, make an order discharging the offender absolutely[2]. This power is not available in respect of an offence the sentence for which is:

(1)   a sentence fixed by law[3];

(2)   the required minimum sentences for threatening with an offensive weapon or an article with a blade or point in public in public[4];

(3)   the required custodial sentence for possession of a firearm or using a person to mind a weapon[5];

(4)   the specified minimum term for a third class A drug trafficking offence[6];

(5)   the specified minimum term for a third domestic burglary[7]; or

(6)   an extended sentence for a violent or sexual offence[8].

A discharge may not be combined with a fine for the same offence[9]. On discharging an offender absolutely, an order for costs or compensation, a restitution order, a deprivation order or an unlawful profits order may be made[10]; and the court may in the case of a discretionary disqualification, and must in the case of an obligatory disqualification, exercise its powers to disqualify[11]. An absolute discharge may be coupled with a recommendation for deportation[12].

1   As to the meaning of 'court' see PARA 1 note 1.

2   Powers of Criminal Courts (Sentencing) Act 2000 s 12(1)(a). See e g *Willcock v Muckle* [1951] 2 KB 844, [1951] 2 All ER 367, DC (court emphatically approved the granting of an absolute discharge by magistrates' court). In these circumstances the court may also discharge the offender conditionally: see PARA 454. In connection with the effect of a discharge see PARA 445.

 Nothing in the Powers of Criminal Courts (Sentencing) Act 2000 s 12 prevents a court, on discharging an offender absolutely or conditionally in respect of an offence, from making an order under the Prosecution of Offences Act 1985 s 21A (criminal courts charge: and CRIMINAL PROCEDURE) or making an order for costs against the offender: Powers of Criminal Courts (Sentencing) Act 2000 s 12(8) (added by the Criminal Justice and Courts Act 2015 Sch 12 para 9).

3   Powers of Criminal Courts (Sentencing) Act 2000 s 12(1) (s 12(1) amended by the Criminal Justice Act 2003 Sch 32 paras 90, 93(a), 124; the Violent Crime Reduction Act 2006 Sch 1 para 6; the Criminal Justice and Immigration Act 2008 Sch 26 paras 40, 41; and the Legal Aid, Sentencing and Punishment of Offenders Act 2012 Sch 19 para 4, Sch 26 para 10; Powers of Criminal Courts (Sentencing) Act 2000 s 12(1) further amended, s 12(1A) added, by the Criminal Justice and Courts Act 2015 Sch 5 para 4).

4   Powers of Criminal Courts (Sentencing) Act 2000 s 12(1), (1A)(a), (c) (as amended and added: see note 3). As to the sentences referred to see the Prevention of Crime Act 1953 ss 1(2B), 1A(5); the Criminal Justice Act 1988 ss 139(6B), 139A(5B), 139AA(7); and CRIMINAL LAW: Powers of Criminal Courts (Sentencing) Act 2000 s 12(1A)(a), (c) (as so added). As to when such a sentence falls to be imposed see PARA 536 note 2.

5   Powers of Criminal Courts (Sentencing) Act 2000 s 12(1), (1A)(b), (f) (as amended and added: see note 3). As to the sentences referred to see the Firearms Act 1968 s 51A(2); the Violent Crime Reduction Act 2006 s 29(4), (6); and CRIMINAL LAW vol 26 (2010) PARAS 614, 656. As to when such a sentence falls to be imposed see PARA 536 note 2.

6   Powers of Criminal Courts (Sentencing) Act 2000 s 12(1), (1A)(d) (as amended and added: see note 3). As to the sentence referred to see the Powers of Criminal Courts (Sentencing) Act 2000 s 110(2); and CRIMINAL LAW vol 26 (2010) PARA 725. As to when such a sentence falls to be imposed see PARA 536 note 2.

7   Powers of Criminal Courts (Sentencing) Act 2000 s 12(1), (1A)(d) (as amended and added: see note 3). As to the sentence referred to see the Powers of Criminal Courts (Sentencing) Act 2000 s 111(2); and CRIMINAL LAW vol 25 (2010) PARA 290. As to when such a sentence falls to be imposed see PARA 536 note 2.

8   Powers of Criminal Courts (Sentencing) Act 2000 s 12(1), (1A)(e) (as amended and added: see note 3). As to the sentences referred to see ss 224A, 225(2), 226(2); and PARAS 34, 35, 37. As to when such a sentence falls to be imposed see PARA 536 note 2.

9   *R v Sanck* (1990) 12 Cr App Rep (S) 155, CA.

10   Powers of Criminal Courts (Sentencing) Act 2000 s 12(7) (amended by the Prevention of Social Housing Fraud Act 2013 Schedule para 8; and by the Criminal Justice and Courts Act 2015 Sch 12 para 9). As to orders for costs and compensation orders see PARA 281 et seq; as to deprivation orders see PARA 470 et seq; as to restitution orders see PARA 492 et seq; as to unlawful profits orders see LANDLORD AND TENANT.

11   Powers of Criminal Courts (Sentencing) Act 2000 s 12(7) (as amended: see note 10).

12   See the Immigration Act 1971 s 6(3); and IMMIGRATION AND ASYLUM vol 57 (2012) PARA 181.

444. Absolute discharge of person not guilty by reason of insanity or under a disability. The court[1] may also make an order for the absolute discharge of an accused where a special verdict of not guilty by reason of insanity[2] is returned[3] or findings have been made that the defendant is under a disability[4] and that he did the act or omission charged against him[5]. The court may make the order if it is of the opinion, having regard to the circumstances, including the nature of the offence and character of the offender, that it is inexpedient to inflict punishment and that an order for absolute discharge wold be most suitable in all the circumstances of the case[6]. The power to order absolute discharge in these circumstances is not available in respect of the offences for which an order for absolute discharge on conviction is unavailable[7].

1   As to the meaning of 'court' see PARA 1 note 1.

2   As to such verdicts see CRIMINAL LAW vol 25 (2010) PARA 30.

3   Criminal Procedure (Insanity) Act 1964 s 5(1)(a), (2)(c) (s 5 substituted, s 5A added, by the Domestic Violence, Crime and Victims Act 2004 s 24(1)).

4   As to such findings see MENTAL HEALTH AND CAPACITY vol 75 (2013) PARA 874.

5   Criminal Procedure (Insanity) Act 1964 ss 5(1)(b), 5A(6)(a) (as substituted and added: see note 3).

6   Powers of Criminal Courts (Sentencing) Act 2000 s 12(1); Criminal Procedure (Insanity) Act 1964 s 5A(6)(b) (as added: see note 3).

7   See the Powers of Criminal Courts (Sentencing) Act 2000 s 12(1); and as to these offences see PARA 443.

445. Effects of discharge. A conviction of an offence for which an order is made discharging the offender[1] is deemed not to be a conviction[2] for any purpose other than the purposes of the proceedings in which the order is made and of any subsequent proceedings which may be taken[3] against him[4]; but where the offender was aged 18 or over[5] at the time of his conviction of the offence in question and is subsequently sentenced for the offence[6], this exemption ceases to apply to that conviction[7].

Except as otherwise provided, a conviction of an offence for which an order is made discharging the offender is in any event disregarded for the purposes of any enactment[8] or instrument[9] which imposes any disqualification or disability[10] upon convicted persons[11], or authorises or requires the imposition of any such disqualification or disability[12].

These provisions do not affect any right of any offender discharged absolutely or conditionally to rely on his conviction in bar of any subsequent proceedings for the same offence[13], or the restoration of any property in consequence of the conviction of any such offender[14].

1 Ie discharging the offender either absolutely (see PARAS 443, 444) or conditionally (see PARA 454): the Powers of Criminal Courts (Sentencing) Act 2000 s 14 (see the text and notes 2–14) applies to both types of discharge.

2 A conviction for which an order is made discharging the offender is treated as a conviction for the purposes of the Rehabilitation of Offenders Act 1974: see PARA 591 note 3.

3 Ie under the Powers of Criminal Courts (Sentencing) Act 2000 s 13 (see PARAS 455–456).

4 Powers of Criminal Courts (Sentencing) Act 2000 s 14(1). See also *Cassidy v Cassidy* [1959] 3 All ER 187, [1959] 1 WLR 1024, DC. This is in contrast to the position where the offender is made subject to a 'common law bind over': see PARA 447. The Powers of Criminal Courts (Sentencing) Act 2000 s 14(1) has effect subject to the Criminal Appeal Act 1968 s 50(1A) (added by the Criminal Justice Act 1982 s 66; amended by the Criminal Justice Act 1991 Sch 11 para 4, Sch 13; and the Powers of Criminal Courts (Sentencing) Act 2000 Sch 9 para 30) (which provides that the Powers of Criminal Courts (Sentencing) Act 2000 s 14 does not prevent an appeal under the Criminal Appeal Act 1968, whether against conviction or otherwise) and the Magistrates' Courts Act 1980 s 108(1A) (see CRIMINAL PROCEDURE vol 28 (2015) PARA 665) (rights of appeal): Powers of Criminal Courts (Sentencing) Act 2000 s 14(6) (which does not prejudice any other enactment that excludes the effect of s 14(1) or s 14(3) (see the text and notes 8–12) for particular purposes).

  In connection with whether a person has to reveal an offence for which he has been conditionally discharged see *R v Patel (Rupal)* [2006] EWCA Crim 2689, [2007] ICR 571, [2007] Crim LR 476.

5 As to the determination of a person's age see the Children and Young Persons Act 1933 s 99; and CHILDREN AND YOUNG PERSONS vol 10 (2012) PARA 1206.

6 Ie under the Powers of Criminal Courts (Sentencing) Act 2000 s 13.

7 Powers of Criminal Courts (Sentencing) Act 2000 s 14(2). The conviction is at the date of the making of an order, not at that of the subsequent passing of sentence: *R v Thomas* (1962) 46 Cr App Rep 466, CA.

8 For these purposes, 'enactment' includes an enactment contained in a local Act: Powers of Criminal Courts (Sentencing) Act 2000 s 14(5).

9 For these purposes, 'instrument' means an instrument having effect by virtue of an Act: Powers of Criminal Courts (Sentencing) Act 2000 s 14(5).

10 A recommendation for deportation is not a disqualification or disability: *R v Akan* [1973] QB 491, [1972] 3 All ER 285, CA. See also *R v Secretary of State for the Home Department, ex p Thornton* [1987] QB 36, [1986] 2 All ER 641, CA (punishments under the Police Discipline Regulations 1977, SI 1977/580, reg 22 (revoked), including dismissal of officer or requirement that he resign, did not amount to imposition of disqualification or disability).

11 Powers of Criminal Courts (Sentencing) Act 2000 s 14(3)(a). This does not prevent a disciplinary tribunal from hearing a complaint based on the matters which formed the basis of the conviction: *R v Statutory Committee of the Pharmaceutical Society of Great Britain, ex p Pharmaceutical Society of Great Britain* [1981] 2 All ER 805, [1981] 1 WLR 886, DC. As to disqualification on conviction see PARA 316.

12 Powers of Criminal Courts (Sentencing) Act 2000 s 14(3)(b). See note 11.

13 Powers of Criminal Courts (Sentencing) Act 2000 s 14(4)(a).

14 Powers of Criminal Courts (Sentencing) Act 2000 s 14(4)(b).

(2) BINDING OVER TO COME UP FOR JUDGMENT

446. Powers of the Crown Court. The Crown Court has power, instead of passing sentence, to respite judgment and require a person who has been convicted of any offence, the penalty for which is not fixed by law, to enter into recognisances, with or without sureties, to come up for judgment when called upon[1]. If the Crown Court is considering binding over an individual to come up for judgment, it should specify any conditions with which the individual is to comply in the meantime and not specify that the individual is to be of good behaviour[2]. A defendant dealt with by binding over to come up for judgment is deemed to be for all purposes a person convicted on indictment[3].

  There are no reports of this power being used recently.

1   See the Senior Courts Act 1981 s 79(2); and COURTS AND TRIBUNALS vol 24 (2010) PARA 720.
    If it is proposed to bring the defendant up for judgment, a notice must be given to him and his
    bail: *R v David* [1939] 1 All ER 782, 27 Cr App Rep 50, CCA.

2   *Criminal Practice Directions 2015* [2015] EWCA Crim 1567, [2015] All ER (D) 134 (Sep)
    CPD VII Sentencing J: Binding Over Orders and Conditional Discharges J.17. As to
    recognisance to keep the peace see further PARAS 447–453. This power, known as the 'common
    law bind over', may be exercised in lieu of sentence only: *R v Ayu* [1958] 3 All ER 636, 43 Cr
    App Rep 31, CCA. It may be used to return an offender to Ireland and keep him there: *R v
    Flaherty* [1958] Crim LR 556, CCA; *R v McCartan* [1958] 3 All ER 140, 42 Cr App Rep 262,
    CCA; *R v Hodges* (1967) 51 Cr App Rep 361, CA. The power to keep an offender out of the
    jurisdiction is one which should be used very sparingly. It is very seldom to be done if the
    offender does not consent and, save in exceptional circumstances (see eg *R v Hodges*), it should
    be used only to ensure that the offender goes to a country of which he is a citizen or in which he
    is habitually resident or where there are very special circumstances in which the receiving
    country is prepared to take him for his own well-being: *R v Ayu*; *R v Williams (Carl)* [1982]
    3 All ER 1092, 75 Cr App Rep 378, CA.
        A magistrates' court may not bind over a defendant to come up for judgment: *R v Crown
    Court at Acton, ex p Bewley* (1988) 10 Cr App Rep (S) 105, DC.

3   *Jephson v Barker and Redman* (1886) 3 TLR 40; *R v Abrahams* (1952) 36 Cr App Rep 147,
    CCA. This is in contrast to the position of the defendant absolutely or conditionally discharged:
    see PARA 445.

(3) BINDING OVER TO KEEP THE PEACE

447. Recognisances to keep the peace at common law. A person convicted of
any indictable offence, whether at common law or by statute, may be ordered, in
addition to or in substitution for any other penalty, to enter into a recognisance,
with or without sureties, to keep the peace or to be of good behaviour for a
reasonable time to be specified in the order, and to be imprisoned until the
recognisances are entered into[1]. It is doubtful whether or not there is power to
order a person to enter into a recognisance for an unlimited period of time, but
the established practice has been to impose a time limit, and this practice ought
to be followed[2]. A court intending to impose a substantial recognisance must
give the defendant an opportunity to make representations and must inquire into
his means before making the order[3]. If the conditions of a recognisance are
broken, it may be forfeited[4].

There is a presumption against the validity of a recognisance entered into by a
person who was at the time mentally disordered[5]. A magistrates' court may bind
over a person under 18 who consents to be bound over[6], although if such a
person refuses to enter into a recognisance, there is no such power to do so[7]. If
the offender is aged 18 or over and under 21 and refuses to enter into a
recognisance, the court has power to commit him[8] to be detained[9].

Magistrates may bind a person over to be of good behaviour to prevent an
apprehended offence, and it is not necessary in such a case for the applicant to
swear that he goes in fear of the person against whom the application is made[10].
Before imposing a binding over order, the court must be satisfied that a breach of
the peace involving violence or an imminent threat of violence has occurred or
that there is a real risk of violence in the future: such violence may be perpetrated
by the individual who will be subject to the order or by a third party as a natural
consequence of the individual's conduct[11]. An order of a magistrates' court
requiring a person to find sureties to keep the peace and to be of good behaviour
should show on its face facts sufficient to give the justices jurisdiction to make
the order, especially when there has been no conviction[12].

It has been held that the power to bind over to prevent an apprehended
offence is exercisable, even though no criminal offence has been committed, if

there was conduct contra bonos mores (ie conduct which has the property of being wrong rather than right in the judgment of the majority of contemporary citizens), and the magistrates have some cause to believe that without a binding over the defendant might repeat his conduct[13].

The power to bind over to be of good behaviour does not meet the requirement of certainty for the purposes of the protection of freedom of expression under the European Convention on Human Rights[14] because it fails to give any reliable indication of what would constitute a breach of the order[15], and in light of this judgment courts should no longer bind an individual over 'to be of good behaviour', and rather than binding an individual over to 'keep the peace' in general terms, the court should identify the specific conduct or activity from which the individual must refrain[16]. When making an order binding an individual over to refrain from specified types of conduct or activities, the details of that conduct or those activities should be specified by the court in a written order, served on all relevant parties, and the court should state its reasons for the making of the order, its length and the amount of the recognisance[17]. The length of the order should be proportionate to the harm sought to be avoided and should not generally exceed 12 months[18]. If there is any possibility that an individual will refuse to enter a recognisance, the court should consider whether there are any appropriate alternatives to a binding over order (for example, continuing with a prosecution): where there are no appropriate alternatives and the individual continues to refuse to enter into the recognisance, the court may commit the individual to custody[19].

1   *Dunn v R* (1848) 12 QB 1031, Ex Ch; *R v Trueman* [1913] 3 KB 164, 9 Cr App Rep 20, CCA (conviction under the Libel Act 1843 s 5 (repealed)). See also *R v Hart* (1809) 30 State Tr 1325 at 1343–1344, HL.

2   *R v Edgar* (1913) 9 Cr App Rep 13, CCA. Cf *Prickett v Gratrex* (1846) 8 QB 1020.

3   *R v Central Criminal Court, ex p Boulding* [1984] QB 813, 79 Cr App Rep 100, DC; *R v Atkinson* (1988) 10 Cr App Rep (S) 470, [1989] Crim LR 457, CA; *R v Crown Court at Nottingham, ex p Brace* (1989) 154 JP 161, CA. See also the *Criminal Practice Directions 2015* [2015] EWCA Crim 1567, [2015] All ER (D) 134 (Sep) CPD VII Sentencing J: Binding Over Orders and Conditional Discharges J.5–J.7.

4   See PARA 449. As to the powers and duties of a court by which a recognisance is forfeited see PARA 186. See also *R v Crown Court at Ipswich, ex p Eris* (1989) Times, 23 February, DC (a judge is not entitled to bind over a defendant to be of good behaviour simply because he has used his criminal trial as a vehicle for airing his views about nuclear power etc; the appropriate response is judicial control of the trial and, if necessary, resort to the procedure for contempt of court).

5   *R v Green-Emmott* (1931) 144 LT 671, 22 Cr App Rep 183, CCA.

6   *Conlan v Oxford* (1983) 79 Cr App Rep 157, 5 Cr App Rep (S) 237, DC.

7   *Veater v G* [1981] 2 All ER 304, sub nom *Veater v Glennon* (1981) 72 Cr App Rep 331, DC).

8   Ie under the Powers of Criminal Courts (Sentencing) Act 2000 s 108(1)(a) (see PARA 551).

9   *Howley v Oxford* (1985) 81 Cr App Rep 246, DC. As to the statutory power to bind over see PARA 448. As to the determination of a person's age see the Children and Young Persons Act 1933 s 99; and CHILDREN AND YOUNG PERSONS vol 10 (2012) PARA 1206.

10   See *R v Wilkins* [1907] 2 KB 380, DC; *Lansbury v Riley* [1914] 3 KB 229, DC; followed in *R v Sandbach, ex p Williams* [1935] 2 KB 192, DC.

11   See the *Criminal Practice Directions 2015* [2015] EWCA Crim 1567, [2015] All ER (D) 134 (Sep) CPD VII Sentencing J: Binding Over Orders and Conditional Discharges J.2.

12   *R (Boylan) v Londonderry County Justices* [1912] 2 IR 374; *R (Mulholland) v Monaghan Justices* [1914] 2 IR 156. See, however, *Hashman v United Kingdom* (Application 25594/94) (2000) 30 EHRR 241, 8 BHRC 104, [2000] Crim LR 185, ECtHR; *Steel v United Kingdom* (1998) 28 EHRR 603, ECtHR.

     Whether the origin of the jurisdiction of justices is derived from the common law, the commission of the peace, or the Justices of the Peace Act 1361 (34 Edw 3 c 1: see MAGISTRATES vol 71 (2013) PARA 402), the practice of making these orders for the purpose of preventing apprehended breaches of the peace is too well established to allow of its propriety being now questioned: *Lansbury v Riley* [1914] 3 KB 229, DC. A magistrates' court may exercise its powers if there is an incitement to commit breaches of the peace generally; it is not necessary that a particular person be threatened: *Lansbury v Riley*. The order may be made if it is apprehended that the defendant will break the law, even though there is no apprehension of violence and even though he may become liable, on forfeiture of the recognisance, to a penalty greater than that fixed for the offence of which he has been convicted (*R v Sandbach, ex p Williams*), and may be made even if the occasion upon which the breach of the peace was feared has passed (*R v Little and Dunning, ex p Wise* (1909) 74 JP 7, DC). Justices have power to bind over a defendant for the future if his disorderly conduct is likely to result in violence, even if no offence has been committed: *R v Morpeth Ward Justices, ex p Ward* (1992) 95 Cr App Rep 215, DC.

13 See *Hughes v Holley* [1987] Crim LR 253, (1986) 86 Cr App Rep 130, DC; see also *R v South Molton Justices, ex p Ankerson* [1988] 3 All ER 989, [1989] 1 WLR 40, DC (not followed, in relation to the requirements for consent in *R v Crown Court at Lincoln, ex p Jude* [1997] 3 All ER 737, [1998] 1 WLR 24, DC)): this is however now doubtful (see *Hashman v United Kingdom* (Application 25594/94) (2000) 30 EHRR 241, 8 BHRC 104, [2000] Crim LR 185, ECtHR, in which it was held that the concept of 'contra bonos mores' was insufficiently precise to comply with the requirements of the Convention for the Protection of Human Rights and Fundamental Freedoms (Rome, 4 November 1950; TS 71 (1953); Cmd 8969) (the European Convention on Human Rights) art 10 (freedom of expression: see RIGHTS AND FREEDOMS vol 88A (2013) PARAS 398–435).

14 Ie under the European Convention on Human Rights art 10.

15 *Hashman v United Kingdom* (Application 25594/94) (2000) 30 EHRR 241, 8 BHRC 104, [2000] Crim LR 185, ECtHR. Cf, however, *Steel v United Kingdom* (1998) 28 EHRR 603, [1998] Crim LR 893 ECtHR (power to bind over to keep the peace meets the requirement of certainty under the Convention).

16 See the *Criminal Practice Directions 2015* [2015] EWCA Crim 1567, [2015] All ER (D) 134 (Sep) CPD VII Sentencing J: Binding Over Orders and Conditional Discharges J.3.

17 See the *Criminal Practice Directions 2015* [2015] EWCA Crim 1567, [2015] All ER (D) 134 (Sep) CPD VII Sentencing J: Binding Over Orders and Conditional Discharges J.4.

18 See the *Criminal Practice Directions 2015* [2015] EWCA Crim 1567, [2015] All ER (D) 134 (Sep) CPD VII Sentencing J: Binding Over Orders and Conditional Discharges J.4.

19 See the *Criminal Practice Directions 2015* [2015] EWCA Crim 1567, [2015] All ER (D) 134 (Sep) CPD VII Sentencing J: Binding Over Orders and Conditional Discharges J.13.

448. Recognisances to keep the peace by statute. Any court of record[1] having a criminal jurisdiction has, as ancillary to that jurisdiction, the power to bind over to keep the peace, and power to bind over to be of good behaviour[2], a person who, or whose case, is before the court[3], by requiring him to enter into his own recognisance or to find sureties or both, and committing him to prison if he does not comply[4].

The power of a magistrates' court[5] on the complaint of any person to adjudge any other person to enter into a recognisance, with or without sureties, to keep the peace or to be of good behaviour towards the complainant is exercised by order on complaint[6], and the facts must be ascertained and the case decided in the same manner as in the hearing of any other complaint[7]. Alternatively, he may be brought before the court following his arrest for a breach of the peace[8], or may simply be present before the court[9]. Before magistrates may exercise their power under these provisions to bind over a defendant to keep the peace, it must be proved on the criminal standard of proof that there has been violence or threats of violence, and it suffices that a consequence of the defendant's conduct is that there is a real risk of violence by a third party[10]. The order should show on its face facts sufficient to give the court jurisdiction to make the order, especially when there has been no conviction[11]. A magistrates' court should require the recognisance to be for a definite period[12].

Consent is not a prerequisite to making an order for a bind over[13]. Where any person ordered by a magistrates' court[14] to enter into a recognisance, with or without sureties, to keep the peace or to be of good behaviour fails to comply with the order, the court may commit him to custody for a period not exceeding six months or until he sooner complies with the order[15]. Where a child or young person is convicted of an offence, the magistrates' court has the power, with the consent of the offender's parent or guardian, to order the parent or guardian to enter into a recognisance to take proper care of him and exercise proper control over him[16].

1   The Crown Court, High Court and Court of Appeal are courts of record: see COURTS AND TRIBUNALS vol 24 (2010) PARA 618.

2   See PARA 447.

3   A person who has attended court to give evidence but who has not been called as a witness is not 'a person who, or whose case, is before the court': *R v Crown Court at Swindon, ex p Pawittar Singh* [1984] 1 All ER 941, 79 Cr App Rep 137, DC. See also *R v Crown Court at Kingston-upon-Thames, ex p Guarino* [1986] Crim LR 325, DC.

4   Justices of the Peace Act 1968 s 1(7) (amended by the Administration of Justice Act 1973 Sch 5 Pt II). Where a court is minded to bind over a person who has appeared before it either as a complainant or a witness, the court must inform the person concerned and give him the opportunity of being heard: *Sheldon v Bromfield Justices* [1964] 2 QB 573, [1964] 2 All ER 131, DC; *R v Hendon Justices, ex p Gorchein* [1974] 1 All ER 168, [1973] 1 WLR 1502, DC. It is not essential to do so in the case of an acquitted defendant but it is good practice: *R v Woking Justices, ex p Gossage* [1973] QB 448, [1973] 2 All ER 621, DC. See also *R v Central Criminal Court, ex p Boulding* [1984] QB 813, 79 Cr App Rep 100, DC; and PARA 447. An order can be made at the court's own motion at any stage of proceedings before the court if it emerges in evidence that there is a likelihood of a breach of the peace: *R v Crown Court at Swindon, ex p Pawittar Singh* [1984] 1 All ER 941, 79 Cr App Rep 137, DC.

5   As to the meaning of 'magistrates' court' see MAGISTRATES vol 71 (2013) PARA 470.

6   Magistrates' Courts Act 1980 s 115(1). The prescribed form of commission of the peace requires justices 'to cause to come before you and to deal according to law with all persons against whom anything is alleged giving just cause under any rule of law or enactment for the time being in force why they should find security to keep the peace or be of good behaviour towards us and our people ...': see the Crown Office (Forms and Proclamations Rules) Order 1992, SI 1992/1730, Schedule Pt II Form A (amended by SI 2005/617). Where a complaint is made under the Magistrates' Courts Act 1980 s 115, the power of the court to remand the defendant for non-appearance under s 55(5) (see MAGISTRATES vol 71 (2013) PARA 550) is not subject to the restrictions imposed by s 55(6): s 115(2). A binding over is not a conviction: *R v County of London Quarter Sessions Appeal Committee, ex p Metropolitan Police Comrs* [1948] 1 KB 670, [1948] 1 All ER 72, DC; *R v London Sessions, ex p Beaumont* [1951] 1 KB 557, [1951] 1 All ER 232, DC. As to the method of taking and recording recognisances see the Magistrates' Courts Rules 1981, SI 1981/552, r 86 (amended by SI 2001/167; SI 2001/610; SI 2003/1236; SI 2005/617); and for the form of order of recognisance to keep the peace see the Magistrates' Courts (Forms) Rules 1981, SI 1981/553, Sch 2 Form 115.

     Proceedings for binding over a person to keep the peace may comply with the requirements of the Convention for the Protection of Human Rights and Fundamental Freedoms (Rome, 4 November 1950; TS 71 (1953); Cmd 8969) (the European Convention on Human Rights) art 5 (right to liberty and security: see RIGHTS AND FREEDOMS vol 88A (2013) PARAS 210–242) and art 6 (right to a fair hearing: see RIGHTS AND FREEDOMS vol 88A (2013) PARAS 243–300) as the legal rules relevant to the concept of breach of the peace provide sufficient guidance and are formulated with the degree of precision required by the Convention: *Steel v United Kingdom* (1998) 5 BHRC 339, ECtHR. However, a binding-over order to prevent future conduct which is contra bonos mores (see PARA 447) does not comply with the Convention since the expression 'to be of good behaviour' is particularly imprecise and offers little guidance to the person bound over as to the type of conduct which will amount to a breach of the order where the defendant has not been charged with a criminal offence and has not been found to have breached the peace: see *Hashman v United Kingdom* (Application 25594/94) (2000) 30 EHRR 241, 8 BHRC 104, [2000] Crim LR 185, ECtHR; and PARA 447.

7   See MAGISTRATES vol 71 (2013) PARA 564 et seq. Before imposing a binding over order, the court must be satisfied that a breach of the peace involving violence or an imminent threat of violence has occurred or that there is a real risk of violence in the future: such violence may be perpetrated by the individual who will be subject to the order or by a third party as a natural consequence of the individual's conduct: see the *Criminal Practice Directions 2015* [2015]

EWCA Crim 1567, [2015] All ER (D) 134 (Sep) CPD VII Sentencing J: Binding Over Orders and Conditional Discharges J.2. The jurisdiction of the justices does not depend on the issue of a summons, nor the existence of a complaint in the prescribed form: *R v Coventry Magistrates' Court, ex p Crown Prosecution* Service (1996) 160 JP 741, [1996] Crim LR 723, DC. As to the right of appeal to the Crown Court see MAGISTRATES vol 71 (2013) PARA 701. As to enforcement of the order and forfeiture of the recognisance see PARAS 452–453. As the jurisdiction may no longer be exercised without notice, no action for malicious prosecution will lie at the suit of a person required to enter into a recognisance: *Everett v Ribbands* [1952] 2 QB 198, [1952] 1 All ER 823, CA. See TORT vol 97 (2010) PARA 627.

8 As to the power of arrest for breach of the peace see POLICE AND INVESTIGATORY POWERS vol 84A (2013) PARA 493. It is doubtful there is any procedure at common law and in practice the drawing up of a 'charge sheet' or other such document can be construed as a complaint under the Magistrates' Courts Act 1980 s 115: *DPP v Speede* [1998] 2 Cr App Rep 108, DC.

9 No formal complaint is necessary if the party is already before the court (*Ex p Davis* (1871) 35 JP 551 per Blackburn J; *R v Hughes* (1879) 4 QBD 614 at 625 per Hawkins J), and a complainant may himself be bound over without being summoned (*R v Wilkins* [1907] 2 KB 380, DC). If the justices are thinking of binding over a complainant or a witness, they should warn him and give him an opportunity to make representations (*Sheldon v Bromfield Justices* [1964] 2 QB 573, [1964] 2 All ER 131, DC; *R v Hendon Justices, ex p Gorchein* [1974] 1 All ER 168, [1973] 1 WLR 1502, DC), but such a warning is not necessary where the person to be bound over is an acquitted defendant (*R v Woking Justices, ex p Gossage* [1973] QB 448, [1973] 2 All ER 621, DC), or has committed the misconduct justifying the order in the face of the court (*R v North London Metropolitan Magistrate, ex p Haywood, R v North London Metropolitan Magistrate, ex p Brown* [1973] 3 All ER 50, [1973] 1 WLR 965, DC).

Whereas an order for binding over under the Magistrates' Courts Act 1980 s 115 may only be made after the case has been heard out completely, an order under the Justices of the Peace Act 1361 (see MAGISTRATES vol 71 (2013) PARAS 401, 402) may be made at any time during the proceedings subject to an opportunity being given to the applicant or his advisers to argue against it; nevertheless there is no jurisdiction to make an order unless the proceedings have reached the stage where it emerges that there might be a breach of the peace in the future: *R v Aubrey-Fletcher, ex p Thompson* [1969] 2 All ER 846, [1969] 1 WLR 872, DC.

10 *Percy v DPP* [1995] 3 All ER 124, [1995] 1 WLR 1382, DC.

11 *R (Boylan) v Londonderry County Justices* [1912] 2 IR 374; *R (Mulholland) v Monaghan Justices* [1914] 2 IR 156.

12 See *R v Edgar* (1913) 77 JP 356.

13 *R v Woking Justices, ex p Gossage* [1973] QB 448, [1973] 2 All ER 621, DC; *R v Crown Court at Lincoln, ex p Jude* [1997] 3 All ER 737, [1998] 1 WLR 24, DC, not following *R v South Molton Justices, ex p Ankerson* [1988] 3 All ER 989, [1989] 1 WLR 40, DC.

14 Ie under the Magistrates' Courts Act 1980 s 115(1): see the text and notes 5–6.

15 Magistrates' Courts Act 1980 s 115(3). See *Veater v G* [1981] 2 All ER 304, [1981] 1 WLR 567, DC. See further PARA 450. The court has power to bind over an offender aged under 18 (and who is not liable to imprisonment or detention under what is now the Powers of Criminal Courts (Sentencing) Act 2000 s 108 (see MAGISTRATES vol 71 (2013) PARA 650)) with his consent either under his own recognisance or by requiring him to provide sureties: *Conlan v Oxford* (1983) 148 JP 97, DC. As to the determination of a person's age see the Children and Young Persons Act 1933 s 99; and CHILDREN AND YOUNG PERSONS vol 10 (2012) PARA 1206.

16 See the Powers of Criminal Courts (Sentencing) Act 2000 s 150; and CHILDREN AND YOUNG PERSONS vol 10 (2012) PARA 1299.

449. Breach of condition of recognisance. If a person fails to satisfy the condition of a recognisance it may be forfeited[1]. Breach of recognisance which renders a person liable to be sentenced for an offence of which he was convicted when he entered into the recognisance must be proved as any other allegation of fact is proved in a criminal court[2]. However, where a breach of recognisance only renders a person liable to forfeiture of the recognisance, the civil standard of proof applies[3]. An appeal lies to the Court of Appeal from a decision of the Crown Court that a defendant has broken a recognisance[4].

1 As to the powers and duties of a court by which a recognisance is forfeited see PARA 186.

2 *R v Smith* [1925] 1 KB 603, 18 Cr App Rep 170, CCA; *R v McGarry* (1945) 30 Cr App Rep 187, CCA; *R v McGregor* [1945] 2 All ER 180, 30 Cr App Rep 155, CCA. In such cases counsel

for the prosecution should be instructed: *R v McGregor*. In *R v David* [1939] 1 All ER 782, 27 Cr App Rep 50, CCA, it was held that the issue as to whether there has been a breach is not one for a jury. Where the prosecution relies on a conviction during the period of the recognisance as constituting the breach, that conviction should, it seems, be strictly proved: see *R v Pine* (1932) 24 Cr App Rep 10, CCA. See also *R v Philbert* [1973] Crim LR 129, CA (breach of condition added to common law bind over that offender returned to West Indies; should be inquiry as to whether breach deliberate or caused by lack of means). The defendant must be given the opportunity of giving evidence in answer to the allegation that he has committed a breach of his recognisance: *R v Pine*. The Crown Court should inform any magistrates' court dealing with an offender of any pending case of breach of recognisance, and the latter court should inquire whether the Crown Court wishes it to take the breach into consideration in passing sentence: *R v Tarbotton* [1942] 1 All ER 198, 28 Cr App Rep 92, CCA.

3   *R v Marlow Justices, ex p O'Sullivan* [1984] QB 381, 78 Cr App Rep 13, DC (doubted, obiter, in *Percy v DPP* [1995] 3 All ER 124 at 134, DC, per Collins J). See also the *Criminal Practice Directions 2015* [2015] EWCA Crim 1567, [2015] All ER (D) 134 (Sep) CPD VII Sentencing J: Binding Over Orders and Conditional Discharges J.9.

4   *R v Smith* [1925] 1 KB 603, 18 Cr App Rep 170, CCA; *R v McGarry* (1945) 30 Cr App Rep 187, CCA; *R v McGregor* [1945] 2 All ER 180, 30 Cr App Rep 155, CCA.

450.   Dispensing with defendant's recognisance. Where a magistrates' court[1] has committed a person to custody in default of finding sureties, the court may, on application by or on behalf of the person committed, and after hearing fresh evidence, reduce the amount in which it is proposed that any surety should be bound or dispense with any of the sureties or otherwise deal with the case as it thinks just[2]. However, this does not apply in relation to a person granted bail in criminal proceedings[3].

1   As to the meaning of 'magistrates' court' see MAGISTRATES vol 71 (2013) PARA 470.

2   Magistrates' Courts Act 1980 s 118(1). These powers are exercisable by any magistrates' court for the same local justice area as the court which made the order: see s 148(2); and MAGISTRATES vol 71 (2013) PARA 470. Where a person has been committed to custody in default of finding sureties and the order to find sureties was made at the instance of another person, an application under s 118 is made by complaint against that other person: Magistrates' Courts Rules 1981, SI 1981/552, r 83. For the forms of summons to vary sureties and recognisance see the Magistrates' Courts (Forms) Rules 1981, SI 1981/553, Sch 2 Forms 116, 117; and MAGISTRATES vol 71 (2013) PARA 403.

The amount of a recognisance fixed by the High Court or the Crown Court may not be altered by a magistrates' court: see the Magistrates' Courts Act 1980 s 119(3) (amended by the Criminal Justice Act 1982 Sch 14 para 55).

3   Magistrates' Courts Act 1980 s 118(2). Magistrates' courts have the power to vary the conditions of bail in criminal proceedings: see the Bail Act 1976 s 3(8); and CRIMINAL PROCEDURE vol 27 (2015) PARA 73.

451.   Fixing and taking recognisances. Where a magistrates' court[1] has power to take any recognisance, the court may, instead of taking it, fix the amount[2] in which the principal and his sureties[3], if any, are to be bound[4]. Thereafter the recognisance may be taken by any such person as may be prescribed[5], namely any justice of the peace, justices' clerk, designated officer for a magistrates' court, police officer not below the rank of inspector, officer in charge of a police station, or, in cases where the person to be bound is in a prison or other place of detention, the governor or keeper of that prison or place[6]. Where the recognisance of any person committed to custody by a magistrates' court or of any surety of such a person is taken by any person other than the court which committed him to custody, the person taking the recognisance must send it to the designated officer for that court or, if the person committed has been committed for trial before the Crown Court, to the appropriate officer of the Crown Court[7].

1   As to the meaning of 'magistrates' court' see MAGISTRATES vol 71 (2013) PARA 470.

2 The designated officer for a magistrates' court which has fixed the amount in which a person (including any surety) is to be bound by a recognisance or, under the Bail Act 1976 s 3(5), (6), (6A) (see CRIMINAL PROCEDURE vol 27 (2015) PARA 73), imposed any requirement to be complied with before a person's release on bail or any condition of bail must issue a certificate showing the amount and conditions, if any, of the recognisance, or as the case may be, containing a statement of the requirement or condition of bail; and a person authorised to take the recognisance or do anything in relation to the compliance with such requirement or condition of bail must not be required to take or do it without production of such a certificate: Magistrates' Courts Rules 1981, SI 1981/552, r 86(2) (substituted by SI 1984/1552; and amended by SI 2001/610; SI 2003/1236; SI 2005/617).

3 In criminal proceedings regard may be had (amongst other things), when considering the suitability of a proposed surety to the surety's financial resources, character, previous convictions and proximity to the person for whom he is to be surety: see the Bail Act 1976 s 8(2); and CRIMINAL PROCEDURE vol 27 (2015) PARA 74. Where a surety seeks to enter into his recognisance before any person authorised to take it, but that person declines to take his recognisance because he is not satisfied of the surety's suitability, the surety may apply to the court which fixed the amount of the recognisance in which the surety was to be bound, or to a magistrates' court, for that court to take his recognisance and that court must, if satisfied of his suitability, take his recognisance: see s 8(5); and CRIMINAL PROCEDURE vol 27 (2015) PARA 74.

4 Magistrates' Courts Act 1980 s 119(1). Nothing in s 119 enables a magistrates' court to alter the amount of recognisance fixed by the High Court or the Crown Court: s 119(3) (amended by the Criminal Justice Act 1982 Sch 14 para 55). As to the enforcement of a recognisance see PARA 447 et seq.

5 Magistrates' Courts Act 1980 s 119(1). Where a recognisance is entered into otherwise than before the court that fixed the amount of it, the same consequences follow as if it had been entered into before that court: s 119(2). References in any Act to the court before which a recognisance was entered into are to be construed accordingly: s 119(2).

6 See the Bail Act 1976 s 8(4)(a); CRIMINAL PROCEDURE vol 27 (2015) PARA 74; and the Magistrates' Courts Rules 1981, SI 1981/552, r 86(1) (amended by SI 2001/167; SI 2005/617). If any person proposed as a surety for a person committed to custody by a magistrates' court produces to the prison governor or keeper of the prison or other place of detention in which the person so committed is detained a certificate to the effect that he is acceptable as a surety, signed by any of the justices composing the court or the clerk of the court and signed in the margin by the person proposed as surety, the governor or keeper must take the recognisance of the person so proposed: Magistrates' Courts Rules 1981, SI 1981/552, r 86(3) (amended by SI 2003/1236).

Where a magistrates' court has, with a view to the release on bail of a person in custody, fixed the amount in which he or any surety of such a person is to be bound or under the Bail Act 1976 s 3(5), (6) or (6A) (see CRIMINAL PROCEDURE vol 27 (2015) PARAS 72, 73) in criminal proceedings, imposed any requirement to be complied with before his release or any condition of bail: (1) the designated officer for the court must give notice to the governor or keeper of the prison or place where that person is detained by sending him such a certificate as is mentioned in the Magistrates' Courts Rules 1981, SI 1981/552, r 86(2) (see note 2); (2) any person authorised to take recognisance of a surety or do anything in relation to the compliance with such requirement must, on taking or doing it, send notice by post to the governor or keeper and, in the case of recognisance of a surety, must give a copy of the notice to the surety: r 87 (amended by SI 1984/1552; SI 2001/610; SI 2003/1236). The governor must then take the defendant's recognisance (if not already taken) and release him, unless he is held for some other cause: see the Magistrates' Courts Rules 1981, SI 1981/552, r 88.

7 Magistrates' Courts Rules 1981, SI 1981/552, r 86(4) (amended by SI 2001/610; SI 2005/617).

452. Discharge of recognisance on complaint of surety. On complaint being made to a justice of the peace by a surety to a recognisance to keep the peace or to be of good behaviour entered into before a magistrates' court[1] that the person bound as principal has been, or is about to be, guilty of conduct constituting a breach of the conditions of the recognisance, the justice may issue a warrant to arrest the principal and bring him before a magistrates' court or a summons requiring the principal to appear before such a court[2]. The magistrates' court before which the principal appears or is brought may, unless it adjudges the recognisance to be forfeited[3], order the recognisance to be discharged[4] and order the principal to enter into a new recognisance, with or without sureties, to keep the peace or to be of good behaviour[5].

1   As to the meaning of 'magistrates' court' see MAGISTRATES vol 71 (2013) PARA 470.

2   Magistrates' Courts Act 1980 s 116(1) (amended by the Courts Act 2003 Sch 8 para 236). The warrant must not, however, be issued unless the complaint is in writing and substantiated on oath: Magistrates' Courts Act 1980 s 116(1).

3   As to forfeiture of recognisance see PARA 453.

4   Where a magistrates' court acting in any local justice area makes an order under the Magistrates' Courts Act 1980 s 116 discharging a recognisance entered into before a magistrates' court acting for any other local justice area, the designated officer for the court that orders the recognisance to be discharged must send a copy of the order to the designated officer for the court acting for that other local justice area: Magistrates' Courts Rules, 1981, SI 1981/552, r 82 (amended by SI 2001/610; SI 2005/617).

5   Magistrates' Courts Act 1980 s 116(2).

453. Forfeiture of recognisance. Where a recognisance to keep the peace or to be of good behaviour has been entered into before a magistrates' court[1] or any recognisance is conditioned for the appearance of a person before a magistrates' court, or for his doing any other thing connected with a proceeding before it[2], and the recognisance appears to the magistrates' court to be forfeited, the court may declare it to be forfeited[3] and adjudge each person bound by it, whether as principal or surety to pay the sum in which he is bound[4]. Where, in the case of a recognisance which is conditioned for the appearance of an accused before a magistrates' court, the accused fails to appear in accordance with the condition, the magistrates' court may declare the recognisance to be forfeited[5], and issue a summons directed to each person bound by the recognisance as surety requiring him to appear before the court on a date specified in the summons to show cause why he should not be adjudged to pay the sum in which he is bound[6], and on that date the magistrates' court may proceed in the absence of any surety if it is satisfied that he has been served with the summons[7]. The magistrates' court which declares the recognisance to be forfeited may, instead of adjudging any person to pay the whole sum in which he is bound, adjudge him to pay part only of the sum or remit the sum[8].

In exercising their discretion under these provisions justices should take into consideration the extent to which the surety has been at fault and should take into account only his own means[9]. The onus is on the surety to show that he was not at fault and to show reasons why the penalty should not be enforced[10]. The burden is a heavy one as the court will presume that the full amount of the surety should be forfeited unless it appears fair that a lesser sum be forfeited or none at all[11].

A person brought before a magistrates' court on an allegation that he has done any act by which a recognisance entered into by him is liable to be forfeited must be told exactly what the breach complained of is, and there should be precise evidence of it[12].

1   Magistrates' Courts Act 1980 s 120(1)(a) (s 120(1), (2) substituted, s 120(1A) added, by the Crime and Disorder Act 1998 s 55). As to the meaning of 'magistrates' court' see MAGISTRATES vol 71 (2013) PARA 470.

2   Magistrates' Courts Act 1980 s 120(1)(b) (as substituted: see note 1).

3   Magistrates' Courts Act 1980 s 120(2)(a) (as substituted: see note 1). Where a recognisance is conditioned to keep the peace or to be of good behaviour, the magistrates' court must not declare it forfeited except by order made on complaint: s 120(2) proviso (as so substituted).

4   Magistrates' Courts Act 1980 s 120(2)(b) (as substituted: see note 1). A recognisance mentioned in s 120 must not be enforced otherwise than in accordance with s 120, and accordingly must not be transmitted to the Crown Court, nor may its forfeiture be certified to the Crown Court: s 120(5).

5   Magistrates' Courts Act 1980 s 120(1A)(a) (as added: see note 1).

6   Magistrates' Courts Act 1980 s 120(1A)(b) (as added: see note 1).

7   Magistrates' Courts Act 1980 s 120(1A) (as added: see note 1).

8   Magistrates' Courts Act 1980 s 120(3). The sum should not exceed that which a surety could reasonably pay within three years: *R v Crown at Birmingham, ex p Rashid Ali; R v Bristol Magistrates' Court, ex p Davies; R v Immigration Appellate Authority, ex p Davies* (1998) 163 JP 145, [1999] Crim LR 504. Justices have a wide power under the Magistrates' Courts Act 1980 s 120 in deciding whether to remit in whole or part a recognisance: *Kaur v DPP* (1999) Times, 5 October, DC.

    Payment of any sum adjudged to be paid under the Magistrates' Courts Act 1980 s 120, including any costs awarded against the defendant, may be enforced, and any such sum must be applied, as if it were a fine and as if the adjudication were a summary conviction of an offence not punishable with imprisonment, and so much of s 85(1) (see MAGISTRATES vol 71 (2013) PARA 674) as empowers a magistrates' court to remit fines does not apply to the sum but so much of it as relates to remission after a term of imprisonment has been imposed applies: s 120(4). However, at any time before the issue of a warrant of commitment to enforce payment of the sum, or before the sale of goods under a warrant of control, to satisfy the sum, the magistrates' court may remit the whole or any part of the sum either absolutely or on such conditions as the court thinks just: s 120(4) (amended by the Tribunals, Courts and Enforcement Act 2007 Sch 13 paras 45, 46).

9   *R v Southampton Justices, ex p Green* [1976] QB 11, [1975] 2 All ER 1073, CA; *R v Horseferry Road Magistrates' Court, ex p Pearson* [1976] 2 All ER 264, [1976] 1 WLR 511, DC; *R v Tottenham Magistrates' Court, ex p Riccardi* (1977) 66 Cr App Rep 150, DC.

10   *R v Southampton Justices, ex p Corker* (1976) 120 Sol Jo 214, DC.

11   *R v Waltham Forest Justices, ex p Parfrey* (1980) 2 Cr App Rep (S) 208, DC; *R v Crown Court at York, ex p Coleman and How* (1987) 86 Cr App Rep 151, [1987] Crim LR 761, DC; *R v Uxbridge Justices, ex p Heward-Mills* [1983] 1 All ER 530, [1983] 1 WLR 56 (obligation of the court to explain to an unrepresented surety that the burden of satisfying the court that the full recognisance should not be forfeited rests on him and that he must lay before the court evidence of his means and lack of culpability). See also *R v Crown Court at Maidstone, ex p Lever; R v Crown Court at Maidstone, ex p Connell* [1995] 2 All ER 35, [1995] 1 WLR 928, CA (lack of culpability of surety in failure of accused to stand trial and failure by police to take action which would have resulted in accused standing trial to be taken into account in exercising of discretion to remit part of recognisance, but this does not justify remission of whole or substantial part); *R v Wells Street Magistrates' Court, ex p Albanese* [1982] QB 333, [1981] 3 All ER 769 (where surety to secure attendance is continuous, failure to notify surety of variation of bail conditions does not affect validity of surety, but fact that such a variation may have caused the surety to act differently, or refused to have continued as a surety if he had been informed, is a matter which should be taken into account by the court when deciding to forfeit the whole of the recognisance) (applied in *R v Crown Court of Inner London, ex p Springall* (1986) 85 Cr App Rep 214, [1987] Crim LR 252, DC). As to ignorance of surety as to the date when accused required to surrender see *R v Crown Court at Reading, ex p Bello* [1992] 3 All ER 353, 92 Cr App Rep 303, CA.

12   *R v McGregor* [1945] 2 All ER 180, 30 Cr App Rep 155, CCA. See also *R v Marlow Justices, ex p O'Sullivan* [1984] QB 381, [1983] 3 All ER 578, DC (breach of recognisance to be proved to civil standard of proof except where defendant liable to sentence for an offence as well).

(4) CONDITIONAL DISCHARGE

454.   Power to order conditional discharge. A court[1] by or before which a person is convicted of an offence may, if it is of the opinion, having regard to the circumstances, including the nature of the offence and character of the offender, that it is inexpedient to inflict punishment, and if it thinks fit, make an order discharging the offender subject to the condition that he commits no offence during such period, not exceeding three years from the date of the order[2], as may be specified therein[3]. This is referred to as an 'order for conditional discharge';

and the period specified in any such order is referred to as the 'period of conditional discharge'[4]. On making an order for conditional discharge, the court may, if it thinks it expedient for the purposes of the offender's reformation, allow any person who consents to do so to give security for the offender's good behaviour[5]. The power to order conditional discharge is not available in respect of the offences for which an order for absolute discharge is unavailable[6] or for:

(1)   breach of a criminal behaviour order[7];
(2)   breach of a sexual harm prevention order or an interim sexual harm prevention order[8];
(3)   breach of an anti-social behaviour order[9]; or
(4)   breach of a sexual offences prevention order or an interim sexual offences prevention order[10].

A discharge may not be combined with a fine for the same offence[11]. On discharging an offender conditionally, an order for costs or compensation, a restitution order, a deprivation order or an unlawful profits order may be made[12]; and the court may in the case of a discretionary disqualification, and must in the case of an obligatory disqualification, exercise its powers to disqualify[13]. The court may make a confiscation order in relation to a person who has been conditionally discharged, and in most cases has a duty to do so[14]. A conditional discharge may also be coupled with a recommendation for deportation[15].

1   As to the meaning of 'court' see PARA 1 note 1. Where an order for conditional discharge is made on appeal, the order is deemed to have been made by the court from which the appeal was brought: Powers of Criminal Courts (Sentencing) Act 2000 s 15(2).
2   The Secretary of State may by order direct that the Powers of Criminal Courts (Sentencing) Act 2000 s 12(1) be amended by substituting, for the maximum period there specified as originally enacted or as previously amended, such period as may be specified in the order: s 15(1). At the date at which this volume states the law no such order had been made.
3   Powers of Criminal Courts (Sentencing) Act 2000 s 12(1)(b). This is subject to the Crime and Disorder Act 1998 s 66ZB(6) (effects of youth cautions: see CHILDREN AND YOUNG PERSONS): Powers of Criminal Courts (Sentencing) Act 2000 s 12(2) (amended by the Legal Aid, Sentencing and Punishment of Offenders Act 2010 Sch 24 para 19). Where a person conditionally discharged is sentenced for the offence in respect of which the order for conditional discharge was made, the order ceases to have effect: Powers of Criminal Courts (Sentencing) Act 2000 s 12(5). In connection with the effect of a conditional discharge see PARA 445.
4   Powers of Criminal Courts (Sentencing) Act 2000 s 12(3).
5   Powers of Criminal Courts (Sentencing) Act 2000 s 12(6). When making such an order, the court should specify the type of conduct from which the offender is to refrain: see the *Criminal Practice Directions 2015* [2015] EWCA Crim 1567, [2015] All ER (D) 134 (Sep) CPD VII Sentencing J: Binding Over Orders and Conditional Discharges J.20.
6   See the Powers of Criminal Courts (Sentencing) Act 2000 s 12(1); and as to these offences see PARA 443.
7   See the Anti-social Behaviour, Crime and Policing Act 2014 s 30(3); and PARA 326.
8   See the Sexual Offences Act 2003 s 103I(4); and PARAS 327, 331.
9   See the Crime and Disorder Act 1998 s 1(11) (repealed); the Anti-social Behaviour, Crime and Policing Act 2014 s 33(1), (2); and PARA 439.
10   See the Sexual Offences Act 2003 s 113(3) (repealed); the Anti-social Behaviour, Crime and Policing Act 2014 s 114; and PARA 442.
11   *R v Sanck* (1990) 12 Cr App Rep (S) 155, CA.
12   Powers of Criminal Courts (Sentencing) Act 2000 s 12(7) (amended by the Prevention of Social Housing Fraud Act 2013 Schedule para 8). As to orders for costs and compensation orders see PARA 281 et seq; as to deprivation orders see PARA 470 et seq; as to restitution orders see PARA 492 et seq; as to unlawful profits orders see LANDLORD AND TENANT.
13   Powers of Criminal Courts (Sentencing) Act 2000 s 12(7) (as amended: see note 12).
14   See *R v Varma* [2012] UKSC 42, [2013] 1 AC 463, [2013] 1 All ER 129.
15   See the Immigration Act 1971 s 6(3); and IMMIGRATION AND ASYLUM vol 57 (2012) PARA 181.

455. Commission of offence by person subject to order for conditional discharge. If it appears to the Crown Court, where that court has jurisdiction, or to a justice of the peace having jurisdiction, that a person in whose case an order for conditional discharge has been made[1] has been convicted by a court[2] in any part of Great Britain of an offence committed during the period of conditional discharge[3], and has been dealt with in respect of that offence[4], the Crown Court or the justice may issue a summons requiring the person to appear at the place and time specified therein or a warrant for his arrest[5]. A justice of the peace may not so issue a summons except on information and may not so issue a warrant except on information in writing and on oath[6]. A summons or warrant so issued must direct the person to whom it relates to appear or be brought before the court by which the order for conditional discharge was made[7].

If a person in whose case an order for conditional discharge has been made by the Crown Court is convicted by a magistrates' court of an offence committed during the period of discharge, the magistrates' court may commit him to custody or release him on bail until he can appear or be brought before the Crown Court[8]; and, if it does so, the magistrates' court must send to the Crown Court a copy of the minute or memorandum of the conviction entered in the register, signed by the designated officer by whom the register is kept[9].

1 See PARA 454.
2 As to the meaning of 'court' see PARA 1 note 1.
3 Powers of Criminal Courts (Sentencing) Act 2000 s 13(1)(a). As to the period of conditional discharge see PARA 454.
4 Powers of Criminal Courts (Sentencing) Act 2000 s 13(1)(b).
5 Powers of Criminal Courts (Sentencing) Act 2000 s 13(1). For these purposes, jurisdiction may be exercised: (1) if the order was made by the Crown Court, by that court (s 13(2)(a)); and (2) if the order was made by a magistrates' court, by a justice of the peace (s 13(2)(b) (amended by SI 2005/886)). As to the information to be supplied see the Criminal Procedure Rules 2015, SI 2015/1490, r 28.10.
6 Powers of Criminal Courts (Sentencing) Act 2000 s 13(3).
7 Powers of Criminal Courts (Sentencing) Act 2000 s 13(4). An order made on appeal is deemed to have been made by the court from which the appeal was brought: see PARA 454 note 1.
8 Powers of Criminal Courts (Sentencing) Act 2000 s 13(5)(a). As to committal for sentence in respect of other offences see PARA 549.
9 Powers of Criminal Courts (Sentencing) Act 2000 s 13(5)(b) (amended by SI 2005/886).

456. Person subject to order for conditional discharge convicted of offence; powers of court. Where it is proved to the satisfaction of the court by which an order for conditional discharge was made[1] that the person in whose case the order was made has been convicted[2] of an offence committed during the period of discharge[3], the court may deal with him, for the offence for which the order was made, in any way in which it could deal with him if he had just been convicted by or before that court of that offence[4].

If a person in whose case an order for conditional discharge was made by a magistrates' court is convicted before the Crown Court of an offence committed during the period of discharge[5], or is dealt with by the Crown Court for any such offence in respect of which he was committed for sentence to the Crown Court[6], the Crown Court may deal with him, for the offence for which the order was made, in any way in which the magistrates' court could deal with him if it had just convicted him of that offence[7]; and, if he is so convicted by another magistrates' court of any offence committed during the period of discharge, that other court may, with the consent of the court which made the order, deal with him, for the offence for which the order was made, in any way in which the court could deal with him if it had just convicted him of that offence[8]. Where an order for conditional discharge has been made by a magistrates' court in the case of an offender under 18 years of age[9] in respect of an offence triable only on indictment in the case of an adult, any powers exercisable by that or any other court[10] in respect of the offender after he has attained the age of 18 are powers to do either or both of:

(1)   impose a fine not exceeding £5,000 for the offence in respect of which the order was made[11]; and

(2)   deal with the offender for that offence in any way in which a magistrates' court could deal with him if it had just convicted him of an offence punishable with imprisonment for a term not exceeding six months[12].

A sentence, even though a nominal sentence, should normally be imposed for the offence for which the order of conditional discharge was made[13].

1   See PARA 454. As to the meaning of 'court' see PARA 1 note1.
2   Ie by a court in Great Britain: Powers of Criminal Courts (Sentencing) Act 2000 s 13(10).
3   As to the period of conditional discharge see PARA 454. In proceedings before the Crown Court, any question whether any person in whose case an order for conditional discharge has been made has been convicted of an offence committed during the period of conditional discharge must be determined by the court and not by the verdict of a jury: Powers of Criminal Courts (Sentencing) Act 2000 s 15(3). As to a conviction in respect of which an invalid sentence was imposed see *R v Green* [1959] 2 QB 127, 42 Cr App Rep 77, CCA.
4   Powers of Criminal Courts (Sentencing) Act 2000 s 13(6).
5   Powers of Criminal Courts (Sentencing) Act 2000 s 13(7)(a).
6   Powers of Criminal Courts (Sentencing) Act 2000 s 13(7)(b).
7   Powers of Criminal Courts (Sentencing) Act 2000 s 13(7).
8   Powers of Criminal Courts (Sentencing) Act 2000 s 13(8).
9   As to the determination of a person's age see the Children and Young Persons Act 1933 s 99; and CHILDREN AND YOUNG PERSONS vol 10 (2012) PARA 1206.
10 Ie under the Powers of Criminal Courts (Sentencing) Act 2000 s 13(6), (7) or (8).
11 Powers of Criminal Courts (Sentencing) Act 2000 s 13(9)(a).
12 Powers of Criminal Courts (Sentencing) Act 2000 s 13(9)(b).
13 Unless a sentence is imposed, the conviction cannot be treated as such for certain purposes: see PARA 445.

(5) DEFERRED SENTENCES

457.   Power to defer.   Both Crown Courts and magistrates' courts[1] may defer passing sentence on an offender for the purpose of enabling the court, or any other court[2] to which it falls to deal with him to have regard, in dealing with him, to his conduct after conviction (including, where appropriate, the making by him of reparation for his offence)[3] or to any change in his circumstances[4]. Deferment may not be combined with remand[5] or with a common law binding over or release on bail[6].

1   In deferring the passing of sentence pursuant to these provisions a magistrates' court is to be regarded as exercising the power of adjourning the trial which is conferred by the Magistrates' Courts Act 1980 s 10(1) (see CRIMINAL PROCEDURE vol 27 (2015) PARA 287) and accordingly ss 11(1), 13(1)–(3A) (non-appearance of the defendant: see CRIMINAL PROCEDURE vol 27 (2015) PARAS 145, 248) apply without prejudice to the Powers of Criminal Courts (Sentencing) Act 2000 s 1(7) (see PARA 459) if the offender does not appear on the date specified under s 1(4) (see PARA 459): s 1D(1) (s 1 substituted, ss 1A–1D added, by the Criminal Justice Act 2003 Sch 23 para 1).
2   As to the meaning of 'court' see PARA 1 note 1.
3   Powers of Criminal Courts (Sentencing) Act 2000 s 1(1)(a) (as substituted: see note 1). The matters to which the court may have regard in respect of the offender's conduct after conviction

also include the extent to which the offender has complied with any requirements with which the offender has undertaken (see s 1(3)(b); and PARA 458) to comply: s 1(2) (as so substituted).

4   Powers of Criminal Courts (Sentencing) Act 2000 s 1(1)(b) (as substituted: see note 1). As to the conditions under which deferment is exercisable see PARA 458; as to the period of deferment see PARA 459. The judge must make clear his intentions to defer the whole or part of a sentence at the time of the original hearing: *R v Jones* [2003] EWCA Crim 1631, [2004] 1 Cr App Rep (S) 154, [2003] Crim LR 732.

Where a court has deferred passing sentence under the Powers of Criminal Courts (Sentencing) Act 2000 s 1 it must forthwith give a copy of the order deferring the passing of sentence and setting out any requirements imposed under s 1(3)(b) to the offender (s 1(5)(a) (as so substituted)), to any local probation board whose officer has been appointed to act as supervisor (s 1(5)(b) (as so substituted)), to any provider of probation services whose officer has been appointed to act as a supervisor in relation to him (s 1(5)(ba) (as so substituted; added by SI 2008/912)), and to a person appointed as supervisor under the Powers of Criminal Courts (Sentencing) Act 2000 s 1A(2)(b) (see PARA 458) (s 1(5)(c) (as so substituted)). As to local probation boards and the provision of probation services see PARAS 666–687. Where a restorative justice requirement is imposed under s 1(3)(b), the duty under s 1(5) to give copies of the order extends to every person who would be a participant in the activity concerned: s 1ZA(5) (s 1(8) amended, s 1ZA added, by the Crime and Courts Act 2013 Sch 16 paras 5, 6).

Nothing in the Powers of Criminal Courts (Sentencing) Act 2000 ss 1, 1A–1D affects the power of the Crown Court to bind over an offender to come up for judgment when called upon (s 1(8)(a) (as so substituted and amended)) or the power of any court to defer passing sentence for any purpose for which it may otherwise lawfully do so (s 1(8)(b) (as so substituted and amended)).

5   See the Powers of Criminal Courts (Sentencing) Act 2000 s 1(6) (as substituted: see note 1) (notwithstanding any enactment, a court which under s 1 defers passing sentence on an offender may not on the same occasion remand him).

6   See *R v Dwyer* (1974) 60 Cr App Rep 39, [1974] Crim LR 610, CA; *R v Ross* (1987) 86 Cr App Rep 337, Crown Ct.

458.   When deferment is exercisable.   Deferment of sentence[1] is exercisable only if:

(1)   the offender consents[2];

(2)   the offender undertakes to comply with any requirements as to his conduct during the period of the deferment that the court considers it appropriate to impose[3]; and

(3)   the court is satisfied, having regard to the nature of the offence and the character and circumstances of the offender, that it would be in the interests of justice to exercise the power[4].

1   As to the power to defer sentence see PARA 457.

2   Powers of Criminal Courts (Sentencing) Act 2000 s 1(3)(a) (s 1 substituted, ss 1A–1D added, by the Criminal Justice Act 2003 Sch 23 para 1). As to consent see *R v Fairhead* [1975] 2 All ER 737, 61 Cr App Rep 102, CA; *R v McQuaide* (1974) 60 Cr App Rep 239, CA.

3   Powers of Criminal Courts (Sentencing) Act 2000 s 1(3)(b) (as substituted: see note 2). The requirements may include requirements as to the residence of the offender during the whole or any part of the period of deferment (s 1A(1) (as so added)) and may, without prejudice to the generality of this provision, include restorative justice requirements (s 1ZA(1) (s 1ZA added by the Crime and Courts Act 2013 Sch 16 para 5)). Any reference in the Powers of Criminal Courts (Sentencing) Act 2000 s 1ZA to a restorative justice requirement is to a requirement to participate in an activity: (1) where the participants consist of, or include, the offender and one or more of the victims (s 1ZA(2)(a) (as so added)); (2) which aims to maximise the offender's awareness of the impact of the offending concerned on the victims (s 1ZA(2)(b) (as so added)); and (3) which gives an opportunity to a victim or victims to talk about, or by other means express experience of, the offending and its impact (s 1ZA(2)(c) (as so added)). In s 1ZA 'victim' means a victim of, or other person affected by, the offending concerned: s 1ZA(7) (as so added). Imposition under s 1(3)(b) of a restorative justice requirement requires, in addition to the offender's consent and undertaking under s 1(3), the consent of every other person who would be a participant in the activity concerned: s 1ZA(3) (as so added). For the purposes of s 1ZA(3), a supervisor appointed under s 1A(2) (see below) does not count as a proposed participant: s 1ZA(4) (as so added). In a case where there is such a restorative justice requirement, a person

running the activity concerned must in doing that have regard to any guidance that is issued, with a view to encouraging good practice in connection with such an activity, by the Secretary of State: s 1ZA(6) (as so added)

Where an offender has undertaken to comply with any requirements under s 1(3)(b) the court may appoint an officer of the local probation board or an officer of a provider of probation service or any other person (if he consents) whom the court thinks appropriate to act as a supervisor in relation to him: s 1A(2), (3) (as so added; s 1A(2) amended by SI 2008/912). It is the duty of such a supervisor to monitor the offender's compliance with the requirements and to provide the court to which it falls to deal with the offender in respect of the offence in question with such information as the court may require relating to the offender's compliance with the requirements: Powers of Criminal Courts (Sentencing) Act 2000 s 1A(4) (as so added).

4   Powers of Criminal Courts (Sentencing) Act 2000 s 1(3)(c) (as substituted: see note 2).

459. Period of deferment.

Where sentence is deferred[1] it must be until such date as may be specified by the court[2], not being more than six months after the date on which the deferment is announced by the court; and, where the passing of sentence has been so deferred, it may not[3] be further deferred[4].

A court which has so deferred passing sentence on an offender may deal with him before the end of the period of deferment if during that period he is convicted in Great Britain of any offence[5]. Where a court has deferred passing sentence on an offender who undertook to comply with one or more requirements[6] in connection with the deferment and the person appointed to act as supervisor[7] in relation to the offender has reported to the court that the offender has failed to comply with one or more of the requirements, the court may issue either a summons requiring the offender to appear before it at a time and place specified or a warrant to arrest him and bring him to the court at a time and place specified[8]; and if the offender so appears or is so brought before the court, and the court is satisfied that he has failed to comply with one or more of the requirements, it may deal with him before the end of the period of deferment[9].

1   As to the power to defer sentence see PARAS 457, 458.
2   As to the meaning of 'court' see PARA 1 note 1.
3   Ie subject to the Powers of Criminal Courts (Sentencing) Act 2000 s 1D(3) (see PARA 460).
4   Powers of Criminal Courts (Sentencing) Act 2000 s 1(4) (s 1 substituted, ss 1A–1D added, by the Criminal Justice Act 2003 Sch 23 para 1). Where a court which has deferred passing sentence on an offender proposes to deal with him on the date originally specified by the court, or where the offender does not appear on the date specified, the court may issue a summons requiring him to appear before the court at a time and place specified in the summons, or may issue a warrant to arrest him and bring him before the court at a time and place specified in the warrant: Powers of Criminal Courts (Sentencing) Act 2000 s 1(7) (as so substituted). See also *R v Ingle* [1974] 3 All ER 811, 59 Cr App Rep 306, CA; *R v Anderson* (1983) 78 Cr App Rep 251, 5 Cr App Rep (S) 338, CA (inherent power to postpone sentence at the end of the deferment period; power should, however, be exercised only where there are strong reasons to do so).
5   Powers of Criminal Courts (Sentencing) Act 2000 s 1C(1) (as added: see note 4). As to the meaning of 'Great Britain' see PARA 4 note 3. If an offender on whom a court has under s 1 deferred passing sentence in respect of one or more offences is during the period of deferment convicted in England and Wales of any offence (the 'later offence') then, without prejudice to s 1C(1) and whether or not the offender is sentenced for the later offence during the period of deferment, the court which passes sentence on him for the later offence may also, if this has not already been done, deal with him for the offence or offences for which the passing of sentence was deferred, except that the power so conferred may not be exercised by a magistrates' court if the court which deferred passing sentence was the Crown Court and the Crown Court, in exercising that power in a case in which the court which deferred passing sentence was a magistrates' court, may not pass any sentence which could not have been passed by a magistrates' court in exercising that power: s 1C(2), (3) (as so added). Where a court which under s 1 has deferred passing sentence on an offender proposes to deal with him by virtue of s 1C(1) before the end of the deferment period, it may issue a summons requiring him to appear

before the court at a time and place specified or a warrant to arrest him and bring him before the court at a time and place specified: s 1C(4) (as so added).

6   Ie requirements imposed under the Powers of Criminal Courts (Sentencing) Act 2000 s 1(3)(b): see PARA 458.

7   Ie under the Powers of Criminal Courts (Sentencing) Act 2000 s 1A(2): see PARA 458.

8   Powers of Criminal Courts (Sentencing) Act 2000 s 1B(2), (3) (as added: see note 4).

9   Powers of Criminal Courts (Sentencing) Act 2000 s 1B(1) (as added: see note 4).

460.   Power to deal with offender. The power of a court[1] to deal[2] with an offender in a case where the passing of sentence has been deferred includes power to deal with him, in respect of the offence for which the passing of sentence has been deferred, in any way in which the court which deferred passing sentence could have dealt with him[3]. Where the passing of sentence in respect of one or more offences has been deferred and a magistrates' court deals with the offender in respect of the offence or any of the offences by committing him to the Crown Court[4] for sentence, the power of the Crown Court to deal with him in respect of the offence or any of the offences includes the power to defer passing sentence on him as if he had been convicted of the offence or offences on indictment[5].

Where the passing of sentence in respect of one or more offences has been deferred, it falls to a magistrates' court to determine a relevant matter[6] and a magistrate is satisfied that a person appointed to act as supervisor[7] is likely to be able to give evidence that may assist the court in determining that matter and that that person will not voluntarily attend as a witness, the justice may issue a summons directed to that person requiring him to attend the court at the time and place thereby appointed to give evidence[8].

1   As to the meaning of 'court' see PARA 1 note 1.

2   Ie the power of the original court (the court which granted the deferral) under the Powers of Criminal Courts (Sentencing) Act 2000 s 1 (see PARA 457) to deal with the offender at the end of the period of deferment and any power of that court under s 1B(1) or s 1C(1) (see PARA 459), or of any court under s 1C(3) (see PARA 459), to deal with the offender.

3   Powers of Criminal Courts (Sentencing) Act 2000 s 1D(2)(a) (s 1 substituted, ss 1A–1D added, by the Criminal Justice Act 2003 Sch 23 para 1). The Powers of Criminal Courts (Sentencing) Act 2000 s 1D(2) includes also, in the case of a magistrates' court, the power conferred by s 3 (see **CRIMINAL PROCEDURE** vol 27 (2015) PARA 292) to commit him to the Crown Court for sentence: s 1D(2)(b) (as so added). As to the sentence to be passed at the end of the period of deferment see *R v George* [1984] 3 All ER 13, 79 Cr App Rep 26, CA; *R v Gilby* [1975] 2 All ER 743, 61 Cr App Rep 112, CA; *R v Smith (Michael Stewart)* (1976) 64 Cr App Rep 116, CA; *R v Smith (Joseph)* (1979) 1 Cr App Rep (S) 339, [1979] Crim LR 251, CA; *R v Benstead* (1979) 1 Cr App Rep (S) 32, [1979] Crim LR 409, CA; *R v Glossop* (1981) 3 Cr App Rep (S) 347, [1982] Crim LR 244, CA; *R v Hope* (1980) 2 Cr App Rep (S) 6, [1980] Crim LR 314, CA; *R v Fletcher* (1982) 4 Cr App Rep (S) 118, CA; *R v Aquilina* [1990] Crim LR 134, (1989) 11 Cr App Rep (S) 431, CA; *A-G's Reference (no 62 of 2011), R v Johnson* [2011] EWCA Crim 2354, (2011) 175 CL & J 582, [2011] All ER (D) 50 (Sep). Counsel who appeared for the offender when sentence was deferred should regard himself as bound to appear when sentence is passed if it is at all possible to do so: *R v Ryan* [1976] Crim LR 508, CA. As to the constitution of the court see *R v Gurney* [1974] Crim LR 472; *R v Jacobs* (1975) 62 Cr App Rep 116, CA.

4   Ie under the Powers of Criminal Courts (Sentencing) Act 2000 s 3.

5   Powers of Criminal Courts (Sentencing) Act 2000 s 1D(3) (as added: see note 3).

6   For these purposes a court determines a relevant matter if it deals with the offender in respect of the offence, or any of the offences, for which the passing of sentence has been deferred or if it determines, for the purposes of the Powers of Criminal Courts (Sentencing) Act 2000 s 1B(1)(b) (see PARA 459) whether the offender has failed to comply with any requirement imposed under s 1(3)(b) (see PARA 458): s 1D(6) (as added: see note 3).

7   Ie under the Powers of Criminal Courts (Sentencing) Act 2000 s 1A(2): see PARA 458.

8   Powers of Criminal Courts (Sentencing) Act 2000 s 1D(4), (5) (as added: see note 3).

(6) DISQUALIFICATION FROM BEING A DIRECTOR OF A COMPANY

461. Disqualification orders. In certain circumstances the court may, and in some circumstances must, make against a person a disqualification order, that is to say an order that he may not be a director of a company, or act as receiver of a company's property, or in any way, whether directly or indirectly be concerned or take part in the promotion, formation or management of a company, unless (in each case) he has the leave of the court, and that he may not act as an insolvency practitioner[1].

1 See the Company Directors Disqualification Act 1986 s 1(1); and COMPANIES vol 15 (2009) PARA 1578.

(7) DEPORTATION

462. Recommendation for deportation. A person who is not a British citizen[1] is liable to deportation from the United Kingdom[2] if, after he has attained the age of 17[3], he is convicted of an offence for which he is punishable with imprisonment, and on his conviction he is recommended for deportation by a court empowered to do so[4].

In considering whether to make a recommendation for deportation the court must first consider whether the offender's continued presence in the United Kingdom would be detrimental to the country[5]. A recommendation should be made only if there exists a genuine and sufficiently serious threat to the requirements of public policy affecting one of the fundamental interests of society[6]: the more serious the crime and the longer the criminal record, the more obvious it is that there should be such an order, although a minor offence would not merit one[7]. The proper approach is for the court first to deal with the offence charged on its merits and to determine the appropriate sentence before considering whether or not a recommendation for deportation is merited[8].

If a person's removal from the United Kingdom in pursuance of a deportation order would be contrary to the United Kingdom's obligations under the European Convention on Human Rights[9] or the Refugee Convention[10], a deportation order should not be made against him[11].

1 As to British citizenship see BRITISH NATIONALITY vol 4 (2011) PARA 405.
2 As to the meaning of 'United Kingdom' see PARA 4 note 3.
3 A person is deemed to have attained the age of 17 at the time of his conviction if, on consideration of any available evidence, he appears to have done so to the court: see the Immigration Act 1971 s 6(3)(a); and IMMIGRATION AND ASYLUM vol 57 (2012) PARA 181. As to the determination of a person's age see the Children and Young Persons Act 1933 s 99; and CHILDREN AND YOUNG PERSONS vol 10 (2012) PARA 1206.
4 See the Immigration Act 1971 s 3(6); and IMMIGRATION AND ASYLUM vol 57 (2012) PARA 181. As to the conditions upon which a court may make a recommendation for deportation see IMMIGRATION AND ASYLUM vol 57 (2012) PARA 181; as to persons against whom deportation orders may not be made see IMMIGRATION AND ASYLUM vol 57 (2012) PARA 184; and as to exemptions from deportation for certain existing residents see IMMIGRATION AND ASYLUM vol 57 (2012) PARA 185. A recommendation for deportation is treated as a sentence for the purpose of any enactment providing an appeal against sentence: see the Immigration Act 1971 s 6(5)(a); and IMMIGRATION AND ASYLUM vol 57 (2012) PARA 181. Provision is also made for the automatic deportation of foreign offenders: see the UK Borders Act 2007 ss 32–38; and IMMIGRATION AND ASYLUM vol 57 (2012) PARAS 182–184.
5 See *R v Caird* (1970) 54 Cr App Rep 499, CA; *R v Nazari* [1980] 3 All ER 880, 71 Cr App Rep 87, CA. The fact that a person is living on social security is not to the country's 'detriment' and should not be taken into account: *R v Serry* (1980) 2 Cr App Rep (S) 336, CA. For guidance

about the exercise of the power to make a recommendation for deportation in the case of an offence relating to immigration status see *R v Ahemed* [2005] EWCA Crim 1954, [2005] Crim LR 974; *R v Benabbas* [2005] EWCA Crim 2113, [2005] Crim LR 976.

6   See Case 30/77 *R v Bouchereau* [1978] QB 732, 66 Cr App Rep 202, ECJ; *R v Kraus* (1982) 4 Cr App Rep (S) 113, CA; *R v Escauriaza* (1988) 87 Cr App Rep 344, 9 Cr App Rep (S) 542, CA; *R v Spura* (1988) 10 Cr App Rep (S) 376, CA. The possibility of re-offending is a very important factor in deciding whether to recommend deportation: *R v Secretary of State for the Home Department, ex p Santillo* [1981] QB 778, 73 Cr App Rep 71 at 785 and 77, CA per Donaldson LJ. In connection with the deportation of citizens of EU member states see also *R v Secretary of State for the Home Department, ex p Dannenberg* [1984] QB 766, [1984] 2 All ER 481, CA; *R v Compassi* (1987) 9 Cr App Rep (S) 270, CA.

7   *R v Nazari* [1980] 3 All ER 880, 71 Cr App Rep 87, CA.

8   *R v Edgehill* [1963] 1 QB 593, 47 Cr App Rep 41, CCA. A judge who recommends deportation in the course of sentencing must give his reasons for making such recommendation: *R v Nazari* [1980] 3 All ER 880, 71 Cr App Rep 87, CA; *R v Secretary of State for the Home Department, ex p Santillo* [1981] QB 778, 73 Cr App Rep 71, CA; *R v Compassi* (1987) 9 Cr App Rep (S) 270, [1987] Crim LR 716, CA; *R v Escauriaza* (1988) 87 Cr App Rep 344, 9 Cr App Rep (S) 542, CA; *R v Rodney* [1996] 2 Cr App Rep (S) 230, [1996] Crim LR 357, CA. It is wrong to postpone passing sentence in order to see whether the Home Secretary will give effect to the recommendation: *R v Edgehill*. A recommendation for deportation may be made in conjunction with a conditional discharge: *R v Akan* [1973] QB 491, 56 Cr App Rep 716, CA.

9   Ie the Convention for the Protection of Human Rights and Fundamental Freedoms (Rome, 4 November 1950; TS 71 (1953); Cmd 8969): see RIGHTS AND FREEDOMS vol 88A (2013) PARA 88.

10 Ie the Convention relating to the Status of Refugees (Geneva, 28 July 1951; TS 39 (1954); Cmd 9171) and Protocol (New York, 31 January 1967; TS 15 (1969); Cmnd 3906): see IMMIGRATION AND ASYLUM vol 57 (2012) PARAS 277–279.

11 See e g *RB (Algeria) v Secretary of State for the Home Department; U (Algeria) v Secretary of State for the Home Department; Othman v Secretary of State for the Home Department* [2009] UKHL 10, [2010] 2 AC 110, [2009] 4 All ER 1045; the Immigration Rules para 380; and IMMIGRATION AND ASYLUM vol 57 (2012) PARA 181.

463.   Automatic deportation.   The Secretary of State is required to make a deportation order[1] in respect of a foreign criminal[2] who is convicted of an offence and sentenced to a period of imprisonment of at least 12 months[3].

1   As to the meaning of 'deportation order' see the UK Borders Act 2007 s 38(4)(c); and IMMIGRATION AND ASYLUM vol 57 (2012) PARA 182.

2   As to the meaning of 'foreign criminal' see the UK Borders Act 2007 s 32(1); and IMMIGRATION AND ASYLUM vol 57 (2012) PARA 182.

3   See the UK Borders Act 2007 s 32(2), (5); and IMMIGRATION AND ASYLUM vol 57 (2012) PARA 182. See *R v Kluxen* [2010] EWCA Crim 1081, [2011] 1 WLR 218, [2011] 1 Cr App Rep (S) 249 at [27] ('it will rarely be that [either of the tests for deportation] is satisfied in the case of an offender none of whose offences merits a custodial sentence of 12 months or more. An offender who repeatedly commits minor offences could conceivably do so, as could a person who commits a single offence involving for example the possession or use of false identity documents for which he receives a custodial sentence of less than 12 months') (recommending that courts should no longer make recommendations when a defendant faces automatic deportation as no useful purpose would be served in doing so).

(8)   DESTRUCTION ORDERS

464.   Destruction under the Animal Welfare Act 2006.   The court by or before which a person is convicted of a specified animal cruelty offence[1] may[2] order the destruction of an animal in relation to which the offence was committed where it is appropriate to do so in the interests of the animal[3]. Where the offence involved fighting[4], the court may order destruction of the animal on grounds other than it being in that animal's interests[5]. There is a right of appeal against a destruction order (which in the case of an offence involving fighting may be exercised only where the order is made in relation to an animal which is owned by a person other than the offender)[6].

1 Ie an offence under the Animal Welfare Act 2006 s 4 (unnecessary suffering: see ANIMALS vol 2 (2008) PARA 826), s 5 (mutilation: see ANIMALS vol 2 (2008) PARA 827), s 6(1), (2) (docking of dogs' tails: see ANIMALS vol 2 (2008) PARA 828), s 7 (administration of poisons: see ANIMALS vol 2 (2008) PARA 829), s 8(1), (2) (fighting: see ANIMALS vol 2 (2008) PARA 830) and s 9 (failure to ensure welfare: see ANIMALS vol 2 (2008) PARAS 754, 761, 821).
2 Ie in addition to the sentencing powers specified for the purposes of those offences by the Animal Welfare Act 2006 s 32 (imprisonment or fine: see ANIMALS vol 2 (2008) PARAS 826–830), s 33 (deprivation: see ANIMALS vol 2 (2008) PARA 851) and s 34 (disqualification for keeping: see ANIMALS vol 2 (2008) PARA 852).
3 See the Animal Welfare Act 2006 s 37(1), (6); and ANIMALS vol 2 (2008) PARA 854.
4 Ie in the case of an offence under the Animal Welfare Act 2006 s 8(1), (2).
5 See the Animal Welfare Act 2006 s 38(1), (5); and ANIMALS vol 2 (2008) PARA 855.
6 See the Animal Welfare Act 2006 ss 37(4), (5), 38(4); and ANIMALS vol 2 (2008) PARAS 854, 855.

465. Dangerous dogs. Where a person is convicted of an offence involving the breeding, sale, exchange, giving away or advertising for sale or exchange of a prohibited dog[1] or an aggravated offence of failing to keep a dog under proper control (ie where the dog has injured a person or assistance dog)[2] the court must[3], unless it is satisfied that the dog in question does not constitute a danger to public safety[4], order the destruction of the dog[5]. Where the court does not make a mandatory destruction order (ie where it is satisfied that the dog does not constitute a danger to public safety) it must make a contingent destruction order under which it must be destroyed unless within a specified period it is either exempted from the prohibition on the breeding of dogs for fighting[6] or is kept under proper control[7]. The court may also[8] make a destruction order at its discretion where a person is convicted of an offence involving the keeping of dangerous dogs[9] or the non-aggravated version of the offence[10] of failing to keep a dog under proper control[11], and where a dangerous dog or a dog bred for fighting is seized but there no prosecution follows[12]. There is a right of appeal against a destruction order (which may be exercised only where the order is made in relation to a dog which is owned by a person other than the offender)[13]. Failure to comply with a destruction order is an offence[14].

1 Ie an offence under the Dangerous Dogs Act 1991 s 1: see ANIMALS vol 2 (2008) PARA 912.
2 Ie the aggravated version of an offence under the Dangerous Dogs Act 1991 s 3(1): see ANIMALS vol 2 (2008) PARA 912.
3 Ie in addition to the sentencing powers specified for the purposes of those offences by the Dangerous Dogs Act 1991 ss 1(7), 3(4), (4A) (see ANIMALS vol 2 (2008) PARA 912) and in addition to the power to make a disqualification order (see PARA 467).
4 See the Dangerous Dogs Act 1991 s 4(1A)(a), (1B); and ANIMALS vol 2 (2008) PARA 912.
5 See the Dangerous Dogs Act 1991 s 4(1)(a); and ANIMALS vol 2 (2008) PARA 912.
6 Ie the prohibition under the Dangerous Dogs Act 1991 s 1(3): see ANIMALS vol 2 (2008) PARA 912.
7 See the Dangerous Dogs Act 1991 s 4A; and ANIMALS vol 2 (2008) PARA 913.
8 See note 3.
9 Ie an offence under an order made under the Dangerous Dogs Act 1991 s 2: see ANIMALS vol 2 (2008) PARA 912.
10 Ie the non-aggravated version of an offence under the Dangerous Dogs Act 1991 s 3(1): see ANIMALS vol 2 (2008) PARA 912.
11 See the Dangerous Dogs Act 1991 s 4(1)(a); and ANIMALS vol 2 (2008) PARA 912.
12 See the Dangerous Dogs Act 1991 s 4B; and ANIMALS vol 2 (2008) PARA 914.
13 See the Dangerous Dogs Act 1991 s 4(2); and ANIMALS vol 2 (2008) PARA 912.
14 See the Dangerous Dogs Act 1991 s 4(8); and ANIMALS vol 2 (2008) PARA 912.

(9) DISQUALIFICATION FROM KEEPING AN ANIMAL

466. Animals generally. Where a person is convicted of a specified animal cruelty offence[1] the court by or before which he is convicted may, instead of or in addition to dealing with him in any other way, make an order disqualifying him, for such period as it thinks fit, from:

(1) owning or keeping animals, participating in the keeping of animals, or being party to an arrangement under which he is entitled to control or influence the way in which animals are kept[2];

(2) dealing in animals[3]; or

(3) transporting or arranging for the transport of animals[4].

Failure to comply with such an order is an offence[5].

Where a person is convicted of a specified offence[6] the court by or before which he is convicted may, instead of or in addition to dealing with him in any other way, make an order cancelling any licence held by him and disqualifying him, for such period as it thinks fit, from holding such a licence[7].

1 Ie an offence under the Animal Welfare Act 2006 s 4 (unnecessary suffering: see ANIMALS vol 2 (2008) PARA 826), s 5 (mutilation: see ANIMALS vol 2 (2008) PARA 827), s 6(1), (2) (docking of dogs' tails: see ANIMALS vol 2 (2008) PARA 828), s 7 (administration of poisons: see ANIMALS vol 2 (2008) PARA 829), s 8 (fighting: see ANIMALS vol 2 (2008) PARA 830), s 9 (failure to ensure welfare: see ANIMALS vol 2 (2008) PARAS 754, 761, 821), s 13(6) (licensing and registration of activities involving animals: see ANIMALS vol 2 (2008) PARA 834) and s 34(9) (breach of disqualification order: see ANIMALS vol 2 (2008) PARA 852).

2 See the Animal Welfare Act 2006 s 34(1), (2); and ANIMALS vol 2 (2008) PARA 852.

3 See the Animal Welfare Act 2006 s 34(3); and ANIMALS vol 2 (2008) PARA 852.

4 See the Animal Welfare Act 2006 s 34(4); and ANIMALS vol 2 (2008) PARA 852.

5 See the Animal Welfare Act 2006 ss 34(9); and ANIMALS vol 2 (2008) PARA 858.

6 Ie the offences referred to in note 1 and an offence under the Animal Welfare Act 2006 s 11 (transfer of animals by way of sale or prize to persons aged under 16: see ANIMALS vol 2 (2008) PARA 832).

7 See the Animal Welfare Act 2006 s 42(1); and ANIMALS vol 2 (2008) PARA 858.

467. Dangerous dogs. Where a person is convicted of an offence involving the breeding of dogs for fighting[1], an offence of failing to keep a dog under proper control[2], or an offence involving the keeping of dangerous dogs[3] the court may[4] order the offender to be disqualified, for such period as the court thinks fit, for having custody of a dog[5]. A person who is subject to a disqualification order may apply, after one year has elapsed, for a direction terminating his disqualification, and the court may grant or refuse such application at its discretion[6]. Failure to comply with a disqualification order is an offence[7].

1 Ie an offence under the Dangerous Dogs Act 1991 s 1: see ANIMALS vol 2 (2008) PARA 912.

2 Ie an offence under the Dangerous Dogs Act 1991 s 3(1): see ANIMALS vol 2 (2008) PARA 912.

3 Ie an offence under an order made under the Dangerous Dogs Act 1991 s 2: see ANIMALS vol 2 (2008) PARA 912.

4 Ie in addition to the sentencing powers specified for the purposes of those offences by the Dangerous Dogs Act 1991 ss 1(7), 3(4), (4A) (see ANIMALS vol 2 (2008) PARA 912) and in addition to the power to make a destruction order (see PARA 465).

5 See the Dangerous Dogs Act 1991 s 4(1)(b); and ANIMALS vol 2 (2008) PARA 912.

6 See the Dangerous Dogs Act 1991 s 4(6), (7); and ANIMALS vol 2 (2008) PARA 912.

7 See the Dangerous Dogs Act 1991 s 4(8); and ANIMALS vol 2 (2008) PARA 912.

(10) DISQUALIFICATION FROM PUBLIC OFFICE

468. Disqualifications from office etc consequent on conviction for certain offences. Conviction of the sale or purchase of a public office renders a person permanently disqualified from holding that office; and on conviction of the common law offence of neglect of duty a public officer becomes disqualified from holding the office in question[1].

A person is disqualified from being or being elected a member of a local authority if, within five years before the day of his election or since his election, he has been convicted[2] of any offence and has had passed on him a sentence of imprisonment (whether suspended or not) for a period of not less than three months without the option of a fine[3]. While detained in a penal institution in pursuance of his sentence or unlawfully at large when he would otherwise be so detained, a convicted person is legally incapable of voting at any parliamentary or local government election[4].

The statutory provisions relating to the effect of rehabilitation[5] do not affect the operation of any enactment by virtue of which, in consequence of any conviction, a person is subject, otherwise than by way of sentence[6], to any disqualification, disability, prohibition or other penalty the period of which extends beyond the rehabilitation period applicable[7] to the conviction[8].

1   See CRIMINAL LAW vol 26 (2010) PARA 467 et seq. As to liability to disqualification from holding public office consequent upon conviction of bribery see CRIMINAL LAW vol 26 (2010) PARA 455 et seq. Other disqualifications affecting specified classes of persons or eligibility for certain offices, membership of certain professions etc which are, or may be, consequent upon conviction or conviction of certain offences are dealt with in the relevant titles in this work.
2   Ie in the United Kingdom, the Channel Islands or the Isle of Man: see the Local Government Act 1972 s 80(1)(d); and LOCAL GOVERNMENT vol 69 (2009) PARA 119. As to the meaning of 'United Kingdom' see PARA 11 note 5. As to the legal status of the Channel Islands and the Isle of Man (which are not within the United Kingdom) see COMMONWEALTH vol 13 (2009) PARA 790 et seq.
3   See the Local Government Act 1972 s 80(1)(d); and LOCAL GOVERNMENT vol 69 (2009) PARA 119.
4   See the Representation of the People Act 1983 s 3(1); and ELECTIONS AND REFERENDUMS vol 37 (2013) PARA 107.
5   Ie the Rehabilitation of Offenders Act 1974 s 4(1): see PARA 591.
6   As to the meaning of 'sentence' for these purposes see PARA 591.
7   Ie applicable in accordance with the Rehabilitation of Offenders Act 1974 s 6 (see PARAS 604, 607, 608): see s 7(1)(d); and PARA 609.
8   See the Rehabilitation of Offenders Act 1974 s 7(1)(d); and PARA 609.

(11) DRINKING BANNING ORDERS

469. Introduction and abolition. The power to make drinking banning orders was introduced in 2006[1] and brought into force on various dates between 2009 and 2010[2]. The purpose of drinking banning orders was to protect other persons from criminal or disorderly conduct by the subject while he is under the influence of alchohol[3], by prohibiting him from doing the things specified in the order[4]. Orders could be made:

(1)   by a court on conviction, where the offender was shown to be under the influence of alcohol at the time of the offence[5];

(2)   by a magistrates' court on complaint by the police or a local authority, where it appeared to the court that the individual had engaged in criminal or disorderly conduct while under the influence of alcohol[6]; or

(3)   in county court proceedings, on application by the police or a local

authority, in respect of a person whose criminal or disorderly conduct while under the influence of alcohol is material to the proceedings[7].

Drinking banning orders have been abolished[8], although the abolition does not affect existing orders[9].

1 See the Violent Crime Reduction Act 2006 ss 1–14 (as originally enacted).

2 See the Violent Crime Reduction Act 2006 (Commencement No 7) Order 2009, SI 2009/1840, arts 2, 3 (bringing the Violent Crime Reduction Act 2006 ss 1–5 into force on 31 August 2009 and bringing ss 9–14 into force for certain purposes on 31 August 2009); the Violent Crime Reduction Act 2006 (Commencement No 8) Order 2010, SI 2010/469, arts 2, 3 (bringing the Violent Crime Reduction Act 2006 ss 6–8 into force for certain purposes on 1 April 2010 and bringing ss 9–14 into force for remaining purposes on 1 April 2010); and the Violent Crime Reduction Act 2006 (Commencement No 9) Order 2010, SI 2010/2541, art 2 (bringing the Violent Crime Reduction Act 2006 ss 6–8 into force for certain purposes on 1 November 2010).

3 See the Violent Crime Reduction Act 2006 ss 1(2), 6(2) (repealed).

4 See the Violent Crime Reduction Act 2006 s 1(1) (repealed).

5 See the Violent Crime Reduction Act 2006 s 6(1) (repealed).

6 See the Violent Crime Reduction Act 2006 s 3(2) (repealed).

7 See the Violent Crime Reduction Act 2006 s 4 (repealed).

8 The Violent Crime Reduction Act 2006 ss 1–14 were repealed by the Anti-social Behaviour, Crime and Policing Act 2014 Sch 11 paras 44, 50: the repeals of ss 6–8, s 9 (for certain purposes) and s 10 (for certain purposes) were brought into force on 20 October 2014 by the Anti-social Behaviour, Crime and Policing Act 2014 (Commencement No 7, Saving and Transitional Provisions) Order 2014, SI 2014/2590; and the repeals of ss 1–5, s 9 (for remaining purposes), s 10 (for remaining purposes) and ss 11–14 were brought into force on 23 March 2015 by the Anti-social Behaviour, Crime and Policing Act 2014 (Commencement No 8, Saving and Transitional Provisions) Order 2015, SI 2015/373.

9 For savings relating to existing orders see the Anti-social Behaviour, Crime and Policing Act 2014 ss 21(1)(g), (2), (4), (5)(a), (c), 33(1), (2)(c), (3), (4).

(12) FORFEITURE/DEPRIVATION ORDERS

470. Deprivation orders in respect of property used, or intended for use, for purposes of crime. Where a person is convicted of an offence and:

(1) the court by or before which he is convicted is satisfied that any property which has been lawfully seized[1] from him, or which was in his possession or under his control[2] at the time when he was apprehended for the offence or when a summons in respect of it was issued, has been used for the purpose of committing[3], or facilitating the commission[4] of, any offence[5], or was intended by him to be used for that purpose[6]; or

(2) the offence, or an offence which the court has taken into consideration in determining his sentence, consists of unlawful possession of property which has been lawfully seized from him[7], or was in his possession or under his control at the time when he was apprehended for the offence of which he has been convicted or when a summons in respect of that offence was issued[8],

the court may make a deprivation order in respect of that property[9]. It may do so whether or not it also deals with the offender in any other way in respect of the offence of which he has been convicted[10] and without regard to any restrictions on forfeiture in an enactment passed before 29 July 1988[11]. The power to make a deprivation order does not apply to real property, the power being necessarily confined to personal property[12].

In considering whether to make a deprivation order, the court must have regard to the value of the property[13] and to the likely financial and other effects on the offender of the making of the order (taken together with any other order that the court contemplates making)[14].

An order so made operates to deprive the offender of his rights, if any, in the property to which it relates, and the property must (if not already in their possession) be taken into the possession of the police[15].

Where a court makes a deprivation order in a case where:

(a)　　the offender has been convicted of an offence which has resulted in a person suffering personal injury, loss or damage[16]; or

(b)　　any such offence is taken into consideration by the court in determining sentence[17],

the court may also make an order that any proceeds which arise from the disposal of the property and which do not exceed a sum specified by the court must be paid to that person[18]. However, the court may so make an order only if it is satisfied that, but for the inadequacy of the means of the offender, it would have made a compensation order under which the offender would have been required to pay compensation of an amount not less than the specified amount[19].

Penalties must be proportionate to the offence[20]. An owner of property cannot be deprived of it where he is not the offender prosecuted[21]. Deprivation orders ought not to be made except in simple, uncomplicated cases: if a person has an interest in an object which is not free from incumbrances, difficulties are likely to arise[22]. It is incumbent upon the prosecution to justify the application for a deprivation order and upon the trial judge to put the prosecution to proof if the prosecution simply states baldly, without any supporting evidence, that it seeks a deprivation order[23]. The money or other matter to be forfeited must relate to the offence of which the accused was convicted[24]. No deprivation order may be made when the property has been used by persons other than the offender to commit an offence[25]: however, property can be the subject of a deprivation order where it was used by another to facilitate the commission of an offence by the offender[26]. A deprivation order may not be made in respect of property which appears to be the proceeds of earlier offences[27], but a deprivation order made in relation to money which is the offender's working capital for future dealings has been held to be properly made[28]. A deprivation order cannot be used as security for a fine; it is to be provided as an additional penalty[29].

An order should not be made unless the court has information as to the value of the property involved and the effect on the offender of making the order[30]. Where several offenders are equally culpable for an offence and receive comparable sentences, a deprivation order against one of them may give rise to an objectionable disparity[31].

When fixing the totality of a sentence, the court must reflect and take account of the financial penalties imposed by any deprivation orders[32].

1　　The power of deprivation in the Powers of Criminal Courts (Sentencing) Act 2000 s 143 does not provide a power of seizure: *Malone v Metropolitan Police Comr* [1980] QB 49, 69 Cr App Rep 4, CA. As to the seizure of property see POLICE AND INVESTIGATORY POWERS vol 84A (2013) PARA 465 et seq.

2　　As to 'possession' and 'control' in the context of forfeiture orders see *R v Hinde* (1977) 64 Cr App Rep 213.

3　　In connection with property 'used for the purpose; see *R v Slater* (1986) 8 Cr App Rep (S) 217 (property must have been used by the defendant, it cannot simply have been used by anyone); and *R v Coleville-Scott* (1991) 12 Cr App Rep (S) 238 (the Powers of Criminal Courts (Sentencing) Act 2000 s 143(1) does not require the user and the offender to be one and the same person). Where a person commits an offence to which s 143(6) applies:

(1)　　by driving, attempting to drive, or being in charge of a vehicle (s 143(6)(a));

(2)　　by failing to comply with a requirement made under the Road Traffic Act 1988 s 7 (provisions of specimens for analysis: see ROAD TRAFFIC vol 90 (2011) PARA 743) or s 7A (specimens of blood taken from persons incapable of consenting: see ROAD TRAFFIC vol 90 (2011) PARA 744) in the course of an investigation into whether the offender had committed an offence while driving, attempting to drive or being in charge of a vehicle (Powers of Criminal Courts (Sentencing) Act 2000 s 143(6)(b) (amended by the Police Reform Act 2002 s 56(6))); or

(3)   by failing, as the driver of a vehicle, to comply with the Road Traffic Act 1988 s 170(2) or (3) (duty to stop and give information or report accident: see ROAD TRAFFIC vol 89 (2011) PARA 448) (Powers of Criminal Courts (Sentencing) Act 2000 s 143(6)(c)),

the vehicle is to be regarded for the purposes of s 143(1) and s 144(1)(b) (see note 15) as used for the purpose of committing the offence (and for the purpose of committing any offence of aiding, abetting, counselling or procuring the commission of the offence): s 143(6) (as so amended).

The Powers of Criminal Courts (Sentencing) Act 2000 s 143(6) applies to:

(a)   an offence under the Road Traffic Act 1988 which is punishable with imprisonment (Powers of Criminal Courts (Sentencing) Act 2000 s 143(7)(a));

(b)   an offence of manslaughter (s 143(7)(b)); and

(c)   an offence under the Offences against the Person Act 1861 s 35 (wanton and furious driving: see ROAD TRAFFIC vol 90 (2011) PARA 775) (Powers of Criminal Courts (Sentencing) Act 2000 s 143(7)(c)).

4   For these purposes, facilitating the commission of an offence is to be taken to include the taking of any steps after it has been committed for the purpose of disposing of any property to which it relates or of avoiding apprehension or detection: Powers of Criminal Courts (Sentencing) Act 2000 s 143(8). The property must be used for the purpose of committing or facilitating the commission of an offence: *R v Lucas* [1976] RTR 235, CA.

5   Powers of Criminal Courts (Sentencing) Act 2000 s 143(1)(a).

6   Powers of Criminal Courts (Sentencing) Act 2000 s 143(1)(b). Lack of such intention or purpose prevents the making of such an order: *R v Ribeyre* (1982) 4 Cr App Rep (S) 165, [1982] Crim LR 538, CA (decided under the Misuse of Drugs Act 1971 s 27 (see MEDICAL PRODUCTS AND DRUGS vol 75 (2013) PARA 526)).

7   Powers of Criminal Courts (Sentencing) Act 2000 s 143(2)(a).

8   Powers of Criminal Courts (Sentencing) Act 2000 s 143(2)(b).

9   Powers of Criminal Courts (Sentencing) Act 2000 s 143(1), (2).

10   Powers of Criminal Courts (Sentencing) Act 2000 s 143(4)(a). As to confiscation orders under the Proceeds of Crime Act 2002 see PARA 189 et seq; and as to forfeiture orders under the Misuse of Drugs Act 1971 see MEDICAL PRODUCTS AND DRUGS vol 75 (2013) PARA 526.

11   Powers of Criminal Courts (Sentencing) Act 2000 s 143(4)(b). The date referred to in the text is the date on which the Criminal Justice Act 1988 was passed (ie received the Royal Assent).

12   *R v Khan* [1982] 3 All ER 969, 76 Cr App Rep 29, [1980] Crim LR 249, CA (deprivation order with regard to a house quashed).

13   Powers of Criminal Courts (Sentencing) Act 2000 s 143(5)(a). See *R v Highbury Corner Stipendiary Magistrates' Court, ex p Di Matteo* [1992] 1 All ER 102, 92 Cr App Rep 263, DC.

14   Powers of Criminal Courts (Sentencing) Act 2000 s 143(5)(b).

15   Powers of Criminal Courts (Sentencing) Act 2000 s 143(3). In relation to property which is in the possession of the police by virtue of s 143:

(1)   the Police (Property) Act 1897 applies, with the following modifications:

(a)   no application may be made under s 1(1) (see POLICE AND INVESTIGATORY POWERS vol 84A (2013) PARA 635) by any claimant of the property after the end of six months from the date on which the deprivation order in respect of the property was made (Powers of Criminal Courts (Sentencing) Act 2000 s 144(1)(a));

(b)   no such application may succeed unless the claimant satisfies the court either that he had not consented to the offender having possession of the property (s 144(1)(b)(i)) or, where an order is made under s 143(1) (see the text and notes 1–6), that he did not know, and had no reason to suspect, that the property was likely to be used for the purpose there mentioned (s 144(1)(b)(ii));

(2)   the power to make regulations under the Police (Property) Act 1897 s 2 (disposal of property in cases where the owner of the property has not been ascertained and no order of a competent court has been made with respect to it: see POLICE AND INVESTIGATORY POWERS vol 84A (2013) PARA 636) includes power to make regulations for disposal in cases where no application under the Powers of Criminal Courts (Sentencing) Act 2000 s 144(1)(a) (see head (1)(a) above) has been made or no such application has succeeded (s 144(2)).

The regulations may not provide for the vesting in the relevant authority of property in relation to which an order has been made under s 145 (see the text and notes 16–19) (s 144(3)), and nothing in the Police (Property) Act 1897 s 2(2A)(a) (see POLICE AND INVESTIGATORY

POWERS vol 84A (2013) PARA 636) or s 2(3) (see POLICE AND INVESTIGATORY POWERS vol 84A (2013) PARA 635) limits the power to make regulations under s 2 by virtue of the Powers of Criminal Courts (Sentencing) Act 2000 s 144(2) (s 144(4)). As to regulations which have been made see the Police (Property) Regulations 1997, SI 1997/1908; and POLICE AND INVESTIGATORY POWERS vol 84A (2013) PARA 637.

A court making an order about property under the Powers of Criminal Courts (Sentencing) Act 2000 s 143 may order that the property be taken into the possession of the Secretary of State (and not of the police): see the UK Borders Act 2007 s 25. See also *Trans Berckx BVBA v North Avon Magistrates' Court* [2011] EWHC 2605 (Admin), 176 JP 28 (orders were invalid where magistrates had not considered the statutory test).

16 Powers of Criminal Courts (Sentencing) Act 2000 s 145(1)(a).
17 Powers of Criminal Courts (Sentencing) Act 2000 s 145(1)(b).
18 Powers of Criminal Courts (Sentencing) Act 2000 s 145(1).
19 Powers of Criminal Courts (Sentencing) Act 2000 s 145(2). An order under s 145 has no effect: (1) before the end of the period specified in s 144(1)(a) (see note 15) (s 145(3)(a)); or (2) if a successful application under the Police (Property) Act 1897 s 1(1) (see POLICE AND INVESTIGATORY POWERS vol 84A (2013) PARA 635) has been made (Powers of Criminal Courts (Sentencing) Act 2000 s 145(3)(b)).
20 See e g *R v Thomson* (1978) 66 Cr App Rep 130; *R v Buddo* (1982) 4 Cr App Rep (S) 268; *R v Scully* (1985) 7 Cr App Rep (S) 119; *R v Joyce* (1989) 11 Cr App Rep (S) 253; *R v Highbury Corner Stipendiary Magistrates' Court, ex p Di Matteo* [1992] 1 All ER 102, 92 Cr App Rep 263, DC. In the case of a crime committed on the spur of the moment, it has been held not appropriate to order deprivation of a car of considerable value: *R v Miele* [1976] RTR 238, CA. Where a car was an integral part of the commission of the offence of handling stolen goods, it has been held appropriate for a deprivation order to be made: *R v Lidster* [1976] RTR 240, [1976] Crim LR 80, CA; and see *R v Boothe* (1987) 9 Cr App Rep (S) 8, [1987] Crim LR 347, CA. When a car is used for the appropriate purposes within the Powers of Criminal Courts (Sentencing) Act 2000 s 143(1), it is appropriate to make a deprivation order, which perhaps should be considered more frequently: *R v Stratton* (1988) Times, 15 January, CA. A deprivation order cannot be made where the use of a motor vehicle was merely incidental to the commission of an offence (*R v Wilmott* (1985) 149 JP 428, CA), but it may be made in respect of an offender convicted of driving while disqualified (*R v Highbury Corner Stipendiary Magistrates' Court, ex p Di Matteo*). Where the applicant disputed ownership of a car in connection with which a deprivation order had been made on the conviction of her husband, since ownership could not be determined by the Crown Court under the Courts Act 1971 s 11 (repealed), the order was quashed and the case remitted to the justices with a direction to hear and determine the matter under the Police (Property) Act 1897: *R v Chester Justices, ex p Smith* [1978] RTR 373, (1978) 67 Cr App Rep 133, DC; and see also *R v Menocal* [1980] AC 598, sub nom *Customs and Excise Comrs v Menocal* (1979) 69 Cr App Rep 148 at 157, HL.
21 See *O'Leary International v Chief Constable of North Wales* [2012] EWHC 1516 (Admin), 176 JP 514, 176 CL & J 370.
22 *R v Troth* (1980) 71 Cr App Rep 1, CA (deprivation order with regard to appellant's rights in lorry quashed; lorry co-owned by himself and his partner; lorry used in their business); *R v Kearney* [2011] EWCA Crim 826, [2011] 2 Cr App Rep (S) 608 (deprivation order could not be made over car owned by finance company).
23 *R v Pemberton* (1982) 4 Cr App Rep (S) 328, [1983] Crim LR 121, CA.
24 *R v Cox (Stephen)* (1986) 8 Cr App Rep (S) 384, CA.
25 *R v Slater* [1986] 3 All ER 786, 8 Cr App Rep (S) 217, CA; *R v Neville* (1987) 9 Cr App Rep (S) 222, [1987] Crim LR 585, CA.
26 *R v Colville-Scott* [1990] 1 WLR 958, 12 Cr App Rep (S) 238, CA. There may be exceptional circumstances suggesting that such an order should not be made because it would have a disproportionately severe impact, such as where the property is a vehicle and the offender is physically disabled: *R v Tavernor* [1976] RTR 242, CA.
27 *R v Neville* (1987) 9 Cr App Rep (S) 222, [1987] Crim LR 585, CA.
28 *R v O'Farrell* (1988) 10 Cr App Rep (S) 74, CA.
29 *R v Kingston-upon-Hull Stipendiary Magistrate, ex p Hartung* [1981] RTR 262, (1981) 72 Cr App Rep 26, DC.
30 *R v Ball* [2002] EWCA Crim 2777, [2003] 2 Cr App Rep (S) 92, [2003] Crim LR 122.
31 *R v Ottey* (1984) 6 Cr App Rep (S) 163, [1984] Crim LR 506, CA; and see also *R v Burgess* [2001] 2 Cr App Rep (S) 5, CA.
32 *R v Joyce* (1989) 11 Cr App Rep (S) 253, CA; *R v Priestly* [1996] 2 Cr App Rep (S) 144, CA. In addition to the totality of the sentence, the court should have regard to the two matters set out

in the Powers of Criminal Courts (Sentencing) Act 2000 s 143(5) (see the text and notes 13–14): see *R v Highbury Corner Stipendiary Magistrates' Court, ex p Di Matteo* [1992] 1 All ER 102, 92 Cr App Rep 263, DC.

(13) NON-PECUNIARY FORFEITURE

471. Non-pecuniary forfeitures. A court, on the conviction of an offender, may order the forfeiture of some article in relation to which the offence was committed[1]. Subject to any enactment relating to customs or excise, anything other than money forfeited on a conviction by a magistrates' court[2] or the forfeiture of which may be enforced by a magistrates' court must be sold or otherwise disposed of in such manner as the court may direct, and the proceeds are applied as if they were a fine imposed under the enactment on which the proceedings for the forfeiture are founded[3].

1   As to deprivation of property used for crime see the Powers of Criminal Courts (Sentencing) Act 2000 s 143; and PARA 470.
2   As to the meaning of 'magistrates' court' see MAGISTRATES vol 71 (2013) PARA 470.
3   Magistrates' Courts Act 1980 s 140.

(14) HOSPITAL AND GUARDIANSHIP ORDERS

472. Making of hospital orders and guardianship orders. The court may make a hospital order[1] where:

(1)   a person is convicted before the Crown Court[2] or a magistrates' court[3] of an offence punishable with imprisonment[4];

(2)   a special verdict of not guilty by reason of insanity[5] is returned[6]; or

(3)   findings have been made that the defendant is under a disability and that he did the act or omission charged against him[7].

In the case of a person who has been convicted[8] the court may alternatively place him under the guardianship of a local social services authority[9] or of such other person approved by a local social services authority as may be so specified[10].

Where a court is minded to make a guardianship order in respect of any offender, it may request the local social services authority for the area in which the offender resides or last resided, or any other local social services authority that appears to the court to be appropriate:

(a)   to inform the court whether it or any other person approved by it is willing to receive the offender into guardianship[11]; and

(b)   if so, to give such information as it reasonably can about how it or the other person could be expected to exercise powers of guardianship[12] in relation to the offender[13],

and that authority must comply with any such request[14].

Hospital and guardianship orders may not be made unless specified conditions are satisfied[15], and where a hospital or guardianship order is made the court may not:

(i)   pass sentence of imprisonment[16], or impose a fine, or make a community order[17] or a youth rehabilitation order[18] in respect of the offence[19];

(ii)   if the order is a hospital order, make a referral order[20] in respect of the offence[21]; or

(ii)   make in respect of the offender an order[22] requiring the parent or guardian of a child or young person to enter into a recognisance to take proper care of him and exercise proper control over him[23],

but the court may make any other order which it otherwise has power to make[24].

A person in respect of whom the Crown Court has made a hospital order after a verdict of not guilty by reason of insanity or after findings that the defendant is under a disability[25] may appeal to the Court of Appeal against the order[26].

1 Ie the court may by order authorise a person's admission to and detention in a hospital specified in the order: Mental Health Act 1983 s 37(4); Criminal Procedure (Insanity) Act 1964 s 5(4) (s 5 substituted, s 5A added, by the Domestic Violence, Crime and Victims Act 2004 s 24(1)). As to the information to be supplied on admission see the Criminal Procedure Rules 2015, SI 2015/1490, r 28.9.

Where a court is minded to make a hospital order or interim hospital order (see PARAS 473, 474) in respect of any person, it may request the clinical commissioning group or local health board for the area in which that person resides or last resided, or the National Health Service Commissioning Board or the National Assembly for Wales or any other clinical commissioning group or local health board that appears to the court to be appropriate, to furnish the court with such information as that clinical commissioning group or local health board or the National Assembly for Wales have or can reasonably obtain with respect to the hospital or hospitals (if any) in their area or elsewhere at which arrangements could be made for the admission of that person in pursuance of the order; and that clinical commissioning group or local health board, or the National Health Service Commissioning Board or the National Assembly for Wales, must comply with any such request: Mental Health Act 1983 s 39(1) (amended by the Health Authorities Act 1995 Sch 1 para 107(1), (5), Sch 3; the National Health Service Reform and Health Care Professions Act 2002 Sch 2 paras 42, 46; the Health and Social Care Act 2012 Sch 5 para 28; and SI 2007/961). A request to the National Health Service Commissioning Board may relate only to services or facilities the provision of which the Board arranges: Mental Health Act 1983 s 39(1ZA) (added by the Health and Social Care Act 2012 Sch 5 para 28). Where the person concerned has not attained the age of 18 years, the information which may be requested under these provisions includes, in particular, information about the availability of accommodation or facilities designed so as to be specially suitable for patients who have not attained the age of 18 years: Mental Health Act 1983 s 39(1A) (added by the Mental Health Act 2007 s 31(1)). See also the Mental Health Act 1983 s 45A(8); and PARA 478. See also *R v Marsden* [1968] 2 All ER 341, 52 Cr App Rep 301, CA (unnecessary that offender should be admitted to hospital in part of country where normally resident). As to the determination of a person's age see the Children and Young Persons Act 1933 s 99; and CHILDREN AND YOUNG PERSONS vol 10 (2012) PARA 1206. As to National Health Service bodies see HEALTH SERVICES vol 54 (2008) PARA 75 et seq. As to the National Assembly for Wales see constitutional and administrative law vol 20 (2014) PARA 351 et seq.

As to the court's power to make a hospital order, guardianship order or interim hospital order in the case of persons suffering from mental illness or severe mental impairment who could otherwise be committed to prison for contempt see the Contempt of Court Act 1981 s 14(4); and CONTEMPT OF COURT vol 22 (2012) PARA 111. As to a court's power to make interim hospital orders, to remand for a report on the offender's mental condition and to remand to hospital for treatment see PARAS 474–476; and as to the Crown Court's power to make, in addition to a hospital order, a restriction order see PARA 477. In connection with requests for medical reports see the Criminal Procedure Rules 2015, SI 2015/1490, r 28.8.

2 In the case of a Crown Court conviction this power does not apply if the sentence for the offence is fixed by law: Mental Health Act 1983 s 37(1). Offences for which the sentence is fixed by law are not excluded in relation to the making of a hospital order by virtue of the Criminal Procedure (Insanity) Act 1964 s 5(2)(a) (seethe text and notes 5–6): s 5A(1)(b) (as added: see note 1). As to the Crown Court's powers to make hospital orders in the case of persons committed to the court to be dealt with see PARA 549. In relation to the making of a hospital order by virtue of the Criminal Procedure (Insanity) Act 1964 s 5(2)(a), the Mental Health Act 1983 s 37 has effect as if the reference in s 37(1) (see the text and notes 3–4) to a person being convicted before the Crown Court included a reference to the case where the Criminal Procedure (Insanity) Act 1964 s 5 applies: s 5A(1)(a) (as so added).

3 Where a person is charged before a magistrates' court with any act or omission as an offence and the court would have power, on convicting him of that offence, to make a hospital order or a guardianship order in his case as being a person suffering from mental illness or severe mental impairment, then, if the court is satisfied that the defendant did the act or made the omission charged, the court may, if it thinks fit, make such order without convicting him: Mental Health

Act 1983 s 37(3). See also *R v Lincolnshire (Kesteven) Justices, ex p O'Connor* [1983] 1 All ER 901, [1983] 1 WLR 335, DC; *R v Ramsgate Justices, ex p Kazmarek* (1984) 80 Cr App Rep 366, DC. This power applies only to an offence punishable on summary conviction with imprisonment and does not apply to an offence triable only on indictment: Mental Health Act 1983 s 37(1); *R v Chippenham Magistrates' Court, ex p Thompson* (1995) 160 JP 207, DC. Provision is made for an appeal against a hospital order made by a magistrates' court: see the Mental Health Act 1983 s 45(1); and MENTAL HEALTH AND CAPACITY vol 75 (2013) PARA 880.

4 Mental Health Act 1983 s 37(1). For these purposes, any reference to an offence punishable on summary conviction with imprisonment is to be construed without regard to any prohibition or restriction imposed by or under any enactment on the imprisonment of young offenders: s 55(2). The court is not prevented from making an order for the admission of an offender to a hospital only because the offence in question is an offence the sentence for which would otherwise fall to be imposed under:

(1) the Prevention of Crime Act 1953 s 1A(5) or s 1(2B) (see CRIMINAL LAW) (Mental Health Act 1983 s 37(1A)(za) (s 37(1A), (1B) added by the Criminal Justice Act 2003 Sch 32 para 38; Mental Health Act 1983 s 37(1A)(za), (aa), (ba) added by the Legal Aid, Sentencing and Punishment of Offenders Act 2012 Sch 19 para 1, Sch 26 para 2; Mental Health Act 1983 s 37(1A)(za), (aa) amended by the Criminal Justice and Courts Act 2015 Sch 5 para 1));

(2) the Firearms Act 1968 s 51A(2) (see CRIMINAL LAW vol 26 (2010) PARA 613) (Mental Health Act 1983 s 37(1A)(a) (as so added))

(3) the Criminal Justice Act 1988 s 139AA(7) (see CRIMINAL LAW), s 139(6B) (see CRIMINAL LAW vol 26 (2010) PARA 653) or s 139A(5B) (see CRIMINAL LAW vol 26 (2010) PARA 654) (Mental Health Act 1983 s 37(1A)(aa) (as so added and amended));

(4) the Powers of Criminal Courts (Sentencing) Act 2000 s 110(2) (see CRIMINAL LAW vol 26 (2010) PARA 725) or s 111(2) (see CRIMINAL LAW vol 26 (2010) PARA 290) (Mental Health Act 1983 s 37(1A)(b) (as so added));

(5) the Criminal Justice Act 2003 s 224A (see PARA 35) (Mental Health Act 1983 s 37(1A)(ba) (as so added));

(6) under any of the Criminal Justice Act 2003 ss 225–228 (see PARA 33 et seq) (or, as from a day to be appointed, ss 225(2), 226(2) (see PARAS 34, 37) (Mental Health Act 1983 s 37(1A)(c) (as so added; prospectively amended by the Criminal Justice and Immigration Act 2008 Sch 26 para 8)); or

(7) the Violent Crime Reduction Act 2006 s 29(4) or (6) (see CRIMINAL LAW vol 26 (2010) PARAS 614, 656) (Mental Health Act 1983 s 37(1A)(d) (as so added; amended by the Violent Crime Reduction Act 2006 Sch 1 para 2)).

The Mental Health Act 1983 s 37(1A) is to be read in accordance with the Criminal Justice Act 2003 s 305(4) (see PARA 536): Mental Health Act 1983 s 37(1B) (as so added).

5 As to such verdicts see CRIMINAL LAW vol 25 (2010) PARA 30.

6 Criminal Procedure (Insanity) Act 1964 ss 5(1)(a), (2)(a), 5A(1)(b) (as substituted: see note 1). Where a hospital order is made under s 5 it is stated that the order may be made with or without a restriction order (s 5(2)(a) (as so substituted)), although where the offence to which the special verdict or the findings relate is an offence the sentence for which is fixed by law, and the court has power to make a hospital order, the court must make a hospital order with a restriction order (whether or not it would have power to make a restriction order apart from this provision): Criminal Procedure (Insanity) Act 1964 s 5(3) (as so substituted). As to the meaning of 'restriction order' see the Mental Health Act 1983 s 41; and PARA 477 (definition applied by the Criminal Procedure (Insanity) Act 1964 s 5(4) (as so substituted)). In these circumstances the court may also make a supervision order or an order for the absolute discharge of the accused: see s 5(2)(b), (c); and PARAS 443, 495.

7 Criminal Procedure (Insanity) Act 1964 s 5(1)(b) (as substituted: see note 1). As to references to a person being or having been found to be under a disability and to have done the act charged against him in respect of an offence see PARA 329 note 1. Where a person is detained in pursuance of a hospital order which the court had power to make by virtue of s 5(1)(b), and the court also made a restriction order, and that order has not ceased to have effect, the Secretary of State, if satisfied after consultation with the responsible clinician that the person can properly be tried, may remit the person for trial, either to the court of trial or to a prison (s 5A(4) (as so added; amended by the Mental Health Act 2007 s 15(4))). As to the 'responsible clinician' for the purposes of the Mental Health Act 1983 see PARA 474 note 17.

8 Ie where the Mental Health Act 1983 s 37(1) (see the text and notes 1–4) applies.

9 For these purposes 'local social services authority' means a council which is a local authority for the purposes of the Local Authority Social Services Act 1970 (see LOCAL GOVERNMENT vol 69

(2009) PARA 23): Mental Health Act 1983 s 145(1). In connection with guardianship see the Criminal Procedure Rules 2015, SI 2015/1490, r 28.9.

10 Mental Health Act 1983 s 37(1).
11 Mental Health Act 1983 s 39A(a) (s 39A added by the Criminal Justice Act 1991 s 27(1)).
12 Ie the powers conferred by the Mental Health Act 1983 s 40(2) (see MENTAL HEALTH AND CAPACITY vol 75 (2013) PARA 867).
13 Mental Health Act 1983 s 39A(b) (as added: see note 11).
14 Mental Health Act 1983 s 39A (as added: see note 11).
15 As to the specified conditions see PARA 473.
16 For these purposes 'sentence of imprisonment' includes any sentence or order for detention: Mental Health Act 1983 s 37(8) (amended by the Youth Justice and Criminal Evidence Act 1999 Sch 4 para 11; the Powers of Criminal Courts (Sentencing) Act 2000 Sch 9 para 90(1), (6); the Criminal Justice Act 2003 Sch 32 paras 37, 38(c); and the Criminal Justice and Immigration Act 2008 Sch 4 para 30).
17 Ie within the meaning of the Criminal Justice Act 2003 Pt 12 (ss 142–305).
18 Ie within the meaning of the Criminal Justice and Immigration Act 2008 Pt 1 (ss 1–8).
19 Mental Health Act 1983 s 37(8)(a) (as amended: see note 16).
20 Ie within the meaning of the Powers of Criminal Courts (Sentencing) Act 2000 (see s 16(2), (3); and PARA 156).
21 Mental Health Act 1983 s 37(8)(b) (as amended: see note 16).
22 Ie an order under the Powers of Criminal Courts (Sentencing) Act 2000 s 150 (see CHILDREN AND YOUNG PERSONS vol 10 (2012) PARA 1299).
23 Mental Health Act 1983 s 37(8)(c) (as amended: see note 16).
24 Mental Health Act 1983 s 37(8) (as amended: see note 16).
25 Ie under the Criminal Procedure (Insanity) Act 1964 s 5 or s 5A.
26 Criminal Appeal Act 1968 s 16A(1)(a) (ss 16A, 16B added by the Domestic Violence, Crime and Victims Act 2004 s 25). Such an appeal lies only with the leave of the Court of Appeal or, if the judge of the court of trial (ie, where the Crown Court comprises justices of the peace, the judge presiding: Criminal Appeal Act 1968 s 51(1) (definition substituted by the Courts Act 1971 Sch 8 para 57(3))) grants a certificate that the case is fit for appeal: Criminal Appeal Act 1968 s 16A(2) (as so added). If on such an appeal the Court of Appeal considers that the appellant should be dealt with differently from the way in which the court below dealt with him:
  (1) it may quash any order which is the subject of the appeal (s 16B(1)(a) (as so added)); and
  (2) it may make such order, whether by substitution for the original order or by variation of or addition to it, as it thinks appropriate for the case and as the court below had power to make (s 16B(1)(b) (as so added)).

473. Conditions for making hospital and guardianship orders. The court may make a hospital or guardianship order[1] if:
  (1) the court is satisfied, on the written or oral evidence of two registered medical practitioners[2], that the offender or person in respect of whom the order is proposed to be made[3] is suffering from mental disorder[4] and that either:
      (a) the mental disorder from which the person is suffering is of a nature or degree which makes it appropriate for him to be detained in a hospital for medical treatment and appropriate medical treatment is available for him[5]; or
      (b) in the case of a person who has attained the age of 16 years, the mental disorder is of a nature or degree which warrants his reception into guardianship[6]; and
  (2) the court is of the opinion, having regard to all the circumstances, including the nature of the offence and the character and antecedents of the person, and to the other available methods of dealing with him, that the most suitable method of disposing of the case is by means of such a hospital or guardianship order[7].

A hospital order may not be made[8] in respect of a conviction unless the court is satisfied on the written or oral evidence of the approved clinician who would have overall responsibility for the offender's case or of some other person representing the managers of the hospital that arrangements have been made for his admission to that hospital, and for his admission to it within the period of 28 days beginning with the date of the making of such an order[9]. In relation to the making of a hospital order following a special verdict or a finding that a person is under a disability[10] it is the duty of the managers of the hospital specified in the order to admit him in accordance with it[11]. A guardianship order may not be made unless the court is satisfied that the local social services authority[12] or person under whose guardianship the person is to be placed is willing to receive the person into guardianship[13].

1   Ie under the Mental Health Act 1983 s 37(1) or the Criminal Procedure (Insanity) Act 1964 s 5 (see PARA 472). In connection with the circumstances in which a hospital order may and may not be made see in particular *R (on the application of Vowles) v Secretary of State for Justice* [2015] EWCA Civ 56, [2015] All ER (D) 69 (Feb).

2   At least one of the registered medical practitioners must have been approved for the purposes of the Mental Health Act 1983 s 12 (see MENTAL HEALTH AND CAPACITY vol 75 (2013) PARA 849): see s 54(1); and MENTAL HEALTH AND CAPACITY vol 75 (2013) PARA 865. The evidence may be given by way of written report, but the court may require the practitioner signing the report to give oral evidence: see s 54(2); and MENTAL HEALTH AND CAPACITY vol 75 (2013) PARA 865. It is desirable in every case where hospital orders and restriction orders (see PARA 477) are being considered that oral evidence should be given by the doctor who will be in charge of the case if the orders are made, or by a doctor fully informed of his views: *R v Blackwood* (1974) 59 Cr App Rep 170, [1974] Crim LR 437, CA. As to medical evidence see further the Mental Health Act 1983 s 54(3); and MENTAL HEALTH AND CAPACITY vol 75 (2013) PARA 865.

3   In relation to the making of any order under the Mental Health Act 1983 by virtue of the Criminal Procedure (Insanity) Act 1964 (see PARA 472), references in the Mental Health Act 1983 to an offender are to be construed as including references to a person in whose case the Criminal Procedure (Insanity) Act 1964 s 5 applies; and references to an offence are to be construed accordingly: s 5A(3) (s 5A added by the Domestic Violence, Crime and Victims Act 2004 s 24(1)).

4   As to the meaning of 'mental disorder' see the Mental Health Act 1983 s 1; and MENTAL HEALTH AND CAPACITY vol 75 (2013) PARA 761 (definition applied (subject to s 86(4): see MENTAL HEALTH AND CAPACITY vol 75 (2013) PARA 761) by s 145(1) (amended by the Mental Health Act 2007 Sch 1 paras 1, 17; and by the Mental Health (Discrimination) Act 2013 Schedule para 1(1))).

5   Mental Health Act 1983 s 37(2)(a)(i) (s 37(2)(a) amended by the Mental Health Act 2007 s 4(1), (5), Sch 1 paras 1, 7). As to the effect of hospital orders see the Mental Health Act 1983 s 40; and MENTAL HEALTH AND CAPACITY vol 75 (2013) PARA 867.

6   Mental Health Act 1983 s 37(2)(a)(ii) (as amended: see note 5). As to the effect of guardianship orders see s 40; and MENTAL HEALTH AND CAPACITY vol 75 (2013) PARA 867. As to the determination of a person's age see the Children and Young Persons Act 1933 s 99; and CHILDREN AND YOUNG PERSONS vol 10 (2012) PARA 1206.

7   Mental Health Act 1983 s 37(2)(b). For an illustrative decision where a hospital order was found to be inappropriate in a case of manslaughter see *R v Welsh* [2011] EWCA Crim 73, [2011] 2 Cr App Rep (S) 79, 119 BMLR 21.

8   Ie under the Mental Health Act 1983 s 37(1) (see PARA 472).

9   Mental Health Act 1983 s 37(4) (amended by the Crime (Sentences) Act 1997 Sch 4 para 12(3), Sch 6; and by the Mental Health Act 2007 s 10(1), (4)). The court may, pending a person's admission within the specified period, give such directions as it thinks fit for his conveyance to, and detention in, a place of safety: Mental Health Act 1983 s 37(4) (as so amended). If within the period of 28 days it appears to the Secretary of State that by reason of an emergency or other special circumstances it is not practicable for the patient to be received into the hospital specified in the order, he may give directions for the admission of the patient to such other hospital as appears to be appropriate instead of the hospital so specified; and, where such directions are given: (1) the Secretary of State must cause the person having the custody of the patient to be informed (s 37(5)(a)); and (2) the hospital order has effect as if the hospital specified in the directions were substituted for the hospital specified in the order (s 37(5)(b)). 'Place of safety', in relation to a person who is not a child or young person, means any police station, prison or remand centre, or any hospital the managers of which are willing temporarily to receive him, and in relation to a child or young person has the same meaning as in the Children and Young

Persons Act 1933: Mental Health Act 1983 s 55(1). For these purposes 'child' and 'young person' have the same meanings as in the Children and Young Persons Act 1933 (see CHILDREN AND YOUNG PERSONS vol 9 (2012) PARA 3): Mental Health Act 1983 s 55(1). As to the meaning of 'place of safety' in the Children and Young Persons Act 1933 see s 107(1); and CHILDREN AND YOUNG PERSONS vol 9 (2012) PARA 632. The period of 28 days referred to in the Mental Health Act 1983 s 37(4), (5) may be reduced by order of the Secretary of State: s 54A (added by the Criminal Justice Act 1991 s 27(2)). At the date at which this volume states the law no such order had been made.

10 Ie under the Criminal Procedure (Insanity) Act 1964 s 5(2)(a) (see PARA 472).

11 Criminal Procedure (Insanity) Act 1964 s 5A(1)(c) (as added: see note 3).

12 See PARA 472 note 9.

13 Mental Health Act 1983 s 37(6). See *R (on the application of Buckowicki) v Northamptonshire County Council* [2007] EWHC 310 (Admin), [2007] All ER (D) 140 (Feb).

474. Interim hospital orders. Before making a hospital order[1] (or dealing in some other way[2]) in respect of a person:

(1)   convicted before the Crown Court[3] of an offence punishable with imprisonment[4] or convicted by a magistrates' court of an offence punishable on summary conviction with imprisonment[5];

(2)   in relation to whom a special verdict of not guilty by reason of insanity has been returned[6]; or

(3)   in relation to whom findings have been made that he is under a disability and that he did the act or omission charged against him[7],

the court[8] may make an interim hospital order[9] if it is satisfied, on the written or oral evidence of two registered medical practitioners[10]:

(a)   that the offender is suffering from mental disorder[11]; and

(b)   that there is reason to suppose that the mental disorder from which the person is suffering is such that it may be appropriate for a hospital order to be made in his case[12].

A hospital order may not be made[13] in respect of a conviction unless the court is satisfied on the written or oral evidence of the approved clinician who would have overall responsibility for the offender's case or of some other person representing the managers of the hospital that arrangements have been made for his admission to that hospital, and for his admission to it within the period of 28 days beginning with the date of the making of such an order[14]. It is submitted that in relation to the making of a hospital order following a special verdict or a finding that a person is under a disability it is the duty of the managers of the hospital specified in the order to admit him in accordance with it[15].

An interim hospital order remains in force for such period, not exceeding 12 weeks, as the court may specify when making the order[16], but may be renewed for further periods of not more than 28 days at a time if it appears to the court, on the written or oral evidence of the responsible clinician, that the continuation of the order is warranted[17]. No such order may, however, continue in force for more than 12 months in all; and the court must terminate the order if it makes a hospital order in respect of the offender or decides, after considering the written or oral evidence of the responsible clinician, to deal with the offender in some other way[18].

If an offender absconds from a hospital in which he is detained in pursuance of an interim hospital order, or while being conveyed to or from such a hospital, he may be arrested without warrant by a constable and must, after being arrested, be brought as soon as practicable before the court that made the order; and the court may thereupon terminate the order and deal with him in any way in which it could have dealt with him if no such order had been made[19].

A person in respect of whom the Crown Court has made an interim hospital order after a verdict of not guilty by reason of insanity or after findings that the defendant is under a disability[20] may appeal to the Court of Appeal against the order[21].

1 Ie under the Mental Health Act 1983 s 37(1) or the Criminal Procedure (Insanity) Act 1964 s 5 (see PARA 472). In connection with the circumstances in which a hospital order may and may not be made see in particular *R (on the application of Vowles) v Secretary of State for Justice* [2015] EWCA Civ 56, [2015] All ER (D) 69 (Feb).

2 Dealing in some other way includes, in the case of a person in respect of whom a special verdict has been returned or a finding of disability has been made, the making of a supervision order or an order for absolute discharge: see the Criminal Procedure (Insanity) Act 1964 s 5(2)(b), (c); PARA 472 note 6; and PARAS 443, 495.

3 As to the powers of the Crown Court to make an interim hospital order in the case of a person committed to the court to be dealt with see PARA 549.

4 Ie other than an offence the sentence for which is fixed by law: Mental Health Act 1983 s 38(1). Offences for which the sentence is fixed by law are not excluded in relation to the making of a hospital order by virtue of the Criminal Procedure (Insanity) Act 1964 s 5 (see PARA 472): s 5A(2)(d)(ii) (s 5A added by the Domestic Violence, Crime and Victims Act 2004 s 24(1)).

5 Mental Health Act 1983 s 38(1).

6 Criminal Procedure (Insanity) Act 1964 s 5A(2)(d)(i) (as added: see note 4). As to such verdicts see CRIMINAL LAW vol 25 (2010) PARA 30; and as to the power to make a hospital order in respect of such findings see PARA 472.

7 Criminal Procedure (Insanity) Act 1964 s 5A(2)(d) (as added: see note 4). As to such findings see CRIMINAL PROCEDURE vol 27 (2015) PARA 357; and as to the power to make a hospital order in respect of such findings see PARA 472.

8 Ie, in the case of a convicted person, the court before or by which he is convicted: Mental Health Act 1983 s 38(1).

9 Ie an order authorising the person's admission to such hospital as may be specified in the order and his detention there: Mental Health Act 1983 s 38(1). For the power to require information as to hospitals before making an order see s 39; and PARA 472 note 1. In the case of an offender who is subject to an interim hospital order, the court may make a hospital order without his being brought before the court if he is represented by an authorised person who is given an opportunity of being heard: s 38(2) (amended by the Legal Services Act 2007 Sch 21 paras 53, 56). 'Authorised person' means a person who, for the purposes of the Legal Services Act 2007, is an authorised person in relation to an activity which constitutes the exercise of a right of audience (within the meaning of the Legal Services Act 2007: see Sch 2 para 3; and LEGAL PROFESSIONS vol 65 (2015) PARA 352): Mental Health Act 1983 s 55(1) (definition added by the Legal Services Act 2007 Sch 21 para 59). See also the Mental Health Act 1983 s 45A(8); and PARA 478.

10 At least one of the registered medical practitioners must have been approved for the purposes of the Mental Health Act 1983 s 12 (see MENTAL HEALTH AND CAPACITY vol 75 (2013) PARA 849) (see s 54(1); and MENTAL HEALTH AND CAPACITY vol 75 (2013) PARA 865), and at least one of the registered medical practitioners whose evidence is taken into account must be employed at the hospital which is to be specified in the order (s 38(3)). See also *R v Blackwood* (1974) 59 Cr App Rep 170, [1974] Crim LR 437, CA; and PARA 473 note 2.

11 Mental Health Act 1983 s 38(1)(a) (amended by the Mental Health Act 2007 Sch 1 paras 1, 8). As to the meaning of 'mental disorder' see PARA 473 note 4.

12 Mental Health Act 1983 s 38(1)(b).

13 Ie under the Mental Health Act 1983 s 37(1) (see PARA 472). Section 38(4) is not expressly limited to hospital orders made in respect of a conviction but such limitation may be inferred from the identical provisions set out in s 37(4) (see PARA 472), which are expressed to be so limited. The Criminal Procedure (Insanity) Act 1964 s 5A(1)(c) makes provision alternative to the Mental Health Act 1983 s 37(4) in respect of a person in relation to whom a special verdict of not guilty by reason of insanity has been returned or findings that he is under a disability have been made (see PARA 472) and it is submitted that a corresponding differentiation in treatment should be made under s 38(4).

14 Mental Health Act 1983 s 38(4) (amended by the Mental Health Act 2007 s 10(1), (5)). The court may, pending a person's admission within the specified period, give such directions as it thinks fit for his conveyance to, and detention in, a place of safety: Mental Health Act 1983 s 38(4) (as so amended). See note 13; and as to the meaning of 'place of safety' see PARA 473

note 9. The period may be reduced by an order made by the Secretary of State: s 54A (added by the Criminal Justice Act 1991 s 27(2)). At the date at which this volume states the law no such order had been made.

15 See the Criminal Procedure (Insanity) Act 1964 s 5A(1)(c); and note 13.

16 Mental Health Act 1983 s 38(5)(a).

17 Mental Health Act 1983 s 38(5)(b) (amended by the Mental Health Act 2007 s 10(1), (5)). 'Responsible clinician', in relation to a person liable to be detained in a hospital within the meaning of the Mental Health Act 1983 Pt 2 (ss 2–34: see MENTAL HEALTH AND CAPACITY), means the approved clinician with overall responsibility for the patient's case: s 55(1) (definition added by the Mental Health Act 2007 s 11(1), (7)).

18 Mental Health Act 1983 s 38(5) (amended by the Crime (Sentences) Act 1997 s 49(1); and the Mental Health Act 2007 s 10(5)). See also the Mental Health Act 1983 s 45A(8); and PARA 478. The power of renewing an interim hospital order may be exercised without the offender being brought before the court if he is represented by counsel or a solicitor and his counsel or solicitor is given an opportunity of being heard: s 38(6).

19 Mental Health Act 1983 s 38(7).

20 Ie under the Criminal Procedure (Insanity) Act 1964 s 5 or s 5A.

21 Criminal Appeal Act 1968 s 16A(1)(a) (ss 16A, 16B added by the Domestic Violence, Crime and Victims Act 2004 s 25). Such an appeal lies only with the leave of the Court of Appeal; or if the judge of the court of trial (ie, where the Crown Court comprises justices of the peace, the judge presiding: Criminal Appeal Act 1968 s 51(1) (definition substituted by the Courts Act 1971 Sch 8 para 57(3))) grants a certificate that the case is fit for appeal: Criminal Appeal Act 1968 s 16A(2) (as so added). If on such an appeal the Court of Appeal considers that the appellant should be dealt with differently from the way in which the court below dealt with him:
   (1)   it may quash any order which is the subject of the appeal (s 16B(1)(a) (as so added)); and
   (2)   it may make such order, whether by substitution for the original order or by variation of or addition to it, as it thinks appropriate for the case and as the court below had power to make (s 16B(1)(b) (as so added)).
The fact that an appeal is pending against an interim hospital order does not affect the power of the court below to renew or terminate the order or to deal with the appellant on its termination (s 16B(2) (as so added)); and where the Court of Appeal quashes such an order but does not pass any sentence or make any other order in its place, the court may (subject to the Criminal Justice and Public Order Act 1994 s 25 (see CRIMINAL PROCEDURE vol 27 (2015) PARA 76)) direct the appellant to be kept in custody or released on bail pending his being dealt with by the court below (Criminal Appeal Act 1968 s 11(5) (added by the Mental Health (Amendment) Act 1982 Sch 3 para 37; and amended by the Mental Health Act 1983 Sch 4 para 23(d); and the Criminal Justice and Public Order Act 1994 Sch 10 para 20)).

475. Remand to hospital for report on mental condition. The Crown Court or a magistrates' court may remand an accused person[1], or a person in respect of whom a special verdict has been returned or a finding of disability has been made[2], to a hospital specified by the court for a report on his mental condition[3], if:

   (1)   the court is satisfied, on the written or oral evidence of a registered medical practitioner[4], that there is reason to suspect that the person in question is suffering from mental disorder[5]; and

   (2)   the court is of the opinion that it would be impracticable for a report on his mental condition to be made if he were remanded on bail[6],

but those powers may not be exercised by the Crown Court in respect of a person who has been convicted[7] before the court if the sentence for the offence of which he has been convicted is fixed by law[8].

A hospital remand may not be made unless the court is satisfied on the written or oral evidence of the approved clinician who would be responsible for making the report or of some other person representing the managers of the hospital that arrangements have been made for his admission to that hospital, and for his admission to it within the period of 28 days beginning with the date of the remand[9]. Where a court has so remanded a person, it may further remand him if it appears to the court, on the written or oral evidence of the approved clinician responsible for making the report, that a further remand is necessary for completing the assessment of the person's mental condition[10]. An accused person may not be remanded or further remanded for more than 28 days at a time or for more than 12 weeks in all; and the court may at any time terminate the remand if it appears to the court that it is appropriate to do so[11].

If a person absconds from a hospital to which he has been remanded, or while being conveyed to or from that hospital, he may be arrested without warrant by any constable and must, after being arrested, be brought as soon as practicable before the court that remanded him; and the court may thereupon terminate the remand and deal with him in any way in which it could have dealt with him if he had not been so remanded[12].

1 For these purposes, an accused person is: (1) in relation to the Crown Court, any person who is awaiting trial before the court for an offence punishable with imprisonment or who has been arraigned before the court for such an offence and has not yet been sentenced or otherwise been dealt with for the offence on which he has been arraigned (Mental Health Act 1983 s 35(2)(a)); (2) in relation to a magistrates' court, any person who has been convicted by the court of an offence punishable on summary conviction with imprisonment and any person charged with such an offence if the court is satisfied that he did the act or made the omission charged or he has consented to the exercise by the court of the powers conferred by s 35 (s 35(2)(b)).

2 Criminal Procedure (Insanity) Act 1964 s 5A(2)(c) (s 5A added by the Domestic Violence, Crime and Victims Act 2004 s 24(1)). As to such verdicts and findings see CRIMINAL LAW vol 25 (2010) PARA 30; CRIMINAL PROCEDURE vol 27 (2015) PARA 357; and as to the power to make a hospital order in respect of such verdicts and findings see PARA 472.

3 Mental Health Act 1983 s 35(1). A person remanded to hospital is entitled to obtain at his own expense an independent report on his mental condition from a registered medical practitioner (or approved clinician) chosen by him and to apply to the court on the basis of it for his remand to be terminated: s 35(8) (amended by the Mental Health Act 2007 s 10(1), (2)). In connection with requests for medical reports see the Criminal Procedure Rules 2015, SI 2015/1490, r 28.8.

4 The practitioner must be approved for the purposes of the Mental Health Act 1983 s 12 (see MENTAL HEALTH AND CAPACITY vol 75 (2013) PARA 849): see s 54(1); and MENTAL HEALTH AND CAPACITY vol 75 (2013) PARA 865. See also *R v Blackwood* (1974) 59 Cr App Rep 170, [1974] Crim LR 437, CA; and PARA 473 note 2.

5 Mental Health Act 1983 s 35(3)(a) (amended by the Mental Health Act 2007 Sch 1 paras 1, 5). As to the meaning of 'mental disorder' see PARA 473 note 4.

6 Mental Health Act 1983 s 35(3)(b).

7 Ie this exclusion does not apply in respect of a person in respect of whom a special verdict has been returned or a finding of disability has been made: Criminal Procedure (Insanity) Act 1964 s 5A(2)(a) (as added: see note 2).

8 Mental Health Act 1983 s 35(3).

9 Mental Health Act 1983 s 35(4) (amended by the Mental Health Act 2007 s 10(1), (2)). As to the information to be supplied on admission see the Criminal Procedure Rules 2015, SI 2015/1490, r 28.9. The court may, pending a person's admission within the specified period, give such directions as it thinks fit for his conveyance to, and detention in, a place of safety: Mental Health Act 1983 s 35(4) (as so amended). As to remands under the Mental Health Act 1983 s 35 see *R (on the application of Bitcon) v West Allerdale Magistrates' Court* [2003] EWHC 2460 (Admin), 147 Sol Jo LB 1028, [2003] All ER (D) 33 (Sep). Where an accused person is so remanded: (1) a constable or any other person directed to do so by the court must convey the accused person to the hospital specified by the court within the period specified in the Mental Health Act 1983 s 35(4) (s 35(9)(a)); and (2) the managers of the hospital must admit him within that period and thereafter detain him in accordance with the provisions of s 35 (s 35(9)(b)). As to the meaning of 'responsible clinician' see PARA 474 note 17. As to the meaning of 'place of safety' see PARA 473 note 9.

10 Mental Health Act 1983 s 35(5) (amended by the Mental Health Act 2007 s 10(2)). The power of further remanding a person may be exercised by the court without his being brought before the court if he is represented by an authorised person who is given an opportunity of being heard: Mental Health Act 1983 s 35(6) (amended by the Legal Services Act 2007 Sch 21 paras 53, 54). As to the meaning of 'authorised person' see PARA 474 note 9.

11 Mental Health Act 1983 s 35(7).
12 Mental Health Act 1983 s 35(10).

476. Remand to hospital for treatment. Instead of remanding an accused person[1] or a person in respect of whom a special verdict has been returned or a finding of disability has been made[2] in custody, the Crown Court may remand such person to a hospital specified by the court if satisfied, on the written or oral evidence of two registered medical practitioners[3], that:

(1)   he is suffering from mental disorder[4] of a nature or degree which makes it appropriate for him to be detained in a hospital for medical treatment[5]; and

(2)   appropriate medical treatment is available for him[6].

However, the court may not so remand a person unless it is satisfied, on the written or oral evidence of the approved clinician who would have overall responsibility for his case or of some other person representing the managers of the hospital, that arrangements have been made for his admission to that hospital and for his admission to it within the period of seven days beginning with the date of the remand[7]. Where a court has so remanded a person it may further remand him if it appears to the court, on the written or oral evidence of the responsible clinician[8], that a further remand is warranted[9]. A person may not be remanded or further remanded for more than 28 days at a time or for more than 12 weeks in all; and the court may at any time terminate the remand if it appears to the court that it is appropriate to do so[10].

If a person absconds from a hospital to which he has been remanded, or while being conveyed to or from that hospital, he may be arrested without warrant by any constable and must, after being arrested, be brought as soon as practicable before the court that remanded him; and the court may thereupon terminate the remand and deal with him in any way in which it could have dealt with him if he had not been so remanded[11].

1   For these purposes, an accused person is any person who is in custody awaiting trial before the Crown Court for an offence punishable with imprisonment (other than an offence the sentence for which is fixed by law) or who at any time before sentence is in custody in the course of a trial before that court for such an offence: Mental Health Act 1983 s 36(2). In relation to a case where the Criminal Procedure (Insanity) Act 1964 s 5 applies (see note 2; and PARA 472), the exclusion in respect of offences the sentence for which are fixed by law does not apply: s 5A(2)(b) (s 5A added by the Domestic Violence, Crime and Victims Act 2004 s 24(1)).

2   Criminal Procedure (Insanity) Act 1964 s 5A(2)(c) (as added: see note 1). As to such verdicts and findings see CRIMINAL LAW vol 25 (2010) PARA 30; CRIMINAL PROCEDURE vol 27 (2015) PARA 357; and as to the power to make a hospital order in respect of such verdicts and findings see PARA 472.

3   At least one of the registered medical practitioners must be approved for the purposes of the Mental Health Act 1983 s 12 (see MENTAL HEALTH AND CAPACITY vol 75 (2013) PARA 849): see s 54(1) (see MENTAL HEALTH AND CAPACITY vol 75 (2013) PARA 865). See also *R v Blackwood* (1974) 59 Cr App Rep 170, [1974] Crim LR 437, CA; and PARA 473 note 2. A person remanded to hospital is entitled to obtain at his own expense an independent report on his mental condition from a registered medical practitioner (or approved clinician) chosen by him and to apply to the court on the basis of it for his remand to be terminated under the Mental Health Act 1983 s 36(6) (see the text and note 10): s 36(7) (amended by the Mental Health Act 2007 s 10(1), (2)). In connection with requests for medical reports see the Criminal Procedure Rules 2015, SI 2015/1490, r 28.8.

4   As to the meaning of 'mental disorder' see PARA 473 note 4.

5   Mental Health Act 1983 s 36(1)(a) (s 36(1)(a) substituted, s 36(1)(b) amended, by the Mental Health Act 2007 s 5, Sch 1 paras 1, 6).

6   Mental Health Act 1983 s 36(1)(b) (as amended: see note 5).

7   Mental Health Act 1983 s 36(3) (amended by the Mental Health Act 2007 s 10(1), (3)). As to the information to be supplied on admission see the Criminal Procedure Rules 2015,

SI 2015/1490, r 28.9. Where an accused person is so remanded: (1) a constable or any other person directed to do so by the court must convey the accused person to the hospital specified by the court within the period specified in the Mental Health Act 1983 s 36(3) (ss 35(9)(a), 36(8)); and (2) the managers of the hospital must admit him within that period and thereafter detain him in accordance with the provisions of s 36 (s 35(9)(b)). If the court is satisfied as described in s 36(3), it may, pending the person's admission, give directions for his conveyance to, and detention in, a place of safety: s 36(3) (as so amended). As to the meaning of 'place of safety' see PARA 473 note 9.

8   As to the meaning of 'responsible clinician' see PARA 474 note 17.

9   Mental Health Act 1983 s 36(4) (amended by the Mental Health Act 2007 s 10(1), (3)). The power of further remanding a person may be exercised by the court without his being brought before the court if he is represented by an authorised person who is given an opportunity of being heard: Mental Health Act 1983 s 36(5) (amended by the Legal Services Act 2007 Sch 21 paras 53, 55). As to the meaning of 'authorised person' see PARA 474 note 9.

10 Mental Health Act 1983 s 36(6).

11 Mental Health Act 1983 ss 35(10), 36(8).

477. Restriction orders. Where a hospital order[1] is made[2] by the Crown Court[3] and it appears to the court, having regard to the nature of the offence, the antecedents of the offender and the risk of his committing further offences if set at large, that it is necessary for the protection of the public from serious harm[4] so to do, the court may further order that the offender be subject to special statutory restrictions[5] (ie may make a 'restriction order')[6]. However, a restriction order may not be made in the case of any person unless at least one of the registered medical practitioners whose evidence is taken into account by the court[7] has given evidence orally before the court[8].

While a person is subject to a restriction order, the responsible medical officer must at such intervals, not exceeding one year, as the Secretary of State may direct, examine and report to the Secretary of State on that person; and every such report must contain such particulars as the Secretary of State may require[9].

1   See PARA 472.

2   These provisions (ie the Mental Health Act 1983 s 41: see the text and notes 3–9) are expressed to be applicable only in relation to a hospital order made in respect of an offender (see s 41(1)); however a hospital order made under the Criminal Procedure (Insanity) Act 1964 s 5(2) in respect of a person in respect of whom a special verdict has been returned or a finding of disability has been made may also be made with or without a restriction order (see s 5(2)(a); and PARA 472).

3   As to the power of the Crown Court to make a restriction order in the case of a person committed to the court to be dealt with see PARA 549.

4   'Serious' in the term 'serious harm' qualifies 'harm' rather than risk. 'Serious harm' is not limited to personal injury, nor need it relate to the public in general. It suffices if a category of persons, or even a single person, is adjudged to be at risk, although the category of persons excludes the offender himself: *R v Birch* (1990) 90 Cr App Rep 78, (1990) 11 Cr App Rep (S) 202, CA.

5   The special restrictions applicable to a person in respect of whom a restriction order is in force are:

    (1)   none of the provisions of the Mental Health Act 1983 Pt II (ss 2–34) (compulsory admission to hospital or guardianship: see MENTAL HEALTH AND CAPACITY) relating to the duration, renewal and expiration of authority for the detention of patients applies; and the patient continues to be liable to be detained by virtue of the relevant hospital order until he is duly discharged under Pt II or absolutely discharged under s 42, s 73, s 74 or s 75 (see MENTAL HEALTH AND CAPACITY vol 75 (2013) PARAS 876, 969–971) (s 41(3)(a));

    (2)   none of the provisions of Pt II relating to community treatment orders and community patients (ie ss 17A–17G: see MENTAL HEALTH AND CAPACITY vol 75 (2013) PARAS 797–803) apply (s 41(3)(aa) (added by the Mental Health (Patients in the Community) Act 1995 Sch 1 para 5; amended by the Mental Health Act 2007 Sch 3 paras 1, 17));

    (3)   no application may be made to the appropriate tribunal in respect of a patient under

the Mental Health Act 1983 s 66 or s 69(1) (see MENTAL HEALTH AND CAPACITY vol 75 (2013) PARAS 960–961) (s 41(3)(b) (amended by SI 2008/2833));

(4)   the following powers are exercisable only with the consent of the Secretary of State:

    (a)   the power to grant leave of absence to the patient under the Mental Health Act 1983 s 17 (see MENTAL HEALTH AND CAPACITY vol 75 (2013) PARA 917) (s 41(3)(c)(i)) and, if leave of absence is so granted, the power to recall the patient under s 17 vests in the Secretary of State as well as the responsible clinician (s 41(3)(c) (amended by the Mental Health Act 2007 s 10(1), (6)));

    (b)   the power to transfer the patient in pursuance of regulations under the Mental Health Act 1983 s 19 or in pursuance of s 19(3) (see MENTAL HEALTH AND CAPACITY vol 75 (2013) PARA 887) (s 41(3)(c)(ii) (amended by the Crime (Sentences) Act 1997 s 49(2))); and

    (c)   the power to order the discharge of the patient under the Mental Health Act 1983 s 23 (see MENTAL HEALTH AND CAPACITY vol 75 (2013) PARA 913) (s 41(3)(c)(iii)); and

(5)   the power of the Secretary of State to recall the patient under s 17 and the power to take the patient into custody and return him under s 18 (see MENTAL HEALTH AND CAPACITY vol 75 (2013) PARA 918) may be exercised at any time (s 41(3)(d)).

In relation to any such patient, s 40(4) has effect as if it referred to Sch 1 Pt II instead of Sch 1 Pt I (see MENTAL HEALTH AND CAPACITY vol 75 (2013) PARA 860 et seq): s 41(3). As to the meaning of 'responsible clinician' see PARA 474 note 17.

6   Mental Health Act 1983 s 41(1). As to the effect of a restriction order and the circumstances in which such an order should be made see *R v Birch* (1990) 90 Cr App Rep 78, (1990) 11 Cr App Rep (S) 202, CA (court not obliged to follow advice of medical witnesses; seriousness of offence committed by offender no more important than other factors to which the Mental Health Act 1983 s 41 required court to have regard); and see the following cases decided under the Mental Health Act 1959: *R v Gardiner* [1967] 1 All ER 895, 51 Cr App Rep 187, CA (if a restriction order is made, the safer course is to make the order without limit of time, unless the medical practitioners are confident that recovery will take place within a fixed period); *R v Haynes* (1981) 3 Cr App Rep (S) 330, [1982] Crim LR 245, CA (no analogy between a restriction order and a determinate sentence of imprisonment). See also *R v Nwohia* [1996] 1 Cr App Rep (S) 170, 26 BMLR 157, CA (without medical evidence that the offender can be cured within a particular period, it is unwise to make a restriction order with limit of time). Before making an order, the court should ascertain that the hospital to which the offender is to be admitted has the facilities for his safe custody: *R v Morris* [1961] 2 QB 237, 45 Cr App Rep 185, CCA; *R v Higginbotham* [1961] 3 All ER 616, 45 Cr App Rep 379, CCA; *R v Cox* [1968] 1 All ER 386, 52 Cr App Rep 130, CA. Arrangements may be made for an offender's admission to a hospital in any part of the country where a vacancy exists: *R v Marsden* [1968] 2 All ER 341, 52 Cr App Rep 301, CA. Except in the rarest cases, it is desirable that the defendant should be represented by counsel: *R v Blackwood* (1974) 59 Cr App Rep 170, [1974] Crim LR 437, CA. The decision whether to make a restriction order is the responsibility of the judge; the judge may make such an order contrary to the recommendations of the medical witnesses: *R v Royse* (1981) 3 Cr App Rep (S) 58, CA; *R v Birch*. A hospital order does not cease to have effect under the Mental Health Act 1983 s 40(5) (see MENTAL HEALTH AND CAPACITY vol 75 (2013) PARA 867) if a restriction order in respect of the patient is in force at the material time: s 41(4). An offender who becomes subject to a restriction order becomes a 'patient' within the meaning of the Mental Health Act 1983 and remains such until such time as he is absolutely discharged: *R v Merseyside Mental Health Review Tribunal, ex p K* [1990] 1 All ER 694, (1989) Times, 15 June, CA. Where a restriction order in respect of a patient ceases to have effect while the relevant hospital order continues in force, the provisions of the Mental Health Act 1983 s 40 and Sch 1 Pt I apply to the patient as if he had been admitted to the hospital in pursuance of a hospital order (without a restriction order) made on the date on which the restriction order ceased to have effect: s 41(5).

7   Ie under the Mental Health Act 1983 s 37(2)(a) (see PARA 473).

8   Mental Health Act 1983 s 41(2).

9   Mental Health Act 1983 s 41(6).

478. Hospital and limitation directions ('hybrid orders'). Where, in the case of a person aged 21 or over convicted before the Crown Court of an offence the sentence for which is not fixed by law[1]:

(1)   the court is satisfied, on the written or oral evidence of two registered

medical practitioners[2], that the offender is suffering from mental disorder[3], that the mental disorder from which the offender is suffering is of a nature or degree which makes it appropriate for him to be detained in a hospital for medical treatment[4], and that appropriate medical treatment is available for him[5]; and

(2)   the court considers making a hospital order[6] in respect of him before deciding to impose a sentence of imprisonment (the 'relevant sentence') in respect of the offence[7],

the court may give both of the following directions, namely:

(a)   a direction that, instead of being removed to and detained in a prison, the offender be removed to and detained in such hospital as may be specified in the direction (a 'hospital direction')[8]; and

(b)   a direction that the offender be subject to special restrictions[9] (a 'limitation direction')[10].

A hospital direction and a limitation direction may not be given in relation to an offender unless the court is satisfied on the written or oral evidence of the approved clinician who would have overall responsibility for his case, or of some other person representing the managers of the hospital, that arrangements have been made for his admission to that hospital[11] and for his admission to it within the period of 28 days beginning with the day of the giving of such directions[12]; and the court may, pending his admission within that period, give such directions as it thinks fit for his conveyance to and detention in a place of safety[13]. If within such period of 28 days it appears to the Secretary of State that by reason of an emergency or other special circumstances it is not practicable for the patient to be received into the hospital specified in the hospital direction, he may give instructions for the admission of the patient to such other hospital as appears to be appropriate instead of the hospital so specified[14].

A hospital direction and a limitation direction given in relation to an offender have effect not only as regards the relevant sentence but also (so far as applicable) as regards any other sentence of imprisonment imposed on the same or a previous occasion[15]. A hospital direction and a limitation direction are sufficient authority:

(i)   for a constable or any other person directed to do so by the court to convey the patient to the hospital specified in the hospital direction within a period of 28 days[16]; and

(ii)   for the managers of the hospital to admit him at any time within that period and thereafter detain him in accordance with these provisions[17].

With respect to any person, a hospital direction has effect as a transfer direction and a limitation direction has effect as a restriction direction[18].

While a person is subject to a hospital direction and a limitation direction the responsible clinician must at such intervals (not exceeding one year) as the Secretary of State may direct examine and report to the Secretary of State on that person; and every report must contain such particulars as the Secretary of State may require[19].

1   Mental Health Act 1983 s 45A(1) (ss 45A, 45B added by the Crime (Sentences) Act 1997 s 46). As to the determination of a person's age see the Children and Young Persons Act 1933 s 99; and CHILDREN AND YOUNG PERSONS vol 10 (2012) PARA 1206.

2   At least one of the registered medical practitioners must have been approved for the purposes of the Mental Health Act 1983 s 12 (see MENTAL HEALTH AND CAPACITY vol 75 (2013) PARA 849): see s 54(1) (amended by the Crime (Sentences) Act 1997 Sch 4 para 12(6)). A direction under these provisions may not be given in relation to an offender unless at least one of the medical practitioners whose evidence is taken into account by the court under the Mental Health Act 1983 s 45A(2) has given evidence orally before the court: s 45A(4) (as so added).

3   Mental Health Act 1983 s 45A(1)(a), (2)(a) (as added (see note 1); s 45A(2)(a) amended by the
    Mental Health Act 2007 Sch 1 paras 1, 9). As to the meaning of 'mental disorder' see PARA 473
    note 4.
4   Mental Health Act 1983 s 45A(2)(b) (as added: see note 1).
5   Mental Health Act 1983 s 45A(2)(c) (as added (see note 1); substituted by the Mental Health
    Act 2007 s 4(1), (6)).
6   See PARA 472.
7   Mental Health Act 1983 s 45A(1)(b) (as added: see note 1); amended by the Criminal Justice
    Act 2003 Sch 32 paras 37, 39, Sch 37 Pt 7).
8   Mental Health Act 1983 s 45A(3)(a) (as added: see note 1). See note 10.
9   Ie subject to the special restrictions set out in the Mental Health Act 1983 s 41 (restriction
    orders) (see PARA 477).
10 Mental Health Act 1983 s 45A(3)(b) (as added: see note 1). Section 38(1), (5) (see PARA 474)
    and s 39 (see PARA 472) have effect as if any reference to the making of a hospital order included
    a reference to the giving of a hospital direction and a limitation direction: s 45A(8) (as so
    added).
11 Mental Health Act 1983 s 45A(5)(a) (as added (see note 1); s 45A(5) amended by the Mental
    Health Act 2007 s 10(1), (8)).
12 Mental Health Act 1983 s 45A(5)(b) (as added and amended: see notes 1, 11).
13 Mental Health Act 1983 s 45A(5) (as added and amended: see notes 1, 11).
14 Mental Health Act 1983 s 45A(6) (as added: see note 1). Where such instructions are given the
    Secretary of State must cause the person having the custody of the patient to be informed and
    the hospital direction has effect as if the hospital specified in the instructions were substituted
    for the hospital specified in the hospital direction: s 45A(7) (as so added).
15 Mental Health Act 1983 s 45A(9) (as added: see note 1).
16 Mental Health Act 1983 s 45B(1)(a) (as added: see note 1).
17 Mental Health Act 1983 s 45B(1)(b) (as added: see note 1).
18 Mental Health Act 1983 s 45B(2) (as added: see note 1). As to transfer directions (ie directions
    under s 47) see MENTAL HEALTH AND CAPACITY vol 75 (2013) PARA 892. As to restriction
    directions (ie directions under s 49) see MENTAL HEALTH AND CAPACITY vol 75 (2013) PARA
    894.
19 Mental Health Act 1983 s 45B(3) (as added (see note 1); amended by the Mental Health
    Act 2007 s 10(1), (9)). As to the meaning of 'responsible clinician' see PARA 474 note 17.

479.   Power to specify hospital units.   Any power to specify a hospital
conferred by the provisions relating to hospital orders[1], to hospital and
limitation directions[2] and to transfer directions[3] includes power to specify a
hospital unit[4]; and where such a unit is specified in relation to any person in the
exercise of such a power, any reference in any enactment[5] to him being, or being
liable to be, detained in a hospital is to be construed accordingly[6]. However, in
the case of a hospital order, this provision does not apply unless the court also
makes a restriction order[7]; and in the case of a transfer direction, this provision
does not apply unless the Secretary of State also gives a restriction direction[8].

1   Crime (Sentences) Act 1997 s 47(1)(a). As to hospital orders (ie orders under the Mental Health
    Act 1983 s 37) see PARA 472. A reference in the Crime (Sentences) Act 1997 s 47 (see the text
    and notes 2–8) to the Mental Health Act 1983 s 37 or s 41 (see PARA 477) includes a reference
    to that provision as it applies by virtue of:
    (1)   the Criminal Procedure (Insanity) Act 1964 s 5 (see PARA 472) (Crime (Sentences)
          Act 1997 s 47(4)(a) (s 47(4) substituted by the Domestic Violence, Crime and Victims
          Act 2004 Sch 10 para 45(1), (3)));
    (2)   the Criminal Appeal Act 1968 s 6 (see CRIMINAL PROCEDURE vol 28 (2015) PARA 767)
          or s 14 (see CRIMINAL PROCEDURE vol 28 (2015) PARA 773) (Crime (Sentences)
          Act 1997 s 47(4)(b) (as so substituted)); or
    (3)   the Armed Forces Act 2006 Sch 4 (see ARMED FORCES vol 3 (2011) PARA 650)
          (including as applied by the Courts-Martial (Appeals) Act 1968 s 16(2)) (Crime
          (Sentences) Act 1997 s 47(4)(c) (substituted by the Armed Forces Act 2006 Sch 16
          para 143)).
2   Crime (Sentences) Act 1997 s 47(1)(b). As to hospital and limitation directions (ie under the
    Mental Health Act 1983 s 45A) see PARA 478.

3 Crime (Sentences) Act 1997 s 47(1)(c). As to transfer directions (ie directions under the Mental Health Act 1983 s 47) see MENTAL HEALTH AND CAPACITY vol 75 (2013) PARA 892.
4 Ie any part of a hospital which is treated as a separate unit: Crime (Sentences) Act 1997 s 47(3).
5 Ie including the Crime (Sentences) Act 1997.
6 Crime (Sentences) Act 1997 s 47(1).
7 Crime (Sentences) Act 1997 s 47(2)(a). A 'restriction order' is an order under the Mental Health Act 1983 s 41 (see PARA 477). As to references to s 41 see note 1.
8 Crime (Sentences) Act 1997 s 47(2)(b). A restriction direction is a direction under s 49 (see MENTAL HEALTH AND CAPACITY vol 75 (2013) PARA 894).

480. Victims' rights where offender is under a hospital order with a restriction order. Where:
(1) a patient is charged with a sexual or violent offence[1] and:
   (a) the patient is convicted of the offence[2]; or
   (b) a verdict is returned that the patient is not guilty of the offence by reason of insanity[3]; or
   (c) a finding is made that the patient is under a disability[4], and he did the act or made the omission charged against him as the offence[5]; and
(2) a hospital order[6] (whether with or without a restriction order[7]) is made in respect of the patient by a court[8] dealing with him for the offence[9],
then the local probation board[10] or provider of probation services[11] must take all reasonable steps to ascertain whether a person who appears to the board to be the victim of the offence or to act for the victim of the offence wishes to make representations about the conditions of the patient's discharge from hospital[12] or to receive the information about any conditions to which the patient is to be subject in the event of his discharge from hospital[13]. Provision is made in connection with the forwarding of any such representations to specified persons (the identity of whom depends on whether a restriction order has[14] or has not[15] been made), and with the giving of any such information where a restriction order has been made[16]. Where a restriction order has not been made, there is provision for the notification of hospital managers of a patient's decisions concerning the making of representations and the receipt of information[17] and of other matters concerning the patient's treatment[18]. Provision is also made in connection with the making of representations and the receipt of information where a restriction order ceases to have effect while a hospital order remains in force[19].

1 Domestic Violence, Crime and Victims Act 2004 s 36(1), (2). For the purposes of ss 35–44B an offence is a sexual or violent offence if it is any of these: (1) murder or an offence specified in the Criminal Justice Act 2003 Sch 15 (see PARAS 23–24); (2) an offence in respect of which the patient or offender is subject to the notification requirements of the Sexual Offences Act 2003 Pt 2 (ss 80–136ZD) (see PARA 498)et seq); (3) an offence against a child within the meaning of the Criminal Justice and Courts Services Act 2000 Pt 2 (ss 26–42) (see CHILDREN AND YOUNG PERSONS vol 9 (2012) PARA 454): Domestic Violence, Crime and Victims Act 2004 s 45(2) (amended by the Mental Health Act 2007 Sch 6 paras 1, 16).
2 Domestic Violence, Crime and Victims Act 2004 s 36(2)(a).
3 Domestic Violence, Crime and Victims Act 2004 s 36(2)(b). As to such verdicts see CRIMINAL LAW vol 25 (2010) PARA 30.
4 Ie under the Criminal Procedure (Insanity) Act 1964 s 4 (see CRIMINAL PROCEDURE vol 27 (2015) PARA 357): Domestic Violence, Crime and Victims Act 2004 s 36(2)(c)(i).
5 Ie under the Criminal Procedure (Insanity) Act 1964 s 4A (see CRIMINAL PROCEDURE vol 27 (2015) PARA 357): Domestic Violence, Crime and Victims Act 2004 s 36(2)(c)(ii).
6 'Hospital order' has the meaning given by the Mental Health Act 1983 s 37(4) (see PARA 472): Domestic Violence, Crime and Victims Act 2004 s 45(1).
7 'Restriction order' has the meaning given by the Mental Health Act 1983 s 41(1) (see PARA 477): Domestic Violence, Crime and Victims Act 2004 s 45(1).

8   'Court' does not include the Court Martial or the Court Martial Appeal Court: Domestic Violence, Crime and Victims Act 2004 s 45(1) (amended by the Armed Forces Act 2006 Sch 16 para 239).

9   Domestic Violence, Crime and Victims Act 2004 s 36(3) (amended by the Mental Health Act 2007 Sch 6 para 2).

10 Ie the local probation board for the area in which the determination mentioned in the Domestic Violence, Crime and Victims Act 2004 s 36(2)(a), (b) or (c) (see the text and notes 1–5) is made: s 36(4) (amended by SI 2008/912). As to local probation boards and the provision of probation services see PARAS 666–687.

11 Ie the provider of probation services operating in the local justice area in which the determination mentioned in the Domestic Violence, Crime and Victims Act 2004 s 36(2)(a), (b) or (c) is made: s 36(4) (amended by SI 2008/912). See note 10. The provider of probation services mentioned in the Domestic Violence, Crime and Victims Act 2004 s 36(4) is the provider of probation services identified as such by arrangements under the Offender Management Act 2007 s 3 (see PARA 669): Domestic Violence, Crime and Victims Act 2004 s 36(4A) (added by SI 2008/912).

12 Domestic Violence, Crime and Victims Act 2004 s 36(4)(a). The representations which may be so made are about whether the patient should be subject to any conditions in the event of his discharge from hospital while a restriction order is in force in respect of him (s 36(5)(a) (s 36(5)(a) amended, s 36(5)(c) added, by the Mental Health Act 2007 Sch 6 paras 1, 2)), if so, what conditions (Domestic Violence, Crime and Victims Act 2004 s 36(5)(b)) and what conditions he should be subject to in the event of his discharge from hospital under a community treatment order (s 36(5)(c) (as so added)). As to the meaning of 'community treatment order' see the Mental Health Act 1983 s 17A; and MENTAL HEALTH AND CAPACITY vol 75 (2013) PARA 797 (definition applied by the Domestic Violence, Crime and Victims Act 2004 s 45(1) (amended by the Mental Health Act 2007 Sch 6 para 16)).

13 Domestic Violence, Crime and Victims Act 2004 s 36(4)(b), (6).

14 If in a case where the Domestic Violence, Crime and Victims Act 2004 s 36 applies the hospital order in respect of the patient was made with a restriction order, a person makes representations about a matter specified in s 36(5) to the local probation board or provider of probation services mentioned in s 36(4) or the relevant probation body, and it appears to the relevant probation body that the person is the victim of the offence or acts for the victim of the offence, the relevant probation body must (provided the restriction order made in respect of the patient is in force) forward the representations to the persons responsible for determining the matter: s 37(1)–(3) (s 37(1) amended by the Mental Health Act 2007 Sch 6 para 4; Domestic Violence, Crime and Victims Act 2004 s 37(2), (4)–(7) amended, s 37(8) substituted, by SI 2008/912).

    For this purpose the 'relevant probation body' is:

(1)   in a case where the patient is to be discharged subject to a condition that he reside in a particular area, which is or is part of the area of a local probation board, that local probation board (Domestic Violence, Crime and Victims Act 2004 s 37(8)(a) (as so substituted));

(2)   in a case where the patient is to be discharged subject to a condition that he reside in a particular area other than one mentioned in s 37(8)(a), the provider of probation services operating in that area that is identified as the relevant probation body by arrangements under the Offender Management Act 2007 s 3 (Domestic Violence, Crime and Victims Act 2004 s 37(8)(b) (as so substituted)); and

(3)   in any other case, if the hospital in which the patient is detained is situated in the area of a local probation board, that area, and if that hospital is not so situated, the provider of probation services operating in the local justice area in which the hospital in which the patient is detained is situated that is identified as the relevant probation body by arrangements under the Offender Management Act 2007 s 3 (Domestic Violence, Crime and Victims Act 2004 s 37(8)(c) (as so substituted)).

    A reference in ss 35–44B to a place in which a person is detained includes a reference to a place in which he is liable to be detained under the Mental Health Act 1983: Domestic Violence, Crime and Victims Act 2004 s 45(3) (added by the Mental Health Act 2007 Sch 6 para 16).

    In such a case the Secretary of State must inform the relevant probation body if he is considering:

(a)   whether to give a direction in respect of the patient under the Mental Health Act 1983 s 42(1) (directions lifting restrictions: see MENTAL HEALTH AND CAPACITY vol 75 (2013) PARA 876) (Domestic Violence, Crime and Victims Act 2004 s 37(4)(a) (as so amended)),

(b)   whether to discharge the patient under the Mental Health Act 1983 s 42(2) (see

MENTAL HEALTH AND CAPACITY vol 75 (2013) PARA 876), either absolutely or subject to conditions (Domestic Violence, Crime and Victims Act 2004 s 37(4)(b) (as so amended)); or

(c) if the patient has been discharged subject to conditions, whether to vary the conditions (s 37(4)(c) (as so amended)),

and the First-tier Tribunal or the Mental Health Review Tribunal for Wales must inform the relevant probation body if:

(i) an application is made to the tribunal by the patient under the Mental Health Act 1983 s 69, 70 or 75 (applications concerning restricted patients: see MENTAL HEALTH AND CAPACITY vol 75 (2013) PARAS 961–962, 965) (Domestic Violence, Crime and Victims Act 2004 s 37(5)(a) (as so amended; further amended by SI 2008/2833)); or

(ii) the Secretary of State refers the patient's case to the tribunal under the Mental Health Act 1983 s 71 (references concerning restricted patients: see MENTAL HEALTH AND CAPACITY vol 75 (2013) PARA 965) (Domestic Violence, Crime and Victims Act 2004 s 37(5)(b) (as so amended)).

If the relevant probation body receives information under s 37(4) or (5) and a person who appears to the relevant probation body to be the victim of the offence or to act for the victim of the offence when his wishes were ascertained under s 36(4), expressed a wish to make representations about a matter specified in s 36(5), or has made representations about such a matter to the relevant probation body or the local probation board or provider of probation services mentioned in s 36(4), the relevant probation body must provide the information to the person: s 37(6), (7) (as so amended).

15 If, in a case where the Domestic Violence, Crime and Victims Act 2004 s 36 applies, the hospital order in respect of the patient was made without a restriction order and:

(1) a person makes representations about a matter specified in s 36(5) to the managers of the relevant hospital (s 37A(1), (2)(a) (ss 36A, 37A, 38A, 38B added by the Mental Health Act 2007 Sch 6 paras 3, 5, 7)); and

(2) it appears to the managers that the person is the victim of the offence or acts for the victim of the offence (Domestic Violence, Crime and Victims Act 2004 s 37A(2)(b) (as so added)),

the managers must forward the representations to the persons responsible for determining the matter (s 37A(3) (as so added)). For this purpose the relevant hospital is the hospital in which the patient is detained, or, if a community treatment order is in force in respect of the patient, the responsible hospital: ss 36A(6), 37A(9), 38A(8), 38B(5) (as so added). As to the meaning of 'managers' see the Mental Health Act 1983 s 145; and MENTAL HEALTH AND CAPACITY vol 75 (2013) PARA 778 (definition applied by the Domestic Violence, Crime and Victims Act 2004 s 45(1) (amended by the Mental Health Act 2007 Sch 6 para 16)). As to the meaning of 'responsible hospital' see the Mental Health Act 1983 s 17A; and MENTAL HEALTH AND CAPACITY vol 75 (2013) PARA 801 (definition applied by the Domestic Violence, Crime and Victims Act 2004 s 45(1) (amended by the Mental Health Act 2007 Sch 6 para 16)).

In such a case the responsible clinician must inform the managers of the relevant hospital if he is considering making:

(a) an order for discharge in respect of the patient under the Mental Health Act 1983 s 23(2) (see MENTAL HEALTH AND CAPACITY vol 75 (2013) PARA 913) (Domestic Violence, Crime and Victims Act 2004 s 37A(4)(a) (as so added));

(b) a community treatment order in respect of the patient (s 37A(4)(b) (as so added)); or

(c) an order under the Mental Health Act 1983 s 17B(4) (see MENTAL HEALTH AND CAPACITY vol 75 (2013) PARA 800) to vary the conditions specified in a community treatment order in force in respect of the patient (Domestic Violence, Crime and Victims Act 2004 s 37A(4)(c) (as so added)).

As to the meaning of 'responsible clinician' see PARA 334 note 17. The First-tier Tribunal or the Mental Health Review Tribunal for Wales must inform the managers of the relevant hospital if an application is made to the tribunal under the Mental Health Act 1983 s 66 or s 69 (see MENTAL HEALTH AND CAPACITY vol 75 (2013) PARAS 955, 960–961) or the patient's case is referred to the tribunal under s 67 (see MENTAL HEALTH AND CAPACITY vol 75 (2013) PARAS 963, 965): Domestic Violence, Crime and Victims Act 2004 s 37A(6) (as so added; amended by SI 2008/2833).

If the managers of the relevant hospital receive information under the Domestic Violence, Crime and Victims Act 2004 s 37A(4) or (6) and a person who appears to the managers to be the victim of the offence or to act for the victim of the offence when his wishes were ascertained under s 36(4) expressed a wish to make representations about a matter specified in s 36(5), or has made representations about such a matter to the managers of the hospital in which the patient was, at the time in question, detained, the managers of the relevant hospital must provide the information to the person: s 37A(7), (8) (as so added; s 37A(7) amended by the Health and Social Care Act 2012 s 39(4)(e)(ii)).

16 If the Domestic Violence, Crime and Victims Act 2004 s 36 applies and a restriction order has been made, a person who appears to the relevant probation body to be the victim of the offence or to act for the victim of the offence when his wishes were ascertained under s 36(4) expressed a wish to receive the information specified in s 36(6), or has subsequently informed the relevant probation body that he wishes to receive that information, then the relevant probation body must, provided the restriction order is in force, take all reasonable steps:

    (1)   to inform that person whether or not the patient is to be subject to any conditions in the event of his discharge (Domestic Violence, Crime and Victims Act 2004 s 38(1), (2), (3)(a), (8) (s 38(1) amended by the Mental Health Act 2007 Sch 6 paras 1, 6; Domestic Violence, Crime and Victims Act 2004 s 38(3), (4), (6), (7), (9) amended by SI 2008/912));

    (2)   if he is, to provide that person with details of any conditions which relate to contact with the victim or his family (Domestic Violence, Crime and Victims Act 2004 s 38(3)(b) (as so amended));

    (3)   if the restriction order in respect of the patient is to cease to have effect, to notify that person of the date on which it is to cease to have effect (s 38(3)(c) (as so amended)); and

    (4)   to provide that person with such other information as the board or the body considers appropriate in all the circumstances of the case (s 38(3)(d) (as so amended)).

As to the meaning of 'relevant probation body' see note 14 (definition applied by s 38(9) (as so amended)).

The Secretary of State must inform the relevant probation body whether the patient is to be discharged (s 38(4)(a) (as so amended)), and if he is, whether he is to be discharged absolutely or subject to conditions (s 38(4)(b) (as so amended)) (and if he is to be discharged subject to conditions, then the Secretary of State must inform the relevant probation body what the conditions are to be (s 38(4)(c) (as so amended))), and if he has been discharged subject to conditions the Secretary of State must inform the relevant probation body of any variation of the conditions by him and of any recall to hospital under the Mental Health Act 1983 s 42(3) (see MENTAL HEALTH AND CAPACITY vol 75 (2013) PARAS 876, 914) (Domestic Violence, Crime and Victims Act 2004 s 38(4)(d) (as so amended)). If the restriction order is to cease to have effect by virtue of action to be taken by the Secretary of State, he must inform the relevant probation body of the date on which the restriction order is to cease to have effect: s 38(4)(e) (as so amended).

If an application is made to the First-tier Tribunal or the Mental Health Review Tribunal for Wales by the patient under the Mental Health Act 1983 s 69, 70 or 75 (applications concerning restricted patients: see MENTAL HEALTH AND CAPACITY vol 75 (2013) PARAS 961–962, 965) or the Secretary of State refers the patient's case to the First-tier Tribunal or the Mental Health Review Tribunal for Wales under s 71 (references concerning restricted patients: see MENTAL HEALTH AND CAPACITY vol 75 (2013) PARA 965), then, instead of the Domestic Violence, Crime and Victims Act 2004 s 38(4) applying, the tribunal must inform the relevant probation body of the matters specified in s 38(4)(a)–(c); and where the patient has been discharged subject to conditions, the tribunal must also inform the relevant probation body of any variation of the conditions by the tribunal: s 38(5), (6)(a), (b) (as so amended; s 38(5) further amended by SI 2008/2833). If the restriction order is to cease to have effect by virtue of action to be taken by the tribunal, the tribunal must inform the relevant probation body of the date on which the restriction order is to cease to have effect: Domestic Violence, Crime and Victims Act 2004 s 38(6)(c). If the patient has been discharged subject to conditions the Secretary of State must inform the relevant probation body of the matters specified in s 38(4)(d), (e): s 38(7) (as so amended). These duties to provide information apply only while the restriction order is in force: s 38(8).

17 If, in a case where the Domestic Violence, Crime and Victims Act 2004 s 36 applies, the hospital order in respect of the patient was made without a restriction order and a person who appears to the local probation board or provider of probation services mentioned in the Domestic Violence, Crime and Victims Act 2004 s 36(4) to be the victim of the offence or to act for the victim of the offence, when his wishes are ascertained under s 36(4), expresses a wish to make representations about a matter specified in s 36(5) (s 36A(1), (2)(a) (s 36A as added (see note 15); s 36A(2)–(5) amended by SI 2008/912)) or to receive the information specified in the Domestic Violence, Crime and Victims Act 2004 s 36(6) (s 36A(2)(b) (as so added and amended)), the local probation board or the provider of probation services must notify the managers of the hospital in which the patient is detained of that person's wish and of that person's name and address (s 36A(3)(a) (as so added and amended)) and notify that person of the name and address of the hospital (s 36A(3)(b) (as so added and amended)). If in such a case

a person who appears to the local probation board or provider of probation services mentioned in s 36(4) to be the victim of the offence or to act for the victim of the offence, subsequently to his wishes being ascertained under s 36(4), expresses a wish to do something specified in s 36A(2)(a) or (b) the local probation board or provider of probation services mentioned in s 36(4) must take all reasonable steps to ascertain whether the hospital order made in respect of the patient continues in force and whether a community treatment order is in force in respect of him (s 36A(4), (5)(a) (as so added and amended)) and, if the board or provider ascertains that the hospital order does continue in force, to notify the managers of the relevant hospital of that person's wish and to notify that person of the name and address of the hospital (s 36A(5)(b) (as so added and amended)). As to the relevant hospital see note 15.

18   If, in a case where the Domestic Violence, Crime and Victims Act 2004 s 36 applies, the hospital order in respect of the patient was made without a restriction order, the responsible clinician must inform the managers of the relevant hospital:

(1)   whether he is to make an order for discharge in respect of the patient under the Mental Health Act 1983 s 23(2) (see MENTAL HEALTH AND CAPACITY vol 75 (2013) PARA 913) (Domestic Violence, Crime and Victims Act 2004 s 38A(1), (2)(a) (as added: see note 15));

(2)   whether he is to make a community treatment order in respect of the patient (Domestic Violence, Crime and Victims Act 2004 s 38A(2)(b) (as so added));

(3)   if a community treatment order is to be made in respect of the patient, what conditions are to be specified in the order (s 38A(2)(c) (as so added));

(4)   if a community treatment order is in force in respect of the patient, of any variation to be made under the Mental Health Act 1983 s 17B(4) (see MENTAL HEALTH AND CAPACITY vol 75 (2013) PARA 800) of the conditions specified in the order (Domestic Violence, Crime and Victims Act 2004 s 38A(2)(d) (as so added));

(5)   if a community treatment order in respect of the patient is to cease to be in force, of the date on which it is to cease to be in force (s 38A(2)(e) (as so added));

(6)   if, following the examination of the patient under the Mental Health Act 1983 s 20 (see MENTAL HEALTH AND CAPACITY vol 75 (2013) PARAS 768, 908–910), it does not appear to the responsible clinician that the conditions set out in s 20(4) are satisfied, of the date on which the authority for the patient's detention is to expire (Domestic Violence, Crime and Victims Act 2004 s 38A(2)(f) (as so added)).

If:

(a)   an application is made to the First-tier Tribunal or the Mental Health Review Tribunal for Wales under the Mental Health Act 1983 s 66 or 69 (see MENTAL HEALTH AND CAPACITY vol 75 (2013) PARAS 955, 960–961) (Domestic Violence, Crime and Victims Act 2004 s 38A(4)(a) (as so added; s 36A(4) amended by SI 2008/2833));

(b)   the patient's case is referred to the First-tier Tribunal or the Mental Health Review Tribunal for Wales under the Mental Health Act 1983 s 67 (see MENTAL HEALTH AND CAPACITY vol 75 (2013) PARAS 963, 965) (Domestic Violence, Crime and Victims Act 2004 s 38A(4)(b) (as so added and amended)); or

(c)   the managers of the relevant hospital refer the patient's case to the First-tier Tribunal or the Mental Health Review Tribunal for Wales under the Mental Health Act 1983 s 68 (see MENTAL HEALTH AND CAPACITY vol 75 (2013) PARA 964) (Domestic Violence, Crime and Victims Act 2004 s 38A(4)(c) (as so added and amended)),

the tribunal must inform the managers of the relevant hospital if it directs that the patient is to be discharged (s 38A(5) (as so added)).

If a person who appears to the managers of the relevant hospital to be the victim of the offence or to act for the victim of the offence when his wishes were ascertained under s 36(4), expressed a wish to receive the information specified in s 36(6), or has subsequently informed the managers of the relevant hospital that he wishes to receive that information, the managers of the relevant hospital order must take all reasonable steps:

(i)   to inform that person whether the patient is to be discharged under the Mental Health Act 1983 s 23 (see MENTAL HEALTH AND CAPACITY vol 75 (2013) PARA 913) or s 72 (see MENTAL HEALTH AND CAPACITY vol 75 (2013) PARAS 967–968) (Domestic Violence, Crime and Victims Act 2004 s 38A(6), (7)(a) (as so added));

(ii)   to inform that person whether a community treatment order is to be made in respect of the patient (s 38A(7)(b) (as so added));

(iii)   if a community treatment order is to be made in respect of the patient and is to specify conditions which relate to contact with the victim or his family, to provide that person with details of those conditions (s 38A(7)(c) (as so added));

(iv)   if a community treatment order is in force in respect of the patient and the conditions specified in the order are to be varied under the Mental Health Act 1983 s 17B(4) (see

MENTAL HEALTH AND CAPACITY vol 75 (2013) PARA 800), to provide that person with details of any variation which relates to contact with the victim or his family (Domestic Violence, Crime and Victims Act 2004 s 38A(7)(d) (as so added));

(v)   if a community treatment order in respect of the patient is to cease to be in force, to inform that person of the date on which it is to cease to be in force (s 38A(7)(e) (as so added));

(vi)   if, following the examination of the patient under the Mental Health Act 1983 s 20 (see MENTAL HEALTH AND CAPACITY vol 75 (2013) PARAS 768, 908–910), the authority for the patient's detention is not to be renewed, to inform that person of the date on which the authority is to expire (Domestic Violence, Crime and Victims Act 2004 s 38A(7)(f) (as so added)); and

(vii)   to provide that person with such other information as the managers of the relevant hospital consider appropriate in all the circumstances of the case (s 38A(7)(g) (as so added)).

19   If in a case where the Domestic Violence, Crime and Victims Act 2004 s 36 applies the hospital order in respect of the patient was made with a restriction order and the restriction order ceases to have effect while the hospital order continues in force (Domestic Violence, Crime and Victims Act 2004 s 38B(1) (s 38B as added: see note 15)), and a person who appears to the relevant probation body to be the victim of the offence or to act for the victim of the offence when his wishes were ascertained under s 36(4), expressed a wish to make representations about a matter specified in s 36(5) or to receive the information specified in s 36(6), or has subsequently informed the relevant probation body that he wishes to make representations about such a matter or to receive that information (s 38B(2) (as so added; s 38B(2), (3), (6) amended by SI 2008/912)), the relevant probation body must take all reasonable steps to notify the managers of the relevant hospital of an address at which that person may be contacted and to notify that person of the name and address of the hospital (Domestic Violence, Crime and Victims Act 2004 s 38B(3) (as so added and amended)). As to the meaning of 'relevant probation body' see note 14 (definition applied by s 38B(6) (as so added and amended)). While the hospital order continues in force, the patient is to be regarded as a patient in respect of whom a hospital order was made without a restriction order; and ss 37A, 38A (see notes 15, 18) are to apply in relation to him accordingly: s 38B(4) (as so added).

481.   Victims' rights where offender is under a hospital direction and a limitation direction.

If a person (the 'offender') is convicted of a sexual or violent offence[1], a relevant sentence[2] is imposed on him in respect of the offence, and a hospital direction[3] and a limitation direction[4] are given in relation to him by a court[5] dealing with him for the offence[6], then the local probation board[7] or provider of probation services[8] must take all reasonable steps to ascertain whether a person who appears to the board or the provider to be the victim of the offence or to act for the victim of the offence wishes[9] to make representations about the conditions of the patient's discharge from hospital[10] or to receive information about any conditions to which the patient is to be subject in the event of his discharge from hospital[11]. Provision is made in connection with the forwarding of any such representations to specified persons[12], with the giving of any such information[13], and in connection with the making of representations and the receipt of information where a limitation direction ceases to have effect while an offender is treated as a patient in respect of whom a hospital order has effect[14].

1   As to sexual or violent offences see PARA 480 note 1.

2   'Relevant sentence' means any of these: (1) a sentence of imprisonment for a term of 12 months or more; (2) a sentence of detention during Her Majesty's pleasure; (3) a sentence of detention for a period of 12 months or more under the Powers of Criminal Courts (Sentencing) Act 2000 s 91 (offenders under 18 convicted of certain serious offences: see PARA 8); (4) a detention and training order for a term of 12 months or more: Domestic Violence, Crime and Victims Act 2004 s 45(1).

3   'Hospital direction' has the meaning given by the Mental Health Act 1983 s 45A(3)(a) (see MENTAL HEALTH AND CAPACITY vol 75 (2013) PARA 864): Domestic Violence, Crime and Victims Act 2004 s 45(1).

4 'Limitation direction' has the meaning given by the Mental Health Act 1983 s 45A(3)(b) (see MENTAL HEALTH AND CAPACITY vol 75 (2013) PARA 864): Domestic Violence, Crime and Victims Act 2004 s 45(1).

5 As to the meaning of 'court' see PARA 480 note 8.

6 Domestic Violence, Crime and Victims Act 2004 s 39(1).

7 Ie the local probation board for the area in which the hospital direction mentioned in the Domestic Violence, Crime and Victims Act 2004 s 39(1) (see the text and notes 1–6) is given: s 39(2) (amended by SI 2008/912). As to local probation boards and the provision of probation services see PARAS 666–687.

8 Ie the provider of probation services operating in the local justice area in which the hospital direction mentioned in the Domestic Violence, Crime and Victims Act 2004 s 39(1) (see the text and notes 1–6) is given: s 39(2) (amended by SI 2008/912). The provider of probation services mentioned in the Domestic Violence, Crime and Victims Act 2004 s 39(2) is the provider of probation services identified as such by arrangements under the Offender Management Act 2007 s 3 (see PARA 669): Domestic Violence, Crime and Victims Act 2004 s 39(2A) (added by SI 2008/912).

9 Domestic Violence, Crime and Victims Act 2004 s 39(2).

10 Domestic Violence, Crime and Victims Act 2004 s 39(2)(a). The representations which may be made are representations about:

(1) whether the offender should, in the event of his discharge from hospital while he is subject to a limitation direction, be subject to any conditions and, if so, what conditions (s 39(3)(a) (s 39(3)(a) amended, s 39(3)(aa) added, by the Mental Health Act 2007 Sch 6 paras 1, 8));

(2) what conditions he should be subject to in the event of his discharge from hospital under a community treatment order (Domestic Violence, Crime and Victims Act 2004 s 39(3)(aa) (as so added));

(3) whether the offender should, in the event of his release from hospital, be subject to any licence conditions or supervision requirements and, if so, what licence conditions or supervision requirements (s 39(3)(b));

(4) if the offender is transferred to a prison or other institution in which he might have been detained if he had not been removed to hospital, whether he should, in the event of his release from prison or another such institution, be subject to any licence conditions or supervision requirements and, if so, what licence conditions or supervision requirements (s 39(3)(c)).

As to the meaning of 'community treatment order' see PARA 480 note 12. 'Licence condition' means a condition in a licence; and 'supervision requirements' means requirements specified in a notice under the Powers of Criminal Courts (Sentencing) Act 2000 s 103(6) (see PARA 12): Domestic Violence, Crime and Victims Act 2004 s 45(1).

11 Domestic Violence, Crime and Victims Act 2004 s 39(2)(b). The specified information for this purpose is any information about any conditions to which the offender is to be subject in the event of his discharge (s 39(4)(a)) and information about any licence conditions or supervision requirements to which the offender is to be subject in the event of his release (s 39(4)(b)).

12 If in a case where the Domestic Violence, Crime and Victims Act 2004 s 39 applies, a person makes representations about a matter specified in s 39(5) to the local probation board or provider of probation services mentioned in s 39(2) or the relevant probation body, and it appears to the relevant probation body that the person is the victim of the offence or acts for the victim of the offence, the relevant probation body must (provided, if the representations are about a matter specified in s 39(3)(a), the limitation direction given in relation to the offender is in force) forward the representations to the persons responsible for determining the matter: s 40(1)–(3) (s 40(2), (4), (6), (7) amended, s 40(8) substituted, by SI 2008/912).

For this purpose the 'relevant probation body' is:

(1) in a case where the offender is to be discharged from hospital subject to a condition that he reside in a particular area, which is or is part of a local probation board, that local probation board (Domestic Violence, Crime and Victims Act 2004 s 40(8)(a) (as so substituted));

(2) in a case where the offender is to be discharged subject to a condition that he reside in a particular area other than one mentioned in s 40(8)(a), the provider of probation services operating in that area that is identified as the relevant probation body by arrangements under the Offender Management Act 2007 s 3 (see PARA 669) (Domestic Violence, Crime and Victims Act 2004 s 40(8)(b) (as so substituted));

(3) in a case where the offender is to be supervised on release by an officer of a local

probation board or an officer of a provider of probation services, that local probation board or that provider of probation services (as the case may be) (s 40(8)(c) (as so substituted)); and

(4)   in any other case, if the hospital, prison or other place in which the offender is detained is situated in the area of a local probation board, that area, and if that hospital, prison or other place is not so situated, the provider of probation services operating in the local justice area in which the hospital, prison or other place in which the patient is detained is situated that is identified as the relevant probation body by arrangements under the Offender Management Act 2007 s 3 (Domestic Violence, Crime and Victims Act 2004 s 40(8)(d) (as so substituted)).

As to a place in which a person is detained see PARA 480 note 14.

In such a case the Secretary of State must inform the relevant probation body if he is considering:

(a)   whether to give a direction in respect of the offender under the Mental Health Act 1983 s 42(1) (directions lifting restrictions: see MENTAL HEALTH AND CAPACITY vol 75 (2013) PARA 876) (Domestic Violence, Crime and Victims Act 2004 s 40(4)(a) (as so amended));

(b)   whether to discharge the offender under the Mental Health Act 1983 s 42(2) (see MENTAL HEALTH AND CAPACITY vol 75 (2013) PARA 876), either absolutely or subject to conditions (Domestic Violence, Crime and Victims Act 2004 s 40(4)(b) (as so amended)); or

(c)   if the offender has been discharged subject to conditions, whether to vary the conditions (s 40(4)(c) (as so amended)),

and the First-tier Tribunal or the Mental Health Review Tribunal for Wales must inform the relevant probation body if:

(i)   an application is made to the tribunal by the offender under the Mental Health Act 1983 s 69, 70 or 75 (applications concerning restricted patients: see MENTAL HEALTH AND CAPACITY vol 75 (2013) PARAS 961–962, 965) (Domestic Violence, Crime and Victims Act 2004 s 40(5)(a) (as so amended; further amended by SI 2008/2833)); or

(ii)   the Secretary of State refers the offender's case to the tribunal under the Mental Health Act 1983 s 71 (references concerning restricted patients: see MENTAL HEALTH AND CAPACITY vol 75 (2013) PARA 965) (Domestic Violence, Crime and Victims Act 2004 s 40(5)(b) (as so amended)).

If the relevant probation body receives information under s 40(4) or (5) and a person who appears to the relevant probation body to be the victim of the offence or to act for the victim of the offence when his wishes were ascertained under s 39(2), expressed a wish to make representations about a matter specified in s 39(3)(a), or has made representations about such a matter to the relevant probation body or the local probation board or provider of probation services mentioned in s 39(2), the relevant probation body must provide the information to the person: s 40(6), (7) (as so amended).

13   If the Domestic Violence, Crime and Victims Act 2004 s 39 applies and a person who appears to the relevant probation body to be the victim of the offence or to act for the victim of the offence when his wishes were ascertained under s 39(2) expressed a wish to receive the information specified in s 39(4), or has subsequently informed the relevant probation body that he wishes to receive that information, then the relevant probation body must, provided the limitation direction is in force, take all reasonable steps:

(1)   to inform that person whether or not the offender is to be subject to any conditions in the event of his discharge (s 41(1), (2), (3)(a), (8) (s 41(2)–(4), (6), (7), (9) amended by SI 2008/912));

(2)   if he is, to provide that person with details of any conditions which relate to contact with the victim or his family (Domestic Violence, Crime and Victims Act 2004 s 41(3)(b) (as so amended));

(3)   if the limitation direction in respect of the offender is to cease to have effect, to notify that person of the date on which it is to cease to have effect (s 41(3)(c) (as so amended));

(4)   to inform that person whether or not the offender is to be subject to any licence conditions or supervision requirements in the event of his release (s 41(3)(d) (as so amended));

(5)   if he is, to provide that person with details of any licence conditions or supervision requirements which relate to contact with the victim or his family (s 41(3)(e) (as so amended)); and

(6) to provide that person with such other information as the board considers appropriate in all the circumstances of the case (s 41(3)(f) (as so amended)).

As to the meaning of 'relevant probation body' see note 12 (definition applied by s 41(9) (as so amended)).

The Secretary of State must inform the relevant probation body whether the patient is to be discharged (s 41(4)(a) (as so amended)), and if he is, whether he is to be discharged absolutely or subject to conditions (s 41(4)(b) (as so amended)) (and if he is to be discharged subject to conditions, then the Secretary of State must inform the relevant probation body what the conditions are to be (s 41(4)(c) (as so amended))), and if he has been discharged subject to conditions the Secretary of State must inform the relevant probation body of any variation of the conditions by him and of any recall to hospital under the Mental Health Act 1983 s 42(3) (see **MENTAL HEALTH AND CAPACITY** vol 75 (2013) PARAS 876, 914) (Domestic Violence, Crime and Victims Act 2004 s 41(4)(d) (as so amended)). If the limitation direction is to cease to have effect by virtue of action to be taken by the Secretary of State, he must inform the relevant probation body of the date on which the limitation direction is to cease to have effect: s 41(4)(e) (as so amended).

If an application is made to the First-tier Tribunal or the Mental Health Review Tribunal for Wales by the patient under the Mental Health Act 1983 s 69, 70 or 75 (applications concerning restricted patients: see **MENTAL HEALTH AND CAPACITY** vol 75 (2013) PARAS 961–962, 965) or the Secretary of State refers the offender's case to the First-tier Tribunal or the Mental Health Review Tribunal for Wales under s 71 (references concerning restricted patients: see **MENTAL HEALTH AND CAPACITY** vol 75 (2013) PARA 965), then, instead of the Domestic Violence, Crime and Victims Act 2004 s 41(4) applying, the tribunal must inform the relevant probation body of the matters specified in s 41(4)(a)–(c); and where the offender has been discharged subject to conditions, the tribunal must also inform the relevant probation body of any variation of the conditions by the tribunal: s 41(5), (6)(a), (b) (as so amended; s 41(5) further amended by SI 2008/2833). If the limitation direction is to cease to have effect by virtue of action to be taken by the tribunal, the tribunal must inform the relevant probation body of the date on which the limitation direction is to cease to have effect: Domestic Violence, Crime and Victims Act 2004 s 41(6)(c). If the offender has been discharged subject to conditions the Secretary of State must inform the relevant probation body of the matters specified in s 41(4)(d), (e): s 41(7) (as so amended). These duties to provide information apply only while the limitation direction is in force: s 41(8).

14 If in a case where the Domestic Violence, Crime and Victims Act 2004 s 39 applies the limitation direction in respect of the offender ceases to be in force and he is treated for the purposes of the Mental Health Act 1983 as a patient in respect of whom a hospital order has effect (Domestic Violence, Crime and Victims Act 2004 s 41A(1) (s 41A added by the Mental Health Act 2007 Sch 6 para 9)), and a person who appears to the relevant probation body to be the victim of the offence or to act for the victim of the offence when his wishes were ascertained under the Domestic Violence, Crime and Victims Act 2004 s 39(2), expressed a wish to make representations about a matter specified in s 39(3) or to receive the information specified in s 39(4), or has subsequently informed the relevant probation body that he wishes to make representations about such a matter or to receive that information (s 41A(2) (as so added; s 41A(2), (3), (6) amended by SI 2008/912)), the relevant probation body must take all reasonable steps to notify the managers of the relevant hospital of an address at which that person may be contacted and to notify that person of the name and address of the hospital (Domestic Violence, Crime and Victims Act 2004 s 41A(3) (as so added and amended)). As to the meaning of 'relevant probation body' see note 12 (definition applied by s 41A(6) (as so added and amended)). As to the meaning of 'relevant hospital' see s 36A(6); and PARA 480 note 15 (definition applied by s 41A(5) (as so added and amended)). As to the managers see PARA 480 note 15. The offender is to be regarded as a patient in respect of whom a hospital order was made without a restriction order; and ss 37A, 38A (see PARA 480) are to apply in relation to him accordingly: s 41A(4) (as so added).

482. Victims' rights where offender is under a transfer direction. If a person (the 'offender') is convicted of a sexual or violent offence[1], a relevant sentence[2] is imposed on him in respect of the offence, and while the offender is serving the sentences the Secretary of State gives a transfer direction[3] in respect of the offender (whether or not he also gives a restriction direction[4] in respect of the offender)[5], then the local probation board[6] or provider of probation services[7] must take all reasonable steps to ascertain whether a person who appears to the board or the provider to be the victim of the offence or to act for the victim of the offence wishes[8] to make representations about the conditions of the offender's discharge from hospital[9] or to receive information about any conditions to which the offender is to be subject in the event of his discharge from hospital[10]. Provision is made in connection with the forwarding of any such representations to specified persons (the identity of whom depends on whether a restriction direction has[11] or has not[12] been given), and with the giving of any such information where a restriction direction has been made[13]. Where a restriction direction has not been given, there is provision for the notification of hospital managers of a patient's decisions concerning the making of representations and the receipt of information[14] and of other matters concerning the patient's treatment[15]. Provision is also made in connection with the making of representations and the receipt of information where a restriction direction ceases to have effect while the transfer direction with which it was given continues in force[16].

1   As to sexual or violent offences see PARA 480 note 1.
2   As to the 'relevant sentence' see PARA 481 note 2.
3   As to transfer directions (ie directions under the Mental Health Act 1983 s 47) see MENTAL HEALTH AND CAPACITY vol 75 (2013) PARA 892 (definition applied by the Domestic Violence, Crime and Victims Act 2004 s 45(1)).
4   As to restriction directions (ie directions under the Mental Health Act 1983 s 49) see MENTAL HEALTH AND CAPACITY vol 75 (2013) PARA 894 (definition applied by the Domestic Violence, Crime and Victims Act 2004 s 45(1)).
5   Domestic Violence, Crime and Victims Act 2004 s 42(1) (s 42(1), (3)(a) amended, s 42(2), (3)(c) added, by the Mental Health Act 2007 Sch 6 paras 1, 10).
6   Ie the local probation board for the area in which the hospital specified in the transfer direction mentioned in the Domestic Violence, Crime and Victims Act 2004 s 42(1) (see the text and notes 1–5) is situated: s 42(2) (s 42(2) amended, s 42(2A) added, by SI 2008/912). As to local probation boards and the provision of probation services see PARAS 666–687.
7   Ie the provider of probation services operating in the local justice area in which the hospital specified in the transfer direction mentioned in the Domestic Violence, Crime and Victims Act 2004 s 42(1) is situated: s 42(2) (as amended: see note 6). The provider of probation services mentioned in s 42(2) is the provider of probation services identified as such by arrangements under the Offender Management Act 2007 s 3 (see PARA 669): Domestic Violence, Crime and Victims Act 2004 s 42(2A) (as so added).
8   Domestic Violence, Crime and Victims Act 2004 s 42(2) (as amended: see note 6).
9   Domestic Violence, Crime and Victims Act 2004 s 42(2)(a) (as amended: see note 6). The representations which may be made are representations about whether the offender should be subject to any conditions in the event of his discharge from hospital at a time when a restriction direction is in force in respect of him, if so, what conditions, and what conditions he should be subject to in the event of his discharge from hospital under a community treatment order: s 42(3)(a)–(c) (as amended and added: see note 5). As to the meaning of 'community treatment order' see PARA 480 note 12.
10   Domestic Violence, Crime and Victims Act 2004 s 42(2)(b), (4).
11   If in a case where the Domestic Violence, Crime and Victims Act 2004 s 42 applies the transfer direction in respect of the patient was given with a restriction direction, a person makes representations about a matter specified in s 42(3) to the local probation board or provider of probation services mentioned in s 42(2) or the relevant probation body, and it appears to the relevant probation body that the person is the victim of the offence or acts for the victim of the offence, the relevant probation body must (provided the restriction direction given in respect of the offender is in force) forward the representations to the persons responsible for determining the matter: s 43(1)–(3) (s 43(1) amended by the Mental Health Act 2007 Sch 6 para 12; Domestic Violence, Crime and Victims Act 2004 s 43(2), (4)–(7) amended, s 43(8) substituted, by SI 2008/912).
      For this purpose the 'relevant probation body' is:
     (1)   in a case where the offender is to be discharged subject to a condition that he reside in a particular area, which is or is part of the area of a local probation board, that local probation board (Domestic Violence, Crime and Victims Act 2004 s 43(8)(a) (as so substituted));

(2) in a case where the offender is to be discharged subject to a condition that he reside in a particular area other than one mentioned in s 43(8)(a), the provider of probation services operating in that area that is identified as the relevant probation body by arrangements under the Offender Management Act 2007 s 3 (see PARA 669) (Domestic Violence, Crime and Victims Act 2004 s 43(8)(b) (as so substituted)); and

(3) in any other case, if the hospital in which the offender is detained is situated in the area of a local probation board, that area, and if that hospital is not so situated, the provider of probation services operating in the local justice area in which the hospital in which the offender is detained is situated that is identified as the relevant probation body by arrangements under the Offender Management Act 2007 s 3 (Domestic Violence, Crime and Victims Act 2004 s 43(8)(c) (as so substituted)).

As to a place in which a person is detained see PARA 480 note 14.

In such a case the Secretary of State must inform the relevant probation body if he is considering:

(a) whether to give a direction in respect of the offender under the Mental Health Act 1983 s 42(1) (directions lifting restrictions: see MENTAL HEALTH AND CAPACITY vol 75 (2013) PARA 876) (Domestic Violence, Crime and Victims Act 2004 s 43(4)(a) (as so amended));

(b) whether to discharge the offender under the Mental Health Act 1983 s 42(2) (see MENTAL HEALTH AND CAPACITY vol 75 (2013) PARA 876), either absolutely or subject to conditions (Domestic Violence, Crime and Victims Act 2004 s 43(4)(b) (as so amended)); or

(c) if the offender has been discharged subject to conditions, whether to vary the conditions (s 43(4)(c) (as so amended)),

and the First-tier Tribunal or the Mental Health Review Tribunal for Wales must inform the relevant probation body if:

(i) an application is made to the tribunal by the offender under the Mental Health Act 1983 s 69, 70 or 75 (applications concerning restricted patients: see MENTAL HEALTH AND CAPACITY vol 75 (2013) PARAS 961–962, 965) (Domestic Violence, Crime and Victims Act 2004 s 43(5)(a) (as so amended; further amended by SI 2008/2833)); or

(ii) the Secretary of State refers the offender's case to the tribunal under the Mental Health Act 1983 s 71 (references concerning restricted patients: see MENTAL HEALTH AND CAPACITY vol 75 (2013) PARA 965) (Domestic Violence, Crime and Victims Act 2004 s 43(5)(b) (as so amended)).

If the relevant probation body receives information under s 43(4) or (5) and a person who appears to the relevant probation body to be the victim of the offence or to act for the victim of the offence when his wishes were ascertained under s 42(2), expressed a wish to make representations about a matter specified in s 42(3), or has made representations about such a matter to the relevant probation body or the local probation board or provider of probation services mentioned in s 42(2), the relevant probation body must provide the information to the person: Domestic Violence, Crime and Victims Act 2004 s 43(6), (7) (as so amended).

12 If, in a case where the Domestic Violence, Crime and Victims Act 2004 s 42 applies, the transfer direction in respect of the patient was made without a restriction direction and:

(1) a person makes representations about a matter specified in s 42(3) to the managers of the relevant hospital (s 43A(1), (2)(a) (s 43A added by the Mental Health Act 2007 Sch 6 para 13)); and

(2) it appears to the managers that the person is the victim of the offence or acts for the victim of the offence (Domestic Violence, Crime and Victims Act 2004 s 43A(2)(b) (as so added)),

the managers must forward the representations to the persons responsible for determining the matter (s 43A(3) (as so added)). As to the meaning of 'relevant probation body' see note 11 (definition applied by s 43A(9) (as so amended)).

As to the meaning of 'managers' see the Mental Health Act 1983 s 145; and MENTAL HEALTH AND CAPACITY vol 75 (2013) PARA 778 (definition applied by the Domestic Violence, Crime and Victims Act 2004 s 45(1) (amended by the Mental Health Act 2007 Sch 6 para 16)).

In such a case the responsible clinician must inform the managers of the relevant hospital if he is considering making:

(a) an order for discharge in respect of the patient under the Mental Health Act 1983 s 23(2) (see MENTAL HEALTH AND CAPACITY vol 75 (2013) PARA 913) (Domestic Violence, Crime and Victims Act 2004 s 43A(4)(a) (as so added));

(b) a community treatment order in respect of the patient (s 43A(4)(b) (as so added)); or

(c) an order under the Mental Health Act 1983 s 17B(4) (see MENTAL HEALTH AND

CAPACITY vol 75 (2013) PARA 800) to vary the conditions specified in a community treatment order in force in respect of the patient (Domestic Violence, Crime and Victims Act 2004 s 43A(4)(c) (as so added)).

As to the meaning of 'responsible clinician' see PARA 474 note 17. The First-tier Tribunal or the Mental Health Review Tribunal for Wales must inform the managers of the relevant hospital if an application is made to the tribunal under the Mental Health Act 1983 s 66 or s 69 (see MENTAL HEALTH AND CAPACITY vol 75 (2013) PARAS 955, 960–961) or the patient's case is referred to the tribunal under s 67 (see MENTAL HEALTH AND CAPACITY vol 75 (2013) PARAS 963, 965): Domestic Violence, Crime and Victims Act 2004 s 43A(6) (as so added; amended by SI 2008/2833).

If the managers of the relevant hospital receive information under the Domestic Violence, Crime and Victims Act 2004 s 43A (4) or (6) and a person who appears to the managers to be the victim of the offence or to act for the victim of the offence when his wishes were ascertained under s 42(2) expressed a wish to make representations about a matter specified in s 42(3), or has made representations about such a matter to the managers of the hospital in which the patient was, at the time in question, detained, the managers of the relevant hospital must provide the information to the person: s 43A(7), (8) (as so added; s 43A(7) amended by the Health and Social Care Act 2012 s 39(4)(e)(ii)).

13 If the Domestic Violence, Crime and Victims Act 2004 s 42 applies and the transfer direction in respect of the patient was given with a restriction direction, a person who appears to the relevant probation body to be the victim of the offence or to act for the victim of the offence when his wishes were ascertained under s 42(2) expressed a wish to receive the information specified in s 42(4), or has subsequently informed the relevant probation body that he wishes to receive that information, then the relevant probation body must, provided the restriction direction is in force, take all reasonable steps:

(1) to inform that person whether or not the offender is to be subject to any conditions in the event of his discharge (Domestic Violence, Crime and Victims Act 2004 s 44(1), (2), (3)(a), (8) (s 44(1) amended by the Mental Health Act 2007 Sch 6 para 14; Domestic Violence, Crime and Victims Act 2004 s 38(3), (4), (6), (7), (9) amended by SI 2008/912));

(2) if he is, to provide that person with details of any conditions which relate to contact with the victim or his family (Domestic Violence, Crime and Victims Act 2004 s 44(3)(b) (as so amended));

(3) if the restriction direction in respect of the offender is to cease to have effect, to notify that person of the date on which it is to cease to have effect (s 44(3)(c) (as so amended)); and

(4) to provide that person with such other information as the board or the body considers appropriate in all the circumstances of the case (s 44(3)(d) (as so amended)).

As to the meaning of 'relevant probation body' see note 11 (definition applied by s 44(9) (as so amended)).

The Secretary of State must inform the relevant probation body whether the offender is to be discharged (s 44(4)(a) (as so amended)), and if he is, whether he is to be discharged absolutely or subject to conditions (s 44(4)(b) (as so amended)) (and if he is to be discharged subject to conditions, then the Secretary of State must inform the relevant probation body what the conditions are to be (s 44(4)(c) (as so amended))), and if he has been discharged subject to conditions the Secretary of State must inform the relevant probation body of any variation of the conditions by him and of any recall to hospital under the Mental Health Act 1983 s 42(3) (see MENTAL HEALTH AND CAPACITY vol 75 (2013) PARAS 876, 914) (Domestic Violence, Crime and Victims Act 2004 s 44(4)(d) (as so amended)). If the restriction direction is to cease to have effect by virtue of action to be taken by the Secretary of State, he must inform the relevant probation body of the date on which the restriction direction is to cease to have effect: s 44(4)(e) (as so amended).

If an application is made to the First-tier Tribunal or the Mental Health Review Tribunal for Wales by the offender under the Mental Health Act 1983 s 69, 70 or 75 (applications concerning restricted patients: see MENTAL HEALTH AND CAPACITY vol 75 (2013) PARAS 961–962, 965) or the Secretary of State refers the offender's case to the First-tier Tribunal or the Mental Health Review Tribunal for Wales under s 71 (references concerning restricted patients: see MENTAL HEALTH AND CAPACITY vol 75 (2013) PARA 965), then, instead of the Domestic Violence, Crime and Victims Act 2004 s 44(4) applying, the tribunal must inform the relevant probation body of the matters specified in s 44(4)(a)–(c); and where the offender has been discharged subject to conditions, the tribunal must also inform the relevant probation body of any variation of the conditions by the tribunal: s 44(5), (6)(a), (b) (as so amended; s 44(5) further amended by SI 2008/2833). If the restriction direction is to cease to have effect by virtue of action to be taken by the tribunal, the tribunal must inform the relevant probation body of the date on which the restriction direction is to cease to have effect: Domestic Violence, Crime and Victims Act 2004 s 44(6)(c). The Secretary of State must inform the relevant probation body of the matters specified in s 44(4)(d), (e): s 44(7) (as so amended). These duties to provide information apply only while the restriction direction is in force: s 44(8).

14 If, in a case where the Domestic Violence, Crime and Victims Act 2004 s 42 applies, the transfer direction in respect of the patient was given without a restriction direction and a person who appears to the local probation board or provider of probation services mentioned in s 42(2) to be the victim of the offence or to act for the victim of the offence, when his wishes are ascertained under s 42(2), expresses a wish to make representations about a matter specified in s 42(3) (s 42A(1), (2)(a) (s 42A added by the Mental Health Act 2007 Sch 6 para 11; Domestic Violence, Crime and Victims Act 2004 s 42A(2)–(5) amended by SI 2008/912)) or to receive the information specified in the Domestic Violence, Crime and Victims Act 2004 s 42(4) (s 42A(2)(b) (as so added and amended)), the local probation board or the provider of probation services must notify the managers of the hospital in which the patient is detained of that person's wish and of that person's name and address (s 42A(3)(a) (as so added and amended)) and notify that person of the name and address of the hospital (s 42A(3)(b) (as so added and amended)). If in such a case a person who appears to the local probation board or provider of probation services mentioned in s 42(2) to be the victim of the offence or to act for the victim of the offence, subsequently to his wishes being ascertained under s 42(2), expresses a wish to do something specified in s 42A(2)(a) or (b) the local probation board or provider of probation services mentioned in s 42(2) must take all reasonable steps to ascertain whether the transfer direction given in respect of the patient continues in force and whether a community treatment order is in force in respect of him (s 42A(4), (5)(a) (as so added and amended)) and, if the board or provider ascertains that the transfer direction does continue in force, to notify the managers of the relevant hospital of that person's wish and to notify that person of the name and address of the hospital (s 42A(5)(b) (as so added and amended)). As to the relevant hospital see PARA 474 note 15 (definition applied by s 42A(6) (as so added)).

15 If, in a case where the Domestic Violence, Crime and Victims Act 2004 s 42 applies, the transfer direction in respect of the patient was made without a restriction direction, the responsible clinician must inform the managers of the relevant hospital:

(1) whether he is to make an order for discharge in respect of the patient under the Mental Health Act 1983 s 23(2) (see MENTAL HEALTH AND CAPACITY vol 75 (2013) PARA 913) (Domestic Violence, Crime and Victims Act 2004 s 44A(1), (2)(a) (s 44A added by the Mental Health Act 2007 Sch 6 para 15));

(2) whether he is to make a community treatment order in respect of the patient (Domestic Violence, Crime and Victims Act 2004 s 44A(2)(b) (as so added));

(3) if a community treatment order is to be made in respect of the patient, what conditions are to be specified in the order (s 44A(2)(c) (as so added));

(4) if a community treatment order is in force in respect of the patient, of any variation to be made under the Mental Health Act 1983 s 17B(4) (see MENTAL HEALTH AND CAPACITY vol 75 (2013) PARA 800) of the conditions specified in the order (Domestic Violence, Crime and Victims Act 2004 s 44A(2)(d) (as so added));

(5) if a community treatment order in respect of the patient is to cease to be in force, of the date on which it is to cease to be in force (s 44A(2)(e) (as so added));

(6) if, following the examination of the patient under the Mental Health Act 1983 s 20 (see MENTAL HEALTH AND CAPACITY vol 75 (2013) PARAS 768, 908–910), it does not appear to the responsible clinician that the conditions set out in s 20(4) are satisfied, of the date on which the authority for the patient's detention is to expire (Domestic Violence, Crime and Victims Act 2004 s 44A(2)(f) (as so added)).

As to the relevant hospital see PARA 474 note 15 (definition applied by s 44A(8) (as so added)).

If:

(a) an application is made to the First-tier Tribunal or the Mental Health Review Tribunal for Wales under the Mental Health Act 1983 s 66 or 69 (see MENTAL HEALTH AND CAPACITY vol 75 (2013) PARAS 955, 960–961) (Domestic Violence, Crime and Victims Act 2004 s 44A(4)(a) (as so added; s 44A(4) amended by SI 2008/2833));

(b) the patient's case is referred to the First-tier Tribunal or the Mental Health Review Tribunal for Wales under the Mental Health Act 1983 s 67 (see MENTAL HEALTH AND CAPACITY vol 75 (2013) PARA 963, 965) (Domestic Violence, Crime and Victims Act 2004 s 44A(4)(b) (as so added and amended)); or

(c) the managers of the relevant hospital refer the patient's case to the First-tier Tribunal or the Mental Health Review Tribunal for Wales under the Mental Health Act 1983 s 68

(see **MENTAL HEALTH AND CAPACITY** vol 75 (2013) PARA 964) (Domestic Violence, Crime and Victims Act 2004 s 44A(4)(c) (as so added and amended)),
the tribunal must inform the managers of the relevant hospital if it directs that the patient is to be discharged (s 44A(5) (as so added)).

If a person who appears to the managers of the relevant hospital to be the victim of the offence or to act for the victim of the offence when his wishes were ascertained under s 42(2), expressed a wish to receive the information specified in s 42(4), or has subsequently informed the managers of the relevant hospital that he wishes to receive that information, the managers of the relevant hospital order must take all reasonable steps:

(i) to inform that person whether the patient is to be discharged under the Mental Health Act 1983 s 23 (see **MENTAL HEALTH AND CAPACITY** vol 75 (2013) PARA 913) or s 72 (see **MENTAL HEALTH AND CAPACITY** vol 75 (2013) PARAS 967–968) (Domestic Violence, Crime and Victims Act 2004 s 44A(6), (7)(a) (as so added));

(ii) to inform that person whether a community treatment order is to be made in respect of the patient (s 44A(7)(b) (as so added));

(iii) if a community treatment order is to be made in respect of the patient and is to specify conditions which relate to contact with the victim or his family, to provide that person with details of those conditions (s 44A(7)(c) (as so added));

(iv) if a community treatment order is in force in respect of the patient and the conditions specified in the order are to be varied under the Mental Health Act 1983 s 17B(4) (see **MENTAL HEALTH AND CAPACITY** vol 75 (2013) PARA 800), to provide that person with details of any variation which relates to contact with the victim or his family (Domestic Violence, Crime and Victims Act 2004 s 44A(7)(d) (as so added));

(v) if a community treatment order in respect of the patient is to cease to be in force, to inform that person of the date on which it is to cease to be in force (s 44A(7)(e) (as so added));

(vi) if, following the examination of the patient under the Mental Health Act 1983 s 20 (see **MENTAL HEALTH AND CAPACITY** vol 75 (2013) PARAS 768, 908–910), the authority for the patient's detention is not to be renewed, to inform that person of the date on which the authority is to expire (Domestic Violence, Crime and Victims Act 2004 s 44A(7)(f) (as so added)); and

(vii) to provide that person with such other information as the managers of the relevant hospital consider appropriate in all the circumstances of the case (s 44A(7)(g) (as so added)).

16 If in a case where the Domestic Violence, Crime and Victims Act 2004 s 42 applies the transfer direction in respect of the patient was given with a restriction direction and the restriction direction ceases to be in force while the transfer direction continues in force (Domestic Violence, Crime and Victims Act 2004 s 44B(1) (s 44B added by the Mental Health Act 2007 Sch 6 para 15)), and a person who appears to the relevant probation body to be the victim of the offence or to act for the victim of the offence when his wishes were ascertained under s 42(2), expressed a wish to make representations about a matter specified in s 42(3) or to receive the information specified in s 42(4), or has subsequently informed the relevant probation body that he wishes to make representations about such a matter or to receive that information (Domestic Violence, Crime and Victims Act 2004 s 44B(2) (as so added; s 44B(2), (3), (6) amended by SI 2008/912)), the relevant probation body must take all reasonable steps to notify the managers of the relevant hospital of an address at which that person may be contacted and to notify that person of the name and address of the hospital (Domestic Violence, Crime and Victims Act 2004 s 44B(3) (as so added and amended)). As to the meaning of 'relevant probation body' see note 11 (definition applied by s 44B(6) (as so added and amended)). As to the meaning of 'relevant hospital' see s 36A(6); and PARA 480 note 15 (definition applied by s 44B(5) (as so added and amended)). As to the managers see PARA 480 note 15. While the transfer direction continues in force the patient is to be regarded as a patient in respect of whom a transfer direction was given without a restriction direction; and ss 43A, 44A (see notes 12, 15) are to apply in relation to him accordingly: s 44B(4) (as so added).

(15) INJUNCTIONS FOR GANG-RELATED VIOLENCE AND DRUG DEALING

483. Purpose of injunctions. The court[1] may, pursuant to the prevention of gang-related[2] violence[3] or drug-dealing activity[4], grant an injunction for either or both of the purposes of:

(1)   prohibiting the respondent[5] from doing anything described in the injunction[6]; or

(2)   requiring the respondent to do anything described in the injunction[7].

The prohibitions included in such an injunction may, in particular, have the effect of prohibiting the respondent from:

(a)   being in a particular place (which includes an area)[8];

(b)   being with particular persons in a particular place[9];

(c)   being in charge of a particular species of animal in a particular place[10];

(d)   wearing particular descriptions of articles of clothing in a particular place[11]; and

(e)   using the internet to facilitate or encourage violence or drug-dealing activity[12].

The requirements included in such an injunction may, in particular, have the effect of requiring the respondent to:

(i)   notify the person who applied for the injunction of the respondent's address and of any change to that address[13];

(ii)   be at a particular place between particular times on particular days[14];

(iii) present himself or herself to a particular person at a place where he or she is required to be between particular times on particular days[15]; and

(iv)   participate in particular activities between particular times on particular days[16].

The prohibitions and requirements included in the injunction must, so far as practicable, be such as to avoid any conflict with the respondent's religious beliefs and any interference with the times, if any, at which the respondent normally works or attends any educational establishment[17], and the injunction may not include a prohibition or requirement that has effect after the end of the period of two years beginning with the day on which the injunction is granted (the 'injunction date')[18]. The court may attach a power of arrest in relation to any prohibition in the injunction or any requirement in the injunction, other than one which has the effect of requiring the respondent to participate in particular activities[19].

1   Ie (except in the Policing and Crime Act 2009 Sch 5A (see PARA 489)) the High Court or a county court or, in respect of a respondent aged under 18, a youth court: s 49(1) (ss 46B, 48(4) added, s 49(1) (definition 'court') substituted, by the Crime and Courts Act 2013 s 18(1), (2), (4), (6), Sch 12 paras 1, 2). This is subject to any provision in rules of court that is or could be made under the Policing and Crime Act 2009 s 48(4) (see below): s 49(1) (as so substituted).
      An appeal lies to the Crown Court against a decision of a youth court made under these provisions (ie under the Policing and Crime Act 2009 Pt 4 (ss 34–50): s 46B(1) (as so added). On such an appeal the Crown Court may make whatever orders are necessary to give effect to its determination of the appeal and whatever incidental or consequential orders appear to it to be just: s 46B(2) (as so added). An order of the Crown Court made on an appeal under s 46B (other than one directing that an application be re-heard by a youth court) is to be treated for the purposes of s 42 (see PARA 487) as an order of a youth court: s 46B(3) (as so added).
      In relation to a respondent attaining the age of 18 after the commencement of proceedings under Pt 4, rules of court may provide for the transfer of the proceedings from a youth court to the High Court or the county court and prescribe circumstances in which the proceedings may or must remain in a youth court: s 48(4) (as so added). As to the determination of a person's age see the Children and Young Persons Act 1933 s 99; and CHILDREN AND YOUNG PERSONS vol 10 (2012) PARA 1206.

2   For these purposes something is 'gang-related' if it occurs in the course of, or is otherwise related to, the activities of a group that:
      (1)   consists of at least three people (Policing and Crime Act 2009 s 34(5)(a) (s 34 substituted, s 35(2)(e) amended, by the Serious Crime Act 2015 s 51, Sch 4 para 84)); and

(2)   has one or more characteristics that enables its members to be identified by others as a group (Policing and Crime Act 2009 s 34(5)(b) (as so substituted)).
       In connection with the identification of a 'gang' for this purpose see *Chief Constable of Greater Manchester v Clader* [2015] All ER (D) 185 (Jul).
3   'Violence' includes a threat of violence and violence against property: Policing and Crime Act 2009 ss 34(6), 49(1) (s 34(6) as substituted: see note 2).
4   'Drug-dealing activity' means the unlawful production, supply, importation or exportation of a controlled drug: Policing and Crime Act 2009 s 34(7) (as substituted: see note 2). As to the meanings of 'production', 'supply' and 'controlled drug' see the Misuse of Drugs Act 1971 37(1); and MEDICAL PRODUCTS AND DRUGS vol 75 (2013) PARAS 481, 492 (definitions applied by the Policing and Crime Act 2009 s 34(7) (as so substituted)).
5   'Respondent' means the person in respect of whom an application for an injunction is made or (as the context requires) the person against whom such an injunction is granted: Policing and Crime Act 2009 s 49(1).
6   Policing and Crime Act 2009 s 34(4)(a) (as substituted: see note 2).
7   Policing and Crime Act 2009 s 34(4)(b) (as substituted: see note 2).
8   Policing and Crime Act 2009 s 35(1), (2)(a), (7).
9   Policing and Crime Act 2009 s 35(2)(b).
10   Policing and Crime Act 2009 s 35(2)(c).
11   Policing and Crime Act 2009 s 35(2)(d).
12   Policing and Crime Act 2009 s 35(2)(e) (as amended: see note 2).
13   Policing and Crime Act 2009 s 35(3)(a).
14   Policing and Crime Act 2009 s 35(3)(b). A requirement of this kind may not be such as to require the respondent to be at a particular place for more than eight hours in any day: s 35(4). Nothing in s 34(2) or (3) affects the generality of s 34(4): s 35(6).
15   Policing and Crime Act 2009 s 35(3)(c).
16   Policing and Crime Act 2009 s 35(3)(d).
17   Policing and Crime Act 2009 s 35(5).
18   Policing and Crime Act 2009 s 36(1), (2).
19   Policing and Crime Act 2009 s 36(6). If the court attaches a power of arrest it may specify that the power is to have effect for a shorter period than the prohibition or requirement to which it relates: s 36(7). 'Specify', in relation to an injunction, means specify in the injunction: s 49(1).

484.   Applications for, and granting of, injunctions.   A court[1] may grant an injunction for the prevention of gang-related violence or drug-dealing activities[2] if it:

(1)   is satisfied on the balance of probabilities that the respondent[3] has engaged in, or has encouraged or assisted, gang-related violence or gang-related drug-dealing activity[4]; and

(2)   thinks it is necessary to grant the injunction for either or both of the purposes of preventing the respondent from engaging in, or encouraging or assisting, gang-related violence or gang-related drug-dealing activity or protecting the respondent from gang-related violence or gang-related drug-dealing activity[5].

An application for an injunction may be made by the chief officer of police for a police area, the chief constable of the British Transport Police Force or a local authority[6]. Before applying for an injunction[7] the applicant must consult any local authority, and any chief police officer, that the applicant thinks it appropriate to consult[8], and any other body or individual that the applicant thinks it appropriate to consult[9]: where the respondent is under the age of 18 (and will be under that age when the application is made), the applicant must also consult the youth offending team[10] in whose area it appears to the applicant that the respondent resides[11]. An application may be made without the respondent being given notice[12].

1   As to the meaning of 'court' see PARA 483 note 1.

2   Ie an injunction under the Policing and Crime Act 2009 s 34 (see the text and notes 3–5; and PARA 483). As to the meanings of 'gang-related', 'violence' and 'drug-dealing activity' see PARA 483 notes 2–4.

3   As to the meaning of 'respondent' see PARA 483 note 5.

4   Policing and Crime Act 2009 s 34(1), (2)(a) (s 34 substituted by the Serious Crime Act 2015 s 51)).

5   Policing and Crime Act 2009 s 34(3) (as substituted: see note 4).

6   Policing and Crime Act 2009 s 37(1). Each of those officers or bodies must have regard to any guidance published under s 47(5) (see PARA 490): s 47(6). As to police forces, police areas and chief officers of police see POLICE AND INVESTIGATORY POWERS vol 84 (2013) PARAS 52 et seq, 123 et seq. In Pt 5 'local authority' means: in relation to England, a district council, a county council, a London borough council, the Common Council of the City of London or the Council of the Isles of Scilly (s 37(2)(a)); and in relation to Wales, a county council or a county borough council (s 37(2)(b)). As to local authorities in England and Wales see LOCAL GOVERNMENT vol 69 (2009) PARA 22 et seq. As to the London boroughs and the City of London see LONDON GOVERNMENT vol 71 (2013) PARAS 15, 16.

7   Ie under the Policing and Crime Act 2009 s 37 (see the text and note 6).

8   Policing and Crime Act 2009 s 38(1), (2)(a).

9   Policing and Crime Act 2009 s 38(2)(b).

10 Ie the youth offending team established under the Crime and Disorder Act 1998 s 39: see CHILDREN AND YOUNG PERSONS vol 10 (2012) PARA 1193.

11 Policing and Crime Act 2009 s 38(2)(aa) (s 38(2)(aa), (3) added by the Crime and Security Act 2010 s 36). If it appears to the applicant that the respondent resides in the area of two or more youth offending teams, the obligation in the Policing and Crime Act 2009 s 38(2)(aa) is to consult such of those teams as the applicant thinks appropriate: s 38(3) (as so added). As to the determination of a person's age see the Children and Young Persons Act 1933 s 99; and CHILDREN AND YOUNG PERSONS vol 10 (2012) PARA 1206.

12 Policing and Crime Act 2009 s 39(1). Such an application is referred to as an application without notice: s 39(2). Section 38(1) (see the text and notes 7–8) does not apply in relation to an application without notice: s 39(3). If an application without notice is made the court must either dismiss the application (s 39(4)(a)) or adjourn the proceedings (s 39(4)(b)), and if the court acts to adjourn proceedings the applicant must comply with the consultation requirement before the date of the first full hearing (s 39(5)). In s 39 'full hearing' means a hearing of which notice has been given to the applicant and respondent in accordance with rules of court: s 39(6).

Rules of court may provide that an appeal from a decision under s 39(4)(a) that an application without notice be dismissed may be made without notice being given to the respondent: s 48(2), (3)(a) (amended by the Crime and Courts Act 2013 Sch 12 para 3).

485. Interim injunctions. If the court[1] adjourns the hearing of an application for an injunction for the prevention of gang-related violence or drug-dealing activity[2] and the respondent[3] was notified of the hearing in accordance with rules of court[4], the court may grant an interim injunction[5] if it thinks that it is just and convenient to do so[6]. The court may also grant an interim injunction if it thinks that it is necessary to do so where an application without notice is made[7] and the proceedings are adjourned (otherwise than at a full hearing)[8]. An interim injunction under these provisions may include any provision which the court has power to include in an injunction[9], including a power of arrest[10].

1   As to the meaning of 'court' see PARA 483 note 1.

2   Ie an injunction under the Policing and Crime Act 2009 s 34 (see PARAS 483, 484). As to the meanings of 'gang-related', 'violence' and 'drug-dealing activity' see PARA 483 notes 2–4.

3   As to the meaning of 'respondent' see PARA 483 note 5.

4   Policing and Crime Act 2009 s 40(1).

5   Any reference in the Policing and Crime Act 2009 Pt 4 (ss 34–50) to an injunction under Pt 4 includes a reference to an interim injunction: s 49(2).

6   Policing and Crime Act 2009 s 40(2).

7   Ie by virtue of the Policing and Crime Act 2009 s 39 (see PARA 484).

8   Policing and Crime Act 2009 s 41(1), (2). As to the meaning of 'full hearing' see PARA 484 note 12 (definition applied by s 41(1)). An interim injunction under s 41 may not have the effect of requiring the respondent to participate in particular activities: s 41(3). Rules of court may

provide that an appeal from a decision to refuse to grant an interim injunction under s 41 may be made without notice being given to the respondent: s 48(2), (3)(a) (amended by the Crime and Courts Act 2013 Sch 12 para 3).
9   See note 2.
10 Policing and Crime Act 2009 ss 40(3), 41(4). In the case of an injunction under s 41 this is subject to s 41(3) (see note 8).

486. Reviews of injunctions. The court[1] may order the applicant[2] and the respondent[3] in proceedings for an injunction for the prevention of gang-related violence or drug-dealing activity[4] to attend one or more review hearings on a specified[5] date or dates[6]. A review hearing is a hearing held for the purpose of considering whether the injunction should be varied or discharged[7]. If any prohibition or requirement in the injunction is to have effect after the end of the period of one year beginning with day on which the injunction is granted, the court must order the applicant and the respondent to attend a review hearing on a specified date within the last four weeks of the one-year period (whether or not the court orders them to attend any other review hearings)[8].

Where the respondent is under the age of 18 on the injunction date and any prohibition or requirement in the injunction is to have effect after the respondent reaches that age and for at least the period of four weeks beginning with his 18th birthday, the court must order the applicant and the respondent to attend a review hearing on a specified date within that period[9].

1   As to the meaning of 'court' see PARA 483 note 1.
2   As to applicants for these purposes see PARA 484.
3   As to the meaning of 'respondent' see PARA 483 note 5.
4   Ie an injunction under the Policing and Crime Act 2009 s 34 (see PARAS 483, 484). As to the meanings of 'gang-related', 'violence' and 'drug-dealing activity' see PARA 483 notes 2–4.
5   As to the meaning of 'specified' see PARA 483 note 19.
6   Policing and Crime Act 2009 s 36(1), (3).
7   Policing and Crime Act 2009 s 36(5).
8   Policing and Crime Act 2009 s 36(4). Section 36(4) does not apply where an injunction is varied (see PARA 487) to include a prohibition or requirement which is to have effect as mentioned in that provision but the variation is made within (or at any time after) the period of four weeks mentioned in it: s 42(4).
9   Policing and Crime Act 2009 s 36(4A) (ss 36(4A), 42(4A) added by the Crime and Security Act 2010 s 35). The Policing and Crime Act 2009 s 36(4A) does not apply where an injunction is varied to include a prohibition or requirement which is to have effect as mentioned in that provision but the variation is made within (or at any time after) the period of four weeks ending with the respondent's 18th birthday: s 42(4A) (as so added). As to the determination of a person's age see the Children and Young Persons Act 1933 s 99; and CHILDREN AND YOUNG PERSONS vol 10 (2012) PARA 1206.

487. Variation and discharge of injunctions. The court[1] may vary or discharge an injunction for the prevention of gang-related violence or drug-dealing activity[2] if a review hearing is held[3] or an application to vary or discharge the injunction is made[4]. An application to vary or discharge the injunction may be made by the person who applied for the injunction[5] or the respondent[6], and the power to vary an injunction includes power to include an additional prohibition or requirement in the injunction[7], to extend the period for which a prohibition or requirement in the injunction has effect[8], and to attach a power of arrest or extend the period for which a power of arrest attached to the injunction has effect[9].

1   As to the meaning of 'court' see PARA 483 note 1.
2   Ie an injunction under the Policing and Crime Act 2009 Pt 4 (ss 34–50). As to the meanings of 'gang-related', 'violence' and 'drug-dealing activity' see PARA 483 notes 2–4.
3   As to review hearings see PARA 486.

4 Policing and Crime Act 2009 s 42(1). If an application to vary or discharge an injunction is dismissed, no further application to vary or discharge it may be made by any person without the consent of the court: s 42(6) (added by the Crime and Security Act 2010 s 37).
5 As to applicants for these purposes see PARA 484. Before applying for the variation or discharge of an injunction such a person must notify the persons consulted under the Policing and Crime Act 2009 s 38(1) or s 39(5) (see PARA 484): s 42(5).
6 Policing and Crime Act 2009 s 42(2). As to the meaning of 'respondent' see PARA 483 note 6.
7 As to prohibitions and requirements see PARA 483.
8 Ie subject to the Policing and Crime Act 2009 s 36(2) (see PARA 483).
9 Policing and Crime Act 2009 s 42(3).

488. Arrest and remand. If a power of arrest is attached to a provision of an injunction for the prevention of gang-related violence or drug dealing[1] a constable may arrest without warrant a person whom he has reasonable cause to suspect to be in breach of the provision[2], and the arrested person must be brought before a relevant judge[3] within the period of 24 hours beginning with the time of the arrest[4]. If the matter is not disposed of when the person is brought before the judge, the judge may remand the person[5].

If the person who applied for the injunction considers that the respondent[6] is in breach of any of its provisions he may apply to a relevant judge for the issue of a warrant for the arrest of the respondent[7]: however a relevant judge may not issue a warrant on such an application unless the judge has reasonable grounds for believing that the respondent is in breach of any provision of the injunction[8]. If a person is brought before a court by virtue of such a warrant but the matter is not disposed of, the court may remand the person[9].

If a person is brought before the relevant judge or the court under these provisions[10] and the judge or court has reason to consider that a medical report will be required, the judge or court may remand the person[11] for the purpose of enabling a medical examination to take place and a report to be made[12], and if the judge or court has reason to suspect that the person is suffering from a mental disorder[13] the judge or court has the same power to make an order[14] remanding the accused for a report on his medical condition as the Crown Court has[15] in the case of an accused person[16].

1 Ie an injunction under the Policing and Crime Act 2009 Pt 4 (ss 34–50). As to the meanings of 'gang-related', 'violence' and 'drug-dealing activity' see PARA 483 notes 2–4. As to the attaching of powers of arrest see PARA 483.
2 Policing and Crime Act 2009 s 43(1), (2). If a constable arrests a person under s 43(2) he must inform the person who applied for the injunction: s 43(3).
3 In the Policing and Crime Act 2009 Pt 4 'relevant judge', in relation to an injunction, means a judge of the court that granted the injunction, except that where the respondent is aged 18 or over but the injunction was granted by a youth court, it means a judge of the county court: s 43(7) (s 43(7), Sch 5 para 1(2) amended by the Crime and Courts Act 2013 s 18(1), (3), (6), Sch 9 para 51, Sch 12 para 5). As to the determination of a person's age see the Children and Young Persons Act 1933 s 99; and CHILDREN AND YOUNG PERSONS vol 10 (2012) PARA 1206.
4 Policing and Crime Act 2009 s 43(4). In calculating when the period of 24 hours mentioned in s 34(4) ends, Christmas Day, Good Friday and any Sunday are to be disregarded: s 43(6).
5 Policing and Crime Act 2009 s 43(5). Where the court (ie the High Court or a county court) has power to remand a person under s 43(5) or s 44(4) (see the text and note 9) the court may, in the case of a person aged 18 or over, remand the person in custody (ie commit him to custody to be brought before the court at the end of the period of remand or at such earlier time as the court may require) (Sch 5 paras 1(1), (2), 2(1)(a) (Sch 5 para 2(1)(a) amended by the Crime and Security Act 2010 s 38)) or remand the person on bail (Policing and Crime Act 2009 Sch 5 para 2(1)(b)). The court may remand the person on bail by taking from him a recognisance, with or without sureties (Sch 5 para 2(2)(a)), and the court may direct that the person's recognisance be conditioned for the person's appearance before that court at the end of the period of remand (Sch 5 para 3(1)(a)) or at every time and place to which during the course of the proceedings the hearing may from time to time be adjourned (Sch 5 para 3(1)(b)): where a recognisance is

conditioned for a person's appearance as mentioned in Sch 5 para 3(1)(b) the fixing of any time for the person next to appear is to be treated as a remand (Sch 5 para 3(2)). Nothing in Sch 5 para 3 affects the power of the court at any subsequent hearing to remand the person afresh: Sch 5 para 3(3). The court may also remand the person on bail by fixing the amount of the recognisances with a view to their being taken subsequently and, in the meantime, committing the person to custody as mentioned in Sch 5 para 2(1)(a) (see above) (Sch 5 para 2(2)(b)): where the court so fixes the amount in which the principal and the sureties, if any, are to be bound, the recognisance may afterwards be taken by such person as may be prescribed by rules of court, with the same consequences as if it had been entered into before the court (Sch 5 para 6).

Where a person is brought before the court after remand the court may further remand the person: Sch 5 para 2(3). The court may not, however, remand a person for a period exceeding eight clear days unless the person is remanded on bail and both that person and the person who applied for the injunction consent to a longer period (Sch 5 para 4(1)(a)): where the court has power to remand a person in custody it may, if the remand is for a period not exceeding three clear days, commit the person to the custody of a constable (Sch 5 para 4(1)(b)). Where the court has power to remand a person in custody it may, if the remand is for a period not exceeding 3 clear days, commit the person to the custody of a constable: Sch 5 para 4(2).

If the court is satisfied that a person who has been remanded is unable by reason of illness or accident to appear or be brought before the court at the expiration of the period of remand the court may, in the absence of the person, further remand the person (Sch 5 para 5(1)): this power may, in the case of a person who was remanded on bail, be exercised by enlarging the person's recognisance and those of any sureties for the person to a later time (Sch 5 para 5(2)). Where a person remanded on bail is bound to appear before the court at any time and the court has no power to remand the person under Sch 5 para 5(1) the court may (in the person's absence) enlarge the person's recognisance and those of any sureties for the person to a later time, the enlargement of the person's recognisance being treated as a further remand: Sch 5 para 5(3), (4). Sch 5 para 4(1) (limit of remand: see above) does not apply to the exercise of the powers conferred by Sch 5 para 5: Sch 5 para 5(5).

The court may when remanding a person on bail under Sch 5 require the person to comply, before release on bail or later, with such requirements as appear to the court to be necessary to secure that the person does not interfere with witnesses or otherwise obstruct the course of justice: Sch 5 para 7.

In Sch 5 'court' means the High Court, the county court or a youth court and includes: (1) in relation to the High Court, a judge of that court; (2) in relation to the county court, a judge of that court; and (3) in relation to a youth court, a judge of that court: Sch 5 para 1(2) (as amended: see note 3).

6   As to the meaning of 'respondent' see PARA 483 note 5.

7   Policing and Crime Act 2009 s 44(1), (2).

8   Policing and Crime Act 2009 s 44(3).

9   Policing and Crime Act 2009 s 44(4). As to remands see Sch 5; and note 5.

10 Ie under the Policing and Crime Act 2009 s 43 or s 44: see the text and notes 1–9.

11 Ie under the Policing and Crime Act 2009 s 43(5) or (as the case may be) s 44(4): see the text and notes 5, 9.

12 Policing and Crime Act 2009 s 45(1), (2). If the person is remanded in custody for the purpose of enabling a medical examination to take place and a report to be made the adjournment may not be for more than three weeks at a time (s 45(3)); and if the person is remanded on bail for that purpose the adjournment may not be for more than four weeks at a time (s 45(4)).

13 Ie within the meaning of the Mental Health Act 1983: see s 1; MENTAL HEALTH AND CAPACITY vol 75 (2013) PARA 761.

14 Ie under the Mental Health Act 1983 s 35: see PARA 475.

15 See note 14.

16 Policing and Crime Act 2009 s 45(5). As to the meaning of 'accused person' see the Mental Health Act 1983 s 35(2); and PARA 475 note 1 (definition applied by the Policing and Crime Act 2009 s 45(5)).

489. Breach by respondents aged under 18. Where an injunction for the prevention of gang-related violence or drug dealing[1] has been granted against a person under the age of 18[2], the person is still under the age of 18[3], and on an application made by the injunction applicant[4], a youth court is satisfied beyond reasonable doubt that the person is in breach of any provision of the injunction[5], that court may make either a supervision order[6] or a detention order[7] in respect of the person[8].

1 Ie an injunction under the Policing and Crime Act 2009 Pt 4 (ss 34–50). As to the meanings of 'gang-related', 'violence' and 'drug-dealing activity' see PARA 483 notes 2–4.

2 Policing and Crime Act 2009 s 56A, Sch 5A Pt 1 para 1(1)(a) (s 56A, Sch 5A added by the Crime and Security Act 2010 s 39; Policing and Crime Act 2009 Sch 5A Pt 1 para 1(1)(a), (b), Sch 5A Pts 2, 3 amended, Sch 5 Pt 1 para 1(1)(aa) added, by the Crime and Courts Act 2013 Sch 12). An order under these provisions may not be made in respect of a person aged 18 or over: Policing and Crime Act 2009 Sch 5A para 1(6) (as so added). As to the determination of a person's age see the Children and Young Persons Act 1933 s 99; and CHILDREN AND YOUNG PERSONS vol 10 (2012) PARA 1206.

3 Policing and Crime Act 2009 Sch 5A para 1(1)(aa) (as added: see note 2).

4 'Injunction applicant', in relation to an injunction under the Policing and Crime Act 2009 Pt 4 or an order under Sch 5A made in respect of such an injunction, means the person who applied for the injunction: Sch 5A para 9 (as added: see note 2).

5 Policing and Crime Act 2009 Sch 5A para 1(1)(b) (as added: see note 2). Before making an application under Sch 5A para 1(1)(b) the injunction applicant must consult the youth offending team consulted under s 38(1) (see PARA 484) or s 39(5) (see PARA 484) in relation to the injunction (Sch 5A para 1(4)(a) (as so added)) and any other person previously so consulted (Sch 5A para 1(4)(b) (as so added)). In considering whether and how to exercise its powers under Sch 5A para 1, the court must consider a report made to assist the court in that respect by the youth offending team referred to in Sch 5A para 1(4)(a): Sch 5A para 1(5) (as so added).

6 Policing and Crime Act 2009 Sch 5A para 1(2)(a) (as added: see note 2). Provision in connection with the making of supervision orders is made by Sch 5A Pt 2 (as so added and amended).

7 Policing and Crime Act 2009 Sch 5A para 1(2)(b) (as added: see note 2). Provision in connection with the making of detention orders is made by Sch 5A Pt 3 (as so added and amended; amended by the Legal Aid, Sentencing and Punishment of Offenders Act 2012 Sch 12 para 58; prospectively amended by the Criminal Justice and Courts Act 2015 Sch 9 para 27). The court may not make a detention order unless it is satisfied, in view of the severity or extent of the breach, that no other power available to the court is appropriate: Policing and Crime Act 2009 Sch 5A para 1(7) (as so added). Where the court makes a detention order it must state in open court why it is satisfied as specified in Sch 5A para 1(7): Sch 5A para 1(8) (as so added).

8 Policing and Crime Act 2009 Sch 5A para 1(2) (as added: see note 2).

490. Guidance and review. The Secretary of State must issue guidance relating to injunctions for the prevention of gang-related violence or drug dealing[1] and may revise any guidance so issued[2]. Before issuing or revising any such guidance the Secretary of State must consult the Lord Chief Justice of England and Wales and such other persons as the Secretary of State thinks appropriate[3]. The Secretary of State must lay any guidance so issued or revised before Parliament[4] and must publish any guidance so issued or revised[5].

The Secretary of State must review the operation of the provisions governing injunctions and must prepare and publish a report on the outcome of the review[6].

1 Ie injunctions under the Policing and Crime Act 2009 Pt 4 (ss 34–50). As to the meanings of 'gang-related', 'violence' and 'drug-dealing activity' see PARA 483 notes 2–4.

2 Policing and Crime Act 2009 s 47(1), (2).

3 Policing and Crime Act 2009 s 47(3).

4 Policing and Crime Act 2009 s 47(4).

5 Policing and Crime Act 2009 s 47(5). See *Statutory Guidance: Injunctions to Prevent Gang-Related Violence* (December 2010), published by the Home Office.

6 Policing and Crime Act 2009 s 50(1). The report was required to have been published before 31 January 2014 (ie the end of the period of three years beginning with the day on which Pt 4 was brought into force by the Policing and Crime Act 2009 (Commencement No 7) Order 2010, SI 2010/1988): Policing and Crime Act 2009 s 50(2), (3).

(16) PARENTING ORDERS

491. Making of parenting orders on conviction. A parenting order is a court order which requires the parent to comply with such requirements as are specified in the order[1] and to attend such counselling or guidance sessions as may be specified[2]. These orders may be made in a number of circumstances including where an anti-social behaviour order[3], a criminal behaviour order[4] or a sexual harm prevention order[5] is made, or where an injunction for prohibiting anti-social behaviour[6] is granted, in respect of a child or young person, where a child or young person is convicted of an offence or where a person is convicted of failing to comply with a school attendance order or of failing to secure the attendance of a pupil at school[7].

1   See the Crime and Disorder Act 1998 s 8(4)(a); and CHILDREN AND YOUNG PERSONS vol 10 (2012) PARA 1279.
2   See the Crime and Disorder Act 1998 s 8(4)(b); and CHILDREN AND YOUNG PERSONS vol 10 (2012) PARA 1279.
3   Anti-social behaviour orders have been abolished: see PARA 439.
4   Ie an order under the Anti-social Behaviour, Crime and Policing Act 2014 s 22: see PARAS 319–326.
5   See PARAS 327–335.
6   Ie an injunction granted under the Anti-social Behaviour, Crime and Policing Act 2014 s 1: see PARAS 371–391.
7   See the Crime and Disorder Act 1998 s 8(1); and CHILDREN AND YOUNG PERSONS vol 10 (2012) PARA 1279. See further CHILDREN AND YOUNG PERSONS vol 10 (2012) PARAS 1280–1282.

(17) RESTITUTION ORDERS

492. Restitution orders. Where goods[1] have been stolen[2], and either a person is convicted of any offence with reference to the theft (whether or not the stealing is the gist of his offence[3]) or a person is convicted of any other offence but such an offence is taken into consideration in determining his sentence[4], the court by or before which the offender is convicted may on the conviction (whether or not the passing of sentence is in other respects deferred) exercise any of the following powers[5]:

(1)   the court may order anyone having possession or control of the stolen goods to restore them to any person entitled to recover them from him[6]; or

(2)   on the application of a person entitled to recover from the person convicted any other goods directly or indirectly representing the first-mentioned goods (as being the proceeds of any disposal or realisation of the whole or part of them or of goods so representing them) the court may order those other goods to be delivered or transferred to the applicant[7]; or

(3)   the court may order[8] that a sum not exceeding the value of the stolen goods be paid, out of any money of the person convicted which was taken out of his possession on his apprehension[9], to any person who, if those goods were in the possession of the person convicted, would be entitled to recover them from him[10].

Where the court has power on a person's conviction to make an order against him both under head (2) and under head (3) above with reference to the stealing of the same goods, the court may make orders under both heads provided that the person in whose favour the orders are made does not thereby recover more than the value of those goods[11].

Where the court on a person's conviction makes an order under head (1) above for the restoration of any goods, and it appears to the court that the person convicted has sold the goods to a person acting in good faith[12], or has borrowed money on the security of them from a person so acting[13], the court may order that there be paid to the purchaser or lender, out of any money of the person convicted which was taken out of his possession on his apprehension, a sum not exceeding the amount paid for the purchase by the purchaser or, as the case may be, the amount owed to the lender in respect of the loan[14].

The court may not exercise these powers, however, unless in the opinion of the court the relevant facts sufficiently appear from evidence given at the trial or the available documents[15], together with admissions made by or on behalf of any person in connection with any proposed exercise of the powers[16].

Unless the court otherwise directs, a restitution order must be suspended until there is no further possibility of an appeal on which the order could be varied or set aside[17].

These powers are exercisable not only where a person is convicted of an offence with reference to the theft of the goods in question but also where, on the conviction of a person of any other offence, the court takes an offence with reference to the theft of those goods into consideration in determining sentence; and where a restitution order is so made against any person in respect of an offence taken into consideration in determining his sentence:

(a) the order ceases to have effect if he successfully appeals against his conviction of the offence or, if more than one, all the offences, of which he was convicted in the proceedings in which the order was made[18]; and

(b) he may appeal against the order as if it were part of the sentence imposed in respect of the offence or, if more than one, any of the offences, of which he was so convicted[19].

1   For the purposes of the Powers of Criminal Courts (Sentencing) Act 2000 ss 148, 149 (see the text and notes 2–19), 'goods', except in so far as the context otherwise requires, includes money and every other description of property (within the meaning of the Theft Act 1968: see CRIMINAL LAW vol 25 (2010) PARA 281) except land, and includes things severed from the land by stealing: Powers of Criminal Courts (Sentencing) Act 2000 s 148(10). In connection with the making of restitution orders see the Criminal Procedure Rules 2015, SI 2015/1490, r 28.7.

2   For these purposes, references to stealing are to be construed in accordance with the Theft Act 1968 s 1(1) (see CRIMINAL LAW vol 25 (2010) PARA 278), read with the provisions of that Act relating to the construction of s 1(1): Powers of Criminal Courts (Sentencing) Act 2000 s 148(8). The provisions of the Theft Act 1968 s 24(1), (4) (see CRIMINAL LAW vol 25 (2010) PARA 299) also apply as they apply in relation to the provisions of the Theft Act 1968 relating to goods which have been stolen: Powers of Criminal Courts (Sentencing) Act 2000 s 148(9).

3   Powers of Criminal Courts (Sentencing) Act 2000 s 148(1)(a).

4   Powers of Criminal Courts (Sentencing) Act 2000 s 148(1)(b).

5   Powers of Criminal Courts (Sentencing) Act 2000 s 148(2). An order may be made under s 148 in respect of money owed by the Crown: s 148(11). Any order under s 148 is to be treated as an order for restitution of property within the meaning of the Criminal Appeal Act 1968 s 30 (effect of orders on appeals: see PARA 493): Powers of Criminal Courts (Sentencing) Act 2000 s 148(7). Where a magistrates' court commits the offender to the Crown Court for sentence it may not make a restitution order, because the power to do so becomes vested in the Crown Court: *R v Blackpool Justices, ex p Charlson and Gregory* [1972] 3 All ER 854, [1972] 1 WLR 1456, DC.

6   Powers of Criminal Courts (Sentencing) Act 2000 s 148(2)(a). An order under s 148 should not normally be made where there are serious competing claims involving third parties as a criminal court is not the correct forum for deciding such issues: see *Stamp v United Dominions Trust (Commercial) Ltd* [1967] 1 QB 418, [1967] 1 All ER 251, DC; *R v Ferguson* [1970] 2 All ER 820, [1970] 1 WLR 1246, CA; *R v Calcutt, R v Varty* (1985) 7 Cr App Rep (S) 385, [1986] Crim LR 266, CA. An order not expressly directed to any named person may be effective: see

    Barclays Bank Ltd v Milne [1963] 3 All ER 663, [1963] 1 WLR 1241. An order may be enforced in the same manner as a judgment: *Barclays Bank Ltd v Milne*.

7   Powers of Criminal Courts (Sentencing) Act 2000 s 148(2)(b). Where no application is made under s 148(2)(b), the court has no power to make an order under that provision: *R v Thibeault* [1983] RTR 316, (1982) 76 Cr App Rep 201, CA.

8   The power conferred by the Powers of Criminal Courts (Sentencing) Act 2000 s 148(2)(c) (see head (3) in the text) is exercisable without any application being made in that behalf or on the application of any person appearing to the court to be interested in the property concerned: s 149(1), (2).

9   See *R v Ferguson* [1970] 2 All ER 820, [1970] 1 WLR 1246, CA (money taken from offender's safe deposit box two weeks after arrest was 'taken out of his possession on his apprehension'). See also *R v Parker* [1970] 2 All ER 458, [1970] 1 WLR 1003, CA (where all the property in respect of which the offender has been convicted has been recovered, it is an incorrect exercise of the discretion to make a restitution order in respect of property which was not the subject of a charge against him). If the issue whether such money belonged to the offender is raised, except in the clearest case, it should be decided in the civil courts: *R v Ferguson*.

10 Powers of Criminal Courts (Sentencing) Act 2000 s 148(2)(c). See also *R v Parker* [1970] 2 All ER 458, [1970] 1 WLR 1003, CA (goods in respect of which offender was convicted were recovered; order for payment in respect of goods stolen at same time invalid).

11 Powers of Criminal Courts (Sentencing) Act 2000 s 148(3).

12 Powers of Criminal Courts (Sentencing) Act 2000 s 148(4)(a).

13 Powers of Criminal Courts (Sentencing) Act 2000 s 148(4)(b).

14 Powers of Criminal Courts (Sentencing) Act 2000 s 148(4). The power conferred by s 148(4) is exercisable without any application being made in that behalf or on the application of any person appearing to the court to be interested in the property concerned: s 149(1), (2).

15 For these purposes 'available documents' means any written statements or admissions which were made for use, and would have been admissible, as evidence at the trial (Powers of Criminal Courts (Sentencing) Act 2000 s 148(6)(a)) and such documents as were served on the offender in pursuance of regulations made under the Crime and Disorder Act 1998 Sch 3 para 1 (see CRIMINAL PROCEDURE vol 27 (2015) PARA 305) (Powers of Criminal Courts (Sentencing) Act 2000 s 148(6)(b) (substituted by the Criminal Justice Act 2003 Sch 3, para 74(1), (5))).

16 Powers of Criminal Courts (Sentencing) Act 2000 s 148(5). See *R v Church* (1970) 55 Cr App Rep 65, CA (a trial comes to a conclusion when sentence is passed and evidence given after sentence is not evidence given at the trial).

17 See PARA 493. Any order made by a magistrates' court must be suspended: (1) in any case until the expiration of the period for the time being prescribed by law for the giving of notice of appeal against a decision of a magistrates' court (Powers of Criminal Courts (Sentencing) Act 2000 s 149(4)(a)); (2) where notice of appeal is given within the period so prescribed, until the determination of the appeal (s 149(4)(b)). However, this provision does not apply where the order is made under s 148(2)(a) or (b) (see the text and notes 6–7) and the court so directs, being of the opinion that the title to the goods to be restored or, as the case may be, delivered or transferred under the order is not in dispute: s 149(4).

18 Powers of Criminal Courts (Sentencing) Act 2000 s 149(3)(a).

19 Powers of Criminal Courts (Sentencing) Act 2000 s 149(3)(b).

493. Suspension of orders for restitution of property.

Unless the Court of Appeal directs to the contrary in any case in which, in its opinion, the title to property is not in dispute, the operation of an order for the restitution of property[1] to a person made by the Crown Court is suspended until (disregarding any power of a court to grant leave to appeal out of time) there is no further possibility of an appeal on which the order could be varied or set aside; and provision may be made[2] for the custody of any property in the meantime[3]. The Court of Appeal may by order annul or vary any order made by the court of trial[4] for the restitution of property to any person, although the conviction is not quashed; and the order, if annulled, does not take effect and, if varied, takes effect as so varied[5]. Where the Supreme Court restores a conviction[6], it may make any order for the restitution of property which the court of trial could have made[7].

1 Any order under the Powers of Criminal Courts (Sentencing) Act 2000 s 148 (orders for restitution: see PARA 492) is to be treated as an order for the restitution of property within the meaning of the Criminal Appeal Act 1968 s 30 (see the text and notes 2–7): Powers of Criminal Courts (Sentencing) Act 2000 s 148(7). See also the Wildlife and Countryside Act 1981 s 31; and OPEN SPACES AND COUNTRYSIDE vol 78 (2010) PARA 693.

2 Ie by rules of court.

3 Criminal Appeal Act 1968 s 30(1) (s 30 substituted by the Criminal Justice Act 1988 Sch 15 paras 20, 28).

4 As to the meaning of 'court of trial' see CRIMINAL PROCEDURE vol 28 (2015) PARA 734.

5 Criminal Appeal Act 1968 s 30(2) (as substituted: see note 3).

6 As to appeals from the Court of Appeal to the Supreme Court see CRIMINAL PROCEDURE vol 28 (2015) PARA 812 et seq.

7 Criminal Appeal Act 1968 s 30(3) (as substituted (see note 3); amended by the Constitutional Reform Act 2005 Sch 9 para 16(1), (2)).

(18) RESTRAINING ORDERS

494. Restraining orders. In the circumstances described below, a court may make a restraining order[1]. Such an order may, for the purpose of protecting the victim or victims[2] of an offence, or any other person mentioned in the order, from conduct which either amounts to harassment[3] or will cause a fear of violence, prohibit the defendant from doing anything described in the order[4], and may be made by a court sentencing or otherwise dealing with a person convicted of any offence[5]. A court may make a restraining order in addition to sentencing the defendant or dealing with him in any other way[6] and may also make a restraining order in respect of a person who is acquitted of an offence before it[7] if it considers it necessary to do so to protect a person from harassment by that person[8]; and such an order may prohibit the defendant from doing anything described in it[9].

A restraining order may have effect for a specified period or until further order[10] and must identify the protected party by name[11]. If without reasonable excuse[12] the defendant does anything which he is prohibited from doing by a restraining order, he is guilty of an offence[13].

A court dealing with a person for an offence under these provisions may vary or discharge the order in question by a further order[14].

1 Protection from Harassment Act 1997 s 5(1). For procedural rules in connection with the making of restraining orders see the Criminal Procedure Rules 2015, SI 2015/1490, Pt 31. The Criminal Justice (European Protection Order) (England and Wales) Regulations 2014, SI 2014/3300, make provision for and in connection with the making of a European Protection Order, applying these provisions with modifications. See also the Criminal Procedure Rules 2015, SI 2015/1490, rr 31.9, 31.10.

2 A restraining order may, where appropriate, be made in order to protect a company: the power to make such an order is not restricted to the protection of individuals: see *R v Buxton* [2010] EWCA Crim 2923, [2011] 1 WLR 857, [2011] 2 Cr App Rep (S) 121.

3 Protection from Harassment Act 1997 s 5(2)(a) (s 5(1), (2) amended, and ss 5(3A), (4A), (7), 5A added, by the Domestic Violence, Crime and Victims Act 2004 s 12, Sch 10 para 43(1), (3); Protection from Harassment Act 1997 s 5(2)(a) amended by the Serious Organised Crime and Police Act 2005 s 125(1), (6)). As to what constitutes 'harassment' see the Protection from Harassment Act 1997 s 7(2); and CRIMINAL LAW vol 26 (2010) PARA 491.

4 Protection from Harassment Act 1997 s 5(2)(b). A restraining order must be drafted in clear and precise terms so there is no doubt as to what the defendant is prohibited from doing: *R v Debnath* [2005] EWCA Crim 3472, [2006] 2 Cr App Rep (S) 169, [2006] Crim LR 451. Orders should be framed in practical terms (eg by reference to specific roads or a specific address) and if necessary a map should be prepared: *R v Debnath*. In considering the terms and extent of a restraining order a court should have regard to considerations of proportionality: *R v Debnath*.

5 Protection from Harassment Act 1997 s 5(1) (as amended: see note 3).

6 Protection from Harassment Act 1997 s 5(1) (as amended: see note 3).

7   Where the Crown Court allows an appeal against conviction, or a case is remitted to the Crown Court under the Protection from Harassment Act 1997 s 5A(3) (see note 8), the reference to a court before which a person is acquitted of an offence is to be read as referring to that court: s 5A(4) (as added: see note 3).

8   Protection from Harassment Act 1997 s 5A(1) (as added: see note 3). A person made subject to an order under s 5A has the same right of appeal against the order as if he had been convicted of the offence in question before the court which made the order, and as if the order had been made under s 5: s 5A(5) (as so added). Where the Court of Appeal allows an appeal against conviction it may remit the case to the Crown Court to consider whether to proceed under this provision: s 5A(3) (as so added).

9   Protection from Harassment Act 1997 s 5A(1) (as added: see note 3).

10   Protection from Harassment Act 1997 ss 5(3), 5A(2) (s 5A(2) as added: see note 3). The prosecutor, defendant or any other person mentioned in the order may apply to the court which made the order for it to be varied or discharged by a further order: s 5(4). Any person mentioned in the order is entitled to be heard on the hearing of such an application: s 5(4A) (as so added). Where an order is expressed as being until further order has been made, an application, or further application, to discharge the order under s 5(4) should be made only where circumstances have changed such that the continuance of the order is no longer necessary or appropriate: *Shaw v DPP* [2005] EWHC 1215 (Admin), [2005] 7 Archbold News 2, [2005] All ER (D) 93 (Apr), DC. A restraining order made for a specified period may be varied by extending the expiry date: see *DPP v Hall* [2005] EWHC 2612 (Admin), [2006] 3 All ER 170, [2006] 1 WLR 1000. Where an order is varied it is desirable that the order as varied is drawn up as a fresh document containing all its terms: *R v Liddle* [2001] EWCA Crim 2512, [2002] 1 Archbold News 2. In proceedings under the Protection from Harassment Act 1997 s 5 or s 5A both the prosecution and the defence may lead, as further evidence, any evidence that would be admissible in proceedings for an injunction under the Protection from Harassment Act 1997 s 3 (see **TORT** vol 97 (2010) PARA 557): s 5(3A) (as so added).

11   *R v Mann* (2000) 144 Sol Jo LB 150, (2000) Times, 11 April, CA.

12   It is for the defendant to raise the evidential issue of reasonable excuse and then for the prosecution to prove lack of that excuse: see *R v Evans (Dorothy)* [2004] EWCA Crim 3102, [2005] 1 WLR 1435, [2005] 1 Cr App Rep 546 (in interpreting the terms of a restraining order the matter of whether a word or phrase in the order was being used in its ordinary sense or a special sense is a question of law in each individual case; if, as a matter of law, the word or phrase was being used in its ordinary sense, it is for the tribunal of fact to apply that meaning to the facts as found).

13   Protection from Harassment Act 1997 s 5(5). A person guilty of this offence is liable on conviction on indictment to imprisonment for a term not exceeding five years or to a fine or to both, or on summary conviction to imprisonment for a term not exceeding six months or to a fine not exceeding the statutory maximum or to both: s 5(6). See *R v Liddle* [1999] 3 All ER 816, [2000] 1 Cr App Rep (S) 131, CA; *R v Lydon* [2005] EWCA Crim 1909, [2006] 1 Cr App Rep (S) 342. As to the standard scale, the statutory maximum, the prescribed sum, and magistrates' powers to levy unlimited fines see PARA 176.

     When sentencing for breach of a restraining order, courts should take into account: (1) the nature of the act giving rise to the breach; (2) the effect on the victim; (3) whether the offence was the first breach or the latest in a series of breaches; (4) the record of the offender, especially his previous response to community penalties; and (5) the need to protect the person named in the order: *R v Pace* [2004] EWCA Crim 2018, [2005] 1 Cr App Rep (S) 370.

14   Protection from Harassment Act 1997 s 5(7) (as added: see note 3).

(19) SUPERVISION ORDERS

495. Making of supervision orders. A 'supervision order' is an order which requires the person in respect of whom it is made (the 'supervised person') to be under the supervision of a social worker or an officer of a local probation board or an officer of a provider of probation services (the 'supervising officer')[1] for a period specified in the order of not more than two years[2]. A supervision order may[3] require the supervised person to submit, during the whole of that period or such part of it as may be specified in the order, to treatment by or under the direction of a registered medical practitioner[4].

The court may make a supervision order where:

(1) a special verdict of not guilty by reason of insanity[5] is returned[6]; or
(2) findings have been made that the defendant is under a disability and that he did the act or omission charged against him[7].

The court must not make a supervision order unless it is satisfied that:

(a) having regard to all the circumstances of the case, the making of such an order is the most suitable means of dealing with the defendant or appellant[8];

(b) the supervising officer intended to be specified in the order is willing to undertake the supervision[9]; and

(c) arrangements have been made for the treatment intended to be specified in the order[10].

A person in respect of whom the Crown Court has made a supervision order after a verdict of not guilty by reason of insanity or after findings that the defendant is under a disability[11] may appeal to the Court of Appeal against the order[12].

1 As to local probation boards and the provision of probation services see PARAS 666–687.
2 Criminal Procedure (Insanity) Act 1964 s 5(4), Sch 1A para 1(1) (s 5 substituted, s 5A, Sch 1A added, by the Domestic Violence, Crime and Victims Act 2004 s 24(1), Sch 2; Criminal Procedure (Insanity) Act 1964 Sch 1A para 1(1) amended by SI 2008/912). The Secretary of State may by order direct that the Criminal Procedure (Insanity) Act 1964 Sch 1A para 1(1) be amended by substituting, for the period for the time being specified there, such period as may be specified in the order: Sch 1A para 1(3) (as so added). An order under Sch 1A para 1(3) may make in Sch 1A para 11(2) (see PARA 497) any amendment which the Secretary of State thinks necessary in consequence of any substitution made by the order: Sch 1A para 1(4) (as so added). At the date at which this volume states the law no such order had been made.
  Before making a supervision order, the court must explain to the supervised person in ordinary language the effect of the order (including any requirements proposed to be included in the order in accordance with Sch 1A para 4, 5 or 8 (see PARA 496) (Sch 1A para 3(2)(a) (as so added))) and that a magistrates' court has power under Sch 1A paras 9–11 (see PARA 497) to review the order on the application either of the supervised person or of the supervising officer (Sch 1A para 3(2)(b) (as so added)). After making an order, the court must forthwith give copies of the order to an officer of a local probation board assigned to the court or an officer of a provider of probation services acting at the court, and he must give a copy to the supervised person (Sch 1A para 3(3)(a) (as so added; amended by SI 2008/912)) and to the supervising officer (Criminal Procedure (Insanity) Act 1964 Sch 1A para 3(3)(b) (as so added)). After making an order, the court must also send to the designated officer for the local justice area in which the supervised person resides or will reside (the 'local justice area concerned') a copy of the order (Sch 1A para 3(4)(a) (as so added)) and such documents and information relating to the case as it considers likely to be of assistance to a court acting for that area in the exercise of its functions in relation to the order (Sch 1A para 3(4)(b) (as so added)).
  Persons in respect of whom supervision orders may be made may be remanded to hospital for a report on their mental condition or for treatment (see the Criminal Procedure (Insanity) Act 1964 s 5A(2); the Mental Health Act 1983 ss 35, 36; and PARAS 475, 476).
3 Ie in accordance with the Criminal Procedure (Insanity) Act 1964 Sch 1A para 4 or Sch 1A para 5 (see PARA 496).
4 Criminal Procedure (Insanity) Act 1964 Sch 1A para 1(2) (as added: see note 2).
5 See CRIMINAL LAW vol 25 (2010) PARA 30.
6 Criminal Procedure (Insanity) Act 1964 ss 5(1)(a), (2)(b) (as substituted: see note 2). In these circumstances the court may also make a hospital order or an order for the absolute discharge of the accused: see s 5(2)(b), (c); and PARAS 443, 472.
7 Criminal Procedure (Insanity) Act 1964 s 5(1)(b) (as substituted: see note 2). See also note 3. As to such findings see CRIMINAL PROCEDURE vol 27 (2015) PARA 357.
8 Criminal Procedure (Insanity) Act 1964 Sch 1A para 2(1) (as added: see note 2).
9 Criminal Procedure (Insanity) Act 1964 Sch 1A para 2(2)(a) (as added: see note 2).
10 Criminal Procedure (Insanity) Act 1964 Sch 1A para 2(2)(b) (as added: see note 2).
11 Ie under the Criminal Procedure (Insanity) Act 1964 s 5 (see the text and notes 2–6).
12 Criminal Appeal Act 1968 s 16A(1)(b) (ss 16A, 16B added by the Domestic Violence, Crime and Victims Act 2004 s 25). Such an appeal lies only with the leave of the Court of Appeal; or if the judge of the court of trial (ie, where the Crown Court comprises justices of the peace, the judge

presiding: Criminal Appeal Act 1968 s 51(1) (definition substituted by the Courts Act 1971 Sch 8 para 57(3))) grants a certificate that the case is fit for appeal: Criminal Appeal Act 1968 s 16A(2) (as so added). If on such an appeal the Court of Appeal considers that the appellant should be dealt with differently from the way in which the court below dealt with him:

    (1)   it may quash any order which is the subject of the appeal (s 16B(1)(a) (as so added)); and

    (2)   it may make such order, whether by substitution for the original order or by variation of or addition to it, as it thinks appropriate for the case and as the court below had power to make (s 16B(1)(b) (as so added)).

496. Requirements to be specified in supervision orders. A supervision order[1] must either:

    (1)   specify the local social services authority area in which the supervised person[2] resides or will reside, and require him to be under the supervision of a social worker of the local social services authority for that area[3]; or

    (2)   specify the local justice area in which that person resides or will reside, and require him to be under the supervision of an officer of a local probation board appointed for or assigned to that area or, as the case may be, an officer of a provider of probation services acting in that area[4].

A supervision order may also, on medical advice[5] include a requirement that the supervised person must submit, during the whole of the period specified in the order or during such part of that period as may be so specified, to treatment by or under the direction of a registered medical practitioner with a view to the improvement of his mental[6] or medical[7] condition[8].

The supervised person must keep in touch with the supervising officer in accordance with such instructions as he may from time to time be given by that officer and must notify him of any change of address[9]. A supervision order may also include requirements as to the residence of the supervised person[10].

1   As to supervision orders see PARA 495.

2   As to the supervised person see PARA 495 note 1.

3   Criminal Procedure (Insanity) Act 1964 Sch 1A para 3(1)(a) (Sch 1A added by the Domestic Violence, Crime and Victims Act 2004 s 24(1), Sch 2).

4   Criminal Procedure (Insanity) Act 1964 Sch 1A para 3(1)(b) (as added (see note 3); amended by SI 2008/912). As to local probation boards and the provision of probation services see PARAS 666–687.

5   See notes 6, 7.

6   The court may order treatment with a view to the improvement of a person's mental condition (ie under the Criminal Procedure (Insanity) Act 1964 Sch 1A para 4) if it is satisfied on the written or oral evidence of two or more registered medical practitioners, at least one of whom is duly registered, that the mental condition of the supervised person is such as requires and may be susceptible to treatment (Sch 1A para 4(2)(a) (as added: see note 3)) but is not such as to warrant the making of a hospital order within the meaning of the Mental Health Act 1983 (Criminal Procedure (Insanity) Act 1964 Sch 1A para 4(2)(b) (as so added)). As to the making of hospital orders within the meaning of the Mental Health Act 1983 see PARA 472. As to registered medical practitioners see the Medical Act 1983 s 55(1); and MEDICAL PROFESSIONS vol 74 (2011) PARA 176.

7   The court may order treatment with a view to the improvement of a person's medical condition (ie under the Criminal Procedure (Insanity) Act 1964 Sch 1A para 5), whether or not it includes a requirement under Sch 1A para 4 (see the text and note 8), if it is satisfied on the written or oral evidence of two or more registered medical practitioners that, because of his medical condition, other than his mental condition, the supervised person is likely to pose a risk to himself or others (Sch 1A para 5(1)(a) (as added: see note 3)), and that the condition may be susceptible to treatment (Sch 1A para 5(1)(b) (as so added)).

8   Criminal Procedure (Insanity) Act 1964 Sch 1A paras 4(1), 5(2) (as added: see note 3). The treatment required under Sch 1A paras 4, 5 by any such order must be such one of the following

kinds of treatment as may be specified in the order, that is to say treatment as a non-resident patient at such institution or place as may be specified in the order (Sch 1A paras 4(3)(a), 5(3)(a) (as so added)) and treatment by or under the direction of such registered medical practitioner as may be so specified (Sch 1A paras 4(3)(b), 5(3)(b) (as so added)), but the nature of the treatment may not be specified in the order except as so mentioned (Sch 1A paras 4(3), 5(3) (as so added)). Where the medical practitioner by whom or under whose direction the supervised person is being treated in pursuance of a requirement under Sch 1A para 4 or Sch 1A para 5 is of the opinion that part of the treatment can be better or more conveniently given in or at an institution or place which is not specified in the order (Sch 1A para 6(1)(a) (as so added)), and is one in or at which the treatment of the supervised person will be given by or under the direction of a registered medical practitioner (Sch 1A para 6(1)(b) (as so added)), he may, with the consent of the supervised person, make arrangements for him to be treated accordingly (Sch 1A para 6(1) (as so added)). Such arrangements may provide for the supervised person to receive part of his treatment as a resident patient in an institution or place of any description: Sch 1A para 6(2) (as so added). Where any such arrangements are made for the treatment of a supervised person:

(1)   the medical practitioner by whom the arrangements are made must give notice in writing to the supervising officer, specifying the institution or place in or at which the treatment is to be carried out (Sch 1A para 6(3)(a) (as so added)); and

(2)   the treatment provided for by the arrangements is deemed to be treatment to which he is required to submit in pursuance of the supervision order (Sch 1A para 6(3)(b) (as so added)).

While the supervised person is under treatment as a resident patient in pursuance of arrangements under Sch 1A para 6, the supervising officer must carry out the supervision to such extent only as may be necessary for the purpose of the revocation or amendment of the order: Sch 1A para 7 (as so added). As to the 'supervising officer' see PARA 495 note 1.

9   Criminal Procedure (Insanity) Act 1964 Sch 1A para 3(5) (as added: see note 3).

10   Criminal Procedure (Insanity) Act 1964 Sch 1A para 8(1) (as added: see note 3). This is subject to Sch 1A para 8(2) (as so added), which provides that before making a supervision order containing any such requirement the court must consider the home surroundings of the supervised person.

497.   Revocation and amendment of supervision orders.   A supervision order[1] which is in force in respect of any person may be revoked by a magistrates' court acting for the local justice area concerned if it appears to the court that, having regard to circumstances which have arisen since the order was made, it would be in the interests of the health or welfare of the supervised person that the order should be revoked, the court may revoke the order[2]. A magistrates' court may so revoke an order only on the application of the supervised person[3] or the supervising officer[4]: however the court by which a supervision order was made may of its own motion revoke the order if, having regard to circumstances which have arisen since the order was made, it considers that it would be inappropriate for the order to continue[5].

Where, at any time while a supervision order is in force in respect of any person, a magistrates' court acting for the local justice area concerned is satisfied that the supervised person proposes to change, or has changed, his residence from the area specified in the order to another local social services authority area or local justice area[6], the court may, and on the application of the supervising officer must, amend the supervision order by substituting the other area for the area specified in the order[7].

A magistrates' court for the local justice area concerned may, on the application of the supervised person or the supervising officer, by order amend a supervision order by cancelling any of the requirements of the order[8] or by inserting in the order (either in addition to or in substitution for any such requirement) any requirement which the court could include if it were the court by which the order was made and were then making it[9].

Where the medical practitioner by whom or under whose direction a supervised person is being treated for his mental condition in pursuance of any requirement of a supervision order is of a specified opinion[10] relating to the person's treatment[11], or is for any reason unwilling to continue to treat or direct the treatment of the supervised person[12], he must make a report in writing to that effect to the supervising officer and that officer must apply[13] to a magistrates' court for the local justice area concerned for the variation or cancellation of the requirement[14].

1 As to supervision orders see PARA 495.
2 Criminal Procedure (Insanity) Act 1964 Sch 1A para 9(1) (Sch 1A added by the Domestic Violence, Crime and Victims Act 2004 s 24(1), Sch 2). On the making under the Criminal Procedure (Insanity) Act 1964 Sch 1A para 9 of an order revoking a supervision order, the designated officer for the local justice area concerned, or (as the case may be) the Crown Court, must forthwith give copies of the revoking order to the supervising officer: Sch 1A para 13(1) (as so added). A supervising officer to whom in accordance with Sch 1A para 13(1) copies of a revoking order are given must give a copy to the supervised person and to the person in charge of any institution in which the supervised person is residing: Sch 1A para 13(2) (as so added). As to the 'supervising officer' see PARA 495 note 1.
3 As to the 'supervised person' see PARA 495 note 1.
4 Criminal Procedure (Insanity) Act 1964 Sch 1A para 9(1) (as added: see note 2).
5 Criminal Procedure (Insanity) Act 1964 Sch 1A para 9(2) (as added: see note 2).
6 Criminal Procedure (Insanity) Act 1964 Sch 1A para 10(1) (as added: see note 2).
7 Criminal Procedure (Insanity) Act 1964 Sch 1A para 10(2) (as added: see note 2). However, the court may not amend under Sch 1A para 10 a supervision order which contains requirements which, in the opinion of the court, cannot be complied with unless the supervised person continues to reside in the area specified in the order unless, in accordance with Sch 1A para 11 (see the text and notes 8–9), it either cancels those requirements (Sch 1A para 10(3)(a) (as so added)), or substitutes for those requirements other requirements which can be complied with if the supervised person ceases to reside in that area (Sch 1A para 10(3)(b) (as so added)).
   On the making under Sch 1A para 10 or Sch 1A para 11 of any order amending a supervision order, the designated officer for the local justice area concerned must forthwith:
   (1) if the order amends the supervision order otherwise than by substituting a new area or a new place for the one specified in the supervision order, give copies of the amending order to the supervising officer (Sch 1A para 14(1)(a) (as so added));
   (2) if the order amends the supervision order in the manner excepted by head (1) above, send to the designated officer for the new local justice area concerned copies of the amending order (Sch 1A para 14(1)(b)(i) (as so added)) and such documents and information relating to the case as he considers likely to be of assistance to a court acting for that area in exercising its functions in relation to the order (Sch 1A para 14(1)(b)(ii) (as so added)).
   In a case falling within head (2) above, the designated officer for that area must give copies of the amending order to the supervising officer: Sch 1A para 14(1) (as so added).
   Where the designated officer for the court making the order is also the designated officer for the new local justice area, head (2) above does not apply (Sch 1A para 14(2)(a) (as so added)), but the designated officers must give copies of the amending order to the supervising officer (Sch 1A para 14(2)(b) (as so added)).
   Where in accordance with Sch 1A para 14(1) or (2) copies of an order are given to the supervising officer, he must give a copy to the supervised person and to the person in charge of any institution in which the supervised person is or was residing: Sch 1A para 14(3) (as so added).
8 Criminal Procedure (Insanity) Act 1964 Sch 1A para 11(1)(a) (as added: see note 2). Sch 1A para 11 is without prejudice to the provisions of Sch 1A para 10 (see the text and notes 6–7) but is subject to Sch 1A para 11(2) (as so added), which provides that the power of a magistrates' court under Sch 1A para 11(1) does not include power to amend an order by extending the period specified in it beyond the end of two years from the day of the original order. As to the making of orders under Sch 1A para 11 see Sch 1A para 14; and note 7.
9 Criminal Procedure (Insanity) Act 1964 Sch 1A para 11(1)(b) (as added: see note 2). See note 8.
10 The opinion referred to in the Criminal Procedure (Insanity) Act 1964 Sch 1A para 12(1) is:
   (1) that the treatment of the supervised person should be continued beyond the period specified in the supervision order (Sch 1A para 12(2)(a) (as added: see note 2));

     (2)   that the supervised person needs different treatment, being treatment of a kind to which he could be required to submit in pursuance of such an order (Sch 1A para 12(2)(b) (as so added));

     (3)   that the supervised person is not susceptible to treatment (Sch 1A para 12(2)(c) (as so added)); or

     (4)   that the supervised person does not require further treatment (Sch 1A para 12(2)(d) (as so added)).

11 Criminal Procedure (Insanity) Act 1964 Sch 1A para 12(1)(a) (as added: see note 2).

12 Criminal Procedure (Insanity) Act 1964 Sch 1A para 12(1)(b) (as added: see note 2).

13 Ie under the Criminal Procedure (Insanity) Act 1964 Sch 1A para 11 (see the text and notes 8–9).

14 Criminal Procedure (Insanity) Act 1964 Sch 1A para 12(1) (as added: see note 2).

8. NOTIFICATION REQUIREMENTS

(1) NOTIFICATION REQUIREMENTS AND ORDERS (SEXUAL OFFENCES)

(i) Notification Requirements

498. The notification requirements and relevant offenders. Provision is made for persons convicted of or cautioned for a range of sexual offences against children to be required to provide the police with specified information about themselves[1]. There are two categories of offender who may be subject to the notification requirements (referred to as 'relevant offenders'): those becoming subject to the requirements on or after 1 May 2004[2] and those subject to the requirements before that date[3]. In either case, a person is subject to the notification requirements if he is or was convicted of or cautioned for a relevant offence[4], found not guilty of such an offence by reason of insanity, or found to be under a disability and to have done the act charged against him in respect of such an offence, and continues to be subject to the requirements for a specified period (the 'notification period'), the length of which is determined by the sentence he is given[5].

Provision is made for the assessment and management of the risks posed by persons who are subject to the notification requirements and other persons who, by reason of offences committed by them, are considered by the responsible authority to be persons who may cause serious harm to the public[6].

1   This provision has effect under the Sexual Offences Act 2003 Pt 2 (ss 80–136ZD), which re-enacted with amendments the scheme originally having effect under the Sex Offenders Act 1997 Pt 1 (ss 1–6) (repealed as from 1 May 2004). For the matters required to be notified, and the means of notification, see PARA 503 et seq. In connection with the notification requirements see the Criminal Procedure Rules 2015, SI 2015/1490, r 28.3.

      The police, as a public authority, may publish such information only if it is in the public interest and there is a pressing need to do so, and they must obtain as much information regarding the matter as is reasonably possible before taking such a highly sensitive decision: *R v Chief Constable of the North Wales Police, ex p Thorpe* [1999] QB 396, sub nom *R v Chief Constable of the North Wales Police, ex p AB* [1998] 3 All ER 310, CA.

      The notification requirements under the Sexual Offences Act 2003 Pt 2 do not impose any obligation other than the requirements set out in PARA 503 et seq, nor do they have any other effect: eg they do not automatically disqualify someone from holding a passenger-carrying vehicle driving licence (see *Secretary of State for Transport, Local Government and the Regions v Snowdon* [2002] EWHC 2394 (Admin), [2003] RTR 216, [2002] 47 LS Gaz R 29).

2   Ie the date on which the Sexual Offences Act 2003 Pt 2 was brought into force by the Sexual Offences Act 2003 (Commencement) Order 2004, SI 2004/874. As to these offenders see PARA 499.

3   Ie under the Sex Offenders Act 1997 Pt 1 (repealed as from 1 May 2004). As to these offenders see PARA 500.

4   As to the offences in respect of which the notification requirements may arise see the Sexual Offences Act 2003 Sch 3; and PARA 329.

5   As to the notification period see PARA 501.

6   See CRIMINAL LAW vol 25 (2010) PARA 97.

499. Persons becoming subject to notification requirements on or after 1 May 2004. A person is subject to the notification requirements[1] for the duration of the notification period[2] (that is to say, he is a 'relevant offender'[3]) if after 1 May 2004[4]:

(1)   he is convicted of a listed offence[5];

(2)   he is found not guilty of such an offence by reason of insanity[6];

(3)   he is found to be under a disability and to have done the act charged against him in respect of such an offence[7]; or

(4)   in England and Wales or Northern Ireland, he is cautioned in respect of such an offence[8].

A person is also subject to the notification requirements where a sexual harm prevention order[9] is made in respect of him[10] or he breaches a sexual risk order or a risk of sexual harm order[11].

1   For the matters required to be notified, and the means of notification, see PARA 503 et seq.

2   As to the notification period see PARA 501. The notification requirement system applies automatically and is, therefore, not part of the system of penalties and is irrelevant to the sentencing exercise; consequently, it would be wrong, for example, to reduce a sentence in order that the offender is subject to the notification requirement for a shorter period: *A-G's Reference (No 50 of 1997)* [1998] 2 Cr App Rep (S) 155, CA. However, placing an offender on the sex offenders register indefinitely without a mechanism for review is a disproportionate interference with the right to respect for private and family life under the Convention for the Protection of Human Rights and Fundamental Freedoms (Rome, 4 November 1950; TS 71 (1953); Cmd 8969) art 8 (see RIGHTS AND FREEDOMS vol 88A (2013) PARAS 317–367) (see *R (on the application of JF (by his litigation friend OF)) v Secretary of State for the Home Department* [2010] UKSC 17, [2011] 1 AC 331, [2010] 2 All ER 707): accordingly, in the light of this decision, provision is now made for reviews (see the Sexual Offences Act 2003 ss 91A–91F; and PARAS 511–512).

    The notification requirement is not an order of the court but a consequence that flows automatically from certain convictions and sentence; however, the court by or before which an offender is convicted may inform the offender of any notification requirement which applies as a consequence of such conviction provided that this is not done in a way which appears to make such information part of the sentence or to clothe it with the authority of a further order by the sentencing court: *R v Longworth* [2006] UKHL 1, [2006] 1 All ER 887, [2006] 1 WLR 313. Special provision is made in respect of young offenders: see PARA 509.

3   Sexual Offences Act 2003 s 80(2).

4   Ie the date on which the Sexual Offences Act 2003 Pt 2 (ss 80–136ZD) was brought into force by the Sexual Offences Act 2003 (Commencement) Order 2004, SI 2004/874.

5   Sexual Offences Act 2003 s 80(1)(a). As to the offences in respect of which the notification requirements may arise see Sch 3; and PARA 329.

6   Sexual Offences Act 2003 s 80(1)(b). As to verdicts of not guilty by reason of insanity see CRIMINAL LAW vol 25 (2010) PARA 30.

7   Sexual Offences Act 2003 s 80(1)(c). As to a reference to a person being or having been found to be under a disability and to have done the act charged against him in respect of an offence see PARA 329 note 1.

8   Sexual Offences Act 2003 s 80(1)(d).

9   As to sexual harm prevention orders and interim sexual harm prevention orders see PARAS 327–335.

10   Regarding sexual harm prevention orders and interim sexual harm prevention orders see the Sexual Offences Act 2003 ss 103G(1)–(4) (ss 103G, 122I added by the Anti-social Behaviour, Crime and Policing Act 2014 Sch 5 paras 2, 4), which provide:

    (1)   that where a sexual harm prevention order or an interim order is made in respect of a defendant who was not a relevant offender immediately before the making of the order, the order causes him to become subject to the notification requirements from the making of the order until the order (as renewed from time to time (other than in the case of an interim order)) ceases to have effect (Sexual Offences Act 2003 s 103G(2)(a), (4) (as so added)), and Pt 2 applies to the defendant subject to the modification that the 'relevant date' is the date of service of the order (s 103G(2)(b), (3) (as so added)); and

    (2)   that where a sexual harm prevention order or interim order is made in respect of a defendant who was a relevant offender immediately before the making of the order (s 103G(1)(a) (as so added)) and the defendant would (apart from these provisions) cease to be subject to the notification requirements of Pt 2 while the order (as renewed from time to time (other than in the case of an interim order)) has effect (s 103G(1)(b) (as so added)), he remains subject to the notification requirements.

11   As to sexual risk orders and interim sexual risk orders see PARAS 392–397; as to risk of sexual harm orders (which have been abolished) see PARA 440). Where a person breaches such an order (ie is convicted of an offence under the Sexual Offences Act 2003 s 122H (breach of sexual risk

order: see PARA 392) or s 128 (breach of risk of sexual harm order (repealed)) (s 122I(1)(a), (2)(a) (as added: see note 10)), is found not guilty of such an offence by reason of insanity (s 122I(1)(b) (as so added)), is found to be under a disability and to have done the act charged against him in respect of such an offence (s 122I(1)(c) (as so added)) or is cautioned in respect of such an offence (s 122I(1)(d) (as so added)), then:

(1)   where the defendant was not a relevant offender immediately before s 122I applied to him, s 122I causes him to become subject to the notification requirements of Pt 2 from the time s 122I first applies to him until the relevant order (as renewed from time to time) ceases to have effect (s 122I(4)(a) (as so added)), and Pt 2 applies to the defendant, subject to the modification that the 'relevant date' is the date on which s 122I first applies to the him (s 122I(4)(b), (5) (as so added)); and

(2)   where a defendant was a relevant offender immediately before s 122I applied to him (s 122I(3)(a) (as so added)), and he would (apart from this provision) cease to be subject to the notification requirements of Pt 2 while the relevant order (as renewed from time to time) has effect (s 122I(3)(b) (as so added)), he remains subject to the notification requirements.

In s 122I 'relevant order' means:

(a)   where the conviction, finding or caution within s 122I(1) is in respect of a breach of a sexual risk order or a risk of sexual harm order, that order (s 122I(6)(a) (as so added)); and

(b)   where the conviction, finding or caution within s 122I(1) is in respect of a breach of an interim sexual risk order or an interim risk of sexual harm order, any sexual risk order or risk of sexual harm order made on the hearing of the application to which the interim order relates or, if no such order is made, the interim order (s 122I(6)(b) (as so added)).

500. Persons subject to notification requirements under former legislation. A person is subject to the notification requirements[1] from 1 May 2004[2] until the end of the notification period[3] (that is to say, he is a 'relevant offender'[4]) if before that date:

(1)   he was convicted[5] of a listed offence[6];

(2)   he was found not guilty of such an offence by reason of insanity[7];

(3)   he was found to be under a disability and to have done the act charged against him in respect of such an offence[8]; or

(4)   in England and Wales or Northern Ireland, he was cautioned in respect of such an offence[9].

A person who, immediately before 1 May 2004, was subject to a restraining order, a sex offender order or an interim order under any of the former statutory provisions imposing notification requirements on a person[10], is subject to the notification requirements as from that date until the order is discharged or otherwise ceases to have effect[11]. Special provision is made in respect of young offenders[12] and persons who are subject to the notification requirements as a result of a conviction, finding or caution for buggery or gross indecency prior to the abolition of criminal liability for consensual homosexual acts with 16- or 17-year olds[13].

1   For the matters required to be notified, and the means of notification, see PARA 503 et seq.

2   Ie the date on which the Sexual Offences Act 2003 Pt 2 (ss 80–136ZD) was brought into force by the Sexual Offences Act 2003 (Commencement) Order 2004, SI 2004/874.

3   As to the notification period see PARA 501. These provisions do not apply to a person whose notification period ended before 1 May 2004: Sexual Offences Act 2003 s 81(2).

4   Sexual Offences Act 2003 s 80(2).

5   Note that 'conviction' in the present context does not include a conviction in respect of which the offender receives a conditional discharge: see *R v Longworth* [2006] UKHL 1, [2006] 1 All ER 887, [2006] 2 Cr App Rep (S) 401.

6   Sexual Offences Act 2003 s 81(1)(a). As to the offences in respect of which the notification requirements may arise see Sch 3; and PARA 329. This provision does not apply to a conviction before 1 September 1997 (ie the date on which the Sex Offenders Act 1997 was brought into force by the Sex Offenders Act 1997 (Commencement) Order 1999, SI 1997/1920) unless, at the

beginning of that day, the person had not been dealt with in respect of the offence (Sexual Offences Act 2003 s 81(3)(a)), or was serving a sentence of imprisonment, or was subject to a community order, in respect of the offence (s 81(3)(b) (amended by the Armed Forces Act 2006 Sch 16 para 206, Sch 17)), or was subject to supervision, having been released from prison after serving the whole or part of a sentence of imprisonment in respect of the offence (Sexual Offences Act 2003 s 81(3)(c)), or was detained in a hospital or was subject to a guardianship order, following the conviction (s 81(3)(d)). A person who would have been within s 81(3)(b) or s 81(3)(d) but for the fact that at the beginning of 1 September 1997 he was unlawfully at large or absent without leave, on temporary release or leave of absence, or on bail pending an appeal, is treated as being within that provision: s 81(6).

'Imprisonment' is to be construed in accordance with the provisions applying the notification requirements to young offenders serving periods of detention: see s 131; and PARA 502. 'Community order' means a community order within the meaning of the Powers of Criminal Courts (Sentencing) Act 2000 as it had effect before 20 November 2003 (ie the date on which the Criminal Justice Act 2003 received the Royal Assent), a corresponding Scottish or Northern Ireland order, or a community supervision order under the Army Act 1955 Sch 5A para 4, the Air Force Act 1955 Sch 5A para 4 or the Naval Discipline Act 1957 Sch 4A para 4 (all repealed): Sexual Offences Act 2003 s 133(1) (amended by the Criminal Justice Act 2003 Sch 32 paras 142, 144). 'Supervision' means supervision in pursuance of an order made for the purpose or, in the case of a person released from prison on licence, in pursuance of a condition contained in his licence: Sexual Offences Act 2003 s 133(1). 'Detained in a hospital' means detained in a hospital under the Mental Health Act 1983 Pt III (ss 35–55) (see MENTAL HEALTH AND CAPACITY vol 75 (2013) PARA 859 et seq) (or corresponding Scottish or Northern Ireland provisions) (including those provisions as they apply by virtue of the Criminal Procedure (Insanity) Act 1964 s 5 (see PARA 444), the Criminal Appeal Act 1968 s 6 (see CRIMINAL PROCEDURE vol 28 (2015) PARA 767) or s 14 (see CRIMINAL PROCEDURE vol 28 (2015) PARA 773), the Armed Forces Act 2006 Sch 4 (see ARMED FORCES vol 3 (2011) PARA 650) (including as applied by the Court Martial Appeals Act 1968 s 16(2) (see ARMED FORCES vol 3 (2011) PARA 668)) the Army Act 1955 s 116A, the Air Force Act 1955 s 116A, or the Naval Discipline Act 1957 s 63A (all repealed), or the Courts-Martial (Appeals) Act 1968 s 16 (see ARMED FORCES vol 3 (2011) PARA 668) or s 23 (repealed)), or the Mental Health Act 1983 s 46 (repealed), the Criminal Procedure (Insanity and Unfitness to Plead) Act 1991 Sch 1 (repealed), or the Criminal Procedure (Insanity) Act 1964 Sch 1 (repealed) (or its Scottish counterpart): Sexual Offences Act 2003 ss 133(1), (1A), 135(4)(a)(i) (s 133(1) amended, and s 133(1A) added, by the Domestic Violence, Crime and Victims Act 2004 Sch 10 para 57(1)–(3); Sexual Offences Act 2003 s 133(1A) amended by the Armed Forces Act 2006 Sch 16 para 209). 'Guardianship order' means a guardianship order under the Mental Health Act 1983 s 37 (see PARA 472; and MENTAL HEALTH AND CAPACITY vol 75 (2013) PARA 864 et seq) or corresponding Scottish or Northern Ireland provisions: Sexual Offences Act 2003 s 133(1).

The Secretary of State may exempt a relevant offender who is subject to the notification requirements arising from the former offence of buggery or gross indecency (ie arising from a conviction, finding or caution in respect of an offence under the Sexual Offences Act 1956 s 12 (repealed) or s 13 (repealed) or a conviction, finding or caution for incitement, conspiracy or attempt to commit such an offence or for aiding, abetting, counselling or procuring the commission of the offence (Sexual Offences Act 2003 Sch 4 para 6(1)), or corresponding Northern Ireland offences, from those requirements on the basis of the abolition of criminal liability for consensual homosexual acts with 16-year olds: see Sch 4 para 1. The offender may apply to the Secretary of State for a decision as to whether it appears that, at the time of the offence, the other party to the act of buggery or gross indecency (or, in the case of an attempt, conspiracy or incitement, to the act of buggery or gross indecency to which the attempt, conspiracy or incitement related (whether or not that act occurred) (Sch 4 para 6(2)) was aged 16 or over and consented to the act (Sch 4 para 2(1)(a)), and if the Secretary of State decides that it appears that the other party to the act was aged 16 or over and consented to it, the offender ceases, from the beginning of the day on which the decision is recorded, to be subject to the requirements of Pt 2 as a result of the conviction, finding or caution in respect of the offence (Sch 4 para 4(1)). This does not affect the operation of Pt 2 as a result of any other conviction, finding, caution or any court order: Sch 4 para 4(2). If the Secretary of State decides, however, that it does not so appear, and if the High Court gives permission, the offender may appeal to that court (Sch 4 para 5(1)), which may either decide that it does so appear and make an order that the offender is to cease to be subject to the notification requirements as a result of the conviction, finding or caution in respect of the offence (Sch 4 para 5(3)(a), (4)) or dismiss the appeal (Sch 4 para 5(3)(b)). There is no appeal from the decision of the High Court: Sch 4 para 5(5). The court may not receive oral evidence on an appeal: Sch 4 para 5(2).

An application for exemption must be in writing and state the name, address and date of birth of the relevant offender (Sch 4 para 2(2)(a)), his name and address at the time of the conviction, finding or caution (Sch 4 para 2(2)(b)), the time when and the place where the conviction or finding was made or the caution was given, so far as known to him (Sch 4 para 2(2)(c)) and, for a conviction or finding, the case number, and such other information as the Secretary of State may require (Sch 4 para 2(2)(d)). An application may include representations by the offender about the other party's consent to the act: Sch 4 para 2(3). In making the decision applied for, the Secretary of State must consider any representations included in the application (Sch 4 para 3(1)(a)) and any available record of the investigation of the offence and of any proceedings relating to it that appears to him to be relevant (Sch 4 para 3(1)(b)), but is not to seek evidence from any witness (Sch 4 para 3(1)). On making the decision the Secretary of State must record it in writing (Sch 4 para 3(2)(a)) and give notice in writing to the relevant offender (Sch 4 para 3(2)(b)).

As to the determination of a person's age see the Children and Young Persons Act 1933 s 99; and CHILDREN AND YOUNG PERSONS vol 10 (2012) PARA 1206.

7 Sexual Offences Act 2003 s 81(1)(b). As to verdicts of not guilty by reason of insanity see CRIMINAL LAW vol 25 (2010) PARA 30. This provision, and the provision made by s 81(1)(c) (see the text and note 8) does not apply to a finding made before 1 September 1997 unless at the beginning of that day the person in question either had not been dealt with in respect of the finding (s 81(4)(a)) or was detained in a hospital following the finding (s 81(4)(b)). A person who would have been within s 81(4)(b) but for the fact that at the beginning of 1 September 1997 he was unlawfully at large or absent without leave, on temporary release or leave of absence, or on bail pending an appeal, is treated as being within that provision: s 81(6).

8 Sexual Offences Act 2003 s 81(1)(c). See note 7. As to references to a person being or having been found to be under a disability and to have done the act charged against him in respect of an offence see PARA 329 note 1.

9 Sexual Offences Act 2003 s 81(1)(d). This provision does not apply to a caution given before 1 September 1997: s 81(5).

10 Ie an order under the Sex Offenders Act 1997 s 5A, the Crime and Disorder Act 1998 s 2 or s 2A (all repealed), or the Scottish or Northern Ireland counterpart of these orders: Sexual Offences Act 2003 s 81(8)(a)–(f).

11 Sexual Offences Act 2003 s 81(7). Despite their partially retrospective effect, the notification requirements are preventive rather than punitive in nature and therefore do not constitute a 'penalty' for the purposes of the Convention for the Protection of Human Rights and Fundamental Freedoms (Rome, 4 November 1950; TS 71 (1973); Cmnd 8969) art 7 (prohibition of retrospective laws: see RIGHTS AND FREEDOMS vol 88A (2013) PARAS 301–316): *Ibbotson v United Kingdom* [1999] Crim LR 153, (1998) 27 EHRR CD 332, ECtHR. The notification requirements clearly interfere with the right to privacy under the Convention for the Protection of Human Rights and Fundamental Freedoms art 8 (see RIGHTS AND FREEDOMS vol 88A (2013) PARAS 317–367), but that interference is likely to be accepted as necessary and proportionate to prevent crime: *Adamson v United Kingdom* (1999) 28 EHRR CD 209, EComHR.

12 See PARA 502.

13 See note 6.

501. The notification period. The notification period for a person in respect of whom the notification requirements arise[1]:

(1)   in the case of a person who, in respect of the offence, is or has been sentenced to imprisonment for life, imprisonment for public protection[2] or imprisonment for a term[3] of 30 months or more, is an indefinite period beginning with the relevant date[4];

(2)   in the case of a person who, in respect of the offence or finding, is or has been admitted to a hospital[5] subject to a restriction order[6], is an indefinite period beginning with the relevant date[7];

(3)   in the case of a person who, in respect of the offence, is or has been sentenced to imprisonment for a term of more than six months but less than 30 months, is ten years (or five years if he is under 18 on the relevant date) beginning with the relevant date[8];

(4)   in the case of a person who, in respect of the offence, is or has been

sentenced to imprisonment for a term of six months or less, is seven years (or three and a half years if he is under 18 on the relevant date) beginning with the relevant date[9];

(5) in the case of a person who, in respect of the offence or finding, is or has been admitted to a hospital without being subject to a restriction order, is seven years (or three and a half years if he is under 18 on the relevant date) beginning with the relevant date[10];

(6) in the case of a person who has been cautioned in respect of the offence[11], is two years (or one year if he is under 18 on the relevant date) beginning with the relevant date[12];

(7) in the case of a person in whose case an order for conditional discharge is made in respect of the offence, is the period of conditional discharge[13]; and

(8) in the case of a person of any other description, is five years (or two and a half years if the person is under 18 at the relevant date) beginning with the relevant date[14].

Where a relevant offender[15] is or has been sentenced in respect of two or more listed offences[16] to consecutive terms of imprisonment[17], these provisions have effect as if he was or had been sentenced, in respect of each of the offences, to a term of imprisonment equal to the aggregate of those terms[18]; and where a relevant offender is or has been sentenced in respect of two or more such offences to partly concurrent terms of imprisonment[19], these provisions have effect as if he was or had been sentenced, in respect of each of the offences, to a term of imprisonment equal to the aggregate of the partly concurrent terms minus the period of overlap[20].

Where a relevant offender who has been found to have been under a disability and to have done the act charged against him in respect of a listed offence[21] is subsequently tried for the offence, the notification period relating to the finding ends at the conclusion of the trial[22].

1 As to the circumstances in which the notification requirements arise in respect of an offender see PARAS 499–500. As to the offences in respect of which the notification requirements may arise see Sch 3; and PARA 329. These provisions apply also to a person who is subject to a notification order by virtue of a conviction for an offence committed overseas: see the Sexual Offences Act 2003 s 98(1)(a), (3)(a); and PARA 515.

2 Ie under the Criminal Justice Act 2003 s 225: see PARA 37.

3 Where an offender has been sentenced to an extended term of imprisonment under the Powers of Criminal Courts (Sentencing) Act 2000 s 85 (repealed) the term for which he is to be regarded as 'sentenced to imprisonment' for these purposes is the 'custodial term' element of the extended sentence, and not the whole length of the extended term: *R v S* [2001] 1 Cr App Rep 111, [2001] 1 Cr App Rep (S) 335, CA.

4 Sexual Offences Act 2003 s 82(1) (amended by the Violent Crime Reduction Act 2006 s 57(1)). The 'relevant date' is:
    (1) in the case of a person within the Sexual Offences Act 2003 s 80(1)(a) or s 81(1)(a) (see PARAS 499–500), the date of conviction (s 82(6)(a));
    (2) in the case of a person within s 80(1)(b) or (c) or s 81(1)(b) or (c) (see PARAS 499–500), the date of the finding (s 82(6)(b));
    (3) in the case of a person within s 80(1)(d) or s 81(1)(d) (see PARAS 499–500), the date of the caution (s 82(6)(c)); and
    (4) in the case of a person within s 81(7) (see PARA 500), the date which, for the purposes of the Sex Offenders Act 1997 Pt 1 (ss 1–6) (repealed as from 1 May 2004), was the relevant date in relation to that person (Sexual Offences Act 2003 s 82(6)(d)).

5 For these purposes, 'admitted to a hospital' means admitted to a hospital under the Mental Health Act 1983 s 37 (see MENTAL HEALTH AND CAPACITY vol 75 (2013) PARA 864 et seq) (or its Scottish or Northern Ireland counterparts) (including those provisions as they apply by virtue of the Criminal Procedure (Insanity) Act 1964 s 5 (see PARA 444), the Criminal Appeal Act 1968 s 6 (see CRIMINAL PROCEDURE vol 28 (2015) PARA 767) or s 14 (see CRIMINAL PROCEDURE

vol 28 (2015) PARA 773), the Armed Forces Act 2006 Sch 4 (see ARMED FORCES vol 3 (2011) PARA 650) (including as applied by the Court Martial Appeals Act 1968 s 16(2) (see ARMED FORCES vol 3 (2011) PARA 668)) the Army Act 1955 s 116A, the Air Force Act 1955 s 116A, or the Naval Discipline Act 1957 s 63A (all repealed), or the Courts-Martial (Appeals) Act 1968 s 16 (see ARMED FORCES vol 3 (2011) PARA 668) or s 23 (repealed)), or the Mental Health Act 1983 s 46 (repealed), the Criminal Procedure (Insanity and Unfitness to Plead) Act 1991 Sch 1 (repealed), or the Criminal Procedure (Insanity) Act 1964 Sch 1 (repealed) (or its Scottish counterpart): Sexual Offences Act 2003 ss 133(1), (1A), 135(4)(a)(i) (s 133(1) amended, and s 133(1A) added, by the Domestic Violence, Crime and Victims Act 2004 Sch 10 para 57(1), (2); Sexual Offences Act 2003 s 133(1A) amended by the Armed Forces Act 2006 Sch 16 para 209).

6 'Restriction order' means an order under the Mental Health Act 1983 s 41 (see MENTAL HEALTH AND CAPACITY vol 75 (2013) PARA 867 et seq) (or its Scottish or Northern Ireland counterparts) (including those provisions as they apply by virtue of the Criminal Procedure (Insanity) Act 1964 s 5, the Criminal Appeal Act 1968 s 6 (see CRIMINAL PROCEDURE vol 28 (2015) PARA 767) or s 14 (see CRIMINAL PROCEDURE vol 28 (2015) PARA 773), the Armed Forces Act 2006 Sch 4 (see ARMED FORCES vol 3 (2011) PARA 650) (including as applied by the Court Martial Appeals Act 1968 s 16(2) (see ARMED FORCES vol 3 (2011) PARA 668)), the Army Act 1955 s 116A, the Air Force Act 1955 s 116A, or the Naval Discipline Act 1957 s 63A (all repealed), or the Courts-Martial (Appeals) Act 1968 s 16 (see ARMED FORCES vol 3 (2011) PARA 668) or s 23 (repealed)), or a direction under the Mental Health Act 1983 s 46 (repealed) or the Criminal Procedure (Insanity and Unfitness to Plead) Act 1991 Sch 1 para 2(1)(b) (repealed) (or its Scottish counterpart): Sexual Offences Act 2003 ss 133(1), (1A), 135(4)(a)(i) (s 133(1) amended, and s 133(1A) added, by the Domestic Violence, Crime and Victims Act 2004 Sch 10 para 57(1), (2); Sexual Offences Act 2003 s 133(1A) amended by the Armed Forces Act 2006 Sch 16 para 209).

7 Sexual Offences Act 2003 s 82(1).

8 Sexual Offences Act 2003 s 82(1), (2). Additional provision is made in connection with young offenders: see PARA 502.

9 Sexual Offences Act 2003 s 82(1), (2).

10 Sexual Offences Act 2003 s 82(1), (2).

11 Ie a person within the Sexual Offences Act 2003 s 80(1)(d) (see PARA 499): s 82(1).

12 Sexual Offences Act 2003 s 82(1), (2).

13 Sexual Offences Act 2003 s 82(1). As to the meanings of 'order for conditional discharge' and 'period of conditional discharge' see the Powers of Criminal Courts (Sentencing) Act 2000 s 12(3) (see PARA 454), the Armed Forces Act 2006 s 185 (see ARMED FORCES vol 3 (2011) PARA 609), and the Army Act 1955 Sch 5A para 2(1), the Air Force Act 1955 Sch 5A para 2(1), and the Naval Discipline Act 1957 Sch 4A para 2(1) (all repealed) (definitions applied by the Sexual Offences Act 2003 s 133(1) (amended by the Armed Forces Act 2006 Sch 16 para 209)).

14 Sexual Offences Act 2003 s 82(1), (2).

15 Ie a relevant offender for the purposes of the Sexual Offences Act 2003 s 80(1)(a) or s 81(1)(a) (see PARAS 499–500).

16 See PARA 329.

17 Sexual Offences Act 2003 s 82(3)(a).

18 Sexual Offences Act 2003 s 82(4)(a).

19 Sexual Offences Act 2003 s 82(3)(b).

20 Sexual Offences Act 2003 s 82(4)(b).

21 Ie has been the subject of a finding within the Sexual Offences Act 2003 s 80(1)(c) or s 81(1)(c) (see PARAS 499–500).

22 Sexual Offences Act 2003 s 82(5).

502. The notification period: young offenders. The statutory provisions imposing notification requirements on persons convicted of or cautioned for sexual offences[1] also apply, as they apply to an equivalent sentence of imprisonment[2], to:

(1) a period of detention which a person is liable to serve under a detention and training order[3] or a secure training order[4];

(2) a period for which a person is ordered to be detained in residential accommodation[5];

(3) a sentence of detention in a young offender institution[6];

(4)   a sentence under a custodial order[7] in respect of certain persons who are subject to the service discipline Acts[8];

(5)   a sentence of detention at Her Majesty's pleasure or for a specified period[9];

(6)   a sentence of custody for life[10];

(7)   a sentence of detention or custody for life under the service discipline Acts[11];

(8)   a sentence of detention for public protection[12]; and

(9)   an extended sentence[13].

1   Ie the Sexual Offences Act 2003 Pt 2 (ss 80–136ZD).
2   References in the Sexual Offences Act 2003 Pt 2 are to be construed accordingly: s 131.
3   As to detention and training orders see PARA 9 et seq. This includes an order under the Armed Forces Act 2006 s 211 (see ARMED FORCES vol 3 (2011) PARA 611): Sexual Offences Act 2003 s 131(a) (s 131(a), (h), (k), (l) amended by the Armed Forces Act 2006 Sch 16 para 208). The notification period in respect of a person subject to a detention and training order is governed by the length only of the detention and training period in the order, and not by reference to the entire term of the order: see *R v Slocombe* [2005] EWCA Crim 2297, [2006] 1 All ER 670, [2006] 1 WLR 328.
4   Sexual Offences Act 2003 s 131(a) (as amended: see note 3). Secure training orders were formerly made under the Criminal Justice and Public Order Act 1994 s 1 (repealed).
5   Sexual Offences Act 2003 s 131(b). The reference in the text to a person being ordered to be detained in residential accommodation is a reference to being ordered to be so detained under the Criminal Procedure (Scotland) Act 1995 s 44(1).
6   Sexual Offences Act 2003 s 131(f). Provision for imposing sentences of detention in young offender institutions is made by the Powers of Criminal Courts (Sentencing) Act 2000 ss 96–98: see PARA 16.
7   Ie within the meaning of the Army Act 1955 s 71AA or Sch 5A para 10(1), the Air Force Act 1955 s 71AA or Sch 5A para 10(1), or the Naval Discipline Act 1957 s 43AA or Sch 4A para 10(1) (all repealed).
8   Sexual Offences Act 2003 s 131(g). As to the service discipline Acts see ARMED FORCES.
9   Sexual Offences Act 2003 s 131(h) (as amended: see note 3). As to these sentences see the Powers of Criminal Courts (Sentencing) Act 2000 ss 90, 91; and PARAS 9, 38; and the Armed Forces Act 2006 ss 209, 218; and ARMED FORCES vol 3 (2011) PARA 611.
10 Sexual Offences Act 2003 s 131(i). As to these sentences see the Powers of Criminal Courts (Sentencing) Act 2000 ss 93, 94; and PARAS 36–37.
11 Sexual Offences Act 2003 s 131(j). As to such sentences see the Army Act 1955 s 71A, the Air Force Act 1955 s 71A, and the Naval Discipline Act 1957 s 43A (all repealed).
12 Sexual Offences Act 2003 s 131(k) (s 131(k), (l) added by the Criminal Justice Act 2003 Sch 32 paras 142, 143; as amended (see note 3)). As to such sentences see the Criminal Justice Act 2003 s 226; and PARA 34: these include sentences of detention for public protection passed as a result of the Armed Forces Act 2006 s 221 (see ARMED FORCES vol 3 (2011) PARA 596).
13 Sexual Offences Act 2003 s 131(l) (as added and amended (see notes 3, 12); amended by the Legal Aid, Sentencing and Punishment of Offenders Act 2012 Sch 22 para 20). As to such sentences see the Criminal Justice Act 2003 s 226B (see PARAS 18–20) and PARA 228 (repealed): these include sentences of detention for public protection passed as a result of the Armed Forces Act 2006 s 222 (see ARMED FORCES vol 3 (2011) PARA 596).

503.   Initial notification.   A relevant offender[1] must, within the period of three days[2] beginning with the relevant date[3], notify to the police[4]:

(1)   his date of birth[5];

(2)   his national insurance number[6];

(3)   his name on the relevant date and, where he used one or more other names on that date, each of those names[7];

(4)   his home address[8] on the relevant date[9];

(5)   his name on the date on which notification is given[10] and, where he uses one or more other names on that date, each of those names[11];

(6)   his home address on the date on which notification is given[12];

(7)   the address of any other premises in the United Kingdom at which, at the time the notification is given, he regularly resides or stays[13];

(8)   specified information about any household in which he resides or stays for a period of at least 12 hours[14];

(9)   specified information about bank accounts and credit cards[15];

(10)   specified information about passports and other forms of identification[16].

Failure without reasonable excuse to comply with these requirements is an offence, as is notifying false information[17].

1   As to the relevant offenders for the purposes of the notification requirements see PARAS 499–500.

2   When determining this period and the three- and six-day periods for the purposes of the Sexual Offences Act 2993 s 84 (see PARA 505) there is to be disregarded any time when the relevant offender is either remanded in or committed to custody by an order of a court or kept in service custody (Sexual Offences Act 2003 ss 83(6)(a), 84(5) (s 83(6)(a) amended by the Criminal Justice and Immigration Act 2008 Sch 26 paras 53, 54)), serving a prison sentence or a term of service detention (Sexual Offences Act 2003 s 83(6)(b)), detained in a hospital (s 83(6)(c)) or outside the United Kingdom (s 83(6)(d)). As to the meaning of 'detained in a hospital' see PARA 500 note 6. As to the meaning of 'United Kingdom' see PARA 4 note 3.

3   As to the relevant date see PARA 501 note 4. For the circumstances in which initial notification need not be made see PARA 504.

4   As to the methods of notification see PARA 508.

5   Sexual Offences Act 2003 s 83(1), (5)(a).

6   Sexual Offences Act 2003 s 83(5)(b).

7   Sexual Offences Act 2003 s 83(5)(c).

8   'Home address' means the address of the relevant offender's sole or main residence in the United Kingdom (Sexual Offences Act 2003 s 83(7)(a)) or where he has no such residence, the address or location of a place in the United Kingdom where he can regularly be found and, if there is more than one such place, such one of those places as the person may select (s 83(7)(b)).

9   Sexual Offences Act 2003 s 83(5)(d).

10   As to when notification is not required to be given see PARA 504.

11   Sexual Offences Act 2003 s 83(5)(e).

12   Sexual Offences Act 2003 s 83(5)(f).

13   Sexual Offences Act 2003 s 83(5)(g).

14   Sexual Offences Act 2003 s 83(5)(h), (5A) (added by the Criminal Justice and Immigration Act 2008 s 142(1), (11)); Sexual Offences Act 2003 (Notification Requirements) (England and Wales) Regulations 2012, SI 2012/1876, reg 10(1). The required information is set out in reg 10(2).

15   See the Sexual Offences Act 2003 (Notification Requirements) (England and Wales) Regulations 2012, SI 2012/1876, reg 12. The requirements of reg 12 are not incompatible with the right to respect for private and family life under the Convention for the Protection of Human Rights and Fundamental Freedoms (Rome, 4 November 1950; TS 71 (1953); Cmd 8969) art 8 (see RIGHTS AND FREEDOMS vol 88A (2013) PARAS 317–367): see *R (on the application of Prothero) v Secretary of State for the Home Department* [2013] EWHC 2830 (Admin), [2014] 1 WLR 1195.

16   See the Sexual Offences Act 2003 (Notification Requirements) (England and Wales) Regulations 2012, SI 2012/1876, reg 14.

17   See the Sexual Offences Act 2003 s 91(1); and PARA 510.

504. Circumstances in which initial notification need not be given. A relevant offender[1] who, as a result of an earlier conviction, finding, caution or court order (the 'earlier event') was subject to the notification requirements[2] immediately before a subsequent conviction, finding or caution[3] is not required to comply with the initial notification requirements arising in respect of the subsequent matter[4] if at that time he had made an initial notification[5] in respect of the earlier event[6] and throughout the initial notification period[7] he remains subject to the notification requirements as a result of that event[8]. A relevant offender in relation to whom a notification order[9] has been made in respect of any conviction, finding or caution[10], and a relevant offender who has complied with the former notification requirements[11] in respect of a previous conviction, finding, caution or order[12], are similarly exempt.

1 As to the relevant offenders for the purposes of the notification requirements see PARAS 499–500.
2 Ie the requirements of the Sexual Offences Act 2003 Pt 2 (ss 80–136ZD).
3 Sexual Offences Act 2003 s 83(2)(a). The text refers to a conviction, finding or caution falling within s 80(1) (see PARA 499).
4 Ie the requirements of the Sexual Offences Act 2003 s 83(1) (see PARA 503).
5 Ie under the Sexual Offences Act 2003 s 83(1).
6 Sexual Offences Act 2003 s 83(2)(b).
7 Ie the initial notification period under the Sexual Offences Act 2003 s 83(1).
8 Sexual Offences Act 2003 s 83(2)(c).
9 As to the meaning of 'notification order' see the Sexual Offences Act 2003 s 97(1); and PARA 515.
10 Sexual Offences Act 2003 s 83(4)(a)–(c).
11 Ie the Sex Offenders Act 1997 s 2(1) (repealed).
12 Sexual Offences Act 2003 s 83(3). The text refers to a conviction, finding or caution within s 81(1) or an order within s 81(7) (see PARA 500): s 83(3).

505. Changes to be notified. A relevant offender[1] who:

(1) uses a name which has not been notified[2] to the police[3];
(2) changes his home address[4];
(3) has resided or stayed, for a period of seven days, or two or more periods in any 12-month period which taken together amount to seven days (a 'qualifying period'[5]) at any premises in the United Kingdom[6] whose address has not been notified[7] to the police[8];
(4) is released from custody pursuant to a court order or from imprisonment[9], service detention or detention in a hospital[10];
(5) has undergone a change in circumstances notified to the police[11] relating to his residence or staying-in a household[12];
(6) has undergone a change in circumstances notified to the police[13] relating to bank accounts and credit cards[14]; or
(7) has undergone a change in circumstances notified to the police[15] relating to passports and other forms of identification[16],

must within three days[17] beginning with such a change notify to the police that name, the new home address, the address of those premises or the prescribed details relating to households, bank accounts and passports and identification, as the case may be, as well as the initial notification requirements[18]. A notification of a change may be given before a name is used, a change of home address or the prescribed change of circumstances occurs or the qualifying period ends, but in that case the relevant offender must also specify the date when the event is expected to occur[19].

Failure without reasonable excuse to comply with the requirement to notify changes is an offence, as is giving false information when notifying a change[20].

1 As to the relevant offenders for the purposes of the notification requirements see PARAS 499–500.
2 Ie under the Sexual Offences Act 2003 s 83(1) (see PARA 503), s 84(1) (see the text and notes 2–12) or the Sex Offenders Act 1997 s 2 (repealed): Sexual Offences Act 2003 s 84(1)(a).
3 Sexual Offences Act 2003 s 84(1)(a).
4 Sexual Offences Act 2003 s 84(1)(b). As to the meaning of 'home address' see PARA 503 note 8.
5 Sexual Offences Act 2003 s 84(6).
6 As to the meaning of 'United Kingdom' see PARA 4 note 3.
7 Ie under the Sexual Offences Act 2003 s 83(1) or s 84(1) or the Sex Offenders Act 1997 s 2 (repealed): Sexual Offences Act 2003 s 84(1)(c).

8   Sexual Offences Act 2003 s 84(1)(c).

9   'Imprisonment' is to be construed in accordance with the provisions applying the notification requirements to young offenders serving periods of detention: see the Sexual Offences Act 2003 s 131; and PARA 502.

10 Sexual Offences Act 2003 s 84(1)(d). As to the meaning of 'detained in a hospital' see PARA 500 note 6.

11 Ie under the Sexual Offences Act 2003 s 83(5)(h) and the Sexual Offences Act 2003 (Notification Requirements) (England and Wales) Regulations 2012, SI 2012/1876, reg 10: see PARA 503.

12 Sexual Offences Act 2003 s 84(1)(ca), (5A) (s 84(1), (2) amended, s 84(1)(ca), (5A) added, by the Criminal Justice and Immigration Act 2008 s 142(1)–(5), (11)); Sexual Offences Act 2003 (Notification Requirements) (England and Wales) Regulations 2012, SI 2012/1876, reg 11(1). The changes to be specified are set out in reg 11(2), (3).

13 Ie under the Sexual Offences Act 2003 (Notification Requirements) (England and Wales) Regulations 2012, SI 2012/1876, reg 12: see PARA 503.

14 See the Sexual Offences Act 2003 (Notification Requirements) (England and Wales) Regulations 2012, SI 2012/1876, reg 13.

15 Ie under the Sexual Offences Act 2003 (Notification Requirements) (England and Wales) Regulations 2012, SI 2012/1876, reg 14: see PARA 503.

16 See the Sexual Offences Act 2003 (Notification Requirements) (England and Wales) Regulations 2012, SI 2012/1876, reg 15.

17 As to the determination of this period see PARA 503 note 2.

18 Sexual Offences Act 2003 s 84(1) (as amended: see note 12). As to the initial notification requirements see s 83(5); and PARA 563. As to the methods of notification see PARA 508.

19 Sexual Offences Act 2003 s 84(2) (as amended: see note 12). However, if the event to which an advance notification relates occurs more than two days before the expected date specified in it, the notification does not affect the duty imposed by s 84(1): s 84(3). Moreover, if advance notification is given and the event to which it relates has not occurred by the end of the three-day period beginning with the expected date specified, the notification does not affect the duty imposed by s 84(1) (s 84(4)(a)) and the relevant offender must, within a six-day period beginning with the expected date specified, notify the police that the event did not occur within the three-day period beginning with the date specified (s 84(4)(b)). As to the determination of this six-day period see PARA 503 note 2.

20 See the Sexual Offences Act 2003 s 91(1); and PARA 510.

506. Periodic re-notification. A relevant offender[1] who has given any initial notification[2], periodic re-notification[3] or a notification of changes[4] is required to notify to the police the information required to be notified[5] on initial notification[6]. Such notification must be given within the applicable period[7]. A person who is a relevant offender from 1 May 2004[8] is also required to notify to the police the information required to be notified[9] on initial notification within the applicable period[10].

These requirements do not apply where within the applicable period the offender has given[11] a notification of change[12]: otherwise failure without reasonable excuse to comply with the requirement for periodic notification is an offence, as is notifying false information when making a periodic notification[13].

1   As to the relevant offenders for the purposes of the notification requirements see PARAS 499–500.

2   Sexual Offences Act 2003 s 85(2)(b). As to the giving of initial notifications see s 83(1); and PARA 503. As to the methods of notification see PARA 508.

3   Sexual Offences Act 2003 s 85(2)(c). As to the giving of periodic re-notifications see s 85(1); and the text and notes 4–12.

4   Sexual Offences Act 2003 s 85(2)(b). As to the notification of changes see s 84(1); and PARA 505.

5   Ie the information required to be notified under the Sexual Offences Act 2003 s 83(5) (see PARA 503).

6   Sexual Offences Act 2003 s 85(1) (s 85(1), (3), (4) amended, s 85(5), (6) added, by the Criminal Justice and Immigration Act 2008 s 142(6)–(9), (11), Sch 26 paras 53, 55).

7   Sexual Offences Act 2003 s 85(1) (as amended: see note 6). For this purpose the applicable period is the period of one year, unless the last home address notified by the relevant offender under s 83(1), s 84(1) or s 85(1) was the address or location of such a place as is mentioned in s 83(7)(b), in which event the applicable period is seven days: s 85(5), (6) (as so added); Sexual Offences Act 2003 (Notification Requirements) (England and Wales) Regulations 2012, SI 2012/1876, reg 9.
    If the applicable period would otherwise end while a relevant offender is remanded in or committed to custody by an order of a court or kept in service custody (Sexual Offences Act 2003 s 85(4)(a) (as so amended)), or serving a sentence of imprisonment or a term of service detention (s 85(4)(b)) or detained in a hospital (s 85(4)(c)) or outside the United Kingdom (s 85(4)(d)), that period is treated as continuing until the end of the period of three days beginning when the offender first ceases to be so remanded, imprisoned, detained or abroad: s 85(3). For this purpose 'imprisonment' is to be construed in accordance with the provisions applying the notification requirements to young offenders serving periods of detention: see s 131; and PARA 502. As to the meaning of 'detained in a hospital' see PARA 500 note 6. As to the meaning of 'United Kingdom' see PARA 4 note 3.
8   The date mentioned in the text is the date on which the Sexual Offences Act 2003 Pt 2 (ss 80–136ZD) was brought into force by the Sexual Offences Act 2003 (Commencement) Order 2004, SI 2004/874. As to the persons who are relevant offenders from that date see PARA 499.
9   See note 5.
10 Sexual Offences Act 2003 s 85(2)(a).
11 Ie under the Sexual Offences Act 2003 s 84(1).
12 Sexual Offences Act 2003 s 85(1) (as amended: see note 6).
13 See the Sexual Offences Act 2003 s 91(1); and PARA 510.

507. Travel outside the United Kingdom. A relevant offender[1] who intends to leave the United Kingdom[2] must give, before he leaves, a notification[3] disclosing the date on which he will leave the United Kingdom[4] and the country (or, if there is more than one, the first country) to which he will travel and his point of arrival[5] in that country[6]. The notification must also disclose (where he holds such information):

(1)   where the offender intends to travel to more than one country outside the United Kingdom, his intended point of arrival in each such additional country[7];

(2)   the dates on which the offender intends to stay in any country to which he intends to travel[8];

(3)   details of the offender's accommodation arrangements in any country to which he intends to travel[9];

(4)   the identity of any carrier or carriers the offender intends to use for the purposes of his departure from and return to the United Kingdom, and of travelling to any other point of arrival[10];

(5)   in a case in which the offender intends to return to the United Kingdom on a particular date, that date[11]; and

(6)   in a case in which the offender intends to return to the United Kingdom at a particular point of arrival, that point of arrival[12].

Where the offender knows the information whose disclosure is compulsory[13] more than seven days before the date of his intended departure, he must give a notification which sets out that information and as much of the additional information[14] as he holds not less than seven days before that date[15] or, if and only if he has a reasonable excuse for not complying with this requirement, as soon as reasonably practicable but not less than 24 hours before that date[16]. Where the offender does not know the information whose disclosure is compulsory more than seven days before the date of his intended departure he must give, not less than 24 hours before that date, a notification which sets out that information and as much of the additional information as he holds[17]. If any of the information given in a notification changes prior to the offender's departure from the United Kingdom, he must give a further notification[18].

An offender giving a notification of departure from or return to the United Kingdom must inform the person to whom he gives the notice of his name and other names he is using[19], his home address[20], and his date of birth[21], as currently notified[22], and an offender giving late notification of compulsory information before leaving the United Kingdom[23] must inform the person to whom he gives the notification of the police station at which he first gave a notification[24] in respect of the journey in question[25].

Where a relevant offender who is required to give a notification concerning travel abroad[26] has left the United Kingdom and subsequently returns, he must within three days of his return give a notification disclosing the date of his return and his point of arrival[27] unless he had previously disclosed this information[28] in his initial notification concerning his travel[29].

Failure without reasonable excuse to comply with any of these requirements is an offence, as is notifying false information[30].

1   As to the relevant offenders for the purposes of the notification requirements see PARAS 499–500.
2   As to the meaning of 'United Kingdom' see PARA 4 note 3.
3   As to the methods of notification see PARA 508.
4   Sexual Offences Act 2003 s 86(2)(a); Sexual Offences Act 2003 (Travel Notification Requirements) Regulations 2004, SI 2004/1220, reg 5(1) (amended by SI 2012/1876). The Sexual Offences Act 2003 (Travel Notification Requirements) Regulations 2004, SI 2004/1220, are made under the Sexual Offences Act 2003 s 86, under which it is provided that specified matters concerning the notification requirements applicable to offenders who travel outside the United Kingdom are to be determined in accordance with regulations.
5   In a case in which a relevant offender will arrive in a country by rail, sea or air, his point of arrival is the station, port or airport at which he will first disembark: Sexual Offences Act 2003 (Travel Notification Requirements) Regulations 2004, SI 2004/1220, reg 4(1), (2). Where he will arrive in a country by any other means his point of arrival is the place at which he will first enter the country: reg 4(3).
6   Sexual Offences Act 2003 s 86(2)(b).
7   Sexual Offences Act 2003 s 86(2)(c) (which provides that a notification under s 86 must disclose any other information prescribed by regulations which the offender holds about his departure from or return to the United Kingdom or his movements while outside the United Kingdom); Sexual Offences Act 2003 (Travel Notification Requirements) Regulations 2004, SI 2004/1220, reg 6(a) (reg 6 substituted by SI 2012/1876).
8   Sexual Offences Act 2003 (Travel Notification Requirements) Regulations 2004, SI 2004/1220, reg 6(b) (as substituted: see note 7).
9   Sexual Offences Act 2003 (Travel Notification Requirements) Regulations 2004, SI 2004/1220, reg 6(c) (as substituted: see note 7).
10 Sexual Offences Act 2003 (Travel Notification Requirements) Regulations 2004, SI 2004/1220, reg 6(d) (as substituted: see note 7).
11 Sexual Offences Act 2003 (Travel Notification Requirements) Regulations 2004, SI 2004/1220, reg 6(e) (as substituted: see note 7).
12 Sexual Offences Act 2003 (Travel Notification Requirements) Regulations 2004, SI 2004/1220, reg 6(f) (as substituted: see note 7).
13 Ie the information required to be disclosed by the Sexual Offences Act 2003 s 86(2)(a), (b) (see the text and notes 1–6).
14 Ie the information required to be disclosed only where it is held by the offender (see the Sexual Offences Act 2003 s 86(2)(c); and the text and notes 7–12).
15 Sexual Offences Act 2003 (Travel Notification Requirements) Regulations 2004, SI 2004/1220, reg 5(2)(a). This is referred to as the 'seven-day notification requirement'.
16 Sexual Offences Act 2003 (Travel Notification Requirements) Regulations 2004, SI 2004/1220, reg 5(2)(b).
17 Sexual Offences Act 2003 (Travel Notification Requirements) Regulations 2004, SI 2004/1220, reg 5(3). This is referred to as the 'special case'.

18 See the Sexual Offences Act 2003 (Travel Notification Requirements) Regulations 2004, SI 2004/1220, reg 7 (amended by SI 2012/1876). This provides that where a relevant offender has given a notification under the Sexual Offences Act 2003 s 86(2) (see the text and notes 1–7) and at any time prior to his intended departure from the United Kingdom the information disclosed in that notification becomes inaccurate or incomplete as a statement of all the information mentioned in s 86(2)(a), (b) (see the text and notes 1–7) and the additional information under the Sexual Offences Act 2003 (Travel Notification Requirements) Regulations 2004, SI 2004/1220, reg 6 (see the text and notes 7–12) which he currently holds, he must, not less than 12 hours before his intended departure from the United Kingdom, give a further notification under the Sexual Offences Act 2003 s 86(2) and may not give such further notification less than 24 hours before the date of his intended departure unless he has reasonable excuse for being unable to give such notification before that time.

19 Sexual Offences Act 2003 (Travel Notification Requirements) Regulations 2004, SI 2004/1220, reg 10(4)(a).

20 Sexual Offences Act 2003 (Travel Notification Requirements) Regulations 2004, SI 2004/1220, reg 10(4)(b). As to the meaning of 'home address' see PARA 503 note 8.

21 Sexual Offences Act 2003 (Travel Notification Requirements) Regulations 2004, SI 2004/1220, reg 10(4)(c).

22 Ie under the Sexual Offences Act 2003 Pt 2 (ss 80–136ZD) (see PARA 503 et seq).

23 Ie under the Sexual Offences Act 2003 (Travel Notification Requirements) Regulations 2004, SI 2004/1220, reg 7 (see note 18).

24 Ie under the Sexual Offences Act 2003 s 86(2) (see the text and notes 1–12).

25 Sexual Offences Act 2003 (Travel Notification Requirements) Regulations 2004, SI 2004/1220, reg 10(5).

26 Ie a notification under the Sexual Offences Act 2003 s 86(2) (see the text and notes 1–7).

27 Sexual Offences Act 2003 s 86(3) (which provides that a notification under s 86 must disclose any information prescribed by regulations about the offender's return to the United Kingdom); Sexual Offences Act 2003 (Travel Notification Requirements) Regulations 2004, SI 2004/1220, regs 8(1), (2), 9.

28 Ie unless his initial notification disclosed a date under the Sexual Offences Act 2003 (Travel Notification Requirements) Regulations 2004, SI 2004/1220, reg 6(e) and a point of arrival under reg 6(f) (see the text and note 12) and his return was on that date and at that point: reg 8(3) (amended by SI 2012/1876).

29 Sexual Offences Act 2003 (Travel Notification Requirements) Regulations 2004, SI 2004/1220, reg 8(3) (as amended: see note 28).

30 See the Sexual Offences Act 2003 s 91(1); and PARA 510.

508. Method of notification. An initial notification[1], a notification of change[2], a periodic re-notification[3] and a notification of departure from[4] or return to[5] the United Kingdom[6] is given by attending at the appropriate police station[7] and giving a notification[8] to any police officer, or to any person authorised for the purpose by the officer in charge of the station[9]. Where an initial notification, a notification of change or a periodic re-notification is given the offender must, if requested by the police officer or authorised person, allow the officer or person to take his fingerprints[10], to photograph[11] any part of him[12], or to do both[13], for the purpose of verifying his identity[14].

Any notification given pursuant to these requirements must be acknowledged in writing in such form as the Secretary of State may direct[15].

1 Ie a notification under the Sexual Offences Act 2003 s 83(1) (see PARA 503).
2 Ie a notification under the Sexual Offences Act 2003 s 84(1) (see PARA 505).
3 Ie a notification under the Sexual Offences Act 2003 s 85(1) (see PARA 506).
4 Ie a notification under the Sexual Offences Act 2003 s 86(2) (see PARA 507).
5 Ie a notification under the Sexual Offences Act 2003 s 86(3) (see PARA 507).
6 As to the meaning of 'United Kingdom' see PARA 4 note 3.
7 Sexual Offences Act 2003 s 87(1)(a); Sexual Offences Act 2003 (Travel Notification Requirements) Regulations 2004, SI 2004/1220, reg 10(1). An appropriate police station for these purposes is such police station in an offender's local police area as the Secretary of State may by regulations prescribe or, if there is more than one, at any of them (Sexual Offences Act 2003 s 87(1)(a)), although a person giving a notification of change in relation to a

prospective change of home address (ie under s 84(1)(b) (see PARA 505)) or in relation to premises in which he has resided or stayed for a qualifying period (ie under s 84(1)(c) (see PARA 505)) may give the notification at a police station that would fall within s 87(1) if the change in home address had already occurred or (as the case may be) if the address of those premises were his home address (s 87(2)), and a person giving a notification under the Sexual Offences Act 2003 (Travel Notification Requirements) Regulations 2004, SI 2004/1220, reg 5(3) (late notification of compulsory information by persons leaving the United Kingdom) or reg 7 (change to such information previously disclosed) (see PARA 507) may attend at any prescribed police station whether or not in his local police area (reg 10(2)). For the prescribed police stations see the Sexual Offences Act 2003 (Prescribed Police Stations) (No 2) Regulations 2015, SI 2015/1523.

'Local police area' means, in relation to a person, the police area in which his home address is situated (Sexual Offences Act 2003 s 88(1), (3)(a)); or in the absence of a home address, the police area in which the home address last notified is situated (s 88(3)(b)); or in the absence of a home address and of any such notification, the police area in which the court which last dealt with the person is situated (s 88(3)(c)). As to police forces and police areas see POLICE AND INVESTIGATORY POWERS vol 84 (2013) PARA 52 et seq. For these purposes, the ways in which a court may be considered last to have dealt with a person are: (1) dealing with a person in respect of a listed sexual offence (see PARA 329) or an insanity or disability finding in respect of such an offence (s 88(4)(a)); (2) dealing with a person in respect of an offence of breach of a risk of sexual harm order (see PARA 440) or of an interim risk of sexual harm order or a finding in respect of such an offence (s 88(4)(b)); (3) making, in respect of a person, a notification order (see PARAS 515–516), an interim notification order (see PARA 517), a sexual harm prevention order or an interim sexual harm prevention order (see PARAS 327–335), or a sexual offences prevention order or an interim sexual offences prevention order (see PARA 442) (s 88(4)(c) (amended by the Anti-social Behaviour, Crime and Policing Act 2014 Sch 11 para 56)); or (4) making, in respect of a person, an order under the Crime and Disorder Act 1998 s 2, s 2A or s 20 (all repealed) (sex offender orders and interim orders made in England and Wales or Scotland) or corresponding Northern Ireland provisions (Sexual Offences Act 2003 s 88(4)(d)). As to verdicts of not guilty by reason of insanity see CRIMINAL LAW vol 25 (2010) PARA 30. As to a finding that a person was under a disability and did the act or omission charged against him in respect of an offence see PARA 329 note 1. For these purposes, 'finding', in relation to an offence, means a finding of not guilty of the offence by reason of insanity or a finding that the person was under a disability and did the act or omission charged against him in respect of the offence: s 88(4).

8　Initial notifications, notifications of change and periodic re-notifications must be given orally: Sexual Offences Act 2003 s 87(1)(b). No such requirement is made in respect of notifications of departure from or return to the United Kingdom.

9　Sexual Offences Act 2003 s 87(1)(b); Sexual Offences Act 2003 (Travel Notification Requirements) Regulations 2004, SI 2004/1220, reg 10(3).

10　Sexual Offences Act 2003 s 87(4)(a). Failure without reasonable excuse to comply with the requirements of s 87(4) (see the text and notes 11–13) or the Sexual Offences Act 2003 (Travel Notification Requirements) Regulations 2004, SI 2004/1220, reg 10(4) (see PARA 507), or notification of false particulars pursuant to reg 10(4) or reg 10(5) (see PARA 507) is an offence: see the Sexual Offences Act 2003 s 91(1); and PARA 510.

11　'Photograph' includes any process by means of which an image may be produced: Sexual Offences Act 2003 s 88(2).

12　Sexual Offences Act 2003 s 87(4)(b).

13　Sexual Offences Act 2003 s 87(4)(c).

14　Sexual Offences Act 2003 s 87(5).

15　Sexual Offences Act 2003 s 87(3).

509.　Parental directions. Where a relevant offender[1] is aged under 18[2] when he is before the court which deals with him in respect of an offence or finding, that court may direct that the obligations that would otherwise be imposed on him in connection with the making of an initial notification[3], a notification of change[4], a periodic re-notification[5] or a notification of departure from or return to the United Kingdom[6] are to be treated instead as obligations on the individual or individuals having parental responsibility[7] for the offender[8]. The police[9] may, by complaint to any magistrates' court whose commission area includes any part of the police area[10], also apply for such a direction in respect of a relevant offender who resides in that area or who they believe is in or is intending to come to it[11], and who they believe is under 18[12]. Where a parental direction is made, the person having parental responsibility for the offender must ensure that the offender attends at the police station with him when a notification is being given[13].

The relevant offender[14], the person having parental responsibility[15], the police for the area in which the offender resides[16] and the police for any other area which they believe that the offender is in, or is intending to come to[17], may apply to the appropriate court[18] for an order varying, renewing or discharging a parental direction[19], and the court may make any order varying, renewing or discharging the direction as it considers appropriate[20].

A failure without reasonable excuse by the parent to give the necessary notification pursuant to a parental direction is an offence[21]. In addition, a notifying parent commits an offence if, without reasonable excuse, he fails to ensure that the young offender attends with him[22].

1   As to the relevant offenders for these purposes see the Sexual Offences Act 2003 ss 80(1)(a)–(c), 81(1)(a)–(c); and PARAS 499–500.
2   As to the determination of a person's age see the Children and Young Persons Act 1933 s 99; and CHILDREN AND YOUNG PERSONS vol 10 (2012) PARA 1206.
3   Ie a notification under the Sexual Offences Act 2003 s 83 (see PARA 503).
4   Ie a notification under the Sexual Offences Act 2003 s 84 (see PARA 505).
5   Ie a notification under the Sexual Offences Act 2003 s 85 (see PARA 506).
6   Ie a notification under the Sexual Offences Act 2003 s 86 (see PARA 507). As to the meaning of 'United Kingdom' see PARA 4 note 3.
7   As to the meaning of 'parental responsibility' see the Children Act 1989 s 3; and CHILDREN AND YOUNG PERSONS vol 9 (2012) PARAS 151–154 (definition applied by the Sexual Offences Act 2003 s 133(1)).
8   Sexual Offences Act 2003 s 89(1), (2)(a) (s 89(1) amended by the Anti-social Behaviour, Crime and Policing Act 2014 Sch 11 para 57). Such a direction takes immediate effect and applies either until the offender attains the age of 18 (Sexual Offences Act 2003 s 89(3)(a)) or for such shorter period as the court may, at the time the direction is given, direct (s 89(3)(b)).
9   Although the Sexual Offences Act 2003 s 89(4) states that the application must be made by a chief officer of police, the application may be made by another suitable person to whom the chief officer has delegated his responsibility (see *R (on the application of the Chief Constable of West Midlands Police) v Birmingham Justices* [2002] EWHC 1087 (Admin), [2003] Crim LR 37, [2002] 28 LS Gaz R 32), and it is therefore broadly correct to refer to the application having to be made by 'the police'. Determination of who is a suitable delegate is for the chief officer, and improper delegation is a matter for the courts: *R (Chief Constable of West Midlands Police) v Birmingham Justices*. This decision was made in relation to an application for an anti-social behaviour order but is equally applicable by its reasoning to an application for an order under the Sexual Offences Act 2003 s 89.
10 As to police forces and police areas see POLICE AND INVESTIGATORY POWERS vol 84 (2013) PARA 52 et seq.
11 Sexual Offences Act 2003 s 89(4)(a).
12 Sexual Offences Act 2003 s 89(4)(b).
13 Sexual Offences Act 2003 s 89(2)(b).
14 Sexual Offences Act 2003 s 90(2)(a).
15 Sexual Offences Act 2003 s 90(2)(b).
16 Sexual Offences Act 2003 s 90(2)(c).
17 Sexual Offences Act 2003 s 90(2)(d).
18 The 'appropriate court' is the Crown Court, where the parental direction was made by the Court of Appeal (Sexual Offences Act 2003 s 90(5)(a)); otherwise, it means the court that made the direction (s 90(5)(b)). An application to the Crown Court must be made in accordance with rules of court (s 90(3)(a)); otherwise, it must be made by complaint (s 90(3)(b)).
19 Sexual Offences Act 2003 s 90(1).
20 Sexual Offences Act 2003 s 90(4). Before making the order the court must hear the applicant and (if they wish to be heard) any of the other persons who may apply for such an order: s 90(4).

21 See the Sexual Offences Act 2003 s 91(1)(a); and PARA 510.
22 See the Sexual Offences Act 2003 s 91(1); and PARA 510.

510. Offences of failing to notify and notifying false information. A person commits an offence if he fails, without reasonable excuse, to comply with:

(1)   the initial notification requirement[1];
(2)   the requirement to notify changes in notified information[2];
(3)   the requirement to notify non-occurrence of changes in notified information in respect of which advance notice has been given[3];
(4)   the requirement periodically to re-notify[4];
(5)   the requirement to allow fingerprints to be taken and/or to be photographed when giving notification[5];
(6)   the requirement, when a parental direction has been made[6], that the parent ensures that the young offender attends with him when notification is given by the parent[7]; or
(7)   any requirement imposed by regulations[8] in respect of travel outside the United Kingdom[9].

A person commits any such offence on the day on which he first fails, without reasonable excuse, to comply with the initial notification requirement[10], the requirement to notify changes in notified information[11], the requirement to notify non-occurrence of changes[12] or the requirement to make a notification under the travel notification regulations[13] and continues to commit it throughout any period during which the failure continues[14].

A person also commits an offence[15] if he notifies to the police any information which he knows to be false in purported compliance with:

(a)   the initial notification requirement[16];
(b)   the requirement to notify changes in notified information[17];
(c)   the requirement periodically to re-notify[18]; or
(d)   any requirements imposed by regulations in respect of travel outside the United Kingdom[19].

A person guilty of any of these offences is liable on conviction on indictment to imprisonment for a term not exceeding five years[20], or on summary conviction to imprisonment for a term not exceeding six months[21] to a fine not exceeding the statutory maximum[22] or to both[23]. Proceedings for an offence may be commenced in any court with jurisdiction in any place where the defendant resides or is found[24].

1   Sexual Offences Act 2003 s 91(1)(a). For the initial notification requirement see s 83(1); and PARA 503.
2   Ie under the Sexual Offences Act 2003 s 84(1): see PARA 505.
3   Ie under the Sexual Offences Act 2003 s 84(4)(b): see PARA 505.
4   Ie under the Sexual Offences Act 2003 s 85(1): see PARA 506.
5   Ie under the Sexual Offences Act 2003 s 87(4): see PARA 508.
6   As to parental directions see PARA 509.
7   Ie under the Sexual Offences Act 2003 s 89(2)(b): see PARA 509.
8   Ie regulations made under the Sexual Offences Act 2003 s 86(1): see the Sexual Offences Act 2003 (Travel Notification Requirements) Regulations 2004, SI 2004/1220; and PARAS 507, 508.
9   See PARAS 507, 508.
10 See the text and note 1.
11 See the text and note 2.
12 See the text and note 4.
13 See the text and notes 8–9.
14 Sexual Offences Act 2003 s 91(3). A person must not, however, be prosecuted under s 91(1) more than once in respect of the same failure: s 91(3).

15 Sexual Offences Act 2003 s 91(1)(b).
16 See PARA 503.
17 See PARA 505.
18 See PARA 506.
19 See PARA 507.
20 Sexual Offences Act 2003 s 91(2)(b). Where more than one offence is committed (eg a failure to notify a change of name and a failure to notify a change of address) and the offences are committed at different times, consecutive sentences are appropriate: *R v Adams (Christopher)* [2003] EWCA Crim 3231, [2004] 2 Cr App Rep (S) 78 (corresponding offences under the Sex Offenders Act 1997 s 3(1) (repealed)).
21 As from a day to be appointed this maximum term of imprisonment is increased to a maximum term of 12 months (see the Criminal Justice Act 2003 ss 281(7), 282(2), (3) (not yet in force)), although this does not affect the penalty for any offence committed before that day (see s 282(4) (not yet in force)). At the date at which this volume states the law no such day had been appointed.
22 As to the standard scale, the statutory maximum, the prescribed sum, and magistrates' powers to levy unlimited fines see PARA 176.
23 Sexual Offences Act 2003 s 91(2)(a).
24 Sexual Offences Act 2003 s 91(4).

511. Review of notification requirements. A qualifying relevant offender[1] may apply[2] to the relevant chief officer of police[3] for a determination that he is no longer subject to the indefinite notification requirements[4], and if he satisfies the chief officer that it is not necessary for the purpose of protecting the public or any particular members of the public from sexual harm for him to remain subject to those requirements[5], he ceases to be subject to them on the date of receipt of the notice of determination[6]. If the chief officer determines that the offender should remain subject to the requirements[7], the notice of the determination must contain a statement of reasons for the determination[8] and inform the offender that he may[9] appeal the determination[10].

If, when determining that the offender should remain subject to the indefinite notification requirements, the chief officer considers that the risk of sexual harm posed by that offender is sufficient to justify a continuation of those requirements for more than[11] eight years[12], he may make a determination to require the offender to remain subject to the requirements for a period not exceeding[13] 15 years[14].

If the court makes an order on appeal[15] that an offender should not remain subject to the indefinite notification requirements, the offender ceases to be subject to the requirements on the date of the order[16].

1 A 'qualifying relevant offender' means a relevant offender who, on the date on which he makes an application for review, is subject to the indefinite notification requirements (Sexual Offences Act 2003 s 91A(2)(a) (ss 91A–91C, 91E, 91F added by SI 2012/1883) and not subject to a sexual harm prevention order under the Sexual Offences Act 2003 s 103A (see PARA 327), an interim sexual harm prevention order under s 103F (see PARA 332), a sexual offences prevention order under s 104(1) (repealed: see PARA 442) or an interim sexual offences prevention order under s 109(3) (repealed: see PARA 442) (s 91A(2)(b) (as so added; amended by the Anti-social Behaviour, Crime and Policing Act 2014 Sch 11 para 58)). As to the relevant offenders for these purposes see the Sexual Offences Act 2003 ss 80(1)(a)–(c), 81(1)(a)–(c); and PARAS 499–500. As to the indefinite notification requirements see note 4.
2 An application for review must be in writing and may be made on or after the qualifying date or, as the case may be, the further qualifying date: Sexual Offences Act 2003 s 91B(1) (as added: see note 1). The qualifying date must not be earlier than the expiry of the fixed period specified in a notification continuation order made in relation to a qualifying relevant offender in accordance with ss 88A–88I (applicable to Scotland only) (s 91B(7) (as so added)): subject to that, the qualifying date is:
   (1)   where the qualifying relevant offender was 18 or over on the relevant date, the day after the end of the 15 year period beginning with the day on which the qualifying relevant offender gives the relevant notification (see below) (s 91B(2)(a) (as so added)); or

(2)   where the qualifying relevant offender was under 18 on the relevant date, the day after the end of the 8 year period beginning with the day on which the qualifying relevant offender gives the relevant notification (s 91B(2)(b) (as so added)).

The further qualifying date is the day after the end of the 8 year period beginning with the day on which the relevant chief officer of police (see note 3) makes a determination under s 91C (see the text and notes 5–10) to require a qualifying relevant offender to remain subject to the indefinite notification requirements (s 91B(3) (as so added)), although this is subject to s 91B(4), (5) (see the text and notes 11–14) and if s 91B(5) applies, the further qualifying date is the day after the end of the period determined thereunder (s 91B(6) (as so added)).

The relevant chief officer of police within 14 days of receipt of an application for review must give an acknowledgment of receipt of the application to the qualifying relevant offender (s 91B(8)(a) (as so added)) and may notify a responsible body (see below) that the application has been made (s 91B(8)(b) (as so added)). Where a responsible body is notified of the application for review under s 91B(8)(b) and holds information which it considers to be relevant to the application, the responsible body must give such information to the relevant chief officer of police within 28 days of receipt of the notification: s 91B(9) (as so added).

In s 91B 'the relevant notification' means the first notification which the relevant offender gives under s 83 (see PARA 503), s 84 (see PARA 505) or s 85 (see PARA 506) when he is first released after being remanded in or committed to custody by an order of a court in relation to the conviction for the offence giving rise to the indefinite notification requirements (s 91B(10)(a) (as so added)), serving a sentence of imprisonment or a term of service detention in relation to that conviction (s 91B(10)(b) (as so added)), or being detained in hospital in relation to that conviction (s 91B(10)(c) (as so added)). For the purposes of Pt 2 'responsible body' means:

(a)   the probation trust for any area that includes any part of the police area concerned (s 91B(11)(a)(i) (as so added));

(b)   in relation to any part of the police area concerned for which there is no probation trust, each provider of probation services which has been identified as a relevant provider of probation services for the purposes of the Criminal Justice Act 2003 s 325 (see CRIMINAL LAW vol 25 (2010) PARA 97), by arrangements under the Offender Management Act 2007 s 3 (see PARA 669) (Sexual Offences Act 2003 s 91B(11)(a)(ii) (as so added));

(c)   the Minister of the Crown exercising functions in relation to prisons (and for this purpose 'prison' has the same meaning as in the Prison Act 1952: see s 53(1); and PRISONS AND PRISONERS vol 85 (2012) PARA 403) (Sexual Offences Act 2003 s 91B(11)(a)(iii) (as so added)); and

(d)   each body mentioned in the Criminal Justice Act 2003 s 325(6), but as if the references in that subsection to the relevant area were references to the police area concerned (Sexual Offences Act 2003 s 91B(11)(a)(iv) (as so added)).

'Risk of sexual harm' means a risk of physical or psychological harm to the public in the United Kingdom or any particular members of the public caused by the qualifying relevant offender committing one or more of the offences listed in Sch 3 (see PARA 329): Sexual Offences Act 2003 s 91B(11)(b).

3   For these purposes the 'relevant chief officer of police' means the chief officer of police for the police area in which a qualifying relevant offender is recorded as residing or staying in the most recent notification given by him under the Sexual Offences Act 2003 s 84(1) (see PARA 505) or s 85(1) (see PARA 506): s 91A(4) (as so added). As to police forces, police areas and chief officers of police see POLICE AND INVESTIGATORY POWERS vol 84 (2013) PARAS 52 et seq, 123 et seq. This is subject to the proviso that if a qualifying relevant offender is recorded as residing or staying at more than one address in the most recent notification given by him under s 84(1) or s 85(1) the 'relevant chief officer of police' means the chief officer of police for the police area in which, during the period of 12 months ending on the day on which the qualifying relevant offender makes an application for review ('the relevant period'), the qualifying relevant offender has resided or stayed on a number of days which equals or exceeds the number of days on which he has resided or stayed in any other police area: s 91A(5)–(7) (as so added).

The Secretary of State must issue guidance to relevant chief officers of police in relation to the determination by them of applications made under s 91B (s 91F(1) (as so added), may from time to time, revise the guidance so issued (s 91F(2) (as so added)) and must arrange for any guidance so issued or revised to be published in such manner as he considers appropriate (s 91F(3) (as so added)).

4   Sexual Offences Act 2003 s 91A(1) (as added: see note 1). The 'indefinite notification requirements' mean the notification requirements of Pt 2 (ss 80–136ZD) for an indefinite period by virtue of s 80(1) (see PARA 499), s 81(1) (see PARA 500) or a notification order made under s 97(5) (see PARA 515): s 91A(2) (as so added).

5 Sexual Offences Act 2003 s 91C(2) (as added: see note 1).
6 Sexual Offences Act 2003 s 91C(4) (as added: see note 1). The chief officer must determine the application for review and give notice of the determination to the qualifying relevant offender within 6 weeks of the latest date on which any body to which a notification has been given under s 91B(8)(b) may give information under s 91B(9) (see note 2): s 91C(1) (as so added). The Secretary of State may by order amend the specified 6-week period (s 91C(5) (as so added)): at the date at which this volume states the law no such order had been made.
7 As to the factors to be taken into account when making a determination see PARA 512.
8 Sexual Offences Act 2003 s 91C(3)(a) (as added: see note 1).
9 Ie in accordance with the Sexual Offences Act 2003 s 91E (see PARA 511).
10 Sexual Offences Act 2003 ss 91C(3)(b), 91E(1) (as added: see note 1). As to appeals see the text and notes 15–16.
11 Ie after the end of the eight year period beginning with the day on which the determination is made: Sexual Offences Act 2003 s 91B(4) (as added: see note 1).
12 Sexual Offences Act 2003 s 91B(4) (as added: see note 1).
13 Ie a period no longer than the 15 year period beginning with the day on which the determination is made: Sexual Offences Act 2003 s 91B(5) (as added: see note 1).
14 Sexual Offences Act 2003 s 91B(5) (as added: see note 1).
15 An appeal under the Sexual Offences Act 2003 s 91E may be made by complaint to a magistrates' court within the period of 21 days beginning with the day of receipt of the notice of determination: s 91E(2) (as so added). A qualifying relevant offender may appeal under s 91E to any magistrates' court in a local justice area which includes any part of the police area for which the chief officer is the relevant chief officer of police: s 91E(3) (as so added).
16 Sexual Offences Act 2003 s 91E(4) (as added: see note 1).

512. Matters to be considered in determining review. In determining an application for review[1] the relevant chief officer of police[2] must have regard to information (if any) received from a responsible body[3], consider the risk of sexual harm posed by the qualifying relevant offender[4] and the effect of a continuation of the indefinite notification requirements[5] on him[6], and take into account:

(1)   the seriousness of the offence in relation to which the qualifying relevant offender became subject to the indefinite notification requirements[7];

(2)   the period of time which has elapsed since the offender committed the offence (or other offences)[8];

(3)   where the offender is subject to the notification requirements under former legislation[9], whether he committed any offence[10] involving failure to comply with those requirements[11];

(4)   whether the offender has committed any offence[12] relating to notification[13];

(5)   the age of the offender at the qualifying date or further qualifying date[14];

(6)   the age of the offender at the time the relevant offence[15] was committed[16];

(7)   the age of any person who was a victim of any such offence (where applicable) and the difference in age between the victim and the offender at the time the offence was committed[17];

(8)   any assessment of the risk posed by the offender which has been made by a responsible body under the arrangements[18] for managing and assessing risk[19];

(9)   any submission or evidence from a victim of the offence giving rise to the indefinite notification requirements[20];

(10) any convictions or findings made by a court[21] in respect of the offender for any of the listed sexual offences[22] other than the relevant offence[23];

(11) any caution which the offender has received for a listed sexual offence[24];

(12) any convictions or findings made by a court outside England and

Wales[25] in respect of the offender for any listed non-sexual offence[26] where the offender's behaviour since the date of such conviction or finding indicates a risk of sexual harm[27];

(13) any other submission or evidence of the risk of sexual harm posed by the offender[28];

(14) any evidence presented by or on behalf of the offender which demonstrates that he does not pose a risk of sexual harm[29]; and

(15) any other matter which the chief officer considers to be appropriate[30].

1 Ie under the Sexual Offences Act 2003 s 91C (see PARA 511).
2 See PARA 511 note 3.
3 Sexual Offences Act 2003 s 91D(1)(a) (s 91D added by SI 2012/1883). As to the meaning of 'responsible body' see PARA 511 note 2.
4 As to the meaning of 'qualifying relevant offender' see PARA 511 note 1.
5 As to the meaning of 'indefinite notification requirements' see PARA 511 note 4.
6 Sexual Offences Act 2003 s 91D(1)(b) (as added: see note 3).
7 Sexual Offences Act 2003 s 91D(1)(c), (2)(a) (as added: see note 3).
8 Sexual Offences Act 2003 s 91D(2)(b) (as added: see note 3).
9 Ie where the offender falls within the Sexual Offences Act 2003 s 81(1) (see PARA 500).
10 Ie any offence under the Sex Offenders Act 1997 s 3 (repealed).
11 Sexual Offences Act 2003 s 91D(2)(c) (as added: see note 3).
12 Ie any offence under the Sexual Offences Act 2003 s 91 (see PARA 510).
13 Sexual Offences Act 2003 s 91D(2)(d) (as added: see note 3).
14 Sexual Offences Act 2003 s 91D(2)(e) (as added: see note 3). As to the qualifying date or further qualifying date see PARA 511 note 2. As to the determination of a person's age see the Children and Young Persons Act 1933 s 99; and CHILDREN AND YOUNG PERSONS vol 10 (2012) PARA 1206.
15 Ie the offence referred to in the Sexual Offences Act 2003 s 91D(2)(a) (see the text and note 7).
16 Sexual Offences Act 2003 s 91D(2)(f) (as added: see note 3).
17 Sexual Offences Act 2003 s 91D(2)(g) (as added: see note 3).
18 Ie arrangements established under the Criminal Justice Act 2003 s 325 (see CRIMINAL LAW vol 25 (2010) PARA 97).
19 Sexual Offences Act 2003 s 91D(2)(h) (as added: see note 3).
20 Sexual Offences Act 2003 s 91D(2)(i) (as added: see note 3).
21 Ie including by a court in Scotland, Northern Ireland or countries outside the United Kingdom: Sexual Offences Act 2003 s 91D(2)(j) (as added: see note 3).
22 Ie the offences listed in the Sexual Offences Act 2003 Sch 3 (see PARA 329).
23 Sexual Offences Act 2003 s 91D(2)(j) (as added: see note 3). As to the 'relevant offence' see note 15.
24 Sexual Offences Act 2003 s 91D(2)(k) (as added: see note 3). This includes a caution for an offence in Northern Ireland or countries outside the United Kingdom: s 91D(2)(k) (as so added). In s 91D a reference to a conviction, finding or caution for an offence committed in a country outside the United Kingdom means a conviction, finding or caution for an act which constituted an offence under the law in force in the country concerned (s 91D(3)(a) (as so added)) and would have constituted an offence listed in Sch 3 or Sch 5 (see PARA 330) if it had been done in any part of the United Kingdom (s 91D(3)(b) (as so added)).
25 Ie a court in Scotland, Northern Ireland or countries outside the United Kingdom: Sexual Offences Act 2003 s 91D(2)(l) (as added: see note 3).
26 Ie the offences listed in the Sexual Offences Act 2003 Sch 5 (see PARA 330).
27 Sexual Offences Act 2003 s 91D(2)(l) (as added: see note 3).
28 Sexual Offences Act 2003 s 91D(2)(m) (as added: see note 3).
29 Sexual Offences Act 2003 s 91D(2)(n) (as added: see note 3).
30 Sexual Offences Act 2003 s 91D(2)(o) (as added: see note 3).

513. Sharing of information for verification purposes. A chief officer of police[1] and the Director of the National Crime Agency[2] are empowered to supply to the Secretary of State[3], for the purpose of verification[4], any information notified to the police pursuant to the requirements relating to initial notification[5], changes to notified information[6], and periodic re-notification[7]. The

Secretary of State[8] may in turn supply a report compiled for these purposes[9] to a chief officer of police[10] and the Serious Organised Crime Agency[11].

These provisions do not affect any other power to supply information[12] or authorise the doing of anything that contravenes data protection laws[13], although, subject to this, the supply of information under these provisions is taken not to breach any restriction on the disclosure of information (however arising or imposed)[14].

1   Sexual Offences Act 2003 s 94(3)(a). As to police forces, police areas and chief officers of police see POLICE AND INVESTIGATORY POWERS vol 84 (2013) PARAS 52 et seq, 123 et seq.

2   Sexual Offences Act 2003 s 94(3)(b) (substituted by the Crime and Courts Act 2013 Sch 8 para 154). As to the National Crime Agency see POLICE AND INVESTIGATORY POWERS vol 84 (2013) PARA 424.

3   Sexual Offences Act 2003 s 94(2)(a). Where appropriate supply may be made to a Northern Ireland Department (s 94(2)(b)) or a person providing services to the Secretary of State or a Northern Ireland Department in connection with a relevant function (s 94(2)(c) (amended by SI 2008/2656; SI 2012/2007)). For these purposes 'relevant function' means a function relating to social security, child support, employment or training, a function relating to passports, or a function under the Road Traffic Act 1988 Pt 3 (ss 87–109C) (licensing of drivers of vehicles: see ROAD TRAFFIC vol 89 (2011) PARA 245 et seq) or a corresponding Northern Ireland enactment: Sexual Offences Act 2003 ss 94(8), 95(5) (s 94(8) amended by SI 2008/2656; SI 2012/2007).

4   Ie for the purposes of the prevention, detection, investigation or prosecution of offences under the Sexual Offences Act 2003 Pt 2 (ss 80–136ZD): s 94(2). In relation to information supplied under this provision to any person, the reference to verifying the information is a reference to checking its accuracy by comparing it with information held either by the Secretary of State or a Northern Ireland Department (where the information is held by him or it in connection with the exercise of a relevant function) (s 94(4)(a)(i) (amended by SI 2008/2656; SI 2012/2007)) or by a person providing services to the Secretary of State or a Northern Ireland Department in connection with a relevant function (where the information is held by that person in connection with the provision of the services) (Sexual Offences Act 2003 s 94(4)(a)(ii)), and compiling a report of that comparison (s 94(4)(b)).

5   Sexual Offences Act 2003 s 94(1)(a). As to initial notification see s 83; and PARA 503. Information under the corresponding provisions of the Sex Offenders Act 1997 s 2(1)–(3) (repealed) may also be notified under these provisions: Sexual Offences Act 2003 s 94(1)(b).

6   For the provisions relating to notifying changes to notified information see the Sexual Offences Act 2003 s 84; and PARA 505.

7   For the provisions relating to periodic re-notification see the Sexual Offences Act 2003 s 85; and PARA 506.

8   Sexual Offences Act 2003 s 95(1)(a). This power may also be exercised, where appropriate, by a Northern Ireland Department or a person providing services to the Secretary of State or a Northern Ireland Department in connection with a relevant function: s 95(1)(b), (c).

9   See note 4.

10 Sexual Offences Act 2003 s 95(2)(a). Such a report may contain any information held by the Secretary of State or a Northern Ireland Department in connection with the exercise of a relevant function (s 95(3)(a) (amended by SI 2008/2656; SI 2012/2007)) or held in connection with the provision of services by a person providing services to the Secretary of State or Northern Ireland Department in connection with a relevant function (Sexual Offences Act 2003 s 95(3)(b)). Where a report contains such information the person to whom it is supplied may retain the information, whether or not used for the purposes of the prevention, detection, investigation or prosecution of an offence under Pt 2 (ss 80–136ZD) (s 95(4)(a)) and may use the information for any purpose related to the prevention, detection, investigation or prosecution of offences (whether or not under Pt 2), but for no other purpose (s 95(4)(b)).

11 Sexual Offences Act 2003 s 95(2)(b) (substituted by the Serious Organised Crime and Police Act 2005 Sch 4 para 195). As to the Serious Organised Crime Agency see POLICE AND INVESTIGATORY POWERS vol 84 (2013) PARA 379 et seq.

12 Sexual Offences Act 2003 ss 94(7), 95(5).

13 Sexual Offences Act 2003 s 94(6). For the relevant data protection laws see the Data Protection Act 1998; and CONFIDENCE AND INFORMATIONAL PRIVACY.

14 Sexual Offences Act 2003 s 94(5).

514. Powers of entry and search. A justice of the peace may issue a warrant authorising a constable[1] to enter premises for the purpose of assessing the risks posed by the relevant offender[2] to which the warrant relates[3] and to search the premises for that purpose[4]. The justice may issue such a warrant only on an application made by a senior police officer[5] of the relevant force[6] and only if the justice is satisfied that:

(1)   the address of each set of premises specified in the application is an applicable address for these purposes[7];

(2)   the relevant offender is not currently detained[8] or is outside the United Kingdom[9];

(3)   it is necessary for a constable to enter and search the premises for the purpose of assessing the risks posed by the relevant offender to which the warrant relates[10]; and

(4)   on at least two occasions a constable has sought entry to the premises in order to search them for that purpose and has been unable to obtain entry for that purpose[11].

1   Ie a constable of the relevant force: Sexual Offences Act 2003 s 96B(1) (s 96B added by the Violent Crime Reduction Act 2006 s 58(1)). For this purpose 'relevant force' means the police force maintained for the police area in which the premises in respect of which the application is made or the warrant is issued are situated: Sexual Offences Act 2003 s 96B(10) (as so added).

2   For these purposes a reference to the relevant offender to whom the warrant relates is a reference to the relevant offender who has in accordance with the Sexual Offences Act 2003 Pt 2 (ss 80–136ZD) notified the police that the premises specified in the warrant are his home address, or in respect of whom there are reasonable grounds to believe that he resides there or may regularly be found there: s 96B(9) (as added: see note 1).

3   Sexual Offences Act 2003 s 96B(1)(a) (as added: see note 1).

4   Sexual Offences Act 2003 s 96B(1)(b) (as added: see note 1). A warrant issued under these provisions must specify the one or more sets of premises to which it relates (s 96B(5) (as so added)) and may authorise the constable executing it to use reasonable force if necessary to enter and search the premises (s 96B(6) (as so added)). It may authorise entry to and search of premises on more than one occasion if, on the application, the justice of the peace is satisfied that it is necessary to authorise multiple entries in order to achieve the purpose mentioned in s 96B(1)(a): s 96B(7) (as so added). Where a warrant issued under s 96B authorises multiple entries, the number of entries authorised may be unlimited or limited to a maximum: s 96B(8) (as so added).

5   For these purposes 'senior police officer' means a constable of the rank of superintendent or above: Sexual Offences Act 2003 s 96B(10) (as added: see note 1).

6   Sexual Offences Act 2003 s 96B(1) (as added: see note 1).

7   Sexual Offences Act 2003 s 96B(2)(a) (as added: see note 1). An address is an applicable address for these purposes if:
     (1)   it is the address which was last notified in accordance with Pt 2 by a relevant offender to the police as his home address (s 96B(3)(a) (as so added)); or
     (2)   there are reasonable grounds to believe that a relevant offender resides there or may regularly be found there (s 96B(3)(b) (as so added)).

8   An offender is currently detained for this purpose if he is:
     (1)   remanded in or committed to custody by order of a court (Sexual Offences Act 2003 s 96B(4)(a));
     (2)   serving a sentence of imprisonment or a term of service detention (s 96B(4)(b)); or
     (3)   detained in a hospital (s 96B(4)(c)).
   As to the meanings of 'imprisonment' and 'detained in a hospital' see PARA 500 note 6.

9   Sexual Offences Act 2003 s 96B(2)(b), (4)(d) (as added: see note 1). As to the meaning of 'United Kingdom' see PARA 4 note 3.

10   Sexual Offences Act 2003 s 96B(2)(c) (as added: see note 1).

11   Sexual Offences Act 2003 s 96B(2)(d) (as added: see note 1).

(ii) Notification Orders

515. Notification orders in respect of offences committed outside the United Kingdom. A notification order may be made in respect of a person who has committed an act which constituted an offence under the law in force in a country outside the United Kingdom[1] and which had it been committed in any part of the United Kingdom would have constituted one of the offences in respect of which the notification requirements arise[2]: for the purposes of the making of notification orders these are known as 'relevant offences'[3]. The police[4] may, by complaint to any magistrates' court whose commission area includes any part of the police area[5] apply for a notification order[6] provided that three specified conditions are met with respect to the defendant[7] and the defendant resides in the police area or the police believe that the defendant is in, or is intending to come to, the police area[8]; and if the specified conditions are met, the court must make the order[9]. Where a notification order is made, the defendant becomes or (as the case may be) remains subject to the notification requirements[10] for the duration of the notification period[11]. A court which makes a notification order in respect of a young offender (that is, a person aged under 18) may make a parental direction[12]. A defendant may appeal to the Crown Court against the making of a notification order[13].

1   Sexual Offences Act 2003 ss 97(6), 99(1)(a). As to the meaning of 'United Kingdom' see PARA 4 note 3. An act punishable under the law in force in a country outside the United Kingdom constitutes an offence under that law for these purposes however described in that law: s 99(2).
2   Sexual Offences Act 2003 s 99(1)(b). As to the notification requirements see PARA 498 et seq. As to the offences in respect of which the notification requirements arise see Sch 3; and PARA 329. Where the offence in question is a foreign offence (ie an act which constituted an offence under the law in force in a country outside the United Kingdom (the 'relevant foreign law') (s 132(4)(a)) and would have constituted an offence subject to a sentencing condition (but not any other offence listed in Sch 3) if it had been done in any part of the United Kingdom (s 132(4)(b)), a person is regarded as convicted under the relevant foreign law of a foreign offence at the time when he is, in respect of the offence, dealt with under that law in a way equivalent to that mentioned in Sch 3 as it applies to the corresponding United Kingdom offence (s 132(6)). In relation to a foreign offence, references to the corresponding United Kingdom offence are references to the offence (or any offence) to which s 132(4)(b) applies in the case of that foreign offence: s 132(5). Where in the case of any person a court exercising jurisdiction under the relevant foreign law makes in respect of a foreign offence a finding equivalent to a relevant finding, the court's finding is for these purposes to be regarded as made at the time when the person is, in respect of the finding, dealt with under that law in a way equivalent to that mentioned in Sch 3 as it applies to the corresponding United Kingdom offence: s 132(7). 'Country' includes territory: s 133(1).
      On an application for a notification order the condition in s 99(1)(b) is to be taken as met unless, not later than three days before the hearing date for the application for the notification order (Magistrates' Courts (Notification Orders) Rules 2004, SI 2004/1052, r 4), the defendant serves on the applicant a notice stating that, on the facts as alleged with respect to the act concerned, the condition is not in his opinion met (Sexual Offences Act 2003 s 99(3)(a)), showing his grounds for that opinion (s 99(3)(b)), and requiring the applicant to prove that the condition is met (s 99(3)(c)), although the court may, if it thinks fit, permit the defendant to require the applicant to prove that the condition is met without service of such a notice (s 99(4)).
3   Sexual Offences Act 2003 ss 98(3)(d), 99(1).
4   Although these provisions refer to a 'chief officer of police' in connection with the making of applications for notification orders, the powers described in the text are exercisable by the police generally (ie by another suitable person to whom the chief officer has delegated his responsibility) (see *R (on the application of the Chief Constable of West Midlands Police) v Birmingham Justices* [2002] EWHC 1087 (Admin), [2003] Crim LR 37, [2002] 28 LS Gaz R 32), and it is therefore broadly correct to refer to the application having to be made by 'the police'. Determination of who is a suitable delegate is for the chief officer, and improper delegation is a matter for the courts: *R (Chief Constable of West Midlands Police) v*

Birmingham Justices. This decision was made in relation to an application for an anti-social behaviour order (see PARA 439) but is equally applicable by its reasoning to an application for a notification order.

5   As to police forces and police areas see POLICE AND INVESTIGATORY POWERS vol 84 (2013) PARA 52 et seq.

6   An application for a notification order may be in the form set out the Magistrates' Courts (Notification Orders) Rules 2004, SI 2004/1052, Sch 1 (r 3(1)(a)).

    Proceedings by complaint are governed by the Magistrates' Courts Act 1980 ss 51–57, under which (as in the case of criminal proceedings) the court is required to give a defendant sufficient opportunity to attend and cannot otherwise proceed in his absence (see MAGISTRATES). Because the proceedings are civil, the rules of civil evidence, not criminal evidence, apply (see *Clingham v Royal Borough of Kensington and Chelsea, R (on the application of McCann) v Crown Court at Manchester* [2002] UKHL 39, [2003] 1 AC 787, [2002] 4 All ER 593, by analogy with the procedure for anti-social behaviour orders with which those proceedings were concerned): thus hearsay evidence, admitted under the statutory procedure for the introduction of such evidence in civil cases, is, depending on its persuasiveness, capable of satisfying the proof required in applications for preventive orders under the Sexual Offences Act 2003 Pt 2 (ss 80–136ZD).

7   Sexual Offences Act 2003 s 97(1)(a). As to these conditions see PARA 516.

8   Sexual Offences Act 2003 s 97(1)(b).

9   Sexual Offences Act 2003 s 97(5). A notification order must state the name of the defendant, that the notification requirements of Pt 2 apply to the defendant, and the date when the order expires: Magistrates' Courts (Notification Orders) Rules 2004, SI 2004/1052, r 3(3) (substituted by SI 2012/2018). As soon as reasonably practicable after a notification order has been made, the designated officer for the court must serve a copy of that order on the defendant: Magistrates' Courts (Notification Orders) Rules 2004, SI 2004/1052, r 3(5) (amended by SI 2005/617). Any copy of an order required to be sent to the defendant under these provisions must be either given to him in person or sent by post to his last known address and, if so given or sent, is deemed to have been received by him, unless the defendant proves that it was not received by him: Magistrates' Courts (Notification Orders) Rules 2004, SI 2004/1052, r 3(5) (as so amended).

10   As to the notification requirements see PARA 498 et seq.

11   Sexual Offences Act 2003 s 98(1)(b). As to the notification period see s 82; and PARA 501. The provisions are modified in their application to persons subject to notification orders, as follows:

    (1)   the 'relevant date' in respect of a person who is subject to a notification order by virtue of a conviction for an offence committed overseas (see s 97(2)(a); and PARA 516) is the date of conviction (s 98(2)(a));
    (2)   the 'relevant date' in respect of a person who is subject to a notification order by virtue of a corresponding finding in connection with an offence committed overseas (see s 97(2)(b), (c); and PARA 516) is the date of the finding (s 98(2)(b));
    (3)   the 'relevant date' in respect of a person who is subject to a notification order by virtue of a caution (see PARA 499) given in connection with an offence committed overseas (see s 97(2)(d); and PARA 516) is the date of the finding (s 98(2)(c));
    (4)   references in s 82 (except in s 82(1)) to a person (or relevant offender) within any provision of s 80 are to be read as references to the defendant (s 98(3)(a));
    (5)   the reference in s 82(1) to s 80(1)(d) is to be read as a reference to s 97(2)(d) (s 98(3)(b));
    (6)   references to an order of any description are to be read as references to any corresponding disposal made in relation to the defendant in respect of an offence or finding by reference to which the notification order was made (s 98(3)(c)); and
    (7)   the reference to offences listed in Sch 3 is to be read as a reference to relevant offences (s 98(3)(d)).

12   See the Sexual Offences Act 2003 s 89(1); and PARA 509. As to the determination of a person's age see the Children and Young Persons Act 1933 s 99; and CHILDREN AND YOUNG PERSONS vol 10 (2012) PARA 1206.

13   Sexual Offences Act 2003 s 101.

516.   Conditions for making notification orders. The first condition which must be satisfied in order for the police[1] to make an application for a notification order[2] in respect of a person is that under the law of a country outside the United Kingdom[3]:

(1)   he has been convicted of a relevant offence[4] (whether or not he has been punished for it)[5];

(2)   a court exercising jurisdiction under that law has made in respect of such an offence a finding equivalent to a finding that he is not guilty by reason of insanity[6] or to a finding that the defendant is under a disability and did the act charged against him in respect of the offence[7]; or

(3)   he has been cautioned in respect of a relevant offence[8].

The second condition is that:

(a)   the first condition is met because of a conviction, finding or caution which occurred on or after 1 September 1997[9];

(b)   the first condition is met because of a conviction or finding which occurred before that date, but the person was dealt with in respect of the offence or finding on or after that date, or has yet to be dealt with in respect of it[10]; or

(c)   the first condition is met because of a conviction or finding which occurred before 1 September 1997, but on that date the person was, in respect of the offence or finding, subject under the law of the country concerned to detention, supervision or any other equivalent disposal[11].

The third condition is that the notification period[12] in respect of the relevant offence has not expired[13].

1   The Sexual Offences Act 2003 s 97 refers to a 'chief officer of police' but the powers described in the text are exercisable by the police generally: see PARA 515 note 4.
2   As to the making of notification orders see PARA 515.
3   As to the meaning of 'United Kingdom' see PARA 4 note 3.
4   As to the meaning of 'relevant offence' see PARA 515.
5   Sexual Offences Act 2003 s 97(2)(a).
6   Sexual Offences Act 2003 s 97(2)(b). As to verdicts of not guilty by reason of insanity see CRIMINAL LAW vol 25 (2010) PARA 30.
7   Sexual Offences Act 2003 s 97(2)(c). As to references to a person being or having been found to be under a disability and to have done the act charged against him in respect of an offence see PARA 329 note 1.
8   Sexual Offences Act 2003 s 97(2)(d).
9   Sexual Offences Act 2003 s 97(3)(a).
10   Sexual Offences Act 2003 s 97(3)(b).
11   Sexual Offences Act 2003 s 97(3)(c). The reference in the text to 'any other equivalent disposal' is a reference to any disposal equivalent to those set out in s 81(3) (read with ss 81(6), 131) (see PARAS 500, 502): s 97(3)(c).
12   Ie the period set out in the Sexual Offences Act 2003 s 82, as modified by s 98(2), (3) (see PARAS 501, 515 note 11).
13   Sexual Offences Act 2003 s 97(4).

517.   Interim notification orders. Where an application for a notification order has not been determined[1], an application for an interim notification order may be made[2] either in the complaint containing the main application[3] or, if the main application has been made, by complaint to the court to which that application has been made by the person who made it[4]. The court may make an interim order if it considers it just to do so[5]. An interim order subjects the defendant to the notification requirements[6] from the date of service of the order[7], so that the initial notification requirement[8] must be complied with within three days of that date[9]. The duration of an interim order is a fixed period specified in the order[10], and it ceases to have effect, if it has not already done so, on the determination of the main application[11]. The applicant or the defendant may by complaint apply to the court which made the interim order for it to be varied, renewed or discharged[12]. A court which makes an interim notification order in respect of a young offender (that is, a person aged under 18) may make a parental direction[13]. A defendant may appeal to the Crown Court against the making of an interim notification order[14].

1 Sexual Offences Act 2003 s 100(1). As to the making of notification orders see PARA 515.
2 An application for an interim notification order may be in the form set out in the Magistrates' Courts (Notification Orders) Rules 2004, SI 2004/1052, Sch 1 (r 3(1)(b)).
3 Sexual Offences Act 2003 s 100(2)(a).
4 Sexual Offences Act 2003 s 100(2)(b).
5 Sexual Offences Act 2003 s 100(3). An interim notification order must state the name of the defendant, that the notification requirements of Pt 2 (ss 80–136ZD) apply to the defendant, and the date when the order expires: Magistrates' Courts (Notification Orders) Rules 2004, SI 2004/1052, r 3(4) (substituted by SI 2012/2018). As soon as reasonably practicable after an interim order has been made, the designated officer for the court must serve a copy of the order on the defendant: Magistrates' Courts (Notification Orders) Rules 2004, SI 2004/1052, r 3(5) (amended by SI 2005/617). Any copy of an order required to be sent to the defendant under these provisions must be either given to him in person or sent by post to his last known address and, if so given or sent, is deemed to have been received by him, unless the defendant proves that it was not received by him: Magistrates' Courts (Notification Orders) Rules 2004, SI 2004/1052, r 3(5) (as so amended).
6 As to the notification requirements see PARA 498 et seq.
7 Sexual Offences Act 2003 s 100(5)(b), (6).
8 As to the initial notification requirement see PARA 503.
9 See the Sexual Offences Act 2003 s 100(5)(b), (6); and PARA 517.
10 Sexual Offences Act 2003 s 100(4)(a).
11 Sexual Offences Act 2003 s 100(4)(b).
12 Sexual Offences Act 2003 s 100(7).
13 See the Sexual Offences Act 2003 s 89(1); and PARA 509. As to the determination of a person's age see the Children and Young Persons Act 1933 s 99; and CHILDREN AND YOUNG PERSONS vol 10 (2012) PARA 1206.
14 Sexual Offences Act 2003 s 101.

(2) NOTIFICATION REQUIREMENTS (TERRORISM OFFENCES)

(i) Application of Notification Requirements

518. Persons who may be the subject of notification requirements in respect of terrorism offences. Provision is made for the imposition of notification requirements on persons dealt with for certain offences having a terrorist connection[1]. Such requirements apply to any person who is aged 16 or over at the time of being dealt with for an applicable offence connected with terrorism[2] and who is made subject in respect of the offence to a sentence or order which triggers the notification requirements[3]. Provision is also made for the application of the notification requirements to persons dealt with outside the United Kingdom for corresponding foreign offences[4] and for the imposition of restrictions on travel outside the United Kingdom on persons subject to the notification requirements[5].

1 See the Counter-Terrorism Act 2008 Pt 4 (ss 40–61); and PARA 519 et seq. For the purposes of the Counter-Terrorism Act 2008 an offence has a terrorist connection if the offence is, or takes place in the course of, an act of terrorism, or is committed for the purposes of terrorism: s 93. As to the meaning of 'terrorism' see the Terrorism Act 2000 s 1; and CRIMINAL LAW vol 25 (2010) PARA 372 (definition applied by the Counter-Terrorism Act 2008 s 92). The imposition of notification requirements in these circumstances is not a disproportionate interference with the right to respect for private and family life under the Convention for the Protection of Human Rights and Fundamental Freedoms (Rome, 4 November 1950; TS 71 (1953); Cmd 8969) art 8

(see **RIGHTS AND FREEDOMS** vol 88A (2013) PARAS 317–367): see *R (on the application of Irfan) v Secretary of State for the Home Department* [2012] EWCA Civ 1471, [2013] QB 885, [2013[2 WLR 1840.

2 Counter-Terrorism Act 2008 s 44(a). As to the applicable offences for these purposes (ie the offences to which Pt 4 applies) see ss 41–43; and PARA 519 (s 40(1)(a)). As to when a person is being 'dealt with' for an offence, and as to the time at which a person is dealt with for an offence, see PARA 519 notes 1, 2. For the purposes of s 44(a) a person is treated as dealt with at the time of the original decision (see PARA 519 note 2) and any subsequent variation of the decision is disregarded: s 61(4)(b). As to the meaning of 'variation' see PARA 527 note 3. As to the determination of a person's age see the Children and Young Persons Act 1933 s 99; and **CHILDREN AND YOUNG PERSONS** vol 10 (2012) PARA 1206.

3 Counter-Terrorism Act 2008 s 44(b). As to the sentences and orders which trigger the notification requirements see ss 44–46; and PARA 520 (s 40(1)(b)): see also Sch 6 (corresponding service offences). As to the notification requirements themselves see ss 47–53; and PARA 521 et seq (s 40(1)(c), (d)).

4 See the Counter-Terrorism Act 2008 ss 40(2)(a), 57, Sch 4; and PARAS 528, 529.

5 See the Counter-Terrorism Act 2008 ss 40(2)(b), 58, Sch 5; and PARA 530.

519. Terrorism offences to which notification applies. The notification requirements in respect of persons dealt with for terrorism offences[1] may be imposed[2] on persons dealt with for:

(1) offences relating to proscribed organisations[3];
(2) offences relating to terrorist property[4];
(3) the failure to disclose information about acts of terrorism[5];
(4) weapons training[6];
(5) directing terrorism, possessing things and collecting information for the purposes of terrorism and inciting terrorism outside the United Kingdom[7];
(6) the use of noxious substances or things[8];
(7) encouragement of terrorism[9];
(8) preparation and training for terrorism[10];
(9) offences relating to radioactive devices and material and nuclear facilities[11];
(10) an offence in respect of which there is[12] extra-territorial jurisdiction[13];
(11) any ancillary offence in relation to the offences listed above[14];
(12) service offences as respects which the corresponding civil offence is any of the offences listed above[15]; and
(13) an offence as to which a court has determined[16] that the offence has a terrorist connection[17].

The notification requirements may be imposed[18] on a person dealt with for an applicable offence at any time[19].

1 As to the meaning of 'terrorism' see PARA 518 note 1. For the purposes of the notification requirements (ie for the purposes of the Counter-Terrorism Act 2008 Pt 4 (ss 40–61)) references to a person being dealt with for or in respect of an offence are to their being sentenced or made subject to a hospital order (or, in relation to foreign proceedings and cases where the notification requirements apply because a notification order (see PARAS 528–529) has been made, being made subject by the foreign court to a sentence or order within Sch 4 para 3(2)(a) or (b)), in respect of the offence; and references to an offence being dealt with are to a person being dealt with in respect of the offence: s 61(1), Sch 4 para 8(a). 'Hospital order' means a hospital order within the meaning of the Mental Health Act 1983 (see PARA 472) or corresponding Scottish or Northern Ireland provisions: Counter-Terrorism Act 2008 s 60.

2 Ie the Counter-Terrorism Act 2008 Pt 4 applies in respect of such persons: s 41(1). The Secretary of State may by order amend s 41(1): s 41(3). An order adding an offence applies only in relation to offences dealt with after the order comes into force (s 41(5)); and an order removing an offence has effect in relation to offences whenever dealt with, whether before or after the order comes into force (s 41(6)). At the date at which this volume states the law no such order had been made. As to when a person is being 'dealt with' for an offence see note 1; references in

Pt 4 to the time at which a person is dealt with for an offence are to the time at which they are first dealt with by a magistrates' court or the Crown Court (or, in relation to foreign proceedings and cases where the notification requirements apply because a notification order (see PARAS 528–529) has been made, by the foreign court of first instance): s 61(2)(a), Sch 4 para 8(b). This is subject to s 61(3)–(7); and is referred to as the 'original decision': s 61(2). For the purposes of s 41(5) a person is treated as dealt with at the time of the original decision and any subsequent variation of the decision is disregarded: s 61(4)(a). As to the meaning of 'variation' see PARA 527 note 3.

Where an offence is removed from the list, a person subject to the notification requirements by reason of that offence being listed (and who is not otherwise subject to those requirements) ceases to be subject to them when the order comes into force: s 41(7).

3   Ie an offence under the Terrorism Act 2000 s 11 or s 12 (see CRIMINAL LAW vol 25 (2010) PARAS 376, 377): Counter-Terrorism Act 2008 s 41(1)(a).

4   Ie an offence under the Terrorism Act 2000 ss 15–18 (see CRIMINAL LAW vol 25 (2010) PARAS 379–382): Counter-Terrorism Act 2008 s 41(1)(a).

5   Ie an offence under the Terrorism Act 2000 s 38B (see CRIMINAL LAW vol 25 (2010) PARA 396): Counter-Terrorism Act 2008 s 41(1)(a).

6   Ie an offence under the Terrorism Act 2000 s 54 (see CRIMINAL LAW vol 25 (2010) PARA 401): Counter-Terrorism Act 2008 s 41(1)(a).

7   Ie an offence under the Terrorism Act 2000 ss 56–61 (see CRIMINAL LAW vol 25 (2010) PARAS 403, 404, 409, 410, 415): Counter-Terrorism Act 2008 s 41(1)(a).

8   Ie an offence under the Anti-terrorism, Crime and Security Act 2001 s 113 (see CRIMINAL LAW vol 25 (2010) PARA 134): Counter-Terrorism Act 2008 s 41(1)(c).

9   Ie an offence under the Terrorism Act 2006 ss 1, 2 (see CRIMINAL LAW vol 25 (2010) PARAS 411, 412): Counter-Terrorism Act 2008 s 41(1)(d).

10 Ie an offence under the Terrorism Act 2006 ss 5, 6, 8 (see CRIMINAL LAW vol 25 (2010) PARAS 401, 402, 405): Counter-Terrorism Act 2008 s 41(1)(d).

11 Ie an offence under the Terrorism Act 2006 ss 9, 10, 11 (see CRIMINAL LAW vol 25 (2010) PARAS 406–408): Counter-Terrorism Act 2008 s 41(1)(d).

12 Ie, in respect of certain offences committed outside the United Kingdom for the purposes of terrorism, by virtue of any of the Terrorism Act 2000 ss 62–63D (see CRIMINAL LAW vol 25 (2010) PARAS 419–425) or the Terrorism Act 2006 s 17 (see CRIMINAL LAW vol 25 (2010) PARA 422). As to the meaning of 'United Kingdom' see PARA 4 note 3.

13 Counter-Terrorism Act 2008 s 41(1)(b), (e).

14 Counter-Terrorism Act 2008 s 41(2). In the Counter-Terrorism Act 2008 'ancillary offence', in relation to an offence, means any of:

(1)   aiding, abetting, counselling or procuring the commission of the offence (s 94(1)(a));

(2)   an offence under the Serious Crime Act 2007 Pt 2 (ss 44–67) (encouraging or assisting crime: see CRIMINAL LAW vol 25 (2010) PARAS 65–72) (including, in relation to times before 1 October 2008 (ie the date on which Pt 2 was brought into force by the Serious Crime Act 2007 (Commencement No 3) Order 2008, SI 2008/2504), an offence of incitement under the law of England and Wales or Northern Ireland) in relation to the offence (Counter-Terrorism Act 2008 s 94(1)(b), (2)); and

(3)   attempting or conspiring to commit the offence (s 94(1)(c)).

15 See the Counter-Terrorism Act 2008 Sch 6 para 1, which provides that Pt 4 applies to a service offence as respects which the corresponding civil offence is an offence within s 41(1) or (2) (see the text and notes 1–14). 'Service offence' means an offence under the Armed Forces Act 2006 s 42 (see ARMED FORCES vol 3 (2011) PARA 587) or under the Army Act 1955 s 70, the Air Force Act 1955 s 70, or the Naval Discipline Act 1957 s 42 (all repealed): Counter-Terrorism Act 2008 s 95(3). The 'corresponding civil offence', in relation to an offence under the Armed Forces Act 2006 s 42, is the corresponding offence under the law of England and Wales within the meaning of s 42; in relation to an offence under the Army Act 1955 s 70 or the Air Force Act 1955 s 70, is the corresponding civil offence within the meaning of either the Army Act 1955 or the Air Force Act 1955 (repealed); and in relation to an offence under the Naval Discipline Act 1957 s 42 (repealed), is the corresponding civil offence within the meaning of s 42: Counter-Terrorism Act 2008 s 95(4).

16 Ie under the Counter-Terrorism Act 2008 s 30 (sentences for offences with a terrorist connection: see PARA 590).

17 Counter-Terrorism Act 2008 s 42(1)(a). As to when an offence has a terrorist connection see PARA 518 note 1. Part 4 also applies to a service offence as to which the service court dealing with the offence has determined in accordance with s 32 (see PARA 590) that the offence has a terrorist connection: Sch 6 para 2(1). In the Counter-Terrorism Act 2008 'service court' means the Court Martial, the Service Civilian Court or the Court Martial Appeal Court: s 95(1). As to

the establishment and procedure of the Court Martial see ARMED FORCES vol 3 (2011) PARAS 633–655; as to the establishment and procedure of the Service Civilian Court see ARMED FORCES vol 3 (2011) PARAS 681–688; as to the Court Martial Appeal Court and the Supreme Court on an appeal brought from the Court Martial Appeal Court see ARMED FORCES vol 3 (2011) PARAS 656–680.

A person to whom the notification requirements apply by virtue of such a determination as is mentioned in s 42(1)(a) or Sch 6 para 2(1) may appeal against it to the same court, and subject to the same conditions, as an appeal against sentence (s 42(2), Sch 6 para 2(2)) and if the determination is set aside on appeal, the notification requirements are treated as never having applied to that person in respect of the offence (s 42(3), Sch 6 para 2(3)). Where an order is made under s 33 removing an offence from the list in Sch 2 (see PARA 590) a person subject to the notification requirements by reason of that offence being so listed (and who is not otherwise subject to those requirements) ceases to be subject to them when the order comes into force: s 42(4).

18 Ie the Counter-Terrorism Act 2008 Pt 4 applies in respect of such persons: s 43(1).

19 See the Counter-Terrorism Act 2008 s 43(1), which provides that Pt 4 applies to a person dealt with for an offence or a service offence before 1 October 2009 (ie the date on which Pt 4 was brought into force by the Counter-Terrorism Act 2008 (Commencement No 4) Order 2009, SI 2009/1493) only if the offence (or the corresponding civil offence) is on that date within the Counter-Terrorism Act 2008 s 41(1) or s 41(2) (see the text and notes 1–14) (s 43(1)(a), Sch 6 paras 3(1)(a), 12(a)) and immediately before that date the person:

    (1)   is imprisoned or detained in pursuance of the sentence passed or order made in respect of the offence (s 43(1)(b)(i), Sch 6 para 3(1)(b)(i));

    (2)   would be so imprisoned or detained but for being unlawfully at large, absent without leave, on temporary leave or leave of absence, or on bail pending an appeal (s 43(1)(b)(ii), Sch 6 para 3(1)(b)(ii)); or

    (3)   is on licence, having served the custodial part of a sentence of imprisonment in respect of the offence (s 43(1)(b)(iii), Sch 6 para 3(1)(b)(iii)).

In relation to a person dealt with for an offence before 1 October 2009:

    (a)   any reference in Pt 4 to a sentence, order or finding under a specified statutory provision includes a sentence or order under any corresponding earlier statutory provision (s 43(2)(a), Sch 6 para 3(2));

    (b)   any reference in Pt 4 to a person being or having been found to be under a disability and to have done the act charged against them in respect of an offence includes a reference to their being or having been found unfit to be tried for the offence (s 43(2)(b)(i)), insane so that their trial for the offence cannot or could not proceed (s 43(2)(b)(ii)) or unfit to be tried and to have done the act charged against them in respect of the offence (s 43(2)(b)(iii)).

For the purposes of s 43(1), (2), Sch 6 para 3(1), (2), a person is dealt with for an offence before 1 October 2009 if the time of the original decision (see note 2) falls before the that date: s 61(5)(a). Where in such a case s 61(3) (see PARA 527) applies for the purposes of any provision of Pt 4, s 61(3) has effect as if the provisions of Pt 4 had been in force at all material times: s 61(5).

520. Sentences and orders triggering notification requirements.

The notification requirements[1] apply to a person who in England and Wales[2]:

    (1)   has been convicted of an applicable terrorism offence[3] and sentenced in respect of the offence to:

        (a)   imprisonment or custody for life[4];

        (b)   imprisonment or detention in a young offender institution for a term of 12 months or more[5];

        (c)   imprisonment or detention in a young offender institution for public protection[6];

        (d)   detention for life or for a period of 12 months or more[7];

        (e)   a detention and training order for a term of 12 months or more[8];

        (f)   detention for public protection[9];

        (g)   an extended sentence of detention[10]; or

        (h)   detention during Her Majesty's pleasure[11]; or

    (2)   has been:

(a) convicted of an applicable terrorism offence carrying a maximum term of imprisonment of 12 months or more[12];

(b) found not guilty by reason of insanity of such an offence[13]; or

(c) found to be under a disability and to have done the act charged against them in respect of such an offence[14],

and made subject in respect of the offence to a hospital order[15].

These provisions apply in a modified form to persons being dealt with for service offences[16].

1 As to the persons who may be the subject of notification requirements in respect of terrorism offences see PARAS 518, 519; as to the notification requirements themselves see PARA 521 et seq.

2 Corresponding provision is made in respect of Scotland and Northern Ireland: see the Counter-Terrorism Act 2008 s 45(2), (3).

3 Ie an offence to which the Counter-Terrorism Act 2008 Pt 4 (ss 40–61) applies in respect of such persons (see PARA 519): s 45(1)(a). The Secretary of State may by order amend the provisions of s 45 referring to a specified term or period of imprisonment or detention: s 46(1). An order reducing a specified term or period has effect only in relation to persons dealt with after the order comes into force (s 46(2)); where an order increases a specified term or period it has effect in relation to persons dealt with at any time, whether before or after the order comes into force and a person who would not have been subject to the notification requirements if the order had been in force when the offence was dealt with (and who is not otherwise subject to those requirements) ceases to be subject to the requirements when the order comes into force (s 46(3)). As to when a person is being 'dealt with' for an offence, and as to the time at which a person is dealt with for an offence, see PARA 519 notes 1, 2. For the purposes of s 46(2) a person is treated as dealt with at the time of the original decision (see PARA 519 note 2) and any subsequent variation of the decision is disregarded: s 61(4)(c). As to the meaning of 'variation' see PARA 527 note 3.

4 Counter-Terrorism Act 2008 s 45(1)(a)(i). As to custody for life see PARAS 36, 37.

5 Counter-Terrorism Act 2008 s 45(1)(a)(ii). As to detention in a young offender institution see PARA 16 et seq.

6 Counter-Terrorism Act 2008 s 45(1)(a)(iii). As to such imprisonment or detention see the Criminal Justice Act 2003 s 225; and PARA 37.

7 Counter-Terrorism Act 2008 s 45(1)(a)(iv). As to such detention see the Powers of Criminal Courts (Sentencing) Act 2000 s 91 (offenders under 18 convicted of certain serious offences); and PARA 8.

8 Counter-Terrorism Act 2008 s 45(1)(a)(v). As to such detention see the Powers of Criminal Courts (Sentencing) Act 2000 s 100 (offenders under 18); and PARA 9.

9 Counter-Terrorism Act 2008 s 45(1)(a)(vi). As to such detention see the Criminal Justice Act 2003 s 226 (serious offences committed by persons under 18); and PARA 34.

10 Counter-Terrorism Act 2008 s 45(1)(a)(via) (added by the Legal Aid, Sentencing and Punishment of Offenders Act 2012 Sch 21 para 33). As to such detention see the Criminal Justice Act 2003 s 226B (extended sentences for persons under 18); and PARAS 18–20.

11 Counter-Terrorism Act 2008 s 45(1)(a)(vii). As to detention during Her Majesty's pleasure see PARA 38.

12 Counter-Terrorism Act 2008 s 45(1)(b)(i). References to an offence carrying a maximum term of imprisonment of 12 months or more are to an offence carrying such a maximum term in the case of a person who has attained the age of 21 (as from the day to be appointed for the coming into force of the Criminal Justice and Court Services Act 2000 s 61 (see PARA 16), 18 in relation to England and Wales) (Counter-Terrorism Act 2008 s 45(4)(a), (5)) and include an offence carrying in the case of such a person a maximum term of life imprisonment and an offence for which in the case of such a person the sentence is fixed by law as life imprisonment (s 45(4)(b)). As to the determination of a person's age see the Children and Young Persons Act 1933 s 99; and CHILDREN AND YOUNG PERSONS vol 10 (2012) PARA 1206.

13 Counter-Terrorism Act 2008 s 45(1)(b)(ii). As to verdicts of not guilty by reason of insanity see CRIMINAL LAW vol 25 (2010) PARA 30.

14 Counter-Terrorism Act 2008 s 45(1)(b)(iii). As to such findings see the Criminal Procedure (Insanity) Act 1964 ss 4, 4A; and see CRIMINAL PROCEDURE vol 27 (2015) PARA 357.

15 Counter-Terrorism Act 2008 s 45(1)(b). As to the meaning of 'hospital order' see PARA 519 note 1.

16 See the Counter-Terrorism Act 2008 Sch 6 paras 4–6, 12(b), 13 (Sch 6 para 5 amended by the Legal Aid, Sentencing and Punishment of Offenders Act 2012 Sch 22 para 38); and see in

particular the Counter-Terrorism Act 2008 Sch 6 para 11, which provides that references in Pt 4 to a sentence of detention do not include a sentence of service detention (as defined by the Armed Forces Act 2006 s 374: see ARMED FORCES vol 3 (2011) PARA 349) or a corresponding sentence passed under (or by virtue of) the Army Act 1955, the Air Force Act 1955 or the Naval Discipline Act 1957 (all repealed). As to the meaning of 'service offence' see PARA 520 note 15.

(ii) Notification Requirements

521. Initial notification and annual renotification under the notification requirements. A person to whom the notification requirements apply[1] must[2] notify to the police[3]:

(1) date of birth[4];

(2) national insurance number[5];

(3) name on the date on which the person was dealt with in respect of the offence (where the person used one or more other names on that date, each of those names)[6];

(4) home address on that date[7];

(5) name on the date on which notification is made (where the person uses one or more other names on that date, each of those names)[8];

(6) home address on the date on which notification is made[9];

(7) address of any other premises in the United Kingdom at which, at the time the notification is made, the person regularly resides or stays[10]; and

(8) any other information prescribed by regulations made by the Secretary of State[11].

This information must, subject to any intervening statutory notifications, be re-notified to the police annually[12] unless the person in question is in custody, imprisoned or detained[13], in which event he must notify the police of this information on his release[14]. Any period of absence from the United Kingdom does not in general affect the requirement for initial notification, although it may affect the requirement for periodic re-notification[15].

Failure without reasonable excuse to comply, or the notification of information known to be false in purported compliance, with these requirements is an offence[16].

1 Ie a person to whom the notification requirements in the Counter-Terrorism Act 2008 Pt 4 (ss 40–61) (see PARAS 518, 519) apply. As to the persons who may be the subject of notification requirements in respect of terrorism offences see PARAS 518–520. These provisions (ie s 47: see the text and notes 2–11) do not apply to a person who is subject to the notification requirements in respect of another offence (and does not cease to be so subject before the end of the period within which notification is to be made) (s 47(5)(a)) and has complied with s 47 in respect of that offence (s 47(5)(b)).

2 Ie within the period of three days beginning with the day on which the person is dealt with in respect of the offence in question: Counter-Terrorism Act 2008 s 47(1). In relation to foreign proceedings and cases where the notification requirements apply because a notification order has been made (see PARAS 528–529), this period begins with the date of service of the notification order: Sch 4 para 8(c). As to when a person is being 'dealt with' for an offence, and as to the time at which a person is dealt with for an offence, see PARA 519 notes 1, 2. In the application of these provisions to a person dealt with for an offence before 1 October 2009 (ie the date on which Pt 4 was brought into force by the Counter-Terrorism Act 2008 (Commencement No 4) Order 2009, SI 2009/1493) (that is to say, an offence where the time of the original decision (see PARA 519 note 2) falls before that date) who, immediately before that date, would be imprisoned or detained in respect of the offence but for being unlawfully at large, absent without leave, on temporary leave or leave of absence, or on bail pending an appeal (Counter-Terrorism Act 2008 ss 47(6)(a), 61(6)(a)), or is on licence, having served the custodial part of a sentence of imprisonment in respect of the offence (s 47(6)(b)), the reference in s 47(1) to the day on which the person is dealt with in respect of the offence must be read as a reference to 1 October 2009 (ss 47(6), 61(6)(b)). In determining the period within which notification is to

be made under s 47 there must be disregarded any time when the person is remanded in or committed to custody by an order of a court (s 47(4)(a)), serving a sentence of imprisonment or detention (s 47(4)(b)), detained in a hospital (s 47(4)(c)) or detained under the Immigration Acts (s 47(4)(d)). 'Detained in a hospital' means detained in a hospital under the Mental Health Act 1983 Pt III (ss 35–55) (see MENTAL HEALTH AND CAPACITY vol 75 (2013) PARA 859 et seq) (or corresponding Scottish or Northern Ireland provisions): Counter-Terrorism Act 2008 s 60. In connection with service detention see PARA 520 note 15; and as to the modified application of the Counter-Terrorism Act 2008 s 47(4), (6) in relation to service offences see Sch 6 paras 8(1)(a), 9. As to the meaning of 'service offence' see PARA 520 note 15.

3   Notification under the Counter-Terrorism Act 2008 s 47 (see the text and notes 4–11), s 48 (notification of change: see PARA 522), s 49 (periodic re-notification: see PARA 521) or s 56 (notification on return after absence from United Kingdom: see PARA 526) must be made by the person attending at a police station in the person's local police area (s 50(1), (2)(a)) and making an oral notification to a police officer or to a person authorised for the purpose by the officer in charge of the station (s 50(2)(b)). The notification must be acknowledged in writing (s 50(4)) and in such form as the Secretary of State may direct (s 50(5)). The person making the notification must, for the purpose of verifying the person's identity and if requested to do so by the police officer or person to whom the notification is made, allow the officer or person to take the person's fingerprints (s 50(6)(a)), photograph (which includes any process by means of which an image may be produced) any part of the person (ss 50(6)(b), 60) or do both these things (s 50(6)(c)). Failure without reasonable excuse to comply with s 50(6) is an offence: s 54(1)(a). As to the punishment of violations of s 50(6) see note 16.

For the purposes of s 50(2) a person's 'local police area' means:
(1)   the police area in which the person's home address is situated (s 51(1)(a));
(2)   in the absence of a home address, the police area in which the home address last notified is situated (s 51(1)(b)); or
(3)   in the absence of a home address and of any such notification, the police area in which the court of trial (or, in relation to foreign proceedings and cases where the notification requirements apply because a notification order has been made (see PARAS 528–529), the court by which the notification order was made) was situated (s 51(1)(c), Sch 4 para 8(d)).

'Home address' means, in relation to a person, the address of the person's sole or main residence in the United Kingdom or, where the person has no such residence, the address or location of a place in the United Kingdom where the person can regularly be found and, if there is more than one such place, such one of those places as the person may select: s 60. As to the meaning of 'United Kingdom' see PARA 4 note 3.

In s 51(1)(c) 'court of trial' means:
(a)   the court by or before which the conviction or finding was made by virtue of which the notification requirements apply to the person (s 51(2)(a)); or
(b)   if that conviction or finding was one substituted on an appeal or reference, the court by or before which the proceedings were taken from which the appeal or reference was brought (s 51(2)(b)).

As to the modified application of s 51(1)(c) in relation to service offences see Sch 6 para 10.

4   Counter-Terrorism Act 2008 s 47(2)(a).
5   Counter-Terrorism Act 2008 s 47(2)(b).
6   Counter-Terrorism Act 2008 s 47(2)(c).
7   Counter-Terrorism Act 2008 s 47(2)(d).
8   Counter-Terrorism Act 2008 s 47(2)(e).
9   Counter-Terrorism Act 2008 s 47(2)(f).
10   Counter-Terrorism Act 2008 s 47(2)(g).
11   Counter-Terrorism Act 2008 s 47(2)(h), (3). At the date at which this volume states the law no regulations had been made for these purposes.
12   See the Counter-Terrorism Act 2008 s 49(1), which requires a person to whom the notification requirements apply to re-notify to the police the information mentioned in s 47(2) (see the text and notes 4–11) within the period of one year after last notifying or re-notifying the information to the police in accordance with s 47 or s 49, one year after last notifying changes in accordance with s 48 (see PARA 522) or one year after last notifying information to the police on the person's return to the United Kingdom in accordance with s 56 (see PARA 526).
13   Ie unless the one-year period referred to in s 49(1) (see the text and note 12) ends at a time when the person is remanded in or committed to custody by an order of a court (s 49(2)(a)), serving a sentence of imprisonment or detention (s 49(2)(b)), detained in a hospital (s 49(2)(c)) or detained under the Immigration Acts (s 49(2)(d)). As to the modified application of s 49(2) in relation to service offences see Sch 6 para 8(1)(c).

14 Counter-Terrorism Act 2008 ss 48(4), 49(3). Any such notification must be accompanied by re-notification of the other information mentioned in s 47(2): s 48(10). 'Release' from imprisonment or detention includes release on licence but not temporary release: s 60. As to the modified application of s 48(4) in relation to service offences see Sch 6 para 8(1)(b).

15 If a person to whom the notification requirements apply is absent from the United Kingdom for any period the period of absence does not affect the obligation under the Counter-Terrorism Act 2008 s 47 (s 55(1), (3)) unless the period of absence begins before the end of the period within which notification must be made under s 47 and the person's absence results from his removal from the United Kingdom, in which case s 47 does not apply (s 55(4)). If a person to whom the notification requirements apply is absent from the United Kingdom for any period s 49 does not apply if the period referred to in s 49(1) (see the text and note 12) ends during the period of absence: s 55(7).

> References in ss 55, 56 to a person's removal from the United Kingdom include:
>
> (1) the person's removal from the United Kingdom in accordance with the Immigration Acts (s 55(9)(a));
> (2) the person's extradition from the United Kingdom (s 55(9)(b)); or
> (3) the person's transfer from the United Kingdom to another country (which includes a territory) pursuant to a warrant under the Repatriation of Prisoners Act 1984 s 1 (Counter-Terrorism Act 2008 ss 55(9)(c), 60).

16 Counter-Terrorism Act 2008 s 54(1)(a), (b). A person guilty of an offence under s 58 is liable on conviction on indictment to imprisonment for a term not exceeding five years or a fine or both or on summary conviction to imprisonment for a term not exceeding 12 months (or, in relation to an offence committed before the commencement of the Criminal Justice Act 2003 s 154(1), six months) or a fine not exceeding the statutory maximum or both: Counter-Terrorism Act 2008 s 54(2), (3). As to the standard scale, the statutory maximum, the prescribed sum, and magistrates' powers to levy unlimited fines see PARA 176.

> A person who fails without reasonable excuse to comply with s 47, s 48, s 49, regulations under s 52(1), or s 56 commits the offence under s 54(1)(a) on the day on which he first fails without reasonable excuse to comply with the provision in question and continues to commit it throughout any period during which the failure continues (although a person must not be prosecuted under s 54(1) more than once in respect of the same failure): s 54(4).

> Proceedings for an offence under s 54 may be commenced in any court having jurisdiction in any place where the person charged with the offence resides or is found: s 54(5).

522. Notification of changes. A person to whom the notification requirements apply[1] must notify the police[2]:

(1) of any name he uses that has not previously been notified to the police[3];

(2) if there is a change of his home address, of the new home address[4];

(3) if he resides or stays for specified minimum periods[5] at premises in the United Kingdom[6] the address of which has previously not been notified to the police, of the address of those premises[7];

(4) if he is released from custody, imprisonment or detention[8]; and

(5) if he is required to notify prescribed information[9], of the prescribed[10] details of any prescribed changes in that information[11].

Notification of changes under these provisions affects the annual re-notification schedule[12], and the requirement to notify changes is itself affected by periods of absence from the United Kingdom[13]. Failure without reasonable excuse to comply, or the notification of information known to be false in purported compliance, with these requirements is an offence[14].

1 Ie a person to whom the notification requirements in the Counter-Terrorism Act 2008 Pt 4 (ss 40–61) (see PARA 518 et seq) apply.

2 Ie before the end of the period of three days beginning with the day on which the event in question occurs: Counter-Terrorism Act 2008 s 48(7) (note, however, s 48(3), and the text and note 5). In determining the period within which notification is to be made under s 48 there must be disregarded any time when the person is remanded in or committed to custody by an order of a court (s 48(8)(a)), serving a sentence of imprisonment or detention (s 48(8)(b)), detained in a hospital (s 48(8)(c)) or detained under the Immigration Acts (s 48(8)(d)). As to the meaning of 'detained in a hospital' see PARA 521 note 2.

As to the means of notification see PARA 521 note 3 (noting s 50(3); and note 7). Notification under s 48 must be accompanied by re-notification of the other information mentioned in s 47(2) (see PARA 521): s 48(10). In connection with service detention see PARA 520 note 15; and as to the modified application of s 48(8) in relation to service offences see Sch 6 para 8(1)(b). As to the meaning of 'service offence' see PARA 520 note 15.

3   Counter-Terrorism Act 2008 s 48(1). References in s 48 to previous notifications are to previous notifications by the person under s 47 (initial notification: see PARA 521), s 48, s 49 (periodic re-notification: see PARA 521) or s 56 (notification on return after absence from United Kingdom: see PARA 526): s 48(9).

4   Counter-Terrorism Act 2008 s 48(2). As to the meaning of 'home address' see PARA 521 note 3.

5   Ie for a period of seven days (Counter-Terrorism Act 2008 s 48(3)(a)) or for two or more periods, in any period of 12 months, that taken together amount to seven days (s 48(3)(b)). Where s 48(3) applies the end of the period of three days beginning with the day on which the event in question occurs for the purposes of s 48(7) (see note 2) is the day with which the period referred to in s 48(3)(a) or s 48(3)(b) (as the case may be) ends: s 48(7).

6   As to the meaning of 'United Kingdom' see PARA 4 note 3.

7   Counter-Terrorism Act 2008 s 48(3). A person making a notification under s 48 in relation to premises referred to in s 48(3) may make the notification at a police station that would be a police station in his local police area for the purposes of s 50(2)(a) (see PARA 521 note 3) if the address of those premises were the person's home address: s 50(3).

8   Counter-Terrorism Act 2008 s 48(4). As to the meaning of 'release' see PARA 521 note 14. The notification requirements arise under this provision if a person is released from custody pursuant to an order of a court (s 48(4)(a)), from imprisonment or detention pursuant to a sentence of a court (s 48(4)(b)), from detention in a hospital (s 48(4)(c)) or from detention under the Immigration Acts (s 48(4)(d)); however s 48(4) does not apply if the person is at the same time required to notify the police under s 47 (s 48(4)). As to the meaning of 'detained in a hospital' see PARA 521 note 2. As to the modified application of the Counter-Terrorism Act 2008 s 48(4) in relation to service offences see Sch 6 para 8(2).

9   Ie information within the Counter-Terrorism Act 2008 s 47(2)(h): see PARA 521.

10   Ie prescribed by regulations made by the Secretary of State: Counter-Terrorism Act 2008 s 48(6). At the date at which this volume states the law no regulations had been made for these purposes.

11   Counter-Terrorism Act 2008 s 48(5).

12   See the Counter-Terrorism Act 2008 s 49; and PARA 521.

13   If a person to whom the notification requirements apply is absent from the United Kingdom for any period s 48 applies in relation to an event that occurs before the period of absence (subject to the proviso that this does not apply in relation to an event that occurs before the period of absence if the period of absence begins before the end of the period within which notification must be made under s 48 and the person's absence results from the person's removal from the United Kingdom), but s 48 does not apply in relation to an event that occurs during the period of absence: s 55(1), (5), (6). As to references to removal from the United Kingdom see PARA 521 note 15.

14   Counter-Terrorism Act 2008 s 54(1)(a), (b). As to the punishment of violations of s 48 see PARA 521 note 16.

523.   Foreign travel: notification of departure. If a person to whom the notification requirements apply[1] intends to leave the United Kingdom[2] for a period of three days or more[3] he must notify to the police:

(1)   the date on which he intends to leave the United Kingdom[4];

(2)   the country (or, if there is more than one, the first country) to which he will travel[5];

(3)   his point of arrival[6] in that country[7];

(4)   where he intends to travel to more than one country outside the United Kingdom, his point of arrival[8] in each such country[9];

(5)   the name of the carrier the person intends to use to leave the United Kingdom and to return to the United Kingdom[10];

(6)   the name of any carrier the person intends to use to travel between countries while outside the United Kingdom[11];

(7)   the address or other place at which the person intends to stay for their first night outside the United Kingdom[12];

(8)   where the person intends to return to the United Kingdom on a particular date, that date[13]; and

(9)   where the person intends to return to the United Kingdom at a particular point of arrival, that point of arrival[14].

Where a person knows any of the required information more than seven days before the date of his intended departure, he must notify such of the required information as he holds not less than seven days before that date[15] or, if he has a reasonable excuse for not complying with the seven day notification requirement, as soon as practicable but in any event not less than twenty-four hours before that date[16]. Where a person has so notified the police[17] but the information so notified does not contain all the required information[18] or at any time prior to his intended departure, the information so notified becomes inaccurate[19], he must notify to the police the remaining required information or the changes to the required information as the case may be prior to departure[20]: similarly, where a person does not know any of the required information more than seven days before the date of his intended departure, he must notify the required information to the police[21] prior to departure[22].

Failure without reasonable excuse to comply, or the notification of information known to be false in purported compliance, with these requirements is an offence[23].

1   Ie a person to whom the notification requirements in the Counter-Terrorism Act 2008 Pt 4 (ss 40–61) (see PARA 518 et seq) apply.

2   As to the meaning of 'United Kingdom' see PARA 4 note 3.

3   Counter-Terrorism Act 2008 s 52(1); Counter-Terrorism Act 2008 (Foreign Travel Notification Requirements) Regulations 2009, SI 2009/2493, reg 3(1). Notification under the Counter-Terrorism Act 2008 s 52 must be given in accordance with the regulations: Counter-Terrorism Act 2008 s 52(4).

4   Counter-Terrorism Act 2008 s 52(2)(a); Counter-Terrorism Act 2008 (Foreign Travel Notification Requirements) Regulations 2009, SI 2009/2493, reg 3(2), (3)(a).

5   Counter-Terrorism Act 2008 s 52(2)(b).

6   Where a person will arrive in a country by rail, sea or air, the point of arrival is the station, port or airport at which the person will first disembark (Counter-Terrorism Act 2008 s 52(2)(c); Counter-Terrorism Act 2008 (Foreign Travel Notification Requirements) Regulations 2009, SI 2009/2493, reg 2(1), (2)); and where a person will arrive in a country by any other means, the point of arrival is the place at which the person will first enter the country (reg 2(3)).

7   Counter-Terrorism Act 2008 s 52(2)(c).

8   Ie other than the point of arrival specified in the Counter-Terrorism Act 2008 s 52(2)(c) (see the text and notes 6–7).

9   Counter-Terrorism Act 2008 s 52(2)(d); Counter-Terrorism Act 2008 (Foreign Travel Notification Requirements) Regulations 2009, SI 2009/2493, reg 3(3)(b)(i). The information required to be notified pursuant to reg 3(3)(b)(i)–(vi) (see the text and notes 10–14) is required to be notified only insomuch as that information is held by the person in question: reg 3(3)(b).

10   Counter-Terrorism Act 2008 (Foreign Travel Notification Requirements) Regulations 2009, SI 2009/2493, reg 3(3)(b)(ii). As to the extent of notification under this requirement see note 9.

11   Counter-Terrorism Act 2008 (Foreign Travel Notification Requirements) Regulations 2009, SI 2009/2493, reg 3(3)(b)(iii). As to the extent of notification under this requirement see note 9.

12   Counter-Terrorism Act 2008 (Foreign Travel Notification Requirements) Regulations 2009, SI 2009/2493, reg 3(3)(b)(iv). As to the extent of notification under this requirement see note 9.

13   Counter-Terrorism Act 2008 (Foreign Travel Notification Requirements) Regulations 2009, SI 2009/2493, reg 3(3)(b)(v). As to the extent of notification under this requirement see note 9.

14   Counter-Terrorism Act 2008 (Foreign Travel Notification Requirements) Regulations 2009, SI 2009/2493, reg 3(3)(b)(vi). As to the extent of notification under this requirement see note 9.

15   Counter-Terrorism Act 2008 (Foreign Travel Notification Requirements) Regulations 2009, SI 2009/2493, reg 4(1)(a). This is referred to as the 'seven day notification requirement': reg 4(1)(a). Notification in accordance with reg 4(1)–(3) or reg 5(2) (see PARA 524) must be made by the person attending at a police station (which in the case of notifications under reg 4(1) or reg 5(2) must be in the person's local police area) (reg 6(1)(a), (2)(a)) and making an

oral notification to a police officer or to a person authorised for the purpose by the officer in charge of the station (reg 6(1)(b), (2)(b)). The person making a notification must inform the police officer or person to whom the notification is made of his name, home address and date of birth: reg 6(3).

16 Counter-Terrorism Act 2008 (Foreign Travel Notification Requirements) Regulations 2009, SI 2009/2493, reg 4(1)(b). As to the means of notification see note 15.

17 Ie in accordance with the Counter-Terrorism Act 2008 (Foreign Travel Notification Requirements) Regulations 2009, SI 2009/2493, reg 4(1) (see the text and notes 15–16).

18 Counter-Terrorism Act 2008 (Foreign Travel Notification Requirements) Regulations 2009, SI 2009/2493, reg 4(2)(a). As to the means of notification see note 15. A person making a notification in accordance with reg 4(2) must also inform the police officer or person to whom the notification is made of the police station at which the person made a notification in accordance with reg 4(1) in respect of the intended departure: reg 6(4).

19 Counter-Terrorism Act 2008 (Foreign Travel Notification Requirements) Regulations 2009, SI 2009/2493, reg 4(2)(b). As to the means of notification see note 15.

20 Ie in accordance with the rule in the Counter-Terrorism Act 2008 (Foreign Travel Notification Requirements) Regulations 2009, SI 2009/2493, reg 4(4), which requires the person to make the relevant notification under reg 4(2) or reg 4(3) (as the case may be) not less than twenty-four hours before the date of his intended departure (the 'twenty-four hour notification requirement') (reg 4(4)(a)) or, if he has a reasonable excuse for not complying with the twenty-four hour notification requirement, as soon as practicable but in any event before the person's departure from the United Kingdom (reg 4(4)(b)).

21 See note 20.

22 Counter-Terrorism Act 2008 (Foreign Travel Notification Requirements) Regulations 2009, SI 2009/2493, reg 4(3). As to the means of notification see note 15.

23 Counter-Terrorism Act 2008 s 54(1)(a), (b). As to the punishment of violations of these provisions see PARA 521 note 16.

524. Foreign travel: notification of return. If a person to whom the notification requirements apply[1] returns to the United Kingdom[2] after leaving the United Kingdom for a period of three days or more[3] he must notify to the police[4], within the period of three days beginning with the day on which he returns to the United Kingdom, the date of his return[5] and his point of arrival in the United Kingdom[6]. This requirement does not, however, apply if the person has previously given notification[7] of his date and point of arrival[8] and his return to the United Kingdom was on that date and at that point of arrival[9].

Failure without reasonable excuse to comply, or the notification of information known to be false in purported compliance, with these requirements is an offence[10].

1 Ie a person to whom the notification requirements in the Counter-Terrorism Act 2008 Pt 4 (ss 40–61) (see PARA 518 et seq) apply.

2 As to the meaning of 'United Kingdom' see PARA 4 note 3.

3 Counter-Terrorism Act 2008 (Foreign Travel Notification Requirements) Regulations 2009, SI 2009/2493, reg 5(1). These regulations are made under the Counter-Terrorism Act 2008 s 52: see PARA 523 note 3.

4 As to the means of notification see PARA 523 note 15.

5 Counter-Terrorism Act 2008 s 52(3); Counter-Terrorism Act 2008 (Foreign Travel Notification Requirements) Regulations 2009, SI 2009/2493, reg 5(2), (3)(a).

6 Counter-Terrorism Act 2008 (Foreign Travel Notification Requirements) Regulations 2009, SI 2009/2493, reg 5(3)(b).

7 Ie in accordance with the Counter-Terrorism Act 2008 (Foreign Travel Notification Requirements) Regulations 2009, SI 2009/2493, reg 4 (see PARA 523).

8 Ie as specified in the Counter-Terrorism Act 2008 (Foreign Travel Notification Requirements) Regulations 2009, SI 2009/2493, reg 3(3)(b)(v), (vi) (see PARA 523).

9 Counter-Terrorism Act 2008 (Foreign Travel Notification Requirements) Regulations 2009, SI 2009/2493, reg 5(4).

10 Counter-Terrorism Act 2008 s 54(1)(a), (b). As to the punishment of violations of these provisions see PARA 521 note 16.

525. Period for which notification requirements apply. The period for which the notification requirements[1] apply depends on the age of the person at the time of his conviction and the sentence he receives in respect of his offence[2]. If a person is aged under 18 at the time of conviction for the offence the period for which the notification requirements apply is ten years, whatever his sentence[3]. If he is aged 18 or over at the time of conviction and receives in respect of the offence a sentence of imprisonment or detention in a young offender institution for a term of five years or more but less than ten years, the period for which the notification requirements apply is 15 years[4]. Finally, the period for which the notification requirements apply is 30 years if the offender is aged 18 or over at the time of conviction and receives in respect of the offence a sentence of:

(1) imprisonment or custody for life[5];

(2) imprisonment or detention in a young offender institution for a term of ten years or more[6];

(3) imprisonment or detention in a young offender institution for public protection[7]; or

(4) detention during Her Majesty's pleasure[8].

The period for which the notification requirements apply begins with the day on which the person is dealt with for the offence[9], and continues to run during any period of absence from the United Kingdom[10]. Provision is made for determining the length of the period in respect of persons sentenced to consecutive[11] and concurrent[12] terms of imprisonment, the extent of the period resulting from a finding of disability[13], whether the period has expired[14] and the period for which the notification requirements apply where a sentence has been varied[15].

These provisions apply in a modified form to persons being dealt with for service offences[16].

1 As to the notification requirements in respect of terrorism offences see the Counter-Terrorism Act 2008 ss 47–52; and PARAS 521–524. As to the persons who may be the subject of notification requirements see PARAS 518–520.

2 See the Counter-Terrorism Act 2008 s 53; and the text and notes 3–9. In relation to foreign proceedings and cases where the notification requirements apply because a notification order has been made (see PARAS 528–529), a reference in s 53 to a sentence or order of any description is to be read as a reference to an equivalent sentence or order of the foreign court: Sch 4 para 8(e). As to the determination of a person's age see the Children and Young Persons Act 1933 s 99; and CHILDREN AND YOUNG PERSONS vol 10 (2012) PARA 1206.

3 Counter-Terrorism Act 2008 s 53(1)(c).

4 Counter-Terrorism Act 2008 s 53(1)(b), (3)(a). As to detention in a young offender institution see PARA 16 et seq. Corresponding provision is made in respect of persons convicted in Scotland and Northern Ireland: see s 53(3)(b), (c).

5 Counter-Terrorism Act 2008 s 53(1)(a), (2)(a). As to custody for life see PARAS 36–37. Corresponding provision is made in respect of persons convicted in Scotland and Northern Ireland: see s 53(2)(b), (c) (s 53(2)(c) amended by SI 2010/976).

6 Counter-Terrorism Act 2008 s 53(2)(b).

7 Counter-Terrorism Act 2008 s 53(2)(c). As to such imprisonment or detention see the Criminal Justice Act 2003 s 225; and PARA 37.

8 Counter-Terrorism Act 2008 s 53(2)(d). As to detention during Her Majesty's pleasure see PARA 38.

9 Counter-Terrorism Act 2008 s 53(4). As to when a person is being 'dealt with' for an offence, and as to the time at which a person is dealt with for an offence, see PARA 519 notes 1, 2.

10 Counter-Terrorism Act 2008 s 55(1), (2).

11 For the purposes of determining the length of the period for which the notification requirements apply a person who has been sentenced in respect of two or more offences to which the Counter-Terrorism Act 2008 Pt 4 (ss 40–61) (see PARA 518) applies to consecutive terms of imprisonment is treated as if sentenced, in respect of each of the offences, to a term of imprisonment equal to the aggregate of the terms: s 53(6)(a).

12 For the purposes of determining the length of the period for which the notification requirements apply a person who has been sentenced in respect of two or more offences to which the Counter-Terrorism Act 2008 Pt 4 applies to concurrent terms of imprisonment (X and Y) that overlap for a period (Z) is treated as if sentenced, in respect of each of the offences, to a term of imprisonment equal to X plus Y minus Z: s 53(6)(b).

13 If a person who is the subject of a finding within the Counter-Terrorism Act 2008 s 45(1)(b)(iii), (2)(b)(iii) or (3)(b)(iii) (finding of disability, etc: see PARA 520) is subsequently tried for the offence, the period resulting from that finding ends either at the conclusion of the trial (if the person is acquitted) (s 53(5)(a)) or when the person is again dealt with in respect of the offence (if he is convicted) (s 53(5)(b)). For the purposes of s 53(5)(b) a person is treated as dealt with at the time of the original decision (see PARA 519 note 2) and any subsequent variation of the decision is disregarded: s 61(4)(d). As to the meaning of 'variation' see PARA 527 note 3.

14 In determining whether the period has expired there must be disregarded any period when the person was remanded in or committed to custody by an order of a court (Counter-Terrorism Act 2008 s 53(7)(a)), serving a sentence of imprisonment or detention (s 53(7)(b)), detained in a hospital (s 53(7)(c)) or detained under the Immigration Acts (Counter-Terrorism Act 2008 s 53(7)(d)). If a person to whom the notification requirements apply is absent from the United Kingdom for any period s 53(7) applies in relation to the period of absence as if it referred to any period when the person was:

    (1)   remanded in or committed to custody by an order of a court outside the United Kingdom (s 55(8)(a));

    (2)   serving a sentence of imprisonment or detention imposed by such a court (s 55(8)(b));

    (3)   detained in a hospital pursuant to an order of such a court that is equivalent to a hospital order (s 55(8)(c)); or

    (4)   subject to a form of detention outside the United Kingdom that is equivalent to detention under the Immigration Acts (s 55(8)(d)).

    As to the meaning of 'hospital order' see PARA 519 note 1. As to the meaning of 'detained in a hospital' see PARA 521 note 2. As to the modified application of the Counter-Terrorism Act 2008 s 53(7) in relation to service offences see Sch 6 para 8(1)(d). As to the meaning of 'service offence' see PARA 520 note 15.

15 See the Counter-Terrorism Act 2008 s 61(3)(d); and PARA 527.

16 See the Counter-Terrorism Act 2008 Sch 6 paras 7, 12(c), 13; and in connection with service detention see PARA 520 note 15.

526. Notification on return to United Kingdom. If before the end of the period for which the notification requirements apply[1] a person to whom the requirements apply[2] returns to the United Kingdom[3] after a period of absence and that person was not required[4] to make an initial notification[5], there has been a change to any of the information last notified[6] to the police[7] and period after which re-notification is required[8] ended during the period of absence[9], the person must notify or (as the case may be) re-notify to the police the information required to be notified on initial notification[10] within the period of three days beginning with the day of return[11].

Failure without reasonable excuse to comply, or the notification of information known to be false in purported compliance, with these requirements is an offence[12]: however these requirements do not apply if:

    (1)   the person subsequently leaves the United Kingdom[13];

    (2)   the period of absence begins before the end of the period within which notification must be made under these provisions[14]; and

    (3)   the person's absence results from the person's removal from the United Kingdom[15].

1 As to the notification requirements in respect of terrorism offences see the Counter-Terrorism Act 2008 ss 47–52; and PARAS 521–524. As to the period for which the notification requirements apply see PARA 525.

2 As to the persons who may be the subject of notification requirements see PARAS 518–520.

3 As to the meaning of 'United Kingdom' see PARA 4 note 3.

4 Ie under the Counter-Terrorism Act 2008 s 47: see PARA 521.

5 Counter-Terrorism Act 2008 s 56(1)(a).

6 Ie in accordance with the Counter-Terrorism Act 2008 s 47, s 48 (notification of changes: see PARA 522), s 49 (periodic re-notification: see PARA 521), or s 56 (see the text and notes 7–15).
7 Counter-Terrorism Act 2008 s 56(1)(b).
8 Ie the period referred to in the Counter-Terrorism Act 2008 s 49(1): see PARA 521.
9 Counter-Terrorism Act 2008 s 56(1)(c).
10 Ie the information mentioned in the Counter-Terrorism Act 2008 s 47(2): see PARA 521.
11 Counter-Terrorism Act 2008 s 56(2). The obligation under s 56 does not affect any obligation to notify information under s 52(3) (regulations requiring notification of return etc: see PARA 524): s 56(5). In determining the period within which notification is to be made under these provisions there must be disregarded any time when the person is remanded in or committed to custody by an order of a court (s 56(3)(a)), serving a sentence of imprisonment or detention (s 56(3)(b)), detained in a hospital (s 56(3)(c)) or detained under the Immigration Acts (s 56(3)(d)). As to the meaning of 'detained in a hospital' see PARA 521 note 2. In connection with service detention see PARA 520 note 15; and as to the modified application of the Counter-Terrorism Act 2008 s 56(3) in relation to service offences see Sch 6 para 8(1)(e). As to the meaning of 'service offence' see PARA 520 note 15.
12 Counter-Terrorism Act 2008 s 54(1)(a), (b). As to the punishment of violations of these provisions see PARA 521 note 16.
13 Counter-Terrorism Act 2008 s 56(4)(a).
14 Counter-Terrorism Act 2008 s 56(4)(b).
15 Counter-Terrorism Act 2008 s 56(4)(c). As to references to removal from the United Kingdom see PARA 521 note 15.

527. Disapplication and variation of requirements on variation of decision.
Where the notification requirements apply[1] and the original decision (ie the dealing with the person for the offence[2]) is varied[3], on appeal or otherwise, then:

(1) if the result is that the conditions for application of the notification requirements to a person in respect of an offence cease to be met (and a conviction of, or finding in relation to, a different offence is not substituted[4]), the notification requirements are treated as never having applied to that person in respect of that offence[5];

(2) if the result is that the conditions for application of the notification requirements to a person in respect of an offence are met where they were not previously met (and a conviction of, or finding in relation to, a different offence is not substituted[6]), the person is treated as dealt with for the offence when the variation takes place[7] and the notification requirements apply accordingly[8];

(3) if a conviction of, or finding in relation to, a different offence is substituted[9], and the conditions for application of the notification requirements were met in respect of the original offence and are also met in respect of the substituted offence[10], the person is treated as if he had been dealt with for the substituted offence at the time of the original decision[11];

(4) if the sentence is varied so as to become one by virtue of which the notification requirements would apply for a different period, the period for which those requirements apply is to be determined as if the sentence as varied had been imposed at the time of the original decision[12]; and

(5) in any other case, the variation is disregarded[13].

1 As to the notification requirements in respect of terrorism offences see the Counter-Terrorism Act 2008 ss 47–52; and PARAS 521–524. As to the persons who may be the subject of notification requirements see PARAS 518–520.
2 See the Counter-Terrorism Act 2008 s 61(2); and PARA 519 note 2.
3 References in the Counter-Terrorism Act 2008 s 61 to the variation of a decision include any proceedings by which the decision is altered, set aside or quashed, or in which a further decision is come to following the setting aside or quashing of the decision: s 61(7).
4 Ie the Counter-Terrorism Act 2008 s 61(3)(c) (see the text and notes 9–11) does not apply.

5 Counter-Terrorism Act 2008 s 61(3)(a).
6 See note 3.
7 Counter-Terrorism Act 2008 s 61(3)(b)(i).
8 Counter-Terrorism Act 2008 s 61(3)(b)(ii).
9 Counter-Terrorism Act 2008 s 61(3)(c)(i).
10 Counter-Terrorism Act 2008 s 61(3)(c)(ii).
11 Counter-Terrorism Act 2008 s 61(3)(c).
12 Counter-Terrorism Act 2008 s 61(3)(d).
13 Counter-Terrorism Act 2008 s 61(3)(e).

(iii) Persons Dealt with Outside the United Kingdom

528. Notification orders. A 'notification order' is an order applying the notification requirements[1] to a person who has been dealt with outside the United Kingdom[2] in respect of a corresponding foreign offence[3], that is to say, constituted an offence under the law in force in a country outside the United Kingdom[4] and corresponds to an applicable terrorism offence[5]. The effect of a notification order is that the notification requirements[6] apply to the person in respect of whom it is made[7].

Notification orders may only be made on application to the High Court[8] by a chief officer of police[9], and the High Court must make the order if it is proved on such an application that the conditions for making the order[10] are met[11].

1 Ie the requirements of the Counter-Terrorism Act 2008 Pt 4 (ss 40–61): see PARA 518 et seq. As to the notification requirements in respect of terrorism offences see ss 47–52; and PARAS 521–524. As to the persons who may be the subject of notification requirements see PARAS 518–520.
2 As to the meaning of 'United Kingdom' see PARA 4 note 3.
3 Counter-Terrorism Act 2008 Sch 4 para 1.
4 Counter-Terrorism Act 2008 Sch 4 para 2(1)(a). As to the meaning of 'country' see PARA 521 note 15. For this purpose an act punishable under the law in force in a country outside the United Kingdom is regarded as constituting an offence under that law however it is described in that law: Sch 4 para 2(2).
5 Counter-Terrorism Act 2008 Sch 4 para 2(1)(b). An 'applicable terrorism offence' is an offence to which Pt 4 applies (see PARA 519), and an act corresponds to an offence to which Pt 4 applies if it would have constituted an offence to which Pt 4 applies by virtue of s 41 if it had been done in any part of the United Kingdom (Sch 4 para 2(3)(a)) or it was, or took place in the course of, an act of terrorism or was done for the purposes of terrorism (Sch 4 para 2(3)(b)). As to the establishment and rebuttal of these conditions see Sch 4 para 2(4); and PARA 529 note 4. As to the meaning of 'terrorism' see PARA 518 note 1.
6 Ie the requirements of the Counter-Terrorism Act 2008 Pt 4.
7 Counter-Terrorism Act 2008 Sch 4 para 7.
8 Counter-Terrorism Act 2008 Sch 4 para 4(3).
9 Counter-Terrorism Act 2008 Sch 4 para 4(1). An application may only be made if the person resides in the chief officer's police area (Sch 4 para 4(2)(a)) or the chief officer believes that the person is in, or is intending to come to, that area (Sch 4 para 4(2)(b)). Corresponding provision is made in respect of applications in Scotland and Northern Ireland: see Sch 4 paras 5, 6 (Sch 4 para 5 amended by SI 2013/602).
10 Ie the conditions in the Counter-Terrorism Act 2008 Sch 4 para 3(2), (4), (5): see PARA 529.
11 Counter-Terrorism Act 2008 Sch 4 para 3(6).

529. Conditions for making notification orders. The first condition for making a notification order[1] in respect of a person is that under the law in force in a country[2] outside the United Kingdom[3] either the person has been convicted of a corresponding foreign offence[4] and has received an equivalent sentence[5] in respect of it[6] or a court exercising jurisdiction under that law has, in respect of a corresponding foreign offence, convicted the person or made a finding[7] of insanity or disability[8] and made the person subject to an order equivalent to a hospital order[9]: however this condition is not met if there was a flagrant denial of the person's right to a fair trial[10].

The second condition is either that the sentence was imposed or order made after 1 October 2009[11] or it was imposed or made before that date and immediately before then the person was imprisoned or detained in pursuance of the sentence or order[12], would have been so imprisoned or detained but for being unlawfully at large or otherwise unlawfully absent, lawfully absent on a temporary basis or on bail pending an appeal[13], or had been released on licence, or was subject to an equivalent form of supervision, having served the whole or part of a sentence of imprisonment for the offence[14].

The third condition is that the period for which the notification requirements would apply in respect of the offence[15] has not expired[16].

1 See PARA 528.
2 As to the meaning of 'country' see PARA 521 note 15.
3 As to the meaning of 'United Kingdom' see PARA 4 note 3.
4 As to the meaning of 'corresponding foreign offence' see the Counter-Terrorism Act 2008 Sch 4 para 2(1)–(3); and PARA 528. On an application for a notification order the condition in Sch 4 para 2(3)(a) or (b) (ie the requirement that the offence corresponds to a United Kingdom offence specified in s 41) is to be taken to be met unless the defendant serves on the applicant, not later than rules of court may provide, a notice stating that, on the facts as alleged with respect to the act concerned, the condition is not in the defendant's opinion met, showing the defendant's grounds for that opinion, and requiring the applicant to prove that the condition is met (Sch 4 para 2(4)(a)) or the court permits the defendant to require the applicant to prove that the condition is met without service of such a notice (Sch 4 para 2(4)(b)).
5 Ie a sentence equivalent to a sentence mentioned in the Counter-Terrorism Act 2008 s 45(1)(a), (2)(a) or (3)(a) (see PARA 520): Sch 4 para 3(2)(a).
6 Counter-Terrorism Act 2008 Sch 4 para 3(1), (2)(a).
7 Ie a finding in relation to the person equivalent to a finding mentioned in the Counter-Terrorism Act 2008 s 45(1)(b)(ii) or (iii), (2)(b)(ii) or (iii) or (3)(b)(ii) or (iii) (see PARA 520): Sch 4 para 3(2)(b)(i).
8 Counter-Terrorism Act 2008 Sch 4 para 3(2)(b)(i).
9 Counter-Terrorism Act 2008 Sch 4 para 3(2)(b)(ii). As to the meaning of 'hospital order' see PARA 519 note 1.
10 Counter-Terrorism Act 2008 Sch 4 para 3(3).
11 Counter-Terrorism Act 2008 Sch 4 para 3(4)(a). 1 October 2009 is the date on which Pt 4 (ss 40–61) (see PARA 518 et seq) was brought into force by the Counter-Terrorism Act 2008 (Commencement No 4) Order 2009, SI 2009/1493.
12 Counter-Terrorism Act 2008 Sch 4 para 3(4)(b)(i).
13 Counter-Terrorism Act 2008 Sch 4 para 3(4)(b)(ii).
14 Counter-Terrorism Act 2008 Sch 4 para 3(4)(b)(iii).
15 Ie in accordance with the Counter-Terrorism Act 2008 s 53 (see PARA 525) as modified by Sch 4 para 8(e).
16 Counter-Terrorism Act 2008 Sch 4 para 3(5).

(iv) Foreign Travel Restriction Orders

530. Foreign travel restriction orders. A 'foreign travel restriction order' is an order prohibiting the person to whom it applies from doing whichever of the following is specified in the order:

(1) travelling to a country[1] outside the United Kingdom[2] named or described in the order[3];

(2) travelling to any country outside the United Kingdom other than a country named or described in the order[4]; and

(3) travelling to any country outside the United Kingdom[5].

Foreign travel restriction orders may only be made by complaint to a magistrates' court[6] by a chief officer of police[7], and the court may make the order if it is satisfied on such an application that the conditions for making the order[8] are met[9]. Orders have effect for a fixed period of not more than six months[10], specified in the order[11]. A person against whom a foreign travel restriction order is made may appeal to the Crown Court against the making of the order[12]. A person who fails to comply with a foreign travel restriction order[13] commits an offence[14].

1 As to the meaning of 'country' see PARA 521 note 15.
2 As to the meaning of 'United Kingdom' see PARA 4 note 3.
3 Counter-Terrorism Act 2008 s 58(a), Sch 5 paras 1(a), 6(1)(a).
4 Counter-Terrorism Act 2008 s 58(b), Sch 5 paras 1(b), 6(1)(b).
5 Counter-Terrorism Act 2008 s 58(c), Sch 5 paras 1(c), 6(1)(c). A foreign travel restriction order containing a prohibition within Sch 5 para 6(1)(c) must require the person to whom it applies to surrender all that person's passports, at a police station specified in the order on or before the date when the prohibition takes effect or within a period specified in the order: Sch 5 para 6(3). 'Passport' means a United Kingdom passport within the meaning of the Immigration Act 1971 (see IMMIGRATION AND ASYLUM vol 57 (2012) PARA 33) or a passport issued by or on behalf of the authorities of a country outside the United Kingdom or by or on behalf of an international organisation, and includes any document that can be used (in some or all circumstances) instead of a passport (Counter-Terrorism Act 2008 s 60), and any passports surrendered must be returned as soon as reasonably practicable after the person ceases to be subject to a foreign travel restriction order containing such a prohibition (Sch 5 para 6(4)).
6 Counter-Terrorism Act 2008 Sch 5 para 3(3). The application must be made to a magistrates' court whose commission area includes any part of the chief officer's police area: Sch 5 para 3(3).
7 Counter-Terrorism Act 2008 Sch 5 para 3(1). An application may only be made if the person resides in the chief officer's police area (Sch 5 para 3(2)(a)) or the chief officer believes that the person is in, or is intending to come to, that area (Sch 5 para 3(2)(b)). Corresponding provision is made in respect of applications in Scotland and Northern Ireland: see Sch 5 paras 4, 5 (Sch 5 para 4 amended by SI 2013/602).
8 Ie the conditions in the Counter-Terrorism Act 2008 Sch 5 para 2(2), (3): see PARA 531.
9 Counter-Terrorism Act 2008 Sch 5 para 2(5).
10 Counter-Terrorism Act 2008 Sch 5 para 7(1).
11 Counter-Terrorism Act 2008 Sch 5 para 7(2). A foreign travel restriction order ceases to have effect if a court (whether the same or another court) makes another foreign travel restriction order in relation to the person to whom the earlier order applies: Sch 5 para 7(3).
12 Counter-Terrorism Act 2008 Sch 5 para 12(1)(a), (2). On an appeal under Sch 5 the court may make such orders as it considers necessary to give effect to its determination of the appeal and such incidental and consequential orders as appear to it to be just: Sch 5 para 12(3). Corresponding provision is made in respect of applications in Scotland and Northern Ireland: see Sch 5 paras 13, 14.
13 Ie a person who does anything he is prohibited from doing by a foreign travel restriction order or fails to comply with a requirement imposed on them by such an order: Counter-Terrorism Act 2008 Sch 5 para 15(1)(a), (b).
14 Counter-Terrorism Act 2008 Sch 5 para 15(1). A person guilty of an offence under Sch 5 para 15 is liable on conviction on indictment to imprisonment for a term not exceeding five years or a fine or both or on summary conviction to imprisonment for a term not exceeding 12 months (or, in relation to an offence committed before the commencement of the Criminal Justice Act 2003 s 154(1), six months) or a fine not exceeding the statutory maximum or both: Counter-Terrorism Act 2008 Sch 5 para 15(2), (3). Where a person is convicted of an offence under Sch 5 para 15 it is not open to the court by or before which he is convicted to make an order for conditional discharge (see PARA 454) in respect of the offence: Sch 5 para 15(4). As to the standard scale, the statutory maximum, the prescribed sum, and magistrates' powers to levy unlimited fines see PARA 176.

531. Conditions for making foreign travel restriction orders. A foreign travel restriction order[1] may be made in respect of a person if the notification requirements[2] apply to him[3] and his behaviour since he was dealt with for the offence[4] by virtue of which those requirements apply makes it necessary for a foreign travel restriction order to be made to prevent him from taking part in terrorism activity[5] outside the United Kingdom[6].

1   See PARA 530.
2   Ie the requirements of the Counter-Terrorism Act 2008 Pt 4 (ss 40–61): see PARA 518 et seq. As to the notification requirements in respect of terrorism offences see ss 47–52; and PARAS 521–524. As to the persons who may be the subject of notification requirements see PARAS 518–520.
3   Counter-Terrorism Act 2008 Sch 5 para 2(1), (2).
4   As to when a person is being 'dealt with' for an offence, and as to the time at which a person is dealt with for an offence, see PARA 519 notes 1, 2. For these purposes a person is treated as dealt with at the time of the original decision and any subsequent variation of the decision is disregarded: Counter-Terrorism Act 2008 s 61(4)(e). As to the meaning of 'variation' see PARA 527 note 3.
5   In the Counter-Terrorism Act 2008 Sch 5 'terrorism activity' means anything that would constitute an offence to which Pt 4 applies by virtue of s 41 (see PARA 519) if done in any part of the United Kingdom or is, or takes place in the course of, an act of terrorism or is for the purposes of terrorism: Sch 5 para 16. As to the meaning of 'United Kingdom' see PARA 4 note 3. As to the meaning of 'terrorism' see PARA 518 note 1.
6   Counter-Terrorism Act 2008 Sch 5 para 2(3). If the person was dealt with for the offence before 1 October 2009 (ie the date on which Pt 4 was brought into force by the Counter-Terrorism Act 2008 (Commencement No 4) Order 2009, SI 2009/1493) the condition in the Counter-Terrorism Act 2008 Sch 5 para 2(3) is not met unless the person has acted in that way since that date: Sch 5 para 2(4). For the purposes of Sch 5 para 2(4) a person is dealt with for an offence before 1 October 2009 if the time of the original decision (see PARA 519 note 2) falls before that date: s 61(5)(b). Where in such a case s 61(3) (see PARA 527) applies for the purposes of any provision of Pt 4, s 61(3) has effect as if the provisions of Pt 4 had been in force at all material times: s 61(5).

532. Variation, renewal and discharge of orders. A magistrates' court may make an order varying, renewing or discharging a foreign travel restriction order[1] if and to the extent that the court considers it appropriate so to do[2]. Such orders may only be made on an application made by complaint to the court[3] by either the chief officer of police[4] or the person subject to the foreign travel restriction order[5], and before making the order the court must hear the person making the application and (if they wish to be heard) the other persons entitled[6] to make such an application[7].

A foreign travel restriction order may be renewed, or varied so as to impose additional prohibitions[8], only if it is necessary to do so for the purpose of preventing the person subject to the order from taking part in terrorism activities[9] outside the United Kingdom[10].

A person subject to a foreign travel restriction order may appeal to the Crown Court against an order[11] varying or renewing the order or a refusal to make an order[12] varying or discharging the foreign travel restriction order[13].

1   As to foreign travel restriction orders see PARA 530.
2   Counter-Terrorism Act 2008 Sch 5 para 8(3). Corresponding provision is made in respect of applications in Scotland and Northern Ireland: see Sch 5 paras 9, 10 (Sch 5 para 9 amended by SI 2013/602).
3   Ie a magistrates' court for the same area as the court that made the order, a magistrates' court for the area in which the person subject to the order resides or, where the application is made by a chief officer of police, any magistrates' court whose commission area includes any part of that chief officer's police area: Counter-Terrorism Act 2008 Sch 5 para 8(2).
4   Ie the chief officer of police on whose application the order was made, the chief officer of police for the area in which the person subject to the order resides or a chief officer of police who believes that the person subject to the order is in, or is intending to come to, the officer's police area: Counter-Terrorism Act 2008 Sch 5 para 8(1)(b)–(d).
5   Counter-Terrorism Act 2008 Sch 5 para 8(1)(a).
6   Ie by virtue of the Counter-Terrorism Act 2008 Sch 5 para 8(1) (see the text and notes 4–5).

7   Counter-Terrorism Act 2008 Sch 5 para 8(4).

8   Any renewed or varied order must contain only the prohibitions necessary for the purpose referred to in the Counter-Terrorism Act 2008 Sch 5 para 11(1) (see the text and notes 9–10): Sch 5 para 11(2).

9   As to the meaning of 'terrorism activity' see PARA 531 note 5.

10   Counter-Terrorism Act 2008 Sch 5 para 11(1). As to the meaning of 'United Kingdom' see PARA 4 note 3.

11   Ie an order under the Counter-Terrorism Act 2008 Sch 5 para 8 (see the text and notes 1–7).

12   See note 11.

13   Counter-Terrorism Act 2008 Sch 5 para 12(1)(b), (2). As to the court's powers on an appeal under Sch 5 para 12 see PARA 530 note 12.

9. SENTENCING PROCEDURE

(1) GENERAL PROCEDURE

533. Proceedings after verdict on trial on indictment. After arriving at a verdict on the trial of an indictment the court will be given details of the defendant's previous convictions[1]. The defendant should be informed of any outstanding charges against him and asked whether he admits any other offences and wishes them to be taken into consideration[2]. The defendant or his advocate may also address the court in mitigation[3]. The court will also consider any pre-sentence reports[4].

1 See CRIMINAL PROCEDURE vol 27 (2015) PARA 426.
2 See CRIMINAL PROCEDURE vol 27 (2015) PARA 427.
3 As to mitigation see PARA 573 et seq.
4 See CRIMINAL PROCEDURE vol 27 (2015) PARA 430.

534. Discretion of court as to sentence. There is a general principle that no-one should be sentenced for criminal conduct in respect of which he has neither accepted it nor been convicted[1]. A convicted person is entitled to humane treatment; excessive fines may not be imposed and unusual punishments may not be inflicted[2]; and no one may be subjected to inhuman or degrading punishment[3].

It is the duty of counsel to familiarise themselves with the maximum sentence for the offence, the relevant sentencing powers of the court and any relevant sentencing guidelines, and, where appropriate, to direct the judge's attention to them[4].

1 See PARA 535; and *R v Khan* [2009] EWCA Crim 389, [2010] 1 Cr App Rep (S) 1, [2009] All ER (D) 117 (Mar).

2 See the Bill of Rights (1688) s 1.

3 See the Convention for the Protection of Human Rights and Fundamental Freedoms (Rome, 4 November 1950; TS 71 (1953; Cmd 8969) (the European Convention on Human Rights) art 3; and RIGHTS AND FREEDOMS vol 88A (2013) PARAS 158–187.

4 See *R v Pepper* [2005] EWCA Crim 1181, [2006] 1 Cr App Rep (S) 111; *R v Cain* [2006] EWCA Crim 3233, [2007] 2 Cr App Rep (S) 135, [2007] Crim LR 310; and see further LEGAL PROFESSIONS vol 66 (2015) PARA 884. As to the duty of counsel to ensure that the court does not exceed its sentencing powers see *R v Clarke* (1974) 59 Cr App Rep 298, [1975] Crim LR 607, CA; *R v Komsta* (1990) 12 Cr App Rep (S) 63, [1990] Crim LR 434, CA; and LEGAL PROFESSIONS vol 66 (2015) PARA 884.

The Criminal Justice Act 1991 s 95 imposes a duty on the Secretary of State to publish annually such information as he considers expedient for the purposes of enabling persons engaged in the administration of justice to become aware of the financial implications of their decisions (s 95(1)(a)), enabling such persons to become aware of the relative effectiveness of different sentences in preventing re-offending (s 95(1)(aa)(i) (s 95(1)(aa) added by the Criminal Justice Act 2003 s 175)) and promoting public confidence in the criminal justice system (Criminal Justice Act 1991 s 95(1)(aa)(ii) (as so added)), or facilitating the performance by such persons of their duty to avoid discriminating against any persons on the ground of race or sex or any other improper ground (s 95(1)(b)). Publication must be effected in such manner as the Secretary of State considers appropriate for the purpose of bringing the information to the attention of the persons concerned: s 95(2).

535. Offences for which offender may be sentenced. The court may sentence an offender only in respect of an offence of which he has been convicted, or which he has admitted by pleading guilty or by asking for it to be taken into consideration[1].

1   *R v Wishart* (1979) 1 Cr App Rep (S) 322, CA; *R v Davies* (1980) 72 Cr App Rep 262, 2 Cr App Rep (S) 364, CA; *R v Davies* [1998] 1 Cr App Rep (S) 380, [1998] Crim LR 75, CA. As to taking offences into consideration see PARAS 618–621.

536. Restrictions on imposition of discretionary custodial sentences.

Where a person is convicted of an offence[1] which is punishable with a custodial sentence[2] the court[3] must not pass a custodial sentence unless it is of the opinion that the offence, or the combination of the offence and one or more offences associated[4] with it, was so serious[5] that neither a fine[6] alone nor a community sentence[7] can be justified for the offence[8]. However, this does not prevent the court from passing a custodial sentence on the offender if he fails either to express his willingness to comply with a requirement which is proposed by the court to be included in a community order and which requires an expression of such willingness[9] or to comply with a pre-sentence drug testing order[10].

1   Ie other than an offence committed before 4 April 2005 (the date on which the Criminal Justice Act 2003 s 152 (see the text and notes 2–10) was brought into force by the Criminal Justice Act 2003 (Commencement No 8 and Transitional and Saving Provisions) Order 2005, SI 2005/950). Provision in connection with offences committed before 4 April 2005 is made by the Powers of Criminal Courts (Sentencing) Act 2000 s 79 (repealed; saved for those purposes by the Criminal Justice Act 2003 (Commencement No 8 and Transitional and Saving Provisions) Order 2005, SI 2005/950, Sch 2 para 5(1), (2)(c)(xii), (3)).

2   Ie other than:
     (1)   a sentence fixed by law (Criminal Justice Act 2003 s 152(1)(a));
     (2)   a life sentence for serious or second listed offences (ie the sentence required by the Criminal Justice Act 2003 ss 224A, 225(2), 226(2): see PARAS 34, 35, 37) (Criminal Justice Act 2003 s 152(1)(b), (1A)(e) (Powers of Criminal Courts (Sentencing) Act 2000 s 164(3)(d) added, Criminal Justice Act 2003 s 152(1)(b) amended, s 305(4)(ba) added, by the Violent Crime Reduction Act 2006 Sch 1 paras 8, 9; Powers of Criminal Courts (Sentencing) Act 2000 s 164(3)(c) amended, Criminal Justice Act 2003 s 152(1)(b) amended, s 305(4)(c), (d) substituted, by the Criminal Justice and Immigration Act 2008 Sch 26 paras 40, 48, 59, 66, 72; Powers of Criminal Courts (Sentencing) Act 2000 s 164(3)(c) amended, s 164(3)(aa), (ba) added, Criminal Justice Act 2003 s 152(1)(b) amended, s 305(4)(za), (aa), (bb) added, by the Legal Aid, Sentencing and Punishment of Offenders Act 2012 Sch 19 paras 7, 11, 14, 15, 22, Sch 26 para 20; Criminal Justice Act 2003 ss 152(1)(b), 305(4)(za), (aa) amended, s 152(1A) added, by the Criminal Justice and Courts Act 2015 Sch 5 paras 14, 16));
     (3)   the required custodial sentence for possession of a firearm or using a person to mind a weapon (ie sentences under the Firearms Act 1968 s 51A(2) or the Violent Crime Reduction Act 2006 s 29(4), (6): see CRIMINAL LAW vol 26 (2010) PARAS 614, 656) (Criminal Justice Act 2003 s 152(1)(b), (1A)(b), (f) (as so amended and added));
     (4)   the specified minimum term for a third class A drug trafficking offence (ie sentences under the Powers of Criminal Courts (Sentencing) Act 2000 s 110(2): see CRIMINAL LAW vol 26 (2010) PARA 725 (Criminal Justice Act 2003 s 152(1)(b), (1A)(d) (as so amended and added));
     (5)   the specified minimum term for a third domestic burglary (ie a sentence under the Powers of Criminal Courts (Sentencing) Act 2000 s 111(2): see CRIMINAL LAW vol 25 (2010) PARA 290) (Criminal Justice Act 2003 s 152(1)(b), (1A)(d) (as so amended and added)); or
     (6)   the required minimum sentences for threatening with an offensive weapon or an article with a blade or point in public in public (ie sentences under the Prevention of Crime Act 1953 ss 1(2B), 1A(5) and the Criminal Justice Act 1988 ss 139(6B), 139A(5B), 139AA(7) (see CRIMINAL LAW) (Criminal Justice Act 2003 s 152(1)(b), (1A)(a), (c) (as so amended and added)).

   In the Criminal Justice Act 2003 Pt 12 (ss 142–305) 'custodial sentence' has the meaning given by the Powers of Criminal Courts (Sentencing) Act 2000 s 76: see the Criminal Justice Act 2003 s 305(1); and PARA 9 note 15.

   A sentence falls to be imposed under s 224A if the court is obliged thereby to pass a sentence of imprisonment for life; a sentence falls to be imposed under s 225(2) if the court is obliged to pass a sentence of imprisonment for life (or, in the case of a person aged at least 18 but under 21, a sentence of custody for life) thereunder; and a sentence falls to be imposed under s 226(2) if the court is obliged to pass a sentence of detention for life thereunder: Powers of Criminal Courts (Sentencing) Act 2000 s 164(3)(c) (s 164(3) substituted by the Criminal Justice Act 2003 Sch 32 paras 90, 124; as so amended); Criminal Justice Act 2003 s 305(4)(bb), (c), (d) (as so added and substituted; s 305(4)(c) amended (until the coming into force of the Criminal Justice and Court Services Act 2000 s 61) by SI 2008/1587). As to the determination of a person's age see the Children and Young Persons Act 1933 s 99; and CHILDREN AND YOUNG PERSONS vol 10 (2012) PARA 1206.

A sentence falls to be imposed under the Firearms Act 1968 s 51A(2) or the Violent Crime Reduction Act 2006 s 29(4) or (6) (see CRIMINAL LAW vol 26 (2010) PARA 656) if it is required by the provision specified and the court is not of the opinion there mentioned: Powers of Criminal Courts (Sentencing) Act 2000 s 164(3)(b), (d) (as so substituted and added); Criminal Justice Act 2003 s 305(4)(a), (ba) (s 305(4)(ba) as so added).

A sentence falls to be imposed under the Powers of Criminal Courts (Sentencing) Act 2000 s 110(2) if it is required by that provision and the court is not of the opinion there mentioned: s 164(3)(a) (as so substituted); Criminal Justice Act 2003 s 305(4)(b).

A sentence falls to be imposed under the Powers of Criminal Courts (Sentencing) Act 2000 s 111(2) if it is required by that provision and the court is not of the opinion there mentioned: s 164(3)(a) (as so substituted); Criminal Justice Act 2003 s 305(4)(b).

A sentence falls to be imposed under the Prevention of Crime Act 1953 ss 1(2B), 1A(5) and the Criminal Justice Act 1988 ss 139(6B), 139A(5B), 139AA(7) if it is required by the provision in question and the court is not of the opinion there mentioned: Powers of Criminal Courts (Sentencing) Act 2000 s 164(3)(aa), (ba) (as so substituted and added; s 164(3)(amended by the Criminal Justice and Courts Act 2015 Sch 5 para 8); Criminal Justice Act 2003 s 305(4)(za), (aa) (as so added and amended).

3   As to the meaning of 'court' see PARA 1 note 1.
4   As to when an offence is 'associated' with another see PARA 9 note 7.
5   As to the seriousness of an offence see PARA 9 note 8.
6   See PARA 174 et seq.
7   As to the meaning of 'community sentence' see PARA 42.
8   Criminal Justice Act 2003 s 152(2). As to pre-sentence reports and other requirements see s 156; and PARA 579. Section 152(2) does not prevent a court, after taking into account such matters, from passing a community sentence even though it is of the opinion that the offence, or the combination of the offence and one or more offences associated with it, was so serious that a community sentence could not normally be justified for the offence: s 166(2).

Prison overcrowding can be a relevant factor where the sentencer's decision is on the cusp, so that there is a real issue as to whether a community sentence could be justified rather than a custodial sentence: *A-G's Reference (No 11 of 2006), R v Scarth* [2006] EWCA Crim 856, [2006] 2 Cr App Rep 705. See also *A-G's Reference (No 19 of 2006), R v Hoyle* [2006] EWCA Crim 1160, [2006] All ER (D) 123 (Apr) (prison overcrowding not a material factor when deciding sentence for case of such gravity that there was no question that a significant term of imprisonment was called for); *R v Seed* [2007] EWCA Crim 254, [2007] 2 Cr App Rep (S) 436, [2007] Crim LR 501 (guidelines in view of prison overcrowding).

9   Criminal Justice Act 2003 s 152(3)(a).
10 Criminal Justice Act 2003 s 152(3)(b).

537.   Restrictions on custodial sentences on persons not legally represented. A magistrates' court on summary conviction or the Crown Court on committal for sentence or on conviction on indictment may not pass a sentence of imprisonment[1] or (in relation to a young offender):

(1)   pass a sentence of detention[2];

(2)   until a day to be appointed[3], pass a sentence of custody for life[4] or detention in a young offender institution[5];

(3)   as from that day, pass a sentence of imprisonment on a person who, when convicted, was aged at least 18 but under 21[6]; or

(4)   make a detention and training order[7],

on or in respect of a person who is not legally represented in that court[8] (and, in relation to a person who is not a young offender in the context described above, has not been previously sentenced[9] to that punishment by a court in any part of the United Kingdom[10]).

These provisions do not apply in respect of an offender if:

(1) representation was made available to him for the purposes of the proceedings[11] but was withdrawn either because of his conduct or because it appeared that his financial resources were such that he was not eligible for such representation[12];

(2) he applied for such representation and the application was refused because it appeared that his financial resources were such that he was not eligible for such representation[13]; or

(3) having been informed of his right to apply for such representation and having had the opportunity to do so, he refused or failed to apply[14].

1 Powers of Criminal Courts (Sentencing) Act 2000 s 83(1).

2 Powers of Criminal Courts (Sentencing) Act 2000 s 83(2)(a). The sentences of detention referred to in the text are sentences under s 90 (see PARA 38) or s 91 (see PARA 8).

3 As from a day to be appointed the Powers of Criminal Courts (Sentencing) Act 2000 s 83(2)(aa) is added, and s 83(2)(b), (c) repealed, by the Criminal Justice and Court Services Act 2000 Sch 7 paras 160, 178. At the date at which this volume states the law no such day had been appointed.

4 Ie a sentence under the Powers of Criminal Courts (Sentencing) Act 2000 s 93 or s 94 (see PARAS 36–37).

5 Powers of Criminal Courts (Sentencing) Act 2000 s 83(2)(b), (c) (prospectively repealed: see note 3). A sentence of detention in a young offender institution is a sentence under s 96: see PARA 16.

6 Powers of Criminal Courts (Sentencing) Act 2000 s 83(2)(aa) (prospectively added: see note 3). As to the determination of a person's age see the Children and Young Persons Act 1933 s 99; and CHILDREN AND YOUNG PERSONS vol 10 (2012) PARA 1206.

7 Powers of Criminal Courts (Sentencing) Act 2000 s 83(2)(d). As to the making of a detention and training order see PARA 9.

8 Powers of Criminal Courts (Sentencing) Act 2000 s 83(1)(a), (2). For these purposes a person is to be treated as legally represented in a court if, but only if, he has the assistance of counsel or a solicitor to represent him in the proceedings in that court at some time after he is found guilty and before he is sentenced: s 83(4). See *R v Hollywood* (1990) 12 Cr App Rep (S) 325, [1990] Crim LR 817, CA (breach of what is now the Powers of Criminal Courts (Sentencing) Act 2000 s 83(1), (4); sentence of imprisonment invalid). See also *R v Wilson* (1995) 16 Cr App Rep (S) 997, [1995] Crim LR 510, CA.

As to the effect of failing to observe the Powers of Criminal Courts (Sentencing) Act 2000 s 83(1) see *R v Birmingham Justices, ex p Wyatt* [1975] 3 All ER 897, [1976] 1 WLR 260, DC; *R v Hollywood* (1990) 12 Cr App Rep (S) 325, CA (sentence invalid). However, on appeal from the Crown Court to the Court of Appeal, the Court of Appeal may uphold the sentence if it considers it was the appropriate one in all the circumstances: *R v McGinlay, R v Ballantyne* (1975) 62 Cr App Rep 156, [1976] Crim LR 78, CA; *R v Hollywood*.

9 For these purposes a previous sentence of imprisonment which has been suspended and which has not taken effect under the Powers of Criminal Courts (Sentencing) Act 2000 s 119 (repealed) or corresponding Northern Ireland provisions is to be disregarded: s 83(5). As to the meaning of 'sentence of imprisonment' see PARA 27 note 4; and note that for these purposes 'sentence of imprisonment' does not include a committal for contempt of court or any kindred offence (s 83(6)).

10 Powers of Criminal Courts (Sentencing) Act 2000 s 83(1)(b). As to the meaning of 'United Kingdom' see PARA 4 note 3.

11 Ie under the Legal Aid, Sentencing and Punishment of Offenders Act 2012 Pt 1 (ss 1–43: see LEGAL AID vol 65 (2015) PARAS 1–169).

12 Powers of Criminal Courts (Sentencing) Act 2000 s 83(3)(a) (s 83(3)(a) amended, s 83(3)(aa) added, by the Criminal Defence Service Act 2006 s 4(2)(c), (3); Powers of Criminal Courts (Sentencing) Act 2000 s 83(3)(a), (aa) amended by the Legal Aid, Sentencing and Punishment of Offenders Act 2012 Sch 5 para 53).

13 Powers of Criminal Courts (Sentencing) Act 2000 s 83(3)(aa) (as added and amended: see note 12).

14 Powers of Criminal Courts (Sentencing) Act 2000 s 83(3)(b) (as added and amended: see note 12).

538. Duty to give reasons for sentence. Any court[1] passing sentence[2] on an offender must state in open court[3], in ordinary language and in general terms, its reasons for deciding on the sentence[4]. In complying with this requirement:

(1) the court must identify any definitive sentencing guidelines[5] relevant to the offender's case, explain how it discharged its duty[6] to follow such guidelines unless satisfied it would be contrary to the interests of justice to do so[7], and where it was satisfied it would be contrary to the interests of justice to follow the guidelines, state why[8];

(2) where, as a result of taking into account guilty pleas[9], the court imposes a punishment on the offender which is less severe than the punishment it would otherwise have imposed, it must state that the sentence has been discounted for the guilty plea if it has[10]; and

(3) where the offender is under 18 and the court imposes a sentence that may only be imposed in the offender's case if the court is of the requisite opinion[11], the court must state why it is of that opinion[12].

1 As to the meaning of 'court' see PARA 1 note 1.
2 In the Criminal Justice Act 2003 Pt 12 Ch 1 (ss 142–176) 'sentence', in relation to an offence, includes any order made by a court when dealing with the offender in respect of his offence, and 'sentencing' is to be construed accordingly: s 142(3).
3 As to the meaning of 'open court' see PARA 30 note 7.
4 Criminal Justice Act 2003 s 174(1), (2) (s 174 substituted by the Legal Aid, Sentencing and Punishment of Offenders Act 2012 s 64(1), (2)). In connection with these requirements see the Criminal Procedure Rules 2015, SI 2015/1490, rr 24.10, 25.16, 28.1 (made pursuant to the Criminal Justice Act 2003 s 174(4)(a) (as so substituted)).
5 For these purposes 'definitive sentencing guidelines' means sentencing guidelines issued by the Sentencing Council for England and Wales under the Coroners and Justice Act 2009 s 120 (see PARA 558) as definitive guidelines, as revised by any subsequent guidelines so issued: Criminal Justice Act 2003 s 174(9) (as substituted: see note 4).
6 Ie any duty imposed on it by the Coroners and Justice Act 2009 s 125 (see PARA 561).
7 Criminal Justice Act 2003 s 174(5), (6)(a) (as substituted: see note 4).
8 Criminal Justice Act 2003 s 174(6)(b) (as substituted: see note 4).
9 Ie any matter referred to in the Criminal Justice Act 2003 s 144(1) (see PARA 564).
10 Criminal Justice Act 2003 s 174(7) (as substituted: see note 4).
11 Ie the opinion mentioned in the Criminal Justice and Immigration Act 2008 s 1(4)(a)–(c) and the Criminal Justice Act 2003 s 148(1) (youth rehabilitation order with intensive supervision and surveillance or with fostering: see PARAS 75–76) or s 152(2) (discretionary custodial sentence: see PARA 9).
12 Criminal Justice Act 2003 s 174(8) (as substituted: see note 4).

539. Duty to explain effect of sentence. Any court[1] passing sentence[2] on an offender must explain to the offender in ordinary language:

(1) the effect of the sentence[3];

(2) the effects of non-compliance with any order that the offender is required to comply with and that forms part of the sentence[4];

(3) any power of the court to vary or review any order that forms part of the sentence[5]; and

(4) where the sentence consists of or includes a fine, the effects of failure to pay the fine[6].

1 As to the meaning of 'court' see PARA 1 note 1.
2 As to the meaning of 'sentence' see PARA 538 note 2. In connection with these requirements see the Criminal Procedure Rules 2015, SI 2015/1490, rr 24.10, 25.16, 28.1 (made pursuant to the Criminal Justice Act 2003 s 174(4)(a), (b) (s 174 substituted by the Legal Aid, Sentencing and Punishment of Offenders Act 2012 s 64(1), (2)).
3 Criminal Justice Act 2003 s 174(1), (3)(a) (as substituted: see note 2). The judge is required simply to explain the effect of the sentence and it does not make the sentence unfair in any sense

which gives rise to a ground of appeal if he simply makes an error in carrying out that function: *R v Giga* [2008] EWCA Crim 703, [2008] 2 Cr App Rep (S) 638, [2008] All ER (D) 134 (Jul).
4   Criminal Justice Act 2003 s 174(3)(b) (as substituted: see note 2).
5   Criminal Justice Act 2003 s 174(3)(c) (as substituted: see note 2).
6   Criminal Justice Act 2003 s 174(3)(d) (as substituted: see note 2).

(2) ATTORNEY-GENERAL'S REFERENCES

540. Reference of sentence for review. If it appears to the Attorney General that the sentencing[1] of a person in a proceeding[2] in the Crown Court has been unduly lenient[3] and that the case in question is one that is susceptible to review[4] he may, with the leave of the Court of Appeal, refer the case to the court for it to review the sentencing of that person[5]. The Court of Appeal will not review any sentence referred to it under these provisions on an erroneous basis[6]. No judge may sit as a member of the Court of Appeal on the hearing of, or may determine any application in proceedings incidental or preliminary to, a reference of a sentence passed by himself[7].

1   As to the sentences which may be reviewed under these provisions see PARA 543. An order deferring the passing of sentence (see PARA 457) is a 'sentence' for these purposes: *A-G's Reference (No 22 of 1992)* [1994] 1 All ER 105, (1993) 97 Cr App Rep 275, CA; *R v L (Deferred Sentence)* [1999] 1 WLR 479, sub nom *A-G's Reference (Nos 36 and 38 of 1998), R v Dean L and Jones* [1999] 2 Cr App Rep (S) 7, CA.
2   For these purposes any two or more sentences are to be treated as passed in the same proceeding if they would be so treated for the purposes of the Criminal Appeal Act 1988 s 11 (see PARAS 627, 629): Criminal Justice Act 1988 s 36(3) (amended by the Criminal Justice Act 2003 Sch 36 para 96(a)).
3   Criminal Justice Act 1988 s 36(1)(a). As to when sentencing has been unduly lenient for these purposes see s 36(2); and PARA 541.
4   Criminal Justice Act 1988 s 36(1)(b). As to the cases which are susceptible to review (i e cases to which Pt IV (ss 35, 36) applies) see the Criminal Justice Act 1988 s 35(3), (4); and PARA 544.
5   Criminal Justice Act 1988 s 36(1). For the court's powers on review see PARA 542. Procedural provision in connection with reviews is made by the Criminal Procedure Rules 2015, SI 2015/1490, rr 41.1–41.8. If the Registrar of Criminal Appeals is given notice of a reference or application to the Court of Appeal under these provisions he must take all necessary steps for obtaining a hearing of the reference or application and obtain and lay before the court in proper form all documents, exhibits and other things which appear necessary for the proper determination of the reference or application: Criminal Justice Act 1988 Sch 3 para 2.
     Where the court grants leave for such a reference, its powers are not confined to increasing the sentence: *A-G's Reference (No 4 of 1989)* [1990] 1 WLR 41, 90 Cr App Rep 366, CA. Subject to rules of court, the jurisdiction of the Court of Appeal under the Criminal Justice Act 1988 s 36 must be exercised by the criminal division of the court: s 35(2).
6   *A-G's Reference (No 14 of 2003) (R v Sheppard)* [2003] EWCA Crim 1459, [2003] LS Gaz R 35, (2003) Times, 18 April. See also *A-G's Reference (No 79 of 2010), R v Haimes* [2010] EWCA Crim 187, (2010) Times, 17 March (a reference to the Attorney-General is not the same as an appeal against sentence; it is a process for the correction of errors leading to unduly lenient sentences).
7   Criminal Justice Act 1988 s 36(4).

541. What amounts to 'undue leniency'. The Attorney General may conclude that a sentence is 'unduly lenient' and therefore susceptible to review[1] if it falls outside the range of sentences which in the light of all the relevant factors (including any sentencing guidelines[2]) could reasonably be considered appropriate[3]. A sentence may be unduly lenient if the sentencing court has imposed a community order where a custodial sentence would be more appropriate[4], has imposed a custodial sentence which is shorter than is appropriate[5], or has failed to make an ancillary order, such as a confiscation order, when such an order should have been made[6]. The sentence may also be unduly lenient if the sentencing judge erred in law as to his sentencing powers[7] or has failed to impose a specified mandatory sentence[8].

1 Ie the condition specified in the Criminal Justice Act 1988 s 36(1)(a) (see PARA 540) may be satisfied: s 36(2). These provisions are without prejudice to the generality of s 36(1): s 36(2).
2 As to sentencing principles and guidelines see PARA 553 et seq.
3 See *A-G's Reference (No 4 of 1989)* [1990] 1 WLR 41, 90 Cr App Rep 366, CA; *A-G's Reference (No 14 of 2015), R v H* [2015] All ER (D) 04 (May), CA; *A-G's Reference (No 21 of 2015), R v Murtagh* [2015] EWCA Crim 953, [2015] 2 Cr App Rep (S) 327, [2015] All ER (D) 25 (May).
4 See eg *A-G's Reference (No 67 of 2008), R v Edwards* [2009] EWCA Crim 132, [2009] 2 Cr App Rep (S) 428.
5 See eg *A-G's Reference (Nos 56, 57 and 58 of 2008), R v Waller* [2009] EWCA Crim 235, [2009] 2 Cr App Rep (S) 356.
6 See eg *A-G's Reference (Nos 114, 115, 116, 144 and 145 of 2002)* [2003] EWCA Crim 3374, 147 Sol Jo LB 1400, [2003] All ER (D) 379 (Nov).
7 Criminal Justice Act 1988 s 36(2)(a) (s 36(2)(a), (b) substituted by the Criminal Justice Act 2003 Sch 32 paras 45, 46).
8 Criminal Justice Act 1988 s 36(2)(b) (as substituted: see note 7). The sentences specified for this purpose are those required by or under:
   (1) the Prevention of Crime Act 1953 s 1A(5) or s 1(2B) (see CRIMINAL LAW) (Criminal Justice Act 1968 s 36(2)(b)(zi) (as so substituted; s 36(2)(b)(zi), (ia) added, s 36(2)(iii) amended, by the Legal Aid, Sentencing and Punishment of Offenders Act 2012 Sch 19 para 2, Sch 26 paras 4, 5; Criminal Justice Act 1968 s 36(2)(b)(zi), (ia) amended by the Criminal Justice and Courts Act 2015 Sch 5 para 2));
   (2) the Firearms Act 1968 s 51A(2) (see CRIMINAL LAW vol 25 (2010) PARA 613) (Criminal Justice Act 1968 s 36(2)(b)(i) (as so substituted));
   (3) the Criminal Justice Act 1988 s 139AA(7), s 139(6B) or s 139A(5B) (see CRIMINAL LAW) (Criminal Justice Act 1968 s 36(2)(b)(ia) (as so substituted, added and amended));
   (4) the Powers of Criminal Courts (Sentencing) Act 2000 s 110(2) (see CRIMINAL LAW vol 26 (2010) PARA 725) or 111(2) (see CRIMINAL LAW vol 25 (2010) PARA 290) (Criminal Justice Act 1968 s 36(2)(b)(ii) (as so substituted));
   (5) the Criminal Justice Act 2003 s 224A (see PARA 35), s 225(2) (see PARA 37) or s 226(2) (see PARA 34) (Criminal Justice Act 1968 s 36(2)(b)(iii) (as so substituted and amended; amended by the Criminal Justice and Immigration Act 2008 Sch 26 paras 22, 23); or
   (6) the Violent Crime Reduction Act 2006 s 29(4) or (6) (see CRIMINAL LAW vol 26 (2010) PARA 656) (Criminal Justice Act 1968 s 36(2)(b)(iv) (as so substituted; added by the Violent Crime Reduction Act 1968 Sch 1 para 3)).

542. Powers of court on review. Where a case has been referred to the Court of Appeal for review[1] the court may:

(1) quash any sentence passed on the person whose sentencing has been referred in the proceeding in question[2]; and

(2) in place of it pass such sentence as the court thinks appropriate for the case and as the court below had power to pass when dealing with that person[3].

The court may only increase sentences which it considers unduly lenient; it is not enough that the sentence was less than the court would have imposed[4]. The court will not intervene unless it is shown that there has been a substantial error in principle in the sentence, so that public confidence would be damaged if the sentence was not altered[5]. Sometimes the Court of Appeal, when increasing an unduly lenient sentence, allows some discount from what it considers the sentence should have been[6].

The term of any sentence passed by the Court of Appeal or the Supreme Court begins to run, unless the court otherwise directs, from the time when it would have begun to run if passed in the proceedings in relation to which the reference was made[7], and the time during which a person whose case has been so referred for review is in custody pending its review and pending any reference to the Supreme Court[8] must be reckoned as part of the term of any sentence to which he is for the time being subject[9].

1 Ie under the Criminal Justice Act 1988 s 36(1): see PARA 540. As to the cases which may be referred see PARA 544.

2 Criminal Justice Act 1988 s 36(1)(i). As to the sentences which may be reviewed see PARA 543. On hearing a reference and quashing a sentence, the Court of Appeal has the same powers as a sentencing court to remand a defendant in custody pending medical reports: _A-G's Reference (No 129 of 2004), R v Ssan_ [2005] EWCA Crim 363, [2005] All ER (D) 159 (Feb).

3 Criminal Justice Act 1988 s 36(1)(ii). The power of the court to pass sentence on a person may be exercised although he is not present: Sch 3 para 8. For examples of sentences which have been increased on review see _A-G's Reference (No 16 of 2007), R v Hargreaves_ [2007] EWCA Crim 1229, [2008] 1 Cr App Rep (S) 152 (supplier of stolen vehicles for use in a robbery guilty of conspiracy to rob); _A-G's Reference (No 68 of 2007), R v Hawkes_ [2007] EWCA Crim 2634, (2007) Times, 11 December, [2007] All ER (D) 328 (Oct) (violent drug dealer keeping weapons on CCTV-controlled premises); _A-G's Reference (No 65 of 2008), R v Pearson_ [2008] EWCA Crim 3135, [2009] 2 Cr App Rep (S) 297 (causing death by dangerous driving). For an example of a sentence which was not increased see _A-G's Reference (Nos 32, 33 and 34 of 2007), R v Bates_ [2007] EWCA Crim 1375, [2008] 1 Cr App Rep (S) 187 (two years' imprisonment for robbery with minimal violence not unduly lenient).

4 _A-G's Reference (No 4 of 1989)_ [1990] 1 WLR 41, 90 Cr App Rep 366, CA; _A-G's Reference (No 132 of 2001), R v Johnson_ [2002] EWCA Crim 1418, [2003] 1 Cr App Rep (S) 190. Nevertheless, it is open to the court to increase a sentence although it is in accordance with the tariff for the offence in question: _A-G's Reference (No 14 of 1998), R v McGregor_ [1999] 1 Cr App Rep (S) 205, CA.

The question of whether a sentence is unduly lenient must be decided not in the light of what has been alleged but what has been proved: _A-G's Reference (No 95 of 1998), R v Highfield_ (1999) Times, 21 April, CA. The Court of Appeal cannot take into account new material which was not available to the sentencing judge (_A-G's Reference (No 19 of 2005), R v Bowden_ [2006] EWCA Crim 785, (2006) Times, 3 May) but it may take into account matters adverse to the offender (_A-G's Reference (No 74 of 2010), R v P_ [2011] All ER (D) 183 (Feb)). Offender rehabilitation is a proper consideration in sentencing and a lenient sentence based on such considerations should not necessarily be increased: see _A-G's Reference (No 92 of 2007), R v Harding_ [2007] EWCA Crim 2634, (2007) Times, 11 December, [2007] All ER (D) 328 (Oct).

5 _A-G's Reference (No 5 of 1989), R v Hill-Trevor_ (1989) 90 Cr App Rep 358, CA; _A-G's Reference (No 132 of 2001), R v Johnson_ [2002] EWCA Crim 1418, [2003] 1 Cr App Rep (S) 190.

6 See eg _A-G's References (Nos 19, 20, 21 of 2001)_ [2001] EWCA Crim 1432, [2002] 1 Cr App Rep (S) 136; _A-G's Reference (Nos 108 and 109 of 2002), R v Fielding, R v Adgebenle_ [2003] EWCA Crim 968, [2003] 2 Cr App Rep (S) 608; _A-G's Reference (No 59 of 2006), R v D_ [2006] EWCA Crim 2096, [2006] All ER (D) 240 (Nov). This is commonly called the 'double jeopardy element', and it does not apply where a reference relates to a case in which the judge made an order under the Criminal Justice Act 2003 s 269(2) (determination of minimum term in relation to mandatory life sentence: see CRIMINAL LAW vol 25 (2010) PARA 97) or, as from a day to be appointed, the Powers of Criminal Courts (Sentencing) Act 2000 s 82A(2) (see PARA 39): see the Criminal Justice Act 1988 s 36(3A), (3B) (s 36(3A) added by the Criminal Justice Act 2003 s 272(1); Criminal Justice Act 1988 s 36(3A) prospectively substituted, s 36(3B) prospectively added, by the Criminal Justice and Immigration Act 2008 s 46(1), (2)). At the date at which this volume states the law no day had been appointed for this purpose. See also _A-G's Reference (No 82 of 2000), R v Vinnicombe_ [2001] EWCA Crim 65, [2001] 2 Cr App Rep (S) 60. The element of double jeopardy is also of limited application where the offence is so serious that the defendant already had a lengthy period of imprisonment to serve: _A-G's Reference (Nos 14 and 15 of 2006)_ [2006] EWCA Crim 1335, [2007] 1 All ER 718, [2007] 1 Cr App Rep (S) 215. In considering double jeopardy the court may take into account matters adverse to the offender (_A-G's Reference (No 74 of 2010), R v P_ [2011] EWCA Crim 873, (2011) Times, 1 April, [2011] All ER (D) 183 (Feb).

7 Criminal Justice Act 1988 Sch 3 para 10 (Sch 3 paras 5, 10 amended by the Constitutional Reform Act 2005 Sch 9 para 48).

8 See PARA 546.

9 Criminal Justice Act 1988 Sch 3 para 5 (as amended: see note 7).

543. Sentences which may be reviewed. In the context of a referral of a sentence to the Court of Appeal for review[1] 'sentence' includes any order made by a court when dealing with an offender[2] including, in particular:

(1) a hospital order[3] with or without a restriction order[4];

(2) a hospital direction and a limitation direction (a hybrid order)[5];

(3) a recommendation for deportation[6];

(4) a confiscation order[7] and an order varying such an order[8];

(5) a declaration of relevance[9] as respects an offence relating to a football match[10]; and

(6) an order for the forfeiture or suspension[11] of a personal licence to supply alcohol[12].

In addition, the following orders have been held to be appealable under the provisions relating to appeals against sentence[13] and, by extension[14], may therefore be considered reviewable for these purposes:

(a) an order that the defendant pay prosecution costs[15];

(b) restitution and compensation orders[16];

(c) an order for disqualification for holding or obtaining a driving licence[17];

(d) an order for driving test made on application for removal of disqualification, being an order in 'subsequent proceedings'[18];

(e) an order revoking parole licence on conviction of an offence[19];

(f) binding over to come up for judgment[20];

(g) an order for deferment of sentence[21]; and

(h) a period specified[22] in connection with a life sentenced passed in a case when the sentence is not fixed by law[23].

The following are not appealable and may therefore be considered reviewable[24]:

(i) an order relating to a requirement to make a payment[25] in connection with the provision of legal services[26]; and

(ii) binding over to keep the peace[27].

1 Ie for the purposes of the Criminal Justice Act 1988 Pt IV (ss 35–36): see PARA 540 et seq.

2 Criminal Appeal Act 1968 s 50(1) (s 50(1) substituted by the Criminal Justice Act 1993 Sch 5 Pt 1); Criminal Justice Act 1988 s 35(6).

3 Ie under the Mental Health Act 1983 Pt III (ss 35–55): see PARA 472 et seq.

4 Criminal Appeal Act 1968 s 50(1)(a) (as substituted: see note 2). As to restriction orders see PARA 477.

5 Criminal Appeal Act 1968 s 50(1)(bb) (as substituted (see note 2); added by the Crime (Sentences) Act 1997 Sch 4 para 6(1)(a)). See the Mental Health Act 1983 Pt III; and (in particular) MENTAL HEALTH AND CAPACITY vol 75 (2013) PARA 863.

6 Criminal Appeal Act 1968 s 50(1)(c) (as substituted: see note 2). See PARA 462; and IMMIGRATION AND ASYLUM vol 57 (2012) PARA 181 et seq.

7 Ie an order under the Proceeds of Crime Act 2002 Pt 2 (ss 6–91) (see PARA 220 et seq), not including a determination under s 10A (see PARA 226): Criminal Appeal Act 1968 s 50(1)(ca) (as substituted (see note 2); s 50(1)(ca), (cb) added by the Proceeds of Crime Act 2002 Sch 11 paras 1, 4(1), (3); Criminal Justice Act 1968 s 50(1)(ca) amended by the Serious Crime Act 2015 Sch 4 para 3). Confiscation orders under the Drug Trafficking Act 1994 and the Criminal Justice Act 1988 (provisions repealed: see PARA 189) and orders varying such orders are also reviewable under these provisions: see the Criminal Justice Act 1968 s 50(1)(d)–(g) (as so substituted; s 50(1)(d), (g) amended by the Drug Trafficking Act 1994 Schs 1, 2)).

8 Criminal Appeal Act 1968 s 50(1)(ca), (cb) (as substituted and added: see notes 2, 7). An order under the Proceeds of Crime Act 2002 is reviewable only if the varying order is made under s 21 (see PARA 275), s 22 (see PARA 276) or s 29 (see PARA 218): Criminal Appeal Act 1968 s 50(1)(cb) (as so substituted and added).

9 Ie within the meaning of the Football Spectators Act 1989 s 23: see PARA 343.

10 Criminal Appeal Act 1968 s 50(1)(h) (as substituted (see note 2); amended by the Violent Crime Reduction Act 2006 Sch 3 para 14(1), (2)).

11 Ie under the Licensing Act 2003 s 129(2): see LICENSING AND GAMBLING vol 67 (2008) PARA 129.
12 Criminal Appeal Act 1968 s 50(1)(i) (as substituted (see note 2); amended by the Licensing Act 2003 Sch 6 paras 38, 42).
13 Ie under the Criminal Appeal Act 1968 s 50(1): see notes 1–12.
14 See the Criminal Justice Act 1988 s 35(6); and note 2.
15 *R v Hayden* [1975] 2 All ER 558, 60 Cr App Rep 304, CA.
16 *R v Parker* [1970] 2 All ER 458, [1970] 1 WLR 1003, CA; *R v Brogan* [1975] 1 All ER 879, 60 Cr App Rep 279, CA. As to restitution orders see the Powers of Criminal Courts (Sentencing) Act 2000 s 148; and PARA 492. As to compensation orders see s 130; and PARA 281.
17 *R v McNulty* [1965] 1 QB 437, [1964] 3 All ER 713, CA (decided under the Criminal Appeal Act 1907 s 21 (repealed)).
18 *R v Bentham* (1981) 3 Cr App Rep (S) 229.
19 *R v Welch* [1982] 2 All ER 824, 75 Cr App Rep 207, CA.
20 *R v Williams* [1982] 3 All ER 1092, 75 Cr App Rep 378, CA.
21 *A-G's Reference (No 22 of 1992)* [1994] 1 All ER 105, 97 Cr App Rep 275, CA; *R v L (Deferred Sentence)* [1999] 1 WLR 479, sub nom *A-G's References (Nos 36 and 38 of 1998), R v Jones (William)* [1999] 2 Cr App Rep (S) 7, CA.
22 Ie under the Powers of Criminal Courts (Sentencing) Act 2000 s 82A: see PARA 39.
23 *R v Dalton* [1995] QB 243, [1995] 2 Cr App Rep 340, CA.
24 See the text and notes 2, 13, 14.
25 Ie under regulations under the Legal Aid, Sentencing and Punishment of Offenders Act 2012 s 23 or s 24: see LEGAL AID vol 65 (2015) PARA 31 et seq.
26 Criminal Appeal Act 1968 s 50(3) (added by the Access to Justice Act 1999 Sch 4 para 3; amended by the Legal Aid, Sentencing and Punishment of Offenders Act 2012 Sch 5 para 3).
27 *R v Randall* (1986) 8 Cr App Rep (S) 433, [1987] Crim LR 254, CA.

544. Cases which may be referred. The cases which may be referred to the Court of Appeal for review[1] are:
(1) any case in which sentence[2] is passed on a person for an offence triable only on indictment[3];
(2) any case in which sentence is passed on a person for any of the following statutory sexual offences which are triable either way (and thus not included under head (1) above)[4]:
    (a) sexual assault[5];
    (b) causing a person to engage in sexual activity without consent[6];
    (c) sexual assault of a child aged under 13[7];
    (d) causing or inciting a child under 13 to engage in sexual activity[8];
    (e) sexual activity with a child[9];
    (f) causing or inciting a child to engage in sexual activity[10];
    (g) engaging in sexual activity in the presence of a child[11];
    (h) causing a child to watch a sexual act[12];
    (i) arranging or facilitating the commission of a child sex offence[13];
    (j) meeting a child following sexual grooming[14];
    (k) sexual activity with a child family member[15];
    (l) paying for the sexual services of a child[16];
    (m) causing or inciting child prostitution or pornography[17];
    (n) controlling a child prostitute or a child involved in pornography[18];
    (o) arranging or facilitating child prostitution or pornography[19];
    (p) causing or inciting prostitution for gain[20];
    (q) trafficking into, out of or within the United Kingdom for sexual exploitation[21];
    (r) trafficking people for exploitation[22]; and
    (s) administering a substance with intent to commit a sexual offence[23],

(3)   any case in which sentence is passed on a person for attempting to commit an offence set out under heads (a) to (h), (j) or (k) above[24] (a 'relevant offence'), inciting the commission of such an offence, or encouraging or assisting[25] such an offence[26];

(4)   any case tried on indictment either following a notice of transfer[27] or in which one or more counts in respect of which sentence is passed relates to a charge which was dismissed[28] and on which further proceedings were brought by means of the preferment of a voluntary bill of indictment[29];

(5)   any case tried on indictment following a notice given[30] in a serious or complex fraud case, or following such a notice, in which one or more of the counts in respect of which sentence is passed relates to a charge which was dismissed[31] on application and on which further proceedings were brought by means of the preferment of a voluntary bill of indictment[32]; and

(6)   any case in which sentence is passed on a person for any of the following statutory offences:

(a)   making threats to kill[33];

(b)   defilement of a girl aged between 14 and 17[34];

(c)   cruelty to persons under 16[35];

(d)   unlawful sexual intercourse with a girl under 16[36];

(e)   indecent assault on a woman or man[37];

(f)   indecent conduct with a child[38];

(g)   production or supply of a controlled drug[39];

(h)   possession of a controlled drug with intent to supply[40];

(i)   cultivation of cannabis plant[41];

(j)   inciting a girl under 16 to have incestuous sexual intercourse[42];

(k)   specified customs offences involving the importation or exportation of controlled drugs or indecent images[43];

(l)   racially or religiously aggravated assault, criminal damage, public disorder or harassment[44];

(m)   trafficking people for exploitation[45];

(n)   offences involving slavery, servitude and forced or compulsory labour[46].

1   Ie under the Criminal Justice Act 1988 Pt IV (ss 35, 36): see PARA 540.

2   As to the sentences which may be reviewed see PARA 543.

3   Criminal Justice Act 1988 s 35(1), (3)(b)(i) (s 35(3), (4) amended by the Criminal Justice and Public Order Act 1994 Sch 9 para 34). For these purposes an offence which is triable only on indictment when committed by an adult is an offence 'triable only on indictment', despite the fact that a person under 18 may be tried summarily for it by virtue of the Magistrates' Courts Act 1980 s 24 (see CRIMINAL PROCEDURE vol 27 (2015) PARA 226): *A-G's Reference (No 3 of 1993)* (1993) 98 Cr App Rep 84, CA.

4   Criminal Justice Act 1988 s 35(3)(b)(ii), (4) (as amended: see note 3); Criminal Justice Act 1988 (Reviews of Sentencing) Order 2006, SI 2006/1116, art 2, Sch 1 para 3. The Criminal Justice Act 1988 (Reviews of Sentencing) Order 2006, SI 2006/1116, Sch 1 para 3 applies the Criminal Justice Act 1988 Pt IV (to the extent that does not apply by virtue of s 35(3)(b)(i) (see the text and note 3) to any case in which sentence is passed on a person for any of the sexual offences listed in the text and notes 5–23.

5   Criminal Justice Act 1988 (Reviews of Sentencing) Order 2006, SI 2006/1116, Sch 1 para 3(a). As to this offence see the Sexual Offences Act 2003 s 3; and CRIMINAL LAW vol 25 (2010) PARA 182.

6   Criminal Justice Act 1988 (Reviews of Sentencing) Order 2006, SI 2006/1116, Sch 1 para 3(b). As to this offence see the Sexual Offences Act 2003 s 4; and CRIMINAL LAW vol 25 (2010) PARA 184.

7 Criminal Justice Act 1988 (Reviews of Sentencing) Order 2006, SI 2006/1116, Sch 1 para 3(c). As to this offence see the Sexual Offences Act 2003 s 7; and CRIMINAL LAW vol 25 (2010) PARA 183. As to the determination of a person's age see the Children and Young Persons Act 1933 s 99; and CHILDREN AND YOUNG PERSONS vol 10 (2012) PARA 1206.

8 Criminal Justice Act 1988 (Reviews of Sentencing) Order 2006, SI 2006/1116, Sch 1 para 3(d). As to this offence see the Sexual Offences Act 2003 s 8; and CRIMINAL LAW vol 25 (2010) PARA 185.

9 Criminal Justice Act 1988 (Reviews of Sentencing) Order 2006, SI 2006/1116, Sch 1 para 3(e). As to this offence see the Sexual Offences Act 2003 s 9; and CRIMINAL LAW vol 25 (2010) PARA 186.

10 Criminal Justice Act 1988 (Reviews of Sentencing) Order 2006, SI 2006/1116, Sch 1 para 3(f). As to this offence see the Sexual Offences Act 2003 s 10; and CRIMINAL LAW vol 25 (2010) PARA 187.

11 Criminal Justice Act 1988 (Reviews of Sentencing) Order 2006, SI 2006/1116, Sch 1 para 3(g). As to this offence see the Sexual Offences Act 2003 s 11; and CRIMINAL LAW vol 25 (2010) PARA 188.

12 Criminal Justice Act 1988 (Reviews of Sentencing) Order 2006, SI 2006/1116, Sch 1 para 3(h). As to this offence see the Sexual Offences Act 2003 s 12; and CRIMINAL LAW vol 25 (2010) PARA 189.

13 Criminal Justice Act 1988 (Reviews of Sentencing) Order 2006, SI 2006/1116, Sch 1 para 3(i). As to this offence see the Sexual Offences Act 2003 s 14; and CRIMINAL LAW vol 25 (2010) PARA 191.

14 Criminal Justice Act 1988 (Reviews of Sentencing) Order 2006, SI 2006/1116, Sch 1 para 3(j). As to this offence see the Sexual Offences Act 2003 s 15; and CRIMINAL LAW vol 25 (2010) PARA 192.

15 Criminal Justice Act 1988 (Reviews of Sentencing) Order 2006, SI 2006/1116, Sch 1 para 3(k). As to this offence see the Sexual Offences Act 2003 s 25; and CRIMINAL LAW vol 25 (2010) PARAS 204, 206, 208.

16 Criminal Justice Act 1988 (Reviews of Sentencing) Order 2006, SI 2006/1116, Sch 1 para 3(l). As to this offence see the Sexual Offences Act 2003 s 47; and CRIMINAL LAW vol 25 (2010) PARA 228.

17 Criminal Justice Act 1988 (Reviews of Sentencing) Order 2006, SI 2006/1116, Sch 1 para 3(m). As to this offence see the Sexual Offences Act 2003 s 48; and CRIMINAL LAW vol 25 (2010) PARA 229.

18 Criminal Justice Act 1988 (Reviews of Sentencing) Order 2006, SI 2006/1116, Sch 1 para 3(n). As to this offence see the Sexual Offences Act 2003 s 49; and CRIMINAL LAW vol 25 (2010) PARA 229.

19 Criminal Justice Act 1988 (Reviews of Sentencing) Order 2006, SI 2006/1116, Sch 1 para 3(o). As to this offence see the Sexual Offences Act 2003 s 50; and CRIMINAL LAW vol 25 (2010) PARA 229.

20 Criminal Justice Act 1988 (Reviews of Sentencing) Order 2006, SI 2006/1116, Sch 1 para 3(p). As to this offence see the Sexual Offences Act 2003 s 52; and CRIMINAL LAW vol 25 (2010) PARA 230.

21 Criminal Justice Act 1988 (Reviews of Sentencing) Order 2006, SI 2006/1116, Sch 1 para 3(q)–(s). As to this offence see the Sexual Offences Act 2003 ss 57–59; and CRIMINAL LAW vol 25 (2010) PARA 254.

22 Criminal Justice Act 1988 (Reviews of Sentencing) Order 2006, SI 2006/1116, Sch 1 para 3(sa) (added by SI 2013/862). As to this offence see the Sexual Offences Act 2003 s 59A; and CRIMINAL LAW.

23 Criminal Justice Act 1988 (Reviews of Sentencing) Order 2006, SI 2006/1116, Sch 1 para 3(t). As to this offence see the Sexual Offences Act 2003 s 61; and CRIMINAL LAW vol 25 (2010) PARA 182.

24 Ie an offence set out in the Criminal Justice Act 1988 (Reviews of Sentencing) Order 2006, SI 2006/1116, Sch 1 para 3(a)–(h), (j) or (k).

25 Ie an offence under the Serious Crime Act 2007 s 44 or s 45 (see CRIMINAL LAW vol 25 (2010) PARAS 65, 66).

26 Criminal Justice Act 1988 (Reviews of Sentencing) Order 2006, SI 2006/1116, Sch 1 para 4 (substituted by SI 2012/1833; amended by SI 2014/1651).

27 Ie a notice given under the Criminal Justice Act 1987 s 4 (repealed) by an authority designated for that purpose by s 4(2) (repealed).

28 Ie under the Criminal Justice Act 1987 s 6 (repealed).

29 Criminal Justice Act 1988 s 35(3)(a) (as amended: see note 3); Criminal Justice Act 1988 (Reviews of Sentencing) Order 2006, SI 2006/1116, Sch 1 para 1.

30 Ie under the Crime and Disorder Act 1998 s 51B (see CRIMINAL PROCEDURE vol 27 (2015) PARA 309).

31 Ie under the Crime and Disorder Act 1998 Sch 3 para 2 (see CRIMINAL PROCEDURE vol 27 (2015) PARA 306).

32 Criminal Justice Act 1988 (Reviews of Sentencing) Order 2006, SI 2006/1116, Sch 1 para 1A (added by SI 2012/1833).

33 Criminal Justice Act 1988 (Reviews of Sentencing) Order 2006, SI 2006/1116, Sch 1 para 2(a). As to this offence see the Offences against the Person Act 1861 s 16; and CRIMINAL LAW vol 25 (2010) PARA 115.

34 Criminal Justice Act 1988 (Reviews of Sentencing) Order 2006, SI 2006/1116, Sch 1 para 2(b). This is an offence under the Criminal Law Amendment Act 1885 s 5(1) (repealed).

35 Criminal Justice Act 1988 (Reviews of Sentencing) Order 2006, SI 2006/1116, Sch 1 para 2(c). As to this offence see the Children and Young Persons Act 1933 s 1; and CRIMINAL LAW vol 25 (2010) PARA 153.

36 Criminal Justice Act 1988 (Reviews of Sentencing) Order 2006, SI 2006/1116, Sch 1 para 2(d). This is an offence under the Sexual Offences Act 1956 s 6 (repealed).

37 Criminal Justice Act 1988 (Reviews of Sentencing) Order 2006, SI 2006/1116, Sch 1 para 2(d). This is an offence under the Sexual Offences Act 1956 s 14 or s 15 or the Offences against the Person Act 1861 s 52 (all repealed) or corresponding Northern Ireland enactments.

38 Criminal Justice Act 1988 (Reviews of Sentencing) Order 2006, SI 2006/1116, Sch 1 para 2(e). This is an offence under the Indecency with Children Act 1960 s 1 (repealed) or the corresponding Northern Ireland enactment.

39 Criminal Justice Act 1988 (Reviews of Sentencing) Order 2006, SI 2006/1116, Sch 1 para 2(f). As to this offence see the Misuse of Drugs Act 1971 s 4(2) or (3); and CRIMINAL LAW vol 26 (2010) PARA 725.

40 Criminal Justice Act 1988 (Reviews of Sentencing) Order 2006, SI 2006/1116, Sch 1 para 2(f). As to this offence see the Misuse of Drugs Act 1971 s 5(3); and CRIMINAL LAW vol 26 (2010) PARA 725.

41 Criminal Justice Act 1988 (Reviews of Sentencing) Order 2006, SI 2006/1116, Sch 1 para 2(f). As to this offence see the Misuse of Drugs Act 1971 s 6(2); and CRIMINAL LAW vol 26 (2010) PARA 730.

42 Criminal Justice Act 1988 (Reviews of Sentencing) Order 2006, SI 2006/1116, Sch 1 para 2(g). This is an offence under the Criminal Law Act 1977 s 54 (repealed) or the corresponding Northern Ireland enactment.

43 Criminal Justice Act 1988 (Reviews of Sentencing) Order 2006, SI 2006/1116, Sch 1 para 2(h). By virtue of Sch 1 para 2(h) the specified offences are offences under the Customs and Excise Management Act 1979 s 50(2) or (3), s 68(2) or s 170(1) or (2) (see CUSTOMS AND EXCISE vol 31 (2012) PARAS 992, 1027, 1175) in so far as those offences are committed in connection with a prohibition or restriction on importation or exportation of either:

   (1)   a controlled drug within the meaning of the Misuse of Drugs Act 1971 s 2 (see MEDICAL PRODUCTS AND DRUGS vol 75 (2013) PARA 481), such prohibition or restriction having effect by virtue of s 3 (see MEDICAL PRODUCTS AND DRUGS vol 75 (2013) PARA 491); or

   (2)   in so far as they relate to or depict a person under the age of 16, indecent or obscene prints, paintings, photographs, books, cards, lithographic or other engravings, or any other indecent or obscene articles, such prohibition and restriction having effect by virtue of the Customs Consolidation Act 1876 s 42.

44 Criminal Justice Act 1988 (Reviews of Sentencing) Order 2006, SI 2006/1116, Sch 1 para 2(i). As to these offences see the Crime and Disorder Act 1998 ss 29–32; and CRIMINAL LAW vol 25 (2010) PARAS 166–167; CRIMINAL LAW vol 26 (2010) PARA 493.

45 Criminal Justice Act 1988 (Reviews of Sentencing) Order 2006, SI 2006/1116, Sch 1 para 2(j) (added by SI 2012/1833). As to these offences see the Asylum and Immigration (Treatment of Claimants, etc) Act 2004 s 4; and IMMIGRATION AND ASYLUM vol 57 (2012) PARA 218.

46 Criminal Justice Act 1988 (Reviews of Sentencing) Order 2006, SI 2006/1116, Sch 1 para 2(k) (added by SI 2014/1651). As to these offences see the Coroners and Justice Act 2009 s 71; and CRIMINAL LAW.

545. Defendant's right to be present at hearing. A person whose sentencing is the subject of a reference to the Court of Appeal[1] is entitled to be present, if he wishes it, on the hearing of the reference, although he may be in custody[2]. A person in custody is not, however, entitled to be present on an application by the

Attorney General for leave to refer a case, or on any proceedings preliminary or incidental to a reference, unless the Court of Appeal gives him leave to be present[3].

1   Ie under the Criminal Justice Act 1988 s 36: see PARA 540.
2   Criminal Justice Act 1988 Sch 3 para 6. A person in custody may attend a hearing by live link: see the Criminal Procedure Rules 2015, SI 2015/1490, r 41.7(2). Where on a reference to the Court of Appeal under the Criminal Justice Act 1988 s 36 or a reference to the Supreme Court under s 36(5) the person whose sentencing is the subject of the reference appears by counsel for the purpose of presenting any argument to the Court of Appeal or the Supreme Court, he is entitled to the payment out of central funds of such funds as are reasonably sufficient to compensate him for expenses properly incurred by him for the purpose of being represented on the reference; and any amount recoverable under this provision must be ascertained, as soon as practicable, by the registrar of criminal appeals or, as the case may be, under Supreme Court Rules: Criminal Justice Act 1988 Sch 3 para 11(1) (Sch 3 para 11(1) renumbered and amended, Sch 3 para 11(2)–(4) added, by the Legal Aid, Sentencing and Punishment of Offenders Act 2012 Sch 7 paras 21, 23; Criminal Justice Act 1988 Sch 3 11(1) further amended by the Constitutional Reform Act 2005 Sch 9 para 48). The Criminal Justice Act 1988 Sch 3 para 11(1) has effect subject to Sch 3 para 11(3) (as so added), which provides that a person is not entitled under Sch 3 para 11(1) to the payment of sums in respect of legal costs (as defined in the Prosecution of Offences Act 1985 s 16A: see CRIMINAL PROCEDURE vol 28 (2015) PARA 828) incurred in proceedings in the Court of Appeal, and regulations under s 20(1A)(d) (see CRIMINAL PROCEDURE vol 28 (2015) PARA 830) (applied so that s 20(1A)–(1C), (3) apply in relation to funds payable out of central funds under the Criminal Justice Act 1988 Sch 3 para 11(1) as they apply in relation to amounts payable out of central funds in pursuance of costs orders made under the Prosecution of Offences Act 1985 s 16 (see CRIMINAL PROCEDURE vol 28 (2015) PARA 827)): Criminal Justice Act 1988 Sch 3 para 11(2), (4) (as so added).
3   Criminal Justice Act 1988 Sch 3 para 7. The court may pass sentence although the offender is not present: see PARA 546.

546. Further reference to Supreme Court. Where the Court of Appeal has concluded its review of a case referred to it[1] the Attorney General or the person to whose sentencing the reference relates may refer a point of law involved in any sentence passed on that person in the proceeding to the Supreme Court for its opinion, and that court must consider the point and give its opinion on it accordingly and either remit the case to the Court of Appeal to be dealt with or deal with it itself[2]. Such a reference may be made only with the leave of the Court of Appeal or the Supreme Court[3], and leave may not be granted unless it is certified by the Court of Appeal that the point of law is of general public importance and it appears to the Court of Appeal or the Supreme Court (as the case may be) that the point is one which ought to be considered by that Court[4]. For the purpose of dealing with a case under this provision the Supreme Court may exercise any powers of the Court of Appeal[5].

1   Ie under the Criminal Justice Act 1988 s 36: see PARA 540.
2   Criminal Justice Act 1988 s 36(5) (s 36(5)–(7), Sch 3 paras 4, 9 amended by the Constitutional Reform Act 2005 Sch 9 para 48). A person whose sentencing is the subject of a reference to the Supreme Court under the Criminal Justice Act 1988 s 36(5) and who is detained pending the hearing of that reference is not entitled to be present on the hearing of the reference or of any proceeding preliminary or incidental thereto except where an order of the Supreme Court authorises him to be present, or where the Supreme Court or the Court of Appeal, as the case may be, gives him leave to be present: Sch 3 para 9 (as so amended).
3   An application to the Court of Appeal for leave to refer a case to the Supreme Court under the Criminal Justice Act 1988 s 36(5) must be made within the period of 14 days beginning with the date on which the Court of Appeal concludes its review of the case; and an application to the Supreme Court for leave must be made within the period of 14 days beginning with the date on which the Court of Appeal concludes its review or refuses leave to refer the case to the Supreme Court: Criminal Justice Act 1988 Sch 3 para 4 (as amended: see note 2).
4   Criminal Justice Act 1988 s 36(6) (as amended: see note 2).
5   Criminal Justice Act 1988 s 36(7) (as amended: see note 2).

(3) GOODYEAR INDICATIONS

547. Advance indications by judge. There is an obvious danger that discussions between counsel and the trial judge with regard to sentencing may put undue pressure on the defendant to plead guilty, and accordingly guidance has been issued about advance indications of sentence by a judge in the Crown Court[1]. The guidance given in relation to the judge provides that:

(1) the judge should not give an advance indication of sentence unless one has been sought by the defendant[2];

(2) an indication should not be sought if there is any uncertainty about the factual basis[3];

(3) indication should normally be confined to the maximum sentence if a plea of guilty were tendered at the stage at which the indication is sought[4];

(4) the judge is entitled in an appropriate case to remind the defence advocate that the defendant is entitled to seek an advance indication of sentence[5];

(5) the judge retains an unfettered discretion to refuse to give such an indication and can reserve his position until such time as he feels able to give an indication[6];

(6) the judge may or may not give reasons[7];

(6) once an indication has been given, it is and remains binding on the judge who has given it, and it also binds any other judge who becomes responsible for the case[8];

(8) if, after a reasonable opportunity to consider his position, the defendant does not plead guilty, the indication ceases to have effect[9];

(9) an indication should not be sought on a basis of hypothetical facts[10]; and

(10) where appropriate, there must be an agreed, written basis of plea[11].

The guidance given in relation to the defence is that:

(a) the process of seeking an indication should normally be started by the defence[12];

(b) the defendant's advocate should not seek an indication without written authority, signed by his client, that he, the client, wishes to seek an indication[13];

(c) the defendant's advocate is personally responsible for ensuring that his client fully appreciates that he should plead not guilty unless he was guilty, and that any indication given remains subject to the entitlement of the Attorney General to refer an unduly lenient sentence to the Court of Appeal, reflects the situation at the time when it was given, and relates only to the matters about which an indication has been sought[14]; and

(d) an indication should not be sought while there is any uncertainty between the prosecution and the defence about an acceptable plea to the indictment or any factual basis relating to the plea[15].

The guidance given in relation to the prosecution is that:

(i) if there is no final agreement about the plea to the indictment, or the basis of plea, and the defence nevertheless proceeds to seek an indication, prosecuting counsel should remind him that normally an indication should not be given until the basis of the plea has been agreed, or the judge has concluded that he could properly deal with the case without the need for a hearing on the facts[16];

(ii) if an indication is sought, the prosecution should normally inquire whether the judge is in possession of all the evidence relied on by the prosecution, including any victim impact statement, as well as any relevant previous convictions of the defendant[17];

(iii) prosecuting counsel should draw the judge's attention to any minimum or mandatory statutory sentencing requirements[18]; and

(iv) prosecuting counsel should not say anything which might create the impression that the sentence indication had the support or approval of the Crown[19].

Guidance is also given in relation to the acceptance of pleas[20], as follows:

(A) justice, save in the most exceptional circumstances, is conducted in public, and this includes the acceptance of pleas by the prosecution and sentencing[21];

(B) the Code for Crown Prosecutors sets out the circumstances in which pleas to a reduced number of charges, or less serious charges, can be accepted[22];

(C) only in the most exceptional circumstances should plea and sentence be discussed in chambers, and where there is such a discussion the prosecution advocate should at the outset, if necessary, remind the judge of the principle that an independent record must be kept: the prosecution advocate should make a full note of such an event, recording all decisions and comments, which should be made available to the prosecuting authority[23];

(D) where there is to be a discussion on plea and sentence and the prosecution advocate takes the view that the circumstances are not exceptional, then it is his duty to remind the judge of the relevant decisions of the Court of Appeal[24] and disassociate himself from involvement in any discussion on sentence[25]; and

(E) when a case is listed for trial and the prosecution forms the view that the appropriate course is to accept a plea before the proceedings commence or continue, or to offer no evidence, the prosecution should whenever practicable, speak with the victim or the victim's family, so that the position can be explained and their views and interests can be taken into account as part of the decision making process: the victim or victim's family should then be kept informed and decisions explained once made at court[26].

Guidance is also given in relation to process[27].

1 See *R v Goodyear* [2005] EWCA Crim 888, [2005] 3 All ER 117, [2005] 2 Cr App Rep 281. Further guidance on the application of *R v Goodyear* has been given in the *Criminal Practice Directions 2015* [2015] EWCA Crim 1567, [2015] All ER (D) 134 (Sep) CPD VII Sentencing C: Indications of Sentence: *R v Goodyear* C.1C.8; and see *R v Kulah* [2007] EWCA Crim 1701, [2008] 1 All ER 16, [2008] 1 WLR 2517. See also *R v Nightingale* [2013] EWCA Crim 405, [2013] 2 Cr App Rep 69.

2 See note 1.
3 See note 1.
4 See note 1.
5 See note 1.
6 See note 1.
7 See note 1. In many cases involving an outright refusal, the judge would probably conclude that it would be inappropriate to give reasons.

8 See note 1. This does not, however, prevent the Attorney-General or the Court of Appeal from increasing a sentence on a reference: see *A-G's Reference (No 48 of 2006)*, *R v Farrow* [2006] EWCA Crim 2396, [2007] 1 Cr App Rep (S) 558; *A-G's Reference (No 112 of 2006)*, *R v Glover* [2006] EWCA Crim 3385, [2007] 2 Cr App Rep (S) 248. A Goodyear indication made in error is not binding on the judge, but revisions must be very much the exception and can only be made in a manner that is fair to the defendant: see *R v Newman* [2010] EWCA Crim 1566, [2011] 1 Cr App Rep (S) 419.

9 See note 1.

10 See note 1.

11 See note 1. Unless there is an agreed, written basis of plea the judge should refuse to give an indication.

12 See note 1.

13 See note 1.

14 See note 1.

15 See note 1. Any agreed basis should be reduced into writing before an indication is sought. Where there is a dispute about a particular fact which defence counsel believes to be immaterial to the sentencing decision, the difference should be recorded, so that the judge can make up his own mind. The judge should never be invited to give an indication on the basis of what would appear to be a plea bargain. The judge is not to be asked to indicate levels of sentence depending on possible different pleas. If the defendant is unrepresented, he is entitled to seek a sentence indication on his own initiative.

16 See note 1; and see also *R v Newton* (1982) 77 Cr App Rep 13, 4 Cr App Rep (S) 388, CA; PARA 14; and CRIMINAL PROCEDURE vol 27 (2015) PARA 378.

17 See note 1.

18 See note 1. Where he would be expected to offer assistance with relevant guideline cases or the Sentencing Guideline Council's views, prosecuting counsel should invite the judge to allow him to do so, and, where applicable, remind the judge that the position of the Attorney General to refer any eventual sentencing decision as unduly lenient was not affected.

19 See note 1.

20 See the *Attorney General's Guidelines on the Acceptance of Pleas* [2001] 1 Cr App Rep 425.

21 See note 20.

22 See note 20. Where this is done the prosecution should be prepared to explain the reasons in open court.

23 See note 20.

24 See *R v Goodyear* [2005] EWCA Crim 888, [2005] 3 All ER 117, [2005] 2 Cr App Rep 281.

25 See note 20. The prosecution advocate should not do or say anything which could be construed as expressly or impliedly agreeing to a particular sentence; and if the offence is one to which the Criminal Justice Act 1988 s 35 (review of unduly lenient sentences: see PARA 540 et seq) applies he should make it clear that the Attorney General may refer the case for review under s 36 (see PARA 540 et seq).

26 See note 20.

27 See note 1. Any sentence indication will normally be sought at the plea and trial preparation hearing (see CRIMINAL PROCEDURE vol 27 (2015) PARA 158) but a defendant may seek an indication at a later stage, or even, in rare cases, during the trial itself. In complicated or difficult cases, no less than seven days' notice of an intention to seek an indication should normally be given in writing to the prosecution and the court. The hearing should normally take place in open court, with a full recording of the entire proceedings, and both sides represented, in the defendant's presence. Any reference to a request for a sentence indication is inadmissible in any subsequent trial. Reporting restrictions should normally be imposed, to be lifted if and when the defendant pleads or is found guilty. It is only in wholly exceptional circumstances that counsel should see the judge in private to discuss pleas or sentence; an example would be where the defendant is unaware that he is dying of cancer: *A-G's Reference (No 44 of 2000)*, *R v Peverett* [2001] 1 Cr App Rep 416, [2001] Crim LR 60, CA. As to private meetings between counsel and the judge see CRIMINAL PROCEDURE vol 27 (2015) PARA 373.

(4) INFORMANTS AND GIVING EVIDENCE FOR THE PROSECUTION

548. Assistance by defendant: reduction in sentence and review of sentence. If a defendant:

(1) following a plea of guilty is either convicted of an offence in proceedings in the Crown Court or is committed to the Crown Court for sentence[1]; and

(2) has, pursuant to a written agreement made with a specified prosecutor[2], assisted or offered to assist the investigator or prosecutor in relation to that or any other offence[3],

then in determining what sentence[4] to pass on the defendant the court may take into account the extent and nature of the assistance given or offered[5].

If the Crown Court has passed a sentence on a person in respect of an offence[6] and the person either:

(a) receives a discounted sentence[7] in consequence of his having offered in pursuance of a written agreement[8] to give assistance to the prosecutor or investigator of an offence, but knowingly fails to any extent to give assistance in accordance with the agreement[9];

(b) receives a discounted sentence in consequence of his having offered in pursuance of a written agreement to give assistance to the prosecutor or investigator of an offence and, having given the assistance in accordance with the agreement, in pursuance of another written agreement gives or offers to give further assistance[10]; or

(c) receives a sentence which is not discounted but in pursuance of a written agreement subsequently gives or offers to give assistance to the prosecutor or investigator of an offence[11],

then a specified prosecutor may at any time refer the case back to the court by which the sentence was passed if the person is still serving his sentence[12] and the specified prosecutor thinks it is in the interests of justice to do so[13]. A case so referred must, if possible, be heard by the judge who passed the sentence to which the referral relates[14]. If the court is satisfied that a person who has received a discounted sentence in consequence of having offered in pursuance of a written agreement to give assistance to the prosecutor or investigator of an offence[15] has knowingly failed to any extent to give assistance in accordance with the agreement, it may substitute for the sentence to which the referral relates such greater sentence (not exceeding that which it would have passed but for the agreement to give assistance) as it thinks appropriate[16]. In a case of a person who either receives a discounted sentence in consequence of having offered in pursuance of a written agreement to give assistance to the prosecutor or investigator of an offence and, having given the assistance in accordance with the agreement, in pursuance of another written agreement gives or offers to give further assistance[17] or receives a sentence which is not discounted but in pursuance of a written agreement subsequently gives or offers to give assistance to the prosecutor or investigator of an offence[18], the court may take into account the extent and nature of the assistance given or offered[19] and substitute for the sentence to which the referral relates such lesser sentence as it thinks appropriate[20]. A person in respect of whom a reference is so made, and the specified prosecutor, may with the leave of the Court of Appeal appeal to the Court of Appeal against the decision of the Crown Court[21].

If in any of these circumstances the court passes a sentence which is less than it would have passed but for the assistance given or offered it must state in open court[22], unless it thinks that it would not be in the public interest to do so, that it has passed a lesser sentence than it would otherwise have passed[23] and what the greater sentence would have been[24]. If, in determining what sentence to pass on the defendant, the court takes into account the extent and nature of the assistance given or offered as so mentioned, that does not prevent the court from also taking account of any other matter which it is entitled by virtue of any other enactment to take account of for the purposes of determining either the sentence[25] or, in the case of a sentence which is fixed by law, any minimum period of imprisonment which an offender must serve[26].

1   Serious Organised Crime and Police Act 2005 s 73(1)(a).
2   As to the specified prosecutors see the Serious Organised Crime and Police Act 2005 s 71; and CRIMINAL LAW vol 25 (2010) PARA 47 (definition applied by ss 73(10), 74(11)(b), 75B(3) (s 75B added by the Coroners and Justice Act 2009 s 113(7)). An agreement with a specified prosecutor may provide for assistance to be given to that prosecutor or to any other prosecutor: Serious Organised Crime and Police Act 2005 s 73(9). The Attorney General may issue guidance to specified prosecutors about the exercise by them of any of their powers under s 73, 74: s 75B(1) (as so added). The Attorney General may from time to time revise any guidance so issued: s 75B(2) (as so added). At the date at which this volume states the law no such guidance had been issued.
3   Serious Organised Crime and Police Act 2005 s 73(1)(b).
4   For these purposes, a reference to a sentence includes, in the case of a sentence which is fixed by law, a reference to the minimum period an offender is required to serve; and a reference to a lesser sentence must be construed accordingly: Serious Organised Crime and Police Act 2005 ss 73(8)(a), 74(15).
5   Serious Organised Crime and Police Act 2005 s 73(2). See the Criminal Procedure Rules 2015, SI 2015/1490, rr 28.1, 28.11. The court's power under the Serious Organised Crime and Police Act 2005 s 73 is unaffected by anything in any enactment which:
    (1)   requires that a minimum sentence is passed in respect of any offence or an offence of any description or by reference to the circumstances of any offender (whether or not the enactment also permits the court to pass a lesser sentence in particular circumstances) (s 73(5)(a)); or
    (2)   in the case of a sentence which is fixed by law, requires the court to take into account certain matters for the purposes of making an order which determines or has the effect of determining the minimum period of imprisonment which the offender must serve (whether or not the enactment also permits the court to fix a lesser period in particular circumstances) (s 73(5)(b)).
    For these purposes a reference to 'imprisonment' includes a reference to any other custodial sentence within the meaning of the Powers of Criminal Courts (Sentencing) Act 2000 s 76 (see PARA 9 note 15): Serious Organised Crime and Police Act 2005 s 73(8)(b).
    The common law principles apply where assistance is given and sentence is passed before the commencement of s 73: *R v Z* [2007] EWCA Crim 1473, [2008] 1 Cr App Rep (S) 344, [2007] All ER (D) 312 (Jun). As to the approach of the court when conducting a review of sentence see *R v P, R v Blackburn* [2007] EWCA Crim 2290, [2008] 2 All ER 684, [2008] 2 Cr App Rep (S) 16 (process is not confined to offenders providing assistance in relation to crimes in which they actually participated or with which they were otherwise linked); *R v Bevens* [2009] EWCA Crim 2554, [2010] 2 Cr App Rep (S) 199 (five-year reduction from life sentence appropriate where offender assisted with investigation of corrupt police officer but refused to assist in investigation involving co-accused); *R v Dougall* [2010] EWCA Crim 1048, [2010] Crim LR 661 (suspended sentence granted taking into account a written agreement); *R v D* [2010] EWCA Crim 1485, [2011] 1 Cr App Rep (S) 424 (further guidance on court's approach when conducting review of sentence); *R v McGarry* [2012] EWCA Crim 255, [2012] 2 Cr App Rep (S) 354 (discount in level of sentence increased to 20% where offender agreed to provide assistance but prosecution chose not to rely on evidence).
6   Serious Organised Crime and Police Act 2005 s 74(1)(a). A person does not fall within s 74(2) (see the text and notes 7–11) if: (1) he was convicted of an offence for which the sentence is fixed by law (s 74(13)(a)); and (2) he did not plead guilty to the offence for which he was sentenced (s 74(13)(b)).
7   A discounted sentence is a sentence passed in pursuance of Serious Organised Crime and Police Act 2005 s 73 (see the text and notes 1–5) or s 74(6) (see the text and notes 17–20): s 74(10).
8   References to a written agreement are references to an agreement made in writing with a specified prosecutor: Serious Organised Crime and Police Act 2005 s 74(11)(a).
9   Serious Organised Crime and Police Act 2005 s 74(1)(b), (2)(a).
10 Serious Organised Crime and Police Act 2005 s 74(2)(b).
11 Serious Organised Crime and Police Act 2005 s 74(2)(c).
12 Serious Organised Crime and Police Act 2005 s 74(3)(a).

13 Serious Organised Crime and Police Act 2005 s 74(3)(b). The Crime and Disorder Act 1998 s 57E (see CRIMINAL PROCEDURE vol 27 (2015) PARA 172) applies to hearings in proceedings relating to a reference under s 74(3) as it applies to sentencing hearings: Serious Organised Crime and Police Act 2005 s 75A (added by the Police and Justice Act 2006 Sch 14 para 62).

14 Serious Organised Crime and Police Act 2005 s 74(4). The court in which proceedings relating to a reference under s 74(3) (s 75(1)(a)), and any other proceedings arising in consequence of them (s 75(1)(b)), will be or are being heard may make such order as it thinks appropriate to exclude from the proceedings any person who is not a member or officer of the court (s 75(2)(a), (4)(a)), a party to the proceedings (s 75(4)(b)), counsel or a solicitor for a party to the proceedings (s 75(4)(c)) or otherwise directly concerned with the proceedings (s 75(4)(d)), and to give such directions as it thinks appropriate prohibiting the publication of any matter relating to the proceedings (including the fact that the reference has been made) (s 75(2)(b)). Such an order may be made only to the extent that the court thinks that it is necessary to do so to protect the safety of any person (s 75(3)(a)) and that it is in the interests of justice (s 75(3)(b)). These provisions do not affect any other power which the court has by virtue of any rule of law or other enactment to exclude any person from proceedings (s 75(5)(a)) or to restrict the publication of any matter relating to proceedings (s 75(5)(b)).

    In relation to any proceedings under s 74, the Secretary of State may, in relation to proceedings in England and Wales, make an order containing provision corresponding to any provision in the Criminal Appeal Act 1968 (subject to any specified modifications): Serious Organised Crime and Police Act 2005 s 74(12)(a) (substituted by SI 2010/976). As to the order that has been made see the Serious Organised Crime and Police Act 2005 (Appeals under Section 74) Order 2006, SI 2006/2135 (amended by SI 2011/1242).

15 Ie a person falling within the Serious Organised Crime and Police Act 2005 s 74(2)(a) (see the text and notes 7–9).

16 Serious Organised Crime and Police Act 2005 s 74(5). Any part of the sentence to which the referral relates which the person has already served must be taken into account in determining when a greater or lesser sentence imposed by s 74(5) has been served: s 74(7). The Criminal Justice Act 2003 s 174(1)(a) (duty to give reasons for sentence: see PARA 538) or s 270 (duty to give reasons for applying or disapplying early release provisions in connection with a person in respect of whom a mandatory life sentence is passed: see CRIMINAL LAW vol 25 (2010) PARA 97), as the case may be, applies to a sentence substituted under the Serious Organised Crime and Police Act 2005 s 74(5) unless the court thinks that it is not in the public interest to disclose that the person falls within s 74(2)(a) (see the text and notes 7–9, 15): s 74(14).

17 Ie a person falling within the Serious Organised Crime and Police Act 2005 s 74(2)(b) (see the text and note 10).

18 Ie a person falling within the Serious Organised Crime and Police Act 2005 s 74(2)(c) (see the text and note 11).

19 Serious Organised Crime and Police Act 2005 s 74(6)(a). Any part of the sentence to which the referral relates which the person has already served must be taken into account in determining when a greater or lesser sentence imposed by s 74(6) has been served: s 74(7). The court's power under this provision is unaffected by anything in any enactment which:

    (1)   requires that a minimum sentence is passed in respect of any offence or an offence of any description or by reference to the circumstances of any offender (whether or not the enactment also permits the court to pass a lesser sentence in particular circumstances) (s 73(5)(a)); or

    (2)   in the case of a sentence which is fixed by law, requires the court to take into account certain matters for the purposes of making an order which determines or has the effect of determining the minimum period of imprisonment which the offender must serve (whether or not the enactment also permits the court to fix a lesser period in particular circumstances) (s 73(5)(b)).

20 Serious Organised Crime and Police Act 2005 s 74(6)(b). See note 19.

21 Serious Organised Crime and Police Act 2005 s 74(8). The Criminal Appeal Act 1968 s 33(3) (limitation on appeal from the criminal division of the Court of Appeal: see CRIMINAL PROCEDURE vol 28 (2015) PARA 812) does not prevent an appeal to the Supreme Court under the Serious Organised Crime and Police Act 2005 s 74: s 74(9).

22 As to the meaning of 'open court' see PARA 30 note 7. The Serious Organised Crime and Police Act 2005 73(3) (see the text and notes 23–24) does not apply if the court thinks that it would not be in the public interest to disclose that the sentence has been discounted; but in such a case the court must give written notice of the matters specified in s 73(3) to both the prosecutor and the defendant: s 73(4). If s 73(3) does not so apply, the Criminal Justice Act 2003 s 174(1)(a) (duty to give reasons for sentence: see PARA 538) and s 270 (duty to give reasons for applying or disapplying early release provisions in connection with a person in respect of whom a

mandatory life sentence is passed: see CRIMINAL LAW vol 25 (2010) PARA 97) do not apply to the extent that the explanation will disclose that a sentence has been discounted pursuant to these provisions: Serious Organised Crime and Police Act 2005 s 73(7).

23   Serious Organised Crime and Police Act 2005 s 73(3)(a).
24   Serious Organised Crime and Police Act 2005 s 73(3)(b).
25   Serious Organised Crime and Police Act 2005 s 73(6)(a).
26   Serious Organised Crime and Police Act 2005 s 73(6)(b).

(5) COMMITTALS FOR SENTENCE

549. Sentencing on committal for sentence. Where an offender is committed by a magistrates' court for sentence[1] for an either-way matter the Crown Court must inquire into the circumstances of the case and may deal with the offender in any manner in which it could deal with him if he had just been convicted of the offence on indictment before the court[2].

Where a magistrates' court commits a person to be dealt with by a Crown Court in respect of certain additional offences which are summary only[3], the Crown Court may, after inquiring into the circumstances of the case, deal with him in any way in which the magistrates' court could deal with him if it had just convicted him of the offence[4].

Where a magistrates' court by which a person aged 14 or over is convicted of an offence is of opinion that, if a hospital order[5] is made, a restriction order[6] should also be made and, instead of making a hospital order or dealing with him in any other manner, commits him to the Crown Court to be dealt with[7], the Crown Court must inquire into the circumstances of the case and:

(1)   if that court would have power to make a hospital order upon the conviction of the offender before the court[8], may make a hospital order in his case, with or without a restriction order[9];

(2)   if the court does not make such an order, may deal with the offender in any other manner in which the magistrates' court might have dealt with him[10].

On sentencing a person committed to the Crown Court the conviction and identity of the offender must be strictly proved unless expressly admitted[11]. If the time for appeal against the conviction has not expired, the court should not proceed to deal with the offender without first ascertaining that he does not intend to appeal against conviction; if he intends to appeal the issue of sentence should be adjourned until after determination of the appeal[12].

The Crown Court has power to impose a confiscation order on an offender who has been committed for sentence following his summary conviction of an offence triable either way[13]. It has no power[14] to remit a case to a magistrates' court where it appears that the defendant pleaded guilty under a material mistake, but it may permit a change of plea and (if such an application is granted) it may remit the case to the magistrates' court[15]. Where the committal order is clearly invalid on its face, the Crown Court should not pass sentence but should remit the case back to the magistrates' court for sentence[16]. An order which is valid on its face can only be challenged in the High Court[17].

1   Ie, in relation to an offender aged 18 or over, under the Powers of Criminal Courts (Sentencing) Act 2000 s 3, s 3A or s 4 (see CRIMINAL PROCEDURE vol 27 (2015) PARAS 292–295) or, in relation to an offender under the age of 18, under the Powers of Criminal Courts (Sentencing) Act 2000 s 3B, s 3C or s 4A (see CRIMINAL PROCEDURE vol 27 (2015) PARAS 234–236): Powers of Criminal Courts (Sentencing) Act 2000 ss 5(1), 5A(1) (s 5 substituted, s 5A added, by the Criminal Justice Act 2003 Sch 3 paras 21, 26, 27).

The powers of a magistrates' court under the Powers of Criminal Courts (Sentencing) Act 2000 s 3 or s 3B are also exercisable by a magistrates' court where it is of the opinion, or it so appears to the court, as mentioned in s 3 or s 3B unless a hospital order is made in the offender's case with a restriction order: Mental Health Act 1983 s 43(4) (substituted by the Criminal Justice Act 2003 Sch 3 para 55(1), (2)). See further MENTAL HEALTH AND CAPACITY vol 75 (2013) PARA 873.

As to the information to be supplied on committal for sentence see the Criminal Procedure Rules 2015, SI 2015/1490, r 28.10.

2   Powers of Criminal Courts (Sentencing) Act 2000 ss 5(1), 5A(1) (as substituted and added: see note 1). In relation to committals under s 4, s 5(1) has effect subject to s 4(4), (5) (see CRIMINAL PROCEDURE vol 27 (2015) PARA 295), and in relation to committals under s 4A, s 5A(1) has effect subject to s 4A(4), (5): ss 5(2), 5A(2) (as so substituted and added). The Magistrates' Courts Act 1980 s 20A(1) (which relates to the effect of an indication of sentence under s 20: see CRIMINAL PROCEDURE vol 27 (2015) PARA 191) does not apply in respect of any specified offence (within the meaning of the Criminal Justice Act 2003 s 224: see PARA 21 et seq) in respect of which the offender is committed under the Powers of Criminal Courts (Sentencing) Act 2000 s 3A(2) or in respect of which the offender is committed under s 4(2) and the court states under s 4(4) that, in its opinion, it also has power to commit the offender under s 3A(2): s 5(3)(a), (b) (as so substituted). As to the powers of the Crown Court on a committal following conviction in a magistrates' court of an offence of absconding by a person released on bail or agreeing to indemnify sureties under the Bail Act 1976 ss 6(6), 9(3) see ss 6(7), s 9(4); and CRIMINAL PROCEDURE vol 27 (2015) PARAS 121, 122.

3   Ie under the Powers of Criminal Courts (Sentencing) Act 2000 s 6 (committal for sentence for offences tried summarily: see CRIMINAL PROCEDURE vol 27 (2015) PARA 296).

4   Powers of Criminal Courts (Sentencing) Act 2000 s 7(1). This includes the statutory limitation on the permissible aggregate term of consecutive sentences for summary offences: *R v Cattell* (1986) 8 Cr App Rep (S) 268, [1986] Crim LR 823, CA; *R v Whitlock* (1991) 13 Cr App Rep (S) 157, CA. The Powers of Criminal Courts (Sentencing) Act 2000 s 7(1) does not apply where under s 6 a magistrates' court commits a person to be dealt with by the Crown Court in respect of a suspended sentence, but in such a case the powers under the Criminal Justice Act 2003 s 193, Sch 12 paras 8, 9 (power of court to deal with suspended sentence: see PARA 117) are exercisable by the Crown Court: Powers of Criminal Courts (Sentencing) Act 2000 s 7(2) (amended by the Criminal Justice Act 2003 Sch 32 paras 90, 92).

Without prejudice to the Powers of Criminal Courts (Sentencing) Act 2000 s 7(1), (2), where under s 6 or under any enactment to which s 6 applies (see s 6(4); and CRIMINAL PROCEDURE vol 27 (2015) PARA 296) a magistrates' court so commits a person, any duty or power which would otherwise fall to be discharged or exercised by the magistrates' court may not be discharged or exercised by that court but must instead be discharged or may instead be exercisable by the Crown Court: see s 7(3); and *R v Brogan* [1975] 1 All ER 879, 60 Cr App Rep 279, CA. Where under the Powers of Criminal Courts (Sentencing) Act 2000 s 6 a magistrates' court commits a person to be dealt with by the Crown Court in respect of an offence triable only on indictment in the case of an adult (being an offence which was tried summarily because of the offender's being under 18 years of age), the Crown Court's powers under s 7(1) in respect of the offender after he attains the age of 18 are powers to do either or both of: (1) impose a fine not exceeding £5,000 (s 7(4)(a)); and (2) deal with the offender in respect of the offence in any way in which the magistrates' court could deal with him if it had just convicted him of an offence punishable with imprisonment for a term not exceeding six months (s 7(4)(b)).

5   As to the meaning of 'hospital order' see PARA 472 note 1.

6   As to restriction orders see PARA 477.

7   Ie under the Mental Health Act 1983 s 43(1): see MENTAL HEALTH AND CAPACITY vol 75 (2013) PARA 873.

8   Ie conviction of such an offence as is described in the Mental Health Act 1983 s 37(1): see PARA 472.

9   Mental Health Act 1983 s 43(2)(a).

10 Mental Health Act 1983 s 43(2)(b). The Crown Court has the same power to make orders under s 35 (remand to hospital: see PARA 475), s 36 (remand to hospital for treatment: see PARA 476) and s 38 (interim hospital orders: see PARA 474) in the case of a person committed to the court under s 43 as the Crown Court has under s 35, s 36 and s 38 in the case of a defendant within the meaning of s 35 or s 36 or of a person convicted before that court as mentioned in s 38: s 43(3).

11 See *R v Evans* [1915] 2 KB 762, 11 Cr App Rep 178, CCA. The offender should either be formally identified as the person convicted by the magistrates' court or asked if he admits being

the person mentioned in the conviction and committed for sentence: *R v Barker* [1951] 1 All ER 479n, 35 Cr App Rep 20, CCA; cf *R v Jeffries* [1963] Crim LR 559, CCA.

12 See *R v Faithful* [1950] 2 All ER 1251, 34 Cr App Rep 220, CCA. There is no right of appeal against committal for sentence: *R v London Sessions Appeal Committee, ex p Rogers* [1951] 2 KB 74, [1951] 1 All ER 343, DC.

13 *R v Pope* [2002] UKHL 26, [2002] 3 All ER 889, [2002] 1 WLR 1966.

14 Ie under the Powers of Criminal Courts (Sentencing) Act 2000 s 5(1) (see the text and notes 1–2).

15 *R v Crown Court at Isleworth, ex p Buda* [2000] 1 Cr App Rep (S) 538, [2000] Crim LR 111, DC.

16 *R v Norfolk Justices, ex p DPP* [1950] 2 KB 558, 34 Cr App Rep 120, DC; *R v Sheffield Crown Court and Sheffield Stipendiary Magistrate, ex p DPP* (1994) 15 Cr App Rep (S) 768, 158 JP 334, DC.

17 *R v Sheffield Crown Court and Sheffield Stipendiary Magistrate, ex p DPP* (1994) 15 Cr App Rep (S) 768, 158 JP 334, DC.

(6) SENTENCING OF CHILDREN AND YOUNG OFFENDERS

550. Overriding objective. Every court[1] in dealing with a child or young person[2] who is brought before it, either as an offender or otherwise, must have regard to the welfare of the child or young person and must in a proper case take steps for removing him from undesirable surroundings, and for securing that proper provision is made for his education and training[3]. It is the principal aim of the youth justice system[4] to prevent offending by children and young persons[5], and it is the duty of all persons and bodies carrying out functions in relation to the youth justice system to have regard to that aim in addition to any other duty to which they are subject[6]. Local authorities are required to secure the provision of youth justice services in their area through the establishment of youth offending teams and the drawing-up of youth justice plans, and the Youth Justice Board has been established in order to oversee this process[7].

1 As to the meaning of 'court' see PARA 1 note 1.

2 As to the meanings of 'child' and 'young person' for the purposes of the Children and Young Persons Act 1933 see CHILDREN AND YOUNG PERSONS vol 9 (2012) PARA 3.

3 See the Children and Young Persons Act 1933 s 44; and CHILDREN AND YOUNG PERSONS vol 10 (2012) PARA 1191 et seq. See also the Criminal Justice Act 2003 s 142A (as from a day to be appointed); the Children Act 1989 s 1; PARA 554; and CHILDREN AND YOUNG PERSONS vol 9 (2012) PARA 364 et seq. As to the determination of a person's age see the Children and Young Persons Act 1933 s 99; and CHILDREN AND YOUNG PERSONS vol 10 (2012) PARA 1206.

4 Ie the system of criminal justice in so far as it relates to children and young persons: Crime and Disorder Act 1998 s 42(1).

5 Crime and Disorder Act 1998 s 37(1). For the purposes of the Crime and Disorder Act 1998 'child' means a person under the age of 14 years and 'young person' means a person who has attained the age of 14 and is under the age of 18, and the age of a person is deemed to be that which it appears to the court to be after considering any available evidence: s 117(1), (3).

6 Crime and Disorder Act 1998 s 37(2). In carrying out any of their duties under s 37, a local authority, a police authority, a local probation board, a provider of probation services, a clinical commissioning group, or a Local Health Board, must act in accordance with any guidance given by the Secretary of State: s 42(3) (amended by the Criminal Justice and Court Services Act 2000 Sch 7 paras 150, 151; the Offender Management Act 2007 Sch 3 para 3; the Health and Social Care Act 2012 Sch 5 para 89; SI 2000/90; SI 2007/961). As to local authorities see PARA 73 note 2; as to police authorities see POLICE AND INVESTIGATORY POWERS vol 84 (2013) PARAS 52 et seq; as to health service bodies see HEALTH SERVICES; and as to local probation boards and the provision of probation services see PARAS 666–687.

7 See the Crime and Disorder Act 1998 ss 38–42; and CHILDREN AND YOUNG PERSONS vol 10 (2012) PARA 1192 et seq.

551. Custodial sentences which may be imposed in respect of young offenders. Until a day to be appointed[1] no court[2] may pass a sentence of imprisonment[3] on a person for an offence if he is aged under 21 when convicted of an offence[4] or commit a person added under 21 to prison for any reason[5]; as from the appointed day no court may pass a sentence of imprisonment on a person for an offence if he is aged under 18 when convicted, or commit a person aged under 18 to prison[6].

A court must in specified cases order detention for life for serious offences committed by dangerous offenders aged under 18 at the time of conviction[7]. A court may order the detention of persons convicted of serious offences if they are under 18 at the time of conviction[8]. In addition, a court may, and sometimes (ie where minimum sentences are specified) must, make a detention and training order in respect of a young offender aged under 18, providing for a period of detention and training followed by a period of supervision[9]. Until a day to be appointed a court may, and sometimes must, sentence a person under 21 to custody for life in specified circumstances[10] and a person aged 18 or over but under 21 may be sentenced to detention in a young offender institution[11].

Detention during Her Majesty's pleasure may, where an offender is convicted of murder, be imposed only if the offender had not attained the age of 18 years at the time of the offence[12]. Detention for specified serious offences, or a detention and training order, may be imposed only on offenders who have not attained 18 years of age at the date of conviction[13]. A sentence of detention in a young offender institution may be passed only if the offender has attained 18 years of age but not 21 years of age at the date of conviction[14].

If there is a dispute about the offender's age the court should apply the *Merton* guidelines[15] and the best course may be to adjourn until the matter can be resolved in the light of further evidence[16]. If on the available evidence an offender is deemed to be of the applicable age, and is dealt with on that basis, the fact he is subsequently found to be under that age does not invalidate the sentence[17]. It is an abuse of the power of adjournment to adjourn a case solely in order to wait for an offender to attain a particular age before which a particular form of sentence could not be imposed[18]. A person under the applicable age at the date of conviction but who attains that age between conviction and sentence should be sentenced as a person under the applicable age and not as an adult[19]. The base line for sentencing in such a case should be the sentence which the offender would be likely to have received if sentenced at the time of the offence; this can be departed from but only with good reason[20].

1 The Powers of Criminal Courts (Sentencing) Act 2000 s 89(1)(a), (b), (2) are amended, so as to reduce the age specified therein from 21 to 18, and s 108 repealed, by the Criminal Justice and Court Services Act 2000 Sch 7 paras 160, 180, 188, Sch 8, as from a day to be appointed, subject to a saving in respect of offences committed before the appointed day (see Sch 27 para 1)). At the date at which this volume states the law no day had been appointed for these purposes.

2 As to the meaning of 'court' see PARA 1 note 1.

3 In the Powers of Criminal Courts (Sentencing) Act 2000 'sentence of imprisonment' does not include a committal in default of payment of any sum of money, for want of sufficient distress to satisfy any sum of money, or for failure to do or abstain from doing anything required to be done or left undone; and references to 'sentencing an offender to imprisonment' are to be read accordingly: s 163.

4 Powers of Criminal Courts (Sentencing) Act 2000 s 89(1)(a) (prospectively amended: see note 1). Nothing in s 89(1) prevents the committal to prison of a person aged under 21 years of age (or, as from a day to be appointed (see note 1), under 18) who is remanded in custody (s 89(2)(a) (as so prospectively amended)), committed in custody for sentence (s 89(2)(b) (s 89(2)(b), (c) amended by the Criminal Justice Act 2003 Sch 3 para 74(1), (3), Sch 37 Pt 4)) or

sent in custody for trial under the Crime and Disorder Act 1998 s 51 or s 51A (see CRIMINAL PROCEDURE vol 27 (2015) PARAS 227, 299) (Powers of Criminal Courts (Sentencing) Act 2000 s 89(2)(c) (as so amended)).

Until a day to be appointed (see note 1), in any case where, but for the Powers of Criminal Courts (Sentencing) Act 2000 s 89(1), a court would have power:

(1) to commit a person under 21 but not less than 18 years of age to prison for default in payment of a fine or any other sum of money (s 108(1)(a) (prospectively repealed: see note 1));

(2) to make an order fixing a term of imprisonment in the event of such a default by such a person (s 108(1)(b) (as so prospectively repealed)); or

(3) to commit such a person to prison for contempt of court or any kindred offence (s 108(1)(c) (as so prospectively repealed)),

the court has power to commit him to be detained or, as the case may be, to make an order fixing a term of detention in the event of default, for a term not exceeding the term of imprisonment; and, for these purposes, the power of a court to order a person to be imprisoned under the Attachment of Earnings Act 1971 s 23 (see CIVIL PROCEDURE vol 12 (2009) PARAS 1465–1466) is to be taken to be a power to commit him to prison (Powers of Criminal Courts (Sentencing) Act 2000 s 108(2) (as so prospectively repealed)). No court may, however, commit such a person to be so detained unless it is of the opinion that no other method of dealing with him is appropriate; and in forming such an opinion the court must take into account all such information about the circumstances of the default or contempt (including any aggravating or mitigating factors) as is available to it (s 108(3)(a) (as so prospectively repealed)) and may take into account any information about the person which is before it (s 108(3)(b) (as so prospectively repealed)). Where a magistrates' court so commits a person to be detained it must state in open court the reason for its opinion that no other method of dealing with him is appropriate (s 108(4)(a) (as so prospectively repealed)) and cause that reason to be specified in the warrant of commitment and to be entered on the register (s 108(4)(b) (as so prospectively repealed)). 'Register' means the register of proceedings before a magistrates' court required by Criminal Procedure Rules to be kept by the designated officer for the court: s 163 (amended by SI 2001/618; SI 2004/2035; SI 2005/886). See *R v Grimsby Justices, ex p Hogg* (1994) 158 JP 1053, DC; *R v Byas* (1995) 159 JP 458, 16 Cr App Rep (S) 869, CA. As from a day to be appointed no court is to commit a person to be detained under the Powers of Criminal Courts (Sentencing) Act 2000 s 108 or make an order thereunder fixing a term of detention (Criminal Justice and Court Services Act 2000 s 61(2) (not yet in force)), and a person aged under 21 who has been committed (before the coming into force of s 61) to be detained under the Powers of Criminal Courts (Sentencing) Act 2000 s 108 or in respect of whom an order thereunder fixing a term of detention has been made (before the coming into force of the Criminal Justice and Court Services Act 2000 s 61) may be detained in a young offender institution, or in a prison, determined by the Secretary of State (s 61(4) (not yet in force)). A determination of the Secretary of State under s 61 may be made in respect of an individual or any description of individuals: s 61(6) (not yet in force). At the date at which this volume states the law no day had been appointed for the commencement of s 61.

A failure to obey an order to enter into a recognisance may not be dealt with as a contempt of court since it is not within the ambit of matters which can be dealt with as such a contempt before a magistrates' court; however, a refusal twice repeated in open court to enter into a recognisance to keep the peace is a 'kindred offence' to contempt of court: *Howley v Oxford* (1985) 81 Cr App Rep 246, [1985] Crim LR 724, DC.

5 Powers of Criminal Courts (Sentencing) Act 2000 s 89(1)(b) (prospectively amended: see note 1). As to the determination of a person's age see the Children and Young Persons Act 1933 s 99; and CHILDREN AND YOUNG PERSONS vol 10 (2012) PARA 1206.

6 See note 1. As from a day to be appointed, a person who has been sentenced to imprisonment and is aged under 21 may be detained either in a prison or in a young offender institution in which there are detained either one or more persons aged at least 18 but under 21 who have been sentenced to a term of detention in a young offender institution, to custody for life or to a custodial order, or one or more persons aged under 21 who have been committed to be detained under the Powers of Criminal Courts (Sentencing) Act 2000 s 108 (see note 4) or in respect of whom an order thereunder fixing a term of detention has been made, as determined by the Secretary of State: Criminal Justice and Courts Service Act 2000 s 61(5) (not yet in force). A determination of the Secretary of State under s 61 may be made in respect of an individual or any description of individuals: s 61(6) (not yet in force).

7 See PARA 34.

8 See PARA 8.

9 See PARA 9.

10 See PARAS 36–37.
11 See PARA 16.
12 See PARA 38.
13 As to the specified serious offences see PARA 8; as to detention and training orders see PARA 9 et seq.
14 See PARA 16.
15 Ie the guidelines set out in *R (on the application of B) v Merton London Borough Council* [2003] EWHC 1689 (Admin), [2003] 4 All ER 280. As to the matters to which the court must have regard in these circumstances see also *R v Bowker* [2007] EWCA Crim 1608, [2008] 1 Cr App Rep (S) 412, [2007] Crim LR 904; and PARA 553.
16 *R v Steed* (1990) 12 Cr App Rep (S) 230, [1990] Crim LR 816, CA.
17 *R v Farndale* (1973) 58 Cr App Rep 336, CA; *R v Brown* (1989) 11 Cr App Rep (S) 263, [1989] Crim LR 750, CA.
18 *Arthur v Stringer* (1987) 84 Cr App Rep 361, (1986) 8 Cr App Rep (S) 329, DC.
19 *R v Danga* [1992] QB 476, [1992] 1 All ER 624, CA.
20 *R v Ghafoor* [2002] EWCA Crim 1857, [2003] 1 Cr App Rep (S) 428, [2002] Crim LR 739 (applied in *R v LM* [2002] EWCA Crim 3047, [2003] 2 Cr App Rep (S) 124, [2003] Crim LR 205; *R v Jones (Martin)* [2003] EWCA Crim 1609, [2004] 1 Cr App Rep (S) 126, [2003] Crim LR 639). Contrast *R v H (Anthony)* [2002] EWCA Crim 2938, 167 JP 30, CA.

(7) VARIATION OF SENTENCE

552. Power to vary. A sentence[1] imposed, or other order[2] made, by the Crown Court when dealing with an offender may be varied or rescinded by the Crown Court within the period of 56 days beginning with the day on which it was imposed or made[3]. This power may not be exercised in relation to any sentence or order if an appeal, or an application for leave to appeal, against that sentence or order has been determined[4]. A sentence or other order may not be varied or rescinded under these provisions except by the court constituted as it was when the sentence or other order was imposed or made, or, where that court comprised one or more justices of the peace, a court so constituted except for the omission of any one or more of those justices[5]. Similar provisions are made in respect of magistrates' courts[6].

Pursuant to these powers the court may vary the sentence by substituting a sentence or order of a different kind to that originally imposed[7]. The power to vary is for slips of the tongue or slips of memory: it is not to be used for fundamental changes of mind[8]. The power may also be used where, for example, the court had overlooked that an offence was 'specified' or 'serious' under statute and therefore required a particular approach to sentencing[9], or where the original sentence might, for example, attract mandatory suspension where a short prison sentence was the judge's intention[10]. Although the power may be used either to increase or reduce the sentence[11], the power to increase should be exercised with care[12]. Making false representations to the court concerning mitigation or the defendant's 'turning over a new leaf', have been held to be grounds for variation[13]; but making false representations about intended compliance with a post-sentence order was not[14].

1 As to the meaning of 'sentence' see PARA 27 note 1.
2 As to the meaning of 'order' see PARA 27 note 2.
3 Powers of Criminal Courts (Sentencing) Act 2000 s 155(1) (s 155(1) amended, s 155(1A) added, by the Criminal Justice and Immigration Act 2008 Sch 8 pars 28). As to when a varied order takes effect see the Powers of Criminal Courts (Sentencing) Act 2000 s 155(4), (6); and PARA 27. Criminal Procedure Rules may, as respects cases where two or more persons are tried separately on the same or related facts alleged in one or more indictments, provide for extending the period fixed by Powers of Criminal Courts (Sentencing) Act 2000 s 155(1) and may (subject to s 155(1)–(6)) prescribe the cases and circumstances in which, and the time within which, any

order or other decision made by the Crown Court may be varied or rescinded by that court: s 155(7) (amended by SI 2004/2035). See the Criminal Procedure Rules 2015, SI 2015/1490, r 28.4.

4   Powers of Criminal Courts (Sentencing) Act 2000 s 155(1A) (as added: see note 3).
5   Powers of Criminal Courts (Sentencing) Act 2000 s 155(4).
6   See the Magistrates' Courts Act 1980 s 142; and CRIMINAL PROCEDURE vol 27 (2015) PARA 285.
7   See *R v Sodhi* (1978) 66 Cr App Rep 260, CA.
8   See *R v Grice* (1978) 66 Cr App Rep 167, CA; *R v Nodjoumi* (1985) 7 Cr App Rep (S) 183, CA.
9   See *R v Reynolds* [2007] EWCA Crim 538, 2 Cr App Rep (S) 553.
10 See *R v Newsome* (1970) 54 Cr App Rep (S) 485.
11 See *R v Hart* (1983) 5 Cr App Rep (S) 25, CA.
12 See *R v Crozier* (1990) 12 Cr App Rep (S) 206 (only in extreme circumstances should the varied sentence be a radical departure from the original (substitution of hospital order for term of imprisonment); *R v Woop* [2002] EWCA Crim 58, 2 Cr App Rep (S) 281.
13 *R v Hart* (1983) 5 Cr App Rep (S) 25; *R v McLean* (1988) 10 Cr App Rep (S) 18.
14 *R v Hudson* [2011] EWCA Crim 906, [2011] 2 Cr App Rep (S) 666.

10. SENTENCING PRINCIPLES

(1) PURPOSES OF SENTENCING

553.   Purposes of sentencing: offenders over 18.   Any court[1] dealing with an offender in respect of his offence must have regard to the following purposes of sentencing[2]:

(1)   the punishment of offenders[3];

(2)   the reduction of crime (including its reduction by deterrence)[4];

(3)   the reform and rehabilitation of offenders[5];

(4)   the protection of the public[6]; and

(5)   the making of reparation by offenders to persons affected by their offences[7].

However, this does not apply:

(a)   in relation to an offender who is aged under 18 at the time of conviction[8];

(b)   to an offence the sentence for which is fixed by law[9];

(c)   to an offence the sentence for which falls to be imposed under specified provisions as to required custodial sentences or dangerous offenders[10]; or

(d)   in relation to the making[11] of a hospital order (with or without a restriction order), an interim hospital order, a hospital direction or a limitation direction[12].

1   As to the meaning of 'court' see PARA 1 note 1.
2   As to the meanings of 'sentence' and 'sentencing' see PARA 538 note 2.
3   Criminal Justice Act 2003 s 142(1)(a). See *R v Skidmore* [2008] EWCA Crim 1539, [2008] All ER (D) 133 (Aug).
4   Criminal Justice Act 2003 s 142(1)(b). See *R v Preddie* [2007] EWCA Crim 1961, [2007] All ER (D) 44 (Sep) (gang violence to be severely punished despite young age of defendants).
5   Criminal Justice Act 2003 s 142(1)(c).
6   Criminal Justice Act 2003 s 142(1)(d).
7   Criminal Justice Act 2003 s 142(1)(e).
8   Criminal Justice Act 2003 s 142(2)(a). As from a day to be appointed this provision is amended by the Criminal Justice and Immigration Act 2008 s 9(2)(a) so as to remove the words 'at the time of the conviction'. At the date at which this volume states the law no such day had been appointed. For the purposes of any provision of the Criminal Justice Act 2003 Pt 12 (ss 142–305) which requires the determination of the age of a person by the court or the Secretary of State, his age is deemed to be that which it appears to the court or (as the case may be) the Secretary of State to be after considering any available evidence: s 305(2). Although the court must take into account the purposes mentioned in heads (1)–(5) in the text where an offender has attained the age of 18 after the commission of the offence, his culpability is to be judged by reference to his age at the time of the offence: *R v Bowker* [2007] EWCA Crim 1608, [2008] 1 Cr App Rep (S) 412, [2007] All ER (D) 122 (Jul). See also *R v Robson* [2006] EWCA Crim 1414, [2007] 1 All ER 506, [2007] 1 Cr App Rep (S) 301. As to the determination of a person's age see the Children and Young Persons Act 1933 s 99; and CHILDREN AND YOUNG PERSONS vol 10 (2012) PARA 1206.
9   Criminal Justice Act 2003 s 142(2)(b).
10   Criminal Justice Act 2003 s 142(2)(c) (amended by the Legal Aid, Sentencing and Punishment of Offenders Act 2012 Sch 26 para 16; Criminal Justice Act 2003 s 142(2)(c) further amended, s 142(2A) added, by the Criminal Justice and Courts Act 2015 Sch 5 para 10). The specified provisions are (by virtue of the Criminal Justice Act 2003 s 142(2A) (as so added)): the Prevention of Crime Act 1953 s 1(2B) or s 1A(5) (minimum sentence for certain offences involving offensive weapons: see CRIMINAL LAW); the Firearms Act 1968 s 51A(2) (minimum sentence for certain firearms offences: see CRIMINAL LAW vol 25 (2010) PARA 613); the Criminal Justice Act 1988 ss 139(6B), 139A(5B), 139AA(7) (minimum sentence for certain offences involving article with blade or point or offensive weapon: see CRIMINAL LAW); the Powers of

Criminal Courts (Sentencing) Act 2000 ss 110(2), 111(2) (minimum sentence for certain drug trafficking and burglary offences: see CRIMINAL LAW vol 25 (2010) PARA 290; CRIMINAL LAW vol 26 (2010) PARA 725); the Criminal Justice Act 2003 s 224A (life sentence for second listed offence for certain dangerous offenders: see PARA 35); ss 225(2), 226(2) (imprisonment or detention for life for certain dangerous offenders: see PARAS 34, 37); and the Violent Crime Reduction Act 2006 s 29(4) or (6) (minimum sentence in certain cases of using someone to mind a weapon: see CRIMINAL LAW vol 26 (2010) PARA 656).

11 Ie under the Mental Health Act 1983 Pt 3 (ss 35–55) (see PARAS 472–479; and MENTAL HEALTH AND CAPACITY vol 75 (2013) PARA 859 et seq).

12 Criminal Justice Act 2003 s 142(2)(d).

554. Purposes of sentencing: offenders under 18. It is the principal aim of the youth justice system[1] to prevent offending by children and young persons[2]. In addition to any other duty to which they are subject, it is the duty of all persons and bodies carrying out functions in relation to the youth justice system to have regard to that aim[3].

As from a day to be appointed the following provisions apply where a court is dealing with an offender aged under 18 in respect of an offence[4].

The court must have regard to:

(1)   the principal aim of the youth justice system which is to prevent offending (or re-offending)[5] by persons aged under 18[6];

(2)   provisions[7] relating to the welfare of the offender[8]; and

(3)   the purposes of sentencing (so far as it is not required to do so by head (1) above)[9].

The purposes of sentencing are:

(a)   the punishment of offenders[10];

(b)   the reform and rehabilitation of offenders[11];

(c)   the protection of the public[12]; and

(d)   the making of reparation by offenders to persons affected by their offences[13].

However, the above provisions do not apply:

(i)   to an offence the sentence for which is fixed by law[14];

(ii)   to an offence the sentence for which falls to be imposed under specified provisions as to required custodial sentences or dangerous offenders[15];

(iii)   in relation to the making[16] of a hospital order (with or without a restriction order), an interim hospital order, a hospital direction or a limitation direction[17].

1   'Youth justice system' means the system of criminal justice in so far as it relates to children and young persons: Crime and Disorder Act 1998 s 42(1).

2   Crime and Disorder Act 1998 s 37(1). As to the meanings of 'child' and 'young person' see PARA 550 note 5.

3   Crime and Disorder Act 1998 s 37(2).

4   Criminal Justice Act 2003 s 142A (prospectively added by the Criminal Justice and Immigration Act 2008 s 9(1)). At the date at which this volume states the law no day had been appointed for the commencement of this provision. As to the determination of a person's age see the Children and Young Persons Act 1933 s 99; and CHILDREN AND YOUNG PERSONS vol 10 (2012) PARA 1206.

5   See the Crime and Disorder Act 1998 s 37(1); and the text and notes 1–2.

6   Criminal Justice Act 2003 s 142A(2)(a) (prospectively added: see note 4).

7   Ie in accordance with the Children and Young Persons Act 1933 s 44 (see CHILDREN AND YOUNG PERSONS vol 10 (2012) PARA 1191 et seq).

8   Criminal Justice Act 2003 s 142A(2)(b) (prospectively added: see note 4).

9   Criminal Justice Act 2003 s 142A(2)(c) (prospectively added: see note 4).

10   Criminal Justice Act 2003 s 142A(3)(a) (prospectively added: see note 4).

11   Criminal Justice Act 2003 s 142A(3)(b) (prospectively added: see note 4).

12   Criminal Justice Act 2003 s 142A(3)(c) (prospectively added: see note 4).

13 Criminal Justice Act 2003 s 142A(3)(d) (prospectively added: see note 4).

14 Criminal Justice Act 2003 s 142A(4)(a) (prospectively added: see note 4).

15 Criminal Justice Act 2003 s 142A(4)(b) (prospectively added (see note 4); s 142A(4)(b) substituted, s 142A(5) added, by the Criminal Justice and Courts Act 2015 Sch 5 para 11). The specified provisions are (by virtue of the Criminal Justice Act 2003 s 142A(5) (as so added)): the Prevention of Crime Act 1953 s 1(2B) or s 1A(5) (minimum sentence for certain offences involving offensive weapons: see CRIMINAL LAW); the Firearms Act 1968 s 51A(2) (minimum sentence for certain firearms offences: see CRIMINAL LAW vol 25 (2010) PARA 613); the Criminal Justice Act 1988 ss 139(6B), 139A(5B), 139AA(7) (minimum sentence for certain offences involving article with blade or point or offensive weapon: see CRIMINAL LAW); the Criminal Justice Act 2003 s 226(2) (detention for life for certain dangerous offenders: see PARA 34); and the Violent Crime Reduction Act 2006 s 29(6) (minimum sentence in certain cases of using someone to mind a weapon: (see CRIMINAL LAW vol 26 (2010) PARA 656).

16 Ie under the Mental Health Act 1983 Pt 3 (ss 35–55) (see PARAS 472–479; and MENTAL HEALTH AND CAPACITY vol 75 (2013) PARA 859 et seq).

17 Criminal Justice Act 2003 s 142A(4)(c) (prospectively added: see note 4).

(2) CONCURRENT AND CONSECUTIVE SENTENCES

555. Totality. The principle of totality comprises two elements[1]:

   (1)   that all courts, when sentencing for more than a single offence, should pass a total sentence which reflects all the offending behaviour before it and is just and proportionate[2]; and

   (2)   it is usually impossible to arrive at a just and proportionate sentence for multiple offending simply by adding together notional single sentences: it is necessary to address the offending behaviour, together with the factors personal to the offender as a whole[3].

There is no inflexible rule governing whether sentences should be structured as concurrent or consecutive components: the overriding principle is that the overall sentence must be just and proportionate[4]. The general approach is[5]:

   (a)   to consider the sentence for each individual offence, with reference to the applicable guidelines;

   (b)   to determine whether the case calls for concurrent or consecutive sentences;

   (c)   to test the overall sentence or sentences against the requirement that they be just and proportionate; and

   (d)   to consider whether the sentence is structured in a way that will be best understood by those affected by it.

As a rule, concurrent sentences will ordinarily be appropriate where offences arise out of the same incident or facts[6] or where there is a series of offences of the same or a similar kind (especially where committed against the same person)[7]; consecutive sentences will ordinarily be appropriate where offences arise out of unrelated facts or incidents[8], where offences are of the same or similar kind but the overall criminality would not sufficiently be reflected by concurrent sentences[9], and where one or more offences qualifies for a statutory minimum sentence and concurrent sentences would improperly undermine that minimum[10].

A sentence should not be ordered to run partly concurrently and partly consecutively to an existing sentence[11]. Consecutive sentences may be passed which in total substantially exceed the maximum for any one of the offences[12]. There is no reason why a sentence should not be imposed which requires an offender to commence to serve an additional period after the minimum period before he could be considered for parole[13].

A magistrates' court[14] imposing imprisonment[15] or detention in a young offender institution[16] on any person may order that the term of imprisonment or detention is to commence on the expiration of any other term of imprisonment or detention imposed by that or any other court[17]. However, where a magistrates' court imposes two or more terms of imprisonment or detention to run consecutively, the aggregate of such terms must not exceed six months (or, as from a day to be appointed, 65 weeks)[18]. Until a day to be appointed[19], if two or more of the terms imposed by the court are imposed in respect of an offence triable either way[20] which was tried summarily[21], the aggregate of the terms so imposed and any other terms imposed by the court may exceed six months but must not exceed 12 months[22]. The limitations imposed by these provisions do not operate to reduce the aggregate of the terms that the magistrates' court may impose in respect of any offences below the term which the court has power to impose in respect of any one of those offences[23]. Where a person has been sentenced by a magistrates' court to imprisonment and a fine for the same offence, a period of imprisonment imposed for non-payment of the fine, or for want of sufficient distress (or, as from a day to be appointed, goods) to satisfy the fine, must not be subject to these limitations[24].

Committal to custody for disobedience of an order of a magistrates' court to do anything other than the payment of money or abstain from doing anything is not a period of imprisonment nor may such committal orders be imposed consecutively[25].

1 See the Sentencing Council Definitive Guideline *Offence Taken into Consideration and Totality* p 5 (General Principles). The guideline is effective from 11 June 2012 and is applicable to all offenders whose cases are dealt with on or after that date. As to guidelines generally see PARA 562.

2 Sentencing Council Definitive Guideline *Offence Taken into Consideration and Totality* p 5 (General Principles). This is so whether the sentences are structured as concurrent or consecutive, and therefore concurrent sentences will ordinarily be longer than a single sentence for a single offence.

3 Sentencing Council Definitive Guideline *Offence Taken into Consideration and Totality* p 5 (General Principles).

4 Sentencing Council Definitive Guideline *Offence Taken into Consideration and Totality* p 5 (General Principles). Where a court passes on a defendant more than one term of imprisonment, it should state in the presence of the defendant whether the terms are to be concurrent or consecutive: *Criminal Practice Directions 2015* [2015] EWCA Crim 1567, [2015] All ER (D) 134 (Sep) CPD VII Sentencing E: Concurrent and Consecutive Sentences E.1. Should this not be done, the court clerk should ask the court, before the defendant leaves court, to do so: para E.1. For the restriction under the Criminal Justice Act 2003 s 265 on consecutive sentences being imposed on early release prisoners who have been recalled to prison see PARA 27.

5 Sentencing Council Definitive Guideline *Offence Taken into Consideration and Totality* pp 6–8 (General Approach).

6 See eg *R v Lawrence (Justin)* (1990) 11 Cr App Rep (S) 580, [1990] RTR 45, CA (applied in *R v Jordan* [1996] 1 Cr App Rep (S) 181, [1996] RTR 221, CA); *R v Poulton* [2002] EWCA Crim 2487; *A-G's Reference (Nos 21 and 22 of 2003)* [2003] EWCA Crim 3089.

7 Sentencing Council Definitive Guideline *Offence Taken into Consideration and Totality* p 6 (General Approach).

8 See eg *R v Kastercum* (1972) 56 Cr App Rep 298, CA; *A-G's Reference (No 1 of 1990)* (1990) 12 Cr App Rep (S) 245; *R v Millen* (1980) 2 Cr App Rep (S) 357; *R v Poulton* [2002] EWCA Crim 2487; *R v Fletcher* [2002] EWCA Crim 834, [2002] 2 Cr App Rep (S) 127, [2002] Crim LR 591; *A-G's Reference (Nos 21 and 22 of 2003)* [2003] EWCA Crim 3089.

9 See eg *R v Jamieson* [2008] EWCA Crim 2761.

10 See eg *R v Raza* (2010) 1 Cr App R (S) 56; *R v Ralphs* [2009] EWCA Crim 2555.

11 *R v Salmon* [2002] EWCA Crim 2088, [2003] 1 Cr App Rep (S) 441, CA.

12 *R v Blake* [1962] 2 QB 377, 45 Cr App Rep 292, CCA; *R v Britten* [1969] 1 All ER 517, 53 Cr App Rep 111, CA.

13   See *R v Hills* [2008] EWCA Crim 1871, [2009] 1 Cr App Rep (S) 441, [2009] Crim LR 116. See also *R v Foy* [1962] 2 All ER 246, 46 Cr App Rep 290, CCA (a fixed-term of imprisonment may not be imposed to run consecutively to a sentence of life imprisonment), *R v Jones* [1962] AC 635 at 647 (affd on appeal on another point sub nom *Jones v DDP* [1962] AC 647, 46 Cr App Rep 129, HL) (although it is undesirable, a life sentence may be made consecutive to a fixed term of imprisonment) and *R v Bird* (2004) Times, 10 December, CA (there is no objection to imposing an extended sentence to run consecutively to a fixed-term one).

14   As to the meaning of 'magistrates' court' see MAGISTRATES vol 71 (2013) PARA 470.

15   As to the meaning of 'impose imprisonment' see PARA 28 note 3. For these purposes a term of imprisonment is deemed to be imposed in respect of an offence if it is imposed as a sentence or in default of payment of a sum adjudged to be paid by the conviction or for want of sufficient goods to satisfy such a sum: Magistrates' Courts Act 1980 s 133(5) (amended by the Tribunals, Courts and Enforcement Act 2007 Sch 13 paras 45, 62). Any reference to a sum adjudged to be paid by a conviction or order of a magistrates' court includes any costs, damages or compensation adjudged to be paid by the conviction or order of which the amount is ascertained by the conviction or order: Magistrates' Courts Act 1980 s 150(3). The provisions of the Magistrates' Courts Act 1980 authorising a magistrates' court on conviction of an offender to pass a sentence or make an order instead of dealing with him in any other way must not be construed as taking away any power to order him to pay costs, damages or compensation: s 150(7).

16   See PARA 16.

17   Magistrates' Courts Act 1980 s 133(1) (amended by the Criminal Justice Act 1982 Sch 14 para 56; the Powers of Criminal Courts (Sentencing) Act 2000 Sch 9 para 76; and by virtue of the Criminal Justice Act 1988 Sch 8 para 2). The Magistrates' Courts Act 1980 s 133(1) is expressed to be subject to the provisions of the Criminal Justice Act 2003 s 265 (restriction on consecutive sentences for released prisoners: see PARA 27), other than so far as relating to a sentence of imprisonment of less than 12 months: see the Magistrates' Courts Act 1980 s 133(1) (as so amended; further amended by the Criminal Justice Act 2003 Sch 32 paras 25, 30); and the Criminal Justice Act 2003 (Commencement No 8 and Transitional and Saving Provisions) Order 2005, SI 2005/950, Sch 2 para 14. The Magistrates' Courts Act 1980 s 133 also does not apply to the activation of a suspended sentence (*R v Chamberlain* (1991) 13 Cr App Rep (S) 525, 156 JP 440, CA).

18   Magistrates' Courts Act 1980 s 133(1) (as amended (see note 17); prospectively further amended by the Criminal Justice Act 2003 s 155(1), (2)). At the date at which this volume states the law no day had been appointed for the coming into force of the amendment made by the Criminal Justice Act 2003. This provision does not prevent the subsequent imposition of a term of imprisonment in default of payment of a fine consecutive to a six-month (or, as from a day to be appointed, 65 week) term which has already been imposed at the same time as the fine: *R v Metropolitan Stipendiary Magistrate for South Westminster, ex p Green* [1977] 1 All ER 353. Where the defendant is already undergoing imprisonment, the warrant of commitment for the subsequent offence must be delivered to the governor or keeper of the prison or place of detention in which he is detained: see the Magistrates' Courts Rules 1981, SI 1981/552, r 97(5).

19   As from a day to be appointed the Magistrates' Courts Act 1980 s 133(2) is repealed, and s 133(3) is amended, by the Criminal Justice Act 2003 s 155(1), (3), (4), Sch 37 Pt 7; and the Magistrates' Courts Act 1980 s 133(2A) is repealed by the Criminal Justice and Court Services Act 2000 Sch 7 paras 58, 66, Sch 8. At the date at which this volume states the law no day had been appointed for the coming into force of any of these amendments.

20   As to the procedural classification of offences see MAGISTRATES vol 71 (2013) PARA 511 et seq.

21   Ie otherwise than in pursuance of the Magistrates' Courts Act 1980 s 22(2): see CRIMINAL PROCEDURE vol 27 (2015) PARA 192.

22   Magistrates' Courts Act 1980 s 133(2) (prospectively repealed: see note 19). See *Re Forrest* [1981] AC 1038, sub nom *Forrest v Brighton Justices* [1981] 2 All ER 711, HL. Until a day to be appointed, in relation to the imposition of terms of detention in a young offender institution, the Magistrates' Courts Act 1980 s 133(2) has effect as if the reference to an offence triable either way were a reference to such an offence or an offence triable only on indictment: s 133(2A) (added by the Criminal Justice Act 1988 Sch 15 paras 65, 70; as so prospectively repealed).

23   Magistrates' Courts Act 1980 s 133(3) (prospectively amended (but not so as to affect the sense of the text): see note 19).

24   Magistrates' Courts Act 1980 s 133(4) (prospectively amended by the Tribunals, Courts and Enforcement Act 2007 Sch 13 paras 45, 62). At the date at which this volume states the law no day had been appointed for the coming into force of this amendment.

25   *Head v Head* [1982] 3 All ER 14, [1982] 1 WLR 1186.

(3) DEROGATORY ASSERTIONS ORDERS

556. Restricting the publication and broadcast of derogatory assertions. A 'derogatory assertions order' is an order restricting the publication or broadcasting of a false or irrelevant assertion made pursuant to the sentencing process which is derogatory to a person's character[1]. The effect of the order is that at any time when the order has effect the assertion must not be published in Great Britain in a written publication available to the public or be included in a relevant programme for reception in Great Britain[2]. A derogatory assertions order cannot be made in relation to an assertion if it appears to the court that the assertion was previously made at the trial at which the person was convicted of the offence or during any other proceedings relating to the offence[3], and the court making the order must have substantial grounds for believing that the assertion is derogatory or false or that the facts asserted in it are irrelevant to the sentence[4]. Publication or broadcast in breach of a derogatory assertions order is an offence punishable by fine on summary conviction[5].

1 See the Criminal Procedure and Investigations Act 1996 s 58(4); and CRIMINAL PROCEDURE vol 27 (2015) PARA 177.
2 See the Criminal Procedure and Investigations Act 1996 s 59(1); and CRIMINAL PROCEDURE vol 27 (2015) PARA 177.
3 See the Criminal Procedure and Investigations Act 1996 s 58(5); and CRIMINAL PROCEDURE vol 27 (2015) PARA 177.
4 See the Criminal Procedure and Investigations Act 1996 s 58(4); and CRIMINAL PROCEDURE vol 27 (2015) PARA 177.
5 See the Criminal Procedure and Investigations Act 1996 s 60; and CRIMINAL PROCEDURE vol 27 (2015) PARA 177.

(4) GUIDELINES

(i) Sentencing Council Guidelines

557. The Sentencing Council for England and Wales. The Sentencing Council for England and Wales ('the Council') is established by statute[1]. The principal function of the Council is to prepare, revise and publish sentencing guidelines[2] and allocation guidelines[3] which the court is required to observe[4]. The Council must also publish a resource assessment in respect of the draft or definitive guidelines it publishes[5].

Resource assessments are required to be published where the Council publishes[6] draft guidelines[7] or issues guidelines[8] as definitive guidelines[9]. A resource assessment in respect of any guidelines is an assessment by the Council of the likely effect of the guidelines on the resources required for the provision of prison places, the resources required for probation provision and the resources required for the provision of youth justice services[10].

The Council must also monitor the operation and effect of its sentencing guidelines[11], publish information relating to sentencing practice[12], and may promote awareness of matters relating to the sentencing of offenders by courts in England and Wales[13]. Matters which the Council may promote include, in particular, the sentences imposed by courts in England and Wales, the cost of different sentences and their relative effectiveness in preventing re-offending and the operation and effect of guidelines[14].

Where the Lord Chancellor refers to the Council any government policy proposal (including a policy proposal of the Welsh Ministers), or government proposal for legislation[15] (including a proposal of the Welsh Ministers for legislation), which the Lord Chancellor considers may have a significant effect on the resources required for the provision of prison places[16], the resources required for probation provision[17] or the resources required for the provision of youth justice services[18], the Council must assess the likely effect of the proposal on the matters such matters[19]. The Council must prepare a report of the assessment (a single report may be prepared of the assessments relating to two or more proposals) and send it to the Lord Chancellor and, if it relates to a proposal of the Welsh Ministers, to the Welsh Ministers[20]. The Council must also make an annual report to the Lord Chancellor[21].

1   Coroners and Justice Act 2009 s 118(1). Provision is made for the constitution and membership of the Council: see s 118(2), Sch 15.
2   See the Coroners and Justice Act 2009 ss 120, 121, 123, 124; and PARAS 558–559. The Lord Chancellor may provide the Council with such assistance as it requests in connection with the performance of its functions: s 133.
3   See the Coroners and Justice Act 2009 ss 122–124; and PARA 560. See note 2.
4   See the Coroners and Justice Act 2009 ss 125–126; and PARA 561.
5   Coroners and Justice Act 2009 s 127(2).
6   Ie under the Coroners and Justice Act 2009 s 120 or s 122: see PARAS 558, 560.
7   Coroners and Justice Act 2009 s 127(1)(a).
8   See note 6.
9   Coroners and Justice Act 2009 s 127(1)(b).
10   Coroners and Justice Act 2009 s 127(3). The resources assessment must be published: (1) in a case within s 127(1)(a), at the time of publication of the draft guidelines (s 127(4)(a)); and (2) in a case within s 127(1)(b), at the time the guidelines are issued or, where the guidelines are issued by virtue of s 123 (see PARAS 558, 560), as soon as reasonably practicable after the guidelines are issued (s 127(4)(b)). The Council must keep under review any resource assessment published under s 127 and, if the assessment is found to be inaccurate in a material respect, publish a revised resource assessment: s 127(5).
11   Coroners and Justice Act 2009 s 128(1)(a). The Council is also required to consider what conclusions can be drawn from the information obtained by virtue of such monitoring: s 128(1)(b). The Council must, in particular, discharge its monitoring duty (ie its duty under s 128(1)(a)) with a view to drawing conclusions about the frequency with which, and extent to which, courts depart from sentencing guidelines, the factors which influence the sentences imposed by courts, the effect of the guidelines on the promotion of consistency in sentencing and the effect of the guidelines on the promotion of public confidence in the criminal justice system: s 128(2). The Council must report on the exercise of these functions in its annual report: see s 128(3); and note 21. 'Sentence', in relation to an offence, includes any order made by a court when dealing with the offender in respect of the offender's offence, and 'sentencing' is to be construed accordingly: s 136.
12   Coroners and Justice Act 2009 s 129(1), which requires the Council to publish, at such intervals as it considers appropriate: (1) in relation to each local justice area, information regarding the sentencing practice of the magistrates' courts acting in that area (s 129(1)(a)); and (2) in relation to each location at which the Crown Court sits, information regarding the sentencing practice of the Crown Court when it sits at that location (s 129(1)(b)).
13   Coroners and Justice Act 2009 s 129(2).
14   Coroners and Justice Act 2009 s 129(2). For these purposes the Council may, in particular, publish any information obtained or produced by it in connection with its functions under 128(1) (see note 11): s 129(3).
15   For these purposes 'legislation' means an Act of Parliament if, or to the extent that, it extends to England and Wales, subordinate legislation made under an Act of Parliament if, or to the extent that, the subordinate legislation extends to England and Wales, and a Measure or Act of the National Assembly for Wales or subordinate legislation made under such a Measure or Act: Coroners and Justice Act 2009 s 132(9).
16   'Prison' includes any youth detention accommodation within the meaning of the Powers of Criminal Courts (Sentencing) Act 2000 s 107(1) (detention and training orders: see PARA 11) but does not include any naval, military or air force prison: Coroners and Justice Act 2009 s 136.
17   'Probation provision' has the meaning given by the Offender Management Act 2007 s 2 (see PARA 669): Coroners and Justice Act 2009 s 136.

18 'Youth justice services' has the meaning given by the Crime and Disorder Act 1998 s 38(4) (see CHILDREN AND YOUNG PERSONS vol 10 (2012) PARA 1192): Coroners and Justice Act 2009 s 136.

19 Coroners and Justice Act 2009 s 132(1)–(3).

20 Coroners and Justice Act 2009 s 132(4), (5). If the Lord Chancellor receives such a report he must, unless it relates only to a proposal of the Welsh Ministers, lay a copy of it before each House of Parliament; if the Welsh Ministers receive such a report they must lay a copy of it before the National Assembly for Wales (s 132(6), (7)), and the Council must publish a report which has been so laid (s 132(8)).

21 The Council must, as soon as practicable after the end of each financial year, make to the Lord Chancellor a report on the exercise of the Council's functions during the year: Coroners and Justice Act 2009 s 119(1). The Lord Chancellor must lay a copy of the report before Parliament (s 119(2)) and the Council must publish the report once a copy has been so laid (s 119(3)). When reporting on the exercise of its functions under s 128 (see note 11) in its annual report for a financial year, the Council must include a summary of the information obtained under s 128(1)(a) and a report of any conclusions drawn by the Council under s 128(1)(b): ss 119(4), 128(3).

The annual report for a financial year must contain a sentencing factors report, which is an assessment made by the Council, using the information available to it, of the effect which any changes in the sentencing practice of courts are having or are likely to have on the resources required for the provision of prison places, the resources required for probation provision and the resources required for the provision of youth justice services (s 130) and a non-sentencing factors report, which is a report by the Council of any significant quantitative effect (or any significant change in quantitative effect) which non-sentencing factors are having or are likely to have on the resources needed or available for giving effect to sentences imposed by courts in England and Wales (s 131(1), (3)). 'Non-sentencing factors' are factors which do not relate to the sentencing practice of the courts, and include the recalling of persons to prison, breaches of community orders (within the meaning of the Criminal Justice Act 2003 s 177: see PARA 45 et seq), suspended sentence orders (within the meaning of s 189(7): see PARA 100 et seq), and youth rehabilitation orders (within the meaning of the Criminal Justice and Immigration Act 2008 Pt 1 (ss 1–8): see PARA 73 et seq), patterns of re-offending, decisions or recommendations for release made by the Parole Board or (as from a day to be appointed) a recall adjudicator as defined in the Criminal Justice Act 2003 s 239A (see PARA 705), the early release under discretionary powers of persons detained in prison, and the remanding of persons in custody: Coroners and Justice Act 2009 s 131(4), (5) (s 131(5) prospectively amended by the Criminal Justice and Courts Act 2015 Sch 3 para 16).

The Council may, at any other time, provide the Lord Chancellor with a non-sentencing factors report, and may publish that report: Coroners and Justice Act 2009 s 131(2).

'Financial year' means a period of 12 months ending with 31 March: s 136.

558. Sentencing guidelines. The Sentencing Council for England and Wales[1] must prepare sentencing guidelines[2] about the discharge of a court's duty[3] in connection with reductions in sentences for guilty pleas[4] and about the application of any rule of law as to the totality of sentences[5]. The Council may also prepare sentencing guidelines about any matter[6], from time to time review and revise any guidelines it has issued[7], and must consider any proposals received from the Lord Chancellor[8] or the Court of Appeal[9] for the preparation or revision of existing or further guidelines[10].

When exercising its functions relating to the making or revision of guidelines the Council must have regard to:

(1) the sentences imposed by courts in England and Wales for offences[11];

(2) the need to promote consistency in sentencing[12];

(3) the impact of sentencing decisions on victims of offences[13];

(4) the need to promote public confidence in the criminal justice system[14];

(5) the cost of different sentences and their relative effectiveness in preventing re-offending[15]; and

(6) the results of the Council's monitoring[16] of the operation and effect of its guidelines[17].

Where the Council has prepared or revised guidelines it must first publish such guidelines or revisions as draft guidelines[18] and must consult about the draft guidelines or draft revisions with appropriate persons[19] before issuing them as definitive guidelines[20].

Where the Council decides to prepare or revise sentencing guidelines[21] and is of the opinion that the urgency of the case makes it impractical to comply with the procedural requirements[22] it may prepare or revise the guidelines without first publishing them[23] as draft guidelines[24] and may amend and issue the guidelines[25] without having fully complied with the consultation requirements[26].

The Lord Chancellor may by order provide for existing guidelines[27] to be treated as guidelines issued by the Sentencing Council for England and Wales under these provisions[28].

1   As to the establishment, functions, constitution etc of the Sentencing Council for England and Wales see PARA 557.
2   In the Coroners and Justice Act 2009 Pt 4 Ch 1 (ss 118–136) 'sentencing guidelines' means guidelines relating to the sentencing of offenders: ss 120(1), 136. A sentencing guideline may be general in nature or limited to a particular offence, particular category of offence or particular category of offender: s 120(2). As to the meanings of 'sentence' and 'sentencing' see PARA 538 note 2.
3   Ie under the Criminal Justice Act 2003 s 144: see PARA 564.
4   Coroners and Justice Act 2009 s 120(3)(a).
5   Coroners and Justice Act 2009 s 120(3)(b).
6   Coroners and Justice Act 2009 s 120(4).
7   Coroners and Justice Act 2009 s 120(9).
8   The Lord Chancellor may propose to the Council that sentencing guidelines be prepared or revised by the Council under the Coroners and Justice Act 2009 s 120 in relation to a particular offence, particular category of offence or particular category of offenders, or in relation to a particular matter affecting sentencing: s 124(1)(a).
9   Where the criminal division of the Court of Appeal is seised of an appeal against, or a reference under the Criminal Justice Act 1988 s 36 (reviews of sentencing: see PARA 540 et seq) with respect to, the sentence passed for an offence (the 'relevant offence') the Court of Appeal may propose to the Council that sentencing guidelines be prepared or revised by the Council under the Coroners and Justice Act 2009 s 120 in relation to the relevant offence or in relation to a category of offences within which the relevant offence falls: s 124(2), (3). Such a proposal may be included in the appeal court's judgment in the appeal: s 124(4).
        For these purposes the Court of Appeal is seised of an appeal against a sentence if the court or a single judge has granted leave to appeal against the sentence under the Criminal Appeal Act 1968 s 9 or s 10 (appeals against sentence: see PARAS 627–629) or, in a case where the judge who passed the sentence granted a certificate of fitness for appeal under s 9 or s 10, notice of appeal has been given, and the appeal has not been abandoned or disposed of (Coroners and Justice Act 2009 s 124(6)) and it is seised of a reference under the Criminal Justice Act 1988 s 36 if it has given leave under s 36(1) and the reference has not been disposed of (Coroners and Justice Act 2009 s 124(7)).
        Section 124 is without prejudice to any power of the appeal court to provide guidance relating to the sentencing of offenders in a judgment of the court: s 124(8).
10 Coroners and Justice Act 2009 s 124(5). If the Council receives a proposal under s 124(1) or (3) to prepare or revise any guidelines it must consider whether to do so: s 124(5).
11 Coroners and Justice Act 2009 s 120(11)(a).
12 Coroners and Justice Act 2009 s 120(11)(b).
13 Coroners and Justice Act 2009 s 120(11)(c).
14 Coroners and Justice Act 2009 s 120(11)(d).
15 Coroners and Justice Act 2009 s 120(11)(e).
16 Ie the monitoring carried out under the Coroners and Justice Act 2009 s 128 (see PARA 557).
17 Coroners and Justice Act 2009 s 120(11)(f).
18 Coroners and Justice Act 2009 s 120(5), (10). The Council is required to publish a resource assessment in respect of draft guidelines: see s 127; and PARA 557.
19 Coroners and Justice Act 2009 s 120(6). The Council is required to consult with the Lord Chancellor (s 120(6)(a)), such persons as the Lord Chancellor may direct (s 120(6)(b)), the Justice Select Committee of the House of Commons (or, if there ceases to be a committee of that

name, such committee of the House of Commons as the Lord Chancellor directs) (s 120(6)(c)) and such other persons as the Council considers appropriate (s 120(6)(d)).

20 Coroners and Justice Act 2009 s 120(7), (8). In the case of the guidelines which it must make under s 120(3) (see the text and notes 1–5), the Council must issue the guidelines or the revised guidelines as definitive guidelines after making any amendments of the guidelines which it considers appropriate (s 120(7)); in any other case, the Council may issue the guidelines or the revised guidelines as definitive guidelines after making such amendments (s 120(8)).

21 Coroners and Justice Act 2009 s 123(1)(a).

22 Coroners and Justice Act 2009 s 123(1)(b). The procedural requirements referred to are the requirements of s 120 (see the text and notes 1–20). The guidelines or revised guidelines must state that the Council was of this opinion and give the Council's reasons for that opinion: s 123(4).

23 Ie under the Coroners and Justice Act 2009 s 120(5) (see the text and note 18).

24 Coroners and Justice Act 2009 s 123(2)(a).

25 Ie under the Coroners and Justice Act 2009 s 120(7) or (8) (see the text and note 20).

26 Coroners and Justice Act 2009 s 123(3)(a). The consultation requirements with which the Council need not comply in these circumstances are the requirements of s 120(6)(b)–(d) (see the text and note 19); thus the Council continues to be required to consult the Lord Chancellor in these circumstances.

27 Ie sentencing or allocation guidelines issued by the Sentencing Guidelines Council as definitive guidelines under the Criminal Justice Act 2003 s 170 and guidelines with respect to sentencing which were included in any judgment of the Court of Appeal given before 27 February 2004 and have not been superseded by sentencing guidelines so issued, to the extent that such guidelines have effect immediately before 6 April 2010 (ie the date on which the Coroners and Justice Act 2009 s 125(1) was brought into force by the Coroners and Justice Act 2009 (Commencement No 4, Transitional and Saving Provisions) Order 2010, SI 2010/816): Coroners and Justice Act 2009 Sch 22 para 28(1)(b), (2). The Sentencing Guidelines Council was established in 2003 under the Criminal Justice Act 2003 s 167(1) (repealed) and has been abolished (see the Coroners and Justice Act 2009 s 135), its functions having been taken over by the Sentencing Council.

28 Coroners and Justice Act 2009 Sch 22 para 28(1)(b). At the date at which this volume states the law no order had been made under these provisions, but the Sentencing Council nevertheless applies certain existing guidelines as indicated in PARA 562.

559. Sentencing ranges. When exercising functions relating to the making or revision of sentencing guidelines[1] the Sentencing Council for England and Wales[2] is to have regard to the desirability of sentencing guidelines[3] which relate to a particular offence being structured[4] so that the guidelines:

(1) if reasonably practicable given the nature of the offence, describe (by reference to one or more of the offender's culpability in committing the offence[5], the harm caused, or intended to be caused or which might foreseeably have been caused, by the offence[6], and such other factors as the Council considers to be particularly relevant to the seriousness of the offence in questions[7]) different categories of case involving the commission of the offence which illustrate in general terms the varying degrees of seriousness with which the offence may be committed[8];

(2) specify the range of sentences (the 'offence range') which, in the opinion of the Council, it may be appropriate for a court to impose on an offender convicted of that offence[9];

(3) specify the sentencing starting point in the offence range[10];

(4) list relevant aggravating or mitigating factors[11]; and

(5) include criteria, and provide guidance, for determining the weight to be given to previous convictions of the offender and such of the other relevant aggravating or mitigating factors[12] as the Council considers to be of particular significance in relation to the offence or the offender[13].

The sentencing starting point in the offence range for a category of case described in the guidelines is:

(a) the sentence within that range which the Council considers[14] to be the appropriate starting point for cases within that category[15]; and

(b) where the guidelines do not describe categories of case, is the sentence within that range which the Council considers[16] to be the appropriate starting point[17].

1 Ie function under the Coroners and Justice Act 2009 s 120 (see PARA 558).

2 As to the establishment, functions, constitution etc of the Sentencing Council for England and Wales see PARA 557.

3 As to the meaning of 'sentencing guidelines' see PARA 558 note 2.

4 Ie in the way described by the Coroners and Justice Act 2009 s 121(2)–(9) (see the text and notes 5–13). The provision made in accordance with s 121(2)–(8) may be different for different circumstances or cases involving the offence: s 121(9).

5 Coroners and Justice Act 2009 s 121(2), (3)(a).

6 Coroners and Justice Act 2009 s 121(3)(b).

7 Coroners and Justice Act 2009 s 121(3)(c).

8 Coroners and Justice Act 2009 s 121(2). If the guidelines describe different categories of case in accordance with s 121(2) they should specify for each category the range of sentences (the 'category range') within the offence range which, in the opinion of the Council, it may be appropriate for a court to impose on an offender in a case which falls within the category (s 121(4)(b)) and the sentencing starting point in the offence range for each of those categories (s 121(5)(b)).

9 Coroners and Justice Act 2009 s 121(4)(a). See also s 121(4)(b); and note 8.

10 Coroners and Justice Act 2009 s 121(5)(a). See also s 121(5)(b); and note 8.

11 Coroners and Justice Act 2009 s 121(6)(a), (b), providing that the guidelines should: (1) to the extent not already taken into account by categories of case described in accordance with s 121(2), list any aggravating or mitigating factors which, by virtue of any enactment or other rule of law, the court is required to take into account when considering the seriousness of the offence and any other aggravating or mitigating factors which the Council considers are relevant to such a consideration (s 121(6)(a)); and (2) list any other mitigating factors which the Council considers are relevant in mitigation of sentence for the offence (s 121(6)(b)). For the purposes of s 121(6)(b) the following are to be disregarded: (a) the requirements of the Criminal Justice Act 2003 s 144 (reduction in sentences for guilty pleas: see PARA 564) (Coroners and Justice Act 2009 s 121(7)(a)); (b) the Serious Organised Crime and Police Act 2005 ss 73, 74 (assistance by defendants: reduction or review of sentence: see PARA 548) and any other rule of law by virtue of which an offender may receive a discounted sentence in consequence of assistance given (or offered to be given) by the offender to the prosecutor or investigator of an offence (Coroners and Justice Act 2009 s 121(7)(b)); and (c) any rule of law as to the totality of sentences (s 121(7)(c)).

12 Ie factors within the Coroners and Justice Act 2009 s 121(6)(a) or (b) (see note 11).

13 Coroners and Justice Act 2009 s 121(6)(c). The provision made in accordance with s 121(6)(c) should be framed in such manner as the Council considers most appropriate for the purpose of assisting the court, when sentencing an offender for the offence, to determine the appropriate sentence within the offence range: s 121(8).

14 Ie before taking account of the factors mentioned in the Coroners and Justice Act 2009 s 121(6) (see the text and notes 11–13) and assuming the offender has pleaded not guilty: s 121(10)(a).

15 Coroners and Justice Act 2009 s 121(10)(a).

16 See note 14.

17 Coroners and Justice Act 2009 s 121(10)(b).

560. Allocation guidelines. The Sentencing Council for England and Wales[1] may prepare, review and revise allocation guidelines[2], and must consider any proposals received from the Lord Chancellor for the preparation or revision of existing or further guidelines[3]. When exercising its functions relating to the making or revision of allocation guidelines the Council must have regard to the need to promote consistency in decisions[4] relating to allocation[5] and the results of the Council's monitoring[6] of the operation and effect of its guidelines[7].

Where the Council has prepared or revised allocation guidelines it must first publish such guidelines or revisions as draft guidelines[8] and must consult about the draft guidelines or draft revisions with appropriate persons[9] before issuing them as definitive guidelines[10].

Where the Council decides to prepare or revise allocation guidelines[11] and is of the opinion that the urgency of the case makes it impractical to comply with the procedural requirements[12] it may prepare or revise the guidelines without first publishing them[13] as draft guidelines[14] and may amend and issue the guidelines[15] without having fully complied with the consultation requirements[16].

1   As to the establishment, functions, constitution etc of the Sentencing Council for England and Wales see PARA 557.
2   Coroners and Justice Act 2009 s 122(2), (6). In Pt 4 Ch 1 (ss 118–136) 'allocation guidelines' means guidelines relating to decisions by a magistrates' court under the Magistrates' Courts Act 1980 s 19 (see CRIMINAL PROCEDURE vol 27 (2015) PARA 190) or the Crown Court under the Crime and Disorder Act 1998 Sch 3 para 7(7) or 8(2)(d) (see CRIMINAL PROCEDURE vol 27 (2015) PARA 351 et seq), as to whether an offence is more suitable for summary trial or trial on indictment: Coroners and Justice Act 2009 s 122(1).
3   Coroners and Justice Act 2009 s 124(1)(b). The Lord Chancellor may propose to the Council that allocation guidelines be prepared or revised by the Council under s 122: s 124(1)(b). If the Council receives such a proposal it must consider whether to do so: s 124(3).
4   Ie decisions of the kind referred to in the Coroners and Justice Act 2009 s 122(1) (see note 2).
5   Coroners and Justice Act 2009 s 122(8)(a).
6   Ie the monitoring carried out under the Coroners and Justice Act 2009 s 128 (see PARA 557).
7   Coroners and Justice Act 2009 s 122(8)(b).
8   Coroners and Justice Act 2009 s 122(3), (7). The Council is required to publish a resource assessment in respect of draft allocation guidelines: see s 127; and PARA 557.
9   Coroners and Justice Act 2009 s 122(4). The Council is required to consult with the Lord Chancellor (s 122(4)(a)), such persons as the Lord Chancellor may direct (s 122(4)(b)), the Justice Select Committee of the House of Commons (or, if there ceases to be a committee of that name, such committee of the House of Commons as the Lord Chancellor directs) (s 122(4)(c)) and such other persons as the Council considers appropriate (s 122(4)(d)).
10 Coroners and Justice Act 2009 s 122(5). The Council may issue the guidelines or the revised guidelines as definitive guidelines after making any amendments of the guidelines which it considers appropriate: s 122(5).
11 Coroners and Justice Act 2009 s 123(1)(a).
12 Coroners and Justice Act 2009 s 123(1)(b). The procedural requirements referred to are the requirements of s 122 (see the text and notes 1–10). The guidelines or revised guidelines must state that the Council was of this opinion and give the Council's reasons for that opinion: s 123(4).
13 Ie under the Coroners and Justice Act 2009 s 122(3) (see the text and note 8).
14 Coroners and Justice Act 2009 s 123(2)(b).
15 Ie under the Coroners and Justice Act 2009 s 122(5) (see the text and note 10).
16 Coroners and Justice Act 2009 s 123(3)(b). The consultation requirements with which the Council need not comply in these circumstances are the requirements of s 122(4)(b)–(d) (see the text and note 9); thus the Council continues to be required to consult the Lord Chancellor in these circumstances.

561. Duty of court to follow guidelines. Every court must[1], in sentencing[2] an offender[3], follow any sentencing guidelines[4] which are relevant to the offender's case[5] and, in exercising any other function relating to the sentencing of offenders, follow any sentencing guidelines which are relevant to the exercise of the function[6]: this duty[7] is, however, subject to:

(1)   the provisions[8] restricting the imposition of community sentences[9];
(2)   the provisions[10] restricting the imposition of discretionary custodial sentences[11];
(3)   the provisions[12] requiring a custodial sentence to be for the shortest term commensurate with the seriousness of the offence[13];

(4) the provisions[14] requiring a fine to reflect the seriousness of an offence[15];

(5) the provisions[16] relating to the imposition of a life sentence for a second listed offence[17];

(6) the provisions[18] relating to the determination of a minimum term in relation to a mandatory life sentence[19];

(7) the provisions[20] imposing a minimum sentence for offences involving offensive weapons[21];

(8) the provisions[22] imposing a minimum sentence for specified firearms offences[23];

(9) the provisions[24] imposing a minimum sentence for offences involving bladed articles etc[25];

(10) the provisions[26] imposing minimum sentences for certain drug trafficking and burglary offences[27]; and

(11) the provisions[28] imposing minimum sentences for certain offences involving firearms[29].

If a court is deciding what sentence to impose on a person ('P') who is guilty of an offence[30] and appropriately structured sentencing guidelines[31] have been issued in relation to that offence[32], the duty imposed on a court[33] to follow any sentencing guidelines which are relevant to the offender's case includes[34]:

(a) in all cases, a duty to impose on P, in accordance with the offence-specific guidelines, a sentence which is within the offence range[35]; and

(b) where the offence-specific guidelines describe categories of case[36], a duty to decide which of the categories most resembles P's case in order to identify the sentencing starting point in the offence range[37].

1 Ie unless the court is satisfied that it would be contrary to the interests of justice to do so: Coroners and Justice Act 2009 s 125(1).
2 As to the meanings of 'sentence' and 'sentencing' see PARA 538 note 2.
3 Nothing in these provisions (ie the Coroners and Justice Act 2009 ss 125, 126: see the text and notes 4–37) is to be taken as restricting any power (whether under the Mental Health Act 1983 or otherwise) which enables a court to deal with a mentally disordered offender in the manner it considers to be most appropriate in all the circumstances: Coroners and Justice Act 2009 s 125(7). In connection with s 125(7) see *A-G's Reference (No 117 of 2014), R v Balogh* [2015] EWCA Crim 44, [2015] 1 WLR 301, [2015] All ER (D) 35 (Feb). For this purpose 'mentally disordered', in relation to a person, means suffering from a mental disorder within the meaning of the Mental Health Act 1983 (see s 1; and MENTAL HEALTH AND CAPACITY vol 75 (2013) PARA 761): Coroners and Justice Act 2009 s 125(8).
4 As to the meaning of 'sentencing guidelines' see PARA 558 note 2. For these purposes 'sentencing guidelines' means definitive sentencing guidelines (Coroners and Justice Act 2009 s 125(8)); and 'definitive sentencing guidelines' means sentencing guidelines issued by the Council under the Coroners and Justice Act 2009 s 120 (see PARA 558) as definitive guidelines, as revised by any subsequent guidelines so issued (s 136).
5 Coroners and Justice Act 2009 s 125(1)(a). See note 4. In relation to an offence committed before 6 April 2010, the requirement is to have regard to guidelines, not to follow them: see Sch 22 para 27; and the Coroners and Justice Act 2009 (Commencement No 4, Transitional and Saving Provisions) Order 2010, SI 2010/816.
6 Coroners and Justice Act 2009 s 125(1)(b). In relation to an offence committed before 6 April 2010, the requirement is to have regard to guidelines, not to follow them: see note 5.
7 Ie the duty imposed by the Coroners and Justice Act 2009 s 125(1) (see the text and notes 1–6).
8 Ie the Criminal Justice Act 2003 s 148(1), (2): see PARA 42.
9 Coroners and Justice Act 2009 s 125(6)(a).
10 Ie the Criminal Justice Act 2003 s 152: see PARA 536.
11 Coroners and Justice Act 2009 s 125(6)(b).
12 Ie the Criminal Justice Act 2003 s 153: see PARA 29.
13 Coroners and Justice Act 2009 s 125(6)(c).

14 Ie the Criminal Justice Act 2003 s 164(2): see PARA 178.

15 Coroners and Justice Act 2009 s 125(6)(d).

16 Ie the Criminal Justice Act 2003 s 224A: see PARA 35.

17 Coroners and Justice Act 2009 s 125(6)(da) (s 125(6)(da), (ea), (fa) added by the Legal Aid, Sentencing and Punishment of Offenders Act 2012 Sch 19 para 23, Sch 26 para 31).

18 Ie the Criminal Justice Act 2003 s 269, Sch 21: see CRIMINAL LAW vol 25 (2010) PARA 97.

19 Coroners and Justice Act 2009 s 125(6)(e).

20 Ie the Prevention of Crime Act 1953 ss 1(2B), 1A(5) (see CRIMINAL LAW).

21 Coroners and Justice Act 2009 s 125(6)(ea) (as added (see note 17); s 125(6)(ea), (fa) amended by the Criminal Justice and Courts Act 2015 Sch 5 para 17(1)).

22 Ie the Firearms Act 1968 s 51A: see CRIMINAL LAW vol 26 (2010) PARAS 614, 626, 628 et seq.

23 Coroners and Justice Act 2009 s 125(6)(f).

24 Ie the Criminal Justice Act 1988 ss 139(6B), 139A(5B), 139AA(7) (see CRIMINAL LAW).

25 Coroners and Justice Act 2009 s 125(6)(fa) (as added and amended: see notes 17, 21).

26 Ie the Powers of Criminal Courts (Sentencing) Act 2000 s 110(2) (see CRIMINAL LAW vol 26 (2010) PARA 725) or s 111(2) (see CRIMINAL LAW vol 25 (2010) PARA 290).

27 Coroners and Justice Act 2009 s 125(6)(g).

28 Ie the Violent Crime Reduction Act 2006 s 29(4) or (6) (see CRIMINAL LAW vol 26 (2010) PARA 656).

29 Coroners and Justice Act 2009 s 125(6)(h).

30 Coroners and Justice Act 2009 s 125(2)(a). Where a court determines the notional determinate term for the purpose of determining in any case:

    (1)   the order to be made under the Powers of Criminal Courts (Sentencing) Act 2000 s 82A (life sentence: determination of tariff: see PARA 39) (Coroners and Justice Act 2009 s 126(2)(a));

    (2)   the appropriate custodial term for the purposes of the Criminal Justice Act 2003 s 226A(6) (extended sentence for certain violent or sexual offences: persons 18 or over: see PARAS 18–20) (Coroners and Justice Act 2009 s 126(2)(c) (s 126(1)(c), (d), (2)(c), (d), (5) amended by the Legal Aid, Sentencing and Punishment of Offenders Act 2012 Sch 21 para 34)); or

    (3)   the appropriate term for the purposes of the Criminal Justice Act 2003 s 226B(4) (extended sentence for certain violent or sexual offences: persons under 18: see PARAS 18–20) (Coroners and Justice Act 2009 s 126(2)(d) (as so amended)),

the provisions of s 125(2)–(5) (see the text and notes 31–37) apply for the purposes of determining the notional determinate term in relation to an offence as they apply for the purposes of determining the sentence for an offence: s 126(3). In s 126 references to the notional determinate term are to the determinate sentence that would have been passed in the case if the need to protect the public and the potential danger of the offender had not required the court to impose a life sentence (in circumstances where the sentence is not fixed by law) or, as the case may be, an extended sentence of imprisonment or detention: s 126(4). In s 126(4) 'life sentence' means a sentence mentioned in the Crime (Sentences) Act 1997 s 34(2)(a)–(c), (f), (g) (see PARA 706): Coroners and Justice Act 2009 s 126(5) (as so amended).

31 Ie sentencing guidelines which are structured in the way described in the Coroners and Justice Act 2009 s 121(2)–(5) (see PARA 559).

32 Coroners and Justice Act 2009 s 125(2)(b).

33 Ie by the Coroners and Justice Act 2009 s 125(1)(a) (see the text and notes 1–5).

34 The Coroners and Justice Act 2009 s 125(3) (except as applied by virtue of s 126(3): see note 30) is subject to any power a court has to impose:

    (1)   an extended sentence of imprisonment by virtue of the Criminal Justice Act 2003 s 226A (see PARAS 18–20) (Coroners and Justice Act 2009 s 126(1)(c) (as amended: see note 30)); or

    (2)   an extended sentence of detention by virtue of the Criminal Justice Act 2003 s 226B (Coroners and Justice Act 2009 s 126(1)(d) (as so amended)).

35 Coroners and Justice Act 2009 s 125(3)(a). Section 125(3)(a) is subject to: (1) the Criminal Justice Act 2003 s 144 (reduction in sentences for guilty pleas: see PARA 564) (Coroners and Justice Act 2009 s 125(5)(a)); (2) the Serious Organised Crime and Police Act 2005 ss 73, 74 (assistance by defendants: reduction or review of sentence: see PARA 548) and any other rule of law by virtue of which an offender may receive a discounted sentence in consequence of assistance given (or offered to be given) by the offender to the prosecutor or investigator of an offence (Coroners and Justice Act 2009 s 125(5)(b)); and (3) any rule of law as to the totality of sentences (s 125(5)(c)).

36 Ie in accordance with the Coroners and Justice Act 2009 s 121(2) (see PARA 559).

37 Coroners and Justice Act 2009 s 125(3)(b). Section 125(3)(b) does not apply if the court is of the
opinion that, for the purpose of identifying the sentence within the offence range which is the
appropriate starting point, none of the categories sufficiently resembles P's case: s 125(4).
Nothing in s 125 imposes on the court a separate duty, in a case within s 125(3)(b), to impose a
sentence which is within the category range: s 125(3).

562. Published guidelines. The Sentencing Council[1] has issued[2] definitive
guidelines[3] relating to:

(1) sentencing for fraud, bribery and money laundering offences[4];
(2) sentencing for environmental offences[5];
(3) sentencing for sexual offences[6];
(4) sentencing for dangerous dog offences[7];
(5) sentencing for drug offences[8];
(6) sentencing for burglary offences[9];
(7) sentencing for assault[10]; and
(8) offences taken into consideration and totality[11].

The Council also applies[12] existing guidelines issued by the former Sentencing
Guidelines Council[13] relating to:

(a) sentencing for corporate manslaughter and health and safety offences
     causing death[14];
(b) sentencing for attempted murder[15];
(c) sentencing for breach of an anti-social behaviour order[16];
(d) sentencing for theft and burglary in a building other than a dwelling[17];
(e) sentencing for causing death by driving[18];
(f) sentencing for assaults on children and child cruelty[19];
(g) sentencing for failure to surrender to bail[20];
(h) sentencing for breach of a protective order[21];
(i) sentencing for domestic violence[22];
(j) sentencing for robbery[23];
(k) sentencing for manslaughter by reason of provocation[24];
(l) youth sentencing[25];
(m) the reduction in sentence for a guilty plea[26];
(n) seriousness[27]; and
(o) aspects of the sentencing framework introduced by the Criminal Justice
     Act 2003[28].

There are also allocation guidelines[29] and guidelines relating to sentencing in
the magistrates' court[30].

1   As to the establishment, functions, constitution etc of the Sentencing Council for England and
    Wales see PARA 557.
2   Ie under the Coroners and Justice Act 2009 s 120 (see PARA 558).
3   As to the meanings of 'sentencing guidelines' and 'definitive sentencing guidelines' see PARAS 558
    note 2, 561 note 4.
4   See the Sentencing Council Definitive Guideline *Fraud, Bribery and Money Laundering Offences*
    (published 23 May 2014), which is applicable to all individual offenders aged 18 and over and
    to organisations who are sentenced on or after 1 October 2014, regardless of the date of the
    offence.
5   See the Sentencing Council Definitive Guideline *Environmental Offences* (published 26 February
    2014), which is applicable to all individual offenders aged 18 and over and to organisations who
    are sentenced on or after 1 July 2014, regardless of the date of the offence.
6   See the Sentencing Council Definitive Guideline *Sexual Offences* (published 12 December 2013),
    which is applicable to all offenders aged 18 and over who are sentenced on or after 1 April
    2014, regardless of the date of the offence. In respect of offenders aged under 18 the former
    Sentencing Guidelines Council's Guideline *Sexual Offences Act 2003* (published on 30 April
    2007) Pt 7 applies (pursuant to powers set out in the Coroners and Justice Act 2009 Sch 22
    para 28: see PARA 558 text and notes 27–28).

7   See the Sentencing Council Definitive Guideline *Dangerous Dog Offences* (published 15 May 2012), which is applicable to all individual offenders aged 18 and over who are sentenced on or after 20 August 2012, regardless of the date of the offence.

8   See the Sentencing Council Definitive Guideline *Drug Offences* (published 24 January 2012), which is applicable to all offenders aged 18 and over who are sentenced on or after 27 February 2012, regardless of the date of the offence.

9   See the Sentencing Council Definitive Guideline *Burglary Offences* (published 13 October 2011), which is applicable to all offenders aged 18 and over who are sentenced on or after 16 January 2012, regardless of the date of the offence.

10 See the Sentencing Council Definitive Guideline *Assault* (published 16 March 2011), which is applicable to all offenders aged 18 and over who are sentenced on or after 13 June 2011, regardless of the date of the offence.

11 See the Sentencing Council Definitive Guideline *Offences Taken into Consideration and Totality* (published 6 March 2012), which is applicable to all offenders whose cases are dealt with on or after 11 June 2012; and PARA 555.

12 Ie pursuant to powers set out in the Coroners and Justice Act 2009 Sch 22 para 28.

13 The Sentencing Guidelines Council has been abolished: see PARA 558 note 27.

14 See the Sentencing Guidelines Council Definitive Guideline *Corporate Manslaughter and Health and Safety Offences Causing Death* (published 9 February 2010), which is applicable to the sentencing of organisations on or after 15 February 2010.

15 See the Sentencing Guidelines Council Definitive Guideline *Attempted Murder* (published 16 July 2009), which is applicable to the sentencing of offenders aged 18 and over convicted of any of the offences dealt with therein who are sentenced on or after 27 July 2009.

16 See the Sentencing Guidelines Council Definitive Guideline *Breach of an Anti-Social Behaviour Order* (published 9 December 2008), which is applicable to the sentencing of offenders convicted of breaching an anti-social behaviour order (ASBO) who are sentenced on or after 5 January 2009.

17 See the Sentencing Guidelines Council Definitive Guideline *Theft and Burglary in a Building other than a Dwelling* (published 9 December 2008), which is applicable to the sentencing of offenders aged 18 or over convicted of theft or burglary in a building other than a dwelling who are sentenced on or after 5 January 2009.

18 See the Sentencing Guidelines Council Definitive Guideline *Causing Death by Driving* (published 15 July 2008), which is applicable to the sentencing of offenders aged 18 or over convicted of any of the offences dealt with therein who are sentenced on or after 4 August 2008.

19 See the Sentencing Guidelines Council Definitive Guideline *Overarching Principles — Assault on Children and Cruelty to a Child* (published 20 February 2008), which is applicable to the sentencing of offenders on or after 3 March 2008.

20 See the Sentencing Guidelines Council Definitive Guideline *Failure to Surrender to Bail* (published 29 November 2007), which is applicable to the sentencing of offenders convicted of failing to surrender to bail who are sentenced on or after 10 December 2007.

21 See the Sentencing Guidelines Council Definitive Guideline *Breach of a Protective Order* (published 7 December 2006), which is applicable to offenders convicted of breach of an order who are sentenced on or after 18 December 2006.

22 See the Sentencing Guidelines Council Definitive Guideline *Overarching Principles — Domestic Violence* (published 7 December 2006), which is applicable to all offences sentenced on or after 18 December 2006.

23 See the Sentencing Guidelines Council Definitive Guideline *Robbery* (published 26 July2006), which is applicable to the sentencing of offenders convicted of robbery who are sentenced on or after 1 August 2006.

24 See the Sentencing Guidelines Council Definitive Guideline *Manslaughter by Reason of Provocation* (published 28 November 2005), which is applicable to offenders convicted of manslaughter by reason of provocation who are sentenced after 28 November 2005.

25 See the Sentencing Guidelines Council Definitive Guideline *Overarching Principles — Sentencing Youths* (published 20 November 2009), which is applicable to the sentencing of offenders on or after 30 November 2009.

26 See the Sentencing Guidelines Council Definitive Guideline *Reduction in Sentence for a Guilty Plea* (revised 20 July 2007), which is applicable to all cases sentenced on or after 23 July 2007.

27 See the Sentencing Guidelines Council Definitive Guideline *Overarching Principles — Seriousness* (published 16 December 2004), which is applicable to all cases involving persons aged 18 or over sentenced on or after that date.

28 See the Sentencing Guidelines Council Definitive Guideline *New Sentences — Criminal Justice Act 2003* (published 16 December 2004), which is applicable to cases involving persons aged 18 or over sentenced on or after that date.

29 See the Sentencing Council Definitive Guideline *Allocation* (published 6 March 2012), which applies to all defendants in the magistrates' court (including youths jointly charged with adults) whose cases are dealt with on or after 11 June 2012. This guideline is not applicable in the youth court. As to allocation guidelines see PARA 560.

30 See the Sentencing Guidelines Council Definitive Guideline *Magistrates' Court Sentencing Guidelines* (published 12 May 2008), which applies to all relevant cases appearing for allocation (mode of trial) or for sentence on or after 4 August 2008. See also the Sentencing Guidelines Council Additional Note to Magistrates' Court Sentencing Guidelines *Knife Crime* (published 4 August 2008), which is applicable as from that date.

(ii) Guidelines by the Court of Appeal

563.   Guidelines. Prior to the establishment of the Sentencing Guidelines Council[1] the authority on sentencing guidelines was the Court of Appeal. The Council has provided[2] a compendium of guideline judgments in relation to the following areas:

(1)   generic sentencing principles;

(2)   homicide and related offences;

(3)   non-fatal offences against the person;

(4)   driving offences relating in death;

(5)   sexual offences;

(6)   drug offences;

(7)   public order offences;

(8)   Theft Acts offences/fraud;

(9)   offences against public justice;

(10) counterfeiting and money laundering;

(11) miscellaneous offences[3].

1 See PARA 635.

2 See the Sentencing Guidelines Council Guideline *Guideline Judgments—Case Compendium* (2005). The Compendium is updated on the Council website.

3 See the Sentencing Guidelines Council Guideline *Guideline Judgments—Case Compendium* (2005).

(5) GUILTY PLEAS

564.   Reduction in sentences for guilty pleas. In determining what sentence to pass on an offender who has pleaded guilty to an offence in proceedings before that or another court[1], a court must take into account:

(1)   the stage in the proceedings for the offence at which the offender indicated his intention to plead guilty[2]; and

(2)   the circumstances in which this indication was given[3].

A reduction in sentence for a plea of guilty should only be applied to the punitive elements of a penalty: the guilty plea reduction has no impact on a sentencing decision in relation to ancillary orders, including orders of disqualification from driving[4]. Where a sentencer is in doubt as to whether a custodial sentence is appropriate the reduction attributable to a guilty plea will be a relevant consideration[5]. Where this is amongst the factors leading to the imposition of a non-custodial sentence there will be no need to apply a further reduction on account of the guilty plea[6]. A similar approach is appropriate where the reduction for a guilty plea is amongst the factors leading to the imposition of a financial penalty or discharge instead of a community order[7]. Alternatively, it may operate to reduce the length of the sentence with the proportion of the sentence calculated by reference to the circumstances in which the guilty plea was indicated, in particular the stage in the proceedings[8].

In the case of an offence the sentence for which falls to be imposed under one of the specified minimum sentence provisions[9], nothing in that provision prevents the court, after taking into account any matter relating to the stage in the proceedings at which the offender indicated his intention to plead guilty and the circumstances in which this indication was given[10], from:

(a)   in the case of an offender aged 18 or over when convicted[11], imposing any sentence which is not less than 80 per cent of that specified in that provision[12]; and

(b)   in the case of a person who is aged at least 16 but under 18 when convicted[13], from imposing any sentence that it considers appropriate[14].

1   As to the meaning of 'court' see PARA 1 note 1.
2   Criminal Justice Act 2003 s 144(1)(a).
3   Criminal Justice Act 2003 s 144(1)(b).
4   See the Sentencing Guidelines Council Definitive Guideline *Reduction in Sentence for a Guilty Plea* (revised 20 July 2007) para 2.6. In connection with the guidelines see PARA 562.
5   *Reduction in Sentence for a Guilty Plea* para 2.3.
6   *Reduction in Sentence for a Guilty Plea* para 2.3.
7   *Reduction in Sentence for a Guilty Plea* para 2.3.
8   See *Reduction in Sentence for a Guilty Plea* para 4.1. See further PARA 565.
9   As to these see note 11 (defendants aged 18 or over when convicted) and note 13 (defendant aged 16 or 17 when convicted).
10   Ie any matter referred to in the Criminal Justice Act 2003 s 144(1) (see the text and notes 1–3).
11   Ie where the Prevention of Crime Act 1953 ss 1(2B), 1A(5) or (6)(a) (see CRIMINAL LAW), the Powers of Criminal Courts (Sentencing) Act 2000 s 110(2) (see CRIMINAL LAW vol 26 (2010) PARA 725) or s 111(2) (see CRIMINAL LAW vol 25 (2010) PARA 290), or the Criminal Justice Act 1988 ss 139(6B), s 139A(5B), 139AA(7) or (8)(a) (see CRIMINAL LAW), is the provision under which the sentence falls to be imposed: Criminal Justice Act 2003 s 144(3) (s 144(2) amended, s 144(3)–(5) added, by the Legal Aid, Sentencing and Punishment of Offenders Act 2012 Sch 26 para 18; Criminal Justice Act 2003 s 144(2)–(5) amended by the Criminal Justice and Courts Act 2015 Sch 5 para 12). As to when such sentences fall to be imposed see PARA 536 note 2. As to the determination of a person's age see the Children and Young Persons Act 1933 s 99; and CHILDREN AND YOUNG PERSONS vol 10 (2012) PARA 1206.
12   Criminal Justice Act 2003 s 144(2) (as amended: see note 11).
13   Ie where the Prevention of Crime Act 1953 ss 1(2B), 1A(6)(b) or the Criminal Justice Act 1988 ss 139(6B), s 139A(5B), 139AA(7), (8)(b) is the provision under which the sentence falls to be imposed.
14   Criminal Justice Act 2003 s 144(4), (5) (as added and amended: see note 11).

565.   Calculating the discount.   The greatest reduction[1] will be where the plea was indicated at the first reasonable opportunity[2]. The level of the reduction will be[3] gauged on a sliding scale ranging from a recommended one third (where the guilty plea was entered at the first reasonable opportunity in relation to the offence for which sentence is being imposed), reducing to a recommended one quarter (where a trial date has been set) and to a recommended one tenth (for a guilty plea entered at the 'door of the court' or after the trial has begun)[4]. Any defendant is entitled to put the prosecution to proof and every defendant who is guilty should be encouraged to indicate that guilt at the first reasonable opportunity[5]. Where the prosecution case is overwhelming it may not be appropriate to give the full reduction that would otherwise be given and, whilst there is a presumption in favour of the full reduction being given where a plea has been indicated at the first reasonable opportunity, the fact that the prosecution case is overwhelming without relying on admissions from the defendant may be a reason justifying departure from the guideline[6]. If, after pleading guilty, there is a Newton hearing and the offender's version is rejected, this should be taken into account in determining the level of sentence[7]. If the not guilty plea was entered and maintained for tactical reasons (eg to retain privileges on remand), a late guilty plea should attract very little, if any, discount[8]. Credit should not be withheld or reduced on the ground that the defendant had no alternative but to plead guilty[9], nor on the ground that the defendant has in error been charged with a less serious offence than appropriate, which restricted the judge's sentencing powers[10]. A judge is entitled to refuse a reduction for a guilty plea where there is an overwhelming case and where a defendant clearly lies as to his involvement in the offence during a Newton hearing[11]. A judge is not required to give credit for a pre-trial guilty plea to a lesser offence that is rejected by the prosecution where, at trail, the offender pleads not guilty to, and is convicted of, that lesser offence[12].

1　See PARA 564.
2　See the Sentencing Guidelines Council Definitive Guideline *Reduction in Sentence for a Guilty Plea* (revised 20 July 2007) para 4.1. In connection with the guidelines see PARA 562.
3　Ie, save where the Criminal Justice Act 2003 s 144(2) (see PARA 564) applies: *Reduction in Sentence for a Guilty Plea* para 4.2.
4　See *Reduction in Sentence for a Guilty Plea* paras 4.2, 4.3(i)–(iii).
5　See *Reduction in Sentence for a Guilty Plea* para 5.2.
6　See *Reduction in Sentence for a Guilty Plea* para 5.3.
7　See *Reduction in Sentence for a Guilty Plea* para 4.3(iv). See also *R v Underwood* [2004] EWCA Crim 2256, [2005] 1 Cr App Rep (S) 478; *Criminal Practice Directions 2015* [2015] EWCA Crim 1567, [2015] All ER (D) 134 (Sep) CPD VII Sentencing B: Determining the Factual Basis of Sentence B.8B.10; and see CRIMINAL PROCEDURE vol 27 (2015) PARA 378.
8　*Reduction in Sentence for a Guilty Plea* para 4.3(v).
9　*R v Forbes* [2005] EWCA Crim 2069, [2005] NLJR 1631; *A-G's References (Nos 14 and 15 of 2006), R v French* [2006] EWCA Crim 1335, [2007] 1 All ER 718, [2007] 1 Cr App Rep (S) 215.
10　*R v Dalby, R v Berry* [2005] EWCA Crim 1292, [2006] 1 Cr App Rep (S) 216, [2005] Crim LR 730.
11　*R v Elicin* [2008] EWCA Crim 2249, [2009] 1 Cr App Rep (S) 561, [2008] All ER (D) 60 (Sep).
12　See *R v Birt* [2010] EWCA Crim 2823, [2011] 2 Cr App Rep (S) 82. See also *R v Razaq* [2011] EWCA Crim 1518 (focus on appeal should be whether overall sentence manifestly excessive); *R v Wilson* [2012] EWCA Crim 386, [2012] 2 Cr App Rep (S) 440 (defendant entitled to discount for guilty plea even where case against him was overwhelming).

566.　First reasonable opportunity. The critical time for determining the reduction for a guilty plea[1] is the first reasonable opportunity for the defendant to have indicated a willingness to plead guilty[2]. This opportunity will vary with a wide range of factors[3]. Examples of circumstances where a determination will have to be made are:

(1)　the first reasonable opportunity may be the first time that a defendant appears before the court and has the opportunity to plead guilty[4], although the court may consider that it would be reasonable to have expected an indication of willingness even earlier, perhaps whilst under interview[5];

(2)　where an offence triable either way is committed to the Crown Court for trial and the defendant pleads guilty at the first hearing in that Court, the reduction will be less than if there had been an indication of a guilty plea given to the magistrates' court (recommended reduction of one third) but more than if the plea had been entered after a trial date had been set (recommended reduction of one quarter), and is likely to be in the region of 30 per cent[6];

(3)　where an offence is triable only on indictment, it may well be that the first reasonable opportunity would have been during the police station stage; where that is not the case, the first reasonable opportunity is likely to be at the first hearing in the Crown Court[7]; and

(4) where a defendant is convicted after pleading guilty to an alternative (lesser) charge to that to which he had originally pleaded not guilty, the extent of any reduction will be determined by the stage at which the defendant first formally indicated to the court willingness to plead guilty to the lesser charge, and the reason why that lesser charge was proceeded with in preference to the original charge[8].

1   See PARA 564.
2   See the Sentencing Guidelines Council Definitive Guideline *Reduction in Sentence for a Guilty Plea* (revised 20 July 2007) Annex para 1. In connection with the guidelines see PARA 562.
3   *Reduction in Sentence for a Guilty Plea* Annex para 1. The key principle is that the purpose of giving a reduction is to recognise the benefits that come from a guilty plea not only for those directly involved in the case in question but also in enabling Courts more quickly to deal with other outstanding cases: Annex para 2.
4   *Reduction in Sentence for a Guilty Plea* Annex para 3(a).
5   *Reduction in Sentence for a Guilty Plea* Annex para 3(b).
6   *Reduction in Sentence for a Guilty Plea* Annex para 3(c).
7   *Reduction in Sentence for a Guilty Plea* Annex para 3(d).
8   *Reduction in Sentence for a Guilty Plea* Annex para 3(e).

567.   Maximum considered too low. The sentencer is bound to sentence for the offence with which the offender has been charged, and to which he has pleaded guilty, and cannot remedy perceived defects (for example an inadequate charge or maximum penalty) by refusal of the guilty plea discount[1].

1   See the Sentencing Guidelines Council Definitive Guideline *Reduction in Sentence for a Guilty Plea* (revised 20 July 2007) Annex para E 5.6. In connection with the guidelines see PARA 562. In connection with reductions for guilty pleas generally see PARA 564.

568.   Defendant requires advice. In some cases the defendant will genuinely not know whether he is guilty or not and will require advice, or sight of the evidence against him, in order to decide: these might include cases where even if the facts are known there is a need for legal advice as to whether an offence is constituted by them, or cases where the defendant genuinely has no recollection of events, and there will be other cases in which the defendant cannot reasonably be expected to make any admission until he and his advisors have seen at least some of the evidence[1]. However, as a rule a defendant does not require legal advice in order to know whether he is guilty or not, and this is taken into account in calculating any guilty plea reduction[2].

1   *R v Caley* [2012] EWCA Crim 2821, [2013] 2 Cr App Rep (S) 305.
2   *R v Caley* [2012] EWCA Crim 2821, [2013] 2 Cr App Rep (S) 305. See PARA 564.

569.   False mitigation. A false or dishonest claim made in mitigation may justify a smaller than usual reduction for the guilty plea[1].

1   See *R v Martin* [2006] EWCA Crim 1035, [2007] 1 Cr App Rep (S) 14. See PARA 564.

570.   Overwhelming prosecution case. Where the prosecution case is overwhelming, it may not be appropriate to give the full reduction[1] that would otherwise be given[2]. Whilst there is a presumption in favour of the full reduction being given where a plea has been indicated at the first reasonable opportunity, the fact that the prosecution case is overwhelming without relying on admissions from the defendant may be a reason justifying departure from the guideline[3].

1   See PARA 564.

2   See the Sentencing Guidelines Council Definitive Guideline *Reduction in Sentence for a Guilty Plea* (revised 20 July 2007) Annex para E 5.3. In connection with the guidelines see PARA 562.

3   *Reduction in Sentence for a Guilty Plea* para E 5.3.

571.   Judicial discretion. The guidelines relating to reductions in sentences for guilty pleas[1] do not remove a judge's discretion, which he may exercise so long as he gives valid reasons for departing from the guidelines[2].

1   See PARA 564.

2   See *R v Last* [2005] EWCA Crim 106, [2005] 2 Cr App Rep (S) 381; *R v Bowering* [2005] EWCA Crim 3215, [2006] 2 Cr App Rep (S) 80; *R v Caley* [2012] EWCA Crim 2821, [2013] 2 Cr App Rep (S) 305.

572.   Reduction and the early guilty plea scheme. Where a guilty plea is anticipated, sentence should normally be passed at an early guilty plea hearing[1]. The parties must prepare accordingly in advance of the hearing[2]. The court must be notified promptly of any difficulty which may mean that sentence cannot be passed at the hearing so that an alternative date can be considered[3].

1   See the *Criminal Practice Directions 2015* [2015] EWCA Crim 1567, [2015] All ER (D) 134 (Sep) CPD I General Matters 3A.7. The magistrates' court or the Crown Court may order an early guilty plea hearing, in accordance with directions given by the presiding judges, where a guilty plea is anticipated, to allow the Crown Court promptly to deal with such a case: See the *Criminal Practice Directions 2015* [2015] EWCA Crim 1567, [2015] All ER (D) 134 (Sep) CPD I General Matters 3A.6.

2   See the *Criminal Practice Directions 2015* [2015] EWCA Crim 1567, [2015] All ER (D) 134 (Sep) CPD I General Matters 3A.7. This may include:
      (1)   addressing any issue arising from a basis of plea;
      (2)   making timely application for a pre-sentence report and, if granted, ensuring that the Probation Service is provided with details of the offence or offences in respect of which the defendant intends to plead guilty, the details of any basis of plea and of the defendant's current address and telephone number;
      (3)   obtaining medical or other material necessary for sentencing; and
      (4)   quantifying costs.

3   See the *Criminal Practice Directions 2015* [2015] EWCA Crim 1567, [2015] All ER (D) 134 (Sep) CPD I General Matters 3A.8.

(6) MITIGATION

573.   Court's powers. Nothing in the statutory provisions relating to the imposition of community sentences[1], the imposition of custodial sentences[2], pre-sentence reports and other requirements[3], or the fixing of fines[4] or youth rehabilitation orders with intensive supervision and surveillance[5] or youth rehabilitation orders with fostering[6]:

(1)   prevents a court[7] from mitigating an offender's sentence[8] by taking into account any such matters as, in the opinion of the court, are relevant in mitigation of sentence[9];

(2)   prevents a court from mitigating any penalty included in an offender's sentence by taking into account any other penalty included in that sentence and, in the case of an offender who is convicted of one or more other offences, from mitigating his sentence by applying any rule of law as to the totality of sentences[10]; or

(3)   is to be taken either as requiring a court to pass a custodial sentence, or any particular custodial sentence, on a mentally disordered offender[11] or

as restricting any power[12] which enables a court to deal with such an offender in the manner it considers to be most appropriate in all the circumstances[13].

Heads (2) and (3) above are without prejudice to the generality of head (1) above[14].

1   Criminal Justice Act 2003 s 166(1)(a). For the relevant statutory provisions see s 148 (see PARA 42) and or s 151(2) or (2B) (see PARAS 47, 77): s 166(1)(a) (s 166(1)(a), (3), (5) amended, s 166(1)(e), (f) added, by the Criminal Justice and Immigration Act 2008 Sch 4 paras 76(7), 79). As to the meaning of 'community sentence' see PARA 42.
2   Criminal Justice Act 2003 s 166(1)(b). For the relevant statutory provisions see s 152, s 153 or s 157; and PARAS 29, 536, 584. As to the meaning of 'custodial sentence' see the Powers of Criminal Courts (Sentencing) Act 2000 s 76; and PARA 9 note 15 (definition applied by the Criminal Justice Act 2003 s 305(1)).
3   Criminal Justice Act 2003 s 166(1)(c). For the relevant statutory provision see s 156; and PARA 579.
4   Criminal Justice Act 2003 s 166(1)(d). For the relevant statutory provision see s 164; and PARA 178.
5   Criminal Justice Act 2003 s 166(1)(e) (as added: see note 1).
6   Criminal Justice Act 2003 s 166(1)(f) (as added: see note 1).
7   As to the meaning of 'court' see PARA 1 note 1.
8   As to the meaning of 'sentence' for these purposes see PARA 538 note 2.
9   Criminal Justice Act 2003 s 166(1).
10 Criminal Justice Act 2003 s 166(3) (as amended: see note 1).
11 For these purposes, 'mentally disordered', in relation to a person, means suffering from a mental disorder within the meaning of the Mental Health Act 1983 (see PARA 333 note 4; and MENTAL HEALTH AND CAPACITY vol 75 (2013) PARA 761): Criminal Justice Act 2003 s 166(6).
12 Ie whether under the Mental Health Act 1983 or otherwise.
13 Criminal Justice Act 2003 s 166(5) (as amended: see note 1).
14 Criminal Justice Act 2003 s 166(4).

574.   Relevant factors. Some factors may indicate that the offender's culpability is unusually low, or that the harm caused by an offence is less than usually serious[1], for example:

(1)   a greater degree of provocation than normally expected[2];
(2)   mental illness or disability[3];
(3)   youth or age, where it affects the responsibility of the individual defendant[4];
(4)   the fact that the offender played only a minor role in the offence[5].

A court, after taking into account such matters as, in its opinion, are relevant in mitigation of sentence, may pass a community sentence even though it is of the opinion that the offence, or the combination of the offence and one or more offences associated[6] with it, was so serious that a community sentence could not normally be justified for the offence[7].

1   See the Sentencing Guidelines Council Definitive Guideline *Overarching Principles — Seriousness* (published 16 December 2004) para 1.24. As to the levels of criminal culpability see PARA 586 note 2.
2   *Overarching Principles: Seriousness* para 1.25.
3   *Overarching Principles: Seriousness* para 1.25. See eg *R v Hall* [2013] EWCA Crim 82, [2013] 2 Cr App Rep (S) 434, [2013] All ER (D) 92 (Feb).
4   *Overarching Principles: Seriousness* para 1.25. In sexual offences the age of the offender and the age of offences cannot be given too much weight, but they are mitigating factors: *A-G's Reference (No 70 of 2008), R v W* [2009] EWCA Crim 100, [2009] 2 Cr App Rep (S) 454, (2009) Times, 2 February. As to the determination of a person's age see the Children and Young Persons Act 1933 s 99; and CHILDREN AND YOUNG PERSONS vol 10 (2012) PARA 1206.
5   *Overarching Principles: Seriousness* para 1.25.
6   As to when an offence is associated with another see PARA 9 note 7.

7   Criminal Justice Act 2003 s 166(2). Section 152(2) (see PARA 536) does not prevent this:
     s 166(2).

575.   Personal mitigating factors.   Personal mitigating factors which may be
considered include the offender's previous good character[1], any assistance he
may have given to the police as to offences committed by others which leads to
their apprehension and prosecution[2], any serious delay between the commission
of the offence and trial[3] (which in some cases could violate the defendant's
Convention right to a fair hearing[4]) and the fact that the crime would not have
been committed but for the activities of an informer or police officer[5] or an agent
provocateur such as a journalist[6]. The cultural background of the complainant
and the defendant in a case of relationship rape was not a mitigating factor in
sentencing[7]. The fact that an offender's business may collapse, leading to the
unemployment of its staff, is not a mitigating factor where the offence relates to
the manner in which the business was conducted[8].

1   See PARA 576.
2   See PARA 577.
3   See eg *R v Tierney* [1982] Crim LR 53, CA; *R v Barrick* (1985) 81 Cr App Rep 78, 7 Cr App
     Rep (S) 142, CA.
4   Ie the right to a fair hearing under the Convention for the Protection of Human Rights and
     Fundamental Freedoms (Rome, 4 November 1950; TS 71 (1953; Cmd 8969) (the European
     Convention on Human Rights) art 6 (see RIGHTS AND FREEDOMS vol 88A (2013) PARAS
     243–300): see *R v Shaw* [2011] EWCA Crim 98, [2011] All ER (D) 65 (Feb) (two-year delay
     between guilty plea and sentence).
5   See eg *R v Underhill* (1979) 1 Cr App Rep (S) 270, CA. Test purchases of drugs by undercover
     police officers in endeavouring to obtain evidence of drug dealing is not a mitigating factor
     where the dealer would have sold in any event (*R v Springer* [1999] 1 Cr App Rep (S) 217,
     [1998] Crim LR 912, CA; *R v Mayeri* [1999] 1 Cr App Rep (S) 304, CA), nor is the use of test
     letters in order to obtain evidence that postal workers are stealing mail (*R v Ramen* (1988) 10
     Cr App Rep (S) 334, CA), and nor is the fact that the defendant suffered anxiety created by a
     'cut-throat' defence (*R v Thomas (Corey)* [2005] EWCA Crim 2023, (2005) Times, 20 October
     (co-defendant had said that the defendant had killed the victim)).
6   See eg *R v Tonnessen* [1998] 2 Cr App Rep (S) 328.
7   *A-G's Reference (No 66 of 2010), R v W* [2011] EWCA Crim 97, [2011] Cr App Rep (S) 285.
8   *A-G's Reference (No 89 of 2006), R v Shaw* [2006] EWCA Crim 2570, [2007] ICR 1047,
     [2007] 1 Cr App Rep (S) 621.

576.   Good character.   Some measure of leniency will ordinarily be extended to
offenders of previous good character, the more so if there is evidence of good
character (for example relating to the offender's employment record or discharge
or family responsibilities) as opposed to a mere absence of previous convictions[1].
'Good character' is of minor relevance in cases involving serious criminal
behaviour such as rape[2], armed robbery[3] or the supply of Class A drugs[4]. The
previous good character of a courier in an offence of importation of drugs is of
less importance than in other cases[5]. It is appropriate to consider positive good
character, such as service to the local community[6].

1   See *R v Howells* [1999] 1 All ER 50, [1999] 1 WLR 307, [1999] 1 Cr App Rep (S) 335. As to
     the appropriateness of imposing a custodial sentence on a female defendant of previous good
     character with dependent children see *R v Mills* [2002] EWCA Crim 26, [2002] 2 Cr App Rep
     (S) 229, [2002] Crim LR 331.
2   *R v Billam* [1986] 1 All ER 985, 82 Cr App Rep 347, CA.
3   *R v Turner* [1975] 61 Cr App Rep 67.
4   See *A-G's Reference (No 17 of 2011), R v Mandale* [2011] EWCA Crim 1319, [2012]
     01 LS Gaz R 15, [2011] All ER (D) 75 (Dec).

5   *R v Aramah* (1982) 76 Cr App Rep 190, [1983] Crim LR 271, CA; *R v Saunders* (1991) 92 Cr
    App Rep 6, CA; and see, in connection with *R v Aramah*, *R v Ronchetti* [1998] 2 Cr App Rep
    (S) 100, [1998] Crim LR 227, CA.
6   *R v Clark (Joan)* (1999) Times, 27 January, CA.

577. Assisting the investigation. The fact that a defendant has assisted a
police investigation may serve to mitigate his sentence, although the assistance
must be given sufficiently early to be potentially useful[1]. The amount of the
reduction will vary from one-half to two-thirds depending on the circumstances[2].
Where a defendant pleads guilty and gives truthful evidence against an
accomplice, he will be given a greater discount in his sentence than if he pleads
guilty but fails to give such evidence[3]. The Court of Appeal may review cases
where a defendant pleads guilty and receives credit for supplying information but
the value of that information is not fully appreciated by the sentencing judge[4]. A
defendant is entitled to receive credit for meritorious behaviour relating to an
earlier unconnected offence[5].

1   *R v Debbag and Izett* (1991) 12 Cr App Rep (S) 733, CA. See also *R v A (Informer: Reduction
    of Sentence)*, *R v B (Informer: Reduction of Sentence)* [1999] 1 Cr App Rep (S) 52, [1998] Crim
    LR 757, (1998) Times, 1 May, CA. As to the factors to be considered in deciding whether a
    sentence should be discounted, and the extent of the discount, see further *R v Lowe* (1977)
    66 Cr App Rep 122, CA; *R v Davies, R v Gorman* (1979) 68 Cr App Rep 319, CA; *R v Rose,
    R v Sapiano* (1980) 2 Cr App Rep (S) 239, CA; *R v Wood* (1987) 9 Cr App Rep (S) 238, [1987]
    Crim LR 715, CA; *R v Sivan* (1988) 87 Cr App Rep 407, 10 Cr App Rep (S) 282, CA
    (disapproving *R v Preston, R v McAleny* (1987) 9 Cr App Rep (S) 155, [1987] Crim LR
    587, CA). See also *R v Aramah* (1982) 76 Cr App Rep 190, [1983] Crim LR 271, CA
    (substantial reduction appropriate for a plea of guilty coupled with considerable assistance to
    the police); *R v Afzal* (1989) Times, 14 October, CA. As to guidelines for sentencing judges
    dealing with confidential police reports about defendants who have given information or
    assistance to the police see *R v X* [1999] 2 Cr App Rep 125, [1999] Crim LR 678, CA. In
    respect of cases where the assistance is given in pursuance of a written agreement with a
    specified prosecutor see also PARA 548.
2   *R v King* (1985) 82 Cr App Rep 120, 7 Cr App Rep (S) 227, CA.
3   *R v Wood* [1997] 1 Cr App Rep (S) 347, [1996] Crim LR 916, CA.
4   *R v A (Informer: Reduction of Sentence), R v B (Informer: Reduction of Sentence)* [1999] 1 Cr
    App Rep (S) 52, [1998] Crim LR 757, (1998) Times, 1 May, CA.
5   *R v Alexander* [1997] 2 Cr App Rep (S) 74, CA.

(7) PRE-SENTENCE REPORTS

578. Definition. A 'pre-sentence report' is a report which, with a view to
assisting the court in determining the most suitable method of dealing with an
offender, is made or submitted by an appropriate officer[1] and contains
information as to such matters, presented in such manner, as may be prescribed
by rules made by the Secretary of State[2]. Subject to any such rules the court may
accept a pre-sentence report given orally in open court[3], although a pre-sentence
report that relates to an offender aged under 18 and is required to be obtained
and considered before the court forms an opinion relating to the risk the offender
occasions to the public[4], must be in writing[5].

1   Criminal Justice Act 2003 s 158(1)(a). In s 158(1), 'appropriate officer' means, where the
    offender is aged 18 or over, an officer of a local probation board or an officer of a provider of
    probation services (s 158(2)(a) (amended by SI 2008/912)); and, where the offender is aged
    under 18, an officer of a local probation board, an officer of a provider of probation services, a
    social worker of a local authority or a member of a youth offending team (Criminal Justice
    Act 2003 s 158(2)(b) (amended by the Children Act 2004 s 64, Sch 5 Pt 4; and SI 2008/912)).
    As to the meanings of 'local probation board' and 'youth offending team' see PARA 73 note 2. As
    to local probation boards and the provision of probation services see PARAS 666–687. As to

youth offending teams see CHILDREN AND YOUNG PERSONS vol 10 (2012) PARA 1193. As to the determination of a person's age see the Children and Young Persons Act 1933 s 99; and CHILDREN AND YOUNG PERSONS vol 10 (2012) PARA 1206.

2   Criminal Justice Act 2003 s 158(1)(b).

3   Criminal Justice Act 2003 s 158(1A) (s 158(1A), (1B) added by the Criminal Justice and Immigration Act 2008).

4   Ie the opinion mentioned in the Criminal Justice Act 2003 s 156(3)(a) (see PARA 580).

5   Criminal Justice Act 2003 s 158(1B) (as added: see note 3).

579.   When required.   In forming an opinion for the purposes of the statutory provisions concerning the imposition of community sentences[1], a court[2] must take into account all such information as is available to it about the circumstances of the offence or (as the case may be) of the offence and the offence or offences associated[3] with it, including any aggravating or mitigating factors[4].

1   Ie in forming any such opinion as is mentioned in the Criminal Justice Act 2003 s 148(1) or (2)(b) (see PARA 42), s 152(2) or s 153(2) (see PARAS 29, 536) (including where a court forms that opinion for the purposes of s 224A(3) (see PARA 35) and (in the case of the opinion mentioned in s 153(2)), for the purposes of s 226A(6) or s 226B(4) (see PARAS 18–20)), or in the Criminal Justice and Immigration Act 2008 s 1(4)(b) or (c) (see PARA 75): Criminal Justice Act 2003 s 156(1), (9), (10) (s 156(1) amended by the Criminal Justice and Immigration Act 2008 Sch 4 para 77(1), (2); Criminal Justice Act 2003 s 156(9), (10) added by the Legal Aid, Sentencing and Punishment of Offenders Act 2012 Sch 19 para 13, Sch 21 para 22). As to the meaning of 'community sentence' see PARA 42. As to the meaning of 'sentence' for these purposes see PARA 538 note 2.

2   As to the meaning of 'court' see PARA 1 note 1.

3   As to an 'associated offence' see PARA 9 note 5.

4   Criminal Justice Act 2003 s 156(1) (as amended: see note 1). The defendant's previous convictions, sentences and cautions (including dates of release and the expiry dates of sentences) appear in the antecedents: see *R v Egan* [2004] EWCA Crim 630, (2004) Times, 9 March. A statement of previous convictions made to a court considering how to deal with an offender may not include any order made by a court with respect to him otherwise than on a conviction: see the Rehabilitation of Offenders Act 1974 s 7(5). As to the meaning of 'conviction' for these purposes see PARA 591 note 3. As to methods of proving previous convictions, if not admitted, see CRIMINAL PROCEDURE vol 27 (2015) PARA 426. If the antecedents report contains anything disputed by the offender, prosecuting counsel must either call admissible evidence to prove the disputed facts or omit them from the evidence: *R v Sargeant* (1974) 60 Cr App Rep 74, [1975] Crim LR 173, CA; *R v Coughlan, R v Young* (1976) 63 Cr App Rep 33, CA.

580.   Procedural requirements for imposing community sentences and discretionary custodial sentences.   In forming an opinion in respect of the passing of a community sentence[1], the court must take into account any information about the offender which is before it[2].

A court must obtain and consider a pre-sentence report[3] before:

(1)   in the case of a custodial sentence[4], forming an opinion[5] in connection with sentencing as to the seriousness of the offence or the necessity of passing a custodial sentence or extended sentence for reasons of public protection[6]; or

(2)   in the case of a community sentence, forming an opinion in accordance with the statutory provisions concerning the imposition of community sentences, community sentences which consist of or include community orders or community sentences which consist of or include one or more youth community orders[7], or any opinion as to the suitability for the offender of the particular requirement or requirements to be imposed by the community order or youth rehabilitation order[8].

However, a court need not obtain a pre-sentence report if, in the circumstances of the case, the court is of the opinion that it is unnecessary to obtain one[9].

1 Ie in forming any such opinion as is mentioned in the Criminal Justice Act 2003 s 148(2)(a) (see PARA 42).

2 Criminal Justice Act 2003 s 156(2) (ss 156(2), (3)(b) amended by the Criminal Justice and Immigration Act 2008 Sch 4 para 77(3), (4), Sch 28 Pt 1).

3 As to the meaning of 'pre-sentence report' see PARA 578.

4 As to the meaning of 'custodial sentence' see the Powers of Criminal Courts (Sentencing) Act 2000 s 76; and PARA 9 note 15 (definition applied by the Criminal Justice Act 2003 s 305(1)).

5 Ie, in the case of a custodial sentence, any such opinion as is mentioned in the Criminal Justice Act 2003 s 152(2) or s 153(2) (see PARAS 29, 536) (including where a court forms that opinion for the purposes of s 224A(3) (see PARA 35)), s 225(1)(b) (see PARA 37), s 226(1)(b) (see PARA 34), s 226A(1)(b) (or s 226B(1)(b) (see PARAS 18–20): Criminal Justice Act 2003 s 156(3)(a), (9) (s 156(3)(a) amended, s 156(9) added, by the Legal Aid, Sentencing and Punishment of Offenders Act 2012 Sch 19 para 13, Sch 21 para 22).

6 Criminal Justice Act 2003 s 156(3)(a) (as amended: see note 5).

7 Ie any such opinion as is mentioned in the Criminal Justice Act 2003 s 148(1) or (2)(b) (see PARA 42) or in the Criminal Justice and Immigration Act 2008 s 1(4)(b) or (c) (see PARA 75): Criminal Justice Act 2003 s 156(3)(b) (as amended: see note 2).

8 Criminal Justice Act 2003 s 156(3)(b) (as amended: see note 2).

9 Criminal Justice Act 2003 s 156(4). As to juveniles see PARA 583.

581. Report not obtained. No custodial or community sentence is invalidated by the failure of a court to obtain and consider a pre-sentence report[1] before forming an opinion in respect of the defendant's suitability for the sentence proposed to be passed[2], but any court on an appeal against such a sentence must obtain a pre-sentence report if none was obtained by the court below[3] (although this does not apply if the court is of the opinion either that the court below was justified in forming an opinion that it was unnecessary to obtain a pre-sentence report[4] or that although the court below was not justified in forming that opinion, in the circumstances of the case at the time it is before the court, it is unnecessary to obtain a pre-sentence report[5]) and must consider any such report obtained by it or by that court[6].

It will usually be appropriate to order a report (although in some cases a recent report may be sufficient) where, for example, the defendant is aged 17 and under, the defendant is aged under 21 and is a first time offender or has not served a prison sentence, or where the defendant falls to be assessed under the 'dangerousness' provisions[7]. It will not usually be appropriate to order a report in cases where the defence has asked for report to assist in determining the length of sentence or in cases involving the supply of Class A drugs, false passports or identity documents, 'third strike' burglary, the cultivation of cannabis, offences in breach of a suspended sentence order (where a breach report is available), high level frauds (in excess of £100,000), or in 'custody inevitable' cases where dangerousness is not a consideration and defendant is not aged under 18[8].

1 As to the meaning of 'pre-sentence report' see PARA 578.

2 Ie an opinion referred to in the Criminal Justice Act 2003 s 156(3) (see PARA 580). See eg *R v Milhailsens* [2010] EWCA Crim 2545 (failure to obtain report did not of itself give rise to an appeal against sentence).

3 Criminal Justice Act 2003 s 156(6)(a).

4 Criminal Justice Act 2003 s 156(7)(a). As to juveniles see PARA 583.

5 Criminal Justice Act 2003 s 156(7)(b).

6 Criminal Justice Act 2003 s 156(6)(b).

7   See the London Group Crown Courts Protocol *Outlining the Process to Support the Early Guilty Plea Scheme and Work Sent Up from Magistrates' Courts from 28 May 2013*, Annex A para 3. As to the 'dangerousness' provisions PARAS 33, 34.

8   *Outlining the Process to Support the Early Guilty Plea Scheme and Work Sent Up from Magistrates' Courts from 28 May 2013*, Annex A para 3.

582. Warning the defendant. If it is not necessarily minded to follow a pre-sentence report[1], the court should warn the defendant when the report is ordered that recommendations in a pre-sentence report are not binding, although a failure to do so will not ground judicial review[2].

When a court purposely postpones sentence for a report to ascertain the offender's suitability for a community sentence, it thereby creates in the offender's mind an expectation of an order if the report is favourable: if the report does recommend a community sentence, the court ought to adopt that alternative as a feeling of injustice is otherwise aroused[3]. It is otherwise if the court makes it clear to the offender that it is not holding out any express or implied promise or expectation that a favourable report will necessarily be adopted[4]. The issue is whether the circumstances created an expectation of a non-custodial sentence which it would be unjust to disappoint[5].

A person released on bail pending an obligatory pre-sentence report, without being warned that a custodial sentence might be passed, is not entitled to assume that a community sentence would be imposed[6]. Given that the court is statutorily obliged to obtain the report and the purpose for which it is required, the judge is not obliged to warn the offender that he is still liable to be sentenced to imprisonment[7]. It is, however, better practice for the court, when adjourning for a pre-sentence report and granting bail, to warn the offender that this does not mean that a non-custodial sentence is likely[8].

The defendant must be clearly told not to assume that a custodial sentence is ruled out where he is further assessed on the suitability of a community sentence after pre-sentence reports[9].

1   As to the meaning of 'pre-sentence report' see PARA 578. As to the admissibility in evidence of a confession contained in a pre-sentence report see *R v Elleray* [2003] EWCA Crim 553, [2003] 2 Cr App Rep 165; and CRIMINAL PROCEDURE vol 28 (2015) PARA 637.

2   See *R v Inner London Crown Court, ex p McCann* (1990) 154 JP 917, DC.

3   *R v Gillam* (1980) 2 Cr App Rep (S) 267, [1981] Crim LR 55, CA; *R v Millwood* (1982) 4 Cr App Rep (S) 281, [1982] Crim LR 832, CA. See also *R v Rennes* (1985) 7 Cr App Rep (S) 343, [1986] Crim LR 193, CA.

4   See *R v Moss* (1983) 5 Cr App Rep (S) 209, CA; *R v Stokes* (1983) 5 Cr App Rep (S) 449, CA; *R v Horton, R v Alexander* (1985) 7 Cr App Rep (S) 299, CA.

5   *R v Norton, R v Claxton* (1989) 11 Cr App Rep (S) 143, [1989] Crim LR 663, CA.

6   *R v Woodin* (1993) 15 Cr App Rep (S) 307, [1994] Crim LR 72, CA; *R v Renan* (1994) 15 Cr App Rep (S) 722, [1994] Crim LR 379, CA.

7   *R v Woodin* (1993) 15 Cr App Rep (S) 307, [1994] Crim LR 72, CA.

8   *R v Renan* (1994) 15 Cr App Rep (S) 722, [1994] Crim LR 379, CA.

9   *R v Chamberlain* (1994) 16 Cr App Rep (S) 473, [1995] Crim LR 85, CA.

583. Juveniles. Where the offender is aged under 18, the court must not form an opinion that it is unnecessary to obtain a pre-sentence report[1] unless there exists a previous pre-sentence report obtained in respect of the offender[2] and the court has had regard to the information contained in that report, or, if there is more than one such report, the most recent report[3].

1   Ie an opinion referred to in the Criminal Justice Act 2003 s 156(4) (see PARA 580) or s 156(7) (see PARA 581). As to the meaning of 'pre-sentence report' see PARA 578.

2   Criminal Justice Act 2003 s 156(5)(a), (8)(a).

3   Criminal Justice Act 2003 s 156(5)(b), (8)(b).

584.   Additional requirements in case of mentally disordered offender.
Without prejudice to the generality of the provisions concerning pre-sentence
reports[1], where an offender is or appears to be mentally disordered[2], the court[3]
must obtain and consider a medical report[4] before passing a custodial sentence[5]
other than one fixed by law[6]. However, this rule does not apply if, in the
circumstances of the case, the court is of the opinion that it is unnecessary to
obtain a medical report[7].

Before passing a custodial sentence other than one fixed by law on an offender
who is or appears to be mentally disordered, a court must consider:

(1)   any information before it which relates to his mental condition (whether
       given in a medical report, a pre-sentence report or otherwise)[8]; and

(2)   the likely effect of such a sentence on that condition and on any
       treatment which may be available for it[9].

1   Criminal Justice Act 2003 s 157(7). As to these provisions see s 156; and PARAS 579, 580. As to
     the meaning of 'pre-sentence report' see PARA 578. In connection with requests for medical
     reports see the Criminal Procedure Rules 2015, SI 2015/1490, r 28.8.
2   For these purposes, 'mentally disordered', in relation to a person, means suffering from a mental
     disorder within the meaning of the Mental Health Act 1983 (see PARA 473; and MENTAL
     HEALTH AND CAPACITY vol 75 (2013) PARA 761): Criminal Justice Act 2003 s 157(5).
3   As to the meaning of 'court' see PARA 1 note 1.
4   For these purposes 'medical report' means a report as to an offender's mental condition made or
     submitted orally or in writing by a registered medical practitioner who is approved for the
     purposes of the Mental Health Act 1983 s 12 (see MENTAL HEALTH AND CAPACITY vol 75
     (2013) PARA 849) by the Secretary of State or by another person by virtue of s 12ZA or s 12ZB
     (see MENTAL HEALTH AND CAPACITY vol 75 (2013) PARA 570) as having special experience in the
     diagnosis or treatment of mental disorder: Criminal Justice Act 2003 s 157(6) (amended by the
     Health and Social Care Act 2012 s 38(5)(d)). As to registered medical practitioners see MEDICAL
     PROFESSIONS vol 74 (2011) PARA 176.
5   As to the meaning of 'custodial sentence' see the Powers of Criminal Courts (Sentencing)
     Act 2000 s 76; and PARA 9 note 15 (definition applied by the Criminal Justice Act 2003
     s 305(1)).
6   Criminal Justice Act 2003 s 157(1). No custodial sentence which is passed in a case to which
     s 157(1) applies is invalidated by the failure of a court to comply with s 157(1), but any court on
     an appeal against such a sentence must obtain a medical report if none was obtained by the
     court below (s 157(4)(a)) and must consider any such report obtained by it or by that court
     (s 157(4)(b)).
7   Criminal Justice Act 2003 s 157(2).
8   Criminal Justice Act 2003 s 157(3)(a).
9   Criminal Justice Act 2003 s 157(3)(b).

585.   Disclosure of pre-sentence reports etc.   Where the court[1] obtains a
pre-sentence report[2], other than a report given orally in open court[3], the court
must give a copy of the report:

(1)   to the offender or his legal representative[4];

(2)   if the offender is aged under 18[5], to any parent or guardian[6] of his who
       is present in court[7]; and

(3)   to the prosecutor[8].

In relation to an offender aged under 18 for whom a local authority[9] has
parental responsibility[10] and who is either in its care[11] or is provided with
accommodation by it in the exercise of any social services functions[12], references
in the above provisions to the offender's 'parent or guardian' are to be read as
references to that authority[13].

If the offender is aged under 18 and it appears to the court that the disclosure
to the offender or to any parent or guardian of his of any information contained
in the report would be likely to create a risk of significant harm[14] to the offender,

a complete copy of the report need not be given to the offender or, as the case may be, to that parent or guardian[15]. In addition, if the prosecutor is not of a description prescribed by order made by the Secretary of State, a copy of the report need not be given to the prosecutor if the court considers that it would be inappropriate for him to be given it[16].

Where:

(a)   a report by an officer of a local probation board[17] or a member of a youth offending team[18] is made to any court (other than a youth court) with a view to assisting the court in determining the most suitable method of dealing with any person in respect of an offence[19]; and

(b)   the report is not a pre-sentence report[20],

the court must give a copy of the report to the offender or his legal representative[21] and, if the offender is aged under 18, to any parent or guardian[22] of his who is present in court[23]. However, if the offender is aged under 18 and it appears to the court that the disclosure to the offender or to any parent or guardian of his of any information contained in the report would be likely to create a risk of significant harm to the offender, a complete copy of the report need not be given to the offender, or as the case may be, to that parent or guardian[24].

1   As to the meaning of 'court' see PARA 1 note 1.
2   As to the meaning of 'pre-sentence report' see PARA 578.
3   As to the meaning of 'open court' see PARA 30 note 7.
4   Criminal Justice Act 2003 s 159(1), (2)(a) (amended by the Legal Services Act 2007 Sch 21 para 147).
5   As to the determination of a person's age see the Children and Young Persons Act 1933 s 99; and CHILDREN AND YOUNG PERSONS vol 10 (2012) PARA 1206.
6   As to the meaning of 'guardian' see the Children and Young Persons Act 1933 s 107(1); and CHILDREN AND YOUNG PERSONS vol 10 (2012) PARA 709 (definition applied by the Criminal Justice Act 2003 s 305(1)).
7   Criminal Justice Act 2003 s 159(2)(b).
8   Criminal Justice Act 2003 s 159(2)(c). The 'prosecutor' is the person having the conduct of the proceedings in respect of the offence: s 159(2)(c). No information obtained by virtue of s 159(2)(c) may be used or disclosed otherwise than for the purpose of determining whether representations as to matters contained in the report need to be made to the court (s 159(5)(a)) or making such representations to the court (s 159(5)(b)).
9   As to the meaning of 'local authority' for the purposes of the Criminal Justice Act 2003 ss 159, 160 see the Children Act 1989 s 105(1); and CHILDREN AND YOUNG PERSONS vol 9 (2012) PARA 155 (definition applied by the Criminal Justice Act 2003 s 159(7)).
10   As to the meaning of 'parental responsibility' for those purposes see the Children Act 1989 s 3; and CHILDREN AND YOUNG PERSONS vol 9 (2012) PARA 151 (definition applied by the Criminal Justice Act 2003 s 159(7)).
11   Criminal Justice Act 2003 s 159(6)(a).
12   Criminal Justice Act 2003 s 159(6)(b). As to the meaning of 'social services functions' in relation to a local authority for those purposes see the Local Authority Social Services Act 1970 s 1A; and see SOCIAL SERVICES AND COMMUNITY CARE vol 95 (2013) PARA 1 (definition applied by the Criminal Justice Act 2003 s 159(7)).
13   Criminal Justice Act 2003 s 159(6).
14   As to the meaning of 'harm' in the Criminal Justice Act 2003 ss 159, 160 see the Children Act 1989 s 31; and CHILDREN AND YOUNG PERSONS vol 9 (2012) PARA 316 (definition applied by the Criminal Justice Act 2003 s 159(7)).
15   Criminal Justice Act 2003 s 159(3).
16   Criminal Justice Act 2003 s 159(4). At the date at which this volume states the law no such order had been made, but by virtue of the Interpretation Act 1978 s 17(2)(b), the Pre-Sentence Report Disclosure (Prescription of Prosecutors) Order 1998, SI 1998/191, continues to have effect for these purposes. The following descriptions of prosecutors are prescribed: (1) a Crown prosecutor; (2) any other person acting on behalf of the Crown Prosecution Service; (3) a person acting on behalf of the Commissioners for Her Majesty's Revenue and Customs; (4) a person acting on behalf of the Secretary of State for Social Security; and (5) a person acting on behalf of

the Director of the Serious Fraud Office. There is no longer a Secretary of State for Social Security; social security matters are now the responsibility of the Secretary of State for Work and Pensions.

17 As to the meaning of 'local probation board' see PARA 73 note 2.

18 As to the meaning of 'youth offending team' see PARA 73 note 2.

19 Criminal Justice Act 2003 s 160(1)(a).

20 Criminal Justice Act 2003 s 160(1)(b).

21 Criminal Justice Act 2003 s 160(2)(a) (amended by the Legal Services Act 2007 Sch 21 para 148).

22 In relation to an offender aged under 18 for whom a local authority has parental responsibility and who is either in its care (Criminal Justice Act 2003 s 160(4)(a)) or is provided with accommodation by them in the exercise of any social services functions (s 160(4)(b)), references in s 160 to his 'parent or guardian' are to be read as references to that authority: s 160(4).

23 Criminal Justice Act 2003 s 160(2)(b).

24 Criminal Justice Act 2003 s 160(3).

(8) SERIOUSNESS AND AGGRAVATING FACTORS

586. Determining the seriousness of the offence. In considering the seriousness of any offence, the court[1] must consider the offender's culpability[2] in committing the offence and any harm[3] which the offence caused, was intended to cause or might foreseeably have caused[4].

In considering the seriousness of an offence (the 'current offence') committed by an offender who has one or more previous convictions[5], the court must treat each previous conviction as an aggravating factor if (in the case of that conviction) the court considers that it can reasonably be so treated having regard, in particular, to:

(1) the nature of the offence to which the conviction relates and its relevance to the current offence[6]; and

(2) the time that has elapsed since the conviction[7].

In considering the seriousness of any offence committed while the offender was on bail, the court must treat the fact that it was committed in those circumstances as an aggravating factor[8].

Assessing the seriousness of an offence is only the first step in the process of determining the appropriate sentence in an individual case[9]. Matching the offence to a type and level of sentence is assisted by the application of the respective threshold tests for custodial and community sentences[10] and by consulting the sentencing guidelines for an offence for guidance on factors that are likely to indicate whether a custodial sentence or other disposal is most likely to be appropriate[11].

1 As to the meaning of 'court' see PARA 1 note 1.

2 Four levels of criminal culpability can be identified for sentencing purposes:
   (1) where the offender has the intention to cause harm, with the highest culpability when an offence is planned: the worse the harm intended, the greater the seriousness (Sentencing Guidelines Council Definitive Guideline *Overarching Principles — Seriousness* (published 16 December 2004) paras 1.6, 1.7(i));
   (2) where the offender is reckless as to whether harm is caused, that is, where he appreciates at least some harm would be caused but proceeds giving no thought to the consequences even though the extent of the risk would be obvious to most people (*Overarching Principles: Seriousness* para 1.7(ii));
   (3) where the offender has knowledge of the specific risks entailed by his actions even though he does not intend to cause the harm that results (*Overarching Principles: Seriousness* para 1.7(iii));
   (4) where the offender is guilty of negligence (*Overarching Principles: Seriousness* para 1.7(iv)).

As to culpability see further PARA 587. Where liability is strict and no culpability needs to be proved for a conviction, the degree of culpability is still important when determining sentence: *Overarching Principles: Seriousness* para 1.7.

As to the meanings of 'sentence' and 'sentencing' see PARA 538 note 2.

3   The harm may be to individual victims, to the community and other types of harm: see further the *Overarching Principles: Seriousness* paras 1.8–1.14.

4   Criminal Justice Act 2003 s 143(1). The culpability of the offender in the particular circumstances of an individual case should be the initial factor in determining the seriousness of an offence. As to the assessment of culpability of harm see *Overarching Principles: Seriousness* paras 1.15–1.29; and note 2. See *A-G's Reference (No 60 of 2009), R v Appleby* [2009] EWCA Crim 2693, [2010] 2 Cr App Rep (S) 311, [2009] All ER (D) 182 (Dec) ('What is now required, without of course diminishing the attention to be paid to the actions of the defendant and his intentions at the time, and the true level of his culpability, is that specific attention must also be paid to the consequences of his crime': per Lord Judge CJ at [13]). The key factor in determining whether sentencing levels should be enhanced in response to prevalence of a particular crime in an area will be the level of harm being caused in the locality: enhanced sentences should be exceptional and in response to exceptional circumstances. It is essential that sentencers have supporting evidence of prevalence from an external source. Sentencers must sentence within the sentencing guidelines once the prevalence has been addressed. See *R v Lanham* [2008] EWCA Crim 2450, [2009] 1 Cr App Rep (S) 592, [2009] Crim LR 125; *Overarching Principles: Seriousness* (2004) paras 1.38–1.39. See also *R v Oosthuizen* [2005] EWCA Crim 1978, [2006] 1 Cr App Rep (S) 385, [2005] Crim LR 979; *R v Wood (Clive)* [2009] EWCA Crim 651, [2009] Crim LR 543, [2009] All ER (D) 49 (Apr); *A-G's Reference (No 60 of 2009), R v Appleby* [2009] EWCA Crim 2693, [2010] 2 Cr App Rep (S) 311, [2009] All ER (D) 182 (Dec).

5   Any reference in the Criminal Justice Act 2003 s 143(2) (see the text and notes 6–7) to a previous conviction is to be read as a reference either to a previous conviction by a court in the United Kingdom (s 143(4)(a)), a previous conviction by a court in another member state of a relevant offence under the law of that State (s 143(4)(aa) (s 143(4)(aa), (c), (6) added, s 143(5) substituted, by the Coroners and Justice Act 2009 Sch 17 para 6, Sch 23 Pt 5)), a previous conviction of a service offence within the meaning of the Armed Forces Act 2006 ('conviction' here including anything that under s 376(1) and (2) is to be treated as a conviction) (Criminal Justice Act 2003 s 143(4)(b) (substituted by the Armed Forces Act 2006 Sch 16 para 216)) or a finding of guilt in respect of a member state service offence (Criminal Justice Act 2003 s 143(4)(c) (as so added)). As to service proceedings generally see ARMED FORCES vol 3 (2011) PARA 505 et seq.

For the purposes of the Criminal Justice Act 2003 s 143:

(1)   an offence is 'relevant' if the offence would constitute an offence under the law of any part of the United Kingdom if it were done in that part at the time of the conviction of the defendant for the current offence (s 143(6)(a) (as so added));

(2)   'member state service offence' means an offence which was the subject of proceedings under the service law of a member state other than the United Kingdom and would constitute an offence under the law of any part of the United Kingdom, or a service offence (within the meaning of the Armed Forces Act 2006: see ARMED FORCES vol 3 (2011) PARA 569), if it were done in any part of the United Kingdom, by a member of Her Majesty's forces, at the time of the conviction of the defendant for the current offence (Criminal Justice Act 2003 s 143(6)(b) (as so added));

(3)   'Her Majesty's forces' has the same meaning as in the Armed Forces Act 2006 (see ARMED FORCES vol 3 (2011) PARA 311) (Criminal Justice Act 2003 s 143(6)(c) (as so added)); and

(4)   'service law', in relation to a member state other than the United Kingdom, means the law governing all or any of the naval, military or air forces of that State (s 143(6)(d) (as so added)).

6   Criminal Justice Act 2003 s 143(2)(a). Section 143(2), (4) (see the text and note 5) do not prevent the court from treating a previous conviction by a court outside both the United Kingdom and any other member state, or a previous conviction by a court in any member state (other than the United Kingdom) of an offence which is not a relevant offence, as an aggravating factor in any case where the court considers it appropriate to do so: s 143(5) (as substituted: see note 5).

7   Criminal Justice Act 2003 s 143(2)(b). See note 6.

8   Criminal Justice Act 2003 s 143(3).

9   *Overarching Principles: Seriousness* para 1.30.

10   *Overarching Principles: Seriousness* para 1.30.

11   See the *Overarching Principles: Seriousness* para 1.37. As to these thresholds see PARAS 42, 536.

587. **Aggravating factors.** Among the factors which indicate a higher than usual level of culpability on the part of the offender are:

(1)   the offence was committed whilst on bail for other offences[1];

(2)   a failure to respond to previous sentences[2];

(3)   the offence was racially or religiously aggravated[3];

(4)   the offence was motivated by, or demonstrated, hostility to the victim based on his sexual orientation (or presumed sexual orientation)[4];

(5)   the offence was motivated by, or demonstrated, hostility based on the victim's disability (or presumed disability)[5];

(6)   a previous conviction or convictions, particularly where a pattern of repeat offending is disclosed[6];

(7)   the planning of an offence[7];

(8)   an intention to commit more serious harm than actually resulted from the offence[8];

(9)   the offenders operated in groups or gangs[9];

(10)   'professional' offending[10];

(11)   commission of the offence for financial gain (where this is not inherent in the offence itself)[11];

(12)   a high level of profit from the offence[12];

(13)   an attempt to conceal or dispose of evidence[13];

(14)   a failure to respond to warnings or concerns expressed by others about the offender's behaviour[14];

(15)   the offence was committed whilst on licence[15];

(16)   the offence was motivated by hostility towards a minority group, or a member or members of it[16];

(17)   the deliberate targeting of vulnerable victim or victims[17];

(18)   the commission of an offence while under the influence of alcohol or drugs[18];

(19)   the use of a weapon to frighten or injure a victim[19];

(20)   deliberate and gratuitous violence or damage to property, over and above what is needed to carry out the offence[20];

(21)   abuse of power[21]; and

(22)   abuse of a position of trust[22].

Factors indicating a more than usually serious degree of harm include:

(a)   multiple victims[23];

(b)   an especially serious physical or psychological effect on the victim, even if unintended[24];

(c)   a sustained assault or repeated assaults on the same victim[25];

(d)   a particularly vulnerable victim[26];

(e)   the location of the offence (for example, in an isolated place)[27];

(f)   the offence is committed against those working in the public sector or providing a service to the public[28];

(g)   the presence of others (for example, relatives, especially children or a partner of the victim)[29];

(h)   additional degradation of the victim (for example, taking photographs of a victim as part of a sexual offence)[30]; and

(i)   in property offences, high value (including sentimental value) of property to the victim, or substantial consequential loss (for example, where the theft of equipment causes serious disruption to a victim's life or business)[31].

Some of these factors are integral features of certain offences; in such cases, the presence of the aggravating factor is already reflected in the offence and cannot be used as justification for increasing the sentence further[32].

1 Sentencing Guidelines Council Definitive Guideline *Overarching Principles — Seriousness* (published 16 December 2004) para 1.22.
2 *Overarching Principles: Seriousness* para 1.22.
3 *Overarching Principles: Seriousness* para 1.22. See PARA 588.
4 *Overarching Principles: Seriousness* para 1.22. See PARA 589.
5 *Overarching Principles: Seriousness* para 1.22. See PARA 589.
6 *Overarching Principles: Seriousness* para 1.22. See eg *A-G's Reference (No 23 of 2011), R v Williams* [2011] EWCA Crim 1496, [2012] 1 Cr App Rep (S) 266.
7 *Overarching Principles: Seriousness* para 1.22. See eg *A-G's Reference (Nos 103, 104 and 105 of 2009), R v Denley* [2010] EWCA Crim 1704, 174 CL & J 284, [2010] All ER (D) 89 (Apr).
8 *Overarching Principles: Seriousness* para 1.22.
9 *Overarching Principles: Seriousness* para 1.22.
10 *Overarching Principles: Seriousness* para 1.22.
11 *Overarching Principles: Seriousness* para 1.22.
12 *Overarching Principles: Seriousness* para 1.22.
13 *Overarching Principles: Seriousness* para 1.22.
14 *Overarching Principles: Seriousness* para 1.22.
15 *Overarching Principles: Seriousness* para 1.22.
16 *Overarching Principles: Seriousness* para 1.22.
17 *Overarching Principles: Seriousness* para 1.22.
18 *Overarching Principles: Seriousness* para 1.22.
19 *Overarching Principles: Seriousness* para 1.22. See *R v Rowland* [2008] EWCA Crim 2188, [2008] All ER (D) 143 (Aug) (air pistol; minor injuries); *R v Maina* [2009] All ER (D) 157 (Nov) (use of knives).
20 *Overarching Principles: Seriousness* para 1.22.
21 *Overarching Principles: Seriousness* para 1.22.
22 *Overarching Principles: Seriousness* para 1.22.
23 *Overarching Principles: Seriousness* para 1.23. See *A-G's Reference (No 85 of 2007), R v Bushell* [2007] EWCA Crim 3218, [2008] 2 Cr App Rep (S) 221, [2007] All ER (D) 159 (Dec), CA (the fact that there were multiple victims had to be relevant to sentencing in cases of causing grievous bodily harm with intent where there was high culpability and a high degree of harm).
24 *Overarching Principles: Seriousness* para 1.23.
25 *Overarching Principles: Seriousness* para 1.23. See eg *A-G's Reference (No 23 of 2011), R v Williams* [2011] EWCA Crim 1496, [2012] 1 Cr App Rep (S) 266.
26 *Overarching Principles: Seriousness* para 1.23.
27 *Overarching Principles: Seriousness* para 1.23.
28 *Overarching Principles: Seriousness* para 1.23.
29 *Overarching Principles: Seriousness* para 1.23. See eg *A-G's Reference (No 23 of 2011), R v Williams* [2011] EWCA Crim 1496, [2012] 1 Cr App Rep (S) 266. Professional football matches are watched by families and professional footballers have become role models, so it is a significant factor where a footballer assaults an opposing player during a televised match: *R v Cotterill* [2007] EWCA Crim 526, [2007] 2 Cr App Rep (S) 391.
30 *Overarching Principles: Seriousness* para 1.23.
31 *Overarching Principles: Seriousness* para 1.23.
32 *Overarching Principles: Seriousness* para 1.21. Where two or more aggravating factors are features of an offence, care needs to be taken to avoid 'double-counting': *Overarching Principles: Seriousness* para 1.21.

588. Racial or religious aggravation as an aggravating factor. Where a court[1] is considering the seriousness of an offence (other than one of the specific racially or religiously aggravated offences[2]) and the offence was racially or religiously aggravated[3], the court must treat that fact as an aggravating factor[4] and state in open court[5] that the offence was so aggravated[6].

1 As to the meaning of 'court' see PARA 1 note 1.

2   Ie other than an offence under the Crime and Disorder Act 1998 ss 29–32 (see CRIMINAL LAW vol 25 (2010) PARAS 166–167, 328; CRIMINAL LAW vol 26 (2010) PARA 493): Criminal Justice Act 2003 s 145(1).

3   As to the meaning of 'racially or religiously aggravated' see the Crime and Disorder Act 1998 s 28; and CRIMINAL LAW vol 25 (2010) PARA 165 (definition applied by the Criminal Justice Act 2003 s 145(3)). In the Crown Court, if evidence to the effect that the offence was racially or religiously aggravated has not been adduced at the trial, the prosecution should seek to adduce such evidence at a Newton hearing; even though the question of racial or religious aggravation has not arisen at the trial, the judge is entitled to interpret the verdict of the jury, and may sentence the defendant on the basis of evidence disclosing such aggravating factors which could have resulted in a more serious charge (although he cannot sentence on the basis that a more serious offence has been committed), but either a Newton hearing should be held to establish any such aggravation or the judge should give notice of his intention to sentence on an aggravated basis: *R v O'Callaghan* [2005] EWCA Crim 317, [2005] 2 Cr App Rep (S) 514, [2005] Crim LR 486. As to Newton hearings see CRIMINAL PROCEDURE vol 27 (2015) PARA 378. Where the prosecution accepts a plea of guilty to assault occasioning actual bodily harm, and does not proceed on a count charging racially aggravated assault occasioning actual bodily harm, it is not open to the sentencer to pass sentence on the basis that the assault was in fact racially aggravated: *R v McGillivray* [2005] EWCA Crim 604, [2005] 2 Cr App Rep (S) 366, [2005] Crim LR 484. The fact that one (or more) of a number of joint offenders has demonstrated racial or religious hostility in the prescribed way does not make the provision applicable to any of them who has not: *R v Davies, R v Ely* [2003] EWCA Crim 3700, [2004] 2 Cr App Rep (S) 148, [2004] Crim LR 677.

4   Criminal Justice Act 2003 s 145(2)(a). The court should determine the sentence which would be appropriate if the offence had not been racially or religiously aggravated, and then add an appropriate amount depending on the circumstances to reflect the racial or religious aggravation: *R v Saunders* [2000] 1 Cr App Rep 458, [2000] 2 Cr App Rep (S) 71, CA; *R v Kelly (Lewis), R v D (Miles) (A Juvenile)* [2001] EWCA Crim 170, [2001] 2 Cr App Rep (S) 73. As to how that amount is to be determined see *R v Saunders* (but note the comments in *A-G's Reference (No 92 of 2003)* [2004] EWCA Crim 924, (2004) Times, 21 April, [2004] All ER (D) 407 (Mar); *R v Kelly, R v Donnolly* above).

5   As to the meaning of 'open court' see PARA 30 note 7.

6   Criminal Justice Act 2003 s 145(2)(b).

589.   Disability or sexual orientation as an aggravating factor. Where the court[1] is considering the seriousness of an offence in circumstances where:

(1)   at the time of committing the offence, or immediately before or after doing so, the offender demonstrated towards the victim of the offence hostility based on the sexual orientation (or presumed sexual orientation) of the victim[2], a disability[3] (or presumed disability) of the victim[4], or the victim being (or being presumed to be) transgender[5]; or

(2)   the offence was motivated (wholly or partly) by hostility towards persons who are of a particular sexual orientation[6], by hostility towards persons who have a disability or a particular disability[7], or by hostility towards persons who are transgender[8],

it must treat the fact that the offence was committed in any of those circumstances as an aggravating factor[9] and must state in open court[10] that the offence was committed in such circumstances[11].

It is immaterial for these purposes[12] whether or not the offender's hostility is also based, to any extent, on any other factor[13].

1   As to the meaning of 'court' see PARA 1 note 1.

2   Criminal Justice Act 2003 s 146(1), (2)(a)(i) (s 146(2)(a)(i), (b)(i) amended, s 146(2)(a)(iii), (b)(iii), (6) added, by the Legal Aid, Sentencing and Punishment of Offenders Act 2012 s 65).

3   Ie any physical or mental impairment: Criminal Justice Act 2003 s 146(5).

4   Criminal Justice Act 2003 s 146(2)(a)(ii).

5   Criminal Justice Act 2003 s 146(2)(a)(iii) (as added: see note 2). References to a person being transgender include references to being transsexual, or undergoing, proposing to undergo or having undergone a process of gender reassignment: s 146(6) (as so added).

6 Criminal Justice Act 2003 s 146(2)(b)(i) (as amended: see note 2).
7 Criminal Justice Act 2003 s 146(2)(b)(ii).
8 Criminal Justice Act 2003 s 146(2)(b)(iii) (as added: see note 2).
9 Criminal Justice Act 2003 s 146(3)(a).
10 As to the meaning of 'open court' see PARA 30 note 7.
11 Criminal Justice Act 2003 s 146(3)(b).
12 Ie for the purposes of the Criminal Justice Act 2003 s 146(2).
13 Criminal Justice Act 2003 s 146(4).

590. Terrorist connection as an aggravating factor. The following provisions apply where a court in England and Wales[1] is considering for the purposes of sentence[2] the seriousness of one of the following offences[3]. The provisions also apply where a service court is considering for the purposes of sentence the seriousness of a service offence as respects which the corresponding civil offence is one of the following offences[4]. The offences are[5]:

(1) the common law offences of murder, manslaughter, culpable homicide, kidnapping and abduction[6];
(2) soliciting murder[7];
(3) maliciously administering poison etc so as to endanger life or inflict grievous bodily harm[8];
(4) causing bodily injury by explosives[9];
(5) using explosives etc with intent to do grievous bodily harm[10];
(6) placing explosives with intent to do bodily injury[11];
(7) making or having gunpowder etc with intent to commit or enable any person to commit any felony mentioned in the Offences against the Person Act 1861[12];
(8) causing explosion likely to endanger life or property[13];
(9) attempting to cause explosion or making or keeping explosive with intent to endanger life or property[14];
(10) making or possession of explosive under suspicious circumstances[15];
(11) the punishment of accessories[16];
(12) the restriction on development etc of certain biological agents and toxins and of biological weapons[17];
(13) hostage-taking[18];
(14) hijacking[19];
(15) destroying, damaging or endangering safety of aircraft[20];
(16) other acts endangering or likely to endanger safety of aircraft[21];
(17) offences in relation to certain dangerous articles[22];
(18) inducing or assisting the commission of an offence under heads (14) to (16) outside the United Kingdom[23];
(19) offences relating to damage to the environment[24];
(20) offences of importing or exporting etc nuclear materials: extended jurisdiction[25];
(21) so far as they apply to an offence specified in heads (1) to (20) and (22) to (32), offences involving preparatory acts and threats[26];
(22) endangering safety at aerodromes[27];
(23) the hijacking of ships[28];
(24) seizing or exercising control of fixed platforms[29];
(25) destroying ships or fixed platforms or endangering their safety[30];
(26) so far as relating to an offence under head (23) or (25), inducing or assisting the commission of an offence outside the United Kingdom[31];
(27) offences against the safety of channel tunnel trains and the tunnel system[32];

(28)   the use etc of chemical weapons[33];
(29)   premises or equipment for producing chemical weapons[34];
(30)   the use etc of nuclear weapons[35];
(31)   hoaxes involving noxious substances or things[36];
(32)   any ancillary offence relating to heads (1) to (31)[37].

If, having regard to the material before it for the purposes of sentencing, it appears to the court that the offence has or may have a terrorist connection, the court must determine whether that is the case[38] and, for that purpose, the court may hear evidence, and must take account of any representations made by the prosecution and the defence, as in the case of any other matter relevant for the purposes of sentence[39].

If the court determines that the offence has a terrorist connection, the court must treat that fact as an aggravating factor and must state in open court that the offence was so aggravated[40].

1   Equivalent provision is made in relation to Scotland: see the Counter-Terrorism Act 2008 s 31.
2   For these purposes 'sentence', in relation to an offence, includes any order made by a court when dealing with a person in respect of the offence: Counter-Terrorism Act 2008 s 30(5).
3   See the Counter-Terrorism Act 2008 s 30(1). As to the meaning of 'terrorism' see the Terrorism Act 2000 s 1; the Terrorism Act 2006 s 20(1); and CRIMINAL LAW vol 25 (2010) PARA 372 (definition applied by the Counter-Terrorism Act 2008 s 92). An offence has a 'terrorist connection' if the offence is, or takes place in the course of, an act of terrorism or is committed for the purpose of terrorism: s 93.
4   See the Counter-Terrorism Act 2008 s 32(1).
5   See the Counter-Terrorism Act 2008 Sch 2. Sections 30, 32 have effect in relation only to offences committed on or after 18 June 2009 (ie the day on which those provisions came into force): ss 30(6), 32(5); Counter-Terrorism Act 2008 (Commencement No 3) Order 2009, SI 2009/1256, art 2(b). The Secretary of State may amend the Counter-Terrorism Act 2008 Sch 2 and any such order is subject to affirmative resolution procedure: see s 33(1), (2). Any order adding an offence to Sch 2 applies only in relation to offences committed after the order comes into force: s 33(2). At the date at which this volume states the law no such orders had been made.
6   See CRIMINAL LAW vol 25 (2010) PARAS 91 et seq, 146 et seq.
7   Ie an offence under the Offences against the Person Act 1861 s 4: see CRIMINAL LAW vol 25 (2010) PARA 114.
8   Ie an offence under the Offences against the Person Act 1861 s 23: see CRIMINAL LAW vol 25 (2010) PARA 132.
9   Ie an offence under the Offences against the Person Act 1861 s 28: see CRIMINAL LAW vol 25 (2010) PARA 135.
10 Ie an offence under the Offences against the Person Act 1861 s 29: see CRIMINAL LAW vol 25 (2010) PARA 136.
11 Ie an offence under the Offences against the Person Act 1861 s 30: see CRIMINAL LAW vol 25 (2010) PARA 140.
12 Ie an offence under the Offences against the Person Act 1861 s 64: see CRIMINAL LAW vol 26 (2010) PARA 666.
13 Ie an offence under the Explosive Substances Act 1883 s 2: see CRIMINAL LAW vol 25 (2010) PARA 137.
14 Ie an offence under the Explosive Substances Act 1883 s 3: see CRIMINAL LAW vol 25 (2010) PARA 138.
15 Ie an offence under the Explosive Substances Act 1883 s 4: see CRIMINAL LAW vol 26 (2010) PARA 666.
16 Ie an offence under the Explosive Substances Act 1883 s 5: see CRIMINAL LAW vol 25 (2010) PARAS 137–138; CRIMINAL LAW vol 26 (2010) PARA 666.
17 Ie an offence under the Biological Weapons Act 1974 s 1: see ARMED CONFLICT AND EMERGENCY vol 3 (2011) PARA 64.
18 Ie an offence under the Taking of Hostages Act 1982 s 1: see CRIMINAL LAW vol 25 (2010) PARA 416.
19 Ie an offence under the Aviation Security Act 1982 s 1: see AIR LAW vol 2 (2008) PARAS 624–625.
20 Ie an offence under the Aviation Security Act 1982 s 2: see AIR LAW vol 2 (2008) PARA 628.
21 Ie an offence under the Aviation Security Act 1982 s 3: see AIR LAW vol 2 (2008) PARA 629.

22 Ie an offence under the Aviation Security Act 1982 s 4: see AIR LAW vol 2 (2008) PARA 630.
23 Ie an offence under the Aviation Security Act 1982 s 6(2): see AIR LAW vol 2 (2008) PARAS 624, 628, 629.
24 Ie an offence under the Nuclear Material (Offences) Act 1983 s 1B: see ENERGY AND CLIMATE CHANGE vol 44 (2011) PARA 976.
25 Ie an offence under the Nuclear Material (Offences) Act 1983 s 1C: see ENERGY AND CLIMATE CHANGE vol 44 (2011) PARA 976.
26 Ie an offence under the Nuclear Material (Offences) Act 1983 s 2: see ENERGY AND CLIMATE CHANGE vol 44 (2011) PARA 976.
27 Ie an offence under the Aviation and Maritime Security Act 1990 s 1: see AIR LAW vol 2 (2008) PARA 631.
28 Ie an offence under the Aviation and Maritime Security Act 1990 s 9: see SHIPPING AND MARITIME LAW vol 94 (2008) PARA 1210.
29 Ie an offence under the Aviation and Maritime Security Act 1990 s 10: see SHIPPING AND MARITIME LAW vol 94 (2008) PARA 1211.
30 Ie an offence under the Aviation and Maritime Security Act 1990 s 11: see SHIPPING AND MARITIME LAW vol 94 (2008) PARA 1212.
31 Ie an offence under the Aviation and Maritime Security Act 1990 s 14(4): see SHIPPING AND MARITIME LAW vol 94 (2008) PARA 1215.
32 Ie an offence under the Channel Tunnel (Security) Order 1994, SI 1994/570, arts 4–9.
33 Ie an offence under the Chemical Weapons Act 1996 s 2: see ARMED CONFLICT AND EMERGENCY vol 3 (2011) PARA 69.
34 Ie an offence under the Chemical Weapons Act 1996 s 11: see ARMED CONFLICT AND EMERGENCY vol 3 (2011) PARAS 68, 75.
35 Ie an offence under the Anti-Terrorism, Crime and Security Act 2001 s 47: see ARMED CONFLICT AND EMERGENCY vol 3 (2011) PARA 91.
36 Ie an offence under the Anti-Terrorism, Crime and Security Act 2001 s 114: see CRIMINAL LAW vol 26 (2010) PARA 792.
37 See the Counter-Terrorism Act 2008 Sch 2.
38 Counter-Terrorism Act 2008 ss 30(1), (2), 32(1), (2).
39 Counter-Terrorism Act 2008 ss 30(3), 32(3).
40 Counter-Terrorism Act 2008 ss 30(4), 32(4).

(9) REHABILITATION OF OFFENDERS

(i) Principles of Rehabilitation

591.   Objectives of the legislation.   The objectives of the Rehabilitation of Offenders Act 1974 are to rehabilitate offenders who have not been reconvicted of any serious offence for periods of time and to penalise the unauthorised disclosure of their previous convictions or cautions[1]. Subject to a number of specified exceptions[2], a person who has become a rehabilitated person for the purposes of the Act in respect of a conviction[3] is to be treated for all purposes in law as a person who has not committed or been charged with or prosecuted for or convicted of or sentenced[4] for the offence or offences which were the subject of that conviction[5] and a person who is given a caution[6] (or an alternative to prosecution in Scotland[7]) for an offence is to be treated, from the time the caution (or alternative) is spent[8], for all purposes in law as a person who has not committed, been charged with or prosecuted for, or been given a caution for the offence[9].

1   See the long title to the Rehabilitation of Offenders Act 1974, as read with the amendments effected by the Criminal Justice and Immigration Act 2008 Sch 10 (new provision for spent cautions).
2   See PARA 609 et seq.
3   For these purposes references to a 'conviction', however expressed, include references to:
    (1)   a conviction by or before a court outside England, Wales and Scotland (Rehabilitation

of Offenders Act 1974 s 1(4)(a) (ss 1(4)(a), 8A(2)(d) amended, s 8AA added, by the Legal Aid, Sentencing and Punishment of Offenders Act 2012 s 139(6), Sch 24 para 2, Sch 25 paras 8, 12, 13)); and

(2)   any finding (other than a finding linked with a finding of insanity) in any criminal proceedings that a person has committed an offence or done the act or made the omission charged (Rehabilitation of Offenders Act 1974 s 1(4)(b) (amended by the Children Act 1989 Sch 15)).

The Rehabilitation of Offenders Act 1974 does not apply to disregarded convictions: see PARA 596.

As to the meaning of 'Great Britain' see PARA 4 note 3. Notwithstanding anything in the Powers of Criminal Courts (Sentencing) Act 2000 s 14 (conviction of a person discharged to be deemed not to be a conviction: see PARA 445) or corresponding Scottish or service law (see the Armed Forces Act 2006 s 187; and ARMED FORCES vol 3 (2011) PARA 609) provisions, a conviction in respect of which an order is made discharging the person concerned absolutely or conditionally is to be treated for these purposes as a conviction and the person in question may become a rehabilitated person in respect of that conviction and the conviction a spent conviction for these purposes accordingly: Rehabilitation of Offenders Act 1974 s 1(4) (amended by the Criminal Justice Act 1991 Sch 11 para 20(b), (c), Sch 13; the Powers of Criminal Courts (Sentencing) Act 2000 Sch 9 para 47; and the Armed Forces Act 2006 Sch 16 para 63).

No order made by a court with respect to any person otherwise than on a conviction may be included in any list or statement of that person's previous convictions given or made to any court which is considering how to deal with him in respect of any offence: Rehabilitation of Offenders Act 1974 s 7(5).

4   For these purposes 'sentence' includes any order made by a court in dealing with a person in respect of his conviction of any offence or offences, other than:

(1)   a surcharge imposed under the Criminal Justice Act 2003 s 161A (see PARA 185) (Rehabilitation of Offenders Act 1974 s 1(3)(za) (added by the Domestic Violence, Crime and Victims Act 2004 Sch 10 para 9));

(2)   an order for committal or any other order made in default of payment of any fine or other sum adjudged to be paid by or imposed on a conviction, or for want of sufficient distress to satisfy any such fine or other sum (which includes a reference to circumstances where there is power to use the procedure in the Tribunals, Courts and Enforcement Act 2007 Sch 12 to recover the fine or other sum from a person, but it appears, after an attempt has been made to exercise the power, that the person's goods are insufficient to pay the amount outstanding (as defined by Sch 12 para 50(3))) (Rehabilitation of Offenders Act 1974 s 1(3)(a), (3A) (s 1(3A) added by the Tribunals, Courts and Enforcement Act 2007 Sch 13 para 38));

(3)   an order dealing with a person in respect of a suspended sentence of imprisonment (Rehabilitation of Offenders Act 1974 s 1(3)(b)); and

(4)   an order under the Prosecution of Offences Act 1985 s 21A (see CRIMINAL PROCEDURE vol 28 (2015) PARA 843) requiring a person to pay a charge in respect of relevant court costs (Rehabilitation of Offenders Act 1974 s 1(3)(c) (added by the Criminal Justice and Courts Act 2015 Sch 12 para 1)).

Where a person has been fined and disqualified from driving there are in fact two sentences: *Munro v Highland Council* 2003 SC 239, 1 Div.

5   Rehabilitation of Offenders Act 1974 s 4(1).

6   As to the meaning of 'caution' see PARA 595 note 1. The Rehabilitation of Offenders Act 1974 does not apply to disregarded cautions: see PARA 596.

7   The provisions of the Rehabilitation of Offenders Act 1974 relating to the unauthorised disclosure of spent cautions (ie s 9A and Sch 2 paras 2–6: see PARAS 593, 598–601, 610–612) apply with modifications to the unauthorised disclosure of spent alternatives to prosecution, which are available only in Scotland: see s 8AA (as added: see note 3) and s 8B (which applies only to Scotland).

8   As to spent cautions see PARA 595.

9   Rehabilitation of Offenders Act 1974 Sch 2 para 3(1) (added by the Criminal Justice and Immigration Act 2008 Sch 10 para 6).

592.   Sentences excluded from rehabilitation. The sentences[1] excluded from rehabilitation[2] are:

(1)   a sentence of imprisonment for life[3];

(2) a sentence of imprisonment, youth custody, detention in a young offender institution or corrective training for a term exceeding 48 months[4];

(3) a sentence of preventive detention[5];

(4) a sentence of detention[6] during Her Majesty's pleasure[7];

(5) a sentence of detention[8] for a term exceeding 48 months passed on young offenders convicted of grave crimes[9];

(6) a sentence of custody for life[10]; and

(7) a sentence of imprisonment for public protection[11], a sentence of detention for public protection[12] or an extended sentence[13], including any such sentence passed as a result of any corresponding service law provisions[14].

Any other sentence is a 'sentence subject to rehabilitation'[15].

1 As to the meaning of 'sentence' see PARA 591 note 4.
2 See PARA 591.
3 Rehabilitation of Offenders Act 1974 s 5(1)(a).
4 Rehabilitation of Offenders Act 1974 s 5(1)(b) (amended by the Criminal Justice Act 1982 Sch 14 para 36; the Criminal Justice Act 1988 Sch 8 para 9(a); Rehabilitation of Offenders Act 1974 s 5(1)(b), (d), (f), (1A) amended by the Legal Aid, Sentencing and Punishment of Offenders Act 2012 s 139(1), (2), Sch 21 para 2).
5 Rehabilitation of Offenders Act 1974 s 5(1)(c) (amended by the Criminal Justice Act 1982 Sch 16).
6 Ie under the Powers of Criminal Courts (Sentencing) Act 2000 s 90 or s 91 (see PARAS 8, 38), under corresponding Scottish provision or under a corresponding service law provision: Rehabilitation of Offenders Act 1974 s 5(1)(d) (amended by the Powers of Criminal Courts (Sentencing) Act 2000 Sch 9 para 48(1), (2); Rehabilitation of Offenders Act 1974 s 5(1)(d), (f) amended, s 5(1A) substituted, by the Armed Forces Act 2006 Sch 16 para 65, Sch 17; Rehabilitation of Offenders Act 1974 s 5(1)(d) as amended (see note 4)). The 'corresponding service law provisions' for these purposes are the Armed Forces Act 2006 ss 209, 218 (see ARMED FORCES vol 3 (2011) PARAS 596, 611) and references to those provisions include references to the Army Act 1955 s 71A(3), (4), the Air Force Act 1955 s 71A(3), (4) and the Naval Discipline Act 1957 s 43A(3), (4) (all repealed): Rehabilitation of Offenders Act 1974 s 5(1A) (Rehabilitation of Offenders Act 1974 s 5(1A) added by the Armed Forces Act 1976 Sch 9 para 20(4); as so substituted and amended).
7 Rehabilitation of Offenders Act 1974 s 5(1)(d) (as amended: see notes 4, 6).
8 Ie under the Powers of Criminal Courts (Sentencing) Act 2000 s 91, under corresponding Scottish provision or under a corresponding service law provision: Rehabilitation of Offenders Act 1974 s 5(1)(d) (as amended: see notes 4, 6). The 'corresponding service law provision' for these purposes is the Armed Forces Act 2006 s 209 and references to that provision include references to the Army Act 1955 s 71A(4), the Air Force Act 1955 s 71A(4) or the Naval Discipline Act 1957 s 43A(4) (all repealed): Rehabilitation of Offenders Act 1974 s 5(1)(d), (1A) (as so amended, added and substituted).
9 Rehabilitation of Offenders Act 1974 s 5(1)(d) (as amended: see notes 4, 6).
10 Rehabilitation of Offenders Act 1974 s 5(1)(e) (added by the Criminal Justice Act 1982 Sch 14 para 36).
11 Ie under the Criminal Justice Act 2003 s 225: see PARA 33.
12 Ie under the Criminal Justice Act 2003 s 226: see PARA 34.
13 Ie under the Criminal Justice Act 2003 s 226A, s 226B (see PARAS 18–20), s 227 (repealed) or s 228 (repealed).
14 Rehabilitation of Offenders Act 1974 s 5(1)(f) (added by the Criminal Justice Act 2003 Sch 32 para 18(1), (2); as amended (see notes 4, 6)). The 'corresponding service law provisions' for this purpose are the Armed Forces Act 2006 ss 219–222 (see ARMED FORCES vol 3 (2011) PARAS 596, 611): Rehabilitation of Offenders Act 1974 s 5(1)(f) (as so added and amended).
15 Rehabilitation of Offenders Act 1974 s 5(1).

593. Inadmissibility in evidence. Notwithstanding the provisions of any other enactment or rule of law to the contrary[1]:

(1) no evidence is admissible in any proceedings before a judicial authority[2]

exercising its jurisdiction or functions in England, Wales or Scotland to prove that any person who has become a rehabilitated person[3] in respect of a conviction[4] has committed or been charged with or prosecuted for or convicted of or sentenced[5] for any offence which was the subject of a spent conviction[6];

(2) no evidence is admissible in any proceedings before a judicial authority exercising its jurisdiction or functions in England and Wales to prove that any person who has become a rehabilitated person in respect of a caution[7] has committed, been charged with or prosecuted for, or been given a caution for the offence[8]; and

(3) a person may not, in any such proceedings, be asked, and, if asked, will not be required to answer, any question relating to his past which cannot be answered without acknowledging or referring to a spent conviction or convictions or a spent caution or any circumstances ancillary thereto[9].

1 These provisions are, however, subject to a number of specified exceptions concerning ongoing judicial processes and the interests of justice and the bringing of defamation actions: see the Rehabilitation of Offenders Act 1974 ss 7, 8; and PARAS 609–613.

2 For these purposes 'proceedings before a judicial authority' includes, in addition to proceedings before any of the ordinary courts of law, proceedings before any tribunal, body or person having power to determine any question affecting the rights, privileges, obligations or liabilities of any person, or to receive evidence affecting the determination of any such question:

    (1) by virtue of any enactment, law, custom or practice (Rehabilitation of Offenders Act 1974 s 4(6)(a), Sch 2 para 2(3) (Sch 2 added by the Criminal Justice and Immigration Act 2008 Sch 10 paras 1, 6));

    (2) under the rules governing any association, institution, profession, occupation or employment (Rehabilitation of Offenders Act 1974 s 4(6)(b)); or

    (3) under any provision of an agreement providing for arbitration with respect to questions arising thereunder (s 4(6)(c)).

3 As to the meaning of 'rehabilitated person' see PARA 591.

4 As to the meaning of 'conviction' see PARA 591 note 3.

5 As to the meaning of 'sentenced' see PARA 591 note 4.

6 Rehabilitation of Offenders Act 1974 s 4(1)(a) (s 4(1)(a), Sch 2 para 2(1)(e) amended by the Legal Aid, Sentencing and Punishment of Offenders Act 2012 Sch 24 para 3, Sch 25 para 5). As to spent convictions see PARA 594; note in connection with disregarded convictions PARA 596.

7 As to the meaning of 'caution' see PARA 595 note 1; note in connection with disregarded cautions PARA 596.

8 Rehabilitation of Offenders Act 1974 Sch 2 para 3(1)(a) (as added: see note 2). Nothing in Sch 2 para 3(1) applies in relation to any proceedings for the offence which are not part of the ancillary circumstances relating to the caution (as to which see note 9): Sch 2 para 3(2) (as so added).

9 Rehabilitation of Offenders Act 1974 s 8(1)(b), Sch 2 para 3(1)(b) (as added: see note 2). For the purposes of ss 4, 7 any of the following are 'circumstances ancillary to a conviction':

    (1) the offence or offences which were the subject of that conviction (s 4(5)(a));

    (2) the conduct constituting that offence or those offences (s 4(5)(b)); and

    (3) any process or proceedings preliminary to that conviction, any sentence imposed in respect of that conviction, any proceedings (whether by way of appeal or otherwise) for reviewing that conviction or any such sentence, and anything done in pursuance of or undergone in compliance with any such sentence (s 4(5)(c)).

    'Ancillary circumstances' in relation to a caution are any circumstances of:

    (a) the offence which was the subject of the caution or the conduct constituting that offence (Sch 2 para 2(1)(a) (as so added));

    (b) any process preliminary to the caution (including consideration by any person of how to deal with that offence and the procedure for giving the caution) (Sch 2 para 2(1)(b) (as so added));

    (c) any proceedings for that offence which take place before the caution is given (including anything which happens after that time for the purpose of bringing the proceedings to an end) (Sch 2 para 2(1)(c) (as so added));

(d)   any judicial review proceedings relating to the caution (Sch 2 para 2(1)(d) (as so added));

(e)   in the case of a youth caution given under the Crime and Disorder Act 1998 s 66ZA (see CHILDREN AND YOUNG PERSONS vol 10 (2012) PARA 1199), anything done in pursuance of or undergone in compliance with a requirement to participate in a rehabilitation programme under s 66ZB(2) or (3) (see CHILDREN AND YOUNG PERSONS vol 10 (2012) PARA 1199) (Rehabilitation of Offenders Act 1974 Sch 2 para 2(1)(e) (as so added; as amended (see note 6)); and

(f)   in the case of a conditional caution (see s 8A(2)(a); and PARA 595 note 1), any conditions attached to the caution or anything done in pursuance of or undergone in compliance with those conditions (Sch 2 para 2(1)(e) (as so added)).

Where the caution relates to two or more offences, references to the 'offence' which was the subject of the caution include a reference to each of the offences concerned: Sch 2 para 2(2) (as so added).

594. Spent convictions.
Where an individual has been convicted[1] of any offence or offences and:

(1)   he did not have imposed on him in respect of that conviction a sentence[2] which is excluded from rehabilitation[3]; and

(2)   he has not had imposed on him[4] in respect of a subsequent conviction during the rehabilitation period applicable to the first-mentioned conviction a sentence which is excluded from rehabilitation[5],

then, after the end of the applicable rehabilitation period[6] that individual, provided he has complied with his sentence[7], is to be treated as a rehabilitated person in respect of the first-mentioned conviction and that conviction is to be treated as spent[8].

1   Ie whether before or after 1 July 1975 (the date on which the Rehabilitation of Offenders Act 1974 was brought into force by s 11(2)). As to the meaning of 'conviction' see PARA 591 note 3. These provisions are subject to s 1(2), (5), (6) (see PARAS 596, 602): s 1(1) (amended by the Protection of Freedoms Act 2012 Sch 9 para 134(2)).
2   As to the meaning of 'sentence' see PARA 591 note 4.
3   Rehabilitation of Offenders Act 1974 s 1(1)(a). As to the sentences excluded from rehabilitation see PARA 592.
4   Ie in accordance with the Rehabilitation of Offenders Act 1974 s 6: see PARA 607.
5   Rehabilitation of Offenders Act 1974 s 1(1)(b).
6   Ie including, where appropriate, any extension under the Rehabilitation of Offenders Act 1974 s 6(4) (see PARA 607) of the period originally applicable to the first-mentioned conviction: s 1(1). As to rehabilitation periods see PARA 604 et seq.
7   These provisions are subject to the Rehabilitation of Offenders Act 1974 s 1(2): see PARA 602.
8   Rehabilitation of Offenders Act 1974 s 1(1).

595. Spent cautions.
A caution[1] is regarded as a spent caution, and the person to whom it was given is afforded protection similar to that relating to spent convictions:

(1)   in the case of a conditional caution[2], at the end of the period of three months from the date on which the caution is given or, if earlier, when the caution ceases to have effect[3]; and

(2)   in any other case, at the time the caution is given[4].

1   For these purposes 'caution' means:
      (1)   a conditional caution, that is to say, a caution given under the Criminal Justice Act 2003 s 22 (conditional cautions for adults: see CRIMINAL PROCEDURE vol 27 (2015) PARA 55) or under the Crime and Disorder Act 1998 s 66A (conditional cautions for children and young persons: see CHILDREN AND YOUNG PERSONS vol 10 (2012) PARA 1199) (Rehabilitation of Offenders Act 1974 s 8A(2)(a) (s 8A, Sch 2 added by the Criminal Justice and Immigration Act 2008 Sch 10 paras 1, 3, 6));
      (2)   any other caution given to a person in England and Wales in respect of an offence

which, at the time the caution is given, that person has admitted (Rehabilitation of Offenders Act 1974 s 8A(2)(b) (as so added));

(3) anything corresponding to a caution falling within head (1) or (2) above (however described) which is given to a person in respect of an offence under the law of a country outside England and Wales (and which is not an alternative to prosecution within the meaning of s 8AA) (s 8A(2)(d) (as so added)).

2   See the Rehabilitation of Offenders Act 1974 s 8A(2)(a); and PARA 595 note 1.

3   Rehabilitation of Offenders Act 1974 Sch 2 para 1(1)(a) (as added (see note 1); amended by the Legal Aid, Sentencing and Punishment of Offenders Act 2012 s 139(1), (7)).

4   Rehabilitation of Offenders Act 1974 Sch 2 para 1(1)(b) (as added: see note 1).

596. Disregarded convictions and cautions. The Rehabilitation of Offenders Act 1974[1] does not apply to any disregarded conviction or caution (that is to say, a conviction or caution for certain homosexual offences which have subsequently been decriminalised by statute)[2], and references in the Act to a conviction or caution do not include references to any such disregarded conviction or caution[3].

1   See PARA 591.

2   Rehabilitation of Offenders Act 1974 s 1(5) (s 1(5), (6) added by the Protection of Freedoms Act 2012 Sch 9 para 134). A 'disregarded conviction' and a 'disregarded caution' is a conviction or caution which has become a disregarded caution by virtue of the Rehabilitation of Offenders Act 1974 Pt 5 Ch 4 (ss 92–101): see s 101.

3   Rehabilitation of Offenders Act 1974 s 1(6) (as added: see note 2).

597. Protected convictions and cautions. Certain of the restrictions on, and modifications of, the statutory protections for rehabilitated persons[1] are disapplied in connection with protected convictions and cautions[2]. A person's conviction[3] is a 'protected conviction' if:

(1) the offence of which the person was convicted was not a listed offence[4];

(2) neither a custodial sentence[5] or a sentence of service detention[6] was imposed in respect of the conviction[7]; and

(3) the person has not been convicted of any other offence at any time[8],

and 11 years (in the case of an adult offender[9]) or five years and six months (in the case of a young offender[10]) or more have passed since the date of the conviction[11].

A caution is a protected caution if it was given to a person for an offence other than a listed offence[12] and six years (in the case of an adult offender[13]) or two years (in the case of a young offender[14]) or more have passed since the date on which the caution was given[15].

1   Ie the Rehabilitation of Offenders Act 1974 (Exceptions) Order 1975, SI 1975/1023, arts 3(1) (see PARAS 614–617), 3A(1) (see PARA 617).

2   Rehabilitation of Offenders Act 1974 (Exceptions) Order 1975, SI 1975/1023, arts 3(2), 3A(1A), 4(2) (art 3A added by SI 2010/1153; Rehabilitation of Offenders Act 1974 (Exceptions) Order 1975, SI 1975/1023, arts 2A, 3(2), 3A(1A), 4(2) added by SI 2013/1198).

3   As to the meaning of 'conviction' see PARA 591 note 3.

4   Rehabilitation of Offenders Act 1974 (Exceptions) Order 1975, SI 1975/1023, art 2A(3)(a) (as added: see note 2). 'Listed offence' means (by virtue of the Rehabilitation of Offenders Act 1974 (Exceptions) Order 1975, SI 1975/1023, art 2A(5) (as so added):

(1) an offence under the Medicines Act 1968 s 67(1A) (see MEDICAL PRODUCTS AND DRUGS vol 75 (2013) PARA 272);

(2) an offence under any of the Mental Health Act 1983 ss 126–129 (see MENTAL HEALTH AND CAPACITY vol 75 (2013) PARAS 1008–1015);

(3) an offence specified in the Disqualification from Caring for Children (England) Regulations 2002, SI 2002/635, Schedule (see CHILDREN AND YOUNG PERSONS vol 10 (2012) PARA 1068);

(4) an offence specified in the Criminal Justice Act 2003 Sch 15 (see PARA 23);

(5) an offence under the Mental Capacity Act 2005 s 44, Sch 1 para 4 or Sch 4 para 4 (see AGENCY vol 1 (2008) PARAS 200, 203, 225–226);

(6)   an offence under the Safeguarding Vulnerable Groups Act 2006 s 7, 9 or 19 (see SOCIAL
       SERVICES AND COMMUNITY CARE vol 95 (2013) PARAS 205–208);

(7)   an offence specified in the Health and Social Care Act 2008 s 17(3)(a), (b) or (c) (see
       SOCIAL SERVICES AND COMMUNITY CARE vol 95 (2013) PARA 101), apart from an
       offence under s 76 (see SOCIAL SERVICES AND COMMUNITY CARE vol 95 (2013) PARA
       227);

(8)   an offence specified in the Safeguarding Vulnerable Groups Act 2006 (Prescribed
       Criteria and Miscellaneous Provisions) Regulations 2009, SI 2009/37, Schedule (see
       SOCIAL SERVICES AND COMMUNITY CARE vol 95 (2013) PARA 164);

(9)   an offence specified in the Childcare (Disqualification) Regulations 2009,
       SI 2009/1547, Sch 2 or 3 (see CHILDREN AND YOUNG PERSONS vol 10 (2012) PARAS
       1119);

(10)   an offence superseded (whether directly or indirectly) by any of the above offences;

(11)   an offence of attempting or conspiring to commit any of the above offences or inciting
       or aiding, abetting, counselling or procuring the commission of any such offence, or an
       offence under the Serious Crime Act 2007 Pt 2 (ss 44–67) (encouraging or assisting
       crime: see CRIMINAL LAW vol 25 (2010) PARAS 65–72) committed in relation to any such
       offence;

(12)   an offence under the law of Scotland or Northern Ireland, or any country or territory
       outside the United Kingdom, which corresponds to any of the above offences;

(13)   an offence under the Armed Forces Act 2006 s 42 (criminal conduct: see ARMED
       FORCES vol 3 (2011) PARA 587) in relation to which the corresponding offence under
       the law of England and Wales (within the meaning of s 42) is any of the above offences;
       or

(14)   an offence under the Army Act 1955 s 70, the Air Force Act 1955 s 70 or the Naval
       Discipline Act 1957 s 42 (all repealed) of which the corresponding civil offence was any
       of the above offences.

5   Ie within the meaning of the Rehabilitation of Offenders Act 1974 s 5(8).
6   See note 5.
7   Rehabilitation of Offenders Act 1974 (Exceptions) Order 1975, SI 1975/1023, art 2A(3)(b), (4)
    (as added: see note 2).
8   Rehabilitation of Offenders Act 1974 (Exceptions) Order 1975, SI 1975/1023, art 2A(3)(c) (as
    added: see note 2).
9   Ie where the person was 18 years or over at the time of the conviction: Rehabilitation of
    Offenders Act 1974 (Exceptions) Order 1975, SI 1975/1023, art 2A(2)(a) (as added: see note 2).
10 Ie where the person was under 18 years at the time of the conviction: Rehabilitation of
    Offenders Act 1974 (Exceptions) Order 1975, SI 1975/1023, art 2A(2)(b) (as added: see note 2).
11 Rehabilitation of Offenders Act 1974 (Exceptions) Order 1975, SI 1975/1023, art 2A(2)(a), (b)
    (as added: see note 2).
12 See note 2.
13 Ie where the person was 18 years or over at the time the caution was given: Rehabilitation of
    Offenders Act 1974 (Exceptions) Order 1975, SI 1975/1023, art 2A(1)(a) (as added: see note 2).
14 Ie where the person was under 18 years at the time the caution was given: Rehabilitation of
    Offenders Act 1974 (Exceptions) Order 1975, SI 1975/1023, art 2A(1)(b) (as added: see note 2).
15 Rehabilitation of Offenders Act 1974 (Exceptions) Order 1975, SI 1975/1023, art 2A(1)(a), (b)
    (as added: see note 2).

598.   Information as to spent convictions and spent cautions.   Subject to a
number of specific exceptions[1], where a question seeking information with
regard to a person's previous convictions[2], cautions[3], offences, conduct or
circumstances is put to him or to any other person otherwise than in proceedings
before a judicial authority[4]:

(1)   the question is to be treated as not relating to spent convictions[5] or
       spent cautions[6] or to any circumstances ancillary to spent convictions or
       cautions[7], and the answer thereto may be framed accordingly[8]; and

(2)   the person questioned may not be subjected to any liability or otherwise
       prejudiced in law by reason of any failure to acknowledge or disclose a
       spent conviction or a spent caution or any circumstances ancillary to a
       spent conviction or caution in his answer to the question[9].

1   See the Rehabilitation of Offenders Act 1974 s 4(4)(a), Sch 2 para 4(a); the Rehabilitation of Offenders Act 1974 (Exceptions) Order 1975, SI 1975/1023; and PARA 609 et seq.
2   As to the meaning of 'conviction' see PARA 591 note 3.
3   As to the meaning of 'caution' see PARA 595 note 1.
4   As to the meaning of 'proceedings before a judicial authority' see PARA 593 note 2.
5   As to spent convictions see PARA 594; note in connection with disregarded convictions PARA 596.
6   As to spent cautions see PARA 595; note in connection with disregarded cautions PARA 596.
7   As to the circumstances ancillary to a conviction or a caution see PARA 593 note 9.
8   Rehabilitation of Offenders Act 1974 s 4(2)(a), Sch 2 para 3(3)(a) (Sch 2 added by the Criminal Justice and Immigration Act 2008 Sch 10 paras 1, 6).
9   Rehabilitation of Offenders Act 1974 s 4(2)(b), Sch 2 para 3(3)(b) (as added: see note 8).

599.   Non-disclosure of spent convictions and spent cautions.   Subject to a number of specific exceptions[1], any obligation imposed on any person by any rule of law or by the provisions of any agreement or arrangement to disclose any matters to any other person does not extend to requiring him to disclose a spent conviction[2] or a spent caution[3] or any circumstances ancillary to a spent conviction or caution[4], whether the conviction or caution is his own or another's[5].

1   See the Rehabilitation of Offenders Act 1974 s 4(4)(b), Sch 2 para 4(b); the Rehabilitation of Offenders Act 1974 (Exceptions) Order 1975, SI 1975/1023; and PARA 612 et seq.
2   As to the meaning of 'conviction' see PARA 591 note 3; as to spent convictions see PARA 594; note in connection with disregarded convictions PARA 596.
3   As to the meaning of 'caution' see PARA 595 note 1; as to spent cautions see PARA 595; note in connection with disregarded cautions PARA 596.
4   As to the circumstances ancillary to a conviction or a caution see PARA 593 note 9.
5   Rehabilitation of Offenders Act 1974 s 4(3)(a), Sch 2 para 3(4) (Sch 2 added by the Criminal Justice and Immigration Act 2008 Sch 10 paras 1, 6).

600.   Protection of employment.   Subject to a number of specific exceptions[1], a conviction[2] or caution[3] which has become spent, or any circumstances ancillary thereto[4], or any failure to disclose a spent conviction or caution or any such circumstances, is not a proper ground for dismissing or excluding a person from any office, profession, occupation or employment, or for prejudicing him in any occupation or employment[5].

1   See the Rehabilitation of Offenders Act 1974 s 4(4)(b), Sch 2 para 4(b); the Rehabilitation of Offenders Act 1974 (Exceptions) Order 1975, SI 1975/1023; and PARA 612 et seq.
2   As to the meaning of 'conviction' see PARA 591 note 3; as to spent convictions see PARA 594; note in connection with disregarded convictions PARA 596.
3   As to the meaning of 'caution' see PARA 595 note 1; as to spent cautions see PARA 595; note in connection with disregarded cautions PARA 596.
4   As to the circumstances ancillary to a conviction or a caution see PARA 593 note 9.
5   Rehabilitation of Offenders Act 1974 s 4(3)(b), Sch 2 para 3(5) (Sch 2 added by the Criminal Justice and Immigration Act 2008 Sch 10 paras 1, 6).

601.   Unauthorised disclosure of spent convictions and spent cautions.   Any person who, in the course of his official duties anywhere in the United Kingdom[1], has or at any time has had custody of or access to any official record[2] or the information contained therein, is guilty of an offence if, knowing or having reasonable cause to suspect that any specified information[3] or caution information[4] he has obtained in the course of those duties is specified information or caution information, he discloses it, otherwise than in the course of those duties, to another person[5]. A person who obtains any specified information or caution information from any official record by means of any fraud, dishonesty or bribe is also guilty of an offence[6].

1   As to the meaning of 'United Kingdom' see PARA 4 note 3.

2   In connection with spent convictions, 'official record' means a record kept for the purposes of its functions by any court, police force, Government department, local or other public authority in Great Britain, or a record kept, in Great Britain or elsewhere, for the purposes of any of Her Majesty's forces, being in either case a record containing information about persons convicted of offences (Rehabilitation of Offenders Act 1974 s 9(1)); and in connection with spent cautions, 'official record' means a record which contains information about persons given a caution for any offence or offences and is kept for the purposes of its functions by any court, police force, Government department or other public authority in England and Wales (s 9A(1)(a) (s 9A added by the Criminal Justice and Immigration Act 2008 Sch 10 paras 1, 4)). As to the meanings of 'conviction' and 'caution' see PARAS 591 note 3, 595 note 1; as to spent convictions and cautions see PARAS 594, 595; note in connection with disregarded convictions and cautions PARA 596.

3   'Specified information' means information imputing that a named or otherwise identifiable rehabilitated living person has committed or been charged with or prosecuted for or convicted of or sentenced for any offence which is the subject of a spent conviction: Rehabilitation of Offenders Act 1974 s 9(1).

4   'Caution information' means information imputing that a named or otherwise identifiable living person has committed, been charged with or prosecuted or cautioned for any offence which is the subject of a spent caution: Rehabilitation of Offenders Act 1974 s 9A(1)(b) (as added: see note 2).

5   Rehabilitation of Offenders Act 1974 ss 9(2), 9A(2) (s 9A as added: see note 2). This is subject to the provisions or terms of any order made under s 9(5) or s 9A(5) (s 9A(5) as so added) (under which the Secretary of State may make such provision as appears to him to be appropriate for excepting the disclosure of specified information or caution information derived from an official record from the provisions of ss 9(2), 9A(2) in such cases or classes of case as may be specified in the order): ss 9(2), 9A(2) (s 9A as so added). At the date at which this volume states the law no such order had been made. A person guilty of an offence under s 9(2) or s 9A(2) is liable on summary conviction to a fine not exceeding level 4 on the standard scale: ss 9(6), 9A(6) (s 9(6) amended by the Criminal Justice Act 1982 ss 38, 46; Rehabilitation of Offenders Act 1974 s 9A as so added). As to the standard scale, the statutory maximum, the prescribed sum, and magistrates' powers to levy unlimited fines see PARA 176.

       In any proceedings for an offence under s 9(2) or s 9A(2) it is a defence for the defendant to show that the disclosure was made to the rehabilitated or named person or to another person at the express request of the rehabilitated or named person or to a person whom he reasonably believed to be the rehabilitated or named person or to another person at the express request of a person whom he reasonably believed to be the rehabilitated or named person: ss 9(3), 9A(3) (s 9A as so added)). Proceedings for an offence under s 9A(2) may not, in England and Wales, be instituted except by or on behalf of the Director of Public Prosecutions: s 9A(8) (as so added).

6   Rehabilitation of Offenders Act 1974 ss 9(4), 9A(4) (s 9A as added: see note 2). A person guilty of an offence under s 9(4) or s 9A(4) is liable on summary conviction to a fine not exceeding level 5 on the standard scale or to imprisonment for a term not exceeding six months (where the offence involves specified information) or 51 weeks (where the offence involves caution information): ss 9(7), 9A(7) (s 9(7) amended by the Criminal Justice Act 1982 ss 38, 46; Rehabilitation of Offenders Act 1974 s 9A as so added).

602.   Compliance with sentence. A person does not become a rehabilitated person[1] in respect of a conviction[2] unless he has served or otherwise undergone or complied with any sentence[3] imposed on him in respect of that conviction[4]. The following do not, however, prevent a person from becoming a rehabilitated person for these purposes:

(1)   failure to pay a fine or other sum[5] adjudged to be paid by or imposed on a conviction, or breach of a condition of a recognisance to keep the peace or be of good behaviour[6];

(2)   breach of any condition or requirement applicable in relation to a sentence which renders the person to whom it applies liable to be dealt with for the offence for which the sentence was imposed, or, where the sentence was a suspended sentence of imprisonment, liable to be dealt with in respect of that sentence, whether or not, in any case, he is in fact so dealt with[7]; or

(3)   failure to comply with any requirement of a suspended sentence supervision order[8].

1   As to the meaning of 'rehabilitated person' see PARA 591.
2   As to the meaning of 'conviction' see PARA 591 note 3; as to spent convictions see PARA 594; note in connection with disregarded convictions PARA 596.
3   As to the meaning of 'sentence' see PARA 591 note 4.
4   Rehabilitation of Offenders Act 1974 s 1(2). Where in respect of a conviction a person was sentenced to imprisonment with an order under the Criminal Law Act 1977 s 47(1) (partly suspended sentence: now repealed), he is to be treated for these purposes as having served the sentence as soon as he completes service of so much of the sentence as was by that order required to be served in prison: Rehabilitation of Offenders Act 1974 s 1(2A) (added by the Criminal Law Act 1977 Sch 9 para 11).
5   The reference to a fine or other sum adjudged to be paid by or imposed on a conviction does not include a reference to an amount payable under a confiscation order made under the Proceeds of Crime Act 2002 Pt 2 (ss 6–91) (see PARA 220 et seq): Rehabilitation of Offenders Act 1974 s 1(2B) (added by the Proceeds of Crime Act 2002 Sch 11 paras 1, 7).
6   Rehabilitation of Offenders Act 1974 s 1(2)(a).
7   Rehabilitation of Offenders Act 1974 s 1(2)(b).
8   Rehabilitation of Offenders Act 1974 s 1(2)(c).

603.   Exclusion for immigration matters. The statutory rehabilitation provisions[1] do not apply in relation to any proceedings in respect of a relevant immigration decision[2] or a relevant nationality decision[3] or otherwise for the purposes of, or in connection with, any such decision[4].

1   Ie the Rehabilitation of Offenders Act 1974 s 4(1) (see PARA 591), s 4(2) (see PARA 598) and s 4(3) (see PARA 599).
2   'Relevant immigration decision' means any decision, or proposed decision, of the Secretary of State or an immigration officer under or by virtue of the Immigration Acts, or rules made under the Immigration Act 1971 s 3 (immigration rules: see IMMIGRATION AND ASYLUM), in relation to the entitlement of a person to enter or remain in the United Kingdom (including, in particular, the removal of a person from the United Kingdom, whether by deportation or otherwise): UK Borders Act 2007 s 56A(2) (s 56A added by the Legal Aid, Sentencing and Punishment of Offenders Act 2012 s 140). 'Immigration officer' means a person appointed by the Secretary of State as an immigration officer under the Immigration Act 1971 Sch 2 para 1 (see IMMIGRATION AND ASYLUM vol 57 (2012) PARA 142): UK Borders Act 2007 s 56A(2) (as so added).
     The references to the Immigration Acts and to the Acts listed in note 3 include references to any provision made under the European Communities Act 1972 s 2(2) (see CONSTITUTIONAL AND ADMINISTRATIVE LAW vol 20 (2014) PARA 156), or of EU law, which relates to the subject matter of the Act concerned: UK Borders Act 2007 s 56A(3) (as so added).
3   UK Borders Act 2007 s 56A(1)(a) (as added: see note 2). 'Relevant nationality decision' means any decision, or proposed decision, of the Secretary of State under or by virtue of the British Nationality Act 1981 (see BRITISH NATIONALITY vol 4 (2011) PARA 421 et seq), the British Nationality (Hong Kong) Act 1990 (see BRITISH NATIONALITY vol 4 (2011) PARA 433) or the Hong Kong (War Wives and Widows) Act 1996 (see BRITISH NATIONALITY vol 4 (2011) PARA 434) in relation to the good character of a person: UK Borders Act 2007 s 56A(2) (as so added).
4   UK Borders Act 2007 s 56A(1)(b) (as added: see note 2).

(ii) Periods of Rehabilitation

604.   Reckoning the rehabilitation period. The rehabilitation period for a sentence[1] is the period beginning with the date of the conviction[2] in respect of which the sentence is imposed[3] and ending at the time specified in relation to that sentence[4]. Where only one sentence is imposed in respect of a conviction, not being a sentence excluded from rehabilitation[5], the rehabilitation period applicable to the conviction is the period applicable[6] to that sentence[7]. Where more than one sentence is imposed in respect of a conviction, whether or not in the same proceedings, and none of the sentences is excluded from rehabilitation, then, if the periods applicable to those sentences differ, the rehabilitation period applicable to the conviction is the longer or the longest, as the case may be, of those periods[8].

There is no rehabilitation period for an order discharging a person absolutely for an offence or any other sentence in respect of a conviction where the sentence is not dealt with in the legislation[9], and, in such cases, references to any rehabilitation period are to be read as if the period of time were nil[10].

1   As to the meaning of 'sentence' see PARA 591 note 4.
2   As to the meaning of 'conviction' see PARA 591 note 3; as to spent convictions see PARA 594; note in connection with disregarded convictions PARA 596.
3   Rehabilitation of Offenders Act 1974 s 5(2)(a) (s 5(2), (4) substituted by the Legal Aid, Sentencing and Punishment of Offenders Act 2012 s 139(4)).
4   Rehabilitation of Offenders Act 1974 s 5(2)(b) (as substituted: see note 3). The end of the rehabilitation periods for both adults and young offenders is specified in the Table in s 5(2): see PARAS 605, 606.
5   Ie by virtue of the Rehabilitation of Offenders Act 1974 s 5(1): see PARA 592.
6   Ie in accordance with the Rehabilitation of Offenders Act 1974 s 5: see PARAS 605–606.
7   Rehabilitation of Offenders Act 1974 s 6(1). This is subject to s 6(2)–(5): see the text and note 8; and PARAS 607, 608.
8   Rehabilitation of Offenders Act 1974 s 6(2). This is subject to s 6(3), (3A)–(5): see PARAS 607, 608.
9   Ie in the Rehabilitation of Offenders Act 1974 s 5(2), Table or under s 5(3) (see PARAS 605–606).
10 Rehabilitation of Offenders Act 1974 s 5(4) (as substituted: see note 3).

605.   Adult offenders. The rehabilitation period[1] applicable in respect of a sentence[2] passed on an adult offender is the period beginning with the date of the conviction[3] in respect of which the sentence is imposed and ending:

(1)   in the case of a custodial sentence[4] of more than 30 months and up to, or consisting of, 48 months, the end of the period of seven years beginning with the day on which the sentence (including any licence period) is completed[5];

(2)   in the case of a custodial sentence of more than six months and up to, or consisting of, 30 months, the end of the period of 48 months beginning with the day on which the sentence (including any licence period) is completed[6];

(3)   in the case of a custodial sentence of six months or less, the end of the period of 24 months beginning with the day on which the sentence (including any licence period) is completed[7];

(4)   in the case of removal from Her Majesty's Service[8], the end of the period of 12 months beginning with the date of the conviction[9] in respect of which the sentence is imposed[10];

(5)   in the case of a sentence of service detention[11], the end of the period of 12 months beginning with the day on which the sentence is completed[12];

(6)   in the case of a fine, the end of the period of 12 months beginning with the date of the conviction in respect of which the sentence is imposed[13];

(7)   in the case of a compensation order[14], the date on which the payment is made in full[15];

(8)   in the case of a community or youth rehabilitation order[16], the end of the period of 12 months beginning with the day provided for by or under the order as the last day on which the order is to have effect[17]; and

(9)   in the case of a relevant order[18], the day provided for by or under the order as the last day on which the order is to have effect[19].

'Custodial sentence' means[20]:

(a)   a sentence of imprisonment[21];

(b)   a sentence of detention in a young offender institution[22];

(c)   a sentence of Borstal training;

(d)   a sentence of youth custody;

(e)   a sentence of corrective training;

(f)   a sentence of detention[23];

(g)   a detention and training order[24]; and

(h)   any sentence of a kind superseded (whether directly or indirectly) by a sentence mentioned in head (f) or (g).

'Sentence of imprisonment' includes a sentence of penal servitude (and 'term of imprisonment' is to be read accordingly)[25], and for these purposes[26]:

(i)   consecutive terms of imprisonment or other custodial sentences are to be treated as a single term;

(ii)   terms of imprisonment or other custodial sentences which are wholly or partly concurrent (that is terms of imprisonment or other custodial sentences imposed in respect of offences of which a person was convicted in the same proceedings) are to be treated as a single term;

(iii)   no account is to be taken of any subsequent variation, made by a court dealing with a person in respect of a suspended sentence of imprisonment, of the term originally imposed;

(iv)   no account is to be taken of any subsequent variation of the day originally provided for by or under an order as the last day on which the order is to have effect;

(v)   no account is to be taken of any detention or supervision ordered by a court[27]; and

(vi)   a sentence imposed by a court outside England and Wales is to be treated as the sentence mentioned in this section to which it most closely corresponds.

1   As to the rehabilitation period generally see PARA 604.

2   As to the meaning of 'sentence' see PARA 591 note 4.

3   See PARA 604.

4   See the text and notes 20–24.

5   Rehabilitation of Offenders Act 1974 s 5(2), Table (s 5(2), (3), (6)–(8) substituted by the Legal Aid, Sentencing and Punishment of Offenders Act 2012 s 139(4))). The Secretary of State may by order amend the Table: Rehabilitation of Offenders Act 1974 s 5(6) (as so substituted). At the date at which this volume states the law no such order had been made.

6   Rehabilitation of Offenders Act 1974 s 5(2), Table (as substituted: see note 5).

7   Rehabilitation of Offenders Act 1974 s 5(2), Table (as substituted: see note 5).

8   'Removal from Her Majesty's service' means a sentence of dismissal with disgrace from Her Majesty's service, a sentence of dismissal from Her Majesty's service or a sentence of cashiering or discharge with ignominy: Rehabilitation of Offenders Act 1974 s 5(8) (as substituted: see note 5).

9   As to the meaning of 'conviction' see PARA 591 note 3; as to spent convictions see PARA 594; note in connection with disregarded convictions PARA 596.

10   Rehabilitation of Offenders Act 1974 s 5(2), Table (as substituted: see note 5).

11   'Sentence of service detention' means (by virtue of the Rehabilitation of Offenders Act 1974 s 5(8) (as substituted: see note 5)): (1) a sentence of service detention (within the meaning given by the Armed Forces Act 2006 s 374 (see ARMED FORCES vol 3 (2011) PARA 583)), or a sentence of detention corresponding to such a sentence, in respect of a conviction in service disciplinary proceedings; or (2) any sentence of a kind superseded (whether directly or indirectly) by such a sentence.

12   Rehabilitation of Offenders Act 1974 s 5(2), Table (as substituted: see note 5).

13   Rehabilitation of Offenders Act 1974 s 5(2), Table (as substituted: see note 5).

14   As to compensation orders see PARA 281.

15   Rehabilitation of Offenders Act 1974 s 5(2), Table (as substituted: see note 5).

16 'Community or youth rehabilitation order' means (by virtue of the Rehabilitation of Offenders Act 1974 s 5(8) (as substituted: see note 5)):

    (1)   a community order under the Criminal Justice Act 2003 s 177 (see PARA 45 et seq);

    (2)   a service community order or overseas community order under the Armed Forces Act 2006;

    (3)   a youth rehabilitation order under the Criminal Justice and Immigration Act 2008 Pt 1 (ss 1–8) (see PARA 73 et seq); or

    (4)   any order of a kind superseded (whether directly or indirectly) by an order mentioned in head (1), (2) or (3).

17 Rehabilitation of Offenders Act 1974 s 5(2), Table (as substituted: see note 5). Where no provision is made by or under a community or youth rehabilitation order for the last day on which the order is to have effect, the rehabilitation period for the order is to be the period of 24 months beginning with the date of conviction: s 5(3) (as so substituted). The Secretary of State may by order amend the number of months for the time being specified in s 5(3): s 5(6) (as so substituted). At the date at which this volume states the law no such order had been made.

18 'Relevant order' means (by virtue of the Rehabilitation of Offenders Act 1974 s 5(8) (as substituted: see note 5)):

    (1)   an order discharging a person conditionally for an offence (see PARAS 454–456);

    (2)   an order binding a person over to keep the peace or be of good behaviour (see PARA 447 et seq);

    (3)   an order under the Street Offences Act 1959 s 1(2A) (see CRIMINAL LAW vol 25 (2010) PARA 251);

    (4)   a hospital order under the Mental Health Act 1983 Pt 3 (ss 35–55) (see PARAS 472–479; and MENTAL HEALTH AND CAPACITY vol 75 (2013) PARA 859 et seq) (with or without a restriction order);

    (5)   a referral order under the Powers of Criminal Courts (Sentencing) Act 2000 s 16 (see PARA 156);

    (6)   an earlier statutory order; or

    (7)   any order which imposes a disqualification, disability, prohibition or other penalty and is not otherwise dealt with in the Rehabilitation of Offenders Act 1974 s 5(2), Table or under s 5(3),

but does not include a reparation order under the Powers of Criminal Courts (Sentencing) Act 2000 s 73 (see PARA 293).

'Earlier statutory order' means (by virtue of the Rehabilitation of Offenders Act 1974 s 5(8) (as so substituted)):

    (a)   an order under the Children and Young Persons Act 1933 s 54 (repealed) committing the person convicted to custody in a remand home;

    (b)   an approved school order under s 57 (repealed); or

    (c)   any order of a kind superseded (whether directly or indirectly) by an order mentioned in any of heads (3)–(5), (a), (b) above.

19 Rehabilitation of Offenders Act 1974 s 5(2), Table (as substituted: see note 5). Where no provision is made by or under a relevant order for the last day on which the order is to have effect, the rehabilitation period for the order is to be the period of 24 months beginning with the date of conviction: s 5(3) (as so substituted).

20 Ie by virtue of the Rehabilitation of Offenders Act 1974 s 5(8) (as substituted: see note 5).

21 See PARA 26 et seq.

22 See PARAS 16–17.

23 Ie under the Powers of Criminal Courts (Sentencing) Act 2000 s 91 (see PARA 8) or the Armed Forces Act 2006 s 209 (see ARMED FORCES vol 3 (2011) PARA 596).

24 under the Powers of Criminal Courts (Sentencing) Act 2000 s 100 or an order under the Armed Forces Act 2006 s 211 (see ARMED FORCES vol 3 (2011) PARA 611).

25 Rehabilitation of Offenders Act 1974 s 5(8) (as substituted: see note 5).

26 Rehabilitation of Offenders Act 1974 s 5(7) (as substituted: see note 5).

27 Ie under the Powers of Criminal Courts (Sentencing) Act 2000 s 104(3) (see PARA 13).

606. Young offenders. The rehabilitation period[1] applicable in respect of a sentence[2] passed on an offender who was aged under 18 at the date of conviction is the period beginning with the date of the conviction[3] in respect of which the sentence is imposed and ending:

    (1)   in the case of a custodial sentence[4] of more than 30 months and up to,

or consisting of, 48 months, the end of the period of 42 months beginning with the day on which the sentence (including any licence period) is completed[5];

(2) in the case of a custodial sentence of more than six months and up to, or consisting of, 30 months, the end of the period of 24 months beginning with the day on which the sentence (including any licence period) is completed[6];

(3) in the case of a custodial sentence of six months or less, the end of the period of 18 months beginning with the day on which the sentence (including any licence period) is completed[7];

(4) in the case of removal from Her Majesty's Service[8], the end of the period of six months beginning with the date of the conviction[9] in respect of which the sentence is imposed[10];

(5) in the case of a sentence of service detention[11], the end of the period of six months beginning with the day on which the sentence is completed[12];

(6) in the case of a fine, the end of the period of six months beginning with the date of the conviction in respect of which the sentence is imposed[13];

(7) in the case of a compensation order[14], the date on which the payment is made in full[15];

(8) in the case of a community or youth rehabilitation order[16], the end of the period of six months beginning with the day provided for by or under the order as the last day on which the order is to have effect[17]; and

(9) in the case of a relevant order[18], the day provided for by or under the order as the last day on which the order is to have effect[19].

1 As to the rehabilitation period generally see PARA 604.
2 As to the meaning of 'sentence' see PARA 591 note 4.
3 See PARA 604.
4 As to the meaning of 'custodial sentence' see PARA 605.
5 Rehabilitation of Offenders Act 1974 s 5(2), Table (s 5(2), (3) substituted by the Legal Aid, Sentencing and Punishment of Offenders Act 2012 s 139(4)).
6 Rehabilitation of Offenders Act 1974 s 5(2), Table (as substituted: see note 4).
7 Rehabilitation of Offenders Act 1974 s 5(2), Table (as substituted: see note 4).
8 As to the meaning of 'removal from Her Majesty's service' see PARA 605 note 8.
9 As to the meaning of 'conviction' see PARA 591 note 3; as to spent convictions see PARA 594; note in connection with disregarded convictions PARA 596.
10 Rehabilitation of Offenders Act 1974 s 5(2), Table (as substituted: see note 4).
11 As to the meaning of 'sentence of service detention' see PARA 605 note 11.
12 Rehabilitation of Offenders Act 1974 s 5(2), Table (as substituted: see note 4).
13 Rehabilitation of Offenders Act 1974 s 5(2), Table (as substituted: see note 4).
14 As to compensation orders see PARA 281 et seq.
15 Rehabilitation of Offenders Act 1974 s 5(2), Table (as substituted: see note 4).
16 As to the meaning of 'community or youth rehabilitation order' see PARA 605 note 16.
17 Rehabilitation of Offenders Act 1974 s 5(2), Table (as substituted: see note 4). Where no provision is made by or under a community or youth rehabilitation order for the last day on which the order is to have effect, the rehabilitation period for the order is to be the period of 24 months beginning with the date of conviction: s 5(3) (as so substituted).
18 As to the meaning of 'relevant order' see PARA 605 note 18.
19 Rehabilitation of Offenders Act 1974 s 5(2), Table (as substituted: see note 4). Where no provision is made by or under a relevant order for the last day on which the order is to have effect, the rehabilitation period for the order is to be the period of 24 months beginning with the date of conviction: s 5(3) (as so substituted).

607. Conviction of offence during rehabilitation period. Where during the rehabilitation period[1] applicable to a conviction[2]:

(1)   the person convicted is convicted of a further offence[3]; and

(2)   no sentence[4] excluded from rehabilitation[5] is imposed on him in respect of the later conviction[6],

if the rehabilitation period applicable[7] to either of the convictions would end earlier than the period so applicable in relation to the other, the rehabilitation period which would[8] end the earlier is extended so as to end at the same time as the other rehabilitation period[9].

Where the rehabilitation period applicable to a conviction is the period applicable[10] to an order imposing on a person any disqualification, disability, prohibition or other penalty, the rehabilitation period applicable to another conviction is not extended[11] by reference to that period[12]. However, if any other sentence is imposed in respect of the first-mentioned conviction for which a rehabilitation period is prescribed[13], the rehabilitation period applicable to another conviction is, where appropriate, extended[14] by reference to the rehabilitation period applicable[15] to that sentence or, where more than one such sentence is imposed, by reference to the longer or longest of the periods so applicable to those sentences, as if the period in question were the rehabilitation period applicable to the first-mentioned conviction[16].

1   As to the rehabilitation period generally see PARA 604.
2   As to the meaning of 'conviction' see PARA 591 note 3; as to spent convictions see PARA 594; note in connection with disregarded convictions PARA 596.
3   Rehabilitation of Offenders Act 1974 s 6(4)(a).
4   As to the meaning of 'sentence' see PARA 591 note 4.
5   Ie under the Rehabilitation of Offenders Act 1974 s 5(1): see PARA 592.
6   Rehabilitation of Offenders Act 1974 s 6(4)(b).
7   Ie in accordance with the Rehabilitation of Offenders Act 1974 s 6: see PARAS 604, 608.
8   Ie apart from the Rehabilitation of Offenders Act 1974 s 6(4).
9   Rehabilitation of Offenders Act 1974 s 6(4).
10   Ie by virtue of the Rehabilitation of Offenders Act 1974 s 5(8), definition 'relevant order' para (g) (see PARA 605 note 18).
11   Ie by virtue of the Rehabilitation of Offenders Act 1974 s 6(4).
12   Rehabilitation of Offenders Act 1974 s 6(5) (amended by the Legal Aid, Sentencing and Punishment of Offenders Act 2012 s 139(1), (5)).
13   Ie by the Rehabilitation of Offenders Act 1974 s 5: see PARAS 604–606.
14   Ie under the Rehabilitation of Offenders Act 1974 s 6(4).
15   Ie in accordance with the Rehabilitation of Offenders Act 1974 s 5.
16   Rehabilitation of Offenders Act 1974 s 6(5) (as amended: see note 12).

608.   Extension of rehabilitation period for breach of discharge or order. Where:

(1)   in respect of a conviction[1] a person was conditionally discharged or a probation order was made and, after the end of the rehabilitation period applicable to the conviction[2], the person is dealt with, in consequence of a breach of conditional discharge or a breach of the order, for the offence for which the order for conditional discharge or probation was made[3]; or

(2)   an order is made[4] requiring an offender to attend meetings in respect of a conviction for loitering or soliciting and after the end of the rehabilitation period applicable to the conviction the offender is dealt with again for the offence for which that order was made[5],

then, if the rehabilitation period applicable to the conviction[6] (taking into account any sentence[7] imposed when he is so dealt with) ends later than the rehabilitation period previously applicable to the conviction, he is to be treated as not having become a rehabilitated person[8] in respect of that conviction; and the conviction is for those purposes to be treated as not having become spent, in relation to any period falling before the end of the new rehabilitation period[9].

1   As to the meaning of 'conviction' see PARA 591 note 3; as to spent convictions see PARA 594; note in connection with disregarded convictions PARA 596.
2   Ie in accordance with the Rehabilitation of Offenders Act 1974 s 6(1) or (2): see PARA 604.
3   Rehabilitation of Offenders Act 1974 s 6(3) (amended by the Criminal Justice and Court Services Act 2000 Sch 7 paras 48, 50).
4   Ie under the Street Offences Act 1959 s 1(2A) (see CRIMINAL LAW vol 25 (2010) PARA 251).
5   Rehabilitation of Offenders Act 1974 s 6(3A)(a), (b) (s 6(3A) added by the Policing and Crime Act 2009 s 18(1), (3)).
6   Ie in accordance with the Rehabilitation of Offenders Act 1974 s 6(2).
7   As to the meaning of 'sentence' see PARA 591 note 4.
8   As to the meaning of 'rehabilitated person' see PARA 591.
9   Rehabilitation of Offenders Act 1974 s 6(3), (3A)(c) (as amended and added: see notes 3, 5). These provisions are without prejudice to the Rehabilitation of Offenders Act 1974 s 6(2): see s 6(3), (3A) (as so amended and added).

(iii) Limitations and Restrictions on Statutory Rehabilitation Provisions

609.   Pardons, enforcement and other ongoing processes.   Although a person who is rehabilitated in respect of a conviction[1] is to be treated for all purposes in law as a person who has not committed or been charged with or prosecuted for or convicted of or sentenced[2] for the offence or offences which were the subject of that conviction[3], such rehabilitation does not affect:

(1)   any right of Her Majesty, by virtue of Her Royal prerogative or otherwise, to grant a free pardon, to quash any conviction or sentence, or to commute any sentence[4];

(2)   the enforcement by any process or proceedings of any fine or other sum adjudged to be paid by or imposed on a spent conviction[5];

(3)   the issue of any process for the purpose of proceedings in respect of any breach of a condition or requirement applicable to a sentence imposed in respect of a spent conviction[6]; or

(4)   the operation of any enactment by virtue of which, in consequence of any conviction, a person is subject, otherwise than by way of sentence, to any disqualification, disability, prohibition or other penalty the period of which extends beyond the applicable rehabilitation period[7].

Although a person who is rehabilitated in respect of caution is to be treated, from the time the caution is spent[8], for all purposes in law as a person who has not committed, been charged with or prosecuted for, or been given a caution for the offence, nothing in the rehabilitation provisions[9] affects the operation of the caution in question[10] or the operation of any enactment by virtue of which, in consequence of any caution, a person is subject to any disqualification, disability, prohibition or other restriction or effect, the period of which extends beyond the rehabilitation period applicable to the caution[11].

1   As to the meaning of 'conviction' see PARA 591 note 3; as to spent convictions see PARA 594; note in connection with disregarded convictions PARA 596.
2   As to the meaning of 'sentences' see PARA 591 note 4.
3   See the Rehabilitation of Offenders Act 1974 s 4(1); and PARA 591.
4   Rehabilitation of Offenders Act 1974 s 7(1)(a).
5   Rehabilitation of Offenders Act 1974 s 7(1)(b).
6   Rehabilitation of Offenders Act 1974 s 7(1)(c).
7   Rehabilitation of Offenders Act 1974 s 7(1)(d). As to the applicable rehabilitation period see s 6; and PARAS 604, 608.
8   As to the meaning of 'caution' see PARA 595 note 1; as to spent cautions see PARA 595; note in connection with disregarded cautions PARA 596.

9   Ie the Rehabilitation of Offenders Act 1974 Sch 2 para 3 (see PARAS 593–600).
10 Rehabilitation of Offenders Act 1974 Sch 2 para 5(a) (Sch 2 added by the Criminal Justice and Immigration Act 2008 Sch 10 paras 1, 6).
11 Rehabilitation of Offenders Act 1974 Sch 2 para 5(b) (as added: see note 10).

610.   Civil and criminal proceedings.   The rehabilitation principle, and the concomitant exclusions of evidence and questioning as to spent convictions and cautions[1], do not affect the determination of any issue, or prevent the admission or requirement of any evidence, relating to a person's previous convictions[2] or cautions[3] or to circumstances ancillary thereto[4]:

(1)   in any criminal proceedings before a court in England, Wales or Scotland (including any appeal or reference in a criminal matter)[5];

(2)   in any service disciplinary proceedings[6] or in any proceedings on appeal from any service disciplinary proceedings[7];

(3)   in any proceedings[8] relating to the making and operation of notification and other orders in connection with sexual offences, or on appeal from any such proceedings[9];

(4)   in any proceedings relating to adoption, the marriage or the formation of a civil partnership by any minor, the exercise of the inherent jurisdiction of the High Court with respect to minors or the provision by any person of accommodation, care or schooling for minors[10];

(5)   in any proceedings brought under the Children Act 1989[11];

(6)   in any proceedings relating to the variation or discharge of a youth rehabilitation order[12], or on appeal from any such proceedings[13];

(7)   in any proceedings in which he is a party or a witness, provided that, on the occasion when the issue or the admission or requirement of the evidence falls to be determined, he consents, notwithstanding the rehabilitation provisions[14], to the determination of the issue or, as the case may be, the admission or requirement of the evidence[15]; or

(8)   in any proceedings brought[16] in connection with the proceeds of criminal memoirs[17].

For these purposes 'service disciplinary proceedings' means any of:

(a)   any proceedings (whether or not before a court) in respect of a service offence[18] except proceedings before a civilian court[19];

(b)   any proceedings under the Army Act 1955, the Air Force Act 1955, or the Naval Discipline Act 1957 (all repealed) (whether before a court-martial or before any other court or person authorised thereunder to award a punishment in respect of any offence)[20];

(c)   any proceedings under any Act previously in force corresponding to any of the Acts mentioned in head (b) above[21];

(d)   any proceedings before a Standing Civilian Court established under the Armed Forces Act 1976[22]; and

(e)   any applicable proceedings under any corresponding enactment or law applying to a force, other than a home force[23], being proceedings in respect of a member of a home force who is or was at that time attached to the first-mentioned force under that section[24].

whether in any event those proceedings take place in England, Wales or Scotland or elsewhere[25].

1   See the Rehabilitation of Offenders Act 1974 s 4(1), Sch 2 para 3(1); and PARAS 591, 593.
2   As to the meaning of 'conviction' see PARA 591 note 3; as to spent convictions see PARA 594; note in connection with disregarded convictions PARA 596.

3   As to the meaning of 'caution' see PARA 595 note 1; as to spent cautions see PARA 595; note in connection with disregarded cautions PARA 596. These provisions (ie the Rehabilitation of Offenders Act 1974 s 7(2) (apart from s 7(2)(b), (d)) (see the text and notes 6–7, 12–13)) apply to the determination of any issue, and the admission or requirement of any evidence, relating to a person's previous cautions or to ancillary circumstances (see note 4) as they apply to matters relating to a person's previous convictions and circumstances ancillary thereto: Sch 2 para 6(2) (Sch 2 added by the Criminal Justice and Immigration Act 2008 Sch 10 paras 1, 6).

4   As to the circumstances ancillary to a conviction or a caution see PARA 593 note 9.

5   Rehabilitation of Offenders Act 1974 s 7(2)(a), Sch 2 para 6(1) (ss 2(5), 7(2)(a) amended by the Legal Aid, Sentencing and Punishment of Offenders Act 2012 Sch 5 para 6, Sch 25 para 3; Rehabilitation of Offenders Act 1974 s 7(2)(a), Sch 2 para 6(1) as added (see note 3)).

6   See the text and notes 19–24.

7   Rehabilitation of Offenders Act 1974 s 7(2)(b). This provision does not apply to a spent caution: see note 3.

8   Ie under the Sexual Offences Act 2003 Pt 2 (ss 80–136) (see PARA 498 et seq).

9   Rehabilitation of Offenders Act 1974 s 7(2)(bb) (added by the Sexual Offences Act 2003 Sch 6 para 19).

10 Rehabilitation of Offenders Act 1974 s 7(2)(c) (s 7(2)(c) substituted, s 7(2)(cc) added, by the Children Act 1989 Sch 13 para 35; Rehabilitation of Offenders Act 1974 s 7(2)(c) amended by the Civil Partnership Act 2004 Sch 27 para 53).

11 Rehabilitation of Offenders Act 1974 s 7(2)(cc) (as added: see note 10).

12 Ie under the Criminal Justice and Immigration Act 2008 Pt 1 (ss 1–8): see PARA 73 et seq.

13 Rehabilitation of Offenders Act 1974 s 7(2)(d) (substituted by the Criminal Justice and Immigration Act 2008 Sch 4 para 22). This provision does not apply to a spent caution: see note 3.

14 Ie notwithstanding the Rehabilitation of Offenders Act 1974 s 4(1): see PARA 591.

15 Rehabilitation of Offenders Act 1974 s 7(2)(f).

16 Ie under the Coroners and Justice Act 2009 Pt 7 (ss 155–172).

17 Rehabilitation of Offenders Act 1974 s 7(2)(h) (added by the Coroners and Justice Act 2009 s 158(1)).

18 Ie within the meaning of the Armed Forces Act 2006 (see s 50; and ARMED FORCES vol 3 (2011) PARA 569). The provisions of s 376(1)–(3) ('conviction' and 'sentence' in relation to summary hearings and the SAC: see ARMED FORCES) apply for the purposes of the Rehabilitation of Offenders Act 1974 as they apply for the purposes of the Armed Forces Act 2006: Rehabilitation of Offenders Act 1974 s 2(6) (as added: see note 5).

19 Rehabilitation of Offenders Act 1974 s 2(5)(za) (s 2(5)(za), (6) added by the Armed Forces Act 2006 Sch 16 para 64). The reference in the text to proceedings before a civilian court is a reference to such proceedings within the meaning of the Armed Forces Act 2006 (see s 374; and ARMED FORCES vol 3 (2011) PARA 345).

20 Rehabilitation of Offenders Act 1974 s 2(5)(a).

21 Rehabilitation of Offenders Act 1974 s 2(5)(b).

22 Rehabilitation of Offenders Act 1974 s 2(5)(bb) (added by the Armed Forces Act 1976 Sch 9 para 20(3)).

23 Ie any proceedings to which the Visiting Forces (British Commonwealth) Act 1933 s 4 (see ARMED FORCES vol 3 (2011) PARA 468) applies or applied at the time of the proceedings.

24 Rehabilitation of Offenders Act 1974 s 2(5)(c).

25 Rehabilitation of Offenders Act 1974 s 2(5) (as amended: see note 5).

611. Interests of justice. If at any stage in any proceedings before a judicial authority[1] in England, Wales or Scotland, not being proceedings to which the rehabilitation principle and the concomitant exclusions of evidence and questioning as to spent convictions[2] and cautions[3] do not apply[4] or (in relation to a spent conviction) proceedings to which the special provisions relating to defamation actions[5] apply, the authority is satisfied, in the light of any considerations which appear to it to be relevant (including any evidence which has been or may thereafter be put before it), that justice cannot be done in the case except by admitting or requiring evidence relating to a person's spent convictions or spent cautions or to circumstances ancillary thereto[6], that authority may admit or, as the case may be, require the evidence in question notwithstanding the rehabilitation principle and exclusions[7] and may determine any issue to which the evidence relates in disregard, so far as necessary, of those provisions[8].

1   As to the meaning of 'proceedings before a judicial authority' see PARA 593 note 2.
2   As to the meaning of 'conviction' see PARA 591 note 3; as to spent convictions see PARA 594; note in connection with disregarded convictions PARA 596.
3   As to the meaning of 'caution' see PARA 595 note 1; as to spent cautions see PARA 595; note in connection with disregarded cautions PARA 596. See the Rehabilitation of Offenders Act 1974 s 4(1), Sch 2 para 3(1); and PARAS 591, 593.
4   Ie by virtue of any of the Rehabilitation of Offenders Act 1974 s 7(2)(a)–(e), Sch 2 para 6(1), (2) (see PARA 610) or of any order for the time being in force under s 7(4) (see PARA 612).
5   Ie the Rehabilitation of Offenders Act 1974 s 8 (see PARA 613).
6   As to the circumstances ancillary to a conviction or a caution see PARA 593 note 9.
7   Ie notwithstanding the provisions of the Rehabilitation of Offenders Act 1974 s 4(1), Sch 2 para 3(1): see note 4; and PARAS 591, 593.
8   Rehabilitation of Offenders Act 1974 s 7(3), Sch 2 para 6(1), (3) (s 7(3) amended by the Legal Aid, Sentencing and Punishment of Offenders Act 2012 Sch 5 para 6; Rehabilitation of Offenders Act 1974 Sch 2 added by the Criminal Justice and Immigration Act 2008 Sch 10 paras 1, 6).

612. Administrative proceedings. The rehabilitation principle, and the concomitant exclusions of evidence and questioning as to spent convictions and cautions[1], do not apply[2] in relation to:

(1)   proceedings in respect of a person's admission to, or disciplinary proceedings against a member of, any of the excepted professions[3];

(2)   proceedings before the Court of Appeal of the High Court in the exercise of their disciplinary jurisdiction in respect of solicitors[4];

(3)   disciplinary proceedings against a constable[5];

(4)   proceedings before the Gambling Commission[6];

(5)   mental health proceedings[7] before any tribunal[8];

(6)   specified proceedings[9] relating to the dealing and use of firearms[10];

(7)   proceedings in respect of the grant, renewal or variation of a licence[11] relating to persons under the age of 18 going abroad for the purpose of performing or being exhibited for profit[12];

(8)   proceedings in respect of a direction prohibiting a person from teaching[13] or of any prohibition or restriction on a person's employment or work which has effect as if it were contained in such a direction[14];

(9)   proceedings in respect of an application for, or cancellation of, the Secretary of State's approval[15] of a place for the medical termination of pregnancies[16];

(10)   proceedings in respect of an application for, or the suspension or cancellation of, registration in respect of a registered activity[17];

(11)   proceedings in respect of an application to the chief officer of police for a certificate[18] as to the fitness of the applicant to acquire or acquire and keep explosives (including consideration as to whether to refuse[19] the application)[20];

(12)   proceedings in respect of the revocation[21] of such certificates[22];

(13)   proceedings in respect of an appeal or application[23] against a decision[24] taken in respect of the refusal or revocation of such certificates[25];

(14)   proceedings relating to a taxi driver licence[26];

(15)   as from a day to be appointed, proceedings before the National Lottery Commission[27] in respect of the grant or revocation of a licence[28] to run

the National Lottery or by way of appeal to the Secretary of State against the revocation of any such licence by the National Lottery Commission[29];

(16) proceedings relating to the registration[30] of care establishments and agencies[31];

(17) proceedings relating to the registration[32] of social workers in Wales[33];

(18) appeals[34] in matters relating to the licensing of workers in the private security industry[35] and specified proceedings relating to the approval of persons to undertake licensable conduct at specified football matches without a licence[36] pursuant to the statutory exemptions[37] from the licensing requirement[38];

(19) proceedings relating to the grant, amendment, variation, suspension or revocation of a poisons licence[39];

(20) proceedings before the Parole Board[40];

(21) recovery proceedings for criminal injuries compensation[41];

(22) specified proceedings[42] for the recovery of the proceeds of criminal conduct[43];

(23) proceedings by way of appeal against, or review of, any decision taken[44], on consideration of a spent conviction or caution[45]; and

(24) proceedings held for the receipt of evidence affecting the determination of any question arising in any of these proceedings[46].

1   See the Rehabilitation of Offenders Act 1974 s 4(1), Sch 2 para 3(1); and PARAS 591, 593. As to the meaning of 'conviction' see PARA 591 note 3; as to spent convictions see PARA 594; note in connection with disregarded convictions PARA 596. As to the meaning of 'caution' see PARA 595 note 1; as to spent cautions see PARA 595; note in connection with disregarded cautions PARA 596.

2   Ie by virtue of the Rehabilitation of Offenders Act 1974 s 7(4), Sch 2 para 6(1), (4), (5) (Sch 2 added by the Criminal Justice and Immigration Act 2008 Sch 10 paras 1, 6) (under which the Secretary of State may by order exclude the application of the Rehabilitation of Offenders Act 1974 s 4(1), Sch 2 para 3(1) in relation to any proceedings specified in the order (other than, in connection with spent convictions, proceedings to which the Rehabilitation of Offenders Act 1974 s 8 (see PARA 613) applies) to such extent and for such purposes as may be so specified).

3   Rehabilitation of Offenders Act 1974 (Exceptions) Order 1975, SI 1975/1023, art 5(1)(a), Sch 3 para 1 (art 5(1) substituted by SI 1986/2268; amended by SI 2008/3259). As to the excepted professions, and a further restriction on the rehabilitation provisions in connection therewith, see Sch 2; and PARA 614.

4   Rehabilitation of Offenders Act 1974 (Exceptions) Order 1975, SI 1975/1023, Sch 3 para 2. As to the disciplining of solicitors see LEGAL PROFESSIONS vol 66 (2015) PARA 662 et seq.

5   Rehabilitation of Offenders Act 1974 (Exceptions) Order 1975, SI 1975/1023, Sch 3 para 3.

6   Rehabilitation of Offenders Act 1974 (Exceptions) Order 1975, SI 1975/1023, Sch 3 para 4. This provision refers to the Gaming Board for Great Britain, which has been abolished and replaced by the Gambling Commission: see the Gambling Act 2005 Pt 2 (ss 20–32); and LICENSING AND GAMBLING vol 67 (2008) PARA 4.

7   Ie proceedings under the Mental Health Act 1983: see MENTAL HEALTH AND CAPACITY vol 75 (2013) PARA 955 et seq.

8   Rehabilitation of Offenders Act 1974 (Exceptions) Order 1975, SI 1975/1023, Sch 3 para 5 (substituted by SI 2008/2683).

9   Ie proceedings under the Firearms Act 1968 in respect of:

(1)   the registration of a person as a firearms dealer, the removal of a person's name from a register of firearms dealers or the imposition, variation or revocation of conditions of any such registration (Rehabilitation of Offenders Act 1974 (Exceptions) Order 1975, SI 1975/1023, Sch 3 para 6(a): see CRIMINAL LAW vol 26 (2010) PARAS 642–645);

(2)   the grant, renewal, variation or revocation of a firearm certificate (Sch 3 para 6(b): see CRIMINAL LAW vol 26 (2010) PARAS 636–639);

(3)   the grant, renewal or revocation of a shot gun certificate (Sch 3 para 6(c): see CRIMINAL LAW vol 26 (2010) PARAS 636–639); or

(4) the grant of a permit under the Firearms Act 1968 s 7(1), 9(2) or 13(1)(c) (Rehabilitation of Offenders Act 1974 (Exceptions) Order 1975, SI 1975/1023, Sch 3 para 6(d): CRIMINAL LAW vol 26 (2010) PARAS 598, 600, 609).

10 Rehabilitation of Offenders Act 1974 (Exceptions) Order 1975, SI 1975/1023, Sch 3 para 6. In connection with firearms dealers see also PARA 616.

11 Ie under the Children and Young Persons Act 1933 s 25: see CHILDREN AND YOUNG PERSONS vol 10 (2012) PARAS 738–740.

12 Rehabilitation of Offenders Act 1974 (Exceptions) Order 1975, SI 1975/1023, Sch 3 para 7. As to the determination of a person's age see the Children and Young Persons Act 1933 s 99; and CHILDREN AND YOUNG PERSONS vol 10 (2012) PARA 1206.

13 Ie a direction given under the Education Act 2002 s 142: see EDUCATION vol 35 (2011) PARA 469.

14 Rehabilitation of Offenders Act 1974 (Exceptions) Order 1975, SI 1975/1023, Sch 3 para 9 (substituted by SI 2006/2143).

15 Ie under the Abortion Act 1967 s 1: see CRIMINAL LAW vol 25 (2010) PARA 122.

16 Rehabilitation of Offenders Act 1974 (Exceptions) Order 1975, SI 1975/1023, Sch 3 para 11(a).

17 Rehabilitation of Offenders Act 1974 (Exceptions) Order 1975, SI 1975/1023, Sch 3 para 11A (added by SI 2013/1198). As to the registration of regulated activities see the Health and Social Care Act 2008 Pt 1 (ss 1–97); and SOCIAL SERVICES AND COMMUNITY CARE vol 95 (2013) PARA 88 et seq.

18 Ie pursuant to the Explosives Regulations 2014, SI 2014/1638, regs 4, 5, 11: see EXPLOSIVES.

19 Ie on any of the grounds specified in the Explosives Regulations 2014, SI 2014/1638, reg 19: see EXPLOSIVES.

20 Rehabilitation of Offenders Act 1974 (Exceptions) Order 1975, SI 1975/1023, Sch 3 para 13(a) (substituted by SI 2014/1638).

21 Ie on any of the grounds specified in the Explosives Regulations 2014, SI 2014/1638, reg 21: see EXPLOSIVES.

22 Rehabilitation of Offenders Act 1974 (Exceptions) Order 1975, SI 1975/1023, Sch 3 para 13(b) (substituted by SI 2014/1638).

23 Ie pursuant to the Explosives Regulations 2014, SI 2014/1638, reg 22: see EXPLOSIVES.

24 Ie a decision taken under the Explosives Regulations 2014, SI 2014/1638, reg 19 or 21: see EXPLOSIVES.

25 Rehabilitation of Offenders Act 1974 (Exceptions) Order 1975, SI 1975/1023, Sch 3 para 13(c) (substituted by SI 2014/1638).

26 Rehabilitation of Offenders Act 1974 (Exceptions) Order 1975, SI 1975/1023, Sch 3 para 16 (substituted by SI 2003/965).

27 As to the National Lottery Commission see LICENSING AND GAMBLING vol 67 (2008) PARA 7 et seq.

28 Ie a licence under the National Lottery etc Act 1993 Pt 1 (ss 1–20): see LICENSING AND GAMBLING vol 68 (2008) PARA 691 et seq.

29 Rehabilitation of Offenders Act 1974 (Exceptions) Order 1975, SI 1975/1023, Sch 3 para 17 (prospectively added by SI 2002/441). At the date at which this volume states the law no day had been appointed for the coming into force of this provision.

30 Ie under the Care Standards Act 2000 Pt II (ss 11–42): see HEALTH SERVICES vol 54 (2008) PARA 755 et seq.

31 Rehabilitation of Offenders Act 1974 (Exceptions) Order 1975, SI 1975/1023, Sch 3 para 17A (added by SI 2014/1707).

32 Ie under the Care Standards Act 2000 Pt IV (ss 54–71): see SOCIAL SERVICES AND COMMUNITY CARE vol 95 (2013) PARA 83 et seq.

33 Rehabilitation of Offenders Act 1974 (Exceptions) Order 1975, SI 1975/1023, Sch 3 para 18 (added by SI 2003/965).

34 Ie proceedings under the Private Security Industry Act 2001 s 11: see TRADE AND INDUSTRY vol 97 (2015) PARA 997.

35 Rehabilitation of Offenders Act 1974 (Exceptions) Order 1975, SI 1975/1023, Sch 3 para 19 (added by SI 2003/965).

36 Ie a licence granted under the Private Security Industry Act 2001 s 8: see TRADE AND INDUSTRY vol 97 (2015) PARA 996.

37 Ie the Private Security Industry Act 2001 s 4: see TRADE AND INDUSTRY vol 97 (2015) PARA 992.

38 Rehabilitation of Offenders Act 1974 (Exceptions) Order 1975, SI 1975/1023, Sch 3 para 23 (added by SI 2006/2143). The proceedings relating to the undertaking of licensable conduct at football matches without a licence are proceedings brought before the Football Association or Football Association Premier League against a decision taken by the body before which the proceedings are brought to refuse to approve a person as able to undertake, in the course of

acting as a steward at a sports ground at which football matches are played or as a supervisor or manager of such a person, such conduct: Rehabilitation of Offenders Act 1974 (Exceptions) Order 1975, SI 1975/1023, Sch 3 para 23 (as so added).

39 Rehabilitation of Offenders Act 1974 (Exceptions) Order 1975, SI 1975/1023, Sch 3 para 19A (added by SI 2015/968). A poisons licence is a licence under the Poisons Act 1952 s 4A (see **MEDICAL PRODUCTS AND DRUGS**).

40 Rehabilitation of Offenders Act 1974 (Exceptions) Order 1975, SI 1975/1023, Sch 3 para 20 (added by SI 2006/2143). As to the Parole Board see PARA 699.

41 Rehabilitation of Offenders Act 1974 (Exceptions) Order 1975, SI 1975/1023, Sch 3 para 21 (added by SI 2006/2143). As to these proceedings see the Criminal Injuries Compensation Act 1995 s 7D; and **CRIMINAL PROCEDURE** vol 28 (2015) PARA 897.

42 Ie proceedings under:
  (1) the Proceeds of Crime Act 2002 Pt 5 Ch 2 (ss 243–288) (civil recovery: see **CRIMINAL PROCEDURE** vol 28 (2015) PARA 911 et seq) (Rehabilitation of Offenders Act 1974 (Exceptions) Order 1975, SI 1975/1023, Sch 3 para 22(a) (added by SI 2006/2143));
  (2) proceedings pursuant to a notice under the Proceeds of Crime Act 2002 s 317(2) (Rehabilitation of Offenders Act 1974 (Exceptions) Order 1975, SI 1975/1023, Sch 3 para 22(b) (as so added)); and
  (3) proceedings pursuant to an application under the Proceeds of Crime Act 2002 Pt 8 (ss 341–416) in connection with a civil recovery investigation (within the meaning of s 341: see **CRIMINAL LAW** vol 26 (2010) PARA 759 et seq) (Rehabilitation of Offenders Act 1974 (Exceptions) Order 1975, SI 1975/1023, Sch 3 para 22(c) (as so added)).

43 Rehabilitation of Offenders Act 1974 (Exceptions) Order 1975, SI 1975/1023, Sch 3 para 22 (as added: see note 42).

44 Ie by virtue of the Rehabilitation of Offenders Act 1974 (Exceptions) Order 1975, SI 1975/1023.

45 Rehabilitation of Offenders Act 1974 (Exceptions) Order 1975, SI 1975/1023, Sch 3 para 14.

46 Rehabilitation of Offenders Act 1974 (Exceptions) Order 1975, SI 1975/1023, Sch 3 para 15.

613.   Defamation actions. The rehabilitation principle, and the concomitant exclusions of evidence and questioning as to spent convictions[1], do not affect any action for libel or slander begun by a rehabilitated person[2] and founded upon the publication of any matter imputing that the claimant has committed or been charged with or prosecuted for or convicted[3] of or sentenced[4] for an offence which was the subject of a spent conviction[5] if the publication complained of took place before the conviction in question became spent[6]. Similarly, those provisions do not in general[7] prevent the defendant in any such action from relying on any defence of justification or fair comment or of absolute or qualified privilege which is available to him, or restrict the matters he may establish in support of any such defence[8], and they do not[9] restrict the matters that a defendant who is relying on a defence of qualified privilege in any such action where malice is alleged against him may establish in rebuttal of the allegation[10].

These exceptions for defamation actions to not apply in relation to spent cautions[11].

1 See the Rehabilitation of Offenders Act 1974 s 4(1); and PARAS 591, 593.
2 As to the meaning of 'rehabilitated person' see PARA 591.
3 As to the meaning of 'convicted' see PARA 591 note 3.
4 As to the meaning of 'sentenced' see PARA 591 note 4.
5 As to spent convictions see PARA 594.
6 Rehabilitation of Offenders Act 1974 s 8(1), (2). The provisions of s 8(3)–(7) (see the text and notes 7–10) are disapplied in any such case: s 8(2).
7 See note 8.
8 Rehabilitation of Offenders Act 1974 s 8(3) (s 8(3), (5) amended by the Defamation Act 2013 s 16). However:
  (1) a defendant in any action to which the Rehabilitation of Offenders Act 1974 s 8 applies may not by virtue of s 8(3) be entitled to rely upon a defence under the Defamation Act 2013 s 2 (see **DEFAMATION**) if the publication is proved to have been made with malice (Rehabilitation of Offenders Act 1974 s 8(5) (s 8(3), (5) amended by the Defamation Act 2013 s 16) to which s 8(3) is expressly made subject); and

(2)   a defendant in any such action may not, by virtue of s 8(3), be entitled to rely on any
matter or adduce or require any evidence for the purpose of establishing (whether under
the Defamation Act 1996 s 14 (see DEFAMATION vol 32 (2012) PARA 600) or otherwise)
the defence that the matter published constituted a fair and accurate report of judicial
proceedings if it is proved that the publication contained a reference to evidence which
was ruled to be inadmissible in the proceedings by virtue of the Rehabilitation of
Offenders Act 1974 s 4(1) (s 8(6) (amended by the Defamation Act 1996 s 14(4)), to
which the Rehabilitation of Offenders Act 1974 s 8(3) is expressly made subject.
Note that s 8(3) will apply without the qualifications imposed by s 8(6) in relation to any
report of judicial proceedings contained in any bona fide series of law reports which does not
form part of any other publication and consists solely of reports of proceedings in courts of law
(s 8(7)(a)) and any report or account of judicial proceedings published for bona fide educational,
scientific or professional purposes, or given in the course of any lecture, class or discussion given
or held for any of those purposes (s 8(7)(b)).

9   Ie without prejudice to the generality of the Rehabilitation of Offenders Act 1974 s 8(3): s 8(4).
10   Rehabilitation of Offenders Act 1974 s 8(4). A rehabilitated person may recover damages for
libel provided he can show that publication of convictions which are to be treated as spent by
virtue of s 1(1) (see PARA 594) was malicious; but an injunction restraining future publication
will be granted only where the evidence of malice is overwhelming: see *Herbage v
Pressdram Ltd* [1984] 2 All ER 769, [1984] 1 WLR 1160, CA. See further see DEFAMATION
vol 32 (2012) PARA 675.
11   See the Rehabilitation of Offenders Act 1974 Sch 2 paras 5, 6; and PARAS 609, 610. As to spent
cautions see PARA 595.

614.   Excepted professions. None of the statutory protections for rehabilitated
persons[1] relating to the asking and answering of questions concerning past
convictions or spent cautions[2] apply in relation to any question asked by or on
behalf of any person, in the course of duties of his office or employment, in order
to assess the suitability of the person to whom the question relates for admission
to any of a number of specified professions, and none of the statutory
protections relating to the non-disclosure of spent convictions or spent cautions
in an employment context[3] apply to the dismissal or exclusion of any person
from any such profession[4]. The professions are:
(1)   health care professional[5];
(2)   barrister or solicitor[6];
(3)   chartered accountant and certified accountant[7];
(4)   actuary[8];
(5)   registered foreign lawyer[9];
(6)   chartered legal executive of other CILEx authorised person[10]; and
(7)   receiver appointed by the Court of Protection[11].
The operation of the rehabilitation provisions is also restricted in relation to
proceedings in respect of a person's admission to, or disciplinary proceedings
against a member of, any of these professions[12].

1   As to the meaning of 'rehabilitated person' see PARA 591.
2   Ie the Rehabilitation of Offenders Act 1974 s 4(2), Sch 2 para 3(3): see PARA 598. As to the
meaning of 'conviction' see PARA 591 note 3; as to spent convictions see PARA 594; note in
connection with disregarded convictions PARA 596. As to the meaning of 'caution' see PARA 595
note 1; as to spent cautions see PARA 595; note in connection with disregarded cautions PARA
596. For the exception from the operation of s 4(2), Sch 2 para 3(3) to apply, the person
questioned must be informed at the time the question is asked that, by virtue of the
Rehabilitation of Offenders Act 1974 (Exceptions) Order 1975, SI 1975/1023, spent convictions
or cautions are to be disclosed: art 3(1)(a) (art 3(1) amended by SI 2008/3259; Rehabilitation of
Offenders Act 1974 (Exceptions) Order 1975, SI 1975/1023, arts 3(1), 4(1) renumbered by
SI 2013/1198).
3   Ie the Rehabilitation of Offenders Act 1974 s 4(3)(b), Sch 2 para 3(5): see PARA 600.
4   Rehabilitation of Offenders Act 1974 s 4(4), Sch 2 para 4 (Sch 2 added by the Criminal Justice
and Immigration Act 2008 Sch 10 paras 1, 6) (providing that the Secretary of State may by
order make such provisions as seem to him appropriate for excluding or modifying the

application of either or both of the Rehabilitation of Offenders Act 1974 s 4(2)(a) or (b) or Sch 2 para 3(2)(a) or (b) in relation to questions put in such circumstances as may be specified in the order and may provide for such exceptions from the provisions of s 4(3) or Sch 2 para 3(4), (5) as seem to him appropriate, in such cases or classes of case, and in relation to convictions of such a description, as may be specified in the order); Rehabilitation of Offenders Act 1974 (Exceptions) Order 1975, SI 1975/1023, arts 3(1)(a)(i), 4(1)(a) (as renumbered and amended: see note 2).

5 Rehabilitation of Offenders Act 1974 (Exceptions) Order 1975, SI 1975/1023, Sch 1 Pt I para 1 (substituted by SI 2012/1957). 'Health care professional' means a person who is a member of a profession regulated by a body mentioned in the National Health Service Reform and Health Care Professions Act 2002 s 25(3) (see MEDICAL PROFESSIONS vol 74 (2011) PARA 48) (and for the purposes of this definition s 25(3A) is to be ignored): Rehabilitation of Offenders Act 1974 (Exceptions) Order 1975, SI 1975/1023, Sch 1 Pt IV (definition added by SI 2012/1957).

6 Rehabilitation of Offenders Act 1974 (Exceptions) Order 1975, SI 1975/1023, Sch 1 Pt I para 2 (amended by SI 2013/1198).

7 Rehabilitation of Offenders Act 1974 (Exceptions) Order 1975, SI 1975/1023, Sch 1 Pt I para 3. For these purposes 'chartered accountant' means a member of the Institute of Chartered Accountants in England and Wales and 'certified accountant' means a member of the Association of Certified Accountants: Sch 1 Pt IV.

8 Rehabilitation of Offenders Act 1974 (Exceptions) Order 1975, SI 1975/1023, Sch 1 Pt I para 14 (Sch 1 Pt I paras 14–17 added by SI 2002/441). For these purposes 'actuary' means a member of the Institute and Faculty of Actuaries: see the Rehabilitation of Offenders Act 1974 (Exceptions) Order 1975, SI 1975/1023, Sch 1 Pt IV (definition added by SI 2002/441; amended by SI 2011/1800).

9 Rehabilitation of Offenders Act 1974 (Exceptions) Order 1975, SI 1975/1023, Sch 1 Pt I para 15 (as added: see note 8). As to the meaning of 'registered foreign lawyer' see the Courts and Legal Services Act 1990 s 89; and LEGAL PROFESSIONS vol 65 (2015) PARA 461 (definition applied by the Rehabilitation of Offenders Act 1974 (Exceptions) Order 1975, SI 1975/1023, Sch 1 Pt IV (definition added by SI 2002/441)).

10 Rehabilitation of Offenders Act 1974 (Exceptions) Order 1975, SI 1975/1023, Sch 1 Pt I para 16 (as added (see note 8); substituted by SI 2014/1707). For these purposes 'chartered legal executive' means a fellow of the Chartered Institute of Legal Executives (see LEGAL PROFESSIONS vol 66 (2015) PARA 1044) and 'CILEx authorised person' means a person authorised by the Chartered Institute of Legal Executives to provide a reserved legal activity in accordance with the Legal Services Act 2007 (see LEGAL PROFESSIONS vol 65 (2015) PARA 352): see the Rehabilitation of Offenders Act 1974 (Exceptions) Order 1975, SI 1975/1023, Sch 1 Pt IV (definitions added by SI 2014/1707).

11 Rehabilitation of Offenders Act 1974 (Exceptions) Order 1975, SI 1975/1023, Sch 1 Pt I para 17 (as added: see note 8).

12 See PARA 612.

615. Excepted offices and employments. None of the statutory protections for rehabilitated persons[1] relating to the asking and answering of questions concerning past convictions or spent cautions[2] apply in relation to any question asked by or on behalf of any person, in the course of duties of his office or employment, in order to assess the suitability of the person to whom the question relates for a number of specified offices and employments, and none of the statutory protections relating to the non-disclosure of spent convictions or spent cautions in an employment context[3] apply in relation to specified offices and employments[4]. The offices and employments are:

(1) judicial appointments[5];

(2) the Director of Public Prosecutions and any office or employment in the Crown Prosecution Service[6];

(3) designated officers for magistrates' courts, for justices of the peace or for local justice areas, justices' clerks and assistants to justices' clerks[7];

(4) persons employed for the purpose of, or to assist the constable of, a police force established under any enactment[8];

(5) any employment which is concerned with the administration of, or is otherwise normally carried out wholly or partly within the precincts of,

a prison, remand centre, removal centre, short-term holding facility, young offender institution or young offenders institution, and members of boards of visitors appointed under the Prison Act 1952[9];

(6) traffic wardens appointed under the Road Traffic Regulation Act 1984[10];

(7) officers of providers of probation services[11];

(8) any office or employment which is concerned with the provision of care services[12] to vulnerable adults[13] or the representation of, or advocacy services for, vulnerable adults by a service that has been approved by the Secretary of State or the Welsh Ministers or created under any enactment, and which is of such a kind as to enable a person, in the course of his normal duties, to have access to vulnerable adults in receipt of such services[14];

(9) any work which is regulated activity relating to vulnerable adults[15];

(10) any employment or other work which is concerned with the provision of health services[16] and which is of such a kind as to enable the holder of that employment or the person engaged in that work to have access to persons in receipt of such services in the course of his normal duties[17];

(11) any employment or other work in England or Wales concerned with the investigation of fraud, corruption or other unlawful activity affecting the national health service[18], or security management[19] in the national health service[20],

(12) any work which is work in a regulated position[21] or work in a further education institution or 16 to 19 academy where the normal duties of that work involve regular contact with persons aged under 18[22];

(13) any work which is regulated activity[23] relating to children[24];

(14) any employment or other work that is carried out at a children's home or residential family centre[25];

(15) any employment or other work which is carried out for the purposes of an adoption service, an adoption support agency, a voluntary adoption agency, a fostering service or a fostering agency and which is of such a kind as to enable a person, in the course of his normal duties, to have contact with children or access to sensitive or personal information about children[26];

(16) any employment or office which is concerned with the management of a childminder agency or any work for a childminder agency which is of such a kind as to require the person engaged in that work to enter day care premises or premises on which child minding is provided and as to enable the person, in the course of his normal duties, to have contact with children for whom child minding or day care is provided or access to sensitive or personal information about children for whom childminding or day care is provided[27];

(17) any employment in the Royal Society for the Prevention of Cruelty to Animals where the person employed or working, as part of his duties, may carry out the humane killing of animals[28];

(18) any employment which is concerned with the monitoring, for the purposes of child protection, of communications by means of the internet[29];

(19) any employment or other work which is normally carried out in premises approved under the Criminal Justice and Court Services Act 2000[30];

(20) any employment or other work which is normally carried out in a hospital used only for the provision of high security psychiatric services[31];

(21) an individual designated under certain provisions of the Traffic Management Act 2004[32];

(22) judges' clerks, secretaries and legal secretaries[33];

(23) court officers and court contractors, who in the course of their work, have to face contact with judges of the Supreme Court, or access to such judges' lodgings[34];

(24) persons who in the course of their work have regular access to personal information relating to an identified or identifiable member of the judiciary[35];

(25) court officers and court contractors who, in the course of their work, attend either the Royal Courts of Justice or the Central Criminal Court[36];

(26) court security officers and tribunal security officers[37];

(27) court contractors who, in the course of their work, have unsupervised access to court-houses, offices and other accommodation used in relation to the courts[38];

(28) contractors, sub-contractors, and any person acting under the authority of such a contractor or sub-contractor, who in the course of their work, have unsupervised access to tribunal buildings, offices and other accommodation used in relation to tribunals[39];

(29) court officers who execute county court warrants[40];

(30) High Court enforcement officers[41];

(31) sheriffs and under-sheriffs[42];

(32) tipstaffs[43];

(33) any other persons who execute High Court writs or warrants who act under the authority of a person listed in heads (29) to (32) above[44];

(34) persons who execute writs of sequestration[45];

(35) civilian enforcement officers[46];

(36) persons who are authorised[47] to execute warrants and any other person other than a constable who is authorised[48] to execute a warrant[49];

(37) persons who execute clamping orders[50];

(38) the Official Solicitor and his deputy[51];

(39) court officers and court contractors who exercise functions in connection with the administration and management of funds in court including the deposit, payment, delivery and transfer in, into and out of any court of funds in court and regulating the evidence of such deposit, payment, delivery or transfer and court officers and court contractors, who receive payments in pursuance of a conviction or order of a magistrates' court[52];

(40) persons working in the Department for Education, the Office for Standards in Education, Children's Services and Skills with access to sensitive or personal information about children or vulnerable adults[53];

(41) the chairman, other members, and members of staff (including any person seconded to serve as a member of staff) of the Disclosure and Barring Service[54];

(42) staff working within the Office of the Public Guardian with access to data relating to children and vulnerable adults[55];

(43) the Commissioner for Older People in Wales, and his deputy, and any person appointed by the Commissioner to assist him in the discharge of his functions or authorised to discharge his functions on his behalf[56];

(44) the Commissioners for the Gambling Commission and any office or employment in their service[57];

(45) individuals seeking authorisation from the Secretary of State for the Home Department to become authorised search officers[58]; and

(46) any employment or other work where the normal duties involve caring for, training, supervising, or being solely in charge of, persons aged under 18 serving in the naval, military or air forces of the Crown or include supervising or managing a person employed or working in such a capacity[59].

1   As to the meaning of 'rehabilitated person' see PARA 591.

2   Ie the Rehabilitation of Offenders Act 1974 s 4(2), Sch 2 para 3(3): see PARA 598. As to the meaning of 'conviction' see PARA 591 note 3; as to spent convictions see PARA 594; note in connection with disregarded convictions PARA 596. As to the meaning of 'caution' see PARA 595 note 1; as to spent cautions see PARA 595; note in connection with disregarded cautions PARA 596. For the exception from the operation of s 4(2), Sch 2 para 3(3) to apply, the person questioned must be informed at the time the question is asked that, by virtue of the Rehabilitation of Offenders Act 1974 (Exceptions) Order 1975, SI 1975/1023, spent convictions or cautions are to be disclosed: art 3(1)(a) (art 3(1) amended by SI 2008/3259; Rehabilitation of Offenders Act 1974 (Exceptions) Order 1975, SI 1975/1023, arts 3(1), 4(1) renumbered by SI 2013/1198).

3   Ie the Rehabilitation of Offenders Act 1974 s 4(3)(b), Sch 2 para 3(5): see PARA 600.

4   Rehabilitation of Offenders Act 1974 (Exceptions) Order 1975, SI 1975/1023, arts 3(1)(a)(ii), 4(1)(b) (arts 3(1), 4(1) renumbered by SI 2013/1198; Rehabilitation of Offenders Act 1974 (Exceptions) Order 1975, SI 1975/1023, arts 3(1)(a)(ii), 4(1)(b) substituted by SI 2001/1192; and amended by SI 2009/1818; SI 2012/1957; SI 2012/3006; SI 2013/1198; SI 2014/1707; SI 2015/317). The 'specified offices and employments' for these purposes include any other work specified in the Rehabilitation of Offenders Act 1974 (Exceptions) Order 1975, SI 1975/1023, Sch 1 Pt II paras 12A, 13, 13A, 14, 14A, 14B, 14C, 14D, 20, 21, 38 (other than in the context of the application of those provisions pursuant to art 4(1)(b)), 40, 43 or (in the context of the application of those provisions pursuant to art 4(1)(b)), 44: arts 3(1)(a)(ii), 4(1)(b) (as so renumbered, substituted and amended). See also PARA 614 note 4.

5   Rehabilitation of Offenders Act 1974 (Exceptions) Order 1975, SI 1975/1023, Sch 1 Pt II para 1. For these purposes 'judicial appointment' means an appointment to any office by virtue of which the holder has power, whether alone or with others, under any enactment or rule of law to determine any question affecting the rights, privileges, obligations or liabilities of any person: Sch 1 Pt IV.

6   Rehabilitation of Offenders Act 1974 (Exceptions) Order 1975, SI 1975/1023, Sch 1 Pt II para 2 (substituted by SI 2002/441). As to the Director of Public Prosecutions and offices and employments in the Crown Prosecution Service see CRIMINAL PROCEDURE vol 27 (2015) PARAS 25, 30 et seq.

7   Rehabilitation of Offenders Act 1974 (Exceptions) Order 1975, SI 1975/1023, Sch 1 Pt II para 4 (substituted by SI 2001/1192; and amended by SI 2005/617; SI 2006/2143). 'Assistants to justices' clerks' has the same meaning as in the Courts Act 2003 s 27(5) (see MAGISTRATES vol 71 (2013) PARA 500): Rehabilitation of Offenders Act 1974 (Exceptions) Order 1975, SI 1975/1023, Sch 1 Pt IV (definition added by SI 2006/2143).

8   Rehabilitation of Offenders Act 1974 (Exceptions) Order 1975, SI 1975/1023, Sch 1 Pt II para 6A (added by SI 2013/1198). As to the establishment of police forces see POLICE AND INVESTIGATORY POWERS vol 84 (2013) PARA 52 et seq.

9   Rehabilitation of Offenders Act 1974 (Exceptions) Order 1975, SI 1975/1023, Sch 1 Pt II para 7 (amended by the Criminal Justice Act 1988 Sch 8 para 3; and by SI 2006/2143). As to boards of visitors appointed under the Prison Act 1952 see s 6; and PRISONS AND PRISONERS vol 85 (2012) PARA 412. 'Removal centre' and 'short-term holding facility' have the meanings given by the

Immigration and Asylum Act 1999 s 147 (see IMMIGRATION AND ASYLUM vol 57 (2012) PARA 192): Rehabilitation of Offenders Act 1974 (Exceptions) Order 1975, SI 1975/1023, Sch 1 Pt IV (definition added by SI 2006/2143).

10 Rehabilitation of Offenders Act 1974 (Exceptions) Order 1975, SI 1975/1023, Sch 1 Pt II para 8. See the Road Traffic Regulation Act 1984 s 95; and ROAD TRAFFIC vol 89 (2011) PARA 639.

11 Ie as defined in the Offender Management Act 2007 (see PARA 666 et seq): Rehabilitation of Offenders Act 1974 (Exceptions) Order 1975, SI 1975/1023, Sch 1 Pt II para 9 (substituted by SI 2014/1707).

12 'Care services' means:
    (1)   accommodation and nursing and personal care in a care home (Rehabilitation of Offenders Act 1974 (Exceptions) Order 1975, SI 1975/1023, Sch 1 Pt IV (definition added by SI 2002/441));
    (2)   personal care or nursing or support for a person to live independently in his own home (Rehabilitation of Offenders Act 1974 (Exceptions) Order 1975, SI 1975/1023, Sch 1 Pt IV (as so amended));
    (3)   social care services (Sch 1 Pt IV (as so amended)); and
    (4)   any services provided in an establishment catering for a person with learning difficulties (Sch 1 Pt IV (as so amended)).
    As to the meaning of 'care home' see the Care Standards Act 2000 s 3; and CHILDREN AND YOUNG PERSONS vol 10 (2012) PARA 994.

13 'Vulnerable adult' has the meaning given by the Safeguarding Vulnerable Groups Act 2006 s 59 (repealed) as it had effect immediately before its repeal by the Protection of Freedoms Act 2012 (ie 10 September 2012, the date on which the repeal was brought into force by the Protection of Freedoms Act 2012 (Commencement No 3) Order 2012, SI 2012/2234): Rehabilitation of Offenders Act 1974 (Exceptions) Order 1975, SI 1975/1023, Sch 1 Pt IV (definition substituted by SI 2012/1957).

14 Rehabilitation of Offenders Act 1974 (Exceptions) Order 1975, SI 1975/1023, Sch 1 Pt II para 12 (substituted by SI 2006/2143).

15 Ie within the meaning of the Safeguarding Vulnerable Groups Act 2006 Sch 4 Pt 2 (see SOCIAL SERVICES AND COMMUNITY CARE vol 95 (2013) PARA 145), including Sch 4 Pt 2 as it had effect immediately before 10 September 2012 (ie the date on which the Protection of Freedoms Act 2012 s 66 was brought into force by the Protection of Freedoms Act 2012 (Commencement No 3) Order 2012, SI 2012/2234): Rehabilitation of Offenders Act 1974 (Exceptions) Order 1975, SI 1975/1023, Sch 1 Pt II para 12A, Pt IV (Sch 1 Pt II para 12A added by SI 2009/1818; amended by SI 2012/1957; SI 2015/317).

16 For these purposes 'health services' means services provided under the National Service Acts 1946–1973 (now consolidated in the National Health Service Act 2006: see HEALTH SERVICES) and similar services provided otherwise than under the National Health Service: Rehabilitation of Offenders Act 1974 (Exceptions) Order 1975, SI 1975/1023, Sch 1 Pt IV.

17 Rehabilitation of Offenders Act 1974 (Exceptions) Order 1975, SI 1975/1023, Sch 1 Pt II para 13 (substituted by SI 2001/1192).

18 In this context 'the national health service' means, in respect of England, the health service continued under the National Health Service Act 2006 s 1(1) (see HEALTH SERVICES vol 54 (2008) PARA 10) and, in respect of Wales, that continued under the National Health Service (Wales) Act 2006 s 1(1) (see HEALTH SERVICES vol 54 (2008) PARA 74): Rehabilitation of Offenders Act 1974 (Exceptions) Order 1975, SI 1975/1023, Sch 1 Pt II para 13A (added by SI 2015/317).

19 'Security management' means activity carried out pursuant to the Secretary of State's security management functions within the meaning given by the National Health Service Act 2006 s 195(3) (see HEALTH SERVICES vol 54 (2008) PARA 41) and, in respect of Wales, the corresponding functions of Welsh Ministers (see HEALTH SERVICES vol 54 (2008) PARA 74): Rehabilitation of Offenders Act 1974 (Exceptions) Order 1975, SI 1975/1023, Sch 1 Pt IV (definition added by SI 2015/317).

20 Rehabilitation of Offenders Act 1974 (Exceptions) Order 1975, SI 1975/1023, Sch 1 Pt II para 13A (added by SI 2015/317).

21 'Regulated position' means a position which is a regulated position for the purposes of the Criminal Justice and Court Services Act 2000 Pt II (ss 26–42) (repealed), other than a position which would not re a regulated position if in s 36(4) 'employment' included unpaid employment: Rehabilitation of Offenders Act 1974 (Exceptions) Order 1975, SI 1975/1023, Sch 1 Pt IV (definition added by SI 2001/1192; amended by SI 2012/1957).

22 Rehabilitation of Offenders Act 1974 (Exceptions) Order 1975, SI 1975/1023, Sch 1 Pt II para 14 (substituted by SI 2001/1192; amended by SI 2012/979). As to the determination of a person's age see the Children and Young Persons Act 1933 s 99; and CHILDREN AND YOUNG PERSONS vol 10 (2012) PARA 1206.

23 Ie within the meaning of the Safeguarding Vulnerable Groups Act 2006 Sch 4 Pt 1 (see CHILDREN AND YOUNG PERSONS vol 9 (2012) PARA 684), including Sch 4 Pt 1 as it had effect immediately before 10 September 2012 (ie the date on which the Protection of Freedoms Act 2012 s 64 was brought into force by the Protection of Freedoms Act 2012 (Commencement No 3) Order 2012, SI 2012/2234): Rehabilitation of Offenders Act 1974 (Exceptions) Order 1975, SI 1975/1023, Sch 1 Pt II para 14A (added by SI 2009/1818; amended by SI 2012/1957; SI 2015/317).

24 Rehabilitation of Offenders Act 1974 (Exceptions) Order 1975, SI 1975/1023, Sch 1 Pt II para 14A (as added and amended: see note 23).

25 Rehabilitation of Offenders Act 1974 (Exceptions) Order 1975, SI 1975/1023, Sch 1 Pt II para 14B (added by SI 2014/1707).

26 Rehabilitation of Offenders Act 1974 (Exceptions) Order 1975, SI 1975/1023, Sch 1 Pt II para 14C (added by SI 2014/1707).

27 Rehabilitation of Offenders Act 1974 (Exceptions) Order 1975, SI 1975/1023, Sch 1 Pt II para 14D (added by SI 2014/1707).

28 Rehabilitation of Offenders Act 1974 (Exceptions) Order 1975, SI 1975/1023, Sch 1 Pt II para 15 (added by SI 2002/441; Rehabilitation of Offenders Act 1974 (Exceptions) Order 1975, SI 1975/1023, Sch 1 Pt II para 15 amended by SI 2006/2143).

29 Rehabilitation of Offenders Act 1974 (Exceptions) Order 1975, SI 1975/1023, Sch 1 Pt II para 19 (added by SI 2002/441).

30 Rehabilitation of Offenders Act 1974 (Exceptions) Order 1975, SI 1975/1023, Sch 1 Pt II para 20 (added by SI 2003/965). The Criminal Justice and Court Services Act 2000 s 9 has been repealed.

31 Rehabilitation of Offenders Act 1974 (Exceptions) Order 1975, SI 1975/1023, Sch 1 Pt II para 21 (added by SI 2003/965). 'High security psychiatric services' has the meaning given by the National Health Service Act 1977 s 4 (repealed): Rehabilitation of Offenders Act 1974 (Exceptions) Order 1975, SI 1975/1023, Sch 1 Pt IV (definition added by SI 2003/965).

32 Rehabilitation of Offenders Act 1974 (Exceptions) Order 1975, SI 1975/1023, Sch 1 Pt II para 22 (added by SI 2006/2143). See the Traffic Management Act 2004 s 2; and ROAD TRAFFIC vol 89 (2011) PARA 635.

33 Rehabilitation of Offenders Act 1974 (Exceptions) Order 1975, SI 1975/1023, Sch 1 Pt II para 23 (added by SI 2006/2143). See the Senior Courts Act 1981 s 98; and COURTS AND TRIBUNALS vol 24 (2010) PARA 757.

34 Rehabilitation of Offenders Act 1974 (Exceptions) Order 1975, SI 1975/1023, Sch 1 Pt II para 24 (added by SI 2006/2143). 'Court officer' means a person appointed by the Lord Chancellor under the Courts Act 2003 s 2(1) (see COURTS AND TRIBUNALS vol 24 (2010) PARA 827); 'court contractor' means a person who has entered into a contract with the Lord Chancellor under the Courts Act 2003 s 2(4) (see COURTS AND TRIBUNALS vol 24 (2010) PARA 827), such a person's sub-contractor, and persons acting under the authority of such a contractor or sub-contractor for the purpose of discharging the Lord Chancellor's general duty in relation to the courts; and 'judges of the Supreme Court' means the Lord Chief Justice, the Master of the Rolls, the President of the Queen's Bench Division, the President of the Family Division, the Chancellor of the High Court, the Lord Justices of Appeal and the puisne judges of the High Court: Rehabilitation of Offenders Act 1974 (Exceptions) Order 1975, SI 1975/1023, Sch 1 Pt IV (definitions added by SI 2006/2143).

35 Rehabilitation of Offenders Act 1974 (Exceptions) Order 1975, SI 1975/1023, Sch 1 Pt II para 25 (added by SI 2006/2143). 'Personal information' means any information which is of a personal or confidential nature and is not in the public domain and it includes information in any form but excludes anything disclosed for the purposes of proceedings in a particular cause or matter: Rehabilitation of Offenders Act 1974 (Exceptions) Order 1975, SI 1975/1023, Sch 1 Pt IV (definition added by SI 2006/2143).

36 Rehabilitation of Offenders Act 1974 (Exceptions) Order 1975, SI 1975/1023, Sch 1 Pt II para 26 (added by SI 2006/2143).

37 Rehabilitation of Offenders Act 1974 (Exceptions) Order 1975, SI 1975/1023, Sch 1 Pt II para 27 (added by SI 2006/2143). 'Court security officers' has the meaning given by the Courts Act 2003 s 51 (see COURTS AND TRIBUNALS vol 24 (2010) PARA 840); and 'tribunal security officers' means persons who, in the course of their work, guard tribunal buildings, offices and other accommodation used in relation to tribunals against unauthorised access or occupation,

against outbreaks of disorder or against damage: Rehabilitation of Offenders Act 1974 (Exceptions) Order 1975, SI 1975/1023, Sch 1 Pt IV (definitions added by SI 2006/2143).

38 Rehabilitation of Offenders Act 1974 (Exceptions) Order 1975, SI 1975/1023, Sch 1 Pt II para 28 (added by SI 2006/2143).

39 Rehabilitation of Offenders Act 1974 (Exceptions) Order 1975, SI 1975/1023, Sch 1 Pt II para 29 (added by SI 2006/2143). 'Tribunals' means any person exercising the judicial power of the State, that is not a court listed in the Courts Act 2003 s 1(1) (see COURTS AND TRIBUNALS vol 24 (2010) PARA 826): Rehabilitation of Offenders Act 1974 (Exceptions) Order 1975, SI 1975/1023, Sch 1 Pt IV (definition added by SI 2006/2143).

40 Rehabilitation of Offenders Act 1974 (Exceptions) Order 1975, SI 1975/1023, Sch 1 Pt II para 30(a) (added by SI 2006/2143).

41 Rehabilitation of Offenders Act 1974 (Exceptions) Order 1975, SI 1975/1023, Sch 1 Pt II para 30(b) (added by SI 2006/2143).

42 Rehabilitation of Offenders Act 1974 (Exceptions) Order 1975, SI 1975/1023, Sch 1 Pt II para 30(c) (added by SI 2006/2143).

43 Rehabilitation of Offenders Act 1974 (Exceptions) Order 1975, SI 1975/1023, Sch 1 Pt II para 30(d) (added by SI 2006/2143).

44 Rehabilitation of Offenders Act 1974 (Exceptions) Order 1975, SI 1975/1023, Sch 1 Pt II para 30(e) (added by SI 2006/2143).

45 Rehabilitation of Offenders Act 1974 (Exceptions) Order 1975, SI 1975/1023, Sch 1 Pt II para 30(f) (added by SI 2006/2143).

46 Rehabilitation of Offenders Act 1974 (Exceptions) Order 1975, SI 1975/1023, Sch 1 Pt II para 30(g) (added by SI 2006/2143). As to the meaning of 'civilian enforcement officers' see the Magistrates' Courts Act 1980 s 125A; and MAGISTRATES vol 71 (2013) PARA 670.

47 Ie under the Magistrates' Courts Act 1980 s 125B(1): see MAGISTRATES vol 71 (2013) PARA 670.

48 Ie under the Magistrates' Courts Act 1980 s 125(2): see MAGISTRATES vol 71 (2013) PARA 670.

49 Rehabilitation of Offenders Act 1974 (Exceptions) Order 1975, SI 1975/1023, Sch 1 Pt II para 30(h) (added by SI 2006/2143).

50 Rehabilitation of Offenders Act 1974 (Exceptions) Order 1975, SI 1975/1023, Sch 1 Pt II para 30(i) (added by SI 2006/2143). As to the meaning of 'clamping orders' see the Courts Act 2003 Sch 5 para 38(2); and MAGISTRATES vol 71 (2013) PARA 662 (definition applied by the Rehabilitation of Offenders Act 1974 (Exceptions) Order 1975, SI 1975/1023, Sch 1 Pt II para 30(i) (as so added)).

51 Rehabilitation of Offenders Act 1974 (Exceptions) Order 1975, SI 1975/1023, Sch 1 Pt II para 31 (added by SI 2006/2143). As to the Official Solicitor see COURTS AND TRIBUNALS vol 24 (2010) PARA 755.

52 Rehabilitation of Offenders Act 1974 (Exceptions) Order 1975, SI 1975/1023, Sch 1 Pt II para 33 (added by SI 2006/2143). 'Funds in court' has the meaning given by the Administration of Justice Act 1982 s 47 (see CIVIL PROCEDURE vol 12 (2009) PARA 1548): Rehabilitation of Offenders Act 1974 (Exceptions) Order 1975, SI 1975/1023, Sch 1 Pt IV (definition added by SI 2006/2143).

53 Rehabilitation of Offenders Act 1974 (Exceptions) Order 1975, SI 1975/1023, Sch 1 Pt II para 34 (added by SI 2007/2149; Rehabilitation of Offenders Act 1974 (Exceptions) Order 1975, SI 1975/1023, Sch 1 Pt II para 34 amended by SI 2007/3324; SI 2010/1836; SI 2012/1957). As to the administration of education see EDUCATION.

54 Rehabilitation of Offenders Act 1974 (Exceptions) Order 1975, SI 1975/1023, Sch 1 Pt II para 38 (added by SI 2007/2149; amended by SI 2012/3006). As to the Disclosure and Barring Service see the Safeguarding Vulnerable Groups Act 2006 s 1; and CHILDREN AND YOUNG PERSONS vol 9 (2012) PARA 672.

55 Rehabilitation of Offenders Act 1974 (Exceptions) Order 1975, SI 1975/1023, Sch 1 Pt II para 39 (added by SI 2007/2149). As to the Office of the Public Guardian see MENTAL HEALTH AND CAPACITY vol 75 (2013) PARAS 751–756.

56 Rehabilitation of Offenders Act 1974 (Exceptions) Order 1975, SI 1975/1023, Sch 1 Pt II para 40 (added by SI 2007/2149). As to the Commissioner for Older People in Wales see DISCRIMINATION vol 33 (2013) PARA 292 et seq.

57 Rehabilitation of Offenders Act 1974 (Exceptions) Order 1975, SI 1975/1023, Sch 1 Pt II para 41 (added by SI 2007/2149). As to the Gambling Commission see LICENSING AND GAMBLING vol 67 (2008) PARA 4.

58 Rehabilitation of Offenders Act 1974 (Exceptions) Order 1975, SI 1975/1023, Sch 1 Pt II para 42 (added by SI 2007/2149).

59 Rehabilitation of Offenders Act 1974 (Exceptions) Order 1975, SI 1975/1023, Sch 1 Pt II para 43 (added by SI 2007/2149).

616. Excepted occupations. None of the statutory protections for rehabilitated persons[1] relating to the asking and answering of questions concerning past convictions or spent cautions[2] apply in relation to any question asked by or on behalf of any person, in the course of duties of his office or employment, in order to assess the suitability of the person to whom the question relates or of any other person to pursue any specified occupation or to pursue it subject to a particular condition or restriction[3]. The specified occupations are:

(1) firearms dealer[4];

(2) any occupation in respect of which an application to the Gambling Commission for a licence, certificate or registration is required by or under any enactment[5];

(3) any occupation which is concerned with the management of a place in respect of which the approval of the Secretary of State is required under the Abortion Act 1967[6];

(4) any occupation which is concerned with carrying on a regulated activity in respect of which a person is required[7] to be registered[8];

(5) any occupation in respect of which the holder, as occupier of premises on which explosives are kept, is required[9] to obtain from the chief officer of police a valid explosives certificate certifying him to be a fit person to acquire or acquire and keep explosives[10];

(6) approved legal services body manager[11];

(7) a regulated immigration adviser[12];

(8) a head of finance and administration of a licensed body[13]; and

(9) a head of legal practice of a licensed body[14].

1   As to the meaning of 'rehabilitated person' see PARA 591.

2   Ie the Rehabilitation of Offenders Act 1974 s 4(2), Sch 2 para 3(3): see PARA 598. As to the meaning of 'conviction' see PARA 591 note 3; as to spent convictions see PARA 594; note in connection with disregarded convictions PARA 596. As to the meaning of 'caution' see PARA 595 note 1; as to spent cautions see PARA 595; note in connection with disregarded cautions PARA 596. For the exception from the operation of s 4(2), Sch 2 para 3(3) to apply, the person questioned must be informed at the time the question is asked that, by virtue of the Rehabilitation of Offenders Act 1974 (Exceptions) Order 1975, SI 1975/1023, spent convictions or cautions are to be disclosed: art 3(1)(a) (art 3(1) amended by SI 2008/3259; Rehabilitation of Offenders Act 1974 (Exceptions) Order 1975, SI 1975/1023, arts 3(1), 4(1) renumbered by SI 2013/1198).

3   Rehabilitation of Offenders Act 1974 (Exceptions) Order 1975, SI 1975/1023, arts 3(1)(a)(iii) (art 3(1) renumbered by SI 2013/1198; Rehabilitation of Offenders Act 1974 (Exceptions) Order 1975, SI 1975/1023, art 3(1)(a)(iii) amended by SI 2013/1198). See also PARA 614 note 4.

4   Rehabilitation of Offenders Act 1974 (Exceptions) Order 1975, SI 1975/1023, Sch 1 Pt III para 1. For these purposes, 'firearms dealer' has the meaning assigned to that expression by the Firearms Act 1968 s 57(4) (see CRIMINAL LAW vol 26 (2010) PARA 582): Rehabilitation of Offenders Act 1974 (Exceptions) Order 1975, SI 1975/1023, Sch 1 Pt IV. The operation of the rehabilitation provisions is also restricted in relation to specified proceedings relating to the dealing and use of firearms: see PARA 612.

5   Rehabilitation of Offenders Act 1974 (Exceptions) Order 1975, SI 1975/1023, Sch 1 Pt III para 2. Schedule 1 Pt III para 2 refers to the Gaming Board for Great Britain, the functions, rights and liabilities of which were transferred to the Gambling Commission under the Gambling Act 2005 and any references to the Board in any instrument are to be treated as a reference to the Commission: see s 21, Sch 5 para 4; and LICENSING AND GAMBLING vol 67 (2008) PARAS 5, 330 et seq.

6   Rehabilitation of Offenders Act 1974 (Exceptions) Order 1975, SI 1975/1023, Sch 1 Pt III para 6(a). See the Abortion Act 1967 s 1; and CRIMINAL LAW vol 25 (2010) PARA 122.

7   Ie under the Health and Social Care Act 2008 Pt 1 (ss 1–97) (see SOCIAL SERVICES AND COMMUNITY CARE vol 95 (2013) PARA 88 et seq).

8   Rehabilitation of Offenders Act 1974 (Exceptions) Order 1975, SI 1975/1023, Sch 1 Pt III para 6(b) (amended by SI 2013/1198).

9   Ie pursuant to the Explosives Regulations 2014, SI 2014/1638, regs 4, 5, 11: see EXPLOSIVES.

10 Rehabilitation of Offenders Act 1974 (Exceptions) Order 1975, SI 1975/1023, Sch 1 Pt III para 8 (amended by SI 2005/1082; SI 2014/1638).

11 Rehabilitation of Offenders Act 1974 (Exceptions) Order 1975, SI 1975/1023, Sch 1 Pt III para 10 (added by SI 2008/3259).

12 Rehabilitation of Offenders Act 1974 (Exceptions) Order 1975, SI 1975/1023, Sch 1 Pt III para 11 (added by SI 2009/1818). By virtue of the Rehabilitation of Offenders Act 1974 (Exceptions) Order 1975, SI 1975/1023, Sch 1 Pt IV (definition added by SI 2009/1818), 'regulated immigration adviser' means any person who provides immigration advice or immigration services as defined in the Immigration and Asylum Act 1999 s 82(1) (see IMMIGRATION AND ASYLUM vol 57 (2012) PARA 204) and is:

    (1)   a registered person under Pt 5 (ss 82–93) (see IMMIGRATION AND ASYLUM vol 57 (2012) PARA 205); or

    (2)   a person who acts on behalf of and under the supervision of such a registered person; or

    (3)   a person who falls within s 84(4)(a), (b) or (c) (see IMMIGRATION AND ASYLUM vol 57 (2012) PARA 205).

13 Rehabilitation of Offenders Act 1974 (Exceptions) Order 1975, SI 1975/1023, Sch 1 Pt III para 12 (added by SI 2011/1800). 'Head of finance and administration of a licensed body' means an individual who is designated as head of finance and administration and whose designation is approved in accordance with licensing rules made under the Legal Services Act 2007 s 83, Sch 11 paras 13, 14 (see LEGAL PROFESSIONS vol 66 (2015) PARA 1083): Rehabilitation of Offenders Act 1974 (Exceptions) Order 1975, SI 1975/1023, Sch 1 Pt IV (definition applied by SI 2011/1800).

14 Rehabilitation of Offenders Act 1974 (Exceptions) Order 1975, SI 1975/1023, Sch 1 Pt III para 13 (added by SI 2011/1800). 'Head of legal practice of a licensed body' means an individual who is designated as head of legal practice and whose designation is approved in accordance with licensing rules made under the Legal Services Act 2007 s 83, Sch 11 paras 11, 12 (see LEGAL PROFESSIONS vol 66 (2015) PARA 1082): Rehabilitation of Offenders Act 1974 (Exceptions) Order 1975, SI 1975/1023, Sch 1 Pt IV (definition applied by SI 2011/1800).

617. Further exclusions and modifications relating to particular matters. Additional restrictions on, and modifications of, the statutory protections for rehabilitated persons[1], are also imposed in connection with:

    (1)   the issuing of firearms and shotgun certificates and related matters[2];

    (2)   the licensing of persons organising or arranging overseas travel for child performers[3];

    (3)   the issuing of explosives certificates[4];

    (4)   taxi driver licences[5];

    (5)   licences relating to the private security industry[6];

    (6)   poisons licences and licences for the production of controlled drugs[7];

    (7)   work with children in a residential context[8];

    (8)   the provision of air traffic services[9];

    (9)   adoption and special guardianship[10];

    (10)   the provision of day care and childminding[11];

    (11)   the provision of financial services[12];

    (12)   organising the National Lottery[13];

    (13)   the provision of social care and care establishments[14];

    (14)   the awarding of public and utilities contracts[15];

    (15)   law enforcement and national security[16];

    (16)   membership of the Master Locksmiths Association[17];

    (17)   the provision of legal services[18]; and

    (18)   barring and safeguarding[19].

1 Ie the Rehabilitation of Offenders Act 1974 s 4, Sch 2.

2 See the Rehabilitation of Offenders Act 1974 (Exceptions) Order 1975, SI 1975/1023, art 3(1)(a)(iv), Sch 2 para 1 (arts 3(1) amended by SI 2008/3259; Rehabilitation of Offenders Act 1974 (Exceptions) Order 1975, SI 1975/1023, arts 3(1), 4(1) renumbered by SI 2013/1198; Rehabilitation of Offenders Act 1974 (Exceptions) Order 1975, SI 1975/1023, art 3(1)(a)(iv) amended by SI 2013/1198; SI 2014/942).

3   See the Rehabilitation of Offenders Act 1974 (Exceptions) Order 1975, SI 1975/1023, Sch 2 para 2.

4   See the Rehabilitation of Offenders Act 1974 (Exceptions) Order 1975, SI 1975/1023, Sch 2 para 3 (substituted by SI 2005/1082; amended by SI 2014/1638).

5   See the Rehabilitation of Offenders Act 1974 (Exceptions) Order 1975, SI 1975/1023, art 4(1)(l), 5(1)(b), (c), (2), Sch 2 para 4 (art 3(1) as amended (see note 1); art 4(1)(l), Sch 2 para 4 added by SI 2003/965; Rehabilitation of Offenders Act 1974 (Exceptions) Order 1975, SI 1975/1023, art 5(2) amended by SI 2001/2816; SI 2008/3259; SI 2015/317).

6   See the Rehabilitation of Offenders Act 1974 (Exceptions) Order 1975, SI 1975/1023, arts 3(1)(k), 4(1)(m), (n), 5(1)(b), (c), (2), Sch 2 para 5 (arts 3(1), 4(1) as amended (see note 1); art 3(1)(k) added by SI 2006/2143 and amended by SI 2006/3290; Rehabilitation of Offenders Act 1974 (Exceptions) Order 1975, SI 1975/1023, art 4(1)(m), Sch 2 para 5 added by SI 2003/965; Rehabilitation of Offenders Act 1974 (Exceptions) Order 1975, SI 1975/1023, art 4(1)(n) added by SI 2006/2143; and amended by SI 2006/3290; Rehabilitation of Offenders Act 1974 (Exceptions) Order 1975, SI 1975/1023, art 5(2) amended by SI 2001/2816; SI 2008/3259; SI 2015/317).

7   See the Rehabilitation of Offenders Act 1974 (Exceptions) Order 1975, SI 1975/1023, art 3(1)(n), Sch 2 para 6 (art 3(1) as amended (see note 1); art 3(1)(n) added by SI 2009/1818; Rehabilitation of Offenders Act 1974 (Exceptions) Order 1975, SI 1975/1023, Sch 2 para 6 added by SI 2015/968).

8   See the Rehabilitation of Offenders Act 1974 (Exceptions) Order 1975, SI 1975/1023, art 3(1)(aa) (art 3(1) as amended (see note 1); art 3(1)(aa) added by SI 1986/1249; substituted by SI 2001/1192).

9   See the Rehabilitation of Offenders Act 1974 (Exceptions) Order 1975, SI 1975/1023, art 3(1)(bb) (art 3(1) as amended (see note 1); art 3(1)(bb) added by SI 2002/441).

10   See the Rehabilitation of Offenders Act 1974 (Exceptions) Order 1975, SI 1975/1023, art 3(1)(e), (ea) (art 3(1) as amended (see note 1); art 3(1)(e) added by SI 2001/1192; Rehabilitation of Offenders Act 1974 (Exceptions) Order 1975, SI 1975/1023, art 3(1)(ea) added by SI 2014/1707).

11   See the Rehabilitation of Offenders Act 1974 (Exceptions) Order 1975, SI 1975/1023, arts 3(1)(f), (fa), 4(1)(ka), 5(1)(b), (c), (2) (arts 3(1), 4(1) as amended (see note 1); art 3(1)(f) added by SI 2001/1192; Rehabilitation of Offenders Act 1974 (Exceptions) Order 1975, SI 1975/1023, arts 3(1)(fa), 4(1)(ka) added by SI 2014/1707; Rehabilitation of Offenders Act 1974 (Exceptions) Order 1975, SI 1975/1023, art 5(2) amended by SI 2001/2816; SI 2008/3259; SI 2015/317).

12   See the Rehabilitation of Offenders Act 1974 (Exceptions) Order 1975, SI 1975/1023, arts 3(1)(g), 4(1)(d)–(j), 5(1)(b), (c), (2) (arts 3(1), 4(1) as amended (see note 1); art 3(1)(g) added by SI 2001/3816; amended by SI 2007/2149; SI 2013/472; SI 2013/1388; Rehabilitation of Offenders Act 1974 (Exceptions) Order 1975, SI 1975/1023, art 4(1)(d) added by SI 1986/2268; Rehabilitation of Offenders Act 1974 (Exceptions) Order 1975, SI 1975/1023, art 4(1)(d) substituted, art 4(1)(e)–(j) added, by SI 2001/3816; Rehabilitation of Offenders Act 1974 (Exceptions) Order 1975, SI 1975/1023, art 4(1)(d), (f), (g), (i), (j) amended by SI 2007/2149; SI 2011/99; SI 2011/1800; SI 2013/472; SI 2013/504; SI 2013/1388; SI 2013/1773; Rehabilitation of Offenders Act 1974 (Exceptions) Order 1975, SI 1975/1023, art 5(2) amended by SI 2001/2816; SI 2008/3259; SI 2015/317).

13   See the Rehabilitation of Offenders Act 1974 (Exceptions) Order 1975, SI 1975/1023, art 3(1)(h) (art 3(1) as amended (see note 1); art 3(1)(h) added by SI 2002/441; amended by SI 2013/2329).

14   See the Rehabilitation of Offenders Act 1974 (Exceptions) Order 1975, SI 1975/1023, arts 3(1)(i), 4(1)(ja), (k), 5(1)(b), (c), (2) (arts 3(1), 4(1) as amended (see note 1); arts 3(1)(i), 4(1)(k) added by SI 2003/965; amended by SI 2012/1957; Rehabilitation of Offenders Act 1974 (Exceptions) Order 1975, SI 1975/1023, art 4(1)(ja) added by SI 2014/1707; Rehabilitation of Offenders Act 1974 (Exceptions) Order 1975, SI 1975/1023, art 5(2) amended by SI 2001/2816; SI 2008/3259; SI 2015/317).

15   See the Rehabilitation of Offenders Act 1974 (Exceptions) Order 1975, SI 1975/1023, art 3(1)(j), (ja) (art 3(1) as amended (see note 1); art 3(1)(j) added by SI 2006/2143; Rehabilitation of Offenders Act 1974 (Exceptions) Order 1975, SI 1975/1023, art 3(1)(j) substituted, art 3(1)(ja) added, by SI 2015/102).

16   See the Rehabilitation of Offenders Act 1974 (Exceptions) Order 1975, SI 1975/1023, arts 3(1)(l), 3ZA, 4ZA, 4A (art 3(1) as amended (see note 1); art 3(1)(l) added by SI 2007/2149; amended by SI 2012/3006; Rehabilitation of Offenders Act 1974 (Exceptions) Order 1975,

SI 1975/1023, arts 3ZA, 4ZA added by SI 2013/1198; and amended by SI 2014/1942; Rehabilitation of Offenders Act 1974 (Exceptions) Order 1975, SI 1975/1023, art 4A added by SI 2012/1957).

17 See the Rehabilitation of Offenders Act 1974 (Exceptions) Order 1975, SI 1975/1023, art 3(1)(m) (art 3(1) as amended (see note 1); art 3(1)(m) added by SI 2009/1818).

18 See the Rehabilitation of Offenders Act 1974 (Exceptions) Order 1975, SI 1975/1023, art 3(1)(o) (art 3(1) as amended (see note 1); art 3(1)(o) added by SI 2011/2865).

19 See the Rehabilitation of Offenders Act 1974 (Exceptions) Order 1975, SI 1975/1023, art 3A (added by SI 2010/1153; amended by SI 2012/1957; SI 2013/1198).

(10) OFFENCES TAKEN INTO CONSIDERATION

618. Consideration of outstanding offences. If the defendant admits other offences outstanding against him and consents to this course[1], the judge in passing sentence may, and often does, take such offences into consideration[2]. Offences taken into consideration have relevance to the overall criminality[3]. In general only offences which are similar to those in respect of which the defendant has been convicted should be taken into consideration[4]. Offences should not be taken into consideration if they are dissimilar, even where the prosecution consents, unless the judge considers it proper to do so[5]; nor should they be taken into consideration if the court would not have jurisdiction to try them[6].

When sentencing an offender who requests offences to be taken into consideration the court should pass a total sentence which reflects all the offending behaviour[7]. The sentence must be just and proportionate and must not exceed the statutory maximum for the conviction offence[8]. The court has discretion as to whether to take offences into consideration or not, and in exercising this discretion the court must take into account the fact that offences taken into consideration are capable of reflecting the offender's overall criminality[9].

Road traffic offences which may involve disqualification or the endorsement of a driving licence ought not to be taken into consideration when passing sentence for a different class of offence[10]. Offences of a disciplinary nature committed in the armed forces ought not to be taken into consideration[11]. A sentence which the judge states takes other offences into consideration is still in law passed only for the offence with which the court is dealing, and may not therefore exceed the maximum for the offence[12]; but the judge may, if taking other offences into consideration, give a longer sentence than he would if he were dealing with the offences mentioned in the indictment[13].

An offence taken into consideration does not amount to a conviction[14]. Although the practice is not to proceed on an offence taken into consideration, the fact that an offence is taken into consideration does not operate as a bar to a further trial[15].

1 See CRIMINAL PROCEDURE vol 27 (2015) PARA 427.

2 See *R v Syres* (1908) 1 Cr App Rep 172, CA; *R v Shapcote (alias Heathcote)* (1909) 3 Cr App Rep 58, CCA; *R v Smith* (1921) 15 Cr App Rep 172, CCA; *R v Lloyd* (1923) 17 Cr App Rep 184, CCA; *R v Towers* (1987) 86 Cr App Rep 355, 9 Cr App Rep (S) 333, CA. If the outstanding charges are not taken into consideration, they should be proceeded with as soon as possible (*R v Carter* (1922) 17 Cr App Rep 51, CCA), and not left until after release from prison (*R v Silverman* (1935) 25 Cr App Rep 101, CCA). The sentence already imposed on the defendant in respect of the earlier charge may be a ground for the mitigation of the sentence for the later one: *R v Aleron* (1909) 2 Cr App Rep 152, CCA; *R v Taylor* (1909) 2 Cr App Rep 158, CCA; *R v Markham* (1909) 2 Cr App Rep 160, CCA; and see *R v Carey, R v Ames* [1938]

1 All ER 515, 26 Cr App Rep 133, CCA. See also *R v MacMillan* (1921) 16 Cr App Rep 3, CCA (outstanding charges taken into consideration by the Court of Criminal Appeal, when the court of trial omitted to do so).

3 *R v Miles* [2006] EWCA Crim 256, (2006) Times, 10 April, [2006] All ER (D) 176 (Mar). Offences which are taken into consideration count for the purposes of compensation orders (see the Powers of Criminal Courts (Sentencing) Act 2000 s 130(1)(a); and PARA 281 et seq) and confiscation orders (see the Proceeds of Crime Act 2002 s 76(3)(c); and PARA 221).

4 *R v McLean* [1911] 1 KB 332, 6 Cr App Rep 26, CCA.

5 *R v McLean* [1911] 1 KB 332, 6 Cr App Rep 26, CCA.

6 *R v Warn* [1937] 4 All ER 327, 26 Cr App Rep 115, CCA; *R v Simons* [1953] 2 All ER 599, 37 Cr App Rep 120, sub nom *R v Simons and Simons* [1953] 1 WLR 1014, CCA. See also *R v Tarbotton* [1942] 1 All ER 198, 28 Cr App Rep 92, CCA (where there is a pending case of breach of recognisance in the Crown Court, a magistrates' court should obtain that court's permission to take into consideration the breach of recognisance).

7 See the Sentencing Council Definitive Guideline *Offences Taken into Consideration and Totality* (published 6 March 2012), which is applicable to all offenders whose cases are dealt with on or after 11 June 2012, p 2. As to guidelines for taking offences into consideration see PARAS 619–621; as to guidelines generally see PARAS 555, 562.

8 *Offences Taken into Consideration and Totality* p 2.

9 *Offences Taken into Consideration and Totality* p 2. The court is likely to consider that the fact that the offender has assisted the police (particularly if the offences would not otherwise have been detected) and avoided the need for further proceedings demonstrates a genuine determination by the offender to 'wipe the slate clean': *Offences Taken into Consideration and Totality* p 2; see *R v Miles* [2006] EWCA Crim 256, (2006) Times, 10 April, [2006] All ER (D) 176 (Mar).

10 *R v Collins* [1947] KB 560, 32 Cr App Rep 27, CCA; *R v Simons* [1953] 2 All ER 599, 37 Cr App Rep 120, sub nom *R v Simons and Simons* [1953] 1 WLR 1014, CCA; and see *R v James* [1970] 3 All ER 263, [1970] 1 WLR 1304, CA.

    An offence for which disqualification is mandatory may properly be taken into consideration on sentencing for a similar offence: *R v Jones* [1970] 3 All ER 815, 55 Cr App Rep 32, CA.

11 *R v Anderson* (1958) 122 JP 282, 42 Cr App Rep 91, CCA. Charges for civil offences awaiting trial by court-martial may, however, be taken into consideration: see *R v Anderson* (where the commanding officer supported the soldier-defendant's request that this course should be followed).

12 See the observations of Lord Goddard CJ in *R v Webb* [1953] 2 QB 390, 37 Cr App Rep 82, CCA. See also *R v Tremayne* (1932) 23 Cr App Rep 191, CCA; *R v Hobson* (1942) 29 Cr App Rep 30, CCA.

13 *R v Batchelor* (1952) 36 Cr App Rep 64, CCA. Sometimes offences taken into consideration add little or nothing to the sentence which the court would otherwise impose, but they may lead to a substantial increase, eg where they show a pattern of criminal activity which suggests careful and deliberate planning rather than casual involvement, or offences committed on bail: *R v Miles* [2006] EWCA Crim 256, (2006) Times, 10 April, [2006] All ER (D) 176 (Mar).

14 *R v Howard* (1990) 92 Cr App Rep 223, 12 Cr App Rep (S) 426, CA.

15 *R v Nicholson (No 2)* (1947) 32 Cr App Rep 127, CCA (disapproving *R v McMinn* (1945) 30 Cr App Rep 138, CCA); *R v Neal* [1949] 2 KB 590, 33 Cr App Rep 189, CCA; *R v Webb* [1953] 2 QB 390, 37 Cr App Rep 82, CCA. See also CRIMINAL PROCEDURE vol 27 (2015) PARA 371. A prosecution for an offence taken into consideration might amount to an abuse of process. As to abuse of process see CRIMINAL PROCEDURE vol 27 (2015) PARA 330.

619. Procedure. A court should generally take offences into consideration[1] only if the following procedural provisions have been satisfied[2]:

(1)   the police or prosecuting authorities have prepared a schedule of offences ('TIC schedule') that they consider suitable for taking into consideration[3];

(2)   a copy of the TIC schedule must be provided to the defendant and his representative before the sentencing hearing;

(3)   at the sentencing hearing the court should ask the defendant in open court whether he admits each of the offences on the TIC schedule and whether he wishes to have them taken into consideration[4];

(4)   if there is any doubt about the admission of a particular offence it

should not be taken into consideration: special care should be taken with vulnerable or unrepresented defendants; and

(5)   if the defendant is committed to the Crown Court for sentence, that procedure must take place again at the Crown Court even if the defendant has agreed to the TIC schedule in the magistrates' court.

1   As to the consideration of outstanding offences see PARA 618.
2   See the Sentencing Council Definitive Guideline *Offences Taken into Consideration and Totality* (published 6 March 2012), which is applicable to all offenders whose cases are dealt with on or after 11 June 2012, p 3. As to guidelines see generally PARAS 555, 562.
3   The TIC schedule should set out the nature of each offence, the date of the offences, relevant detail about the offences and any other brief details that the court should have been aware of: *Offences Taken into Consideration and Totality* p 3.
4   See eg *Anderson v DPP* [1978] AC 964; *R v Davies* [1980] 2 Cr App Rep (S) 364 (the appropriate time for the defendant to be asked whether he wishes other offences to be taken into consideration is when he is before the court which is to sentence him, even where he has previously asked the magistrates' court to take those offences into consideration before committal).

620.   Offences that cannot be taken into consideration.   It is generally undesirable for offences to be taken into consideration[1]:

(1)   where the offence is likely to attract a greater sentence than the conviction offence[2];

(2)   where it is in the public interest that the offence should be the subject of a separate charge;

(3)   where the offender would avoid a prohibition, ancillary order or similar consequence which it would have been appropriate to impose on conviction;

(4)   where the offence constitutes the breach of an earlier sentence[3];

(5)   where the offence is a specified offence[4] but the conviction offence is not; or

(6)   where the offence is not founded on the same facts or evidence or is part of a series of offences of the same or a similar character (unless the court is satisfied that it is in the interests of justice to do so).

The magistrates' court cannot take into consideration an indictable-only offence, and the Crown Court can take into account summary offences provided they are not founded on the same facts or evidence or is part of a series of offences of the same or a similar character as the indictable conviction offence[5].

1   See the Sentencing Council Definitive Guideline *Offences Taken into Consideration and Totality* (published 6 March 2012), which is applicable to all offenders whose cases are dealt with on or after 11 June 2012, pp 2–3. As to the consideration of outstanding offences see PARA 618. As to guidelines see generally PARAS 555, 562.
2   See *R v Lavery* [2008] EWCA Crim 2499, [2009] 3 All ER 295 (although there is no reason in principle why an offence to be taken into consideration, which was of a more serious nature than the conviction offence or offences, should not result in a higher sentence than would otherwise have been the case, it is open to a judge to refuse to take an offence into consideration if to do so would be to distort the sentencing exercise and lead to an unjust result, and that the public interest required that the offence be charged).
3   See eg *R v Webb* [1953] 2 QB 390, 37 Cr App Rep 82, CCA.
4   Ie for the purposes of the Criminal Justice Act 2003 s 224 (see PARA 21).
5   *Offences Taken into Consideration and Totality* p 3.

621.   Sentencing guidelines.   The sentence imposed on an offender should, in most cases, be increased to reflect the fact that other offences have been taken into consideration[1]. The court should determine the sentencing starting point for the conviction offence, referring to the relevant definitive sentencing guidelines[2], no regard being had at this stage to the presence of offences to be taken into consideration, and consider whether there are any aggravating or mitigating factors[3] that justify an upward or downward adjustment from the starting point[4]. The presence of offences to be taken into consideration should generally be considered an aggravating feature that justifies an upward adjustment from the starting point, and where there are several offences to be taken into consideration it may be appropriate to move outside the category range, although this must be considered in the context of the case and subject to the principle of totality[5]. The court must then continue through the sentencing process including[6]:

(1)   considering whether the frank admission of a number of offences is an indication of an offender's remorse or determination and/or demonstration of steps taken to address addiction or offending behaviour;

(2)   applying any reduction for a guilty plea[7] to the overall sentence;

(3)   considering the principle of totality[8]; and

(4)   considering ancillary orders[9] in relation to all or any of the offences to be taken into consideration.

1   See the Sentencing Council Definitive Guideline *Offences Taken into Consideration and Totality* (published 6 March 2012), which is applicable to all offenders whose cases are dealt with on or after 11 June 2012, pp 3–4. As to the consideration of outstanding offences see PARA 618.
2   As to the definitive sentencing guidelines see PARAS 557–563.
3   As to mitigation see PARAS 573–577; as to aggravating factors see PARAS 586–590.
4   Guideline *Offences Taken into Consideration and Totality* p 3.
5   Guideline *Offences Taken into Consideration and Totality* p 4. The court is limited to the statutory maximum for the conviction offence: *Offences Taken into Consideration and Totality* p 4. As to the standard scale, the statutory maximum, the prescribed sum, and magistrates' powers to levy unlimited fines see PARA 176.
6   *Offences Taken into Consideration and Totality* p 4.
7   As to guilty pleas see PARAS 564–572.
8   As to the principle of totality see PARA 555.
9   Eg compensation orders (see PARA 281: in the magistrates' court the total compensation cannot exceed the limit for the conviction offence) and restitution orders (see PARA 492): see further *R v Crutchley* (1994) 15 Cr App Rep (S) 627 (it is not open to the court to make a compensation order relating to admitted offences taken into consideration); *R v Hose* (1995) 16 Cr App Rep (S) 682 (compensation order should only be made for the value represented by the counts with which the defendant has been convicted).

(11) VICTIM PERSONAL STATEMENTS AND IMPACT STATEMENTS

622. Victim Personal Statements. Victims of crime, and where appropriate, their relatives, are invited to make a statement, known as a Victim Personal Statement ('VPS'), which the court is required to take into account when determining sentence[1]. If the court is presented with a VPS the following approach[2] should be adopted[3]:

(1)   the VPS and any evidence in support should be considered and taken into account by the court, prior to passing sentence;

(2)   evidence of the effects of an offence on the victim contained in the VPS or other statement, must be in proper form[4] and served in good time upon the defendant's solicitor or the defendant, if he is not represented;

(3)   except where inferences can properly be drawn from the nature of or

circumstances surrounding the offence, a sentencing court must not make assumptions unsupported by evidence about the effects of an offence on the victim;

(4) in all cases it will be appropriate for a VPS to be referred to in the course of the sentencing hearing and/or in the sentencing remarks[5]; and

(5) the court must pass what it judges to be the appropriate sentence having regard to the circumstances of the offence and of the offender, taking into account, so far as the court considers it appropriate, the impact on the victim: however the opinions of the victim or the victim's close relatives as to what the sentence should be are therefore not relevant, unlike the consequences of the offence on them, and victims should be advised of this and if, despite the advice, opinions as to sentence are included in the statement, the court should pay no attention to them.

1 See the *Criminal Practice Directions 2015* [2015] EWCA Crim 1567, [2015] All ER (D) 134 (Sep) CPD VII Sentencing F: Victim Personal Statements F.1. The VPS or other statement may be made at any time prior to the disposal of the case: *Criminal Practice Directions 2015* [2015] EWCA Crim 1567, [2015] All ER (D) 134 (Sep) CPD VII Sentencing F: Victim Personal Statements F.2. For guidance in, and as to the purpose of, the making of Victim Personal Statements see *R v Perkins* [2013] EWCA Crim 323, [2013] Crim LR 533; and the Ministry of Justice *Code of Practice for Victims of Crime* (October 2013) (made pursuant to the Domestic Violence, Crime and Victims Act 2004 ss 32–34: see CRIMINAL PROCEDURE vol 28 (2015) PARA 901).

2 Ie subject to the further guidance given by the Court of Appeal in *R v Perkins* [2013] EWCA Crim 323, [2013] Crim LR 533.

3 See the *Criminal Practice Directions 2015* [2015] EWCA Crim 1567, [2015] All ER (D) 134 (Sep) CPD VII Sentencing F: Victim Personal Statements F.3.

4 Ie, must be a witness statement made under the Criminal Justice Act 1967 s 9 (see CRIMINAL PROCEDURE vol 28 (2015) PARA 627) or an expert's report: *Criminal Practice Directions 2015* [2015] EWCA Crim 1567, [2015] All ER (D) 134 (Sep) CPD VII Sentencing F: Victim Personal Statements F.3.

5 Subject to the court's discretion, the contents of the VPS may be summarised and in an appropriate case even read out in open court: *Criminal Practice Directions 2015* [2015] EWCA Crim 1567, [2015] All ER (D) 134 (Sep) CPD VII Sentencing F: Victim Personal Statements F.3.

623. Community Impact Statements. The police may prepare a community impact statement to make the court aware of particular crime trends in the local area and the impact of these on the local community, and such statements should be considered and taken into account by the court prior to passing sentence[1]. The court must pass what it judges to be the appropriate sentence having regard to the circumstances of the offence and of the offender, taking into account, so far as the court considers it appropriate, the impact on the community: however, opinions as to what the sentence should be are not relevant and, if they are included in the statement, the court must ignore them[2].

1 See the *Criminal Practice Directions 2015* [2015] EWCA Crim 1567, [2015] All ER (D) 134 (Sep) CPD VII Sentencing H: Community Impact Statements H.1, H.3. The statement must be in proper form, that is a witness statement made under the Criminal Justice Act 1967 s 9 (see CRIMINAL PROCEDURE vol 28 (2015) PARA 627) or an expert's report: *Criminal Practice Directions 2015* [2015] EWCA Crim 1567, [2015] All ER (D) 134 (Sep) CPD VII Sentencing H: Community Impact Statements H.2.

2 See the *Criminal Practice Directions 2015* [2015] EWCA Crim 1567, [2015] All ER (D) 134 (Sep) CPD VII Sentencing H: Community Impact Statements H.4.

624. Impact Statements for Businesses. If the victim, or one of the victims, of a crime is a business or enterprise (including charities but excluding public sector bodies), of any size, a nominated representative may make an Impact Statement for Business ('ISB'), which gives a formal opportunity for the court to be informed how a crime has affected a business[1]. The court must pass what it judges to be the appropriate sentence having regard to the circumstances of the offence and of the offender, taking into account, so far as the court considers it appropriate, the impact on the victims: however, opinions as to what the sentence should be are not relevant and, if they are included in the statement, the court must ignore them[2].

1 See the *Criminal Practice Directions 2015* [2015] EWCA Crim 1567, [2015] All ER (D) 134 (Sep) CPD VII Sentencing I: Impact Statements for Businesses I.1. The statement must be in proper form, that is a witness statement made under the Criminal Justice Act 1967 s 9 (see CRIMINAL PROCEDURE vol 28 (2015) PARA 627) and may be made at any time prior to the disposal of the case: *Criminal Practice Directions 2015* [2015] EWCA Crim 1567, [2015] All ER (D) 134 (Sep) CPD VII Sentencing I: Impact Statements for Businesses I.3.

2 See the *Criminal Practice Directions 2015* [2015] EWCA Crim 1567, [2015] All ER (D) 134 (Sep) CPD VII Sentencing I: Impact Statements for Businesses CPD VII Sentencing I: Impact Statements for Businesses I.9.

11. APPEALS

625. Right of appeal. Appeal, usually with leave[1] of the Court of Appeal, lies against the majority[2] of sentences[3] passed in the Crown Court; and, if leave is given, the sentence may be altered by the Court of Appeal[4]. The Court of Appeal will normally interfere only if the sentence was defective in law, or improperly took material into account, or was manifestly excessive or wrong in principle[5].

The Court of Appeal may also review sentences which appear to have been unduly lenient if the Attorney General refers such cases to it[6].

1 An appeal against sentence lies only with leave of the Court of Appeal unless the judge who passed the sentence grants a certificate that the case is fit for appeal: see the Criminal Appeal Act 1968 s 11(1), (1A); PARA 627; and CRIMINAL PROCEDURE vol 28 (2015) PARA 739. For the powers of a single judge to grant leave see CRIMINAL PROCEDURE vol 28 (2015) PARA 745. As to the power of the Criminal Cases Review Commission to refer a sentence to the Court of Appeal for review see PARA 633; and CRIMINAL PROCEDURE vol 28 (2015) PARA 796 et seq. There is an appeal as of right against a sentence for contempt of court: see the Administration of Justice Act 1960 s 13; and CONTEMPT OF COURT vol 22 (2012) PARA 118.
2 As to the right of appeal against sentence see PARAS 626–629.
3 As to the meaning of 'sentence' for this purpose see the Criminal Appeal Act 1968 s 50(1); and PARA 626.
4 See the Criminal Appeal Act 1968 s 11; and PARAS 627, 630.
5 See PARA 631.
6 See PARA 540 et seq.

626. Sentences which may be appealed. In the context of an appeal against sentence[1], 'sentence' includes any order made by a court when dealing with an offender[2] including, in particular:

(1)   a hospital order[3] with or without a restriction order[4];
(2)   an interim hospital order[5];
(3)   a hospital direction and a limitation direction (a 'hybrid order')[6];
(4)   a recommendation for deportation[7];
(5)   a confiscation order[8] and an order varying such an order[9];
(6)   a declaration of relevance[10] as respects an offence relating to a football match[11]; and
(7)   an order for the forfeiture or suspension[12] of personal licence to supply alcohol[13].

The following do not fall within the meaning of 'sentence' for this purpose:

(a)   an order[14] for the repayment of the costs of legal aid[15];
(b)   a financial reporting order[16];
(c)   a victim surcharge[17];
(d)   binding over to keep the peace[18]; and
(e)   deferment of sentence[19].

Where there are two or more defendants and an order is made upon sentence which the court has power to make in respect of one of the defendants only, the other defendant has no right of appeal against that order even if he is in fact affected by it[20].

1 Ie for the purposes of the Criminal Appeal Act 1968: see PARAS 625, 627 et seq.
2 Criminal Appeal Act 1968 s 50(1) (s 50(1) substituted by the Criminal Justice Act 1993 Sch 5 Pt 1).
3 Ie under the Mental Health Act 1983 Pt III (ss 35–55): see PARA 472 et seq; and MENTAL HEALTH AND CAPACITY vol 75 (2013) PARA 864.
4 Criminal Appeal Act 1968 s 50(1)(a) (as substituted: see note 2). As to restriction orders see PARA 477.

5 Criminal Appeal Act 1968 s 50(1)(b) (as substituted: see note 2). As to interim hospital orders see the Mental Health Act 1983 Pt III; PARA 474; and MENTAL HEALTH AND CAPACITY vol 75 (2013) PARA 864.

6 Criminal Appeal Act 1968 s 50(1)(bb) (as substituted (see note 2); added by the Crime (Sentences) Act 1997 Sch 4 para 6(1)(a)). See the Mental Health Act 1983 Pt III; and MENTAL HEALTH AND CAPACITY vol 75 (2013) PARA 863.

7 Criminal Appeal Act 1968 s 50(1)(c) (as substituted: see note 2). See PARA 462; and IMMIGRATION AND ASYLUM vol 57 (2012) PARA 181 et seq.

8 Ie an order under the Proceeds of Crime Act 2002 Pt 2 (ss 6–91) (see PARA 189 et seq), excluding a determination under s 10A (see PARA 226): Criminal Appeal Act 1968 s 50(1)(ca) (as substituted (see note 2); s 50(1)(ca), (cb) added by the Proceeds of Crime Act 2002 Sch 11 paras 1, 4(1), (3); Criminal Appeal Act 1968 s 50(1)(ca) amended by the Serious Crime Act 2015 Sch 4 para 3). 'Sentence' also includes an order under the Drug Trafficking Act 1994 other than one made by the High Court (provisions repealed) or an order under the Criminal Justice Act 1988 Pt VI (ss 71–103) (repealed): Criminal Appeal Act 1968 s 50(1)(d), (e) (as so substituted; s 50(1)(d), (g) amended by the Drug Trafficking Act 1994 Sch 1).

9 Criminal Appeal Act 1968 s 50(1)(cb) (as substituted and added: see notes 2, 8). An order varying a confiscation order under the Proceeds of Crime Act 2002 is appealable under these provisions only if the varying order is made under s 21 (see PARA 275), s 22 (see PARA 276) or s 29 (see PARA 218): Criminal Appeal Act 1968 s 50(1)(cb) (as so substituted and added). 'Sentence' also includes an order varying a confiscation order under the Drug Trafficking Act 1994 other than one made by the High Court (provisions repealed), an order varying a confiscation order under the Criminal Justice Act 1988 Pt VI (repealed) and an order made by the Crown Court varying a confiscation order which was made by the High Court by virtue of the Drug Trafficking Act 1994 s 19 (repealed): Criminal Appeal Act 1968 s 50(1)(f), (g) (as so substituted; s 50(1)(g) as amended (see note 8)).

10 Ie within the meaning of the Football Spectators Act 1989 s 23: see PARA 343.

11 Criminal Appeal Act 1968 s 50(1)(h) (as substituted (see note 2); amended by the Football (Offences and Disorder) Act 1999 s 7(2)(b); and by the Violent Crime Reduction Act 2006 Sch 3 para 14(1), (2)).

12 Ie under the Licensing Act 2003 s 129(2): see LICENSING AND GAMBLING vol 67 (2008) PARA 129.

13 Criminal Appeal Act 1968 s 50(1)(i) (as substituted (see note 2); amended by the Licensing Act 2003 Sch 6 paras 38, 42).

14 Ie under regulations under the Legal Aid, Sentencing and Punishment of Offenders Act 2012 s 23 or s 24 (see LEGAL AID vol 65 (2014) PARAS 46, 47, 143).

15 Criminal Appeal Act 1968 s 50(3) (added by the Access to Justice Act 1999 Sch 4 para 3; amended by the Legal Aid, Sentencing and Punishment of Offenders Act 2012 Sch 5 para 3).

16 As to financial reporting orders see PARAS 336–340.

17 As to victim surcharges see PARA 185.

18 *R v Randall* (1986) 8 Cr App Rep (S) 433, [1987] Crim LR 254, CA.

19 As to the power to defer see PARA 457.

20 *R v Ioannou* [1975] 3 All ER 400, 61 Cr App Rep 257, CA (owner of restaurant could not appeal against disqualification of licence-holder of premises).

627. Appeal against sentence following conviction on indictment. A person who has been convicted of an offence on indictment[1] may appeal to the Court of Appeal against any sentence (not being a sentence fixed by law)[2] passed on him for the offence, whether passed on his conviction or in subsequent proceedings[3]. Where the Crown Court has passed on an offender[4] two or more sentences[5] in the same proceeding[6], an appeal or application for leave to appeal against any one of those sentences is to be treated as an appeal or application in respect of both or all of them[7]. Where different orders, each of which is a sentence for present purposes, are made in separate proceedings, two appeals may be made against sentence[8].

The court has jurisdiction to entertain an appeal against sentence[9] even if it has already reviewed the sentence upon a reference by the Attorney General[10], although its earlier decision would generally constitute as much an end to the sentencing process as would its decision upon an application[11] by the defendant[12].

It is the duty of the Director of Public Prosecutions to appear for the prosecution, when directed by the court to do so on any appeal to the criminal division of the Court of Appeal[13].

An appeal against sentence[14] lies only with the leave of the Court of Appeal[15]; but, if within 28 days from the date on which the sentence was passed the judge who passed the sentence grants a certificate that the case is fit for appeal[16], an appeal lies without the leave of the Court of Appeal[17]. The court may treat an application for leave to appeal as the hearing of the appeal[18].

The giving of notice of appeal does not in general suspend the operation of any sentence or order of the court of trial but, subject to any direction which the Court of Appeal may give to the contrary, the time during which an appellant is in custody pending the determination of his appeal is reckoned as part of the term of any sentence to which he is for the time being subject[19].

Procedural provision is also made in connection with appeals against sentence[20].

1   All proceedings on indictment in England and Wales are brought in the Crown Court: see CRIMINAL PROCEDURE vol 27 (2015) PARA 184. As to appeals against sentence where the conviction was not on indictment see PARA 628.

2   As to the meaning of 'sentence' for these purposes see PARA 626. The reference to a sentence fixed by law does not include a reference to an order made under the Criminal Justice Act 2003 s 269(2) or (4) (see CRIMINAL LAW vol 25 (2010) PARA 97) in relation to a life sentence (as defined by s 277 (see CRIMINAL LAW vol 25 (2010) PARA 97)) that is fixed by law: Criminal Appeal Act 1968 s 9(1A) (added by the Criminal Justice Act 2003 s 271(1)). If a statutory provision which requires the imposition of a sentence of life imprisonment is incompatible with the Convention for the Protection of Human Rights and Fundamental Freedoms (Rome, 4 November 1950; TS 71 (1953); Cmd 8969) (the European Convention on Human Rights) art 3 (the prohibition of torture and inhuman or degrading treatment or punishment: see RIGHTS AND FREEDOMS vol 88A (2013) PARAS 158–187) or art 5 (the right to liberty and security: see RIGHTS AND FREEDOMS vol 88A (2013) PARAS 210–242) then, at least until Parliament has had the opportunity to consider its response to the court's declaration of incompatibility, the sentence is not fixed by law for the purposes of the Criminal Appeal Act 1968 s 9(1); alternatively the exclusion of sentences fixed by law is itself subject to an implied exception where the statutory provision fixing the sentence was incompatible with the Convention: *R (on the application of Lichniak) v Secretary of State for the Home Department, R (on the application of Pyrah) v Secretary of State for the Home Department* [2001] EWHC 294 (Admin), [2002] QB 296, [2001] 4 All ER 934, DC and CA (point not considered in *R v Lichniak, R v Pyrah* [2002] UKHL 47, [2003] 1 AC 903, [2002] 4 All ER 1122).

3   Criminal Appeal Act 1968 s 9(1) (numbered as such by the Criminal Justice Act 1988 Sch 15 paras 20, 21). As to appeals where the convicted person has died see CRIMINAL PROCEDURE vol 28 (2015) PARA 821.

4   Ie in dealing with the offender either on his conviction on indictment or in a proceeding to which the Criminal Appeal Act 1968 s 10(2) (see PARA 628) applies: s 11(2) (amended by the Courts Act 1971 Sch 8 para 57(1); and the Criminal Justice Act 1988 Sch 15 paras 20, 23(1)).

5   Ie two or more sentences against which an appeal lies under the Criminal Appeal Act 1968 s 9(1) or s 10 (see PARA 628).

6   For the purposes of the Criminal Appeal Act 1968 s 11, any two or more sentences are to be treated as passed in the same proceeding if they are passed on the same day, or they are passed on different days but the court in passing any one of them states that it is treating that one together with the other or others as substantially one sentence: s 11(7) (added by the Criminal Justice Act 2003 s 319(1), (3)).

7   Criminal Appeal Act 1968 s 11(2) (as amended: see note 4).

8   *R v Neal (John Frederick)* [1999] 2 Cr App Rep (S) 352, [1999] Crim LR 509, CA (defendant convicted of drug trafficking offence and sentenced to imprisonment; confiscation order later made in postponed proceedings; earlier appeal against sentence of imprisonment not a bar to appeal against confiscation order).

9   Ie under the Criminal Appeal Act 1968 s 9.
10 Ie under the Criminal Justice Act 1988 s 36: see PARA 540 et seq.
11 See note 9.
12 See *R v Hughes* [2009] EWCA Crim 841, [2010] 1 Cr App Rep (S) 146, [2009] All ER (D) 141 (May).
13 See the Prosecution of Offences Act 1985 s 3(2)(f)(ii); and CRIMINAL PROCEDURE vol 28 (2015) PARA 741.
14 Ie under the Criminal Appeal Act 1968 s 9 or s 10: s 11(1) (amended by the Criminal Justice Act 1982 s 29(2)).
15 Criminal Appeal Act 1968 s 11(1) (as amended: see note 14). Applications are normally considered in the first instance by a single judge: see CRIMINAL PROCEDURE vol 28 (2015) PARA 745. Certain of the Court of Appeal's powers in respect of appeals to it may be exercised by a single judge or by the Registrar of Criminal Appeals: see ss 31, 31A–31C; and CRIMINAL PROCEDURE vol 28 (2015) PARA 742 et seq.
16 Where such a certificate has been granted, the Court of Appeal may not give a direction under the Criminal Appeal Act 1968 s 29(1) that time spent in custody is not to be reckoned as part of sentence: see s 29(2)(b) (amended by the Criminal Justice Act 1988 Sch 15 paras 20, 27); and CRIMINAL PROCEDURE vol 28 (2015) PARA 738.
17 Criminal Justice Act 1968 s 11(1A) (added by the Criminal Justice Act 1982 s 29(2)(a); amended by the Criminal Justice and Immigration Act 2008 Sch 8 paras 1, 3).
18 See *R v Jowsey* (1915) 11 Cr App Rep 241, 84 LJKB 2118, CCA; *R v Thomas* (1941) 28 Cr App Rep 21, CCA. Consent of counsel is required to such course or, if the appellant is not represented, he must be given the opportunity to request the case to be restored to the list: see CRIMINAL PROCEDURE vol 28 (2015) PARA 759. As to information which may be required by the court see CRIMINAL PROCEDURE vol 28 (2015) PARA 753.
19 See the Criminal Appeal Act 1968 s 29; and CRIMINAL PROCEDURE vol 28 (2015) PARAS 737, 738.
20 See the Criminal Appeal Act 1968 ss 18–23A; and CRIMINAL PROCEDURE vol 28 (2015) PARA 747 et seq. See also CRIMINAL PROCEDURE vol 28 (2015) PARAS 798, 822 (the royal prerogative of mercy); and the Criminal Appeal Act 1968 s 44A (appeals in cases of death: see CRIMINAL PROCEDURE vol 28 (2015) PARA 821).

628.   Appeal against sentence of the Crown Court after summary conviction. The proceedings from which an appeal against sentence after summary conviction[1] lies are those where an offender convicted of an offence by a magistrates' court:

(1) is committed by the court to be dealt with for his offence before the Crown Court[2]; or

(2) appears or is brought before the Crown Court to be further dealt with for an offence in respect of which he had been made the subject of a conditional discharge or a community order or had been given a suspended sentence[3].

An offender dealt with for an offence before the Crown Court in such a proceeding[4] may appeal to the Court of Appeal against any sentence passed on him for the offence by the Crown Court[5].

1   Ie an appeal against sentence when a person is dealt with by the Crown Court (otherwise than on appeal from a magistrates' court) for an offence of which he was not convicted on indictment: Criminal Appeal Act 1968 s 10(1) (amended by the Courts Act 1971 Sch 8 para 57(1)). There is no right of appeal to the Court of Appeal from proceedings in the Crown Court on appeal from a magistrates' court since those proceedings do not fall within the Criminal Appeal Act 1968. As to appeals to the Crown Court from a magistrates' court against summary conviction and sentence see CRIMINAL PROCEDURE vol 28 (2015) PARA 665 et seq; and as to when the Crown Court may be asked to state a case on a point of law for the opinion of the High Court see CRIMINAL PROCEDURE vol 28 (2015) PARA 687 et seq.
2   Criminal Appeal Act 1968 s 10(2)(a) (amended by the Courts Act 1971 Sch 8 para 57(1)). As to the committal of a person convicted by a magistrates' court to the Crown Court for sentence see CRIMINAL PROCEDURE vol 27 (2015) PARAS 292–298; as to committal in connection with an offence committed during the period of an order for conditional discharge see PARA 455; and in connection with hospital orders see PARA 472 et seq. Invalidity of the committal to the Crown

Court does not constitute a ground of appeal; application for judicial review should be made to quash the committal: *R v Warren* [1954] 1 All ER 597, 38 Cr App Rep 44, CCA; *R v Brown* [1963] Crim LR 647, CCA; *R v Jones* [1969] 2 QB 33, 53 Cr App Rep 87, CA. See also *R v Finch* (1962) 47 Cr App Rep 58, CCA; *R v Birtles* [1975] 3 All ER 395, [1975] 1 WLR 1623, CA. The charges committed to the Crown Court should be clear from the record so that they are apparent on a subsequent appeal to the Court of Appeal: *R v Hooper* [1967] 1 All ER 766n, [1967] 1 WLR 657, CA.

3   Criminal Appeal Act 1968 s 10(2)(b) (substituted by the Criminal Justice and Immigration Act 2008 Sch 4 para 4). An offender may appeal against his sentence under these provisions if he has been given a suspended sentence (see PARA 100) or has been made the subject of an order for conditional discharge (see PARA 454) or a youth rehabilitation order within the meaning of the Criminal Justice and Immigration Act 2008 Pt 1 (ss 1–8) (see PARA 73) or a community order within the meaning of the Criminal Justice Act 2003 Pt 12 (ss 142–305) (see PARA 45 et seq): see the Criminal Appeal Act 1968 s 10(2)(b) (as so substituted); and see further the text and note 5.
    As to dealing with an offence committed by a person subject to an order for conditional discharge see PARA 456.

4   Ie a proceeding to which the Criminal Appeal Act 1968 s 10(2) applies: see the text and notes 1–3.

5   Criminal Appeal Act 1968 s 10(3) (substituted by the Criminal Justice Act 2003 s 319(1), (2)).

629.   Appeal against sentence imposed by Crown Court for summary offence by person committed for trial on indictment of offence triable either way. A person who on conviction on indictment has also been convicted of a summary offence[1] may appeal to the Court of Appeal against any sentence passed on him[2] for the summary offence, whether on his conviction or in subsequent proceedings[3]. Where following conviction on indictment a person has been convicted of a summary offence[4], an appeal or application for leave to appeal against any sentence for the offence triable either way[5] for which he was committed for trial is to be treated also as an appeal or application in respect of any sentence for the summary offence; and an appeal or application for leave to appeal against any sentence for the summary offence is to be treated also as an appeal or application in respect of the offence triable either way[6].

1   Ie under the Crime and Disorder Act 1998 Sch 3 para 6 (see CRIMINAL PROCEDURE vol 28 (2015) PARA 769): Criminal Appeal Act 1968 s 9(2) (added by the Criminal Justice Act 1988 Sch 15 para 21; amended by the Crime and Disorder Act 1998 Sch 8 para 12; the Access to Justice Act 1999 s 58(3); and by the Criminal Justice Act 2003 Sch 3 para 44(1), (3), Sch 37 Pt 4)).

2   Ie under the Crime and Disorder Act 1998 Sch 3 para 4 (see CRIMINAL PROCEDURE vol 27 (2015) PARA 308) or, as the case may be, the Criminal Justice Act 1988 s 41(7) (repealed): Criminal Appeal Act 1968 s 9(2) (as added and amended: see note 1).

3   Criminal Appeal Act 1968 s 9(2) (as added and amended: see note 1). As to time limits for appealing and appeals out of time see s 18; and CRIMINAL PROCEDURE vol 28 (2015) PARA 749.

4   Ie under the Criminal Justice Act 1988 s 41 (repealed).

5   If the appellant or applicant was convicted on indictment of two or more offences triable either way, references to the offence triable either way are to be construed, in relation to the summary offence of which he was convicted under the Criminal Justice Act 1988 s 41 following conviction on indictment, as references to the offence triable either way specified in the notice relating to that summary offence which was given under s 41(2) (repealed): Criminal Appeal Act 1968 s 11(2B) (s 11(2A), (2B) added by the Criminal Justice Act 1988 Sch 15 paras 20, 23(2)).

6   Criminal Appeal Act 1968 s 11(2A) (as added: see note 5).

630.   Variation of sentence. On an appeal against sentence[1], if the Court of Appeal considers that the sentence was wrong in principle or manifestly excessive, it may:

(1)   quash any sentence or order which is the subject of the appeal[2]; and

(2)   in place of it pass such sentence or make such order as it thinks

appropriate for the case and as the court below had power to pass or make when dealing with him for the offence[3].

Where the Court of Appeal exercises its power[4] to quash a confiscation order[5] it may, instead of proceeding[6] to pass a new sentence, direct the Crown Court to proceed afresh under the relevant enactment (ie the enactment under which the order was made)[7]. When proceeding afresh[8] the Crown Court must comply with any directions the Court of Appeal may make[9]. Where the Court of Appeal quashes a confiscation order (the 'quashed order')[10] and[11] directs the Crown Court to proceed afresh under the relevant enactment, these provisions do not prevent any sum paid by the appellant pursuant to the quashed order being a sum which is recoverable from the Secretary of State as a debt owing to the appellant, but the Court of Appeal may direct that any such sum is not to be repaid until such time as the Crown Court makes a confiscation order, or decides not to make such an order, when[12] proceeding afresh[13]. These provisions also do not prevent an amount which would otherwise fall to be repaid as a result of the order being quashed being set against an amount which the appellant is required to pay by virtue of a confiscation order made by the Crown Court in those proceedings[14].

The court must exercise its powers so that, taking the case as a whole, the appellant is not more severely dealt with on appeal than he was dealt with by the court below[15]. No statutory guidance is given as to what constitutes greater severity in sentences which are not of a like nature: however, a hospital order is not more severe than a sentence of imprisonment because of the curative element[16]; an immediate sentence of imprisonment has been held to be more severe than a suspended sentence of the same period[17]; a sentence of life imprisonment is more severe than a fixed term of any length[18]; and six years' disqualification for driving and an order requiring the appellant to pass a driving test has been held to be not more severe than eight years' disqualification without such order[19].

Where the Crown Court has failed to order disqualification for driving until the appropriate driving test has been passed[20], the Court of Appeal does not have power on an unsuccessful appeal to make such an order, because to do so would result in the appellant being dealt with more severely on appeal than by the court below[21].

1   Ie under the Criminal Appeal Act 1968 s 9 or s 10: see PARAS 627–629. As to the meaning of 'sentence' see PARA 626. The court cannot interfere with a sentence fixed by law: see PARA 627.

2   Criminal Appeal Act 1968 s 11(3)(a). The effect of quashing a sentence is to make the sentence void only for the future, not from its commencement: *Hancock v Prison Comrs* [1960] 1 QB 117, [1959] 3 All ER 513. As to bail where an interim hospital order is quashed see CRIMINAL PROCEDURE vol 27 (2015) PARA 114.

3   Criminal Appeal Act 1968 s 11(3)(b). Any power of the criminal division of the Court of Appeal to pass a sentence includes a power to make a recommendation for deportation in cases where the court from which the appeal lies had power to make such a recommendation: s 50(2). As to the reduction of a sentence where the appellant gives evidence against his co-accused see *R v A* [2006] EWCA Crim 1803, [2007] 1 Cr App Rep (S) 347, [2006] All ER (D) 348 (Jun).

4   Ie under the Criminal Appeal Act 1968 s 11(3)(a) (see the text and notes 1–2).

5   Ie an order made under the Proceeds of Crime Act 2002 s 6 (see PARA 221 et seq), the Drug Trafficking Offences Act 1986 s 1 (repealed), the Criminal Justice Act 1988 s 71 (repealed) or the Drug Trafficking Act 1994 s 2 (repealed)).

6   Ie under the Criminal Appeal Act 1968 s 11(3)(b) (see the text and note 3).

7   Criminal Appeal Act 1968 ss 11(3A), (3D), 11A(4) (ss 11(3A)–(3D), 11A added by the Coroners and Justice Act 2009 s 140).

8   Ie pursuant to the Criminal Appeal Act 1968 s 11(3A) (see the text and notes 4–7).

9   Criminal Appeal Act 1968 s 11(3B) (as added: see note 7). The Court of Appeal must exercise the power to give such directions so as to ensure that any confiscation order made in respect of the appellant by the Crown Court does not deal more severely with the appellant than the order quashed under s 11(3)(a): s 11(3C) (as so added).
10 See note 4.
11 Ie under the Criminal Appeal Act 1968 s 11(3A) (see the text and notes 4–7).
12 See note 8.
13 Criminal Appeal Act 1968 s 11A(1), (2) (as added: see note 7).
14 Criminal Appeal Act 1968 s 11A(3) (as added: see note 7).
15 Criminal Appeal Act 1968 s 11(3). The power to increase sentence was abolished by the Criminal Appeal Act 1966 s 4(2) (repealed). As to the Court of Appeal's review of other sentences passed in the same proceedings see PARA 627. In the case of committals to the Crown Court for sentence, the court's powers on appeal are limited to what the Crown Court could have ordered: see the Criminal Appeal Act 1968 s 11(3)(b); and the text and note 3.
    The court must look at the case as a whole as well as considering each separate sentence: *R v Marsden* (28 February 1972, unreported), CA. The court may increase one sentence in an appropriate case where convictions have been quashed on other counts: see CRIMINAL PROCEDURE vol 28 (2015) PARA 768. The periods of imprisonment imposed by the Crown Court on separate indictments may be adjusted so as to give the Court of Appeal power to make a suspended sentence supervision order: see *R v Baker* (1988) 10 Cr App Rep (S) 409, CA. As to adjustments in sentence by reason of disparity in sentences of co-defendants etc see PARA 631.
    Up to the time when that officer has amended the records of the court of trial, the Court of Appeal may alter a sentence which it has passed: *R v Cross* [1973] QB 937, 57 Cr App Rep 660, CA.
16 *R v Bennett* [1968] 2 All ER 753, 52 Cr App Rep 514, CA. When a hospital order is so made, an order under the Mental Health Act 1983 s 41 (restricting discharge: see PARA 477) should also be made in appropriate cases: see *R v Gardiner* [1967] 1 All ER 895, 51 Cr App Rep 187, CA.
17 See *R v Taylor* (1968) 53 Cr App Rep 175, CA; *R v March* [1970] 2 All ER 536n, [1970] 1 WLR 998, CA. See also *R v Kruger* [1973] Crim LR 133, CA (reduction in a sentence of imprisonment was balanced by a recommendation for deportation); *R v Reynolds* [2007] EWCA Crim 538, [2007] 4 All ER 369, [2008] 1 WLR 1075 (alteration of sentence imposed under the provisions relating to dangerous offenders in the Criminal Justice Act 2003 Pt 12 Ch 5 (ss 224–236) (see PARA 21 et seq)).
18 *R v Gills* [1967] Crim LR 247, CA; *R v Whittaker* [1967] Crim LR 431, CA; *R v Sieh* [1969] Crim LR 99, CA; *R v Stofile* [1969] Crim LR 325, CA.
19 See *R v Murphy* [1989] RTR 236, 89 Cr App Rep 176, CA.
20 Ie in circumstances where the court is required so to order by the Road Traffic Offenders Act 1988 s 36 (see ROAD TRAFFIC vol 90 (2011) PARA 892).
21 *R v Murphy* [1989] RTR 236, 89 Cr App Rep 176, CA; *R v Lauder* (1999) 163 JP 721, CA.

631.   Principles on which Court of Appeal interferes with a sentence. The Court of Appeal may interfere with a sentence[1] where (inter alia):

(1)   the sentence is defective in law[2];

(2)   the sentence improperly took material into account[3];

(3)   the sentence was passed on an incorrect factual basis[4]; and

(4)   where the public interest would normally require a substantial penalty[5].

It is not enough that the sentence is more severe than the Court of Appeal would have imposed; it must be much too severe or the wrong form of sentence[6]. Where there is more than one view of the facts, the judge is entitled to form his own view of them provided that it is consistent with the verdict and supported by the evidence given; he does not have to sentence the defendant on the most favourable view of the facts[7].

1   As to the meaning of 'sentence' see PARA 626. As to the principles which should be considered by the trial judge in determining sentence see PARA 553 et seq.
2   Eg because the sentence exceeds the prescribed maximum, because a procedural requirement has not been satisfied or because a specified statutory pre-condition is not satisfied: see *R v Jackson* [1974] QB 517, [1974] 2 All ER 211, CA; *R v Marquis* [1974] 2 All ER 1216, 59 Cr App Rep 228, CA. Under this heading, the Court of Appeal can interfere with an invalid sentence even

though there is a statutory prohibition on an appeal against the type of sentence in question: *R v Wehner* [1977] 3 All ER 553, 65 Cr App Rep 1, CA; *R v Cain* [1985] AC 46, [1984] 2 All ER 737, HL.

3 Eg *R v Wilson* [1980] 1 All ER 1093, 70 Cr App Rep 219, CA. The Court of Appeal has power to hear additional evidence, such as up-to-date medical or prison reports or changed family circumstances or employment prospects (see the Criminal Appeal Act 1968 s 23; and CRIMINAL PROCEDURE vol 28 (2015) PARA 753) but the case law is insufficiently developed to provide a clear indication of when the Court of Appeal will interfere with a sentence on the basis solely of such additional material: cf *R v Thomas* [1983] Crim LR 493, CA, and *R v Waddingham* (1983) 5 Cr App Rep (S) 66, [1983] Crim LR 492, CA.

4 See eg *R v Reeves* (1983) 5 Cr App Rep (S) 188, CA. Within this consideration are also included cases where a wrong aggregation of sentences has been made: *R v Hussain* [1962] Crim LR 712, CCA. The Court of Appeal will not interfere with a sentence on the basis simply of a change in the legislation or the tariff since the time of the sentence: *R v Graham (Edward)* [1999] 2 Cr App Rep (S) 312, [1999] Crim LR 677, CA.

5 See eg *R v Withers* (1935) 25 Cr App Rep 53, CCA (offence prevalent in locality: on this see further *R v Lanham* [2008] EWCA Crim 2450, [2009] 1 Cr App Rep (S) 592, [2009] Crim LR 125); *R v Hollis* [1965] Crim LR 378, CCA (offence of small financial value by railway employee but conviction resulting in loss of job and house); *R v Saunders* [1972] Crim LR 194, CA (conviction for shoplifting; five previous convictions); *R v Anderson* (1972) 56 Cr App Rep 863, CA (persistent shoplifting).

6 See eg *R v Socratous* (1984) 6 Cr App Rep (S) 33, [1984] Crim LR 301, DC; *R v Rahiem* [2007] EWCA Crim 653, [2007] All ER (D) 224 (Feb) (court would not interfere where defence counsel advised that sentence was 'on the high side'). See also *R v King, R v Simpkins* (1973) 57 Cr App Rep 696, CA (wrong in principle to give consideration to defendant's political utterances); *R v Longman* [1974] Crim LR 374, CA (sentence within statutory maximum but in excess of maximum prescribed by subsequent legislation in force at time of trial: sentence wrong in principle); *R v Mark* (1974) Times, 16 October, CA (sentence wrong in principle, grossly excessive and harsh); *R v Stewart* [2007] EWCA Crim 1621, [2007] All ER (D) 10 (Sep) (imprisonment for public protection); *R v Gbedje* [2007] EWCA Crim 730, [2007] 2 Cr App Rep (S) 585, [2007] All ER (D) 165 (Mar), CA; *R v Khan* [2009] EWCA Crim 389, [2010] 1 Cr App Rep (S) 1, [2009] All ER (D) 117 (Mar) (manifestly excessive); *R v Christie* [2012] EWCA Crim 35, [2012] 2 Cr App Rep (S) 273 (although fine imposed for careless driving was manifestly excessive, period of disqualification was not). It has, however, been held that in cases involving widespread public disorder, sentences beyond the range of sentences recommended in guidelines for conventional offending are inevitable: see *R v Blackshaw* [2011] EWCA Crim 2312, [2012] 1 WLR 1126, [2011] All ER (D) 144 (Oct).

7 *R v Solomon and Triumph* (1984) 6 Cr App Rep (S) 120, [1984] Crim LR 433, CA.

632. Appeals to the Crown Court. A person convicted by a magistrates' court may appeal to the Crown Court against his sentence whether or not he pleaded guilty[1], and a person ordered by a magistrates' court to enter into a recognisance or to be of good behaviour may appeal to the Crown Court against such order[2]. Provision is also made for the review of decisions made by the Crown Court in its appellate capacity[3].

1 See the Magistrates' Courts Act 1980 s 108; and CRIMINAL PROCEDURE vol 28 (2015) PARA 665. For the relevant procedure see CRIMINAL PROCEDURE vol 28 (2015) PARA 667 et seq.
2 See the Magistrates' Courts (Appeals from Binding Over Orders) Act 1956; and CRIMINAL PROCEDURE vol 28 (2015) PARA 665.
3 See CRIMINAL PROCEDURE vol 28 (2015) PARAS 687–700.

633. Reference of sentence to Court of Appeal by Criminal Cases Review Commission. Where a person has been convicted of an offence the Criminal Cases Review Commission[1] may (whether or not they refer the conviction) at any time refer to the Court of Appeal (in the case of a conviction on indictment) or the Crown Court (in the case of a summary conviction) any sentence (not being a sentence fixed by law)[2] imposed on, or in subsequent proceedings relating to, the conviction, and any such reference is treated for all purposes as an appeal by the person[3] against the sentence and any other sentence (not being a sentence fixed by law) imposed on, or in subsequent proceedings relating to, the conviction or any associated conviction[4].

1 As to the Criminal Cases Review Commission see CRIMINAL PROCEDURE vol 28 (2015) PARAS 790–794.
2 As to the meaning of 'sentence' for the purposes of the bringing of appeals against sentence see PARA 626.
3 Ie under the Criminal Appeal Act 1968 s 9: see PARAS 627, 629.
4 See the Criminal Appeal Act 1995 ss 9, 11; and CRIMINAL PROCEDURE vol 28 (2015) PARAS 795–797.

634. Appeals and references from Court of Appeal to Supreme Court. An appeal lies to the Supreme Court from any decision of the Court of Appeal on an appeal[1] against sentence if a point of law of general public importance is involved in the decision and it appears to the Court of Appeal that it ought to be considered by the Supreme Court[2]. The Court of Appeal may also refer to the Supreme Court a point of law referred to it by the Attorney General[3].

1 Ie under the Criminal Appeal Act 1968: see PARA 625 et seq.
2 See the Criminal Appeal Act 1968 s 33(1)–(3); and CRIMINAL PROCEDURE vol 28 (2015) PARAS 812–820. The Court of Appeal or the Supreme Court must give leave for such an appeal to be brought: see s 33(2); and CRIMINAL PROCEDURE vol 28 (2015) PARA 812. There is no appeal to the Supreme Court from a decision of the Court of Appeal to refuse leave: see s 33(3); and CRIMINAL PROCEDURE vol 28 (2015) PARA 812.
3 See the Criminal Justice Act 1972 s 36; and CRIMINAL PROCEDURE vol 28 (2015) PARA 799 et seq.

635. Prosecution rights of appeal. The prosecution has a right of appeal to the Court of Appeal and the Supreme Court in respect of the making or otherwise of a confiscation order under the Proceeds of Crime Act 2002[1]. The prosecution may also appeal against a decision of the Crown Court to reduce the sentence of a person who has given assistance in a criminal investigation[2] and against a decision of the court to make a football banning order[3].

1 See the Proceeds of Crime Act 2002 ss 31–33; and PARAS 243–245.
2 See the Serious Organised Crime and Police Act 2005 s 74(8); and PARA 548.
3 See the Football Spectators Act 1989 s 14A(5A); and PARA 344.

12. OFFENDER MANAGEMENT

(1) CRIMINAL RECORD CHECKS

(i) Criminal Conviction Certificates and Criminal Record Certificates

636. Criminal conviction certificates. A 'criminal conviction certificate' is a certificate[1] which gives the prescribed details[2] of every conviction[3] or conditional caution[4] of the applicant which is recorded in central records[5], or states that there are no such convictions and conditional cautions[6]. As from a day to be appointed[7] a criminal conviction certificate may also contain details as to the applicant's immigration status[8].

1 'Certificate' means any one or more documents issued in response to a particular application, but does not include any documents issued in response to a request under the Police Act 1997 s 116A(1) (see PARA 645), an application as mentioned in s 116A(4)(a) or (5)(a) (see PARA 645), or a request under s 120AC (see PARA 650) or s 120AD (see PARA 645): s 126(1) (ss 112(2)(a), (b), 126(1) (definition 'certificate') amended by the Protection of Freedoms Act 2012 s 84, Sch 9 para 118).

2 The following details of a conviction are prescribed (by virtue of the Police Act 1997 (Criminal Records) Regulations 2002, SI 2002/233, reg 4B(1) (reg 4B added by SI 2014/239)) for these purposes:
   (1) the date of conviction;
   (2) the convicting court;
   (3) the offence; and
   (4) the method of disposal for the offence, including any ancillary order made.
   The following details of a conditional caution (see note 4) are prescribed (by virtue of the Police Act 1997 (Criminal Records) Regulations 2002, SI 2002/233, reg 4B(2) (as so added)) for these purposes:
   (a) the date on which the conditional caution was given;
   (b) the offence; and
   (c) the attached conditions.

3 'Conviction' means a conviction within the meaning of the Rehabilitation of Offenders Act 1974 (see PARA 591 note 3), other than a spent conviction (see PARA 594): Police Act 1997 s 112(3).

4 'Conditional caution' means a caution given under the Criminal Justice Act 2003 s 22 (conditional cautions for adults: see CRIMINAL PROCEDURE vol 27 (2015) PARA 55) or the Crime and Disorder Act 1998 s 66A (conditional cautions for children and young persons: see CHILDREN AND YOUNG PERSONS vol 10 (2012) PARA 1199), other than one that is spent for the purposes of the Rehabilitation of Offenders Act 1974 Sch 2 (see PARA 595) (Police Act 1997 s 112(3) (s 112(2)(a) amended, s 112(3) (definition 'conditional caution') added, by the Criminal Justice and Immigration Act 2008 s 50(2))); and 'caution' means a caution given to a person in England and Wales or Northern Ireland in respect of an offence which, at the time when the caution is given, he has admitted (Police Act 1997 s 126(1)).

5 Police Act 1997 s 112(2)(a) (as amended: see note 4). As to the meaning of 'central records' see PARA 637 note 4.

6 Police Act 1997 s 112(2)(b) (as amended: see note 4).

7 The Police Act 1997 s 113CD (see note 8) is added, as from a day to be appointed, by the Policing and Crime Act 2009 s 94. At the date at which this volume states the law no day had been appointed for the coming into force of this provision.

8 As from a day to be appointed where:
   (1) an application for a criminal conviction certificate under the Police Act 1997 s 112 (see PARA 641 et seq), an application for a criminal record certificate under s 113A (see PARAS 637, 641) or an application for an enhanced criminal record certificate under s 113B (see PARA 638 et seq) contains a request for the information referred to herein (ie information under s 113CD) (s 113CD(1)(a) (prospectively added: see note 7));
   (2) in the case of an application for a certificate under s 112, the application contains a statement that the information is sought for the purposes of employment with a person specified in the application (s 113CD(1)(b) (as so prospectively added)); and
   (3) the applicant pays in the prescribed manner any additional fee prescribed in respect of the application (s 113CD(1)(c) (as so prospectively added)),

the certificate must state whether according to records held by the Secretary of State the applicant is subject to immigration control (s 113CD(2)(a) (as so prospectively added)) or that records held by the Secretary of State do not show whether the applicant is subject to immigration control (s 113CD(2)(b) (as so prospectively added)). For these purposes a person is subject to immigration control if under the Immigration Act 1971 (see IMMIGRATION AND ASYLUM) the person requires leave to enter or remain in the United Kingdom: Police Act 1997 s 113CD(8) (as so prospectively added). If the records show that the applicant is subject to immigration control, the certificate must state whether according to the records the applicant has been granted leave to enter or remain in the United Kingdom (s 113CD(3)(a) (as so prospectively added)) or that the records do not show whether the applicant has been granted leave to enter or remain in the United Kingdom (s 113CD(3)(b) (as so prospectively added)); and if the records show that the applicant has been granted leave to enter or remain in the United Kingdom, the certificate must state whether according to the records the applicant's leave to enter or remain in the United Kingdom is current (s 113CD(4)(a) (as so prospectively added)) or that the records do not show whether the applicant's leave to enter or remain in the United Kingdom is current (s 113CD(4)(b) (as so prospectively added)). If the records show that the applicant has been granted leave to enter or remain in the United Kingdom and that it is current, the certificate must also state any conditions to which the leave to enter or remain is subject and which relate to the applicant's employment: s 113CD(5) (as so prospectively added).

A certificate under s 113CD must contain such advice as the Secretary of State thinks appropriate about where to obtain further information about the matters mentioned in s 113CD(2)–(5): s 113CD(6) (as so prospectively added).

For these purposes a person's leave to enter or remain in the United Kingdom is current unless it is invalid (s 113CD(7)(a) (as so prospectively added)) or it has ceased to have effect (whether by reason of curtailment, revocation, cancellation, passage of time or otherwise) (s 113CD(7)(b) (as so prospectively added)).

637.   Criminal record certificates. A 'criminal record certificate' is a certificate[1] which gives the prescribed details[2] of every relevant matter[3] relating to the applicant which is recorded in central records[4] or states that there is no such matter[5]. As from a day to be appointed a criminal record certificate may contain details as to the applicant's immigration status[6].

1   As to the meaning of 'certificate' see PARA 636 note 1.
2   By virtue of the Police Act 1997 (Criminal Records) Regulations 2002, SI 2002/233, reg 5, the prescribed details for these purposes are:
    (1)   in the case of a conviction including a spent conviction:
        (a)   the date of conviction;
        (b)   the convicting court;
        (c)   the offence; and
        (d)   the method of disposal for the offence including details of any order made under the Criminal Justice and Court Services Act 2000 Pt 2 (ss 26–42) (protection of children: see CHILDREN AND YOUNG PERSONS); and
    (2)   in the case of a caution, reprimand or warning:
        (a)   the date of caution, reprimand or warning;
        (b)   the place where the caution, reprimand or warning was issued; and
        (c)   the offence which the person issued with a caution, reprimand or warning had admitted.
    'Reprimand' and 'warning' mean a reprimand or a warning given to a child or young person in accordance with the Crime and Disorder Act 1998 s 65 (see CHILDREN AND YOUNG PERSONS vol 10 (2012) PARA 1197): Police Act 1997 (Criminal Records) Regulations 2002, SI 2002/233, reg 2.
3   Ie: (1) in relation to a person who has one conviction only, a conviction of an offence within the Police Act 1997 s 113A(6D) (see below), a conviction in respect of which a custodial sentence or a sentence of service detention was imposed, or a current conviction; (2) in relation to any other person, any conviction; (3) a caution given in respect of an offence within s 113A(6D); and (4) a current caution: s 113A(6), 113B(9) (ss 113A, 113B added by the Serious Organised Crime and Police Act 2005 s 163(2); Police Act 1997 s 113A(6) (definition 'relevant matter') substituted, s 113(6D)–(6F) added, by SI 2013/1200 (made pursuant to the power conferred on the Secretary of State by the Police Act 1997 s 113A(7), (8) (added by the Safeguarding Vulnerable Groups Act 2006 Sch 9 para 14(1), (2)) by order to amend the definitions 'relevant matter' and 'central records' (see note 4))).

By virtue of the Police Act 1997 s 113(6D) (as so added), the offences referred to above are:
(a) murder;
(b) an offence under the Medicines Act 1968 s 67(1A) (prescribing, etc a medicinal product in contravention of certain conditions) (see MEDICAL PRODUCTS AND DRUGS vol 75 (2013) PARA 272);
(c) an offence under the Mental Health Act 1983 ss 126–129 (see MENTAL HEALTH AND CAPACITY vol 75 (2013) PARAS 1008–1015);
(d) an offence specified in the Disqualification from Caring for Children (England) Regulations 2002, SI 2002/635, Schedule (see CHILDREN AND YOUNG PERSONS vol 10 (2012) PARA 1068);
(e) an offence specified in the Criminal Justice Act 2003 Sch 15 (specified offences for the purposes of Pt 12 Ch 5 (dangerous offenders) (see PARA 23);
(f) an offence under the Mental Capacity Act 2005 s 44 (ill-treatment or neglect), Sch 1 para 4 (applications and procedure for registration), or Sch 4 para 4 (duties of attorney in event of incapacity of donor) (see AGENCY vol 1 (2008) PARAS 200, 203, 225–226);
(g) an offence under the Safeguarding Vulnerable Groups Act 2006 ss 7, 9 or 19 (offences in respect of regulated activity) (see SOCIAL SERVICES AND COMMUNITY CARE vol 95 (2013) PARAS 205–208);
(h) an offence specified in the Health and Social Care Act 2008 s 17(3)(a), (b) or (c) (cancellation of registration), apart from an offence under s 76 (disclosure of confidential personal information) (see SOCIAL SERVICES AND COMMUNITY CARE vol 95 (2013) PARAS 101, 227);
(i) an offence specified in the Safeguarding Vulnerable Groups Act 2006 (Prescribed Criteria and Miscellaneous Provisions) Regulations 2009, SI 2009/37, Schedule (see SOCIAL SERVICES AND COMMUNITY CARE vol 95 (2013) PARA 164);
(j) an offence specified in the Childcare (Disqualification) Regulations 2009, SI 2009/1547, Sch 2 or 3 (see CHILDREN AND YOUNG PERSONS vol 10 (2012) PARAS 1119);
(k) an offence which has been superseded (directly or indirectly) by any of the above offences;
(l) an offence of attempting or conspiring to commit any of the above offences or inciting or aiding, abetting, counselling or procuring the commission of any such offence, or an offence under the Serious Crime Act 2007 Pt 2 (encouraging or assisting crime: see CRIMINAL LAW vol 25 (2010) PARAS 65–72) committed in relation to any such offence;
(m) an offence under the law of Scotland or Northern Ireland or any territory outside the United Kingdom which corresponds to any of the above offences;
(n) any offence under the Armed Forces Act 2006 s 42 (criminal conduct: see ARMED FORCES vol 3 (2011) PARA 587) in relation to which the corresponding offence under the law of England and Wales is any of the above offences; and
(o) an offence under the Army Act 1955 s 70, the Air Force Act 1955 s 70 or the Naval Discipline Act 1957 s 42 (all repealed) of which the corresponding civil offence is any of the above offences.
For these purposes (by virtue of the Police Act 1997 s 113(6E), 6(F) (as so added)):
(i) 'conviction' has the same meaning as in the Rehabilitation of Offenders Act 1974 (see PARA 591 note 3), and includes a spent conviction (see PARA 594);
(ii) 'caution' includes a caution which is spent for the purposes of Sch 2 (see PARA 595) but excludes a disregarded caution within the meaning of the Protection of Freedoms Act 2012 Pt 5 Ch 4 (see PARA 596);
(iii) a person's conviction is a current conviction if the person was aged 18 or over on the date of the conviction and that date fell within the 11 year period ending with the day on which the certificate is issued, or the person was aged under 18 on the date of conviction and that date fell within the period of 5 years and 6 months ending with the day on which the certificate is issued;
(iv) a caution given to a person is a current caution if the person was aged 18 or over on the date it was given and that date fell within the 6 year period ending with the day on which the certificate is issued, or the person was aged under 18 on the date it was given and that date fell within the 2 year period ending with the day on which the certificate is issued; and
(v) 'custodial sentence' and 'sentence of service detention' have the same meaning as in the Rehabilitation of Offenders Act 1974 s 5(8) (see PARA 605).
4 Police Act 1997 s 113A(3)(a) (as added: see note 3). 'Central records' for these purposes means information in any form relating to convictions, cautions, reprimands and warnings on a names database held by the Secretary of State for the use of constables: ss 112(3), 113A(6), 113B(9)

(ss 113A(6), 113B(9) as so added); Police Act 1997 (Criminal Records) Regulations 2002, SI 2002/233, reg 9 (substituted by SI 2007/700; amended by SI 2012/2669; SI 2014/239).
5   Police Act 1997 s 113A(3)(b) (as added: see note 3).
6   See the Police Act 1997 s 113CD; and PARA 636 notes 7, 8.

638. Enhanced criminal record certificates. An 'enhanced criminal record certificate' is a certificate[1] which gives the prescribed details of every relevant matter[2] relating to the applicant which is recorded in central records[3] and specified additional information where applicable[4] or states that there is no such matter or information[5].

An enhanced criminal record certificate must also include such suitability information relating to children and vulnerable adults as may be prescribed[6]. 'Suitability information relating to children'[7] is:

(1)   whether the applicant is barred[8] from regulated activity[9] relating to children[10];

(2)   whether the applicant is subject to a direction[11] prohibiting him from participation in school management[12].

'Suitability information relating to vulnerable adults'[13] is whether the applicant is barred from regulated activity relating to vulnerable adults[14].

As from a day to be appointed an enhanced criminal record certificate may also contain details as to the applicant's immigration status[15]. Additional information may also accompany enhanced criminal record certificates[16].

1   As to the meaning of 'certificate' see PARA 636 note 1.
2   As to the relevant matters for these purposes see PARA 637 note 3. At the date at which this volume states the law no details had been prescribed for these purposes.
3   As to the meaning of 'central records' see PARA 637 note 4.
4   Police Act 1997 s 113B(3)(a) (ss 113B–113D added by the Serious Organised Crime and Police Act 2005 s 163(2)). Before issuing an enhanced criminal record certificate DBS must request any relevant chief officer to provide any information which the chief officer reasonably believes to be relevant for the purpose described in the statement under the Police Act 1997 s 113B(2) (see PARA 641) and in the chief officer's opinion, ought to be included in the certificate and any information so provided must be given in the certificate: see s 113B(4); and PARA 640.
     'DBS' means the Disclosure and Barring Service established by the Protection of Freedoms Act 2012 s 87(1) (see SOCIAL SERVICES AND COMMUNITY CARE vol 95 (2013) PARA 237): Police Act 1997 s 126(1) (definition added by SI 2012/3006).
5   Police Act 1997 s 113B(3)(b) (as added: see note 4).
6   Police Act 1997 ss 113BA(1), 113BB(1) (ss 113BA–113BC added by the Safeguarding Vulnerable Groups Act 2006 Sch 9 para 14(1), (4)).
7   The Secretary of State may by order made by statutory instrument amend the Police Act 1997 s 113BA for the purpose of altering the meaning of 'suitability information relating to children': s 113BC(1)(a) (as added: see note 6). At the date at which this volume states the law no such order had been made.
8   As to the meaning of 'barred' see the Safeguarding Vulnerable Groups Act 2006 s 3; and CHILDREN AND YOUNG PERSONS vol 9 (2012) PARA 682 (definition applied by the Police Act 1997 ss 113BA(3), (4), 113BB(3), (4) (as added: see note 6)).
9   As to the meaning of 'regulated activity' see the Safeguarding Vulnerable Groups Act 2006 s 5; and CHILDREN AND YOUNG PERSONS vol 9 (2012) PARA 684 (definition applied by the Police Act 1997 s 113BA(3), (4), 113BB(3), (4) (as added: see note 6)).
10   Police Act 1997 s 113BA(2)(a) (as added: see note 6). As to the meaning of 'children' see the Safeguarding Vulnerable Groups Act 2006 s 60; and CHILDREN AND YOUNG PERSONS vol 9 (2012) PARA 672 (definition applied by the Police Act 1997 s 113BA(3), (4) (as so added)).
11   Ie under the Education and Skills Act 2008 s 128 (prohibition on participation in management of independent educational institution in England: see EDUCATION vol 35 (2011) PARA 504) or the Education Act 2002 s 167A (prohibition on participation in management of independent school in Wales: see EDUCATION vol 35 (2011) PARA 470).
12   Police Act 1997 s 113BA(2)(e) (as added (see note 6); further added by the Education and Inspections Act 2006 s 170(2); and amended by the Education and Skills Act 2008 Sch 1 para 12).

13 The Secretary of State may by order made by statutory instrument amend the Police Act 1997 s 113BB for the purpose of altering the meaning of 'suitability information relating to vulnerable adults': s 113BC(1)(b) (as added: see note 6). At the date at which this volume states the law no such order had been made.

14 Police Act 1997 s 113BB(2)(a) (as added: see note 6). As to the meaning of 'vulnerable adult' see the Safeguarding Vulnerable Groups Act 2006 s 59; and SOCIAL SERVICES AND COMMUNITY CARE vol 95 (2013) PARA 145 (applied by the Police Act 1997 s 113BB(3), (4) (as so added)).

15 See the Police Act 1997 s 113CD; and PARA 636 notes 7, 8.

16 See PARA 640.

639. Purposes for which enhanced criminal record certificates may be required. The purposes for which an enhanced criminal record certificate[1] may be required[2] are:

(1) considering the applicant's suitability to work with children[3];

(2) considering the applicant's suitability to work with vulnerable adults[4];

(3) obtaining or holding an operating licence[5] or a personal licence[6] for the provision of gambling services[7];

(4) considering an individual's suitability for a position as Commissioner for the Gambling Commission[8] and for any office or employment in the Commissioners' service[9];

(5) obtaining or holding a licence[10] to run or promote the National Lottery[11];

(6) considering the suitability of any person appointed by the Commissioner for Older People in Wales to assist him in the discharge of his functions or authorised to discharge his functions on his behalf[12];

(7) considering the applicant's suitability for work as a person who provides immigration advice or services[13] and is a registered person[14], or a person who acts on behalf of and under the supervision of such a registered person, or a person who is exempt[15];

(8) considering the applicant's suitability to obtain or retain a licence[16] where the question relates to any person who as a result of his role in the body concerned is required to be named in the application for such a licence (or would have been so required if that person had had that role at the time the application was made)[17];

(9) considering an individual's suitability to have in their possession, to acquire or to transfer, prohibited weapons or ammunition[18];

(10) assessing the suitability of a person for any office or employment which relates to national security[19]; and

(11) considering the applicant's suitability to obtain or hold a taxi driver licence[20].

1 As to the meaning of 'enhanced criminal record certificate' see PARA 638. As to the duty of DBS to issue certificates see PARA 642.

2 Ie in accordance with a statement made by a registered person under the Police Act 1997 s 113B(2)(b): see PARA 641. As to registered persons see PARAS 646–653.

3 Police Act 1997 (Criminal Records) Regulations 2002, SI 2002/233, reg 5A(a) (reg 5A added by SI 2006/748; and the Police Act 1997 (Criminal Records) Regulations 2002, SI 2002/233, reg 5A(a), (b) substituted by SI 2014/955). The circumstances referred to in the Police Act 1997 (Criminal Records) Regulations 2002, SI 2002/233, reg 5A(a) are set out in full in reg 5C (added by SI 2013/2669; amended by SI 2014/955; SI 2014/2122). As to the meaning of 'children' see the Safeguarding Vulnerable Groups Act 2006 s 60; and CHILDREN AND YOUNG PERSONS vol 9 (2012) PARA 672.

4 Police Act 1997 (Criminal Records) Regulations 2002, SI 2002/233, reg 5A(b) (as added and substituted: see note 3). The circumstances referred to in the Police Act 1997 (Criminal Records) Regulations 2002, SI 2002/233, reg 5A(b) are set out in full in reg 5B (added by SI 2013/1194;

amended by SI 2014/955; SI 2014/2103; SI 2015/643). As to the meaning of 'vulnerable adult' see the Safeguarding Vulnerable Groups Act 2006 s 59; and SOCIAL SERVICES AND COMMUNITY CARE vol 95 (2013) PARA 145.

5   Ie under the Gambling Act 2005 Pt 5 (ss 65–126) (see LICENSING AND GAMBLING vol 67 (2008) PARA 349 et seq) for the purposes of that Act.
6   Ie under the Gambling Act 2005 Pt 6 (ss 127–139) (see LICENSING AND GAMBLING vol 67 (2008) PARA 400 et seq) for the purposes of that Act.
7   Police Act 1997 (Criminal Records) Regulations 2002, SI 2002/233, reg 5A(c), (d) (as added (see note 3); substituted by SI 2007/1892).
8   See LICENSING AND GAMBLING vol 67 (2008) PARA 4 et seq.
9   Police Act 1997 (Criminal Records) Regulations 2002, SI 2002/233, reg 5A(e) (as added (see note 3); and substituted by SI 2007/1892).
10   Ie under the National Lottery etc Act 1993 s 5 or 6: see LICENSING AND GAMBLING vol 68 (2008) PARAS 691–692, 694.
11   Police Act 1997 (Criminal Records) Regulations 2002, SI 2002/233, reg 5A(f) (as added: see note 3).
12   Police Act 1997 (Criminal Records) Regulations 2002, SI 2002/233, reg 5A(v) (as added (see note 3); further added by SI 2007/1892; amended by SI 2009/1882).
13   Ie as defined in the Immigration and Asylum Act 1999 s 82(1) (see IMMIGRATION AND ASYLUM vol 57 (2012) PARA 204).
14   Ie under the Immigration and Asylum Act 1999 Pt 5 (ss 82–93) (see IMMIGRATION AND ASYLUM vol 57 (2012) PARAS 204–208).
15   Police Act 1997 (Criminal Records) Regulations 2002, SI 2002/233, reg 5A(x) (as added (see note 3); further added by SI 2009/1882). The text refers to a person who is exempt under the Immigration and Asylum Act 1999 s 84(4)(a)–(c) (see IMMIGRATION AND ASYLUM vol 57 (2012) PARA 205).
16   Ie under the Misuse of Drugs Regulations 2001, SI 2001/3998, reg 5 (see MEDICAL PRODUCTS AND DRUGS vol 75 (2013) PARAS 493–494, 496), or Council Regulation (EC) 2004/273 (OJ L47, 18.2.2004, p 1) on drug precursors, art 3(2), or Council Regulation (EC) 2005/111 (OJ L22, 26.1.2005, p 1) art 6(1).
17   Police Act 1997 (Criminal Records) Regulations 2002, SI 2002/233, reg 5A(y) (as added (see note 3); further added by SI 2009/1882).
18   Police Act 1997 (Criminal Records) Regulations 2002, SI 2002/233, reg 5A(zd) (as added (see note 3); further added by SI 2012/3016). The reference in the text to prohibited weapons and ammunition is a reference to prohibited weapons and ammunition to which the Firearms Act 1968 s 5 (see CRIMINAL LAW vol 25 (2010) PARA 613) applies.
19   Police Act 1997 (Criminal Records) Regulations 2002, SI 2002/233, reg 5A(ze) (as added (see note 3); further added by SI 2013/2669).
20   Police Act 1997 (Criminal Records) Regulations 2002, SI 2002/233, reg 5A(zf) (as added (see note 3); further added by SI 2014/955).

640. Additional information to accompany enhanced criminal record certificates.

Before issuing an enhanced criminal record certificate[1] the DBS[2] must request any relevant chief officer[3] to provide any information[4] which the chief officer reasonably believes to be relevant[5] for the purposes of the application[6] and which in the chief officer's opinion, ought to be included in the certificate[7].

1   As to the meaning of 'enhanced criminal record certificate' see PARA 638. As to the duty to issue certificates see PARA 642.
2   Ie the Disclosure and Barring Service: see PARA 638 note 4.
3   'Relevant chief officer' means any chief officer of a police force who is identified by DBS for the purposes of making a request under the Police Act 1997 s 113B(4): s 113B(9) (s 113B added, s 119(2), (3) amended, by the Serious Organised Crime and Police Act 2005 ss 163(2), 165(1), Sch 14 para 4(b); Police Act 1997 s 113B(4) amended, ss 113B(4A), (9) (definition 'relevant chief officer'), 119(2A) added, by the Protection of Freedoms Act 2012 s 82(1), (3), Sch 9 para 110; Police Act 1997 s 113B(4), (9) (definition 'relevant chief officer') amended by SI 2012/3006). In exercising functions under the Police Act 1997 s 113B(4) a relevant chief officer must have regard to any guidance for the time being published by the Secretary of State: s 113B(4A) (as so added).
     Reference to a police force in the Police Act 1997 s 113B include (by virtue of s 113B(10) (as so added)) any of:

(1)   the Royal Navy Police (Police Act 1997 s 113B(10)(a) (as so added; substituted by the Armed Forces Act 2006 Sch 16 para 149));

(2)   the Royal Military Police (Police Act 1997 s 113B(10)(c) (as so added));

(3)   the Royal Air Force Police (s 113B(10)(d) (as so added));

(4)   the Ministry of Defence Police (s 113B(10)(e) (as so added));

(5)   the British Transport Police (s 113B(10)(h) (as so added));

(6)   the Civil Nuclear Constabulary (s 113B(10)(i) (as so added));

(7)   the States of Jersey Police Force (s 113B(10)(j) (as so added));

(8)   the salaried police force of the Island of Guernsey (s 113B(10)(k) (as so added));

(9)   the Isle of Man Constabulary (s 113B(10)(l) (as so added)); and

(10)   a body with functions in any country or territory outside the British Islands which correspond to those of a police force in any part of the United Kingdom (s 113B(10)(m) (as so added)).

and any reference to the chief officer of a police force includes the person responsible for the direction of a body so mentioned. As to the Ministry of Defence Police see POLICE AND INVESTIGATORY POWERS vol 84 (2013) PARA 27. As to the British Transport Police see RAILWAYS AND TRAMWAYS vol 86 (2013) PARA 287.

For these purposes each of the following must also be treated as if it were a police force:

(a)   the Commissioners for Her Majesty's Revenue and Customs (and for this purpose a reference to the chief officer of a police force must be taken to be a reference to any one of the Commissioners) (s 113B(11)(a) (as so added));

(b)   the National Crime Agency (and for this purpose a reference to the chief officer of a police force must be taken to be a reference to the Director General of the Agency) (s 113B(11)(b) (as so added; amended by the Crime and Courts Act 2013 Sch 8 para 60)); and

(c)   such other department or body as is prescribed (and regulations may prescribe in relation to the department or body the person to whom a reference to the chief officer is to be taken to refer) (Police Act 1997 s 113B(11)(c) (as so added)).

The Police Act 1997 (Criminal Records) Regulations 2009, SI 2009/460, have been made for the purposes of the Police Act 1997 s 113B(11)(c). As to Her Majesty's Revenue and Customs see CUSTOMS AND EXCISE vol 31 (2012) PARA 921 et seq. As to the National Crime Agency see POLICE AND INVESTIGATORY POWERS vol 84 (2013) PARA 424.

4   See *R (on the application of X) v Chief Constable of the West Midlands Police* [2004] EWCA Civ 1068, [2005] 1 All ER 610, [2005] 1 WLR 65, in which it was held that:

(1)   information should be disclosed under these provisions even if it only might be true;

(2)   a chief officer is not required to give an opportunity for a person to make representations prior to his performing his statutory duty of disclosure;

(3)   making available, in accordance with the law, information which a responsible employer would want to know before making a decision as to whether to employ a person as a social worker is not contrary to the Convention for the Protection of Human Rights and Fundamental Freedoms (Rome, 4 November 1950; TS 71 (1953); Cmd 8969) (the European Convention on Human Rights) art 8.2 (right to respect for private and family life, home and correspondence: see RIGHTS AND FREEDOMS vol 88A (2013) PARAS 317–367); and

(4)   these provisions properly confer the responsibility of forming an opinion on the chief officer and, if he has properly formed the opinion that certain information might be relevant, it is not for the courts to interfere.

See also *R (on the application of L) v Metropolitan Police Comr* [2007] EWCA Civ 168, [2007] 4 All ER 128, [2008] 1 WLR 681 (non-criminal matters may be disclosed under these provisions if relevant to the applicant's suitability for a position caring or supervising children); *R (on the application of Pinnington) v Chief Constable of Thames Valley Police* [2008] EWHC 1870 (Admin), [2008] All ER (D) 405 (Jul) (in circumstances where the information disclosed by the police under an enhanced criminal record certificate is in dispute the question for the court is to decide whether the opinion formed by the police officer who had disclosed that information had been reasonably open to him); *R (on the application of C) v Chief Constable of Greater Manchester Police* [2011] EWCA Civ 175, [2011] 2 FLR 383 (police disclosure of sexual abuse allegation which had not resulted in conviction was disproportionate and unlawful); *R (on the application of A) v Chief Constable of Kent Constabulary* [2013] EWHC 424 (Admin), 131 BMLR 231 (disclosure of allegations made against burse unlawful and in breach of art 8 rights); *R (on the application of T) v Chief Constable of Greater Manchester* [2013] EWCA Civ 25, [2015] AC 49, [2013] 2 All ER 813 (statutory scheme requiring disclosure incompatible with claimants' rights).

5   Ie for the purpose described in the Police Act 1997 s 113B(2): see PARA 641.

6 Police Act 1997 s 113B(4)(a) (as added and amended: see note 3). The chief officer of police must comply with the request as soon as possible: s 119(2) (as so amended). Where, in connection with the provision of up-date information under s 116A (see PARA 645), the chief officer of a police force receives a request for information of the kind mentioned in s 113B(4), the chief officer of police must comply with it as soon as practicable: s 119(2A) (as so added). DBS may require the chief officer of a police force to make available such information as it may specify for the purpose of deciding whether to make a request to that chief officer under s 113B(4): s 119(1B) (added by the Safeguarding Vulnerable Groups Act 2006 Sch 9 para 14(1), (7); amended by the Protection of Freedoms Act 2012 Sch 9 para 110; and SI 2012/3006). No proceedings lie against DBS by reason of an inaccuracy in the information made available or provided to him in accordance with these requirements: Police Act 1997 s 119(5) (amended by SI 2012/3006). DBS must pay to the appropriate local policing body or police authority such fee as it thinks appropriate for information provided in accordance with this requirement: Police Act 1997 s 119(3) (as so amended; amended by the Greater London Authority Act 1999 Sch 27 para 112, Sch 34 Pt VII; the Criminal Justice and Police Act 2001 s 134(2); the Police Reform and Social Responsibility Act 2011 Sch 16 para 223; and SI 2012/3006). For the purposes of the Police Act 1997 s 119 references to a 'police force' include any body mentioned in s 113B(10)(a)–(i), (11) (see note 3), references to a 'chief officer' are construed accordingly; and in the case of such a body the reference in s 119(3) to the 'appropriate local policing body or police authority' must be construed as a reference to such body as is prescribed: s 119(6), (7)) (added by the Serious Organised Crime and Police Act 2005 s 165; Police Act 1997 s 119(7) amended by the Police Reform and Social Responsibility Act 2011 Sch 16 para 223).

7 Police Act 1997 s 113B(4)(b) (as added and amended: see note 3).

(ii) Obtaining Certificates

A. APPLICATION AND ISSUE

641. Applying for certificates. An application for a criminal record certificate[1], an enhanced criminal record certificate[2] or a criminal conviction certificate[3], and any associated request[4], must be made in a form and manner determined by DBS[5]. In order for a certificate to be issued an applicant must be aged 16 or over[6]. Evidence of identity is also required[7].

An application for a criminal record certificate or an enhanced criminal record certificate, other than one made in relation to Crown employment or a judicial appointment[8], must be accompanied by a statement by the registered person[9]. In the case of an application for a criminal record certificate the statement must be to the effect that the certificate[10] is required for the purposes of a question about spent convictions or cautions (an 'exempted question')[11]. In the case of an application for an enhanced criminal record certificate the statement must be to the effect that the certificate is required for the purposes[12] of an exempted question asked for a prescribed purpose[13]. In either case the application must be countersigned by a registered person[14] unless it is transmitted electronically[15].

An application for a criminal record certificate relating to a person's suitability for an appointment by or under the Crown must be accompanied by a statement by a Minister of the Crown that the certificate is required for the purposes of an exempted question asked in the course of considering the applicant's suitability for an appointment by or under the Crown[16], and an application for an enhanced criminal record certificate in relation to such an appointment or to a proposed judicial appointment must be accompanied by a statement by a Minister of the Crown, or a person nominated by a Minister of the Crown, that the certificate is required for the purposes of an exempted question asked in the course of considering the applicant's suitability for a judicial appointment or an appointment by or under the Crown to a position of such description as may be prescribed[17].

DBS may, in appropriate circumstances, treat an application for a criminal record certificate as an application for an enhanced criminal record certificate and vice versa[18].

1　As to the meaning of 'criminal record certificate' see PARA 637.

2　As to the meaning of 'enhanced criminal record certificate' see PARA 638.

3　As to the meaning of 'criminal conviction certificate' see PARA 636.

4　Ie a request under the Police Act 1997 s 116A(1) (see PARA 645), s 120AC(1) (see PARA 650) or s 120AD(2) (see PARA 645): Police Act 1997 s 125B(3) (s 125B added by the Policing and Crime Act 2009 s 97(1); Police Act 1997 s 125B(3) added by the Protection of Freedoms Act 2012 Sch 9 para 117).

5　Police Act 1997 s 125B(1) (as added (see note 4); amended by SI 2012/3006). Such a determination may, in particular, impose requirements about the form or manner in which an electronic application is to be signed or countersigned: Police Act 1997 s 125B(2) (as so added). As to DBS (ie the Disclosure and Barring Service) see PARA 638 note 4.

　　For the prescribed form for applications for criminal record certificates and enhanced criminal record certificates see the Police Act 1997 (Criminal Records) Regulations 2002, SI 2002/233, reg 3, Sch 2 (amended by SI 2003/137) and the Police Act 1997 (Criminal Records) (Welsh Language) Regulations 2003, SI 2003/117, reg 2, Schedule. Prior to submitting an application for a criminal record certificate or an enhanced criminal record certificate to DBS, a registered person must use all reasonable endeavours to ensure that the mandatory data fields are completed to the Secretary of State's satisfaction on the prescribed form and that the data supplied is accurate: Police Act 1997 (Criminal Records) (Registration) Regulations 2006, SI 2006/750, reg 7(e)(i) (amended by SI 2012/3006).

　　Any person who holds records of convictions or cautions for the use of police forces generally must make those records available to DBS for the purpose of enabling it to carry out a relevant function: Police Act 1997 s 119(1) (amended by the Criminal Justice and Police Act 2001 s 134; the Safeguarding Vulnerable Groups Act 2006 Sch 9 para 14; and SI 2012/3006). For these purposes 'relevant function' is a function of DBS: (1) in relation to any application for a certificate or for registration; (2) in relation to any request under the Police Act 1997 s 116A(1) (see PARA 645); and (3) in relation to the determination of whether a person should continue to be a registered person: Police Act 1997 s 119(8) (added by the Safeguarding Vulnerable Groups Act 2006 Sch 9 para 14(1), (7)(d); amended by the Protection of Freedoms Act 2012 Sch 9 para 110; and SI 2012/3006). As to references to a 'police force' and associated expressions see the Police Act 1997 s 119(6); and PARA 640 notes 3, 6.

　　The provisions of the Police Act 1997 relating to the issue, etc, of certificates are modified in their application to the Channel Islands and the Isle of Man: see the Police Act 1997 (Criminal Records) (Guernsey) Order 2009, SI 2009/3215 (amended SI 2012/1762); the Police Act 1997 (Criminal Records) (Jersey) Order 2010, SI 2010/765 (amended by SI 2012/2591); and the Police Act 1997 (Criminal Records) (Isle of Man) Order 2010, SI 2010/764 (amended by SI 2012/2598). As to the making of application see the Police Act 1997 (Criminal Records and Registration) (Jersey) Regulations 2010, SI 2010/1087 (amended by SI 2010/2701; SI 2011/717; SI 2012/2108; SI 2012/2668); the Police Act 1997 (Criminal Records and Registration) (Guernsey) Regulations 2009, SI 2009/3297 (amended by SI 2010/2700; SI 2011/718; SI 2012/2107; SI 2012/2666); and the Police Act 1997 (Criminal Records and Registration) (Isle of Man) Regulations 2011, SI 2011/2296 (amended by SI 2012/2109; SI 2012/2667).

6　See PARA 642.

7　See PARA 644.

8　In connection with applications made in relation to Crown employment or a judicial appointment see the text and notes 16–17.

9　Police Act 1997 ss 113A(2)(b), 113B(2)(b) (ss 113A, 113B added by the Serious Organised Crime and Police Act 2005 s 163(2); Police Act 1997 s 113B(2)(b) amended by the Safeguarding Vulnerable Groups Act 2006 Sch 9 para 14(1), (3)). As to the 'registered person' see PARAS 646–653. As to fees see PARA 642 note 7.

　　Prior to making a statement under the Police Act 1997 s 113A(2)(b) or s 113B(2)(b) in relation to an application for a criminal record certificate or an enhanced criminal record certificate, a registered person or his authorised agent must verify the identity of the applicant and in so doing comply with such conditions as DBS thinks fit and has notified to the registered person in writing: Police Act 1997 (Criminal Records) (Registration) Regulations 2006, SI 2006/750, reg 7(f) (amended by SI 2012/3006). Where a registered person uses the services of another person to verify the identity of applicants, the registered person must ensure the suitability of that person to conduct such checks, provide appropriate training and guidance to that person; and ensure that that person discharges his duties in accordance with such conditions as DBS thinks fit under the Police Act 1997 (Criminal Records) (Registration) Regulations 2006, SI 2006/750, reg 7(f): reg 7(g) (amended by SI 2012/3006).

Where a registered person has made a statement under the Police Act 1997 s 113A(2)(b) or s 113B(2)(b) in relation to an application for a criminal record certificate or an enhanced criminal record certificate any charges levied in connection with the services it provides under Pt 5 (ss 112–127) must be:

(1) notified in writing to DBS who may publish details of any such charges in such manner as he thinks fit (Police Act 1997 (Criminal Records) (Registration) Regulations 2006, SI 2006/750, reg 7(d)(i) (amended by SI 2012/3006)); and

(2) set out in any documentation the registered person publishes which relates to the services it provides under the Police Act 1997 Pt 5 (Police Act 1997 (Criminal Records) (Registration) Regulations 2006, SI 2006/750, reg 7(d)(ii)).

10 As to the meaning of 'certificate' see PARA 636 note 1.

11 Police Act 1997 s 113A(2)(b) (as added: see note 9). By virtue of ss 113A(6), 113B(9) (as so added; s 113A(6) amended by the Criminal Justice and Immigration Act 2008 s 50(1), (3)), 'exempted question' means a question which:

(1) so far as it applies to convictions, is a question in relation to which the Rehabilitation of Offenders Act 1974 s 4(2)(a) or (b) (effect of rehabilitation: see PARA 598) has been excluded by an order of the Secretary of State under s 4(4) (see PARA 614); and

(2) so far as it applies to cautions, is a question to which Sch 2 para 3(3) or (4) (see PARAS 598, 599) has been excluded by an order of the Secretary of State under Sch 2 para 4 (see PARA 614).

Prior to submitting an application for a criminal record certificate or an enhanced criminal record certificate to the Secretary of State, a registered person must use all reasonable endeavours to ensure that the certificate is requested for an exempted question or, as the case may be, a prescribed purpose: Police Act 1997 (Criminal Records) (Registration) Regulations 2006, SI 2006/750, reg 7(e)(ii) (amended by SI 2012/3006).

12 As to the purposes for which enhanced criminal record certificates may be required see PARA 639.

13 Police Act 1997 s 113B(2)(b) (as added amended: see note 9).

14 Police Act 1997 ss 113A(2)(a), 113B(2)(a) (as added: see note 9).

15 See the Police Act 1997 ss 113A(2A), 113B(2A) (as added (see note 9); further added by SI 2009/203; amended by SI 2012/3006), which provide that an application for a criminal record certificate or an enhanced criminal record certificate need not be countersigned by a registered person if it is transmitted to DBS electronically by a registered person who satisfies conditions determined by DBS and is transmitted in accordance with requirements determined by DBS. Any electronic system used by the registered person for the purposes of countersigning applications under the Police Act 1997 s 113A or s 113B must comply with such specifications as DBS may notify in writing to the registered body: Police Act 1997 (Criminal Records) (Registration) Regulations 2006, SI 2006/750, reg 7(k) (amended by SI 2012/3006). As to the registered body see PARA 646 et seq.

16 Police Act 1997 s 114(2). The provisions of s 113A(3)–(6) (see PARAS 637, 642), s 120AC (see PARA 650) and s 120AD (see PARA 645) apply in relation to s 114 with any necessary modifications: s 114(3) (amended by the Protection of Freedoms Act 2012 Sch 9 para 106).

17 Police Act 1997 s 116(2) (amended by the Criminal Justice Act 2003 Sch 35 paras 1, 5). The Police Act 1997 s 113B(3)–(11) (see PARAS 637–640), ss 113BA–113BC (see PARA 638), s 120AC and s 120AD apply in relation to s 116 with any necessary modifications: s 116(3) (amended by the Serious Organised Crime and Police Act 2005 Sch 14 paras 1, 3; and the Protection of Freedoms Act 2012 Sch 9 para 107).

18 See the Police Act 1997 ss 113A(5), 113B(7), (8) (as added (see note 9); amended by SI 2012/3006), which provide that DBS may treat an application for a criminal record certificate as an application for an enhanced criminal record certificate as an application for a criminal record certificate if:

(1) in its opinion the certificate is required for a prescribed purpose (see PARA 639);

(2) the registered person provides it with the statement required by the Police Act 1997 s 113B(2); and

(3) the applicant consents and pays to DBS the amount (if any) by which the fee payable in relation to an application for an enhanced criminal record certificate exceeds the fee paid in relation to the application for a criminal record certificate,

and that DBS may treat an application for an enhanced criminal record certificate as an application for a criminal record certificate if in its opinion the certificate is not required for a prescribed purpose (in which event DBS must refund to the applicant the amount (if any) by which the fee paid exceeds the fee payable for a criminal record certificate).

642. Duty of DBS to issue certificates. DBS[1] must issue a criminal record certificate[2] or an enhanced criminal record certificate[3] (including a criminal record certificate relating to Crown employment and an enhanced criminal record certificate relating to Crown employment or a judicial appointment), and must issue a criminal conviction certificate[4], to any individual who makes an application[5], provided that individual is aged 16 or over at the time he makes the application[6] and pays the prescribed fee in the prescribed manner[7].

1   Ie the Disclosure and Barring Service: see PARA 638 note 4.
2   As to the meaning of 'criminal record certificate' see PARA 637.
3   As to the meaning of 'enhanced criminal record certificate' see PARA 638.
4   As to the meaning of 'criminal conviction certificate' see PARA 636.
5   Police Act 1997 ss 112(1)(a), 113A(1)(a), 113B(1)(a), 114(1)(a), 116(1)(a) (ss 113A, 113B added by the Serious Organised Crime and Police Act 2005 s 163(2); Police Act 1997 ss 112(1)(aa), 113A(1)(aa), 113B(1)(aa), 114(1)(aa), 116(1)(aa), 125B(3) added by the Protection of Freedoms Act 2012 s 80(1), Sch 9 para 117; Police Act 1997 ss 112(1), (4), 113A(1), 113B(1), 114(1), 116(1), 125B(1) amended by SI 2012/3006).
    Applications, and associated requests (ie a request under the Police Act 1997 s 116A(1) (see PARA 645), s 120AC(1) (see PARA 650) or s 120AD(2) (see PARA 645)), must be made in a form and manner determined by DBS: Police Act 1997 s 125B(1), (3) (s 125B added by the Policing and Crime Act 2009 s 97(1); Police Act 1997 s 125B(1) as so amended, s 125B(3) as so added)). Such a determination may, in particular, impose requirements about the form or manner in which an electronic application is to be signed or countersigned: s 125B(2) (as so added).
    Where an applicant has received a criminal conviction certificate, DBS may refuse to issue another certificate to that applicant during such period as may be prescribed: Police Act 1997 s 112(4) (as so amended). At the date at which this volume states the law no period had been prescribed for these purposes.
6   Police Act 1997 ss 112(1)(aa), 113A(1)(aa), 113B(1)(aa), 114(1)(aa), 116(1)(aa) (as added: see note 5).
7   Police Act 1997 ss 112(1)(b), 113A(1)(b), 113B(1)(b), 114(1)(b), 116(1)(b) (ss 113A, 113B as added: see note 5). A fee of £26 is payable in respect of a criminal record certificate and a fee of £44 is payable in respect of an enhanced criminal record certificate (see the Police Act 1997 (Criminal Records) Regulations 2002, SI 2002/233, reg 4(a), (b) (reg 4 substituted by SI 2003/1418; SI 2006/748; amended by SI 2009/2428; SI 2011/719)), although no fee is payable in relation to an application made by a volunteer (Police Act 1997 (Criminal Records) Regulations 2002, SI 2002/233, reg 4 (as so substituted)). The fee payable in relation to an application under the Police Act 1997 s 113A or s 113B which is accompanied by a statement under s 113A(2)(b) or s 113B(2)(b) (see PARA 641) must be invoiced by DBS and is payable on account within 15 days of the invoice date: Police Act 1997 (Criminal Records) (Registration) Regulations 2006, SI 2006/750, reg 7(c) (amended by SI 2012/3006). In connection with fees under these provisions see also the Police Act 1997 (Criminal Records) (Fees) Order 2004, SI 2004/1007 (amended by SI 2013/1196).
    At the date at which this volume states the law no fee had been prescribed in respect of criminal conviction certificates.
    'Volunteer' means a person engaged in an activity which involves spending time, unpaid (except for travel and other approved out-of-pocket expenses), doing something which aims to benefit some third party other than or in addition to a close relative: Police Act 1997 (Criminal Records) Regulations 2002, SI 2002/233, reg 2. If an application is made by a volunteer the registered person must, prior to submitting the application, use all reasonable endeavours to ensure that the applicant falls within this definition: Police Act 1997 (Criminal Records) (Registration) Regulations 2006, SI 2006/750, reg 7(e)(iii). As to the 'registered person' see PARAS 646–653.
    Anything authorised or required by any provision of the Police Act 1997 Pt V (ss 112–127) to be prescribed must be prescribed by regulations made by the Secretary of State: s 125(1).

643. Correction of inaccuracies. Where an applicant[1] for a criminal record certificate[2], an enhanced criminal record certificate[3] or a criminal conviction certificate[4] believes that the information contained in the certificate[5] is inaccurate, he may make an application in writing to DBS[6] for a new certificate[7]. Where a person other than the applicant believes that the information contained in such a certificate is inaccurate he may make an application in writing to DBS for a decision as to whether or not the information is inaccurate[8]. Where a person believes that the wrong up-date information[9] has been given[10] in relation to the person's certificate, he may make an application in writing to DBS for corrected up-date information[11]. DBS must consider any such application; and where it is of the opinion that the information in the certificate is inaccurate, or that the wrong up-date information has been given, it must issue a new certificate or (as the case may be) corrected up-date information[12].

1   Ie under the Police Act 1997 ss 112–116: see PARA 641 et seq.
2   As to the meaning of 'criminal record certificate' see PARA 637.
3   As to the meaning of 'enhanced criminal record certificate' see PARA 638.
4   As to the meaning of 'criminal conviction certificate' see PARA 636.
5   As to the meaning of 'certificate' see PARA 636 note 1.
6   Ie the Disclosure and Barring Service: see PARA 638 note 4.
7   Police Act 1997 s 117(1) (amended by SI 2012/3006). Evidence of identity is required: see PARA 644.
8   Police Act 1997 s 117(1A) (s 117(1A), (1B), (2A) added, s 117(2) amended, by the Protection of Freedoms Act 2012 s 82(4), Sch 9 para 108; Police Act 1997 s 117(1A), (1B), (2) amended by SI 2012/3006).
9   As to the meaning of 'up-date information' see the Police Act 1997 s 116A; and PARA 645 note 3 (definition applied by s 117(2A) (as added: see note 8)).
10   Ie under the Police Act 1997 s 116A (see PARA 645).
11   Police Act 1997 s 117(1B) (as added and amended: see note 8). 'Corrected up-date information', in relation to a certificate, means information which includes information that the wrong up-date information was given in relation to the certificate on a particular date and new up-date information in relation to the certificate: s 117(2A) (as added: see note 8).
12   Police Act 1997 s 117(2) (as added and amended: see note 8).

644. Evidence of identity. DBS[1] may refuse to issue a criminal conviction certificate[2], a criminal record certificate[3] or an enhanced criminal record certificate[4], or consider an application for an updated certificate[5], for a corrected or replacement certificate[6], for the removal of irrelevant information from a certificate[7] or for a person's registration as a countersignatory[8], unless the application is supported by such evidence of identity as DBS may require[9]. In particular, DBS may refuse to issue a certificate or consider an application for a replacement unless the applicant has his fingerprints taken at the prescribed place and in the prescribed manner[10] and pays the prescribed fee to such person as may be prescribed[11]; and as from a day to be appointed DBS may[12], in particular, refuse to issue a certificate to a person unless the application is supported by prescribed evidence that the person's identity has been verified by a third person determined by DBS[13].

1   Ie the Disclosure and Barring Service: see PARA 638 note 4.
2   As to the meaning of 'criminal conviction certificate' see PARA 636.
3   As to the meaning of 'criminal record certificate' see PARA 637.
4   As to the meaning of 'enhanced criminal record certificate' see PARA 638.
5   Ie under the Police Act 1997 s 116A(4)(a) or (5)(a): see PARA 645.
6   Ie under the Police Act 1997 s 117: see PARA 643.
7   Ie under the Police Act 1997 s 117A: see PARA 655.
8   Ie under the Police Act 1997 s 120: see PARA 647.
9   Police Act 1997 s 118(1) (s 118(1) amended, s 118(2A) added, by the Serious Organised Crime and Police Act 2005 s 164; Police Act 1997 s 118(1) further amended, ss 118(4), 119(4) amended, by the Protection of Freedoms Act 2012 Sch 9 paras 109, 110; Police Act 1997 ss 118(1), (2), (2ZA), (2A), 119(4) further amended SI 2012/3006). For the purpose of verifying evidence of identity supplied in pursuance of these provisions DBS may obtain such information

as it thinks is appropriate from data held by the United Kingdom Passport Agency, the Driver and Vehicle Licensing Agency, Driver and Vehicle Licensing Northern Ireland, the Secretary of State in connection with keeping records of national insurance numbers or such other persons or for such purposes as is prescribed: Police Act 1997 s 118(2A) (as so added). At the date at which this volume states the law no additional persons or purposes had been prescribed.

10   Police Act 1997 s 118(2)(a) (as amended: see note 9). Regulations dealing with the taking of fingerprints may make provision requiring their destruction in specified circumstances and by specified persons: s 118(3).

Where DBS requires an application to be supported by evidence of identity in the form of fingerprints he must notify the applicant of his requirement and of the fact that any fingerprints taken from the applicant and provided to DBS in pursuance of the requirement may be the subject of a speculative search within the meaning of the Police and Criminal Evidence Act 1984 Pt V (ss 53–65) (see POLICE AND INVESTIGATORY POWERS vol 84A (2013) PARAS 575–579): Police Act 1997 (Criminal Records) Regulations 2002, SI 2002/233, reg 11(1), (9) (reg 11(1), (2), (2A), (3), (4) amended by SI 2012/3006). An applicant in receipt of such notification must notify DBS of whether he wishes to proceed with his application and, if so, must notify DBS that he consents to the taking of his fingerprints and either that he proposes to attend at a police station (the 'specified police station') for the purpose of having his fingerprints taken or that he proposes to have his fingerprints taken by the registered person countersigning or acting as the registered person in relation to his application (although a person can only have his fingerprints taken by the registered person with the consent of DBS): Police Act 1997 (Criminal Records) Regulations 2002, SI 2002/233, reg 11(2), (2A) (reg 11(2) amended, reg 11(2A) added, by SI 2009/460; as so amended). As to the 'registered person' see PARAS 646–653. DBS may require the police officer in charge of the specified police station, or any other police station it reasonably determines, to take the applicant's fingerprints at the specified station at such reasonable time as the officer may direct and notify the applicant: Police Act 1997 (Criminal Records) Regulations 2002, SI 2002/233, reg 11(3) (as so amended).

Fingerprints taken pursuant to these provisions must be destroyed as soon as is practicable after the identity of the applicant is established to the satisfaction of DBS, and where fingerprints are destroyed any copies of the fingerprints must also be destroyed and any chief officer of police controlling access to computer data relating to the fingerprints must make access to the data impossible as soon as it is practicable to do so: reg 11(4), (5) (as so amended). Any applicant who asks to be allowed to witness the destruction of his fingerprints or copies of them has a right to witness it: reg 11(6). If access to computer data relating to fingerprints is not destroyed and the applicant to whose fingerprints the data relates asks for a certificate that it has been complied with, such a certificate must be issued to him, not later than the end of the period of three months beginning with the day on which he asks for it, by the responsible chief officer of police (ie the chief officer of police in whose area the computer data were put on to the computer) or a person authorised by him or on his behalf for these purposes: reg 11(7), (9).

In the case of an applicant under the age of 18 years the consent of the applicant's parent or guardian to the taking of the applicant's fingerprints is also required: reg 11(8).

Any person who holds records of fingerprints for the use of police forces generally must make those records available to DBS for the purpose of enabling it to carry out its functions in relation to any application for a certificate or for an updated certificate or for registration or the determination of whether a person should continue to be a registered person: Police Act 1997 s 119(4) (amended by the Criminal Justice and Police Act 2001 s 134; as so amended). As to references to a 'police force' see the Police Act 1997 s 119(6); and PARA 640 notes 3, 6. See also s 119(5); and PARA 640 note 6.

11   Police Act 1997 s 118(2)(b) (as amended: see note 9). Regulations prescribing a fee for the purposes of s 118(2)(b) must make provision for a refund in cases of an application under s 117 (see PARA 643) or s 117A (see PARA 655) where a new certificate is issued: s 118(4) (as so amended). At the date at which this volume states the law no fee had been prescribed.

12   Ie by virtue of the Police Act 1997 s 118(1) (see the text and notes 1–9).

13   Police Act 1997 s 118(2ZA) (prospectively added by the Policing and Crime Act 2009 s 95; as amended (see note 9)). At the date at which this volume states the law no day had been appointed for the coming into force of this provision. This provision applies whether or not the third person charges a fee for the verification: Police Act 1997 s 118(2ZA) (as so prospectively added).

645. Updating certificates. DBS[1] must, on the request of a relevant person[2], give up-date information[3] to that person about a criminal conviction certificate, a criminal record certificate or an enhanced criminal record certificate, which is subject to up-date arrangements[4]. This is subject to the proviso that DBS may impose conditions about the information to be supplied in connection with such a request for the purpose of enabling the Secretary of State to decide whether the person is a relevant person[5] and any other information to be supplied in connection with such a request[6].

DBS, by notice given in writing, may require a person who has a certificate which is subject to up-date arrangements under these provisions to attend at a place and time specified in the notice to provide fingerprints for the sole purpose of enabling DBS to verify whether information in the possession of DBS that DBS considers may be relevant to the person's certificate does relate to that person[7].

1   Ie the Disclosure and Barring Service: see PARA 638 note 4.

2   'Relevant person' means (by virtue of the Police Act 1997 s 116A(11) (ss 116A, 118(3A), (3B), 120AD added by the Protection of Freedoms Act 2012 ss 79(3), 83, Sch 9 para 109)):
    (1)   in relation to a criminal conviction certificate (see PARA 636), the individual whose certificate it is or any person authorised by the individual;
    (2)   in relation to a criminal record certificate (see PARA 637), the individual whose certificate it is or any person who is authorised by the individual and is seeking the information for the purposes of an exempted question; and
    (3)   in relation to an enhanced criminal record certificate (see PARA 638), the individual whose certificate it is or any person who is authorised by the individual and is seeking the information for the purposes of an exempted question asked for a purpose prescribed under the Police Act 1997 s 113B(2)(b) (see PARA 641).
    As to the meaning of 'exempted question' see s 113A; and PARA 641 (definition applied by s 116A(11) (as so added)). As to the form and manner of making requests see s 125B(3); and PARA 641.

3   For these purposes 'up-date information' means:
    (1)   in relation to a criminal conviction certificate or a criminal record certificate, information that there is no information recorded in central records which would be included in a new certificate but is not included in the current certificate (Police Act 1997 ss 116A(8)(a)(i), 120AD(4) (as added: see note 2)) or advice to apply for a new certificate or (as the case may be) request another person to apply for such a certificate (s 116A(8)(a)(ii) (as so added));
    (2)   in relation to an enhanced criminal record certificate which includes suitability information relating to children or vulnerable adults, information that there is no information recorded in central records, no information of the kind mentioned in s 113B(4) (see PARA 640), and no information of the kind mentioned in s 113BA(2) (see PARA 638) or (as the case may be) s 113BB(2) (see PARA 638), which would be included in a new certificate but is not included in the current certificate (s 116A(8)(b)(i) (as so added)) or advice to apply for a new certificate or (as the case may be) request another person to apply for such a certificate (s 116A(8)(b)(ii) (as so added)); and
    (3)   in relation to any other enhanced criminal record certificate information that there is no information recorded in central records, nor any information of the kind mentioned in s 113B(4), which would be included in a new certificate but is not included in the current certificate (s 116A(8)(c)(i) (as so added)) or advice to apply for a new certificate or (as the case may be) request another person to apply for such a certificate (s 116A(8)(c)(ii) (as so added)).
    As to the meaning of 'central records' see s 113A; and PARA 637 note 4 (definition applied by s 116A(11) (as so added)). If up-date information is given under s 116A(8)(a)(i), (8)(b)(i) or (8)(c)(i) and the certificate to which that information relates is one which: (a) in the case of a criminal conviction certificate, states that there are no convictions or conditional cautions of the applicant recorded in central records; (b) in the case of a criminal record certificate, is as described in s 120AC(3) (see PARA 650); or (c) in the case of an enhanced criminal record certificate, is as described in section 120AC(4) (see PARA 650), the up-date information must include that fact: s 116A(9), (10) (as so added).
    If:
    (a)   DBS gives up-date information in relation to a criminal record certificate or enhanced criminal record certificate (s 120AD(1)(a) (as so added; ss 116A(1), (2), (4)(a), (c), (5)(a), (c), (7), 118(3A), (3B), 120AD(1)(a), (2)(a), (b) amended by SI 2012/3006));

(b) the up-date information is advice to apply for a new certificate or (as the case may be) request another person to apply for such a certificate (Police Act 1997 s 120AD(1)(b) (as so added)); and

(c) the person whose certificate it is in respect of which the up-date information is given applies for a new criminal record certificate or (as the case may be) enhanced criminal record certificate (s 120AD(1)(c) (as so added)),

DBS must, in response to a request made within the prescribed period (see below) by the person who is acting as the registered person in relation to the application, send to that person a copy of any certificate issued in response to the application if the registered person:

(i) has countersigned the application or transmitted it to DBS under s 113A(2A) or s 113B(2A) (s 120AD(2)(a) (as so added and amended));

(ii) has informed DBS that the applicant for the new certificate has not, within such period as may be prescribed, sent a copy of it to a person of such description as may be prescribed (s 120AD(2)(b) (as so added and amended)); and

(iii) no prescribed circumstances apply (s 120AD(2)(c) (as so added)).

The power under s 120AD(2)(b) to prescribe a description of person may be exercised to describe the registered person or any other person: s 120AD(3) (as so added). A person acting as a registered person in relation to an application of a type described in s 120AD(1)(c) may only be issued with a copy of a criminal record certificate or (as the case may be) enhanced criminal record certificate issued further to that application where a request is made not less than 28 days from the date of issue of the certificate (Police Act 1997 (Criminal Records) Regulations 2002, SI 2002/233, reg 7(a) (reg 7 added by SI 2013/1194)), a request is made not more than 3 months from the date of issue of the certificate or, where a dispute is raised under the Police Act 1997 s 117 (see PARA 643) or s 117A (see PARA 655) in respect of that certificate, the conclusion of that dispute (Police Act 1997 (Criminal Records) Regulations 2002, SI 2002/233, reg 7(b) (as so added)), the certificate is not the subject of a pending review under the Police Act 1997 s 117 (disputes about accuracy of certificates) (Police Act 1997 (Criminal Records) Regulations 2002, SI 2002/233, reg 7(c) (as so added)), the certificate is not the subject of a pending review under the Police Act 1997 s 117A (other disputes about s 113B(4) information) (Police Act 1997 (Criminal Records) Regulations 2002, SI 2002/233, reg 7(d) (as so added)), and any statement made by the registered person in respect of the application for the certificate described in the Police Act 1997 s 120AD(1)(a) (see PARA 645) continues to apply (Police Act 1997 (Criminal Records) Regulations 2002, SI 2002/233, reg 7(e) (as so added)).

As to the meaning of 'registered person' see PARA 646 note 1; and as to 'acting as the registered person' see PARA 646.

4 Police Act 1997 s 116A(1) (as added and amended: see notes 2, 3). For these purposes a certificate is subject to up-date arrangements if condition A, B or C below is met and the arrangements have not ceased to have effect in accordance with a notice given under s 118(3B) (see note 7): s 116A(3) (as so added).

Condition A is that:

(1) the individual who applied for the certificate made an application at the same time to DBS for the certificate to be subject to up-date arrangements (s 116A(4)(a) (as so added and amended));

(2) the individual has paid in the prescribed manner any prescribed fee (s 116A(4)(b) (as so added));

(3) DBS has granted the application for the certificate to be subject to up-date arrangements (s 116A(4)(c) (as so added and amended)); and

(4) the period of 12 months beginning with the date on which the grant comes into force has not expired (s 116A(4)(d) (as so added)).

Condition B is that:

(a) the individual whose certificate it is has made an application to DBS to renew or (as the case may be) further renew unexpired up-date arrangements in relation to the certificate (s 116A(5)(a) (as so added and amended));

(b) the individual has paid in the prescribed manner any prescribed fee (s 116A(5)(b) (as so added))

(c) DBS has granted the application (s 116A(5)(c) (as so added and amended));

(d) the grant has come into force on the expiry of the previous up-date arrangements (s 116A(5)(d) (as so added)); and

(e) the period of 12 months beginning with the date on which the grant has come into force has not expired (s 116A(5)(e) (as so added)).

Condition C is that:

(i) the certificate was issued under s 117(2) (see PARA 643) or s 117A(5)(b) (see PARA 655) (s 116A(6)(a) (as so added)); and

(ii)   the certificate which it superseded was subject to up-date arrangements immediately
before it was superseded (s 116A(6)(b)(i) (as so added)) and would still be subject to
those arrangements had it not been superseded (s 116A(6)(b)(ii) (as so added)).

DBS must not grant an application as mentioned in s 116A(4)(c) or (5)(c) unless any fee
prescribed under s 116A(4)(b) or (as the case may be) s 116A(5)(b) has been paid in the manner
so prescribed: s 116A(7) (as so added and amended)). The fees payable in relation to an
application for a certificate to be subject to up-date arrangements under s 116A are £13 in the
case of a fee as mentioned in s 116A(4)(b) and £13 in the case of a fee as mentioned in
s 116A(5)(b): Police Act 1997 (Criminal Records) Regulations 2002, SI 2002/233, reg 6(1)
(reg 6 added by SI 2013/1194). However no fee is payable in relation to an application made by
a volunteer or an application for a criminal conviction certificate, a criminal record certificate or
an enhanced criminal record certificate to be subject to up-date arrangements where the person
making the request already holds any such a certificate that is subject to up-date arrangements:
Police Act 1997 (Criminal Records) Regulations 2002, SI 2002/233, reg 6(2) (as so added).

5   Police Act 1997 s 116A(2)(a) (as added and amended: see notes 2, 3).
6   Police Act 1997 s 116A(2)(b) (as added and amended: see notes 2, 3).
7   Police Act 1997 s 118(3A) (as added and amended: see notes 2, 3). If a person fails to comply
with a requirement imposed under s 118(3A), DBS by notice given in writing may inform that
person that, from a date specified in the notice, the person's certificate is to cease to be subject to
up-date arrangements: s 118(3B) (as so added and amended).

B. REGISTRATION OF COUNTERSIGNATORIES

646.   Acting as countersignatory. A person acts as the 'registered person'[1] in
relation to an application for a criminal record certificate[2] or an enhanced
criminal record certificate[3] if he countersigns the application[4] or transmits it[5] to
DBS[6].

1   For the purposes of the Police Act 1997 Pt V (ss 112–127) a 'registered person' is a person who
is listed in a register to be maintained by DBS for the purposes of Pt V: see s 120(1) (ss 113A(9),
113B(12), 120(1) amended by SI 2012/3006); and PARAS 647–653. As to DBS (ie the Disclosure
and Barring Service) see PARA 638 note 4.
2   As to the meaning of 'criminal record certificate' see PARA 637.
3   As to the meaning of 'enhanced criminal record certificate' see PARA 638.
4   Ie in accordance with the Police Act 1997 s 113A(2) or, as the case may be, s 113B(2): see PARA
641.
5   Ie in accordance with the Police Act 1997 s 113A(2A) or, as the case may be, s 113B(2A): see
PARA 641.
6   Police Act 1997 ss 113A(9), 113B(12) (ss 113A, 113B added by the Serious Organised Crime
and Police Act 2005 s 163(2); Police Act 1997 ss 113A(9), 113B(12) added by SI 2009/203; as
amended (see note 1)).

647.   Inclusion in the register of countersignatories. DBS must[1] include in the
register of countersignatories[2] any person who:
(1)   applies to it in writing to be registered[3];
(2)   is either:
    (a)   a body corporate or unincorporate[4];
    (b)   a person who is appointed to an office by virtue of any enactment
            and who, in the case of an individual, is aged 18 or over[5]; or
    (c)   an individual aged 18 or over who employs others in the course of
            a business[6];
(3)   satisfies DBS that it is likely to ask exempted questions[7] or is likely to
        act as the registered person[8] in relation to applications[9] for criminal
        record certificates[10] or enhanced criminal record certificates[11] at the
        request of bodies or individuals asking exempted questions[12]; and
(4)   where the applicant is a person other than a body applying for
        registration, satisfies DBS that he is likely to ask exempted questions[13].
Evidence of identity may also be required[14].

A person's registration in the register of countersignatories is conditional upon:

(i)   payment of the requisite fees and notification of specified charges[15];

(ii)   the registered person using all reasonable endeavours to ensure that the application is in order[16];

(iii)   the applicant's identity being properly verified[17];

(iv)   compliance with the code of practice[18];

(v)   the provision of any information relating to his eligibility and suitability[19];

(vi)   the notification of any change to the details in the information recorded on the register[20];

(vii) the number of applications dealt with by a registered person not being fewer than 100 in any 12 month period[21]; and

(viii) compliance with the requirements concerning powers of entry and inspection[22],

and DBS may remove from the register any registered person who fails to comply with these conditions[23].

1   Ie subject to regulations under the Police Act 1997 s 120ZA (further provision about registration: see below) and under s 120AA (refusal, cancellation and suspension of registration: see PARA 652) and to s 120A (refusal and cancellation of registration: see PARA 651): s 120(2), (2A) (s 120(2) substituted, ss 120ZA, 120AA added, by the Criminal Justice Act 2003 Sch 35 paras 1, 6, 7, 9; Police Act 1997 s 120(2), (4)(b), (c) amended, s 120(2A) added, by the Protection of Freedoms Act 2012 s 80(2), Sch 9 para 112; Police Act 1997 ss 120(2), 120ZA(2)(e), (3), (4)(b), (5), (6), 120AA(3) amended by SI 2012/3006). Regulations under the Police Act 1997 s 120ZA may in particular make provision for:

    (1)   the payment of fees (s 120ZA(1), (2)(a) (as so added));

    (2)   the information to be included in the register (s 120ZA(2)(b) (as so added));

    (3)   the registration of any person to be subject to conditions (s 120ZA(2)(c) (as so added)): provision which may be made by virtue of this head includes provision for the registration or continued registration of any person to be subject to prescribed conditions or, if the regulations so provide, such conditions as DBS thinks fit (s 120ZA(3)(a) (as so added and amended)) and for DBS to vary or revoke those conditions (s 120ZA(3)(b) (as so added and amended)), and the conditions so imposed may in particular include conditions requiring a registered person, before acting as the registered person in relation to an application at an individual's request, to verify the identity of that individual in the prescribed manner (s 120ZA(4)(a) (as so added; ss 120(5)(b), 120ZA(2)(d), (4)(a), (b) amended by SI 2009/203)), conditions requiring an application under the Police Act 1997 s 113A or s 113B to be transmitted by electronic means to DBS by the person who acts as the registered person in relation to the application (s 120ZA(4)(b) (as so added and amended; amended by the Serious Organised Crime and Police Act 2005 Sch 14 para 7)), and conditions requiring a registered person to comply with any code of practice for the time being in force under the Police Act 1997 s 122 (see PARA 654) (s 120ZA(4)(c) (as so added));

    (4)   the nomination by a body corporate or unincorporate (s 120ZA(2)(d)(i) (as so added)), or a person appointed to an office by virtue of any enactment (s 120ZA(2)(d)(ii) (as so added)), of the individuals authorised to act for it or, as the case may be, him in relation to the countersigning of applications under Pt V (ss 112–127) or the transmitting of applications under s 113A(2A) or s 113B(2A) (s 120ZA(2)(d) (as so added and amended)); and

    (5)   the refusal by DBS, on such grounds as may be specified in or determined under the regulations, to accept or to continue to accept the nomination of a person as so authorised (s 120ZA(2)(e) (as so added and amended)).

    As to DBS (ie the Disclosure and Barring Service) see PARA 638 note 4.

2   Ie the register maintained by DBS for the purposes of the Police Act 1997 Pt V: see s 120(1).

3   Police Act 1997 s 120(2)(a) (as substituted and amended: see note 1). The fee payable by a person on application for inclusion in the register is £300: Police Act 1997 (Criminal Records) (Registration) Regulations 2006, SI 2006/750, reg 5. Persons holding records of convictions or

cautions for the use of police forces generally must make those records available to DBS for these purposes: see the Police Act 1997 s 119(1); and PARA 641.

4 Police Act 1997 s 120(2)(b), (4)(a) (s 120(2)(b) as substituted: see note 1).

5 Police Act 1997 s 120(4)(b) (as amended: see note 1).

6 Police Act 1997 s 120(4)(c) (as amended: see note 1).

7 Police Act 1997 s 120(5)(a) (as amended: see note 1). As to the meaning of 'exempted question' see the Police Act 1997 s 113A; and PARA 641 (definition applied by the Police Act 1997 s 120(7) (s 120(5)(b), (7) amended by the Serious Organised Crime and Police Act 2005 Sch 14 para 6)).

8 As to the meaning of 'act as the registered person' see PARA 646.

9 Ie applications under the Police Act 1997 s 113A or s 113B: see PARA 641.

10 As to the meaning of 'criminal record certificate' see PARA 637.

11 As to the meaning of 'enhanced criminal record certificate' see PARA 638.

12 Police Act 1997 s 120(5)(b) (as amended: see notes 1, 7).

13 Police Act 1997 s 120(6) (as amended: see note 1).

14 See the Police Act 1997 s 118; and PARA 644.

15 The requisite fees are those payable under the Police Act 1997 (Criminal Records) (Registration) Regulations 2006, SI 2006/750, reg 5 (see note 3), reg 6 (see PARA 649), the fees and charges payable and notifiable in relation to an application under the Police Act 1997 s 113A or s 113B which is accompanied by a statement under s 113A(2)(b) or s 113B(2)(b) (see PARA 641), and any payments incurred for any applications knowingly submitted after DBS removing or suspending the registered person from the register (see PARAS 651, 652): Police Act 1997 (Criminal Records) (Registration) Regulations 2006, SI 2006/750, reg 7(a)–(d), (m) (regs 7(d), (e)–(g), (j)–(m), 9 amended by SI 2012/3006).

16 Police Act 1997 (Criminal Records) (Registration) Regulations 2006, SI 2006/750, reg 7(e), (k) (as amended: see note 15). As to the registered person's duties in this regard see reg 7(e)(i)–(iii); and PARAS 641, 642.

17 Police Act 1997 (Criminal Records) (Registration) Regulations 2006, SI 2006/750, reg 7(f), (g) (as amended: see note 15). As to the registered person's duties in this regard see PARA 641 note 9.

18 Police Act 1997 (Criminal Records) (Registration) Regulations 2006, SI 2006/750, reg 7(h). As to the code of practice see the Police Act 1997 s 122; and PARA 654.

19 See the Police Act 1997 (Criminal Records) (Registration) Regulations 2006, SI 2006/750, reg 7(i) (as amended: see note 15); and PARA 651.

20 See the Police Act 1997 (Criminal Records) (Registration) Regulations 2006, SI 2006/750, reg 7(j) (as amended: see note 15); and PARA 649.

21 See the Police Act 1997 (Criminal Records) (Registration) Regulations 2006, SI 2006/750, reg 7(l) (as amended: see note 15) (amended by SI 2009/203); and PARA 652.

22 See the Police Act 1997 (Criminal Records) (Registration) Regulations 2006, SI 2006/750, reg 8(1); and PARA 727.

23 Police Act 1997 s 120AA(2)(c), (3)(b) (as added and amended: see note 1); Police Act 1997 (Criminal Records) (Registration) Regulations 2006, SI 2006/750, reg 9 (as amended: see note 15). DBS may also suspend such a person's registration for such period not exceeding six months as DBS thinks fit: Police Act 1997 s 120AA(3)(a) (as so added and amended). The powers of suspension and removal are subject to s 120AB: see PARA 652.

648. Nomination of authorised individuals. A body or statutory office-holder[1] applying for registration in the register of countersignatories[2] must submit with the application the names of the individuals authorised to act for the body or statutory office-holder in relation to the countersigning or transmission of such applications[3], and a registered body or person[4] who is a statutory office-holder must submit to DBS[5] the names of any individuals so authorised after the registration of the body or the statutory office-holder, whether or not in substitution for any name previously submitted[6]. DBS may refuse to accept, or to continue to accept, the nomination of an individual as so authorised if in its opinion that individual is not a suitable person to have access to information[7] which has become, or is likely to become, available to him as a result of the registration of the body or the statutory office-holder which nominated him[8], or if the maximum number of names for that registered body or statutory office-holder are already registered[9].

1   'Statutory office-holder' means a person appointed to an office by virtue of any enactment: Police Act 1997 (Criminal Records) (Registration) Regulations 2006, SI 2006/750, reg 2.
2   Ie registration under the Police Act 1997 s 120 (see PARA 647): Police Act 1997 (Criminal Records) (Registration) Regulations 2006, SI 2006/750, reg 4(1) (regs 4(1), 10(1) amended by SI 2009/203). As to acting as countersignatory see PARA 646.
3   Police Act 1997 (Criminal Records) (Registration) Regulations 2006, SI 2006/750, reg 4(1) (as amended: see note 2). As to the countersigning and transmission of applications see the Police Act 1997 ss 113A, 113B; and PARA 641.
4   As to the registration of bodies for these purposes see PARA 648. As to the meaning of 'registered person' see PARA 646 note 1.
5   Ie the Disclosure and Barring Service: see PARA 638 note 4.
6   Police Act 1997 (Criminal Records) (Registration) Regulations 2006, SI 2006/750, reg 4(2) (regs 4(2)–(5), 10(1)–(3) amended by SI 2012/3006).
7   In determining for these purposes whether an individual is a suitable person to have access to any information DBS may have regard, in particular, to the matters specified in the Police Act 1997 s 120A(3) (see PARA 651): Police Act 1997 (Criminal Records) (Registration) Regulations 2006, SI 2006/750, reg 4(4) (as amended: see note 6).
8   Police Act 1997 (Criminal Records) (Registration) Regulations 2006, SI 2006/750, reg 4(3) (as amended: see note 6). Where DBS refuses to accept, or to continue to accept, the nomination of an individual under these provisions it must notify the body or the statutory office-holder concerned, and that body or statutory office-holder may submit the name of another individual in substitution: reg 4(5) (as so amended).
9   Police Act 1997 (Criminal Records) (Registration) Regulations 2006, SI 2006/750, reg 10(1) (as amended: see notes 2, 6). For this purpose the maximum number of names for a registered body or statutory office-holder is that specified administratively DBS: reg 10(2) (as so amended). Where more than the maximum number of names have been registered, DBS may remove from the register such number of names as is necessary to bring the registered body's or statutory office-holder's number of registered names to the maximum number permitted: reg 10(3) (as so amended).

649. Information to be included in the register. The register of countersignatories[1] must include the following information:

(1)   the name and address of each registered person[2] and any telephone or facsimile number or electronic mailing address which has been notified to DBS for communication purposes[3];

(2)   the date on which the name of that person was first listed in the register[4];

(3)   the number assigned to that person on being so listed[5];

(4)   the nature of the exempted questions[6], if any, that that person is likely to ask[7];

(5)   in the case of a registered body[8]:

    (a)   whether that body is likely to countersign applications[9] at the request of bodies or individuals asking exempted questions and, if so, the nature of those questions[10];

    (b)   the name and address of any individual for the time being nominated to act for a registered body in relation to the countersigning of applications under these provisions[11] and any telephone or facsimile number or electronic mailing address which has been notified to DBS for communication purposes[12];

    (c)   the date on which the name of that individual was first listed in the register[13];

    (d)   the number assigned to that individual on being so listed[14]; and

    (e)   a specimen of the signature of that individual[15];

(6)   in the case of each registered person who is a statutory office holder[16]:

    (a)   the name and address of any individual for the time being nominated[17] as being authorised to act for the statutory office holder in relation to the countersigning or transmission of applications[18] and any telephone or facsimile number or electronic mailing address which has been notified to DBS for communications purposes[19];

(b)   the date on which the name of that individual was first listed on the register[20];

(c)   the number assigned to that individual on being listed[21]; and

(d)   a specimen of the signature of that individual[22]; and

(7)   in respect of each registered person other than a body, a specimen of any signature which will be used by that person for the purposes of countersigning[23] applications[24].

Any change to the details in the information recorded on the register must be notified to DBS[25].

1   Ie the register maintained by DBS for the purposes of the Police Act 1997 Pt 5 (ss 112–127) (see PARA 646 et seq): Police Act 1997 (Criminal Records) (Registration) Regulations 2006, SI 2006/750, reg 2 (regs 2, 3(1)(a), (e)(ii), (f)(i), 7(b), (j) amended by SI 2012/3006). As to acting as countersignatory see PARA 646; and as to inclusion in the register of countersignatories see PARA 647. As to DBS (ie the Disclosure and Barring Service) see PARA 638 note 4.

2   As to the meaning of 'registered person' see PARA 646 note 1.

3   Police Act 1997 (Criminal Records) (Registration) Regulations 2006, SI 2006/750, reg 3(1)(a) (as amended: see note 1).

4   Police Act 1997 (Criminal Records) (Registration) Regulations 2006, SI 2006/750, reg 3(1)(b).

5   Police Act 1997 (Criminal Records) (Registration) Regulations 2006, SI 2006/750, reg 3(1)(c).

6   'Exempted question' means a question in relation to which the Rehabilitation of Offenders Act 1974 s 4(2)(a) or (b) (effect of rehabilitation: see PARA 598) has been excluded by an order of the Secretary of State under s 4(4) (see PARA 614): Police Act 1997 (Criminal Records) (Registration) Regulations 2006, SI 2006/750, reg 2 (as amended: see note 1). Cf also the meaning of 'exempted question' in the Police Act 1997 Pt V: see s 113A; and PARA 641.

7   Police Act 1997 (Criminal Records) (Registration) Regulations 2006, SI 2006/750, reg 3(1)(d).

8   As to the registration of bodies for these purposes see PARA 648.

9   Ie under the Police Act 1997 s 113A (see PARA 637 et seq) or s 113B (see PARA 638 et seq).

10 Police Act 1997 (Criminal Records) (Registration) Regulations 2006, SI 2006/750, reg 3(1)(e)(i) (reg 3(e)(i), (f)(i) amended by SI 2009/203).

11 Ie under the Police Act 1997 Pt V.

12 Police Act 1997 (Criminal Records) (Registration) Regulations 2006, SI 2006/750, reg 3(1)(e)(ii) (as amended: see note 1). There is payable by a registered person which is a body a fee of £5 in respect of the second and each subsequent name entered in the register in accordance with reg 3(1)(e)(ii): reg 6(1). The fee payable under reg 6(1) or 6(2) in respect of the second and each subsequent name entered in the register must be invoiced by DBS to the person and payable on account within 15 days of the invoice date: reg 7(b) (as so amended).

13 Police Act 1997 (Criminal Records) (Registration) Regulations 2006, SI 2006/750, reg 3(1)(e)(iii).

14 Police Act 1997 (Criminal Records) (Registration) Regulations 2006, SI 2006/750, reg 3(1)(e)(iv).

15 Police Act 1997 (Criminal Records) (Registration) Regulations 2006, SI 2006/750, reg 3(1)(e)(v).

16 As to the meaning of 'statutory office-holder' see PARA 648 note 1.

17 Ie in accordance with the Police Act 1997 (Criminal Records) (Registration) Regulations 2006, SI 2006/750, reg 4: see PARA 648.

18 See note 11.

19 Police Act 1997 (Criminal Records) (Registration) Regulations 2006, SI 2006/750, reg 3(1)(f)(i) (as amended: see notes 1, 10). There is payable by a registered person which is a statutory office-holder a fee of £5 in respect of the second and each subsequent name entered in the register in accordance with reg 3(1)(f)(i): reg 6(2). See note 12.

20 Police Act 1997 (Criminal Records) (Registration) Regulations 2006, SI 2006/750, reg 3(1)(f)(ii).

21 Police Act 1997 (Criminal Records) (Registration) Regulations 2006, SI 2006/750, reg 3(1)(f)(iii).

22 Police Act 1997 (Criminal Records) (Registration) Regulations 2006, SI 2006/750, reg 3(1)(f)(iv).

23 See note 9.
24 Police Act 1997 (Criminal Records) (Registration) Regulations 2006, SI 2006/750, reg 3(1)(g).
25 Police Act 1997 (Criminal Records) (Registration) Regulations 2006, SI 2006/750, reg 7(j) (as amended: see note 1).

650. Information on progress of application. DBS[1] must, in response to a request from a person who is acting as the registered person[2] in relation to an application[3] for a criminal record certificate or an enhance criminal record certificate, inform that person whether or not a certificate has been issued in response to the application[4]. If, at the time such a request is made, a certificate has been issued, then:

(1)   in the case of a criminal record certificate[5], if it was a certificate stating that there is no relevant matter[6] recorded in central records[7], DBS may inform the person who made the request that the certificate was such a certificate[8]; and

(2)   in the case of an enhanced criminal record certificate[9], if it was a certificate stating that there is no relevant matter recorded in central records and no additional information[10] is provided[11] and, where the certificate is required to include suitability information relating to children or vulnerable adults[12], it is a certificate containing no suitability information indicating that the person to whom the certificate is issued is barred from regulated activity relating to children or to vulnerable adults[13] or is subject to a direction[14] prohibiting him from participation in school management[15], DBS may inform the person who made the request that the certificate was such a certificate[16].

If no certificate has been issued, DBS must inform the person who made the request of such other matters relating to the processing of the application as it considers appropriate[17].

1   Ie the Disclosure and Barring Service: see PARA 638 note 4.
2   As to the meaning of 'registered person' see PARA 646 note 1; and as to 'acting as the registered person' see PARA 646.
3   Ie an application under the Police Act 1997 s 113A (see PARA 641) or s 113B (see PARA 641). Subject to s 120AC(2)–(4) (see below), nothing in s 120AC permits DBS to inform a person who is acting as the registered person in relation to an application under s 113A or s 113B of the content of any certificate issued in response to the application: s 120AC(6) (s 120AC added by the Protection of Freedoms Act 2012 s 79(3); Police Act 1997 s 120AC(1), (3)–(7) amended by SI 2012/3006).
4   Police Act 1997 s 120AC(1) (as added and amended: see note 3). As to the form and manner of making requests see the Police Act 1997 s 125B(3); and PARA 641. DBS may refuse a request under s 120AC(1) if it is made after the end of a prescribed period beginning with the day on which the certificate was issued: s 120AC(7) (as so added and amended).
5   Ie in the case of a certificate under the Police Act 1997 s 113A.
6   As to the meaning of 'relevant matter' see the Police Act 1997 s 113A(6); and PARA 637 note 3 (definition applied by s 120AC(8) (as added: see note 3)).
7   As to the meaning of 'central records' see the Police Act 1997 s 113A(6); and PARA 637 note 4 (definition applied by s 120AC(8) (as added: see note 3)).
8   Police Act 1997 s 120AC(2), (3) (as added and amended: see note 3).
9   Ie in the case of a certificate under the Police Act 1997 s 113B.
10 Ie information provided in accordance with the Police Act 1997 s 113B(4) (see PARA 640).
11 Police Act 1997 s 120AC(4)(a) (as added: see note 3).
12 Ie if the Police Act 1997 s 113BA(1) or s113BB(1) applies to the certificate: s 120AC(4)(b) (as added: see note 3). 'Suitability information' means information required to be included in a certificate under s 113B by virtue of s 113BA or s 113BB: s 120AC(8) (as so added).
13 Police Act 1997 s 120AC(4)(b)(i) (as added: see note 3). For the purposes of s 120AC(4)(b), as to the meanings of 'barred' and 'regulated activity' see the Safeguarding Vulnerable Groups Act 2006 ss 3, 5; and SOCIAL SERVICES AND COMMUNITY CARE (definitions applied by the Police Act 1997 s 120AC(9) (as so added)).

14 Ie under the Education and Skills Act 2008 s 128 (prohibition on participation in management
    of independent educational institution in England: see EDUCATION vol 35 (2011) PARA 504) or
    the Education Act 2002 s 167A (prohibition on participation in management of independent
    school in Wales: see EDUCATION vol 35 (2015) PARA 420).

15 Police Act 1997 s 120AC(4)(b)(ii) (as added: see note 3).

16 Police Act 1997 s 120AC(4) (as added and amended: see note 3).

17 Police Act 1997 s 120AC(5) (as added and amended: see note 3).

651. Refusal and cancellation of registration of unsuitable persons. A
person's registration in the register of countersignatories[1] is conditional upon the
provision of information reasonably required in order to consider the continuing
eligibility and suitability of registered persons and the eligibility and suitability of
applicants for registered person status[2]. DBS may refuse to include a person in
the register if it appears to it that the registration of that person is likely to make
it possible for information to become available to an individual who, in DBS's
opinion, is not a suitable person to have access to that information[3], and may
remove a person from the register if it appears to DBS that the registration of
that person is likely to make it possible for information to become available to
an individual who, in DBS's opinion, is not a suitable person to have access to
that information[4], or that the registration of that person has resulted in
information becoming known to such an individual[5].

DBS may also refuse an application for registration[6] made by an individual
who has previously been a registered person[7] and has been removed from the
register (otherwise than at that individual's own request)[8], and an application
made by a body corporate or unincorporate which has previously been a
registered person[9] and has been removed from the register (otherwise than at its
own request)[10].

1   Ie the register maintained for the purposes of the Police Act 1997 Pt 5 (ss 112–127) (see PARA
    646 et seq). As to inclusion in the register see PARA 647.

2   Police Act 1997 (Criminal Records) (Registration) Regulations 2006, SI 2006/750, reg 7(i)(i),
    (ii). Registration is also conditional upon the continuing ability of registered persons to make
    payments of fees on behalf of applicants under the Police Act 1997 Pt 5: Police Act 1997
    (Criminal Records) (Registration) Regulations 2006, SI 2006/750, reg 7(i)(iii).
       It is the duty of the chief officer of any police force to comply, as soon as practicable after
    receiving it, with any request by DBS to provide it with information which is available to the
    chief officer, relates to an applicant for registration, a registered person or an individual who is
    likely to have access to information in consequence of a particular application for registration,
    or a particular registered person, acting as the registered person in relation to applications under
    Pt V, and concerns a matter which DBS has notified to the chief officer to be a matter which, in
    its opinion, is relevant to the determination of the suitability of individuals for having access to
    the information that may be provided in consequence of a person acting as the registered person
    in relation to applications under these provisions: Police Act 1997 s 120A(4) (s 120A added by
    the Criminal Justice and Police Act 2001 s 34(1); Police Act 1997 s 120A(4) amended by
    SI 2009/203; SI 2012/3006). DBS must pay to the appropriate police authority such fee as it
    thinks appropriate for information provided in accordance with this requirement: Police
    Act 1997 s 119(3) (as so amended; amended by the Greater London Authority Act 1999 Sch 27
    para 112, Sch 34 Pt VII; the Criminal Justice and Police Act 2001 s 134(2); the Police Reform
    and Social Responsibility Act 2011 Sch 16 para 223; and SI 2012/3006). See also the Police
    Act 1997 s 119(5)–(7); and PARA 640 note 6. As to the meaning of 'registered person' see PARA
    646 note 1; and as to 'acting as the registered person' see PARA 646. As to DBS (ie the Disclosure
    and Barring Service) see PARA 638 note 4.

3   Police Act 1997 s 120A(1) (s 120A added by the Criminal Justice and Police Act 2001 s 134(1);
    Police Act 1997 s 120A(1)–(3) amended by SI 2012/3006). In determining for these purposes
    whether an individual is a suitable person to have access to any information, DBS may have
    regard, in particular, to:
       (1)   any information relating to that person which concerns a relevant matter (within the

meaning of the Police Act 1997 s 113A: see PARA 637) (s 120A(3)(a), (5) (as so added and amended; s 120A(5) further amended by the Serious Organised Crime and Police Act 2005 Sch 14 para 8));

(2)   any information relating to the person of the following kinds:

     (a)   whether the person is barred from regulated activity (Police Act 1997 s 120A(3)(b), (3A)(a) (as so added; s 120A(3)(b) substituted, s 120A(3A), (3D), (7), (8) further added, by the Policing and Crime Act 2009 s 96)); and

     (b)   whether the person is subject to a direction under the Education Act 2002 s 167A (prohibition on participation in management of independent school: see EDUCATION vol 35 (2015) PARA 420) (Police Act 1997 s 120A(3A)(d) (as so added)); and

(3)   any information provided to DBS under s 120A(4) (see below) (s 120A(3)(c) (as so added and amended)).

For the purposes of s 120A(3A), as to the meanings of 'barred' and 'regulated activity' see the Safeguarding Vulnerable Groups Act 2006 ss 3, 5; and SOCIAL SERVICES AND COMMUNITY CARE (definitions applied by the Police Act 1997 s 120A(3D) (as so added; s 120A(3D) amended, s 120AA(4)–(6) added, by the Protection of Freedoms Act 2012 s 81, Sch 9 para 42)).

The Secretary of State may by order made by statutory instrument amend the Police Act 1997 s 120A(3A) for the purpose of altering the information specified therein that subsection: s 120A(7), (8) (as so added). At the date at which this volume states the law no such order had been made.

4   Police Act 1997 s 120A(2)(a) (as added and amended: see note 3).
5   Police Act 1997 s 120A(2)(b) (as added and amended: see note 3). In the event of DBS removing or suspending the registered person from the register, that person must pay for any applications knowingly submitted after such removal or suspension: Police Act 1997 (Criminal Records) (Registration) Regulations 2006, SI 2006/750, reg 7(m) (amended by SI 2012/3006).
6   Ie an application under the Police Act 1997 s 120 (see PARA 647).
7   Police Act 1997 s 120AA(4)(a), (6) (as added (see note 3); s 120AA(6) amended by SI 2012/3006).
8   Police Act 1997 s 120AA(4)(b) (as added: see note 3).
9   Police Act 1997 s 120AA(5)(a) (as added: see note 3).
10   Police Act 1997 s 120AA(5)(b) (as added: see note 3).

652. Refusal and suspension of unused registrations. The number of applications[1] in relation to which a registered person has acted as a registered person[2] in any 12 month period must not be fewer than 100[3], and DBS[4] may remove from the register any registered person who fails to comply with this requirement[5].

Where a registered person:

(1)   is, in the opinion of DBS, no longer likely to wish to act as the registered person in relation to applications[6]; or

(2)   has, in any period of 12 months during which he was registered, acted as the registered person in relation to fewer applications than the minimum number specified in respect of him by such regulations[7],

DBS may suspend that person's registration for such period not exceeding six months as the it thinks fit or remove that person from the register[8].

1   Ie applications for inclusion in the register maintained for the purposes of the Police Act 1997 Pt 5 (ss 112–127) (see PARA 646 et seq). As to inclusion in the register see PARA 647.
2   As to acting as a registered person see PARA 646; and as to the meaning of 'registered person' see PARA 646 note 1.
3   Police Act 1997 (Criminal Records) (Registration) Regulations 2006, SI 2006/750, reg 7(l) (amended by SI 2009/203).
4   Ie the Disclosure and Barring Service: see PARA 638 note 4.
5   Police Act 1997 (Criminal Records) (Registration) Regulations 2006, SI 2006/750, reg 9 (regs 7(m), 9 amended by SI 2012/3006). In the event of DBS removing or suspending the registered person from the register, that person must pay for any applications knowingly submitted after such removal or suspension: Police Act 1997 (Criminal Records) (Registration) Regulations 2006, SI 2006/750, reg 7(m) (as so amended). These provisions are made pursuant to the Police Act 1997 s 120AA(1) (ss 120AA, 120AB added by the Criminal Justice Act 2003

Sch 35 paras 1, 9; Police Act 1997 ss 120AA(1), (2), 120AB(8) amended by SI 2009/203; Police Act 1997 ss 120AA(1)–(3), 120AB(1)–(6), (8) further amended by SI 2012/3006), which provides that regulations may make provision enabling DBS in prescribed cases to refuse to register a person who, in its opinion, is likely to act as the registered person in relation to fewer applications in any period of 12 months than a prescribed minimum number.

6 Police Act 1997 s 120AA(2)(a) (as added and amended: see note 5).

7 Police Act 1997 s 120AA(2)(b) (as added and amended: see note 5).

8 Police Act 1997 s 120AA(3) (as added and amended: see note 5).

Before cancelling or suspending a person's registration under s 120AA, DBS must send him written notice of (or transmit electronically) his intention to do so: s 120AB(1), (7) (as so added). Every such notice must give DBS's reasons for proposing to cancel or suspend the registration and inform the person concerned of his right under to make representations under s 120AB(3) (which provides that a person who receives such a notice may, within 21 days of service, make representations in writing to DBS as to why the registration should not be cancelled or suspended): s 120AB(2), (3) (as so added and amended). After considering any such representations, DBS must give the registered person written notice that at the end of a further period of six weeks beginning with the date of service (or such other period as may be substituted by DBS), the person's registration will be cancelled or suspended or that he does not propose to take any further action: s 120AB(4), (9) (as so added and amended)). If no representations are received within the period mentioned in s 120AB(3), DBS may cancel or suspend the person's registration at the end of the period so mentioned: s 120AB(5) ((as so added and amended)).

These provisions do not prevent DBS from imposing on the registered person a lesser sanction than that specified in the notice thereunder and do not apply where DBS is satisfied, in the case of a registered person other than a body, that the person has died or is incapable, by reason of physical or mental impairment, of acting as the registered person in relation to applications, or the registered person has requested to be removed from the register: s 120AB(6), (8) (as so added and amended).

653. Inspections of registered persons and premises. A person authorised in writing for the purpose by DBS[1] may require any person appearing to be a registered person[2] or a nominated individual[3] to produce to it any documents for the purpose of assessing whether the registered person or nominated individual has complied with the conditions of registration[4], and it is a condition of a person's registration that, for this purpose only, he must allow a person authorised in writing for the purpose by DBS to enter any premises[5] owned or occupied by any person appearing to that person to be a registered person or a nominated individual[6].

1 Ie the Disclosure and Barring Service: see PARA 638 note 4.

2 As to the meaning of 'registered person' see PARA 646 note 1. As to registration generally see PARA 646 et seq.

3 Ie an individual nominated in accordance with the Police Act 1997 (Criminal Records) (Registration) Regulations 2006, SI 2006/750, reg 4: see PARA 648.

4 Police Act 1997 (Criminal Records) (Registration) Regulations 2006, SI 2006/750, reg 8(2) (reg 8(1), (2), (4) amended by SI 2012/3006). As to the conditions of registration see PARA 647.

5 Ie other than premises occupied exclusively for residential purposes as a private dwelling: Police Act 1997 (Criminal Records) (Registration) Regulations 2006, SI 2006/750, reg 8(1) (as amended: see note 4).

6 Police Act 1997 (Criminal Records) (Registration) Regulations 2006, SI 2006/750, reg 8(1) (as amended: see note 4). A person exercising such power of entry may do so only at a reasonable hour (reg 8(3)), must comply with any reasonable request (whether before or after entry is gained to the premises) by any person present on the premises to state the purpose for which the power is being exercised, show the authorisation by DBS for his exercise of the power, and produce evidence of his identity (reg 8(4) (as so amended)), and must make a record of the date and time of his entry, the period for which he remained there and his conduct while there (reg 8(5)). If the person exercising the power is requested to do so by any person present on the premises at the time of entry, he must provide that person with a copy of the record made under reg 8(5).

(iii) Administration and Compliance

654. Code of practice. The Secretary of State must publish, and may from time to time revise, a code of practice in connection with the use of information provided[1] to registered persons[2]; and if DBS[3] thinks that the person who acted as the registered person[4] in relation to an application[5] for a criminal record certificate[6] or an enhanced criminal record certificate[7] has either acted as the registered person at the request of a body which, or individual who, has failed to comply with the code of practice[8] or (until a day to be appointed) failed to comply with such code of practice[9], it may suspend or cancel the person's registration[10].

1   Ie under the Police Act 1997 Pt 5 (ss 112–127).
2   Police Act 1997 s 122(1). See the *Code of Practice for Registered Persons and Other Recipients of Disclosure Information* (revised April 2009), published by the Home Office. As to the meaning of 'registered person' see PARA 646 note 1. As to registration see PARA 646 et seq. The reference in the Police Act 1997 s 122(1) to the use of information provided to registered persons under Pt V includes a reference to the use of information provided in accordance with s 116A(1) (see PARA 645) to relevant persons (within the meaning thereof) who are not registered persons under Pt V: s 122(1A) (s 122(1A) added, s 122(3)(a) prospectively repealed, by the Protection of Freedoms Act 2012 Sch 9 paras 113, 114, Sch 10 Pt 6). The Secretary of State must lay before Parliament the code of practice under the Police Act 1997 s 122 as soon as practicable after publication and after revision: s 122(2). At the date at which this volume states the law no day had been appointed for the coming into force of the repeal of s 122(3)(a).
3   Ie the Disclosure and Barring Service: see PARA 638 note 4.
4   As to acting as a registered person see PARA 646.
5   Ie an application under the Police Act 1997 s 113A or s 113B: see PARA 641.
6   As to the meaning of 'criminal record certificate' see PARA 637.
7   As to the meaning of 'enhanced criminal record certificate' see PARA 638.
8   Police Act 1997 s 122(3)(b) (s 122(3) amended, s 122(3A), (3B) added, by the Safeguarding Vulnerable Groups Act 2006 s 29; Police Act 1997 ss 120AB(7), 122(3) further amended by SI 2009/203; Police Act 1997 ss 120AB(1)–(6), (8), 122(3), (3A), (3B) further amended by SI 2012/3006).
9   Police Act 1997 s 122(3)(a) (as amended and prospectively repealed: see notes 2, 8).
10   Police Act 1997 s 122(3A)(b), (c) (as added: see note 8). Before cancelling or suspending a person's registration under s 122, DBS must send him written notice of (or transmit electronically) its intention to do so: ss 122(3B), 120AB(1), (7) (s 122(3B) as added and amended (see note 8); s 120AB added by the Criminal Justice Act 2003 Sch 35 paras 1, 9; as so amended). Every such notice must give DBS's reasons for proposing to cancel or suspend the registration and inform the person concerned of his right to make representations under the Police Act 1997 s 120AB(3) (which provides that a person who receives such a notice may, within 21 days of service, make representations in writing to DBS as to why the registration should not be cancelled or suspended): s 120AB(2), (3) (as so added and amended). After considering any such representations, DBS must give the registered person written notice that at the end of a further period of six weeks beginning with the date of service (or such other period as may be substituted by the Secretary of State), the person's registration will be cancelled or suspended or that he does not propose to take any further action: s 120AB(4), (9) (as so added and amended). If no representations are received within the period mentioned in s 120AB(3), DBS may cancel or suspend the person's registration at the end of the period so mentioned: s 120AB(5) (as so added and amended).

     These provisions do not prevent DBS from imposing on the registered person a lesser sanction than that specified in the notice thereunder and do not apply where DBS is satisfied, in the case of a registered person other than a body, that the person has died or is incapable, by reason of physical or mental impairment, of acting as the registered person in relation to applications, or the registered person has requested to be removed from the register: s 120AB(6), (8) (as so added and amended).

655. Monitoring. There is an independent monitor for the purposes of the statutory provisions governing criminal record checks[1] whose responsibility is to review[2]:

(1)   a sample of cases in which an enhanced criminal record certificate[3] has included[4] potentially relevant information which ought to be so included[5];

(2)   a sample of cases in which the chief officer of a police force has decided that information must not be included[6] in a certificate or report[7]; and

(3)   a sample of cases in which the chief officer of a police force has decided that information should be disclosed or not disclosed to DBS[8] for the purpose of the provision[9] by DBS of up-date information[10].

The independent monitor must in relation to each year make a report to the Secretary of State about the performance of police forces in exercising their functions under these provisions[11] and may make recommendations to the Secretary of State as to:

(a)   any guidance issued by the Secretary of State or which the monitor thinks it would be appropriate for the Secretary of State to issue[12];

(b)   any changes to any enactment which the monitor thinks may be appropriate[13].

If a person believes that information provided[14] and included in a certificate[15] is not[16] relevant[17] or ought not to be included in the certificate[18], he may apply in writing to the independent monitor for a decision as to whether the information is such information[19], and on receiving such an application the independent monitor must ask such chief officer of a police force as the independent monitor considers appropriate[20] to review whether the information concerned is information which the chief officer reasonably believes to be[21] relevant[22] and in the chief officer's opinion, ought to be included in the certificate[23]. If following such a review the independent monitor considers that any of the information concerned is information which is irrelevant or ought not to be included[24] he must inform DBS of that fact[25] and on being so informed, DBS must issue a new certificate[26].

1   Ie for the purposes of the Police Act 1997 Pt V (ss 112–127): see PARA 636 et seq. The independent monitor is a person appointed by the Secretary of State for such period, not exceeding three years, as the Secretary of State decides (although a person may be appointed for a further period or periods) and on such terms as the Secretary of State decides: s 119B(2), (3) (s 119B added by the Safeguarding Vulnerable Groups Act 2006 s 28). The Secretary of State may terminate the appointment of the independent monitor before the end of the three-year period specified by giving the monitor notice of the termination not less than three months before it is to take effect: Police Act 1997 s 119B(4) (as so added).
    The chief officer of a police force must provide to the independent monitor such information as the monitor reasonably requires in connection with the exercise of his functions under these provisions or under s 117A (see PARA 655): s 119B(9) (as so added; ss 117A, 119B(8A) added, s 119B(9) amended, by the Protection of Freedoms Act 2012 s 82(5), Sch 9 para 111).

2   Ie in order to ensure compliance with the Convention for the Protection of Human Rights and Fundamental Freedoms (Rome, 4 November 1950; TS 71 (1953); Cmd 8969) art 8 (right to respect for private and family life, home and correspondence: see RIGHTS AND FREEDOMS vol 88A (2013) PARAS 317–367): Police Act 1997 s 119B(6) (as added: see note 1).

3   Ie a certificate issued under the Police Act 1997 s 113B: see PARAS 638, 642.

4   Ie pursuant to the Police Act 1997 s 113B(4)(b): see PARA 640.

5   Police Act 1997 s 119B(5)(b) (as added: see note 1).

6   Ie pursuant to the Police Act 1997 s 113B(4)(b).

7   Police Act 1997 s 119B(5)(c) (as added (see note 1); s 119B(5)(c) amended, s 119B(5)(ca) added, by the Protection of Freedoms Act 2012 Sch 9 para 111, Sch 10 Pt 6).

8   Ie the Disclosure and Barring Service: see PARA 638 note 4.

9   Ie under the Police Act 1997 s 116A: see PARA 645.

10 Police Act 1997 s 119B(5)(ca) (as added (see notes 1, 7); ss 117A(5)(a), (b), (6), 119B(5)(ca) amended by SI 2012/3006).

11 Police Act 1997 s 119B(7) (as added: see note 1).

12 Police Act 1997 s 119B(8)(a) (as added: see note 1).

13 Police Act 1997 s 119B(8)(b) (as added: see note 1).

14 Ie in accordance with the Police Act 1997 s 113B(4).

15 Ie under the Police Act 1997 s 113B or s 116.

16 Ie for the purpose described in the statement under the Police Act 1997 s 113B(2) or (as the case may be) s 116(2).

17 Police Act 1997 ss 117A(1)(a), 119B(8A) (as added: see note 1).

18 Police Act 1997 s 117A(1)(b) (as added: see note 1).

19 Police Act 1997 s 117A(2) (as added: see note 1).

20 In connection with references to a police force see the Police Act 1997 s 113B(10), (11); and PARA 640 notes 3, 6 (provisions applied by s 117A(8) (as added: see note 1)). In exercising functions under s 117A(3), the chief officer concerned must have regard to any guidance for the time being published under s 113B(4A) (see PARA 640): s 117A(4) (as so added).

21 Ie for the purpose described in the statement under the Police Act 1997 s 113B(2) or (as the case may be) s 116(2).

22 Police Act 1997 s 117A(3)(a) (as added: see note 1).

23 Police Act 1997 s 117A(3)(b) (as added: see note 1).

24 Ie it is information that falls within the Police Act 1997 s 117A(1)(a) or (b) (see the text and notes 14–18). In deciding for these purposes whether information is information which falls within s 117A(1)(a) or (b), the independent monitor must have regard to any guidance for the time being published under s 113B(4A): s 117A(6) (as added: see note 1).

25 Police Act 1997 s 117A(5)(a) (as added and amended: see notes 1, 10).

26 Police Act 1997 s 117A(5)(b) (as added and amended: see notes 1, 10). In issuing such a certificate, DBS must proceed as if the information which falls within s 117A(1)(a) or (b) had not been provided under s 113B(4): s 117A(6) (as so added and amended).

656. Falsification of certificates. A person commits an offence[1] if, with intent to deceive, he:

(1)   makes a false certificate[2];

(2)   alters a certificate[3];

(3)   uses a certificate which relates to another person in a way which suggests that it relates to himself[4]; or

(4)   allows a certificate which relates to him to be used by another person in a way which suggests that it relates to that other person[5].

A person also commits an offence if he knowingly makes a false statement for the purpose of obtaining, or enabling another person to obtain, a certificate[6].

1 A person who is guilty of an offence under these provisions is liable on summary conviction to imprisonment for a term not exceeding six months or to a fine not exceeding level 5 on the standard scale or to both: Police Act 1997 s 123(3). As to the standard scale, the statutory maximum, the prescribed sum, and magistrates' powers to levy unlimited fines see PARA 176.

2 Police Act 1997 s 123(1)(a). The 'certificate' referred to in the text is a certificate under Pt V (ss 112–127), ie a criminal record certificate, an enhanced criminal record certificate or (as from a day to be appointed) a criminal conviction certificate: see PARA 636 et seq. As to the meaning of 'certificate' see PARA 636 note 1.

3 Police Act 1997 s 123(1)(b).

4 Police Act 1997 s 123(1)(c).

5 Police Act 1997 s 123(1)(d).

6 Police Act 1997 s 123(2).

657. Unauthorised disclosure. Subject to a number of specified exceptions[1]:

(1)   a member, officer or employee of a body registered as a registered person[2] commits an offence[3] if he discloses information provided following an application[4] for a criminal record certificate[5] or an enhanced criminal record certificate[6], unless he discloses it in the course of his duties:

      (a)   to another member, officer or employee of the registered body[7];

(b) to a member, officer or employee of a body at the request of which the registered body acted as the registered person[8] in relation to the application[9]; or

(c) to an individual at whose request the registered body acted as the registered person in relation to the relevant application[10];

(2) where information is provided[11] following an application for a criminal record certificate or an enhanced criminal record certificate, in relation to which the person who acted as the registered person did so at the request of an unregistered body[12], a member, officer or employee of the body commits an offence if he discloses the information, unless he discloses it in the course of his duties to another member, officer or employee of that body[13];

(3) where information is provided[14] following an application for a criminal record certificate or an enhanced criminal record certificate in relation to which an individual acted as the registered person, or in relation to which the person who acted as the registered person did so at the request of an individual, the individual commits an offence if he discloses the information, unless he discloses it to an employee of his for the purpose of the employee's duties, and an employee of the individual commits an offence if he discloses the information unless he discloses it in the course of his duties to another employee of the individual[15]; and

(4) where information provided[16] on an application for a criminal record certificate or an enhanced criminal record certificate is disclosed to a person and the disclosure is an offence under these provisions[17] the person to whom the information is disclosed commits an offence if he discloses it to any other person[18].

These provisions[19] do not apply to a disclosure of information contained in a certificate[20] which is made:

(i) with the written consent of the applicant for the certificate[21];

(ii) to a government department[22];

(iii) to a person appointed to an office by virtue of any enactment[23];

(iv) in accordance with an obligation to provide information under or by virtue of any enactment[24]; or

(v) by an employment agency or an employment business[25], whether or not in response to an exempted question, for the purpose of consideration by an educational institution[26], an alternative provision Academy that is not an 'educational institution' for this purpose[27], an institution within the further education sector[28] or a 16 to 19 academy, of a person's suitability for a position at that institution or academy[29].

Provision is also made in connection with unauthorised disclosures by persons exercising functions delegated by DBS[30].

1 See the Police Act 1997 s 124(5), (6); and the text and notes 19–29. Nothing in ss 112–119 (see PARA 636 et seq) prejudices any power which exists apart from the Police Act 1997 to disclose information or to make records available: s 127.

2 Ie registered under the Police Act 1997 s 120: see PARA 647. As to the meaning of 'registered person' see PARA 646 note 1. As to registration see PARA 646 et seq.

3 A person who is guilty of an offence under these provisions is liable on summary conviction to imprisonment for a term not exceeding six months or to a fine not exceeding level 3 on the standard scale or to both: Police Act 1997 s 124(7). As to the standard scale, the statutory maximum, the prescribed sum, and magistrates' powers to levy unlimited fines see PARA 176.

4 Ie an application under the Police Act 1997 s 113A or s 113B: see PARA 641.

5 As to the meaning of 'criminal record certificate' see PARA 637.

6 As to the meaning of 'enhanced criminal record certificate' see PARA 638.

7   Police Act 1997 s 124(1)(a) (s 124(1)–(4), (6) amended by the Serious Organised Crime and Police Act 2005 Sch 14 paras 1, 12; Police Act 1997 s 124(1)(b), (c), (2), (3) further amended by SI 2009/203).

8   As to acting as a registered person see PARA 646.

9   Police Act 1997 s 124(1)(b) (as amended: see note 7).

10 Police Act 1997 s 124(1)(c) (as amended: see note 7).

11 Ie under the Police Act 1997 s 113A or s 113B.

12 Ie a body which is not registered under the Police Act 1997 s 120.

13 Police Act 1997 s 124(2) (as amended: see note 7).

14 See note 11.

15 Police Act 1997 s 124(3) (as amended: see note 7).

16 See note 11.

17 Or would be an offence but for the application of the exceptions specified in the Police Act 1997 s 124(6)(a), (d), (e) or (f): see the text and notes 19–29.

18 Police Act 1997 s 124(4) (as amended (see note 7); further amended by the Protection of Freedoms Act 2012 Sch 9 para 115, Sch 10 Pt 6).

19 Ie the Police Act 1997 s 124(1)–(4) (see the text and notes 1–18).

20 See note 11.

21 Police Act 1997 s 124(6)(a) (as amended: see note 7).

22 Police Act 1997 s 124(6)(b) (as amended: see note 7).

23 Police Act 1997 s 124(6)(c) (as amended: see note 7).

24 Police Act 1997 s 124(6)(d) (as amended: see note 7).

25 The references to an 'employment agency' and an 'employment business' are references to such an agency or business within the meanings given by the Employment Agencies Act 1973 s 13 (see TRADE AND INDUSTRY vol 97 (2015) PARA 974): Police Act 1997 (Criminal Records) Regulations 2002, SI 2002/233, reg 12(2) (reg 12 added by SI 2006/2181).

26 Ie an institution which is exclusively or mainly for the provision of full-time education to children: see the Criminal Justice and Court Services Act 2000 s 42(1).

27 Ie an institution which is not an institution exclusively or mainly for the provision of full-time education to children.

28 Ie within the meaning given by the Further and Higher Education Act 1992 s 91(3): see EDUCATION vol 35 (2015) PARA 555.

29 Police Act 1997 s 124(6)(e), (f) (as amended: see note 7); Police Act 1997 (Criminal Records) Regulations 2002, SI 2002/233, reg 12(1) (as added (see note 25); amended by SI 2012/979).

30 See PARA 658.

658. Disclosure of information obtained in connection with delegated functions.   Subject to a number of specified exceptions[1] any person who is engaged in the discharge of functions conferred on DBS[2] commits an offence[3] if he discloses information which has been obtained by him in connection with those functions and which relates to a particular person unless he discloses the information, in the course of his duties:

(1)   to another person engaged in the discharge of those functions[4];

(2)   to the chief officer of a police force[5] in connection with a request[6] to provide information to DBS[7]; or

(3)   to an applicant[8] who is entitled[9] to the information disclosed to him[10].

These provisions do not apply to a disclosure of information which is made:

(a)   with the written consent of the person to whom the information relates[11];

(b)   to a government department[12];

(c)   to a person appointed to an office by virtue of any enactment[13];

(d)   in accordance with an obligation to provide information under or by virtue of any enactment[14]; or

(e)   for some other purpose specified in regulations made by the Secretary of State[15].

Where information is disclosed to a person and the disclosure is an offence[16], or would be such an offence but for head (a), (d) or (e) above[17], the person to whom the information is disclosed commits an offence if he discloses it to any other person[18].

1   See the Police Act 1997 s 124A(3); and the text and notes 11–15.
2   Ie functions conferred by the Police Act 1997 Pt V (ss 112–127) (see PARA 636 et seq). As to DBS (ie the Disclosure and Barring Service) see PARA 638 note 4.
3   Police Act 1997 s 124A(1) (s 124A added by the Criminal Justice Act 2003 Sch 35 paras 1, 11; Police Act 1997 s 124A(1) amended by SI 2012/3006). A person who is guilty of an offence under these provisions is liable on summary conviction to imprisonment for a term not exceeding six months or to a fine not exceeding level 3 on the standard scale or to both: Police Act 1997 s 124A(4), (5) (as so added). As to the standard scale, the statutory maximum, the prescribed sum, and magistrates' powers to levy unlimited fines see PARA 176.
4   Police Act 1997 s 124A(1)(a) (as added: see note 3).
5   For these purposes the reference to a 'police force' includes any body mentioned in the Police Act 1997 s 113B(10)(a)–(i), (11) (see PARA 640); and the reference to a 'chief officer' must be construed accordingly: s 124A(6) (as added (see note 3); further added by the Serious Organised Crime and Police Act 2005 s 165(3)).
6   Ie under the Police Act 1997 Pt V.
7   Police Act 1997 s 124A(1)(b) (as added and amended: see note 3).
8   For these purposes the reference to an applicant includes a person who makes a request under the Police Act 1997 s 116A(1) (see PARA 645), s 120AC(1) (see PARA 650) or s 120AD(2) (see PARA 645): s 124A(6A) (s 124A(1)(c) amended, s 124A(6A) added, by the Protection of Freedoms Act 2012 Sch 9 para 116).
9   Ie under the Police Act 1997 Pt V.
10 Police Act 1997 s 124A(1)(c) (as added: see note 3).
11 Police Act 1997 s 124A(3)(a) (as added: see note 3).
12 Police Act 1997 s 124A(3)(b) (as added: see note 3).
13 Police Act 1997 s 124A(3)(c) (as added: see note 3).
14 Police Act 1997 s 124A(3)(d) (as added: see note 3).
15 Police Act 1997 s 124A(3)(e) (as added: see note 3). At the date at which this volume states the law no other such purpose had been specified.
16 Police Act 1997 s 124A(2)(a) (as added: see note 3). The text refers to an offence under s 124A(1): see the text and notes 1–10.
17 Police Act 1997 s 124A(2)(b) (as added: see note 3).
18 Police Act 1997 s 124A(2) (as added: see note 3).

(iv) Disregarded Convictions and Cautions

659.   Disregarding of convictions or cautions involving buggery or gross indecency between men.   A conviction of, or a caution for, an offence of buggery or gross indecency between men[1] may be treated[2] as a disregarded conviction or caution if the conduct constituting the offence was consensual and would now be lawful[3]. The effects of such a conviction or caution being disregarded are:

(1)   that the person in question[4] is to be treated for all purposes in law as if he has not committed[5], been charged with[6], been convicted of[7], or been prosecuted[8], sentenced[9] or cautioned for[10], the offence;

(2)   that the conviction or caution or any connected circumstances is not a proper ground for dismissal or exclusion from any office or employment[11];

(3)   that no evidence or information relating to the conviction or caution is to be given in judicial or other proceedings[12]; and

(4)   that details of the conviction or caution contained in official records are deleted[13].

Nothing in the provisions relating to the disregarding of convictions or cautions affects any right of Her Majesty, by virtue of Her Royal prerogative or otherwise, to grant a free pardon, to quash any conviction or sentence, or to commute any sentence[14].

1 As to the offences a conviction of, or caution for, which may be disregarded under these provisions, and as to the meanings of 'conviction' and 'caution', see the Protection of Freedoms Act 2012 ss 92(1)(a)–(c), 101; and PARA 660.

2 Ie on the application of the person subject to the conviction or caution: see the Protection of Freedoms Act 2012 s 92(1); and PARA 665.

3 Ie if the other person involved in the conduct constituting the offence consented to it and was aged 16 or over (Protection of Freedoms Act 2012 s 92(3)(a)) and any such conduct now would not be an offence under the Sexual Offences Act 2003 s 71 (sexual activity in a public lavatory: see CRIMINAL LAW vol 25 (2010) PARA 269) (which includes an offence under the Armed Forces Act 2006 s 42 (criminal conduct: see ARMED FORCES vol 3 (2011) PARA 587) which is such an offence by virtue of the Sexual Offences Act 2003 71) (Protection of Freedoms Act 2012 ss 92(3)(b), 101(4)).

4 Ie the person who has the disregarded conviction or caution: Protection of Freedoms Act 2012 s 96(1).

5 Protection of Freedoms Act 2012 s 96(1)(a).

6 Protection of Freedoms Act 2012 s 96(1)(b).

7 Protection of Freedoms Act 2012 s 96(1)(c).

8 Protection of Freedoms Act 2012 s 96(1)(b).

9 Protection of Freedoms Act 2012 s 96(1)(d). 'Sentence' includes any punishment awarded, and any order made by virtue of the Army Act 1955 Sch 5A, the Air Force Act 1955 Sch 5A or the Naval Discipline Act 1957 Sch 4A (all repealed) in respect of a finding that a person is guilty of an offence in respect of conduct which was the subject of service disciplinary proceedings: Protection of Freedoms Act 2012 s 101(1).

10 Protection of Freedoms Act 2012 s 96(1)(e).

11 See the Protection of Freedoms Act 2012 s 96(5); and PARA 661.

12 See the Protection of Freedoms Act 2012 s 96(2)–(4); and PARAS 662, 663.

13 See the Protection of Freedoms Act 2012 s 95; and PARA 664.

14 Protection of Freedoms Act 2012 s 97.

660. Offences a conviction of or caution for which may be disregarded. The offences a conviction[1] of, or a caution[2] for, may be disregarded[3] are the offences of buggery[4] or gross indecency between men[5], corresponding offences under earlier legislation[6] and under the Service Discipline Acts[7], and inchoate offences[8].

1 'Conviction' includes (by virtue of the Protection of Freedoms Act 2012 s 101(1), (2)):

    (1)   a finding that a person is guilty of an offence in respect of conduct which was the subject of service disciplinary proceedings;

    (2)   a conviction in respect of which an order has been made discharging the person concerned absolutely or conditionally (notwithstanding the Powers of Criminal Courts (Sentencing) Act 2000 s 14 (see PARA 445) and the Armed Forces Act 2006 s 187 (see ARMED FORCES vol 3 (2011) PARA 609) (which deem a conviction of a person discharged not to be a conviction) or any corresponding earlier enactment); and

    (3)   a finding in any criminal proceedings (including a finding linked with a finding of insanity) that a person has committed an offence or done the act or made the omission charged.

'Service disciplinary proceedings' means any proceedings (whether in England and Wales or elsewhere) under the Naval Discipline Act 1866, the Army Act 1881, the Air Force Act 1917, the Army Act 1955, the Air Force Act 1955 or the Naval Discipline Act 1957 (all repealed) (whether before a court-martial or before any other court or person authorised under the enactment concerned to award a punishment in respect of an offence), or proceedings before a Standing Civilian Court established under the Armed Forces Act 1976 (repealed): Protection of Freedoms Act 2012 s 101(1).

2 'Caution' means a caution given to a person in England and Wales in respect of an offence which, at the time the caution is given, that person has admitted, or a reprimand or warning given under the Crime and Disorder Act 1998 s 65 (reprimands and warnings for persons aged under 18: see CHILDREN AND YOUNG PERSONS vol 10 (2012) PARA 1197): Protection of Freedoms Act 2012 s 101(1).

3 Ie for the purposes of the Protection of Freedoms Act 2012 Pt 5 Ch 4 (ss 92–101) (see PARAS 659, 661–665). As to the meaning and effect of a disregarded conviction or caution see PARA 659; as to how and when a conviction or caution becomes disregarded see PARA 665.

4 Ie an offence under the Sexual Offences Act 1956 s 12 (repealed): Protection of Freedoms Act 2012 s 92(1)(a).

5 Ie an offence under the Sexual Offences Act 1956 s 13 (repealed): Protection of Freedoms Act 2012 s 92(1)(b).

6 Ie a corresponding earlier offence under the Offences against the Person Act 1861 s 61 (repealed) or the Criminal Law Amendment Act 1885 s 11 (repealed): Protection of Freedoms Act 2012 s 92(1)(c).

7 The references in the Protection of Freedoms Act 2012 s 92(1) (see the text and notes 1–6) to offences under particular provisions are to be read as including references to offences under the Naval Discipline Act 1866 s 45, the Army Act 1881 s 41, the Air Force Act 1917 s 41, the Army Act 1955 s 70, the Air Force Act 1955 s 70 and the Naval Discipline Act 1957 s 42 (all repealed) which are such offences by virtue of those provisions: Protection of Freedoms Act 2012 s 101(3).

8 For these purposes a reference to an 'offence' includes a reference to an attempt, conspiracy or incitement to commit that offence, and a reference to aiding, abetting, counselling or procuring the commission of that offence: Protection of Freedoms Act 2012 s 101(5). In the case of an attempt, conspiracy or incitement, references to the conduct constituting the offence are references to the conduct to which the attempt, conspiracy or incitement related (whether or not that conduct occurred): s 101(6). For these purposes an attempt to commit an offence includes conduct which consisted of frequenting with intent to commit the offence any river, canal, street, highway, place of public resort or other location mentioned in the Vagrancy Act 1824 s 4 (see CRIMINAL LAW vol 26 (2010) PARA 773) (as it then had effect) in connection with frequenting by suspected persons or reputed thieves, and was itself an offence under s 4: Protection of Freedoms Act 2012 s 101(7).

661. Protection of employment, etc. A disregarded conviction or caution[1], or any circumstances ancillary to it[2], is not a proper ground for dismissing or excluding a person from any office, profession, occupation or employment[3] or prejudicing the person in any way in any office, profession, occupation or employment[4].

1 Ie a conviction or caution which has become disregarded for the purposes of the Protection of Freedoms Act 2012 Pt 5 Ch 4 (ss 92–101) (see PARAS 659–660, 662–665). Note that these provisions do not effect Royal pardons and similar matters (ie they are subject to s 97; see PARA 659) but otherwise apply despite any enactment or rule of law to the contrary (s 96(6)). As to the meaning and effect of a disregarded conviction or caution see PARA 659; as to how and when a conviction or caution becomes disregarded see PARA 665.

2 For the purposes of the Protection of Freedoms Act 2012 s 96, circumstances ancillary to a conviction or caution are any circumstances of:
  (1) the offence which was the subject of the conviction or caution (ss 96(7), 98(2)(a), (3)(a));
  (2) the conduct constituting the offence (s 98(2)(b), (3)(b));
  (3) any process or proceedings preliminary to the conviction (s 98(2)(c)), any process preliminary to the caution (including consideration by any person of how to deal with the offence and the procedure for giving the caution) (s 98(3)(c)), any proceedings for the offence which take place before the caution is given (s 98(3)(d)), and anything which happens after the caution is given for the purpose of bringing any such proceedings to an end (s 98(3)(e));
  (4) any sentence imposed in respect of the conviction (s 98(2)(d));
  (5) any proceedings (whether by way of appeal or otherwise) for reviewing the conviction or any such sentence (s 98(2)(e));
  (6) anything done in pursuance of, or undergone in compliance with, any such sentence (s 98(2)(f));
  (7) any judicial review proceedings relating to the caution (s 98(3)(f)); and
  (8) in the case of a warning under the Crime and Disorder Act 1998 s 65 (reprimands and warnings for persons aged under 18: see CHILDREN AND YOUNG PERSONS vol 10 (2012) PARA 1197), anything done in pursuance of, or undergone in compliance with, a

requirement to participate in a rehabilitation programme under s 66(2) (see CHILDREN AND YOUNG PERSONS vol 10 (2012) PARA 1198) (Protection of Freedoms Act 2012 s 98(3)(g)).

As to the meanings of 'conviction' and 'caution' see PARA 660. As to the meaning of 'sentence' see PARA 659 note 9.

3   Protection of Freedoms Act 2012 ss 92(5), 96(5)(a).
4   Protection of Freedoms Act 2012 s 96(5)(b).

662. Inadmissibility of evidence of disregarded convictions and cautions. No evidence is admissible in any proceedings before a judicial authority[1] exercising its jurisdiction or functions in England and Wales to prove that a person has committed, been charged with, been convicted of, or been prosecuted, sentenced or cautioned for, an offence[2] the conviction of or caution for which has become[3] disregarded[4], and such a person is not, in any such proceedings, to be asked (and, if asked, is not to be required to answer) any question relating to his past which cannot be answered without acknowledging or referring to the conviction or caution or any circumstances ancillary to it[5].

1   For the purposes of the Protection of Freedoms Act 2012 s 96 'proceedings before a judicial authority' includes (in addition to proceedings before any of the ordinary courts of law) proceedings before any tribunal, body or person having power:
     (1)   by virtue of any enactment, law, custom or practice (s 98(1)(a));
     (2)   under the rules governing any association, institution, profession, occupation or employment (s 98(1)(b)); or
     (3)   under any provision of an agreement providing for arbitration with respect to questions arising under that agreement (s 98(1)(c)),
   to determine any question affecting the rights, privileges, obligations or liabilities of any person, or to receive evidence affecting the determination of any such question.
2   Ie that the person has done, or undergone, anything within the Protection of Freedoms Act 2012 s 92(1)(a)–(e) (see PARA 659). As to the meanings of 'conviction' and 'caution' see PARA 660.
3   Ie for the purposes of the Protection of Freedoms Act 2012 Pt 5 Ch 4 (ss 92–101) (see PARAS 659–661, 663–665). Note that these provisions do not effect Royal pardons and similar matters (ie they are subject to s 97; see PARA 659) but otherwise apply despite any enactment or rule of law to the contrary (s 96(6)). As to the meaning and effect of a disregarded conviction or caution see PARA 659; as to how and when a conviction or caution becomes disregarded see PARA 665.
4   Protection of Freedoms Act 2012 s 96(2)(a).
5   Protection of Freedoms Act 2012 s 96(2)(b). As to the circumstances ancillary to a conviction or caution see PARA 661 note 2.

663. Protection of information about disregarded convictions and cautions. Where a question is put to a person, other than in proceedings before a judicial authority[1], seeking information[2] with respect to the previous convictions[3], cautions[4], offences, conduct or circumstances of any person:

     (1)   the question is to be treated as not relating to any disregarded conviction or caution[5], or any circumstances ancillary to it[6]; and

     (2)   the person questioned is not to be subjected to any liability or otherwise prejudiced in law by reason of any failure to acknowledge or disclose that conviction or caution or any circumstances ancillary to it in answering the question[7].

Any obligation imposed on any person by any enactment or rule of law or by the provisions of any agreement or arrangement to disclose any matters to any other person is not to extend to requiring the disclosure of a disregarded conviction or caution or any circumstances ancillary to it[8].

1   See PARA 662.
2   'Information' includes documents; and 'document' includes information recorded in any form and, in relation to information recorded otherwise than in legible form, references to its

provision or production include providing or producing a copy of the information in legible form: Protection of Freedoms Act 2012 s 101(1).

3   As to the meaning of 'conviction' see PARA 660 note 1.

4   As to the meaning of 'caution' see PARA 660 note 2.

5   Ie a conviction or caution which has become disregarded for the purposes of the Protection of Freedoms Act 2012 Pt 5 Ch 4 (ss 92–101) (see PARAS 659–662, 664–665). Note that these provisions do not effect Royal pardons and similar matters (ie they are subject to s 97; see PARA 659) but otherwise apply despite any enactment or rule of law to the contrary (s 96(6)). As to the meaning and effect of a disregarded conviction or caution see PARA 659; as to how and when a conviction or caution becomes disregarded see PARA 665.

6   Protection of Freedoms Act 2012 s 96(3)(a). The answer to the question may be framed accordingly: s 96(3)(a). As to the circumstances ancillary to a conviction or caution see PARA 661 note 2.

7   Protection of Freedoms Act 2012 s 96(3)(b).

8   Protection of Freedoms Act 2012 s 96(4).

664.   Deletion from official records.   Where a conviction[1] or caution[2] has become disregarded[3] the Secretary of State must by notice[4] direct the relevant data controller[5] to delete[6] details, contained in relevant official records, of that conviction or caution[7]. Such notice may be given at any time after the Secretary of State has decided that the conduct constituting the offence was consensual and would now be lawful[8], but no deletion may have effect before the applicable notification requirements and time limits have been complied with[9]. Subject to that, the relevant data controller must delete the details as soon as reasonably practicable[10] and having done so, must give notice to the person who has the disregarded conviction or caution that the details of it have been deleted[11].

1   As to the meaning of 'conviction' see PARA 660 note 1.

2   As to the meaning of 'caution' see PARA 660 note 2.

3   Ie for the purposes of the Protection of Freedoms Act 2012 Pt 5 Ch 4 (ss 92–101) (see PARAS 659–663, 665). As to the meaning and effect of a disregarded conviction or caution see PARA 659; as to how and when a conviction or caution becomes disregarded see PARA 665.

4   'Notice' means notice in writing: Protection of Freedoms Act 2012 s 101(1).

5   'Relevant data controller' means:
    (1)   in relation to the names database, any chief officer of police of a police force in England and Wales who is a data controller in relation to the details concerned (Protection of Freedoms Act 2012 s 95(5)); and
    (2)   in relation to other relevant official records (by virtue of s 95(5), (6) and the Protection of Freedoms Act 2012 (Relevant Official Records) Order 2012, SI 2012/2279, art 3):
        (a)   the chief officer of police of a police force in England and Wales in relation to the records kept locally by that force for the use of constables;
        (b)   the chief constable of the British Transport Police in relation to the records kept locally by the British Transport Police for the use of constables;
        (c)   the chief constable of the Ministry of Defence Police in relation to the records kept by the Ministry of Defence Police for the use of constables;
        (d)   the Provost Marshal for the Royal Navy Police in relation to the records kept by the Royal Navy Police for the use of members of a service police force;
        (e)   the Provost Marshal for the Royal Military Police in relation to the records kept by the Royal Military Police for the use of members of a service police force;
        (f)   the Provost Marshal for the Royal Air Force Police in relation to the records kept by the Royal Air Force Police for the use of members of a service police force;
        (g)   the Secretary of State for Justice in relation to the records of magistrates' courts dating from 1992 kept by Her Majesty's Courts and Tribunals Service; and
        (h)   the Secretary of State for Justice in relation to the records of the Crown Court kept by Her Majesty's Courts and Tribunals Service.
    As to police forces in England and Wales see POLICE AND INVESTIGATORY POWERS vol 84 (2013) PARA 52 et seq. As to the British Transport Police see RAILWAYS AND TRAMWAYS vol 86 (2013) PARA 287. As to the Ministry of Defence Police see POLICE AND INVESTIGATORY POWERS vol 84 (2013) PARA 27. As to Her Majesty's Courts and Tribunals Service see COURTS AND TRIBUNALS vol 24 (2010) PARA 828. 'The names database' means the names database held by the Secretary of State for the use of constables (Protection of Freedoms Act 2012 s 95(5)

(amended by the Crime and Courts Act 2013 Sch 8 para 185)); 'official records' means records containing information about persons convicted of, or cautioned for, offences and kept by any court, police force, government department or local or other public authority in England and Wales for the purposes of its functions (Protection of Freedoms Act 2012 s 95(5)); and 'relevant official records' means (by virtue of s 95(5) and the Protection of Freedoms Act 2012 (Relevant Official Records) Order 2012, SI 2012/2279, art 2):

    (i)   records kept locally by a police force for the use of constables;

    (ii)   records kept locally by the British Transport Police for the use of constables;

    (iii) records kept by the Ministry of Defence Police for the use of constables;

    (iv) records kept by the Royal Navy Police for the use of members of a service police force;

    (v)   records kept by the Royal Military Police for the use of members of a service police force;

    (vi) records kept by the Royal Air Force Police for the use of members of a service police force;

    (vii) records of magistrates' courts dating from 1992 kept by Her Majesty's Courts and Tribunals Service; and

    (viii) records of the Crown Court kept by Her Majesty's Courts and Tribunals Service.

6   In relation to any records forming part of the names database which are not held electronically and the relevant official records referred to in note 5 heads (i)–(viii), 'delete' means record with the details of the conviction or caution concerned the fact that it is a disregarded conviction or caution and the effect of it being such a conviction or caution: Protection of Freedoms Act 2012 s 95(5); Protection of Freedoms Act 2012 (Relevant Official Records) Order 2012, SI 2012/2279, art 4.

7   Protection of Freedoms Act 2012 s 95(1).

8   Ie at any time after Condition A in the Protection of Freedoms Act 2012 s 92(3) (see PARA 665) is met: Protection of Freedoms Act 2012 s 95(2).

9   Ie before Condition B in the Protection of Freedoms Act 2012 s 92(3) is met: Protection of Freedoms Act 2012 s 95(2).

10   Protection of Freedoms Act 2012 s 95(3).

11   Protection of Freedoms Act 2012 s 95(4).

665. When a conviction or caution becomes disregarded. A person who has been convicted of, or cautioned for, an offence a conviction of or a caution for which may be disregarded[1], may apply to the Secretary of State[2] for the conviction or caution to become a disregarded conviction or caution[3]. On receiving such an application the Secretary of State must decide whether it appears that the other person involved in the conduct constituting the offence consented to it and was aged 16 or over[4] and that any such conduct now would not be[5] an offence of sexual activity in a public lavatory[6]. If the Secretary of State decides these matters in the affirmative 'Condition A' has been met[7]. The Secretary of State must record his decision[8] in writing[9] and give notice of it to the applicant[10], and the conviction or caution will become a disregarded conviction or caution when the period of 14 days beginning with the day on which such notice was given has ended[11] (ie after 'Condition B' has also been met)[12].

The applicant may appeal to the High Court[13] if the Secretary of State does not decide condition A in the affirmative[14], and if the High Court decides that it appears as mentioned in condition A, it must make an order to that effect[15] and any conviction or caution to which such an order relates becomes a disregarded conviction or caution when the period of 14 days beginning with the day on which the order was made has ended[16]. If the High Court does not so decide it must dismiss the appeal[17]. There is no further appeal[18].

1   Ie for the purposes of the Protection of Freedoms Act 2012 Pt 5 Ch 4 (ss 92–101) (see PARAS 659–664). As to the meaning and effect of a disregarded conviction or caution see PARA 659; as to the offences a conviction of, or a caution for, may be disregarded, and as to the meanings of 'conviction' and 'caution', see PARA 660.

2   An application must be in writing (Protection of Freedoms Act 2012 s 93(1)) and must state the name, address and date of birth of the applicant (s 93(2)(a)), the name and address of the

applicant at the time of the conviction or caution (s 93(2)(b)), so far as known to the applicant, the time when and the place where the conviction was made or the caution given and, for a conviction, the case number (s 93(2)(c)), and such other information as the Secretary of State may require (s 93(2)(d)). It may also include representations by the applicant or written evidence about the matters mentioned in condition A in s 92: s 93(3).

3   Protection of Freedoms Act 2012 s 92(1).
4   Protection of Freedoms Act 2012 s 92(3)(a). In considering whether to make a decision of the kind mentioned in s 92(3), the Secretary of State must, in particular, consider any representations or evidence included in the application (s 94(1)(a)) and any available record of the investigation of the offence and of any proceedings relating to it that the Secretary of State considers to be relevant (s 94(1)(b)). However he may not hold an oral hearing for the purpose of deciding whether to make a decision of the kind mentioned in s 92(3): s 94(2).
      The Secretary of State may appoint persons to advise whether, in any case referred to them by the Secretary of State, the Secretary of State should decide as mentioned in s 92(3): s 100(1). He may disclose to a person so appointed such information (including anything within s 94(1)(a) or (b)) as he considers relevant to the provision of such advice: s 100(2). The Secretary of State may pay expenses and allowances to a person so appointed: s 100(3). See also s 93(3); and note 2.
5   Ie under the Sexual Offences Act 2003 s 71 (sexual activity in a public lavatory: see CRIMINAL LAW vol 25 (2010) PARA 269) (which includes an offence under the Armed Forces Act 2006 s 42 (criminal conduct: see ARMED FORCES vol 3 (2011) PARA 587) which is such an offence by virtue of the Sexual Offences Act 2003 71) (Protection of Freedoms Act 2012 ss 92(3)(b), 101(4)).
6   Protection of Freedoms Act 2012 s 92(3)(b).
7   Protection of Freedoms Act 2012 s 92(3).
8   Ie the Secretary of State's decision that it appears as mentioned in condition A (Protection of Freedoms Act 2012 s 94(3)(a)) or a different decision in relation to the matters mentioned in that condition (s 94(3)(b)). A decision under s 94(3)(b) is appealable: see s 99; and the text and notes 13–18.
9   Protection of Freedoms Act 2012 s 94(4)(a).
10 Protection of Freedoms Act 2012 ss 92(4)(a), 94(4)(b).
11 Protection of Freedoms Act 2012 s 92(4)(b).
12 Protection of Freedoms Act 2012 s 92(2).
13 Ie if the High Court gives permission for such an appeal: Protection of Freedoms Act 2012 s 99(1)(b).
14 Ie if the Secretary of State makes a decision in relation to the matters in condition A makes a decision of the kind mentioned in the Protection of Freedoms Act 2012 s 94(3)(b) (see note 8): s 99(1)(a).
15 Protection of Freedoms Act 2012 s 99(3). On such an appeal, the High Court must make its decision only on the basis of the evidence that was available to the Secretary of State: s 99(2).
16 Protection of Freedoms Act 2012 s 99(5).
17 Protection of Freedoms Act 2012 s 99(4).
18 Protection of Freedoms Act 2012 s 99(6).

(2) PROVISION OF PROBATION SERVICES

(i) Introduction

666. Purposes of probation. The purposes of probation[1] are the purposes of providing for:

(1)   courts to be given assistance in determining the appropriate sentences to pass, and making other decisions, in respect of persons charged with or convicted of offences[2];

(2)   the giving of assistance to persons determining whether conditional cautions[3] should be given and which conditions to attach to conditional cautions[4];

(3)   the supervision and rehabilitation of persons charged with or convicted of offences[5], including in particular:

(a)   giving effect to community orders[6] and suspended sentence orders[7];

(b)   assisting in the rehabilitation of offenders who are being held in prison[8];

(c)   supervising persons released from prison on licence[9]; and

(d)   providing accommodation in approved premises[10],

(4)   the giving of assistance to persons remanded on bail[11];

(5)   the supervision and rehabilitation of persons to whom conditional cautions are given[12]; and

(6)   the giving of information to victims[13] of persons charged with or convicted of offences[14].

1   The Secretary of State may by regulations extend the purposes referred to in the Offender Management Act 2007 s 1(1) (see the text and notes 2–14) to include other purposes relating to persons charged with or convicted of offences or persons to whom conditional cautions are given: s 1(5). At the date at which this volume states this power had not been exercised.

2   Offender Management Act 2007 s 1(1)(a).

3   Ie within the meaning of the Criminal Justice Act 2003 Pt 3 (ss 22–27) (see CRIMINAL PROCEDURE vol 27 (2015) PARA 55).

4   Offender Management Act 2007 s 1(1)(b), (4) (s 1(1)(b), (4) amended by the Criminal Justice and Immigration Act 2008 Sch 4 para 99, Sch 26 para 83).

5   Offender Management Act 2007 s 1(1)(c). This purpose also applies in relation to persons who are convicted of an offence under the law of a country outside England and Wales and receive a sentence which is to any extent to be served or carried out in England and Wales, as it applies in relation to persons convicted of offences: s 1(3).

6   'Community order' means (by virtue of the Offender Management Act 2007 s 1(4) (as amended: see note 4)):

    (1)   a community order within the meaning of the Criminal Justice Act 2003 (see s 177; and PARA 45 et seq); and

    (2)   a youth rehabilitation order under the Criminal Justice and Immigration Act 2008 Pt 1 (see s 1; and PARA 73 et seq).

7   Offender Management Act 2007 s 1(2)(a). 'Suspended sentence order' refers to an order within the meaning of the Criminal Justice Act 2003 s 189 (see PARA 100): Offender Management Act 2007 s 1(4). Where the purpose of providing for the supervision and rehabilitation of convicted offenders is extended to persons convicted abroad (see s 1(3); and note 5), this provision should be read as referring to any sentence corresponding to a community order or a suspended sentence order which is to be carried out in England and Wales: s 1(2)(a).

8   Offender Management Act 2007 s 1(2)(b). 'Prison' includes a young offender institution (see PARA 16; and PRISONS AND PRISONERS vol 85 (2012) PARA 487), a secure training centre (see PRISONS AND PRISONERS vol 85 (2012) PARA 491 et seq) and a secure college (see PRISONS AND PRISONERS): s 1(4) (amended by the Criminal Justice and Courts Act 2015 Sch 9 para 25).

9   Offender Management Act 2007 s 1(2)(c).

10 Offender Management Act 2007 s 1(2)(d).

11 Offender Management Act 2007 s 1(1)(d).

12 Offender Management Act 2007 s 1(1)(e).

13 'Victim' includes a person claiming to be a victim of a person charged with or convicted of an offence: Offender Management Act 2007 s 1(4).

14 Offender Management Act 2007 s 1(1)(f).

667.   Aims of probation. The aims of probation are:

(1)   the protection of the public[1];

(2)   the reduction of re-offending[2];

(3)   the proper punishment of offenders[3];

(4)   ensuring offenders' awareness of the effects of crime on the victims of crime and the public[4]; and

(5)   the rehabilitation of offenders[5].

1   Offender Management Act 2007 s 2(4)(a).

2   Offender Management Act 2007 s 2(4)(b).

3   Offender Management Act 2007 s 2(4)(c).

4   Offender Management Act 2007 s 2(4)(d).

5   Offender Management Act 2007 s 2(4)(e).

668.   Extension of probation arrangements to service proceedings abroad.
Independently of the transfer of responsibility for the making of arrangements
for the provision of probation services from local probation boards to probation
trusts and other public bodies[1] it continues to be provided that a local probation
board[2] may, in pursuance of arrangements made with the Secretary of State,
carry out activities anywhere in the world in relation to persons who are or have
been subject to proceedings before the Court Martial, the Summary Appeal
Court or the Service Civilian Court[3]. Any activities carried out in relation to such
persons must correspond to activities which the board is required or authorised
to carry out in relation to persons who have been charged with or convicted of
criminal offences[4].

1   Local probation boards were responsible for making arrangements for the provision of
    probation services in England and Wales under the Criminal Justice and Court Services Act 2000
    Pt 1 Ch 1 (ss 1–10). Those provisions have been repealed insofar as they relate to the provision
    of probation services in England and Wales and replaced by the Offender Management Act 2007
    Pt 1 (ss 1–15), under which such responsibility is transferred to probation trusts and other
    public bodies: however the Criminal Justice and Court Services Act 2000 s 5A (added by the
    Armed Forces Act 2006 Sch 16 para 178 and substituted by s 327) (local probation boards and
    service justice: see the text and notes 2–4) remains in force.
2   Local probation boards were established under the Criminal Justice and Court Services
    Act 2000 s 4 (repealed).
3   Criminal Justice and Court Services Act 2000 s 5A(1) (as added and substituted: see note 1).
4   Criminal Justice and Court Services Act 2000 s 5A(2) (as added and substituted: see note 1).

(ii)   Provision of Probation Services

669.   Arrangements for the making of probation provision.   It is the function
of the Secretary of State to ensure that sufficient provision[1] is made throughout
England and Wales:
(1)   for the probation purposes[2];
(2)   for enabling functions conferred by any enactment on providers of
       probation services, or on officers of a provider of probation services[3], to
       be performed[4]; and
(3)   for the performance of any function of the Secretary of State under any
       enactment which is expressed to be a relevant function[5].
The Secretary of State must discharge this function in relation to any
probation provision by making and carrying out contractual and other
arrangements with any other person for the making of that provision[6]. Such
arrangements may in particular authorise or require the person with whom the
Secretary of State is making the arrangements:
(a)   to co-operate with other providers of probation services or persons who
       are concerned with the prevention or reduction of crime or with giving
       assistance to the victims of crime[7];
(b)   to authorise individuals[8] to act as officers of a provider of probation
       services[9]; or
(c)   to make contractual or other arrangements with third parties for
       purposes connected with the probation provision to be made[10].
Arrangements under these provisions relating to 'restricted probation
provision' (that is, probation provision which is made for the probation
purposes[11] or for enabling functions conferred by any enactment on providers of
probation services, or on officers of a provider of probation services, to be
performed[12] and relates to the giving of assistance to any court in determining

the appropriate sentence to pass, or making any other decision, in respect of a person charged with or convicted of an offence[13]) may only be made with a probation trust or other public body[14].

1   Any provision which the Secretary of State considers should be made for these purposes is a 'probation provision': Offender Management Act 2007 s 2(1). The Secretary of State must have regard to the aims of the probation service (see s 2(4); and PARA 667) in the exercise of his functions under these provisions so far as they may be exercised for any of the probation purposes (see PARA 666) (s 2(3)): he is not, however, required to take any action in relation to the making of probation provision if it appears to him that appropriate provision is being or will be made by any person acting otherwise than in pursuance of arrangements under s 3 (s 2(5)). The Secretary of State must have regard to the annual plan published under s 8(2) (see PARA 672)) for any year in discharging his functions under s 2(1) during that year: s 8(3)(a). 'Year' means a period of 12 months ending with 31 March: s 8(7).

2   Offender Management Act 2007 s 2(1)(a).

3   'Provider of probation services' means:
    (1)   a person with whom the Secretary of State has made arrangements that are in force under s 3(2) (see the text and notes 4–6) (s 3(6)(a)); or
    (2)   the Secretary of State (in relation to probation provision which is the subject of arrangements that are in force under s 3(5)) (see PARA 671) (s 3(6)(b)).
    'Officer of a provider of probation services' means an individual who is for the time being authorised (s 9(1)); and an individual may be authorised to act as an officer of a particular provider of probation services (the 'relevant provider') by the Secretary of State (s 9(2)(a)) or (unless the relevant provider is the Secretary of State) a provider of probation services (whether the relevant provider or any other provider) who is authorised to do so by the Secretary of State (s 9(2)(b), (3)). 'Officer', in relation to a particular provider of probation services, means a person so authorised to act as an officer of that provider: s 9(1).

4   Offender Management Act 2007 s 2(1)(b). 'Enactment' includes subordinate legislation within the meaning of the Interpretation Act 1978 (see s 21(1); and STATUTES AND LEGISLATIVE PROCESS vol 96 (2012) PARAS 608, 1030).

5   Offender Management Act 2007 s 2(1)(c). The reference to a 'relevant function' is a reference to any function of the Secretary of State under any enactment which is expressed to be a function to which s 2(1)(c) applies: s 2(1)(c). The Secretary of State may make provision for the performance of any function to which s 2(1)(c) applies by making arrangements under s 3(2) providing for the delegation of that function to the other person: s 3(4).

6   Offender Management Act 2007 ss 2(2), 3(1), (2). See PARA 670 (power to establish probation trusts) and PARA 671 (making of probation provision by Secretary of State). The Secretary of State must have regard to the annual plan published under s 8(2) (see PARA 672) for any year in discharging his functions under s 2(2) during that year (s 8(3)(a)), and in carrying out his functions under these provisions in relation to arrangements under s 3(2) with another person (the 'provider'), must have regard to the need to take reasonable steps to avoid (so far as practicable) the risk that the provision, in pursuance of the arrangements, of assistance to a court or to the Parole Board for England and Wales (or, as from a day to be appointed, to a recall adjudicator as defined by the Criminal Justice Act 2003 s 239A (see PARA 705)), and the carrying out, in pursuance of the arrangements, of any other activities, might be adversely affected by any potential conflict between the provider's obligations in relation to those activities and the financial interests of the provider: Offender Management Act 2007 s 3(7) (prospectively amended by the Criminal Justice and Courts Act 2015 Sch 3 para 14). The Secretary of State must also ensure that arrangements under the Offender Management Act 2007 s 3(2) or (5) for the supervision or rehabilitation of persons convicted of offences state that the Secretary of State has, in making the arrangements, complied with the duty under the Equality Act 2010 s 149 (public sector equality duty: see DISCRIMINATION vol 33 (2013) PARAS 266–272) as it relates to female offenders and identify anything in the arrangements that is intended to meet the particular needs of female offenders: Offender Management Act 2007 s 3(6A)(a) (ss 3(6A), 4(3) added by the Offender Rehabilitation Act 2014 s 10, Sch 4 para 8).
    In exercising his powers under the Offender Management Act 2007 s 3(2) and s 3(5) (see PARA 671) the Secretary of State must also have regard to the need to secure, so far as practicable, that guidelines published under s 10 (see PARA 672) have the same effect in relation to every provider of probation services whose officers perform work to which they relate (s 10(4)), and in exercising his powers under s 3(2), must have regard to the need to secure, so far as practicable, that the arrangements in force from time to time provide for the national

standards to have the same effect in relation to every provider of probation services carrying out the activities to which the standards apply (s 7(3)). As to the publication of national standards see s 7(1); and PARA 672.

7   Offender Management Act 2007 s 3(3)(a).

8   Ie under the Offender Management Act 2007 s 9(2): see note 3.

9   Offender Management Act 2007 s 3(3)(b).

10 Offender Management Act 2007 s 3(3)(c). Such contractual or other arrangements include in particular:
    (1)   for provision to be made, or for activities to be carried out, by third parties on behalf of that other person (s 3(3)(c)(i)); or
    (2)   for individuals who are not members of that other person's staff to act as officers of a provider of probation services (s 3(3)(c)(ii)).

11 As to the probation purposes see PARA 666.

12 Ie probation provision which is made for a purpose mentioned in the Offender Management Act 2007 2(1)(a) or (b) (see PARA 669): s 4(2)(a).

13 Offender Management Act 2007 s 4(2)(b). The provision described in s 4(2)(b) includes provision which relates to the making of an application by an officer to a court under the Criminal Justice Act 2003 Sch 8 para 13, 14, 17, 19A or 20 (revocation or amendment of community orders: see PARA 57 et seq), Sch 12 paras 13, 15, 17 or 18 (amendment of suspended sentence orders: see PARA 105 et seq), or Sch 19A para 10 (revocation or amendment of supervision default orders: see PARA 741): Offender Management Act 2007 s 4(3) (as added: see note 6).

14 Offender Management Act 2007 s 4(1). Section 4 may be repealed by order of the Secretary of State (s 15(1)), and such power of repeal includes power to provide for s 4 to cease to have effect for such purposes as may be specified in the order (s 15(2)). At the date at which this volume states the law no such order had been made.

670.   Power to establish probation trusts. The Secretary of State may by order establish a probation trust for purposes specified in the order[1]. The purposes of a probation trust must include the making or performance by the trust[2] of contracts with the Secretary of State[3], and may include all or any of the following purposes:

(1)   the making and performance by the trust of contracts with another probation trust or any other person which provide for the carrying out by the trust of activities which contribute to the achievement of any of the probation purposes[4];

(2)   the making or performance by the trust of contracts with the Secretary of State for the carrying out by the trust of activities anywhere in the world which are to be carried out in connection with persons who are or have been subject to proceedings in service courts and correspond to activities which, if carried out in connection with persons charged with or convicted of offences, would contribute to the achievement of any of the probation purposes[5]; and

(3)   any other purpose specified for these purposes by regulations made by the Secretary of State[6].

A number of trusts were previously established by the Secretary of State pursuant to these provisions[7] but all of them have been dissolved[8], and at the date at which this volume states the law there are no trusts established for these purposes.

1   Offender Management Act 2007 s 5(1)(a): the Secretary of State may also by order alter the name or purposes of, or dissolve, a probation trust: s 5(1)(b), (c). As to the establishment and constitution of probation trusts see further s 5(6), Sch 1. A purpose specified for a probation trust under s 5(1)(a) may be expressed in more specific terms than those used in s 5(2) or (3)(a) or (b) (see the text and notes 2–5) or in regulations under s 5(3)(c) (see the text and note 6): s 5(4).

2   Ie under the Offender Management Act 2007 s 3(2): see PARA 669. A purpose specified under these provisions which relates to the making or performance of contracts includes the carrying

out of any activities relating to a contract of a relevant kind (including activities taking place before it is made or after it is terminated): s 5(5). Arrangements made by the Secretary of State under s 3(2) with a probation trust must, and arrangements so made by the Secretary of State with a person other than a probation trust may if the Secretary of State thinks fit, require the trust or that person to publish an annual plan for each year in which it expects to carry out any specified activities (ie activities of a description specified in those arrangements for this purpose): s 8(4)–(6). 'Annual plan' means a plan setting out the way in which the probation trust or other person (as the case may be) proposes to carry out any specified activities during the year to which the plan relates: s 8(6).

3   Offender Management Act 2007 s 5(2).
4   Offender Management Act 2007 s 5(3)(a). As to the probation purposes see s 1; and PARA 666.
5   Offender Management Act 2007 s 5(3)(b).
6   Offender Management Act 2007 s 5(3)(c).
7   See the Offender Management Act 2007 (Establishment of Probation Trusts) Order 2008, SI 2008/598; the Offender Management Act 2007 (Establishment of Probation Trusts) Order 2009, SI 2009/504; and the Offender Management Act 2007 (Establishment of Probation Trusts) Order 2010, SI 2010/195.
8   See the Offender Management Act 2007 (Dissolution of Probation Trusts) Order 2014, SI 2014/2704.

671.   Making of probation provision by the Secretary of State.   If instead of making arrangements[1] for the making of probation provision[2] by probation trusts[3], other public bodies or other persons, the Secretary of State considers it appropriate to make any probation provision himself, he must make arrangements for the making of that probation provision[4].

1   Ie under the Offender Management Act 2007 s 3(2): see PARA 669.
2   As to the meaning of 'probation provision' see PARA 669 note 1.
3   As to the establishment and purposes of probation trusts see PARA 670.
4   Offender Management Act 2007 s 3(5). For the avoidance of doubt the members of staff through whom the Secretary of State may act in making and carrying out such arrangements include prison officers or other persons employed at a prison: s 3(5). The Secretary of State must have regard to the annual plan published under s 8(2) (see PARA 672) for any year in making or carrying out arrangements under s 3(5) for that year: s 8(3)(b). As to the meaning of 'year' see PARA 669 note 1. See also ss 3(6A), (7), 10(4); and PARA 669 note 6.

672.   Supplementary powers and duties of the Secretary of State.   The Secretary of State:

(1)   may make payments[1] to a probation trust[2] or towards expenditure incurred by any other person for any purpose falling within the probation purposes[3];

(2)   may publish guidelines about any qualifications, experience or training required to perform the work of an officer of a provider of probation services[4], and must publish such guidelines in relation to work involving the supervision of offenders and other work requiring direct contact with offenders (including offenders held in custody)[5];

(3)   must at least once in every year[6] consult the Welsh Ministers[7], and such other persons as he thinks fit, about the provision that should be made for the purposes of the probation provision[8] for the following year[9];

(4)   must before the end of each year publish an annual plan for the following year which sets out the way in which he proposes to discharge his functions relating to the making of probation provision[10] during that year and carry out any arrangements which he expects to be in force[11] for the carrying out of such provision himself for that year[12]; and

(5)   must continue to publish national standards for the management of offenders[13].

1   Ie other than payments falling to be made in pursuance of arrangements under the Offender
    Management Act 2007 s 3(2) (see PARA 669): s 6(1). Payments under s 6 may be made on
    conditions (which may require repayment in specified circumstances): s 6(2).
2   As to the establishment and purposes of probation trusts see PARA 670.
3   Offender Management Act 2007 s 6(1). As to the purposes of the probation service see PARA
    666.
4   As to the meanings of 'provider of probation services' and 'officer of a provider of probation
    services' see PARA 669 note 3.
5   Offender Management Act 2007 s 10(1), (2). Guidelines under s 10 may make different
    provision for different purposes: s 10(3). At the date at which this volume states the law no
    guidelines had been published.
6   As to the meaning of 'year' see PARA 669 note 1.
7   As to the Welsh Ministers and the Welsh Assembly Government see the Government of Wales
    Act 2006 Pt 2 (ss 45–92); and CONSTITUTIONAL AND ADMINISTRATIVE LAW vol 20 (2014) PARA
    373 et seq.
8   Ie the purposes mentioned in the Offender Management Act 2007 s 2(1): see PARA 669.
9   Offender Management Act 2007 s 8(1).
10 Ie functions under the Offender Management Act 2007 s 2(1), (2): see PARA 669.
11 Ie under the Offender Management Act 2007 s 3(5): see PARA 671.
12 Offender Management Act 2007 s 8(2). Regard must be had to this plan in the carrying out of
    the Secretary of State's functions: see s 8(3); and PARAS 669 notes 1, 6, 671 note 4.
13 Offender Management Act 2007 s 7(1). The national standards may in particular include
    standards relating to the management of offenders held in custody: s 7(2). See *National
    Standards for the Management of Offenders* (applicable from 1 February 2015), published by
    the Ministry of Justice and the National Offender Management Service.

(iii)   Approval of Premises for Probation Purposes

A. POWERS OF SECRETARY OF STATE

673.   Approval of premises by the Secretary of State. The Secretary of State
may approve premises in which accommodation is provided for persons granted
bail in criminal proceedings[1] or for or in connection with the supervision or
rehabilitation of persons convicted of offences[2], and may make payments in
connection with the operation of approved premises or constructing, enlarging
or improving premises, if they are approved premises or the works are being
carried out with a view to the premises becoming approved premises, to any
person who incurs expenditure on the activities in question[3].

1   Ie within the meaning of the Bail Act 1976: see s 1; and CRIMINAL PROCEDURE vol 27 (2015)
    PARA 67.
2   Offender Management Act 2007 s 13(1). 'Approved premises' means premises which are for the
    time being approved (s 13(1)), and references in any Act or subordinate legislation (within the
    meaning of the Interpretation Act 1978: see s 21(1); and STATUTES AND LEGISLATIVE PROCESS
    vol 96 (2012) PARAS 608, 1030) to an approved bail hostel or an approved probation hostel are
    to be read as a reference to approved premises (Offender Management Act 2007 s 13(6)).
3   Offender Management Act 2007 s 13(3). Such payments may be made on conditions (including
    conditions requiring repayment in specified circumstances) (s 13(4)), and the power to make
    those payments is without prejudice to the powers of the Secretary of State under ss 2–6 (see
    PARAS 669–671) (s 13(5)).

B. REQUIREMENTS APPLICABLE TO ALL APPROVED PREMISES

674.   Residence conditions. A provider of approved premises[1] must not allow
any person to become a resident[2] of approved premises or, where that person is a
resident, allow them to continue to reside there, unless:
   (1)   they are on bail[3];

(2)   they are serving a community sentence[4] or are subject to a suspended sentence order[5];

(3)   they are on licence[6];

(4)   they are subject to statutory supervision[7]; or

(5)   the Secretary of State considers that residence at the approved premises is necessary for the protection of the public[8]; or

(6)   the Secretary of State considers that the person ought to receive supervision or treatment and that residence at the approved premises is necessary in order to enable them to receive it[9].

1   As to the approval of premises by the Secretary of State see PARA 673.
2   'Resident', in relation to approved premises, means a person who lives in the approved premises otherwise than in the course of their employment, and 'reside' is construed accordingly: Offender Management Act 2007 (Approved Premises) Regulations 2014, SI 2014/1198, reg 4.
3   Offender Management Act 2007 (Approved Premises) Regulations 2014, SI 2014/1198, reg 5(1)(a). 'Bail' means bail in criminal proceedings within the meaning of the Bail Act 1976 (see s 1; and CRIMINAL PROCEDURE vol 27 (2015) PARA 67): Offender Management Act 2007 (Approved Premises) Regulations 2014, SI 2014/1198, reg 4.
4   As to the meaning of 'community sentence' see the Criminal Justice Act 2003 s 147; and PARA 42 (definition applied by the Offender Management Act 2007 (Approved Premises) Regulations 2014, SI 2014/1198, reg 4).
5   Offender Management Act 2007 (Approved Premises) Regulations 2014, SI 2014/1198, reg 5(1)(b). As to the meaning of 'suspended sentence order' see the Criminal Justice Act 2003 s 189; and PARA 100 (definition applied by the Offender Management Act 2007 (Approved Premises) Regulations 2014, SI 2014/1198, reg 4).
6   Offender Management Act 2007 (Approved Premises) Regulations 2014, SI 2014/1198, reg 5(1)(c). 'Licence' includes temporary release in accordance with the Prison Rules 1999, SI 1999/728, r 9 (see PARA 691): Offender Management Act 2007 (Approved Premises) Regulations 2014, SI 2014/1198, reg 4.
7   Offender Management Act 2007 (Approved Premises) Regulations 2014, SI 2014/1198, reg 5(1)(d). 'Statutory supervision' means supervision by virtue of the Criminal Justice Act 2003 s 256B (see PARA 745): Offender Management Act 2007 (Approved Premises) Regulations 2014, SI 2014/1198, reg 4.
8   Offender Management Act 2007 (Approved Premises) Regulations 2014, SI 2014/1198, reg 5(1)(e).
9   Offender Management Act 2007 (Approved Premises) Regulations 2014, SI 2014/1198, reg 5(1)(f).

675.   Number and age of residents.   Except with the prior consent of the Secretary of State a provider of approved premises[1] must not allow:

(1)   the number of residents[2] at any approved premises at any time to exceed such number as may be approved in respect of those premises by the Secretary of State[3]; or

(2)   any person to be present on approved premises if they are outside such age limits as may be approved by the Secretary of State in respect of the premises[4].

1   As to the approval of premises by the Secretary of State see PARA 673.
2   As to the meaning of 'resident' see PARA 674 note 2.
3   Offender Management Act 2007 (Approved Premises) Regulations 2014, SI 2014/1198, reg 5(2).
4   Offender Management Act 2007 (Approved Premises) Regulations 2014, SI 2014/1198, reg 5(3).

676.   Management and control.   Each provider of approved premises[1] must:

(1)   ensure that the premises are maintained in a condition which is satisfactory having regard to their purpose[2];

(2)   ensure that the premises are run in a manner which promotes protection of the public and the reduction of re-offending[3];

(3)   ensure that at least two members of staff are present at all times[4];

(4)   exercise effective control over all expenditure incurred in connection with the premises and prepare such statements of accounts as the Secretary of State may require[5];

(5)   prepare house rules for the premises governing the conduct of residents[6], which must comply with any requirements of the Secretary of State as to the content of such rules[7]; and

(6)   bring the house rules to the attention of every resident of the premises and take all appropriate measures to ensure that they are complied with by all such residents[8].

The provider is responsible for the appointment, training, discipline and dismissal of the staff of the premises[9].

All approved premises must be managed by a management committee[10].

1   As to the approval of premises by the Secretary of State see PARA 673.
2   Offender Management Act 2007 (Approved Premises) Regulations 2014, SI 2014/1198, reg 6(1)(a)(i).
3   Offender Management Act 2007 (Approved Premises) Regulations 2014, SI 2014/1198, reg 6(1)(a)(ii).
4   Offender Management Act 2007 (Approved Premises) Regulations 2014, SI 2014/1198, reg 6(1)(a)(iii).
5   Offender Management Act 2007 (Approved Premises) Regulations 2014, SI 2014/1198, reg 6(1)(b).
6   As to the meaning of 'resident' see PARA 674 note 2.
7   Offender Management Act 2007 (Approved Premises) Regulations 2014, SI 2014/1198, reg 6(1)(c).
8   Offender Management Act 2007 (Approved Premises) Regulations 2014, SI 2014/1198, reg 6(1)(d).
9   Offender Management Act 2007 (Approved Premises) Regulations 2014, SI 2014/1198, reg 6(2).
10 Offender Management Act 2007 (Approved Premises) Regulations 2014, SI 2014/1198, reg 14. Provision is made for the constitution and meetings of management committees: see regs 15, 16.

677. Admissions. Each provider of approved premises[1] must adopt an admissions policy for the premises[2], which must comply with the residence conditions[3] and any requirements of the Secretary of State as to the admissions policies of approved premises[4], and must notify the courts for the local justice area in which the premises are situated of the terms of such policy[5].

1   As to the approval of premises by the Secretary of State see PARA 673.
2   Offender Management Act 2007 (Approved Premises) Regulations 2014, SI 2014/1198, reg 7(1).
3   Ie the Offender Management Act 2007 (Approved Premises) Regulations 2014, SI 2014/1198, reg 5(1): see PARA 674.
4   Offender Management Act 2007 (Approved Premises) Regulations 2014, SI 2014/1198, reg 7(2).
5   Offender Management Act 2007 (Approved Premises) Regulations 2014, SI 2014/1198, reg 7(3).

678. Residence requirements. A 'residence requirement' is a requirement to reside[1] at approved premises[2] by virtue of:

(1)   a requirement of any court order[3];

(2)   any condition of a licence[4]; or

(3)   any requirement imposed under statutory supervision[5].

Where a person is subject to a residence requirement the provider of the approved premises must not require that person to end his residence before the expiry of the residence requirement unless:

(a)   an emergency has arisen[6]; or

(b)   the resident has broken the house rules and that breach has been reported to the applicable person[7].

Where a provider intends to require a resident who is subject to a residence requirement to end their residence at the approved premises, it must give reasonable notice of that intention:

(i)   in the case of a resident who is on bail[8], to the court which granted bail[9];

(ii)   in the case of a resident who is serving a community sentence[10] or is subject to a suspended sentence order[11], to the person responsible for supervising that sentence[12];

(iii) in the case of a resident who is on licence, to the person responsible for supervising that licence[13];

(iv)   in the case of a resident who is subject to statutory supervision, to the person providing the supervision[14].

1   As to the meaning of 'reside' see PARA 674 note 2.
2   As to the approval of premises by the Secretary of State see PARA 673.
3   Offender Management Act 2007 (Approved Premises) Regulations 2014, SI 2014/1198, reg 8(1)(a).
4   Offender Management Act 2007 (Approved Premises) Regulations 2014, SI 2014/1198, reg 8(1)(b). As to the meaning of 'licence' see PARA 674 note 6.
5   Offender Management Act 2007 (Approved Premises) Regulations 2014, SI 2014/1198, reg 8(1)(c). As to the meaning of 'statutory supervision' see PARA 674 note 7.
6   Offender Management Act 2007 (Approved Premises) Regulations 2014, SI 2014/1198, reg 8(2)(a).
7   Offender Management Act 2007 (Approved Premises) Regulations 2014, SI 2014/1198, reg 8(2)(b). If the residence requirement is imposed by virtue of a requirement of a court order (ie in a case to which reg 8(1)(a) applies) the breach must be reported to the court which made the order, and if it is imposed by virtue of any condition of a licence (ie in a case to which reg 8(1)(b) applies) or a requirement imposed under statutory supervision (ie in a case to which reg 8(1)(c) applies) the breach must be reported to the Secretary of State: reg 8(2)(b).
8   As to the meaning of 'bail' see PARA 674 note 3.
9   Offender Management Act 2007 (Approved Premises) Regulations 2014, SI 2014/1198, reg 8(3)(a).
10 As to the meaning of 'community sentence' see PARA 674 note 4.
11 As to the meaning of 'suspended sentence order' see PARA 674 note 5.
12 Offender Management Act 2007 (Approved Premises) Regulations 2014, SI 2014/1198, reg 8(3)(b).
13 Offender Management Act 2007 (Approved Premises) Regulations 2014, SI 2014/1198, reg 8(3)(c).
14 Offender Management Act 2007 (Approved Premises) Regulations 2014, SI 2014/1198, reg 8(3)(d).

679.   Absconding. A person in charge of approved premises[1] who believes that a resident[2] may have absconded must immediately notify:

(1)   in the case of a resident who is on bail[3] and is required as a condition of that bail to reside at the approved premises, the court which granted bail and the police[4];

(2)   in the case of a resident required by or under any provision of a community sentence[5] or suspended sentence order[6] to reside at the approved premises, the person responsible for supervising that sentence[7];

(3)   in the case of a resident required by virtue of any condition of a licence[8] to reside at the approved premises, the person responsible for supervising that licence[9];

(4)   in the case of a resident required by virtue of any requirement to reside at approved premises imposed as part of statutory supervision[10], the person providing the supervision[11].

1   As to the approval of premises by the Secretary of State see PARA 673.
2   As to the meaning of 'resident' see PARA 674 note 2.
3   As to the meaning of 'bail' see PARA 674 note 3.
4   Offender Management Act 2007 (Approved Premises) Regulations 2014, SI 2014/1198, reg 9(a).
5   As to the meaning of 'community sentence' see PARA 674 note 4.
6   As to the meaning of 'suspended sentence order' see PARA 674 note 5.
7   Offender Management Act 2007 (Approved Premises) Regulations 2014, SI 2014/1198, reg 9(b).
8   As to the meaning of 'licence' see PARA 674 note 6.
9   Offender Management Act 2007 (Approved Premises) Regulations 2014, SI 2014/1198, reg 9(c).
10   As to the meaning of 'statutory supervision' see PARA 674 note 7.
11   Offender Management Act 2007 (Approved Premises) Regulations 2014, SI 2014/1198, reg 9(c).

680.   Medical care and advice. Each provider of approved premises[1] must ensure that facilities are available for the provision to residents[2] of any necessary medical and dental treatment[3], and may appoint a health care professional to assist it in discharging these functions[4].

1   As to the approval of premises by the Secretary of State see PARA 673.
2   As to the meaning of 'resident' see PARA 674 note 2.
3   Offender Management Act 2007 (Approved Premises) Regulations 2014, SI 2014/1198, reg 11(1).
4   Offender Management Act 2007 (Approved Premises) Regulations 2014, SI 2014/1198, reg 11(2).

681.   Expenses, administration and inspection. The Secretary of State may determine the maximum sum that each provider of approved premises[1] may charge residents[2] in respect of the expenses of the resident's maintenance[3]. Each provider must arrange for the keeping of all registers and records required by the Secretary of State and cause to be sent to the Secretary of State such returns, statements and other information as may be required by the Secretary of State from time to time[4].

Each provider must arrange for approved premises to be open at all times to inspection by or on behalf of the Secretary of State and must, in connection with any such inspection, make available for examination the books and records of the premises[5].

1   As to the approval of premises by the Secretary of State see PARA 673.
2   As to the meaning of 'resident' see PARA 674 note 2.
3   Offender Management Act 2007 (Approved Premises) Regulations 2014, SI 2014/1198, reg 10.
4   Offender Management Act 2007 (Approved Premises) Regulations 2014, SI 2014/1198, reg 12.
5   Offender Management Act 2007 (Approved Premises) Regulations 2014, SI 2014/1198, reg 13.

(iv)   Inspections of Probation Services

682.   The inspectorate. There is an inspectorate and chief inspector of probation in England and Wales[1]. The principal function of the chief inspector is to secure that provision made in pursuance of arrangements for ensuring the provision of probation services is inspected by a member of the inspectorate[2] in accordance with criteria specified by the Secretary of State[3]. The Secretary of State may also give directions, in connection with the probation purposes[4], conferring further functions on the chief inspector and the other members of the inspectorate[5].

1   Ie Her Majesty's Inspectorate of Probation for England and Wales and its chief inspector, which were originally established under the Probation Service Act 1993 s 23 (repealed) and are continued in being by the Criminal Justice and Court Services Act 2000 s 6(1) (ss 6(1), (4), 7(1), (6) amended by the Offender Management Act 2007 s 12(2), (3), Sch 5 Pt 1). References to the chief inspector are to Her Majesty's Chief Inspector of the Probation for England and Wales; and references to the members of the inspectorate are to the chief inspector and the other members of Her Majesty's Inspectorate of Probation for England and Wales: Criminal Justice and Court Services Act 2000 s 6(4) (as so amended).
        The power to appoint a person to be chief inspector or one of the other members of the inspectorate is exercisable by the Secretary of State, who may also determine the number of members of the inspectorate and the remuneration and allowances or other amounts to be paid by him in respect of the members of the inspectorate: Criminal Justice and Court Services Act 2000 s 6(2), (3).
2   Criminal Justice and Court Services Act 2000 s 7(1) (as amended: see note 1). A report of such an inspection must be sent to the Secretary of State (Criminal Justice and Court Services Act 2000 s 7(3)): the Secretary of State may give directions as to the information to be given in the report and the form in which it is to be given, and the time by which the report is to be given (s 7(4)), and must lay a copy of the report before each House of Parliament (s 7(5)).
3   See the Criminal Justice and Court Services Act 2000 s 7(2) (empowering the Secretary of State to direct the members of the inspectorate to assess the provision made by reference to criteria specified in directions).
4   As to the probation purposes see PARA 666.
5   Criminal Justice and Court Services Act 2000 s 7(6) (as amended: see note 1).

683.   Delegation of functions.   A member of the inspectorate[1] may delegate any of his functions (to such extent as he may determine) to another public authority[2], although if a member of the inspectorate so delegates the carrying out of an inspection it is nevertheless to be regarded[3] as carried out by that member[4].

1   As to the inspectorate and its membership and functions see PARA 682.
2   Criminal Justice and Court Services Act 2000 Sch 1A para 1(1) (Sch 1A added by the Police and Justice Act 2006 s 31(2)). 'Public authority' includes any person certain of whose functions are functions of a public nature: Criminal Justice and Court Services Act 2000 Sch 1A para 1(3) (as so added).
3   Ie for the purposes of the Criminal Justice and Court Services Act 2000 s 7 (see PARA 682) and Sch 1A (see PARAS 684–687).
4   Criminal Justice and Court Services Act 2000 Sch 1A para 1(2) (as added: see note 2).

684.   Inspection programmes and frameworks.   The chief inspector[1] must from time to time, or at such times as the Secretary of State may specify by order[2], prepare an inspection programme[3] and an inspection framework[4] after consulting the Secretary of State and[5]:

(1)   Her Majesty's Chief Inspector of Prisons[6];
(2)   Her Majesty's Chief Inspector of Constabulary[7];
(3)   Her Majesty's Chief Inspector of the Crown Prosecution Service[8];
(4)   Her Majesty's Chief Inspector of Education, Children's Services and Skills[9];
(5)   the Auditor General for Wales[10];
(6)   the Care Quality Commission[11]; and
(7)   any other person or body specified by an order made by the Secretary of State[12],

and must send to each of those persons or bodies a copy of each programme or framework once it is prepared[13]. Nothing in any inspection programme or framework is to be read as preventing the inspectorate from making visits without notice[14].

1 As to references to the chief inspector see PARA 682 note 1.

2 At the date at which this volume states the law no such orders had been made.

3 Ie a document setting out what inspections the chief inspector proposes to carry out: Criminal Justice and Court Services Act 2000 Sch 1A para 2(1)(a) (Sch 1A added by the Police and Justice Act 2006 s 31(2)). The Secretary of State may by order specify the form that inspection programmes or inspection frameworks are to take (Criminal Justice and Court Services Act 2000 Sch 1A para 2(4) (as so added)): at the date at which this volume states the law no such order had been made.

4 Ie a document setting out the manner in which the chief inspector proposes to carry out his functions of inspecting and reporting: Criminal Justice and Court Services Act 2000 Sch 1A para 2(1)(b) (as added: see note 3).

5 Ie subject to any agreement made between the chief inspector and the specified person or body to waive the requirement in such cases or circumstances as may be specified in the agreement: Criminal Justice and Court Services Act 2000 Sch 1A para 2(3) (as added: see note 3).

6 Criminal Justice and Court Services Act 2000 Sch 1A para 2(2)(a) (as added: see note 3). As to Her Majesty's Chief Inspector of Prisons see PRISONS AND PRISONERS vol 85 (2012) PARA 409.

7 Criminal Justice and Court Services Act 2000 Sch 1A para 2(2)(b) (as added: see note 3). As to Her Majesty's Chief Inspector of Constabulary see POLICE AND INVESTIGATORY POWERS vol 84 (2013) PARA 152.

8 Criminal Justice and Court Services Act 2000 Sch 1A para 2(2)(c) (as added: see note 3). As to Her Majesty's Chief Inspector of the Crown Prosecution Service see CRIMINAL PROCEDURE vol 27 (2015) PARA 26.

9 Criminal Justice and Court Services Act 2000 Sch 1A para 2(2)(e) (as added: see note 3). As to Her Majesty's Chief Inspector of Education, Children's Services and Skills see EDUCATION vol 36 (2015) PARA 1128 et seq.

10 Criminal Justice and Court Services Act 2000 Sch 1A para 2(2)(i) (as added: see note 3). As to the Auditor General for Wales see CONSTITUTIONAL AND ADMINISTRATIVE LAW vol 20 (2014) PARA 400.

11 Criminal Justice and Court Services Act 2000 Sch 1A para 2(2)(g) (as added (see note 3); substituted by the Health and Social Care Act 2008 Sch 5 para 74). As to the Care Quality Commission see SOCIAL SERVICES AND COMMUNITY CARE vol 95 (2013) PARA 217 et seq.

12 Criminal Justice and Court Services Act 2000 Sch 1A para 2(2)(j) (as added: see note 3). At the date at which this volume states the law no further persons or bodies had been specified.

13 Criminal Justice and Court Services Act 2000 Sch 1A para 2(2) (as added: see note 3).

14 Criminal Justice and Court Services Act 2000 Sch 1A para 2(5) (as added: see note 3).

685. Inspections by other organisations within inspectorate's remit. The chief inspector[1] may, by notice or otherwise[2], instruct specified persons or bodies[3] not to carry out, or not to carry out in a particular manner, a proposed inspection of a manager or other person working at approved premises[4] if he considers that the proposed inspection would impose an unreasonable burden, or would do so if carried out in that particular manner[5]. The persons or bodies referred to[6] are Her Majesty's Chief Inspector of Prisons[7], Her Majesty's Chief Inspector of Education, Children's Services and Skills[8], and the Care Quality Commission[9].

Where a notice is so given, the proposed inspection is not to be carried out, or (as the case may be) is not to be carried out in the manner mentioned in the notice[10], although the Secretary of State, if satisfied that the proposed inspection would not impose an unreasonable burden or would not do so if carried out in a particular manner, may give consent to the inspection being carried out, or being carried out in that manner[11].

1 As to references to the chief inspector see PARA 682 note 1.

2   These provisions are subject to the Criminal Justice and Court Services Act 2000 Sch 1A para 3(7) (Sch 1A added by the Police and Justice Act 2006 s 31(2)), which provides that the Secretary of State may by order specify cases or circumstances in which a notice need not, or may not, be given under these provisions.

The Secretary of State may by order make provision supplementing that made by these provisions including in particular:

(1)   provision about the form of notices (Criminal Justice and Court Services Act 2000 Sch 1A para 3(10)(a) (as so added));

(2)   provision prescribing the period within which notices are to be given (Sch 1A para 3(10)(b) (as so added));

(3)   provision prescribing circumstances in which notices are, or are not, to be made public (Sch 1A para 3(10)(c) (as so added));

(4)   provision for revising or withdrawing notices (Sch 1A para 3(10)(d) (as so added)); and

(5)   provision for setting aside notices not validly given (Sch 1A para 3(10)(e) (as so added)).

At the date at which this volume states the law no such order had been made.

3   As to these see the text and notes 7–9.

4   Criminal Justice and Court Services Act 2000 Sch 1A para 3(1)(a) (as added: see note 2); Her Majesty's Inspectorate of the National Probation Service for England and Wales (Specified Organisations) Order 2007, SI 2007/1172, art 2(c). As to the approval of premises see PARA 673 et seq.

5   Criminal Justice and Court Services Act 2000 Sch 1A para 3(1)(b) (as added: see note 2).

6   The Secretary of State may by order amend the Criminal Justice and Court Services Act 2000 Sch 1A para 3(2) (see the text and notes 7–9): Sch 1A para 3(3) (as added: see note 2). At the date at which this volume states the law no such order had been made.

7   Criminal Justice and Court Services Act 2000 Sch 1A para 3(2)(a) (as added: see note 2). As to Her Majesty's Chief Inspector of Prisons see PRISONS AND PRISONERS vol 85 (2012) PARA 409.

8   Criminal Justice and Court Services Act 2000 Sch 1A para 3(2)(b) (as added: see note 2). As to Her Majesty's Chief Inspector of Education, Children's Services and Skills see EDUCATION vol 36 (2015) PARA 1128 et seq.

9   Criminal Justice and Court Services Act 2000 Sch 1A para 3(2)(d) (as added (see note 2); substituted by the Health and Social Care Act 2008 Sch 5 para 74). As to the Care Quality Commission see SOCIAL SERVICES AND COMMUNITY CARE vol 95 (2013) PARA 217 et seq.

10 Criminal Justice and Court Services Act 2000 Sch 1A para 3(8) (as added: see note 2).

11 Criminal Justice and Court Services Act 2000 Sch 1A para 3(9) (as added: see note 2).

686.   Cooperation and assistance. Where it is appropriate to do so for the efficient and effective discharge of its functions, the inspectorate may co-operate with:

(1)   Her Majesty's Chief Inspector of Prisons[1];

(2)   Her Majesty's Chief Inspector of Constabulary[2];

(3)   Her Majesty's Chief Inspectorate of the Crown Prosecution Service[3];

(4)   Her Majesty's Chief Inspector of Education, Children's Services and Skills[4];

(5)   the Auditor General for Wales[5];

(6)   the Care Quality Commission[6]; and

(7)   any other person or body specified by an order made by the Secretary of State[7].

The chief inspector[8] may if he thinks it appropriate to do so provide assistance to any other public authority[9] for the purpose of the exercise by that authority of its functions[10].

1   Criminal Justice and Court Services Act 2000 Sch 1A para 4(a) (Sch 1A added by the Police and Justice Act 2006 s 31(2)). As to Her Majesty's Chief Inspector of Prisons see PRISONS AND PRISONERS vol 85 (2012) PARA 409.

2   Criminal Justice and Court Services Act 2000 Sch 1A para 4(b) (as added: see note 1). As to Her Majesty's Chief Inspector of Constabulary see POLICE AND INVESTIGATORY POWERS vol 84 (2013) PARA 152.

3   Criminal Justice and Court Services Act 2000 Sch 1A para 4(c) (as added: see note 1). As to Her Majesty's Chief Inspector of the Crown Prosecution Service see CRIMINAL PROCEDURE vol 27 (2015) PARA 26.

4   Criminal Justice and Court Services Act 2000 Sch 1A para 4(e) (as added: see note 1). As to Her Majesty's Chief Inspector of Education, Children's Services and Skills see EDUCATION vol 36 (2015) PARA 1128 et seq.

5   Criminal Justice and Court Services Act 2000 Sch 1A para 4(i) (as added: see note 1). As to the Auditor General for Wales see CONSTITUTIONAL AND ADMINISTRATIVE LAW vol 20 (2014) PARA 400.

6   Criminal Justice and Court Services Act 2000 Sch 1A para 4(g) (as added (see note 1); substituted by the Health and Social Care Act 2008 Sch 5 para 74). As to the Care Quality Commission see SOCIAL SERVICES AND COMMUNITY CARE vol 95 (2013) PARA 217 et seq.

7   Criminal Justice and Court Services Act 2000 Sch 1A para 4(j) (as added: see note 1). At the date at which this volume states the law no further persons or bodies had been specified.

8   As to references to the chief inspector see PARA 682 note 1.

9   As to the meaning of 'public authority' see PARA 683 note 2.

10 Criminal Justice and Court Services Act 2000 Sch 1A para 6(1) (as added: see note 1). The chief inspector may also do anything he thinks appropriate to facilitate the carrying out of an inspection under the Local Government Act 1999 s 10 (inspection of best value authorities: see LOCAL GOVERNMENT vol 69 (2009) PARA 699): Criminal Justice and Court Services Act 2000 Sch 1A para 6(1A) (Sch 1A para 6(1A) added, Sch 1A Para 6(2) substituted, by the Local Audit and Accountability Act 2014 Sch 12 para 46). Anything done under the Criminal Justice and Court Services Act 2000 Sch 1A para 6 may be done on such terms (including terms as to payment) as the chief inspector thinks fit: Sch 1A para 6(2) (as so added and substituted).

687. Joint action and joint inspection programmes. The inspectorate may act jointly with another public authority[1] where it is appropriate to do so for the efficient and effective discharge of the inspectorate's functions[2], and pursuant to this power the chief inspector[3] must prepare a joint inspection programme[4], acting jointly with:

(1)   Her Majesty's Chief Inspector of Prisons[5];

(2)   Her Majesty's Chief Inspector of Constabulary[6]; and

(3)   Her Majesty's Chief Inspector of the Crown Prosecution Service[7].

Before preparing a joint inspection programme the chief inspector must consult the Secretary of State and[8]:

(a)   Her Majesty's Chief Inspector of Prisons[9];

(b)   Her Majesty's Chief Inspector of Constabulary[10];

(c)   Her Majesty's Chief Inspector of the Crown Prosecution Service[11];

(d)   Her Majesty's Chief Inspector of Education, Children's Services and Skills[12];

(e)   the Auditor General for Wales[13];

(f)   the Care Quality Commission[14]; and

(g)   any other person or body specified by an order made by the Secretary of State[15],

and must send to each of those persons or bodies a copy of each programme once it is prepared[16]. Nothing in any joint inspection programme is to be read as preventing the inspectorate from making visits without notice[17].

The inspectorate may also inspect any aspect of the Crown Court or magistrates' courts in relation to their criminal jurisdiction which could have been inspected by Her Majesty's Inspectorate of Court Administration immediately before its abolition[18].

1   As to the meaning of 'public authority' see PARA 683 note 2.

2   Criminal Justice and Court Services Act 2000 Sch 1A para 5(1) (Sch 1A added by the Police and Justice Act 2006 s 31(2)).

3   As to references to the chief inspector see PARA 682 note 1.

4   Ie a document setting out what inspections the inspectorate proposes to carry out in the exercise of the power conferred by the Criminal Justice and Court Services Act 2000 Sch 1A para 5(1) (see the text and notes 1–2) and what inspections the chief inspectors listed in heads (1)–(4) in the text (or their inspectorates) propose to carry out in the exercise of any corresponding powers conferred on them: Sch 1A para 5(2) (as added: see note 2). A joint inspection programme must be prepared from time to time or at such times as the Secretary of State, the Lord Chancellor and the Attorney General may jointly direct (Sch 1A para 5(4) (as so added)), and the Secretary of State, the Lord Chancellor and the Attorney General may by a joint direction specify the form that a joint inspection programme is to take (Sch 1A para 5(6) (as so added)).

5   Criminal Justice and Court Services Act 2000 Sch 1A para 5(3)(a) (as added: see note 2). As to Her Majesty's Chief Inspector of Prisons see PRISONS AND PRISONERS vol 85 (2012) PARA 409.

6   Criminal Justice and Court Services Act 2000 Sch 1A para 5(3)(b) (as added: see note 2). As to Her Majesty's Chief Inspector of Constabulary see POLICE AND INVESTIGATORY POWERS vol 84 (2013) PARA 152.

7   Criminal Justice and Court Services Act 2000 Sch 1A para 5(3)(c) (as added: see note 2). As to Her Majesty's Chief Inspector of the Crown Prosecution Service see CRIMINAL PROCEDURE vol 27 (2015) PARA 26.

8   Ie subject to any agreement made between the chief inspector and the specified person or body to waive the requirement in such cases or circumstances as may be specified in the agreement: Criminal Justice and Court Services Act 2000 Sch 1A paras 2(3), 5(5) (as added: see note 2).

9   Criminal Justice and Court Services Act 2000 Sch 1A para 2(2)(a) (as added: see note 2).

10   Criminal Justice and Court Services Act 2000 Sch 1A para 2(2)(b) (as added: see note 2).

11   Criminal Justice and Court Services Act 2000 Sch 1A para 2(2)(c) (as added: see note 2).

12   Criminal Justice and Court Services Act 2000 Sch 1A para 2(2)(e) (as added: see note 2). As to Her Majesty's Chief Inspector of Education, Children's Services and Skills see EDUCATION vol 36 (2011) PARA 1359.

13   Criminal Justice and Court Services Act 2000 Sch 1A para 2(2)(i) (as added: see note 2). As to the Auditor General for Wales see CONSTITUTIONAL AND ADMINISTRATIVE LAW vol 20 (2014) PARA 400.

14   Criminal Justice and Court Services Act 2000 Sch 1A para 2(2)(g) (as added (see note 2); substituted by the Health and Social Care Act 2008 Sch 5 para 74). As to the Care Quality Commission see SOCIAL SERVICES AND COMMUNITY CARE vol 95 (2013) PARA 217 et seq.

15   Criminal Justice and Court Services Act 2000 Sch 1A para 2(2)(j) (as added: see note 2). At the date at which this volume states the law no further persons or bodies had been specified.

16   Criminal Justice and Court Services Act 2000 Sch 1A para 2(2) (as added: see note 2).

17   Criminal Justice and Court Services Act 2000 Sch 1A para 2(5) (as added: see note 2).

18   Criminal Justice and Court Services Act 2000 Sch 1A para 7(1) (as added (see note 2); Sch 1A para 7 further added by SI 2012/2401). Her Majesty's Inspectorate of Court Administration was established under the Courts Act 2003 s 58 and was abolished as from 18 September 2012 by the Public Bodies (Abolition of Her Majesty's Inspectorate of Courts Administration and the Public Guardian Board) Order 2012, SI 2012/2401, art 2. The Criminal Justice and Court Services Act 2000 Sch 1A para 7(1) applies only if the inspection includes matters other than any aspect of the Crown Court or magistrates' courts: Sch 1A para 7(2) (as so added). The power of the inspectorate under Sch 1A para 7 is in addition to the power under Sch 1A para 5 (see the text and notes 1–17) to act jointly with another public authority: Sch 1A para 7(3) (as so added).

13. RELEASE AND RECALL OF PRISONERS

(1) OVERVIEW OF EARLY RELEASE PROVISIONS

688. General overview of early release and recall arrangements. The current regimes that govern the release of prisoners on licence, and the supervision of prisoners after release, derive from the Crime (Sentences) Act 1997 (if the prisoner is serving an indeterminate sentence)[1] or the Criminal Justice Act 2003 (if the prisoner is serving a determinate sentence)[2]. Transitional provisions govern the release and supervision of prisoners serving determinate sentences for offences committed before 4 April 2005 (that is, before the main provisions of the Criminal Justice Act 2003 were commenced)[3].

Accordingly, subject to any relevant statutory guidance:

(1)   a prisoner serving a determinate sentence has his or her release on licence, and supervision after release, determined under the Criminal Justice Act 2003[4] (but modified significantly with regard to release dates and release conditions in the case of prisoners who were sentenced in respect of offences committed before 4 April 2005[5]); and

(2)   the release of prisoners serving an indeterminate sentence (once the minimum term has been served[6]) is determined in accordance with the Crime (Sentences) Act 1997[7].

The processes referred to under head (1) above generally take their course without the Parole Board being involved (if the prisoner was sentenced after 4 April 2005 and is not serving an extended determinate sentence) but the processes referred to under both heads (1) and (2) above generally require the Parole Board to be involved where there is a discretionary element to a prisoner's release (that is, where an assessment of risk to the public is required, either because of the nature of the sentence being served or where the prisoner is recalled and subsequently becomes eligible for re-release)[8].

Release is available on extraordinary grounds for any prisoner regardless of these usual factors (for instance, on compassionate grounds or for medical reasons)[9].

The process of recall (and subsequent release after recall) is governed by the Criminal Justice Act 2003 in respect of all prisoners serving determinate terms released on licence after 4 April 2005 whether or not the prisoners were released previously before that date[10], except that such prisoners sentenced in respect of offences committed before 4 April 2005 are subject to transitional provisions (which have themselves been incorporated into the 2003 Act)[11], and the recall of prisoners serving indeterminate sentences continues to be governed by the Crime (Sentences) Act 1997[12].

1   Ie under the Crime (Sentences) Act 1997 Pt II Ch II (ss 28–34) (life sentences) (see PARAS 697, 706 et seq). Note that this includes life sentences imposed for a second listed offence under the Criminal Justice Act 2003 s 224A (see PARA 35).

2   Ie under the Criminal Justice Act 2003 Pt 12 Ch 6 (ss 237–268) (sentencing: release, licences and recall) (see PARAS 696, 699, 709 et seq). A determinate prison sentence is where the court sets a fixed length for the prison sentence: see PARA 26 et seq. Note that this includes an extended determinate sentence imposed under the Criminal Justice Act 2003 s 246A (see PARA 716).

3   See the Criminal Justice Act 2003 Pt 12 Ch 6.

4   Ie in accordance with the Criminal Justice Act 2003 Pt 12 Ch 6.

5   Ie subject to the transitional provisions contained in the Criminal Justice Act 2003 ss 267A, 267B, Schs 20A, 20B: see PARA 722 et seq.

6   See note 1.

7　Ie in accordance with the Crime (Sentences) Act 1997 Pt II Ch II (in respect of life prisoners within the meaning of Pt II Ch II): see PARA 706 et seq.

8　Ie the Parole Board acting under the Criminal Justice Act 2003 s 239 (see PARA 699) in respect of the functions conferred on it by Pt 12 Ch 6 in respect of fixed-term prisoners and by the Crime (Sentences) Act 1997 Pt II Ch II in respect of prisoners serving indeterminate sentences.

　　The decisions made by the Parole Board may be challenged under common law requirements of procedural fairness or under the Convention for the Protection of Human Rights and Fundamental Freedoms (1950) (Rome, 4 November 1950; TS 71 (1953); Cmd 8969; ETS no 5) (the European Convention on Human Rights ('ECHR')): see PARA 700. The Convention guarantees, in particular, that a person may be deprived of his liberty only according to specified circumstances (which include lawful detention after conviction by a competent court) and in accordance with a procedure prescribed by law (see art 5.1); and that a person deprived of his liberty by arrest or detention is entitled to take proceedings by which the lawfulness of his detention may be decided speedily by a court and his release ordered if the detention is not lawful (see art 5.4): see RIGHTS AND FREEDOMS vol 88A (2013) PARA 210 et seq. Where a sentence imposed is conclusive of the lawfulness of the detention, the supervision required by art 5.4 is incorporated in the original decision so the administrative implementation of a determinate sentence does not engage art 5.4 (unless 'new issues' arise that affect the lawfulness of the detention, such as a prisoner's recall for breach of his licence conditions after release, which necessarily implies that the punitive element of a sentence has been served); however, where the law imposes a sentence of an indeterminate character, 'new issues' arise when the prisoner becomes eligible for release following expiry of the tariff,and his dangerousness has to be determined, so that art 5.4 is engaged and must be satisfied before the lawfulness of the continued detention can be attributable, under art 5.1(a), to the original sentence: see *De Wilde, Ooms and Versyp v Belgium* (1971) 1 EHRR 373, ECtHR; *Winterwerp v Netherlands* (1979) 2 EHRR 387, ECtHR; *Van Droogenbroeck v Belgium* (1982) 4 EHRR 443, ECtHR; *Weeks v United Kingdom* (1987) 10 EHRR 293, ECtHR (life sentences); *Thynne, Wilson and Gunnell v United Kingdom* (1990) 13 EHRR 666, ECtHR (discretionary life sentences); *Hussain v United Kingdom* (1996) 22 EHRR 1, ECtHR; *Stafford v United Kingdom* (2002) 35 EHRR 1121, 13 BHRC 260, ECtHR (mandatory life sentences); and see *R v Offen* [2001] 2 All ER 154, [2001] 1 WLR 253, CA (automatic life sentences); *R (on the application of Smith) v Parole Board, R (on the application of West) v Parole Board* [2005] UKHL 1, [2005] 1 All ER 755, [2005] 1 WLR 350; *R (on the application of Black) v Secretary of State for Justice* [2009] UKHL 1, [2009] AC 949, [2009] 4 All ER 1; *R (on the application of James) v Secretary of State for Justice* [2009] UKHL 22, [2010] 1 AC 553, [2009] 4 All ER 255 (indeterminate sentences of imprisonment for public protection).

　　The European Convention on Human Rights art 5.4, being concerned with the means of determining the lawfulness of the individual's detention and not with the conditions in which the prisoner is held, is not engaged where a serving prisoner is transferred from open to closed conditions (see *R (on the application of Davies) v Secretary of State for Justice* [2008] EWHC 397 (Admin), [2008] All ER (D) 44 (Mar)), although conditions of confinement generally may engage the European Convention on Human Rights art 3 (prohibition of torture or inhuman or degrading treatment or punishment: see RIGHTS AND FREEDOMS vol 88A (2013) PARA 158 et seq) or art 8 (right to respect for private and family life, home and correspondence: see RIGHTS AND FREEDOMS vol 88A (2013) PARAS 317 et seq, 351 et seq), and decisions made by the Parole Board, particularly those relating to licence conditions, may also raise issues under art 8 (see eg *R (on the application of Craven) v Secretary of State for the Home Department* [2001] EWHC Admin 850, [2001] All ER (D) 74 (Oct); and PARA 736).

9　As to compassionate release see PARAS 696, 697. See also the Royal Prerogative of Mercy (cited in PARA 695). As to transfers on medical grounds see PARAS 693, 694. Rules made by the Secretary of State under the Prison Act 1952 s 47 (see PRISONS AND PRISONERS vol 85 (2012) PARAS 403, 404) may also provide for the temporary release of convicted and sentenced prisoners: see PARAS 691, 692. As to the release of certain determinate sentence prisoners to make best use of the places available for detention see PARA 698.

10　See PARA 717 et seq.

11　See PARAS 726, 728; and see note 5.

12　See PARA 708.

689.　Release, supervision and recall of persons aged under 18 or aged between 18 and 21.　Although statute provides for young offenders to be sentenced under provisions that are distinct from those applied to adult offenders[1], young persons detained in a young offender institution or secure training centre[2] (or, if the

Secretary of State so directs, a prison) are released on licence, and subject to supervision and recall after release, according to almost identical mechanisms as adult prisoners[3].

1 See PARA 8 et seq; and CHILDREN AND YOUNG PERSONS vol 10 (2012) PARA 1300 et seq.
2 As to young offender institutions and secure training centres see PRISONS AND PRISONERS vol 85 (2012) PARAS 487 et seq, 491 et seq.
3 As to special provision made for the supervision of young offenders after release see PARA 745.

690. Persons detained in England and Wales in pursuance of a sentence of the International Criminal Court. Where the United Kingdom[1] is designated by the International Criminal Court ('ICC')[2] as the state in which a person ('the prisoner') is to serve a sentence of imprisonment imposed by the ICC, and where the Secretary of State[3] informs the ICC that the designation is accepted, the Secretary of State must issue a warrant authorising the bringing of the prisoner to England and Wales or Northern Ireland, the detention of the prisoner there in accordance with the sentence of the ICC, and the taking of the prisoner to a specified place where he is to be detained[4]. A prisoner subject to such a warrant authorising his detention is to be treated[5] as if he were subject to a sentence of imprisonment imposed in exercise of its criminal jurisdiction by a court in the part of the United Kingdom in which he is to be detained[6]. The operation of certain domestic statutory provisions is excluded in relation to a person detained in pursuance of a sentence of the ICC[7]; and this exclusion affects the early release or release on licence of ICC prisoners[8].

1 As to the meaning of 'United Kingdom' see PARA 4 note 3.
2 Ie the International Criminal Court established by the Statute of the International Criminal Court (Rome, 17 July 1998; Cm 5590) (see INTERNATIONAL RELATIONS LAW vol 61 (2010) PARA 437 et seq): see the International Criminal Court Act 2001 s 1(1).
3 As to the Secretary of State for these purposes see INTERNATIONAL RELATIONS LAW vol 61 (2010) PARA 29.
4 See the International Criminal Court Act 2001 s 42(1), (3); and INTERNATIONAL RELATIONS LAW vol 61 (2010) PARA 450. As to enforcement of sentences imposed by the International Criminal Court see the Agreement between the government of the United Kingdom of Great Britain and Northern Ireland and the International Criminal Court on the enforcement of sentences imposed by the International Criminal Court (London, 8 November 2007; TS 1 (2008); Cm 7306); and INTERNATIONAL RELATIONS LAW vol 61 (2010) PARA 450.
5 Ie for all purposes, subject to the International Criminal Court Act 2001 s 42(5) and Sch 7 (see the text and notes 7–8): see s 42(4); and INTERNATIONAL RELATIONS LAW vol 61 (2010) PARA 450. The Repatriation of Prisoners Act 1984 (see PRISONS AND PRISONERS vol 85 (2012) PARA 463 et seq) and the Crime (Sentences) Act 1997 Sch 1 (transfers of prisoners within the British Islands: see PRISONS AND PRISONERS vol 85 (2012) PARA 455 et seq) do not apply to a person detained in pursuance of a sentence of the ICC: see the International Criminal Court Act 2001 s 42(5); and INTERNATIONAL RELATIONS LAW vol 61 (2010) PARA 450. As to transfer of such a person within the United Kingdom see ss 44, 45; and INTERNATIONAL RELATIONS LAW vol 61 (2010) PARA 451.
6 See the International Criminal Court Act 2001 s 42(4); and INTERNATIONAL RELATIONS LAW vol 61 (2010) PARA 450.
7 See the International Criminal Court Act 2001 Sch 7; and INTERNATIONAL RELATIONS LAW vol 61 (2010) PARA 450. See also the text and note 8.
8 Specifically, the following provisions of the law of England and Wales do not apply in relation to a person detained in England and Wales in pursuance of a sentence of the ICC (see the International Criminal Court Act 2001 Sch 7 para 3(1) (amended by the Criminal Justice Act 2003 s 304, Sch 32 para 139(1), (3); and by the Legal Aid, Sentencing and Punishment of Offenders Act 2012 s 111(2), Sch 14 para 4)):
    (1) the Prison Act 1952 s 28 (power to discharge prisoners temporarily on grounds of ill health: see PARA 692);
    (2) any provision of rules under the Prison Act 1952 s 47 (prison rules: see PRISONS AND PRISONERS vol 85 (2012) PARA 403 et seq) permitting temporary release on licence (see PARA 691);

(3)   the Criminal Justice Act 1982 s 32 (order to release certain determinate sentence prisoners to make best use of places available for detention: see PARA 698) or the Criminal Justice Act 2003 ss 243A–264 (early release of prisoners: see PARA 712 et seq);

(4)   the Crime (Sentences) Act 1997 Pt II Ch II (ss 28–34) (life sentences) (see PARAS 697, 706 et seq).

Nor does the Criminal Justice Act 1961 s 23(3) (discharge at weekend or on a holiday: see PARA 746) apply in relation to such a person: see Sch 7 para 2(1)(c).

(2) OTHER POWERS OF RELEASE

(i) Temporary Release

691. Temporary release. Rules made by the Secretary of State[1] under the Prison Act 1952[2] may provide for the temporary release of convicted and sentenced prisoners (that is, for the temporary release of persons detained in a prison[3], remand centre[4], young offender institution[5] secure training centre[6] or secure college, not being persons committed in custody for trial before the Crown Court or committed to be sentenced or otherwise dealt with by the Crown Court or remanded in custody by any court)[7].

Accordingly, the Secretary of State may[8] release temporarily certain classes of prisoner or inmate[9]. Such a prisoner or inmate may be released for any period or periods and subject to any conditions[10], but only for the following purposes[11]:

(1)   on compassionate grounds or for the purpose of receiving medical treatment[12];

(2)   to engage in employment or voluntary work[13];

(3)   to receive instructions or training which cannot reasonably be provided in the prison or young offender institution (as the case may be)[14];

(4)   to enable him to participate in any proceedings before any court, tribunal or inquiry[15];

(5)   to enable him to consult with his legal adviser in circumstances where it is not reasonably practicable for the consultation to take place in the prison or young offender institution (as the case may be)[16];

(6)   to assist any police officer in any enquiries[17];

(7)   to facilitate the prisoner's transfer between prisons or (as the case may be) the inmate's transfer between the young offender institution and another penal establishment[18];

(8)   to assist him in maintaining family ties or in his transition from life in custody to freedom[19].

A prisoner or an inmate may not be temporarily released in this way unless the Secretary of State is satisfied that there would not be an unacceptable risk of his committing offences whilst released or otherwise of his failing to comply with any condition upon which he is released[20]. Furthermore, the Secretary of State must not release a prisoner or an inmate under these provisions if, having regard to[21]:

(a)   the period or proportion of his sentence which the prisoner or inmate has served[22]; and

(b)   the frequency with which the prisoner or inmate has been granted temporary release[23],

the Secretary of State is of the opinion that the release of the prisoner or inmate would be likely to undermine public confidence in the administration of justice[24].

If a prisoner or an inmate has been temporarily released under these provisions during the relevant period[25] and has been sentenced to imprisonment, detention or custody for a criminal offence committed whilst at large following that release, he must not be temporarily released in this way unless his release, having regard to the circumstances of his conviction, would not, in the opinion of the Secretary of State, be likely to undermine public confidence in the administration of justice[26].

A prisoner or an inmate who is temporarily released in this way may be recalled at any time whether the conditions of his release have been broken or not[27].

The Prison Service Instructions System makes further provision with regard to release on temporary licence[28].

1   As to the Secretary of State for these purposes see PRISONS AND PRISONERS vol 85 (2012) PARA 408.

2   Ie under the Prison Act 1952 s 47 (prison rules: see PRISONS AND PRISONERS vol 85 (2012) PARA 403 et seq): see s 47(5); and PRISONS AND PRISONERS vol 85 (2012) PARA 404.

3   As to the meaning of 'prison' for the purposes of the Prison Act 1952 see PRISONS AND PRISONERS vol 85 (2012) PARA 403.

4   As to remand centres see PRISONS AND PRISONERS vol 85 (2012) PARAS 485, 486.

5   As to young offender institutions see PRISONS AND PRISONERS vol 85 (2012) PARA 487 et seq.

6   As to secure training centres see PRISONS AND PRISONERS vol 85 (2012) PARA 491 et seq. As to temporary release from a secure training centre see PRISONS AND PRISONERS vol 85 (2012) PARA 496.

7   See the Prison Act 1952 s 47(5); and PRISONS AND PRISONERS vol 85 (2012) PARA 404. See also note 9.

     Any provision of rules under the Prison Act 1952 s 47(5) permitting temporary release on licence does not apply in relation to a person detained in England and Wales in pursuance of a sentence of the International Criminal Court: see the International Criminal Court Act 2001 Sch 7 paras 1, 3(1); and PARA 690. As to the meanings of 'England' and 'Wales' see PARA 4 note 3.

8   Ie in accordance with the Prison Rules 1999, SI 1999/728, r 9(2)–(11) or the Young Offender Institution Rules 2000, SI 2000/3371, r 5(2)–(11), as the case may be (see the text and notes 10–27): Prison Rules 1999, SI 1999/728, r 9(1) (amended by SI 2014/2169); Young Offender Institution Rules 2000, SI 2000/3371, r 5(1) (amended by SI 2014/2169). The Secretary of State's power under these provisions is subject to the Prison Rules 1999, SI 1999/728, r 9(1A) (added by SI 2014/2169); and the Young Offender Institution Rules 2000, SI 2000/3371, r 5(1A) (added by SI 2014/2169), which provide that a prisoner or inmate who has the relevant deportation status must not be released under the Prison Rules 1999, SI 1999/728, r 9 or the Young Offender Institution Rules 2000, SI 2000/3371, r 5 unless he is located in open conditions immediately before the time of release. Any reference to a prisoner or inmate who has the relevant deportation status is to be read in accordance with the Prison Rules 1999, SI 1999/728, r 7(1E), (1F) (see PRISONS AND PRISONERS vol 85 (2012) PARA 437) or the Young Offender Institution Rules 2000, SI 2000/3371, r 4(6), (7) (see PRISONS AND PRISONERS vol 85 (2012) PARA 440): Prison Rules 1999, SI 1999/728, r 9(11)(c) (added by SI 2014/2169); and the Young Offender Institution Rules 2000, SI 2000/3371, r 5(12)(a) (added by SI 2014/2169).

9   See the Prison Rules 1999, SI 1999/728, r 9(1) (as amended: see note 8); and the Young Offender Institution Rules 2000, SI 2000/3371, r 5(1) (as so amended). The provision made by Prison Rules 1999, SI 1999/728, r 9, or the Young Offender Institution Rules 2000, SI 2000/3371, r 5, as the case may be, applies to prisoners or inmates other than persons committed in custody for trial or to be sentenced or otherwise dealt with before or by any Crown Court or remanded in custody by any court: Prison Rules 1999, SI 1999/728, r 9(9); Young Offender Institution Rules 2000, SI 2000/3371, r 5(9). See also the Prison Act 1952 s 47(5) (cited in the text and notes 1–7); and see the text and note 28.

     The decision whether or not to grant an application for temporary release from prison is a decision entrusted by prison rules to the Secretary of State alone, although the decision will, in practice, normally be made on behalf of the Secretary of State by the prison governor: *Lexi Holdings plc v Luqman* [2008] EWHC 151 (Ch), (2008) Times, 19 February, [2008] All ER (D) 22 (Jan) (application by contemnor); and see note 28. Even though continued detention is generally justified, the denial of temporary release may engage the Convention for the Protection of Human Rights and Fundamental Freedoms (1950) (Rome, 4 November 1950; TS 71 (1953); Cmd 8969; ETS no 5) (the European Convention on Human Rights) art 8 (right to respect for private and family life, home and correspondence: see RIGHTS AND FREEDOMS vol 88A (2013)

PARAS 317 et seq, 351 et seq); any restriction on a prisoner's Convention rights, including those guaranteed under art 8, could be justified as flowing, inter alia, from the necessary and inevitable consequences of imprisonment or from an adequate link between the restriction and the circumstances of the prisoner in question, but this does not preclude a subsequent breach of art 8 arising from refusal of temporary leave from prison in an appropriate case so that any such refusal must be justifiable in accordance with art 8.2: see *Ploski v Poland* [2002] ECHR 26761/95, ECtHR; *Dickson v United Kingdom* (2007) 46 EHRR 927, [2007] 3 FCR 877, ECtHR; and *R (on the application of MP) v Secretary of State for Justice, R (on the application of P) v Governor of HMP Downview* [2012] EWHC 214 (Admin), [2012] 09 LS Gaz R 17, [2012] All ER (D) 81 (Feb). See also note 24.

10 Prison Rules 1999, SI 1999/728, r 9(2); Young Offender Institution Rules 2000, SI 2000/3371, r 5(2).

11 Prison Rules 1999, SI 1999/728, r 9(3); Young Offender Institution Rules 2000, SI 2000/3371, r 5(3).

12 Prison Rules 1999, SI 1999/728, r 9(3)(a); Young Offender Institution Rules 2000, SI 2000/3371, r 5(3)(a). As to the temporary and conditional discharge of prisoner and his removal for ill health see also PARA 692.

13 Prison Rules 1999, SI 1999/728, r 9(3)(b); Young Offender Institution Rules 2000, SI 2000/3371, r 5(3)(b).

14 Prison Rules 1999, SI 1999/728, r 9(3)(c); Young Offender Institution Rules 2000, SI 2000/3371, r 5(3)(c).

15 Prison Rules 1999, SI 1999/728, r 9(3)(d); Young Offender Institution Rules 2000, SI 2000/3371, r 5(3)(d).

16 Prison Rules 1999, SI 1999/728, r 9(3)(e); Young Offender Institution Rules 2000, SI 2000/3371, r 5(3)(e).

17 Prison Rules 1999, SI 1999/728, r 9(3)(f); Young Offender Institution Rules 2000, SI 2000/3371, r 5(3)(f).

18 Prison Rules 1999, SI 1999/728, r 9(3)(g); Young Offender Institution Rules 2000, SI 2000/3371, r 5(3)(g).

19 Prison Rules 1999, SI 1999/728, r 9(3)(h); Young Offender Institution Rules 2000, SI 2000/3371, r 5(3)(h). See also *R (on the application of MP) v Secretary of State for Justice, R (on the application of P) v Governor of HMP Downview* [2012] EWHC 214 (Admin), [2012] 09 LS Gaz R 17, [2012] All ER (D) 81 (Feb); and note 28.

20 Prison Rules 1999, SI 1999/728, r 9(4); Young Offender Institution Rules 2000, SI 2000/3371, r 5(4).

21 Prison Rules 1999, SI 1999/728, r 9(5); Young Offender Institution Rules 2000, SI 2000/3371, r 5(6).
   Where at any time an offender is subject concurrently to a detention and training order and to a sentence of detention in a young offender institution, he must be treated for the purposes of r 5(6) and r 5(7) as if he were subject only to the one of them that was imposed on the later occasion: see r 5(5). As to detention and training orders see PARA 9 et seq.

22 Prison Rules 1999, SI 1999/728, r 9(5)(a); Young Offender Institution Rules 2000, SI 2000/3371, r 5(6)(a). See note 21. For the purposes of any reference in the Prison Rules 1999, SI 1999/728, r 9, or in the Young Offender Institution Rules 2000, SI 2000/3371, r 5, as the case may be, to a prisoner's sentence or an inmate's sentence, consecutive terms and terms which are wholly or partly concurrent are to be treated as a single term: Prison Rules 1999, SI 1999/728, r 9(10) (substituted by SI 2005/3437); Young Offender Institution Rules 2000, SI 2000/3371, r 5(10) (substituted by SI 2005/3438). Any reference to a sentence of imprisonment is to be construed as including any sentence to detention or custody: Prison Rules 1999, SI 1999/728, r 9(11)(a).
   Where the Prison Rules 1999, SI 1999/728, r 9(10), or the Young Offender Institution Rules 2000, SI 2000/3371, r 5(10), as the case may be, does not apply to require all the sentences the prisoner or inmate is serving to be treated as a single term, then the Secretary of State must have regard to the period or portion of any such sentence which he has served: Prison Rules 1999, SI 1999/728, r 9(5)(a); Young Offender Institution Rules 2000, SI 2000/3371, r 5(6)(a).

23 Prison Rules 1999, SI 1999/728, r 9(5)(b); Young Offender Institution Rules 2000, SI 2000/3371, r 5(6)(b). See note 21. The Prison Act 1952 s 47(5) and rules made thereunder (see the text and notes 1–7) confer a wide discretion on the Secretary of State to grant temporary leave, and do not restrict it to the period leading up to release: see *R (on the application of MP) v Secretary of State for Justice, R (on the application of P) v Governor of HMP Downview* [2012] EWHC 214 (Admin), [2012] 09 LS Gaz R 17, [2012] All ER (D) 81 (Feb); and see note 28.

24 Prison Rules 1999, SI 1999/728, r 9(5); Young Offender Institution Rules 2000, SI 2000/3371, r 5(6). See note 21. Cases concerning temporary leave from prison have identified factors which could be in play under the European Convention on Human Rights art 8.2 (see note 9), such as the risk of absconding and re-offending, and the fact that mother and child are already separated, by virtue of the sentence of imprisonment; the risk of 'offending public opinion' (see *Dickson v United Kingdom* (2007) 46 EHRR 927, [2007] 3 FCR 877, ECtHR) may be covered in the concerns encapsulated in the Prison Rules 1999, SI 1999/728, r 9(5) so that, while offending public opinion is capable of being a relevant factor in considering whether to grant temporary release, a refusal of temporary release could not, consistently with the European Convention on Human Rights art 8.2, be based solely on this factor: *R (on the application of MP) v Secretary of State for Justice, R (on the application of P) v Governor of HMP Downview* [2012] EWHC 214 (Admin), [2012] 09 LS Gaz R 17, [2012] All ER (D) 81 (Feb).

25 For these purposes, the 'relevant period' is:

    (1) in the case of a prisoner or an inmate serving a determinate sentence of imprisonment, detention or custody, the period he has served in respect of that sentence, unless, notwithstanding the Prison Rules 1999, SI 1999/728, r 9(10), or the Young Offender Institution Rules 2000, SI 2000/3371, r 5(10), as the case may be (see note 22), the sentences he is serving do not fall to be treated as single term, in which case it is the period since he was last released in relation to one of those sentences under the Criminal Justice Act 1991 Pt II (ss 32–51) (repealed) or the Powers of Criminal Courts (Sentencing) Act 2000 s 100 (ie in relation to detention and training orders: see PARA 9 et seq) or the Criminal Justice Act 2003 Pt 12 Ch 6 (ss 237–268) (sentencing: release, licences and recall) (see PARAS 696, 699, 709 et seq) (Prison Rules 1999, SI 1999/728, r 9(7)(a) (r 9(7)(a), (b) amended by SI 2005/3437); Young Offender Institution Rules 2000, SI 2000/3371, r 5(7)(a) (r 5(7)(a), (b) amended by SI 2005/3438)); or

    (2) in the case of a prisoner or an inmate serving an indeterminate sentence of imprisonment, detention or custody, if he has been previously released on licence under the Criminal Justice Act 1991 Pt II (repealed) or the Crime (Sentences) Act 1997 Pt II (ss 28–34) (life sentences) (see PARAS 697, 706 et seq) or the Criminal Justice Act 2003 Pt 12 Ch 6, the period since the date of his last recall in respect of that sentence or, where the prisoner or inmate has not been so released, the period he has served in respect of that sentence (Prison Rules 1999, SI 1999/728, r 9(7)(b) (as so amended); Young Offender Institution Rules 2000, SI 2000/3371, r 5(7)(b) (as so amended)); or

    (3) (only in the case of a prisoner detained for any other reason) the period for which he has been detained for that reason (Prison Rules 1999, SI 1999/728, r 9(7)(c)).

However, where a prisoner falls within two or more of heads (1) to (3) above, or where an inmate falls within both head (1) and head (2) above, the 'relevant period', in the case of that prisoner or inmate, is determined by whichever of the applicable heads produces the longer period: Prison Rules 1999, SI 1999/728, r 9(7); Young Offender Institution Rules 2000, SI 2000/3371, r 5(7). See note 21. Any reference to release on licence or otherwise under the Criminal Justice Act 1991 Pt II (repealed) includes any release on licence under any legislation providing for early release on licence: Prison Rules 1999, SI 1999/728, r 9(11)(b); Young Offender Institution Rules 2000, SI 2000/3371, r 5(11).

26 Prison Rules 1999, SI 1999/728, r 9(6); Young Offender Institution Rules 2000, SI 2000/3371, r 5(7). See note 21.

27 Prison Rules 1999, SI 1999/728, r 9(8); Young Offender Institution Rules 2000, SI 2000/3371, r 5(8). If, immediately before the relevant time, a prisoner or inmate has been released under the Prison Rules 1999, SI 1999/728, r 9 or the Young Offender Institution Rules 2000, SI 2000/3371, r 5 and the prison or young offender institution has received notice that the prisoner or inmate has the relevant deportation status, the prisoner or inmate must be recalled unless the prisoner or inmate was released from open conditions: Prison Rules 1999, SI 1999/728, r 9(8A) (r 9(8A), (8B) added by SI 2014/2169); Young Offender Institution Rules 2000, SI 2000/3371, r 5(8A) (r 5(8A), (8B) added by SI 2014/2169). If a prisoner or inmate has been released under the Prison Rules 1999, SI 1999/728, r 9 or the Young Offender Institution Rules 2000, SI 2000/3371, r 5 (whether before or after the relevant time) and the prison or young offender institution receives notice after the relevant time that the prisoner or inmate has the relevant deportation status, the prisoner must be recalled unless the period for which the prisoner or inmate has been released is due to expire on the day on which the prison or young offender institution receives that notice or the prisoner or inmate was released from open conditions: Prison Rules 1999, SI 1999/728, r 9(8B) (as so added); Young Offender Institution Rules 2000, SI 2000/3371, r 5(8B) (as so added). Any reference to the relevant time is to be read in accordance with the Prison Rules 1999, SI 1999/728, r 7(1G) (see PRISONS AND PRISONERS vol 85 (2012) PARA 437) or the Young Offender Institution Rules 2000,

SI 2000/3371, r 4(8) (see PRISONS AND PRISONERS vol 85 (2012) PARA 440): Prison Rules 1999, SI 1999/728, r 9(11)(d) (added by SI 2014/2169); and the Young Offender Institution Rules 2000, SI 2000/3371, r 5(12)(b) (added by SI 2014/2169).

    It is an offence to remain unlawfully at large after temporary release in pursuance of rules made under the Prison Act 1952 s 47(5) (cited in the text and notes 1–7): see the Prisoners (Return to Custody) Act 1995 s 1; and PRISONS AND PRISONERS vol 85 (2012) PARA 429. As to the concept of 'custody' as an element of the common law offence of escape from lawful custody see *R v Dhillon* [2005] EWCA Crim 2996, [2006] 1 WLR 1535, [2006] 1 Cr App Rep 237 (escape from hospital having been taken there for treatment from police station); and CRIMINAL LAW vol 26 (2010) PARA 698. For the purposes of the common law offence, 'custody' is to be construed as a matter of common sense and ordinary language so that, while temporary release lasted and the prisoner was not subject to any supervision, he was not in custody and therefore could not be guilty of the offence at common law: *R v Montgomery* [2007] EWCA Crim 2157, [2008] 2 All ER 924, [2008] 1 WLR 636 (prisoner who simply failed to return to prison at the end of a period of temporary release for employment could not be said to have escaped from lawful custody at common law; however, because he had been released under the provisions of the Prison Rules 1999, SI 1999/728, r 9, the prisoner could have been charged under the Prisoners (Return to Custody) Act 1995 s 1).

28   As to the system of central policy instructions and guidance contained eg in Prison Service Orders (PSOs) and Prison Service Instructions (PSIs) see PRISONS AND PRISONERS vol 85 (2012) PARA 406. A prisoner may not assert a substantive legitimate expectation that any particular scheme for administering the grant of temporary release will remain in force, only that he will be treated fairly in accordance with the published criteria: *R v Secretary of State for the Home Department, ex p Hargreaves* [1997] 1 All ER 397, [1997] 1 WLR 906, CA. See further *Lexi Holdings plc (in Administration) v Luqman* [2008] EWHC 151 (Ch), (2008) Times, 19 February, [2008] All ER (D) 22 (Jan) (PSO 6300 guidance, purporting to require permission of sentencing judge before granting temporary release on licence of prisoner serving a term of imprisonment for civil contempt, unlawful); *R (on the application of Adelana) v Governor of HMP Downview* [2008] EWHC 2612 (Admin), [2008] All ER (D) 275 (Oct) (application for temporary release refused on ground of ineligibility pursuant to PSO 6300; policy restricting temporary leave for prisoners in default of confiscation orders declared unlawful); and *R (on the application of MP) v Secretary of State for Justice, R (on the application of P) v Governor of HMP Downview* [2012] EWHC 214 (Admin), [2012] 09 LS Gaz R 17, [2012] All ER (D) 81 (Feb) (Childcare Resettlement Leave ('CRL') is a type of temporary licence available under the Prison Rules 1999, SI 1999/728, r 9, to prisoners who have sole caring responsibility for a child under 16, and the thorough risk assessment and decision-making process in PSO 6300 is capable of meeting the requirements of release on CRL at any stage of the sentence and not only when prisoners were in the final stages of their custodial term).

692.   Temporary and conditional discharge of prisoner and removal for ill health. In addition to the general power to release a prisoner temporarily[1], there is power available to the Secretary of State[2] to order a temporary and conditional discharge of a prisoner on grounds of ill health[3]. Accordingly, if the Secretary of State is satisfied that by reason of the condition of the prisoner's health it is undesirable to detain him in prison[4] but that, since his condition is due in whole or in part to the prisoner's own conduct in prison, it is desirable that his release should be temporary and conditional only, the Secretary of State may, if he thinks fit, and having regard to the circumstances of the case, by order authorise the temporary discharge of the prisoner for such period and subject to such conditions as may be stated in the order[5]. Any prisoner so discharged must comply with any conditions in the order of temporary discharge and must return to prison at the expiration of the period stated in the order (or of such extended period as may be fixed by any subsequent order of the Secretary of State), and he may be arrested without warrant and returned to prison if he fails to do either[6]. Where a prisoner under sentence is discharged in pursuance of an order of temporary discharge, the currency of the sentence is suspended from the day on which he is discharged from prison under the order to the day on which he is received back into prison[7].

1 See PARA 691.
2 As to the Secretary of State for these purposes see PRISONS AND PRISONERS vol 85 (2012) PARA 408.
3 See the Prison Act 1952 s 28; and the text and notes 4–7. No provision of s 28 applies in relation to a person detained in England and Wales in pursuance of a sentence of the International Criminal Court: see the International Criminal Court Act 2001 Sch 7 para 3(1); and PARA 690. As to the meanings of 'England' and 'Wales' see PARA 4 note 3.
4 As to the meaning of 'prison' for the purposes of the Prison Act 1952 see PRISONS AND PRISONERS vol 85 (2012) PARA 403.
5 Prison Act 1952 s 28(1). The power, previously under the Prisoners (Temporary Discharge for Ill-health) Act 1913 (repealed), was once used liberally in the case of hunger-striking prisoners, but is now not used. The Prison Act 1952 s 28 does not apply to remand centres, young offender institutions or secure training centres: see s 43(5), (5A); and PRISONS AND PRISONERS vol 85 (2012) PARAS 485, 487, 491.
   As to the removal to hospital of mentally disordered prisoners see MENTAL HEALTH AND CAPACITY vol 75 (2013) PARA 892 et seq.
6 Prison Act 1952 s 28(3).
7 Prison Act 1952 s 28(4). The day on which he is discharged from prison is to be reckoned but the day on which he is received back into prison is not to be reckoned as part of the sentence: see s 28(4).

(ii) Transfer to Hospital, etc

693. Escorted removal of appellant for medical investigation, observation or treatment. If the Secretary of State[1] is satisfied that an appellant who is in custody and is to be taken to, kept in custody at, and brought back from, any place at which he is entitled to be present for the purposes of the Criminal Appeal Act 1968[2], requires medical investigation or observation, or medical or surgical treatment of any description, the Secretary of State may direct him to be taken to a hospital or other suitable place for that purpose[3]. Where any person is directed in this way to be taken to any place he must, unless the Secretary of State otherwise directs, be kept in custody while being so taken, while at that place, and while being taken back to the prison in which he is required in accordance with law to be detained[4].

1 As to the Secretary of State for these purposes see PRISONS AND PRISONERS vol 85 (2012) PARA 408.
2 Ie if the Secretary of State is satisfied that a person detained in accordance with the Prison Act 1952 s 22(1) (see PRISONS AND PRISONERS vol 85 (2012) PARA 587): s 22(2)(b) (amended by the Criminal Justice Act 1982 s 77, Sch 14 para 5). The reference in the text to an appellant is to an appellant within the meaning of the Criminal Appeal Act 1968 Pt I (ss 1–32) (appeal to Court of Appeal in criminal cases: see CRIMINAL PROCEDURE vol 28 (2015) PARA 734 et seq): see the Prison Act 1952 s 22(1); and PRISONS AND PRISONERS vol 85 (2012) PARA 587.
3 Prison Act 1952 s 22(2)(b) (as amended: see note 2).
4 See the Prison Act 1952 s 22(2). As to legal custody see PRISONS AND PRISONERS vol 85 (2012) PARA 426.

694. Transfer from custody of mentally disordered persons. Persons detained in custody (whether serving a sentence of imprisonment or not) who are suffering from mental disorder may at the direction of the Secretary of State[1] be transferred to hospital for treatment[2].

If a prisoner or an inmate is removed to hospital on account of mental disorder, the governor must at once inform next of kin or a spouse (if he knows his or her address) and also any other person whom the prisoner or inmate may reasonably have asked should be informed[3].

1 As to the Secretary of State for these purposes see MENTAL HEALTH AND CAPACITY vol 75 (2013) PARA 568.

2   See the Mental Health Act 1983 ss 47–49; and MENTAL HEALTH AND CAPACITY vol 75 (2013) PARA 892 et seq.
3   See the Prison Rules 1999, SI 1999/728, r 22(1); the Young Offender Institution Rules 2000, SI 2000/3371, r 29(1); and PRISONS AND PRISONERS vol 85 (2012) PARA 547.

(iii) Royal Prerogative of Mercy

695.   Release by prerogative.   The royal prerogative of mercy may be extended at any time to a person sentenced to imprisonment or other form of detention[1]. The prerogative, although sparingly exercised for reasons of constitutional propriety associated with the inviolability of the judicial process and general non-interference by executive action, is not restricted by the fact that an appeal is pending before, or has been dismissed by, the Criminal Division of the Court of Appeal[2]. It may rarely be exercised in the form of a pardon; more commonly, prisoners benefit from a reduction of the whole or a part of the court's sentence[3]. The occasions for clemency might be, for example: medical grounds; fresh evidence indicating a wrongful conviction revealed too late or unavailable for consideration by the court of trial but insufficiently conclusive to justify a pardon; to mitigate the consequences of some irregularity at a summary trial[4]; to compensate a prisoner for physical injury suffered in prison through no fault of his own; as a reward for supplying valuable information to the authorities investigating serious crime; or for exceptionally meritorious conduct by the prisoner during his imprisonment[5].

1   As to pardon and reprieves generally see CONSTITUTIONAL AND ADMINISTRATIVE LAW vol 20 (2014) PARA 139 et seq. As to the possibility of a claim for compensation arising out of the issue of a pardon see the Criminal Justice Act 1988 s 133; CRIMINAL PROCEDURE vol 28 (2015) PARA 823; and *R (on the application of Clark) v Secretary of State for Justice* [2015] EWHC 2383 (Admin), [2015] All ER (D) 61 (Aug).
2   See the Criminal Appeal Act 1968 s 49; and CRIMINAL PROCEDURE vol 28 (2015) PARA 822.
3   See CONSTITUTIONAL AND ADMINISTRATIVE LAW vol 20 (2014) PARA 139 et seq; and CRIMINAL PROCEDURE vol 28 (2015) PARA 822. Although it is probably right to say that the formulation of criteria for the exercise of the prerogative of mercy by the grant of a free pardon is entirely a matter of policy and not justiciable. such a decision of the Secretary of State has been reviewed on the basis that he had failed to appreciate the full extent of his powers: see *R v Secretary of State for the Home Department, ex p Bentley* [1994] QB 349, [1993] 4 All ER 442, DC. As to the granting of a pardon under the Convention on the Transfer of Sentenced Persons 1983 (as to which see PRISONS AND PRISONERS vol 85 (2012) PARA 463) see *R (on the application of Shields) v Secretary of State for Justice* [2008] EWHC 3102 (Admin), [2010] QB 150, [2009] 3 All ER 265 (Secretary of State had the power and jurisdiction, in the instant case, to consider the grant of a pardon, which was a flexible process intended in very rare cases to secure justice which the concluded court process could not achieve). See also JUDICIAL REVIEW vol 61 (2010) PARA 607.
4   If an irregularity is such as to make the whole proceedings null and void, the Secretary of State may order a prisoner to be released, but this is, strictly speaking, not an exercise of the prerogative of mercy.
5   See eg *R (on the application of Ghartey) v Secretary of State for the Home Department* [2001] EWHC Admin 199, [2001] 1 PLR 145, [2001] All ER (D) 69 (Mar).

(iv) Release on Compassionate Grounds

696.   Power to release fixed-term prisoners on compassionate grounds.   The Secretary of State[1] may at any time release on licence[2] a fixed-term prisoner[3] if he is satisfied that exceptional circumstances exist which justify the prisoner's release on compassionate grounds[4].

1   As to the Secretary of State for these purposes see PRISONS AND PRISONERS vol 85 (2012) PARA 408.
2   As to the duration of licences, and as to licence conditions, see PARAS 735–737.

3   As to the meaning of 'fixed-term prisoner' for the purposes of the Criminal Justice Act 2003 Pt 12 Ch 6 (ss 237–268) (sentencing: release, licences and recall) see PARA 709. As to equivalent provision made for life prisoners see the Crime (Sentences) Act 1997 s 30; and PARA 697.

4   Criminal Justice Act 2003 s 248(1). Any provision made by ss 243A–264 does not apply in relation to a person detained in England and Wales in pursuance of a sentence of the International Criminal Court: see the International Criminal Court Act 2001 Sch 7 para 3(1); and PARA 690. As to the meanings of 'England' and 'Wales' see PARA 4 note 3.

    As to the release on compassionate grounds of young offenders serving under detention and training orders see the Powers of Criminal Courts (Sentencing) Act 2000 s 102(3); *R (on the application of A) v Governor of Huntercombe Young Offender Institution* [2006] EWHC 2544 (Admin), 171 JP 65, 171 JPN 345, [2006] All ER (D) 226 (Oct); and PARA 11. The Secretary of State also may at any time release on compassionate grounds a person committed to prison for defaulting on a fine or for contempt: see PARA 729 et seq.

697.   Power to release life prisoners on compassionate grounds. The Secretary of State[1] may at any time release on licence[2] a life prisoner[3] if he is satisfied that exceptional circumstances exist which justify the prisoner's release on compassionate grounds[4]. However, before releasing a life prisoner in this way, the Secretary of State must consult the Parole Board[5], unless the circumstances are such as to render such consultation impracticable[6].

The Prison Service Instructions System makes further provision with regard to compassionate release on medical grounds[7].

1   As to the Secretary of State for these purposes see PRISONS AND PRISONERS vol 85 (2012) PARA 408.

2   As to the duration of licences, and as to licence conditions, see PARAS 735–737.

3   As to the meaning of 'life prisoner' for the purposes of the Crime (Sentences) Act 1997 Pt II Ch II (ss 28–34) (life sentences) see PARA 706. As to equivalent provision made for fixed-term prisoners see the Criminal Justice Act 2003 s 248(1); and PARA 696.

    The Crime (Sentences) Act 1997 Pt II Ch II does not apply in relation to a person detained in England and Wales in pursuance of a sentence of the International Criminal Court: see the International Criminal Court Act 2001 Sch 7 para 3(1); and PARA 690. As to the meanings of 'England' and 'Wales' see PARA 4 note 3.

4   Crime (Sentences) Act 1997 s 30(1). The statutory power that is available to the Secretary of State under s 30 means that, if the position were reached, in England and Wales, where the continued imprisonment of a prisoner was held to amount to inhuman or degrading treatment, so as to engage the Convention for the Protection of Human Rights and Fundamental Freedoms (Rome, 4 November 1950; TS 71 (1953); Cmd 8969) (the European Convention on Human Rights) art 3 (prohibition of torture or inhuman or degrading treatment or punishment: see RIGHTS AND FREEDOMS vol 88A (2013) PARA 158 et seq), there was no reason why, having particular regard to the requirement to comply with the Convention, the statutory power could not be used to release the prisoner on compassionate grounds: *R v Bieber* [2008] EWCA Crim 1601, [2009] 1 All ER 295, [2009] 1 WLR 223 (treatment of prisoner serving mandatory life sentence for the offence of murder where a whole life term (reduced on appeal to a minimum term of 37 years) was specified is not incompatible with the European Convention on Human Rights art 3 provided that the offender is not detained beyond a period justified on the grounds of punishment and deterrence).

5   As to the constitution and functions of the Parole Board, continued by the Criminal Justice Act 2003 s 239(1), see PARA 699.

6   Crime (Sentences) Act 1997 s 30(2). The provision made by s 30 does not require that matters should be investigated further by the Parole Board where the Secretary of State had not considered that a prisoner could be released on compassionate grounds: *R (on the application of Spinks) v Secretary of State for the Home Department* [2005] EWCA Civ 275, [2005] All ER (D) 297 (Jan). While the power to release on compassionate grounds has to be exercised so as not to provoke a breach of the European Convention on Human Rights art 3 (see note 4), on the proper construction of the Crime (Sentences) Act 1997 s 30, the Parole Board has no role to play in disciplining the Secretary of State for actual, current breaches of the European Convention on Human Rights art 3; that supervisory role is to be played by the court, which is in a position to determine whether an actual breach of art 3 is in progress and, if so, to require its termination: *R (on the application of Spinks) v Secretary of State for the Home Department*. See also *R (on the application of AS) v Secretary of State for Justice* [2009] EWHC 1315 (Admin), [2009] All

ER (D) 108 (Jun) (Secretary of State had failed to give adequate reasons for his decision not to release indeterminate sentence prisoner suffering from terminal cancer; and had failed to have regard to the medical evidence which was before him). See also the text and note 7.

7　As to the system of central policy instructions and guidance contained e g in Prison Service Orders (PSOs) and Prison Service Instructions (PSIs) see PRISONS AND PRISONERS vol 85 (2012) PARA 406. Although the Crime (Sentences) Act 1997 s 30 gives the Secretary of State a general discretion, his decision to adopt a policy on how applications under s 30 should be dealt with meant that he had created a procedural legitimate expectation that the policy would be complied with, unless there were reasons not to do so: see *R (on the application of AS) v Secretary of State for Justice* [2009] EWHC 1315 (Admin), [2009] All ER (D) 108 (Jun) (Secretary of State had failed to fulfil the procedural legitimate expectation that he would obtain an up-to-date medical report addressing the issues of life expectancy and the effect of the claimant's condition on his ability to commit offences).

(v) Administrative Power of Release

698.   Order to release certain determinate sentence prisoners to make best use of places available for detention.   The Secretary of State[1] may order that persons of any class specified in the order who are serving a sentence of imprisonment[2], other than[3]:

(1)　imprisonment for life[4], imprisonment for public protection[5] or an extended sentence[6]; or

(2)　imprisonment to which they were sentenced: (a) for an excluded offence[7]; (b) for attempting to commit such an offence[8]; (c) for conspiracy to commit such an offence[9]; or (d) for aiding or abetting, counselling, procuring or inciting the commission of such an offence[10]; or

(3)　imprisonment to which they were sentenced for an offence of criminal conduct under the Armed Forces Act 2006[11] as respects which the corresponding offence under the law of England and Wales[12] is[13]: (a) an excluded offence[14]; (b) an attempt to commit an excluded offence[15]; (c) conspiracy to commit an excluded offence[16]; or (d) aiding or abetting, counselling, procuring or inciting the commission of an excluded offence[17],

are to be released from prison at such time earlier (but not more than six months earlier) than they would otherwise be so released as may be fixed by the order[18]; but the Secretary of State must not make such an order unless he is satisfied that it is necessary to do so in order to make the best use of the places available for detention[19]. Nor may any person be released in this way if he is subject to more than one sentence of imprisonment[20] and at least one of the terms that he has to serve is for an offence mentioned in head (2) or in head (3) above[21].

Such an order:

(i)　may define a class of persons in any way[22];

(ii)　may relate to one or more specified prisons, or to prisons of a specified class (however defined), or to prisons generally[23]; and

(iii)　may make the time at which a person of any specified class is to be released depend on any circumstances whatever[24]; and

(iv)　must be made by statutory instrument[25].

Where a person who is to be released from prison in pursuance of such an order is a person serving a sentence of imprisonment in respect of whom an extended sentence certificate[26] was issued when the sentence was passed, his release must be a release on licence[27], irrespective of whether at the time of his release he could have been released on licence[28]. Where a person is released from prison in pursuance of such an order his sentence expires on his release[29].

Such an order, that persons of a specified class are to be released from prison at a time earlier than they would otherwise be released[30], does not remain in force after the expiration of six months beginning with the date on which it is made[31]. However, this is without prejudice to the power of the Secretary of State to revoke the order or to make a further such order[32].

1 As to the Secretary of State for these purposes see PRISONS AND PRISONERS vol 85 (2012) PARA 408.

2 References in these provisions to a sentence of imprisonment include a sentence of detention (other than a sentence of service detention within the meaning of the Armed Forces Act 2006: see s 374; and ARMED FORCES vol 3 (2011) PARA 349), including a detention and training order and an order under the Armed Forces Act 2006 s 211 (see ARMED FORCES vol 3 (2011) PARA 611): Criminal Justice Act 2003 s 32(1A)(a) (s 32(1A) added by the Armed Forces Act 2006 s 378(1), Sch 16 para 94(1), (3); and substituted by the Criminal Justice and Courts Act 2015 Sch 9 para 8).

3 Criminal Justice Act 1982 s 32(1). No provision of s 32 applies in relation to a person detained in England and Wales in pursuance of a sentence of the International Criminal Court: see the International Criminal Court Act 2001 s 42(6), Sch 7 paras 1, 3(1); and PARA 690. As to the meanings of 'England' and 'Wales' see PARA 4 note 3.

4 References in these provisions to a sentence of imprisonment for life include custody for life and detention at Her Majesty's pleasure: Criminal Justice Act 2003 s 32(1A)(b) (as added and substituted: see note 2).

5 References in these provisions to a sentence of imprisonment for public protection are to a sentence under the Criminal Justice Act 2003 s 225 (see PARA 37) or s 226 (see PARA 34), including a sentence passed as a result of the Armed Forces Act 2006 s 219 (see ARMED FORCES vol 3 (2011) PARA 611) or s 221 see ARMED FORCES vol 3 (2011) PARA 596): Criminal Justice Act 2003 s 32(1A)(c) (as added and substituted: see note 2).

6 Criminal Justice Act 1982 s 32(1)(a) (amended by the Criminal Justice Act 2003 s 304, Sch 32 Pt 1 paras 34, 35; and the Criminal Justice and Courts Act 2015 Sch 9 para 8). References to an extended sentence are to a sentence under the Criminal Justice Act 2003 s 226A, s 226B (see PARAS 18–20), s 227 (repealed) or s 228 (repealed), including a sentence passed as a result of the Armed Forces Act 2006 s 219A, s 220, s 221A or s 222 (see ARMED FORCES vol 3 (2011) PARA 611): Criminal Justice Act 2003 s 32(1A)(d) (as added and substituted: see note 2).

7 Criminal Justice Act 1982 s 32(1)(b)(i). For these purposes, 'excluded offence' means:
   (1) an offence (whether at common law or under any enactment) specified in the Criminal Justice Act 1982 s 32, Sch 1 Pt I (see heads (a) to (c) below) (s 32(2)(a)); and
   (2) an offence under an enactment specified in Sch 1 Pt II (see heads (i) to (xxiii) below) (s 32(2)(b)); and
   (3) an offence specified in Sch 1 Pt III (s 32(2)(c)), being offences under the Customs and Excise Management Act 1979 ss 50(2), (3), 68(2), 170 (see MEDICAL PRODUCTS AND DRUGS vol 75 (2013) PARAS 487, 491) in connection with a prohibition or restriction on importation or exportation of a controlled drug which has effect by virtue of the Misuse of Drugs Act 1971 s 3 (see MEDICAL PRODUCTS AND DRUGS vol 75 (2013) PARA 491) (see the Criminal Justice Act 1982 Sch 1 Pt III).
The offences referred to in head (1) above are:
   (a) manslaughter (Sch 1 Pt I para 1);
   (b) kidnapping (Sch 1 Pt I para 3);
   (c) assault of any description (Sch 1 Pt I para 4).
The enactments referred to in head (2) above are:
   (i) the Malicious Damage Act 1861 ss 35, 47, 48 (ss 47, 48 repealed) (criminal damage: see CRIMINAL LAW vol 25 (2010) PARAS 326, 337) (Criminal Justice Act 1982 Sch 1 Pt II para 1);
   (ii) the Offences Against the Person Act 1861 s 16 (making threats to kill: see CRIMINAL LAW vol 25 (2010) PARA 115), s 18 (wounding with intent to do grievous bodily harm or to resist apprehension: see CRIMINAL LAW vol 25 (2010) PARAS 128–129), s 20 (wounding or inflicting grievous bodily harm: see CRIMINAL LAW vol 25 (2010) PARA 130), s 21 (garrotting: see CRIMINAL LAW vol 25 (2010) PARA 131), s 23 (endangering life or causing harm by administering poison: see CRIMINAL LAW vol 25 (2010) PARA 133), s 28 (burning, maiming, etc by explosion: see CRIMINAL LAW vol 25 (2010) PARA 135), s 29 (causing explosions or casting corrosive fluids with intent to do grievous bodily harm: see CRIMINAL LAW vol 25 (2010) PARA 136) (see the Criminal Justice Act 1982 Sch 1 Pt II paras 2–8);

(iii)   the Explosive Substances Act 1883 s 2 (causing explosion likely to endanger life or property: see CRIMINAL LAW vol 25 (2010) PARA 137) (Criminal Justice Act 1982 Sch 1 Pt II para 9);

(iv)   the Infant Life (Preservation) Act 1929 s 1 (child destruction: see CRIMINAL LAW vol 25 (2010) PARA 118) (Criminal Justice Act 1982 Sch 1 Pt II para 10);

(v)   the Infanticide Act 1938 s 1(1) (infanticide: see CRIMINAL LAW vol 25 (2010) PARA 113) (Criminal Justice Act 1982 Sch 1 Pt II para 11);

(vi)   the Firearms Act 1968 s 17(1) (use of firearms and imitation firearms to resist arrest: see CRIMINAL LAW vol 26 (2010) PARA 630) (Criminal Justice Act 1982 Sch 1 Pt II para 15);

(vii)   the Theft Act 1968 s 8 (robbery: see CRIMINAL LAW vol 25 (2010) PARA 289), s 10 (aggravated burglary: see CRIMINAL LAW vol 25 (2010) PARA 291) (see the Criminal Justice Act 1982 Sch 1 Pt II paras 16, 17);

(viii)   the Misuse of Drugs Act 1971 s 4 (production or supply of a controlled drug: see CRIMINAL LAW vol 26 (2010) PARA 725; and MEDICAL PRODUCTS AND DRUGS vol 75 (2013) PARA 492), s 5(3) (possession of a controlled drug with intent to supply it to another: see MEDICAL PRODUCTS AND DRUGS vol 75 (2013) PARA 495), s 20 (assisting in, or inducing the commission outside the United Kingdom of, an offence relating to drugs punishable under a corresponding law: see CRIMINAL LAW vol 26 (2010) PARA 732; and MEDICAL PRODUCTS AND DRUGS vol 75 (2013) PARA 504) (see the Criminal Justice Act 1982 Sch 1 Pt II paras 18–20);

(ix)   the Criminal Damage Act 1971 s 1(2)(b) (criminal damage, including arson, with intent to endanger life: see CRIMINAL LAW vol 25 (2010) PARA 329) (Criminal Justice Act 1982 Sch 1 Pt II para 21);

(x)   the Road Traffic Act 1972 s 1 (repealed) (causing death by reckless driving) (Criminal Justice Act 1982 Sch 1 Pt II para 22);

(xi)   the Customs and Excise Management Act 1979 s 85(2) (shooting at naval or revenue vessels: see CRIMINAL LAW vol 26 (2010) PARA 484) (Criminal Justice Act 1982 Sch 1 Pt II para 23);

(xii)   the Aviation Security Act 1982 ss 1, 2, 3, 6 (hijacking, destroying or damaging an aircraft or endangering its safety in flight and ancillary offences: see AIR LAW vol 2 (2008) PARA 624 et seq) (see the Criminal Justice Act 1982 Sch 1 Pt II paras 24, 25);

(xiii)   the Drug Trafficking Offences Act 1986 s 23A (repealed) (acquisition, possession or use of proceeds of drug trafficking), s 24 (assisting another to retain the benefit of drug trafficking) (repealed) (see the Criminal Justice Act 1982 Sch 1 Pt II paras 25A, 26 (Sch 1 Pt II paras 25A, 29A–29C added by the Criminal Justice Act 1993 s 74(2), (3); the Criminal Justice Act 1982 Sch 1 Pt II para 26 added by the Drug Trafficking Offences Act 1986 s 24(6)));

(xiv)   the Public Order Act 1986 s 1 (riot: see CRIMINAL LAW vol 26 (2010) PARA 487), s 2 (violent disorder: see CRIMINAL LAW vol 26 (2010) PARAS 488), s 3 (affray: see CRIMINAL LAW vol 26 (2010) PARA 489) (see the Criminal Justice Act 1982 Sch 1 Pt II paras 27–29 (Sch 1 Pt II paras 27–29 added by the Public Order Act 1986 s 40(2), Sch 2 para 4));

(xv)   the Criminal Justice Act 1988 s 93A (repealed) (assisting another to retain the benefit of criminal conduct), s 93B (repealed) (acquisition, possession or use of proceeds of criminal conduct), s 93C (repealed) (concealing or transferring proceeds of criminal conduct), s 134 (torture: see CRIMINAL LAW vol 25 (2010) PARA 172) (Criminal Justice Act 1982 Sch 1 Pt II paras 29A–29C, 30 (Sch 1 Pt II paras 29A–29C as so added; Sch 1 Pt II para 30 added by the Criminal Justice Act 1988 s 170(1), Sch 15 para 91));

(xvi)   the Road Traffic Act 1988 s 1 (causing death by dangerous driving: see ROAD TRAFFIC vol 90 (2011) PARA 720), s 3A (causing death by careless driving when under the influence of drink or drugs: see ROAD TRAFFIC vol 90 (2011) PARA 731) (see the Criminal Justice Act 1982 Sch 1 Pt II (entry added by the Road Traffic (Consequential Provisions) Act 1988 s 4, Sch 3 para 24; and amended by the Road Traffic Act 1991 s 48, Sch 4 para 17));

(xvii)   the Criminal Justice (International Co-operation) Act 1990 s 14 (repealed) (concealing or transferring proceeds of drug trafficking) (see the Criminal Justice Act 1982 Sch 1 Pt II (entry added by the Criminal Justice (International Co-operation) Act 1990 s 31(1), Sch 4 para 3));

(xviii)   the Aviation and Maritime Security Act 1990 s 1 (endangering safety at aerodromes: see AIR LAW vol 2 (2008) PARA 631), s 9 (hijacking of ships: see SHIPPING AND MARITIME LAW vol 94 (2008) PARA 1210), s 10 (seizing or exercising control of fixed platforms: see SHIPPING AND MARITIME LAW vol 94 (2008) PARA 1211), ss 11–14 (destroying ships or fixed platforms or endangering their safety, endangering safe navigation, threats and ancillary offences: see SHIPPING AND MARITIME LAW vol 94 (2008) PARAS 1212–1215) (see the Criminal Justice Act 1982 Sch 1 Pt II (entry added by the Aviation and Maritime Security Act 1990 s 53(1), Sch 3 para 7));

(xix) the Channel Tunnel (Security) Order 1994, SI 1994/570, art 4 (hijacking of Channel Tunnel trains: see RAILWAYS AND TRAMWAYS vol 86 (2013) PARA 328), art 5 (seizing or exercising control of the Channel Tunnel system: see RAILWAYS AND TRAMWAYS vol 86 (2013) PARA 328), arts 6–8 (other offences relating to Channel Tunnel trains or the tunnel system: see RAILWAYS AND TRAMWAYS vol 86 (2013) PARA 328) (see the Criminal Justice Act 1982 Sch 1 Pt II (entry added by SI 1994/570));

(xx) the Drug Trafficking Act 1994 s 49 (repealed) (concealing or transferring the proceeds of drug trafficking), s 50 (repealed) (assisting another person to retain the benefit of drug trafficking), s 51 (repealed) (acquisition, possession or use of proceeds of drug trafficking) (see the Criminal Justice Act 1982 Sch 1 Pt II (entry added by the Drug Trafficking Act 1994 s 65(1), Sch 1 para 7));

(xxi) the Proceeds of Crime Act 2002 s 327 (concealing criminal property etc: see CRIMINAL LAW vol 26 (2010) PARA 744), s 328 (arrangements relating to criminal property: see CRIMINAL LAW vol 26 (2010) PARA 745), s 329 (acquisition, use and possession of criminal property: see CRIMINAL LAW vol 26 (2010) PARA 746) (see the Criminal Justice Act 1982 Sch 1 Pt II (entry added by the Proceeds of Crime Act 2002 s 456, Sch 11 paras 1, 13));

(xxii) the Sexual Offences Act 2003 ss 1, 2 (rape, assault by penetration: see CRIMINAL LAW vol 25 (2010) PARAS 178, 180), s 4 (causing a person to engage in sexual activity without consent), where the activity caused involved penetration within s 4(4)(a)–(d) (see CRIMINAL LAW vol 25 (2010) PARA 184), ss 5, 6 (rape of a child under 13, assault of a child under 13 by penetration: see CRIMINAL LAW vol 25 (2010) PARAS 179, 181), s 8 (causing or inciting a child under 13 to engage in sexual activity), where an activity involving penetration within s 8(2)(a)–(d) was caused (see CRIMINAL LAW vol 25 (2010) PARA 185), s 30 (sexual activity with a person with a mental disorder impeding choice), where the touching involved penetration within s 30(3)(a)–(d) (see CRIMINAL LAW vol 25 (2010) PARA 214), s 31 (causing or inciting a person, with a mental disorder impeding choice, to engage in sexual activity), where an activity involving penetration within s 31(3)(a)–(d) was caused (see CRIMINAL LAW vol 25 (2010) PARA 214) (see the Criminal Justice Act 1982 Sch 1 Pt II (entry added by the Sexual Offences Act 2003 s 139, Sch 6 para 27));

(xxiii) the Domestic Violence, Crime and Victims Act 2004 s 5 (causing or allowing a child or vulnerable adult to die or suffer serious physical harm: see CRIMINAL LAW vol 25 (2010) PARA 117) (see the Criminal Justice Act 1982 Sch 1 Pt II (entry added by the Domestic Violence, Crime and Victims Act 2004 s 58(1), Sch 10 para 16; and amended by the Domestic Violence, Crime and Victims (Amendment) Act 2012 s 3, Schedule para 1)).

Further to head (xxii) above, see the Violent Crime Reduction Act 2006 s 55 (continuity of sexual offences law); and CRIMINAL LAW vol 25 (2010) PARA 174. As to the meaning of 'United Kingdom' see PARA 4 note 3.

8   Criminal Justice Act 1982 s 32(1)(b)(ii).

9   Criminal Justice Act 1982 s 32(1)(b)(iii).

10 Criminal Justice Act 1982 s 32(1)(b)(iv). The reference in s 32(1)(b)(iv) to (or to conduct amounting to) the common law offence of inciting the commission of another offence, has effect (as from the day that offence is abolished) as a reference to (or to conduct amounting to) offences under the Serious Crime Act 2007 Pt 2 (ss 44–67) (see CRIMINAL LAW vol 25 (2010) PARAS 65–72): s 63(1), Sch 6 Pt 1 para 8.

11 Ie an offence under the Armed Forces Act 2006 s 42 (see ARMED FORCES vol 3 (2011) PARA 587): Criminal Justice Act 1982 s 32(1)(c) (added by the Armed Forces Act 2006 Sch 16 para 94(1), (2)).

12 Ie within the meaning of the Armed Forces Act 2006 s 42 (see ARMED FORCES vol 3 (2011) PARA 587): Criminal Justice Act 1982 s 32(1)(c) (as added: see note 11).

13 Criminal Justice Act 1982 s 32(1)(c) (as added: see note 11). The provision made by s 32(1)(c) is modified so that the reference to an offence under the Armed Forces Act 2006 s 42 (see ARMED FORCES vol 3 (2011) PARA 587) includes an SDA civil offence; and the reference to the corresponding offence under the law of England and Wales includes the corresponding civil offence: see the Armed Forces Act 2006 (Transitional Provisions etc) Order 2009, SI 2009/1059, art 205, Sch 1 para 23. For these purposes, 'SDA civil offence' means an offence under the Army

Act 1955 s 70 (repealed), the Air Force Act 1955 s 70 (repealed) or the Naval Discipline Act 1957 s 42 (repealed): see the Armed Forces Act 2006 (Transitional Provisions etc) Order 2009, SI 2009/1059, art 2(4), (5).

14 Criminal Justice Act 1982 s 32(1)(c)(i) (as added: see note 11).

15 Criminal Justice Act 1982 s 32(1)(c)(ii) (as added: see note 11). The Armed Forces Act 2006 s 48 (attempts, conspiracy, encouragement and assistance and aiding and abetting outside England and Wales: see ARMED FORCES vol 3 (2011) PARA 587) applies for the purposes of the Criminal Justice Act 1982 s 32(1)(c)(ii)–(iv) (see also heads (3)(c), (d) in the text) as if the reference in the Armed Forces Act 2006 s 48(3)(b) to 'any of the following provisions of that Act' were a reference to the Criminal Justice Act 1982 s 32(1)(c)(ii)–(iv): s 32(2A) (added by the Armed Forces Act 2006 Sch 16 para 94(1), (4); and amended by the Serious Crime Act 2007 s 60, Sch 5 para 1).

16 Criminal Justice Act 1982 s 32(1)(c)(iii) (as added: see note 11). See also note 15.

17 Criminal Justice Act 1982 s 32(1)(c)(iv) (as added: see note 11). The reference in s 32(1)(c)(iv) to (or to conduct amounting to) the common law offence of inciting the commission of another offence, has effect (as from the day that offence is abolished) as a reference to (or to conduct amounting to) offences under the Serious Crime Act 2007 Pt 2 (ss 44–67) (see CRIMINAL LAW vol 25 (2010) PARAS 65–72): s 63(1), Sch 6 Pt 1 para 8. See also note 15.

18 Criminal Justice Act 1982 s 32(1). At the date at which this volume states the law, no such order had been made.

19 Criminal Justice Act 1982 s 32(1).

20 Criminal Justice Act 1982 s 32(3)(a).

21 Criminal Justice Act 1982 s 32(3)(b) (amended by the Armed Forces Act 2006 Sch 16 para 94(1), (5)).

22 Criminal Justice Act 1982 s 32(4)(a).

23 Criminal Justice Act 1982 s 32(4)(b).

24 Criminal Justice Act 1982 s 32(4)(c).

25 Criminal Justice Act 1982 s 32(8).

26 Ie within the meaning of the Powers of Criminal Courts Act 1973 s 28(4) (repealed): Criminal Justice Act 1982 s 32(5).

27 Ie under the Criminal Justice Act 1967 s 60 (repealed) (release on licence of persons serving determinate sentences): Criminal Justice Act 1982 s 32(5).

28 Criminal Justice Act 1982 s 32(5). The text refers to the application of s 32(5) irrespective of whether at the time of the prisoner's release he could have been released on licence under the Criminal Justice Act 1967 s 60 (repealed) (see note 27) by virtue of s 60(3) (repealed) (ie where the Secretary of State had power to direct that a person serving a sentence of imprisonment in respect of whom an extended sentence certificate was issued when the sentence was passed, or that a person serving a sentence of imprisonment for a term of 18 months or more who was under the age of 21 when the sentence was passed, may, instead of being granted remission of any part of his sentence under the prison rules, be released on licence at any time on or after the day on which he could have been discharged from prison if the remission had been granted): Criminal Justice Act 1982 s 32(5).

29 Criminal Justice Act 1982 s 32(6) (amended by the Criminal Justice and Courts Act 2015 Sch 9 para 8).

30 Ie an order under the Criminal Justice Act 1982 s 32: see s 32(13).

31 Criminal Justice Act 1982 s 32(13).

32 Criminal Justice Act 1982 s 32(13).

(3) THE PAROLE BOARD AND RECALL ADJUDICATORS

(i) The Parole Board

A. ESTABLISHMENT AND FUNCTIONS

699. Constitution and functions of the Parole Board. The Parole Board continues to be[1], by that name, a body corporate[2]. As such, it is constituted in accordance with Chapter 6 of Part 12 of the Criminal Justice Act 2003[3], and it has the functions conferred on it[4]:

(1)   in respect of fixed-term prisoners, by or under that Chapter[5]; and

(2) in respect of life prisoners, by Chapter II of Part II of the Crime (Sentences) Act 1997[6].

It is the duty of the Board to advise the Secretary of State[7] with respect to any matter referred to it by him which is to do with the early release or recall of prisoners[8].

In dealing with cases[9] as respects which it makes recommendations under head (1) or head (2) above, the Board must consider[10]:

(a) any documents given to it by the Secretary of State[11]; and

(b) any other oral or written information obtained by it[12].

If, in any particular case, the Board thinks it necessary to interview the person to whom the case relates before reaching a decision, the Board may authorise one of its members to interview him and must consider the report of the interview made by that member[13]. The Board must deal with cases as respects which it gives directions under head (1) or head (2) above on consideration of all such evidence as may be adduced before it[14]. Without prejudice to these procedural provisions[15], the Secretary of State may make rules with respect to the proceedings of the Board, including proceedings authorising cases to be dealt with by a prescribed number of its members or requiring cases to be dealt with at prescribed times[16].

The Secretary of State may also give to the Board directions as to the matters to be taken into account by it in discharging any functions under head (1) above or under head (2) above[17]; and in giving any such directions the Secretary of State must have regard to: (i) the need to protect the public from serious harm from offenders[18]; and (ii) the desirability of preventing the commission by them of further offences and of securing their rehabilitation[19]. The Secretary of State may by order[20] provide that, following a referral by the Secretary of State of the case of a discretionary release prisoner[21], the Parole Board[22]:

(A) must direct the prisoner's release if it is satisfied that conditions specified in the order are met[23]; or

(B) must do so unless it is satisfied that conditions specified in the order are met[24].

The Prison Service Instructions System gives guidance and deals with basic matters of policy relating to the process of parole release and recall[25].

1 The Parole Board for England and Wales was established in 1968 under the Criminal Justice Act 1967 s 59 (repealed) with the primary function of advising the Secretary of State in relation to the exercise of his powers to release prisoners on licence under the 1967 Act (although the Secretary of State was under no obligation to comply with the advice given). The Board was constituted a body corporate under the Criminal Justice and Public Order Act 1994 (see s 149, substituting the Criminal Justice Act 1991 s 32(1) (repealed)) and, as such, has the status of an Executive Non-Departmental Public Body (ENDPB). The respective roles of the Secretary of State and Parole Board have changed as they have developed over time: see note 17.

2 Criminal Justice Act 2003 s 239(1). As to membership, proceedings etc of the Board see s 239(7), Sch 19. There must be transparency not only in the appointment process to the Board, but also in any stipulation of the qualities to be looked for in candidates, because departmental sponsorship arrangements were capable of giving rise to the perception that the Board was not independent: *R (on the application of Brooke) v Parole Board, R (on the application of Murphy) v Parole Board* [2008] EWCA Civ 29, [2008] 3 All ER 289, [2008] 1 WLR 1950 (ministers should not require that lay members demonstrate qualities that are not relevant to the Board's functions but which are likely to affect the Board's decisions). See further note 17.

   The Parole Board is subject to investigation by the Parliamentary Commissioner for Administration: see the Parliamentary Commissioner Act 1967 s 4(1), Sch 2; and **CONSTITUTIONAL AND ADMINISTRATIVE LAW**.

3 Criminal Justice Act 2003 s 239(1)(a). As to Pt 12 Ch 6 (ss 239–268) (sentencing: release, licences and recall) see also PARAS 696, 709 et seq.

4   Criminal Justice Act 2003 s 239(1)(b) (amended by the Criminal Justice and Courts Act 2015 Sch 3 para 6).

5   Criminal Justice Act 2003 s 239(1)(b).

6   See the Criminal Justice Act 2003 s 239(1)(b). As to the Crime (Sentences) Act 1997 Pt II Ch II (ss 28–34) (life sentences), and as to life prisoners within the meaning of Pt II Ch II, see PARA 706 et seq.

7   As to the Secretary of State for these purposes see PRISONS AND PRISONERS vol 85 (2012) PARA 408.

8   Criminal Justice Act 2003 s 239(2). See *R (on the application of Brooke) v Parole Board, R (on the application of Murphy) v Parole Board* [2008] EWCA Civ 29 at [47], [2008] 3 All ER 289 at [47], [2008] 1 WLR 1950 at [47] per Lord Phillips of Worth Matravers CJ (whatever uncertainty there may be as to the scope of the Board's advisory functions, there is no doubt that the major part of the Board's duties is judicial in nature, involving the adjudication, in respect of different types of sentence, on whether the continued detention of prisoners is lawful or whether they are entitled to be released under licence). See also note 14; and PARA 700.

9   The Criminal Justice Act 2003 s 239(3) does not deprive the Parole Board of its judicial power to exclude a document or documents provided by the Secretary of State (see head (a) in the text) from consideration by the panel of the Parole Board making the decision whether to direct release: *R (on the application of McGetrick) v Parole Board* [2013] EWCA Civ 182, [2013] 3 All ER 636, [2013] 1 WLR 2064. Such a decision to exclude is likely to be taken only in rare circumstances and, if taken at all, will be taken by a Panel of the Parole Board at an interlocutory hearing conducted in accordance with the Criminal Justice Act 2003 s 293(4) (see the text and note 14).

10   Criminal Justice Act 2003 s 239(3). The wording of s 239 does not qualify the inherent power of the Parole Board to decide what if any weight is to be given to any evidence it considers, eg evidence contained in any document given to it by the Secretary of State (see head (a) in the text): see *R (on the application of McGetrick) v Parole Board* [2013] EWCA Civ 182 at [33], [2013] 3 All ER 636, [2013] 1 WLR 2064 per Pill LJ; and see note 9.

11   Criminal Justice Act 2003 s 239(3)(a). See notes 9, 10.

12   Criminal Justice Act 2003 s 239(3)(b).

13   Criminal Justice Act 2003 s 239(3). As to whether procedural fairness requires the Board to consider whether further evidence should be obtained, or whether to hold an oral hearing, see PARA 700.

14   Criminal Justice Act 2003 s 239(4). In rare cases, a panel of the Parole Board can decide, when dealing with cases in respect of which it makes recommendations, that one or more documents provided by the Secretary of State are excluded from consideration by the panel which is to make a recommendation under s 239(3) (see note 9): *R (on the application of McGetrick) v Parole Board* [2013] EWCA Civ 182, [2013] 3 All ER 636, [2013] 1 WLR 2064. As to procedure before the Board, and the scope for the Board to regulate its own procedure, see PARA 700.

     The Parole Board exercises a quasi-judicial function but there is no requirement that, in performing its function, it has to follow a criminal trial procedure, or anything like it, so long as it conducts its deliberations fairly: *R v Parole Board, ex p Harris* (15 September 1997, unreported). See also *R (on the application of Allen) v Parole Board* [2012] EWHC 3496 (Admin), [2012] All ER (D) 73 (Dec) (Parole Board was engaged in a different legal exercise to the sentencing judge, asking a different legal question, applying a different legal standard of proof, using a different juridical approach, and taking account of different (and ample) evidence and materials when properly determining an issue which the sentencing judge expressly said he was not able to decide himself).

     The Board is required to have before it all information that bears on its consideration of the risk to the public of the prisoner committing further offences if he is released: *R (on the application of Roberts) v Parole Board* [2005] UKHL 45, [2005] 2 AC 738, sub nom *Roberts v Parole Board* [2006] 1 All ER 39 (the Board should be in a position to know all the relevant information about the progress that the prisoner has made during his sentence; in some situations, the risk that will exist could relate to circumstances that did not exist at the time of sentence). The information before the Board may include material provided by the Secretary of State containing factual allegations about the prisoner's pre-trial conduct, which formed part of the original prosecution case against him, but in relation to which he was never convicted ('untried material'): *R (on the application of McGetrick) v Parole Board* [2013] EWCA Civ 182 at [9], [39], [2013] 3 All ER 636, [2013] 1 WLR 2064 per Pill LJ (the weight, if any, to be given to that evidence is a matter for the Board but, if it concludes that the allegations relied on at trial are relevant, but that it cannot fairly determine whether or not they have been made out, little or no weight should be given to such allegations and the Board's view of any reports that relied on them would be affected accordingly). See also *R (on the application of Wyles) v Parole Board* [2006] EWHC 493 (Admin), [2006] All ER (D) 233 (Jan) (prisoner released on life licence was charged with causing grievous bodily harm with intent, but acquitted; nevertheless, circumstances of the incident for which he was charged had a sufficient causal connection with the index offence that the claimant might pose a risk to the public if released); cf *R (on the application of Headley) v Parole Board* [2009] EWHC 663 (Admin), [2009] All ER (D) 307 (Jul) (allegations made by ex-wife which appeared to have some bearing on the index offence ought to have given rise to opportunity for cross examination). Where an initial sentence was substituted or varied on appeal prior to the application for parole, the Parole Board should take into account that new judgment, as well as any fresh sentencing reports and other relevant material before making its assessment: *R (on the application of Martin) v Parole Board* [2003] EWHC 1512 (Admin), (2003) Times, 15 May, [2003] All ER (D) 89 (May).

15 Ie without prejudice to the Criminal Justice Act 2003 s 239(3), (4) (see the text and notes 9–14): see s 239(5).

16 Criminal Justice Act 2003 s 239(5). In exercise of the power conferred by s 239(5), the Secretary of State has made the Parole Board Rules 2011, SI 2011/2947 (see PARA 700).

17 Criminal Justice Act 2003 s 239(6). Directions may have been issued to the Board by the Secretary of State under the Criminal Justice Act 1991 s 32(6) (which is repealed, but re-enacted in identical terms as the Criminal Justice Act 2003 s 239(6)). As to the way in which the Secretary of State should treat the Parole Board's recommendations see *R v Secretary of State for the Home Department, ex p Draper* [2000] All ER (D) 79, DC (rules of procedural fairness did not require the Home Secretary to issue a 'minded to refuse' letter indicating the views of the Board and the Home Secretary's reasons for rejecting the Board's view, where there was no new evidence or new points being raised before the Home Secretary that had not been before the Board); *R (on the application of Burgess) v Secretary of State for the Home Department* [2000] All ER (D) 1682, DC (notwithstanding the increased emphasis on the sexual element in the index offence, there was nothing material before the Secretary of State which had not been before the Parole Board); and see *R (on the application of Hill) v Secretary of State for the Home Department* [2007] EWHC 2164 (Admin), [2007] All ER (D) 112 (Sep) (Secretary of State had to maintain an even-handed approach to the exercise of his discretion in relation to the transfer of prisoners following an apparent change in policy); and *R (on the application of Banfield) v Secretary of State for Justice* [2007] EWHC 2605 (Admin), [2007] All ER (D) 116 (Oct) (in any given case what the court has to do is to determine whether the Secretary of State's decision was lawful). See also *R (on the application of Oletunde Adetoro) v Secretary of State for Justice* [2012] EWHC 2576 (Admin), [2012] All ER (D) 162 (Sep) (there was an unfairness inherent in the procedure adopted by the Secretary of State where, having held out as his decision one reached in which he accepted the recommendation of the Parole Board, he then acted upon arguments advanced privately by one party to change his mind, without inviting submissions from the prisoner).

The power of the Secretary of State to give directions to the Board (conferred by the Criminal Justice Act 2003 s 239(6) or under predecessor legislation) was construed as a power to give guidance to the Board as to the matters to be taken into account, in so far as they were legally relevant, in order to assist the Board to reach a structured decision on the question which it was its duty to decide (ie whether to direct the release of a prisoner in accordance with the law): *R (on the application of Girling) v Parole Board* [2006] EWCA Civ 1779, [2007] QB 783, [2007] 2 All ER 688. Construed in this way, directions do not infringe the independence of the Board, but the Secretary of State is not entitled to direct the Board how it was to decide a particular case, or class of case, or to direct it to have regard to an irrelevant consideration, or not to have regard to a relevant consideration, since that would be to impugn the Board's independence and interfere with its functions as a court in contravention of the common law and the Convention for the Protection of Human Rights and Fundamental Freedoms (Rome, 4 November 1950; TS 71 (1953); Cmd 8969) (the European Convention on Human Rights) art 5.4 (see RIGHTS AND FREEDOMS vol 88A (2013) PARA 210 et seq): *R (on the application of Girling) v Parole Board* (Secretary of State's directions objectionable insofar as they purported to tell the Parole Board how to decide whether or not a prisoner should be released); and see also *Sturnham v Secretary of State for Justice* [2012] EWCA Civ 452, [2013] 2 AC 254, [2012] 3 WLR 476 (affd [2013] UKSC 47, [2013] 2 AC 254, [2013] 4 All ER 177) (Board simply referring to unobjectionable part of Secretary of State's guidance when stating that it had taken into account 'the matters specified in the Secretary of State's directions').

In *R (on the application of Brooke) v Parole Board, R (on the application of Murphy) v Parole Board* [2008] EWCA Civ 29, [2008] 3 All ER 289, [2008] 1 WLR 1950, the Court of Appeal gave guidance in relation to areas of policy and practice that required attention, having found that neither the Secretary of State nor his department had adequately addressed the need for the Parole Board to be and to be seen to be free of influence in relation to the performance of its judicial functions, given that these latter functions have gradually assumed greater importance over time. See also *R (on the application of Morales) v Parole Board* [2011] EWHC 28 (Admin), [2011] 1 WLR 1095, [2011] All ER (D) 94 (Jan) (tribunal which lacked power to summon witnesses nevertheless had independence necessary to constitute a court); and *R (on the application of D'Cunha) v Parole Board* [2011] EWHC 128 (Admin), 175 CL & J 111, [2011] All ER (D) 105 (Feb) (Board obliged to follow Secretary of State's directions when it gave advice on the suitability of a prisoner for transfer to open conditions).

In *Clift v United Kingdom* (2010) Times, 21 July, [2010] ECHR 7205/07, ECtHR, the Secretary of State's continuing role in deciding upon the releases under the Criminal Justice Act 1991 provisions of prisoners sentenced to determinate terms of 15 years or more for offences committed before 4 April 2005 was held by the European Court of Human Rights to violate the European Convention on Human Rights art 5 in conjunction with art 14 (rights and fundamental freedoms to be secured without discrimination on any ground: see RIGHTS AND FREEDOMS vol 88A (2013) PARA 506 et seq) because there was no objective justification for treating prisoners serving determinate terms of less than 15 years more favourably; in the case of such prisoners, the Secretary of State was required by the Parole Board (Transfer of Functions) Order 1998, SI 1998/3218, art 2 (lapsed) to act in accordance with a Parole Board recommendation for release. Effect was given to the judgment of the European Court of Human Rights by an amendment to the Criminal Justice Act 1991 s 35 (power to release long-term prisoners) (repealed) which required the Secretary of State to give effect to a recommendation for release of any long term prisoner: see the Coroners and Justice Act 2009 s 145(2) (repealed). See also *R (on the application of Mills) v Secretary of State for the Home Department* [2005] EWHC 2508 (Admin), [2005] All ER (D) 307 (Oct) (Board's powers were circumscribed by its specific statutory duties and any specific matters which might have been referred to it by the Secretary of State under the Criminal Justice Act 1991 (now repealed)); and *R (on the application of Foley) v Parole Board for England and Wales* [2012] EWHC 2184 (Admin), [2012] All ER (D) 09 (Aug) (no longer any objective justification for the different tests applied by the Parole Board to those serving indeterminate sentences and those serving determinate sentences of 15 years or more).

18 Criminal Justice Act 2003 s 239(6)(a). As to when there is a significant risk of serious harm to members of the public for the purposes of Pt 12 Ch 5 (ss 224–236): see PARAS 33–34.

19 Criminal Justice Act 2003 s 239(6)(b).

20 An order under the Legal Aid, Sentencing and Punishment of Offenders Act 2012 s 128 may:

    (1)   amend the Crime (Sentences) Act 1997 s 28 (duty to release IPP prisoners and others: see PARA 707) (Legal Aid, Sentencing and Punishment of Offenders Act 2012 s 128(3)(a));

    (2)   amend the Criminal Justice Act 2003 s 244A (release on licence of s 236A prisoners (ie prisoners serving sentences under s 236A (see PARA 32), including one imposed as a result of the Armed Forces Act 2006 s 224A (see ARMED FORCES): see PARA 714) (Legal Aid, Sentencing and Punishment of Offenders Act 2012 s 128(3)(ba), (6) (s 128(2)(ba) added, s 128(3), (6) amended, by the Criminal Justice and Courts Act 2015 Sch 1 para 25));

    (3)   amend the Criminal Justice Act 2003 s 246A (release on licence of extended sentence prisoners: see PARA 716) (Legal Aid, Sentencing and Punishment of Offenders Act 2012 s 128(3)(b));

    (4)   amend the Criminal Justice Act 2003 s 267B, Sch 20B para 6 (duty to release on direction of Parole Board (transitional provisions): see PARA 725), Sch 20B para 15 (release on licence of certain extended sentence prisoners on direction of Parole Board (transitional provisions): see PARA 726), Sch 20B para 25 (duty to release Criminal Justice Act 1967 sentence prisoners unconditionally (transitional provisions): see PARA 727) or the Criminal Justice Act 2003 Sch 20B para 28 (duty to release Criminal Justice Act 1967 sentence prisoners on licence (transitional provisions): see PARA 727) (Legal Aid, Sentencing and Punishment of Offenders Act 2012 s 128(3)(c));

    (5)   make provision in relation to any person whose case is disposed of by the Parole Board on or after the day on which the regulations come into force (even if the Secretary of State referred that person's case to the Board before that day) (Legal Aid, Sentencing and Punishment of Offenders Act 2012 s 128(3)(d));

    (6)   make different provision in relation to each of the categories of discretionary release prisoner mentioned in s 128(2) (see note 21) (s 128(3)(e)); and

    (7)   include consequential provision (s 128(3)(f)); and

    (8)   as from a day to be appointed, amend the Crime (Sentences) Act 1997 s 32 (recall of IPP prisoners and others while on licence and further release: see PARA 708) (Legal Aid,

Sentencing and Punishment of Offenders Act 2012 s 128(3)(aa) (prospectively added by the Criminal Justice and Courts Act 2015 s 11(3)). At the date at which this volume states the law no day had been appointed for this purpose.

21 For these purposes, 'discretionary release prisoner' means: (1) an IPP prisoner; (2) an extended sentence prisoner; or (3) a section 236A prisoner; or (4) a person to whom the Criminal Justice Act 2003 Sch 20B para 4 (duty to make automatic initial release (transitional provisions): see PARA 725), Sch 20B para 15, Sch 20B para 24 (duty to release Criminal Justice Act 1967 sentence prisoners unconditionally (transitional provisions): see PARA 727) or Sch 20B para 27 (duty to release Criminal Justice Act 1967 extended sentence prisoners on licence (transitional provisions): see PARA 727) applies: Legal Aid, Sentencing and Punishment of Offenders Act 2012 s 128(2) (as amended: see note 20). 'IPP prisoner' means a prisoner who is serving one or more of the following sentences and is not serving any other life sentence (i e a life sentence within the meaning the Crime (Sentences) Act 1997 s 34: see PARA 706):

    (a)   a sentence of imprisonment for public protection or detention in a young offender institution for public protection under the Criminal Justice Act 2003 s 225 (see PARA 37), including one imposed as a result of the Armed Forces Act 2006 s 219 (person aged at least 18 but under 21 convicted by Court Martial of offence of criminal conduct corresponding to a serious offence: see ARMED FORCES vol 3 (2011) PARA 611) (Legal Aid, Sentencing and Punishment of Offenders Act 2012 s 128(6));

    (b)   a sentence of detention for public protection under the Criminal Justice Act 2003 s 226 (see PARA 34; and CHILDREN AND YOUNG PERSONS vol 10 (2012) PARA 1300), including one imposed as a result of the Armed Forces Act 2006 s 221 (required custodial sentences for dangerous offenders: see ARMED FORCES vol 3 (2011) PARA 611) (Legal Aid, Sentencing and Punishment of Offenders Act 2012 s 128(6)).

'Extended sentence prisoner' means a prisoner who is serving a sentence under the Criminal Justice Act 2003 s 226A (extended sentence for certain violent or sexual offences (persons 18 or over): see PARAS 18–20) or s 226B (extended sentence for certain violent or sexual offences (persons under 18): see PARAS 18–20), including one imposed as a result of the Armed Forces Act 2006 s 219A (extended sentence for certain violent or sexual offenders aged 18 or over: see ARMED FORCES) or s 221A (extended sentence for certain violent or sexual offenders aged under 18: see ARMED FORCES): Legal Aid, Sentencing and Punishment of Offenders Act 2012 s 128(6).

22 Legal Aid, Sentencing and Punishment of Offenders Act 2012 s 128(1).

23 Legal Aid, Sentencing and Punishment of Offenders Act 2012 s 128(1)(a).

24 Legal Aid, Sentencing and Punishment of Offenders Act 2012 s 128(1)(b).

25 As to the system of central policy instructions and guidance contained eg in Prison Service Orders (PSOs) and Prison Service Instructions (PSIs) see PRISONS AND PRISONERS vol 85 (2012) PARA 406.

B. PROCEDURE

700. General procedural matters relating to the Parole Board. The Secretary of State[1] may[2] make rules with respect to the proceedings of the Parole Board[3], including proceedings authorising cases to be dealt with by a prescribed number of its members or requiring cases to be dealt with at prescribed times[4]. In exercise of the power so conferred, the Secretary of State has made the Parole Board Rules 2011[5], which:

    (1)   cover general procedures which are required in Parole Board proceedings, including the appointment of panels, information and reports to be prepared by the Secretary of State and the giving of directions[6];

    (2)   set out the timetable and rules for proceedings without a hearing where the Parole Board determines the initial release of a prisoner serving an indeterminate sentence[7];

    (3)   set out the timetable and rules for proceedings with a hearing by an oral panel[8]; and

    (4)   contain miscellaneous provisions about time limits, the transmission of documents and procedural errors[9].

The fairness of the procedure before the Board is to be judged according to the common law rules of procedural fairness and the applicable articles of the European Convention on Human Rights[10]. Fairness may require the Board, of its own initiative, to consider whether further evidence should be obtained, such as where there is a factual dispute and the material before it is inadequate to resolve the issue[11]. However, neither the common law duty of procedural fairness nor the obligations imposed by the Convention require the Board to hold an oral hearing in every case[12]. The Convention requires that any proceedings by which the lawfulness of a prisoner's detention is decided must be determined speedily by a court[13], but as to what constitutes speedy determination will depend on the circumstances of the case[14].

Within such constraints, it seems that the Parole Board has power to regulate its own procedure[15].

1   As to the Secretary of State for these purposes see PRISONS AND PRISONERS vol 85 (2012) PARA 408.
2   Ie without prejudice to the Criminal Justice Act 2003 s 239(3), (4): see s 239(5); and PARA 699.
3   As to the constitution and functions of the Parole Board, continued by the Criminal Justice Act 2003 s 239(1), see PARA 699.
4   See the Criminal Justice Act 2003 s 239(5); and PARA 699.
5   Ie the Parole Board Rules 2011, SI 2011/2947, which contain provisions for the commencement, application and interpretation of the Rules (see Pt 1 (rr 1–3)). The 2011 Rules came into force on 3 January 2012 (see r 1(1)); and they revoke the Parole Board Rules 2004 (see the Parole Board Rules 2011, SI 2011/2947, r 1(2)). This revocation does not, however, affect anything done under the Parole Board Rules 2004 before 3 January 2012: see the Parole Board Rules 2011, SI 2011/2947, r 1(3). Although the Parole Board Rules 2004 were made under the Criminal Justice Act 1991 s 32(5) (revoked), which was couched in almost identical terms to the Criminal Justice Act 2003 s 239(5), they were not made by statutory instrument.
     The Parole Board Rules 2011, SI 2011/2947, apply where the Secretary of State refers a case to the Parole Board relating to the release or recall of a prisoner: r 3(1). However:
     (1)   Rule 7(3) (service of information and reports: see PARA 701) applies only where the Secretary of State refers a case to the Board relating to the initial release of a prisoner serving an indeterminate sentence (r 3(2)); and
     (2)   Pt 3 (rr 16–18) (see head (2) in the text) applies only where the Secretary of State refers a case to the Board relating to the release of a prisoner serving an indeterminate sentence (r 3(3)).
     A reference to a period of time (in the case of the initial release of a prisoner serving an indeterminate sentence) applies as set out in the Parole Board Rules 2011, SI 2011/2947 and (in all other cases) applies as if it was a reference to such period of time as the chair may in each case determine: r 3(4). As to the meaning of 'Board' for these purposes see PARA 701 note 2; as to the meaning of 'chair' for these purposes see PARA 701 note 10; and as to the meaning of 'indeterminate sentence' see PARA 701 note 6.
6   See the Parole Board Rules 2011, SI 2011/2947, Pt 2 (rr 4–15); and PARA 701. As to the information and reports to be sent to the Parole Board by the Secretary of State see r 7, Schs 1, 2; and PARA 701.
7   See the Parole Board Rules 2011, SI 2011/2947, Pt 3; and PARA 702.
8   See the Parole Board Rules 2011, SI 2011/2947, Pt 4 (rr 19–26); and PARAS 703, 704.
9   See the Parole Board Rules 2011, SI 2011/2947, Pt 5 (rr 27–29); and PARA 701 et seq.
10   Ie the Convention for the Protection of Human Rights and Fundamental Freedoms (Rome, 4 November 1950; TS 71 (1953); Cmd 8969) and, in this context, especially art 5.4 (ie that everyone who is deprived of his liberty by arrest or detention is entitled to take proceedings by which the lawfulness of his detention is to be decided speedily by a court and his release ordered if the detention is not lawful: see RIGHTS AND FREEDOMS vol 88A (2013) PARA 210 et seq).
11   See *R v Parole Board, ex p Davies* (27 November 1996, unreported), DC; and *R (on the application of Emirsoylu) v Parole Board* [2007] EWHC 2007 (Admin), [2007] All ER (D) 82 (Aug) (Parole Board should decide whether it required further evidence in the light of the information it already had before it, including the expressed stance of the parties, but it should also reach its view in the light of the impact of the factual issue it had determined, and what it could get from the reports it already had and what it would get from any further reports). Cf note 12.

12 Under earlier authorities, it was held that the Board had a discretion conferred by statute whether to hold an oral hearing and it will be acting illegally if it refuses to consider a request for such a hearing: *R v Parole Board, ex p Davies* (27 November 1996, unreported), DC (considering the Criminal Justice Act 1991 s 32(3) (repealed), which was enacted in identical terms to the Criminal Justice Act 2003 s 239(3) (see PARA 699)). See also *R v Parole Board, ex p Mansell* [1996] COD 327, DC; *R v Parole Board, ex p Downing* [1997] COD 149, DC. The position now is that, while the common law duty of procedural fairness does not require the Parole Board to hold an oral hearing in every case where a determinate sentence prisoner resisted recall, the Board's duty is not as restricted as had hitherto been assumed: see *R (on the application of Smith) v Parole Board, R (on the application of West) v Parole Board* [2005] UKHL 1, [2005] 1 All ER 755, [2005] 1 WLR 350 (on the facts of the case, the Board had breached its duty of procedural fairness by failing to offer the prisoner an oral hearing of his representations against revocation of his licence, and was accordingly in breach of the European Convention on Human Rights art 5.4 (see note 10)). While an oral hearing is most obviously necessary to achieve a just decision in a case where facts are in issue which may affect the outcome, there are other cases in which an oral hearing may well contribute to achieving a just decision, on the facts of the case: *R (on the application of Smith) v Parole Board, R (on the application of West) v Parole Board* (important facts, whether or not, in dispute, might be open to explanation or mitigation, or might lose some of their significance in the light of other new facts). The Board's task in assessing risk might well be greatly assisted by exposure to the prisoner, or by the questioning of those who had dealt with him, as it could often be very difficult to address effective representations without knowing the points which were troubling the decision maker: *R (on the application of Smith) v Parole Board, R (on the application of West) v Parole Board*. See also *R (on the application of Yusuf) v Parole Board* [2010] EWHC 1483 (Admin), [2011] 1 WLR 63, [2010] All ER (D) 166 (Jun) (oral hearing would be convened where the circumstances required evidence to be given orally for a lifer whose minimum term had not expired and whose transfer to open conditions was in issue); *Roose v Parole Board* [2010] EWHC 1780 (Admin), (2010) Times, 1 September, [2010] All ER (D) 194 (Jul) (in an exceptional case, the court may think it appropriate to decide whether procedural fairness required an oral hearing on the basis of documents and information which the prisoner or his representatives could have put before the Board but did not do so); and as for an example of 'those rare cases' in which an oral hearing is necessary to achieve a just result, notwithstanding that there was no apparent dispute of fact or discernible issue of law advanced by the prisoner see *R (on the application of Chester) v Parole Board* [2011] EWHC 800 (Admin), [2011] All ER (D) 126 (Apr). However, in *Osborn v Parole Board* [2010] EWCA Civ 1409, [2010] All ER (D) 185 (Dec), Moses LJ referred with approval [at 54] to the Parole Board's practice of refusing an oral hearing in cases 'where there is no realistic prospect of the Board's judgment being affected by an oral hearing'.

Strasbourg jurisprudence draws a distinction between the administrative implementation (ie by a tribunal such as the Parole Board) of a determinate sentence of the court, and the determination of the length of a life-sentence prisoner's imprisonment beyond the minimum term, which was otherwise indeterminate and had to be determined by a court: see *R (on the application of Giles) v Parole Board* [2003] UKHL 42 at [25]–[26], [2004] 1 AC 1 [25]–[26], [2003] 4 All ER 429 at [25]–[26] per Lord Hope of Craighead; and RIGHTS AND FREEDOMS vol 88A (2013) PARA 317 et seq. See also *R (on the application of K) v Parole Board* [2006] EWHC 2413 (Admin), [2006] NLJR 1561, [2006] All ER (D) 75 (Oct) (Board failed to advise child applicant, not assisted by adult, that an oral hearing was possible and he was not visited by the Board, despite being told he would be, before decision made); *R (on the application of Black) v Secretary of State for Justice* [2009] UKHL 1, [2009] AC 949, [2009] 4 All ER 1 (decision when to release a prisoner subject to an indeterminate sentence engaged the European Convention on Human Rights art 5); *R (on the Application of Jacob) v Parole Board* [2010] EWHC 2475 (Admin) (Parole Board has power to make a provisional decision on a prisoner's parole application without his representations if they are not submitted within the time limit under the applicable rules, which are sufficient to ensure fairness overall).

13 Ie in accordance with the European Convention on Human Rights art 5.4 (see note 10).

14 As to delay and claims made against the Parole Board in relation to prisoner's rights under the European Convention on Human Rights art 5.4 (see note 10) see *R (on the application of James) v Secretary of State for Justice* [2009] UKHL 22, [2010] 1 AC 553, [2009] 4 All ER 255 (provided the Parole Board has been given the basic dossier under the Parole Board Rules, the Board's inability to obtain the further reports from those responsible for providing such reports does not amount to a breach of the European Convention on Human Rights art 5.4 on the part of the Parole Board unless and until the point has been reached when the delay in providing information has continued for such a long period that continued detention has become arbitrary

because the absence of such material does not preclude the Board from taking a decision as to the necessity of continued detention). However, delay to a hearing due to lack of resources (and *a fortiori* where the delay is due to error or omission on the part of the Parole Board or its staff or members) is capable of being a breach of the European Convention on Human Rights art 5.4: see *R (on the application of Pennington) v Parole Board* [2009] EWHC 2296 (Admin), 153 Sol Jo (no 37) 38, [2009] All ER (D) 126 (Sep), where the authorities were reviewed at [17] per Pelling QC (sitting as a judge of the High Court). Accordingly, delays to a hearing occasioned by a lack of resources (and a fortiori where the delay is due to error or omission on the part of the Board or its staff or members) are capable of being a breach of the European Convention on Human Rights art 5.4: see *R (on the application of Betteridge) v Parole Board* [2009] EWHC 1638 (Admin), [2009] All ER (D) 202 (Jul); *R (on the application of Noorkoiv) v Secretary of State for the Home Department* [2002] EWCA Civ 770 at [15], [30], [45], [2002] 4 All ER 515, [2002] 1 WLR 3284 per Buxton LJ; *R (on the application of Robson) v Parole Board* [2008] EWHC 248 (Admin) at [32], [2008] All ER (D) 200 (Jan) at [32] per Cranston J. However, delays resulting from the Parole Board's own reasonable actions (eg in requiring further information before a case is listed for hearing) do not amount to a breach of the European Convention on Human Rights art 5.4: see *R (on the application of D) v Life Sentence Review Comrs (Northern Ireland)* [2008] UKHL 33, [2008] 4 All ER 992, [2008] 1 WLR 1499; *R (on the application of Robson) v Parole Board* at [36] per Cranston J; and *R (on the application of Betteridge) v Parole Board* at [22] per Collins J. See also *R (on the application of Black) v Secretary of State for Justice* [2009] UKHL 1, [2009] AC 949, [2009] 4 All ER 1.

On the point as to whether the Parole Board should be held liable for delay caused by the failure of others to provide reports as directed see *R (on the application of Smith (Craig)) v Secretary of State for Justice* [2008] EWHC 2998 (Admin), [2008] All ER (D) 70 (Dec); and see also *R (on the application of Pennington) v Parole Board* (although it was reasonable for the Parole Board to delay fixing a hearing until addendum reports were received, delay cannot be characterised as a 'reasonable action' such that the European Convention on Human Rights art 5.4 is not breached). As to prioritisation of overdue cases see *R (on the application of Alcock) v Parole Board* [2009] EWHC 2401 (Admin), [2009] All ER (D) 18 (Sep) (Board's procedure was adequate, being designed to bring to the fore cases meriting hearing sooner rather than later; no basis of a claim for damages); *R (on the application of Hoole) v Parole Board* [2010] EWHC 186 (Admin), [2010] All ER (D) 100 (Feb) (correct approach to the decision whether to prioritise a prisoner's case was to make an assessment of the effects of continued incarceration on third parties by reference to the prospects of release, after the alleged compassionate circumstances had been examined). As to damages see *R (on the application of Pennington) v Parole Board* [2010] EWHC 78 (Admin), [2010] All ER (D) 69 (Feb). See also *R (on the application of Johnson) v Secretary of State for the Home Department* [2007] EWCA Civ 427, [2007] 3 All ER 532, [2007] 1 WLR 1990 (delay by the parole Board in its consideration of a case after the prisoner with a determinate sentence became eligible for parole breached the European Convention on Human Rights art 5.4 so that, provided only he could demonstrate that an earlier consideration of his case would have resulted in his earlier release, he was entitled to compensation); *R (on the application of Faulkner) v Secretary of State for Justice* [2010] EWCA Civ 1434, (2011) Times, 23 February, [2010] All ER (D) 178 (Dec) (affd [2013] UKSC 23, [2013] 2 AC 254, [2013] 2 All ER 1013) (unjustified delay by Parole Board in conducting review prevented the appellant from having the lawfulness of his continued detention decided in accordance with the European Convention on Human Rights art 5.4, for which prisoner entitled to damages); *R (on the application of Flinders) v Director of High Security* [2011] EWHC 1630 (Admin), [2011] All ER (D) 02 (Jul) (Board had failed to explain its delay in holding a review of the prisoner's case and acknowledged that the delay constituted a breach of his rights under the European Convention on Human Rights art 5.4; however, there was no proper foundation to infer that the delay in convening the parole hearing had had any additional adverse effect upon the prisoner sufficient to justify an award of damages); and see *Sturnham v Secretary of State for Justice* [2012] EWCA Civ 452 at [22], [2013] 2 AC 254, [2012] 3 WLR 476 per Laws LJ (affd [2013] UKSC 47, [2013] 2 AC 254, [2013] 4 All ER 177) (in a European Convention on Human Rights art 5.4 delay case, just satisfaction is ordinarily achieved by a declaration unless the violation involves an additional outcome for the claimant which requires an award of damages).

There is a second element to the requirement of speediness under the European Convention on Human Rights art 5.4: indeterminate sentence prisoners have a right to a prompt review of the lawfulness of their detention determined at regular intervals because the justification for their detention, namely continued dangerousness, is susceptible to change over time; the Parole Board must conduct these periodic reviews to assess continuing dangerousness at reasonable intervals, but the question of whether the periods between reviews are reasonable is to be determined in the light of the circumstances of each case: *Oldham v United Kingdom* (2000) 31 EHRR 813, ECtHR; *Blackstock v United Kingdom* (2005) 42 EHRR 55, (2005) Times, 29 June, [2005] All ER (D) 218 (Jun). See also *R (on the application of MacNeill) v HMP Lifer Panel* [2001] EWCA Civ 448, [2001] All ER (D) 248 (Mar) (European Court of Human Rights had not given a ruling on the maximum period of time between reviews applicable to all cases, and recognised that what was reasonable depended on the facts and circumstances of the individual case). The decision as to the appropriate interval between reviews is not one which under the Convention needs to be taken by a court for the purposes of the European Convention on Human Rights art 5.4 and it can properly be taken by the Secretary of State, who has a discretion to refer a case to the Parole Board before the expiry of the statutory two years minimum, whether an early review is recommended by the Parole Board or of his own motion: *Oldham v United Kingdom*; *R (on the application of Spence) v Secretary of State for the Home Department* [2003] EWCA Civ 732, 147 Sol Jo LB 660, [2003] All ER (D) 354 (May); and see *R (on the application of Day) v Secretary of State for the Home Department* [2004] EWHC 1742 (Admin), [2004] All ER (D) 274 (Jun) (authority indicates that there are aspects of the release procedures which properly remain administrative procedures under the control of the Secretary of State; the European Convention on Human Rights art 5 does not require the Parole Board to be charged with the fixing of a review date). The Secretary of State's decision to fix the period before the next review can be challenged by judicial review, however, whereby the court may not merely determine whether the decision was reasonable but also reach its own decision as to the appropriate review period: see *R (on the application of Loch) v Secretary of State for Justice* [2008] EWHC 2278 (Admin), [2008] All ER (D) 39 (Oct) (while there was no formal presumption that an interval of more than a year was unreasonable and non-compliant, the court should approach the question on the basis that where there was an interval of more than a year it was generally for the decision maker to show, by reference to the facts, that it was reasonable and thus compliant); *R (on the application of Ashford) v Secretary of State for Justice* [2008] EWHC 2734 (Admin), [2008] All ER (D) 203 (Oct) (in the circumstances of the case, the Secretary of State's decision not to bring forward the claimant's Parole Board hearing had been reasonable and pragmatic); *R (on the application of Johnson) v Secretary of State for Justice* [2009] EWHC 3336 (Admin), [2009] All ER (D) 195 (Dec) (reasonableness of the interval between reviews necessarily had to be related to the assessment of risk and due weight and regard had to be had to the decision maker; but any decision had to be made in the context of preventing unjustified detention and, the greater the period between reviews, the more cogent the reasons would have to be if the court was not to be persuaded that it was unreasonably long in that context); *R (on the application of Gray) v Secretary of State for Justice* [2010] EWHC 2 (Admin), [2010] 04 LS Gaz R 14, [2010] All ER (D) 53 (Jan) (claim for judicial review allowed to the extent that Parole Board had violated the claimant's right to a speedy hearing, to consider whether it was safe to release him); *R (on the application of NW and YW) v Secretary of State for Justice* [2010] EWHC 2485 (Admin), [2010] All ER (D) 75 (Aug) (in assessing the Parole Board's decision that had set the period between parole review meetings, the court had to determine whether: (1) a need for monitoring and progress had been identified; (2) a sensible timetable had been proposed; (3) the Secretary of state had approached the task with flexibility; and (4) whether the 'public protection' test was irrelevant); *R (on the application of Harrison) v Secretary of State for Justice* [2009] EWHC 1769 (Admin), [2009] All ER (D) 236 (Jul) (European Convention on Human Rights art 5.4 not infringed; decision to delay review was open to criticism because it was not specific as to the reasons for setting a date beyond a 12-month bench mark but there were clear reasons within the material which had been before the Secretary of State to justify it; and the Secretary of State had expressed an intention to review the claimant's case, and, if appropriate, to have the claimant's next hearing brought forward); *R (on the application of Parratt) v Secretary of State for Justice* [2013] EWHC 17 (Admin), [2013] All ER (D) 142 (Jan) (European Convention on Human Rights art 5.4 not infringed where the review period set at 15 months had been calculated having regard to what the claimant would need to do in order to persuade the Parole Board that it was safe to order his release, it having been by no means clear that the claimant would have been ready for release had the review period been fixed at 12 months).

15 See the Criminal Justice Act 2003 s 239(7), Sch 19 para 1(2); and PARA 699 note 2. See also *R (on the application of Roberts) v Parole Board* [2005] UKHL 45, [2005] 2 AC 738, sub nom *Roberts v Parole Board* [2006] 1 All ER 39 (although the appointment of special advocates should remain wholly exceptional, the Board was permitted to direct their use if the need to have regard to all the evidence in assessing risk relevant to a prisoner's parole review required the protection of a source from the prisoner and his legal representatives) (considering predecessor legislation to the Criminal Justice Act 2003 Sch 19 para 1(2)); *R (on the application of Brooks) v Parole Board* [2004] EWCA Civ 80, 148 Sol Jo LB 233, [2004] All ER (D) 142

(Feb) (Parole Board able to rely on hearsay evidence, following *R (on the application of Sim) v Parole Board* [2003] EWCA Civ 1845, [2004] QB 1288, [2004] 2 WLR 1170); and *R (on the application of Gardner) v Parole Board* [2006] EWCA Civ 1222, (2006) Times, 29 September, [2006] All ER (D) 12 (Sep) (Board had power to exclude prisoner from part of a hearing). In a different context the suggestion, raised in judicial review proceedings, that a special advocate should have been appointed during the substantive proceedings where no such suggestion had been previously raised by the claimant's representatives attracted criticism in *R (on the application of Sher) v Chief Constable of Greater Manchester Police* [2010] EWHC 1859 (Admin), [2011] 2 All ER 364, [2010] All ER (D) 212 (Jul). As to the general procedural rules applicable to the Parole Board see PARA 701 et seq.

701.   General procedural rules applicable to Parole Board proceedings. Where the Secretary of State[1] refers to the Parole Board[2] a case relating to the release or recall of a prisoner[3], the chairman[4] must appoint:

(1)   a single member of the Board to constitute a panel[5] to deal with a case where the Board is to consider the initial release of a prisoner serving an indeterminate sentence[6]; and

(2)   one or more members of the Board to constitute a panel[7], in any other case[8].

A person appointed under head (1) above may not in the same case sit on a panel appointed under head (2) above[9].

The Chairman must appoint one member of each panel to act as chair of that panel[10].

Directions may be given, varied or revoked (before the appointment of a panel) by a member of the Parole Board or (after the appointment of a panel) by the chair[11].

A party may be represented by any person appointed by the party[12]; but the following may not act as a representative[13]: (a) any person who is detained or is liable to be detained under the Mental Health Act 1983[14]; (b) any person serving a sentence of imprisonment[15]; (c) any person who is on licence having been released from a sentence of imprisonment[16]; or (d) any person with a conviction for an offence which remains unspent under the Rehabilitation of Offenders Act 1974[17]. Within five weeks of a case being referred to the Parole Board[18], a party must notify the Board and the other party of the name, address and occupation of any person appointed to act as their representative[19]. Where a prisoner does not appoint a person to act as their representative, the Board may, with the prisoner's agreement, appoint a person to do so[20].

The Secretary of State must serve on the Parole Board[21] and, subject to the rules that provide for the Secretary of State to withhold information and reports[22], the prisoner or their representative[23]:

(i)   where a case relates to the initial release of a prisoner, the information[24] and the reports[25] that are specified for this purpose[26];

(ii)   where a case relates to the recall following release of a prisoner, the information[27] and the reports[28] that are specified for that purpose[29]; and

(iii)   in either case, any other information which the Secretary of State considers relevant to the case[30].

Where the Board has a duty to advise the Secretary of State, the Secretary of State must serve on the Board and, subject again to the rules that provide for the Secretary of State to withhold information and reports[31], the prisoner or their representative, any information or reports which the Secretary of State considers relevant to the case[32].

Information about the proceedings and the names of persons concerned in the proceedings must not be made public[33].

A prisoner who wishes to make representations to the Parole Board must serve them on the Board and the Secretary of State within 12 weeks of the case being referred to the Board[34]; and any documentary evidence that a prisoner wishes to present at their hearing must be served on the Board and the Secretary of State at least 14 days before the date of the hearing[35].

A chair may adjourn proceedings to obtain further information or for such other purpose as the chair considers appropriate[36]. Where the chair adjourns a hearing without a further hearing date being fixed, the chair must give the parties at least three weeks' notice of the date, time and place of the resumed hearing[37] (or such shorter notice period as the parties agree)[38].

Where a panel has been appointed under head (2) above, a decision of the majority of the members of the panel is to be the decision of the panel[39]. Where the Secretary of State refers a case to the Parole Board relating to a prisoner serving a determinate sentence, the Board may make a decision without a hearing[40]. Similarly, where the Board has a duty to advise the Secretary of State with respect to any matter referred to it by the Secretary of State which is to do with the early release or recall of a prisoner, the Board may advise the Secretary of State without a hearing[41].

Where there has been an error of procedure, such as a failure to comply with a rule[42], the error does not invalidate any steps taken in the proceedings unless the panel so directs[43], and the panel may remedy the error[44].

1 As to the Secretary of State for these purposes see PRISONS AND PRISONERS vol 85 (2012) PARA 408.
2 For these purposes, 'Board' means the Parole Board, continued by the Criminal Justice Act 2003 s 239(1) (see PARA 699): Parole Board Rules 2011, SI 2011/2947, r 2.
3 Ie where the Parole Board Rules 2011, SI 2011/2947, apply: see r 3; and PARA 700.
4 For these purposes, 'chairman' means the chairman of the Board appointed under the Criminal Justice Act 2003 s 239(7), Sch 19 para 2 (see PARA 699 note 2): Parole Board Rules 2011, SI 2011/2947, r 2.
5 For these purposes, 'single member' means a member of the Parole Board who has been appointed to constitute a panel in accordance with Parole Board Rules 2011, SI 2011/2947, r 5(1) (see head (1) in the text); and 'panel' means a panel appointed in accordance with r 5(1) or r 5(2) (see head (2) in the text): r 2.
6 Parole Board Rules 2011, SI 2011/2947, r 5(1). For these purposes, 'indeterminate sentence' means a sentence of imprisonment listed under the Crime (Sentences) Act 1997 s 34(2) (see PARA 706): Parole Board Rules 2011, SI 2011/2947, r 2. See further Pt 3 (rr 16–18) (which sets out the timetable and rules for proceedings without a hearing where the Parole Board determines the initial release of a prisoner serving an indeterminate sentence); and PARA 702.
7 See note 5.
8 Parole Board Rules 2011, SI 2011/2947, r 5(2) (substituted by SI 2014/240).
9 Parole Board Rules 2011, SI 2011/2947, r 5(4) (renumbered and amended by SI 2014/240)
10 Parole Board Rules 2011, SI 2011/2947, r 5(3). Accordingly, for these purposes, 'chair' means a chairman of a panel appointed under r 5(3): r 2.
11 Parole Board Rules 2011, SI 2011/2947, r 10(1). Such directions may relate to:
   (1)   the timetable for the proceedings (r 10(2)(a));
   (2)   the service of information or a report (r 10(2)(b));
   (3)   whether any information or report should be withheld (r 10(2)(c));
   (4)   the submission of evidence (r 10(2)(d));
   (5)   the attendance of a witness or observer (r 10(2)(e)).
   Within seven days of being notified of a direction under r 10(2)(c) (see head (3) above), either party may appeal against that direction to the chairman, who must notify the other party of the appeal (r 10(3)); and within seven days of being notified that a party has appealed under r 10(3), the other party may make representations on the appeal to the chairman (r 10(4)). For these purposes, 'party' means either a prisoner or the Secretary of State: r 2.

A party may apply in writing for a direction to be given, varied or revoked (r 10(5)); and such an application must specify any direction sought (r 10(6)(a)), and must be served on the other party (r 10(6)(b)). Where a party has applied in writing for a direction to be given, varied or revoked, either party may make written representations about the application (r 10(7)(a)); and, where the chair thinks it necessary, and subject to r 11(4)(b), either party may make oral submissions at a directions hearing (r 10(7)(b)). The power to give directions may be exercised in the absence of the parties (r 10(8)); but the Board must serve notice on the parties of any directions given, varied or revoked as soon as practicable (r 10(9)).

A chair may hold a directions hearing: r 11(1). He must give the parties at least 14 days' notice of the date, time and place fixed for any such hearing (r 11(2)), which must be held in private (r 11(3)). At such a hearing, unless the chair directs otherwise, the chair is to sit alone (r 11(4)(a)); and a prisoner who is represented may not attend (r 11(4)(b)).

In the Parole Board Rules 2011, SI 2011/2947, except where the initial release of a prisoner serving an indeterminate sentence is being considered (see PARA 702), a reference to a period of time applies as if it was a reference to such period of time as the chair may in each case determine: see r 3(4); and PARA 700 note 5. Where the time prescribed by or under the Parole Board Rules 2011, SI 2011/2947, for doing any act expires on a Saturday, Sunday or public holiday, the act will be in time if it is done on the next working day: r 27. Any document required or authorised by the Parole Board Rules 2011, SI 2011/2947, to be served or otherwise transmitted to any person may be transmitted by electronic means, sent by pre-paid post or delivered (in the case of a document directed to the Board or the chair) to the office of the Board, or (in any other case) to the last known address of the person to whom the document is directed: r 28.

12 Parole Board Rules 2011, SI 2011/2947, r 6(1).
13 Parole Board Rules 2011, SI 2011/2947, r 6(2).
14 Parole Board Rules 2011, SI 2011/2947, r 6(2)(a). As to persons liable to be detained under the Mental Health Act 1983 see MENTAL HEALTH AND CAPACITY vol 75 (2013) PARA 766 et seq.
15 Parole Board Rules 2011, SI 2011/2947, r 6(2)(b). As to prisoners and their sentences see PARAS 706, 709 et seq.
16 Parole Board Rules 2011, SI 2011/2947, r 6(2)(c). As to release on licence see PARA 707 et seq.
17 Parole Board Rules 2011, SI 2011/2947, r 6(2)(d). As to the effect of the Rehabilitation of Offenders Act 1974 see PARA 591 et seq.
18 Where the Board is to consider the release of a prisoner serving a determinate sentence, the release following a recall of a prisoner serving an indeterminate sentence or is to advise the Secretary of State, the case is deemed to be referred to the Board on the date it receives the information and reports specified in the Parole Board Rules 2011, SI 2011/2947, r 7 (see the text and notes 21–32): r 4.
19 Parole Board Rules 2011, SI 2011/2947, r 6(3).
20 Parole Board Rules 2011, SI 2011/2947, r 6(4).
21 Where the Secretary of State refers a case to the Board relating to the initial release of a prisoner serving an indeterminate sentence, he must serve the information and reports mentioned in the Parole Board Rules 2011, SI 2011/2947, r 7(1) within eight weeks of the case being referred to the Board: rr 3(2), 7(3).
22 Ie subject to the Parole Board Rules 2011, SI 2011/2947, r 8: r 7(1). The Secretary of State may withhold any information or report from the prisoner and their representative where the Secretary of State considers (r 8(1)):
    (1)   that its disclosure would adversely affect: (a) national security (r 8(1)(a)(i)); (b) the prevention of disorder or crime (r 8(1)(a)(ii)); or (c) the health or welfare of the prisoner or any other person (r 8(1)(a)(iii)); and
    (2)   that withholding the information or report is a necessary and proportionate measure in the circumstances of the case (r 8(1)(b)).
Where any information or report is withheld, the Secretary of State must record it in a separate document (r 8(2)(a)), must serve it only on the Board (r 8(2)(b)), and must explain to the Board in writing why it has been withheld (r 8(2)(c)). Where any information or report is withheld from the prisoner, the Secretary of State must, unless the chair directs otherwise, serve it as soon as practicable on:
    (a)   the prisoner's representative, if the representative is a barrister or solicitor (r 8(3)(a)(i)), a registered medical practitioner (r 8(3)(a)(ii)), or a person whom the chair directs is suitable by virtue of their experience or professional qualification (r 8(3)(a)(iii)); or
    (b)   a special advocate who has been appointed by the Attorney General to represent the prisoner's interests (r 8(3)(b)).
A prisoner's representative or a special advocate may not disclose any information or report disclosed in accordance with r 8(3) without the consent of the chair (r 8(4)); and, where the

chair decides that any information or report withheld by the Secretary of State under r 8(1) should be disclosed to the prisoner or their representative, the Secretary of State may withdraw the information or report (r 8(5)). If the Secretary of State withdraws any information or report in accordance with r 8(5), nobody who has seen that information or report may sit on a panel which determines the case: r 8(6). As to the provision of medical attention see PRISONS AND PRISONERS vol 85 (2012) PARA 547. As to registered medical practitioners generally see MEDICAL PROFESSIONS vol 74 (2011) PARA 210 et seq. See also *R (on the application of Roberts) v Parole Board* [2005] UKHL 45, [2005] 2 AC 738, sub nom *Roberts v Parole Board* [2006] 1 All ER 39 (although the appointment of special advocates should remain wholly exceptional, the Board was permitted to direct their use if the need to have regard to all the evidence in assessing risk relevant to a prisoner's parole review required the protection of a source from the prisoner and his legal representatives); and *R (on the application of Gardner) v Parole Board* [2006] EWCA Civ 1222, (2006) Times, 29 September, [2006] All ER (D) 12 (Sep) (Board had power to exclude prisoner from part of a hearing) (both cases decided before the Parole Board Rules were issued as a statutory instrument).

23 Parole Board Rules 2011, SI 2011/2947, r 7(1).

24 Ie the information specified in the Parole Board Rules 2011, SI 2011/2947, r 7, Sch 1 Pt A: r 7(1)(a). Accordingly, the following information related to the prisoner is required for submission to the Board by the Secretary of State on a reference to the Board to determine the initial release of a prisoner:

    (1)   the full name of the prisoner (Sch 1 Pt A para 1);

    (2)   the date of birth of the prisoner (Sch 1 Pt A para 2);

    (3)   the prison in which the prisoner is detained, details of any other prisons in which the prisoner has been detained and the date and the reason for any transfer (Sch 1 Pt A para 3);

    (4)   the date on which the prisoner was given the current sentence, details of the offence and any previous convictions (Sch 1 Pt A para 4);

    (5)   the comments, if available, of the trial judge when passing sentence (Sch 1 Pt A para 5);

    (6)   if available, the conclusions of the Court of Appeal in respect of any appeal by the prisoner against conviction or sentence (Sch 1 Pt A para 6); and

    (7)   the parole history, if any, of the prisoner, including details of any periods spent on licence during the current sentence (Sch 1 Pt A para 7).

For these purposes, 'prison' includes a young offender institution or any other institution where a prisoner is or has been detained: r 2. As to the establishment of young offender institutions see PRISONS AND PRISONERS vol 85 (2012) PARA 487 et seq. Although the Parole Board exercises a quasi-judicial function, it is engaged in a different legal exercise to the sentencing judge: see further PARA 699 note 14.

25 Ie the reports specified in the Parole Board Rules 2011, SI 2011/2947, r 7, Sch 1 Pt B: see r 7(1)(a). Accordingly, the following reports related to the prisoner are required for submission to the Board by the Secretary of State on a reference to the Board to determine the initial release of a prisoner:

    (1)   if available, the pre-trial and pre-sentence reports examined by the sentencing court on the circumstances of the offence (Sch 1 Pt B para 1);

    (2)   any reports on a prisoner who was subject to a transfer direction under the Mental Health Act 1983 s 47 (see MENTAL HEALTH AND CAPACITY vol 75 (2013) PARA 892 et seq) (Parole Board Rules 2011, SI 2011/2947, Sch 1 Pt B para 2);

    (3)   any current reports on the prisoner's risk factors, reduction in risk and performance and behaviour in prison, including views on suitability for release on licence as well as compliance with any sentence plan (Sch 1 Pt B para 3);

    (4)   an up-to-date risk management report prepared for the Board by an officer of the supervising local probation trust, including information on the following where relevant (see Sch 1 Pt B para 4):

        (a)   details of the home address, family circumstances and family attitudes towards the prisoner (Sch 1 Pt B para 4(a));

        (b)   alternative options if the offender cannot return home (Sch 1 Pt B para 4(b));

        (c)   the opportunity for employment on release (Sch 1 Pt B para 4(c));

        (d)   the local community's attitude towards the prisoner, if known (Sch 1 Pt B para 4(d));

        (e)   the prisoner's attitude to the index offence (Sch 1 Pt B para 4(e));

        (f)   the prisoner's response to previous periods of supervision (Sch 1 Pt B para 4(f));

        (g)   the prisoner's behaviour during any temporary leave during the current sentence (Sch 1 Pt B para 4(g));

    (h)   the prisoner's attitude to the prospect of release and the requirements and objectives of supervision (Sch 1 Pt B para 4(h));

    (i)   an assessment of the risk of reoffending (Sch 1 Pt B para 4(i));

    (j)   a programme of supervision (Sch 1 Pt B para 4(j));

    (k)   if available, an up-to-date victim personal statement setting out the impact the index offence has had on the victim and the victim's immediate family (Sch 1 Pt B para 4(k));

    (l)   a view on suitability for release (Sch 1 Pt B para 4(l)); and

    (m)   recommendations regarding any non-standard licence conditions (Sch 1 Pt B para 4(m)).

The word 'current' in the context of the Parole Board Rules should not be given an inflexible meaning, eg it did not mean that there had to be a very close connection in time between the compilation of the reports required and the date of the oral hearing, and a report could be a current report within the Parole Board Rules even if made some time before the hearing, provided that it still provided a proper and reasonable appraisal of the prisoner as at the time of the hearing (although some reports should be updated annually): *R (on the application of Flinders) v Director of High Security* [2011] EWHC 1630 (Admin), [2011] All ER (D) 02 (Jul) (considering the Parole Board Rules 2004, specifically 'current material' pursuant to r 6 and Schedule Pt B para 3: see now the Parole Board Rules 2011, SI 2011/2947, r 7, Sch 1 Pt B para 3 (see head (3) above) which is set out in very similar but not identical terms). See also *R (on the application of Brooks) v Parole Board* [2004] EWCA Civ 80, 148 Sol Jo LB 233, [2004] All ER (D) 142 (Feb) (Parole Board able to rely on hearsay evidence) (case decided before the Parole Board Rules were issued as a statutory instrument); and *R (on the application of Broadbent) v Parole Board for England and Wales* [2005] EWHC 1207 (Admin), (2005) Times, 22 June, [2005] All ER (D) 437 (May) (where a prisoner has been charged with a criminal offence whilst on licence, the possible injustice of hearing evidence before the trial of that charge had to be weighed against the need for the Parole Board to preserve its jurisdiction to determine whether the claimant should be returned to prison until the determination of the criminal matter; it was for the Parole Board to make its own assessment of the claimant's risk of re-offending on the basis of all the information before it, and not every allegation of the commission of a further offence whilst subject to licence would automatically justify a breach of licence and recall to custody).

    Further to head (4)(e) above, prisoners who deny their offences should not automatically be refused release by the Parole Board, because denial might be ascribed to a variety of reasons and any admission of guilt was unlikely to be more than one of many factors to which undue weight should not be given; however, denial of guilt may make the task of risk assessment particularly difficult, especially if that denial is coupled with a refusal to address offending behaviour: see *R v Secretary of State for the Home Department, ex p Zulfikar* (1995) Times, 26 July, DC; *R v Secretary of State for the Home Department, ex p Zulfikar (No 2)* (1 May 1996, unreported), DC; *R v Secretary of State for the Home Department, ex p Hepworth, Fenton-Palmer and Baldonzy* [1997] EWHC Admin 324; and see *R v Parole Board and Home Secretary, ex p Oyston* [2000] EWCA Crim 3552, [2000] All ER (D) 274, CA (Parole Board is free to consider the risk that a prisoner may pose when he denies guilt of his index offence but a decision that is solely based on denial of the index offending is unlawful).

    Further to head (4)(k) above, see PARA 704 note 10.

26   Parole Board Rules 2011, SI 2011/2947, r 7(1)(a).

27   Ie the information specified in the Parole Board Rules 2011, SI 2011/2947, Sch 2 Pt A: r 7(1)(b). Accordingly, the following information related to the prisoner is required for submission to the Board by the Secretary of State on a reference to the Board to determine the release of a recalled prisoner:

    (1)   the full name of the prisoner (Sch 2 Pt A para 1);

    (2)   the date of birth of the prisoner (Sch 2 Pt A para 2);

    (3)   the prison in which the prisoner is detained, details of other prisons in which the prisoner has been detained and the date and reason for any transfer (Sch 2 Pt A para 3);

    (4)   the date on which the prisoner was given the current sentence, details of the offence and any previous convictions (Sch 2 Pt A para 4);

    (5)   the parole history, if any, of the prisoner, including details of any periods spent on licence during the current sentence (Sch 2 Pt A para 5);

    (6)   if available, the details of any sentence plan prepared for the prisoner which has previously been disclosed to the prisoner (Sch 2 Pt A para 6);

    (7)   the details of any previous recalls of the prisoner including the reasons for such recalls and subsequent re-release on licence (Sch 2 Pt A para 7);

    (8)   the statement of reasons for the most recent recall which was given to the prisoner,

including the outcome of any criminal charges laid against the prisoner prior to or subsequent to the point at which they were recalled (Sch 2 Pt A para 8).
As to recall and re-release see PARA 717 et seq.

28 Ie the reports specified in the Parole Board Rules 2011, SI 2011/2947, Sch 2 Pt B: r 7(1)(b). Accordingly, the following reports related to the prisoner are required for submission to the Board by the Secretary of State on a reference to the Board to determine the release of a recalled prisoner:

    (1)   any reports considered by the Secretary of State in deciding to recall the prisoner (Sch 2 Pt B para 1);

    (2)   if available, any pre-sentence report examined by the sentencing court on the circumstances of the offence (Sch 2 Pt B para 2);

    (3)   any details of convictions prior to the index offence (Sch 2 Pt B para 3);

    (4)   a copy of the prisoner's licence at the point at which the Secretary of State decided to recall the prisoner (see Sch 2 Pt B para 4).

29 Parole Board Rules 2011, SI 2011/2947, r 7(1)(b).

30 Parole Board Rules 2011, SI 2011/2947, r 7(1)(c).

31 Ie subject to the Parole Board Rules 2011, SI 2011/2947, r 8 (see note 22): r 7(2).

32 Parole Board Rules 2011, SI 2011/2947, r 7(2).

33 Parole Board Rules 2011, SI 2011/2947, r 14. The characterisation of Parole Board proceedings as being administrative rather than judicial in respect of recommendations for early release in the case of determinate sentence prisoners (see PARA 700 note 12) indicates that the protection of judicial privilege may not be available in such cases; but quaere whether a Parole Board hearing is a 'court' for the purposes of the law of contempt of court (ie by analogy with mental health review tribunals: see CONTEMPT OF COURT vol 22 (2012) PARA 39). See also *R (on the application of Brooke) v Parole Board, R (on the application of Murphy) v Parole Board* [2008] EWCA Civ 29 at [47], [2008] 3 All ER 289 at [47], [2008] 1 WLR 1950 at [47] per Lord Phillips of Worth Matravers CJ (cited in PARA 699 note 8).

34 Parole Board Rules 2011, SI 2011/2947, r 9(1).

35 Parole Board Rules 2011, SI 2011/2947, r 9(2).

36 Parole Board Rules 2011, SI 2011/2947, r 12(1). The Parole Board has power to gather its own evidence, and procedural fairness may require the Board to consider whether further evidence should be obtained: see the Criminal Justice Act 2003 s 239(3); and PARA 699.

37 Parole Board Rules 2011, SI 2011/2947, r 12(2)(a).

38 Parole Board Rules 2011, SI 2011/2947, r 12(2)(b).

39 Parole Board Rules 2011, SI 2011/2947, r 13(1). A panel that is unable to reach a decision in accordance with r 13(1) must be dissolved by the chairman, who must then appoint a new panel: r 13(2). The Crime (Sentences) Act 1997 places the power to take the decision on the Parole Board: see PARA 707 et seq. Though it is presented with reports from, inter alios, prison staff, it is not obliged to accept those views even if they are unanimous, unless in taking a different course it is acting irrationally in that its decision is unsupported by any of the other material presented to it: *R v Parole Board, ex p Telling* (1993) Times, 10 May, DC; *R v Secretary of State for the Home Department and the Parole Board, ex p Evans* (2 November 1994, unreported), DC (Board rejected the clear, emphatic and unanimous views of report writers; the Divisional Court held that in such a case the reasons should have included an explanation in sufficiently clear terms and sufficiently full to ensure that the basis for the difference between them could be understood). See also *R (on the application of D'Cunha) v Parole Board* [2011] EWHC 128 (Admin), 175 CL & J 111, [2011] All ER (D) 105 (Feb); and PARA 704 note 29.

40 Parole Board Rules 2011, SI 2011/2947, r 15(1). As to whether procedural fairness requires the Board to consider whether to hold an oral hearing see PARA 700.

41 Parole Board Rules 2011, SI 2011/2947, r 15(2).

42 Parole Board Rules 2011, SI 2011/2947, r 29.

43 Parole Board Rules 2011, SI 2011/2947, r 29(a).

44 Parole Board Rules 2011, SI 2011/2947, r 29(b).

702. Parole Board proceedings without a hearing to consider initial release of indeterminate sentence prisoners. Within 14 weeks of a case relating to the initial release of an indeterminate sentence prisoner[1] being referred to the Parole Board[2] by the Secretary of State[3], a single member[4] must consider the case without a hearing[5]; and he must either[6]:

    (1)   decide that the case should be referred to an oral panel[7]; or

(2)   make a provisional decision that the prisoner is unsuitable for release[8].

The decision of the single member must be recorded in writing with reasons for the decision[9], and provided to the parties within a week of the date of the decision[10].

Where a single member has made a provisional decision under head (2) above that a prisoner is unsuitable for release, the prisoner may request that an oral panel hear the case[11]. A prisoner who requests such a hearing must, within 19 weeks of the case being referred to the Parole Board, serve notice giving full reasons for their request on the Board and the Secretary of State[12]. If no notice has been served in this way[13] after the expiry of the period so permitted[14], the provisional decision becomes final[15]; and that decision must be provided to the parties within 20 weeks of the case being referred to the Board[16]. If notice is duly served[17], however, a single member decides whether or not to hold a hearing[18]. The single member who made the provisional decision under head (2) above that a prisoner is unsuitable for release may not in the same case decide whether to grant such a hearing, however[19].

Where a single member has referred a case to an oral panel for consideration under head (1) above, or where a hearing has been ordered pursuant to a request by the prisoner[20], the case must be considered by an oral panel within 26 weeks of the case being referred to the Board[21].

1   The Parole Board Rules 2011, SI 2011/2947, Pt 3 (rr 16–18) applies only where the Secretary of State refers a case to the Board relating to the release of a prisoner serving an indeterminate sentence: see r 3(3); and PARA 700 note 5. As to the meaning of 'Board' for these purposes see PARA 701 note 2; and as to the meaning of 'indeterminate sentence' see PARA 701 note 6.
      In the Parole Board Rules 2011, SI 2011/2947, where the initial release of a prisoner serving an indeterminate sentence is being considered, a reference to a period of time applies as set out in the Parole Board Rules 2011, SI 2011/2947: see r 3(4); and PARA 700 note 5. Where the time prescribed by or under the Parole Board Rules 2011, SI 2011/2947, for doing any act expires on a Saturday, Sunday or public holiday, the act will be in time if it is done on the next working day: see r 27; and PARA 701 note 11.
2   Ie the Parole Board, continued by the Criminal Justice Act 2003 s 239(1): see the Parole Board Rules 2011, SI 2011/2947, r 2; and PARA 701 note 2. As to the date when a case is deemed to be referred to the Parole Board see PARA 701 note 18.
3   As to the Secretary of State for these purposes see PRISONS AND PRISONERS vol 85 (2012) PARA 408.
4   As to the meaning of 'single member' for these purposes see PARA 701 note 5.
5   Parole Board Rules 2011, SI 2011/2947, r 16(1).
6   Parole Board Rules 2011, SI 2011/2947, r 16(2).
7   Parole Board Rules 2011, SI 2011/2947, r 16(2)(a). For these purposes, 'oral panel' means a panel which determines a case or matter at a hearing: r 2.
8   Parole Board Rules 2011, SI 2011/2947, r 16(2)(b).
9   Parole Board Rules 2011, SI 2011/2947, r 16(3)(a). As to reasons see PARA 704 note 29.
10 Parole Board Rules 2011, SI 2011/2947, r 16(3)(b).
      Any document required or authorised by the Parole Board Rules 2011, SI 2011/2947, to be served or otherwise transmitted to any person may be transmitted by electronic means, sent by pre-paid post or delivered (in the case of a document directed to the Board or the chair) to the office of the Board, or (in any other case) to the last known address of the person to whom the document is directed: see r 28; and PARA 701 note 11.
11 Parole Board Rules 2011, SI 2011/2947, r 17(1).
12 Parole Board Rules 2011, SI 2011/2947, r 17(2).
13 Ie in accordance with the Parole Board Rules 2011, SI 2011/2947, r 17(2) (see the text and note 12): r 17(3).
14 Parole Board Rules 2011, SI 2011/2947, r 17(3). The text refers to expiry of the period permitted by r 17(2) (see the text and note 12): r 17(3).
15 Parole Board Rules 2011, SI 2011/2947, r 17(3)(a).
16 Parole Board Rules 2011, SI 2011/2947, r 17(3)(b).
17 Ie served in accordance with the Parole Board Rules 2011, SI 2011/2947, r 17(2) (see the text and note 12): r 17(4).

18   Parole Board Rules 2011, SI 2011/2947, r 17(4). As to when an oral hearing must be held in order to meet the demands of the Convention for the Protection of Human Rights and Fundamental Freedoms (Rome, 4 November 1950; TS 71 (1953); Cmd 8969) (the European Convention on Human Rights) art 5.4 (see RIGHTS AND FREEDOMS vol 88A (2013) PARA 210 et seq) or the requirements of procedural fairness under common law see PARA 700 note 12.

19   Parole Board Rules 2011, SI 2011/2947, r 17(5). The text refers to a hearing requested by the prisoner under r 17(1) (see the text and note 11): r 17(5).

20   Ie a request by the prisoner under the Parole Board Rules 2011, SI 2011/2947, r 17(1) (see the text and note 11): r 18.

21   Parole Board Rules 2011, SI 2011/2947, r 18.

703.   Parole Board proceedings with a hearing: rules as to timings, attendance etc.

Where the Secretary of State[1] refers a case to the Parole Board[2] relating to the release or recall of a prisoner[3], provision is made for the hearing (where a hearing is directed)[4].

Accordingly, the hearing must be held within 26 weeks of a case being referred to the Parole Board[5]. The panel[6] must consult the parties when fixing the date of the hearing[7]. The Board must notify the parties of the date on which the case is due to be heard within five working days of a case being listed[8]; and the panel must give the parties[9] at least three weeks' notice of the date, time and place scheduled for the hearing[10] (or such shorter notice as the parties agree)[11]. If applicable, the panel also must give the parties notice that the hearing is to be held via video link, telephone conference or other electronic means[12].

A prisoner who wishes to attend his hearing must notify the Parole Board and the Secretary of State within 23 weeks of the case being referred to the Board[13].

A party who wishes to call a witness at a hearing must make a written application to the Parole Board (a copy of which must be served on the other party) within 20 weeks of the case being referred to the Board[14]. A chair[15] may grant or refuse an application to call a witness[16] but he must communicate this decision to the parties[17] and he must give reasons in writing for any such refusal[18]. Where the panel intends to call a witness, the chair must notify the parties in writing within 21 weeks of the case being referred to the Board[19]. Where a witness is called, whether by a party[20] or by the panel[21], it is the duty of the person calling the witness to notify the witness at least two weeks before the hearing of the date of the hearing and the need to attend[22].

A party who wishes to be accompanied by an observer must make a written application to the panel (a copy of which must be served on the other party) within 20 weeks of the case being referred to the Parole Board[23]. A chair may grant or refuse such an application and must communicate this decision to the parties[24]. However, before granting such an application, the Board must obtain the agreement (where the hearing is being held in a prison[25]) of the prison governor or prison director[26] or the agreement (in any other case) of the person who has the authority to agree[27].

1   As to the Secretary of State for these purposes see PRISONS AND PRISONERS vol 85 (2012) PARA 408.

2   Ie the Parole Board, continued by the Criminal Justice Act 2003 s 239(1): see the Parole Board Rules 2011, SI 2011/2947, r 2; and PARA 701 note 2. As to the date when a case is deemed to be referred to the Parole Board see PARA 701 note 18.

3   Ie where the Parole Board Rules 2011, SI 2011/2947, generally apply: see r 3; and PARA 700.

4   Parole Board Rules 2011, SI 2011/2947, r 19(1). Specifically, the provision made by Pt 4 (rr 19–26) (proceedings with a hearing) applies to hearings: r 19(1).

5   Parole Board Rules 2011, SI 2011/2947, r 20(1). In the Parole Board Rules 2011, SI 2011/2947, except where the initial release of a prisoner serving an indeterminate sentence is being considered (see PARA 702), a reference to a period of time applies as if it was a reference to such period of time as the chair may in each case determine: see r 3(4); and PARA 700 note 5. Where

the time prescribed by or under the Parole Board Rules 2011, SI 2011/2947, for doing any act expires on a Saturday, Sunday or public holiday, the act will be in time if it is done on the next working day: see r 27; and PARA 701 note 11.

6 Any reference in the Parole Board Rules 2011, SI 2011/2947, Pt 4 to a 'panel' is to an oral panel: r 19(2). As to the meaning of 'oral panel' see PARA 702 note 7.

7 Parole Board Rules 2011, SI 2011/2947, r 20(2). As to the meaning of 'party' for these purposes see PARA 701 note 11.

8 Parole Board Rules 2011, SI 2011/2947, r 20(3). Any document required or authorised by the Parole Board Rules 2011, SI 2011/2947, to be served or otherwise transmitted to any person may be transmitted by electronic means, sent by pre-paid post or delivered (in the case of a document directed to the Board or the chair) to the office of the Board, or (in any other case) to the last known address of the person to whom the document is directed: see r 28; and PARA 701 note 11.

9 Parole Board Rules 2011, SI 2011/2947, r 20(4).

10 Parole Board Rules 2011, SI 2011/2947, r 20(4)(a).

11 Parole Board Rules 2011, SI 2011/2947, r 20(4)(b).

12 Parole Board Rules 2011, SI 2011/2947, r 20(5).

13 Parole Board Rules 2011, SI 2011/2947, r 21.

14 Parole Board Rules 2011, SI 2011/2947, r 22(1). A written application to call a witness must include the witness's name, address and occupation (r 22(2)(a)) and must explain why the witness is being called (r 22(2)(b)). In addition to the prisoner and the panel, other people who may be present at the hearing might include witnesses such as the prisoner's offender manager or a prison psychologist.

Parties may apply to the county court or High Court for a witness summons under CPR 34.4 (witness summons in aid of inferior court or tribunal: see CIVIL PROCEDURE vol 11 (2009) PARA 1006). For these purposes, 'inferior court or tribunal' means any court or tribunal that does not have power to issue a witness summons in relation to proceedings before it: see CPR 34.4(3); and CIVIL PROCEDURE vol 11 (2009) PARA 1006.

15 As to the meaning of 'chair' for these purposes see PARA 701 note 10.

16 Parole Board Rules 2011, SI 2011/2947, r 22(3).

17 Parole Board Rules 2011, SI 2011/2947, r 22(3).

18 Parole Board Rules 2011, SI 2011/2947, r 22(4).

19 Parole Board Rules 2011, SI 2011/2947, r 22(5). Written notification from the panel that it intends to call a witness must include the witness's name, address and occupation (r 22(6)(a)); and must explain why the witness is being called (r 22(6)(b)).

20 Ie under the Parole Board Rules 2011, SI 2011/2947, r 22(1) (see the text and note 14): r 22(7).

21 Ie under the Parole Board Rules 2011, SI 2011/2947, r 22(5) (see the text and note 19): r 22(7).

22 Parole Board Rules 2011, SI 2011/2947, r 22(7).

23 Parole Board Rules 2011, SI 2011/2947, r 23(1).

24 Parole Board Rules 2011, SI 2011/2947, r 23(2).

25 As to the meaning of 'prison' for these purposes see PARA 701 note 24.

26 Parole Board Rules 2011, SI 2011/2947, r 23(3)(a). As to governors see PRISONS AND PRISONERS vol 85 (2012) PARA 417; and as to directors of contracted-out prisons see PRISONS AND PRISONERS vol 85 (2012) PARA 522.

27 Parole Board Rules 2011, SI 2011/2947, r 23(3)(b).

704. Parole Board proceedings with a hearing: rules as to procedure. A Parole Board hearing[1] must be held at the prison[2] where the prisoner is detained or at such other place as the chair[3], with the agreement of the Secretary of State[4], directs[5], except where[6] a chair exercises his power to direct instead that a hearing is to be held via video link, telephone conference or other electronic means[7]. A hearing must be held in private[8] but, in addition to any witness and observer whose attendance has been duly approved[9], the chair may admit any other person to the hearing[10]. He may, however, impose conditions on that person's admittance[11].

At the beginning of the hearing, the chair must explain the order of proceeding which the panel[12] proposes to adopt[13], and he must invite each party present to state their view as to the suitability of the prisoner for release[14]. The panel:

(1)　　must avoid formality in the proceedings[15];

(2)　　may ask any question to satisfy itself of the level of risk of the prisoner[16]; and

(3)　　must conduct the hearing in a manner it considers most suitable to the clarification of the issues before it and to the just handling of the proceedings[17].

The parties are entitled to:

(a)　　take such part in the proceedings as the panel thinks fit[18];

(b)　　hear each other's evidence[19];

(c)　　put questions to each other[20];

(d)　　call a witness who has been granted permission to give evidence[21]; and

(e)　　question any witness or other person appearing before the panel[22].

If, in the chair's opinion, any person at the hearing is behaving in a disruptive manner, the chair may require that person to leave[23], but the chair may permit a person who was required to leave in this way to return on such conditions as may be specified by the chair[24].

A panel may produce or receive in evidence any document or information whether or not it would be admissible in a court of law[25]. However, no person is to be compelled to give any evidence or produce any document which they could not be compelled to give or produce on the trial of an action[26]. The chair may require any person present to leave the hearing where evidence which has been directed to be withheld from the prisoner or their representative is to be considered[27]. After all the evidence has been given, the prisoner must be given an opportunity to address the panel[28].

The panel's decision determining a case must be:

(i)　　recorded in writing with reasons[29];

(ii)　　signed by the chair[30]; and

(ii)　　provided to the parties not more than 14 days after the end of the hearing[31].

The recorded decision however, must refer only to the matter which the Secretary of State referred to the Board[32].

1　The provision made by the Parole Board Rules 2011, SI 2011/2947, Pt 4 (rr 19–26) (proceedings with a hearing) applies to hearings: see r 19(1); and PARA 703. References to the Parole Board are to the Board continued by the Criminal Justice Act 2003 s 239(1): see the Parole Board Rules 2011, SI 2011/2947, r 2; and PARA 701 note 2.

2　As to the meaning of 'prison' for these purposes see PARA 701 note 24.

3　As to the meaning of 'chair' for these purposes see PARA 701 note 10.

4　As to the Secretary of State for these purposes see PRISONS AND PRISONERS vol 85 (2012) PARA 408.

5　Parole Board Rules 2011, SI 2011/2947, r 24(1).

6　The Parole Board Rules 2011, SI 2011/2947, r 24(1) (see the text and notes 1–5) does not apply where a hearing is held in accordance with r 24(3) (see the text and note 7): r 24(2).

7　Parole Board Rules 2011, SI 2011/2947, r 24(3).

8　Parole Board Rules 2011, SI 2011/2947, r 24(4).

9　Ie approved in accordance with the Parole Board Rules 2011, SI 2011/2947, r 22 (witnesses: see PARA 703) or r 23 (observers: see PARA 703): r 24(5). At the hearing, the parties may not challenge the attendance of any witness or observer whose attendance has been approved pursuant to r 22 or r 23: r 24(6). As to the meaning of 'party' for these purposes see PARA 701 note 11.

10　Parole Board Rules 2011, SI 2011/2947, r 24(5)(a). In addition to the prisoner and the panel, and representatives of the parties (see PARA 701 note 11), the victim of the crime (or one of their relatives) might attend the start of the hearing to read a 'victim personal statement', explaining how the crime has affected them and their immediate family, and if they want conditions attached to the prisoner's release (see Sch 1 Pt B para 4(k); and PARA 701 note 25).

11　Parole Board Rules 2011, SI 2011/2947, r 24(5)(b).

12 Any reference in the Parole Board Rules 2011, SI 2011/2947, Pt 4 to a 'panel' is to an oral panel: see r 19(2); and PARA 703 note 6. As to the meaning of 'oral panel' see PARA 702 note 7.

13 Parole Board Rules 2011, SI 2011/2947, r 25(1)(a).

14 Parole Board Rules 2011, SI 2011/2947, r 25(1)(b).

15 Parole Board Rules 2011, SI 2011/2947, r 25(2)(a). The informality required by head (1) in the text is reflected in the nature of evidence that may be admitted: see further the text and note 25.

16 Parole Board Rules 2011, SI 2011/2947, r 25(2)(b). As to whether there is a burden on the prisoner to persuade the Parole Board that it is safe to recommend release see *R v Lichniak, R v Pyrah* [2002] UKHL 47, [2003] 1 AC 903, [2002] 4 All ER 1122 (process was administrative and defensible: Board would have before it any material going to show that a prisoner was not dangerous; if the Board was thought to show an exaggerated degree of caution, it could be challenged).

17 Parole Board Rules 2011, SI 2011/2947, r 25(2)(c).

18 Parole Board Rules 2011, SI 2011/2947, r 25(3)(a).

19 Parole Board Rules 2011, SI 2011/2947, r 25(3)(b).

20 Parole Board Rules 2011, SI 2011/2947, r 25(3)(c).

21 Parole Board Rules 2011, SI 2011/2947, r 25(3)(d).

22 Parole Board Rules 2011, SI 2011/2947, r 25(3)(e).

23 Parole Board Rules 2011, SI 2011/2947, r 25(4).

24 Parole Board Rules 2011, SI 2011/2947, r 25(5).

25 Parole Board Rules 2011, SI 2011/2947, r 25(6). As to evidence before the Parole Board see generally PARA 699 note 14. The Parole Board has power to gather its own evidence, and procedural fairness may require the Board to consider whether further evidence should be obtained: see the Criminal Justice Act 2003 s 239(3); and PARAS 699, 700.

26 Parole Board Rules 2011, SI 2011/2947, r 25(7).

27 Parole Board Rules 2011, SI 2011/2947, r 25(8). See *R (on the application of Gardner) v Parole Board* [2006] EWCA Civ 1222, (2006) Times, 29 September, [2006] All ER (D) 12 (Sep) (Board had power to exclude prisoner from part of a hearing) (case decided before the Parole Board Rules were issued as a statutory instrument).

28 Parole Board Rules 2011, SI 2011/2947, r 25(9).

29 Parole Board Rules 2011, SI 2011/2947, r 26(1)(a). See *R v Parole Board and Home Secretary, ex p Oyston* [2000] EWCA Crim 3552, [2000] All ER (D) 274, CA (whilst the Board had to focus in each case on the question of risk, it should, in its decision letter, identify in general terms the matters which it had considered on both sides in carrying out the balancing exercise, and its reasons for striking the balance, summarising the considerations which had led to its decision), applied in *R (on the application of Tinney) v Parole Board* [2005] EWHC 863 (Admin), [2005] All ER (D) 280 (Apr) (Board failed to identify in broad terms matters judged by it as pointing towards continuing risk of reoffending). See also *R v Secretary of State for the Home Department and the Parole Board, ex p Evans* (2 November 1994, unreported), DC (where the Board rejected clear, emphatic and unanimous views of report writers, the reasons should have included an explanation in sufficiently clear terms and sufficiently full to ensure that the basis for the difference between them could be understood). The duty to give reasons requires that they are intelligible and deal with the substantial points that have been raised: *R v Parole Board, ex p Gittens* (1994) Times, 3 February, DC; *R v Parole Board, ex p Lodomez* (1994) 26 BMLR 162, [1994] COD 525, DC. See also *R (on the application of D'Cunha) v Parole Board* [2011] EWHC 128 (Admin), 175 CL & J 111, [2011] All ER (D) 105 (Feb) (it was not necessary for the Board, in meeting the requirement to give reasons for its decisions, to include in its decision letter a specific section setting out in detail what the views of each expert were and its reasons for rejecting them, in particular in which respects the Board disagreed with each witness and upon what basis).

30 Parole Board Rules 2011, SI 2011/2947, r 26(1)(b).

31 Parole Board Rules 2011, SI 2011/2947, r 26(1)(c). In the Parole Board Rules 2011, SI 2011/2947, except where the initial release of a prisoner serving an indeterminate sentence is being considered (see PARA 702), a reference to a period of time applies as if it was a reference to such period of time as the chair may in each case determine: see r 3(4); and PARA 700 note 5. Where the time prescribed by or under the Parole Board Rules 2011, SI 2011/2947, for doing any act expires on a Saturday, Sunday or public holiday, the act will be in time if it is done on the next working day: see r 27; and PARA 701 note 11. Any document required or authorised by the Parole Board Rules 2011, SI 2011/2947, to be served or otherwise transmitted to any person may be transmitted by electronic means, sent by pre-paid post or delivered (in the case of a

document directed to the Board or the chair) to the office of the Board, or (in any other case) to the last known address of the person to whom the document is directed: see r 28; and PARA 701 note 11.

32 Parole Board Rules 2011, SI 2011/2947, r 26(2).

(ii) Recall Adjudicators

705. Appointment of recall adjudicators. As from a day to be appointed[1] the Secretary of State[2] may[3] appoint the Parole Board[4] or another person as a 'recall adjudicator'[5]. The Secretary of State may, in particular, appoint a person to carry out all or only some of the functions of a recall adjudicator[6], to carry out such functions only in relation to a specified area[7], and to carry out such functions only in relation to a specified description of case[8]. The Secretary of State may also appoint a recall adjudicator ('the chief recall adjudicator') to oversee the activities of recall adjudicators[9], and recall adjudicators must carry out their functions in accordance with guidance issued from time to time by the chief recall adjudicator[10].

The Secretary of State may make rules with respect to the proceedings of recall adjudicators[11].

1 The Criminal Justice Act 2003 s 239A (see the text and notes 2–11) is added, as from a day to be appointed, by the Criminal Justice and Courts Act 2015 s 8(1), (2). At the date at which this volume states the law no day has been appointed for this purpose.

2 As to the Secretary of State for these purposes see PRISONS AND PRISONERS vol 85 (2012) PARA 408.

3 Ie for the purposes of the Criminal Justice Act 2003 Pt 12 Ch 6 (ss 237–268) (sentencing: release, licences and recall) (see also PARAS 696, 699, 710 et seq): s 239A(1) (prospectively added: see note 1).

4 As to the constitution and functions of the Parole Board, continued by the Criminal Justice Act 2003 s 239(1), see PARA 699.

5 Criminal Justice Act 2003 s 239A(1), (2) (prospectively added: see note 1). The Secretary of State may make payments to a recall adjudicator: s 239A(9) (as so prospectively added). A person is not to be regarded as acting on behalf of the Crown, or as enjoying any status, immunity or privilege of the Crown, by virtue of an appointment under these provisions: s 239A(10) (as so prospectively added).

6 Criminal Justice Act 2003 s 239A(3)(a) (prospectively added: see note 1).

7 Criminal Justice Act 2003 s 239A(3)(b) (prospectively added: see note 1).

8 Criminal Justice Act 2003 s 239A(3)(c) (prospectively added: see note 1).

9 Criminal Justice Act 2003 s 239A(5) (prospectively added: see note 1).

10 Criminal Justice Act 2003 s 239A(8) (prospectively added: see note 1). The chief recall adjudicator may, in particular, issue guidance with respect to the carrying out of the functions of recall adjudicators and make recommendations to the Secretary of State about the termination of appointments under these provisions: s 239A(6) (as so prospectively added). Before issuing guidance the chief recall adjudicator must consult the recall adjudicators and the Secretary of State: s 239A(7) (as so prospectively added).

11 Criminal Justice Act 2003 s 239A(4) (prospectively added: see note 1). At the date at which this volume states the law no such rules had been made.

(4) PRISONERS SERVING INDETERMINATE SENTENCE

(i) Definition of 'Life Prisoner'

706. Meaning of 'life prisoner' for the purposes of the Crime (Sentences) Act 1997. For the purposes of the provisions of the Crime (Sentences) Act 1997 that govern the early release of prisoners serving life sentences[1], 'life prisoner' means a person serving one or more life sentences[2], where 'life sentence' means any of the following imposed for an offence, whether committed before or after 1 October 1997[3], namely[4]:

(1)   a sentence of imprisonment for life[5];

(2)   a sentence of detention during Her Majesty's pleasure or for life[6];

(3)   a sentence of custody for life[7];

(4)   a sentence of imprisonment or detention in a young offender institution for public protection[8];

(5)   a sentence of detention for public protection[9].

This definition of 'life prisoner' includes a transferred life prisoner[10].

1   Ie for the purposes of the Crime (Sentences) Act 1997 Pt II Ch II (ss 28–34) (life sentences) (see also PARAS 697, 707 et seq): see s 34(1) (amended by the Criminal Justice and Court Services Act 2000 Sch 7 Pt II paras 135, 138, 145, 148, Sch 8; and the Criminal Justice Act 2003 s 273(4)). The amendment made by the Criminal Justice and Court Services Act 2000 has effect only in relation to life sentences passed after 30 November 2000 (the date on which the Criminal Justice and Court Services Act 2000 obtained Royal Assent): see ss 60, 80(3)(b), Sch 7 Pt II paras 135, 138, 145, 148.

    The Crime (Sentences) Act 1997 Pt II Ch II does not apply in relation to a person detained in England and Wales in pursuance of a sentence of the International Criminal Court: see the International Criminal Court Act 2001 Sch 7 para 3(1); and PARA 690. As to the meanings of 'England' and 'Wales' see PARA 4 note 3.

2   See the Crime (Sentences) Act 1997 s 34(1) (as amended: see note 1). See also the text and note 10. Where a person has been sentenced to one or more life sentences and to one or more terms of imprisonment, nothing in the Crime (Sentences) Act 1997 Pt II Ch II requires the Secretary of State to release the person in respect of any of the life sentences unless and until the Secretary of State is required to release him in respect of each of the terms: s 34(4) (added by the Crime and Disorder Act 1998 s 101(2)). Where the terms of two or more sentences passed before 30 September 1998 (ie before the commencement of the Crime and Disorder Act 1998 s 101: see the Crime and Disorder Act 1998 (Commencement No 2 and Transitional Provisions) Order 1998, SI 1998/2327, art 2(1)(v)) have been treated, by virtue of the Criminal Justice Act 1991 s 51(2) (repealed), as a single term for the purposes of Pt II (ss 32–51) (repealed), they must continue to be so treated after that commencement: see the Crime and Disorder Act 1998 s 120(1), Sch 9 para 11(1). Subject to Sch 9 para 11(1), s 101 applies where one or more of the sentences concerned were passed after that commencement: see Sch 9 para 11(2). As to the statutory scheme substantially contained in the Criminal Justice Act 1991 Pt II see PARA 722 note 2.

3   Ie whether committed before or after the commencement of the Criminal Justice Act 1991 Pt II: see s 34(2); and the Crime (Sentences) Act 1997 (Commencement No 2 and Transitional Provisions) Order 1997, SI 1997/2200, art 2(1)(f).

4   Crime (Sentences) Act 1997 s 34(2).

5   Crime (Sentences) Act 1997 s 34(2)(a). As to sentences of imprisonment for life see PARA 688 note 1.

6   Crime (Sentences) Act 1997 s 34(2)(b) (s 34(2)(b), (c) amended by the Powers of Criminal Courts (Sentencing) Act 2000 Sch 9 para 183(1), (2)). Head (2) in the text refers specifically to a sentence of detention at Her Majesty's pleasure (passed on a person under 18 convicted of murder or any other offence the sentence for which is fixed by law as life imprisonment) under the Powers of Criminal Courts (Sentencing) Act 2000 s 90 (see PARA 38; and CHILDREN AND YOUNG PERSONS vol 10 (2012) PARA 1308) and to a sentence of detention for life (passed on a person aged under 18 who has committed a serious offence) under s 91 (detention for a serious offence for a specified period: see PARA 8; and CHILDREN AND YOUNG PERSONS vol 10 (2012) PARA 1307): see the Crime (Sentences) Act 1997 s 34(2)(b) (as so amended). See also PARA 689.

    For these purposes, a sentence of detention for life under the Armed Forces Act 2006 s 209 (person under 18 convicted of serious offence (power to detain for specified period): see ARMED FORCES vol 3 (2011) PARA 611) (Crime (Sentences) Act 1997 s 34(2)(f) (s 34(2)(f), (g) added by the Armed Forces Act 2006 Sch 16 para 142(1), (2)(c))) and a sentence of detention at Her Majesty's pleasure under the Armed Forces Act 2006 s 218 (person aged under 18 convicted of murder (mandatory detention at Her Majesty's pleasure): see ARMED FORCES vol 3 (2011) PARA 611) are also included (Crime (Sentences) Act 1997 s 34(2)(g) (as so added)).

7   Crime (Sentences) Act 1997 s 34(2)(c) (as amended: see note 6). Head (3) in the text refers specifically to a sentence of custody for life (passed on a person aged under 21 convicted of murder or any other serious offence, or in certain other cases on a person aged between 18 and 21 where the offence would attract a sentence of imprisonment for life if committed by a person aged 21 years or over) under the Powers of Criminal Courts (Sentencing) Act 2000 ss 93, 94

(prospectively repealed) (see PARAS 36, 37; and CHILDREN AND YOUNG PERSONS vol 10 (2012) PARA 1309): see the Crime (Sentences) Act 1997 s 34(2)(c) (as so amended).

8   Crime (Sentences) Act 1997 s 34(2)(d) (s 34(2)(d), (e) added by the Criminal Justice Act 2003 Sch 18 para 3; Crime (Sentences) Act 1997 s 34(2)(d) amended by the Armed Forces Act 2006 Sch 16 para 142(1), (2)(a), Sch 17; and the Legal Aid, Sentencing and Punishment of Offenders Act 2012 s 117(10)(b), (11)). Head (4) in the text refers specifically to a sentence for public protection under the Criminal Justice Act 2003 s 225 (see PARA 37) either of imprisonment or detention in a young offender institution (where the offender is aged at least 18 but under 21), including one passed as a result of the Armed Forces Act 2006 s 219 (person aged at least 18 but under 21 convicted by Court Martial of offence of criminal conduct corresponding to a serious offence: see ARMED FORCES vol 3 (2011) PARA 611): Crime (Sentences) Act 1997 s 34(2)(d) (as so added and amended).

9   Crime (Sentences) Act 1997 s 34(2)(e) (as added (see note 8); and amended by the Armed Forces Act 2006 Sch 16 para 142(1), (2)). Head (5) in the text refers specifically to a sentence of detention for public protection (where the offender has committed a serious offence but is aged under 18) imposed under the Criminal Justice Act 2003 s 226 (see PARA 34; and CHILDREN AND YOUNG PERSONS vol 10 (2012) PARA 1300), including one passed as a result of the Armed Forces Act 2006 s 221 (required custodial sentences for dangerous offenders: see ARMED FORCES vol 3 (2011) PARA 611): Crime (Sentences) Act 1997 s 34(2)(e) (as so added and amended).

10   Ie a transferred life prisoner as defined by the Criminal Justice Act 2003 s 273 (see PRISONS AND PRISONERS vol 85 (2012) PARA 463): Crime (Sentences) Act 1997 s 34(1) (as amended: see note 1).

(ii) Release

707. Duty to release certain life prisoners. As soon as a life prisoner[1], in respect of whom a minimum term order[2] has been made[3], has served the relevant part of his sentence[4], and the Parole Board[5] has directed his release[6], it is the duty of the Secretary of State[7] to release him on licence[8]. The Parole Board must not give such a direction with respect to such a life prisoner, however, unless the Secretary of State has referred the prisoner's case to the Board[9], and unless the Board is satisfied that it is no longer necessary for the protection of the public that the prisoner should be confined[10].

Such a life prisoner may require the Secretary of State to refer his case to the Parole Board at any time[11]:

(1)   after he has served the relevant part of his sentence[12]; and

(2)   where there has been a previous reference[13] of his case to the Board, after the end of the period of two years beginning with the disposal of that reference[14]; and

(3)   where he is also serving a sentence of imprisonment or detention for a term, after he has served: (a) until a day to be appointed, one-half of that sentence; or (b) as from that day, the requisite custodial period[15].

If a life prisoner is serving two or more life sentences:

(a)   the duty to release him[16] does not apply unless a minimum term order has been made in respect of each of those sentences[17]; and

(b)   the involvement of the Parole Board[18] does not apply in relation to his case until he has served the relevant part of each of them[19].

Special provision has been made by the Parole Board Rules[20] setting out the timetable and rules for proceedings with or without a hearing where the Parole Board determines the initial release of a prisoner serving an indeterminate sentence[21].

1   Ie a life prisoner to whom the Crime (Sentences) Act 1997 s 28 applies (see s 28(1A), (1B); and the text and notes 2–3, 16–19): s 28(5)(a) (s 28(1A), (1B) added, s 28(5)(a) substituted, by the Criminal Justice and Court Services Act 2000 Sch 7 Pt II paras 135, 136(a), 145, 148). As to the meaning of 'life prisoner' for the purposes of the Crime (Sentences) Act 1997 Pt II Ch II (ss 28–34) (life sentences) see PARA 706. The amendment made by the Criminal Justice and

Court Services Act 2000 has effect only in relation to life sentences passed after 30 November 2000 (the date on which the Criminal Justice and Court Services Act 2000 obtained Royal Assent): see ss 60, 80(3)(b), Sch 7 Pt II paras 135, 136, 145, 148; and see also note 17.

The Crime (Sentences) Act 1997 Pt II Ch II does not apply in relation to a person detained in England and Wales in pursuance of a sentence of the International Criminal Court: see the International Criminal Court Act 2001 Sch 7 para 3(1); and PARA 690. As to the meanings of 'England' and 'Wales' see PARA 4 note 3.

2   For these purposes 'minimum term order' means an order under:
    (1)   the Powers of Criminal Courts (Sentencing) Act 2000 s 82A(2) (determination of minimum term in respect of life sentence that is not fixed by law: see PARA 39) (Crime (Sentences) Act 1997 s 28(8A)(a) (s 28(8A) added by the Criminal Justice Act 2003 s 275(1), (4))); or
    (2)   the Criminal Justice Act 2003 s 269(2) (determination of minimum term in relation to mandatory life sentence: see CRIMINAL LAW vol 25 (2010) PARA 97) (Crime (Sentences) Act 1997 s 28(8A)(b) (as so added)).

In relation to head (1) above, if a court passes a life sentence in circumstances where the sentence is not fixed by law (a 'discretionary life sentence'), the court must, unless it orders otherwise, order that s 28(5)–(8) apply to the offender as soon as he has served the part of the sentence which is specified in the order: see the Powers of Criminal Courts (Sentencing) Act 2000 s 82A (life sentences (determination of tariffs)); and PARA 39.

In relation to head (2) above, where a court passes a life sentence in circumstances where the sentence is fixed by law (a 'mandatory life sentence'), it must order that the Crime (Sentences) Act 1997 s 28(5)–(8) are to apply to the offender as soon as he has served the part of his sentence which is specified in the order: see the Criminal Justice Act 2003 s 269. Further to this purpose, the Crime (Sentences) Act 1997 s 28 is modified in relation to an 'existing prisoner' (where 'existing prisoner' means a person serving one or more mandatory life sentences passed before 18 December 2003 (ie before the day on which s 269 came into force)), and associated provision is made: see the Criminal Justice Act 2003 s 336, Sch 22 (amended by the Constitutional Reform Act 2005 ss 40(4), 59(5), Sch 9 Pt 1 para 82(1), (6), Sch 11 Pt 1 para 1(2); and the Criminal Justice Act 2003 (Mandatory Life Sentences: Appeals in Transitional Cases) Order 2005, SI 2005/2798 (amended by SI 2011/1242).). See also *Re Mohammed Riaz* [2004] EWHC 74 (QB) (in fixing tariff, court must have regard to exceptional circumstances, including exceptional progress made in prison); *Re Brown (reference under paragraph 6 of Schedule 22 to the Criminal Justice Act 2003)* [2006] EWHC 518 (QB), [2006] All ER (D) 280 (Mar); *Re Cadman (application under para 3 of Sch 22 to the Criminal Justice Act 2003)* [2006] EWHC 586 (QB), [2006] 3 All ER 1255, (2006) Times, 26 May; *Re Waters* [2006] EWHC 355 (QB), [2006] 3 All ER 1251; *Re Bingham (application under para 3 of Sch 22 to the Criminal Justice Act 2003)* [2006] EWHC 2591 (QB), [2006] All ER (D) 262 (Oct); *Re Grimson (application under para 3 of Sch 22 to the Criminal Justice Act 2003)* [2008] EWHC 1038 (QB), [2008] All ER (D) 339 (May); *Re Sharif (application under para 3 of Sch 22 to the Criminal Justice Act 2003)* [2012] EWHC 868 (QB), [2012] All ER (D) 129 (Apr); and see *R (on the application of Hammond) v Secretary of State for the Home Department* [2005] UKHL 69, [2006] 1 AC 603, [2006] 1 All ER 219 (fairness would not, in many cases, require an oral hearing, to which many existing prisoners might in any event waive their right). As to appeals see eg *R v Sullivan, R v Gibbs, R v Elener* [2004] EWCA Crim 1762, [2005] 1 Cr App Rep 23, [2004] All ER (D) 133 (Jul) (applied in *R v Walker* [2005] EWCA Crim 82, [2005] 2 Cr App Rep (S) 328, [2005] All ER (D) 138 (Mar)).

3   Crime (Sentences) Act 1997 s 28(1A) (as added (see note 1); and substituted by the Criminal Justice Act 2003 s 275(1), (2)).

4   Crime (Sentences) Act 1997 s 28(5)(a) (as substituted: see note 1). In determining for the purpose of s 28(5) whether a life prisoner to whom s 28 applies has served the 'relevant part' of his sentence, no account is to be taken of any time during which he was unlawfully at large within the meaning of the Prison Act 1952 s 49 (see PRISONS AND PRISONERS vol 85 (2012) PARA 429): Crime (Sentences) Act 1997 s 28(8). In relation to a life prisoner in respect of whom a minimum term order has been made, any reference in s 28 to the relevant part of such a prisoner's sentence is a reference to the part of the sentence specified in the order: s 28(1A) (as added and substituted: see note 3). In relation to an 'existing prisoner' see note 2.

5   As to the constitution and functions of the Parole Board, continued by the Criminal Justice Act 2003 s 239(1), see PARA 699.

6   Crime (Sentences) Act 1997 s 28(5)(b). The text refers to the Parole Board directing release under s 28: see s 28(5)(b).

7   As to the Secretary of State for these purposes see PRISONS AND PRISONERS vol 85 (2012) PARA 408.

8 Crime (Sentences) Act 1997 s 28(5). As to the duration of licences granted to life prisoners see PARA 733; and as to licence conditions see PARA 734. The introduction of the Crime (Sentences) Act 1997 s 28 followed the decision of the European Court of Human Rights in *Hussain v United Kingdom* (1996) 22 EHRR 1, ECtHR. The sentence of detention at Her Majesty's pleasure, imposed in respect of offenders convicted of murder committed when they were aged 17 or under, was held to comprise both a punitive and preventative component, so that when the sentence entered the preventative phase, it attracted the guarantees of the Convention for the Protection of Human Rights and Fundamental Freedoms (Rome, 4 November 1950; TS 71 (1953); Cmd 8969) ('the European Convention on Human Rights) art 5.4 (ie that everyone who is deprived of his liberty by arrest or detention is entitled to take proceedings by which the lawfulness of his detention is to be decided speedily by a court and his release ordered if the detention is not lawful: see RIGHTS AND FREEDOMS vol 88A (2013) PARA 210 et seq).

The predecessor legislation to the Crime (Sentences) Act 1997 s 28 (contained in the Criminal Justice Act 1991 s 34 (now repealed)) was a response to earlier applications before the European Court of Human Rights: see eg *Thynne, Wilson and Gunnell v United Kingdom* (1990) 13 EHRR 666, ECtHR. The applicants were all prisoners serving discretionary life sentences (ie prisoners convicted of offences for which the sentence was not fixed by law). See also *R v Secretary of State for the Home Department, ex p Furber* [1998] 1 All ER 23, [1998] 1 Cr App Rep (S) 208; *R v M, R v L* [1998] 2 All ER 939, [1999] 1 WLR 485, CA.

The introduction of the Criminal Justice Act 2003 assimilated the position of mandatory life sentence prisoners with that of discretionary life sentence prisoners and those detained at Her Majesty's pleasure which was itself the result of judicial determinations revisiting the characterisation of the sentence. In *Stafford v United Kingdom* (2002) 35 EHRR 1121, 13 BHRC 260, ECtHR, the European Court of Human Rights departed from its earlier distinction (in *Thynne, Wilson and Gunnell v United Kingdom*; and *Wynne v United Kingdom* (1994) 19 EHRR 333, ECtHR) between the mandatory and discretionary life sentences and held that the mandatory life sentence, like the discretionary life sentence, comprises punitive and preventative elements and that once the punitive element has been served, continued detention engages the European Convention on Human Rights art 5 and thus requires review by an independent tribunal for the purposes of art 5.4 (as to the position with regard to prisoners serving sentences of imprisonment for public protection see *James v United Kingdom* [2013] 56 EHRR 12, 33 BHRC 617, [2012] All ER (D) 109 (Sep)). This position was confirmed domestically in *R (on the application of Anderson) v Secretary of State for the Home Department* [2002] UKHL 46, [2003] 1 AC 837, [2002] 4 All ER 1089, which acknowledged that the European Court of Human Rights had held that the tariff fixing exercise was a sentencing exercise, there being no distinction in that regard between mandatory life prisoners, discretionary life prisoners and juvenile murderers, and that the Secretary of State should pay no part in fixing the tariff of a convicted murderer, even if he did no more than confirm what the judges had recommended, since the rule of law depended on a complete functional separation of the judiciary from the executive. Because it was not possible to read the Crime (Sentences) Act 1997 s 29 (which dealt with the release of life prisoners 'other' than those falling within s 28) as precluding participation by the Secretary of State, s 29 was declared incompatible with the right under the European Convention on Human Rights art 6 (the right to a fair hearing: see RIGHTS AND FREEDOMS vol 88A (2013) PARAS 243–300) to have a sentence imposed by an independent and impartial tribunal. Accordingly, the Criminal Justice Act 2003 was enacted to repeal the Crime (Sentences) Act 1997 s 29, to amend s 28 to include mandatory life sentence prisoners amongst those who must be released upon the direction of the Parole Board, and to provide for the judicial determination of the minimum term to be served prior to consideration of release by the Parole Board (see the Criminal Justice Act 2003 ss 269, 276, Sch 21 (determination of minimum term in relation to mandatory life sentence), Sch 22 (mandatory life sentences: transitional cases)).

9 Crime (Sentences) Act 1997 s 28(6)(a).

10 Crime (Sentences) Act 1997 s 28(6)(b). The test in s 28(6)(b) requires the Parole Board to be satisfied that the prisoner does not present a substantial risk of re-offending in a manner which is dangerous to life or limb or of committing serious sexual offences: *R v Secretary of State for the Home Department, ex p Benson* [1989] COD 329, (1988) Times, 8 November, DC; *R v Parole Board, ex p Bradley* [1990] 3 All ER 828, [1991] 1 WLR 134, DC; and see *R v Parole Board, ex p Watson* [1996] 2 All ER 641 at 650, [1996] 1 WLR 906 at 916, CA, per Sir Thomas Bingham MR (in exercising its practical judgment, the Board is bound to [...] balance[e] the hardship and injustice of continuing to imprison a man who is unlikely to cause serious injury to the public against the need to protect the public against a man who is not unlikely to cause to such injury; in other than a clear case, this is bound to be a difficult and very anxious judgment but in the final balance the Board is bound to give preponderant weight to the need to protect

innocent members of the public against any significant risk of serious injury). See also *Sturnham v Secretary of State for Justice* [2012] EWCA Civ 452, [2013] 2 AC 254, [2012] 3 WLR 476 (affd [2013] UKSC 47, [2013] 2 AC 254, [2013] 4 All ER 177) (approving *R v Parole Board, ex p Bradley*) (the test for release under Crime (Sentences) Act 1997 is the same irrespective of the type of indeterminate sentence under consideration and in the case of prisoners sentenced to imprisonment for public protection (IPP), there does not need to be an equivalence of risk at the point when IPP was imposed and when release is being considered); but c f *R v Parole Board, ex p Curley* (22 October 1999, unreported) (mandatory life sentence prisoners, including those detained at Her Majesty's pleasure (HMP), have their sentence imposed as a matter of law, rather than on a finding of 'dangerousness', so the Board will require cogent evidence of 'dangerousness' before being satisfied that an HMP prisoner poses more than a minimal risk of danger to life and limb).

While the Secretary of State has power to give directions, so as to provide the Parole Board with guidance as to the legally relevant matters to be taken into account to assist it to reach a structured decision on the question it was duty bound to decide, what he could not do was give mandatory directions as this would usurp the Board's judicial function: *R (on the application of Girling) v Parole Board* [2006] EWCA Civ 1779, [2007] QB 783, [2007] 2 All ER 688 (considering the Criminal Justice Act 1991s 32(6): see now the power exercisable under the Criminal Justice Act 2003 s 239(6); and PARA 699 note 17).

In so far as it is relevant to do so, the Parole Board applies the civil standard of proof (see *R (on the application of Brooks) v Parole Board* [2004] EWCA Civ 80, 148 Sol Jo LB 233, [2004] All ER (D) 142 (Feb)). However, because it is concerned with the assessment of risk (i e a more than minimal risk of further grave offences being committed in the future), ultimately the burden of proof has no real part to play: see *R (on the application of Sim) v Parole Board* [2003] EWCA Civ 1845 at [42], [2004] QB 1288 at [42], [2004] 2 WLR 1170 at [42] per Keene LJ (the concept of a burden of proof is inappropriate where one is involved in risk evaluation); and *R (on the application of Brooks) v Parole Board* at [28] per Kennedy LJ; cf *R v Hodgson* (1967) 52 Cr App Rep 113, [1968] Crim LR 46, CA. Prisoners who deny their offences should not automatically be refused release, though the fact of that denial may make the task of risk assessment particularly difficult: see *R v Secretary of State for the Home Department, ex p Hepworth, Fenton-Palmer and Baldonzy* [1997] EWHC Admin 324; *R v Parole Board and Home Secretary, ex p Oyston* [2000] All ER (D) 274, CA (Parole Board is free to consider the risk that a prisoner may pose in the event of an escape when he denies guilt of his index offence but a decision that is solely based on denial of the index offending is unlawful). See also Butterfield J in *R v Secretary of State for the Home Department, ex p Lillycrop* (1996) Times, 13 December: 'We consider that the Parole Board must approach its consideration of any application for parole on the basis that the applicant has committed the offences of which he has been convicted. It is not the function of the Parole Board to investigate possible miscarriages of justice or to give effect in their considerations to any personal misgivings they may have about the correctness of any particular conviction. That being so, where the pattern of offending behaviour is such that there is a significant risk of a further offence being committed, particularly an offence of a violent or sexual nature, and an applicant has not demonstrated by his conduct in prison that such risk has been reduced to an acceptable level, then a recommendation for parole is unlikely to be made. Part of that conduct in prison to which a panel of the Parole Board will inevitably and rightly look will be the extent to which an applicant has examined the behaviour which has led to his imprisonment. Where because of denial that the offence has been committed no such examination has taken place it will be more difficult for an applicant to satisfy the Board that the risk he posed when he was sentenced to a term of imprisonment has been reduced to an acceptable level. We repeat and emphasise that each case must turn on its own particular facts'.

As to what material is relevant for the Parole Board to consider when making its evaluation, it is not confined to material which would be admissible in criminal or disciplinary proceedings, nor need it follow procedures prescribed in relation to those types of proceedings: see *R (on the application of West) v Parole Board* [2002] EWCA Civ 1641, [2003] 1 WLR 705, (2002) Times, 21 November, [2002] All ER (D) 194 (Nov); *R (on the application of Sim) v Parole Board*; *R (on the application of Brooks) v Parole Board*. As to whether procedural fairness requires that an oral hearing take place see generally PARA 700 note 12.

Though the Board only has power to direct release, it is the duty of the Board to advise the Secretary of State with respect to any matter referred to it by him which is to do with the early release or recall of prisoners. In practice, it is invited by the Secretary of State to advise whether a prisoner serving an indeterminate sentence should be transferred to an open prison or should have his case next referred to the Board in less than the statutory period (see head (2) in the text). As to open prisons see PRISONS AND PRISONERS vol 85 (2012) PARA 482. In relation to all advice given, the Secretary of State is entitled to take a different course, though any unreasonable failure to follow a recommendation by the Board will be susceptible to judicial review: see eg *R (on the application of Hill) v Secretary of State for the Home Department* [2007] EWHC 2164 (Admin), [2007] All ER (D) 112 (Sep) (Secretary of State's practice differed markedly depending on whether the Parole Board recommendation was for a transfer to open conditions or against: in the former case, he rarely accepted the recommendation but, in the latter, he almost always did so; the Secretary of State should act even-handedly and either accept the Parole Board's advice every time, save in exceptional circumstances, or he could look carefully in each case at every piece of advice whether positive or negative). Where the Secretary of State does reject a recommendation he must, as a matter of fairness, address the reasons given by the Board for taking the view with which he is disagreeing: *R v Secretary of State for the Home Department, ex p Murphy* [1997] COD 478. Where a panel of the Parole Board determines that it is safe to release a prisoner but is unable to direct release because suitable release arrangements have not been put in place, the panel has discharged the function of the Parole Board under the Crime (Sentences) Act 1997 s 28(5) (see the text and notes 4–8), and is functus officio: *R v Parole Board, ex p Robinson* (29 July 1999, unreported). Any future panel convened to consider the prisoner's case may not re-open the issue of risk, but must direct release once suitable arrangements are in place: *R v Parole Board, ex p Robinson*.

The detention of prisoners with indeterminate sentences for public protection who have completed their tariff terms is not unlawful in itself, since the provisions of the Crime (Sentences) Act 1997 require that the Parole Board is satisfied that it is no longer necessary for the protection of the public that they are confined, and it is not possible to describe a prisoner who remains detained in accordance with those provisions as unlawfully detained under the common law: *R (on the application of James) v Secretary of State for Justice, R (on the application of Lee) v Secretary of State for Justice, R (on the application of Wells) v Secretary of State for Justice* [2009] UKHL 22, [2010] 1 AC 553, [2009] 4 All ER 255 (parole review is a matter of form rather than substance). Notwithstanding this, the continuing detention of a post-tariff indeterminate sentence prisoner does engage the European Convention on Human Rights art 5.4: *Thynne, Wilson and Gunnell v United Kingdom* (1990) 13 EHRR 666, ECtHR; *Stafford v United Kingdom* (2002) 35 EHRR 1121, 13 BHRC 260, ECtHR; *R (on the application of James) v Secretary of State for Justice, R (on the application of Lee) v Secretary of State for Justice, R (on the application of Wells) v Secretary of State for Justice; R (on the application of Noorkoiv) v Secretary of State for the Home Department* [2002] EWCA Civ 770, [2002] 4 All ER 515, [2002] 1 WLR 3284 (policy of referring life sentence prisoners to the Parole Board after expiry of the tariff period). A breach by the Secretary of State of his public law duty to provide such courses as would enable prisoners with indeterminate sentences for public protection to demonstrate their safety for release does not result in post-tariff detentions being unlawful at common law or under the European Convention on Human Rights art 5 provided the system has not broken down to the extent that the causal link between the initial sentence and the continued detention is broken: *R (on the application of James) v Secretary of State for Justice, R (on the application of Lee) v Secretary of State for Justice, R (on the application of Wells) v Secretary of State for Justice*. However, see *James v United Kingdom, Lee v United Kingdom, Wells v United Kingdom* (2012) 33 BHRC 617, [2012] All ER (D) 109 (Sep), ECtHR (there had been a violation of the European Convention on Human Rights art 5.1 in respect of the applicants' detention following the expiry of their tariff periods and until steps were taken to progress them through the prison system with a view to providing them with access to appropriate rehabilitative courses).

11   Crime (Sentences) Act 1997 s 28(7). The provision made by s 28(7) has effect as if any reference of a prisoner's case made to the Parole Board under the Criminal Justice Act 1991 s 32(2) or s 34(4) (both repealed) had been made under the Crime (Sentences) Act 1997 s 28(6) (see the text and notes 9–10); and as if any such reference made under the Criminal Justice Act 1991 s 39(4) (repealed) had been made under the Crime (Sentences) Act 1997 s 32(4) (recall of life prisoners on licence: see PARA 708): see s 56(1), Sch 5 para 5.

A prisoner to whom s 28 applies is entitled to require the Secretary of State to have his first parole review conducted immediately upon the expiry of the relevant part or punitive period, or as soon as practicable thereafter: *R v Secretary of State for the Home Department, ex p Norney* (1995) Times, 6 October, DC; *Noorkoiv v Secretary of State for the Home Department (No 2)* [2002] EWCA Civ 770, [2002] 4 All ER 515, [2002] 1 WLR 3284. The prisoner is entitled, under the European Convention on Human Rights art 5.4 to have such a review conducted speedily: see note 8.

12   Crime (Sentences) Act 1997 s 28(7)(a). In determining for the purpose of s 28(7) whether a life prisoner to whom s 28 applies has served the relevant part of his sentence, no account is to be

taken of any time during which he was unlawfully at large within the meaning of the Prison Act 1952 s 49 (see PRISONS AND PRISONERS vol 85 (2012) PARA 429): Crime (Sentences) Act 1997 s 28(8).

13 For these purposes, 'previous reference' means a reference either under the Crime (Sentences) Act 1997 s 28(6) (see the text and notes 9–10) or under s 32(4): s 28(7). Following a review, the Board may recommend that the prisoner's case should be heard sooner than the statutory period but the Secretary of State is not obliged to accept any such recommendation, although his refusal to do so may be susceptible to challenge by way of judicial review: see note 10.

14 Crime (Sentences) Act 1997 s 28(7)(b). Under the European Convention on Human Rights art 5.4 (see note 8), prisoners serving an indeterminate sentence are entitled to have the lawfulness of their detention determined at regular intervals because the justification for detention, namely continued dangerousness, is susceptible to change over time: *Oldham v United Kingdom* (2000) 31 EHRR 813, ECtHR (and see relevant cases listed in PARA 700). The Secretary of State has a discretion to refer a case before the expiry of two years, whether an early review is recommended by the Parole Board or of his own motion because the European Convention on Human Rights art 5.4 does not require the decision on the timing of reviews to be taken by a Court; the determination of what the appropriate interval between reviews should be can properly be taken by the Secretary of State who must take into account the circumstances of the particular prisoner's case: see *R (on the application of Spence) v Secretary of State for the Home Department* [2003] EWCA Civ 732, 147 Sol Jo LB 660, [2003] All ER (D) 354 (May); and PARA 700 note 14.

15 Crime (Sentences) Act 1997 s 28(7)(c) (amended by the Crime and Disorder Act 1998 Sch 8 para 130(2); prospectively amended by the Criminal Justice and Courts Act 2015 s 11(1), (4)). For these purposes 'the requisite custodial period; means (by virtue of the Criminal Justice Act 2003 s 268(1A) (added by the Criminal Justice and Courts Act 2015 s 14(2)):

    (1)   in relation to a person serving an extended sentence imposed under the Criminal Justice Act 2003 s 226A or s 226B (see PARAS 18–20), the requisite custodial period for the purposes of s 246A (see PARA 716);

    (2)   in relation to a person serving an extended sentence imposed under s 227 (repealed) or s 228 (repealed), the requisite custodial period for the purposes of s 247 (see PARA 716);

    (3)   in relation to a person serving a sentence imposed under s 236A (see PARA 32), the requisite custodial period for the purposes of s 244A (see PARA 714);

    (4)   in relation to any other fixed-term prisoner, the requisite custodial period for the purposes of s 243A (see PARA 712) or s 244 (see PARA 713) (as appropriate).

At the date at which this volume states the law no day had been appointed for the coming into force of the amendment referred to as prospective.

16 Ie the general provisions of the Crime (Sentences) Act 1997 s 28 (see the text and notes 1–15): s 28(1B)(a) (s 28(1B) as added (see note 1); s 28(1B)(a) amended by the Criminal Justice Act 2003 s 275(1), (3)).

17 Crime (Sentences) Act 1997 s 28(1B)(a) (as added and amended: see notes 1, 16). Section 28(1B) is to be read with modifications where a person serving any life sentence passed after 30 November 2000 is also serving a 'pre-commencement life sentence', being a life sentence passed before that date or any sentence passed before commencement by reason of which the prisoner is a transferred life prisoner within the meaning of the Crime (Sentences) Act 1997 s 33 (repealed) (life prisoners transferred to England and Wales: see PARA 706 note 10; and note 2): see the Criminal Justice and Court Services Act 2000 s 74, Sch 7 Pt II paras 146–148.

18 Ie the provisions of the Crime (Sentences) Act 1997 s 28(5)–(8) (see the text and notes 4–15): s 28(1B)(b) (as added: see note 1).

19 Crime (Sentences) Act 1997s 28(1B)(b) (as added: see note 1).

20 Ie the Parole Board Rules 2011, SI 2011/2947 (see PARA 700).

21 See the Parole Board Rules 2011, SI 2011/2947, Pt 3 (rr 16–18); and PARA 702. As to general procedure before a Parole Board see also PARA 701.

(iii) Recall

708. Recall of life prisoners while on licence. The Secretary of State[1] may, in the case of any life prisoner[2] who has been released on licence under the provisions of the Crime (Sentences) Act 1997 that so provide[3], revoke his licence and recall him to prison[4]. A person recalled to prison in this way[5]:

    (1)   may make representations in writing with respect to his recall[6]; and

(2) on his return to prison, must be informed of the reasons for his recall and of his right to make representations[7].

The Secretary of State must refer the case of any life prisoner recalled in this way to the Parole Board[8]; and where, on such a reference, the Board directs his immediate release on licence, the Secretary of State must give effect to the direction[9].

On the revocation of the licence of any life prisoner in this way, he is liable to be detained in pursuance of his sentence and, if at large, is deemed to be unlawfully at large[10].

A person recalled to prison under these provisions commits an offence[11] if he has been notified of the recall orally or in writing[12] and while unlawfully at large fails, without reasonable excuse, to take all necessary steps to return to prison as soon as possible[13].

1   As to the Secretary of State for these purposes see PRISONS AND PRISONERS vol 85 (2012) PARA 408.

2   As to the meaning of 'life prisoner' for the purposes of the Crime (Sentences) Act 1997 Pt II Ch II (ss 28–34) (life sentences) see PARA 706.

3   Ie who has been released on licence under the Crime (Sentences) Act 1997 Pt II Ch II (see also PARAS 697, 707, 733 et seq): s 32(1) (substituted by the Criminal Justice and Immigration Act 2008 s 31(1), (2)).
      The Crime (Sentences) Act 1997 Pt II Ch II does not apply in relation to a person detained in England and Wales in pursuance of a sentence of the International Criminal Court: see the International Criminal Court Act 2001 Sch 7 para 3(1); and PARA 690. As to the meanings of 'England' and 'Wales' see PARA 4 note 3.

4   Crime (Sentences) Act 1997 s 32(1) (as substituted: see note 3). The provision made by s 32 is compatible with the right to liberty guaranteed by the Convention for the Protection of Human Rights and Fundamental Freedoms (Rome, 4 November 1950; TS 71 (1953); Cmd 8969) (the European Convention on Human Rights) art 5 (see RIGHTS AND FREEDOMS vol 88A (2013) PARA 210 et seq): see *R (on the application of Hirst) v Secretary of State for the Home Department* [2006] EWCA Civ 945, [2006] 4 All ER 639, [2006] 1 WLR 3083 (provided the circumstances under which the original sentence was imposed were sufficiently reflected in those that pertained at the time when the recall order was made, the recall of a prisoner subject to a discretionary life sentence did not contravene the European Convention on Human Rights art 5.1.

5   Crime (Sentences) Act 1997 s 32(3) (amended by the Criminal Justice and Immigration Act 2008 s 31(1), (3)). The Crime (Sentences) Act 1997 s 32(3) has effect as if any life prisoner recalled to prison under the Criminal Justice Act 1991 s 39(1), (2) (repealed) had been recalled to prison under the Crime (Sentences) Act 1997 s 32: see s 56(1), Sch 5 para 7(1) (amended by the Criminal Justice and Immigration Act 2008 s 149, Sch 28 Pt 2). For these purposes, 'life prisoner' has the same meaning as in the Crime (Sentences) Act 1997 Pt II Ch II: see Sch 5 para 13.

6   Crime (Sentences) Act 1997 s 32(3)(a).

7   Crime (Sentences) Act 1997 s 32(3)(b). Whether or not reasons given for a recall decision are adequate or prompt is highly fact specific: see *R (on the application of Hirst) v Secretary of State for the Home Department* [2005] EWHC 1480 (Admin), (2005) Times, 4 July, [2005] All ER (D) 223 (Jun); *R (on the application of FM) v Secretary of State for Justice* [2012] EWHC 2630 (QB), 176 CL & J 594, [2012] All ER (D) 176 (Sep). As to the approach taken to requests made to the Secretary of State to rescind a recall see *R (on the application of FM) v Secretary of State for Justice* (it seems highly restrictive to differentiate between a plain and obvious error undermining the original correctness of the decision to recall and a refusal, virtually without exception, to countenance any request to rescind based on a change in the judgement made about management of risk).

8   Crime (Sentences) Act 1997 s 32(4) (amended by the Criminal Justice and Immigration Act 2008 s 31(1), (4)). As to the constitution and functions of the Parole Board, continued by the Criminal Justice Act 2003 s 239(1) see PARA 699. The Crime (Sentences) Act 1997 s 32(4) has effect as if any life prisoner recalled to prison under the Criminal Justice Act 1991 s 39(1), (2) (repealed with savings: see PARA 688) had been recalled to prison under the Crime (Sentences) Act 1997 s 32 (see Sch 5 para 7(1) (as amended: see note 5)); and as if any

    representations made by a life prisoner under the Criminal Justice Act 1991 s 39(3) had been made under the Crime (Sentences) Act 1997 s 32(3) (see the text and notes 5–7) (Sch 5 para 7(2)).

9   Crime (Sentences) Act 1997 s 32(5) (substituted by the Criminal Justice Act 2003 s 304, Sch 32 Pt 1 paras 82, 84). As from a day to be appointed the Parole Board may not direct a person's immediate release on licence under the Crime (Sentences) Act 1997 s 32(5) unless it is satisfied that it is no longer necessary for the protection of the public that the life prisoner should remain in prison: s 32(5A) (prospectively added by the Criminal Justice and Courts Act 2015 s 11(2), (5)). At the date at which this volume states the law no such day had been appointed. The Parole Board must direct release where it concludes that the circumstances giving rise to the recall do not demonstrate any causal connection with the original purpose in imposing the indeterminate sentence; where the circumstances leading to recall demonstrate nothing more than a risk of non-violent offending, they are incapable of justifying detention pursuant to a sentence whose purpose is to protect the public from offences dangerous to life or limb: see e g *Stafford v United Kingdom* (2002) 35 EHRR 1121, 13 BHRC 260, ECtHR; and see PARA 688 note 8. Where a panel of the Parole Board determines that it is safe to release a prisoner but is unable to direct release because suitable release arrangements have not been put in place, the panel has discharged the function of the Parole Board under the Crime (Sentences) Act 1997 s 28(5) (see PARA 707), and is functus officio: *R v Parole Board, ex p Robinson* (29 July 1999, unreported). Any future panel convened to consider the prisoner's case may not re-open the issue of risk, but must direct release once suitable arrangements are in place: *R v Parole Board, ex p Robinson*. See also PARA 707 note 10.

10 Crime (Sentences) Act 1997 s 32(6).

11 A person who is guilty of such an offence is liable on conviction on indictment to imprisonment for a term not exceeding 2 years or a fine (or both) (Crime (Sentences) Act 1997 s 32ZA(5)(a) (s 32ZA added by the Criminal Justice and Courts Act 2015 s 12(1), (3))) or on summary conviction to imprisonment for a term not exceeding 12 months or a fine (or both) (Crime (Sentences) Act 1997 s 32ZA(5)(b) (as so added)). In relation to an offence committed before the coming into force of the Criminal Justice Act 2003 s 154(1) (general limit of magistrates' courts' power to impose imprisonment: not yet in force) the reference in the Crime (Sentences) Act 1997 s 32ZA(5)(b) to 12 months is to be read as a reference to 6 months: s 32ZA(6) (as so added). In relation to an offence committed before the coming into force of the Legal Aid, Sentencing and Punishment of Offenders Act 2012 s 85 (removal of limit on certain fines on conviction by magistrates' court: see PARA 176), the reference in the Crime (Sentences) Act 1997 s 32ZA(5)(b) to a fine is to be read as a reference to a fine not exceeding the statutory maximum: s 32ZA(7) (as so added). As to the standard scale, the statutory maximum, the prescribed sum, and magistrates' powers to levy unlimited fines see PARA 176.

12 Crime (Sentences) Act 1997 s 32ZA(1)(a) (as added: see note 11). A person is to be treated for these purposes as having been notified of the recall if written notice of the recall has been delivered to an appropriate address (s 32ZA(2)(a) (as so added)) and a period specified in the notice has elapsed (s 32ZA(2)(b) (as so added)). 'An appropriate address' means an address at which, under the person's licence, he is permitted to reside or stay (s 32ZA(3)(a) (as so added)) or an address nominated, in accordance with the person's licence, for these purposes (s 32ZA(3)(b) (as so added)). A person is also to be treated for these purposes as having been notified of the recall if his licence requires him to keep in touch in accordance with any instructions given by an officer of a provider of probation services (s 32ZA(4)(a) (as so added)), he has failed to comply with such an instruction (s 32ZA(4)(b) (as so added)), and he has not complied with such an instruction for at least 6 months (s 32ZA(4)(c) (as so added)).

13 Crime (Sentences) Act 1997 s 32ZA(1)(b) (as added: see note 11).

(5) PRISONERS SERVING DETERMINATE SENTENCE FOR OFFENCE COMMITTED ON OR AFTER 4 APRIL 2005

(i) Definition of 'Fixed-term Prisoner'; and Treatment of Concurrent and Consecutive Terms

709. Meaning of 'fixed-term prisoner' for the purposes of the Criminal Justice Act 2003. For the purposes of the provisions of the Criminal Justice Act 2003 that govern the early release, and recall, of prisoners[1], 'fixed-term prisoner' means a person:

(1)　　serving a sentence of imprisonment for a determinate term[2]; or

(2)　　serving a determinate sentence of detention[3].

For these purposes also, unless the context otherwise requires, 'prisoner' includes a person serving a sentence falling within head (2) above[4]; and 'prison' includes any place where a person serving such a sentence is liable to be detained[5].

1　Ie for the purposes of the Criminal Justice Act 2003 Pt 12 Ch 6 (ss 237–268) (sentencing: release, licences and recall) (see also PARAS 696, 699, 710 et seq): s 237(1).

2　Criminal Justice Act 2003 s 237(1)(a). As to the meaning of 'sentence of imprisonment' generally see PARA 27 note 4). References in Pt 12 Ch 6 to a sentence of imprisonment include such a sentence passed by a service court: see s 237(1B)(a) (s 237(1B), (1C) added by the Armed Forces Act 2006 Sch 16 para 219). However, nothing in the Criminal Justice Act 2003 s 237(1B) has the effect that s 240ZA (time remanded in custody to count as time served: terms of imprisonment and detention: see PARA 30) or s 265 (commencement of Crown Court sentence: see PARA 27), provision equivalent to which is made by the Armed Forces Act 2006, or the Criminal Justice Act 2003 s 240A (time remanded on bail to count as time served: terms of imprisonment and detention: see PARA 31), applies to a service court: s 237(1C) (as so added; amended by the Criminal Justice and Immigration Act 2008 s 21(1), (2); and the Legal Aid, Sentencing and Punishment of Offenders Act 2012 s 110(1), (2)(a), (b)).

In determining for the purposes of the Criminal Justice Act 2003 Pt 12 Ch 6 whether a person to whom s 240ZA applies, or to whom a direction under s 240A relates, either has served (or would, but for his release, have served) a particular proportion of his sentence, or has served a particular period, the number of days specified in s 240ZA, or in the direction under s 240A, are to be treated as having been served by him as part of that sentence or period: s 241(1) (amended by the Legal Aid, Sentencing and Punishment of Offenders Act 2012 ss 89(2), 110(1), (3), (4)(a), (b), Sch 10 paras 12, 20). For this purpose, the reference to the Criminal Justice Act 2003 s 240ZA includes the Armed Forces Act 2006 s 246 (crediting of time in service custody: terms of imprisonment and detention: see ARMED FORCES vol 3 (2011) PARA 596): Criminal Justice Act 2003 s 241(1A) (added by the Armed Forces Act 2006 Sch 16 para 220; and amended by the Legal Aid, Sentencing and Punishment of Offenders Act 2012 s 110(1), (3), (5)). For the purposes of the Criminal Justice Act 2003 ss 240ZA, 240A, 241 'sentence of imprisonment' does not include a committal in default of payment of any sum of money (other than one adjudged to be paid on a conviction), for want of sufficient distress to satisfy any sum of money, or for failure to do or abstain from doing anything required to be done or left undone (see s 305(1); and PARA 27 note 4 (definition applied and modified by s 242(1) (amended by the Criminal Justice and Immigration Act 2008 s 21(1), (6); and the Legal Aid, Sentencing and Punishment of Offenders Act 2012, s 110(1), (7)))); and references in the Criminal Justice Act 2003 ss 240ZA, 240A, 241 to sentencing an offender to imprisonment, and to an offender's sentence, are to be read accordingly (see s 242(1) (as so amended)).

3　Criminal Justice Act 2003 s 237(1)(b) (amended by the Legal Aid, Sentencing and Punishment of Offenders Act 2012 ss 117(1), (2)(a), (b), 125(4), Sch 20 paras 1, 2(1), (2); and by the Criminal Justice and Courts Act 2015 Sch 1 para 15). Head (2) in the text refers to the following sentences:

(1)　　a determinate sentence of detention under the Powers of Criminal Courts (Sentencing) Act 2000 s 91 (sentence of detention for a specified period passed on a person aged under 18 who has committed a serious offence: see PARA 8; and CHILDREN AND YOUNG PERSONS vol 10 (2012) PARA 1307) or s 96 (prospectively repealed) (detention in young offender institution for a person aged between 18 and 21: see PARA 16) (Criminal Justice Act 2003 s 237(1)(b) (as so amended)); or

(2)　　a sentence imposed under s 226A (extended sentence for certain violent or sexual offences (persons 18 or over): see PARAS 18–20), s 226B (extended sentence for certain violent or sexual offences (persons under 18): see PARAS 18–20), s 227 (repealed with savings), s 228 (repealed with savings), or s 236A (special custodial sentence for certain offenders of particular concern: see PARA 32) (s 237(1)(b) (as so amended)).

References in Pt 12 Ch 6 to a sentence of detention under the Powers of Criminal Courts (Sentencing) Act 2000 s 96 (see head (1) above) or under the Criminal Justice Act 2003 s 226A (see head (2) above), s 227 (see head (2) above) or s 236A (see head (2) above) are references to a sentence of detention in a young offender institution: s 237(3) (added by the Legal Aid, Sentencing and Punishment of Offenders Act 2012 s 117(1), (3); and amended by Sch 20 paras 1, 2(1), (3); and by the Criminal Justice and Courts Act 2015 Sch 1 para 15). References in the Criminal Justice Act 2003 Pt 12 Ch 6:

(a)   to a sentence of detention under the Powers of Criminal Courts (Sentencing) Act 2000 s 91 include a sentence of detention under the Armed Forces Act 2006 s 209 (offenders under 18 convicted of certain serious offences (power to detain for a specified period): see ARMED FORCES vol 3 (2011) PARA 611) (Criminal Justice Act 2003 s 237(1B)(b) (s 237(1B) as added: see note 2));

(b)   to a sentence under the Criminal Justice Act 2003 s 226A include a sentence under s 226A passed as a result of the Armed Forces Act 2006 s 219A (extended sentence for certain violent or sexual offenders aged 18 or over: see ARMED FORCES) (Criminal Justice Act 2003 s 237(1B)(ba) (s 237(1B) as so added; s 237(1B)(ba), (bb) added by the Legal Aid, Sentencing and Punishment of Offenders Act 2012 Sch 22 Pt 2 para 21));

(c)   to a sentence under the Criminal Justice Act 2003 s 226B include a sentence under s 226B passed as a result of the Armed Forces Act 2006 s 221A (extended sentence for certain violent or sexual offenders aged under 18: see ARMED FORCES) (Criminal Justice Act 2003 s 237(1B)(bb) (as so added));

(d)   to a sentence under the Criminal Justice Act 2003 s 227 include a sentence under s 227 passed as a result of the Armed Forces Act 2006 s 220 (repealed) (certain violent or sexual offences (offenders aged 18 or over): see ARMED FORCES vol 3 (2011) PARA 611) (Criminal Justice Act 2003 s 237(1B)(c) (as so added));

(e)   references to a sentence under the Criminal Justice Act 2003 s 228 include a sentence under s 228 passed as a result of the Armed Forces Act 2006 s 222 (repealed) (certain violent or sexual offences (offenders aged under 18): see ARMED FORCES vol 3 (2011) PARA 611) (Criminal Justice Act 2003 s 237(1B)(d) (as so added)); and

(f)   references to a sentence under s 236A include a sentence under s 236A passed as a result of s 224A (Criminal Justice Act 2003 s 237(1B)(e) (as so added; further added by the Criminal Justice and Courts Act 2015 Sch 1 para 15)).

4   Criminal Justice Act 2003 s 237(2). Accordingly, for the purposes of Pt 12 Ch 6, 'prisoner' is to be read in accordance with s 237(2): see s 268.

5   Criminal Justice Act 2003 s 237(2). Accordingly, for the purposes of Pt 12 Ch 6, 'prison' is to be read in accordance with s 237(2): see s 268.

710. Treatment of concurrent terms under the Criminal Justice Act 2003.
Where a person (the 'offender') has been sentenced to two or more terms of imprisonment[1] which are wholly or partly concurrent[2], and where the sentences were passed on the same occasion (or, where they were passed on different occasions, the person has not been released under Chapter 6 of Part 12 of the Criminal Justice Act 2003[3] at any time during the period beginning with the first and ending with the last of those occasions)[4], then:

(1)   nothing in Chapter 6 of Part 12 of the Criminal Justice Act 2003[5] requires the Secretary of State[6] to release the offender in respect of any of the terms unless and until he is required to release him in respect of each of the others[7];

(2)   the offender's release is to be unconditional if the provisions governing the automatic unconditional release of prisoners serving less than 12 months so requires[8] in respect of each of the sentences (and in any other case is to be on licence)[9];

(3)   the Secretary of State's statutory power to release on home detention curfew[10] does not authorise him to release the offender on licence[11] in respect of any of the terms unless and until the statutory provisions authorise him[12] to do so in respect of each of the others to which those provisions apply[13];

(4)   on and after his release under Chapter 6 of Part 12 of the Criminal Justice Act 2003[14] (unless that release is unconditional), the offender is to be on licence[15]: (a) until the last date on which the offender is required to be on licence in respect of any of the terms[16]; and (b) subject to such conditions as are required by Chapter 6 of Part 12 in respect of any of the sentences[17].

1   For this purpose, 'term of imprisonment' includes:

(1)   a determinate sentence of detention under the Powers of Criminal Courts (Sentencing) Act 2000 s 91 (sentence of detention for a specified period passed on a person aged under 18 who has committed a serious offence: see PARA 8; and **CHILDREN AND YOUNG PERSONS** vol 10 (2012) PARA 1307) or s 96 (prospectively repealed) (detention in young offender institution for a person aged between 18 and 21: see PARA 16) (Criminal Justice Act 2003 s 263(4) (amended by the Legal Aid, Sentencing and Punishment of Offenders Act 2012 ss 117(1), (7)(a), (b), 125(4), Sch 20 paras 1, 11)); or

(2)   a determinate sentence of detention under the Criminal Justice Act 2003 s 227 (repealed with savings) or s 228 (repealed with savings) (s 263(4) (as so amended)); or

(3)   a sentence of detention in a young offender institution under the Powers of Criminal Courts (Sentencing) Act 2000 s 96 (prospectively repealed) or under the Criminal Justice Act 2003 s 226A (extended sentence for certain violent or sexual offences (persons 18 or over): see PARAS 18–20), s 226B (extended sentence for certain violent or sexual offences (persons under 18): see PARAS 18–20), s 227 or s 236A (special custodial sentence for certain offenders of particular concern: see PARA 32) (s 263(4) (as so amended; amended by the Criminal Justice and Courts Act 2015 Sch 1 para 22)).

References in the Criminal Justice Act 2003 Pt 12 Ch 6 (ss 237–268) (sentencing: release, licences and recall) (see also PARAS 696, 699, 709, 711 et seq) to a sentence of detention under the Powers of Criminal Courts (Sentencing) Act 2000 s 96 (prospectively repealed) (see head (1) above) or under the Criminal Justice Act 2003 s 226A (see head (3) above), s 227 (see head (2) above) or s 236A (see head (3) above) are references to a sentence of detention in a young offender institution: see s 237(3); and PARA 709 note 3.

The Criminal Justice Act 2003 ss 243A–264 do not apply in relation to a person detained in England and Wales in pursuance of a sentence of the International Criminal Court: see the International Criminal Court Act 2001 Sch 7 paras 3(1); and PARA 690. As to the meanings of 'England' and 'Wales' see PARA 4 note 3.

2   Criminal Justice Act 2003 s 263(1)(a) (amended by the Armed Forces Act 2006 Sch 16 para 226, Sch 17). See note 1.

3   Ie under the Criminal Justice Act 2003 Pt 12 Ch 6: s 263(1)(b).

4   Criminal Justice Act 2003 s 263(1)(b). See note 1. See *R v Secretary of State for the Home Department and the Governor of HMP Swaledale, ex p Francois* [1999] 1 AC 43, [1998] 1 All ER 929, HL (considering the position under the Criminal Justice Act 1991, whose provisions concerning the treatment of consecutive or concurrent terms of imprisonment were held not to have the effect of imposing a heavier penalty than the one that was applicable at the time the criminal offence was committed, even if sentences were imposed by different courts on different occasions, since the sentence was not changed, although a longer part of the original sentence would be spent in prison owing to the change in period of early release).

5   Ie nothing in the Criminal Justice Act 2003 Pt 12 Ch 6: s 263(2)(a).

6   As to the Secretary of State for these purposes see **PRISONS AND PRISONERS** vol 85 (2012) PARA 408.

7   Criminal Justice Act 2003 s 263(2)(a). See note 1.

8   Ie if the Criminal Justice Act 2003 s 243A (unconditional release of prisoners serving less than 12 months: see PARA 712) so requires: s 263(2)(aa) (added by the Legal Aid, Sentencing and Punishment of Offenders Act 2012 s 111(2), Sch 14 paras 5, 13(a))). However, see also the Criminal Justice Act 2003 s 256AA (which imposes supervision requirements on offenders aged over 18 on their day of release from sentences of more than 1 day but less than 2 years imposed after 1 February 2015); and PARA 741.

9   Criminal Justice Act 2003 s 263(2)(aa) (as added: see note 8). See note 1. As to the duration and conditions of licences see PARA 735 et seq.

10   Ie the Criminal Justice Act 2003 s 246 (power to release fixed-term prisoners before required term: see PARA 715): s 263(2)(b) (amended by the Legal Aid, Sentencing and Punishment of Offenders Act 2012 s 116(1), (8), Sch 14 paras 5, 13(b)).

11   Ie under the Criminal Justice Act 2003 s 246: s 263(2)(b) (as amended: see note 10).

12   Ie unless and until the Criminal Justice Act 2003 s 246 authorises the Secretary of State: see s 263(2)(b) (as amended: see note 10).

13   Criminal Justice Act 2003 s 263(2)(b) (as amended: see note 10). See note 1.

14   Ie under the Criminal Justice Act 2003 Pt 12 Ch 6: s 263(2)(c) (amended by the Legal Aid, Sentencing and Punishment of Offenders Act 2012 Sch 14 paras 5, 13(c)).

15   Criminal Justice Act 2003 s 263(2)(c) (as amended: see note 14). See note 1.

16   Criminal Justice Act 2003 s 263(2)(c)(i) (s 263(2)(c)(i), (ii) added by the Legal Aid, Sentencing and Punishment of Offenders Act 2012 s 116(1), (9)). See note 1.

17   Criminal Justice Act 2003 s 263(2)(c)(ii) (as added: see note 16). See note 1.

711. Treatment of consecutive terms under the Criminal Justice Act 2003. Where a person (the 'offender') has been sentenced to two or more terms of imprisonment[1] which are to be served consecutively on each other[2], and where the sentences were passed on the same occasion (or, where they were passed on different occasions, the person has not been released under Chapter 6 of Part 12 of the Criminal Justice Act 2003[3] at any time during the period beginning with the first and ending with the last of those occasions)[4], then nothing in Chapter 6 of Part 12 of the Criminal Justice Act 2003[5] requires the Secretary of State[6] to release the offender until he has served a period equal in length to the aggregate of the length of the custodial periods in relation to each of the terms of imprisonment[7].

The offender's release under these provisions is to be unconditional if the aggregate length of the terms of imprisonment is less than 12 months[8] and the statutory duty to release certain prisoners serving less than 12 months[9] so requires in respect of each of the sentences[10], but in any other case is to be on licence[11]. When the offender is released under these provisions (whether unconditionally or on licence), the offender is to be subject to supervision requirements[12] if so required in respect of one or more of the sentences[13].

A court sentencing a person to a term of imprisonment[14] may not order or direct that the term is to commence on the expiry of any other sentence of imprisonment from which he has been released[15] either under Chapter 6 of Part 12 of the Criminal Justice Act 2003[16] or under Part II of the Criminal Justice Act 1991[17].

1   The Criminal Justice Act 2003 s 264 applies to:
    (1)   a determinate sentence of detention under the Powers of Criminal Courts (Sentencing) Act 2000 s 91 (sentence of detention for a specified period passed on a person aged under 18 who has committed a serious offence: see PARA 8; and CHILDREN AND YOUNG PERSONS vol 10 (2012) PARA 1307) or s 96 (prospectively repealed) (detention in young offender institution for a person aged between 18 and 21: see PARA 16) (Criminal Justice Act 2003 s 264(7) (amended by the Legal Aid, Sentencing and Punishment of Offenders Act 2012 ss 111(2), 117(1), (8)(a), (b), 125(4), Sch 14 paras 5, 14(f), Sch 20 paras 1, 12(1), (3); and by the Criminal Justice and Courts Act 2015 Sch 1 para 23)); or
    (2)   a determinate sentence of detention under the Criminal Justice Act 2003 s 227 (repealed with savings) or s 228 (repealed with savings) (s 264(7) (as so amended)); or
    (3)   a sentence of detention in a young offender institution under the Powers of Criminal Courts (Sentencing) Act 2000 s 96 (prospectively repealed) or under the Criminal Justice Act 2003 s 226A (extended sentence for certain violent or sexual offences (persons 18 or over): see PARAS 18–20), s 226B (extended sentence for certain violent or sexual offences (persons under 18): see PARAS 18–20), s 227 or s 236A (special custodial sentence for certain offenders of particular concern: see PARA 32) (s 264(7) (as so amended)),
  as s 264 applies to a term of imprisonment (s 264(7) (as so amended)). References in Pt 12 Ch 6 (ss 237–268) (sentencing: release, licences and recall) (see also PARAS 696, 699, 709 et seq, 712 et seq) to a sentence of detention under the Powers of Criminal Courts (Sentencing) Act 2000 s 96 (prospectively repealed) (see head (1) above) or under the Criminal Justice Act 2003 s 226A (see head (3) above), s 227 (see head (2) above) or s 236A (see head (2) above) are references to a sentence of detention in a young offender institution: see s 237(3); and PARA 709 note 3.
    The Criminal Justice Act 2003 ss 243A–264 do not apply in relation to a person detained in England and Wales in pursuance of a sentence of the International Criminal Court: see the International Criminal Court Act 2001 Sch 7 para 3(1); and PARA 690. As to the meanings of 'England' and 'Wales' see PARA 4 note 3.
2   Criminal Justice Act 2003 s 264(1)(a).
3   Ie under the Criminal Justice Act 2003 Pt 12 Ch 6: s 264(1)(b).
4   Criminal Justice Act 2003 s 264(1)(b). See *R v Secretary of State for the Home Department and the Governor of HMP Swaledale, ex p Francois* [1999] 1 AC 43, [1998] 1 All ER 929, HL.
5   Ie nothing in the Criminal Justice Act 2003 Pt 12 Ch 6: s 264(2) (amended by the Legal Aid, Sentencing and Punishment of Offenders Act 2012 Sch 14 paras 5, 14(a)).

6   As to the Secretary of State for these purposes see PRISONS AND PRISONERS vol 85 (2012) PARA 408.

7   Criminal Justice Act 2003 s 264(2) (as amended: see note 5). For these purposes, 'custodial period' means (by virtue of s 264(6) (substituted by the Criminal Justice and Courts Act 2015 Sch 1 para 23)):

    (1)   in relation to an extended sentence imposed under the Criminal Justice Act 2003 s 226A or s 226B), two-thirds of the appropriate custodial term determined by the court under, as the case may be, s 226A or s 226B;

    (2)   in relation to an extended sentence imposed under s 227 or s 228, one-half of the appropriate custodial term determined by the court under, as the case may be, s 227 or s 228;

    (3)   in relation to a sentence imposed under s 236A, one-half of the appropriate custodial term determined by the court under s 236A; and

    (4)   in relation to any other sentence, one-half of the sentence.

8   Criminal Justice Act 2003 s 264(3B)(a) (ss 264(3B)–(3E), 265B added by the Offender Rehabilitation Act 2014 s 5).

9   Ie the duty under the Criminal Justice Act 2003 s 243A (see PARA 712).

10   Criminal Justice Act 2003 s 264(3B)(a) (as added: see note 8).

11   If the offender is released on licence under these provisions he is to be on licence, on and after the release, until he would, but for the release, have served a term equal in length to the aggregate length of the terms of imprisonment (s 264(3C)(a) (as added: see note 8)) and is to be subject to supervision requirements under s 256AA (see PARA 741) if (and only if) 256AA so requires in respect of one or more of the sentences (s 264(3C)(b)(i) (as so added)) and the aggregate length of the terms of imprisonment is less than 2 years (s 264(3C)(b)(i) (as so added)). If the offender is subject to supervision requirements under s 256AA, the supervision period for those purposes begins on the expiry of the period during which the offender is on licence by virtue of s 264(3C)(a): s 264(3D) (as so added).

    If: (1) the offender is released on licence under these provisions (s 264B(1)(a) (as so added)), the aggregate length of the terms of imprisonment mentioned in s 264(1)(a) (see the text and notes 1–2) is less than 12 months (s 264B(1)(b) (as so added)) and those terms include one or more terms of imprisonment ('short transitional terms') which were imposed in respect of an offence committed before 1 February 2015 (ie the day on which the Offender Rehabilitation Act 2014 s 1 was brought into force by the Offender Rehabilitation Act 2014 (Commencement No 2) Order 2015, SI 2015/40) as well as one or more terms imposed in respect of an offence committed on or after that day (Criminal Justice Act 2003 s 264B(1)(c) (as so added)), the offender is to be on licence until the offender would, but for the release, have served a term equal in length to the aggregate of the custodial period (see note 7) in relation to each of the short transitional terms (s 264B(2)(a), (3) (as so added)), and the full length of each of the other terms (s 264B(3)(b) (as so added)).

12   Ie under the Criminal Justice Act 2003 s 256B (see PARA 745).

13   Criminal Justice Act 2003 s 264(3E) (as added: see note 8).

14   For this purpose 'sentence of imprisonment' includes:

    (1)   a sentence of detention under the Powers of Criminal Courts (Sentencing) Act 2000 s 91 (sentence of detention for a specified period passed on a person aged under 18 who has committed a serious offence: see PARA 8; and CHILDREN AND YOUNG PERSONS vol 10 (2012) PARA 1307) or s 96 (prospectively repealed) (detention in young offender institution for a person aged between 18 and 21: see PARA 16) (Criminal Justice Act 2003 s 265(2) (amended by the Legal Aid, Sentencing and Punishment of Offenders Act 2012 ss 117(1), (9)(a), (b), Sch 20 paras 1, 13; and by the Criminal Justice and Courts Act 2015 Sch 1 para 24)); or

    (2)   a sentence of detention under the Criminal Justice Act 2003 s 227 or s 228 (see s 265(2) (as so amended)); or

    (3)   a sentence of detention in a young offender institution under the Powers of Criminal Courts (Sentencing) Act 2000 s 96 (prospectively repealed) or under the Criminal Justice Act 2003 s 226A, s 226B, s 227 or s 236A (s 265(2) (as so amended)),

and 'term of imprisonment' is to be read accordingly (s 265(2) (as so amended)). As to references to a sentence of detention under the Powers of Criminal Courts (Sentencing) Act 2000 s 96 (prospectively repealed) (see head (1) above) or under the Criminal Justice Act 2003 s 226A (see head (3) above), s 227 (see head (2) above) or s 236A (see head (2) above) see note 1.

15   Criminal Justice Act 2003 s 265(1).

16   Criminal Justice Act 2003 s 265(1)(a) (s 265(1)(a), (b) substituted by the Criminal Justice and Immigration Act 2008 s 20(1), (4)(a)).

17   Criminal Justice Act 2003 s 265(1)(b) (as substituted: see note 16). As to the Criminal Justice Act 1991 Pt II (ss 32–51) (repealed with savings) see PARA 688.

(ii) Release

712. Early release of prisoners serving a sentence of under 12 months. If a fixed-term prisoner[1]:

(1)   is serving a sentence which is for a term of 1 day[2];

(2)   is serving a sentence which is for a term of less than 12 months[3] and is aged under 18 on the last day of the requisite custodial period[4]; or

(3)   is serving a sentence which is for a term of less than 12 months[5] and the sentence was imposed in respect of an offence committed before 1 February 2015[6],

it is the duty of the Secretary of State[7] to release him unconditionally as soon as he has served the requisite custodial period[8].

1   As to the meaning of 'fixed-term prisoner' for the purposes of the Criminal Justice Act 2003 Pt 12 Ch 6 (ss 237–268) (sentencing: release, licences and recall) see PARA 709.
2   Criminal Justice Act 2003 s 243A(1)(a) (s 243A added by the Legal Aid, Sentencing and Punishment of Offenders Act 2012 s 111(1); Criminal Justice Act 2003 s 243A(1), (1A) substituted, s 243A(3) amended, by the Offender Rehabilitation Act 2014 s 1, Sch 3 para 17).
3   Criminal Justice Act 2003 s 243A(1)(b)(i) (as added and substituted: see note 2).
4   Criminal Justice Act 2003 s 243A(1)(b)(ii) (as added and substituted: see note 2). 'The requisite custodial period' is either one-half of the sentence (in relation to a person serving one sentence) or the period determined under s 263(2) (see PARA 710) or s 264(2) (see PARA 711) (in relation to a person serving two or more concurrent or consecutive sentences: s 243A(3) (as so added and amended).
5   Criminal Justice Act 2003 s 243A(1A)(a) (as added and substituted: see note 2).
6   Criminal Justice Act 2003 s 243A(1A)(b) (as added and substituted: see note 2). 1 February 2015 is the day on which the Offender Rehabilitation Act 2014 s 1 was brought into force by the Offender Rehabilitation Act 2014 (Commencement No 2) Order 2015, SI 2015/40.
7   As to the Secretary of State for these purposes see PRISONS AND PRISONERS vol 85 (2012) PARA 408.
8   Criminal Justice Act 2003 s 243A(2) (as added: see note 2). This is subject to s 256B (supervision of young offenders after release: see PARA 745) and Sch 20B para 8 (transitional cases): s 243A(4) (as so added).

713. Early release of fixed-term prisoners serving a sentence of 12 months or more. As soon as a fixed-term prisoner[1], who is serving a sentence which is for a term of 12 months or more[2], other than[3]:

(1)   a prisoner of particular concern who is serving a special sentence sentence[4];

(2)   a prisoner who is serving an extended determinate sentence[5];

(3)   a prisoner who is serving an extended sentence under predecessor legislation[6];

(4)   a prisoner who has been released on home detention curfew and recalled under the Criminal Justice Act 2003[7],

has served the requisite custodial period specified for these purposes[8], it is the duty of the Secretary of State to release that person on licence[9].

1   As to the meaning of 'fixed-term prisoner' for the purposes of the Criminal Justice Act 2003 Pt 12 Ch 6 (ss 237–268) (sentencing: release, licences and recall) see PARA 709. Sections 243A–264 do not apply in relation to a person detained in England and Wales in pursuance of a sentence of the International Criminal Court: see the International Criminal Court Act 2001 Sch 7 para 3(1); and PARA 690. As to the meanings of 'England' and 'Wales' see PARA 4 note 3.
2   Ie other than a prisoner to whom the Criminal Justice Act 2003 s 243A (unconditional release of prisoners serving less than 12 months: see PARA 712) applies: s 244(1) (amended by the Legal

Aid, Sentencing and Punishment of Offenders Act 2012 ss 111(2), 125(1), (2), Sch 14 paras 5, 6(1), (2); and by the Criminal Justice and Courts Act 2015 Sch 1 para 5).

3   Criminal Justice Act 2003 s 244(1) (as amended: see note 2).

4   Ie other than a prisoner to whom the Criminal Justice Act 2003 s 244A (release on licence of prisoners serving sentence under s 236A: see PARAS 32, 714) applies: s 244(1) (as amended: see note 2).

5   Ie other than a prisoner to whom the Criminal Justice Act 2003 s 246A (release on licence of prisoners serving extended sentence under s 226A or s 226B: see PARA 716) applies: s 244(1) (as amended: see note 2).

6   Ie other than a prisoner to whom the Criminal Justice Act 2003 s 247 (release on licence of prisoners serving extended sentence under s 227 or s 228 (both repealed with savings): see PARA 716) applies: s 244(1) (as amended: see note 2).

7   Ie other than a determinate sentence prisoner who has been released on licence and recalled under the Criminal Justice Act 2003 s 254 (see PARA 717), whose further release must be dealt with in accordance with ss 255B, 255C (re-release following recall: see PARA 719).

8   For the purposes of the Criminal Justice Act 2003 s 244 the 'requisite custodial period' means (by virtue of s 244(3) (amended by the Legal Aid, Sentencing and Punishment of Offenders Act 2012 Sch 14 paras 5, 6(1), (3)(a))):

(1)   one-half of his sentence, in relation to a prisoner serving one sentence (Criminal Justice Act 2003 s 244(3)(a) (amended by the Legal Aid, Sentencing and Punishment of Offenders Act 2012 s 117(1), (4), Sch 14 paras 5, 6(1), (3)(b); and by the Offender Rehabilitation Act 2014 Sch 3 para 18)); and

(2)   the period determined under the Criminal Justice Act 2003 s 263(2) (concurrent terms: see PARA 710) and s 264(2) (consecutive terms: see PARA 711), in relation to a person serving two or more concurrent or consecutive sentences (s 244(3)(d) (amended by the Legal Aid, Sentencing and Punishment of Offenders Act 2012 s 89(2), Sch 10 paras 12, 21(1)–(3)).

The Secretary of State may by order provide that any reference in the Criminal Justice Act 2003 s 244(3)(a) (see head (1) above) to a particular proportion of a prisoner's sentence is to be read as a reference to such other proportion of a prisoner's sentence as may be specified in the order: s 267. At the date at which this volume states the law, no such order had been made. As to the Secretary of State for these purposes see PRISONS AND PRISONERS vol 85 (2012) PARA 408.

9   Criminal Justice Act 2003 s 244(1) (as amended: see note 2). The release on licence referred to in the text takes place under s 244: see s 244(1) (as so amended). The provision made by s 244(1) does not apply, however, if the prisoner has been released early on licence incorporating a home detention curfew condition under s 246 (see PARA 715) or s 248 (see PARA 696) and recalled under s 254 (see PARA 717): s 244(1A) (added by the Legal Aid, Sentencing and Punishment of Offenders Act 2012 s 114(2); amended by the Offender Rehabilitation Act 2014 s 9). Provision for the release of such persons as are mentioned in the Criminal Justice Act 2003 s 244(1A) is made instead by s 255B and s 255C: s 244(1A) (as so added).

The provision made by the Criminal Justice Act 2003 s 244 is subject to the transitional arrangements contained in s 267B, Sch 20B para 5 (initial duty to release on licence: see PARA 725), Sch 20B para 6 (duty to release on direction of Parole Board: see PARA 725), Sch 20B para 8 (duty to release extended sentence prisoners on licence: see PARA 725), Sch 20B para 25 (duty to release Criminal Justice Act 1967 sentence prisoners unconditionally: see PARA 727) and the Criminal Justice Act 2003 Sch 20B para 28 (duty to release Criminal Justice Act 1967 sentence prisoners on licence: see PARA 727), which displace the Criminal Justice Act 2003 s 244: s 244(4) (added by the Legal Aid, Sentencing and Punishment of Offenders Act 2012 s 121(6), Sch 17 paras 1, 2).

714.   Release on licence of offenders of particular concern.   Where a prisoner is serving a special custodial sentence for an offender of particular concern[1] the Secretary of State[2] must refer his case to the Parole Board[3] as soon as he has served the requisite custodial period[4] and, where there has been a previous reference of the prisoner's case to the Board under these provisions and the Board did not direct his release, not later than the second anniversary of the disposal of that reference[5]. It is the duty of the Secretary of State to release the prisoner on licence as soon as he has served the requisite custodial period[6] and the Board has directed his release under these provisions[7]. It is the duty of the Secretary of State to release the prisoner on licence as soon as he has served the appropriate custodial term, unless he has previously been released on licence under these provisions and has been[8] recalled[9].

1   Ie a sentence imposed under the Criminal Justice Act 2003 s 236A (and PARA 32).
2   As to the Secretary of State for these purposes see PRISONS AND PRISONERS vol 85 (2012) PARA 408.
3   As to the constitution and functions of the Parole Board, continued by the Criminal Justice Act 2003 s 239(1), see PARA 699 et seq.
4   Criminal Justice Act 2003 s 244A(1), (2)(a) (s 244A added by the Criminal Justice and Courts Act 2015 Sch 1 para 6). 'The requisite custodial period' means one-half of the appropriate custodial term (in relation to a person serving one sentence) and the period determined under the Criminal Justice Act 2003 ss 263(2), 264(2) (see PARAS 710, 711) (in relation to a person serving two or more concurrent or consecutive sentences); and 'the appropriate custodial term' means the term determined as such by the court under s 236A: s 244A(6) (as so added).
5   Criminal Justice Act 2003 s 244A(2)(b) (as added: see note 4).
6   Criminal Justice Act 2003 s 244A(3)(a) (as added: see note 4).
7   Criminal Justice Act 2003 s 244A(3)(b) (as added: see note 4). The Board must not give such a direction unless the Secretary of State has referred the prisoner's case to the Board and the Board is satisfied that it is not necessary for the protection of the public that he should be confined: s 244A(4) (as so added).
8   Ie under the Criminal Justice Act 2003 s 254 (provision for the release of such persons being made by ss 255A–255C): see PARA 717.
9   Criminal Justice Act 2003 s 244A(5) (as added: see note 4).

715. Power to release fixed-term prisoners before required term on home detention curfew. The Secretary of State[1] may[2] release on licence[3] incorporating a home detention curfew condition[4] a fixed-term prisoner[5], at any time during the period of 135 days[6] ending with the day on which the prisoner will have served the requisite custodial period specified for these purposes[7], except where[8]:

(1)   the sentence is an extended sentence imposed for certain violent or sexual offences or a special custodial sentence for an offender of particular concern[9];

(2)   the sentence is for a term of four years or more[10];

(3)   the sentence is imposed for an offence of remaining at large after temporary release[11];

(4)   the prisoner is subject to a hospital order, hospital direction or transfer direction[12];

(5)   the sentence was imposed[13] in a case where the prisoner has failed to comply with a curfew requirement of a community order[14];

(6)   the prisoner is subject to the notification requirements of Part 2 of the Sexual Offences Act 2003[15];

(7)   the prisoner is liable to removal from the United Kingdom[16];

(8)   the prisoner has been released on licence incorporating a home detention curfew condition[17] at any time, and has been recalled to prison[18] for failure to comply with a condition included in his licence, and where the revocation has not been cancelled[19];

(9)   the prisoner is a short-term prisoner who has at any time been released on licence[20] and has been recalled to prison[21] (and the revocation of the licence has not[22] been cancelled)[23];

(10)   the prisoner has been released on licence during the currency of the sentence on compassionate grounds[24], and has been recalled to prison[25];

(11)   the prisoner has at any time been returned to prison under a 'return to custody' order[26];

(12)   in the case of a prisoner whose time remanded in custody has been counted as time served[27], or to whom a direction regarding crediting of

periods of remand relates[28], the interval between the date on which the sentence was passed and the date on which the prisoner will have served the requisite custodial period is less than 14 days[29].

1 As to the Secretary of State for these purposes see PRISONS AND PRISONERS vol 85 (2012) PARA 408.

2 Ie subject to the Criminal Justice Act 2003 s 246(2)–(4) (see note 5; and the text and notes 8–25): s 246(1). Sections 243A–264 do not apply in relation to a person detained in England and Wales in pursuance of a sentence of the International Criminal Court: see the International Criminal Court Act 2001 Sch 7 para 3(1); and PARA 690. As to the meanings of 'England' and 'Wales' see PARA 4 note 3.

3 Ie under the Criminal Justice Act 2003 s 246: s 246(1)(a) (amended by the Legal Aid, Sentencing and Punishment of Offenders Act 2012 Sch 10 para 23(1), (2)(a)).

4 A curfew condition complying with the Criminal Justice Act 2003 s 253 (home detention curfew: see PARA 737) must be included in a licence under s 246: see s 250(5); and PARA 737. As to the meaning of 'curfew condition' see PARA 737 note 4. As to the duration and conditions of licences see PARA 735 et seq. There is no requirement for the discretion to release and recall in respect of home detention curfew to be exercised on the recommendation of a judicial body such as the Parole Board because home detention curfew operates during the part of the sentence when custody is compulsory and before the point at which a prisoner would be released or become eligible for release on the Board's recommendation: *R (on the application of Benson) v Secretary of State for Justice* [2007] EWHC 2055 (Admin), [2007] All ER (D) 120 (Aug); *Mason v Secretary of State for Justice* [2008] EWHC 1787 (QB), [2009] 1 All ER 1128, [2009] 1 WLR 509; *R (on the application of McAlinden) v Secretary of State for the Home Department* [2010] EWHC 1557 (Admin), [2010] All ER (D) 24 (Jul). Accordingly, the review of the lawfulness of detention demanded by the Convention for the Protection of Human Rights and Fundamental Freedoms (Rome, 4 November 1950; TS 71 (1953); Cmd 8969) (the European Convention on Human Rights) art 5.4 (see RIGHTS AND FREEDOMS vol 88A (2013) PARA 210 et seq), at least up to that point, had already been conducted by the sentencing court so that, during the compulsory part of the sentence, release or recall under the home detention curfew policy is simply the administrative implementation of the original sentence: *Mason v Secretary of State for Justice, R (on the application of Whiston) v Secretary of State for Justice* [2012] EWCA Civ 1374, [2014] QB 306, [2013] 2 WLR 1080 (release on home detention curfew is much more closely integrated with the original sentence than is release as of right once the custodial period has been completed). The exercise of the discretion to release and recall under home detention curfew remains reviewable on general public law principles, however: *Mason v Secretary of State for Justice.*

5 As to the meaning of 'fixed-term prisoner' for the purposes of the Criminal Justice Act 2003 Pt 12 Ch 6 (ss 237–268) (sentencing: release, licences and recall) see PARA 709. The provision made by s 246(1)(a) (see the text and notes 3–7) does not apply in relation to a prisoner, however, unless:
    (1)   the length of the requisite custodial period is at least six weeks (s 246(2)(a)); and
    (2)   he has served: (a) at least four weeks of that period (s 246(2)(b)(i) (s 246(2)(b) substituted by the Criminal Justice and Immigration Act 2008 s 24)); and (b) at least one-half of that period (Criminal Justice Act 2003 s 246(2)(b)(ii) (as so substituted)).
    For these purposes the 'requisite custodial period', in relation to a person serving any sentence, has the meaning given by s 243A(3)(a) or (b) (unconditional release of prisoners serving less than 12 months: see PARA 712) or (as the case may be) s 244(3)(a) or (d) (release on licence of prisoners serving 12 months or more: see PARA 713 note 8): s 246(6) (definition amended by the Legal Aid, Sentencing and Punishment of Offenders Act 2012 s 89(2), Sch 10 paras 12, 23(1), (6)(b), Sch 14 paras 5, 7). As to the calculation of sentences see PARAS 710, 711.
    The Secretary of State may by order amend the number of weeks for the time being specified in the Criminal Justice Act 2003 s 246(2)(a) (see head (1) above), or in s 246(2)(b)(i) (see head (2)(a) above) (s 246(5)(b)); and he may by order amend the fraction for the time being specified in s 246(2)(b)(ii) (see head (2)(b) above) (s 246(5)(c) (amended by the Legal Aid, Sentencing and Punishment of Offenders Act 2012 Sch 10 paras 12, 23(1), (5)(b))). At the date at which this volume states the law, no such order had been made in relation to the Criminal Justice Act 2003 s 246(2)(a), (b)(i), (ii).

6 The Secretary of State may by order amend the number of days for the time being specified in the Criminal Justice Act 2003 s 246(1)(a): s 246(5)(a) (amended by the Legal Aid, Sentencing and Punishment of Offenders Act 2012 Sch 10 paras 12, 23(1), (5)(a)). At the date at which this volume states the law, no such order had been made.

7   Criminal Justice Act 2003 s 246(1)(a) (as amended : see note 3).
8   Criminal Justice Act 2003 s 246(4). The provision made by s 246(1) (see the text and notes 1–7) does not apply in the circumstances specified in s 246(4) (see heads (1) to (12) in the text): s 246(4).
9   Criminal Justice Act 2003 s 246(4)(a) (amended by the Legal Aid, Sentencing and Punishment of Offenders Act 2012 s 125(4), Sch 20 paras 1, 5(1), (2); and by the Criminal Justice and Courts Act 2015 Sch 1 para 7). Head (1) in the text refers to a sentence imposed under the Criminal Justice Act 2003 s 226A (extended sentence for certain violent or sexual offences (persons 18 or over): see PARAS 18–20), s 227 (repealed with savings), s 228 (repealed with savings) or s 236A (special custodial sentences for offenders of particular concern: see PARA 32): see s 246(4)(a) (as so amended).
10 Criminal Justice Act 2003 s 246(4)(aa) (added by the Legal Aid, Sentencing and Punishment of Offenders Act 2012 s 112(1), (2))). Where the Criminal Justice Act 2003 s 246(4)(aa) applies to a prisoner who is serving two or more terms of imprisonment, the reference to the term of the sentence is:
    (1)   if the terms are partly concurrent, a reference to the period which begins when the first term begins and ends when the last term ends (s 246(4ZA)(a) (s 246(4ZA) added by the Legal Aid, Sentencing and Punishment of Offenders Act 2012 s 112(1), (5)));
    (2)   if the terms are to be served consecutively, a reference to the aggregate of the terms (Criminal Justice Act 2003 s 246(4ZA)(b) (as so added)).
    For the purposes of s 246, 'term of imprisonment' includes a determinate sentence of detention under:
    (a)   the Powers of Criminal Courts (Sentencing) Act 2000 s 91 (sentence of detention for a specified period passed on a person aged under 18 who has committed a serious offence: see PARA 8; and CHILDREN AND YOUNG PERSONS vol 10 (2012) PARA 1307) or s 96 (prospectively repealed) (detention in young offender institution for a person aged between 18 and 21: see PARA 16) (Criminal Justice Act 2003 s 246(6) (definition of 'term of imprisonment' added by the Legal Aid, Sentencing and Punishment of Offenders Act 2012 s 112(1), (6); amended by Sch 20 paras 1, 5(1), (3); and by the Criminal Justice and Courts Act 2015 Sch 1 para 7)); or
    (b)   the Criminal Justice Act 2003 s 226A, s 226B, s 227, s 228 or s 236A (s 246(6) (definition of 'term of imprisonment' as so added and amended)).
11 Criminal Justice Act 2003 s 246(4)(b). Head (3) in the text refers to a sentence for an offence under the Prisoners (Return to Custody) Act 1995 s 1 (see PRISONS AND PRISONERS vol 85 (2012) PARA 429): see s 246(4)(b).
12 Criminal Justice Act 2003 s 246(4)(c). Head (4) in the text refers to orders or directions under the Mental Health Act 1983 s 37 (hospital orders: see MENTAL HEALTH AND CAPACITY vol 75 (2013) PARA 864; and PARAS 472, 473), s 45A (hospital and limitation directions: see PARA 478), or s 47 (transfer directions: see MENTAL HEALTH AND CAPACITY vol 75 (2013) PARA 892): Criminal Justice Act 2003 s 246(4)(c).
13 Ie by virtue of the Criminal Justice Act 2003 s 179, Sch 8 para 9(1)(b), (c) (community order made by magistrates' court: see PARA 55) or Sch 8 para 10(1)(b), (c) (community order made by Crown Court: see PARA 56): see s 246(4)(d).
14 Criminal Justice Act 2003 s 246(4)(d). The reference in head (5) in the text to a community order includes a service community order or overseas community order under the Armed Forces Act 2006 (see ss 178, 182; and ARMED FORCES vol 3 (2011) PARAS 602, 608): Criminal Justice Act 2003 s 246(4A)(a) (s 246(4A) added by the Armed Forces Act 2006 s 378(1), Sch 16 para 221).
15 Criminal Justice Act 2003 s 246(4)(e). As to the notification requirements of the Sexual Offences Act 2003 Pt 2 (ss 80–136) see PARA 498 et seq.
16 Criminal Justice Act 2003 s 246(4)(f). As to persons liable to removal from the United Kingdom see PARA 749. As to the meaning of 'United Kingdom' see PARA 4 note 3.
17 Ie under the Criminal Justice Act 2003 s 246: see s 246(4)(g) (amended by the Legal Aid, Sentencing and Punishment of Offenders Act 2012 s 112(1), (3)). See note 10.
18 Ie under the Criminal Justice Act 2003 s 255(1)(a) (see PARA 718): s 246(4)(g) (as amended: see note 17).
19 Criminal Justice Act 2003 s 246(4)(g) (as amended: see note 17). The text refers to a revocation that has not been cancelled under s 255(3) (see PARA 718): s 246(4)(g) (as so amended).
20 Ie under the Criminal Justice Act 1991 s 34A (repealed).
21 Ie under the Criminal Justice Act 1991 s 38A(1)(a) (repealed).
22 Ie under the Criminal Justice Act 1991 s 38A(3) (repealed).
23 Criminal Justice Act 2003 s 246(4)(ga) (added by the Criminal Justice and Courts Act 2015 s 15(4)).

24 Ie under the Criminal Justice Act 2003 s 248 (see PARA 696): s 246(4)(h) (amended by the Legal Aid, Sentencing and Punishment of Offenders Act 2012 s 112(1), (4)).

25 Criminal Justice Act 2003 s 246(4)(h) (as amended: see note 24). The text refers to a recall to prison under s 254 (see PARA 717): s 246(4)(h) (as so amended).

26 Criminal Justice Act 2003 s 246(4)(ha) (added by the Legal Aid, Sentencing and Punishment of Offenders Act 2012 s 112(1), (4)). See note 10. Head (11) in the text refers to a prisoner who has at any time been returned to prison under the Criminal Justice Act 1991 s 40 (repealed) or the Powers of Criminal Courts (Sentencing) Act 2000 s 116 (repealed with savings): Criminal Justice Act 2003 s 246(4)(ha) (as so added).

27 Ie a person to whom the Criminal Justice Act 2003 s 240ZA (time remanded in custody to count as time served: terms of imprisonment and detention: see PARA 30) applies: s 246(4)(i) (amended by the Legal Aid, Sentencing and Punishment of Offenders Act 2012 s 110(1), (9)(a), Sch 10 paras 12, 23(1), (4)). The reference in head (12) in the text to the Criminal Justice Act 2003 s 240ZA includes the Armed Forces Act 2006 s 246 (crediting of time in service custody: terms of imprisonment and detention: see ARMED FORCES vol 3 (2011) PARA 596): Criminal Justice Act 2003 s 246(4A)(b) (s 246(4A) as added (see note 14); s 246(4A)(b) amended by the Legal Aid, Sentencing and Punishment of Offenders Act 2012 s 110(1), (9)(b)).

28 Ie a person to whom a direction under the Criminal Justice Act 2003 s 240A (time remanded on bail to count as time served: terms of imprisonment and detention: see PARA 31) relates: s 246(4)(i) (as amended: see note 27).

29 Criminal Justice Act 2003 s 246(4)(i) (as amended: see note 27). The Secretary of State may by order amend the number of days for the time being specified in s 246(4)(i): s 246(5)(a) (as amended: see note 6). At the date at which this volume states the law, no such order had been made.

716. Early release of fixed-term prisoners: extended sentences. In relation to a prisoner who is serving an extended determinate sentences ('EDS') imposed for certain violent or sexual offences[1], it is the duty of the Secretary of State[2] to release him on licence[3] as soon as he has served the requisite custodial period[4] specified for these purposes if:

(1)   the sentence was imposed before 13 April 2015[5];

(2)   the appropriate custodial term is less than ten years[6]; and

(3)   the sentence was not imposed in respect of a listed offence[7].

In any other case it is the duty of the Secretary of State to release the prisoner on licence in accordance with the following provisions[8]:

(a)   the Secretary of State must refer the prisoner's case to the Parole Board[9]: (i) as soon as the prisoner has served the requisite custodial period[10]; and (ii) where there has been a previous such reference of the prisoner's case to the Board[11] and where the Board did not direct his release, not later than the second anniversary of the disposal of that reference[12];

(b)   it is the duty of the Secretary of State to release the prisoner on licence[13] as soon as[14]: (i) the prisoner has served the requisite custodial period[15]; and (ii) the Board has directed his release[16]; and

(c)   it is the duty of the Secretary of State to release the prisoner on licence[17] as soon as the prisoner has served the appropriate custodial term (unless the prisoner has previously been released on licence[18] and recalled)[19].

In relation to a prisoner who is serving an extended sentence imposed for certain violent or sexual offences under predecessor legislation[20], it is the duty of the Secretary of State to release him on licence[21] as soon as he has served the requisite custodial period[22].

1   Ie an extended sentence imposed under the Criminal Justice Act 2003 s 226A (extended sentence for certain violent or sexual offences (persons 18 or over): see PARAS 18–20) or s 226B (extended sentence for certain violent or sexual offences (persons under 18): see PARAS 18–20): s 246A(1) (s 246A added by the Legal Aid, Sentencing and Punishment of Offenders Act 2012 s 125(1), (3)).

    The Criminal Justice Act 2003 ss 243A–264 do not apply in relation to a person detained in England and Wales in pursuance of a sentence of the International Criminal Court: see the International Criminal Court Act 2001 Sch 7 para 3(1); and PARA 690. As to the meanings of 'England' and 'Wales' see PARA 4 note 3.

2   As to the Secretary of State for these purposes see PRISONS AND PRISONERS vol 85 (2012) PARA 408.

3   Ie under the Criminal Justice Act 2003 s 246A: s 246A(2) (as added: see note 1). As to the duration and conditions of licences see PARA 735 et seq.

4   For the purposes of the Criminal Justice Act 2003 s 246A, the 'requisite custodial period' means:
    (1)   two-thirds of the appropriate custodial term, in relation to a person serving one sentence (s 246A(8)(a) (as added: see note 1)); and
    (2)   the period determined under s 263(2) (concurrent terms: see PARA 710) and s 264(2) (consecutive terms: see PARA 711), in relation to a person serving two or more concurrent or consecutive sentences (s 246A(8)(b) (as so added)),
where 'appropriate custodial term' means the term determined as such by the court, as appropriate, under s 226A or s 226B (s 246A(8) (as so added)).

5   Criminal Justice Act 2003 s 246A(2)(a) (as added (see note 1); ss 246A(2)(a)–(c), 247(7) substituted, ss 246A(3), 247(2)(a) amended, by the Criminal Justice and Courts Act 2015 ss 4, 14(3)). 13 April 2015 is the date on which s 4 was brought into force by the Criminal Justice and Courts Act 2015 (Commencement No 1, Saving and Transitional Provisions) Order 2015, SI 2015/778.

6   Criminal Justice Act 2003 s 246A(2)(b) (as added and substituted: see notes 1, 5).

7   Criminal Justice Act 2003 s 246A(2)(c) (as added and substituted: see notes 1, 5). The text refers to an offence listed in Sch 15B Pts 1–3 (offences listed for the purposes of ss 224A, 226A, 246A: see PARA 25) of or in respect of offences that include one or more offences listed in Sch 15B Pts 1–3: s 246A(2)(b) (as so added and substituted).

8   Criminal Justice Act 2003 s 246A(3) (as added and amended: see notes 1, 5). The text refers to the prisoner's release on licence in accordance with s 246A(4)–(7) (see heads (a) to (c) in the text): s 246A(3) (as so added and amended).

9   See the Criminal Justice Act 2003 s 246A(4) (as added: see note 1). As to the constitution and functions of the Parole Board, continued by s 239(1), see PARA 699 et seq.

10   Criminal Justice Act 2003 s 246A(4)(a) (as added: see note 1).

11   Ie where there has been a previous reference of the prisoner's case to the Board under the Criminal Justice Act 2003 s 246A(4): s 246A(4)(b) (as added: see note 1).

12   Criminal Justice Act 2003 s 246A(4)(b) (as added: see note 1).

13   Ie under the Criminal Justice Act 2003 s 246A: s 246A(5) (as added: see note 1).

14   Criminal Justice Act 2003 s 246A(5) (as added: see note 1).

15   Criminal Justice Act 2003 s 246A(5)(a) (as added: see note 1).

16   Criminal Justice Act 2003 s 246A(5)(b) (as added: see note 1). The text refers to the prisoner's release on licence under s 246A following a direction of the Parole Board under s 246A: s 246A(5)(b) (as so added). The Board must not give a direction under s 246A(5), however, unless: (1) the Secretary of State has referred the prisoner's case to the Board (s 246A(6)(a) (as so added)); and (2) the Board is satisfied that it is no longer necessary for the protection of the public that the prisoner should be confined (s 246A(6)(b) (as so added)).

17   Ie under the Criminal Justice Act 2003 s 246A: s 246A(7) (as added: see note 1).

18   Ie under the Criminal Justice Act 2003 s 246A: s 246A(7) (as added: see note 1).

19   Criminal Justice Act 2003 s 246A(7) (as added: see note 1). The text refers to a person who has been recalled under s 254 (recall of prisoners after release on licence: see PARA 717): s 246A(7) (as so added). Provision for the release of such persons is made by s 255C (release after recall: see PARA 719): s 246A(7) (as so added).

20   Ie imposed under the Criminal Justice Act 2003 s 227 (repealed with savings) or s 228 (repealed with savings): s 247(1).
    In its application to a person serving a sentence imposed before 14 July 2008, s 247 is subject to the transitional arrangements contained in s 267B, Sch 20B para 15 (release on licence of certain extended sentence prisoners on direction of Parole Board: see PARA 726), which modifies s 247 for those purposes: s 247(8) (added by the Legal Aid, Sentencing and Punishment of Offenders Act 2012 s 121(6), Sch 17 paras 1, 3). As to the significance of the date of 14 July 2008 see PARA 722 note 11.

21   Criminal Justice Act 2003 s 247(1), (2).

22   Criminal Justice Act 2003 s 247(2)(a) (as amended (see note 5); amended by the Criminal Justice and Immigration Act 2008 ss 25(1), (2)(a), 149, Sch 28 Pt 2). In this context 'the requisite custodial period' means:

(1) one-half of the appropriate custodial term, in relation to a person serving one sentence (Criminal Justice Act 2003 s 247(7) (as so substituted)); and

(2) the period determined under s 263(2) (see PARA 710) and s 264(2) (see PARA 711), in relation to a person serving two or more concurrent or consecutive sentences (s 247(7) (as so substituted)),

and the 'appropriate custodial term' means the period determined by the court as the appropriate custodial term under s 227 or s 228: s 247(7).

The Secretary of State may by order provide that any reference in s 247(2) to a particular proportion of a prisoner's sentence is to be read as a reference to such other proportion of a prisoner's sentence as may be specified in the order: s 267. At the date at which this volume states the law, no such order had been made.

(iii) Recall

717. General power under the Criminal Justice Act 2003 to revoke licence and recall released person to prison. The Secretary of State[1] may, in the case of any determinate sentence prisoner who has been released on licence under the Criminal Justice Act 2003[2], revoke his licence and recall him to prison[3]. A person recalled to prison in this way[4]:

(1) may make representations in writing with respect to his recall[5]; and

(2) on his return to prison, he must be informed of the reasons for his recall and of his right to make representations[6].

When a person's licence is revoked, he is liable to be detained in pursuance of his sentence and, if at large, is to be treated as being unlawfully at large[7]. Such a revocation[8] may be cancelled, however, by the Secretary of State, after considering any representations under head (1) above, or any other matters[9], but only if he is satisfied that the person recalled has complied with all the conditions specified in the licence[10]. Where the revocation of a person's licence is so cancelled, the person is to be treated as if the recall[11] had not happened[12].

1 As to the Secretary of State for these purposes see PRISONS AND PRISONERS vol 85 (2012) PARA 408.

2 Ie released on licence under the Criminal Justice Act 2003 Pt 12 Ch 6 (ss 237–268) (sentencing: release, licences and recall) (see also PARAS 696, 699, 709 et seq, 718 et seq): s 254(1). As to the duration and conditions of licences see PARA 735 et seq. Indeterminate sentence prisoners are released and recalled under the Crime (Sentences) Act 1997 Pt II Ch II (ss 28–34) (life sentences): see PARA 708. The Criminal Justice Act 2003 ss 243A–264 do not apply in relation to a person detained in England and Wales in pursuance of a sentence of the International Criminal Court: see the International Criminal Court Act 2001 Sch 7 para 3(1); and PARA 690. As to the meanings of 'England' and 'Wales' see PARA 4 note 3.

3 Criminal Justice Act 2003 s 254(1). A person recalled to prison under s 254 or s 255 (see PARA 718) commits an offence if he has been notified of the recall orally or in writing (s 255ZA(1)(a) (s 255ZA added by the Criminal Justice and Courts Act 2015 s 12(2), (3)) and while unlawfully at large fails, without reasonable excuse, to take all necessary steps to return to prison as soon as possible (Criminal Justice Act 2003 s 255ZA(1)(b) (as so added)). A person is to be treated for the purposes of s 255ZA(1)(a) as having been notified of the recall if written notice of the recall has been delivered to an appropriate address (s 255ZA(2)(a) (as so added)) and a period specified in the notice has elapsed (s 255ZA(2)(b) (as so added)). In s 255ZA(2) 'an appropriate address' means an address at which, under the person's licence, the person is permitted to reside or stay (s 255ZA(3)(a) (as so added)) or an address nominated, in accordance with the person's licence, for these purposes (s 255ZA(3)(b) (as so added)). A person is also to be treated for the purposes of s 255ZA(1)(a) as having been notified of the recall if his licence requires him to keep in touch in accordance with any instructions given by an officer of a provider of probation services (s 255ZA(4)(a) (as so added)), he has failed to comply with such an instruction (s 255ZA(4)(b) (as so added)), and he has not complied with such an instruction for at least 6 months (s 255ZA(4)(c) (as so added)). A person who is guilty of an offence under s 255ZA is liable on conviction on indictment to imprisonment for a term not exceeding 2 years or a fine (or both) (s 255ZA(5)(a) (as so added)) or on summary conviction to imprisonment for a term not exceeding 12 months or a fine (or both) (s 255ZA(5)(b) (as so added)). In relation to an

offence committed before the coming into force of s 154(1) (general limit of magistrates' courts' power to impose imprisonment: not yet in force) the reference in the Criminal Justice Act 2003 s 255ZA(5)(b) to 12 months is to be read as a reference to 6 months: s 255ZA(6) (as so added). In relation to an offence committed before the coming into force of the Legal Aid, Sentencing and Punishment of Offenders Act 2012 s 85 (removal of limit on certain fines on conviction by magistrates' court: see PARA 176), the reference in the Criminal Justice Act 2003 s 255ZA(5)(b) to a fine is to be read as a reference to a fine not exceeding the statutory maximum: s 255ZA(7) (as so added). As to the standard scale, the statutory maximum, the prescribed sum, and magistrates' powers to levy unlimited fines see PARA 176.

Nothing in s 254 applies in relation to a person recalled under s 255 (recall of prisoners released early under home detention curfew: see PARA 718), however: s 254(7) (amended by the Criminal Justice and Immigration Act 2008 s 29(1)(b)). Subject to this provision, s 254 governs the recall process in all cases of release after 4 April 2005: *R (on the application of Uttley) v Secretary of State for the Home Department* [2004] UKHL 38, [2004] 4 All ER 1, [2004] 1 WLR 2278; *R (on the application of Stellato) v Secretary of State for the Home Department* [2007] UKHL 5, [2007] 2 AC 70, [2007] 2 All ER 737; and see *R (on the application of Buddington) v Secretary of State for the Home Department* [2006] EWCA Civ 280, [2006] 2 Cr App Rep (S) 715, [2006] All ER (D) 402 (Mar); *R (on the application of Young) v Secretary of State for Justice* [2009] EWHC 2675 (Admin), [2009] All ER (D) 20 (Nov). As to the recall process in cases of release made before 4 April 2005 see PARAS 726, 728.

Recall occurs when the Secretary of State issues a determination to that effect, and is a natural corollary to revocation: *Roberts v Secretary of State for the Home Department* [2005] EWCA Civ 1663, [2006] 1 WLR 843, (2005) Times, 2 December (considering wording of the Criminal Justice Act 1991 s 39 (repealed)).

A prisoner recalled under the Criminal Justice Act 2003 s 254 is entitled to have the lawfulness of a decision to recall him determined speedily by a court: see *R (on the application of Smith) v Parole Board, R (on the application of West) v Parole Board* [2005] UKHL 1, [2005] 1 All ER 755, [2005] 1 WLR 350; the Convention for the Protection of Human Rights and Fundamental Freedoms (Rome, 4 November 1950; TS 71 (1953); Cmd 8969) (the European Convention on Human Rights) art 5.4 (ie everyone who is deprived of his liberty by arrest or detention is entitled to take proceedings by which the lawfulness of his detention is to be decided speedily by a court and his release ordered if the detention is not lawful: see RIGHTS AND FREEDOMS vol 88A (2013) PARA 210 et seq); and see PARA 700.

4 Criminal Justice Act 2003 s 254(2).
5 Criminal Justice Act 2003 s 254(2)(a). The right to make representations at any stage is a guard against arbitrary detention and it can be exercised on recall and before physical return to prison: *Roberts v Secretary of State for the Home Department* [2005] EWCA Civ 1663, [2006] 1 WLR 843, (2005) Times, 2 December (considering wording of the Criminal Justice Act 1991 s 39 (repealed)).
6 Criminal Justice Act 2003 s 254(2)(b).
7 Criminal Justice Act 2003 s 254(6). As to prisoners unlawfully at large see PRISONS AND PRISONERS vol 85 (2012) PARA 429.
8 Ie a revocation under the Criminal Justice Act 2003 s 254 (see the text and notes 1–3): s 254(2A) (s 254(2A)–(2C) added by the Legal Aid, Sentencing and Punishment of Offenders Act 2012 s 113(1)).
9 Criminal Justice Act 2003 s 254(2A) (as added: see note 8).
10 Criminal Justice Act 2003 s 254(2B) (as added: see note 8).
11 Ie the recall under the Criminal Justice Act 2003 s 254(1) (see the text and notes 1–3): s 254(2C) (as added: see note 8).
12 Criminal Justice Act 2003 s 254(2C) (as added: see note 8).

718.   Specific power to revoke licence and recall fixed-term prisoner released early under home detention curfew. If it appears to the Secretary of State[1], as regards a fixed-term prisoner[2] released on licence[3] incorporating a home detention curfew condition[4]:

(1)   that he has failed to comply with the curfew condition included in his licence[5]; or

(2)   that his whereabouts can no longer be electronically monitored at the place for the time being specified in the curfew condition included in his licence[6],

the Secretary of State may, if the curfew condition is still in force, revoke the licence and recall the person to prison[7]. A person whose licence incorporating a home detention curfew condition[8] is revoked in this way[9]:

(a) may make representations in writing with respect to the revocation[10]; and

(b) on his return to prison, must be informed of the reasons for the revocation and of his right to make representations[11].

The Secretary of State, after considering any representations under head (a) above or any other matters[12], may cancel a revocation so made[13]; and, where the revocation of a person's licence is cancelled in this way, the person is to be treated for the purposes of his release under home detention curfew[14] as if he had not been recalled[15] to prison[16].

On the revocation of a person's licence following his release under home detention curfew[17], he is liable to be detained in pursuance of his sentence and, if at large, is to be treated as being unlawfully at large[18].

1 As to the Secretary of State for these purposes see PRISONS AND PRISONERS vol 85 (2012) PARA 408.

2 As to the meaning of 'fixed-term prisoner' for the purposes of the Criminal Justice Act 2003 Pt 12 Ch 6 (ss 237–268) (sentencing: release, licences and recall) see PARA 709. The Criminal Justice Act 2003 ss 243A–264 do not apply in relation to a person detained in England and Wales in pursuance of a sentence of the International Criminal Court: see the International Criminal Court Act 2001 Sch 7 para 3(1); and PARA 690. As to the meanings of 'England' and 'Wales' see PARA 4 note 3.

3 Ie released on licence under the Criminal Justice Act 2003 s 246 (power to release prisoners before required term: see PARA 715): see s 255(1). A curfew condition complying with s 253 (home detention curfew: see PARA 737) must be included in a licence under s 246: see s 250(5); and PARA 737. As to the meaning of 'curfew condition' see PARA 737 note 4. As to the duration and conditions of licences see PARA 735 et seq.

4 Criminal Justice Act 2003 s 255(1).

5 Criminal Justice Act 2003 s 255(1)(a) (amended by the Offender Rehabilitation Act 2014 s 9(3)). There is no requirement for the case of a prisoner recalled under the Criminal Justice Act 2003 s 255 to have that decision reviewed by a court since release prior to completion of the requisite period is a matter of administrative discretion: *R (on the application of Benson) v Secretary of State for Justice* [2007] EWHC 2055 (Admin), [2007] All ER (D) 120 (Aug); *Mason v Secretary of State for Justice* [2008] EWHC 1787 (QB), [2009] 1 All ER 1128, [2009] 1 WLR 509; *R (on the application of McAlinden) v Secretary of State for the Home Department* [2010] EWHC 1557 (Admin), [2010] All ER (D) 24 (Jul). The power available under the Criminal Justice Act 2003 s 255 is not only applicable where there has been a breach of a curfew condition: see *R (on the application of Ramsden) v Secretary of State for the Home Department, R (on the application of Naylor) v Secretary of State for the Home Department* [2006] EWHC 3502 (Admin) at [32], [2006] All ER (D) 167 (Dec) at [32] per Toulson J (obiter).

The consequences of recall are quite different under the Criminal Justice Act 2003 s 254 and s 255 because s 254 (general power to revoke licence and recall released person to prison: see PARA 717) is a stronger power and therefore subject to the scrutiny of the Parole Board, which decides in the first instance whether the recall should be confirmed, and, if so, determines when the prisoner should be released (see PARA 719 et seq), whilst under s 255 the Parole Board has no involvement and his recall continues until the point at which the prisoner becomes entitled to automatic release under s 244 (duty to release fixed-term prisoners: see PARA 713). On the proper construction of s 254 and s 255, it is clear that mutual exclusivity was not intended by the drafters so that the existence of powers under s 255 does not preclude the use of the powers under s 254: see *R (on the application of Ramsden) v Secretary of State for the Home Department, R (on the application of Naylor) v Secretary of State for the Home Department* at [32] per Toulson J (obiter). The guiding principle must be that, as with any exercise of public powers, the holder has to consider whether it is necessary and appropriate to use them in the particular circumstances; given that one set of powers is, in a practical sense, stronger than the other set, the stronger power should only be used if he judges that the public interest requires it but it would not be right for the weaker power to be ignored and so become a dead letter in circumstances where it may be adequate: see *R (on the application of Ramsden) v Secretary of*

State for the Home Department, R (on the application of Naylor) v Secretary of State for the Home Department at [32] per Toulson J (obiter).

6　Criminal Justice Act 2003 s 255(1)(b). As to the home detention curfew scheme condition see note 3; and see also note 5.

7　Criminal Justice Act 2003 s 255(1). The licence is revoked and the recall made, as mentioned in the text, under s 255: s 255(1). A person recalled under these provisions commits an offence if he fails to answer the recall: see s 255ZA; and PARA 718 note 3.

　　Because the procedure under s 255 incorporates an appeal process, and because any decision made under s 255 is amenable to judicial review under general public law principles, revocation under s 255 does not engage the guarantees of the Convention for the Protection of Human Rights and Fundamental Freedoms (Rome, 4 November 1950; TS 71 (1953); Cmd 8969) (the European Convention on Human Rights) art 5.4 (i e that everyone who is deprived of his liberty by arrest or detention is entitled to take proceedings by which the lawfulness of his detention is to be decided speedily by a court and his release ordered if the detention is not lawful: see RIGHTS AND FREEDOMS vol 88A (2013) PARA 210 et seq), whose requirements are satisfied by the original sentencing court to the extent that a judicial body such as the Parole Board is not required to consider the matter: *R (on the application of Benson) v Secretary of State for Justice* [2007] EWHC 2055 (Admin), [2007] All ER (D) 120 (Aug) (judicial review of decision to recall prisoner for alleged breach of home detention curfew scheme conditions; European Convention on Human Rights art 5.4 does not apply); *R (on the application of McAlinden) v Secretary of State for the Home Department* [2010] EWHC 1557 (Admin), [2010] All ER (D) 24 (Jul); *R (on the application of Whiston) v Secretary of State for Justice* [2014] UKSC 39, [2015] AC 176, [2014] 4 All ER 251.

8　Ie a licence under the Criminal Justice Act 2003 s 246 (power to release prisoners before required term: see PARA 715): s 255(2).

9　Criminal Justice Act 2003 s 255(2). The text refers to a licence that has been revoked under s 255: s 255(2).

10　Criminal Justice Act 2003 s 255(2)(a). As to the making of representations with respect to recall see PARA 717 note 5.

11　Criminal Justice Act 2003 s 255(2)(b).

12　See *R (on the application of Davies) v Secretary of State for the Home Department* [2000] All ER (D) 1856, (2000) Independent, 23 November, CA (ample material was available to enable a reasonable Secretary of State to take the view that it was necessary to revoke the applicant's licence and the applicant's denial and contradiction of that material was insufficient in the circumstances to require the Secretary of State to make any further enquiries before acting on it).

13　Criminal Justice Act 2003 s 255(3) (amended by the Legal Aid, Sentencing and Punishment of Offenders Act 2012 s 113(2)).

14　Ie for the purposes of the Criminal Justice Act 2003 s 246: s 255(4).

15　Ie under the Criminal Justice Act 2003 s 255: s 255(4).

16　Criminal Justice Act 2003 s 255(4).

17　Ie on the revocation of a person's licence under the Criminal Justice Act 2003 s 246: s 255(5).

18　Criminal Justice Act 2003 s 255(5). As to prisoners unlawfully at large see PRISONS AND PRISONERS vol 85 (2012) PARA 429.

(iv) Further Release

719. Fixed-term recalls and re-release following recall. The Secretary of State[1] must, on recalling a person who is serving a determinate sentence (other than an extended sentence prisoner[2]), consider whether the person is suitable for automatic release[3]. A person is suitable for automatic release only if the Secretary of State is satisfied that he will not present a risk of serious harm to members of the public if he is released at the end of the automatic release period[4]: however, as from a day to be appointed it is provided that a person is not suitable for automatic release if it appears to the Secretary of State that he is highly likely to breach a condition included in his licence if released at the end of the automatic release period[5] and for that reason, the Secretary of State considers that it would not be appropriate to release him at the end of that period[6].

A determinate sentence prisoner (other than an extended sentence prisoner) who has been recalled must be dealt with:

(1)   in accordance with the automatic release provisions[7], if he is suitable for automatic release[8];

(2)   in accordance with the alternative provisions[9] otherwise[10].

although this is subject to the provisions relating to unconditional release[11].

Further to head (1) above, a prisoner who is suitable for automatic release:

(a)   must, on return to prison, be informed that he will be released[12]; and

(b)   must, at the end of the automatic release period[13], be released by the Secretary of State on licence under Chapter 6 of Part 12 of the Criminal Justice Act 2003[14], unless he has already been released before that date[15].

The Secretary of State may, at any time after such a prisoner is returned to prison, release him again on licence[16]; however, the Secretary of State must not release a person in this way unless he is satisfied that it is not necessary for the protection of the public that the prisoner should remain in prison until the end of the period mentioned in head (b) above[17]; and as from a day to be appointed the Secretary of State must not release a person in this way if it appears to the Secretary of State that, if released, the person is highly likely to breach a condition included in his licence[18] and for that reason, the Secretary of State considers that it is not appropriate so to release him[19]. If a prisoner who is suitable for automatic release makes representations with respect to his recall[20] before the end of the period mentioned in head (b) above, the Secretary of State must refer his case to the Parole Board[21] (or, as from a day to be appointed, a recall adjudicator[22]) on the making of those representations[23].

Where head (1) above does not apply, either because the prisoner is an extended sentence prisoner[24] or because he is not considered suitable for automatic release[25], the Secretary of State may, at any time after such a prisoner is returned to prison, release him again on licence under Chapter 6 of Part 12 of the Criminal Justice Act 2003[26]. However, the Secretary of State must not release such a person in this way unless he is satisfied that it is not necessary for the protection of the public that the person should remain in prison[27]; and as from a day to be appointed the Secretary of State must not release a person in this way if it appears to the Secretary of State that, if released, the person is highly likely to breach a condition included in his licence[28] and for that reason, the Secretary of State considers that it is not appropriate so to release him[29].

The Secretary of State must refer such a case to the Parole Board (or, as from a day to be appointed, a recall adjudicator)[30]:

(i)   if the prisoner makes representations in writing with respect to his recall[31] before the end of the period of 28 days beginning with the date on which he returns to custody[32], on the making of those representations[33]; or

(ii)   if, at the end of that period, the prisoner has not been released again[34] and has not made such representations, at that time[35].

1   As to the Secretary of State for these purposes see PRISONS AND PRISONERS vol 85 (2012) PARA 408.

2   A prisoner is an 'extended sentence prisoner' for these purposes if he is serving an extended sentence imposed under the Criminal Justice Act 2003 s 226A (extended sentence for certain violent or sexual offences (persons 18 or over): see PARAS 18–20), s 226B (extended sentence for certain violent or sexual offences (persons under 18): see PARAS 18–20), s 227 (repealed with savings) or s 228 (repealed with savings), or under the Powers of Criminal Courts (Sentencing) Act 2000 s 85 (repealed): Criminal Justice Act 2003 s 255A(7) (ss 255A–255C substituted by the Legal Aid, Sentencing and Punishment of Offenders Act 2012 s 114(1); Criminal Justice Act 2003 s 255A(7) amended by the Legal Aid, Sentencing and Punishment of Offenders Act 2012 s 125(4), Sch 20 para 7). The reference to the Powers of Criminal Courts (Sentencing)

Act 2000 s 85 includes, in accordance with s 165, Sch 11 para 1(3), a reference to a sentence under the Crime and Disorder Act 1998 s 58 (repealed): Criminal Justice Act 2003 s 255A(7) (as so substituted).

The Criminal Justice Act 2003 ss 243A–264 do not apply in relation to a person detained in England and Wales in pursuance of a sentence of the International Criminal Court: see the International Criminal Court Act 2001 Sch 7 para 3(1); and PARA 690. As to the meanings of 'England' and 'Wales' see PARA 4 note 3.

3   Criminal Justice Act 2003 s 255A(2) (as substituted: see note 2). 'Automatic release' means release at the end of the automatic release period: s 255A(8) (as so substituted; ss 255A(4), (5), 255B(1)(b) amended, s 255A(8)–(10) added, by the Offender Rehabilitation Act 2014 s 9(4)). In the case of a person recalled under the Criminal Justice Act 2003 s 254 (see PARA 717) while on licence under a provision of Pt 12 Ch 6 (ss 237–268) (sentencing: release, licences and recall) (see also PARAS 696, 699, 709 et seq, 720 et seq): other than s 246 (see PARA 715), 'the automatic release period' means the period of 14 days beginning with the day on which the person returns to custody (where the person is serving a sentence of less than 12 months) (s 255A(9)(a) (as so substituted and added)) or the period of 28 days beginning with that day (where the person is serving a sentence of 12 months or more) (s 255A(9)(b) (as so substituted and added)). In the case of a person recalled under s 254 while on licence under s 246, 'the automatic release period' means whichever of the period described in s 255A(9)(a) or (b) (as appropriate), and the requisite custodial period which the person would have served under s 243A or s 244 but for the earlier release, ends later: s 255A(10) (as so substituted and added). A person returns to custody for this purpose when that person, having been recalled, is detained (whether or not in prison) in pursuance of the sentence: s 255A(6) (as so substituted).

The provision made by s 255A applies for the purpose of identifying which of s 255B (see the text and notes 12–23) or s 255C (see the text and notes 24–35) governs the further release of a person who has been recalled under s 254: s 255A(1) (as so substituted).

4   Criminal Justice Act 2003 s 255A(4) (as substituted and amended: see notes 2, 3). As to the phrase 'risk of serious harm' in this context see *R (on the application of Bektas) v Probation Service* [2009] EWHC 2359 (Admin) at [23], [2009] All ER (D) 69 (Aug) at [23] per Rabinder Singh QC (sitting as a deputy High Court judge) (the provision is negatively expressed but the Secretary of State must be satisfied that the prisoner would not pose a risk if released). See also *R (on the application of Oakes) v Secretary of State for Justice* [2009] EWHC 3470 (Admin), [2010] All ER (D) 150 (Mar); affd [2010] EWCA Civ 1169, [2011] 1 WLR 321, [2010] All ER (D) 211 (Oct). Compare the phrase 'the protection of the public' which is used in the Criminal Justice Act 2003 s 255C(3) (see the text and note 27).

5   Criminal Justice Act 2003 s 255A(4A)(a) (as substituted (see note 2); ss 255A(4A), 255B(3A), (4A)–(4C), 255C(3A), (4A)–(4C), 256AZA prospectively added, ss 255B(2), (4), 255C(2), (4) prospectively amended, ss 255B(5), 255C(5) prospectively substituted, by the Criminal Justice and Courts Act 2015 ss 9(2)–(4), 10(1)). At the date at which this volume states the law no day had been appointed for this purpose.

As from a day to be appointed the Secretary of State may by order change the test to be applied by the Secretary of State in deciding under the Criminal Justice Act 2003 s 255A whether a person is suitable for automatic release: s 256AZA(1)(a) (as so prospectively added). An order under s 256AZA(1) may, in particular apply to persons recalled before the day on which it comes into force as well as to persons recalled on or after that day and amend Pt 12 Ch 6: s 256AZA(2) (as so prospectively added). At the date at which this volume states the law no such order had been made.

6   Criminal Justice Act 2003 s 255A(4A)(b) (as substituted and prospectively added: see notes 2, 5).

7   Ie in accordance with the Criminal Justice Act 2003 s 255B (see the text and notes 11–22): s 255A(5)(a) (as substituted: see note 2).

8   Criminal Justice Act 2003 s 255A(5)(a) (as substituted: see note 2).

9   Ie in accordance with the Criminal Justice Act 2003 s 255C (see the text and notes 23–34): s 255A(5)(b) (as substituted: see note 2).

10   Criminal Justice Act 2003 s 255A(5)(b) (as substituted: see note 2).

11   Criminal Justice Act 2003 s 255A(5) (as substituted and amended: see notes 2, 3).

12   Criminal Justice Act 2003 s 255B(1)(a) (as substituted: see note 2). The release takes place under s 255B but is subject to s 255B(8), (9): see s 255B(1)(a) (as so substituted). Accordingly, if the Secretary of State, after the prisoner has been informed that he is to be released under s 255B, receives further information about the prisoner, whether or not relating to any time before the prisoner was recalled (s 255B(8) (as so substituted)), then, if the Secretary of State determines, having regard to that and any other relevant information, that the prisoner is not suitable for automatic release (s 255B(9) (as so substituted)):

(1) the Secretary of State must inform the prisoner that he is not to be released under s 255B (s 255B(9)(a) (as so substituted)); and

(2) the provisions of s 255C apply to the prisoner as if the Secretary of State had determined, on the prisoner's recall, that he was not suitable for automatic release (s 255B(9)(b) (as so substituted)).

13 Ie at the end of the period defined in the Criminal Justice Act 2003 s 255A(9), (10) (see note 3): s 255B(1)(b) (as substituted and amended: see notes 2, 3).

14 Ie under the Criminal Justice Act 2003 Pt 12 Ch 6: s 255B(1)(b) (as substituted and amended: see notes 2, 3). As to the duration and conditions of licences see PARA 735 et seq.

15 Criminal Justice Act 2003 s 255B(1)(b) (as substituted and amended: see notes 2, 3). The text refers to a prisoner who has already been released under s 255B(2) (see the text and note 16) or s 255B(5) (see note 23): s 255B(1)(b) (as so substituted and amended).

16 Criminal Justice Act 2003 s 255B(2) (as substituted and prospectively amended: see notes 2, 5). Section 255B(2) is subject to s 255B(3), (3A) (see the text and notes 17–19): s 255B(2) (as so substituted and prospectively amended).The prisoner is released again on licence as mentioned in the text under Pt 12 Ch 6: s 255B(2) (as so substituted and prospectively amended).

As from a day to be appointed the Secretary of State may by order change the tests to be applied by the Secretary of State in deciding whether to release a person under s 255B(2): s 256AZA(1)(b) (as so prospectively added). See also s 256AZA(2); and note 5. At the date at which this volume states the law no such order had been made.

17 Criminal Justice Act 2003 s 255B(3) (as substituted: see note 2).

18 Criminal Justice Act 2003 s 255B(3A)(a) (as substituted and prospectively added: see notes 2, 5).

19 Criminal Justice Act 2003 s 255B(3A)(b) (as substituted and prospectively added: see notes 2, 5).

20 Ie if he makes representations under the Criminal Justice Act 2003 s 254(2) (see PARA 717): s 255A(4) (as substituted and prospectively amended: see notes 2, 5).

21 As to the constitution and functions of the Parole Board, continued by the Criminal Justice Act 2003 s 239(1), see PARA 699.

22 As to recall adjudicators see PARA 705.

23 Criminal Justice Act 2003 s 255B(4) (as substituted and prospectively amended: see notes 2, 5). Until a day to be appointed, where on such a reference the Parole Board directs the prisoner's immediate release on licence under Pt 12 Ch 6, the Secretary of State must give effect to the direction (s 255B(5) (as so substituted and prospectively amended)); as from that day, on such a reference the recall adjudicator must determine the reference by directing the person's immediate release on licence under Pt 12 Ch 6 (s 255B(4A)(a) (as so substituted and prospectively amended)), directing his release on licence thereunder as soon as conditions specified in the direction are met (s 255B(4A)(b) (as so substituted and prospectively amended)), or giving no direction as to his release (s 255B(4A)(c) (as so substituted and prospectively amended)). The recall adjudicator must not give a direction under s 255B(4A)(a) or (b) unless satisfied that it is not necessary for the protection of the public that the person should remain in prison until the end of the period mentioned in s 255B(1)(b): s 255B(4B) (as so substituted and prospectively amended). The recall adjudicator must not give a direction under s 255B(4A)(a) or (b) if it appears to the recall adjudicator that, if released, the person is highly likely to breach a condition included in P's licence (s 255B(4C)(a) (as so substituted and prospectively amended)) and for that reason, the recall adjudicator considers that it is not appropriate to give the direction (s 255B(4C)(b) (as so substituted and prospectively amended)). The Secretary of State must give effect to any direction under s 255B(4A)(a) or (b): s 255B(5) (as so substituted and prospectively substituted).

If the prisoner who is suitable for automatic release is recalled before the date on which he would (but for the earlier release) have served the requisite custodial period for the purposes of s 243A (unconditional release of prisoners serving less than 12 months: see PARA 712) or (as the case may be) s 244 (release on licence of prisoners serving 12 months or more: see PARA 713) (s 255B(6) (as so substituted)), then:

(1) if the prisoner is released under s 255B before that date, his licence must include a curfew condition complying with s 253 (home detention curfew: see PARA 737) (s 255B(7)(a) (as so substituted)); and

(2) the prisoner is not to be so released, despite s 255B(1)(b) (see head (b) in the text) and s 255B(5), unless the Secretary of State is satisfied that arrangements are in place to enable that condition to be complied with (s 255B(7)(b) (as so substituted)).

As from a day to be appointed the Secretary of State may by order change the tests to be applied by the recall adjudicator in deciding how to determine a reference under s 255B(4): s 256AZA(1)(c) (as so prospectively added). See also s 256AZA(2); and note 5. At the date at which this volume states the law no such order had been made.

24 Criminal Justice Act 2003 s 255C(1)(a) (as substituted: see note 2).
25 Criminal Justice Act 2003 s 255C(1)(b) (as substituted: see note 2).
26 Criminal Justice Act 2003 s 255C(2) (as substituted and prospectively amended: see notes 2, 5).
Section 255C(2) is subject to s 255C(3), (3A) (see the text and notes 27–29): s 255C(2) (as so
substituted and prospectively amended).
    As from a day to be appointed the Secretary of State may by order change the tests to be
applied by the Secretary of State in deciding whether to release a person under s 255C(2):
s 256AZA(1)(b) (as so prospectively added). See also s 256AZA(2); and note 5. At the date at
which this volume states the law no such order had been made.
27 Criminal Justice Act 2003 s 255C(3) (as substituted: see note 2). As to the use of the expression
'protection of the public' for these purposes see *R (on the application of Oakes) v Secretary of
State for Justice* [2010] EWCA Civ 1169, [2011] 1 WLR 321, [2010] All ER (D) 211 (Oct).
28 Criminal Justice Act 2003 s 255C(3A)(a) (as substituted and prospectively added: see
notes 2, 5).
29 Criminal Justice Act 2003 s 255C(3A)(b) (as substituted and prospectively added: see
notes 2, 5).
30 Criminal Justice Act 2003 s 255C(4) (as substituted and prospectively amended: see notes 2, 5).
Until a day to be appointed, where on such a reference the Parole Board directs the prisoner's
immediate release on licence under Pt 12 Ch 6, the Secretary of State must give effect to the
direction (s 255C(5) (as so substituted and prospectively amended)); as from that day, on such a
reference the recall adjudicator must determine the reference by directing the person's immediate
release on licence under Pt 12 Ch 6 (s 255C(4A)(a) (as so substituted and prospectively
amended)), directing his release on licence thereunder as soon as conditions specified in the
direction are met (s 255C(4A)(b) (as so substituted and prospectively amended)), or giving no
direction as to his release (s 255C(4A)(c) (as so substituted and prospectively amended)). The
recall adjudicator must not give a direction under s 255C(4A)(a) or (b) unless satisfied that it is
not necessary for the protection of the public that the person should remain in prison:
s 255C(4B) (as so substituted and prospectively amended). The recall adjudicator must not give
a direction under s 255C(4A)(a) or (b) if it appears to the recall adjudicator that, if released, the
person is highly likely to breach a condition included in P's licence (s 255C(4C)(a) (as so
substituted and prospectively amended)) and for that reason, the recall adjudicator considers
that it is not appropriate to give the direction (s 255C(4C)(b) (as so substituted and
prospectively amended)). The Secretary of State must give effect to any direction under
s 255C(4A)(a) or (b): s 255C(5) (as so substituted and prospectively substituted).
    If the prisoner mentioned in the text is recalled before the date on which he would (but for
the earlier release) have served the requisite custodial period for the purposes of s 243A or (as
the case may be) s 244 (release on licence of prisoners serving 12 months or more: see PARA 713)
(s 255C(6) (as so substituted)), then: (1) if the prisoner is released under s 255C before that date,
his licence must include a curfew condition complying with s 253 (home detention curfew: see
PARA 737) (s 255C(7)(a) (as so substituted)); and (2) the prisoner is not to be so released, despite
s 255C(5), unless the Secretary of State is satisfied that arrangements are in place to enable that
condition to be complied with (s 255C(7)(b) (as so substituted)).
    As from a day to be appointed the Secretary of State may by order change the tests to be
applied by the recall adjudicator in deciding how to determine a reference under s 255C(4):
s 256AZA(1)(c) (as so prospectively added). See also s 256AZA(2); and note 5. At the date at
which this volume states the law no such order had been made.
31 Ie if he makes representations under the Criminal Justice Act 2003 s 254(2) (see PARA 717):
s 255C(4)(a) (as substituted: see note 2).
32 For the purposes of the Criminal Justice Act 2003 s 255C, a prisoner to whom s 255C applies
returns to custody when, having been recalled, he is detained (whether or not in prison) in
pursuance of the sentence: s 255C(8) (as substituted: see note 2).
33 Criminal Justice Act 2003 s 255C(4)(a) (as substituted: see note 2).
34 Ie under the Criminal Justice Act 2003 s 255C(2) (see the text and note 26): s 255C(4)(b) (as
substituted: see note 2).
35 Criminal Justice Act 2003 s 255C(4)(b) (as substituted: see note 2).

**720.   Review following Parole Board's decision not to recommend immediate
release of recalled prisoner.** Until a day to be appointed[1], where a case is
referred to the Parole Board[2] of a recalled prisoner:

    (1)   who is suitable for automatic release[3]; or

    (2)   who does not fall within head (1) above[4], but who, within 28 days of

his return to custody, either: (a) has made representations[5]; or (b) did not made representations and has not been released[6],

and the Board does not direct his immediate release on licence under Chapter 6 of Part 12 of the Criminal Justice Act 2003[7], the Board must either[8]:

(i)   fix a date for the person's release on licence[9]; or

(ii)   determine the reference by making no direction as to his release[10],

and where the Board has fixed a date under head (i) above, it is the duty of the Secretary of State[11] to release the person on licence on that date[12].

1   The Criminal Justice Act 2003 s 256 (see the text and notes 2–12) is repealed, as from a day to be appointed, by the Criminal Justice and Courts Act 2015 s 9(5). At the date at which this volume states the law no day had been appointed for this purpose.

2   As to the constitution and functions of the Parole Board, continued by the Criminal Justice Act 2003 s 239(1), see PARA 699.

3   Ie on a reference under the Criminal Justice Act 2003 s 255B(4) (see PARA 719): s 256(1) (amended by the Legal Aid, Sentencing and Punishment of Offenders Act 2012 ss 114(4), (5), 116(1), (3)(a); prospectively repealed (see note 1)). As to the meaning of 'automatic release' for these purposes see PARA 719 note 3. The Criminal Justice Act 2003 ss 243A–264 do not apply in relation to a person detained in England and Wales in pursuance of a sentence of the International Criminal Court: see the International Criminal Court Act 2001 Sch 7 para 3(1); and PARA 690. As to the meanings of 'England' and 'Wales' see PARA 4 note 3.

4   Ie on a reference under the Criminal Justice Act 2003 s 255C(4) of a prisoner who is not considered suitable for automatic release or who is an extended sentence prisoner (see PARA 719): s 256(1) (as amended and prospectively repealed: see notes 1, 3). As to the meaning of 'extended sentence prisoner' for these purposes see PARA 719 note 2.

5   Ie where the Criminal Justice Act 2003 s 255C(4)(a) applies (see PARA 719): s 256(1) (as amended: see note 3).

6   Ie where the Criminal Justice Act 2003 s 255C(4)(b) applies (see PARA 719): s 256(1) (as amended and prospectively repealed: see notes 1, 3).

7   Ie under the Criminal Justice Act 2003 Pt 12 Ch 6 (ss 237–268) (sentencing: release, licences and recall) (see also PARAS 696, 699, 709 et seq, 722 et seq): see s 256(1) (as amended and prospectively repealed: see notes 1, 3). As to the duration and conditions of licences see PARA 735 et seq.

8   Criminal Justice Act 2003 s 256(1) (as amended and prospectively repealed: see notes 1, 3).

9   Criminal Justice Act 2003 s 256(1)(a) (prospectively repealed: see note 1). Any date fixed under s 256(1)(a) must not be later than the first anniversary of the date on which the decision is taken: s 256(2) (amended by the Criminal Justice and Immigration Act 2008 ss 30(1), (3), 149, Sch 28 Pt 2).

10 Criminal Justice Act 2003 s 256(1)(b) (substituted by the Criminal Justice and Immigration Act 2008 s 30(1), (2); amended by the Legal Aid, Sentencing and Punishment of Offenders Act 2012 s 116(1), (3)(b); prospectively repealed (see note 1)). See notes 2, 9.

11 As to the Secretary of State for these purposes see PRISONS AND PRISONERS vol 85 (2012) PARA 408.

12 Criminal Justice Act 2003 s 256(4).

721.   Further review.   Until a day to be appointed the Secretary of State[1] must, not later than the first anniversary of the determination of a reference by the Parole Board[2], refer the person's case to the Board; as from that day, where a case has been referred to a recall adjudicator[3] and the person has not been released, the Secretary of State must refer the person's case back to a recall adjudicator no later than the review date[4]. However, at any time before that anniversary (or, as from the appointed day, the review date), the Secretary of State may refer the case to the Board (or, as from the appointed day, the recall adjudicator)[5]; and the Board (or adjudicator) may at any time recommend to the Secretary of State that a person's case be so referred[6]. On such a reference, the Board (or adjudicator) must determine the reference by[7]:

(1)   directing the person's immediate release[8] on licence[9];

(2) until the appointed day, fixing a date for his release on licence; as from that day, directing his release on licence as soon as conditions specified in the direction are met[10]; or

(3) making no direction as to his release[11].

Until the appointed day, where the Board makes a direction under head (1) above for the person's immediate release on licence, the Secretary of State must give effect to the direction[12], and where the Board fixes a release date under head (2) above, the Secretary of State must release the person on licence on that date[13]; as from that day the Secretary of State must give effect to any direction under head (1) or (2) above[14].

1 As to the Secretary of State for these purposes see PRISONS AND PRISONERS vol 85 (2012) PARA 408.

2 Ie a determination by the Parole Board under either the Criminal Justice Act 2003 s 256(1) (see PARA 720) or s 256A(4) (see the text and notes 7–11): s 256A(1) (s 256A added by the Criminal Justice and Immigration Act 2008 s 30(6); Criminal Justice Act 2003 s 256A(1), (4)(b), (5) prospectively substituted, s 256A(1A), (1B), (4A), (4B), (6) prospectively added, s 256A(2)–(4) prospectively amended, by the Criminal Justice and Courts Act 2015 s 9(6)).

As from a day to be appointed the Secretary of State may by order change the tests to be applied by the recall adjudicator in deciding how to determine a reference under the Criminal Justice Act 2003 s 256A(1) or (2): s 256AZA(1)(c) (as so prospectively added). See also s 256AZA(2); and PARA 719 note 5. At the date at which this volume states the law no such order had been made.

3 Ie under the Criminal Justice Act 2003 s 255C(4) (see PARA 719) or s 256A: s 256A(1) (as added and prospectively substituted: see note 2). As to recall adjudicators see PARA 705.

4 Criminal Justice Act 2003 s 256A(1) (as added and prospectively substituted: see note 2). In the case of a person serving one sentence of imprisonment, 'the review date' is the first anniversary of the determination by the recall adjudicator on the reference mentioned in s 256A(1): s 256A(1A) (as so added and prospectively added). In the case of a person serving more than one sentence of imprisonment, 'the review date' is either the first anniversary of the determination by the recall adjudicator on the reference mentioned in s 256A(1) (s 256A(1B)(a) (as so added and prospectively added)), or, if later, the day on which the person has served the requisite custodial period and, if the sentences include a life sentence, the minimum term (s 256A(1B)(b) (as so added and prospectively added)). In s 256A(1B)(b) 'life sentence' means a sentence mentioned in the Crime (Sentences) Act 1997 s 34(2) (see PARA 706) and 'the minimum term' means the part of the sentence specified in the minimum term order (as defined by s 28 (see PARA 707)): s 256A(6) (as so added and prospectively added).

5 Criminal Justice Act 2003 s 256A(2) (as added and prospectively amended: see note 2).

6 Criminal Justice Act 2003 s 256A(3) (as added and prospectively amended: see note 2).

7 Criminal Justice Act 2003 s 256A(4) (as added and prospectively amended: see note 2).

8 Ie under the Criminal Justice Act 2003 Pt 12 Ch 6 (ss 237–268) (sentencing: release, licences and recall) (see also PARAS 696, 699, 709 et seq, 722 et seq).

9 Criminal Justice Act 2003 s 256A(4)(a) (as added (see note 2); s 256A(4)(a), (c), (5) amended by the Legal Aid, Sentencing and Punishment of Offenders Act 2012 s 116(1), (4)). As from the appointed day the recall adjudicator must not give a direction under the Criminal Justice Act 2003 s 256A(4)(a) or (b) unless satisfied that it is not necessary for the protection of the public that the person should remain in prison (s 256A(4A) (as so added and prospectively added)), and must not give such a direction if it appears to him that, if released, the person is highly likely to breach a condition included in the person's licence and for that reason, he considers that it is not appropriate to give the direction (s 256A(4B) (as so added and prospectively added)).

10 Criminal Justice Act 2003 s 256A(4)(b) (as added and prospectively substituted: see note 2). See note 9.

11 Criminal Justice Act 2003 s 256A(4)(c) (as added and amended: see notes 2, 9).

12 Criminal Justice Act 2003 s 256A(5)(a) (as added and amended: see note 2, 9).

13 Criminal Justice Act 2003 s 256A(5)(b) (as added and amended: see note 2, 9).

14 Criminal Justice Act 2003 s 256A(5) (as added and amended: see note 2, 9).

(6) PRISONERS SERVING DETERMINATE SENTENCE FOR OFFENCE COMMITTED BEFORE 4 APRIL 2005

(i) Transitional Arrangements for Early Release and Recall

722. Overview of transitional early release and recall arrangements. For a diminishing number of historical cases, where a prisoner is or was sentenced to a determinate term for an offence that was committed before 4 April 2005[1], the regimes that govern early release and recall are subject to transitional provisions[2]. The Legal Aid, Sentencing and Punishment of Offenders Act 2012 brought into effect a simplified transitional regime[3] which applies the Criminal Justice Act 2003 provisions that govern early release and recall[4] to any person serving a determinate sentence for an offence committed before 4 April 2005[5], whenever that sentence was or is imposed[6], as follows:

(1)　　where such a person has been released on licence under Part II of the Criminal Justice Act 1991 or under the Criminal Justice Act 1967, the Criminal Justice Act 2003 provisions apply with modifications[7]; but

(2)　　where such a person has not been released from prison on licence previously (or where such a person has been released but recalled in certain circumstances), the Criminal Justice Act 2003 provisions are subject to new transitional provisions[8].

Head (2) above applies to two broad categories of case:

(a)　　certain persons serving 'Criminal Justice Act 1967 sentences'[9];

(b)　　certain persons serving 'Criminal Justice Act 1991 sentences'[10].

The regime applicable under head (b) above applies also to certain 'Criminal Justice Act 2003 sentences' which are extended sentences[11].

1　As to an overview of early release and recall arrangements for prisoners sentenced to a determinate term for an offence that was committed on or after 4 April 2005 see PARA 688.

2　It is only with the passing of the Legal Aid, Sentencing and Punishment of Offenders Act 2012 that the provision for such transitional cases has been addressed in a systematic and holistic manner: see the text and notes 3–11.

　　Before the Criminal Justice Act 2003 was amended by the Legal Aid, Sentencing and Punishment of Offenders Act 2012, a very complex regime had grown up piecemeal to govern the early release of prisoners serving determinate sentences for offences committed before 4 April 2005, evolving from the successive transitional and provisional arrangements that were put in place each time the sentencing regime itself was reformed. The statutory scheme substantially contained in the Criminal Justice Act 1991 Pt II (ss 32–51), which regulated the release of determinate sentence prisoners under that Act, subject to significant amendment by the Crime and Disorder Act 1998 and the Powers of Criminal Courts (Sentencing) Act 2000, was repealed by the Criminal Justice Act 2003 ss 303(a), 332, Sch 37 Pt 7, with effect from 4 April 2005: see the Criminal Justice Act 2003 (Commencement No 8 and Transitional and Saving Provisions) Order 2005, SI 2005/950, art 2(1), Sch 1. However, transitional and saving provisions were made which preserved the effect of the Criminal Justice Act 1991 Pt II so that it could be applied to certain historical cases: see the Criminal Justice Act 2003 (Commencement No 8 and Transitional and Saving Provisions) Order 2005, SI 2005/950, Sch 2. The Criminal Justice Act 1991 had itself made transitional and saving arrangements in relation to release and recall provisions put in place by the Criminal Justice Act 1967, affecting prisoners sentenced to a term of more than 12 months before 1 October 1992 (ie before the Criminal Justice Act 1991 came into force) ('existing prisoners'): see the Criminal Justice Act 1991 s 101(1), Sch 12. These preserved regimes were further amended significantly by the Criminal Justice and Immigration Act 2008 (see note 11). As to criticism of the 'legislative morass' that resulted see especially *R (on application of Noone) v Governor of Drake Hall Prison* [2010] UKSC 30 at [86], [2010] 4 All ER 463 at [86], [2010] 1 WLR 1743 at [86] per Lord Judge LCJ. These transitional arrangements have been simplified and codified, but their effect preserved, by the Legal Aid, Sentencing and Punishment of Offenders Act 2012 Pt 3 Ch 4 (ss 108–121): see note 3.

3 The Legal Aid, Sentencing and Punishment of Offenders Act 2012 Pt 3 Ch 4 introduced the regime that now applies to the release of a prisoner sentenced to a determinate term for an offence that was committed before 4 April 2005. The Act achieves this by making amendments to the Criminal Justice Act 2003, most notably to Pt 12 Ch 6 (ss 237–268) (sentencing: release, licences and recall) (see PARAS 696, 699, 709 et seq, 723 et seq), including the adding of ss 243A, 267A, 267B, Schs 20A, 20B (see PARA 723 et seq), so that all the transitional release and recall provisions that are to continue to apply to prisoners sentenced to determinate terms for offences committed before 4 April 2005 (see note 2) are brought together on the face of the Criminal Justice Act 2003, along with the release and recall provisions that continue to apply to prisoners sentenced to determinate terms for offences committed on or after 4 April 2005. Prisoners sentenced to a determinate term imposed on or after the commencement date of the Legal Aid, Sentencing and Punishment of Offenders Act 2012 Pt 3 Ch 4 (ie on or after 3 December 2012: see note 9) will be serving a 'Criminal Justice Act 2003 sentence' for the purposes of the release regime regardless of the date of their offence (ie even where the offences for which they are sentenced were committed before 4 April 2005): see note 11.

4 Ie the Criminal Justice Act 2003 Pt 12 Ch 6.

5 The Criminal Justice Act 2003 s 267A, Sch 20A paras 3–9 apply in relation to any person serving a sentence for an offence committed before 4 April 2005, whenever that sentence was imposed: see Sch 20A para 2; and PARA 724.

6 See the Legal Aid, Sentencing and Punishment of Offenders Act 2012 s 121(1); and PARA 724. In accordance with s 121(1), the repeal of the Criminal Justice Act 1991 Pt II (ss 32–51) which is made by the Criminal Justice Act 2003 s 303(a) has effect in relation to any person mentioned in the Legal Aid, Sentencing and Punishment of Offenders Act 2012 s 121(1): see s 121(3)(a); and PARA 724.

7 See the transitional regime that is contained in the Criminal Justice Act 2003 s 267A, Sch 20A (added by the Legal Aid, Sentencing and Punishment of Offenders Act 2012 s 121(5), Sch 16 paras 1–3); and PARA 724.

8 See the transitional regime that is contained in the Criminal Justice Act 2003 s 267B, Sch 20B (added by the Legal Aid, Sentencing and Punishment of Offenders Act 2012 s 121(6), Sch 17 paras 1, 9, 10); and see also PARA 725 et seq.

9 Ie certain persons serving a 'Criminal Justice Act 1967 sentence', to whom the Criminal Justice Act 2003 Sch 20B Pt 3 (Sch 20B paras 23–33) (cited in PARAS 723, 727, 728) applies: see Sch 20B para 23(1) (as added: see note 8). The provision made by Pt 3 does not apply, however, to a person who:
   (1) has been released on licence (Sch 20B para 23(2)(a) (as so added));
   (2) has been recalled to prison (Sch 20B para 23(2)(b) (as so added)); and
   (3) (whether or not having returned to custody on the commencement date (Sch 20B para 23(2)(c) (as so added)).
As to prisoners unlawfully at large see PRISONS AND PRISONERS vol 85 (2012) PARA 429. For the purposes of Sch 20B, a 'Criminal Justice Act 1967 sentence' is a sentence imposed before 1 October 1992: see Sch 20B para 1(8) (as so added). For these purposes:
   (a) the 'commencement date' means the date on which the Legal Aid, Sentencing and Punishment of Offenders Act 2012 s 121 came into force (ie 3 December 2012: see the Legal Aid, Sentencing and Punishment of Offenders Act 2012 (Commencement No 4 and Saving Provisions) Order 2012, SI 2012/2906, art 2(d)) (Criminal Justice Act 2003 Sch 20B para 1(2) (as so added)); and
   (b) 1 October 1992 is the date on which the Criminal Justice Act 1991 Pt II (see note 2) came into force (see the Criminal Justice Act 2003 Sch 20B para 2 (as so added)).

10 Ie certain persons serving a 'Criminal Justice Act 1991 sentence', to whom the Criminal Justice Act 2003 Sch 20B Pt 2 (Sch 20B paras 3–22) applies: Sch 20B para 3(1) (as added: see note 8). The provision made by Pt 2 does not apply, however, to a person who:
   (1) has been released on licence under the Criminal Justice Act 1991 Pt II (see note 2) (Criminal Justice Act 2003 Sch 20B para 3(3)(a) (as so added));
   (2) has been recalled to prison (Sch 20B para 3(3)(b) (as so added)); and
   (3) (whether or not having returned to custody in consequence of that recall) is unlawfully at large on 3 December 2012 (ie 'the commencement date') (Sch 20B para 3(3)(c) (as so added)).
For the purposes of Sch 20B, a 'Criminal Justice Act 1991 sentence' is a sentence which is imposed:
   (a) on or after 1 October 1992 but before 4 April 2005 (Criminal Justice Act 2003 Sch 20B para 1(9)(a) (as so added)); or
   (b) on or after 4 April 2005 but before 3 December 2012 ('the commencement date') (Sch 20B para 1(9)(b) (as so added)), and is either: (i) imposed in respect of an offence

committed before 4 April 2005 (Sch 20B para 1(9)(b)(i) (as so added)); or (ii) for a term of less than 12 months (Sch 20B para 1(9)(b)(ii) (as so added)).

For these purposes, 4 April 2005 is the date on which Pt 12 Ch 6 came into force: Sch 20B para 2 (as so added)). Where an offence is found to have been committed over a period of two or more days, or at some time during a period of two or more days, it is to be taken for the purposes of Sch 20B to have been committed on the last of those days: Sch 20B para 1(11) (as so added).

11 Accordingly, the Criminal Justice Act 2003 Sch 20B Pt 2 applies also to a person serving a Criminal Justice Act 2003 sentence (Sch 20B para 3(2) (as added: see note 8)) which is an extended sentence imposed before 14 July 2008 under either s 227 (repealed with savings) or s 228 (repealed with savings): Sch 20B para 3(2)(b) (as so added).

For the purposes of Sch 20B, a 'Criminal Justice Act 2003 sentence' is a sentence which is imposed:

(1)   on or after the commencement date (Sch 20B para 1(10)(a) (as so added)); or

(2)   on or after 4 April 2005 but before 3 December 2012 ('the commencement date') (Sch 20B para 1(10)(b) (as so added)), and is both: (a) imposed in respect of an offence committed on or after 4 April 2005 (Sch 20B para 1(10)(b)(i) (as so added)); and (b) for a term of 12 months or more (Sch 20B para 1(10)(b)(ii) (as so added)).

723. Treatment of concurrent and consecutive terms: transitional arrangements. Where:

(1)   a person is serving two or more sentences of imprisonment imposed on or after 1 October 1992[1]; and

(2)   either the sentences were passed on the same occasion[2] (or, where they were passed on different occasions, the person has not been released under Part II of the Criminal Justice Act 1991[3] or under Chapter 6 of Part 12 of the Criminal Justice Act 2003[4] at any time during the period beginning with the first and ending with the last of those occasions)[5],

then:

(a)   if each of the sentences of imprisonment mentioned in head (1) above is a Criminal Justice Act 1991 sentence[6], the usual Criminal Justice Act 2003 provisions governing the treatment of concurrent[7] and consecutive terms[8] do not apply in relation to the sentences[9]; and

(b)   where two or more of the sentences mentioned in head (1) above are to be served consecutively on each other[10], and: (i) one or more of those sentences is a Criminal Justice Act 1991 sentence[11]; and (ii) one or more of them is a Criminal Justice Act 2003 sentence[12], the Criminal Justice Act 2003 provisions governing the treatment of consecutive terms[13] do not affect the length of the period which the person serving two or more such sentences must serve in prison in respect of the Criminal Justice Act 1991 sentence or sentences[14].

If the person serving two or more sentences of imprisonment is also serving one or more Criminal Justice Act 1967 sentences, however, then head (b) above does not apply[15]. Accordingly, where head (2) above applies, but in relation to two or more sentences of imprisonment imposed before 1 October 1992[16], then:

(A)   where each of the sentences of imprisonment is a Criminal Justice Act 1967 sentence[17], or if: (aa) one or more of those sentences is a Criminal Justice Act 1967 sentence[18]; and (bb) one or more of them is a Criminal Justice Act 1991 sentence[19], then the Criminal Justice Act 2003 provisions governing the treatment of concurrent[20] and consecutive terms[21] do not apply in relation to those sentences[22]; and

(B)   where two or more of the sentences are to be served consecutively on each other[23], and: (aa) one or more of those sentences is a Criminal Justice Act 1967 sentence[24]; and (bb) one or more of them is a Criminal Justice Act 2003 sentence[25], the Criminal Justice Act 2003 provisions governing the treatment of consecutive terms[26] do not affect the length of the period which the person serving two or more sentences of imprisonment must serve in prison in respect of the Criminal Justice Act 1967 sentence or sentences[27].

1   Criminal Justice Act 2003 s 267B, Sch 20B para 20 (s 267B, Sch 20B added by the Legal Aid, Sentencing and Punishment of Offenders Act 2012 s 121(6), Sch 17 paras 1, 9, 10). As to the application of the Criminal Justice Act 2003 Sch 20B Pt 2 (Sch 20B paras 3–22), and as to the significance of the date of 1 October 1992, see PARA 722 note 9.
2   Criminal Justice Act 2003 Sch 20B para 20(a) (as added: see note 1).
3   Ie under the Criminal Justice Act 1991 Pt II (ss 32–51) (repealed: see PARA 722 note 2): Criminal Justice Act 2003 Sch 20B para 20(b) (as added: see note 1).
4   Ie under the Criminal Justice Act 2003 Pt 12 Ch 6 (ss 237–268) (sentencing: release, licences and recall) (see also PARAS 696, 699, 709 et seq, 724 et seq): Sch 20B para 20(b) (as added: see note 1).
5   Criminal Justice Act 2003 Sch 20B para 20(b) (as added: see note 1).
6   Criminal Justice Act 2003 Sch 20B para 21(1) (as added: see note 1). As to the meaning of 'Criminal Justice Act 1991 sentence' see PARA 722 note 10.
7   Ie the Criminal Justice Act 2003 s 263 (see PARA 710): Sch 20B para 21(2) (as added: see note 1). With effect from 3 December 2012, s 263 is subject to the transitional arrangements contained in Sch 20B para 21 (see also the text and notes 6, 8–9), Sch 20B paras 31, 32 (see the text and notes 16–22): see s 263(5); and PARA 710.
8   Ie the Criminal Justice Act 2003 s 264 (see PARA 711): Sch 20B para 21(2) (as added: see note 1). With effect from 3 December 2012, s 264 is subject to the transitional arrangements contained in Sch 20B paras 21, 22 (see also the text and notes 6–7, 9–15), Sch 20B paras 31, 32 and 33 (see the text and notes 16–27): see s 264(8); and PARA 711.
9   Criminal Justice Act 2003 Sch 20B para 21(2) (as added: see note 1). For the purposes of any reference in Pt 12 Ch 6, however expressed, to the term of imprisonment to which the person serving two or more sentences of imprisonment has been sentenced (or which, or part of which, that person has served), the terms are to be treated as a single term: Sch 20B para 21(3) (as so added). If one or more of the sentences is a section 85 extended sentence:
    (1)   for the purpose of determining the single term mentioned in Sch 20B para 21(3), the extension period or periods is or are to be disregarded (Sch 20B para 21(4)(a) (as so added)); and
    (2)   the period for which the person serving two or more such sentences is to be on licence in respect of the single term is to be increased in accordance with Sch 20B para 21(5) (Sch 20B para 21(4)(b) (as so added)).
Accordingly, that period is to be increased: (a) if only one of the sentences is a section 85 extended sentence, by the extension period (Sch 20B para 21(5)(a) (as so added)); (b) if there is more than one such sentence and they are wholly or partly concurrent, by the longest of the extension periods (Sch 20B para 21(5)(b) (as so added)); (c) if there is more than one such sentence and they are consecutive, by the aggregate of the extension periods (Sch 20B para 21(5)(c) (as so added)).
A 'section 85 extended sentence' is an extended sentence under the Powers of Criminal Courts (Sentencing) Act 2000 s 85 (repealed) and includes, in accordance with s 165, Sch 11 para 1(3), a reference to a sentence under the Crime and Disorder Act 1998 s 58 (repealed): Criminal Justice Act 2003 Sch 20B para 1(5) (as so added). In relation to a 'section 85 extended sentence', the 'custodial term' and the 'extension period' have the meanings given by the Powers of Criminal Courts (Sentencing) Act 2000 s 85 (repealed with savings): Criminal Justice Act 2003 Sch 20B para 1(6) (as so added).
For the purposes of the Criminal Justice Act 2003 Sch 20B, 30 September 1998 is the date on which certain provisions of the Crime and Disorder Act 1998 came into force (further amending the sentencing regime, including the introduction of extended sentences, and making significant adjustments to the recall regime); and 14 July 2008 is the date on which certain provisions of the Criminal Justice and Immigration Act 2008 other than s 26 (repealed) came into force: Criminal Justice Act 2003 Sch 20B para 2 (as so added). By virtue of the Criminal Justice and Immigration Act 2008, all determinate sentence prisoners who are recalled after 14 July 2008 are subject to recall under the Criminal Justice Act 2003 s 254 (see PARA 717).
10   Criminal Justice Act 2003 Sch 20B para 22(1) (as added: see note 1).
11   Criminal Justice Act 2003 Sch 20B para 22(1)(a) (as added: see note 1).
12   Criminal Justice Act 2003 Sch 20B para 22(1)(b) (as added: see note 1). As to the meaning of 'Criminal Justice Act 2003 sentence' see PARA 722 note 11.

13 Ie the Criminal Justice Act 2003 s 264 (see PARA 711): Sch 20B para 22(2) (as added: see note 1).

14 Criminal Justice Act 2003 Sch 20B para 22(2) (as added: see note 1). Nothing in Pt 12 Ch 6 requires the Secretary of State to release such a person serving two or more sentences of imprisonment until that person has served a period equal in length to the aggregate of the length of the periods which he must serve in relation to each of the sentences mentioned in Sch 20B para 22(1) (see head (b) in the text): Sch 20B para 22(3) (as so added). If the prisoner is subject to supervision requirements under s 256AA (by virtue of s 264(3C)(b)) (see PARA 711), s 256AA(4)(b) (end of supervision period: see PARA 741) applies in relation to him as if the reference to the requisite custodial period were to the period described in Sch 20B para 22(3): Sch 20B para 22(3A) (added by the Offender Rehabilitation Act 2014 s 5(6), (7)). As to the Secretary of State for these purposes see PRISONS AND PRISONERS vol 85 (2012) PARA 408.

15 Criminal Justice Act 2003 Sch 20B para 22(4) (as added: see note 1). In the circumstances mentioned in the text, the provisions of Sch 20B paras 32, 33 (see the text and notes 18–27) apply instead of Sch 20B para 22 (see the text and notes 10–14): Sch 20B para 22(4) (as so added). As to the meaning of 'Criminal Justice Act 1967 sentence' see PARA 722 note 9.

16 Ie the provisions of the Criminal Justice Act 2003 Sch 20B paras 31–33 (see the text and notes 17–27) apply where:
    (1)   a person is serving two or more sentences of imprisonment (Sch 20B para 30 (as added: see note 1)); and
    (2)   either: (a) the sentences were passed on the same occasion (Sch 20B para 30(a) (as so added)); or (b) where they were passed on different occasions, the person has not been released under the Criminal Justice Act 1991 Pt II (repealed: see PARA 722 note 2) or under the Criminal Justice Act 2003 Pt 12 Ch 6 at any time during the period beginning with the first and ending with the last of those occasions (Sch 20B para 30(b) (as so added)).

17 Criminal Justice Act 2003 Sch 20B para 31(1) (as added: see note 1).

18 Criminal Justice Act 2003 Sch 20B para 32(1)(a) (as added: see note 1).

19 Criminal Justice Act 2003 Sch 20B para 32(1)(b) (as added: see note 1).

20 Ie the Criminal Justice Act 2003 s 263 (see PARA 710): Sch 20B paras 31(2), 32(2) (as added: see note 1).

21 Ie the Criminal Justice Act 2003 s 264: see Sch 20B paras 31(2), 32(2) (as added: see note 1).

22 Criminal Justice Act 2003 Sch 20B paras 31(2), 32(2) (as added: see note 1). Where Sch 20B para 31 applies (see the text and notes 16–17), then for the purposes of any reference in Pt 12 Ch 6, however expressed, to the term of imprisonment to which the person serving two or more sentences of imprisonment has been sentenced (or which, or part of which, that person has served), the terms are to be treated as a single term: Sch 20B para 31(3) (as so added).

Where Sch 20B para 32 applies, however (see the text and notes 16, 18–19), then the terms mentioned in heads (A)(aa) and (A)(bb) in the text are to be treated as a single term for those purposes (Sch 20B para 32(3)(a) (as so added)), and that single term is to be treated as if it were a Criminal Justice Act 1967 sentence (Sch 20B para 32(3)(b) (as so added)). If one or more of the sentences is a section 85 extended sentence:
    (1)   for the purpose of determining the single term mentioned in Sch 20B para 32(3), the extension period or periods is or are to be disregarded (Sch 20B para 32(4)(a) (as so added)); and
    (2)   the period for which the person serving two or more sentences of imprisonment is to be on licence in respect of the single term is to be increased in accordance with Sch 20B para 32(5) (Sch 20B para 32(4)(b) (as so added)).

Accordingly, that period is to be increased: (a) if only one of the sentences is a section 85 extended sentence, by the extension period (Sch 20B para 32(5)(a) (as so added)); (b) if there is more than one such sentence and they are wholly or partly concurrent, by the longest of the extension periods (Sch 20B para 32(5)(b) (as so added)); (c) if there is more than one such sentence and they are consecutive, by the aggregate of the extension periods (Sch 20B para 32(5)(c) (as so added)).

If the person serving two or more sentences of imprisonment is also serving a Criminal Justice Act 2003 sentence, Sch 20B para 32(3) is to be applied before the period mentioned in s 263(2)(c) (concurrent terms: see PARA 710) or Sch 20B para 33(3) (consecutive terms: see note 27) is calculated: Sch 20B para 32(6) (as so added).

23 Criminal Justice Act 2003 Sch 20B para 33(1) (as added: see note 1).

24 Criminal Justice Act 2003 Sch 20B para 33(1)(a) (as added: see note 1).

25 Criminal Justice Act 2003 Sch 20B para 33(1)(b) (as added: see note 1).

26 Ie the Criminal Justice Act 2003 s 264 (see PARA 711): Sch 20B para 33(2) (as added: see note 1).

27 Criminal Justice Act 2003 Sch 20B para 33(2) (as added: see note 1). Nothing in Pt 12 Ch 6 requires the Secretary of State to release the person serving two or more sentences of

imprisonment until that person has served a period equal in length to the aggregate of the length of the periods which he must serve in relation to each of the sentences mentioned in Sch 20B para 33(1) (see the text and note 23): Sch 20B para 33(3) (as so added). If the prisoner is subject to supervision requirements under s 256AA (by virtue of s 264(3C)(b)) (see PARA 711), s 256AA(4)(b) (end of supervision period: see PARA 741) applies in relation to him as if the reference to the requisite custodial period were to the period described in Sch 20B para 33(3): Sch 20B para 33(4) (added by the Offender Rehabilitation Act 2014 s 5(8)).

(ii) Application of Criminal Justice Act 2003 Provisions governing Early Release and Recall

724. Application of the Criminal Justice Act 2003 early release and recall arrangements to sentences for offence committed before 4 April 2005. As from 3 December 2012[1], the usual Criminal Justice Act 2003 provisions that govern early release and recall[2] apply with modifications to any person serving a sentence for an offence committed before 4 April 2005[3], whenever that sentence was or is imposed[4]. Subject to such modifications:

(1) where the person has been released on licence under Part II of the Criminal Justice Act 1991[5] or under the Criminal Justice Act 1967[6] before 3 December 2012[7], the person is to be treated as if the release had been under the Criminal Justice Act 2003 provisions[8]; and

(2) where a person has been recalled under Part II of the Criminal Justice Act 1991[9] before 3 December 2012[10], the person is to be treated as if the recall had been under the Criminal Justice Act 2003[11].

Further provision is made in relation to: (a) persons removed from prison, before 3 December 2012, who were liable to removal from the United Kingdom[12]; and (b) persons extradited to the United Kingdom before 3 December 2012[13].

In relation to certain other historical cases, where a person has not been released from prison on licence previously (or where such a person has been released but recalled in certain circumstances), the Criminal Justice Act 2003 provisions that govern early release and recall[14] are displaced by other transitional arrangements[15].

1 The Criminal Justice Act 2003 s 267A, Sch 20A (application of the Criminal Justice Act 2003 Pt 12 Ch 6 to pre-4 April 2005 cases) are added by the Legal Aid, Sentencing and Punishment of Offenders Act 2012 s 121(5), Sch 16 paras 1–3; and s 121(1), (3) makes related provision, as from 3 December 2012 ('the commencement date'), being the day appointed under s 151(1) (see the Legal Aid, Sentencing and Punishment of Offenders Act 2012 (Commencement No 4 and Saving Provisions) Order 2012, SI 2012/2906, art 2(d), (n)).

2 Ie the Criminal Justice Act 2003 Pt 12 Ch 6 (ss 237–268) (sentencing: release, licences and recall) (see also PARAS 696, 699, 709 et seq, 725 et seq): Legal Aid, Sentencing and Punishment of Offenders Act 2012 s 121(1).

3 Ie the Criminal Justice Act 2003 Sch 20A paras 3–9 (see the text and notes 5–13) are applied in relation to any person serving a sentence for an offence committed before 4 April 2005, whenever that sentence was imposed: Sch 20A para 2 (as added: see note 1). As to the significance of the date of 4 April 2005 see PARA 722 note 10. As to the provision made by Sch 20A para 7 (rules made by virtue of the Criminal Justice Act 1991 s 42 (repealed) have effect as if made by virtue of the Criminal Justice Act 2003 s 257) see PRISONS AND PRISONERS vol 85 (2012) PARA 404.

4 See the Legal Aid, Sentencing and Punishment of Offenders Act 2012 s 121(1). In accordance with s 121(1), the repeal of the Criminal Justice Act 1991 Pt II (ss 32–51) (repealed), which is made by the Criminal Justice Act 2003 s 303(a) (see PARA 722 note 2) has effect in relation to any person mentioned in the Legal Aid, Sentencing and Punishment of Offenders Act 2012 s 121(1): s 121(3)(a).

5 Ie under the Criminal Justice Act 1991 Pt II (see note 4): Criminal Justice Act 2003 Sch 20A para 5(1) (as added: see note 1).

6 Ie under the Criminal Justice Act 1967 s 60 (repealed) (release on licence of persons serving determinate sentences): Criminal Justice Act 2003 Sch 20A para 5(1) (as added: see note 1). Any

period which would, but for the repeal of the Criminal Justice Act 1967 s 67 (repealed) (computation of sentences of imprisonment passed in England and Wales), be a 'relevant period' within the meaning of s 67 (see s 67(1A) (reduction of sentences by period spent in custody etc)) is to be treated, for the purposes of the Criminal Justice Act 2003 s 240ZA (time remanded in custody to count as time served: terms of imprisonment and detention: see PARA 30), as if it were a period for which the offender was remanded in custody in connection with the offence: Sch 20A para 3 (as so added).

7   Ie before the 'commencement date', which means the date on which the Legal Aid, Sentencing and Punishment of Offenders Act 2012 s 121 came into force (see note 1): Criminal Justice Act 2003 Sch 20A paras 1, 5(1) (as added: see note 1). As to the application and modification of the definition of 'custodial period' in s 264(6) (consecutive terms) for these purposes see Sch 20A para 10; and PARA 711 note 7.

8   Criminal Justice Act 2003 Sch 20A para 5(1) (as added: see note 1). The text refers to the person being treated as if the release had been under Pt 12 Ch 6: Sch 20A para 5(1) (as so added).

   In particular, the following provisions apply (Sch 20A para 5(2) (as so added)):
   (1)   a licence under the Criminal Justice Act 1991 s 34A (repealed) (power to release short-term prisoners on licence) is to be treated as if it were a licence under the Criminal Justice Act 2003 s 246 (power to release fixed-term prisoners before required term: see PARA 715) (Sch 20A para 5(3) (as so added));
   (2)   a licence under the Criminal Justice Act 1991 s 36 (repealed) (power to release prisoners on compassionate grounds) is to be treated as if it were a licence under the Criminal Justice Act 2003 s 248 (power to release fixed-term prisoners on compassionate grounds: see PARA 696) (Sch 20A para 5(4) (as so added));
   (3)   any condition of a licence specified under the Criminal Justice Act 1991 s 37 (repealed) (duration of licences granted to short-term prisoners) is to have effect as if it were included under the Criminal Justice Act 2003 s 250 (licence conditions: see PARA 736), whether or not the condition is of a kind which could otherwise be included under s 250 (Sch 20A para 5(5) (as so added));
   (4)   where the licence is, on the commencement date, subject to a suspension under the Criminal Justice Act 1991 s 38(2) (repealed) (effect of breach of licence conditions by short-term prisoners), the suspension continues to have effect for the period specified by the court despite the repeal of s 38 (Criminal Justice Act 2003 Sch 20A para 5(6) (as so added));
   (5)   a licence under the Criminal Justice Act 1991 s 40A (repealed) (release on licence following return to prison) is to be treated as if it were a licence under the Criminal Justice Act 2003 Pt 12 Ch 6, except that in respect of any failure before or after 3 December 2012 (ie before or after 'the commencement date': see note 7) to comply with the conditions of the licence, the person is liable to be dealt with in accordance with the Criminal Justice Act 1991 s 40A(4)–(6), despite the repeal of s 40A, and is not liable to be dealt with in any other way (Criminal Justice Act 2003 Sch 20A para 5(7) (as so added)); and
   (6)   Sch 20A para 5(1) does not affect the duration of the licence (Sch 20A para 5(8) (as so added)).
   Further to head (1) above, s 246 applies for the purposes of Sch 20A, with modifications made to the operation of s 246(4): Sch 20A para 4 (as so added; Sch 20A para 4 amended by the Criminal Justice and Courts Act 2015 s 15(7)).

9   Ie under the Criminal Justice Act 1991 Pt II (see note 4): Criminal Justice Act 2003 Sch 20A para 6(1) (as added: see note 1).

10   Ie before the 'commencement date' (see note 7): Criminal Justice Act 2003 Sch 20A para 6(1) (as added: see note 1).

11   Criminal Justice Act 2003 Sch 20A para 6(1) (as added: see note 1). The text refers to the person being treated as if the recall had been under s 254 (general power to recall of prisoners after release on licence: see PARA 717): Sch 20A para 6(1) (as so added).

   In particular, the following provisions apply (Sch 20A para 6(2) (as so added)):
   (1)   if the Secretary of State has not referred the person's case to the Board under the Criminal Justice Act 1991 s 39(4) (repealed) (recall of long-term and life prisoners while on licence) or s 44A (repealed) (re-release of prisoners serving extended sentences), the Secretary of State must refer the case under the Criminal Justice Act 2003 s 255C(4) (see PARA 719) (Sch 20A para 6(3) (as so added));
   (2)   if the Secretary of State has referred the person's case to the Board under the Criminal Justice Act 1991 s 39(4) (repealed) or s 44A (repealed), that reference is to be treated as if it had been made under the Criminal Justice Act 2003 s 255C(4) (Sch 20A para 6(4) (as so added));

   (3)   until a day to be appointed, a determination of a reference under the Criminal Justice Act 1991 s 39(4) (repealed) or s 44A (repealed), is to be treated as a determination under the Criminal Justice Act 2003 s 256(1) (further review following Parole Board's decision not to recommend immediate release of recalled prisoner: see PARA 720) (Sch 20A para 6(5) (as so added; prospectively repealed by the Criminal Justice and Courts Act 2015 s 9(7))); and

   (4)   if the person is released on licence, the duration of that licence is determined in accordance with the Criminal Justice Act 2003 s 249 (duration of licences granted to fixed-term prisoners: see PARA 735), subject to the transitional arrangements in s 267B, Sch 20B para 17 (duration of licences granted to prisoners serving certain Criminal Justice Act 1991 sentences: see PARA 738), Sch 20B para 19 (duration of licences granted to prisoners serving certain extended sentences: see PARA 738) and Sch 20B para 26 (duration of licences granted to prisoners serving Criminal Justice Act 1967 sentences: see PARA 739) (Sch 20A para 6(6) (as so added)).

As to the Secretary of State for these purposes see PRISONS AND PRISONERS vol 85 (2012) PARA 408.

12 See the Criminal Justice Act 2003 Sch 20A para 8.
13 Criminal Justice Act 2003 Sch 20A para 9.
14 Ie the Criminal Justice Act 2003 Pt 12 Ch 6.
15 Criminal Justice Act 2003 s 267B, Sch 20B; and PARAS 722, 725 et seq.

(iii) Early Release and Recall administered under Transitional Arrangements

A. RELEASE UNDER TRANSITIONAL ARRANGEMENTS WHERE CRIMINAL JUSTICE ACT 1991 SENTENCES AND CERTAIN EXTENDED SENTENCES APPLY

725. Initial duty to release. As soon as a prisoner[1]:

   (1)   who is serving a 'Criminal Justice Act 1991 sentence'[2], or who is serving an extended 'Criminal Justice Act 2003 sentence' (as defined for these purposes)[3]; and

   (2)   who meets the statutory conditions for automatic release on licence[4],

has served two-thirds of the sentence, it is the duty of the Secretary of State[5] to release the person on licence[6]. Where these transitional provisions apply[7], they apply in place of the usual Criminal Justice Act 2003 provisions[8] which govern the release on licence of prisoners serving 12 months or more[9]. After a person who falls within heads (1) and (2) above[10] has served one-half of the sentence, the Secretary of State must, if directed to do so by the Parole Board[11], release the person on licence[12]. However, the Board must not give such a direction unless the Board is satisfied that it is no longer necessary for the protection of the public that the person should be confined[13]. Where such a direction is given by the Parole Board under transitional provisions[14], they apply in place of the usual Criminal Justice Act 2003 provisions[15] which govern the release on licence of prisoners serving 12 months or more[16].

As soon as a person who[17]:

   (a)   has been convicted of an offence committed on or after 30 September 1998 but before 4 April 2005[18];

   (b)   is serving a section 85 extended sentence in respect of that offence[19];

   (c)   has not previously been released from prison on licence in respect of that sentence[20]; and

   (d)   does not fall within heads (1) and (2) above[21],

has served one-half of the custodial term, it is the duty of the Secretary of State to release the person on licence[22]. Where this transitional provision applies[23], it displaces the usual Criminal Justice Act 2003 provisions[24] which govern, as the case may be, the unconditional release of prisoners serving less than 12 months, and the release on licence of those serving 12 months or more[25].

1   Ie a person to whom the Criminal Justice Act 2003 s 267B, Sch 20B para 4 applies (see note 4): Sch 20B para 5(1) (s 267B, Sch 20B added by the Legal Aid, Sentencing and Punishment of Offenders Act 2012 s 121(6), Sch 17 paras 1, 9, 10). As to the application of the Criminal Justice Act 2003 Sch 20B Pt 2 (Sch 20B paras 3–22) see PARA 722 notes 10, 11.

2   Ie where the Criminal Justice Act 2003 Sch 20B Pt 2 applies to a person by virtue of Sch 20B para 3(1): see PARA 722. As to persons to whom Pt 2 does not apply, and as to the meaning of 'Criminal Justice Act 1991 sentence' for these purposes, see PARA 722 note 10.

3   Ie where the Criminal Justice Act 2003 Sch 20B Pt 2 applies to a person by virtue of Sch 20B para 3(2): see PARA 722. As to the meaning of 'Criminal Justice Act 2003 sentence' for these purposes see PARA 722 note 11.

4   Ie is a person to whom the Criminal Justice Act 2003 Sch 20B para 4 applies: Sch 20B para 5(1) (as added: see note 1). The provision made by Sch 20B para 4 applies to a person in relation to whom (see Sch 20B para 4(1) (as so added)):

(1)   all the conditions in Sch 20B para 4(2) are met (Sch 20B para 4(1)(a) (as so added)), namely that:

(a)   the person has been convicted of an offence committed before 4 April 2005 (Sch 20B para 4(2)(a) (as so added));

(b)   the person is serving a sentence of imprisonment imposed in respect of that offence on or after 1 October 1992 but before 3 December 2012 (Sch 20B para 4(2)(b) (as so added));

(c)   the sentence (or, in the case of a section 85 extended sentence, the 'custodial term') is for a term of four years or more (Sch 20B para 4(2)(c) (as so added)); and

(d)   the person has not previously been released from prison on licence in respect of that sentence (Sch 20B para 4(2)(d) (as so added)); and

(2)   the condition in any one or more of the following heads (a) to (c) below is met (see Sch 20B para 4(2)(b) (as so added)), namely:

(a)   that the offence (or one of the offences) in respect of which the sentence was imposed is: (i) an offence specified in s 224, Sch 15 Pt 1 (violent offences) or Sch 15 Pt 2 (sexual offences) (see PARAS 23, 24) as Sch 15 had effect on 4 April 2005 (Sch 20B para 4(3)(a) (as so added)); (ii) an offence under any of the Terrorism Act 2000 s 11 or s 12 (offences relating to proscribed organisations: see CRIMINAL LAW vol 25 (2010) PARAS 376–377), ss 15–18 (offences relating to terrorist property: see CRIMINAL LAW vol 25 (2010) PARAS 379–382), s 54 (weapons training: see CRIMINAL LAW vol 25 (2010) PARA 401) and ss 56–63 (directing terrorism, possessing things and collecting information for the purposes of terrorism, eliciting, publishing or communicating information about members of armed forces etc and terrorist bombing and finance offences: see CRIMINAL LAW vol 25 (2010) PARAS 403–404, 409–410, 415, 418–420) (Criminal Justice Act 2003 Sch 20B para 4(3)(b) (as so added)); (iii) an offence under any of the Anti-terrorism, Crime and Security Act 2001 s 47 (offence of causing nuclear explosion: see ARMED CONFLICT AND EMERGENCY vol 3 (2011) PARA 91), s 50 (assisting or inducing certain weapons-related acts overseas: see ARMED CONFLICT AND EMERGENCY vol 3 (2011) PARA 97) or s 113 (use of noxious substances or things: see CRIMINAL LAW vol 25 (2010) PARA 134) (Criminal Justice Act 2003 Sch 20B para 4(3)(c) (as so added)); (iv) an offence under the Sexual Offences Act 1956 s 12 (buggery) (repealed) (Criminal Justice Act 2003 Sch 20B para 4(3)(d) (as so added)); (v) an offence of aiding, abetting counselling, procuring or inciting the commission of an offence listed in any of heads (2)(a)(ii) to (2)(a)(iv) above (Sch 20B para 4(3)(e) (as so added)); or (vi) an offence of conspiring or attempting to commit an offence listed in any of heads (2)(a)(ii) to (2)(a)(iv) above (Sch 20B para 4(3)(f) (as so added));

(b)   that the person has served one-half of the sentence (or, in the case of a section 85 extended sentence, one-half of the 'custodial term') before 9 June 2008 (Sch 20B para 4(4) (as so added));

(c)   that: (i) the person is serving the sentence by virtue of having been transferred to the United Kingdom in pursuance of a warrant under the Repatriation of Prisoners Act 1984 s 1 (see PRISONS AND PRISONERS vol 85 (2012) PARA 463) (Criminal Justice Act 2003 Sch 20B para 4(5)(a) (as so added)); (ii) the warrant was issued before 9 June 2008 (Sch 20B para 4(5)(b) (as so added)); and (iii) the offence (or one of the offences) for which the person is serving the sentence corresponds to murder or to any offence specified in Sch 15 Pt 1 (violent offences) or Sch 15 Pt 2 (sexual offences) as Sch 15 had effect on 4 April 2005 (Sch 20B para 4(5)(c) (as so added)).

The date of 3 December 2012 is known for these purposes as the 'commencement date', being the date on which the Legal Aid, Sentencing and Punishment of Offenders Act 2012 s 121 came into force on the day appointed under s 151(1) (see the Legal Aid, Sentencing and Punishment of Offenders Act 2012 (Commencement No 4 and Saving Provisions) Order 2012, SI 2012/2906, art 2(d), (o)): Criminal Justice Act 2003 Sch 20B para 1(1), (2) (as so added). For the purposes of Sch 20B, 9 June 2008 is the date on which the Criminal Justice and Immigration Act 2008 s 26 (repealed), which amended the Criminal Justice Act 1991 ss 33, 35, 37 (all repealed) and added s 37ZA (repealed) (duration and conditions of licences under section 33(1A) etc), came into force: Criminal Justice Act 2003 Sch 20B para 2 (as so added). As to the meanings of a 'section 85 extended sentence' and the 'custodial term' for these purposes see PARA 723 note 9. As to the meaning of 'United Kingdom' see PARA 4 note 3. As to the significance of the date of 1 October 1992 see PARA 722 note 9; and as to the significance of the date of 4 April 2005 see PARA 722 note 10.

5   As to the Secretary of State for these purposes see PRISONS AND PRISONERS vol 85 (2012) PARA 408.

6   Criminal Justice Act 2003 Sch 20B para 5(1) (as added: see note 1). The release mentioned in the text is made under Sch 20B para 5: Sch 20B para 5(1) (as so added). If the person is serving a section 85 extended sentence, the reference in Sch 20B para 5(1) to two-thirds of the sentence is a reference to two-thirds of the 'custodial term': Sch 20B para 5(2) (as so added). As to the duration and conditions of licences for these purposes see PARA 738 et seq.

7   Ie where the Criminal Justice Act 2003 Sch 20B para 5(1), (2) applies (see the text and notes 1–6): Sch 20B para 5(3) (as added: see note 1).

8   Ie in place of the Criminal Justice Act 2003 s 244 (release on licence of prisoners serving 12 months or more: see PARA 713): Sch 20B para 5(3) (as added: see note 1).

9   Criminal Justice Act 2003 Sch 20B para 5(3) (as added: see note 1).

10 Ie after a person to whom the Criminal Justice Act 2003 Sch 20B para 4 applies (see note 4): Sch 20B para 6(1) (as added: see note 1).

11 As to the constitution and functions of the Parole Board, continued by the Criminal Justice Act 2003 s 239(1), see PARA 699.

12 Criminal Justice Act 2003 Sch 20B para 6(1) (as added: see note 1). The release mentioned in the text is made under Sch 20B para 6: Sch 20B para 6(1) (as so added). If the person is serving a section 85 extended sentence, the reference in Sch 20B para 6(1) to one-half of the sentence is a reference to one-half of the 'custodial term': Sch 20B para 6(3) (as so added).

13 Criminal Justice Act 2003 Sch 20B para 6(2) (as added: see note 1).

14 Ie where the Criminal Justice Act 2003 Sch 20B para 6(1)–(3) applies (see the text and notes 10–13): Sch 20B para 6(4) (as added: see note 1).

15 Ie in place of the Criminal Justice Act 2003 s 244: Sch 20B para 6(4) (as added: see note 1).

16 Criminal Justice Act 2003 Sch 20B para 6(4) (as added: see note 1).

17 Ie as soon as a person to whom the Criminal Justice Act 2003 Sch 20B para 7 applies (see heads (a) to (d) in the text): Sch 20B para 8(1) (as added: see note 1).

18 Criminal Justice Act 2003 Sch 20B para 7(1)(a) (as added: see note 1). As to the significance of the date of 30 September 1998 see PARA 723 note 9.

19 Criminal Justice Act 2003 Sch 20B para 7(1)(b) (as added: see note 1).

20 Criminal Justice Act 2003 Sch 20B para 7(1)(c) (as added: see note 1).

21 Criminal Justice Act 2003 Sch 20B para 7(1)(d) (as added: see note 1). Head (d) in the text refers to a person to whom Sch 20B para 4 does not apply (see note 4): Sch 20B para 7(1)(d) (as so added).

22 Criminal Justice Act 2003 Sch 20B para 8(1) (as added: see note 1). The release mentioned in the text is made under Sch 20B para 8: Sch 20B para 8(1) (as so added).

23 Ie where the Criminal Justice Act 2003 Sch 20B para 8(1) applies (see the text and notes 17–22): Sch 20B para 8(2) (as added: see note 1).

24 Ie in place of either the Criminal Justice Act 2003 s 243A (unconditional release of prisoners serving less than 12 months: see PARA 712) or s 244 (release on licence of prisoners serving 12 months or more: see PARA 713): Sch 20B para 8(2) (as added: see note 1).

25 Criminal Justice Act 2003 Sch 20B para 8(2) (as added: see note 1).

726.   Release after recall.   As soon as a person[1]:

(1)   who has been convicted of an offence committed before 30 September 1998[2];

(2)   who is serving a sentence of imprisonment imposed in respect of that offence on or after 1 October 1992[3];

(3)   whose sentence is for a term of 12 months or more[4];

(4)   who has been released on licence under Part II of the Criminal Justice Act 1991[5]; and

(5)   who has been recalled before 14 July 2008 (and has not been recalled after that date)[6],

would (but for the earlier release) have served three-quarters of the sentence, it is the duty of the Secretary of State[7] to release the person unconditionally[8].

As soon as a person who[9]:

(a)   has been convicted of an offence committed on or after 30 September 1998 but before 4 April 2005[10];

(b)   is serving a sentence of imprisonment for a term of 12 months or more imposed in respect of that offence[11];

(c)   has been released on licence under Part II of the Criminal Justice Act 1991[12]; and

(d)   has been recalled before 14 July 2008 (and has not been recalled after that date)[13],

would (but for the earlier release) have served three-quarters of the sentence, it is the duty of the Secretary of State to release the person on licence[14].

Where a person who[15]:

(i)   has been convicted of an offence committed on or after 30 September 1998 but before 4 April 2005[16];

(ii)   is serving a section 85 extended sentence in respect of that offence[17];

(iii)   has been released on licence under Part II of the Criminal Justice Act 1991[18]; and

(iv)   has been recalled before 14 July 2008 (and has not been recalled after that date)[19],

it is the duty of the Secretary of State to release the person on licence as soon as the person would (but for the earlier release) have served the period found by adding[20]:

(A)   one-half of the custodial term (where the prisoner is serving a sentence with a custodial term of less than 12 months)[21] or three-quarters of the custodial term (where the prisoner is serving a sentence with a custodial term of 12 months or more)[22]; and

(B)   the extension period[23].

Where a person is serving an extended Criminal Justice Act 2003 sentence imposed before 14 July 2008 (which is not a section 85 extended sentence)[24], that person's release on licence is governed by the usual Criminal Justice Act 2003 provisions[25], but with modifications[26].

1   Ie a person to whom the Criminal Justice Act 2003 s 267B, Sch 20B para 9 applies (see heads (1) to (5) in the text): Sch 20B para 10 (s 267B, Sch 20B added by the Legal Aid, Sentencing and Punishment of Offenders Act 2012 s 121(6), Sch 17 paras 1, 9, 10). The provisions of the Criminal Justice Act 2003 Sch 20B para 9 do not apply if the court by which the person was sentenced ordered that the Powers of Criminal Courts (Sentencing) Act 2000 s 86 (repealed) (extension of periods in custody and on licence in the case of certain sexual offences committed before 30 September 1998) should apply: Criminal Justice Act 2003 Sch 20B para 9(2) (as so added). References in Sch 20B to the Powers of Criminal Courts (Sentencing) Act 2000 s 86 (repealed) include, in accordance with s 165, Sch 11 para 1(3), the Criminal Justice Act 1991 s 44 (extended sentences for sexual or violent offenders) (repealed), as originally enacted: Criminal Justice Act 2003 Sch 20B para 1(7). As to the application of the Criminal Justice Act 2003 Sch 20B Pt 2 (Sch 20B paras 3–22) see PARA 722 notes 10, 11.

2   Criminal Justice Act 2003 Sch 20B para 9(1)(a) (as added: see note 1). As to the significance of the date of 30 September 1998 see PARA 723 note 9.

3   Criminal Justice Act 2003 Sch 20B para 9(1)(b) (as added: see note 1). The provisions of Sch 20B Pt 2 apply to certain persons serving a 'Criminal Justice Act 1991 sentence' or a specified extended sentence falling within the definition of a 'Criminal Justice Act 2003 sentence': see PARA 722. As to the significance of the date of 1 October 1992 see PARA 722 note 9. As to the meaning of 'Criminal Justice Act 1991 sentence' for these purposes see PARA 722 note 10; and as to the meaning of 'Criminal Justice Act 2003 sentence' for these purposes see PARA 722 note 11.

4   Criminal Justice Act 2003 Sch 20B para 9(1)(c) (as added: see note 1).

5   Criminal Justice Act 2003 Sch 20B para 9(1)(d) (as added: see note 1). As to the Criminal Justice Act 1991 Pt II (ss 32–51) (repealed) see PARA 722 note 2.

6   Criminal Justice Act 2003 Sch 20B para 9(1)(e) (as added: see note 1). As to the significance of the date of 14 July 2008 see PARA 722 note 11.

7   As to the Secretary of State for these purposes see PRISONS AND PRISONERS vol 85 (2012) PARA 408.

8   Criminal Justice Act 2003 Sch 20B para 10 (as added: see note 1).

9   Ie a person to whom the Criminal Justice Act 2003 Sch 20B para 11 applies (see heads (a) to (d) in the text): Sch 20B para 12 (as added: see note 1). The provisions of Sch 20B para 11 do not apply, however, if:
    (1)   the person has been released and recalled more than once (Sch 20B para 11(2) (as so added)); or
    (2)   the sentence is a section 85 extended sentence (Sch 20B para 11(3) (as so added)).
    Where head (2) above applies, Sch 20B para 13 (see the text and notes 15–19) applies to such a case instead of Sch 20B para 11: Sch 20B para 11(3) (as so added). As to the meaning of a 'section 85 extended sentence' for these purposes see PARA 723 note 9.

10 Criminal Justice Act 2003 Sch 20B para 11(1)(a) (as added: see note 1). See note 9. As to the significance of the date of 4 April 2005 see PARA 722 note 10.

11 Criminal Justice Act 2003 Sch 20B para 11(1)(b) (as added: see note 1). See note 9.

12 Criminal Justice Act 2003 Sch 20B para 11(1)(c) (as added: see note 1). See note 9.

13 Criminal Justice Act 2003 Sch 20B para 11(1)(d) (as added: see note 1). See note 9.

14 Criminal Justice Act 2003 Sch 20B para 12 (as added: see note 1). As to the duration and conditions of licences for these purposes see PARA 738 et seq.

15 Ie a person to whom the Criminal Justice Act 2003 s 267B, Sch 20B para 13 applies (see heads (i) to (iv) in the text): Sch 20B para 14(1) (as added: see note 1). The provision made by Sch 20B para 13 does not apply, however, if the person has been released and recalled more than once: Sch 20B para 13(2) (as so added).

16 Criminal Justice Act 2003 Sch 20B para 13(1)(a) (as added: see note 1).

17 Criminal Justice Act 2003 Sch 20B para 13(1)(b) (as added: see note 1).

18 Criminal Justice Act 2003 Sch 20B para 13(1)(c) (as added: see note 1). See note 15.

19 Criminal Justice Act 2003 Sch 20B para 13(1)(d) (as added: see note 1). See note 15.

20 Criminal Justice Act 2003 Sch 20B para 14(1), (2) (as added: see note 1).

21 Criminal Justice Act 2003 Sch 20B para 14(1)(a) (as added: see note 1). As to the meaning of 'custodial term' for these purposes see PARA 723 note 9.

22 Criminal Justice Act 2003 Sch 20B para 14(2)(a) (as added: see note 1).

23 Criminal Justice Act 2003 Sch 20B para 14(1)(b), (2)(b) (as added: see note 1). As to the meaning of 'extension period' for these purposes see PARA 723 note 9.

24 Ie where a person is serving an extended sentence imposed before 14 July 2008 under either the Criminal Justice Act 2003 s 227 (repealed with savings) or s 228: Sch 20B para 15(1) (as added: see note 1).

25 Ie the Criminal Justice Act 2003 s 247 (release on licence of prisoners serving extended sentence under s 227 or s 228 (both repealed with savings): see PARA 716) applies: Sch 20B para 15(2) (as added: see note 1).

26 Criminal Justice Act 2003 Sch 20B para 15(1), (2) (as added: see note 1). The specified modifications are that:
    (1)   the Secretary of State must not release the prisoner under s 247(2) (see PARA 716) unless the Parole Board has directed his release under s 247(2) (see s 247(2)(b) as originally enacted) (Sch 20B para 15(3) (as so added));
    (2)   the Parole Board must not give a direction under s 247(3) (as originally enacted) unless the Board is satisfied that it is no longer necessary for the protection of the public that the person should be confined (Sch 20B para 15(4) (as so added)); and
    (3)   as soon as the prisoner has served the appropriate custodial term, the Secretary of State

must release the prisoner on licence, unless he has previously been recalled under s 254 (recall of prisoners after release on licence: see PARA 717) (Sch 20B para 15(5) (as so added)).

As to the constitution and functions of the Parole Board, continued by s 239(1), see PARA 699.

B. RELEASE UNDER TRANSITIONAL ARRANGEMENTS WHERE CRIMINAL JUSTICE ACT 1967 SENTENCES APPLY

727. Initial duty to release. As soon as a person[1]:

(1) who is serving a Criminal Justice Act 1967 sentence of imprisonment imposed before 1 October 1992[2];

(2) whose sentence is for a term of more than 12 months[3]; and

(3) who has not previously been released from prison on licence in respect of that sentence[4],

has served two-thirds of the sentence[5], it is the duty of the Secretary of State[6] to release that person unconditionally[7]; and the Secretary of State must, if directed to do so by the Parole Board[8], release on licence a person who falls within heads (1) to (3) above[9], after he has served one-third of the sentence or six months (whichever is longer)[10]. However, the Board must not give such a direction unless the Board is satisfied that it is no longer necessary for the protection of the public that the person should be confined[11]. Where these transitional provisions apply[12], they displace the usual Criminal Justice Act 2003 provisions[13] which govern the release on licence of prisoners serving 12 months or more[14].

As soon as a person[15]:

(a) who is serving a Criminal Justice Act 1967 sentence of imprisonment imposed before 1 October 1992[16];

(b) whose sentence is for a term of more than 12 months[17];

(c) on the passing of whose sentence an extended sentence certificate was issued[18];

(d) who has not previously been released from prison on licence in respect of that sentence[19],

has served two-thirds of the sentence[20], it is the duty of the Secretary of State to release the person on licence[21]. After a person who falls within heads (a) to (d) above[22] has served one-third of the sentence or six months, whichever is longer, the Secretary of State must, if directed to do so by the Parole Board, release the person on licence[23]. The Board must not give such a direction, however, unless it is satisfied that it is no longer necessary for the protection of the public that the person should be confined[24]. Where these transitional provisions apply[25], they displace the usual Criminal Justice Act 2003 provisions[26] which govern the release on licence of prisoners serving 12 months or more[27].

1 Ie a person to whom the Criminal Justice Act 2003 s 267B, Sch 20B para 24 applies (see heads (1) to (3) in the text): Sch 20B para 25(1) (s 267B, Sch 20B added by the Legal Aid, Sentencing and Punishment of Offenders Act 2012 s 121(6), Sch 17 paras 1, 9, 10). The Criminal Justice Act 2003 Sch 20B para 24 does not apply if, on the passing of the sentence, an extended sentence certificate (see note 18) was issued: Sch 20B para 24(3) (as so added). As to the application of Sch 20B Pt 3 (Sch 20B paras 23–33) see PARA 722 note 9.

2 Criminal Justice Act 2003 Sch 20B para 24(1)(a) (as added: see note 1). As to the meaning of 'Criminal Justice Act 1967 sentence' for these purposes, and as to the significance of the date of 1 October 1992, see PARA 722 note 9.

3 Criminal Justice Act 2003 Sch 20B para 24(1)(b) (as added: see note 1).

4 Criminal Justice Act 2003 Sch 20B para 24(1)(c) (as added: see note 1).

5 Criminal Justice Act 2003 Sch 20B para 25(1)(a) (as added: see note 1).

6 As to the Secretary of State for these purposes see PRISONS AND PRISONERS vol 85 (2012) PARA 408.

7 Criminal Justice Act 2003 Sch 20B para 25(1) (as added: see note 1). The release mentioned in the text is made under Sch 20B para 25: Sch 20B para 25(1) (as so added).

8 As to the constitution and functions of the Parole Board, continued by the Criminal Justice Act 2003 s 239(1), see PARA 699.

9 Ie a person falling within the Criminal Justice Act 2003 Sch 20B para 24(1) (see heads (1) to (3) in the text): Sch 20B para 25(2) (as added: see note 1).

10 Criminal Justice Act 2003 Sch 20B para 25(2) (as added: see note 1). The release mentioned in the text is made under Sch 20B para 25: Sch 20B para 25(2) (as so added). As to the duration and conditions of licences for these purposes see PARA 738 et seq.

11 Criminal Justice Act 2003 Sch 20B para 25(3) (as added: see note 1).

12 Ie where the Criminal Justice Act 2003 Sch 20B para 25(1)–(3) applies (see the text and notes 1–11): Sch 20B para 25(4) (as added: see note 1).

13 Ie in place of the Criminal Justice Act 2003 s 244 (release on licence of prisoners serving 12 months or more: see PARA 713): Sch 20B para 25(4) (as added: see note 1).

14 Criminal Justice Act 2003 Sch 20B para 25(4) (as added: see note 1).

15 Ie a person to whom the Criminal Justice Act 2003 Sch 20B para 27(1) applies (see heads (a) to (d) in the text): Sch 20B para 28(1) (as added: see note 1).

16 Criminal Justice Act 2003 Sch 20B para 27(1)(a) (as added: see note 1).

17 Criminal Justice Act 2003 Sch 20B para 27(1)(b) (as added: see note 1).

18 Criminal Justice Act 2003 Sch 20B para 27(1)(c) (as added: see note 1). For these purposes, 'extended sentence certificate' means a certificate that was issued under the Powers of Criminal Courts Act 1973 s 28 (punishment of persistent offenders) (repealed by the Criminal Justice Act 1991 ss 5(2)(a), 101(2), Sch 13) stating that an extended term of imprisonment was imposed on the person under the Powers of Criminal Courts Act 1973 s 28: Criminal Justice Act 2003 Sch 20B para 27(3) (as so added).

19 Criminal Justice Act 2003 Sch 20B para 27(1)(d) (as added: see note 1).

20 Criminal Justice Act 2003 Sch 20B para 28(1)(a) (as added: see note 1).

21 Criminal Justice Act 2003 Sch 20B para 28(1) (as added: see note 1). The release mentioned in the text is made under Sch 20B para 28: Sch 20B para 28(1) (as so added).

22 Ie after a person falling within the Criminal Justice Act 2003 Sch 20B para 27(1) (see heads (a) to (d) in the text): Sch 20B para 28(2) (as added: see note 1).

23 Criminal Justice Act 2003 Sch 20B para 28(2) (as added: see note 1). The release mentioned in the text is made under Sch 20B para 28: Sch 20B para 28(2) (as so added).

24 Criminal Justice Act 2003 Sch 20B para 28(3) (as added: see note 1).

25 Ie where the Criminal Justice Act 2003 Sch 20B para 28(1)–(3) apply (see the text and notes 20–24): Sch 20B para 28(4) (as added: see note 1).

26 Ie in place of the Criminal Justice Act 2003 s 244: Sch 20B para 28(4) (as added: see note 1).

27 Criminal Justice Act 2003 Sch 20B para 28(4) (as added: see note 1).

728. Release after recall. As soon as a person[1]:

(1) who is serving a Criminal Justice Act 1967 sentence of imprisonment imposed before 1 October 1992[2];

(2) whose sentence is for a term of more than 12 months[3];

(3) who has been released on licence under Part II of the Criminal Justice Act 1991[4]; and

(4) who has been recalled before 14 July 2008 (and has not been recalled after that date)[5],

would (but for the earlier release) have served two-thirds of the sentence[6], it is the duty of the Secretary of State to release the person unconditionally[7].

As soon as a person[8]:

(a) who is serving a Criminal Justice Act 1967 sentence of imprisonment imposed before 1 October 1992[9];

(b) whose sentence is for a term of 12 months or more[10];

(c) on the passing of whose sentence an extended sentence certificate was issued[11];

(d) who has been released on licence under Part II of the Criminal Justice Act 1991[12]; and

(e)   who has been recalled before 14 July 2008 (and has not been recalled after that date)[13],

would (but for the earlier release) have served two-thirds of the sentence[14], it is the duty of the Secretary of State to release the person on licence[15].

1   Ie as soon as a person to whom the Criminal Justice Act 2003 s 267B, Sch 20B para 24(2) applies (see heads (1) to (4) in the text): Sch 20B para 25(1) (s 267B, Sch 20B added by the Legal Aid, Sentencing and Punishment of Offenders Act 2012 s 121(6), Sch 17 paras 1, 9, 10). The Criminal Justice Act 2003 Sch 20B para 24 does not apply if, on the passing of the sentence, an extended sentence certificate was issued: Sch 20B para 24(3) (as so added). As to the meaning of 'extended sentence certificate' see PARA 727 note 18. As to extended sentence certificates see further the text and notes 8–15. As to the application of Sch 20B Pt 3 (Sch 20B paras 23–33) see PARA 722 note 9.
2   Criminal Justice Act 2003 Sch 20B para 24(2)(a) (as added: see note 1). As to the meaning of 'Criminal Justice Act 1967 sentence' for these purposes, and as to the significance of the date of 1 October 1992, see PARA 722 note 9.
3   Criminal Justice Act 2003 Sch 20B para 24(2)(b) (as added: see note 1).
4   Criminal Justice Act 2003 Sch 20B para 24(2)(c) (as added: see note 1). In Sch 20B Pt 3, references to release under the Criminal Justice Act 1991 Pt II (ss 32–51) (repealed) (see PARA 722 note 2) include release under the Criminal Justice Act 1967 s 60 (repealed with savings) (release on licence of persons serving determinate sentences): Criminal Justice Act 2003 Sch 20B para 23(3) (as so added).
5   Criminal Justice Act 2003 Sch 20B para 24(2)(d) (as added: see note 1). As to the significance of the date of 14 July 2008 see PARA 722 note 11. If a person has been released under the Criminal Justice Act 1991 s 34A (repealed) and recalled under s 38A(1)(b) (repealed), or if a person has been released under the Criminal Justice Act 2003 s 246 (power to release fixed-term prisoners before required term: see PARA 715), and recalled under s 255(1)(b) (ie where it is no longer possible to monitor whereabouts of a prisoner released on licence subject to a curfew condition: see PARA 718), the release and recall are to be disregarded for the purposes of Sch 20B para 24: Sch 20B para 24(4) (as so added).
6   Criminal Justice Act 2003 Sch 20B para 25(1)(b) (as added: see note 1).
7   Criminal Justice Act 2003 Sch 20B para 25(1) (as added: see note 1). Such a release as is mentioned in the text is made under Sch 20B para 25: Sch 20B para 25(1) (as so added).
8   Ie as soon as a person to whom the Criminal Justice Act 2003 Sch 20B para 27(2) applies (see heads (a) to (e) in the text): Sch 20B para 28(1) (as added: see note 1).
9   Criminal Justice Act 2003 Sch 20B para 27(2)(a) (as added: see note 1).
10   Criminal Justice Act 2003 Sch 20B para 27(2)(b) (as added: see note 1).
11   Criminal Justice Act 2003 Sch 20B para 27(2)(c) (as added: see note 1).
12   Criminal Justice Act 2003 Sch 20B para 27(2)(d) (as added: see note 1). See note 4.
13   Criminal Justice Act 2003 Sch 20B para 27(2)(e) (as added: see note 1).
14   Criminal Justice Act 2003 Sch 20B para 28(1)(b) (as added: see note 1).
15   Criminal Justice Act 2003 Sch 20B para 28(1) (as added: see note 1). Such a release as is mentioned in the text is made under Sch 20B para 28: Sch 20B para 28(1) (as so added).

(7) FINE DEFAULTERS AND CONTEMNORS

(i) Prisoner Committed or Detained on or after 4 April 2005

729.   Early release of contemnors.   As soon as a person who has been committed to prison for contempt of court or any kindred offence[1] has served one-half of the term for which he was committed, it is the duty of the Secretary of State[2] to release him unconditionally[3]. Where such a person is also serving one or more sentences of imprisonment[4], however, the Secretary of State is not so required[5] to release him until he is also required to release him in respect of that sentence or each of those sentences[6].

The Secretary of State also may at any time release unconditionally such a person if he is satisfied that exceptional circumstances exist which justify the person's release on compassionate grounds[7].

1   Ie a person to whom the Criminal Justice Act 2003 s 258 applies: see s 258(1)(b), (2). These
     provisions apply not only to contemnors (s 258(1)(b)) but also to fine defaulters (see s 258(1)(a);
     and PARA 730). The Criminal Justice Act 2003 ss 243A–264 do not apply in relation to a person
     detained in England and Wales in pursuance of a sentence of the International Criminal Court:
     see the International Criminal Court Act 2001 Sch 7 para 3(1); and PARA 690. As to the
     meanings of 'England' and 'Wales' see PARA 4 note 3.
2   As to the Secretary of State for these purposes see PRISONS AND PRISONERS vol 85 (2012) PARA
     408.
3   Criminal Justice Act 2003 s 258(1)(b), (2). Section 258(2) does not apply to a person within
     s 258(1)(a) if the sum in question is a sum of more than £10m ordered to be paid under a
     confiscation order made under the Proceeds of Crime Act 2002 Pt 2 (ss 6–91) (see PARA 189 et
     seq): Criminal Justice Act 2003 s 258(2B) (s 258(2B), (2C) added by the Serious Crime Act 2015
     s 10(3)). The Secretary of State may by order amend the amount for the time being specified in
     the Criminal Justice Act 2003 s 258(2B): s 258(2C) (as so added). At the date at which this
     volume states the law no such order had been made.
        The provision made by s 258(2) is subject to the transitional arrangements contained in
     s 267B, Sch 20B para 35 (duty to release fine defaulters and contemnors unconditionally: see
     PARA 731): see s 258(2A) (added by the Legal Aid, Sentencing and Punishment of Offenders
     Act 2012 s 121(6), Sch 17 paras 1, 5(1), (2)). Where the transitional provisions do not apply, the
     Criminal Justice Act 2003 s 258 applies to any person who was, before 4 April 2005, committed
     to prison or to be detained under the Powers of Criminal Courts (Sentencing) Act 2000 s 108
     (detention of persons aged at least 18 but under 21 for default or contempt: see PARA 551) for
     contempt of court or any kindred offence: see the Legal Aid, Sentencing and Punishment of
     Offenders Act 2012 s 121(2)(b); and PARA 731 note 10.
4   The reference in the Criminal Justice Act 2003 s 258(3) to sentences of imprisonment includes
     sentences of detention:
     (1)   under the Powers of Criminal Courts (Sentencing) Act 2000 s 91 (sentence of detention
            for a specified period passed on a person aged under 18 who has committed a serious
            offence: see PARA 8; and CHILDREN AND YOUNG PERSONS vol 10 (2012) PARA 1307) or
            s 96 (prospectively repealed) (detention in young offender institution for a person aged
            between 18 and 21: see PARA 16) (Criminal Justice Act 2003 s 258(3A) (added by the
            Legal Aid, Sentencing and Punishment of Offenders Act 2012 s 117(1), (6); and
            amended by s 125(4), Sch 20 paras 1, 8)); or
     (2)   under the Criminal Justice Act 2003 s 226A (extended sentence for certain violent or
            sexual offences (persons 18 or over): see PARAS 18–20), s 226B (extended sentence for
            certain violent or sexual offences (persons under 18): see PARAS 18–20), s 227 (repealed
            with savings), s 228 (repealed with savings) or s 236A (special custodial sentence for
            certain offenders of particular concern: see PARA 32) (see s 258(3A) (as so added and
            amended; further amended by the Criminal Justice and Courts Act 2015 Sch 1
            para 19)).
5   Ie nothing in the Criminal Justice Act 2003 s 258 or in the transitional arrangements contained
     in Sch 20B para 35 (duty to release fine defaulters and contemnors unconditionally: see note 3)
     so requires: s 258(3) (amended by the Legal Aid, Sentencing and Punishment of Offenders
     Act 2012 Sch 17 paras 1, 5(1), (3)).
6   Criminal Justice Act 2003 s 258(3) (as amended see note 5).
7   Criminal Justice Act 2003 s 258(4). As to the release of determinate sentence prisoners on
     compassionate grounds see PARA 696.

730.   Early release of fine defaulters.   As soon as a person who has been
committed to prison in default of payment of a sum adjudged to be paid by a
conviction[1] has served one-half of the term for which he was committed, it is the
duty of the Secretary of State[2] to release him unconditionally[3]. Where such a
person is also serving one or more sentences of imprisonment[4], however, the
Secretary of State is not so required[5] to release him until he is also required to
release him in respect of that sentence or each of those sentences[6].

The Secretary of State also may at any time release unconditionally such a
person if he is satisfied that exceptional circumstances exist which justify the
person's release on compassionate grounds[7].

1   Ie a person to whom the Criminal Justice Act 2003 s 258 applies: s 258(1)(a), (2). These
     provisions apply not only to fine defaulters (see s 258(1)(a)) but also to contemnors (see

s 258(1)(b); and PARA 729) (although as a general rule the early release provisions that apply to criminal defaulters are not applicable to civil defaulters). The Criminal Justice Act 2003 ss 243A–264 do not apply in relation to a person detained in England and Wales in pursuance of a sentence of the International Criminal Court: see the International Criminal Court Act 2001 Sch 7 para 3(1); and PARA 690. As to the meanings of 'England' and 'Wales' see PARA 4 note 3.

2 As to the Secretary of State for these purposes see PRISONS AND PRISONERS vol 85 (2012) PARA 408.

3 Criminal Justice Act 2003 s 258(1)(a), (2). Section 258(2) does not apply to a person within s 258(1)(a) if the sum in question is a sum of more than £10m ordered to be paid under a confiscation order made under the Proceeds of Crime Act 2002 Pt 2 (ss 6–91) (see PARA 189 et seq): Criminal Justice Act 2003 s 258(2B) (s 258(2B), (2C) added by the Serious Crime Act 2015 s 10(3)). The Secretary of State may by order amend the amount for the time being specified in the Criminal Justice Act 2003 s 258(2B): s 258(2C) (as so added). At the date at which this volume states the law no such order had been made.

The provision made by s 258(2) is subject to the transitional arrangements contained in s 267B, Sch 20B para 35 (duty to release fine defaulters and contemnors unconditionally: see PARA 732): s 258(2A) (added by the Legal Aid, Sentencing and Punishment of Offenders Act 2012 s 121(6), Sch 17 paras 1, 5(1), (2)). Where the transitional provisions do not apply, the Criminal Justice Act 2003 s 258 applies to any person who was, before 4 April 2005, committed to prison or to be detained under the Powers of Criminal Courts (Sentencing) Act 2000 s 108 (see PARA 551) in default of payment of a sum adjudged to be paid by a conviction: see the Legal Aid, Sentencing and Punishment of Offenders Act 2012 s 121(2)(a); and PARA 732 note 10.

4 As to the meaning of references in the Criminal Justice Act 2003 s 258(3) to sentences of imprisonment see PARA 729 note 4.

5 Ie nothing in the Criminal Justice Act 2003 s 258 or in the transitional arrangements contained in Sch 20B para 35 (duty to release fine defaulters and contemnors unconditionally: see note 3) so requires: s 258(3) (amended by the Legal Aid, Sentencing and Punishment of Offenders Act 2012 Sch 17 paras 1, 5(1), (3)).

6 Criminal Justice Act 2003 s 258(3) (as amended see note 5).

7 Criminal Justice Act 2003 s 258(4). As to the release of determinate sentence prisoners on compassionate grounds see PARA 696.

(ii) Prisoner Committed or Detained before 4 April 2005

731. Early release of contemnors. As soon as a person[1]:

(1)   who has been committed to prison or to be detained under the Powers of Criminal Courts (Sentencing) Act 2000[2] for contempt of court or any kindred offence[3];

(2)   who was so committed or detained before 4 April 2005[4]; and

(3)   whose term for which he was so committed or detained is 12 months or more[5],

has served two-thirds of the term, it is the duty of the Secretary of State[6] to release the person unconditionally[7].

These transitional provisions governing the early release of contemnors[8], where they apply, displace the usual Criminal Justice Act 2003 provisions[9] governing the same[10].

1 Ie as soon as a person to whom the Criminal Justice Act 2003 s 267B, Sch 20B para 35 applies (see heads (1) to (3) in the text): Sch 20B para 35(2) (s 267B, Sch 20B added by the Legal Aid, Sentencing and Punishment of Offenders Act 2012 s 121(6), Sch 17 paras 1, 9, 10).

2 Ie under the Powers of Criminal Courts (Sentencing) Act 2000 s 108 (prospectively repealed) (detention of persons aged at least 18 but under 21 for default or contempt: see PARA 551): Criminal Justice Act 2003 Sch 20B para 35(1)(a) (as added: see note 1).

3 Criminal Justice Act 2003 Sch 20B para 35(1)(a)(ii) (as added: see note 1).

4 Criminal Justice Act 2003 Sch 20B para 35(1)(b) (as added: see note 1). As to the significance of the date of 4 April 2005 see PARA 722 note 10.

5 Criminal Justice Act 2003 Sch 20B para 35(1)(c) (as added: see note 1).

6 As to the Secretary of State for these purposes see PRISONS AND PRISONERS vol 85 (2012) PARA 408.

7 Criminal Justice Act 2003 Sch 20B para 35(2) (as added: see note 1).

8 Ie the provision made by the Criminal Justice Act 2003 Sch 20B para 35(2) (see the text and notes 1–7): Sch 20B para 35(3) (as added: see note 1).
9 Ie the Criminal Justice Act 2003 s 258(2) (early release of contemnors: see PARA 729): Sch 20B para 35(3) (as added: see note 1).
10 See the Criminal Justice Act 2003 Sch 20B para 35(3) (as added: see note 1). Where the transitional provisions do not apply, s 258 (see PARA 729) applies to any person who was, before 4 April 2005, committed to prison or to be detained under the Powers of Criminal Courts (Sentencing) Act 2000 s 108 for contempt of court or any kindred offence: see the Legal Aid, Sentencing and Punishment of Offenders Act 2012 s 121(2)(b). See also PARA 722 note 11.

732. Early release of fine defaulters. As soon as a person[1]:

(1) who has been committed to prison or to be detained under the Powers of Criminal Courts (Sentencing) Act 2000[2] in default of payment of a sum adjudged to be paid by a conviction[3];

(2) who was so committed or detained before 4 April 2005[4]; and

(3) whose term for which he was so committed or detained is 12 months or more[5],

has served two-thirds of the term, it is the duty of the Secretary of State[6] to release the person unconditionally[7].

These transitional provisions governing the early release of fine defaulters[8], where they apply, displace the usual Criminal Justice Act 2003 provisions[9] governing the same[10].

1 Ie as soon as a person to whom the Criminal Justice Act 2003 s 267B, Sch 20B para 35 applies (see heads (1) to (3) in the text): Sch 20B para 35(2) (s 267B, Sch 20B added by the Legal Aid, Sentencing and Punishment of Offenders Act 2012 s 121(6), Sch 17 paras 1, 9, 10).
2 Ie under the Powers of Criminal Courts (Sentencing) Act 2000 s 108 (prospectively repealed) (detention of persons aged at least 18 but under 21 for default or contempt: see PARA 551): Criminal Justice Act 2003 Sch 20B para 35(1)(a) (as added: see note 1).
3 Criminal Justice Act 2003 Sch 20B para 35(1)(a)(i) (as added: see note 1).
4 Criminal Justice Act 2003 Sch 20B para 35(1)(b) (as added: see note 1). As to the significance of the date of 4 April 2005 see PARA 722 note 10.
5 Criminal Justice Act 2003 Sch 20B para 35(1)(c) (as added: see note 1).
6 As to the Secretary of State for these purposes see PRISONS AND PRISONERS vol 85 (2012) PARA 408.
7 Criminal Justice Act 2003 Sch 20B para 35(2) (as added: see note 1).
8 Ie the provision made by the Criminal Justice Act 2003 Sch 20B para 35(2) (see the text and notes 1–7): Sch 20B para 35(3) (as added: see note 1).
9 Ie the Criminal Justice Act 2003 s 258(2) (early release of fine defaulters: see PARA 730): Sch 20B para 35(3) (as added: see note 1).
10 See the Criminal Justice Act 2003 Sch 20B para 35(3) (as added: see note 1). Where the transitional provisions do not apply, s 258 (early release of fine defaulters: see PARA 730) applies to any person who was, before 4 April 2005, committed to prison or to be detained under the Powers of Criminal Courts (Sentencing) Act 2000 s 108 in default of payment of a sum adjudged to be paid by a conviction: see the Legal Aid, Sentencing and Punishment of Offenders Act 2012 s 121(2)(a). See also PARA 722 note 11.

(8) CONDITIONS OF RELEASE; SUPERVISION

(i) Prisoner serving Indeterminate Sentence

733. Duration of licences granted to life prisoner. Where a life prisoner[1], other than a prisoner falling within heads (1) and (2) below[2], is released on licence[3], the licence must, unless previously revoked[4], remain in force until his death[5]. However, where a prisoner who[6]:

(1) is serving one or more preventive sentences[7]; and

(2) is not serving any other life sentence[8],

has been released on licence under Chapter II of Part II of the Crime (Sentences) Act 1997[9], and where the qualifying period has expired[10], the Secretary of State[11] must, if directed to do so by the Parole Board[12], order that the licence is to cease to have effect[13]. Where:

(a) the prisoner has been released on licence under Chapter II of Part II of the Crime (Sentences) Act 1997[14];

(b) the qualifying period has expired[15]; and

(c) if he has made a previous application[16], a period of at least 12 months has expired since the disposal of that application[17],

the prisoner may make an application to the Parole Board[18]. Where such an application is made, the Parole Board must[19]:

(i) if it is satisfied that it is no longer necessary for the protection of the public that the licence should remain in force, direct the Secretary of State to make an order that the licence is to cease to have effect[20]; or

(ii) otherwise dismiss the application[21].

Where a prisoner falling within heads (1) and (2) above[22] is released on licence, the licence remains in force until his death unless either it is previously revoked[23], or it ceases to have effect in accordance with an order made by the Secretary of State[24].

1   As to the meaning of 'life prisoner' for the purposes of the Crime (Sentences) Act 1997 Pt II Ch II (ss 28–34) (life sentences) see PARA 706.

2   Ie other than a prisoner to whom the Crime (Sentences) Act 1997 s 31A applies (see the text and notes 6–21): s 31(1) (amended by the Criminal Justice Act 2003 s 230, Sch 18 para 1(1), (2); and the Criminal Justice and Immigration Act 2008 s 149, Sch 28 Pt 2). The Crime (Sentences) Act 1997 Pt II Ch II does not apply in relation to a person detained in England and Wales in pursuance of a sentence of the International Criminal Court: see the International Criminal Court Act 2001 Sch 7 para 3(1); and PARA 690. As to the meanings of 'England' and 'Wales' see PARA 4 note 3.

3   As to licence conditions imposed on life prisoners see PARA 734.

4   Ie under the Crime (Sentences) Act 1997 s 32 (see PARA 708): s 31(1) (as amended: see note 2).

5   Crime (Sentences) Act 1997 s 31(1) (as amended: see note 2).

6   Crime (Sentences) Act 1997 s 31A(1), (2) (s 31A added by the Criminal Justice Act 2003 s 230, Sch 18 para 2).

7   Crime (Sentences) Act 1997 s 31A(1)(a) (as added: see note 6). For these purposes, 'preventive sentence' means a sentence of imprisonment or detention in a young offender institution for public protection under the Criminal Justice Act 2003 s 225 (see PARA 37) or a sentence of detention for public protection under s 226 (see PARA 34; and CHILDREN AND YOUNG PERSONS vol 10 (2012) PARA 1300), including such a sentence of imprisonment or detention passed as a result of the Armed Forces Act 2006 s 219 (person aged at least 18 but under 21 convicted by Court Martial of offence of criminal conduct corresponding to a serious offence: see ARMED FORCES vol 3 (2011) PARA 611) or s 221 (required custodial sentences for dangerous offenders: see ARMED FORCES vol 3 (2011) PARA 611): Crime (Sentences) Act 1997 s 31A(5) (s 31A as so added; definition of 'preventive sentence' in s 31A(5) amended by the Armed Forces Act 2006 s 378(1), Sch 16 para 141; and the Legal Aid, Sentencing and Punishment of Offenders Act 2012 s 117(10)(a)). As to young offender institutions see PRISONS AND PRISONERS vol 85 (2012) PARA 487 et seq.

8   Crime (Sentences) Act 1997 s 31A(1)(b) (as added: see note 6).

9   Crime (Sentences) Act 1997 s 31A(2)(a) (as added: see note 6). The text refers to release on licence under Pt II Ch II (see also PARAS 697, 706 et seq, 734 et seq): s 31A(2)(a) (as so added).

10   Crime (Sentences) Act 1997 s 31A(2)(b) (as added: see note 6). For these purposes, the 'qualifying period', in relation to a prisoner who has been released on licence, means the period of 10 years beginning with the date of his release: s 31A(5) (as so added).

11   As to the Secretary of State for these purposes see PRISONS AND PRISONERS vol 85 (2012) PARA 408.

12   As to the constitution and functions of the Parole Board, continued by the Criminal Justice Act 2003 s 239(1), see PARA 699.

13   Crime (Sentences) Act 1997 s 31A(2) (as added: see note 6).

14 Crime (Sentences) Act 1997 s 31A(3)(a) (as added: see note 6). The text refers to release on licence under Pt II Ch II: s 31A(3)(a) (as so added).

15 Crime (Sentences) Act 1997 s 31A(3)(b) (as added: see note 6).

16 Ie a previous application to the Parole Board under the Crime (Sentences) Act 1997 s 31A(3): s 31A(3)(c) (as added: see note 6).

17 Crime (Sentences) Act 1997 s 31A(3)(c) (as added: see note 6).

18 Crime (Sentences) Act 1997 s 31A(3) (as added: see note 6). The text refers to an application which is made under s 31A(3): s 31A(3) (as so added).

19 Crime (Sentences) Act 1997 s 31A(4) (as added: see note 6).

20 Crime (Sentences) Act 1997 s 31A(4)(a) (as added: see note 6).

21 Crime (Sentences) Act 1997 s 31A(4)(b) (as added: see note 6).

22 Ie where a prisoner to whom the Crime (Sentences) Act 1997 s 31A applies (see the text and notes 6–21): s 31(1A) (added by the Criminal Justice Act 2003 Sch 18 para 1(1), (3)).

23 Ie under the Crime (Sentences) Act 1997 s 32(1), (2) (see PARA 708): s 31(1A) (as added: see note 22).

24 Crime (Sentences) Act 1997 s 31(1A) (as added: see note 22). The text refers to an order made by the Secretary of State under s 31A (see s 31A(2) (see the text and notes 11–13) and s 31A(4)(a) (see head (i) in the text)): see s 31(1A) (as so added).

734. Licence conditions imposed on life prisoner. A life prisoner[1] subject to a licence[2] must comply with such conditions as may for the time being be specified in the licence[3]. The Secretary of State[4] may make rules for regulating the supervision of any description of such persons[5].

The Secretary of State must not include a condition in a life prisoner's licence on release, insert a condition in such a licence or vary or cancel a condition of such a licence except in accordance with recommendations of the Parole Board[6] or where required to do so by an order[7] relating to compulsory electronic monitoring conditions[8].

1 As to the meaning of 'life prisoner' for the purposes of the Crime (Sentences) Act 1997 Pt II Ch II (ss 28–34) (life sentences) see PARA 706. The Crime (Sentences) Act 1997 Pt II Ch II does not apply in relation to a person detained in England and Wales in pursuance of a sentence of the International Criminal Court: see the International Criminal Court Act 2001 Sch 7 para 3(1); and PARA 690. As to the meanings of 'England' and 'Wales' see PARA 4 note 3.

2 As to the duration of licences granted to life prisoners see PARA 733.

3 Crime (Sentences) Act 1997 s 31(2) (amended by the Crime and Disorder Act 1998 ss 119, 120(2), Sch 8 para 131(1), Sch 10). The conditions so specified must include on the prisoner's release conditions as to his supervision by (see the Crime (Sentences) Act 1997 s 31(2A) (added by the Crime and Disorder Act 1998 Sch 8 para 131(2))):

    (1)   an officer of a local probation board appointed for or assigned to the local justice area within which the prisoner resides for the time being or (as the case may be) an officer of a provider of probation services acting in the local justice area within which the prisoner resides for the time being (Crime (Sentences) Act 1997 s 31(2A)(a) (s 31(2A) as so added; s 31(2A)(a) amended by the Criminal Justice and Court Services Act 2000 s 74, Sch 7 Pt I para 4(1)(a), (2); and by SI 2005/886; SI 2008/912));

    (2)   where the prisoner is under the age of 22, a social worker of the local authority within whose area the prisoner resides for the time being (Crime (Sentences) Act 1997 s 31(2A)(b) (s 31(2A) as so added; s 31(2A)(b) amended by the Children Act 2004 s 64, Sch 5 Pt 4)); or

    (3)   where the prisoner is under the age of 18, a member of a youth offending team established by that local authority under the Crime and Disorder Act 1998 s 39 (see **CHILDREN AND YOUNG PERSONS** vol 10 (2012) PARA 1193) (Crime (Sentences) Act 1997 s 31(2A)(c) (s 31(2A) as so added)).

As to the provision of probation services in England and Wales see PARAS 666–687. As to local justice areas see **MAGISTRATES** vol 71 (2013) PARA 475.

    In relation to a life prisoner who is liable to removal from the United Kingdom (within the meaning given by the Criminal Justice Act 2003 s 259: see PARA 749 note 3), the Crime (Sentences) Act 1997 s 31(2) has effect as if s 31(2A) were omitted: s 31(6) (amended by the Crime and Disorder Act 1998 Sch 8 para 131(3); and the Criminal Justice Act 2003 s 304, Sch 32 Pt 1 paras 82, 83(1), (4)). As to the meaning of 'United Kingdom' see PARA 4 note 3.

4   As to the Secretary of State for these purposes see PRISONS AND PRISONERS vol 85 (2012) PARA
    408.
5   Crime (Sentences) Act 1997 s 31(2) (as amended: see note 3). At the date at which this volume
    states the law, no such rules had been made.
6   As to the constitution and functions of the Parole Board, continued by the Criminal Justice
    Act 2003 s 239(1), see PARA 699.
7   Ie an order under the Criminal Justice and Court Services Act 2000 s 62A (see PARA 742).
8   Crime (Sentences) Act 1997 s 31(3) (substituted by the Criminal Justice and Courts Act 2015
    Sch 2 para 1).

(ii) Prisoner serving Determinate Sentence for Offence Committed on or after 4 April 2005

A. DURATION OF LICENCES

735. Duration of licences granted to fixed-term prisoner. Where a fixed-term
prisoner[1] (other than one who is serving a sentence of less than 12 months[2]) is
released on licence[3], the licence must, subject to any revocation[4], remain in force
for the remainder of his sentence[5].
   Where a fixed-term prisoner who is serving a sentence of less than 12 months[6]
is released on licence, the licence must, subject to any revocation[7], remain in
force until the date on which, but for the release, the prisoner would have served
one-half of the sentence[8].

1   As to the meaning of 'fixed-term prisoner' for the purposes of the Criminal Justice Act 2003
    Pt 12 Ch 6 (ss 237–268) (sentencing: release, licences and recall) see PARA 709.
2   Ie other than one to whom the Criminal Justice Act 2003 s 243A (unconditional release of
    prisoners serving less than 12 months: see PARA 712) applies (see the text and notes 6–8):
    s 249(1) (amended by the Legal Aid, Sentencing and Punishment of Offenders Act 2012
    ss 89(2), 111(2), Sch 10 paras 12, 24(a), Sch 14 paras 5, 8(1), (2)). The Criminal Justice
    Act 2003 ss 243A–264 do not apply in relation to a person detained in England and Wales in
    pursuance of a sentence of the International Criminal Court: see the International Criminal
    Court Act 2001 Sch 7 para 3(1); and PARA 690. As to the meanings of 'England' and 'Wales' see
    PARA 4 note 3.
3   As to licence conditions imposed on fixed-term prisoners see PARA 736.
4   Ie under either the Criminal Justice Act 2003 s 254 (recall of prisoners after release on licence:
    see PARA 717) or s 255 (recall of early release prisoners: see PARA 718): s 249(1) (as amended:
    see note 2).
5   Criminal Justice Act 2003 s 249(1) (as amended: see note 2). The provision made by s 249(1) is
    subject to s 249(3): s 249(1) (as so amended). Accordingly, it has effect subject to s 263(2) (see
    PARA 710), s 264(3C)(a) (see PARA 711) and s 264B (see PARA 711): s 249(3) (amended by the
    Legal Aid, Sentencing and Punishment of Offenders Act 2012 Sch 10 paras 12, 24(c), Sch 14
    paras 5, 8(1), (4); and by the Offender Rehabilitation Act 2014 s 5(4)). As from 3 December
    2012, the Criminal Justice Act 2003 s 249 is subject also to the transitional arrangements
    contained in s 267B, Sch 20B para 17 (duration of licence where offence committed before
    4 April 2005: see PARA 738), Sch 20B para 19 (duration of licence where extended sentence
    imposed for offence committed before 4 April 2005: see PARA 738) and Sch 20B para 26
    (duration of licence where sentence imposed before 1 October 1992: see PARA 739): s 249(5)
    (added by the Legal Aid, Sentencing and Punishment of Offenders Act 2012 s 121(6), Sch 17
    paras 1, 4); the Legal Aid, Sentencing and Punishment of Offenders Act 2012 (Commencement
    No 4 and Saving Provisions) Order 2012, SI 2012/2906, art 2(d), (o).
6   Ie a prisoner to whom the Criminal Justice Act 2003 s 243A (unconditional release of prisoners
    serving less than 12 months: see PARA 712) applies: s 249(1A) (added by the Legal Aid,
    Sentencing and Punishment of Offenders Act 2012 Sch 14 paras 5, 8(1), (3)). See note 2.
7   Ie under either the Criminal Justice Act 2003 s 254 or s 255: s 249(1A) (as added: see note 6).
8   Criminal Justice Act 2003 s 249(1A) (as added: see note 6). The provision made by s 249(1A) is
    subject to s 249(3) (see note 5): s 249(1A) (as so added).

B. LICENCE CONDITIONS

736. Licence conditions imposed on fixed-term prisoner. Any licence granted on release under Chapter 6 of Part 12 of the Criminal Justice Act 2003[1] in respect of a fixed-term prisoner[2] serving a sentence of imprisonment[3] or detention in a young offender institution[4]:

(1)   must include the standard conditions[5];

(2)   must include any electronic monitoring conditions required[6] by order[7]; and

(2)   may include any other electronic monitoring, drug testing or polygraph condition[8], and such other conditions of a kind prescribed by the Secretary of State for these purposes as the Secretary of State may for the time being specify in the licence[9].

A licence granted on the release of a fixed-term prisoner under these provisions must also include a curfew condition[10].

A person subject to any such licence granted on release[11] must comply with such conditions as may for the time being be specified in the licence[12]. However, where:

(a)   the licence relates to a sentence of imprisonment passed by a service court[13]; and

(b)   the person is residing outside the British Islands[14],

the conditions specified in the licence apply to him only so far as it is practicable for him to comply with them where he is residing[15].

1   Ie any licence under the Criminal Justice Act 2003 Pt 12 Ch 6 (ss 237–268) (sentencing: release, licences and recall) (see also PARAS 696, 699, 709 et seq, 737 et seq): s 250(4) (amended by the Legal Aid, Sentencing and Punishment of Offenders Act 2012 ss 111(2), 117(1), (5), 125(4), Sch 14 paras 5, 9, Sch 20 paras 1, 6(1), (2); and by the Criminal Justice and Courts Act 2015 Sch 1 para 17). The Criminal Justice Act 2003 ss 243A–264 do not apply in relation to a person detained in England and Wales in pursuance of a sentence of the International Criminal Court: see the International Criminal Court Act 2001 Sch 7 para 3(1); and PARA 690. As to the meanings of 'England' and 'Wales' see PARA 4 note 3.

2   As to the meaning of 'fixed-term prisoner' for the purposes of the Criminal Justice Act 2003 Pt 12 Ch 6 (sentencing: release, licences and recall) see PARA 709.

3   Ie including a sentence imposed under the Criminal Justice Act 2003 s 226A (extended sentence for certain violent or sexual offences (persons 18 or over): see PARAS 18–20), s 227 (repealed with savings) or s 236A (special custodial sentence for certain offenders of particular concern: see PARA 32): s 250(4) (as amended: see note 1).

4   Criminal Justice Act 2003 s 250(4) (as amended: see note 1). The text refers to any sentence of detention in a young offender institution:

    (1)   under the Powers of Criminal Courts (Sentencing) Act 2000 s 91 (sentence of detention for a specified period passed on a person aged under 18 who has committed a serious offence: see PARA 8; and **CHILDREN AND YOUNG PERSONS** vol 10 (2012) PARA 1307) or s 96 (prospectively repealed) (detention in young offender institution for a person aged between 18 and 21: see PARA 16) (Criminal Justice Act 2003 s 250(4) (as so amended)); or

    (2)   under the Criminal Justice Act 2003 s 226A, s 226B (extended sentence for certain violent or sexual offences (persons under 18): see PARAS 18–20), s 227 (repealed with savings), s 228 (repealed with savings) or s 236A (s 250(4) (as so amended)).

    References in Pt 12 Ch 6 to a sentence of detention under the Powers of Criminal Courts (Sentencing) Act 2000 s 96 (see head (1) above) or under the Criminal Justice Act 2003 s 226A (see head (2) above), s 227 (see head (2) above) or s 236A (see head (2) above) are references to a sentence of detention in a young offender institution: see s 237(3); and PARA 709 note 3. As to young offender institutions see **PRISONS AND PRISONERS** vol 85 (2012) PARA 487 et seq.

5   Criminal Justice Act 2003 s 250(4)(a). For these purposes, the 'standard conditions' means such conditions as may be prescribed for the purposes of s 250 as standard conditions; and 'prescribed' means prescribed by the Secretary of State by order: s 250(1). In exercising his powers to prescribe standard conditions, or the other conditions referred to in s 250(4)(b)(ii)

(see the text and note 9), the Secretary of State must have regard to the following purposes of the supervision of offenders while on licence under Pt 12 Ch 6 (s 250(8)):

(1)   the protection of the public (s 250(8)(a));
(2)   the prevention of re-offending (s 250(8)(b)); and
(3)   securing the successful re-integration of the prisoner into the community (s 250(8)(c)).

As to the Secretary of State for these purposes see PRISONS AND PRISONERS vol 85 (2012) PARA 408. In exercise of the powers conferred upon him by ss 250(1), (4)(b)(ii), 330(3), the Secretary of State has made the Criminal Justice (Sentencing) (Licence Conditions) Order 2015, SI 2015/337. Accordingly, the standard conditions prescribed for the purposes of the Criminal Justice Act 2003 s 250(1) are that the prisoner must (by virtue of the Criminal Justice (Sentencing) (Licence Conditions) Order 2015, SI 2015/337, art 3):

(a)   be of good behaviour and not behave in a way which undermines the purpose of the licence period;
(b)   not commit any offence;
(c)   keep in touch with the supervising officer in accordance with instructions given by the supervising officer;
(d)   receive visits from the supervising officer in accordance with instructions given by the supervising officer;
(e)   reside permanently at an address approved by the supervising officer and obtain the prior permission of the supervising officer for any stay of one or more nights at a different address;
(f)   not undertake work, or a particular type of work, unless it is approved by the supervising officer and notify the supervising officer in advance of any proposal to undertake work or a particular type of work; and
(g)   not travel outside the United Kingdom, the Channel Islands or the Isle of Man except with the prior permission of your supervising officer or for the purposes of immigration deportation or removal.

As to deportation or removal from the United Kingdom in accordance with the Immigration Act 1971 or the Immigration and Asylum Act 1999 see IMMIGRATION AND ASYLUM vol 57 (2012) PARA 177 et seq. As to the meaning of 'United Kingdom' see PARA 4 note 3).

Further to head (a) above, see *R (on the application of McDonagh) v Secretary of State for Justice* [2010] EWHC 369 (Admin), [2010] All ER (D) 165 (Mar) (words 'to be well behaved' in the context of a condition of release on licence meant at least to conduct oneself not merely lawfully but in a way that did not adversely affect, annoy, hinder, inconvenience or distress another or others in relation to their lawful activities or performance of their lawful duties, whether by action, omission or by a course of conduct; there was more than sufficient material available to the probation service and the Secretary of State for them to conclude that the prisoner was 'attempting to flee the scene of what was potentially a very serious road traffic accident').

6   Ie any condition which is required by order under the Criminal Justice and Court Services Act 2000 s 62A (electronic monitoring: see PARA 742): Criminal Justice Act 2003 s 250(4)(aa) (s 250(4)(aa) added, s 250(4)(b)(i) amended, by the Criminal Justice and Court Services Act 2000 Sch 2 para 4).

7   Criminal Justice Act 2003 s 250(4)(aa) (as added: see note 6). The standard conditions that must be included in an offender's licence in accordance with s 250(4)(a) where the offender is subject to an electronic monitoring condition under the Criminal Justice and Court Services Act 2000 s 62 or s 62A are (by virtue of the Criminal Justice (Sentencing) (Licence Conditions) Order 2015, SI 2015/337, art 4):

(1)   allow an electronic device to be fitted to their person;
(2)   allow the installation of any equipment associated with electronic monitoring;
(3)   not damage or tamper with the electronic device or equipment associated with electronic monitoring;
(4)   ensure at all times that the electronic device is sufficiently charged;
(5)   immediately report to the supervising officer if the electronic device or equipment associated with electronic monitoring is not working correctly;
(6)   allow any person nominated by the supervising officer to check whether the electronic device or equipment associated with electronic monitoring is working correctly.

8   Criminal Justice Act 2003 s 250(4)(b)(i) (as amended (see note 6); amended by the Offender Rehabilitation Act 2014 ss 12(2), 28(5)). The conditions referred to are any other condition authorised by the Criminal Justice and Court Services Act 2000 s 62, s 64 or s 64A (see PARAS 742, 743) or the Offender Management Act 2007 s 28 (see PARA 744): Criminal Justice Act 2003 s 250(4)(b)(i) (as so amended). The conditions that are the standard conditions that must be included in an offender's licence in accordance with s 250(4)(a) where the offender is

subject to a drug testing requirement under the Criminal Justice and Court Services Act 2000 s 64 are that while subject to a drug testing requirement an offender must attend a place notified to the offender by the supervising officer, and comply with the required form of testing and must not frustrate the drug testing process: Criminal Justice (Sentencing) (Licence Conditions) Order 2015, SI 2015/337, art 5. The conditions that are the standard conditions that must be included in an offender's licence in accordance with the Criminal Justice Act 2003 s 250(4)(a) where the offender is subject to a polygraph condition under the Offender Management Act 2007 s 28 are that while subject to a polygraph condition an offender must attend a polygraph testing session and examination as instructed by the supervising officer, and comply with the process, comply with any instruction given during a polygraph session by the person conducting the polygraph, and must not frustrate the polygraph testing process: Criminal Justice (Sentencing) (Licence Conditions) Order 2015, SI 2015/337, art 6.

9   Criminal Justice Act 2003 s 250(4)(b)(ii). The conditions of a kind prescribed for the purposes of s 250(4)(b)(ii) are (by virtue of the Criminal Justice (Sentencing) (Licence Conditions) Order 2015, SI 2015/337, art 7) those concerning:
    (1)   residence at a specified place;
    (2)   restriction of residency;
    (3)   making or maintaining contact with a person;
    (4)   participation in, or co-operation with, a programme or set of activities;
    (5)   possession, ownership, control or inspection of specified items or documents;
    (6)   disclosure of information;
    (7)   a curfew arrangement (ie an arrangement under which an offender is required to remain at a specified place for a specified period of time which is not an arrangement contained in a curfew condition imposed by virtue of the Criminal Justice Act 2003 s 250(5) (see PARA 736));
    (8)   freedom of movement; and
    (9)   supervision in the community by the supervising officer, or other responsible officer, or organisation.

    Until a day to be appointed it is provided that in respect of a prisoner serving an extended sentence imposed under s 226A or s 226B, other than a sentence that meets the conditions in s 246A(2) (release without direction of the Board: see PARA 716), or in respect of a prisoner serving a sentence imposed under s 236A, the Secretary of State must not include a condition referred to in s 250(4)(b)(ii) in any licence granted either on initial release or after recall to prison, or vary or cancel any such condition included in the licence, unless the Board directs him to do so: s 250(5A), (5B) (s 250(5A) added by the Legal Aid, Sentencing and Punishment of Offenders Act 2012 Sch 20 paras 1, 6(1), (3); Criminal Justice Act 2003 s 250(5A) substituted and amended, s 250(5B) added, by the Criminal Justice and Courts Act 2015 s 15(5), Sch 1 para 17; Criminal Justice Act 2003 s 250(5A), (5B) prospectively further amended, s 250(5C) prospectively added, by the Criminal Justice and Courts Act 2015 Sch 3 para 7). As from the appointed day it is provided that where a prisoner serving an extended sentence imposed under the Criminal Justice Act 2003 s 226A or s 226B, other than a sentence that meets the conditions in s 246A(2), or in respect of a prisoner serving a sentence imposed under s 236A, then: (a) in the case of a licence granted when the prisoner is initially released, the Secretary of State must not include a condition referred to in s 250(4)(b)(ii) in any licence granted either on initial release or after recall to prison, or vary or cancel any such condition included in the licence, unless the Board directs him to do so (s 250(5A), (5B) (as so added, substituted, amended and prospectively amended)); and (b) in the case of a licence granted when the prisoner is released after recall to prison, the Secretary of State must not include a condition referred to in s 250(4)(b)(ii) in the licence, either on release or subsequently, or vary or cancel any such condition included in the licence, unless a recall adjudicator directs the Secretary of State to do so (s 250(5C) (as so prospectively added)). At the date at which this volume states the law no day had been appointed for these purposes. As to recall adjudicators see PARA 705.

10   See the Criminal Justice Act 2003 s 250(5); and PARA 737. The text refers to a curfew condition complying with s 253 (see PARA 737): see s 250(5). As to the meaning of 'curfew condition' see PARA 737 note 4.

11   Ie any licence under the Criminal Justice Act 2003 Pt 12 Ch 6: s 252(1) (s 252(1) numbered as such, s 252(2) added, by the Armed Forces Act 2006 s 378(1), Sch 16 para 224).

12   Criminal Justice Act 2003 s 252(1) (as renumbered: see note 11). See *R (on the application of Carman) v Secretary of State for the Home Department* [2004] EWHC 2400 (Admin), (2004) Times, 11 October, [2004] All ER (D) 591 (Jul) (per curiam) (challenges to licence conditions should be unusual; licence conditions and assessment of risk are matters of fine judgment for those in the prison and probation services, which were experienced in such matters, and the courts must be steadfastly astute not to interfere save in the most exceptional case); cf *R (on the*

application of Craven) v Secretary of State for the Home Department [2001] EWHC Admin 850, [2001] All ER (D) 74 (Oct) (imposition of an exclusion zone on the movements of a convicted murderer, in order to minimise the risk of accidental contact between him and the family of his victim ought to be considered as being capable of being necessary in a democratic society under the Convention for the Protection of Human Rights and Fundamental Freedoms (Rome, 4 November 1950; TS 71 (1953); Cmd 8969; ETS no 5) (the European Convention on Human Rights) art 8 (right to respect for private and family life, home and correspondence: see RIGHTS AND FREEDOMS vol 88A (2013) PARAS 317 et seq, 351 et seq)).

13 Criminal Justice Act 2003 s 252(2)(a) (s 252(2) as added (see note 11); s 252(2)(a) amended by the Legal Aid, Sentencing and Punishment of Offenders Act 2012 Sch 10 paras 12, 27(a)). As to the meaning of 'service court' see the Criminal Justice Act 2003 s 305(1); and PARA 1 note 1.

14 Criminal Justice Act 2003 s 252(2)(c) (as added: see note 11).

15 Criminal Justice Act 2003 s 252(2) (as added: see note 11).

737. Home detention curfew conditions applied where prisoner released on licence before required term. A licence granted on the release of a fixed-term prisoner[1] before the required term[2] must also include a curfew condition[3].

The curfew condition[4] may specify different places or different periods for different days, but may not specify periods which amount to less than nine hours in any one day (excluding for this purpose the first and last days of the period for which the condition is in force)[5].

The curfew condition is to remain in force until the date when the released person would (but for his release) fall to be released either unconditionally[6] or on licence in due course[7].

1 As to the meaning of 'fixed-term prisoner' for the purposes of the Criminal Justice Act 2003 Pt 12 Ch 6 (ss 237–268) (sentencing: release, licences and recall) see PARA 709.

2 Ie a licence under the Criminal Justice Act 2003 s 246 (power to release fixed-term prisoners before required term: see PARA 715): s 250(5). The Criminal Justice Act 2003 ss 243A–264 do not apply in relation to a person detained in England and Wales in pursuance of a sentence of the International Criminal Court: see the International Criminal Court Act 2001 Sch 7 para 3(1); and PARA 690. As to the meanings of 'England' and 'Wales' see PARA 4 note 3.

3 Criminal Justice Act 2003 s 250(5). The text refers to a curfew condition complying with s 253 (see the text and notes 4–8): s 250(5).

4 For the purposes of the Criminal Justice Act 2003 Pt 12 Ch 6 a 'curfew condition' is a condition which:
   (1) requires the released person to remain, for periods for the time being specified in the condition, at a place for the time being so specified (which may be premises approved by the Secretary of State under the Offender Management Act 2007 s 13 (see PARA 673)) (Criminal Justice Act 2003 s 253(1)(a) (amended by SI 2008/912)); and
   (2) includes a requirement, imposed under the Criminal Justice and Court Services Act 2000 s 62 (see PARA 742) to submit to electronic monitoring of his whereabouts during the periods for the time being so specified (Criminal Justice Act 2003 s 253(1)(b) (amended by the Criminal Justice and Court Services Act 2015 Sch 2 para 5)).
   However, nothing in the Criminal Justice Act 2003 s 253 is to be taken to require the Secretary of State to ensure that arrangements are made for the electronic monitoring of the whereabouts of released persons in any particular part of England and Wales: s 253(6). As to the Secretary of State for these purposes see PRISONS AND PRISONERS vol 85 (2012) PARA 408.

5 Criminal Justice Act 2003 s 253(2).

6 Ie released unconditionally under the Criminal Justice Act 2003 s 243A (unconditional release of prisoners serving less than 12 months: see PARA 712): s 253(3) (amended by the Legal Aid, Sentencing and Punishment of Offenders Act 2012 s 111(2), Sch 14 paras 5, 10).

7 Criminal Justice Act 2003 s 253(3) (as amended: see note 6). The text refers the date when the released person would (but for his release) fall to be released on licence under s 244 (duty to release fixed-term prisoners: see PARA 713): s 253(3) (as so amended).

(iii) Prisoner serving Determinate Sentence for Offence Committed before 4 April 2005

738.   Duration of licences granted to prisoner serving Criminal Justice Act 1991 sentences and certain extended sentences. Where certain prisoners convicted of an offence committed before 4 April 2005[1] are released on licence for the first time under transitional provisions[2], or in accordance with the automatic release provisions of the Criminal Justice Act 2003[3], the licence remains in force until the date on which the person would (but for the release) have served three-quarters of the sentence[4]. The class of prisoners subject to this provision include persons serving a 'Criminal Justice Act 1991 sentence'[5] (or serving a specified extended sentence which falls within the definition of a 'Criminal Justice Act 2003 sentence' for these purposes[6]), and who:

(1)   are persons meeting the statutory conditions for automatic release on licence[7]; or

(2)   are persons: (a) who have been convicted of an offence committed before 4 April 2005[8]; (b) who are serving a sentence of imprisonment imposed in respect of that offence on or after 1 October 1992 but before 3 December 2012[9]; (c) whose sentence is for a term of 12 months or more but less than four years[10]; and (d) who has not previously been released from prison on licence in respect of that sentence[11]; or

(3)   are persons: (a) who have been convicted of an offence committed before 4 April 2005[12]; (b) who are serving a sentence of imprisonment imposed in respect of that offence on or after 1 October 1992[13]; (c) whose sentence is for a term of 12 months or more[14]; (d) who has been released on licence under Part II of the Criminal Justice Act 1991[15]; and (e) who has been recalled before 14 July 2008 (and has not been recalled after that date)[16].

Where a person who[17]:

(i)   has been convicted of an offence committed on or after 30 September 1998 but before 4 April 2005[18];

(ii)   is serving a section 85 extended sentence imposed in respect of that offence[19]; and

(iii) has not previously been released from prison on licence in respect of that sentence[20],

is released on licence, the licence remains in force until the end of the period found by adding[21]:

(A)   one-half of the custodial term (where the prisoner is released on licence and the custodial term is less than 12 months)[22] or three-quarters of the custodial term (where the prisoner is released on licence and the custodial term is 12 months or more)[23]; and

(B)   the extension period[24].

These transitional provisions, governing the duration of licences granted to prisoners serving Criminal Justice Act 1991 sentences and certain extended sentences[25], where they apply, displace the usual Criminal Justice Act 2003 provisions[26] governing the same[27].

The Prison Service Instructions System gives guidance and deals with basic matters of policy relating to the process of parole release and recall, including licences granted to fixed-term prisoners[28].

---

1   Ie where a person to whom the Criminal Justice Act 2003 s 267B, Sch 20B para 16 applies (see heads (1) to (3) in the text): Sch 20B para 17(1) (s 267B, Sch 20B added by the Legal Aid,

Sentencing and Punishment of Offenders Act 2012 s 121(6), Sch 17 paras 1, 9, 10). As to the application of the Criminal Justice Act 2003 Sch 20B Pt 2 (Sch 20B paras 3–22), and as to the significance of the date of 4 April 2005, see PARA 722 notes 10, 11.

The Criminal Justice Act 2003 Sch 20B para 16 does not apply if the person has been released and recalled more than once: Sch 20B para 16(4) (as so added). If a person has been released under the Criminal Justice Act 1991 s 34A (repealed) and recalled under s 38A(1)(b) (repealed), or if a person has been released under the Criminal Justice Act 2003 s 246 (power to release fixed-term prisoners before required term: see PARA 715), and recalled under s 255(1)(b) (ie where it is no longer possible to monitor whereabouts of a prisoner released on licence subject to a curfew condition: see PARA 718), the release and recall are to be disregarded for the purposes of Sch 20B para 16: Sch 20B para 16(6) (as so added).

Nor does Sch 20B para 16 apply if:

(1) the person is serving a section 85 extended sentence (Sch 20B para 16(5)(a) (as so added)); or

(2) the court by which the person was sentenced ordered that the Powers of Criminal Courts (Sentencing) Act 2000 s 86 (repealed) (extension of periods in custody and on licence in the case of certain sexual offences committed before 30 September 1998) should apply (Criminal Justice Act 2003 Sch 20B para 16(5)(b) (as so added)).

References in Sch 20B to the Powers of Criminal Courts (Sentencing) Act 2000 s 86 (repealed) include, in accordance with s 165, Sch 11 para 1(3), the Criminal Justice Act 1991 s 44 (extended sentences for sexual or violent offenders) (repealed), as originally enacted: Criminal Justice Act 2003 Sch 20B para 1(7). As to the meaning of a 'section 85 extended sentence' for these purposes, and as to the significance of the date of 30 September 1998, see PARA 723 note 9. As to the duration of licences granted to prisoners serving extended sentences see further the text and notes 17–27.

2   Ie released on licence under the Criminal Justice Act 2003 Sch 20B para 5 or Sch 20B para 6 (see PARA 725): Sch 20B para 17(1) (as added: see note 1).

3   Ie under the Criminal Justice Act 2003 s 244 (release on licence of prisoners serving 12 months or more: see PARA 713): Sch 20B para 17(1) (as added: see note 1).

4   Criminal Justice Act 2003 Sch 20B para 17(1) (as added: see note 1). The provision made by Sch 20B para 17(1) is subject to any revocation under s 254 (recall of prisoners while on licence: see PARA 717): Sch 20B para 17(2) (as so added).

5   Ie where the Criminal Justice Act 2003 Sch 20B Pt 2 applies to a person by virtue of Sch 20B para 3(1): see PARA 722. As to the meaning of 'Criminal Justice Act 1991 sentence' for these purposes see PARA 722 note 10.

6   Ie where the Criminal Justice Act 2003 Sch 20B Pt 2 applies to a person by virtue of Sch 20B para 3(2): see PARA 722. As to the meaning of 'Criminal Justice Act 2003 sentence' for these purposes see PARA 722 note 11.

7   Ie where the Criminal Justice Act 2003 Sch 20B para 4 applies to a person (see PARA 725 note 4): Sch 20B para 16(1) (as added: see note 1).

8   Criminal Justice Act 2003 Sch 20B para 16(2)(a) (as added: see note 1).

9   Criminal Justice Act 2003 Sch 20B para 16(2)(b) (as added: see note 1). The date of 3 December 2012 is known for these purposes as the 'commencement date', being the date on which the Legal Aid, Sentencing and Punishment of Offenders Act 2012 s 121 came into force on the day appointed under s 151(1) (see the Legal Aid, Sentencing and Punishment of Offenders Act 2012 (Commencement No 4 and Saving Provisions) Order 2012, SI 2012/2906, art 2(d), (o)): Criminal Justice Act 2003 Sch 20B para 1(1), (2) (as so added). As to the significance of the date of 1 October 1992 see PARA 722 note 9.

10   Criminal Justice Act 2003 Sch 20B para 16(2)(c) (as added: see note 1).

11   Criminal Justice Act 2003 Sch 20B para 16(2)(d) (as added: see note 1).

12   Criminal Justice Act 2003 Sch 20B para 16(3)(a) (as added: see note 1).

13   Criminal Justice Act 2003 Sch 20B para 16(3)(b) (as added: see note 1).

14   Criminal Justice Act 2003 Sch 20B para 16(3)(c) (as added: see note 1).

15   Criminal Justice Act 2003 Sch 20B para 16(3)(d) (as added: see note 1). As to the Criminal Justice Act 1991 Pt II (ss 32–51) (repealed) see PARA 722 note 2.

16   Criminal Justice Act 2003 Sch 20B para 16(3)(e) (as added: see note 1). As to the significance of the date of 14 July 2008 see PARA 722 note 11.

17   Ie a person to whom the Criminal Justice Act 2003 Sch 20B para 18 applies (see heads (i) to (iii) in the text): Sch 20B para 19(1), (2) (as added: see note 1).

18   Criminal Justice Act 2003 Sch 20B para 18(a) (as added: see note 1).

19   Criminal Justice Act 2003 Sch 20B para 18(b) (as added: see note 1).

20   Criminal Justice Act 2003 Sch 20B para 18(c) (as added: see note 1).

21 Criminal Justice Act 2003 Sch 20B para 19(1), (2) (as added: see note 1). The provision made by Sch 20B para 19(1), (2) is subject to any revocation under s 254: Sch 20B para 19(3) (as so added).

22 Criminal Justice Act 2003 Sch 20B para 19(1)(a) (as added: see note 1). As to the meaning of 'custodial term' for these purposes see PARA 722 note 9.

23 See the Criminal Justice Act 2003 Sch 20B para 19(2)(a) (as added: see note 1).

24 See the Criminal Justice Act 2003 Sch 20B para 19(1)(b), (2)(b) (as added: see note 1). As to the meaning of 'extension period' for these purposes see PARA 722 note 9.

25 Ie the provision made by the Criminal Justice Act 2003 Sch 20B para 17(1), (2) (see the text and notes 1–16) or Sch 20B para 19(1)–(3) (see the text and notes 17–24): Sch 20B paras 17(3), 19(4) (as added: see note 1).

26 Ie the Criminal Justice Act 2003 s 249 (duration of licence: see PARA 735): Sch 20B paras 17(3), 19(4) (as added: see note 1).

27 Criminal Justice Act 2003 Sch 20B paras 17(3), 19(4) (as added: see note 1). Accordingly. as from 3 December 2012, s 249 is subject to the transitional arrangements contained in Sch 20B para 17 (see also the text and notes 1–16) and Sch 20B para 19 (see also the text and notes 17–24): see s 249(5); the Legal Aid, Sentencing and Punishment of Offenders Act 2012 (Commencement No 4 and Saving Provisions) Order 2012, SI 2012/2906, art 2(d), (o); and PARA 735.

28 As to the system of central policy instructions and guidance contained eg in Prison Service Orders (PSOs) and Prison Service Instructions (PSIs) see PRISONS AND PRISONERS vol 85 (2012) PARA 406.

739. Duration of licences granted to prisoner serving Criminal Justice Act 1967 sentences. Where certain persons who are serving Criminal Justice Act 1967 sentences[1] are released on licence under transitional provisions upon direction by the Parole Board[2], the licence remains in force until the date on which the person would (but for the release) have served two-thirds of the sentence[3].

These transitional provisions governing the duration of licences[4], where they apply, displace the usual Criminal Justice Act 2003 provisions[5] governing the same[6].

The Prison Service Instructions System gives guidance and deals with basic matters of policy relating to the process of parole release and recall, including licences granted to fixed-term prisoners[7].

1 Ie where a person to whom the Criminal Justice Act 2003 s 267B, Sch 20B para 24(1) applies (see PARA 727): Sch 20B para 26(1) (s 267B, Sch 20B added by the Legal Aid, Sentencing and Punishment of Offenders Act 2012 s 121(6), Sch 17 paras 1, 9, 10). As to the meaning of 'Criminal Justice Act 1967 sentence' for these purposes, and as to the application of the Criminal Justice Act 2003 Sch 20B Pt 3 (Sch 20B paras 23–33), see PARA 722 note 9.

2 Ie released on licence under the Criminal Justice Act 2003 Sch 20B para 25(2) (see PARA 727): Sch 20B para 26(1) (as added: see note 1). As to the constitution and functions of the Parole Board, continued by s 239(1), see PARA 699.

3 Criminal Justice Act 2003 Sch 20B para 26(1) (as added: see note 1). The provision made by Sch 20B para 26(1) is subject to any revocation under s 254 (recall of prisoners while on licence: see PARA 717): Sch 20B para 26(2) (as so added).

4 Ie the provision made by Sch 20B para 26(1), (2) (see the text and notes 1–3): Sch 20B para 26(3) (as added: see note 1).

5 Ie the Criminal Justice Act 2003 s 249 (duration of licence: see PARA 735): Sch 20B para 26(3) (as added: see note 1).

6 Criminal Justice Act 2003 Sch 20B para 26(3) (as added: see note 1). Accordingly, as from 3 December 2012, s 249 is subject to the transitional arrangements contained in Sch 20B para 26 (see also the text and notes 1–5): see s 249(5); the Legal Aid, Sentencing and Punishment of Offenders Act 2012 (Commencement No 4 and Saving Provisions) Order 2012, SI 2012/2906, art 2(d), (o); and PARA 735.

7 As to the system of central policy instructions and guidance contained eg in Prison Service Orders (PSOs) and Prison Service Instructions (PSIs) see PRISONS AND PRISONERS vol 85 (2012) PARA 406.

740. Variation under transitional arrangements of licences granted on discretionary release by the Parole Board. Until a day to be appointed the Secretary of State[1] must not[2]:

(1)   include on release, or subsequently insert, a condition in a Parole Board licence[3]; or

(2)   vary or cancel any such condition[4],

except in accordance with directions of the Parole Board[5], and any licence is a 'Parole Board licence' if it falls within head (a) or head (b) below[6], namely:

(a)   if the licence is or was granted to a person on his or her release (at any time) on the recommendation or direction of the Parole Board[7], and if that person has not been released otherwise than on such a recommendation or direction[8]; or

(b)   if the licence is or was granted to a person on his or her release (at any time)[9], and if one of two conditions ('condition A' or 'condition B') is met[10].

As from the appointed day:

(i)   in the case of a Parole Board licence granted when the prisoner is initially released, the Secretary of State must not include a prescribed condition[11] in the licence, either on release or subsequently[12], or vary or cancel any such condition[13], unless the Board directs the Secretary of State to do so[14]; and

(ii)   in the case of a Parole Board licence granted when the prisoner is released after recall to prison, the Secretary of State must not include a prescribed condition in the licence, either on release or subsequently[15], or vary or cancel any such condition[16], unless a recall adjudicator directs the Secretary of State to do so[17].

The Prison Service Instructions System gives guidance and deals with basic matters of policy relating to the process of parole release and recall, including licences granted to fixed-term prisoners[18].

1   As to the Secretary of State for these purposes see PRISONS AND PRISONERS vol 85 (2012) PARA 408.

2   Criminal Justice Act 2003 s 267B, Sch 20B para 34(6) (s 267B, Sch 20B added by the Legal Aid, Sentencing and Punishment of Offenders Act 2012 s 121(6), Sch 17 paras 1, 9, 10; Criminal Justice Act 2003 Sch 20B para 34(6) prospectively substituted, Sch 20B para 34(7) prospectively added, by the Criminal Justice and Courts Act 2015 Sch 3 para 10). At the date at which this volume states the law no day had been appointed for these purposes.

3   Criminal Justice Act 2003 Sch 20B para 34(6)(a) (as added: see note 2). The reference is to a Parole Board Licence which was granted to a person serving a 1967 Act sentence, a 1991 Act sentence, or a 2003 Act sentence (see PARA 722 notes 9–11) which is an extended sentence imposed under s 227 (repealed with savings) or s 228 (repealed with savings) before 14 July 2008: Sch 20B para 34(1), (Sch 20B para 34(1), (6)(a) (amended by the Criminal Justice and Court Services Act 2015 s 15(9)). As to 'Parole Board licences' see the text and notes 6–10.

4   Criminal Justice Act 2003 Sch 20B para 34(6)(b) (as added: see note 2).

5   Criminal Justice Act 2003 Sch 20B para 34(6) (as added: see note 2). As to the constitution and functions of the Parole Board, continued by s 239(1), see PARA 699.

6   Criminal Justice Act 2003 Sch 20B para 34(1) (as added: see note 2). The text refers to a licence which falls within either Sch 20B para 34(2) (see head (a) in the text) or Sch 20B para 34(3) (see head (b) in the text): Sch 20B para 34(1) (as so added).

7   Criminal Justice Act 2003 Sch 20B para 34(2)(a) (as added: see note 2).

8   Criminal Justice Act 2003 Sch 20B para 34(2)(b) (as added: see note 2).

9   Criminal Justice Act 2003 Sch 20B para 34(3)(a) (as added: see note 2).

10   Criminal Justice Act 2003 Sch 20B para 34(3)(b) (as added: see note 2). For the purposes of head (b) above, 'condition A' is that, before 2 August 2010, the Board exercised the function under the Criminal Justice Act 1991 s 37(5) (duration and conditions of licences) (repealed) of making recommendations as to any condition to be included or inserted as a condition in a

licence granted to the person so mentioned (including by making a recommendation that no condition should be included in such a licence) (Criminal Justice Act 2003 Sch 20B para 34(4) (as so added)); and 'condition B' is that, before 2 August 2010, the person mentioned in head (b) above was released on licence under the Criminal Justice Act 1991 s 33(2) (repealed) (release of long-term prisoner who has served two-thirds of his sentence), s 33(3) (repealed) (re-release of recalled short-term or long-term prisoner who has served three-quarters of his sentence), s 33(3A) (repealed) (duty to release short-term and long-term prisoners) or s 35(1) (repealed) (release on licence of long-term prisoner who has served one-half of his sentence) (Criminal Justice Act 2003 Sch 20B para 34(5)(a) (as so added)) and the Parole Board exercised the function under the Criminal Justice Act 1991 s 37(5) of making recommendations: (1) as to any condition to be included or inserted as a condition in a licence granted to the person so mentioned (including by making a recommendation that no condition should be included in such a licence) (Criminal Justice Act 2003 Sch 20B para 34(5)(b)(i) (as so added)); or (2) as to the variation or cancellation of any such condition (including a recommendation that the condition should not be varied or cancelled) (Sch 20B para 34(5)(b)(ii) (as so added)). For the purposes of Sch 20B, 2 August 2010 is the date on which the Coroners and Justice Act 2009 s 145 came into force: Criminal Justice Act 2003 Sch 20B para 2 (as added: see note 2).

11 Ie a condition referred to in the Criminal Justice Act 2003 s 250(4)(b)(ii) (see PARA 736): Sch 20B para 34(6)(a) (prospectively substituted: see note 2).

12 Criminal Justice Act 2003 Sch 20B para 34(6)(a) (prospectively substituted: see note 2).

13 Criminal Justice Act 2003 Sch 20B para 34(6)(b) (prospectively substituted: see note 2).

14 Criminal Justice Act 2003 Sch 20B para 34(6) (prospectively substituted: see note 2).

15 Criminal Justice Act 2003 Sch 20B para 34(7)(a) (prospectively added: see note 2).

16 Criminal Justice Act 2003 Sch 20B para 34(7)(b) (prospectively added: see note 2).

17 Criminal Justice Act 2003 Sch 20B para 34(7) (prospectively added: see note 2).

18 As to the system of central policy instructions and guidance contained eg in Prison Service Orders (PSOs) and Prison Service Instructions (PSIs) see PRISONS AND PRISONERS vol 85 (2012) PARA 406.

(iv) Supervision after Release

741. Supervision after end of sentence of prisoners serving less than two years. Where a person ('the offender') has served a fixed-term sentence which was for a term of more than one day but less than two years, except where:

(1)   the offender was aged under 18 on the last day of the requisite custodial period[1];

(2)   the sentence was an extended sentence[2];

(3)   the sentence was a special custodial sentence imposed[3] on an offender of particular concern[4]; or

(4)   the sentence was imposed in respect of an offence committed before 1 February 2015[5],

the offender must comply with the supervision requirements (ie the requirements for the time being specified in a notice given to the offender by the Secretary of State[6]) during the supervision period[7], except at any time when the offender is:

(a)   in legal custody[8];

(b)   subject to a licence[9]; or

(c)   subject to DTO supervision[10].

The purpose of the supervision period is the rehabilitation of the offender[11], and the only requirements that the Secretary of State may specify in such a notice[12] are:

(i)   a requirement to be of good behaviour and not to behave in a way which undermines the purpose of the supervision period[13];

(ii)   a requirement not to commit any offence[14];

(iii)   a requirement to keep in touch with the supervisor[15] in accordance with instructions given by the supervisor[16];

(iv) a requirement to receive visits from the supervisor in accordance with instructions given by the supervisor[17];

(v) a requirement to reside permanently at an address approved by the supervisor and to obtain the prior permission of the supervisor for any stay of one or more nights at a different address[18];

(vi) a requirement not to undertake work[19], or a particular type of work, unless it is approved by the supervisor and to notify the supervisor in advance of any proposal to undertake work or a particular type of work[20];

(vii) a requirement not to travel outside the British Islands, except with the prior permission of the supervisor or in order to comply with a legal obligation (whether or not arising under the law of any part of the British Islands)[21];

(viii) a requirement to participate in activities in accordance with any instructions given by the supervisor[22];

(ix) a drug testing requirement[23]; and

(x) a drug appointment requirement[24].

Where it appears on information to a justice of the peace that a person has failed to comply with a supervision requirement imposed under these provisions the justice may issue a summons requiring the offender to appear at the place and time specified in the summons[25] or if the information is in writing and on oath, issue a warrant for the offender's arrest[26]. If it is proved to the satisfaction of the court that the person has failed without reasonable excuse to comply with a supervision requirement imposed under these provisions the court may order the person to be committed to prison for a period not exceeding 14 days[27], order the person to pay a fine not exceeding level 3 on the standard scale[28], or make a supervision default order[29]. There is a right to appeal[30].

1 Criminal Justice Act 2003 s 256AA(1)(a) (ss 256AA–256AC, Sch 19A added by the Offender Rehabilitation Act 2014 ss 2, 3, Sch 2). As to 'the requisite custodial period' see the Criminal Justice Act 2003 s 243A(3); and PARA 712 (definition applied by s 256AA(1)(a) (as so added)).

2 Criminal Justice Act 2003 s 256AA(1)(b) (as added: see note 1). An 'extended sentence' is a sentence imposed under s 226A or s 226B (see PARAS 18–20): s 256AA(1)(b) (as so added).

3 Ie imposed under the Criminal Justice Act 2003 s 236A (see PARA 32).

4 Criminal Justice Act 2003 s 256AA(1)(ba) (as added (see note 1); s 256AA(1)(ba) added, s 256AC(11) amended, by the Criminal Justice and Courts Act 2015 Sch 1 para 18, Sch 12 para 14).

5 Criminal Justice Act 2003 s 256AA(1)(c) (as added: see note 1). 1 February 2015 is the day on which the Offender Rehabilitation Act 2014 s 2 (see note 1) was brought into force by the Offender Rehabilitation Act 2014 (Commencement No 2) Order 2015, SI 2015/40.

6 Criminal Justice Act 2003 s 256AA(3) (as added: see note 1). As to the Secretary of State for these purposes see PRISONS AND PRISONERS vol 85 (2012) PARA 408.

7 'The supervision period' is the period which begins on the expiry of the sentence (Criminal Justice Act 2003 s 256AA(4)(a) (as added: see note 1)) and ends on the expiry of the period of 12 months beginning immediately after the offender has served the requisite custodial period (as defined in s 244(3): see PARA 713 note 8) (s 256AA(4)(b) (as so added)). Section 256AA has effect subject to s 264(3C)(b), (3D) (see PARA 711): s 256AA(12) (as so added).

8 Criminal Justice Act 2003 s 256AA(2)(a) (as added: see note 1). As to legal custody see PRISONS AND PRISONERS vol 85 (2012) PARA 426.

9 Criminal Justice Act 2003 s 256AA(2)(b) (as added: see note 1). The reference to a licence is a reference to a licence under Pt 12 Ch 6 (ss 237–268) (sentencing: release, licences and recall) (see PARAS 696, 699, 709 et seq) or the Crime (Sentences) Act 1997 Pt II (ss 28–34) (life sentences) (see PARAS 697, 706 et seq).

10 Criminal Justice Act 2003 s 256AA(2)(c) (as added: see note 1). 'DTO supervision' means supervision under a detention and training order (including an order under the Armed Forces Act 2006 s 211 (detention for specified period): see ARMED FORCES vol 3 (2011) PARA 611), or

an order under the Powers of Criminal Courts (Sentencing) Act 2000 s 104(3)(aa) (breach of supervision requirements of detention and training order: see PARA 13): Criminal Justice Act 2003 s 256AA(11) (as so added).

11 Criminal Justice Act 2003 s 256AA(5) (as added: see note 1). The Secretary of State must have regard to that purpose when specifying requirements under s 256AA: s 256AA(6) (as so added).

12 The Secretary of State may by order add requirements that may be specified in a notice under the Criminal Justice Act 2003 s 256AA, remove or amend such requirements, make provision about such requirements, including about the circumstances in which they may be imposed, and make provision about instructions given for the purposes of such requirements: s 256AB(4) (as added: see note 1). An order under s 256AB(4) may amend the Criminal Justice Act 2003: s 256AB(5) (as so added). At the date at which this volume states the law no such orders had been made.

13 Criminal Justice Act 2003 s 256AB(1)(a) (as added: see note 1).

14 Criminal Justice Act 2003 s 256AB(1)(b) (as added: see note 1).

15 For these purposes 'the supervisor', in relation to a person subject to supervision requirements under the Criminal Justice Act 2003 s 256AA, means a person who is for the time being responsible for discharging the functions conferred by Pt 12 Ch 6 on the supervisor in accordance with arrangements made by the Secretary of State: s 256AA(8) (as so added). In relation to a person subject to supervision requirements under s 256AA following a sentence of detention under the Powers of Criminal Courts (Sentencing) Act 2000 s 91 (see PARA 8), the supervisor must be an officer of a provider of probation services (Criminal Justice Act 2003 s 256AA(9)(a) (as so added)) or a member of the youth offending team established by the local authority in whose area the offender resides for the time being (s 256AA(9)(b) (as so added)). In relation to any other person, the supervisor must be an officer of a provider of probation services: s 256AA(10) (as so added). As to the provision of probation services in England and Wales see PARAS 666–687. As to youth offending teams established by local authorities under the Crime and Disorder Act 1998 s 39 see CHILDREN AND YOUNG PERSONS vol 10 (2012) PARA 1193. The supervisor must have regard to the purpose of the supervision period (see the Criminal Justice Act 2003 s 256AA(5); and the text and note 11) when carrying out functions in relation to the requirements: s 256AA(7) (as so added).

16 Criminal Justice Act 2003 s 256AB(1)(c) (as added: see note 1).

17 Criminal Justice Act 2003 s 256AB(1)(d) (as added: see note 1).

18 Criminal Justice Act 2003 s 256AB(1)(e) (as added: see note 1).

19 'Work' includes paid and unpaid work: Criminal Justice Act 2003 s 256AB(6) (as added: see note 1).

20 Criminal Justice Act 2003 s 256AB(1)(f) (as added: see note 1).

21 Criminal Justice Act 2003 s 256AB(1)(g) (as added: see note 1).

22 Criminal Justice Act 2003 s 256AB(1)(h) (as added: see note 1). Where a requirement is imposed under s 256AB(1)(h), s 200A(5)–(10) (see PARA 131) apply in relation to the requirement (reading references to the responsible officer as references to the supervisor): s 256AB(2) (as so added).

23 Criminal Justice Act 2003 s 256AB(1)(i) (as added: see note 1). As to drug testing requirements see s 256D; and PARA 745. Section 256AB(1)(i) has effect subject to the restrictions in s 256D(2): s 256AB(3) (as so added).

24 Criminal Justice Act 2003 s 256AB(1)(j) (as added: see note 1). As to drug appointment requirements see s 256E; and PARA 745. Section 256AB(1)(j) has effect subject to the restrictions in s 256E(2): s 256AB(3) (as so added).

25 Criminal Justice Act 2003 s 256AC(1)(a) (as added: see note 1). Any summons or warrant issued under s 256AC must direct the person to appear or be brought before a magistrates' court acting for the local justice area in which the offender resides (s 256AC(2)(a) (as so added)) or if it is not known where the person resides, before a magistrates' court acting for the same local justice area as the justice who issued the summons or warrant (s 256AC(2)(b) (as so added)). Where the person does not appear in answer to a summons issued under s 256AC(1)(a), the court may issue a warrant for the person's arrest: s 256AC(3) (as so added).

26 Criminal Justice Act 2003 s 256AC(1)(b) (as added: see note 1).

27 Criminal Justice Act 2003 s 256AC(4)(a) (as added: see note 1). Where the person is under the age of 21 an order under s 256AC(4)(a) in respect of him must be for committal to a young offender institution instead of to prison (s 256AC(7)(a) (as so added)) but the Secretary of State may from time to time direct that a person committed to a young offender institution by such an order is to be detained in a prison or remand centre instead (s 256AC(7)(b) (as so added)). A person committed to prison or a young offender institution by an order under s 256A(4)(a) is to be regarded as being in legal custody: s 256AC(8) (as so added).

28 Criminal Justice Act 2003 s 256AC(4)(b) (as added: see note 1). A fine imposed under s 256AC(4)(b) is to be treated, for the purposes of any enactment, as being a sum adjudged to be paid by a conviction: s 256AC(9) (as so added). As to the standard scale, the statutory maximum, the prescribed sum, and magistrates' powers to levy unlimited fines see PARA 176.

29 Criminal Justice Act 2003 s 256AC(4)(c) (as added: see note 1). A supervision default order is an order imposing on the person in question an unpaid work requirement (as defined by s 199: see PARA 133) or a curfew requirement (as defined by s 204: see PARA 123): s 256AC(4)(c)(i), (ii) (as so added). Section 177(3) (obligation to impose electronic monitoring requirement: see PARA 136) applies in relation to a supervision default order that imposes a curfew requirement as it applies in relation to a community order that imposes such a requirement: s 256AC(5) (as so added). If the court deals with the person under s 256AC(4), it must revoke any supervision default order which is in force at that time in respect of that person: s 256AC(6) (as so added). Provision for the requirements, breach, revocation and amendment of supervision default orders is made by s 256AC(10), Sch 19A (as so added).

30 A person dealt with under the Criminal Justice Act 2003 s 256AC may appeal to the Crown Court against the order made by the court under s 256AC and an order made by the court under the Prosecution of Offences Act 1985 s 21A (criminal courts charge: see CRIMINAL PROCEDURE) when dealing with the person under the Criminal Justice Act 2003 s 256AC: s 256AC(11) (as added and amended: see notes 1, 4).

742. Condition for electronic monitoring of compliance with any other condition of release. Where a sentence of imprisonment[1] has been imposed on a person and, by virtue of any enactment[2]:

(1)   the Secretary of State[3] is required to, or may, release[4] the person from prison[5]; and

(2)   the release is required to be, or may be, subject to conditions (whether conditions of a licence or any other conditions, however expressed)[6],

those conditions may include electronic monitoring conditions[7]. The Secretary of State may make rules about the conditions that may be imposed in this way[8].

For these purposes, 'sentence of imprisonment' includes:

(a)   a detention and training order[9];
(b)   a sentence of detention in a young offender institution[10];
(c)   a sentence of detention at Her Majesty's pleasure[11];
(d)   a sentence of detention for a specified period imposed on an offender aged under 18 convicted of a serious offence[12];
(e)   a sentence of custody for life[13];
(f)   a sentence of detention for public protection[14];
(g)   an extended sentence for a violent or sexual offence[15];
(h)   a sentence of detention imposed on an offender aged under 18 convicted by the Court Martial of certain serious offences or murder[16]; and
(i)   a detention and training order imposed by the Court Martial or the Service Civilian Court[17].

The Secretary of State may by order provide that the power to impose an electronic monitoring condition under these provisions must be exercised[18].

The Prison Service Instructions System gives guidance and deals with basic matters of policy relating to licences granted to fixed-term prisoners[19].

1   Ie a sentence of imprisonment that is specified for these purposes in the Criminal Justice and Court Services Act 2000 s 62(5) (see heads (a) to (i) in the text).

2   See the Criminal Justice and Court Services Act 2000 s 62(1).

3   As to the Secretary of State for these purposes see PRISONS AND PRISONERS vol 85 (2012) PARA 408.

4   For the purposes of the Criminal Justice and Court Services Act 2000 Pt III (ss 43–70) (dealing with offenders), except in s 69 (repealed), references to 'release' include temporary release (as to which see PARA 691): s 70(3).

5   Criminal Justice and Court Services Act 2000 s 62(1)(a). 'Prison' is construed according to the type of sentence which has been imposed (see heads (a) to (i) in the text): s 62(5).

6   Criminal Justice and Court Services Act 2000 s 62(1)(b). As to licence conditions imposed on
     life prisoners see PARA 734; and as to licence conditions imposed on fixed-term prisoners see
     PARAS 736, 737.

7   Criminal Justice and Court Services Act 2000 s 62(2) (s 62(2) substituted, s 62(2A), (2B), (5A),
     62A, 62B added, by the Criminal Justice and Courts Act 2015 s 7). For these purposes
     'electronic monitoring condition' means a condition requiring the person to submit to either or
     both of the following: electronic monitoring of his compliance with another condition of release;
     and electronic monitoring of his whereabouts (other than for the purpose of monitoring
     compliance with another condition of release): Criminal Justice and Court Services Act 2000
     ss 62(5A), 62A(5) (as so added). An electronic monitoring condition imposed under these
     provisions must include provision for making a person responsible for the monitoring (s 62(2A)
     (as so added)), and a person may not be made responsible for the monitoring unless the person
     is of a description specified in an order made by the Secretary of State (s 62(2B) (as so added)).
     At the date at which this volume states the law no such orders had been made.
          The Secretary of State must issue a code of practice relating to the processing of data
     gathered in the course of monitoring persons under electronic monitoring conditions imposed
     under s 62: s 62B(1) (as so added). A failure to observe a code issued under this section does not
     of itself make a person liable to any criminal or civil proceedings: s 62B(2) (as so added).

8   Criminal Justice and Court Services Act 2000 s 62(4). At the date at which this volume states the
     law, no such rules had been made.

9   Criminal Justice and Court Services Act 2000 s 62(5)(a). As to detention and training orders see
     PARA 9 et seq.

10   Criminal Justice and Court Services Act 2000 s 62(5)(b). As to determinate sentences of
     detention in a young offender institution see PARAS 688, 689.

11   Criminal Justice and Court Services Act 2000 s 62(5)(c). Head (c) in the text refers to sentences
     of detention at Her Majesty's pleasure imposed under the Powers of Criminal Courts
     (Sentencing) Act 2000 s 90 (PARA 38; and CHILDREN AND YOUNG PERSONS vol 10 (2012) PARA
     1308): Criminal Justice and Court Services Act 2000 s 62(5)(c).

12   Criminal Justice and Court Services Act 2000 s 62(5)(d). Head (d) in the text refers to sentences
     of detention imposed under the Powers of Criminal Courts (Sentencing) Act 2000 s 91 (power
     to impose sentence of detention for a specified period on a person aged under 18 who has
     committed a serious offence: see PARA 8; and CHILDREN AND YOUNG PERSONS vol 10 (2012)
     PARA 1307): Criminal Justice and Court Services Act 2000 s 62(5)(d).

13   Criminal Justice and Court Services Act 2000 s 62(5)(e). Head (e) in the text refers to sentences
     of custody for life imposed under the Powers of Criminal Courts (Sentencing) Act 2000 ss 93, 94
     (both prospectively repealed) (see PARAS 36, 37; and CHILDREN AND YOUNG PERSONS vol 10
     (2012) PARA 1309) on a person aged under 21 convicted of murder or any other serious offence,
     or in certain other cases on a person aged between 18 and 21 where the offence would attract a
     sentence of imprisonment for life if committed by a person aged 21 years or over: Criminal
     Justice and Court Services Act 2000 s 62(5)(e).

14   Criminal Justice and Court Services Act 2000 s 62(5)(f) (added by the Criminal Justice Act 2003
     Sch 32 Pt 1 paras 133, 136(1), (3); amended by the Armed Forces Act 2006 s 378(1), Sch 16
     para 184(a); and the Legal Aid, Sentencing and Punishment of Offenders Act 2012 ss 126, 127,
     Sch 21 Pt 1 paras 16, 17, Sch 22 Pt 2 paras 17, 18). Head (f) in the text refers to sentences of
     detention for public protection under the Criminal Justice Act 2003 s 226 (see PARA 34; and
     CHILDREN AND YOUNG PERSONS vol 10 (2012) PARA 1300), including one imposed as a result of
     the Armed Forces Act 2006 s 221 (required custodial sentences for dangerous offenders: see
     ARMED FORCES vol 3 (2011) PARA 611): Criminal Justice and Court Services Act 2000 s 62(5)(f)
     (as so added and amended).

15   Criminal Justice and Court Services Act 2000 s 62(5)(f) (as added and amended: see note 15).
     Head (g) in the text refers to extended sentences of detention imposed under the Criminal Justice
     Act 2003 s 226B (extended sentence for certain violent or sexual offences (persons under 18):
     see PARAS 18–20), including a sentence passed as a result of the Armed Forces Act 2006 s 221A
     (extended sentence for certain violent or sexual offenders aged under 18: see ARMED FORCES)
     and a sentence imposed under the Criminal Justice Act 2003 s 228 (repealed with savings)
     (extended sentence for certain violent or sexual offences (persons under 18)), including a
     sentence passed as a result of the Armed Forces Act 2006 s 222 (repealed) (certain violent or
     sexual offences (offenders aged under 18): see ARMED FORCES vol 3 (2011) PARA 611): Criminal
     Justice and Court Services Act 2000 s 62(5)(f) (as so added and amended).

16   Criminal Justice and Court Services Act 2000 s 62(5)(g) (s 62(5)(g), (h) added by the Armed
     Forces Act 2006 Sch 16 para 184(b)). Head (h) in the text refers to sentences imposed under the
     Armed Forces Act 2006 s 209 (detention for specified period: see ARMED FORCES vol 3 (2011)

PARA 611) or s 218 (person aged under 18 convicted of murder sentenced to be detained during Her Majesty's pleasure: see ARMED FORCES vol 3 (2011) PARA 611): Criminal Justice and Court Services Act 2000 s 62(5)(g) (as so added).

17 Criminal Justice and Court Services Act 2000 s 62(5)(h) (as added: see note 16). Head (i) in the text refers to orders under the Armed Forces Act 2006 s 211 (detention for specified period: see ARMED FORCES vol 3 (2011) PARA 611): Criminal Justice and Court Services Act 2000 s 62(5)(h) (as so added).

18 Criminal Justice and Court Services Act 2000 s 62A(1) (as added: see note 7). An order under s 62A may:

   (1) require an electronic monitoring condition to be included for so long as the person's release is required to be, or may be, subject to conditions or for a shorter period (s 62A(2)(a) (as so added)); and

   (2) make provision generally or in relation to a case described in the order (s 62A(2)(b) (as so added)).

   An order under s 62A may, in particular:

   (a) make provision in relation to cases in which: compliance with a condition imposed on a person's release is monitored by a person specified or described in the order (s 62A(3)(a) (as so added));

   (b) make provision in relation to persons selected on the basis of criteria specified in the order or on a sampling basis (s 62A(3)(b) (as so added)); and

   (c) make provision by reference to whether a person specified in the order is satisfied of a matter (s 62A(3)(c) (as so added)).

   An order under s 62A may not make provision about a case in which the sentence imposed on the person is:

   (i) a detention and training order (s 62A(4)(a) (as so added));

   (ii) a sentence of detention under the Powers of Criminal Courts (Sentencing) Act 2000 s 91 (Criminal Justice and Court Services Act 2000 s 62A(4)(b) (as so added));

   (iii) a sentence of detention under the Armed Forces Act 2006 s 209 (detention of offenders under 18 convicted of certain offences) (Criminal Justice and Court Services Act 2000 s 62A(4)(c) (as so added)); or

   (iv) an order under the Armed Forces Act 2006 s 211 (Criminal Justice and Court Services Act 2000 s 62A(4)(d) (as so added)).

19 As to the system of central policy instructions and guidance contained e g in Prison Service Orders (PSOs) and Prison Service Instructions (PSIs) see PRISONS AND PRISONERS vol 85 (2012) PARA 406.

743. Drug testing requirements for monitoring compliance with conditions following release on licence. In circumstances where:

   (1) the Secretary of State[1] releases[2] from prison[3] a person aged 18 or over on whom a sentence of imprisonment[4] has been imposed[5];

   (2) the release is subject to conditions (whether conditions of a licence or any other conditions, however expressed)[6]; and

   (3) the Secretary of State is satisfied that the misuse by the person of a specified class A drug or a specified class B drug[7] caused or contributed to an offence of which he has been convicted or is likely to cause or contribute to the commission of further offences by him[8], and that he is dependent on, or has a propensity to misuse, a specified class A drug or a specified class B drug[9],

then, for the purpose of determining whether the person is complying with any of the conditions referred to in head (2), those conditions may include the requirement[10] that the person must provide, when instructed[11] to do so by an officer of a local probation board, an officer of a provider of probation services, or a person authorised by the Secretary of State, any sample mentioned in the instruction for the purpose of ascertaining whether he has any specified Class A drug or specified Class B drug in his body[12].

For these purposes, 'sentence of imprisonment' includes:

   (a) a detention and training order[13];

   (b) a sentence of detention in a young offender institution[14];

(c)   a sentence of detention at Her Majesty's pleasure[15];

(d)   a sentence of detention for a specified period imposed on an offender aged under 18 for a serious offence[16];

(e)   until a day to be appointed[17], a sentence of custody for life[18];

(f)   a sentence of detention imposed on an offender aged under 18 convicted by the Court Martial of certain serious offences or murder[19]; and

(g)   a detention and training order imposed by the Court Martial or the Service Civilian Court[20].

1   As to the Secretary of State for these purposes see PRISONS AND PRISONERS vol 85 (2012) PARA 408.

2   As to the meaning of 'release' for these purposes see PARA 742 note 4.

3   'Prison' is construed according to the type of sentence which has been imposed (see heads (a) to (g) in the text): Criminal Justice and Court Services Act 2000 s 64(5).

4   Ie a sentence of imprisonment that is specified for these purposes in the Criminal Justice and Court Services Act 2000 s 64(5) (see heads (a) to (g) in the text).

5   Criminal Justice and Court Services Act 2000 s 64(1)(a) (ss 64(1)(a), (2)–(4), 70(1) amended, s 64(1)(c), (1A) added, by the Offender Rehabilitation Act 2014 s 11, Sch 3 para 13).

6   Criminal Justice and Court Services Act 2000 s 64(1)(b).

7   For the purposes of the Criminal Justice and Court Services Act 2000 Pt III 'Class A drug' and 'Class B drug' have the same meaning as in the Misuse of Drugs Act 1971 (see CRIMINAL LAW vol 26 (2010) PARA 723; and MEDICAL PRODUCTS AND DRUGS vol 75 (2013) PARA 483); and 'specified', in relation to a Class A drug or a Class B drug, means specified by an order made by the Secretary of State: Criminal Justice and Court Services Act 2000 s 70(1) (as amended: see note 5). Pursuant to this power the Secretary of State has made the Criminal Justice (Specified Class A Drugs) Order 2001, SI 2001/1816; and the Criminal Justice (Specified Class B Drugs) Order 2015, SI 2015/9.

8   Criminal Justice and Court Services Act 2000 s 64(1)(c), (1A)(a) (as added: see note 5).

9   Criminal Justice and Court Services Act 2000 s 64(1A)(b) (as added: see note 5).

10   Criminal Justice and Court Services Act 2000 s 64(2) (as amended: see note 5).

11   The function of giving such an instruction is to be exercised in accordance with guidance given from time to time by the Secretary of State; and rules made by the Secretary of State may regulate the provision of samples in pursuance of such an instruction: Criminal Justice and Court Services Act 2000 s 64(4) (as amended: see note 5). At the date at which this volume states the law, no such regulations had been made.

12   Criminal Justice and Court Services Act 2000 s 64(3) (as amended (see note 5); amended by SI 2008/912). As to the provision of probation services in England and Wales see PARAS 666–687.

13   Criminal Justice and Court Services Act 2000 s 64(5)(a). As to detention and training orders see PARA 9 et seq.

14   Criminal Justice and Court Services Act 2000 s 64(5)(b). As to determinate sentences of detention in a young offender institution see PARAS 688, 689.

15   Criminal Justice and Court Services Act 2000 s 64(5)(c). Head (c) in the text refers to sentences of detention at Her Majesty's pleasure imposed under the Powers of Criminal Courts (Sentencing) Act 2000 s 90 (see PARA 38; and CHILDREN AND YOUNG PERSONS vol 10 (2012) PARA 1308): Criminal Justice and Court Services Act 2000 s 64(5)(c).

16   Criminal Justice and Court Services Act 2000 s 64(5)(d). Head (d) in the text refers to sentences of detention imposed under the Powers of Criminal Courts (Sentencing) Act 2000 s 91 (power to impose sentence of detention for a specified period on a person aged under 18 who has committed a serious offence: see PARA 8; and CHILDREN AND YOUNG PERSONS vol 10 (2012) PARA 1307): Criminal Justice and Court Services Act 2000 s 64(5)(d).

17   The Criminal Justice and Court Services Act 2000 s 64(5)(e) is repealed by the Criminal Justice Act 2003 s 332, Sch 37 Pt 7, as from a day to be appointed under s 336(3). However, at the date at which this volume states the law, no such day had been appointed.

18   Criminal Justice and Court Services Act 2000 s 64(5)(e) (prospectively repealed: see note 16). Head (e) in the text refers to sentences of custody for life imposed under the Powers of Criminal Courts (Sentencing) Act 2000 ss 93, 94 (both prospectively repealed) (see PARAS 36, 37; and CHILDREN AND YOUNG PERSONS vol 10 (2012) PARA 1309) on a person aged under 21 convicted of murder or any other serious offence, or in certain other cases on a person aged between 18

and 21 where the offence would attract a sentence of imprisonment for life if committed by a person aged 21 years or over: Criminal Justice and Court Services Act 2000 s 64(5)(e) (prospectively repealed).

19 Criminal Justice and Court Services Act 2000 s 64(5)(g) (s 64(5)(g), (h) added by the Armed Forces Act 2006 Sch 16 para 185(b)). Head (f) in the text refers to sentences imposed under the Armed Forces Act 2006 s 209 (detention for specified period: see ARMED FORCES vol 3 (2011) PARA 611) and s 218 (person aged under 18 convicted of murder sentenced to be detained during Her Majesty's pleasure: see ARMED FORCES vol 3 (2011) PARA 611): see the Criminal Justice and Court Services Act 2000 s 64(5)(g) (as so added).

20 Criminal Justice and Court Services Act 2000 s 64(5)(h) (as added: see note 18). Head (g) in the text refers to orders imposed under the Armed Forces Act 2006 s 211 (detention for specified period: see ARMED FORCES vol 3 (2011) PARA 611): Criminal Justice and Court Services Act 2000 s 64(5)(h) (as so added).

744. Polygraph conditions for certain offenders released on licence. The Secretary of State[1] may include a polygraph condition[2] in the licence of a person[3] who is serving a relevant custodial sentence[4] in respect of a relevant sexual offence[5] who[6]:

(1) is released on licence by the Secretary of State under any enactment[7]; and

(2) is not aged under 18 on the day on which he is released[8].

For these purposes, 'relevant custodial sentence' means:

(a) a sentence of imprisonment for a term of 12 months or more (including an extended sentence of detention)[9];

(b) a sentence of detention in a young offender institution for a term of 12 months or more[10];

(c) a sentence of detention at Her Majesty's pleasure[11];

(d) a sentence of detention for a period of 12 months or more imposed on an offender aged under 18 for a serious offence[12];

(e) a sentence of custody for life[13];

(f) a sentence of detention for public protection[14].

For these purposes, 'relevant sexual offence' means a specified sexual offence[15].

Evidence of any matter mentioned in heads (i) and (ii) below may not be used in any proceedings against a released person for an offence[16], those matters being: (i) any statement made by the released person while participating in a polygraph session[17]; or (ii) any physiological reactions of the released person while being questioned in the course of a polygraph examination[18].

1 As to the Secretary of State for these purposes see PRISONS AND PRISONERS vol 85 (2012) PARA 408.

2 For the purposes of the Offender Management Act 2007 s 28, a 'polygraph condition' is a condition which requires the released person:

(1) to participate in polygraph sessions conducted with a view to: (a) monitoring his compliance with the other conditions of his licence (s 29(1)(a)(i)); or (b) improving the way in which he is managed during his release on licence (s 29(1)(a)(ii));

(2) to participate in those polygraph sessions at such times as may be specified in instructions given by an appropriate officer (s 29(1)(b)); and

(3) while participating in a polygraph session, to comply with instructions given to him by the person conducting the session (the 'polygraph operator') (s 29(1)(c)).

In head (2) above, 'appropriate officer' means an officer of a provider of probation services or an officer of a local probation board (s 29(4)); and such an officer, when giving instructions as mentioned in head (2) above, must have regard to any guidance issued by the Secretary of State (s 29(5)). As to the provision of probation services in England and Wales see PARAS 666–687.

A 'polygraph session' is a session during which the polygraph operator conducts one or more polygraph examinations of the released person, and interviews the released person in preparation for, or otherwise in connection with, any such examination: s 29(2). For the purposes of s 29(2), a 'polygraph examination' is a procedure in which:

(i) the polygraph operator questions the released person (s 29(3)(a));

    (ii)   the questions and the released person's answers are recorded (s 29(3)(b)); and

    (iii)   physiological reactions of the released person while being questioned are measured and recorded by means of equipment of a type approved by the Secretary of State (s 29(3)(c)).

The Secretary of State may make rules relating to the conduct of polygraph sessions (s 29(6), (8)). The rules may, in particular:

    (A)   require polygraph operators to be persons who satisfy such requirements as to qualifications, experience and other matters as are specified in the rules (s 29(7)(a));

    (B)   make provision about the keeping of records of polygraph sessions (s 29(7)(b)); and

    (C)   make provision about the preparation of reports on the results of polygraph sessions (s 29(7)(c)).

In exercise of the power conferred by s 29(6), the Secretary of State has made the Polygraph Rules 2009, SI 2009/619.

3   Offender Management Act 2007 s 28(1). The text refers to the licence of a person to whom s 28 applies (see s 28(2); and the text and notes 4–8): s 28(1).

4   Ie a sentence that is specified in the Offender Management Act 2007 s 28(3) ('relevant custodial sentence') (see heads (a) to (f) in the text): s 28(2).

5   Ie a sentence that is specified in the Offender Management Act 2007 s 28(4) ('relevant sexual offence') (see note 14): s 28(2).

6   Offender Management Act 2007 s 28(2).

7   Offender Management Act 2007 s 28(2)(a).

8   Offender Management Act 2007 s 28(2)(b).

9   Offender Management Act 2007 s 28(3)(a) (amended by the Legal Aid, Sentencing and Punishment of Offenders Act 2012 s 126, Sch 21 Pt 1 para 32(1), (2)). Head (a) in the text includes a sentence of imprisonment imposed under the Criminal Justice Act 2003 s 226A (extended sentence for certain violent or sexual offences (persons 18 or over): see PARAS 18–20) or s 227 (repealed with savings): Offender Management Act 2007 s 28(3)(a) (as so amended).

10   Offender Management Act 2007 s 28(3)(b). As to determinate sentences of detention in a young offender institution see PARAS 688, 689.

11   Offender Management Act 2007 s 28(3)(c). Head (c) in the text refers to sentences of detention at Her Majesty's pleasure imposed under the Powers of Criminal Courts (Sentencing) Act 2000 s 90 (see PARA 38; and CHILDREN AND YOUNG PERSONS vol 10 (2012) PARA 1308): Offender Management Act 2007 s 28(3)(c).

12   Offender Management Act 2007 s 28(3)(d). Head (d) in the text refers to sentences of detention imposed under the Powers of Criminal Courts (Sentencing) Act 2000 s 91 (power to impose sentence of detention for a specified period on a person aged under 18 who has committed a serious offence: see PARA 8; and CHILDREN AND YOUNG PERSONS vol 10 (2012) PARA 1307): Offender Management Act 2007 s 28(3)(d).

13   Offender Management Act 2007 s 28(3)(e). Head (e) in the text refers to sentences of custody for life imposed under the Powers of Criminal Courts (Sentencing) Act 2000 ss 93, 94 (both prospectively repealed) (see PARAS 36, 37; and CHILDREN AND YOUNG PERSONS vol 10 (2012) PARA 1309) on a person aged under 21 convicted of murder or any other serious offence, or in certain other cases on a person aged between 18 and 21 where the offence would attract a sentence of imprisonment for life if committed by a person aged 21 years or over: Offender Management Act 2007 s 28(3)(e).

14   Offender Management Act 2007 s 28(3)(f) (amended by the Legal Aid, Sentencing and Punishment of Offenders Act 2012 Sch 21 Pt 1 para 32(1), (3)). Head (f) in the text refers to sentences of detention for public protection imposed under the Criminal Justice Act 2003 s 226 (see PARA 34; and CHILDREN AND YOUNG PERSONS vol 10 (2012) PARA 1300), s 226B (extended sentence for certain violent or sexual offences (persons under 18): see PARAS 18–20) or s 228 (repealed with savings): Offender Management Act 2007 s 28(3)(f) (as so amended).

15   Offender Management Act 2007 s 28(4). For these purposes, 'relevant sexual offence' means an offence that is specified in the Criminal Justice Act 2003 s 224, Sch 15 Pt 1 (violent offences) and Sch 15 Pt 2 (sexual offences) (see PARAS 23, 24): Offender Management Act 2007 s 28(4)(a). The definition includes equivalent offences under the law of Scotland (see s 28(4)(b)), and under the law of Northern Ireland (see s 28(4)(c)).

16   Offender Management Act 2007 s 30(1).

17   Offender Management Act 2007 s 30(2)(a). For these purposes, 'polygraph session' has the same meaning as in s 29 (see note 2): s 30(3).

18   Offender Management Act 2007 s 30(2)(b). For these purposes, 'polygraph examination' has the same meaning as in s 29 (see note 2): s 30(3).

745. Supervision of young offenders after release. Where a person ('the offender') is released under Chapter 6 of Part 12 of the Criminal Justice Act 2003[1] and:

(1)   he is, at the time of the release, serving a sentence of detention[2] which is for a term of less than 12 months[3] and is aged under 18 on the last day of the requisite custodial period[4]; or

(2)   he is, at the time of the release, serving a sentence of detention[5] which is for a term of less than 12 months[6] and the sentence was imposed in respect of an offence committed before 1 February 2015[7],

he is to be under the supervision of:

(a)   an officer of a provider of probation services[8];

(b)   a social worker of a local authority[9]; or

(c)   a member of the youth offending team[10].

The supervision period begins on the offender's release and ends three months later (whether or not the offender is detained for a breach of his supervision requirements[11] or otherwise during that period)[12]. During the supervision period, the offender must comply with such requirements, if any, as may for the time being be specified in a notice from the Secretary of State[13]. Such requirements that may be specified in such a notice include:

(i)   requirements to submit to electronic monitoring of the offender's compliance with any other requirements specified in the notice[14];

(ii)   requirements to submit to electronic monitoring of the offender's whereabouts (otherwise than for the purpose of securing compliance with requirements specified in the notice)[15]; and

(iii) where the offender is aged 18 or over, drug testing requirements[16] and drug appointment requirements[17].

Where a young offender is under supervision[18] and it appears on information to a justice of the peace that the offender has failed to comply with any of his supervision requirements[19], the justice may[20] either issue a summons requiring the offender to appear at the place and time specified in the summons[21] or (if the information is in writing and on oath) issue a warrant for the offender's arrest[22].

If it is proved to the satisfaction of the court that the offender has failed to comply with any of his supervision requirements[23], the court may[24] order the offender to be detained, in prison or such youth detention accommodation as the Secretary of State may determine, for such period, not exceeding 30 days, as the court may specify[25], or the court may order the offender to pay a fine not exceeding level 3 on the standard scale[26].

The Prison Service Instructions System gives guidance and deals with basic matters of policy relating to the supervision of young offenders[27].

1   Ie under the Criminal Justice Act 2003 Pt 12 Ch 6 (ss 237–268) (sentencing: release, licences and recall) (see also PARAS 696, 699, 709 et seq, 735 et seq, 749 et seq): s 256B(1) (ss 256B, 256C added by the Legal Aid, Sentencing and Punishment of Offenders Act 2012 s 115). The Criminal Justice Act 2003 ss 243A–264 do not apply in relation to a person detained in England and Wales in pursuance of a sentence of the International Criminal Court: see the International Criminal Court Act 2001 Sch 7 para 3(1); and PARA 690. As to the meanings of 'England' and 'Wales' see PARA 4 note 3.

2   Ie a term of detention under the Powers of Criminal Courts (Sentencing) Act 2000 s 91 (power to impose sentence of detention for a specified period on a person aged under 18 who has committed a serious offence: see PARA 8; and CHILDREN AND YOUNG PERSONS vol 10 (2012) PARA 1307): Criminal Justice Act 2003 s 256B(1)(a) (as so added; s 256B(1), (7)(c), (9) substituted, ss 256B(1A), (7A), 256D, 256E added, ss 256B(2)(c), 256C(4)(b) amended, by the Offender Rehabilitation Act 2014 s 4, Sch 1 para 2, Sch 3 para 21)).

3   Criminal Justice Act 2003 s 256B(1)(a) (as added and substituted: see notes 1, 2).

4   Criminal Justice Act 2003 s 256B(1)(b) (as added and substituted: see notes 1, 2). As to 'the requisite custodial period' see s 243A(3); and PARA 712 (definition applied by s 256B(1)(b) (as so added and substituted)).

5   Ie a sentence of detention under the Powers of Criminal Courts (Sentencing) Act 2000 s 91 or s 96 (prospectively repealed) (detention in young offender institution for a person aged between 18 and 21: see PARA 16): Criminal Justice Act 2003 s 256B(1A)(a) (as added: see notes 1, 2).

6   Criminal Justice Act 2003 s 256B(1A)(a) (as added: see notes 1, 2).

7   Criminal Justice Act 2003 s 256B(1A)(b) (as added: see notes 1, 2). 1 February 2015 is the day on which the Offender Rehabilitation Act 2014 s 1 (reduction of cases in which prisoners released unconditionally: see PARA 712) was brought into force by the Offender Rehabilitation Act 2014 (Commencement No 2) Order 2015, SI 2015/40.

8   Criminal Justice Act 2003 s 256B(2)(a) (as added: see note 1). Where the supervision is to be provided by an officer of a provider of probation services, he must be an officer acting in the local justice area in which the offender resides for the time being: s 256B(3) (as so added). As to local justice areas see MAGISTRATES vol 71 (2013) PARA 475. As to the provision of probation services in England and Wales (see PARAS 666–687).

9   Criminal Justice Act 2003 s 256B(2)(b) (as added: see note 1). Where the supervision is to be provided by a social worker of a local authority, he must be a social worker of the local authority within whose area the offender resides for the time being: s 256B(4)(a) (as so added).

10 Criminal Justice Act 2003 s 256B(2)(c) (as added and amended: see notes 1, 2). Where the supervision is to be provided by a member of a youth offending team, he must be a member of a youth offending team established by the local authority within whose area the offender resides for the time being: s 256B(4)(b) (as so added). As to youth offending teams established by local authorities under the Crime and Disorder Act 1998 s 39 see CHILDREN AND YOUNG PERSONS vol 10 (2012) PARA 1193.

11 Ie detained under the Criminal Justice Act 2003 s 256C (see the text and notes 18–26): s 256B(5) (as added: see note 1).

12 Criminal Justice Act 2003 s 256B(5) (as added: see note 1).

13 Criminal Justice Act 2003 s 256B(6) (as added: see note 1). As to the Secretary of State for these purposes see PRISONS AND PRISONERS vol 85 (2012) PARA 408.

14 Criminal Justice Act 2003 s 256B(7)(a) (as added (see note 1); s 256B(7)(a), (b) amended by the Criminal Justice and Courts Act 2015 Sch 2 para 6). The Secretary of State may make rules about the requirements that may be imposed by virtue of the Criminal Justice Act 2003 s 256B(7)(a) or (b): s 256B(9) (as added and substituted: see notes 1, 2). At the date at which this volume states the law no such rules had been made.

15 Criminal Justice Act 2003 s 256B(7)(b) (as added and amended: see notes 1, 14). See note 14.

16 Criminal Justice Act 2003 s 256B(7)(c)(i) (as added and substituted: see notes 1, 2). 'Drug testing requirement', in relation to an offender subject to supervision under these provisions, means a requirement that, when instructed to do so by the supervisor, the offender provide a sample mentioned in the instruction for the purpose of ascertaining whether the offender has a specified Class A drug or a specified Class B drug in his body: s 256D(1) (as so added). As to the meanings of 'specified Class A drug' and 'specified Class B drug' see the Criminal Justice and Court Services Act 2000 s 70(1); and PARA 743 note 7 (definitions applied by the Criminal Justice Act 2003 s 256D(6) (as so added)). A drug testing requirement may be imposed on an offender subject to supervision under these provisions only if the Secretary of State is satisfied that the misuse by the offender of a specified class A drug or a specified class B drug caused or contributed to an offence of which the offender has been convicted or is likely to cause or contribute to the commission of further offences by the offender (ss 256B(7A), 256D(2)(a), (3)(a) (as so added)) and that the offender is dependent on, or has a propensity to misuse, a specified class A drug or a specified class B drug (s 256D(3)(b) (as so added)), and the requirement is being imposed for the purpose of determining whether the offender is complying with any other supervision requirement (s 256D(2)(b) (as so added)). An instruction given for the purpose of a drug testing requirement must be given in accordance with guidance given from time to time by the Secretary of State: s 256D(4) (as so added). The Secretary of State may make rules regulating the provision of samples in accordance with such an instruction: s 256D(5) (as so added). At the date at which this volume states the law no such rules had been made.

17 Criminal Justice Act 2003 s 256B(7)(c)(ii) (as added and substituted: see notes 1, 2). 'Drug appointment requirement', in relation to an offender subject to supervision under these provisions, means a requirement that the offender, in accordance with instructions given by the supervisor, attend appointments with a view to addressing the offender's dependency on, or propensity to misuse, a controlled drug: s 256E(1) (as so added). As to the meaning of 'controlled drug' see the Misuse of Drugs Act 1971 s 2(1); and MEDICAL PRODUCTS AND DRUGS vol 75 (2013) PARA 481 (definition applied by the Criminal Justice Act 2003 s 256E(8) (as so

added)). A drug appointment requirement may be imposed on an offender subject to supervision under these provisions only if the supervisor has recommended to the Secretary of State that such a requirement be imposed on the offender (ss 256B(7A), 256E(2)(a) (as so added)) and the Secretary of State is satisfied that the misuse by the offender of a controlled drug caused or contributed to an offence of which the offender has been convicted or is likely to cause or contribute to the commission of further offences by the offender (256E(2)(b), (3)(a) (as so added)), that the offender is dependent on, or has a propensity to misuse, a controlled drug (256E(3)(b) (as so added)), that the dependency or propensity requires, and may be susceptible to, treatment (256E(3)(c) (as so added)), and that arrangements have been made, or can be made, for the offender to have treatment (256E(3)(d) (as so added)). The requirement must specify the person with whom the offender is to meet or under whose direction the appointments are to take place (who must be a person who has the necessary qualifications or experience) (256E(4)(a), (5) (as so added)) and where the appointments are to take place (256E(4)(b) (as so added)). The only instructions that the supervisor may give for the purposes of the requirement are instructions as to the duration of each appointment (256E(6)(a) (as so added)) and when each appointment is to take place (256E(6)(b) (as so added)). For these purposes references to a requirement to attend an appointment do not include a requirement to submit to treatment: 256E(7) (as so added).

18 Ie under the Criminal Justice Act 2003 s 256B (see the text and notes 1–17): s 256C(1) (as added: see note 1).

19 Ie with requirements under the Criminal Justice Act 2003 s 256B(6) (see the text and note 13): s 256C(1) (as added: see note 1).

20 Criminal Justice Act 2003 s 256C(1) (as added: see note 1).

21 Criminal Justice Act 2003 s 256C(1)(a) (as added: see note 1). Any summons issued under s 256C must direct the offender to appear: (1) before a court acting for the local justice area in which the offender resides (s 256C(2)(a) (as so added)); or (2) if it is not known where the offender resides, before a court acting for same local justice area as the justice who issued the summons (s 256C(2)(b) (as so added)). Where the offender does not appear in answer to a summons issued under s 256C(1)(a), the court may issue a warrant for the offender's arrest: s 256C(3) (as so added). For these purposes, 'court' means (if the offender has attained the age of 18 years at the date of release) a magistrates' court other than a youth court or (if the offender is under the age of 18 years at the date of release) a youth court: s 256C(8) (as so added). As to youth courts see CHILDREN AND YOUNG PERSONS vol 10 (2012) PARA 1225 et seq.

22 Criminal Justice Act 2003 s 256C(1)(b) (as added: see note 1). Any warrant issued under s 256C must direct the offender to be brought: (1) before a court acting for the local justice area in which the offender resides (s 256C(2)(a) (as so added)); or (2) if it is not known where the offender resides, before a court acting for same local justice area as the justice who issued the warrant (s 256C(2)(b) (as so added)).

23 Ie with requirements under the Criminal Justice Act 2003 s 256B(6): s 256C(4) (as added: see note 1).

24 Criminal Justice Act 2003 s 256C(4) (as added: see note 1).

25 Criminal Justice Act 2003 s 256C(4)(a) (as added: see note 1). An offender detained in pursuance of an order under s 256C(4)(a) is to be regarded as being in legal custody: s 256C(5) (as so added). An offender may appeal to the Crown Court against any order made under s 256C(4)(a): s 256C(7) (as so added). As to legal custody see PRISONS AND PRISONERS vol 85 (2012) PARA 426.

26 Criminal Justice Act 2003 s 256C(4)(b) (as added and amended: see notes 1, 2). As to the standard scale, the statutory maximum, the prescribed sum, and magistrates' powers to levy unlimited fines see PARA 176. A fine imposed under s 256C(4)(b) is to be treated, for the purposes of any enactment, as being a sum adjudged to be paid by a conviction: s 256C(6) (as so added). An offender may appeal to the Crown Court against any order made under s 256C(4)(b): see s 256C(7) (as so added).

27 As to the system of central policy instructions and guidance contained eg in Prison Service Orders (PSOs) and Prison Service Instructions (PSIs) see PRISONS AND PRISONERS vol 85 (2012) PARA 406.

(9) DISCHARGE

746. Formalities. Once the legal requirements for release have been met, discharge from prison is largely an administrative matter in relation to which the Prison Service Instructions System gives guidance and sets out basic matters of policy[1].

A prisoner who would[2] be discharged on any Sunday, Christmas Day, Good Friday or on any day which is a bank holiday in England and Wales[3] (and, in the case of a person who is serving a term of more than five days, any Saturday) is discharged on the next preceding day which is not one of those days[4]. Any power conferred by or under any enactment to release a person from a prison or other institution to which the Prison Act 1952 applies[5] may be exercised notwithstanding that he is not for the time being detained in that institution; and a person so released[6] must, after his release, be treated in all respects as if he had been released from that institution[7].

The Secretary of State[8] may make such payments to or in respect of persons released or about to be released from prison as he may, with Treasury consent, determine[9]. Where necessary, a prisoner or an inmate may be provided with suitable and adequate clothing on his release[10].

In general, a discharged prisoner is not subject to any legal disabilities as such, but there are restrictions upon his possession of firearms for a certain period after release[11].

1 As to the system of central policy instructions and guidance contained eg in Prison Service Orders (PSOs) and Prison Service Instructions (PSIs) see PRISONS AND PRISONERS vol 85 (2012) PARA 406.

2 Ie apart from the Criminal Justice Act 1961 s 23(3): s 23(3) (amended by the Criminal Justice Act 1982 s 77, Sch 14 para 10; and the Legal Aid, Sentencing and Punishment of Offenders Act 2012 s 89(2), Sch 10 para 2(a)). For these purposes, references to prisons and prisoners include references respectively to a young offender institution, secure training centres, secure colleges and remand centres and to persons detained in them: Criminal Justice Act 1961 s 23(4) (amended by the Criminal Justice and Public Order Act 1994 s 168(2), Sch 10 para 11; by virtue of the Criminal Justice Act 1988 s 123, Sch 8 para 1; and by the Criminal Justice and Courts Act 2015 Sch 9 para 6). As from a day to be appointed under the Criminal Justice and Court Services Act 2000 s 80(1), the Criminal Justice Act 1961 s 23(4) is amended so that the reference to 'remand centres' is omitted: s 23(4) (as so amended; prospectively further amended by the Criminal Justice and Court Services Act 2000 s 74, Sch 7 Pt II para 33). However, at the date at which this volume states the law, no such day had been appointed. As to remand centres see PRISONS AND PRISONERS vol 85 (2012) PARAS 485, 486. As to young offender institutions see PARA 16 et seq; and PRISONS AND PRISONERS vol 85 (2012) PARA 487 et seq. As to secure training centres and secure colleges see PRISONS AND PRISONERS vol 85 (2012) PARA 491 et seq.

The Criminal Justice Act 1961 s 23(3) does not apply in relation to a person detained in England and Wales in pursuance of a sentence of the International Criminal Court: see the International Criminal Court Act 2001 Sch 7 para 2(1)(c); and PARA 690. As to the meanings of 'England' and 'Wales' see PARA 4 note 3.

3 Ie under the Banking and Financial Dealings Act 1971 (see TIME vol 97 (2015) PARAS 320–321): Criminal Justice Act 1961 s 23(3) (as amended: see note 2); Interpretation Act 1978 s 17(2).

4 Criminal Justice Act 1961 s 23(3) (as amended: see note 2); Interpretation Act 1978 s 17(2).

5 As to the application of the Prison Act 1952 see PRISONS AND PRISONERS vol 85 (2012) PARA 403 et seq.

6 Ie released by virtue of the Criminal Justice Act 1967 s 71: see s 71.

7 Criminal Justice Act 1967 s 71.

8 As to the Secretary of State for these purposes see PRISONS AND PRISONERS vol 85 (2012) PARA 408.

9 Prison Act 1952 s 30 (substituted by the Criminal Justice Act 1967 s 66(3)).

10 See the Prison Rules 1999, SI 1999/728, r 23(6); the Young Offender Institution Rules 2000, SI 2000/3371, r 19(4); and PRISONS AND PRISONERS vol 85 (2012) PARA 541.

11 As to the possession and sale of firearms by persons convicted of crime see CRIMINAL LAW vol 26 (2010) PARAS 625–626.

(10) REMOVAL OF PRISONERS FROM THE UNITED KINGDOM

(i) Life Sentence Prisoners

747. Life sentence prisoner liable to removal from the United Kingdom. The Secretary of State[1] may remove from prison[2] a life prisoner[3]:

(1)　in respect of whom a minimum term order[4] has been made[5]; and

(2)　who is liable to removal from the United Kingdom[6],

at any time after the prisoner has served the relevant part of the sentence[7].

If such a prisoner is removed from prison in this way[8]:

(a)　he is so removed only for the purpose of enabling the Secretary of State to remove him from the United Kingdom under powers conferred by the Immigration Act 1971 or by the Immigration and Asylum Act 1999[9]; and

(b)　so long as remaining in the United Kingdom, he remains liable to be detained in pursuance of his sentence[10].

So long as the prisoner, having been removed from prison[11], remains in the United Kingdom but has not been returned to prison, any duty or power of the Secretary of State to release him[12] is exercisable in relation to him as if he were in prison[13].

The Prison Service Instructions System gives guidance relating to foreign national prisoners who are liable to deportation[14].

1　As to the Secretary of State for these purposes see PRISONS AND PRISONERS vol 85 (2012) PARA 408.

2　Ie under the Crime (Sentences) Act 1997 s 32A: s 32A(1) (s 32A added by the Legal Aid, Sentencing and Punishment of Offenders Act 2012 s 119).

3　As to the meaning of 'life prisoner' for the purposes of the Crime (Sentences) Act 1997 Pt II Ch II (ss 28–34) (life sentences) see PARA 706. The Crime (Sentences) Act 1997 Pt II Ch II does not apply in relation to a person detained in England and Wales in pursuance of a sentence of the International Criminal Court: see the International Criminal Court Act 2001 Sch 7 para 3(1); and PARA 690. As to the meanings of 'England' and 'Wales' see PARA 4 note 3.

4　'Minimum term order' is defined for the purposes of the Crime (Sentences) Act 1997 s 28 (duty to release certain life prisoners): see s 28(8A); and PARA 707 note 2.

5　Crime (Sentences) Act 1997 s 32A(1)(a) (as added: see note 2). If the prisoner who falls within heads (1) and (2) in the text is serving two or more life sentences: (1) s 32A does not apply to him unless a minimum term order has been made in respect of each of those sentences (s 32A(2)(a) (as so added)); and (2) the Secretary of State may not remove him from prison under s 32A until he has served the relevant part of each of them (s 32A(2)(b) (as so added)).

6　Crime (Sentences) Act 1997 s 32A(1)(b) (as added: see note 2). For these purposes, 'liable to removal from the United Kingdom' has the meaning given by the Criminal Justice Act 2003 s 259 (persons liable to removal from the United Kingdom: see PARA 749 note 3): Crime (Sentences) Act 1997 s 32A(5) (as so added). As to the meaning of 'United Kingdom' see PARA 4 note 3.

7　Crime (Sentences) Act 1997 s 32A(1) (as added: see note 2). The provision made by s 32A(1) applies whether or not the Parole Board has directed the prisoner's release under s 28 (duty to release certain life prisoners: see PARA 707): s 32A(1) (as so added). As to the constitution and functions of the Parole Board, continued by the Criminal Justice Act 2003 s 239(1), see PARA 699.

8　Crime (Sentences) Act 1997 s 32A(3) (as added: see note 2). The text refers to a prisoner removed from prison under s 32A: s 32A(3) (as so added).

9　Crime (Sentences) Act 1997 s 32A(3)(a) (as added: see note 2). Head (a) in the text refers to powers conferred by the Immigration Act 1971 ss 4, 5, Sch 2 (control on entry etc) or Sch 3 (deportation) (see IMMIGRATION AND ASYLUM vol 57 (2012) PARA 177 et seq) or by the Immigration and Asylum Act 1999 s 10 (removal of certain persons unlawfully in the United Kingdom: see IMMIGRATION AND ASYLUM vol 57 (2012) PARA 179): Crime (Sentences) Act 1997 s 32A(3)(a) (as so added).

10 Crime (Sentences) Act 1997 s 32A(3)(b) (as added: see note 2).

11 Ie having been removed from prison under the Crime (Sentences) Act 1997 s 32A: s 32A(4) (as added: see note 2).

12 Ie under the Crime (Sentences) Act 1997 s 28 or under s 30 (power to release life prisoners on compassionate grounds: see PARA 697): s 32A(4) (as added: see note 2).

13 Crime (Sentences) Act 1997 s 32A(4) (as added: see note 2).

14 As to the system of central policy instructions and guidance contained eg in Prison Service Orders (PSOs) and Prison Service Instructions (PSIs) see PRISONS AND PRISONERS vol 85 (2012) PARA 406.

748.   Re-entry into the United Kingdom of life sentence prisoner removed previously. If a person, having been removed from prison[1], is removed from the United Kingdom[2] but then enters the United Kingdom[3]:

(1)   he is liable to be detained in pursuance of his sentence from the time of his entry into the United Kingdom[4];

(2)   if no direction was given by the Parole Board[5] before his removal from prison, the usual provisions that govern a life prisoner's release[6] apply to him[7];

(3)   if such a direction was given before that removal, the prisoner is to be treated as if he had been recalled to prison while on licence[8].

A person who is liable to be detained by virtue of head (1) above[9] is, if at large, to be taken for the purposes of the Prison Act 1952[10] to be unlawfully at large[11]. Head (1) above does not prevent the prisoner's further removal from the United Kingdom[12].

1 Ie under the Crime (Sentences) Act 1997 s 32A (see PARA 747): s 32B(1) (s 32B added by the Legal Aid, Sentencing and Punishment of Offenders Act 2012 s 119). The Crime (Sentences) Act 1997 Pt II Ch II (ss 28–34) (life sentences) does not apply in relation to a person detained in England and Wales in pursuance of a sentence of the International Criminal Court: see the International Criminal Court Act 2001 Sch 7 para 3(1); and PARA 690. As to the meanings of 'England' and 'Wales' see PARA 4 note 3.

2 Crime (Sentences) Act 1997 s 32B(1) (as added: see note 1). As to the meaning of 'United Kingdom' see PARA 4 note 3.

3 Crime (Sentences) Act 1997 s 32B(2) (as added: see note 1).

4 Crime (Sentences) Act 1997 s 32B(2)(a) (as added: see note 1).

5 Ie under the Crime (Sentences) Act 1997 s 28(5) (see PARA 707): s 32B(2)(b) (as added: see note 1). As to the constitution and functions of the Parole Board, continued by the Criminal Justice Act 2003 s 239(1), see PARA 699.

6 Ie the Crime (Sentences) Act 1997 s 28 (duty to release certain life prisoners: see PARA 707): s 32B(2)(b) (as added: see note 1).

7 Crime (Sentences) Act 1997 s 32B(2)(b) (as added: see note 1).

8 Crime (Sentences) Act 1997 s 32B(2)(c) (as added: see note 1). The text refers to the prisoner being treated as if he had been recalled to prison under s 32 (recall of life prisoners while on licence: see PARA 708): s 32B(2)(c) (as so added).

9 Ie by virtue of the Crime (Sentences) Act 1997 s 32B(2)(a) (see head (1) in the text): s 32B(3) (as added: see note 1).

10 Ie for the purposes of the Prison Act 1952 s 49 (persons unlawfully at large: see PRISONS AND PRISONERS vol 85 (2012) PARA 429): Crime (Sentences) Act 1997 s 32B(3) (as added: see note 1).

11 Crime (Sentences) Act 1997 s 32B(3) (as added: see note 1).

12 Crime (Sentences) Act 1997 s 32B(4) (as added: see note 1).

(ii) Fixed-term Prisoners

A. OFFENCES COMMITTED ON OR AFTER 4 APRIL 2005

749. Fixed-term prisoner liable to or eligible for removal from the United Kingdom. Where a fixed-term prisoner[1], who has served at least one-half of the requisite custodial period[2], is liable to[3] (or, as from a day to be appointed, eligible for[4]) removal from the United Kingdom, the Secretary of State may remove him from prison[5] at any time during the period of 270 days ending with the day on which the prisoner will have served the requisite custodial period[6]. If a fixed-term prisoner serving an extended sentence or a special custodial sentence for an offender of particular concern[7] is liable to removal from the United Kingdom[8], and has not been removed from prison[9] during the specified period of 270 days[10], the Secretary of State may remove the prisoner from prison[11] at any time after the end of that period[12].

Until a day to be appointed a prisoner removed from prison in this way:

(1)   is so removed only for the purpose of enabling the Secretary of State to remove him from the United Kingdom under powers conferred by the Immigration Act 1971 or by the Immigration and Asylum Act 1999[13]; and

(2)   so long as remaining in the United Kingdom, remains liable to be detained in pursuance of his sentence until he has served the requisite custodial period[14].

As from the appointed day a prisoner removed from prison in this way:

(a)   if liable to removal from the United Kingdom, is so removed only for the purpose of enabling the Secretary of State to remove him from the United Kingdom under powers conferred by the Immigration Act 1971 or by the Immigration and Asylum Act 1999[15];

(b)   if eligible for removal from the United Kingdom, is so removed only for the purpose of enabling the prisoner to leave the United Kingdom in order to reside permanently outside the United Kingdom[16]; and

(b)   in either case, so long as remaining in the United Kingdom, remains liable to be detained in pursuance of his sentence until he has served the requisite custodial period[17].

So long as a prisoner who is removed from prison in this way remains in the United Kingdom but has not been returned to prison, any duty or power of the Secretary of State to release him[18] is exercisable in relation to him as if he were in prison[19].

In relation to certain historical cases, the usual Criminal Justice Act 2003 provisions[20] are displaced by transitional arrangements[21].

The Prison Service Instructions System gives guidance relating to foreign national prisoners who are liable to deportation[22].

1   As to the meaning of 'fixed-term prisoner' for the purposes of the Criminal Justice Act 2003 Pt 12 Ch 6 (ss 237–268) (sentencing: release, licences and recall) see PARA 709.

2   The Criminal Justice Act 2003 s 260(1) (see the text and notes 2–6) is subject to s 260(2): s 260(1) (amended by the Criminal Justice and Immigration Act 2008 s 34(1), (3), (4)(a); and by SI 2008/978). Accordingly, the Criminal Justice Act 2003 s 260(1) does not apply in relation to a prisoner unless he has served at least one-half of the requisite custodial period: s 260(2) (substituted by the Criminal Justice and Immigration Act 2008 s 34(1), (3), (5)). The Secretary of State may by order amend the fraction for the time being specified in the Criminal Justice Act 2003 s 260(2): s 260(6)(c) (amended by the Criminal Justice and Immigration Act 2008

ss 34(1), (3), (8)(c)). As to the Secretary of State for these purposes see PRISONS AND PRISONERS vol 85 (2012) PARA 408. At the date at which this volume states the law, no such order had been made.

The Criminal Justice Act 2003 ss 243A–264 do not apply in relation to a person detained in England and Wales in pursuance of a sentence of the International Criminal Court: see the International Criminal Court Act 2001 Sch 7 para 3(1); and PARA 690. As to the meanings of 'England' and 'Wales' see PARA 4 note 3.

3   For the purposes of the Criminal Justice Act 2003 Pt 12 Ch 6 a person is liable to removal from the United Kingdom if:

     (1)   he is liable to deportation under the Immigration Act 1971 s 3(5) (grounds of public good or relationship to person ordered to be deported: see IMMIGRATION AND ASYLUM vol 57 (2012) PARA 181) and he has been notified of a decision to make a deportation order against him (Criminal Justice Act 2003 s 259(a));

     (2)   he is liable to deportation under the Immigration Act 1971 s 3(6) (recommendation by sentencing court: see IMMIGRATION AND ASYLUM vol 57 (2012) PARA 181) (Criminal Justice Act 2003 s 259(b));

     (3)   he has been notified of a decision to refuse him leave to enter the United Kingdom (s 259(c));

     (4)   he is an illegal entrant within the meaning of the Immigration Act 1971 s 33(1) (see IMMIGRATION AND ASYLUM vol 57 (2012) PARA 176) (Criminal Justice Act 2003 s 259(d)); or

     (5)   he is liable to removal under the Immigration and Asylum Act 1999 s 10 (removal of certain persons unlawfully in the United Kingdom: see IMMIGRATION AND ASYLUM vol 57 (2012) PARA 179) (Criminal Justice Act 2003 s 259(e)).

As to the meaning of 'United Kingdom' see PARA 4 note 3.

4   As from a day to be appointed, to be 'eligible for removal from the United Kingdom' a person must show, to the satisfaction of the Secretary of State, that he has the settled intention of residing permanently outside the United Kingdom if removed from prison under the Criminal Justice Act 2003 s 260: s 259A(1), (2) (ss 259A, 260(4)(aa) prospectively added, s 260(1), (4)(a), (b) prospectively amended, s 260(3A) prospectively repealed, by the Criminal Justice and Immigration Act 2008 s 34, Sch 28 Pt 2). At the date at which this volume states the law no day had been appointed for this purpose. The person must not be one who is liable to removal from the United Kingdom: Criminal Justice Act 2003 s 260(3) (as so prospectively added).

5   Ie under the Criminal Justice Act 2003 s 260: see s 260(1) (as amended and prospectively amended: see notes 2, 4).

6   Criminal Justice Act 2003 s 260(1) (as amended and prospectively amended: see notes 2, 4). The Secretary of State may by order amend the number of days for the time being specified in s 260(1): s 260(6)(a) (amended by the Criminal Justice and Immigration Act 2008 ss 34(1), (3), (8)(a), 149, Sch 28 Pt 2). In exercise of the powers conferred by s 260(6)(a), the Secretary of State has made the Early Removal of Fixed-Term Prisoners (Amendment of Eligibility Period) Order 2008, SI 2008/978.

7   Ie an extended sentence imposed under the Criminal Justice Act 2003 s 226A (extended sentence for certain violent or sexual offences (persons 18 or over): see PARAS 18–20) or s 226B (extended sentence for certain violent or sexual offences (persons under 18): see PARAS 18–20) or a sentence under s 236A (see PARA 32): s 260(2A) (s 260(2A), (2B) added by the Legal Aid, Sentencing and Punishment of Offenders Act 2012 Sch 20 paras 1, 9(1), (2); Criminal Justice Act 2003 s 260(2A), (5) amended by the Criminal Justice and Courts Act 2015 Sch 1 para 20).

8   Criminal Justice Act 2003 s 260(2A)(a) (as added: see note 7).

9   Ie under the Criminal Justice Act 2003 s 260: s 260(2A)(b) (as added: see note 7).

10   Criminal Justice Act 2003 s 260(2A)(b) (as added: see note 7). The text refers to the period mentioned in s 260(1) (see the text and notes 1–6): s 260(2A)(b) (as so added).

11   Ie under the Criminal Justice Act 2003 s 260: s 260(2A) (as added: see note 6).

12   Criminal Justice Act 2003 s 260(2A) (as added: see note 7). The provision so made by s 260(2A) applies whether or not the Parole Board (or, as from a day to be appointed, a recall adjudicator) has directed the prisoner's release under Pt 12 Ch 6: s 260(2B) (as so added; amended by the Criminal Justice and Courts Act 2015 s 15(6); prospectively amended by Sch 3 para 8). At the date at which this volume states the law no day had been appointed for this purpose. As to the constitution and functions of the Parole Board, continued by the Criminal Justice Act 2003 s 239(1), see PARA 699. As to recall adjudicators see PARA 705.

13   Criminal Justice Act 2003 s 260(4)(a). Head (1) in the text refers to powers conferred by the Immigration Act 1971 ss 4, 5, Sch 2 (control on entry etc) or Sch 3 (deportation) (see IMMIGRATION AND ASYLUM vol 57 (2012) PARA 177 et seq) or by the Immigration and Asylum

Act 1999 s 10 (removal of certain persons unlawfully in the United Kingdom: see IMMIGRATION AND ASYLUM vol 57 (2012) PARA 179): Criminal Justice Act 2003 s 260(4)(a).

14 Criminal Justice Act 2003 s 260(4)(b).

15 Criminal Justice Act 2003 s 260(4)(a) (prospectively amended: see note 4). Head (a) in the text refers to powers conferred by the Immigration Act 1971 ss 4, 5, Sch 2 or by the Immigration and Asylum Act 1999 s 10: Criminal Justice Act 2003 s 260(4)(a) (as so prospectively amended).

16 Criminal Justice Act 2003 s 260(4)(aa) (prospectively added: see note 4).

17 Criminal Justice Act 2003 s 260(4)(b) (prospectively amended: see note 4).

18 Ie under the Criminal Justice Act 2003 s 243A (unconditional release of prisoners serving less than 12 months: see PARA 712), s 244 (duty to release fixed-term prisoners: see PARA 713), s 244A (release on licence of prisoners serving sentence under s 236A), s 246A (release on licence of prisoners serving extended sentence under s 226A or s 226B: see PARA 716), s 247 (release on licence of prisoner serving extended sentence under s 227 or s 228: see PARA 716) or s 248 (power to release fixed-term prisoners on compassionate grounds: see PARA 696): s 260(5) (amended by the Legal Aid, Sentencing and Punishment of Offenders Act 2012 ss 116(1), (5), Sch 14 paras 5, 11(a), Sch 20 paras 1, 9(1), (3); as amended (see note 7)).

19 Criminal Justice Act 2003 s 260(5) (as amended: see notes 7, 16). As to exercise of the Secretary of State's powers under the Criminal Justice Act 1991 (repealed) see *R (on the application of Clift) v Secretary of State for the Home Department, R (on the application of Hindawi) v Secretary of State for the Home Department* [2006] UKHL 54, [2007] 1 AC 484, [2007] 2 All ER 1; and *Clift v United Kingdom* (2010) Times, 21 July, [2010] ECHR 7205/07, ECtHR. See also *R (on the application of Hindawi) v Parole Board* [2012] EWHC 3894 (Admin), [2012] All ER (D) 153 (Dec) (judicial review of Board's risk assessment, that, if deported to Jordan where the monitoring capacity was inadequate, claimant might become active in and/or incite terrorist activities, although the risk he presented if released in the UK was minimal: Board entitled to conclude that the claimant might present a greater risk in Jordan than in the UK and further, the failure to consider how the Jordanian authorities would respond did not render the decision irrational).

20 Ie the Criminal Justice Act 2003 s 260 (see the text and notes 1–19).

21 The transitional arrangements contained in the Criminal Justice Act 2003 s 267B, Sch 20B paras 36, 37 (early removal of prisoners liable to removal from the United Kingdom: see PARA 751) make further provision about early removal of certain prisoners: s 260(8) (added by the Legal Aid, Sentencing and Punishment of Offenders Act 2012 s 121(6), Sch 17 paras 1, 6).

22 As to the system of central policy instructions and guidance contained eg in Prison Service Orders (PSOs) and Prison Service Instructions (PSIs) see PRISONS AND PRISONERS vol 85 (2012) PARA 406.

750. Re-entry into the United Kingdom of fixed-term prisoner removed before serving the requisite custodial period. If a person who, after being removed from prison[1], has been removed from the United Kingdom[2] before he has served the requisite custodial period[3], but enters the United Kingdom at any time before his sentence expiry date[4], he is liable to be detained in pursuance of his sentence from the time of his entry into the United Kingdom until whichever is the earlier of[5]:

(1)   the end of a period (the 'further custodial period') beginning with that time and equal in length to the outstanding custodial period[6]; and

(2)   his sentence expiry date[7];

and such a person may be further removed from the United Kingdom[8].

A person who is liable to be detained in this way[9] is, if at large, to be taken for the purposes of the Prison Act 1952[10] to be unlawfully at large[11].

1   Ie under the Criminal Justice Act 2003 s 260 (see PARA 749): s 261(1). The Criminal Justice Act 2003 ss 243A–264 do not apply in relation to a person detained in England and Wales in pursuance of a sentence of the International Criminal Court: see the International Criminal Court Act 2001 Sch 7 para 3(1); and INTERNATIONAL RELATIONS LAW vol 61 (2010) PARA 450. As to the meanings of 'England' and 'Wales' see PARA 4 note 3.

2   As to the meaning of 'United Kingdom' see PARA 4 note 3.

3   Criminal Justice Act 2003 s 261(1).

4   In relation to a person to whom the Criminal Justice Act 2003 s 261 applies (see s 261(1); and the text and notes 1–3), 'sentence expiry date' means the date on which, but for his release from

prison and removal from the United Kingdom, he would have served the whole of the sentence: s 261(6) (definition of 'sentence expiry date' amended by the Legal Aid, Sentencing and Punishment of Offenders Act 2012 Sch 14 paras 5, 12(1), (3)(b)).

5   Criminal Justice Act 2003 s 261(2).
6   Criminal Justice Act 2003 s 261(2)(a), (6). In relation to a person to whom s 261 applies 'outstanding custodial period' means the period beginning with the date of his removal from the United Kingdom and ending with the date on which he would, but for his removal, have served the requisite custodial period: s 261(6). Where, in the case of a person returned to prison by virtue of s 261(2), the further custodial period ends before the sentence expiry date, either s 243A (unconditional release of prisoners serving less than 12 months: see PARA 712), s 244 (release on licence of prisoners serving 12 months or more: see PARA 713), s 244A (release on licence of s 236A prisoners (ie prisoners serving sentences under s 236A (see PARAS 32, 714), s 246A (initial release of fixed-term prisoners (extended sentences): see PARA 716) or s 247 (release on licence of prisoners serving extended sentence under s 227 or s 228 (both repealed with savings): see PARA 716) (as the case may be) has effect in relation to that person as if the reference to the requisite custodial period were a reference to the further custodial period: s 261(5)(b) (added and amended by the Legal Aid, Sentencing and Punishment of Offenders Act 2012 s 116, Sch 14 para 12(1), (2), Sch 20 paras 1, 10(1), (2); amended by the Criminal Justice and Courts Act 2015 s 14(5), Sch 1 para 21). See note 3.
7   Criminal Justice Act 2003 s 261(2)(b).
8   Criminal Justice Act 2003 s 261(4). The provision made by s 261(2) (see the text and notes 4–7) does not prevent the further removal from the United Kingdom of a person falling within s 261(2): s 261(4).
9   Ie by virtue of the Criminal Justice Act 2003 s 261(2) (see the text and notes 4–7): s 261(3).
10   Ie for the purposes of the Prison Act 1952 s 49 (persons unlawfully at large: see PRISONS AND PRISONERS vol 85 (2012) PARA 429): Criminal Justice Act 2003 s 261(3).
11   Criminal Justice Act 2003 s 261(3).

B. OFFENCES COMMITTED BEFORE 4 APRIL 2005

751. Early removal of extended sentence prisoner liable to removal from United Kingdom.

If a person who[1]:

(1)   has served one-half of a sentence of imprisonment[2]; and
(2)   has not been released on licence under Chapter 6 of Part 12 of the Criminal Justice Act 2003[3],

is liable to removal from the United Kingdom[4], and has not been removed from prison under the usual Criminal Justice Act 2003 provisions[5] during the specified period of 270 days[6], the Secretary of State[7] may remove the person from prison under those provision[8] at any time after the end of that period[9].

1   Ie if a person to whom the Criminal Justice Act 2003 s 267B, Sch 20B para 36 applies (see heads (1) and (2) in the text): Sch 20B para 37(1) (s 267B, Sch 20B added by the Legal Aid, Sentencing and Punishment of Offenders Act 2012 s 121(6), Sch 17 paras 9, 10).
2   Criminal Justice Act 2003 Sch 20B para 36(1)(a) (as added: see note 1). The reference in head (1) in the text to one-half of a sentence is:
    (1)   in the case of a section 85 extended sentence, a reference to one-half of the custodial term (Sch 20B para 36(2)(a) (as so added)); and
    (2)   in the case of an extended sentence imposed under s 227 (repealed with savings) or s 228 (repealed with savings), a reference to one-half of the appropriate custodial term (Sch 20B para 36(2)(b) (as so added)).
     As to the meanings of a 'section 85 extended sentence' and the 'custodial term' for these purposes see PARA 723 note 9.
3   Criminal Justice Act 2003 Sch 20B para 36(1)(b) (as added: see note 1). The text refers to release on licence under Pt 12 Ch 6 (ss 237–268) (sentencing: release, licences and recall) (see also PARAS 696, 699, 709 et seq, 735 et seq, 749, 750): Sch 20B para 36(1)(b) (as so added).
4   Criminal Justice Act 2003 Sch 20B para 37(1)(a) (as added: see note 1). As to the meaning of 'United Kingdom' see PARA 4 note 3.
5   Ie under the Criminal Justice Act 2003 s 260 (persons liable to removal from the United Kingdom: see PARA 749): Sch 20B para 37(1)(b) (as added: see note 1).

6 Criminal Justice Act 2003 Sch 20B para 37(1)(b) (as added: see note 1). The text refers to the period mentioned in s 260(1): Sch 20B para 37(1)(b) (as so added).

7 As to the Secretary of State for these purposes see PRISONS AND PRISONERS vol 85 (2012) PARA 408.

8 Ie under the Criminal Justice Act 2003 s 260: Sch 20B para 37(1) (as added: see note 1).

9 Criminal Justice Act 2003 Sch 20B para 37(1) (as added: see note 1). The provision made by Sch 20B para 37(1) applies whether or not the Parole Board (or, as from a day to be appointed, the recall adjudicator) has directed the person's release under the applicable provisions of Pt 12 Ch 6: Sch 20B para 37(2) (as so added; prospectively amended by the Criminal Justice and Courts Act 2015 Sch 3 para 11). At the date at which this volume states the law no day had been appointed for the coming into force of the amendment made by the Criminal Justice and Courts Act 2015. As to the constitution and functions of the Parole Board, continued by the Criminal Justice Act 2003 s 239(1), see PARA 699. As to recall adjudicators see PARA 705.

INDEX

Sentencing

References are to paragraph numbers; superior figures refer to notes

References are to paragraph numbers; superior figures refer to notes

References are to paragraph numbers; superior figures refer to notes

Words and Phrases

Words in parentheses indicate the context in which the word or phrase is used

accommodation provided by or on behalf
　of a local authority 84n[4]
account monitoring order 313
act of terrorism 420n[2]
activity requirement—
　(supervision order) 386
　(youth rehabilitation order) 139
alcohol abstinence and monitoring
　requirement 135
alcohol treatment requirement 122
anti-social behaviour 372
associated (offences) 75n[2]
attendance centre 5n[8]
attendance centre order 5
attendance centre requirement—
　(community order) 134
　(suspended sentence order) 134
　(youth rehabilitation order) 143
automatic release 719n[3]
authorising officer 414n[2]
British passport 424n[2]
care services 615n[12]
cash 210n[2]
caution—
　(Protection of Freedoms Act 2012)
　　660n[2]
　(Rehabilitation of Offenders Act 1974)
　　591n[6]
caution information 601n[4]
central records 637n[4]
certificate 636n[1]
child 327n[4], 392n[4], 550n[5]
community impact statement 623
community sentence 42
compensation order 281
conditional caution 636n[4]
conviction—
　(Protection of Freedoms Act 2012)
　　660n[1]
　(rehabilitation of offenders) 591n[3],
　　636n[3]
criminal behaviour order 319
criminal conduct 225
criminal conviction certificate 636
criminal investigation 200n[3]
criminal lifestyle 229
criminal record certificate 637
curfew condition 737n[4]
curfew requirement—
　(community order) 123
　(generally) 31n[12]

curfew requirement—*continued*
　(supervision order) 387
　(suspended sentence order) 123
　(youth rehabilitation order) 145
custodial sentence 9n[15], 605n[4]
customer information 311n[4]
damage 282
declaration of relevance 343
deprivation order 470
derogatory assertions order 556
detention order 390
determinate prison sentence 688n[2]
discretionary release prisoner 699n[21]
document 355n[24]
domestic violence protection notice 413
domestic violence protection order 413
drug appointment requirement 745n[17]
drug rehabilitation requirement 124
drug testing requirement 151, 745n[16]
drug trafficking offence 366n[1]
drug treatment requirement 150
drug-dealing activity 483n[4]
education requirement 153
electronic monitoring condition 31n[8]
electronic monitoring requirement—
　(community order) 136
　(supervision requirement) 388
　(suspended sentence order) 136
　(youth rehabilitation order) 155
enforcement officer 114n[8]
England 4n[3]
enhanced criminal record certificate 638
exclusion order 349
exclusion requirement—
　(community order) 126
　(suspended sentence order) 126
　(youth rehabilitation order) 146
extended sentence 35n[11]
extended sentence of imprisonment or
　detention 18
extended sentence prisoner 699n[21], 719n[2]
extradited prisoner 30n[7]
financial circumstances order 180
financial information order 311
financial institution 311n[3]
financial penalty deposit requirement 184
financial year 211n[2]
fine 174
fixed-term prisoner 709
football banning order 341

References are to paragraph numbers; superior figures refer to notes